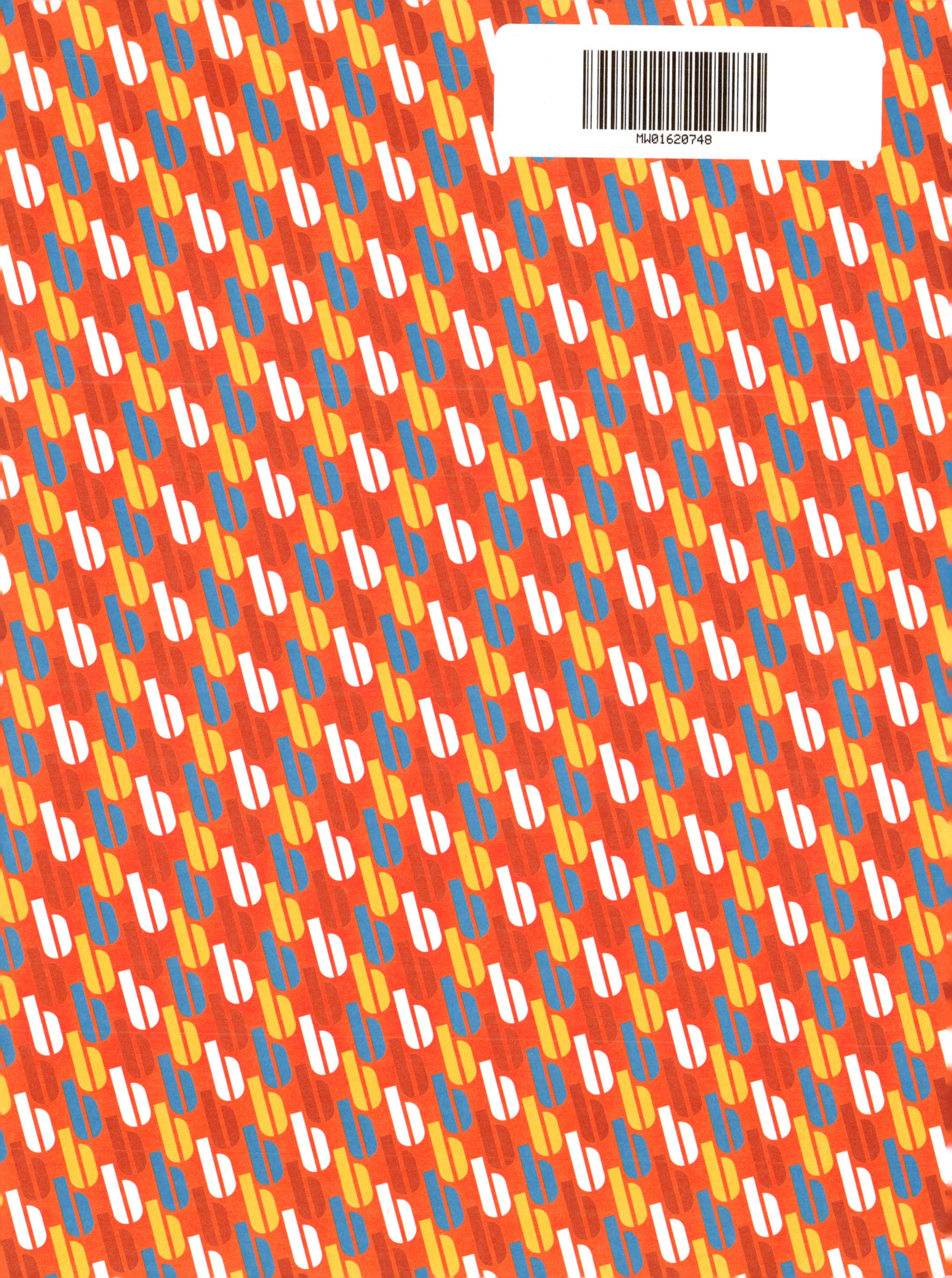
MW01620748

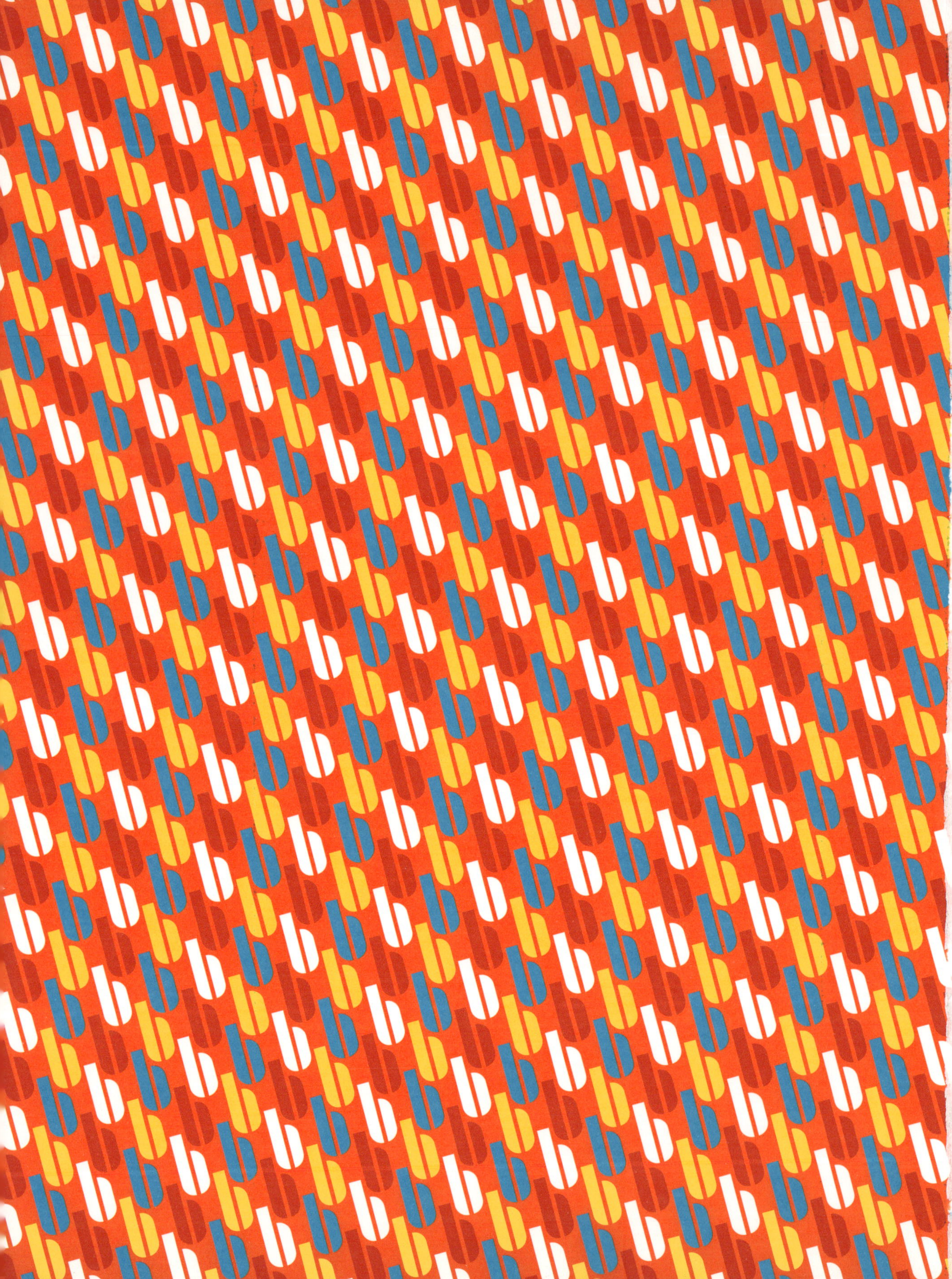

bauha
typog
at 100

us

raphy

INTRODUCTION BY
ELLEN LUPTON

Letterform Archive

conte

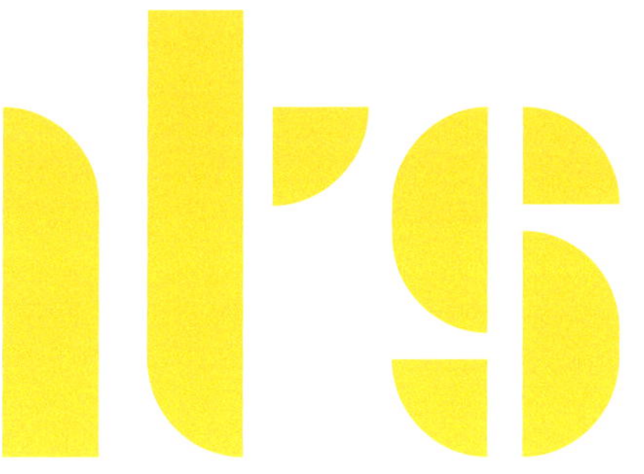

ABOUT THE EXHIBITION

The Bauhaus looms large as one of the most influential legacies in twentieth-century graphic design. Known for its bold sans serif typefaces, crisp asymmetrical grids, and clean use of negative space, the school emerged as the forebearer of a new look—one that seized the tools of mass production in the creation of a radical new art. Today, just over one hundred years after the Bauhaus's opening in 1919, the school's visual hallmarks—its minimalism and utility, enlivened by experimentation—have, for many, come to define modernity as it appears on the printed page. ●

But the Bauhaus did not start off as a school of graphic design, and its initial forays into the genre indicate more nuanced origins. German architect Walter Gropius founded the institution as a utopian collective in which students and professors collaborated and socialized, regardless of gender or class. The school's many workshops aimed to merge instruction in craft and fine art, uniting architecture, painting, and sculpture with printing, pottery, and woodworking into a nineteenth-century ideal of art as a harmonious whole. As such, many of the Bauhaus's early lithograph and letterpress prints veer toward the expressionistic—even the mystic—in their organic approaches to line and letter. ●

While design and typography were not taught at the Bauhaus at first, they were rapidly put into practice as Gropius and his instructors embraced advances in photography and printing. Under a rotating host of directors, masters László Moholy-Nagy, Herbert Bayer, and Joost Schmidt each made their marks on the school's design pedagogy, channeling constructivism's geometric forms, as well as its optimism for industry, into printed vehicles that helped share Bauhaus teachings and sell the products created in its workshops. Here is where Bauhaus typography took on its distinctive form—its rejection of serifs and capitals, embrace of experimental alphabets, insistence on universal clarity, and innovation in layering and hierarchy. ●

The Bauhaus closed due to Nazi pressure in 1933, having made countless contributions to modernist architecture, industrial design, and graphic design. Drawn from the collection of Letterform Archive, this exhibition explores the school's unique legacy in graphic design and typography through artifacts of its own making—its books, magazines, course materials, product catalogs, stationery, promotional fliers, and other ephemera—as well as through objects created by its many characters before and after their time at the school. Finally, it seeks to understand what this inheritance might signal a century later—to draw a throughline from the Bauhaus's iconic dots and rules, as well as the gestural marks of its lesser-known beginnings, to the bold shape of typography today. ●

Clockwise from top right: Students on a balcony at the Bauhaus Dessau; Bauhaus Dessau masters; Herbert Bayer; (left to right) students Marcel Breuer, Marta Erps-Breuer, Katt Both, and Ruth Hollos-Consemüller; the printing workshop in Weimar; László Moholy-Nagy. Top left, middle right, and bottom right courtesy of Bauhaus-Archiv Berlin. Top right and bottom left courtesy of Bauhaus Dessau Foundation.

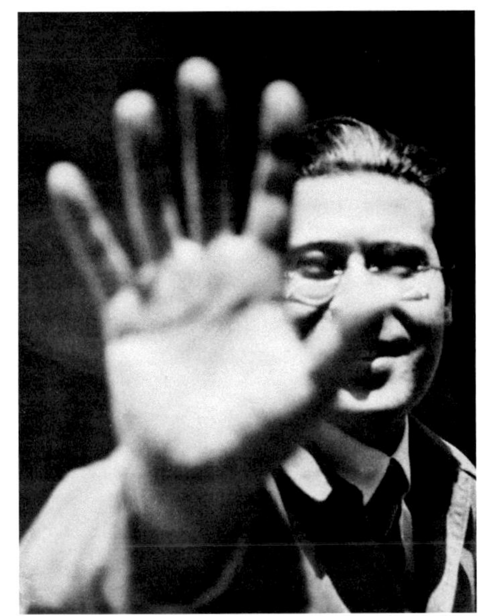

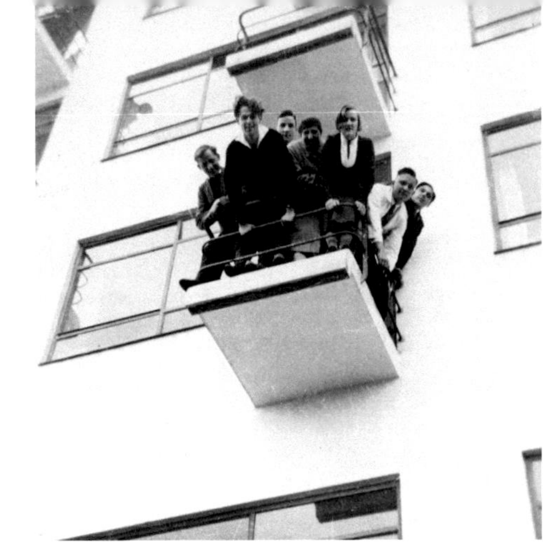

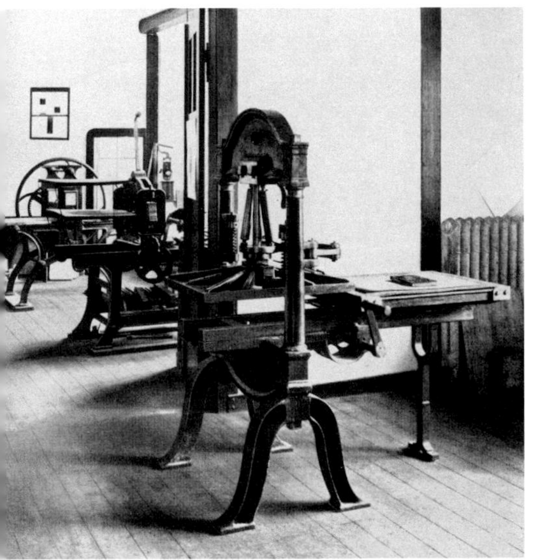

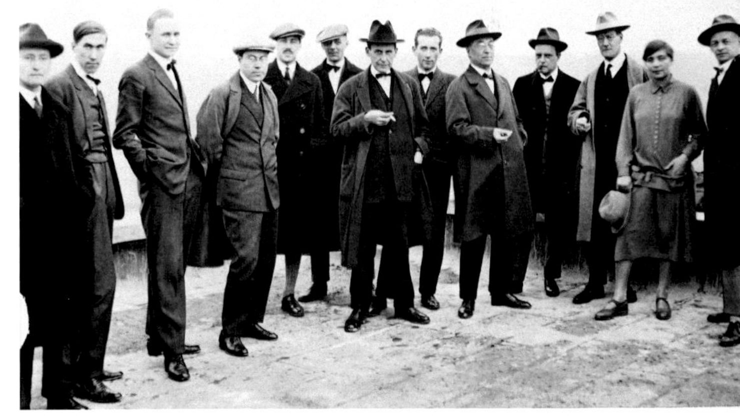

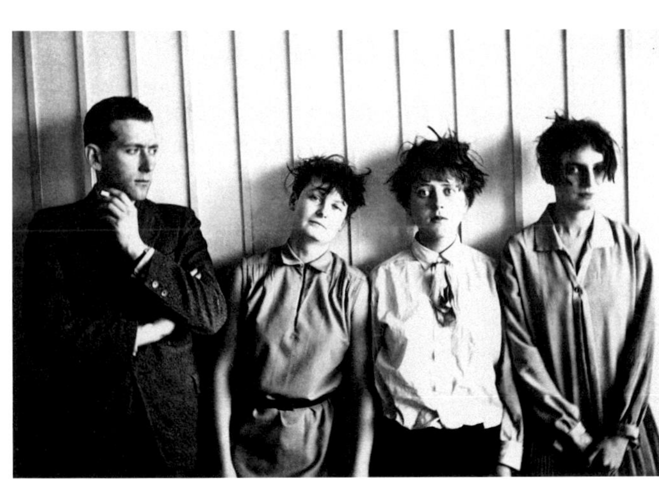

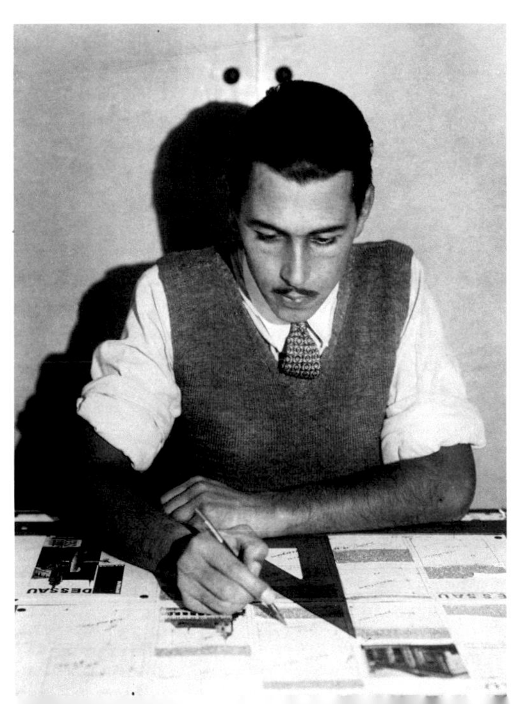

CURATOR'S FOREWORD

ROB SAUNDERS

It wasn't hard to settle on Bauhaus typography for the first show in our first exhibition space. Our little jewel box gallery is opening just after the one hundredth anniversary of the school, and we knew we had plenty of gems to fill it. ●

Based on the Archive's collection, the selection of material from 1919 to 1933, while the school was active, includes most of our Bauhaus holdings from that time, whereas in selecting material from before and after that period, cocurator Henry Cole Smith and I had more to choose from. The result is a concise selection that represents Bauhaus typography over the last hundred years through the lens of Letterform Archive's curatorial vision. ●

As a young designer forty years ago, when I began to collect graphic design (including some of the objects in this show), I certainly wouldn't have copped to a curatorial vision. But by the time Letterform Archive opened in 2015, an early staff member, Kate Robinson Beckwith, saw enough of a pattern in the collection to coin a term for it: *letterformy*. For me, it means graphic design with letterforms that are innovative, inspiring, or influential in their form or use. Each member of the team might define it a little differently, but there's usually a consensus when an object is letterformy enough to belong here at the Archive. ●

So what does a letterformy Bauhaus exhibition look like? For one thing, it's as fascinated with the more expressionist, handmade aesthetic of the school's early days as it is with the better-known New Typography of masters László Moholy-Nagy, Herbert Bayer, and Joost Schmidt. For another, it includes work of the Bauhauslers before and after their time at the school, as well as later echoes of their influence on letterforms and graphic design around the world. ●

In the excitement surrounding the centennial of the Bauhaus, there have been dozens of shows and books on various aspects of the school's legacy. This exhibition is our contribution to these larger conversations. We had a lot of fun putting it together, and we hope that you enjoy it. ●

Oskar Schlemmer, bookplate "From the library of Tut and Oskar Schlemmer" ("Aus der Bücherei von Tut und Oskar Schlemmer"), circa 1942, linocut, shown at actual size (4⅝ × 3⅞ inches/117 × 97 mm), Baden-Baden, Germany.

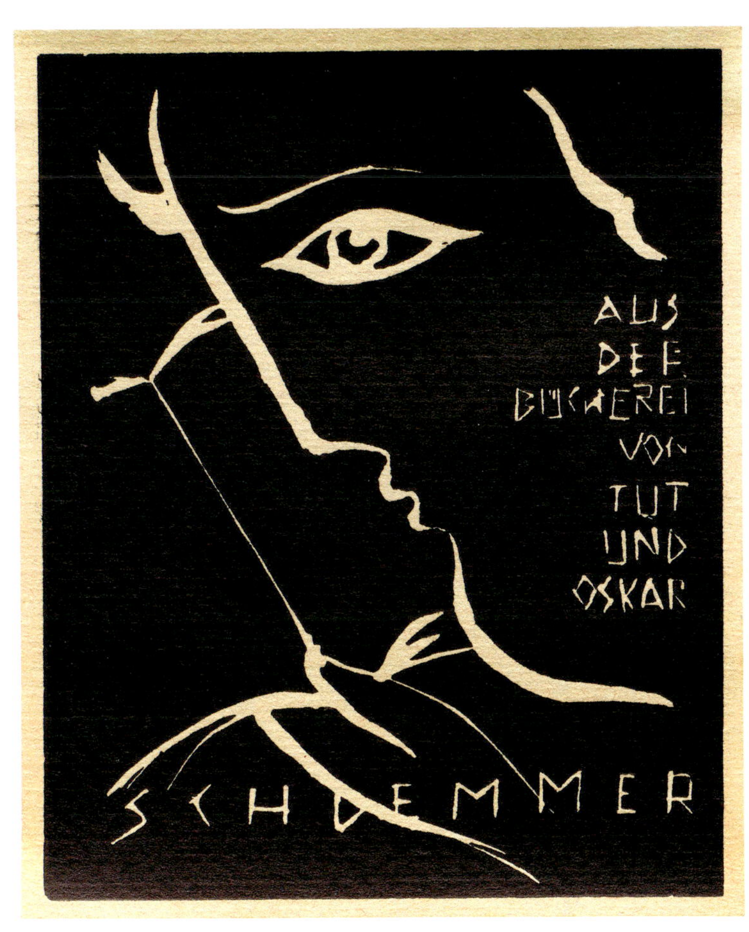
AUS
DER
BÜCHEREI
VON
TUT
UND
OSKAR
SCHLEMMER

INTRODUCTION

ELLEN LUPTON

What is Bauhaus typography? Is it a style? A philosophy? A finite set of artifacts from a fixed historical moment? Narrowly defined, Bauhaus typography is any text drawn, carved, specified, printed, published, written, or edited by Bauhaus students or faculty between 1919 and 1933, the school's years of operation. Yet after the school closed under Nazi pressure, former students and faculty continued to teach and work for decades, feeding the public's hunger for Bauhaus wisdom and spreading it internationally as they traveled to new opportunities and academic posts abroad. Ultimately, many artists and designers passed through the Bauhaus briefly, or were friends with Bauhaus people, or read Bauhaus books and manifestos. These people—who published their own manifestos and exhibited their own work—helped create Bauhaus typography, too. They changed the place and were changed by it. ●

What does Bauhaus typography look like? In the collective imagination, graphic design at the Bauhaus is a crisp constellation of geometric shapes, primary colors, abstract photographs, and stark page layouts. Although those enduring tropes crystallized after the arrival of László Moholy-Nagy in 1923, printed letters flourished at the Bauhaus before and after his time at the school. Graphic design at the Bauhaus took many forms—spiritual, practical, experimental, and pedagogical. Typography was both a creative field and a tool for survival, as graphic design enabled the production of publications, posters, and exhibitions that told the Bauhaus story, sold its products, and kindled its transcendent status. ●

This book and exhibition tell the leaky story of Bauhaus typography through artifacts collected by Letterform Archive. Together, these concrete remnants of history point to the amorphous scope of the school's typographic legacy—its theory, its techniques, its remarkable people, and its slippery status as myth and reality. ●

Lyonel Feininger, detail from *Cathedral* (*Kathedrale*), cover of *Program of the Weimar State Bauhaus* (*Programm des Staatlichen Bauhauses in Weimar*), a.k.a. the Bauhaus manifesto, 1919, woodcut and letterpress, 12⅝ × 7¾ inches (320 × 198 mm), Weimar.

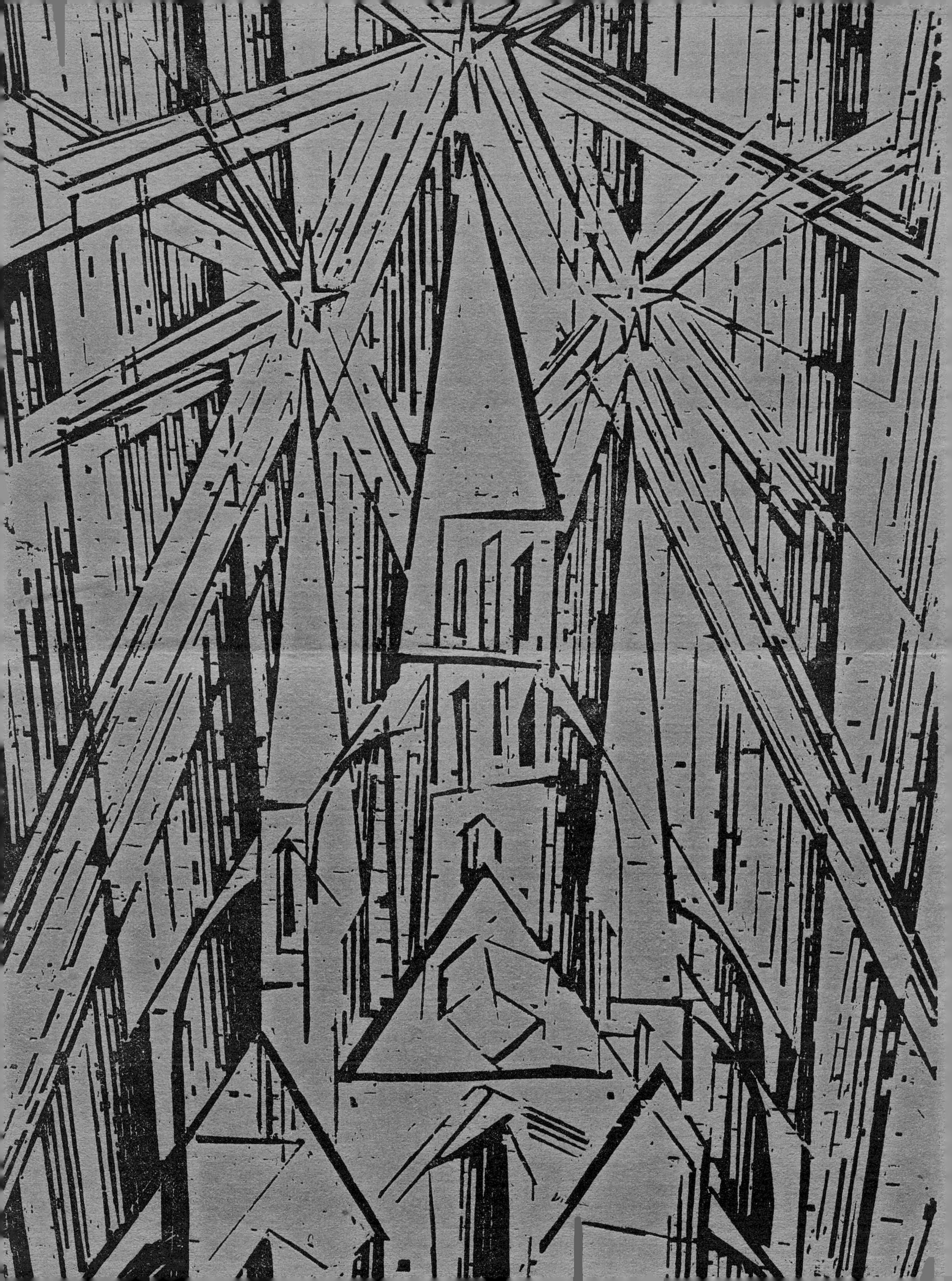

RIGHT
Lyonel Feininger, *Postcard 2, Weimar State Bauhaus Exhibition 1923* (*Karte 2, Staatliches Bauhaus Weimar Ausstellung 1923*), lithograph, 6 × 4¼ inches (151 × 107 mm), Weimar.

BELOW
Lyonel Feininger, *Postcard 1, Weimar State Bauhaus Exhibition 1923* (*Karte 1, Staatliches Bauhaus Weimar Ausstellung 1923*), lithograph, 5⅞ × 4⅛ inches (150 × 105 mm), Weimar.

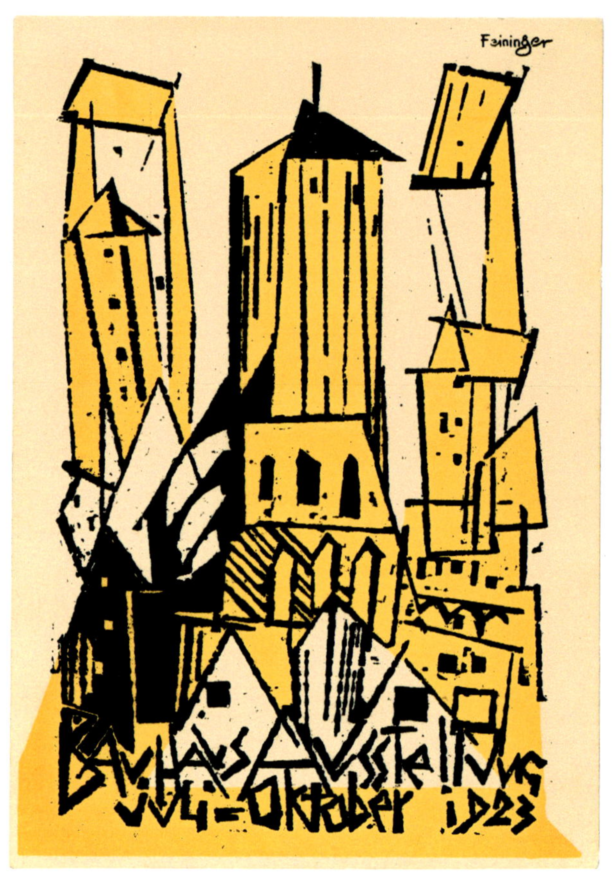

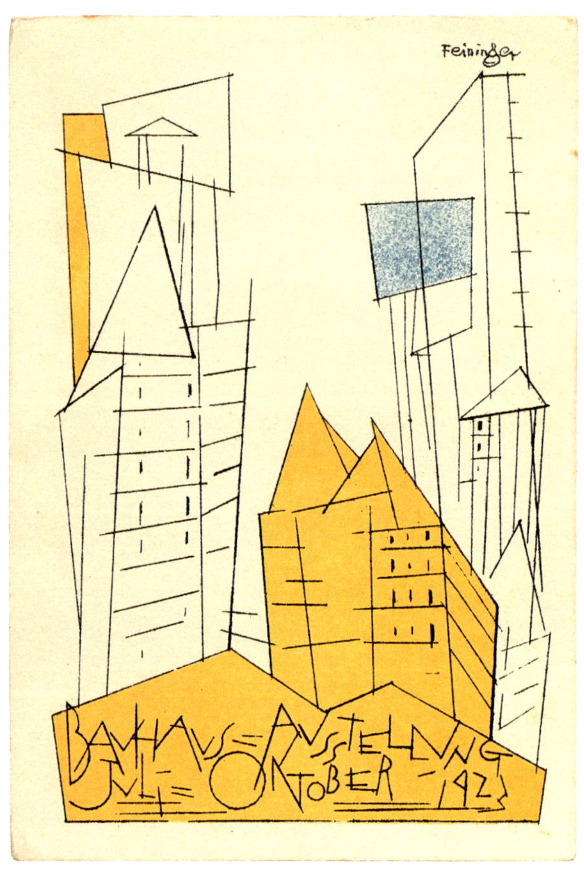

Manifesto

The Bauhaus began in 1919 with Walter Gropius's manifesto, which aimed to unify all forms of visual art beneath the roof of architecture: "The new building of the future . . . will unite every discipline, architecture and sculpture and painting, and . . . will one day rise heavenwards from the million hands of craftsmen as a clear symbol of a new belief to come."[1] Gropius's soaring sentiments echoed the turn-of-the-century theory of the *Gesamtkunstwerk*, or total work of art, and embraced long-standing romantic ideals about the social virtues of medieval craft. ●

An image of a gothic cathedral—nearly full-bleed—adorns the cover of the Bauhaus manifesto (see page 11). This expressionist woodcut set the tone for early Bauhaus graphics; it was created by Lyonel Feininger, born in New York City in 1871, who took charge of the printmaking workshop as Gropius's first faculty hire. The folded broadside also outlines the school's course of study (see pages 38–39). Diverse craft-based workshops sought to train weavers, metalworkers, and cabinetmakers as well as "etchers, wood engravers, lithographers, art printers, and enchasers [*ziselöre*, decorative engravers]." These printing techniques reflect the school's early focus on artistic printing (*kunstdruck*). The manifesto was produced using ordinary commercial printing techniques, which were not available on the Bauhaus premises. The typography is fussy and awkward, but the choice of a roman serif typeface (Ohio by Schriftguss AG) rather than traditional Germanic Fraktur makes the design modern and readable. ●

Even though the Weimar printshop favored artistic genres such as lithography and etching, the school knew from the start that printing could be good for business. In 1923 Gropius charged the young institution with mounting a major exhibition defending the Bauhaus to the skeptical citizens of Weimar. Posters, books, products, signage, and ephemera helped promote this do-or-die event. Students and faculty designed twenty lithograph postcards for the 1923 exhibition (see pages 74–97). With styles ranging from swirling lettering to constructivist abstraction, this collection of postcards shows the diversity of Bauhaus thought. In his own postcards, Feininger reiterated the gothic cathedral as a symbol for the school's roots and ambitions. ●

1 A facsimile and English translation of the Bauhaus manifesto is included in *Weimar State Bauhaus 1919–1923* (*Staatliches Bauhaus in Weimar 1919–1923*), facsimile edition, edited by Lars Müller, and with an essay by Astrid Bähr (Zurich: Lars Müller Publishers, 2019).

Johannes Itten (lettering artist/author), Friedl Dicker (typesetter), *Utopia: Documents of Reality* (*Utopia: Dokumente der Wirklichkeit*), 1921, letterpress and lithograph with photolithograph tip-on, 12¾ × 9⅞ inches (323 × 249 mm), Weimar.

Utopia

As leader of the preliminary course from 1919 to 1923, Johannes Itten of Switzerland was the school's spiritual guide, defining its early utopian phase. The preliminary course sought to strip away conventions, plunging students into fresh acts of expressive abstraction and physical making. Line, shape, and texture were conduits to self-knowledge and personal renewal. The preliminary course laid the ground for foundational programs around the world, which are still widely implemented today. ●

Itten was a zealous promoter of Mazdaznan, an eclectic religious movement founded by Otto Hanisch, a German-born American. Culling beliefs from Zarathustrian, Christian, and Hindu traditions, Mazdaznan demanded a bodily regimen of sexual abstinence, cleansing enemas, and controlled breathing, as well as a vegetarian diet laden with garlic and onions. These rigors aimed to achieve more than personal wellness; Mazdaznan promoted deplorable racial views and sought to purify the so-called white race.[2] (The doctrine considered Jews to be white.) Some of Itten's own students followed him to the Bauhaus and formed a substantial Mazdaznan colony at the school, where Itten promoted the religion's wellness aspects along with its white supremacist views, with Gropius's initial support. Eventually, however, tensions around Mazdaznan developed. Gropius feared that Itten's mystical bent endangered the Bauhaus's reputation as a serious school for the applied arts. The teacher's polarizing philosophy had also produced a schism within the student body (half of which continuously smelled of garlic and onion, to the apparent annoyance of the other half). While it is not clear if the Bauhaus director also recognized parallels between Mazdaznan's eugenics principles and those of the then-nascent Nazi party, strain between the two men resulted in Itten's departure in 1923. ●

2 Ulrich Linse, "Johannes Itten and Mazdaznan at the Bauhaus," Bauhaus Imaginista website, April 10, 2019, http://www.bauhaus-imaginista.org/articles/4787/johannes-itten-and-mazdaznan-at-the-bauhaus?0bbf55ceffc3073.

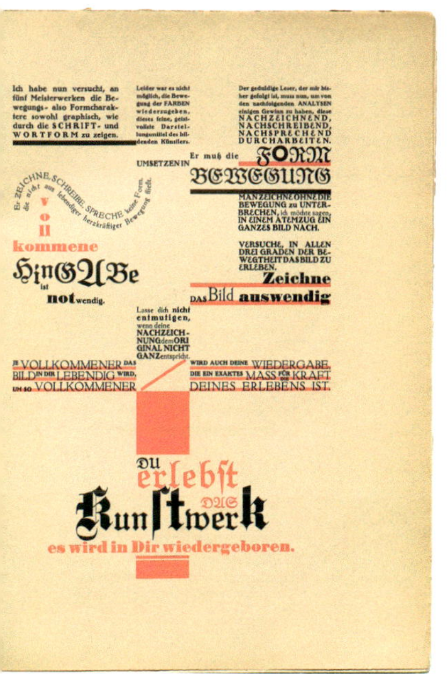

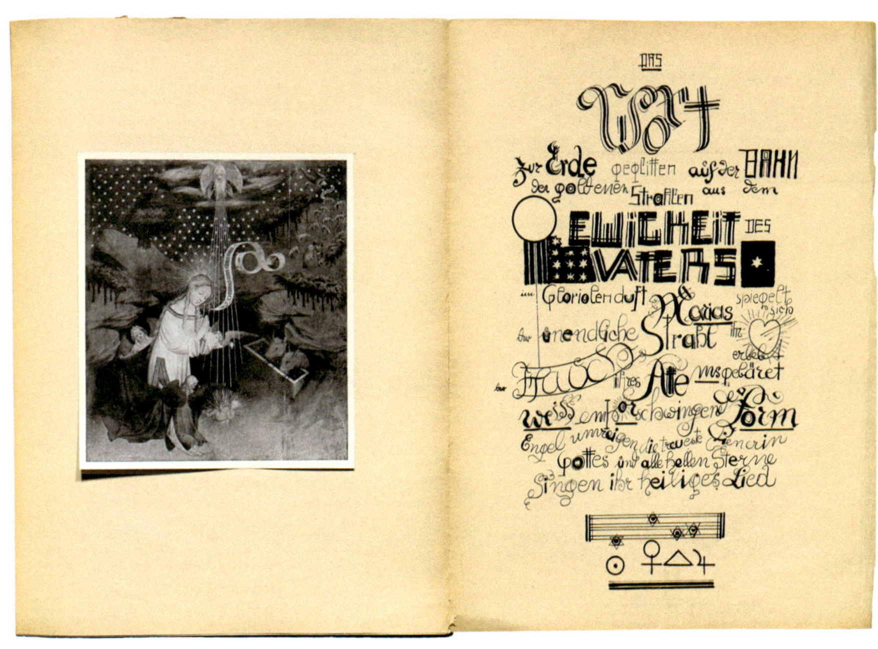

Before he left, Itten made a profound impact on the school's first students. His most extraordinary pupil and collaborator was Friedl Dicker. (She took the name Dicker-Brandeis after marrying Pavel Brandeis in 1936.) An Austrian by birth, she had already completed a degree in photography when she began studying painting with Itten at his private Vienna art school in 1916. A follower of Mazdaznan, she came with him to the Bauhaus in the fall of 1919. Dicker, who also studied with Wassily Kandinsky and Paul Klee at the Bauhaus, was highly regarded by the faculty for her achievements in painting, drawing, photography, printmaking, and more. She was invited to instruct new members in the preliminary course, becoming the first student to teach at the school. The work of Klee was especially influential on her practice as an artist and educator. ●

Dicker collaborated with Itten on the most ambitious typographic work of the school's early years: a series of prints created for the almanac *Utopia: Documents of Reality* (*Utopia: Dokumente der Wirklichkeit*; see above and pages 52–57), published by German art historian Bruno Adler. The prints were based on a drawing exercise from Itten's preliminary course in which students trace the structure of Old Masters paintings in search of the works' essential spiritual movement. (As in all of Itten's exercises, abstract analysis unleashed personal feelings. According to one famous anecdote, Itten yelled at a roomful of students who failed to weep while studying a lantern slide of a medieval altarpiece.[3]) In *Utopia*, Itten endeavored to explain his Old Masters exercise with text, spelling out his process in lines, blocks, and curving waves of words. ●

The project includes ten red-and-black letterpress prints inspired by Hieronymus Bosch's painting *John the Baptist in the Desert* (circa 1489) and a set of lithographs featuring hand-drawn text inspired by five historical works of art. The colophon names Itten as the project's primary author

3 Rainer K. Wick, *Teaching at the Bauhaus* (Ostfildern-Ruit, Germany: Hatje Cantz, 2000), 110.

Johannes Itten (lettering artist/author), Friedl Dicker (typesetter), annotated proof of *Utopia: Documents of Reality* (*Utopia: Dokumente der Wirklichkeit*), 1921, letterpress and pencil, 12¾ × 9⅞ inches (323 × 249 mm), Weimar. Collection of Bauhaus-Archiv Berlin.

but gives design credit to Dicker: "Typesetting and printing directed by Friedl Dicker." While the lithographs were likely drawn in Itten's own hand, the letterpress prints fell to Dicker, Itten's trusted student and acolyte. This interpretation and transformation required hours of meticulous labor to design and produce. Dicker wrote to her friend Anny Wottiz in 1920 or '21, "I typeset an essay from Itten for two weeks and am so weak I can scarcely say when I can come from there . . . Two days later. Today I set six Itten pages."[4] ●

A press sheet for the last print in the series, marked up with pencil corrections by Itten and/or Dicker, exists in the collection of the Bauhaus-Archiv in Berlin (see right). It is a window into an intimate process of editing, design, and production. The Weimar printshop had no letterpress facilities, so Dicker typeset the work elsewhere. Her selection of fonts—from Germanic Fraktur to delicate roman capitals and high-contrast advertising faces—approximates the range of Itten's lettering in the lithographs. The text begins, "I have now tried to show the movement characters in the form of five masterpieces, both graphically and by means of the written and word form." The text goes on to describe the patience required to experience this typographic "tracing" of historical paintings. The typography demands much of its readers. The final line reads, "You inherit the artwork. It is reborn in you." Dicker's visual translations of Itten's words are one of the Bauhaus's most formidable works of typography. ●

After leaving the Bauhaus in 1923, Dicker worked as an artist and a designer in Berlin, Prague, and Hronov, a town in the present-day Czech Republic. Between 1943 and 1944, she taught art to children in the Theresienstadt ghetto and concentration camp. The exercises she conducted with these children included collages inspired by Old Masters paintings as well as rhythmic and observational drawing. Dicker saved over 4,000 artworks created by her students before she was deported to Auschwitz and murdered in 1944; they are preserved today in the Jewish Museum in Prague. Among her students who survived, several became founders of the new disciplines of art therapy and child psychology, seeding another Bauhaus legacy. ●

4 Letter from Friedl Dicker to Anny Wottiz, 1920 or 1921, from Elena Makarova, "The Letters and Life of Friedl Dicker-Brandeis," http://www.makarovainit.com/friedl/letters.html, translation by Julia Reinhard Lupton. See also Elena Makarova, *Friedl Dicker-Brandeis: Vienna 1898–Auschwitz 1944* (Los Angeles: Tallfellow/Every Picture Press, 2001); Elizabeth Otto, "Passages with Friedl Dicker-Brandeis: From the Bauhaus through Theresienstadt," *Passagen des Exils/Passages of Exile*, ed. Burcu Dogramaci and Elizabeth Otto (Munich: Edition Text + Kritik, 2017), 230–251.

Ich habe nun versucht, an fünf Meisterwerken die Bewegungs- also Formcharaktere sowohl graphisch, wie durch die SCHRIFT- und WORTFORM zu zeigen.

Leider war es nicht möglich, die Bewegung der FARBEN wiederzugeben, dieses feine, geistvollste Darstellungsmittel des bildenden Künstlers.

Der geduldige Leser, der mir bisher gefolgt ist, muss nun, um von den nachfolgenden ANALYSEN einigen Gewinn zu haben, diese NACHZEICHNEND, NACHSCHREIBEND, NACHSPRECHEND DURCHARBEITEN.

Er muß die FORM UMSETZEN IN BEWEGUNG

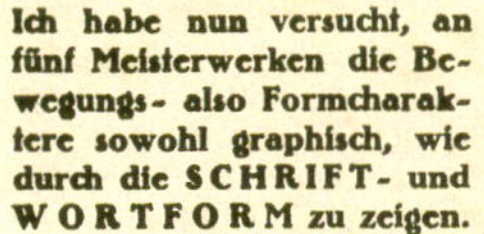

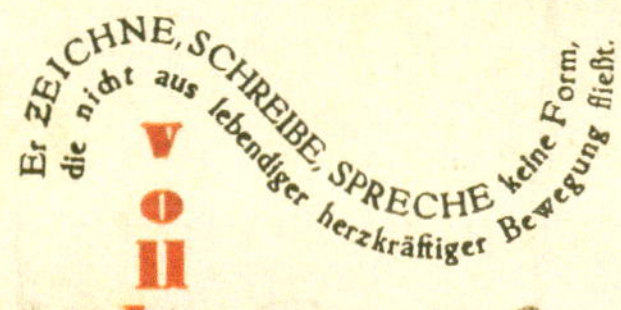

Er ZEICHNE, SCHREIBE, SPRECHE keine Form, die nicht aus lebendiger herzkräftiger Bewegung fließt.

MAN ZEICHNE OHNE DIE BEWEGUNG zu UNTERBRECHEN, ich möchte sagen, IN EINEM ATEMZUG EIN GANZES BILD NACH.

vollkomme

HinGABe ist notwendig.

VERSUCHE, IN ALLEN DREI GRADEN DER BEWEGTHEIT DAS BILD ZU ERLEBEN.

Zeichne DAS Bild auswendig

Lasse dich nicht entmutigen, wenn deine NACHZEICHNUNG dem ORIGINAL NICHT GANZ entspricht.

Je vollkommener DAS Bild IN DIR lebendig wird, umso vollkommener WIRD AUCH DEINE Wiedergabe, die ein EXAKTES Mass FÜR DIE Kraft deines Erlebens ist.

DAS Kunstwerk

es wird in Dir wiedergeboren.

László Moholy-Nagy (layout designer), exhibition catalog for *Weimar State Bauhaus 1919–1923* (*Staatliches Bauhaus in Weimar 1919–1923*), 1923, letterpress and lithograph, 9¾ × 10 inches (248 × 256 mm), Weimar and Munich.

New Typography, 1923

Hungarian artist László Moholy-Nagy replaced Itten in 1923, invigorating the advanced preliminary course with his constructivist ideas. He also took over the metal workshop, where his students included Marcel Breuer, Marianne Brandt, and Wilhelm Wagenfeld, creators of the school's most iconic objects of industrial design. ●

A self-taught artist, Moholy-Nagy drew images of wartime anguish while serving as an officer in World War I. Although he had studied law, he found respite in visual art and decided to become a painter. Traveling across eastern Germany to Berlin in 1920, he moved from town to town, earning meager sums as a letterer and sign painter. Along the way, he contracted Spanish influenza, a horrific disease that nearly killed him. In Berlin, Moholy-Nagy created abstract paintings, wrote about constructivist theory, and became a close friend of the German artist Kurt Schwitters. He was intrigued by Schwitters's Dada antics and complex collages as well as by his experimental typography. Moholy-Nagy's own path led not to the doubting voice of Dada, however, but to the optimism of constructivism, which seized on the new tools of industry as a means of both artistic and civic revolution. He wrote in 1922, "This is our century: technology, machine, Socialism."[5] ●

At the Bauhaus, Moholy-Nagy formed an intense relationship with Gropius. The eager young painter helped his sophisticated mentor reroute the school's expressionist energies into a constructivist philosophy and aesthetic. While Moholy-Nagy brought avant-garde ideas to the Bauhaus, he at first knew little about design or pedagogy. Gropius was a confident leader who gave Moholy-Nagy wide leeway in shaping a new future for the Bauhaus. ●

Graphic design was a crucial tool for building that future. An ambitious exhibition catalog accompanied the 1923 exhibition in Weimar, *Staatliches Bauhaus in Weimar 1919–1923* (see above and pages 100–103). Together, Gropius and Moholy-Nagy edited the book, which includes essays, manifestos, diagrams, and reproductions of paintings, sculptures, objects, buildings, models, and pedagogical exercises. (The catalog features scant examples of graphic design, which—although ultimately crucial to the school's legacy—had not yet emerged as a proper field of study at the Bauhaus.) Moholy-Nagy designed the book, which involved conveying his intended layouts and

5 On the life of László Moholy-Nagy, see Sibyl Moholy-Nagy, *Moholy-Nagy: Experiment in Totality* (Cambridge: MIT Press, 1950), quotation, 19.

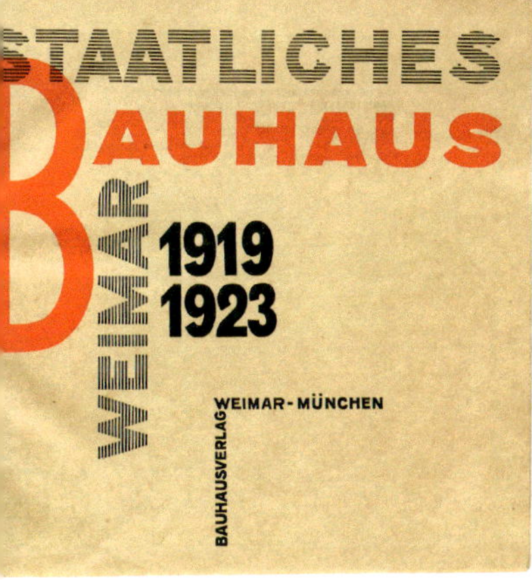

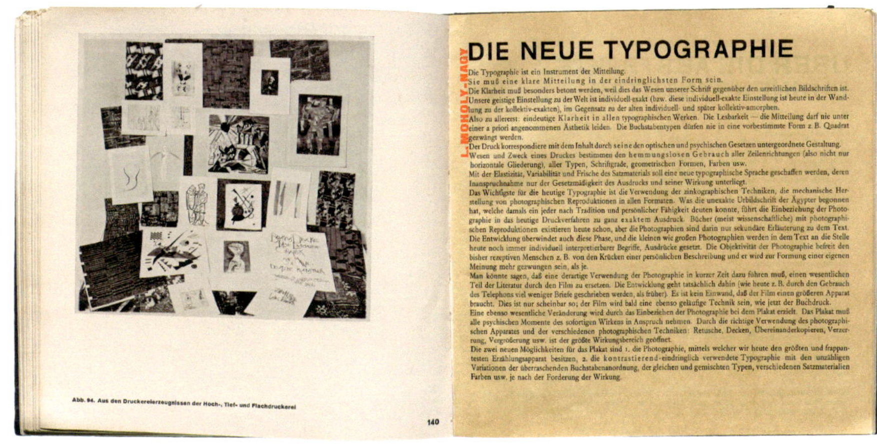

Abb. 94. Aus den Druckereierzeugnissen der Hoch-, Tief- und Flachdruckerei

140

L. MOHOLY-NAGY

DIE NEUE TYPOGRAPHIE

Die Typographie ist ein Instrument der Mitteilung.
Sie muß eine klare Mitteilung in der eindringlichsten Form sein.
Die Klarheit muß besonders betont werden, weil dies das Wesen unserer Schrift gegenüber den urzeitlichen Bildschriften ist.
Unsere geistige Einstellung zu der Welt ist individuell-exakt (bzw. diese individuell-exakte Einstellung ist heute in der Wandlung zu der kollektiv-exakten), im Gegensatz zu der alten individuell- und später kollektiv-amorphen.
Also zu allererst: eindeutige Klarheit in allen typographischen Werken. Die Lesbarkeit — die Mitteilung darf nie unter einer a priori angenommenen Ästhetik leiden. Die Buchstabentypen dürfen nie in eine vorbestimmte Form z. B. Quadrat gezwängt werden.
Der Druck korrespondiere mit dem Inhalt durch seine den optischen und psychischen Gesetzen untergeordnete Gestaltung.
Wesen und Zweck eines Druckes bestimmen den hemmungslosen Gebrauch aller Zeilenrichtungen (also nicht nur horizontale Gliederung), aller Typen, Schriftgrade, geometrischen Formen, Farben usw.
Mit der Elastizität, Variabilität und Frische des Satzmaterials soll eine neue typographische Sprache geschaffen werden, deren Inanspruchnahme nur der Gesetzmäßigkeit des Ausdrucks und seiner Wirkung unterliegt.
Das Wichtigste für die heutige Typographie ist die Verwendung der zinkographischen Techniken, die mechanische Herstellung von photographischen Reproduktionen in allen Formaten. Was die unexakte Urbildschrift der Ägypter begonnen hat, welche damals ein jeder nach Tradition und persönlicher Fähigkeit deuten konnte, führt die Einbeziehung der Photographie in das heutige Druckverfahren zu ganz exaktem Ausdruck. Bücher (meist wissenschaftliche) mit photographischen Reproduktionen existieren heute schon, aber die Photographien sind darin nur sekundäre Erläuterung zu dem Text. Die Entwicklung überwindet auch diese Phase, und die kleinen wie großen Photographien werden in dem Text an die Stelle heute noch immer individuell interpretierbarer Begriffe, Ausdrücke gesetzt. Die Objektivität der Photographie befreit den bisher rezeptiven Menschen z. B. von den Krücken einer persönlichen Beschreibung und er wird zur Formung einer eigenen Meinung mehr gezwungen sein, als je.
Man könnte sagen, daß eine derartige Verwendung der Photographie in kurzer Zeit dazu führen muß, einen wesentlichen Teil der Literatur durch den Film zu ersetzen. Die Entwicklung geht tatsächlich dahin (wie heute z. B. durch den Gebrauch des Telephons viel weniger Briefe geschrieben werden, als früher). Es ist kein Einwand, daß der Film einen größeren Apparat braucht. Dies ist nur scheinbar so; der Film wird bald eine ebenso geläufige Technik sein, wie jetzt der Buchdruck.
Eine ebenso wesentliche Veränderung wird durch das Einbeziehen der Photographie bei dem Plakat erzielt. Das Plakat muß alle psychischen Momente des sofortigen Wirkens in Anspruch nehmen. Durch die richtige Verwendung des photographischen Apparates und der verschiedenen photographischen Techniken: Retusche, Decken, Übereinanderkopieren, Verzerrung, Vergrößerung usw. ist der größte Wirkungsbereich geöffnet.
Die zwei neuen Möglichkeiten für das Plakat sind 1. die Photographie, mittels welcher wir heute den größten und frappantesten Erzählungsapparat besitzen, 2. die kontrastierend-eindringlich verwendete Typographie mit den unzähligen Variationen der überraschenden Buchstabenanordnung, der gleichen und gemischten Typen, verschiedenen Satzmaterialien Farben usw. je nach der Forderung der Wirkung.

type choices (Breite Grotesk and Venus) to the printer, who oversaw the details of the typesetting and printing. Knowing little about typography, Moholy-Nagy plunged in with naive gusto. Excessively wide text blocks fill the book's nearly square pages. Departing from convention, headlines and bylines meet at dynamic right angles—but they have little space to breathe. ●

Moholy-Nagy also designed a brand signet for Bauhausverlag, an independent publishing house responsible for creating portfolios of art prints for the Bauhaus as well as overseeing the 1923 catalog. The signet consists of an overlapping circle, square, and triangle, all rendered in different line weights, which together form an arrow pointing left (see top left on page 62). Bauhausverlag was supposed to publish the Bauhausbücher series, but the venture eventually went bankrupt, leaving the Bauhaus to work with a commercial publisher. ●

Moholy-Nagy knew that avant-garde artists—from Schwitters to El Lissitzky—were transforming the medium of print. Moholy-Nagy's own essay in that 1923 catalog, "The New Typography" ("Die neue Typographie"), is considered the first use of that now famous phrase. He wrote, "The new typography is a simultaneous experience of vision and communication." In his view, typography is functional. Typography is active and present, not passive and invisible. Lines of type can employ different angles, weights, and styles. Type and photography should be used together. Moholy-Nagy's readers included the young German typographer Jan Tschichold, who visited the 1923 Bauhaus exhibition and purchased the catalog—an experience that profoundly changed him.[6] ●

A manifesto is a call for action. It doesn't always spell out what work must be done or what it should look like. Beatriz Colomina writes in her pamphlet-sized book *Manifesto Architecture*, "The manifesto precedes the work. It is a blueprint for the future."[7] From Italian poet Filippo Tommaso Marinetti's 1909 declaration of futurism in a Paris newspaper to the self-published journals of Swiss architect Le Corbusier, manifestos spurred modernism into action. These founding avant-garde texts relied on printing and mass media to spread their messages. Moholy-Nagy wrote his own manifesto for the new typography without fully understanding what this new medium could become. ●

6 Paul Stirton, *Jan Tschichold and the New Typography: Graphic Design Between the World Wars* (New Haven: Yale University Press, 2019).

7 Beatriz Colomina, *Manifesto Architecture: The Ghost of Mies* (Berlin: Sternberg Press, 2014), unpaginated.

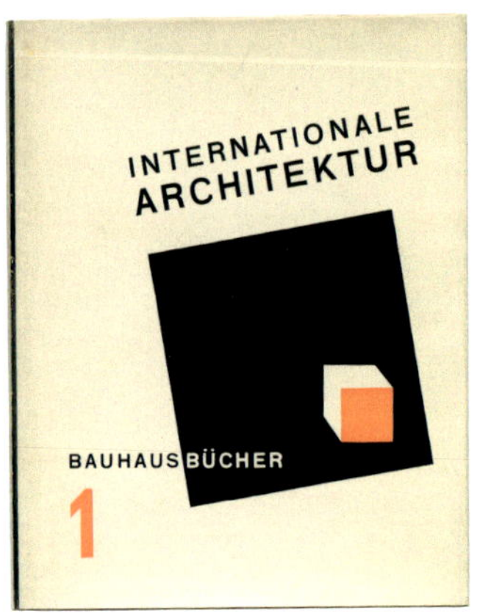

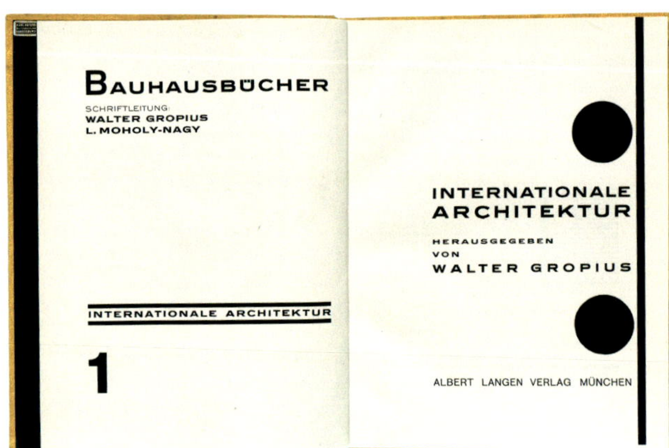

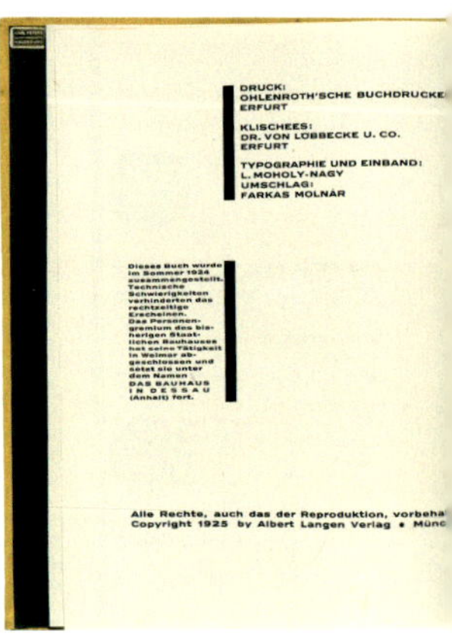

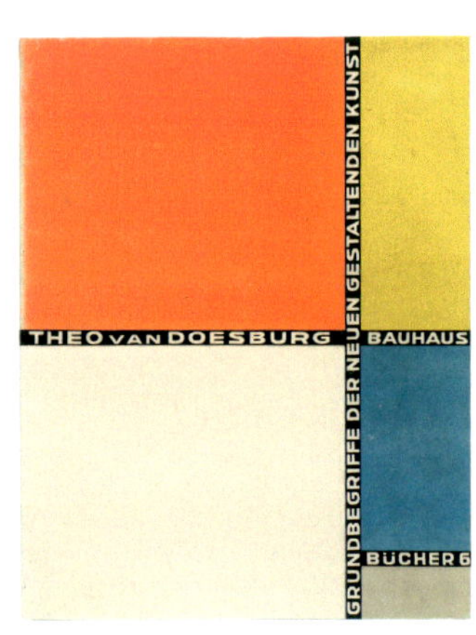

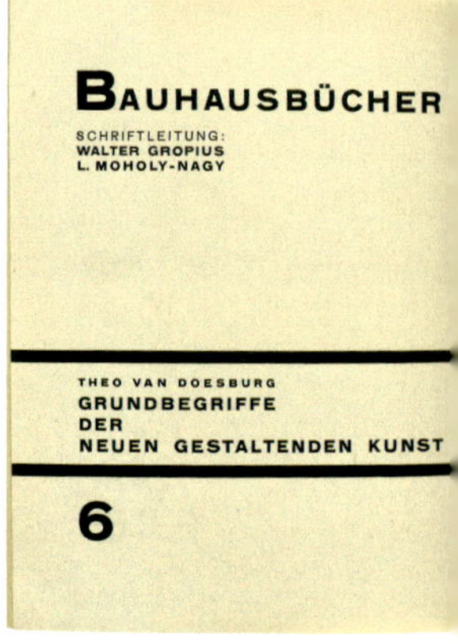

Theo van Doesburg (jacket designer/author), László Moholy-Nagy (layout designer), *Principles of Neo-Plastic Art* (*Grundbegriffe der neuen gestaltenden Kunst*), Bauhaus Book 6, 1925, letterpress, 9 × 7¼ inches (230 × 183 mm), Munich.

8

Handwerks abweichen, genau vertraut sein, wenn auch die Modellstücke mit der Hand ausgearbeitet werden. Denn aus der Eigenart der Maschine entwickelt sich die neue, eigene »Echtheit« und »Schönheit« ihrer Erzeugnisse, während die unlogische Imitation handwerklicher Produkte mittels der Maschine immer den Makel des Surrogats trägt.

Das Bauhaus vertritt die Ansicht, daß der Gegensatz zwischen Industrie und Handwerk weniger durch den Unterschied des Werkzeugs gekennzeichnet wird, als vielmehr durch die Arbeits**teilung** dort und die Arbeits**einheit** hier. Handwerk und Industrie sind aber in ständiger Annäherung begriffen. Das Handwerk der Vergangenheit hat sich verändert, das zukünftige Handwerk wird in einer neuen Werkeinheit aufgehen, in der es Träger der **Versuchsarbeit für die industrielle Produktion** sein wird. Spekulative Versuche in Laboratoriumswerkstätten werden für die produktive Durchführungsarbeit der Fabriken Modelle — Typen — schaffen.

●

Die in den Bauhauswerkstätten endgültig durchgearbeiteten Modelle werden in fremden Betrieben vervielfältigt, mit denen die Werkstätten in Arbeitsverbindung stehen.

Die Bauhausproduktion bedeutet also keine Konkurrenz für Industrie und Handwerk, sondern schafft vielmehr für diese einen neuen Aufbaufaktor. Denn das Bauhaus führt dem realen Werk- und Wirtschaftsleben schöpferisch begabte Menschen über die Praxis zu, die der Industrie und dem Handwerk Vorarbeit zur Produktion abnehmen sollen.

Die vervielfältigten Produkte nach Modellen des Bauhauses sollen ihre Preiswürdigkeit lediglich durch Ausnutzung aller modernen ökonomischen Mittel der Typisierung (Serienherstellung durch die Industrie) und durch den Umsatz erreichen. Der Gefahr einer Minderung der Güte der Produkte in Material und Ausführung gegenüber den Modellen durch die maschinelle Vervielfältigung wird mit allen Mitteln begegnet. **Das Bauhaus kämpft gegen Ersatz, minderwertige Arbeit und kunstgewerblichen Dilettantismus für eine neue Qualitätsarbeit.**

BAUHAUSWERKSTÄTTEN

TISCHLEREI
METALLWERKSTATT
WEBEREI
TÖPFEREI
HOLZ- U. STEINBILDHAUEREI
WANDMALEREI
GLASWERKSTATT
DRUCKEREI
REKLAMEABTEILUNG
BÜHNENWERKSTATT
ARCHITEKTURABTEILUNG

Dieser Band enthält Abbildungen von den Erzeugnissen der ersten vier Werkstätten

László Moholy-Nagy (layout designer), *New Works from Bauhaus Workshops* (*Neue Arbeiten der Bauhauswerkstätten*), Bauhaus Book 7, 1925, letterpress, 9¼ × 7¼ inches (235 × 183 mm), Munich.

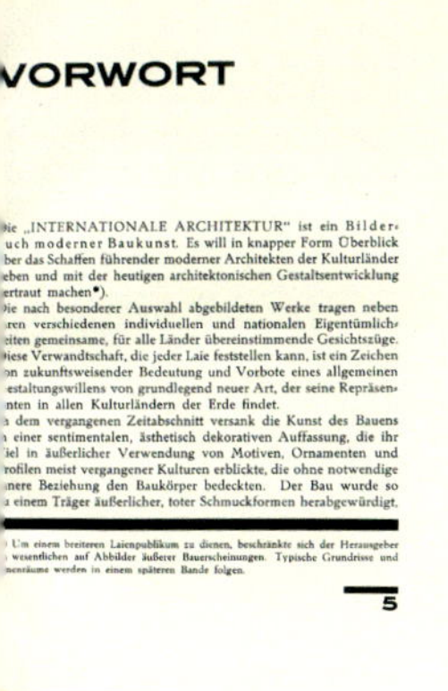

VORWORT

ie „INTERNATIONALE ARCHITEKTUR" ist ein Bilder-
uch moderner Baukunst. Es will in knapper Form Überblick
ber das Schaffen führender moderner Architekten der Kulturländer
eben und mit der heutigen architektonischen Gestaltsentwicklung
ertraut machen*).
ie nach besonderer Auswahl abgebildeten Werke tragen neben
ren verschiedenen individuellen und nationalen Eigentümlich-
eiten gemeinsame, für alle Länder übereinstimmende Gesichtszüge.
iese Verwandtschaft, die jeder Laie feststellen kann, ist ein Zeichen
on zukunftsweisender Bedeutung und Vorbote eines allgemeinen
estaltungswillens von grundlegend neuer Art, der seine Repräsen-
nten in allen Kulturländern der Erde findet.
dem vergangenen Zeitabschnitt versank die Kunst des Bauens
einer sentimentalen, ästhetisch dekorativen Auffassung, die ihr
iel in äußerlicher Verwendung von Motiven, Ornamenten und
rofilen meist vergangener Kulturen erblickte, die ohne notwendige
nere Beziehung den Baukörper bedeckten. Der Bau wurde so
einem Träger äußerlicher, toter Schmuckformen herabgewürdigt.

Um einem breiteren Laienpublikum zu dienen, beschränkte sich der Herausgeber
wesentlichen auf Abbilder äußerer Bauerscheinungen. Typische Grundrisse und
nenräume werden in einem späteren Bande folgen.

5

Farkas Molnár (jacket designer), László Moholy-Nagy (layout designer), *International Architecture* (*Internationale Architektur*), Bauhaus Book 1, 1925, letterpress, 9½ × 7⅜ inches (240 × 187 mm), Munich.

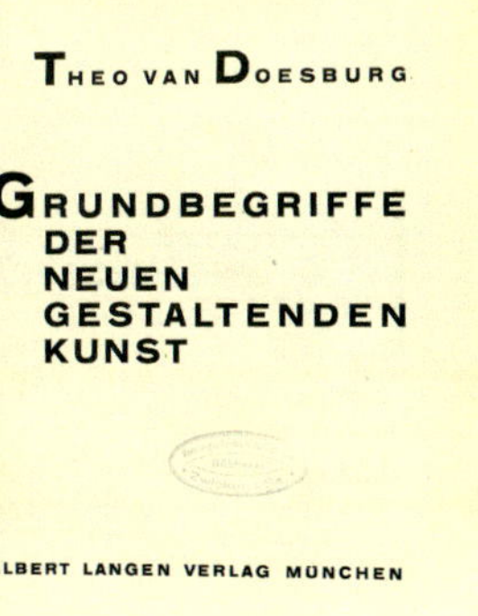

Bauhausbücher

How should the new typography look, feel, and speak? The answer became clearer as Moholy-Nagy tackled more projects. The most ambitious of all was the Bauhausbücher (Bauhaus Books) series. Moholy-Nagy designed the branding, the format, and nearly all the covers and interiors of these legendary volumes. He also coedited the series with Gropius. The first eight Bauhaus Books appeared at once in 1925, followed by six more between 1926 and 1930. Printed and distributed by Albert Langen Verlag in Munich, the Bauhaus Books were modestly produced in hardcover and paperback editions. They were intended to be used, not collected as rarefied objects.[8] ●

As a series, the Bauhausbücher offer an encyclopedic education in avant-garde theory and practice. Authored by contemporary artists from inside and outside the Bauhaus, the series emphasizes ideas over lavish reproductions. The books cover a wide range of disciplines, from painting, architecture, and theater to design and pedagogy. They were written in the voices of creators and first-person observers, not distant acolytes. In the words of Sibyl Moholy-Nagy (an architecture historian and László's wife from 1935 until his death in 1946), "Pictorial material, theoretical content, and typographical form were documents of a new, unified, visual education [. . .] Their texts served to annihilate the beaux-arts spirit."[9] ●

The Bauhausbücher advanced the school's image as an intellectual authority on contemporary theory and practice. Moholy-Nagy received credit on the copyright page for the books' *typographie* (design) and for their *einband* (cover) and often the *umshlagentwurf* (jacket), the latter of which were sometimes designed by the books' authors. The page designs feature boldface sans serif typography for the titles and headings; most of the volumes employ more traditional book faces for the body copy. Moholy-Nagy experimented with heavy black rules, giving them different roles from book to book: underscore, overscore, sidescore. (Herbert Bayer designed Bauhausbücher 9, whose lighter, more open pages make lesser use of rules.) Moholy-Nagy didn't have much choice regarding typefaces, but he was skilled at working with what was available. These included oldstyle serifs like Alt-Medieval and sans serifs like Breite Fette Grotesk. The books hold together as a series not because of a consistent typographic system but because of their distinctive, compact format and their sense of typographic play and experiment. ●

8 See Adrian Sudhalter, "Walter Gropius and László Moholy-Nagy: Bauhaus Book Series, 1925–30," in *Bauhaus 1919–1933: Workshops for Modernity*, ed. Barry Bergdoll and Leah Dickerman (New York: Museum of Modern Art, 2009). These books can be downloaded for free (in German) at http://www.openculture.com/2015/10/download-original-bauhaus-books-journals-for-free.html.

9 *Experiment in Totality*, 37–38.

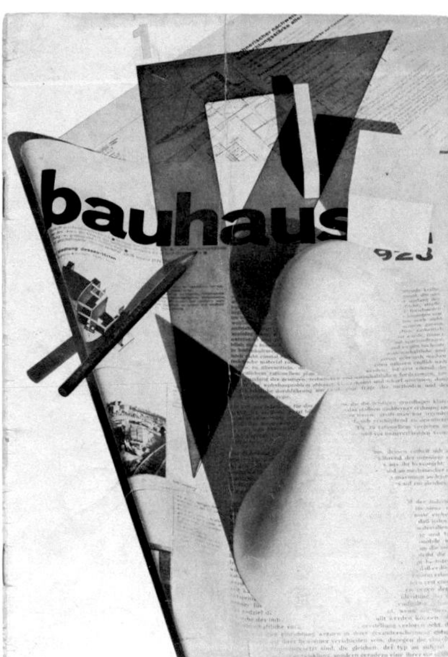

LEFT
Herbert Bayer (designer/editor), *bauhaus: magazine for design* (*bauhaus: zeitschrift für gestaltung*), vol. 2, no. 1, 1928, letterpress, 11¾ × 8¼ inches (296 × 210 mm), Dessau.

RIGHT
Herbert Bayer, letterhead for the Bauhaus Dessau (as featured in Jan Tschichold, *The New Typography*), 1925, letterpress, 11⅝ × 8¼ inches (294 × 210 mm), Dessau.

Dessau Printshop

In 1925, the Bauhaus moved from Weimar to Dessau, a city near Berlin. The school's new building, sheathed in a gridded glass skin, opened in 1926 and was designed by Walter Gropius and financed by the city government. ●

Herbert Bayer, who attended the Bauhaus as a student from 1921 to 1923, returned to the school in 1925 as a young master. In Weimar, he had discovered his interest in graphic design, a discipline not formally recognized in those early years. Gropius liked Bayer and encouraged him to explore graphic design on his own.[10] When he returned to the Bauhaus, this time in Dessau, Bayer joined the faculty and established a new printing workshop. Housed in the basement printshop was metal type for setting text and a platen press and rotary press for printing.[11] This working printshop helped broadcast the theories, activities, and products of the Bauhaus. Bayer designed letterheads, catalogs, party invitations, and posters for lectures and exhibitions. The workshop also did jobs for local clients. The students learned by doing. They worked in the shop alongside Bayer, who preferred hands-on production over theoretical exercises. ●

Bayer's product catalogs mirrored the functional, geometric forms of the lamps, chairs, teapots, and other goods designed at the school. His letterheads were especially innovative (see right). Interspersed across the page, lines of type divided the white space into zones for typing. Occupying the bottom of each letterhead is a manifesto proclaiming the need to abolish capital letters. Bayer denounced uppercase characters as redundant, inefficient, and archaic. For Bayer and other progressive designers in the 1920s, business stationery was a crucial component of standardized communication. A well-designed letterhead showed commitment to standards in

10 Gwen F. Chanzit, *From Bauhaus to Aspen: Herbert Bayer and Modernist Design in America* (Boulder, CO: Johnson Books, 1987).
11 Michael Siebenbrodt and Lutz Schöbe, *Bauhaus: 1919–1933, Weimar-Dessau-Berlin* (New York: Parkstone International, 2012).

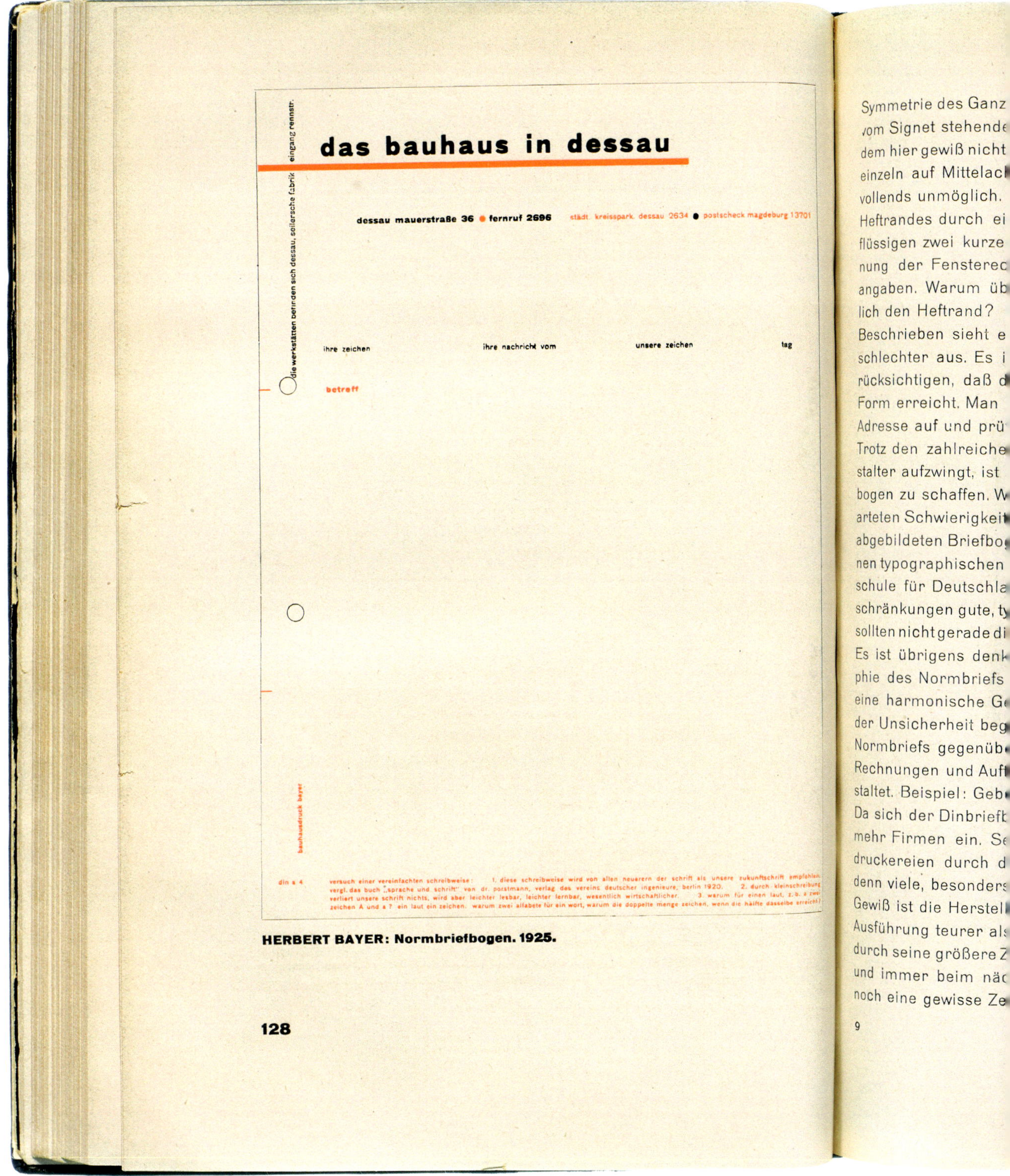

die werkstätten befinden sich dessau, seilersche fabrik eingang rennstr.

das bauhaus in dessau

dessau mauerstraße 36 ● fernruf 2696 städt. kreisspark. dessau 2634 ● postscheck magdeburg 13701

ihre zeichen ihre nachricht vom unsere zeichen tag

betreff

bauhausdruck bayer

din a 4 versuch einer vereinfachten schreibweise: 1. diese schreibweise wird von allen neuerern der schrift als unsere zukunftschrift empfohlen. vergl. das buch „sprache und schrift" von dr. porstmann, verlag des vereins deutscher ingenieure, berlin 1920. 2. durch kleinschreibung verliert unsere schrift nichts, wird aber leichter lesbar, leichter lernbar, wesentlich wirtschaftlicher. 3. warum für einen laut, z. b. a zwei zeichen A und a? ein laut ein zeichen. warum zwei alfabete für ein wort, warum die doppelte menge zeichen, wenn die hälfte dasselbe erreicht?

HERBERT BAYER: Normbriefbogen. 1925.

128

Symmetrie des Ganz
vom Signet stehende
dem hier gewiß nicht
einzeln auf Mittelac
vollends unmöglich.
Heftrandes durch ei
flüssigen zwei kurze
nung der Fensterec
angaben. Warum üb
lich den Heftrand?
Beschrieben sieht e
schlechter aus. Es i
rücksichtigen, daß d
Form erreicht. Man
Adresse auf und prü
Trotz den zahlreiche
stalter aufzwingt, ist
bogen zu schaffen. W
arteten Schwierigkeit
abgebildeten Briefbo
nen typographischen
schule für Deutschla
schränkungen gute, t
sollten nicht gerade di
Es ist übrigens denk
phie des Normbriefs
eine harmonische G
der Unsicherheit beg
Normbriefs gegenüb
Rechnungen und Auf
staltet. Beispiel: Geb
Da sich der Dinbrieft
mehr Firmen ein. Se
druckereien durch d
denn viele, besonders
Gewiß ist die Herstel
Ausführung teurer als
durch seine größere Z
und immer beim näc
noch eine gewisse Ze

9

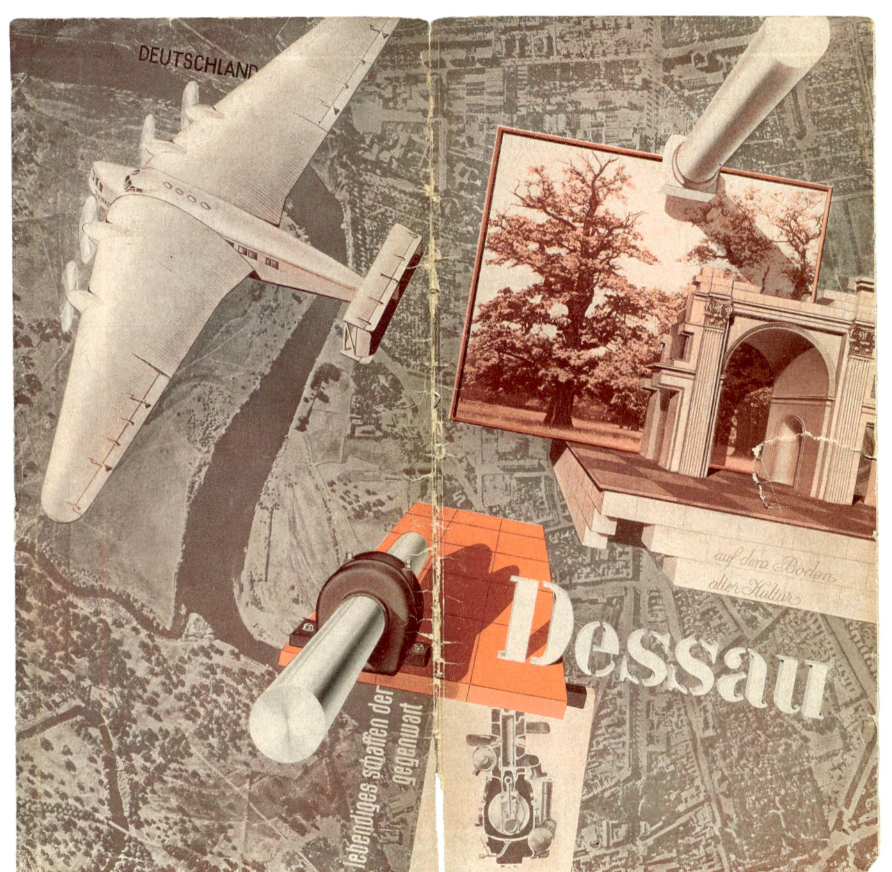
DEUTSCHLAND
auf dem Boden alter Kultur
Dessau
lebendiges schaffen der gegenwart

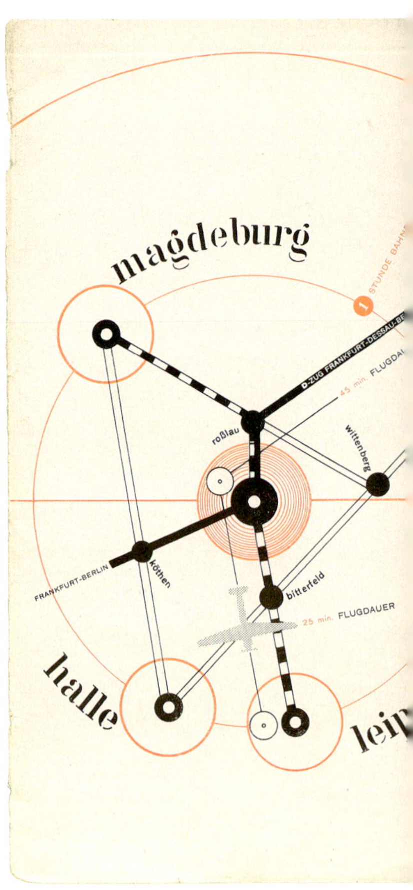
magdeburg
halle
roßlau
wittenberg
köthen
bitterfeld
FRANKFURT-BERLIN
D-ZUG FRANKFURT-DESSAU-BE
45 min. FLUGDAU
25 min. FLUGDAUER

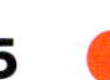

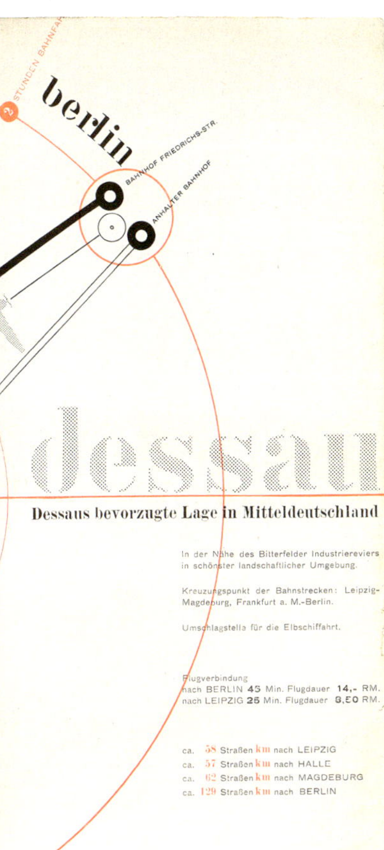

Joost Schmidt, tourist brochure for the city of Dessau, 1931, letterpress, 9½ × 4⅞ inches (241 × 122 mm) folded, 9½ × 9¾ inches (241 × 244 mm) unfolded, Dessau.

design and manufacturing that were affecting everything from household goods to urban plans. Bayer became friends with Jan Tschichold, who featured one of Bayer's Bauhaus letterheads (see page 23) in his 1928 book *The New Typography*, whose title echoes Moholy-Nagy's 1923 essay by the same name. ●

Also teaching in the Dessau printshop was Joost Schmidt, a German artist who joined the sculpture workshop as a student in Weimar. Schmidt designed playful typographic advertisements and promotional pieces for prominent office supply company YKO in 1924, as well as extraordinary posters and ephemera for the Bauhaus. In Dessau, he became a young master in the plastic arts workshop (formerly the sculpture workshop). He began teaching a mandatory two-semester course called Typefaces and Lettering in 1925, which he transformed into a more conceptual and comprehensive course in elementary design. Inspired by the philosophically rich preliminary course curricula developed by Josef Albers, Paul Klee, and Wassily Kandinsky, Schmidt devised pedagogical exercises similar to those assigned in many design programs today, such as creating multiple interpretations of a single letterform, arranged in a nine-square grid. ●

Schmidt became director of the printing workshop when Bayer left in 1928, and he stayed until the Dessau campus closed in 1932. His 1931 brochure for the city of Dessau (see left and page 209) features experiments with photomontage and information graphics, depicting the city as a growing economic hub central to the German economy, as well as Didone-style lettering applied via metal stencil plates common in French and German architectural drafting of the period. Schmidt's kindness and commitment made him well-liked by students. His elementary design course was both analytical and expressive, building on Bauhaus ideals that stretched back to Itten. Expanding on an abstract geometric language, he sought to combine intellectual study with personal feeling and freedom from historical conventions. He deplored traditional and decorative typefaces as the "junkyard of culture."[12] ●

12 For a detailed account of Schmidt's teaching, see *Teaching at the Bauhaus*.

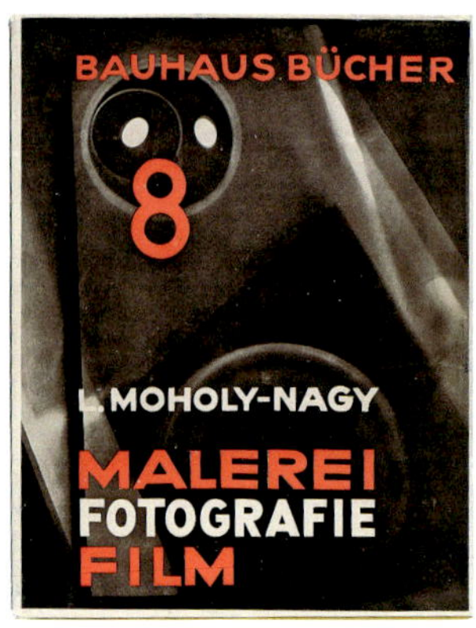
BAUHAUSBÜCHER
8
L. MOHOLY-NAGY
MALEREI
FOTOGRAFIE
FILM

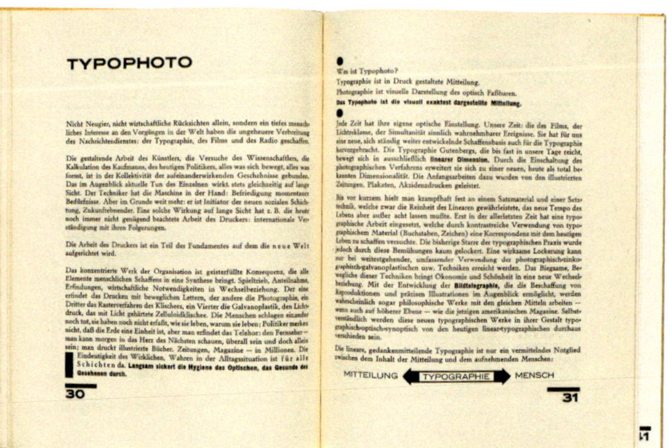
TYPOPHOTO
MITTEILUNG
TYPOGRAPHIE
MENSCH
30
31

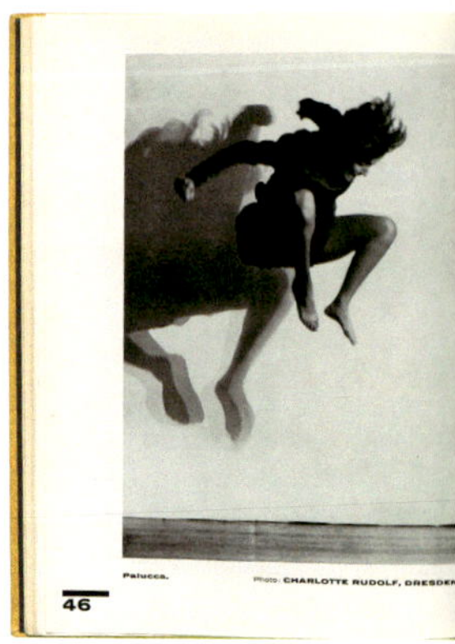
46

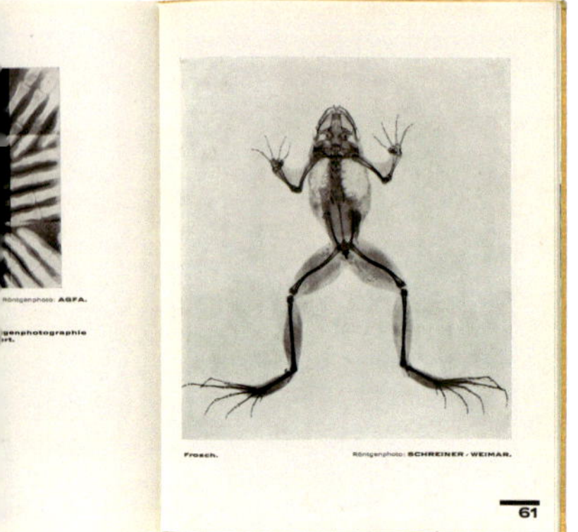
61

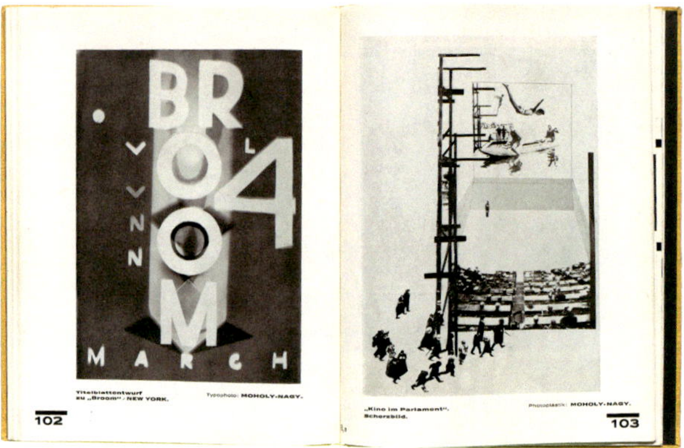
BROOM
MARCH
102
103

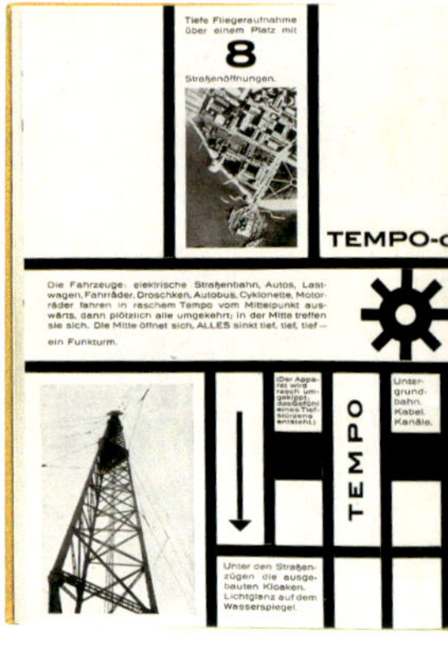
8
TEMPO-O
TEMPO

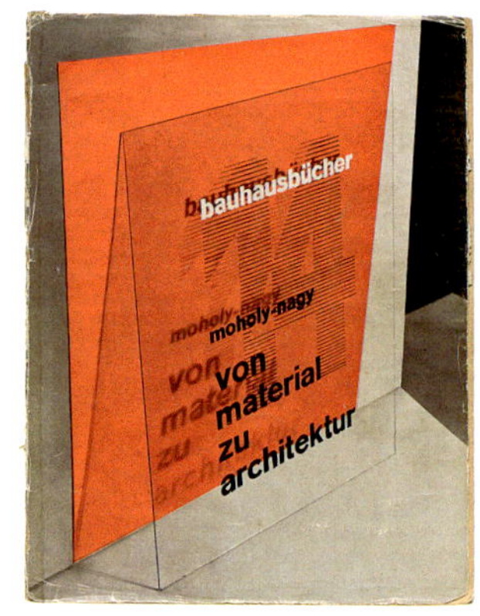
bauhausbücher
moholy-nagy
von
material
zu
architektur

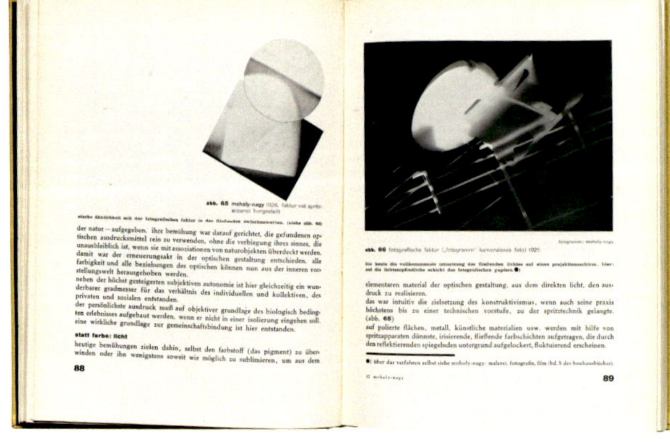
88
89

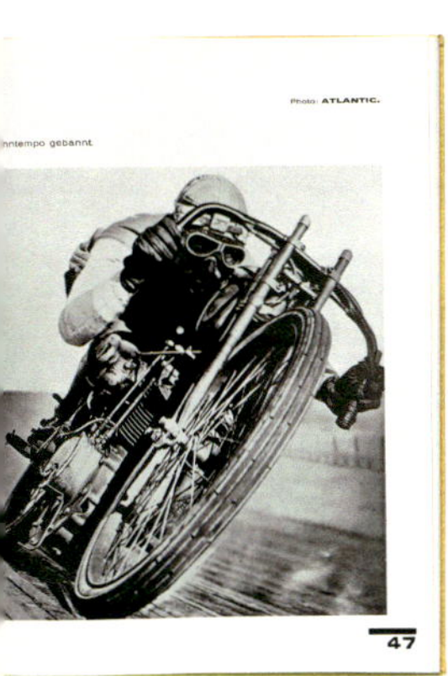

László Moholy-Nagy (designer/coauthor), Lucia Moholy (uncredited coauthor), *Painting, Photography, Film* (*Malerei, Fotografie, Film*), Bauhaus Book 8, 1925, letterpress, 9¼ × 7½ inches (235 × 188 mm), Munich.

Typophoto

Two of the most influential titles in the Bauhausbücher series were authored by Moholy-Nagy: *Painting, Photography, Film* (*Malerei, Fotografie, Film*, 1925) and *From Material to Architecture* (*Von Material zu Architektur*, 1929), published in English as *The New Vision* (1947). In these volumes, the medium of photography is a throughline uniting art, design, and modern life. ●

A photogram, or cameraless photograph, appears on the cover of *Painting, Photography, Film* (see top left). Invented by English scientist William Fox Talbot in the nineteenth century, this technique was expanded on by Moholy-Nagy and Lucia Moholy, a gifted photographer whose portraits, product shots, and architectural views are the visual bedrock of the Bauhaus legacy. Gropius took possession of Moholy's negatives when he left the school and continued to use them for over a decade to promote the Bauhaus without crediting her. According to Elizabeth Otto and Patrick Rössler, László and Lucia wrote *Painting, Photography, Film* together, but László took sole credit as the author. ●

Before she met László in 1920, Lucia worked as an editor in the publishing industry and began creating photography. The couple married in 1921. During the Weimar years, Lucia studied with a commercial photographer and later completed courses focused on photography and print production at the Leipzig Academy for Graphic and Book Arts. Her overall knowledge of the publishing business surely helped the Bauhausbücher series succeed. Her deep creative and technical command of photography drive the content of *Painting, Photography, Film*.[13] ●

A photogram reduces photography to an elemental process: capturing light on a surface. Several photograms in *Painting, Photography, Film* include letterforms. The book defines the photogram as a form of "production"—generating a new experience directly through the means or apparatus of making—as opposed to the mere "reproduction" of existing sensations. For Moholy-Nagy and Moholy, production was a process of rebuilding the human organism. New technologies such as the gramophone, talking films, television, and X-rays were extending the biological senses into new realms, fundamentally changing human life. ●

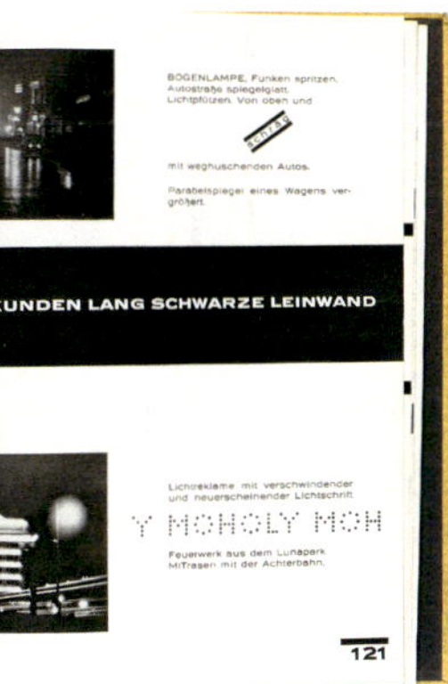

László Moholy-Nagy (designer/author), *From Material to Architecture* (*Von Material zu Architektur*), Bauhaus Book 14, 1929, letterpress, 9¼ × 7⅜ inches (236 × 185 mm), Munich.

In the 1920s, photography was similarly remaking the tools of mass communication while expanding the capacities of the human eye. The essays in *Painting, Photography, Film* are followed by a portfolio of full-page images, including posters and montages credited to Moholy-Nagy as well as press photos and scientific images showing photography's broad reach. The book demanded that photography do more than re-create romantic, painterly views of nature. This modern medium could reveal the unseen, exposing the interior of a frog or capturing the light trails of cars and trains passing at night.[14] ●

13 Elizabeth Otto and Patrick Rössler, *Bauhaus Women: A Global Perspective* (London: Herbert Press, 2019).

14 All quotes from the English edition, László Moholy-Nagy, *Painting, Photography, Film* (London: Lund Humphries, 1969).

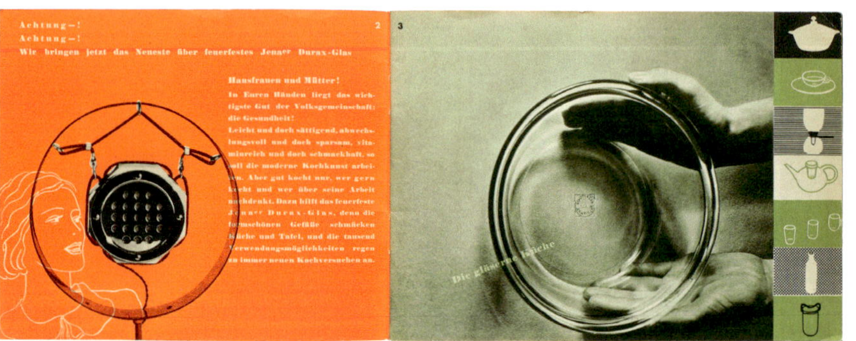

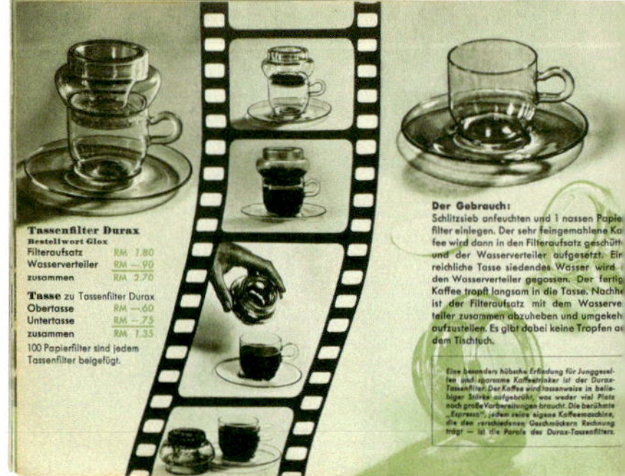

"Typophoto" is the main essay about typography in *Painting, Photography, Film*. This essay demands that the new typography do more than break up the linear composition of text. Type must merge with photography in order to bring a new age of objectivity to mass media. A book or magazine—once constrained by the cultural barriers of language—could now be cleansed and opened up by the objective light of photography. Class distinctions would fall away as the truth of the everyday revealed itself equally to all: "The hygiene of the optical, the health of the visible is slowly filtering through." Photography should be used as typographical material, appearing side-by-side with words or replacing words altogether in the form of phototext—"a precise form of representation so objective as to permit of no individual interpretation." ●

On the cover of *From Material to Architecture*, type and photo converge in a single image (see bottom left on page 26). The book's title has been painted on a sheet of glass and then photographed in a still-life setup to become the cover of the book. (The rectangle of orange ink was probably added in the printing process.) The sheet of glass reveals itself to be both transparent and reflective, absent and present. The letterforms cast their own shadow, modeling the photographic medium. Always fascinated by light, shadow, and transparency, Moholy-Nagy explored shadow typography in several works, from photograms, posters, and book jackets to dimensional exhibition signage. ●

In *Painting, Photography, Film*, Moholy-Nagy wrote, "The future of typographic methods lies with the photomechanical process." He was right. The rapidly growing medium of offset lithography (tracked in contemporary trade magazines such as *Offset*; see pages 200–205) allowed type and image to mix more easily than they did in traditional letterpress printing. ●

Moholy-Nagy explored the fluid dance of type and image in the commercial work he produced after leaving the Bauhaus in 1928. His studio's brochure for Jena Glass is a cinematic product guide built from layers of type and image. Celebrating the materiality and potential transparency of type, image, and glass, it explored diverse effects (such as printing a photograph in green ink behind the product description) and narrative devices (simulating a filmstrip of the product in use). Throughout this brochure, words, illustrations, diagrams, and photographs annotate each other in a manner that is more educational and explanatory than experimental and abstract. On these pages, Bauhaus theories joined up with practice. ●

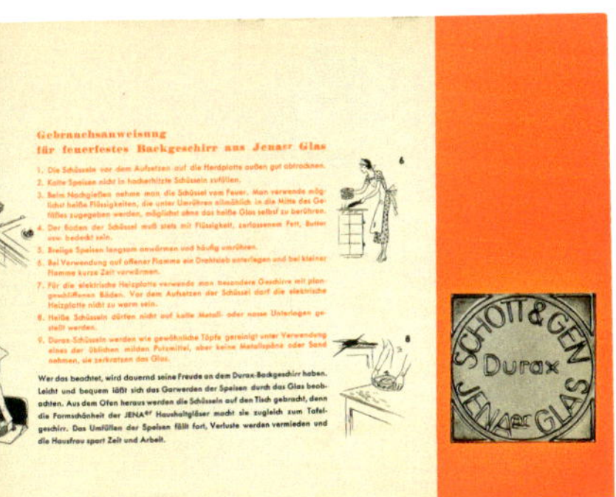

Gebrauchsanweisung
für feuerfestes Backgeschirr aus Jenaer Glas

1. Die Schüsseln vor dem Aufsetzen auf die Herdplatte außen gut abtrocknen.
2. Kalte Speisen nicht in hocherhitzte Schüsseln zufüllen.
3. Beim Nachgießen nehme man die Schüssel vom Feuer. Man verwende möglichst heiße Flüssigkeiten, die unter Umrühren allmählich in die Mitte des Gefäßes zugegeben werden, möglichst ohne das heiße Glas selbst zu berühren.
4. Der Boden der Schüssel muß stets mit Flüssigkeit, zerlassenem Fett, Butter usw. bedeckt sein.
5. Breiige Speisen langsam anwärmen und häufig umrühren.
6. Bei Verwendung auf offener Flamme ein Drahtsieb unterlegen und bei kleiner Flamme kurze Zeit verwärmen.
7. Für die elektrische Heizplatte verwende man besondere Geschirre mit plangeschliffenen Böden. Vor dem Aufsetzen der Schüssel darf die elektrische Heizplatte nicht zu warm sein.
8. Heiße Schüsseln dürfen nicht auf kalte Metall- oder nasse Unterlagen gestellt werden.
9. Durax-Schüsseln werden wie gewöhnliche Töpfe gereinigt unter Verwendung eines der üblichen milden Putzmittel, aber keine Metallspäne oder Sand nehmen, sie zerkratzen das Glas.

Wer das beachtet, wird dauernd seine Freude an dem Durax-Backgeschirr haben. Leicht und bequem läßt sich das Garwerden der Speisen durch das Glas beobachten. Aus dem Ofen heraus werden die Schüsseln auf den Tisch gebracht, denn die Formschönheit der JENAer Haushaltgläser macht sie zugleich zum Tafelgeschirr. Das Umfüllen der Speisen fällt fort, Verluste werden vermieden und die Hausfrau spart Zeit und Arbeit.

Studio of László Moholy-Nagy, product catalog for Jena Glass, circa 1934, letterpress, 5⅞ × 8¼ inches (148 × 210 mm), Leipzig and Berlin.

Beyond Bauhaus Typography

The Bauhaus was a porous place. It admitted—and sent forth—a wide range of people and ideas. Bauhaus theories borrowed and amplified ideas from multiple avant-garde movements, from Theo van Doesburg's de Stijl to El Lissitzky's constructivism. Swiss designer Max Bill studied there briefly in 1928; he went on to run his own school in Ulm, Germany, where he designed products and graphics that pushed past the Bauhaus while still reflecting the school's light. Piet Zwart was offered a teaching position at the Bauhaus in 1929 but ended up coming only for a short visit.[15] His work had already absorbed—and surpassed—Bauhaus design principles. ●

The Bauhaus remains today an open idea and a contested myth. Some designers working in the 1920s thought the Bauhaus was arrogant and self-important.[16] In Germany in the 1920s and '30s, the egalitarian universalism of the Bauhaus was attacked by nationalists hawking their poisoned promises of racial purity. Even before the Bauhaus was closed by the Nazis in 1933, it had become a flattened icon for functional design, and yet the school's strongest educators—from Itten, Klee, and Kandinsky to Moholy-Nagy, Albers, and Schmidt—pursued humanistic, even spiritual, paths through their teaching. Moholy-Nagy left, in part, because he thought the school was becoming too focused on practical concerns. Later, postmodernists poked fun at its repression of history and ornament, as well as its ideological fervor.[17] ●

Today, the Bauhaus faces new tests of purity. The modernist legacy is Eurocentric, patriarchal, and exclusionary. Although some design educators say, "It's time to throw the Bauhaus under the bus," others keep finding new ideas in the school's layered history.[18] The people who lived, worked, wrote, and taught within the Bauhaus's glowing orb of influence struggled with the conflicts and possibilities of their time. They looked boldly forward—and also sideways—at the dangerous present. They left behind their own trails of light and shadow—traces to be read, interpreted, and questioned. ●

15 Bruno Monguzzi provides a detailed biography of Piet Zwart in *Piet Zwart: The Typographical Work*, trans. Sharon Krengel (Milan: Rassegna, 1979).

16 The remembrances collected in Eckard Neumann's book *Bauhaus and Bauhaus People* (New York: Van Nostrand Reinhold, 1993) reflect on the Bauhaus myth with both love and skepticism. In *Jan Tschichold and the New Typography*, Paul Stirton recounts how annoyed members of the Ring (a group of artists working in advertising, led by Kurt Schwitters) were by the Bauhaus's chilly response to an invitation to exhibit with them.

17 Tom Wolfe, *From Bauhaus to Our House* (New York: Farrar, Straus & Giroux, 1981).

18 Designers and educators Silas Munro and Ramon Tejada conducted the workshop "It's Time to Throw the Bauhaus Under the Bus" at Otis College of Art and Design in 2019.

BAUHAUS TIMELINE

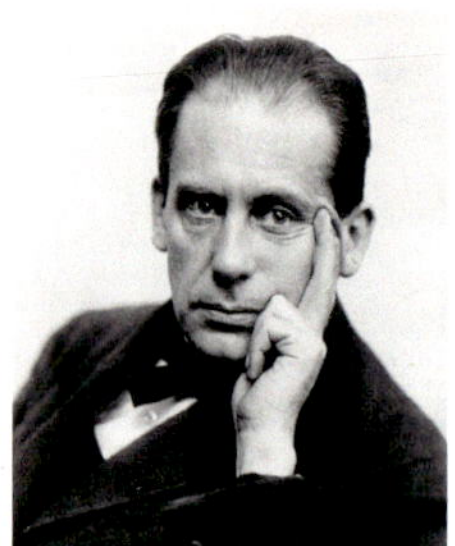

Walter Gropius

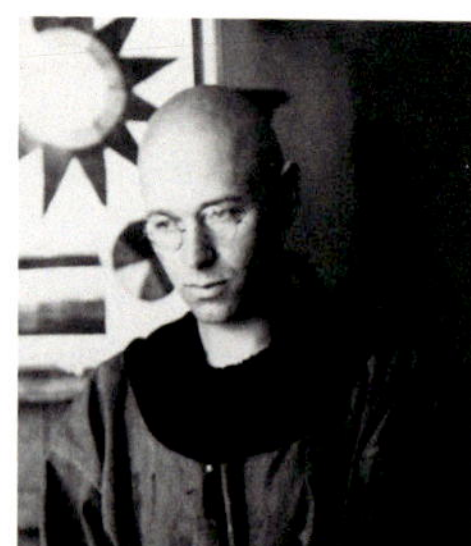

Johannes Itten
Courtesy of Bauhaus-Archiv Berlin

German architect Walter Gropius founds the Staatliches (State) Bauhaus in Weimar. Established as an egalitarian utopia during the liberal upswell in Germany after World War I, the school seeks to revive nineteenth-century ideas about craft using the tools of modern mass production. More than 160 students enroll the first semester.

Gropius recruits American Lyonel Feininger, German Gerhard Marcks, and Swiss Johannes Itten to become the first Bauhaus masters. He also hires German music educator Gertrud Grunow, who was the first—and remains the only—woman to teach at the Bauhaus Weimar.

Itten develops the Bauhaus's preliminary course, a revolutionary approach to foundational visual studies that explores line, shape, and color in the expression of formal and spiritual ideas.

Feininger creates *Cathedral*, the woodcut on the cover of Gropius's Bauhaus manifesto, as an emblem of *Gesamtkunstwerk*, the unification of craft and fine art into a "total work of art."

1919

Swiss-born painter Paul Klee comes to teach at the Bauhaus. He stays for more than a decade, bringing abstract geometry and expressive style.

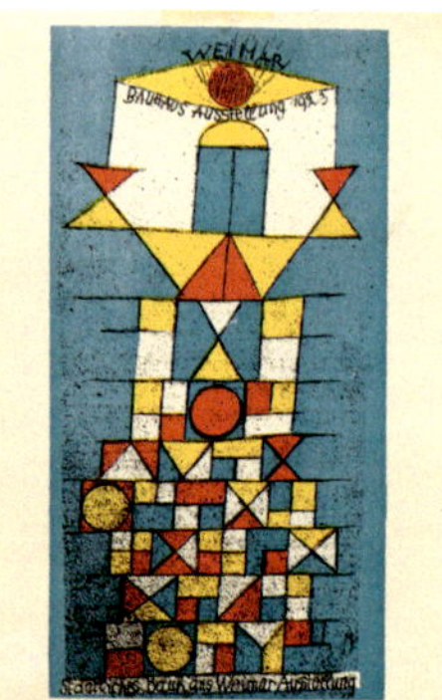

Postcard by Paul Klee

1920

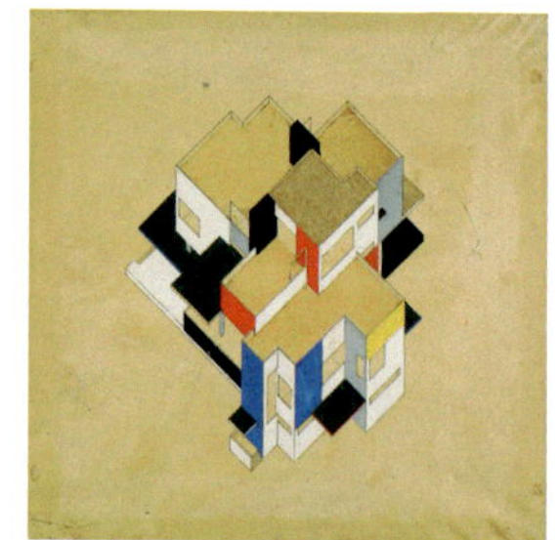

Rendering by Theo van Doesburg

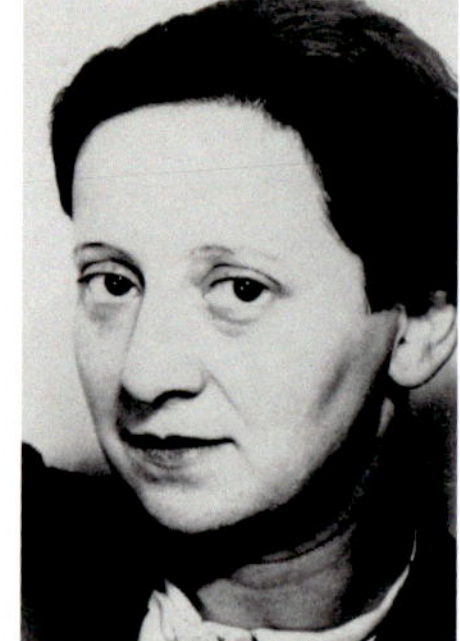

Friedl Dicker

De Stijl cofounder Theo van Doesburg moves to Weimar. While he did not teach at the Bauhaus, he did much to introduce objectivity, industrial production, and the use of a limited visual palette to the lexicon of local artists and students.

Austrian artist and Bauhaus student Friedl Dicker typesets a section of an essay by Itten in *Utopia*. It is a feat in experimental letterpress, showcasing cantilevered, undulating, and otherwise expressively set text.

Designer and artist El Lissitzky arrives in Germany, introducing Russian constructivism to future Bauhaus instructor László Moholy-Nagy. He serves as the Russian cultural ambassador to Weimar for two years.

Adolf Hitler becomes chairman of the National Socialist Party, a far-right, nationalist political party with racist and xenophobic views. As a result of post-WWI reparations, the value of German currency begins to plummet.

1921

LOCATION: WEIMAR

DIRECTOR: WALTER GROPIUS

1922

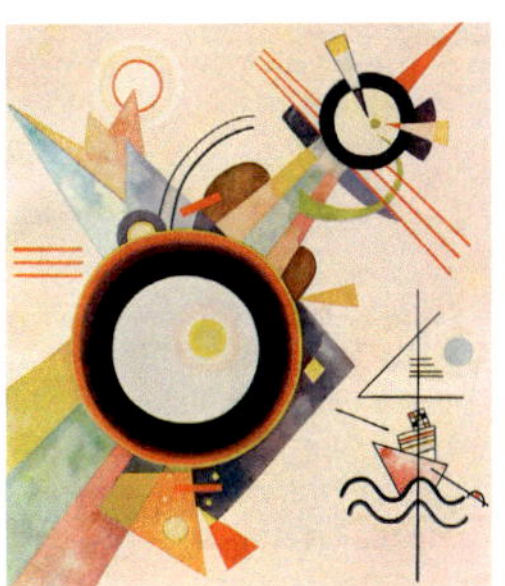

Painting by Wassily Kandinsky

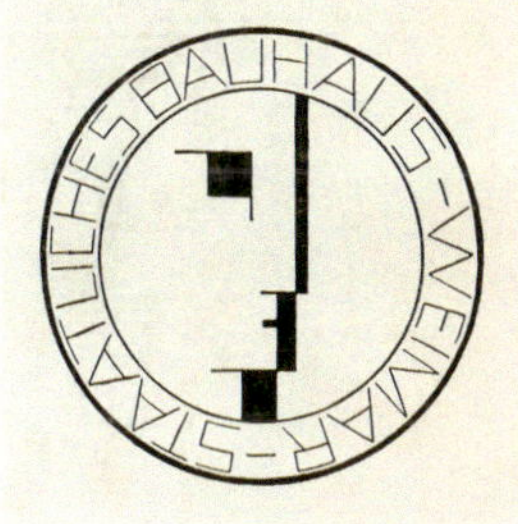

Bauhaus logo by Oskar Schlemmer

Famed Russian painter Wassily Kandinsky joins the faculty. His quest to forge color, form, sound, and motion into a spiritual ideal influenced the Bauhaus's early mysticism. German theatrician Lothar Schreyer also comes to establish a stage workshop.

Itten resigns, ostensibly over resistance to Gropius's aim of creating products but also in no small part due to his own belief in Mazdaznan, an ascetic religion associated with eugenics and white supremacy. With his departure, the school's focus shifts from the expressionistic and metaphysical to the utilitarian and replicable. Grunow, a fellow esoteric, leaves shortly after.

German artist Oskar Schlemmer—a newly appointed master of mural painting—reprises an earlier graphic to make the Bauhaus logo: a face reduced to geometric shapes in black and white.

To raise money, the Bauhaus issues the first of five planned print portfolios, *Bauhaus Prints, New European Graphics* (*Bauhaus-Drucke, neue europäische Graphik*).

1923

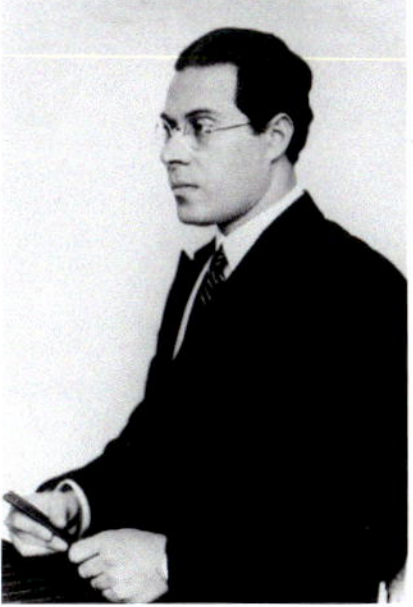

László Moholy-Nagy

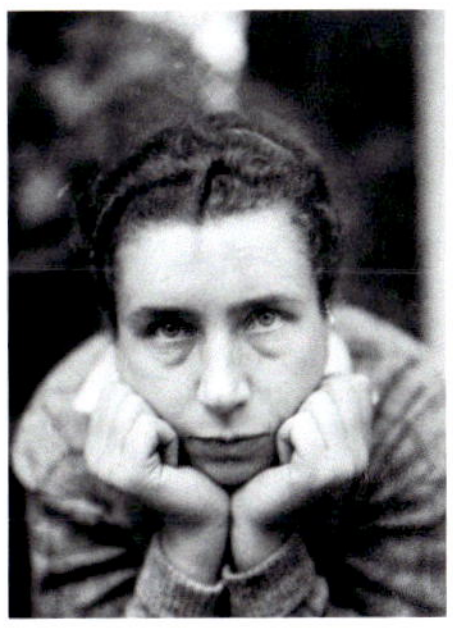

Lucia Moholy
Courtesy of Bauhaus-Archiv Berlin

Hungarian artist László Moholy-Nagy arrives from Berlin to lead the preliminary course. He uses the tools of mass production to remake the Bauhaus's typographic image in print. His wife and fellow photographer, Lucia Moholy, accompanies him and begins to document life at the school.

The Bauhaus puts on an exhibition to justify its funding to the local government. The show is a publicity success but a political failure.

Schlemmer takes over the stage workshop from Schreyer, whose abstruse plays prompted student protest. Performed the week of the Bauhaus exhibition's opening, Schlemmer's *Triadic Ballet* (*Triadisches Ballett*) adapts Bauhaus design to the body with elemental costumes and geometric choreography.

The Bauhaus debuts the Haus am Horn, its first architectural achievement. It was designed by master Georg Muche with student assistance, including a kitchen by Benita Koch-Otte and a children's room by Alma Siedhoff-Buscher.

1924

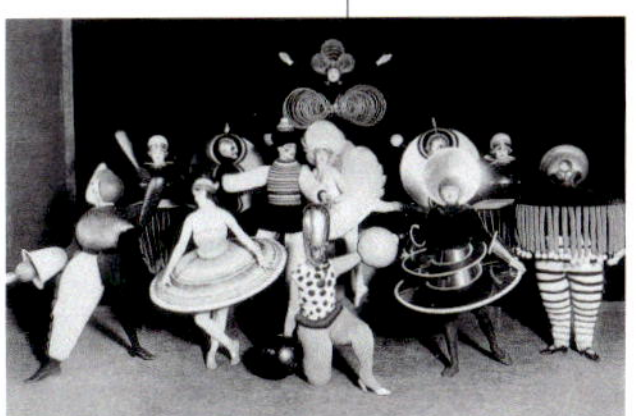

Triadic Ballet by Oskar Schlemmer

Faced with increasing conservatism from government funders, Gropius establishes Bauhaus GmbH to produce and sell works designed in the school's student workshops, including weaving, woodworking, furniture, metalsmithing, and more.

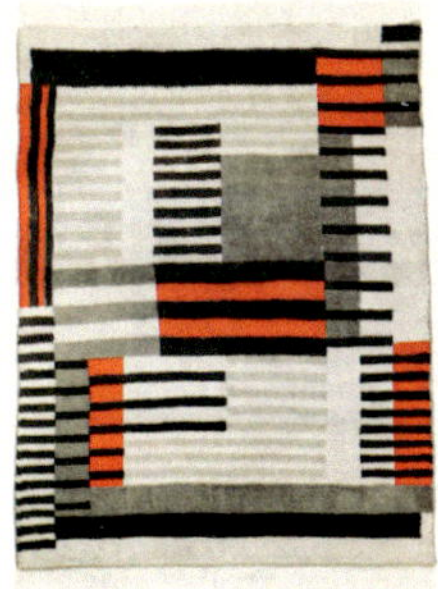

Weaving by Anni Albers

1925

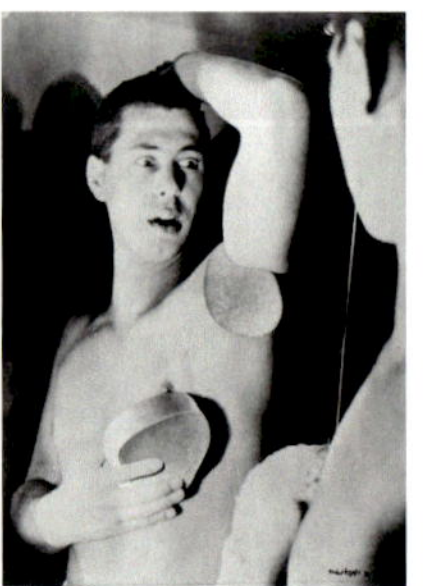

Herbert Bayer
Courtesy of Bauhaus-Archiv Berlin

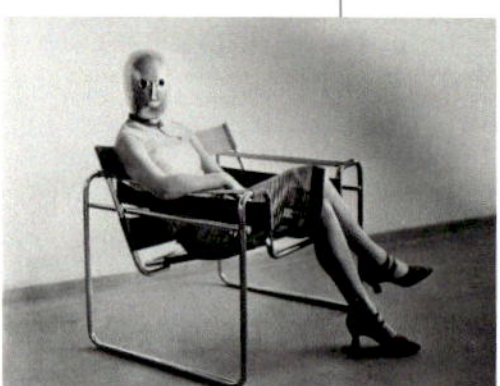
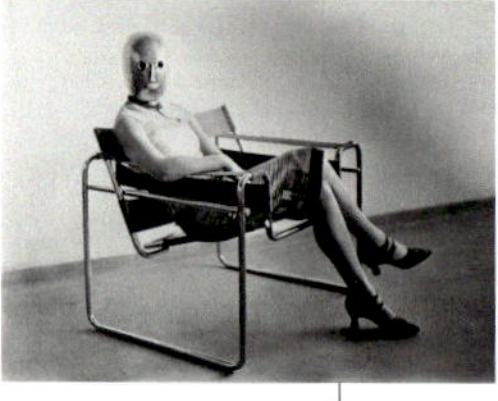

Marcel Breuer's Wassily chair
Courtesy of Bauhaus-Archiv Berlin

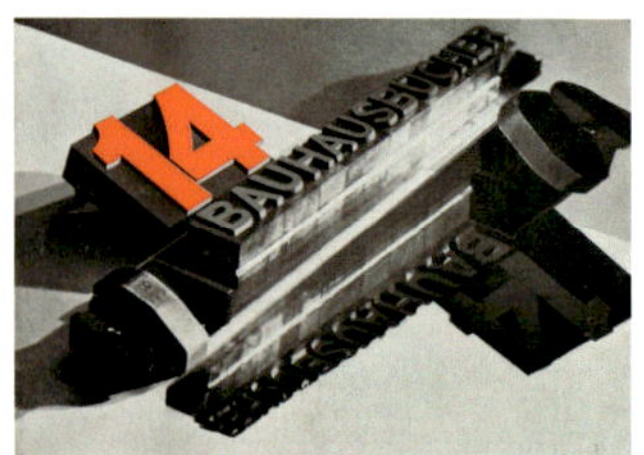

Cover of a Bauhaus Books catalog

Despite the success of the 1923 exhibition, the conservative government in Weimar cuts the Bauhaus's funding. Gropius moves the school to the more liberal city of Dessau. Marcks is the only master who does not make the move.

Gropius and Moholy-Nagy simultaneously publish the first eight Bauhaus Books, which they devised in order to share the pedagogies of the school's masters and peers far and wide. They ultimately produce fourteen titles in the series.

Bauhaus student Herbert Bayer joins the faculty as a junior master, leading the newly formed print and advertising workshop, the school's first official program in design. He drafts Universal Type, an alphabet with only lowercase letters that would become practically synonymous with the school's typography, and begins setting the school's print materials solely in lowercase letters.

After studying sculpture at the Bauhaus, a German World War I veteran named Joost Schmidt begins leading the lettering workshop. Hungarian student Marcel Breuer likewise joins the faculty and begins development of the Wassily chair, one of the school's most famous outputs.

1926

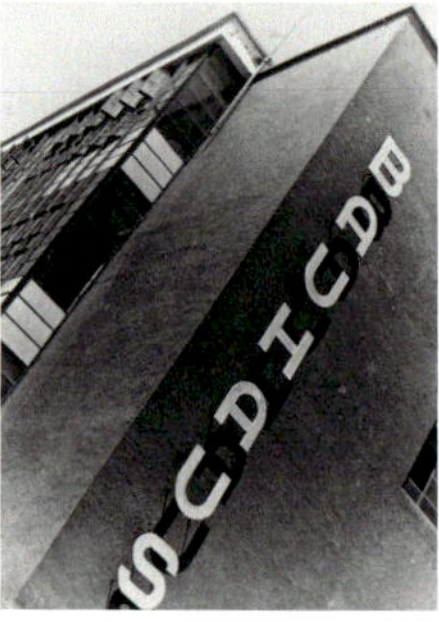

Bauhaus Dessau

Gropius unveils the school's new building in Dessau, which his firm designed. It features a revolutionary glass facade to allow light—and views—into the school's workshops. Bayer creates the school's famous signage.

The school begins publishing *bauhaus*, a quarterly magazine that reports on the school's functions, pedagogy, and contributions to larger conversations in art and architecture, as well as student life. It is published fairly consistently until 1933.

German artist and Bauhaus master Josef Albers begins to experiment with a sans serif, modular stencil alphabet in which each letterform is composed of some combination of a circle, square, and triangle. It becomes another iconic example of Bauhaus typography.

1927

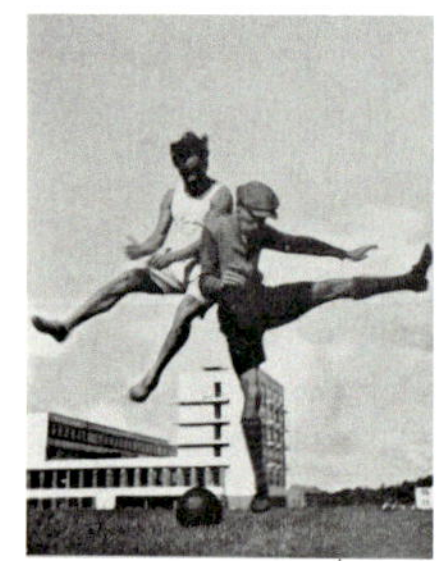

Student life

Josef Albers's modular alphabet

While architecture had been an ambition of the Bauhaus from the beginning, there is no formal course of study for the discipline until Gropius establishes the architecture workshop in 1927. He appoints Swiss architect Hannes Meyer to lead it.

German textile artist Gunta Stölzl becomes the only official woman Bauhaus master. She oversees the weaving workshop for nearly a decade.

American Alfred H. Barr Jr., future founder of the Museum of Modern Art (MoMA), visits the Bauhaus.

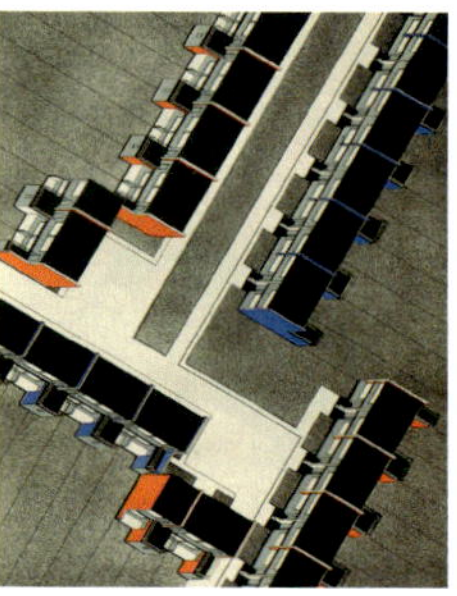

Rendering by Walter Gropius

LOCATION: DESSAU

DIRECTOR: WALTER GROPIUS

TYPOGRAPHIC MASTERS: LÁSZLÓ MOHOLY-NAGY AND HERBERT BAYER

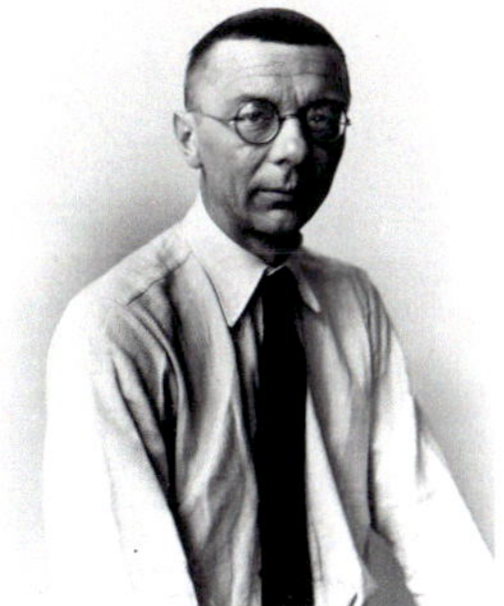

Joost Schmidt
Courtesy of Bauhaus-Archiv Berlin

Meyer takes over the directorship from Gropius, who had grown wary of the political upheaval and wished to pursue a private practice in architecture. A strict functionalist, Meyer was immune to aesthetics and realigned the school to meet social needs through architecture and industry.

In the wake of political strife and Meyer's shifts to the curriculum, Moholy-Nagy and Bayer leave the Bauhaus and set up independent studios in Berlin.

When Bayer leaves, Schmidt becomes head of the print and advertising workshop and oversees the sculpture workshop as well.

Five years after attending the 1923 Bauhaus exhibition, German-born designer Jan Tschichold synthesizes Bauhaus and constructivist ideas in his book *The New Typography*. In its pages, he champions asymmetry, white space, and sans serif type, laying the groundwork for one of the major design movements of the twentieth century, International Typographic Style, also known as Swiss Style.

1928

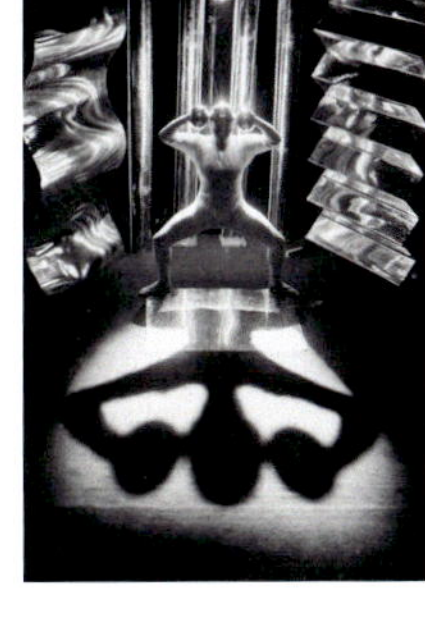

Metallic Festival
Courtesy of Bauhaus-Archiv Berlin

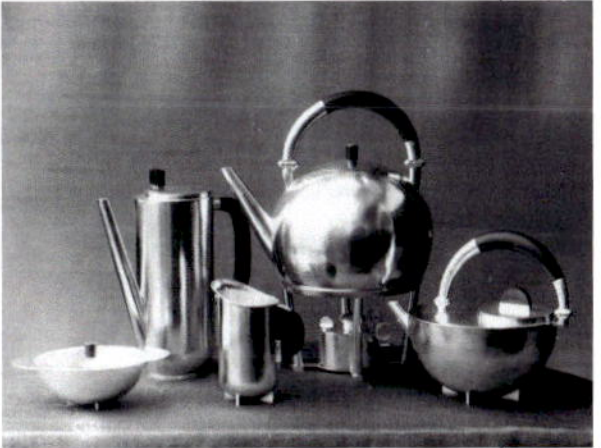

Tea set by Marianne Brandt
Courtesy of Bauhaus-Archiv Berlin

The Bauhaus was famous for its costume parties, where students and masters mingled. The most spectacular example is the 1929 Metallic Festival (Metallisches Fest), hosted to celebrate the departing metalsmithing teacher Marianne Brandt, whose tea sets and lamps would become landmarks of Bauhaus industrial design. Attendees wore outfits made of metal and danced under an installation of reflective orbs.

The school pairs up with an industrial partner to manufacture a Bauhaus line of wallpaper. One of many products sold by the school, the wallpaper proves wildly successful and helps fund the school as government support wanes. It is still in production today.

1929

Schlemmer and Klee resign from the Bauhaus, citing Meyer's rejection of their more individualistic, less utilitarian work.

A record 201 students enroll in the Bauhaus's winter session.

Accused of turning the school into a communist haven, Meyer, the director, is fired and goes to Moscow, taking several students with him. Leading German architect Ludwig Mies van der Rohe takes his place. He has little choice but to make the Bauhaus more traditional to appease Dessau's rising National Socialist Party.

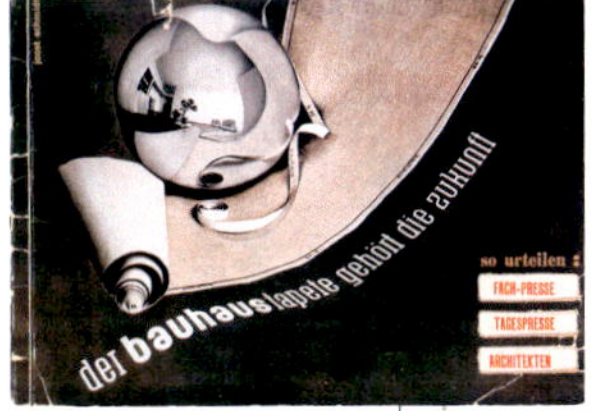

Wallpaper catalog by Joost Schmidt
Courtesy of Bauhaus-Archiv Berlin

1930

DIRECTOR: HANNES MEYER

DIRECTOR: LUDWIG MIES VAN DER ROHE

TYPOGRAPHIC MASTER: JOOST SCHMIDT

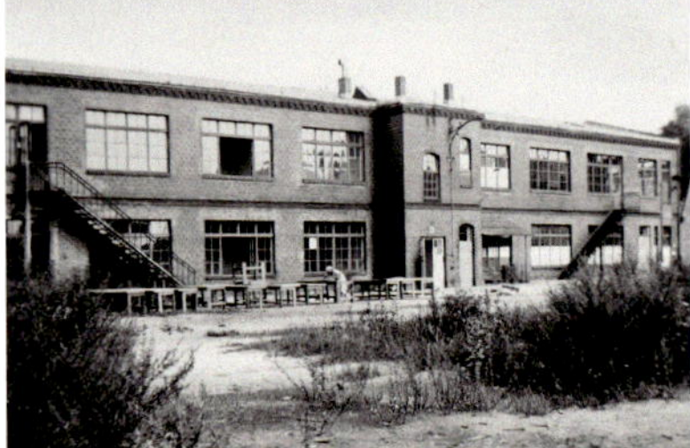

Bauhaus Berlin
Courtesy of Bauhaus-Archiv Berlin

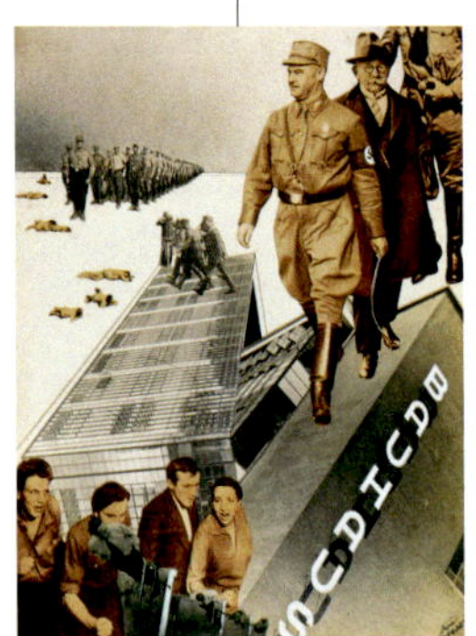

Collage by Bauhaus student Iwao Yamawaki
Courtesy of Bauhaus-Archiv Berlin

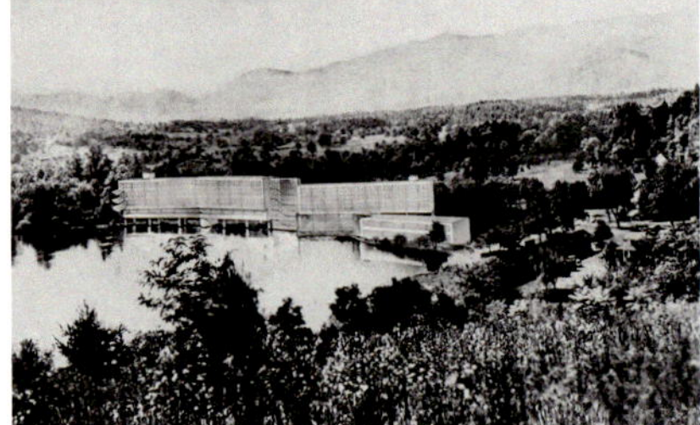

Black Mountain College

1932

The National Socialist Party wins a majority in the Dessau government. The city council votes to cut off all funding to the Bauhaus.

Mies van der Rohe reopens the Bauhaus as a privately funded institution in an abandoned telephone factory in Berlin. It is a skeletal operation focused on architecture. Several instructors, including Schmidt and Feininger, do not make the move to Berlin.

1933

In January, Hitler becomes chancellor of Germany.

In April, the Gestapo raids the Bauhaus Berlin under claims that it promotes “degenerate art” and “cosmopolitan modernism,” a thinly veiled anti-Semitic claim. Mies van der Rohe and the Bauhaus faculty vote not to reopen the school. There are only nineteen students enrolled.

Many Bauhauslers begin struggling to work in Germany, at first due to their foreigner status and eventually due to their association with the school. The exodus begins, with Moholy-Nagy moving to the Netherlands and Albers relocating to the United States to lead Black Mountain College, where Feininger later teaches as well. Many Jewish students and teachers also flee Nazi rule, establishing Bauhaus outposts as far afield as Tel Aviv. Some are not able to leave, including Friedl Dicker, who dies at Auschwitz in 1944.

1934

After the dissolution of the school, former Bauhaus masters Gropius, Schmidt, and Bayer are drawn into the creation of the *German People, German Labor* (*Deutsches Volk, Deutsche Arbeit*) exhibition, commissioned by the Nazis as nationalistic propaganda. Schmidt and Bayer contribute to additional Nazi projects before being blacklisted for working at the Bauhaus. Schmidt's career won't begin to recover until just before his death in 1948.

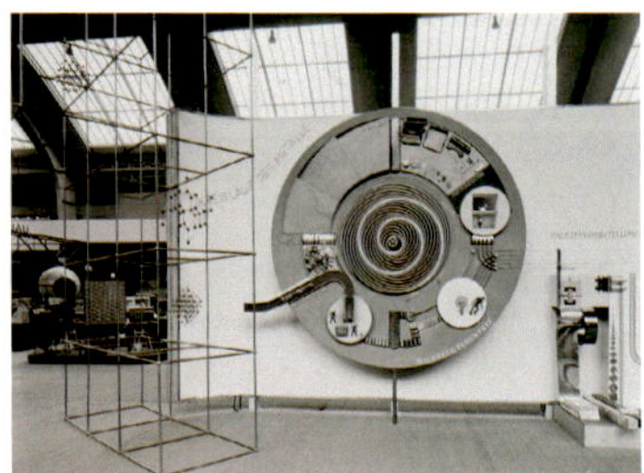

***German People, German Labor* exhibition**
Courtesy of Bauhaus-Archiv Berlin

LOCATION: BERLIN

DIRECTOR: LUDWIG MIES VAN DER ROHE

TYPOGRAPHIC MASTER: JOOST SCHMIDT

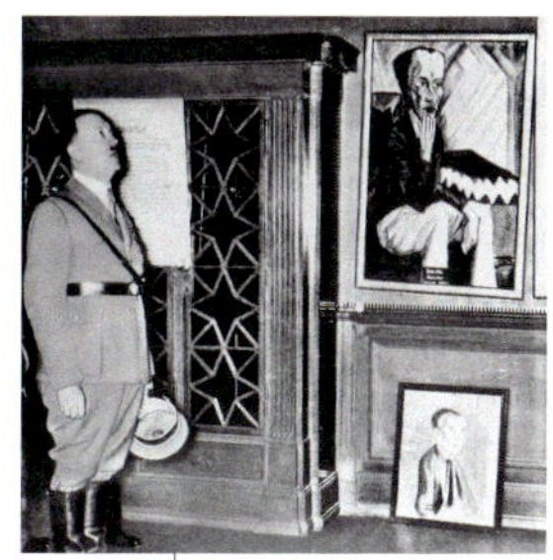

Hitler at the *Degenerate Art Exhibition*

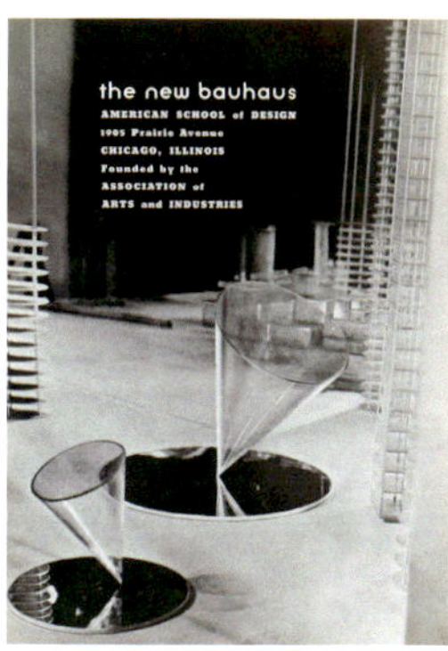

Prospectus for the New Bauhaus

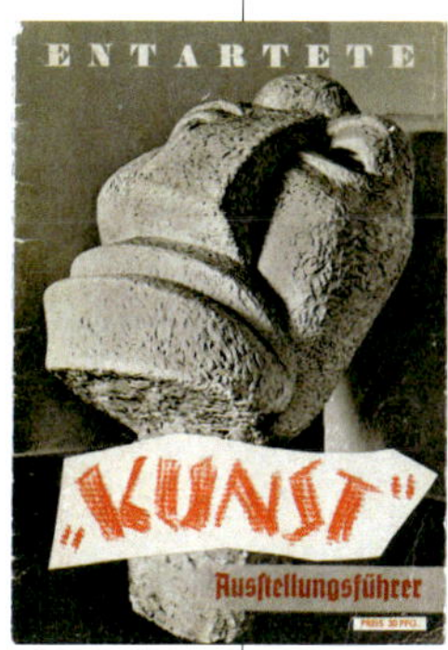

Catalog for the *Degenerate Art Exhibition*

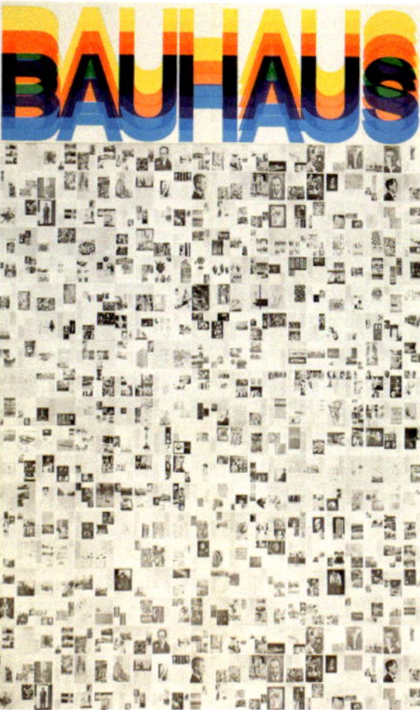

Promotional poster for MIT's *Bauhaus* book

1937

After a stint in London, Gropius and Breuer move to Boston to teach at the newly founded Harvard School of Design, where they will make major contributions to U.S. architecture and design.

Moholy-Nagy moves to Chicago to begin the New Bauhaus; it is briefly shuttered due to lack of funding but reopens in 1939 as the School of Design. He teaches there until his death at age fifty-one in 1946.

Mies van der Rohe also moves to Chicago, where he leads the Illinois Institute of Technology and designs its new campus. He also becomes a noted architect in the States, with achievements such as the Seagram Building in New York.

Back in Germany, the Nazis display confiscated modernist artwork in the *Degenerate Art Exhibition* (*Entartete Kunst Ausstellung*). It includes many pieces by Bauhaus masters, students, and disciples.

1938

At Gropius's urging, Barr hires Bayer to organize the first Bauhaus exhibition in the United States at MoMA. A year before the outbreak of World War II, Bayer is able to leave Germany, where he faced Nazi scrutiny for his Bauhaus association. He has a long career in advertising in America and dies in California in 1985.

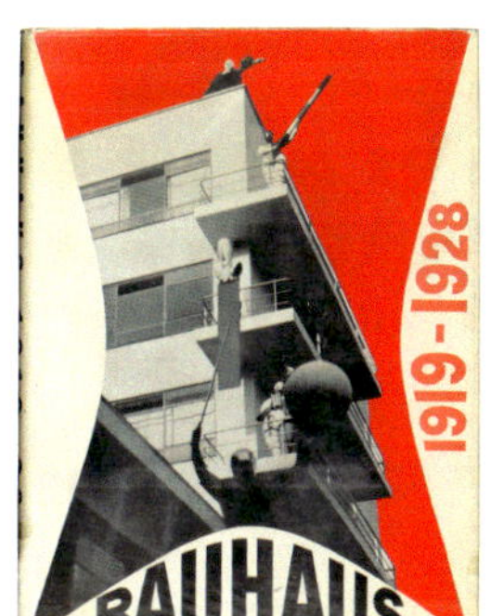

MoMA exhibition catalog

1969

Former Bauhaus directors Gropius and Mies van der Rohe pass away in the United States fifty years after the founding of the school and more than thirty after the Nazis forced its closure.

To mark the semicentennial anniversary, the German exhibition *50 Years Bauhaus* (*50 Jahre Bauhaus*) travels across Europe and North America, with an exhibition catalog designed by Bayer. MIT Press also publishes *Bauhaus: Weimar, Dessau, Berlin, Chicago*, a detailed and definitive multivolume overview of the school's legacy. These books and exhibitions—along with the instructors, students, and contemporaries who carried the school's teachings around the world—serve to further cement the Bauhaus's legacy, as do the collections at institutions such as the Bauhaus-Archiv in Berlin and the Bauhaus Dessau Foundation.

early vision

Under the directorship of German architect Walter Gropius, the Bauhaus formed in 1919 when the Weimar Saxon Grand-Ducal Art School merged with the Weimar Academy of Fine Art. From the school's inception, its pedagogy, the organization of its courses, and the nature of its individual programs evolved under a changing cast of faculty and directors. Even the location of the school proved impermanent, moving from Weimar to Dessau in 1925 and then to Berlin in 1932. ●

In graphic design and typography, the most consequential turnover might have come in 1923, when Swiss painter Johannes Itten ceded his post as instructor of the preliminary course to a young Hungarian artist named László Moholy-Nagy. In this transition, Itten's mysticism and emphasis on German expressionism and Arts and Crafts—prevalent for decades in Europe—gave way to Moholy-Nagy's embrace of universal clarity and artistic use of the tools of mass production. ●

These pedagogical shifts found immediate expression in school documents and publications, from Gropius's 1919 manifesto to Herbert Bayer's single-page syllabi. Meanwhile, monographs like Itten's *Utopia* preserve the ideology of the early instructors, and ephemera such as brochures, invitations, and tickets to festivals and performances provide a window into the vibrant social life integral to the Bauhaus. While the school's legacy has largely been consolidated under a singular aesthetic, the artifacts in this chapter both locate the starting points of the dominant sensibility and attest to a more faceted origin story. ●

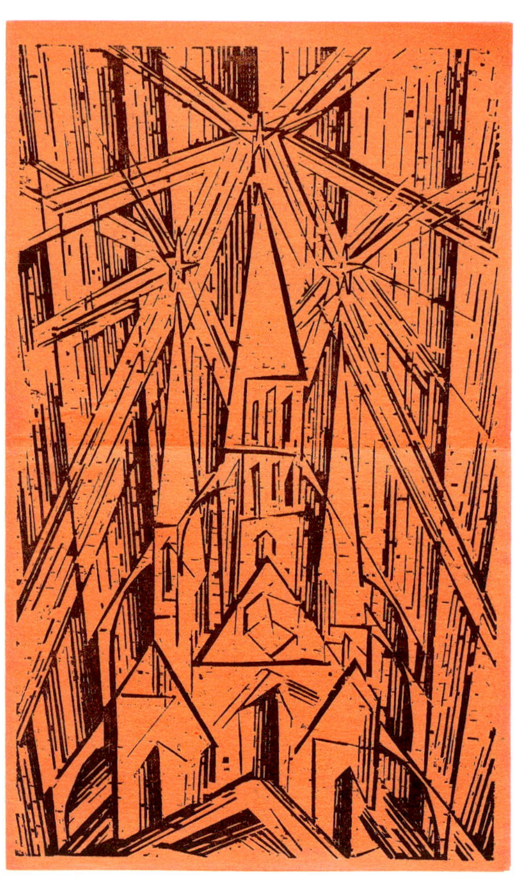

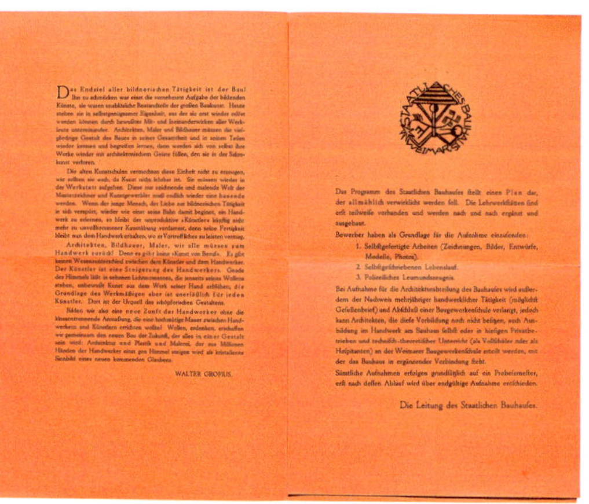

Das Endziel aller bildnerischen Tätigkeit ist der Bau! Ihn zu schmücken war einst die vornehmste Aufgabe der bildenden Künste, sie waren unablösliche Bestandteile der großen Baukunst. Heute stehen sie in selbstgenügsamer Eigenheit, aus der sie erst wieder erlöst werden können durch bewußtes Mit- und Ineinanderwirken aller Werkleute untereinander. Architekten, Maler und Bildhauer müssen die vielgliedrige Gestalt des Baues in seiner Gesamtheit und in seinen Teilen wieder kennen und begreifen lernen, dann werden sich von selbst ihre Werke wieder mit architektonischem Geiste füllen, den sie in der Salonkunst verloren.

Die alten Kunstschulen vermochten diese Einheit nicht zu erzeugen, wie sollten sie auch, da Kunst nicht lehrbar ist. Sie müssen wieder in der Werkstatt aufgehen. Diese nur zeichnende und malende Welt der Musterzeichner und Kunstgewerbler muß endlich wieder eine bauende werden. Wenn der junge Mensch, der Liebe zur bildnerischen Tätigkeit in sich verspürt, wieder wie einst seine Bahn damit beginnt, ein Handwerk zu erlernen, so bleibt der unproduktive »Künstler« künftig nicht mehr zu unvollkommener Kunstübung verdammt, denn seine Fertigkeit bleibt nun dem Handwerk erhalten, wo er Vortreffliches zu leisten vermag.

Architekten, Bildhauer, Maler, wir alle müssen zum Handwerk zurück! Denn es gibt keine »Kunst von Beruf«. Es gibt keinen Wesensunterschied zwischen dem Künstler und dem Handwerker. Der Künstler ist eine Steigerung des Handwerkers. Gnade des Himmels läßt in seltenen Lichtmomenten, die jenseits seines Wollens stehen, unbewußt Kunst aus dem Werk seiner Hand erblühen, die Grundlage des Werkmäßigen aber ist unerläßlich für jeden Künstler. Dort ist der Urquell des schöpferischen Gestaltens.

Bilden wir also eine neue Zunft der Handwerker ohne die klassentrennende Anmaßung, die eine hochmütige Mauer zwischen Handwerkern und Künstlern errichten wollte! Wollen, erdenken, erschaffen wir gemeinsam den neuen Bau der Zukunft, der alles in einer Gestalt sein wird: Architektur und Plastik und Malerei, der aus Millionen Händen der Handwerker einst gen Himmel steigen wird als kristallenes Sinnbild eines neuen kommenden Glaubens.

WALTER GROPIUS.

Das Programm des Staatlichen Bauhauses stellt einen Plan dar, der allmählich verwirklicht werden soll. Die Lehrwerkstätten sind erst teilweise vorhanden und werden nach und nach ergänzt und ausgebaut.

Bewerber haben als Grundlage für die Aufnahme einzusenden:

1. Selbstgefertigte Arbeiten (Zeichnungen, Bilder, Entwürfe, Modelle, Photos).
2. Selbstgeschriebenen Lebenslauf.
3. Polizeiliches Leumundszeugnis.

Bei Aufnahme für die Architekturabteilung des Bauhauses wird außerdem der Nachweis mehrjähriger handwerklicher Tätigkeit (möglichst Gesellenbrief) und Abschluß einer Baugewerkenschule verlangt, jedoch kann Architekten, die diese Vorbildung noch nicht besitzen, auch Ausbildung im Handwerk am Bauhaus selbst oder in hiesigen Privatbetrieben und technisch-theoretischer Unterricht (als Vollschüler oder als Hospitanten) an der Weimarer Baugewerkenschule erteilt werden, mit der das Bauhaus in ergänzender Verbindung steht.

Sämtliche Aufnahmen erfolgen grundsätzlich auf ein Probesemester, erst nach dessen Ablauf wird über endgültige Aufnahme entschieden.

Die Leitung des Staatlichen Bauhauses.

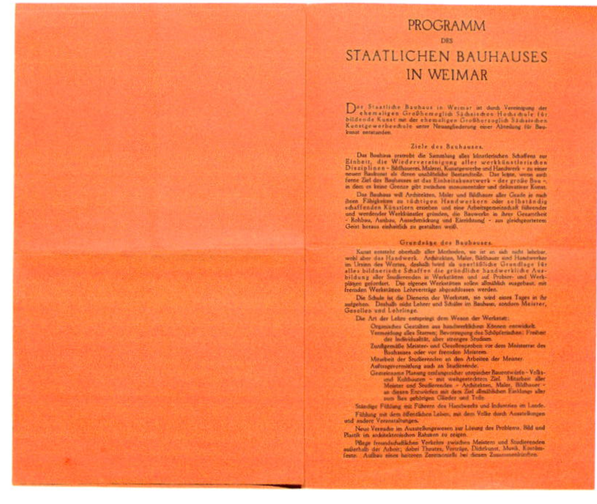

PROGRAMM
DES
STAATLICHEN BAUHAUSES
IN WEIMAR

Das Staatliche Bauhaus in Weimar ist durch Vereinigung der ehemaligen Großherzoglich Sächsischen Hochschule für bildende Kunst mit der ehemaligen Großherzoglich Sächsischen Kunstgewerbeschule unter Neuangliederung einer Abteilung für Baukunst entstanden.

Ziele des Bauhauses.

Das Bauhaus erstrebt die Sammlung alles künstlerischen Schaffens zur Einheit, die Wiedervereinigung aller werkkünstlerischen Disziplinen – Bildhauerei, Malerei, Kunstgewerbe und Handwerk – zu einer neuen Baukunst als deren unablösliche Bestandteile. Das letzte, wenn auch ferne Ziel des Bauhauses ist das Einheitskunstwerk – der große Bau –, in dem es keine Grenze gibt zwischen monumentaler und dekorativer Kunst.

Das Bauhaus will Architekten, Maler und Bildhauer aller Grade je nach ihren Fähigkeiten zu tüchtigen Handwerkern oder selbständig schaffenden Künstlern erziehen und eine Arbeitsgemeinschaft führender und werdender Werkkünstler gründen, die Bauwerke in ihrer Gesamtheit – Rohbau, Ausbau, Ausschmückung und Einrichtung – aus gleichgeartetem Geist heraus einheitlich zu gestalten weiß.

Grundsätze des Bauhauses.

Kunst entsteht oberhalb aller Methoden, sie ist an sich nicht lehrbar, wohl aber das Handwerk. Architekten, Maler, Bildhauer sind Handwerker im Ursinn des Wortes, deshalb wird als unerläßliche Grundlage für alles bildnerische Schaffen die gründliche handwerkliche Ausbildung aller Studierenden in Werkstätten und auf Probier- und Werkplätzen gefordert. Die eigenen Werkstätten sollen allmählich ausgebaut, mit fremden Werkstätten Lehrverträge abgeschlossen werden.

Die Schule ist die Dienerin der Werkstatt, sie wird eines Tages in ihr aufgehen. Deshalb nicht Lehrer und Schüler im Bauhaus, sondern Meister, Gesellen und Lehrlinge.

Die Art der Lehre entspringt dem Wesen der Werkstatt:

Organisches Gestalten aus handwerklichem Können entwickelt.

Vermeidung alles Starren; Bevorzugung des Schöpferischen; Freiheit der Individualität, aber strenges Studium.

Zunftgemäße Meister- und Gesellenproben vor dem Meisterrat des Bauhauses oder vor fremden Meistern.

Mitarbeit der Studierenden an den Arbeiten der Meister.

Auftragsvermittlung auch an Studierende.

Gemeinsame Planung umfangreicher utopischer Bauentwürfe – Volks- und Kultbauten – mit weitgestecktem Ziel. Mitarbeit aller Meister und Studierenden – Architekten, Maler, Bildhauer – an diesen Entwürfen mit dem Ziel allmählichen Einklangs aller zum Bau gehörigen Glieder und Teile.

Ständige Fühlung mit Führern der Handwerke und Industrien im Lande.

Fühlung mit dem öffentlichen Leben, mit dem Volke durch Ausstellungen und andere Veranstaltungen.

Neue Versuche im Ausstellungswesen zur Lösung des Problems, Bild und Plastik im architektonischen Rahmen zu zeigen.

Pflege freundschaftlichen Verkehrs zwischen Meistern und Studierenden außerhalb der Arbeit; dabei Theater, Vorträge, Dichtkunst, Musik, Kostümfeste. Aufbau eines heiteren Zeremoniells bei diesen Zusammenkünften.

Umfang der Lehre.

Die Lehre im Bauhaus umfaßt alle praktischen und wissenschaftlichen Gebiete des bildnerischen Schaffens.

A. Baukunst,
B. Malerei,
C. Bildhauerei

einschließlich aller handwerklichen Zweiggebiete.

Die Studierenden werden sowohl handwerklich (1) wie zeichnerisch-malerisch (2) und wissenschaftlich-theoretisch (3) ausgebildet.

1. Die handwerkliche Ausbildung – sei es in eigenen, allmählich zu ergänzenden, oder fremden durch Lehrvertrag verpflichteten Werkstätten – erstreckt sich auf:
   a) Bildhauer, Steinmetzen, Stukkatöre, Holzbildhauer, Keramiker, Gipsgießer,
   b) Schmiede, Schlosser, Gießer, Dreher,
   c) Tischler,
   d) Dekorationsmaler, Glasmaler, Mosaiker, Emallöre,
   e) Radierer, Holzschneider, Lithographen, Kunstdrucker, Ziselöre,
   f) Weber.

Die handwerkliche Ausbildung bildet das Fundament der Lehre im Bauhause. Jeder Studierende soll ein Handwerk erlernen.

2. Die zeichnerische und malerische Ausbildung erstreckt sich auf:
   a) freies Skizzieren aus dem Gedächtnis und der Fantasie,
   b) Zeichnen und Malen nach Köpfen, Akten und Tieren,
   c) Zeichnen und Malen von Landschaften, Figuren, Pflanzen und Stilleben,
   d) Komponieren,
   e) Ausführen von Wandbildern, Tafelbildern und Bilderschreinen,
   f) Entwerfen von Ornamenten,
   g) Schriftzeichnen,
   h) Konstruktions- und Projektionszeichnen,
   i) Entwerfen von Außen-, Garten- und Innenarchitekturen,
   k) Entwerfen von Möbeln und Gebrauchsgegenständen.
3. Die wissenschaftlich-theoretische Ausbildung erstreckt sich auf:
   a) Kunstgeschichte – nicht im Sinne von Stilgeschichte vorgetragen, sondern zur lebendigen Erkenntnis historischer Arbeitsweisen und Techniken,
   b) Materialkunde,
   c) Anatomie – am lebenden Modell,
   d) physikalische und chemische Farbenlehre,
   e) rationelles Malverfahren,
   f) Grundbegriffe von Buchführung, Vertragsabschlüssen, Verdingungen,
   g) allgemein interessante Einzelvorträge aus allen Gebieten der Kunst und Wissenschaft.

Einteilung der Lehre.

Die Ausbildung ist in drei Lehrgänge eingeteilt:

I. Lehrgang für Lehrlinge,
II. „ „ Gesellen,
III. „ „ Jungmeister.

Die Einzelausbildung bleibt dem Ermessen der einzelnen Meister im Rahmen des allgemeinen Programms und des in jedem Semester neu aufzustellenden Arbeitsverteilungsplanes überlassen.

Um den Studierenden eine möglichst vielseitige, umfassende technische und künstlerische Ausbildung zuteil werden zu lassen, wird der Arbeitsverteilungsplan zeitlich so eingeteilt, daß jeder angehende Architekt, Maler oder Bildhauer auch an einem Teil der anderen Lehrgänge teilnehmen kann.

Aufnahme.

Aufgenommen wird jede unbescholtene Person ohne Rücksicht auf Alter und Geschlecht, deren Vorbildung vom Meisterrat des Bauhauses als ausreichend erachtet wird, und soweit es der Raum zuläßt. Das Lehrgeld beträgt jährlich 180 Mark (es soll mit steigendem Verdienst des Bauhauses allmählich ganz verschwinden). Außerdem ist eine einmalige Aufnahmegebühr von 20 Mark zu zahlen. Ausländer zahlen den doppelten Betrag. Anfragen sind an das Sekretariat des Staatlichen Bauhauses in Weimar zu richten.

APRIL 1919.

Die Leitung des
Staatlichen Bauhauses in Weimar:
Walter Gropius.

1919

LYONEL FEININGER (cover artist)
WALTER GROPIUS (author)

Program of the Weimar State Bauhaus (*Programm des Staatlichen Bauhauses in Weimar*), a.k.a. the Bauhaus manifesto, woodcut and letterpress, 12⅝ × 7¾ inches (320 × 198 mm), Weimar.

This document by Walter Gropius served as the founding manifesto and outline of the first curriculum of the Bauhaus. The most general problem that the Bauhaus sought to address, in varying and conflicting ways during its existence, was the unification of fine and applied arts, especially in the face of new industrial technology. It was to this end that Gropius wrote in his program of the need to "reunify all the disciplines of practical art—sculpture, painting, handicrafts, and the crafts—as inseparable components of a new architecture." At that time, however, Gropius's vision for this unification was influenced by the Romantic notion of the *Gesamtkunstwerk*, or the idea that multiple art forms could come together to create a "total work of art." First expressed by German composer Richard Wagner in 1849, this idea became a cornerstone of the British Arts and Crafts and French art nouveau movements in the late nineteenth century. In Germany, it re-emerged in groups like the state-funded Deutscher Werkbund, established in 1907 to promote partnerships between artisans and manufacturers. This emphasis on craft and a revival of the gothic tradition explains the surprising look of the manifesto, especially the *Cathedral* print by German American painter Lyonel Feininger on the cover, in contrast to the later industrial, geometric modernism for which the Bauhaus became famous. As it was created during the economic strife following World War I, with workers surging to organize after the success of the leftist Bolshevik revolution in Russia and the fall of the conservative kaiser in Germany, Feininger's monument was seen by many Bauhauslers as a cathedral of socialism. ●

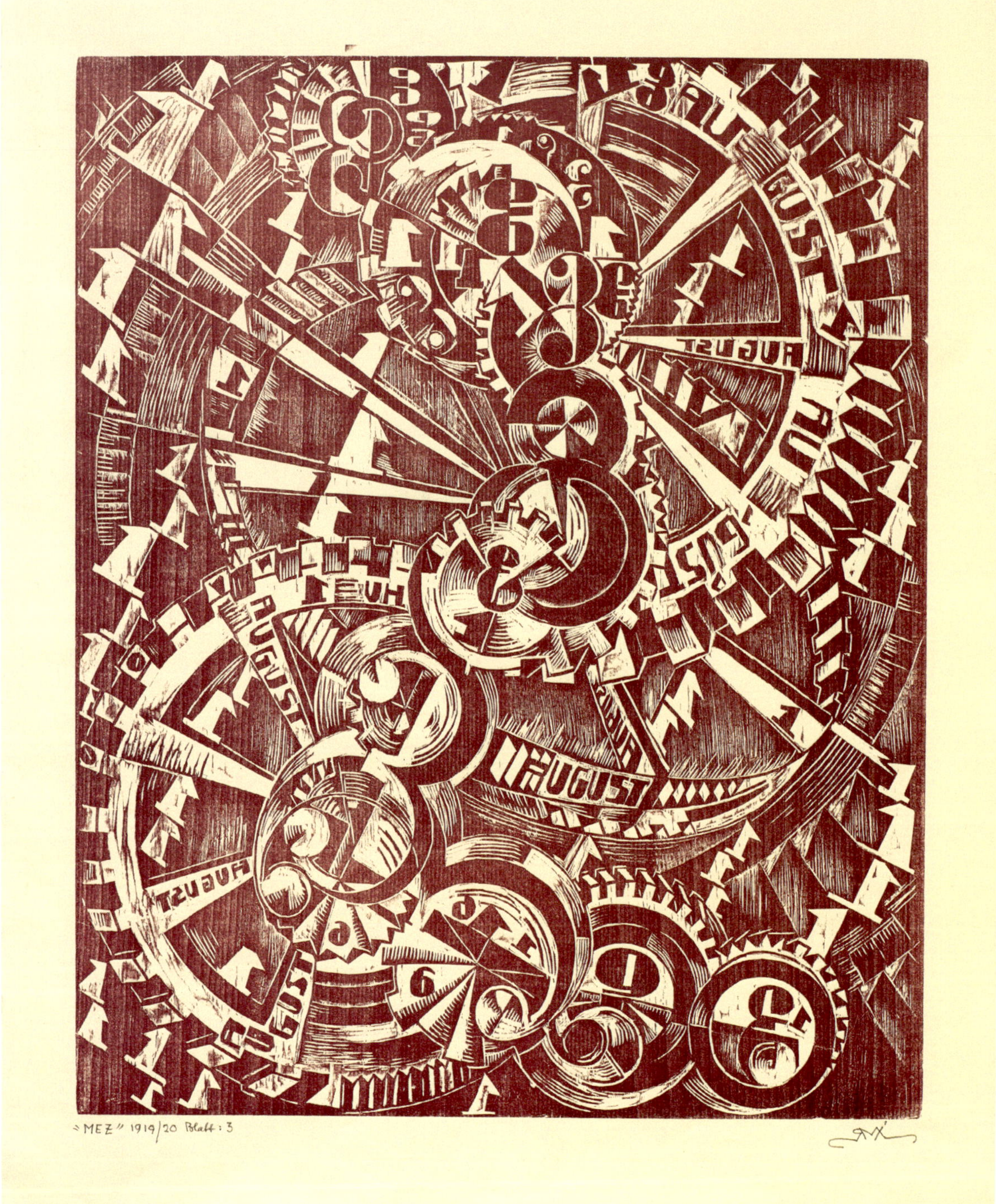

"MEZ" 1919/20 Blatt: 3

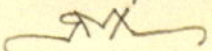

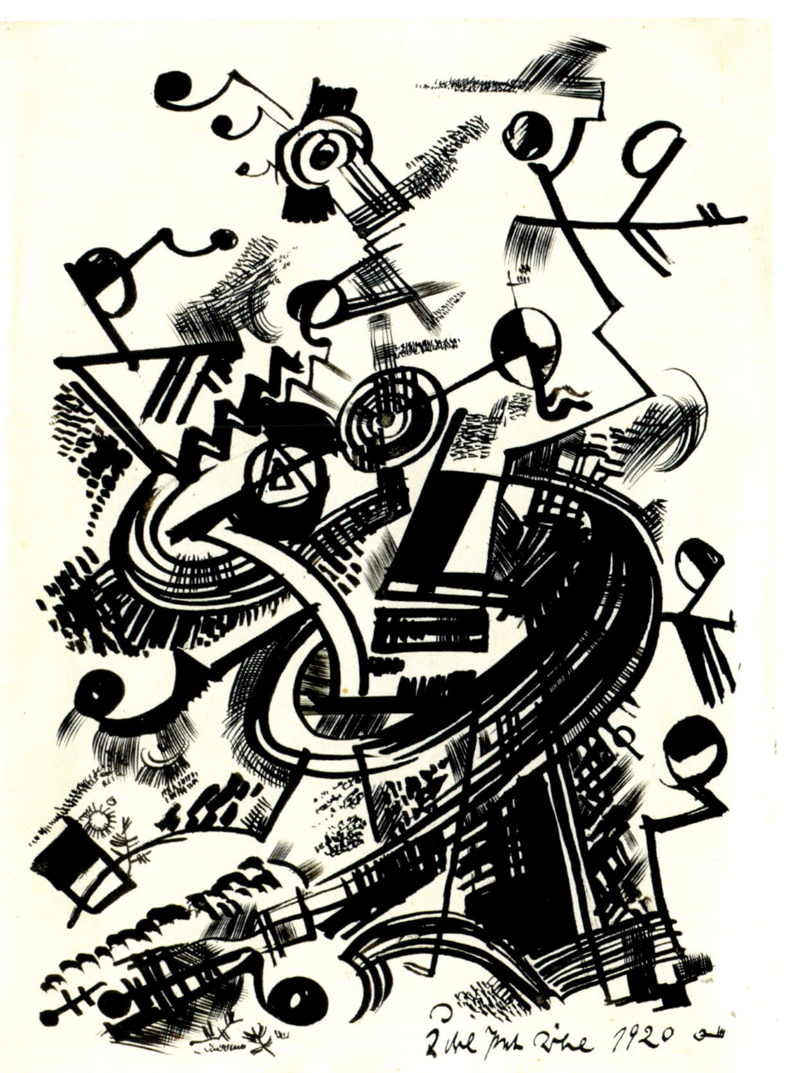

1920

KARL PETER RÖHL

Untitled, ink on paper, 12¼ × 9½ inches (310 × 240 mm), Weimar.

1919

ROBERT MICHEL

Print 3 from the *CET* (*MEZ*) series, woodcut, 21⅜ × 17½ (543 × 445 mm), Weimar.

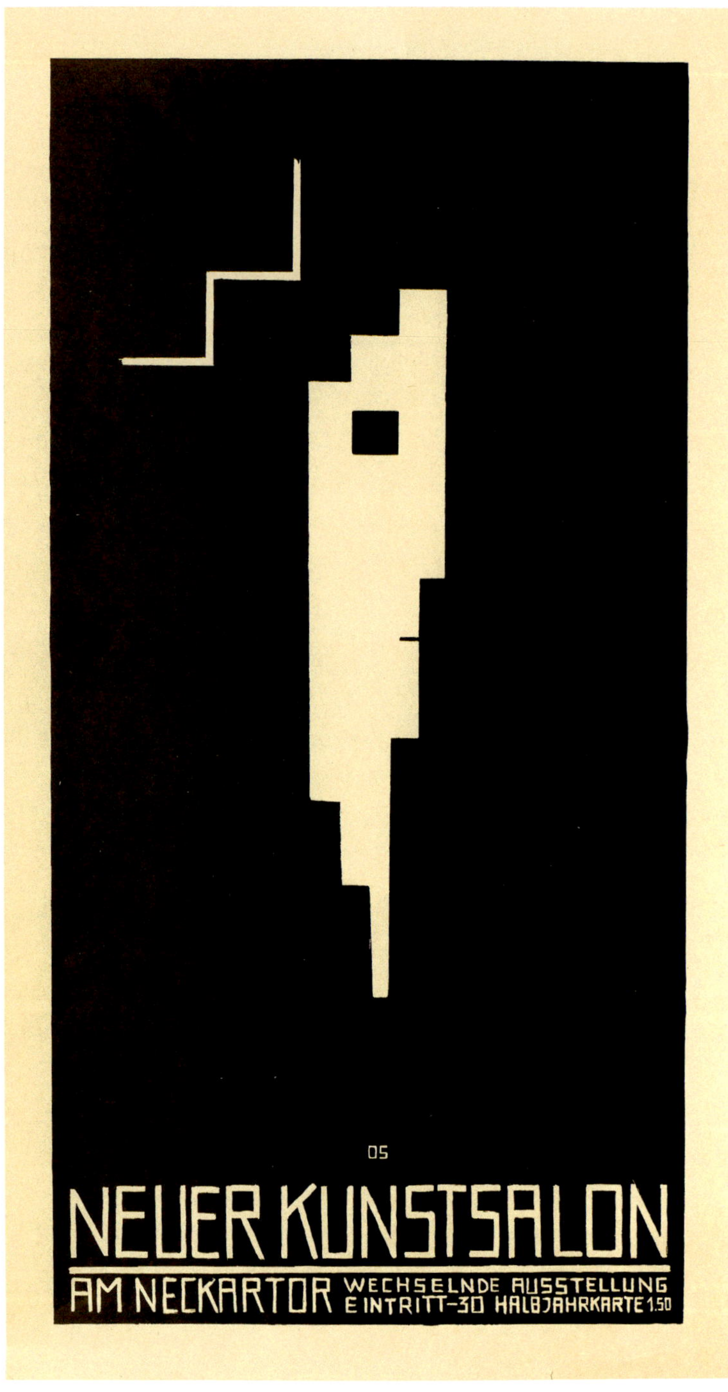

1913

OSKAR SCHLEMMER

Later facsimile edition poster for *New Art Salon* (*Neuer Kunstsalon*) showing an early version of the Bauhaus logo seen at right, lithograph, 22½ × 12¼ inches (570 × 310 mm), Stuttgart, Germany.

1921

OSKAR SCHLEMMER

Promotional prospectus for the *Bauhaus Prints, New European Graphics* (*Bauhaus-Drucke, neue europäische Graphik*) portfolios, lithograph and letterpress, 9⅞ × 7½ inches (250 × 191 mm), Weimar.

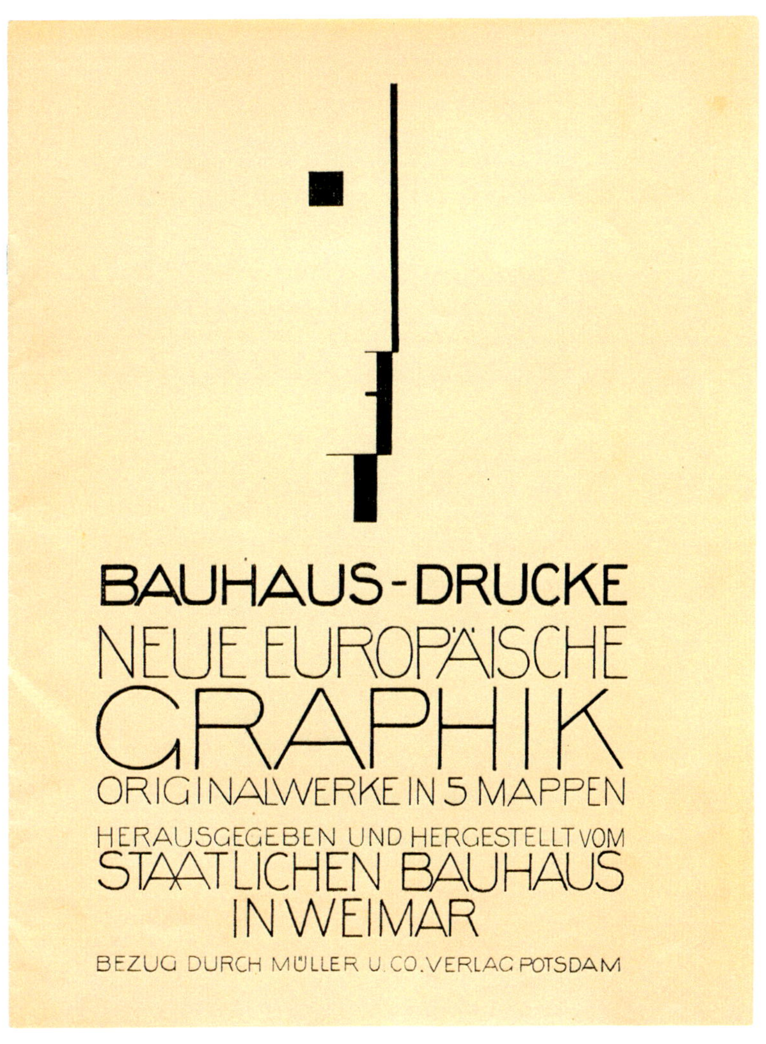

1920

LOTHAR SCHREYER (designer/author)
MAX OLDEROCK and **MAX BILLERT** (woodcutters)

Crucifixion: Performance Score VII (*Kreuzigung: Spielgang Werk VII*), woodcut with hand coloring, 12⅝ × 17⅜ inches (320 × 440 mm), Hamburg.

From 1921 to 1923, German artist Lothar Schreyer established the Bauhaus's theater program, which Gropius saw as parallel to the school's ambitions in architecture. Controversial among students, the theatrician and editor of the expressionist magazine *Der Sturm* was one of the contingent of artists who brought mystical, esoteric sensibilities to the Weimar curriculum. Shortly before his appointment, he printed the play *Crucifixion* (*Kreuzigung*), which dramatizes a modern struggle for spiritual transcendence, in a limited edition. More than a simple playscript, the book attempts to translate the multisensory experience of the stage performance to the printed page. The three characters and their actions are represented by stylized symbols, and each hand-colored leaf (printed only on the recto pages) is structured like a three-tiered musical staff, with the top line representing the actors' lines, the middle line their tone and volume, and the bottom line their movement. Schreyer did not intend the scheme to be technical but rather intuitive and expressive, and—as prefatory notes insist—"anyone can read the play who can hear word-tones within himself and see the movement of color-forms," and "only those who are not professional actors" can perform it. In this light, the variable, organic woodcut symbols and letterforms—sharp and angular, reminiscent of the Viennese Secessionist or German expressionist styles that preceded it—stretch and condense as required by the rhythm of the performance and the duration of each measure, naturally guiding the eye of the reader just as the movements and speech of the actors would guide the audience in a live rendition. ●

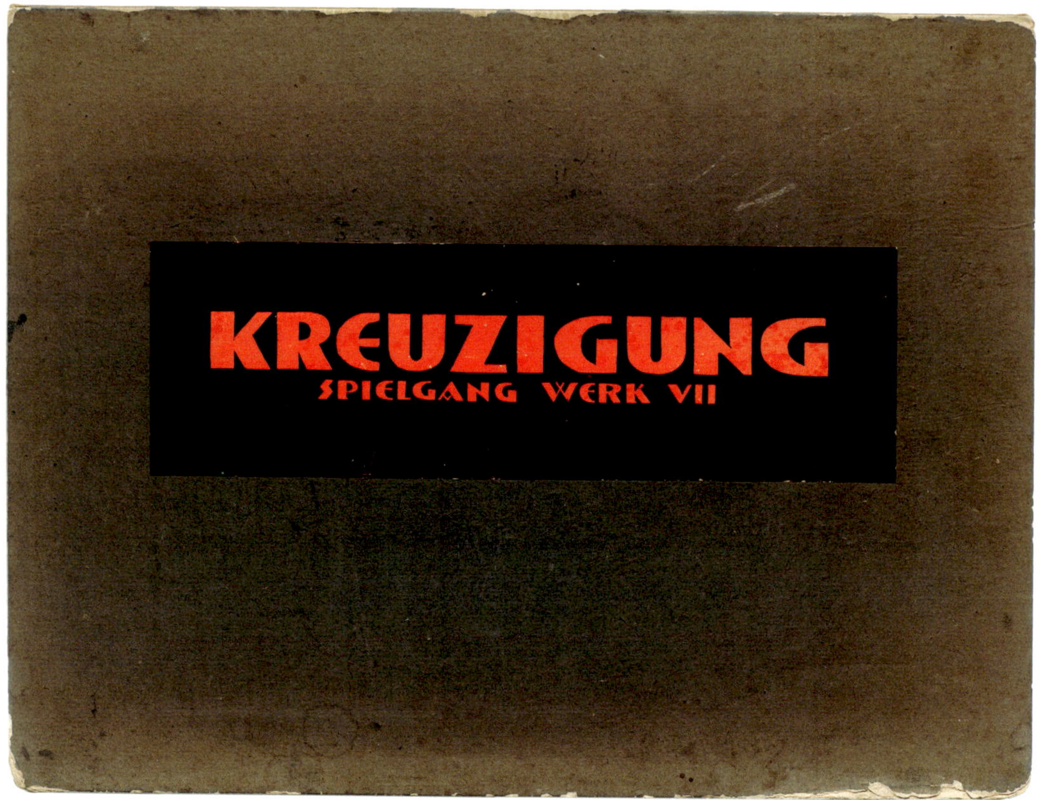

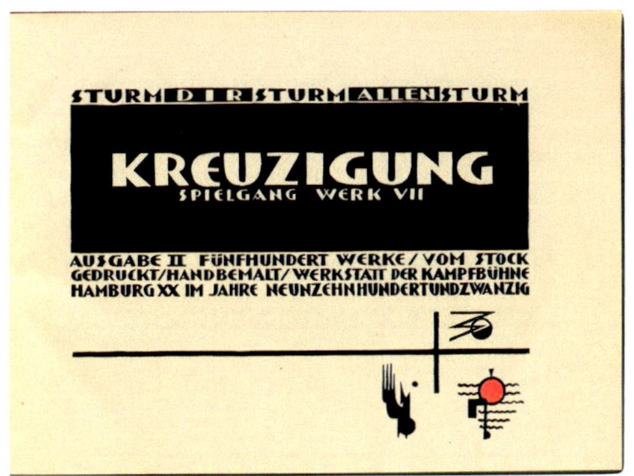
STURM DIR STURM ALLEN STURM
KREUZIGUNG
SPIELGANG WERK VII
AUSGABE II FÜNFHUNDERT WERKE / VOM STOCK
GEDRUCKT/HANDBEMALT/ WERKSTATT DER KAMPFBÜHNE
HAMBURG XX IM JAHRE NEUNZEHNHUNDERTUNDZWANZIG

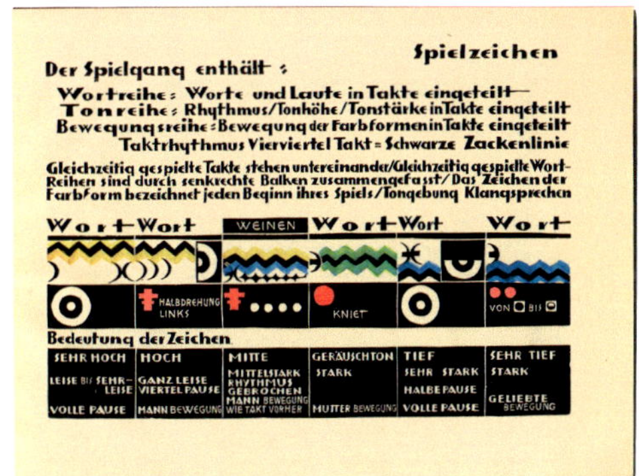
Spielzeichen
Der Spielgang enthält :
Wortreihe: Worte und Laute in Takte eingeteilt
Tonreihe: Rhythmus/Tonhöhe/Tonstärke in Takte eingeteilt
Bewegungsreihe: Bewegung der Farbformen in Takte eingeteilt
Taktrhythmus Vierviertel Takt = Schwarze Zackenlinie
Gleichzeitig gespielte Takte stehen untereinander/Gleichzeitig gespielte Wort-
Reihen sind durch senkrechte Balken zusammengefasst/ Das Zeichen der
Farbform bezeichnet jeden Beginn ihres Spiels/Tongebung Klangsprechen
Wort Wort
WEINEN
Wort Wort
Wort
HALBDREHUNG LINKS
KNIET
VON BIS
Bedeutung der Zeichen
SEHR HOCH
LEISE BIS SEHR-LEISE
VOLLE PAUSE
HOCH
GANZ LEISE
VIERTEL PAUSE
MANN BEWEGUNG
MITTE
MITTELSTARK
RHYTHMUS GEBROCHEN
MANN BEWEGUNG
WIE TAKT VORHER
GERÄUSCHTON
STARK
MUTTER BEWEGUNG
TIEF
SEHR STARK
HALBE PAUSE
VOLLE PAUSE
SEHR TIEF
STARK
GELIEBTE BEWEGUNG

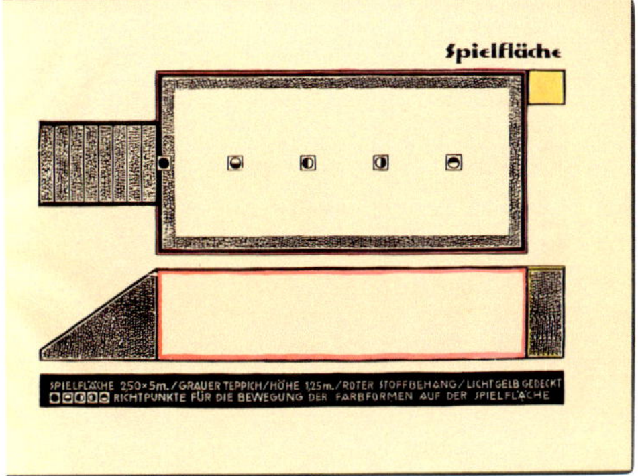
Spielfläche
SPIELFLÄCHE 2,50×5m./GRAUER TEPPICH/HÖHE 1,25m./ROTER STOFFBEHANG/LICHT GELB GEDECKT
RICHTPUNKTE FÜR DIE BEWEGUNG DER FARBFORMEN AUF DER SPIELFLÄCHE

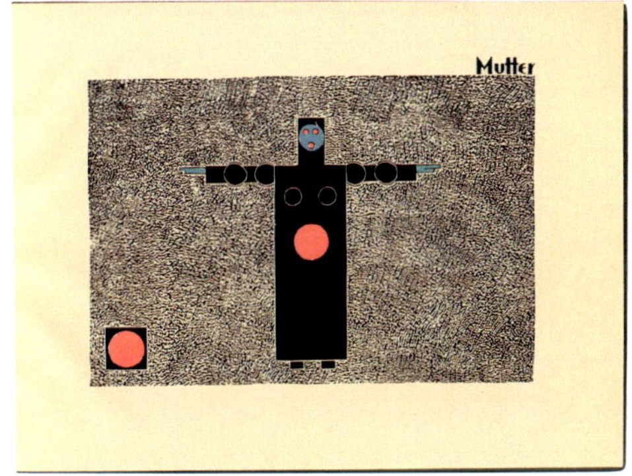
Mutter

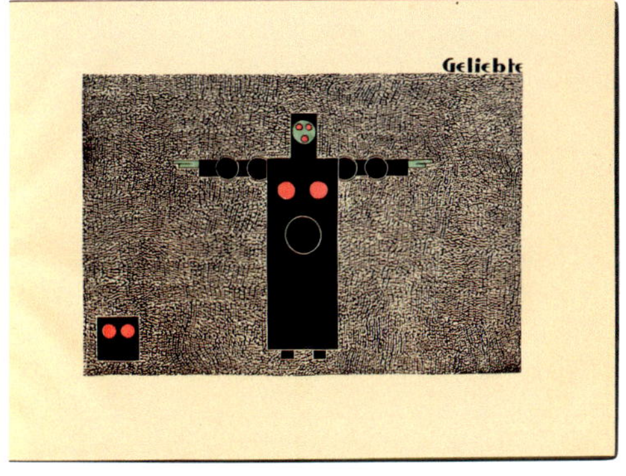
Geliebte

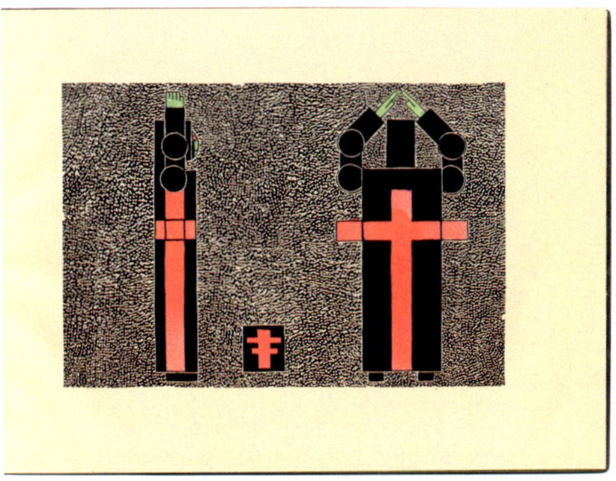

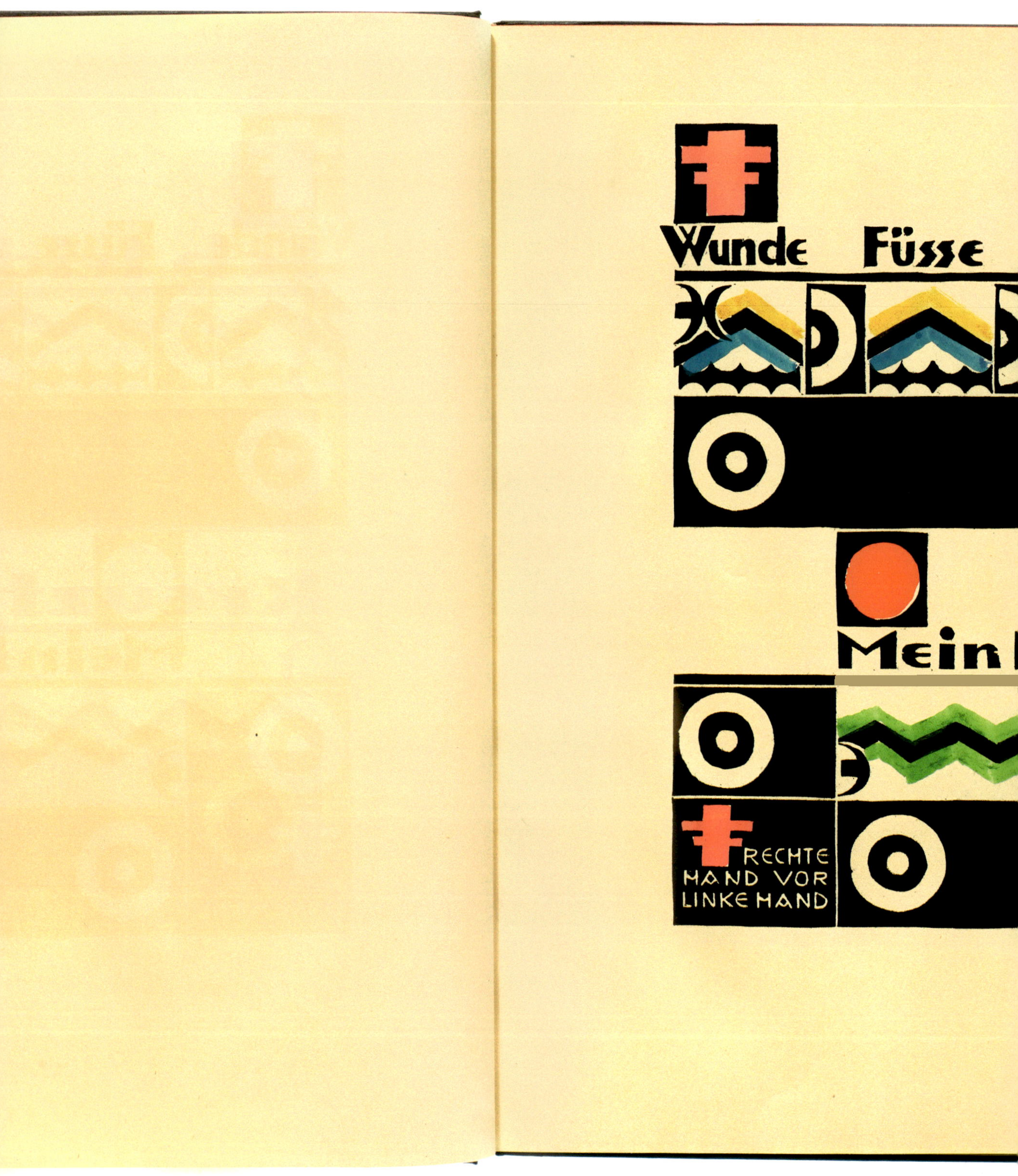
Wunde Füsse
Mein
RECHTE
HAND VOR
LINKE HAND

XIII

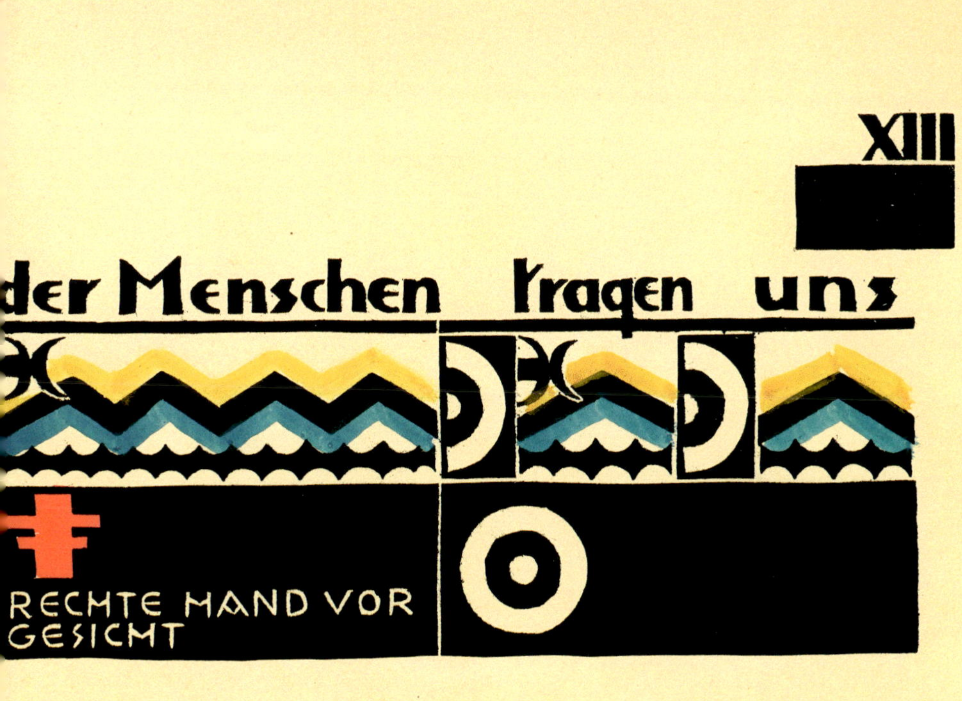
der Menschen fragen uns
RECHTE HAND VOR GESICHT

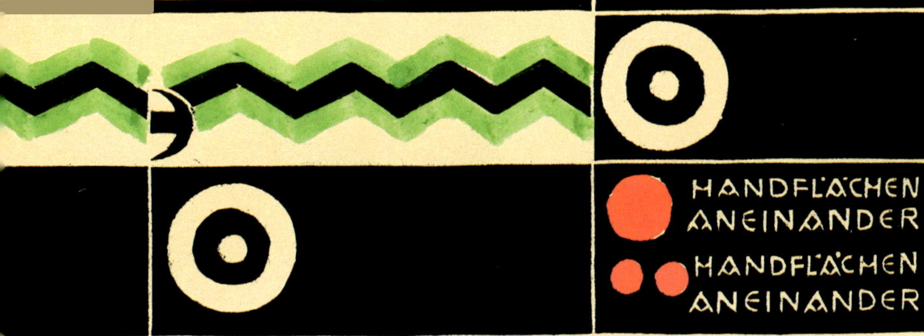
erz ist Blut
HANDFLÄCHEN ANEINANDER
HANDFLÄCHEN ANEINANDER

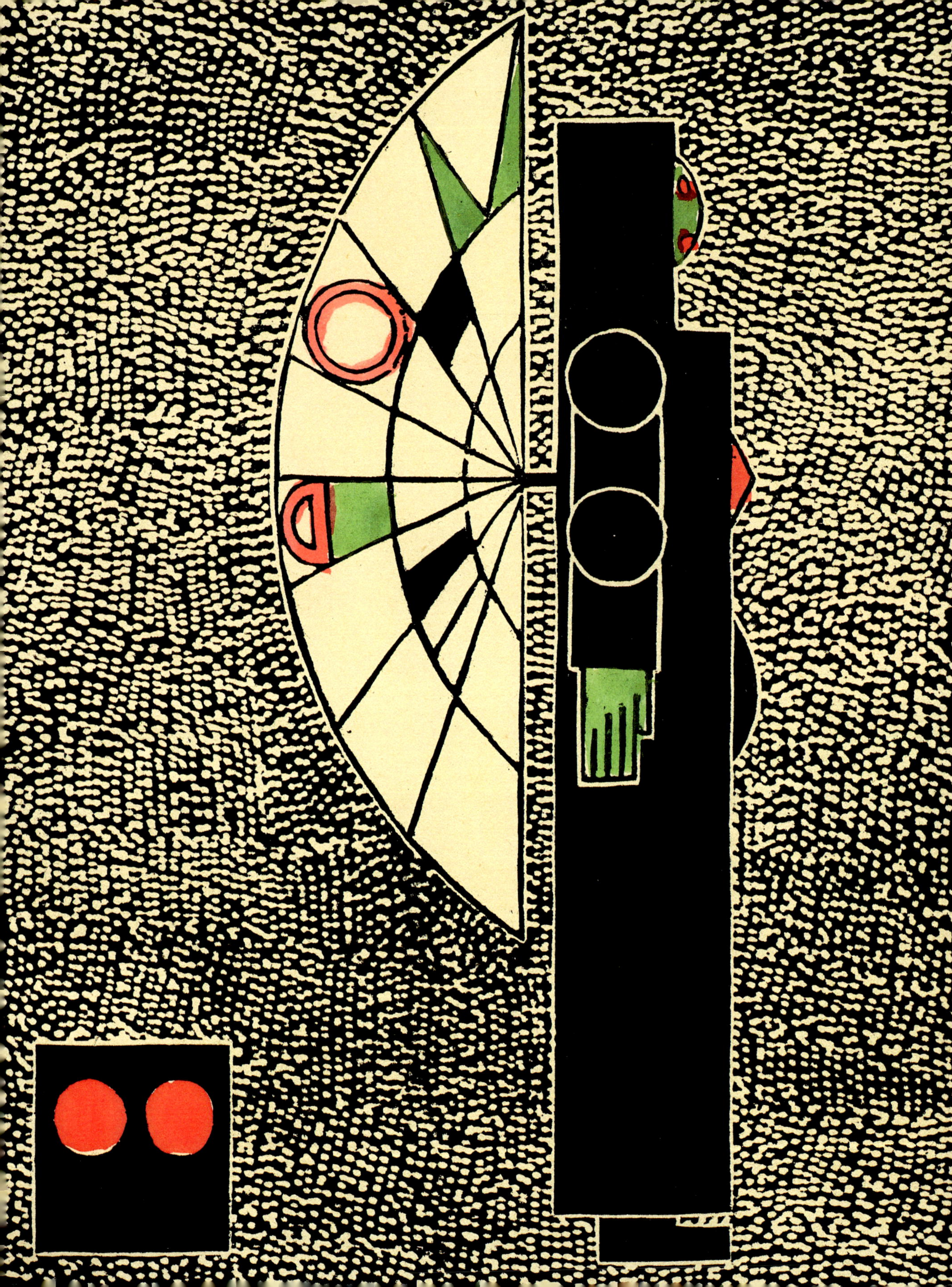

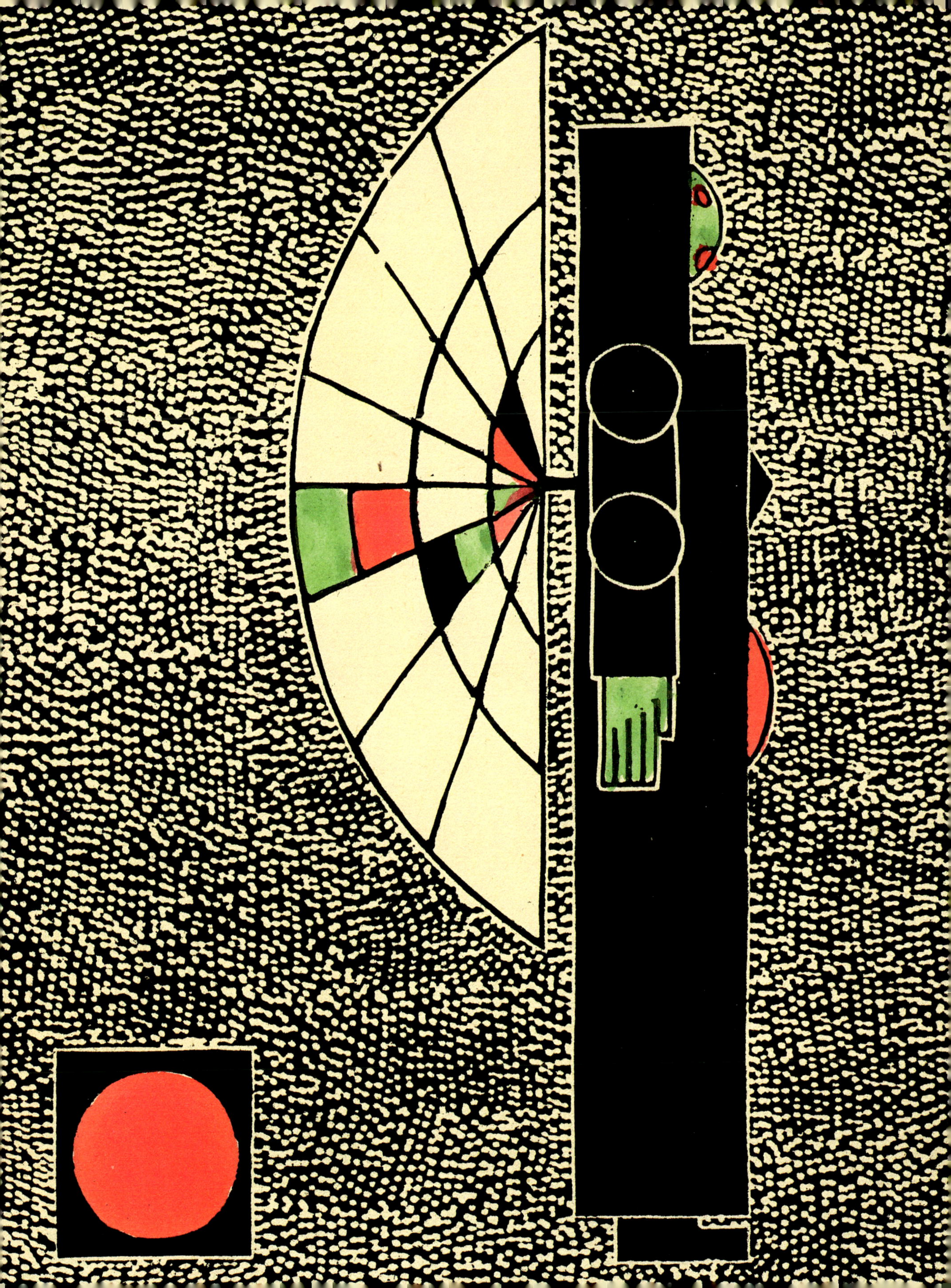

1920

KARL PETER RÖHL (lettering artist)

Announcement for the Bauhaus Evenings (Bauhaus Abende) events series, linocut, 9 × 5⅞ inches (229 × 148 mm), Weimar.

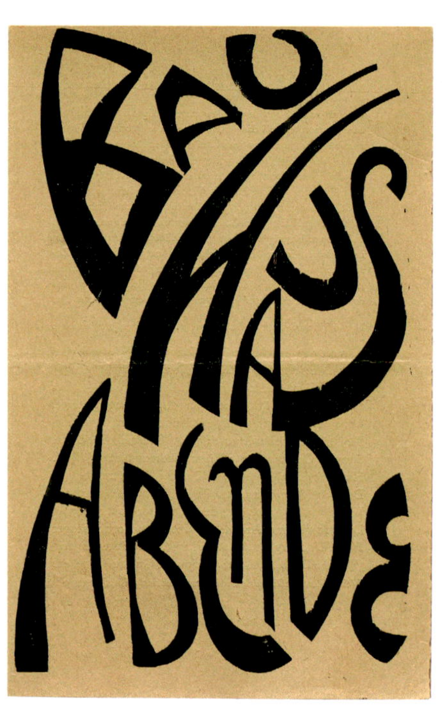

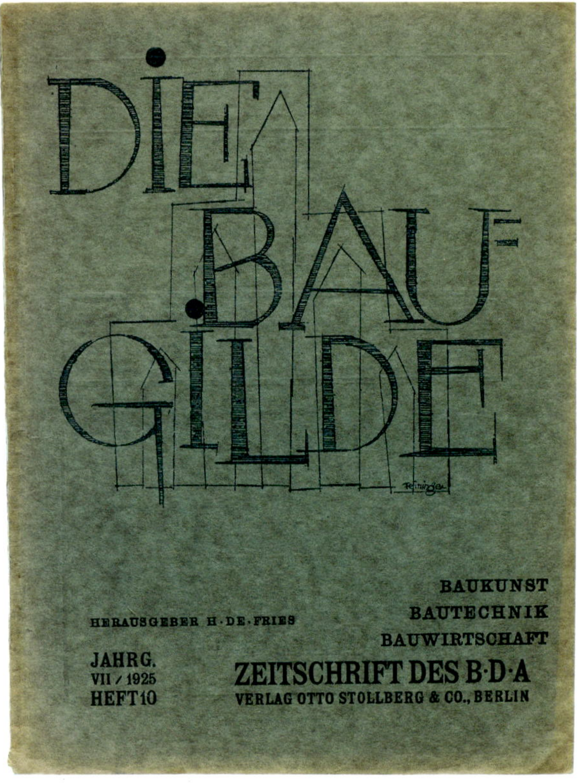

1925

LYONEL FEININGER (cover designer)

Architecture Guild (*Die Baugilde*), vol. 7, no. 10, a magazine for the Association of German Architects, letterpress, 12 × 9⅛ inches (305 × 233 mm), Berlin.

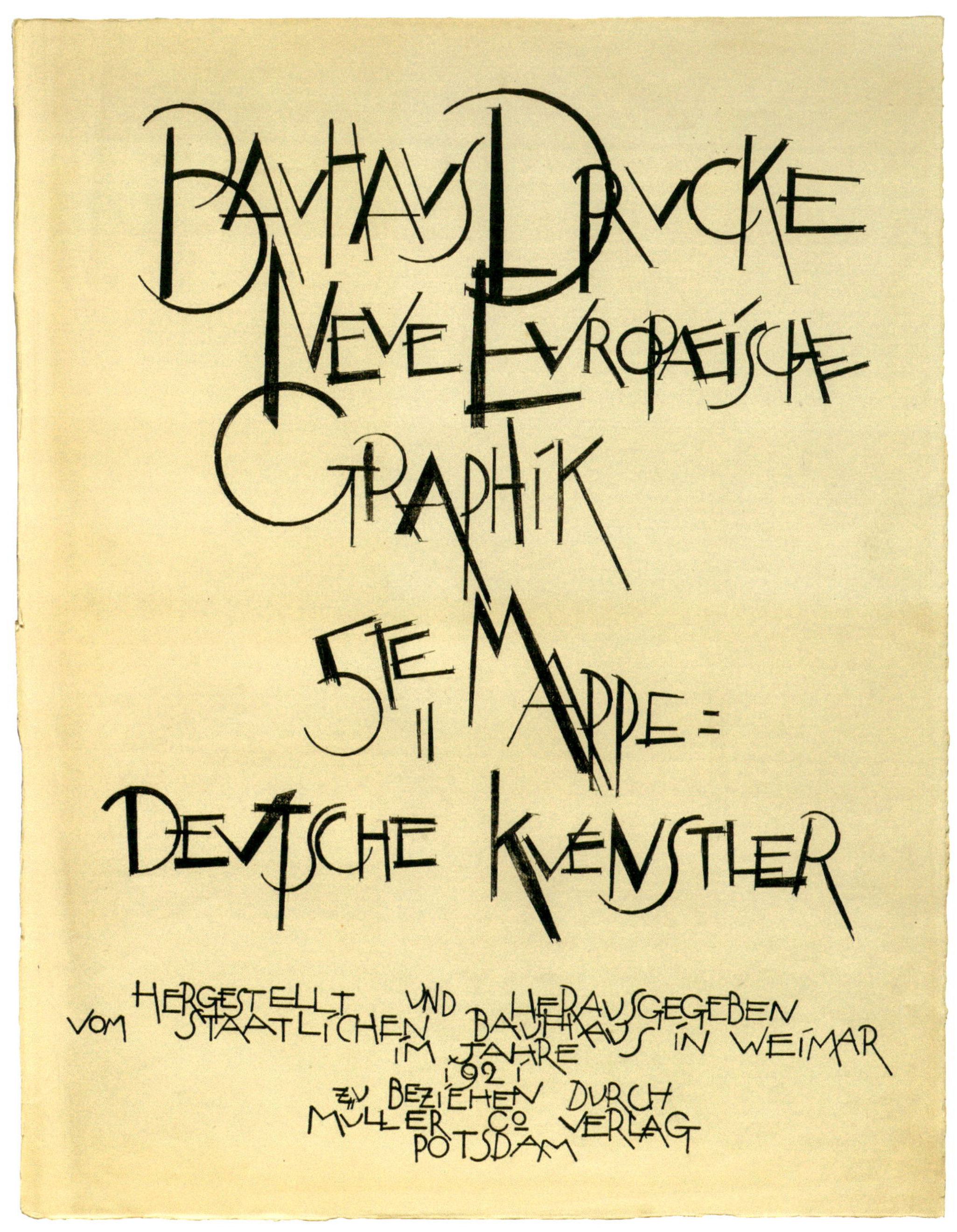

1921

LYONEL FEININGER (lettering artist)

Title page for the fifth portfolio of the *Bauhaus Prints, New European Graphics* (*Bauhaus-Drucke, neue europäische Graphik*) portfolio series, lithograph, 22¼ × 17¾ inches (565 × 450 mm), Potsdam, Germany.

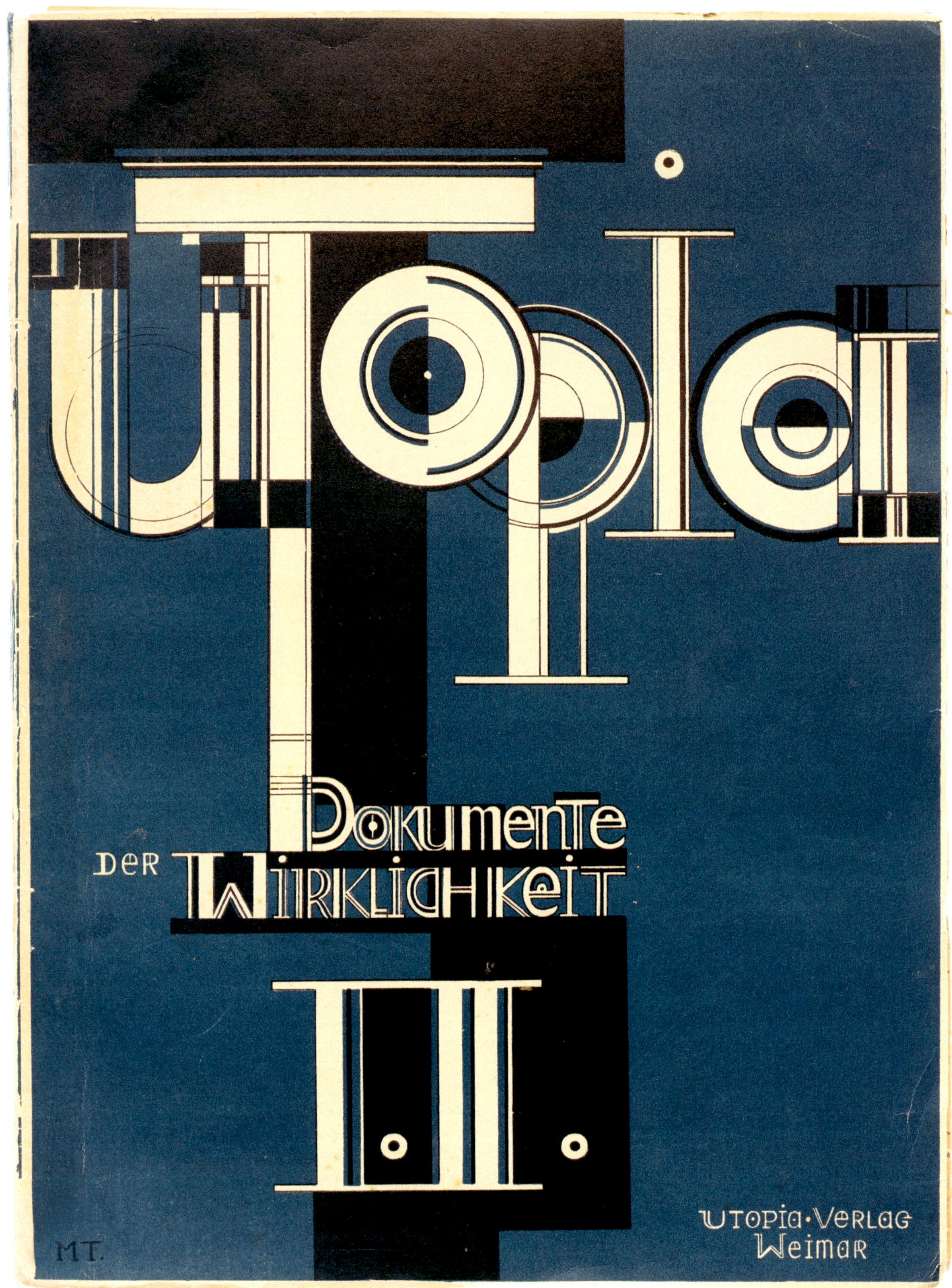
Utopia
Dokumente der Wirklichkeit
MT.
Utopia-Verlag
Weimar

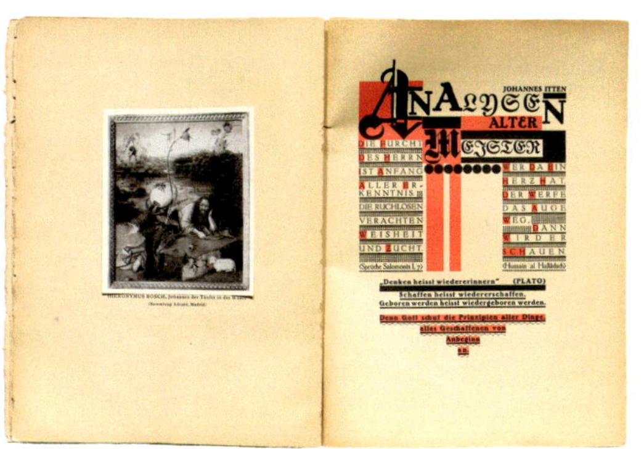

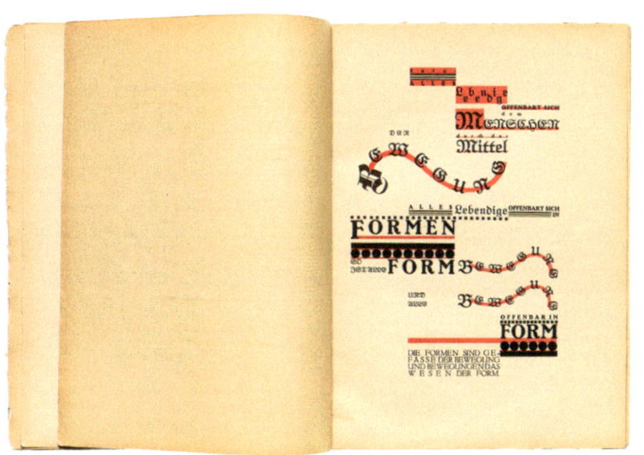

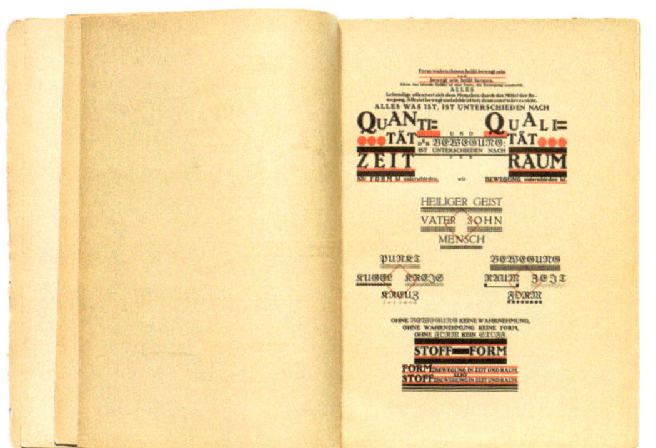

1921

JOHANNES ITTEN (lettering artist/author)
MARGIT TÉRY-ADLER (cover designer)
FRIEDL DICKER (typesetter)

Utopia: Documents of Reality (*Utopia: Dokumente der Wirklichkeit*), lithograph and letterpress with photolithograph tip-ons and tissue paper tip-ins, 12¾ × 9⅞ inches (323 × 249 mm), Weimar.

While not published by the Bauhaus, this book by early master Johannes Itten captures a lesser-known expressive and gestural aesthetic that was nonetheless part of the school in its Weimar years. The book contains a section of reproductions of classical paintings accompanied by lithograph reproductions of Itten's commentary (see top right on page 15 and pages 56–57). His analysis appears in remarkably dense and chaotic hand-lettered compositions, the likes of which are rarely seen in graphic design history until the punk and grunge movements of the late twentieth century. *Utopia* is also a collaborative work, including two student contributions. Hungarian-born Margit Téry-Adler (the wife of the book's publisher, Bruno Adler) designed the cover (see far left), which features geometric-constructivist lettering that contrasts with Itten's irregular organic handwriting inside, and Austrian artist Friedl Dicker rendered one of Itten's essays into striking typographic compositions (see near left and pages 54–55). Dicker's improvisational pages form a typeset complement to Itten's lettering, combining several weights, sizes, and styles of blackletter and roman type—ranging from Unger-Fraktur and Fette Gotisch to Normande, Tiemann-Mediäval, and Bernhard-Antiqua—in red and black ink, plus rules, blocks, and dots, to form structural, Dada-esque configurations. ●

Wir behaupteten oben, daß alle Stoffe Darstellungsmittel sind.
Nun sind aber alle STOFFE — FORMEN.
ALSO IST DIE

Form —
Darstellungsmittel

Wenn dem so ist und das Wesentliche der FORM in ihrem geistig seelischen Ursprung begründet liegt, welcher nie begriffen werden kann, so ergibt sich ohne Mühe der

SCHLUSS:

Die **Darstellungsmittel** sind **ebensowenig lehrbar** wie **Form lehrbar** ist. **Lehren** und **lernen** heißt begriffen haben und begreifen werden.
Die Behauptung, FORM wäre lehrbar, kann also nur einem niedern Verstande als wahr erscheinen.

Frage: Ist ein Lehren und Begreifen überhaupt

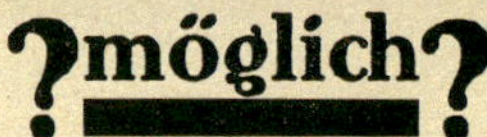

Eines Dinges GRUND ergründen werden wir

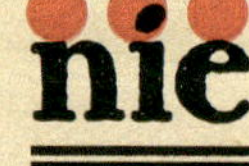

Weder Stoff, noch Form, noch Bewegung
sind lehrbar, begreifbar,

allein

Wahrnehmung
IST
wahrnehmbar

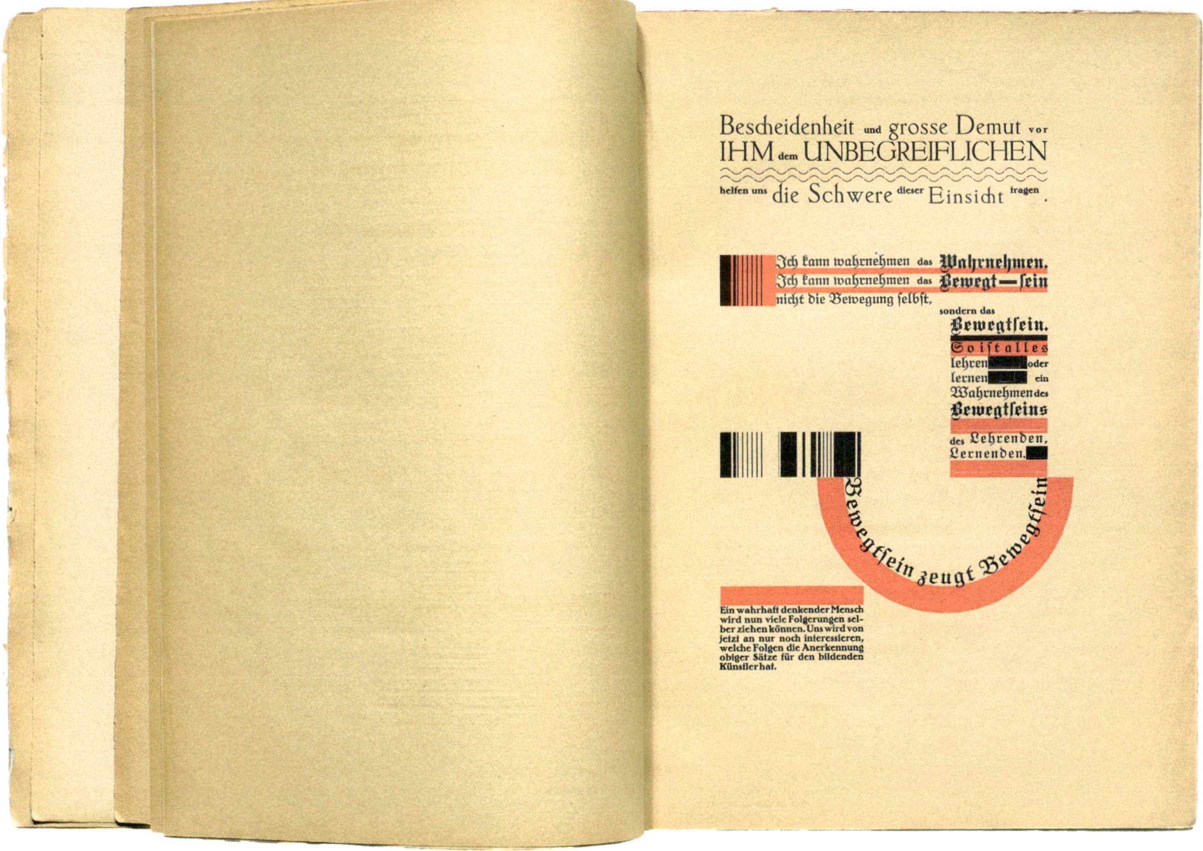
Bescheidenheit und grosse Demut vor
IHM dem UNBEGREIFLICHEN
helfen uns die Schwere dieser Einsicht tragen.
Ich kann wahrnehmen das Wahrnehmen.
Ich kann wahrnehmen das Bewegt—sein
nicht die Bewegung selbst,
sondern das
Bewegtsein.
So ist alles
lehren oder
lernen ein
Wahrnehmen des
Bewegtseins
des Lehrenden,
Lernenden.
Bewegtsein zeugt Bewegtsein
Ein wahrhaft denkender Mensch wird nun viele Folgerungen selber ziehen können. Uns wird von jetzt an nur noch interessieren, welche Folgen die Anerkennung obiger Sätze für den bildenden Künstler hat.

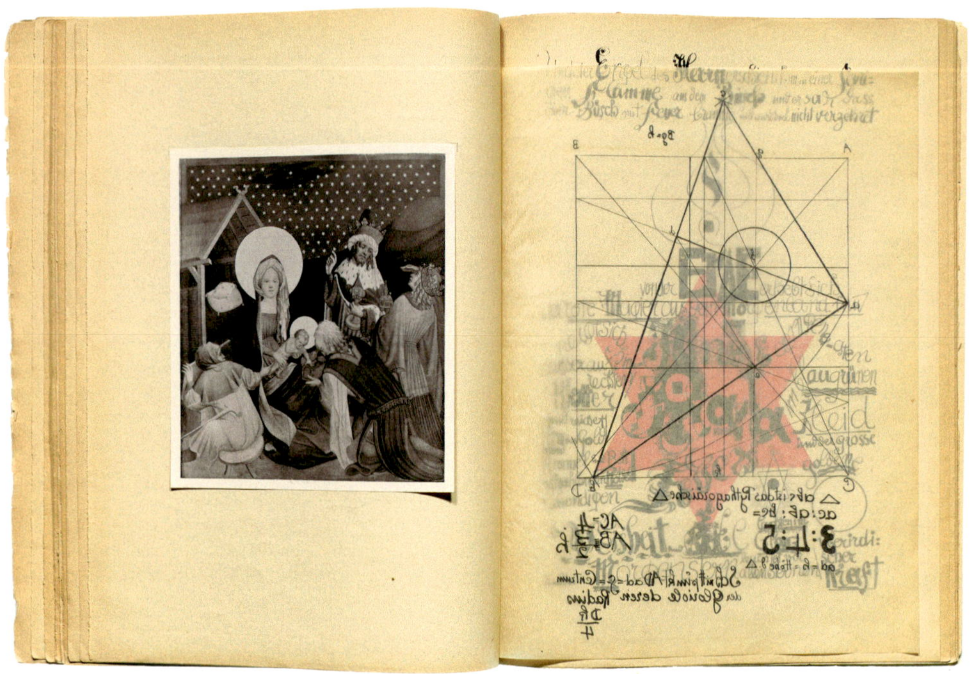

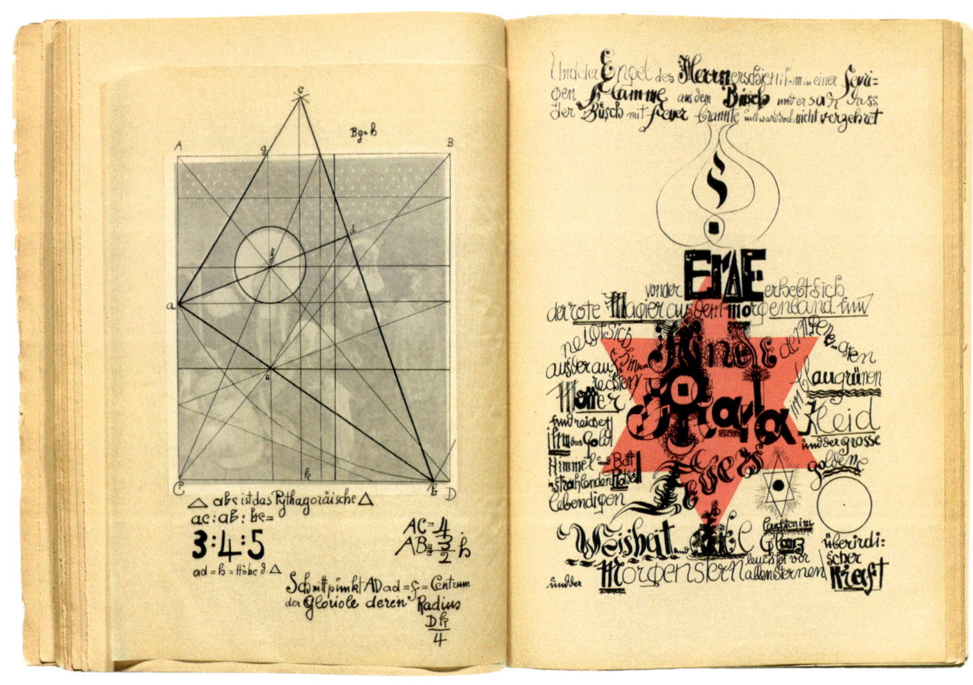
△ abc ist das Pythagoräische △
ac : ab : bc =
3 : 4 : 5
ad = h = Höhe d △
Schnittpunkt AD ad = f = Centrum der Gloriole deren Radius
DK
4
Und der Engel des Herrn erschien ihm in einer feurigen Flamme aus dem Busch
der Busch mit Feuer brannte und ward doch nicht verzehret

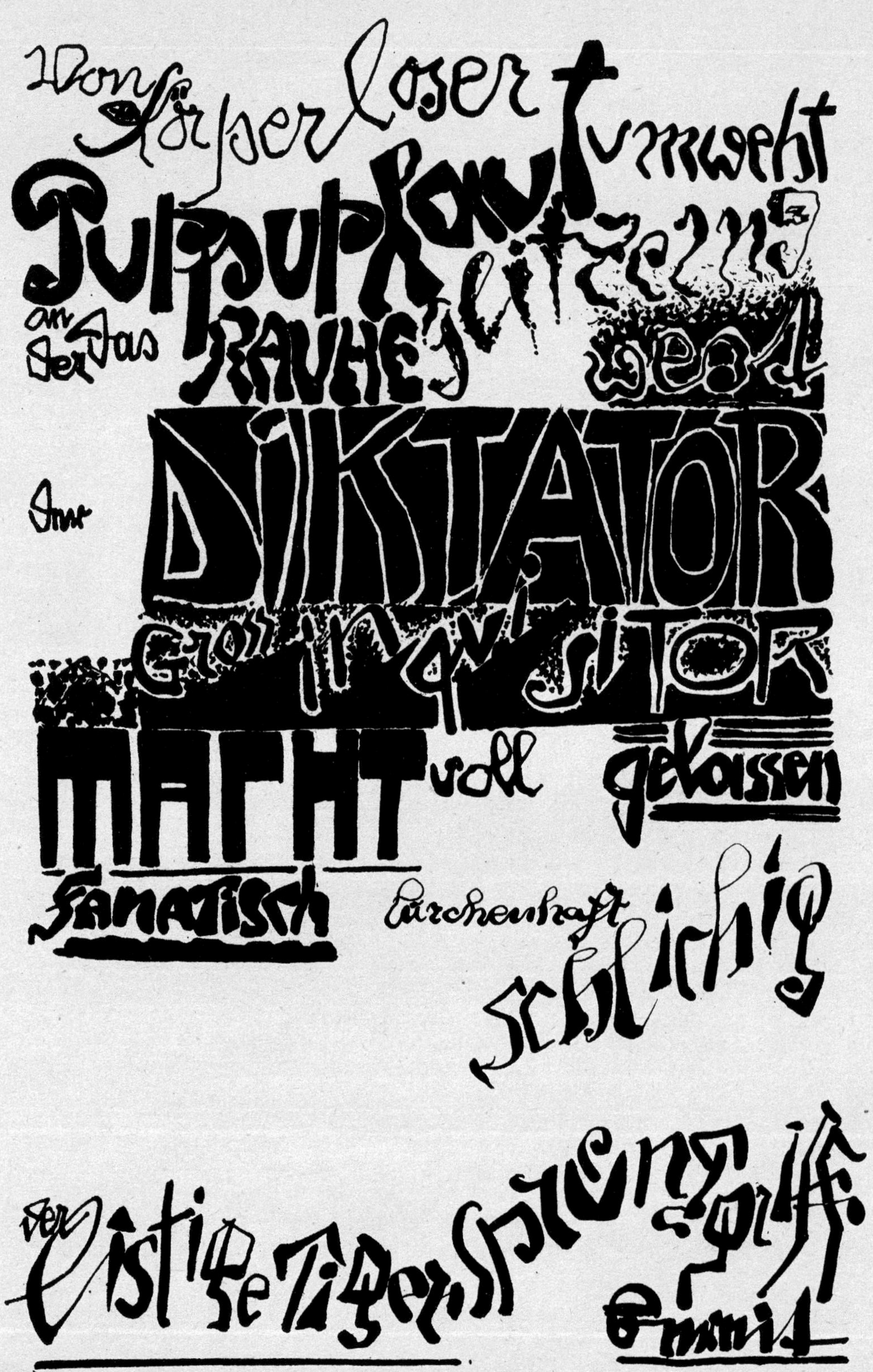
umweht
RAUHE
DIKTATOR
voll
gelassen
fanatisch

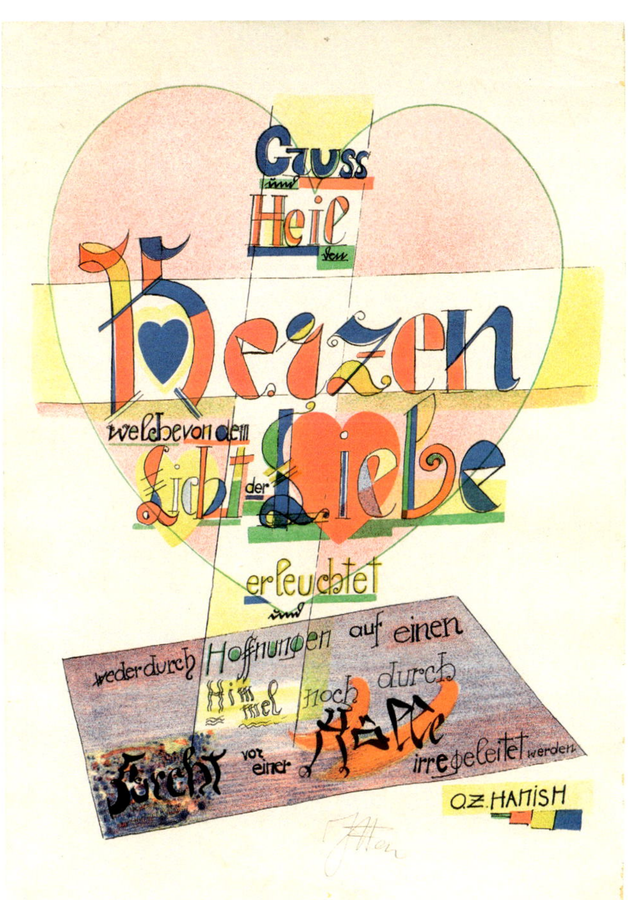

1921

JOHANNES ITTEN

Greetings and Blessings to the Hearts . . . (*Gruss und Heil den Herzen . . .*), from the first portfolio of the *Bauhaus Prints, New European Graphics* (*Bauhaus-Drucke, neue europäische Graphik*) portfolio series, lithograph, 13¾ × 9¾ inches (350 × 248 mm), Weimar.

Created for the first Bauhaus portfolio (one of five planned collections of graphic prints, four of which were produced from 1921 to 1924), this lithograph by Johannes Itten testifies to the spiritual as well as artistic practices that he brought to the Bauhaus as the first master of the preliminary course. The print interprets a phrase by Otto Hanisch, the founder of the mystical neo-Zoroastrian religion Mazdaznan, of which Itten was a follower. It reads: "Greetings and blessings to the hearts that are enlightened by the light of love and are not misled by hopes for heaven or fear of hell." While this particular saying is benign, Mazdaznan also urged belief in malevolent ideas such as racial hierarchy and white supremacy, which Itten espoused on at least one occasion. Itten's course at the Bauhaus included analyses of masterworks (evidenced in his *Utopia*, see pages 52–57) and studies of material and color, but it also began with breathing exercises and encouraged students to explore inner forces. The expressive elements of his pedagogy come through in the palette, composition, and freestyle lettering of this lithograph. With Itten's resignation in 1923 and his replacement by László Moholy-Nagy, these elements largely disappeared from mainstream depictions of the Bauhaus as the paragon of austere, clean-lined rationalism. ●

1930

JOHANNES ITTEN

A 1962 binding and release of sheets from Itten's original 1930 publication, *Diary* (*Tagebuch*), lithograph, 15⅛ × 20½ inches (385 × 521 mm), Zurich.

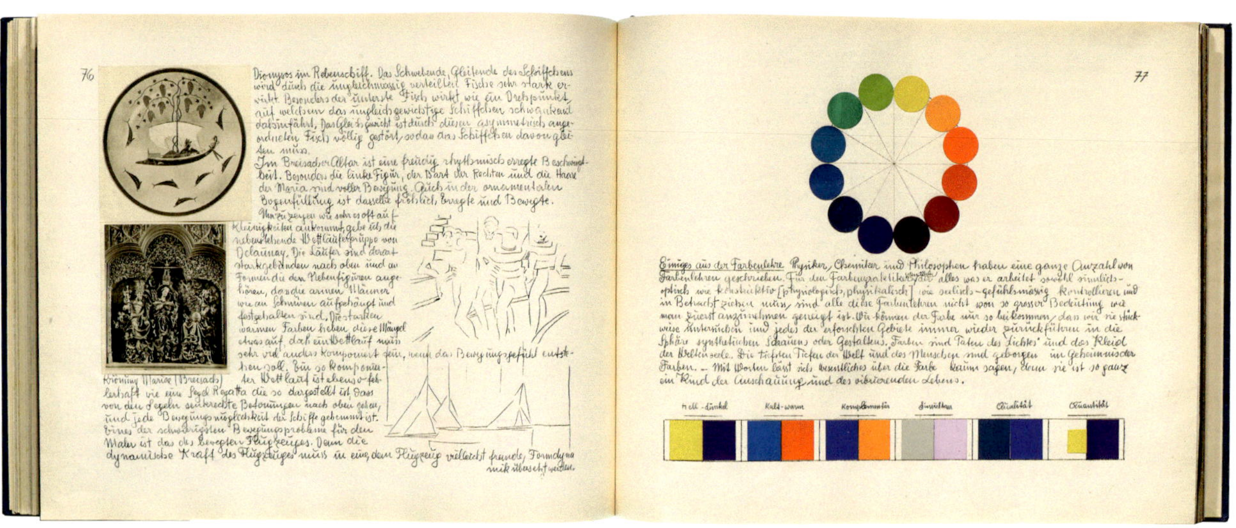

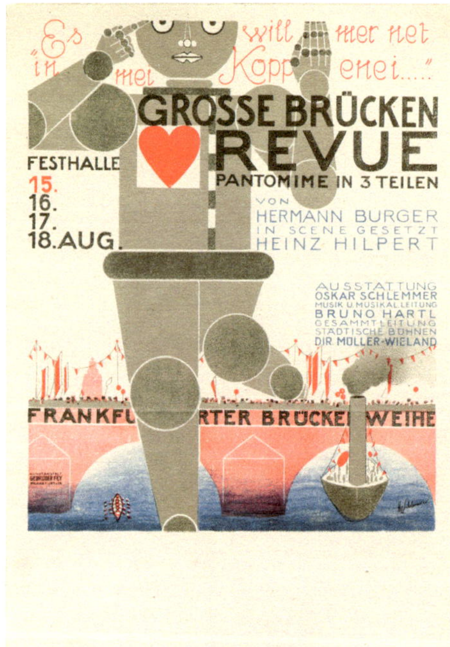

1925

OSKAR SCHLEMMER

Postcard for *Great Bridges Revue, Pantomime in 3 Parts* (*Grosse Brücken Revue, Pantomime in 3 Teilen*), lithograph, 5¾ × 4⅛ inches (147 × 106 mm), Frankfurt.

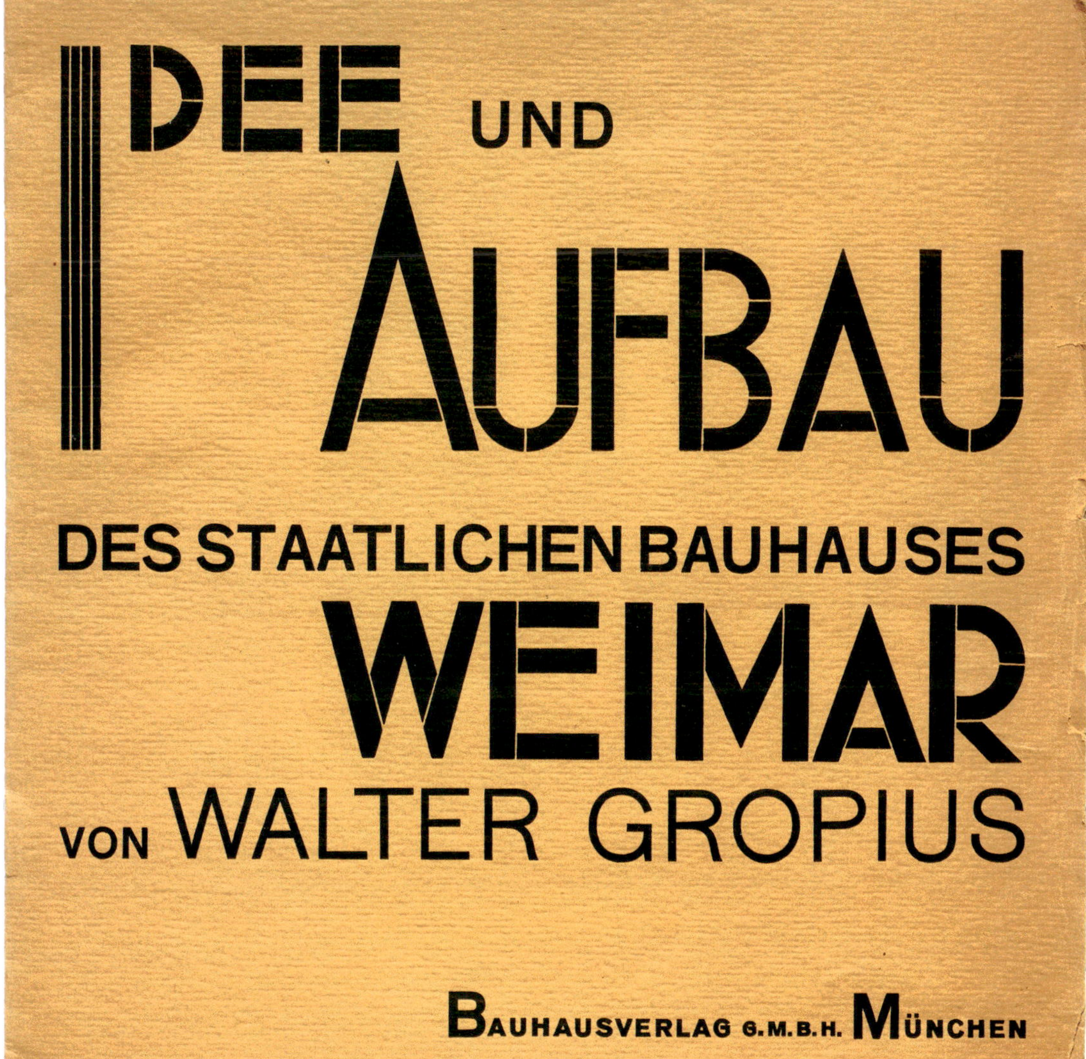
IDEE UND
AUFBAU
DES STAATLICHEN BAUHAUSES
WEIMAR
VON WALTER GROPIUS
BAUHAUSVERLAG G.M.B.H. MÜNCHEN

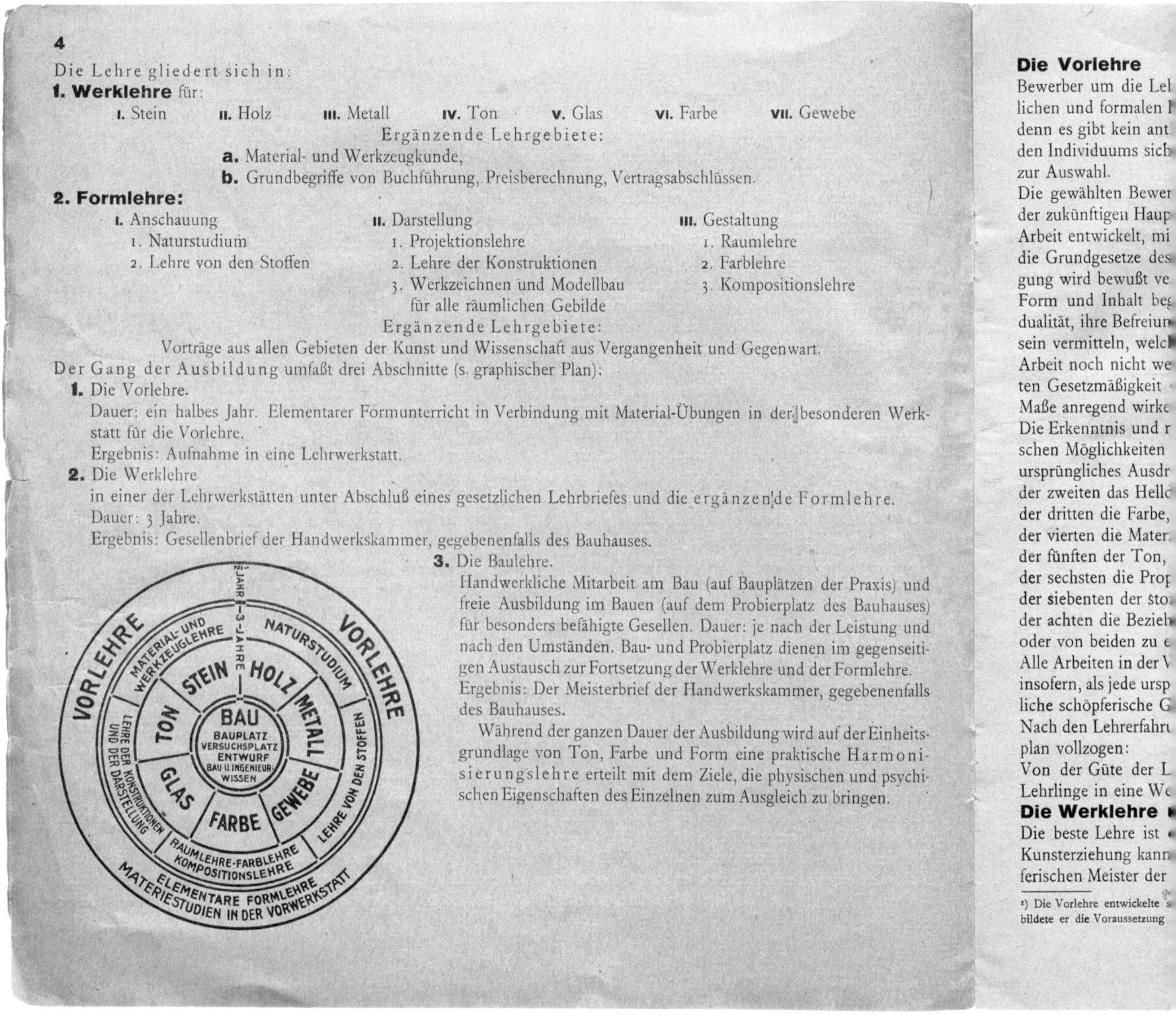

4

Die Lehre gliedert sich in:

1. Werklehre für:

I. Stein **II.** Holz **III.** Metall **IV.** Ton **V.** Glas **VI.** Farbe **VII.** Gewebe

Ergänzende Lehrgebiete:

a. Material- und Werkzeugkunde,
b. Grundbegriffe von Buchführung, Preisberechnung, Vertragsabschlüssen.

2. Formlehre:

I. Anschauung
1. Naturstudium
2. Lehre von den Stoffen

II. Darstellung
1. Projektionslehre
2. Lehre der Konstruktionen
3. Werkzeichnen und Modellbau für alle räumlichen Gebilde

III. Gestaltung
1. Raumlehre
2. Farblehre
3. Kompositionslehre

Ergänzende Lehrgebiete:

Vorträge aus allen Gebieten der Kunst und Wissenschaft aus Vergangenheit und Gegenwart.

Der Gang der Ausbildung umfaßt drei Abschnitte (s. graphischer Plan):

1. Die Vorlehre.
Dauer: ein halbes Jahr. Elementarer Formunterricht in Verbindung mit Material-Übungen in der besonderen Werkstatt für die Vorlehre.
Ergebnis: Aufnahme in eine Lehrwerkstatt.

2. Die Werklehre
in einer der Lehrwerkstätten unter Abschluß eines gesetzlichen Lehrbriefes und die ergänzende Formlehre.
Dauer: 3 Jahre.
Ergebnis: Gesellenbrief der Handwerkskammer, gegebenenfalls des Bauhauses.

3. Die Baulehre.
Handwerkliche Mitarbeit am Bau (auf Bauplätzen der Praxis) und freie Ausbildung im Bauen (auf dem Probierplatz des Bauhauses) für besonders befähigte Gesellen. Dauer: je nach der Leistung und nach den Umständen. Bau- und Probierplatz dienen im gegenseitigen Austausch zur Fortsetzung der Werklehre und der Formlehre.
Ergebnis: Der Meisterbrief der Handwerkskammer, gegebenenfalls des Bauhauses.

Während der ganzen Dauer der Ausbildung wird auf der Einheitsgrundlage von Ton, Farbe und Form eine praktische Harmonisierungslehre erteilt mit dem Ziele, die physischen und psychischen Eigenschaften des Einzelnen zum Ausgleich zu bringen.

Die Vorlehre
Bewerber um die Le[...]
lichen und formalen [...]
denn es gibt kein ant[...]
den Individuums sich[...]
zur Auswahl.
Die gewählten Bewer[...]
der zukünftigen Haup[...]
Arbeit entwickelt, mi[...]
die Grundgesetze des[...]
gung wird bewußt ve[...]
Form und Inhalt beg[...]
dualität, ihre Befreiun[...]
sein vermitteln, welc[...]
Arbeit noch nicht we[...]
ten Gesetzmäßigkeit [...]
Maße anregend wirke[...]
Die Erkenntnis und r[...]
schen Möglichkeiten [...]
ursprüngliches Ausdr[...]
der zweiten das Hell[...]
der dritten die Farbe,
der vierten die Mater[...]
der fünften der Ton,
der sechsten die Pro[...]
der siebenten der Sto[...]
der achten die Bezieh[...]
oder von beiden zu e[...]
Alle Arbeiten in der V[...]
insofern, als jede ursp[...]
liche schöpferische G[...]
Nach den Lehrerfahru[...]
plan vollzogen:
Von der Güte der L[...]
Lehrlinge in eine We[...]
Die Werklehre [...]
Die beste Lehre ist [...]
Kunsterziehung kann[...]
ferischen Meister der [...]

[1]) Die Vorlehre entwickelte [...]
bildete er die Voraussetzung [...]

1923

LÁSZLÓ MOHOLY-NAGY (designer)
WALTER GROPIUS (author)

Idea and Structure of the Weimar State Bauhaus (*Idee und Aufbau des Staatlichen Bauhauses Weimar*), an evolved Bauhaus manifesto published as an excerpt from the *Weimar State Bauhaus 1919–1923* exhibition catalog (see pages 100–103), letterpress, 9⅞ × 9⅞ inches (250 × 250 mm), Munich.

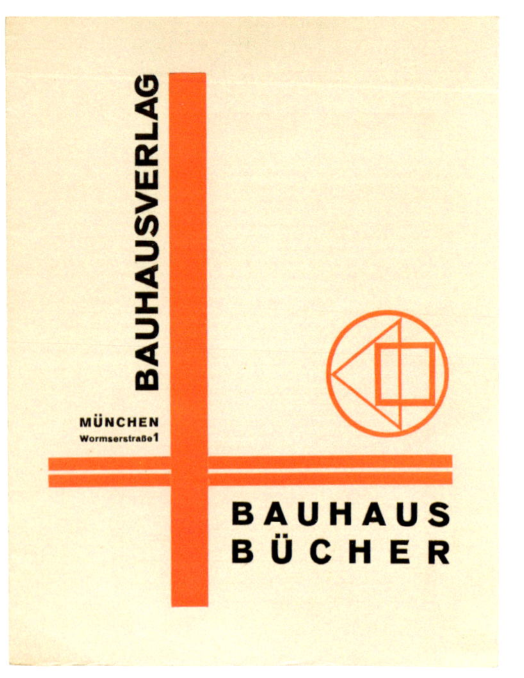

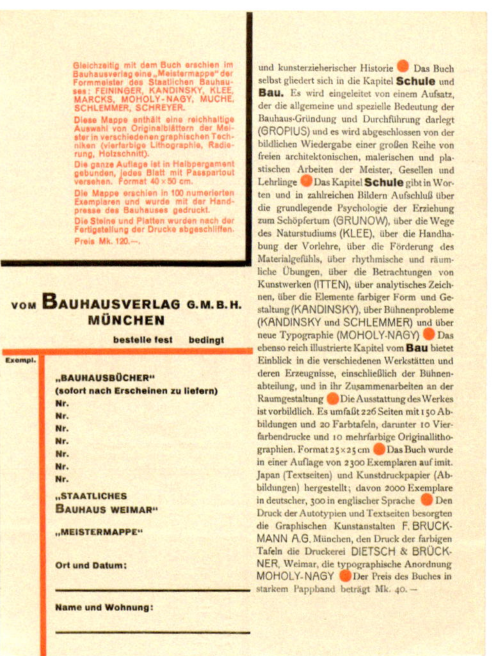

Gleichzeitig mit dem Buch erschien im Bauhausverlag eine „Meistermappe" der Formmeister des Staatlichen Bauhauses: FEININGER, KANDINSKY, KLEE, MARCKS, MOHOLY-NAGY, MUCHE, SCHLEMMER, SCHREYER.

Diese Mappe enthält eine reichhaltige Auswahl von Originalblättern der Meister in verschiedenen graphischen Techniken (vierfarbige Lithographie, Radierung, Holzschnitt).

Die ganze Auflage ist in Halbpergament gebunden, jedes Blatt mit Passpartout versehen. Format 40 × 50 cm.

Die Mappe erschien in 100 numerierten Exemplaren und wurde mit der Handpresse des Bauhauses gedruckt.

Die Steine und Platten wurden nach der Fertigstellung der Drucke abgeschliffen.

Preis Mk. 120.—.

VOM **BAUHAUSVERLAG** G.M.B.H.
MÜNCHEN

bestelle fest bedingt

Exempl.

„BAUHAUSBÜCHER"
(sofort nach Erscheinen zu liefern)
Nr.
Nr.
Nr.
Nr.
Nr.
Nr.
Nr.

„STAATLICHES
BAUHAUS WEIMAR"

„MEISTERMAPPE"

Ort und Datum:

Name und Wohnung:

und kunsterzieherischer Historie ● Das Buch selbst gliedert sich in die Kapitel **Schule** und **Bau.** Es wird eingeleitet von einem Aufsatz, der die allgemeine und spezielle Bedeutung der Bauhaus-Gründung und Durchführung darlegt (GROPIUS) und es wird abgeschlossen von der bildlichen Wiedergabe einer großen Reihe von freien architektonischen, malerischen und plastischen Arbeiten der Meister, Gesellen und Lehrlinge ● Das Kapitel **Schule** gibt in Worten und in zahlreichen Bildern Aufschluß über die grundlegende Psychologie der Erziehung zum Schöpfertum (GRUNOW), über die Wege des Naturstudiums (KLEE), über die Handhabung der Vorlehre, über die Förderung des Materialgefühls, über rhythmische und räumliche Übungen, über die Betrachtungen von Kunstwerken (ITTEN), über analytisches Zeichnen, über die Elemente farbiger Form und Gestaltung (KANDINSKY), über Bühnenprobleme (KANDINSKY und SCHLEMMER) und über neue Typographie (MOHOLY-NAGY) ● Das ebenso reich illustrierte Kapitel vom **Bau** bietet Einblick in die verschiedenen Werkstätten und deren Erzeugnisse, einschließlich der Bühnenabteilung, und in ihr Zusammenarbeiten an der Raumgestaltung ● Die Ausstattung des Werkes ist vorbildlich. Es umfaßt 226 Seiten mit 150 Abbildungen und 20 Farbtafeln, darunter 10 Vierfarbendrucke und 10 mehrfarbige Originallithographien. Format 25 × 25 cm ● Das Buch wurde in einer Auflage von 2300 Exemplaren auf imit. Japan (Textseiten) und Kunstdruckpapier (Abbildungen) hergestellt; davon 2000 Exemplare in deutscher, 300 in englischer Sprache ● Den Druck der Autotypien und Textseiten besorgten die Graphischen Kunstanstalten F. BRUCKMANN A.G. München, den Druck der farbigen Tafeln die Druckerei DIETSCH & BRÜCKNER, Weimar, die typographische Anordnung MOHOLY-NAGY ● Der Preis des Buches in starkem Pappband beträgt Mk. 40.—

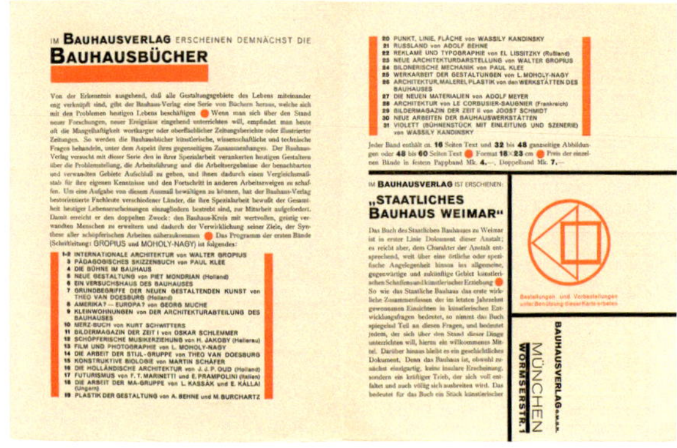

1924

LÁSZLÓ MOHOLY-NAGY

Prospectus for Bauhaus Books (Bauhausbücher), letterpress, 9 × 7 inches (230 × 180 mm) folded, 9 × 14¼ inches (230 x 360 mm) unfolded, Munich.

When László Moholy-Nagy joined the school in 1923 and reformed its typography, there proved no document too insignificant for his graphic approach. This 1924 prospectus for the Bauhaus Books (all published volumes of which appear on pages 106–135) advertises an even more ambitious series than was produced. The brochure promises a surprising number of publications: thirty-one volumes, all advertised with titles and authors, more than double the fourteen books that were ultimately printed by 1930. Still, series editors Moholy-Nagy and Walter Gropius were confident enough in 1924 to include a form—which could be mailed as a postcard—with space to preorder up to seven books (see bottom left). While the brochure was soon obsolete, it remains an excellent example of Moholy-Nagy's typographic sensibility for the Bauhaus's printed matter, with its asymmetric grid of thick horizontal and vertical lines in two colors, a bold sans serif type, Venus, for headlines and emphasis, and large red bullet points that break up text blocks. He reprised this approach two years later in an updated brochure (right), which includes covers and sample images for each title. ●

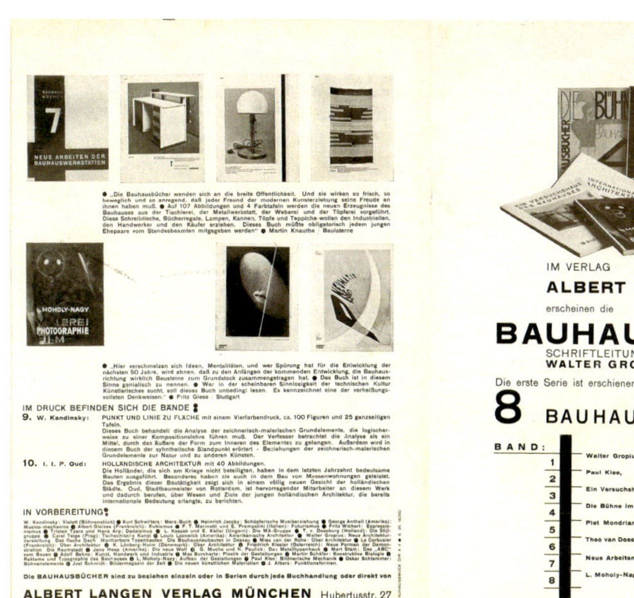

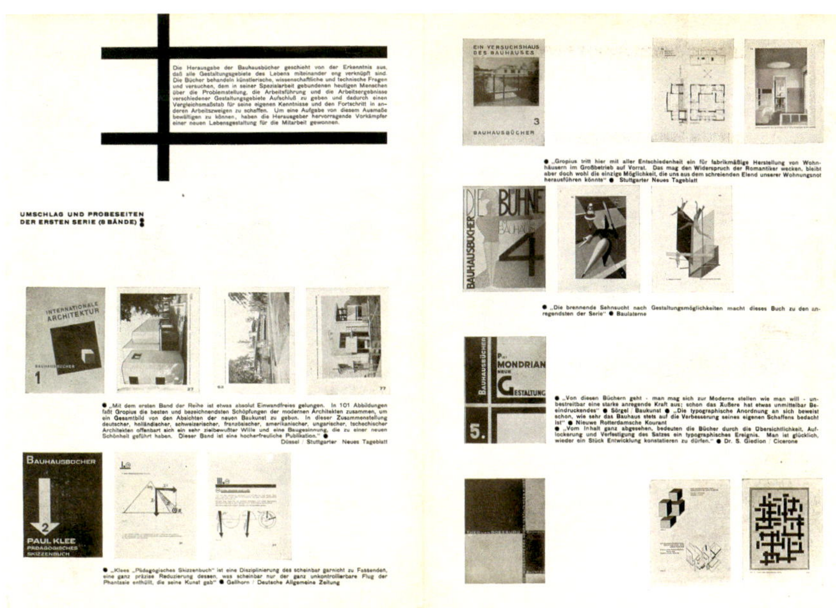

1926

LÁSZLÓ MOHOLY-NAGY

Prospectus for Bauhaus Books (Bauhausbücher), letterpress, 11¾ × 8⅜ inches (297 × 211 mm) folded, 11¾ × 16¾ inches (297 x 422 mm) unfolded, Munich.

1924

LÁSZLÓ MOHOLY-NAGY (designer)
C. AUGUST EMGE (author)

The Idea of the Bauhaus: Art and Reality (*Die Idee des Bauhauses: Kunst und Wirklichkeit*), letterpress, 9 × 6¼ inches (228 × 158 mm), Berlin.

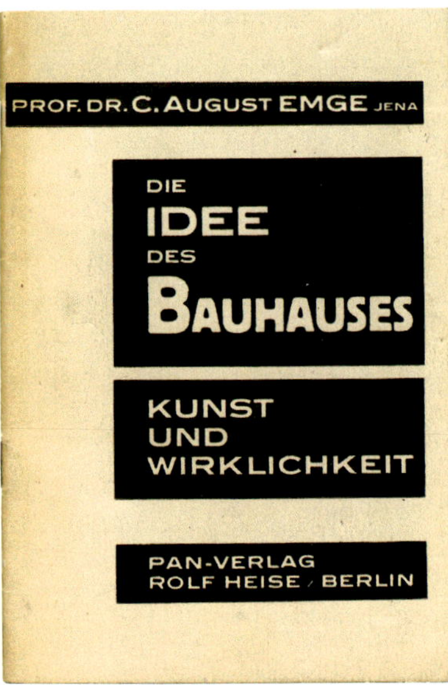

1925

HERBERT BAYER

"Work Plan for First Principles" ("Arbeitsplan der Grundlehre"), syllabus for the preliminary course, letterpress, 11½ × 8⅛ inches (292 × 207 mm), Dessau.

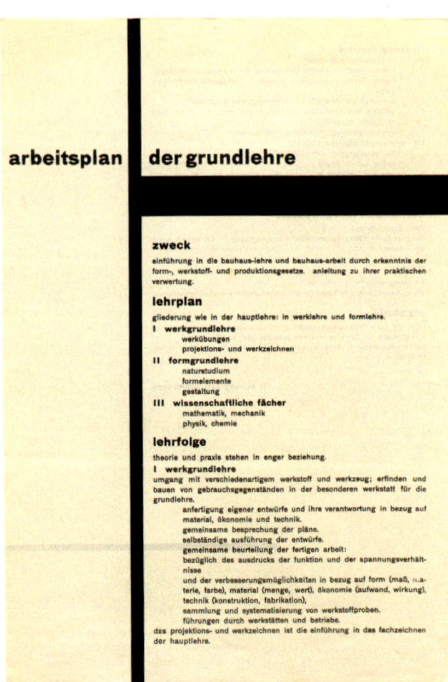

arbeitsplan der grundlehre

zweck

einführung in die bauhaus-lehre und bauhaus-arbeit durch erkenntnis der form-, werkstoff- und produktionsgesetze. anleitung zu ihrer praktischen verwertung.

lehrplan

gliederung wie in der hauptlehre: in werklehre und formlehre.

I werkgrundlehre
werkübungen
projektions- und werkzeichnen

II formgrundlehre
naturstudium
formelemente
gestaltung

III wissenschaftliche fächer
mathematik, mechanik
physik, chemie

lehrfolge

theorie und praxis stehen in enger beziehung.

I werkgrundlehre
umgang mit verschiedenartigem werkstoff und werkzeug; erfinden und bauen von gebrauchsgegenständen in der besonderen werkstatt für die grundlehre.
anfertigung eigener entwürfe und ihre verantwortung in bezug auf material, ökonomie und technik.
gemeinsame besprechung der pläne.
selbständige ausführung der entwürfe.
gemeinsame beurteilung der fertigen arbeit:
bezüglich des ausdrucks der funktion und der spannungsverhältnisse
und der verbesserungsmöglichkeiten in bezug auf form (maß, materie, farbe), material (menge, wert), ökonomie (aufwand, wirkung), technik (konstruktion, fabrikation),
sammlung und systematisierung von werkstoffproben.
führungen durch werkstätten und betriebe.
das projektions- und werkzeichnen ist die einführung in das fachzeichnen der hauptlehre.

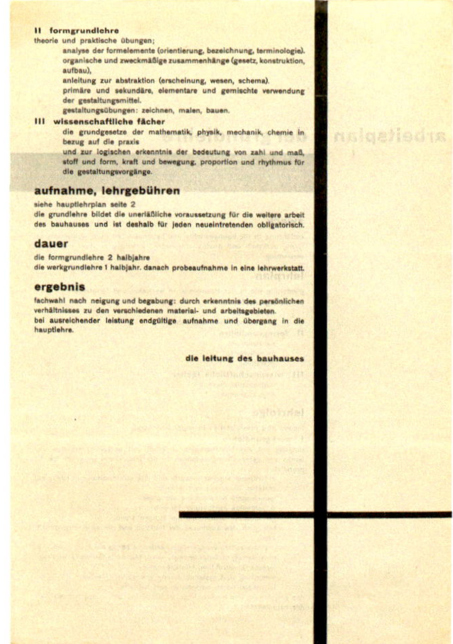

II formgrundlehre
theorie und praktische übungen;
analyse der formelemente (orientierung, bezeichnung, terminologie).
organische und zweckmäßige zusammenhänge (gesetz, konstruktion, aufbau),
anleitung zur abstraktion (erscheinung, wesen, schema).
primäre und sekundäre, elementare und gemischte verwendung der gestaltungsmittel.
gestaltungsübungen: zeichnen, malen, bauen.

III wissenschaftliche fächer
die grundgesetze der mathematik, physik, mechanik, chemie in bezug auf die praxis
und zur logischen erkenntnis der bedeutung von zahl und maß, stoff und form, kraft und bewegung, proportion und rhythmus für die gestaltungsvorgänge.

aufnahme, lehrgebühren

siehe hauptlehrplan seite 2
die grundlehre bildet die unerläßliche voraussetzung für die weitere arbeit des bauhauses und ist deshalb für jeden neueintretenden obligatorisch.

dauer

die formgrundlehre 2 halbjahre
die werkgrundlehre 1 halbjahr. danach probeaufnahme in eine lehrwerkstatt.

ergebnis

fachwahl nach neigung und begabung: durch erkenntnis des persönlichen verhältnisses zu den verschiedenen material- und arbeitsgebieten.
bei ausreichender leistung endgültige aufnahme und übergang in die hauptlehre.

die leitung des bauhauses

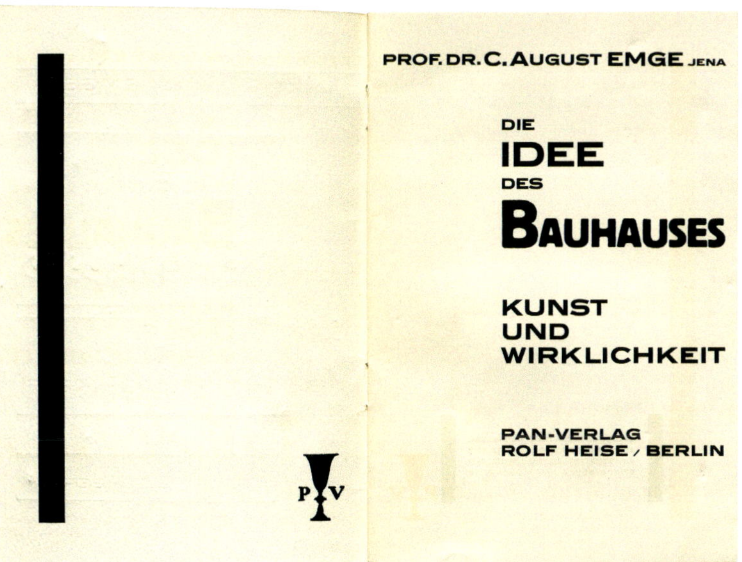

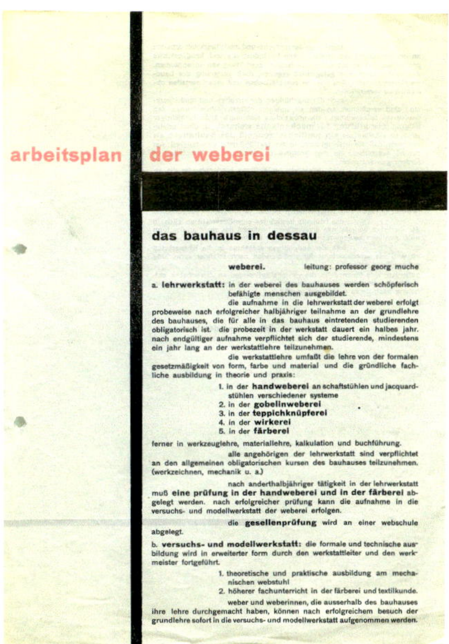

arbeitsplan der weberei

das bauhaus in dessau

weberei. leitung: professor georg muche

a. **lehrwerkstatt:** in der weberei des bauhauses werden schöpferisch befähigte menschen ausgebildet.

die aufnahme in die lehrwerkstatt der weberei erfolgt probeweise nach erfolgreicher halbjähriger teilnahme an der grundlehre des bauhauses, die für alle in das bauhaus eintretenden studierenden obligatorisch ist. die probezeit in der werkstatt dauert ein halbes jahr. nach endgültiger aufnahme verpflichtet sich der studierende, mindestens ein jahr lang an der werkstattlehre teilzunehmen.

die werkstattlehre umfaßt die lehre von der formalen gesetzmäßigkeit von form, farbe und material und die gründliche fachliche ausbildung in theorie und praxis:

1. in der **handweberei** an schaftstühlen und jacquardstühlen verschiedener systeme
2. in der **gobelinweberei**
3. in der **teppichknüpferei**
4. in der **wirkerei**
5. in der **färberei**

ferner in werkzeuglehre, materiallehre, kalkulation und buchführung.

alle angehörigen der lehrwerkstatt sind verpflichtet an den allgemeinen obligatorischen kursen des bauhauses teilzunehmen. (werkzeichnen, mechanik u. a.)

nach anderthalbjähriger tätigkeit in der lehrwerkstatt muß **eine prüfung in der handweberei und in der färberei** abgelegt werden. nach erfolgreicher prüfung kann die aufnahme in die versuchs- und modellwerkstatt der weberei erfolgen.

die **gesellenprüfung** wird an einer webschule abgelegt.

b. **versuchs- und modellwerkstatt:** die formale und technische ausbildung wird in erweiterter form durch den werkstattleiter und den werkmeister fortgeführt.

1. theoretische und praktische ausbildung am mechanischen webstuhl
2. höherer fachunterricht in der färberei und textilkunde.

weber und weberinnen, die ausserhalb des bauhauses ihre lehre durchgemacht haben, können nach erfolgreichem besuch der grundlehre sofort in die versuchs- und modellwerkstatt aufgenommen werden.

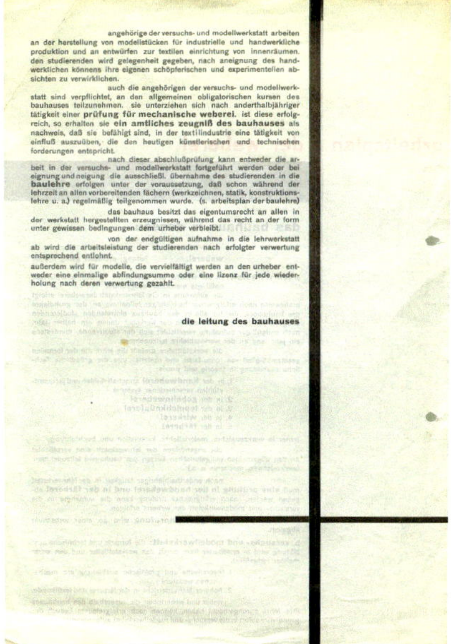

angehörige der versuchs- und modellwerkstatt arbeiten an der herstellung von modellstücken für industrielle und handwerkliche produktion und an entwürfen zur textilen einrichtung von innenräumen. den studierenden wird gelegenheit gegeben, nach aneignung des handwerklichen könnens ihre eigenen schöpferischen und experimentellen absichten zu verwirklichen.

auch die angehörigen der versuchs- und modellwerkstatt sind verpflichtet, an den allgemeinen obligatorischen kursen des bauhauses teilzunehmen. sie unterziehen sich nach anderthalbjähriger tätigkeit einer **prüfung für mechanische weberei**. ist diese erfolgreich, so erhalten sie **ein amtliches zeugniß des bauhauses** als nachweis, daß sie befähigt sind, in der textilindustrie eine tätigkeit von einfluß auszuüben, die den heutigen künstlerischen und technischen forderungen entspricht.

nach dieser abschlußprüfung kann entweder die arbeit in der versuchs- und modellwerkstatt fortgeführt werden oder bei eignung und neigung die ausschließl. übernahme des studierenden in die **baulehre** erfolgen unter der voraussetzung, daß schon während der lehrzeit an allen vorbereitenden fächern (werkzeichnen, statik, konstruktionslehre u. a.) regelmäßig teilgenommen wurde. (s. arbeitsplan der baulehre)

das bauhaus besitzt das eigentumsrecht an allen in der werkstatt hergestellten erzeugnissen, während das recht an der form unter gewissen bedingungen dem urheber verbleibt.

von der endgültigen aufnahme in die lehrwerkstatt ab wird die arbeitsleistung der studierenden nach erfolgter verwertung entsprechend entlohnt.

außerdem wird für modelle, die vervielfältigt werden an den urheber entweder eine einmalige abfindungssumme oder eine lizenz für jede wiederholung nach deren verwertung gezahlt.

die leitung des bauhauses

1925

HERBERT BAYER

"Work Plan of the Weaving Mill" ("Arbeitsplan der Weberei"), syllabus for the weaving workshop, letterpress, 11½ × 8¼ inches (292 × 210 mm), Dessau.

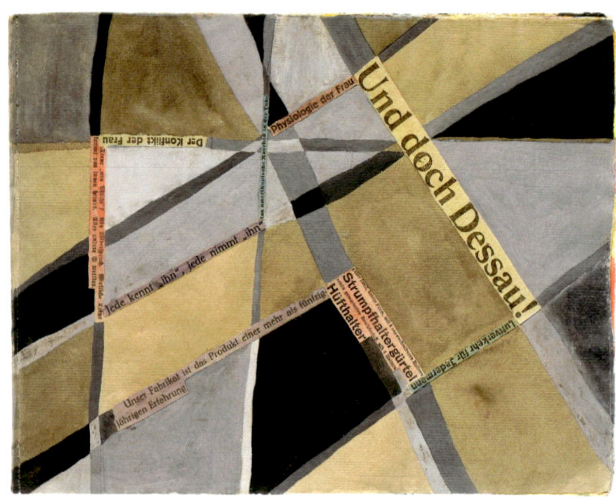
Und doch Dessau!
Physiologie der Frau
Der Konflikt der Frau
Jede kennt „ihn“, jede nimmt „ihn“
Strumpfhaltergürtel
Hüfthalter
Unser Fabrikat ist das Produkt einer mehr als fünfzig-
jährigen Erfahrung

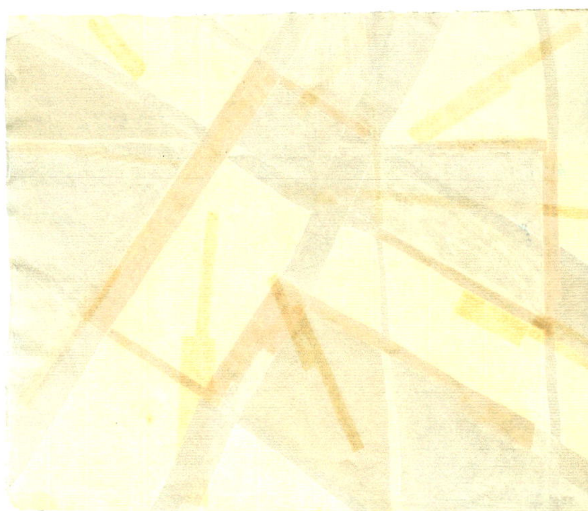

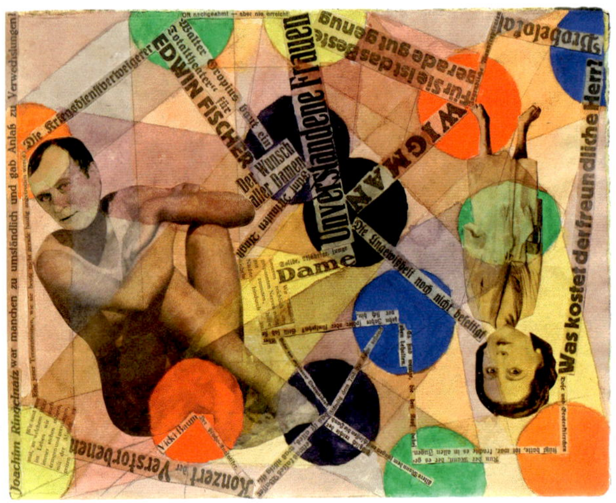
Joachim Ringelnatz war manchen zu umständlich und gab Anlaß zu Verwechslungen
Die Kriegsdienstverweigerer
EDWIN FISCHER
Der Wunsch aller Damen
Unverstandene Frauen
WIGMAN
Für sie ist das Beste gerade gut genug
Probefoto!
Dame
Was kostet der freundliche Herr?
Konzert
Verstorbenen

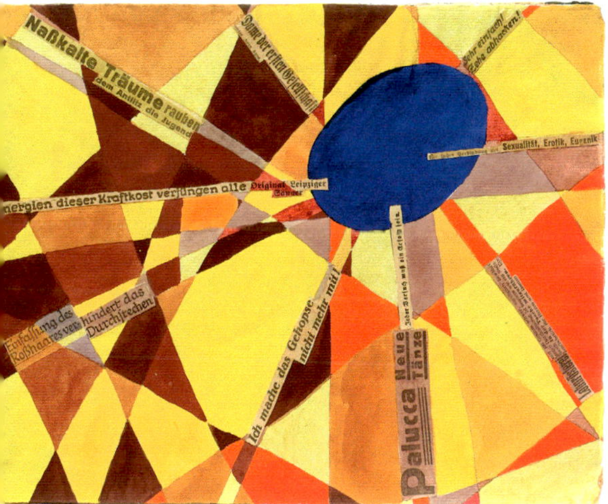

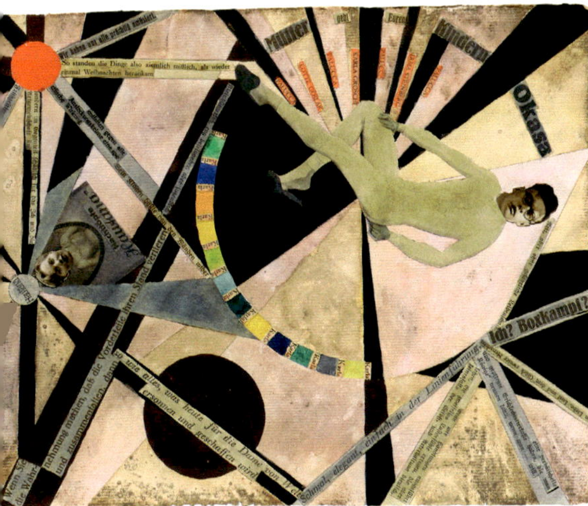

1927

FELIX KLEE

After All, Dessau! (*Und doch, Dessau!*), collage and watercolor, 9¼ × 12 inches (234 × 304 mm), Breslau, Germany (present-day Wrocław, Poland).

Felix Klee sent this eccentric letter to German dancer Karla Grosch in 1927, perhaps in celebration of her teaching appointment at the Bauhaus. It consists of five pages of dynamic pictorial and text collage, laid over watercolor backgrounds of intersecting lines and planes. Felix, son of German Bauhaus master Paul Klee, studied at the school during its Weimar years. Grosch began teaching gymnastics at the Bauhaus in Dessau in 1928 under director Hannes Meyer, who insisted that the institution provide a physical education in addition to technical and artistic schooling. Grosch also became a kind of adopted daughter of the Klee family and lived in their house on the Dessau campus. She remained at the Bauhaus until 1932 and was frequently involved in its theater and dance productions as a choreographer and performer. Grosch and Gunta Stölzl, master of the weaving workshop, were the only women teachers at the Bauhaus in Dessau. Felix Klee's montage booklet—an interpersonal handmade object rather than a public printed one—constitutes a marked contrast to the clean, readable, universally addressed documents most associated with the Bauhaus. Instead, the found texts bear either private or incidental meanings, the typefaces are a cacophony of decorative styles—including Herold, Bernhard-Kursiv, Etienne, Tages-Antiqua, Altfraktur, and Block-Fraktur—rather than a harmony of simple sans serifs, and their topsy-turvy placements seem chosen by instinct rather than by a rational program. ●

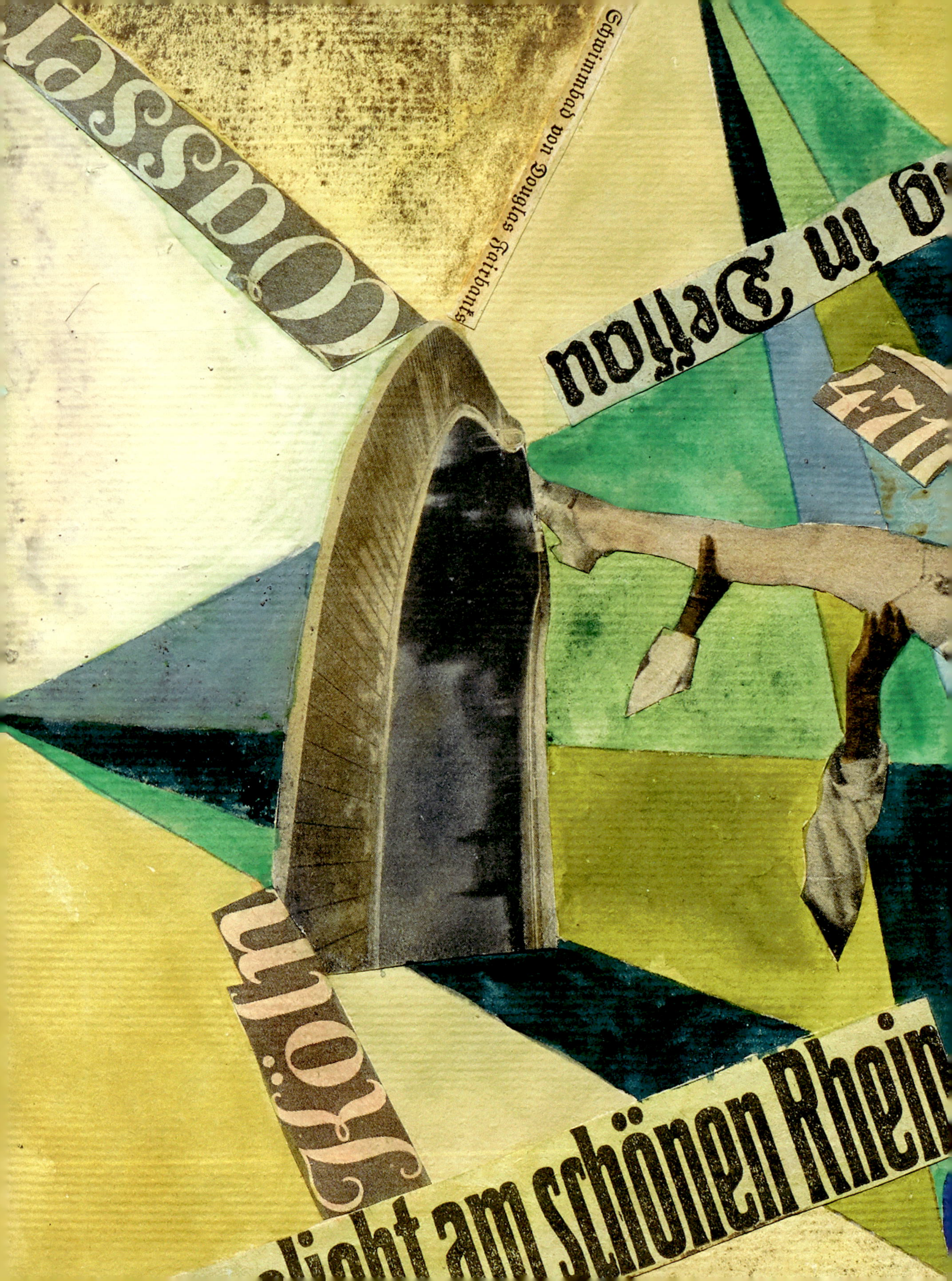

Schwimmbad von Douglas Fairbanks
in Dessau
471
Köln
licht am schönen Rhein

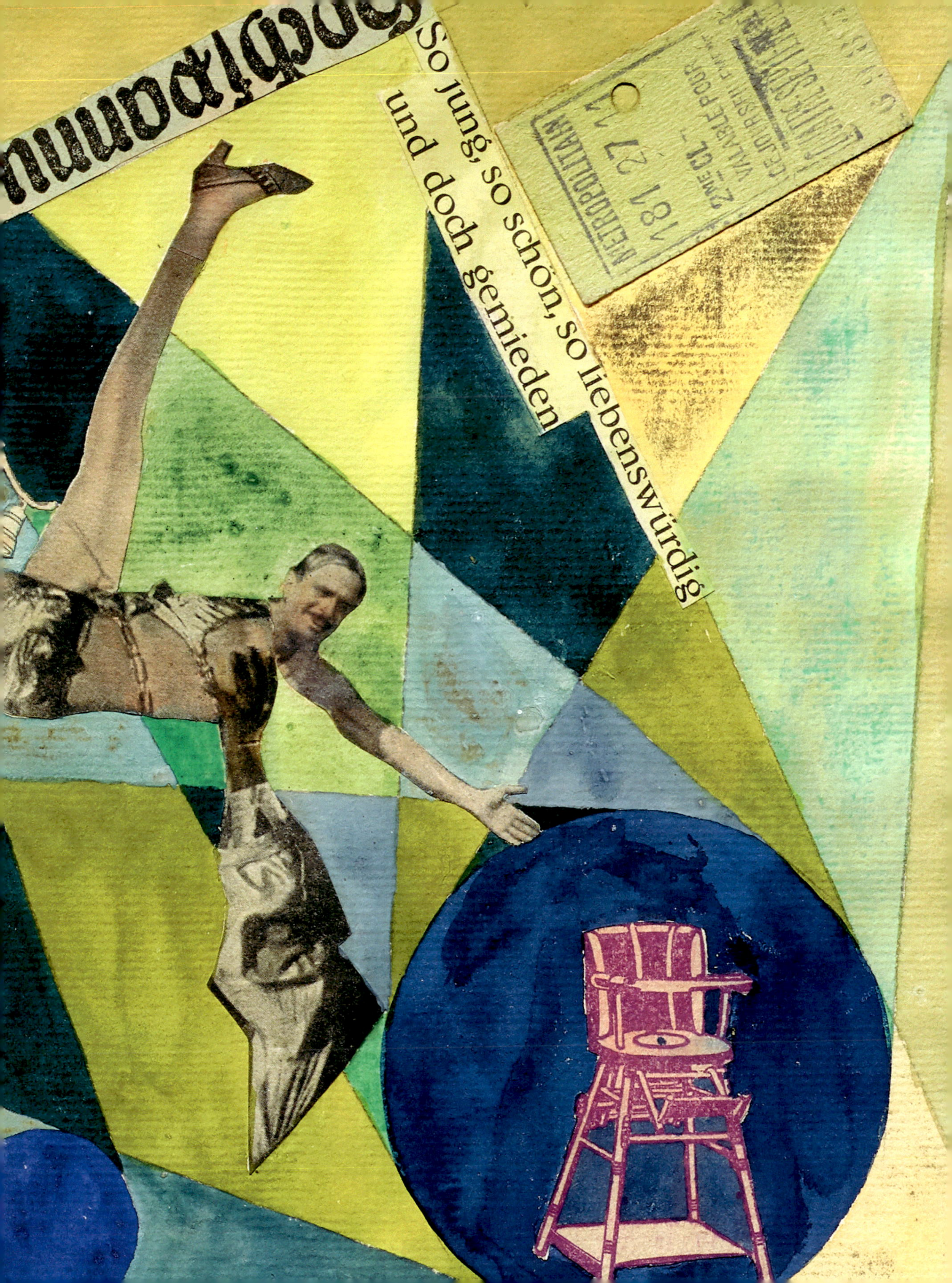
So jung, so schön, so liebenswürdig
und doch gemieden

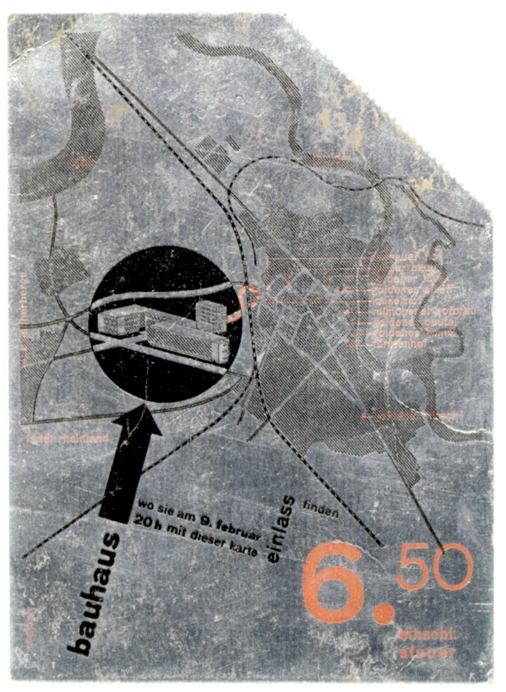

1929

JOHAN NIEGEMAN

LEFT

Ticket for the Bauhaus-Carnival Metallic Festival (Bauhaus-Fasching Metallisches Fest), letterpress, $5\frac{1}{2} \times 4\frac{1}{8}$ inches (140 × 105 mm), Dessau.

RIGHT

Invitation for the Bauhaus-Carnival Metallic Festival (Bauhaus-Fasching Metallisches Fest), letterpress, $4\frac{1}{4} \times 5\frac{7}{8}$ inches (107 × 148 mm), Dessau.

Designed by Dutch architect Johan Niegeman, who taught for two years at the Bauhaus, these two pieces of ephemera from the 1929 Metallic Festival (Metallisches Fest) are evidence of the many parties and celebrations that were an essential component of the life and community of the school. Photographs from these carnivalesque occasions show flamboyant decorations and extravagant costumes. The Metallic Festival in particular proved one of the Bauhaus's most memorable gatherings, with attendees dressed in tin foil, frying pans, and other reflective materials. The themes of these parties often carried over to the design of print materials such as invitations, admission tickets, and posters, as seen in the metallic-coated paper stock and multiple ink colors of the invitation and ticket here. Communal solidarity through social events and levity was explicitly incorporated into the philosophy of the school from its inception. Indeed, the principles of the Bauhaus as stated in Walter Gropius's founding manifesto include "Encouragement of friendly relations between masters and students outside of work; therefore plays, lectures, poetry, music, costume parties" and "Establishment of a cheerful ceremonial at these gatherings." While the basic pedagogical relationship of master and apprentice remained, the Bauhaus idea of a more communal, solidaristic school—where teachers and students lived, worked, and played as social peers, and where accomplished students could themselves become junior masters and teach their discipline—offered a compelling alternative to the traditional hierarchies in arts education. It remains influential today. ●

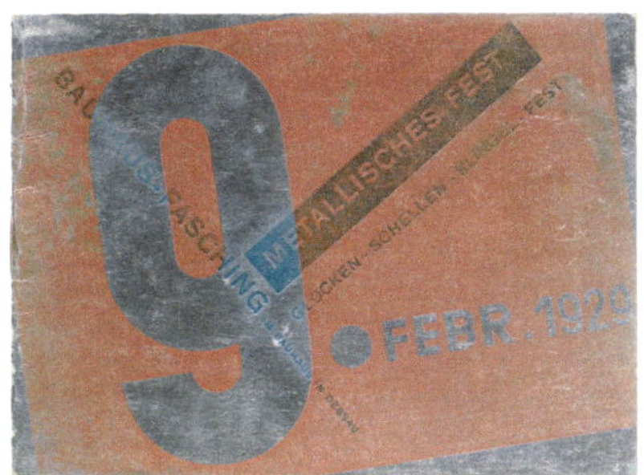

METALLISCHES FEST 9.II.1929

sie werden bestimmt **zum metallischen fest** am **9. 2. 1929** erwartet, das brauchen wir wohl nicht an die grosse **glocke** zu hängen ●

punkt **20 uhr** blasen wir nur etwas ins **goldene horn** und mit **pauken** und **trompeten** bricht in den räumen des bauhauses das **goldene zeitalter** herein ●

3 kapellen sorgen dafür, dass ihr **drehbankherz** nicht verrostet, da walzen erlaubt ist, jedoch nicht für **dampfwalzen.** legen sie nicht alles auf die **goldwage,** wenn wir etwa mit **improvisationen, vorträgen u. theater** ihnen ein U- für ein T-eisen vormachen, es braucht deshalb noch nicht alles **blech** zu sein, was glänzt. seien sie der **schmied** ihres glückes und wählen sie die **goldene** mittelstrasse, legen sie ihr **eisen** bei uns ins feuer und bestellen sie sofort auf angebotener karte bis zum **20. I. 1929** ihre eintrittskarten (die keine **nieten** sind), die wir ihnen per nachnahme zusenden werden, in der hoffnung, dass sie nicht im moment **drahtlos** sind. wir halten **an- und umkleideräume** bereit, in denen sie ihre fassade und andere metallische weichteile genügend polieren können. wo - wenn sie noch nicht glühend sind - sie so in **harnisch** geraten, dass sie aus ihrer normierten haut fahren, um sich in eines von den unten angegebenen glänzenden kostümen zu werfen. kohldampf brauchen sie nicht zu schieben. sie finden ein warmes und ein kaltes büfett vor. in **schnaps-schlössern** und **löt-ecken** können sie ihren **brand** im fliessverfahren abschrecken mit danziger **goldwasser, kupferberg-gold nirosta**-schnäpsen usw.

sind sie ein herr, kommen sie als:

schellenkönig (oder -as) - glöckner (aber bringen sie notre dame mit) - geheimer legierungsrat - zinn- oder bleisoldat (besser noch: belötzinn-soldat) - grosse kanone - schaumschläger - rauschgold (der goldrausch ist an der theke zu bekommen) - eiserner gustav - gehörnter siegfried - quecksilber - quacksalber - klinkenputzer - blechredner - haken (der sich beizeiten krümmen will) - schellenbaum - armleuchter - metall-lurch - klimperkasten - erzgauner - magnetiseur - kneifzange - glockengiesser - gasometer - schienenstrang (um darüber zu schlagen) - badeofen - funkturm - glockenschwengel - reissverschluss - grünspan - stahlskelett - blaukopf -, gustav nagel - trinkbecker - kar-nickel - goldiger kragenknopf - posaunenengel - nürnberger trichter - kolbenventil - stahlross - corrosionsrat - laufkran - wolfram - kobalt - alter freund und kupferstecher - essenschieber - lenkstange - eisenbahnverkehrsamt - magnet - anker - öltank - büchsenöffner - kurbelgetriebe - puffer - eiserner bestand - goldbarsch - goldener bulle - conglomerat - schimmelpfennig - saxo-von der seite - rocher de bronce (für herren in höherer stellung) - thermometer - ventilator - fleischwolf - bleistift - franz blei - schnapsschloss - silberfuchs - goldfasan - gussform (kussform) - glühfaden - usw.

sind sie eine dame, kommmen sie als:

versunkene glocke (oder festgemauert in der erde) - schellendame - singende säge - loses oder angezogenes schräubchen - flügel- oder schraubenmutter - stimmgabel - goldmine - bronzebüste (halter) - gezinkte flebbe - silber-lamm (ée) - maiglöckchen - silberwölkchen - heftzwecke radioaktive substanz - leichtmetall - weichmetall - edelmetall - türklingel - kuhglocke - glockenspiel - häckelnadel - nadelkissen - nagelfeile - antenne - drückfutter - bratpfanne - kaffeemühle - leuchtboje - glockenboje - elektroliese - goldenes kalb - goldammer - goldkäfer (neckischer) - tauchergiocke - klingelzeichen - sardinendose - goldplombe - bare münze - goldenes herz - kugellager - silbrig - goldig.

kommen sie nicht als:

bronce-statue (bavaria, berolina, siegesallee) - bronze- und steinzeitliches fossil - heizschlange - normalprofil - kratzbürste - überdrehte schraube - plombierter zahn der zeit - gold- und dämellack - versetzte niete - fünftes rad am wagen - plätteisen - kanonenofen - schall und rauch - knurrbremse - hemmschuh - ungeschliffener bolzen - schwert an meiner linken - kannegiesser - blindgänger - eiserne jungfrau - jungfrau von orleans - schwertlilie - prinz karneval - blechmusikant (sind schon vorhanden) - gebläse - mutter mit quadratischem kopf - klingelbeutel - klingelbolle - käseglocke - zwischen hammer und ambos - drahtzieher - wellblechbaracke - badewanne - wetterfahne - lautsprecher - reibeisen - vernageltes, verbohrtes, verlötetes, verrostetes, patiniertes, verschrobenes, gestauchtes, plombiertes, kon- und reserviertes subjekt - platoniker (soll heissen: platiniker) - eisernes kreuzworträtsel ●

wir wiederholen die wichtigsten daten nochmals ●

tag ihrer glanzvollen erscheinung:	**9. februar 1929,**
anfang der metallorgie:	**20 h,**
verhuttungsort:	**dessau bauhaus,** friedrichsallee 12.
handlungen:	improvisationen auf der bühne, tänze, vorträge.
attraktionen:	verraten wir ihnen nicht.
tombola:	nietliche erwerbung von kunst-u. bauhausprodukten.
ausstellung:	bauhausarbeiten (letzte novitäten, derniers cris). (auch am 10. februar ab 11 uhr noch geöffnet).

eintrittspreise siehe bestellkarte.

wir bitten, die beigelegte postkarte ausgefüllt bis spätestens **20. januar 1929** zurückzusenden.

bitte nageln sie auch darin ihre betten fest, sonst liegen sie nachher auf der strasse, wir übernehmen keine verantwortung, wenn sie dort unter die räder geraten ●

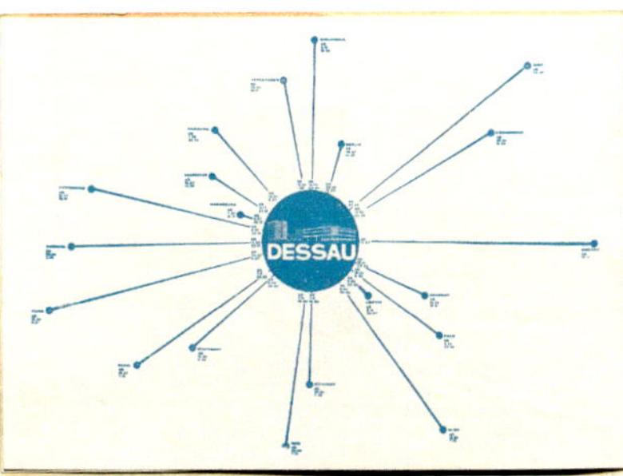

the first exhibi

In 1923, four years after the school opened, the state government of Germany's Thuringia required the Bauhaus to mount a public exhibition to reveal what was under way in its workshops and to justify its continued funding. Held in the first year of Moholy-Nagy's professorship, the resulting show encapsulates a major turning point in the institution's pedagogical and aesthetic development. ●

Since joining the faculty, Moholy-Nagy had begun to shift the curriculum from expressionist and fine-art concerns toward international constructivism. He had encountered this abstract yet architectural style in the work of Russian designer El Lissitzky, whom he had met in Berlin in 1921. At its core was a rigorous engagement with modern technology, intended to disseminate radical political ideas to the public. To make this change clear, Gropius debuted a new credo for the school at the opening of the exhibition: "Art and technology—a new unity." ●

The show also occasioned two of the school's most remarkable print productions: a series of lithograph postcards announcing the event, designed by teachers and students, and the accompanying exhibition catalog. Wide-ranging in their approaches to letterform, illustration, and layout, these publications reveal the school's early expressionism and emergent modernity. ●

While successful in terms of publicity, the exhibition was not the panacea it was intended to be, as the state cut the Bauhaus's funding, forcing it to relocate to the more liberal Dessau in 1925 and to seek new sources of financial support. ●

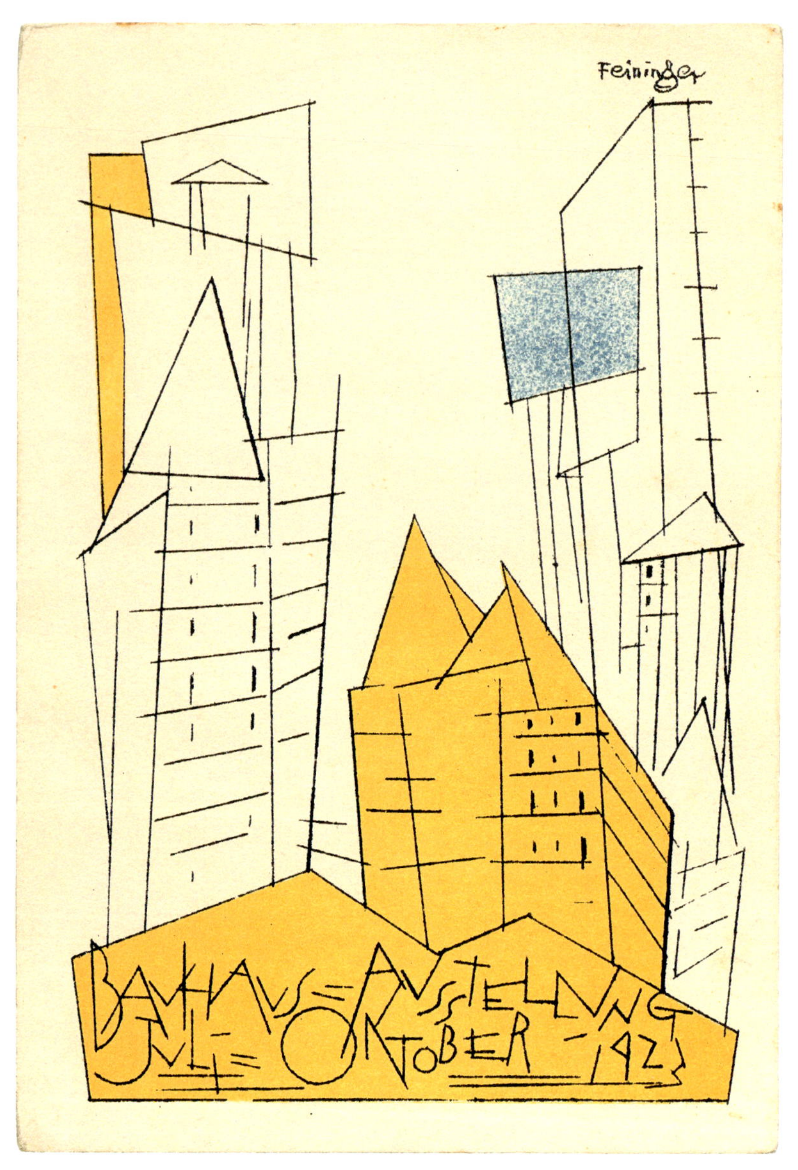
Feininger
BAUHAUS=AUSSTELLUNG
JULI=OKTOBER 1923

1923

LYONEL FEININGER

Postcard 1, Weimar State Bauhaus Exhibition 1923 (*Karte 1, Staatliches Bauhaus Weimar Ausstellung 1923*), lithograph, shown at actual size (5⅞ × 4⅛ inches/150 × 105 mm), Weimar.

Walter Gropius commissioned this set of postcards to promote the first major Bauhaus exhibition, held in Weimar in 1923, but the postcards themselves constitute one of the major early design statements of the school. Designed around a unit of basic information, with each card featuring the name and dates of the exhibition (which shifted during production), these twenty postcards by fourteen artists are a testament to the true diversity of the early Bauhaus style. They feature the work of masters, many of them accomplished painters (Wassily Kandinsky, Paul Klee, László Moholy-Nagy, Lyonel Feininger, Gerhard Marcks, and Oskar Schlemmer) as well as those who were students at the time (Herbert Bayer, Paul Häberer, Dörte Helm, Ludwig Hirschfeld-Mack, Farkas Molnár, Kurt Schmidt, and Georg Teltscher). The various designers were specialists in disparate and often multiple disciplines at the school, leading to a wide variety of results, particularly in approach to letterforms. The postcards also display the divergent influences on the early Bauhaus—roughly, the expressionistic and painterly, and the rational and geometric. The uniform execution by lithograph from hand drawing, however, gives them all a sense of freedom and informality. ●

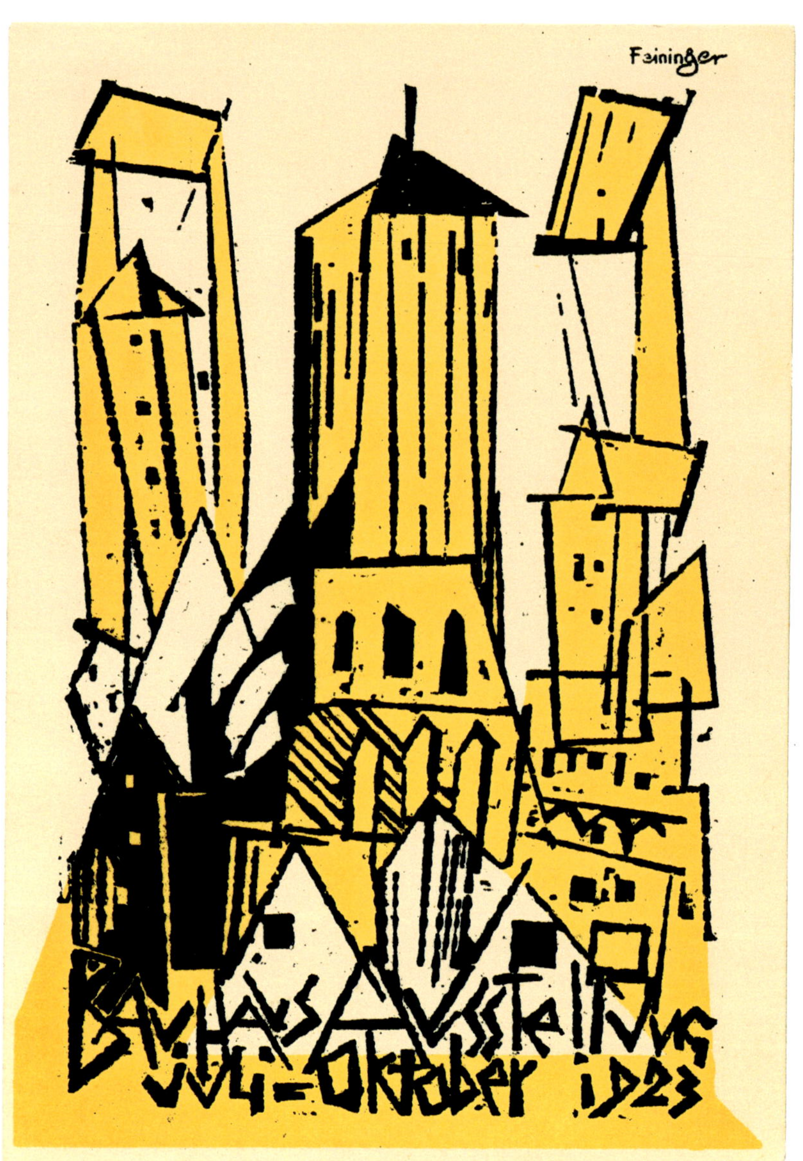

1923

LYONEL FEININGER

Postcard 2, Weimar State Bauhaus Exhibition 1923 (*Karte 2, Staatliches Bauhaus Weimar Ausstellung 1923*), lithograph, shown at actual size (6 × 4¼ inches/151 × 107 mm), Weimar.

1923

WASSILY KANDINSKY

Postcard 3, Weimar State Bauhaus Exhibition 1923 (*Karte 3, Staatliches Bauhaus Weimar Ausstellung 1923*), lithograph, shown at actual size (5⅞ × 4⅛ inches/150 × 105 mm), Weimar.

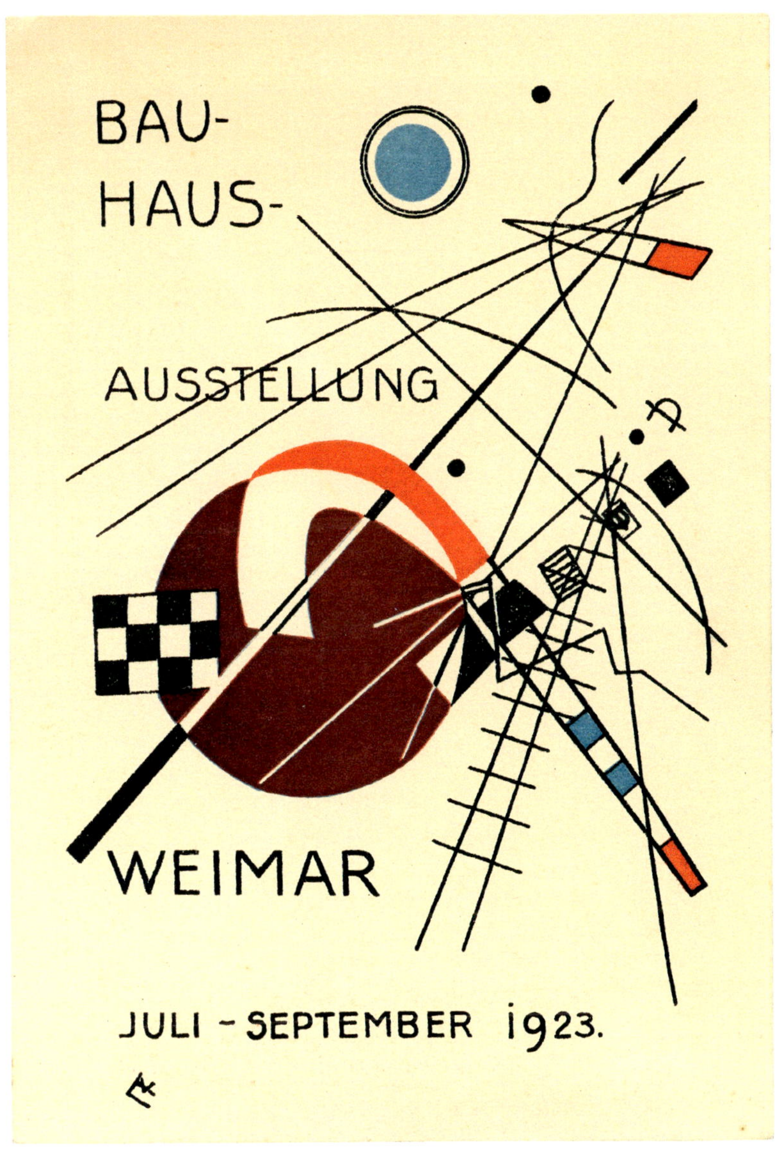

1923

PAUL KLEE

Postcard 4, Weimar State Bauhaus Exhibition 1923 (*Karte 4, Staatliches Bauhaus Weimar Ausstellung 1923*), lithograph, shown at actual size (5⅞ × 4 inches/150 × 104 mm), Weimar.

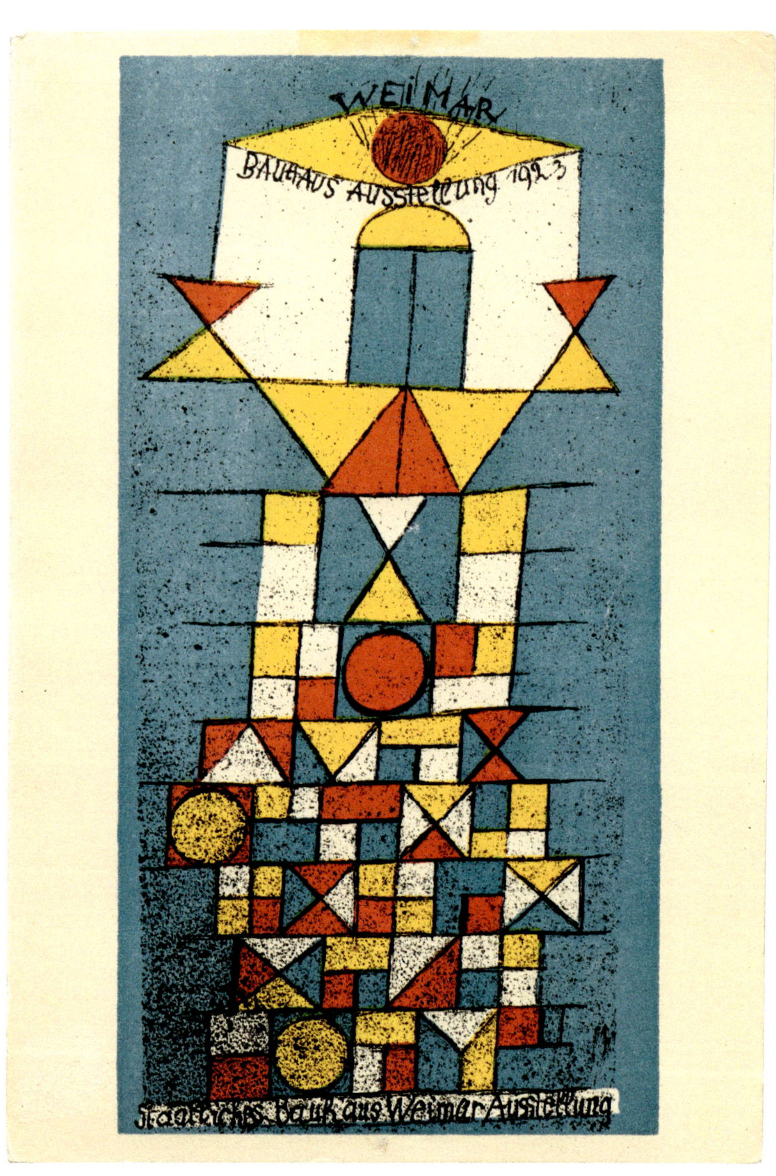

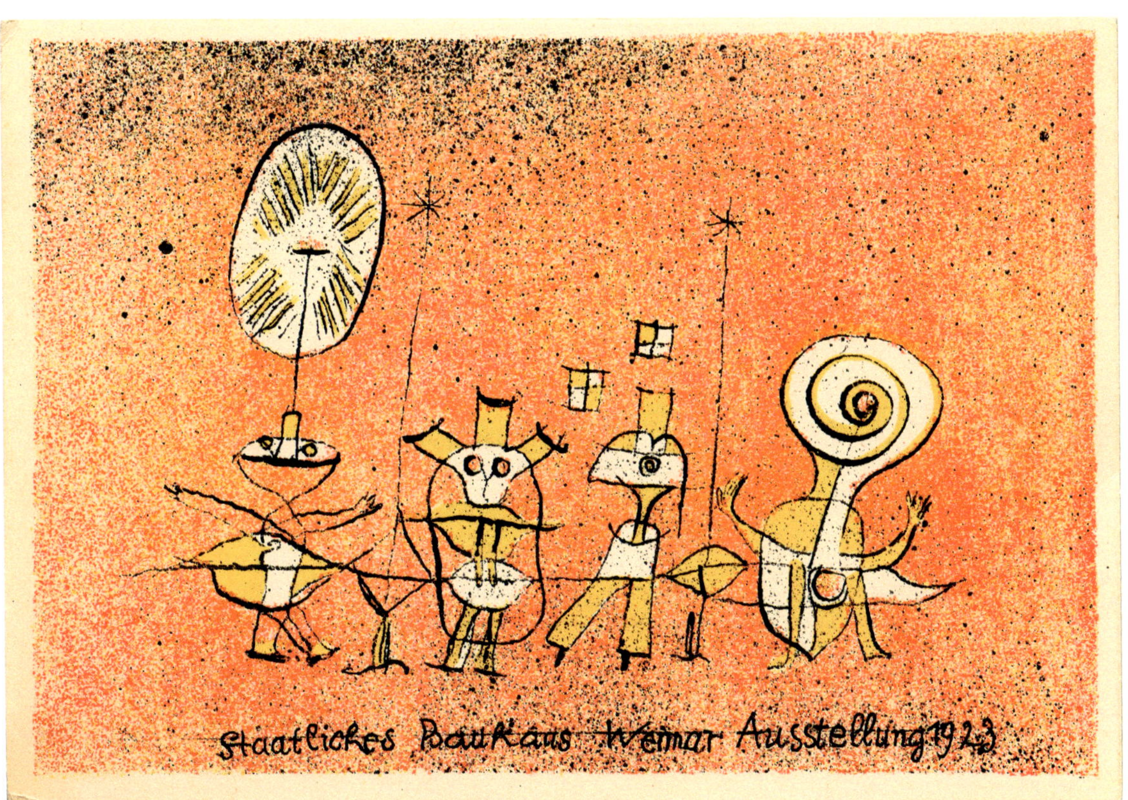

1923

PAUL KLEE

Postcard 5, Weimar State Bauhaus Exhibition 1923 (*Karte 5, Staatliches Bauhaus Weimar Ausstellung 1923*), lithograph, shown at actual size (4⅛ × 6 inches/105 × 151 mm), Weimar.

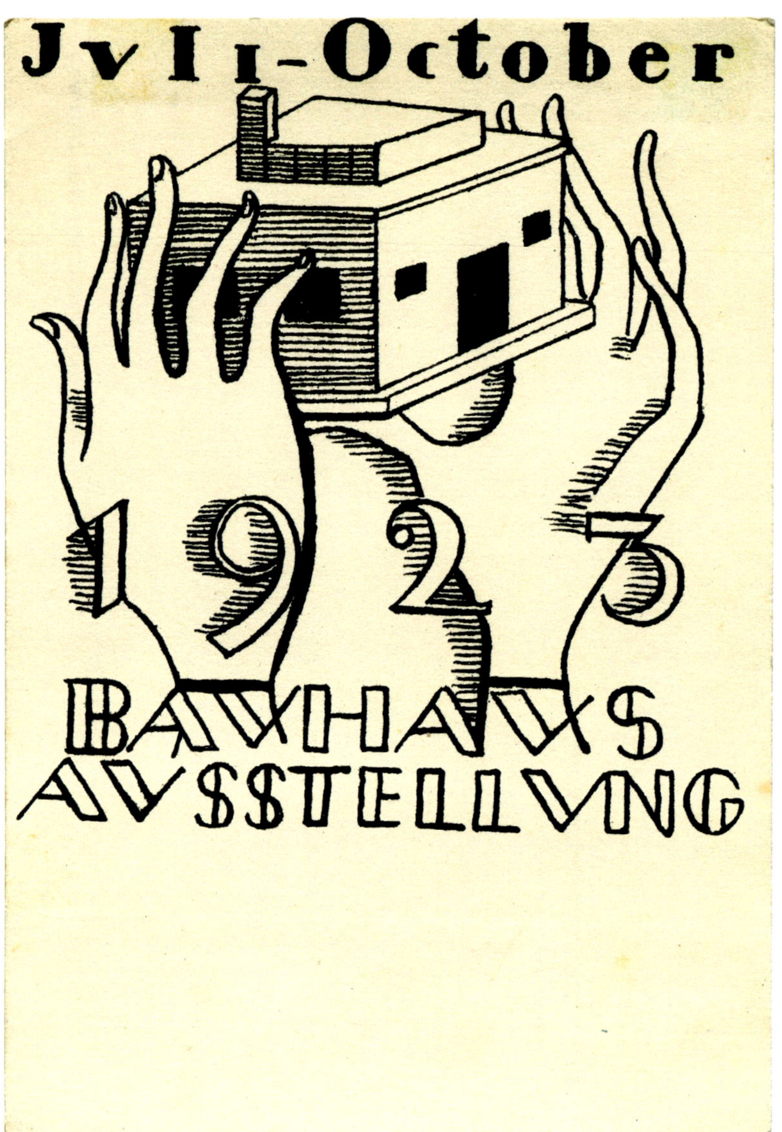

1923

GERHARD MARCKS

Postcard 6, Weimar State Bauhaus Exhibition 1923 (*Karte 6, Staatliches Bauhaus Weimar Ausstellung 1923*), lithograph, shown at actual size (5⅞ × 4⅛ inches/150 × 106 mm), Weimar.

1923

LÁSZLÓ MOHOLY-NAGY

Postcard 7, Weimar State Bauhaus Exhibition 1923 (*Karte 7, Staatliches Bauhaus Weimar Ausstellung 1923*), lithograph, shown at actual size (5⅝ × 3¾ inches/142 × 94 mm), Weimar.

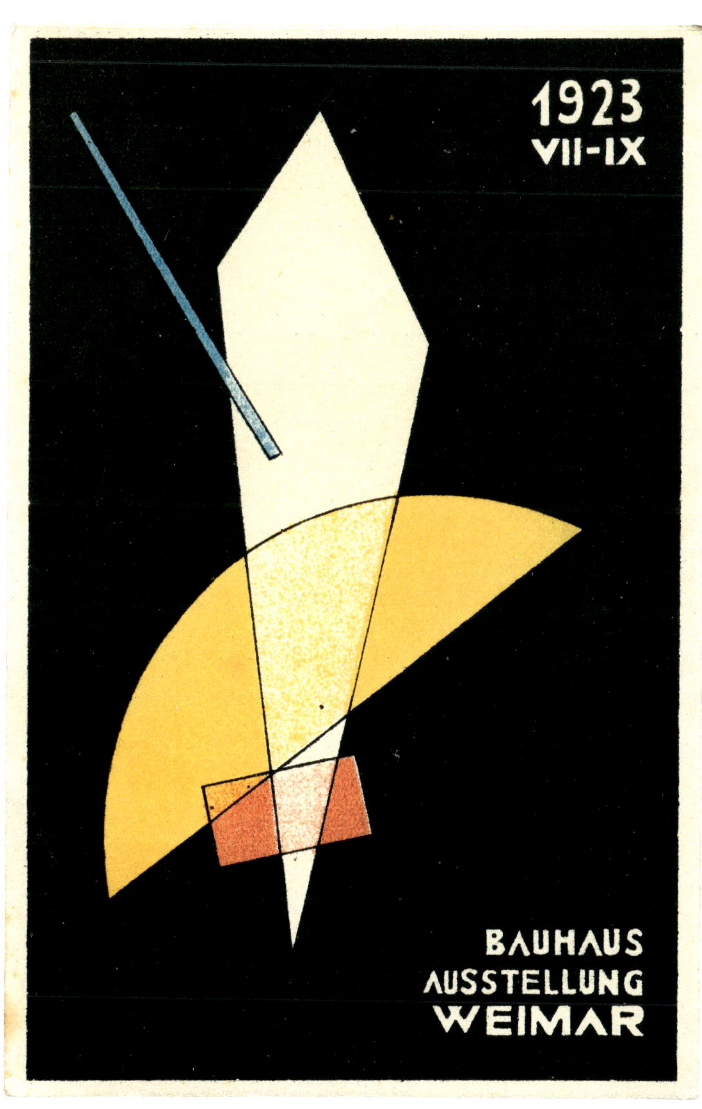

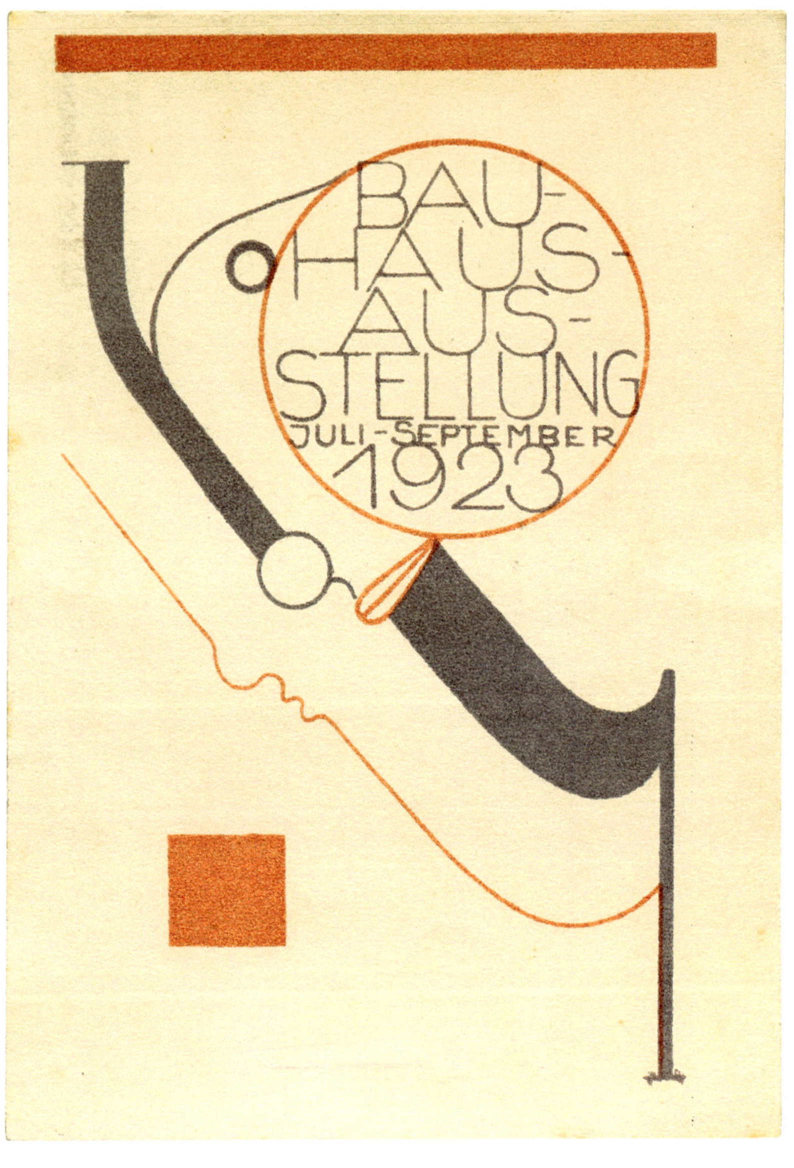
BAU-
HAUS-
AUS-
STELLUNG
JULI-SEPTEMBER
1923

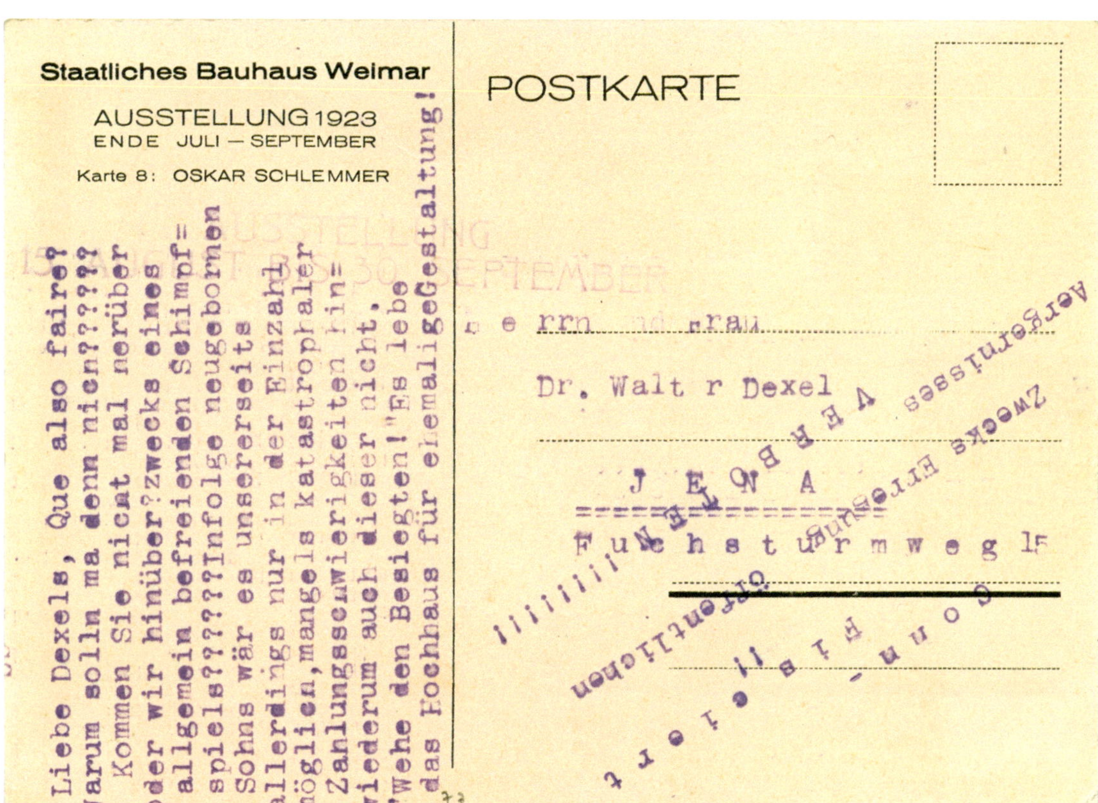

1923

OSKAR SCHLEMMER

Postcard 8, Weimar State Bauhaus Exhibition 1923 (*Karte 8, Staatliches Bauhaus Weimar Ausstellung 1923*), with a message from Schlemmer to graphic designer Walter Dexel, lithograph, shown at actual size (5⅞ × 4¼ inches/150 × 107 mm), Weimar.

1923

RUDOLF BASCHANT

Postcard 9, Weimar State Bauhaus Exhibition 1923 (*Karte 9, Staatliches Bauhaus Weimar Ausstellung 1923*), lithograph, shown at actual size (5⅞ × 4⅛ inches/150 × 106 mm), Weimar.

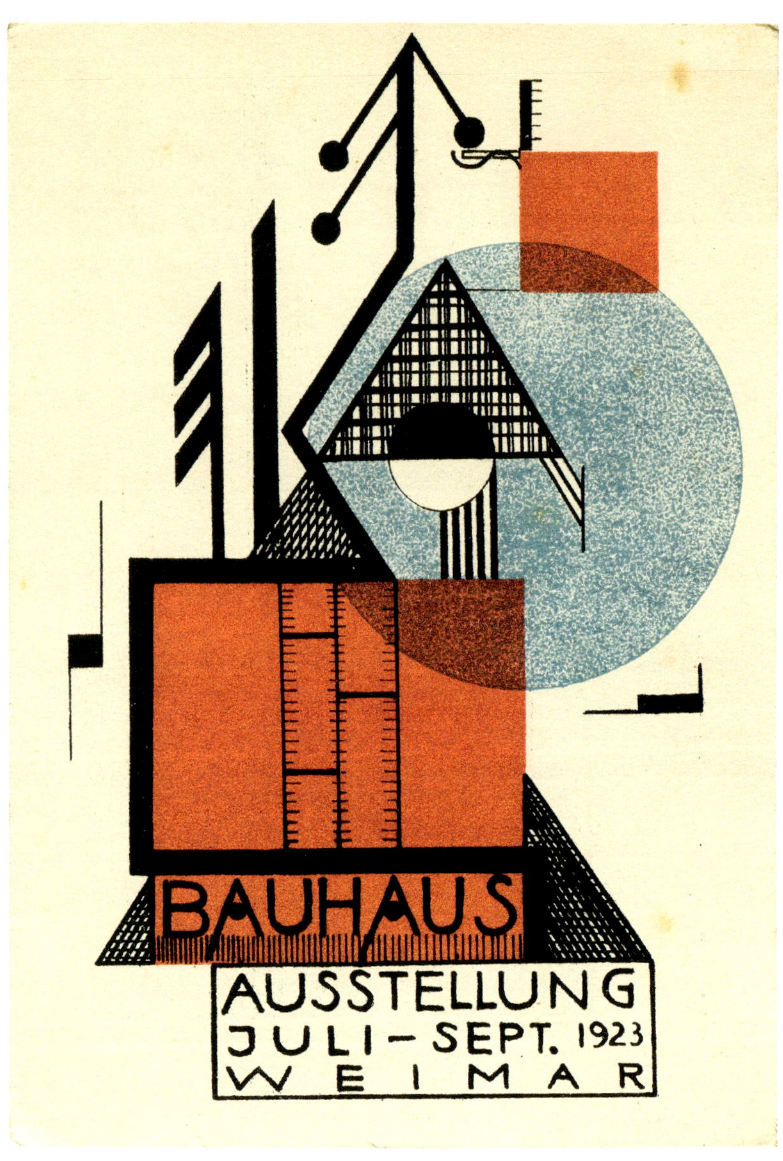

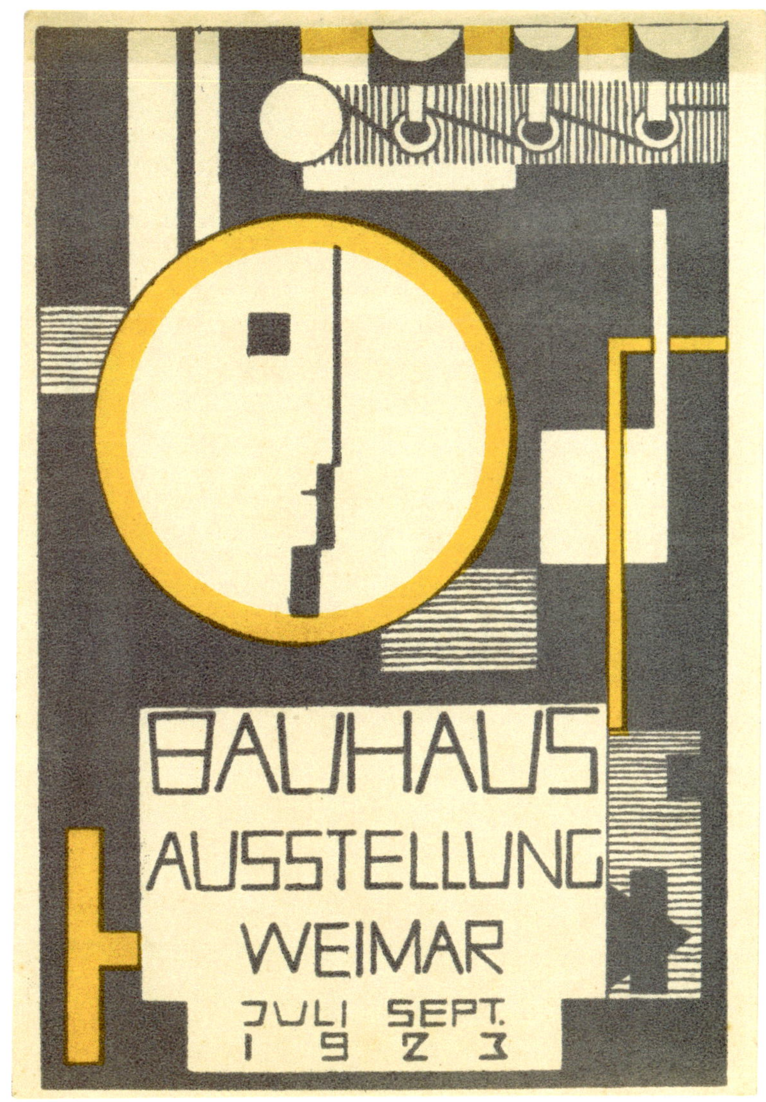

1923

RUDOLF BASCHANT

Postcard 10, Weimar State Bauhaus Exhibition 1923 (*Karte 10, Staatliches Bauhaus Weimar Ausstellung 1923*), lithograph, shown at actual size (5¾ × 4 inches/145 × 100 mm), Weimar. Collection of the Museum of Modern Art, New York, NY, U.S.A.

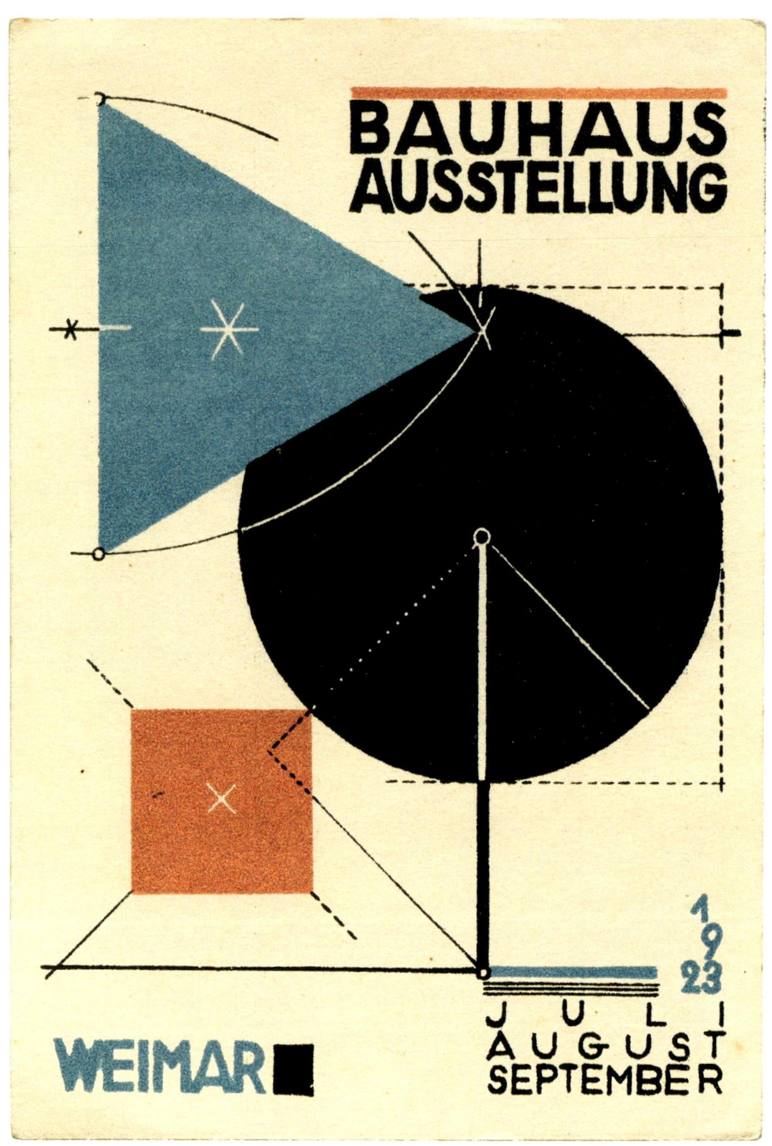

1923

HERBERT BAYER

Postcard 11, Weimar State Bauhaus Exhibition 1923 (*Karte 11, Staatliches Bauhaus Weimar Ausstellung 1923*), lithograph, shown at actual size (5⅞ × 4 inches/150 × 101 mm), Weimar.

1923

HERBERT BAYER

Postcard 12, Weimar State Bauhaus Exhibition 1923 (*Karte 12, Staatliches Bauhaus Weimar Ausstellung 1923*), lithograph, shown at actual size (5⅞ × 4 inches/150 × 101 mm), Weimar.

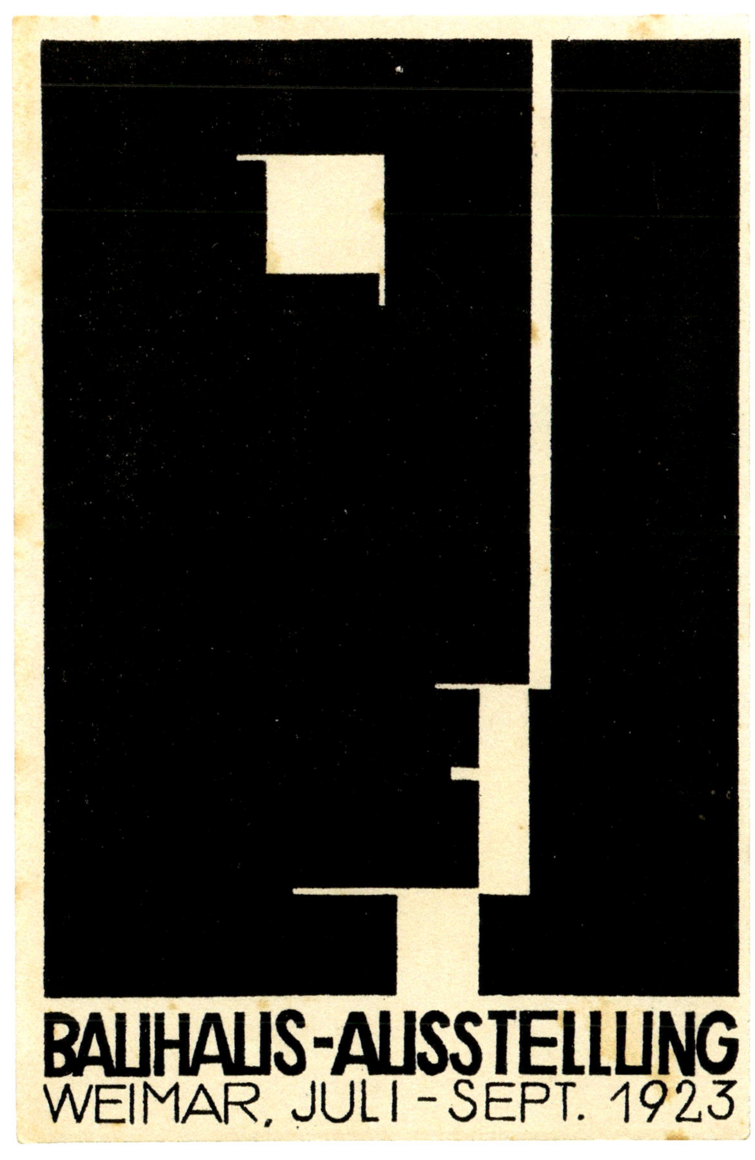

1923

PAUL HÄBERER

Postcard 13, Weimar State Bauhaus Exhibition 1923 (*Karte 13, Staatliches Bauhaus Weimar Ausstellung 1923*), lithograph, shown at actual size (4⅛ × 6 inches/105 × 152 mm), Weimar.

German student Paul Häberer's postcard depicts one of the 1923 exhibition's main attractions: the Haus am Horn, designed by German artist Georg Muche, the youngest Bauhaus master. Built by Gropius's firm at a site off campus, the house marked the school's first architectural achievement. Bauhaus teachers and students furnished and decorated the interior, including light fixtures by László Moholy-Nagy and furniture by Hungarian Marcel Breuer. Häberer's postcard is itself a playful testament to the complementarity of the school's architectural and typographic aesthetics. Rather than the full name *Bauhaus*, Häberer puts the syllable *Bau* on the facade of his drawing, letting the building itself stand for the *haus* in the school's name. Another reading could see the structure's strong horizontal and vertical shape as representative of the letter *H*, especially with the *Aus* of *Ausstellung* set below on its own line in larger letters. Meanwhile, the postcard shown at right is the only one in the suite of twenty that was designed by a woman, the German painter Dörte Helm. While many women students were pushed into the weaving workshop, a few resisted and made work outside the school's textiles department. In addition to Helm, Benita Koch-Otte designed the Haus am Horn's influential kitchen, while Alma Siedhoff-Buscher contributed popular furniture and toys for the children's room. The application of the women's design skills to only the implements of cooking and child-rearing, however, betrays the persistence of sexism. ●

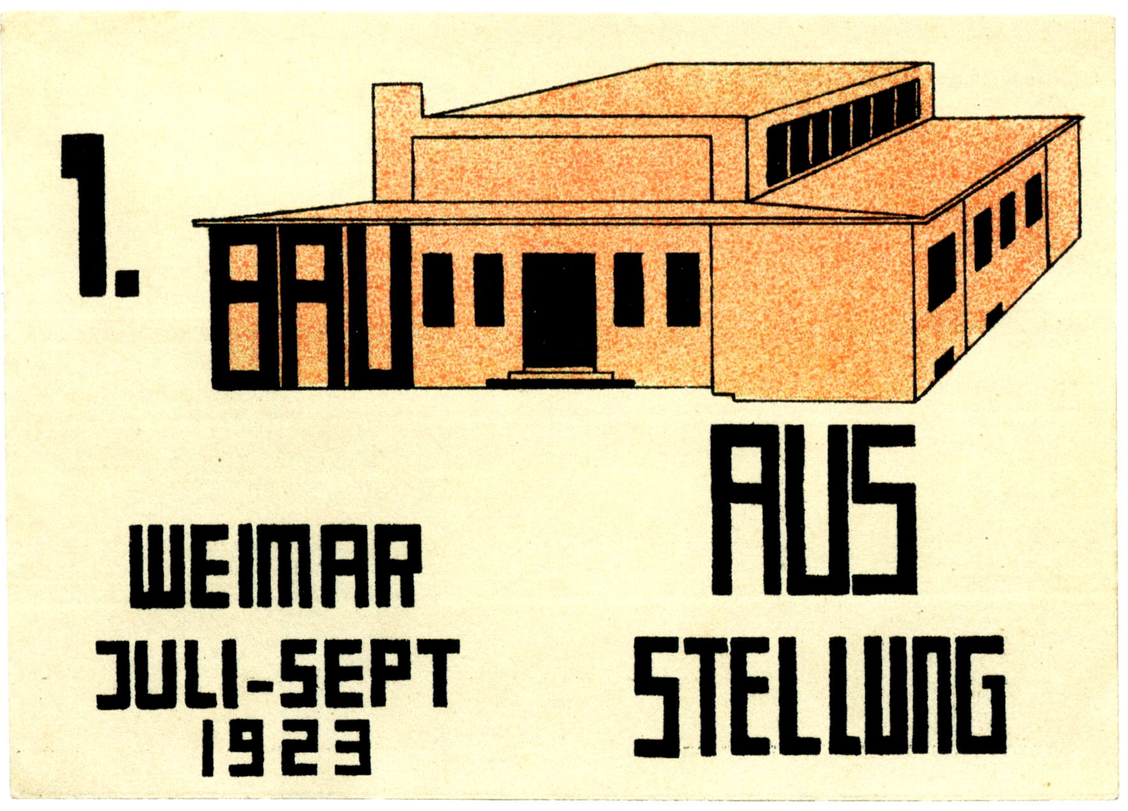

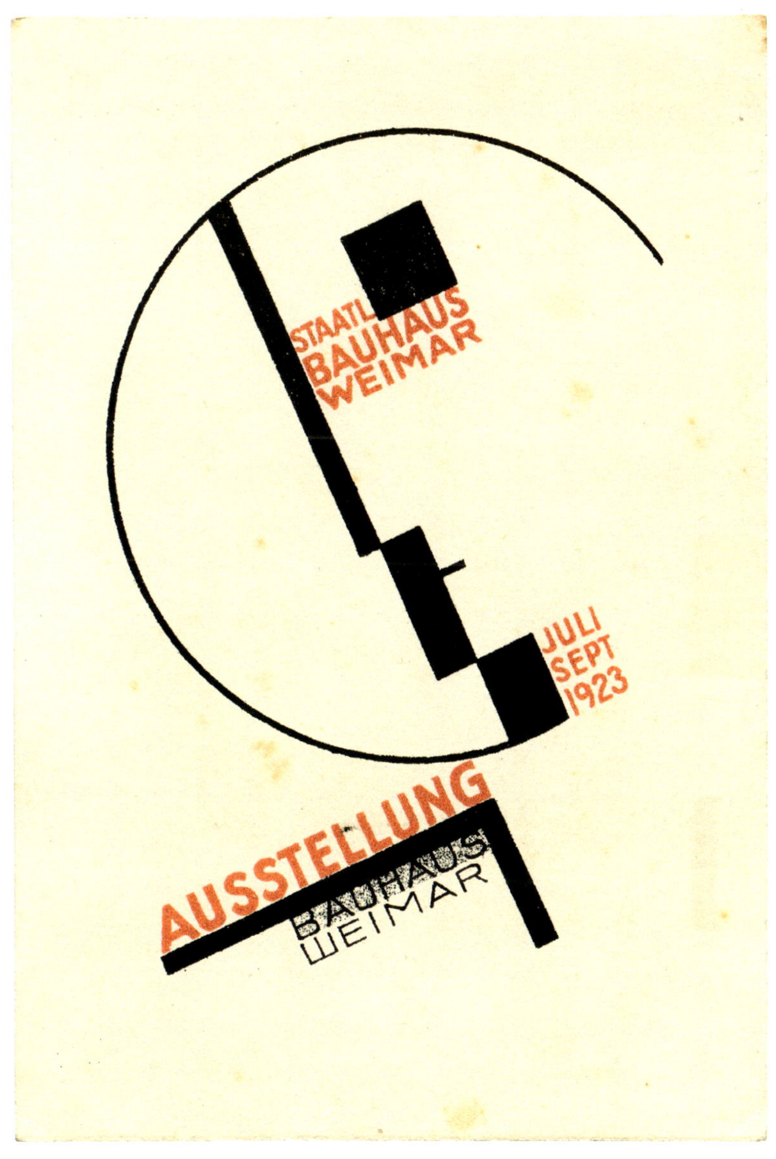

1923

DÖRTE HELM

Postcard 14, Weimar State Bauhaus Exhibition 1923 (*Karte 14, Staatliches Bauhaus Weimar Ausstellung 1923*), lithograph, shown at actual size (5⅞ × 4 inches/150 × 104 mm), Weimar.

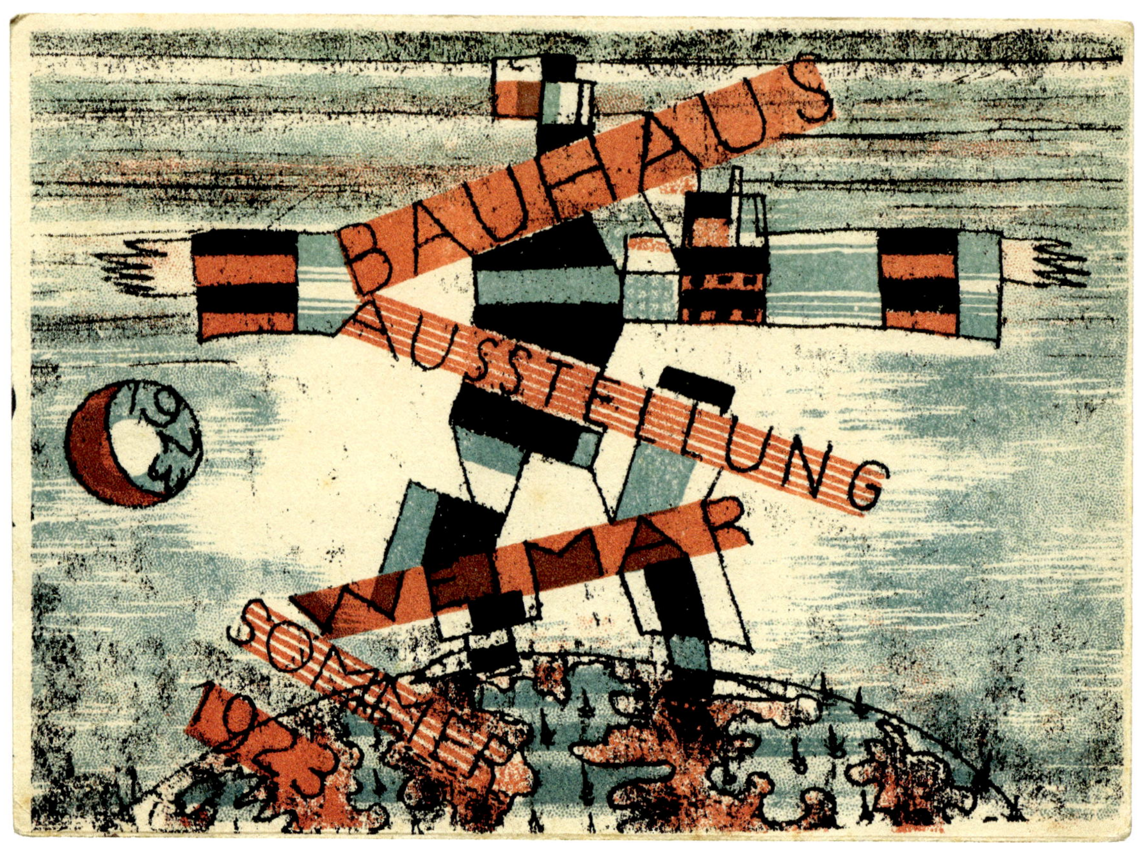

1923

LUDWIG HIRSCHFELD-MACK

Postcard 15, Weimar State Bauhaus Exhibition 1923 (*Karte 15, Staatliches Bauhaus Weimar Ausstellung 1923*), with the backside showing a stamped notice of the delayed exhibition opening, lithograph, shown at actual size (4⅜ × 6 inches/110 × 154 mm), Weimar.

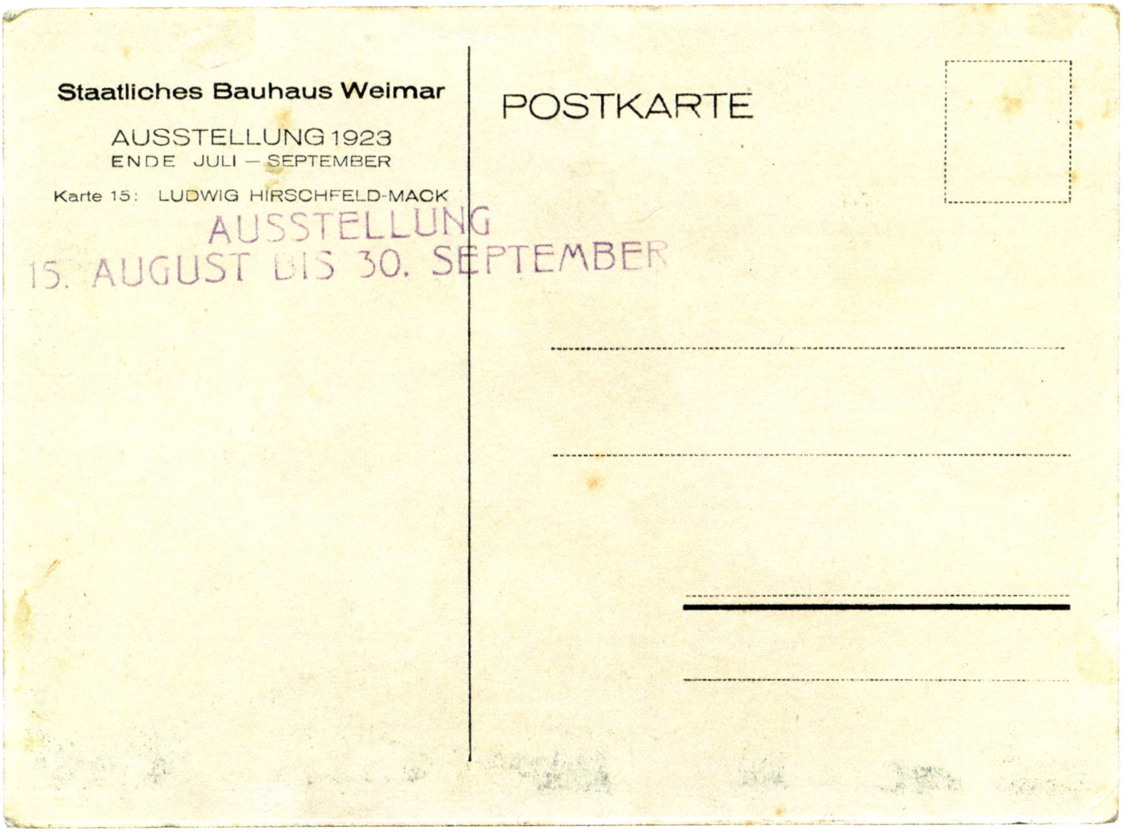

Staatliches Bauhaus Weimar

AUSSTELLUNG 1923
ENDE JULI – SEPTEMBER

Karte 15: LUDWIG HIRSCHFELD-MACK

AUSSTELLUNG
15. AUGUST BIS 30. SEPTEMBER

POSTKARTE

1923

LUDWIG HIRSCHFELD-MACK

Postcard 16, Weimar State Bauhaus Exhibition 1923 (*Karte 16, Staatliches Bauhaus Weimar Ausstellung 1923*), lithograph, shown at actual size (4 × 5⅞ inches/103 × 150 mm), Weimar.

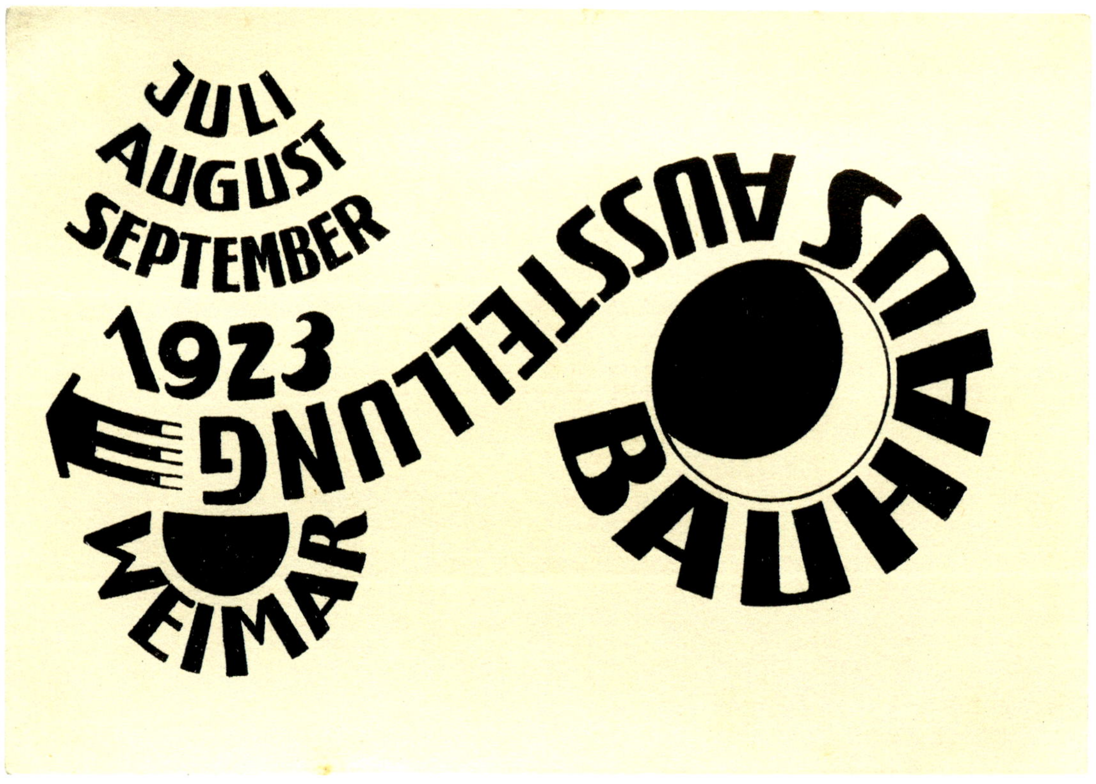

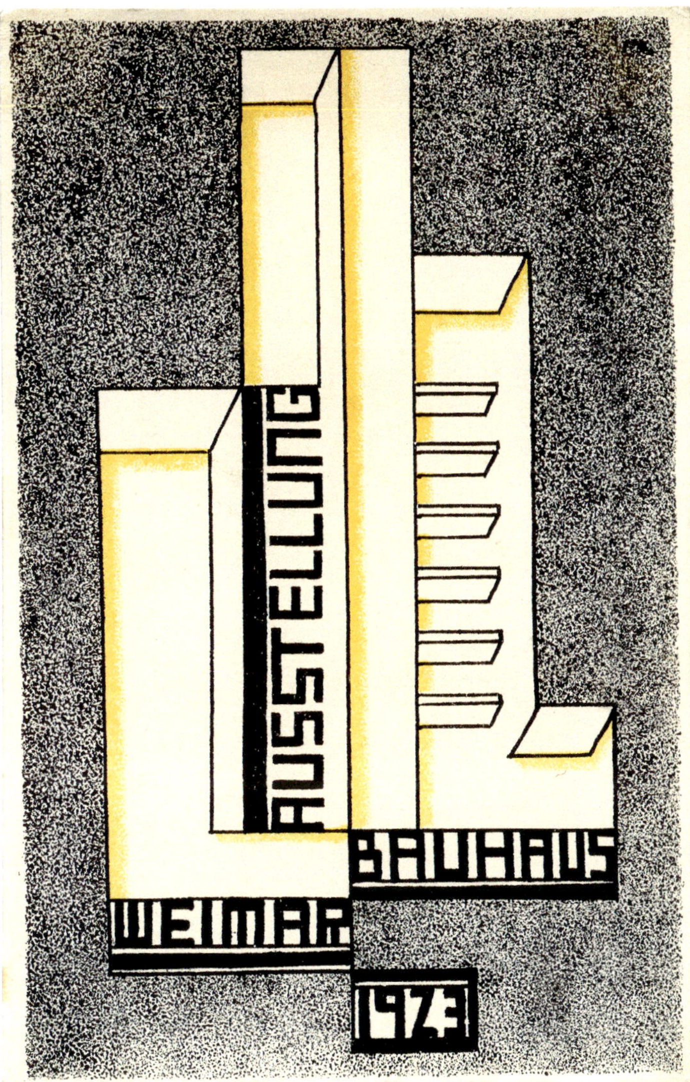

1923

FARKAS MOLNÁR

Postcard 17, Weimar State Bauhaus Exhibition 1923 (*Karte 17, Staatliches Bauhaus Weimar Ausstellung 1923*), lithograph, shown at actual size (5⅝ × 3¾ inches/144 × 94 mm), Weimar.

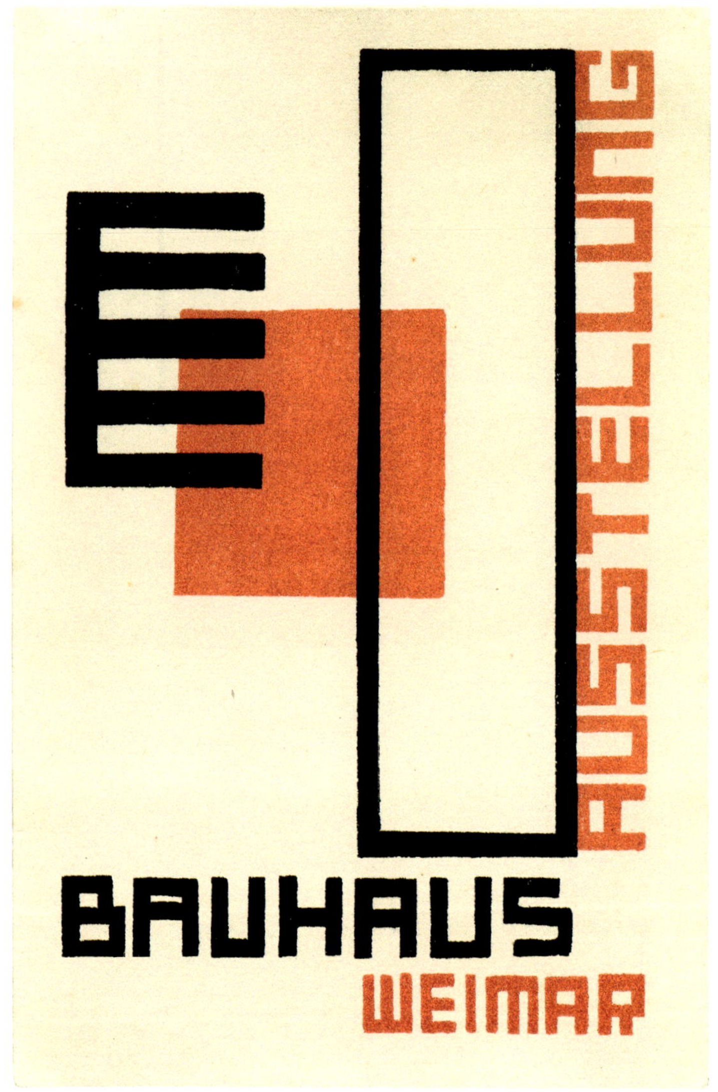

1923

KURT SCHMIDT

Postcard 18, Weimar State Bauhaus Exhibition 1923 (*Karte 18, Staatliches Bauhaus Weimar Ausstellung 1923*), lithograph, shown at actual size (5⅝ × 3¾ inches/142 × 94 mm), Weimar.

1923

KURT SCHMIDT

Postcard 19, Weimar State Bauhaus Exhibition 1923 (Karte 19, Staatliches Bauhaus Weimar Ausstellung 1923), lithograph, shown at actual size (5½ × 3¾ inches/140 × 94 mm), Weimar.

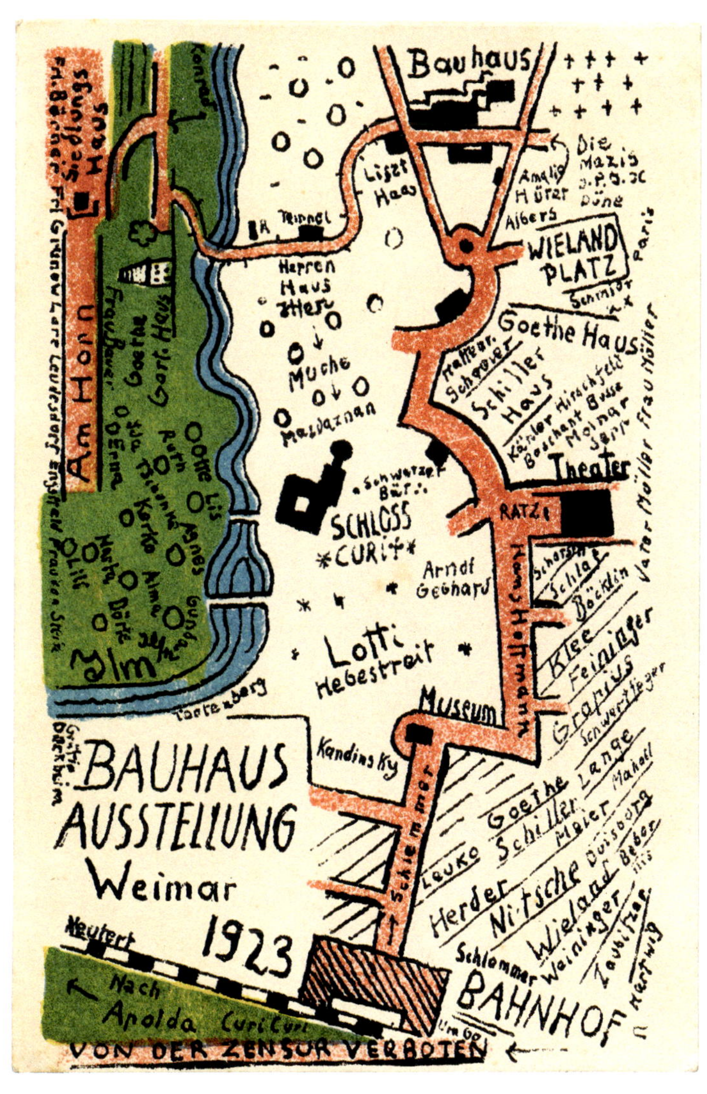

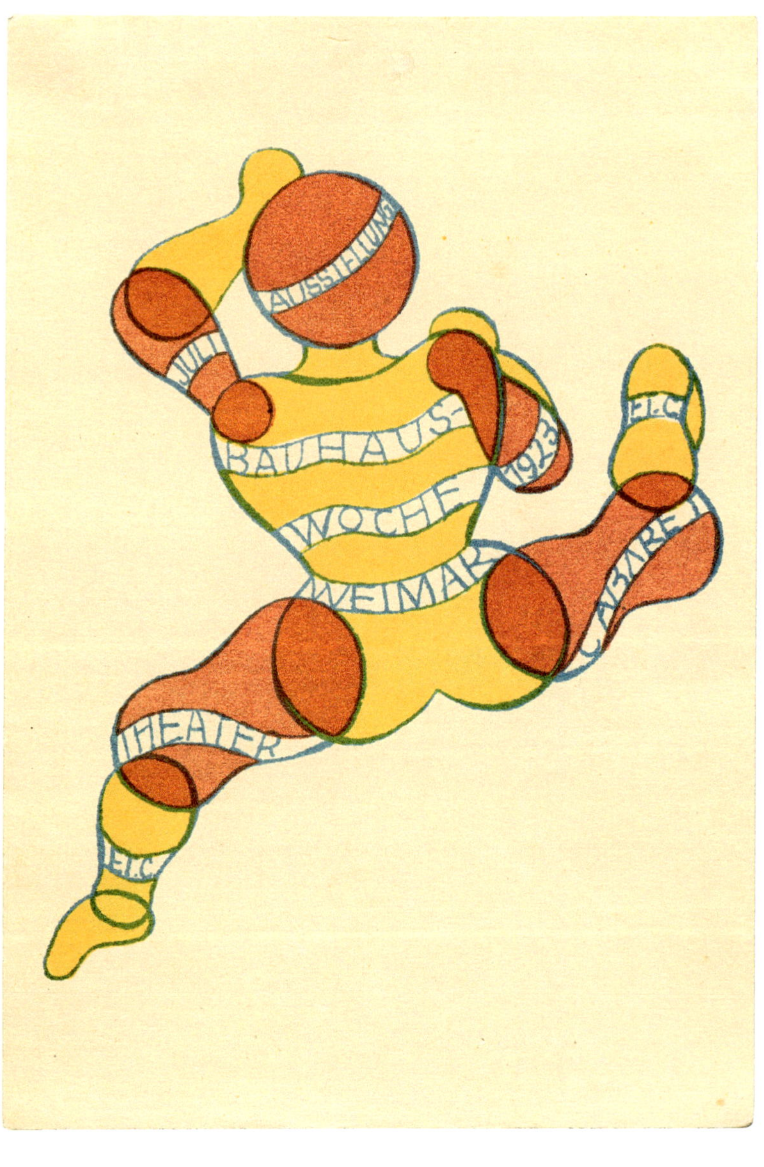
AUSSTELLUNG
JULI
BAUHAUS-
1923
WOCHE
WEIMAR
F.L.C.
CABARET
THEATER
F.L.C.

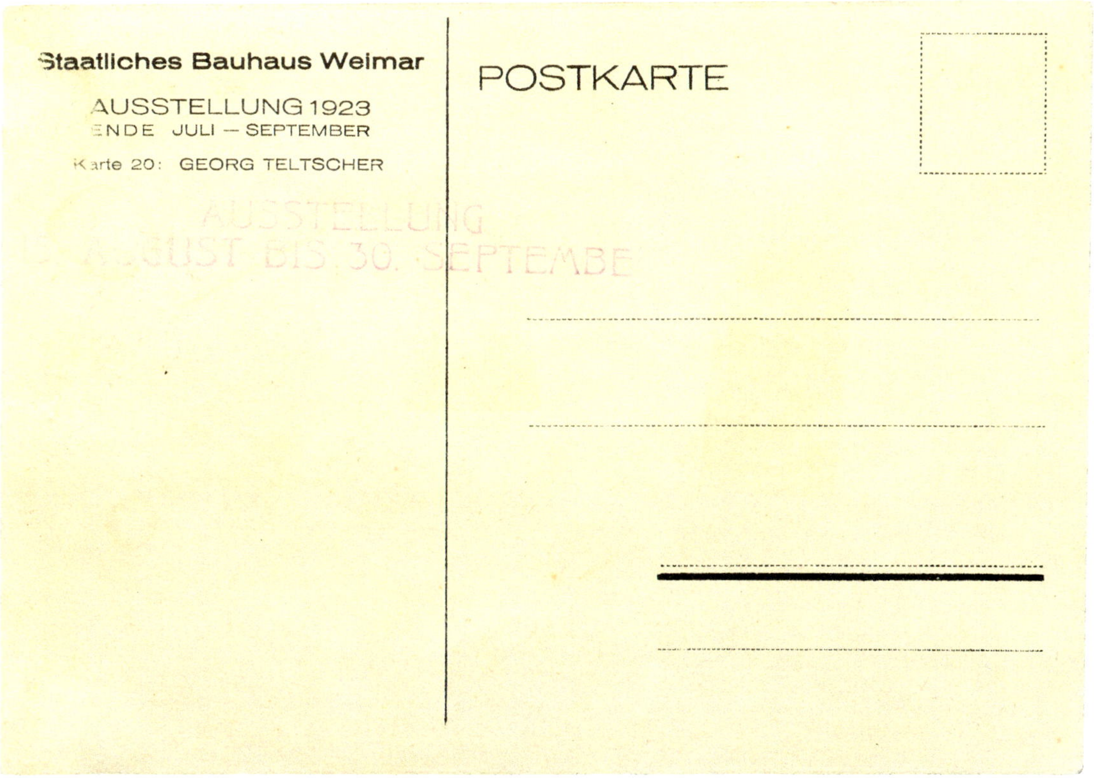

Staatliches Bauhaus Weimar

AUSSTELLUNG 1923
ENDE JULI – SEPTEMBER

Karte 20: GEORG TELTSCHER

POSTKARTE

1923

GEORG TELTSCHER

Postcard 20, Weimar State Bauhaus Exhibition 1923 (*Karte 20, Staatliches Bauhaus Weimar Ausstellung 1923*), lithograph, shown at actual size (5⅞ × 4 inches/150 × 104 mm), Weimar.

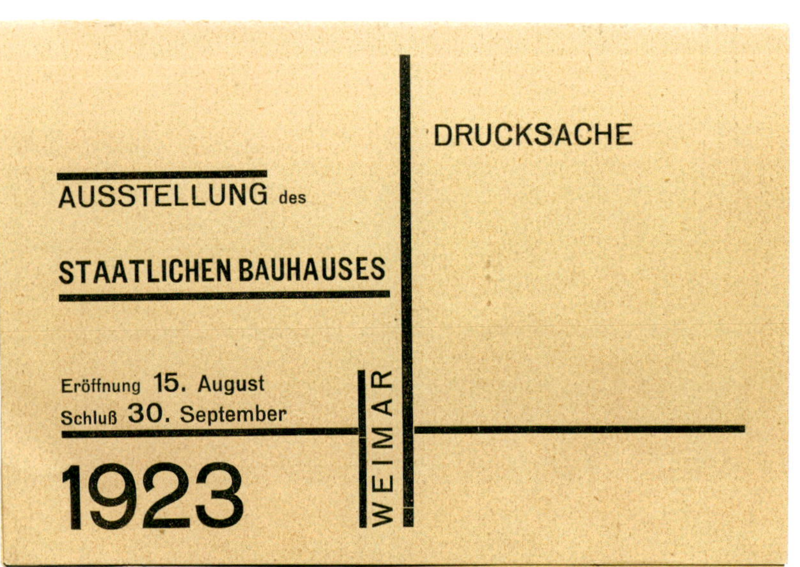

Arbeiten aus der Form- und Gestaltungslehre Klee. (Raum 37).
Arbeiten aus der Harmonisierungslehre Grunow. (Ra um 37).
Arbeiten aus dem Farbkursus Kandinsky. (Raum 38).

d) **Internationale Architekturausstellung.** (Raum 39 und Flure). Entwürfe und Modelle des staatlichen Bauhauses (Leitung GROPIUS), **Deutschland:** W. GROPIUS mit A. MEYER, DÖCKER-STUTTGART, HÄRING-BERLIN, MENDELSSOHN-BERLIN, MIES VAN DER ROHE-BERLIN, POELZIG-POTSDAM, SCHAROUN-INSTERBURG, STAM-BERLIN, BRUNO TAUT-MAGDEBURG, MAX TAUT-BERLIN. **Amerika:** F. L. WRIGHT. **Dänemark:** LÖNBERG-HOLM. **Frankreich:** LE CORBUSIER-SAUGNIER. **Holland:** VAN ANROIJ, DUDOK, HARDEVELD, VAN LONGHEM, OUD, RADEMAKER und MEIJER, RIETVELD, JAN WILS. **Russische Architekten. Tschechoslowakei:** CHOCHOL, FRAGNER, HONZIK, KREJCAR, KONLE, LINHART, OBRTEL.

e) **Plakate und Photoarchiv:** (Raum 2).

f) **Verkaufsraum für Erzeugnisse der Werkstätten,** (Raum 4).

2. **Im Landesmuseum, Museumsplatz.**
Malerische und plastische Einzelwerke der Meister, Gesellen und Lehrlinge des Bauhauses.

3. **Einfamilienwohnhaus am Horn (oberhalb Goethes Gartenhaus).**
Leitung: G. Muche und die Architekturabteilung des Bauhauses.
Neue Wohnprobleme, neue Techniken, Aufbau und gesamte Innenausstattung unter Mitwirkung der deutschen Industrie durch die Werkstätten des staatlichen Bauhauses. M. BREUER: Wohn- und Damenzimmer; DIEKMANN: Speise- und Herrenzimmer; A. BUSCHER - E. BRENDEL: Kinderzimmer; B. OTTE - E. GEBHARDT: Küche.

Zu allen Veranstaltungen der Bauhauswoche sind Karten zu haben.

In BERLIN:	Invalidendank, Unter den Linden.
	In sämtlichen Filialen des Kaufhauses A. Wertheim.
	Im Buch- und Kunstheim Twardy, Potsdamerstraße 12.
In FRANKFURT a. M.:	Musikalienhandlung C. Andre, Steinweg 7.
In HAMBURG:	Tietz, Jungfernstieg.
In MÜNCHEN:	Graphisches Kabinett G. m. b. H. Barerstraße 46.
	Theaterkartenkiosk am Lenbachplatz.
In LEIPZIG:	F. Jost, Peterssteinweg.
	C. A. Klemm, Neumarkt 26.
In WEIMAR:	**In der Buchhandlung Thelemann, Schillerstr. 15.**

BAUHAUSWO

MITTWOCH, 15. AU
hauses. 8h abends.
Einheit / Vortrag mit

DONNERSTAG, 16.
synthetische Kunst / V
im „Deutschen Nat
DAS TRIADISCHE BA
8h abends.

FREITAG, 17. AUG.:
der modernen Bauku
der **„Erholung"** / E
Mechanisches Kabar
F. W. Bogler, M. Br
Schmidt, K. Schwer
von **H. H. Stuckensch**
Zugabfahrt: ab Wein

SONNABEND, 18. A
einem vom Staatlich
in **Helds Lichtspiel**
gesellschaft, **Carl Koc**
abteilung: Mikrosko
8h abends. Konzer
lieder (Erstaufführur
furt a. M. / am Kla
BUSONI: 6 Klavierst
Petri, Berlin.

SONNTAG, 19. AUG
theater: Leitung **H. S**
6 Soloinstrumente u
kapelle / **STRAVINSK**
der Vorleser: **K. Eb**
furt a. M.; der Teufel:
J. Petersen, Frankfur
kapelle (7 Soloinstru
aufführung.
Abends Lampionfest
L. Hirschfeld-Mack,
Liszthaus, Belvedere
Schützengasse).

Privatquartier wird
nungskommission de

1923

WALTER DEXEL

Program for the *Exhibition of the State Bauhaus* (*Ausstellung des Staatlichen Bauhauses*), letterpress, 4¼ x 6⅜ inches (109 x 161 mm) folded, 6⅜ × 8½ inches (161 × 217 mm) unfolded, Weimar.

PROGRAMM

E

h vorm. Eröffnung im Vestibül des Bau-
OPIUS: Kunst und Technik, eine neue
ildern in der „Erholung" Karlsplatz 11.

: 4^{h} nachm. W. KANDINSKY: Über
n der „Erholung" Karlsplatz. Aufführung
ater" Schlemmer, Burger, Hötsel:
mit der Weimarischen Staatskapelle,

vorm. J. P. OUD: Die Entwicklung
Holland / Vortrag mit Lichtbildern in
werkstatt des staatlichen Bauhauses:
ufführung im „Jenaer Stadttheater"
O. Schlemmer, Kurt Schmidt, Joost
, G. Teltscher, A. Weininger Musik
3^{h} abends:
0, Rückfahrt: ab Jena $11^{\underline{35}}$.

10^{30h} vorm, Filmaufführung nach
haus zusammengestellten Programm
, Marienstraße 1. Comenius Film-
iehungsfilm und Filme der Ufa-Kultur-
Zeitlupen- und Zeitrafferaufnahmen.

ationaltheater. HINDEMITH, Marien-
oran: Beatrice Lauer-Kottlar, Frank-
mma Lübbeke-Job, Frankfurt a. M.
4 Uraufführungen) am Klavier: Egon

vorm. Matinee im Deutschen National-
HEN, / KRENEK: Concerto grosso /
chorchester der Weimarischen Staats-
Geschichte vom Soldaten / Personen /
rlin; der Soldat: F. Odemar, Frank-
ramm, Frankfurt a. M.; die Prinzessin:
nd Mitglieder der Weimarischen Staats-
. Wiederholung der Frankfurter-Erst-

rwerk, 2 Reflektorische Spiele von
uskapelle und Tanz / Treffpunkt $8^{\underline{30}}$
anz und Aufführung in der „Armbrust"

htzeitiger Anmeldung von der Woh-
auses besorgt.

AUSSTELLUNG

1. In den Räumen des Staatlichen Bauhauses, Kunstschulstraße.

a) **Raumgestaltungen:**
Ausgestaltung des Vestibüls im Hauptgebäude: Joost Schmidt u. J. Hartwig.
Ausgestaltung des kleinen Treppenhauses: H. Bayer, Wandmalerei.
Ausgestaltung der Flure und Ausstellungsräume durch die Werkstatt für Wandmalerei.
Ausgestaltung der Durchfahrt nach der Belvedereallee: P. Keler, Wandmalerei und W. Molnár, Architekturabteilung.
Ausgestaltung des Vestibüls im Werkstattgebäude: O. Schlemmer, J. Hartwig, H. Müller; Steinbildhauerei und Wandmalerei.
Warteraum / Raumgestaltung / Versuchsarbeiten verschiedener Werkstätten. Leitung: Itten, später Albers. (Raum 26).
Arbeitsraum / Raumgestaltung / W. Gropius. (Raum 25).

b) **Erzeugnisse der Werkstätten des staatlichen Bauhauses:**
Tischlerei: Formmeister Gropius; Technischer Meister Weidensee. (Raum 45).
Holz- und Steinbildhauerei: Formmeister Schlemmer; Technischer Meister Hartwig. (Werkstattgebäude).
Wandmalerei: Formmeister Kandinsky; Technischer Meister Beberniss. (Werkstatt der Wandmalerei).
Glaswerkstatt: Formmeister Klee; Technische Leitung Albers.
Metallwerkstatt: Formmeister Moholy-Nagy; Technischer Meister Dell. (Raum 40 und 45).
Töpferei: Formmeister Marcks; Technischer Meister Krehan. (Raum 40 und 45).
Weberei: Formmeister Muche; Technischer Meister Börner. (Raum 40 und 45).
Druckerei: Formmeister Feininger; Technischer Meister Zaubitzer. (Raum 2 und 38).
Bühnenwerkstatt: Formmeister Schreyer, später Schlemmer. (Raum 38).

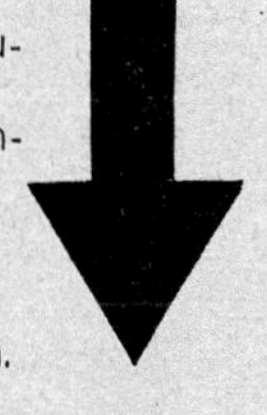

c) **Theoretische Arbeiten:**
Arbeiten aus der Vorlehre Itten. (Raum 36).
Arbeiten aus d. Analytischen Naturzeichnen Kandinsky. (Raum 37).

1923

HERBERT BAYER (cover designer)
LÁSZLÓ MOHOLY-NAGY (layout designer/coeditor)
WALTER GROPIUS (coeditor)

Exhibition catalog for *Weimar State Bauhaus 1919–1923* (*Staatliches Bauhaus in Weimar 1919–1923*), letterpress and lithograph, 9¾ × 10 inches (248 × 256 mm), Weimar and Munich.

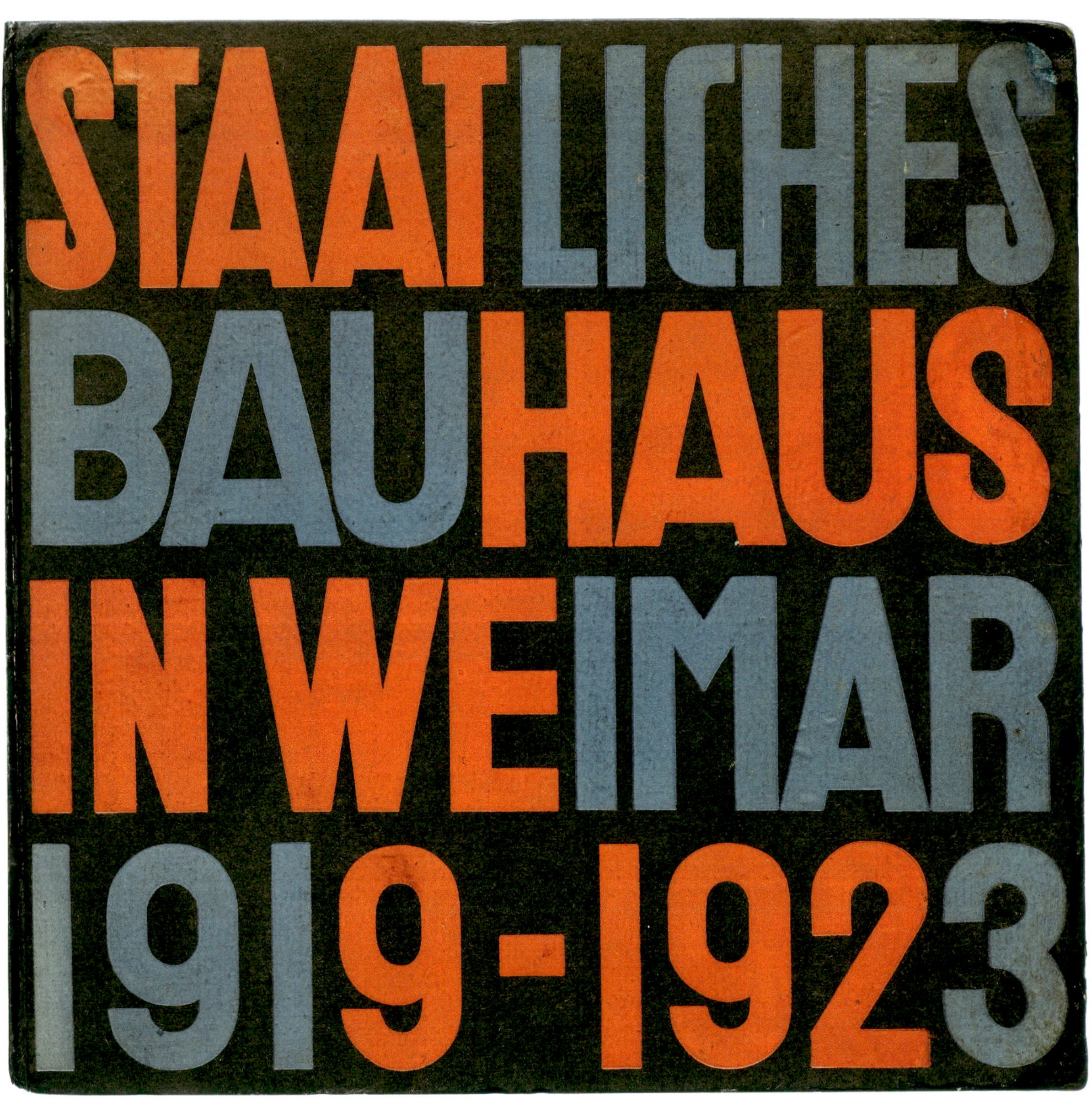

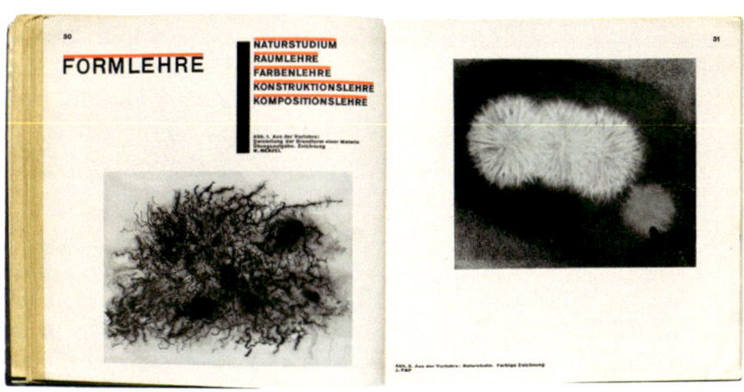

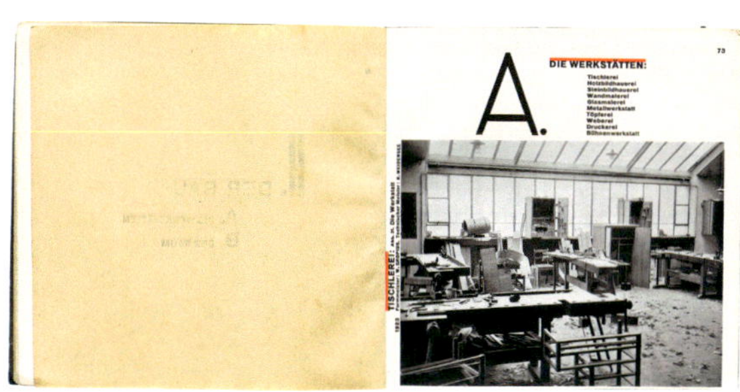

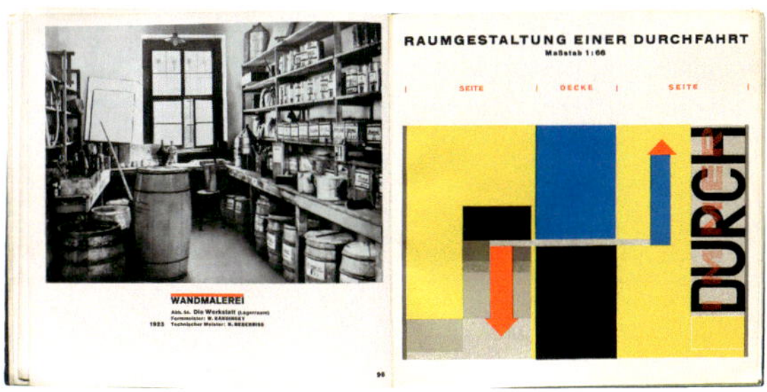

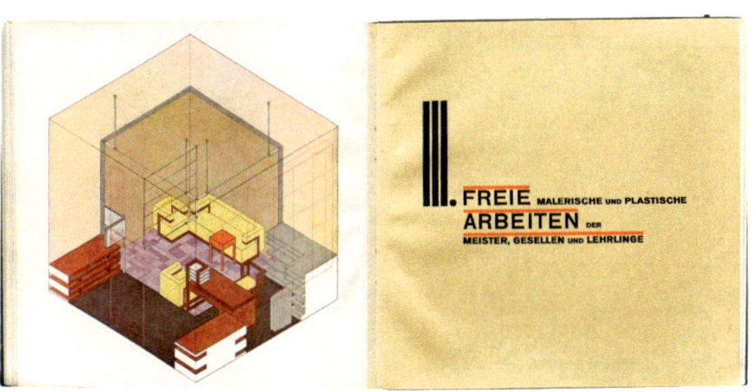

This book represents a number of Bauhaus firsts: It is the catalog for the school's first exhibition, its first statement issued in book form, and the first publication from the school's own publishing house, the Bauhausverlag, which was founded to print it. The catalog records the pedagogies of masters such as German artist Paul Klee and Russian painter Wassily Kandinsky, as well as German musician Gertrud Grunow, who taught a course on various forms of harmonization—the relationships within and between sound, color, and motion—and was the only woman on the teaching staff during the Weimar years. Gropius increasingly saw the Bauhaus's wares as a potential revenue stream, so the exhibition catalog also operated as a calling card for the school's weavings, pottery, furniture, and more. (The next year, he would establish Bauhaus GmbH to sell these products through industry partners, with students providing cheap labor.) The catalog's hand-lettered cover, by Austrian-born Herbert Bayer, then still a student, is a nascent example of his interest in geometric letterforms, which found further expression in his Universal Type (see pages 204–205). The interior design, by László Moholy-Nagy, and in particular his title page, represents one of the first definitive statements of Bauhaus typography (see top left on page 19). In fact, the title of Moholy-Nagy's essay in the catalog, "The New Typography," is the first appearance of the phrase that came to encompass the entire modernist emphasis on asymmetrical layouts, sans serif typefaces, and geometric shapes in page design. ●

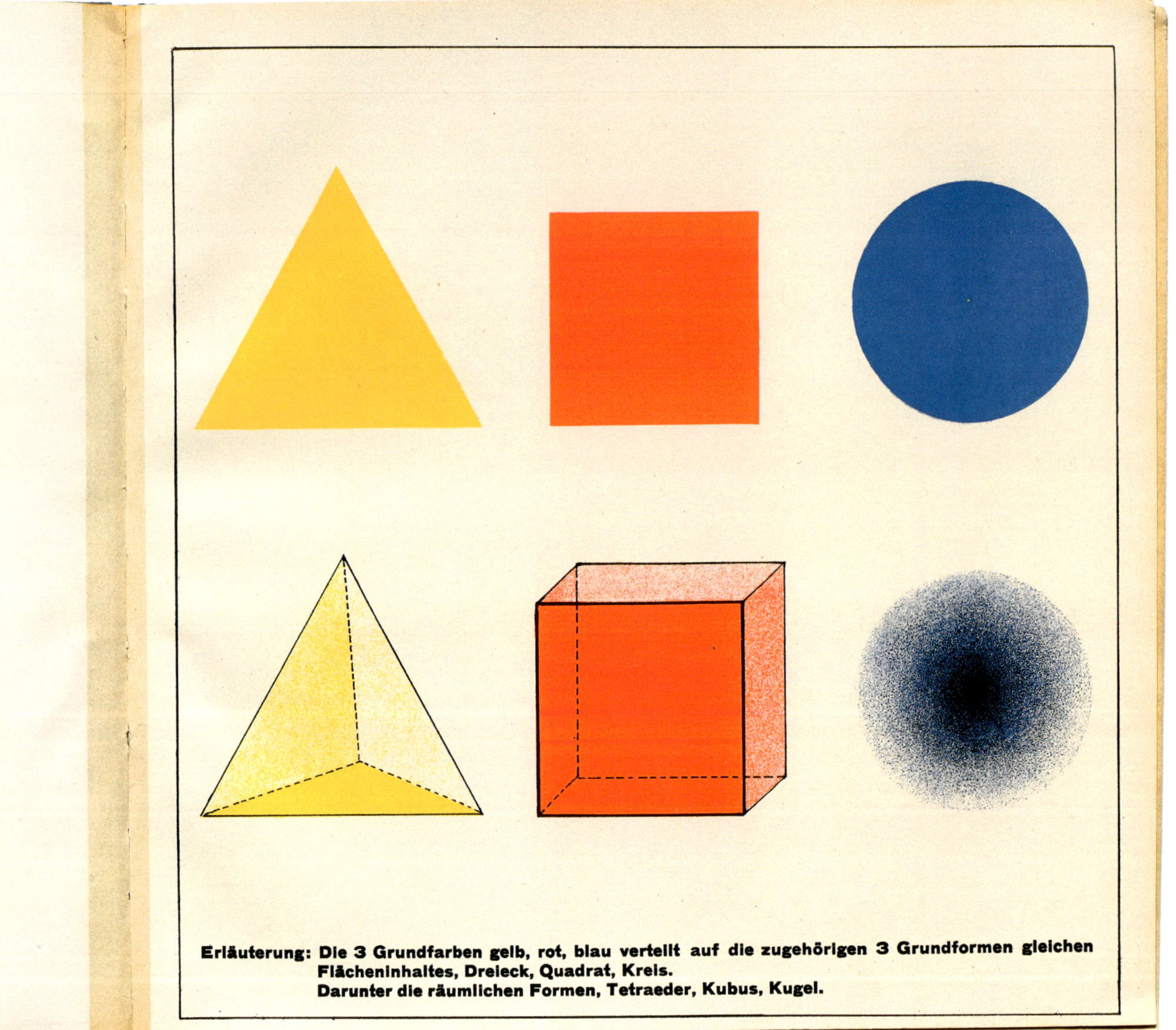
Erläuterung: Die 3 Grundfarben gelb, rot, blau verteilt auf die zugehörigen 3 Grundformen gleichen
Flächeninhaltes, Dreieck, Quadrat, Kreis.
Darunter die räumlichen Formen, Tetraeder, Kubus, Kugel.

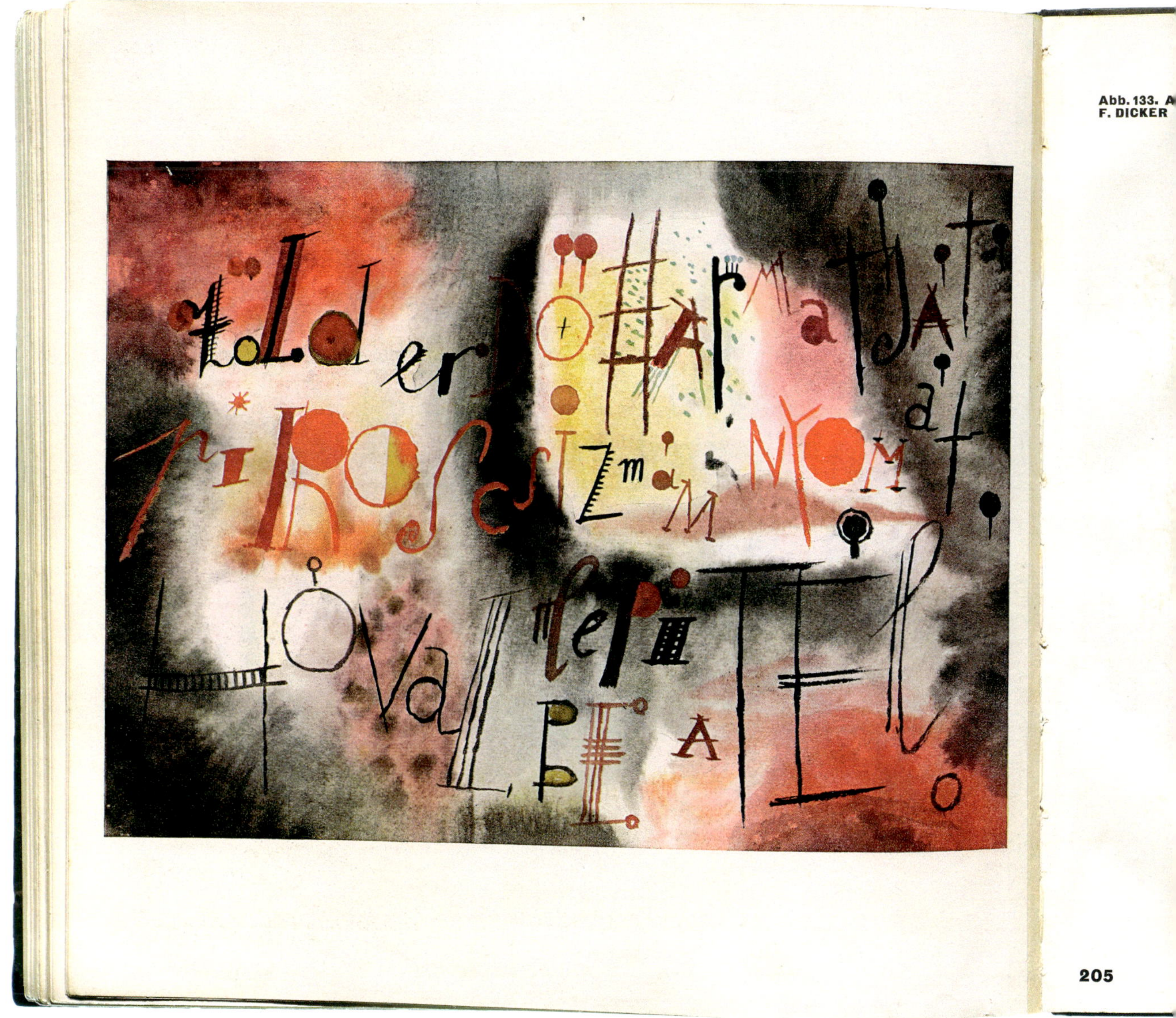
Abb. 133. A
F. DICKER
205

bauha
public

In 1923, Walter Gropius and László Moholy-Nagy began devising the Bauhaus's most ambitious publishing project: the Bauhausbücher, or Bauhaus Books series. The fourteen volumes issued between 1925 and 1930 (of more than thirty that were planned) served to condense and deliver Bauhaus pedagogy to a wider audience, as well as to make connections with allied avant-garde movements and like-minded artists, such as Kazimir Malevich's suprematism or Piet Mondrian and Theo van Doesburg's de Stijl. Within the Bauhaus's fluctuating history, the Bauhausbücher are an exceptional example of consistency and unity, with most cover designs and layouts executed by Moholy-Nagy, and all published in both paperback and hardcover in a similar size by one publisher, Albert Langen. ● December of 1926 saw the advent of the school's other major serial publication: *bauhaus* magazine. While the Bauhaus Books collected the instructors' most essential ideas for posterity, the quarterly magazine kept an international readership up to date on happenings at the school, the aesthetic and ideological debates of its time, and the cutting-edge products of industrial design—from lamps and tea sets to furniture and wallpapers—developed in its workshops and sold to the public. Indeed, *bauhaus* is possibly the richest primary source for understanding the school during some of its most vigorous years. Its changing format, design, and typography also track the successive tenures of the three major Bauhaus typographers: László Moholy-Nagy, Herbert Bayer, and Joost Schmidt. ●

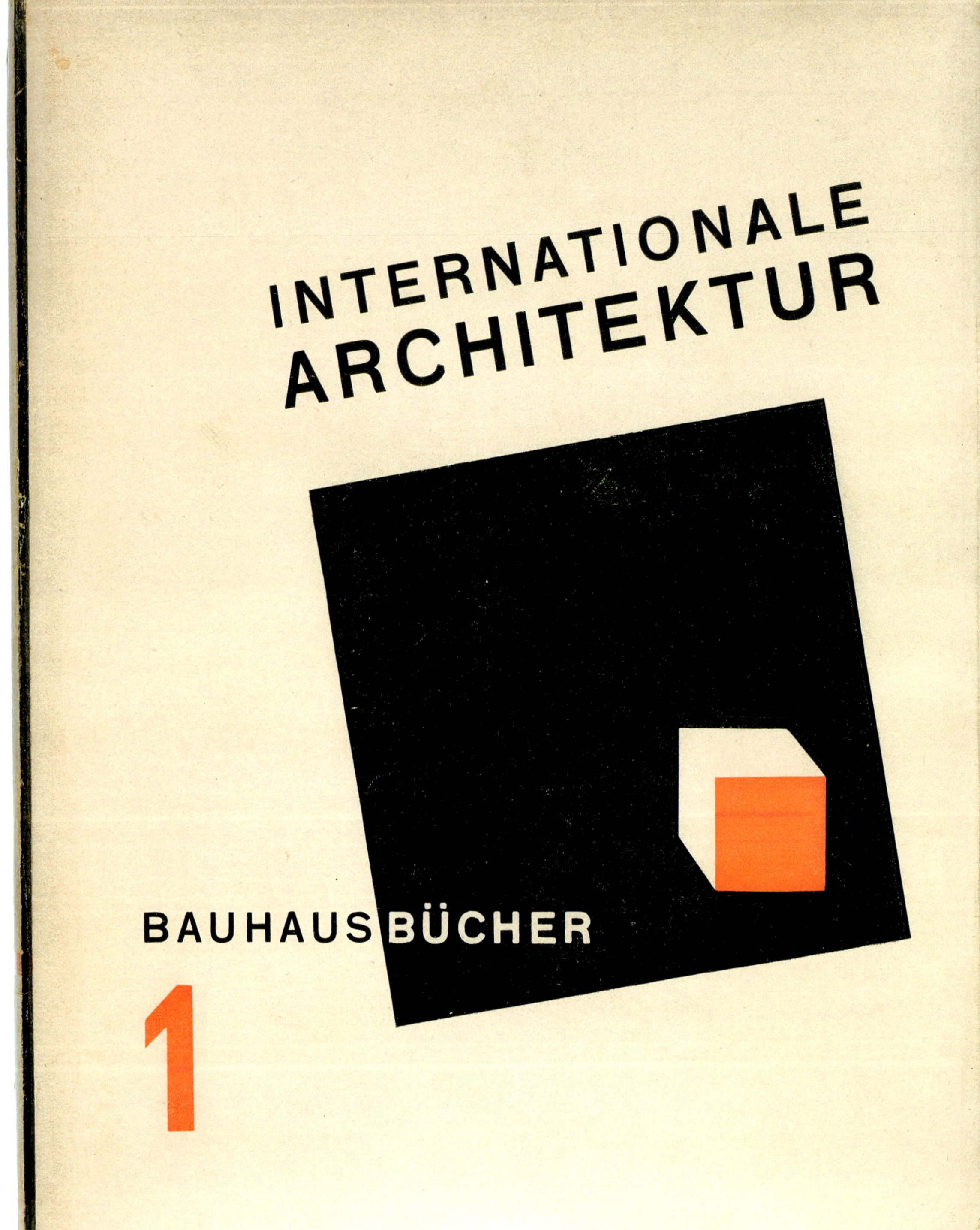
INTERNATIONALE
ARCHITEKTUR
BAUHAUSBÜCHER
1

1925

FARKAS MOLNÁR (jacket designer)
LÁSZLÓ MOHOLY-NAGY (cover and layout designer)
WALTER GROPIUS (author)

International Architecture (*Internationale Architektur*), Bauhaus Book 1, letterpress, 9⅜ × 7⅜ inches (237 × 187 mm), Munich.

After delays due to the school's ouster from Weimar, Gropius and Moholy-Nagy published the first eight Bauhaus Books simultaneously in 1925. In an early instance of branding and product standardization, each book bears the series name and volume number on a jacket otherwise designed to express the individual title's themes, with all hardcovers bound in yellow cloth and stamped in red ink. Type was set primarily in sans serifs like Breite Grotesk, Industria, and Venus, with the occasional appearance of serifs like Genzsch-Antiqua. Some titles were instead lettered by hand to emulate grotesque typefaces, such as the cover of Bauhausbücher 1. The books were printed using letterpress methods instead of the stone lithography of the Bauhaus's earlier portfolios and postcards. As such, Moholy-Nagy's design for them—bold type, thick rules, and heavy use of photography—is meant to mimic the mechanical precision of their production. ●
Despite the titles' uniformity, their topics and authors ranged widely. The first, Gropius's *International Architecture*, details the austerity of International Style, while Oskar Schlemmer's *The Theater of the Bauhaus* captures the whimsical kineticism of the school's costumes and stagecraft. Masters Klee, Kandinsky, and Moholy-Nagy himself documented their pedagogies in book form, as did artists from outside the Bauhaus. Immediately, the series stood out as one of the first multivolume efforts to track the voices of the modern movement. ●
With thousands of each Bauhausbücher title in print, Moholy-Nagy's plan for mass dissemination of the school's ideas was realized. After he and Gropius departed in 1928, the books slowed in publication, then ceased after 1930. ●

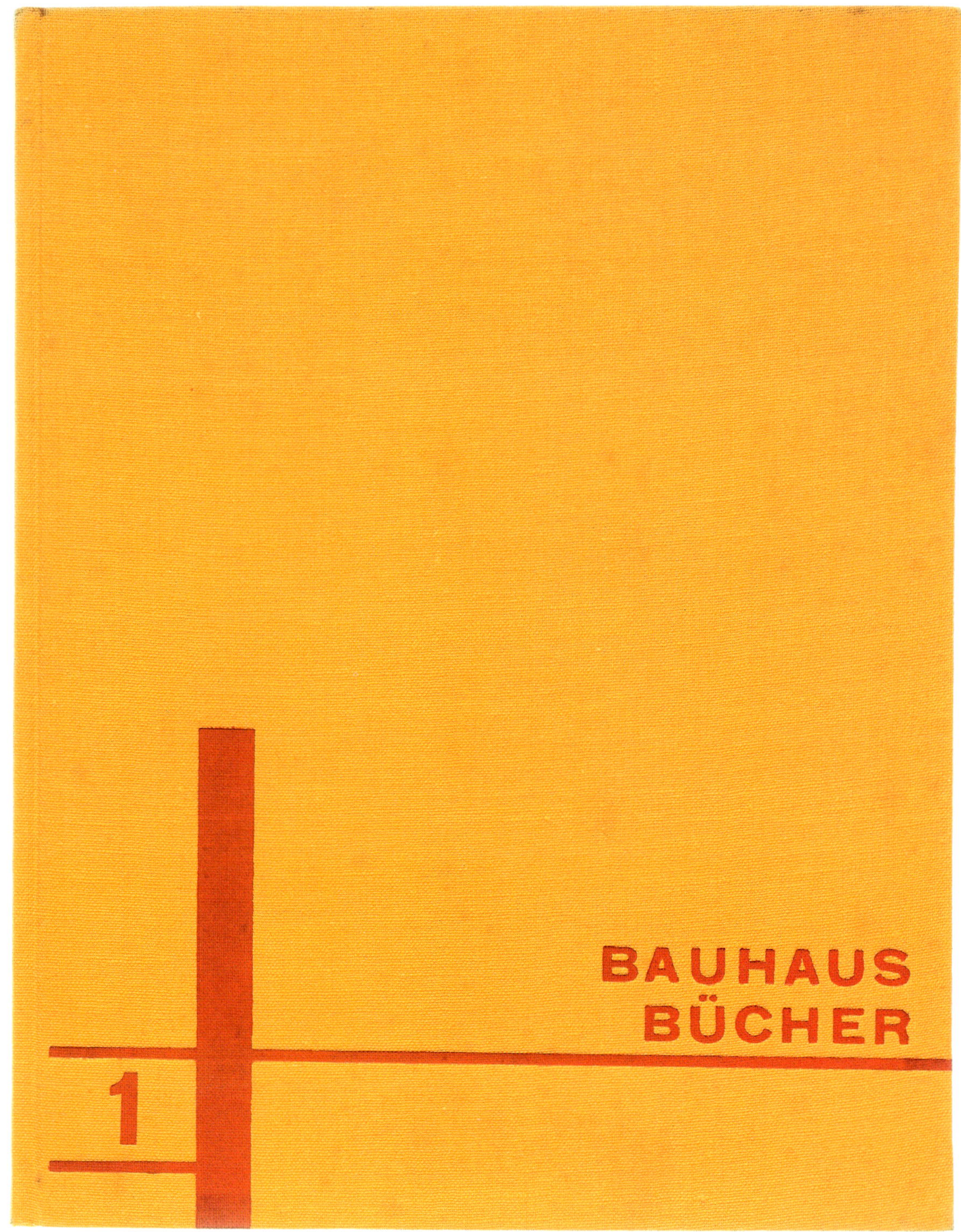
BAUHAUS
BÜCHER
1

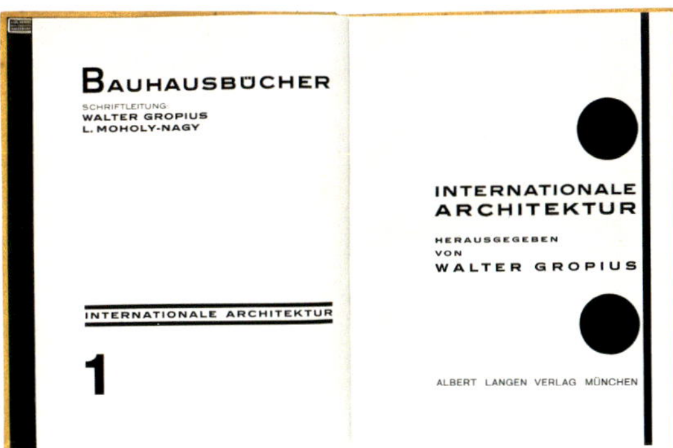

BAUHAUSBÜCHER
SCHRIFTLEITUNG
WALTER GROPIUS
L. MOHOLY-NAGY

INTERNATIONALE ARCHITEKTUR

1

INTERNATIONALE ARCHITEKTUR
HERAUSGEGEBEN VON
WALTER GROPIUS

ALBERT LANGEN VERLAG MÜNCHEN

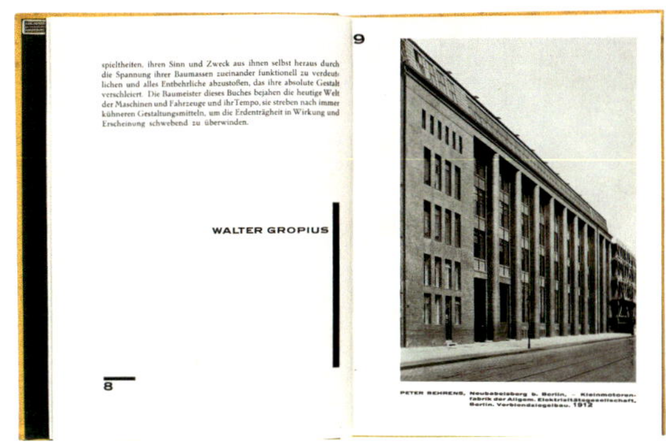

spieltheiten, ihren Sinn und Zweck aus ihnen selbst heraus durch die Spannung ihrer Baumassen zueinander funktionell zu verdeutlichen und alles Entbehrliche abzustoßen, das ihre absolute Gestalt verschleiert. Die Baumeister dieses Buches bejahen die heutige Welt der Maschinen und Fahrzeuge und ihr Tempo, sie streben nach immer kühneren Gestaltungsmitteln, um die Erdenträgheit in Wirkung und Erscheinung schwebend zu überwinden.

WALTER GROPIUS

8

9

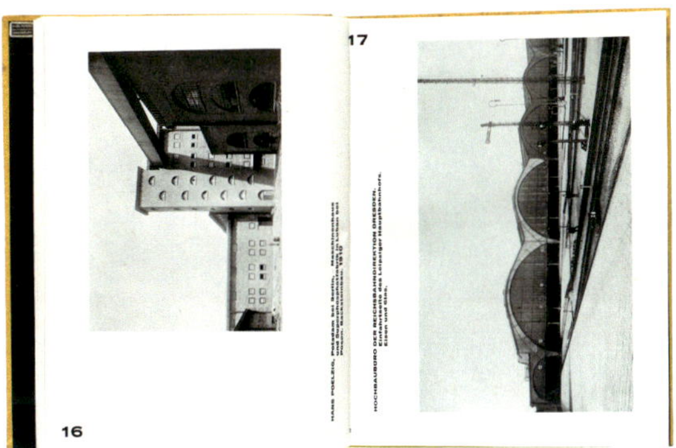

16

17

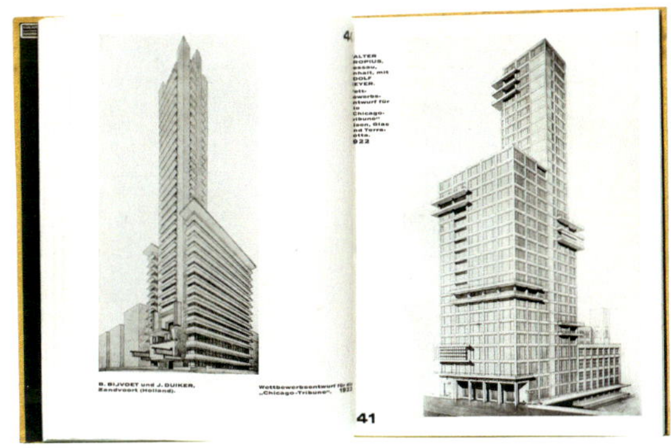

41

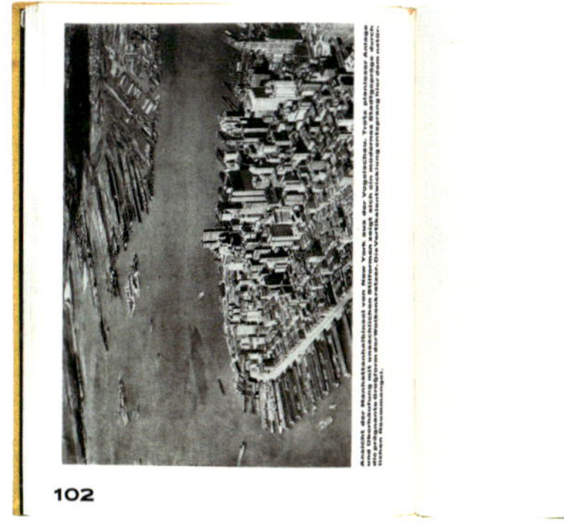

102

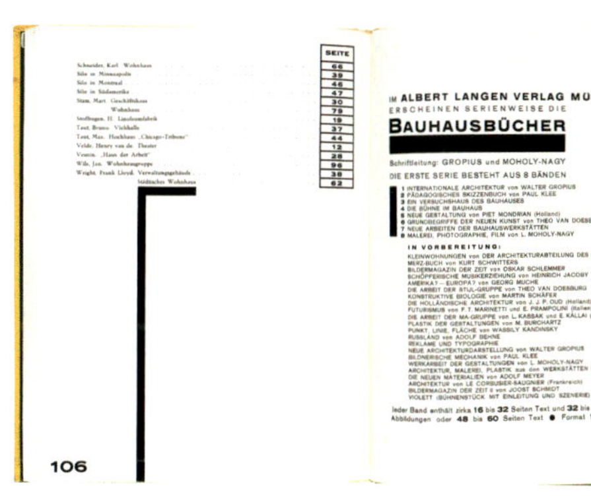

106

IM ALBERT LANGEN VERLAG MÜNCHEN
ERSCHEINEN SERIENWEISE DIE
BAUHAUSBÜCHER

Schriftleitung: GROPIUS und MOHOLY-NAGY

DIE ERSTE SERIE BESTEHT AUS 8 BÄNDEN

1 INTERNATIONALE ARCHITEKTUR von WALTER GROPIUS
2 PÄDAGOGISCHES SKIZZENBUCH von PAUL KLEE
3 EIN VERSUCHSHAUS DES BAUHAUSES
4 DIE BÜHNE IM BAUHAUS
5 NEUE GESTALTUNG von PIET MONDRIAN (Holland)
6 GRUNDBEGRIFFE DER NEUEN KUNST von THEO VAN DOESBURG (Holland)
7 NEUE ARBEITEN DER BAUHAUSWERKSTÄTTEN
8 MALEREI, PHOTOGRAPHIE, FILM von L. MOHOLY-NAGY

IN VORBEREITUNG:

KLEINWOHNUNGEN von DER ARCHITEKTURABTEILUNG DES BAUHAUSES
MERZ-BUCH von KURT SCHWITTERS
BILDERMAGAZIN DER ZEIT von OSKAR SCHLEMMER
SCHÖPFERISCHE MUSIKERZIEHUNG von HEINRICH JACOBY
AMERIKA? — EUROPA? von GEORG MUCHE
DIE ARBEIT DER STIJL-GRUPPE von THEO VAN DOESBURG
KONSTRUKTIVE BIOLOGIE von MARTIN SCHÄFER
DIE HOLLÄNDISCHE ARCHITEKTUR von J. J. P. OUD (Holland)
FUTURISMUS von F. T. MARINETTI und E. PRAMPOLINI (Italien)

Jeder Band enthält zirka 16 bis 32 Seiten Text und 32 bis 96 ganzseitige Abbildungen oder 48 bis 60 Seiten Text • Format 18 × 23 cm •

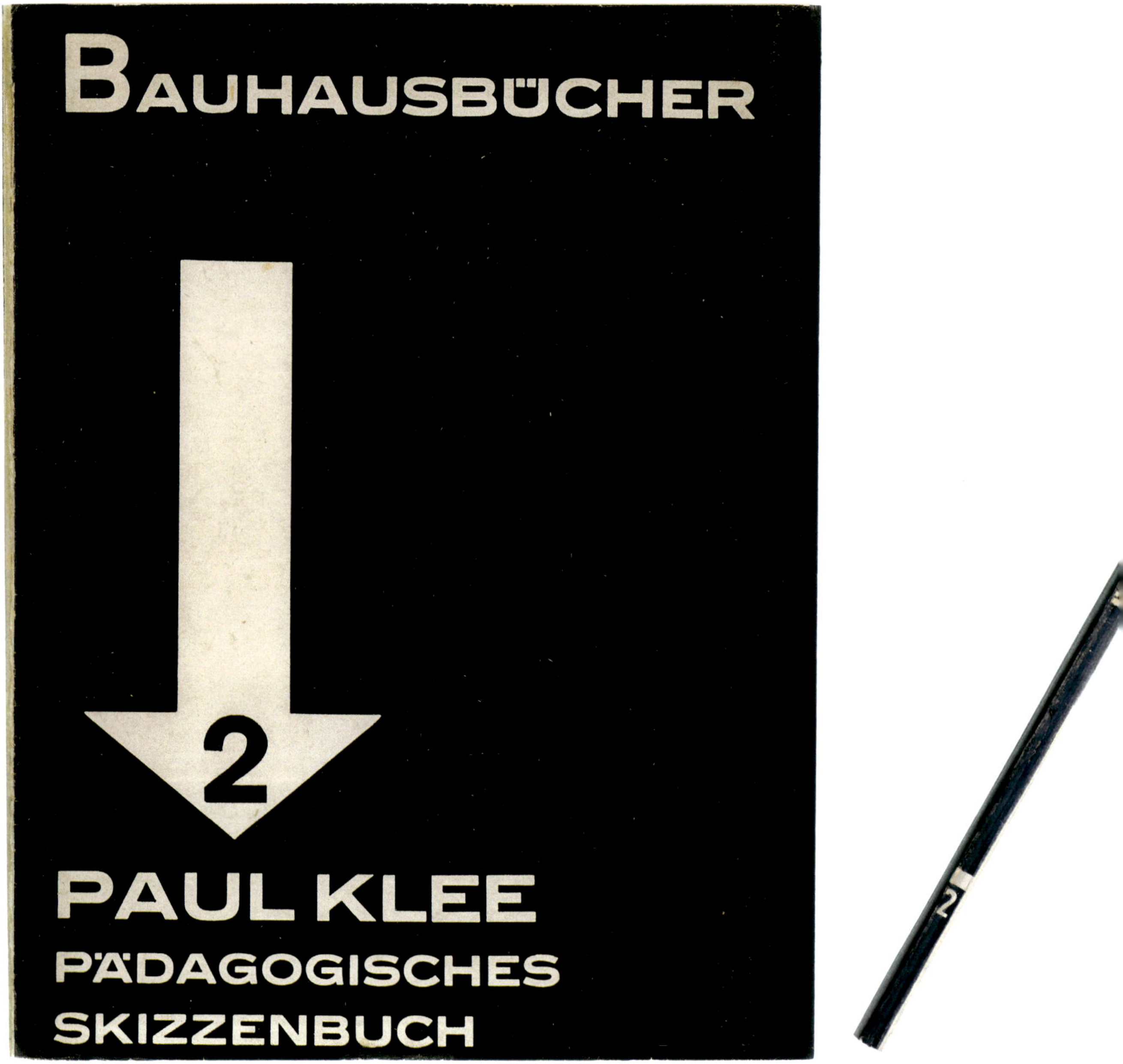

BAUHAUSBÜCHER

2

PAUL KLEE
PÄDAGOGISCHES
SKIZZENBUCH

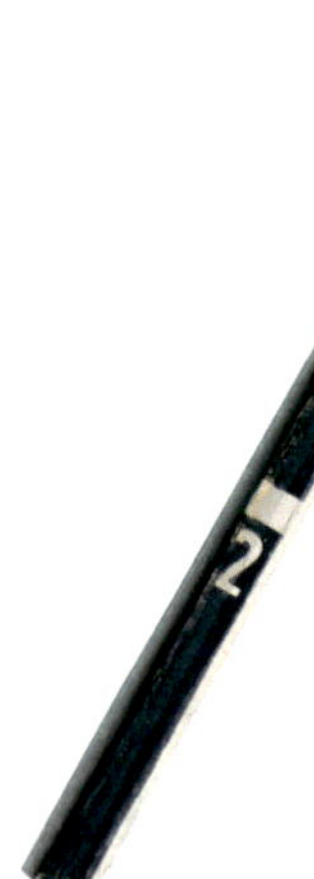

1925

LÁSZLÓ MOHOLY-NAGY (designer)
PAUL KLEE (author)

Pedagogical Sketchbook (*Pädagogisches Skizzenbuch*), Bauhaus Book 2, letterpress, 9 × 7 inches (229 × 180 mm), Munich.

KLEE: PÄDAGOGISCHES SKIZZ
ALBERT LANGEN VERLAG
MÜNCHEN

BAUHAUSBÜCHER

SCHRIFTLEITUNG:
W. GROPIUS
L. MOHOLY-NAGY

2

PAUL KLEE
PÄDAGOGISCHES SKIZZENBUCH

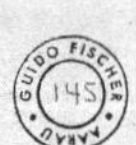

PAUL KLEE

PÄDAGOGI-
SCHES
SKIZZEN-
BUCH

ALBERT LANGEN VERLAG MÜNCHEN

OHLENROTH'SCHE
BUCHDRUCKEREI
ERFURT

KLISCHEES
VON LÜBBECKE u. Co
ERFURT

UMSCHLAGENTWURF
UND
TYPOGRAPHIE
VON
L. MOHOLY-NAGY

Dieses Buch wurde im Sommer 1924 zusammengestellt. Technische Schwierigkeiten verhinderten das rechtzeitige Erscheinen. Das Personengremium des bisherigen Staatlichen Bauhauses hat seine Tätigkeit in Weimar abgeschlossen und setzt sie unter dem Namen: DAS BAUHAUS IN DESSAU (ANHALT) fort.

COPYRIGHT 1925 BY ALBERT LANGEN, MÜNCHEN

URSPRÜNGLICHE GRUNDLAGE ZU EINEM
TEIL DES THEORETISCHEN UNTERRICHTES
AM STAATLICHEN BAUHAUS ZU WEIMAR

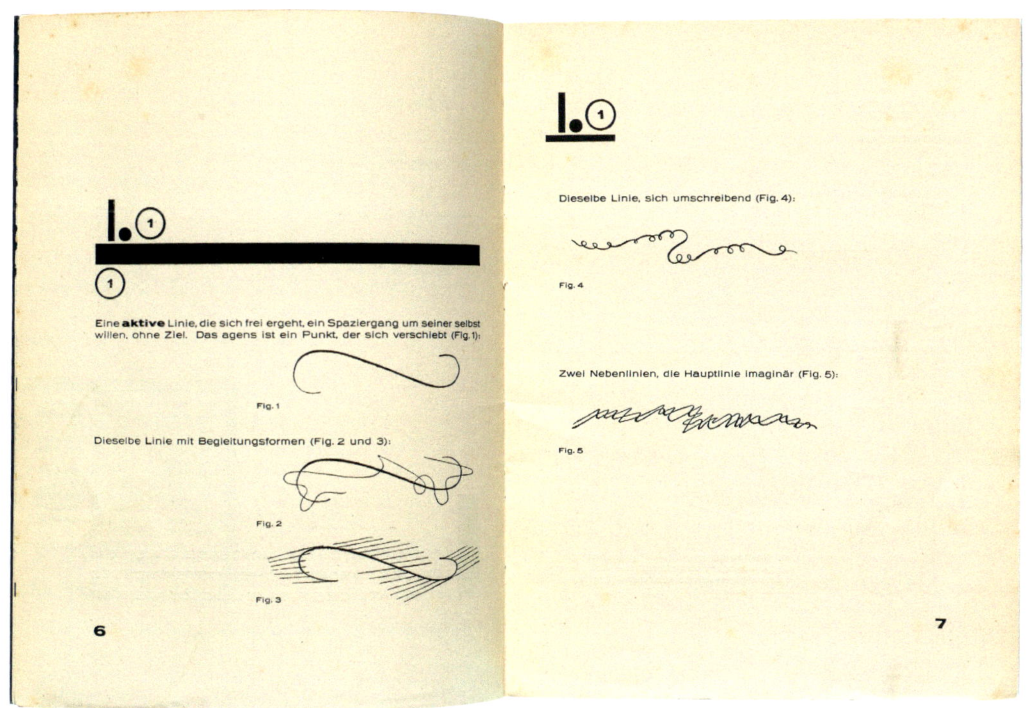

Swiss-born artist Paul Klee was one of the longest-serving professors at the Bauhaus, teaching from 1923 to 1931. His *Pedagogical Sketchbook* (*Pädagogisches Skizzenbuch*) is a prime artifact of the fine arts–dominant teaching of the early school. As playful and expressive as Klee's paintings and drawings, his book begins with simple elements of visual form—the first figure shows "an **active** line on a walk, moving freely, without goal" (emphasis his)—and builds to more complex lessons in structure, kinetics, and chromatics. The cumulative effect is what Sibyl Moholy-Nagy calls, in the conclusion to her 1953 English translation, an "adventure in seeing." While *Pedagogical Sketchbook* was compiled from Klee's handwritten notebook pages and lecture plans, Moholy-Nagy supplements the drawn figures with simple, sans serif captioning and a unique compound wayfinding glyph. Incorporating bold tally marks and circled Arabic numerals for chapter and section numbers at the top left of each page (see above), the folios provide a kind of rational scaffolding for an otherwise expressive and intuitive book. ●

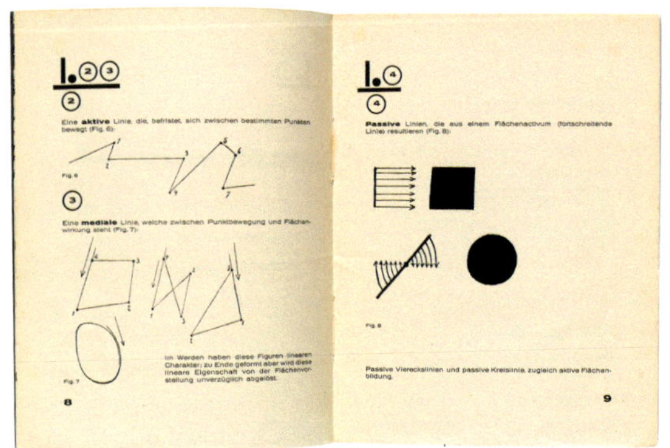

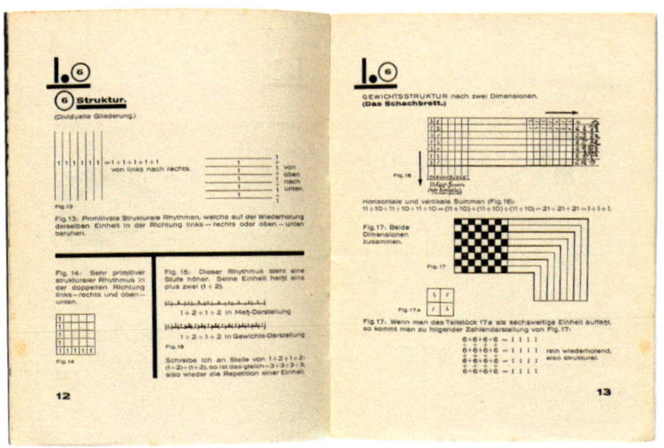

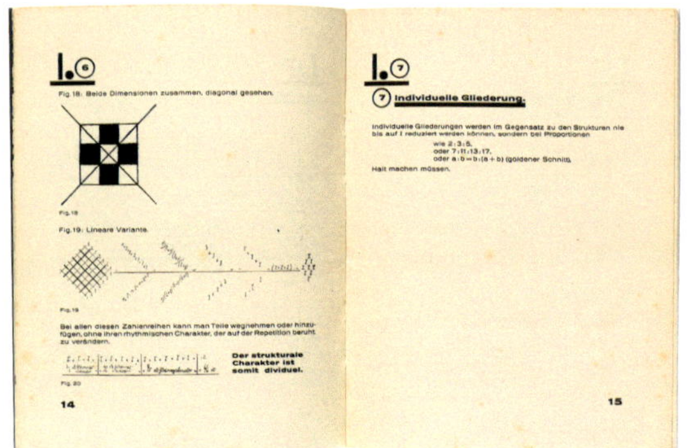

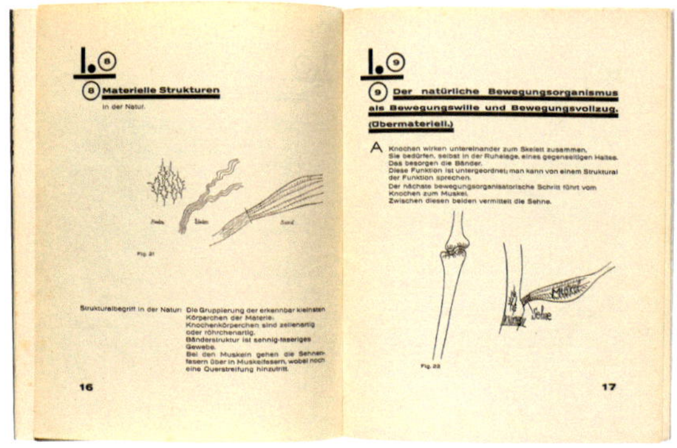

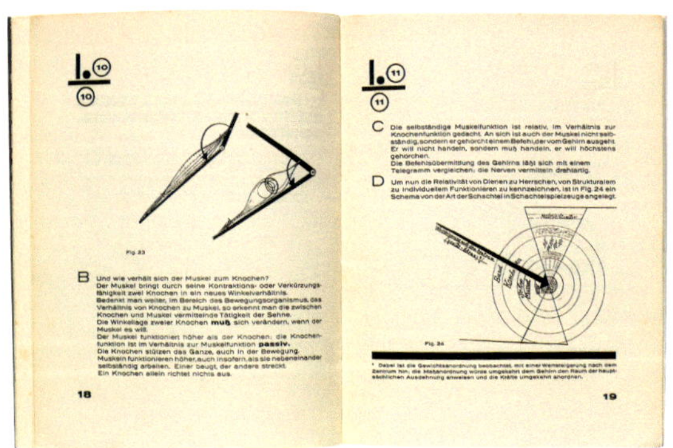

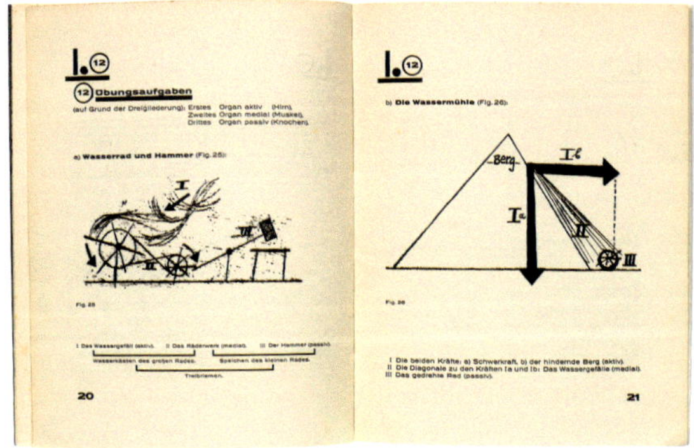

DIE DREI FÄLLE:

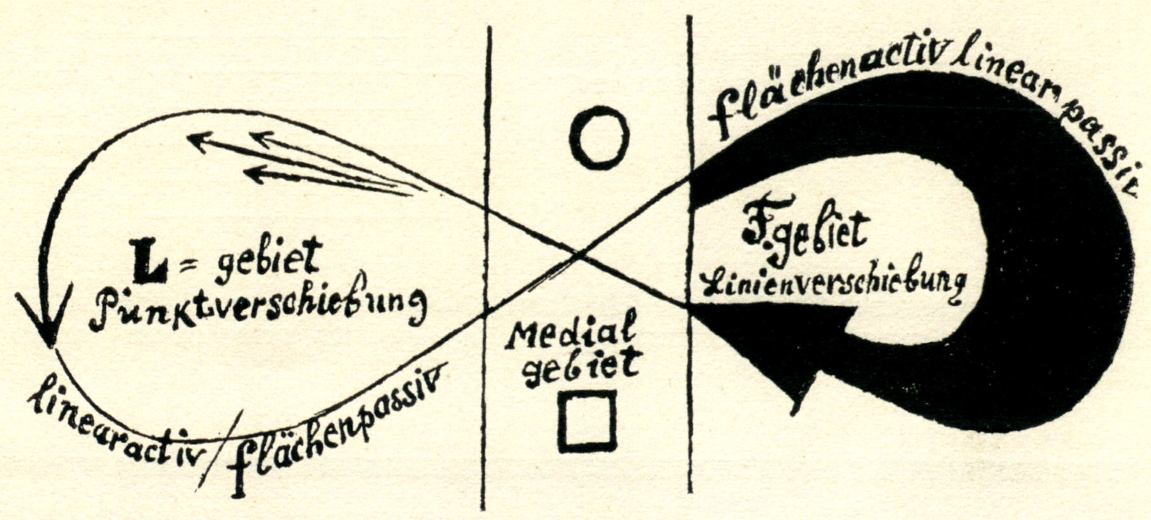

Fig. 12

Sprachliche Erläuterung
zu den Begriffen aktiv, medial und passiv:

aktiv: ich fälle (der Mann fällte mit der Axt den Baum),

medial: ich falle (der Baum fiel unter dem Hieb des Mannes),

passiv: ich werde gefällt (der Baum liegt gefällt).

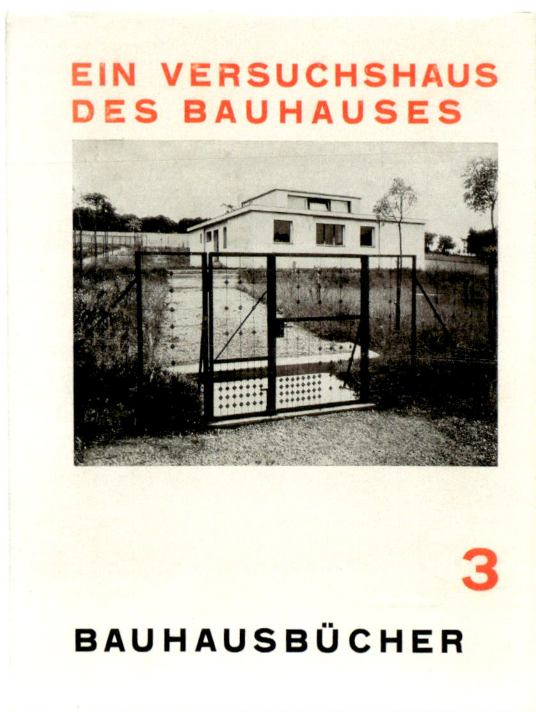

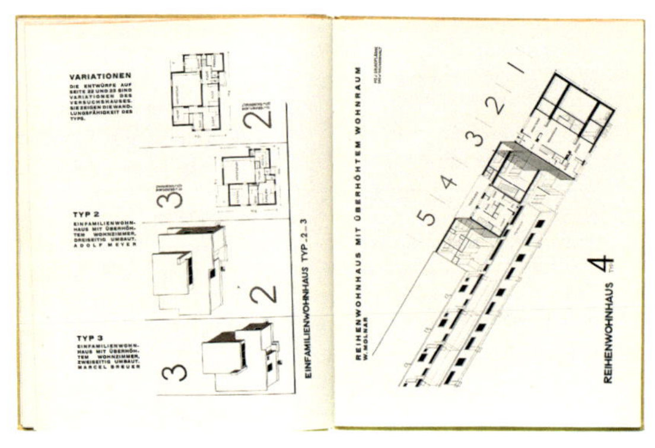

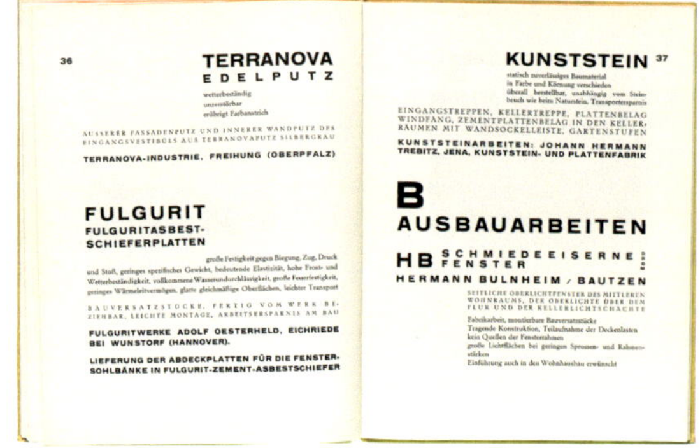

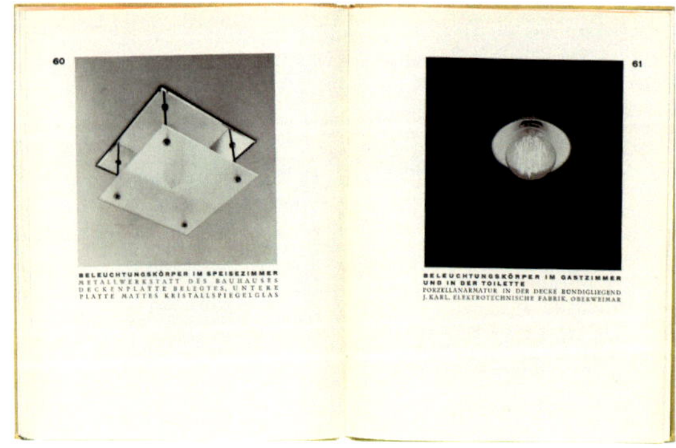

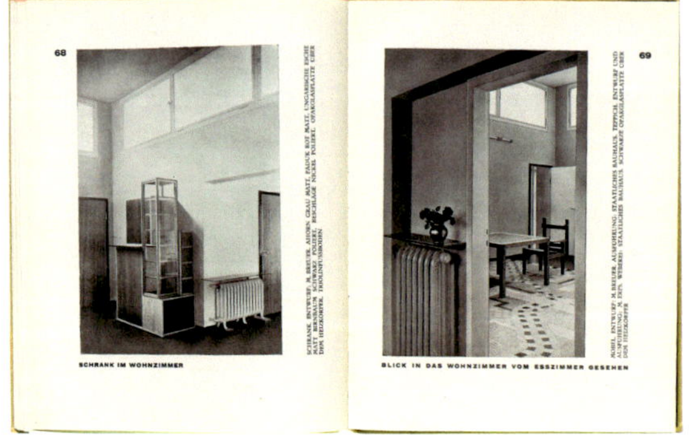

1925

ADOLF MEYER (jacket designer/editor)
LÁSZLÓ MOHOLY-NAGY (cover and layout designer)

A Bauhaus Experimental House (*Ein Versuchshaus des Bauhauses*), Bauhaus Book 3, letterpress, 9¼ × 7¼ inches (235 × 185 mm), Munich.

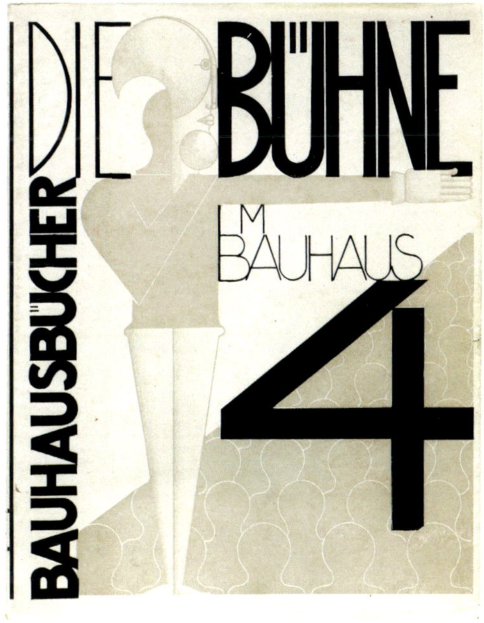

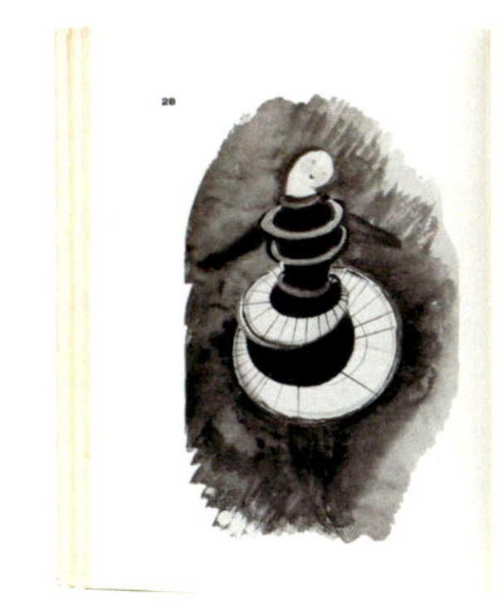

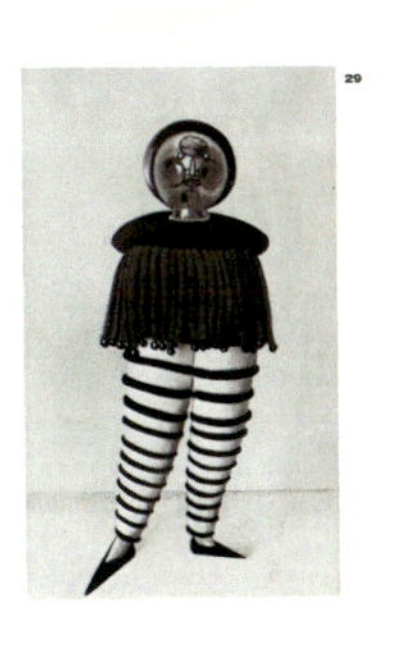

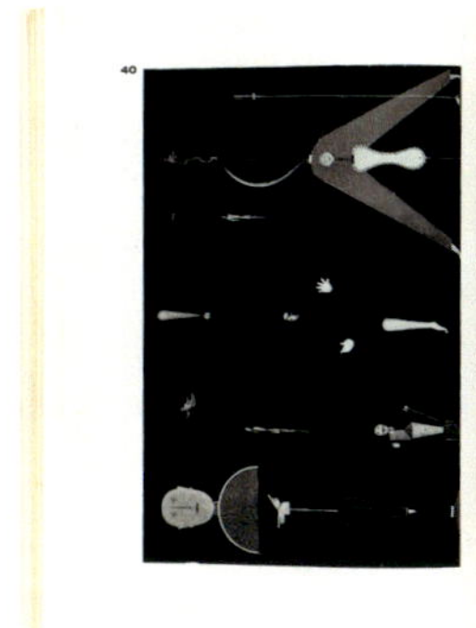

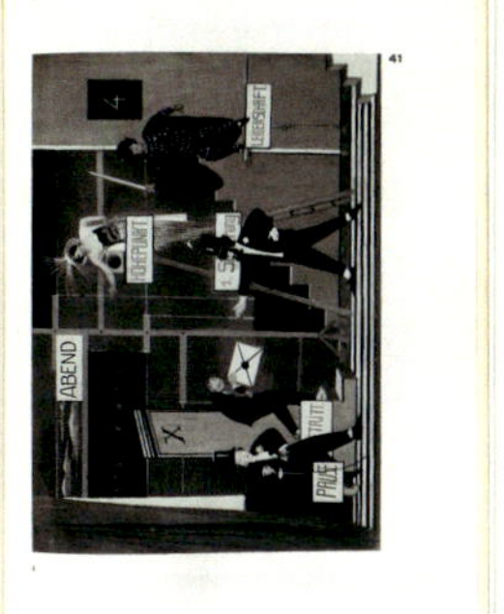

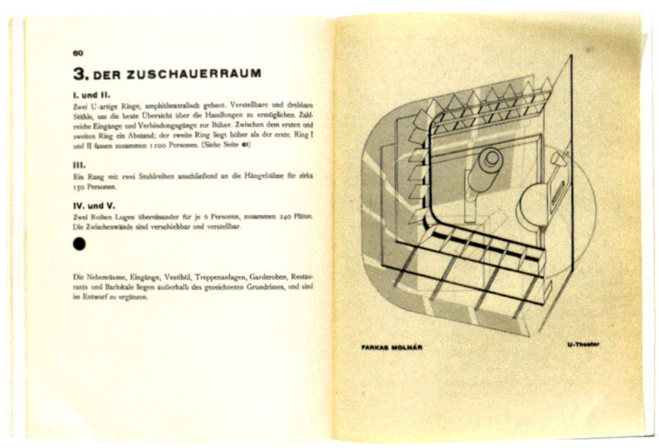

60

3. DER ZUSCHAUERRAUM

I. und II.

Zwei U-artige Ringe, amphitheatralisch gebaut. Verstellbare und drehbare Stühle, um die beste Übersicht über die Handlungen zu ermöglichen. Zahlreiche Eingänge und Verbindungsgänge zur Bühne. Zwischen dem ersten und zweiten Ring ein Abstand; der zweite Ring liegt höher als der erste. Ring I und II fassen zusammen 1100 Personen. (Siehe Seite 61)

III.

Ein Rang mit zwei Stuhlreihen anschließend an die Hängebühne für zirka 150 Personen.

IV. und V.

Zwei Reihen Logen übereinander für je 6 Personen, zusammen 240 Plätze. Die Zwischenwände sind verschiebbar und verstellbar.

●

Die Nebenräume, Eingänge, Vestibül, Treppenanlagen, Garderoben, Restaurants und Barlokale liegen außerhalb des gezeichneten Grundrisses, und sind im Entwurf zu ergänzen.

FARKAS MOLNÁR — U-Theater

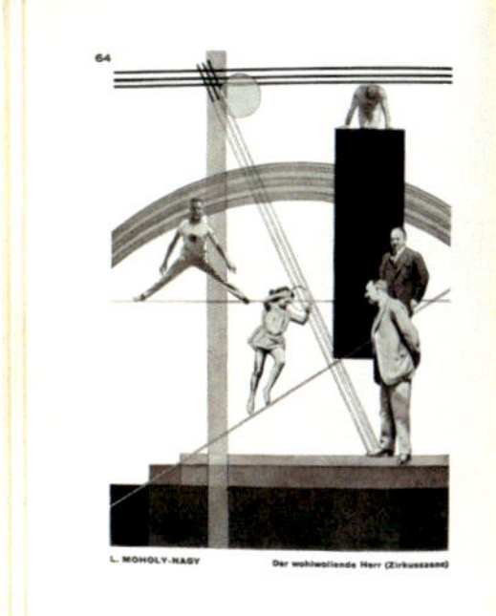

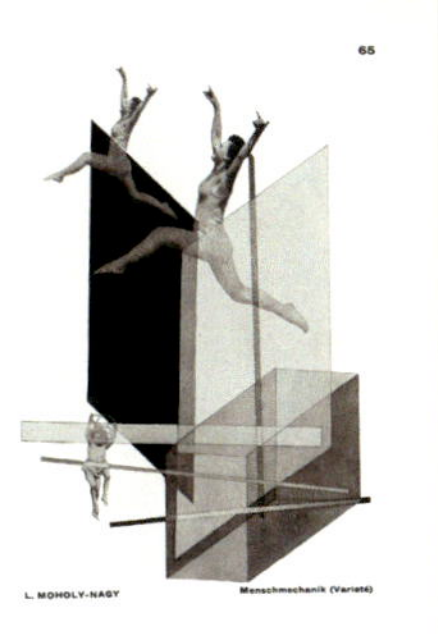

1925

OSKAR SCHLEMMER (cover designer/editor)
LÁSZLÓ MOHOLY-NAGY (layout designer)

The Theater of the Bauhaus (*Die Bühne im Bauhaus*), Bauhaus Book 4, letterpress, 9¼ × 7¼ inches (235 × 185 mm), Munich.

44

MOHOLY-NAGY

Nebenstehend die PARTITUR-SKIZZE einer MECHANISCHEN EXZENTRIK (siehe Seite **47**) für ein Varieté ● Die Bühne ist in drei Teile gegliedert. Der untere Teil für größere Formen und Bewegungen: I. BÜHNE. Die II. BÜHNE (oben) mit aufklappbarer Glasplatte für kleinere Formen und Bewegungen. (Die Glasplatte ist zugleich präparierte PROJEKTIONSWAND für von der Rückseite der Bühne projizierte Filmvorführungen.) Auf der III. (ZWISCHEN-)BÜHNE mechanische Musikapparate; meist ohne Resonanzkasten, nur mit Schalltrichtern (Schlag-, Geräusch- und Blas-Instrumente). Einzelne Wände der Bühne sind doppelt mit weißer Leinwand bespannt, die farbige Lichter aus Scheinwerfern und Lichtbäumen durchlassen und zerstreuen ● Die 1. und 2. Kolonne der Partitur bedeuten in senkrecht abwärtsgehender Kontinuität Form- und Bewegungsvorgänge ● Die 3. Kolonne zeigt nacheinander folgende Lichtwirkungen: Die Breite der Streifen bedeutet die Dauer. Schwarz = Finsternis. Die in den breiten Streifen vorhandenen schmalen vertikalen Streifen sind gleichzeitige Teilbeleuchtungen der Bühne. Die 4. Kolonne ist für Musik vorgesehen; hier nur in den Absichten angedeutet. Die farbigen Vertikalstreifen bedeuten verschiedenartig heulende Sirenentöne, die einen großen Teil der Vorgänge begleiten ● Die Gleichzeitigkeit ist in der Partitur aus der Horizontale zu lesen ●

FOLGE:

1. KOLONNE	2. KOLONNE	3. U. 4. KOLONNE
PFEILE STÜRZEN LAMELLEN ÖFFNEN SICH KREISE ROTIEREN ELEKTRO-APPARATE BLITZ DONNER GITTERSYSTEME VON FARBEN SCHIESSEN AUF - AB HIN - HER PHOSPHORESZENZ RIESEN-APPARATE SCHWINGEN BLITZEN GITTER WEITER RÄDER EXPLOSIONEN GERÜCHE CLOWNERIE MENSCHMECHANIK	PFEILE STÜRZEN LAMELLEN ÖFFNEN SICH KREISE ROTIEREN KINO AUF TAGESWAND RÜCKWÄRTS GEDREHT AKTION TEMPO WILD	SIND OHNE SCHLAGWORTE DEUTLICH

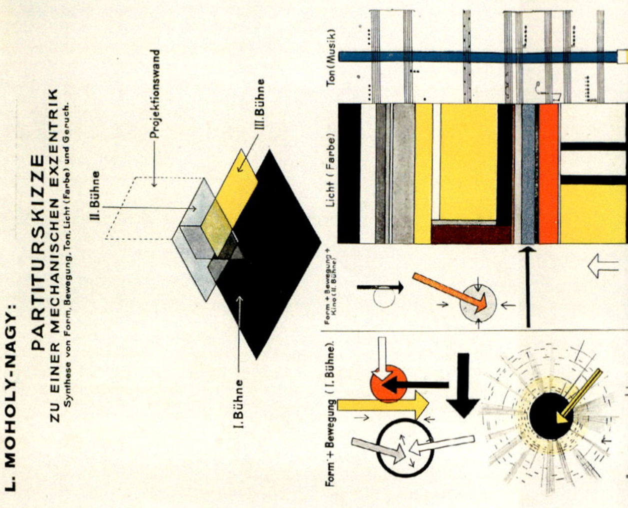

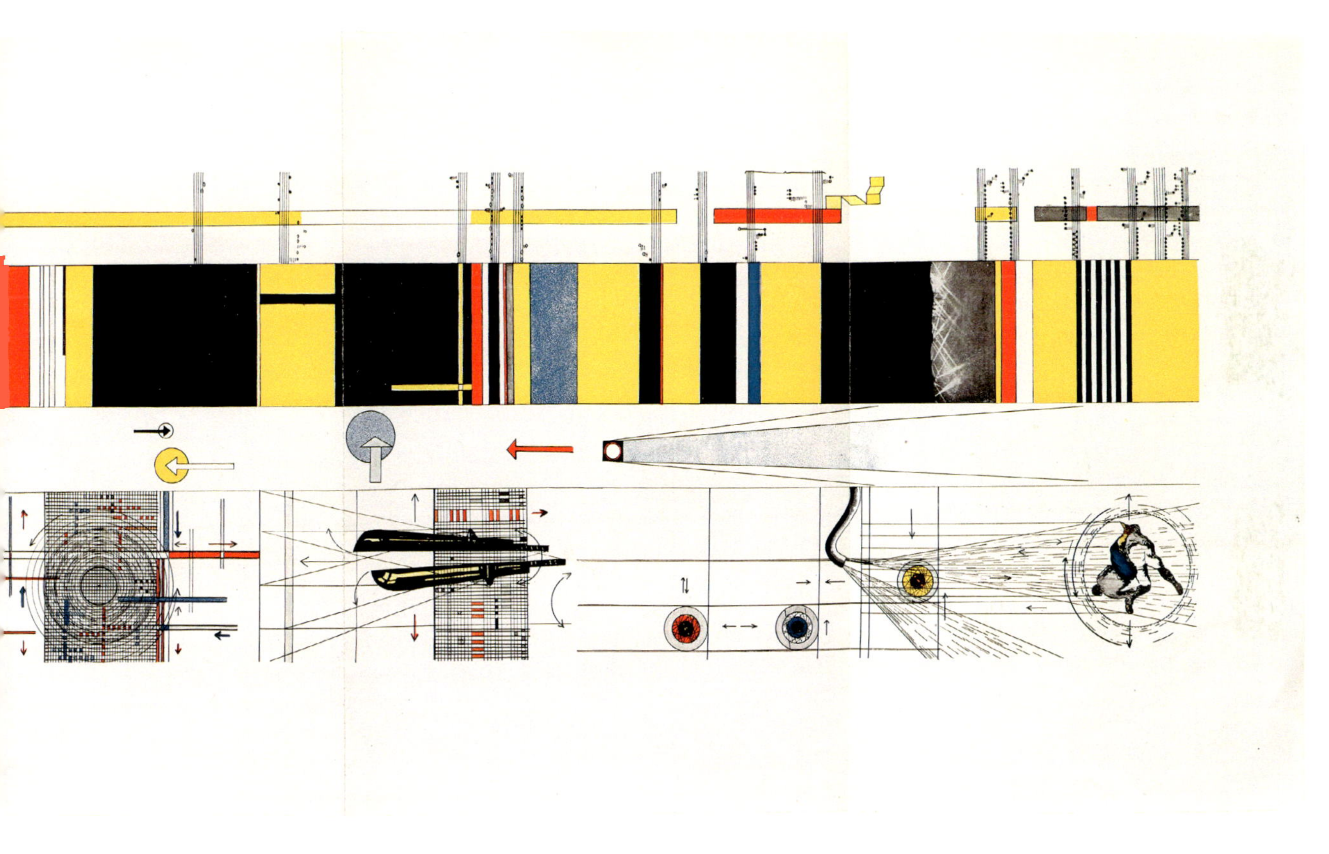

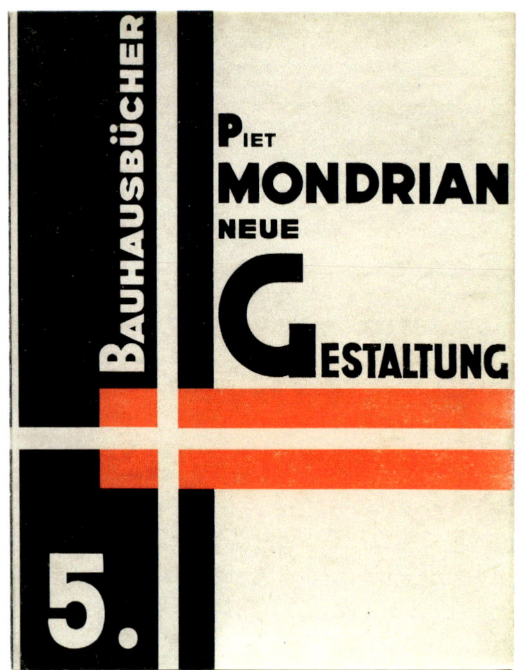

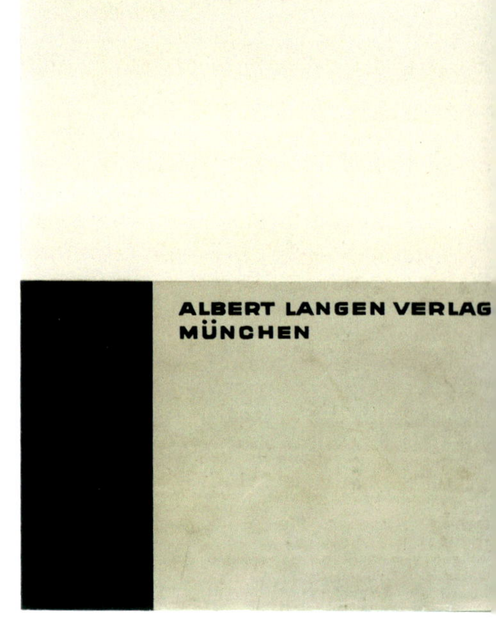

1925

LÁSZLÓ MOHOLY-NAGY (designer)
PIET MONDRIAN (author)

New Design: Neoplasticism (*Neue Gestaltung: Neoplastizismus*), Bauhaus Book 5, letterpress, 9 x 7¼ inches (229 x 183 mm), Munich.

1925

LÁSZLÓ MOHOLY-NAGY (designer)
WALTER GROPIUS (editor)

New Works from Bauhaus Workshops (*Neue Arbeiten der Bauhauswerkstätten*), Bauhaus Book 7, letterpress, 9¼ × 7⅜ inches (236 × 186 mm), Munich.

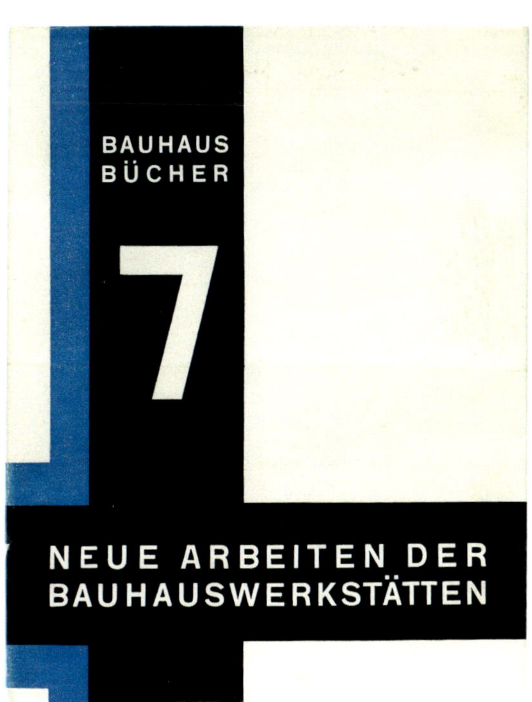

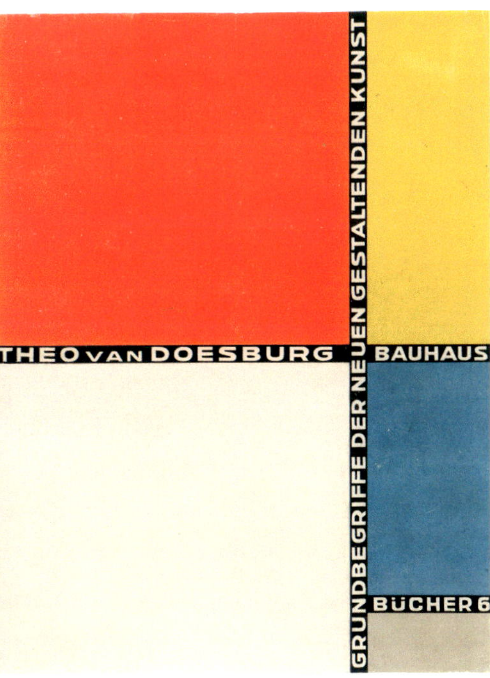

1925

THEO VAN DOESBURG (cover designer/author)
LÁSZLÓ MOHOLY-NAGY (layout designer)

Principles of Neo-Plastic Art (*Grundbegriffe der neuen gestaltenden Kunst*), Bauhaus Book 6, letterpress, 9 × 7¼ inches (230 × 183 mm), Munich.

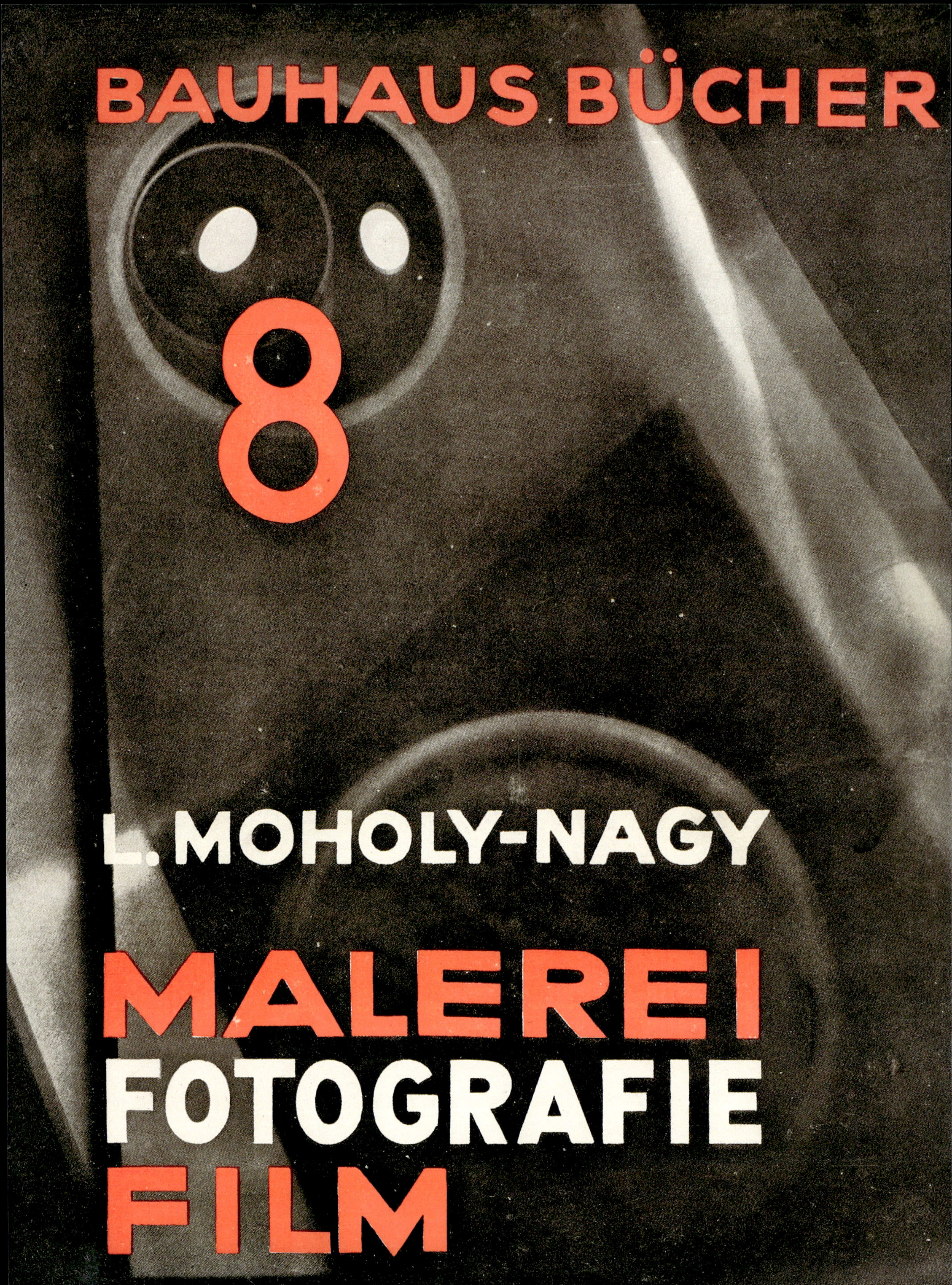

BAUHAUS BÜCHER

8

L. MOHOLY-NAGY

MALEREI FOTOGRAFIE FILM

1925

LÁSZLÓ MOHOLY-NAGY (designer/coauthor)
LUCIA MOHOLY (uncredited coauthor)

Painting, Photography, Film (*Malerei, Fotografie, Film*), Bauhaus Book 8, letterpress, 9¼ × 7⅜ inches (235 × 186 mm), Munich.

László Moholy-Nagy applied his typographic techniques to all the Bauhausbücher that he designed, but in the titles he authored in the series, he gave them full expression. Here, in *Painting, Photography, Film* (*Malerei, Fotografie, Film*), which he coauthored with his wife at the time, Lucia Moholy, he uses bold type liberally for emphasis and, for passages requiring even more attention, institutes a heavy rule on the left margin to indent the text. Bold circles punctuate section breaks; smaller ones mark footnotes. While not jarring today, the inclusion of painting alongside photography and film in the title would have struck readers as provocative, even scandalous. However, the intention was not to debase painting but rather to elevate photography and film to the same level of artistic consideration. The book's most famous section is likely "Dynamic of the Metropolis," described as a "sketch of a manuscript for a film." It is an example of *typophoto*, a term invented by Moholy-Nagy to characterize "the visually most exact rendering of communication," accomplished by synthesizing typography and photography in hybrid compositions. This chapter-as-storyboard runs over several pages in a dynamic montage of typography, photography, and symbols, cut together with Moholy-Nagy's signature bold rules, echoed by heavy lines of text set in the extra-wide Industria typeface. The operative concept is tempo, and that word appears throughout to characterize the variable pacing and filmic quality of the reading experience. It is Moholy-Nagy's definitive experiment in what the new typography can achieve. ●

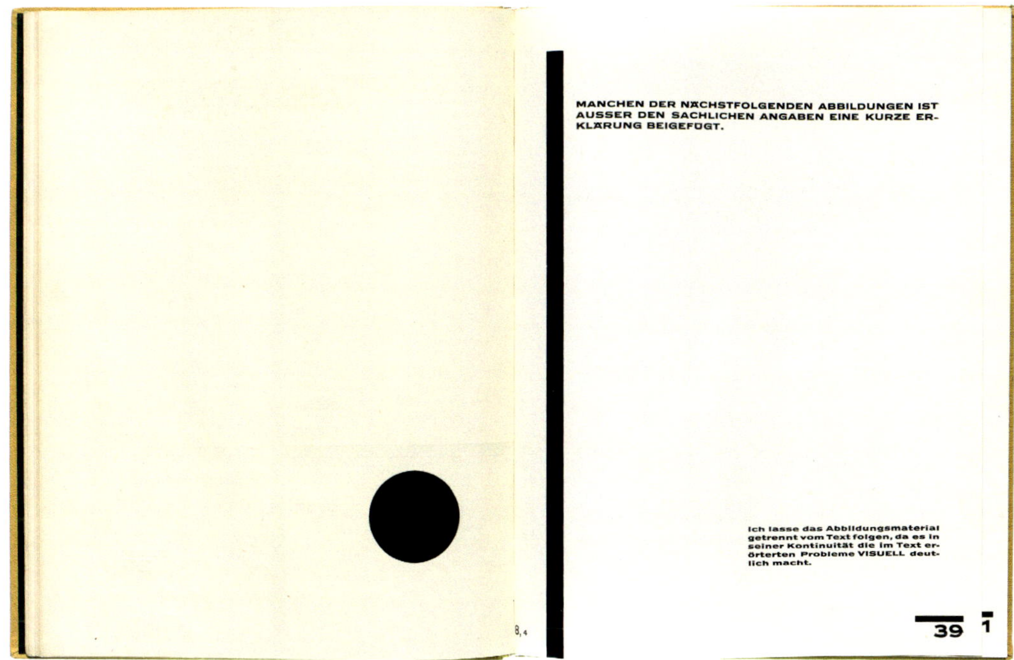

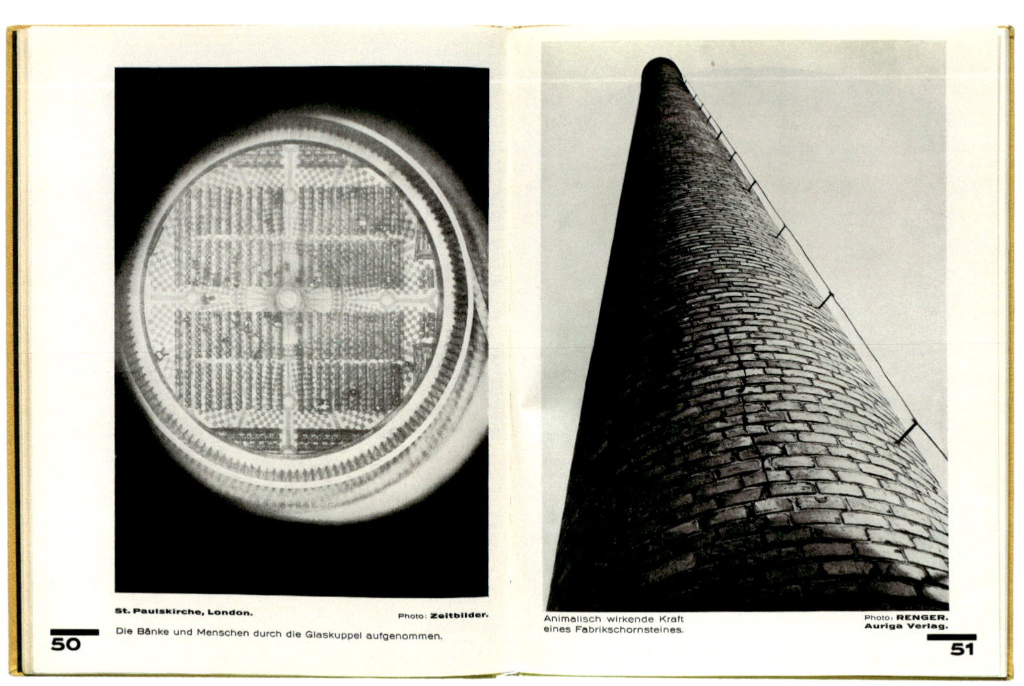
St. Paulskirche, London.
Photo: Zeitbilder.
Die Bänke und Menschen durch die Glaskuppel aufgenommen.
50
Animalisch wirkende Kraft
eines Fabrikschornsteines.
Photo: RENGER.
Auriga Verlag.
51

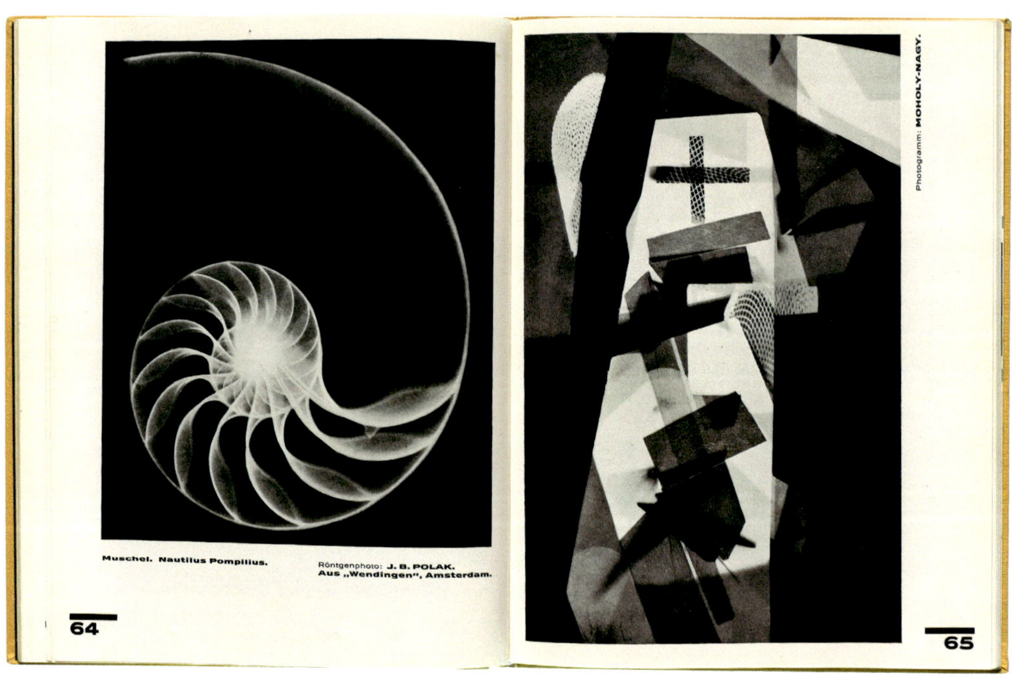
Muschel. Nautilus Pompilius.
Röntgenphoto: J. B. POLAK.
Aus „Wendingen", Amsterdam.
64
Photogramm: MOHOLY-NAGY.
65

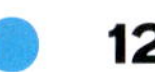

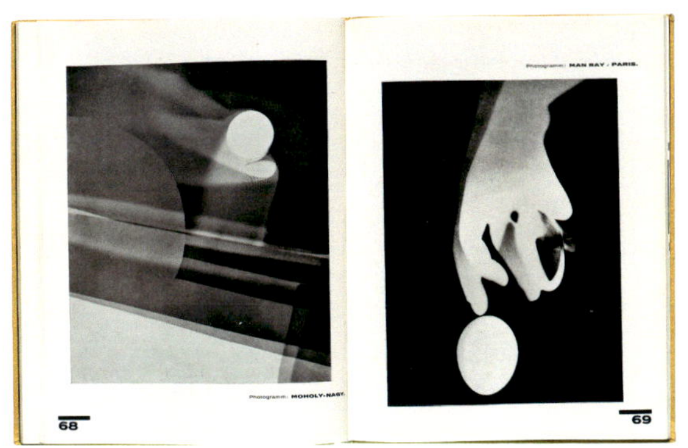

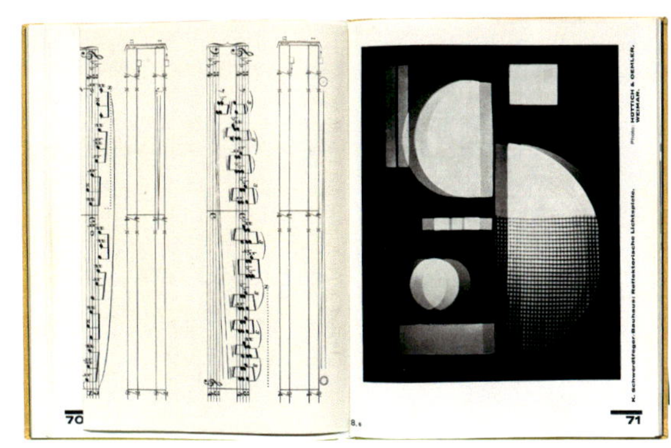

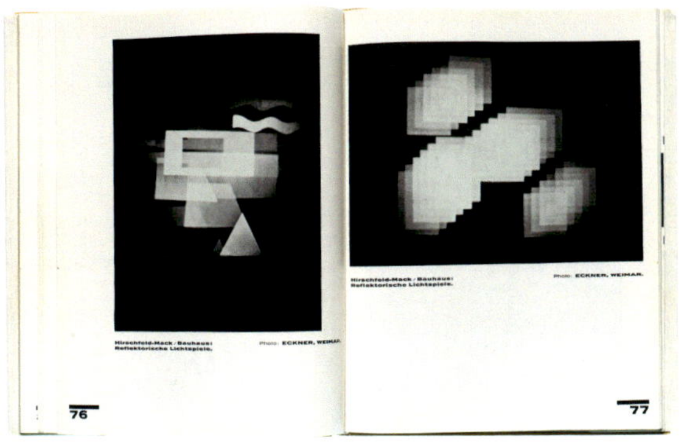

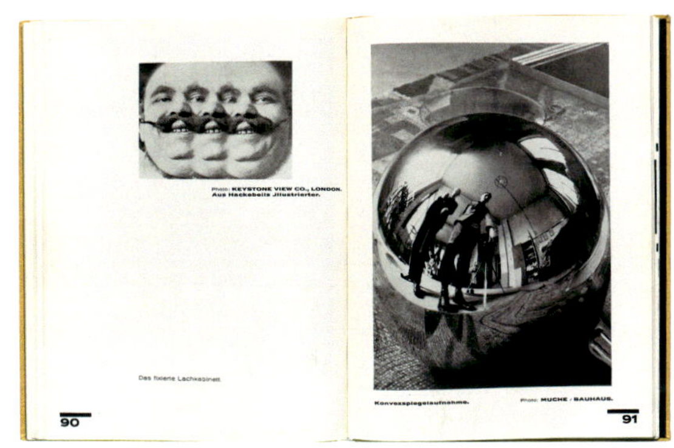

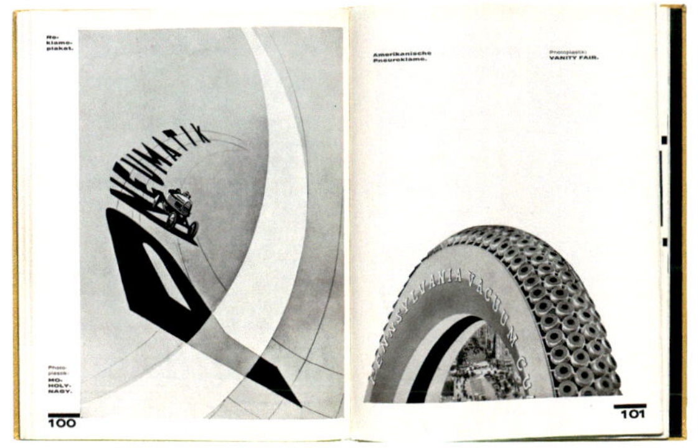

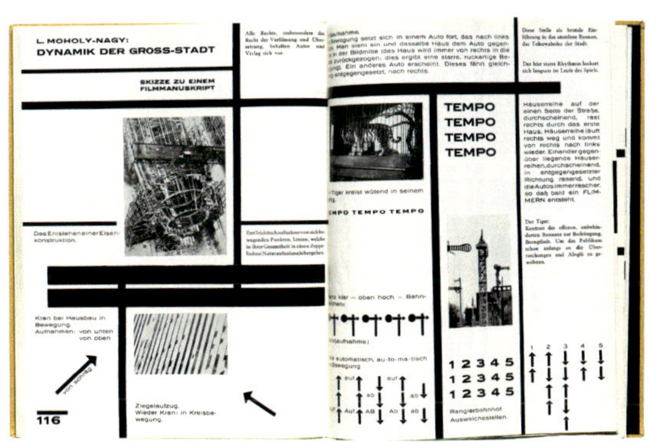

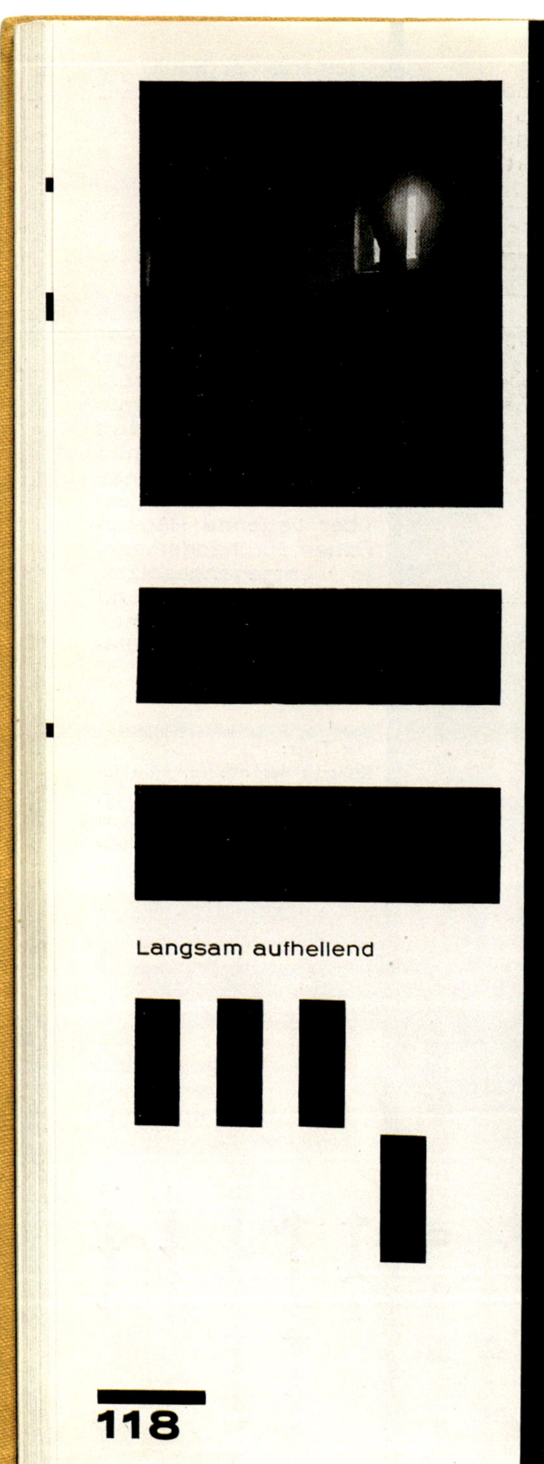

Langsam aufhellend

Lagerräume und Keller.

Finsternis

FINSTERNIS

Eisenbahn.
Landstraße (mit Fuhrwerken).
Brücken. Viadukt. Unten Wasser, Schiffe in Wellen. Darüber der schwebende Zug.
Zugaufnahme von einer Brücke aus: von oben; von unten. (**Der Bauch des Zuges,** wie er dahin fährt; aus einem Graben zwischen den Schienen aufgenommen.)
Ein Wächter salutiert. Glasige Augen. Großaufnahme: Auge.

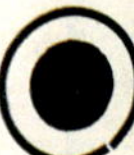

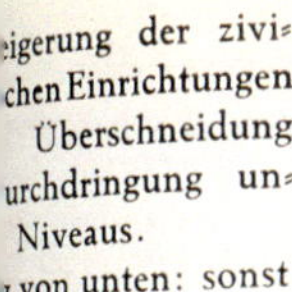

-igerung der zivi-
-chen Einrichtungen
Überschneidung
-urchdringung un-
Niveaus.
- von unten: sonst
-btes.

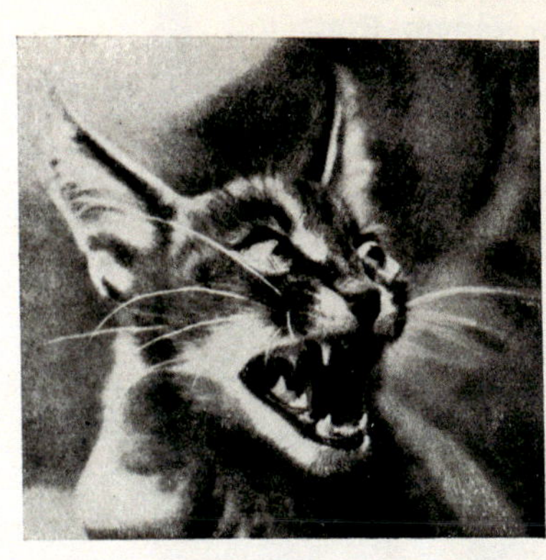

-ufzug in
-n Warenhaus
Negergroom.
-f.
-ektive ver-

-unkel.
-ick. Tumult.
-n Eingang an-
-ndenen
-e.
-n dem Glas-
-g eine Glas-
-honzelle mit
-honierendem.
-CHblick. Auf-
-e des Erdge-
-ssesdurch die
-latten.

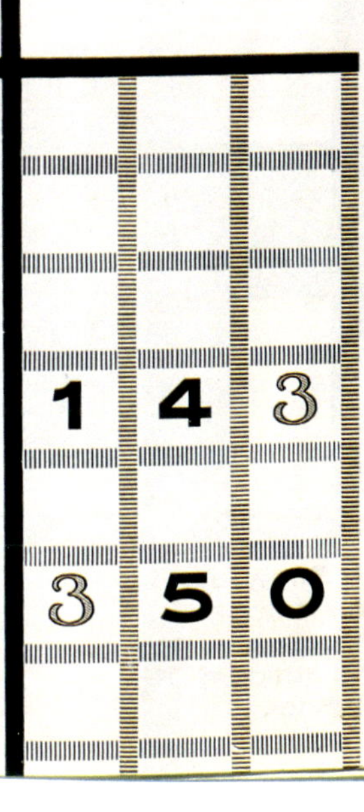

-tion für mühsames
-onieren. Traumhaft
-Glas-Glas); gleich-
-wird man durch die
-e Drehung auf die
-ng des erscheinen-
-gzeugs vorbereitet.

TEMPO-O
TEMPO-O
TEM
TEM
TEM
PO-O-PO-o-O TEM PO

EIN LUCHS WÜTEND.

Die Räder. Sie drehen sich bis zum verwaschenen Vibrieren.

auf ab auf

↑ ↓ ↑

Das GESICHT des Telephonierenden (Großaufnahme) — eingerieben mit phosphoreszierendem Material, damit keine Silhouette entsteht — dreht sich GANZ DICHT an dem Aufnahmeapparat vorüber; rechts, überseinem Kopf (durchscheinend) zieht ein von weitem kommender Flieger in einer Spirale.

119

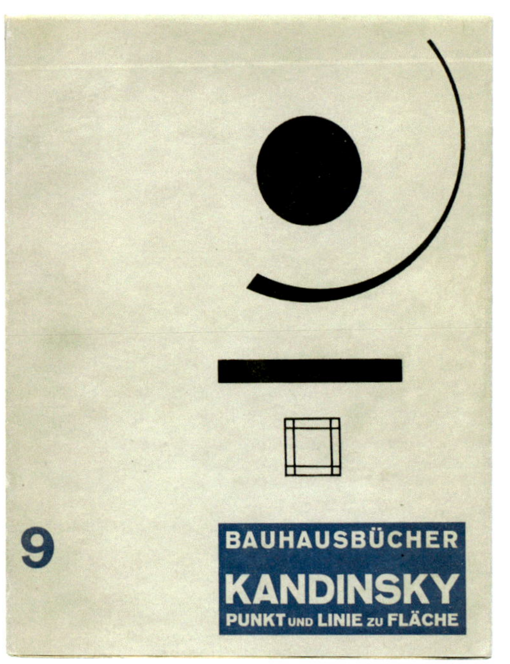

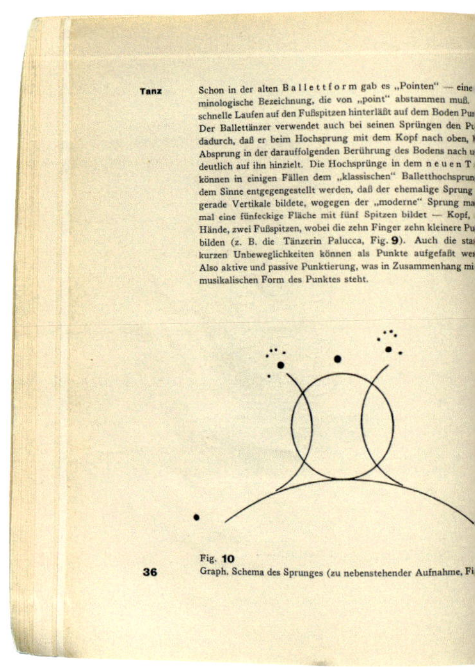

Tanz

Schon in der alten Ballettform gab es „Pointen" — eine
minologische Bezeichnung, die von „point" abstammen muß.
schnelle Laufen auf den Fußspitzen hinterläßt auf dem Boden Pu
Der Ballettänzer verwendet auch bei seinen Sprüngen den Pu
dadurch, daß er beim Hochsprung mit dem Kopf nach oben,
Absprung in der darauffolgenden Berührung des Bodens nach u
deutlich auf ihn hinzielt. Die Hochsprünge in dem neuen T
können in einigen Fällen dem „klassischen" Balletthochsprun
dem Sinne entgegengestellt werden, daß der ehemalige Sprung
gerade Vertikale bildete, wogegen der „moderne" Sprung ma
mal eine fünfeckige Fläche mit fünf Spitzen bildet — Kopf,
Hände, zwei Fußspitzen, wobei die zehn Finger zehn kleinere Pu
bilden (z. B. die Tänzerin Palucca, Fig. **9**). Auch die sta
kurzen Unbeweglichkeiten können als Punkte aufgefaßt we
Also aktive und passive Punktierung, was in Zusammenhang mi
musikalischen Form des Punktes steht.

Fig. **10**
Graph. Schema des Sprunges (zu nebenstehender Aufnahme, Fi

36

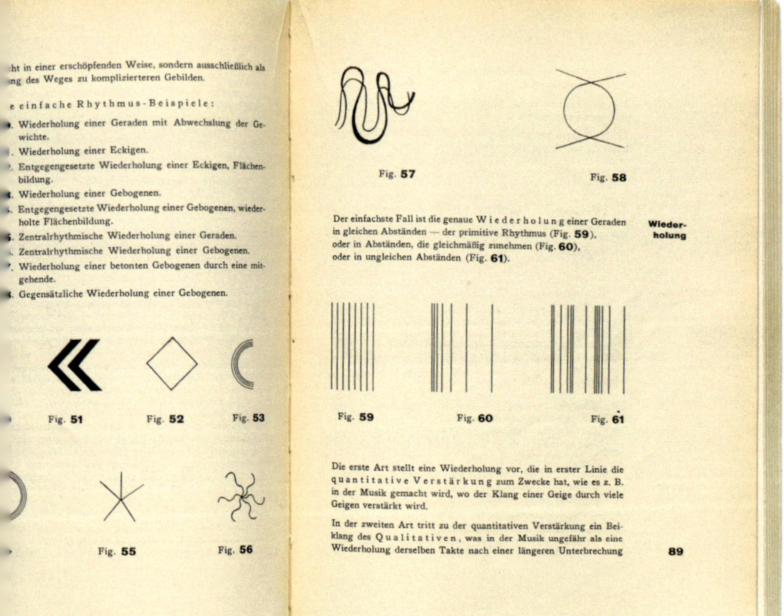

cht in einer erschöpfenden Weise, sondern ausschließlich als
ng des Weges zu komplizierteren Gebilden.

e einfache Rhythmus-Beispiele:

. Wiederholung einer Geraden mit Abwechslung der Gewichte.
. Wiederholung einer Eckigen.
. Entgegengesetzte Wiederholung einer Eckigen, Flächenbildung.
. Wiederholung einer Gebogenen.
. Entgegengesetzte Wiederholung einer Gebogenen, wiederholte Flächenbildung.
. Zentralrhythmische Wiederholung einer Geraden.
. Zentralrhythmische Wiederholung einer Gebogenen.
. Wiederholung einer betonten Gebogenen durch eine mitgehende.
. Gegensätzliche Wiederholung einer Gebogenen.

Fig. **51** Fig. **52** Fig. **53**

Fig. **55** Fig. **56**

Fig. **57** Fig. **58**

Wiederholung

Der einfachste Fall ist die genaue Wiederholung einer Geraden in gleichen Abständen — der primitive Rhythmus (Fig. **59**),
oder in Abständen, die gleichmäßig zunehmen (Fig. **60**),
oder in ungleichen Abständen (Fig. **61**).

Fig. **59** Fig. **60** Fig. **61**

Die erste Art stellt eine Wiederholung vor, die in erster Linie die quantitative Verstärkung zum Zwecke hat, wie es z. B. in der Musik gemacht wird, wo der Klang einer Geige durch viele Geigen verstärkt wird.

In der zweiten Art tritt zu der quantitativen Verstärkung ein Beiklang des Qualitativen, was in der Musik ungefähr als eine Wiederholung derselben Takte nach einer längeren Unterbrechung

89

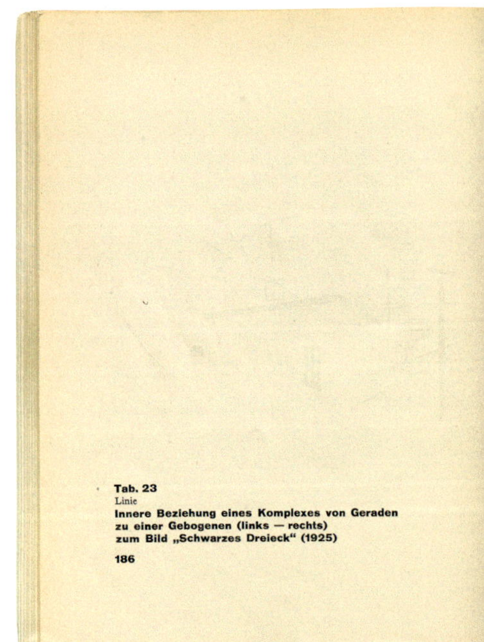

Tab. 23
Linie
Innere Beziehung eines Komplexes von Geraden zu einer Gebogenen (links — rechts) zum Bild „Schwarzes Dreieck" (1925)

186

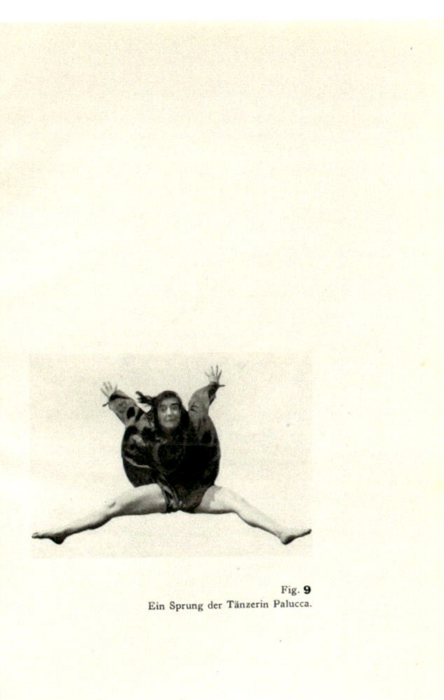

Fig. 9
Ein Sprung der Tänzerin Palucca.

1926

HERBERT BAYER (designer)
WASSILY KANDINSKY (author)

Point and Line to Plane (*Punkt und Linie zu Fläche*), Bauhaus Book 9, letterpress, 9 × 7 inches (230 × 180 mm), Munich.

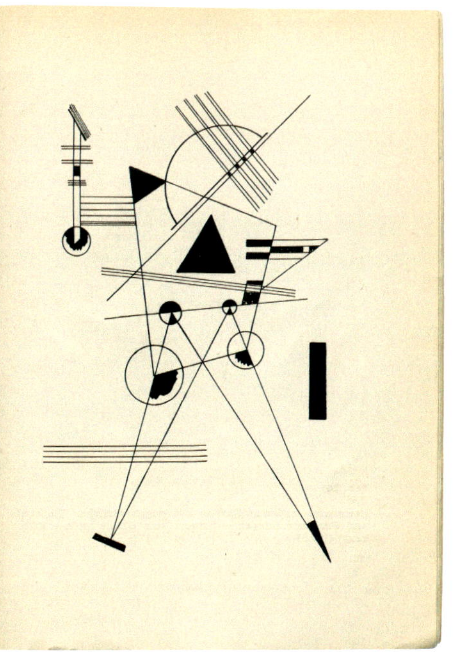

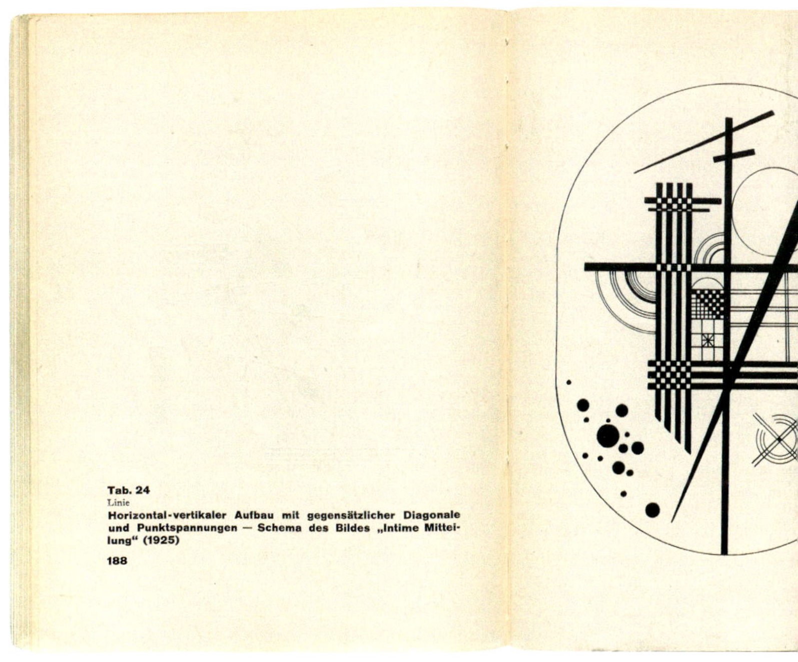

Tab. 24
Linie
Horizontal-vertikaler Aufbau mit gegensätzlicher Diagonale und Punktspannungen — Schema des Bildes „Intime Mitteilung" (1925)
188

1925

LÁSZLÓ MOHOLY-NAGY (designer)
J. J. P. OUD (author)

Dutch Architecture (*Holländische Architektur*), Bauhaus Book 10, letterpress, 9⅞ × 7⅜ inches (250 × 187 mm), Munich.

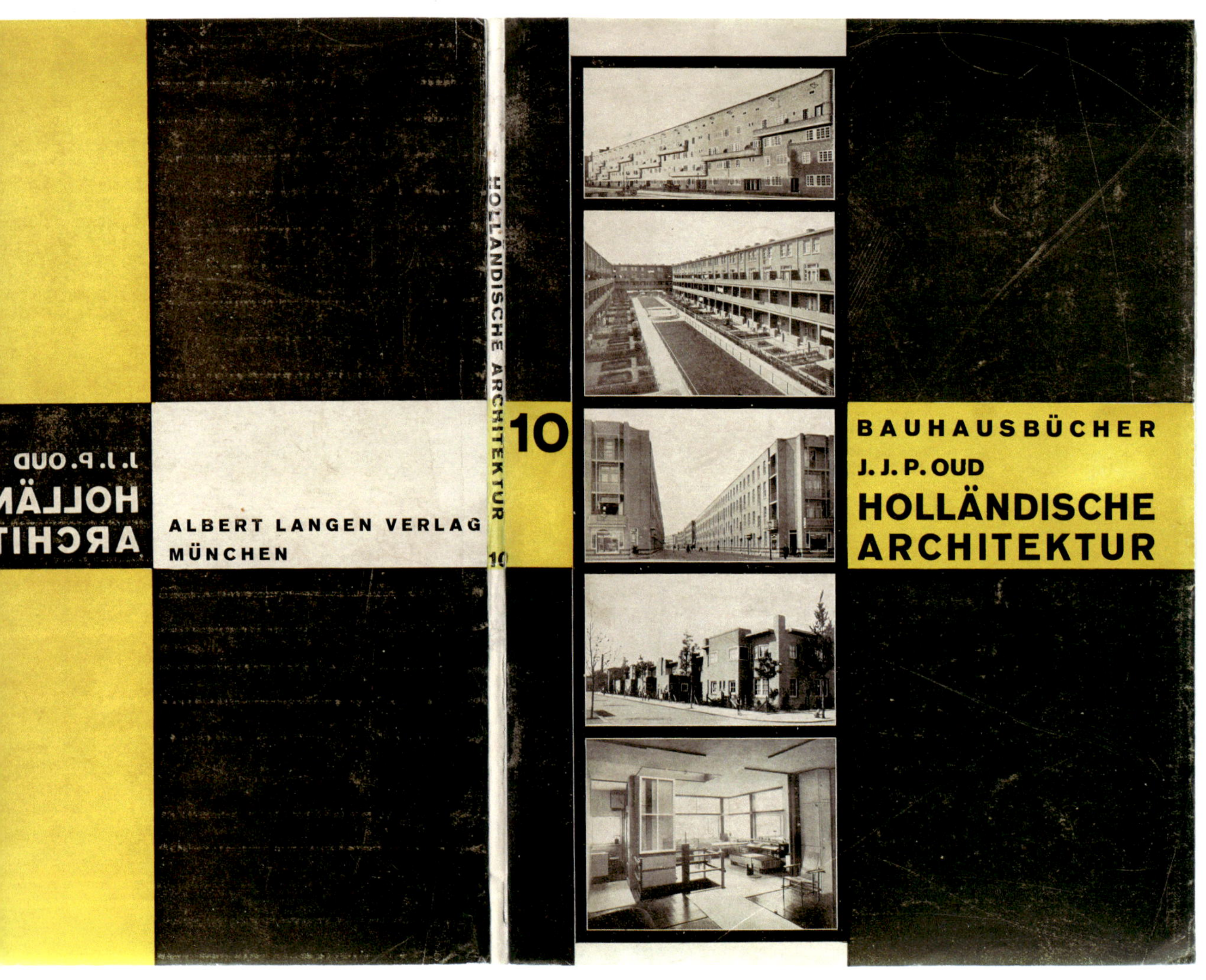

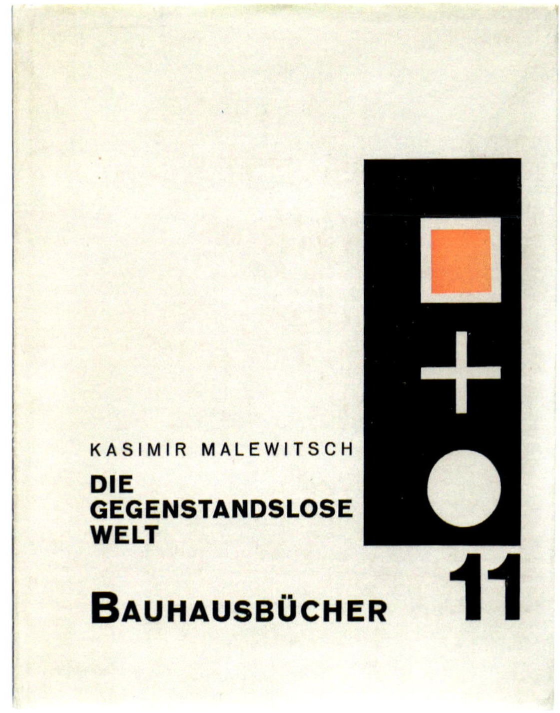

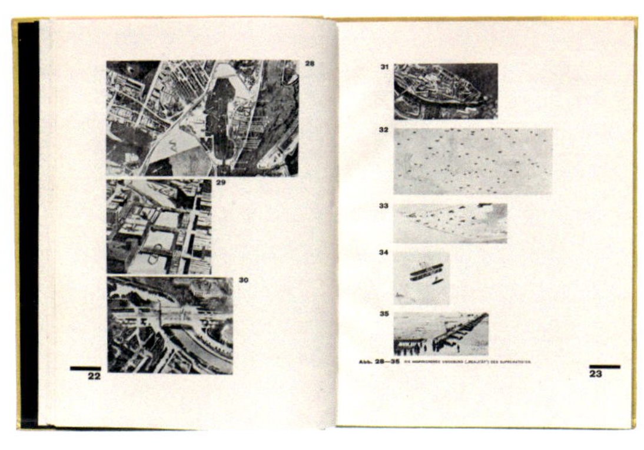

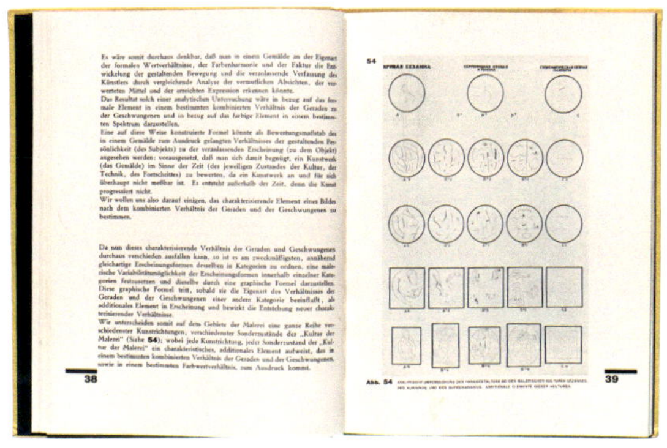

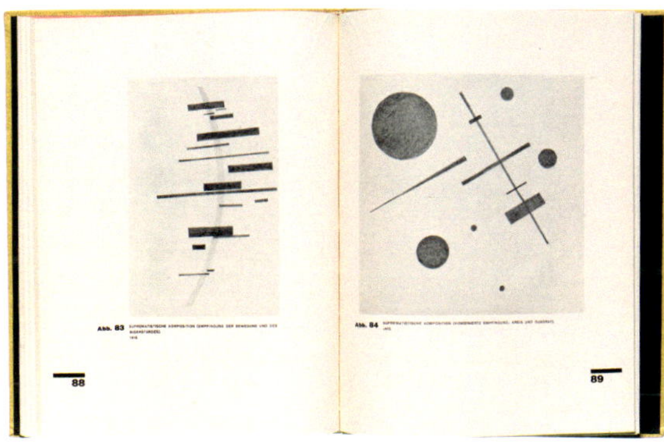

1927

LÁSZLÓ MOHOLY-NAGY (designer)
KAZIMIR MALEVICH (author)

The Non-Objective World (*Die gegenstandslose Welt*), Bauhaus Book 11, letterpress, 9⅜ × 7⅜ inches (237 × 185 mm), Munich.

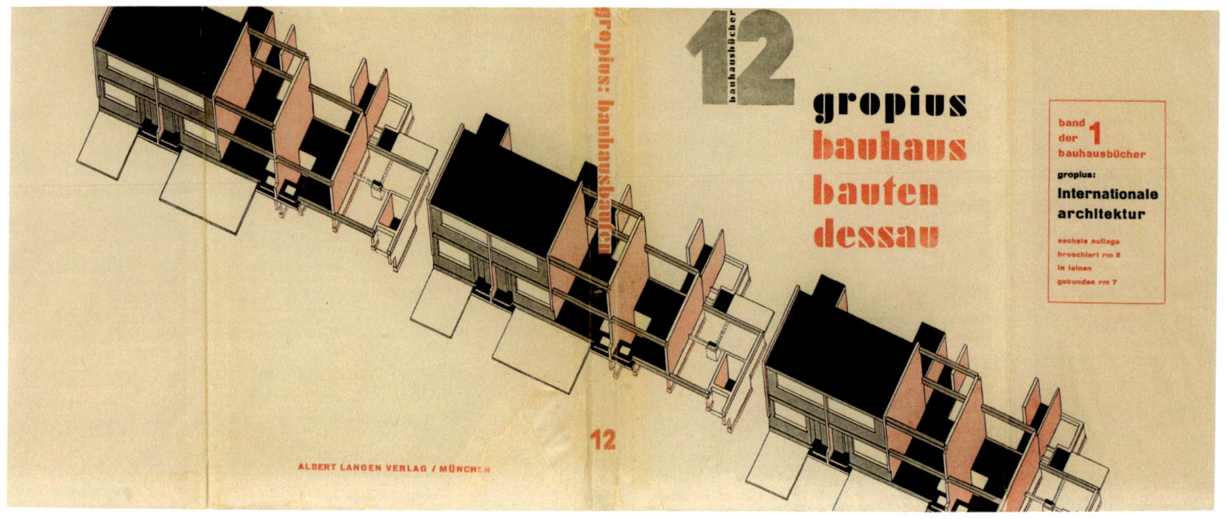

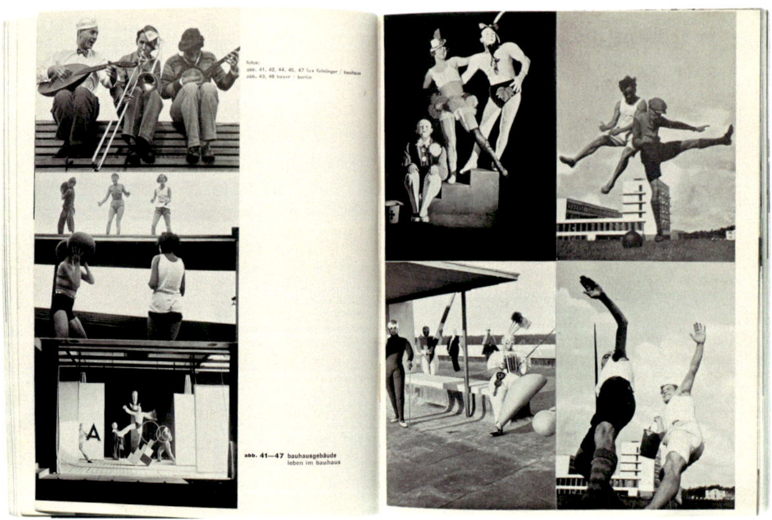

1930

LÁSZLÓ MOHOLY-NAGY (designer)
WALTER GROPIUS (author)

Bauhaus Buildings Dessau (*Bauhausbauten Dessau*), Bauhaus Book 12, letterpress, 9 × 7 inches (229 × 180 mm), Munich.

133

1928

LÁSZLÓ MOHOLY-NAGY (designer)
ALBERT GLEIZES (author)

Cubism (*Kubismus*), Bauhaus Book 13, letterpress, 9 × 7⅛ inches (231 × 182 mm), Munich.

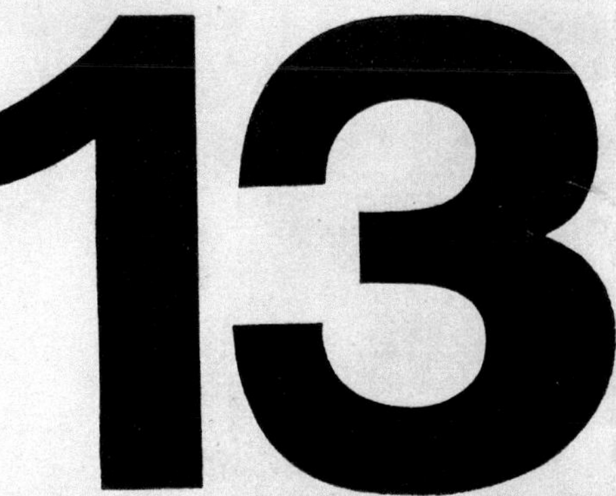

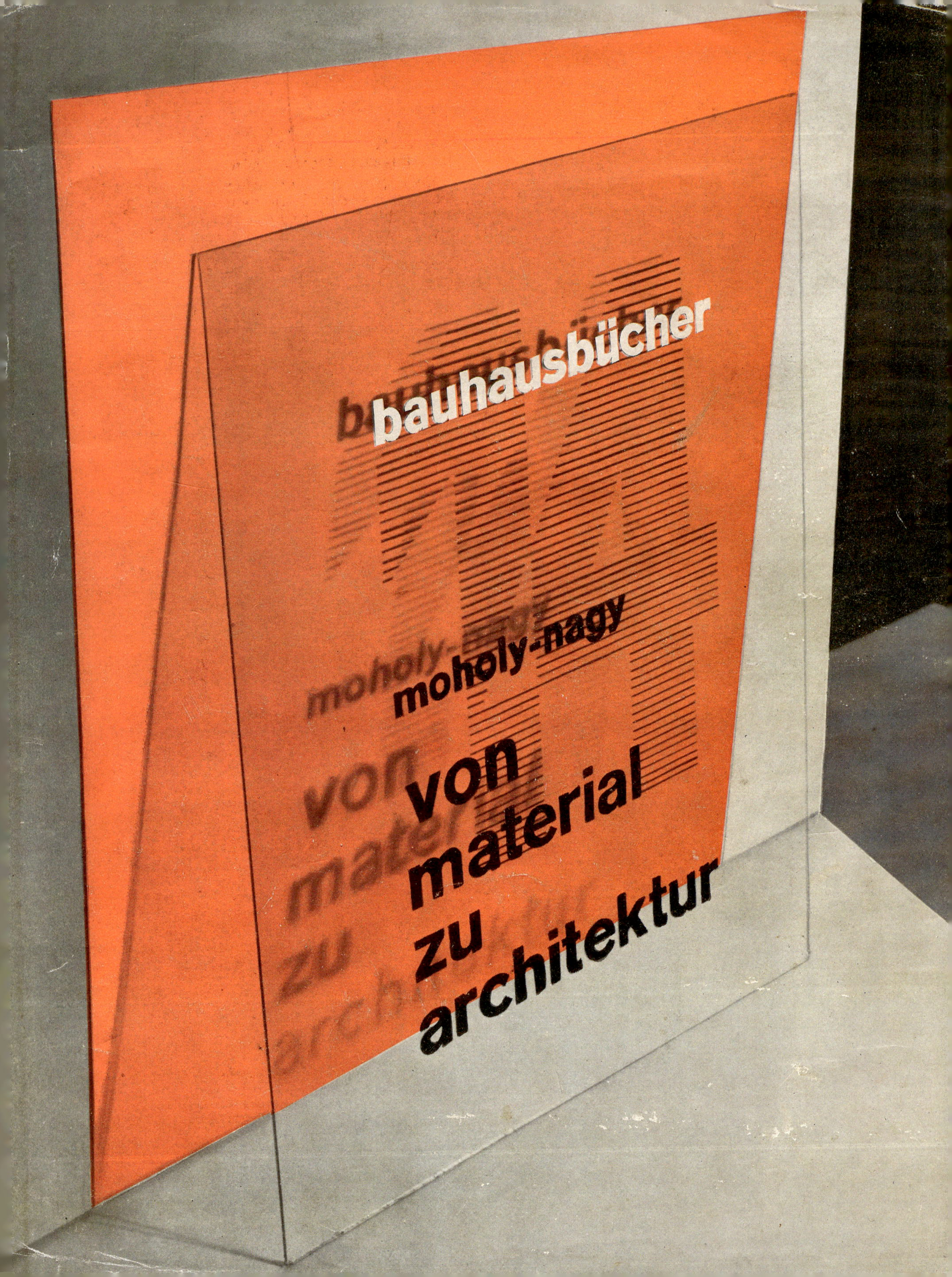

bauhausbücher

14

moholy-nagy

von
material
zu
architektur

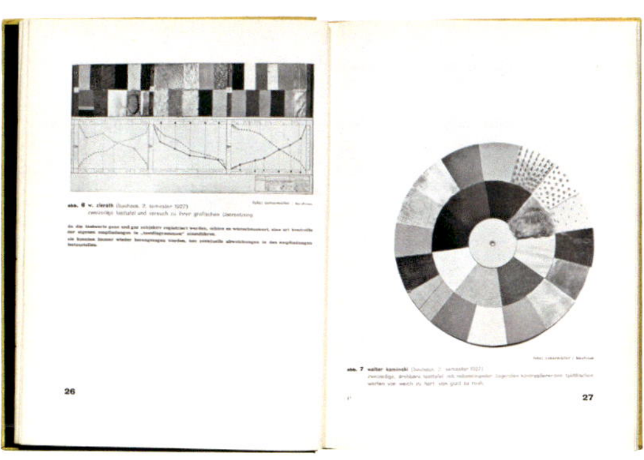

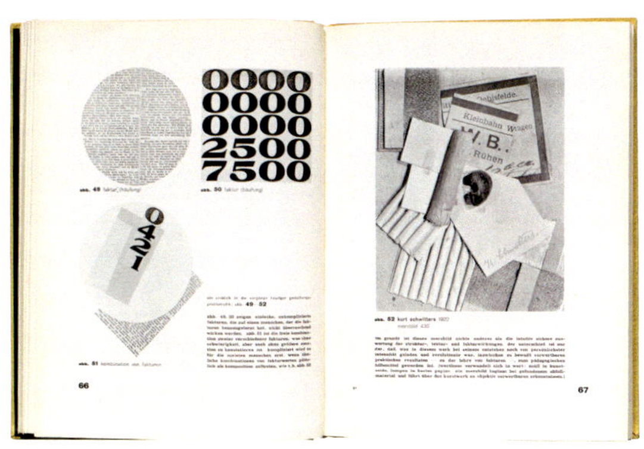

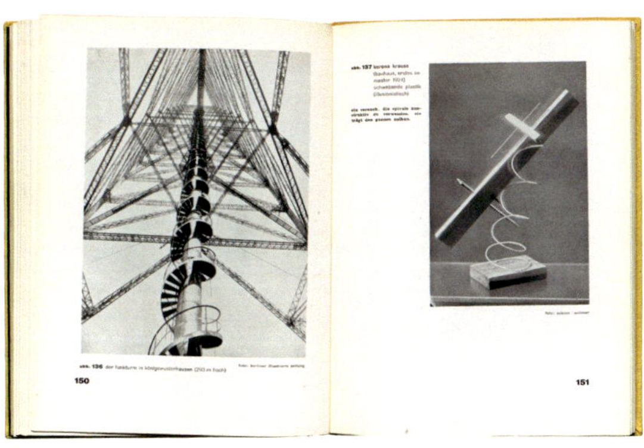

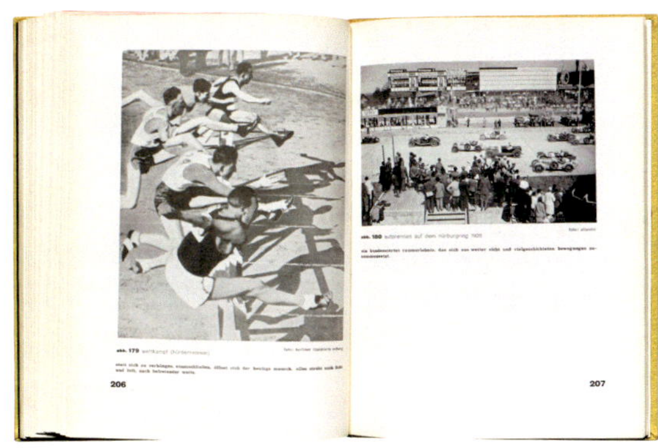

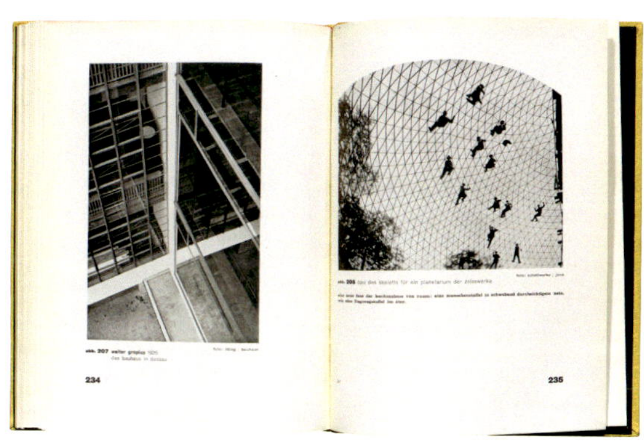

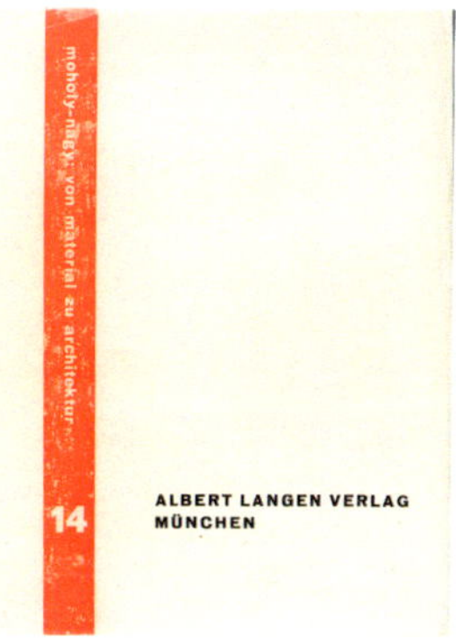

1929

LÁSZLÓ MOHOLY-NAGY (designer/author)

From Material to Architecture (*Von Material zu Architektur*), Bauhaus Book 14, letterpress, 9⅜ × 7⅛ inches (237 × 182 mm), Munich.

bauhaus 1

1926

die zeitschrift erscheint vierteljährlich ● bezugspreis: jährlich mk 2.—; einzelnummer 60 pfennig ●
mitglieder des „kreis der freunde des bauhauses" erhalten die zeitschrift kostenlos ●
schriftleitung: walter gropius und l. moholy-nagy ●
geschäftsstelle: bauhaus dessau ●

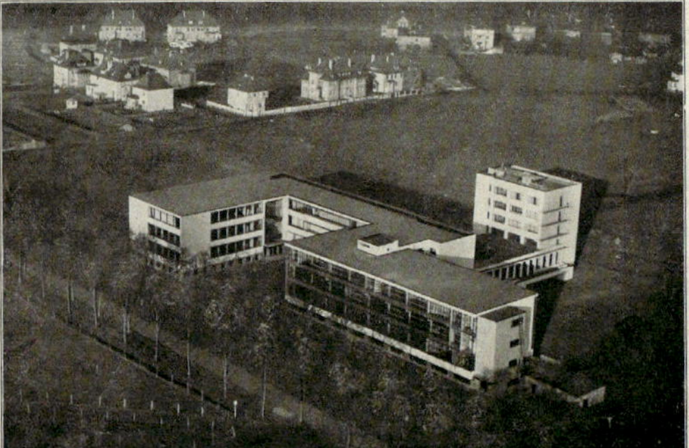

bauhausneubau dessau — junkers luftbild

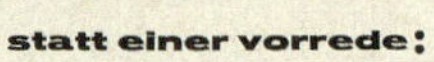

statt einer vorrede:

walter gropius: bauhaus-chronik 1925/1926

weihnachten 1924 auflösungserklärung des staatlichen bauhauses weimar durch die meister des bauhauses.

april 1925 die stadt dessau, ein zentrum des mitteldeutschen braunkohlenreviers mit aufsteigender wirtschaftlicher entwicklung, faßt den beschluß, geleitet von dem kulturellen weitblick seiner stadtverwaltung, das bauhaus zu übernehmen.

alle bisherigen meister — feininger, gropius, kandinsky, klee, moholy, muche, schlemmer — verbleiben am bauhaus, mit ausnahme von marcks, der — da die keramische abteilung, die er leitet, aus räumlichen und finanziellen gründen nicht mit übernommen werden kann — eine berufung nach halle annimmt.

5 ehemalige bauhaus-studierende — albers, bayer, breuer, scheper, schmidt — werden als meister an das bauhaus berufen. mit ihrem eintritt erfährt das bauhaus-programm eine wesentliche änderung.

bauhausneubau dessau

architekt w. gropius

der bau wurde ende september vor. js. begonnen, der rohbau wurde am 21. 3. 26 fertiggestellt. das atelierhaus wurde am 1. september, die übrigen räume des bauhauses wurden am 15. oktober bezogen.

der gesamte bau bedeckt rund 2600 qm grundfläche und enthält 32000 cbm umbauten raums. bauherr ist der magistrat der stadt dessau. der preis pro cbm umbauten raums bleibt unter m. 26,-

der gesamte baukomplex besteht aus 3 teilen:

1 das **fachschulgebäude,** enthaltend die berufsschule (lehr- und verwaltungsräume, lehrerzimmer, bibliothek, fysiksaal, modellräume), [illegible]

ganz ausgebautes souterrain, hochparterre und zwei obergeschosse. im ersten und zweiten obergeschoß führt eine auf 4 pfeilern über eine fahrstraße gespannte brücke, in der unten die bauhausverwaltung, oben die architekturabteilung untergebracht ist, zu dem bau

2 **laboratoriums-werkstätten** und lehrräume des bauhauses. im souterrain die bühnenwerkstatt, druckerei, färberei, bildhauerei, pack- und lagerräume, hausmannswohnung und heizkeller mit vorgelagertem kohlenbunker.

im hochparterre die tischlerei und die ausstellungsräume, großes vestibül, daran anschließend die aula mit der vorgelagerten, überhöhten bühne.

im 1. obergeschoß die weberei, die räume für die grundlehre, ein großer vortragsraum und die verbindung von bau 1 zu bau 2 durch die brücke.

im 2. obergeschoß die wandmalereiwerkstatt, metallwerkstatt, sowie zwei vortragssäle, die durch klappwand zu einem großen ausstellungssaal verändert werden können. daran anschließend die zweite brückenetage mit den räumen für die architekturabteilung und baubüro gropius.

die aula im erdgeschoß dieses baues führt in einem eingeschossigen trakt zu bau

3 **atelierhaus,** das die wohlfahrtseinrichtungen des instituts enthält. die bühne zwischen aula und speisesaal kann bei vorführungen nach beiden seiten geöffnet werden, so daß die zuschauer auf beiden

bauhausneubau - westseite — foto lucia moholy

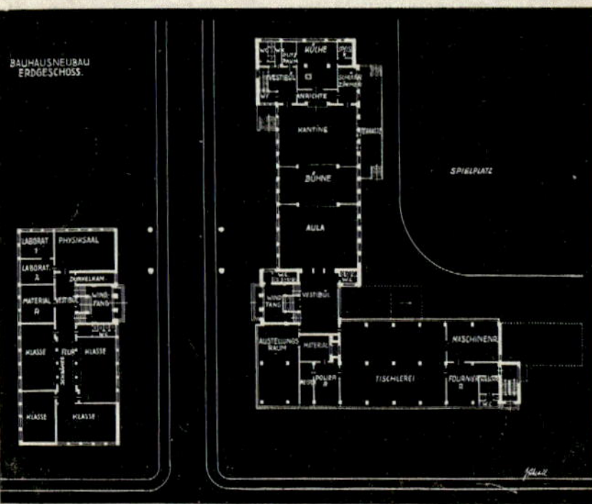

bauhausneubau dessau - grundriß des erdgeschosses

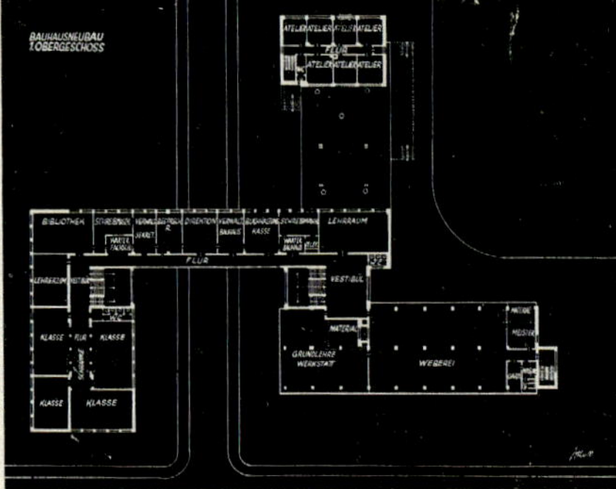

und des 1. obergeschosses

1926

LÁSZLÓ MOHOLY-NAGY (designer/editor)

bauhaus: magazine for design (*bauhaus: zeitschrift für gestaltung*), vol. 1, no. 1, letterpress, 16½ × 11⅝ inches (418 × 295 mm), Dessau.

The Bauhaus's eponymous magazine was the school's primary organ for broadcasting its activities to the international design and arts communities. In its four full years of publication, with a yearlong break in 1930, the quarterly showcased various Bauhaus projects and functions, contemporary design criticism, and features on student life. Its first volume took the form of a simple double-sided trifold, but the next year, with the addition of advertising, it expanded to forty pages in a standard magazine size. While at first edited by various masters, second Bauhaus director Hannes Meyer appointed Hungarian art critic Ernst Kállai to direct its publication in 1928, when Moholy-Nagy and Bayer left. The eleven issues of the first three volumes appear in the following pages. ●

***bauhaus* established one of the school's most enduring typographic hallmarks: the eschewal of uppercase letters. Photography was also crucial to initial designer Moholy-Nagy's typographic style and the presentation of the magazine. And while many documented life at the school (including Erich Consemüller, T. Lux Feininger, Irene Bayer, and Lotte Stam-Beese), a large number of the images featured in the magazine—of the Bauhaus building, events, and people—were taken by Czech-born photographer Lucia Moholy, Moholy-Nagy's wife at the time. While most images in the magazine are fastidiously credited, either to Moholy or to other photographers, she would later struggle to receive credit for—or even possession—of her work, indicating that women's artistic contributions at the school were sometimes erased, despite its egalitarian claims. ●**

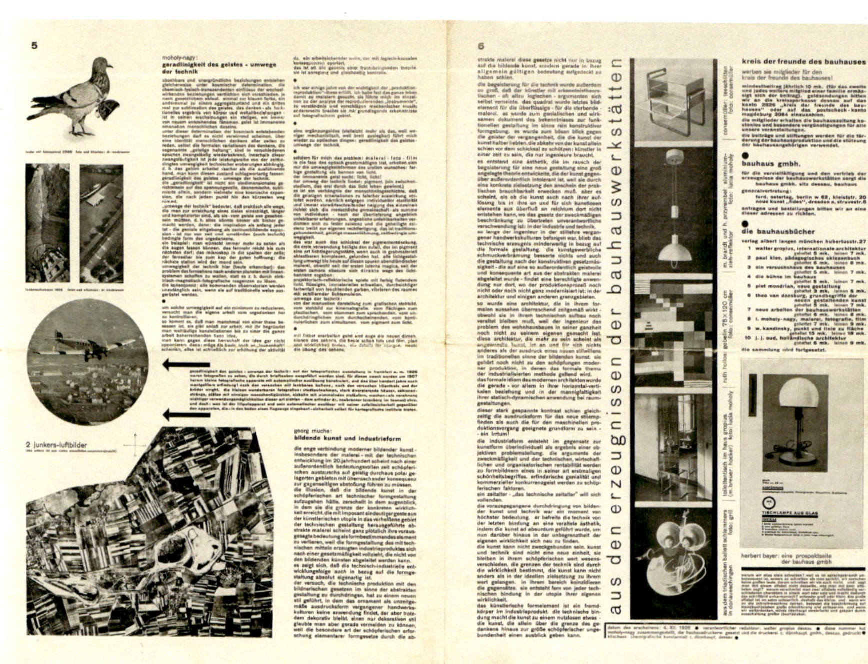
5

moholy-nagy:

geradlinigkeit des geistes - umwege der technik

2 junkers-luftbilder

georg muche:

bildende kunst und industrieform

6

aus den erzeugnissen der bauhauswerkstätten

kreis der freunde des bauhauses

werben sie mitglieder für den kreis der freunde des bauhauses!

mindestbeitrag jährlich 10 mk. (für das zweite und jedes weitere mitglied einer familie ermässigt sich der beitrag). geldsendungen bitten wir an die kreissparkasse dessau auf das konto 2826 „kreis der freunde des bauhauses" oder auf das postscheck-konto magdeburg 2084 einzuzahlen.

die mitglieder erhalten die bauhauszeitung kostenlos und besondere vergünstigungen für alle unsere veranstaltungen.

die beiträge und stiftungen werden für die förderung der bauhausproduktion und die stützung der bauhausangehörigen verwendet.

bauhaus gmbh.

für die vervielfältigung und den vertrieb der erzeugnisse der bauhauswerkstätten sorgt die bauhaus gmbh. sitz dessau, bauhaus

generalvertretung:

ferd. ostertag, berlin w 62, kleiststr. 20

neue kunst „fides", dresden a, struvestr. 6

anfragen und bestellungen bitten wir an eine dieser adressen zu richten.

die bauhausbücher

verlag albert langen münchen hubertusstr. 27

1 walter gropius, internationale architektur geheftet 5 mk. leinen 7 mk.
2 paul klee, pädagogisches skizzenbuch geheftet 6 mk. leinen 8 mk.
3 ein versuchshaus des bauhauses geheftet 5 mk. leinen 7 mk.
4 die bühne im bauhaus geheftet 5 mk. leinen 7 mk.
5 piet mondrian, neue gestaltung geheftet 3 mk. leinen 5 mk.
6 theo van doesburg, grundbegriffe der neuen gestaltenden kunst geheftet 5 mk. leinen 7 mk.
7 neue arbeiten der bauhauswerkstätten geheftet 6 mk. leinen 8 mk.
8 l. moholy-nagy, malerei, fotografie, film geheftet 7 mk. leinen 9 mk.
9 w. kandinsky, punkt und linie zu fläche geheftet 15 mk. leinen 18 mk.
10 j. j. oud, holländische architektur geheftet 6 mk. leinen 9 mk.

die sammlung wird fortgesetzt.

herbert bayer: eine prospektseite der bauhaus gmbh

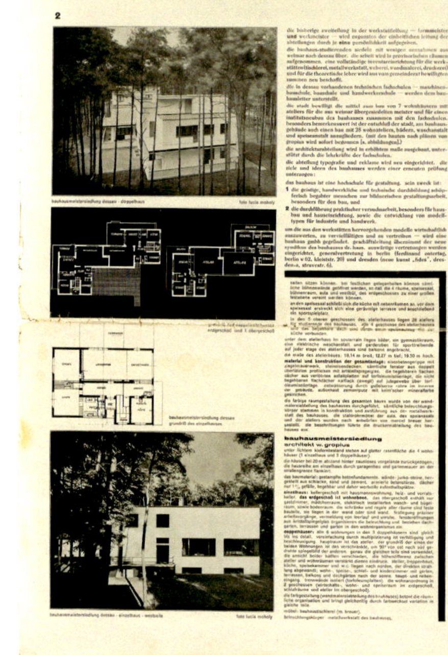
2

bauhausmeistersiedlung

architekt w. gropius

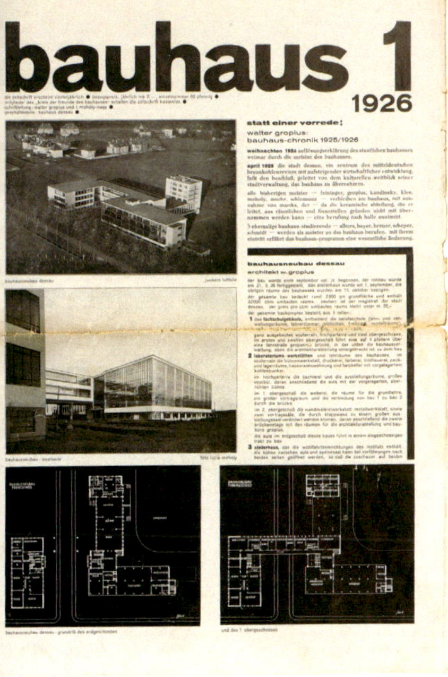

bauhaus 1

1926

statt einer vorrede:

walter gropius:
bauhaus-chronik 1925/1926

bauhausneubau dessau

architekt w. gropius

Published in December 1926, the first issue of *bauhaus* magazine celebrates Gropius's new Bauhaus building in Dessau, designed with the flat rectangular surfaces, hard right angles, asymmetrical layouts, glass facades, and lack of ornamentation characteristic of Bauhaus architecture. Similarly, Moholy-Nagy's typography for the issue relies on ninety-degree angles, asymmetry, and simplicity for its organization and effect. Like Gropius's large glass windows, occasional areas of unprinted space let light into the page. The use of oldstyle serif typefaces, like Alt-Medieval, and sans serifs, like Breite Grotesk, also brighten the layout, in contrast to the dense blocks of blackletter Fraktur common in Germany (and preferred by the rising Nazi party) at the time. Near the bottom of page 6, under a reproduction of a catalog page for a table lamp, is Moholy-Nagy's justification for *bauhaus* magazine's most distinctive act of typographic simplification: the use of only lowercase letters: "Why use two alphabets to say what you can with just one? Why do we meld two alphabets of completely different characters into one word or sentence and make the text unharmonious?" The suggestion is even more unorthodox in the context of traditional German orthography, in which all nouns are capitalized. ●

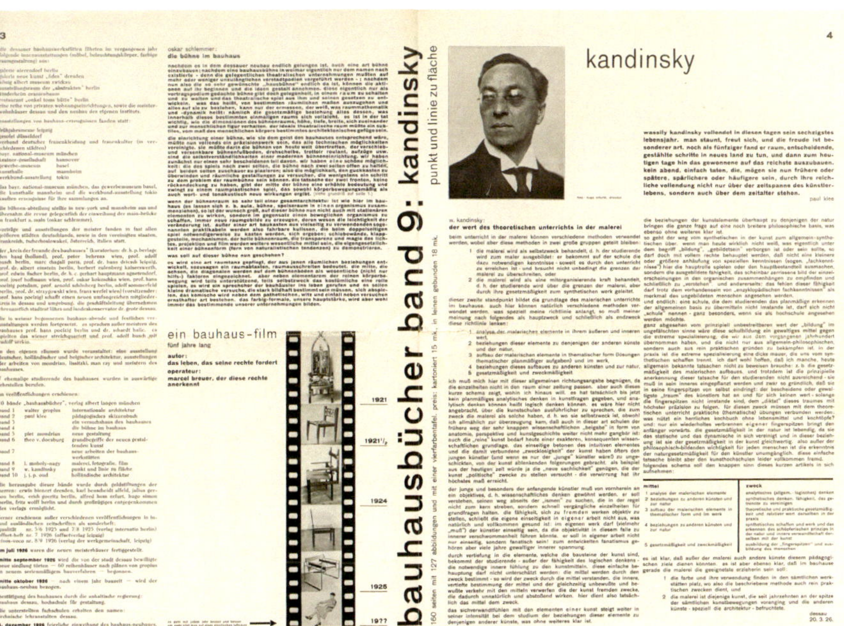

3

oskar schlemmer:
die bühne im bauhaus

ein bauhaus-film
fünf jahre lang

autor:
das leben, das seine rechte fordert

operateur:
marcel breuer, der diese rechte anerkennt

1921

1921½

1924

1925

1927

bauhausbücher band 9: kandinsky

punkt und linie zu fläche

4

kandinsky

1927

LÁSZLÓ MOHOLY-NAGY (designer)
OSKAR SCHLEMMER (editor)

bauhaus: magazine for design (*bauhaus: zeitschrift für gestaltung*), vol. 1, no. 3, letterpress, 16½ × 11⅝ inches (418 × 295 mm), Dessau.

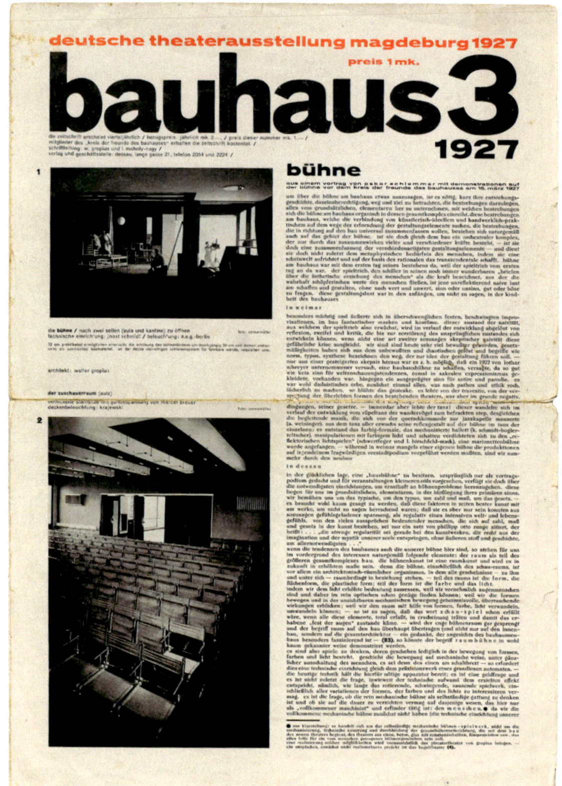
deutsche theaterausstellung magdeburg 1927
preis 1 mk.
bauhaus 3
1927
bühne

bauhaus 2
1927
aus der siedlung dessau-törten
walter gropius
systematische vorarbeit
für rationellen wohnungsbau

1927

LÁSZLÓ MOHOLY-NAGY (designer/editor)

bauhaus: magazine for design (*bauhaus: zeitschrift für gestaltung*), vol. 1, no. 2, letterpress, 16½ × 11⅝ inches (418 × 295 mm), Dessau.

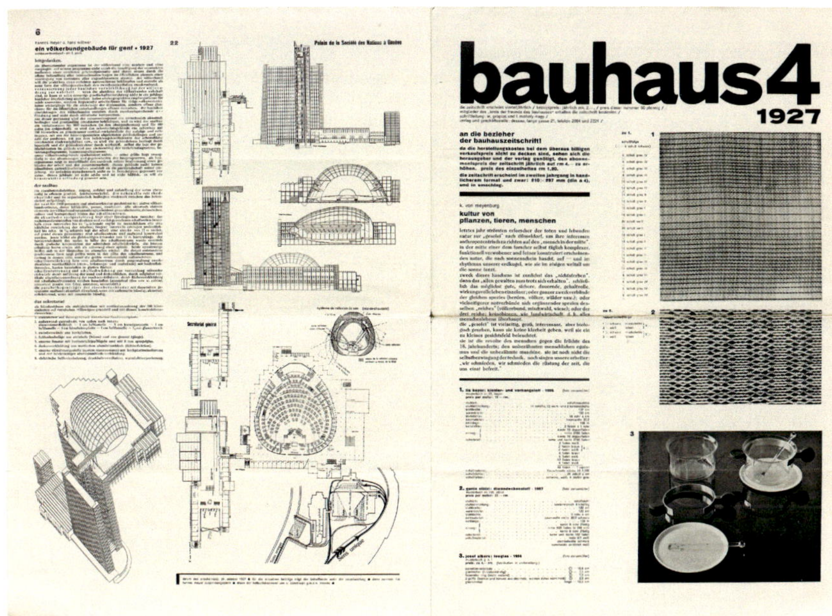

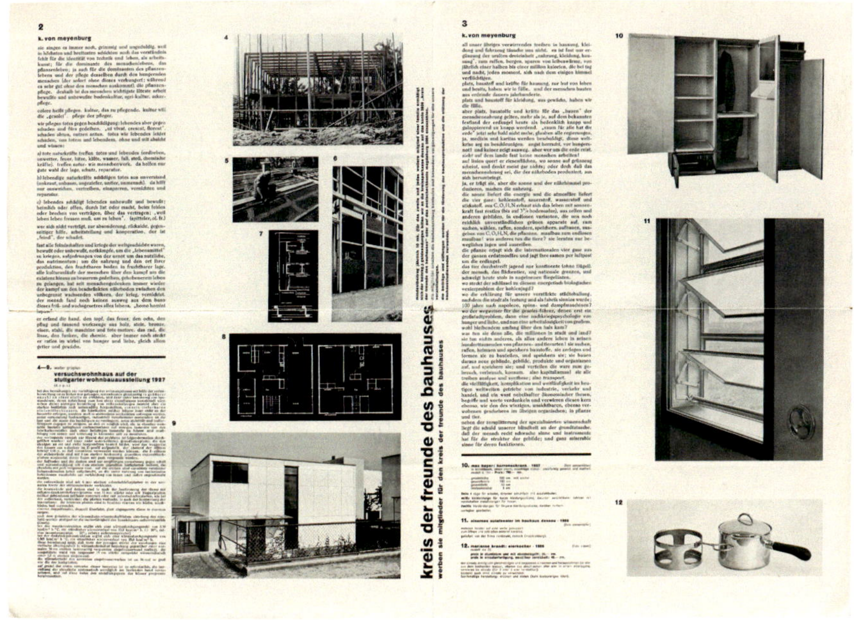

1927

HANNES MEYER (designer/editor)

bauhaus: magazine for design (*bauhaus: zeitschrift für gestaltung*), vol. 1, no. 4, letterpress, 16½ × 11⅝ inches (418 × 295 mm), Dessau.

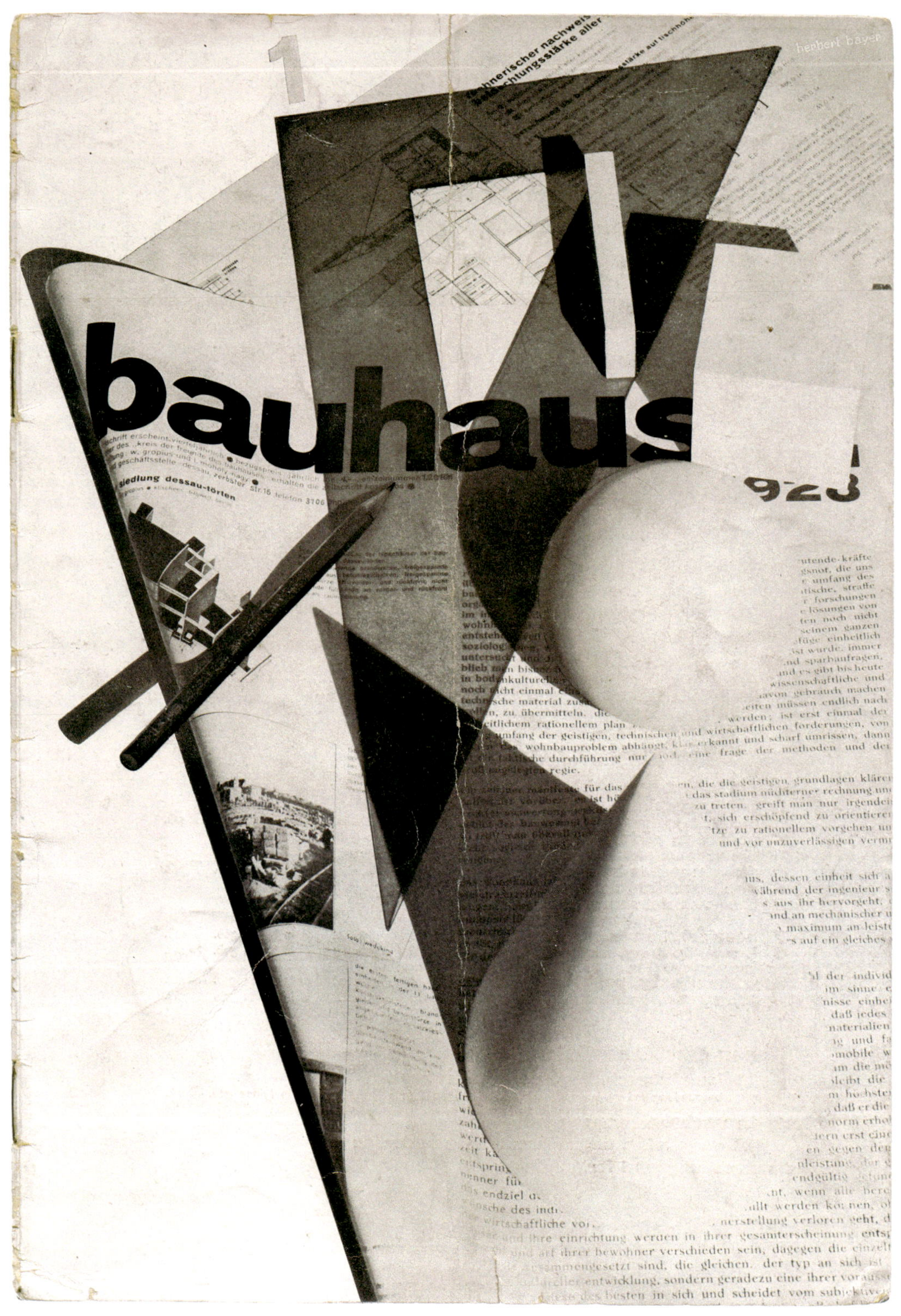
1
herbert bayer
bauhaus
1928
siedlung dessau-törten

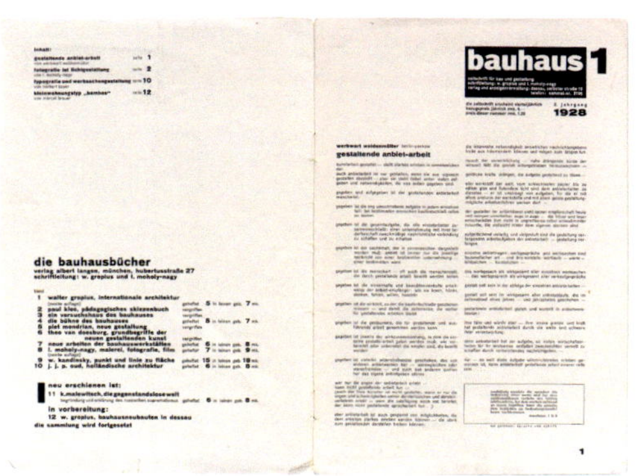
bauhaus 1

1928

die bauhausbücher

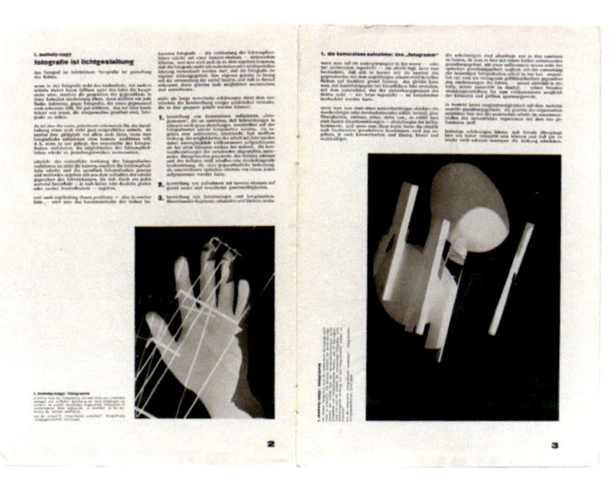

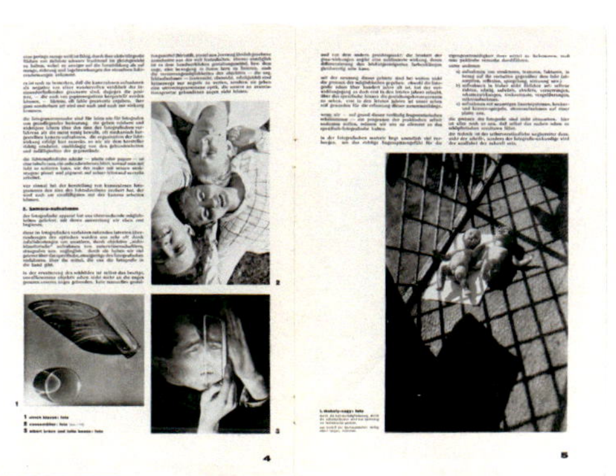

1928

HERBERT BAYER (designer/editor)

bauhaus: magazine for design (*bauhaus: zeitschrift für gestaltung*), vol. 2, no. 1, letterpress, 11¾ × 8¼ inches (296 × 210 mm), Dessau.

Published in 1928, the first issue of the second year of *bauhaus* is the only one designed by Herbert Bayer, who became head of the print and advertising workshop in 1925. In its second year, *bauhaus* changed formats, abandoning the large trifold newspaper for a stapled magazine in a standard paper size. Bayer's famous cover design for this issue creatively establishes continuity with the magazine's old format by using a photograph of a previous issue in place of the logotype, overlaid by draftsman's tools and geometric blocks. While Bayer continued using the Breite Grotesks that had become a signature type family for the Bauhaus, he introduced advertisements to the magazine and simplified the interior typography, mostly forgoing Moholy-Nagy's bold lines, dots, and arrows. His article "Typography and Advertisement Design" in the issue explains why: "An example for the spread of Bauhaus style is shown by the commission statistics of a Frankfurt printing shop: nearly 50% of all printing jobs commissioned in one year were requested to be in Bauhaus style. We are increasingly seeing more coarse dots, thick bars, or even ornaments and imitations of nature through typography. This brought us back to square one." As the school's reputation grew, Bauhaus designers became increasingly self-conscious about their aesthetics being reduced to mere formalism, easily imitated, and emptied of its initial political radicalism. ●

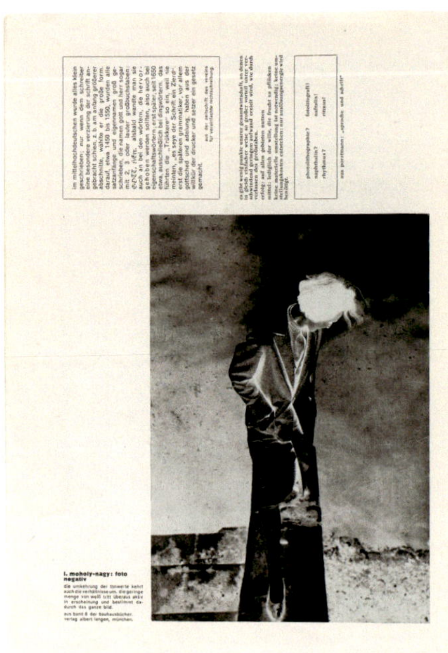

l. moholy-nagy: foto negativ

6

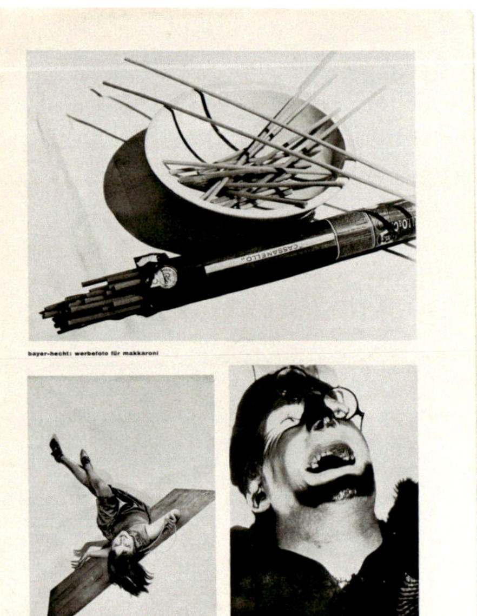

bayer-hecht: werbefoto für makkaroni

consemüller: foto

bayer-hecht: foto

7

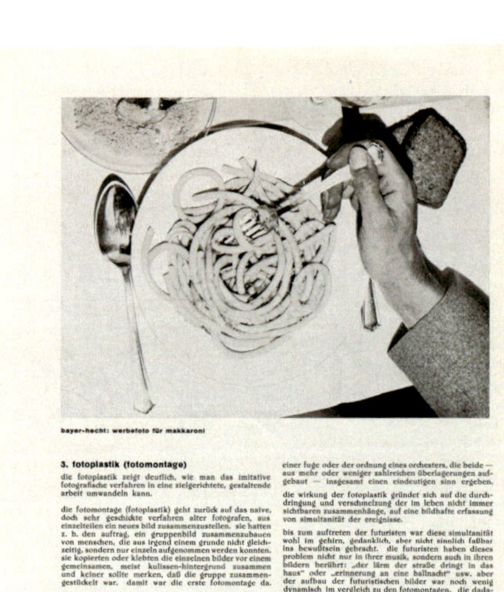

bayer-hecht: werbefoto für makkaroni

3. fotoplastik (fotomontage)

die fotoplastik zeigt deutlich, wie man das imitative fotografische verfahren in eine zielgerichtete, gestaltende arbeit umwandeln kann.

die fotomontage (fotoplastik) geht zurück auf das naive, doch sehr geschickte verfahren alter fotografen, aus einzelteilen ein neues bild zusammenzustellen. sie hatten z. b. den auftrag, ein gruppenbild zusammenzubauen von menschen, die aus irgend einem grunde nicht gleichzeitig, sondern nur einzeln aufgenommen werden konnten. sie kopierten oder klebten die einzelnen bilder vor einem gemeinsamen, meist kulissen-hintergrund zusammen und keiner sollte merken, daß die gruppe zusammengestückelt war. damit war die erste fotomontage da.

die dadaisten haben den sinn der fotomontage erweitert; sie klebten, — teils um zu verblüffen, teils um zu demonstrieren, teils um optische gedichte zu schaffen — verschiedene fototeile zusammen. aus den zusammengefügten bildteilen ergab sich oft irgendein schwer enträtselbarer sinn, der trotzdem aufrührerisch wirken konnte. diesen bildern lag eine wirklichkeitsvortäuschung fern, sie zeigten brutal den entstehungsprozeß, die zerlegung von einzelfotos, den rohen schnitt der schere. diese „fotomontagen" waren die wahren schwestern der futuristischen, bruitistischen musik, die — aus geräuschfetzen zusammengesetzt — aus vielen einzelelementen zusammengeballtes, wie z. b. das aufregende erlebnis eines stadterwachens und ähnliches vermitteln wollten.

demgegenüber ist die fotoplastik eine art organisierter spuk. sie hat ein deutliches sinn- und bildzentrum, das — obwohl oft aus verschiedenen optischen und gedanklichen überlagerungen, verschränkungen bestehend — eine klare übersicht der gesamtsituation ermöglicht. sie entspricht darin annähernd dem aufbau einer fuge oder der ordnung eines orchesters, die beide — aus mehr oder weniger zahlreichen überlagerungen aufgebaut — insgesamt einen eindeutigen sinn ergeben.

die wirkung der fotoplastik gründet sich auf die durchdringung und verschmelzung der im leben nicht immer sichtbaren zusammenhänge, auf eine bildhafte erfassung von simultanität der ereignisse.

bis zum auftreten der futuristen war diese simultanität wohl im gehirn, gedanklich, aber nicht sinnlich faßbar ins bewußtsein gebracht. die futuristen haben dieses problem nicht nur in ihrer musik, sondern auch in ihren bildern berührt: „der lärm der straße dringt in das haus" oder „erinnerung an eine ballnacht" usw. aber der aufbau der futuristischen bilder war noch wenig dynamisch im vergleich zu den fotomontagen. die dadaistische fotomontage dagegen war in ihrer unbändigkeit, in ihren großen sprüngen meist viel zu individuell, um rasch erfaßt werden zu können. sie wollte zuviel: sie wollte auf der fläche, in dem statischen zustand schon eine kinetik präsentieren, die dem film vorbehalten sein mußte. die aufgabe war über das maß gespannt, das sehen versagte.

der unterschied zwischen fotomontage und fotoplastik zeigt sich schon in der technik. ähnlich der fotomontage ist die fotoplastik aus verschiedenen fotografien zusammenmontiert, geklebt, retuschiert, auf eine fläche zusammengedrängt. aber sie versucht maß zu halten in der darstellung von simultanität. die fotoplastik ist klar, übersichtlich und verwendet die fotografischen elemente in einem konzentrierten, von allem störenden beiwerk entledigten zustand. sie zeigt geballte situationen, die assoziativ ungemein rasch weitergesponnen werden können.

die sparsamere art ermöglicht eine leichtere faßbarkeit, oft ein aufblitzen des sonst verborgenen sinnes.

8

durch das vertrauen in die objektivität einer fotografie, die nicht zu erlauben scheint, eine begebenheit subjektiv zu deuten, entstehen aus der zusammenfügung der fotografischen elemente mit linien und anderen ergänzungen unerwartete spannungen, die über die bedeutung der einzelnen teile weit hinausgehen. durch rein zeichnerische oder malerische darstellung derselben formen würde kaum eine ähnliche wirkung zu erreichen sein, denn gerade die ineinanderschaltung von fotografisch dargestellten geschehniselementen, die einfachen bis komplizierten überlagerungen formen sich zu einer merkwürdigen einheit — die sich auf optisch vorgeschriebenem wege — wie auf einem schienenstrang der ideen bewegt. diese einheit kann in ihren ergebnissen erheiternd, ergreifend, niederschmetternd, satirisch, visionär, revolutionär usw. wirken.

die fotoplastik ist oft ausdruck einer gedanklich kaum faßbaren weite vielfältigster verbindungen, oft bitterster spaß, oft blasfemie. oft zeigt sich darin die böse seite der kreatur; oft aber auch das bäumen gegen das unzulängliche: clownesk und witzig, tragisch und ernst.

die fotoplastik beruht auf augen- und gehirngymnastik, konzentrierter als sie dem großstädter täglich zuteil wird.

beispiel: man fährt in der straßenbahn, sieht durch ein fenster hinaus. hinten fährt ein auto. auch die fenster dieses autos sind durchsichtig. hindurch sieht man einen laden, der wiederum durchsichtige fenster hat. darin menschen, käufer und verkäufer. ein anderer mensch öffnet die tür. am laden vorbei gehen passanten. der verkehrspolizist hält einen radfahrer an. das alles erfaßt man in einem einzigen augenblick, weil die scheiben durchsichtig sind und alles in der blickrichtung geschieht.

ein ähnlicher vorgang spielt sich in der fotoplastik ab, — auf einer anderen ebene — nicht als summierung, sondern als synthese: gedankliches - assoziatives und visuelles - sinnliches bilden hier die überlagerungen und durchdringungen.

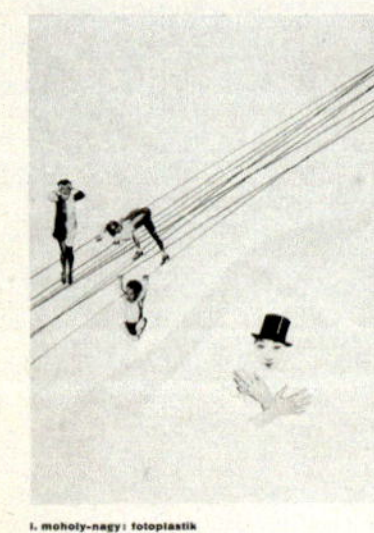

l. moholy-nagy: fotoplastik

auf diesem wege kann man mit fotografischen mitteln erlebnisse und gedankenzusammenhänge geben, die mit andern mitteln nicht in dem gleichen maße erreicht werden können. visuelles und gedankliches sind hier im augenblick zugänglich, müssen im augenblick zugänglich sein, wenn die wirkung erreicht werden soll. darum ist eine ausgewogene komposition des gedanklichen und optischen hier eine besonders wichtige komponente. der bildmäßige aufbau dieser fotoplastiken ist aber nicht komposition im früheren sinne, nicht selbstzweck der formalharmonischen lösung, sondern komposition, geformt in der richtung des gesetzten zieles: der ideendarstellung.

die geschwindigkeit der optischen aufnahme und der assoziationen kann außerordentlich groß sein, wenn ein wissen von der heutigen zeit, von verschiedenen kulturen, politischen begebenheiten, zeitproblemen usw. als voraussetzung da ist. darum kann ein fotoplastisches blatt von einem eskimo nicht erfaßt werden. ein gegenstandsloses bild dagegen kann einem jeden, ohne vorbedingungen, zugänglich werden, da es nicht auf kenntnissen, sondern auf biologischen, in jedem menschen vorhandenen gesetzmäßigkeiten des rein optischen erlebnisses aufgebaut ist.

es ist möglich, daß auch manche stadtmenschen die fotoplastiken erst nur schwer packen können. menschen, die immer geistesgegenwärtig sein müssen, die z. b. oft in schwierigen situationen ein auto lenken, werden viel leichter reagieren können als diejenigen, die nicht gewöhnt sind, das leben um sich herum scharf zu beobachten, auf die anzeichen des im anzug befindlichen zu achten.

eine demonstration hat darum zweckmäßig erst mit einfachen überlagerungen zu beginnen und sie wird durch treffende, zusammenfassende titel dem verständnis entgegenkommen können.

jedes blatt hat einen titel, mitunter auch mehrere. die treffendsten titel werden oft vom betrachter gefunden. durch einen guten titel wird oft das ganze groteske oder absurde bild zur sinnvollen, „überzeugenden wahrheit".

die fotoplastik kann verschiedenartig verwendet werden.

eine von vielen möglichkeiten: als szenenverdichtung ganzer abläufe in teater oder film: dramen und filmmanuskripte können in einer einzigen solchen blattdarstellung zusammengefaßt sein.

eine andere art der verwendung: zur illustration eines begriffes oder gefühls.

als propaganda-illustration, reklame, plakat.

als zeitsatire, usw.

der witz der zukunft wird wahrscheinlich nicht mit grafischen illustrationen, sondern mit fotoplastischen arbeiten auftreten, ebenso werden kinoplakate in zukunft mit fotografischen, fotoplastischen mitteln hergestellt, die dem wesen des films fraglos besser entsprechen als die noch heute üblichen kinoplakate, die nach filmsituationen gezeichnet und poetisch koloriert sind.

●

mit der auswertung dieser neuen wirkungsbereiche beginnt man erst heute und man wird bald merken, daß ein jedes noch so spröde erscheinende material nach langsamem ertasten seiner eigenart knetbar wird.

bauhausbücher im verlag albert langen, münchen
band 8 (zweite auflage)
l. moholy-nagy: malerei, fotografie, film
geheftet rmk. 7.— in leinen gebunden rmk. 9.—

9

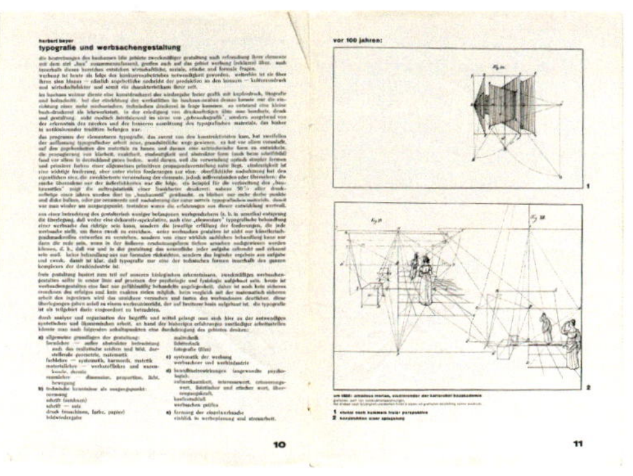
herbert bayer
typografie und werbsachengestaltung
vor 100 jahren:
10
11

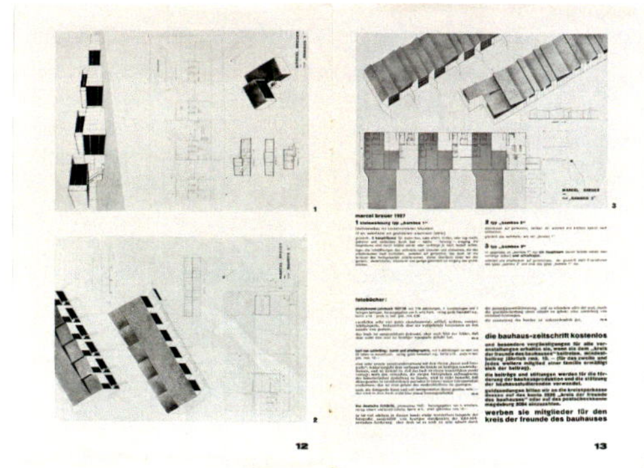
marcel breuer 1927
die bauhaus-zeitschrift kostenlos
werben sie mitglieder für den kreis der freunde des bauhauses
12
13

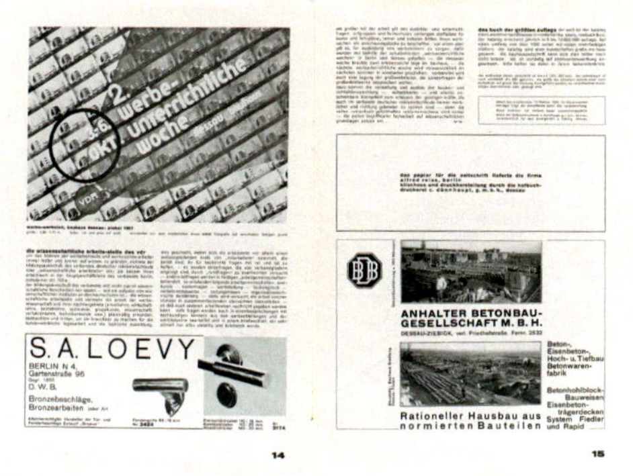
2. werbe-
unterrichtliche
woche
S.A.LOEVY
BERLIN N 4,
Gartenstraße 96
D.W.B.
Bronzebeschläge,
Bronzearbeiten
ANHALTER BETONBAU-
GESELLSCHAFT M. B. H.
Rationeller Hausbau aus normierten Bauteilen
14
15

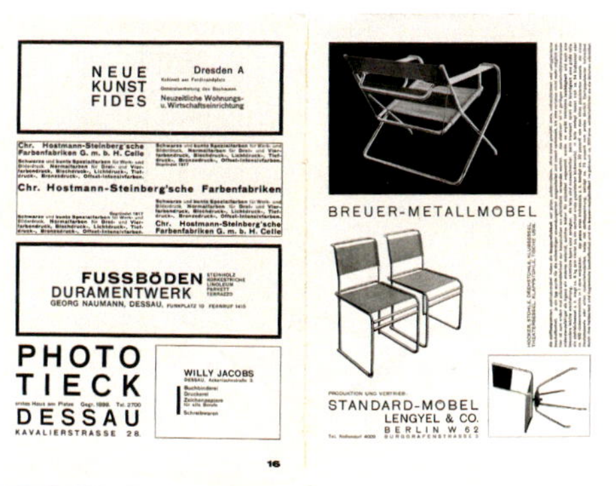
NEUE KUNST FIDES
Dresden A
Chr. Hostmann-Steinberg'sche Farbenfabriken
FUSSBÖDEN
DURAMENTWERK
GEORG NAUMANN, DESSAU
PHOTO TIECK DESSAU
KAVALIERSTRASSE 28.
WILLY JACOBS
BREUER-METALLMÖBEL
STANDARD-MÖBEL
LENGYEL & CO.
BERLIN W 62
16

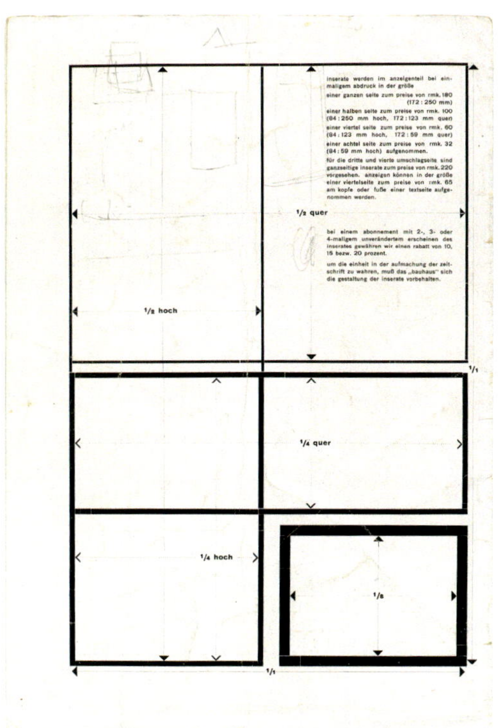
inserate werden im anzeigenteil bei einmaligem abdruck in der größe
einer ganzen seite zum preise von rmk. 180 (172 : 250 mm)
einer halben seite zum preise von rmk. 100 (84 : 250 mm hoch, 172 : 123 mm quer)
einer viertel seite zum preise von rmk. 60 (84 : 123 mm hoch, 172 : 59 mm quer)
einer achtel seite zum preise von rmk. 32 (84 : 59 mm hoch) aufgenommen.
für die dritte und vierte umschlagseite sind ganzseitige inserate zum preise von rmk. 220 vorgesehen. anzeigen können in der größe einer viertelseite zum preise von rmk. 65 am kopfe oder fuße einer textseite aufgenommen werden.
1/2 quer
bei einem abonnement mit 2-, 3- oder 4-maligem unverändertem erscheinen des inserates gewähren wir einen rabatt von 10, 15 bezw. 20 prozent.
um die einheit in der aufmachung der zeitschrift zu wahren, muß das „bauhaus" sich die gestaltung der inserate vorbehalten.
1/2 hoch
1/1
1/4 quer
1/4 hoch
1/8

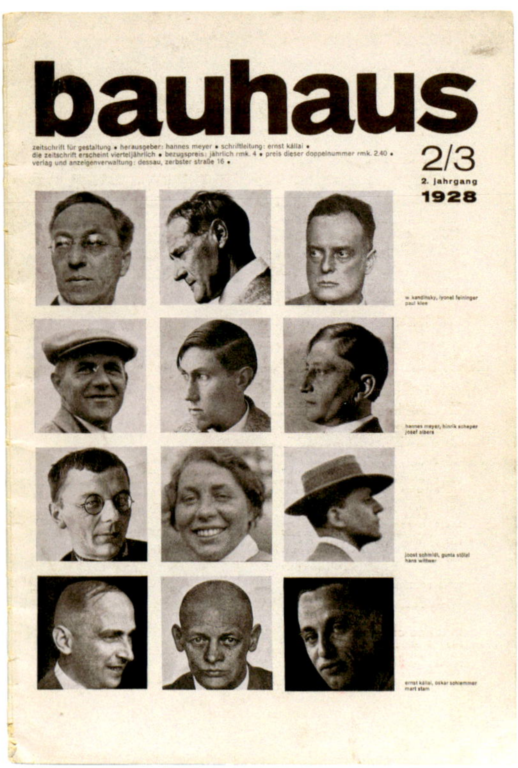

bauhaus

zeitschrift für gestaltung • herausgeber: hannes meyer • schriftleitung: ernst kállai •
die zeitschrift erscheint vierteljährlich • bezugspreis: jährlich rmk. 4 • preis dieser doppelnummer rmk. 2.40 •
verlag und anzeigenverwaltung: dessau, zerbster straße 16 •

2/3
2. jahrgang
1928

w. kandinsky, lyonel feininger
paul klee

hannes meyer, hinnerk scheper
josef albers

joost schmidt, gunta stölzl
hans wittwer

ernst kállai, oskar schlemmer
mart stam

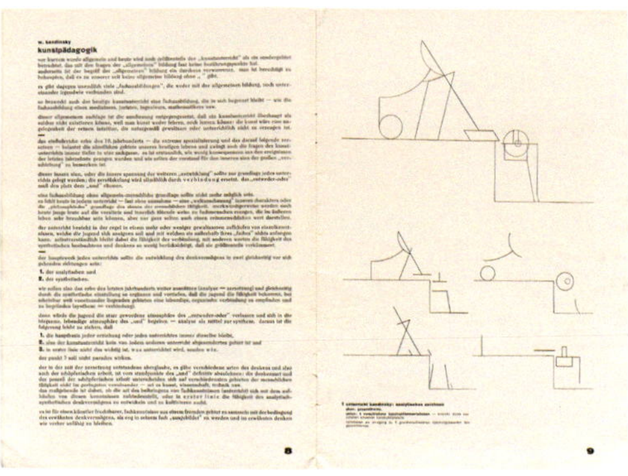

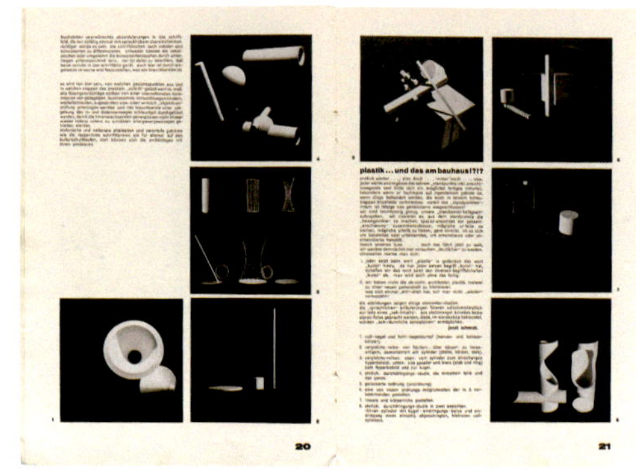

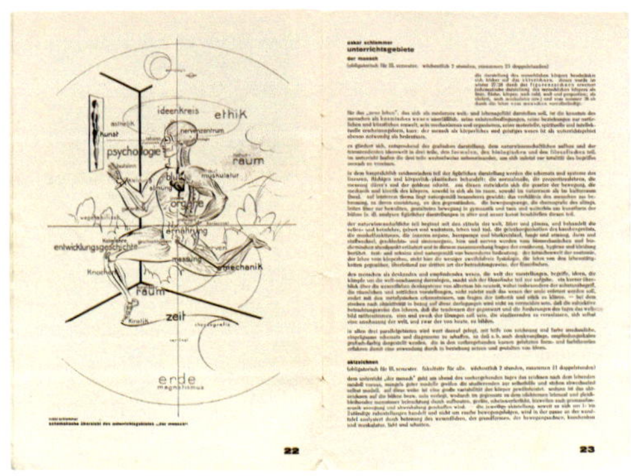

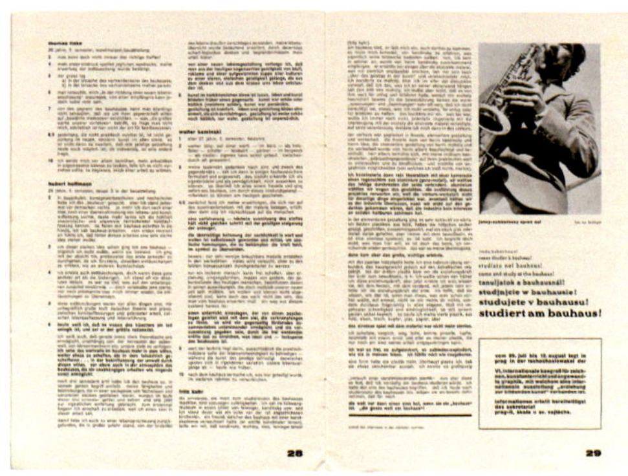

1928

DESIGNER UNKNOWN (likely Joost Schmidt)
HANNES MEYER (editor)

bauhaus: magazine for design (*bauhaus: zeitschrift für gestaltung*), vol. 2, no. 2/3, letterpress, 11¾ × 8¼ inches (296 × 210 mm), Dessau.

1928

DESIGNER UNKNOWN (likely Joost Schmidt)
HANNES MEYER (editor)

bauhaus: magazine for design (*bauhaus: zeitschrift für gestaltung*), vol. 2, no. 4, letterpress, 11¾ × 8¼ inches (296 × 210 mm), Dessau.

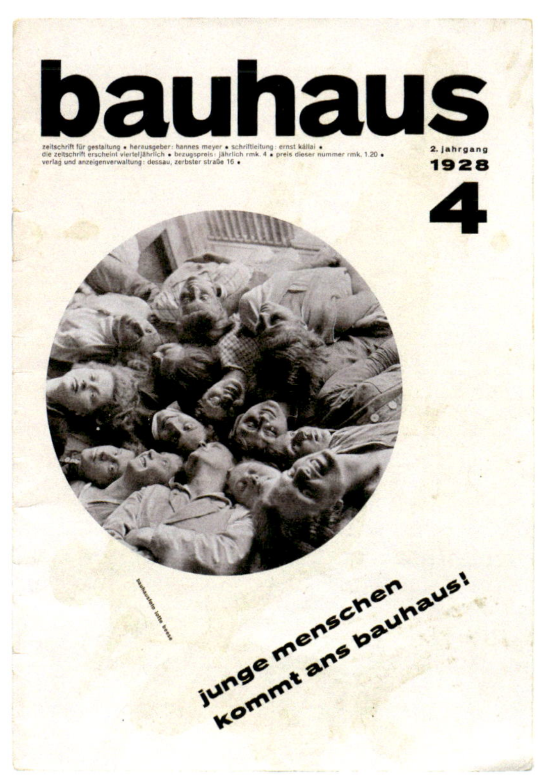

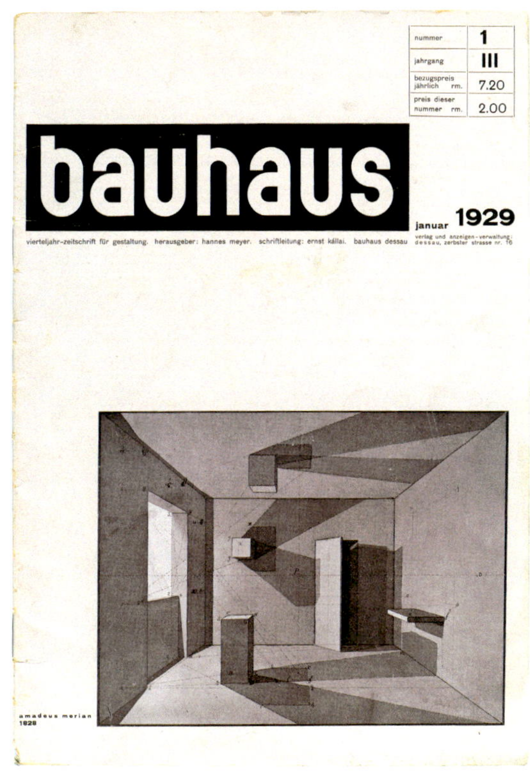

1929

JOOST SCHMIDT (designer)
ERNST KÁLLAI (editor)

bauhaus: magazine for design (*bauhaus: zeitschrift für gestaltung*), vol. 3, no. 1, letterpress, 11¾ × 8¼ inches (296 × 210 mm), Dessau.

nummer	2
jahrgang	III
bezugspreis jährlich rm.	7.20
preis dieser nummer rm.	2.00

bauhaus

april -juni **1929**

vierteljahr-zeitschrift für gestaltung. herausgeber hannes meyer. schriftleitung: ernst kállai. bauhaus dessau

verlag und anzeigen-verwaltung: dessau, zerbster strasse nr. 16

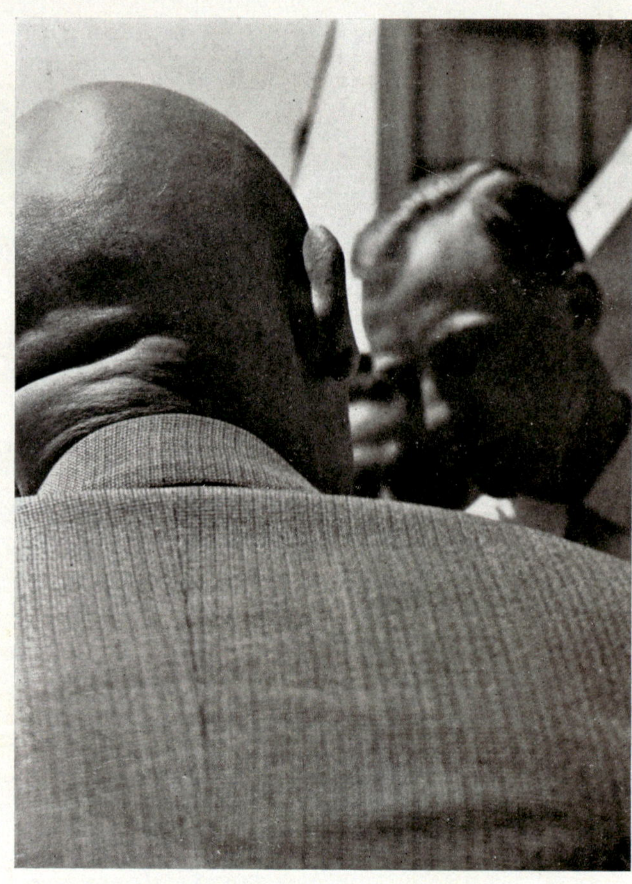

foto lux feininger

1929

3. jahrgang nr. 2.—
einzelheft preis rmk. 2.—

inhalt

28 abbildungen

die bauhausbücher

verlag albert langen, münchen, hubertusstr. 27
schriftleitung: w. gropius und l. moholy-nagy

band 1 walter gropius, internationale architektur (zweite auflage) geh. 5, in leinen geb. 7 rmk.
band 2 paul klee, pädagogisches skizzenbuch vergriffen
band 3 ein versuchshaus des bauhauses vergriffen
band 4 die bühne des bauhauses geh. 5, in leinen geb. 7 rmk.
band 5 piet mondrian, neue gestaltung vergriffen
band 6 theo van doesburg, grundbegriffe der neuen gestaltenden kunst vergriffen
band 7 neue arbeiten der bauhauswerkstätten geh. 6, in leinen geb. 8 rmk.
band 8 l. moholy-nagy, malerei, photographie, film (zweite auflage) geh. 7, in leinen geb. 9 rmk.
band 9 w. kandinsky, punkt und linie zur fläche (zweite auflage) geh. 15, in leinen geb. 18 rmk.
band 10 j. j. p. oud, holländische architektur geh. 6, in leinen geb. 8 rmk.
band 11 k. malewitsch, die gegenstandslose welt, begründung und erklärung des russischen suprematismus geh. 6, in leinen geb. 8 rmk.

neu erschienen ist:

band 13 a. gleizes, kubismus geh. 8, in leinen geb. 10 rmk.

in kürze erscheinen:

band 12 w. gropius, bauhausneubauten in dessau
band 14 l. moholy-nagy, von kunst zu leben

die sammlung wird fortgesetzt

die bauhaus-zeitschrift erscheint vierteljährlich
bezugspreis jährlich rmk. 7.20
einzelnummer rmk. 2.—
preis dieser nummer rmk. 2.—

abonnements bei dem verlag oder durch den buchhandel

verlag und anzeigenverwaltung: dessau, zerbster str. 16
postscheckkonto: magdeburg 16662
telefon sammel-nr. 3106
für den anzeigenteil verantwortlich: paul jesch, dessau.

bezugs- und zahlungsbedingungen:
abonnements haben geltung bis ende des laufenden kalenderjahres. abonnements, die 30 tage vor ablauf d. laufenden kalenderjahres beim verlage schriftlich nicht gekündigt sind, gelten als um das nächste kalenderjahr verlängert. erteilte rechnungen sind so zeitig zu begleichen, daß der verlag spätestens 8 tage nach rechnungsdatum über die rechnungsbeträge verfügen kann. überfällige forderungen erhöhen sich um mahn- und inkassospesen. ausfall der zeitschriftenlieferung ohne verschulden des verlages (streik, höhere gewalt usw.) berechtigt nicht zum verlangen nach minderung des bezugspreises oder schadenersatzleistung. erfüllungsort und gerichtsstand für beide teile ist dessau.

sendungen an die redaktion: bauhaus dessau
für die redaktion verantwortlich: ernst kállai, dessau.
für unverlangte beiträge und rezensionsexemplare keinerlei gewähr.

alle rechte vorbehalten

generalvertretung des bauhauses
architekturbedarf dresden-a.
kabinett am ferdinandplatz.
technische spezialabteilung
der neuen kunst fides g. m. b. h.
moderne wohnungs- und wirtschaftseinrichtungen

bauhauserzeugnisse in der tschechoslowakei durch architekt krejcar, prag II. cernà ul. c. 12a.

RED internationale monatsschrift für moderne gestaltung.
schriftleiter: k. teige.
prag II. cerna 12a. tschechoslowakei.
ein heft 0.85 rmk.
jahresabonnement (10 hefte) 8.50 rmk.

bauhaus zeitschrift für gestaltung

herausgeber: hannes meyer
schriftleitung: ernst kállai

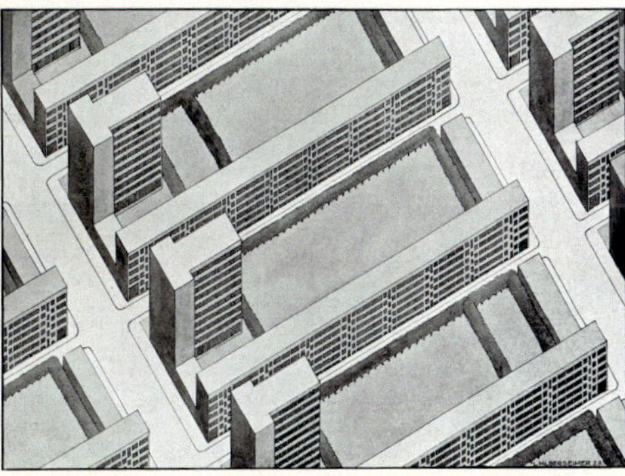

gesamtübersicht

l. hilberseimer

kleinstwohnungen

größe, grundriß und städtebauliche anordnung.

über nichts herrscht größere unklarheit als über die größe einer wohnung. man ist traditionell gewohnt, durch die übliche zimmerteilung die größe einer wohnung nach der anzahl der zimmer zu bestimmen. so gibt es ein, eineinhalb, zwei, zweieinhalb, drei, dreieinhalb usw. -zimmerwohnungen. nichts ist falscher als mit solchen dehnbaren begriffen wie zimmer und ihre anzahl die größe und art einer wohnung festzulegen.

heute bestimmt man die wohnungsgröße nach der größe der wohnfläche. so sollen nach den neuesten bestimmungen der berliner wohnungsfürsorgegesellschaft kleinstwohnungen eine fläche von 48, 54, 62 qm haben, wobei 48 qum einer eineinhalb-zimmer-wohnung, 54 qum einer zwei-zimmer-wohnung, 62 qum einer zweieinhalb-zimmer-wohnung, entspricht. aber auch diese flächenbemessung ist genau wie die bemessung nach zimmern von traditionellen gewohnheiten abhängig und für eine freiere grundrißgestaltung, die auf das wirkliche bedürfnis der bewohner eingeht, ist damit noch keine basis geschaffen.

die an sich richtige methode, die größe nach der fläche zu bemessen, scheitert an der willkürlichen annahme dieser fläche, die von der alten zimmerteilung abhängig ist.

bei festlegung der flächengröße für eine wohnung muß die erste überlegung die sein, wieviel personen darin unterzubringen und wie die räume auf der fläche zu verteilen sind. es ist zu ermitteln: die wohnungsgröße für 1, 2, 3, 4, 5, 6 usw. personen, wobei zu berücksichtigen ist, daß jede wohnung, gleichgültig für wieviel personen sie gedacht ist, den nötigen wohn- und schlafraum, bad und küche haben muß.

1

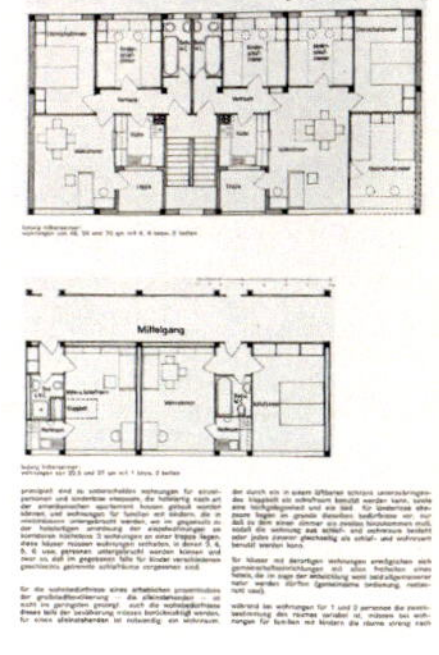

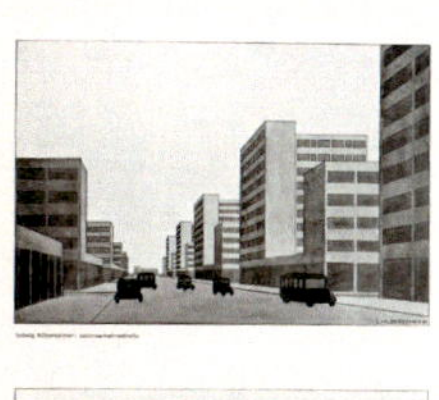

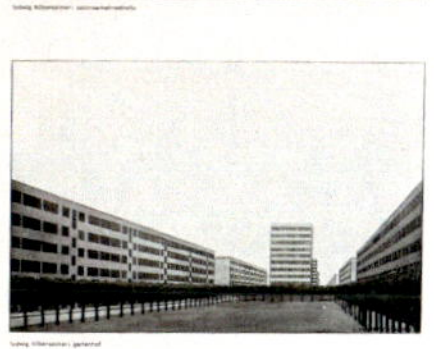

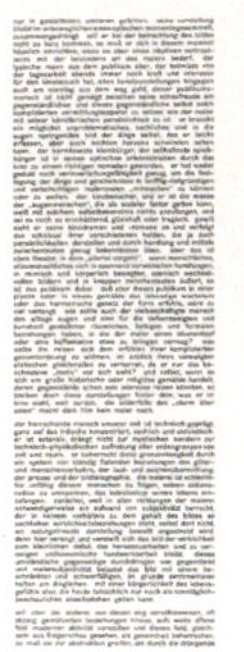

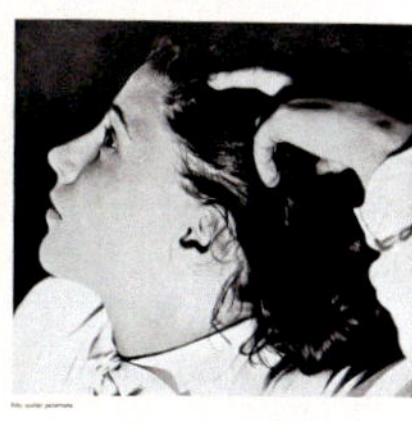

1929

JOOST SCHMIDT (designer)
ERNST KÁLLAI (editor)

bauhaus: magazine for design (*bauhaus: zeitschrift für gestaltung*), vol. 3, no. 2, letterpress, 11¾ × 8¼ inches (296 × 210 mm), Dessau.

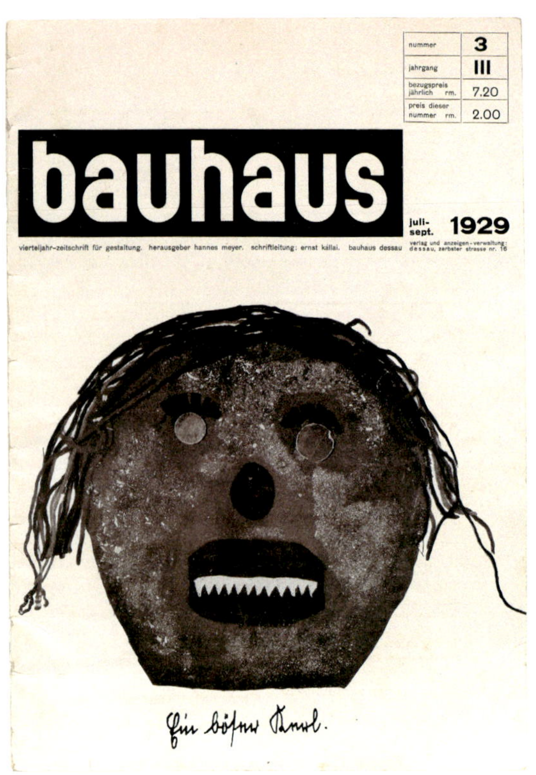

1929

JOOST SCHMIDT (designer)
ERNST KÁLLAI (editor)

bauhaus: magazine for design (*bauhaus: zeitschrift für gestaltung*), vol. 3, no. 3, letterpress, 11¾ × 8¼ inches (296 × 210 mm), Dessau.

In 1929, the design of *bauhaus* fell to Joost Schmidt, a former student and a junior master of lettering. The previous year had been pivotal for the Bauhaus and for Bauhaus typography in particular. Swiss architect Hannes Meyer had taken over the directorship of the school, marking a further shift from fine arts toward industrial production and functionalism. Amid these pedagogical upheavals, László Moholy-Nagy and Herbert Bayer—up to that point the main typographic figures—left the school. When Schmidt took over *bauhaus*, he mostly continued in the direction set by Bayer. His most distinctive flourish was the new cover layout and hand-lettered *bauhaus* logotype, set as white text in a black rectangle, for the magazine's third volume. Drawing from one of his own alphabet models, he moved the identity of the magazine toward the idealized geometric letterforms that many modernists aspired to, as opposed to the generic sans serif typefaces available at the time. Issue three of the third volume also records Schmidt's interdisciplinary pedagogy as the new typography teacher. It begins with photographs of the informational exhibition *Gas and Water* (*Gas und Wasser*), including a trade stand for radiator and aeronautical company Junkers & Co., collaboratively carried out by the workshops for print and advertising, sculpture, carpentry, and metal, under Schmidt's direction. In this project, the Bauhaus ambitions for typography—as a tool for the communication of information to the public, with accessible and compelling presentation, and in partnership with other disciplines—were realized. ●

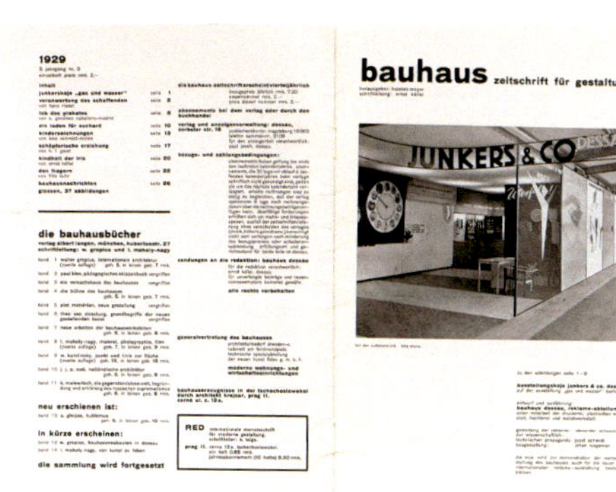
1929
bauhaus zeitschrift für gestaltung
JUNKERS & CO DESSAU
die bauhausbücher
neu erschienen ist:
in kürze erscheinen:
die sammlung wird fortgesetzt

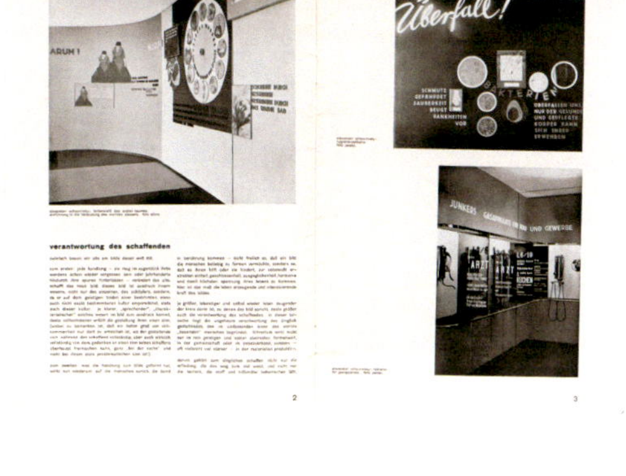
Überfall!
verantwortung des schaffenden

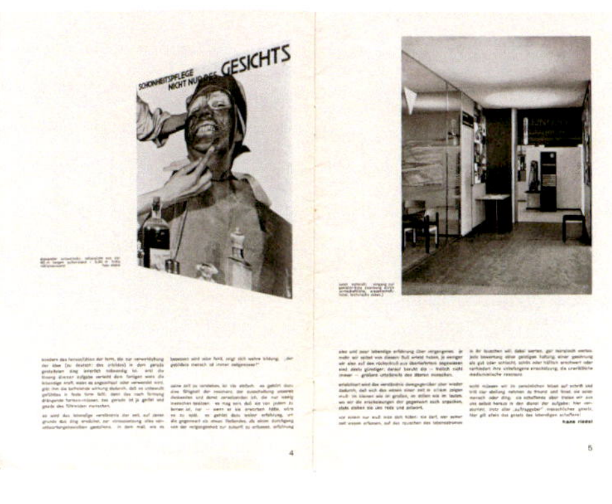
SCHÖNHEITSPFLEGE NICHT NUR DES GESICHTS

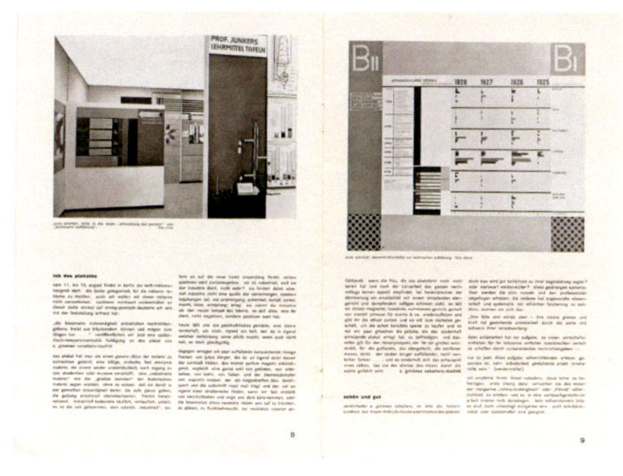
PROF. JUNKERS LEHRMITTEL TAFELN

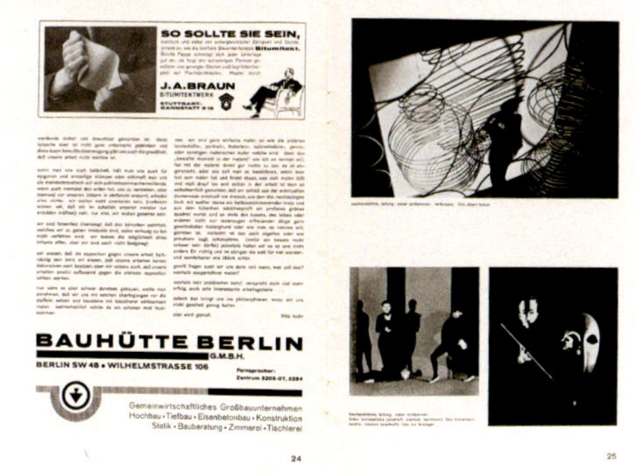
SO SOLLTE SIE SEIN,
J.A.BRAUN
BAUHÜTTE BERLIN
BERLIN SW 48 • WILHELMSTRASSE 106

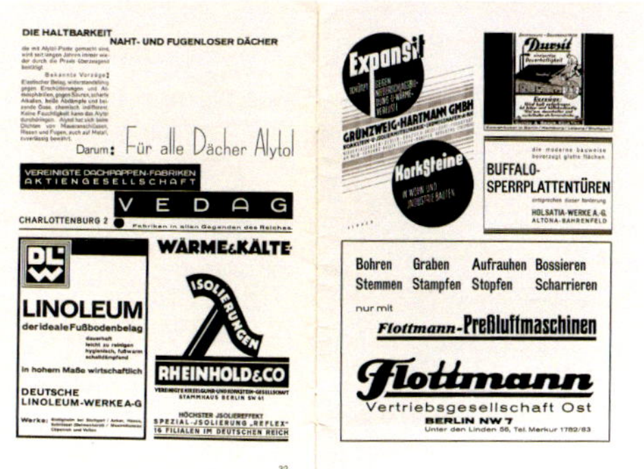
DIE HALTBARKEIT NAHT- UND FUGENLOSER DÄCHER
Darum: Für alle Dächer Alytol
VEREINIGTE DACHPAPPEN-FABRIKEN AKTIENGESELLSCHAFT
VEDAG
CHARLOTTENBURG 2
LINOLEUM
der ideale Fußbodenbelag
DEUTSCHE LINOLEUM-WERKE A-G
WÄRME&KÄLTE
RHEINHOLD&CO
Expansit
GRÜNZWEIG+HARTMANN GMBH
BUFFALO-SPERRPLATTENTÜREN
Bohren Graben Aufrauhen Bossieren
Stemmen Stampfen Stopfen Scharrieren
nur mit
Flottmann-Preßluftmaschinen
Flottmann
Vertriebsgesellschaft Ost
BERLIN NW 7

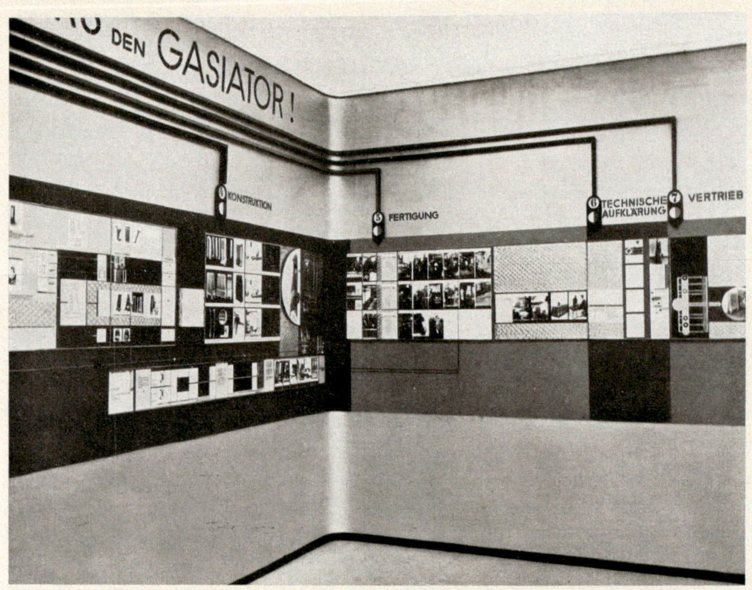

joost schmidt: werbung für den gasheizofen „gasiator" durch wirtschaftliche, wissenschaftliche, technische daten aus der arbeitsmethode von junkers. fotos stone.

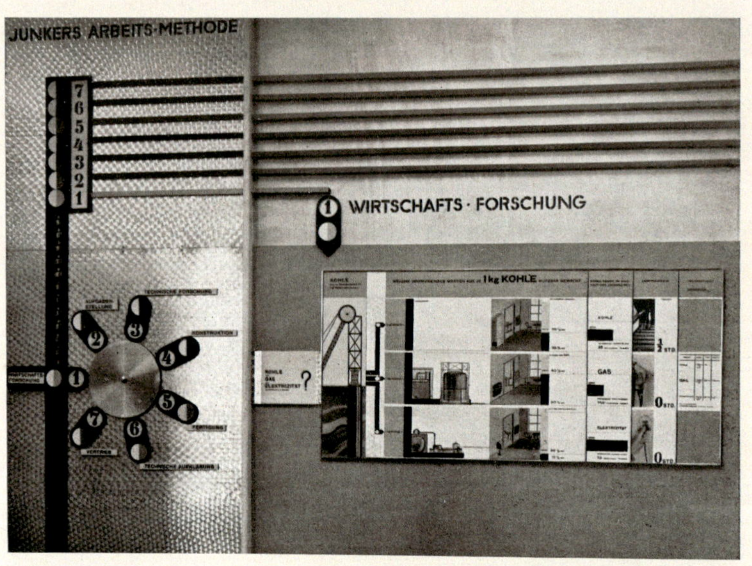

6

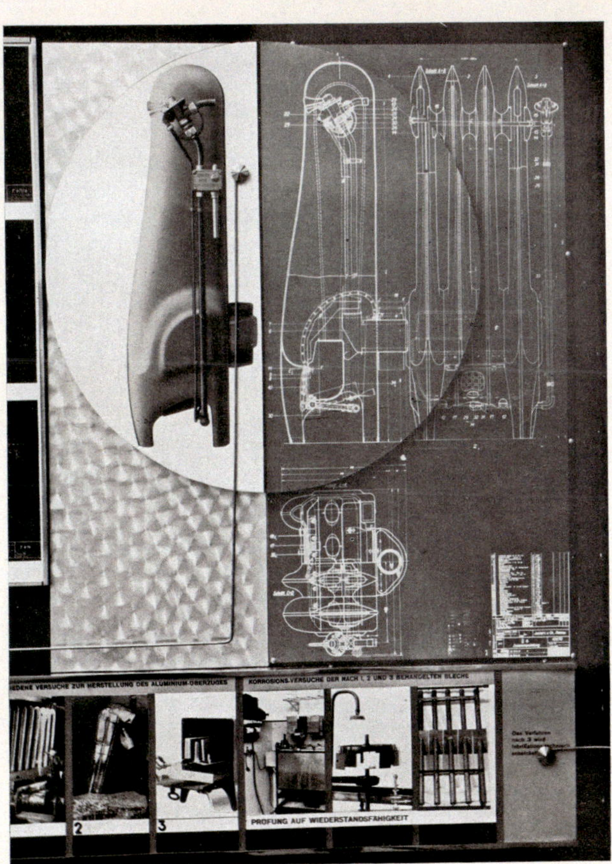

joost schmidt: teil des demonstrationsbildbandes der gasiatorkoje. foto stone

gruß an den welt-reklame-kongreß der weltstadt berlin!
am werbewesen wird die welt genesen!

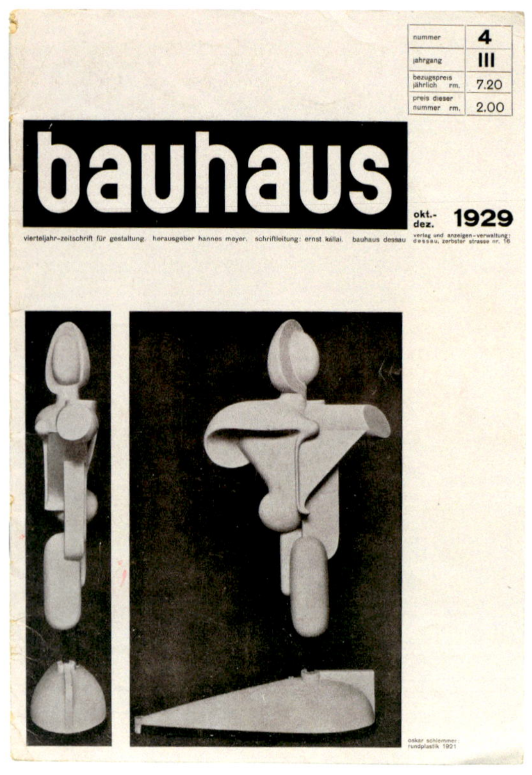

nummer 4
jahrgang III
bezugspreis jährlich rm. 7.20
preis dieser nummer rm. 2.00

bauhaus

okt.-dez. 1929

vierteljahr-zeitschrift für gestaltung. herausgeber hannes meyer. schriftleitung: ernst kállai. bauhaus dessau

verlag und anzeigen-verwaltung: dessau, zerbster strasse nr. 16

oskar schlemmer rundplastik 1921

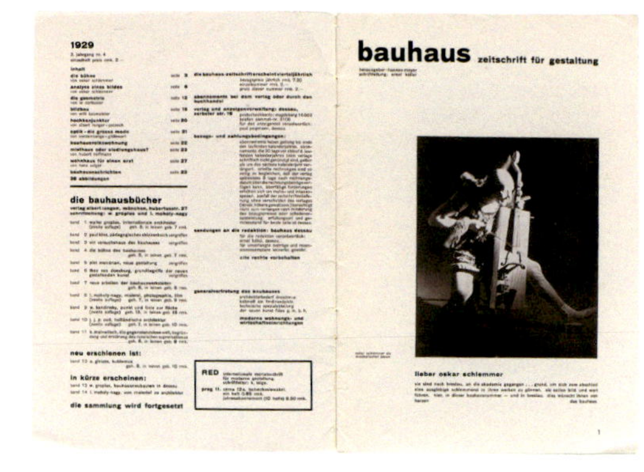

1929

die bauhausbücher

bauhaus zeitschrift für gestaltung

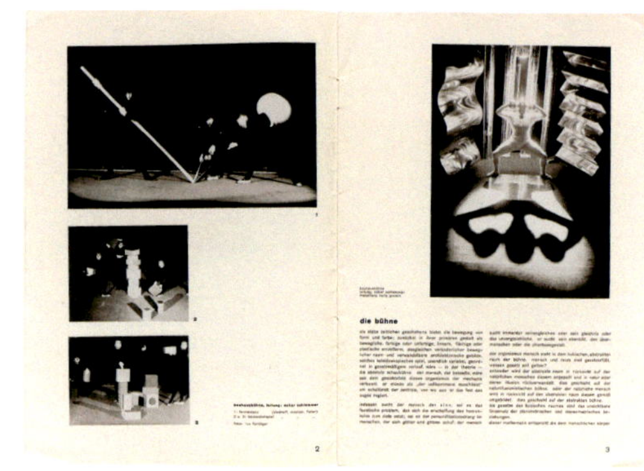

die bühne

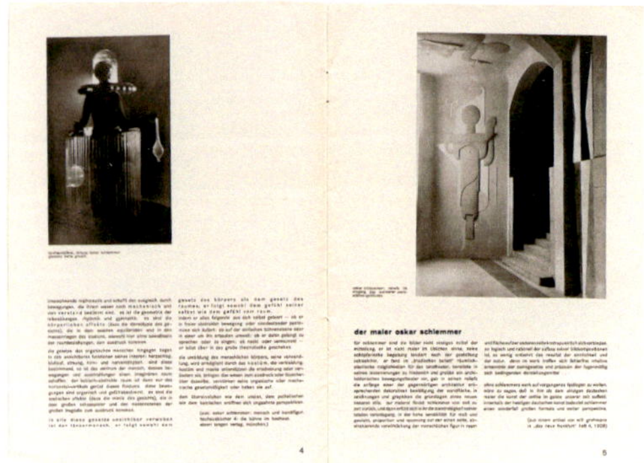

der maler oskar schlemmer

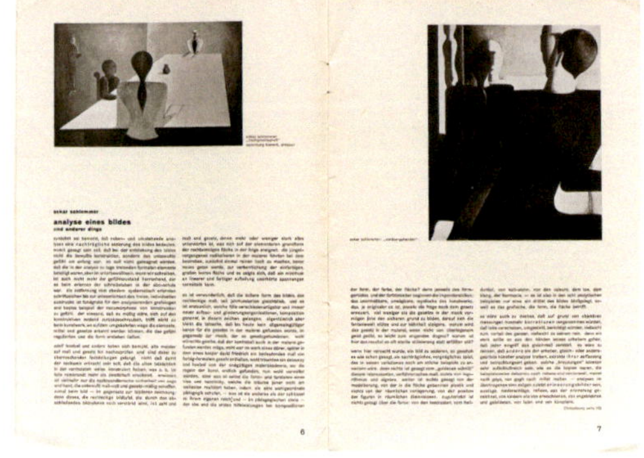

analyse eines bildes

1929

JOOST SCHMIDT (designer)
ERNST KÁLLAI (editor)

bauhaus: magazine for design (*bauhaus: zeitschrift für gestaltung*), vol. 3, no. 4, letterpress, 11¾ × 8¼ inches (296 × 210 mm), Dessau.

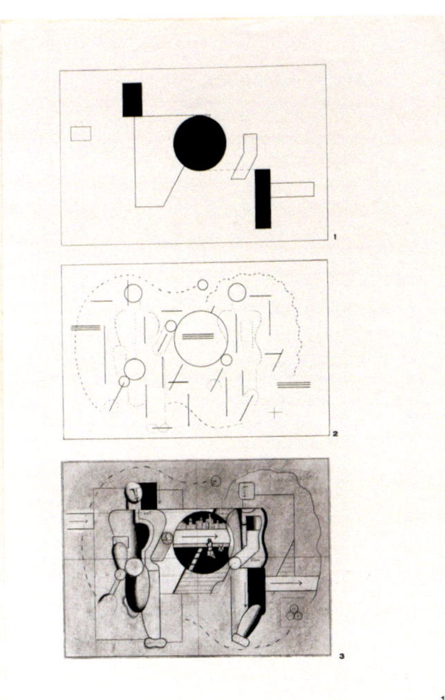

14

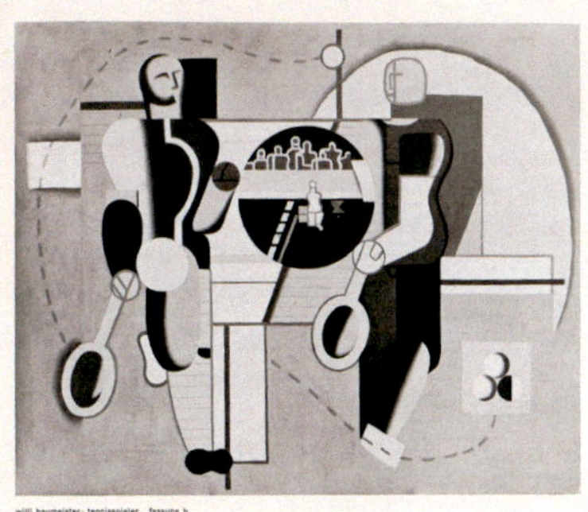

willi baumeister: tennisspieler. fassung b.

zu den abbildungen:

1) verteilung der reinen weiß- und schwarzflächen.

2) beziehungen der kreisformen. abwandlung in verwandte formen: ellipse, tropfen, violin und die 3 freieren kurven, die das bild umkreisen. die senkrechten, wagrechten und schrägen.

3) weiß durchzieht das bild horizontal, getreppt von links oben nach rechts unten. (wagrechte pfeile) schwarz vertikal, gleichfalls von links oben in steiler treppe. (senkrechte pfeile) die linke figur hat rot als dominante, die rechte blau, die zuschauer gelb. die rote hat helleres blau als umgebung, die blaue ein entsprechend abgeschwächtes rot. die verankerungen behalten durch kontraste ihre stärke. die verflechtung in weiterer differenzierung ist in einem kurzen resümé nicht klarzulegen.

bildbau

jedes werk beruht auf gesetzen und gibt gesetze.
die ersteren sind die mittel und hilfsmittel. in der malerei sind sie mechanismen der fläche, der farbe.

die mittel, d. h. ihre kombinationen sind unendlich. z. b. beziehungen und kontrast zum format, zur fläche. beziehungen und kontraste unter sich. masse und intensitäten.

eine fläche wird einwandfrei demonstriert und verspannt vergleichsweise wie ein papierdrachen. durch die zwei diagonalen oder durch das kreuz der beiden mittellinien. aber unsre augen suchen im bild einen drall und wollen bewegungen folgen. bewegung hat aber richtung und ist der symmetrie gegensätzlich. deshalb kommen wir zum „freien gleichgewicht".

geht man von einem unterbau von mathematik und geometrie aus, so kann es vorkommen, daß die komposition weniger das erreicht, was sie beabsichtigt, da der wert des errechneten netzes alsbald aufgehoben wird durch die ausspielung der farben in ihrem unendlich differenzierten fächer.- bekanntlich entstehen mathematik und geometrie sehr oft absichtslos. die wissenschaft beweist nicht a priori das bild. und die kunst hat nicht die absicht, die wissenschaft zu beweisen.

15

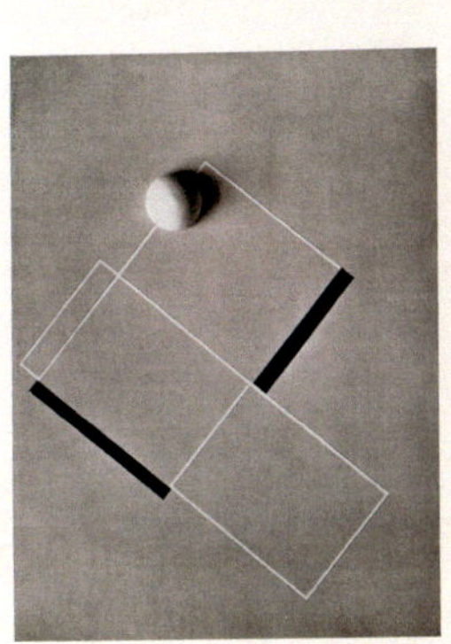

vordemberge-gildewart
komposition no. 26

carl buchheister, komposition nr. 25a

die verwendung des rechten winkels ist bewußt geworden. alle senkrechten gehen eine resonanz ein mit den beiden senkrechten der bildbegrenzung. alle wagrechten mit den beiden wagrechten. bezeichnend ist die verlegung der schwerpunkte in die obere bildhälfte. die vorliebe für das unstatische, leichte, ist damit gekennzeichnet.

es gibt eine zentrale anordnung, die vom bildrand abrückt und so den „ausschnitt" vermeidet.

ist ein durchgehender geistiger und formal-farbiger ausdruck entstanden, so sind alle mittel gerechtfertigt. die verbotstafeln der früheren generation haben uns nicht hindern können. seien wir nun vorsichtig mit verboten für die andern. in aller freiheit entstand das gebundenste, beste.

jede kunst ist romantik, zauberei, erfindung. die illusion angeführt durch vorstellung und einbildungskraft trägt alle andern mittel der malerei. (dies ist auch gültig für die „abstrakte" „elementare" malerei.)

w. baumeister

exakte gestaltung

die äußerung der menschlichen gefühle und sinne kann sich nur auf abstraktem wege entwickeln. diese entwicklung erfaßt nur die äußerungen. unsere gefühle und sinne bleiben immer die gleichen, und wenn sie sich auch von epoche zu epoche, von volk zu volk zu wandeln scheinen

16

und wenn ihre funktionen auch verschleiert und getrübt sind, so liegt der grund hierfür in unserer erziehung. unsere ideen, unsere geistigen konzeptionen unterscheiden sich immer von der wirklichkeit, wir müssen sie berichtigen und genau bestimmen. hierzu brauchen wir ein genaues mittel. je reiner unser mittel ist, um so näher kommt unsere äußerung dem exakten. eins der schönsten mittel, das dem menschen zu gebote steht, ist die mathematik. es ist klar, daß die mathematik uns nicht die absolute wahrheit sagt. aber sie ist sicherlich ein mittel, das unseren sinnen gleichgeordnet ist. wenn wir unsere empfindungen äußern wollen und sie der mathematik unterordnen, gehen wir sicher, die möglichkeiten des irrtums auf ein mindestmaß zu beschränken. oft glaubt man, daß die kunst dieses exakte wissen entbehren könne und daß die erschaffung eines kunstwerkes ganz einfach der genialität einer persönlichkeit zuzuschreiben sei. gewiß, man muß vor allen dingen ein künstler sein. selbstverständlich ist es nicht das mittel, das schöpferisch tätig ist, aber es kann die äußerung exakter gestalten. wenn ein musiker seine gefühle äußern will, greift er zum ton. der ton ist physikalisch und gehorcht bestimmten gesetzen. das gleiche gilt für die farbe. aber abgesehen von physikalischem wert, nimmt diese immer, sobald wir sie darstellen wollen, eine fläche ein und ist somit der geometrie unterworfen. ebenso verhält es sich mit dem raum und ich glaube, daß man nicht mehr daran zweifeln kann, daß die künste mathematische offenbarungen ästhetischer absicht sind.

g. vantongerloo

17

typog
maste

raphic
rs

Of the many instructors that helped shape the Bauhaus, László Moholy-Nagy, Herbert Bayer, and Joost Schmidt did the most to establish the school's legacy in typography and graphic design. Each spent only a few years as lead instructors, but their individual impacts were enduring, and they continued to make diverse commercial work that ultimately furthered the Bauhaus's reputation. ●

Ironically, the school did not offer official instruction in design or typography until 1925, six years after it was founded. Still, when he joined in 1923, Moholy-Nagy charged ahead with a typographic identity for the school, infusing Bauhaus ephemera and publications with Russian constructivism. When Bayer took the helm of the new print and advertising workshop in 1925, he simplified Moholy-Nagy's more chaotic tendencies across stationery, catalogs, and order forms, and he brought in paid commissions from local clients. In 1928, lettering instructor Joost Schmidt inherited the directorship of the print and advertising workshop, which by then included photography, and also began instruction in sculpture. After leading students in complex multidisciplinary projects, he departed just before the school was forced to move from Dessau to Berlin in 1933. ●

Moholy-Nagy and Bayer ultimately took their design principles to the United States, while Schmidt continued to work in Germany as a designer and mapmaker before being blacklisted by the Nazis. Examples of the three artists' work from before, during, and after their time at the school appear here, providing an in-depth look at their ongoing contributions to design and the Bauhaus story. ●

MA

AKTIVISTA FOLYÓIRAT

Moholy-Nagy: Üvegarchitektura

1922

LÁSZLÓ MOHOLY-NAGY (cover designer)

MA, vol. 7, no. 5/6, letterpress, 12¼ × 9¼ inches (310 × 236 mm), Vienna.

Before his 1920 move to Berlin and 1923 arrival at the Bauhaus, László Moholy-Nagy participated in revolutionary avant-garde art groups in his native Hungary. This cover design for the magazine *MA* (*Today*, also an acronym for *Magyar Aktivizmus*, or Hungarian activism) shows the geometric, constructivist, quasi-architectural aesthetics that likely drew Gropius's attention. Moholy-Nagy's early activism led to his belief that the goal of unifying art and technology was the mass dissemination of radical ideas to a new collectivist public—a viewpoint he translated into a set of visual principles at the Bauhaus. ●

In 1928, Swiss architect Hannes Meyer succeeded Gropius at the school, and Moholy-Nagy found himself at odds with Meyer's strict utilitarianism. He left and set up a design studio in Berlin while carrying on with photography, film, stage and exhibition design, painting, and sculpture. In 1929, an English translation of his Bauhausbücher *From Material to Architecture* appeared under the title *The New Vision*; it became a seminal text in photography and art. Before moving to Amsterdam, London, and finally Chicago, he established the design for the esteemed women's magazine *The New Line* (*Die neue Linie*) and contributed to publications and exhibitions on image-making. In the United States, he devised the pedagogy for one of his most enduring accomplishments, the School of Design in Chicago, before his death in 1946. ●

1931

LÁSZLÓ MOHOLY-NAGY (cover designer)

The New Line (*Die neue Linie*), vol. 3, no. 4, letterpress, 14⅜ × 10⅝ inches (365 × 270 mm), Leipzig and Berlin.

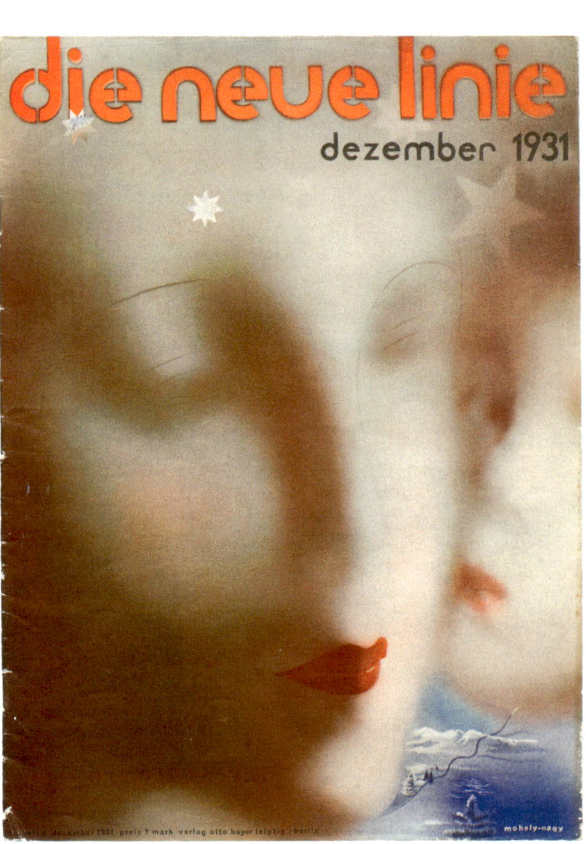

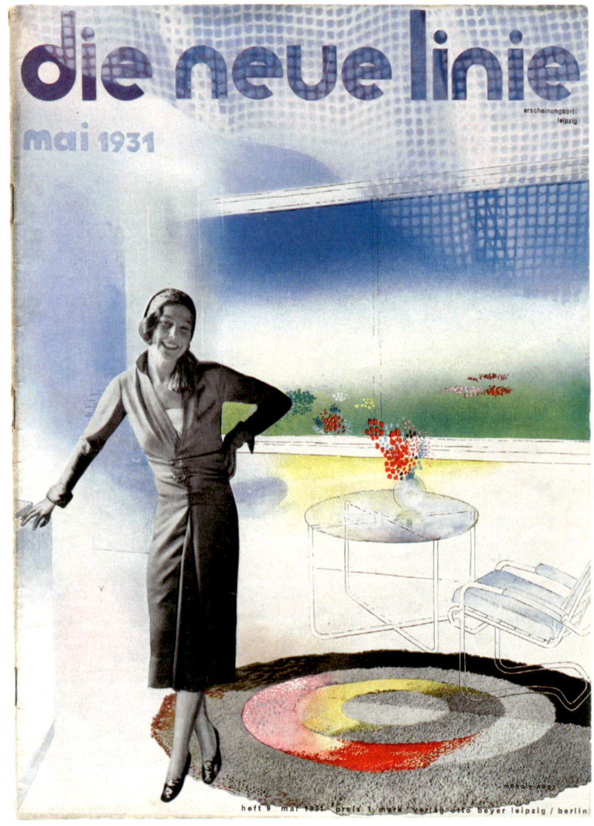

1931

LÁSZLÓ MOHOLY-NAGY (cover designer)

The New Line (*Die neue Linie*), vol. 2, no. 9, letterpress, 14⅜ × 10⅝ inches (365 × 270 mm), Leipzig and Berlin.

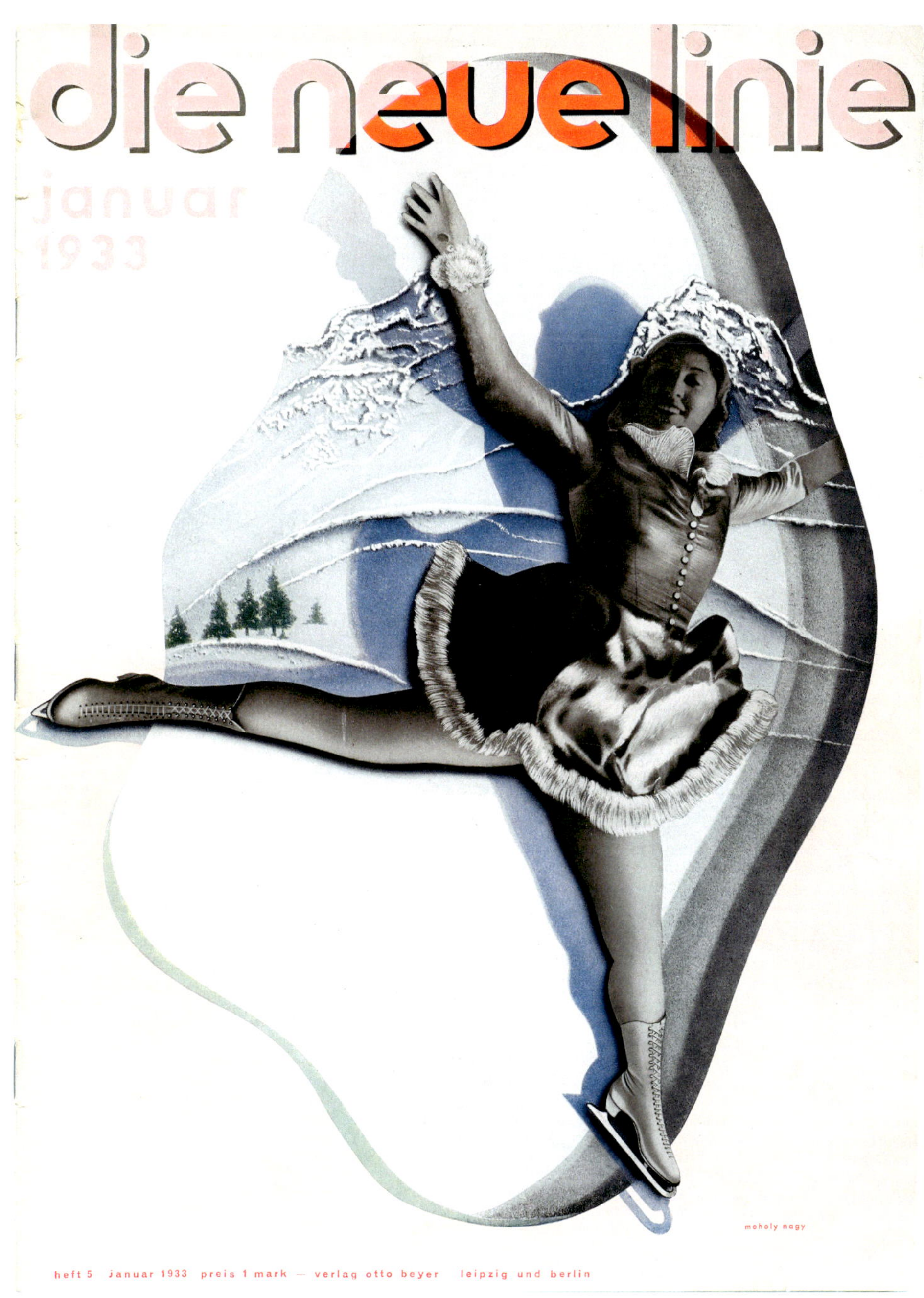

1933

LÁSZLÓ MOHOLY-NAGY (cover designer)

The New Line (*Die neue Linie*), vol. 4, no. 5, letterpress, 14⅜ × 10⅝ inches (365 × 270 mm), Leipzig and Berlin.

1936

LÁSZLÓ MOHOLY-NAGY

1937 New Year's card, letterpress, 5 × 7½ inches (125 × 192 mm), London.

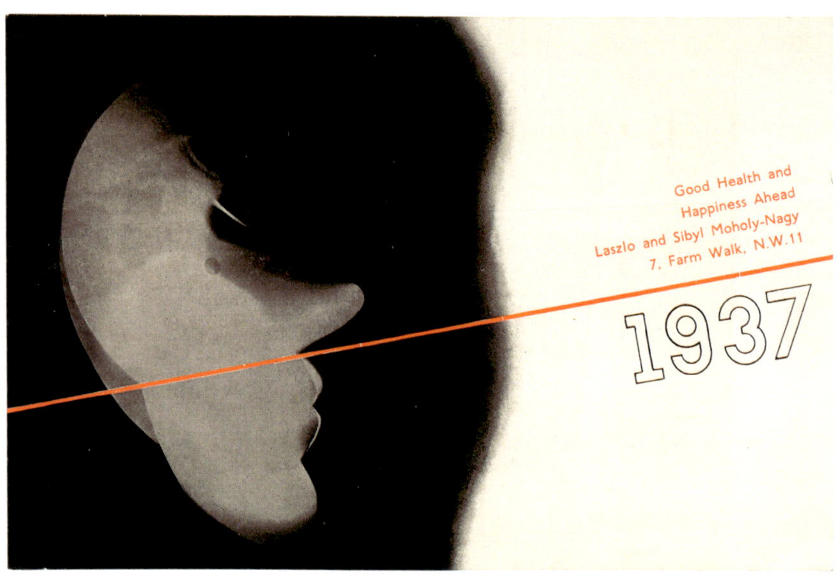

CIRCA 1934

STUDIO OF LÁSZLÓ MOHOLY-NAGY

Product catalog for Jena Glass, letterpress, 5⅞ × 8¼ inches (148 × 210 mm), Leipzig and Berlin.

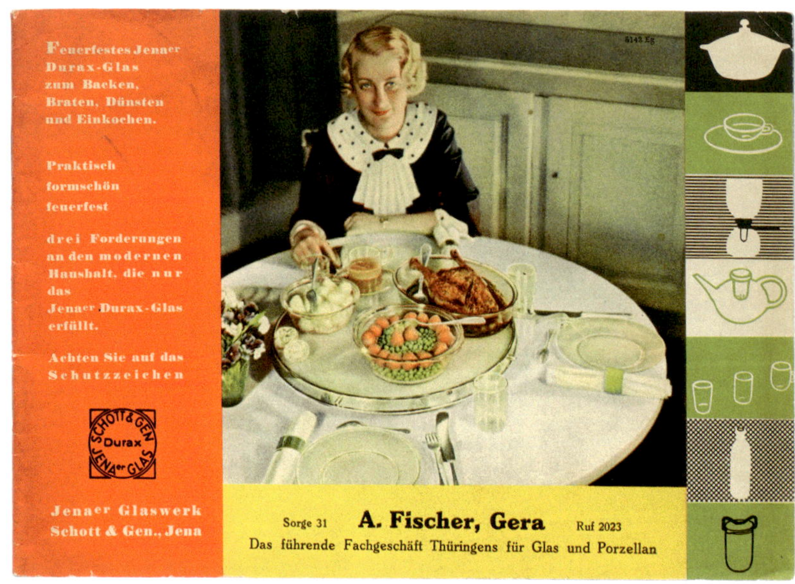

1936

LÁSZLÓ MOHOLY-NAGY (designer/editor)

Telehor: The International Review, New Vision issue, letterpress, 11¾ × 8⅜ inches (298 × 211 mm), Brno, present-day Czech Republic.

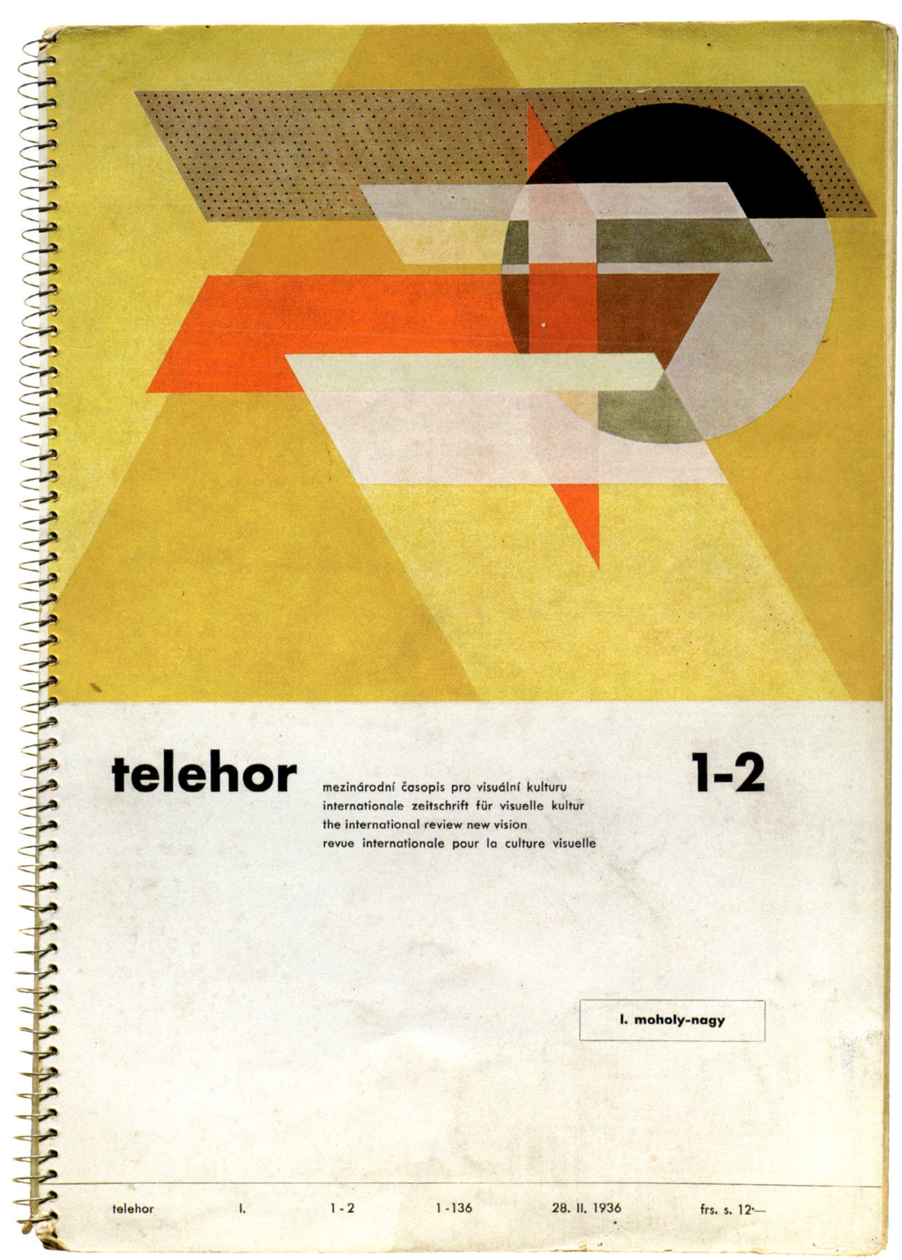

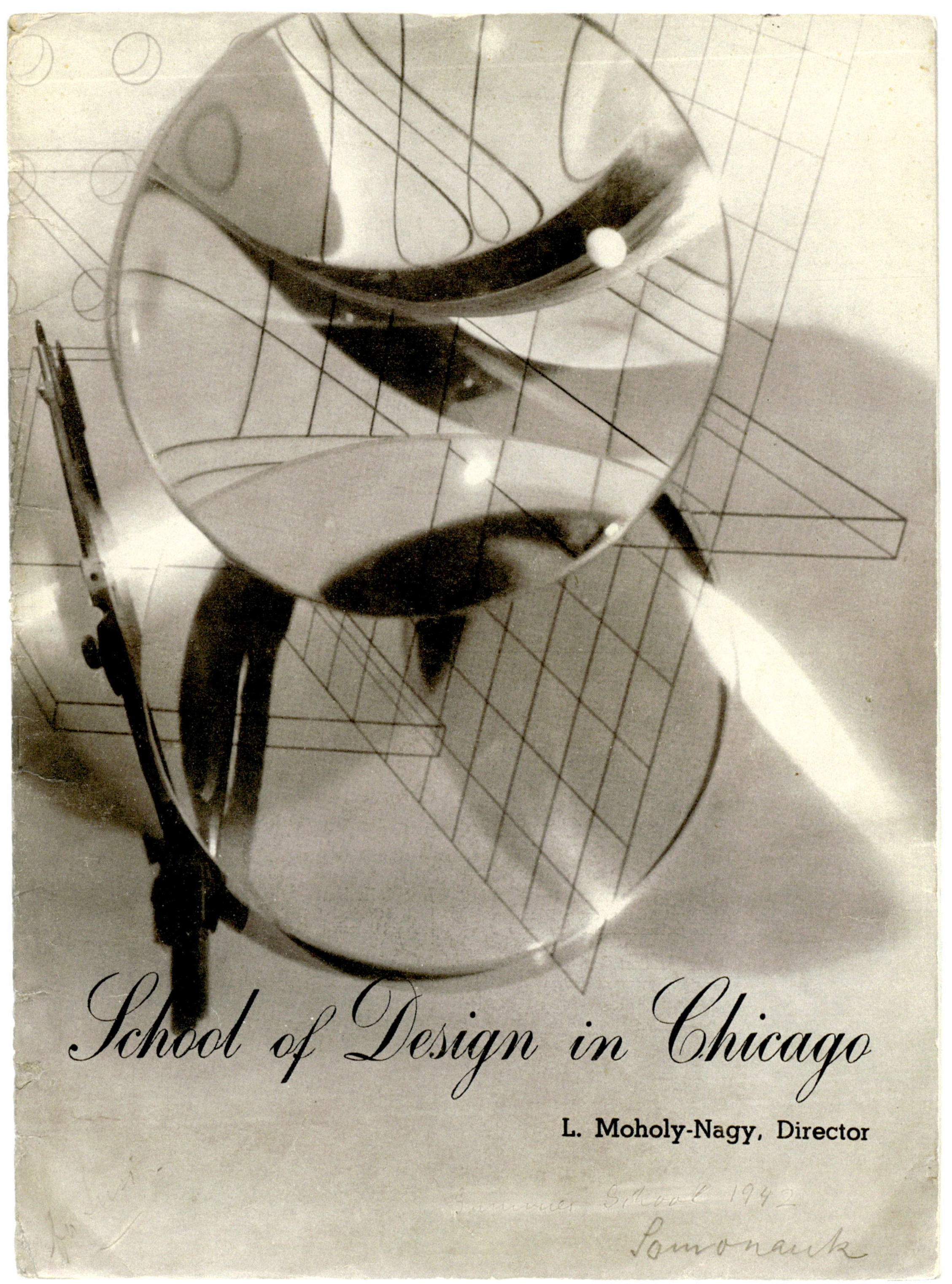
School of Design in Chicago
L. Moholy-Nagy, Director

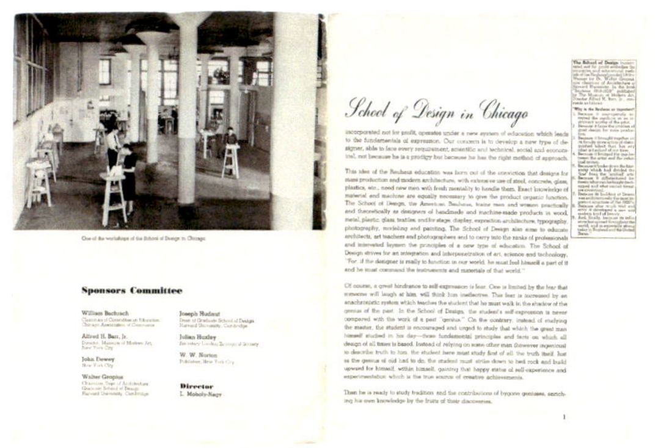

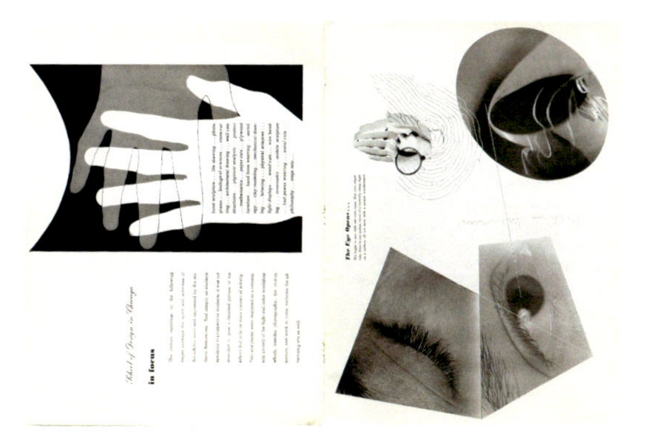

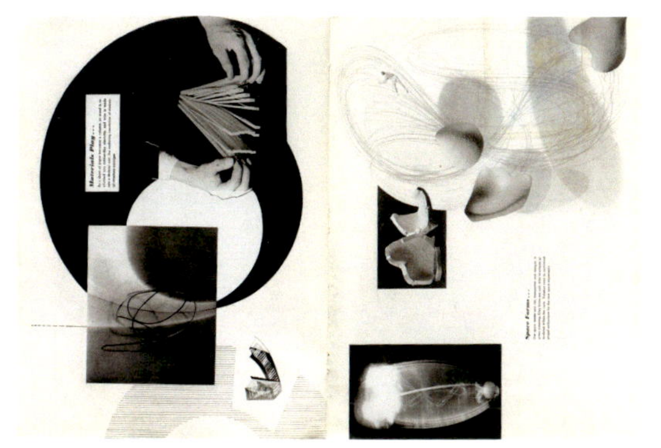

CIRCA 1943

LÁSZLÓ MOHOLY-NAGY (designer/editor)

Course catalog for the School of Design in Chicago, letterpress, 12 × 9 inches (304 × 230 mm), Chicago.

After Adolf Hitler came to power in 1933, and Germany became increasingly inhospitable to experimental artists, political leftists, and foreigners, many former Bauhaus masters immigrated to the United States. In 1937, at the recommendation of Walter Gropius (who had himself recently arrived in Boston), László Moholy-Nagy moved to Chicago to found a design school, initially called the New Bauhaus. After a brief closure, it reopened in 1939 as the Chicago School of Design, with funding from American Walter Paepcke, chairman of the Container Corporation of America (CCA) and a patron of design. (Paepcke later commissioned Herbert Bayer to design the *World Geo-Graphic Atlas*; see pages 192–197). The course catalog displayed here, designed by Moholy-Nagy himself, showcases Bauhaus design principles even in the absence of the school's original name (and in spite of the catalog's use of Typo Script and workhorse slab serifs, such as Stymie). The influence of his typophoto techniques, exemplified in the abstract photographic cover, reappears in photomontage pages designed by students, one of which explores an analogy between the structure of letterforms and the visual tenets of modernist chair design (see pages 166–167). Today known as the Institute of Design at the Illinois Institute of Technology, it became, in 1949, the first school in the United States to offer a PhD in design. ●

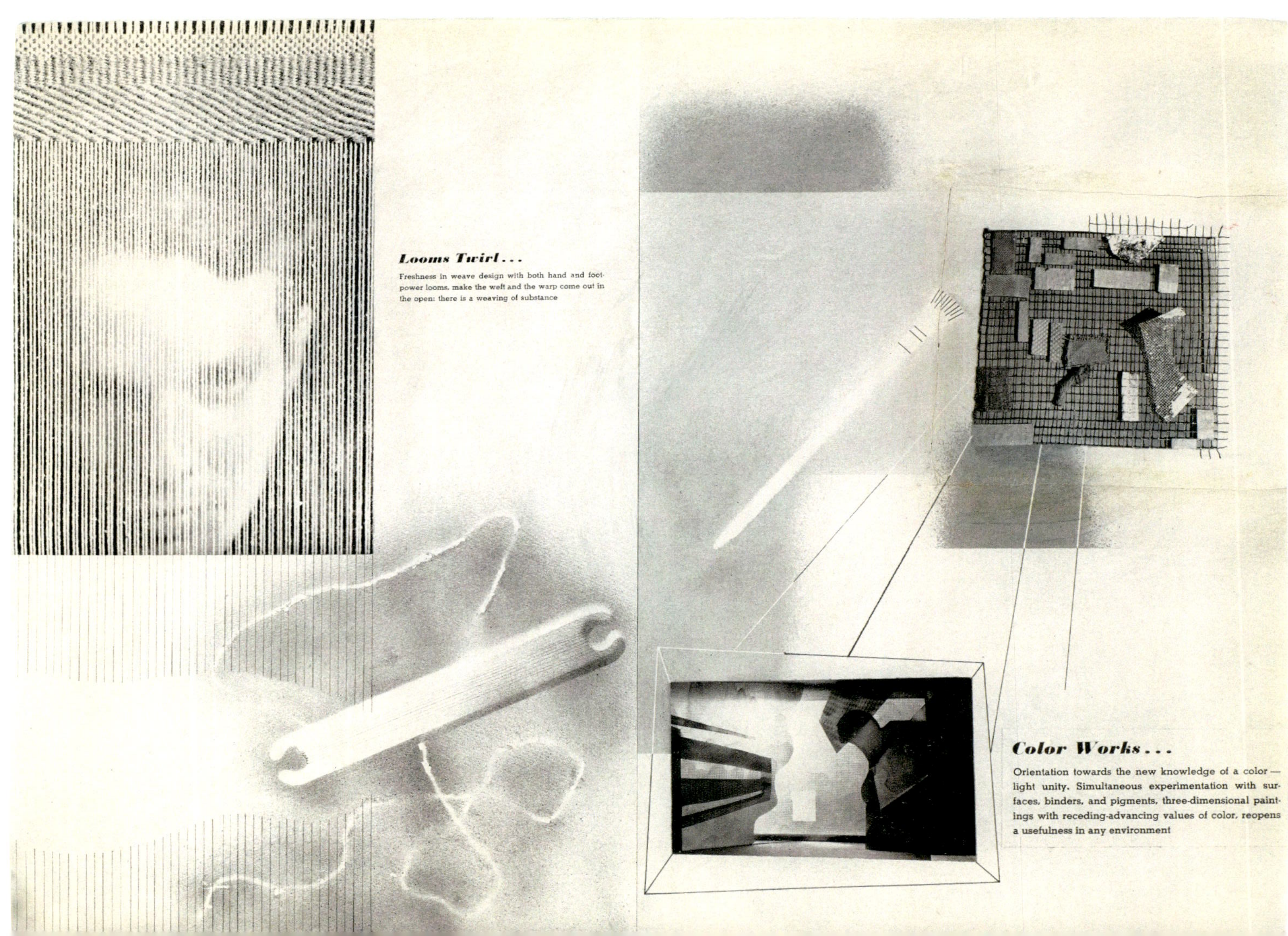
Looms Twirl . . .
Freshness in weave design with both hand and foot-power looms, make the weft and the warp come out in the open: there is a weaving of substance
Color Works . . .
Orientation towards the new knowledge of a color — light unity. Simultaneous experimentation with surfaces, binders, and pigments, three-dimensional paintings with receding-advancing values of color, reopens a usefulness in any environment

Mastered Technique = Freedom of Creation

Out of the indivisibility of idea and execution, control and exactness is evolved; discipline merges with fantasy and genuine results for application begin to appear

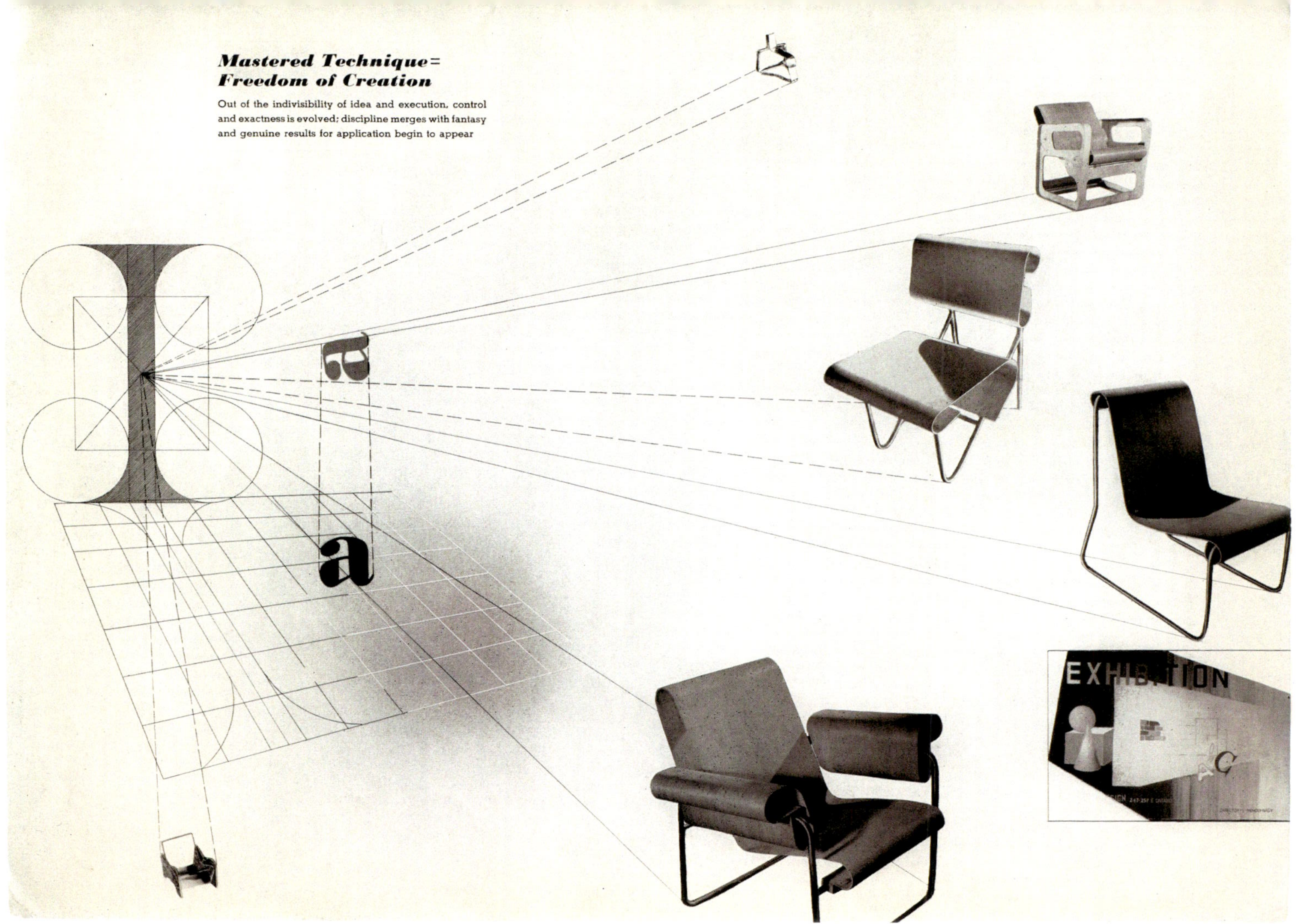

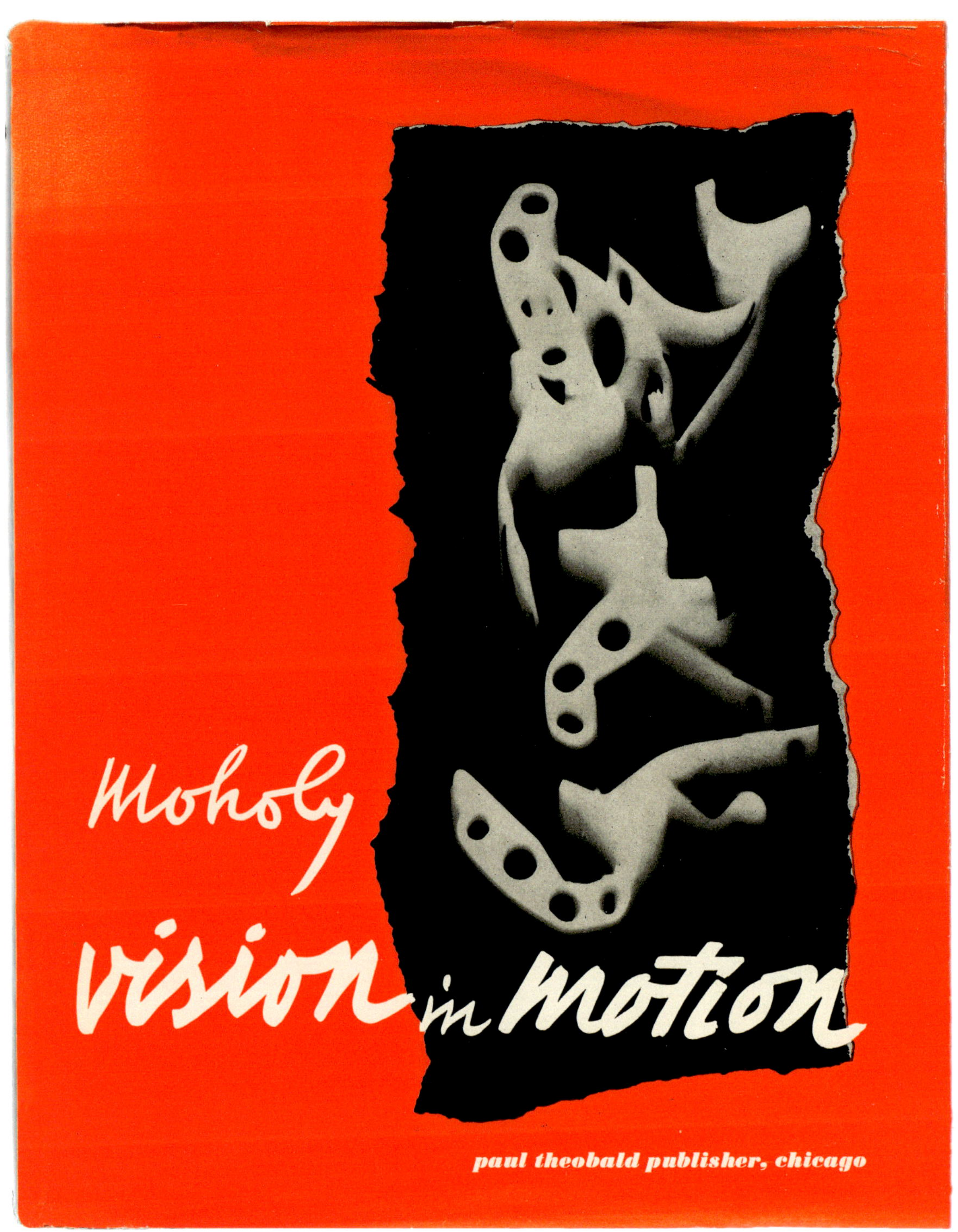
Moholy
vision in motion
paul theobald publisher, chicago

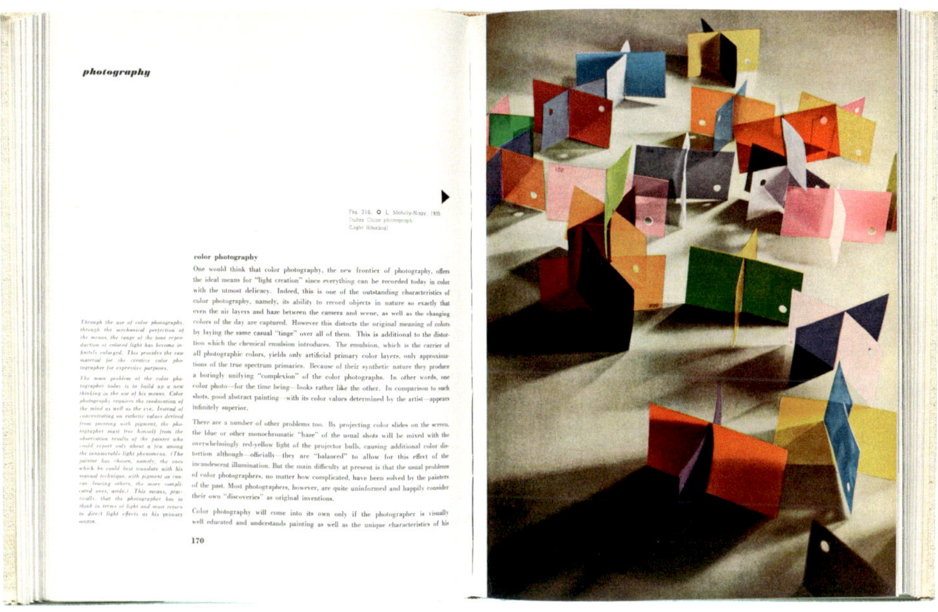

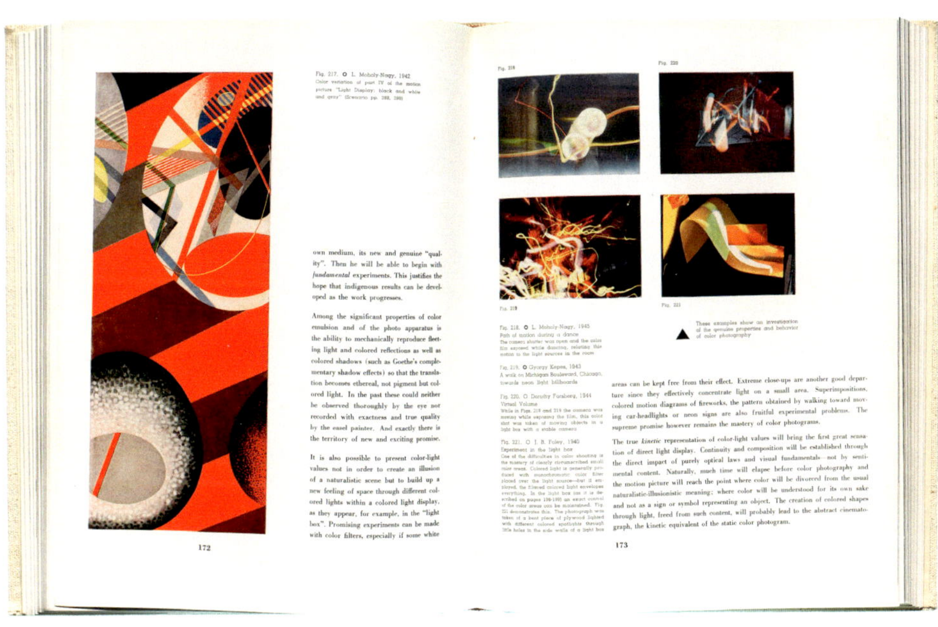

1947

LÁSZLÓ MOHOLY-NAGY (designer/author)

Vision in Motion, a posthumously published expansion of his book *The New Vision*, letterpress, 11⅛ × 9 inches (283 × 228 mm), Chicago.

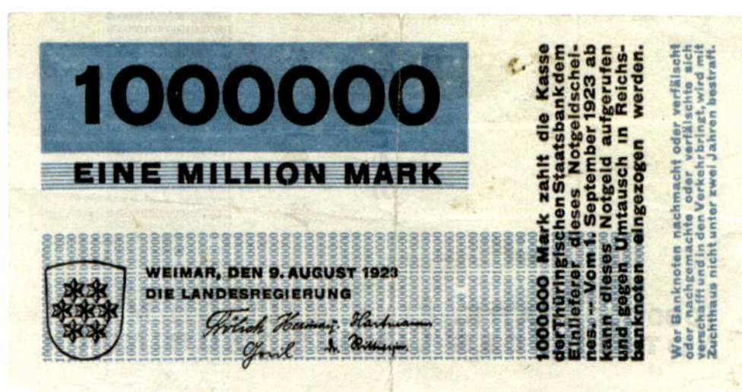

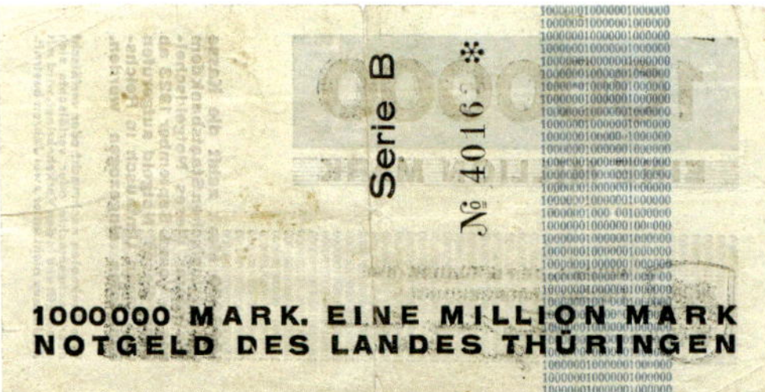

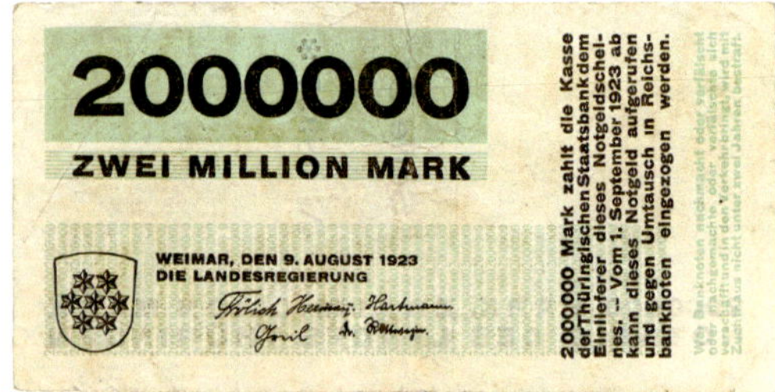

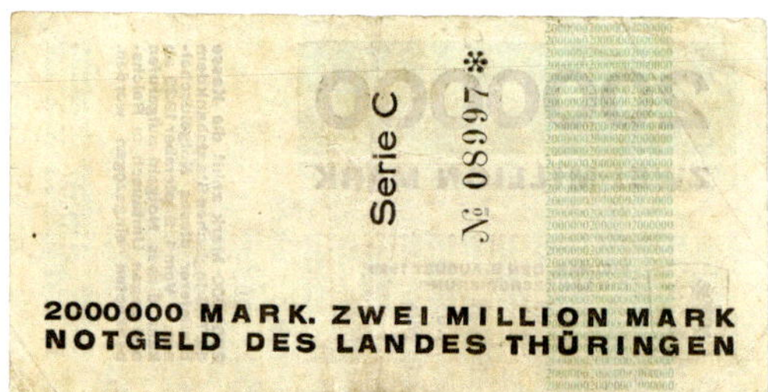

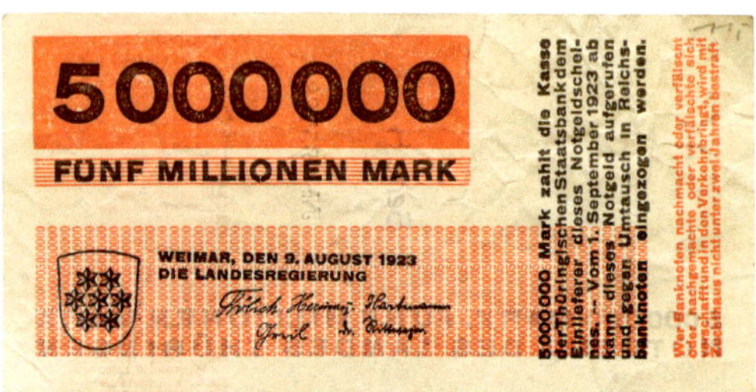

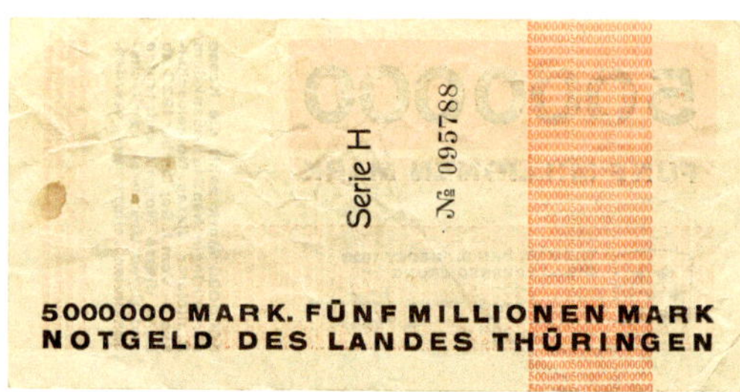

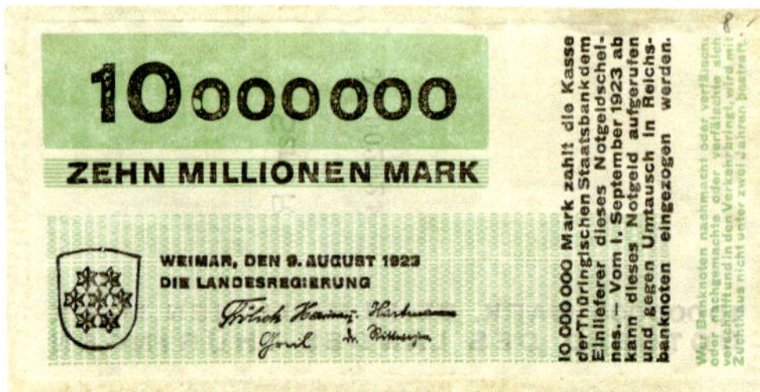

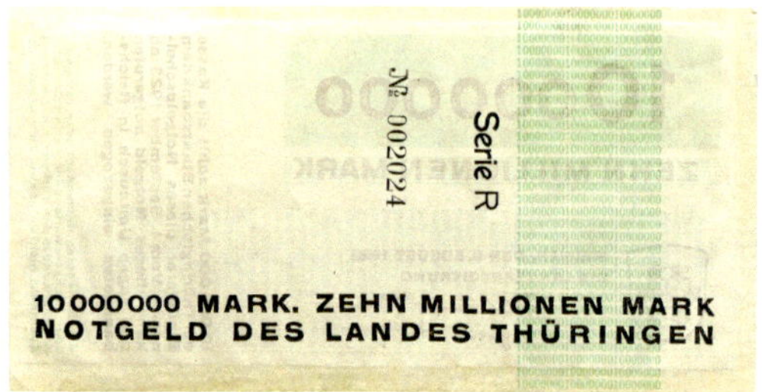

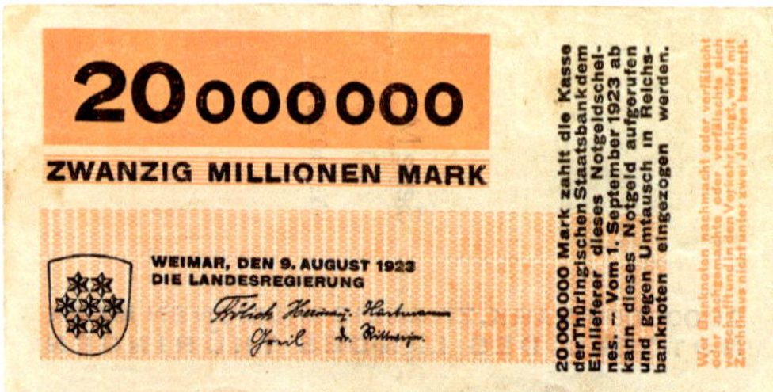

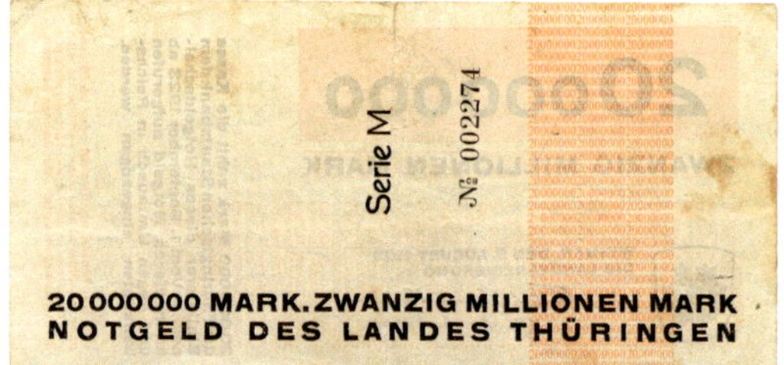

1923

HERBERT BAYER

Inflation currency for the Thuringian state government (front and back), letterpress, 2¾ × 5½ inches (70 × 140 mm), Weimar.

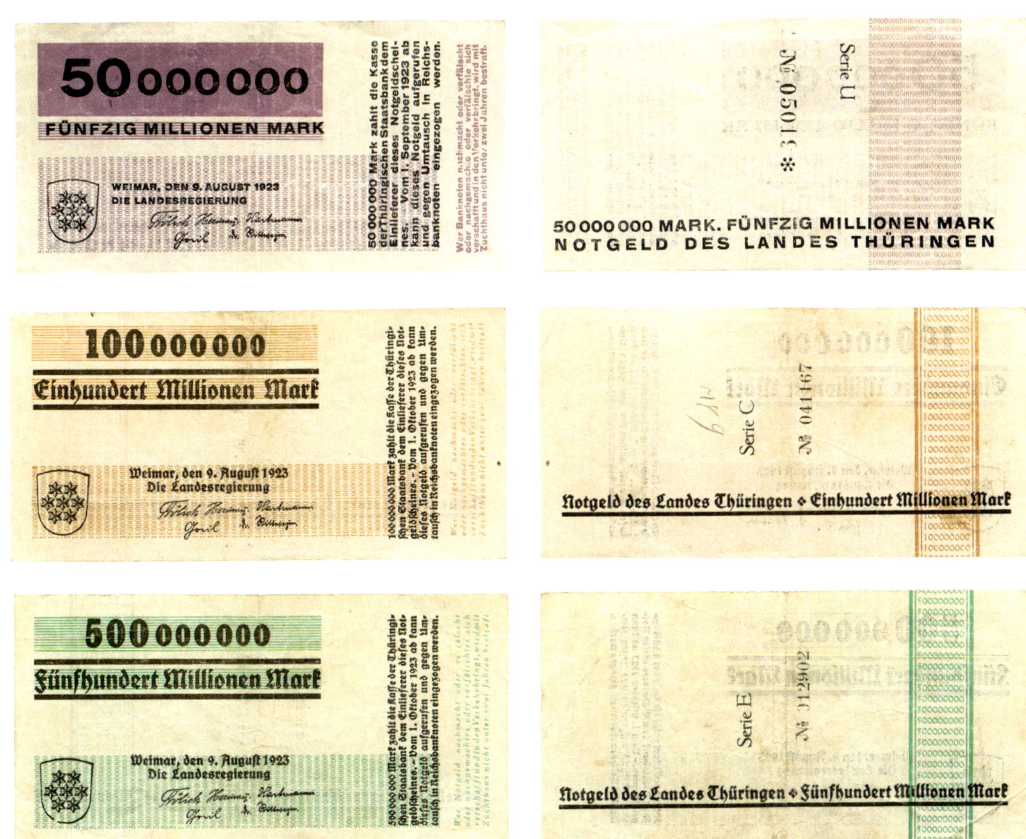

Austrian-born Herbert Bayer was only twenty-three—and still a student at the Bauhaus—when the state commissioned this *notgeld* (emergency money). Its astronomical denominations reflect the German hyperinflation crisis after World War I. Designed nearly overnight for immediate printing, and relying on only the type available at the press, Bayer's banknotes are unique in their simplicity, with mainly Breite Grotesk (the bold sans serif commonly used at the Bauhaus) and none of the ornamentation, dense pattern, or portraiture that decorate most legal tender. The design's only nonfunctional aspect is its use of color: While each note was printed in black and one of several choices of second ink, each denomination appears in the full range of hues, so a bill's color does not indicate its value. ● After leaving the Bauhaus in 1928, Bayer worked in Berlin for the Dorland advertising agency while freelancing for magazines such as *The New Line* (*Die neue Linie*) and *Vogue Paris*; his 1938 move to America saw him apply his penchants for photomontage and infographics to *Life*, *Fortune*, General Electric, the Container Corporation of America, and many other publications and businesses. ●

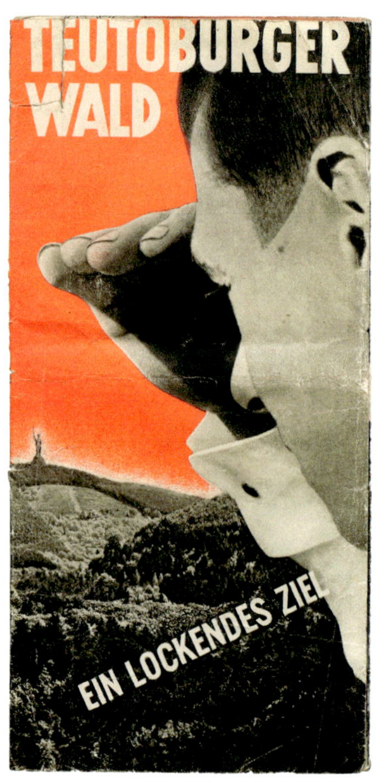

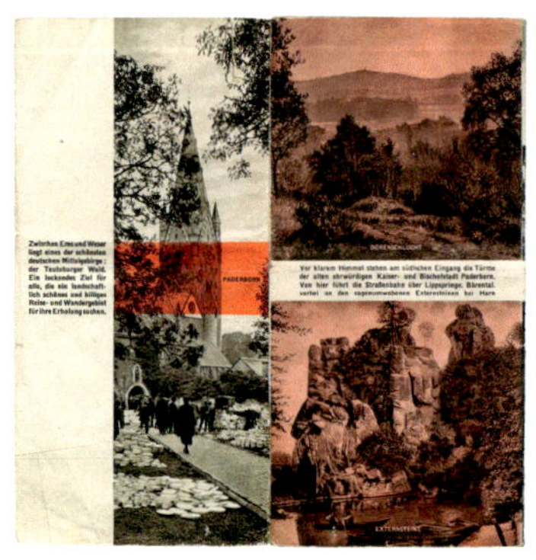

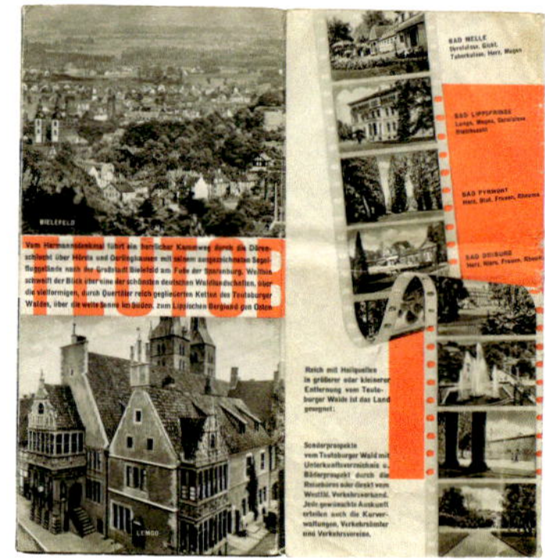

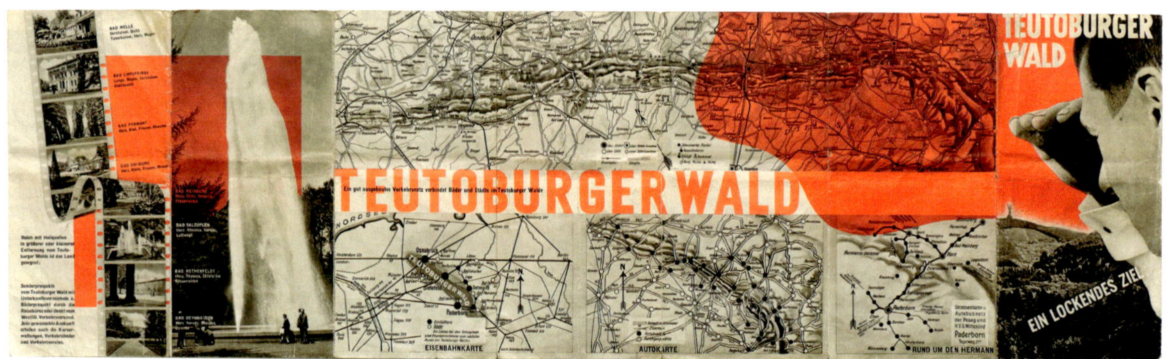

1926

HERBERT BAYER

Tourism brochure for the Teutoburg Forest (Teutoburger Wald), letterpress, 8¼ × 4⅛ inches (210 × 105 mm) folded, 8¼ × 28⅜ inches (210 × 720 mm) unfolded, Leipzig.

DESSAU

Kostenlose Auskunft erteilt das Verkehrsbüro des Gemeinnützigen Vereins Dessau e. V.
Kavalierstraße 28,
neben dem Kaffee „Altes Theater" (F. 3800)
Geöffnet werktäglich 9-19 Uhr.
Führer von Dessau und Umgeg. mit Karten.
Nachweis von Hotel- und Privat-Unterkunft.
Vorverkauf v. Einlaßkarten z. Friedrich-Theater und zu allen bedeutenden Veranstaltungen.
Alle Eisenbahn-, Schiffs- und Flugkarten.
Amtliche Preise - Kein Aufschlag
Reisegepäck-, Reise- und Flug-Unfallversicherung.
Beschaffung von Paß-Visa.
Vorbereitung von Kongressen und Tagungen.

Herausgegeben vom Gemeinnützigen Verein Dessau

Dessau, Hauptstadt des Freistaates Anhalt mit über 78000 Einwohnern, liegt an der Elbe und Mulde in deren fruchtbarer, wasserreicher Niederung. Seit Jahrhunderten Residenz der anhaltischen Fürsten und Herzöge, war Dessau lange Zeit hauptsächlich Beamtenstadt und Pensionopolis. Seit kurzem dagegen vollzieht sich der große Umformungsprozeß zu einer wirtschaftlich-industriell wie künstlerisch und kulturell führenden Stadt, die sich den anderen mitteldeutschen Hauptplätzen gleichberechtigt zur Seite zu stellen vermag.

Will man Dessau eine „Industriestadt" nennen, so steht ihr mit gleichem Rechte auch der Titel einer „Kunststadt" zu. Das Friedrich-Theater, Erbe des einstigen Hoftheaters, führt dessen hohe Tradition im Einklang mit den Gegebenheiten der Gegenwart und ihres künstlerischen Schaffens fort, sein Ruf wird weithin gehört und beachtet.

1

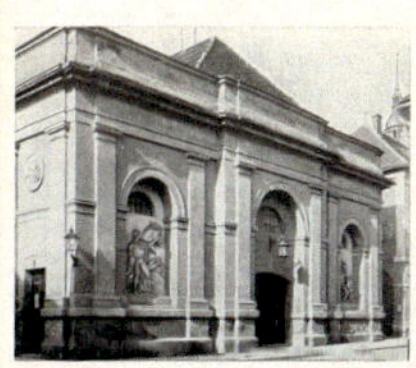

Friedrich-Theater

Sammlungen, wie die Anhaltische Landes-Gemälde-Galerie und das Museum für Naturkunde und Vorgeschichte enthalten über das lokale Maß weit hinausgehendes künstlerisches wie wissenschaftliches Material und die große Anhaltische Landesbücherei ist für die Stadt Dessau und das Land Anhalt ein wissenschaftliches Zentrum ersten Ranges.

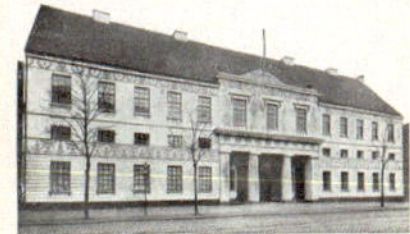

Palais Reina (Georgs-Palais) Gemäldegalerie

2

Besondere Bedeutung hat für den künstlerischen Ruf Dessaus auch das Bauhaus — Hochschule für Gestaltung — gewonnen, durch dessen Tätigkeit im Sinne der Erforschung und Beeinflussung moderner Kulturtendenzen Dessau im Brennpunkt des internationalen Kunstinteresses steht.

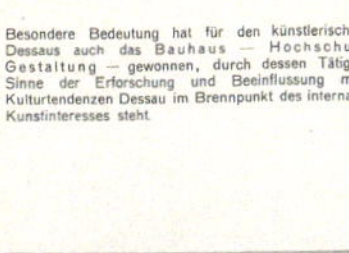

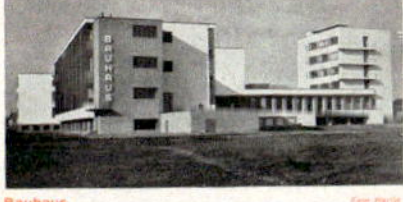

Bauhaus

Eine leistungsfähige Industrie gibt der Silhouette der Stadt ein eigenes Gepräge. Werke von Rang und Weltbedeutung haben hier ihren Sitz; z. B. die Deutsche Continental-Gas-Gesellschaft, die Junkers-Werke, deren Flugplatz im Westen der Stadt sich ausbreitet, Maschinenbau-Betriebe, wie „Bamag" und Polysius, Brauereien, wie Schultheiß-Patzenhofer u. a., Zuckerraffinerien, eine Waggonfabrik und holzindustrielle Werke.

3

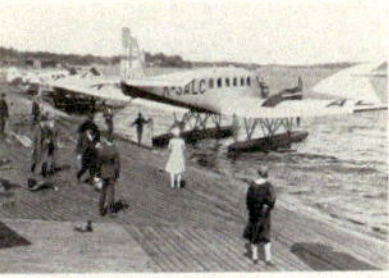

Junkers-Flugzeug

Altes und Neues reichen sich in der Stadt die Hand. Aus der Zeit nach dem Mittelalter haben die spätgotische Marienkirche aus dem 16. Jahrhundert wie das Herzogliche Schloß (Renaissance und Rokoko) neben schönen alten Bürgerhäusern am Großen Markt Anspruch auf Beachtung.

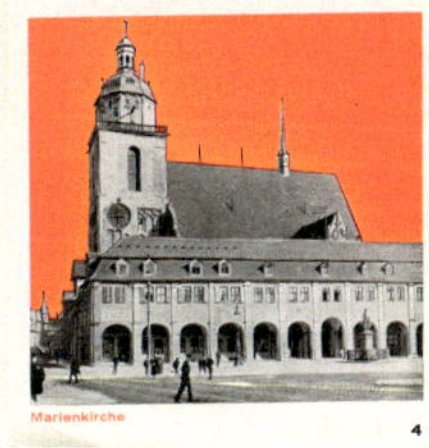

Marienkirche

4

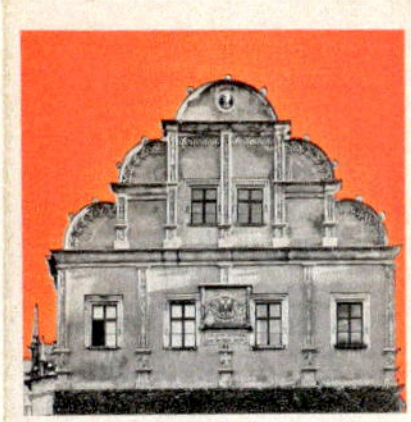

Herzogliches Schloß, Westgiebel

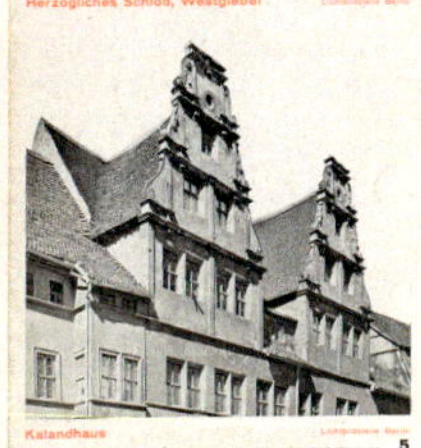

Kalandhaus

5

DESSAU

die Stadt alter Kultur und neuer Arbeitsstätten

Erst um 1800 hebt sich das bis dahin bescheidene Kunstniveau der Stadt; damals ist sie ein Kulturzentrum ersten Ranges gewesen, dominierend die Künste (Friedrich Wilhelm Freiherr v. Erdmannsdorff, der Architekt des Frühklassizismus in Deutschland) und die Pädagogik (Basedows Philanthropin, dessen Reliquien die Landesbücherei aufbewahrt). Nach 1800 verliert sich das meiste davon, doch baut Carlo Ignazio Pozzi noch wertvolle spätklassizistische Bauten (Säulenhalle des Alten Theaters, Palais Reina).

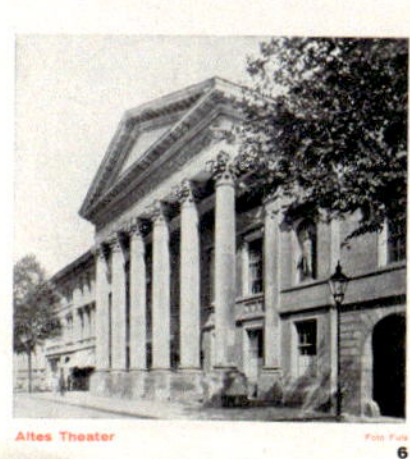

Altes Theater

6

Als in späteren Jahrzehnten die Stadt wuchs, erstanden auch neue Großbauten (Rathaus, Mausoleum).

Mausoleum

Aber erst in unserem Jahrhundert nahm Dessau den großen Aufschwung nach jeglicher Richtung. Damals schuf es soziale und hygienische Anlagen, wie Schwimmhalle und Krematorium, baute Alfred Messel das nach ihm benannte Messelhaus, heute städtisches Repräsentationsgebäude. Und gegenwärtig ist auf Grund großzügiger Eingemeindungspolitik Groß-Dessau zur Stadt der Siedlungen geworden; rings um die Altstadt legt sich ein Kranz weitausgedehnter Siedlungsviertel, in denen vom althergebrachten bis zum modernsten flachgedeckten Betonbau alle Typen des Siedlungshauses vertreten sind.

7

Mit seiner wasser- und waldreichen Umgebung ist Dessau engstens verknüpft. Von allen Teilen der Stadt ist man in kurzem inmitten der um 1800 angelegten wundervollen Parkanlagen (Georgium, Beckerbruch, Kühnau, Luisium), die alle den Einfluß der klassizistischen und romantischen Gedankenwelt darlegen. Darüber hinaus ziehen sich an Elbe und Mulde meilenweite, wildreiche Forsten hin — ein Grüngürtel, den manche andre Stadt Dessau neiden kann.

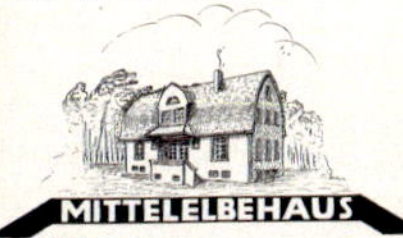

Jugendherberge

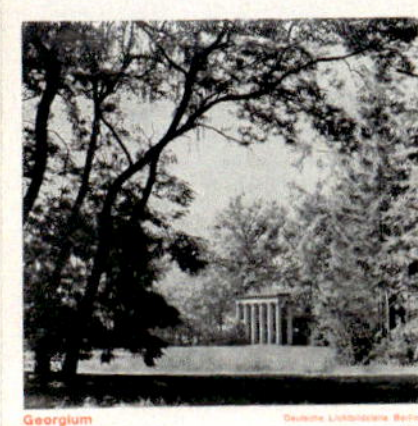

Georgium

8

Zu den bekanntesten Ausflugszielen gehören die Parks von Oranienbaum — eine regelmäßige Barockschöpfung mit großer Achse durch Stadt, Schloß und Park und „englischen" Erweiterungen um 1800 — und besonders der von Wörlitz. Hier ist um 1800 ein gartenkünstlerisches Paradies erstanden. Das Zeitalter der Empfindsamkeit, Klassizismus und gotische Romantik haben im wasserdurchzogenen Park und seinen Gebäuden ein Idyll ohnegleichen geschaffen.

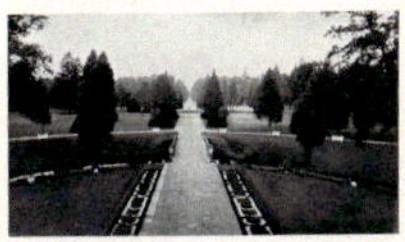

Oranienbaum

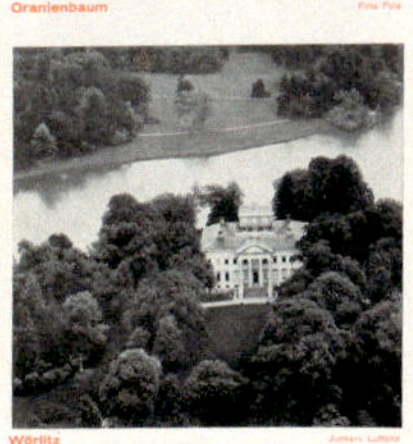

Wörlitz

9

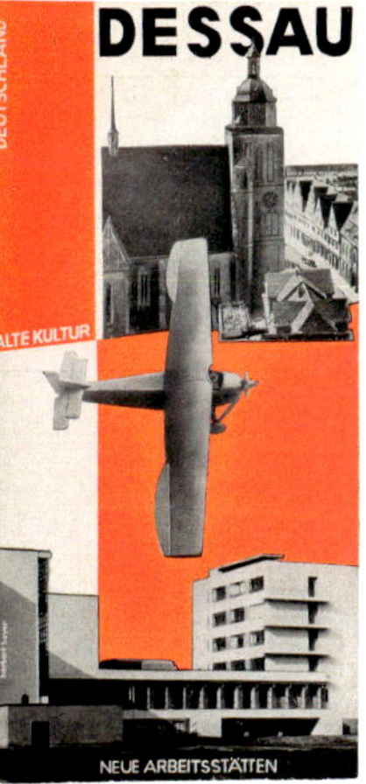

1926

HERBERT BAYER

Tourism brochure for the city of Dessau, "Dessau, Germany, Old Culture, New Workplaces" ("Dessau, Deutschland, alte Kultur, neue Arbeitsstätten"), letterpress, 8¼ × 4⅛ inches (210 × 105 mm) folded, 8¼ x 16½ inches (210 × 418 mm) unfolded, Dessau.

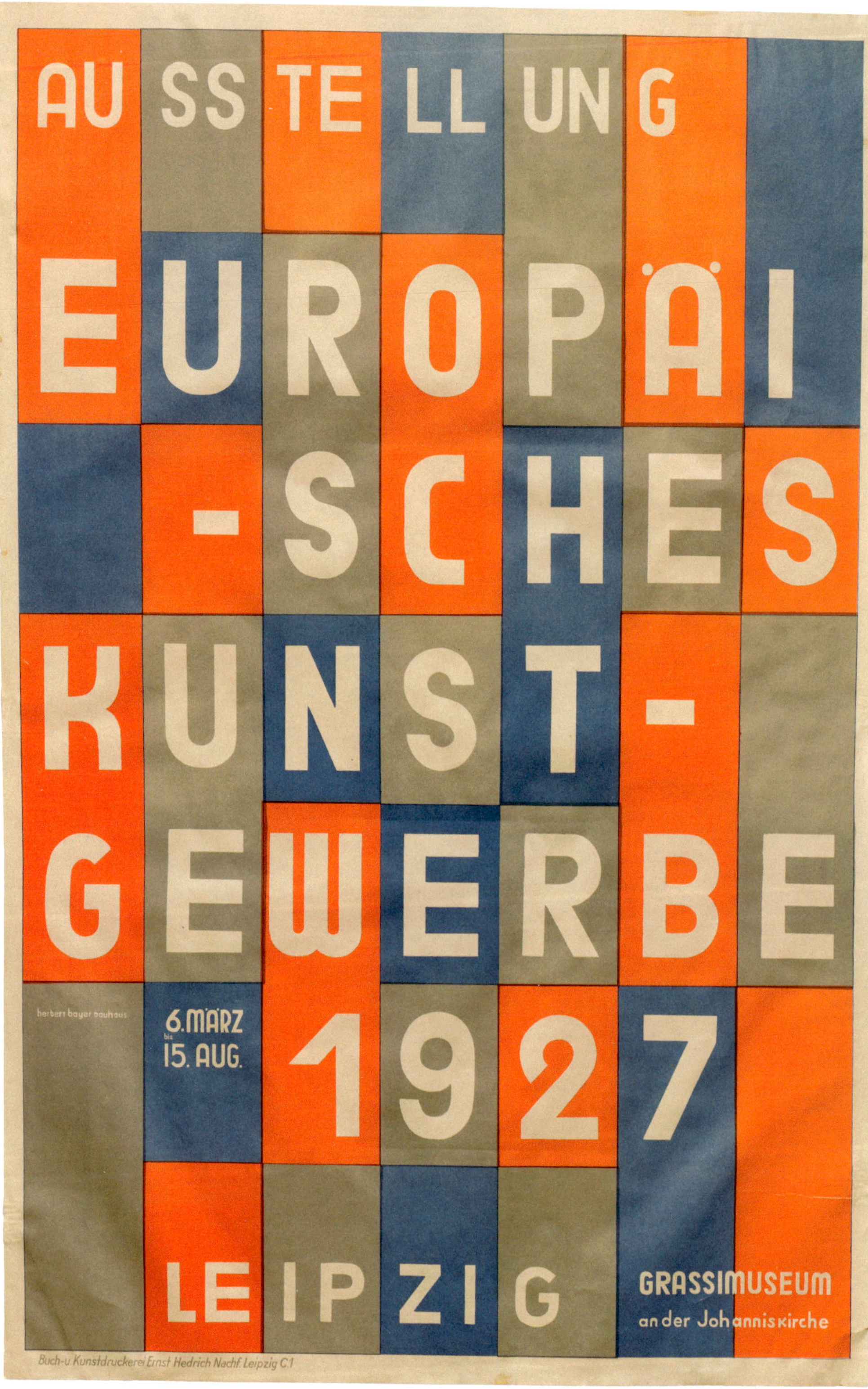
AU SS TE LL UN G
EUROPÄI
-SCHES
KUNST-
GEWERBE
herbert bayer bauhaus
6. MÄRZ
bis
15. AUG.
1927
LEIPZIG
GRASSIMUSEUM
an der Johanniskirche
Buch-u. Kunstdruckerei Ernst Hedrich Nachf. Leipzig C.1

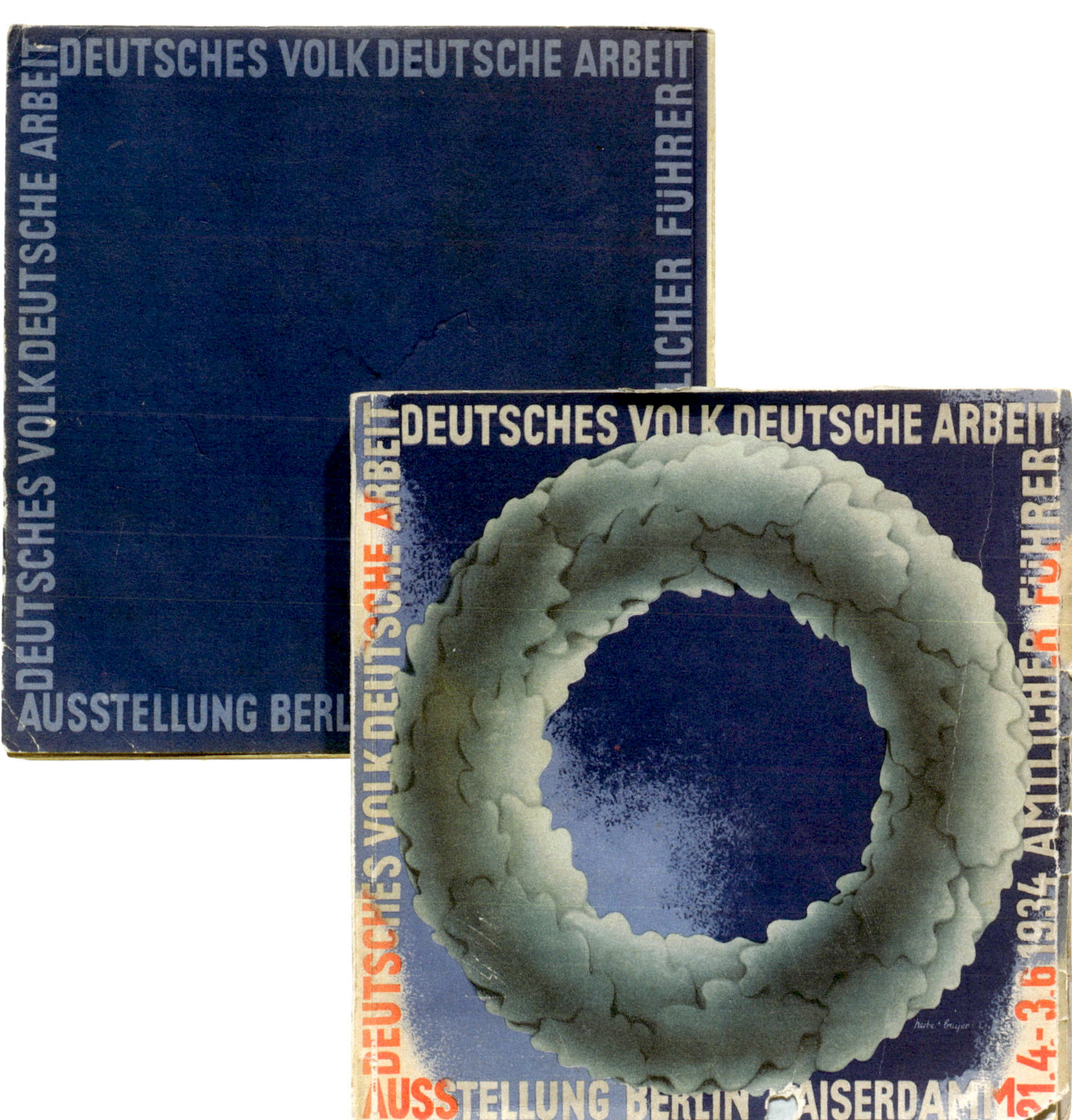

1934

HERBERT BAYER

Front and back cover of the exhibition catalog for *German People, German Labor* (*Deutsches Volk, Deutsche Arbeit*), lithograph, 8¼ × 8¼ inches (208 × 208 mm), Berlin.

1927

HERBERT BAYER

Exhibition poster for the *European Applied Arts Exhibition* (*Ausstellung europäisches Kunstgewerbe*), lithograph, 35¼ × 23¼ inches (895 × 590 mm), Leipzig.

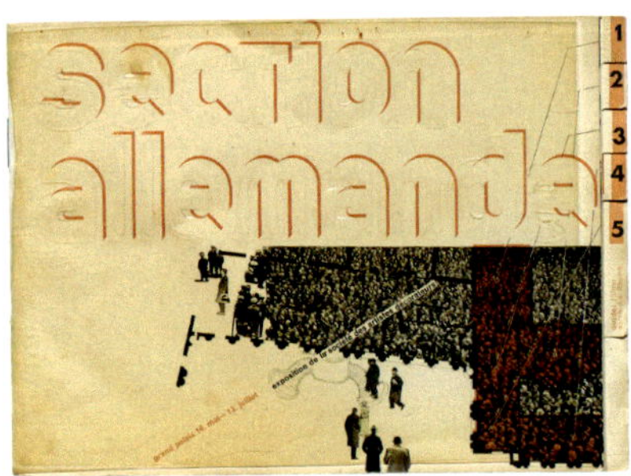

1930

HERBERT BAYER

Section Allemande, catalog for the German section of the *Exhibition of the Society of Decorative Artists* (*Exposition de la Société des Artistes Décorateurs*), letterpress with embossed cellophane cover, 5⅞ × 8¼ inches (149 × 210 mm), Berlin.

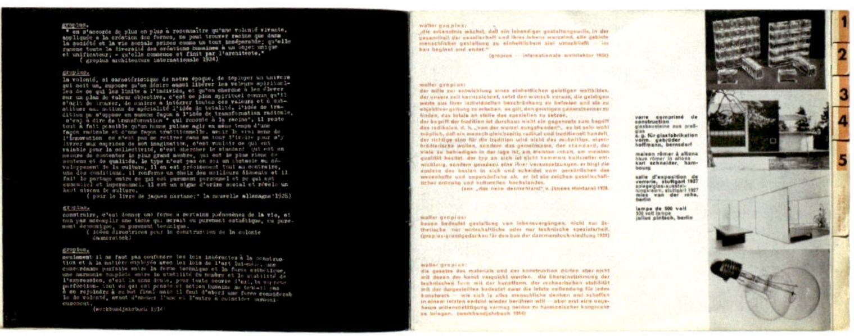

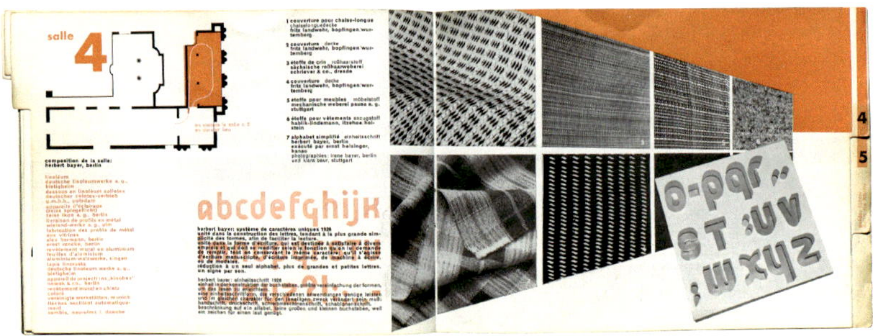

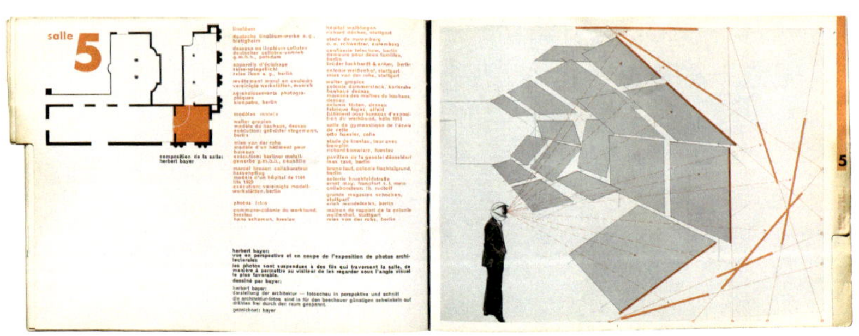

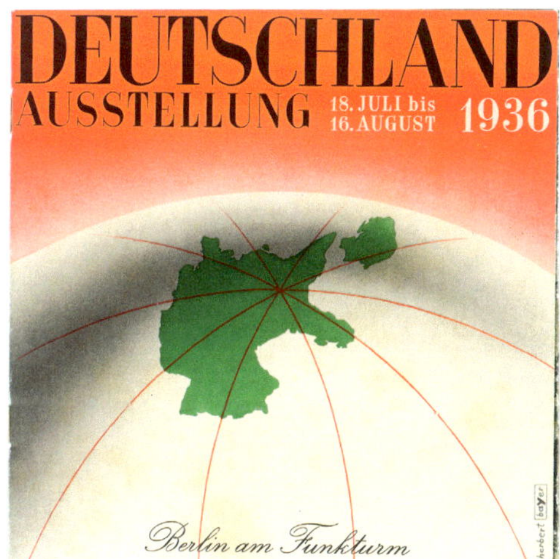

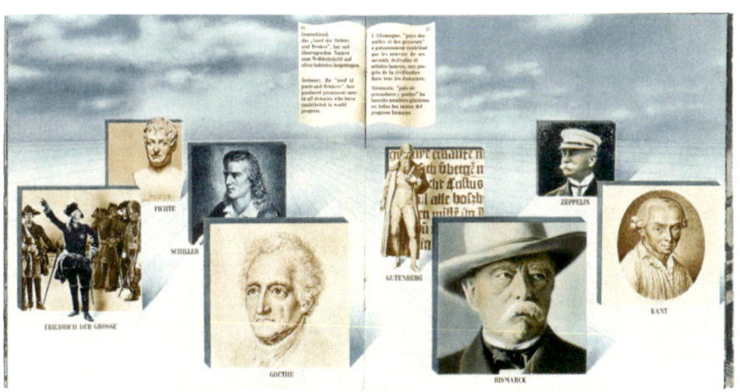

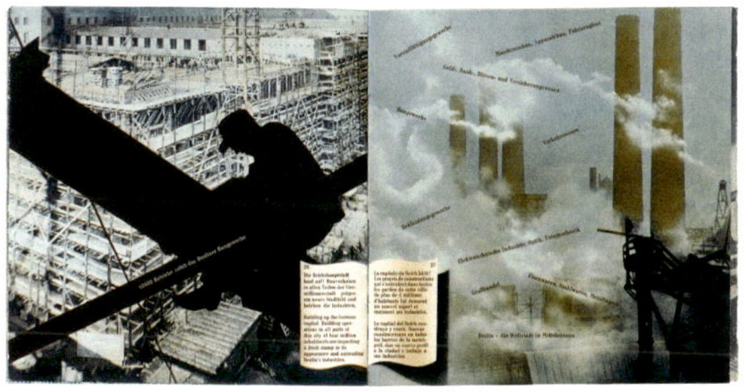

1936

HERBERT BAYER

Catalog for the *Germany Exhibition* (*Deutschland Ausstellung*), lithograph, 8¼ × 8⅜ inches (212 × 214 mm), Berlin.

After his time at the Bauhaus, Bayer worked as a commercial designer in Berlin for ten years. Later, he recalled this period with regret as his "advertising purgatory," likely because—among his many commissions—he executed several projects for Nazi propaganda campaigns. This work mostly took the form of exhibition catalogs, such as books for the *German People, German Labor* exhibition (see page 175) and the *Germany Exhibition*, shown here, which coincided with the 1936 Olympics in Berlin. (Walter Gropius, Joost Schmidt, and other Bauhauslers were also pressed into contributing to these and similar projects.) While there is no evidence that Bayer was sympathetic to Nazi ideology—his wife and daughter were Jewish, and he considered himself apolitical—his participation remains an uncomfortable part of his legacy. Ultimately, his efforts to remain neutral did not spare him persecution: By 1937, he was out of favor with the German government, and at least one of his paintings was included in the Nazis' *Degenerate Art Exhibition* (*Entartete Kunst Ausstellung*), a showing of confiscated modernist works. In 1938, Gropius arranged for Bayer to organize the first Bauhaus exhibition in the United States at the Museum of Modern Art (see page 184), in part to fund his move out of Germany. ●

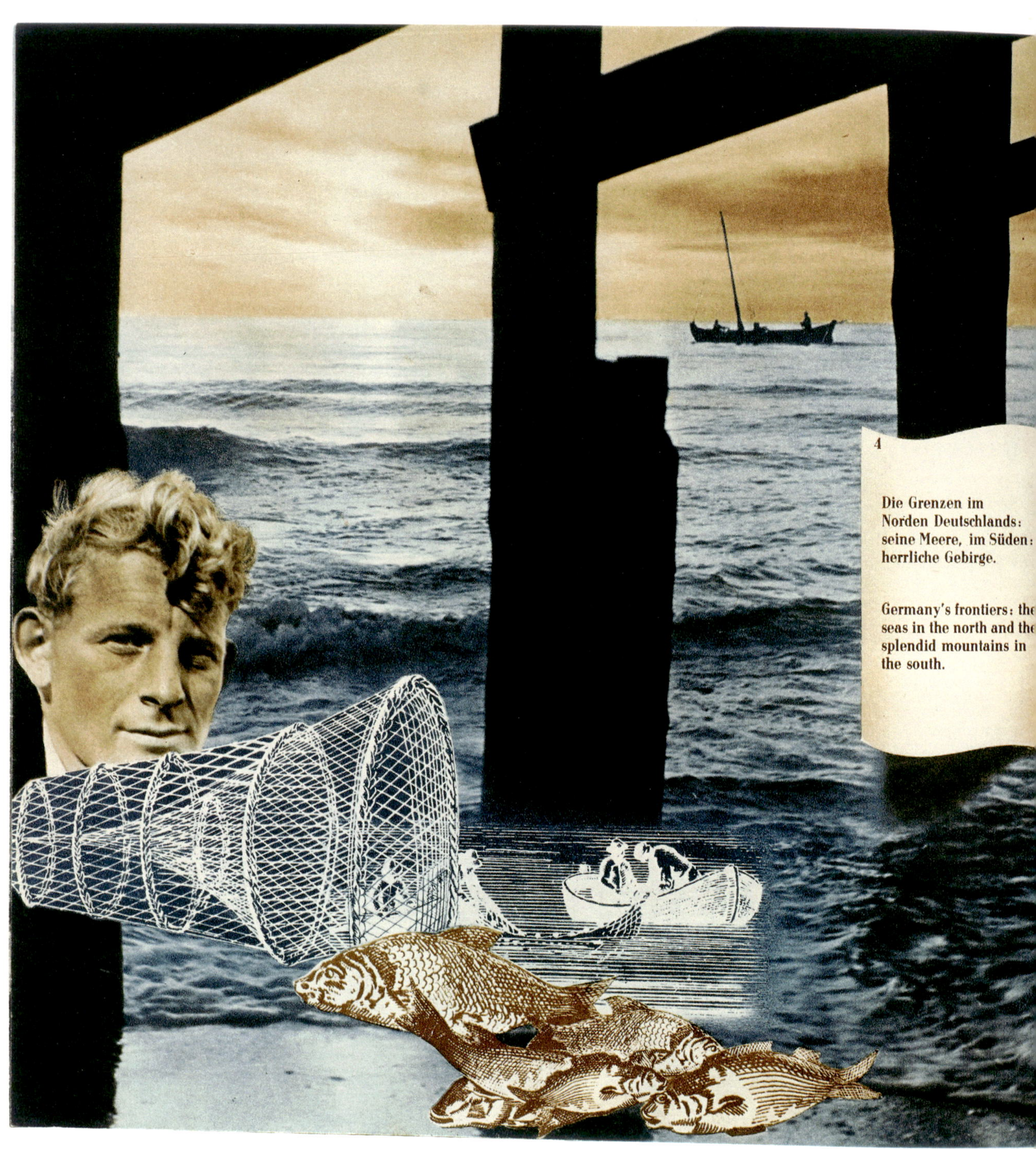
4
Die Grenzen im
Norden Deutschlands:
seine Meere, im Süden:
herrliche Gebirge.
Germany's frontiers: the
seas in the north and the
splendid mountains in
the south.

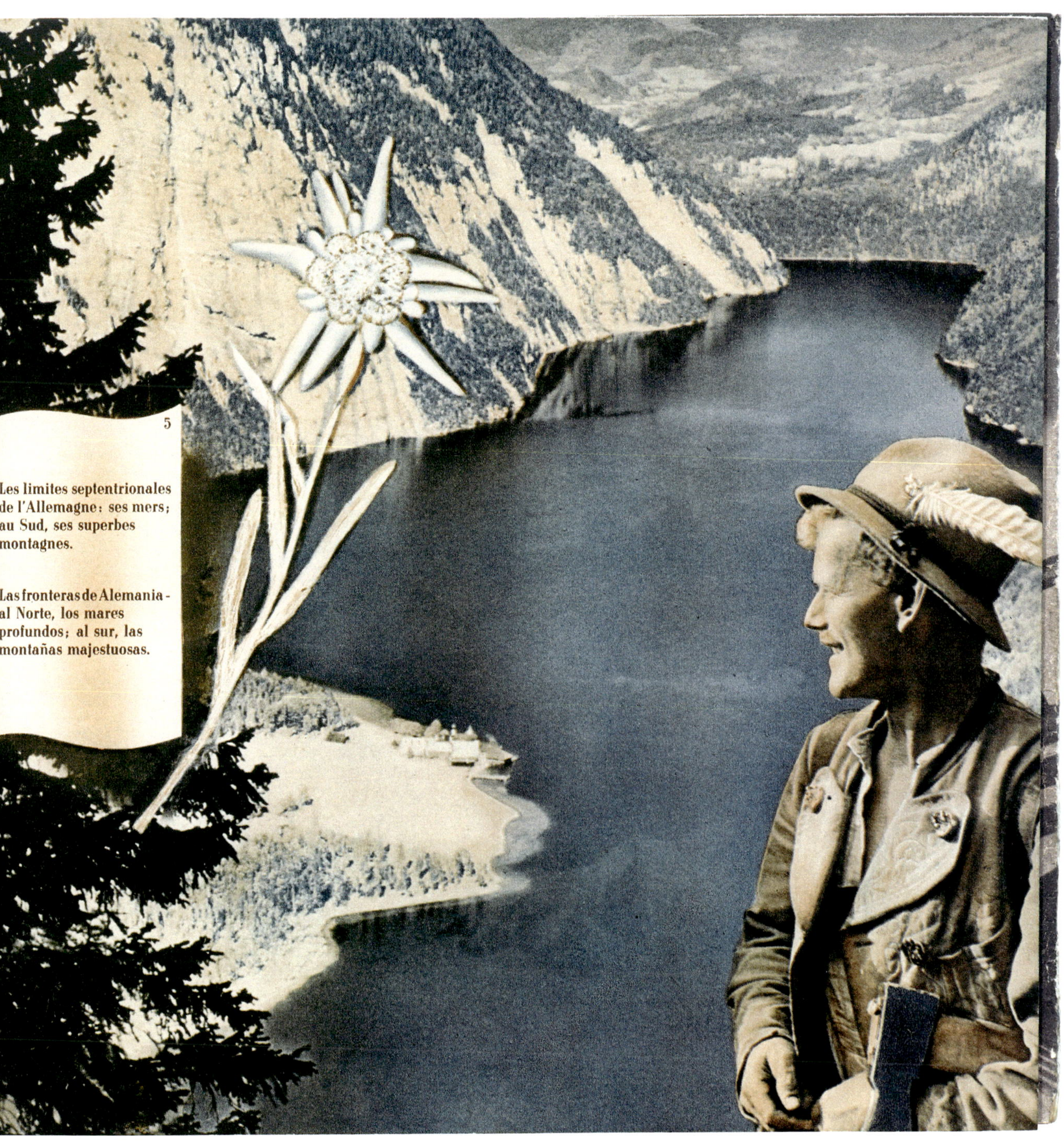
5
Les limites septentrionales de l'Allemagne: ses mers; au Sud, ses superbes montagnes.
Las fronteras de Alemania - al Norte, los mares profundos; al sur, las montañas majestuosas.

1931

HERBERT BAYER (cover designer)

The New Line (*Die neue Linie*), vol. 2, no. 10, letterpress, 14⅜ × 10⅝ inches (365 × 270 mm), Leipzig and Berlin.

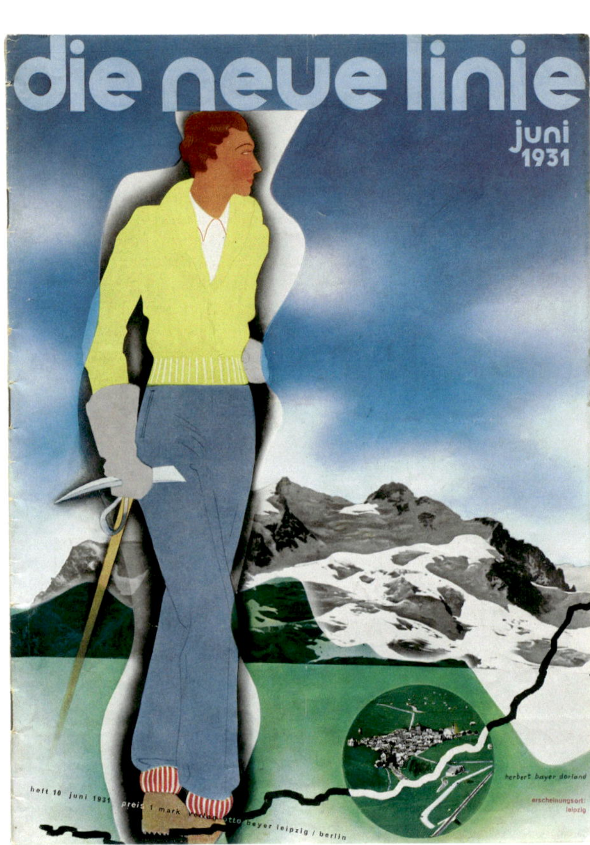

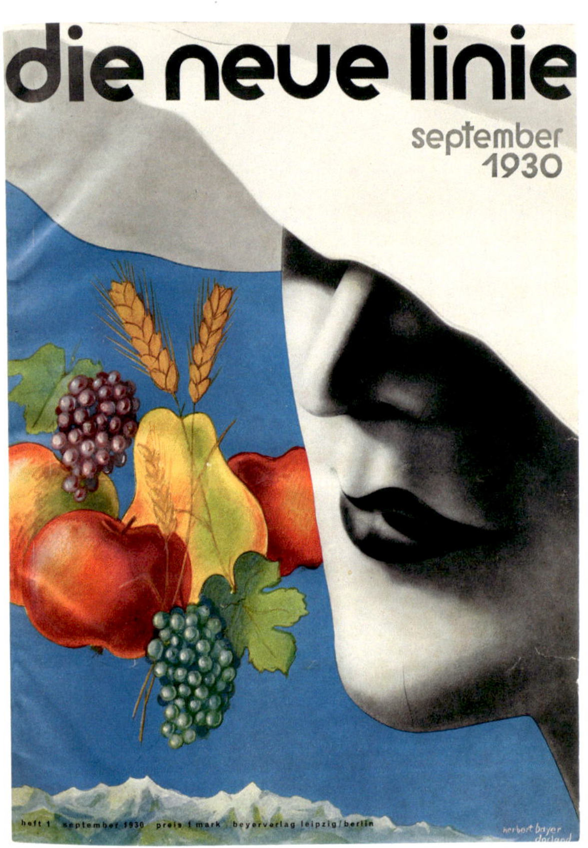

1930

HERBERT BAYER (cover designer)

The New Line (*Die neue Linie*), vol. 2, no. 1, letterpress, 14⅜ × 10⅝ inches (365 × 270 mm), Leipzig and Berlin.

1936

HERBERT BAYER (cover designer)

The New Line (*Die neue Linie*), vol. 7, no. 11, letterpress, 14⅜ × 10⅝ inches (365 × 270 mm), Leipzig and Berlin.

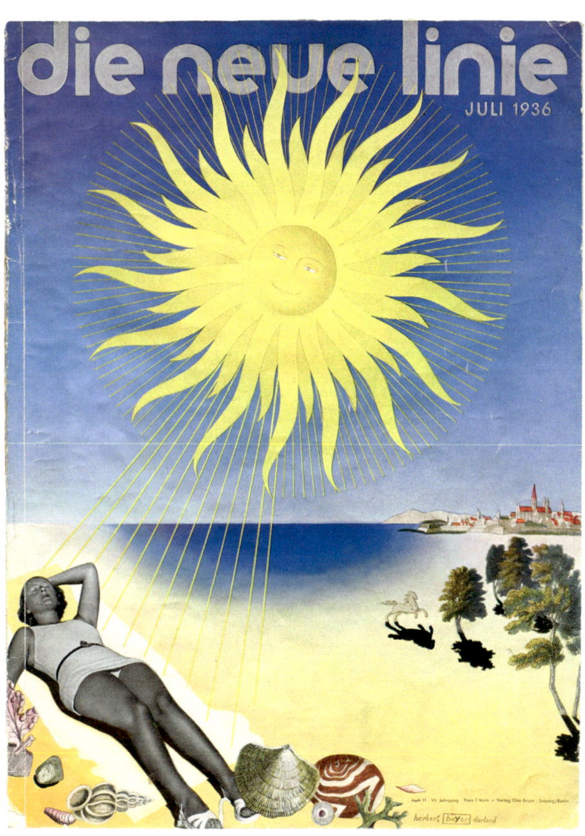

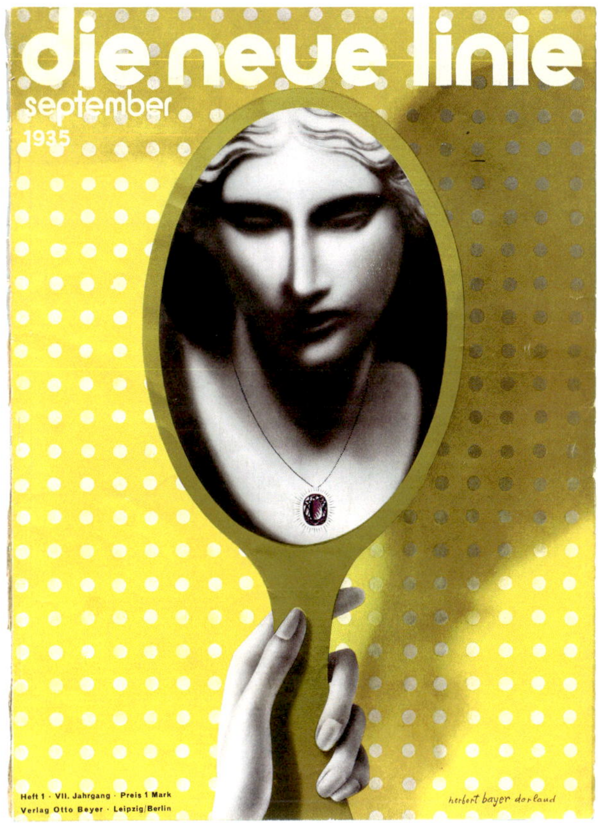

1935

HERBERT BAYER (cover designer)

The New Line (*Die neue Linie*), vol. 7, no. 1, letterpress, 14⅜ × 10⅝ inches (365 × 270 mm), Leipzig and Berlin.

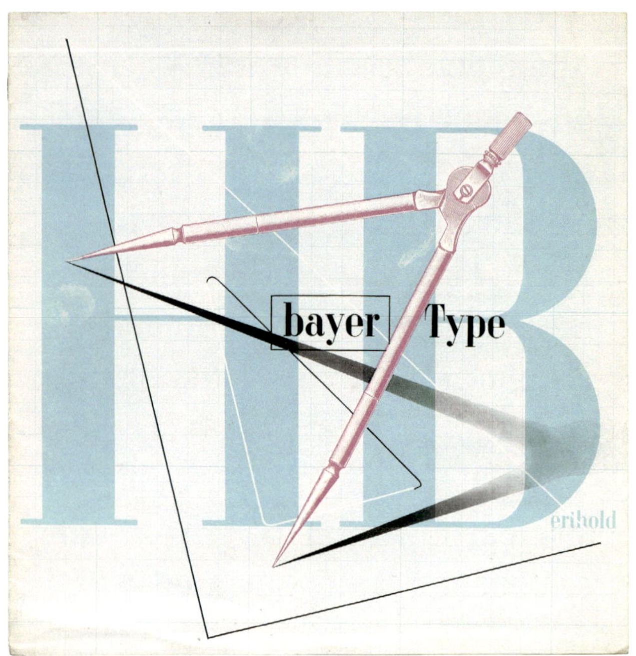

1933

HERBERT BAYER (type designer/type specimen designer)
Type specimen for Bayer Type, letterpress, 8⅛ × 8⅛ inches (206 × 206 mm), Berlin.

Herbert Bayer's idealistic vision for his Universal Type—a geometrically derived, sans serif, single-case alphabet designed during his time at the Bauhaus—never made it beyond initial draft proposals (see pages 204–205). However, he applied some of its principles to a more traditional antiqua typeface, released in 1933 as a metal font by Berthold Type Foundry and called Bayer Type, shown in the specimen here. While Bayer Type does have serifs and a set of capital letters, it still demonstrates Bayer's belief that modern typefaces for the machine age should abandon what he saw as an unnecessary basis in calligraphy or handwriting. As such, the letters of Bayer Type get their shape from simple geometric forms, as demonstrated by the use of circles in the diagram of the lowercase *a* at bottom left. Bayer Type turned out to be a success, and Bayer himself used it on the cover of the *Germany Exhibition* catalog (see page 177). ●

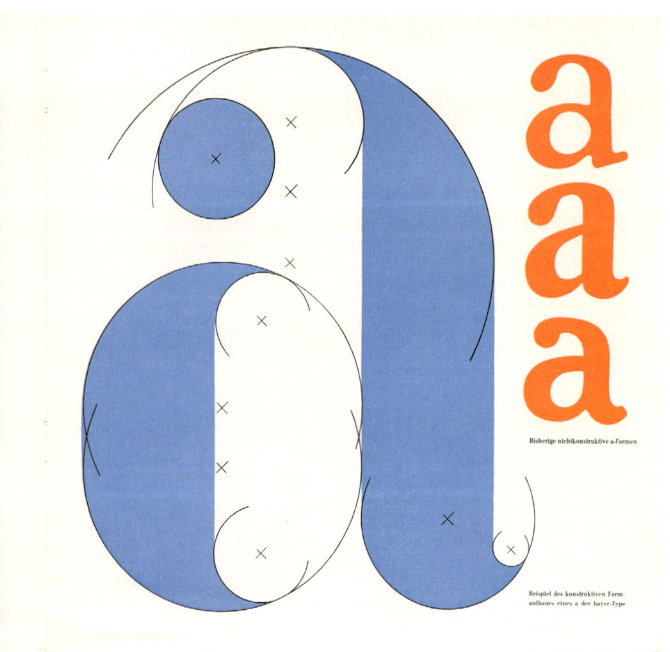

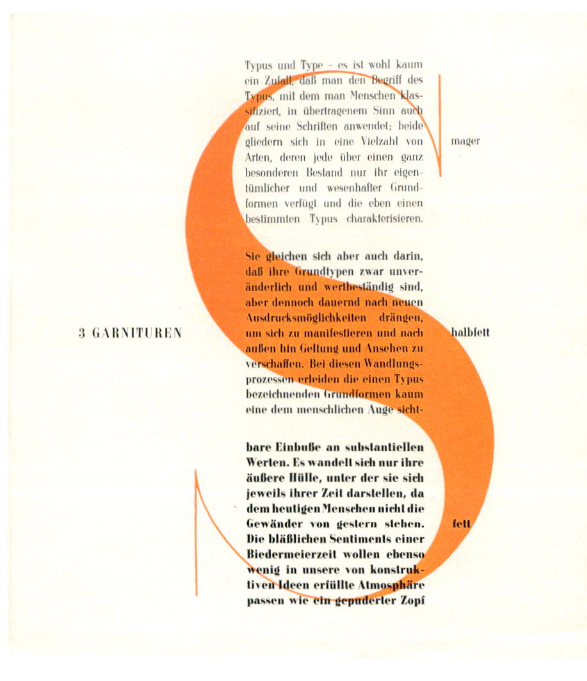

Typus und Type – es ist wohl kaum ein Zufall, daß man den Begriff des Typus, mit dem man Menschen klassifiziert, in übertragenem Sinn auch auf seine Schriften anwendet; beide gliedern sich in eine Vielzahl von Arten, deren jede über einen ganz besonderen Bestand nur ihr eigentümlicher und wesenhafter Grundformen verfügt und die eben einen bestimmten Typus charakterisieren.

mager

3 GARNITUREN

Sie gleichen sich aber auch darin, daß ihre Grundtypen zwar unveränderlich und wertbeständig sind, aber dennoch dauernd nach neuen Ausdrucksmöglichkeiten drängen, um sich zu manifestieren und nach außen hin Geltung und Ansehen zu verschaffen. Bei diesen Wandlungsprozessen erleiden die einen Typus bezeichnenden Grundformen kaum eine dem menschlichen Auge sicht-

halbfett

bare Einbuße an substantiellen Werten. Es wandelt sich nur ihre äußere Hülle, unter der sie sich jeweils ihrer Zeit darstellen, da dem heutigen Menschen nicht die Gewänder von gestern stehen. Die bläßlichen Sentiments einer Biedermeierzeit wollen ebenso wenig in unsere von konstruktiven Ideen erfüllte Atmosphäre passen wie ein gepuderter Zopf

fett

Alle guten Schriftformen wachsen aus einer erlebten Vergangenheit in eine lebendige Gegenwart hinein. So offenbaren sich auch in der neuen bayer -Type deutlich die Beständigkeit und der Wandel. Sie ist eine Antiqua von klassischer Haltung, jedoch was sie von allen anderen Schriften ihrer Gattung sichtbar unterscheidet, ist ihr entschiedener Wille zur Gegenwart

Gesetzt in bayer-Type halbfett, 36 Punkt

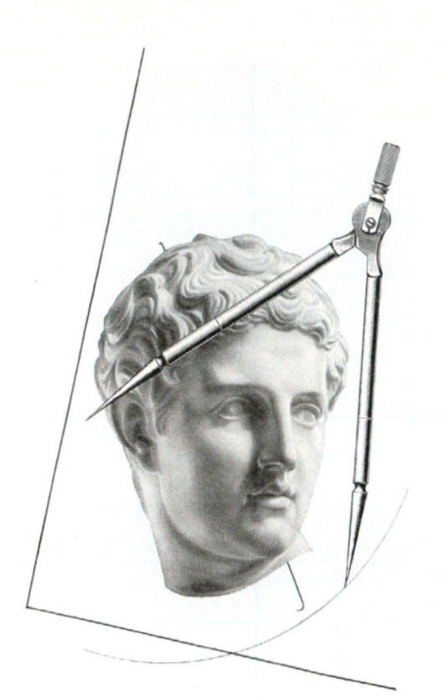

A a B b C c D d E

e f g h

F i G j H k I l J

m n o p

K q L r M s N t O

u v w x

P y Q z R ä S ö T

ü f ß fi

U fl V ff W æ X œ Y

Die Figuren der bayer-Type halbfett

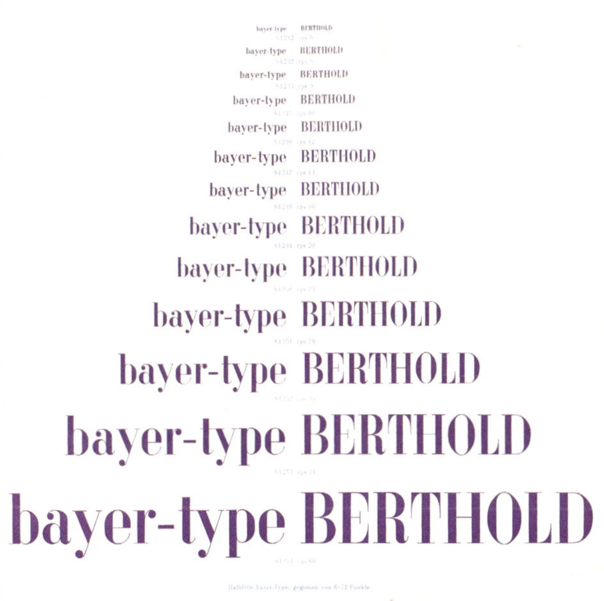

Halbfette bayer-Type, gegossen von 6–72 Punkte

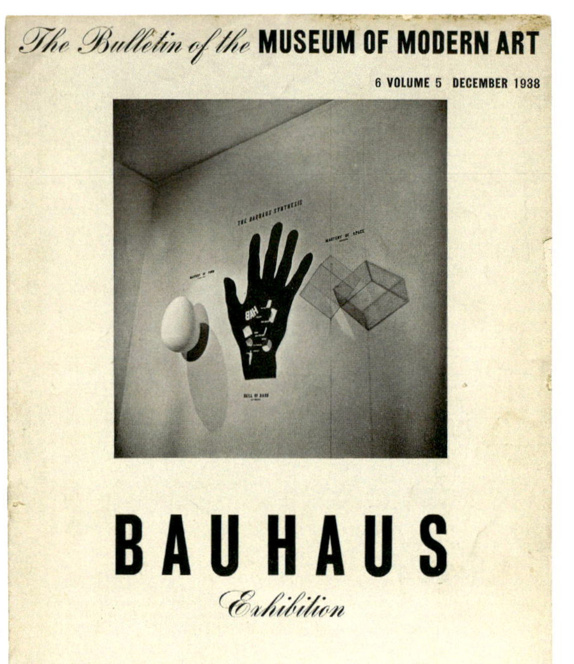

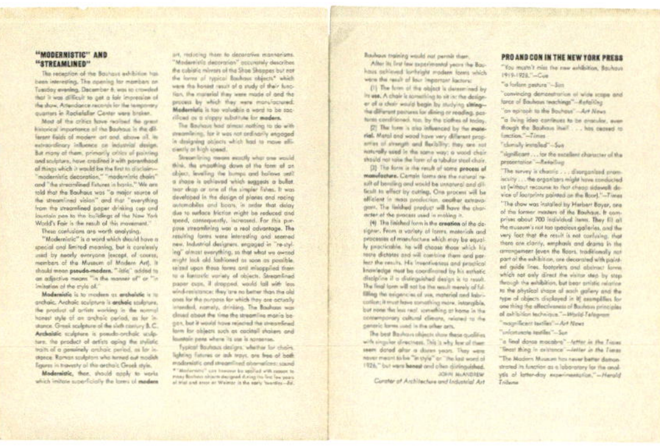

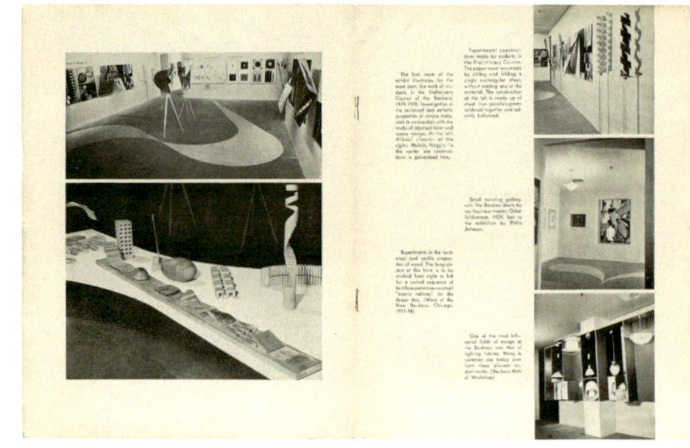

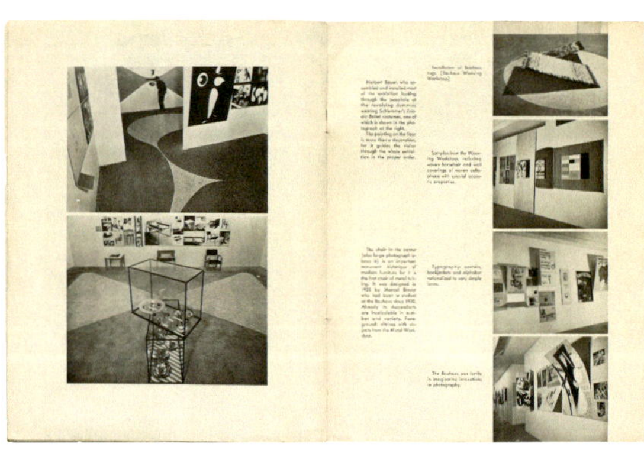

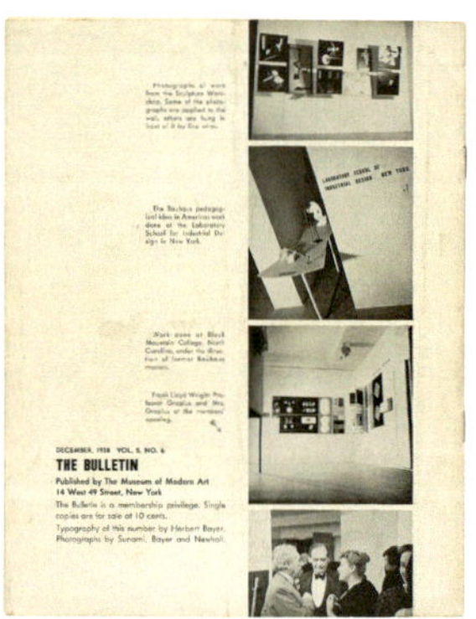

1938

HERBERT BAYER

The Bulletin of the Museum of Modern Art: Bauhaus Exhibition, vol. 5, no. 6, the first major Bauhaus show in the United States, letterpress, 9⅜ × 7⅜ inches (238 × 186 mm), New York.

1939

HERBERT BAYER (cover designer/contributor)

PM, vol. 6, no. 2, an issue of the art direction magazine that includes an insert composed by Bayer on design in advertising, letterpress, 7⅞ × 5⅜ inches (201 × 137 mm), New York.

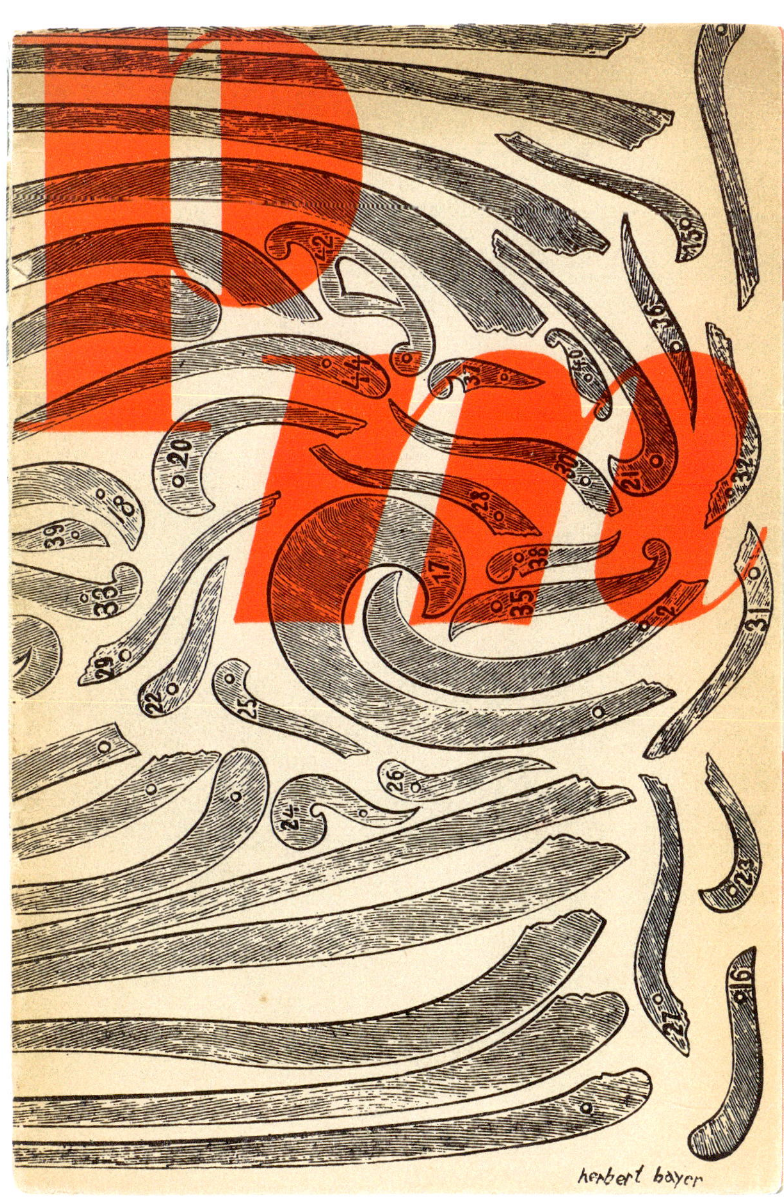

1942

HERBERT BAYER (cover designer)

Fortune, June 1942 issue, offset, 13⅝ × 10⅝ inches (345 × 270 mm), New York.

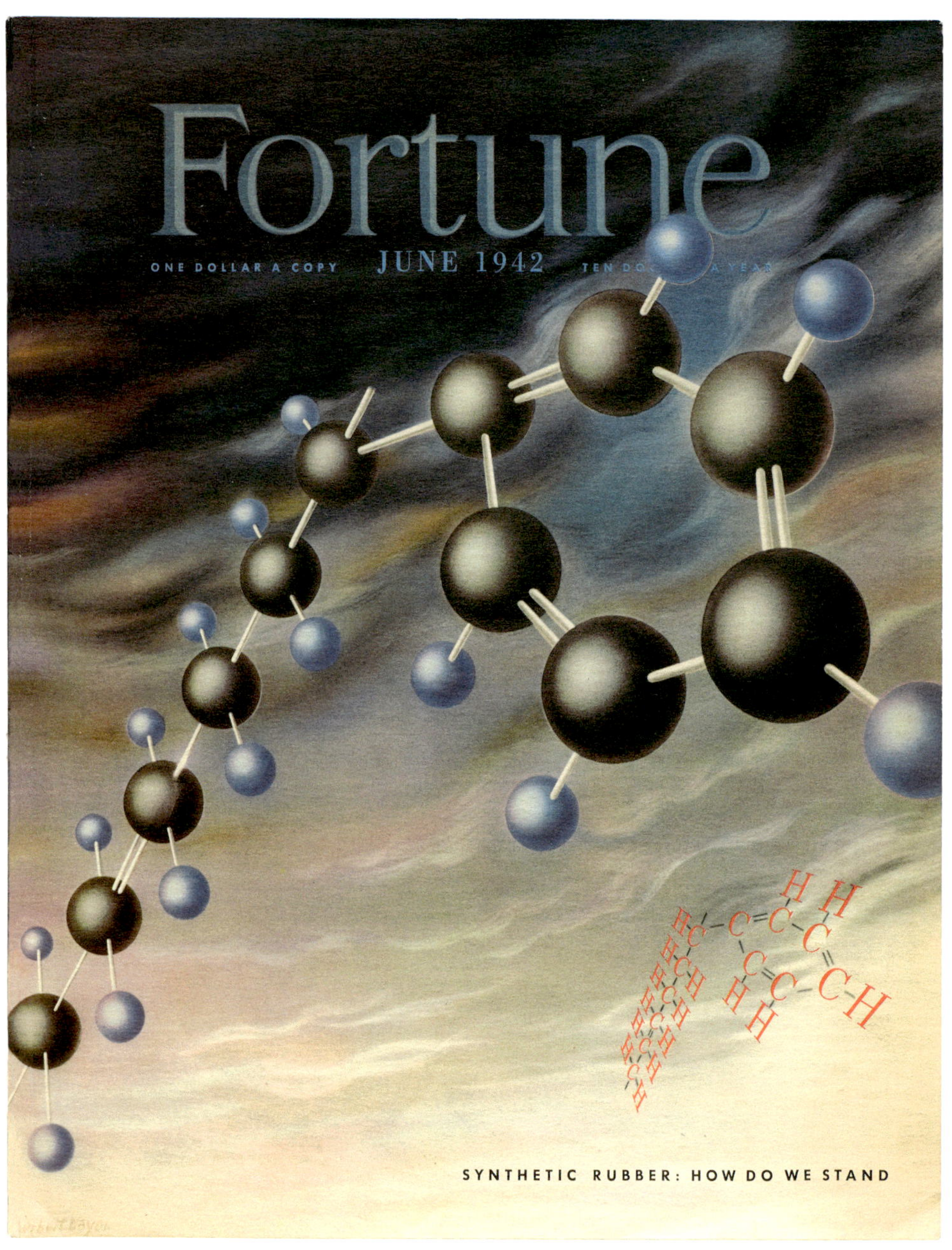

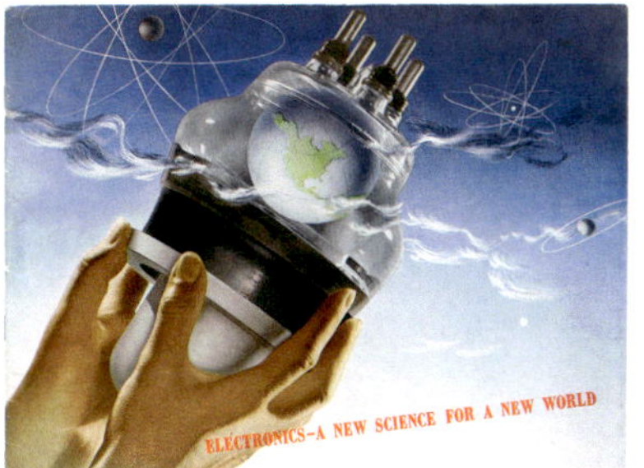

1942

HERBERT BAYER

Pamphlet for General Electric, letterpress, 8¼ × 11⅛ inches (210 × 283 mm), New York.

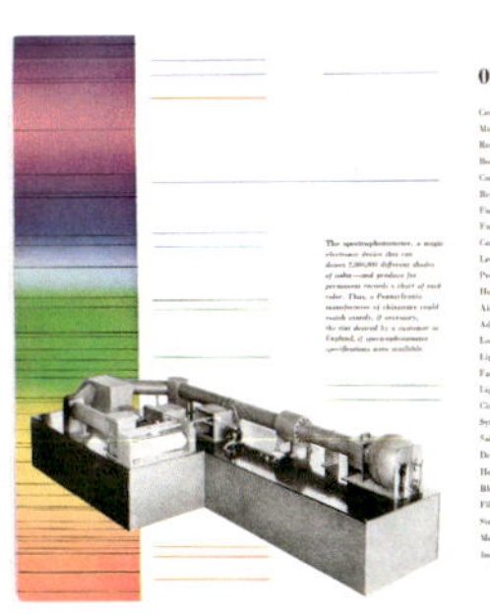

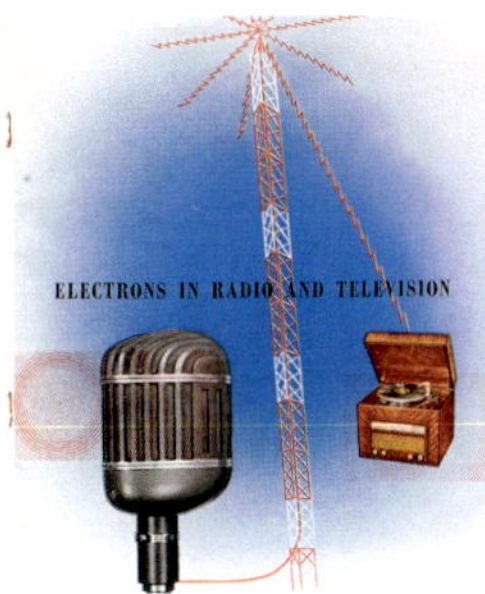

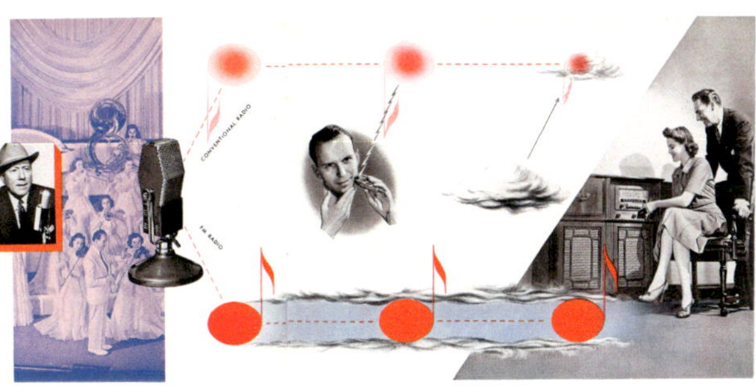

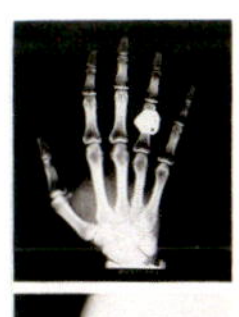

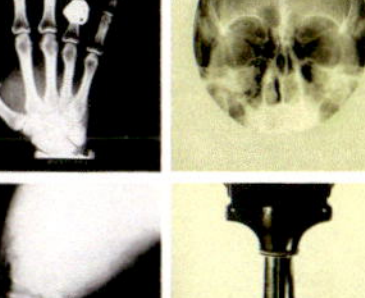

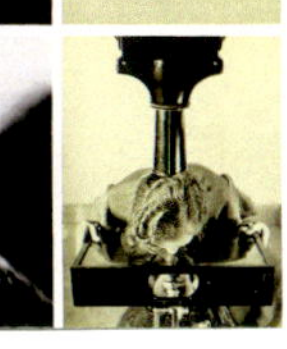

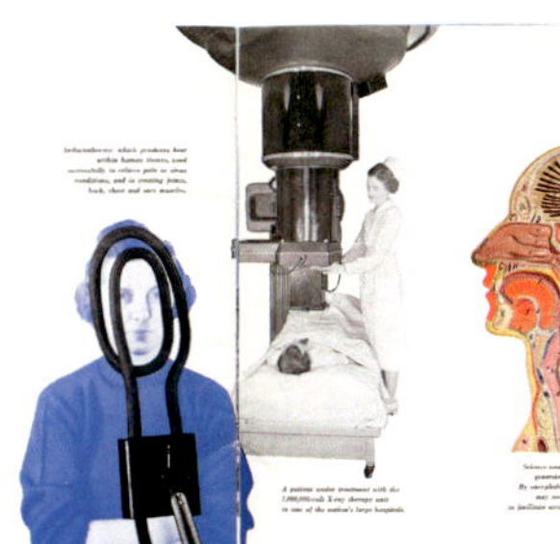

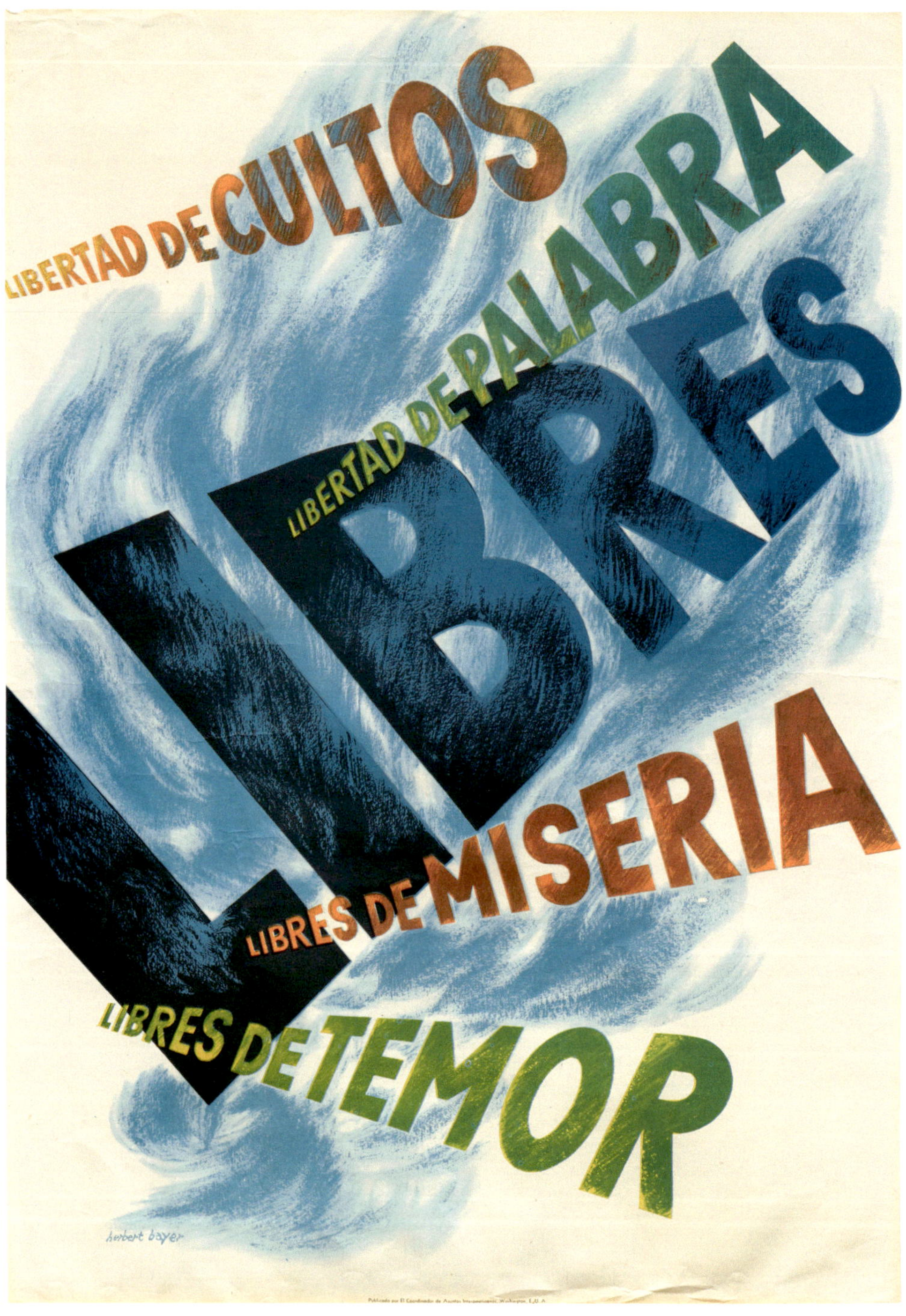

1942

HERBERT BAYER

Freedom of Worship, Freedom of Speech, Free of Misery, Free of Fear (*Libertad de Cultos, Libertad de Palabra, Libres de Miseria, Libres de Temor*), World War II Allied Forces propaganda poster for use in Latin America, offset, 19⅞ × 14¼ inches (504 × 360 mm), Washington, D.C.

1944

HERBERT BAYER

Proof for Cohama Ties advertisement, letterpress, 13⅞ × 11⅛ inches (353 × 283 mm), New York.

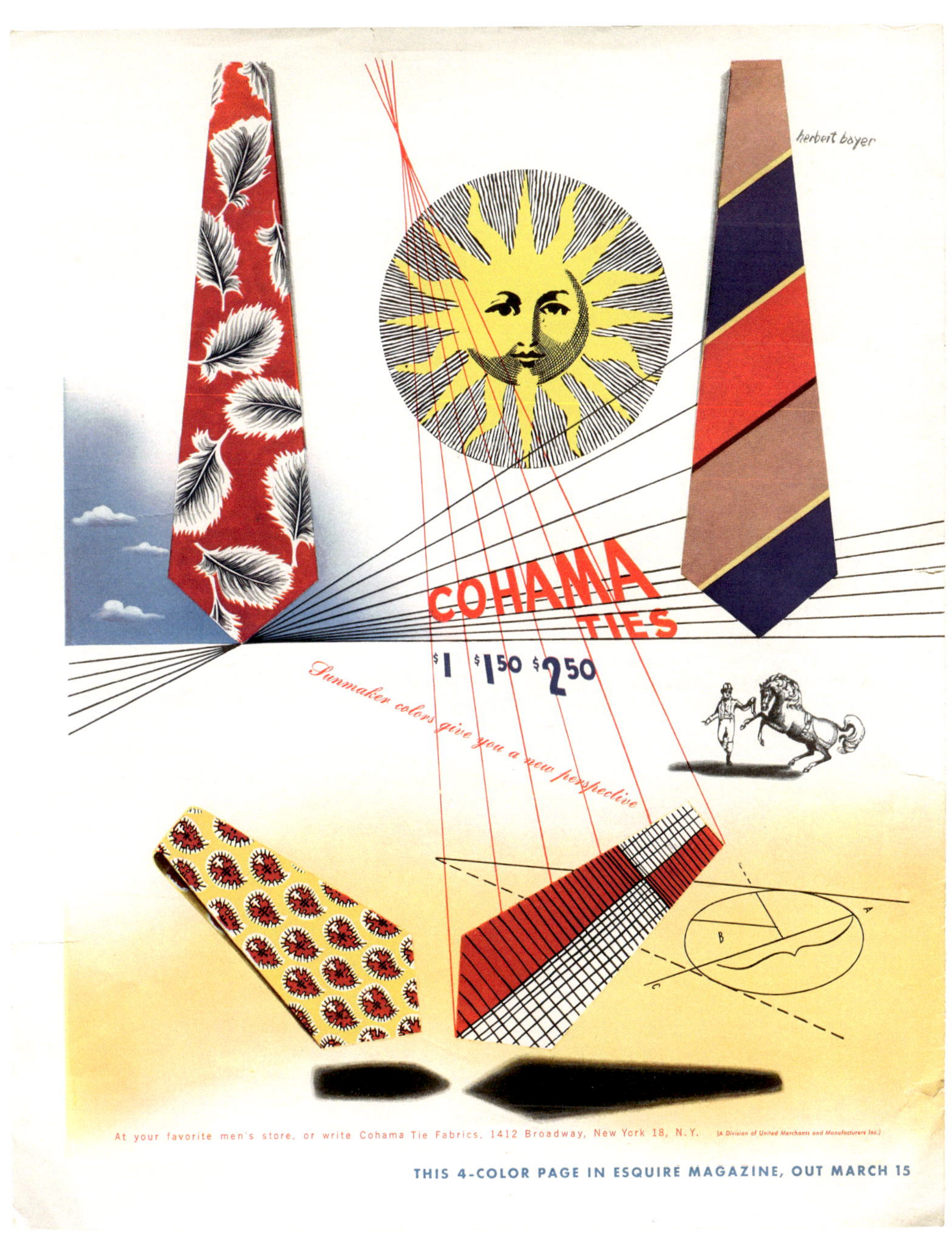

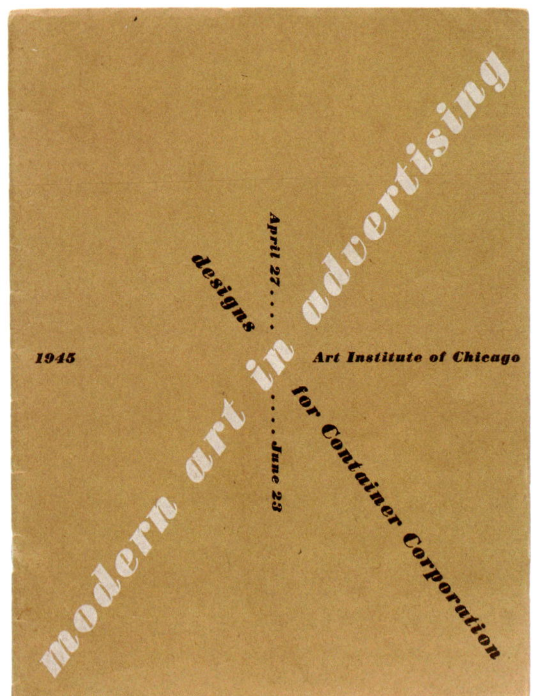

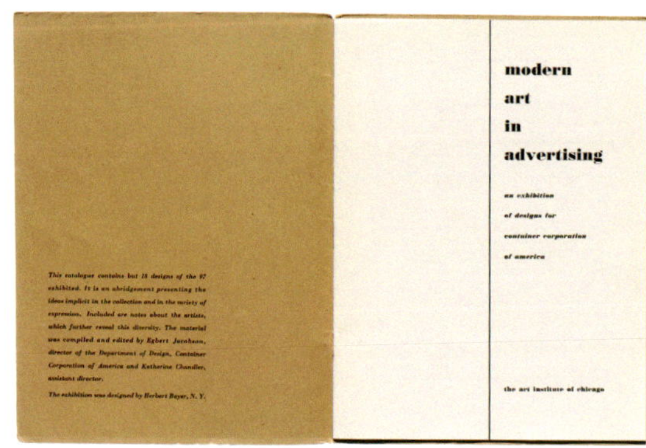

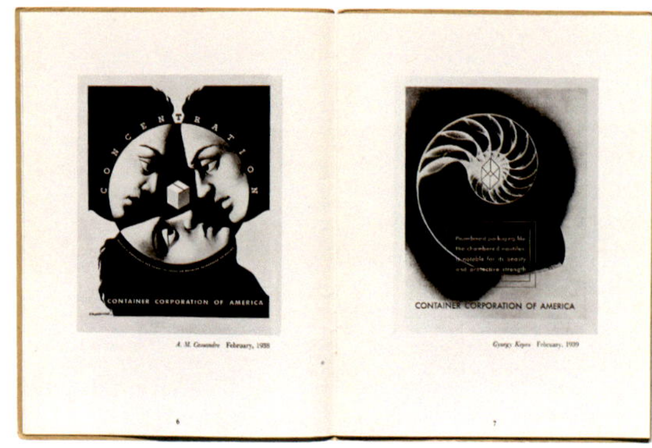

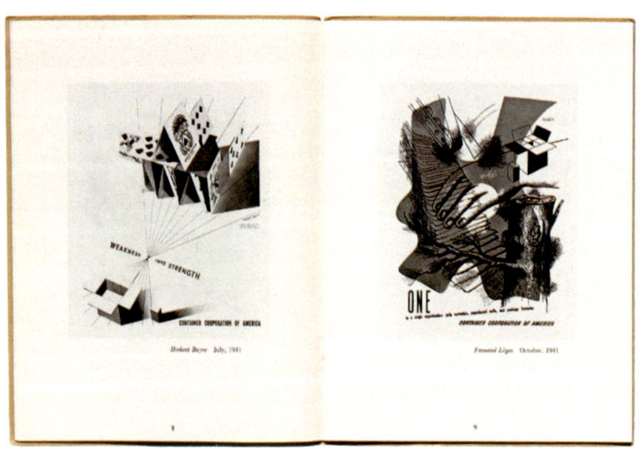

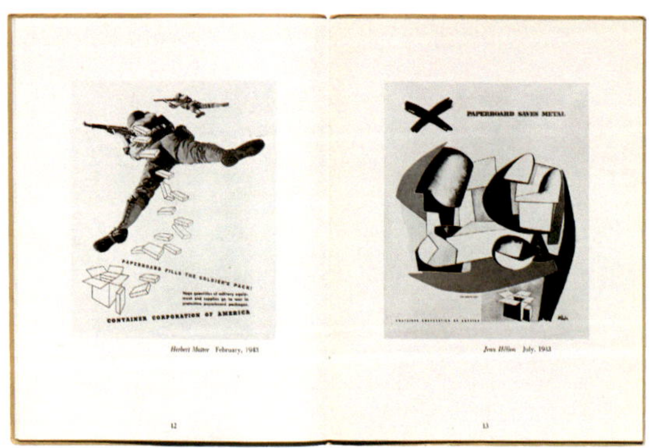

1945

HERBERT BAYER

Exhibition catalog for *Modern Art in Advertising: Designs for Container Corporation*, letterpress, 9¼ × 7 inches (235 × 178 mm), Chicago.

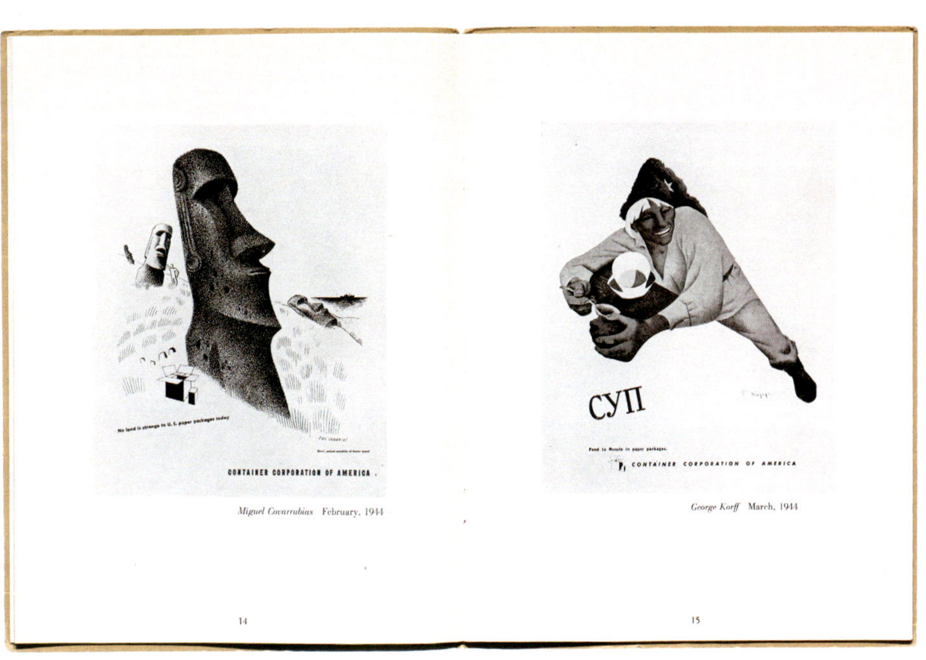

Miguel Covarrubias February, 1944

George Korff March, 1944

14

15

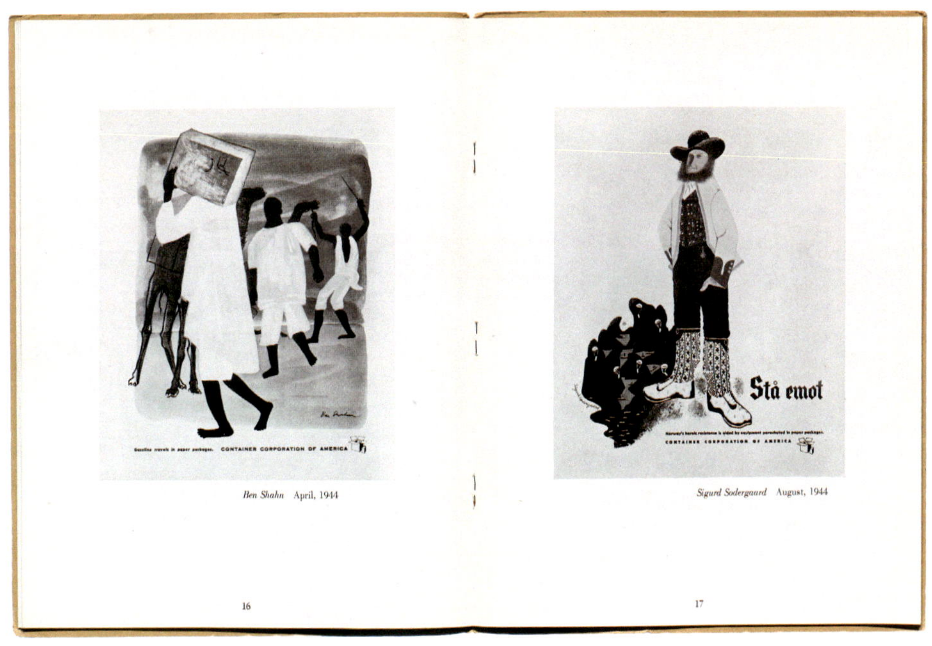

Ben Shahn April, 1944

Sigurd Sodergaard August, 1944

16

17

1953

HERBERT BAYER (designer/editor)

World Geo-Graphic Atlas, letterpress and lithograph, 15¾ × 11 inches (400 × 280 mm), Chicago.

After immigrating to the United States, Herbert Bayer did some of his most significant design work stateside for the Container Corporation of America (CCA). He served first as a consultant and later as director of the design department, implementing a number of successful advertising campaigns, including the "Great Ideas of Western Man" series, in which he directed artists such as René Magritte and Milton Glaser in the creation of posters based on famous quotations. In 1953, he was tasked with compiling and designing the *World Geo-Graphic Atlas* to commemorate the company's twenty-fifth anniversary. Truly a monumental work, for Bayer it serves as a culmination of many of the techniques and interests he had pursued as a professional designer since leaving the Bauhaus. Choosing Futura for both display and text, he wields typography, photomontage, illustration, information design, and infographics in a rational and systematic way for utmost clarity and comprehension. As a whole, the atlas represents precisely the kind of simple, functional, and legible design system theorized earlier at the Bauhaus.

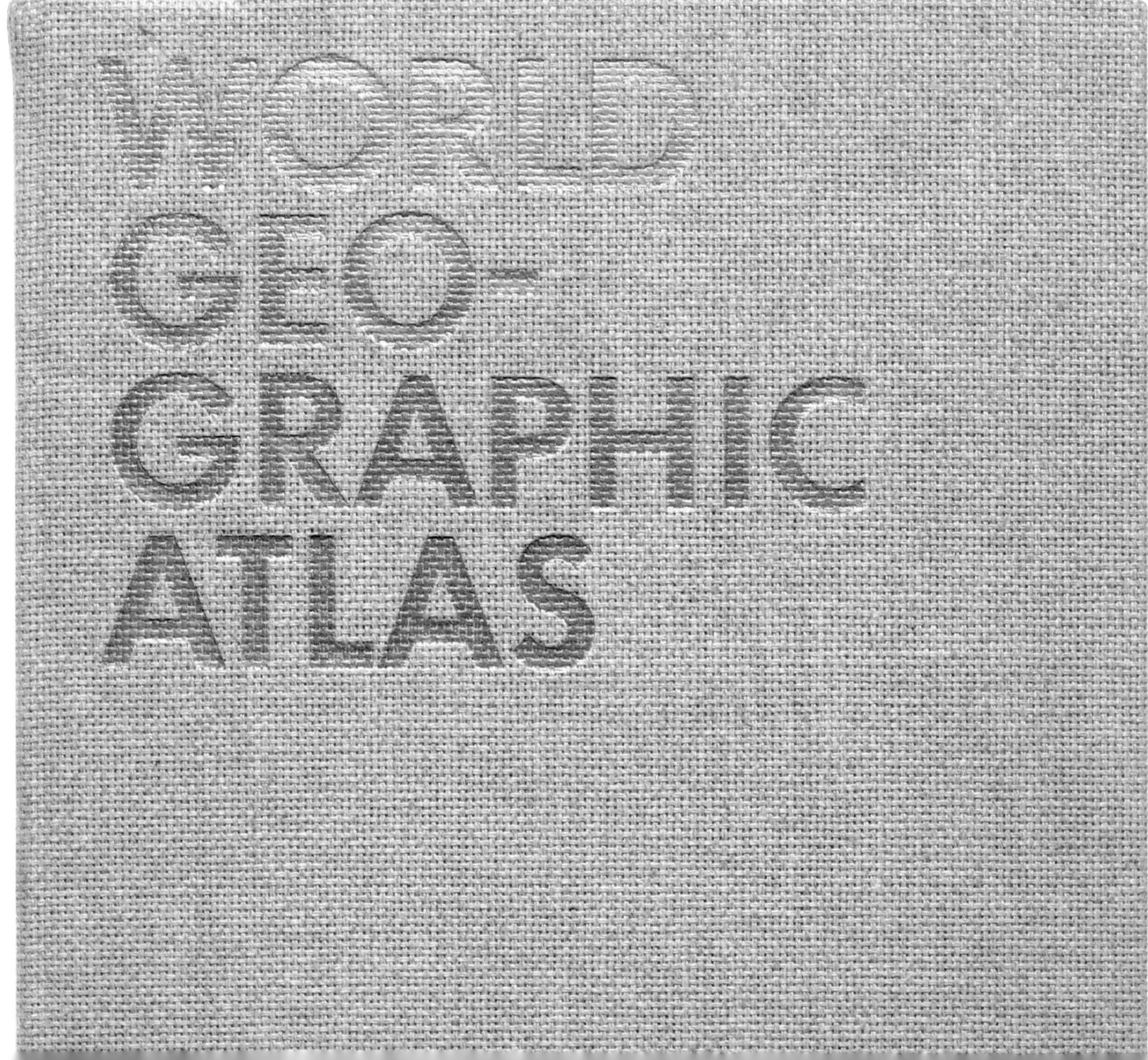

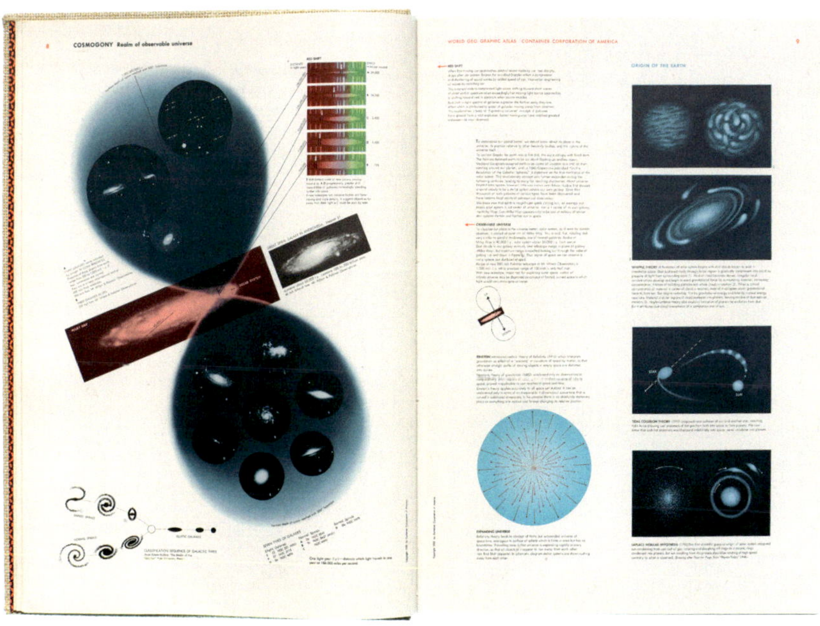

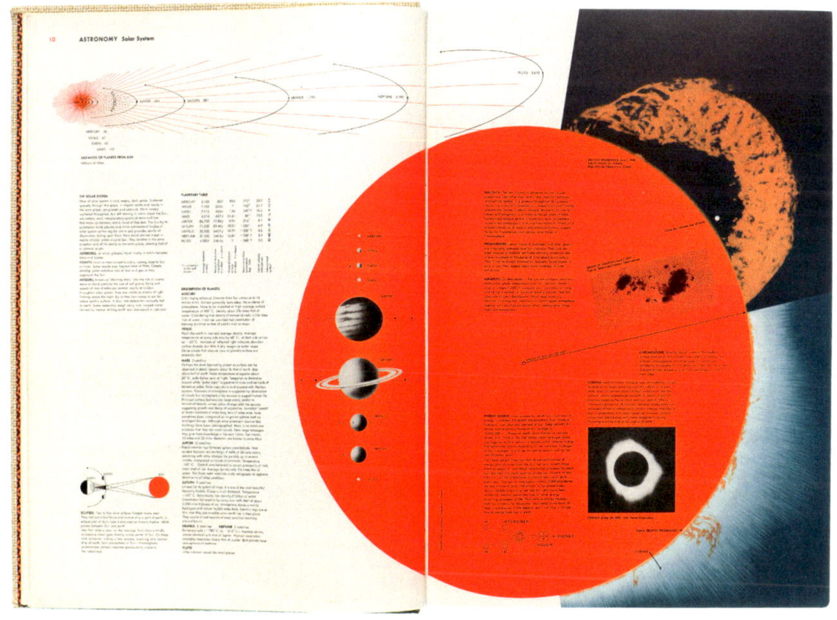

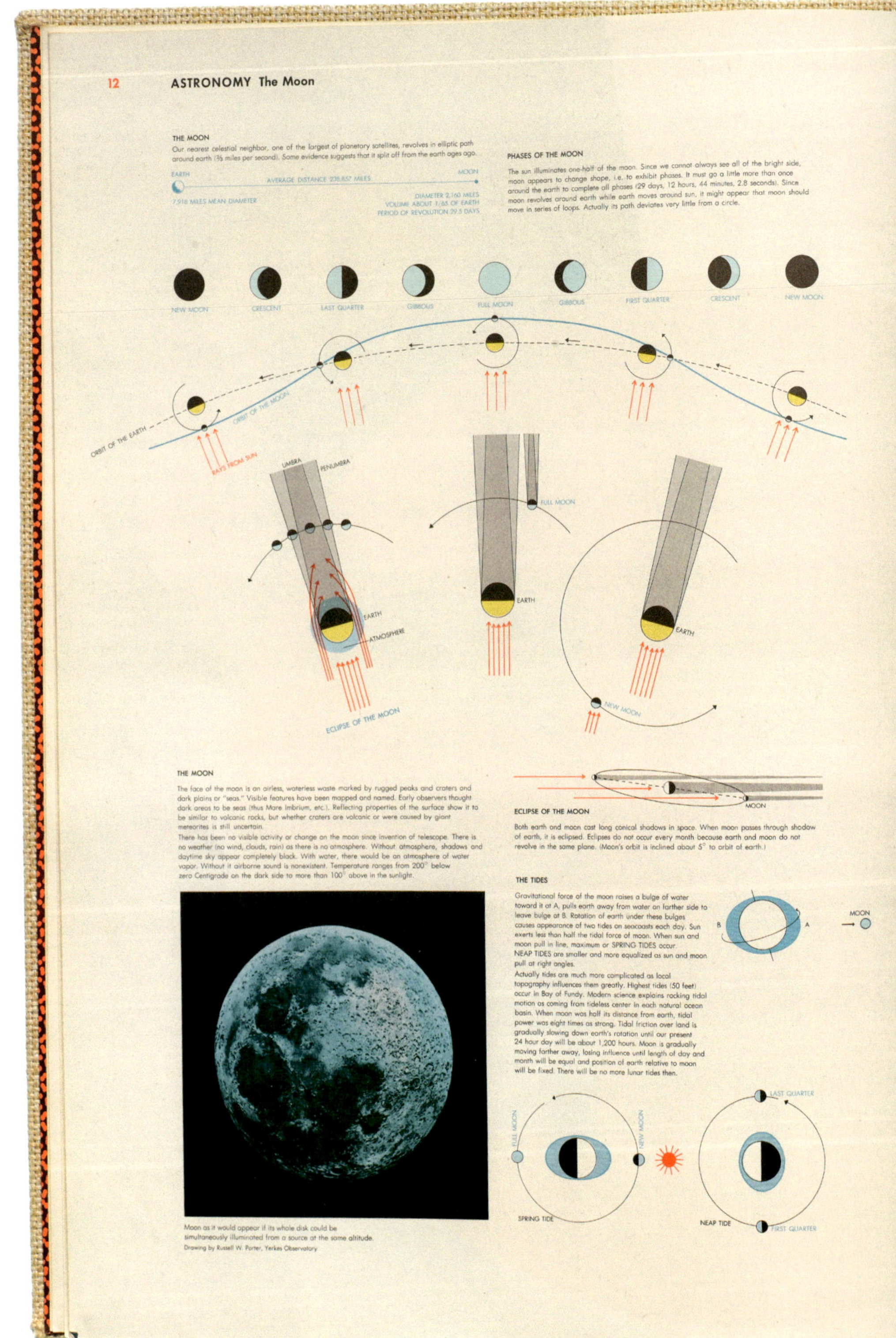
12
ASTRONOMY The Moon
THE MOON
Our nearest celestial neighbor, one of the largest of planetary satellites, revolves in elliptic path around earth (⅗ miles per second). Some evidence suggests that it split off from the earth ages ago.
EARTH
AVERAGE DISTANCE 238,857 MILES
MOON
7,918 MILES MEAN DIAMETER
DIAMETER 2,160 MILES
VOLUME ABOUT 1/65 OF EARTH
PERIOD OF REVOLUTION 29.5 DAYS
PHASES OF THE MOON
The sun illuminates one-half of the moon. Since we cannot always see all of the bright side, moon appears to change shape, i.e. to exhibit phases. It must go a little more than once around the earth to complete all phases (29 days, 12 hours, 44 minutes, 2.8 seconds). Since moon revolves around earth while earth moves around sun, it might appear that moon should move in series of loops. Actually its path deviates very little from a circle.
NEW MOON
CRESCENT
LAST QUARTER
GIBBOUS
FULL MOON
GIBBOUS
FIRST QUARTER
CRESCENT
NEW MOON
ORBIT OF THE EARTH
ORBIT OF THE MOON
RAYS FROM SUN
UMBRA
PENUMBRA
EARTH
ATMOSPHERE
ECLIPSE OF THE MOON
FULL MOON
EARTH
EARTH
NEW MOON
THE MOON
The face of the moon is an airless, waterless waste marked by rugged peaks and craters and dark plains or "seas." Visible features have been mapped and named. Early observers thought dark areas to be seas (thus Mare Imbrium, etc.). Reflecting properties of the surface show it to be similar to volcanic rocks, but whether craters are volcanic or were caused by giant meteorites is still uncertain.
There has been no visible activity or change on the moon since invention of telescope. There is no weather (no wind, clouds, rain) as there is no atmosphere. Without atmosphere, shadows and daytime sky appear completely black. With water, there would be an atmosphere of water vapor. Without it airborne sound is nonexistent. Temperature ranges from 200° below zero Centigrade on the dark side to more than 100° above in the sunlight.
MOON
ECLIPSE OF THE MOON
Both earth and moon cast long conical shadows in space. When moon passes through shadow of earth, it is eclipsed. Eclipses do not occur every month because earth and moon do not revolve in the same plane. (Moon's orbit is inclined about 5° to orbit of earth.)
THE TIDES
Gravitational force of the moon raises a bulge of water toward it at A, pulls earth away from water on farther side to leave bulge at B. Rotation of earth under these bulges causes appearance of two tides on seacoasts each day. Sun exerts less than half the tidal force of moon. When sun and moon pull in line, maximum or SPRING TIDES occur.
NEAP TIDES are smaller and more equalized as sun and moon pull at right angles.
Actually tides are much more complicated as local topography influences them greatly. Highest tides (50 feet) occur in Bay of Fundy. Modern science explains rocking tidal motion as coming from tideless center in each natural ocean basin. When moon was half its distance from earth, tidal power was eight times as strong. Tidal friction over land is gradually slowing down earth's rotation until our present 24 hour day will be about 1,200 hours. Moon is gradually moving farther away, losing influence until length of day and month will be equal and position of earth relative to moon will be fixed. There will be no more lunar tides then.
B
A
MOON
FULL MOON
NEW MOON
SPRING TIDE
LAST QUARTER
NEAP TIDE
FIRST QUARTER
Moon as it would appear if its whole disk could be simultaneously illuminated from a source at the same altitude.
Drawing by Russell W. Porter, Yerkes Observatory

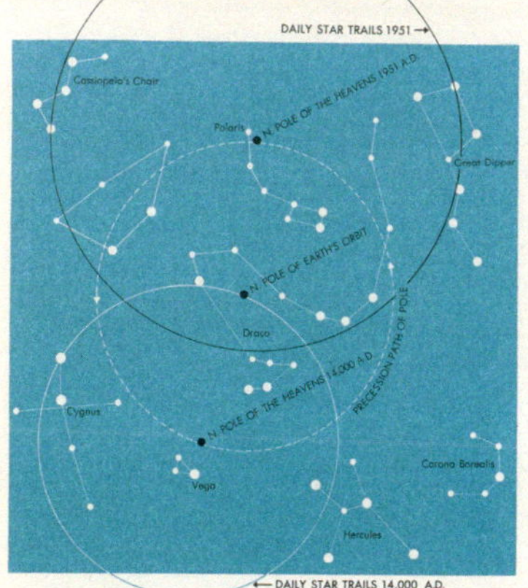

PRECESSION

is the motion of the earth's axis comparable to the wobbling movement of a spinning top. Due to the motion of the celestial poles among the stars, the sky seems to turn in the opposite direction around the celestial poles. It takes 26,000 years to complete the full circle. The north pole of the heavens is now near Polaris; but Alpha Draconis was polestar of ancient Egyptians. About 14,000 A.D. stars will circle daily around the bright star Vega.

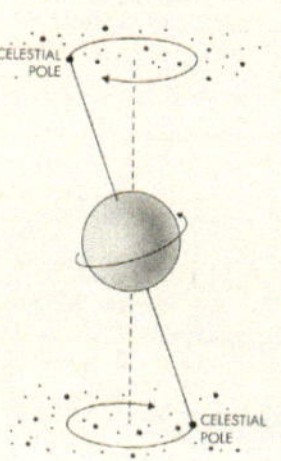

26,000 YEARS TO COMPLETE CIRCLE

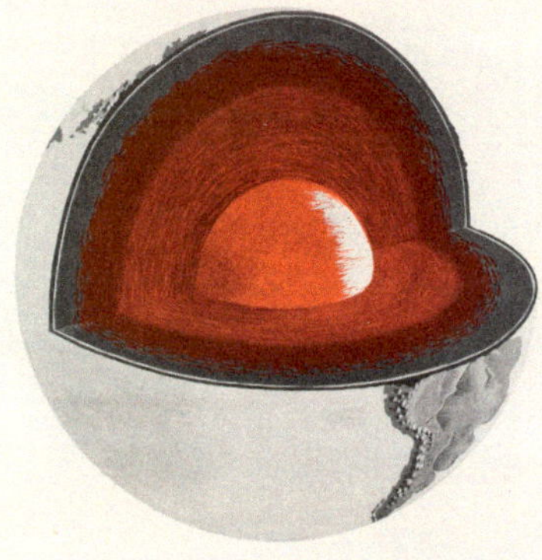

Outer crust of sedimentary layers and solidified granites 30 miles deep. At 40 miles, may be layer of basaltic glass. Various layers with abrupt structural changes follow. Core of about 2,000 miles radius, assumed to be of molten metallic iron. All global concepts are still weighed by hypothesis.

THE EARTH

The earth is at least 3 billion years old. Its surface conditions of temperature and atmosphere have been nearly the same for at least one billion years. Seismologists using earthquake waves and their refractions as sounding devices have discovered various concentric shells inside globe, the outer crust forming our continents and ocean floors. Layers may indicate that earth was once molten. Folding and fracturing to which crust was subjected indicate dynamic internal activity, of which we have no tangible knowledge. Volcanoes probably do not reach to the core, but draw molten lava from localized intrusions at 20-40 mile depths (see p. 16, fig. 6). In deep mines, temperature increases 2°F. every 100 feet down. Temperature at the core is believed to be several thousand degrees.

Pressure at 22 mile depths is 73 tons per square inch; at 300 miles 1,176 tons; at the center 21,000 tons. (Pressure at sea level about 15 pounds per square inch.)

Measurements of the Earth, see page 25

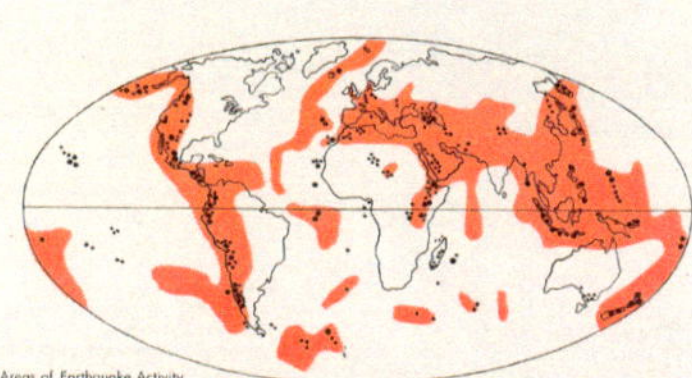

Areas of Earthquake Activity

Distribution of Volcanoes

After a map prepared by the American Geographical Society

EARTHQUAKES

Most great destructive earthquakes are of tectonic nature, being caused by steady cooling and shrinking, and in turn, faulting and folding of globe's crust. Earthquakes are accompanied by shaking and trembling of the earth and by fore- and after-shocks, often of long duration. Volcanic earthquakes are usually accompanied by eruptions. Waves are recorded by seismographic instruments.

Particularly seismic are regions of recent mountain upheaval where crust shows symptoms of weakness.

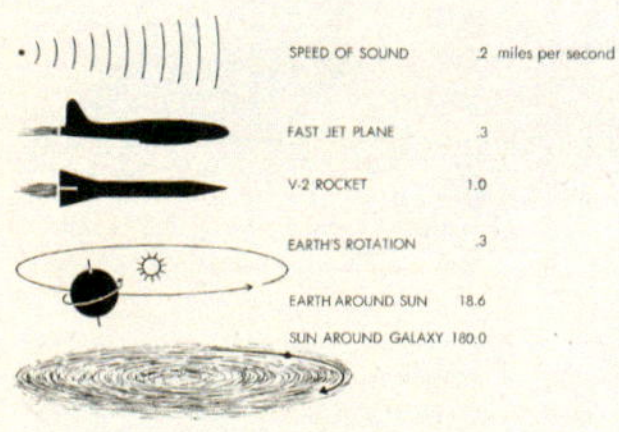

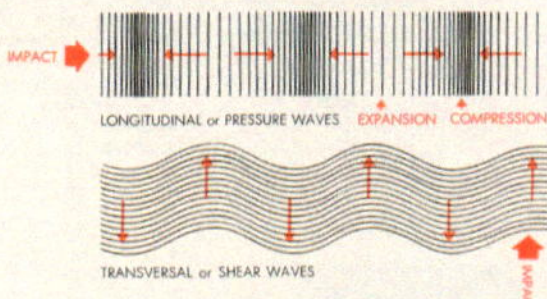

CONTINENTAL DRIFT HYPOTHESIS

This hypothesis contends that during early stages of our planet, a huge chunk broke away to become the moon. The hole left on earth would be today's Pacific basin. Mean density of moon 3.3 compared to that of earth 5.5 suggests that moon took none of earth's heavy iron core away, that moon is made of granite and basalt of earth's outer layers. Leftover land masses still floating on bed of molten basalt drifted apart due to centrifugal forces, until cooling of rocks stopped drifting, settling continents at their present position. (Controversies over Drift Hypothesis have been renewed as no other convincing explanations have been suggested.)

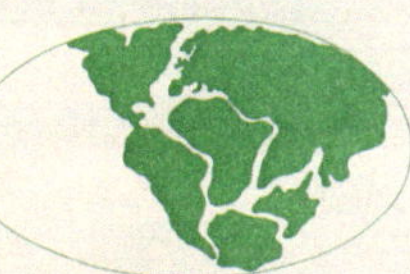

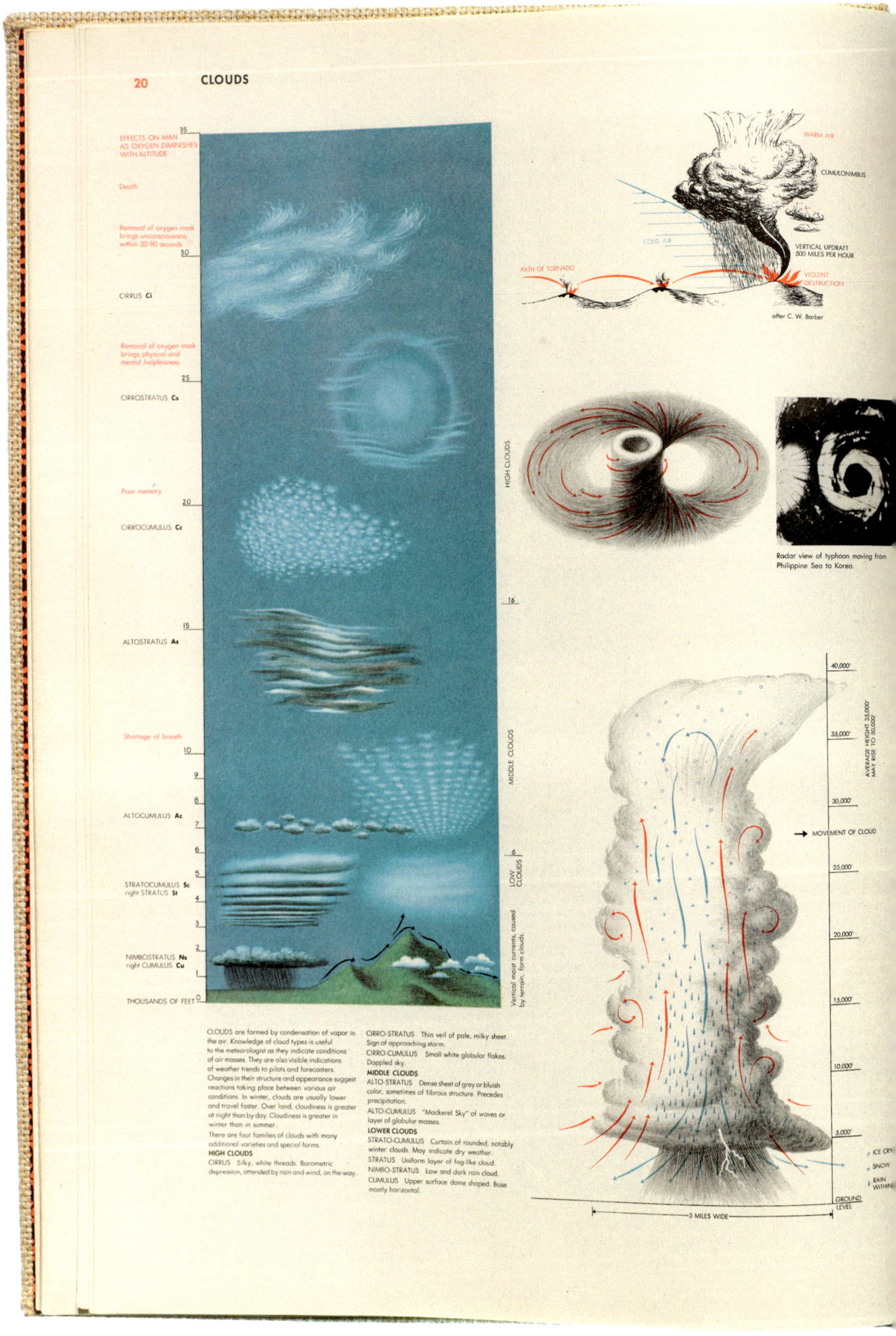
20
CLOUDS
EFFECTS ON MAN
AS OXYGEN DIMINISHES
WITH ALTITUDE
Death
Removal of oxygen mask
brings unconsciousness
within 30-90 seconds
CIRRUS Ci
Removal of oxygen mask
brings physical and
mental helplessness
CIRROSTRATUS Cs
Poor memory
CIRROCUMULUS Cc
ALTOSTRATUS As
Shortage of breath
ALTOCUMULUS Ac
STRATOCUMULUS Sc
right STRATUS St
NIMBOSTRATUS Ns
right CUMULUS Cu
THOUSANDS OF FEET
35
30
25
20
15
10
9
8
7
6
5
4
3
2
1
0
HIGH CLOUDS
16
MIDDLE CLOUDS
6
LOW CLOUDS
Vertical moist currents, caused by terrain, form clouds.
CLOUDS are formed by condensation of vapor in the air. Knowledge of cloud types is useful to the meteorologist as they indicate conditions of air masses. They are also visible indications of weather trends to pilots and forecasters. Changes in their structure and appearance suggest reactions taking place between various air conditions. In winter, clouds are usually lower and travel faster. Over land, cloudiness is greater at night than by day. Cloudiness is greater in winter than in summer.
There are four families of clouds with many additional varieties and special forms.
HIGH CLOUDS
CIRRUS Silky, white threads. Barometric depression, attended by rain and wind, on the way.
CIRRO-STRATUS Thin veil of pale, milky sheet. Sign of approaching storm.
CIRRO-CUMULUS Small white globular flakes. Dappled sky.
MIDDLE CLOUDS
ALTO-STRATUS Dense sheet of grey or bluish color, sometimes of fibrous structure. Precedes precipitation.
ALTO-CUMULUS "Mackerel Sky" of waves or layer of globular masses.
LOWER CLOUDS
STRATO-CUMULUS Curtain of rounded, notably winter clouds. May indicate dry weather.
STRATUS Uniform layer of fog-like cloud.
NIMBO-STRATUS Low and dark rain cloud.
CUMULUS Upper surface dome shaped. Base mostly horizontal.
WARM AIR
CUMULONIMBUS
COLD AIR
VERTICAL UPDRAFT
500 MILES PER HOUR
PATH OF TORNADO
VIOLENT
DESTRUCTION
after C. W. Barber
Radar view of typhoon moving from
Philippine Sea to Korea.
40,000'
35,000'
30,000'
25,000'
20,000'
15,000'
10,000'
5,000'
GROUND
LEVEL
AVERAGE HEIGHT 35,000'
MAY RISE TO 50,000'
MOVEMENT OF CLOUD
SNOW
3 MILES WIDE

←TORNADO (Twister)
The small diameter (average 1000 feet), but most violent storm, travels as funnel-shaped, upward spiralling wind column 20-50 miles p.h., leaving behind narrow path of destruction. Normally occurs in spring and summer, when polar and tropical air meet. Moves in northeastward direction in America. Runs its entire course of 30-40 miles in short time and may pass one place in a minute. Tornadoes appear first in storm cloud above and when fully developed, extend down to the ground. Over the sea, they are called waterspouts.

TRAVELING DISTURBANCES
Interaction of all climatic phenomena (such as the world wind system, temperature variations, distribution of land and water areas, local variations, etc.) results in movements (300 to 500 miles per day) of large air masses, and creates regions of high and low pressure. Observation and measurement of these are the basis of meteorological weather forecasting.

When two air masses of different temperature and pressure meet, a "Front" is created. Front is dividing line between air masses. There are many variations of frontal types.

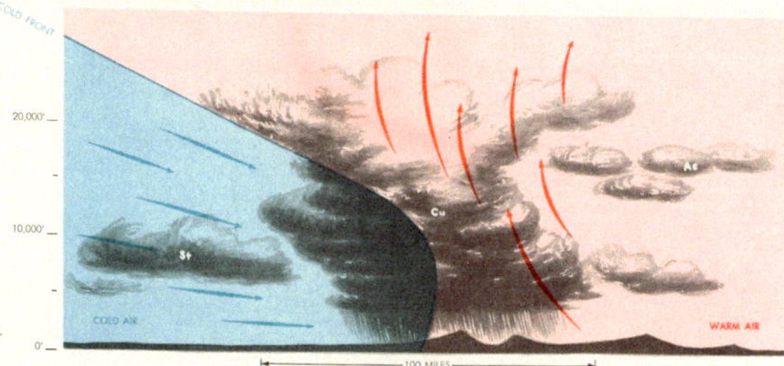

COLD FRONT TYPE Cold air mass overtakes and flows under warm, lighter air, forcing it up. Cumulus and Cumulonimbus clouds and drop of temperature usually announce approaching cold front. Frontal thunderstorms are characteristic. When front passes, weather usually clears.

←CYCLONE (Called Typhoon in the Pacific, Hurricane in the Atlantic)
Most destructive of storms; originates over tropical oceans, moves to temperate zones. On its way, it grows larger, but becomes less violent. Great amount of condensation over warm oceans supplies heat, which causes rapid rising of air. Spiral upward winds around entirely windless center (the storm eye, about 15 miles diameter) may exceed 200 miles p.h. Outward winds blow counter-clockwise down and return to the eye. Hurricanes occur mostly during summer and autumn, may grow to 400 miles diameter. In the Western Hemisphere, their path is usually across West Indies, Southeastern U.S. states, then eastward over the Atlantic. Sometimes, they move along Gulf Coast or north towards Great Lakes. (see p. 180)

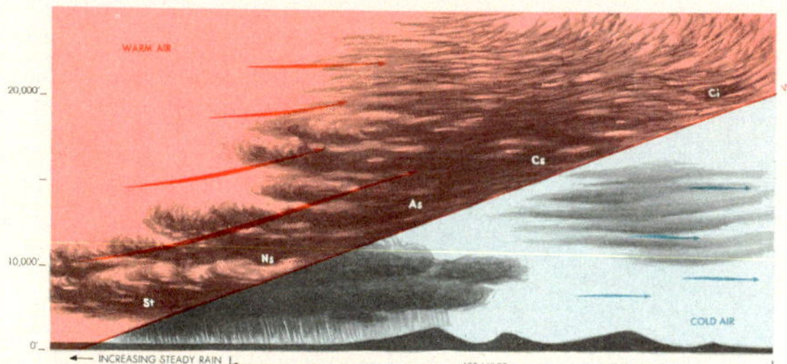

IDEAL WARM FRONT Warm air moves in, overtakes mass of cold air, and rises along front line. A certain sequence of cloud types is characteristic. Temperature changes occur in cold air while warm air mass will remain constant. Weather usually clears after passing of front.

Sources:
C. W. Barber
Weather Science
Pitman
U.S. Weather Bureau
"Scientific American," June, 1950
G. T. Renner and H. A. Bauer
The Air We Live In
Macmillan

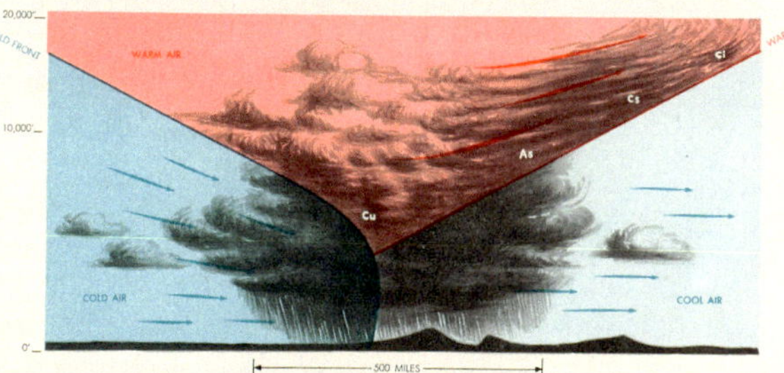

OCCLUDED FRONT TYPE Fast moving cold front overtakes warm front, forcing its air up. Normally there is a temperature difference between preceding cool and advancing cold air mass. Weather of occluded front is combination of that of warm and cold fronts. Weather clears after passage of occlusion.

←**CUMULONIMBUS CLOUD CuN (clouds of vertical development)**
The THUNDER CLOUD grows from small cumulus cloud to towering cumulonimbus. Air is taken in through base and through sides of cloud. Air in the cloud, being warmer than the outside, rises with great speed and turbulence. As updraft passes through cold altitudes, its vapor forms into raindrops. At a height of 20-25,000 feet rain within cloud becomes snow. Warm updrafts (up to seventy miles p.h.) and cold downdrafts (up to fifty miles p.h.) flow past each other in cloud. Cold air, and with it gusty winds, spread over ground. Lightning and thunder occur. Feathery appearance of cloud's top not to be mistaken for cirrus cloud.

Air turbulence of thunderstorms is great hazard to planes. Safest level for flying seems to be below 10,000 feet.

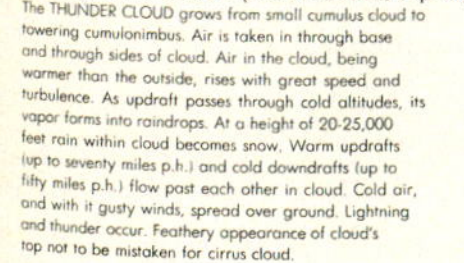

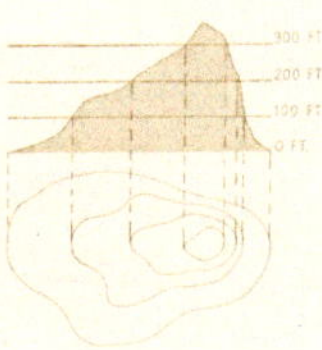

TOPOGRAPHY OF THE ATMOSPHERE
Principle of contour lines used in mapping land elevations. Lines connect points of equal elevation.

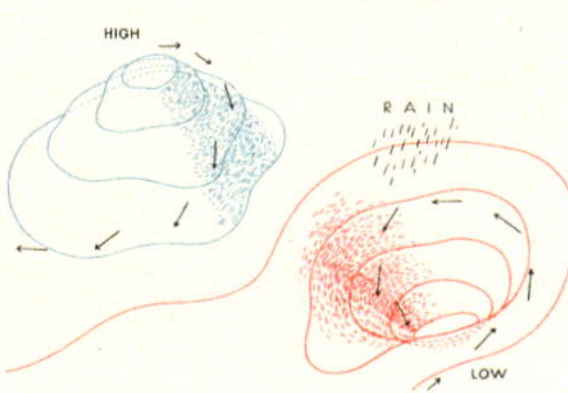

Air hill and valley as measured by same principle of contour lines. Called isobars because they connect points of equal pressure.
(see World Pressure and Temperature, Pages 28, 29)

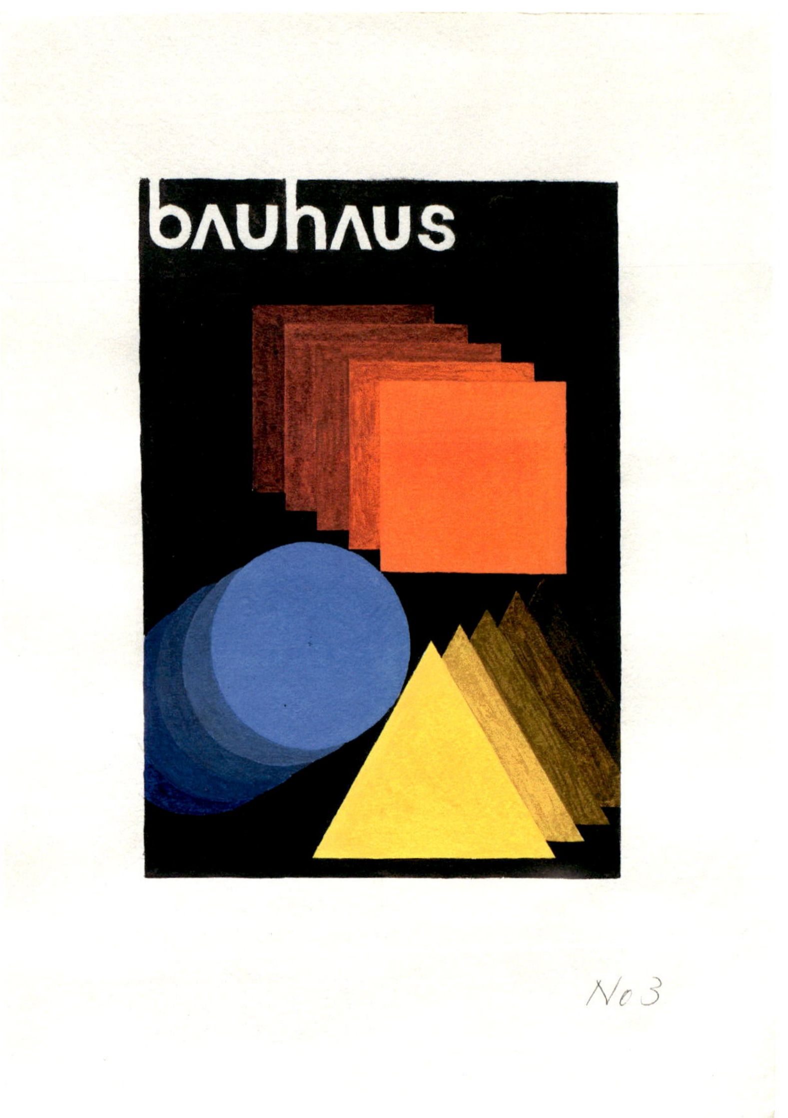

1968

HERBERT BAYER

Exhibition poster maquette for *50 Years Bauhaus* (*50 Jahre Bauhaus*), gouache on paper, 13¼ × 9⅜ inches (337 × 238 mm), Aspen, Colorado.

1968

HERBERT BAYER

Exhibition poster for *50 Years Bauhaus* (*50 Jahre Bauhaus*), offset, 33 × 23⅜ inches (840 × 592 mm), Stuttgart, Germany.

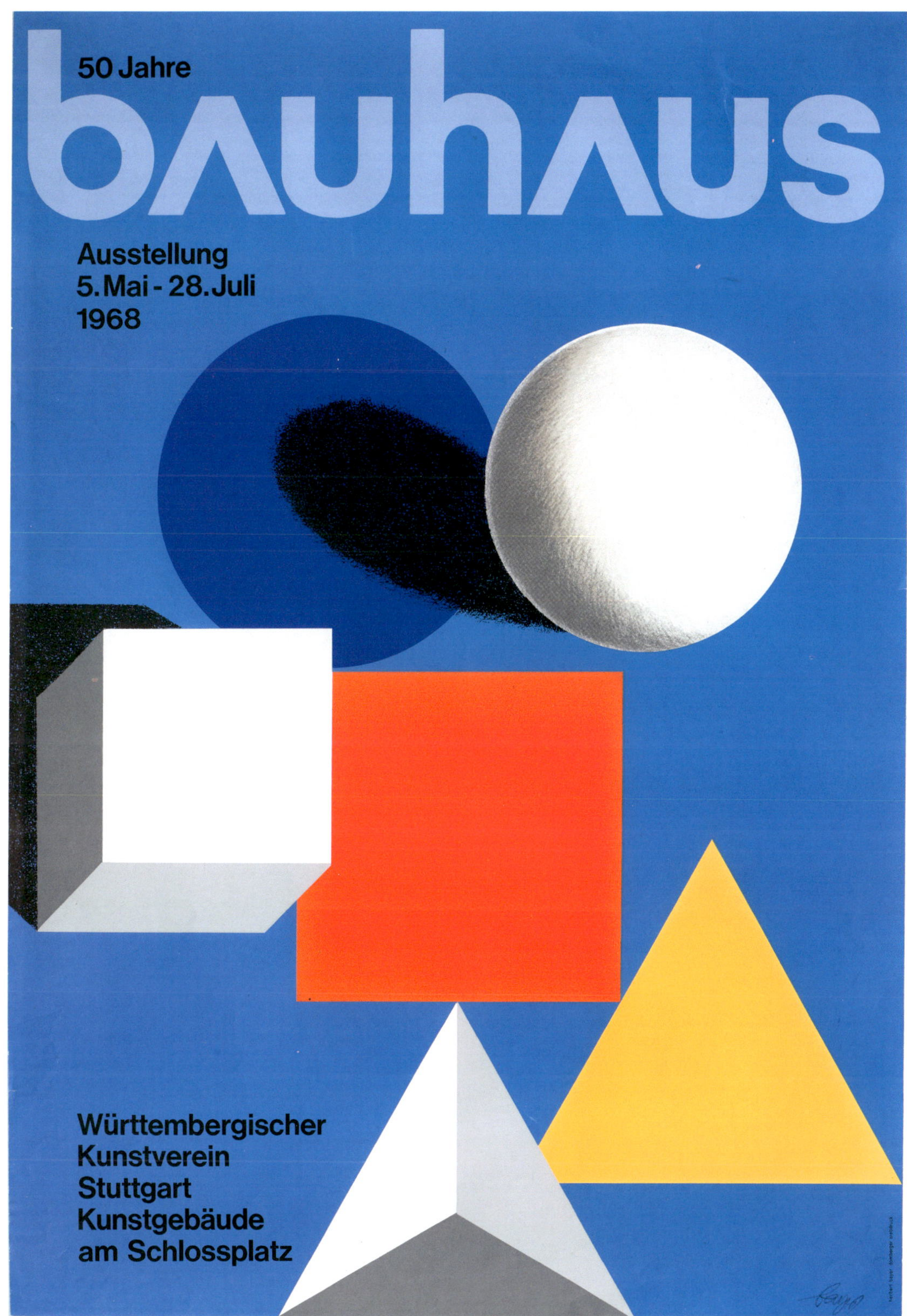
50 Jahre
bauhaus
Ausstellung
5. Mai - 28. Juli
1968
Württembergischer
Kunstverein
Stuttgart
Kunstgebäude
am Schlossplatz

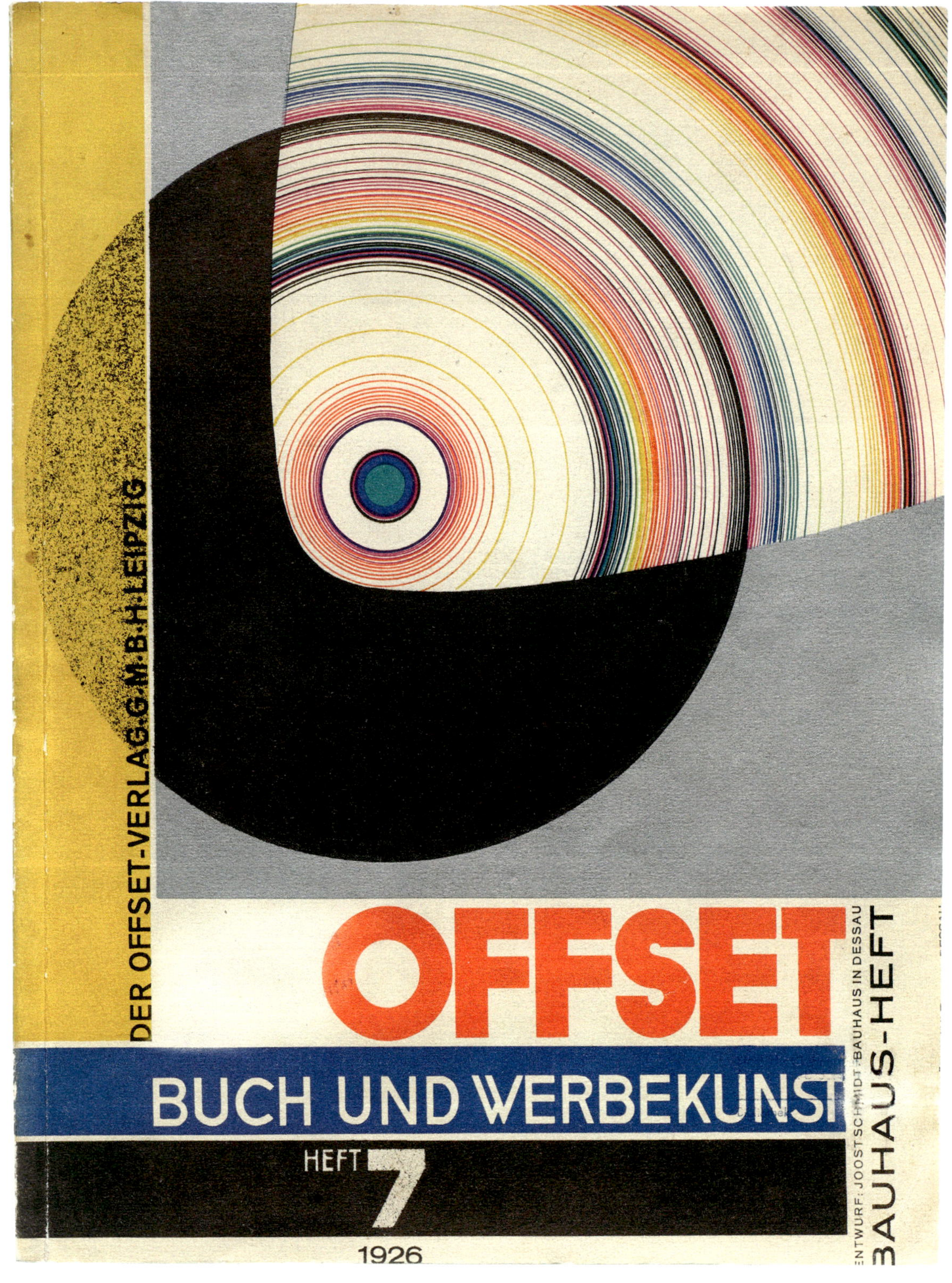
DER OFFSET-VERLAG G.M.B.H. LEIPZIG
OFFSET
BUCH UND WERBEKUNST
HEFT 7
1926
ENTWURF: JOOST SCHMIDT · BAUHAUS IN DESSAU
BAUHAUS-HEFT

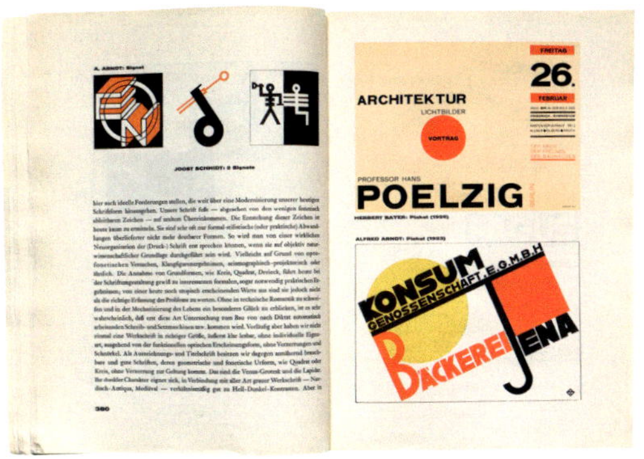

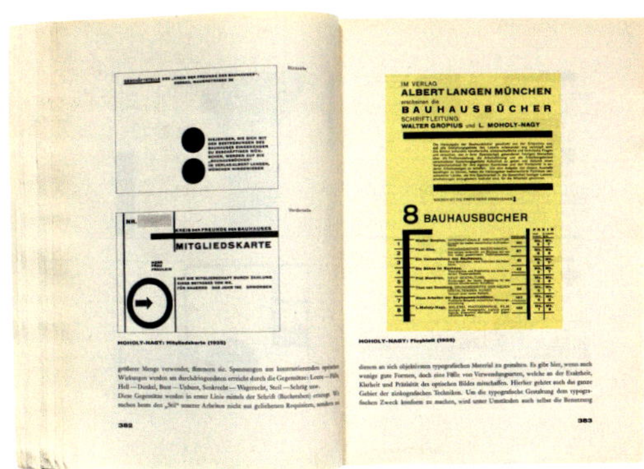

Joost Schmidt designed this 1926 cover for the special Bauhaus issue of *Offset*, a trade magazine that showcased the newly affordable four-color printing. The cover titling represents a geometric ideal that couldn't be fulfilled by type, as fonts in this highly rationalized genre didn't exist until Erbar-Grotesk and Futura came along later in 1926 and in 1927. He created the now-iconic design when he was a Bauhaus teacher of lettering, just one year after finishing the school's sculpture course and two years before taking over its print and advertising workshop. ●
Schmidt's tenure at the Bauhaus is overshadowed by those of Moholy-Nagy and Bayer. (This was perhaps by his own hand due to his need to disassociate from the institution to avoid Nazi persecution within Germany; in contrast, his predecessors could promote themselves as ambassadors of Bauhaus ideas abroad.) Nonetheless, Schmidt's impact on the school's typography is undisputed. To his students, he was "Schmidtchen," a kind yet rigorous teacher who constructed experimental, modular stencil type and geometric, condensed letterforms. ●
These pages show how Schmidt's typography changed in step with the school's aesthetics, with his early organic letterforms yielding to the polished sans serifs, layered photomontage, and crisp infographics of the Bauhaus's later years. ●

1926

JOOST SCHMIDT (cover designer)

Offset: Book and Advertising Art, Bauhaus Issue (*Offset: Buch und Werbekunst, Bauhaus-heft*), vol. 3, no. 7, offset and letterpress, 11⅞ × 9 inches (301 × 230 mm), Leipzig.

▶

nischen Möglichkeiten und den
die Mittel der Typografie außer-
Bedürfnissen entsprechend, anders

usgleich der Buchstabenabstände,
r und -fachleute auch für Schreib-
nmte Zwischenwerte, Restflächen,
schließen. Besonders bei der oft
die ausgeglichene Zeile als einzig
.

n.

Schriftform. Sie geht mehr in die
. Heute, bei anders gearteter Le-
s durch fette Schriften), wie über-
d.

olger (nur auf die Schriftzeichen
en, als das Buch noch ein „Schrift-
Presseerzeugnis wurde. Seitdem
. Dafür kommt der Typograf, der

Form neu erfinden, weil er meist
zu gehen, muß er sich auf die Ele-
studieren, um zu erkennen, warum
uns gehört.

anerkennen, daß eins nur tragend,
er Fabrik tragend ist, die General-
die Minister oder die Ingenieure
Auswertung des Einzelnen. Dem-
weißen, passiven Untergrund selb-
leiben nicht bloß übrig, sondern
Plastik die Leerräume positiv ge-

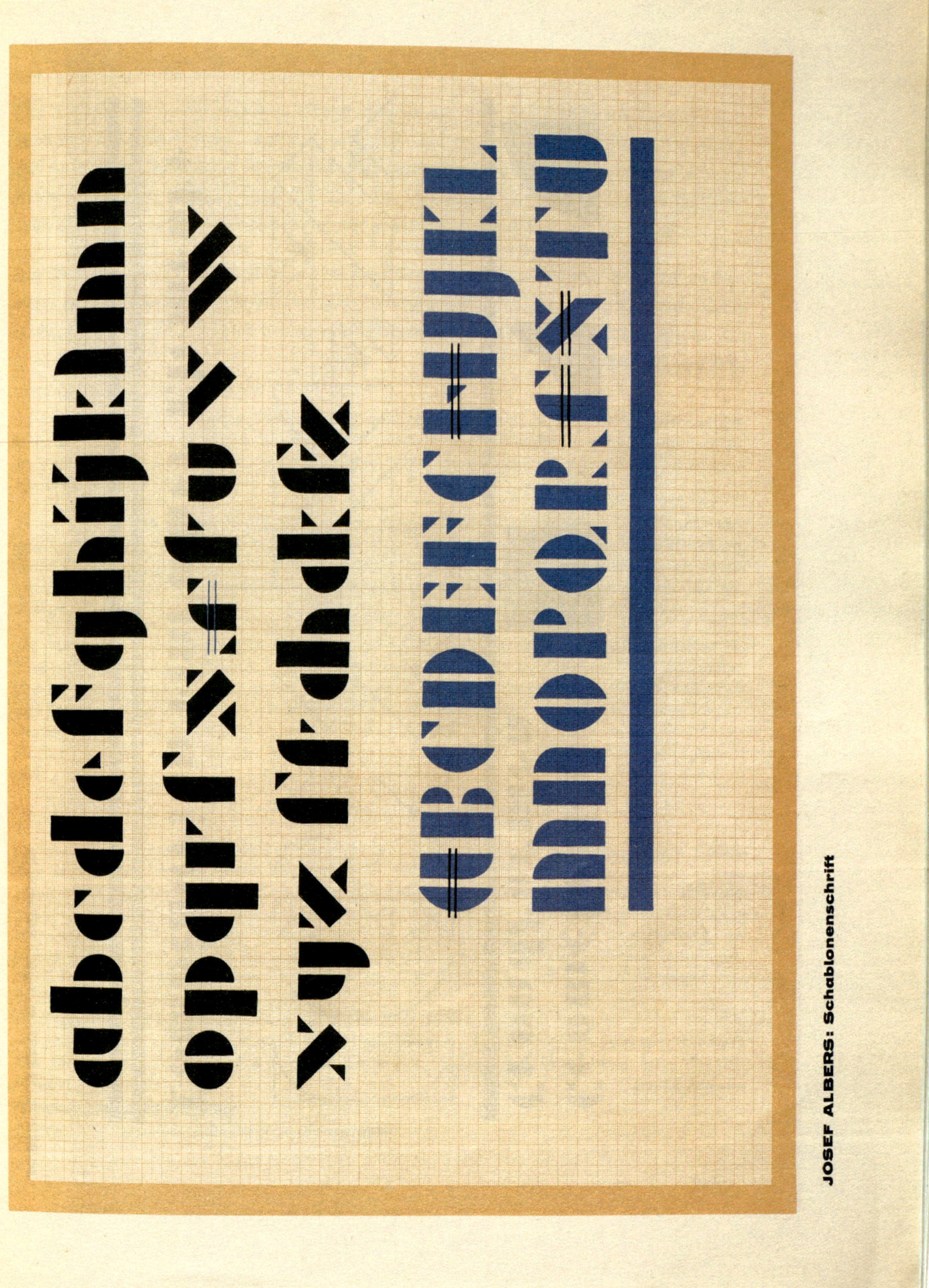

JOSEF ALBERS: Schablonenschrift

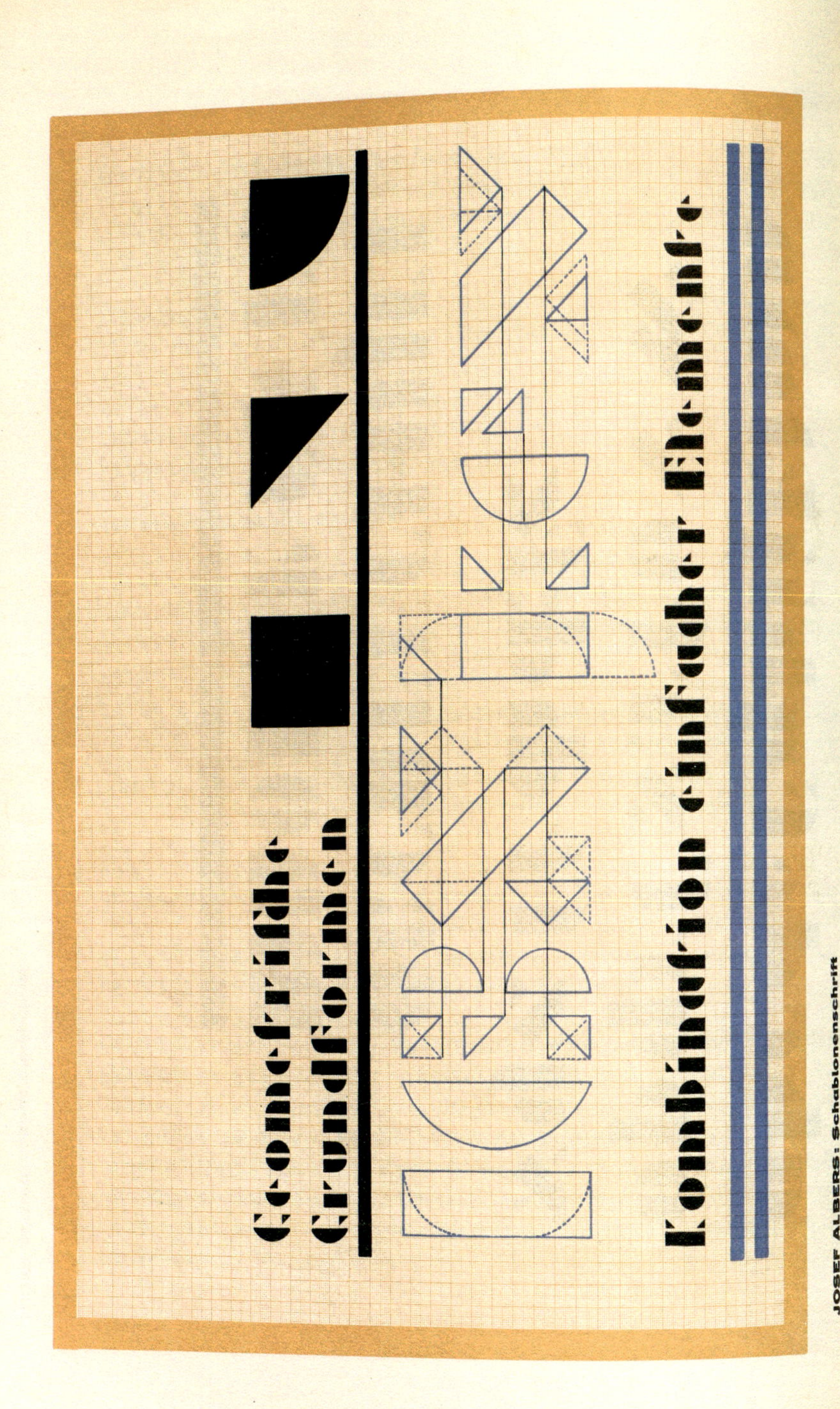

JOSEF ALBERS: Schablonenschrift

Das organisierte S
Schwarz-Grau-Weiß
die neue Form bes
Klarheit geordnet, z
kehr regieren, also

Ein Versuch, die T
men, ist die Schab
nicht, endgültig zu

ZUR SCHABLONE

Sie will eine Reklame-
lesbar ist. Die Deutlich
am wenigsten wohl be
schrift steigert die Lesb

Sie ist, wie zum Teil
gebaut, und zwar aus
dessen Radius der Qu
bunden nebeneinander
flächigen Elemente.

Das durchgehende Ma
Abstände innerhalb de
Quadrats) = $^2/_3$ der
sind überall gleich gro
Der Stegüberstand ist
gleichen Elementen er
exakt schneidbar.

Die Zeile erhält kein

Die ungleich groß wi
über das Schriftfeld v
Damit ist der Blocksat
rechts oder gar nicht,
links erleichtert den L
nächste Zeile oft falsc
den Zeile irrt das Aug
durch senkrechte Aus
Die Typisierung der B
den Buchstaben aus se
und wir erhalten gl
seitigstes Betonungsm

*) nicht nur im materiel

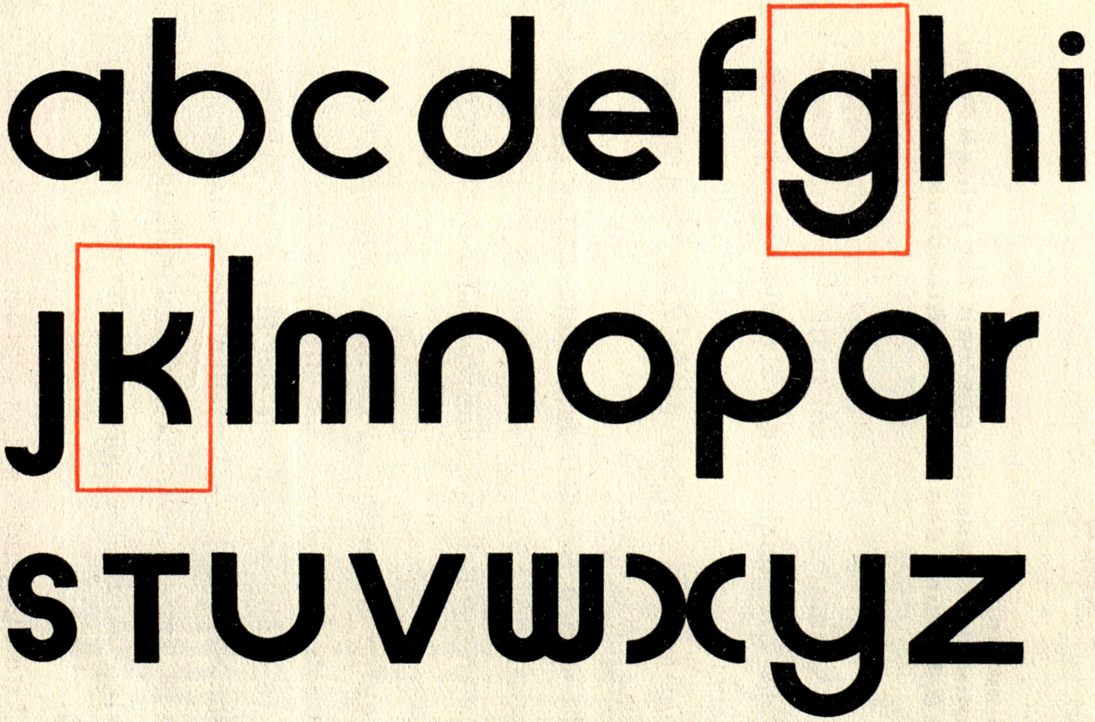

abcdefghi
jklmnopqr
stuvwxyz

d

HERBERT BAYER: Abb. 1. Alfabet
„g“ und „k“ sind noch als
unfertig zu betrachten

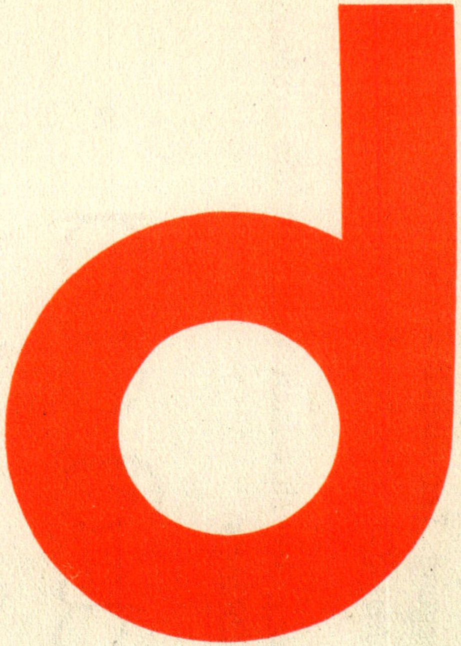

Beispiel eines Zeichens
in größerem Maßstab
Präzise optische Wirkung

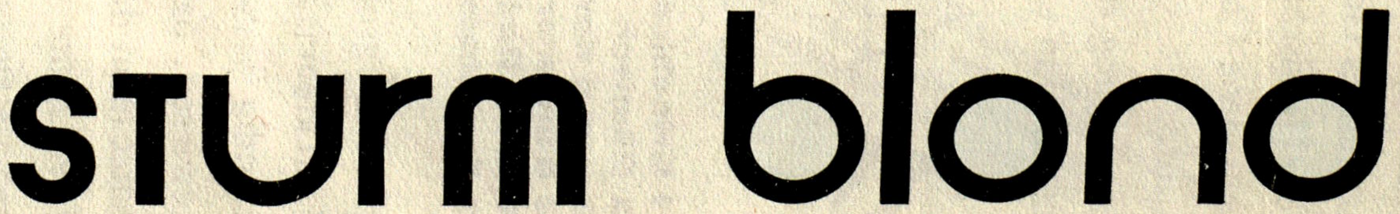

sturm blond

Abb. 2. Anwendung

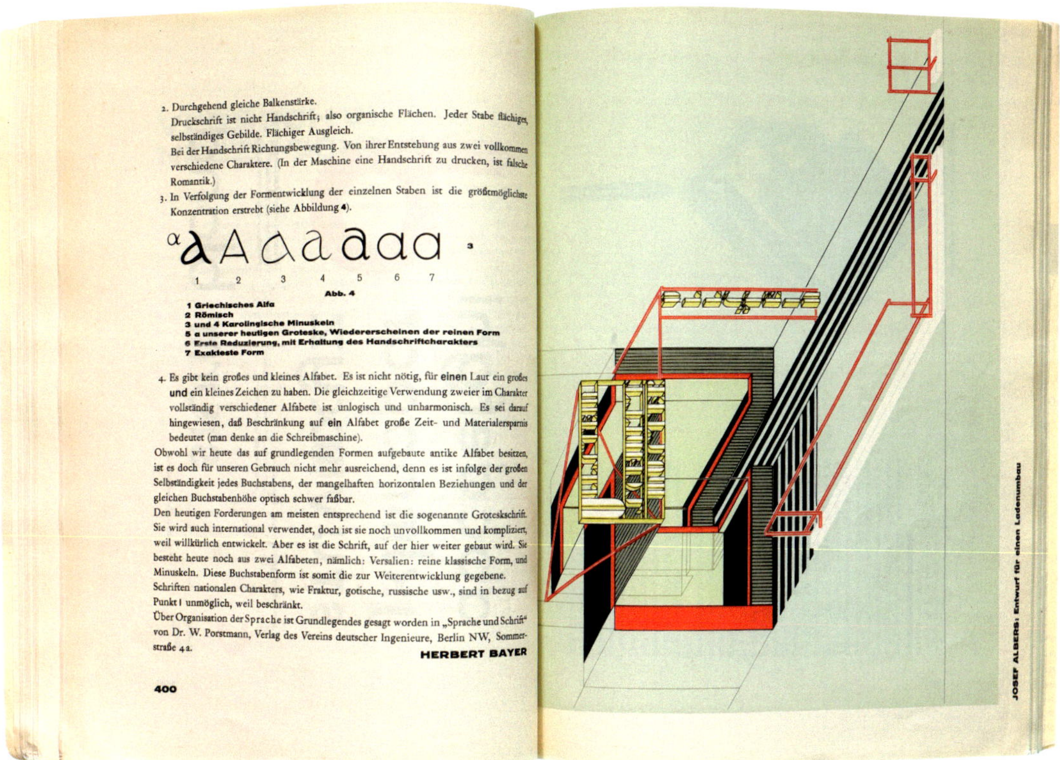

2. Durchgehend gleiche Balkenstärke.
   Druckschrift ist nicht Handschrift; also organische Flächen. Jeder Stabe flächiges, selbständiges Gebilde. Flächiger Ausgleich.
   Bei der Handschrift Richtungsbewegung. Von ihrer Entstehung aus zwei vollkommen verschiedene Charaktere. (In der Maschine eine Handschrift zu drucken, ist falsche Romantik.)
3. In Verfolgung der Formentwicklung der einzelnen Staben ist die größtmöglichste Konzentration erstrebt (siehe Abbildung **4**).

Abb. 4

1 Griechisches Alfa
2 Römisch
3 und 4 Karolingische Minuskeln
5 a unserer heutigen Groteske, Wiedererscheinen der reinen Form
6 Erste Reduzierung, mit Erhaltung des Handschriftcharakters
7 Exakteste Form

4. Es gibt kein großes und kleines Alfabet. Es ist nicht nötig, für **einen** Laut ein großes **und** ein kleines Zeichen zu haben. Die gleichzeitige Verwendung zweier im Charakter vollständig verschiedener Alfabete ist unlogisch und unharmonisch. Es sei darauf hingewiesen, daß Beschränkung auf **ein** Alfabet große Zeit- und Materialersparnis bedeutet (man denke an die Schreibmaschine).

Obwohl wir heute das auf grundlegenden Formen aufgebaute antike Alfabet besitzen, ist es doch für unseren Gebrauch nicht mehr ausreichend, denn es ist infolge der großen Selbständigkeit jedes Buchstabens, der mangelhaften horizontalen Beziehungen und der gleichen Buchstabenhöhe optisch schwer faßbar.

Den heutigen Forderungen am meisten entsprechend ist die sogenannte Groteskschrift. Sie wird auch international verwendet, doch ist sie noch unvollkommen und kompliziert, weil willkürlich entwickelt. Aber es ist die Schrift, auf der hier weiter gebaut wird. Sie besteht heute noch aus zwei Alfabeten, nämlich: Versalien: reine klassische Form, und Minuskeln. Diese Buchstabenform ist somit die zur Weiterentwicklung gegebene.

Schriften nationalen Charakters, wie Fraktur, gotische, russische usw., sind in bezug auf Punkt **1** unmöglich, weil beschränkt.

Über Organisation der Sprache ist Grundlegendes gesagt worden in „Sprache und Schrift" von Dr. W. Porstmann, Verlag des Vereins deutscher Ingenieure, Berlin NW, Sommerstraße 4a.

HERBERT BAYER

400

In addition to showcasing Bauhaus projects printed in multiple colors, this issue of *Offset* includes early coverage of two experimental Bauhaus alphabet designs. The first is one of several stencil alphabets designed by German-born painter Josef Albers, who was a student and then a professor at the Bauhaus. His typeface is modular, meaning that a limited set of identical shapes mix and match to make up all letters (see pages 202–203). In this case, Albers built his alphabet out of three forms: a square, a triangle, and a quarter-circle. The other typeface featured in the issue, Universal Type, is Herbert Bayer's attempt at a completely rational typeface—one derived from geometry rather than handwriting and therefore ostensibly better adapted to industrial production (see above and left). It also eliminates the use of two sets of distinct characters for uppercase and lowercase. The design was especially radical in light of the rise of National Socialism, which presented Fraktur as the only so-called authentically German style (as opposed to the Latinate class of antiqua typefaces or grotesque sans serifs). While neither typeface design ever saw production in metal, both greatly influenced later experimental alphabets and inspired several revivals. In the late 1960s and early 1970s, almost every phototype and transfer lettering company came out with their own take on the minimalist, geometric style. Ads, album covers, book jackets, and posters of the era were filled with typefaces like Harry (Mary Goldstein, VGC, 1966), Burko (David Burke, Headliners, 1967), Blippo (Joe Taylor, FotoStar, 1969), Pump (Bob Newman, Letraset, 1970), and Bauhaus (Ed Benguiat, Photo-Lettering, 1969). The latter became ITC Bauhaus, a large and popular family that, despite its name, is the furthest departure from its Universal Type inspiration. ●

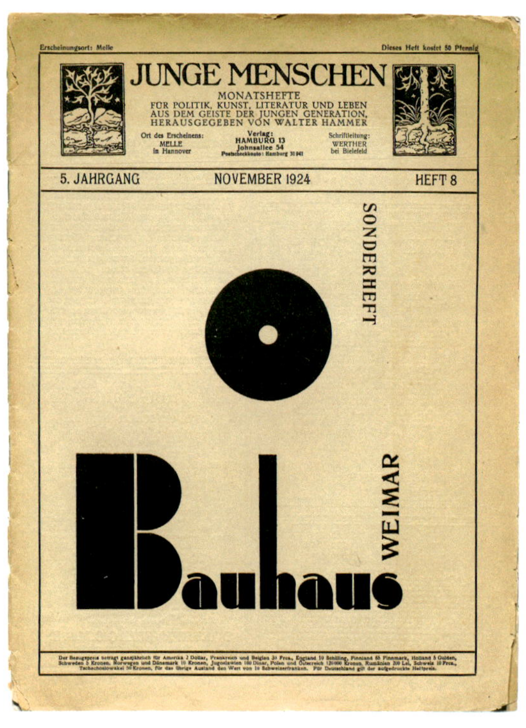

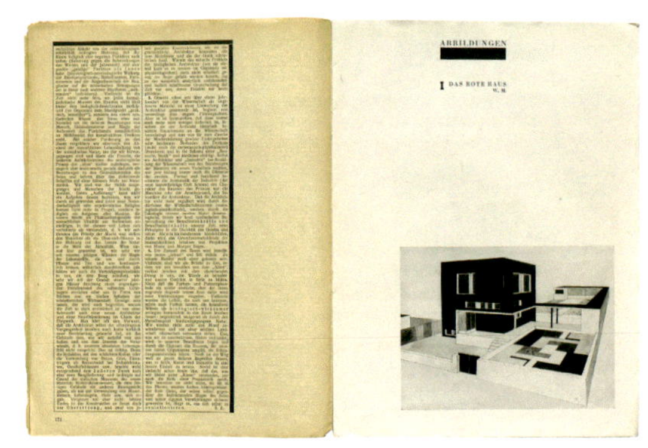

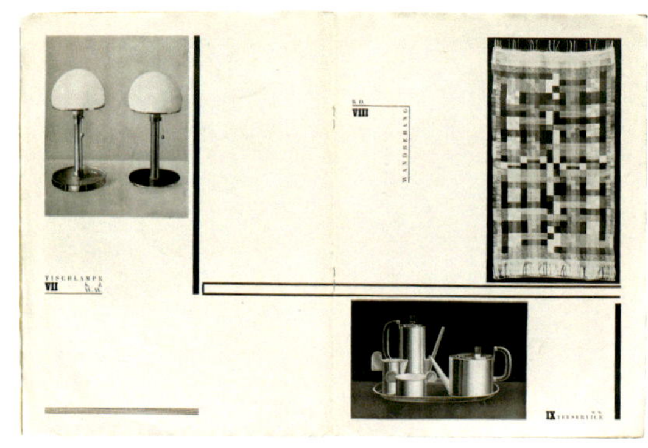

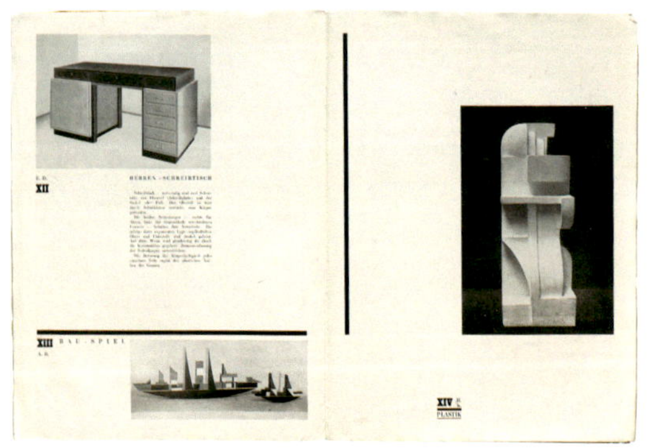

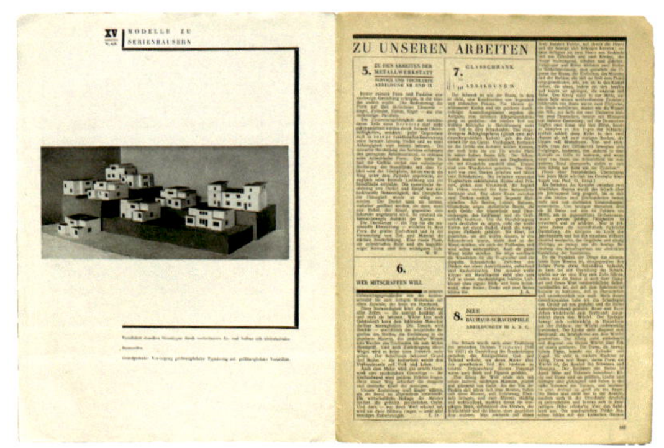

1924

JOOST SCHMIDT

Young People (*Junge Menschen*), *Special Issue: Bauhaus Weimar*, vol. 5, no. 8, letterpress, 12 × 9⅛ inches (305 × 232 mm), Hamburg.

1924

JOOST SCHMIDT

Ticket for the Celebration of the Fifth Bauhaus Year (Feier des fünften Bauhaus Jahres), lithograph, shown at actual size (6 × 4¾ inches/150 × 120 mm), Weimar.

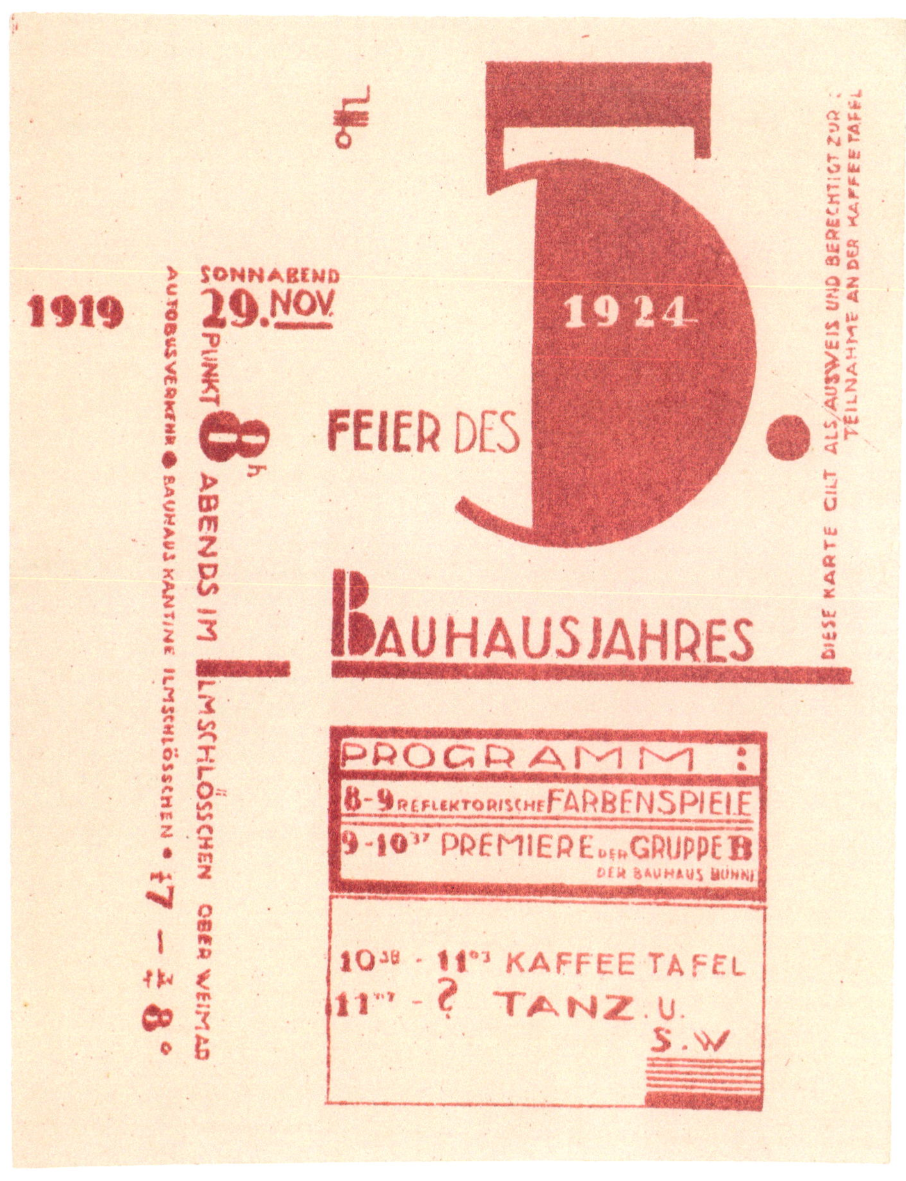

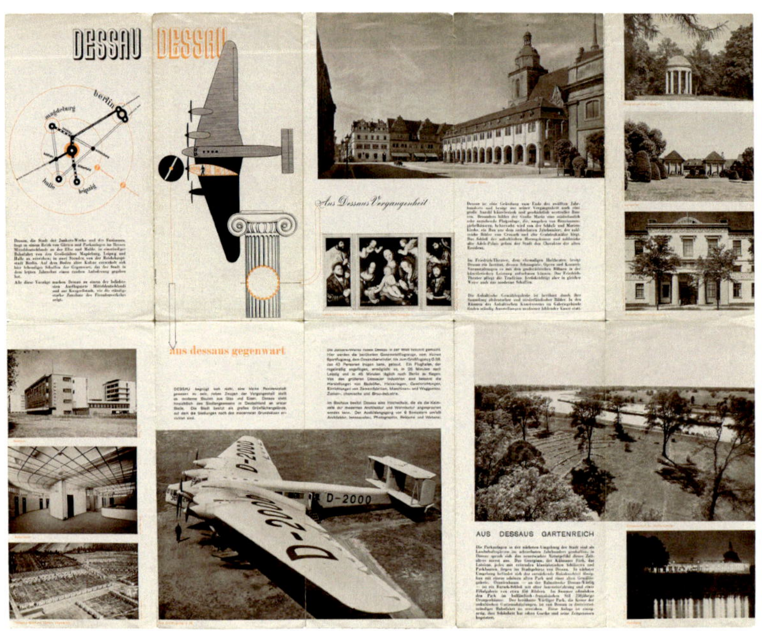

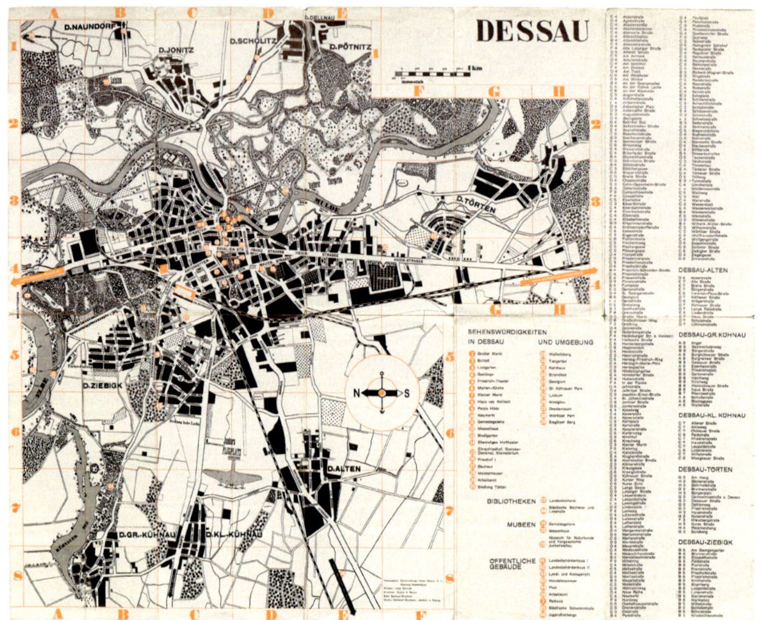

1930

JOOST SCHMIDT

Tourism brochure for the city of Dessau, letterpress and lithograph, 9 × 4⅞ inches (230 × 122 mm) folded, 23½ × 18¾ inches (600 x 475 mm) unfolded, Dessau.

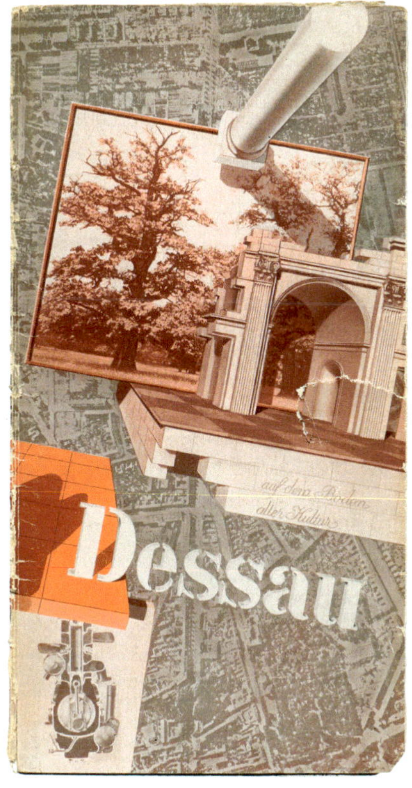

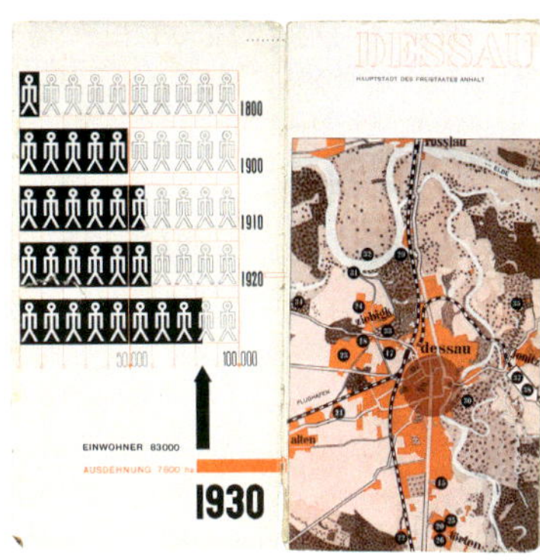

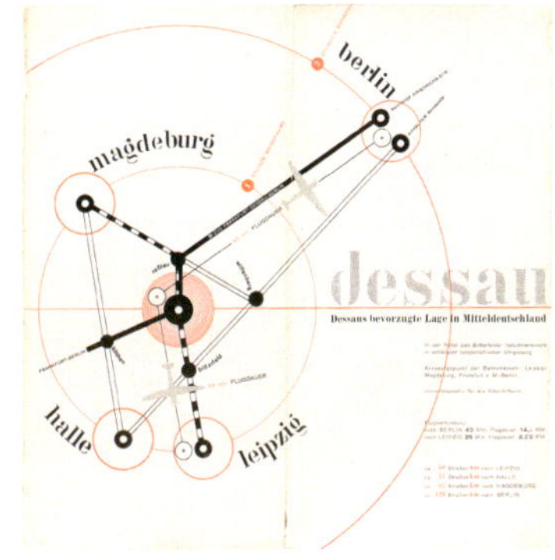

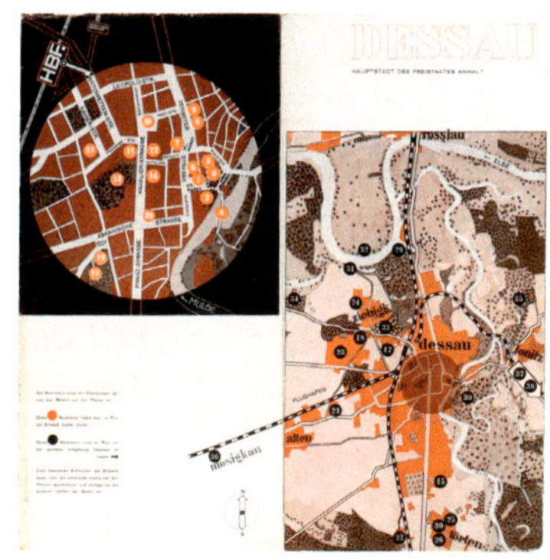

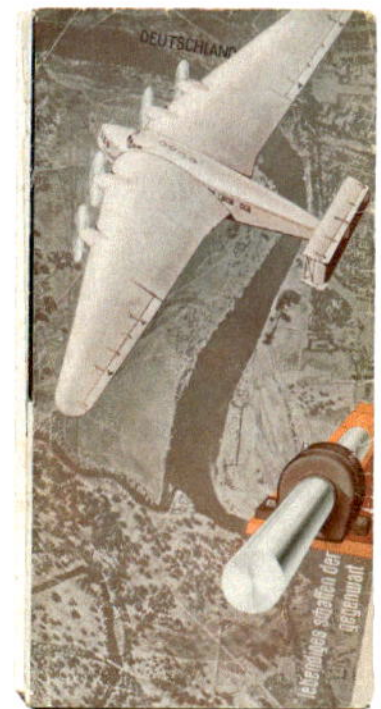

1931

JOOST SCHMIDT

Tourism brochure for the city of Dessau, letterpress, 9½ × 4⅞ inches (241 × 122 mm) folded, 9½ × 9¾ inches (241 x 244 mm) unfolded, Dessau.

1926

JOOST SCHMIDT (cover designer)

The Form (*Die Form*), vol. 1, no. 14, an influential craft and trade publication, letterpress, 11¾ × 8¼ inches (297 × 210 mm), Berlin.

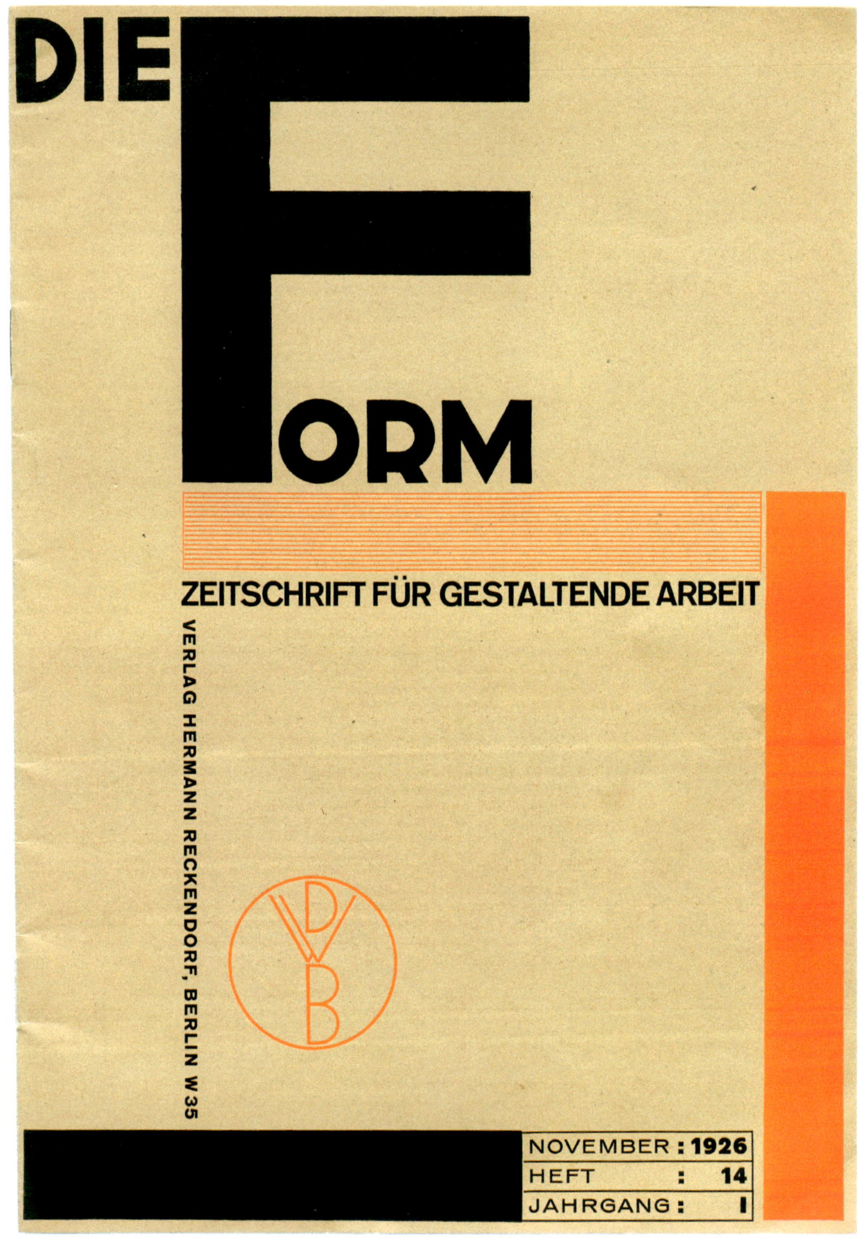

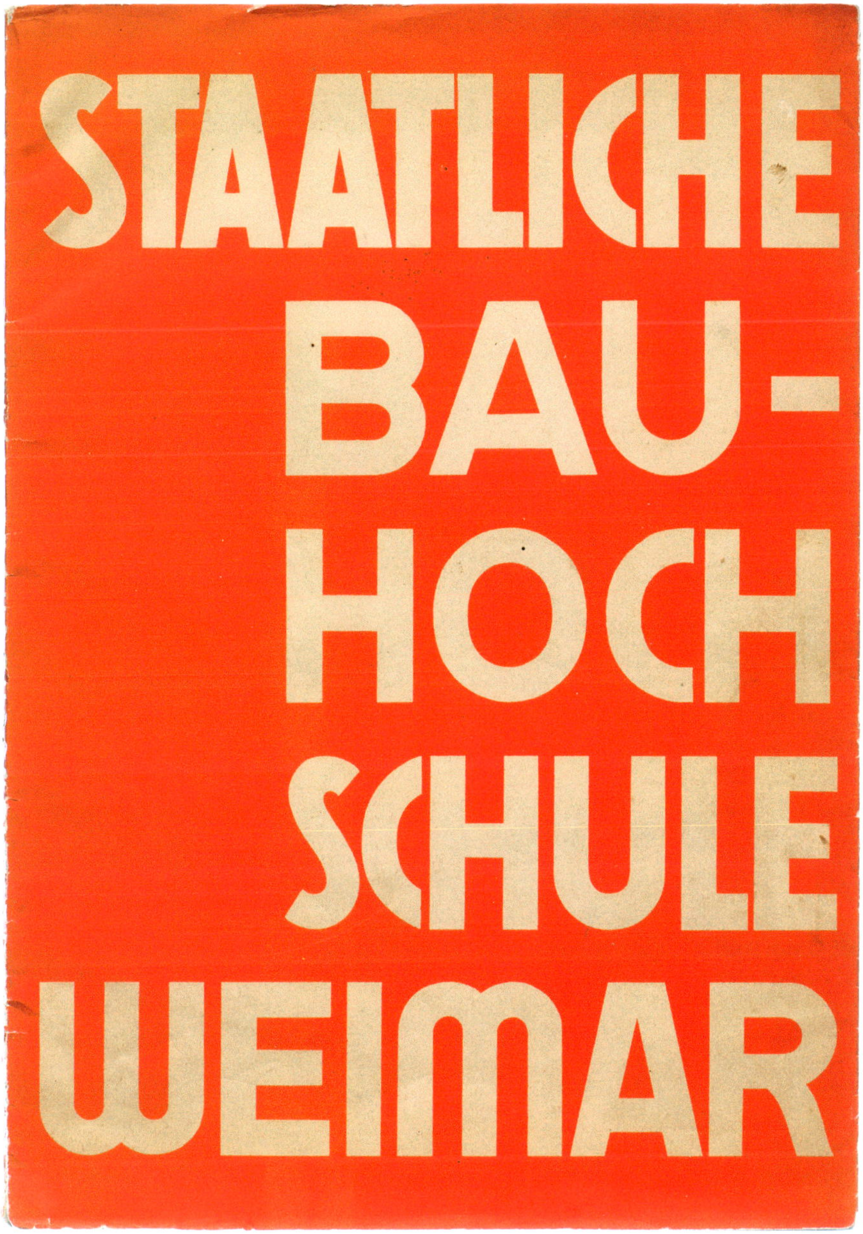

STAATLICHE
BAU-
HOCH
SCHULE
WEIMAR

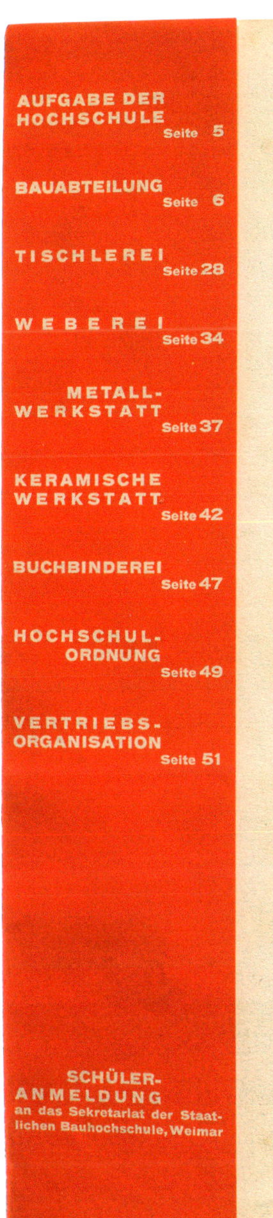

SCHÜLER-ANMELDUNG
an das Sekretariat der Staatlichen Bauhochschule, Weimar

1929

DESIGNER UNKNOWN (likely Joost Schmidt)

Course curriculum book for the Weimar Architecture and Building College (Staatliche Bauhochschule Weimar), letterpress, 11¾ × 8⅜ inches (297 × 214 mm), Weimar.

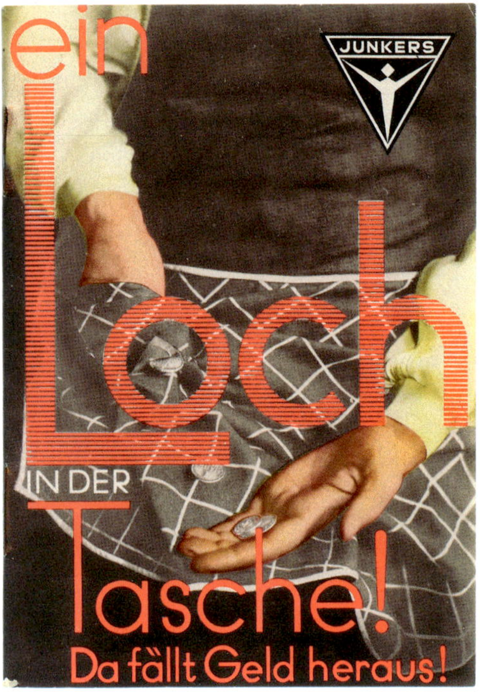
ein
Loch
IN DER
Tasche!
Da fällt Geld heraus!
JUNKERS

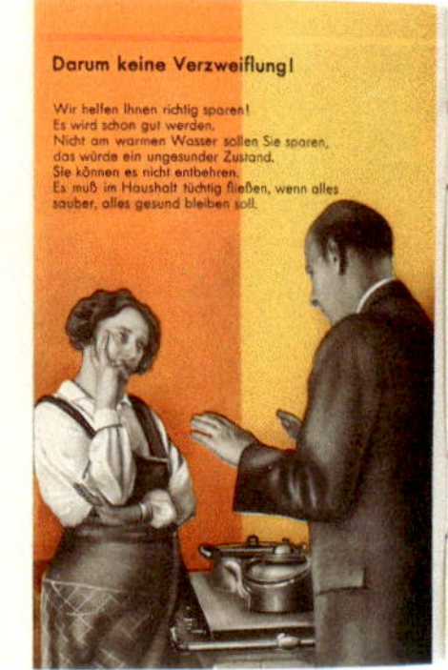
Darum keine Verzweiflung!
Wir helfen Ihnen richtig sparen!
Es wird schon gut werden.
Nicht am warmen Wasser sollen Sie sparen,
das würde ein ungesunder Zustand.
Sie können es nicht entbehren.
Es muß im Haushalt tüchtig fließen, wenn alles
sauber, alles gesund bleiben soll.

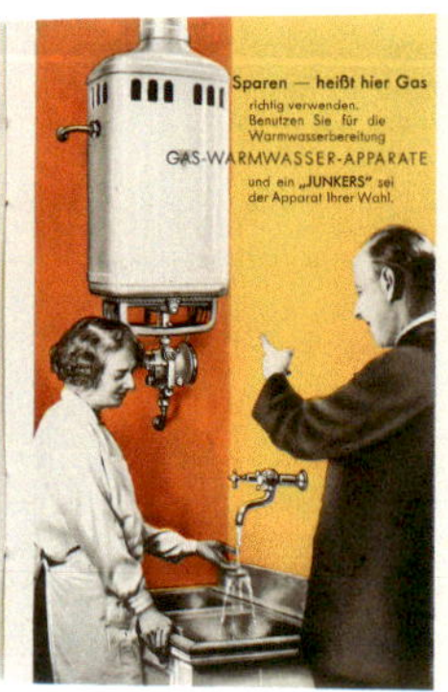
Sparen — heißt hier Gas
richtig verwenden.
Benutzen Sie für die
Warmwasserbereitung
GAS-WARMWASSER-APPARATE
und ein „JUNKERS" sei
der Apparat Ihrer Wahl.

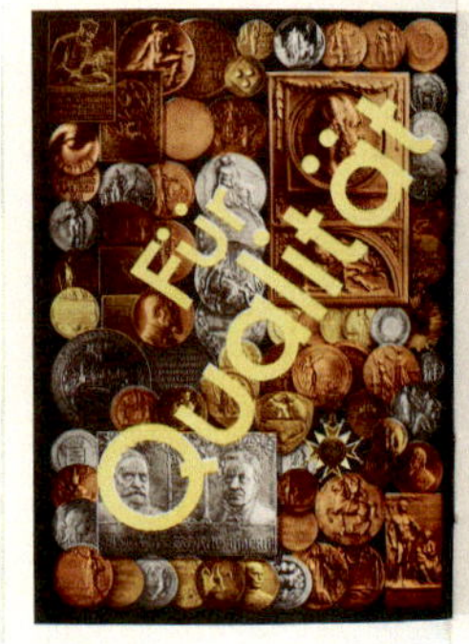
Für
Qualität

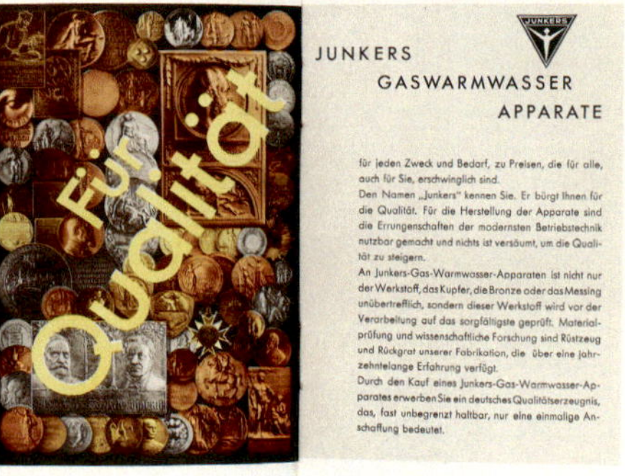
JUNKERS
GASWARMWASSER
APPARATE
für jeden Zweck und Bedarf, zu Preisen, die für alle, auch für Sie, erschwinglich sind.
Den Namen „Junkers" kennen Sie. Er bürgt Ihnen für die Qualität. Für die Herstellung der Apparate sind die Errungenschaften der modernsten Betriebstechnik nutzbar gemacht und nichts ist versäumt, um die Qualität zu steigern.
An Junkers-Gas-Warmwasser-Apparaten ist nicht nur der Werkstoff, das Kupfer, die Bronze oder das Messing unübertrefflich, sondern dieser Werkstoff wird vor der Verarbeitung auf das sorgfältigste geprüft. Materialprüfung und wissenschaftliche Forschung sind Rüstzeug und Rückgrat unserer Fabrikation, die über eine jahrzehntelange Erfahrung verfügt.
Durch den Kauf eines Junkers-Gas-Warmwasser-Apparates erwerben Sie ein deutsches Qualitätserzeugnis, das, fast unbegrenzt haltbar, nur eine einmalige Anschaffung bedeutet.

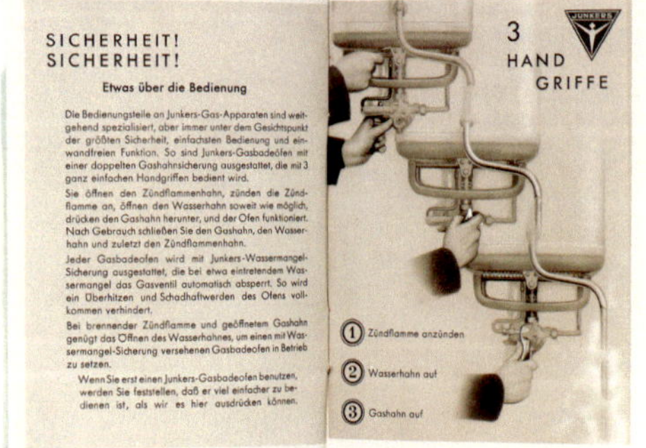
SICHERHEIT!
SICHERHEIT!
Etwas über die Bedienung
Die Bedienungsteile an Junkers-Gas-Apparaten sind weitgehend spezialisiert, aber immer unter dem Gesichtspunkt der größten Sicherheit, einfachsten Bedienung und einwandfreien Funktion. So sind Junkers-Gasbadeöfen mit einer doppelten Gashahnsicherung ausgestattet, die mit 3 ganz einfachen Handgriffen bedient wird.
Sie öffnen den Zündflammenhahn, zünden die Zündflamme an, öffnen den Wasserhahn soweit wie möglich, drücken den Gashahn herunter, und der Ofen funktioniert. Nach Gebrauch schließen Sie den Gashahn, den Wasserhahn und zuletzt den Zündflammenhahn.
Jeder Gasbadeofen wird mit Junkers-Wassermangel-Sicherung ausgestattet, die bei etwa eintretendem Wassermangel das Gasventil automatisch absperrt. So wird ein Überhitzen und Schadhaftwerden des Ofens vollkommen verhindert.
Bei brennender Zündflamme und geöffnetem Gashahn genügt das Öffnen des Wasserhahnes, um einen mit Wassermangel-Sicherung versehenen Gasbadeofen in Betrieb zu setzen.
Wenn Sie erst einen Junkers-Gasbadeofen benutzen, werden Sie feststellen, daß er viel einfacher zu bedienen ist, als wir es hier ausdrücken können.
3
HAND
GRIFFE
① Zündflamme anzünden
② Wasserhahn auf
③ Gashahn auf

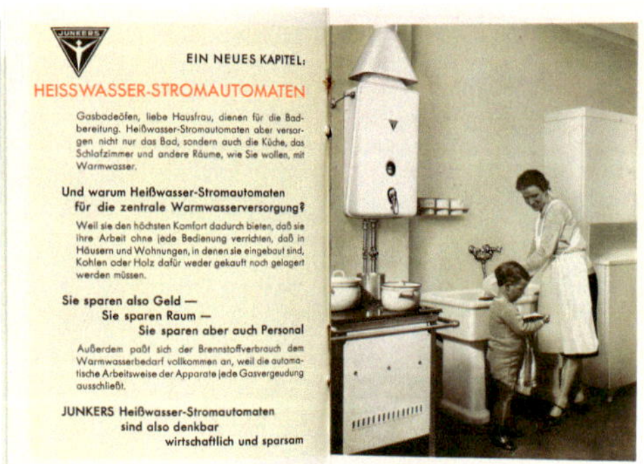
EIN NEUES KAPITEL:
HEISSWASSER-STROMAUTOMATEN
Gasbadeöfen, liebe Hausfrau, dienen für die Badbereitung. Heißwasser-Stromautomaten aber versorgen nicht nur das Bad, sondern auch die Küche, das Schlafzimmer und andere Räume, wie Sie wollen, mit Warmwasser.
Und warum Heißwasser-Stromautomaten für die zentrale Warmwasserversorgung?
Weil sie den höchsten Komfort dadurch bieten, daß sie ihre Arbeit ohne jede Bedienung verrichten, daß in Häusern und Wohnungen, in denen sie eingebaut sind, Kohlen oder Holz dafür weder gekauft noch gelagert werden müssen.
Sie sparen also Geld —
Sie sparen Raum —
Sie sparen aber auch Personal
Außerdem paßt sich der Brennstoffverbrauch dem Warmwasserbedarf vollkommen an, weil die automatische Arbeitsweise der Apparate jede Gasvergeudung ausschließt.
JUNKERS Heißwasser-Stromautomaten
sind also denkbar
wirtschaftlich und sparsam

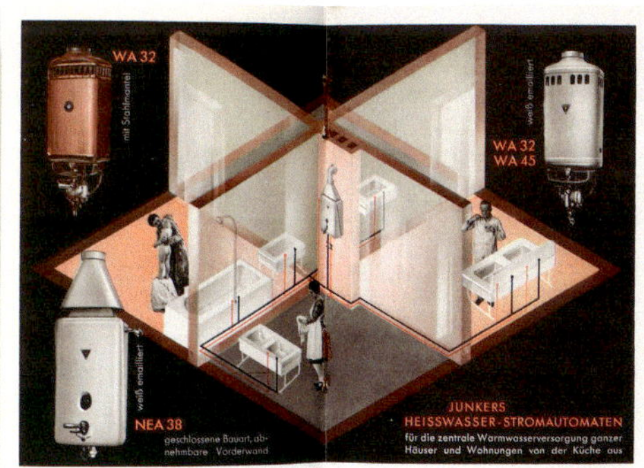

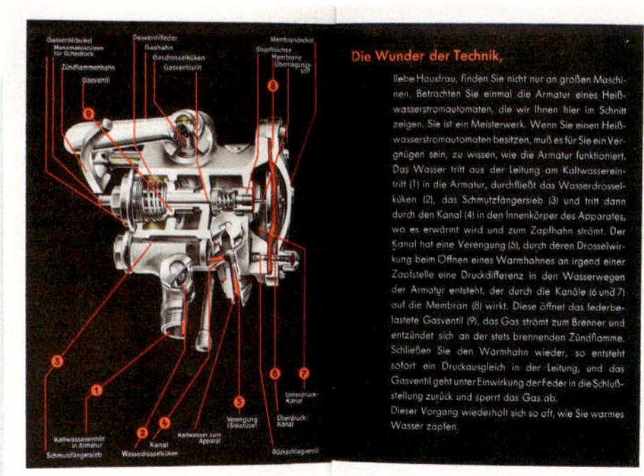

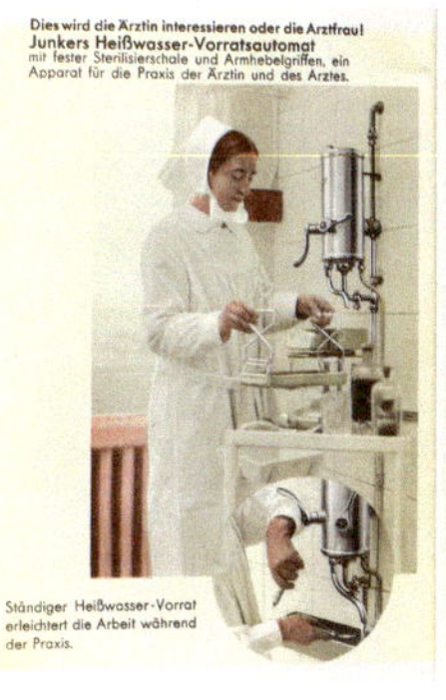

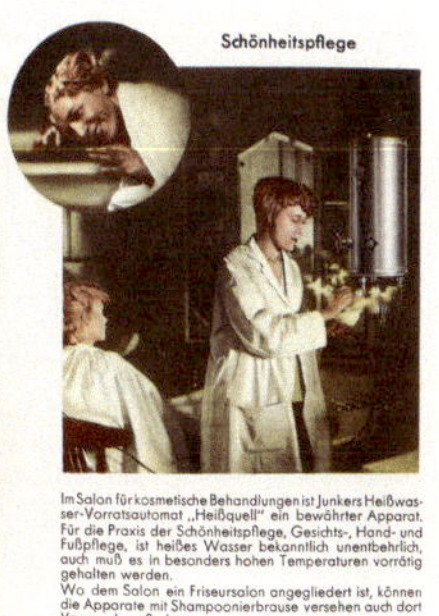

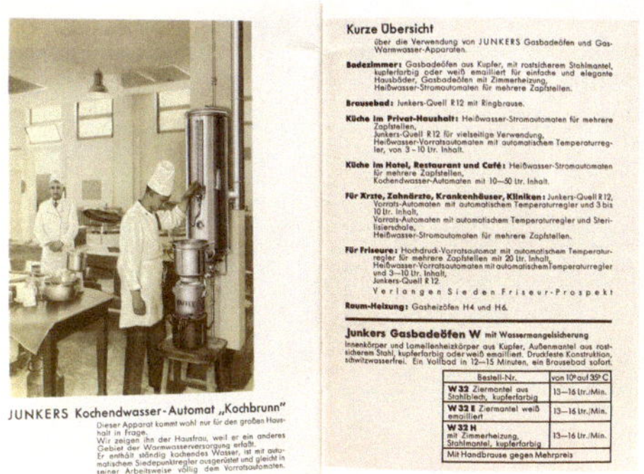

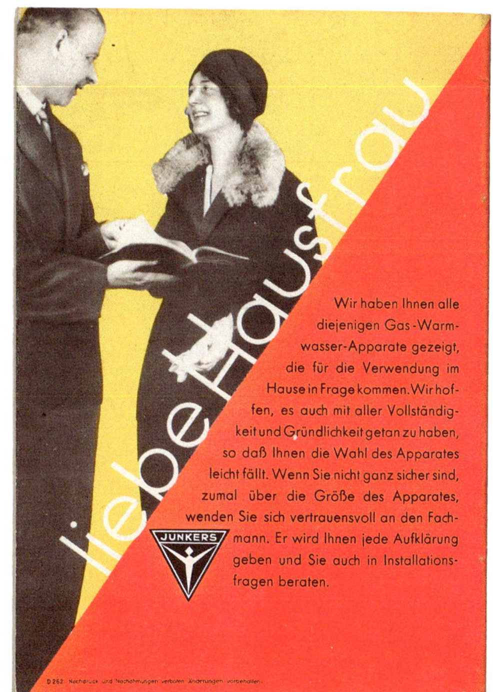

CIRCA 1930s

JOOST SCHMIDT

"A Hole in the Pocket! Money Falls Out!" ("Ein Loch in der Tasche! Da fällt Geld heraus!"), product catalog for water heaters manufactured by Junkers & Co., letterpress, 5¾ × 4⅛ inches (146 × 105 mm), Dessau.

towar
a new
typog

While influential, the Bauhaus was just one nexus at which the modernist revolution in typography and design occurred. Throughout Europe, avant-garde artists were applying the aesthetics of abstraction to commercial advertising, while others—typographers and designers by trade—simply sought a new, streamlined system of communication for the machine age. This broader movement, sometimes labeled the New Typography after Moholy-Nagy's 1923 essay and Jan Tschichold's 1928 book of the same name, was a loosely associated and highly international network of designers working in a similarly spare, geometric style—an aesthetic that would inform typographic discourse for much of the century. While not directly affiliated with the Bauhaus, many of these designers engaged in active dialogue with its teachers, students, and ideas. ●

The objects in the following pages represent only a small cross-section of activities and figures adjacent to the Bauhaus. Some, like the 1920s advertising monograph *Captivated Gaze* or Tschichold's *The New Typography*, serve as anthologies of the broader New Typography movement. Others, such as the work of Dutch designer Piet Zwart and Czech artist Karel Teige, represent contemporaneous commercial and artistic designs from outside Germany, though both men lectured at the Bauhaus. And German painter and gallerist Walter Dexel, while not a student of the school, organized several exhibitions that were hosted by the Bauhaus or featured Bauhaus artists. Finally, original type specimens of Futura and geometric ornaments show the influence of modernist ideas on the tools as well as the products of typography. ●

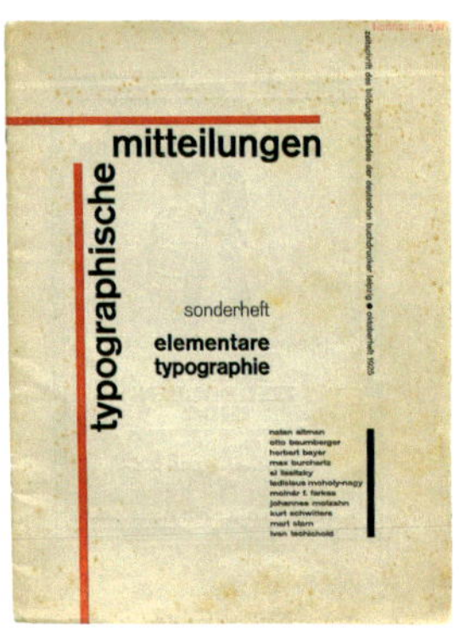

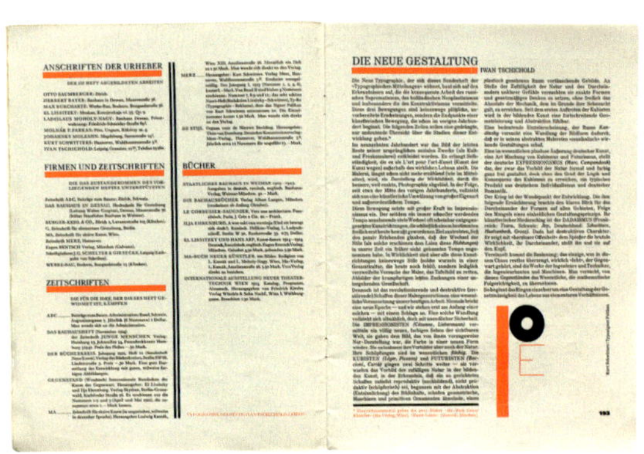

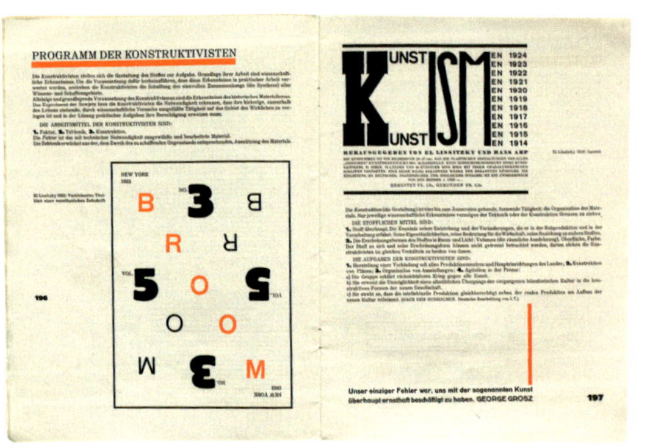

1925

JAN TSCHICHOLD (designer/editor)

Typographic Notes, Fundamental Typography Special Issue (*Typographische Mitteilungen, Sonderheft Elementare Typographie*), October 1925 issue, letterpress, 12¼ × 9¼ inches (310 × 236 mm), Leipzig.

German-born designer Jan Tschichold created the October 1925 special issue of *Typographic Notes*, a trade magazine for printers, typesetters, and typographers, before the 1928 publication of *The New Typography* solidified his reputation as a founder of typographic modernism. Its cover features a variety of sans serif typefaces, including Akzidenz-Grotesk and Aurora-Grotesk, while the interior text is set in a utilitarian serif, punctuated by extrabold grotesque numerals. The issue sparked a debate in the German print community, dividing those liberated by the new emphasis on asymmetry, simplicity, empty space, and sans serifs from the traditionalists who preferred symmetrical layouts, Fraktur type, and nonphotographic illustration. It also attests to the importance of two events in Tschichold's early life: his befriending of the Russian constructivist El Lissitzky and his attendance at the first Bauhaus exhibition in 1923. Tschichold hints at the impact of the former by adopting a Russianized version of his name, Iwan, on the insert's cover; the latter finds expression in the inclusion of several pieces of early Bauhaus ephemera. In turn, the issue was noticed by those at the Bauhaus; notably, this copy bears the ownership stamp of Swiss architect Hannes Meyer, the school's second director. ●

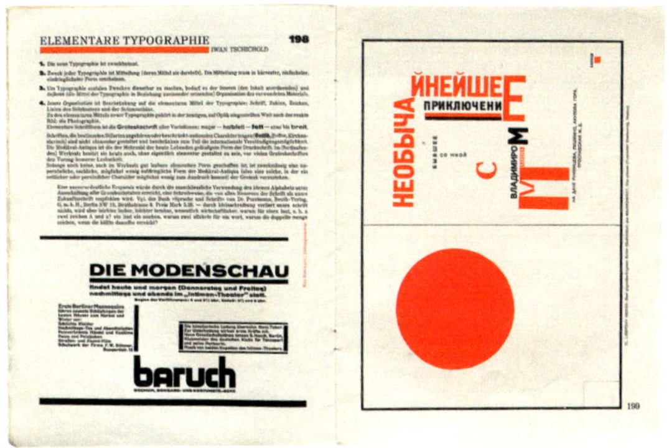
ELEMENTARE TYPOGRAPHIE
IWAN TSCHICHOLD
198
DIE MODENSCHAU
baruch
НЕОБЫЧАЙНЕЙШЕ
ПРИКЛЮЧЕНИ
199

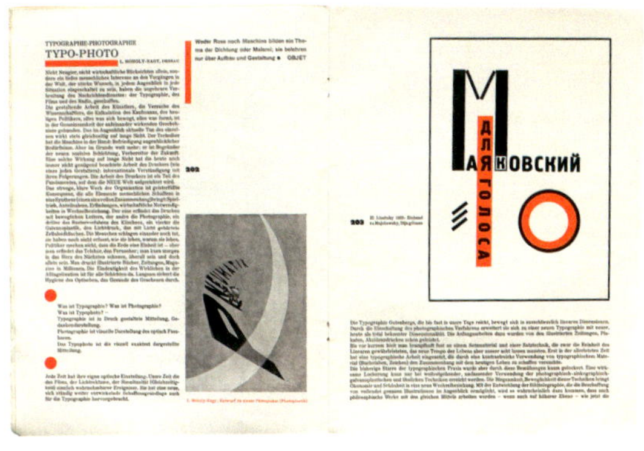
TYPO-PHOTO
202
МАЯКОВСКИЙ
ДЛЯ ГОЛОСА
203

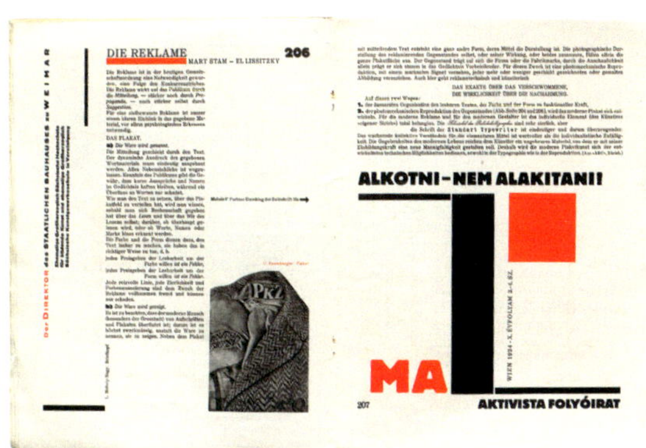
DIE REKLAME
MART STAM – EL LISSITZKY
206
ALKOTNI-NEM ALAKITANI!
MA
AKTIVISTA FOLYÓIRAT
207

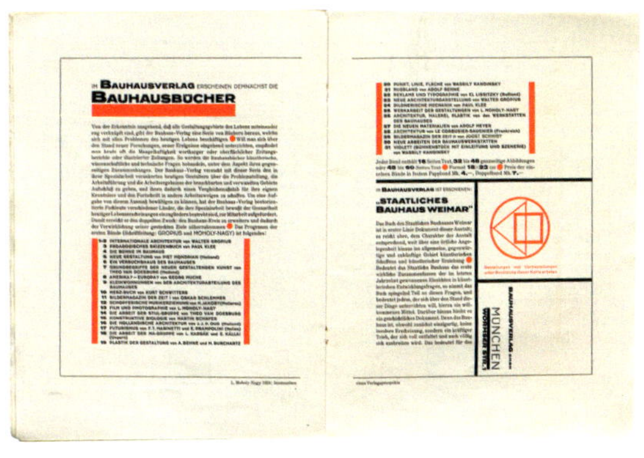
BAUHAUSVERLAG
BAUHAUSBÜCHER
„STAATLICHES BAUHAUS WEIMAR"
MÜNCHEN

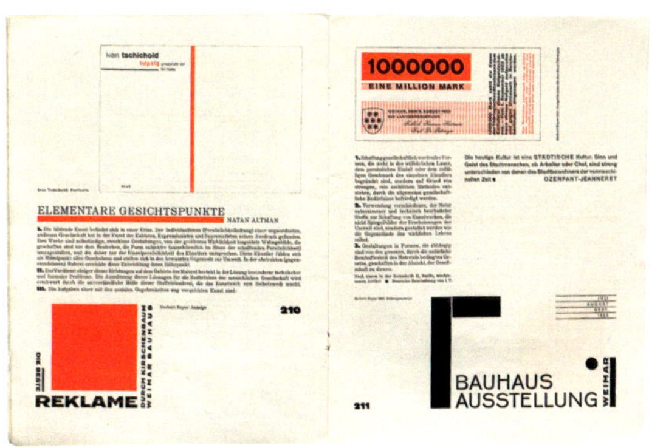
ivan tschichold
ELEMENTARE GESICHTSPUNKTE
NATAN ALTMAN
210
REKLAME
1000000
EINE MILLION MARK
211
BAUHAUS AUSSTELLUNG
WEIMAR

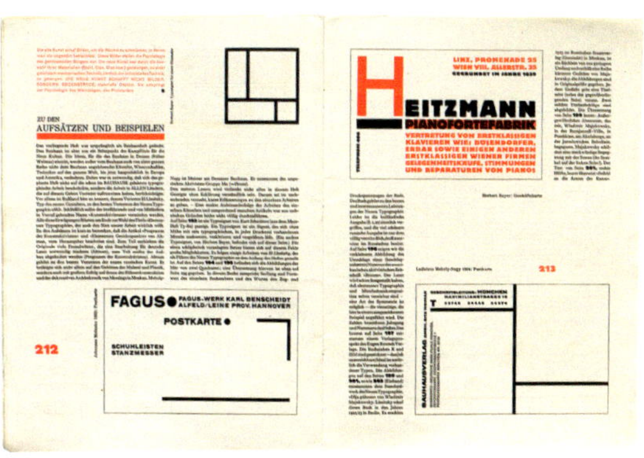
AUFSÄTZEN UND BEISPIELEN
FAGUS
POSTKARTE
212
HEITZMANN
PIANOFORTEFABRIK
213

1928

JAN TSCHICHOLD (designer/author)

The New Typography (Die neue Typographie), letterpress, shown at actual size (8⅜ × 5⅞ inches/212 × 150 mm), Berlin.

Piggybacking on the notoriety he gained with *Typographic Notes* (see pages 216–217), Jan Tschichold published his most important book, *The New Typography*, in 1928. Synthesizing theory and praxis, *The New Typography* is part fervent manifesto for modernist typographical severity and part practical guide on typeface selection, spacing, standardization, and other minutiae. As in the earlier magazine supplement, Tschichold illustrates his arguments using reproductions of cutting-edge designs by artists of the international avant-garde, including Bauhaus figures, as well as his own work. He ensures that the book embodies its own teachings, from its asymmetrical title page and solid black frontispiece to the use of Aurora-Grotesk, a nondescript sans serif text face, uncommon for book printing at the time. He also ascribed to notions about the integration of photography with typography, on view in his designs for various books and exhibitions for the New Photography movement (see pages 224–227), of which Moholy-Nagy was a contributor. Tschichold's ideas were important for the subsequent practice of modernist graphic design, particularly in the aesthetic known as Swiss Style or International Typographic Style, which became dominant at midcentury and remains highly influential today. Tschichold himself, on the other hand, came to disavow the extremism of his modernist convictions after World War II and returned to a more classical style. His later traditionalism is most recognizable in his designs for Penguin Books in England. ●

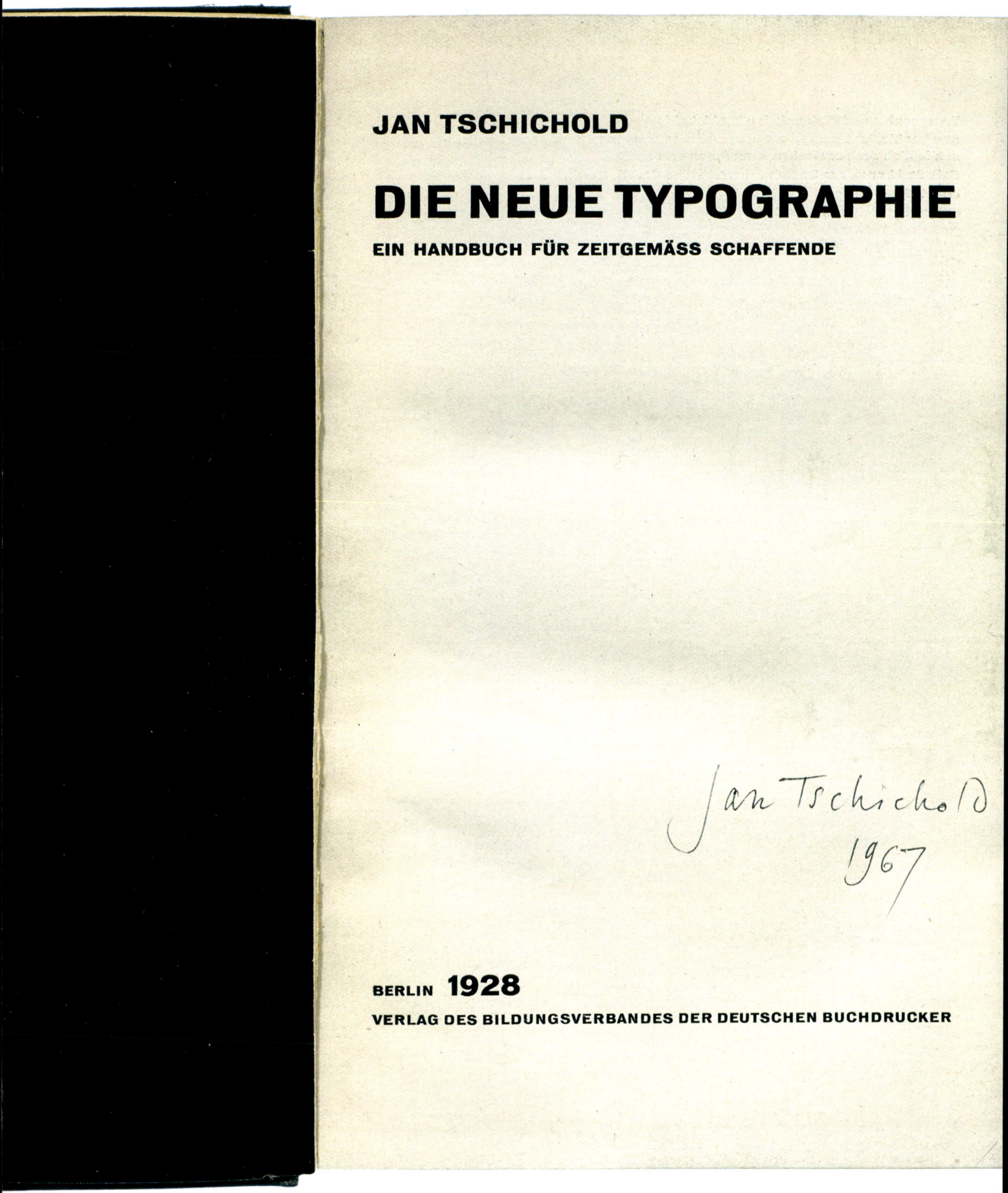

JAN TSCHICHOLD

DIE NEUE TYPOGRAPHIE

EIN HANDBUCH FÜR ZEITGEMÄSS SCHAFFENDE

Jan Tschichold
1967

BERLIN **1928**

VERLAG DES BILDUNGSVERBANDES DER DEUTSCHEN BUCHDRUCKER

deren Ausgangs-
selbst sind auch
ewissem Betracht
de von Czeschka

er F. T. Marinetti,
ftakt zu der Um-
geben.
Milano 1909, ver-

sich vor allem
g des passéisti-
Papier, seinem
nerven, Apolls,
üse, mit seinen
Buch muß der
s sein. Besser:
die sogenannte
ensatz steht zu
werden, wenn
e Farben und
Kursiv für eine
n, **fett** für die
ypographisch-

expressive)
sorthographie
ach und nach
Fesseln und

n Rausch in
und Echos,
nden auszu-
vandelten sie

Lettre d'une jolie femme
à un monsieur passéiste

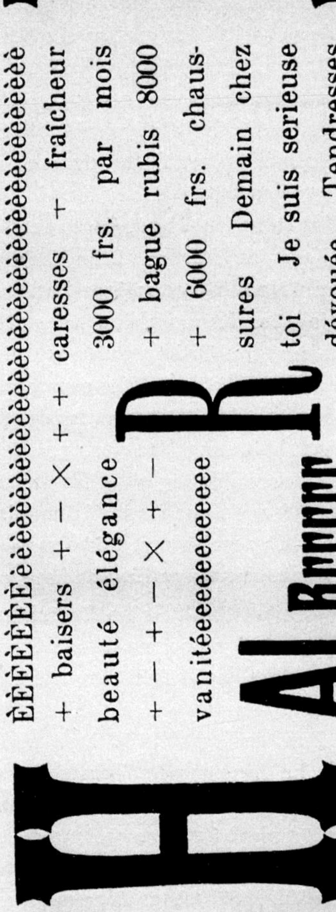

F. T. MARINETTI: Gedicht aus dem Buche „Les Mots en liberté futuristes" (Milano 1919)

55

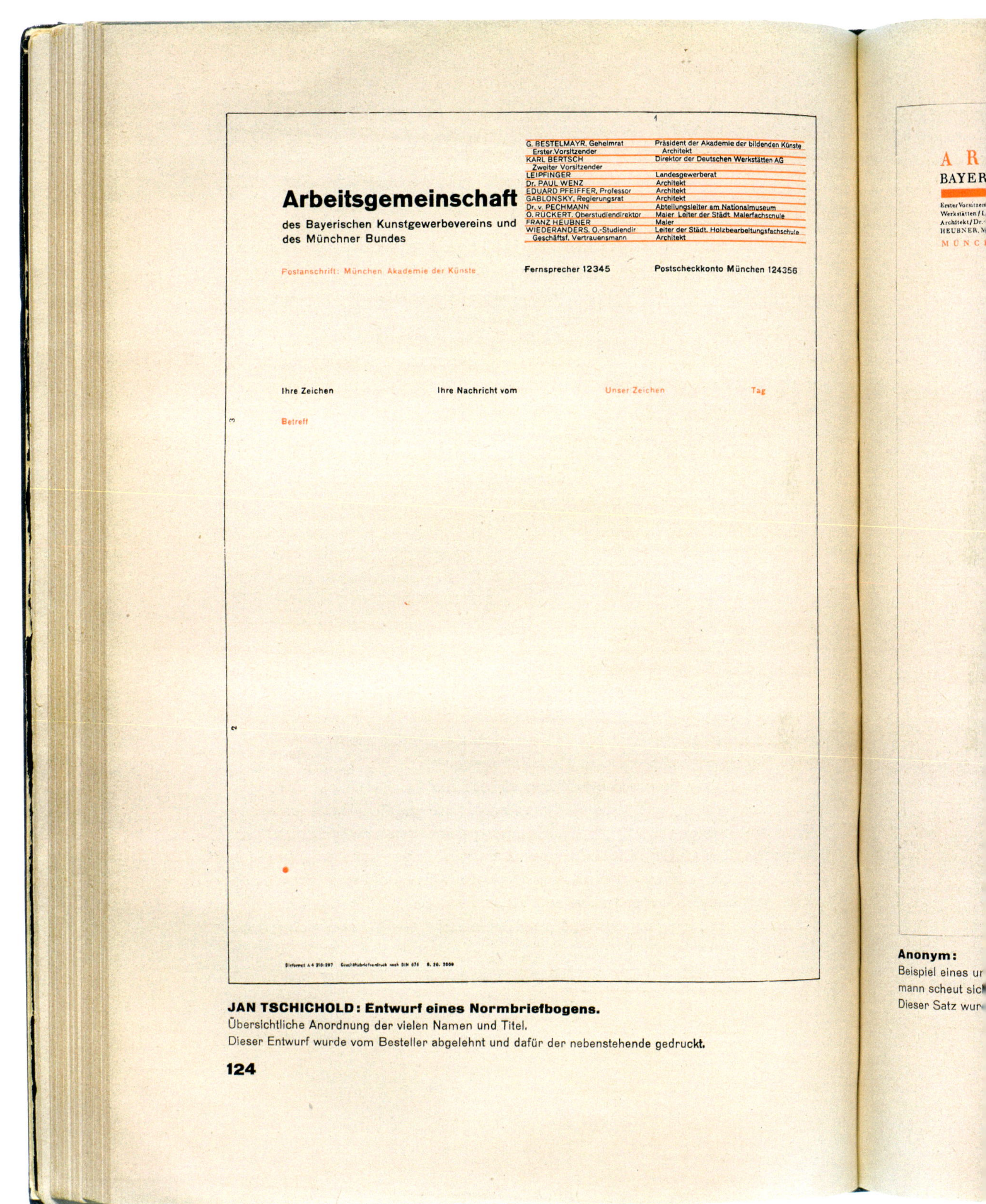

1

Arbeitsgemeinschaft

des Bayerischen Kunstgewerbevereins und
des Münchner Bundes

G. BESTELMAYR, Geheimrat Erster Vorsitzender	Präsident der Akademie der bildenden Künste Architekt
KARL BERTSCH Zweiter Vorsitzender	Direktor der Deutschen Werkstätten AG
LEIPFINGER	Landesgewerberat
Dr. PAUL WENZ	Architekt
EDUARD PFEIFFER, Professor	Architekt
GABLONSKY, Regierungsrat	Architekt
Dr. v. PECHMANN	Abteilungsleiter am Nationalmuseum
O. RÜCKERT, Oberstudiendirektor	Maler, Leiter der Städt. Malerfachschule
FRANZ HEUBNER	Maler
WIEDERANDERS, O.-Studiendir Geschäftsf. Vertrauensmann	Leiter der Städt. Holzbearbeitungsfachschule Architekt

Postanschrift: München Akademie der Künste

Fernsprecher 12345

Postscheckkonto München 124356

Ihre Zeichen

Ihre Nachricht vom

Unser Zeichen

Tag

3

Betreff

2

JAN TSCHICHOLD: Entwurf eines Normbriefbogens.
Übersichtliche Anordnung der vielen Namen und Titel.
Dieser Entwurf wurde vom Besteller abgelehnt und dafür der nebenstehende gedruckt.

124

Anonym:

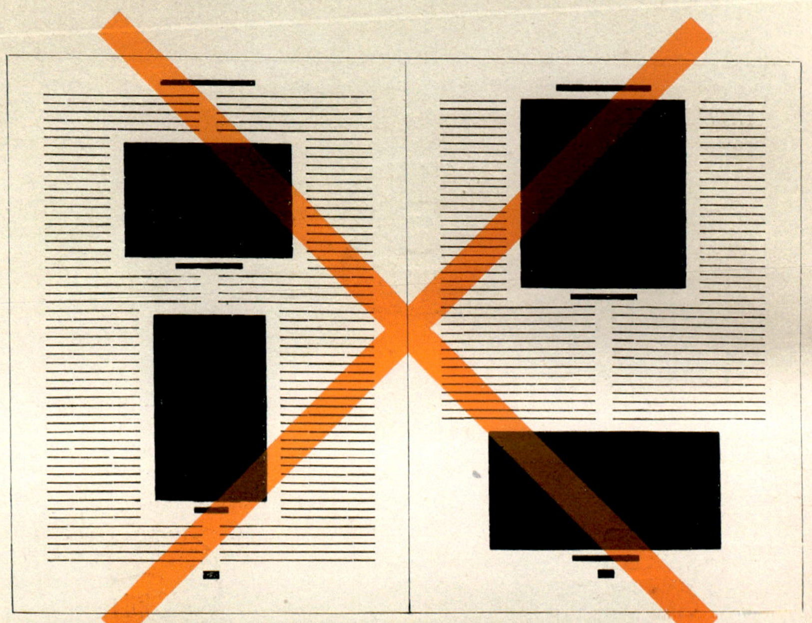

Schema der bisherigen Anordnung von Klischees in Zeitschriften.
Schematische, sinnlos gewordene Mittelachsengruppierung.
„Dekorativ", unpraktisch und unökonomisch **(= unschön).**

Auf Mitte geschlossene lebende Kolumnentitel sollten vermieden werden. Sie würden neben den asymmetrischen Abschnittiteln unharmonisch wirken. Am besten stellt man sie — besser ohne irgendwelche Linien darunter! — nach außen und zeichnet sie durch Grotesk aus. Wenn schon eine Linie verwendet werden soll, vermeide man fettfeine und Doppellinien. Einfache stumpffeine bis sechspunktfette sind dann am besten.

Ein vernünftig denkender Mensch kann sich nur wundern, zu welchen unmöglichen Folgen die Starrheit des Mittelachsenprinzips hinsichtlich der Klischeeanordnung geführt hat. An den zwei hier abgebildeten Schemen habe ich versucht, den Unterschied zwischen der alten Zwangsjacke und einer vernünftigen Anordnung der Klischees darzulegen. Ich habe dabei absichtlich Klischees von verschiedenen, zum Teil zufälligen Breiten fingiert, weil man mit solchen wohl immer (in Zukunft infolge der Normung allerdings in geringerem Maße) wird rechnen müssen. Normbreite Klischees würden, wozu es keines Beweises bedarf, das Problem noch sehr vereinfachen. Auf welch kompliziertem Wege man es bisher zu lösen versuchte, geht aus der linken Abbildung deutlich hervor. Krampfhaft sind die Abbildungen auf Mitte gestellt worden, wodurch das teure und umständliche Verschmälern des Spaltensatzes notwendig wurde. Das neue Schema rechts spricht für

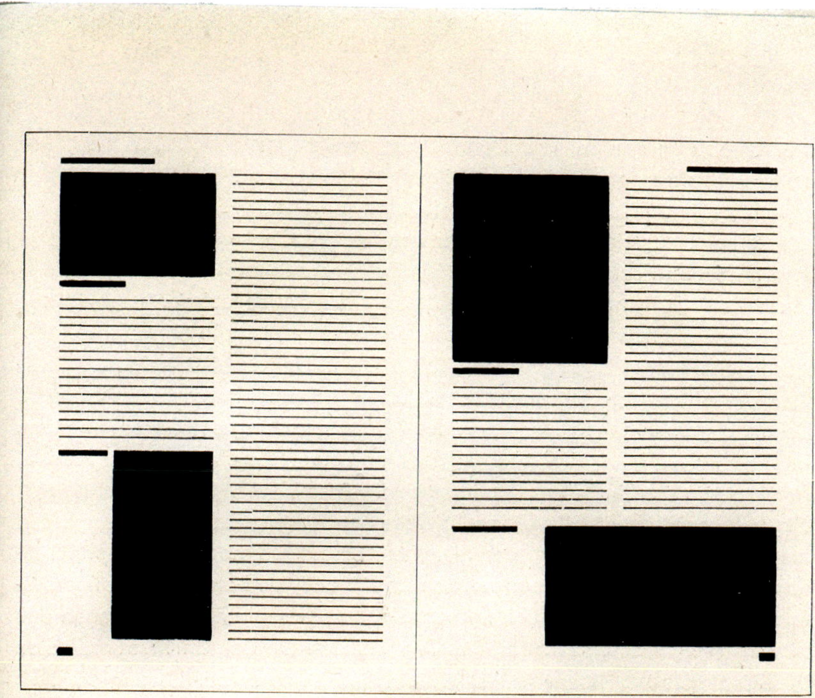

Schema für eine richtige Einordnung derselben Klischees in denselben Satzspiegel.
Konstruktiv, sinngemäß und ökonomisch **(= schön).**

sich selbst; es ist offenbar, um wieviel einfacher und dabei schöner diese neue Form ist. Als Kontrastform zu den meist dunklen Klischees und dem Grau der Schrift wirken die, neben den nicht die volle Spalten- oder Spiegelbreite erreichenden Klischees verbleibenden weißen Flächen erfreulich, während der frühere um die Klischees herumgeführte Satz, oft von nur Konkordanzbreite, geradezu den Eindruck von Geiz erweckt.

Nach Möglichkeit müssen die Klischees in engster Nähe des zugehörigen Textes stehen.

Ebenso wie die Abschnittitel, sollten auch die Unterschriften der Abbildungen (wie in diesem Buch) nicht mehr auf Mitte gestellt werden, sondern, wenn sie darunter stehen, im allgemeinen links beginnen. Eine Auszeichnung durch fette oder halbfette Grotesk intensiviert den Gesamteindruck der Seite. Daß man sie vielfach auch seitwärts stellen kann, geht ebenfalls aus dem Schema der neuen Klischeegruppierung hervor.

Bei den Klischees selbst sollte man das unschöne „Rändchen" unbedingt vermeiden. Das glatt abgeschnittene Klischee wirkt angenehmer und frischer. Die merkwürdigen Wolken, auf denen nicht nur kleinere Gegenstände, sondern auch schwere Maschinen zu schweben pflegen, sind aus ästhetischen Gründen und der Druckschwierigkeiten wegen bedingungslos abzulehnen.

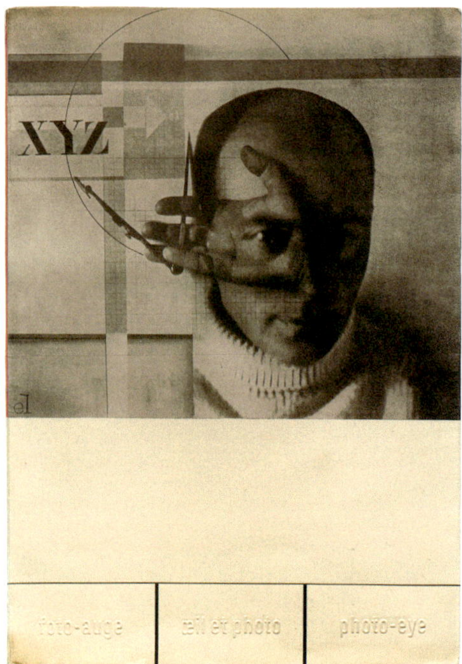

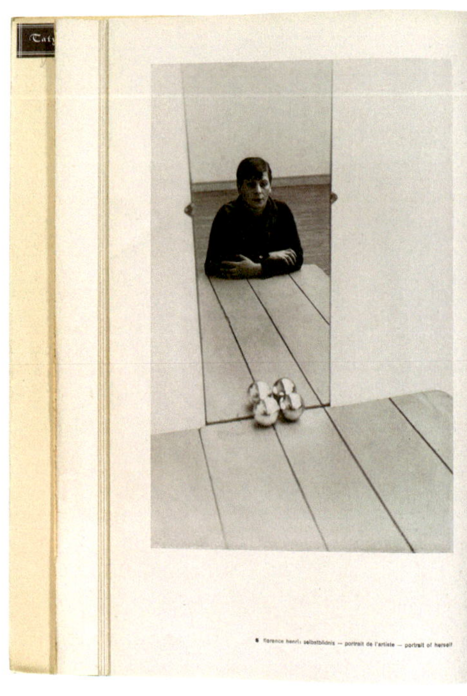

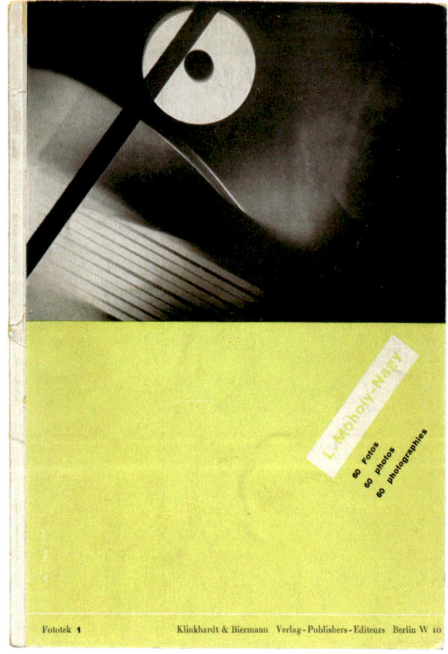

1930

JAN TSCHICHOLD (designer)
LÁSZLÓ MOHOLY-NAGY (photographer/author)

Fototek 1: 60 Fotos, letterpress, 9⅞ × 6⅞ inches (251 × 175 mm), Berlin.

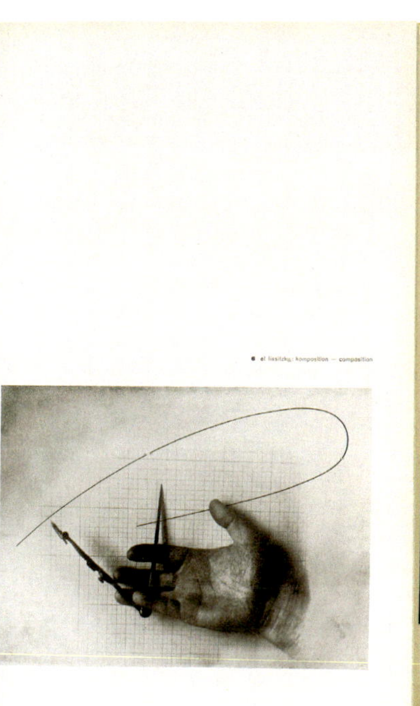

1929

JAN TSCHICHOLD (designer/editor)
EL LISSITZKY (photomontage artist)

Photo-Eye (Foto-Auge): 76 Photos of the Period, in conjunction with the pivotal contemporary photography exhibition *Fifo* (*Film und Foto*), letterpress, 11⅝ × 8¼ inches (295 × 210 mm), Stuttgart, Germany.

1935

JAN TSCHICHOLD (designer/author)

Typographic Design (*Typographische Gestaltung*), letterpress, 8½ × 6⅛ inches (215 × 155 mm), Basel.

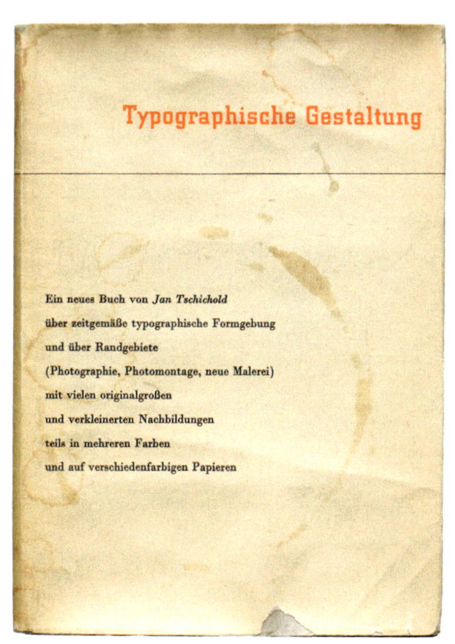

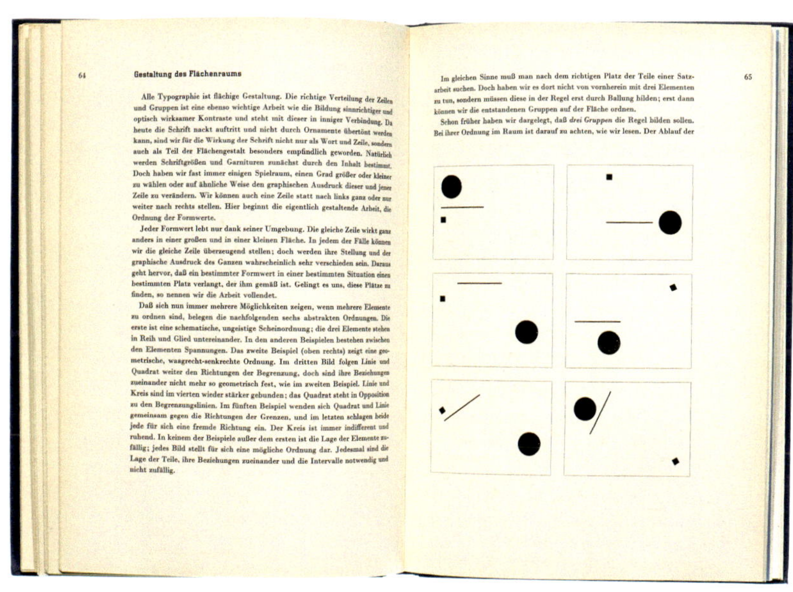

64

Gestaltung des Flächenraums

Alle Typographie ist flächige Gestaltung. Die richtige Verteilung der Zeilen und Gruppen ist eine ebenso wichtige Arbeit wie die Bildung sinnrichtiger und optisch wirksamer Kontraste und steht mit dieser in inniger Verbindung. Da heute die Schrift nackt auftritt und nicht durch Ornamente übertönt werden kann, sind wir für die Wirkung der Schrift nicht nur als Wort und Zeile, sondern auch als Teil der Flächengestalt besonders empfindlich geworden. Natürlich werden Schriftgrößen und Garnituren zunächst durch den Inhalt bestimmt. Doch haben wir fast immer einigen Spielraum, einen Grad größer oder kleiner zu wählen oder auf ähnliche Weise den graphischen Ausdruck dieser und jener Zeile zu verändern. Wir können auch eine Zeile statt nach links ganz oder nur weiter nach rechts stellen. Hier beginnt die eigentlich gestaltende Arbeit, die Ordnung der Formwerte.

Jeder Formwert lebt nur dank seiner Umgebung. Die gleiche Zeile wirkt ganz anders in einer großen und in einer kleinen Fläche. In jedem der Fälle können wir die gleiche Zeile überzeugend stellen; doch werden ihre Stellung und der graphische Ausdruck des Ganzen wahrscheinlich sehr verschieden sein. Daraus geht hervor, daß ein bestimmter Formwert in einer bestimmten Situation einen bestimmten Platz verlangt, der ihm gemäß ist. Gelingt es uns, diese Plätze zu finden, so nennen wir die Arbeit vollendet.

Daß sich nun immer mehrere Möglichkeiten zeigen, wenn mehrere Elemente zu ordnen sind, belegen die nachfolgenden sechs abstrakten Ordnungen. Die erste ist eine schematische, ungeistige Scheinordnung; die drei Elemente stehen in Reih und Glied untereinander. In den anderen Beispielen bestehen zwischen den Elementen Spannungen. Das zweite Beispiel (oben rechts) zeigt eine geometrische, waagrecht-senkrechte Ordnung. Im dritten Bild folgen Linie und Quadrat weiter den Richtungen der Begrenzung, doch sind ihre Beziehungen zueinander nicht mehr so geometrisch fest, wie im zweiten Beispiel. Linie und Kreis sind im vierten wieder stärker gebunden; das Quadrat steht in Opposition zu den Begrenzungslinien. Im fünften Beispiel wenden sich Quadrat und Linie gemeinsam gegen die Richtungen der Grenzen, und im letzten schlagen beide jede für sich eine fremde Richtung ein. Der Kreis ist immer indifferent und ruhend. In keinem der Beispiele außer dem ersten ist die Lage der Elemente zufällig; jedes Bild stellt für sich eine mögliche Ordnung dar. Jedesmal sind die Lage der Teile, ihre Beziehungen zueinander und die Intervalle notwendig und nicht zufällig.

65

Im gleichen Sinne muß man nach dem richtigen Platz der Teile einer Satzarbeit suchen. Doch haben wir es dort nicht von vornherein mit drei Elementen zu tun, sondern müssen diese in der Regel erst durch Ballung bilden; erst dann können wir die entstandenen Gruppen auf der Fläche ordnen.

Schon früher haben wir dargelegt, daß *drei Gruppen* die Regel bilden sollen. Bei ihrer Ordnung im Raum ist darauf zu achten, wie wir lesen. Der Ablauf der

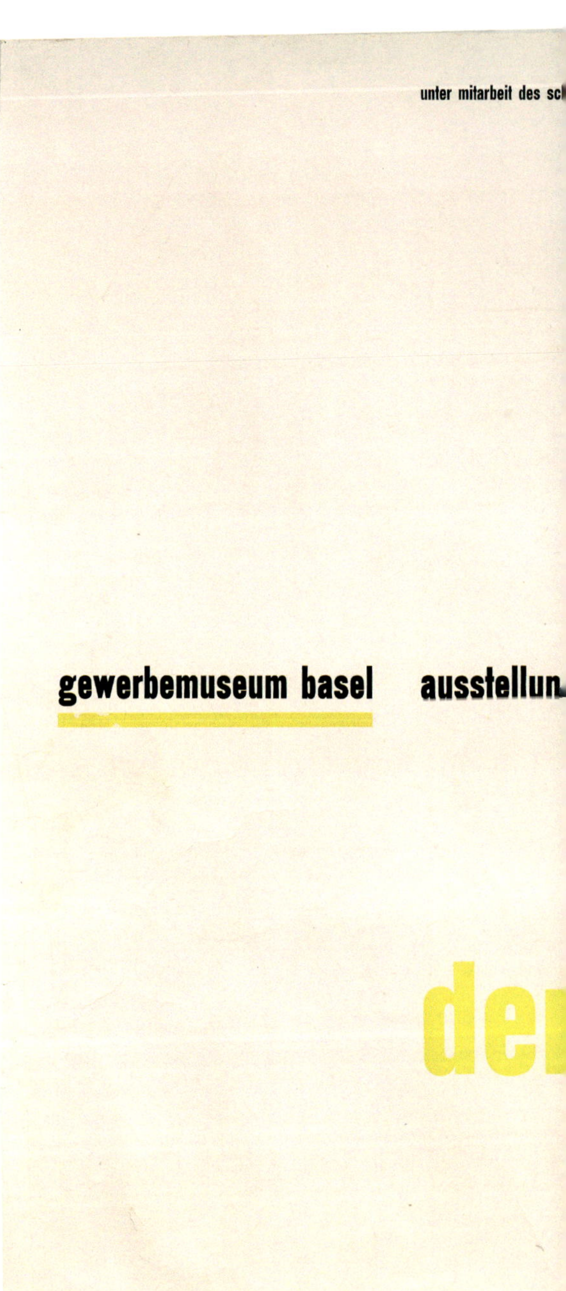

1938

JAN TSCHICHOLD

Exhibition poster for *The Professional Photographer* (*Der Berufsphotograph*), letterpress, 25¼ × 36 inches (640 × 915 mm), Basel.

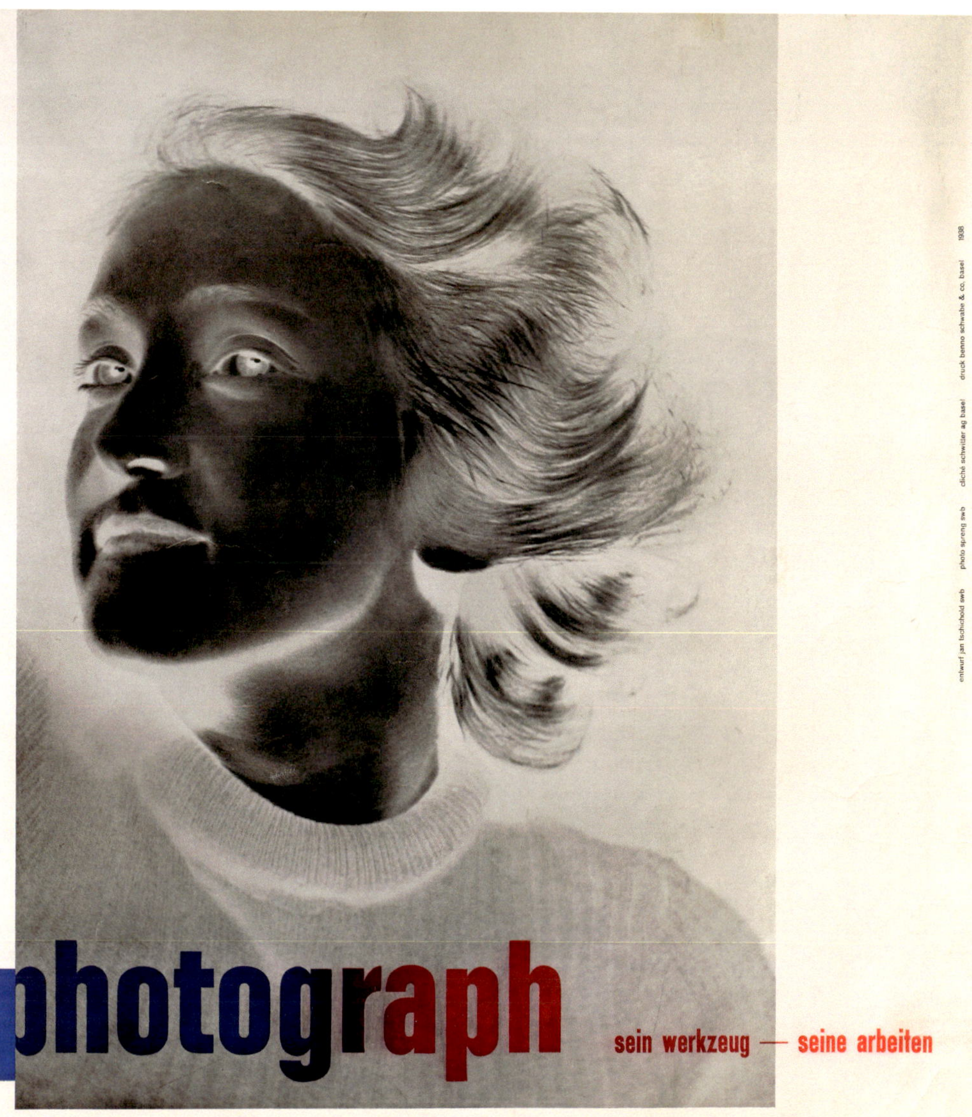

chen photographen-verbandes
berufsphotograph
sein werkzeug — seine arbeiten
8. mai — 6. juni
werktags 14-19
mittwochs 14-19 19-21
sonntags 10-12 14-19
eintritt frei
entwurf jan tschichold swb
photo spreng swb
cliché schwitter ag basel
druck benno schwabe & co. basel
1938

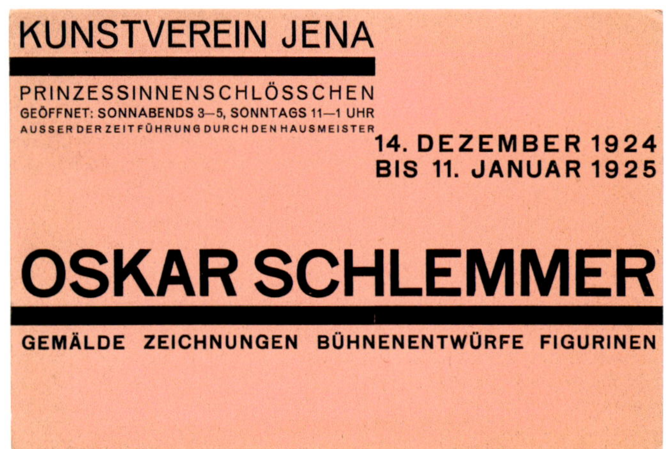

1924

WALTER DEXEL

Announcement for the Oskar Schlemmer exhibition, letterpress, 4⅛ × 6⅜ inches (105 × 160 mm), Jena, Germany.

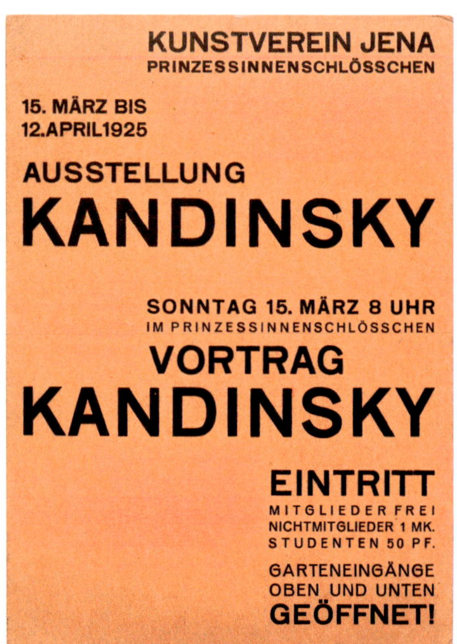

1925

WALTER DEXEL

Announcement for the Wassily Kandinsky exhibition, letterpress, 5¾ × 4⅛ inches (147 × 105 mm), Jena, Germany.

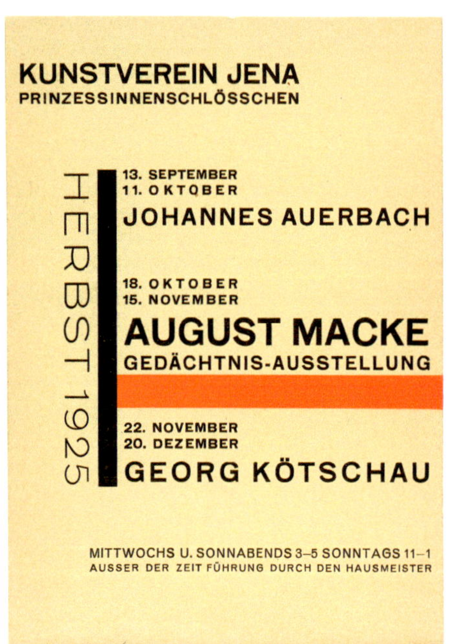

1925

WALTER DEXEL

Announcement for the August Macke exhibition, letterpress, 5¾ × 4⅛ inches (146 × 106 mm), Jena, Germany.

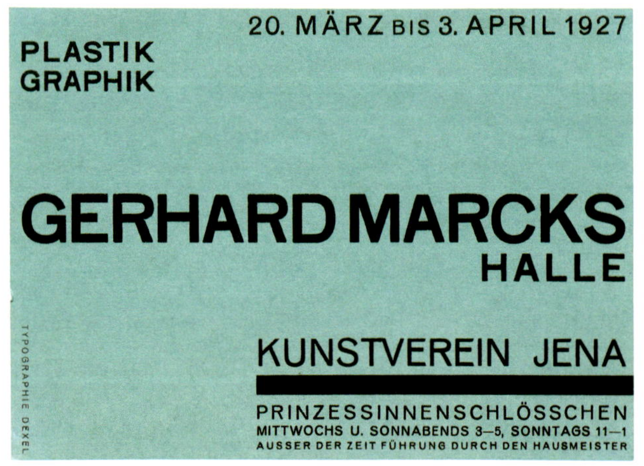

1927

WALTER DEXEL

Announcement for the Gerhard Marcks exhibition, letterpress, 4⅛ × 5¾ inches (104 × 147 mm), Jena, Germany.

1928

WALTER DEXEL

Exhibition poster mechanical for *New Ways of Photography* (*Neue Wege der Photographie*), paper on board, 13⅞ × 10 inches (352 × 252 mm), Jena, Germany.

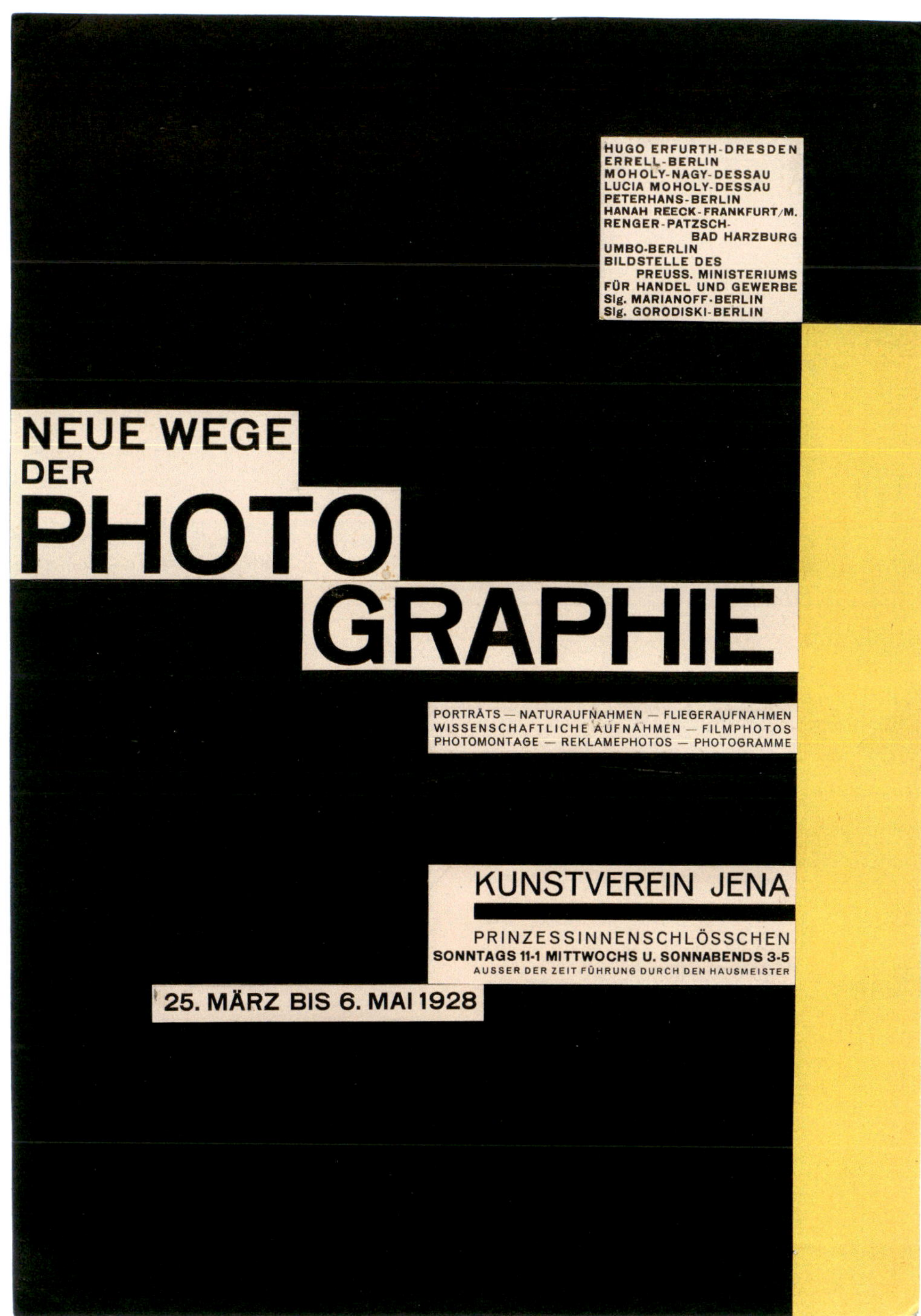

1945

MAX BILL

Exhibition poster for *USA Builds* (*USA Baut*), lithograph, 49¼ × 35 inches (125 × 89 cm), Zurich.

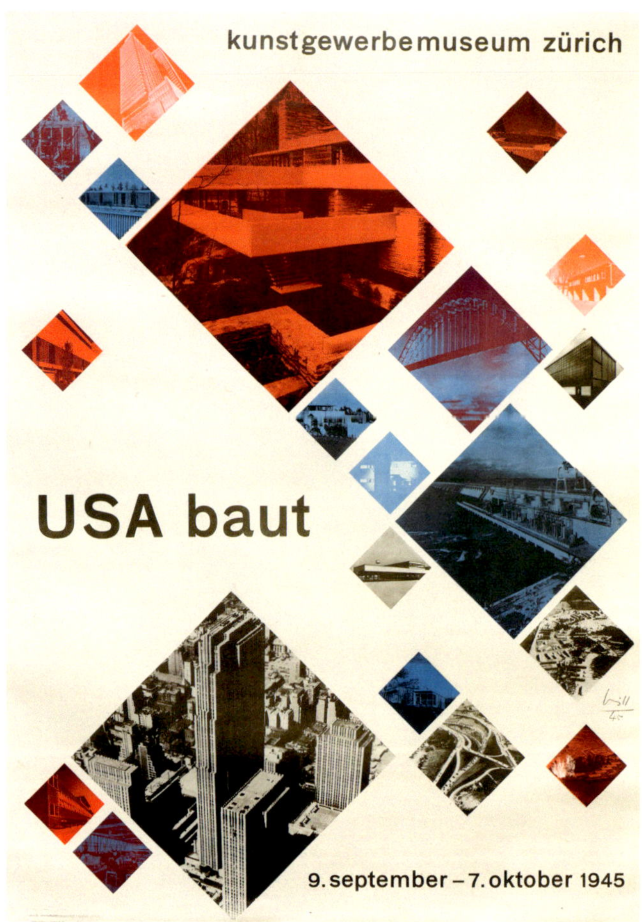

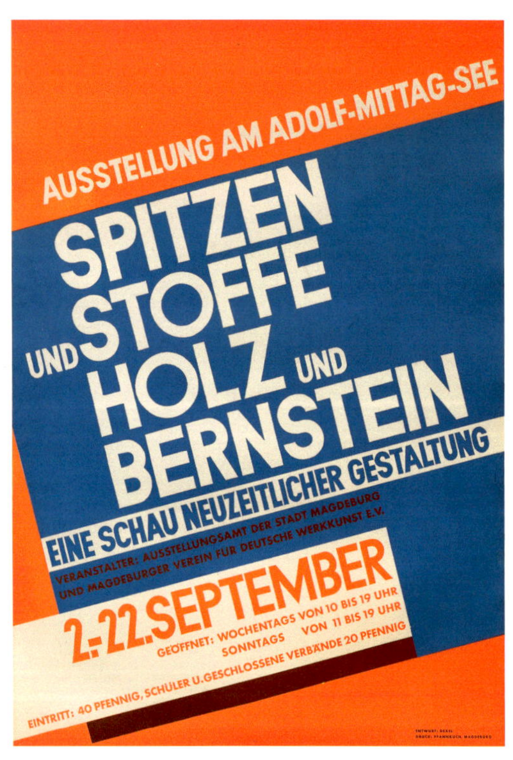

1929

WALTER DEXEL

Exhibition poster for *Lace and Fabrics, Wood and Amber* (*Spitzen und Stoffe, Holz und Bernstein*), lithograph, 33⅜ × 23¼ inches (848 × 590 mm), Magdeburg, Germany.

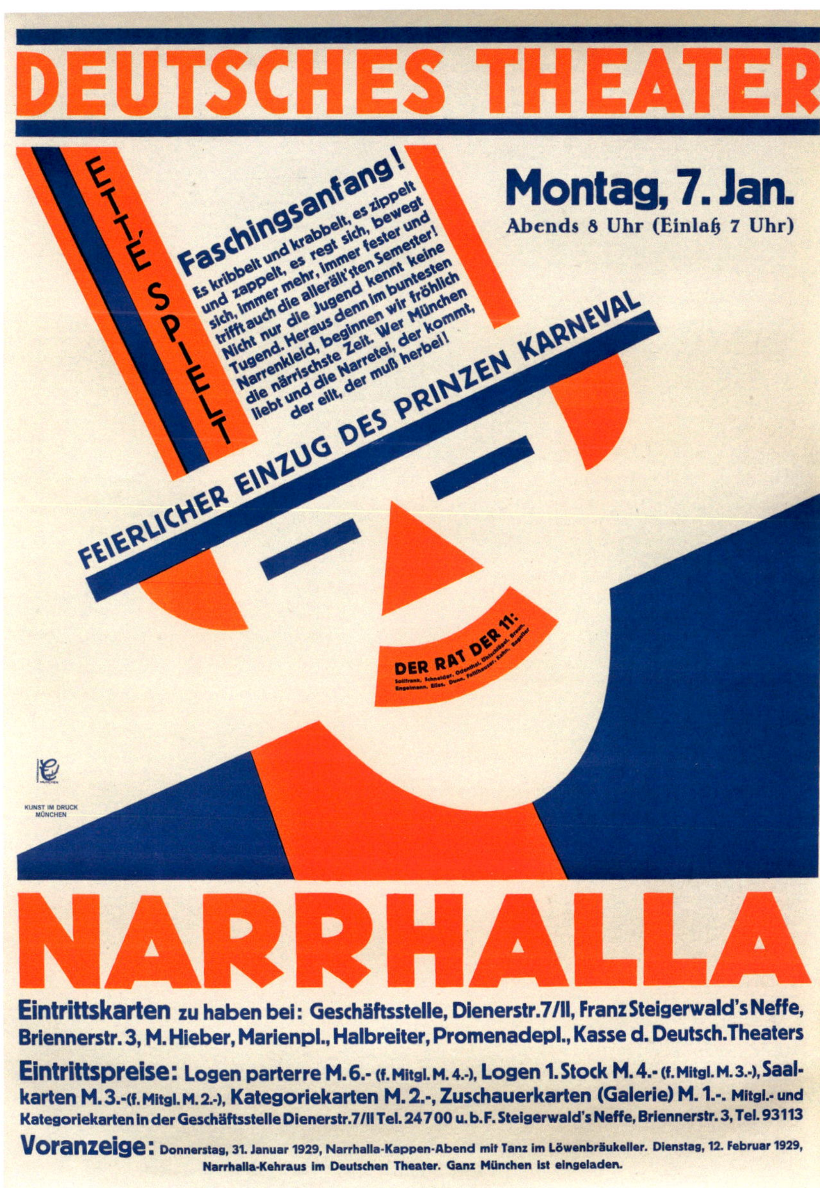

1929

ENGELMANN

Poster for Narrhalla, a theatrical event during the German carnival season, lithograph, 46⅞ × 33½ inches (119 × 85 cm), Munich.

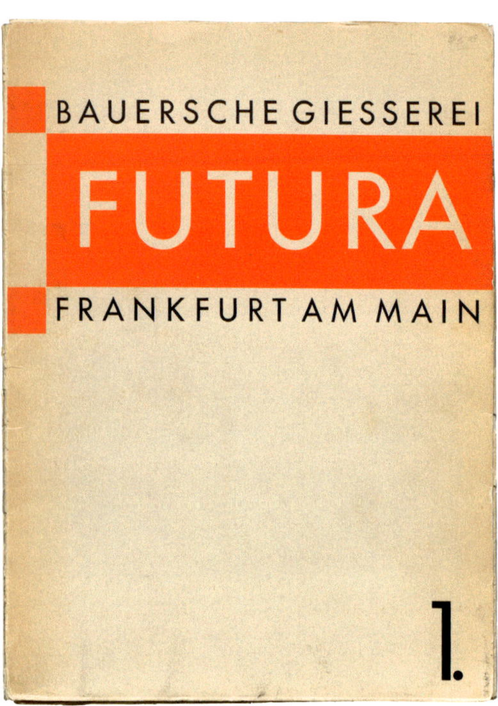

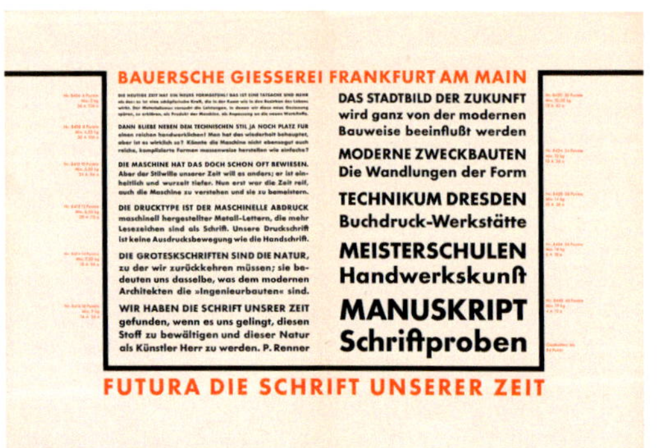

1927

PAUL RENNER (type designer/type specimen designer)

Type specimen for Futura, letterpress, 10⅜ × 7¾ inches (265 × 198 mm), Frankfurt.

Today, Futura is one of the most popular typefaces, used everywhere by advertisers and artists alike. But at the time of its release in 1927—represented here by the typeface's first specimen from the Bauer Type Foundry, featuring uses such as the concert announcement by Hans Leistikow at right—Futura was on the cutting edge of experimental, geometrically derived typefaces. Eschewing the lettering origins of most sans serifs (grotesques) of the era, Renner based Futura on elemental circles, squares, and triangles in a bid for modernity suitable to the machine era. Though the timing of its release meant that it appeared in only one or two late Bauhaus productions, there are certainly similarities between Paul Renner's Futura and alphabets theorized at the school. Take, for instance, the alternate glyphs, present in this first brochure but absent from subsequent offerings: The alternates for *n* and *m* have straight tops, while the variants for *a* and *g*—a double-story with an open bowl and a circle with a triangular descender, respectively—are even more adventurous (see the line of alternate glyphs shown below each weight on page 235). The original lowercase *r* consists simply of a vertical line and a small circle (it was later replaced by a less geometric version). Experimental and abstract solutions like these recall some of Herbert Bayer's designs for his Universal Type (see page 204). While Bauer dropped the more radical lettershapes, the immediate popularity of Futura (along with that of Erbar-Grotesk, which was developed nearly simultaneously) proved the mainstream demand for geometric styles. A flood of competitors rushed in, including Berthold-Grotesk (1928), Bernhard Gothic (Lucian Bernhard, ATF, 1929), Elegant Grotesk (Hans Möring, Stempel, 1928), Kabel (Rudolf Koch, Klingspor, 1927), Nobel (Amsterdam, 1929), Metro (1929), Tempo (Robert Hunter Middleton, Ludlow, 1930), and Vogue (Intertype, 1930). The widespread availability and use of these typefaces altered the landscape of graphic design in ways the Bauhaus never could on its own. ●

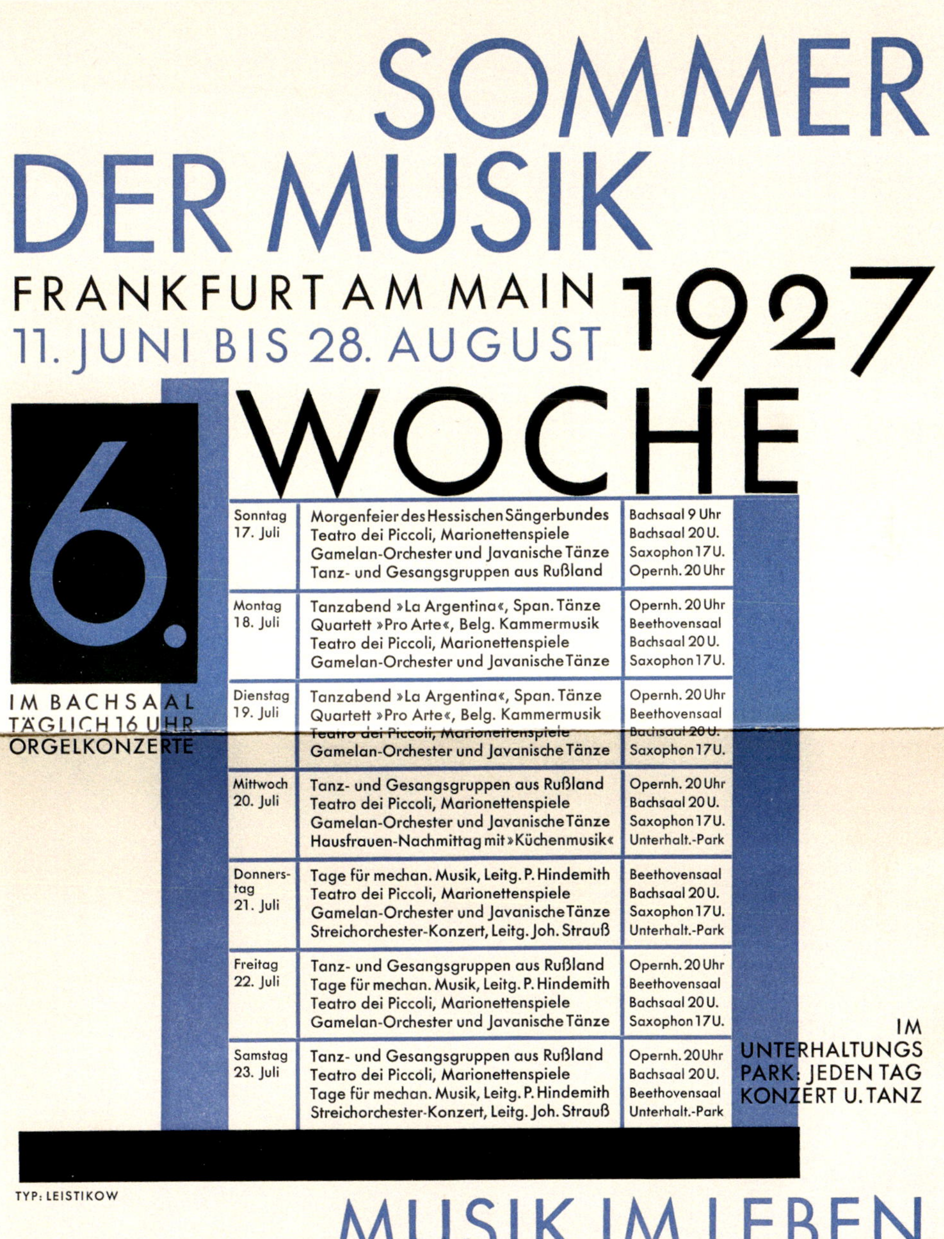
SOMMER
DER MUSIK
FRANKFURT AM MAIN 1927
11. JUNI BIS 28. AUGUST
6. WOCHE
Sonntag 17. Juli
Morgenfeier des Hessischen Sängerbundes — Bachsaal 9 Uhr
Teatro dei Piccoli, Marionettenspiele — Bachsaal 20 U.
Gamelan-Orchester und Javanische Tänze — Saxophon 17 U.
Tanz- und Gesangsgruppen aus Rußland — Opernh. 20 Uhr
Montag 18. Juli
Tanzabend »La Argentina«, Span. Tänze — Opernh. 20 Uhr
Quartett »Pro Arte«, Belg. Kammermusik — Beethovensaal
Teatro dei Piccoli, Marionettenspiele — Bachsaal 20 U.
Gamelan-Orchester und Javanische Tänze — Saxophon 17 U.
Dienstag 19. Juli
Tanzabend »La Argentina«, Span. Tänze — Opernh. 20 Uhr
Quartett »Pro Arte«, Belg. Kammermusik — Beethovensaal
Teatro dei Piccoli, Marionettenspiele — Bachsaal 20 U.
Gamelan-Orchester und Javanische Tänze — Saxophon 17 U.
Mittwoch 20. Juli
Tanz- und Gesangsgruppen aus Rußland — Opernh. 20 Uhr
Teatro dei Piccoli, Marionettenspiele — Bachsaal 20 U.
Gamelan-Orchester und Javanische Tänze — Saxophon 17 U.
Hausfrauen-Nachmittag mit »Küchenmusik« — Unterhalt.-Park
Donnerstag 21. Juli
Tage für mechan. Musik, Leitg. P. Hindemith — Beethovensaal
Teatro dei Piccoli, Marionettenspiele — Bachsaal 20 U.
Gamelan-Orchester und Javanische Tänze — Saxophon 17 U.
Streichorchester-Konzert, Leitg. Joh. Strauß — Unterhalt.-Park
Freitag 22. Juli
Tanz- und Gesangsgruppen aus Rußland — Opernh. 20 Uhr
Tage für mechan. Musik, Leitg. P. Hindemith — Beethovensaal
Teatro dei Piccoli, Marionettenspiele — Bachsaal 20 U.
Gamelan-Orchester und Javanische Tänze — Saxophon 17 U.
Samstag 23. Juli
Tanz- und Gesangsgruppen aus Rußland — Opernh. 20 Uhr
Teatro dei Piccoli, Marionettenspiele — Bachsaal 20 U.
Tage für mechan. Musik, Leitg. P. Hindemith — Beethovensaal
Streichorchester-Konzert, Leitg. Joh. Strauß — Unterhalt.-Park
IM BACHSAAL TÄGLICH 16 UHR ORGELKONZERTE
IM UNTERHALTUNGSPARK: JEDEN TAG KONZERT U. TANZ
TYP: LEISTIKOW
MUSIK IM LEBEN DER VÖLKER
INTERNAT. AUSSTELLUNG

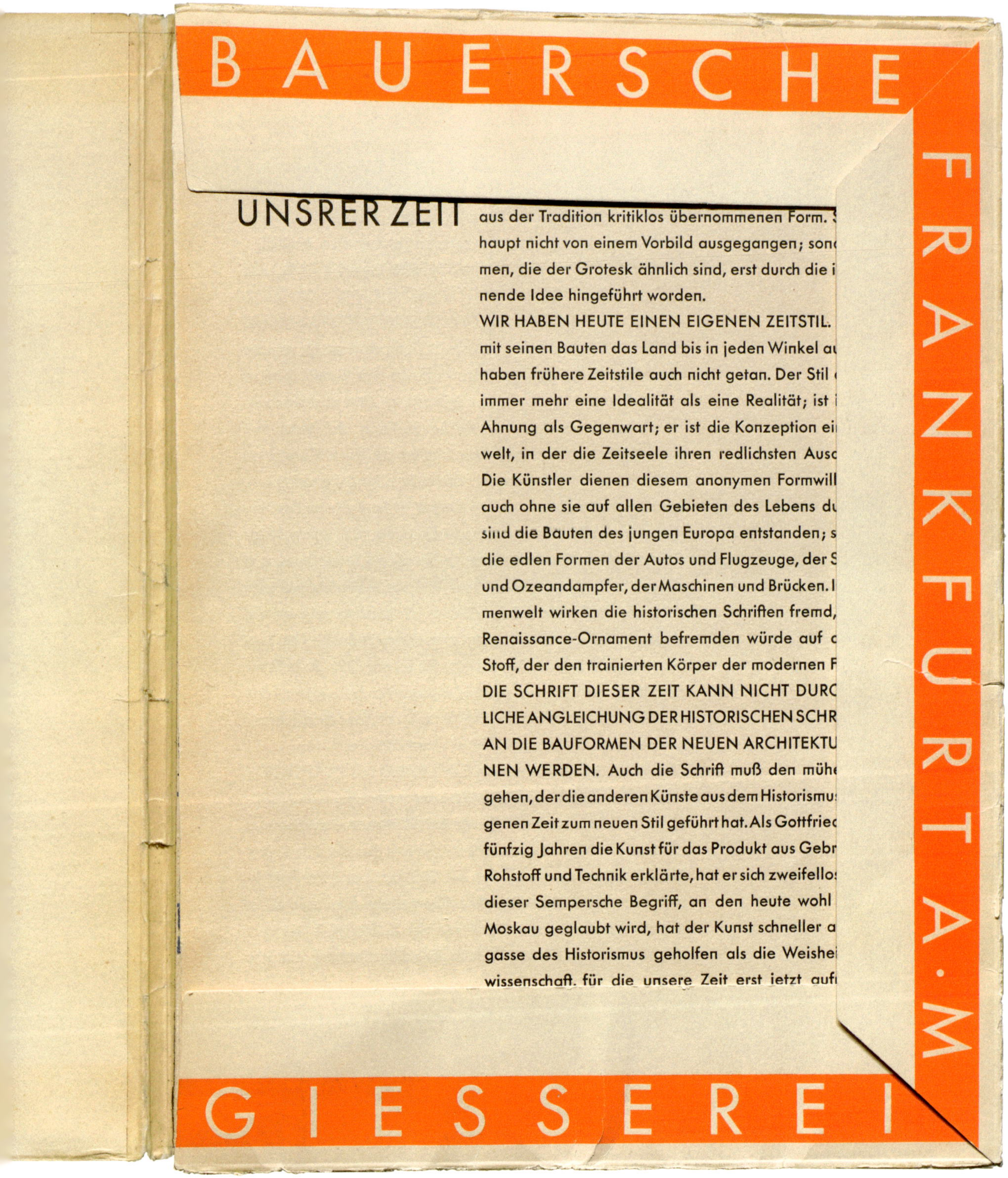

BAUERSCHE

FRANKFURT A·M

GIESSEREI

UNSRER ZEIT

aus der Tradition kritiklos übernommenen Form. S
haupt nicht von einem Vorbild ausgegangen; sond
men, die der Grotesk ähnlich sind, erst durch die i
nende Idee hingeführt worden.
WIR HABEN HEUTE EINEN EIGENEN ZEITSTIL.
mit seinen Bauten das Land bis in jeden Winkel a
haben frühere Zeitstile auch nicht getan. Der Stil
immer mehr eine Idealität als eine Realität; ist i
Ahnung als Gegenwart; er ist die Konzeption ei
welt, in der die Zeitseele ihren redlichsten Ausc
Die Künstler dienen diesem anonymen Formwill
auch ohne sie auf allen Gebieten des Lebens du
sind die Bauten des jungen Europa entstanden; s
die edlen Formen der Autos und Flugzeuge, der S
und Ozeandampfer, der Maschinen und Brücken. I
menwelt wirken die historischen Schriften fremd,
Renaissance-Ornament befremden würde auf d
Stoff, der den trainierten Körper der modernen F
DIE SCHRIFT DIESER ZEIT KANN NICHT DURC
LICHE ANGLEICHUNG DER HISTORISCHEN SCHR
AN DIE BAUFORMEN DER NEUEN ARCHITEKTU
NEN WERDEN. Auch die Schrift muß den mühe
gehen, der die anderen Künste aus dem Historismus
genen Zeit zum neuen Stil geführt hat. Als Gottfried
fünfzig Jahren die Kunst für das Produkt aus Gebr
Rohstoff und Technik erklärte, hat er sich zweifellos
dieser Sempersche Begriff, an den heute wohl
Moskau geglaubt wird, hat der Kunst schneller a
gasse des Historismus geholfen als die Weishei
wissenschaft, für die unsere Zeit erst jetzt auf

RENNER FUTURA BAUERSCHE GIESSEREI, FRANKFURT A.M.

mager

A B C D E F G H I J K L M N O P
Q R S T U V W X Y Z Ä Ö Ü Æ Œ Ç
a b c d e f g h i j k l m n o p q r ſ s t u v w
x y z ä ö ü ch ck ff fi fl ft ſſ ſi ſt ß æ œ ç
1 2 3 4 5 6 7 8 9 0 & . , - : ; · ! ? (' « » § † *

Auf besonderen Wunsch liefern wir auch nachstehende Figuren

a g m n ä & 1 2 3 4 5 6 7 8 9 0

Sie sind im Gradverzeichnis jeweils in der letzten Zeile verwendet

halbfett

A B C D E F G H I J K L M N O P
Q R S T U V W X Y Z Ä Ö Ü Æ Œ Ç
a b c d e f g h i j k l m n o p q r ſ s t u v w
x y z ä ö ü ch ck ff fi fl ft ſſ ſi ſt ß æ œ ç
1 2 3 4 5 6 7 8 9 0 & . , - : ; · ! ? (' « » § † *

Auf besonderen Wunsch liefern wir auch nachstehende Figuren

a g m n ä & 1 2 3 4 5 6 7 8 9 0

FUTURA · DIE SCHRIFT UNSERER ZEIT

RENNER

PROF. DR. E
PREETOR
in der Neuen Rund

WILLY H
in der Literarische

FUTUR

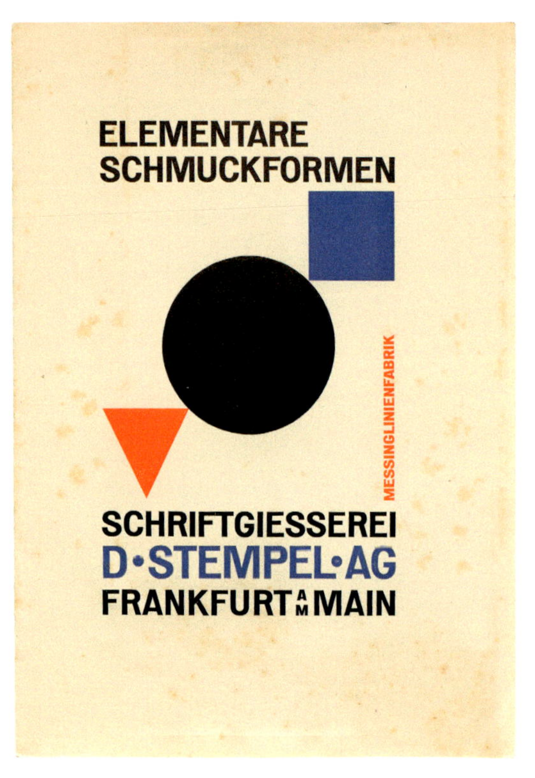
ELEMENTARE
SCHMUCKFORMEN
MESSINGLINIENFABRIK
SCHRIFTGIESSEREI
D·STEMPEL·AG
FRANKFURT A M MAIN

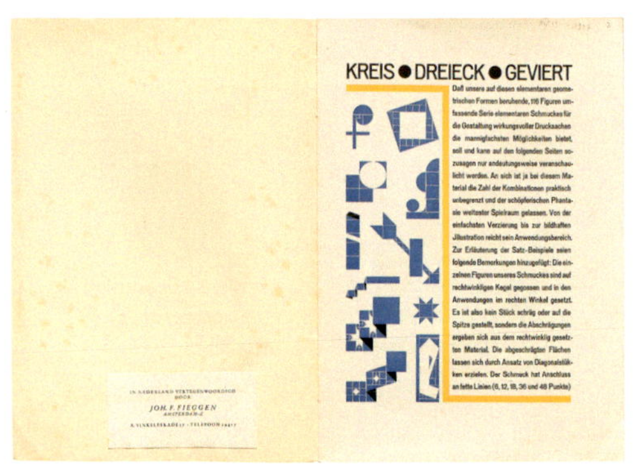
KREIS ● DREIECK ● GEVIERT

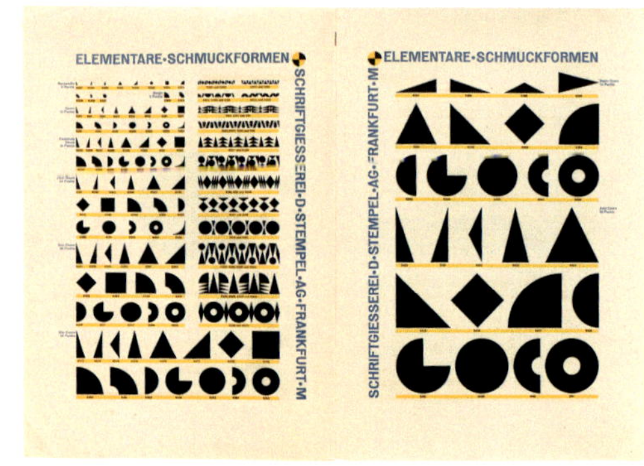
ELEMENTARE·SCHMUCKFORMEN
SCHRIFTGIESSEREI·D·STEMPEL·AG·FRANKFURT·M
ELEMENTARE·SCHMUCKFORMEN
SCHRIFTGIESSEREI·D·STEMPEL·AG·FRANKFURT·M

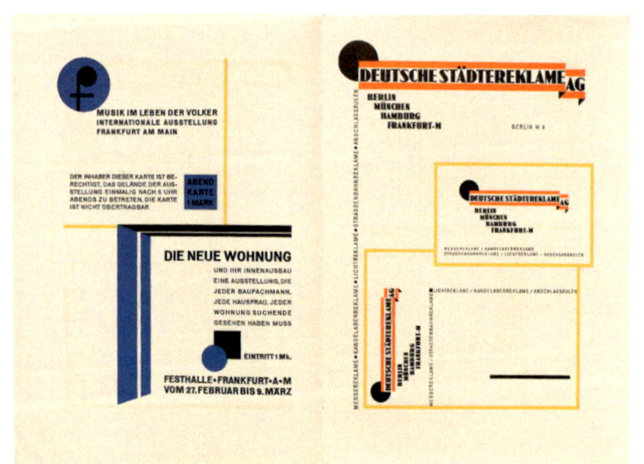
MUSIK IM LEBEN DER VOLKER
INTERNATIONALE AUSSTELLUNG
FRANKFURT AM MAIN
DIE NEUE WOHNUNG
EINTRITT 1 Mk.
FESTHALLE·FRANKFURT·A·M
VOM 27. FEBRUAR BIS 9. MÄRZ
DEUTSCHE STÄDTEREKLAME AG
BERLIN
MÜNCHEN
HAMBURG
FRANKFURT·M

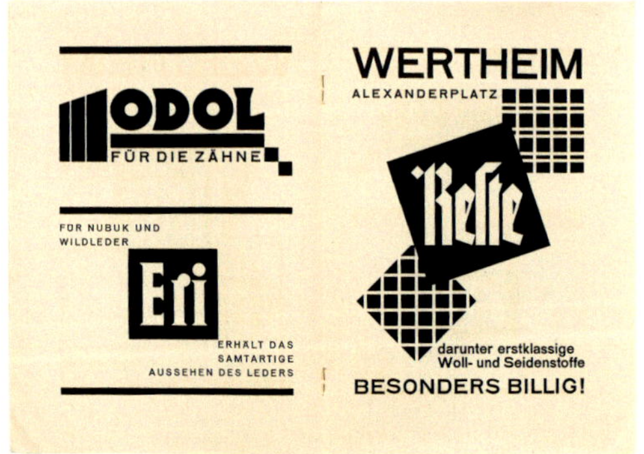
ODOL
FÜR DIE ZÄHNE
FÜR NUBUK UND
WILDLEDER
Eri
ERHÄLT DAS
SAMTARTIGE
AUSSEHEN DES LEDERS
WERTHEIM
ALEXANDERPLATZ
Reste
darunter erstklassige
Woll- und Seidenstoffe
BESONDERS BILLIG!

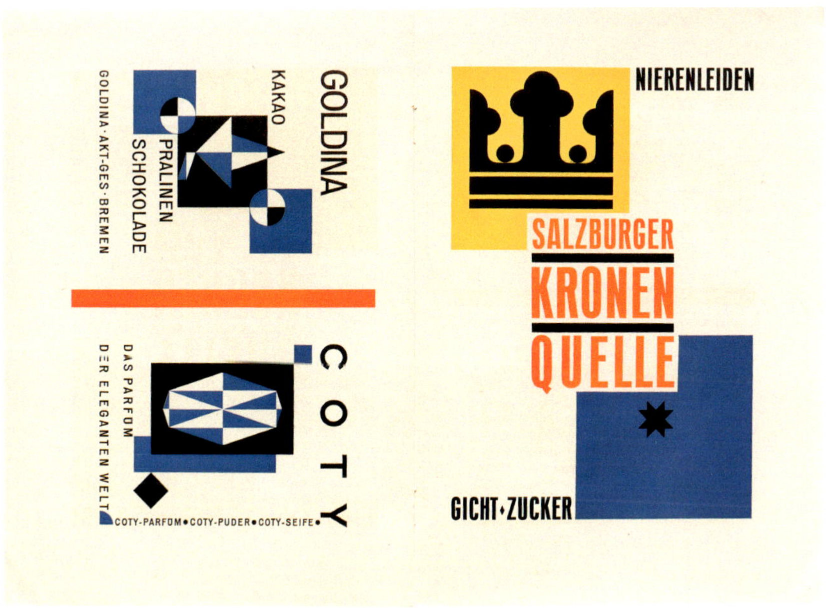

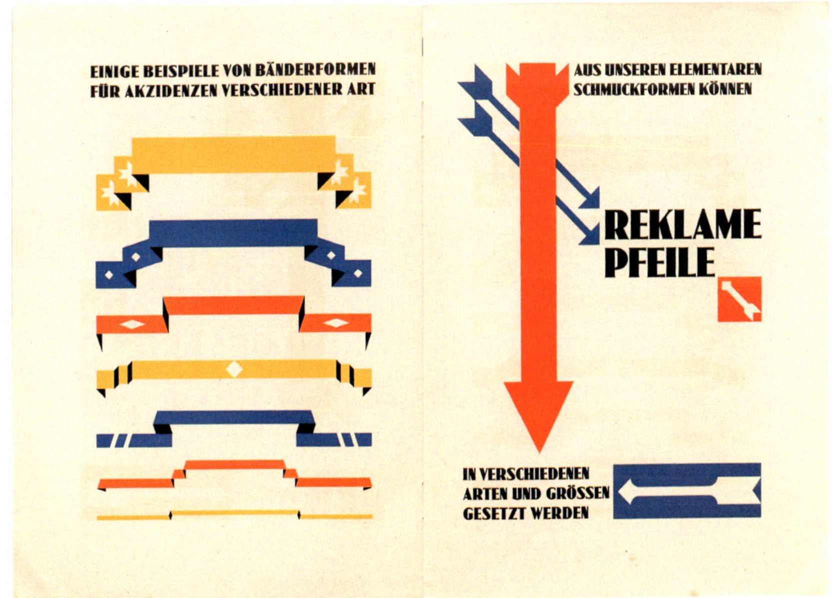

1927

D STEMPEL AG (foundry)

Type specimen for Elemental Decorative Forms (Elementare Schmuckformen), letterpress, 11½ × 8¼ inches (292 × 210 mm), Frankfurt.

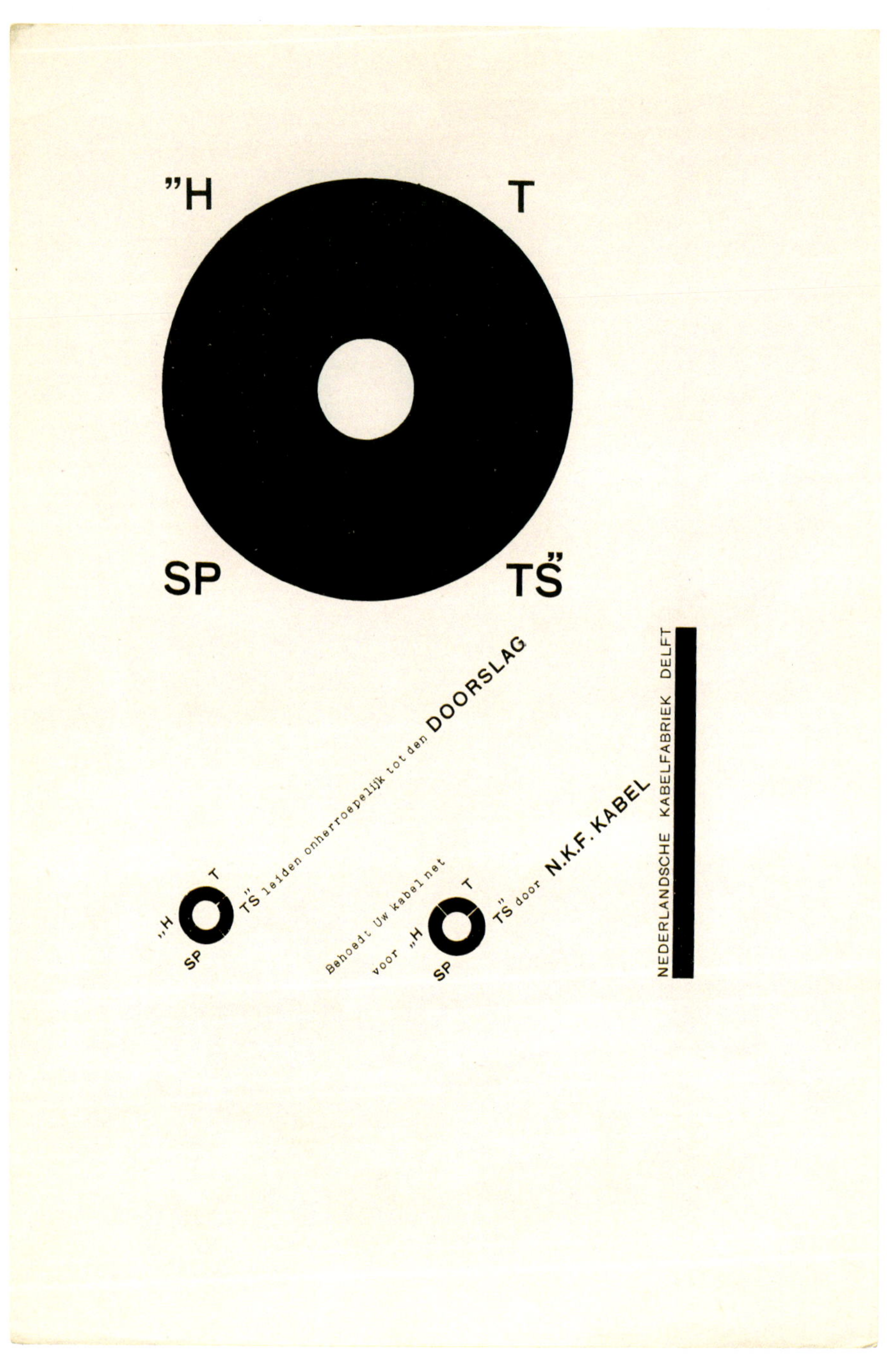

CIRCA 1920

PIET ZWART

Advertisements for Dutch cable company N.K.F. Delft, letterpress, 12½ × 8½ inches (318 × 215 mm), Delft.

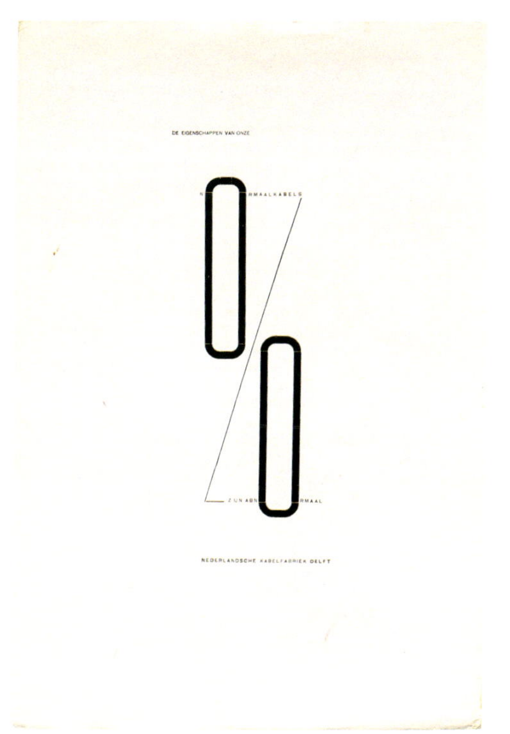
DE EIGENSCHAPPEN VAN ONZE
N RMAALKABELS
ZIJN ABN RMAAL
NEDERLANDSCHE KABELFABRIEK DELFT

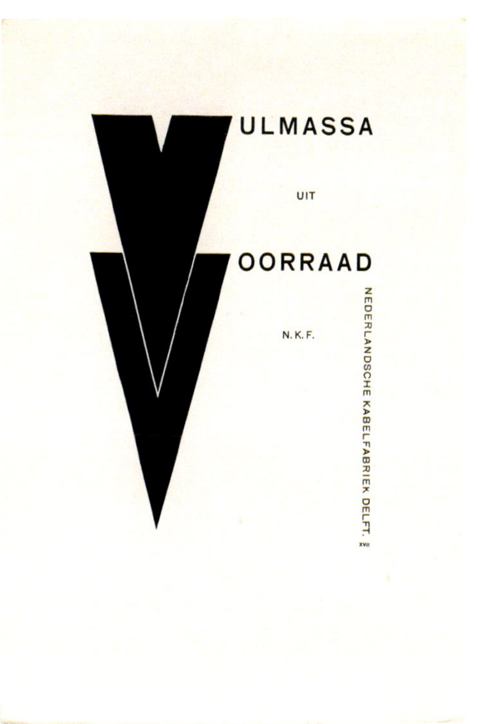
ULMASSA
UIT
OORRAAD
N.K.F.
NEDERLANDSCHE KABELFABRIEK DELFT.
XVII

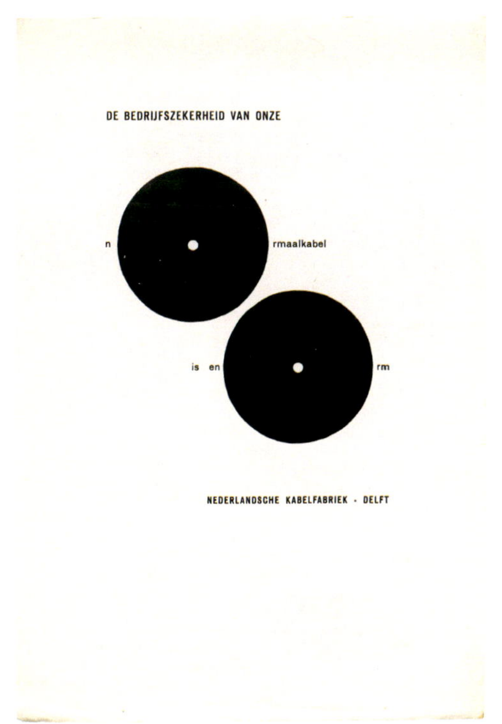
DE BEDRIJFSZEKERHEID VAN ONZE
n rmaalkabel
is en rm
NEDERLANDSCHE KABELFABRIEK · DELFT

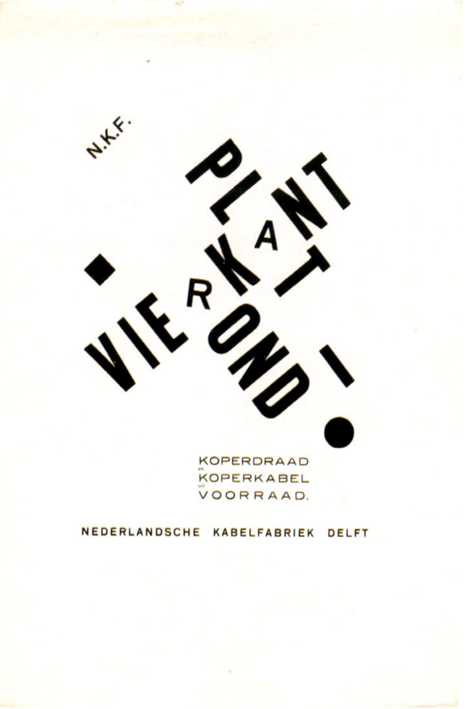
N.K.F.
KOPERDRAAD
KOPERKABEL
VOORRAAD.
NEDERLANDSCHE KABELFABRIEK DELFT

1934

PIET ZWART

“For Happy Days: Lucky Telegrams” (“Voor blijde dagen: Geluktelegrammen”), poster advertising decorative telegrams for the Dutch postal service PTT, collage and letterpress, 27¾ × 19½ inches (705 × 495 mm), Rotterdam.

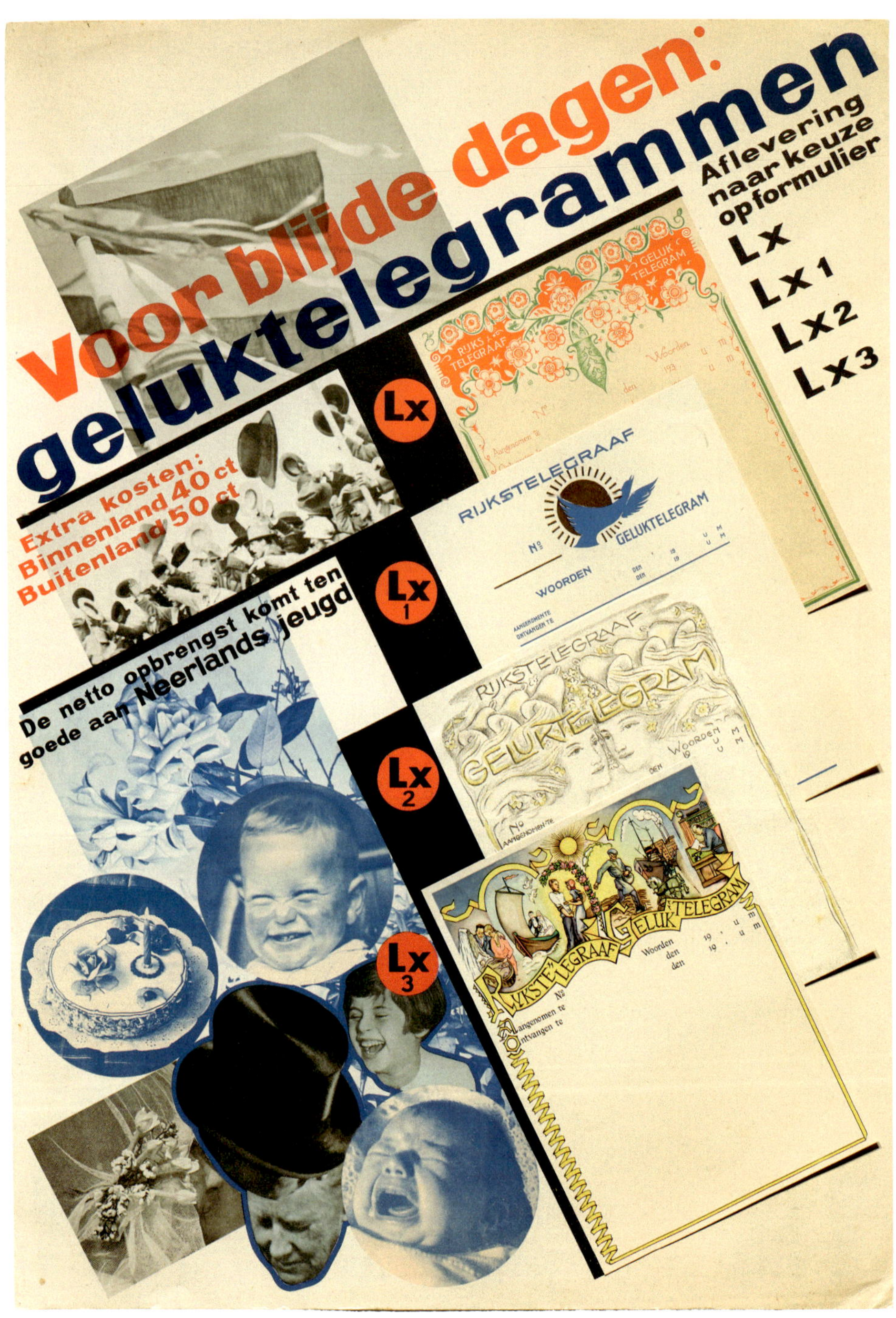

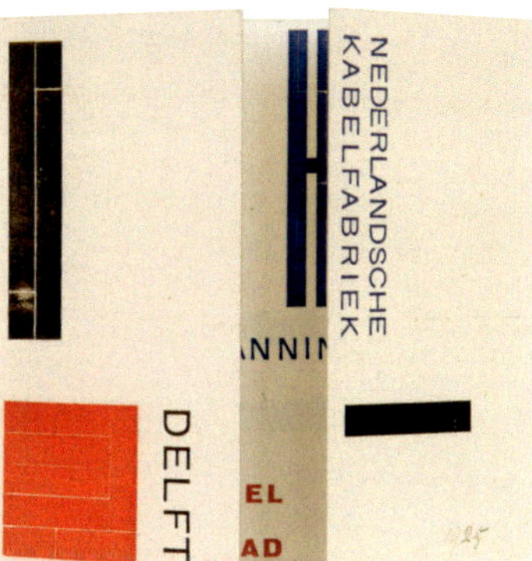

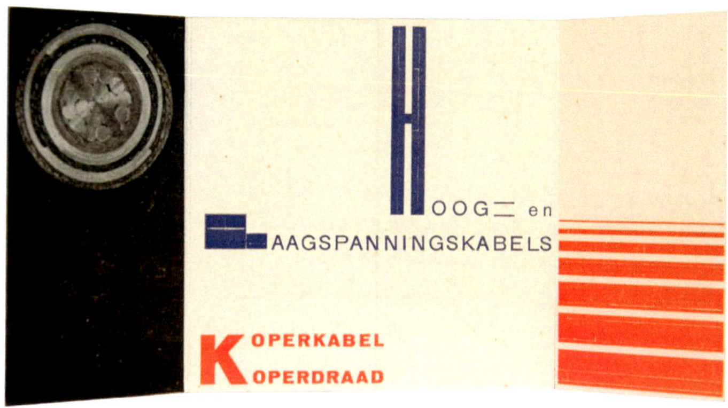

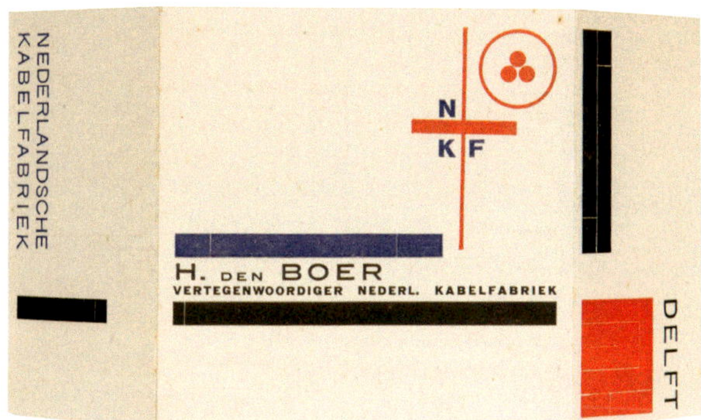

CIRCA 1920s

PIET ZWART

Business card for Dutch cable company N.K.F. Delft, letterpress, 3⅛ × 3⅛ inches (80 × 80 mm) folded, 3⅛ × 6⅜ inches (80 × 160 mm) unfolded, Delft.

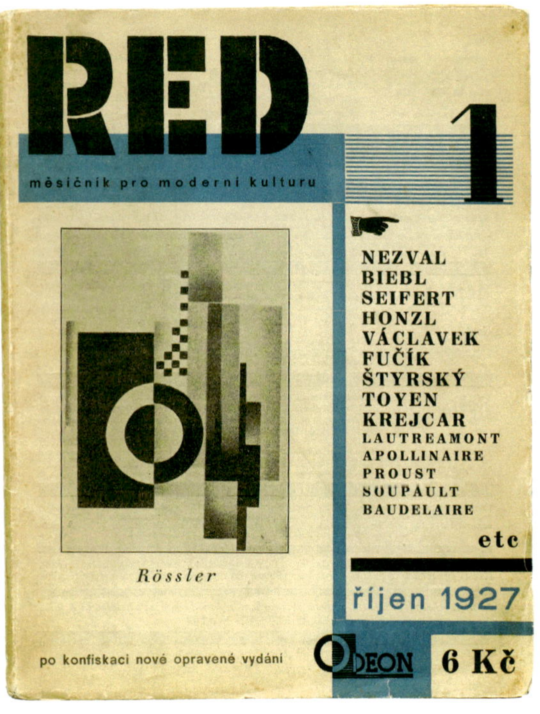

1927

KAREL TEIGE (designer/editor)

ReD: Monthly for Modern Culture (*ReD: Měsíčník pro moderní kulturu*), vol. 1, no. 1, letterpress, 9⅛ × 7¼ inches (232 × 185 mm), Prague.

During Hannes Meyer's term as director of the Bauhaus from 1928 to 1930, he invited a number of guest lecturers and instructors to teach on a wide range of subjects. Among them was Czech typographer, collagist, and modernist theorist Karel Teige, whose successive Devětsil and Poetism movements combined tendencies from Russian constructivism and French surrealism. These two seemingly disparate influences are on display here in his designs for the magazine *ReD* (short for *Revue Devětsilu*)—which published a special Bauhaus issue, coedited by Meyer, in 1930—and two books of poetry by fellow Czech surrealist Konstantin Biebl. Teige's book design for *With a Ship that Imports Tea and Coffee* (*S lodí jež dováží čaj a kávu*) is particularly unique (see pages 244–245), with several pages of Teige's constructivist compositions of typographic lines and ornaments accompanying the more traditionally typeset poems. Among the many examples of constructivist typographic image, Teige's are uniquely loose and playful, weaving in words like *java* and *jazz* and replacing the typical red accent color with a flamboyant pink. ●

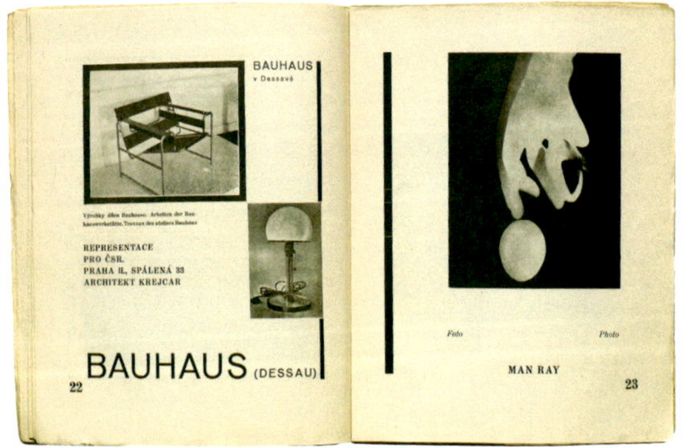

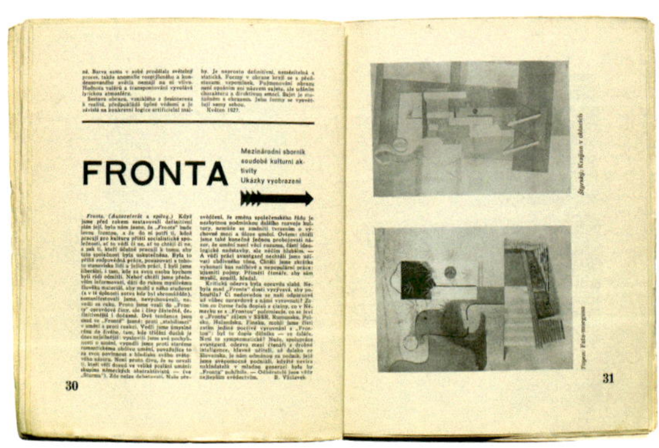

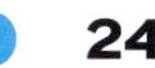

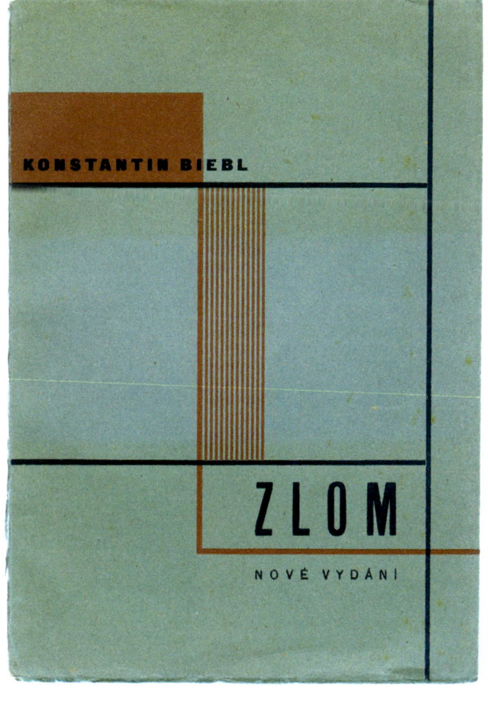

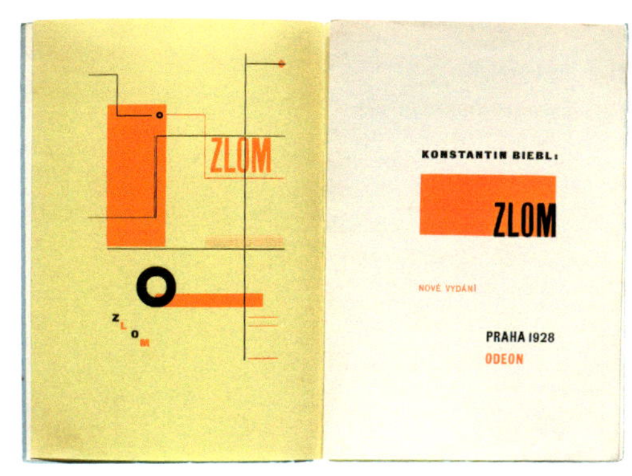

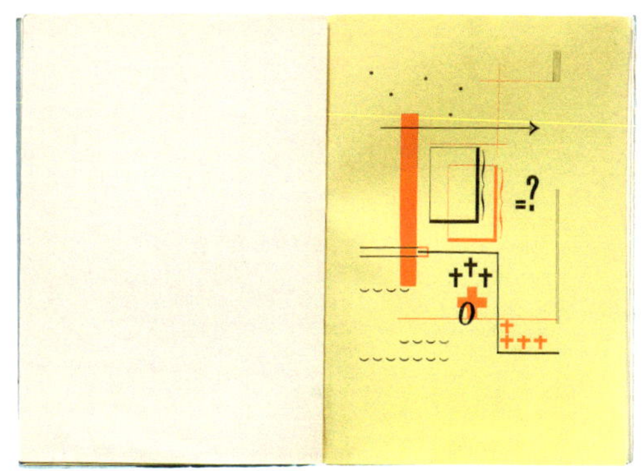

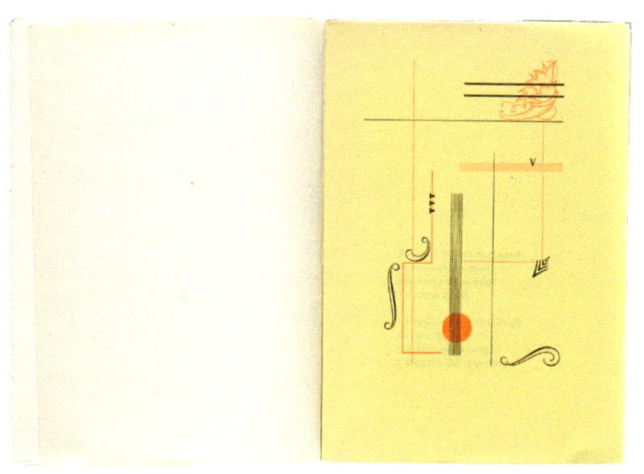

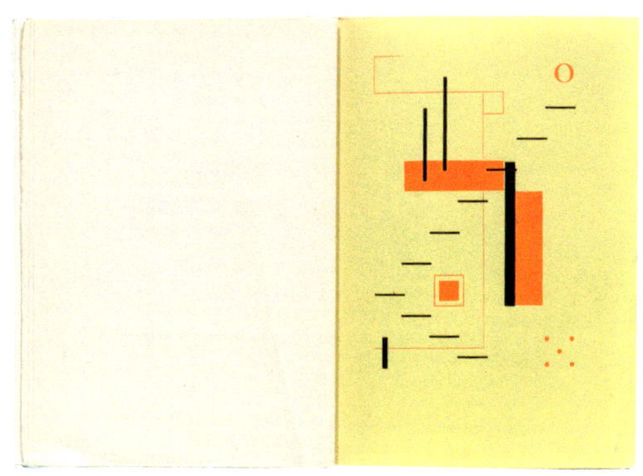

1928

KAREL TEIGE (designer)
KONSTANTIN BIEBL (author)

Rupture (*Zlom*), letterpress, 7¾ × 5⅝ inches (198 × 141 mm), Prague.

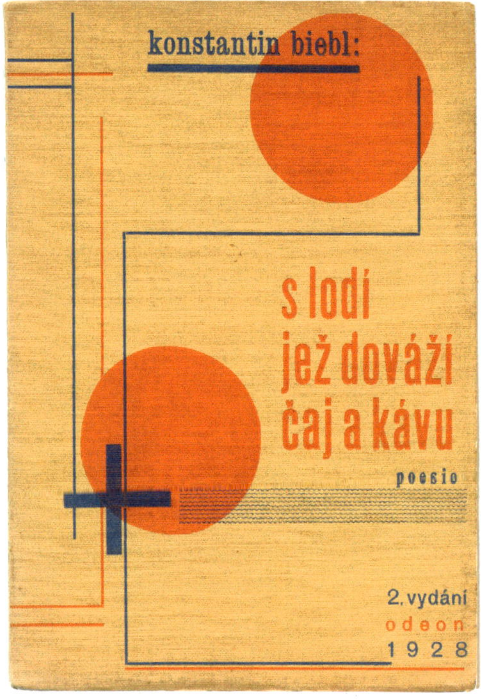

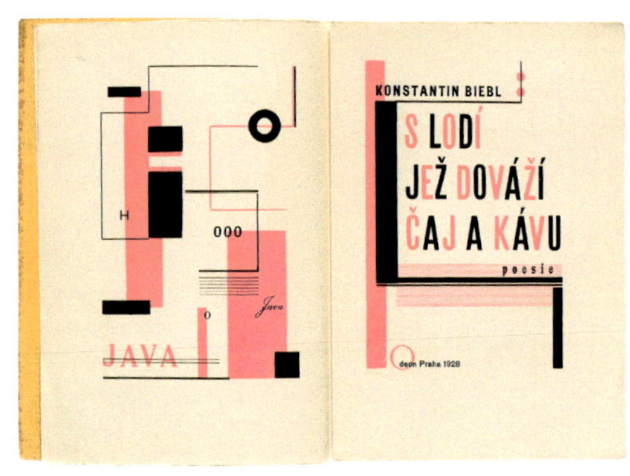

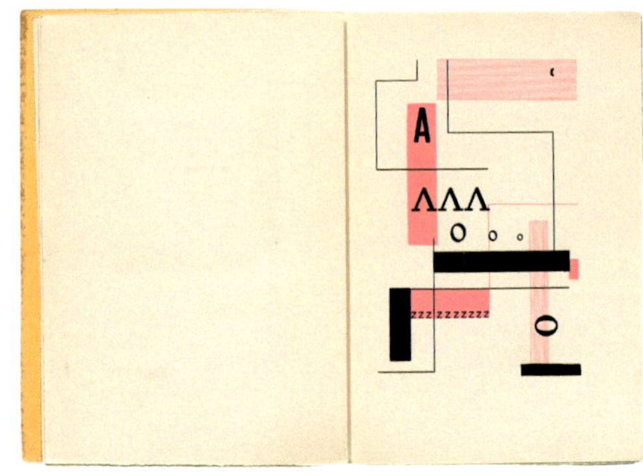

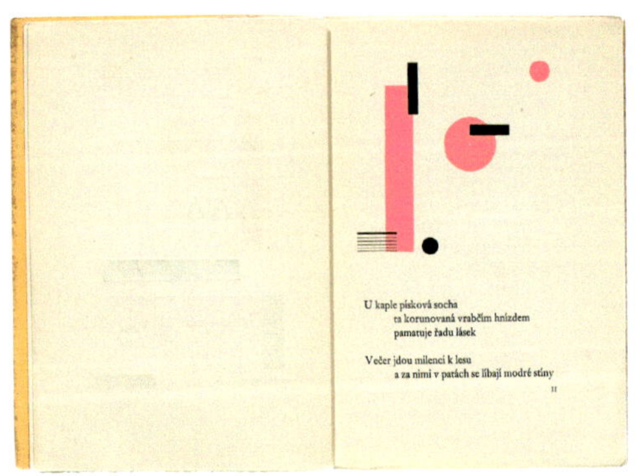

U kaple písková socha
ta korunovaná vrabčím hnízdem
pamatuje řadu lásek

Večer jdou milenci k lesu
a za nimi v patách se líbají modré stíny

11

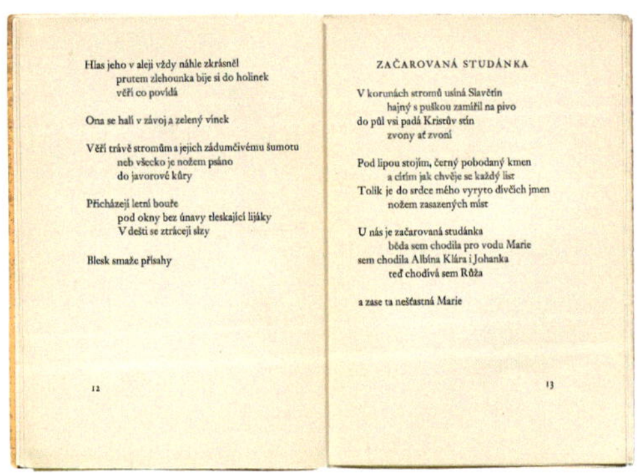

Hlas jeho v aleji vždy náhle zkrásněl
prutem zlehounka bije si do holinek
věří co povídá

Ona se halí v závoj a zelený vínek

Věří trávě stromům a jejich zádumčivému šumotu
neb všecko je nožem psáno
do javorové kůry

Přicházejí letní bouře
pod okny bez únavy tleskající lijáky
V dešti se ztrácejí slzy

Blesk smaže přísahy

12

ZAČAROVANÁ STUDÁNKA

V korunách stromů usíná Slavětín
hajný s puškou zamířil na pivo
do půl vsi padá Kristův stín
zvony ať zvoní

Pod lipou stojím, černý pobodaný kmen
a cítím jak chvěje se každý list
Tolik je do srdce mého vyryto dívčích jmen
nožem zasazených míst

U nás je začarovaná studánka
běda sem chodila pro vodu Marie
sem chodila Albína Klára i Johanka
teď chodívá sem Růža

a zase ta nešťastná Marie

13

1928

KAREL TEIGE (designer)
KONSTANTIN BIEBL (author)
With a Ship that Imports Tea and Coffee (*S lodí jež dováží čaj a kávu*), letterpress, 7⅞ × 5½ inches (200 × 140 mm), Prague.

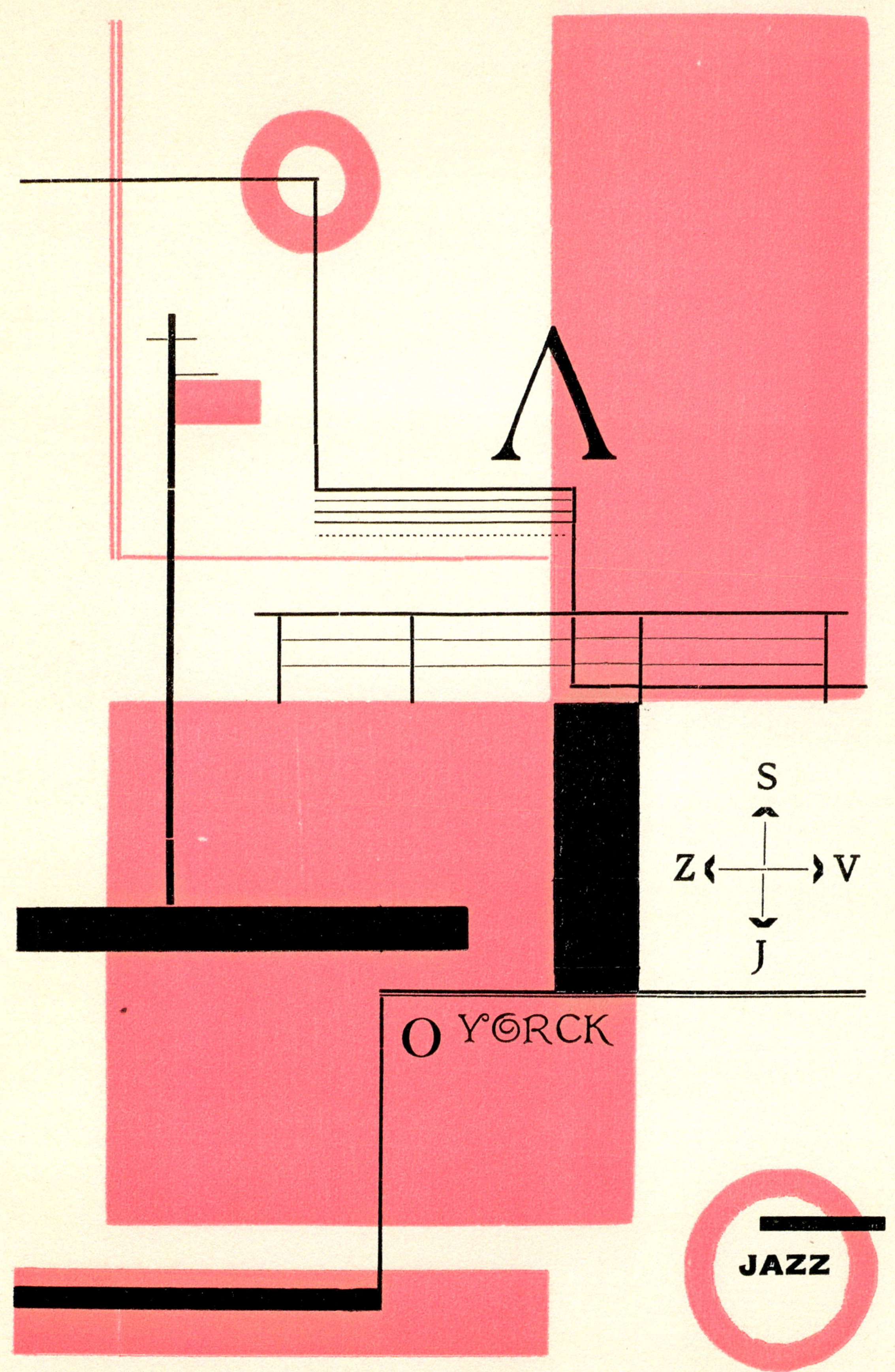
Λ
S
Z
V
J
O YORCK
JAZZ

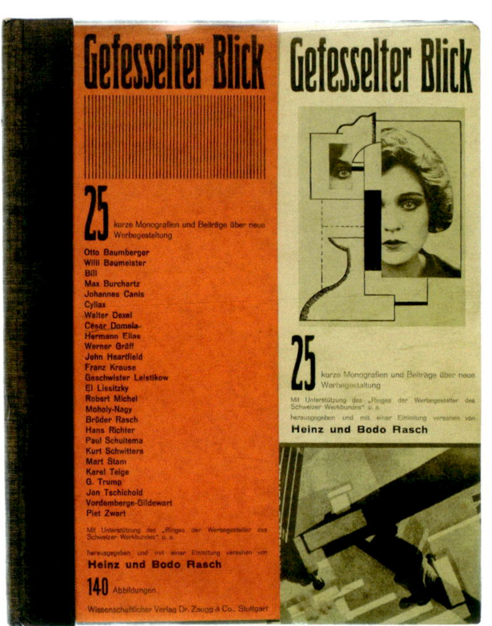

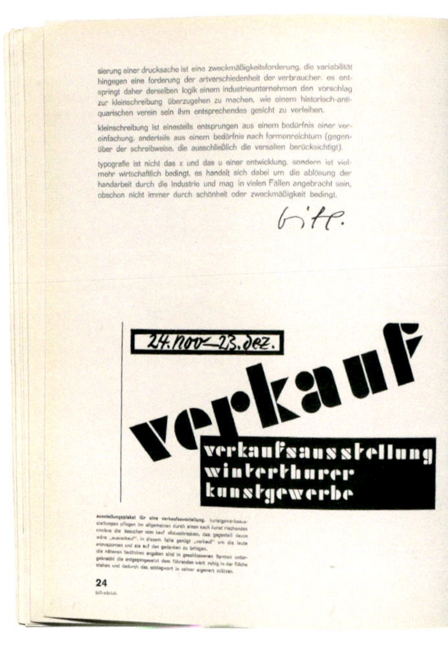
sierung einer drucksache ist eine zweckmäßigkeitsforderung, die variabilität hingegen eine forderung der artverschiedenheit der verbraucher. es entspringt daher derselben logik einem industrieunternehmen den vorschlag zur kleinschreibung überzugehen zu machen, wie einem historisch-antiquarischen verein sein ihm entsprechendes gesicht zu verleihen.

kleinschreibung ist einesteils entsprungen aus einem bedürfnis einer vereinfachung, anderteils aus einem bedürfnis nach formenreichtum (gegenüber der schreibweise, die ausschließlich die versalien berücksichtigt).

typografie ist nicht das x und das u einer entwicklung, sondern ist vielmehr wirtschaftlich bedingt, es handelt sich dabei um die ablösung der handarbeit durch die Industrie und mag in vielen Fällen angebracht sein, obschon nicht immer durch schönheit oder zweckmäßigkeit bedingt.

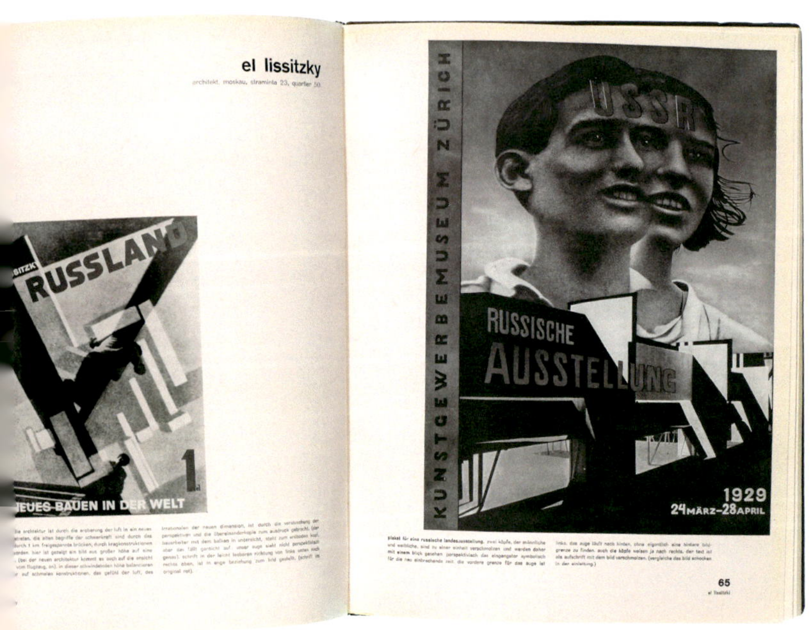

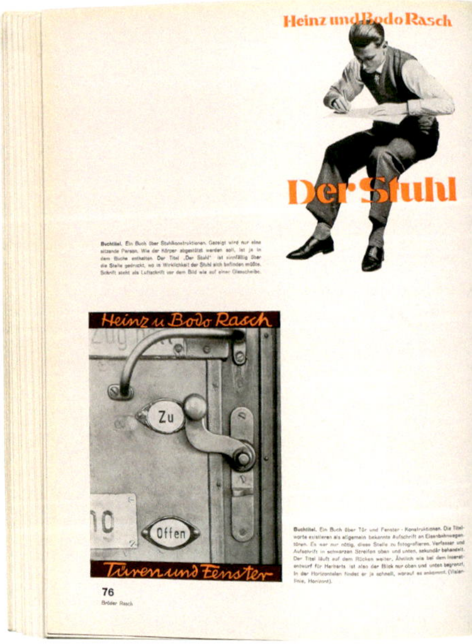

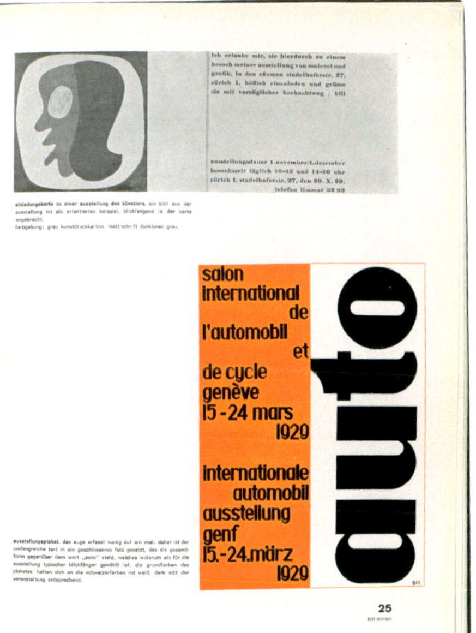

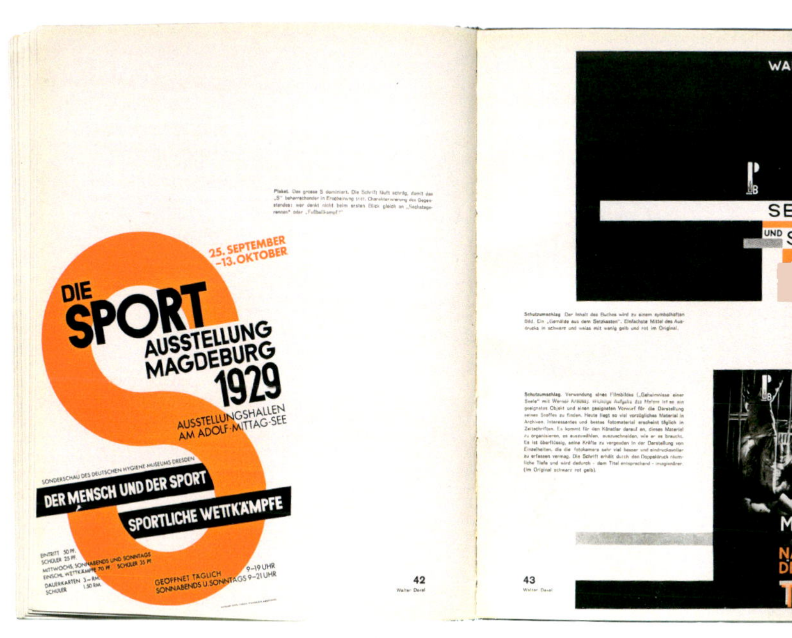

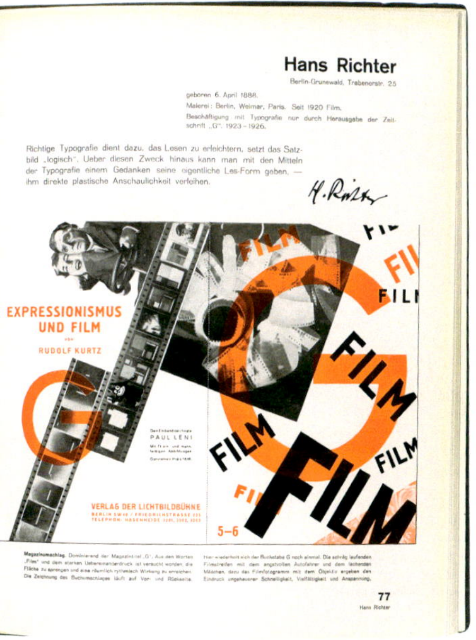

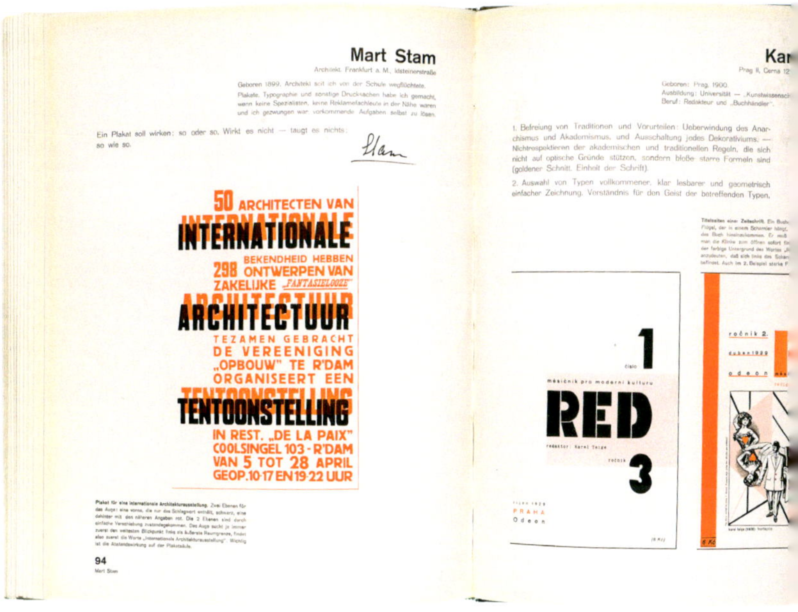

1930

HEINZ RASCH (designer/editor)
BODO RASCH (designer/editor)

Captivated Gaze: 25 Short Monographs and Articles on New Advertising Designers (*Gefesselter Blick: 25 kurze Monografien und Beiträge über neue Werbegestaltung*), letterpress, 10¼ × 8½ inches (260 × 215 mm), Stuttgart, Germany.

beyon
the ba

After the Bauhaus was labeled degenerate in the press and raided by the Nazis in 1933, third director Ludwig Mies van der Rohe succumbed to political pressure and permanently closed its doors. Thirty years later, the rector of the Hochschule für Gestaltung Ulm (HfG), a German institution modeled on the Bauhaus, asked in the school's magazine *Ulm*: "Is the Bauhaus relevant today?" For the HfG, the question had an urgent, political significance, as it had just endured a smear campaign reminiscent of the one directed at the Bauhaus. ●

Today, just over one hundred years since the Bauhaus's founding, one can survey a wide range of design objects and conclude that the school is as relevant as ever. The following pages include just a small sample of items bearing traces of its influence. Some of their designers, such as American Elaine Lustig Cohen, were collectors of Bauhaus design and explicitly made use of Bauhaus principles in their work. Others, such as some designers featured in *Emigre* magazine, while evidently rejecting the ascetic purity of the New Typography, seem to echo the edgier, more expressive designs of Johannes Itten and the early Weimar years. ●

Overall, the Bauhaus's impact on graphic design is not reducible to a single style. Instead, the Bauhaus idea encompasses broader methods of experimentation, simplification, and imagination that are as applicable to today's digital era as they were to the machine age. And, as funding for the arts and education continues to be cut, as corporate design ceaselessly prefers the safety of proven solutions, and as fascist ideologies resurface worldwide, we may also conclude that the forces that once suppressed the Bauhaus are just as alive as its formal lessons. ●

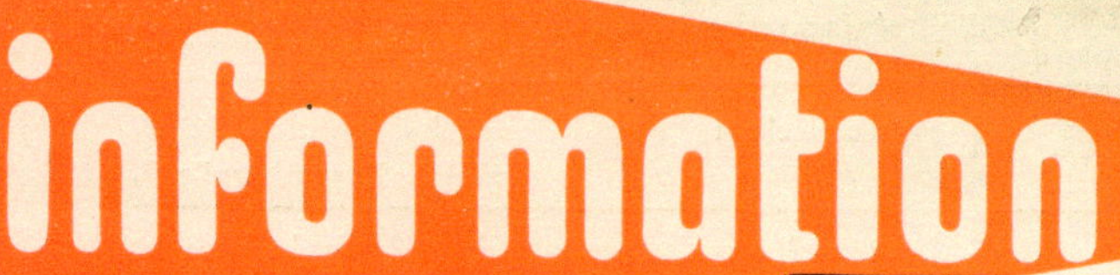

wirtschaft — wissenschaft
erziehung — technik — kunst

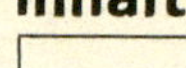

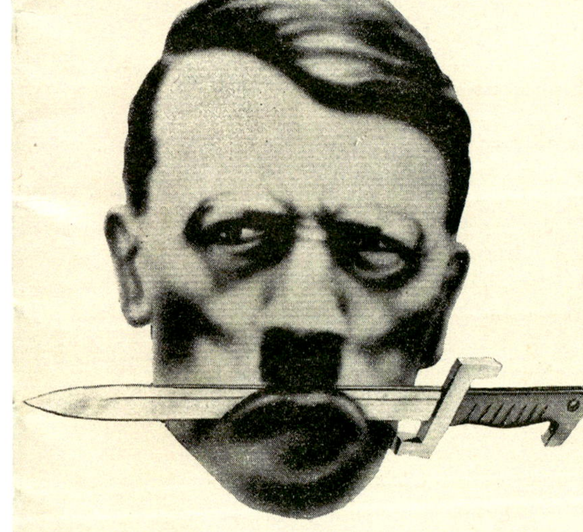

preis fr. -.60 **august / september 1932** heft

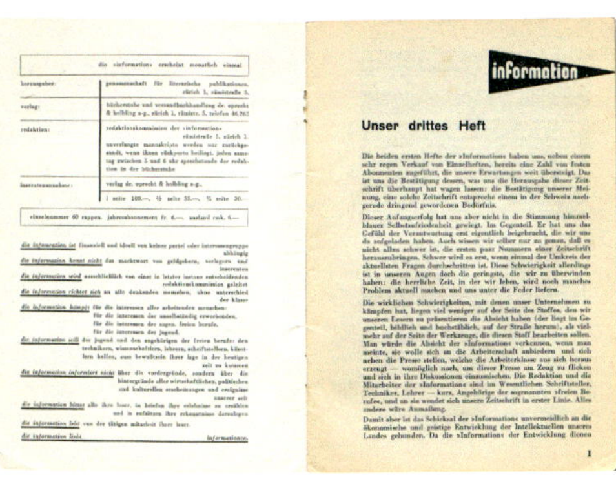
information

Unser drittes Heft

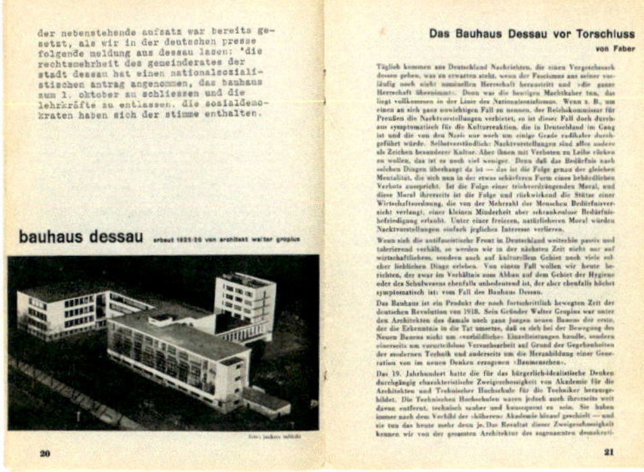
der nebenstehende aufsatz war bereits gesetzt, als wir in der deutschen presse folgende meldung aus dessau lasen: 'die rechtsmehrheit des gemeinderates der stadt dessau hat einen nationalsozialistischen antrag angenommen, das bauhaus zum 1. oktober zu schliessen und die lehrkräfte zu entlassen. die sozialdemokraten haben sich der stimme enthalten.

bauhaus dessau

Das Bauhaus Dessau vor Torschluss

von Faber

20

21

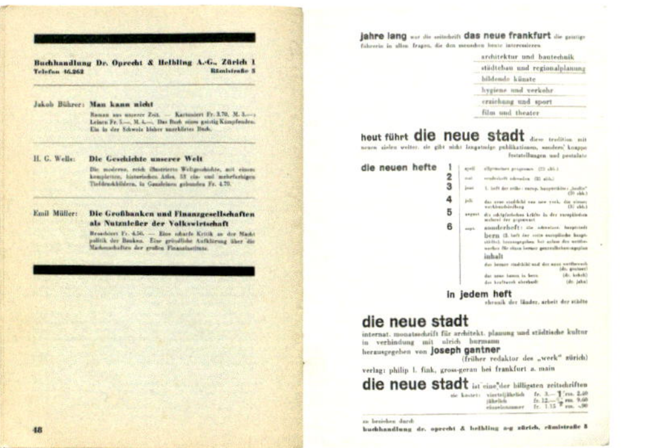
jahre lang ... das neue frankfurt

heut führt die neue stadt

die neuen hefte

in jedem heft

die neue stadt

die neue stadt

48

1932

MAX BILL (designer)

Information, vol. 1, no. 3, letterpress, 8¼ × 5¾ inches (209 × 147 mm), Zurich.

Swiss designer Max Bill enrolled as a student at the Bauhaus in 1927, studying architecture, metalworking, painting, and stage design until his return to Switzerland in 1929. Bill remained vigorously committed to the radical ideas and avant-garde aesthetics of the Bauhaus after his time there, eventually bringing them to bear in the typography and layout for the Swiss magazine *Information*. The cover designs clearly show the influence of Bauhaus typography, especially the *bauhaus* magazine under the direction of Joost Schmidt (see pages 146–155), with its knocked-out, lowercase, sans serif logo lettering and all-lowercase sans serif type set in boxes. On the other hand, Bill's lettering for the *Information* logo is somewhat unprecedented—from our contemporary perspective, its spurless forms and rounded terminals might read more like an artifact of the early computer age than the pretelevisual one. Overall, Bill's striking logo design, minimalist typography, and political photomontage complemented the magazine's radical Marxist and antifascist writing as the Nazis took over Germany. In 1932, on the cover of the third issue, a caricature of Hitler grimaces with a knife in his teeth, while a feature article inside details the recent closure of the Bauhaus Dessau, which was shuttered for political reasons. Bill later returned to Germany in 1953 and cofounded the Hochschule für Gestaltung Ulm (see pages 252–253), a new design school based on the Bauhaus, and served as its first rector. ●

ulm 1

Vierteljahresbericht
der Hochschule für Gestaltung, Ulm
Oktober 1958

Preis pro Nummer DM 1.–/SFr 1.–/ÖS 7.50
Jahresabonnement DM 4.–/SFr 4.–/ÖS 30
portofrei

Quarterly bulletin
of the Hochschule für Gestaltung, Ulm
October 1958

Price per issue 2s6d/$0.50
Yearly subscription 10s/$2.00 post paid

Bulletin trimestriel
de la Hochschule für Gestaltung, Ulm
Octobre 1958

Prix du numéro 125 frs/L 175
Abonnement annuel 500 frs/L 700 port payé

Hochschule für Gestaltung

Die Hochschule für Gestaltung bildet Fachkräfte aus für zwei entscheidende Aufgaben der technischen Zivilisation:
die Gestaltung industrieller Produkte
(Abteilung Produktform und Abteilung Bauen);
die Gestaltung bildhafter und sprachlicher Mitteilungen
(Abteilung visuelle Kommunikation und Abteilung Information).

Die Hochschule für Gestaltung bildet damit Gestalter heran für die Gebrauchs- und Produktionsgüterindustrie sowie für die modernen Kommunikationsmittel Presse, Film, Funk und Werbung. Diese Gestalter müssen über die technologischen und wissenschaftlichen Fachkenntnisse verfügen, die für eine Mitwirkung in der heutigen Industrie erforderlich sind. Gleichzeitig müssen sie die kulturellen und gesellschaftlichen Konsequenzen ihrer Arbeit erfassen und berücksichtigen.

Die Hochschule für Gestaltung ist als eine Schule für höchstens 150 Studierende konzipiert, um ein günstiges Zahlenverhältnis zwischen Studierenden und Dozenten zu gewährleisten.

Dozenten und Studierende kommen aus verschiedenen Ländern und geben der Hochschule einen internationalen Charakter.

The Hochschule für Gestaltung educates specialists for two different tasks of our technical civilization:
The design of industrial products
(industrial design department and building department);
The design of visual and verbal means of communication
(visual communication department and information department).

The school thus educates designers for the production and consumer goods industries as well as for present-day means of communication: press, films, broadcasting, television, and advertising. These designers must have at their disposal the technological and scientific knowledge necessary for collaboration in industry today. At the same time they must grasp and bear in mind the cultural and sociological consequences of their work.

The Hochschule für Gestaltung is conceived as a school for a maximum number of 150 students, in order to ensure a favourable proportion between the number of students and faculty. Faculty and students come from many different countries, thus giving the school an international character.

La Hochschule für Gestaltung s'attache à former des spécialistes appelés à remplir deux tâches d'importance décisive dans notre civilisation technique:
la création dans le domaine des produits industriels
(section «Industrial Design» et section «Industrialisation du Bâtiment»);
la création dans le domaine de la communication visuelle et verbale
(section «Communication Visuelle» et section «Information»).

La Hochschule für Gestaltung forme des créateurs qui s'appliquent tant à l'étude d'objets industriels de consommation et de production, qu'à celle des moyens modernes de communication (presse, film, radiodiffusion, télévision, publicité). Ces créateurs devront posséder les connaissances techniques et théoriques aujourd'hui nécessaires à une collaboration fructueuse avec l'industrie. Ils devront aussi considérer et mesurer la portée des conséquences sociales et culturelles de leur travail.

La Hochschule für Gestaltung est conçue de manière à recevoir un maximum de 150 étudiants, afin d'assurer une proportion numérique favorable aux rapports entre étudiants et professeurs, qui viennent de tous les horizons et donnent à l'Ecole son caractère international.

1958

ANTHONY FROSHAUG (designer)

Ulm 1, letterpress, 11 × 11¾ inches (281 × 299 mm), Ulm.

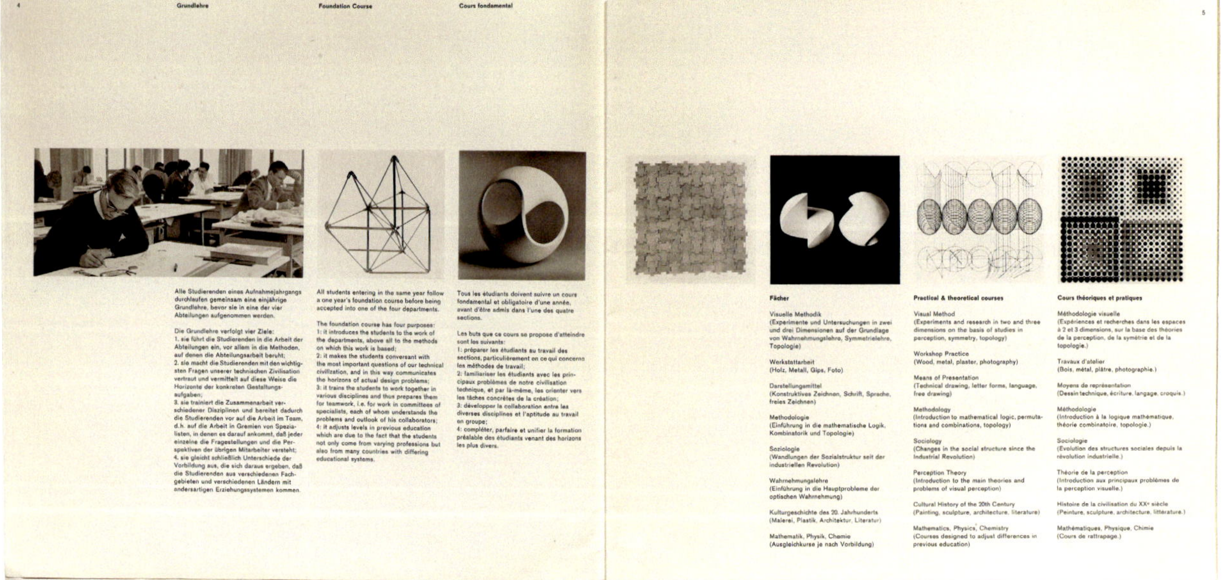

4 **Grundlehre** **Foundation Course** **Cours fondamental**

Alle Studierenden eines Aufnahmejahrgangs durchlaufen gemeinsam eine einjährige Grundlehre, bevor sie in eine der vier Abteilungen aufgenommen werden.

Die Grundlehre verfolgt vier Ziele:
1. sie führt die Studierenden in die Arbeit der Abteilungen ein, vor allem in die Methoden, auf denen die Abteilungsarbeit beruht;
2. sie macht die Studierenden mit den wichtigsten Fragen unserer technischen Zivilisation vertraut und vermittelt auf diese Weise die Horizonte der konkreten Gestaltungsaufgaben;
3. sie trainiert die Zusammenarbeit verschiedener Disziplinen und bereitet dadurch die Studierenden vor auf die Arbeit im Team, d.h. auf die Arbeit in Gremien von Spezialisten, in denen es darauf ankommt, daß jeder einzelne die Fragestellungen und die Perspektiven der übrigen Mitarbeiter versteht;
4. sie gleicht schließlich Unterschiede der Vorbildung aus, die sich daraus ergeben, daß die Studierenden aus verschiedenen Fachgebieten und verschiedenen Ländern mit andersartigen Erziehungssystemen kommen.

All students entering in the same year follow a one year's foundation course before being accepted into one of the four departments.

The foundation course has four purposes:
1: it introduces the students to the work of the departments, above all to the methods on which this work is based;
2: it makes the students conversant with the most important questions of our technical civilization, and in this way communicates the horizons of actual design problems;
3: it trains the students to work together in various disciplines and thus prepares them for teamwork, i.e. for work in committees of specialists, each of whom understands the problems and outlook of his collaborators;
4: it adjusts levels in previous education which are due to the fact that the students not only come from varying professions but also from many countries with differing educational systems.

Tous les étudiants doivent suivre un cours fondamental et obligatoire d'une année, avant d'être admis dans l'une des quatre sections.

Les buts que ce cours se propose d'atteindre sont les suivants:
1: préparer les étudiants au travail des sections, particulièrement en ce qui concerne les méthodes de travail;
2: familiariser les étudiants avec les principaux problèmes de notre civilisation technique, et par là-même, les orienter vers les tâches concrètes de la création;
3: développer la collaboration entre les diverses disciplines et l'aptitude au travail en groupe;
4: compléter, parfaire et unifier la formation préalable des étudiants venant des horizons les plus divers.

5

Fächer

Visuelle Methodik
(Experimente und Untersuchungen in zwei und drei Dimensionen auf der Grundlage von Wahrnehmungslehre, Symmetrielehre, Topologie)

Werkstattarbeit
(Holz, Metall, Gips, Foto)

Darstellungsmittel
(Konstruktives Zeichnen, Schrift, Sprache, freies Zeichnen)

Methodologie
(Einführung in die mathematische Logik, Kombinatorik und Topologie)

Soziologie
(Wandlungen der Sozialstruktur seit der industriellen Revolution)

Wahrnehmungslehre
(Einführung in die Hauptprobleme der optischen Wahrnehmung)

Kulturgeschichte des 20. Jahrhunderts
(Malerei, Plastik, Architektur, Literatur)

Mathematik, Physik, Chemie
(Ausgleichkurse je nach Vorbildung)

Practical & theoretical courses

Visual Method
(Experiments and research in two and three dimensions on the basis of studies in perception, symmetry, topology)

Workshop Practice
(Wood, metal, plaster, photography)

Means of Presentation
(Technical drawing, letter forms, language, free drawing)

Methodology
(Introduction to mathematical logic, permutations and combinations, topology)

Sociology
(Changes in the social structure since the Industrial Revolution)

Perception Theory
(Introduction to the main theories and problems of visual perception)

Cultural History of the 20th Century
(Painting, sculpture, architecture, literature)

Mathematics, Physics, Chemistry
(Courses designed to adjust differences in previous education)

Cours théoriques et pratiques

Méthodologie visuelle
(Expériences et recherches dans les espaces à 2 et 3 dimensions, sur la base des théories de la perception, de la symétrie et de la topologie.)

Travaux d'atelier
(Bois, métal, plâtre, photographie.)

Moyens de représentation
(Dessin technique, écriture, langage, croquis.)

Méthodologie
(Introduction à la logique mathématique, théorie combinatoire, topologie.)

Sociologie
(Evolution des structures sociales depuis la révolution industrielle.)

Théorie de la perception
(Introduction aux principaux problèmes de la perception visuelle.)

Histoire de la civilisation du XXe siècle
(Peinture, sculpture, architecture, littérature.)

Mathématiques, Physique, Chimie
(Cours de rattrapage.)

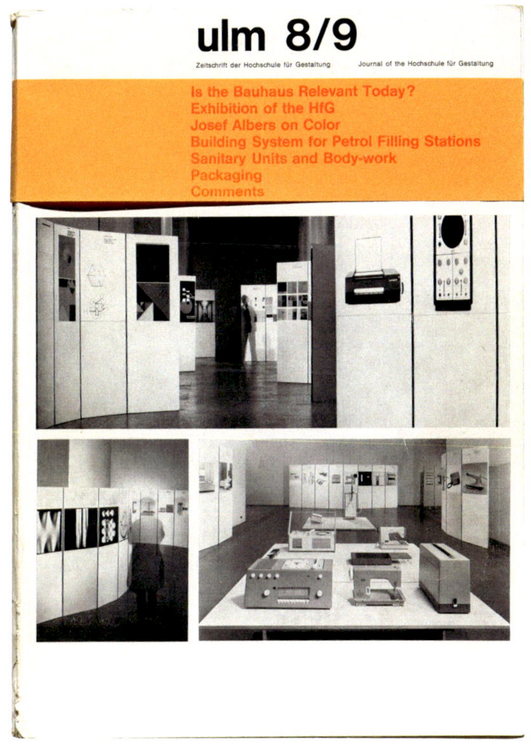

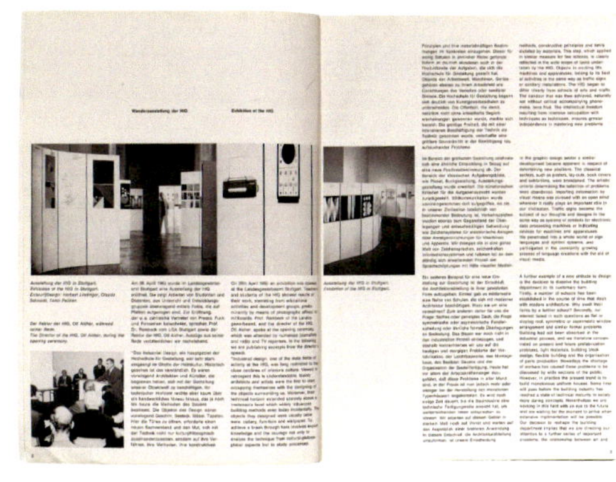

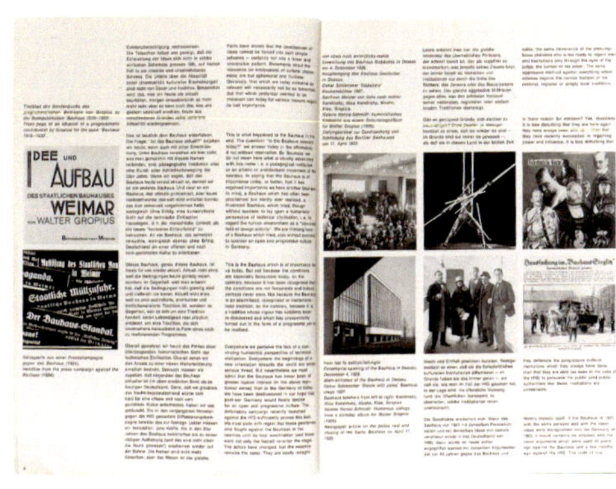

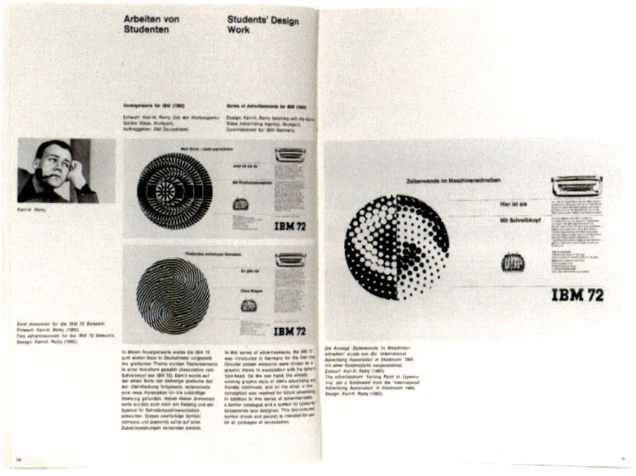

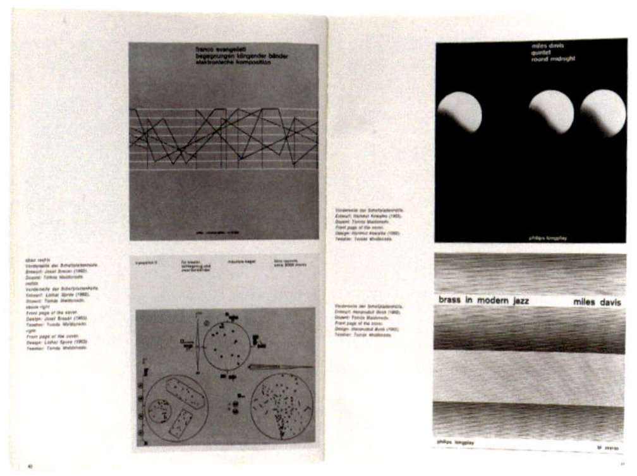

1963

DESIGNER UNKNOWN

Ulm 8/9, the issue in which the rector asked, “Is the Bauhaus relevant today?,” letterpress, 11¾ × 8½ inches (297 × 215 mm), Ulm.

1931

IRMGARD SÖRENSEN-POPITZ (cover designer)

The New Line (*Die neue Linie*), vol. 2, no. 12, letterpress, 14⅜ × 10⅝ inches (365 × 270 mm), Leipzig and Berlin.

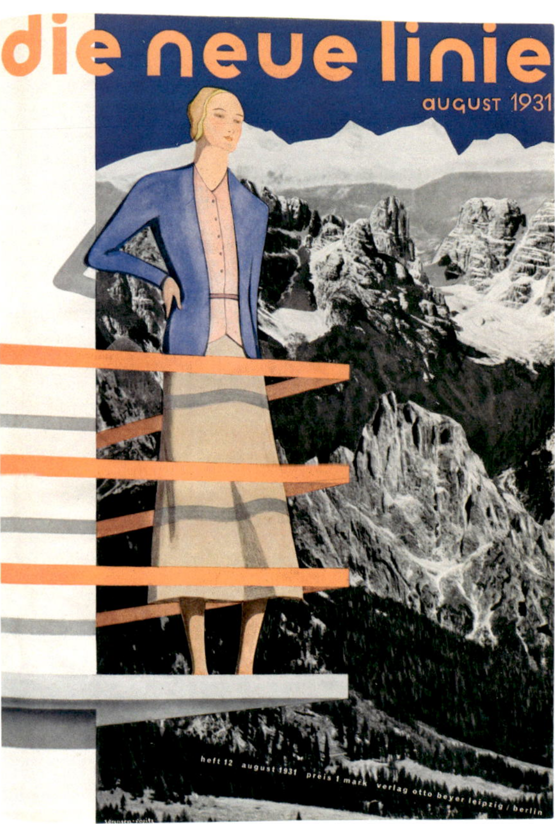

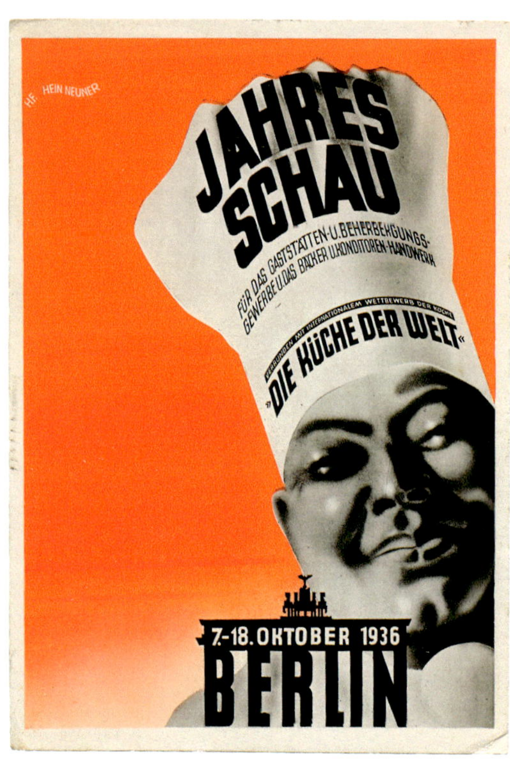

1936

HEIN NEUNER
HANNES F. NEUNER

Postcard announcement for an annual show of the culinary and hospitality industries, gravure, 5⅞ × 4⅛ inches (149 × 105 mm), Berlin.

CIRCA 1950s

HANS-JOACHIM "HAJO" ROSE

Hajo Rose letterhead, letterpress, 11⅝ × 8¼ inches (296 × 210 mm), Leipzig.

While many Bauhaus students went on to lead professional design careers, examples of their work are scarce because many were employed in advertising, where the output was ephemeral and often not credited. After leaving the Bauhaus, German Hannes F. Neuner worked for Bayer and later Moholy-Nagy before starting a studio with his brother, Hein, where they designed this announcement for a restaurant industry show (far left). The second example (near left) is by German designer Irmgard Sörensen-Popitz, who often signed her name Söre Popitz and was perhaps the only woman to practice graphic design professionally after studying at the Bauhaus. While she left after only one semester, she was able to learn from Moholy-Nagy, Albers, Klee, and Kandinsky in the preliminary course. Instead of staying on at the school and being pushed into the weaving workshop, as many women students were, she struck out as a designer in Leipzig, where she worked on the popular women's magazine *The New Line* (*Die neue Linie*), to which Bayer and Moholy-Nagy also contributed. Popitz's 1931 cover here—with its stylishly dressed woman standing on the balcony of a modern building set against a photograph of snowy mountains—could be considered an homage to Moholy-Nagy's covers for the magazine (see pages 160–161). The final example (below) is Hans-Joachim "Hajo" Rose's personal letterhead. The German designer studied under Joost Schmidt and was one of the few students to move to the Bauhaus's final location in Berlin and graduate in 1933, the year it closed. Afterward, Rose worked for Moholy-Nagy before teaching at the Nieuwe Kunstschool in the Netherlands, which was headed by another former Bauhaus student, German-born artist Paul Citroen. ●

Hajo Rose

Werbegrafik · Industrielle Farb- und Formgebung

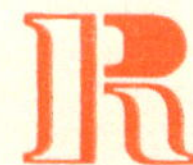

Leipzig S 3

Kurt-Eisner-Str. 56

Ihre Zeichen

Ihre Nachricht vom

Betrifft

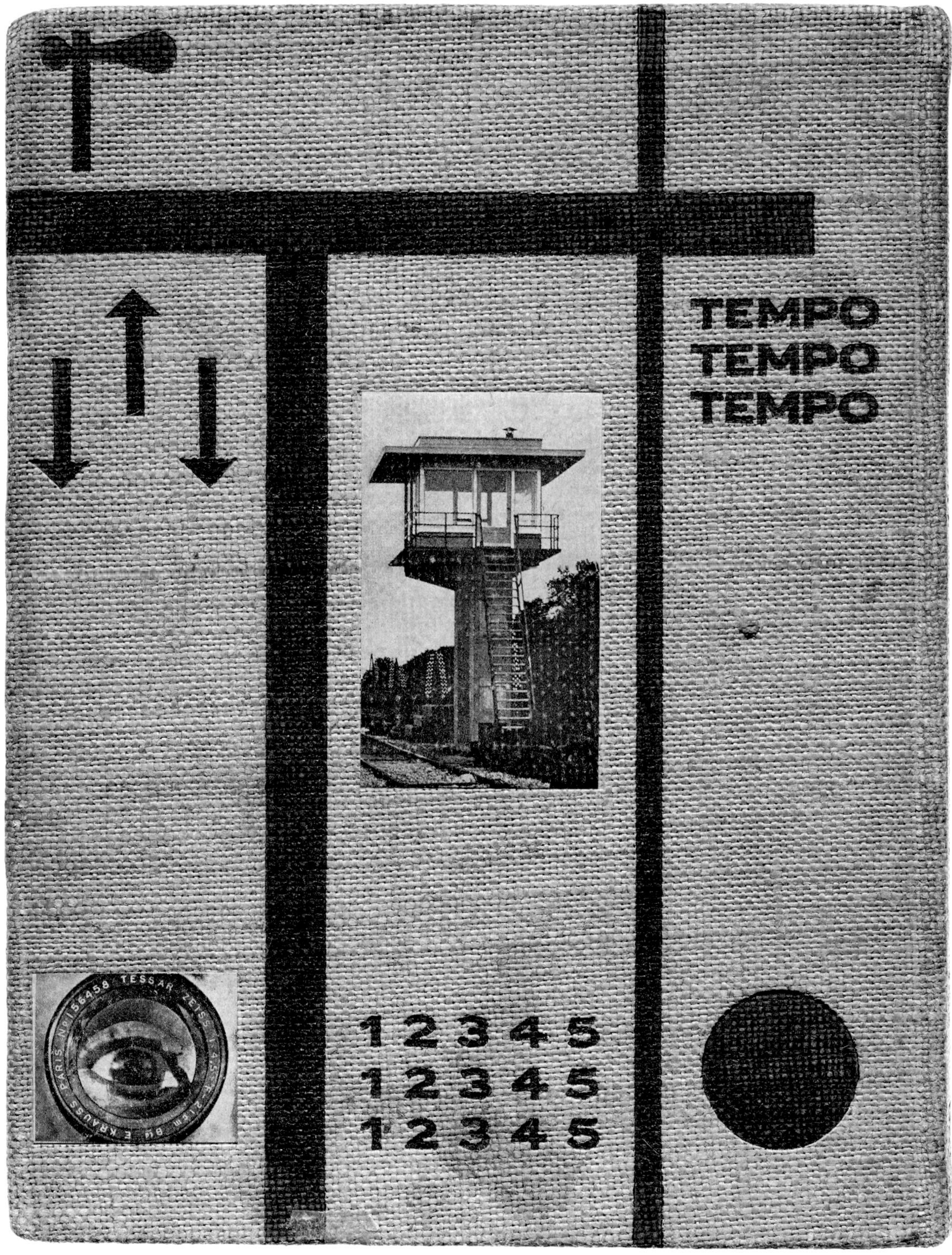
TEMPO
TEMPO
TEMPO
TESSAR ZEISS
1 2 3 4 5
1 2 3 4 5
1 2 3 4 5

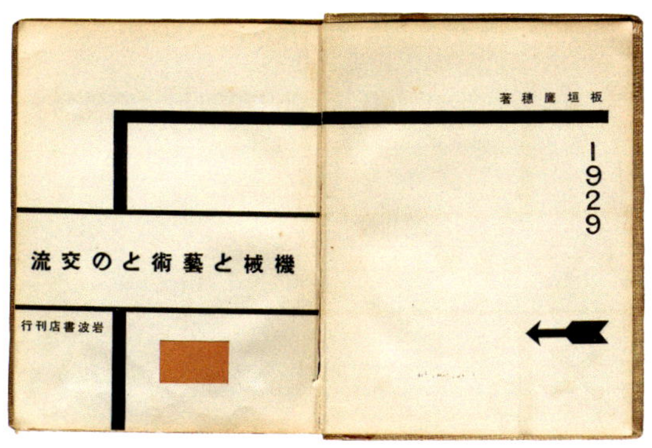

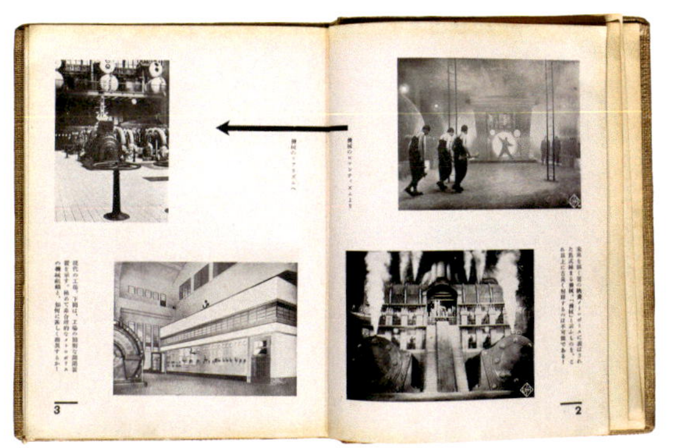

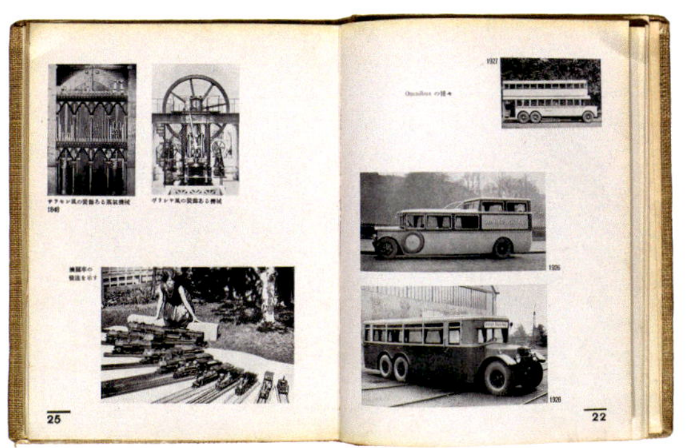

1929

MASAO HORINO (designer)
TAKAO ITAGAKI (author)

Cultural Exchange Between Machine and Art (*Kikai to geijutsu tono kōryū*), letterpress with a linen cover and inlaid photos, 7¾ × 6 inches (198 × 154 mm), Tokyo.

With essays by art historian Takao Itagaki, this 1929 linen-bound Japanese book testifies to the Bauhaus's swift permeation beyond German borders. Borrowing heavily from graphic motifs in Moholy-Nagy's *Painting, Photography, Film* (see pages 122–127) and released in the same year as a Japanese translation of *From Material to Architecture*, this avant-garde title includes photo essays on the architecture and machine aesthetics of the modern era. The Bauhaus's international legacy is often understood as a result of the exodus presaging World War II, but the school had attracted foreign students and visitors from its inception. The author of *Cultural Exchange Between Machine and Art* learned of the Bauhaus during his visit to western Europe in the early 1920s and brought word back to his island nation; Japanese students Takehiko Mizutani and Iwao and Michiko Yamawaki enrolled at the Bauhaus in the ensuing years and returned with training in furniture design, architecture, and textiles. While modernism in Japan was in no doubt influenced by Western ideas, it is perhaps more accurate to see this as a cultural exchange, as the West had, in the late nineteenth century, grown enamored of Japanese art—in particular, its graphic woodblock prints. Indeed, Itten drew from Japanese as well as Chinese ink drawings and calligraphy in his preliminary course, and one of Gropius's early commissions—the Sommerfeld House in Berlin—emulates the architectural style of Nara, Japan. ●

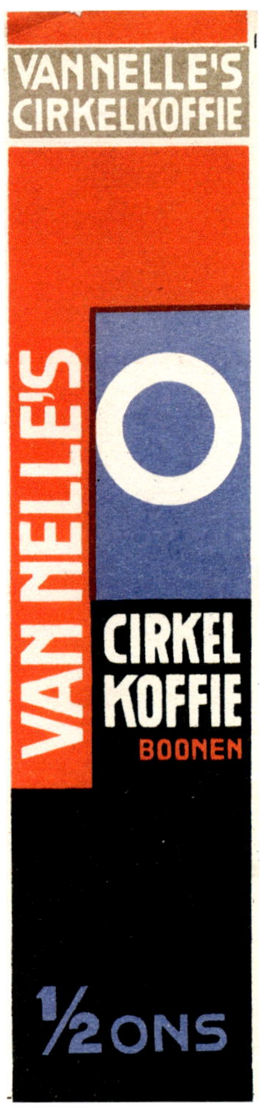

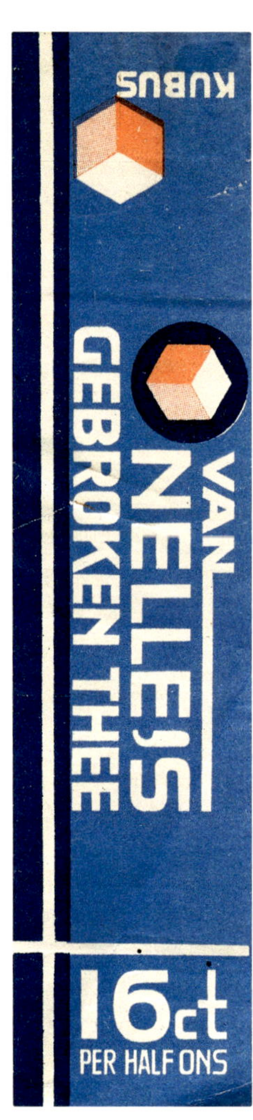

Bauhaus graphic designers executed a great deal of their professional work in advertising, and it is arguably in this area that the school's typographic approach had the largest and most lasting impact. For those original theorists and practitioners, modern advertising was a kind of positive propaganda, a form of communication that would educate the masses about the latest technological, artistic, social, and political innovations. For some designers working in the years during and immediately after the Bauhaus (such as the Dutchman Jacob Jongert in these designs for Van Nelle in the 1930s), the simple, geometric forms and primary color palette of the Bauhaus helped distinguish a brand's products from its competitors. In contrast to the decorative lettering, ornamental borders, and detailed illustrations that were common in packaging design at the time, systems like Jongert's gave a company and its products a unified image of simple, timeless modernity. Like Joost's and Bayer's lettering, Jongert's signature style for Van Nelle incorporated some strict geometry, but mixed it with aspects of grotesque type styles, adapting the proportions to fit the dimensions of each application. Later in the century, in the wake of continuing industrial innovation, burgeoning mass media, and the rise of consumerism, the visual identity of a brand became crucial for communicating a world of associations to the consumer at a glance, and the theories of visual communication that had been developed at the Bauhaus were adopted and expanded into a rigorous science. Examples of corporate identity manuals from Caterpillar, Mobil, and Westinghouse (see pages 260–261) illustrate the persistent influence of geometric letterforms, clever unions of typography and photography, and elemental graphics and logo designs. ●

CIRCA 1930

JACOB JONGERT

Cirkel coffee label for Van Nelle, letterpress, shown at actual size (6 × 1½ inches/152 × 37 mm), Rotterdam.

CIRCA 1930

JACOB JONGERT

Kubus tea label for Van Nelle, letterpress, shown at actual size (6⅜ × 1½ inches/160 × 37 mm), Rotterdam.

CIRCA 1930

JACOB JONGERT

Storage tin for Van Nelle coffee and tea, lithograph on tin, 14⅝ × 16⅛ × 11 inches (370 × 410 × 280 mm), Rotterdam.

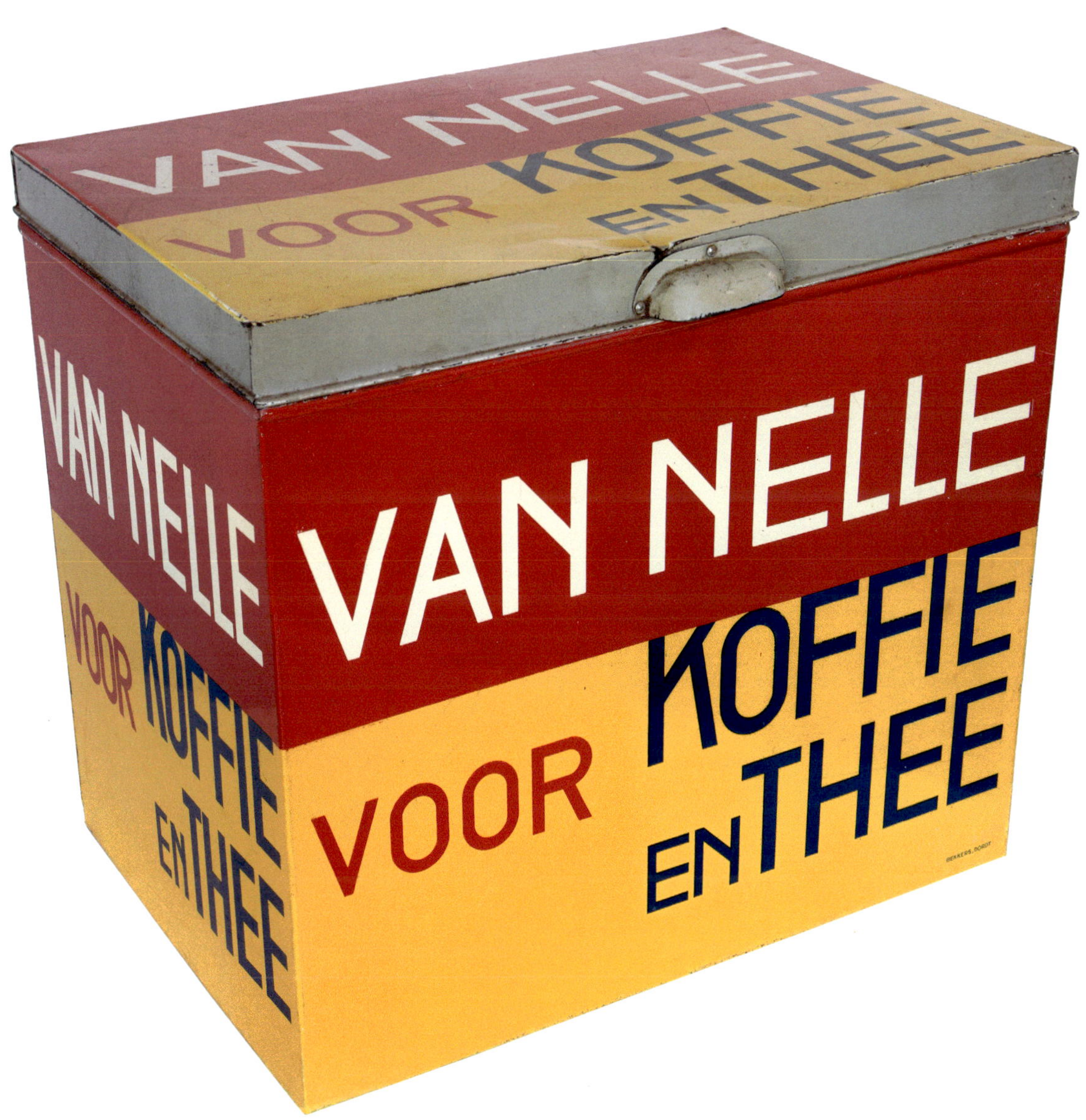

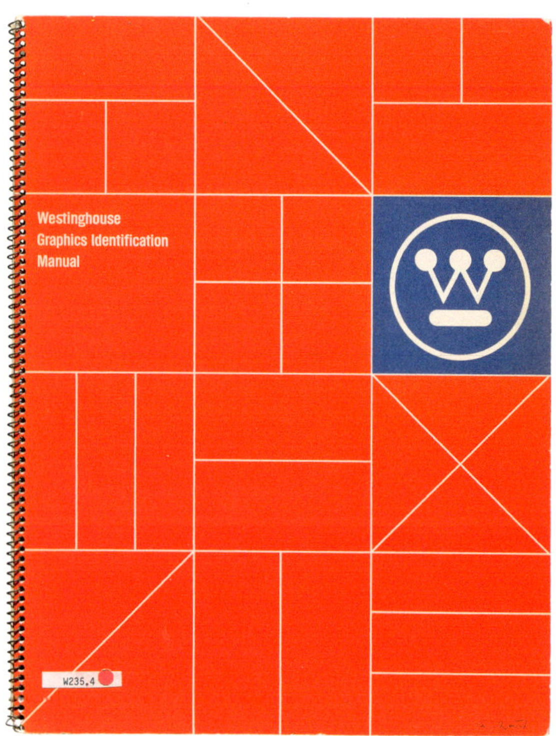

1961

PAUL RAND

Westinghouse Graphics Identification Manual, offset, 10⅞ × 8⅜ inches (276 × 214 mm), Pittsburgh.

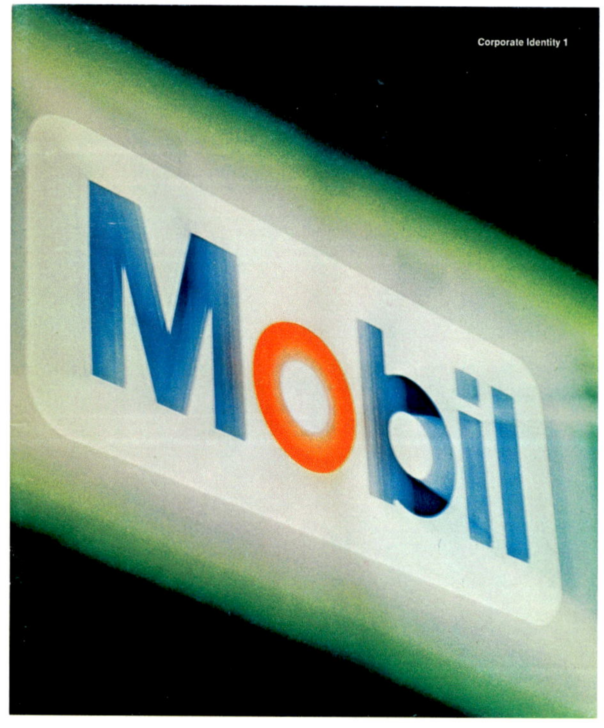

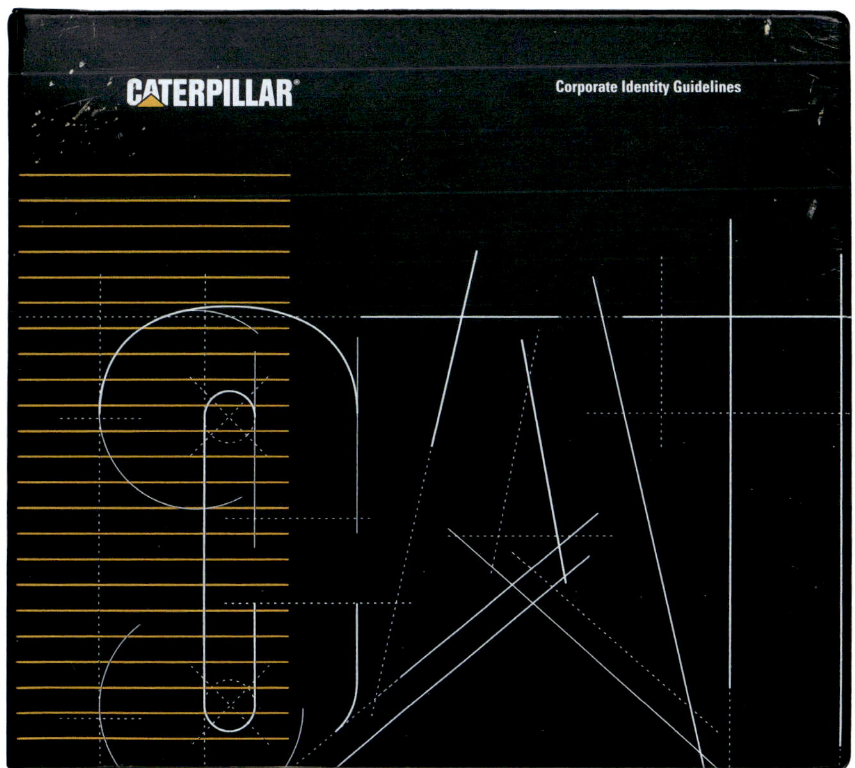

1989

DEAN WILCOX FOR LANDOR ASSOCIATES

Caterpillar Corporate Identity Guidelines, screen print, 11¾ × 13¼ × 2⅜ inches (300 × 335 × 60 mm), Peoria, Illinois.

1968

CHERMAYEFF & GEISMAR ASSOCIATES, INC.

Mobil Corporate Identity 1, offset, 10 × 8½ inches (255 × 215 mm), New York.

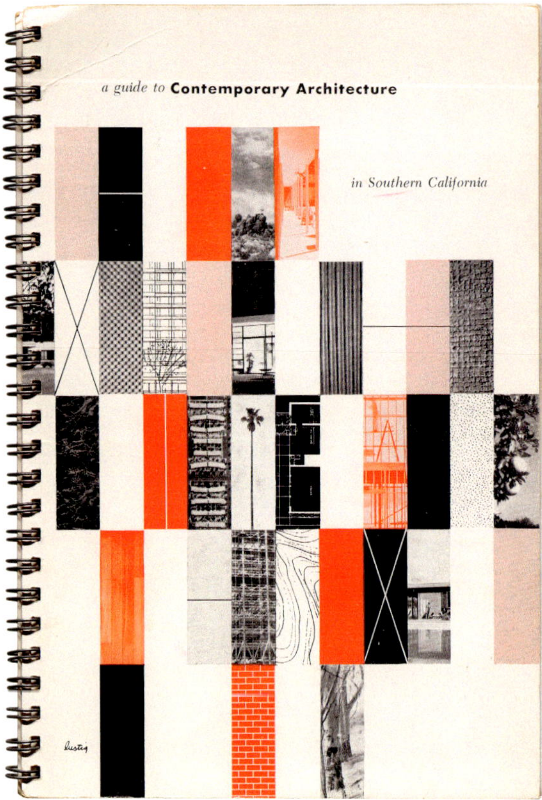

1951

ALVIN LUSTIG (cover designer)

A Guide to Contemporary Architecture in Southern California, letterpress, 9 × 6 inches (228 × 152 mm), Los Angeles.

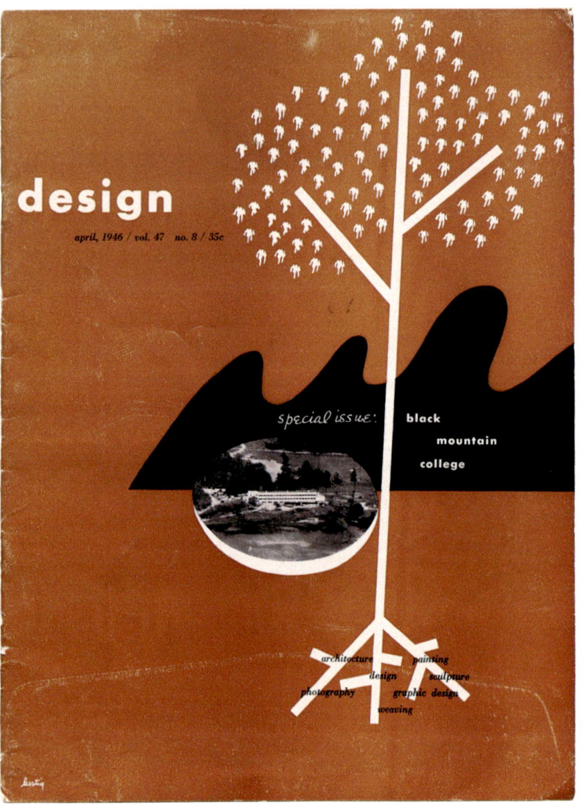

1946

ALVIN LUSTIG (cover designer)

Design, vol. 47, no. 8, letterpress, 12 × 9 inches (306 × 230 mm), Columbus, Ohio.

1960

ELAINE LUSTIG COHEN

"On a Hilltop in Jerusalem," brochure for the National Museum of Israel, offset, 5½ × 8½ inches (140 × 215 mm) folded, 22 × 17 inches (558 × 430 mm) unfolded, New York.

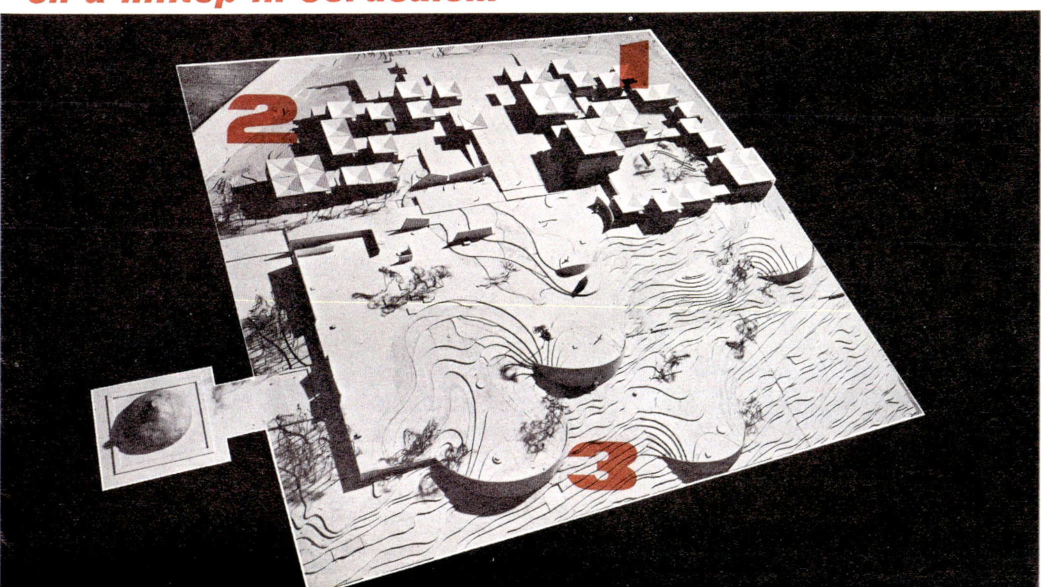

An American designer committed to the clean, modern aesthetic imported from Europe before midcentury, Alvin Lustig is most recognized for his book covers for publisher New Directions, some with illustrations reminiscent of Bauhaus painters such as Klee and Kandinsky. His advertising work also made use of modernist techniques, such as photomontage and constructivist typographic treatments. The grid on his cover for *A Guide to Contemporary Architecture in Southern California* echoes Bayer's poster for the *European Applied Arts Exhibition* (see page 174), with photographs in place of letters. His cover for *Design* magazine evokes the Bauhaus by way of North Carolina's Black Mountain College, an experimental art school and spiritual successor where Bauhaus masters Lyonel Feininger and Josef Albers taught. Near the end of Lustig's life, when his eyesight was failing, his wife Elaine Lustig Cohen helped him carry out his work. She then embarked on her own design career, for which she received an AIGA Medal in 2011. While certainly influenced by Lustig's playful sensibility, Lustig Cohen pushed her work further in the new typographic style of the Bauhaus and Jan Tschichold—a style inspired by her collection of books and ephemera of the European avant-garde. Her regard for Bauhaus typography shows in her pamphlet for the National Museum of Israel (now the Israel Museum), on which she printed bold orange numerals over a black-and-white photo of an architectural model. While Lustig Cohen made a successful career in design, women remained a rarity in the field for decades. ●

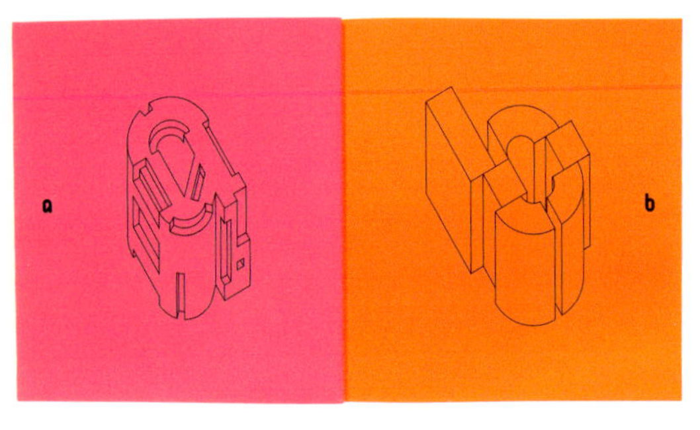
a
b

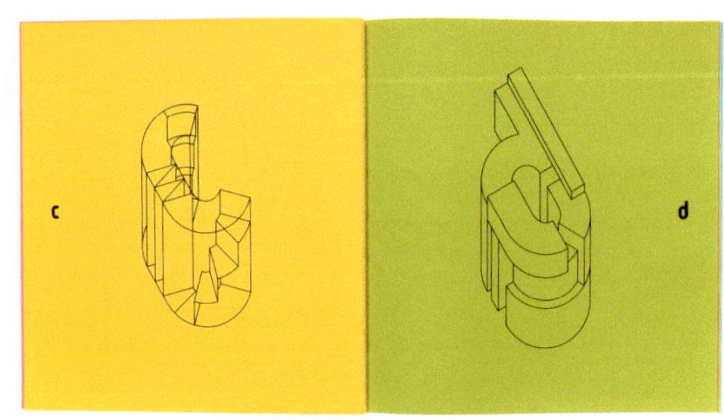
c
d

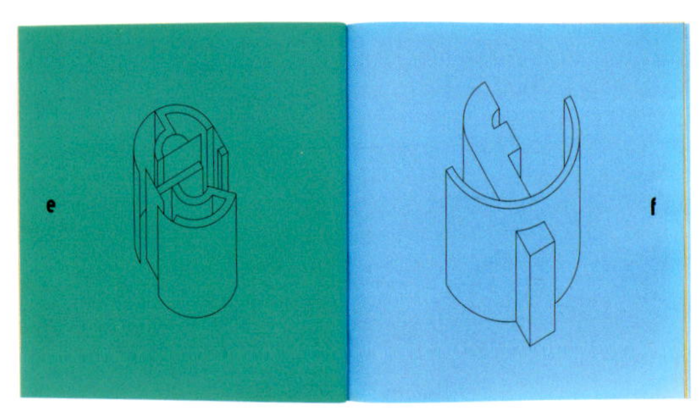
e
f

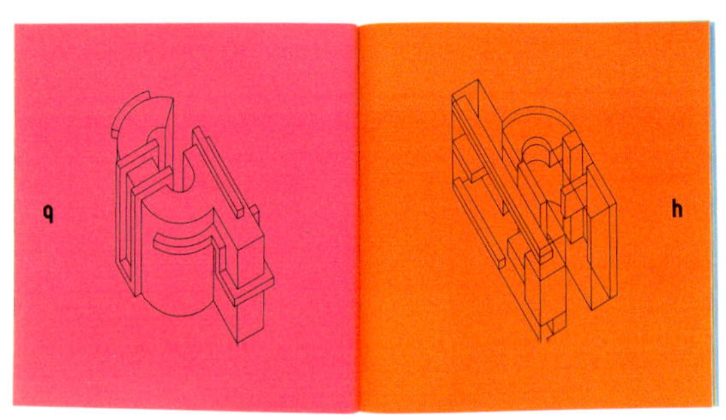
g
h

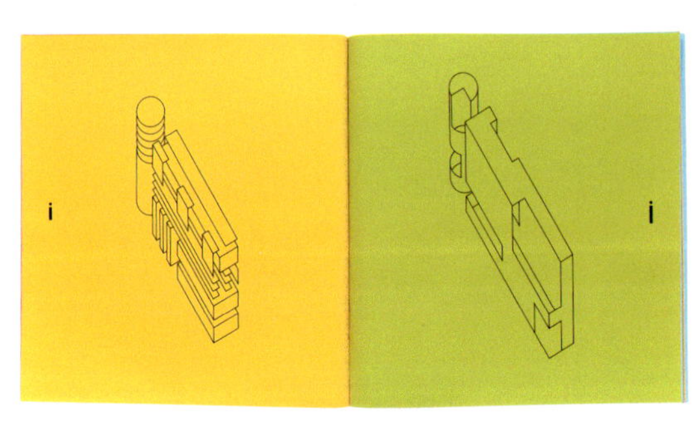
i
j

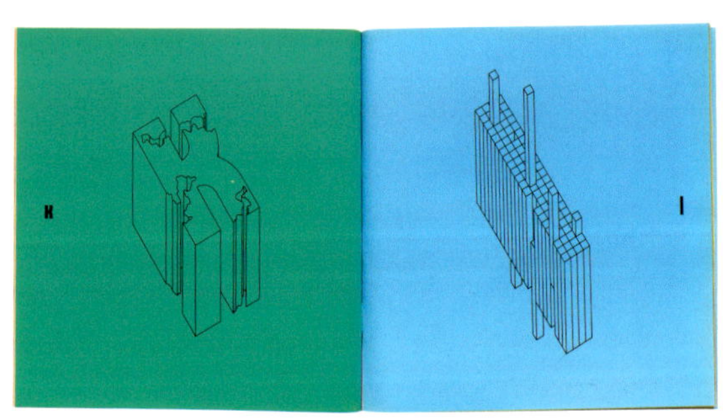
k
l

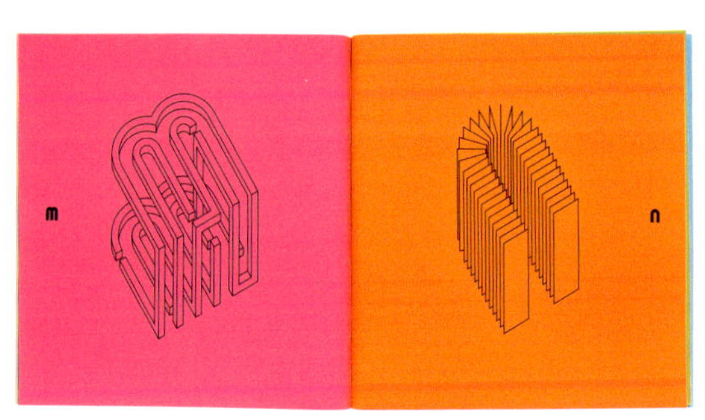
m
n

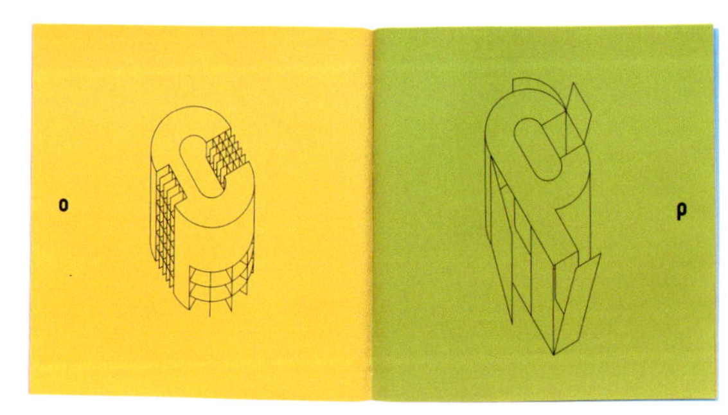
o
p

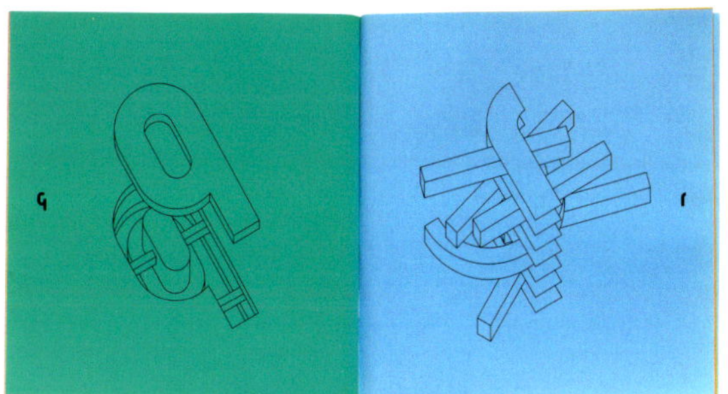

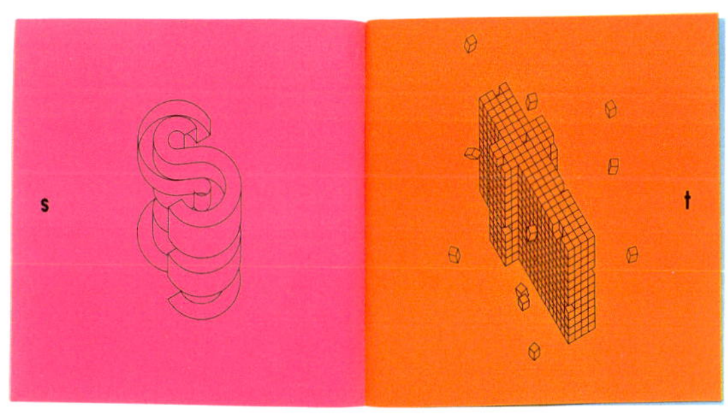

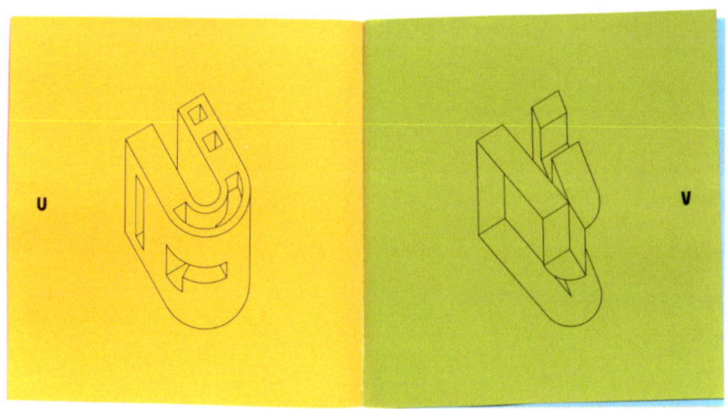

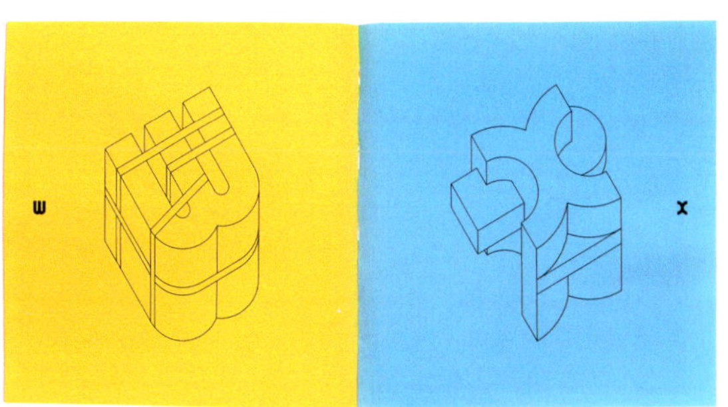

1988

TAKENOBU IGARASHI

The Igarashi ABC Book, offset, 9⅞ × 9½ inches (250 mm × 240 mm), Tokyo.

Japanese designer Takenobu Igarashi created this alphabet book for the 1988 International Design Conference in Aspen as an homage to Herbert Bayer, who lived in Aspen for almost thirty years as director of the Container Corporation of America's design division. Each page of the book features a small black letter in Bayer's 1925 Universal alphabet, plus a larger outline illustration of the letter in three dimensions. In each case, the isometric letterform is playfully transformed, augmented, or deconstructed, with its surfaces hollowed into windows, ramps, or mazes; bisected by arcs; or exploded into cross-sections of blocks and planes. Igarashi became well known for his unique approach to adding structural dimension to letterforms, which otherwise can seem quintessentially flat on paper. In the case of Bayer's alphabet, however, it is tempting to see Igarashi's transformations as a form of reverse engineering in which he rediscovers the Bauhaus's clean-lined architectural style at the heart of the geometric typography that was drafted alongside it—especially given that one of the most prominent realizations of Bayer's alphabet designs appears on the side of Walter Gropius's Bauhaus building in Dessau (see page 32). ●

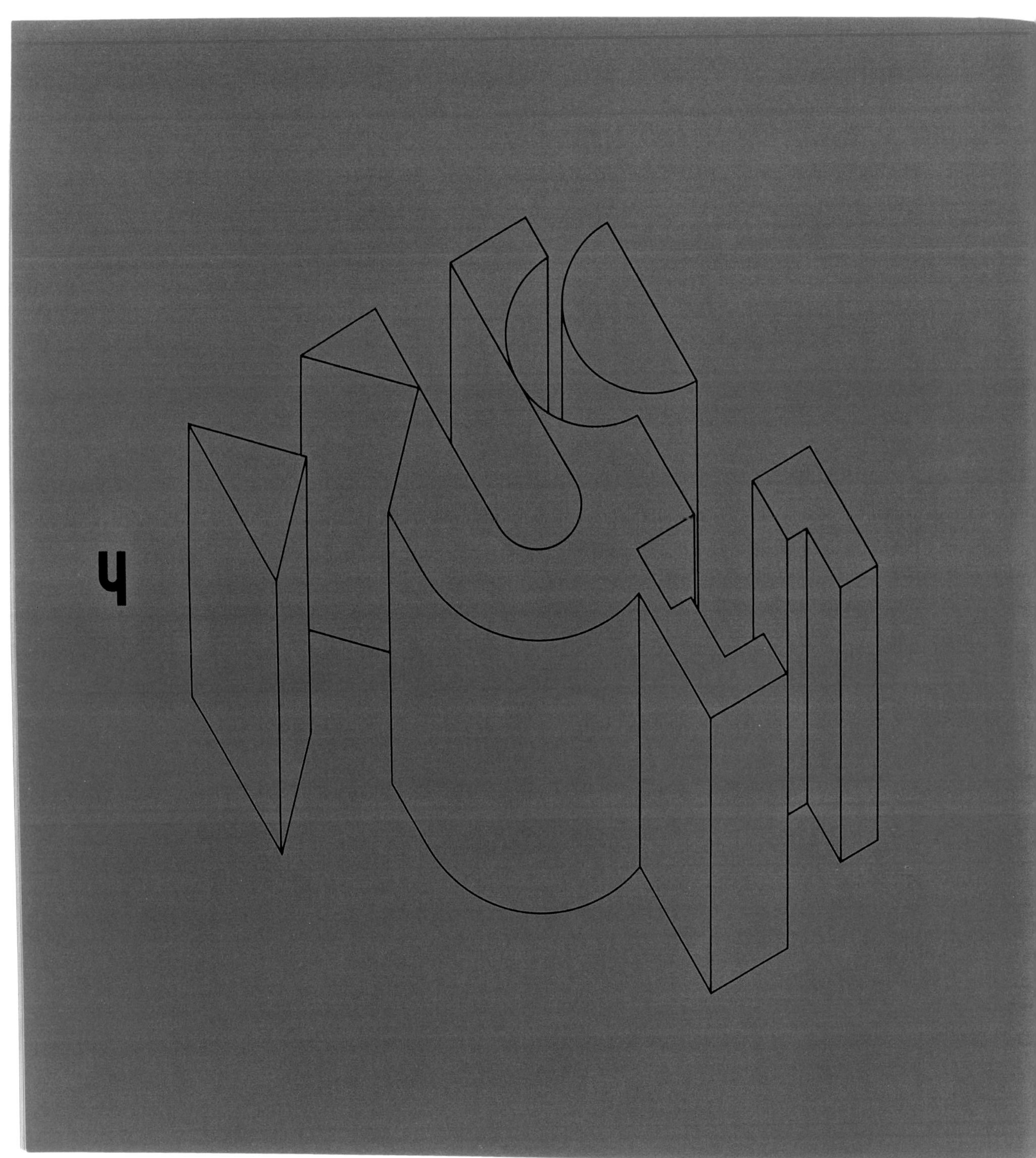
4

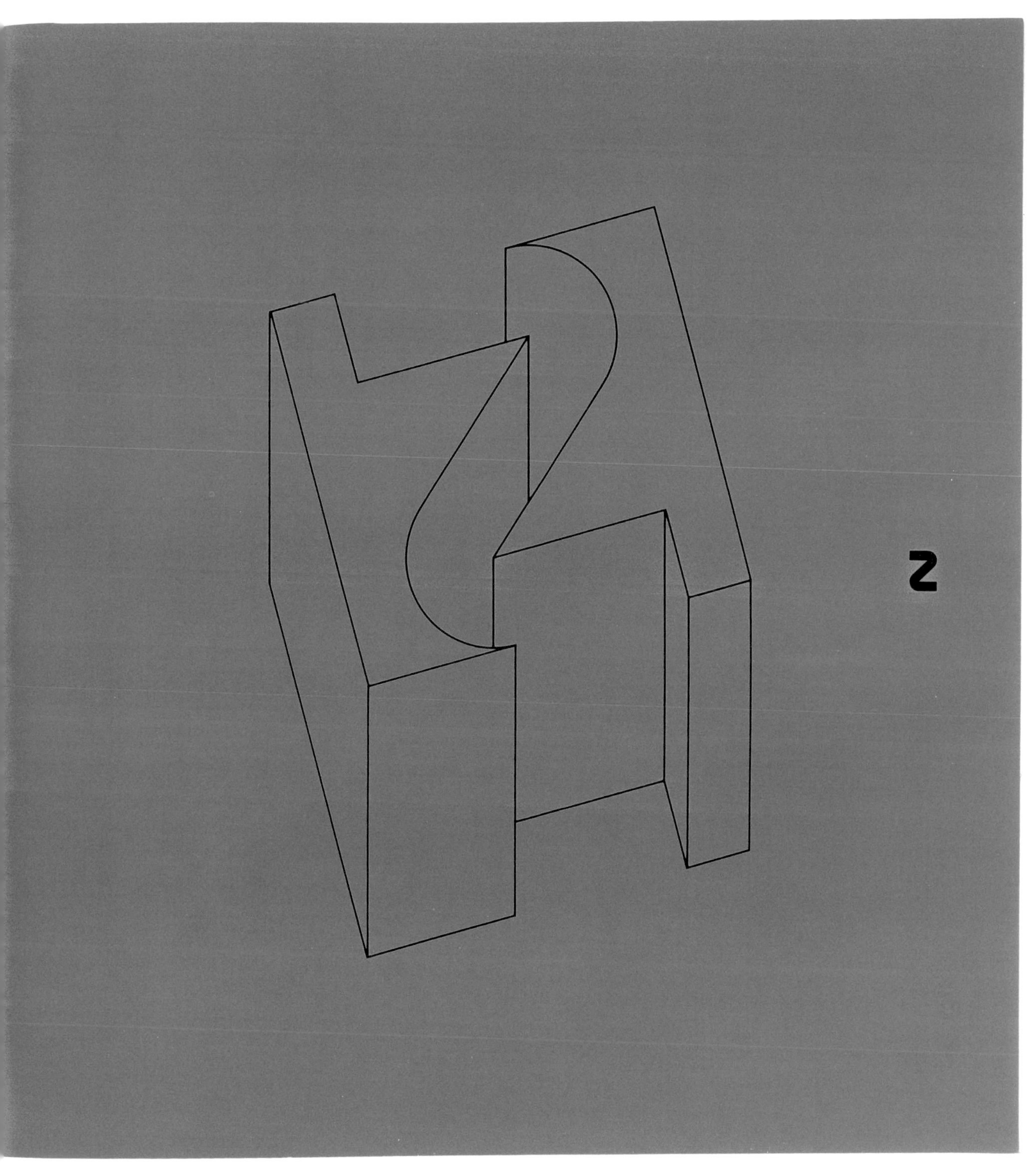
2

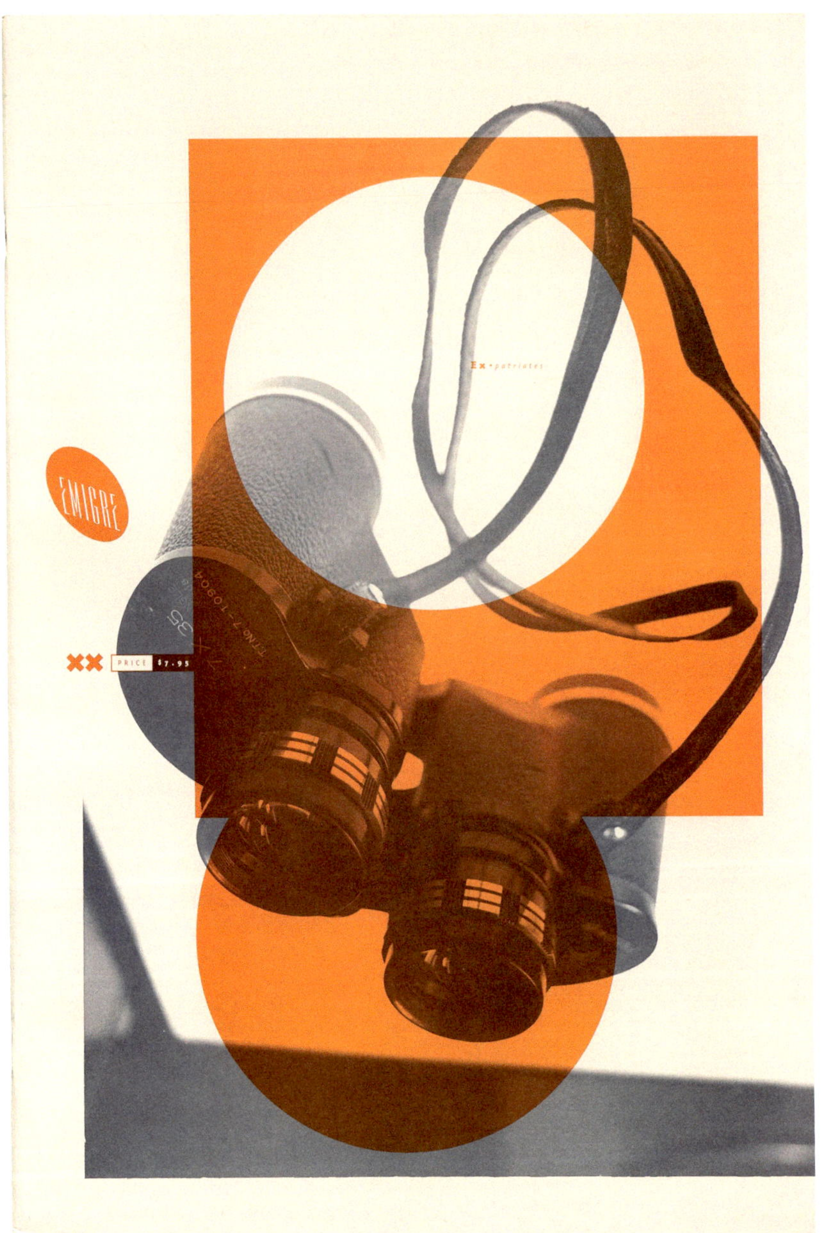

1991

RUDY VANDERLANS (cover designer)

Emigre #20: Expatriates, offset, 16¾ × 11¼ inches (425 × 285 mm), Berkeley, California.

1999

RUDY VANDERLANS (layout designer)

Emigre #49: The Everything Is for Sale Issue, offset, 10⅞ × 8⅜ inches (276 × 213 mm), Berkeley, California.

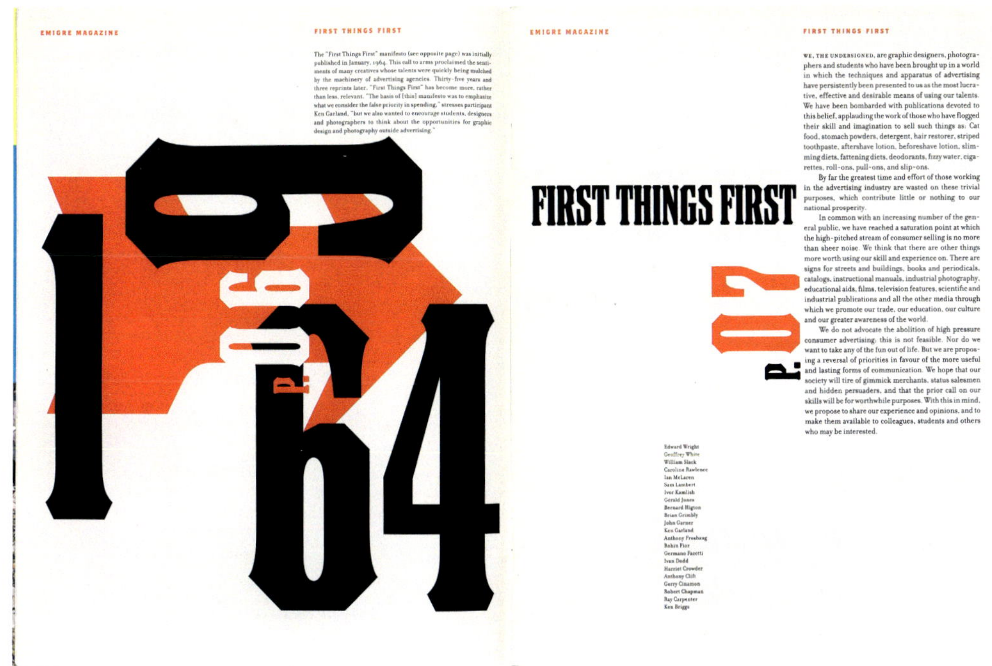

EMIGRE MAGAZINE

FIRST THINGS FIRST

The "First Things First" manifesto (see opposite page) was initially published in January, 1964. This call to arms proclaimed the sentiments of many creatives whose talents were quickly being mulched by the machinery of advertising agencies. Thirty-five years and three reprints later, "First Things First" has become more, rather than less, relevant. "The basis of [this] manifesto was to emphasize what we consider the false priority in spending," stresses participant Ken Garland, "but we also wanted to encourage students, designers and photographers to think about the opportunities for graphic design and photography outside advertising."

1964

P. 06

EMIGRE MAGAZINE

FIRST THINGS FIRST

P. 07

Edward Wright
Geoffrey White
William Slack
Caroline Rawlence
Ian McLaren
Sam Lambert
Ivor Kamlish
Gerald Jones
Bernard Higton
Brian Grimbly
John Garner
Ken Garland
Anthony Froshaug
Robin Fior
Germano Facetti
Ivan Dodd
Harriet Crowder
Anthony Clift
Gerry Cinamon
Robert Chapman
Ray Carpenter
Ken Briggs

FIRST THINGS FIRST

WE, THE UNDERSIGNED, are graphic designers, photographers and students who have been brought up in a world in which the techniques and apparatus of advertising have persistently been presented to us as the most lucrative, effective and desirable means of using our talents. We have been bombarded with publications devoted to this belief, applauding the work of those who have flogged their skill and imagination to sell such things as: Cat food, stomach powders, detergent, hair restorer, striped toothpaste, aftershave lotion, beforeshave lotion, slimming diets, fattening diets, deodorants, fizzy water, cigarettes, roll-ons, pull-ons, and slip-ons.

By far the greatest time and effort of those working in the advertising industry are wasted on these trivial purposes, which contribute little or nothing to our national prosperity.

In common with an increasing number of the general public, we have reached a saturation point at which the high-pitched stream of consumer selling is no more than sheer noise. We think that there are other things more worth using our skill and experience on. There are signs for streets and buildings, books and periodicals, catalogs, instructional manuals, industrial photography, educational aids, films, television features, scientific and industrial publications and all the other media through which we promote our trade, our education, our culture and our greater awareness of the world.

We do not advocate the abolition of high pressure consumer advertising: this is not feasible. Nor do we want to take any of the fun out of life. But we are proposing a reversal of priorities in favour of the more useful and lasting forms of communication. We hope that our society will tire of gimmick merchants, status salesmen and hidden persuaders, and that the prior call on our skills will be for worthwhile purposes. With this in mind, we propose to share our experience and opinions, and to make them available to colleagues, students and others who may be interested.

In 1984, the same year that Apple debuted the Macintosh computer, Rudy VanderLans and Zuzana Licko published the first issue of *Emigre*, a magazine that focused on new (and newly accessible) digital technologies and their applications in graphic design. Through incisive articles as well as groundbreaking layouts and typefaces developed by Licko and others for Emigre Fonts, the magazine sought to redefine the theory and practice of design for the digital age. The occasionally wild, maximalist, rule-breaking, grid-defying postmodern designs featured in *Emigre* might seem like the polar opposite of the utilitarian, austere, and geometric Bauhaus layouts. This break was intentional, as many postmodern designers reacted against the hegemony of rigid, modernist simplicity, which had evolved from a fringe idea to become practically synonymous with "good design" by the end of the twentieth century. The Bauhaus idea, however, represents not merely a style but also a set of principles, including uniting the arts with new technologies of production. In this way, the innovative designers associated with *Emigre* were possibly more aligned with the Bauhaus spirit than anyone imitating the school's decades-old aesthetics. It is also true that the Bauhaus was not a monolith: Johannes Itten's expressive lettering in *Utopia* (see pages 52–57) or Felix Klee's chaotic collage (see pages 66–69) can be seen as forgotten Bauhaus precursors to the postmodernist and punk aesthetics in some issues of *Emigre* (see pages 270–271). ●

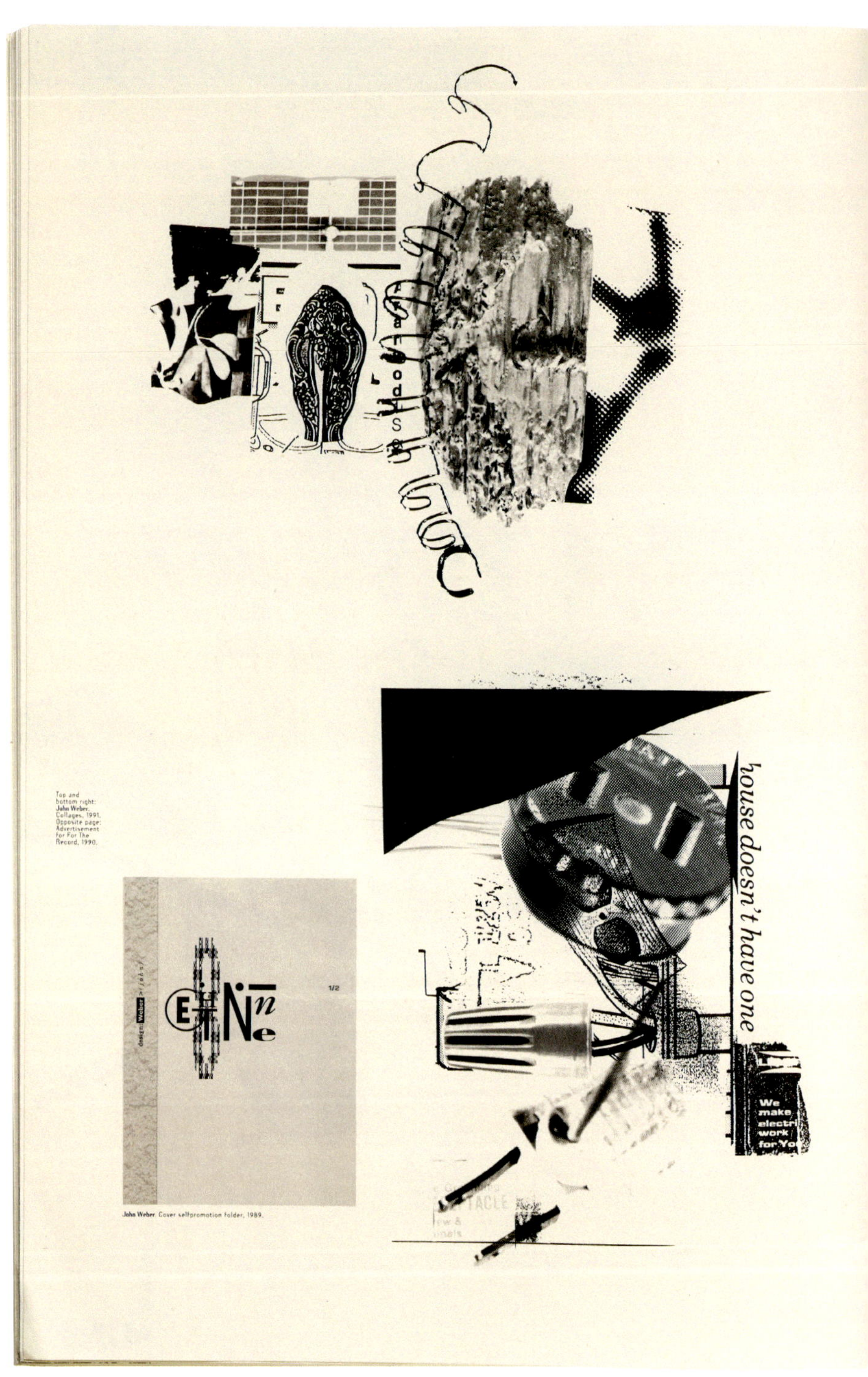
house doesn't have one
We
make
electri
work
for Yo
1/2
Top and bottom right: **John Weber.** Collages, 1991. Opposite page: Advertisement for For The Record, 1990.
John Weber. Cover selfpromotion folder, 1989.

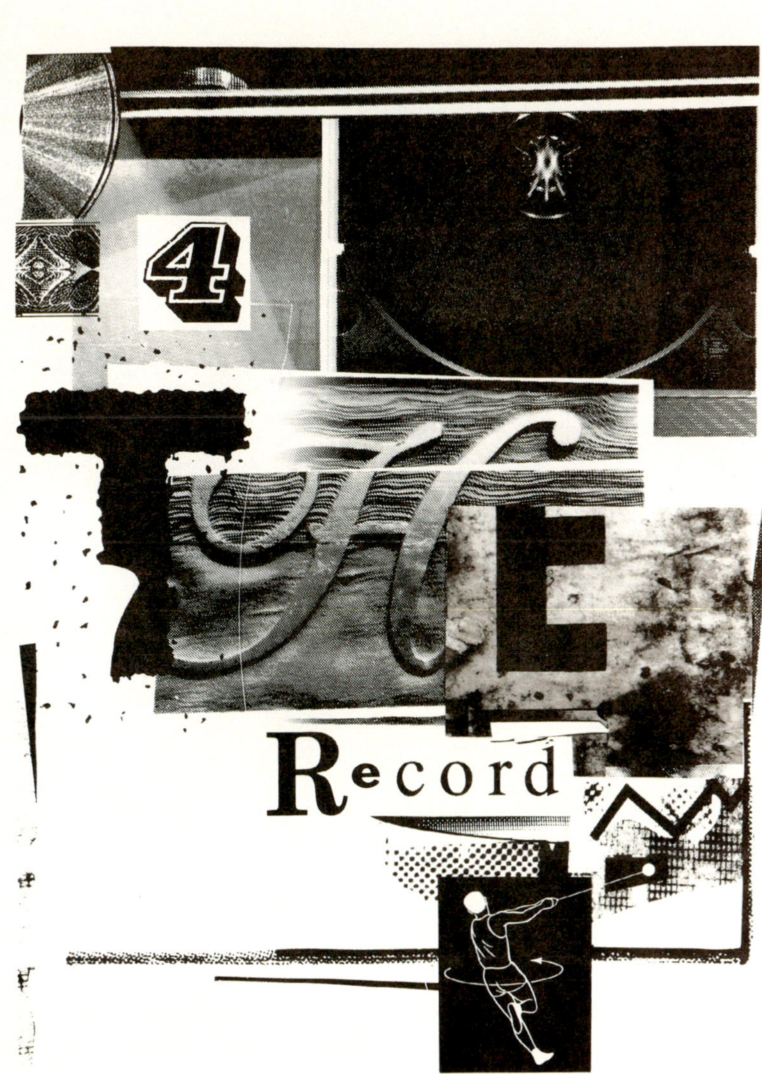

1991

RUDY VANDERLANS (layout designer)
JOHN WEBER (artist)

Emigre #19: Starting from Zero, offset, 16¾ × 11¼ inches (425 × 285 mm), Berkeley, California.

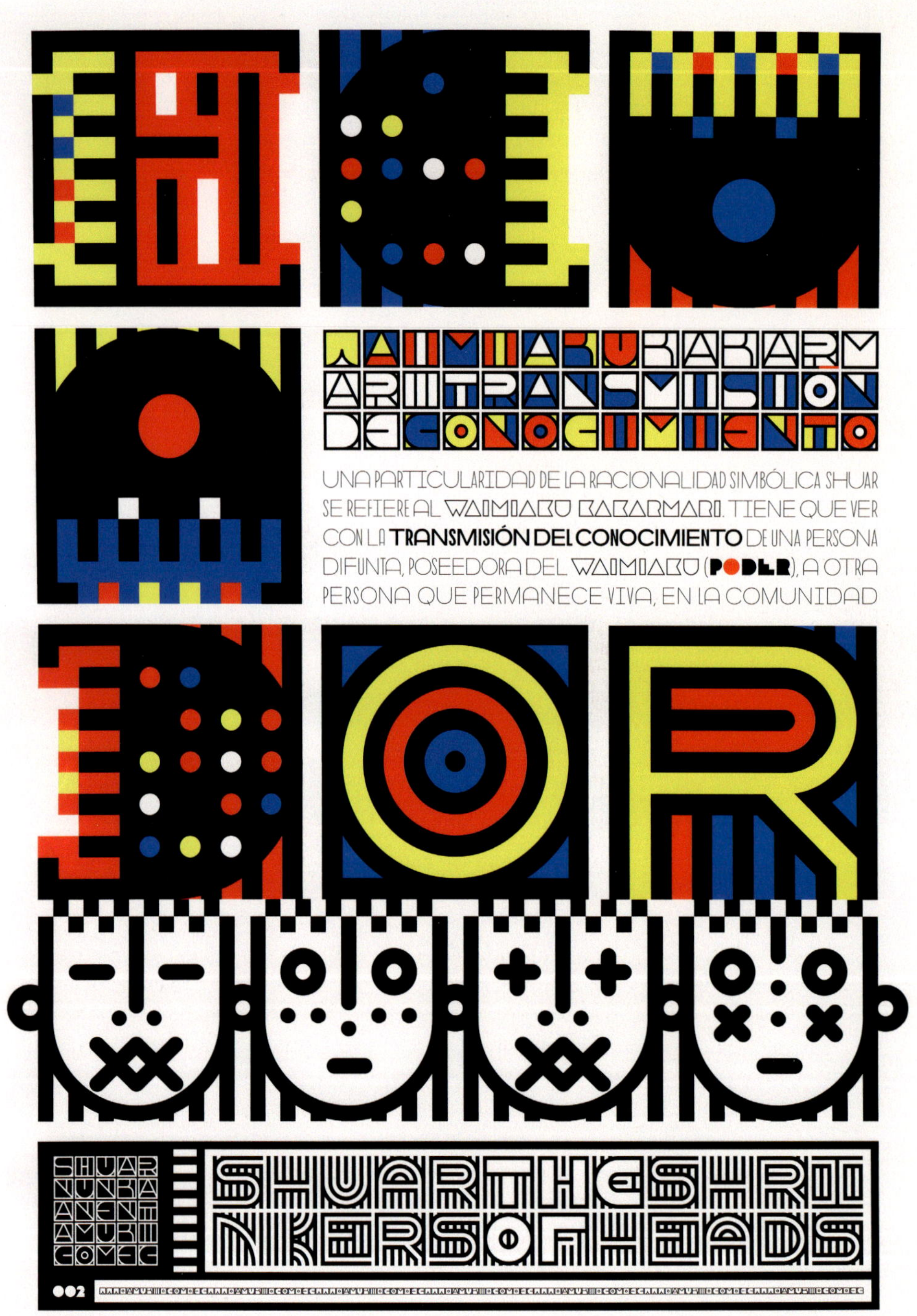

2020

VANESSA ALEXANDRA ZÚÑIGA TINIZARAY

Waimiaku Kakarmari, Transmission of Knowledge, from the *Ecuador, the Land of the Shuar* poster series, digital printing, 33¼ × 24 inches (845 × 610 mm), Loja, Ecuador.

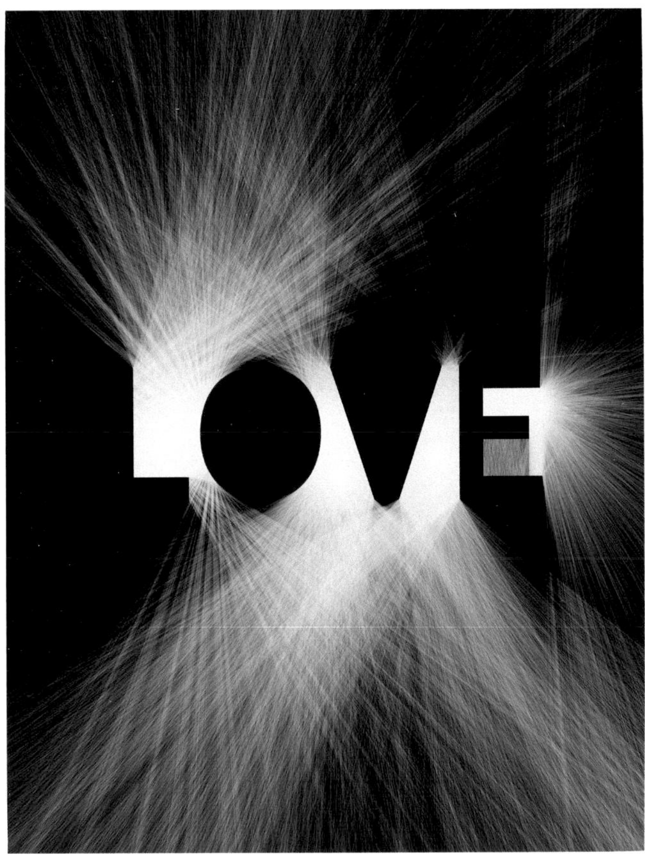

2020

ZACH LIEBERMAN

love reflect #2, digital printing, 22 × 17 inches (558 × 432 mm), New York.

A century later, the Bauhaus's typographical influence continues to ricochet around the world. "I am interested in a history of the Bauhaus that shows how the ideas morphed and blossomed," says New York City digital artist Zach Lieberman, who explains that his *love reflect* posters (see above) operate "in the realm of simulation—what it would look like to have rays of light bouncing around letterforms. I am interested in the letterforms as shapes, as blobs, and trying to twist them and bend them this way and that." His work—which recalls the light experiments of László Moholy-Nagy and Lucia Moholy—participates in a tradition of inquiry that includes Bauhaus typographers objectifying letterforms. A continent away, Ecuadorian designer Vanessa Alexandra Zúñiga Tinizaray says, "If I had to rescue from the Bauhaus a methodology, it would be experimentation, analog and digital." Tinizaray's *Ecuador, the Land of the Shuar* poster series (see left) references the animal symbology in the facial paintings of Amazonian indigenous peoples through stylized jaguars, anacondas, and monkeys, alongside square-bound letterforms that evoke wood carvings, fabric patterns, and digital pixels (and echo the constructed Bauhaus alphabets, with shapes and lines stacked like buildings within a modular grid). She explains, "The geometric relationship and the cosmovision of the ancestral peoples are united; the original peoples simplified in signs what they observed and applied them to objects, homes, textiles, and facial paintings, all of which had a specific use." Here, Tinizaray expresses that the Bauhaus's desire to simplify and unify form with function was not unique to Europe, nor to modernism—a counternarrative that will perhaps inspire a broader discussion of the Bauhaus in the next one hundred years. ●

All objects collection of Letterform Archive unless noted.
All images © Letterform Archive unless noted.

All artwork still in copyright is registered with the artists' estates, heirs, or appointed licensing agencies. The publisher has made every attempt to locate the proper heirs and agencies for artwork still in copyright. Please contact Letterform Archive Books with any questions or corrections pertaining to credit or copyright.

Front Matter (pages 1–35)
Credit, Copyright & Image Sources

page 7 (clockwise from top left): Photograph by Lucia Moholy © 2021 Artists Rights Society (ARS), New York / VG Bild-Kunst, Bonn / Image courtesy and collection of Bauhaus-Archiv Berlin • Image courtesy of Bauhaus Dessau Foundation (I 18980 F) • Image courtesy of Bauhaus-Archiv Berlin / Collection of Bauhaus-Archiv Berlin / Musée National d'Art Moderne / Centre de Création Industrielle, Centre Georges Pompidou, Paris / Legacy of Nina Kandinsky • Photograph by Irene Bayer / Image courtesy and collection of Bauhaus-Archiv Berlin • Photograph by Erich Consemüller © Dr. Stephan Consemüller / Image courtesy of Bauhaus Dessau Foundation (I 46052/1-2) • Uncredited photograph reproduced from *Weimar State Bauhaus 1919–1923* **pages 11–12:** Cathedral and *Postcards 1–2, Weimar State Bauhaus Exhibition 1923* by Lyonel Feininger © 2021 Artists Rights Society (ARS), New York / VG Bild-Kunst, Bonn **page 15:** *Utopia* by Johannes Itten © 2021 Artists Rights Society (ARS), New York / ProLitteris, Zurich **page 17:** *Utopia* by Johannes Itten © 2021 Artists Rights Society (ARS), New York / ProLitteris, Zurich / Proof typeset by Friedl Dicker / Image courtesy and collection of Bauhaus-Archiv Berlin **page 22:** Cover for *bauhaus: magazine for design* vol. 2, no. 1 by Herbert Bayer © 2021 Artists Rights Society (ARS), New York / VG Bild-Kunst, Bonn **page 30 (left to right):** Photograph by Louis Held / Wikimedia Commons / Collection of Kunstmuseum Moritzburg Halle • Photograph by Paula Stockmar / Image courtesy and collection of Bauhaus-Archiv Berlin • *Postcard 4, Weimar State Bauhaus Exhibition 1923* by Paul Klee • Axonometric projection in color by Theo van Doesburg / Wikimedia Commons / Collection of Het Nieuwe Instituut • Uncredited photograph / Wikimedia Commons **page 31 (left to right):** *Image with Arrow Shape* by Wassily Kandinsky / Reproduced from *Weimar State Bauhaus 1919–1923* • Bauhaus logo by Oskar Schlemmer / Reproduced from *Bauhaus: 1919–1928* • Photograph by Hugo Erfurth / Wikimedia Commons • Photograph by Lucia Moholy © 2021 Artists Rights Society (ARS), New York / VG Bild-Kunst, Bonn / Image courtesy and collection of Bauhaus-Archiv Berlin • Photograph by Ernst Schneider / Apic / Contributor / Getty Images / Collection of Hulton Archive • *Smyrna Rug* by Anni Albers © 2021 The Josef and Anni Albers Foundation / Artists Rights Society (ARS), New York / Reproduced from *Offset: Book and Advertising Art, Bauhaus Issue* **page 32 (left to right):** Photomontage by Herbert Bayer / © 2021 Artists Rights Society (ARS), New York / VG Bild-Kunst, Bonn / Image courtesy and collection of Bauhaus-Archiv Berlin • Photograph by László Moholy-Nagy © the Museum of Modern Art / Licensed by SCALA / Art Resource, NY / Collection of the Museum of Modern Art, NY, U.S.A. / Jan Tschichold Collection, Gift of Philip Johnson • Photograph by Erich Consemüller © Dr. Stephan Consemüller / Image courtesy of Bauhaus-Archiv Berlin / Private collection • Bauhaus Dessau facade photograph by Iwao Yamawaki © Yamawaki Iwao & Michiko Archives / Circa 1931 / Image © the Museum of

Modern Art / Licensed by SCALA / Art Resource, NY / Collection of the Museum of Modern Art, NY, U.S.A. / Thomas Walther Collection, Abbott-Levy Collection funds, by exchange • Photograph by T. Lux Feininger © Estate of T. Lux Feininger / Reproduced from *Bauhaus Buildings Dessau* • Alphabet by Josef Albers / Reproduced from *Offset: Book and Advertising Art, Bauhaus Issue* • Rendering of the residential buildings at Torten-Dessau by Walter Gropius © 2021 Artists Rights Society (ARS), New York / VG Bild-Kunst, Bonn / Reproduced from *Offset: Book and Advertising Art, Bauhaus Issue* **page 33 (left to right):** Photograph by Heinz Loew / Image courtesy and collection of Bauhaus-Archiv Berlin • Photograph by Robert Binnemann / Image courtesy and collection of Bauhaus-Archiv Berlin • Photograph by Lucia Moholy © 2021 Artists Rights Society (ARS), New York / VG Bild-Kunst, Bonn / Image courtesy and collection of Bauhaus-Archiv Berlin • "The Future Belongs to Bauhaus Wallpaper" brochure by Joost Schmidt / Image courtesy and collection of Bauhaus-Archiv Berlin **page 34 (left to right):** Photograph by Howard Dearstyne / Image courtesy and collection of Bauhaus-Archiv Berlin • *Attack on the Bauhaus* by Iwao Yamawaki © Yamawaki Iwao & Michiko Archives / Collage, ink, 1932 / Image courtesy and collection of Bauhaus-Archiv Berlin • Uncredited photograph / Wikimedia Commons / Collection of Harvard Art Museums • *German People, German Labor* exhibition design by Walter Gropius © 2021 Artists Rights Society (ARS), New York / VG Bild-Kunst, Bonn / Image courtesy of and collection Bauhaus-Archiv Berlin **page 35 (left to right):** Cover of the prospectus for the New Bauhaus by László Moholy-Nagy / Reproduced from *Printing Art Quarterly*, vol. 67, no. 2 • Cover of the catalog for the *Degenerate Art Exhibition* / Wikimedia Commons • Getty Images / Heritage Images / Contributor / Collection of Hulton Archive • Promotional poster designed by Muriel Cooper for the book *Bauhaus: Weimar, Dessau, Berlin, Chicago* © Massachusetts Institute of Technology, by permission of the MIT Press • Front cover of *Bauhaus: 1919–1928* designed by Herbert Bayer © the Museum of Modern Art / Licensed by SCALA / Art Resource, NY / Collection of the Museum of Modern Art, NY, U.S.A.

Main Text (pages 36–273) Copyright & Image Sources

Design and artwork credits appear in the caption for the work itself; see artist names or work titles in the index (pages 274–277) for where they appear.

page 38 (left): Lyonel Feininger © 2021 Artists Rights Society (ARS), New York / VG Bild-Kunst, Bonn **page 40:** Robert Michel / © 2021 Artists Rights Society (ARS), New York / VG Bild-Kunst, Bonn **pages 44–49:** Lothar Schreyer / © Michael Schreyer **pages 50 (left) and 51:** Lyonel Feininger © 2021 Artists Rights Society (ARS), New York / VG Bild-Kunst, Bonn **pages 53–58 and 59 (top):** Johannes Itten © 2021 Artists Rights Society (ARS), New York / ProLitteris, Zurich **pages 66–69:** Felix Klee / © Estate of Felix Klee **pages 74 and 76:** Lyonel Feininger © 2021 Artists Rights Society (ARS), New York / VG Bild-Kunst, Bonn **page 80:** Gerhard Marcks / © 2021 Artists Rights Society (ARS), New York / VG Bild-Kunst, Bonn **page 85:** Rudolf Baschant / Image © the Museum of Modern Art / Licensed by SCALA / Art Resource, NY **pages 86–87:** Herbert Bayer © 2021 Artists Rights Society (ARS), New York / VG Bild-Kunst, Bonn **pages 90–91, 92:** Ludwig Hirschfeld-Mack © Kaj Delugan **pages 100, 142, 172, 174–181, and 185:** Herbert Bayer © 2021 Artists Rights Society (ARS), New York / VG Bild-Kunst, Bonn **pages 238–240:** Piet Zwart © 2021 Artists Rights Society (ARS), New York / c/o Pictoright Amsterdam **page 254 (right):** Irmgard Sörensen-Popitz © Bauhaus Dessau Foundation (I 44174) / Loan from Wilma Stöhr **pages 256–257:** Masao Horino / © Estate of Masao Horino **page 260 (top):** © Westinghouse Electric Corporation **page 260 (bottom):** Courtesy of ExxonMobil Corporation **page 261:** © Caterpillar Corporation **pages 264–267:** © Takenobu Igarashi **pages 268–271:** © Emigre **page 272:** © Vanessa Alexandra Zúñiga Tinizaray **page 273:** © Zach Lieberman

Acknowledgments

Thank you to Kate Long and Paola Zanol for collections assistance, 42-line and April Harper for digitization, Thomas Bollier for color correction, Stephen Coles for typography consultation, Laura Serra for German consultation, Nancy Wolfe for permissions consultation, and Lisa K. Marietta, Mark Nichol, and Kevin Broccoli for editorial assistance. We are also grateful to Ellen Lupton for her introduction and kind counsel.

About Letterform Archive

Founded in 2015 in San Francisco, Letterform Archive is a nonprofit center for design inspiration. Letterform Archive Books produces exquisite titles based on its collection of more than 75,000 artifacts, as well as bold new books on design, type, and lettering.

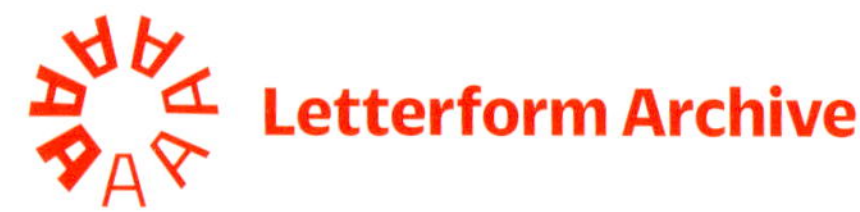

2339 Third Street, Floor 4R
San Francisco, CA 94107
letterformarchive.org

Publisher	Rob Saunders
Associate Publisher	Lucie Parker
Associate Managing Editor & Production Coordinator	Molly O'Neil Stewart
Associate Acquisitions Editor & Marketing Coordinator	Chris Westcott

Design	James Williams, The Common Era
Text	Henry Cole Smith

Bauhaus Typography at 100 is the official catalog for the 2021–2022 Letterform Archive exhibition of the same name, cocurated by Rob Saunders and Henry Cole Smith.

Set in Joschmi, an Adobe typeface by Flavia Zimbardi based on an unfinished stencil alphabet by Joost Schmidt; Christian Schwartz's FF Bau, a revival of a nineteenth-century grotesque from Leipzig foundry Schelter & Giesecke that was a typeface of choice of the Bauhaus Dessau; and Monotype Grotesque, designed in 1926 by Frank Hinman Pierpont.

Introduction © Ellen Lupton

© 2021 Letterform Archive Books
All rights reserved, including the right of reproduction in whole or in part or in any form.

Available through ARTBOOK | D.A.P.
75 Broad Street, Suite 630
New York, NY 10004
www.artbook.com

ISBN: 978-0-9983180-9-7

Library of Congress Control Number: 2021937582

10 9 8 7 6 5 4 3 2
2022 2023 2024 2025

Printed in China by 1010 Printing

Western Whitewater

From the Rockies to the Pacific

A River Guide for Raft, Kayak, and Canoe

Jim Cassady • Bill Cross • Fryar Calhoun

NORTH FORK PRESS

Disclaimer

This book is a guide to the West's finest rivers, not an instruction manual on how to run them. A guide book can no more teach you how to run a river than a road map can teach you how to drive. Before you run any river, you should learn whitewater skills and safety techniques from a qualified instructor.

River sports are inherently hazardous, involving potential risks that include loss of equipment, injury or death. You are responsible for your own safety, and you assume all risk for your actions. This book does not constitute a recommendation for any person to run any river, and it is no substitute for experience, skill, prudence, common sense, and first-hand observation.

We have tried to make this book as accurate as possible; however, there will inevitably be mistakes and omissions regarding the location, rating, or description of rapids or other features. Our river descriptions do not point out every rapid or hazard. Whitewater difficulty ratings for rivers and rapids are inherently imprecise and subjective. The authors have not run or seen every river in this guide; some of our information, though based on the best available sources both written and oral, is second-hand.

Rivers and rapids are constantly changing, so descriptions that were accurate when they were written may no longer be correct when you run the river. Fluctuations in water levels can dramatically alter the difficulty of any river or rapid. In addition, obstacles and hazards like rocks, falls and logs can and will shift and change from year to year. New dangers may arise or develop at any time. Be prepared. Always trust your own eyes and your own judgment first and foremost. Scout carefully before running any river or rapid, and seek additional advice and information from people who have recently boated the river you are considering.

Boaters should not rely exclusively on the information contained in this book; they should consult local guide books, local river runners, and govenment agencies. For more information on river safety, refer to the **Introduction** in this guide.

We do not guarantee the accuracy of information on land ownership and public access. When in doubt about land ownership and legal access, inquire locally. Nothing we say should be construed as an invitation to trespass.

The authors and publisher assume no responsibility or liability whatsoever with respect to personal injury, property damage, loss of time or money, or any other loss or damage caused directly or indirectly by the information contained in this book.

Western Whitewater from the Rockies to the Pacific

Copyright © 1994 Jim Cassady, Bill Cross, and Fryar Calhoun

Printed in the United States of America by Edwards Brothers, Ann Arbor, MI

Maps by Melissa LiCon
Hydrographs by Tony Finnerty
Cover design by Caroline Sutour
Page design and typesetting (Adobe Garamond) by Fryar Calhoun

ISBN 0-9613650-4-8
Library of Congress Catalog Card Number: 93-093680

Cover Photo: Cataraft on the Animas River, Colorado; Turret Peak in background
Photographers: Amy Wiley and Chuck Wales (ProFiles West)

North Fork Press
P.O. Box 3580
Berkeley, CA 94703-0580

This book is dedicated to
Grace Signorelli-Cassady
Polly Greist
and the memory of Erick J. Pinkham

Table of Contents

List of Maps

Preface

From the Rockies to the Pacific, from Canada to Mexico, the American West is home to the most outstanding collection of whitewater rivers on the planet. No doubt this statement betrays a certain home-town bias. But as we see it, the West is unique. Nowhere else can river runners find such a remarkable combination of vast wilderness areas, spectacular and diverse landscapes ranging from high mountains to rugged desert, extensive public lands, and beautiful yet accessible rivers. There are more than enough superb whitewater rivers here for a lifetime of boating.

Rivers define the West. To the Indians they were a sacred source of sustenance as well as an avenue for travel and trade. The history of white exploration begins with Lewis and Clark—a journey almost entirely by river. Later, settlers in this largely arid region built their first towns and cities along life-giving waterways. Twentieth-century politicians and engineers tapped and transformed the West's rivers in the name of growth, prosperity, and profit. Without rivers, the West as we know it would dry up and blow away.

In the last few decades Western rivers have seen the birth and boom of a new sport: whitewater boating. Beginning with a few hardy adventurers who braved the rapids in primitive kayaks and military surplus rafts in the 1940's and 1950's, river running has blossomed into one of the West's top outdoor sports. Hundreds of thousands go boating every year. In 1993 more than 260,000 people ran the Arkansas River in Colorado, the West's most popular whitewater river. Many hire commercial outfitters to guide them safely downriver, while tens of thousands more have learned to run the rapids on their own.

Whitewater sport today has many faces, and this guide is written with *all* river runners in mind: rafters, kayakers, and canoeists in particular, but also drift boaters, inflatable kayakers, innertubers, riverboarders, and so on. We include runs suitable for virtually any skill level, from rank novice to daring expert. Although this book is primarily directed to private, do-it-yourself boaters, it includes plenty of useful information for those who prefer to float with a commercial outfitter and even for armchair adventurers whose craft of choice is memory or imagination.

Why We Wrote This Book

Why a guide book to Western rivers? We've had plenty of time to ask ourselves that question in the seven years it has taken to complete this project. The simplest answer is that we wanted such a book, and it looked as if the only way to have it was to write it.

Beyond that, we offer two answers—one practical, one philosophical. The philosophical reason is simple. The book grows out of our love of rivers and whitewater. It constitutes our tribute to and celebration of the West's great rivers.

The practical answer is that we saw the need for a high-quality guide that would put the best Western rivers between the covers of a single book. As whitewater sport has boomed, so has the number of whitewater guide books. Good sources are now available for most of the West's individual states, for some of its regions, and for a number of its individual rivers. What has been missing is a single source—a menu, if you will, for the smorgasbord of Western rivers.

Our book is not intended as a substitute for local guide books and maps. Just the opposite: one of our book's services is its comprehensive listing of local guides and maps. We encourage boaters to buy and consult local guides, both for their wealth of additional detail and for their coverage of more rivers than we have been able to include here. Perhaps our book will help some boaters decide what rivers they want to run and thus which local guides they need.

How We Wrote This Book

Let's get the reader's most likely question out of the way: no, we didn't run all these rivers. The three of us have boated quite a few Western rivers, but we haven't even seen all the rivers in this book, and we are far from having run them all. It seems most unlikely that anyone who took time to run them all would have time to write a book about them. For that matter, running a river once is far from enough to make someone an expert on it. So to meet the challenge of writing a guide book covering some 160 rivers and over 6,000 river miles, we turned to the experts.

We combined our own first-hand information with an exhaustive review of all available printed material, numerous research and scouting trips, and extensive interviews with local boaters. We drafted chapters—Bill Cross doing the lion's share—and passed them around among ourselves for revision and editing. Then we circulated copies of each chapter to a carefully chosen set of local readers—private boaters, commercial outfitters, and managing agencies. We also contacted local river preservation groups for information on conservation issues. After reviewing the readers' responses and sometimes conducting follow-up interviews, we produced revised drafts, most of which we then sent to one or more readers for another review. At the end of the process, many of the typeset chapters were sent out for a final review.

Quite clearly, this book would not have been possible without the help of the hundreds of readers who very generously contributed their time and expertise to this project (see our **Acknowledgements**). It is as close to a summary of the best current knowledge about Western rivers as our imperfect efforts can make it.

We include much more than whitewater information. Rivers, after all, are not just a collection of rapids, and river running is far more than a thrill sport. Whenever possible, we try to give readers a broader sense of the rivers and their settings: the unique blend of geography, scenery, geology, plants, animals, history, and sense of place that makes each river unique and special. The depth and breadth of this information varies considerably between chapters. Bigger, longer, better-known, and more popular rivers get more detailed coverage. So it shouldn't be surprising that the longest chapter is on the Grand Canyon of the Colorado.

Along with the joy of running rivers goes a responsibility to treat them with care and to help defend them from further development. (To put it in a nutshell, we believe that the West has enough dams and reservoirs.) In our chapters, we talk about dams and diversions past, present, and future. We include specific information on threats to the rivers covered in this guide as well as more general information on river conservation. State, regional, and national river conservation organizations are listed in an appendix at the back of the book. Local groups working to protect specific rivers are mentioned in the appropriate chapters.

Of the hundreds of local experts we contacted during the research and writing of this book, the vast majority were not only helpful but encouraging. Occasionally, we ran across private boaters who objected to publicizing rivers because popularity diminishes the solitude that is part of the wilderness experience. While we understand this point of view, we don't agree. It's the old choice: use 'em or lose 'em. If rivers are kept "secret," only the dam builders will know about them. Recreational boating use is one of the best ways to prevent more short-sighted dam projects.

The problem isn't too many boaters, it's too many dams, which means too few rivers. Sure, at first glance our table of contents seems to show an abundance of rivers. But these are just the remnants. Thousands of miles of outstanding Western whitewater rivers have been lost to dams and diversions. Not all the dams were necessary in the past, and it's doubtful that *any* of the ones now being proposed are really needed or worth what they will cost. For one thing, the good dam sites have long since been taken.

Rivers throughout the West continue to face serious threats from more dams, diversions, development, dewatering, pollution, channelization, overlogging, overgrazing, and other abuses. The best defense is a large, vocal group of river advocates—what some have called a "constituency of users." The most committed advocates are usually those who have actually run the rivers and experienced their beauty first hand. The tradeoff may be a bit less solitude on your favorite run, but the alternative may be no river at all.

It's true that some popular rivers are overused. One goal of this book is to encourage boaters to spread out over a wider field of rivers. By alerting boaters to the many fine lesser-known rivers around the West, we hope to do our bit to ease crowding and competition for permits on the West's one or two dozen most popular runs.

Writing this book has been a time-consuming process, to say the least—one that took several years longer than we anticipated. We knew it was a big project when we started, but looking back, we certainly underestimated its size and duration. The review and revision process, essential to the quality of the book, also took a lot of extra time. Most of our chapters have been rewritten at least five times. Many have been revised to reflect changes that took place during our years of writing the book—dams have been built, rivers have been saved, new rapids have formed. We hope that our readers will forgive us for the long wait and find the book useful.

Acknowledgments

This book would have been impossible without the generous help and advice of hundreds of friends and fellow river runners throughout the West. At the risk of inadvertently leaving out some names, we wish to acknowledge those who shared their knowledge and offered their encouragement and support. For the book's merits, much of the credit goes to these friends, collaborators, and advisors. Blame the authors for its shortcomings.

We should like to acknowledge and thank:

Melissa LiCon, the creative and patient graphic artist who executed the maps; Tony Finnerty, the skilled and genial hydrologist who produced the hydrographs; Polly Greist for help in drafting several chapters, advice on language, and endless support and patience; Caroline Sutour for designing the cover, listening to far too many discussions of the book in particular and rivers in general, and brewing the superb French roast coffee that kept our meetings going; Beth Rundquist and Dale Fuller, constant sources of encouragement and advice; James E. Cross for supporting and believing in a project he did not see completed; F. F. and Lorene Calhoun and Mr. and Mrs. Harold Skramstad for their long-time support in our publishing projects; Richard Cross for legal advice; Dr. and Mrs. Elwood C. Greist for a place to bed down and a pickup truck in need;

The fine photographers whose work appears in these pages; the boaters who contributed their river stories to this book; Curt Smith for assisting in our photo search and for advice on publishing; Steve Jones for information on many rivers; Ron Lodders for help with rivers in Greater Yellowstone and Montana; Judy Theodorson for information on a number of Region I rivers; Stephen Maurer for patient help with several Southwestern rivers; Richard Ely for aid with geological questions; Mike Martell for his constant encouragement and support;

Organizations: Friends of the River, Idaho Rivers United, National Organization for River Sports, Rivers Council of Washington, Pacific Rivers Council, Project Raft, River City Whitewater Club, and the staffs of the map rooms of the libraries of the University of California at Berkeley and Southern Oregon State College;

Idaho and Northern Rockies: Grant Amaral, Les Bechdel, Bob Blackadar, Rick Blanchard, Ron Blanchard, Jim Boyle, Jo Cassin, Sarah Coleman, Cort Conley, Joe Daly, Pat Dillon, Bob Ekey, Guy Erb, Mike Garcia, Todd Gehrke, David Gonzalez, Gregg Goodyear, Verne Huser, Steve Jones, John Jurries, Tary King, Stan Kolby, Paul Kopczynski, Aurele Lamontagne, Greg Lawley, Dan Lewis, Dick Linford, Ron Lodders, Randy McBride, Don McClaran, Mike McLeod, Rena Margulis, Greg Moore, Jack Nichol, Jerry Nichols, John Ochi, Julia Page, Liz Paul, Don Perkins, Dave Rhinehart, Scott Spiker, Charley Stevenson, Darwon Stoneman, Judy Theodorson, Doug Tims, Fran Tonsmeire, Joe Tonsmeire, Ted Weigold, Tom Whittaker, Peter White, Wendy Wilson, Steve Zeman; BLM, Boise District (John Benedict, Barry Rose); BLM, Cottonwood RA (LuVerne Grussing); BLM, Dillon RA (Joe Ashor); BLM, Jarbidge-Bruneau RA (Jeff Ross); BLM, Judith RA (Chuck Otto); BLM, Lewistown District (Buck Damone); Bitterroot NF, West Fork RD; Boise NF, Emmett RD (James Ciardelli, Dave Hale); Bridger-Teton NF, Jackson RD (Jan Langerman); Challis NF, Middle Fork RD (Ted Anderson); Clearwater NF, North Fork RD, (Duane Annis); Flathead NF; Glacier National Park (Jim Bellamy, Charle Logan, Kyle Johnson); Idaho Dept. of Parks & Recreation (Dave Lindsay); Idaho Dept. of Water Resources (Bill Ondrechen); Idaho Panhandle NF, Avery RD (Jaime Schmidt), Priest Lake RD; Kootenai NF (Chuck Harris); Montana Dept. of Fish, Wildlife & Parks (David Todd, Doug Habermann, Woody Baxter, Lee Bastian); Salmon NF, North Fork RD (Troy Cooper); Shoshone NF, Wapiti RD (Francis Carlson), Clarks Fork RD; Targhee NF (Ted Kellogg, Wayne Jenkins); Hells Canyon National Recreation Area (Arthur Seamans, Mike Cole);

Colorado Rockies: Fletcher Anderson, John Arnett, Eric Bader, Jim Blackburn, Claire Carren, Carol Chamber, Ed Conning, Donn Hicks, Tim Hillmer, Hank Hotze, Steve Kachur, Tom Karnuta, Eric Leaper, Dan Lewis, Len Loomans, Stephen G. Maurer, Greg Moore, Sandra Morad, John Moran, David Neff, Rick Perkins, Dick Prouty, Ron Schermacher, Jerry Stocking, Jim Stohlquist, Chuck Wales, Wayne Walls, Bill White, Nancy Wiley, Chan Zwanzig; Arapaho-Roosevelt NF, Estes-

Poudre RD (Martha Moran), Redfeather RD (Karen Roth); Arkansas Headwaters Recreation Area (Steve Reese, Casey Swanson); BLM, Craig District (Dave Cooper); BLM, Glenwood Springs RA (Francisco Mendoza); BLM, Great Divide RA (Brad Holbrook, Shirley Bye-Jech); BLM, Kremmling RA (Rich Rosene); BLM, Taos RA (Tom Mottl, Heidi Mottl); BLM, Uncompaghre Basin RA (Karen Tucker, Brian Hopkins); Cañon City Dept. of Parks (John Nichols); Medicine Bow NF, Hayden RD (Michael B. Murphy, Joe Remick); Rio Grande NF, Creede RD (Mike Blakeman, Greg Coln); Routt NF, North Park RD (Larry Ross, Kevin McCombe); San Juan NF (Ralph Swain), Pagosa Springs RD; White River NF, Dillon RD (Tom Healy, Paul Semmer), Eagle RD (Rich Doak), Sopris RD (Nancy Berry, Mike Keneally); Pike NF, South Platte RD;

Canyon Country: Susan Bassett, Jim Blackburn, Robert Canning, the Colletts, Diane Cross, Regan Dale, Charlie DeLorme, Richard Ely, Loie Belknap Evans, Don Fritch, Kathy Fritch, Michael Ghiglieri, Don Hatch, Ted Hatch, Bart Henderson, Donn Hicks, Dee Holliday, Liz Hymans, Tom Klema, Patty McCleary, Mark S. McCaffrey, Rena Margulis, Stephen G. Maurer, Allen Monroe, Melanie Morrison, Rob Pitagora, Pete Reznick, Spreck Rosekrans, Barry Smith, Rich Zwaal; Ashley NF, Flaming Gorge RD (Mike Stubbs, Fred Houston); BLM, Craig District (Dave Cooper); BLM, Grand Junction District (Brian Hopkins); BLM, Grand RA (Alex Van Hemert); BLM, Moab District (Russ Van Koch, Trish Lindeman, Bob Milton); BLM, Price River RA (Terry Humphrey, Dennis Willis); BLM, San Juan RA (Thomas Christensen, Leah Quesenberry); BLM, San Rafael RA (Tom Gnocek); Bureau of Reclamation (Lilas Lendell, Rick Gold, Brad Vickers, Steve Thompson); Canyonlands National Park (Jim Braggs); Dinosaur National Monument (David Stimson, Ann Excell); Glen Canyon Environmental Studies (Dave Wegner, Bill Vernieu); Grand Canyon National Park (Susan Cherry, Kim Crumbo); Library of the Museum of Northern Arizona.

Southwestern Border: Steve Evans, Steve Harris, Jimboat Hudson, Larry Humphreys, Kelly Kellstedt, Thoron Lane, Rena Margulis, George Marsik, Stephen G. Maurer, Spreck Rosekrans, M. H. Salmon, Jim Slingluff, Richard A. Vinson; Apache-Sitgreaves NF, Clifton RD (Bob Chavez); Big Bend National Park (Marcos Paredes, Dennis Vasquez, Pat Grediagin); Big Bend Natural History Association (Sarah Bourbon); Big Bend Ranch State Natural Area (Luis Armendariz); BLM, Las Cruces District (Mark Hakkila); BLM, Safford District (Steve Knox, Deb Smith, John Collins); Gila NF (Ron Henderson), Glenwood RD (Bill Britton, Tom Dwyer); Prescott NF, Verde RD (Wes Girard); Salt River Project (Frederick Bermudez, Dan Phillips); Tonto NF (Pete Weinel); White Mountain Apache Tribe Game & Fish (John Caid);

California: Rick Batts, Rick Demarest, Ann Dwyer, Steve Evans, Jim Faust, Bob Goodman, Mike Grant, Marty McDonnell, Bill McGinnis, Ron Stork, David Wickander, Rich Zwaal; BLM, Folsom RA (Jim Eicher, John Scull); and all the people and agencies who originally helped us with *California Whitewater*;

Pacific Northwest: John Achio, Al Ainsworth, Jon Almquist, Jeff Bennett, Duane Bolfer, Matt Davidson, Tim Davis, Bob Doppelt, Stuart Ellis, Jib Ellison, Tony Finnerty, Casey Garland, Jim Greenleaf, Hank Hays, Calvin Henry, Peter Hitt, Verne Huser, Gary Korb, Gary Lane, Glen Lewman, Paul McHugh, Dennis Myers, Sandie Nelson, Deb Nicely, Doug North, Judo Patterson, Joel Ryan, Cindy Scherrer, Steve Scherrer, Val Shaull, Morgan Smith, Pat Sumption, James Thomson, Royce Ward, Kent Wickham, Craig Wright; BLM, Boise District (John Benedict); BLM, Prineville District (Max Linn, SuZan Meiners, Tom Farnam, Karen Perault); BLM, Vale District (Rich Law), Baker RA (Kevin McCoy, Marsha Garoutte); Columbia Gorge National Scenic Area (Steve Mellor); Deschutes NF, Sisters RD (Stephen Couche); Gifford Pinchot NF, Packwood RD (Jack Thorne, Mike Rowan, Tom Kogut), Randle RD (Mark Kreiter); Mt. Baker-Snoqualmie NF, Darrington RD (Denis Yoshina, Pat Cook, Carol Rinehart, Matt Krogh), Mt. Baker RD (Jim Chu), North Bend RD (Kathy White, Bill Sobieralski), Skykomish RD (Pat Toman); Mt. Hood NF (Linda de La Rosa), Bear Springs RD (Linda Batten); Mt. St. Helens National Volcanic Monument and Gifford Pinchot NF (Hans Castren); North Cascades National Park (Galen Stark); Ochoco NF (Sue Kocis); Olympic National Park (Maurie Sprague, Hank Warren); Siskiyou NF (Kenneth Vines), Gold Beach RD; Umpqua NF, North Umpqua RD (Ron Murphy); Wallowa-Whitman NF (Robin Rose), Eagle Cap RD (Lloyd Swanger); Washington State Parks Dept.; Wenatchee NF, Lake Wenatchee RD (Corky Broaddus); Willamette NF, McKenzie RD (Susan Skalski, Dave Rodriguez).

Introduction

This guide book features more than 160 rivers in twelve Western states. Most have their own chapters; some three dozen are covered more briefly in the section near the back of the book, **More Western Rivers.**[1] We divide the West into six geographic regions: Idaho and the Northern Rockies, Colorado Rockies, Canyon Country, Southwestern Border, California, and the Pacific Northwest.

We tour the West in a clockwise loop, beginning with the great wilderness rivers of Idaho and the Northern Rocky Mountain region of northwestern Wyoming and western Montana. Then we survey the rivers of the central Rocky Mountains in Colorado, southern Wyoming, and northern New Mexico. Next we visit the West's interior desert: first, the spectacular Canyon Country of Utah and the Four Corners area; then, the rivers of the arid border states of Arizona, New Mexico, and western Texas.

Moving west to California, we journey northward along the Sierra Nevada and Coast Ranges. Finally, we reach the volcanic peaks of the Cascade Range in Oregon and Washington and end our tour in the farthest reaches of the Pacific Northwest—the remote rain forest of Washington's lush Olympic Peninsula.

This tour of Western rivers is a study in diversity, and nothing shows that diversity more than the names people have given to the rivers. Some carry the original Indian names, while others were renamed by white explorers and settlers. (Names like Henrys Fork and Clarks Fork have dropped their apostrophes over the years.) Many rivers have been known by more than one name at different times. Of all the rivers in this book, there are only a few pairs: the Salmon in Idaho and the California Salmon; the Green in Utah and the Green in Washington; the Montana Smith and the California Smith; the Clarks Fork of the Yellowstone and the Clark Fork, a major tributary of the Columbia; the White in Canyon Country and the White in Oregon. But we didn't try to count all the Bear Creeks and Big Creeks mentioned in the various chapters.

[1]Counting rivers means defining our terms. Most people would agree that the Middle Fork Salmon is a different river from the Main Salmon. But is the Lower Salmon really a different river from the Main Salmon? Technically, no; both are stretches of the main stem of the Salmon. But they are different river trips, and long ones at that, so each gets its own chapter. Looking at things this way helped us to organize our book into regions that make sense for planning river trips. That seemed more important than trying to cover longer rivers like the Snake and the Colorado from top to bottom without a break. What's more, dams and reservoirs often chop rivers up into segments.

The number of different river trips we cover in this book is considerably more than 200. Some chapters have two, three, or more separate sections. We divide a river into sections when it changes dramatically in difficulty or character, or when natural or man-made breaks occur. (Examples: falls or unrunnable stretches of river, popular access points, dams, reservoirs.)

River Safety

Considering the powerful natural forces with which river runners contend, whitewater boating enjoys a very good safety record. Nevertheless, every year some more boaters—novices and experts alike—become injury or death statistics. While it is impossible and, in fact, undesirable to eliminate all risk from the sport, every boater should seek to minimize the risks.

As we state in our disclaimer at the front of the book, this is a guide to Western rivers, not an instruction manual on how to run them. **On the river, you are responsible for your own safety.** The keys to safe boating are adequate skills, proper equipment and, above all, good judgment—none of which this book can provide. It's up to you.

Be prudent. Don't run a whitewater river without knowing what you are doing. Seek competent advice and qualified instruction first, and make sure your equipment is appropriate for the river and the conditions. Here are some principles of safe river running:

- Be sure your skills and experience are equal to the river and the conditions. Be realistic about your skills and limitations. Don't boat beyond your abilities.

- When you're learning, move up the whitewater difficulty scale very gradually. Before attempting Class IV, for example, you should be able to handle Class III water easily, not just survive it. Proper learning takes time and patience. There are plenty of less difficult runs suitable for honing your skills (see our **Regional Index of Easier Runs** near the back of the book).

- Be in good physical condition.
- Never boat alone.
- Wear a snugly-adjusted life jacket at all times when you are on or near the river. High-flotation jackets are best. Crotch straps help prevent the jacket from coming off over your head.
- Helmets are a must for kayakers in all levels of whitewater. They are recommended for canoeists and rafters in many circumstances.
- Protect your feet with sturdy footwear that won't come off in the river.
- Be a good swimmer. Know how to float in a whitewater river: feet first and elevated, in the deepest channel, and never just in front of a boat. Know when and how to swim for an eddy.
- Be adept in self-rescue, including swimming a rapid, escape from a capzied boat, and (hard-shell boaters) the Eskimo roll.
- Know how to avoid hypothermia and how to deal with it. Hypothermia is a serious risk any time water and air temperatures add up to less than 120°. Wear a wet suit or dry suit when conditions warrant.
- Beware of high water. Most rivers undergo a profound and dangerous change when their flows rise. Never run a river at or near flood stage.
- Know how to recognize and react to river hazards such as holes, snags, wrap rocks, undercuts, rock sieves, horizon lines across the river, etc.
- Never run a rapid unless you can see a clear path through it.
- When in doubt, stop and scout. Still in doubt? Portage.
- Know the risks of pins and entrapments and how to avoid them. Pins kill more kayakers than any other kind of mishap. Foot entrapments are another leading cause of death.
- Know the dangers of brush and trees in the river, known as "strainers" and "sweepers." These are deadly hazards. Stay clear. Be especially alert for snags after winter or spring high water.
- Know the dangers of man-made obstacles: bridge abutments, fences, and especially weirs and low dams. Boaters can be recycled endlessly in the "keeper" reversals below weirs.
- Beware of entrapment in loose lines.
- Use sturdy equipment in good repair. Carry personal and group safety gear: knife, carabiners, pulleys, toss bags, safety line, spare paddles or oars, repair kit, etc.
- Carry a first aid kid and know how to use it. Learn or review first aid and CPR. Avoid rattlesnakes, poison ivy, poison oak, and other hazards, but know how to deal with emergencies if someone is unlucky.
- Mixing alcohol or other drugs with whitewater can be deadly.
- Use caution on shore and on the road. Many injuries and deaths occur off the river—on side hikes, on shuttle roads, in camp—when boaters let their guard down.
- Tell someone where you are going, when you expect to return, and what to do (including where to call) if you don't.

How to Use This Guide

Each river chapter begins with an information section that provides all the basic facts and figures. The various entries or categories (**Difficulty**, **Length**, etc.) are discussed just below. Some entries (for example, **Side Hikes** and **Fishing**) are not present in every chapter.

The information section is followed by an essay on the river and other topics such as the geology of the river canyon, scenery and wildlife, and human history. We also include information on river conservation, dams and dam threats past and future, and groups working to protect the river.

If there are other runs upstream, downstream, on tributaries, or on other nearby streams, we mention them toward the end of the essay. Then comes either a **Mile by Mile Guide** or, for rivers covered in less detail, a briefer and more compact **River Guide**.

Put-in, Take-out, Elevation

Elevation in feet above sea level is listed in parentheses after put-ins and take-outs. The difference between these figures represents the total vertical drop of the run. Elevations in this guide range from 9,240' at the put-in for the Upper Animas in Colorado to 75' at the take-out for Oregon's Sandy River.

Higher elevation usually implies more severe weather, especially in the earlier and later parts of the boating season. This in turn often translates into lower temperatures and a greater risk of hypothermia. What's more, boaters who are not acclimated to high altitudes may suffer from lack of oxygen, which in turn can affect judgement, stamina and performance.

Difficulty

Rivers in this guide are rated on the international scale of I to VI. (See sidebar on the next page.) We rate rivers, or portions of rivers, according to their most difficult typical rapids. For example, the Upper Animas in Colorado is rated Class V, though of course it has numerous Class II, III, and IV rapids as well.

When there are one or two uncharacteristically tough rapids, we indicate this by a subscript in Arabic numerals instead of Roman. For example, the Skykomish in Washington is rated Class III$_5$, reflecting the presence of a big Class V drop in an otherwise intermediate run.

A "p" indicates one or more portages, as in the case of California's Lower Kern, rated IVp. A plus or minus sign is roughly equivalent to "low" or "high"; thus a Class III- is a "low Class III," while a Class III+ is a "high Class III."

How We Rate Rapids and Rivers

Our ratings are meant to be realistic judgments of difficulty **at moderate flows.**

We have attempted to rate rapids and rivers realistically—that is, in terms that reflect the accomplishments of modern whitewater sport. This means, among other things, that we don't overrate rapids to protect boaters. But we also don't downgrade rapids simply because more people are running them these days.[2]

In our ratings, we assume moderate flows. Difficulty changes with the flow; how much depends on the river and the rapid. Most rivers become more difficult at higher flows; that is often—but not always—the case with individual rapids. In general, Class III rivers require Class IV skills at high flows, and so on—but there are definitely exceptions.[3]

Rating the difficulty of a river, even of a rapid, is a tricky and subjective business and a

[2]It may be true that the concept of Class V has been stretched at its upper limit—first by kayakers, more recently by rafters. As anyone who has run the North Fork Payette in Idaho, Gore Canyon in Colorado, or the Upper Tuolumne in California can testify, there are rapids that should be rated not only V but V+, V–VI, VI, p (portage), and/or U (unrunnable). These distinctions are relevant only to experts, however, and should be of little concern to most boaters.

[3]In some instances, but by no means all, we qualify our rating of a river by referring to different flows. For example, we rate the Middle Fork Salmon "III+ (IV at high water)" and the South Fork Salmon "V (IV at low flows)." When the difficulty of a rapid varies quite widely with flow, in some instances but by no means all, we show the rating as III–IV, IV–V, and so on. In theory, rapids rated III–IV or IV–V vary more with the flow than rapids rated simply III+ or IV+. Examples are Double Drop (III–IV) and Little Niagara (III–IV) on the Selway, where big hydraulics develop at higher water levels. An extreme example is Table Rock Rapid (IV–VI) on California's Trinity River; at low flows boats can reach a safe channel, but at higher flows they are swept toward a dangerous undercut rock.

source of endless debate. Experienced boaters looking at the same river, even the same rapid, may perceive different challenges and hazards—especially if they are in different kinds of boats, or even if they hail from different parts of the country. Moreover, whitewater equipment and technique are always evolving, and the rivers themselves are constantly changing.

The truth is that no simple code can adequately convey a river's unique combination of potential difficulties—especially when you consider complicating factors such as degree of risk, possibility for recovery after the rapid, and variations in flow, season, weather, and water temperature. Here are some important considerations in evaluating difficulty:

- Slight fluctuations in water level can change a river or rapid dramatically. Most rivers become more difficult at high flows, and mistakes are more likely to have serious consequences. However, some rivers and rapids are more dangerous at low water, when undercuts or rock sieves can increase the danger of pins and entrapments and when some holes become "keepers."

- Rapids may change from year to year, and new ones can develop overnight. There can always be a new snag or fallen tree.

- Is there a recovery pool after the rapid, or does it lead to more whitewater with little chance to stop? Would a swimmer[4] be in danger, or could he make it to shore?

- Is there a road out? A trail? Emergency help? Remote rivers flowing through isolated wilderness should be approached with caution. Aid is often difficult or impossible to obtain in case of accident, and the importance of injuries is magnified.

- The danger of hypothermia increases at high water; during spring snowmelt; whenever the river is cold; at high elevations; and in the off-season, when days are short and air temperatures may be even lower than water temperatures.

[4]"Swimming" is a whitewater euphemism for being swept downstream in a life jacket. Nothing remotely resembling swimming takes place until the usually unwilling victim is through the rapid itself.

Rating the Rapids

- **Class I** is merely moving water with a few riffles—small waves and no obstacles.
- **Class II** rapids have bigger waves but no major obstructions in the channel.
- **Class III** rapids are longer and rougher than Class II, and they have considerably bigger hydraulics (waves, holes, and currents). Route-finding is sometimes necessary, though Class III rapids generally require only a few maneuvers. Advanced and expert boaters can usually "read and run" them, but less experienced river runners should scout. Class III rapids may seem easy to passengers who have been guided by experts—for example, on a commercial raft trip—but intermediate and even advanced boaters sometimes run into trouble on Class III rapids.
- **Class IV** rapids are generally steeper, longer, and more heavily obstructed than Class III rapids. They are often "technical" runs requiring a number of turns and lateral moves. Preliminary scouting of all Class IV rapids is definitely recommended unless the boater is highly skilled and knows the river intimately. Few want to try it, but when they must, boaters can usually "swim" Class IV rapids without high risk of major injury.
- **Class V** rapids look different—and bigger—even to the uninitiated. In addition to strong currents, big waves, boulders, and holes powerful enough to hold or flip boats, Class V rapids usually have one or more major vertical drops. Everyone scouts Class V rapids, even experts. Many are routinely portaged even though they are runnable at certain water levels. An accident in a Class V rapid risks injury to boaters as well as damage or loss of equipment.
- **Class VI** rapids—magnified versions of Class V, with additional problems and hazards—are usually considered unrunnable. For most boaters they are. But at certain water levels, teams of experts taking all precautions can and have run Class VI rapids. Nevertheless, even in the best of circumstances, risks include not only injury but loss of life. Definitely not recommended.
- **Class U or p** rapids or falls (unrunnable or portage) should never be attempted. This judgment, like any classification of rapids, is subjective to a degree. In fact, a few that we label "U" or "p" have been run. Nevertheless, we consider them unsafe at any flow.

Length

Number of river miles from put-in to take-out. Where alternate accesses make shorter or longer runs possible, we say so.

Gradient

Average gradient or slope of each run, in vertical feet of drop per river mile (ft./mi.). We sometimes indicate stretches which have a significantly greater drop than the overall average.

Usually, the steeper the gradient, the more difficult the run. But there are many exceptions to this rough generalization. True, most rivers with gradients above 60 ft./mi. will be Class V; but even low-gradient runs like the Grand Canyon (8 ft./mi.) can have Class V rapids. In the Grand Canyon, the Colorado River's enormous volume "makes up" for its low gradient. In general, large-volume rivers with a given gradient will be more difficult than small-volume rivers with a comparable gradient.

A key consideration in evaluating gradient is the manner in which the river loses elevation. Pool-and-drop rivers lose most of their elevation in distinct rapids separated by flatter stretches, while continuous-gradient rivers tend to drop more steadily, spreading the energy of their descent more evenly throughout the run. The former are like staircases (with the steps sometimes far apart); the latter are like ramps. Pool-and-drop rivers are typically more difficult than continuous-gradient rivers with comparable gradients.

Drainage

Size of the watershed drained by the river and its tributaries, measured in square miles at some point on or near the run. A river's drainage is the total land area from which all runoff eventually finds its way to a single point on the river (human meddling notwithstanding). The drainage area increases as one proceeds downstream; each side creek drainage along the way adds to the total area.

Average Annual Discharge

Total flow of water past a given point along the river in an average year. Discharge, or runoff, is measured in acre-feet (af), usually at a government-operated gauging station.

Discharge figures are most useful for judging a river's relative size. In this book, the lowest discharge is the Gila River's 100,000 acre-feet per year (afy), and the highest is 27,500,000 afy on the Snake River below Hells Canyon. Generally, larger drainage areas produce more discharge and therefore larger rivers; but discharge varies dramatically according to the location of a watershed and the type and amount of precipitation it receives. For example, the Gila in arid southwestern New Mexico produces an average of just over 100,000 afy from a watershed of 1,800 square miles (55 af/sq.mi.). In the opposite corner of the West, Washington's Olympic Peninsula, the Wynoochee River gushes 385,000 afy from an upper watershed of only 41 square miles (a whopping 9,390 af/sq. mi.).

Peak Recorded Flow

Size and date of the biggest flood ever recorded, in cubic feet per second (cfs). Typically measured at the same gauging station from which we get our drainage and discharge figures. Peak recorded flows are usually weather-induced, stemming from torrential rainstorms or the sudden melting of record snow-packs.

Hydrographs

Flows at a particular point on a river in a hypothetical "average" year. Horizontal (bottom) scale shows the months and days of the year. Vertical (left) scale shows flow in cubic feet per second (cfs). The curved line representing the river's flow pattern is produced by plotting the long-term average flow for each date and then connecting the dots.[5]

An important point: rivers often peak at levels much higher than the average peaks shown on these hydrographs. Long-term averages, like those in our hydrographs, mask the brief surges of any individual year.

In the real world, there is rarely if ever such a thing as an "average" year. In any particular year a river's flow will usually vary from this average, sometimes substantially.[6] In other

---

[5]The area beneath the line represents total runoff in an average year. In other words, if you calculate this area and convert from cubic feet to acre-feet, the result should be the same as the average annual discharge.

[6]For many rivers, the hydrograph for a single year would be quite "spiky," with lots of variation from the relatively smooth average curve in our hydrographs. An extreme example would be rivers fed almost exclusively by rainfall—like many along the Pacific Coast—*(Cont.)*

words, you can't use our hydrographs to predict what the flow will be in a given year. But you can get a good idea of the river's typical pattern and how it compares with other rivers. And if you use the hydrographs in conjunction with current snowpack reports and/or weather forecasts, you can make general predictions about how the river is likely to behave in a given year. This can help in trip planning, especially for rivers where permit dates must be chosen far in advance.

Flow Gauge Conversion Tables

A few chapters include tables for converting flow gauge readings in feet to cubic feet per second (cfs). **These tables should be used only as rough guidelines.** We have done our best to ensure their accuracy, but future changes in the riverbed can render the gauge readings inaccurate, and relocation or recalibration of gauges can make these tables obsolete.

Season

Most likely period for good boating in an "average" year.[7] Because the timing of rainfall and snowmelt varies considerably from year to year, the actual boatable period in any given season may be longer, shorter, earlier, or later than the range we estimate. On many rivers dams alter the natural runoff pattern, curtailing the season in some instances and extending it in others.

Generally speaking, in the American West boating seasons are earlier for low-elevation rivers, for rivers near the Pacific Coast, and for Southwestern rivers. Seasons are later for high-alititude runs and for those in interior and northern regions.

On many rivers the boating season is limited by weather rather than by water levels. Large rivers like the Main Salmon and the Snake offer runnable flows year-round, but severe winter weather precludes boating in the off-season. Some tough-hided boaters may feel that we have started the seasons too late or ended them too early. These hardy types may choose to boat outside the periods we recommend, but they should beware of hypothermia and be prepared for adverse conditions. In particular, overnight floats and descents of difficult rivers are best scheduled when days are longer and the weather is milder.

Recommended Levels

The range of flows in cubic feet per second (cfs) which we think boaters will find most rewarding. **These numbers are intended as general guidelines only.** We believe that many boaters would find the run frustratingly slow and rocky at flows below our recommended minimum or frighteningly high and swift at levels higher than our recommended maximum. Nevertheless, most rivers can be—and have been—successfully navigated at flows well outside the ranges we suggest.

Our high and low numbers are by no means intended as absolute maximums and minimums. We have specifically avoiding estimating those limits. There is no precise high or low flow at which a river suddenly becomes "unrunnable." Much depends on the boater's skill, experience, and equipment. This is clearly an area for individual judgment, and opinions may differ widely.[8]

Never assume that a given flow is safe just because it falls within our recommended range. Accidents can happen at any water level, and boaters must always excercise caution. Particularly at the higher end of our recommended range, many rivers become extremely powerful and potentially hazardous.

(*Note 6 cont.*) where the vagaries of weather in any given season can produce sudden high runoff followed by dry periods with virtually no flow. In contrast, rivers fed by large, steadily-flowing springs show the least variation.

[7] Our season often includes the period of peak snowmelt, but that doesn't mean it's necessarily all right to go boating at high water. On many rivers it's advisable to avoid peak periods. *Never run a river at flood stage.*

Boaters can consult reports on snowpacks and water conditions published monthly in most Western states by the Soil Conservation Service, a division of the U.S. Department of Agriculture. (In California snow surveys are conducted by the state Department of Water Resources.) Used with weather forecasts and information from our hydrographs and **Season** entries, these reports can help boaters anticipate a river's flows in a given year.

[8] Another reason we avoid stating absolute minimums is the danger that promoters of dams and diversions may misuse this information to argue that a river can be largely dewatered without harming whitewater recreation. If bumping down a rocky streambed at bare minimum flows were the only form of river running available, whitewater boating would not be nearly so enjoyable and popular.

Flow Information

Where reliable flow readings are available, we list the sources. These include flow tapes, ranger stations, local outfitters, and river running supply stores.[9] Be aware of when and how often gauge readings are updated; flows can change much more quickly than tapes.

Special Hazards

All sorts of unpleasant dangers—from weirs, waterfalls, and log jams to rattlesnakes, irascible ranchers, and poison ivy.[10] **Never assume that this book can warn you of all the hazards on a river—it can't.** In addition to our inadvertent mistakes and omissions, there are always new problems to watch for, including rearranged rapids and trees, snags, or strainers in the channel. Be particularly alert for changes made by high water in winter and spring.

Permits

This entry is about permits for private river runners, not about the different kind of permit often held by commercial outfitters. Permits for private float trips are required on many popular rivers and are usually distributed by a government agency that manages public land along the river. In many cases the agency allocates a limited number of launch dates, often by a lottery and/or a waiting list. In other instances permits are required but use is not limited; that is, they are available for the asking. Where permits are not currently required, we say so.

Our information on permits is the most recent available as this book goes to press. But regulations change, and new permit systems are periodically put into place on rivers when use increases substantially. We advise boaters always to check with the managing agency for updated information. These agencies can sometimes give boaters advice on how to improve their chances of getting a permit.

[9]Waterline, a phone service just expanding into the West from the Northeastern U.S., may eventually offer flow information (usually in feet, not cfs) on many Western rivers on a pay-per-call basis or via a paid subscription. For more information call (800) 945-3376.

[10]Recently, there have been reports of a deadly water-borne disease thought to have been transmitted by an amoeba in more than one hot spring near Western rivers. Boaters should check with the managing agency or other local sources about the quality of water in and around the river they plan to float.

Where permits are avilable for the asking, or where simple self-registration of the trip is requested, some boaters may be tempted to float the river without complying. In such cases **we strongly urge all boaters to obtain the permit or register the trip.** Often, when a dam or diversion is proposed, the managing agency is asked to estimate non-commercial boating use. All too frequently, private boaters are significantly undercounted, and that weakens the case for preserving the river. A registration system provides a valuable record of public use.

Managing Agency

Most Western rivers fall under the jurisdiction of one (or more) of three federal agencies: the U.S. Forest Service (USFS), Bureau of Land Management (BLM), and National Park Service (NPS). A smaller number come under state or county management, often through an agency with a name like Fish and Wildlife or Parks and Recreation.

In recent years, a growing number of agencies have added staff members with titles like "Recreation Resource Specialist," "Recreation Planner," or even "River Ranger." These people can be valuable resources for up-to-date information on regulations, river hazards, water levels, road conditions, shuttle driver references, campsites, side hikes, fishing, and so on. Many are boaters themselves.

Commercial Raft Trips

Some readers may wish to float with a commerical outfitter, either because they lack the skills and equipment to make a particular run, or because they want to leave the logistics, cooking, and grunt work to someone else. We indicate whether guided trips are currently available and how to obtain a list of outfitters (usually from the managing agency, which normally regulates commercial river running). You can also call the outfitters' national organization, America Outdoors, (800) 524-4814. Another source is Lloyd Armstead, *Whitewater Rafting in Western North America: A Guide to Rivers and Professional Outfitters* (see **Bibliography**). We do not recommend or endorse any particular outfit.

Land Ownership

Boaters should always try to avoid trespassing on private land. For this reason, we have included this entry to indicate whether the land along a river is public, private, or some mixture of the two. We have done our best to ensure the accuracy of our information, but we do not guarantee it. Boaters should consult a BLM or Forest Service map or other sources for detailed information. Be aware that maps may contain errors and land ownership can change. Ask the managing agency and/or inquire locally.

Scenery

Our subjective assessment of the scenic quality of the river and its canyon.

Solitude

Our subjective assessment of a river's isolation from the sights and sounds of civilization—roads, railroads, houses, and even other river runners. This entry does not measure the presence or absence of human development; it simply indicates whether such things, if they exist, are conspicuous from the river. A highway or railroad that is set far back from the river bank and screened by heavy vegetation does not preclude a good solitude rating.

Wilderness

Here we indicate whether or not the river canyon has a *wilderness character*, which we define as the absence of roads, railroads, towns, vacation homes, and other human developments. Our definition is emphatically *not* limited to officially designated Wilderness Areas.

Fishing

On some rivers we rate the prospects for fishing in the main river or side streams. We do not include information on fishing regulations or permits; these are the angler's responsibility.

Wildlife

On some rivers we note the relative abundance of wildlife, including any unusual or especially interesting animals.

Weather

On some rivers we provide very general information on weather. Weather is especially variable in the early and later parts of the boating season and at higher elevations. Unusual weather patterns can produce rain, snow, or freezing weather on many rivers even in midsummer. Be prudent and prepared.

Water

What the water looks like and how cold or warm it usually is. (We do not recommend drinking the water from any river or side stream unless it is purified and filtered for microorganisms like giardia.[11])

Water temperature is the most important single factor in hypothermia risk. Prudent boaters wear wet suits or dry suits on any river when water temperature or weather conditions merit extra protection. Kayakers wear them more often than rafters. For rafters, wet or dry suits are advisable in almost all weather on Class IV and V runs and anywhere else where long "swims" are a possibility.

Camping

Prospects for camping on or near the river, either at wilderness sites on shore or at developed campgrounds along the river or nearby. On many rivers the number of wilderness campsites is drastically reduced at high flows, when many beaches and flats are flooded. Many managing agencies have strict no-impact camping rules; inquire about specific regulations for the river you plan to float.[12] Conscientious boaters should practice no-impact camping whether it is officially prescribed or not.

---

[11]**Warning:** As a practical matter, no water from any river, creek, or spring in the West can be considered safe for drinking without being first chemically treated, filtered with an advanced "micro-pore" device, and/or boiled, largely because of the widespread presence of giardia. Regarding hot springs, see previous footnote.

As for the quality and availability of water, readers of this guide are advised that although we have tried to get things right, we take no legal responsibility for the accuracy of the information we present. The reader bears full responsibility for planning ahead for water needs and supplies and for assessing the safety of any water source.

[12]The latest development on many important rivers is much stricter regulation of the transport and disposal of solid human waste (feces). More and more managing agencies are prohibiting the old system of lining ammo boxes with plastic bags because there is no legal and environmentally sound way to dispose of the bags. Some are experimenting with special coin- operated machines to clean unlined ammo boxes. Be sure you know what is required before you plan your trip.

Side Hikes

General prospects for side hiking, as well as any particularly outstanding hikes. Side hikes—usually up side canyons but occasionally on other trails or routes—can be the highlight of a river trip.

Side Excursions

Interesting side trips in the surrounding area: scenic overlooks, waterfalls, hot springs (see warning in footnote to **Water**), National Parks and Wilderness Areas, historic towns, and so on.[13]

Guides and References

These listings of additional sources of printed information are usually quite brief. More detailed information can be found in the **Bibliography** at the end of this book. We sometimes list books that are no longer in print, in the hope that boaters can locate used copies or find them in a library. Our list of references is not always complete, especially for popular rivers like the Grand Canyon which are covered by numerous books.

We encourage readers to consult these additional guides and references, many of which are specific to a particular river and contain far more detail than we have been able to include. Unfortunately, whitewater guide books often have fairly small press runs and frequently go out of print.

We occasionally recommend a local source for further information—usually a boating shop or a commerical outfit whose staff knows the river well and has indicated a willingness to field calls and questions from private boaters.

Maps

We list all sorts of maps—specialized river maps, U.S. Geological Survey topo maps, maps published by the BLM and the USFS, and road maps published by automobile clubs or travel bureaus. (Our notation "USGS 1:100" refers to the 1:100,000 series published by both the USGS and the BLM.) Many USFS and BLM maps can be ordered from the river managing agencies. USGS maps can be bought in some retail stores or ordered from USGS Map Sales, Box 25286, Denver Federal Center, Bldg. 810, Denver CO 80225; (303) 236-7477.

Auto Shuttle

Mileages and estimated driving times one way, put-in to take-out. Not given for all rivers. In some cases we list a contact for shuttle services. Occasionally, other services like air shuttles and boat tows are mentioned here.

Logistics

How to get to the river area and find access points and shuttle roads. Many shuttles are complicated, and describing them in words can be difficult. There is no substitute for a good local map and for advice from locals and managing agencies who know the area. Keep in mind that access points may change: new ones are sometimes developed, and old ones are occasionally closed.

We did our best to get all these directions right, but no doubt we blew a few. If so, we apologize. Please vent your frustration by writing us with the correct information, so we can fix it in a future edition.

Mile by Mile Guide

On rivers with maps we provide a relatively detailed **Mile Guide**; on rivers without maps this information appears in more condensed and abbreviated paragraph form in a **River Guide**. Our purpose is to give boaters an idea of what to expect as they head downriver: the name and location of major rapids, access points, side creeks, landmarks, points of interest, side hikes, and so on.

For significant rapids we normally give the name, rating, and location, and we often provide a brief description. In some cases we include information on landmarks to help boaters recognize when they are approaching a big drop. **Our descriptions are not intended as instructions for running a rapid.** That judgment is always left to the boater, who should keep in mind that rapids change, water levels fluctuate, and opinions often differ as to the best and safest approach.

We sometimes point out rapids which boaters may want to scout or portage; however,

[13] Guides to better-known areas like National Parks are readily available and too numerous to list even in our **Bibliography**. A recent book that could come in handy in lesser-known areas is Michael Hodgson, *America's Secret Recreation Areas: Your Guide to the Unexplored Lands of the Bureau of Land Management.* Its full citation is in our **Bibliography**.

this decision is always the boater's responsibility. Depending on their ability and familiarity with the river, they may need to scout and/or portage more or less frequently than we indicate. Remember the rule: **"If in doubt, stop and scout. Still in doubt? Portage."**

We do not pretend to have included anything like a comprehensive list of rapids in our **Mile Guides**. On any given run, we normally list only the more difficult rapids. Rapids rated Class III and below are normally left out of mile guides to Class IV runs, and Class IV rapids appear infrequently—or not at all—in guides to Class V runs. Better-known rivers are described in more detail than those where only a few experts have ventured. Boaters running Class V rivers should be prepared for plenty of scouting and portaging; for these rivers we rarely mention specific portages, we point out only the biggest rapids, and sometimes we list no individual rapids at all.

River miles start with mile 0 at the put-in and correspond to the mileages shown on our river maps. On continuous rivers that are divided into different sections because of difficulty, character, or popular access points, we sometimes start the mileage over at zero at the alternate put-in(s). In such cases we usually show [in brackets] the total mileage from the uppermost put-in, which normally corresponds to mileage on the map.

The location of rapids and other important features by mile is always approximate, even if it's expressed in tenths of a mile. The point is to give boaters some idea of how far one thing is from another. **Readers are urged to take mileage as only a rough indication.** Don't blunder into a big rapid just because you expect it to be a quarter mile or a half mile downstream.

Finally, the terms "right" and "left" are always used assuming the observer is facing downstream.

Abbreviations

AAA	American Automobile Association
af	acre-feet
BLM	Bureau of Land Management
cfs	Cubic feet per second
CG	Campground
DFW	Department of Fish & Wildlife
DWR	Department of Water Resources
ft./mi.	feet per mile
NF	National Forest
NOAA	National Oceanic & Atmospheric Administration
NORS	National Organization for River Sports
NPS	National Park Service
NRA	National Recreation Area
NWS	National Weather Service
RA	Resource Area (BLM)
RD	Ranger District (USFS)
USFS	United States Forest Service
USGS	United States Geological Service

Region I.
Idaho and the Northern Rockies

Idaho, Montana, Wyoming

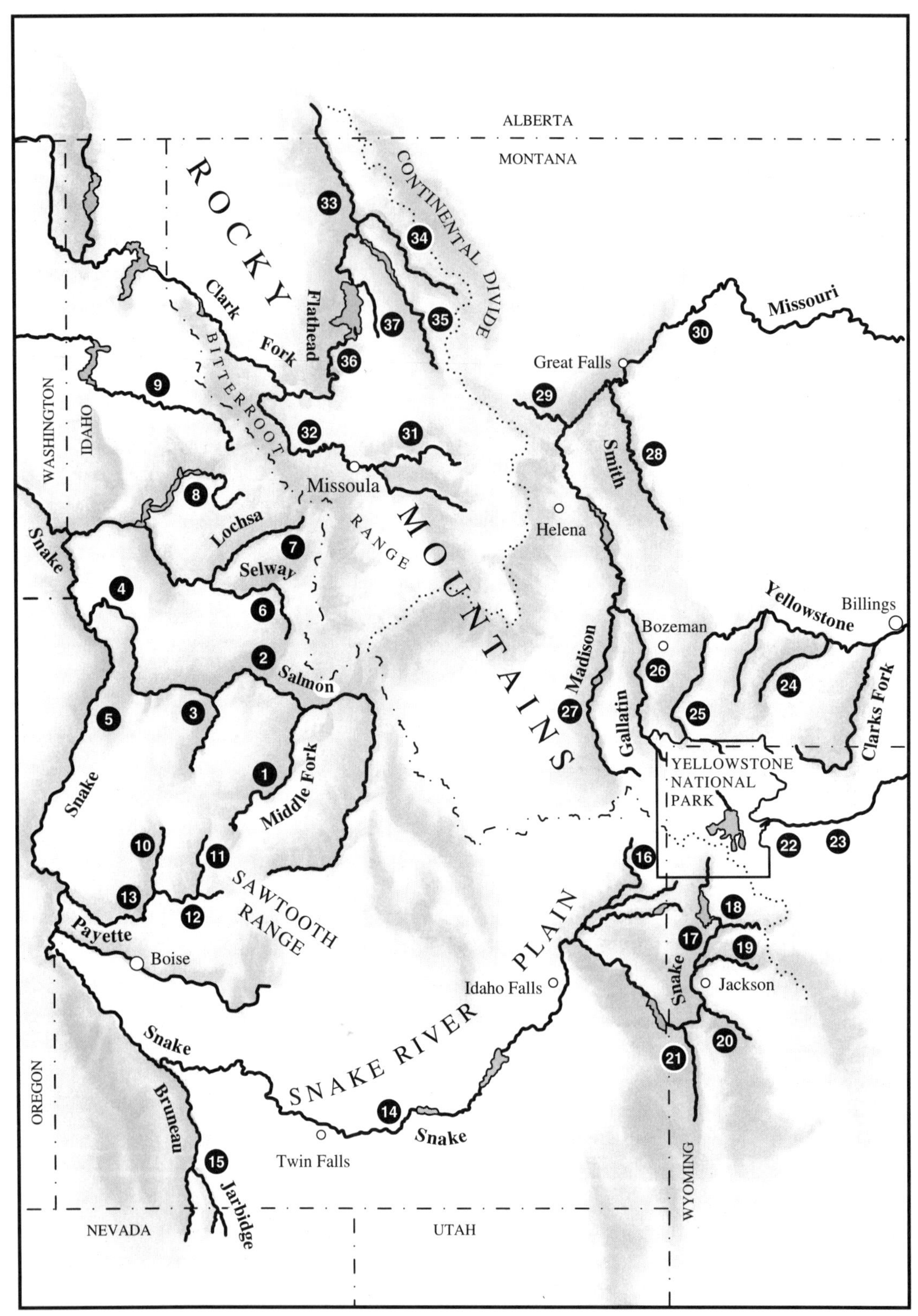

Idaho and the Northern Rockies

Rivers of Idaho and the Northern Rockies

1. Middle Fork Salmon
2. Main Salmon
3. South Fork Salmon
4. Lower Salmon
5. Hells Canyon of the Snake
6. Selway
7. Lochsa
8. North Fork Clearwater
9. St. Joe
10. North Fork Payette
11. Deadwood
12. South Fork Payette
13. Main Payette
14. Middle Snake
15. Jarbidge and Bruneau
16. Henrys Fork
17. Upper Snake
18. Buffalo Fork
19. Gros Ventre
20. Hoback
21. Greys
22. North Fork Shoshone
23. Main Shoshone
24. Stillwater
25. Yellowstone
26. Gallatin
27. Madison
28. Smith
29. Dearborn
30. Missouri
31. Blackfoot
32. Clark Fork
33. North Fork Flathead
34. Middle Fork Flathead
35. South Fork Flathead
36. Lower Flathead
37. Swan

Idaho and the Northern Rockies

The name Idaho has nearly mystical meaning for whitewater boaters. The state's vast, roadless wild lands, rugged mountains, and heavy snowfall combine to create some of the West's most outstanding wilderness rivers. Just to the east, neighboring portions of Montana and Wyoming also boast a wealth of fine whitewater rivers. Taken together, the Idaho and Northern Rockies region holds more miles of boatable whitewater than any other region in the West.

Most famous among these rivers are three Idaho classics: the Middle Fork of the Salmon, the Main Salmon, and the Selway. Cutting through the heart of the immense central Idaho wilderness, these legendary rivers lure boaters from around the nation with a remarkable combination of outstanding scenery, deep solitude, abundant wildlife, and superb whitewater.

But the region holds much more than just these well-known rivers. In this section of our guide, we describe over 45 runs. Many have as much to offer as the celebrated "big name" rivers. In Montana, for example, the Flathead River drainage holds remote wilderness runs that rival those of Salmon-Selway country in Idaho.

Idaho and the Northern Rockies, as we define the region, includes all of Idaho, the northwest corner of Wyoming, and western Montana. Roughly half of the runs we describe are in Idaho itself.

The Rocky Mountains are the heart of this region. Running from northwest to southeast, the Rockies, along with associated ranges like Idaho's Bitterroots and Sawtooths, form a vast terrain of snowy peaks, dense forests, and deep canyons. The Rockies are not as high here as they are farther south in Colorado: no peaks exceed 14,000', and only the Wind River Range in Wyoming has summits over 13,000'. But the northern part of the range is substantially wetter than the southern part: some spots on the west slope of the Bitterroots along the Idaho-Montana border get more than 50" of precipitation in an average year.

The result is a remarkable number of large rivers, especially in the Snake and Columbia River drainages on the wetter west side of the Continental Divide. The region's mightiest rivers—the Salmon, the Flathead, and especially the Snake—all flow westward toward the Pacific Ocean. Watersheds in the Missouri basin, on the east side of the Continental Divide, receive much less rain and snow.

Our Region I has well-defined boundaries. The Northern Rockies are separated from the Colorado Rockies to the south by the Great Divide Basin in southern Wyoming. Here the range essentially disappears for a distance of some 100 miles. This wide breach in the mountains offered an easy travel route for early pioneers and, later, the transcontinental railway. The relatively arid basin, which holds little interest for whitewater river runners, marks the logical southern limit of the Idaho and Northern Rockies region.

To the east the region extends to the edge of the Great Plains, where the rivers become broad and slow. The region's northern boundary is the Canadian border. Fine whitewater rivers abound north of the border, but they are beyond the scope of this guide.

To the west we use the Washington and Oregon borders as a dividing line between the Idaho and Northern Rockies region and the Pacific Northwest. Admittedly, this division is somewhat arbitrary. For example, the Bruneau and Jarbidge rivers in southwestern Idaho have more in common with the nearby Owyhee River in Oregon than they do with other Idaho rivers.[1] The Hells Canyon section of the Snake River, which marks the Idaho-Oregon state line, could reasonably be placed in either region.

This sprawling region contains an enormous diversity of river landscapes: the jagged peaks and rugged granite canyons of central Idaho; the lush forests of the Idaho panhandle; the glacial valleys and ice-sculpted summits of northern Montana; the broad volcanic highlands of the Yellowstone plateau in northwestern Wyoming; the craggy heights of the Grand Tetons; and the vertical basalt chasms of the arid Snake River plain in southern Idaho.

These were the inspiring and intimidating landscapes that lured and often thwarted some of the West's earliest white explorers, begin-

[1]In fact, all three of these rivers—the Bruneau, Jarbidge and Owyhee—are somewhat anomalous. Their long, wild desert gorges are reminiscent of Canyon Country rivers, but their location clearly marks them as Northwestern rivers.

Fork Clearwater, the South Fork Flathead, and others. Fine whitewater runs have been lost, and native salmon fisheries have been devastated.

Recently, local river conservation movements have begun to assert themselves, especially in Idaho. The very popular Payette River near Boise was recently saved from destruction by a grassroots movement that turned back proposals to dam the river for hydropower. This important victory may herald a turning point, as more people in the region recognize the tremendous value of their remaining free-flowing rivers.

Though it is relatively small in numbers, the local boating community in this lightly-populated region is very big in commitment and enthusiasm. Kayaks, canoes, and rowing frames are a common sight on cartops in the most popular boating areas, including towns and cities like Riggins, McCall, Salmon, Boise, Jackson, West Glacier, Bozeman, Missoula, and Billings.

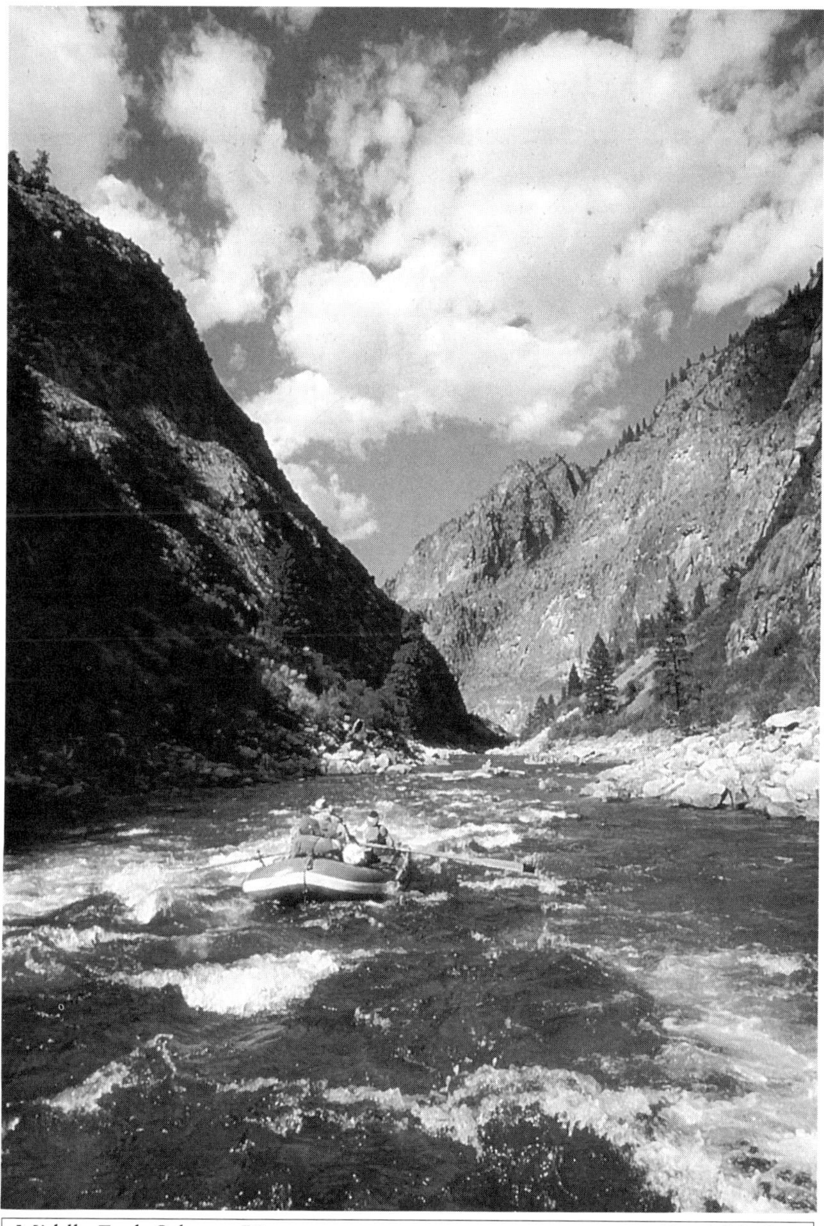

Middle Fork Salmon River *Daniel Bolster*

ning with Lewis and Clark in 1805. The rivers still echo with a rich history, beginning with the native peoples who fished and camped here and continuing through the years to include trappers, prospectors, settlers, dam-builders, pioneering whitewater boaters, and many others.

This region contains some of the nation's longest sections of National Wild and Scenic Rivers. Nevertheless, many great rivers have been lost to dams and other water development. Massive hydropower projects have flooded long stretches of the Snake, the North

Middle Fork Salmon River

Boundary Creek to Main Salmon Confluence

Difficulty: III+ (IV at high water).
Length: 100 miles (96 on Middle Fork, 4 on Main Salmon).
Gradient: 27 ft./mi. overall. 40 from put-in to Indian Creek (mile 25); 23 thereafter.
Put-in: Boundary Creek (5,630').
Take-out: Cache Bar, Main Salmon (3,020' at confluence).
Drainage Area: 290 sq. mi. (est.) at put-in; 770 sq. mi. at Middle Fork Lodge (mile 34).
Average Annual Discharge: 1,098,000 af.
Peak Recorded Flow: 20,900 cfs (Middle Fork Lodge gauge, June 16, 1974).
Season: Late May–August. Flows usually peak between late May and late June, then drop quickly. The road to the put-in is usually snowed in until late May or early June. Hardy boaters have been known to launch in early May on Marsh Creek, near the northernmost point of Highway 21, about 17 miles northwest of Stanley—usually in kayaks or small rafts, since most portage Dagger Falls. They must be prepared for cold, wet weather, log jams, and a river that can rise quickly to flood stage.
Recommended Levels: 1,500–5,000 cfs at the Middle Fork Lodge gauge (mile 34). Flows at the put-in are considerably lower. At moderately high water (4,500 cfs), only experienced boaters with advanced skills should run the river. High water (over 6,000 cfs) demands even more precautions. When the river drops below 2.5' on the gauge (1,080 cfs), flows on the upper section are skimpy for rafts, and many parties fly in to an alternate put-in at Indian Creek (mile 25). Below 2' (690 cfs) most boaters fly in.
Flow Information: Middle Fork RD, (208) 879-5204; Idaho DWR, (208) 327-7865.
Kayaks: Kayaks can bump down the upper stretch in late summer when flows are too low for rafts, but they'll have a hard time carrying enough gear and provisions unless they join up with rafts flown in to Indian Creek.
Special Hazards: Remote area; evacuation could be difficult in case of injury. Some radio phones for emergencies at USFS guard stations and private ranches and airstrips.
Permits: Required year-round. Launch dates by reservation only during the control period, June 1–Sept. 3; at other times, first come first served. Maximum group size 24; maximum trip length 8 days. For private trips during the control period, request application forms after Oct. 1. Applications accepted Dec. 1–Jan. 31 (fee) as part of a four-river permit process that includes the Main Salmon, Selway, and Snake (Hell's Canyon). Lottery held in February. No waiting list, but boaters may obtain canceled launch dates by calling the Middle Fork RD after the lottery. For trips outside the control period, request application form at least one month before launch date. Middle Fork permits are difficult to get; in recent years 6,000 applicants have competed for 372 launch

Flow Gauge
Middle Fork Lodge (Mile 34)

Feet	Flow (cfs)	Feet	Flow (cfs)
1.5	375	6.0	6,380
2.0	690	6.5	7,530
2.3	915	7.0	8,760
2.5	1,080	7.5	10,100
3.0	1,570	8.0	11,500
3.5	2,150	8.5	13,000
4.0	2,820	9.0	14,500
4.5	3,570	9.5	16,200
5.0	4,410	10.0	18,000
5.5	5,340		

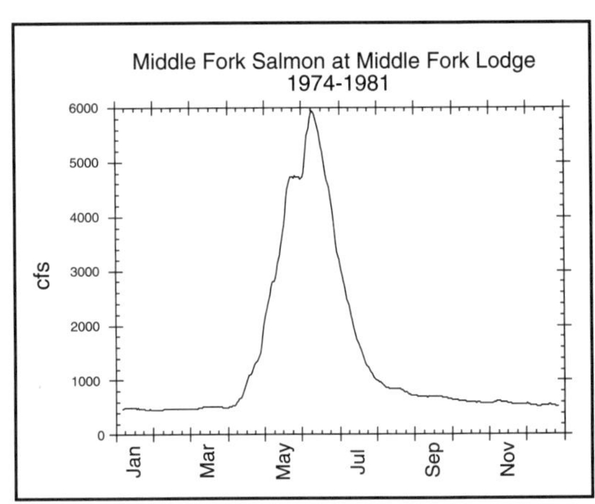

dates. Odds vary dramatically with the date requested. July is the most popular month.

Managing Agency: Middle Fork RD, Challis NF, P.O. Box 750, Challis, ID 83226; (208) 879-5204.

Commercial Raft Trips: Two or three launch daily during permit season. For a list contact the managing agency or Idaho Outfitters & Guides Assn., P.O. Box 95, Boise, ID 83701; (208) 342-1919.

Scenery: Excellent. Deep canyon and rugged, forested mountains. The landscape becomes drier over the course of the run.

Solitude: Very good. A few private ranches or lodges and a fair number of boating parties. No motorized craft allowed.

Wilderness: Roadless. Trails follow one or both banks from the launch site all the way to Big Creek (mile 78). The entire Middle Fork is protected as a National Wild and Scenic River. Most of the surrounding land is part of the Frank Church–River of No Return Wilderness, and all of it is National Forest.

Fishing: Fine trout fishing—cutthroat (locally "Redside"), rainbow, Dolly Varden—in side streams and river, especially at lower flows. Dams on the Columbia have reduced former salmon and steelhead runs to a trickle. Barbless hooks, catch-and-release only.

Water: Cold and clear.

Camping: Excellent. More than 100 riverside campsites, some with pit toilets (slowly being phased out). Many fine beaches and sand bars except at high flows. Good grassy benches above river level. Campsites, which must be reserved with the ranger at the put-in, are marked in the USFS map-guides.

Side Hikes: Excellent. Among the many good hikes are those up Soldier Creek (mile 12), Rapid River (18), Pistol Creek (21.7), Indian Creek (25), Marble Creek (32), Loon Creek (49.5), and both Big Creek and the Waterfall Creek Trail around mile 78.

Side Excursions: Dagger Falls just upstream from the put-in.

Guides and References:

- Moore and McClaran, *Idaho Whitewater.*
- Amaral, *Idaho: The Whitewater State.*
- Garren, *Idaho River Tours.*
- Quinn, *Handbook to the Middle Fork of the Salmon River.*
- Carrey and Conley, *The Middle Fork—A Guide.* Includes the river's colorful history.
- DuBois, *An Innocent on the Middle Fork.* Personal account of an early descent.

Maps:

- **USGS 7.5':** *Big Soldier Mtn, Soldier Creek, Artillery Dome, Big Baldy, Pungo Mtn, Little Soldier Mtn, Sliderock Ridge, Norton Ridge, Ramey Hill, Bear Creek Point, Aparejo Point, Puddin Mtn, Aggipah Mtn, Butts Creek Point, Long Tom Mtn, Square Top.*
- **USGS 1:100:** *Pistol Creek, Challis, Bighorn Crags.*
- **USFS:** *Middle Fork of the Salmon River.* Waterproof map-guide, good for rapids, campsites, trails, and topography. Order from Middle Fork RD.
- **USFS:** *Frank Church–River of No Return Wilderness* (North Half and South Half). For the entire run, you need both halves (order from Middle Fork RD).
- **USFS:** *Challis NF* (West Half), *Salmon NF.*
- *Middle Fork Salmon River Map & Camp Guide* (Backeddy Books, P.O. Box 301, Cambridge, ID 83610). Waterproof.
- *Riverguide Bandana to the Middle Fork Salmon* (Rivers & Mountains). Cloth map.

Auto Shuttle: 210 miles; 5–6 hours one way. About a quarter on unpaved roads. For references contact Chambers of Commerce in Challis, (208) 879-2771; Stanley, (208) 774-2279; Salmon, (208) 756-4935.

Logistics: To reach the **put-in** about 90 miles northeast of Boise, turn west off Idaho Highway 21 about 24 miles northwest of Stanley or 37 miles north of Lowman. Follow unpaved USFS Road 579 for about 10 miles, then bear right on Road 568 and drive 13 more miles to **Boundary Creek Boat Ramp** and Campground.

To reach the **take-out**, return to Highway 21 and turn left toward Stanley. At Stanley, turn left (north) on Idaho Highway 75. Just south of Challis, turn left (north) on U.S. 93. About 22 miles past the town of Salmon, at North Fork, turn left (west) onto USFS Road 030, the "Salmon River Road." The take-out at **Cache Bar Boat Ramp** and Campground is about 40 miles downstream. (See **Main Salmon** chapter for more details.)

MIDDLE FORK SALMON

Salmon River country is the heartland of Idaho whitewater. The pristine Middle Fork, the mighty Main Salmon, and the difficult but increasingly popular South Fork provide the kind of scenic wilderness boating that has made Idaho rivers legendary.

A trip down the Middle Fork Salmon—narrower, steeper, and more technically demanding than the Main Salmon—is one of the finest wilderness floats in the country. No roads reach the river between the Boundary Creek launch site and the confluence with the Main Salmon. Wildlife is abundant in the rugged canyon, especially early in the season when the surrounding peaks, some above 9,000', are still covered with snow. Bighorn sheep and bald and golden eagles are among the finest sights.

The Middle Fork begins at the confluence of Bear Valley Creek and Marsh Creek, only ten miles upstream from the Boundary Creek put-in. Both creeks are major tributaries draining the northern slopes of the Sawtooth Range and the upper end of Sawtooth Valley. Just to the east is the Main Salmon watershed; to the west is the South Fork Payette drainage. At first the Middle Fork is narrow, but as it slices northward through the granite bedrock of the Idaho Batholith, the combined flow of scores of tributaries turns it into a big river.

Most of the rapids are fairly easy, but a few passages—notably Velvet Falls (mile 5) and the big rapids in the final gorge—require more attention. At low and moderate midsummer levels, the Middle Fork is challenging, but not threatening, to intermediates with average experience. Rain and cold weather are always possible, so it's worth bringing along a wet suit even in midsummer (and hoping you don't have to put it on).

During peak runoff the river changes character. Rapids in the steep upper section become nearly continuous, making it hard to land and easy for parties to become separated. (After a high-water raft trip on the Middle Fork a few years ago, a friend reported, "Choosing our first campsite was no problem. When we all finally made the same eddy, that was it.") Less seasoned boaters might consider flying in to Indian Creek (mile 25). Downstream, in the final gorge known as the "Impassable Canyon"—impassable to horseback parties, not to boaters—the swollen river crashes through huge waves and holes. Sudden rainstorms can accelerate snowmelt and produce flood conditions in a matter of hours. A high-water trip on the Middle Fork is no place for the inexperienced.

Archaeologists date human artifacts found in Middle Fork country back to 8,000 years ago. Pictographs in caves and on rock walls along the river are the principal legacy of these early inhabitants. When whites arrived in the nineteenth century, the nearly inaccessible canyon and the surrounding countryside were sparsely populated by a tribe of Northern Shoshone called "Tukudeka" (Sheepeaters).

The discovery of gold on Loon Creek in 1869 provoked a brief rush into the area, with tragic results for the Indians. In February 1879, shortly after the unsuccessful uprisings of the Nez Perce and the Bannocks elsewhere in Idaho, the murder of five Chinese miners was blamed on the Tukudeka—probably unjustifiably. The U.S. Cavalry spent all summer and part of the fall in pursuit of a small group of Sheepeaters who had been joined by a few escaped Bannocks. Finally, the ragged band of 50 Indians, including only 15 warriors, surrendered and were led away from their homeland. The so-called Sheepeater War was Idaho's last Indian conflict. (For more on the history of the Middle Fork, see Carrey and Conley, *The Middle Fork—A Guide.*)

River running came later to the Middle Fork than to the Main Salmon. Harry Guleke floated a log raft down its lower reaches, probably below Indian Creek, in the mid-1920's. In 1926 Henry Weidner's party of canoeists took three months to make their way downstream, doubtless with many portages. The next run of the entire river was made in 1936 by a group led by Bus Hatch, Frank Swain, and Dr. Russell Frazier, who piloted wooden rowboats down both the Middle Fork and the Main Salmon all the way to Riggins.

By the end of the Second World War only a few parties had floated the Middle Fork. The availability of inflatable rafts from military surplus, combined with a renewed surge of public interest in the outdoors, soon led to more trips. The first commercial outfitters on the river began taking customers down the Middle Fork in the late 1940's.[1]

---

[1]Running the Middle Fork used to be even more of an expedition. Until 1960 boaters had to put in on Bear Valley Creek, which meant running or portaging Dagger Falls. Then the U.S. Fish and Wildlife Service made things easier by extending the road all the way to the river in order to construct a fish ladder at the falls. A few years later, the Forest Service built a steep wooden launch ramp just downstream at Boundary Creek.

In 1968 the Middle Fork Salmon became one of the charter members of the National Wild and Scenic Rivers System. River use had increased to around 2,500 boaters a year and was growing fast. Garbage and human waste were becoming problems at the campsites. A few deaths, including some on professionally-guided trips, added to the concerns. (In an article in the Los Angeles Times—reprinted in Verne Huser's *River Reflections*—Tom Brokaw quoted a local as saying, "That river swallows people. Some it gives back, some it don't.") As a result, in the mid-1970's the Forest Service began to control river access more closely and to apply a strict minimum-impact camping policy which, over the years, has done wonders to return the river environment to its natural state.

Interest in the Middle Fork probably peaked in 1979, the year that President Jimmy Carter and his wife made a well-publicized trip down the river in outfitter Norm Guth's sweep boat. Today, some 10,000 people float the Middle Fork every year—about 40 percent in private parties, and the balance with commercial outfitters.

Upstream Run

Some boaters still enjoy the excellent day trip down Marsh Creek and the upper part of the Middle Fork. No permit is required. There's a fairly short window for boating: Marsh Creek is runnable only in the early season, but the access road over Cape Horn Summit to Dagger Falls and Boundary Creek (see **Logistics**) must be free of snow. The 15-mile run begins at any of several sites near the confluence of Cape Horn and Marsh Creeks, just off Idaho Highway 21 northwest of Stanley. The first five miles are on Marsh Creek; then the Bear Creek confluence marks the beginning of the Middle Fork proper. Downstream are strong Class III rapids leading all the way to Dagger Falls, a Class V staircase. Most boaters take out on the left above the rapid; those who run Dagger take out on the left at the Boundary Creek Boat Ramp.

Mile by Mile Guide

0 Boundary Creek Boat Ramp, just above **First Bend Rapid** (II+). USFS permit control and campsite assignments. (No launching at the old ramp upstream, just below **Dagger Falls.** Adventurous boaters who want to run Class V Dagger Falls can put in at the campground just above the falls. But they still must stop at the Boundary Creek launch ramp to pick up their permits.) For the next 30 miles, the Middle Fork slices through the exposed granitic and metamorphic bedrock of the Idaho Batholith. A trail follows the left bank to White Creek Pack Bridge (mile 48).

2.9 **SULPHUR SLIDE** (III). At the end of a long pool, the river turns left into a steep, rocky pitch. Tricky entry at low water.

3.7 **RAMSHORN** (III). A right-hand bend leads to a narrow chute. Ramshorn Creek enters downstream on the left.

5.1 **VELVET FALLS** (IV-). At the mouth of Velvet Creek, which enters on the right, boaters face a river-wide ledge with a powerful reversal. Most try to miss it by tucking in behind the huge boulder overhanging the left bank. A Class II rapid just upstream obscures the sound of the falls—hence the name "Velvet"—so don't be caught unawares.

7 Trail Flat Hot Springs and Camp (left bank). Large site often shows evidence of use by horseback parties. Hot spring at river's edge is washed out at higher flows.

11.3 **POWERHOUSE** (III). A rocky opening section leads into a sharper drop and S-turn. Big hydraulics at high flows. An old stamp mill and waterwheel for crushing gold ore may still be seen on the right bank.

12 Soldier Creek enters on the right. Trail up the creek begins several hundred yards downstream. Large campsite on river left, downstream from Joe Bump Cabin.

13 Sheepeater Hot Springs and Camp (left bank). Springs on the bench above the camp. Scout Camp, a smaller site, is just upstream on the same side. Half a dozen more campsites in the next five miles.

18 The Rapid River, a major tributary, enters on the right. A trail follows the right bank of the Middle Fork to Big Creek (mile 78). Another trail leads up the Rapid River.

19.4 Dolly Lake, a large campsite and fishing hole on the right. Just downstream is a short Class III- drop at the mouth of Cannon Creek, which enters on the left.

21.7 **PISTOL CREEK (III).** Tight S-turn; more difficult at higher flows. Scout right. Large campsite at the mouth of Pistol Creek, entering on the left below the rapid. Trail up the creek, which also provides a good side hike, is a major entry point for backpackers in Middle Fork country. Half a mile downstream on the left are the Middle Fork Ranch and Airstrip (private). For the next 35 miles—until the **Tappan** rapids—the river is much slower and easier.

25 Indian Creek Guard Station (USFS) on the left. Airstrip and boat ramp are often used for fly-in trips late in the season. Two trails lead from the left bank up ridges overlooking the Indian Creek watershed.

32 Marble Creek enters on the left. Trail up the creek. Short Class III- drop as the river turns right. Two campsites, one on each bank. Sunflower Flat Campsite and Hot Springs are on the right a mile downstream.

34 Middle Fork Lodge (private) on the right. Pack bridge across the river. Flow gauge on the left bank a few hundred yards upstream.

35.5 Little Creek Guard Station (USFS) on the right. Pack bridge. A campsite on the left at the mouth of Sunflower Creek, just downstream from the old Hood Ranch where a gravel bar divides the river, has a hot springs nearby.

40.5 Cougar Creek enters on the right, just upstream from Cougar Creek Ranch (private). Mahoney Airstrip (USFS) on the left.

46 Whitey Cox Camp and Hot Springs on the right bank, where the river curves right and a lone Ponderosa pine towers over a small beach. Cox, a miner, is buried between the beach and the hot springs.

48 White Creek Pack Bridge. The left bank trail ends here, but the Middle Fork Trail on the right continues to Big Creek.

49.5 Loon Creek enters on the right. Simplot Ranch and Loon Creek Airstrip (private). Hot springs less than a mile up the creek.

52 Hospital Bar Campsite and Hot Springs —the last hot water on the Middle Fork— on the left, just after a sharp right bend. The name comes from an old ranchers' practice of keeping sick and crippled livestock here. Three smaller campsites nearby.

56.5 Tappan Ranch (private) at the mouth of Grouse Creek, which enters on the right.

57.4 **TAPPAN 1 (II+).** The first of four Tappan rapids, just above a sharp left bend. The three others are spaced nearly evenly through the next mile. The second is the biggest: **TAPPAN FALLS (III+)**, where the river turns right into a pool, then drops over a boulder-studded ledge into a big reversal. Routes vary with the flow, but most boaters run the right side. Scout right. Third is **TAPPAN 2 (III)**, where boats must skirt a big boulder in midstream, then avoid another boulder (hole at higher flows). Finally comes **TAPPAN 3 (III)**, where the river bends right and a boulder blocks the center of the channel.

60 Camas Creek enters on the right. Trail up the creek to the old Yellowjacket Mine.

62.8 **APAREJO POINT (III-).** The river turns left, and the rapid is just below the mouth of Aparejo Creek, which enters on the right. This narrow gorge was once a proposed dam site.

66.2 Bernard Bridge. Old Mormon Ranch upstream on the right. Flying B Ranch and Airstrip (private) on the left.

67.5 **HAYSTACK (III).** The river bends left around the Flying B Airstrip, then turns right into a 150-yard maze through big boulders and holes. Most of the trouble is on the inside of the curve. Scout from the right. At high water, consider stopping well upstream on the right and hiking over the bluff to scout.

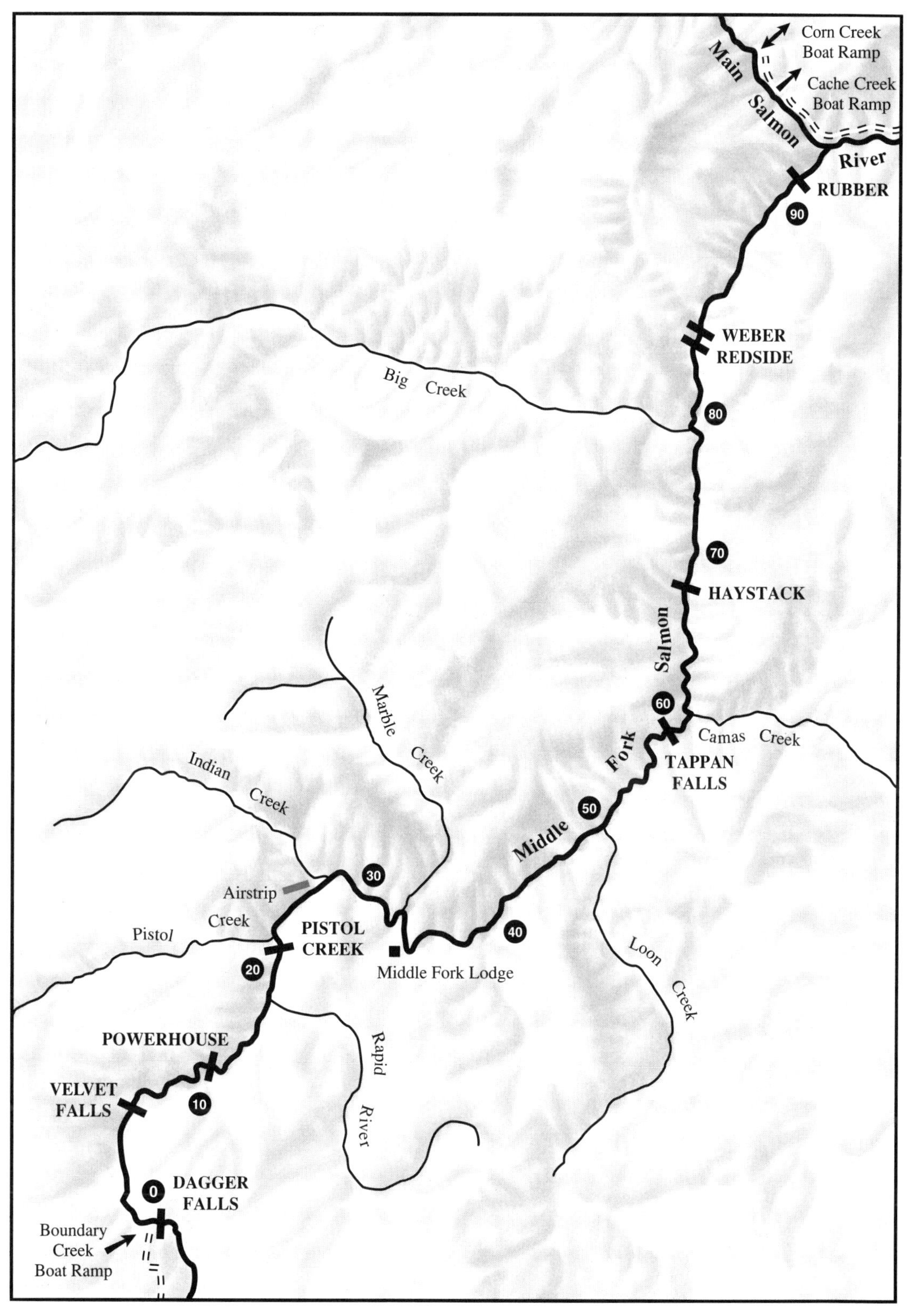

Middle Fork Salmon

67.6 Bernard Creek Guard Station and Airstrip (USFS) on the left, below the mouth of Bernard Creek. Trail up the creek. Bernard Creek and Haystack Rapid mark the beginning of the "Impassable Canyon." The creek was named for Captain Ruben Bernard, who led the Army pursuit in the Sheepeater War.

74.2 Rattlesnake Cave on the right, at the mouth of Rattlesnake Creek. Pictographs on the wall of the shallow cave above the right bank of the creek. Smoke from the fires of earlier campers has damaged the cave paintings, and no camping has been permitted here for years.

77.8 Waterfall Creek Falls cascades into the river (right bank). The Waterfall Trail across its mouth and up the creek can be very dangerous when the creek is high.

78 Big Creek, a major tributary, enters on the left. Boaters have been known to carry hard-shell and inflatable kayaks up the trail along Big Creek to run the Class IV and IV+ drops in its final section. The Middle Fork Trail (right bank) ends here, and the Waterfall Trail leads from river right up a ridge on the right bank of Waterfall Creek.

79.5 Elk Bar, a popular campsite, on the left.

80.3 Veil Falls tumbles into the river from the right. Short hike to the falls and to pictographs in the large cave, referred to as Veil or Cathedral Cave. You may see Indian artifacts around here, but it is illegal—as well as wrong—to remove them.

80.8 **PORCUPINE** (III-). A short drop at the mouth of Wall Creek, which enters on the left. (A few old-timers refer to this rapid as Wall Creek and claim the real Porcupine Rapid is what is now called Redside.)

82.5 **REDSIDE** (III+). At the mouth of Golden Creek, which enters on the left, the river turns sharply right and drops across a ledge divided in midstream by a slope-shouldered boulder. Routes vary with the flow. Scout on the left. The name "Redside" refers to the markings below the gills of cutthroat trout.

82.9 **WEBER** (III+). Another short, sharp drop with a boulder in the middle. Named for a guide who had a less than successful run here. (Some old-timers consider this the real Redside Rapid.) Downstream on the right is Mist Falls. A bit farther, below a Class II rapid, boaters can stop to see pictographs on a sheer rock wall on the left.

86.2 Parrott Placer Mine (right bank). Large campsite. Named for a crotchety hermit who lived in the Impassable Canyon from 1917 to 1942. Remains of his cabin can be seen a mile and a half downstream, near the small left-bank campsite at the mouth of Nugget Creek.

88.5 **UPPER AND LOWER CLIFFSIDE** (III). The first rapid is just below the mouth of Cradle Creek, which enters on the left. The river bends right around a sheer cliff, pauses in a big pool, then curves left through the rock-strewn lower rapid, which has big holes on the right at higher flows.

91.3 **RUBBER** (III+). Just below the mouth of Reese Creek, which enters on the left. A sharp drop among boulders at lower flows; biggest hydraulics on the river at high water.

92.3 **HANCOCK** (III). The river curves right through a rock garden guarded by a big boulder, the "Shark's Fin," in midstream. Several more rapids in the next three miles. A mile downstream is **DEVIL'S TOOTH** (III), and half a mile below that comes **HOUSE ROCK** (III). Both can be tricky. Finally, the whitewater tapers off with **JUMP-OFF** (III-) and **GOAT CREEK** (II+).

96.2 Confluence with the Main Salmon. Stoddard Pack Bridge is about half a mile downstream. In the four miles of the Main Salmon leading to Cache Bar, there are several minor rapids which can develop big waves at high flows.

100 **TAKE-OUT.** Cache Bar Boat Ramp and Campground (right bank). Corn Creek, put-in for the wilderness section of the Main Salmon, is five miles downstream.

Main Salmon River

Corn Creek to Carey Creek, Spring Bar, or Riggins

Difficulty: III. **Gradient:** 12 ft./mi.
Length: 82 miles to Carey Creek, 94 to Spring Bar, 103 to Riggins.
Put-in: Corn Creek Boat Ramp (2,930'), or alternate sites upstream (see essay).
Take-out: Carey Creek Boat Ramp (1,940'), or alternate sites downstream (see **Mile Guide**).
Drainage Area and Average Annual Discharge: 13,550 sq. mi. and 8,300,000 af.
Peak Recorded Flow: 130,000 cfs (June 17, 1974) at White Bird, 30 miles below Riggins.
Season: April–October. Runnable flows but cold weather the rest of the year, and some slush ice in winter. Runoff usually peaks between late May and mid-June, often above 50,000 cfs and sometimes over 90,000.
Recommended Levels: 2,000–25,000 cfs at Corn Creek. The river is never too low for boating. High water begins around 20,000. Extremely powerful above 40,000.
Flow Information: North Fork RD, (208) 865-2383, provides the flow at Corn Creek. Idaho DWR, (208) 327-7865, gives the flow at White Bird, 30 miles below Riggins. No hydrograph available for Corn Creek gauge, but see the White Bird gauge hydrograph in the **Lower Salmon** chapter. This gauge reading includes the South Fork Salmon and Little Salmon, both major tributaries. Flows on the Main Salmon will be somewhat lower.
Special Hazards: Remote area; evacuation could be difficult from some spots.
Permits: Required between Corn Creek and Vinegar Creek (mile 79) June 20—Sept. 7. The Main Salmon application is part of a four-river permit system, along with the Middle Fork Salmon, Selway, and Snake. Request application forms after Oct. 1. Applications accepted Dec. 1–Jan. 31 (fee); lottery in February. About one in 10 applicants gets a launch date in the initial lottery. July is the most popular month. Call after the lottery for unused dates or cancellations, which are more frequent than you might expect. Four non-commercial launches allowed daily. Group limit 30, maximum trip length 10 days.

Lucky or persistent boaters may be able to arrange consecutive permits for a continuous run of some 200 miles down both the Middle Fork and Main Salmon.
Managing Agency: North Fork RD, Salmon NF, P.O. Box 180, North Fork, ID 83466; (208) 865-2383.
Commercial Raft Trips: About 30 outfitters. For a list contact the managing agency.
Land Ownership: Almost all National Forest.
Scenery: Excellent. Deep, rugged canyon.
Solitude: Very good. Some isolated ranches, occasional jet boats.
Wilderness: Yes, except for occasional private ranches. Nearly roadless (see essay). The Main Salmon was added to the National Wild and Scenic Rivers System in 1980, and the surrounding land is part of the Frank Church–River of No Return Wilderness.
Fishing: Generally poor in summer, except for trout in larger side streams. Good steelhead runs October to March.
Wildlife: Abundant in spring.
Water: River not recommended for drinking. Purify water from side streams and/or carry water (available at Corn Creek launch site).
Camping: Excellent on large beaches and bars, except at high flows when many sites are flooded.
Side Hikes: Many excellent USFS trails lead up creeks and ridges.
Guides and References:
- Amaral, *Idaho: The Whitewater State.*
- Moore & McClaran, *Idaho Whitewater.*
- Garren, *Idaho River Tours.*
- Carrey & Conley, *River of No Return.* An excellent river history.

Maps:
- **USGS 7.5':** *Butts Creek Point, Square Top, Waugh Mtn, Devils Teeth Rapids, Arctic Point, Sheep Hill, Hida Point, Whitewater Ranch, Sheepeater Mtn, Fivemile Bar, Mackay Bar, Cottontail Point, Johnson Butte, Carey Dome.*
- **USGS 1:100:** *Bighorn Crags, Elk City, Warren.*
- **USFS:** *The Salmon: A Wild and Scenic River.* Waterproof. Order from North Fork RD.
- **USFS:** *Frank Church–River of No Return Wilderness* (North Half). Order from North Fork RD.

- **USFS:** *Payette NF.* Covers the entire run. Order from Payette NF, P.O. Box 1026, McCall, ID 83638.
- *River of No Return–Waterproof Map & Camp Guide* (Backeddy Books, P.O. Box 301, Cambridge, ID 83610). Similar to USFS Salmon map, but includes river mileages.
- *Riverguide Bandana to the Main Salmon* (Rivers & Mountains). Cloth map.

Auto Shuttle: Long and arduous. 410 miles (9–10 hours) one way to Carey Creek. For references contact Salmon Chamber of Commerce, 200 Main St., Salmon, ID 83467; (208) 756-4935.

Logistics: Two shuttle routes: a northern route through Montana and a southern route through Lowman, Idaho.

To reach the **put-in,** follow U.S. 93 to the wide place in the road called North Fork, 22 miles north of the town of Salmon. Turn west on USFS Road 030, the "Salmon River Road," which crosses the river twice and ends some 45 miles downstream at Corn Creek. The last 30 miles are unpaved, rocky, and rough.

To reach the **take-out** from the put-in via the *northern route,* return to U.S. 93 and drive north to Lolo, Montana. Turn west on U.S. 12, cross back into Idaho, then at Kooskia turn south on Route 13 to Grangeville. Continue south on U.S. 95 to Riggins (a possible take-out). At the south end of town turn east across the Little Salmon River onto USFS Road 103, which leads up the Main Salmon about 10 miles to an alternate take-out, Spring Bar, and a little over 20 miles to the popular take-out at Carey Creek. The *southern route* is more complicated: consult a map, and drive through Stanley and McCall on U.S. 93, take Idaho Highways 75 and 21, USFS Road 528, Idaho Highway 55, and finally U.S. 95 to Riggins, then follow the directions above.

The Main Salmon is a big-water river. Rolling rapids punctuate deep, calm pools which grow longer toward the end of the run. During peak runoff standing waves and holes can become monstrous, and only experienced boaters should attempt the run. Later in the summer, at moderate and lower levels, the Salmon is a perfect introduction to the pleasures of a long wilderness river trip: splashing through big but hardly terrifying rapids, camping on luxurious sandy beaches beside cold green water, perhaps spying bighorn sheep perched on pine-studded granite crags. With no upstream dams to block the movement of sediment, the Main Salmon renews its superb beaches every year. Hot springs, though less numerous than on the Middle Fork, add to the luxury of the trip.

The Salmon, one of the longest undammed rivers in the lower 48 states, is the longest river entirely within a single state. From its headwaters in the mountains of south central Idaho to its confluence with the Snake just below the Washington-Oregon border, the Salmon traces a zig-zag course of over 400 miles.

Rising near Galena Summit in the Sawtooth Range, the Salmon flows north some 175 miles to its confluence with the North Fork at the foot of the Bitterroot Range. Here the river turns west. Boaters who follow it downstream on the run described in this chapter travel through the heart of the largest essentially roadless wilderness in the lower 48 states. Along the way, the Middle and South Forks join the main stem of the river.

The massive Salmon River Canyon, carved in relatively recent geological time—the last one to ten million years—is one of the deepest in North America, measuring over 6,000' from river bottom to the tops of the tallest surrounding peaks. The rugged mountain scenery gradually changes from pine forest, interrupted by somber black granite gorges, to the drier, more open slopes of the high desert.

Some 145 miles below the North Fork, at the confluence with the Little Salmon, the river turns north along the eastern flank of the Seven Devils Mountains. In its lower reaches—below the run described here—the Salmon traverses an arid wilderness canyon on its way to meet the Snake (see the **Lower Salmon** chapter).

Human habitation in the Salmon River area dates back more than 8,000 years. Pictographs—rock paintings—still exist, some from ancient times and others more recent. Those at Legend Creek (mile 4.4) show figures on horseback, so they can hardly be older than the mid-eighteenth century, when horses were introduced to this region. The shadowy prehistoric inhabitants may have been the ancestors of the Northern Shoshone and Nez Perce, who

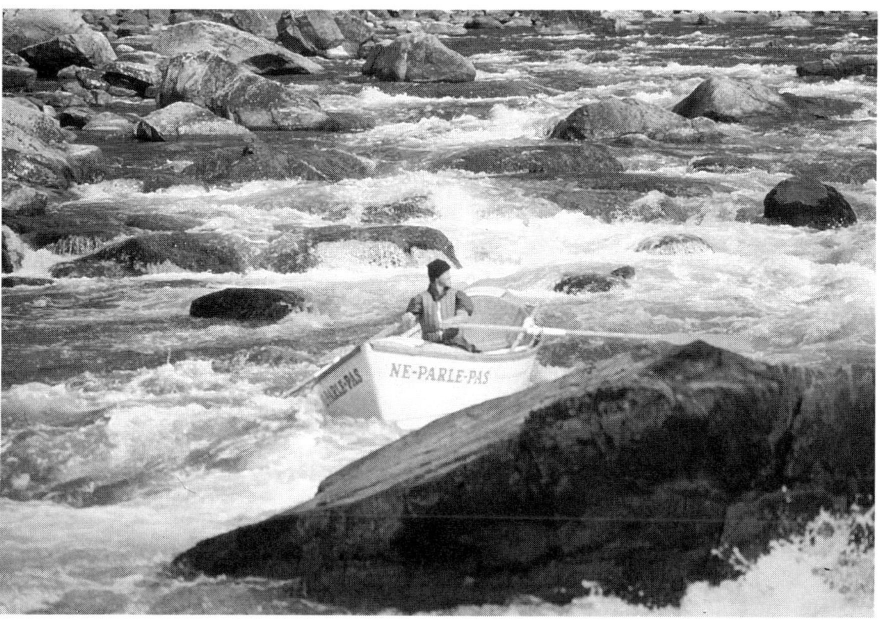

Dory in Growler Rapid, Main Salmon River *Verne Huser*

greeted the first white explorers of the Lewis and Clark expedition.

Despite warnings from the Shoshone that the river could neither be hiked nor navigated in canoes, Clark spent a few days in August 1805 in an attempt to explore the canyon on horseback and foot. Seventeen arduous miles below the North Fork he turned back, and the expedition headed north in search of an alternate route to the Pacific. Today, river runners driving the northern shuttle route across Lost Trail and Lolo Passes retrace almost exactly the path used then by Lewis and Clark.

The Shoshone called the river Tom-Agit-Pah, or "Big Fish Water." Clark named the river in honor of Lewis, his fellow explorer, and bestowed the name "Salmon" on a bountiful side creek. Mapmakers of the period confused matters by calling the main river the Salmon, in addition to showing it flowing in the wrong direction. They eventually got the river turned around, but the name stuck.

Boating on the Salmon goes back a long way. The first known river runners were four Hudson's Bay Company trappers who set off in a small hide canoe in March 1832. Two drowned, and the two survivors had to hike overland to Fort Nez Perce near the Snake-Columbia confluence in Washington, where they arrived "quite naked" a month later. Later in the nineteenth century, river runners shooting the rapids in wooden scows were more successful. Trappers, hunters, prospectors, and eventually a few hardy settlers learned to navigate the Salmon. John McKay, a reclusive Scottish prospector, is said to have floated the river 20 times from 1872 to 1911, building a new boat for each trip. The discovery of gold in the 1860's added impetus to the explorations. As elsewhere in the West, miners used dynamite to ease some of the most difficult passages. Before it was blasted, Salmon Falls—today a Class III rapid—was a major obstacle.[1]

By the turn of the twentieth century, a few pioneering boatmen had learned to make their livings floating hunting parties into the wilderness and hauling supplies downriver to miners and ranchers. For each trip they built heavy wooden scows with huge wooden sweep oars mounted fore and aft. Best known among the early boatmen was Harry "Cap" Guleke, who first ran the river in 1896 and made his last trip in 1937 at the age of 79.[2]

Inflatable boats first ran the Salmon in 1929, but it was after World War II that surplus military rubber rafts transformed river running on the Salmon (as elsewhere). In the 1950's only a handful of people floated the river below Corn Creek. Those numbers grew steadily, from some 300 in 1960, to about 3,000 in 1975, to over 5,000 annually in the early 1990's.

[1]Johnny Carrey's and Cort Conley's book *River of No Return*, which narrates these stories in detail, will enrich any trip down the Salmon. (See **Bibliography**.)

[2]The nickname "River of No Return" first appeared in the 1920's and referred to these early one-way floats in wooden scows. Outfitters still use the name, which also served as the title of a 1954 film starring Marilyn Monroe and Robert Mitchum. The nickname properly refers only to the Main Salmon, although it is sometimes incorrectly applied to the Middle Fork.

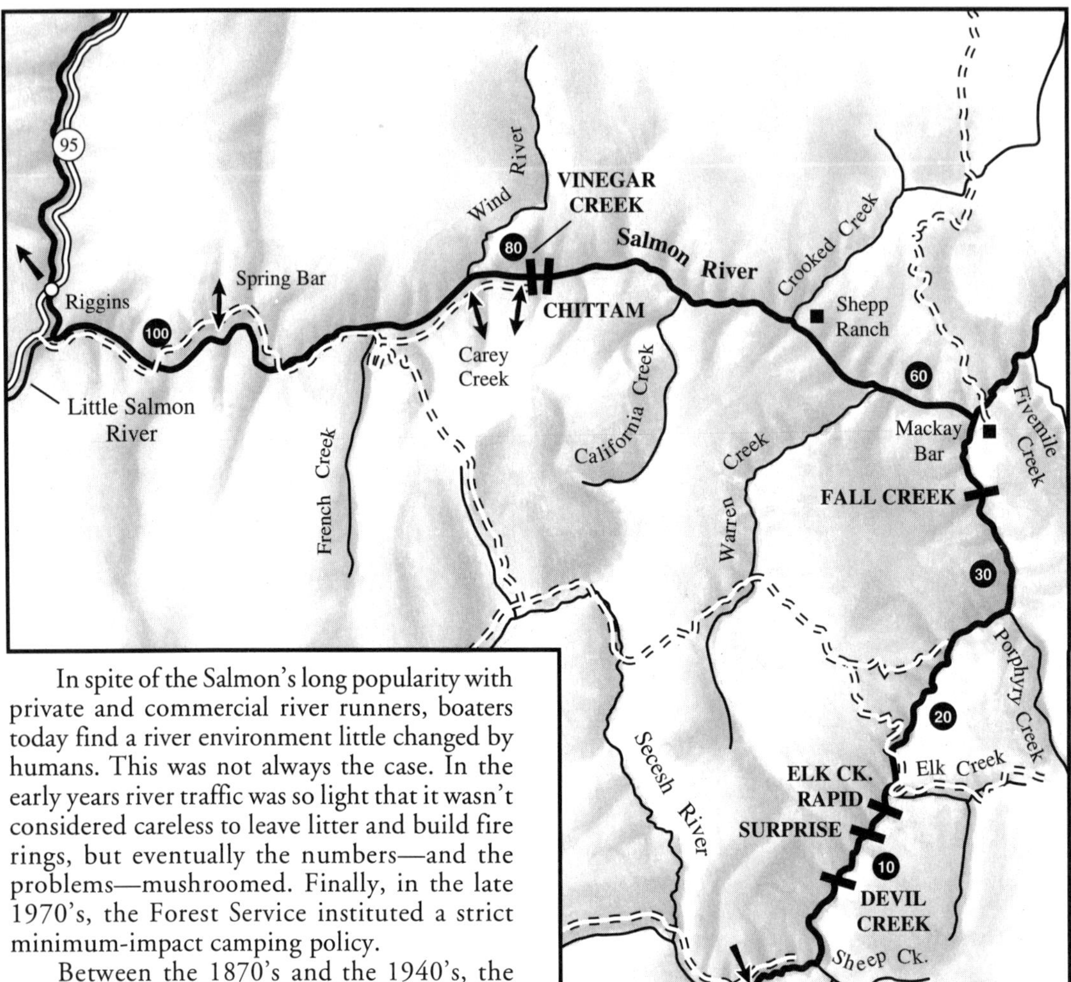

Main Salmon (West) and South Fork Salmon

In spite of the Salmon's long popularity with private and commercial river runners, boaters today find a river environment little changed by humans. This was not always the case. In the early years river traffic was so light that it wasn't considered careless to leave litter and build fire rings, but eventually the numbers—and the problems—mushroomed. Finally, in the late 1970's, the Forest Service instituted a strict minimum-impact camping policy.

Between the 1870's and the 1940's, the Salmon River Canyon was surveyed several times for railroads, roads, and dams. Fortunately, these proposals were deemed impractical and were never realized. Although rough dirt roads lead into the upper and lower reaches of the canyon, the 79-mile central section from Corn Creek to Vinegar Creek remains essentially roadless. Rough tracks reach the river in only two places. The scattered ranches and lodges are generally accessible only by boat, plane, or pack train. Today only an occasional jet boat or bush plane reminds river travelers of the motorized world outside.

The river still has the same relentless force that quickly overwhelmed the earliest explorers. Boaters without the requisite experience and proper equipment should avoid high water, which usually dominates the month of June. Wet suits are strongly recommended at high flows, and it's a good idea to bring one along even in midsummer, since cold rainstorms lasting several days can blow in at any time.

Other Runs

The Main Salmon can be floated above and below the roadless section without a permit. Far upstream near Stanley, more than 150 miles above Corn Creek, is the "Piece of Cake" or "Sunbeam" run, a 13-mile Class III reach from Basin Creek to Torreys Hole. Five miles below Basin Creek is the run's biggest ***HAZARD:*** the old Sunbeam Dam, which was breached in the 1930's to allow fish a passageway. Before you attempt this section, scout the dam carefully from U.S. Highway 93, which follows the left bank. Beware of sharp rocks and

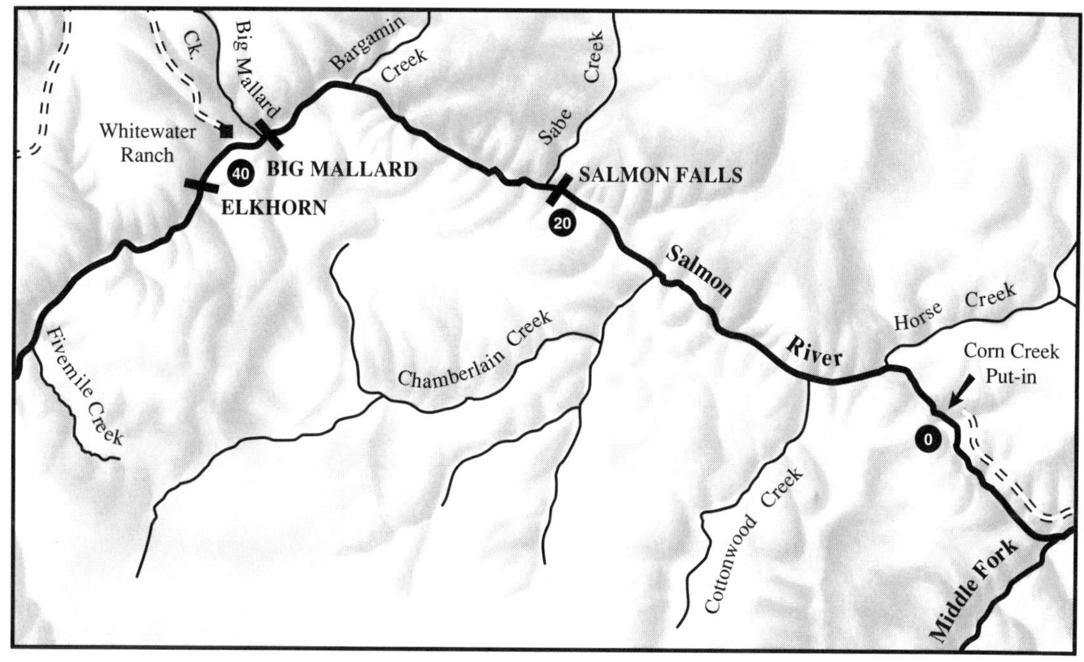

Main Salmon (East)

rebar in the narrow, tricky passage down the right side. To avoid the dam, launch at an access three quarters of a mile downstream.

Then there are the extensions of the Main Salmon run described in this chapter. Not far upstream from Corn Creek, many boaters enjoy a six-mile Class III run from Spring Creek to Panther Creek. The put-in is some 20 miles downriver from North Fork, and the take-out is roughly a dozen miles above the Middle Fork confluence. Boaters can also float the last 21 miles of the Main Salmon run between Carey Creek (mile 82) and Riggins without a permit. (See end of **Mile Guide.**)

Mile by Mile Guide

0 Corn Creek Boat Ramp and USFS check point (right bank). End of the road. Trail follows the right bank to Lantz Bar.

3.5 Horse Creek enters on the right. Campsite. Good side hike. About a mile downstream, look for pictographs on the right bank, above the high-water mark where Legend Creek (often dry) enters on the right.

5.5 Springs on the left at Fern Creek.

8 **RAINIER (III-).** Here boaters may encounter the first big waves of the trip. Rainier Creek enters on the right below the rapid.

11 Lantz Bar, with a USFS Guard Station and campsite on the right. Little Squaw Creek enters on the right (popular side hike). Trail leads downriver to Big Squaw Creek.

13 **DEVIL'S TEETH (III).** Large boulders in the channel. According to legend, pioneering boatman Johnny McKay knocked them out of Satan's mouth with a sweep oar when he met the evil one here. Scout from the left.

15.5 Chamberlain Creek enters on the left. Good side hike.

19.5 Cub Creek enters on the left. Three-mile-long Black Canyon, named for its dark granite walls, begins downstream.

20.5 **SALMON FALLS (III).** Big boulders offer a choice of slots. Scout right. In the early days the rapid—then called "Black Canyon Falls"—was much more difficult, but dynamiting by miners tamed it considerably. Upstream is an old proposed dam site.

21.5 Sabe Creek enters on the right. Good hike.

22.5 Barth Hot Springs, just below Hot Springs Creek on the left. The 134° water bubbles over slippery rocks and is tolerable only when mixed with the cold river. Downstream on the left is a large, popular campsite. The eddy can be tough to catch, especially at high flows.

27 Dillinger Creek on the left. Another old Army Corps dam site.

32 Bargamin Creek (side hike) and Campground on the right. A half mile downstream Bailey Creek enters on the right, just above **BAILEY (III)**.

33.5 Myers Creek and Allison Ranch on the right. Airstrip. A mile downstream is **SPLIT ROCK (III)**.

37 **BIG MALLARD (III+)**. The river swings left into one of the biggest rapids on the trip. Routes vary with the level; at lower flows many run between the left bank and the boulder (hole) blocking the left center of the channel. Stop upstream on the left to scout. Big Mallard Creek enters on the right below the rapid. Good campsites on the right bank above and below the rapid.

39 Whitewater Campground and Whitewater Ranch on the right. Airstrip. Mallard Creek Road, a rough dirt track, leads north to Elk City.

40.5 **ELKHORN (III)** appears as the river bends left. Huge boulder (hole) at the bottom. Approach with caution at high flows. About a mile downstream is **GROWLER (III-)**, named for a bad-tempered hermit who lived in a stone cabin at Slide Creek below the rapid.

42.5 Pack bridge serves Campbell's Ferry Ranch (left bank). Crude airstrip. Hand-hewn log buildings on the right flat were built by miner Jim Moore around the turn of the century. Downstream is **WHIPLASH**, a normally modest rapid that becomes one of the roughest on the river at high flows.

45.5 Lemhi Creek enters on the left. Downstream on the left is Lemhi Bar, a placer claim once worked by Chinese miners.

52.5 Fivemile Creek enters on the left. On the left bank are Buckskin Bill's cabin and lookout tower. Bill, whose real name was Sylvan Hart, retreated here during the depression of the 1930's and stayed until his death in 1982. He grew his own food, made his own clothes, fashioned handmade flintlock rifles, and entertained generations of river travelers with tales of his life and tours of his estate.

55.5 Mackay Bar Bridge. A rough dirt road on the right bank leads north to Dixie.

56 Mackay Bar, on the left, is a staging area for hunting and fishing expeditions. Airstrip. Half a mile downstream, the South Fork Salmon enters on the left.

66 Shepp Ranch, on the right bank upstream from Crooked Creek. Airstrip. A trail follows the right bank down to Sheep Creek.

74 Sheep Creek enters on the right. Trail.

78.5 **CHITTAM (III)**. Just below Chittam Creek, which enters on the right. A rough ride through boulders and holes. The biggest hole is toward the bottom of the rapid, where the current forces boats toward the left wall. More difficult at high flows. Scout right. "Chittam" refers to the bark of the cascara tree, which was used as a laxative.

79 Vinegar Creek Boat Ramp, on the left, is the first possible take-out. Especially popular with jet boaters. Unpaved road from Riggins ends here. Just downstream is **VINEGAR CREEK (III)**, a sharp drop into big waves. Farther downstream the river becomes slower and flatter.

82 Carey Creek Boat Ramp, the most popular **TAKE-OUT**, is on the left just below the Wind River Pack Bridge and the Wind River, which enters on the right. A gravel road follows the next 21 miles from Carey Creek to Riggins, providing frequent access. Some boaters continue 12

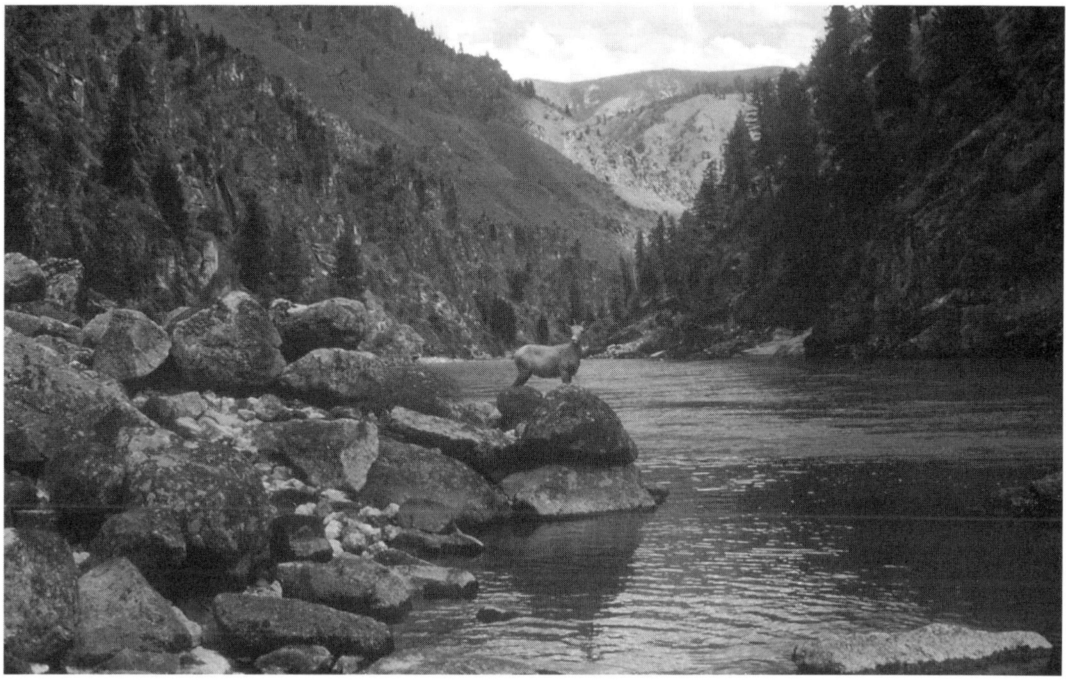

Bighorn sheep on Main Salmon *Bill Cross*

miles to the Spring Bar Boat Ramp (right bank). Others float 10 more miles and take out on the left bank above or in the town of Riggins. The Little Salmon River enters from the left at Riggins.

In this stretch the Salmon is broad and slow, with occasional straightforward Class II and III rapids, notably **RUBY (III)**, about two miles below Spring Bar, and **LAKE CREEK (III-)**, a mile farther downstream where a bridge crosses the river. Beyond Riggins lies the **Lower Salmon** (see that chapter).

I had been in hot water before on river trips, but never quite like this. There we were, a half dozen pink bodies being slowly parboiled in an Avon Adventurer under a star-studded Salmon River sky.

Those were the days before self-bailing rafts, when a boat held water whether you wanted it to or not. We had floated our empty paddle raft under a rivulet of scalding water pouring off the rocks at Barth Hot Springs. As the boat filled with searing spring water, we added a few bailing buckets full of icy snowmelt dipped from the river. In less than fifteen minutes we were soaking in our very own hypalon jacuzzi.

The eddy was big and powerful, and the rocks where we had anchored the bow line were smooth and slippery. Once in a while a big surge swirled through the eddy, and the raft tugged hard at its mooring. We speculated on what would happen if the line slipped off the rocks: we had no paddles and no life jackets, and the boat was swamped with about a ton of hot water. We imagined ourselves being swept down the Salmon River in the middle of the night, stark naked in a steaming, brim-full raft. What a way to go!

The setting seemed complete—as good as it gets—and then, slowly and silently, an enormous full moon lifted over the ridge behind us. Pine trees five miles away suddenly stood out in perfect silhouette. The scene around us came alive as brilliant moonlight sparkled on the waves and shimmered in the wisps of steam curling off the rocks and our bodies.

It was a perfect moment, as flawless and full as any I have known on the river.

—Bill Cross

South Fork Salmon River

Secesh River Confluence to Vinegar Creek, Main Salmon

Difficulty: V (IV at low flows).
Length: 58 miles (36 on South Fork, 22 on Main Salmon). Longer and shorter runs possible.
Gradient: 40 ft/mi. on South Fork.
Put-in: Mouth of Secesh River (3,600').
Take-out: Vinegar Creek Boat Ramp on Main Salmon River (1,960').
Drainage Area and Average Annual Discharge: 1,000 sq. mi. (est.) and 1,200,000 af.
Season: June–early August. The shuttle road is often blocked by snow until mid-June. High water normally lasts through late May and most of June. Wet suits a must.
Recommended Levels: 1,000–4,000 cfs (1.5' to 5') on the Krassel gauge. Minimum 1'. High water begins around 4.5'. Very hazardous above 6'. The gauge is above the confluences with the Secesh and the East Fork of the South Fork, so readings do not include flows of these major tributaries. Our recommendations attempt to take this into account.
Flow Information: Krassel gauge is not on the Idaho flow phone, but readings are usually available from the USFS, (208) 634-0600.
Special Hazards: Extremely difficult at high water. Possible portage at Fall Creek Rapid.
Rafts: Self-bailers strongly recommended.
Permits: Not presently required on the South Fork, but required on the Main Salmon June 20–Sept. 8. As of 1992, boaters are asked to register at a voluntary sign-in box just downstream from the Secesh confluence. Check with the USFS for updated information.
Managing Agency: Krassel RD, Payette NF, P.O. Box 1026, McCall, ID 83638; (208) 634-0600.
Commercial Raft Trips: None at present.
Land Ownership: Mostly National Forest; a few private cabins and ranches.
Scenery: Excellent. Deep, forested canyon.
Solitude: Excellent.
Wilderness: Yes. Only a couple of rough dirt roads reach the river.
Fishing: Good for trout.
Water: Clear and cold. Probably drinkable; purify to be sure. Drinking water is available at Ponderosa Campground (USFS), located along the Secesh on the road to the put-in.
Camping: Good.
Guides and References:
- Amaral, *Idaho: The Whitewater State.*
- Moore & McClaran, *Idaho Whitewater.* Both books have good coverage of this run and runs on upstream tributaries.

Maps:
- **USGS 7.5':** *Williams Peak, Parks Peak, Pilot Peak, Burgdorf Summit, Chicken Peak.*
- **USGS 1:100:** *Warren.* Covers entire run.
- **USFS:** *Payette NF.* Covers entire run.

Auto Shuttle: 100 miles (3 hours) one way. **Contact:** Gravity Sports, (208) 634-8530; Class VI Whitewater, (208) 634-2075; or Canyons, Inc., (208) 634-4303. Contact the managing agency for more references.
Logistics: To reach the **put-in,** drive to McCall (110 miles north of Boise on Idaho Highway 55) and turn east on Lick Creek Road. Continue roughly 35 miles—past Little Payette Lake and Lake Fork Campground, over Lick Creek Summit (6,700') and then down the Secesh River—to the South Fork Salmon. All but the first few miles were unpaved until 1992, when the Forest Service began a three-year project to pave the road. The summit is often blocked by snow until mid-June. Contact the USFS for road conditions and advice on alternate routes.

To reach the **take-out,** return to McCall, drive north 46 miles on Idaho 55 and U.S. 95 to Riggins, then follow directions in **Main Salmon** chapter to Vinegar Creek Boat Ramp or other takeouts above Riggins.

The secret is out: the South Fork Salmon is one of this country's finest expert wilderness runs. For years this Idaho gem was overshadowed by the celebrated Middle Fork and Main Salmon, and none but top kayakers dared to test the South Fork's nearly continuous rapids. Only recently have rafters—usually in self-bailing boats—made this demanding run. Today the river is receiving increasing attention, and the South Fork Salmon is on its way to becoming a whitewater classic. Unlike its famous neighbors, the South Fork is much less frequently boated and currently can be run without a permit.

The South Fork, like the Middle Fork, drains central Idaho's Salmon River Mountains and flows north to feed the Main Salmon. Though the South Fork's watershed is smaller and lies lower than that of the Middle Fork, its forested granite canyon is similar in appearance. The South Fork is roughly equal in size to the Middle Fork above Big Creek and has a similar season. However, the road to the South Fork put-in is usually snowed in a little longer than the Middle Fork road.

Within a mile of the South Fork put-in, three rivers merge: the South Fork of the Salmon, the East Fork of the South Fork, and the Secesh.[1] The East Fork usually carries the most water, the Secesh the least. All three tributaries offer tight, technical advanced and expert runs of their own, many of which could be combined with the run described here for an even longer trip. For more information on these runs, refer to the Idaho guide books listed above.

Below this triple confluence the South Fork enters a remote wilderness canyon where an occasional rough dirt road and a few scattered ranches and cabins are the only evidence of humanity. The scenery is outstanding, wildlife is abundant and varied, and several hot springs offer steamy relief for shivering boaters. Almost all the surrounding land is in Payette National Forest, and for nine miles near the end of the run the South Fork flows through the Frank Church–River of No Return Wilderness. Efforts to protect the entire South Fork canyon as wilderness have met stubborn resistance from logging and mining interests.[2]

The South Fork was once one of the most productive salmon streams in the Northwest, accounting for at least a fifth and possibly as much as half of the Columbia River's total chinook run. Then, in the 1950's and early 60's, the Forest Service permitted widespread logging and road-building on the watershed's steep slopes. Severe erosion of the fragile granitic soils resulted, climaxing during the great flood of December 1964. Sediment loads skyrocketed, and the coarse gravels of the original riverbed were smothered beneath ten to fifteen feet of mud. With the salmon nesting habitat destroyed, the chinook run collapsed. In 1965 the Forest Service placed a moratorium on logging in the basin and began a watershed restoration program. Though the efforts have reduced sediment loads, the salmon fishery has thus far recovered only slightly.

Difficult Class IV and V rapids are scattered throughout the run. The biggest drop, Fall Creek Rapid, comes just a few miles above the Main Salmon confluence. Portages may be necessary at Fall Creek and Devil Creek, but portaging the latter is very tough, especially with rafts. Boaters sometimes divide the run at the South Fork Guard Station (mile 16).

Because of the South Fork's relatively narrow riverbed, the whitewater varies markedly with changes in flow. At low water the river is rocky and technical, mostly Class IV with a few medium Class V's. At high flows the whitewater is huge and nearly continuous, though some rapids develop sneak chutes at these levels. Above 6' on the Krassel gauge, the river is extremely dangerous: enormous hydraulics develop and long, nasty swims become a serious risk. Boaters unfamiliar with the run should make their first trip at levels under 3' on the gauge.

---

[1]Pronounced "SEE-sesh," and named for miners from the Confederate States (secessionists) who once worked claims here. In a battle of words, the name "Yankee Fork" was bestowed on a tributary of the upper Main Salmon.

[2]The USFS has determined that the South Fork Salmon, including the entire run described in this chapter, is eligible for National Wild and Scenic River status.

Mile by Mile Guide

*See map in the **Main Salmon** chapter.*

***Note:** Most of this run's numerous rapids are Class III and IV; only the Class V's are listed in this mile guide.*

0 PUT-IN. Confluence of the Secesh River and the South Fork. The mouth of the East Fork of the South Fork is a mile upstream. A dirt road follows the left bank for the next 3 miles, then a pack trail continues. Put in anywhere between the Secesh and the end of the road.

3 The left bank road ends and steep walls close in for the next 7 miles.

4.5 Sheep Creek enters on the right. Few campsites for the next 5 miles.

8.5 **DEVIL CREEK (V). Recognition:** Watch for a cable crossing about a quarter mile above the rapid. Stop on the left well above Devil Creek, which enters at the rapid as a small waterfall on the left. Use care crossing the creek while scouting. **The rapid:** Big boulders—holes at higher water—litter the channel. In general the best runs are down the right, avoiding bigger drops and a nasty hole on the left. Cliffs on both banks make portaging very difficult. Downstream the gradient steepens; numerous challenging rapids.

10 Good campsites reappear. The trail fords the river, climbs the right bank, and continues downstream high above the river. For the next 6 miles, any emergency hike out should be to the east.

12 **SURPRISE** (V-). Some unexpected rocks and holes wait at the bottom of this long, complex boulder garden, which turns into a collection of big holes at high flows. **Recognition:** Two column-like cliffs rise on either side of the river a few hundred yards above the rapid. These landmarks give the rapid its alternate name, **Citadel**.

14 **ELK CREEK** (V-). The river becomes suspiciously easy just above this very long, two-part rapid. After some lead-in whitewater, the river surges down a narrow drop next to a stairstep cliff on the left, then widens and runs through a gauntlet of big holes. Downstream Elk Creek enters on the right, and a dirt road appears on the right.

16 **RIVER ACCESS** at the bridge where unpaved USFS Road 340 crosses the river, leading west from the left bank to McCall via the ghost town of Warren. South Fork Guard Station (USFS) is above the river on the right. A trail leads downriver high above the left bank; for the next 10 miles, any hike out should be to the west. Downstream the rapids ease for a few miles.

21.5 Foot bridge across the river below Grouse Creek, entering on the right. At a left-hand bend downstream, look for a popular campsite at the top of a large field on the left.

22.5 Emergency river access where a road reaches the left bank at an old bridge site near an abandoned pulp burner. Hettinger Ranch and Airstrip are out of sight above the left bank. Two miles downstream, the South Fork enters the River of No Return Wilderness.

26 Just after Porphyry Creek enters on the right, the trail crosses a foot bridge to the right bank and continues downstream. Downriver the canyon narrows and the whitewater builds.

32 **FALL CREEK** (V–VI), also called **Triple Falls** and **List, Lean, and Fall.** Three big drops in half a mile. **Recognition:** The conservative approach is to stop above the first drop and scout the entire series from the right bank. Watch for a white "eyebrow" formation of rock, which comes into view high on the right canyon wall before the first drop. If necessary, use the right bank trail to portage.

The rapid: The first drop features a large boulder and a big breaking wave on the right. At the second drop boaters generally stay left to avoid a rock in the center and a log jam to the right. In the final section the river churns through a long series of steep chutes and big holes, beginning with a big drop at the top and ending where the current slams into the left wall. Fall Creek Rapid is most difficult at moderately high water. At high flows a sneak chute develops on the right in the third drop.

Downstream, the canyon opens and the rapids ease as the South Fork leaves the River of No Return Wilderness.

34 Badley Ranch Pack Bridge. Badley Ranch is on the left just downstream.

36 Confluence with the Main Salmon. Mackay Bar Resort is less than a half mile up the Main Salmon, with supplies, rough road access and an airstrip. To reach the resort, stop well above the confluence and follow the right bank trail up over a low ridge. The final 22 miles on the Main Salmon to the Vinegar Creek Boat Ramp are relatively flat, but usually go quickly because of the much larger flow. See **Main Salmon** mile guide for details.

"Pool and drop," Rocky Rossi had said on the phone. "It's a classic pool and drop. So bring a 12-foot boat." I heard the message second-hand from Jim Cassady, who left a rambling invitation on my answering machine. The idea was to take a self-bailing SOTAR and a crack paddle crew on what might or might not become the first successful raft descent of the South Fork of Idaho's Salmon River. We would meet five kayakers from Utah and Colorado, including Rocky, who would shoot a video of the trip. Our paddle crew was four seasoned guides—Cassady, Joe Willie Jones, Rene Goddard, and Larry Busby—and me.

Snow was falling on that wet, gray day in early June 1985 when we bounced along a Forest Service road on the way to the South Fork. It was peak runoff time; the Secesh, a major tributary, was roaring toward its confluence with the South Fork like a liquid avalanche. "Maybe this isn't such a good idea," some of us mused out loud.

Then the sun broke through, and we coasted down to the confluence of three magnificent mountain rivers. In the space of a mile, the Secesh, the East Fork of the South Fork, and the South Fork itself join forces in a swollen green current threading through a wonderland of pine and sculpted rock. It was hard to imagine a lovelier spot.

While the kayakers paddled off to wait for us downstream, we suited up and started pumping up the raft. (Cassady, in a burst of good sense, had ignored Rocky's advice and had brought a 14-foot SOTAR.) I was beginning to feel the fear returning when I noticed an aging cowboy astride a little Honda motorcycle coming slowly my way, holding three horses on a leash. He let the Honda's motor die, reached into a pocket of his grimy denim jacket, and lit a cigarette. He let out a lungful of smoke before tilting back the sweat-stained hat on his graying head and offering a "Howdy." We howdied back. "Goin' down the river?" he asked. "Yep," we said. He nodded thoughtfully, drew on his cigarette again, and after a moment added in a noncommittal voice, "Well, it's runnin' a bit high."

Conflicting impulses warred within me as that weather-worn cowboy sucked on his cigarette. One part of me wanted him to tell us how insane we were to launch ourselves on an unknown river at high water without a rescue raft. The other part of me stood cowboy cool, denying the fear that was tying bowlines in my intestines. But he just sat wordlessly on his incongruous little motorcycle while we put in.

The river was an almost eddyless torrent. The gauge above the triple confluence read five and a half feet, over 6,000 cfs. As we sped along downstream, rain-swollen tributaries funneled more water into the river. The rapids merged into a seamless succession of huge holes, mammoth pour-overs, and immense standing waves. On one of many eight-foot drops, a wall of water washed Captain Cassady out of the raft. John Armstrong, a kayaker from Utah, was knocked out of his boat and swam almost a mile before he dragged himself ashore.

On the third morning, someone gently raised the question of "pool and drop." As usual, we had heaved the raft up onto the bank because there was no eddy to tie it in. We were familiar, we said, with the drop. But where was the pool?

As it turned out, the pool was downstream, at the confluence with the Main Salmon. But in between, we faced some very serious drops. In one stretch the gradient averaged 90 feet per mile. Then came the last big rapid, Fall Creek, a half-mile gauntlet of crashing waves, gaping holes, deadly log jams, and seething drops.

Three of the kayakers chose to portage. Armstrong managed to run it by executing a series of amazing braces. Colorado kayaker John Moran punched through the enormous compression wave which recoiled off the cliff at the rapid's entrance and sailed magically into calm water with a triumphant paddle twirl. Under Cassady's direction, we ferried the raft to the opposite bank, lined past the compression wave, and then worked our way back above a giant pyramid rock with a frightening whirlpool hole below it. Expert captaining and a crew driven by fear propelled the boat precisely along the line our captain called, and we squirted out into calm water below the rapid. All that was left was the shrieking and shouting—that and a couple of dozen miles on the broad, bloated Main Salmon.

We couldn't be sure we had made the first successful raft run, but we were fairly confident that no one else had taken a raft all the way down at high water. Self-bailers were just becoming popular, and without one the chance of flips and long, cold, nasty swims seemed too great. In 1986 Rocky Rossi's company, Gravity Sports Films of Salt Lake City, released a video of our South Fork trip entitled "Somewhere in Idaho." (Sad to say, Rocky died that same year.) Just remember that—Rocky's opinion to the contrary—the South Fork drops, but it sure doesn't pool.

—David Bolling. Adapted from an article in ***River Runner*** (now ***Paddler***), July-August 1986.

Lower Salmon River

White Bird to Hellers Bar, Snake River

Difficulty: III (IV above 25,000 cfs).
Length: 73 miles (53 on Salmon, 20 on Snake). Longer and shorter trips possible.
Put-in: Hammer Creek Boat Ramp (1,420').
Take-out: Hellers Bar (820').
Gradient: 10 ft./mi. on Salmon, 4 ft./mi. on Snake.
Drainage Area and Average Annual Discharge: 13,550 sq. mi. and 8,300,000 af.
Peak Recorded Flow: 130,000 cfs at White Bird (June 17, 1974).
Season: May–Oct. Usually peaks late May to mid-June, often above 50,000 cfs. Big water normally extends through June. Low flows of 3,000 to 6,000 late August through winter.
Recommended Levels: 2,000–40,000 cfs. Never too low. High water begins around 25,000.
Flow Information: Idaho DWR, (208) 327-7865.
Special Hazards: High water (Slide Rapid).
Permits: Non-limited self-issue permits at the Hammer Creek and Pine Bar launch sites. Currently, registration is voluntary for the Lower Salmon, but permits are mandatory on the Snake. Contact the BLM for updates.
Managing Agency: BLM, Cottonwood Resource Area, Route 3, Box 181, Cottonwood, ID 83522; (208) 962-3245.
Commercial Raft Trips: For a list, contact BLM or Idaho Outfitters & Guides Assn., P.O. Box 95, Boise, ID 83701; (208) 342-1919.
Land Ownership: Roughly four-fifths public. See BLM map for details.
Solitude: Very good until the Snake, where jet boat traffic is often heavy.
Scenery: Very good. Big desert canyon, few trees.

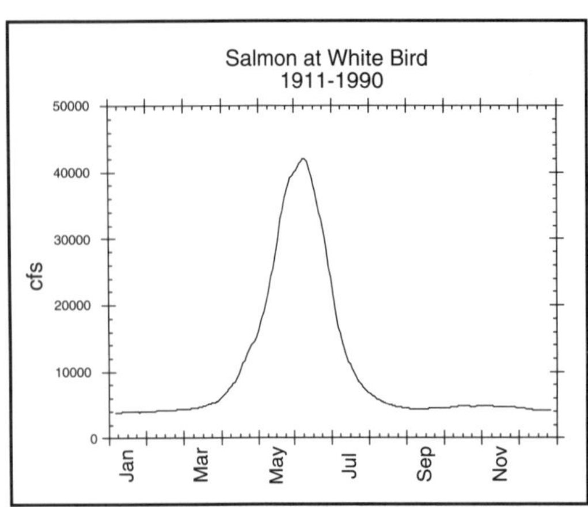

Wilderness: Mostly. A few rough roads.
Fishing: Fair for bass and trout.
Water: Don't drink without purifying. Side streams are scarce, especially late in the season.
Camping: Excellent. Many large beaches, but few trees and little shade. Tarp shelters can help.
Guides and References:

- Moore & McClaran, *Idaho Whitewater.*
- Amaral, *Idaho: The Whitewater State.*
- Garren, *Idaho River Tours.*
- Carrey & Conley, *River of No Return.* River history covers entire Salmon.

Maps:

- **USGS 7.5':** *White Bird, Fenn, Moughmer Point, Boles, Westlake, Hoover Point, Rattlesnake Ridge, Cactus Mtn, Deadhorse Ridge, Wapshilla Creek, Jim Creek Butte, Limekiln Rapids.*
- **USGS 1:100:** *Grangeville, Orofino.*
- **BLM:** *Lower Salmon River Guide,* available from BLM Cottonwood office. Mile guide and strip maps showing access, campsites, and land ownership.
- *Riverguide Bandana to the Snake and Lower Salmon* (Rivers & Mountains). Cloth map.

Auto Shuttle: 125 miles (4 hours) one way. Contact BLM for list of shuttle services.
Logistics: To reach the **put-in** about 90 miles SE of Lewiston, turn west off U.S. 95 a mile south of White Bird and follow signs to Hammer Creek Boat Ramp. Upstream put-ins include Skookumchuck Campground, 4.5 miles south of White Bird, and Slate Creek Boat Ramp, 10 miles south of White Bird.

To reach the **take-out,** take U.S. 95 northwest to Lewiston, turn west on U.S. 12 into Washington, then turn south on Highway 129. From Asotin drive upstream along the road (first paved, then gravel) that follows the Snake roughly 25 miles to Hellers Bar.

To reach **river accesses** at **Pine Bar** (mile 10) and **Rock Creek** (mile 14), follow U.S. 95 to Cottonwood, then drive south 10 miles on a paved and gravel road along Grave Creek and Rock Creek to the river. The road continues 4 miles up the right bank to Pine Bar. The intermediate access at **Eagle Creek** (mile 39) is via a rough dirt road; contact the BLM for directions.

Surrounded by more famous Idaho runs, the Lower Salmon—featuring big, roller-coaster rapids and dramatically desolate scenery—sees relatively little boating, and permits are available for the asking. With typical peak flows in excess of 40,000 cfs, the Lower Salmon provides plenty of big-water action—in fact, more than many boaters can handle. In late summer the river is much tamer and provides a good multi-day trip when many others are too low to float.

The run described here begins some 30 miles below Riggins, the last take-out for the Main Salmon. Between Riggins and White Bird U.S. 95 follows the river, providing frequent access for short floats, even day trips, on this Class II+ to III+ stretch. The Lower Salmon proper lies below White Bird, where the river leaves the highway and curves for some 50 miles through a largely wilderness canyon to its confluence with the Snake at the Oregon-Idaho border.

If hydropower developers had prevailed 30 years ago, 700'-high Nez Perce Dam would now block the Snake a mile below the Salmon confluence, backing water some 60 miles up each river. The Hammer Creek put-in would be under 50 feet of water. Fortunately, the dam was not built, and the Salmon remains one of the longest undammed rivers in the lower 48 states.

The Battle of White Bird

The Lower Salmon's rich history includes one particularly bloody page—the Battle of White Bird, one of the most lopsided Indian victories in U.S. history. In 1877, during the forced relocation of the Nez Perce from their ancestral homelands, fighting broke out not far from the Hammer Creek put-in, near the mouth of what is now known as White Bird Creek. On June 17, some 70 Nez Perce led by 70-year-old Chief White Bird engaged about 100 U.S. troops and volunteers. Firing from high ground, the Indians killed more than a third of their enemies and suffered no losses themselves.

After the battle, the Nez Perce staged a brilliant retreat through Idaho, Wyoming and Montana, eluding the Army for nearly four months. Their dramatic flight included a successful crossing of the Salmon at flood stage near Billy Creek (mile 36) in early July 1877. When General Howard's forces attempted to follow the Nez Perce across the river, the powerful current overwhelmed them. As Howard recounted: "The river here a perfect torrent, lost us our raft, which tumbled down the rapids at a swift rate with all on board, for three or four miles." (See David Lavender, ***Let Me Be Free: The Nez Perce Tragedy****).*

The Battle of White Bird was the last victory for the Nez Perce. Although Chief White Bird and a few others managed to escape to Canada, most of the Nez Perce were captured and sent to a reservation in Oklahoma, where many perished. History buffs may enjoy a side excursion to Nez Perce National Historic Park, a few miles from the Hammer Creek put-in.

Like Hells Canyon of the Snake, the Lower Salmon is a big pool-and-drop river whose difficulty climbs as flows increase. At moderate flows the big waves are exhilarating but relatively forgiving, but above 25,000 cfs the river is solid Class IV. Even hairball boaters should think twice before running above 50,000 cfs, when massive hydraulics and monster waves develop where there are only easy chutes in late summer.

Slide Rapid (mile 49) deserves special mention. Above 25,000 or 30,000 cfs this constricted drop develops enormous hydraulics that can easily flip large rafts. Because this rapid is very difficult to portage, most boaters avoid the lower portion of the run at high water, either by using an alternate upstream take-out or by postponing their trips. At low and moderate flows, Slide Rapid is considerably easier, and Snow Hole Rapid is the biggest challenge on the run.

The Lower Salmon canyon alternates between grassy, open slopes and narrow, brooding gorges of dark basalt. Hot summer days and the rugged terrain discourage side hiking. Once the water warms up in midsummer, most find swimming a more pleasant way to spend the afternoons. Few roads penetrate the canyon below White Bird, and the resulting solitude is one of the run's prime attractions. Jet boats are relatively uncommon on the Lower Salmon, at least until fall. But there is usually heavy jet boat traffic during the 20 miles on the Snake.

Boaters can divide the Lower Salmon into shorter segments by using intermediate accesses at Pine Bar, Rock Creek and Eagle Creek (see **Mile Guide**). Trips of various lengths are possible, including runs as short as one day. The Lower Salmon is sometimes floated in conjunction with part of the Hells Canyon run on the nearby Snake. After running 30 miles of the Snake, boaters make an overland shuttle on a steep gravel road from Pittsburg Landing to White Bird. In this way they can enjoy the greater solitude and more interesting rapids of the Lower Salmon while still ending up at Hellers Bar, the standard take-out for the Hells Canyon run.

Mile by Mile Guide

0 **PUT-IN** on the left bank at Hammer Creek Boat Ramp. Drinking water, camping. File a self-issue permit to float the Snake River, and register (voluntary) to float the Lower Salmon. A poor dirt road follows the right bank for 4 miles.

7 Abandoned cabin marks Shorts Bar (right bank). Pictographs near the downstream end of the bar. Few campsites for the next 5 miles. Below Shorts Bar is the first of five rapids in narrow, three-mile-long **Green Canyon.** The second and fourth rapids, **WRIGHT-WAY** and **DEMON'S DROP,** are moderate Class III's. **PINE BAR (III),** a steep boulder garden, is the last and usually the toughest of the series.

10 Just below Pine Bar Rapid, Pine Bar Recreation Site offers good **RIVER ACCESS** on the right. Boaters can take out here after running Green Canyon, or put in to run the lower river. Gravel road follows the right bank for the next 5 miles.

14 Rock Creek enters on the right. Alternate **RIVER ACCESS.** A road ascends the creek to Cottonwood on U.S. 95.

15 Rice Creek Bridge, where the road leaves the river. Rice Creek enters on the left.

19 The river enters narrow **Cougar Canyon,** a five-mile gorge with many Class II rapids. Near the end of this reach is **BUNG HOLE** (mile 24), where huge waves develop at flows over 15,000 cfs.

25–30 **Snow Hole Canyon** begins just beyond White House Bar, a large camping beach on the right. A series of well-spaced Class III rapids leads to the big drop that gives the canyon its name. First comes an unnamed rapid with a large hole on the right; then **BODACIOUS BOUNCE,** a series of huge, clean haystacks; then **HALF & HALF,** where every other boat is said to be eaten by big holes at the bottom; then **THE GOBBLER,** a straight shot. A little under a mile past Gobbler is the toughest rapid of the series (see below).

29.5 **SNOW HOLE (III+). Recognition:** A smooth rock wall comes into view on the right at the bottom of a Class II chute. Snow Hole Rapid is at the horizon line less than 100 yards downstream. Scout on the left. **The rapid:** House rocks and huge holes. Look for a narrow run just right of center.

32.5 Maloney Creek enters on the right. A mile downstream around a blind left bend is **CHINA (III).** Big holes in the center and right. About two miles downstream is the site of the Nez Perce crossing near Billy Creek (see sidebar).

39 Eagle Creek enters on the right, just below **EAGLE CREEK RAPID (III-).** Possible **RIVER ACCESS** using a rough dirt road that follows the creek out of the canyon. **Take out here to avoid Slide Rapid at higher flows.** A jeep road follows the right bank for the next five miles, serving BLM campgrounds along the river.

44.5 **WAPSHILLA (III),** just above the mouth of Wapshilla Creek on the right.

47.5–53 **Blue Canyon.** Recognize the entrance by spotting a house high on the right bank. Campsites are scarce in this section. At mile 49, just below a power line across the river, lies **SLIDE RAPID,** created around 1950 by a rockslide. Class III at lower flows, but much more difficult above 15,000 cfs as big waves and hydraulics develop. **Above 25,000–30,000 cfs Slide is extremely dangerous and capable of flipping the largest rafts.** Very difficult to portage due to near-vertical walls. Immediately downstream is **SLUICEBOX (III-);** two miles farther comes **CHECKERBOARD (III-).** Just below Checkerboard is the last rapid, **EYE OF THE NEEDLE (III),** with a house rock and big waves.

53 Confluence with the Snake River, which enters from the left. End of Blue Canyon. From here to the Hellers Bar **TAKE-OUT,** boaters must navigate 20 miles of slow water with only a few small rapids and riffles. See the following chapter on **Hells Canyon of the Snake** for details.

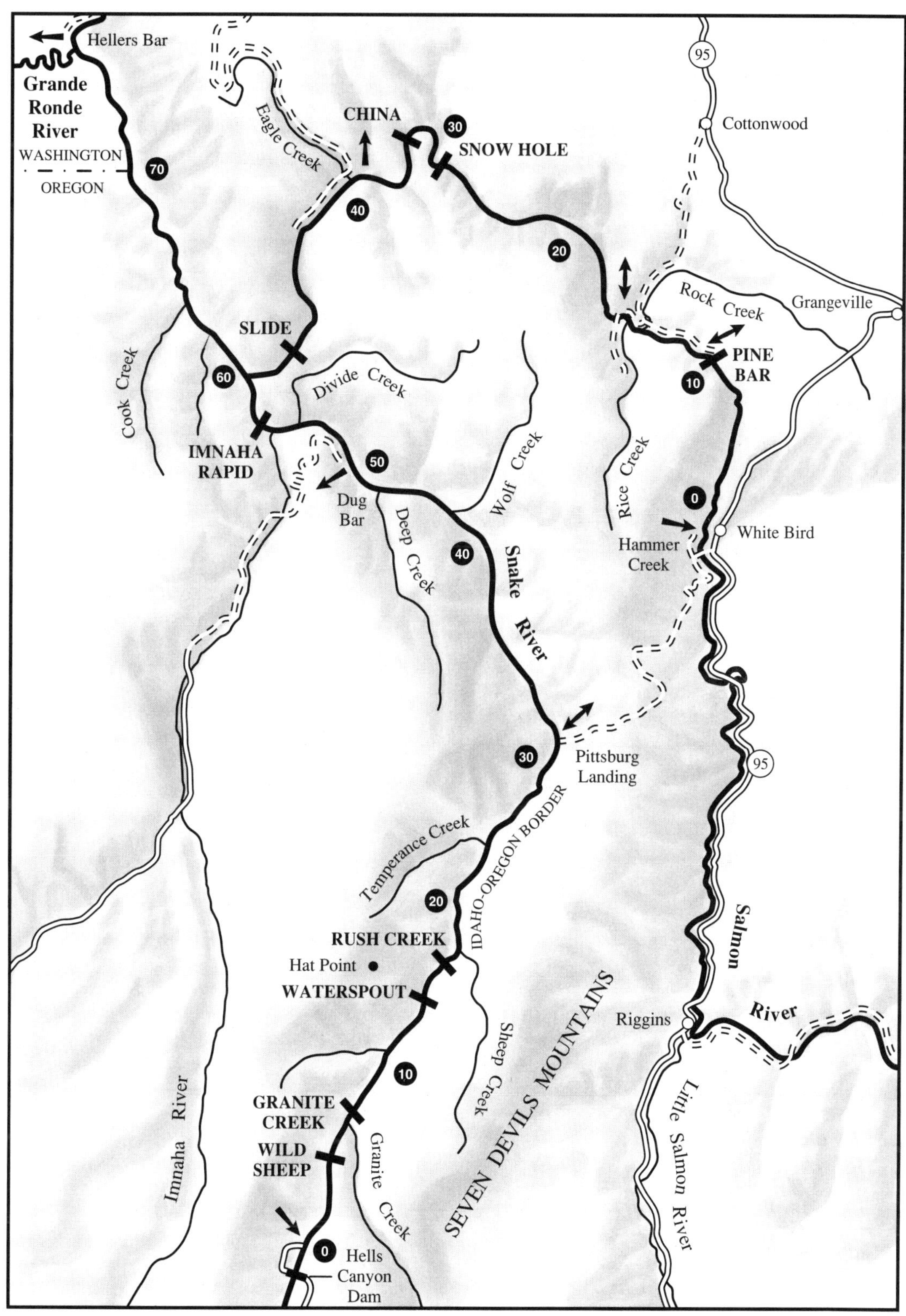

Hells Canyon of the Snake and Lower Salmon

Hells Canyon of the Snake

Hells Canyon Dam to Hellers Bar

Difficulty: III4. **Gradient:** 8 ft./mi.
Length: 79 miles. Shorter trips possible.
Put-in: Hells Canyon Dam (1,470').
Take-out: Hellers Bar (820').
Drainage Area and Average Annual Discharge: 92,960 sq. mi. and 27,500,000 af.
Peak Recorded Flow: 195,000 cfs (June 18, 1974) at Hellers Bar.
Season: April–Nov. Since the upstream dams were built, flows have historically been highest in March and April, tapering off to low levels in late summer. However, releases may be increased in the future to aid salmon runs. For current information, contact the managing agency. Releases from Hells Canyon Dam can fluctuate widely, so camp well above river level and tie boats securely.
Recommended Levels: 5,000–40,000 cfs. High water begins around 30,000. Skilled boaters can run at higher levels, but danger increases. Flows at put-in vary from 5,000 to over 50,000 and average roughly 8,000 to 35,000. At mile 59 the Salmon adds significant volume: 50,000 cfs or more in late spring and early summer.
Flow Information: Idaho Power Co. tape gives the release from Hells Canyon Dam: (800) 521-9102; in Idaho, (800) 422-3143.
Rafts: Large boats (16' and up) at high flows. Afternoon upstream winds can be a problem in the flat lower sections.
Open Canoes: Even experts should think twice before attempting the big rapids at the start of the run. The 47 miles below Pittsburg Landing are good canoeing water, and no advance permit reservations are required.
Permits: Required from Hells Canyon Dam to Rush Creek (mile 16) from the Friday before Memorial Day through Sept. 15. Snake permits are the easiest to get in the four-rivers lottery (which includes the Main and Middle Salmon and the Selway). Apply Dec. 1–Jan. 31; lottery in early February. Odds are best for trips in May or September, worst for July and August. Call for unassigned dates after the lottery. Launch dates must be confirmed by March 15; call for uncomfirmed dates beginning March 16. Group limit 30. Advance permits not required for trips starting at Pittsburg Landing (mile 32).
Managing Agency: Hells Canyon National Recreation Area, P.O. Box 699, Clarkston, WA 99403; (509) 758-1957.
Commercial Raft Trips: Yes. For a list contact Idaho Outfitters & Guides Association, P.O. Box 95, Boise ID 83701; (208) 342-1919.
Land Ownership: Mostly public.
Scenery: Excellent. Massive, arid canyon.
Solitude: Fair. Numerous jet boats, especially below Rush Creek. The lower river is often crowded on summer weekends.
Wilderness: Mostly. A few roads.
Fishing: Good for trout, bass, and catfish; fair for steelhead and salmon. Catch and release for white sturgeon.
Wildlife: Bighorn sheep, elk, bear, eagle, osprey.
Water: Undrinkable. The river gets warm (70°) in summer. Purify water from side streams. No drinking water at the put-in.
Camping: Dam releases have eroded the beaches, so camping is mostly on grassy benches above the river. Beaches reappear below the Salmon confluence. No camping at the Hells Canyon put-in; one night only at Granite and Saddle Creeks. Toilets at some sites. Campfires prohibited July 1–Sept. 15. Because of fluctuating flows, camp high above the river.
Side Hikes: Several trails follow the river and climb side creeks (Granite Creek is a favorite).
Side Excursions: Many in Hells Canyon NRA, including Hat Point, which overlooks the river on the Oregon side.
Guides and References:

- **USFS:** *The Wild and Scenic Snake River.* Excellent map-guide on water-resistant paper. Order from NRA in Clarkston.
- Garren, *Idaho River Tours* or *Oregon River Tours.* (Same write-up in both books.)
- Amaral, *Idaho: The Whitewater State.*
- Moore & McClaran, *Idaho Whitewater.*
- Quinn, *Hells Canyon of the Snake River.* Wire-bound strip maps.
- *Riverguide Bandana to the Snake and Lower Salmon.* (Rivers & Mountains). Cloth map.
- Carrey, Conley, & Barton, *Snake River of Hells Canyon.* Excellent guide to local history.
- Palmer, *The Snake River: Window to the West.* Politics, conservation, personal essays; includes a chapter on Hells Canyon.

• Ashworth, *Hells Canyon: The Deepest Gorge on Earth.* Conservation history.

Maps: USGS 7.5': Not recommended (more than 10 sheets necessary).
• **USGS 1:100:** *Riggins, Grangeville.*
• *Hells Canyon National Recreation Area.* Order from managing agency.

Auto Shuttle: 280 miles (8 hours) one way. For references contact Hells Canyon NRA.

Logistics: The primary **put-in** is just below Hells Canyon Dam on the Idaho-Oregon border, some 22 miles north of Copperfield, Oregon via Idaho Highway 71. Two alternate shuttle routes lead from here to the Hellers Bar **take-out.** The longer paved route (280 miles one way) skirts the canyon on the Idaho side: south on Idaho 71 to Cambridge, north on U.S. 95 to Lewiston, south on Washington 129 to Asotin, then upriver on the paved and gravel road along the Snake some 24 miles to the Hellers Bar or Grande Ronde boat ramps. A shorter summer-only route (190 miles one way) skirts the canyon on the Oregon side: south on Idaho 71 to Copperfield, southwest 7 miles on Oregon 86, north on Wallowa Mountain Loop Road (USFS Road 39), west on Oregon 350 to Joseph, north on Oregon 82 to Enterprise, north on Oregon 3 and Washington 129 to Asotin, then upriver to Hellers Bar (see above).

To reach the **alternate access at Pittsburg Landing** (mile 32), follow U.S. 95 to White Bird, Idaho, turn west, cross the Salmon, and follow USFS Road 493 18 miles to the Snake. This route is also used by boaters who leave the Snake at Pittsburg Landing and shift their float to the Lower Salmon.

To reach the **alternate access at Dug Bar** (mile 51), follow the directions above for the Oregon route from Hells Canyon Dam to Hellers Bar—but instead of turning west on Highway 350 to Joseph, turn east and drive to Imnaha, then continue down the Imnaha River another 25 miles to the Snake.

In Nez Perce mythology, Coyote dug the great chasm of the Snake in a single day to protect the people on the west side of the river from the Seven Devils, a band of evil spirits dwelling in the towering mountain range just to the east. That single day symbolizes the geological blink of an eye in which the river carved most of Hells Canyon, by some measurements the deepest gorge in North America.

Until a million years ago or so, the Owyhee Mountains acted as a natural dam between the ancient Snake and its modern outlet to the Columbia, holding back the river as a vast freshwater lake in what is now southwestern Idaho. When it finally breached this barrier the Snake roared northward, cutting a new canyon and briefly creating what must have been the wildest whitewater in the world.

Hells Canyon[1] is one of the most imposing river canyons in the West. The gorge, roughly ten miles across, is not as sudden or dramatic as the Grand Canyon, and the rim peaks are rarely visible from the river. But when these heights do come into view, the sense of depth is tremendous. The Snake lies,on the average, 5,500' below the nearby ridges. He Devil Mountain, tallest of the Seven Devils at 9,393', towers some 8,000' above the river near the put-in.

The river itself is on a scale in keeping with this monumental landscape. At the put-in below Hells Canyon Dam, the Snake is already the biggest river in this book, with twice the average flow of the Salmon and considerably more water than the Colorado in Grand Canyon. Sixty miles downstream the Salmon joins the Snake at one of the most majestic confluences in the West, bringing the total flow to an average of 35,000 cfs, and often over 100,000 when the Salmon is high. (Before dams tamed the Snake, the combined flow at peak runoff sometimes topped 200,000 cfs.) Below Hells Canyon the Clearwater and other rivers swell the Snake even further; by the end of its journey the Snake is the largest tributary of the Columbia, with a drainage area roughly the size of Oregon.

The Hells Canyon area was once home to Shoshone and Nez Perce. In the late nineteenth century white settlers drove the Indians out and began ranching and mining in the canyon. Today, boaters can explore archaeological sites and old homesteads, all part of the canyon's rich, colorful history.

[1]The river's name is probably due to white explorers who misinterpreted as "snake" the sign made by the Shoshone, who identified themselves in sign language by moving the hand in a swimming motion, signifying that they lived near the river with many fish. The name "Hells Canyon," in use since the 1950's, is borrowed from Hells Canyon Creek, which enters the river at the put-in. In the old days this section was known as Snake River Canyon or Box Canyon, though a few local boosters liked to call it the "Grand Canyon of the Snake." This and other historical information can be found in William Ashworth, *Hells Canyon* (see **Bibliography**).

HELLS CANYON OF THE SNAKE

The Snake's sheer size was enough to convince early explorers that it must offer the hoped-for freshwater passage to the Pacific. In its most easily scouted reaches—above and below Hells Canyon—the Snake was for the most part placid and well suited for canoes and barges. Unfortunately for these flatwater paddlers, the less visible sections, including Hells Canyon, boasted some of the West's roughest rapids. Some old-timers claim that the undammed Snake was tougher than the Grand Canyon. In a little over 15 miles, river runners faced six major rapids, including two—Squaw Creek and Buck Creek—that pioneer boater and mapmaker Les Jones rated 9 on the 10-point Western Scale. (Jones rated Lava Falls on the Colorado a 10.)

But the same characteristics that gave the Snake great whitewater—big volume, good gradient, and a narrow canyon—proved irresistible to hydropower developers. In the 1950's the Idaho Power Company buried over 100 miles of river and all but two of the biggest rapids beneath the slack waters of Brownlee, Oxbow, and Hells Canyon Reservoirs. Then two utilities and the Department of the Interior proposed still more dams, including the notorious Nez Perce Dam. At its projected site a mile below the Snake-Salmon confluence, this 700'-high behemoth would have flooded the lower 60 miles of the Salmon and an equal distance on the Snake. Its reservoir would have extended all the way to the base of Hells Canyon Dam.

In 1967 the U.S. Supreme Court, guided by Justice William O. Douglas, stunned dam builders with a landmark conservation decision. The court ordered the government to consider not just the three competing dam proposals, but also a fourth alternative, at that time almost unthinkable: that the public interest might best be served by no dams at all. In the end, none of the dams was built. In 1975 a citizens' movement won National Wild and Scenic River designation for 68 miles of the Snake and National Recreation Area status for over 600,000 acres of adjacent land. Recently there has been talk of making Hells Canyon a national park.[2]

Trips down Hells Canyon start out with a bang, then ease into a long, lazy float. Though it has only two major rapids, the river should be treated with respect, especially at high flows. Boaters have only five miles to warm up for Wild Sheep and Granite Creek, the remaining two of the original six big drops. At high flows these rapids, if misjudged, can flip the largest rafts. Those with lightweight craft can portage these drops. After this brief climax, the remaining 71 miles are mostly serene afterglow—save for the jet boats roaring through the canyon with loads of sightseers.[3]

Steamboat on the Snake

The first verifiable descent of Hells Canyon stands out as one of the most implausible and remarkable river trips ever undertaken. In 1869 the owners of the 136' steamboat ***Shoshone,*** *frustrated by her unprofitable operation on the Snake near Boise, determined to have the ship brought downstream to more lucrative territory near Lewiston. On April 20, 1870, veteran steamboat captain Sebastian Miller piloted the 300-ton sternwheeler over the lip of Hells Canyon's first big drop. By the time she reached the pool below she was eight feet shorter and missing her paddle wheel but, remarkably, still afloat and capable of being repaired. Seven days later the* ***Shoshone*** *steamed into Lewiston, having successfully run every major drop in the canyon at spring high water.*

Seven years later the Snake witnessed another remarkable feat of navigation, when Chief Joseph and his large band of Nez Perce crossed the river near Dug Bar (mile 51). In mid-May the Indians were ordered to leave their ancestral lands in the Wallowa Valley in northeastern Oregon and relocate to a reservation on the Clearwater River in Idaho. Joseph's pleas for more time fell on deaf ears, so his people were forced to cross both the Snake and Salmon at spring flood. On the Oregon side the Nez Perce constructed boats out of animal skins to ferry the old, young, infirm, and all the tribe's possessions and provisions across to Idaho. Although many horses and cattle were swept downstream and drowned, no human lives were lost. Today a Forest Service sign commemorates the site (see **Mile Guide***).*

[2]Nevertheless, hydro developers continued to push for dams on the unprotected lower reaches of the Snake near the end of Hells Canyon. Fortunately, Congress passed legislation in 1988 prohibiting dams on this stretch.

[3]Under the canyon's controversial management policy, downriver floaters must compete for a limited number of permits, while power boaters ply these waters under unlimited self-issue permits. As a result, jet boat traffic has tripled in the past decade and continues to increase, while the number of non-motorized users holds relatively steady. Recently the Forest Service has proposed a limit on the growth of jet boat traffic.

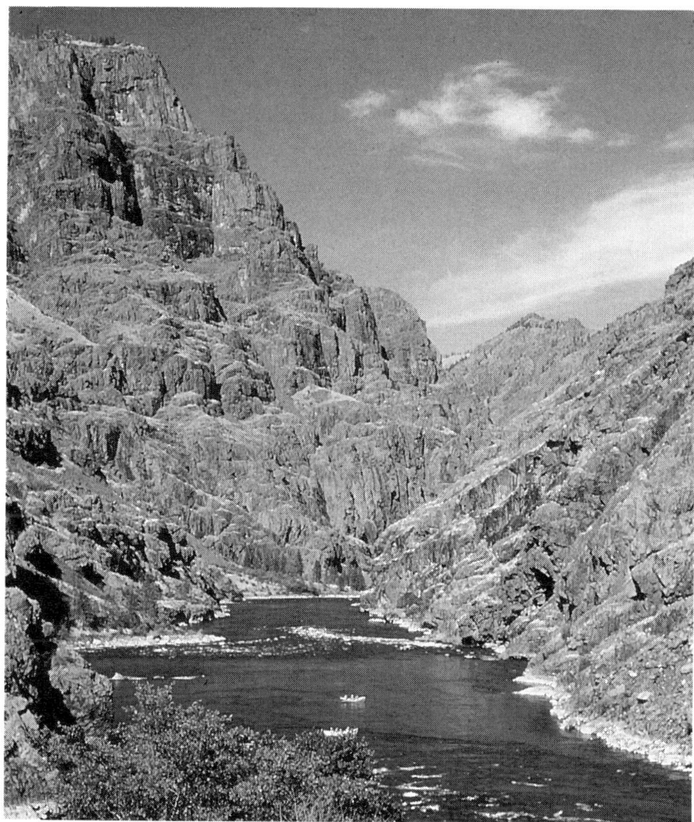

Hells Canyon of the Snake *Bill Cross*

To avoid the slower water and occasional crowds of the lower canyon, many boaters take out at Pittsburg Landing (mile 32). Roughly half of all float trips end here. Some switch their trips to the Lower Salmon at this point, making a short overland shuttle and then running down the Salmon to its confluence with the Snake. This itinerary offers more whitewater than the straight Hells Canyon float and still ends at the standard Hellers Bar take-out on the Snake (see **Lower Salmon** chapter).

Those continuing down the Snake below Pittsburg Landing should float early in the day to avoid the strong upstream winds which often develop in the afternoon.

Mile by Mile Guide

See map just before this chapter.

0 Hells Canyon Creek **PUT-IN** on the left bank, about three quarters of a mile below the dam. No overnight camping. Several Class II rapids in the first 5 miles.

5 Battle Creek enters on the left. Historic Barton Cabin is just above the creek. A trail begins to parallel the left bank, often high above the river.

5.8 **WILD SHEEP** (IV). Downstream from Wild Sheep Creek, which enters on the left. Scout from left-bank trail. Several routes (depending on flow), but all must contend with a big hole (rocks at low flows) at the top center and big diagonal waves at the bottom. More difficult at higher flows.

7.3 Granite Creek enters on the right. Good campsites (one night only). A steep trail climbs the creek into the Seven Devils Mountains. Another follows the right bank to Pittsburg Landing (mile 32).

7.8 **GRANITE CREEK** (IV) where Cache Creek enters on the left. A massive hole (boulder at low flows) blocks the center. Boats can skirt it on either side, but the left run is more common. More difficult at higher flows; **Class V above 50,000 cfs.** Scout right. Pictographs can be found above the trail near the scouting site. Several moderate rapids in the next ten miles, followed by milder water.

11 Saddle Creek enters on the left. Trail up the creek. Good campsite (one night only). A mile downstream Bernard Creek (good hike) enters on the right at **BERNARD CREEK RAPID** (II+), followed by **NO-NAME** or **LOWER BERNARD** (III).

13.5 **WATERSPOUT** (III), where Waterspout Creek enters on the left. Scout left. More difficult at lower flows, when a boulder blocks the channel and a big wave develops.

15.5 **RUSH CREEK (III).** Located where Rush Creek enters on the left, just below a Class II+ rapid. Watch for a big rock/hole at the top center. More difficult at higher flows. Downstream on the right is Johnson Bar, one of the few flat spots in the canyon. Jet boats are more common below this point. Many Class II rapids from here to Pittsburg Landing.

17.5 Sheep Creek enters on the right, just below a Class II rapid. Trail up the creek. Below this point navigation markers indicate miles from the river's mouth.

23 Temperance Creek enters on the left near a private ranch. Trail up the creek. Just upstream on the right is Big Bar, a large flat with a rough airstrip.

26 Kirkwood Creek and Kirkwood Historic Ranch on the right (drinking water, emergency help, radio phone). Boaters can tour a small museum at this 1930's-era homestead. A mile and a half downstream, Kirby Creek enters on the right, adjacent to the private Kirby Creek Resort.

32 Lower Pittsburg Landing on the right bank. **RIVER ACCESS.** Improvements planned for this site in the early 1990's include piped water and campsites. Downstream is mostly flatwater. Many trips take out here or shift to the Lower Salmon.

33 Pleasant Valley, an open area on the right bank. River access on the right just below a Class II rapid. Downstream the canyon narrows, marking the site of the proposed 1950's-era Pleasant Valley Dam, which would have flooded the Snake all the way back to the put-in.

41.5 Copper Creek Resort (private) on the left (radio phone). A mile and a half downstream, Wolf Creek enters on the right.

48 Deep Creek enters on the left. Site of an 1887 massacre of 31 Chinese gold miners by thieves looking for a rumored stash. The white perpetrators were set free by a local jury.

50.5 A sign marks the site where Chief Joseph and the Nez Perce forded the Snake at high water in the spring of 1877. Just downstream is a the lightly-used Dug Bar **RIVER ACCESS** on the left. A rough dirt road leads to Enterprise, Oregon.

55 Imnaha River enters on the left. Just above the confluence is the Mountain Chief Mine tunnel, which runs 600' through the ridge between the two rivers. Below the confluence is **IMNAHA (III).** Below the rapid on the left is Eureka Bar, site of intense mining activity in the early 1900's; today, only the mill's foundations remain. From here to the take-out there are only a few Class II and II+ rapids.

57.5 Paint high on the canyon wall marks the site of the once-proposed High Mountain Sheep Dam. Plans included automated fish tramways to lift migrating salmon over the 670' barrier.

58.5 Confluence with the Salmon River, which enters on the right. Downstream the gradient drops to 4 ft./mi.

60 Paint marks the site of the once-proposed Nez Perce Dam. Flatwater next 7 miles.

67 Wallowa Whitman National Forest ends on the left. A mile downstream the river splits twice around Cochran Islands. Until recently, the left bank from mile 67 to the take-out at mile 78 was mostly private land. In 1992 the Riverlands Conservancy of Portland and the Trust for Public Land purchased some 8,500 acres on this bank, then transferred the land to the USFS and BLM.

71 Oregon-Washington border on the left. About two miles downstream is Class II+ **WILD GOOSE.** A large iron ring on the left bank above the rapid was used by the 125' river steamer *Imnaha* to winch her way upstream on her run from Lewiston to Eureka Bar. The *Imnaha* was launched in June 1903 and sank the following November some 20 miles upstream.

78 The Grande Ronde River enters on the left. Just downstream is the **TAKE-OUT** at the Grande Ronde or Hellers Bar boat ramps on the left.

Selway River

Paradise to Race Creek

Difficulty: IV. **Gradient:** 28 ft./mi.
Length: 47 miles.
Put-in: Paradise Launch Site (3,050').
Take-out: Race Creek Campground (1,725').
Drainage Area and Average Annual Discharge: 1,910 sq. mi. and 2,760,000 af.
Peak Recorded Flow: 48,900 cfs at Lowell (May 29, 1948).
Season: May–July. Usually peaks between mid-May and mid-June. Most boating is after peak runoff. Before peak, weather and water can be dangerously cold, and the put-in road is often blocked by snow. Usually too low by early August, but in wet years boats can scrape down after the permit season ends July 31.
Recommended Levels: 800–3,000 cfs at Paradise. At moderate levels, flows at Paradise are roughly a quarter to a fifth of flows at the take-out. At higher flows boaters face very big water below Moose Creek (mile 26).
Flow Information: Idaho DWR tape, (208) 327-7865, gives Lowell flow in cfs. USFS, (406) 821-3269, gives Paradise flow in feet. Conversion table below gives a rough correlation between the Paradise and Lowell gauges.
Special Hazards: High water; rapid changes in flow; cold water and weather; logs; remote canyon. The rapids below Moose Creek become nearly continuous at high water, so a mishap could lead to a long, nasty swim.

Paradise Gauge Feet	Paradise Gauge Cfs	Lowell Gauge Cfs
1.0	860	1,000
1.5	990	3,000
2.0	1,140	5,000
2.5	1,470	7,500
3.0	1,610	8,750
3.5	2,000	10,750
4.0	2,430	12,500
4.5	2,905	14,750
5.0	3,410	16,300
5.5	3,965	18,000
6.0	4,560	20,300
7.0	5,845	24,250
8.0	7,685	28,000

Permits: Required May 15–July 31; perhaps the most difficult to obtain in the nation. Roughly 2,000 applications for 62 non-commercial launches (overall odds 30 to 1). Competition is heaviest for the last week of June and the first three weeks of July. The Selway is part of the Idaho four-river permit system. Request application forms after Oct. 1, apply Dec. 1–Jan. 31 (fee). Call after the lottery for unused dates or cancellations. Maximum group size 16. In especially dry or wet years, boaters can run before or after the permit period.
Managing Agency: West Fork RD, Bitterroot NF, 6735 West Fork Rd., Darby, MT 59829; (406) 821-3269.
Commercial Raft Trips: Three outfitters. Only 16 trips per season, usually booked well in advance. Contact the USFS for a list.
Land Ownership: Almost all National Forest.
Scenery: Excellent. Heavily forested canyon.
Solitude: Unsurpassed. With only one launch allowed per day, it's possible to float the entire run without seeing any other boaters.
Wilderness: Yes. A few private ranches.
Fishing: Excellent for trout (cutthroat and rainbow), whitefish.
Wildlife: Abundant. Black bear, deer, osprey, moose, bighorn sheep.
Water: Cold and clear.
Camping: Very good; better as you move downstream. Many beaches are flooded at high water.

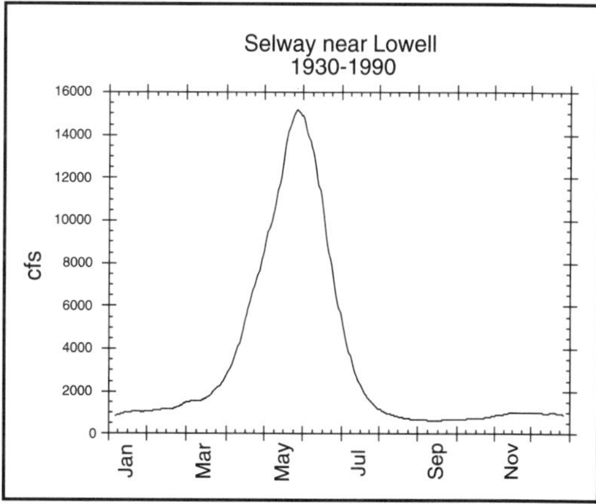

Side Hikes: A USFS trail follows the run, often near the bank, sometimes well above the river. Many other trails climb creeks and ridges.
Side Excursions: Selway Falls, a mile below the take-out.
Guides and References:
- **USFS:** *Floating the Wild Selway.* Water-resistant map-guide. Order from West Fork RD.
- Moore & McClaran, *Idaho Whitewater.*
- Amaral, *Idaho: The Whitewater State.*
- Garren, *Idaho River Tours.*

Maps: USGS 7.5': *Burnt Strip Mtn, Spot Mtn, Gardiner Peak, Dog Creek, Moose Ridge, Mink Peak, Fog Mtn, Selway Falls.*
- **USGS 1:100:** *Nez Perce Pass, Hamilton, Kooskia.*
- **USFS:** *Selway-Bitterroot Wilderness.* Covers entire run. Order from West Fork RD.
- **USFS:** *Bitterroot NF* and *Nez Perce NF.*

Auto Shuttle: About 275 miles (6–7 hours) one way. Contact West Fork RD for a list of shuttle services.
Logistics: The preferred shuttle is via U.S. 12 and U.S. 93, which skirt the north and east flanks of the Selway-Bitterroot Wilderness. To reach the **put-in** from Conner, Montana (a few miles south of Darby and a little over 60 miles south of Missoula), turn off U.S. 93 onto Road 473 ("West Fork Road"). Drive about 12 miles to the West Fork Ranger Station. Half a mile beyond the station, turn right onto USFS Road 468 and climb 16 miles to Nez Perce Pass (6,588') on the Idaho-Montana border. (The pass can be blocked by snow as late as mid-June; call the Forest Service for road conditions.) From the pass descend 15 miles to the Selway, turn right on USFS Road 6223, and drive some 15 miles downstream to the Paradise put-in.

To reach the **take-out** from Conner, drive north about 60 miles on U.S. 93 to Lolo, Montana, then west 113 miles on U.S. 12 to Lowell, Idaho. In Lowell turn left off U.S. 12, cross the Lochsa, and follow USFS Road 223 (first paved, then gravel) up the Selway 20 miles to the take-out just below Race Creek Campground.

A trip down Idaho's Selway is one of the rarest, purest, most exhilarating river experiences in the West. The Selway is the least often run of the nation's famous wilderness rivers, due to a Forest Service policy that permits fewer than 1,300 boaters to float the river each year. With only one launch allowed per day, the fortunate few who obtain private permits or places on a commercial trip are guaranteed one of the most pristine river journeys anywhere. You may see more bears than other boaters.

The Selway[1] is actually the southern branch of the Middle Fork of the Clearwater, one of Central Idaho's largest rivers. From 9,000' headwaters in the Bitterroot Range, the Selway flows north and then west to Lowell, Idaho, where it merges with its sister stream, the Lochsa, to form the Middle Fork Clearwater. In its 90-mile journey the Selway is joined by dozens of tributaries carrying abundant runoff from the wet western slope of the Bitterroots.

Though it begins on a ridge just seven miles north of the Main Salmon's Corn Creek put-in, the Selway has little in common with its giant neighbor. The Selway's lush, intimate canyon and short, intense season contrast with the Main Salmon's more open landscape and reliable summer-long flows. Heavy precipitation in the Selway drainage produces a thick, dark green mantle of fir, hemlock, cedar, and pine. Patches of newer growth show the traces of wildfires that periodically strike the canyon. The watershed's luxuriant vegetation and clean granite soils filter the heavy runoff, keeping the Selway pure and clear.

The Selway cuts through the heart of the vast Selway-Bitterroot Wilderness, which has protected the river canyon since 1936. The river's headwaters lie within the adjoining Frank Church-River of No Return Wilderness, and the Selway itself is a charter member (1968) of the National Wild and Scenic Rivers Sytem. The 47-mile run described here remains virtually untouched by civilization. The river teems with fish, wildlife is remarkably abundant, crystalline side creeks appear at every turn, and graceful, aromatic old-growth cedars shade beaches of clean, white sand.

Floats begin at Paradise Launch Site, just 32 miles from the headwaters. Here the Selway

[1]Academic authorities say the river is named for Thomas Selway, who ran sheep in the area near the turn of the century. Local river runners claim that Selway derives from the Nez Perce word "Sal-wah," meaning "smooth water" or "easy canoeing water." (Those hotshot Nez Perce—always underrating rivers!)

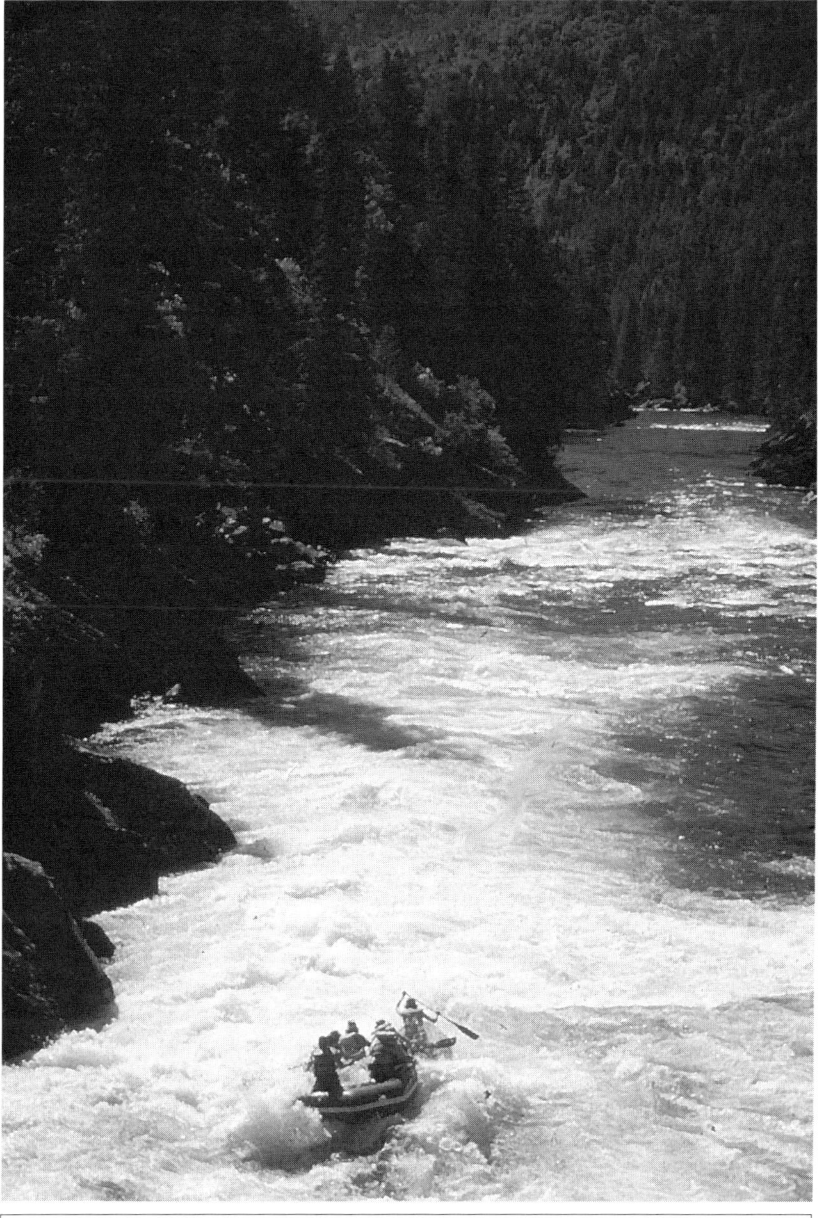

Wolf Creek Rapid, Selway River *Jock Montgomery*

is an icy flow of fresh snowmelt, its waters hardly warmed in their brief journey down the north-facing upper canyon. From Paradise the Selway runs north for 25 miles to meet its largest tributary, Moose Creek, then turns west and churns with increased power through rock-strewn rapids. Not far downstream from the Race Creek take-out, the river pours over imposing Class VI Selway Falls.

As recently as the late 1970's the Selway, along with a handful of other Western rivers, was seen as one of the ultimate tests in technical whitewater. Today, although far more difficult runs are commonplace, the Selway remains a significant benchmark of wilderness river running skills. At lower flows it is deceptively easy, but a number of rapids change character radically at levels around 4' to 5' (about 2,500 to 3,500 cfs) on the Paradise gauge.

Flow is the trickiest thing about the Selway. Snowmelt season is usually brief and unpredictable. A sudden hot spell or a warm rain can quickly raise the river to dangerous levels. The river's many large tributaries roughly quadruple or quintuple the flow between put-in and take- out. Except at low water, boaters face a run that begins as a technical mountain torrent, then gradually builds into a powerful river with impressive hydraulics. At high flows all but seasoned experts should stay away.

In addition to demanding rapids and fluctuating flows, the Selway's potential hazards include logs, icy water, and unpredictable weather that can turn cold and rainy well into June. Early-season trips usually face all these challenges at once (plus possible snow on the road to the put-in). The Selway canyon is extremely remote and lightly travelled, so evacuation in case of mishap can be very difficult.

Other Runs

Above and below the run described in this chapter, boaters can float short sections of the Selway without a permit. The upper river is boatable for about a dozen miles above Paradise Launch Site, with rocky, technical rapids and a short season. A road follows the right bank, allowing easy scouting and access.

It is more common for boaters to run the lower river from below Selway Falls to the Lochsa River confluence at Lowell. The Lower Selway's 13 ft./mi. gradient produces Class II to easy Class III rapids, though some big waves develop at high flows. The canyon is lush and scenic, much like the end of the main run. This 15-mile lower stretch enjoys a longer season than the main Selway run. USFS Road 223 follows the right bank, providing easy scouting and access. Floating begins as far up as Gedney Creek Campground, a half mile below the falls. Among the intermediate accesses is Boyd Creek Campground, about halfway through the run. For more information, see the Idaho guide books listed above.

Mile by Mile Guide

0 **PUT-IN** at Paradise Launch Site below the mouth of White Cap Creek, a major tributary entering on the right. USFS guard station just up the creek at the end of the road. Trail follows the right bank downriver into the Selway-Bitterroot Wilderness. The first six miles are studded with rocky Class II and III rapids, some around blind curves.

3.5–5 A series of Class II+–III boulder gardens: **SLALOM SLIDE** (mile 3.5), **GALLOPING GERTIE** (4), **WASHER WOMAN** (4.2), **COUGAR BLUFF** (4.5), and **HOLY SMOKES** (5).

6.5 Running Creek Ranch (private) and airstrip on the left, just beyond a suspension bridge where the trail crosses to the left bank. Running Creek enters on the left below the ranch. From here to Ham Rapid (mile 22.5), the gradient eases. Rapids are less frequent and generally milder.

8.5 North Star Ranch (private) on the right.

10.5 Goat Creek enters on the left. A half mile downstream is **GOAT CREEK RAPID (III)**, a long boulder slalom. Watch for logs here in the early season.

13 Shearer Guard Station (USFS) and airstrip on the left.

14 Ditch Creek enters on the left. Just downstream at a pack bridge, the trail crosses to the right bank for the remainder of the run. Selway Lodge and airstrip (private) on the left.

15.5 Bear Creek, a major tributary, enters on the right. By now the river is usually noticeably bigger than at the put-in. Minor rapids continue for 2.5 miles to Pettibone Creek, which also enters on the right.

22.5 **HAM (IV-). Recognition:** A little less than a mile past Magpie Creek, which enters on the left, there is an unnamed Class III-rapid that must not be confused with **Ham,** which is at the end of the short, quiet stretch following the unnamed rapid. Scout left. **The rapid:** A long pitch with two drops divided by midstream boulders. More difficult at higher flows.

25.5 Suspension bridge. Moose Creek Ranger Station is out of sight above the right bank. Its good airstrip is the last fly-out point on the river. Good camps on the right at the bridge and just downstream on the left. About 1/4 mile downstream Moose Creek, the Selway's largest tributary, enters on the right and increases the flow by as much as half. A hike up the creek leads to the Moose Creek Cedar Grove, a lovely stand of virgin western red cedar. The 3 miles below Moose Creek are the toughest of the trip. All the rapids can be scouted from the trail on the right.

26.5 **DOUBLE DROP (III–IV).** Two big drops in a left bend. At high water it's important to miss a big hole at the second drop; most boaters work left. Just over half a mile downstream, around a sharp right bend, is **WA-POOTS (III–IV).** Easy at low flows, but at higher levels the current pushes boats toward a big boulder on the right.

27.5 **LADLE (IV+).** Probably the toughest rapid on the run. **Recognition:** At a left bend a few hundred yards below Wa-Poots. Stop before the bend to scout from the trail on the right. **The rapid:** Emerg-

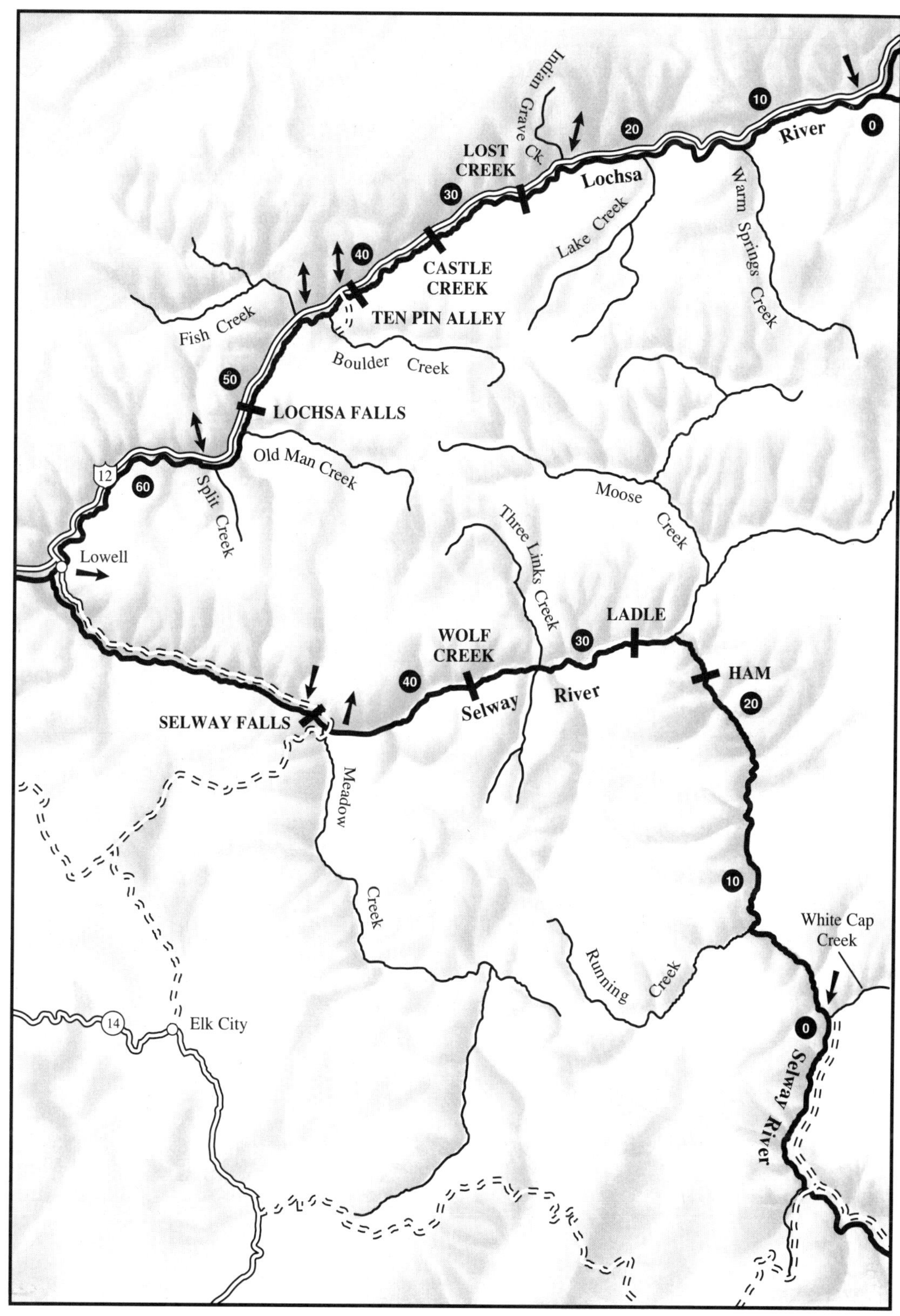

Selway and Lochsa

ing from a fairly narrow channel, the river fans out into a long, wide boulder garden (the "bowl" of the ladle), then narrows farther downstream (the "handle"). Route-finding can be a problem, especially at low flows. The rapid is usually run close to the right bank, avoiding a big hole just right of center at the top. Several big waves and holes develop at high water. Consider stationing rescue parties downstream; long, nasty, even fatal swims are a serious risk.

28 **LITTLE NIAGARA (III–IV).** A sheer rock wall on the right pinches the river into a short drop divided by a house-sized boulder. Straightforward at low flows, but big hydraulics develop at higher levels. At high flows it's difficult to eddy up, so stop well upstream to scout.

Below Little Niagara are three Class III's (IV at higher flows) in quick succession. First is **PUZZLE CREEK (III)**, where at high flows a big hole develops at the bottom in river center. Immediately downstream is **NO SLOUCH,** with big waves and holes. At moderate and high flows most boaters run left. Ending the series is **MIRANDA JANE,** below the mouth of Halfway Creek on the right.

31 **OSPREY (III).** Below the rapid Meeker Creek enters on the right. Class II from here to Wolf Creek.

33 Marten Creek enters on the left. A mile downstream a pack bridge crosses the river where Three Links Creek enters on the right and Mink Creek on the left.

37.5 **WOLF CREEK (IV).** At a left bend where Wolf Creek enters on the left. Easier at lower flows; big hydraulics at higher levels. Scout right.

40 **TEE KEM FALLS (III).** At a left bend where Jims Creek enters on the left. At low flows the rapid is tight, with a big rock in the center; at higher levels watch for big diagonal waves off the left bank.

42.5 **RENSHAW (III).** At the mouth of Renshaw Creek, which enters on the right. Watch for an undercut cliff on the left.

47 **TAKE-OUT** on the right just below Race Creek Campground. A dirt road follows the right bank downstream. ***HAZARD.*** Don't miss the take-out; a little over a mile downstream is Class VI **SELWAY FALLS.**

Lochsa River

White Sand Creek to Lowell

1. White Sand CG to Indian Grave Creek
III; 24 miles; 28 ft./mi.

2. Indian Grave Creek to Split Creek Pack Bridge
IV-; 29 miles; 35 ft./mi.

3. Split Creek Pack Bridge to Lowell
II+; 15 miles; 18 ft./mi.

Put-in: White Sand Creek (3,420').
Take-out: Lowell (1,450').
Drainage Area and Average Annual Discharge: 1,180 sq. mi. and 2,103,000 af.
Peak Recorded Flow: 35,100 cfs at Lowell (June 8, 1964).
Season: May–early August. Peaks in late May or June. Lower sections have higher flows and a longer season.
Recommended Levels: *Runs 1 & 3:* 1,000–6,000 cfs at Lowell. *Run 2:* 1,000–4,000 at Lowell. Very powerful and hazardous around 8,000 and up.
Flow Information: Idaho DWR, (208) 327-7865. Or call the managing agency.
Special Hazards: At high water the rapids become continuous and eddies are scarce. Logs.
Permits: Not presently required.
Managing Agency: Lochsa RD, Clearwater NF, P.O. Box 398, Kooskia, ID 83539; (208) 926-4275.
Land Ownership: Almost all National Forest.
Commercial Raft Trips: Yes. For a list, contact Idaho Outfitters & Guides Association, P.O. Box 95, Boise, ID 83701; (208) 342-1919.

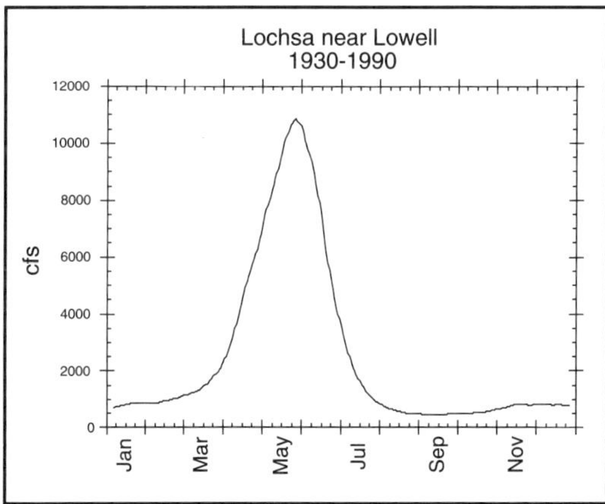

Scenery: Very good.
Solitude: Good, even though U.S. Highway 12 follows the entire run.
Wilderness: No.
Wildlife: Abundant. Deer, bear, elk, moose.
Water: Clear and cold. Drinking water available at several USFS campgrounds along river.
Camping: Many USFS campgrounds along the river.
Side Hikes: Many Forest Service trails climb creeks and ridges, and several lead into the Selway-Bitterroot Wilderness south of the river. See **Mile Guide.**
Guides and References:
- Moore & McClaran, *Idaho Whitewater.*
- Amaral, *Idaho: The Whitewater State.*
- **USFS:** *Lochsa Whitewater Rafting.* Free from Clearwater NF.

Maps:
- **USGS 7.5':** *Rocky Point, Cayuse Junction, Tom Beal Peak, Bear Mtn, Greystone Butte, Holly Creek, Greenside Butte, Huckleberry Butte, McLendon Butte, Coolwater Mtn, Lowell.*
- **USGS 1:100:** *Missoula West, Hamilton, Kooskia.*
- **USFS:** *Clearwater NF.* Also, *Selway-Bitterroot Wilderness* covers run from put-in to Split Creek Pack Bridge (mile 53).

Auto Shuttle: All paved; same mileages as river.
Logistics: U.S. 12 provides frequent access to the entire run, which begins some 55 miles southwest of Missoula. For access points not mentioned in this chapter, refer to the USFS pamphlet *Lochsa Whitewater Rafting* listed above. The **put-in** at **White Sand Campground** is on the right bank about 1/4 mile below the confluence of White Sand Creek and the Crooked Fork of the Lochsa. The turn-off to the campground is roughly 45 miles southwest of Lolo, Montana and 95 miles northwest of Kooskia, Idaho on U.S. 12. The intermediate accesses at **Indian Grave Creek** and **Split Creek Pack Bridge** are both on the right bank off U.S. 12. The **lowermost take-out** is at the town of Lowell, Idaho, where the Selway joins the Lochsa.

LOCHSA

The Lochsa, like the neighboring Selway and North Fork Clearwater, drains the wet western slope of Idaho's scenic Bitterroot Range.[1] Abundant snowmelt gathers in White Sand Creek and the Crooked Fork, and the Lochsa itself begins where these two streams meet. From this confluence the river runs swiftly southwest down a deep, narrow valley. After a journey of some 70 miles the Lochsa meets the Selway at the town of Lowell to form the Middle Fork of the Clearwater.

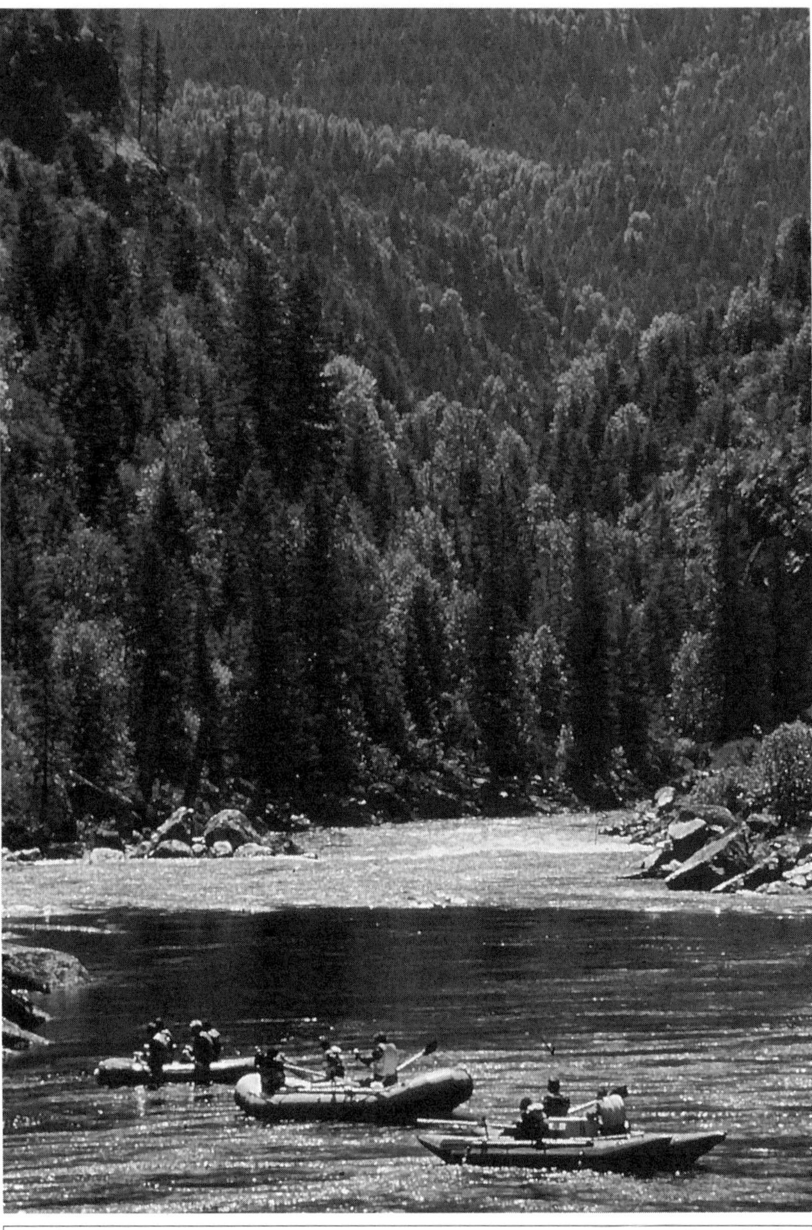

Lochsa River *Scott Spiker*

With continuous rapids, fine scenery, clean water, and easy road access, the Lochsa is one of Idaho's most popular non-permit rivers. In spite of occasional logging scars and U.S. Highway 12, which follows the entire run described here, the Lochsa has a relatively secluded feeling. Wildlife abounds on steep, heavily forested riverside slopes, which in many places still show scars from the great wildfire of 1910. A fringe of verdant undergrowth lines the river, while thick ranks of cedar and hemlock rise just behind. The Lochsa was designated as one of the nation's first Wild and Scenic Rivers in 1968. This timely action saved the Lochsa, Selway, and Middle Fork Clearwater from inundation behind the proposed Pennys Cliff Dam some 20 miles below the Lochsa-Selway confluence.

The Lochsa offers a wide range of whitewater, and frequent access from the nearby highway allows boaters to choose the stretches best suited to their skills and tastes. We have divided the river into three basic sections. The first, from White Sand Creek to Indian Grave Creek, features swift and somewhat technical water in a broad canyon where the river sometimes runs wide and shallow and divides around islands. The middle section from Indian Grave Creek to

[1]The range takes its name from the bitterroot, a small plant with a pink flower and an edible root (said to taste something like a turnip) used by local Indians. The plant's latin name, *Lewisia pygmaea,* is after explorer Meriwether Lewis. The bitterroot is the Montana state flower.

Split Creek is rough, steep, and generally narrow, with challenging Class III and IV drops and good surfing waves. Below Split Creek is a mild stretch of easy Class II water in a broader canyon as the Lochsa approaches its confluence with the Selway at the town of Lowell.

At high water the Lochsa shows an entirely different side of its character. During heavy snow melt—which often lasts through most of June—the Lochsa can turn into a thundering torrent, and each section can jump a full class in difficulty. Boaters will understand why the Nez Perce called this river "Loc-sah," or "rough water." Big waves and holes develop, and long, cold swims become a serious threat.

Because its canyon offers the most direct passage through the heart of the rugged Bitterroot Range, the Lochsa has long served as a corridor for human travel. Much of the area's history centers on early journeys through the canyon. The original inhabitants, the Nez Perce, favored a rugged route that parallels the river along a high ridge a few miles to the north—the so-called "Lolo Trail." For hundreds of years they used the trail for expeditions eastward into the rich buffalo hunting grounds of Montana. In 1877 they toiled for the last time up this arduous path, fleeing from the U.S. Army action that forced them from their ancestral lands.

In September 1805 Lewis and Clark struggled down the Lolo Trail from the east. Thwarted in their efforts to descend the Salmon River, the explorers crossed over the Bitterroots to what is now Montana, then recrossed the great mountain barrier at 5,235' Lolo Pass near the Lochsa's headwaters. The expedition then struggled down the west flank of the Bitterroots, one step ahead of deep winter snows. The explorers would later recall the difficult trek down the Lolo Trail as the most daunting moment in their long journey to the Pacific.

The Lochsa remains an important travel route. U.S. 12, the "Lewis and Clark Highway," follows the entire length of the Lochsa's main stem. Even today, between I-90 to the north and I-84 to the south—a distance of over 250 miles—the Lochsa offers the only year- round passage across central Idaho.

Middle Fork Clearwater

Below the Lochsa-Selway confluence at Lowell, the Middle Fork Clearwater meanders through some 25 miles of Class II water down to Kooskia, where it joins the South Fork Clearwater. The canyon and riverbed are wider on these lower reaches, and the forest is somewhat drier and more open. U.S. 12 follows this section, allowing easy access and scouting. The Middle Fork Clearwater enjoys a summer-long season and makes a fine trip for open canoes. The Nez Perce called this section of river "Koos khee-ich-khee-ich" or "very clear water" (from which the town of Kooskia takes its name).

Mile by Mile Guide

*See map in **Selway** chapter. Note: This guide lists only a few of this run's many popular accesses.*

0 **PUT-IN. White Sand Campground** (right bank). Powell Ranger Station is about 1.5 miles downstream on the right; Powell Campground is a half mile farther. Below Powell CG U.S. 12 joins the right bank and follows the river all the way to Lowell.

5 Whitehouse Campground on the right as a pack bridge crosses the river. Just downstream is Wendover Campground. Below Wendover CG watch for a more difficult rapid in a narrower section of canyon.

12 Warm Springs Pack Bridge just above Warm Springs Creek, which enters on the left. A trail leads from the bridge up the creek about a mile to Jerry Johnson Hot Springs.

16 Class II+ rapid marks the site of Colgate Warm Springs on the right.

20 Lake Creek enters on the left. A mile downstream Mocus Pack Bridge crosses the river. A trail climbs steeply to Mocus Point.

24.5 **RIVER ACCESS** on the right near the mouth of **Indian Grave Creek.** Beginning of Run 2. The whitewater becomes more challenging downstream. **Only the largest rapids are listed below.** Boaters running this stretch for the first time should scout frequently.

27.5 **LOST CREEK** (IV-). Also called **Rocky Corner.** Located at a sweeping right bend where Lost Creek enters on the right. Long and technical; numerous rocks and holes. A mile downstream, Eagle Mountain Pack Bridge crosses the river (alternate **RIVER ACCESS**).

32.5 **LONE PINE** (IV-). Also called **Onno's Hole.** More difficult at lower flows, when a **dangerous hole** develops in the center. A solitary pine rising from a butte on the right serves as a landmark.

33 **CASTLE CREEK** (IV). Just below the mouth of Castle Creek, which enters on the right. Nearly a half mile long, this rocky, twisting rapid is generally considered the toughest on the river. Big holes at higher flows. Scouting recommended. Downstream, at a sharp left bend, watch for **TRIPLE HOLE RAPID.** Below this rapid is a **RIVER ACCESS,** often used as a put-in during high water.

37 **LOG JAM RAPID** (IV-) at a sharp left bend. More difficult at high water, when a big log pile blocks the right channel at the bottom.

41 **TEN PIN ALLEY** (IV-). At a sharp right bend. This long, technical rapid can be run several different ways. Scout right.

41.7 Wilderness Gateway Bridge leads to a large campground on the left bank. **RIVER ACCESS** several hundred yards downstream on the right bank.

45 **RIVER ACCESS** near the mouth of Fish Creek, which enters on the right. The run from here to Split Creek Pack Bridge is less technical than the stretch upstream, and has more of a pool-and-drop character. The big waves and steep, clean chutes make this section a favorite.

47–
53 **Black Canyon.** Six miles of narrow, rugged canyon with many of the Lochsa's best rapids. The canyon begins just below a sharp left bend where Big Stew Creek enters on the left. The first major rapid is **HOUSE WAVE** (III+), mile 47, where a huge wave forms at high flows. A half mile downstream is **SNAG** (IV-), also called **Grim Reaper,** with a big pourover at the bottom left. Other challenging drops follow. Near mile 50, short but powerful **LOCHSA FALLS** (IV) is generally run on the right. Old Man Creek enters on the left at mile 51. Not far downstream is **TERMINATION** (IV-), where the current piles into the wall at the bottom. Finally come the big holes of **SPLIT CREEK** (III+).

53 **RIVER ACCESS** at **Split Creek Pack Bridge,** located about half a mile below the mouth of Split Creek, which enters on the left. Downstream the rapids gradually ease, but the canyon doesn't start to open up until a few miles above Lowell.

60 Glade Creek Campground on the right, followed in a half mile by Apgar Campground. About a mile below the second campground, where Hellgate Creek enters on the left, watch for **HELLGATE** (II+), the toughest rapid below Split Creek (big hole at high flows). Just over a mile downstream is a popular **ALTERNATE TAKE-OUT** on the right.

68 **TAKE-OUT** on the left at the bridge at Lowell, where the Selway River enters from the left.

North Fork Clearwater River

Kelly Creek to Aquarius Campground

1. **Kelly Creek (2,750') to Weitas Creek (2,320').** III-; 14 miles; 30 ft./mi.

2. **Weitas Creek to Aquarius CG (1,675').** III+5; 30 mi.; 21 ft./mi.

Shorter runs possible on both stretches.

Drainage Area and Average Annual Discharge: 1,360 sq. mi. / 2,636,000 af at Aquarius CG.
Season: May–July above Weitas Creek, May–August below. Usually peaks mid-May to early June around 10,000–16,000 cfs, then gradually drops to below 1,000 by early August.
Recommended Levels: 1,000–8,000 cfs.
Flow Information: Idaho DWR, (208) 327-7865; flow at Canyon Gauge (take-out).
Special Hazards: Irish Railroad Rapid. Logs.
Permits: Not presently required.
Managing Agency: North Fork RD, Clearwater NF, P.O. Box 2139, Orofino, ID 83544; (208) 476-3775.
Commercial Raft Trips: Not allowed.
Land Ownership: All National Forest.
Scenery: Excellent. Steep, forested canyon.
Solitude: Very good. Light boating use.
Wilderness: No. Little-used road follows the river.
Guides and References:
- Amaral, *Idaho: The Whitewater State.* Includes upstream runs.
- Moore & McClaran, *Idaho Whitewater.*

Maps:
- **USGS 7.5':** *Junction Mtn, Pot Mtn, Clarke Mtn, The Nub, Sheep Mtn, Thompson Point.*
- **USFS:** *Clearwater NF.* Covers all runs.

Logistics: The drive to the river is very long and far from gas stations, so be sure you can get there and back. From Orofino, Idaho, follow U.S. 12 southeast about 7 miles to Greer, then turn east on Idaho Highway 11 and drive about 40 miles to Headquarters. Take paved USFS Road 247 north to the river, cross the bridge, and bear right to the **take-out at Aquarius Campground.** A USFS road follows the right bank upstream, providing easy scouting and frequent access. Here is a partial list of **alternate accesses** (and miles upstream from Aquarius CG): just below Quartz Creek (9), just above Ermine Creek (14), Washington Creek CG (20), Orogrande Creek (26), Whitefish Rock (27), Weitas Creek CG (30), Kelly Forks CG (44), and Junction Creek Pack Bridge (45).

Despite its abundant runoff, lush scenery, solitude, and fine intermediate whitewater, the North Fork Clearwater is one of Idaho's most obscure rivers. Its extremely remote location and a state prohibition on commercial rafting keep use light. Only a handful of local river runners make the long drive into the canyon, while out-of-state boaters usually head for sister streams to the south, the Lochsa and Selway.

The North Fork Clearwater and its northern neighbor, the St. Joe, have the wettest watersheds in our Idaho and Northern Rockies region. Both drain the western slopes of the Bitterroot Range in north central Idaho. Average annual precipitation of 60" produces heavy runoff and thick forests, with lofty red cedar and hemlock towering over an understory of ferns, mosses, and moisture-loving shrubs. The river still runs clear despite heavy logging in the watershed.

The runs described here take in the river's middle reaches in the Clearwater Mountains, a belt of moderate-elevation peaks west of the Bitterroots. The North Fork flows generally west toward its confluence with the Main Clearwater. Along the way it loops through a giant S-curve 44 river miles long that stretches just 19 miles as the crow flies, and it cuts a V-shaped canyon up to 3,000' deep. Scenic trails climb the steep slopes, while many sandy beaches and Forest Service campgrounds offer good overnight possibilities.

In the 30 miles from Weitas Creek to Aquarius Campground, the North Fork tumbles through Class III and III+ rapids and one big Class V-, Irish Railroad. Most boaters sneak or portage this big drop—or avoid it altogether by taking out upstream at Washington Creek Campground or launching downstream at Ermine Creek. Upstream, between Kelly Creek and Weitas Creek Campground, the gradient is steeper and flows are somewhat lower. A road follows the right bank from Kelly Forks Campground to Aquarius Campground, providing frequent access and letting boaters scout first to choose the sections best suited to their skills. At high flows the North Fork is cold, swift and very powerful.

North Fork Clearwater River Guide

Kelly Creek to Weitas CG

Put in at Kelly Forks CG (mile 0) at the confluence of the North Fork Clearwater and Kelly Creek. (An **alternate put-in** is just over a mile up Kelly Creek at Junction Creek Pack Bridge.) This lightly-used section is mostly swift Class II+ to III-. **Be alert for logs.** Noe Creek CG provides an **alternate access** at mile 8.

Weitas CG to Aquarius CG

At mile 14 a bridge crosses the river to Weitas CG (**fair alternate access**). Weitas Creek, a major tributary, enters on the left. Downstream the difficulty increases; be prepared for some Class III+ drops (Class IV at higher flows). A popular **alternate access** known as "Whitefish Rock" is on the right at mile 17. About half a mile farther are the big waves of **WHITEFISH (III+).** Just below the rapid, a bridge crosses the river as Orogrande Creek enters on the left; Bungalow Ranger Station is on the left, and a good **alternate access** known as "Bungalow" is on the right near mile 18. At mile 24 a bridge crosses the river to Washington Creek CG. There is a good **alternate access** on the right at the bridge; **take out here to avoid Irish Railroad Rapid** 4 miles downstream.

At **mile 28** big boulders clog the channel at the North Fork's biggest drop, **IRISH RAILROAD (V-).** At high flows a massive hole forms in the center; many boaters sneak down the right. **To avoid this rapid, put in downstream at Ermine Creek.** The five miles below Irish Railroad are fairly steep, with several strong Class III+ drops (IV at some flows).

Below the **alternate river access at Ermine Creek** (mile 30), the whitewater is mostly Class III for the remainder of the run. **Quartz Creek** enters on the right at mile 35 (**fair alternate access**). Skull Creek enters on the right at mile 37, and downstream are several strong rapids in the final stretch. **Take out** on the right at **Aquarius Campground** (mile 44). Downstream the river passes under the Road 247 bridge and flows another couple of miles before entering the backwaters of Dworshak Reservoir.

Upstream Runs

Above Kelly Forks Campground the North Fork and its major tributary, Kelly Creek, offer advanced runs with shorter seasons. For more information on these sections refer to Amaral, *Idaho: The Whitewater State.*

Upper North Fork–Black Canyon: Above Kelly Creek the North Fork is small, steep and swift, with many Class III and IV rapids. The five miles immediately above Kelly Creek pass through a spectacular steep-sided cut known as **Black Canyon.** Numerous **logs pose a major hazard**—scout first from a road on the right bank. Hidden Creek CG offers a put-in 11 miles above Kelly Forks CG, but other sites are possible.

Kelly Creek: This large tributary sometimes has slightly more water than the North Fork at their confluence. USFS Road 255 follows the right bank upstream from Kelly Forks CG to Moose Creek, providing scouting and a choice of accesses. The 11-mile run averages 40 ft./mi., with numerous Class III+ rapids and an occasional Class IV. **Be alert for logs.**

The Impact of Dworshak Dam

Below Aquarius Campground the North Fork Clearwater enters Dworshak Reservoir. Dworshak Dam, two miles above the river's mouth, rises 717' from the riverbed and floods over 50 miles of the lower river for purposes of flood control and hydropower.

Since its completion in 1971, Dworshak has proved to be one of the West's most damaging dams. At one time the North Clearwater and its tributaries were among the finest fishing streams in the nation. Now, with the salmon and steelhead cut off from their spawning grounds, the river supports only a modest population of trout. The reservoir also destroyed some 15,000 acres of prime deer and elk range.

With gradients ranging from 10 to 20 ft./mi., the lower North Fork once offered one of the longest easy whitewater runs in Idaho. Today, extended Class I and II floats through such forested terrain are almost unknown in the state. In exchange flatwater boaters have been given a pencil-thin reservoir 53 miles long and just a few hundred yards wide for much of its length.

The debate over Dworshak Dam in the early 1960's contributed significantly to the change in consciousness that culminated in the 1968 National Wild and Scenic Rivers Act. The Forest Service has found the remaining reaches of the North Clearwater and its tributaries eligible for designation as National Wild and Scenic Rivers.

St. Joe River

Spruce Tree Campground to Avery

Difficulty: II, with two Class III+ sections.
Length: 41 miles. Longer and shorter runs possible. **Gradient:** 31 ft./mi.
Put-in: Spruce Tree Campground (3,750').
Take-out: Avery (2,480').
Drainage Area: 472 sq. mi. near Avery.
Season: May–July; a few weeks longer below Gold Creek (mile 12). Typically peaks in May. Rainfall may cause sudden high flows.
Recommended Levels: 1,000–6,000 cfs.
Flow Information: Idaho DWR, (208) 327-7865; flow at Calder. Flows at Avery, 20 miles upstream, are roughly half; on the upper river they are are considerably less.
Permits: Not presently required.
Managing Agency: Avery RD, Idaho Panhandle NF, HC Box 1, Avery, ID 83802; (208) 245-4517.
Commercial Raft Trips: One outfitter in recent years. For a current list, contact Idaho Outfitters & Guides Assn., P.O. Box 95, Boise, ID 83701; (208) 342-1919.
Land Ownership: All National Forest.
Scenery: Very good. Densely forested canyon with some striking gorges.
Wilderness: No. A road follows the river except in the uppermost reaches.
Guides and References:

- Amaral, *Idaho: The Whitewater State.*
- Moore & McClaran, *Idaho Whitewater.*
- *St. Joe River Float Trips.* Small pamphlet available from the managing agency.

Maps:

- **USFS:** *Idaho Panhandle NF (St. Joe NF).*

Auto Shuttle: Mostly paved; same mileages as river.
Logistics: The St. Joe is in the Idaho panhandle southeast of Coeur d'Alene. The **take-out** is on the right bank in Avery, Idaho. The easiest approach is from the west: follow Idaho Highway 3 to St. Maries, then drive upstream along the north bank some 50 miles on St. Joe River Road (Forest Highway 50) to Avery. (Alternatively, boaters can approach Avery from the north via unpaved USFS Road 456, which runs about 30 miles south from I-90 at Wallace, Idaho across a 5,000' pass that may be blocked by snow.) USFS Road 218 follows the right bank from Avery all the way upstream to the **put-in** at Spruce Tree Campground, providing short shuttles and many alternate accesses (most boaters use USFS campgrounds).

Boaters can take another route to reach the upper river from the east: USFS Roads 282 and 388 run from St. Regis, Montana (on I-90) to Gold Creek on the St. Joe; refer to the USFS map for details. This route crosses a 5,800' pass that may be blocked by snow.

The crystalline St. Joe[1], like the Selway, Lochsa, and North Fork Clearwater to the south, drains the wet western slopes of the Bitterroot Range. From its source at St. Joe Lake near the Montana border, the river runs northeast some 120 miles across the Idaho panhandle to Lake Coeur d'Alene near the Washington border. Along the way it cuts a scenic canyon through the northern end of the Bitterroot and Clearwater Mountains.

The mountains here are lower and somewhat gentler than they are farther south, and the moderate elevations (few peaks exceed 7,000') give the St. Joe a somewhat shorter season than its neighbors to the south. The moist climate produces a thick mantle of forest, which in turn supports abundant wildlife and helps keeps the river clear, cold, and teeming with fish. (Anglers will find both cutthroat trout and whitefish.) The upper half of the St. Joe, including the entire 41-mile reach from Spruce Tree Campground to Avery, was added to the National Wild and Scenic Rivers System in 1978.

A lightly-used Forest Service road follows the river for most of its length, providing frequent access and allowing boaters to choose among various sections. Boaters can run short stretches or make an extended trip using Forest Service campgrounds along the river. Most of the St. Joe below Spruce Tree is Class II to III-, with the exception of two steeper and narrower sections—the popular Tumbledown Falls and Skookum Canyon Runs—where the difficulty rises to III+ (IV at high flows). Be alert for possible **log hazards** all along the St. Joe.

[1]The river was named the St. Joseph in 1842 by Father Pierre-Jean DeSmet, a Catholic missionary who sought to convert local Indians.

St. Joe River Guide

Note: Only a few of the many river access points are mentioned here.

Upper St. Joe: Spruce Tree Campground to Avery

1. Spruce Tree CG to Gold Creek

At the **put-in** (Spruce Tree Campground, mile 0), less than 30 miles from its headwaters, the St. Joe is still a small river. The first stretch is a lovely, forested 12-mile run that offers intermediate whitewater—mostly Class II+ and a few easy III's. The current is swift, with a gradient of 35 ft./mi. Choose a convenient **take-out** around Gold Creek, which enters on the right at mile 12, or about a mile downstream at Conrad Crossing Campground.

2. Tumbledown Falls Run: Gold Creek to Bluff Creek

Below Gold Creek the St. Joe has more flow and a longer season. From Gold Creek (mile 12) to Bluff Creek (mile 19) the river encounters harder rock, and the gradient increases to 41 ft./mi. Here the St. Joe carves a beautiful gorge with moss-covered walls and deep pools.

Several Class III rapids provide a warm-up for the roughest spot, **TUMBLEDOWN FALLS (III+)**, at mile 16. On its own, this drop over a ledge is not especially difficult; however, a quarter mile of rough water precedes the main drop, and just above the falls the river bends sharply left, driving boats toward a nasty reversal on the right side of the ledge. Boaters must fight momentum and the current to reach a clean chute on the left. Scout from the road before running.

Below the falls watch for a **possible log hazard** and more Class III drops. The next **possible take-out** is a difficult carry up the right bank at mile 19, just below the Bluff Creek Bridge (USFS Road 509).

3. Bluff Creek to Turner Flat CG

Rapids in the 13.5 miles from Bluff Creek to the **take-out** at Turner Flat Campground (mile 32.5) are Class II and easier, with a gradient of only 25 ft./mi.

4. Skookum Canyon: Turner Flat CG to Packsaddle CG

Action picks up again in short but powerful **Skookum Canyon (III+)**. Almost all the whitewater on this 4.5-mile run is confined to the narrow two miles from Tourist Creek (mile 34) to Skookum Creek (mile 36). **Take out** on the right at Packsaddle CG (mile 37).

5. Packsaddle CG to Avery

This 4-mile stretch is Class II with a mild gradient of 20 ft./mi. **Take out** on the right at the small town of Avery.

Lower St. Joe: Avery to Lake Coeur d'Alene

The North Fork of the St. Joe enters from the right at Avery, adding considerable flow. After a few Class II riffles in the first half dozen miles, the river settles in for a long, easy float to Lake Coeur d'Alene. With pleasant scenery, easy road access, and a summer-long season, part or all of this 65-mile section may appeal to novice canoeists or anyone looking for a drift trip. Innertubing is also popular here in the summer. Lush stands of cottonwood along the lower river account for its nickname, "The Shadowy St. Joe." For more information contact the St. Maries Ranger District, (208) 245-2531.

Upper St. Joe: Heller Creek Run

Adventurous experts may consider running the St. Joe's uppermost reaches, beginning at Heller Creek—a remote access just a dozen miles below the river's source. From here to Spruce Tree Campground, the St. Joe cascades through a spectacular 17-mile wilderness run studded with Class IV drops and **frequent log jams.** However, even experts who are equal to these challenges may have trouble catching the run with adequate flow: snow usually blocks the rough road to Heller Creek until mid-June or early July, by which time most of the snowmelt is over in the tiny upstream basin (less than 40 square miles). A trail follows the right bank through this section, allowing scouting, emergency access, and scenic hiking for those who would rather enjoy the upper river from dry land.

Payette River

The Payette, Boise's backyard river, offers more than a hundred miles of fine boating within a short drive of Idaho's capital city. The main Payette and its principal tributaries—the North Fork, the South Fork, and the Deadwood River—boast a wide variety of whitewater, from placid Class I to thundering Class V+. The spectacular, dangerous hairball run down the North Fork below Smiths Ferry may be the most famous, but the Payette has runs to match every taste and skill level.

From its scenic alpine watershed in west central Idaho, the Payette flows south and west to join the Snake River. The North Fork rises between the watersheds of the Little Salmon and South Fork Salmon, while the South Fork Payette drains the lofty Sawtooth Range. Two smaller branches, the Deadwood River and the Middle Fork Payette, lie between the larger forks. The North and South Forks join near the hamlet of Banks to form the Main Payette.[1]

A combination of summer-long flows and proximity to Boise makes the Payette one of Idaho's most popular rivers. Dam releases on the North Fork and Deadwood extend the boating season, so river running is possible somewhere in the Payette system from April to September. Despite heavy use on some sections, permits are not required. In addition to the runs covered in detail here, there are several novice floats, including portions of the Main Payette below the standard take-out at Beehive Bend and a scenic Class I run on the Middle Fork below Pine Tree Ranch.

The Payette system is threatened by numerous dams and diversions, including expansion of an existing hydro project on the Horseshoe Bend section of the lower Payette (downstream from the Main Payette run in this chapter) and new hydro projects on both the North and South Forks. The North Fork proposal would dewater the spectacular Class V+ run from Murray Creek to Banks. In 1991 conservationists won a major victory when Idaho Governor Cecil Andrus signed a law banning any new hydro dams on the river. But the protection plan is not airtight. Later that year, the Idaho State Land Board approved the Horseshoe Bend project, which had already been licensed by the federal government.[2]

Bills have been introduced in Congress to protect the North Fork. The Forest Service has found eligible for membership in the National Wild and Scenic Rivers System the last 12 miles of the North Fork, all of the Canyon run and most of the Swirly Canyon run on the South Fork, and the entire stretch of the Deadwood described in the following pages.

Payette River — General Data

Managing Agencies: *Upper North Fork and Main Payette:* BLM, Boise District, 3948 Development Ave., Boise, ID 83705; (208) 384-3300. *Other runs:* Lowman RD, Boise NF, Lowman, ID 83637; (208) 259-3361.

Commercial Raft Trips: On some sections. Contact Idaho Outfitters & Guides Assn., P.O. Box 95, Boise, ID 83701; (208) 342-1919.

Camping: Many USFS campgrounds on or near the runs described here. Refer to *Boise NF* map.

Guides and References:
- Moore & McClaran, *Idaho Whitewater.*
- Amaral, *Idaho: The Whitewater State.*
- A good local source of information is Idaho River Sports, 1521 N. 13th, Boise, ID 83702; (208) 336-4844.

Maps: USFS: *Boise NF*. Covers all runs.

[1]The river is named for François Payette, a Canadian trapper and, in 1818, the first white to explore the area.

[2]For more information contact Idaho Rivers United. (See appendix for address.)

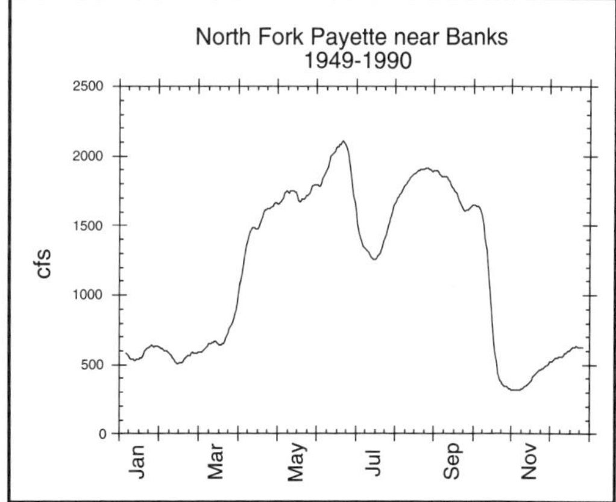

North Fork Payette River

Cabarton Bridge to Banks

1. Cabarton Bridge (4,710')
to above Smiths Ferry (4,520').
III; 9 miles; 21 ft./mi.

2. Below Smiths Ferry (4,485')
to Banks (2,795').
V+; 16 miles; 105 ft./mi.

Drainage Area and Average Annual Discharge: 933 sq. mi. and 1,010,000 af near Banks.
Peak Recorded Flow: 8,830 cfs (May 11, 1947).
Season: June–Sept. After an initial peak in late spring, the river usually drops until late summer, when irrigation releases begin. Flows are typically strong in August and September; then the river drops quickly. *See hydrograph on previous page.*
Recommended Levels: *Run 1:* 1,000–3,000 cfs. *Run 2:* 1,000–2,500 cfs. Very dangerous over 2,500.
Flow Information: Idaho DWR, (208) 327-7865, or BuRec, (208) 334-1466. Flow at Cascade.
Scenery: Very good. Forested canyon upstream; gradually becomes drier toward Banks.
Wilderness: No.
Solitude: *Run 1:* Very good. *Run 2:* Fair.
Land Ownership: Mixed National Forest, BLM, and private.
Maps:
- **USGS 7.5':** *Run 1:* Alpha, Smiths Ferry. *Run 2:* Smiths Ferry, Packer John Mtn, Banks.

Logistics: Accesses are between Boise and McCall on or near Idaho Highway 55, which follows the river closely in the lower run (short shuttles and frequent access).

The **lowermost take-out at Banks** is on river right at the confluence of the North and South Forks. **Smiths Ferry** is about 18 miles upstream. There are several possible **put-ins for the lower run** about 2.5 miles below Smiths Ferry. The **take-out for the upper run** is about a mile upstream from Smiths Ferry. The turnoff to **the upper put-in at Cabarton Bridge** is some 9 miles north of Smiths Ferry and a quarter mile south of the highway bridge over Clear Creek; turn west off the highway and drive about a mile and a half to the river.

The North Fork Payette is one of Idaho's most spectacular whitewater rivers. Upstream is the scenic Cabarton run, perfect for boaters with intermediate skills. But **below Smiths Ferry, the North Fork is emphatically for daring experts only.** In its final 16 miles the river plummets some 1,700 vertical feet—nearly a third of a mile—through a nonstop cascade of steep, technical Class V rapids.

Seen from Highway 55, which runs alongside this section, the North Fork seems to be a wild confusion of boiling foam. Yet the chaotic appearance masks the river's most remarkable feature: its consistency. Though the whitewater hovers near the limits of navigation by experts, it becomes truly unrunnable only at high flows.

This daunting stretch of the North Fork Payette wasn't kayaked until the 1970's and was first rafted in 1987. With a gradient of more than 100 ft./mi., the river is both powerful and highly technical. The already narrow riverbed has been further constricted by riprap tumbled into the channel during construction of the highway and railroad that parallel the run. Many of the rocks are sharp, and eddies are scarce in some sections. The nearly continuous whitewater makes physical condition and stamina almost as important as boating skill. Swims can be long and bruising. The individual drops generally rate Class V, but the overall experience is so demanding that a V+ rating is more appropriate. At flows above 2,500 cfs the run approaches Class VI.

However, boaters have two key factors in their favor. First, the water is relatively warm: late summer irrigation releases from Cascade Reservoir, some 20 miles upstream, provide flows near 70° through most of August and September. Most boaters avoid the North Fork during its other runnable period, a surge of icy snowmelt in spring. (In heavy snowpack years, boatable flows can last through most of the spring and summer.)

Second, boaters can stop any time—provided they can catch an eddy. When discretion

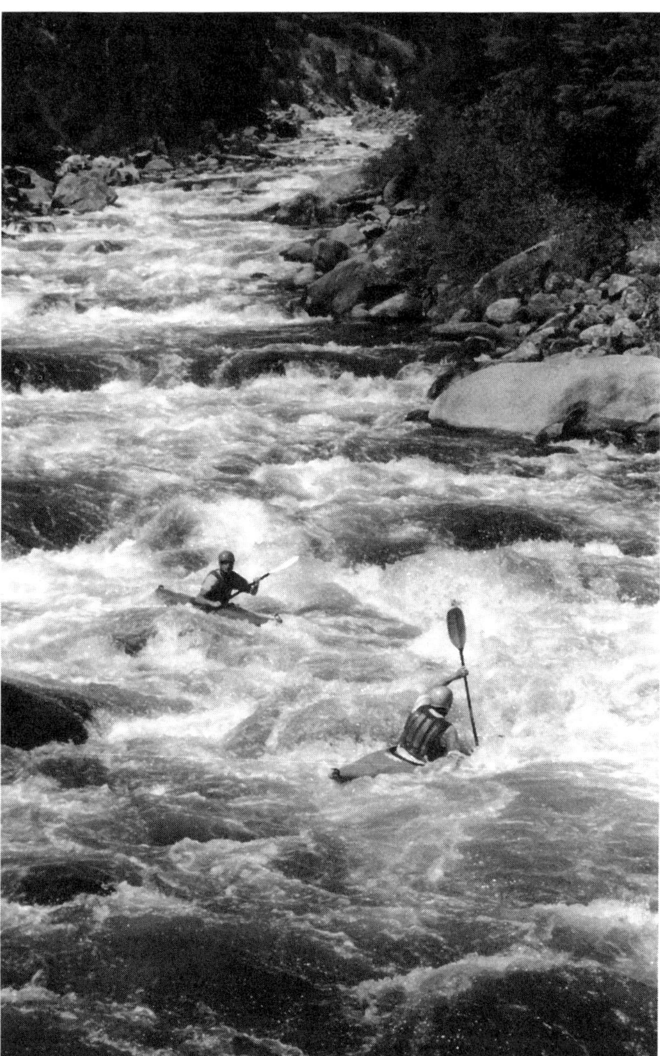

North Fork Payette below Smiths Ferry *Greg Moore*

seems the better part of valor, it is usually only a short scramble up the bank to the highway, which also allows short shuttles and easy scouting of most sections. Beware of rubbernecking motorists, some of whom stop in the middle of the road to gape at those damn fool whitewater maniacs.

Experts planning to run the North Fork below Smiths Ferry for the first time should warm up on the last five miles below Hounds Tooth Rapid (see **Mile Guide**). This Class IV to IV+ section provides them with a good *apéritif* as well as a chance to consider once again whether they really want to run the Class V+ rapids just upstream.

Those who prefer more forgiving whitewater can enjoy the excellent Class III run upstream, from Cabarton Bridge to above Smiths Ferry. Warm water (dam releases), enjoyable rapids, fine scenery, a short shuttle, and a long season make this section one of Idaho's most popular floats. The highway is well away from the river, and the railroad detracts only slightly from the sense of solitude. Even farther upstream is the 2.5-mile Class II3 "Town Run" through McCall, which has a very brief spring season.

North Fork Payette Mile Guide

Cabarton Bridge to above Smiths Ferry

0 PUT-IN on river left below Cabarton Bridge. Downstream the North Fork enters a 7-mile-long canyon. The railroad joins the river about a mile below the put-in.

2.5 **TRESTLE (III)**, where the railroad crosses the river. Usually the toughest rapid in this section.

7 Highway 55 joins the river and crosses to the right bank. The river flows down a rocky mini-gorge to the last rapid, **HOWARDS PLUNGE (III)**. Then the canyon opens and the river stills. The TAKE-OUT is just downstream on the right near mile 9. Then comes flatwater to Smiths Ferry Bridge a mile downstream. Flatwater continues about 2.5 more miles.

Below Smiths Ferry to Banks

0 PUT-IN at any of several popular access points on the right bank roughly 2.5 miles below Smiths Ferry. Downstream the river curves to the right, accelerating through Class III and IV drops before plunging into nearly continuous Class V.

Experts only. *Only the biggest rapids are listed here.* Scout frequently, and portage when in doubt.

1 After the first big drop, **STEEPNESS**, the river surges into **NUTCRACKER (V)**. Watch for a big hole at the top. Not far downstream is **DISNEYLAND**, followed in about a mile by **S-TURN**.

4.5 Big Eddy, a long, quiet pool, provides a rare break in the action. Alternate **RIVER ACCESS** on the right. Downstream a foot bridge crosses the river, signaling the beginning of the most difficult sequence of big drops. First is the narrow washboard of **SLIDE**, followed by **BAD JOSÉ** and **KNOW WHERE TO RUN**.

5.5 **BOUNCER DOWN THE MIDDLE (V)**, one of this run's longest and most difficult rapids. Boaters try to stay right of some nasty holes in the center, then—as the river bends right—they attempt to work left and avoid a big hole at the bottom. Downstream is **PECTORALIS MAJOR**.

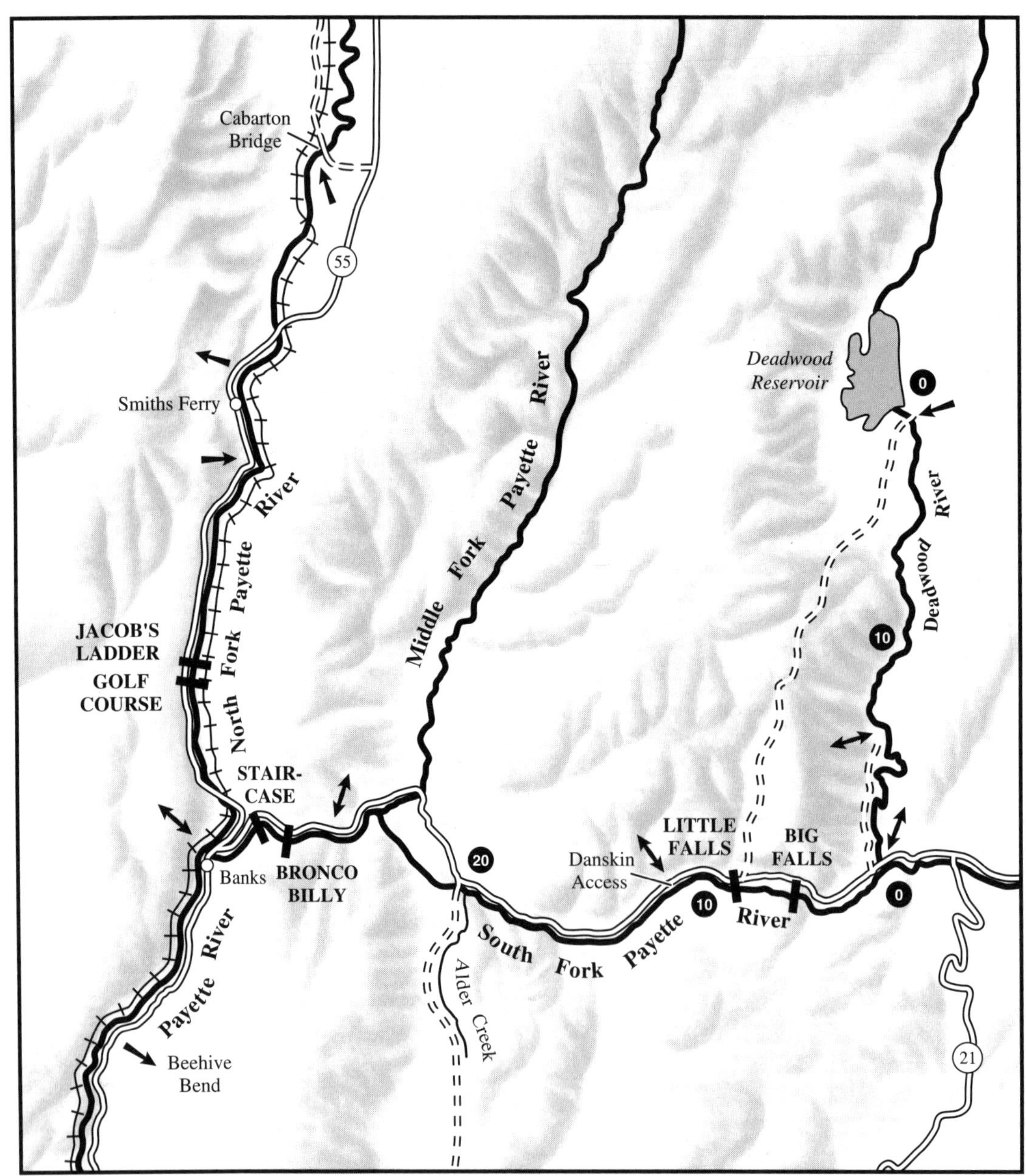

Payette River System

7 In one mile the North Fork drops over 200' through the toughest whitewater on the run—two extremely steep, technical, back-to-back Class V+ rapids, **JACOBS LADDER** and **GOLF COURSE.** Big holes lurk everywhere, and descriptions of these complex rapids are no substitute for thorough scouting. Scout from the highway before attempting these rapids, which are located near milepost 86.4 across from Swinging Bridge CG. Consider portaging along the highway.

8 Swinging Bridge. Popular **RIVER ACCESS.** The next major rapid is **SCREAMING LEFT TURN**, followed by a long series of big drops and holes known as **THE JAWS.**

10.5 **HOUNDS TOOTH (IV+).** Two big rocks cleave the current. Alternate **RIVER ACCESSES** above and below the drop. Downstream the rapids ease somewhat.

12.5 Highway 55 crosses the river. Not far downstream is **OTTERS RUN (IV).** Below a railroad bridge comes a final stretch with two steep Class IV+ rapids, **JUICER** and **CRUNCH.**

16 A bridge crosses the North Fork, and the South Fork Payette enters from the left. Use the **TAKE-OUT** on river right opposite the settlement of Banks, or continue down the Main Payette.

Deadwood River

Deadwood Dam to South Fork Payette

1. Deadwood Dam (5,150')
to Deadwood River Road (4,285').
V_P; 14 miles; 58 ft./mi.

2. Deadwood River Road to South Fork Payette Confluence (3,675').
IV; 9 miles; 65 ft./mi.

Drainage Area and Average Annual Discharge: 112 sq. mi. and 172,500 af.
Peak Recorded Flow: 2,580 cfs near Deadwood Dam (July 14, 1953).
Season: Variable summer dam releases, any time from early June through Sept. Depending on snowpack, season lasts one to 3 months.
Recommended Levels: 700–1,500 cfs.
Flow Information: Idaho DWR, (208) 327-7865, or BuRec, (208) 334-1466. Flow below Deadwood Reservoir.
Land Ownership: All National Forest.
Scenery: Excellent. **Solitude:** Excellent.
Wilderness: Yes.
Maps: USGS 7.5': *Deadwood Reservoir, Scott Creek, Pine Flat.*
Auto Shuttle: The shuttle for the upper run is long; consider hiring a local driver.
Logistics: To reach the **lower take-out** at the Deadwood-South Fork Payette confluence, follow the Banks-Lowman Highway east from Idaho 55 at Banks or west from Idaho 21 at Lowman. To reach the **intermediate access**, turn north at the confluence onto unpaved Deadwood River Road (USFS 024GB), marked "Julie Creek Trail," and drive some 10 miles up the west side of the Deadwood canyon. To reach the **upper put-in** from the Deadwood-South Fork confluence, drive about 6.5 miles down the South Fork on the Banks-Lowman Highway, then turn north onto USFS 555, also known as Scott Mountain Road. (This turnoff is about 25 miles east of Banks.) The rough, slow road winds a little over 25 miles to Deadwood Reservoir. Put in where the road crosses the river below the dam.

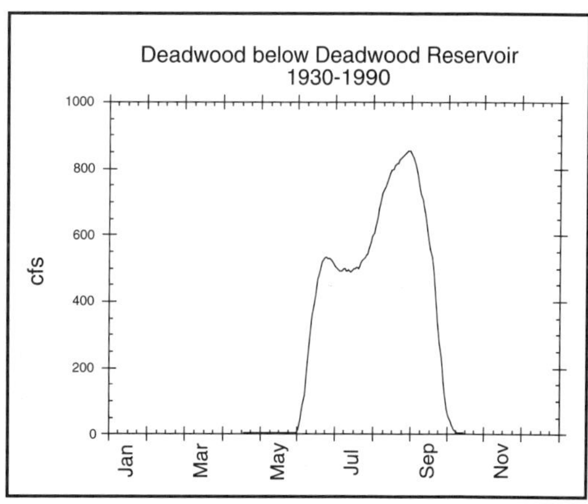

The Deadwood River is the only wilderness run in the Payette system. Those who are up to its considerable challenges will enjoy unspoiled forest scenery, deep solitude, and abundant wildlife. The first 14 miles below Deadwood Dam are truly roadless, while the final nine miles to the South Fork confluence are nearly so; only a lightly used, unpaved Forest Service road follows the lower river, usually high above the right bank.

This run is for experts only. Boaters face cold water, isolation, a steep gradient, and technical Class IV and V rapids. Hiking out from the upper run would be very difficult. Though it is a major tributary of the South Fork Payette, the Deadwood is still a small, low-volume river. **Strainers** are the key hazard; true to its name, the river is full of **log jams.** Numerous portages are likely, so this run is suitable only for lightweight craft. Logs can shift at any time; if possible, ask local boaters about conditions before running. However, don't rely on second-hand information. Scout any time you cannot see a clear passage.

A dirt road provides intermediate access nine miles above the South Fork confluence, dividing the Deadwood into upper and lower runs. Despite its slightly lower gradient, the upper reach is actually more challenging than the lower. Boaters can run the entire 23 miles—upper plus lower—in one long day, but the slow shuttle and frequent portages make this a demanding effort. Those who attempt the full run should get an early start and hire a driver if possible. One-day runs of the lower river are popular because of the much shorter shuttle.

Deadwood River Mile Guide

Note: Experts only. Only the biggest rapids are listed here. Frequent scouting is a must.

0 **PUT-IN** below Deadwood Dam (see **Logistics**). A mile and a half downstream, Whitehawk Creek enters on the left. Not far below the creek, the river's gradient and difficulty increase. **Watch for a portage around a log jam near mile 2.5.**

6 Scott Creek enters on the right.

8.5 Lorenzo Creek enters on the left. **About a mile downstream is the most dangerous rapid on the run.** Recognize it by big logs poking out of the water at a horizon line. Scout and **portage** on the right.

14 **RIVER ACCESS.** Deadwood River Road meets the river, then continues downstream, usually high above the right bank. **The next 3 miles are very steep and difficult** in a narrow section of the canyon.

23 **RIVER ACCESS.** The Banks-Lowman Highway crosses the Deadwood at the South Fork Payette confluence. Take out here or continue down the South Fork.

South Fork Payette River

Grandjean to Banks

1. Grandjean Run: Grandjean (4,995') to Lowman (3,800').
III+; 29 miles; 40 ft./mi.

2. Canyon Run: Deadwood River (3,675') to Danskin (3,220').
IVp; 12 miles; 38 ft./mi.

3. Swirly Canyon Run: Danskin to Deer Creek (2,945').
II+; 15 miles; 19 ft./mi.

4. Staircase Run: Deer Creek to Banks (2,795').
IV-; 5 miles; 30 ft./mi.

Drainage Area and Average Annual Discharge: 456 sq. mi. and 650,000 af at Lowman, above Deadwood confluence; est. 1,200 sq. mi. and 1,350,000 af at Banks.

Season: *Run 1:* May–early July. *Runs 2 & 3:* May–August. *Run 4:* April–Sept. *See hydrograph on following page.*

Recommended Levels: 1,000–3,000 cfs.

Flow Information: DWR tape, (208) 327-7865. Estimate flows as follows: *Run 1:* Use South Fork flow at Lowman. *Runs 2 & 3:* Combine Lowman flow with Deadwood flow below the reservoir. *Run 4:* Subtract North Payette at Cascade from Payette at Horseshoe Bend.

Special Hazards: Big Falls on Run 2. Logs, primarily on Run 1.
Land Ownership: Mostly National Forest in first two runs, mixed thereafter.
Wilderness: No.
Scenery: Very good; best on Run 2.
Solitude: Good; best on Run 2.
Maps:
- USGS 7.5': *Lowman, Pine Flat, Grimes Pass, Garden Valley, Banks.*

Auto Shuttle: Roughly same as river mileages. Contact Cascade Raft Co., (208) 462-3292.
Logistics: *Run 1:* Take out at the town of Lowman, which is roughly 70 miles northeast of Boise. To reach the many **alternate put- ins,** drive upstream along Idaho Highway 21. To reach the **upper put-ins near Grandjean,** bear right on USFS Road 524 some 20 miles above Lowman.

Lower Runs: **The lowermost take-out is at Banks.** Upstream access is via the Banks-Lowman Highway, which follows the right bank for some 35 miles between Idaho 55 at Banks and Idaho 21 at Lowman. (Boaters can approach from either end of this road.) **Deer Creek Bridge site** is 5 miles east of Banks. The **Danskin access** is about 23 miles east of Banks at a turnout just east of Danskin Station. **Deadwood River access** is near Deadwood Campground at the Deadwood confluence, some 32 miles east of Banks and 3 miles west of Lowman.

No wonder the South Fork of the Payette is a favorite among Boise boaters, with its fine scenery, easy road access, enticing riverside hot springs, and the most varied whitewater in the Payette system. Beginning as a sparkling mountain torrent in the rugged Sawtooth Wilderness, the South Fork tumbles down to its confluence with the Deadwood River below the small town of Lowman. The dam-regulated Deadwood enters from the north, boosting summer flows on the South Fork's lower runs.

Aside from one portage, the South Fork is continuously boatable for 61 miles. But most river runners make day trips down one of the four runs described here.

The lightly-used Grandjean-to-Lowman stretch offers good whitewater during a short boating season. Highway 21 and a Forest Service road follow the river, providing many alternate access points. Boaters can launch as far upstream as Grandjean, but they must scout for logs in the channel, especially in the first few miles. More popular runs are below Canyon Creek (mile 4) and Helende Campground (mile 18). The eight miles from Helende to Lowman show the scars of a major wildfire that swept through the upper canyon in 1989. This chapter has no mile guide or map for the Grandjean Run, and it is not shown on the Payette map. Many Class III and III+ rapids punctuate this stretch, and a few drops rate Class IV at certain flows. Watch for logs throughout; if in doubt, scout.

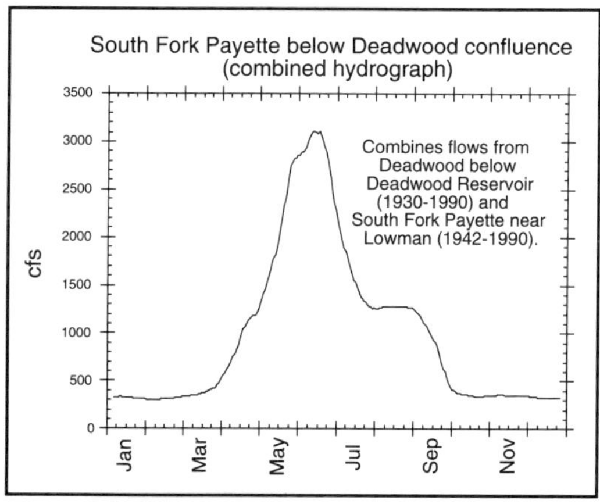

Below the Deadwood River confluence is the Canyon Run, the most challenging reach of the South Fork. Here the canyon is deep and scenic, with dramatic outcrops of dark, jagged rock. A mandatory portage makes this run best suited to lightweight craft. The road climbs high above the river, giving boaters a stronger sense of solitude than on other runs.

Next up is Swirly Canyon, where the river ambles through a narrow, scenic gorge. Turbulent eddy lines and unpredictable currents give this milder section its name. Watch out for low cables and pipes over the river, especially at higher flows. Below Swirly Canyon the river glides through lovely Garden Valley, where the Middle Fork Payette enters. The South Fork finishes with a bang at the Staircase Run, a five-mile joyride through some of Idaho's best-loved rapids. Most trips end at the North Fork confluence at Banks, but boaters can continue down the Main Payette.

South Fork Payette Mile Guide

Canyon Run

0 **PUT-IN** on the right bank just above the Deadwood River confluence, across the highway from Deadwood Campground. Downstream, the road climbs high on the right as the South Fork Payette enters a scenic canyon. Half a mile below the put-in, the South Fork enters mile-long Oxbow Bend, where miners diverted the river through a tunnel on the right bank. **OXBOW RAPID (III+)** is near the beginning of the bend.

3 Pine Flats Hot Springs on the right, just below Pine Flats Campground. Not far downstream is **GATEWAY (III+)**. A bigger and longer rapid, **S-TURN (IV-)**, is at mile 5.

5.7 **BIG FALLS (VI).** ***HAZARD. PORTAGE.*** Below a right bend, a series of runnable drops leads into an unrunnable 30' cascade. **Mandatory portage on the left.** Eddy up well above the falls. Just below the portage is **BLACKADAR'S DROP (III+)**. In 1978 the famous kayaker Dr. Walt Blackadar died when his boat was trapped by a log caught in this rapid. A commemorative plaque is on the right above the drop. This is the deepest point in the canyon.

7 **LONE PINE (III+)**. A solitary pine stands above the right bank between the river and the highway, which has returned almost to river level at this point. More difficult at higher flows, when a nasty hole develops.

7.8 Big Pine Creek enters on the right. Just downstream is a possible **RIVER ACCESS** at a highway turnout on the right. About 200 yards below this access, at a left bend, is **LITTLE FALLS (IV+)**, an abrupt ledge. A half mile below the falls is the last major rapid, **SURPRISE (IV)**, with a hole at the bottom that sometimes flips rafts. A steep **RIVER ACCESS,** often used by kayakers, is at the left bend below Surprise.

12 **RIVER ACCESS.** A short, steep trail leads to a large turnout a couple of hundred yards upstream from Danskin Station, a small building located a few hundred yards above Danskin Creek and not visible from the river.

Swirly Canyon

12 Danskin access. (See above.) No rapids above Class II+ for the next 15 miles. The road is often out of sight above the right bank.

17 Alternate **RIVER ACCESS** where a steep trail climbs the right bank to the highway near Hot Springs Campground, which is not visible from the river.

20 Alder Creek enters on the left just above the Alder Creek Bridge, a popular alternate **RIVER ACCESS.** For the next 4 miles the South Fork drifts quietly through broad Garden Valley, where the road is well away from the river.

24 The Middle Fork Payette enters on the right as the road returns to the right bank. Alternate **RIVER ACCESS** on the right about 200 yards below the confluence. Downstream, the canyon narrows.

26.5 Old bridge pilings mark the Deer Creek Bridge site, where Deer Creek enters on the left. A popular **RIVER ACCESS** is a quarter mile downstream on the right.

Staircase Run

27.2 **BRONCO BILLY (IV-)**, just below a hot springs and a creek entering on the right. Big reversal at the bottom. Just downstream are **DOGLEG (III+)** and **TIGHT AND RIGHT,** followed by the "Play Wave," used for the surfing contest at the annual Payette Whitewater Rodeo.

29.3 **STAIRCASE (IV)**, the toughest rapid on the run. A long boulder maze. Easy scout from the road. A mile below Staircase is the last rapid, **SLALOM.**

31.5 Highway 55 bridge and North Fork confluence at Banks. Ferry across the North Fork to the **TAKE-OUT** on the right bank, or continue down the Main Payette.

Main Payette River

Banks to Beehive Bend

Difficulty: III-.
Gradient: 14 ft./mi.
Length: 7 miles.
Put-in: Banks (2,795').
Take-out: Beehive Bend (2,700').
Drainage Area and Average Annual Discharge: 2,230 sq. mi. and 2,395,000 af.
Peak Recorded Flow: 27,000 cfs (Dec. 23, 1964).
Season: April–September.
Recommended Levels: 2,000–6,000 cfs.
Flow Information: Idaho DWR, (208) 327-7865. Flow at Horseshoe Bend.

Scenery: Good. A wildfire burned through much of this lightly forested canyon in 1992.
Solitude: Fair. **Wilderness:** No.
Logistics: Idaho Highway 55 follows this run closely, providing short shuttles. The **take-out at Beehive Bend,** marked by a "Sportsmans Access" sign, is just off Highway 55 some 7 miles north of the junction with Idaho Highway 52 at Horseshoe Bend. The **put-in** is 7 miles upriver on the right bank across from the hamlet of **Banks** (see **Logistics** for North Fork Payette).

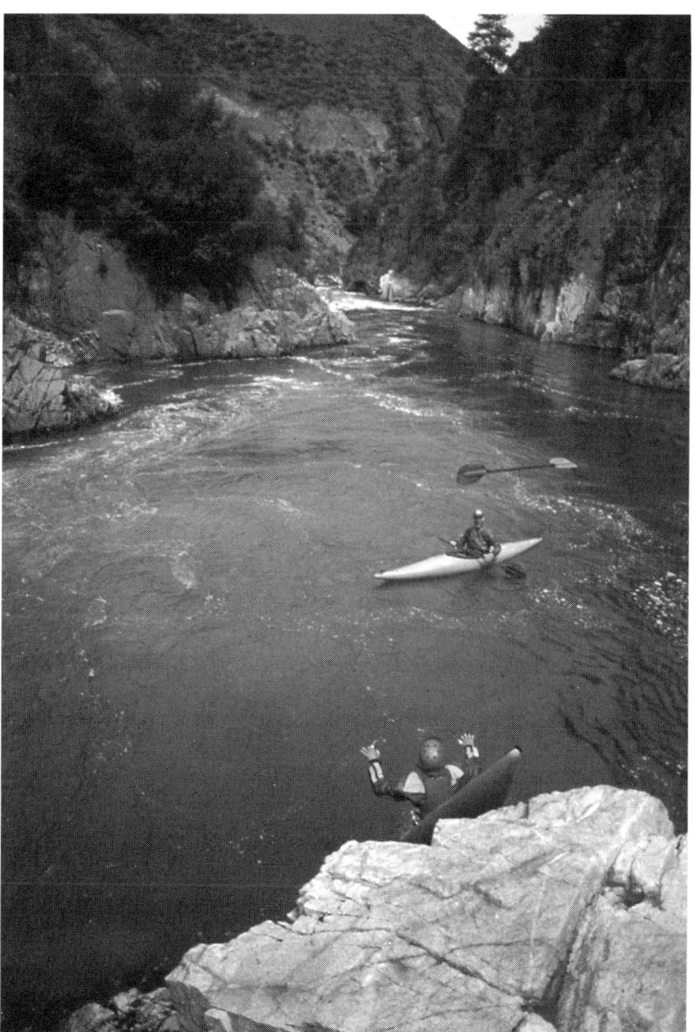

Kayakers on the South Fork Payette *Steve Bly*

Far from the madding crowd this is not. The Main Payette may be the most popular river in Idaho. Hordes of weekend warriors enjoy its boisterous but forgiving rapids, summer-long flows, and proximity to Boise. Boating here is a social experience: a busy highway on one bank, a railroad on the other, and countless rafts, kayaks, and canoes in between. For camaraderie, this is the place. If it's seclusion and escape you want, head upstream to the runs on the Payette tributaries described earlier.

Beginning at the confluence of the North and South Forks, the Main Payette offers seven miles of easy Class III. Intermediates should launch at the confluence; expert and advanced boaters can tack this section on to their runs down either of the forks.

The first two miles provide an easy warm-up. From mile 2.5 to mile 5.5 the river runs through four or five Class III drops. The roughest spots are **MIKES HOLE,** at mile 3.5 where Fleming Creek enters on the left, and **MIXMASTER** and **A.M.F.** near the end of the run. The usual **take-out** is on the left bank at Beehive Bend.

Middle Snake River

The Middle Snake is the lifeblood of southern Idaho's agricultural heartland. As a consequence this 500-mile arc of river, from the Wyoming border in the east to the Oregon border in the west, is dotted with dams and diversions. Yet enough free-flowing stretches remain to attract river runners to the "Mid-Snake," as the river is sometimes called.

At the eastern end of the Middle Snake is a quiet float known as the "South Fork of the Snake" (though it is actually the main stem of the river), and at the western end is an equally placid reach known as the Birds of Prey Run. In between lie the intermediate rapids of the Wiley Reach, the big-water drops of the Murtaugh Run, and the massive hydraulics of the experts-only Milner Run.[1]

This long stretch of the Snake was shaped by relatively recent volcanic activity. Beginning about ten million years ago, repeated lava flows from the north pushed the river southward and created the Snake River Plain, a plateau of volcanic rock that borders the river for 250 miles. No streams cross the plain; all water sinks into the porous rock and becomes part of the vast Snake River Aquifer. In fact, no major tributaries enter the Snake from the north for 261 miles, from the Henrys Fork east of Idaho Falls to the Malad River west of Twin Falls.

The Snake itself leaks prodigious amounts of water into the aquifer. Before it reaches the plain the river's year-round average flow is about 7,000 cfs; at Milner, some 200 miles downstream, it is just 2,850 cfs. Not all the loss is due to leakage; much of the Snake's flow is diverted to seemingly endless fields of potatoes and sugar-beets. Milner Dam, just above the Milner and Murtaugh runs, feeds some 2,600 miles of irrigation canals. By midsummer the Snake is often drained nearly dry below this point.

The water leaked to the aquifer flows underground to the southwest, finally emerging as artesian springs at the western edge of the Snake River Plain. In the Thousand Springs area west of Twin Falls, artesian flow swells the Snake from a moderate-sized river to one of the West's master streams in just a few miles. By some estimates, artesian flow accounts for some 85 percent of the Snake's flow at this point (see sidebar).

The region's volcanic history also explains the violent pool-and-drop rapids of the Central Snake's middle reaches. The most dramatic example is Shoshone Falls, the "Niagara of the West." At a height of 212', the falls actually surpass Niagara by 45'. (A proposed increase in the diversion around the falls may largely dewater this spectacular cataract.)

[1]Several runs covered here are threatened by hydroelectric projects. The conservation group Idaho Rivers United is campaigning for federal and state protection of these sections of the Snake. (See appendix for address.)

Middle Snake—General Data

Permits: Not required at this time.

Commercial Raft Trips: On most runs. Contact Idaho Outfitters & Guides Assn., P.O. Box 95, Boise, ID 83701; (208) 342-1919.

Guides and References:

- Amaral, *Idaho: The Whitewater State.* Covers all runs except the "South Fork."
- Moore & McClaran, *Idaho Whitewater.* Covers all runs.
- Palmer, *The Snake River: Window to the West.* Politics, conservation, essays.

The Snake-Colorado Project

Abundant artesian flow at Thousand Springs west of Twin Falls explains the siting for one of the most audacious water diversions ever envisioned—the Snake-Colorado Project. Proposed in the early 1960's by the Bureau of Reclamation, the project would pump 2.4 million acre-feet of "surplus" water out of the Snake each year and send it over 500 miles south to Lake Mead on the Colorado to slake the thirsts of southern California and Arizona. In 1963 the Bureau estimated that this engineering marvel could be built for only $1.4 billion. Today's price tag is anyone's guess. For years the proposal sat on a back burner, but in 1990 the Los Angeles County Board of Supervisors called for new federal feasibility studies of this project and of a second massive aqueduct to divert water from the Columbia River to Shasta Reservoir on California's Sacramento River. The governors of Idaho, Oregon and Washington denounced the schemes.

"South Fork" Snake River

Palisades Dam to Byington

Difficulty: II-.
Length: 41 miles. Shorter runs possible.
Gradient: 9 ft./mi.
Put-in: Palisades Dam (5,365').
Take-out: Byington Access (5,015').
Season: April–Nov. Season limited by weather; runnable flows all year, controlled by Palisades Dam. Releases can fluctuate suddenly. Typically peaks from 18,000 to 25,000 cfs in late June or early July.
Recommended Levels: 1,500–20,000 cfs.
Flow Information: Call Idaho DWR, (208) 327-7900, for flow "near Irwin" or "at Heise."
Special Hazards: Weir below take-out.
Managing Agency: Palisades RD, Targhee NF, P.O. Box 398-B, Route 1, Idaho Falls, ID 83401; (208) 523-1412. Also BLM, 940 Lincoln Rd., Idaho Falls, ID 83401; (208) 524-7500.
Land Ownership: Mixed USFS, BLM, and private. Refer to *South Fork Snake Boater's Guide.*
Scenery: Very good. Lightly forested canyon.
Wilderness: Partial. Highway or dirt road along some sections.
Solitude: Good first 15 miles, excellent thereafter.
Guides and References: *South Fork of the Snake River Boater's Guide* (available from BLM and USFS).
Maps: *Targhee NF* covers most of this run.
Logistics: Shuttles are via U.S. 26. The **upper put-in** is off U.S. 26 just below Palisades Dam, about 55 miles east of Idaho Falls. Convenient **intermediate accesses** are at Spring Creek, on the left bank at the U.S. 26 bridge west of Swan Valley, and **Conant Valley** two miles downstream, just off U.S. 26 (a good put-in for lower river floats).

To reach the **Byington take-out,** turn north off U.S. 26 toward the hamlet of Poplar (the turnoff is about 1.4 miles east of the Heise turnoff, some 25 miles east of Idaho Falls). Drive north 1.1 miles, turn right and drive to the boat ramp on the left bank. For other accesses refer to the *Boater's Guide* listed above.

East of the city of Idaho Falls, the Snake flows through wooded bottomlands and a secluded canyon in a gentle reach known as the "South Fork of the Snake." In fact this is the river's main stem, but locals refer to the stretch above the confluence with the Henrys Fork as the "South Fork." Palisades Reservoir separates this section from Alpine Canyon just upstream in Wyoming.

The "South Fork" run has strong current and mostly Class II rapids, but high flows in spring produce tricky currents and standing waves that can swamp open canoes. The scenery includes lush riparian woodland where birds and other wildlife abound. The river teems with cutthroat and brown trout as well as whitefish, making this section popular with anglers.

The first nine miles below Palisades Dam are narrow and hold the strongest riffles. Though U.S. 26 is near, this initial stretch offers good scenery, with views of the 8,000' Caribou Mountains to the west. Near mile 9 the river broadens and begins flowing among large islands. At mile 12, Fall Creek Falls appears on the left. U.S. 26 crosses at **mile 13,** with the **Spring Creek Access** just above the bridge on the left. Downstream the highway follows the river closely for two miles to **Conant Valley Access.**

Below Conant Valley is the most popular float. The Snake leaves the highway and winds through a scenic canyon bounded by rock walls and forested slopes. Though farms and ranches are just above the rim to the west, this stretch has a wilderness flavor. Much of the land is public, and camping is excellent. At **mile 29** a dirt road begins to follow the right bank, providing **alternate accesses.** But a take-out on the right means a longer, rougher shuttle, so most boaters continue to the **Byington Access** on the left at **mile 41.** Below this point the river winds through open farmland. ***HAZARD.* If you continue downstream, beware of a dangerous diversion a little over a mile below the Byington take-out.**

Milner and Murtaugh Runs

1. Milner Run: Milner Dam (4,070')
to above Star Falls.
V; 6.5 miles; 25 ft./mi.
(70 ft./mi. first 1.5 miles).

2. Murtaugh Run: Murtaugh Bridge
to Twin Falls Reservoir (3,510').
IV5; 13 miles; 25 ft./mi.

Season: Varies widely. Usually best April–mid-June and Sept.–Nov. and too low in mid-summer due to irrigation diversions. In dry years there may be no boating season. In years when snowmelt fills upstream reservoirs, peak flows reach 10,000 to 20,000 cfs.

Under a new agreement, Milner Dam will release boatable flows on as many as 12 weekend days per summer in years of adequate runoff. For updated information, contact managing agency or Idaho River Sports in Boise, (208) 336-4844.

Recommended Levels: *Run 1:* 1,500–10,000 cfs. *Run 2:* 1,500–20,000 cfs.

Flow Information: Idaho DWR, (208) 327-7865, or BuRec, (208) 678-0461; flow at Milner.

Special Hazards: Star Falls (mandatory portage) below take-out on Milner Run. Pair-A-Dice Rapid on Murtaugh Run.

Managing Agency: BLM, Shoshone District, 400 W. F Street, P.O. Box 2-B, Shoshone, ID 83352; (208) 886-2206.

Land Ownership: Some BLM, mostly private.

Scenery: Excellent. Steep-walled basalt gorges.

Solitude: Very good. **Wilderness:** No.

Guides and References:
- *Murtaugh Section of the Snake River* (BLM). Available from Shoshone office.

Maps: USGS 7.5': *Milner, Milner Butte, Murtaugh, Eden, Kimberly, Twin Falls.*

Logistics: *Milner Run:* Take Exit 194 from I-84 east of Twin Falls and drive south 3 miles on Ridgeway Road to a T-intersection where the routes divide. To reach the **take-out,** turn right and drive west 1 mile, then south 1.2 miles, then west 2.5 miles; then south to the access on the right above Star Falls (may require 4-wheel drive). To reach the **put-in,** turn left at the T-intersection, drive east 1.5 miles, then south 1.2 miles; then bear right at the Y and descend to the put-in bridge.

Murtaugh Run: To reach the **take-out,** take Exit 182 from I-84, drive south 1.1 miles on Highway 50 (stop at Hansen Bridge to look at Pair-A-Dice Rapid); turn right on Addison Ave., drive west 3 miles, then turn right on 3500 East and drive north about 2.5 miles, winding down to **Twin Falls Park take-out.** To reach the **put-in,** return to I- 84 and drive east to Exit 188; then drive south 3 miles, then east 1.2 miles, then south another 3 miles to the put-in on the right bank at the bridge. (An alternate put-in one mile upstream, just below Star Falls, involves a long carry around the big drop.)

Milner Run

The Milner Run, the most difficult section of the entire Snake, is emphatically for **experts only.** Big volume and steep gradient produce some of the largest hydraulics in the West. The run is often reduced to a trickle by upstream diversions, and it could be de-watered entirely by a proposed hydroelectric diversion. But in average and wet years, with springtime peaks of 10,000 cfs and up and a drop of nearly 100' in one wild mile, this run has overwhelming power.

Sharp ledges in the basalt gorge produce a continuum of enormous waves and massive holes flanked by swirling eddies. **Boaters should scout the entire mile and a half of whitewater before putting in.**

After a mile and a half of furious rapids, the river suddenly becomes flat for the remaining five miles. An alternate take-out on the left at mile 1.5 avoids the flatwater but involves a long carry. ***HAZARD.*** **Take out on the right well above STAR FALLS,** a beautiful but lethal 40' double drop. Or make a very difficult portage and continue down the Murtaugh Run.

Murtaugh Run

The Murtaugh Run is a popular day trip for advanced boaters—when it has water. Too often, this is not the case. There was no boating season at all during the drought of the late 1980's and early 1990's. In an average year, spring snowmelt can swell the river to 10,000

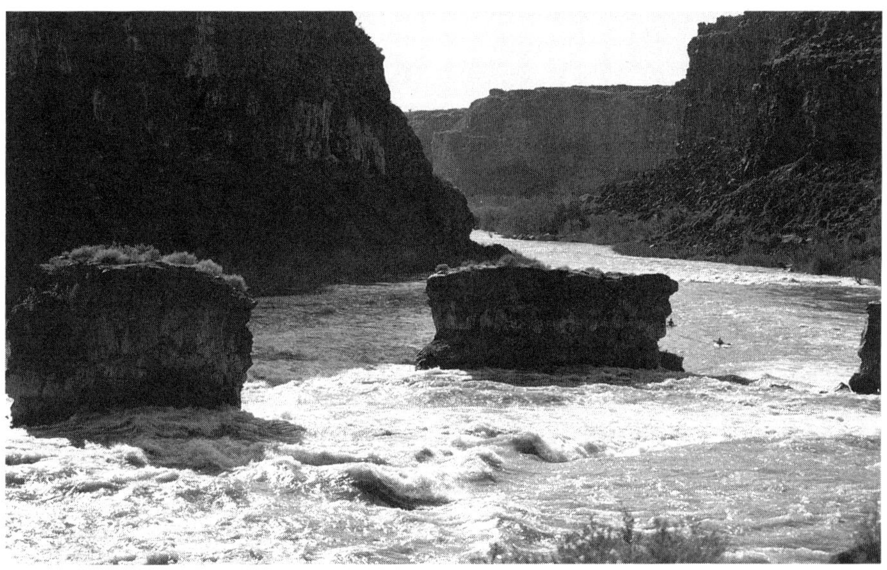
Let's Make a Deal Rapid, Murtaugh Run, Middle Snake *Tom Whittaker*

to 20,000 cfs. But in midsummer, dam releases are usually cut to a trickle.[2] Many springs cascade from the walls, particularly in the lower part of the run.

The 400'-deep canyon cuts through jagged volcanic basalt, and sharp ledges produce big holes at all flows. The Murtaugh Run is very difficult at low water when the river is confined to the narrow, boulder-choked inner gorge; many drops are steep and technical, and entrapment dangers exist. The run is easiest around 5,000 cfs and again becomes more difficult at higher flows. The surfing is some of the finest in Idaho. Around 9,000 cfs the waves grow enormous and the eddies become turbulent. For rafters large self-bailers are recommended at high flows. **Above 15,000 this run approaches Class V; those whose big-water skills are unequal to the challenge should stay away.**

The easiest **put-in** is at **Murtaugh Bridge.** (Eager boaters can add one mile and two good rapids by choosing a very difficult put-in below **STAR FALLS**; see **Logistics.**) Below the bridge the action begins immediately. Near mile 2.5 the river pools before plunging over **MAYBELLINE (IV).**

Class III rapids continue to mile 7, where a pair of rock islands on the right mark the beginning of the rough stuff. Just downstream are the big hydraulics of **MISTY (IV),** followed in the next two miles by three Class IV rapids: **JUNKYARD** (look for rubbish on the bank), **HORSESHOE,** and a long series of undulating rollers at **SINE WAVES.** Below Sine Waves, near mile 9.5, the high Hansen Bridge appears downstream, signaling the approach of **PAIR-A-DICE (V; commonly portaged at higher flows).** Here the Snake divides around two rock islands, with a possible run down the center. ***HAZARD.*** **At all costs avoid the right channel, which thunders into an enormous 20'-wide keeper reversal.** Most boaters land in a small cove on the upstream side of the left island to scout and, frequently, portage over the island (alternate portage on the left bank).

Below Hansen Bridge is a riverwide ledge known as **THE HOOKER (IV; V at low flows),** typically run far right. Just downstream at mile 10.3 is another big drop, **LET'S MAKE A DEAL (IV; IV+ at high flows),** where huge blocks of lava divide the river into five "doors." The doors become more difficult as you move to the right. Door 2 is most popular, and Doors 4 and 5 on the far right are not recommended (except possibly at low flows). The big blocks were deposited here about 15,000 years ago by the catastrophic "Bonneville Flood."

After two smaller rapids, **REDSHANK** and **DUCK BLIND,** the run ends with the superb surfing waves of **THE IDAHO CONNECTION** (mile 11.5). Twin Falls Reservoir begins just downstream, and kayakers sometimes paddle up from the take-out to surf. ***HAZARD.*** **Don't miss the take-out on the left at mile 13—Twin Falls,** the 80' waterfall from which the city takes its name, **is only a few hundred yards downstream.**

[2]Boatable releases on summer weekends are possible; see **Season.** Idaho Rivers United (see earlier footnote) is campaigning for adequate minimum flows.

Wiley Reach

Lower Salmon Falls Dam to Bliss Bridge

Difficulty: II+ **Gradient:** 13 ft./mi.
Length: 7.5 miles.
Put-in: Below Lower Salmon Falls Dam (2,745').
Take-out: Below Bliss Bridge (2,650').
Season: All year.
Recommended Levels: 1,500–20,000 cfs.
Flow Information: Idaho DWR, (208) 327-7865. Use the flow at Murphy.
Managing Agency: BLM, Shoshone District (see **Milner and Murtaugh Runs**).
Scenery: Good. Shallow, semi-arid valley.
Solitude: Good. **Wilderness:** No.
Side Excursions: Hagerman Fossil Beds National Monument. Malad Gorge State Park.
Maps: USGS 7.5': *Hagerman, Bliss.*
Logistics: To reach the **take-out,** take Exit 141 from I-84 and drive a half mile west on U.S. 20/26 to Bliss; turn left (south) on the old highway and descend a mile into the canyon, then turn right on Shoestring Road and drive a mile downstream. Where Shoestring Road turns left toward Bliss Bridge, continue straight ahead and follow signs to the **BLM access** on the right bank below the bridge.

To reach the **put-in,** return upstream on Shoestring Road one mile, then bear right and drive upriver about 4 miles, turn right on U.S. 30, and cross the Malad River. To reach the **lower put-in,** turn right on a dirt road 200 yards past the Malad and descend to the Snake. To reach the **upper put-in,** drive south about two more miles on U.S. 30, then bear right and drive to the put-in some 500 yards below the dam.

The Wiley Reach of the Snake offers pleasant scenery and a sprinkling of big, friendly roller-coaster rapids. Also known as the Hagerman or Bliss Run, this section is best in spring and early summer, when high flows produce big waves.

Boaters can put in just below Lower Salmon Falls Dam or a mile downstream near the mouth of the Malad River (sometimes shown on maps as the Big Wood River). The roughest spot, **PILLAR (III-)**, is about a half mile below the Malad confluence. This 500-yard stretch of big, cresting rollers takes its name from a support pillar standing in the river above the rapid—a remnant of a washed-out canal crossing. Enjoyable Class II to II+ rapids continue intermittently to the take-out on the right bank about a third of a mile below Bliss Bridge.

The proposed Wiley Dam would flood this entire run.

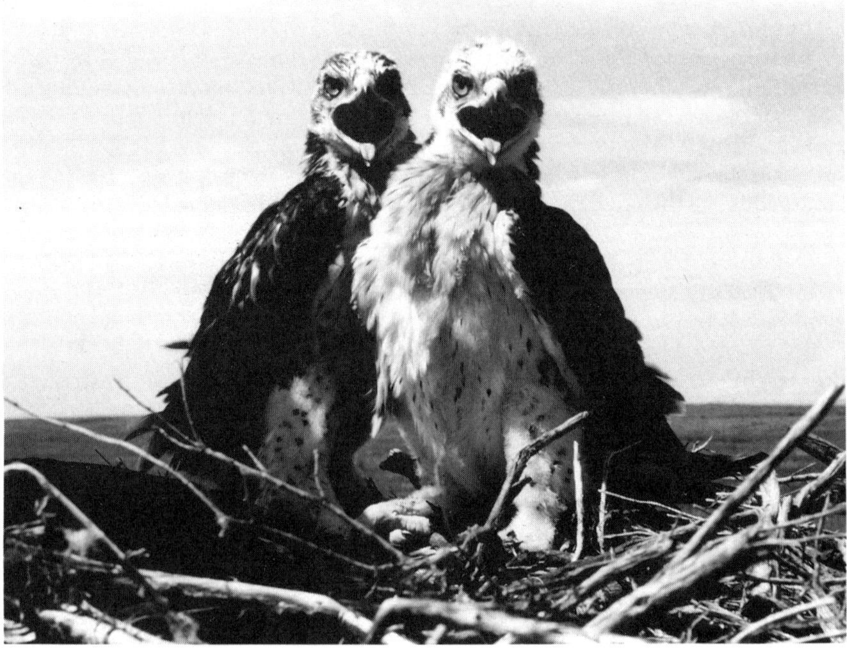

Fledgling ferruginous hawks *BLM, Boise District*

Upper and Lower Birds of Prey Runs

Black Butte Boat Ramp to Walters Ferry Bridge

1. Upper: Black Butte Boat Ramp (2,330') to above Swan Falls Dam.
I; 19 miles; 1 ft./mi.

2. Lower: Below Swan Falls Dam to Walters Ferry Bridge (2,245').
II-; 16 miles; 3 ft./mi.

Season: All year. Dam releases fluctuate, so camp high and tie boats securely.

Flow Information: Idaho DWR, (208) 327-7865; flow at Murphy.

Managing Agency: BLM, Boise District, 3948 Development Ave., Boise, ID 83705; (208) 384-3300.

Land Ownership: Mostly public. A few private parcels.

Scenery: Very good. High desert.

Solitude: Very good. Some motor boats.

Wilderness: Mostly. A few ranches and dirt roads.

Guides and References: *Snake River Birds of Prey Area* (BLM). Available from Boise office.

Maps: USGS 1:100: *Triangle, Murphy.*

Logistics: The runs are south of Boise. **Black Butte Boat Ramp,** on the right bank a few miles north of Grand View, is reached via unpaved roads off Idaho Highway 67; contact the BLM for directions. To reach **Swan Falls Dam,** drive to Kuna (southwest of Boise), then follow Swan Falls Road south some 18 miles to accesses above and below the dam on the right bank. **Walters Ferry** is on the left bank just below the Idaho Highway 45 bridge over the Snake south of Nampa. Contact the BLM for directions to the alternate take-out near the Old Guffey Railroad Bridge.

The Birds of Prey Runs take boaters through scenic terrain that is home to one of the world's largest concentrations of raptors—hawks, eagles, falcons and owls. Imposing basalt cliffs on this remote section of river in southwestern Idaho provide ideal nesting sites, while the surrounding sagebrush plains provide habitat for prey. Established in 1971, the Snake River Birds of Prey Area now covers 482,000 acres.

In recent years the bird population has numbered roughly 700 breeding pairs from some 14 species. Prairie falcons are most common, but sightings include golden eagles, bald eagles, red-tailed hawks, peregrine falcons and at least five species of owls. Most are not year-round residents, avoiding the canyon during summer heat. Mid-March to mid-June is the best time for bird watching. Binoculars are a must. *Please do not disturb the birds or their nesting areas.*

Boaters can choose between two runs—a flat upper stretch and a lower run that has some mild Class II riffles in the first few miles. Open canoes are well suited to these waters. Upstream winds can be a major problem, especially for rafts. Jet boats occasionally break the silence.

Swan Falls Dam separates the two runs in the deepest part of the canyon, but a 150-yard portage path around the west side of the dam allows a continuous run. The scenery is best near the end of the upper run and the beginning of the lower. You can shorten the lower run—and avoid several miles of slow water and open terrain—by taking out on the right near the Old Guffey Railroad Bridge ten miles below the dam.

Jarbidge and Bruneau Rivers

Jarbidge Forks to Hot Creek

Difficulty: IV5+.
Length: 69 miles (29 on Jarbidge, 40 on Bruneau). Shorter trips possible using intermediate access at Indian Hot Springs (mile 29).
Gradient: *Jarbidge:* 45 ft./mi. *Bruneau:* 28 ft./mi.
Put-in: Jarbidge Forks (Confluence of East and West Forks Jarbidge, 4,980').
Take-out: Below Hot Creek on Bruneau (2,600').
Drainage Area and Average Annual Discharge: 2,630 sq. mi. and 297,800 af.
Peak Recorded Flow: 6,860 cfs (May 15, 1984).
Season: Variable; some time mid-April to late June. Typically peaks in mid-to-late May, but this is also highly variable. Flow can change quickly.
Recommended Levels: 800–2,000 cfs at take-out. Minimum 300 for inflatable kayaks, inner-tubes, etc. **Much more difficult at higher flows.**
Flow Information: Idaho DWR, (208) 327-7865; flow at "Hot Springs" (Hot Creek take-out). Flows at Jarbidge put-in are much lower.
Rafts: Self-bailers (no large rafts) recommended on the Jarbidge. Pack light (probable portages).
Special Hazards: Extreme isolation in rugged, sheer-walled canyon. Difficult recommended portage at Jarbidge Falls. High water. Log jams on Jarbidge.
Permits: Not required, but privates must register with the managing agency. Group limit 15.
Managing Agency: BLM, 2620 Kimberly Rd., Twin Falls, ID 83301; (208) 736-2350.
Commercial Raft Trips: A few outfitters. Contact Idaho Outfitters & Guides Assn., P.O. Box 95, Boise, ID 83701; (208) 342-1919.

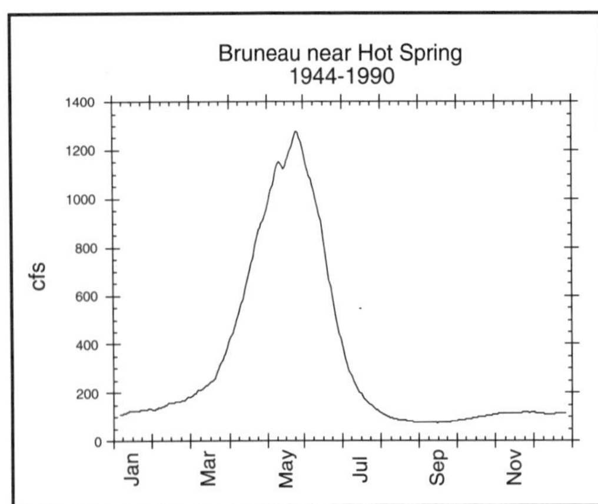

Land Ownership: Mostly BLM; some private.
Scenery: Excellent.
Solitude: Excellent. **Wilderness:** Yes.
Weather: High desert climate. Cold and snow possible in early season.
Water: Often cloudy; Jarbidge runs clear at lower flows. Undrinkable. Carry water or purify.
Camping: Good sites, but harder to find at high water. OK to camp at put-in. Watch for poison ivy.
Side Hikes: See **Mile Guide.**
Side Excursions: Scenic Overlook above river mile 62, accessible from shuttle road. Historic Gold Rush town of Jarbidge, Nevada 15 miles above the put-in.
Guides and References:
- Amaral, *Idaho: The Whitewater State.*
- Moore & McClaran, *Idaho Whitewater.*
- *Bruneau-Jarbidge River Guide* (BLM). Available from managing agency.

Maps:
- **USGS 7.5':** *Dishpan, Poison Butte, The Arch, Inside Lakes, Indian Hot Springs, Stiff Tree Draw, Winter Camp, Austin Butte, Crowbar Gulch, Hot Spring.*
- **USGS 1:100:** *Sheep Creek, Glenns Ferry.*

Auto Shuttle: 74 miles (about two hours) one way, mostly unpaved. **Contact:** Jumbo's Sinclair gas station or other businesses in Bruneau, Idaho. The BLM may also be able to recommend shuttle drivers.
Logistics: Some roads lack signs, and many dirt tracks crisscross this desert south of Boise and west of Twin Falls. If possible, confirm directions with locals or the BLM.

Several approaches to the **put-in** are possible. From the east, follow U.S. 93 to Rogerson, Idaho, turn west onto Jarbidge Road, and drive about 40 miles to the intersection with the Clover-Three Creek Road (sometimes called Bruneau-Three Creek Road). Bear left and follow Jarbidge Road another 9 miles to Murphy Hot Springs on the East Fork Jarbidge, then drive two miles downstream and put in at the confluence of the East and West Forks. Alternate routes to this put-in are via unpaved roads from Nevada Highway 225 or Idaho Highway 51 to the west, or directly from the take-out.

To reach the **take-out,** drive east on Jarbidge Road from the put-in, turn left (north) on Clover-Three Creek Road (not recommended when wet), and drive some 60 miles to the intersection with Blackstone-Grasmere Road. Turn left across the Bruneau, drive 1/4 mile, bear left again, drive 1.5 miles up the hill to the top, then turn left onto a rough dirt road that descends to the take-out.

For those driving to the take-out first, follow Idaho 51 to the town of Bruneau, Idaho, roughly 20 miles south of I-84, then drive 8 miles southeast on Hot Springs Road to the intersection with Blackstone-Grasmere Road. Turn right across the bridge and follow directions as above.

The **intermediate access at Indian Hot Springs** serves as a take-out for the Jarbidge or a put-in for the Bruneau and requires 4-wheel drive. Turn west off Clover-Three Creek Road some 27 miles north of Jarbidge Road or about 36 miles southeast of the town of Bruneau. The turnoff is a mile south of the point where Clover-Three Creek Road crosses the East Fork of the Bruneau (also called Clover Creek). From this turnoff drive west roughly 15 miles to the canyon rim, then make the final descent to the river. For more information refer to maps and contact the BLM.

Desert gorges carved by the Jarbidge and Bruneau in southwestern Idaho are among the most dramatic and spectacular canyons in the West. In this geologic wonderland soaring cliffs rise hundreds of feet from the river's edge. Boaters can combine the runs for a total 69-mile float that ranks as one of the West's great wilderness river trips.

In the Northwest only the nearby chasms of Oregon's Owyhee River rival the incredible vertical defiles of the Jarbidge and Bruneau. All three rivers have cut deep clefts into broad plateaus of rhyolite and basalt that were laid down by repeated volcanic eruptions between 8 and 12 million years ago. The rhyolite often weathers into fanciful pillars and spires known as "hoodoos," while the harder basalt forms unearthly, slot-like canyons of dark stone.

Like their sister river the Owyhee, the Jarbidge and Bruneau are relatively small, short-season tributaries of the Snake that rise high in the Humboldt National Forest of northeastern Nevada. Of the three, the Jarbidge drains the highest and wettest area—the beautiful Jarbidge Mountains and Jarbidge Wilderness, where 10,000' peaks tower over deep glacial canyons.

The East and West Forks of the Jarbidge run north toward Idaho, descending rapidly from forested slopes to desert canyons. At their confluence just north of the state line, where boating typically begins, the two forks have already

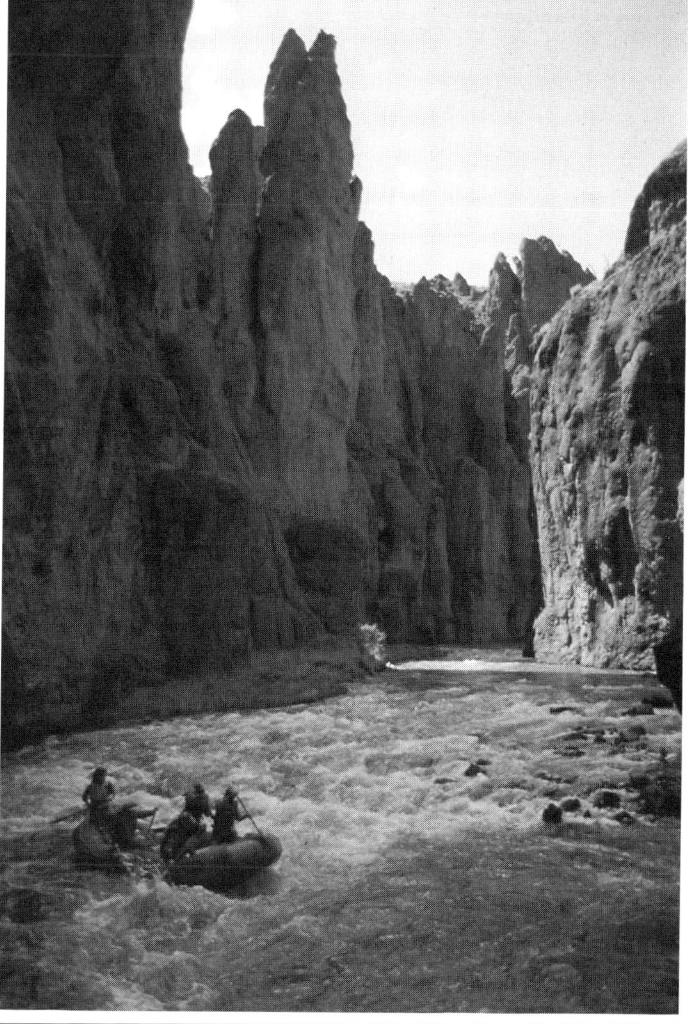

Bruneau River *Steve Bly*

carved 700' into the arid volcanic plateau. Downstream the main stem of the Jarbidge cuts even deeper, nearly doubling the depth of its canyon as it tumbles toward its meeting with the West Fork of the Bruneau. This confluence marks the beginning of the Bruneau River proper.

The West Fork Bruneau, with a lower and drier drainage, carries less water than the Jarbidge, but by geographic convention the longer Bruneau keeps its name when the two rivers join. Below this confluence the main stem of the Bruneau continues down its own impressive canyon, which finally opens some 20 miles above the junction with the Snake.

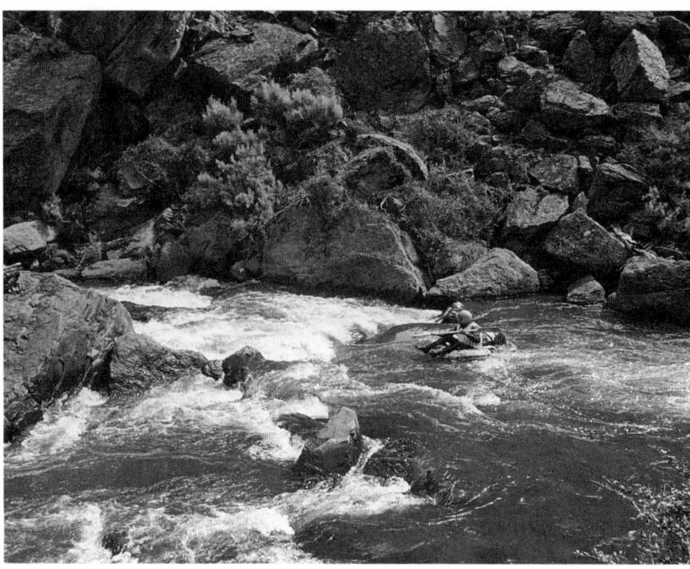

Adventurous tuber on the Jarbidge *Ted Weigold*

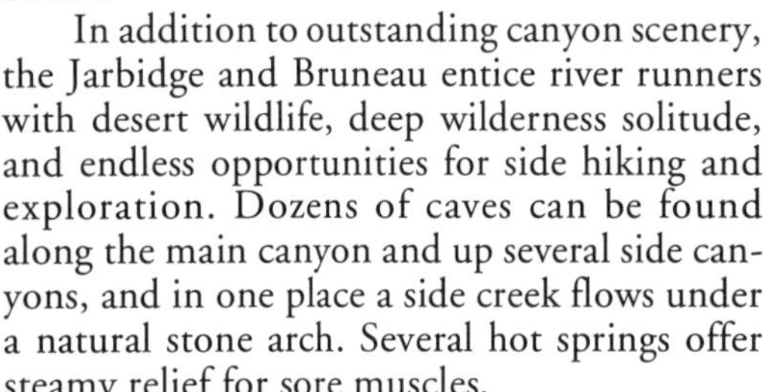

In addition to outstanding canyon scenery, the Jarbidge and Bruneau entice river runners with desert wildlife, deep wilderness solitude, and endless opportunities for side hiking and exploration. Dozens of caves can be found along the main canyon and up several side canyons, and in one place a side creek flows under a natural stone arch. Several hot springs offer steamy relief for sore muscles.

Guarded by sheer walls and stone parapets, the Bruneau and Jarbidge resisted exploration until long after the surrounding territory was mapped and surveyed. Among the first whites to peer into these gorges was Peter Skene Ogden, who explored the plateau country in 1826. Ogden and his company of trappers nearly perished of thirst in the high desert terrain along the rim, stymied from reaching the river by the canyon's sheer rock walls.

Even to the Shoshone who inhabited these lands for centuries, the gorges were a forbidding and mysterious realm. According to Shoshone legend, the "Jarbidge"[1] was a strange monster or beast that Indian braves pursued into a cave deep in the canyons. When the braves blocked the cave entrance with boulders, the Jarbidge was trapped inside. Even today, in these deeply shadowed chasms such legends seem plausible enough.

For modern canyon explorers, the Jarbidge provides plenty of excitement even without an encounter with its fearsome namesake. The 30 miles above the Bruneau confluence challenge expert wilderness boaters with a combination of low volume, steep gradient, narrow boulder-choked drops, possible log jams, a probable portage around Class V+ Jarbidge Falls, and at least two other rapids with slots that could prove too narrow for many boats, especially at lower flows. At high water the Jarbidge becomes a raging torrent that even experts should avoid.

After some 29 miles the Jarbidge merges with the West Fork Bruneau. An intermediate access at Indian Hot Springs, just below the confluence, allows boaters to break the trip into two separate runs. The access can be reached only by 4-wheel-drive vehicles.

Boaters should not be lulled by the lower gradient on the Bruneau, which is more of a pool-and-drop river than the relatively constant-gradient Jarbidge. Nevertheless, rafters in particular usually have an easier time on the Bruneau because the chutes are wider and there are normally no portages. The most serious challenge on the Bruneau is a rocky Class IV gauntlet known as Five Mile Rapids, where the gradient briefly reaches 80 ft./mi.

River runners must approach the Jarbidge and Bruneau with extra caution: even a minor mishap in these extremely rugged and isolated canyons could have serious conse-

[1] "Jarbidge" is the anglicized spelling of a Shoshone word—more closely approximated as "Tsau-hau-bitts" or "Ja-ha-bich"—which means "monster" or "devil." "Bruneau" is of French derivation, and may come either from the name of a French trapper, Baptiste Bruneau, or from a combination of the French words "brun" and "eau," meaning "brown water."

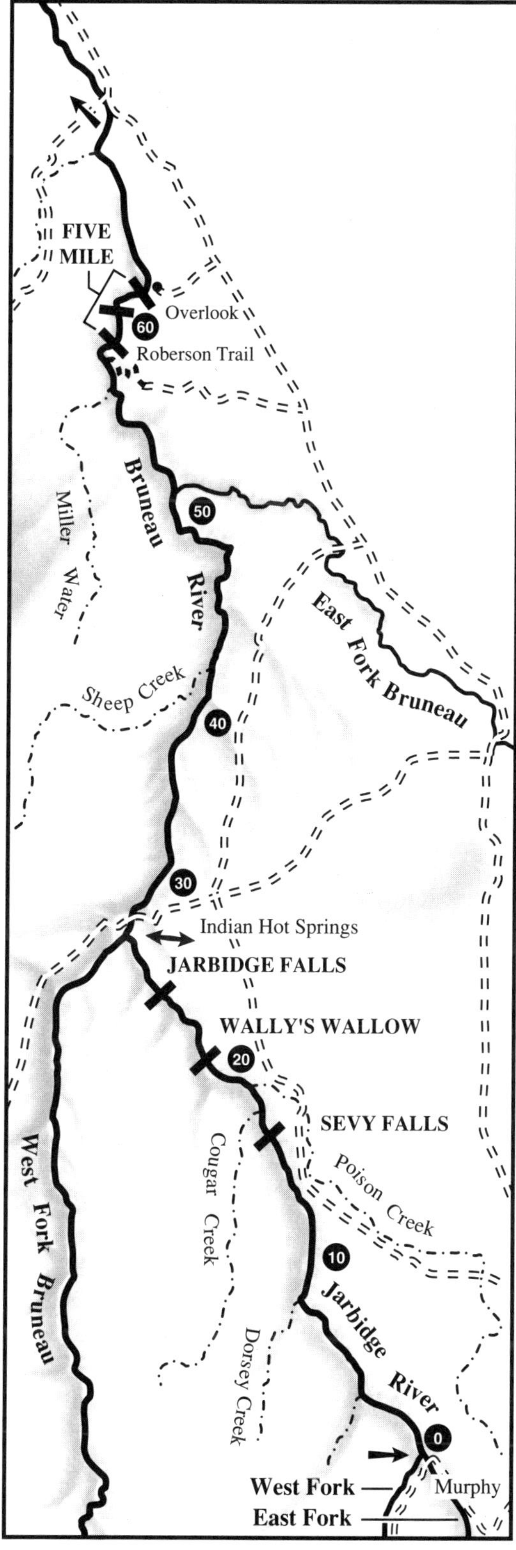

Jarbidge and Bruneau

quences. A couple of steep trails, one jeep track, and the river itself are the only ways out of the sheer-walled gorge. Help is a long way off and river traffic is light.

Those who scoff at such hazards might enjoy a hairball descent of the West Fork Bruneau—steeper and smaller than the Jarbidge and rarely run due to very difficult rapids, log hazards, poor access and a very short season. Trips begin either at Rowland, Nevada (accessible by two-wheel drive) or several miles downstream at Blackrock Crossing, Idaho (4-wheel drive required). At least three portages are usually necessary on the extremely demanding descent to Indian Hot Springs. For more information on this run, refer to the guide books listed above.

Some river runners might be tempted to join the growing number of adventurers who wait until July—when flows typically range from 150 to 500 cfs on the Bruneau and even less on the Jarbidge—to explore these rivers with inflatable kayaks, micro-cats, or combination innertube/backpack rigs. Boaters willing to do a little lining, scraping and pushing in the rocky spots can enjoy midsummer runs on a relative trickle of clear, sun-warmed water.[2]

[2]The Bruneau and Jarbidge, along with part of the upper Owyhee watershed, are threatened by a proposed Air Force bombing range west of the Bruneau (in addition to the present Saylor Creek Bombing Range just east of the river). This would mean more deafening high-speed flights over the canyons, the closure of large tracts of proposed wilderness lands, and potential ecological damage. It could also dash hopes of adding the Jarbidge and Bruneau to the National Wild amd Scenic Rivers System. The BLM recommended these rivers for Wild and Scenic protection back in 1975, but Congress has not acted. For more information contact Idaho Rivers United. (See appendix for address.)

Mile by Mile Guide

Jarbidge River

0 PUT-IN. Confluence of the East and West Forks of the Jarbidge. The first 3 miles are steep (55 ft./mi.), with nearly continuous Class II to III- riffles and rapids. **Watch for log jams.**

3.3 Columbet Creek enters on the left. Good side hike.

8.5 Dorsey Creek enters on the left. Good side hike. Tougher rapids downstream.

10.2 *HAZARD.* Use caution at a large, permanent-looking **log jam**. Numerous hoodoos in this section.

16.5 **SEVY FALLS (IV).** Steep, narrow chutes among big boulders. **Scouting mandatory; possible portage** if logs are in the tight channels. This rapid marks the beginning of 1.5 miles of Class III–IV whitewater. **Watch for logs.**

18 Cougar Creek enters on the left. Side hike up the creek into Arch Canyon, with caves and a natural bridge some 3 miles up.

19.2 Poison Creek on the right. The canyon opens slightly for the next 1.5 miles.

20.8 **WALLY'S WALLOW (IV+). Recognition:** Watch for a boulder slide as the canyon walls close in. **Mandatory scout; possible portage. The rapid:** Narrow chutes and steep drops between huge boulders. The next 5 miles have many Class III and IV rapids; continuous and very difficult at high flows.

25.5 **JARBIDGE FALLS (V+).** ***HAZARD.*** **Usually portaged.** A long, steep boulder maze. **Recognition:** Rockslide on right bank creates the rapid, and a house rock nearly blocks the river. Pull to the left bank well before the rock. Watch for poison ivy on the left-bank portage trail. About a mile downstream the canyon walls become less vertical and the gradient eases.

28.5 West Fork Bruneau enters from the left. Good hiking. This is the deepest section of the canyon (about 1,100').

Bruneau River

29.2 Indian Hot Springs. **RIVER ACCESS.** 4-wheel drive roads reach both banks, and a dilapidated bridge crosses the river. Rough road on the right provides an intermediate access (see **Logistics**). Put in here to run only the Bruneau. Hot spring water can be caught in an old porcelain tub for a soak. A pack trail follows the river, often high above the left bank, for the next 5 miles. A mile below the hot springs, the walls close in and the gradient increases in spectacular Bruneau Canyon.

30.5 **CAVE RAPID (III+).** *HAZARD.* Watch for an **undercut boulder** and a large, permanent-looking **log jam.** Class II and III rapids continue at intervals downstream.

36.5 Aptly-named Cave Draw enters on the left via a narrow opening. Good hiking.

41.8 Sheep Creek enters on the left. Good side hike; many caves farther up the creek. Half a mile up the creek on the north bank, a steep foot trail climbs to a jeep track on the rim.

50.3 East Fork Bruneau, also called Clover Creek, enters on the right. Below here the canyon is a little less vertical.

52 From the mouth of a small side canyon on the left, the Austin Trail, a very steep foot path, climbs to a rough dirt road on the west rim.

56.3 Miller Water, a side canyon on the left, offers good hiking.

58 **EMERGENCY RIVER ACCESS.** Roberson Trail fords the river, climbing out to dirt roads on both the east and west rims.

58.5 **FIVE MILE RAPIDS (IV).** 3 miles of technical, nearly continuous Class III and IV rapids at a gradient of almost 80 ft./mi., followed by two miles of milder rapids and easier gradient. **Recognition:** The first rapid, **BONEYARD,** begins about a quarter mile below a sharp right bend. Downstream, the walls gradually recede and the rapids ease to Class III.

65.7 A tricky Class III rapid as the river splits around an island. Scout left.

68 Hot Creek enters on the left. Several warm springs bubble from the Bruneau's left bank in the next half mile. The best place for a soak is a grotto on the left bank a few hundred feet above the take-out.

68.7 **TAKE-OUT.** BLM site on the left where the canyon opens up. ***HAZARD.*** **Don't continue downstream.** Two dangerous **diversion dams** in the next two miles. **Fences** are sometimes strung across the river.

Henrys Fork

Macks Inn Bridge to Ashton Bridge

1. Coffee Pot Rapids: Macks Inn Bridge (6,375') to McCrea Bridge.
III; 6 miles; 12 ft./mi.

2. Box Canyon: Island Park Dam to Last Chance.
II; 4 miles; 16 ft./mi.

3. Last Chance to Osborne Bridge.
I; 6 miles; 8 ft./mi.

4. Osborne Bridge to Riverside CG.
II; 6.5 miles; 9 ft./mi.

5. Riverside CG to East Hatchery Ford.
III; 4.5 miles; 25 ft./mi.

6. Cardiac Canyon: East Hatchery Ford to above Upper Mesa Falls.
VI_P; 6.5 miles; 50 ft./mi.

7. Below Lower Mesa Falls to Ashton Bridge (5,160').
III-; 13 miles; 18 ft./mi.

Drainage Area and Average Annual Discharge: 481 sq. mi. / 448,500 af at Island Park Dam; 1,040 sq. mi. / 1,087,000 af near Ashton Bridge.
Season: April–Oct.
Recommended Levels: 600–2,000 cfs.
Flow Information: Idaho DWR, (208) 327-7900; release from Island Park Reservoir and flow "at Ashton" (near take-out).
Special Hazards: Portages and lethal waterfalls in Run 6, Cardiac Canyon. **Daring experts only in Cardiac Canyon.**
Permits: Not presently required.
Managing Agency: Targhee NF, P.O. Box 208, St. Anthony's, ID 83445; (208) 624-3151.

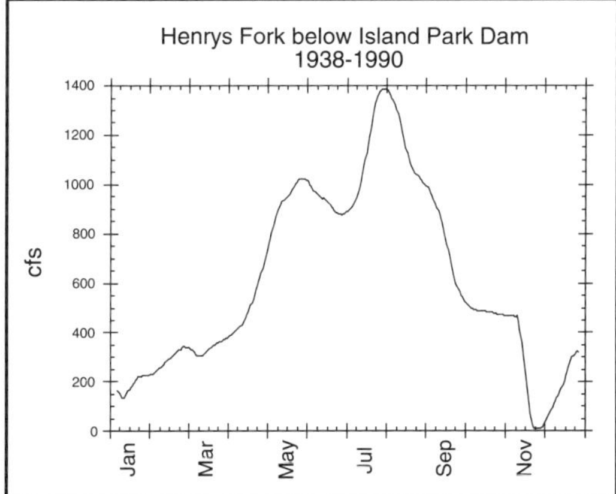

Commercial Raft Trips: No.
Land Ownership: *Run 1:* Mixed public and private. *Runs 2–6:* Mostly public. *Run 7:* Private.
Scenery: Very good. Forest, meadow, and canyon.
Solitude: Fair to very good, depending on run.
Wilderness: Partial.
Guides and References:

- Amaral, *Idaho: The Whitewater State.* Covers Runs 1, 2, 5–7.
- Moore & McClaran, *Idaho Whitewater.* Covers Runs 1 and 7.
- Charles Brooks, *The Henry's Fork.* Focuses on fishing, but includes history, access, etc.

Maps: *Targhee NF (Island Park, Ashton, Teton Basin, and Palisades RDs).* Covers all runs.
Side Excursions: Big Springs, source of most of the Henrys Fork's flow, some 5 miles east of Macks Inn, reached via USFS Road 59. Upper and Lower Mesa Falls Overlooks, reached via Mesa Falls Road (USFS Road 294) and/or Idaho Highway 47. See essay for descriptions.
Logistics: Most accesses are on or near U.S. 20 between the towns of Ashton and Macks Inn, Idaho, northeast of Idaho Falls. **Macks Inn Bridge** (U.S. 20) is 33 miles north of Ashton. To reach **McCrea Bridge,** drive south on U.S. 20 3.5 miles from Macks Inn, then west on USFS Road 30 two miles to the river. To reach **Island Park Dam,** turn west off U.S. 20 5.5 miles south of Macks Inn. **Last Chance** is located where U.S. 20 approaches the left bank 4 miles south of the Island Park turnoff.

Osborne Bridge is the U.S. 20 bridge 14 miles south of Macks Inn. To reach **Riverside Campground,** turn east off U.S. 20 3.5 miles south of Osborne Bridge or 15 miles north of Ashton. To reach **East Hatchery Ford,** follow U.S. 20 north 8 miles from Ashton (U.S. 20) Bridge or south 8 miles from Osborne Bridge, then drive east 3 miles on USFS Road 351.

Ashton Bridge is the U.S. 20 bridge 2.5 miles north of Ashton. To reach the **put-ins below Lower Mesa Falls,** take Idaho Highway 47 east from Ashton 8 miles to the turnoff to **Warm River Bridge** (alternate access) or another 7 miles to **Grandview Campground.**

> *I gave my heart to the mountains the minute I stood beside this river with its spray in my face and watched it thunder into foam, smooth to green glass over sunken rocks, shatter to foam again. I was fascinated by how it sped by and yet was always there; its roar shook both the earth and me.... By such a river it is impossible to believe that one will ever be tired or old. Every sense applauds it. Taste it, feel its chill on the teeth: it is purity absolute. Watch its racing current, its steady renewal of force: it is transient and eternal. And listen again to its sounds: get far enough away so that the noise of falling tons of water does not stun the ears, and hear how much is going on underneath—a whole symphony of smaller sounds, hiss and splash and gurgle, the small talk of side channels, the whisper of blown and scattered spray gathering itself and beginning to flow again, secret and irresistible, among the wet rocks.*
>
> —Wallace Stegner on the Henrys Fork in *The Sound of Mountain Water*

First and foremost, the Henrys Fork is known as a fishing river. Many consider it one of the two or three finest trout streams in the lower 48 states. For boaters the principal attraction on many stretches is scenery, though challenging rapids enliven the pace in several sections. One reach—Cardiac Canyon—is for daring experts only.

The Henrys Fork, occasionally referred to as the North Fork of the Snake, winds across a high plateau that was once home to the Shoshone. White men first laid eyes on the river in 1810, when Andrew Henry and his band of trappers were pursued over the Continental Divide and into the Henrys Fork basin by Blackfeet Indians. This experience led to the construction of Henrys Fort on the banks of the Henrys Fork—the first American fort built west of the Continental Divide. But the Shoshone who lived in the area around the fort were not openly hostile toward the whites—at least not until many years later when their lands were usurped and they were forced onto a reservation.

The Henrys Fork flows south from its headwaters in Henrys Lake, a shallow body of water cupped in an ancient caldera west of Yellowstone National Park and just south of the Montana-Idaho border. At first the Henrys Fork is a small stream—much too small to account for the heavy snowmelt from the surrounding high peaks of the Continental Divide. Most of the water percolates through the porous volcanic soil into underground channels and wells back to the surface at the hundreds of springs that dot the Henrys Fork basin.

Principal among these is Big Springs, the main source of the Henrys Fork. Here crystal-clear water surges smoothly out of the ground at the rate of about 750 cfs, turning the stream into a river. Like many other spring-fed rivers, the Henrys Forks has a relatively constant flow, rarely flooding and seldom falling too low for boating, though flows are manipulated somewhat by dams at Henrys Lake and Island Park Reservoir to meet summer irrigation demands.

In its upper reaches the Henrys Forks is bounded by dense stands of lodgepole pine, broken by expansive meadows offering inspiring views of distant peaks. River runners may spot moose, trumpeter swans, bald eagles, osprey, and other wildlife. Clusters of fishing cabins alternate with long sections of undeveloped Forest Service land. The river's lower reaches cut through remote, rugged volcanic gorges, where boaters willing to deal with difficult access can find more solitude.

Each year thousands of anglers flock to the Henrys Fork to try for trout that commonly weigh over six pounds and occasionally tip the scales at more than 15. Relations between boaters and anglers are generally good, and can remain so with mutual consideration. Boaters should give anglers and their lines a wide berth when possible and keep noise to a minimum. (See our appendix on **River Etiquette.**)

Also, it may be best to avoid certain sections of river during peak angling periods, most notably the annual "Green Drake Madness" of mid-to-late June. Named for a fly that hatches at this time, the madness strikes fish and fishermen alike. There seem to be as many anglers as trout, and boaters may encounter impassable webs of fishing line anywhere from Island Park Dam to Riverside Campground (especially in the "Last Chance" area).

The Henrys Fork is simultaneously being threatened by a proposed hydropower project and considered for state and federal protection. For more information, contact Idaho Rivers United (see appendix for address).

Henrys Fork River Guide

Note that runs 2 through 5 can be run consecutively, while runs 1 and 7 must be run separately.

1. Macks Inn to McCrea Bridge

This secluded 6-mile run is mostly Class I, with one section of good Class III. The **put-in** is at the U.S. 20 bridge near Macks Inn. Boaters can add 4.5 miles of Class I water by starting upstream at the Big Springs Water Trail (see **Side Excursions**). Three miles below Macks Inn the river curves slowly left, the walls close in, the gradient increases, and the water churns through a long set of Class III drops known as **COFFEE POT. Take out** at McCrea Bridge or McCrea Bridge Campground. Downstream the river empties into Island Park Reservoir.

2. Island Park Dam to Last Chance

This four-mile section includes the fine scenery and Class II rapids of Box Canyon, the last whitewater on the Henrys Fork for more than ten miles. **Put in** on the left bank at **Box Canyon Boat Launch** just below the dam. A quarter mile farther, the Buffalo River enters on the left; just downstream is some good Class II rock-dodging. Boaters can **take out** at the first access (where U.S. 20 approaches the left bank at Last Chance) or continue downriver.

3. Last Chance to Osborne Bridge

This six-mile Class I reach is the most popular with anglers. The broad river meanders slowly through open terrain and around islands and shallows. Much of the run is through Harriman State Park. **Take out** at Osborne (U.S. 20) Bridge or continue downstream.

4. Osborne Bridge to Riverside CG

First come four miles of flatwater through the remainder of Harriman State Park. Then the residential development of Pinehaven appears on the right. Soon the gradient steepens and riffles and small rapids resume. **Take out** on the right at Riverside Campground, or continue downstream to more challenging water.

5. Riverside CG to East Hatchery Ford

Class III whitewater begins just below the campground as the Henrys Fork enters a shallow, scenic canyon. **Don't miss the take-out at Hatchery Ford!** Experts-only Cardiac Canyon is just downstream.

6. Cardiac Canyon: East Hatchery Ford to above Upper Mesa Falls

***HAZARD.* This Class VI run is only for teams of hardy experts willing to take substantial risks.** Below Hatchery Ford the Henrys Fork dives into Cardiac Canyon, a heart-stopping millrace of challenging rapids and lethal waterfalls. Two or more arduous portages add to the difficulty of this dangerous run. About 2.5 miles below the ford is **SHEEP FALLS,** a narrow cataract between steep rock walls that **requires a grueling portage** on the left. Not far downstream, boaters must **portage again at LOWER SHEEP FALLS.** Then, 6.5 miles below the ford, the river vaults over Upper Mesa Falls, a lethal 114' vertical drop. ***HAZARD.* Be absolutely sure to take out above UPPER MESA FALLS on the left bank.** Scout the take-out carefully before running this section, and be sure that you are scouting the Upper Falls, not Lower Mesa Falls a mile downstream.

7. Below Lower Mesa Falls to Ashton Bridge

The difficult put-in for this run deters most boaters. However, the reward for those with light craft, a good length of rope, and patience is a scenic float through moderate rapids in a secluded, 600'-deep gorge. **Be certain to put in *below* the deadly 65' drop of LOWER MESA FALLS.** Beginning at Grandview Campground, boaters must drive south on a rough, unmarked dirt road, then park and lower themselves and their boats down a very steep slope to the river.

The whitewater, generally Class II+ to III-, is mostly confined to the first few miles. The biggest rapid, **SURPRISE FALLS,** is an abrupt drop about a mile into the run. Six miles below the put-in, the Warm River (which isn't) enters on the left. An **alternate take-out** is just downstream on the right where a bridge crosses the river.

Below Warm River the walls recede, and the remaining six miles to the U.S. 20 bridge near Ashton have only occasional riffles. **Take out** at the boat ramp near the bridge. Ashton Reservoir is just downstream.

Upper Snake River

1. Flagg Canyon: Yellowstone Park Entrance (6,850') to Flagg Ranch.
III; 3 miles; 17 ft./mi.

2. Jackson Lake Dam to Moose.
II-; 25 miles; 11 ft./mi.

3. South Park Bridge to West Table Creek.
II-; 17 miles; 12 ft./mi.

4. Snake River Canyon: West Table Creek to Sheep Gulch (5,630').
III (IV above 15,000 cfs); 8 miles; 14 ft./mi.

Drainage Area and Average Annual Discharge: 486 sq. mi. and 700,000 af at Flagg Ranch; 3,465 sq. mi. and 3,365,000 af in Snake River Canyon (Run 4).

Season: Flagg Canyon, where the Snake's flow is natural undammed runoff, is boatable from late April to early August. Other runs, partially regulated by Jackson Lake Dam, are boatable all year; season limited by weather.

Recommended Levels: *Runs 1 & 2:* 500–4,000 cfs. *Runs 3 & 4:* 1,000–10,000 cfs. On Run 4 high water begins around 5,000, and the run becomes more difficult as flows increase (Class IV above about 15,000).

Flow Information: (307) 733-5452; inflow and outflow at Jackson Lake (Runs 1 and 2, respectively) and the flow near Alpine (Run 4).

Special Hazards: Logs and brush, especially Run 2.

Permits: Required from Teton NP for Runs 1 & 2; available at local ranger stations. Self-registration for Runs 3 & 4.

Managing Agencies: *Runs 1 & 2:* Grand Teton National Park, Drawer 170, Moose, WY 83012; (307) 733-2880. *Runs 3 & 4:* USFS, Bridger-Teton NF, P.O. Box 1888, Jackson, WY 83001; (307) 739-5500.

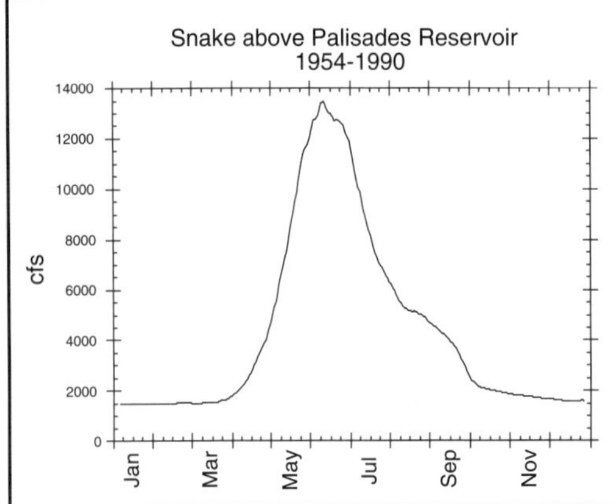

Commercial Raft Trips: Yes. For a list of outfitters, contact the managing agencies.

Land Ownership: *Runs 1, 2, & 4* are all National Forest and/or National Park. *Run 3* is part National Forest, part private.

Scenery: Excellent on Runs 1 & 2; good on Runs 3 & 4.

Solitude: Good on Runs 1 & 2; fair on Runs 3 & 4.

Wilderness: *Run 1:* Yes. *Run 2:* Partial. *Runs 3 & 4:* No.

Wildlife: Moose are especially common. Also beaver, deer, eagle, water fowl.

Camping: Many campgrounds. No river camping in Teton National Park.

Side Excursions: Yellowstone and Grand Teton National Parks. Snake River Overlook in Jackson Hole.

Guides and References:

- Lewis, *Paddle and Portage: The Floater's Guide to Wyoming Rivers.*
- Huser and Belknap, *Snake River Guide.*
- *Floating the Snake River in the John D. Rockefeller Memorial Parkway* (NPS). Covers Run 1. Available from Park Service.
- *Floating the Snake River in Grand Teton National Park* (NPS). Covers Run 2. Available from Park Service.
- *Snake River Floater's Guide* (USFS). Covers Runs 3 & 4. Available from USFS.
- Crandall, *Grand Teton: The Story Behind The Scenery.* Geology, history.
- Palmer, *The Snake River: Window to the West.* Focus on water politics.
- Good local sources of information are Technical Sports and Jackson Hole Kayak School, both located at 1035 W. Broadway, P.O. Box 8695, Jackson, WY 83001, (307) 733-2471.

Maps:

- **USGS 7.5':** *Run 1:* Flagg Ranch. *Run 2:* Moran, Jenny Lake, Moose. *Run 3:* Camp Davis, Munger Mtn, Pine Creek. *Run 4:* Pine Creek, Ferry Peak.
- **USGS 1:100:** *Run 2:* Jackson Lake. *Runs 3 & 4:* Jackson.
- **USFS:** *Bridger-Teton NF* (two sheets) covers all runs. *Grand Teton NP* covers Run 2.

- *Riverguide Bandana to the Upper Snake* (Rivers & Mountains). Cloth map.

Auto Shuttle: *Run 1:* 2 miles one way. *Run 2:* 27 miles one way. *Runs 3 & 4:* same mileages as river.

Logistics: *Run 1:* The **put-in** is just off U.S. 89 a half mile south of the south entrance to Yellowstone Park. To reach the **take-out,** drive south 2.5 miles to the bridge over the Snake at Flagg Ranch.

Run 2: To reach the **Jackson Lake Dam put-in,** follow U.S. 89 to Jackson Lake Junction, 35 miles north of Jackson. Drive southwest one mile on Teton Park Road, then bear left to the boat launch on the left bank below the dam. The **intermediate access at Pacific Creek** is just off U.S. 89 a half mile north of Moran Junction. **Deadmans Bar** is just off U.S. 89 about 9 miles south of Moran Junction and just north of the Snake River Overlook. To reach the **Moose take-out,** follow U.S. 89 to Moose Junction, 14 miles north of Jackson, turn east on Teton Park Road and cross the river to Park Service Headquarters. The boat landing is on the right bank just above the bridge.

Runs 3 & 4: U.S. 89/26 follows both runs, so several alternate accesses are possible. **South Park Bridge Boat Ramp** is at the U.S. 89/26 bridge some 8 miles south of Jackson. **West Table Creek access** is about 24 miles south of Jackson. **Sheep Gulch take-out** is about 7.5 miles downstream from West Table Creek and 3 miles east of Alpine Junction.

The Snake is the longest river in this book, stretching 1,040 miles from Yellowstone National Park in Wyoming to the Columbia River in Washington. The Upper Snake takes in the entire reach in Wyoming, from headwaters at the Continental Divide to Palisades Reservoir near the Idaho border. The whole section can be boated except for the uppermost stretch in Yellowstone National Park, where river running is prohibited by the Park Service (see sidebar in **Yellowstone** chapter). From Yellowstone Park the Snake flows southward through a short whitewater reach known as Flagg Canyon, pauses in Jackson Lake, then glides south through Jackson Hole and finally cuts west through turbulent Snake River Canyon.

Although the Upper Snake has many faces, most people know only one—a serene river draped in majestic, sweeping curves at the feet of those fairy-tale pinnacles, the Tetons. The scene is a classic Western panorama, like Old Faithful or Half Dome. At times, floating the Snake through Jackson Hole (Run 2, below Jackson Lake) is a little like drifting through a postcard.

In most valleys the river is clearly the creator of the scene. In Jackson Hole the Snake seems like an afterthought—a smooth reflecting pool set before the jagged Tetons. But appearances can be deceptive: the river was here long before the Tetons, which are one of the youngest of the Rocky Mountain ranges. Their steep eastern escarpment is an active fault zone that began moving a few million years ago. Today, seven spectacular peaks soar to more than 12,000', while the

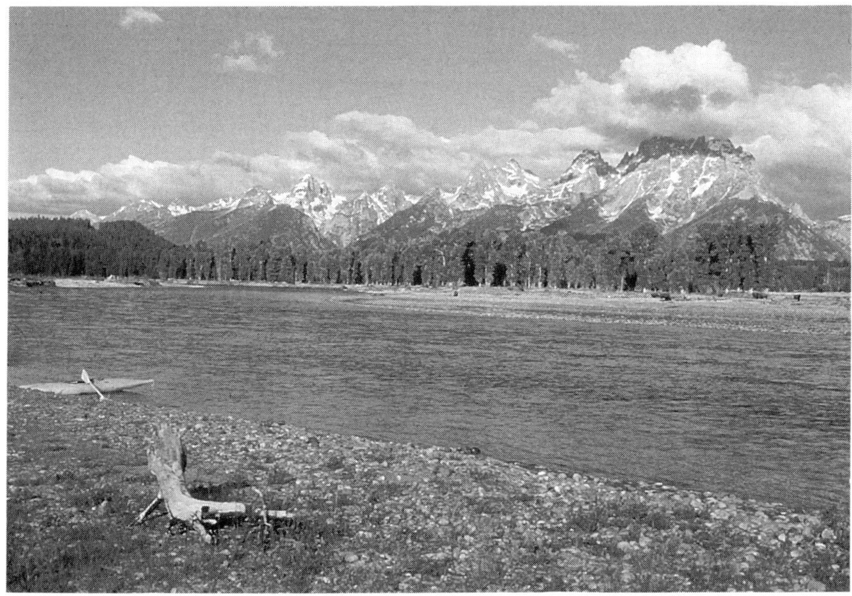

Tetons and Snake River near Deadmans Bar *Dan Lewis*

Snake sidesteps the Tetons to the east and slides smoothly southward through the cobbled glacial deposits of Jackson Hole.

Until fairly recently, humans were only seasonal visitors to this high valley. Bands of Indians camped and hunted here only in summer. In the early 1800's white trappers and explorers first glimpsed the Tetons and the Upper Snake. Among them were some evidently lonely French Canadian trappers who, viewing the peaks from their less angular Western perspective, named them "Les Trois Tétons"—literally, "The Three Nipples." In 1829 the "hole" or valley east of the peaks was named for trapper David Jackson. Since 1929 much of the valley has been protected by Grand Teton National Park, which today draws some three million visitors every year.

The Snake River is one of the Park's premier attractions. A combination of outstanding scenery, abundant wildlife, and summer-long flows[1] make this one of the most popular stretches of river in the West. When commercial floating began in 1956, fewer than 500 souls made the run below Jackson Lake. Today, commercial outfitters carry some 70,000 people down the river every year. Private boaters in large numbers also enjoy some or all of the float from Jackson Lake Dam to Moose (**Run 2**).

In 1811 French Canadian trappers named what is now called the Snake River Canyon (**Run 4**) "la maudite rivière enragée"—"the accursed mad river"—giving it a nickname and a reputation that endure today. The most remarkable descent of the "Mad River" reach was that of Lt. Gustavus C. Doane of the U.S. Cavalry, who in 1867 was ordered to explore the Snake from source to mouth in mid-winter. Using a 22' boat and supported by a team with pack horses on shore, Doane and his men struggled downriver from Yellowstone. In early December they reached the infamous "Mad River Canyon" (today's Snake River Canyon), where they battled not only whitewater but also rapidly forming ice that threatened to trap the boat in the river's pools. Short of provisions and reduced to eating their own horses, the team abandoned the river in mid-December.[2]

[1]Although originally natural, Jackson Lake was dammed in 1916 for irrigation storage. Today its surface elevation varies by as much as 39' as it is drawn down each summer.

[2]Verne Huser's excellent anthology, *River Reflections*, contains excerpts from Doane's journal.

Flagg Canyon

The Upper Snake first swells to boatable size near the southern boundary of Yellowstone National Park. However, river running is prohibited in the park, so **Run 1** begins just outside it. Downstream the river cuts through a narrow volcanic gorge known as Flagg Canyon, where most of the rapids are compressed into a single mile of river. Spring high water can build big, rolling waves up to 8' high. Most boaters **take out** at the highway bridge at Flagg Ranch. Easy water continues for six miles down to Jackson Lake, where the river enters Teton National Park, but due to access problems this lower section is lightly used.

Grand Teton National Park

Although this stretch (**Run 2**) is mostly flat, novices should not be lulled by the easy whitewater rating. The Snake below Pacific Creek (mile 4.5) provides plenty of challenge in the form of **strainers, log hazards,** cold water, high flows in spring, braided channels (some of which are dead ends), and even an occasional temperamental moose. In particular, the final ten miles from Deadmans Bar to Moose wreak havoc every year on the unskilled and unprepared—hence the Class II- rating despite the lack of any true "rapids." Before embarking, check with the Park Service for updates on river conditions, channel changes and log hazards. If in doubt, stick to the 4.5-mile Class I stretch from Jackson Lake to Pacific Creek.

For 30 miles below Teton Park the river flows in braided channels, its course constantly shifting as it winds across glacial cobble deposits. This reach is often confined between dikes erected by the Army Corps of Engineers. Many boaters avoid this stretch; as a result, it can be a rewarding float for those who want to get away from the crowds and see some wildlife. Beware of complex channels and **log hazards.** (This chapter contains no mile guide or further information on this 30-mile stretch.)

South Park Bridge to West Table Creek

Some eight miles south of Jackson, the river returns to a relatively straight course and enters a more scenic valley. Boating increases again at South Park Bridge Boat Ramp, where the river enters Bridger-Teton National Forest and Run 3 begins. This 17-mile reach to West Table Creek has easy to moderate water and is paralleled by a highway. Frequent access allows a variety of runs. Braided channels and **log hazards** make the final eight miles below Pritchard Creek more challenging than the rating of the rapids indicates. See the **Mile Guide** for details.

Snake River Canyon

Saving the best whitewater for last, the upper Snake boils to a climax in Snake River Canyon (**Run 4**), sometimes called "Alpine Canyon" or the "Grand Canyon of the Snake." Here the river turns west and cuts through the rugged Snake River Range. Swollen by upstream tributaries, the Snake becomes a big-water river. At peak snowmelt in June, flows can reach 20,000 cfs. Anything above 15,000 cfs means huge waves and a full Class IV rating. Lunch Counter, the best-known drop, is a popular surfing spot. Exciting whitewater and easy access from the nearby highway make this the most popular stretch on the entire Snake River: nearly 100,000 user-days are recorded annually. On summer weekends the boat ramps at West Table Creek and Sheep Gulch can be quite crowded.

Mile by Mile Guide

1. Flagg Canyon: Yellowstone Park to Flagg Ranch

0 The **PUT-IN** is on the right bank a half mile south of the south entrance to the park. Downstream the highway is out of sight above the right bank.

0.3 **Flagg Canyon** begins at a sharp right bend. Downstream is more than a quarter mile of rough water; big waves at peak runoff. The rapids moderate as the walls recede.

2.7 The **TAKE-OUT** is on the right below the U.S. 89 bridge. Downstream the Snake leaves the highway and runs easily for 6.5 miles through an open valley to Jackson Lake. Boaters making this run must paddle 3 miles across the lake to take out at Lizard Creek Campground

2. Jackson Lake Dam to Moose

0 The upper **PUT-IN** is on the left bank below Jackson Lake Dam. Good water for novices from here to Pacific Creek: flat, slow Class I.

2 Alternate **RIVER ACCESS** at Cattlemens Bridge. Downstream is lovely Oxbow Bend.

4.5 Pacific Creek enters on the left. **RIVER ACCESS** just downstream on the left. Half a mile farther, the Buffalo Fork enters on the left. The next 10 miles (Class I+) require more attention: the current increases, and the channel becomes more braided.

8.5 Spread Creek enters on the left.

15 **RIVER ACCESS** at Deadmans Bar on the left. Snake River Overlook is high on the left. **Novices should not float below this point.** The following 10 miles (Class II-) are considerably more challenging, with numerous **log jams**, braided channels, swift current, and small waves.

17.5- **No stopping.** Critical eagle nesting hab-
18.5 itat on both banks. The **alternate access** at Schwabacher Landing on the left, mile 20.5, is very hard to reach from the river due to heavily braided channels.

25 **TAKE-OUT.** Moose Boat Landing on the right above the bridge. Park Service Headquarters is on the right.

3. South Park Bridge to West Table Creek

Frequent access along the highway allows a variety of runs in this 17-mile Class II- stretch. The most popular accesses are South Park Bridge (mile 0), Astoria Boat Ramp (mile 8), Pritchard Creek Boat Ramp (mile 9), and West Table Creek (mile 17).

A mile below the confluence with the Hoback River, boaters should watch for **KING RAPID,** an S-turn which rates Class II+ at low and moderate flows and washes out at high water. The 8 miles below Pritchard Creek are generally more challenging than the first 9 miles, with braided channels and **log hazards.**

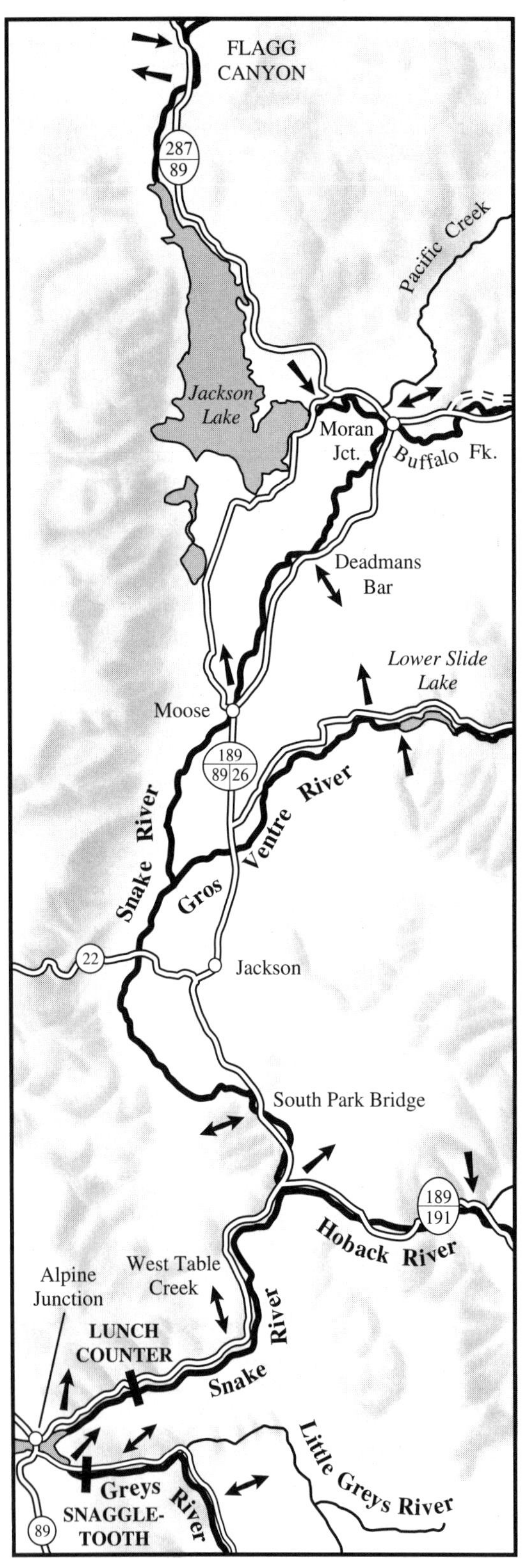

Upper Snake and Tributaries

4. Snake River Canyon: West Table Creek to Sheep Gulch

0 **PUT-IN.** West Table Creek boat landing (right bank). U.S. 89/26 follows the right bank.

1 Station Creek Campground (USFS) on the right. Rapids begin just downstream as the Snake enters narrow **Snake River Canyon.** *HAZARD.* About two miles below Station Creek at a right bend, watch for **THREE OAR DEAL,** where a very powerful keeper reversal develops on the left side at high water.

4 Wolf Creek and Wolf Creek Campground (USFS) on the right, just below **WOLF CREEK RAPID.**

5.5 **KAHUNA** (III). Big waves. More difficult below about 7,000 cfs.

6 **LUNCH COUNTER** (III+), where many come to dine and some get eaten. Big waves build to 8' or 10' at moderate flows. Washes out above about 11,000 cfs. Excellent surfing at high flows here and downstream at Cottonwood Rapid and The Narrows. After a quarter-mile breather, more big waves lead into **ROPE** (III-).

7 Little Cottonwood Creek Campground (USFS) on the right. A half mile downstream is the last major drop, **COTTONWOOD RAPID,** where Cottonwood Creek enters on the right.

8 Sheep Gulch **TAKE-OUT** on the right. (The take-out is actually well above Sheep Gulch.) When full, Palisades Reservoir is only a quarter mile downstream. A mile below Sheep Gulch, the Snake plunges down a 30'-wide slot known as **THE NARROWS** (III); however, the drop is exposed only when the reservoir is drawn down, and boaters descending this far must then make a long, arduous flatwater paddle to the next possible take-out at Palisades Marina. About a mile below The Narrows, the canyon opens and the Greys River enters the reservoir from the south at Alpine Junction near the Idaho border.

Tributaries of the Upper Snake

The Buffalo Fork, Gros Ventre, Hoback, and Greys are all tributaries of the Upper Snake near Jackson Hole. They drain parts of five subranges of the Rocky Mountains: the Absaroka, Wind River, Gros Ventre, Wyoming, and Salt River Ranges. All four rivers are moderate in size, and all enter the Snake from the east between Jackson Lake and the Wyoming-Idaho border.

These streams offer good boating for those who want to escape the crowds that sometimes gather on the Snake (especially on summer weekends). Here are runs for every taste, from the gentle Buffalo Fork to steep and challenging sections of the Gros Ventre and Greys. The most popular runs are on the rivers' lower reaches, closer to the Snake, where flows are more substantial. The trips described here are all within easy reach of the Jackson Hole area.

- All the runs described here are covered in greater detail in a local guide book, Dan Lewis, *Paddle and Portage: The Floater's Guide to Wyoming Rivers.*
- Good local sources of information are Technical Sports and Jackson Hole Kayak School, both located at 1035 W. Broadway, P.O. Box 8695, Jackson, WY 83001, (307) 733-2471.
- **Managing Agency:** Bridger-Teton NF, P.O. Box 1888, Jackson, WY 83301; (307) 739-5500.
- *See map in previous chapter.*

Buffalo Fork

Difficulty: I+. No whitewater, but many logs.
Length: 12 miles. **Gradient:** 10 ft./mi.
Put-in: Turpin Meadows (6,905').
Take-out: Above U.S. 287 Bridge.
Season: May through mid-August.
Recommended Levels: 400–2,500 cfs.
Drainage Area and Average Annual Discharge: 323 sq. mi. and 402,100 af near take-out.
Flow Information: (307) 733-5452.
Permits: Not presently required.
Commercial Raft Trips: No.
Land Ownership: Mostly National Forest.
Wilderness: Partial. Occasional roads, ranches.
Maps: USGS 7.5': *Rosies Ridge, Davis Hill.*
- **USGS 1:100:** *Jackson Lake.*
- **USFS:** *Bridger-Teton NF (Buffalo RD).*

Logistics: To reach the **take-out,** follow U.S. 26/287 east from Moran Junction about 3 miles, turn left on Buffalo Valley Road, drive about two miles, then bear right on a dirt road that leads down to the river. To reach the **alternate take-out** two miles upstream, continue another mile up Buffalo Valley Road and turn right on another dirt road that leads to the river. To reach the **put-in,** continue east on Buffalo Valley Road roughly 7 miles to the bridge over the river at **Turpin Meadows.**

The Buffalo Fork, a small, scenic tributary of the Snake, rises along the Continental Divide in the Absaroka Range east of Grand Teton National Park. The river's North and South Forks tumble over spectacular waterfalls in their descent through the Teton Wilderness area, then merge to form the main Buffalo Fork just before it leaves the wilderness.

A pretty flatwater float begins at the first road access at Turpin Meadows and runs some 12 miles to either of two recommended take-outs located a couple of miles upstream from the U.S. 26/287 bridge, not far above the Teton National Park boundary. Here the cold, clear Buffalo Fork winds peacefully through open forest and frequent meadows, with abundant wildlife and occasional views of the spectacular Teton range to the west.

Although the Buffalo Fork is a flatwater run, boaters must be alert for **log hazards and log jams** that may need to be portaged. Route-finding can be a challenge: the channel divides frequently around large islands, and the river's winding course may change from year to year.

Continued on next page

Buffalo Fork River Guide

Put in at the bridge over the Buffalo Fork at Turpin Meadows (mile 0). Five meandering miles later, the river approaches Buffalo Valley Road on the right, then veers away again. The highway follows the left bank briefly at mile 8.5. Soon the highway and river diverge again and the Buffalo Fork crosses over to Buffalo Valley Road and the **first take-out,** on the right bank at mile 10.5. The **second recommended take-out** is another 1.5 miles downstream on the right. Boaters can continue 2.5 miles downstream to an **alternate take-out** at the highway bridge (mile 14.5), but this access is more difficult. **Boating is prohibited farther downstream where the Buffalo Fork passes through Grand Teton National Park.**

Gros Ventre River

1. Warden Bridge (7,285') to Lower Slide Lake.
II–III; 8 miles; 47 ft./mi.
Shorter runs possible.

2. Lower Slide Lake to Teton National Park Boundary.
IV; 3 miles; 75 ft./mi.

Season: May–late July.
Recommended Levels: 400–2,000 cfs.
Permits: Not presently required.
Commercial Raft Trips: No.
Land Ownership: Mostly National Forest.
Scenery: Excellent. Forested alpine valley.
Wilderness: No, but nearby road is usually unobtrusive.
Maps:
- **USGS 7.5':** *Run 1:* Upper Slide Lake, Grizzly Lake, Mt. Leidy. *Run 2:* Shadow Mtn.
- **USGS 1:100:** *Jackson Lake.*
- **USFS:** *Bridger-Teton NF (Jackson RD).*

Logistics: To reach the river, follow combined U.S. 191/89/26 to Gros Ventre Junction, 7 miles north of Jackson. Turn northeast on Gros Ventre Road and drive about 10 miles (passing the hamlet of Kelly) to the eastern boundary of Teton National Park. The **take-out for the lower run** is located where the road approaches the right bank near the park boundary. To reach the **put-in for the lower run,** continue up Gros Ventre Road a little over two miles. Bear right on an unpaved road which leads about a half mile down to the put-in, which is at a bridge over the river at the outlet of Lower Slide Lake.

To reach the **upper run,** continue up Gros Ventre Road, which soon becomes dirt. The **lowermost take-out for the upper run** is on the north shore of Lower Slide Lake, about 1.5 miles above Atherton Creek CG near the mouth of Horsetail Creek. There are **several alternate river accesses** upstream as the road generally follows first the north and then the south bank of the river. Intermediate accesses include Red Hills CG and Crystal Creek CG. The **uppermost recommended put-in** is at Warden Bridge, reached by turning left on a short spur road some 7.5 miles beyond Crystal Creek CG.

The Gros Ventre River enters the Snake from the east at the southern end of Teton National Park. The river drains the high summits of the Gros Ventre and Wind River Ranges, including one flank of Triple Divide Peak, the unique point where the West's three great drainages—the Columbia, Missouri, and Colorado—intersect. The Gros Ventre Wilderness area protects much of the river's watershed, and the Forest Service has found the river eligible for National Wild and Scenic status.

The river takes its name (pronounced "grow VAHNT") from an Indian tribe sometimes known as the Atsina, but more commonly referred to as "Gros Ventre"—literally "big belly," an unflattering moniker bestowed by French trappers. In fact the tribe had average abdomens, but the Atsina referred to themselves in sign language by sweeping both hands across their stomachs, and apparently something got lost in the translation. To complete the confusion, the Gros Ventre were not a Wyoming tribe at all; their original territory covered parts of northern Montana and southern Saskatchewan.

Twice in the course of its journey to the Snake, the Gros Ventre stills—at Upper and Lower Slide Lakes, where landslides form nat-

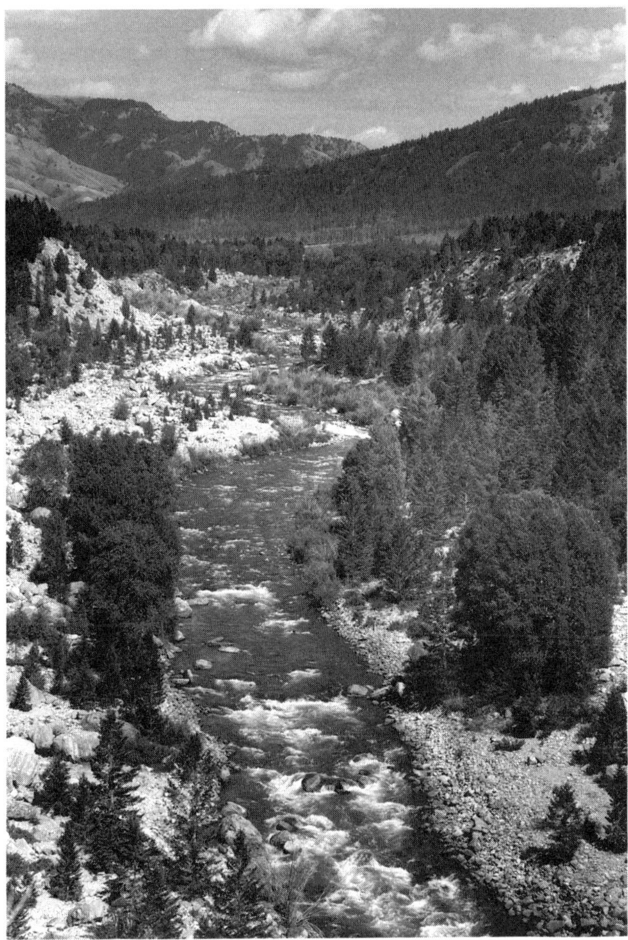

Gros Ventre below Lower Slide Lake *Dan Lewis*

ural dams across the river. The genesis of Lower Slide Lake, the larger of the two, stands as the most dramatic event in the history of Jackson Hole.

On June 23, 1925 one of the largest landslides in U.S. history—some 50 million cubic yards—thundered a mile and a half down the southern slope of the Gros Ventre Valley, blocking the river with a pile of earth and debris some two miles long and over 200' high.

Lower Slide Lake formed behind the natural dam, and for two years the barrier held as water seeped through it. But in May 1927 spring high water finally overtopped the slide, and the Gros Ventre quickly cut an outlet channel deep into the loose debris, releasing a devastating flood. Six people died when an 8' wall of water all but obliterated the hamlet of Kelly three miles downstream. Today the slide area, maintained as a geologic exhibit, is well worth a side trip.

Lower Gros Ventre

River runners enjoying the short (2.7 miles) lower run on the Gros Ventre are in fact riding down the outlet channel first carved through the slide in 1927. Although the way has been worn somewhat smoother since then, the river is still peppered with big, angular boulders that produce nearly continuous Class III and IV whitewater. The Gros Ventre drops 70' in the first half mile below the Lower Slide Lake outlet and 40' in the following half mile. This scenic run is fairly secluded because the road sits high above the right bank. **Boating is prohibited downstream in Grand Teton National Park, so you must take out at the park boundary.**

Upper Gros Ventre

For longer and less difficult runs, boaters can explore the scenic upper reaches of the Gros Ventre. Unpaved Gros Ventre Road generally follows the river, providing several alternate accesses. River runners should be alert for **log hazards and changeable rapids.**

The **highest recommended put-in** is at **Warden Bridge** (mile 0), described in **Logistics**; farther upstream the river is slow and meandering, with frequent log obstacles and lower flows. Not far below Warden Bridge the river stills for nearly a mile in Upper Slide Lake. The lake's outlet is a milder version of the lower Gros Ventre run, with rocky Class III rapids and a total drop of 50' in the first mile. Downstream the gradient moderates to about 30 ft./mi., and Class II and III whitewater continues as the river skirts the Grey Hills on the right. The Gros Ventre passes through a small gorge just above where Slate Creek enters on the right at mile 5.

Two miles below Slate Creek, a good **access** can be found on the left at **Crystal Creek Campground** (mile 7), where Crystal Creek enters on the left. Another **access** is just downstream at **Red Hills Campground**—take out here if you wish to avoid a flatwater paddle on Lower Slide Lake. At mile 8 the road crosses the river, and the last three miles are Class II down to the backwaters of Lower Slide Lake. A half mile of flatwater paddling brings boaters to the **final take-out** on the north shore of the lake near Horsetail Creek.

Hoback River

Granite Creek to Snake River Confluence

Difficulty: III. **Gradient:** 30 ft./mi.
Length: 13 miles. Longer and shorter runs possible.
Season: May–late July.
Recommended Levels: 500–2,500 cfs.
Permits: Not presently required.
Commercial Raft Trips: No.
Land Ownership: Mostly public first half of run, mostly private second half.
Scenery: Very good. Steep, forested canyon.
Wilderness: No. Highway follows entire run.
Maps: USGS 7.5': *Bull Creek, Camp Davis.*
- **USGS 1:100:** *Jackson.*
- **USFS:** *Bridger-Teton NF—Kemmerer, Greys River, & Big Piney RDs (Bridger Division—West Half).*

Logistics: The **take-out** is at a secondary road bridge upstream from the confluence of the Hoback and Snake Rivers, not far from the intersection of U.S. Highways 191/189 and 26/89 at Hoback Junction, 12 miles south of Jackson. To reach **upriver accesses,** drive east on 191/189 some 12 miles to the bridge over the river at the mouth of Granite Creek, which enters from the north; just before the highway crosses the river, turn left on Granite Creek Road and put in at the parking area. **Alternate accesses** are possible at several points along 191/189, including some sites upstream from Granite Creek.

Although it is cut off from the Continental Divide by the watersheds of the Gros Ventre to the north and the Green to the southeast, the Hoback River nonetheless drains high-elevation territory that includes several peaks around 11,000'.

The Hoback offers exciting Class III boating in its descent through Hoback Canyon. During spring and early summer, the river carries sediment from upstream erosion. A U.S. highway follows the river closely, detracting somewhat from the solitude and scenery.

The river takes its name (pronounced HOE-back) from John Hoback, a member of Andrew Henry's expedition which "discovered" and named the Henrys Fork of the Snake in Idaho in 1810 (see **Henrys Fork** chapter). The following year Hoback and two other trappers decided to return to St. Louis. While rowing down the Missouri, they met William Price Hunt and his large exploring party coming upstream, bound for Astoria at the mouth of the Columbia River. Hoback and his friends offered to show Hunt the way west to the Snake River. The expedition ascended the Wind River, crossed the Continental Divide, and descended to the Snake along this stream, which Hunt named "Hoback's River" in honor of his temporary guide.

Hoback River Guide

The most common **put-in** is near the U.S. 191/189 bridge over the Hoback at the mouth of Granite Creek (mile 0). The highway follows the river, offering alternate accesses both above and below Granite Creek. **BOULDER SLALOM,** roughly a mile below Granite Creek, is the most difficult rapid of the run. Hoback Campground (USFS) is on the right at mile 4. At mile 5 the highway crosses to the left bank, then recrosses at mile 6 and stays on the right bank for the rest of the run. Stinking Springs is on the right bank near the second highway bridge. Below Stinking Springs the canyon opens and the gradient eases somewhat. At mile 7.5 a small bridge crosses the river at Camp Davis. In the next few miles several minor ranch bridges cross the river. Willow Creek enters on the left at mile 8.8.

At mile 10.5, where the highway approaches the right bank, watch for a small, sharp drop known as **FIRST LEDGE,** followed in a little under a mile by **SHERRIE'S LEDGE.** The final difficult spot is **LOG JAM,** a rocky drop at a sharp left bend at mile 12.7. The **take-out** at mile 13.2 is at a secondary road bridge just upstream from the confluence with the Snake. Hoback Junction is above the river on the right. Boaters may continue downstream on the Snake (see **Upper Snake River:** South Park Bridge to Table Creek).

Greys River

1. Sheep Creek (6,790') to Lynx Creek CG.
II; 22 miles; 29 ft./mi.

2. Lynx Creek CG to Squaw Creek Bridge.
III+; 7.5 miles; 41 ft./mi.

3. Squaw Creek Bridge to Bridge CG (5,690').
IV5; 2.5 miles; 55 ft./mi.

Drainage Area and Average Annual Discharge: 448 sq. mi. and 482,000 af at Bridge CG.
Season: May–late July
Recommended Levels: 600–2,000 cfs.
Flow Information: No source known for readings of the gauge at Bridge CG.
Special Hazards: Logs. Snaggletooth Rapid.
Permits: Not presently required.
Commercial Raft Trips: No.
Land Ownership: Almost all National Forest.
Scenery: Excellent. Forested alpine canyon.
Solitude: Very good.
Wilderness: No. A road follows the river.
Maps:

- **USGS 7.5':** *Run 1:* Park Creek, Blind Bull Creek, Man Peak, Deer Creek. *Run 2:* Deer Creek, Pine Creek, Ferry Peak. *Run 3:* Ferry Peak.
- **USGS 1:100:** *Ashton, Jackson.*
- **USFS:** *Bridger-Teton NF—Kemmerer, Greys River, & Big Piney RDs (Bridger Division—West Half).*

Auto Shuttle: Roughly same mileages as river.
Logistics: The turnoff to the Greys is located just south of Alpine Junction (the intersection of U.S. Highways 89 and 26 just east of the Wyoming-Idaho border). From the south side of Palisades Reservoir, turn east off U.S. 89 onto USFS Road 138, which follows the Greys upstream and provides frequent access. The following is a partial list of accesses, in ascending (upstream) order, with the approximate mileage from U.S. 89 in parentheses: Bridge Campground (2.3 miles); Squaw Creek Bridge (4.5); Forks Campground (8); Lynx Creek Campground (12); Cabin Creek Road bridge just below Sheep Creek (32).

The Greys—the next Snake River tributary south of the Hoback—flows through one of the loveliest river canyons in Wyoming, a long, narrow north-south valley between the parallel Wyoming and Salt River Ranges. The Wyoming Range, which culminates at 11,363' Wyoming Peak near the headwaters of the Greys, is on the east side of the valley, and beyond this range lies the watershed of the Green River. To the west is the Salt River Range, only slightly less imposing than the Wyoming Range, with 10,763' Rock Lake Peak as its highest point.

The beauty of the landscape is one of the chief attractions of the Greys. Boaters, hikers, and just plain tourists will enjoy its lush alpine scenery and fine views of snow-capped peaks. Camping is excellent at several riverside campgrounds, and the trout fishing is superb. Though boatable flows rarely extend beyond midsummer, the valley is well worth a visit in autumn when riverside trees put on a dazzling display of color.

The Greys was originally named "John Day's River," in honor of the same member of William Price Hunt's 1810 Astoria expedition after whom an Oregon river is still named. The Wyoming river was eventually renamed after a local trapper, John Grey.

A Forest Service road follows the entire length of the Greys, providing frequent access and allowing boaters to scout and choose the sections best suited to their skills. Boating is generally limited to the sections below Sheep Creek, a major tributary which joins the Greys some 35 miles above Palisades Reservoir. Above Sheep Creek flows are skimpier and log hazards are more frequent.

For most of its length the Greys is a fairly mild river, with continuous gradient and frequent log hazards. In its lower reaches, however, the Greys becomes steeper, and in its final descent below Squaw Creek the river roars through several Class IV rapids and one big Class V drop. Below Bridge Campground the river eases to Class I and soon glides into Palisades Reservoir, which covers the confluence of the Greys and the Snake.

Greys River Guide

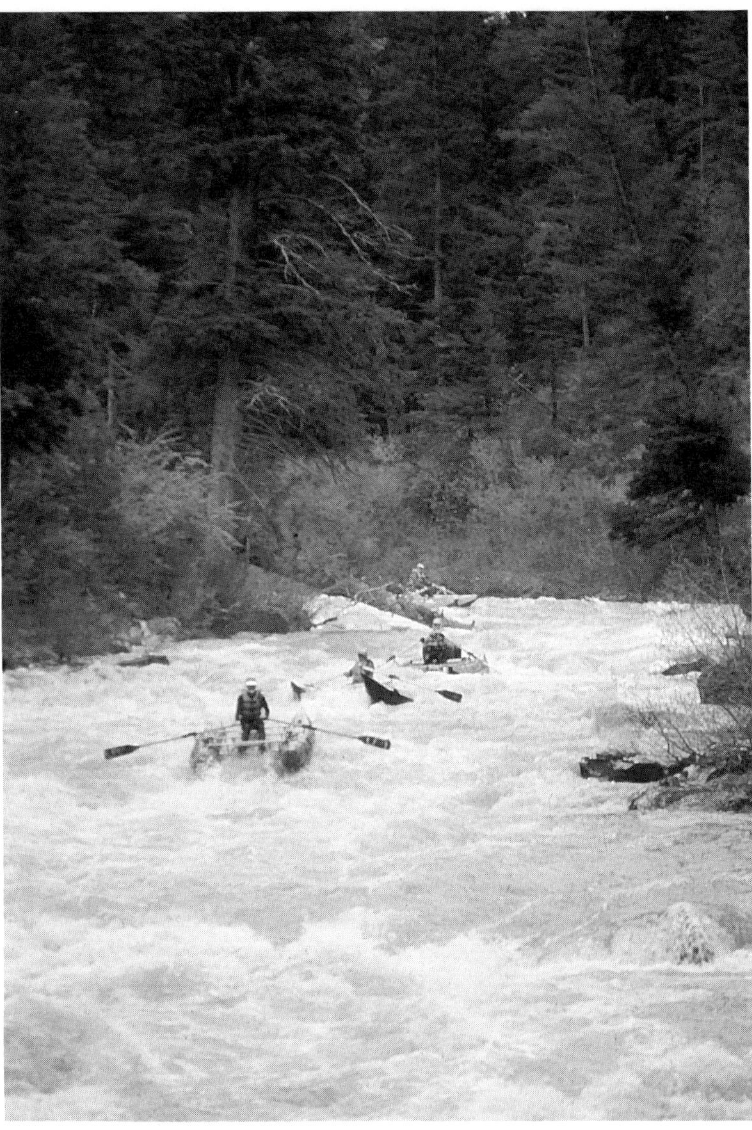

Snaggletooth Rapid, Greys River *Dan Lewis*

Downstream from the bridge just below **Sheep Creek** (mile 0), the Greys drops swiftly and steadily northward through easy Class II rapids. A bridge crosses at mile 4, and Deadmans Creek enters on the right at mile 8. Here the river turns westward at a bend known as The Elbow, but after a couple of miles it resumes its northerly course.

Moose Flat Campground is on the right at mile 11. Another bridge crosses at mile 14, just below the mouth of White Creek, which enters on the left. Murphy Creek enters on the left at mile 19, just above another minor bridge. **Lynx Creek Campground** provides a good **river access** on the right at mile 22.

Below Lynx Creek Campground the gradient accelerates and the difficulty increases to Class III with some Class IV. At mile 26 the Little Greys River enters on the right, adding considerably to the flow. Here the Greys turns due west for the remainder of the run. A good **alternate access** is located at **Forks Campground,** on the right bank immediately downstream from the Little Greys confluence. Class III water continues to the next **access at Squaw Creek Bridge** (mile 29.5, where Squaw Creek enters on the left). **Only expert boaters should continue beyond this point.**

The two and a half miles from Squaw Creek Bridge to Bridge Campground are for experts only. This stretch has several Class IV pitches and, toward the end, one big Class V drop known as **SNAGGLETOOTH.** The entire section should be scouted carefully from the road that runs along the north (right) bank. Snaggletooth has a big hole and should be approached with caution, especially at higher flows. A swim here would be nasty and dangerous.

Take out at Bridge Campground. Downstream, the river eases to Class I, then finally stills in the backwaters of Palisades Reservoir.

Shoshone River

North Fork and Main Shoshone

North Fork Shoshone
Sleeping Giant Campground (6,580')
to Buffalo Bill Reservoir (5,370').
III+; 38 miles; 32 ft./mi.

Main Shoshone
1. Shoshone Canyon:
Below Buffalo Bill Dam (5,120')
to De Maris Hot Springs.
IV+ up to 1,800 cfs; V above 1,800.
4 miles; 50 ft./mi.

2. Red Rock Canyon:
Below Demaris Hot Springs
to Billings Highway Bridge (4,815').
II; 4 miles; 26 ft./mi.

3. Lower Canyon: Billings Highway Bridge
to Powell Highway Bridge (4,660').
II3; 7 miles; 22 ft./mi.

Drainage Area and Average Annual Discharge: *North Fork:* 775 sq. mi. and 627,000 af near take-out. *Main Shoshone:* 1,538 sq. mi. and 809,000 af at De Maris Springs.

Season: *North Fork:* May–July above the Elk Fork confluence at Wapiti, a little longer below. Flows at the Wapiti gauge (below the Elk Fork) typically peak in June and usually fall below 1,000 cfs by early August. *Main Shoshone:* Mid-April to mid-October. Runnable releases year-round from Buffalo Bill Dam. Usually peaks in early to midsummer.

Recommended Levels: *North Fork:* 600–3,000 cfs. *Main Shoshone:* 400–2,000 cfs in Shoshone Canyon, 700–4,000 cfs on lower runs.

Flow Information: *North Fork:* NWS, (307) 635-9901; flow in vertical feet "near Wapiti." Convert to cfs according to the table below. *Main Shoshone:* BuRec in Billings, (800) 253-8295; release from Buffalo Bill Reservoir.

Permits: Not currently required.

Managing Agency: *North Fork:* Wapiti RD, Shoshone NF, 225 W. Yellowstone Ave., P.O. Box 2140, Cody, WY 82414; (307) 527-6241. *Main Shoshone:* BLM, 1714 Stampede Ave., Cody, WY 82414; (307) 587-2216.

North Fork Shoshone near Wapiti

Feet	Cfs	Feet	Cfs
2.5	424	4.5	3,881
3.0	848	5.0	5,900
3.5	1,495	5.5	8,258
4.0	2,430		

Commercial Raft Trips: Yes. For references contact the managing agencies.

Land Ownership: *North Fork:* National Forest first 27 miles, mostly private thereafter. *Main Shoshone:* Mostly private; some BLM.

Wilderness: No.

Guides and References:
- Lewis, *Paddle and Portage: The Floater's Guide to Wyoming Rivers.*

Maps: USFS: *Shoshone NF (North Half)* covers the entire North Fork run.
- **USGS 7.5':** *Main Shoshone:* Shoshone Canyon, Cody, Corbett Dam.

Logistics: *North Fork:* The Yellowstone Highway (U.S. 14/16/20) follows the North Fork, providing frequent access and short shuttles. *Main Shoshone:* Two alternate put-ins for the upper run. (1) **The uppermost put-in below Buffalo Bill Dam is used almost exclusively by kayakers** because it involves a steep scramble down from the highway (but see below about Hayden Bridge being reopened). From Cody follow U.S. 20 west about 6 miles toward Buffalo Bill Dam. Stop at a turnout just before the first highway tunnel and carry boats down some 50' to a lower paved road along the left bank. Just upstream on the opposite bank is the Buffalo Bill Powerhouse. Boaters can put in anywhere along the lower road. When flows above the powerhouse are sufficient, most carry upstream some 3/4 mile and put in just below a small tunnel on the lower road (immediately above **Kop Drop**

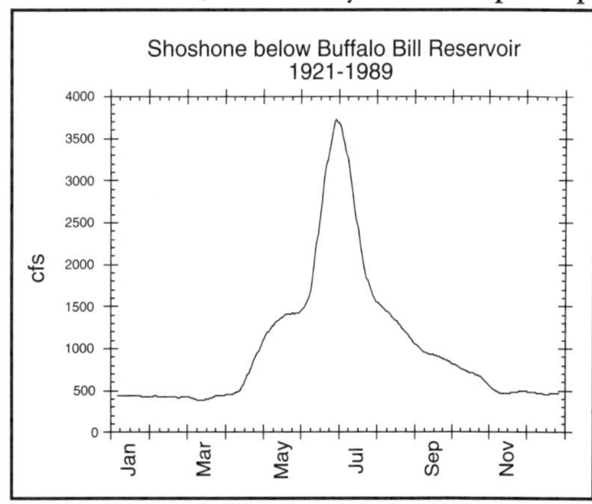

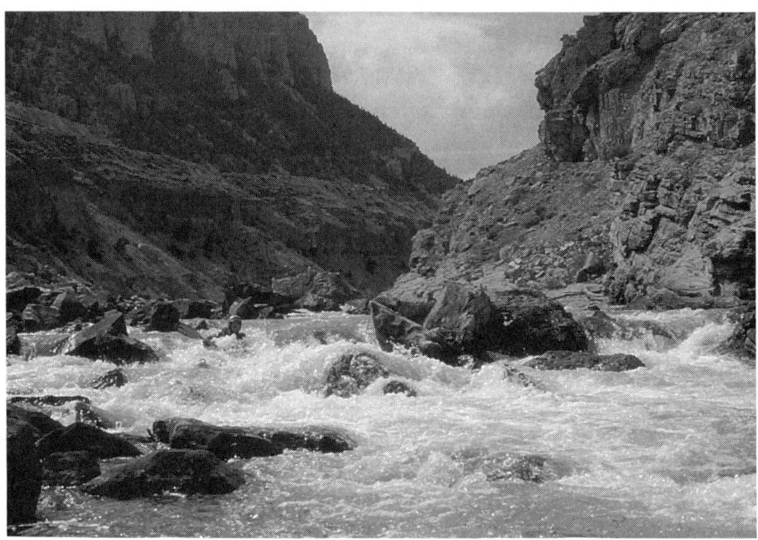

Entrance Exam, Shoshone Canyon *Ron Lodders*

rapid). **Do not go farther upstream:** there is a very dangerous rock sieve rapid just above **Kop Drop.** (2) **The lower put-in is at Hayden Bridge,** two miles downstream from Buffalo Bill Dam. Follow U.S. 20 west from Cody some 5 miles, take the power plant turnoff *before* the highway crosses the river, and put in on the right bank near the old Hayden Bridge. The bridge, which was closed for years, may be reopened in the near future, allowing boaters to drive upriver on the dam access road to the upper put-in (thereby avoiding the scramble down from the highway).

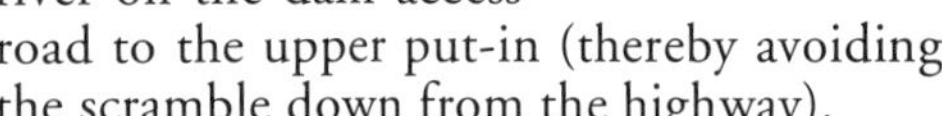

To reach **the put-in below De Maris Springs,** drive about two miles west from Cody on the Yellowstone Highway, then turn right at a sign for Old Trail Town and drive just under a mile to the river. The access is on the right bank at the remains of a rickety bridge. Contact Wyoming River Trips, (307) 587-6661, for permission to use this site. The **Billings Highway (U.S. 120) bridge** is just north of Cody; the state plans to develop a new access on the right bank above the bridge. **The last take-out** is on BLM land on the left bank above the **Powell Highway (U.S. 14A) bridge** northeast of Cody.

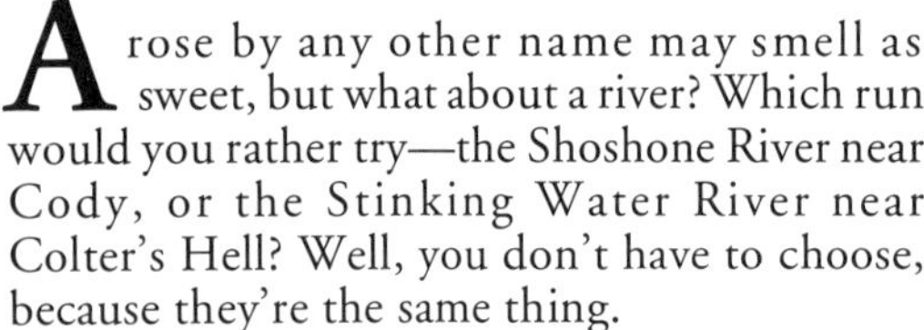

A rose by any other name may smell as sweet, but what about a river? Which run would you rather try—the Shoshone River near Cody, or the Stinking Water River near Colter's Hell? Well, you don't have to choose, because they're the same thing.

"Stinking Water" was thought up in 1807 by trapper and explorer John Colter, one of the West's famous mountain men. Colter was the first white to see the area around modern Cody in northwestern Wyoming, where the odor from sulphurous hot springs inspired his original name for the spot. When Colter regaled fellow trappers with his tales of hot pools and steaming vapors, they generally regarded him as an outrageous liar but humored him by referring to this fantastic place as "Colter's Hell."

The original names lasted less than a century. In the late 1890's, two men who enjoyed hunting and camping along the Stinking Water concocted the idea of damming the river near the mouth of its canyon and diverting water for irrigation. History has all but forgotten George W. Beck, but his partner was none other than the Wild West's most famous hunter and showman, Buffalo Bill Cody. For promotion—and to ensure his partner's enthusiasm—Beck proposed "Cody" as the name for the new town to be built below the dam in the Colter's Hell area. The river got its new name in 1902 when local residents, humiliated by the Stinking Water appellation, prevailed upon the state legislature to rename the river after the Shoshone Indians. (By the way, many locals pronounce the name "shuh-SHOWN.")

Despite vast infusions of capital from Buffalo Bill, the new town's growth was pitifully slow, and the irrigation scheme foundered. Beck and Cody eventually abandoned the water project, ceding their rights to the fledgling Bureau of Reclamation. Under the leadership of John Wesley Powell, the Bureau constructed Buffalo Bill Dam as part of the Shoshone Project for irrigation in the Bighorn River basin. Upon completion in 1910, the 328'-high dam was the tallest in the world.[1] It still stands today, separating the main stem near Cody from the North and South Forks upstream.

[1] David Lavender, *The Rockies,* illuminates the early history of the Shoshone River basin and other Rocky Mountain regions.

North Fork Shoshone

Rising in the Absaroka Range[2] near the eastern boundary of Yellowstone Park, the North Fork Shoshone rushes eastward down a steep, heavily forested canyon once praised by Teddy Roosevelt as "the most scenic 50 miles in America."

In its swift descent toward the high plains, the North Fork passes a series of striking volcanic rock formations with inspired names like Chimney Rock, Hanging Rock, Camel Rock, The Palisades, and even Laughing Pig Rock. Forest Service campgrounds and clusters of summer cabins detract little from the outstanding scenery. Wildlife is abundant—grizzlies have been sighted on the upper river—and the North Fork is a blue-ribbon trout stream.

As it cuts steadily downward through deep deposits of volcanic gravel, the North Fork maintains a continuous gradient and has few eddies. The relatively soft banks are easily eroded, and trees frequently become undermined and fall into the river. As a result, **logs** pose the most serious hazard on the run. Boaters should also be alert for sharp volcanic rock and undercut boulders.

The Yellowstone Highway (combined U.S. 14/16/20) follows the North Fork closely, offering easy access and scouting and allowing boaters to pick the sections best suited to their skills and tastes. Numerous alternate accesses include Forest Service campgrounds in the upper reaches and Fish & Game fishing accesses below the National Forest boundary.

[2]According to Mae Urbanek, *Wyoming Place Names*, "Absaroka" ("bird people") was the Crow Indians' original name for themselves.

[3]"Wapiti" (pronounced WAH-pitty) is an Indian word for elk.

North Fork Shoshone River Guide

The 38 miles described here offer a variety of whitewater and scenery. The first 20 miles to the confluence with the Elk Fork are the most popular and challenging. During peak snowmelt this section is icy and swift, but by late July flows are normally too low for boating. The **uppermost put-in** is at a turnout just below **Sleeping Giant Campground** (mile 0), four miles east of Yellowstone Park. The river is small here, but several tributaries add flow in the first ten miles. **MORMON CREEK RAPID (III+)** at mile 2.5 is usually the toughest on the North Fork. Boaters can avoid this drop by putting in at **Eagle Creek Campground.** After descending swiftly to **Rex Hale Campground,** an alternate access at mile 13, the river eases somewhat as the gradient diminishes and the channel widens. Many boaters **take out** at **Clearwater Campground** (mile 18).

The Elk Fork enters from the right near Wapiti[3] Campground and Ranger Station (mile 20), adding considerable flow and extending the season on the lower North Fork to late summer in most years. Downstream the North Fork cuts through softer volcanic ash, with fewer and generally easier rapids. An exception is at mile 23 (a half mile below Horse Creek Picnic Area): **DEVILS ELBOW (III)**, an S-turn that surges into undercut cliffs on the left. At mile 26, just below Laughing Pig Rock, the valley opens as the river leaves the National Forest. The hamlet of **Wapiti** is on the right near the highway bridge at mile 31 (**river access**). The seven-mile stretch below Wapiti is rarely floated. The lowermost take-outs are fishing accesses and a state campground near the upper end of Buffalo Bill Reservoir.

Main Shoshone

Some eight miles east of Cody, the North Fork and the much smaller South Fork Shoshone come together to form the river's main stem. The confluence is now covered by Buffalo Bill Reservoir, so today the Main Shoshone begins where the river emerges from the base of the dam. In the next 16 miles the Shoshone offers whitewater runs at both ends of the difficulty scale. Reservoir releases give this stretch a summer-long season in most years. Because the river never freezes, hard-core boaters could run the Main Shoshone year-round.

Shoshone Canyon

The North and South Forks run through open valleys for several miles above Buffalo Bill Reservoir, but below the dam the river plunges down a deep, narrow chasm between Rattlesnake Mountain and Cedar Mountain. George Beck and Bill Cody recognized this gorge as an ideal dam site, but they probably didn't realize that the canyon was formed by an earthquake fault. At one time the river flowed smoothly east from the confluence down to the valley around Cody, but a north-south fault gradually built a ridge, or anticline, directly across the river's course. The river cut into the mountain as it rose, eventually producing the dramatic cleft known as Shoshone Canyon.[4]

The river's passage through Shoshone Canyon is anything but smooth. In the four miles below the dam the river drops 300 frothy feet, cutting through hard Precambrian granites and schists at the heart of the anticline. Expert boaters—almost exclusively kayakers—often run this turbulent section, beginning either just below Buffalo Bill Dam or two miles downstream at **Hayden Bridge** (old U.S. 20).

According to a 1992 agreement, dam operators must (except in critical drought years) maintain a minimum flow of (a) 100 cfs in the first mile of river from Buffalo Bill Dam to the Buffalo Bill Powerhouse and (b) 350 cfs below the powerhouse. Since the water is released from the bottom of the reservoir, this stretch doesn't freeze in winter. Hardy off-season boaters can warm their hands in the hot springs.

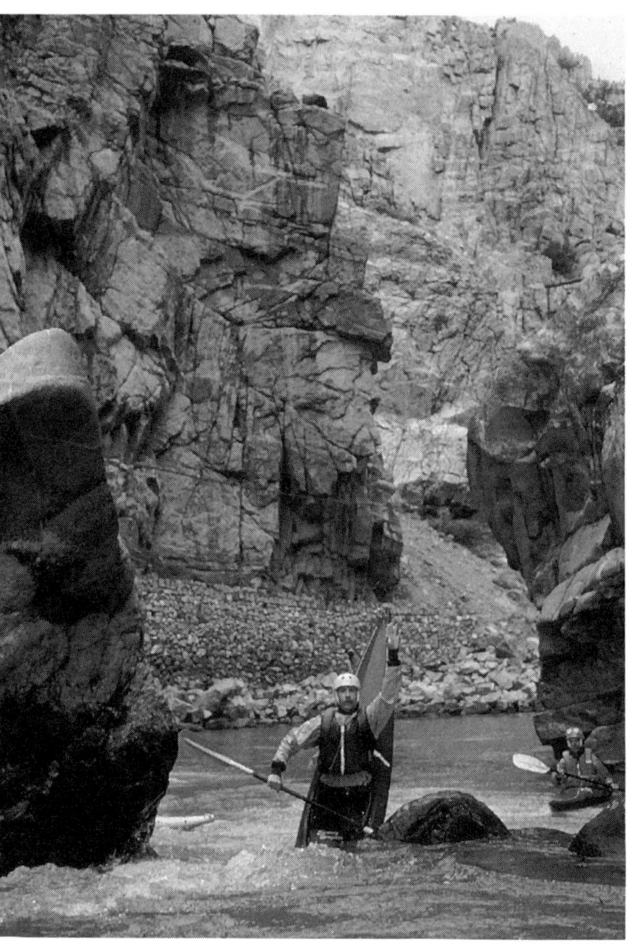

Pop-up on the Shoshone *Ron Lodders*

Shoshone Canyon River Guide

Many kayakers launch at the **uppermost put-in** (mile 0) on the left bank a few hundred yards below Buffalo Bill Dam (see **Logistics**). The action starts immediately with two big rapids: **KOP DROP (IV+; VI at high water)**, a 10' to 12' plunge that becomes unrunnable at flows above 800 to 1,000 cfs, when a keeper hydraulic develops. After a short pool comes **HEAD JOB (IV+)**, where the river drops over a complex of ledges with an undercut boulder on the left. ***HAZARD.*** **Do not launch above Kop Drop**: a dangerous rock sieve is just upstream. Boaters can avoid both **Kop Drop** and **Head Job** by putting in a bit farther downstream.

Below Head Job the whitewater eases to Class III+ and III. Near mile 1 a new bridge crosses the river to the Buffalo Bill Powerhouse on the right. The powerhouse usually adds at least 250 cfs, so boaters can launch here when flows are too skimpy upstream. The S-turn rapid just under the new bridge is the last significant drop on the uppermost section. The next mile down to the highway bridge is mostly Class II. Not far below the highway bridge is the old Hayden Bridge (mile 2.2), an **alternate access** on the right.

Class II water continues for another half mile below Hayden Bridge. Then the bedrock suddenly changes from hard granite to softer limestone, and the most difficult whitewater begins. ***HAZARD.*** Proceed with caution: the river has carved many **undercuts** in the soft rock, making swims very dangerous.

The big action starts with three powerful rapids in quick succession. First is a boulder garden known as **ENTRANCE EXAM (III+)**,

---

[4]William Fritz, *Roadside Geology of the Yellowstone Country,* includes several interesting pages on Shoshone Canyon.

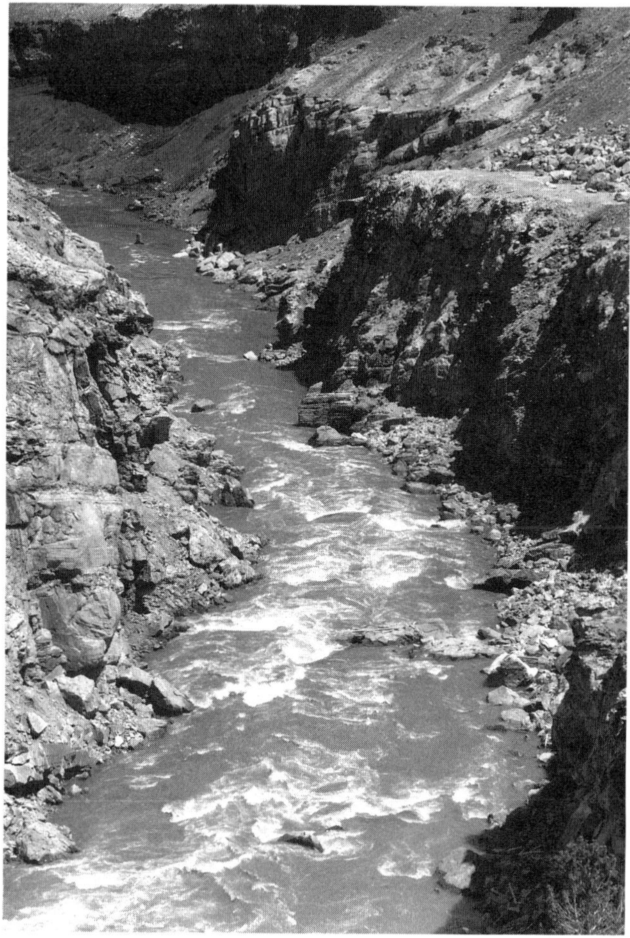
Pinball Rapid, Shoshone River *Dan Lewis*

followed immediately by **CUSTOMS (IV+ to V)**, a big drop over ledges with a hole on the left. At flows above about 1,200 cfs, Customs develops a dangerous river-wide reversal. Last in the series is **IRON CURTAIN (IV+)**, a very narrow dogleg—first left, then hard right—where the river smashes against the left wall. Approach this trio of rapids with extreme caution: trouble at the top could mean a long, nasty swim. Scout carefully from the right or, preferably, scout the entire series **before** running this section by pulling off U.S. 20 and walking to the edge of the canyon.

After **Iron Curtain** is a short pool, followed by **POWERHOUSE (III+)**, a boulder garden. Just downstream a large siphon pipe crosses the river, marking the location (on the right) of the Hart Mountain Power Station, which usually adds about 300 cfs to the flow. Just below the power station is a hot spring on the left. Below the siphon is about a quarter mile of easy water leading up to the last two rapids: **NINTENDO (III+)**, where rocks have fallen into the river from the left wall, followed by **PINBALL (IV)**, a long, complex rock garden at a left bend. Pinball has many ugly **undercuts,** making it a terrible place for a swim. Below Pinball is the **DeMaris Hot Springs take-out** on the right bank at the old bridge.

Parts of Shoshone Canyon can be scouted from the highway, but some spots cannot be seen from the road. Anyone planning a run should first ask local boaters for information, if possible.

Red Rock Canyon

Many boaters running the main stem of the Shoshone stick to the much milder runs below De Maris Hot Springs. Here the river winds easily through a shallow but scenic canyon, cutting through the colorful sedimentary strata of the Chugway Formation. The four miles from De Maris Hot Springs to the take-out just above the U.S. 120 bridge are easy Class II with good current, steady gradient, and pleasant scenery. The highway and the city of Cody are out of sight above the right bank. Local outfitters have dubbed this section "Red Rock Canyon."

Lower Canyon

Below Highway 120 are seven more miles of mostly easy water through a somewhat more open section known as the "Lower Canyon." Watch for one Class III drop where the river plunges abruptly over the remains of an old diversion dam, producing big waves at higher flows. (This passage is not far downstream from an oil refinery that sits high on the left bank.) The recommended **take-out** is on the left just above the Highway 14A bridge. **Don't miss the take-out;** a mile downstream is a mandatory portage at the Corbett diversion dam.

Boaters interested in continuing farther down the Shoshone should consult Dan Lewis, *Paddle and Portage* (see **Guides and References**).

Stillwater River

Woodbine Campground to Firemans Point

1. Woodbine Run: Woodbine CG (5,150') to Old Nye Picnic Area.
V; 4 miles; 75 ft./mi.

2. Buffalo Jump Run: Old Nye Picnic Area to Moraine.
II3; 8 miles; 22 ft./mi.

3. Upper Stillwater: Moraine to Cliff Swallow.
III; 7.5 miles; 37 ft./mi.

4. Lower Stillwater: Cliff Swallow to Firemans Point (3,620').
II; 26 miles; 30 ft./mi.

Drainage Area and Average Annual Discharge: 193 sq. mi. / 261,500 af near the Woodbine Run take-out; 975 sq. mi. / 694,800 af at the Absarokee gauge on the Lower Stillwater.

Season: Longer as you head downstream. *Runs 1 & 2:* May–June, sometimes a bit longer. *Run 3:* May to late July. *Run 4:* May–August above Rosebud Creek, all summer below.

Recommended Levels: *Woodbine Run (Run 1):* about 3.5' to 4.5' on the informal gauge at Chrome Chute (see **Flow Information**); very powerful and dangerous above 5' on that gauge. *Runs 2 and 3 (Upper Stillwater):* good above about 3.3' on the Absarokee gauge. *Run 4 (Lower Stillwater):* good above about 2.5' on the Absarokee gauge.

Flow Information: NWS, (406) 657-6988, or USGS, (406) 449-5263; flow in vertical feet at Absarokee (pronounced "ab-SAR-o-kee"). This gauge is on the Lower Stillwater below Rosebud Creek (a major tributary), so it substantially overestimates flows on the upper river. Convert from feet to cfs according to the table below. (The table is based on 1992 information; it could become inaccurate if the riverbed changes at the gauge site.)

An informal gauge is painted on the bridge at Chrome Chute, but there is no known cfs conversion for it and no known correlation to the Absarokee gauge.

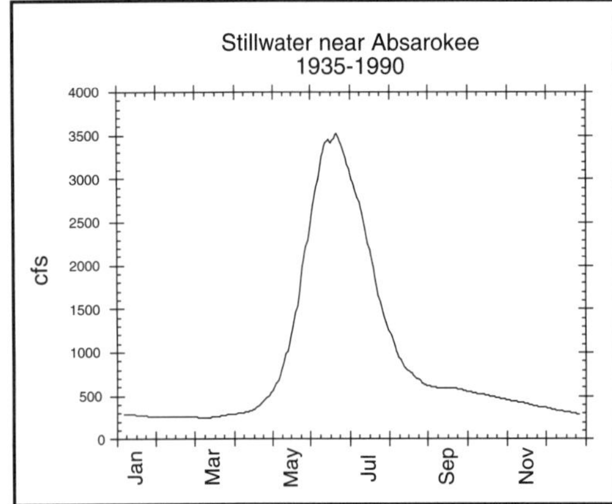

Special Hazards: Logs. Low bridges, especially at high flows. Woodbine and Chrome Chute rapids.

Permits: Not required.

Land Ownership: Mostly private. Some USFS land on Run 1; several state-owned accesses on downstream runs.

Scenery: Very good (forested canyon) on Run 1. Good on lower runs down to Cliff Swallow; more open thereafter.

Solitude: Good. Roads and highways follow most sections, and ranches dot the shore in places, but overall the river has a fairly secluded feel. **Wilderness:** No.

Side Hikes: A trail leads upriver from the road end near Woodbine Campground into the Absaroka Beartooth Wilderness. Another trail climbs steeply from Woodbine Campground to Woodbine Creek Falls.

Guides and References:
- Thompson, *Floating and Recreation on Montana Rivers.*
- Fischer, *Floater's Guide to Montana.*
- Good local sources for information are the Jackson Hole Kayak School, P.O. Box 8695, Jackson, WY, (307) 733-2471; and the Beartooth Paddlers Society in Billings.

Maps: USGS 7.5': *Cathedral Point, Nye, Beehive, Cow Face Hill, Sandborn Creek, Absarokee, Whitebird School.*
- **USFS:** *Custer NF (Beartooth Division).* Shows all runs.

Logistics: Paved or gravel roads follow the entire river, providing short shuttles and many accesses. Montana Highway 78 follows the

Stillwater at Absarokee

Feet	Cfs	Feet	Cfs
2.5	936	4.0	2,830
3.0	1,420	4.5	3,770
3.5	2,060	5.0	4,900

lower river from Columbus (off I-90) upstream to Absarokee. To reach the **Firemans Point, Swinging Bridge, White Bird, and Red Barn** (also called Riverside Inn) **accesses,** turn west on short spur roads off Highway 78. To reach the **Absaroka, Cliff Swallow, and Moraine accesses,** follow 78 upriver (south) to Absarokee, turn west on Road 420, and continue upriver. To reach **Absaroka Campground/Johnson Bridge,** turn right 1.5 miles west of Absarokee. To reach **Cliff Swallow,** continue west (upriver) another 9 miles to Cliff Swallow Campground on the right bank. To reach **Moraine,** continue upriver another 7 miles.

To reach the **Woodbine Run,** drive south from Absarokee on Montana 78 some 3 miles, turn west on Montana 419, and drive about 20 miles to the bridge over the river. (Buffalo Jump Campground, an **alternate access,** is at this bridge.) A good **take-out** for the Woodbine Run is at the Old Nye Picnic Area (USFS), about 4.5 miles upriver from the bridge. An **alternate take-out** is a mile farther upstream where a rough dirt road descends to the left bank. (This may be private property; inquire locally and ask permission if appropriate.) To reach the **put-in,** continue upriver another 2.5 miles, then bear left toward **Woodbine Campground** and put in on the left bank immediately below the bridge.

Names can be deceptive.[1] The Stillwater is actually one of Montana's liveliest whitewater rivers. The Woodbine Run is for experts only, while the rest of the river varies from exciting Class III to brisk, delightful Class II. In its upper reaches the crystal-clear Stillwater runs down a relatively steep, forested canyon. Farther downstream the canyon opens and the river flows through riparian woodlands bounded by hills, bluffs and ranchlands.

The Stillwater is one of nearly a dozen outstanding rivers that rise in the high country in and around Yellowstone National Park. From headwaters among 11,000' peaks in the Beartooth Mountains near the northeastern corner of the park, the Stillwater rushes northeastward some 70 miles to its confluence with the Yellowstone River west of Billings. The heavily forested upper watershed is almost entirely protected by the Absaroka Beartooth Wilderness.[2]

Most boating takes place below the wilderness boundary[3] where roads generally follow the river. Though most of the river bank is private, good access is possible at several public campgrounds, allowing boaters to choose from a wide variety of runs. The river generally has boatable flows from May to late July in most years, though the season can extend longer into the summer, particularly on the lower runs. Boaters should be constantly alert for log hazards and low bridges on this river.

Despite its fine whitewater, enjoyable scenery, and relatively long season, the Stillwater—like many other rivers in south-central Montana—receives little attention from boaters outside the immediate area. It is primarily a popular backyard run for a growing local boating community in and around Billings. Three major tributaries—the West Fork of the Stillwater, and the East and West Forks of Rosebud Creek—offer very difficult short-season runs favored by local experts.

---

[1]According to Roberta Cheney, *Names on the Face of Montana*, the name Stillwater derives from a local Indian legend. When a maiden named Weeluna died tragically, her body was placed high in a tree. A violent storm washed the body out of the tree and into the raging river, whereupon Weeluna's beloved, Nemidji, dived into the river to rescue the body. The current swept him away with Weeluna's body clasped in his arms. When the flood finally subsided, a quiet bayou or side channel was left behind, apart from the rush and roar of the main river. The tribe named this peaceful backwater the "Hallowed Place" or "Stillwater."

[2]The free-flowing Stillwater does face threats. Not long ago the Federal Energy Regulatory Commission (FERC) granted a permit to the owners of Beartooth Ranch to build a hydropower project on the lower river. The river got an unexpected reprieve when actor Mel Gibson bought the ranch and let the permit expire. Another threat comes from the chromite mine on the upper river; mine operators have sought an exemption from Clean Water Act requirements designed to protect the river's water quality.

[3]Adventurous experts occasionally run very demanding sections of the upper Stillwater inside the wilderness, packing boats and gear upriver on a trail that begins at the end of the road.

Stillwater River Guide

Woodbine Run

The uppermost run[4] begins at the bridge near Woodbine Campground, where the road ends (mile 0). **The first three miles are for experts only.** The Stillwater cascades down a narrow, boulder-choked course featuring two Class V rapids. The first, **WOODBINE,** is nearly a mile long with a total drop of 120'. This is powerful, technical water peppered with sticky holes—not the place for a swim. Scout from the left bank before you put in.

After Woodbine the Stillwater flattens out through a meadow for a little over a mile. At mile 2.5 the river roars back to life, plunging down a shorter Class V gauntlet, **CHROME CHUTE,** which begins where the river vaults over the remains of an old boulder dam. The left side is a near-vertical 10' to 12' falls; the right side is less steep but shallower. Next, the river churns under a bridge, and boaters must keep to the right to avoid two big holes in the left and center; at higher flows they are huge and hard to miss. The rapid, which is named for the Mouat chrome mine above the left bank, ends in a run-out through rocks and holes.

Chrome Chute is full of sharp, jagged rocks tumbled into the river by mining operations. It can be scouted on the way to the put-in by bearing left down the road that leads to the bridge in the middle of the rapid. This bridge is also the site of an informal flow gauge that boaters should check before they decide whether to launch (see **Flow Information**).

A few hundred yards below Chrome Chute, a power line crosses the river, marking the site of a **possible take-out** where a rough spur road reaches the left bank (this site may be private—inquire locally). A **public take-out** is a mile farther downstream at the Old Nye Picnic Area on the left.

Buffalo Jump Run

These eight miles from the Old Nye access to Moraine get only light use. The section is named for Buffalo Jump Campground, which provides an **alternate access** about halfway through the run on the left at the Highway 419 bridge. Beware of a low bridge two miles below the Old Nye put-in. The run is mostly Class I, with two short stretches of Class II: one at the beginning of the run, the other just below the Highway 419 bridge at Buffalo Jump. The West Fork of the Stillwater enters on the left below the highway bridge, adding significantly to the flow.

[4]Kayakers sometimes add an additional rapid by continuing up to the end of the road along the left bank, then hiking a short way upstream to launch.

Upper Stillwater

The run begins at the popular **Moraine Campground access.** The next 7.5 miles to Cliff Swallow are the most popular section of the Stillwater, with busy, semi-continuous Class III whitewater. The added flow of the West Fork Stillwater helps extend the season on this section. ***HAZARD.*** Be especially alert for **low bridges** that may require portage, especially at higher flows.

A few rapids in this stretch deserve mention. First is **MORAINE (III)**, a boulder garden about half a mile below the Moraine put-in. Not far downstream is **CASTLE ROCK (III)**, another boulder garden just above Castle Rock Campground (**alternate access**). A couple of miles farther is **DALLAS HOLE,** where a pair of rocks on the left create big holes at higher flows; approach with caution at high water. The last significant rapid is **ROSCOE'S (III-)**, a short, sharp drop about 100 yards below a bridge and about a mile and a half above the end of the run. Big, enjoyable waves form here at higher flows. The most popular **take-out** is at Cliff Swallow Campground, on the right bank half a mile below the Road 420 bridge.

Lower Stillwater

Below Cliff Swallow the river eases to mostly Class II for the remaining 26 miles. Accesses include **Absaroka Campground/Johnson Bridge,** nearly 12 miles below Cliff Swallow; the bridge at **Red Barn** ("Riverside Inn" on maps), a couple of miles farther; **White Bird,** roughly 20 miles below Cliff Swallow; **Swinging Bridge,** a mile below White Bird; and the **take-out** on the left bank just above the bridge at **Firemans Point,** a mile above the Yellowstone confluence. The stretch from Cliff Swallow to Absaroka gets only light use, while the reach from White Bird to Firemans Point gets the most. Rosebud Creek enters from the right between Absaroka Campground and Red Barn, adding substantially to the flow. Look for good surfing waves at Swinging Bridge, but beware of a big hole at high water.

Yellowstone River

Gardiner to Carbella

1. Gardiner (5,220') to Corwin Springs (5,080').
III- first 3 miles, then II.
8 miles; 16 ft./mi.

2. Yankee Jim Canyon: Joe Brown Creek (5,005') to Carbella (4,880').
III; 5 miles; 25 ft./mi.

Drainage Area and Average Annual Discharge: 2,623 sq. mi. and 2,253,000 af at Corwin Springs.
Peak Recorded Flow: 32,000 cfs (June 14, 1918).
Season: All summer. Typically peaks in early June. Often stays high well into July.
Recommended Levels: 1,000–10,000 cfs. Never too low. Big waves in Yankee Jim Canyon above 10,000 cfs.
Flow Information: USGS, (406) 449-5263, or NWS, (406) 657-6988; flow at Corwin Springs.
Permits: Not presently required.
Managing Agency: Montana Dept. of Fish, Wildlife, & Parks, 1400 S. 19th, Bozeman, MT 59715; (406) 994-4042.
Commercial Raft Trips: Yes. For references contact the managing agency.
Land Ownership: Mixed public and private; refer to *Gallatin NF* map.
Scenery: Very good. Beautiful mountain views.
Solitude: Good.
Wilderness: No. Highway follows the river.
Fishing: Blue-ribbon trout stream.
Water: Cold and clear.

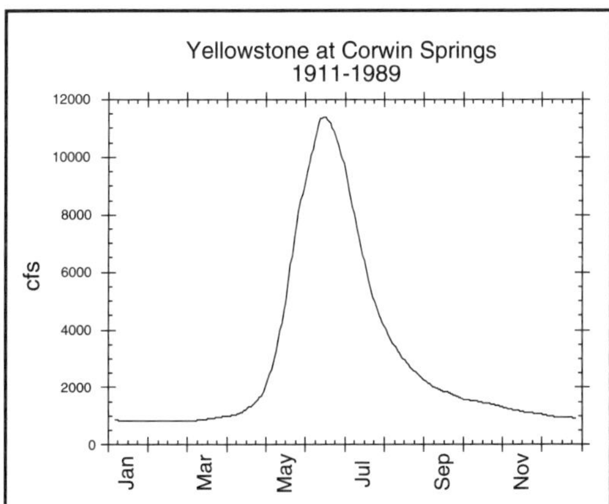

Camping: USFS campgrounds in the area.
Side Excursions: Yellowstone National Park. Absaroka Beartooth Wilderness.
Guides and References:
- *Upper Yellowstone River Guide* (Montana Fish, Wildlife & Parks). Useful map-pamphlet; free from the Bozeman office.
- Fischer, *Floater's Guide to Montana.*
- Thompson, *Floating and Recreation on Montana Rivers.*
- Hughes, *Yellowstone River and its Angling.*
- Fritz, *Roadside Geology of the Yellowstone Country.*

Maps:
- **USGS 7.5':** *Gardiner, Electric Peak, Dome Mtn., Miner.*
- **USFS:** *Gallatin NF.* Covers all runs. See **Gallatin** chapter for address.
- *Montana Afloat: The Yellowstone River.* Map shows accesses, roads, some rapids; notes on history, fishing, flows, etc. Covers river from Gardiner to Big Timber. Available at sporting goods and angling shops.

Auto Shuttle: About same mileages as river.
Logistics: U.S. 89 follows the river north of Yellowstone National Park, providing short shuttles and many alternate accesses in addition to those listed here (for a complete list see the *Upper Yellowstone River Guide*).

The **upper put-in** is in **Gardiner,** some 50 miles south of Livingston on U.S. 89. As of 1992 boaters could launch on the left bank behind the TWRS bunkhouse (large brown building), just below the mouth of the Gardiner River and about a quarter mile above the U.S. 89 bridge. Inquire locally for updates about this access. An **alternate put-in** is on the right bank 3 miles downstream at McConnell Landing; turn west off U.S. 89 at milepost 3. **Two accesses** are located at **Corwin Springs,** about 8 miles below Gardiner: on the left bank just above the bridge (turn west off U.S. 89), or on the right bank farther upstream. The **Carbella take-out** (BLM) is on the right bank about ten miles below Corwin Springs; turn west off U.S. 89 onto Tom Miner Road, drive 50 yards, then turn right and drive just over half a mile to the river.

Yellowstone National Park is one of the West's most fertile sources of rivers. Icy torrents radiate in every direction: the Clarks Fork of the Yellowstone and Shoshone to the east, the Snake to the south, the Fall River to the southwest, the Madison and Gallatin to the northwest, and the Yellowstone[1] itself to the north. The lion's share of the runoff feeds the 680-mile-long Yellowstone, the nation's longest undammed river outside Alaska.[2]

The river's headwaters actually lie just south of the nation's first national park, in the southern Absaroka Range. Just inside the park, the river glides into Yellowstone Lake, where snowmelt gathers from the Continental Divide. As it leaves the lake, the river is big enough to boat, but doing so invites a hefty fine because the Park Service prohibits river running inside the park.

The forbidden sections within Yellowstone Park begin with 20 miles of easy rapids and riffles below the lake, but then the bottom drops out. The river vaults over the Upper and Lower Falls of the Yellowstone—109' and 308', respectively. From the foot of the Lower Falls the river plunges into the spectacular, turbulent Grand Canyon of the Yellowstone. Then below Tower Junction the river crashes through Black Canyon, another blend of sublime scenery and violent rapids.

These Class V and VI wilderness sections are among the world's most outstanding whitewater runs, but the Park Service has placed them strictly off limits. A few experts have occasionally made the descents (apart from the waterfalls, of course), but they have often been caught and fined. Park Service managers argue that river running would intrude on the wilderness, increase search and rescue expenses, and lead to fatalities. (See sidebar.)

Law-abiding citizens have to wait for the river to leave the park at Gardiner. The 102-mile "Upper Yellowstone" section from here to Big Timber is Montana's most popular fishing and floating river. The first 60 miles from Gardiner to Livingston flow through Paradise Valley, a picturesque alpine bowl between the Gallatin and Absaroka Ranges. U.S. 89 follows this reach, providing frequent access. The river can be crowded on weekends. Because thermal activity keeps the river from freezing, some hardy boaters float here year-round. This section's fine scenery was not affected by the great Yellowstone wildfires of 1988.[3]

The first 18 miles below the Park contain all of the Yellowstone's legal whitewater. The action begins with three miles of Class II+ water (III at high flows) below Gardiner. Some boaters take out after this short run, while others float through five more miles of easy Class II to Corwin Springs. Nearly five miles of flatwater lead to Yankee Jim Canyon,[4] a narrow four-mile cut through dark Precambrian rock. The difficulty of Yankee Jim's whitewater varies widely with the flow (see **Mile Guide**). All the major rapids can easily be scouted from the highway. The canyon is a popular run for squirt boaters.

The Yellowstone below Carbella offers good boating, though it is no longer a whitewater river. (The 85 miles from Carbella to Big Timber are known as the "Mellowstone".) Downstream, below Livingston, the Yellowstone runs east some 500 miles through foothills and prairie to meet the broad Missouri. Aside from occasional irrigation diversions, the river is free-flowing and boatable the whole way. Open canoeists enjoy the Lower Yellowstone's peaceful waters, abundant wildlife and rich history.[5]

---

[1]French explorers named the river "Roche Jaune," which was later translated to "Yellow Stone."

[2]The title is far from secure. Though the Bureau of Reclamation has temporarily shelved plans to flood Paradise Valley by building a 300'-high dam above Livingston, this proposal remains a serious long-term threat.

[3]The Grand Canyon and Black Canyon sections in the park were only partly burned, but the upper watershed above Yellowstone Lake was hit hard. In total about half the watershed above Gardiner burned—some 580,000 acres or 900 square miles.

[4]The name comes from pioneer "Yankee Jim" George, who blasted a toll road through the canyon in the 1870's and for a few years collected tolls from miners and tourists bound for Yellowstone Park. In the mid-1880's the Northern Pacific Railroad laid track through the canyon up to Corwin Springs, and his road was soon obsolete. Jim never got over his bitterness. When President Theodore Roosevelt toured the park in 1903, he sent a message downriver asking Jim to come up and meet him. Yankee Jim's reply: "You know where I live, Teddy."

[5]For general information on the lower river refer to Fischer, *Floater's Guide to Montana*, and Thompson, *Floating and Recreation on Montana Rivers,* which covers the entire Yellowstone. For details on the section below Billings see *Treasure of Gold*, available from the Montana Dept. of Fish, Wildlife and Parks.

Mile by Mile Guide

0 **PUT-IN** at Gardiner(see **Logistics**). U.S. 89 crosses the river and follows the right bank downstream. The first 3 miles are Class III.

3 **RIVER ACCESS.** McConnell Landing on the right. Easier water downstream.

8 Bridge over the river at Corwin Springs. A popular **RIVER ACCESS** is on the left bank, a quarter mile above the bridge. Flat water from here to Joe Brown Creek.

12.5 Joe Brown Creek. **RIVER ACCESS** on the right bank. **Yankee Jim Canyon** begins just downstream.

13–17 Yankee Jim Canyon has three major rapids. First is **YANKEE JIM'S REVENGE** (III-), also known as **Boat Eater** because a big wave routinely flips rafts at high water. Then comes **THE SPHINX (III)**, with a house rock (hole at high flows) in river center. At low water this is the toughest rapid in Yankee Jim Canyon; at very high flows it washes out. Last is **BOXCAR (III)**, with big standing waves in a narrow gorge. At 15,000 cfs and up, Boxcar develops a huge wave at the bottom that can be hard to avoid.

17 Tom Miner Bridge. Carbella **TAKE-OUT** is about a half mile downstream on the right.

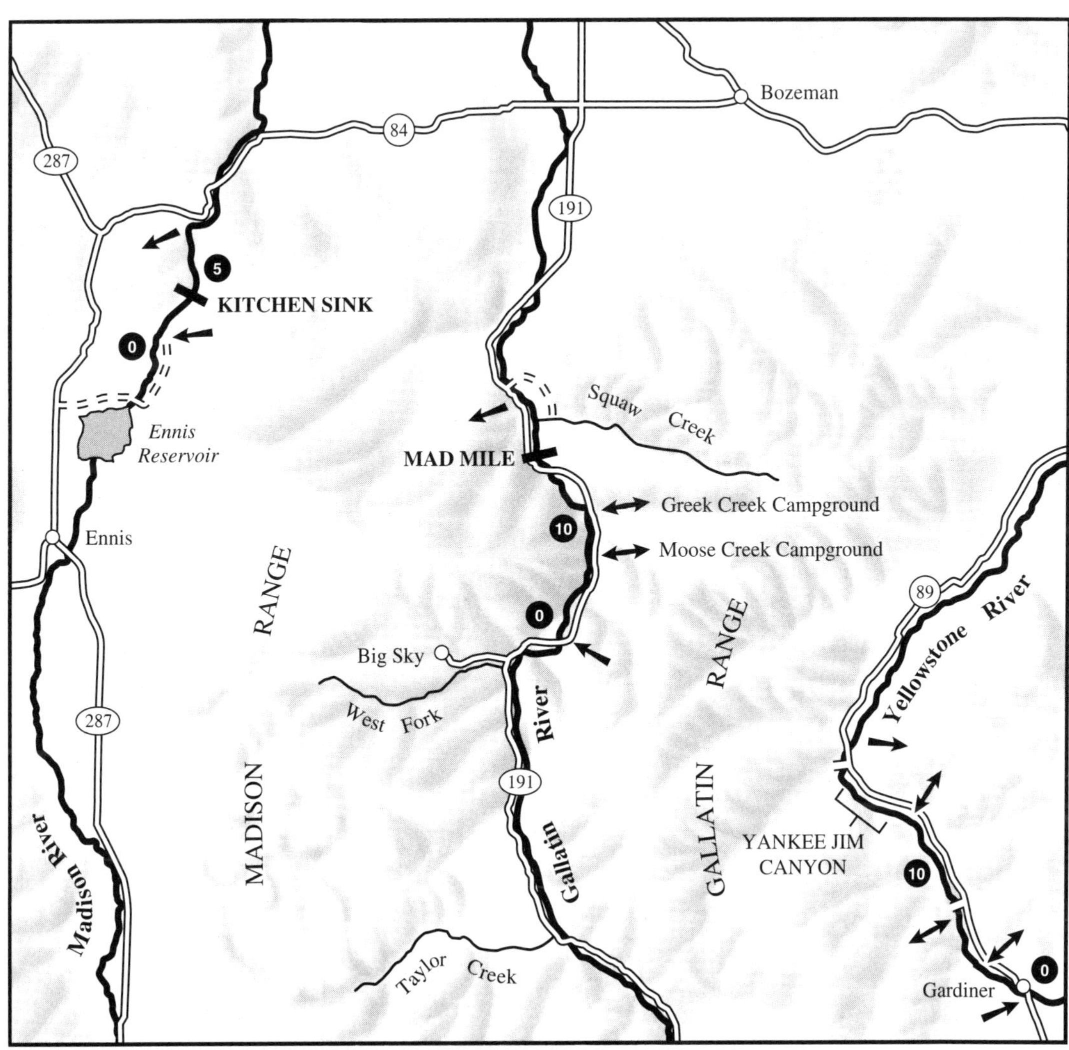

Yellowstone, Gallatin, and Madison

The Forbidden Rivers of Yellowstone Park

"*Notice:* Effective immediately, the National Park Service will permanently close the Colorado River in Grand Canyon, the Rio Grande in Big Bend, the Green and Colorado Rivers (including Cataract Canyon) in Canyonlands National Park, the Yampa and Green Rivers (including Gates of Lodore) in Dinosaur National Monument, and the Snake River in Grand Teton National Park."

No, it's not true. But imagine if it were! The boating community would be outraged if it were confronted with the closure of the premier rivers of America's national parks. Yet the Park Service in Yellowstone National Park has managed to close, by its own tally, more than 400 miles of boatable water.

Closed rivers include—to name only the most visible—the spectacular Black Canyon of the Yellowstone, the Lewis River Canyon, the Lamar River, and many other single and multi-day Class II to V wilderness runs. Yellowstone harbors the largest collection of unexplored rivers in the lower 48 states.

The amazing thing is that boaters who are usually quick to protect access to rivers have so far raised no significant objections to the Park Service's policy. The only reasons for this arbitrary decision to remain uncontested are ignorance and inertia. River runners have a defensive mind set; they concentrate on saving rivers, and opening up new rivers usually doesn't occur to them. The result is that so far, no serious challenge has been mounted to a decision that predates the modern river conservation movement.

Congress closed all Yellowstone rivers to boating in 1950, long before the explosion in recreational paddling gave political voice to lovers of wild rivers. The initial closure was to protect fisheries from anglers in boats. But it was perpetuated in a November 1986 Park Service assessment that whitewater boating might conflict with other resource uses, primarily fishing. Even more incredibly, the Park Service concluded that the impact of recreational boating on the riparian environment and protected wildlife justified a complete closure of all rivers in the park. Yet this same agency permits snowmobilers, horseback riders, backpackers, and fishermen to roam the back country and even the banks of the same rivers which it concludes are threatened by boats! Boaters wouldn't object to the closure of some sites and/or rivers during the crucial nesting season of endangered raptors. But as things stand, the bureaucrats won't even allow boating on Yellowstone rivers that are near heavily-traveled roads.

Since the Park Service's ostensible reasons for forbidding boating don't stand up, it appears that the closure policy is really motivated by a desire to maintain the status quo and to protect more "traditional" recreational uses of the park—a grandfather clause, in short. This isn't good enough. The Park Service has a duty to nurture the environmental resources of Yellowstone by sponsoring the recreational alternatives that are most compatible with conservation mandates. Whitewater boating is surely one of those alternatives. It's up to the river running community to insist upon access to the beautiful wild rivers of America's oldest national park.

—Ron Lodders

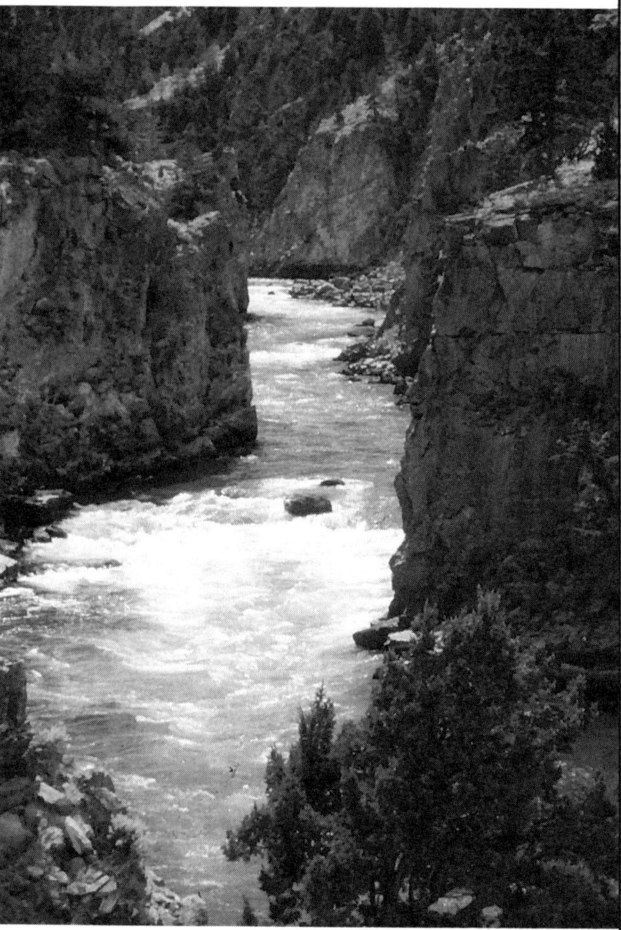

Black Canyon of the Yellowstone *Ron Lodders*

Gallatin River

1. Jack Smith Bridge (5,920') to Greek Creek (5,610').
II+3; 9 miles; 34 ft./mi.
2. Greek Creek to Squaw Creek Bridge (5,280').
III+; 7 miles; 45 ft./mi.

Drainage Area and Average Annual Discharge: 825 sq. mi. / 587,600 af near Squaw Creek.
Peak Recorded Flow: 9,100 cfs (June 17, 1974).
Season: May through July. Usually peaks in late May or early June.
Recommended Levels: 800–4,000 cfs.
Flow Information: USGS, (406) 449-5263; flow near Gallatin Gateway (5 miles below Squaw Creek). Convert feet to cfs using table below.
Permits: Not presently required.
Managing Agency: Gallatin NF, Federal Bldg., Box 130, Bozeman, MT 59771; (406) 587-6920.
Commercial Raft Trips: Yes. Contact the managing agency for references.
Land Ownership: Mostly National Forest.
Scenery: Very good. **Solitude:** Good.
Wilderness: No. Highway follows the river.
Fishing: Excellent for trout.
Water: Cold and clear.
Camping: Many USFS campgrounds along the river.
Side Hikes: Several USFS trails, including one up Cascade Creek to Lava Lake in the Spanish Peaks Wilderness.
Side Excursions: Yellowstone National Park.
Guides and References:
- Fischer, *Floater's Guide to Montana.* Includes novice runs on the lower river.
- Thompson, *Floating and Recreation on Montana Rivers.*
- A good local source of information is Yellowstone Raft Co. on U.S. 191 north of Big Sky, (406) 995-4613.

Gallatin near Gallatin Gateway

Feet	Cfs	Feet	Cfs
1.8	631	4.0	3,280
2.0	784	4.5	4,180
2.5	1,240	5.0	5,200
3.0	1,810	6.0	6,830
3.5	2,490		

Maps:
- **USGS 7.5':** *Hidden Lake, Garnet Mtn.*
- **USFS:** *Gallatin NF* shows all runs.

Auto Shuttle: Paved; about same mileages as river.
Logistics: U.S. 191 follows the Gallatin, providing more accesses than those listed here. The **Jack Smith (U.S. 191) Bridge** is some 40 miles south of I-90, 18 miles north of Yellowstone Park, and about two miles downriver from Big Sky Junction. The **Greek Creek access** is about 8 miles downstream. The **35-mph Bridge access** is at the trail head parking area on the left bank about 200 yards above the U.S. 191 bridge. The **Squaw Creek access** is on the left bank between the highway and the river, just upstream from the bridge leading to Squaw Creek Ranger Station (about two miles above the National Forest boundary). The **last take-out** is at the U.S. 191 bridge at the mouth of Gallatin Canyon, 7 miles downstream from Squaw Creek.

Rising in the rugged northwest corner of Yellowstone National Park in Wyoming, the Gallatin River flows north into Montana, carving a narrow canyon between the Gallatin and Madison Ranges. Best known as a blue-ribbon trout stream, the Gallatin is also the backyard run for an active boating community in Bozeman. The annual Gallatin Whitewater Festival has increased the river's visibility, and now out-of-state boaters also enjoy the Gallatin's fine forest scenery,[1] easy access, and wide variety of whitewater. The entire stretch described here is

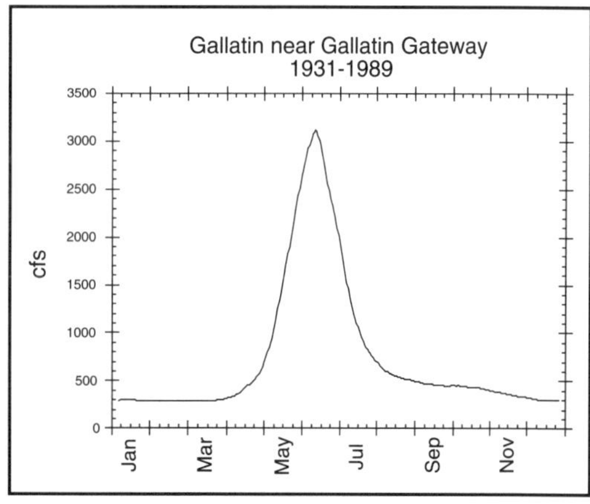

under consideration for National Wild and Scenic River status.

In its lower reaches the Gallatin is a broad river, flowing easily through an agricultural valley and joining with the Madison and Jefferson Rivers to form the mighty Missouri (see sidebar). The whitewater runs are far upstream in Gallatin National Forest. Here the river tumbles through a steep-sided canyon cloaked in lodgepole pine, spruce, and hemlock. U.S. Highway 191 parallels the upper Gallatin, often quite close to the river, allowing boaters to scout from the road and choose sections with adequate flow and appropriate difficulty.

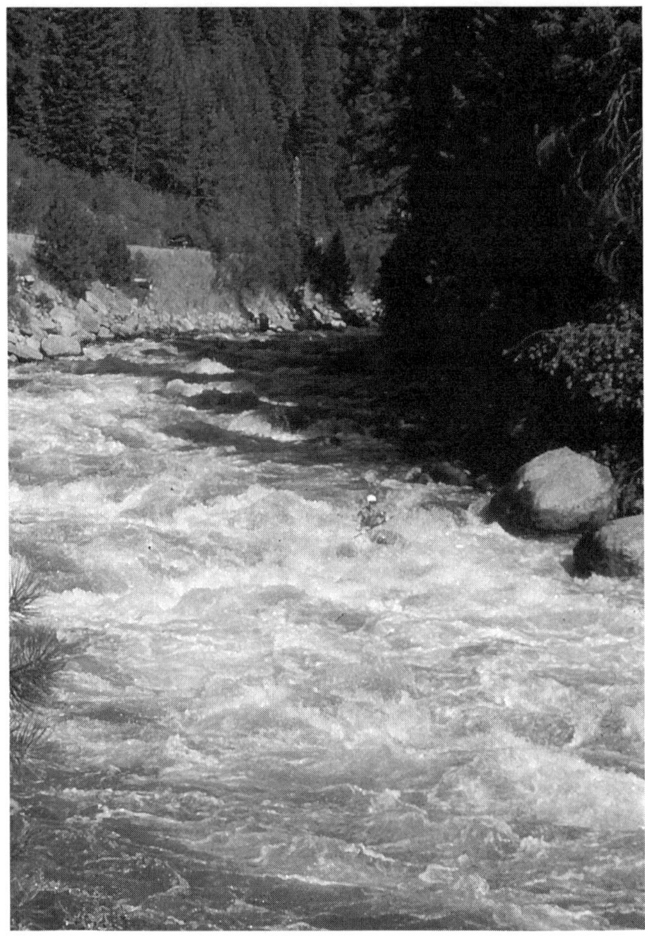

Screaming Left Turn, Gallatin River *Judy Theodorson*

Boating is prohibited on the uppermost reaches of the Gallatin in Yellowstone National Park, but the loss is mostly theoretical: until Taylor Creek joins the river just below the park boundary, the Gallatin is more of a big stream than a river.

The stretch from Taylor Creek to Big Sky Junction offers over 20 miles of Class II water early in the season but is rarely runnable after mid-July. Be alert for occasional **strainers** and fair-sized waves at high water. More tributaries swell the river just above Red Cliff Campground, a popular alternate access eight miles below Taylor Creek.

At Big Sky Junction the West Fork enters, and the Gallatin becomes a full-fledged river. Downstream the whitewater grows somewhat more challenging as the river cuts into older, harder rock formations in Gallatin Canyon. Two miles below Big Sky, U.S. 191 crosses the Gallatin at Jack Smith Bridge. The nine-mile run from here to Greek Creek is Class II and II+ with one III. A popular put-in at Moose Creek (mile 6.5) avoids the Class III rapid.

Below Greek Creek the canyon narrows and more Class III rapids appear. The whitewater peaks in the narrow, V-shaped heart of Gallatin Canyon. This chasm is carved deep into the basement rocks underlying the Gallatin and Madison Ranges: ancient blocks of gneiss with sinuous patterns of dark and light layers, sliced through at angles by striking white and black veins.[2] For more than two miles the river churns through nearly continuous rapids, including famous Mad Mile and House Rock. Most boaters take out not far downstream.

The seven miles from Squaw Creek Bridge (mile 16) to the mouth of the canyon hold nothing above Class II+, although a **weir** below Spanish Creek (a possible portage) demands scouting. The few boaters who run this section usually take out at the U.S. 191 bridge or at Williams Bridge, a little over a mile farther downstream. Below the mouth of the canyon, diversion dams and log jams make boating unrewarding for many miles.

Farther downstream the Gallatin offers flatwater floating from below the confluence with the East Fork (near Manhattan) all the way to the Missouri River.[3]

[1]The 1988 Yellowstone wildfires did not affect the Gallatin Canyon outside the national park.

[2]Alt and Hyndman, *Roadside Geology of Montana,* includes a discussion of Gallatin Canyon.

[3]For more on these sections refer to Fischer, *The Floater's Guide to Montana,* and Thompson, *Floating and Recreation on Montana Rivers.*

Mile by Mile Guide

*See map in **Yellowstone** chapter.*

0 **PUT-IN.** Jack Smith (U.S. 191) Bridge. Mostly Class II and II+ rapids to Greek Creek. U.S. 191 follows the entire run.

3.5 Portal Creek enters on the right in the middle of **PORTAL CREEK RAPID (III)**, the most difficult spot on the run to Greek Creek. Scout right.

6.5 Moose Creek Campground on the right. Popular **RIVER ACCESS.**

8 Swan Creek enters on the right.

9 Greek Creek Campground, a popular **RIVER ACCESS** on the right. Downstream the difficulty increases.

10 **SCREAMING LEFT TURN (III).** The river turns sharply left, and a large dark rock juts out from the left bank. Good run-out pool. About a half mile downstream is **HILARITY HOLE (III)**, where boaters stay left to avoid a keeper hole hidden at the bottom of the wave train at moderate and high flows.

12 So-called "35-mph Bridge" (U.S. 191). A large, popular **RIVER ACCESS** is on the left bank upstream from the bridge. Stop here to avoid the rough water downstream and/or to make the scenic hike up Cascade Creek.

Downstream is the beginning of **MAD MILE (III+)**, a bit longer than its name indicates. Half a mile below the bridge is the biggest rapid, **HOUSE ROCK (IV-)**. After slowing in a large pool, the current accelerates and plows into a huge rock dead center in the channel. A diagonal wave shoves unwary boaters into the boulder. The standard run is down the left. Stop at the pool upstream to scout on the left and check for **logs** that sometimes lodge here.

Below House Rock, the Mad Mile continues in a long section of steep, technical rock gardens that become hole fields at higher flows.

14 **RIVER ACCESS** on the right where a short dirt road leads up to the highway. Popular with private boaters.

16 **TAKE-OUT** on the left just above Squaw Creek Bridge, over a mile downstream from the mouth of Squaw Creek. No eddy; difficult landing for rafts at higher flows. Boaters can also continue downstream (see end of essay).

Lewis and Clark

" ... At the junction of the S.E. fork of the Missouri ... the country opens suddonly to extensive and beatifull plains and meadows which appear to be surrounded in every direction with distant and lofty mountains; supposing this to be the three forks of the Missouri I halted the party ... "

With this journal entry of July 27, 1805, Meriwether Lewis marked the arrival of the "Voyage of Discovery"—led by himself and fellow explorer William Clark—at the long anticipated triple confluence that forms the Missouri River. The site had been described to the explorers by Mandan Indians who lived far downstream. Having navigated the Missouri up to this point, the expedition paused while its leaders decided which fork to follow upstream. They quickly settled on the western fork as the largest and the only one leading in the direction of their ultimate goal, the Pacific Ocean.

Lewis and Clark also seized the opportunity to flatter their sponsors by naming the three tributaries after prominent members of the administration: the large western fork for President Thomas Jefferson, the medium-sized middle fork for Secretary of State James Madison, and the smaller eastern branch for Secretary of the Treasury Albert Gallatin. After deciding to ascend the Jefferson, Lewis and Clark sought to ingratiate themselves further by naming that river's three main forks after their President's most notable virtues: Wisdom, Philosophy, and Philanthropy. Fortunately, these names did not survive. The names for the Missouri forks did stick, however.

The classic work on the Lewis and Clark expedition is David Lavender, *The Way to the Western Sea.*

Madison River

Bear Trap Canyon

Difficulty: III4+.
Length: 8.5 mi. Longer runs possible.
Gradient: 28 ft./mi.
Put-in: Madison Powerhouse (4,700').
Take-out: Warm Springs Creek (4,450').
Drainage Area and Average Annual Discharge: 2,186 sq. mi. and 1,287,000 af near put-in.
Peak Recorded Flow: 9,550 cfs (June 12, 1970).
Season: All summer. Dam releases normally range from 1,000 to 2,500 cfs. High water in June.
Recommended Levels: 1,000–2,500 cfs. Very difficult above 4,000.
Flow Information: Montana Power Co. Hotline, (800) 247-9131 x 199; flow below Ennis Lake. A sign posted near the launch site gives the flow in cfs.
Special Hazards: Kitchen Sink Rapid. High water.
Permits: Not presently required.
Managing Agency: BLM, Dillon RA, 1005 Selway Dr., Dillon, MT 59725; (406) 683-2337.
Commercial Raft Trips: Yes. For references contact the BLM.
Land Ownership: All BLM except the take-out, which is private land with public use permitted.
Scenery: Excellent.
Solitude: Excellent.
Wilderness: Yes.
Camping: Public campgrounds at Red Mountain and along the lower river. No overnight camping for boaters in Bear Trap Canyon.

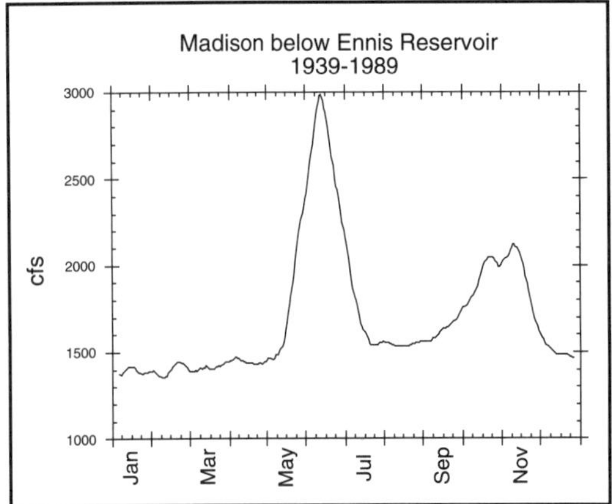

Side Excursions: Yellowstone National Park. Earthquake Lake on upper Madison. Bear Trap Hot Springs on shuttle route.
Guides and References:
- *Bear Trap Canyon Floater's Guide* (BLM). Useful map-pamphlet showing topography, land ownership and roads, but no rapid locations.
- Fischer, *Floater's Guide to Montana.*
- Thompson, *Floating and Recreation on Montana Rivers.*
- Brooks, *The Living River: A Fisherman's Intimate Profile of the Madison River Watershed.*

Maps:
- **USGS** 7.5': *Ennis Lake, Norris, Bear Trap Creek.*
- **USFS:** *Lee Metcalf Wilderness.*
- **USFS:** *Gallatin NF.*
- *Montana Afloat: The Madison River.* Accesses, roads, some rapids, fishing, flows, etc. Available at many sporting goods and angling shops or from Montana Afloat, 4106 Fox Farm Road, Missoula, MT 59802..

Auto Shuttle: 23 miles one way (7 on dirt).
Logistics: To reach the **put-in,** follow U.S. 287 to McAllister, about 6 miles north of Ennis in southwestern Montana. Turn east toward Ennis Reservoir and drive along the north shore to the bridge over the narrow outlet arm of the lake. Immediately beyond the bridge, bear left and drive 3 miles to the launch site just above Madison Powerhouse. Boaters can also use the more difficult **alternate put-in** on the right bank at the Fall Creek Day Use Area, just above Double Drop Rapid.

To reach the **take-out,** return to McAllister and drive north on U.S. 287 about 10 miles to the hamlet of Norris. Turn right on Montana Highway 84 and drive east about 6 miles to the take-out where the highway first meets the river, or continue about two miles to an **alternate access** at the Norris-Bozeman (Highway 84) bridge.

Running Bear Trap Canyon on the Madison in southwestern Montana should be on the wish lists of many boaters. Outstanding scenery, deep solitude, warm water (at the right time of year), and one big rapid combine to make Bear Trap one of Montana's most popular whitewater runs and one of the Rockies' best one-day wilderness trips.

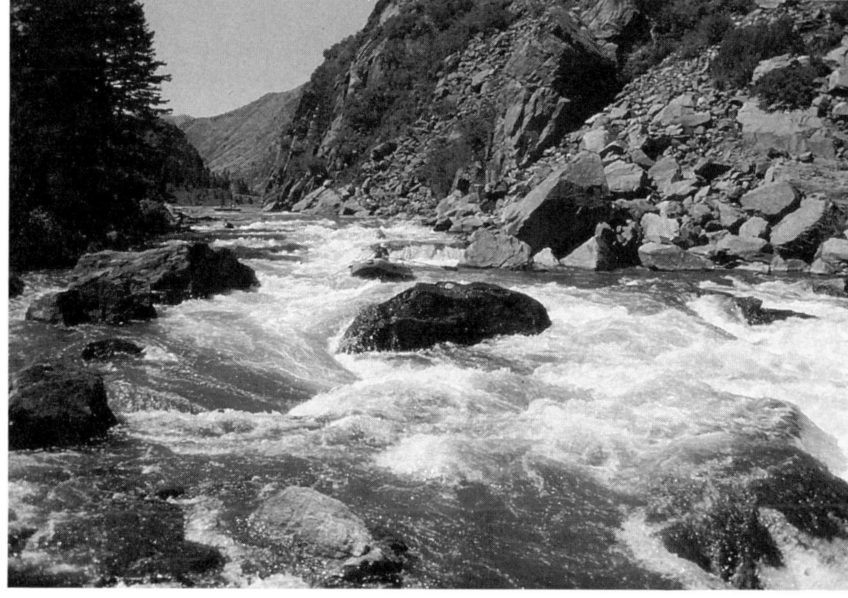

Kitchen Sink Rapid, Bear Trap Canyon, Madison River *Joe Ashor / BLM*

The Madison is born at the meeting of two tributaries in the fiery geothermal heart of Yellowstone National Park. The Gibbon River drains Norris Geyser Basin, while the larger Firehole River begins as frigid snowmelt on the Continental Divide but soon picks up hot water from Old Faithful and other geysers. From the confluence the Madison flows west out of the park, then north to Three Forks, Montana, where it joins the Jefferson and Gallatin Rivers to form the Missouri.[1]

Until this century the Madison ran free from headwaters to mouth, but today three small dams interrupt its flow. In 1900 Madison Dam was built as a small hydroelectric project, creating Ennis Reservoir which now marks the division between the upper and lower Madison. Fifteen years later Hegben Dam began generating electricity farther upstream, just outside Yellowstone Park.

The third dam was particularly impressive for its construction timetable—about one minute. On August 17, 1959, one of the biggest earthquakes ever felt in the Rocky Mountains (magnitude 7.1) shook western Yellowstone and dislodged a mountainside about five miles below Hegben Dam. 80 million tons of earth thundered into the Madison canyon, blocking the river and burying at least 28 people at a riverside campground. Today the long, narrow finger of water backed up behind the slide is known as Earthquake Lake or Quake Lake. The scene of the cataclysm, something of a tourist attraction, makes an interesting side trip.

Upper Madison

Despite its notoriety because of the earthquake, the upper Madison is most famous for its fishing. For more than 50 miles below Earthquake Lake, the river runs ice cold, crystal clear and thick with trout. Anglers in hip boots crowd the shore, while others cast lines from canoes or drift boats. Panoramic views of the nearby Gravelly and Madison Ranges attract some boaters to this generally mild reach, though the heavy fishing use means some crowding and potential conflict between river runners and anglers.

U.S. 287 follows the upper river, providing many alternate accesses. Be aware that **the mile-long section below Quake Lake is a treacherous experts-only run** with a dangerous combination of sharp rocks and powerful hydraulics. (Local kayakers call this reach the "River X Run" or the "Quake Lake Run-out.") Eight miles of the upper river are currently under consideration as a potential addition to the National Wild and Scenic Rivers System.

[1]The Madison was named by Lewis and Clark in 1805 after Secretary of State James Madison. See the sidebar in the **Gallatin** chapter.

Bear Trap Canyon

Below Ennis Reservoir the fishing gives way to challenging whitewater. As the river spreads out in the shallow reservoir, the summer sun raises water temperatures into the high 60's and occasionally above 70° in the later part of the season. Though the trout find the tepid conditions unappealing, whitewater boaters are rarely heard to complain.

Leaving the reservoir, the Madison plunges into Bear Trap Canyon, a narrow cut through the northern end of the Madison Range. Over millions of years the Spanish Peaks Fault has gradually raised the mountains directly across the river's path.[2] Pressed between cliffs soaring to 1,500' and surrounded by the 6,000-acre Bear Trap Wilderness Area, this remote stretch of river offers unspoiled scenery and an abundance of wildlife.

Most of the whitewater action in Bear Trap comes in four big rapids, with plenty of easy water in between for recovery. Class IV+ Kitchen Sink, located about a third of the way into the run, rates a full class above anything else. The next roughest rapid, Double Drop, can be run only by launching at the more difficult upper put-in (see **Logistics** and **Mile Guide**). At high flows (about 2,500 cfs and up) the rapids become much more difficult, and Kitchen Sink approaches Class V. Boaters in lightweight craft can portage Kitchen Sink if necessary. Many river runners stop at Bear Trap Hot Springs on the shuttle route after a cold day on the river.

Lower Madison

Below the Norris-Bozeman Bridge on Montana Highway 84, the Madison winds easily past imposing grey cliffs in a gradually widening valley. These final 18 miles to the Missouri make a pleasant novice run, though upstream winds and **sweepers**—trees in the channel—can pose some problems. This section is popular with the college and Budweiser crowds. Intermediate access is possible at the Greycliff and Cobblestone recreation sites.

---

[2]Alt and Hyndman, *Roadside Geology of Montana,* covers the Madison.

Mile by Mile Guide

*See map in **Yellowstone** chapter.*

0 **PUT-IN.** BLM launch site on the right bank just above Madison Powerhouse. The road on the right bank ends here as the river enters Bear Trap Canyon Wilderness. A trail follows the right bank throughout the run.

A more difficult **alternate put-in** is about 1/3 mile upstream at the Fall Creek Day use Area. The upper put-in adds one challenging technical rapid, **DOUBLE DROP** (IV-), with no time for warm-up. The upper put-in is often not an option due to insufficient flows above the powerhouse, which normally adds 1,000 cfs to the river.

2 **WHITE HORSE** (III), a long series of big waves. **Recognition:** A big rock divides the current at a horizon line. Scouting trail on the left.

3.2 **KITCHEN SINK** (IV+), so named because it has everything but! This long, technical rapid—the most difficult on the run by far—has big drops and waves, tight turns, and plenty of rocks. **Recognition:** A prominent rock outcrop descends steeply to the river on the left. According to the BLM, at least eight people have died in this rapid. Scout and/or portage along the trail on the right.

4.3 **GREEN WAVE** (III). Also called **The Dumplings** and **Youthful Folly.** Big boulders scattered in the channel. Scout left. Good play hole at bottom right. Just downstream, Bear Trap Creek enters on the right. Easy water from here on.

8 A gravel road reaches the right bank as Bear Trap Canyon Wilderness ends.

8.5 **TAKE-OUT** on the left bank where Montana Highway 84 approaches the river near the mouth of Warm Springs Creek (private land, but use is permitted). Boaters can continue about 2.5 miles downstream to an **alternate take-out** at the Norris-Bozeman bridge on Highway 84, or another 18 miles to the Missouri River (easy water, but watch for **sweepers**).

Smith River

Camp Baker to Eden Bridge

Difficulty: II-.
Length: 61 miles. **Gradient:** 15 ft./mi.
Put-in: Camp Baker (4,380').
Take-out: Eden Bridge (3,445').
Drainage Area and Average Annual Discharge: 846 sq. mi. and 125,000 af at put-in.
Season: Variable. May–mid-July; occasionally Sept.–Oct. as well. Usually peaks in late May or early June and falls too low for normal boating from early July to sometime in September; however, many boaters scrape down the river at very low levels.
Recommended Levels: 250–1,500 cfs on the Fort Logan gauge, but many run at lower flows.
Flow Information: USGS, (406) 449-5263; flow "near Fort Logan." The gauge is actually about a mile above the Camp Baker put-in. Flows at the put-in are 50% to 100% higher because Sheep Creek, a major tributary, enters there. Managing agency can also provide flow information.
Special Hazards: Fences (with "floater gates") across the river.
Permits: Required. Applications available in January; lottery in mid-February; first-come, first-served thereafter. Call for cancellations or available dates. Group size limit 15.
Managing Agency: Montana Dept. of Fish, Wildlife & Parks, 4600 Giant Springs Rd., P.O. Box 6610, Great Falls, MT 59406; (406) 454-3441.
Commercial Raft Trips: Yes. For a list of outfitters, contact the managing agency.
Land Ownership: About 80% private, 20% public. Left bank is almost entirely private.
Scenery: Excellent. Thick forest, spectacular limestone canyon.
Solitude: Good in June; very good in other months.
Wilderness: Mostly. Some cabins, summer homes, and isolated ranches.
Fishing: Excellent. Blue-ribbon trout stream; catch and release encouraged. Special regulations.
Water: Murky at peak runoff, clear at low flows. Undrinkable. Bring water or purify.
Camping: Excellent. More than 50 designated sites. Register for sites at put-in.
Side Excursions: Waterfalls on the Missouri at Great Falls, Montana. Giant Springs near Great Falls—one of the world's largest.
Guides and References:
- Fischer, *Floater's Guide to Montana.*
- Thompson, *Floating and Recreation on Montana Rivers.*

Maps:
- **USGS 7.5':** *Devils Footstool, Ellis Canyon, Lingshire NE, Millegan, Boston Coulee School, Spanish Coulee School.*
- **USGS 1:100:** *Canyon Ferry Dam, Great Falls South.*
- **USFS:** *Lewis & Clark NF.* Shows first 52 miles and part of shuttle.
- *Montana Afloat: The Smith River.* Available from managing agency, sports and fishing shops, or Montana Afloat, 4106 Fox Farm Road, Missoula, MT 59802.

Auto Shuttle: Length varies depending on route. Contact managing agency for shuttle service references.
Logistics: To reach the **put-in,** follow U.S. 89 to White Sulphur Springs, Montana, about halfway between Bozeman and Great Falls. Turn west onto Road 360 (Fort Logan Road) and drive northeast some 15 miles. Turn right onto Road 586 and drive north roughly 10 miles, then turn left and drive about a mile, cross the bridge over the Smith, and bear right to the Camp Baker launch site.

Two alternate routes lead to the **take-out at Eden Bridge** (Road 330). The shorter route is over a dirt road that can be rough and may be impassable when wet. From the put-in, return to Road 360 and bear right; follow this road first west, then north about 68 miles; turn right on Road 330 and drive about 2.5 miles to Eden Bridge. The longer route is mostly paved. From the put-in, return to White Sulphur Springs and drive north on U.S. 89 roughly 100 miles to Great Falls, then south on I-15 some 11 miles to Ulm, then take Route 330 south about 20 miles to Eden Bridge. Either way is long; allow half a day.

SMITH

Like a small but perfectly-cut gem, the emerald-green Smith outshines many larger rivers. This magnificent stream appeals to river runners and anglers alike. Great scenery, superb fishing, and miles of easy near-wilderness floating make the Smith one of the jewels of the Northern Rockies. Its only real drawback is skimpy summer flows.

With a relatively low watershed—only two isolated peaks exceed 9,000'—the Smith, one of the Missouri's smaller tributaries, rarely produces big water.[1] But size is not the only measure of a river. The Smith excels in its rare combination of easy water and rugged near-wilderness scenery. By the time most rivers wind down to Class II, the landscape has softened as well, and gentle terrain often means encroaching civilization. The Smith is a welcome exception.

Here is a river seemingly custom-made for open canoes, crafts without equal for easy running on extended Class II. This isn't to say that boaters in other craft don't enjoy the Smith; rafts, drift boats, and kayaks are also seen on the river.

Rising in the Castle Mountains between Bozeman and Great Falls, the Smith flows north between the Little Belt and Big Belt Mountains, reaching the Missouri just upstream from Great Falls. Boating typically begins at Camp Baker, several miles northwest of White Sulphur Springs, and extends to the Eden Bridge about 20 miles upstream from the Missouri confluence. Few boaters venture above or below this section because of even scantier flows in the upstream reach and less inspiring scenery downstream.

The Smith takes its time on its way downstream: the standard run takes 61 river miles to cover 30 air miles. The many loops and bends make the paddling interesting.

From Camp Baker to Eden Bridge, the Smith runs through easy riffles and placid pools. In the first 15 miles the rolling grasslands gradually change to rocky cliffs and spires until the river is secluded within a steep limestone canyon. Wildlife abounds in riverside forest and meadows. The Smith is one of Montana's finest trout streams, attracting anglers from all over the state. Catch-and-release fishing is strongly encouraged to help preserve this superb fishery.

Although much of the land is private, the canyon is nearly wilderness for much of its length. But several subdivisions of vacation cabins—many sited only a few feet from the river—intrude on the run near its midway point, and other developments menace the Smith.[2] Many of the riverside campsites used by boaters are on private land leased by the Montana Department of Fish, Wildlife and Parks.

Occasional livestock fences spanning the river pose a potential hazard for boaters, though most or all are equipped with "floater gates"—usually plastic pipes hanging down from a cable, similar to gates in kayak races. These contraptions are navigable by boaters but impervious to bovines. Be alert for fragments of barbed wire which are often swept downriver in high water and deposited along the bank.

The Smith has a relatively short boating season; what most people would consider barely runnable flows usually last only from May until early July. However, during the rest of the summer many local boaters and anglers redefine "runnable" and "boatable" down to 100 cfs and below. Upstream irrigation diversions diminish flows on the Smith somewhat—but no one knows by how much, since the diversions are not measured.

The Smith attracted so much attention in recent years that the river became overcrowded—especially on summer weekends and holidays—so in 1993 the Montana Department of Fish, Wildlife and Parks instituted a permit system limiting the number of daily launches.

---

[1]Lewis and Clark, who first saw the river in 1805, named tributaries of the Missouri after members of Jefferson's administration (see sidebar in **Gallatin** chapter). This lesser branch was named for the Secretary of the Navy, Robert Smith.

[2]Because of extensive private land holdings along the river, development poses a real threat. Although the Smith is a prime candidate for National Wild and Scenic protection, local landowners have opposed the designation. Public agencies and private groups are exploring conservation easements, land swaps, and purchases to preserve open space. To help, contact Friends of the Smith River, P.O. Box 8832, Missoula, MT 59807.

Mile by Mile Guide

0 **PUT-IN** on the left bank at Camp Baker. Overnight camping allowed. No drinking water. Sheep Creek enters on the right, adding substantially to the flow. A mile and a half downstream, Eagle Creek enters on the right. The first 18 miles are mostly private land with only occasional public campsites.

4.3 Spring Creek enters on the right. Spring Creek Campsite is a quarter mile downstream on the left.

9.5 Rock Creek enters on the left at a right bend. Campsite and a trail up the creek.

16.5 Tenderfoot Creek enters on the right. Just over a mile downstream, the right bank enters Lewis and Clark National Forest. Much of the right bank is public land to mile 40. Campsites are more common in this section. Several private roads reach the left bank between here and the take-out.

19.5 Cabins on the left. A larger and more visible group of cabins is two miles downstream on the left.

25 Sunset Cliff campsite on the right. Side hikes.

33 Trout Creek, a small tributary, enters on the left.

36.5 Trails reach the river at Sunset and Fraunhofer Boat Camps.

40 The river leaves the National Forest. Downstream the land is mostly private, with fewer campsites. Deep Creek enters a half mile downstream on the right.

46 Four campsites in the next mile.

49 A pair of easy Class II rapids are the most challenging on the trip. Rattlesnake Bend Campsite, located between the rapids, is the last designated camp above the take-out.

59.3 Hound Creek enters on the left.

61 Eden Bridge. **TAKE-OUT** on the left.

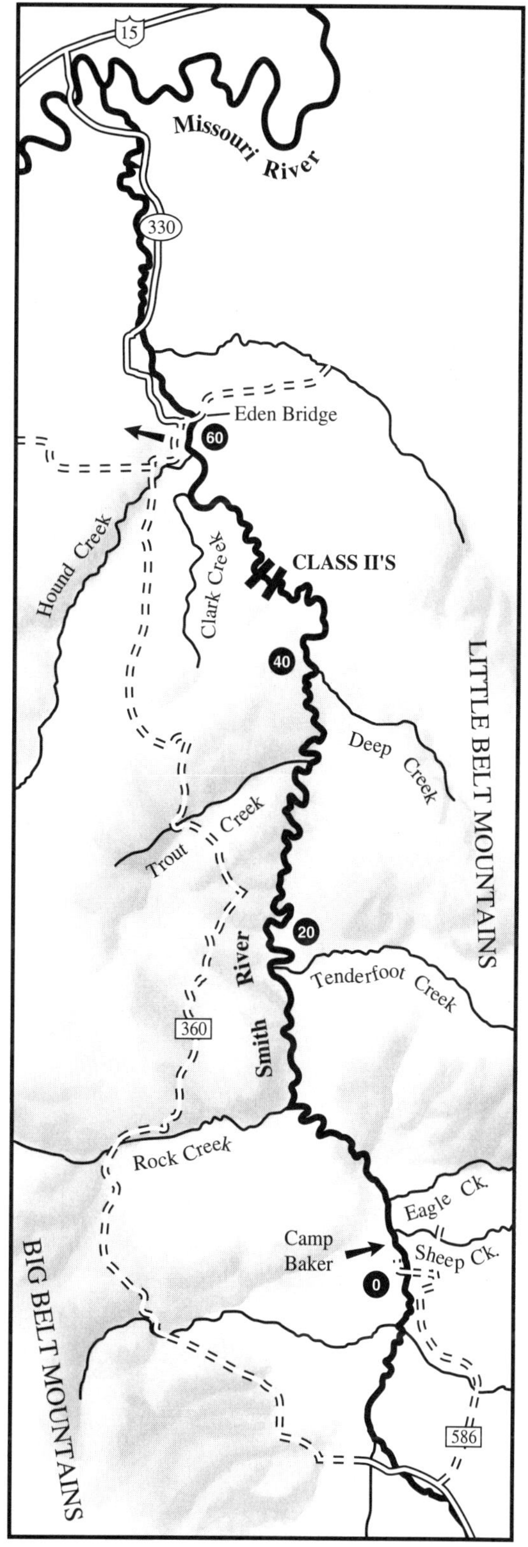

Smith

Dearborn River

Wolf Creek to Missouri River Confluence

Difficulty: II+.
Length: 19 miles. Longer runs possible.
Gradient: 20 ft./mi.
Season: May–July.
Put-in: U.S. 287 Bridge (3,800').
Take-out: Missouri River Confluence (3,430').
Recommended Levels: 800–3,000 cfs (estimate).
Flow Information: No gauge. Boaters can try to estimate by looking across to the mouth of the Dearborn from the right bank of the Missouri River (reached via the Missouri River Recreation Road near the take-out).
Permits: Not presently required.
Managing Agency: Montana Dept. of Fish, Wildlife & Parks, 4600 Giant Springs Rd., P.O. Box 6610, Great Falls, MT 59406; (406) 454-3441.
Land Ownership: Almost all private.
Scenery: Excellent.
Solitude: Excellent.
Wilderness: Yes, except near the end of the run.

Guides and References:
- Fischer, *Floater's Guide to Montana.*
- Thompson, *Floating and Recreation on Montana Rivers.*

Maps:
- **USGS 7.5':** *Coburn Mtn, Mid Canon.*
- **USGS 1:100:** *Dearborn River, Great Falls South.*

Logistics: Put in at the **U.S. 287 bridge** over the Dearborn, some 13 miles north of I-15 near Wolf Creek. Be aware that the landowner at this put-in site has sometimes caused serious problems for boaters in the past.

Take out at **Dearborn State Recreation Area,** located on the right bank of the Missouri about 300 yards below the Dearborn-Missouri confluence (reached via the Missouri River Recreation Road). **Alternate take-outs** are farther down the Missouri. To hire shuttle drivers, try the Craig Store.

Rising among 8,000' and 9,000' peaks along the Continental Divide in west central Montana, the diminutive Dearborn follows a short, swift eastward course to join with its parent stream, the mighty Missouri. Situated midway between two of Montana's largest cities, Helena and Great Falls, the Dearborn might logically be one of the state's more popular rivers. Yet this scenic stream gets only light to moderate use, primarily from open canoeists.

Although the Dearborn is runnable for some 46 miles above its mouth, most floating is limited to the final 19 miles. An upper reach from Dearborn Canyon Road to Montana Highway 200 offers some 13 miles of very scenic intermediate boating with a portage around Dearborn Falls, about two thirds of the way down. This section has a short season that usually lasts only until late June or early July.

The 11 miles from Highway 200 to U.S. 287 offer more water but less inspiring whitewater and scenery as the river runs mostly through fairly open ranchland. The Middle and South Forks of the Dearborn join the main stem near the beginning of this reach.

Below U.S. 287 the Dearborn gets it all together, combining good flows with excellent scenery. For 19 miles the river winds through an intimate and secluded canyon as it descends to the Missouri. Wildlife is abundant, and for most of the run civilization seems far away. The whitewater is generally moderate and forgiving, but extra caution is advised due to the isolation and difficulty hiking out in the event of a mishap.

Though the canyon generally has a strong wilderness flavor, almost all the riverside land is private. This lack of public land makes overnight trips awkward.[1] On the other hand, a one-day run of the full 19 miles can be very demanding. (Be sure to get an early start.) Toward the end of the run, several developments invade the otherwise pristine landscape. National Wild and Scenic designation has been mentioned for the Dearborn. The Montana Department of Fish, Wildlife, and Parks is working with landowners to improve access and install float gates in fences on the Lower Dearborn.[2]

Dearborn River Guide

For the first couple of miles below the **put-in** at the U.S. 287 bridge (mile 0), the river runs through an open valley, paralleling the ridge of Elephant Mountain on the left. Then the Dearborn turns abruptly east and cuts through the ridge, entering a narrow canyon that continues almost to the take-out.

At mile 5 the river winds through a tight horseshoe bend to the left, marking the beginning of a sinuous ten-mile section that advances less than four air miles. Flat Creek enters on the left at mile 6. Dirt roads ford the river at mile 15 and again at mile 17; a foot bridge and power line across the river at the second ford provide good landmarks. Finally, at mile 19.5 the Dearborn passes under the Great Northern Railroad and enters the wide Missouri. **Take out** downstream on the right bank of the Missouri at Dearborn State Recreation Area, or continue down the Missouri.

History

Lewis and Clark first spied the mouth of the Dearborn during their journey up the Missouri in 1805. On their voyage to the Pacific, the Corps of Discovery wasted no time naming things—especially tributaries of the Missouri—after members of the national administration that was financing their expedition. In this instance the lucky bureaucrat was Henry Dearborn, Secretary of War under Thomas Jefferson.

In his journal Lewis describes the Dearborn at its mouth as "a handsome, bold and clear stream, eighty yards wide" and observes that "it appears as if it might be navigated but to what extent must be conjectural." Eager to press on up the Missouri to its three forks (see **Gallatin** chapter), the expedition could spare little time scouting tributaries.

Ironically, the company's key objective, the Continental Divide, lay less than 20 miles to the west. A short haul up the Dearborn's Middle Fork would have brought them to Rogers Pass, one of the lowest and easiest passes anywhere along the Divide. From there it would have been a straight shot down the Blackfoot, Clark Fork, and Pend Oreille Rivers to the Columbia.

The explorers might have suspected the easy crossing. Several months earlier, along the lower Missouri, Mandan Indians had told Lewis and Clark of a Missouri tributary that offered quick passage over the mountains, but the explorers either ignored the advice or didn't recognize the Dearborn when they saw it. Instead they pressed on up the Missouri (which promptly led them *east,* away from their objective) and then struggled westward by a remarkably roundabout and difficult route that included three crossings of the rugged Bitterroot Mountains. Only on the return trip did Lewis take advantage of the Dearborn-Blackfoot connection, crossing easily between the two basins at what is now called Lewis and Clark Pass.[3]

[1]In theory at least, a Montana stream access law passed in 1985 gives boaters the right to camp within the bounds of the normal high-water mark, provided that "the camping is necessary for the enjoyment of the water resource and it is done out of sight of, or more than 500 yards from, any occupied dwelling." In practice, boaters should recognize two caveats. First, the Dearborn offers few good campsites between the normal high-water marks. Second, landowners may not have heard of the 1985 law, may not appreciate being informed of its requirements, and may have a very different view as to whether camping is necessary for the enjoyment of the Dearborn. Tact and diplomacy are called for. As always, shotguns take precedence over legal arguments.

[2]In the late 1980's, Montana Fish, Wildlife and Parks denied a petition by some landowners to close the river to recreational boating.

[3]Detailed information on Lewis and Clark is found in David Lavender, *The Way to the Western Sea,* and Bernard DeVoto, *The Course of Empire* and *The Journals of Lewis and Clark.*

Missouri River

Fort Benton to Robinson Bridge

Difficulty: I+. **Gradient:** 2.5 ft./mi.
Length: 149 miles. Longer and shorter trips possible.
Put-in: Fort Benton (2,615').
Take-out: Robinson Bridge (2,240').
Drainage Area and Average Annual Discharge: 41,000 sq. mi. and 6,821,000 af at take-out.
Season: May–Sept. Typically peaks in June above 25,000 cfs and recedes to late-summer lows of 3,500 to 6,000 cfs.
Recommended Levels: Runnable at all flows.
Flow Information: Contact BLM in Lewiston.
Special Hazards: Isolation; cables and ferries.
Permits: Not presently required; boaters are asked to register at the put-in. Use limits are possible in the near future.
Managing Agency: BLM, Lewiston District, Airport Road, Lewiston, MT 59457; (406) 538-7461. Provides printed information and advice on weather, flows, etc.
Commercial Trips: A few outfitters. Contact the BLM for references.
Land Ownership: Mostly private first 50 miles; mixed but mostly public thereafter. Refer to BLM *Upper Missouri* maps (see below).
Scenery: Very good.
Solitude: Generally very good; can be crowded on holiday weekends. Motorboats.
Wilderness: Mostly. A few roads and jeep trails reach the river.
Guides and References:
- Thompson, *Floating and Recreation on Montana Rivers.*
- *Highlights of the Upper Missouri National Wild & Scenic River* (BLM). Pamphlet with overview of human and natural history.
- Vestal, *The Missouri.* River history.
- Schultz, *Floating on the Missouri* and Neihardt, *The River and I,* narrate descents from Fort Benton in 1901 and 1908.

Maps: *Upper Missouri National Wild & Scenic River.* In two parts—*Fort Benton to Flat Creek* and *Flat Creek to Robinson Bridge.* Available from the BLM. Waterproof; accesses, topography, land ownership, history, etc.
Auto Shuttle: Length and time vary depending on route and run. Up to 175 miles, partly paved. For shuttle service references contact the BLM.
Logistics: The **put-in at Fort Benton** is about 40 miles northeast of Great Falls on U.S. 87. The popular **alternate put-in** at Coal Banks Landing is 40 miles farther downstream near Virgelle. The **take-out at Robinson Bridge** (James Kipp State Park) can be reached via two shuttle routes. The southern route runs through Lewistown, Montana, via Montana 80, U.S. 87, and U.S. 191. The northern route runs through Havre, Montana, via U.S. 87, U.S. 2, Montana 66, and U.S. 191.

"The hills and river clifts which we passed today exhibit a most romantic appearance. The bluffs of the river rise to the hight of from 2 to 300 feet and in most places nearly perpendicular; they are formed of remarkable white sandstone ... As we passed on it seemed as if those scenes of visionary inchantment would never have end ..."

On May 31, 1805, Meriwether Lewis recorded this description of the White Cliffs of the Missouri as seen from a campsite 55 miles below what is now Fort Benton. Lewis and Clark's expedition ascended this section of the Missouri during the second year of their journey to the Pacific. Their exploration of the "Upper Missouri" is the key to the story of a river rich in history.[1]

To reach this campsite under the White Cliffs, the expedition had ascended more than 2,000 miles from the river's mouth at St. Louis By this time Lewis and Clark hoped they were not far from the river's headwaters. Just four days later they got their first glimpse of the distant Rocky Mountains. Poling and hauling their boats upstream was hard labor, particularly during spring runoff. Yet it was easy going compared to what lay ahead. Thirty miles above Fort Benton they encountered the Great Falls, where the Missouri plunges more than 500' in seven miles. The expedition spent a month portaging that obstacle.

[1]Most whitewater devotees would call this reach the "Lower Missouri," reserving the name "Upper" for the first hundred or so miles from Three Forks to Great Falls. But at 2,725 miles the Missouri is the longest river in the United States, so in the larger scheme of things this placid stretch in central Montana isn't that far from the headwaters.

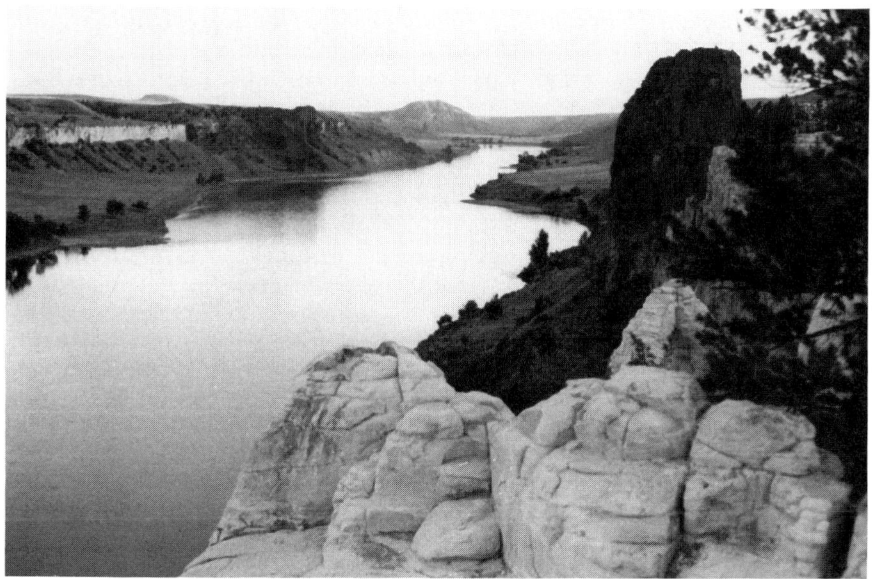

Missouri River — *BLM, Lewiston District*

Today the Upper Missouri is part of the Lewis and Clark National Historic Trail, and river runners can camp in the same sites used by the explorers. At first glance the vistas seem little changed since Lewis and Clark described them in 1805. But look again at Lewis's journal: "I do not think I exaggerate when I estimate the number of Buffaloe ... at one view to amount to 3000." In 1805 the riverside plains and hills abounded with wildlife, including buffalo, wolves, and grizzly bears, animals that are not seen today. The Missouri was in free spring flood as well, almost certainly running higher than it has since dams restrained its muddy exuberance.

Then there were the Indians: the Cree, the Assiniboine, and especially the Blackfeet, whose territory included the Missouri above the White Cliffs. Early trappers and explorers feared the Blackfeet above all other northwestern tribes; their hostility toward whites kept the Upper Missouri region essentially closed for 25 years after Lewis and Clark's first voyage. Yet in the end not even the Blackfeet could resist the white invasion. Devastated by smallpox and the decline of the buffalo, the tribe ceded much of its territory in the 1870's.

Missouri River steamboats fueled the settlement of Montana and northern Idaho in the late 1800's. In 1860 the steamer Chippewa made the first successful run all the way upstream to Fort Benton, which rapidly grew into a commercial center and jumping-off point for miners and settlers. Steamboat pilots nicknamed the river "Old Misery" for its treacherous rapids and shifting sandbars. Modern river runners may have trouble spotting the rapids that daunted early navigators; to eyes accustomed to judging rocks and holes, the Missouri's "rapids" barely count as riffles.

In this century engineers set to work curbing the Missouri's floods and straightening its wandering channel. Fort Peck Dam in eastern Montana, one of the largest earthfill dams in the world, was built in the 1930's as a work relief project. It inundates over 100 miles of river below Robinson Bridge. In fact, of the Missouri's 2,725 miles, only the 149 from Fort Benton to Robinson Bridge are protected in their natural, free-flowing state. After a fierce struggle, this stretch was added to the National Wild and Scenic Rivers System in 1976.

At Great Falls the Missouri leaves the mountains and enters the "Big Sky" country of the semi-arid high plains. Junipers and pines dot the shallow canyon slopes, while lush cottonwoods add color to riverside bottoms. Wildlife along the Missouri, abundant by modern standards, includes bighorn sheep, elk, and a variety of waterfowl. Sediment-laden tributaries transform the river into the "Big Muddy," a broad brown behemoth winding through expansive pastel landscapes.

Until recent geologic time the Upper Missouri followed a very different course. Before the last ice age the river flowed steadily northeast from Fort Benton, eventually joining other rivers that emptied into Hudson Bay and the Arctic Ocean. Some 10,000 to 15,000 years ago, enormous ice-age glaciers forced the river to turn southeast near Coal Banks Landing. As a result, the recently carved valley below Coal Banks has a more rugged appearance.

Downstream from Fort Benton the Upper Missouri is a gentle giant, well suited to open canoes, which have an advantage on flatwater and in headwinds. Rafts, on the other hand, can be very hard to move against upstream breezes. One of the greatest hazards on the river is man-made: low-hanging cables at several ferry crossings, which can snag and capsize boats. The ferries themselves pose an additional hazard and should be given a wide berth. Ferry crossings include Loma (mile 21), Virgelle (mile 39), and Stafford (mile 102).

The most scenic and popular run on the Upper Missouri is the 47-mile stretch from Coal Banks Landing (mile 41) to Judith Landing (mile 88). Alternate accesses allow trips of almost any length. In addition to Fort Benton, Coal Banks Landing, Judith Landing, and Robinson Bridge, access is possible at the Loma and Stafford Ferries. The Loma access is often used for one-day trips.

Typically, river parties take five to eight days for the full 149 miles, with a slower pace leaving more time for exploration. Camping is good on broad beaches, but during windy weather boaters should avoid camping under the brittle cottonwoods along the river banks. Please respect private property, which makes up about a quarter of the riverside land.

Missouri River Guide

Below Fort Benton (mile 0) the Missouri gradually leaves most signs of civilization behind—most, but unfortunately not all. The BLM allows motorboats full run of this section, and although they are limited to wakeless speeds in many places, their drone carries far over the Missouri's placid water. Also, instead of buffalo roaming the plains there are now cattle—decidedly less romantic creatures who leave their distinctive marks on many a campsite. Bring a shovel.

With these notable exceptions, the Missouri largely regains its original wilderness character by the time it reaches Coal Banks Landing (mile 41) near the hamlet of Virgelle. Downstream the river flows for over 30 miles through the White Cliffs section. Here, falling water has worn intricate sculptures into soft, nearly snow-white sandstone deposited by an ancient ocean some 60 to 80 millions years ago.

At mile 88 the Judith River enters on the right just above Judith Landing, a popular access on the left bank at the only bridge on the run. Downstream the river enters the elaborately eroded badlands of the Missouri River Breaks, which continue for the remainder of the run. Sinuous side canyons and twisting coulees (a word for a gully or draw) are the settings for interesting side hikes.

Cow Island (mile 126) marks the site where, in 1877, members of the Nez Perce tribe crossed the Missouri while fleeing the U.S. Army. From here Chiefs Joseph and Looking Glass led their people north toward the sanctuary of Canada, but cavalry units attacked and captured them just 40 miles short of the border. Chief Joseph's speech of surrender, one of the most moving oratories in American history, ends with the famous words: "I will fight no more forever." The battle site near Chinook, Montana, is a worthwhile side excursion just off the northern shuttle route for this run.

Below Cow Island the canyon widens, and for the last 20 miles the Missouri runs through a more open valley to the take-out at James Kipp State Park, where Robinson Bridge (U.S. 191) crosses the river. A few boaters continue downstream through the Charles M. Russell National Wildlife Refuge, home to elk and other wildlife. Fort Peck Reservoir stills the Missouri about 20 miles below Robinson Bridge.

There are also runs upstream on the Missouri above Great Falls, notably from below Holter Dam to Cascade. For more information refer to Thompson, *Floating and Recreation on Montana Rivers.*

Blackfoot River

River Junction to Johnsrud Park

Difficulty: II+. **Gradient:** 16 ft./mi.
Length: 38.5 miles. Longer and shorter runs possible.
Put-in: River Junction Campground at confluence with North Fork Blackfoot (4,020').
Take-out: Johnsrud Park (3,415').
Drainage Area and Average Annual Discharge: 2,290 sq. mi. and 1,195,000 af.
Peak Recorded Flow: 19,200 cfs (June 10, 1964) near Bonner (mouth).
Season: May–August. High water can last into July, and boaters can often scrape down through September. Shorter season for upstream runs above the North Fork.
Recommended Levels: 800–4,000 cfs.
Flow Information: USGS, (406) 449-5263; flow in vertical feet near Bonner (about 5 miles below Johnsrud Park). Convert to cfs using the table below.
Permits: Not presently required.
Managing Agency: Montana Dept. of Fish, Wildlife & Parks, 3201 Spurgin Road, Missoula, MT 59801; (406) 542-5500.
Commercial Raft Trips: Yes. For references contact the managing agency.
Land Ownership: Mostly private, but much is open to public use (see essay).
Scenery: Very good. Forested valley.
Solitude: Very good to fair, depending on run (see essay and **Mile Guide**).
Wilderness: No.
Fishing: Good for trout on upper river.
Water: Cold and clear.
Camping: Several riverside campgrounds.
Guides and References:

- Fischer, *Floater's Guide to Montana.*
- Thompson, *Floating and Recreation on Montana Rivers.*

Blackfoot near Bonner			
Feet	Cfs	Feet	Cfs
2.5	831	5.5	4,490
3.0	1,260	6.0	5,320
3.5	1,800	6.5	6,230
4.0	2,400	7.0	7,200
4.5	3,030	8.0	9,390
5.0	3,730		

Maps:

- **USGS 7.5':** *Chamberlain Mtn, Ovando, Woodworth, Bata Mtn, Greenough, Potomac, Sunflower Mtn.*
- **USFS:** *Lolo NF* covers river from Russell M. Gates access to Johnsrud Park.
- *Montana Afloat: The Blackfoot River.* Map-guide shows accesses, roads, some rapids. Available at sports shops or from Montana Afloat, 4106 Fox Farm Road, Missoula, MT 59802.

Auto Shuttle: All short, mostly paved.
Logistics: All access is via Montana Highway 200, which runs east from I-90 near Missoula. There are many accesses other than those mentioned in this chapter. To reach the **River Junction** access, follow Highway 200 east from I-90 about 40 miles, then turn south on a side road that crosses Scotty Brown Bridge in about a mile. The road continues roughly 8 more miles to the put-in at River Junction Campground and Access. The **Russell M. Gates State Recreation Area** access, previously known as the "County Line Access," is on Montana Highway 200 roughly 35 miles east of I-90 (4 miles east of the intersection with Montana 83). The **Roundup Bar Bridge** access is located where Highway 200 crosses the Blackfoot some 27 miles east of I-90. **Johnsrud Park** is just north of the McNamara Bridge (Highway 200) over the Blackfoot about 11 miles east of I-90. For other accesses, contact the managing agency and refer to the *Montana Afloat* map listed above.

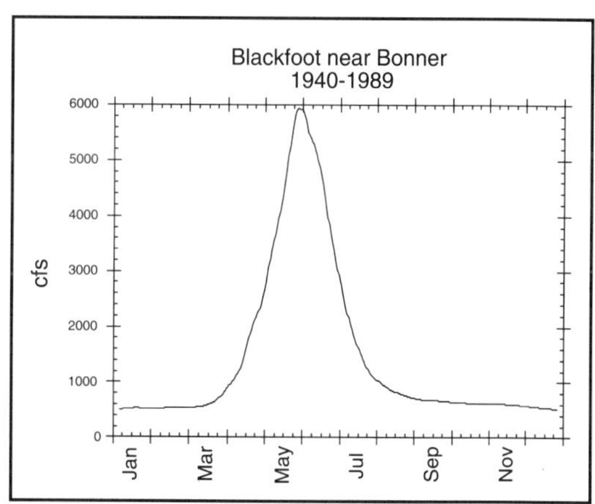

BLACKFOOT

In a region of high peaks and rugged north-south ridges, the Blackfoot River's gentle east-west valley has long served as a corridor for human travel—first by American Indians, then by white explorers and trappers, later by motorists on a state highway. More recently, a different breed of traveller has come to the Blackfoot, one for whom the river itself is the final destination. Whitewater boaters in increasing numbers are enjoying the Blackfoot's fine scenery and enjoyable but forgiving whitewater.

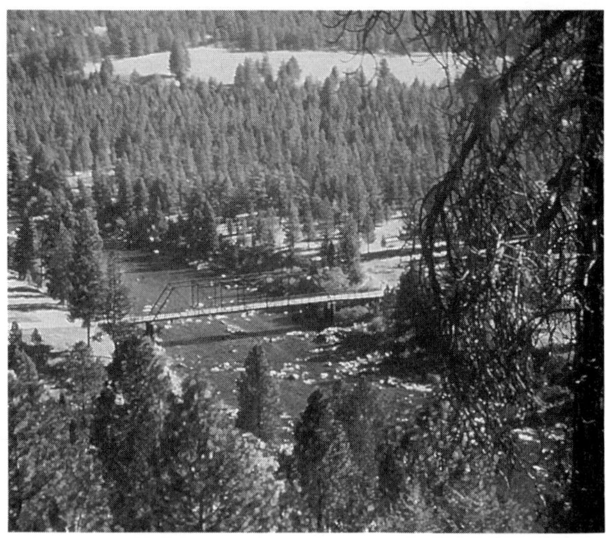

Blackfoot River *Montana Fish, Wildlife & Parks*

From its headwaters along the Continental Divide in western Montana, the Blackfoot descends the west slope of the Rockies, joining the Clark Fork at Missoula. In its upper reaches the Blackfoot flows placidly through meadows and open valleys. Farther downstream the current quickens as the river cuts through a broad canyon, but the terrain and the whitewater never grow very rugged.

As a result river runners find a variety of easy and intermediate rapids on the Blackfoot, with the more challenging whitewater coming toward the downstream end. For the first 45 miles below Lincoln—near the upstream limit of floating—the gradient is only 7 ft./mi. In the remaining 60 miles to the Clark Fork the Blackfoot picks up steam, dropping at an average of 16 ft./mi.

Throughout its length the Blackfoot offers outstanding forest scenery and excellent fishing. Though Montana Highway 200 follows the river, it is generally out of sight and earshot; only in the last 11 miles below Johnsrud Park is the highway conspicuous. Although most of the riverside land is private, little has been developed, thanks in part to conservation easements. Also, an agreement between landowners (including Champion Lumber) and public agencies has opened much of the riverside land to public use as part of the Blackfoot River Recreation Corridor.[1]

The Blackfoot is one of Montana's most popular rivers.[2] For the Missoula boating community the Blackfoot is a favorite backyard run as well as the site of an annual whitewater festival in June. Open canoeists in particular enjoy this technical but generally forgiving stream. (Novice canoeists should stick to the seven-mile flatwater run from Ninemile Prairie to Whitaker Bridge.) Students from the nearby University of Montana often spend an afternoon on the river, sometimes in varying states of (un)dress and (un)consciousness. On summer weekends the Blackfoot's lower reaches, closer to town, can be crowded.

Most boating on the Blackfoot takes place below River Junction, where the North Fork joins the main stem. This major tributary adds enough flow to keep the downstream reaches runnable all summer in most years. Not far below River Junction, the scenic cliffs of five-mile-long Box Canyon pinch the Blackfoot into a narrow course, but the river remains fairly easy. There is one Class II+ rapid on this stretch at mile 8, not far above Scotty Brown Bridge. Otherwise, the first 12 miles below River Junction rate only I+ at most flows, Class II at high water.

[1]The corridor runs from the Missoula County Line, 12 miles below the River Junction put-in, to Johnsrud Park. Many regulations apply, but basically boaters are allowed to use the land up to 50' on either side of the normal high-water mark in this stretch of river. Elsewhere, bank use is limited to the area within the normal high-water mark.

[2]That doesn't mean the river doesn't have problems. Because it continues to be threatened by too much timber cutting and cattle grazing as well as mining, stream diversions, and over-fishing, in 1992 the Blackfoot made the list of the nation's ten most endangered rivers published by the national conservation organization American Rivers (see appendix for address). Although the Blackfoot is the river described in Norman Maclean's book *A River Runs Through It,* its once-pristine banks have so many clearcuts that the successful film of the same name was shot on other streams. A sign of hope is recent improvement in the Blackfoot fishery thanks to stricter fishing regulations and stream enhancement projects.

The Blackfoot's real whitewater and most popular boating sections lie below Russell M. Gates State Recreation Area (previously known as the "County Line Access"), mile 12. In the next 26 miles to Johnsrud Park, Class II+ action (Class III at higher flows) alternates with easier water. The whitewater climaxes at Thibodeau Rapids, just a few miles before the standard take-out at Johnsrud.

Below Johnsrud Park the river runs through 10 miles of pleasant Class I+ water (II at higher flows), suitable for novices at lower flows. This is the Blackfoot's most heavily-used section; on summer weekends it is often crowded with innertubes, canoes, and other river craft. Highway 200 closely parallels this stretch. All floaters must take out at the Bonner Weigh Station on the left bank; just downstream is a **dangerous diversion dam.** A foot bridge that crosses the river a little over a mile above the weigh station serves as a good landmark.

Upstream Runs

The 55 miles above the North Fork confluence (not covered in this chapter's **Mile Guide**) offer good scenery and solitude for those willing to carry around frequent **log jams.** From the town of Lincoln downstream to the Route 271 bridge (Cedar Meadow River Access), the Blackfoot is an oversized meadow stream clogged with logs and brush, winding sedately through 43 miles of loops and meanders while advancing just 16 air miles. By midsummer flows are often skimpy on this lightly-used section.

Below the Cedar Meadow Access the river enters a narrow canyon, and the gradient increases to 19 ft./mi. The 11-mile run from Cedar Meadow to the North Fork confluence is swift Class I+ and has a somewhat longer season than the upstream reaches. Be alert for **logs.**

History

In 1806, Meriwether Lewis finally found the easy way across the Continental Divide—the Blackfoot River. On the return leg of their historic journey to the Pacific, Lewis and Clark took separate paths through what is now Montana. On July 3 Lewis set out from the future site of Missoula, ascended the Blackfoot, crossed the divide at what is now Lewis and Clark Pass, and reached Great Falls on July 11. He needed only eight days to do what had taken two months on their circuitous westbound route the previous year (see **Dearborn River** essay).

Lewis didn't discover the Blackfoot crossing; he heard about it from Indians who had used it for centuries. The Nez Perce called the river "Coakahlerisk Kit," or "the river of the road to the Buffalo," in recognition of the easy passage it afforded through the mountains to rich hunting grounds on the plains east of the Rockies.[3]

Although Lewis adopted the Nez Perce name for the river, it was later renamed after the Blackfeet Indians.[4] Once masters of Northern Montana's high plains, the Blackfeet guarded their territory against all outsiders, including the various western tribes—Nez Perce, Shoshone, Kootenai, and Flathead—who used the Blackfoot River trail to cross the Rockies on buffalo hunting forays. The river is sometimes called the Big Blackfoot, to distinguish it from the Little Blackfoot a few miles to the south.

[3]Lewis didn't get the crossing exactly right: while the Indians followed the river all the way to its headwaters at Rogers Pass, Lewis turned up a side creek and ended up a bit farther north at Lewis and Clark Pass, a more difficult crossing some 800' higher. The engineers who planned Highway 200 from Missoula to Great Falls followed the Indian trail almost precisely.

[4]Black*feet* is often corrupted to the singular Black*foot*—as in the case of the river's name. For more on the Blackfeet, see the **Missouri River** essay.

Mile by Mile Guide

0 **PUT-IN.** River Junction Campground and access on the Blackfoot's left bank at the confluence with the North Fork Blackfoot. A mile and a half downstream, Warren Creek enters on the right as the river enters five-mile-long Box Canyon.

8.3 The most difficult rapid in the first 12 miles rates II+ at most flows. A quarter mile downstream is Scotty Brown Bridge, just below Monture Creek, which enters on the right. Steep **alternate RIVER ACCESS** is surrounded by private land.

11.5 Cottonwood Creek enters on the right. Just downstream, Highway 200 follows the right bank for two miles.

12.5 **RIVER ACCESS.** Russell M. Gates State Recreation Area (formerly known as

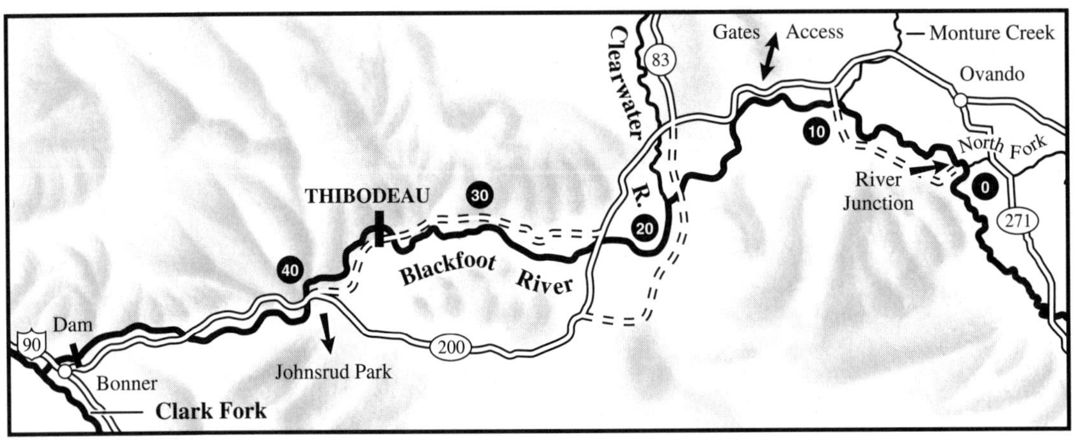

Blackfoot

"County Line Access") on the right. This is a popular put-in for the Blackfoot's whitewater runs. Camping. About a mile downstream, the highway leaves the river again.

15 Bear Creek bridge site. No access. Many Class II and II+ rapids (easy III's at higher flows) from here to Clearwater Bridge.

18.5 **RIVER ACCESS.** Clearwater Bridge, just above the mouth of the Clearwater River, which enters from the right. About 2.5 miles of easy water before the next rapid. The valley opens into broad Ninemile Prairie, which continues for the next 10 miles, mostly on the right.

23 **RIVER ACCESS.** Roundup Bar Bridge (Highway 200). The rock garden just upstream is a favorite play spot for kayakers. A dirt road generally follows the Blackfoot from here to Johnsrud Park, first on the right bank, later on the left. The river is more heavily used below this point. The next few miles contain a number of rocky Class II+ to III- rapids.

24.3 Elk Creek enters on the left. Watch for a Class II rapid at Sunset Bridge pilings a half mile downstream. Then the river eases to Class I until below Whitaker Bridge.

28.5 **RIVER ACCESS.** Riverbend Campground on the right, near where Ninemile Prairie ends and the canyon closes in again. Good put-in for a 4-mile novice float to Whitaker Bridge. Some boaters put in at Ninemile Prairie Campground, two miles upstream on the right—a steeper and more difficult access point.

30.5 Belmont Creek enters on the right. A half mile downstream, distinctive Goose Rock rises out of the river. A mile below that, Red Rock is a landmark on the left.

32.5 **RIVER ACCESS.** Whitaker Bridge. The dirt road crosses from the right to the left bank. Rougher water downstream.

33.5 **THIBODEAU RAPIDS (III-).** Just downstream from Thibodeau Campground (left bank) is the Blackfoot's most famous rapid, a series of drops through a jumble of rocks.

38.5 **TAKE-OUT.** Johnsrud Park, a popular access on the left bank just below Gold Creek, which enters on the right. Just downstream is McNamara Bridge (Highway 200). See the essay for information on downstream runs.

Clark Fork

Alberton Gorge

Difficulty: III (IV at high flows).
Length: 17.5 miles. Longer and shorter trips possible. **Gradient:** 15 ft./mi.
Put-in: St. John's Fishing Access (2,910').
Take-out: Forest Grove (2,650').
Drainage Area and Average Annual Discharge: 9,003 sq. mi. and 4,000,000 af.
Peak Recorded Flow: 52,800 cfs (May 23, 1948) near put-in.
Season: May–Sept. Typically peaks between late May and mid-June. Minimum flows in August and September are rarely less than 1,800 cfs.
Recommended Levels: 1,800–15,000 cfs. Difficulty increases steadily with flow; at high water big hydraulics develop, rapids become more continuous, and eddies wash out. Intimidating above 10,000 cfs, very hazardous above 20,000.
Flow Information: USGS, (406) 449-5263; flow at St. Regis, a few miles below the take-out.
Special Hazards: Cold water. Big hydraulics at high water; long swims possible.
Permits: Not presently required.
Managing Agency: Montana Dept. of Fish, Wildlife & Parks, 3201 Spurgin Road, Missoula, MT 59801; (406) 542-5500.
Commercial Raft Trips: Yes. For references contact Trail Head (see **Guides and References**).
Land Ownership: Mostly private; scattered state and USFS land.
Scenery: Very good.
Solitude: Good. **Wilderness:** No.

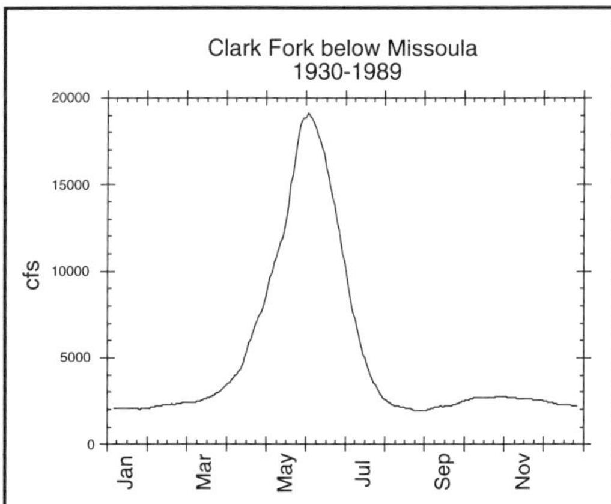

Fishing: Fair for rainbow trout.
Water: Clear except at high flows. Undrinkable.
Camping: Several USFS campgrounds in the area; state campground at Forest Grove take-out.
Side Hikes: Historic Mullan Trail follows the river.
Guides and References:
- Fischer, *Floater's Guide to Montana.*
- Thompson, *Floating and Recreation on Montana Rivers.*
- A good local source of information is Trail Head, 110 E. Pine, Missoula, MT 59802, (406) 543-6966.

Maps:
- **USGS 7.5':** *Stark South, Tarkio, Williams Peak, Lozeau.*
- **USFS:** *Lolo NF.*
- *Montana Afloat: The Clark Fork River.* Map-guide available in sports shops or from Montana Afloat, 4106 Fox Farm Rd., Missoula, MT 59802.

Auto Shuttle: 14 miles (15 minutes) one way. For shuttle service references, contact Trail Head (see **Guides and References**).
Logistics: Two alternate put-ins are located 30 to 35 miles west of Missoula on I-90. **The upper put-in** is on the right bank at **St. Johns Fishing Access,** 3 miles west of Alberton at the I-90 *eastbound* rest area. (Boaters westbound on I-90 from Missoula must drive a couple of miles past the access, take the Cyr exit, and return eastbound to the rest area.) A popular **alternate put-in** is some two miles downstream at **Cyr Bridge:** take the Cyr exit from I-90 *westbound,* cross the river, turn left, and descend the hill to the boat ramp on the left bank, upstream from the old highway bridge and downstream from the I-90 bridge.

To reach the **Forest Grove take-out,** drive downstream (west) on I-90 some 8 miles from Cyr, take the Tarkio exit, and turn right, then immediately left onto the frontage road (old U.S. 10). Drive down-river 5 miles to the Forest Grove Fishing Access on the right bank a half mile below the I-90 bridge over the river. For information on the **alternate take-out** at Tarkio, refer to the **Mile Guide.**

CLARK FORK

By sheer area the Missouri basin dominates Montana, collecting watery tribute from the more than four fifths of the state that lies east of the Continental Divide. But it is the smaller Clark Fork basin, on the wetter west side of the Continental Divide, that produces Montana's largest river.

Technically, the Clark Fork rises from a point on the Divide near Butte, Montana. But in fact this great river system has thousands of small beginnings all along the Continental Divide and Bitterroot Crest. The Clark Fork is a relatively unassuming stream until it reaches Missoula, where the Blackfoot and Bitterroot Rivers more than double its flow. Then, about 120 miles below Missoula, the Flathead joins the Clark Fork, swelling it into one of the West's great rivers. (Though the Flathead has more flow, the longer Clark Fork keeps its name at their confluence.) Shortly after crossing into the Idaho panhandle, the Clark Fork empties into Lake Pend Oreille. Its name changes to the Pend Oreille River as it leaves the lake on its final journey to the Columbia.

The Clark Fork, named for William Clark of the Lewis and Clark expedition of 1804–1806, is sometimes referred to as the Clark Fork of the Columbia. This helps to distinguish it from the Clarks Fork of the Yellowstone River in south central Montana, with which it is routinely confused.[1]

Tremendous open-pit mines were dug in the Clark Fork's headwaters area around Butte and Anaconda, which was long a center of copper mining. Toxic runoff from the mines and tailings flows into creeks which carry it into the Clark Fork. The country around Butte—and the Clark Fork for some distance below the mines—make up one of the largest EPA Superfund toxic clean-up areas in the nation. Things aren't quite as bad as they were a couple of decades ago, and in the long run the situation should improve. But right now, the upper river is still seriously troubled.[2]

The Clark Fork offers over 200 miles of boating, mostly on mild Class I and II water. Interstate 90 follows the river for much of its course, though it is often well away from the river. With the exception of Milltown Dam, located at the Blackfoot River confluence just east of Missoula, the river runs free for some 250 miles from the upstream limits of navigation to a series of dams on the lower river near the Idaho border.

About halfway through its relatively sedate journey across northwestern Montana, the Clark Fork loses its composure. Some 30 miles below Missoula the steep, lofty ridges of spectacular Alberton Gorge[3] constrict the river into a narrow course, producing a nine-mile gauntlet of renowned big-water rapids. Montana and Idaho boaters come here to test their skills against big drops like Tumbleweed, Boat Eater, and Fang—rapids with the power to flip the biggest rafts and maytag the cockiest kayakers.

The difficulty of the whitewater in Alberton Gorge varies widely with the flow. Peak flows of 15,000 to 30,000 cfs in late May and early June produce a non-stop racecourse of pounding waves and monster holes. Long, nasty swims are a serious risk in these conditions. By contrast, in late summer when flows diminish to a mild 1,500 to 3,000 cfs, most of the rapids ease to Class II+ or III-. At lower flows this run makes a long day, so many boaters launch at Cyr Bridge (mile 2.5).

With superb roller-coaster whitewater, excellent scenery, and easy access from I-90, it's no surprise that Alberton Gorge is Montana's most popular whitewater run. In fact, crowds of boaters are more likely to detract from the outdoor experience than is the highway, which is generally well away from the river. Anyone with an interest in solitude should avoid weekends, especially in July and August.

Upstream and Downstream Runs

Boaters can explore many miles of milder water on the Clark Fork above and below Alberton Gorge. Floating is possible as far upstream as Warm Springs near Anaconda, though flows are often skimpy until the Little Blackfoot River joins the Clark Fork at Garrison. Also, water quality is relatively poor on the upper river, where toxic runoff from mining

[1]The Clarks Fork of the Yellowstone is also named for William Clark. Names like Clarks Fork and Henrys Fork were originally spelled with apostrophes—as in "Clark's Fork"—but modern geographers have dropped the possessive form. Lewis and Clark originally named the Bitterroot River the Clark's Fork, and called the Clark Fork the East Fork of Clark's Fork. Subsequent mapmakers changed all that when they discovered that the East Fork was longer than Clark's Fork.

[2]For information contact the Clark Fork-Pend Oreille Coalition, P.O. Box 7593, Missoula, MT 59807, (406) 542-0539; or P.O. Box 1096, Sandpoint, ID 83864.

[3]The gorge is named for the Alberts family, early settlers, and is also known as Fish Creek Gorge and Cyr Canyon.

operations rendered the river virtually sterile as recently as 20 years ago. Today, though the situation has improved, relatively few boaters float the river's upper reaches.

Boating use increases farther downstream as the Clark Fork approaches Missoula. The 40-odd miles above Missoula offer good scenery as the river winds between the Sapphire Mountains and the Garnet Range. However, this section is peppered with strainers and log hazards. Milltown Dam interrupts the river's journey not far above Missoula. Below the dam the Clark Fork provides another 45 miles of easy floating through Missoula and down to the town of Alberton, just above the gorge. Although it is relatively innocuous at most flows, this section can be hazardous at high water. At all times boaters must be alert for diversions and weirs.

Below Alberton Gorge the Clark Fork reverts to mild, scenic Class I and II water. This stretch extends some 55 miles from the Forest Grove access to beyond the town of Paradise, where the Flathead River joins the Clark Fork.[4]

At one time the lowermost reaches of the Clark Fork held rapids far more violent than those of Alberton Gorge. As it approached the Idaho border, the river thundered through narrow chasms and long reaches of wild water at Thompson Falls, Noxon Rapids, and Cabinet Gorge. Today three hydroelectric dams silence the lower river's roar. In the interest of wringing every possible watt from the river, the Army Corps of Engineers continues to consider additional dams in Alberton Gorge.[5]

Glacial Lake Missoula

If you think the Clark Fork has big water, consider the tale of Lake Missoula.

About 15,000 years ago, all of Alberton Gorge lay deep under water, flooded by a freshwater lake known to geologists as Glacial Lake Missoula. The lake was formed when a vast ice age glacier, spreading southward from British Columbia, dammed the Clark Fork at the present site of Pend Oreille Lake in the Idaho panhandle. Over several years the lake grew, ultimately reaching depths of some 2,000' at the ice dam and nearly 1,500' far upstream at Alberton Gorge. At its peak volume, Glacial Lake Missoula held almost as much water as modern Lake Ontario.

Ultimately, the glacial dam failed when the giant ice plug essentially floated off the ground in the rising water. Then, in the space of just a few days, the entire contents of the lake—some 500 cubic miles of water—drained down the Clark Fork, Pend Oreille, and Columbia Rivers to the Pacific, producing the greatest flood in geologic history.

Remarkably, the cataclysm of Glacial Lake Missoula was repeated at least three dozen times over a period of several hundred years, as the glacier repeatedly dammed the Clark Fork and the Clark Fork in turn ruptured each ice dam. Today a perfect record of these events is exposed in a roadcut at Ninemile, a few miles upstream from Alberton Gorge. Thirty-six distinct layers of silt, each laid down on the bottom of Glacial Lake Missoula, record the lake's periodic filling and draining.

For more on the history of Lake Missoula, refer to Alt and Hyndman, *Roadside Geology of Montana.*

---

[4]For more information on all of these easier sections of the Clark Fork, refer to Fischer, *Floater's Guide to Montana,* and/or Thompson, *Floating and Recreation on Montana Rivers.*

[5]For more information contact the Clark Fork–Pend Oreille Coalition (see earlier footnote).

Mile by Mile Guide

0 **PUT-IN.** St. John's Fishing Access on the right bank. (Alternate put-in at Cyr Bridge, mile 2.5). Just downstream are the big waves of **REST STOP,** whose difficulty varies from Class II at low water to Class IV at high flows when a giant hole develops in river center. For more warm-up before this rapid, boaters can launch 5 miles upstream at the Petty Creek access.

2.5 **RIVER ACCESS.** I-90 crosses the Clark Fork. Just downstream on the steep left bank is the Cyr Bridge Access, a popular alternate put-in with a launch ramp for rafts. Cyr is the name of an old railroad siding. Just below the Cyr access the old highway crosses the river. Intermediate rapids for the next couple of miles as the river enters Alberton Gorge.

4.5 **SHELF (III-).** A ledge of sharp rocks extends diagonally across the river. Good center slot. A few hundred yards downstream is **CLIFFSIDE (III-),** where steep cliffs tower above the right bank as waves

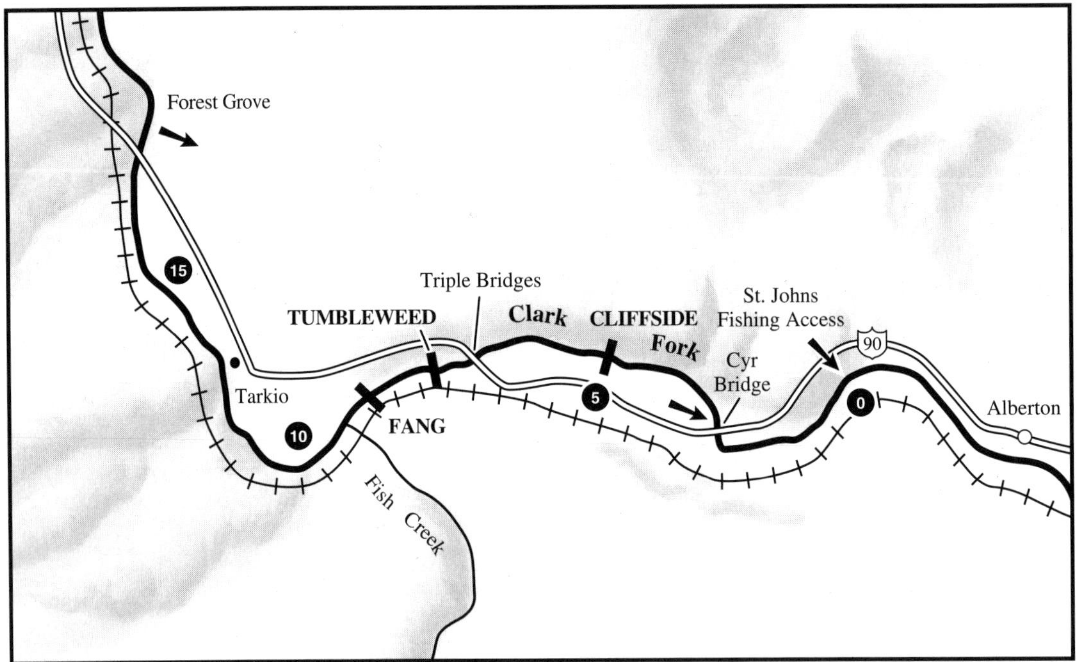

Clark Fork

sweep into the right wall. Rapids continue downstream.

6.7 **TRIPLE BRIDGES (II+)**. Fine surfing in this open wave-train rapid where the old railroad, the old highway, and the interstate cross the Clark Fork. Downstream are the toughest rapids in the narrow heart of **Alberton Gorge.** ***HAZARD.* At high flows the next two miles have nearly continuous whitewater, and trouble early on can mean a long, dangerous swim.** An initial moderate rapid is located almost directly under the I-90 bridges, followed by a second drop, **THUNDER ROCK (II+)**, a quarter mile downstream. Pull to the left bank in the big pool below Thunder Rock to scout the next rapid, Tumbleweed.

7.3 **TUMBLEWEED (III; IV at high flows)**. The most dangerous and difficult rapid on the run. The river narrows and a house rock creates a massive hole on the right. Just downstream is "Surfer Joe," a river-wide surfing wave by a favorite lunch stop on the right. Then comes **BOAT EATER (II; III at high flows)**, where the canyon opens briefly and towering waves form at high water. The canyon narrows again at **ROLLER COASTER (II+)**. Soon comes the last big rapid, **FANG (III)**, a relatively straight shot with huge waves at high flows and a good endo spot at low water.

9.3 Kayakers often take out on the right via a short, steep trail. For road directions to this point, contact Trail Head (see **Guides and References**).

9.5 Fish Creek enters on the left, marking the end of the big rapids. The mouth of the creek is a very popular and sometimes crowded stopping place. A steep trail, used by some kayakers as a take-out, climbs up to Fish Creek Road on the left.

12.5 Tarkio, an old railroad siding on the right. A rough, steep private road on the right bank provides **possible river access.** However, permission is required, and 4-wheel drive is recommended. The Montana Department of Fish, Wildlife & Parks has long-term plans to develop an improved public access at this point. Downstream the river is scenic and mild.

17 I-90 crosses the river. The Forest Grove **TAKE-OUT** is half a mile downstream on the right.

Flathead River

The Flathead drains the western slope of the Rockies in and near Glacier National Park in northwestern Montana. Glaciers shaped this region during the ice age, and today the river's three forks flow for the most part down lush, U-shaped valleys between parallel mountain ridges. After the three forks join, the main Flathead leaves the mountains and winds southward across a wide, flat valley. Near Kalispell the river empties into Flathead Lake, the largest body of fresh water west of the Mississippi. Below the lake the Lower Flathead rolls through drier canyons toward its confluence with the Clark Fork.

The Flathead system is a boating region unto itself, with over 275 miles of river ranging from peaceful Class I to pounding Class V. The river's three forks, its main stem, and one major tributary (the Swan) have enough spectacular scenery and challenging rapids to fill several boating seasons. What's more, each branch has its own distinct character.

The Flathead's North, Middle and South Forks traverse a region of deep wilderness. Much of the watershed is protected by Glacier National Park and the Bob Marshall and Great Bear wilderness areas. In 1976, 219 miles of the Flathead's three forks were added to the National Wild and Scenic Rivers System. This pristine environment shelters an abundance of wildlife, including the legendary grizzly bear. Boaters may encounter grizzlies anywhere on the three forks. Take special precautions to protect food, and contact the Forest Service or Park Service for tips on camping in grizzly country.

Most of the Flathead's whitewater is mild to intermediate, and often the rapids themselves do not pose the biggest dangers. Log hazards are common on the forks—especially during or after high or rising water—and can move from year to year, so inquire locally before floating, and scout when in doubt. Hypothermia can also be a serious threat due to the combination of cold water, relatively high elevations and unpredictable weather.

The river takes its name from the Flathead Indians, who were named by Lewis and Clark in a mistaken reference to a custom actually practiced by some other tribes along the Pacific Coast: the infant's head was deformed by lashing a padded board to its forehead. The Flathead tribe itself apparently never adopted this practice, but the misnomer was never corrected. Today the Flatheads share a reservation with the Kootenai tribe along the Lower Flathead.

Flathead River — General Data

Managing Agencies: Flathead NF, 1935 Third Avenue East, Kalispell, MT 59901, (406) 755-5401; and Glacier National Park, West Glacier, MT 59936, (406) 888-5441. North and Middle Forks are mixed USFS and National Park, South Fork is all USFS.

Commercial Raft Trips: On most runs. For references contact the Forest Service.

Guides and References:

- *Three Forks of the Flathead River Floating Guide.* Best guide to the Flathead forks. Spiral-bound. Order from Glacier Natural History Assn., West Glacier, MT, 59936; (406) 888-5441. They also have dozens of books on the natural and cultural history of the area.
- Fischer, *Floater's Guide to Montana.*
- Thompson, *Floating and Recreation on Montana Rivers.*
- Gildart, *Flathead Country.*
- Palmer, *Endangered Rivers.* River conservation history.
- A good local source of information is Glacier Raft Co., P.O. Box 218, West Glacier, MT 59936; (406) 888-5454.

Maps:

- *Three Forks of the Flathead River.* Glacier Natural History Assn. Similar to spiral-bound version above, but in folded map format.
- **USFS:** *Flathead NF,* in two sheets. *North Half* shows the North Fork, Middle Fork below Spruce Park, Swan, and Lower Flathead. *South Half* shows the Middle Fork, South Fork, Swan, and Lower Flathead. Available from Flathead NF (see **Managing Agencies**).
- **USGS:** *Glacier National Park* sheet shows the North Fork and the Middle Fork below Bear Creek at 1:100,000.

North Fork Flathead River

Canadian Border to Blankenship Bridge

Difficulty: I+, III-. **Gradient:** 15 ft./mi.
Length: 58 miles. Shorter runs possible.
Put-in: Canada–U.S. border (3,970').
Take-out: Blankenship Bridge (3,100').
Drainage Area and Average Annual Discharge: 427 sq. mi. and 676,000 af at put-in; 1,548 sq. mi. and 2,152,000 af near take-out.
Season: Mid-May through August on upper reaches, all summer on lower stretches. Peaks late May to mid-June. On average, flows more than triple between put-in and mouth. Drops below 500 at put-in and below 2,000 at take-out by early August. Above Ford access (mile 14) the river is often too low by early August, but below this point it is usually runnable all summer.
Recommended Levels: 1,000–10,000 cfs.
Flow Information: USGS, (406) 449-5263; flow "near Columbia Falls" (near take-out). Or call Glacier View RD, (406) 892-4372.
Special Hazards: Logs. Cold water. High flows in late spring.
Permits: Not required for boating, but a backcountry permit is required to camp on Glacier National Park land (left bank).
Land Ownership: Left bank all National Park, right bank mixed private and National Forest.
Scenery: Excellent. Wide valley with stunning mountain views. **Solitude:** Very good.
Wilderness: No, but roads are generally well back from the river.
Fishing: Excellent; best in late summer.
Wildlife: Abundant. **Water:** Clear and cold.
Camping: Good. Protect food from bears.
Side Hikes: Kintla Creek, Glacier View Mountain, others (see **Mile Guide**).

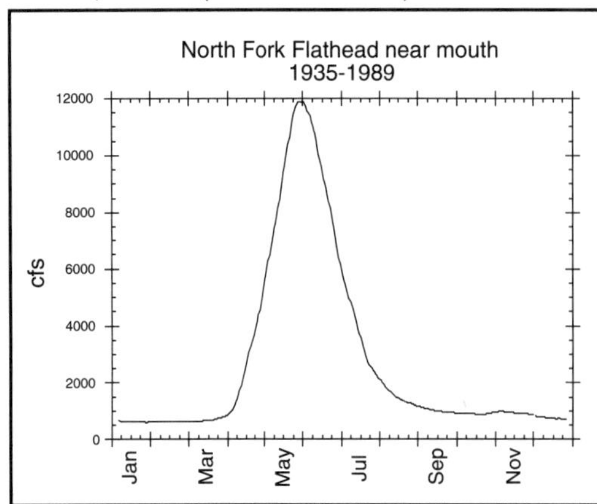

Auto Shuttle: Roughly same mileages as river, mostly unpaved. To hire shuttles try Glacier Raft Co., (406) 888-5454, or Polebridge Mercantile, (406) 888-5916.
Logistics: To reach the **take-out at Blankenship Bridge,** follow Route 486 north some 9 miles from Columbia Falls, then bear right on USFS Road 116 and drive just over two miles to the bridge. Upstream access is via unpaved North Fork Road (extension of Route 486), which generally follows the west bank. Popular **accesses** in ascending order are Glacier Rim, Big Creek, Polebridge, Ford, and the Canadian border. The shuttle from Blankenship Bridge to the border is about 50 miles one way. For details refer to *Flathead NF* and/or *Three Forks of the Flathead* maps.

The North Fork of the Flathead offers a rare combination of relatively easy water and rugged alpine scenery. From its headwaters in British Columbia, the North Fork flows southward down a broad glacial valley bounded by high mountain ridges. To the west is the heavily-forested Whitefish Range, and to the east is the spectacular Livingston Range, whose lofty spires form the Continental Divide in Glacier National Park. Aside from a few rapids near its mouth, the North Fork takes boaters on an easy glide past an almost unbroken procession of majestic peaks.

For 58 miles, from the Canadian border to the Middle Fork confluence at Blankenship Bridge, the North Fork follows the western boundary of Glacier Park, giving boaters a glimpse of Glacier's remote, quiet northwestern corner. The deep riverside forest shelters an abundance of wildlife, including moose, eagle, and grizzly bear. The North Fork is an angler's paradise: its emerald waters teem with cutthroat trout and Dolly Varden. The river has a strong wilderness flavor despite a gravel road on the west (right) bank and a rough dirt track along parts of the east bank. These lightly-used routes are generally well away from the river.

Local geology accounts for the North Fork's mild nature. During the last ice age, glaciers flowed westward out of today's Glacier Park and down into the North Fork Valley. As the climate warmed, the glaciers retreated, leaving behind broad deposits of cobbles and gravels on the valley floor. Over thousands of years, the North Fork has worked and reworked the cobbles into a smooth riverbed with few exposed obstacles. As a result, for most if its distance the river is Class I with an occasional Class II riffle.

The whitewater is mostly confined to a 12-mile stretch from Big Creek to Glacier Rim, not far above the river's mouth. Here the North Fork leaves its broad valley and cuts through a series of ridges. The constriction, increased gradient, and bedrock outcrops produce several Class II and III- rapids. At high water open canoes may have trouble with large waves on this section. Aside from these rapids, the North Fork's chief hazards are logs and seasonal high water.

The North Fork grows substantially over the course of the run described here. Glaciers in the Livingston Range feed a number of large streams that enter from the east; in summer these streams help maintain boatable flows on all but the uppermost reaches of the North Fork. On average, the flow more than triples between the Canadian border and the mouth.

In the 1950's and 60's the Army Corps of Engineers sought permission to build Glacier View Dam some 20 miles above the river's mouth. The dam would have drowned some 25 miles of river and nearly 20,000 acres of Glacier Park. Conservationists finally prevailed in 1976, when the North Fork was designated a National Wild and Scenic River.[1]

[1]Today the river faces threats from logging and energy development. To help protect the North Fork, contact the North Fork Preservation Assn., P.O. Box 4, Polebridge, MT 59928; (406) 756-4780.

North Fork Flathead Mile Guide

0 **PUT-IN** on the right bank near the Canadian border. The North Fork Road is away from the right bank for the first 11 miles.

3 Spruce Creek enters on the left. Downstream, a **log jam** often blocks the river at low flows, requiring a short **portage.** A dirt road generally follows the left bank for the next 25 miles. Kishenehn Ranger Station is on the left at mile 4.

8 Trail Creek enters on the right. A mile downstream, Kintla Creek, a major glacier-fed tributary, enters on the left just above a pair of small rapids. A dirt road leads about 3 miles up the creek to Kintla Lake. The river is usually runnable all summer below this point.

14 **RIVER ACCESS.** Ford Access, just below Ford Work Center (USFS) on the right.

24 **RIVER ACCESS.** Polebridge Access on the right bank at a bridge over the river. NPS Ranger Station on the left. Bowman Creek enters on the left above the bridge. The gradient eases from here to Big Creek (mile 42). **Be alert for log hazards.**

30.5 Quartz Creek enters on the left. Two miles downstream, Coal Creek enters on the right and Logging Creek on the left.

39.5 Camas Bridge crosses the river soon after Camas Creek enters on the left. Trail from North Fork Road near the bridge to the top of Glacier View Mountain (6,097'). The road is closer to the right bank for the next 14 miles. Below the bridge the river enters a canyon between the Apgar Mountains to the east and the Smoky Range to the west. Glacier View Dam site is about a mile below the bridge (see essay).

42 Big Creek enters on the right. Popular **RIVER ACCESS** and campground just downstream on the right. Class II rapids begin downstream.

47 **GREAT NORTHERN (III-).**

49.5 **UPPER FOOL HEN (III)**, the toughest rapid on the river. Canoe-swamping waves at high flows. After **LOWER FOOL HEN** there is mostly flatwater to the take-out.

52 Canyon Creek enters on the right as the canyon begins to open. Glacier Rim **RIVER ACCESS** is a mile and a half downstream on the right.

58 Confluence with the Middle Fork Flathead, which enters from the left. Just downstream, Blankenship Bridge crosses the river. **TAKE OUT** on the left or continue downstream (see **Middle Fork Flathead**).

Middle Fork Flathead River

Schafer Meadows to Blankenship Bridge

1. Schafer Meadows (4,795') to Bear Creek (3,850').
IV; 26 miles; 35 ft./mi.

2. Bear Creek to Moccasin Creek (3,290').
II+; 31 miles; 18 ft./mi.

3. Moccasin Creek to West Glacier (3,150').
III; 9 miles; 18 ft./mi.

4. West Glacier to Blankenship Bridge (3,100').
II; 6 miles; 8 ft./mi.

Drainage Area and Average Annual Discharge: 1,128 sq. mi. and 2,114,000 af.
Peak Recorded Flow: 140,000 cfs (June 9, 1964) near West Glacier.
Season: *Run 1:* Late May–late July. *Runs 2–4:* Glacial tributaries usually maintain boatable flows all summer. Typically peaks between late May and mid-June and drops below 2,000 cfs by late July.
Recommended Levels: 1,000–8,000 cfs.
Flow Information: USGS, (406) 449-5263; flow near West Glacier. Or call Hungry Horse RD, (406) 387-5243.
Special Hazards: High water. Hypothermia. Isolation. Logs. Grizzlies.
Permits: Not presently required. Group limit 10 in designated Wilderness Areas (Run 1). Back-country permit required to camp on National Park land.
Land Ownership: *Run 1:* All National Forest. *Runs 2–4:* Right bank National Park; left bank mostly National Forest above West Glacier, mostly private below.

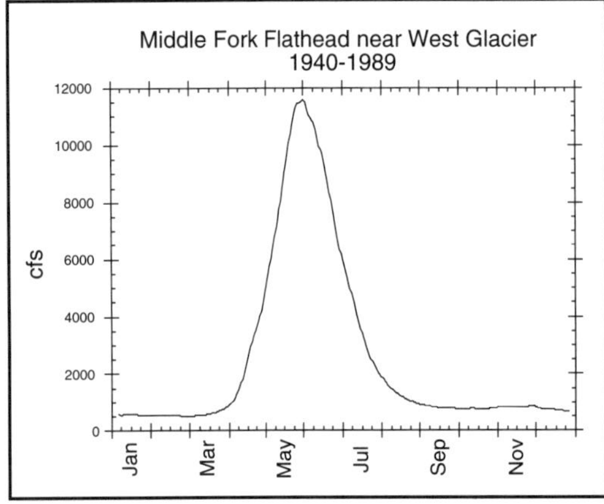

Scenery: Excellent.
Solitude: Excellent above Bear Creek, good below.
Wilderness: *Run 1:* Yes. *Runs 2–4:* No.
Fishing: Good. Cutthroat trout, bull trout, whitefish. **Wildlife:** Abundant.
Water: Cold and clear except at high flows.
Camping: Scattered sites in steep canyon.
Side Hikes: Many USFS trails; see *Flathead NF* map.
Logistics: Access to *Run 1* is by pack train or light plane; for information contact the USFS. U.S. Highway 2 follows the river from Bear Creek to West Glacier *(Runs 2–4)*, providing **accesses at Bear Creek, Essex, Paola Creek, Cascadilla Creek, and Moccasin Creek** (see **Mile Guide** and *Flathead NF* map). **West Glacier** access is about a mile off U.S. 2; follow signs toward Glacier View Golf Course, then drive around the east side of the course to the river. To reach the **take-out at Blankenship Bridge,** turn off U.S. 2 between West Glacier and Hungry Horse and drive west 3 to 4 miles. To hire shuttles, contact outfitters in West Glacier.

The Middle Fork Flathead is two contrasting rivers. Not far below its Continental Divide headwaters south of Glacier National Park, the upper Middle Fork traces a rugged course through one of the West's most pristine wilderness areas. These 28 miles from Schafer Meadows to Bear Creek tumble through unblemished scenery in a steep, remote canyon. Below Bear Creek lies the other Middle Fork, a milder river with a U.S. highway nearby. Though not so stunningly beautiful as its upstream sister, this section is pretty enough, and it attracts far more use due to its easy access and popular commercial raft trips.

At one time the Middle Fork's magnificent wilderness run was slated for destruction by a proposed Army Corps of Engineers dam at Spruce Park. Leading the fight to save the river were two pioneering conservationists, John and Frank Craighead. Best known for their studies of grizzlies, the Craigheads were among the first to propose a federal river protection program, a dream eventually realized as the National Wild and Scenic Rivers System.[1]

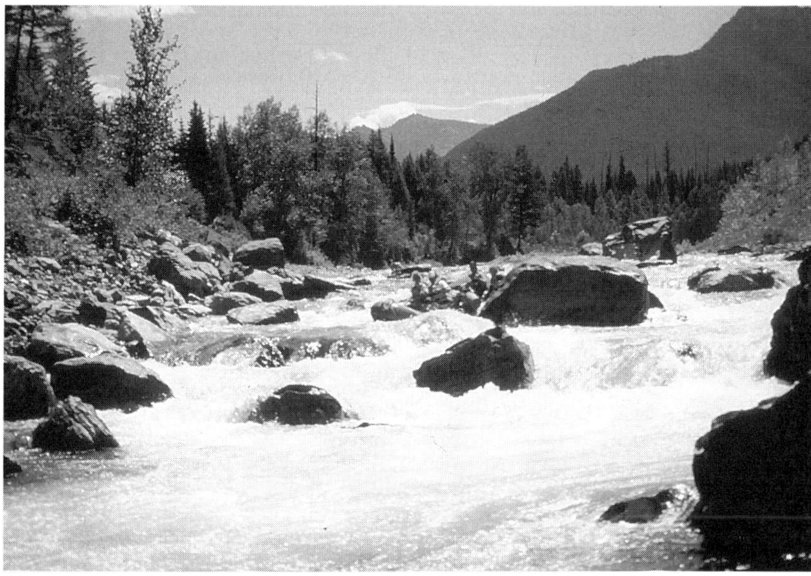

Wilderness Run, Upper Middle Fork Flathead *Glacier Raft Co.*

Today the Middle Fork Flathead is one of the most protected rivers in the nation. The entire river was designated Wild and Scenic in 1976. In addition, the upper watershed is sheltered by the million-acre Bob Marshall Wilderness and the 285,000-acre Great Bear Wilderness, while Glacier National Park protects the right bank below Bear Creek. These vast preserves make the Middle Fork a wildlife haven. Almost anywhere along the river, boaters may spot deer, moose, elk, and other large animals—including the fearsome namesake of the Great Bear Wilderness, the grizzly.

Wilderness Run

The Middle Fork Wilderness Run (Run 1) is always an adventure, beginning with the trip to the put-in. Access is possible by pack train, but most groups fly in to a remote airstrip at Schafer Meadows. From there boaters traverse 28 miles of wilderness down to Bear Creek. The only signs of civilization are a pack trail and three remote ranger stations. At lower flows boaters can pack in to Granite Creek, ten miles into the run. Apparently, many boaters believe the demanding logistics are worth the effort: use on the Wilderness Run is increasing.

The scenery and whitewater reflect the river's geologic history. Though heavily glaciated in the past, the Middle Fork valley is not a classic U-shaped trough. Instead, the river has carved a steep canyon through the Lewis Overthrust Belt, a giant slab of sedimentary rock some one billion years old. This soft rock erodes easily, producing steep slopes and a constantly changing riverbed. Boaters must be alert for new or altered rapids as well as frequent log hazards from undercut trees, especially at high or rising water.

Particular caution is needed at Three Forks and Spruce Park, two series of very demanding rapids located near the beginning and end of the run. Other hazards include isolation, cold water, unpredictable weather, and variable flows. At high flows several rapids rate Class V and the whitewater becomes nearly continuous, so long swims are a risk. Once peak snowmelt is over, flows drop quickly.

Bear Creek to Blankenship Bridge

U.S. Highway 2 follows the Middle Fork here, remaining relatively unobtrusive while offering easy access and short shuttles. From Bear Creek to Essex the rapids are mostly Class II and II+. Many groups add this short section to their trips down the upstream wilderness run, in order to see the goat lick a few miles below Bear Creek (see **Mile Guide**). From Essex to Nyack the river is mostly Class II, while below Nyack is a six-mile flatwater reach, "Nyack Flats," that most boaters avoid because of frequent log hazards. The best whitewater lies below Moccasin Creek, where the narrow constriction of John Stevens Canyon produces seven rapids in quick succession. This section gets heavy use from local outfitters. The last six miles from West Glacier to Blankenship Bridge offer pleasant floating and one small rapid.

---

[1]Tim Palmer, *Endangered Rivers*, includes information on the Craigheads and their efforts to save the Middle Fork Flathead.

Downstream Runs

Below Blankenship Bridge the Middle Fork is a big-volume, low-gradient river.[2] The 14 miles from Blankenship to the U.S. 2 bridge have good current and occasional riffles. The first six miles have a semi-wilderness flavor, after which U.S. 2 follows the river for several miles. Nine miles below Blankenship Bridge the South Fork enters, marking the beginning of the Main Flathead. Downstream the river is flatter and slower, but be alert for unpredictable releases from Hungry Horse Reservoir on the South Fork. In another couple of miles the Flathead leaves the mountains and enters a broad, flat valley. The first easy take-out is at Teakettle Access, near the U.S. 2 bridge east of Columbia Falls. Farther downstream, as the river approaches Flathead Lake, numerous islands and oxbows (abandoned meanders) provide prime wildlife habitat. These lower sections are popular with locals, who use several accesses between Columbia Falls and the lake.

[2]There is some uncertainty about whether the section from the North Fork confluence to the South Fork confluence is the lowermost reach of the Middle Fork or the uppermost reach of the main stem.

Middle Fork Flathead Mile Guide

0 **PUT-IN.** Schafer Meadows. A trail leads a quarter mile from the airstrip to the right bank. A pack trail follows the right bank from here to Bear Creek, generally within a half mile of the river.

2.5–4.5 **THREE FORKS SERIES (IV).** A steep (60 ft./mi.) set of rapids where the river jogs north for two miles. Watch for **log jams.** Few eddies at high water; boulder-choked at low flows. Beware of sharp rocks along the wall. At mile 5 Morrison Creek enters on the right (trail up creek).

10 Granite Creek enters on the right. Pack trail leads half a dozen miles up the creek to USFS road, providing emergency exit or **alternate access** when flows are too low upstream. Granite Cabin (USFS) is a half mile downstream on the right.

13 Twentyfivemile Creek enters on the right just above a Class III rapid. Just downstream is a rocky spot where **logs** often hang up and block the channel.

15.5 Hotel Rock, where **logs** often block the left channel. Just downstream is the **LUNCH CREEK SERIES (III-).**

19 Long Creek enters on the left.

20.3 Spruce Park Guard Station on the right, in the meadows of Spruce Park. Not far downstream, the canyon narrows and the river runs through the **SPRUCE PARK SERIES (IV)**, a long stretch of rapids with three difficult drops and a steep boulder garden with big holes and waves at higher flows. Scout left. Very difficult to portage. Easier water from here to Bear Creek.

26 **RIVER ACCESS.** Bear Creek enters on the right, a mile after the river leaves the Great Bear Wilderness. Take out on the right below the creek, or continue to the alternate take-out at Essex. U.S. 2 follows the Middle Fork from here to West Glacier. The right bank is all Glacier National Park.

28 The river bends left through **STAIRCASE (III-)**, followed by **GOAT LICK (II+).** Nearby is the Walton Goat Lick, where erosion has exposed mineral salts that attract mountain goats. Photo opportunity, but no stopping allowed.

30.5 Town of Essex, with famous Isaac Walton Inn, on the left. Popular **RIVER ACCESS** on the left below the U.S. 2 bridge. Walton Ranger Station is on the right bank.

38 Paola Creek **RIVER ACCESS** on the left.

41 At a right bend is **BROWN'S HOLE (II+)**, the toughest rapid between Essex and Moccasin Creek. At high flows it becomes a Class III+ raft-flipper that most boaters skirt on the right.

49 Cascadilla Creek **RIVER ACCESS** on the left. Take out here to avoid Nyack Flats, a six-mile reach of slow current and braided, log-strewn channels.

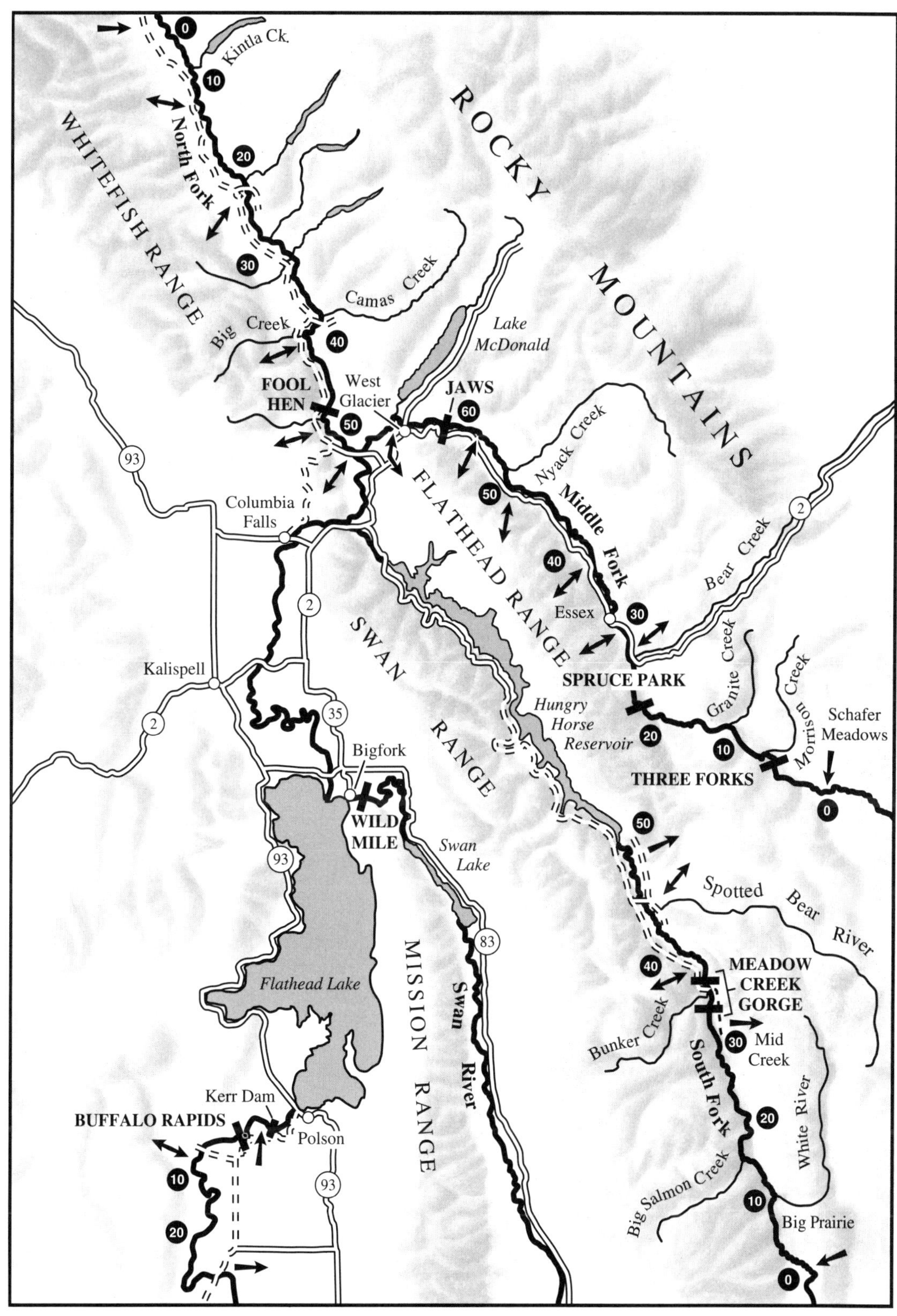

Flathead River System

56.5 Moccasin Creek **RIVER ACCESS**, a popular put-in on the left. Boats must be floated or dragged several hundred yards down the creek to the river. This put-in avoids most of Nyack Flats. Just downstream, Harrison Creek enters on the right.

59 Lincoln Creek enters on the right. John Stevens Canyon begins just downstream.

60.5-63.5 A series of seven rapids that become more turbulent and difficult at high water. The rapids range from II to III- except for the third one, which is considerably stronger. First is **TUNNEL**, where the railroad enters a tunnel, followed by **BONECRUSHER.** After a short breather comes **SCREAMING RIGHT** and the toughest, **JAWS (III+)**, followed in quick succession by **WATERFALL, NARROWS, REPEATER**, and **C.B.T.** ("Could Be Trouble"). After a short breather comes **PUMPHOUSE.**

64.5 Going-to-the-Sun Road crosses the Middle Fork at West Glacier. The West Glacier **RIVER ACCESS** is on the left, a half mile below the bridge. Downstream, U.S. 2 leaves the river. McDonald Creek enters on the right a mile below the access.

69 **DEVIL'S ELBOW (II+)**, a narrow constriction and a sharp right bend.

70.5 Confluence with the North Fork Flathead just upstream from Blankenship Bridge. **TAKE-OUT** on the left. Or continue downstream (see end of essay).

South Fork Flathead River

Big Prairie to Upper Twin Creek

1. Big Prairie (4,620') to Mid Creek.
II; 31 miles; 22 ft./mi.

2. Mid Creek to Cedar Flats.
IVp; 4 miles; 35 ft./mi.

3. Cedar Flats to Spotted Bear.
II; 9.5 miles; 14 ft./mi.

4. Spotted Bear to Upper Twin Creek (3,575').
II-; 6 miles; 13 ft./mi.

Drainage Area and Average Annual Discharge: 1,160 sq. mi. and 1,674,000 af.
Season: Typically peaks late May to mid-June and drops quickly to less than than 2,000 cfs by early to mid-July.
Recommended Levels: 1,000–5,000 cfs.
Flow Information: USGS, (406) 449-5263; flow "above Twin Creek." Flows on upper runs are lower. Gauge includes Spotted Bear River.
Special Hazards: Log hazards on all runs. Run 2 has dangerous constrictions and difficult portages (see **Mile Guide**).
Permits: Not presently required.
Land Ownership: All National Forest.
Scenery: Excellent. Heavily-forested canyon.
Solitude: Excellent above Spotted Bear, very good below.
Wilderness: *Runs 1–3:* Yes. *Run 4:* No.
Fishing: Excellent.
Water: Cold and clear.
Camping: Good. USFS campground at Spotted Bear.
Side Hikes: Many, including Big Salmon Creek (see **Mile Guide** and *Flathead NF* map).
Logistics: Access to the **put-in at Big Prairie** is by trails leading roughly 30 miles from Montana Highway 83. Contact the Forest Service regarding pack services. To reach **other**

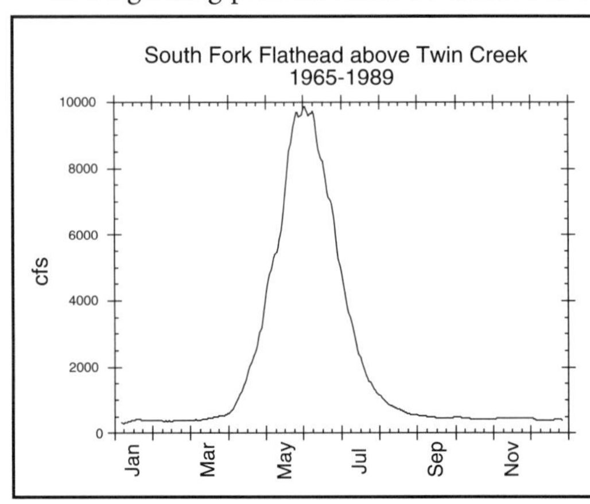

accesses, turn south off U.S. 2 at Hungry Horse and follow a winding USFS road up the west side of Hungry Horse Reservoir. Continue past the reservoir and about a mile beyond an airstrip to the intersection with USFS Road 2826. Here the routes diverge. **1) To reach the Upper Twin Creek and Spotted Bear accesses,** turn left, cross the bridge and drive a half mile to USFS Road 38. To reach **Upper Twin Creek,** turn left and drive downriver 3 miles; to reach **Spotted Bear (also called South Fork Access),** turn right and drive upstream 3⁄4 mile, then bear right on a spur road to the river. **2) To reach Cedar Flats and Mid Creek,** bear right on Road 2826. Drive about 10 miles to the Cedar Flats access trail on the left, or an additional two miles to the Meadow Creek Trailhead, which is some 3 hiking miles from the Mid Creek Access. Contact the Forest Service regarding pack-out services.

The South Fork Flathead flows through a gentle, pristine landscape, giving boaters a glimpse of what much of western Montana was once like. Crystalline water, excellent fishing, fine camping, abundant wildlife, and wilderness seclusion make the South Flathead one of the finest floats in the Northern Rockies.

The river runs northwest down a long trench between the Swan Range to the west and the Flathead Range to the east. These high parallel ridges, which continue almost to the mouth, give rise to a succession of large tributaries that steadily swell the South Fork over the course of its long journey to meet the Middle Fork at Hungry Horse.

Until 1952, the South Fork ran free. Then the Army Corps of Engineers built 564'-high Hungry Horse Dam five miles above the mouth, drowning nearly 40 miles of river and 22,000 acres of lush valley. Fortunately, the remainder of the South Fork is now protected as a National Wild and Scenic River, while the Bob Marshall Wilderness shelters the upper watershed.

Boating use is generally light, especially on the remote upper river, where access is by trail only. Most boaters pack in by horse or mule train to Big Prairie, though some groups add seven miles of flatwater by starting farther upstream at the confluence of Youngs and Danaher Creeks. This "upper upper" section is often too low by early July.

From Big Prairie to Big Salmon Creek the river is mostly Class I; from Big Salmon to Mid Creek, Class II. Below Mid Creek the gorges begin, and most boaters leave the river and pack out about three miles to Meadow Creek Trailhead. Logs are a potential hazard throughout the upper section, especially at high water. The season is longer below the White River confluence, some ten miles below Big Prairie. All of the South Fork above Meadow Creek Gorge is usually too low by mid-July.

The upper and lower reaches of the South Fork are separated by one of the West's most exotic chasms, Meadow Creek Gorge. Sculpted limestone bedrock squeezes the South Fork down to a slender ribbon of water rushing through a deep, shadowy defile. Swift current, sheer walls, difficult rapids, possible portages, and the danger of log jams make **Meadow Creek Gorge an experts-only passage.** At least two slots are too narrow for most rafts and pose a bridging hazard for hard boats. Most boaters should enjoy the gorge as a scenic attraction only.

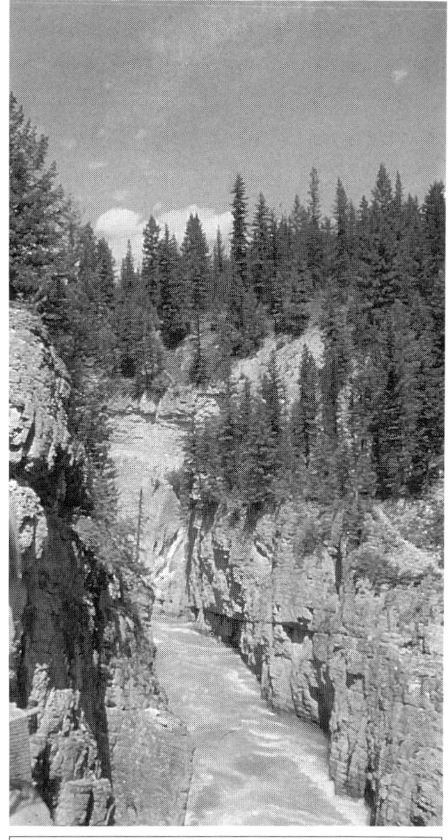

South Fork Flathead *Curt Smith*

The 15 miles below Meadow Creek Gorge offer fine scenery, easy water, and a longer season. Boaters can put in at Cedar Flats, using a short trail from Meadow Creek Road to the river. The run from here to Spotted Bear makes an excellent Class II one-day trip. The final section from Spotted Bear to Upper Twin Creek is somewhat less secluded, with nearby roads and easier access.

South Fork Flathead Mile Guide

0 **PUT-IN.** Big Prairie, accessible only by pack trail. A USFS Work Center is about a quarter mile up from the right bank. Pack trails generally follow both banks—sometimes near the river and sometimes up to a mile away—from here to Meadow Creek.

8.5 A trail leads from the left bank to Holbrook Guard Station (USFS). A mile downstream, the White River enters on the right, adding substantially to the flow.

14 A pack trail fords the river, leading half a mile from the left bank to Salmon Forks Guard Station (USFS). Half a mile downstream, Big Salmon Creek enters on the left, and a trail climbs about a mile up the creek to Big Salmon Lake. Little Salmon Creek enters on the left two miles downstream.

23 Pack bridge. Black Bear Guard Station (USFS) on the left. Class II rapid just downstream.

26 Black Bear Creek enters on the right. Downstream the South Fork leaves its broad valley and enters a canyon that continues to Meadow Creek Gorge. Class II to II+ rapids near mile 27.

30 Mid Creek enters on the right. ***HAZARD.*** About a mile downstream, just below a narrow rapid, a Forest Service sign marks the **last possible take-out above Meadow Creek Gorge** (three-mile hike or pack out).

31–35 **MEADOW CREEK GORGE (IV–Vp).** The next four miles, for **daring experts only,** contain narrow gorges, dramatic constrictions less than 5' wide, dangerous undercuts, few eddies, possible portages, and at least seven major rapids. Though the gorge is generally more difficult at high flows, some spots may be more treacherous at low water. Long swims are possible, and logs lodged here can create lethal hazards. Scout the entire section carefully from the right bank before entering, then proceed with extreme caution.

Immediately below a difficult rapid at mile 33 is **THE CRACK,** where the river narrows to less than 5'. Portage is possible only at low flows when the eddy just upstream is catchable. Downstream the gorge opens briefly as Bunker Creek enters on the left. Boaters can hike out here via trails up either bank. Just upstream the river leaves the wilderness, and downstream a dirt road is on the left, usually far from the river.

Just below Bunker Creek (mile 33.5), a rapid leads around a blind right bend, under the Meadow Creek Pack Bridge, and into the final spectacular mile of the gorge. Confined by sheer 100' walls, the river rushes down a narrow, twisting course and around several blind bends. There are at least three major rapids, almost no eddies, and no way out but downstream. Logs are again a major potential hazard; boaters must scout carefully before entering. After about a mile, the gorge opens and the rapids ease.

35.3 Cedar Flats **RIVER ACCESS** on the left. Harrison Creek enters on the right. An airstrip is above the right bank. Easy water the rest of the way.

44 The Spotted Bear River enters on the right, near a ranger station and campground. Spotted Bear **RIVER ACCESS** (also called South Fork Access) is less than a mile downsteam on the right.

49.5 Watch for a rapid at a sharp left bend. A mile downstream, Upper Twin Creek enters on the right, marking the last **TAKE-OUT** above Hungry Horse Reservoir.

Lower Flathead River

Buffalo Rapids Run

Difficulty: III.
Length: 7 miles. Longer runs possible.
Gradient: 10 ft./mi.
Put-in: Kerr Dam (2,700').
Take-out: Buffalo Bridge (2,630').
Drainage Area and Average Annual Discharge: 7,096 sq. mi. and 8,455,000 af.
Season: May–Oct. (Kerr Dam releases). After big water in late spring, flows diminish to late summer lows of roughly 3,000 to 8,000 cfs. Dam releases can change suddenly.
Recommended Levels: 2,000–20,000 cfs. Never too low. Generally more difficult at lower flows; some rapids wash out at high water.
Flow Information: Call Montana Power, (406) 833-4450, for the release from Kerr Dam.
Permits: Required by the Flathead Indian Reservation; for sale at sports stores. For information call the reservation, (406) 675-2700.
Land Ownership: Flathead Indian Reservation.
Scenery: Very good. Lightly-forested canyon.
Solitude: Very good.
Wilderness: No, but roads and civilization are far away.
Fishing: Poor for trout, good for pike.
Water: Blue-green and clear but undrinkable.
Logistics: To reach the **put-in,** follow U.S. 93 to Polson at the south end of Flathead Lake. Paved roads lead generally west some 6 miles to the put-in a few hundred yards below Kerr Dam. From there follow unpaved roads south and west some 10 miles to the **take-out** at Buffalo Bridge (refer to *Flathead NF* map).

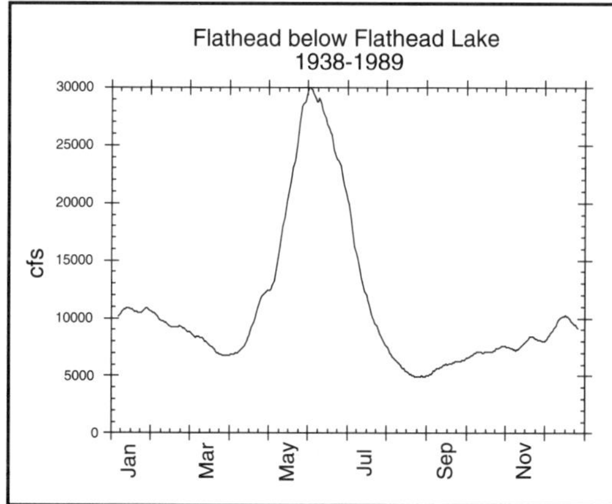

Ice-age glaciers retreating from the Flathead Valley left behind the Polson Moraine, a broad deposit of rocky debris that forms a natural dam on the Flathead River and creates Flathead Lake. Below the moraine the river cuts through the glacial debris, then sweeps down an impressive bedrock canyon. Kerr Dam controls the releases to the river, spilling water from the top of the lake that is pleasantly warm in summer and early fall.

The seven-mile Buffalo Rapids Run below Kerr Dam offers good intermediate whitewater climaxing with with the big waves and holes of Buffalo Rapids itself. Unlike many runs, this section becomes more difficult at moderate and low flows; it washes out somewhat at higher levels. Above about 25,000 cfs many rapids are less difficult, though powerful currents and suctions can pose hazards for swimmers and big water always deserves extra care. At intermediate levels large waves and holes develop, while at low flows some sharp drops and rocks appear. This popular run is entirely within the Flathead Indian Reservation.

Downstream Runs

Below Buffalo Bridge the Flathead rolls peacefully for some 65 miles to its confluence with the Clark Fork near Paradise, Montana. There is a good 21-mile run from Buffalo Bridge to Sloan Bridge; here the river sweeps through a shallow but isolated valley. Though the gradient is only 3 ft./mi., there are some easy Class II ledge drops. Upstream winds can be a problem. Boaters enjoy the abundant birdlife and fine views of the Mission Range. Few river runners float below Sloan Bridge, partly because the terrain is more open and less inspiring, and partly because of motorboat traffic.

Lower Flathead Mile Guide

0 Put in on the left bank below Kerr Dam (private land, but public access allowed). About a mile downstream at a broad left bend is **THE LEDGE (II–III)**, where the river drops over a rock shelf. This drop is sharper and more difficult at low flows; it washes out at high water.

1.8 **PINBALL (II).** Scattered boulders create a rock garden at low flows and big waves and holes at moderate levels. Partially washed out at high water. Next is **EAGLE WAVE,** a long rapid with rock dodging at low flows and roller-coaster waves at higher levels.

3.5 **BUFFALO RAPIDS (III).** The gorge narrows and the river zig-zags through a left-right S-turn. At moderate flows watch for a big hole or wave near the bottom. The standard run is down the left. Scout from the trail on the left. Downstream the canyon opens.

7 Buffalo Bridge. **RIVER ACCESS** on the right. Take out here or continue downstream (see end of essay).

Swan River

Wild Mile

Difficulty: IV+; V at high flows.
Length: 1 mile.
Gradient: 120 ft./mi.
Put-in: Bigfork Dam (3,000').
Take-out: Powerhouse at Flathead Lake (2,880').
Season: May–July.
Recommended Levels: 800–5,000 cfs.
Flow Information: Call the Glacier Kayak Club, (406) 258-3355.
Special Hazards: Sharp rocks; wet suits advised.
Permits: Not presently required.
Solitude: Good except some crowded summer weekends. Road nearby but not obtrusive.
Scenery: Good—but who has time to notice?
Wilderness: No.
Logistics: The run is near the town of Bigfork at the northern end of Flathead Lake. The **put-in** is just below Bigfork Dam, a mile east of town, while the **take-out** is a mile downstream near the dam powerhouse at the southeast corner of town.

Rising near the south end of Montana's Mission Range, the Swan flows north down a narrow, heavily-forested valley just east of Flathead Lake, parallel to the path of its larger and more remote sister stream, the South Fork Flathead. Approaching the lake, the river turns west through a two-mile-long, 700'-deep gunsight notch in the northern end of the Mission Range before it empties into the lake at the town of Bigfork.

Bigfork Dam blocks the river in the middle of this cut, but below the dam, in a spectacular mile-long finale, the Swan plunges some 120 vertical feet through continuous Class IV+ rapids. The run ends near the powerhouse that returns water diverted from the river at Bigfork Dam. This very challenging section, dubbed the "Wild Mile" by local boaters, is by far the most popular whitewater run on the Swan. At high flows it becomes solid Class V, and long, nasty swims are a serious risk. At any water level, challenges include a scarcity of eddies and an abundance of sharp rocks. Wet suits are strongly recommended as protection from both cold water and jagged rocks.

The Wild Mile is popular with local boaters, who often run this short section after work. The access and shuttle are quick and easy, allowing river runners to repeat the run several times in a row. The Wild Mile is the site of the annual Bigfork whitewater festival.

Upstream, Montana Highway 83 follows the Swan for most of its length and provides frequent access, but most of the river is lightly used, primarily because of numerous log jams in its upstream whitewater reaches.[1]

[1]For information on runs farther upstream on the Swan, refer to Fischer, *The Floater's Guide to Montana* or Thompson, *Floating and Recreation on Montana Rivers.*

Region II. Colorado Rockies

Colorado, Wyoming, New Mexico

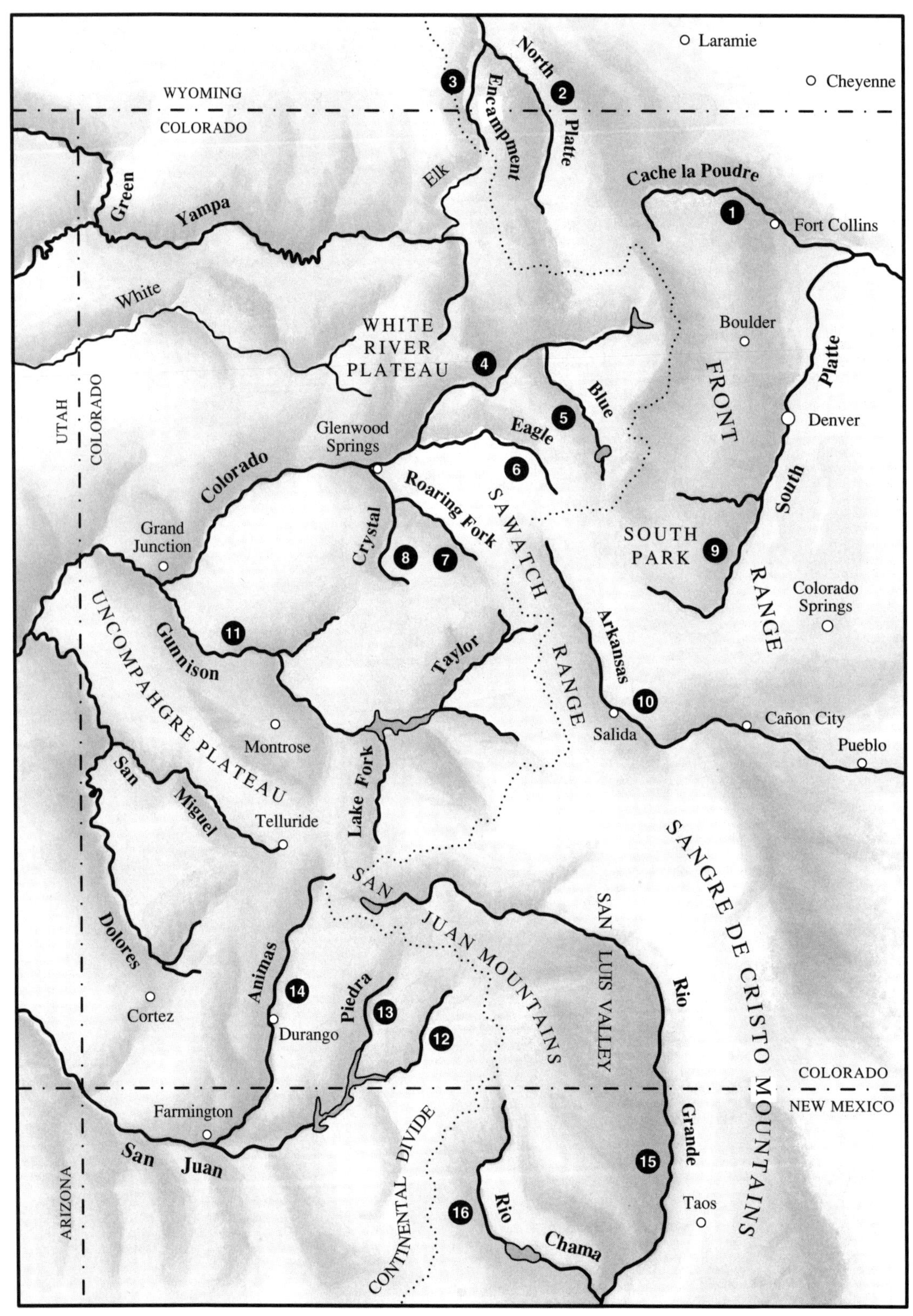

Colorado Rockies

Rivers of the Colorado Rockies

1. Cache la Poudre
2. North Platte
3. Encampment
4. Upper Colorado
5. Blue
6. Eagle
7. Roaring Fork
8. Crystal
9. South Platte
10. Arkansas
11. Gunnison
12. Upper San Juan
13. Piedra
14. Animas
15. Rio Grande
16. Rio Chama

Colorado Rockies

Boating in the Colorado Rockies is a breathtaking experience—literally. This region, which includes the mountainous heart of Colorado as well as neighboring portions of Wyoming and New Mexico, is by far the highest area in the West. Of the 67 peaks in the West over 14,000', 52 are in Colorado. The put-ins for two river runs in this region—the Upper Animas and Upper Rio Grande—are over 9,000'. Even the lowest spots are high: the bottom of the awesome Black Canyon of the Gunnison is more than a mile above sea level.

Like most of the 5,000-mile-long Rocky Mountain range, the Colorado Rockies are really a collection of distinct subranges, including the Sawatch, Front, Park, Gore, Medicine Bow, Sangre de Cristo, San Juan and others. Most were formed by powerful tectonic forces between 70 and 40 million years ago. The great San Juan Range in southwestern Colorado—largest of the subranges—is an eroded volcanic plateau formed 20 to 35 million years ago.

Running down the spine of the Colorado Rockies is the Continental Divide, which separates the Colorado basin to the west from the Rio Grande and Mississippi drainages to the east. Storms moving in from the Pacific drop most of their moisture on the west side of the Rockies, and as a result the rivers of the west slope carry roughly three times as much water in total as their counterparts on the east side. Even runoff on the west slope is not especially heavy, however: most of the snowfall in the Rockies is light powder which is great for skiing but produces less water than the dense, wet snow of the Pacific Coast states.

The rivers of the Colorado Rockies are generally small, steep, constricted, and technically demanding. Broad rivers and extended moderate floats are the exception rather than the rule. Also, wilderness runs are few and far between because roads, highways, and railroads in this rugged terrain generally follow river canyons.

In these conditions the kayak was long the craft of choice on the region's rivers. The Colorado Rockies are home to many of the West's greatest wildwater kayakers. Until fairly recently, rafting and canoeing were often left out in the cold. But with improvements in technique and the advent of self-bailing boats, rafters are successfully running many of the region's most demanding rivers. The canoe, traditionally an Eastern craft, is catching on throughout the West, including the Colorado Rockies.

The northern limit of our Colorado Rockies region is the Great Divide Basin in southern Wyoming, a 100-mile breach in the Rocky Mountains. The only Wyoming rivers included in this region are the Encampment and North Platte, both of which begin in Colorado and have runs that extend only a short way into Wyoming.

At the region's eastern limit the Rockies give way to the Great Plains. Here the rivers of the east slope turn flat as their gradients fall off to just a few feet per mile. The southern ends of the San Juan and Sangre de Cristo Ranges mark the lower boundary of the Colorado Rockies. Farther south, both elevation and precipitation diminish as the Rockies fade out. The only New Mexico rivers included in the Colorado Rockies region are the Rio Grande and Rio Chama, both of which have their headwaters in Colorado.

The region's western boundary is a matter of geology and aesthetics. The same rivers that tumble down the west slope of the Colorado Rockies extend westward into the Canyon Country. In western Colorado, where they leave the Rockies behind and enter "red rock" territory, all the major rivers—the Yampa, Colorado, Dolores, San Juan and others—metamorphose into muddy desert streams.

The rivers of the Colorado Rockies have suffered many abuses. Mining, especially in the mineral-rich San Juan Range, has left many river canyons scarred and polluted. Highways mar a number of canyons, and hydroelectric dams have drowned several fine runs, most notably some outstanding sections of the Gunnison River.

But the greatest damage has come from diversions of water from the west side of the Continental Divide to the east side. In Colorado, as in California, the distribution of water and people is badly out of balance: the west slope of the Rockies has 70 percent of the water, but 80 percent of the people and most of the agricultural land are on the east side of the range. The result has been the development of an elaborate system of dams, ditches, and tunnels that each year suck more than 600,000 acre-feet of water (about 200 billion gallons, or twice the average

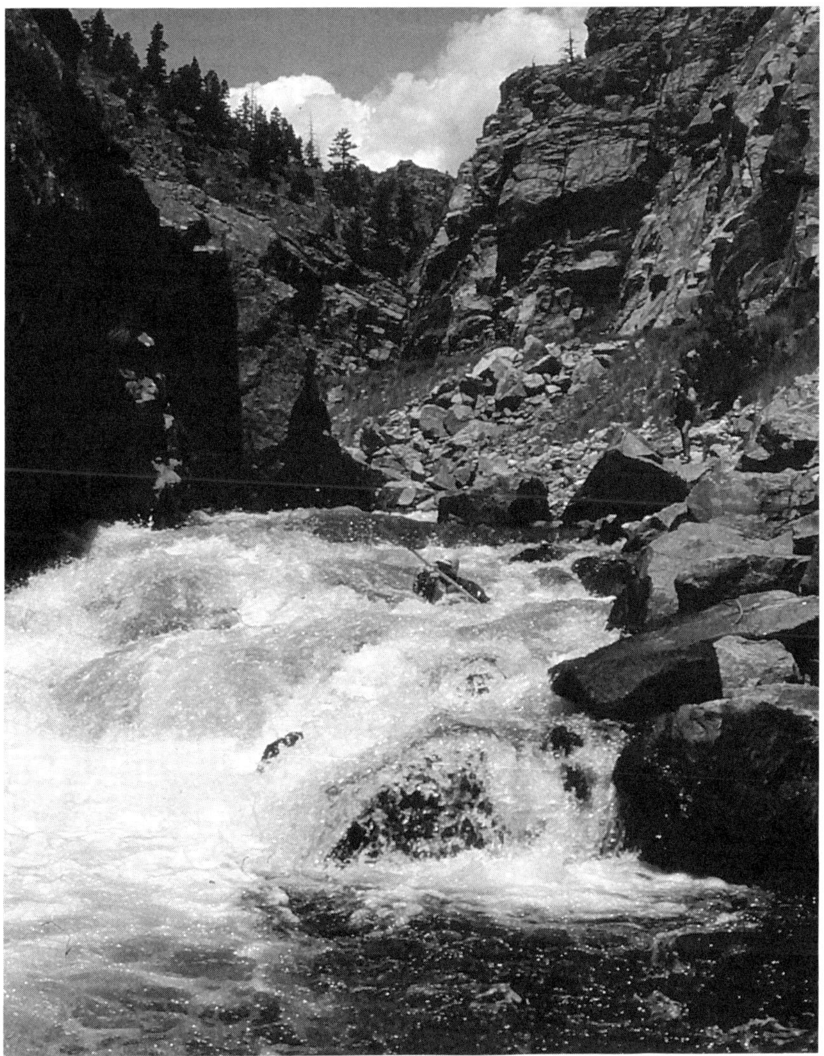

The Narrows, Cache la Poudre River *Martha Moran*

Scenic protection of the Gunnison and other rivers is being discussed. The dramatic growth in the sport over the past 15 years has helped to foster a new appreciation for the remaining wild rivers of the Colorado Rockies both in the public at large and among a growing population of river runners.

Ironically, the same appreciation that may save some rivers from dams and developments has put others at risk of being loved to death. Boating use has skyrocketed as "whitewater fever" has swept the Colorado Rockies. Commercial rafting is concentrated on a relatively few rivers, most notably the hugely popular Arkansas, which ranks as the West's most frequently-boated river with 260,000 user-days (both commercial and private) in 1993—over half the total user-days for the entire region. Much of the remaining commercial boating is on the Upper Colorado, Cache la Poudre, Animas, Rio Grande, and Rio Chama.

Though non-commercial boaters also frequent these very popular runs, private use is spread somewhat more evenly among the area's rivers. As a result, private boaters do not presently face the kinds of use restrictions that are so common in the neighboring Canyon Country and Idaho–Northern Rockies regions. In the Colorado Rockies today, private use is limited on only one river, the Chama. Still, the number of private river runners continues to grow, especially in towns like Salida, Aspen, Durango, Glenwood Springs, and Steamboat Springs.

flow of the Piedra River) from the Upper Colorado and its tributaries to slake the ever-growing thirst of east slope farms and cities.

More rivers are in danger. City dwellers and farmers on the east slope continue to press for more diversions and larger storage reservoirs. Colorado is one of the most laggard states in the West in terms of river protection. As of 1993 the Cache la Poudre is the only National Wild and Scenic River in the state—and even here a new dam has been proposed that would flood the Poudre right up to the Wild and Scenic boundary. Other seriously threatened rivers include the Gunnison, Animas, Yampa, and Blue.

There are some brighter notes. An EPA decision derailed the massive Two Forks Dam project on the South Platte. National Wild and

Cache la Poudre River

Big South Campground to Picnic Rock

1. Spencer Heights Run: Big South CG (8,430') to Sleeping Elephant CG.
Vp; 5 miles; 120 ft./mi.

2. Kinikinik Run: Sleeping Elephant CG to below Fish Hatchery.
IIp; 6.5 miles; 30 ft./mi.

3. Rustic and Mountain Park Runs: Below Fish Hatchery to Narrows Picnic Area.
IV; 19 miles; 60 ft./mi.

4. The Narrows: Narrows Picnic Area to Upper Landing.
V–VIp; 3 miles; 130 ft./mi.

5. Mishawaka, Poudre Park, and Bridges Runs: Upper Landing to Munroe Tunnel Headgate.
IV–III; 10 miles; 60 ft./mi.

6. Filter Plant Run: Filter Plant Access to Picnic Rock Access (5,250').
II3; 3 miles; 30 ft./mi.

Drainage Area and Average Annual Discharge: 1,056 sq. mi. and approx. 300,000 af near canyon mouth.

Season: May through August, with the flow gradually dropping to about 500 cfs in the lower runs by the end of summer. High flows are generally from late May to late June. Sometimes too low for rafts in August.

Recommended Levels: 500–2,000 cfs, though kayakers often boat at lower flows. Most sections are much more difficult around 2,000 cfs and above.

Flow Information: An informal gauge, visible from the highway, is painted on a rock at Pine View Falls on Run 5, over 40 miles below Big South Campground (see **Mile Guide**). Table below gives a rough conversion for this gauge.

Poudre at Pine View Falls

Feet	Cfs	Feet	Cfs
1.5	300	3.5	1,300
2.0	500	4.0	1,800
3.0	1,000	4.5	2,500

Special Hazards: Diversion dams and weirs. Bridges. High flows. Log hazards. Poudre Falls. The Narrows.

Permits: Not presently required.

Managing Agency: Estes-Poudre RD, Arapaho-Roosevelt NF, 1311 South College, Fort Collins, CO 80526; (303) 498-2770.

Commercial Raft Trips: Yes. For references contact the managing agency.

Land Ownership: Mostly National Forest and State, with some private parcels. Refer to *Roosevelt NF* map. Ongoing land swaps under the Wild and Scenic River management plan are bringing more riverside land into public ownership.

Scenery: Excellent.

Solitude: Fair. Highway close by.

Wilderness: No. Highway follows all runs; cabins and summer homes.

Fishing: Excellent. Some sections are designated Colorado Wild Trout River.

Water: Clear and very cold.

Camping: Many Forest Service campgrounds along the river.

Side Hikes: Big South Trail follows the first part of the Poudre's remote upper canyon from Highway 14 above Poudre Falls to Rocky Mountain National Park. Also, scenic trails climb Greyrock Mountain and Roaring Creek near Kinikinik.

Side Excursions: Poudre Falls, an unrunnable drop a mile and a half above Tunnel Rest Area. Also in the area are Rocky Mountain National Park and several wilderness areas.

Guides and References:
- Maddox, *River Guide to the Cache la Poudre.*
- Brief coverage in Wheat, *Floater's Guide to Colorado,* and Rennicke, *Rivers of Colorado.*
- A good source for up-to-date information is Poudre River Kayaks, 1524 W. Oak, Fort Collins, CO 80521; (303) 484-8480.

Maps:
- **USGS 7.5':** *Boston Peak, Kinikinik, Rustic, Big Narrows, Poudre Park, Laporte.*
- **USGS 1:100:** *Fort Collins.* Covers all runs.
- **USFS:** *Roosevelt NF.*

Logistics: Colorado Highway 14 follows the river west of Fort Collins, providing frequent access and easy shuttles. Some accesses are small highway turnouts where boaters must exercise caution in driving, parking, and loading and unloading boats. Several sites have become congested in recent years. Although many popular accesses are at USFS campgrounds and picnic areas, the Forest Service is trying to move accesses outside developed campgrounds. Some access points may change over the next few years as the Forest Service and Colorado State Parks designate new sites or upgrade existing ones. Contact these agencies for up-to-date information.

The Cache la Poudre is all tumultuous action from its headwaters high in Rocky Mountain National Park to the canyon mouth above Fort Collins. Then the river abruptly flattens out, emerges quietly from its 2,000'-deep granite canyon, and glides smoothly across the high plains to its confluence with the South Platte near Greeley, Colorado.

Other rivers in the South Platte system mirror the Cache la Poudre's all-or-nothing character so far as whitewater is concerned. From headwaters along the Continental Divide, these rivers tumble quickly down the steep east face of the Front Range, the great palisade of the Rockies that rises abruptly out of the prairie in an unbroken wall from Colorado Springs to the Wyoming border.

In their mountain canyons the Cache la Poudre and its lesser-known sister streams to the south—such as the Big Thompson River, Boulder Creek, and Clear Creek—cascade through miles of advanced, expert, and unrunnable whitewater. Only occasionally do they slow to a pace suitable for novices or even for intermediate boaters until they leave their canyons and empty onto the plains.

The Cache la Poudre[1]—known simply as "the Poudre" to local boaters, and pronounced "POO-der"—is one of Colorado's most popular rivers. Its excellent scenery and superb whitewater are within easy driving distance of Fort Collins and Denver. Though not a wilderness river, the Poudre is just far enough from Denver to have escaped the worst of the developments that scar many other Front Range rivers.

In 1986, 75 miles of the Poudre were designated as Colorado's first—and to date, only—National Wild and Scenic River. Unfortunately, nine critical miles of river were left unprotected, including the two most popular boating sections, the Bridges and Filter Plant Runs. These sections are threatened by a $1 billion hydroelectric and water storage project proposed by the Northern Colorado Water Conservancy District. The 416'-high dam would destroy the Bridges and Filter Plant Runs along with the lower reaches of the North Fork Poudre.

The Poudre is no stranger to water development projects, and as is sometimes the case, the engineers give even as they take away. The Poudre's flow and season are enhanced by diversions from the upper basins of the Colorado, the North Platte, and—most notably—the Laramie River. Each year some 16,000 acre-feet are shunted from the Laramie through a two-mile tunnel into the Poudre near Tunnel Picnic Area. Downstream, of course, the engineers take away again, diverting much of the flow for irrigation and municipal use near Fort Collins.

Traditionally, the Poudre has been a kayak river—a steep, technical stream where large conventional rafts have often run into trouble. Today, however, small, nimble self-bailing rafts are tackling the Poudre successfully, and commercial and private rafting use is growing rapidly. Regardless of their craft, all boaters must contend with narrow, boulder-choked passages at low flows and big holes and pushy hydraulics at high water. With a constricted, steep-sided channel, the Poudre becomes markedly more challenging with increasing flow.

Like many Front Range rivers, the Poudre's runs are fairly short, separated or interrupted by unnavigable obstacles both natural and man-made. Colorado Highway 14 follows the river closely, providing frequent access and allowing boaters to choose from a wide variety of runs. The six sections listed here are suggestions only; boaters can choose most any stretch that suits them. Local boaters use a bewildering array of names to refer to the various runs.

The upper Poudre gets relatively light use. The uppermost reach covered in our mile guide is the Class Vp Spencer Heights run, which be-

[1] In 1824 French-speaking trappers gave the river its name, which translates literally as "hide the powder"—a reference to gunpowder stashed near the river.

gins about a mile above spectacular (and unrunnable) Poudre Falls. Below Sleeping Elephant Campground the whitewater eases in the Class II Kinikinik run, which includes a mandatory portage around a deadly weir. Downstream the canyon narrows, the gradient steepens, and the river accelerates through rougher rapids in the more popular Class IV Rustic and Mountain Park runs. The Mountain Park run ends at the infamous Narrows, where the river plunges 400' in three miles. Though most boaters avoid this section, experts tackle short stretches of the Narrows (see **Mile Guide**).

Below the Narrows lie many miles of popular advanced whitewater: the Mishawaka and Poudre Park Runs, followed by the very popular Bridges Run, which ends not far above a diversion dam. Finally, near the canyon mouth, the Poudre flows through a heavily-used three-mile stretch of easy intermediate water known as the Filter Plant Run. This lowest run includes the site of the Northern Colorado Water Conservancy District's proposed dam.

Upstream Run

Expert kayakers occasionally tackle the "Big South" run, a very demanding and lightly-used section of the upper Poudre upstream from the Spencer Heights run. This spectacular Class V+ wilderness reach begins near the boundary of Rocky Mountain National Park and extends to near the Highway 14 bridge above Poudre Falls. To reach the put-in points, boaters must carry their boats and gear down access trails that descend from Long Draw Reservoir or Peterson Lake to the river. The run includes more than half a dozen mandatory portages and **severe log hazards.** This section was first run by kayakers John Moran, Dave Neff, and Jeff Parker in 1985. Other expert runs in the area include short-season portions of the North and South Forks of the Poudre.

Mile by Mile Guide

Note: This mile guide lists only some of the many possible accesses. Mileage numbers in brackets are cumulative from Big South Campground and correspond to mileages on our map.

HAZARD. Many bridges across the Poudre have dangerous ***pilings in the current.*** *This guide does* ***not*** *list all bridges, nor are they shown on our map. Use caution.*

Spencer Heights Run

0 **PUT-IN** near Highway 14 bridge and Big South Campground. **The next 2.5 miles are for daring experts only.** The gradient is 165 ft./mi., and there is a dangerous portage around Poudre Falls. **No one should attempt this section at high flows.**

1 **POUDRE FALLS (U).** *HAZARD. PORTAGE.* A beautiful but potentially lethal cascade. Mandatory portage is dangerous, involving a must-catch eddy in Class IV water above the drop. **RIVER ACCESS.** Alternate put-in below the falls. **Very difficult whitewater downstream.** Highway 14 crosses the river below the falls. Just below the bridge is a Class V rapid known as **BONEYARD** or **MEATGRINDER.**

3 **RIVER ACCESS.** Tunnel Picnic Area (USFS). Put in near here to avoid the very difficult water just upstream. At this point the Laramie-Poudre Tunnel discharges water diverted from the upper Laramie River, increasing the Poudre's flow. Class III water downstream.

4 Small settlement of Spencer Heights on the left. Many boaters take out a mile downstream (see put-in for next run).

Kinikinik Run

0 [5] **PUT-IN** at a turnout not far from Sleeping Elephant Campground on the left bank. Class I and II for several miles; rarely boated. Sheep Creek enters on the right a mile downstream.

3.5 [8.5] Roaring Creek enters on the left (side hike) at the small resort of Kinikinik. Downstream on the left is Big Bend Campground.

5 [10] *HAZARD. PORTAGE.* Not far below Big Bend CG is a deadly **diversion weir** with a keeper hydraulic, marked by a warning sign. Mandatory portage on a service road on the left. (Long-term plans call for the installation of a runnable chute here.) Below the weir the river passes a fish hatchery on the left.

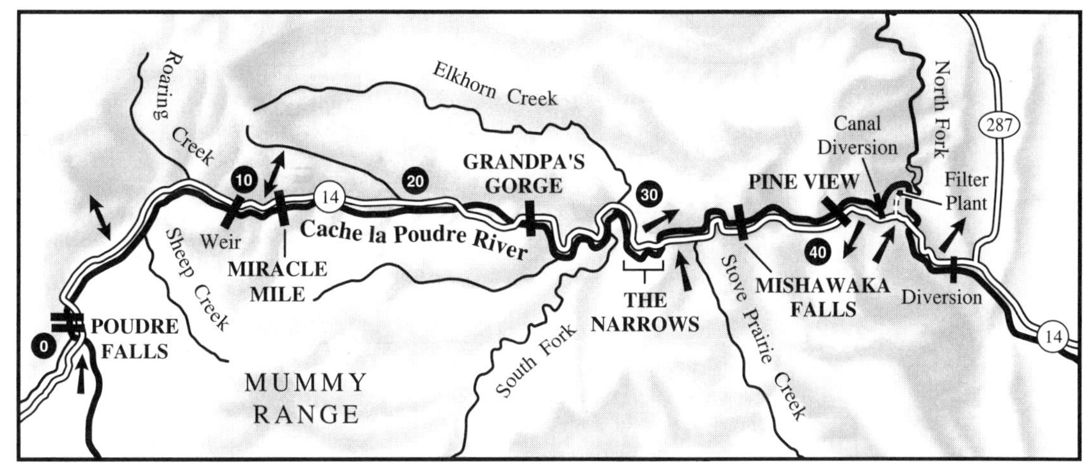

Cache la Poudre

6.5 [11.5] **TAKE-OUT** at a small turnout below the fish hatchery and upstream from the Home Moraine Geologic Site, which has an information display.

Rustic and Mountain Park Runs

0 [11.5] **PUT-IN** at the turnout described just above. Not far downstream is a pair of Class III rapids where the canyon narrows and the river tumbles over an old glacial moraine. A third of a mile farther are the big waves and holes of **MIRACLE MILE (IV)**, also called **White Mile** (actually a quarter mile long.)

3 [14.5] Hamlet of Idylwilde on the left is a popular **RIVER ACCESS.** Put in here to avoid the rapids upstream.

4 [15.5] Arrowhead Lodge on the left. Just downstream is Profile Rock on the right wall. The canyon opens for several miles and the highway is often away from the river. Be alert for a ledge drop where a bridge crosses the river at mile 5.

7.5 [19] Resorts of Glen Echo and Rustic on the left. **RIVER ACCESS** with permission.

9.7 [21.2] *HAZARD. POSSIBLE PORTAGE.* The highway crosses over a new and very dangerous **low bridge.** At normal flows rafts can barely squeeze under it. At higher levels the bridge could be a death trap. Stop well upstream and scout first to check clearance. If in doubt, carry around. This concrete calamity was completed in 1990 by the Colorado State Highway Dept. Popular alternate **RIVER ACCESSES** on both banks just below the bridge. This is the end of the Upper Rustic run and beginning of the Lower Rustic run.

11.5 [23] The canyon suddenly narrows and the rapids intensify. Highway 14 crosses the river, marking the site of **GRANDPA'S GORGE (IV).** A mile farther downstream, Pingree Park Road crosses the river.

14 [25.5] Kelley Flats Campground on both banks. Three quarters of a mile downstream, Bennett Creek enters on the right. Below the creek are a small bridge and a long Class IV rapid.

15.5 [27] Mountain Park Campground on the right. **RIVER ACCESS.** Bridge across the river at the lower end of the campground. Some boaters consider this the end of the Lower Rustic Run and beginning of the Mountain Park Run. Just beyond the bridge are a pair of Class IV drops.

17 [28.5] South Fork of the Cache la Poudre enters on the right. A mile and a half downstream, Elkhorn Creek enters on the left.

19 [30.5] **TAKE-OUT.** Narrows Campground on the left. *HAZARD.* Take out here to avoid The Narrows just downstream.

The Narrows

These three amazing miles begin with the Class V–VI cataracts—and **portages**—of the **Upper Narrows.** Downstream the frenzy eases slightly in the **Middle Narrows,** a frequently-run mile-long Class IV reach. Below the highway bridge is the Class V **Lower Narrows,** which is run less often and may or may not be passable depending on the flow. The Middle and Lower Narrows are choked with large boulders, and the Lower Narrows is full of big, sticky holes. Scout all sections carefully from the highway, and do *not* attempt them at high flows.

Mishawaka, Poudre Park, & Bridges Runs

0 [34] **PUT-IN** on the right bank at Upper Landing, **below** the Lower Narrows near Stevens Gulch Campground. Stove Prairie Creek enters downstream on the right.

1.3–2.8 An action-packed stretch with at least four Class IV drops, including **TUNNEL (IV)** just above the highway tunnel at mile 2.

3 [37] **MISHAWAKA FALLS (IV).** Just downstream on the right is Mishawaka Inn. **RIVER ACCESS** with permission. This is the end of the Upper and beginning of the Lower Mishawaka run. The next 4 miles are Class III.

4 [38] Ansel Watrous Campground, where Youngs Gulch enters on the right (good side hike). Great play hole near the upper campground. Alternate **RIVER ACCESS** at the Diamond Rock Picnic Area about a mile downstream.

6 [40] **RIVER ACCESS.** Poudre Park Picnic Area. Beginning of the **Poudre Park Run.** A bridge crosses the river half a mile downstream, just above the town of Poudre Park. ***HAZARD.*** The next several miles have many small bridges. Pilings are often right in the current, some bridges have dangerous metal fixtures, and the old pilings of several washed-out bridges are just below the surface. Use extra caution around these hazards.

7.5 [41] **CARDIAC CORNER (IV)** at a right bend just below a bridge.

8 [41.5] **PINE VIEW FALLS (IV; IV+ at high flows),** a steep double drop (visible from Highway 14) just below the site of the former Pine View Lodge, which burned down in 1991. Scout on the right. An informal flow gauge is marked here (see **Flow Information**). Popular **RIVER ACCESSES** just above and below the rapid, which is considered the beginning of the Bridges Run.

8.5 [42.5] Greyrock Trail foot bridge crosses the river. ***HAZARD.*** Just over a half mile downstream is **KILLER BRIDGE (III+),** followed by **RED HOUSE HOLE (III)** and then another bridge.

10 [44] **TAKE-OUT.** A sharp right bend marks the most popular, convenient, and crowded take-out. ***HAZARD.*** An unrunnable **diversion dam** is three quarters of a mile downstream at the Munroe Tunnel headgate. An unrunnable **weir** is about a mile farther.

Filter Plant Run

0 [46.5] **PUT-IN** on the right bank about 200 yards downstream from where a spur road leaves Highway 14 to serve the old Fort Collins Filtration Plant. The put-in is about a mile and a half below the Munroe Tunnel Headgate and about half a mile below the filter plant itself. Long-term plans call for the Colorado Department of Parks to develop a new park and put-in at the old filter plant. Class II and II+ rapids in the first mile.

1 [47.5] Highway 14 crosses the river. Just downstream is the proposed site of a 416' dam (see essay). About a quarter mile downstream, at the end of a pool, is **MAD DOG (III-),** a short drop and the biggest rapid on the run.

3 [49.5] **TAKE-OUT.** Picnic Rock Access on the left (parking fee). ***HAZARD.*** A diversion dam blocks the river a few hundred yards downstream at the headgate of the Poudre Valley Canal. Below the diversion the Poudre leaves its canyon and glides through an open valley toward Fort Collins.

North Platte River

Routt to Saratoga

1. Northgate Canyon:
Routt Launch Site (7,810') to Sixmile Gap.
III+; 10 miles; 21 ft./mi.

2. Sixmile Gap to Pickaroon CG
or Prospect Creek.
II-; 9 miles; 22 ft./mi.

3. Pickaroon CG to Sanger Bridge
or Bennett Peak CG.
I; 12 or 18 miles; 17 ft./mi.

4. Bennett Peak CG to Saratoga (6,780').
I; 24 miles; 13 ft./mi.

Drainage Area and Average Annual Discharge: 1,431 sq. mi. and 324,000 af.

Peak Recorded Flow: 6,720 cfs (June 11, 1923) near put-in.

Season: May to mid-July; varies considerably depending on snowpack and weather. The season is somewhat longer below Pickaroon. The river often peaks twice, first in early May and again—at higher levels—in June. Snow in North Park basin (8,000') melts first, more or less all at once; the surrounding slopes and mountains melt later.

Recommended Levels: 1,000–4,000 cfs.

Flow Information: Call North Park RD, (303) 723-4707; or "WaterTalk", (303) 831-7135, **6*9***. Flow is posted at Routt put-in. The Northgate gauge is a half mile upstream from the launch site.

Special Hazards: Hypothermia. Narrow Falls at high flows.

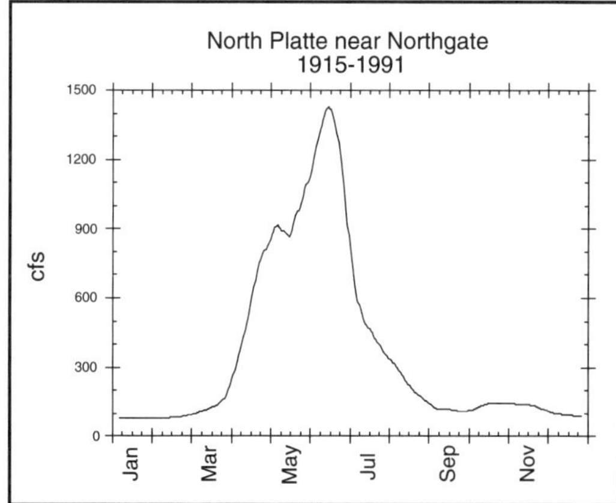

Permits: Not presently required. Maximum group size 25 in wilderness area.

Managing Agency: North Park RD, Routt NF, P.O. Box 158, Walden, CO 80480; (303) 723-8204.

Commercial Raft Trips: Yes. For a list of outfitters, contact the managing agency.

Land Ownership: *Above Pickaroon:* mostly National Forest. *Pickaroon to Bennett Peak:* mixed private and National Forest/BLM. *Below Bennett Peak:* almost all private.

Scenery: Excellent. Steep, forested canyon. Drier, more open landscape on lower runs.

Solitude: Good weekends, very good weekdays.

Wilderness: Yes on Runs 1-2, partial on Runs 3-4.

Fishing: Excellent. Named Wild Trout River in Colorado and Blue Ribbon Trout Stream in Wyoming. Inquire about special regulations.

Wildlife: Deer, elk, eagles, bighorn sheep, etc.

Water: Clear and cold.

Camping: Excellent in Northgate Canyon. USFS campgrounds at Sixmile Gap, Pickaroon, other sites. BLM campsites at Bennett Peak and Corral Creek.

Side Excursions: Hot springs in Saratoga.

Guides and References:

- Lewis, *Paddle and Portage: The Floater's Guide to Wyoming Rivers.*
- Wheat, *Floater's Guide to Colorado.*
- Information sheets available from USFS.

Maps:

- **USGS 7.5':** *Runs 1 & 2:* Northgate, Horatio Rock, Elkhorn Point, Overlook Hill. *Runs 3 & 4:* Overlook Hill, Barcus Peak, Ryan Park, Cow Creek, Finley Reservoir, Saratoga.
- **USGS 1:100:** Saratoga (shows all runs).
- **USFS:** *Routt NF* (first 5 miles), *Medicine Bow NF* (all but first two miles).
- *A Fisherman's and River Runner's Map/Guide to the Upper North Platte River* (Wyoming Game & Fish). Detailed maps. Available at local sports stores or from Wyoming Game & Fish, 5400 Bishop Blvd., Cheyenne, WY 82006; (307) 777-4601.

Auto Shuttle: About 25 minutes one way from Routt to Sixmile.

Logistics: To reach the **put-in at the Routt Launch Site,** turn east off Colorado Highway 125 about a mile northwest of the bridge over the North Platte, some 5 miles south of the Wyoming border, and follow the unpaved road a half mile to the river. To reach **Sixmile Gap,** follow Wyoming Highway 230 north 4 miles past the state line and turn east on Road 492, which leads two miles to the campground and a steep trail to the river (tough for rafts). **Pickaroon access** (the BLM calls this the Prospect Creek Access) can be reached in two ways: (1) a rough 4-wheel-drive road on the west side leading north from Highway 230 near Big Creek Ranch; (2) long routes on the east side via either Foxpark and USFS Road 512, or French Creek Road and Road 512 (all are usually snowed in until mid-June). Access may be possible at the private **Sanger Bridge** (permission and fee required); turn north off Highway 230 onto French Creek Road, 3 miles east of Riverside, and drive north and east some 10 miles to the river. To reach the **Bennett Peak access,** continue past Sanger Bridge a couple of miles, then turn left on unpaved Bennett Peak Road (BLM Road 3404) and drive north some 7 miles. The **Saratoga access** is at the highway bridge over the river.

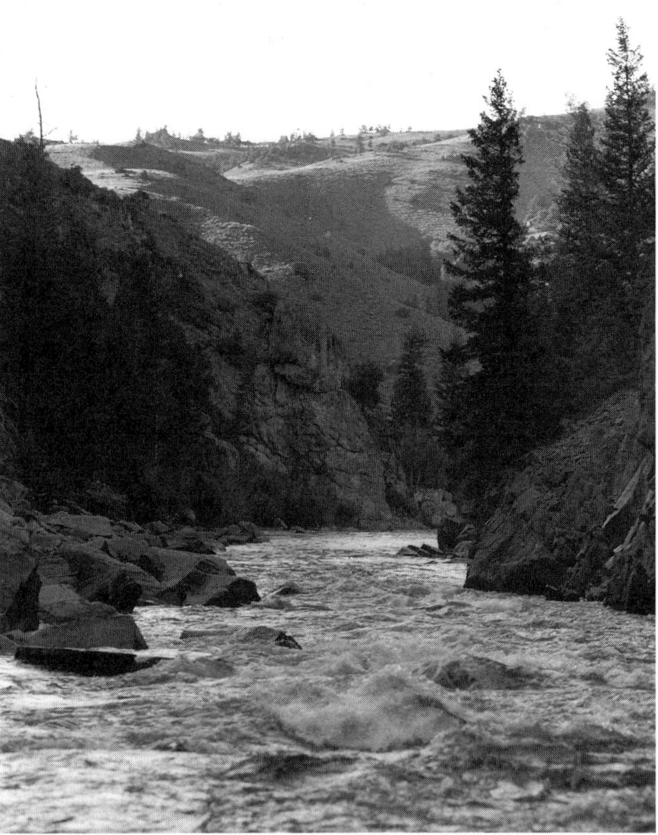

Stovepipe Rapid, North Platte *Dan Lewis*

Snow may block roads to Routt, Sixmile, and Pickaroon accesses in the early season. Contact the Forest Service for road conditions and detailed shuttle directions.

For most of its length the Platte is a shallow, muddy river gliding through braided channels across vast prairies—hardly the stuff of whitewater legend. The Indians called it "Mini Nebrathka," or "spreading waters." In 1739 French explorers named it "La Rivière de Platte"—the "flat river."[1] Early pioneers quipped that the Platte was "a thousand miles long and six inches deep." But upstream, near its Rocky Mountain headwaters, the North Fork of the Platte tumbles from a spectacular valley in a frothy run that is far from flat.

Here in Northgate Canyon river runners will find some of the finest wilderness boating in the Colorado-Wyoming Rockies. At the heart of the canyon, between Elkhorn Creek and Sixmile Gap, lies a four-mile stretch of challenging Class III to III+ rapids. Above and below this section the whitewater is considerably easier, giving boaters a chance to admire Northgate's rugged slopes and lush forests. For 19 miles below the Routt launch site, the river flows through the Platte River Wilderness Area.

The North Platte does not spring from a single headwater lake or stream; instead, it coalesces from hundreds of small creeks and feeders. Snowmelt from four Rocky Mountain subranges—the Parks, the Rabbit Ears, the Never Summers, and the Medicine Bows—merges in North Park, a spectacular alpine basin in northern Colorado. Local Indian tribes named this basin the "Bull Pen," after the vast herds of buffalo and elk that once gathered here. In North Park the collected waters flow serenely north until, just before crossing into Wyoming, the river enters Northgate Canyon. Here the North Platte instantly changes char-

[1]From Mae Urbanek, *Wyoming Place Names.*

acter, churning through boulder-studded rapids as it cuts deep into the west flank of the Medicine Bow Mountains.

Although the put-in for the Northgate run is straightforward enough, take-outs are more complicated. Access at Sixmile Gap is by a steep trail that will deter many rafters. Many boaters prefer nearly to double the mileage by continuing to the Pickaroon or Prospect Creek accesses. Although this gives river runners a chance to enjoy an overnight at one of the canyon's excellent campsites, getting a shuttle vehicle to these sites can be a challenge (see **Logistics**).

Below Pickaroon the river flattens out and gradually enters more open terrain with ranches and back roads, though scenic slopes continue to just below Bennett Peak (mile 36.5). Below Brush Creek (mile 38) the North Platte runs smoothly through braided channels in the open bottomlands of Saratoga Valley, bounded at times by scenic bluffs and cottonwood groves. Boaters who get as far as Saratoga can stop for a soak in the town's well-known hot springs.

From Saratoga to Interstate 80 the river wanders through 40 miles of sagebrush flats, broken by occasional cottonwood groves and sandstone bluffs. Open canoes are the craft of choice here. (Before boating, inquire locally about public access; some groups have reported disputes with a landowner, but the Wyoming Game & Fish Department has acquired several public easements.) Far downstream, well east of Casper, is a pretty Class I float through Wendover Canyon from Glendo Dam to Guernsey Reservoir.[2]

[2]For more information on the lower reaches of the North Platte, refer to Dan Lewis, *Paddle and Portage.*

Mile by Mile Guide

Note: The last 15 miles of this run are not shown on the map.

0 **PUT-IN.** Routt Launch Site (left bank). Downstream the walls close in quickly. The whitewater begins with **WINDY HOLE (III)**, some three quarters of a mile below the put-in and around the first left-hand bend. At high flows watch for a big hole at the bottom right center. Easier water follows for several miles.

2.5 Threemile Creek enters on the left at the private Ginger Quill Ranch.

5 Colorado-Wyoming border.

6.3 A mile below a sharp bend to the right, Elkhorn Creek enters on the right. Just downstream is the narrow heart of **Northgate Canyon,** where the gradient increases to 45 ft./mi. A third of a mile below Elkhorn Creek is **COWPIE (III+)**, technical at low flows and developing big rollers at high water. Rocky drops continue for the next mile, culminating with **NARROW FALLS (III+)**, located beneath a vertical rock face on the left. Stop in the eddy above the falls on the left to scout. The rapid features a straight shot down a series of big, turbulent waves. Downstream the rapids ease for a while.

9.5 **TOOTSIE ROLL (III)**, followed immediately by the big waves of **STOVEPIPE (III). RIVER ACCESS.** A steep trail (not recommended for heavy rafts) climbs about 200 yards up the left bank from the foot of Stovepipe Rapid to Sixmile Gap Campground. Downstream the whitewater eases. A Forest Service trail follows the left bank for 7 miles below Sixmile Campground.

18 **DOUGLAS (II)**, the last rapid worth naming, is only waves. Douglas Creek, a major tributary, enters on the right a half mile downstream (side hike). **RIVER ACCESS** at Pickaroon Campground on the right bank just below Douglas Creek, or a little over a quarter mile farther downstream on the left bank at the Prospect Creek Road access, where a 4-wheel-drive road from Highway 230 reaches the river (see **Logistics**). A dirt road generally follows the right bank for five miles below Douglas Creek.

22 The river leaves Medicine Bow National Forest and enters mostly private land. About ¾ mile downstream, Mullen Creek enters on the right at the A Bar A Ranch. A mile below the ranch, the dirt road crosses to the left bank.

27 Big Creek, a major tributary, enters on the left. A mile and a half downstream, French Creek enters on the right.

30.5 Sanger Ranch (private) on the right. Possible **RIVER ACCESS** a half mile downstream where French Creek Road crosses the river (permission and fee required—see **Logistics**). A couple of miles below the bridge the river enters a shallow, 5-mile-long canyon as it winds around Bennett Peak on the left.

36.5 Bennett Peak Campground and **RIVER ACCESS** on the right.

38 Brush Creek enters on the right as the canyon opens. Two miles downstream, Brush Creek Road crosses the river.

46.5 Confluence with the Encampment River, which enters on the left.

50 Highway 130 bridge.

60 Railroad bridge on the outskirts of Saratoga. **TAKE-OUT** just downstream at the park, or farther down at the highway bridge. Below Saratoga lie some 40 miles of Class I water to Interstate 80 (see end of essay).

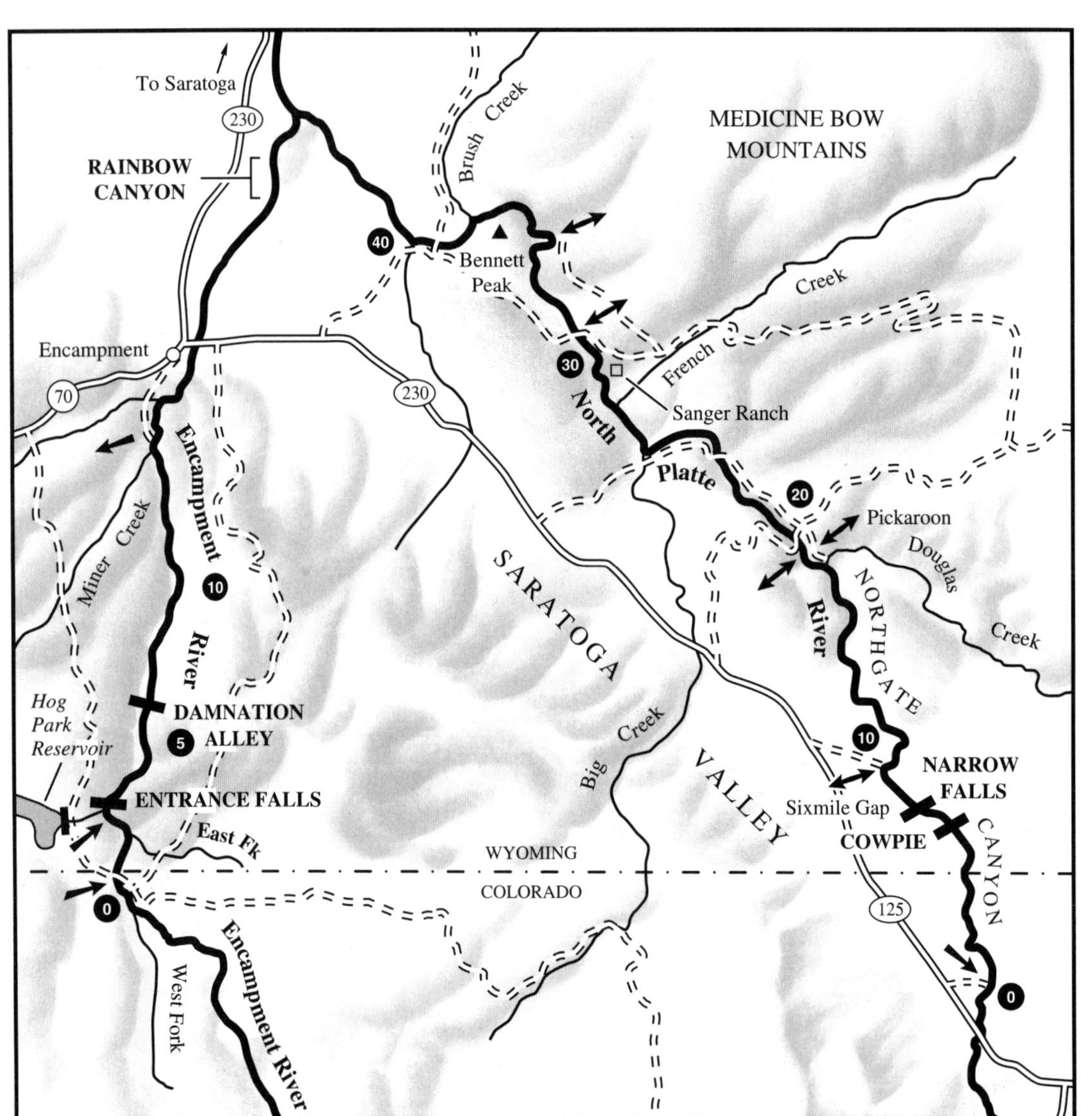

North Platte and Encampment

Encampment River

Commissary Park to Encampment

Difficulty: V. **Length:** 16 miles.
Gradient: 72 ft./mi. overall; 150 ft./mi. for 3 miles below Box Canyon Creek (mile 6.3).
Put-in: Road 496 bridge, Colorado-Wyoming border (8,370').
Take-out: Foot bridge below I.O.O.F. Camp (7,240') near town of Encampment.
Drainage Area and Average Annual Discharge: About 70 sq. mi. and 85,000 af at put-in; 225 sq. mi. and about 200,000 af at take-out.
Season: June–early July, but varies considerably depending on snowpack and reservoir releases. Road often blocked by snow until mid-June. Diversions to the Encampment from the Little Snake River may lengthen the natural season (see essay).
Recommended Levels: 800–3,000 cfs at take-out. Flows at take-out may be two to five times higher than at put-in.
Flow Information: No flow reading regularly available by phone. Managing agency may have information.
Special Hazards: Continuous difficult whitewater, especially at Damnation Alley. Log hazards. Isolation. Cold water. High altitude.
Permits: Not presently required. Maximum group size 15.
Managing Agency: Hayden RD, Medicine Bow NF, P.O. Box 187, Encampment, WY 82325; (307) 327-5481.
Commercial Raft Trips: None at this time.
Land Ownership: Almost all public.
Scenery: Excellent. Forested granite canyon.
Solitude: Excellent.
Wilderness: Yes. Most of the run is in the Encampment River Wilderness Area.
Fishing: Excellent.
Wildlife: Abundant.
Water: Clear and ice cold.
Camping: Allowed at put-in. Also, a USFS campground at Hog Park Reservoir. Many good riverside sites for those willing to float with gear for an overnight trip.
Side Hikes: USFS trail follows the entire run.
Side Excursions: Mt. Zirkel Wilderness. Historic town of Encampment; Grand Encampment Museum. Hot springs in Saratoga.
Guides and References:
- Wheat, *Floater's Guide to Colorado.* The author made the first known descent of the Encampment in 1978.
- Lewis, *Paddle and Portage: The Floater's Guide to Wyoming Rivers.*

Maps:
- **USGS 7.5':** *Dudley Creek, Encampment.*
- **USFS:** *Medicine Bow NF.*

Auto Shuttle: 25 miles (45 minutes) one way.
Logistics: The **take-out** is on the left (west) bank at a foot bridge just downstream from the I.O.O.F. (Odd Fellows) Camp, located about two miles south of the town of Encampment, Wyoming. To reach the bridge, drive west out of Encampment on Wyoming Highway 70. Just outside town, bear left on unpaved Carbon County Road 353. This road descends to and crosses the North Fork of the Encampment, then climbs about a half mile up a hill to a "Y"; bear left, descend a steep drainage to the river, then bear right and continue upstream past the BLM campground to the parking lot and foot bridge.

To reach the **put-in,** drive southwest from Encampment on Highway 70 roughly 6 miles, then turn left on USFS Road 550 and drive south 15 miles to the intersection of Roads 550 and 496 (possible **alternate put-in**). Turn left on 496 and drive 4 miles to where the road crosses the Encampment in Commissary Park, just inside the Colorado state line. The best parking area is a couple of hundred yards north of the bridge; turn onto a small spur road designated "496.1K."

Boaters can also reach the put-in via unpaved roads from Colorado Highway 125 to the east or from Steamboat Springs, Colorado, to the south. From Highway 125 at Cowdry, Colorado, drive west on a paved county road that eventually becomes USFS Road 80 and leads to the put-in described above. Consult Colorado highway maps and the *Routt NF* map. An **alternate put-in** may be possible on Hog Park Creek downstream from Hog Park Dam when releases are sufficient (see essay). The access is at or downstream from the point where Road 496 crosses the creek (see directions above).

ENCAMPMENT

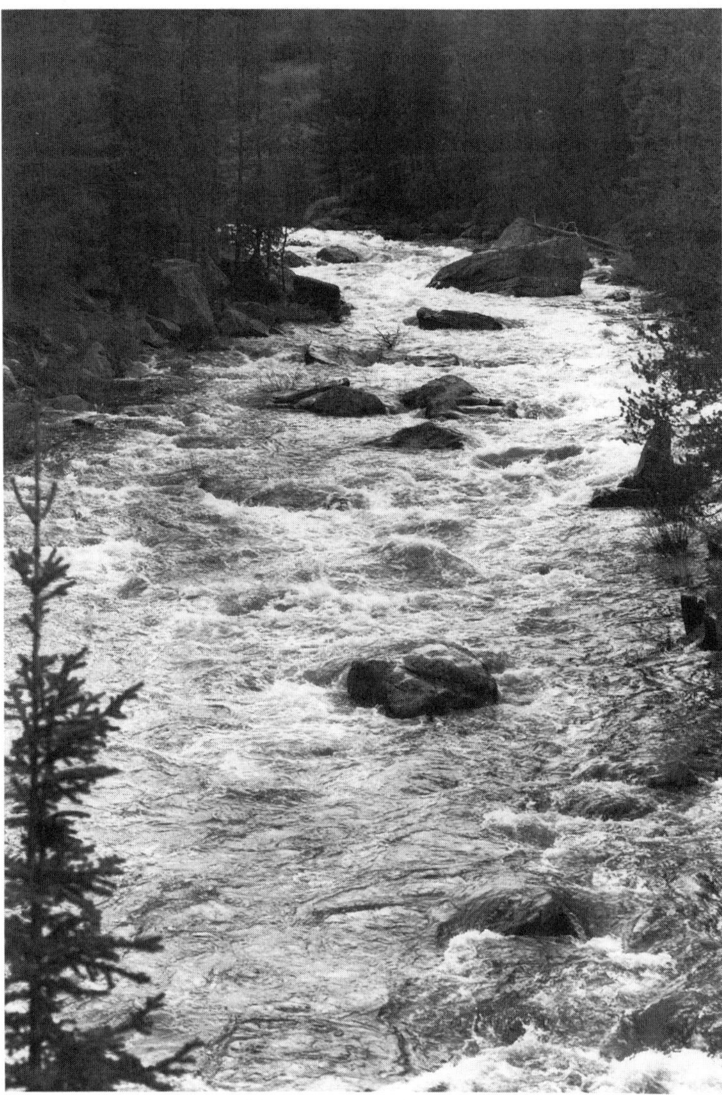

Entrance Falls, Encampment River *Dan Lewis*

The Encampment is short but spectacular. The river dances and shimmers a mere 40 miles from headwaters to mouth, tracing one of the wildest and most captivating courses in the Colorado-Wyoming Rockies. It is a relatively new whitewater discovery, introduced by river runner Doug Wheat in his excellent 1983 book, *The Floater's Guide to Colorado.* Today the Encampment remains primarily the domain of top-notch kayakers, though the river has also been tackled by expert rafters in self-bailers and catarafts.

For those experts with the stamina and skill, the Encampment is the ultimate Rocky Mountain joy ride. Others should regard this pristine river and its spectacular rapids as scenery only, best appreciated from the excellent trail that follows the entire run.[1]

One of the biggest challenges for boaters is catching the Encampment with adequate—but not excessive—flow. Depending on snowpack and spring weather, the brief season may come any time from May to mid-July. As a further complication, snow sometimes blocks the roads to the put-in as late as mid-June. **All boaters should avoid the river at high flows.**

Although it is the North Platte's largest tributary, the Encampment is still a small river at its mouth, contributing a year-round average of only 250 cfs to the Platte. Remarkably, boating begins a mere ten miles from the river's headwaters; flows here are less than half those at the mouth. A mile upstream from the put-in, the West and Main Forks of the Encampment join, carrying icy snowmelt northward from the nearby peaks of the Sierra Madre Range in northern Colorado. River runners launch their craft into this oversized creek at Commissary Park, a grassy swale on the Colorado-Wyoming border, two miles east of the Continental Divide and more than a mile and a half above sea level. Immediately downstream, the river crosses into Wyoming.

[1]Boaters looking for a milder trip might consider a short run through Rainbow Canyon, located on the lower Encampment just above the confluence with the North Platte. This generally quiet float offers good scenery in a semi-wilderness setting. However, the land is almost entirely private, and several diversion weirs, cables, and fences cross the river, adding an element of hazard and detracting from the run. Diversions can substantially reduce flows in this section. Also, there have been problems with landowners regarding access; for current information contact the Wyoming Game & Fish Department in Laramie at (307) 745-4046.

The Encampment grows rapidly in the first three miles below the put-in, swollen first by the added flow of the East Fork, then by the waters of Hog Park Creek. A recently completed diversion from the Little Snake River adds to the Encampment's natural flow, as water is shunted through a tunnel under the Continental Divide to Hog Park Reservoir. River runners on the Encampment may enjoy a longer season as a result of this redirection of water. Later in the season, the put-in may shift from Commissary Park to Hog Park Creek (mile 2.8) when flows permit (see **Logistics**).

Below Hog Park Creek the gradient steepens, the whitewater becomes more difficult, and the tempo increases to a frenetic pace. By the time the river passes Box Canyon (mile 6.3), all but the hardiest experts will be flirting with exhaustion. But the river is just getting warmed up. Below Box Canyon the Encampment sprints with dizzying speed through a narrow granite gorge, dropping 440' in just three miles. Near the head of this inner canyon the river puts on its most dazzling display, leaping and foaming through a rocky Class V gauntlet known as Damnation Alley. This and other challenging sections should be scouted thoroughly, though the heavily forested banks make this difficult in places. If in doubt, portage along the bank or along the maintained trail on the right. Below Cascade Creek (mile 9.3) the Encampment finally slows somewhat, giving boaters a chance to catch their breath and uncurl white knuckles from paddle or oars.

The scenery in the inner canyon is outstanding: crystalline water, chiseled granite slopes cloaked in fir and pine, and sometimes a herd of bighorn sheep gazing serenely down at the strange creatures in their colorful boats. Most of the run is protected from roads and other intrustions by the 10,400-acre Encampment River Wilderness Area, designated in 1984. Boaters will see only one small ranch in the 15 miles from Commissary Park to the Odd Fellows Camp take-out.

River runners with an interest in history will appreciate the town of Encampment, with its many turn-of-the-century buildings and excellent Grand Encampment Museum. The settlement took its original name, "Camp le Grand," from a yearly gathering of Indians and fur trappers; the name was later translated to Grand Encampment. In 1898 the town boomed spectacularly, fueled by the discovery of copper in the nearby Sierra Madre Range and by the Union Pacific Railroad's insatiable appetite for railroad ties cut from the surrounding forest. During high water each spring, loggers known as "tie hacks" launched tens of thousands of freshly cut ties into the river at Hog Park, sending them bobbing and spinning down to the North Platte. Log "drovers" had the harrowing task of breaking up jams that formed at rapids and other bottlenecks in the narrow canyon. But Grand Encampment's heady days were short-lived: a drop in copper prices, combined with disastrous smelter fires, turned boom to bust in only a decade.

Mile by Mile Guide

This guide mentions only a few of this run's many rapids. Scout frequently; watch for ***log hazards.***

0 **PUT-IN** near the bridge over the river in Commissary Park at the Colorado-Wyoming border. **Experts only.** A trail follows the left bank downstream. The tiny river winds about a mile through Commissary Park before entering a steep-sided canyon. The East Fork Encampment enters from the right about a mile and a half below the bridge, adding substantially to the flow and marking the beginning of the Encampment River Wilderness.

2.8 Hog Park Creek, a major tributary, enters on the left. A rough jeep trail leads up the creek to USFS Road 496. Just above the creek the trail crosses a foot bridge, staying on the right bank for the rest of the run. Just below the creek is the first large rapid, **ENTRANCE FALLS (IV+)**; scout on the right. *Anyone who has any trouble or doubt here should hike out.* Downstream the gradient increases, and the river becomes much more difficult. ***HAZARD.*** Watch for **logs,** including one that may block part of the river not far below Hog Park Creek.

4.7 Dudley Creek enters on the right.

6.3 Box Canyon Creek enters on the right. Downstream the canyon closes in and the whitewater intensifies, climaxing at

DAMNATION ALLEY (V). This long rapid begins about half a mile below Box Canyon Creek, some 100 yards downstream from an impressive but runnable 6' drop. It is critical to stop no more than 50 yards below this drop to scout Damnation Alley thoroughly from the right-bank trail. The Alley itself is roughly an eighth of a mile long and ranges from a highly technical boulder garden at low flow to a chaos of pounding reversals at high water. This is no place to swim: below the Alley is about a mile of difficult, nearly continuous whitewater, including a tricky ledge (scout right). Difficult rapids continue for the next 3 miles.

9.3 Cascade Creek enters on the right, marking the end of the roughest whitewater. Billie Creek enters on the right half a mile downstream.

11 At a broad left bend, a trail on the right climbs up Purgatory Gulch to Blackhall Mountain Road. Half a mile downstream, the Wilderness Area ends and the river passes Water Valley Ranch on the left (private). Soldier Creek enters on the left below the ranch. Watch for a possible hydraulic at the site of an old diversion dam near here; this can be a good play spot, but beware of metal debris. Much flatwater from here to the take-out.

15.5 Miner Creek enters on the left. The I.O.O.F. Camp is just downstream on the left. The **TAKE-OUT** is at the foot bridge below the camp. An **alternate take-out** is 4.5 miles farther downstream at the Highway 230 bridge; however, be alert for cables, barbed wire fences and diversion weirs in this lower stretch.

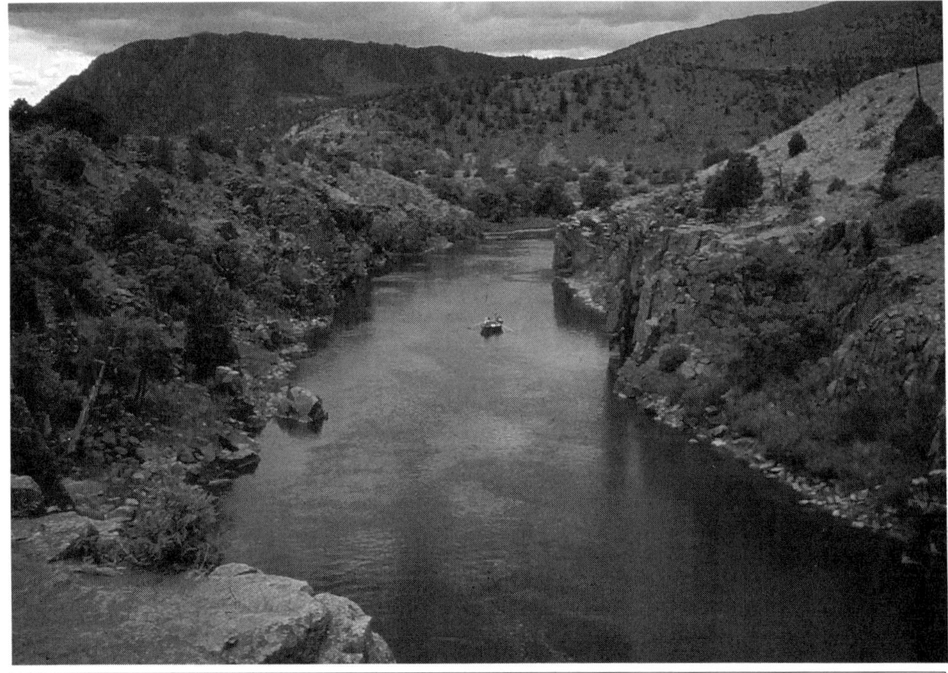

Upper Colorado River *BLM, Kremmling RA*

Upper Colorado River

Kremmling to New Castle

1. Gore Canyon:
Kremmling (7,310') to Pumphouse.
V+; 11 miles; 35 ft./mi. (100+ in Gore Canyon).

2. Pumphouse Run:
Pumphouse to State Bridge.
II+; 15 miles; 15 ft./mi.

3. State Bridge to Dotsero (6,120').
II+; 45 miles; 15 ft./mi.

4. Upper Glenwood Canyon.
I; 8 miles (partly on reservoir).

5. Shoshone Power Plant (5,910')
to Grizzly Creek.
III+; 2 miles; 45 ft./mi.

6. Lower Glenwood and South Canyons:
Grizzly Creek to New Castle (5,500').
II+; 19 miles; 17 ft./mi.

Drainage Area and Average Annual Discharge: *Gore Canyon:* 2,382 sq. mi./768,000 af. *Glenwood Springs:* 6,013 sq. mi./2,623,000 af.

Season: *Gore Canyon:* Mid-July through September. Season begins well after peak snowmelt, which typically occurs in late May or early June. *Other runs:* April through October. High water in June; usually drops below 1,000 cfs by mid-August.

Recommended Levels: *Gore Canyon:* 600–2,000 cfs. *Other runs:* 800–10,000 cfs.

Flow Information: "WaterTalk", (303) 831-7135). 5*7* for flow at Kremmling (*Runs 1-3*); 5*4* for flow near Dotsero *(Run 5)*; 5*6* for flow below Glenwood Springs *(Run 6)*.

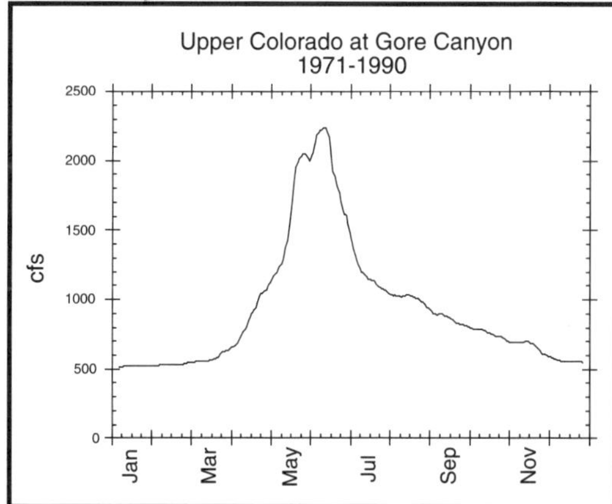

Special Hazards: All of Gore Canyon. Other runs may have hazardous bridges.

Permits: Not presently required.

Managing Agency: *Runs 1 & 2:* BLM, P.O. Box 68, Kremmling, CO 80459; (303) 724-3437. *Runs 3, 4, & 6:* BLM, P.O. Box 1009, Glenwood Springs, CO 81602; (303) 945-2341. *Runs 4 & 5:* Eagle RD, White River NF, P.O. Box 720, Eagle, CO 81631; (303) 328-6388.

Commercial Raft Trips: Yes. For references contact the managing agencies.

Land Ownership: Mixed public and private. Refer to *Upper Colorado River Recreation Area* visitor guide and maps (BLM).

Scenery: Excellent to good. Transition from Rockies to canyon country.

Solitude: Varies. Best in Gore Canyon, worst on Pumphouse Run (heavy commercial use).

Wilderness: *Runs 1 & 2:* Partial (railroad, minor roads). *Other runs:* No.

Fishing: Very good. Designated Wild Trout River above State Bridge.

Water: Cold and clear upstream, becoming muddier toward Glenwood Springs.

Camping: Good on BLM land from the Pumphouse to Dotsero.

Side Hikes: A trail beginning at the Pumphouse access leads 1.5 miles up Gore Canyon. Trails climb Dead Horse and Grizzly Creeks in Glenwood Canyon.

Guides and References:

- *Upper Colorado River Recreation Area: Kremmling to Glenwood Canyon* (BLM). Includes maps; best source for this section.
- Wheat, *Floater's Guide to Colorado.*
- *Glenwood Canyon of the Colorado River* (BLM). Photocopy map with notes.
- Rennicke, *Rivers of Colorado* and *River Days.* Essays.

Maps:

- **USFS:** *Routt NF; White River NF.*
- **USGS 7.5':** *Kremmling, Sheephorn Mtn, Radium, McCoy, State Bridge, Blue Hill, Burns North, Burns South, Sugarloaf Mtn, Dotsero, Shoshone, Glenwood Springs, Storm King Mtn, New Castle.*
- **BLM 1:100:** Vail, Glenwood Springs, Steamboat Springs.

Auto Shuttle: Roughly same as river miles except Gore Canyon shuttle, which is longer. For shuttle services contact Rancho del Rio Resort at mile 11 on Pumphouse Run.

Logistics: As of 1993 the only legal **put-in for Gore Canyon** is at the Colorado Highway 9 bridge just south of Kremmling. However, boaters using this access must paddle 5 miles of flatwater down to the head of the canyon. The BLM is trying to secure new public accesses farther downriver. For current information contact the BLM in Kremmling.

To reach the **Pumphouse access,**turn west off Highway 9 onto Trough Road a half mile south of the bridge over the Colorado near Kremmling, drive about 10 miles, turn right on Pumphouse Road, and descend to the river. Along the way, stop at Inspiration Point to look down into Gore Canyon.

Access at State Bridge is either at State Bridge Lodge (private, fee) or on the left bank below the Colorado Highway 131 bridge (public). Unpaved Trough Road connects State Bridge and the Pumphouse, providing **alternate accesses** at Radium Recreation Site (take Grand County Road 11 off Trough Road) and at Yarmony Bridge (see essay).

Dotsero is located where I-70 crosses the Colorado just above the mouth of the Eagle River. A minor road generally follows the river between State Bridge and Dotsero, providing several alternate accesses. **Shoshone Power Plant boat ramp** is about 7 miles east of Glenwood Springs on I-70. **Grizzly Creek access** is about a mile and a half downriver. Construction of I-70 has eliminated many alternate accesses. A popular take-out area is just below South Canyon Rapid on the right. (Check with the BLM in Glenwood Springs for up-to-date information.)

The West's most famous river, the Colorado, springs to life along the spine of the Continental Divide and flows west by southwest across the state of Colorado. This is only the first leg of its 1,440-mile journey to the Gulf of California,[1] and it hasn't always been called the Colorado this far upriver. Throughout the white settlement of the West in the nineteenth century, it was known as the Grand River—hence Colorado place names like Grand Junction (at the confluence of the Grand and the Gunnison) and Grand County. The Colorado River proper began at the confluence of the Green and the Grand in eastern Utah. In 1921 the Colorado Legislature, in a fit of boosterism, renamed the Grand after its state of origin.[2]

The Colorado and its uppermost tributaries—the Fraser, the Blue, and the Eagle—drain a salient or pocket where the Continental Divide departs from its usual north-south course and bulges eastward toward Denver.[3] Most of the precipitation in Colorado falls on this wetter west side of the Rockies, but most of the people live on the drier east side. As a result, snow falling west of the Continental Divide in Rocky Mountain National Park barely melts before dams and tunnels shunt it through the mountains toward Denver. The largest of these trans-Divide diversions, the Colorado-Big Thompson Project, takes much of the Upper Colorado's flow—over 200,000 acre-feet per year. The Fraser and the Blue are also heavily tapped by diversions.

Gore Canyon

The dam situation could be even worse. Not far downstream from its headwaters, the Colorado passes one of the West's major unused dam sites. After meandering placidly

[1]The Colorado is the sixth longest river in the continental United States. Its huge watershed, which measures 242,000 square miles at its mouth and includes western Colorado, southwestern Wyoming, most of Utah, almost all of Arizona, and part of New Mexico, California, and Nevada, represents a remarkable eight percent of the surface area of the lower 48 states. Because most of its drainage area is arid, the total yearly flow is not enormous: an average of 13 million acre-feet.

[2]According to geographic convention, the Green was considered the true "source" of the Colorado because it was longer than the Grand. So the renaming of the river by the Colorado Legislature had the effect of creating a new, full-length Colorado River and shifting its headwaters from the Wind River Range in Wyoming to the Rockies near Denver.

[3]See Region II map. At the salient's northeast corner are the headwaters of the Upper Colorado itself. Then the Divide runs south along the peaks of the Front Range west of Denver, its western slopes drained first by the Fraser, then by the Blue. Near Breckenridge the Divide bends southwest around the headwaters of the Eagle before resuming its southerly course.

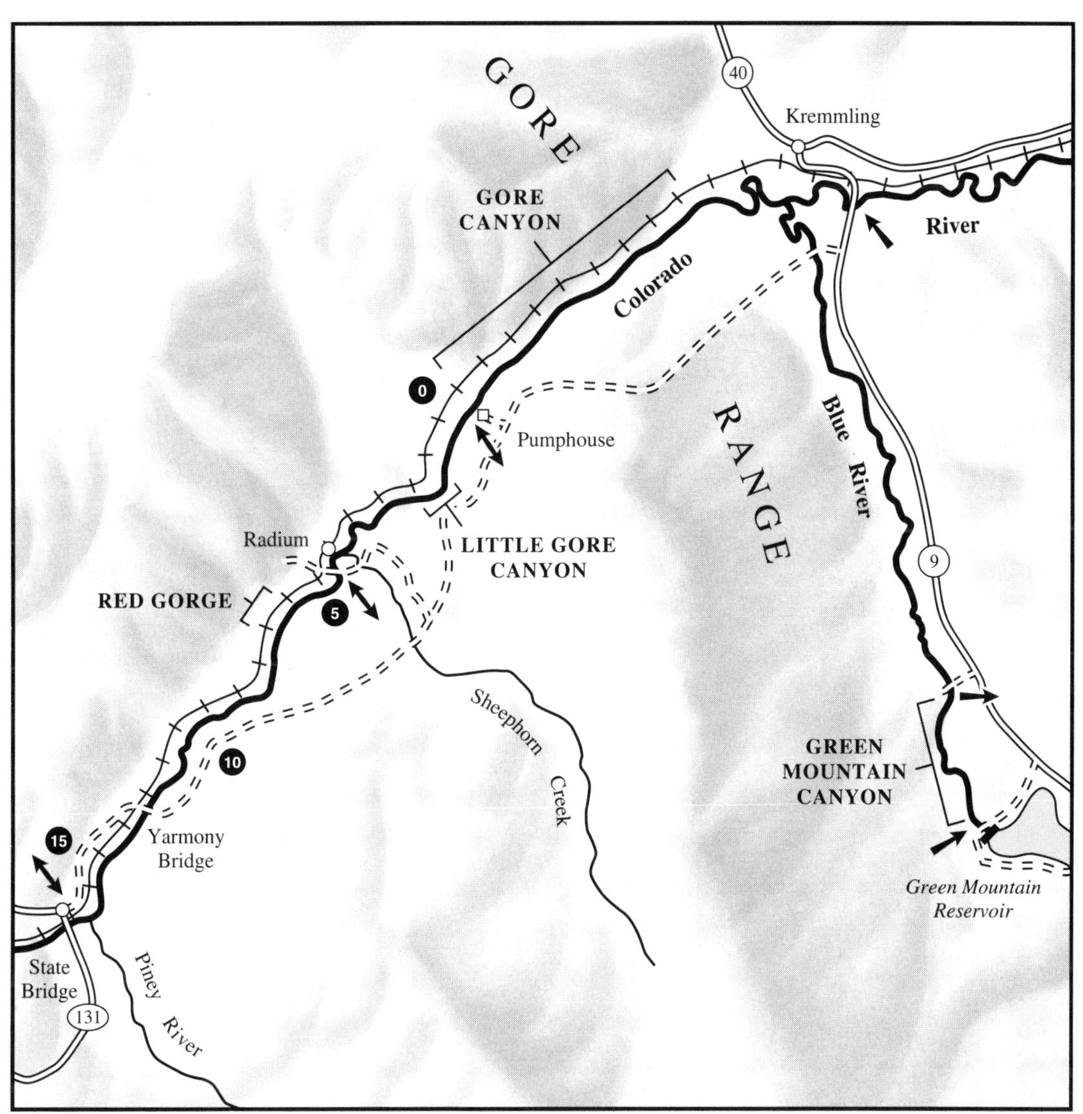

Upper Colorado and Lower Blue

across the broad alpine amphitheater of Middle Park and past the mouth of the Blue River, the Colorado runs smack into the Gore Range[4], a wall of 11,000' peaks standing like an enormous natural dam across the river's path. The river was here before the most recent uplift of these mountains and held to its course as the range rose around it, carving in the process the five-mile-long, 2,500'-deep gash known as Gore Canyon.

A man-made plug in that spectacular abyss would turn the broad flatlands of Middle Park into one of the biggest reservoirs in Colorado. Around the turn of the century the U.S. Reclamation Service (predecessor of the Bureau of Reclamation) proposed to do just that, but the Denver & Rio Grande railroad also sought to exploit Gore Canyon as the easiest passage through the mountains. Fortunately, the railroad won the ear of President Teddy Roosevelt, and track-laying prevailed over dam-building.

Today the Colorado runs free and very wild through Gore Canyon, which has by far the most difficult whitewater on the entire river from its headwaters to its mouth. Here one can plainly see the ongoing battle between water and stone as the river hews a pounding, jarring passage through bedrock of granite, gneiss, and schist. In a little over five miles the Colorado drops 340' with a peak gradient of 120 ft./mi. The current vaults over vertical falls and boils

[4]Named for Lord George Gore, a British explorer who led an expedition to the area in the 1850's.

into dark undercuts. Huge, jagged boulders—tumbled into the river decades ago by blasting for the railway—litter the channel.

Gore Canyon was first run in 1962 by the legendary kayaker Walter Kirschbaum in a canvas-decked boat. It was first paddled without portage by either Roger Paris or Dr. Walt Blackadar in the late 1970's. Rob Wise led the first raft descent in 1977. Today, the annual Gore Canyon Whitewater Race sees kayakers and rafters vying for the fastest downriver time; the winning kayaker usually paddles the canyon in about 20 minutes, while rafters make the descent in just under half an hour.

Gore Canyon should be attempted only at low to moderate flows, and only by teams of experts prepared for scouting and portages. Even at low water in late summer and fall, Gore overwhelms many excellent boaters. Above 2,000 cfs the run is very powerful and treacherous and should be attempted only by the most daring experts. **The following description includes only a few of the biggest Class V drops in Gore Canyon.** Many difficult spots have never been named.

Put in at the Highway 9 bridge south of Kremmling, or at downstream sites if available (see **Logistics**). Five miles of flatwater lead to the dramatic canyon entrance. The first rapid inside the canyon is a rocky 9' drop known as **APPLESAUCE** (V-) (also called **Gateway** or **Pearly Gates**). Watch for a horizon line and a big eddy on the left just above the drop. Not far downstream is the most difficult passage in the canyon, **GORE RAPID (V+)**, a third of a mile of continuous, constricted whitewater that includes three especially notable drops: **THE GORE,** with a treacherous undercut, followed quickly by **DOUBLE POUROVER** or **TWIN HOLES,** and finally the 8' drop of **PYRITE FALLS.** Scout carefully and consider portaging. A swim here would be devastating.

Downstream is a series of three railroad tunnels on the right in the deepest part of the canyon. Beside the second tunnel is a 12' vertical plunge known as **TUNNEL FALLS (V+),** which is hard to spot from upstream and can be portaged on the left. Below the falls is a short, technical rapid leading to a horizon line that announces **TOILET BOWL** (V), a very nasty and deceptive river-wide keeper hydraulic. Immediately downstream is the last major rapid, **KIRSCHBAUM** (V), a long, complex, rocky slalom. Easier water leads to the **take-out** on the left at the **Pumphouse access,** 11 miles below the Highway 9 put-in.

Pumphouse to Dotsero

The **Pumphouse access** marks the start of the Pumphouse Run, Colorado's second most popular stretch of river (after Browns Canyon of the Arkansas). Here, below Gore Canyon, the Colorado reverts to a moderate and pastoral character, winding for the most part through a shallow, semi-arid valley sparsely mantled in sagebrush, juniper, and pinyon pine. Two short mini-canyons—carved from the same dark bedrock as Gore—and a wealth of big waves at high water provide some scenery and excitement. Numerous bridge pilings and abutments, especially below State Bridge, may prove as challenging as the rapids. Also, watch for occasional undercut walls. A fair amount of flatwater separates the roller coaster rides.

During peak season, June through August, the Pumphouse Run is thronged with commercial rafting outfitters and clients on the 15-mile jaunt to State Bridge. Boaters looking for more privacy may prefer part or all of the 45 miles from State Bridge to Dotsero. A busy railroad follows the entire 60 miles, and a lightly-travelled dirt road paralleling many sections provides frequent access.

From the Pumphouse (mile 0) the river flows through open terrain for a mile and a half before entering short but scenic **Little Gore Canyon.** Here is found **NEEDLE EYE (II+),** where big midstream reversals form at higher flows. At mile 4.5 a bridge crosses the river at the hamlet of Radium, and just downstream on the left is an **alternate access at Radium Recreation Area.**

A mile and a half below Radium the walls of **Red Gorge** close in, rising to over 1,500' before opening up again about a mile downstream. Look for **YARMONY (II+)** near the middle of the gorge (mile 6.7), with a big boulder/hole on the right. **Rancho del Rio** resort is on the left at mile 11 (private access, fee). A half mile downstream the shuttle road crosses the river at **Yarmony Bridge (access).** The Piney River enters on the left at mile 14.5. At mile 15 the hamlet of **State Bridge** is on the right, with **accesses** at State Bridge Lodge (private, fee) or on the left bank below the Colorado Highway 131 bridge (public).

Below State Bridge the highway parallels the right bank for some seven miles, after which an unpaved road follows the river much of the way to Dotsero, crossing it several times and providing accesses. The hamlet of Bond is on the right at mile 18, and McCoy Waterwheel is on the left at mile 22. **Catamount Bridge (access)** crosses the river where Big Alkali Creek enters on the left at mile 30. Just downstream is **ALKALI (II).** Five miles farther, the road crosses the river again at **Burns (access).** About a mile below this bridge is **RODEO (III-)**, two abrupt drops among sharp rocks. It was formed by a landslide and is the biggest rapid on the run.

The BLM's **Pinball Point access** is on the right at mile 39. ***HAZARD.*** Just over a mile downstream is a dangerous **railroad bridge** at a left bend. Use caution again at Twin Bridges (mile 43) where the road and railroad both cross. **HORSE CREEK (II+)** is at mile 48. The road crosses the river for the last time (**access**) at mile 51, then follows the right bank for the final seven miles to the **Dotsero take-out** where I-70 crosses the Colorado and the Eagle enters on the left. Few boaters continue down the mild stretch below Dotsero; I-70 follows this section closely, and the river slows and stills as it approaches Shoshone Dam some nine miles downstream.

Glenwood Canyon, South Canyon, and Downstream Runs

This section is shown on the map in the ***Crystal*** *chapter.*

Below Dotsero the river gradually enters **Glenwood Canyon,** a narrow, cliff-lined gorge carved through colorful layers of sandstone, limestone, and granite. At one time Glenwood may have been Colorado's finest wilderness canyon. Today it is home to a dam, a diversion, a railroad, and a highway recently widened into a four-lane interstate. Construction of I-70 has caused a host of problems, including access closures, parking restrictions, shuttle delays, and alteration of the bank and the streambed. Some accesses are being improved. As a result our information on this section is subject to change. Still, Glenwood Canyon does offer fine scenery and whitewater.

At the heart of Glenwood Canyon, the Colorado has carved nearly 3,000' down through sedimentary rock to expose ancient granite bedrock, whose resistance to erosion produces powerful rapids. But the biggest whitewater in Glenwood was lost years ago to Shoshone Dam. Completed in 1909 to supply electricity to Denver, the dam creates a long slackwater pool at the top of Glenwood Canyon and diverts some 1,400 cfs through a tunnel, returning it to the river at Shoshone Powerhouse two and a half miles downstream.

At high flows, when overflow water escapes past the dam, spectacular Class V and VI drops appear in the normally dry diversion section. **Boating here is not recommended.** Although these big rapids have been run by adventurous experts, the uppermost drop in particular is extremely dangerous, and the entire section has been marred and altered by highway construction. Most boaters should simply admire these rapids from shore when the water is up.

River running resumes at a concrete boat ramp just below Shoshone Powerhouse. In the next mile the river runs though a series of big-water rapids before calming again as it reenters softer strata. The drops include **UPPER SUPERSTITION, LOWER SUPERSTITION, THE WALL, TOMBSTONE,** and **MAN-EATER.** At low and moderate flows these are relatively straightforward Class III to III+ drops, but at high water they run together and develop some of the biggest hydraulics and waves in the state, warranting extra caution and a full Class IV rating. A popular **access at Grizzly Creek,** two miles below the powerhouse, allows boaters to repeat the run. Bicycle shuttles are easy on the bike path that follows the right bank through this section.

Below Grizzly Creek the whitewater eases, and less experienced boaters can begin their float trips. Glenwood Canyon continues for some five miles, then opens as the Colorado passes Glenwood Springs and the mouth of the Roaring Fork on the left. State Highway 82 crosses the Colorado here. Just below the Roaring Fork confluence is an **alternate access** on the right at **Two Rivers Park.**

About three miles below Glenwood Springs, the walls rise again as the river enters **South Canyon,** a scenic cut through tilted rock strata. Here the whitewater surges briefly back to life before the canyon opens and the rapids ease. Six miles below Glenwood Springs, a pair of bridges across the river where South Canyon Creek enters on the left mark the site of **SOUTH CANYON RAPID (II+).** Although this is the largest rapid below Grizzly Creek, it is generally straightforward except for big waves that develop at high flows and a potentially dangerous bridge pier on the right. Most boaters **take out** downstream on the right, either immediately below the rapid at a steep site, or a few hundred yards farther down at an easier spot (check with the BLM in Glenwood Springs for information on these accesses).

Two miles below South Canyon Rapid, the railroad crosses the river (beware of **hazardous bridge abutments**). Then Canyon Creek enters on the right, and the canyon begins to open.

About a mile below Canyon Creek is **Tibbetts Landing,** a good **access** on the right that can be reached from I-70 eastbound. By the time the river reaches the town of New Castle, 19 miles below Grizzly Creek, the whitewater has faded and only a few easy riffles remain. **New Castle Park** (right bank) offers a good **take-out,** or a put-in for boaters interested in the easy water downstream.

The Colorado meanders placidly for 15 miles from New Castle to Rifle, with occasional riffles breaking the calm. This scenic one-day float offers a surprising amount of solitude despite the proximity of the railroad and I-70. Another 50 miles from Rifle to DeBeque can be floated,[5] but beware of diversion weirs in these lower reaches. Several towns in this section are developing river parks and alternate accesses.

---

[5]Earl Perry, *Rivers of Colorado,* has detailed information on the section from Rifle to DeBeque, but the book has been out of print since the early 1980's.

Captain Samuel Adams Explores the Colorado

The first "descent" of Gore Canyon is one of the strangest river stories in Western lore. The adventure was led by "Captain" Samuel Adams, a smooth-talking young man obsessed with exploring the Colorado ever since he saw the broad, flat lower river from a steamboat near Yuma, California, in 1865. Others dismissed the river as an obstacle, but Adams saw in its rolling waters limitless potential for navigation, commerce, and agriculture, imagining river banks abounding with irrigated crops. For Adams, the Colorado was to be the Mississippi of the West, a thoroughfare between the Atlantic and the Pacific.

In 1869 Adams learned that Major John Wesley Powell was about to embark on the very exploration of which Adams had so long dreamed. In May Adams appeared at Powell's put-in camp at Green River, Wyoming, hoping to talk his way onto the expedition. But the Major concluded that the Captain would be a windbag and a nuisance and sent him packing.

Adams raced for the laurels. Apparently deciding that one arm of the river was as good as another, he hurried south to Breckenridge, where he talked ten men into joining him for the first descent of the Grand River, as the Colorado above the Green River confluence was then known. On July 12, 1869, starting from an elevation of about 10,000' on the upper reaches of the Blue (a tributary of the Grand), Adams set forth with four wooden boats hastily built at the launch site, bound for glory and the Gulf of California.

It says a lot about Adams' perseverance that it took the river a month to stop him. Descending the Blue to its confluence with the Grand, the expedition lost two boats and a good part of its provisions, and five men deserted. Only six men floated into the jaws of Gore Canyon (which Adams called "Grand Canyon"). For a week they struggled to line the remaining two boats through the raging whitewater; in the end both were swept away and smashed to splinters, whereupon three more men walked out. Adams and his last two men managed to run several miles below Gore Canyon by building two log rafts, each of which was wrecked on a rock. Finally, on August 13, 1869, somewhere upstream from the Eagle River confluence, Adams reluctantly gave up his quest—but not his vision. His diary entry said,

"I am fully satified that we had come over the worst part of our rout in 95 miles we had descended about 4500 feet. The vallies were open up river, the mountains bec[ame] smooth the pine and cedar larger everything indic[ated] that a prosperous passage was ahead of us had we been in a position to have gone on."

Adams insisted that at the end of the run, he could almost see the narrow gap to the southwest that was all that remained between him and the flat reaches of the Lower Colorado. This was sheer fantasy. In fact, that "narrow gap" above the Lower Colorado was some 800 miles away. True, Gore Canyon was the worst of the whitewater, but between Adams and his goal were the big rapids of Glenwood Canyon, Westwater Canyon, Cataract Canyon, and the Grand Canyon.

Undaunted, Adams spent much of the next decade unsuccessfully trying to publicize his "explorations," to persuade Congress to reward him, to contradict the findings of Powell's successful journey down the Colorado, and to convince the public that the Colorado was a highway for commerce rather than an obstacle to the development of the West. He finally retreated to Beaver Falls, Pennsylvania, where he practiced law and died in 1915 at the age of 87, still claiming that he had been wronged by an ungrateful nation.

—Adams' story is told in Wallace Stegner, *Beyond the Hundredth Meridian,* and Doug Wheat, *The Floater's Guide to Colorado.*

Blue River

1. Dillon Dam (8,760')
to Green Mountain Reservoir (7,960').
III; 21 miles; 40 ft./mi. Shorter runs possible.

2. Green Mountain Canyon:
Green Mountain Dam (7,690')
to Spring Creek Road Bridge (7,500').
III-; 4 miles; 45 ft./mi.

Drainage Area and Average Annual Discharge: 600 sq. mi. and 220,000 af below Green Mountain Reservoir.
Season: Varies with dam releases. Generally May to mid-July on upper run, June through September in Green Mountain Canyon.
Recommended Levels: 400–2,000 cfs.
Flow Information: "WaterTalk," (303) 831-7135; **5*1*** for flow below Dillon Reservoir, **5*2*** for flow below Green Mountain Reservoir.
Special Hazards: Very cold water. Low bridges on upper run.
Permits: Not presently required.
Managing Agency: Dillon RD, P.O. Box 620, Silverthorne, CO 80498; (303) 468-5400.
Commercial Raft Trips: Yes. For references contact the managing agency.
Land Ownership: Mixed private and National Forest. **Solitude:** Good.
Scenery: Excellent alpine setting; clear water.
Wilderness: No on upper run, yes on lower.
Guides and References:
- Wheat, *Floater's Guide to Colorado.*
- *Blue River Whitewater Boating* (USFS). Photocopied information pamphlet.

Maps: USGS 7.5': *Run 1:* Dillon, Willow Lakes, Squaw Creek. *Run 2:* King Creek.
- **USFS:** *Dillon RD.*

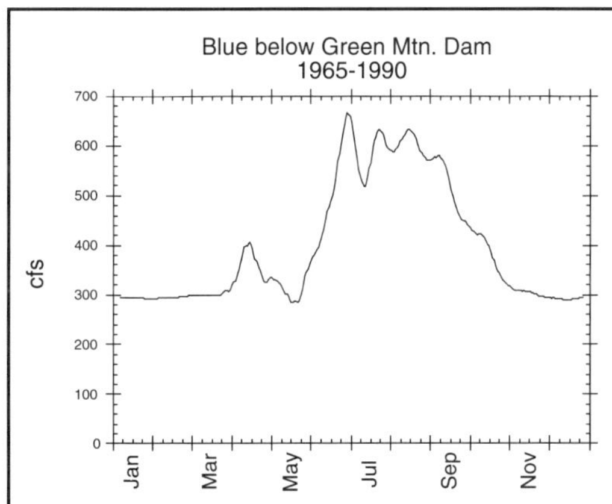

Logistics: *Upper Run:* Access to most of the run between Dillon Dam and Green Mountain Reservoir is via Colorado Highway 9 north of I-70 near Silverthorne. (The only area not served by Highway 9 is the short Blue River Park section, which is located between Dillon Dam and I-70 at the south end of Silverthorne.) Downstream from (north of) I-70, the highway follows the river all the way to Green Mountain Reservoir, providing easy shuttles. The unnamed **put-in** on Forest Service land for the **Boulder Canyon** stretch (see essay) is 4 miles north of I-70 on Highway 9. The **intermediate access at Sutton Wildlife Area** is roughly 7 miles north of I-70 and just upriver from Blue River Campground. **Columbine Landing** is on the left bank just above one of the highway bridges over the river, about 10 miles north of I-70 and 3 miles downriver from Blue River Campground. **Take-outs at Green Mountain Reservoir** are reached via a spur road off Highway 9. Refer to the *Arapaho NF* map for details.

Lower Run: To reach the **put-in for Green Mountain Canyon,** follow Highway 9 to the north end of Green Mountain Reservoir. Turn onto the dam access road, drive about two miles, cross the dam and bear right down to the put-in. To reach the **take-out** return to the highway, turn left, drive north about 2.5 miles, turn left again onto Spring Creek Road and drive about a mile to the bridge over the Blue.

The Blue, like many other rivers in the Upper Colorado basin, is heavily tapped for agricultural and urban use. By the time the various players are finished wrangling over water rights and acre-feet, many miles of the Blue lie deep under water. Fortunately for river runners, however, some lovely scenery and good whitewater remain—including beautiful Green Mountain Canyon, one of the best short runs in the Denver area.

Geography wants the river to run west from its Continental Divide headwaters, but Denver wants it to run east. The city's solution is Dillon Reservoir, completed in 1963. Dillon diverts much of the Blue's flow into a 24-mile-long trans-Divide tunnel leading to the South Platte basin and, ultimately, the faucets and sprinklers of greater Denver.

About the only thing keeping some water in the Blue is downstream agricultural demand, which pre-dates urban water claims. But the Blue in its natural state doesn't suit the ranchers, either: the river runs high in late spring, but the irrigators want their water in middle and late summer. The ranchers' solution is Green Mountain Reservoir, which since 1942 has blocked the river a few miles above Kremmling.

Dillon Dam to Green Mountain Reservoir

The longest remaining run on the Blue lies between the two reservoirs, in a 20-mile-long valley bounded by the Gore Range on the west and the Williams Fork Mountains on the east. Flows here are often sporadic; adequate releases from Dillon Dam are usually early in the season. The water comes from the bottom of the reservoir and is extremely cold. Most of this run is Class I and II, with some Class III near the midpoint. Highway 9 follows the river, providing accesses and easy shuttles. Most boaters float only short sections, not the full 20 miles. Two reaches in particular receive most of the attention.

The first popular stretch is a very short run at **Blue River Park,** just south of Silverthorne between Dillon Dam and the I-70 bridge. This half-mile romp features an artificial rapid which was created in 1981 as a whitewater slalom course. Boaters normally repeat this run several times rather than continue downriver. Immediately downstream is a diversion weir, followed by Class I–II riffles along the outskirts of Silverthorne. Trailer parks, gravel pits, and a sewage treatment plant mar these first four miles below I-70. Efforts are being made to increase their potential for river recreation.

The other popular stretch is scenic **Boulder Canyon,** some ten miles north of Silverthorne. Here steep slopes confine the river to a narrow course for two miles, and the Blue plunges quickly through its largest rapids. Boaters can choose from **alternate put-ins: (1) An upper access** at an unnamed left-bank site on Forest Service land along Highway 9, four miles north of I-70. Putting in here allows a long Class II warm-up before reaching the canyon itself and lengthens the run to Columbine Landing to 7.5 miles. (2) **A lower put-in** four miles farther downstream at the Sutton Wildlife Area fishing access, on the left bank just above Blue River Campground, starts boaters right at the head of Boulder Canyon for a 3.5-mile run.

Blue River Campground marks the approximate beginning of Boulder Canyon. The real action begins about a half mile downstream where Boulder Creek enters on the left. The Blue abruptly rounds a blind right bend and barrels through **BOULDER CREEK RAPID (III+)**, the biggest on the river. Class II and III drops continue for another couple of miles before the Blue enters a broad valley and the whitewater fades. The popular **Columbine Landing take-out** is on the left bank just above the Highway 9 bridge near the mouth of the canyon.

Below Columbine Landing the Blue continues through eight miles of an open valley and Class I–II water leading into Green Mountain Reservoir. **Few boaters run this stretch** because **portages** are usually required at **diversion weirs** and at a **low pipeline crossing** about five miles below Columbine Landing. Since the surrounding land is almost all private, portaging could lead to trouble with landowners.

Aside from Boulder Creek Rapid, **low bridges** present the greatest hazard on the Blue between Dillon Dam and Green Mountain Reservoir, especially at higher flows when the river runs dangerously close to their undersides. Approach with caution. If in doubt, portage.

Green Mountain Canyon

Emerging from its icy rest behind Green Mountain Dam, the Blue cuts through a steep, V-shaped canyon between the summits of Green and Little Green Mountains. This short but enchanting four-mile run (shown on the map in the **Upper Colorado** chapter) offers fine wilderness boating within a relatively brief drive of Denver. Here the Blue tumbles through enjoyable Class II and easy Class III whitewater that challenges intermediates but also leaves them time to admire the outstanding scenery. No roads or trails penetrate the canyon, making this a favorite place for city-weary boaters to unwind. Those familiar with this short reach have learned to linger and play. Consider bringing along a fishing rod: the first couple of miles below the dam are gold-medal trout water.

Upstream diversions keep the flows low, so this run is best suited to kayaks, canoes, and small rafts. Below the standard **take-out** at the Spring Creek Road Bridge, the river meanders through an open valley for some ten miles to its confluence with the Colorado near Kremmling.

Eagle River

Minturn to Dotsero

1. Minturn (7,970') **to Avon** (7,410').
IV5; 7 miles; 65 ft./mi.

2. Avon to Eagle (6,550').
III; 22 miles; 40 ft./mi.

3. Eagle to above Dotsero (6,140').
II; 16 miles; 27 ft./mi.

Drainage Area and Average Annual Discharge: 950 sq. mi. and 424,000 af near Gypsum.
Season: May through July. This unregulated river typically peaks in June, then rapidly recedes to unrunnable levels by late summer.
Recommended Levels: 750–2,000 cfs. Difficulty increases dramatically at higher flows.
Flow Information: "WaterTalk" system, (303) 831-7135; **5*14*** for flow below Gypsum.
Special Hazards: Dowds Junction Chutes. Low pipeline below Minturn. Cold water.
Permits: Not presently required.
Managing Agency: *(1) Above Edwards:* Holy Cross RD, White River NF, P.O. Box 190, Minturn, CO, 81645; (303) 827-5715. *(2) Below Edwards:* BLM, Glenwood Springs RA, P.O. Box 1009, Glenwood Springs, CO, 81602; (303) 945-2341.
Commercial Raft Trips: Yes. For a list of outfitters, contact the BLM in Glenwood Springs.
Land Ownership: Mixed public and private above Eagle, mostly private below. Refer to *White River NF* map or contact BLM.
Scenery: Good. Mountain valley, wooded banks.
Solitude: Good. **Wilderness:** No.
Guides: Wheat, *Floater's Guide to Colorado.*
Maps: USGS 7.5': *Minturn, Edwards, Wolcott, Eagle, Gypsum, Dotsero.*
• **USFS:** *White River NF.* Covers all runs.

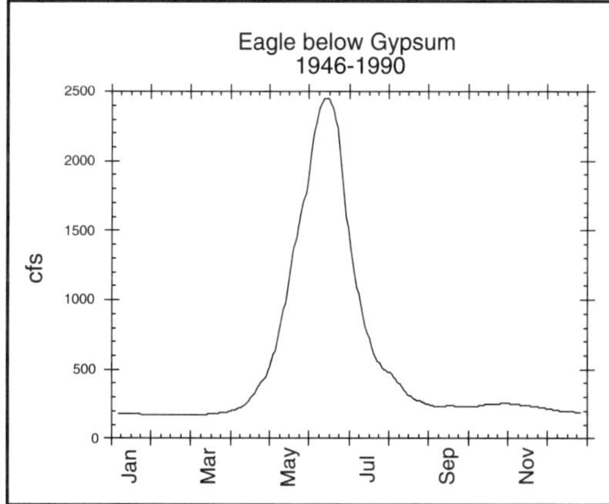

Logistics: Accesses just above and below Minturn are off U.S. 24 south of I-70. I-70 and old U.S. 6/24 follow the Eagle from Dowds Junction to Dotsero, providing numerous alternate accesses and short, easy shuttles. For specific sites, refer to the essay and contact the USFS and BLM.

Gathering snowmelt from the Sawatch and Gore Ranges, the Eagle River cascades more than 4,000 vertical feet in just 60 miles from its headwaters on the Continental Divide to its confluence with the Colorado at Dotsero. In this short reach the Eagle offers the full range of whitewater—suicidal to serene and everything in between.

Unlike many west slope rivers, the Eagle feeds no major reservoir, and trans-Divide diversions swallow only a moderate part of its flow. So the Eagle shows the wild mood swings of a largely untamed mountain river, from the gushing exuberance of peak snowmelt in June to the lazy doldrums of low water in late summer.

The Eagle shares its valley with a railroad, several towns, an interstate highway, and the sprawling Vail ski resort just up Gore Creek. Surprisingly, the river still enjoys a degree of solitude. For much of its length the Eagle runs through an intimate, tree-lined inner canyon, recessed within the broader valley that carries the car and train traffic. It's no wilderness run, but it's better than it looks on the map.

Redcliff Gorge

Experts only. Daring boaters find plenty of privacy on the run above Minturn, but at the risk of their lives. At its confluence with Homestake Creek near Redcliff, about seven miles above Minturn, the Eagle plunges into a dark, forbidding chasm—the kind of place that sends sane boaters into a dead faint and makes hairball kayakers salivate. In four miles the river plummets 500 vertical feet through a continuum of cataracts rating up to Class VI, with any number of constantly changing **log hazards** and a Class VI **low bridge hazard** with metal debris in the river below the bridge. This run has a small watershed and a short season. Interested boaters should inquire locally and refer to Doug Wheat, *The Floater's Guide to Colorado.* The vast majority should stay away.

Minturn to Avon

The whitewater is less threatening but still difficult below Minturn, where the Eagle makes a gradual transition from narrow alpine gorge to broad mountain valley. There are **at least two major hazards.** The first is a **low pipeline** across the river on the downstream side of a minor bridge, about 1.5 miles below Minturn and a quarter mile above the I-70 bridge. This is a serious hazard for kayaks at higher flows and for rafts at all levels. Stop well upstream and scout carefully. Take out here to avoid the big rapid just downstream.

About 400 yards below the bridge is the second hazard, legendary **DOWDS JUNCTION CHUTES** (V), also called **Minturn Chutes.** This tumultuous quarter mile begins at the mouth of Gore Creek west of Vail, where I-70 crosses the Eagle. The river, unnaturally constricted between the highway on the left and the railroad on the right, vaults over a series of thundering, river-wide holes. Logs and debris often accumulate at a hazardous railroad bridge just downstream, and the current sweeps directly into the log jam. Several lives have been lost here. Scout the rapid thoroughly from the left bank and approach it with extreme caution, particularly at higher flows (2,000 cfs and up).

To run the Chutes, **put in off U.S. 24,** either above Minturn at the mouth of Cross Creek, or below town, about a third of a mile above the I-70 bridge. The higher put-in allows a couple of miles of Class IV- warm-up (watch for debris in the river). The lower put-in is only a few hundred yards above the Chutes. You can avoid the rapid by putting in downstream on the left bank—a wise move, especially at high water.

Below the Chutes the Eagle runs through steady Class III and IV water punctuated by big holes. Boaters must maneuver around bridge pilings and other man-made hazards. A possible **take-out** for this section is the wooden bridge at Avon, five miles below Dowds Junction.

Avon to Eagle

Below Avon the river valley gradually widens and becomes drier, but challenging whitewater continues through much of this section. I-70 and U.S. 6/24 provide many alternate accesses, allowing boaters to choose runs suited to their skills and tastes. Five miles of rapids below Avon lead into a brief section of calm water where Lake Creek enters on the left near the trailer-park settlement of Edwards.

I-70 crosses the river eight miles below Avon. Three miles farther downstream is the hamlet of Wolcott on the left bank. A third of a mile below Wolcott the railroad crosses to the left bank, marking the site of **BRIDGE RAPID** (III), followed shortly by **HIDDEN RAPID** (III). Downstream is a good **access** on the left at the BLM's **Wolcott Campground.**

Just under a mile below Wolcott Campground, I-70 crosses to the right bank, marking the site of **INTERSTATE (III).** Downstream the Eagle cuts through the sedimentary deposits of Red Canyon. Near the end of Red Canyon, about 2.5 miles below the I-70 bridge, is **DIVERSION** (III); then the rapids gradually fade. The best **take-out** is at a new boating access on the right bank at the **Eagle County Fairgrounds.** Not far upstream is the site of an old diversion weir with hazardous concrete rubble and rebar. Plans call for removing the remaining debris. Inquire locally and approach this section with caution.

Eagle to Dotsero

*See map in **Crystal** chapter.*

The final 16 miles from the Eagle County Fairgrounds to the Colorado confluence offer pleasant scenery and generally easy water. The entire stretch is bounded by the interstate on the right and the railroad on the left. In the eight miles from Eagle to the town of Gypsum (good intermediate **access at Gypsum Campground**), the river drops steadily through an open valley at 35 ft./mi. In the final eight miles below Gypsum, the gradient eases to less than 20 ft./mi. and the river meanders lazily through a valley bounded by bluffs. The **last good take-out** is on the right a mile above the Colorado confluence, at a BLM site known as Lava Flow. Just downstream is **LAVA FLOW** (II+); however, boaters running this rapid will not be able to take out at the Colorado confluence below Dotsero (no access). The next public access is on the right bank of the Colorado, 2.5 flatwater miles below the confluence at the BLM's Burnt Tree Ridge site.

Roaring Fork

Slaughterhouse Bridge to Glenwood Springs

1. Slaughterhouse Bridge (7,700') to Upper Woody Creek Bridge.
IV+6 (V6 over 1,500 cfs); 5 miles; 80 ft./mi.

2. Upper Woody Creek Bridge to Basalt.
III4 (IV over 2,000 cfs); 12 miles; 60 ft./mi.

3. Basalt to Carbondale.
II (III over 4,000 cfs); 13 miles; 45 ft./mi.

4. Carbondale to Glenwood Springs (5,725').
II (III above 4,000 cfs); 13 miles; 25 ft./mi.

Drainage Area and Average Annual Discharge: 185 sq. mi. and 175,000 af at Aspen; 1,451 sq. mi. and 943,000 af at Glenwood Springs.
Peak Recorded Flow: 19,000 cfs at Glenwood Springs (July 1, 1957).
Season: May–July above Carbondale, several weeks longer below. Typically peaks in June.
Recommended Levels: *Run 1:* 600–1,500 cfs; *Run 2:* 800–2,000; *Runs 3 & 4:* 1,000–4,000.
Flow Information: "WaterTalk", (303) 831-7135; **5*30*** for flow "near Aspen" (slightly underestimates *Run 1* flow; **5*31*** for flow "below Maroon Creek" (gives approximate flow on *Run 2,* underestimates flow on *Run 3*); **5*32*** for flow "at Glenwood Springs" (*Run 4*).
Special Hazards: Slaughterhouse Falls (*Run 1*).
Permits: Not required.
Managing Agency: White River NF, P.O. Box 948, Glenwood Springs, CO 81602; (303) 945-2521.
Commercial Raft Trips: Yes, except Run 1. For references contact Colorado State Parks, Chatfield Office Center, 13787 S. Highway 85, Littleton, CO 80125; (303) 791-1954.

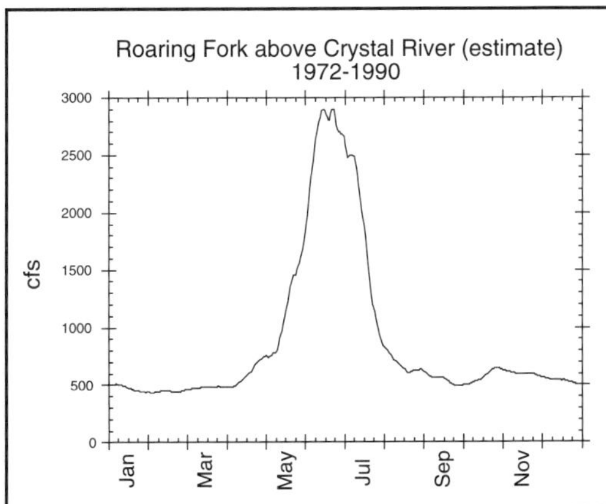

Land Ownership: Almost all private.
Scenery: Very good. Small canyon above Basalt, broader valley below.
Solitude: Good, though civilization isn't far away.
Wilderness: No.
Fishing: Gold Medal Trout Stream below Carbondale.
Water: Cold and clear but not drinkable.
Camping: USFS campgrounds above Aspen and up the Crystal River. Several private campgrounds along Highway 82.
Side Excursions: Aspen resort. Three wilderness areas in upper watershed.
Guides and References:
- *A Guide to the Roaring Fork, Fryingpan, and Crystal Rivers* (USFS). Map-guide.
- Wheat, *Floater's Guide to Colorado.*
- Chronic, *Roadside Geology of Colorado.*

Maps: USGS 7.5': *Aspen, Highland Peak, Woody Creek, Basalt, Leon, Carbondale, Cattle Creek, Glenwood Springs.*
- **USFS:** *White River NF.*

Logistics: Colorado Highway 82 follows the river from Aspen to Glenwood Springs, providing easy shuttles and frequent access. To reach **Slaughterhouse Bridge,** turn north off Highway 82 onto Cemetery Road just west of Aspen and drive a little over a mile to the river. To reach **Upper Woody Creek Bridge,** turn east off Highway 82 about three quarters of a mile north of the Snowmass Village turnoff, then drive about a quarter mile to the river. (Alternate route: take Cemetery Road downriver from Slaughterhouse Bridge.) **Access near Carbondale** is either at Groome's Campground (private, fee), on the right bank just below the Highway 133 bridge, or half a mile downstream at the old Sutank Bridge, not far above the Crystal River confluence. **Access in Glenwood Springs** is at one of two sites: (1) Veltus Park (difficult for rafts) on the left (west) bank of the Roaring Fork, a half mile above the Colorado confluence; or (2) Two Rivers Park on the right bank of the Colorado, just downstream from the Roaring Fork confluence.

ROARING FORK

If asked to name their state's most beautiful river, many Colorado boaters would choose the Roaring Fork, whose watershed embraces some of the finest scenery in the Rockies. Near its Continental Divide headwaters the river gathers snowmelt from two spectacular wilderness areas on the west flank of the Sawatch Range, the state's highest mountains. Then, true to its name, the river roars exuberantly down to Aspen. Here it winds quietly for several miles through alpine meadows, momentarily overshadowed by the glitter and glamour of America's most famous ski resort.

The Roaring Fork comes into its own again as it leaves Aspen behind. Swollen by waters rushing down from the magnificent Maroon Bells Snowmass Wilderness, the Roaring Fork tumbles headlong into a scenic mountain canyon that reverberates with the thunder of expert whitewater. Farther downstream the river's mood moderates, but its lower reaches continue to offer outstanding scenery and breathtaking views of the peaks where it was born. It's not surprising that the Roaring Fork is one of Colorado's most popular whitewater rivers.

Ice-age glaciers helped shape the watershed of the Roaring Fork and the character of its whitewater. A river of ice once filled the entire upper canyon, reaching as far as the present site of Aspen before retreating again when the climate warmed. The melting glacier left behind a large moraine of rock lying like a natural dam across the river's path. The river pooled behind the moraine and, over time, filled the lake with sediment to produce the broad meadows seen today above Aspen. Novice boaters sometimes enjoy floating through these lush, grassy flats.

Just downstream, the river tumbles abruptly over the edge of the moraine, funneling into a natural spillway that ranks as one of the premier expert whitewater runs in the region. This dangerous and demanding section is known as the Slaughterhouse Run, taking its inauspicious name from a bridge just northwest of Aspen that serves as the put-in access.

Below Slaughterhouse Bridge the Roaring Fork plunges into a narrow canyon, pinched between massive Red Mountain on the right and smaller Red Butte on the left. The Roaring Fork is only a small river at this point, made even smaller by a trans-Divide diversion upstream. Big boulders litter the riverbed, splitting the current into narrow, complex channels and chutes navigable only by experts in kayaks or self-bailing rafts. Less than a mile into the run, a treacherous waterfall forces most boaters to portage.

The river churns through five steep, boulder-choked miles before the action lets up near Upper Woody Creek Bridge. The run becomes much more difficult as flows increase. Above 2,000 cfs, even experts should approach it with extreme caution.

Below the Slaughterhouse Run the river moderates somewhat, though the gradient remains steep most of the way to Basalt. Several large tributaries increase the flow, and the rapids in this middle section take on more of a big-water flavor. Many commercial rafters use the section from Upper Woody Creek Bridge to Basalt.

At Basalt the Fryingpan River joins the Roaring Fork, bringing water from the Continental Divide to the east. At one time the Fryingpan contributed substantial volume, but trans-Divide diversions to the Arkansas River basin have severely depleted its flow. Even so, boaters occasionally find enough water to enjoy a scenic 13-mile advanced run on the Fryingpan from Ruedi Reservoir to Basalt. The last five miles above the Roaring Fork confluence are the most rewarding.

The Roaring Fork is milder in its final 26 miles from Basalt to Glenwood Springs. The river's gradient eases as it enters a broader, more open valley. The lightly-used section from Basalt to Carbondale winds across broad terraces of glacial cobbles and gravels washed down from the upper watershed. The current often runs in braided channels and divides around islands, especially in the four miles from Catherine Bridge to Carbondale. Route-finding can be a problem here, and as a result most boaters avoid this section.

At Carbondale the Crystal River joins the Roaring Fork, nearly doubling the flow. Below Carbondale the Roaring Fork again winds easily through glacial deposits, with outstanding upstream views of Mt. Sopris towering above the landscape. Just above Glenwood Springs the canyon walls close in again, and the river rolls through a series of big-water, joy-ride rapids known as the "Cemetery Run." Many boaters float just this section, using a bridge halfway between Carbondale and Glenwood Springs as a put-in.

Mile by Mile Guide

*See map in **Crystal** chapter.*

1. Slaughterhouse Bridge to Upper Woody Creek Bridge

Note: Only a few of this run's many Class IV–V+ rapids are mentioned here.

0 **PUT-IN** on the right bank at Slaughterhouse Bridge. An old railbed—now a foot and bike path—follows the right bank downstream. Before launching, use this path to **scout the entire first mile,** where the river drops a total of 100'. A hundred yards below the put-in is the first rapid, **ENTRANCE EXAM (IV+).** If you fail the exam, *do not continue.* Things get tougher downstream.

0.6 The river slows briefly before thundering over **SLAUGHTERHOUSE FALLS (VI). Recognition:** The river turns right into a large eddy, then sharply left just downstream from a mass of grey rock on the left. **The rapid:** A 6' drop over a dangerously undercut ledge with a treacherous reversal. Several people have drowned here. Scout and **portage** on the right.

Below the falls Maroon Creek enters on the left, adding considerable flow. From here to Upper Woody Creek Bridge the river is steep, technical Class IV+ (V at high water).

2.5 Abandoned bridge is the site of an annual kayak competition. An emergency trail climbs the left bank to Aspen Airport. Downstream, a short section of easy water gives boaters a breather before the action begins again.

4.5 Upper Woody Creek Bridge. **RIVER ACCESS.** Take out on the right or continue downstream.

2. Upper Woody Creek Bridge to Basalt

4.5 Upper Woody Creek Bridge. Brush Creek enters on the left just downstream, and Woody Creek enters on the right at mile 6. The river is still steep, but the channel is not as constricted or boulder-choked as it is upstream. Class II and III rapids continue most of the way to Basalt.

8.5 Lower Woody Creek Bridge, a popular **RIVER ACCESS.** A dirt road leads a quarter mile to Highway 82 above the left bank.

12.5 **TOOTHACHE (IV).** A long, steep rapid visible from the highway. Just downstream is **SNOWMASS (III+),** where the river pounds through big holes at a left bend. Below the rapid Snowmass Bridge provides a **RIVER ACCESS** at mile 13, and just below the bridge Snowmass Creek enters on the left.

14.5 Wingo Bridge (Highway 82). Difficult **RIVER ACCESS.** Half a mile downstream is a railroad bridge. Fun but straightforward rapids continue to Basalt.

17 The Fryingpan River enters on the right at Basalt. **RIVER ACCESS** downstream on the right along Highway 82.

3. Basalt to Carbondale

17 Basalt **RIVER ACCESS** (see above). Few boaters float the Basalt-to-Carbondale stretch (see essay). Sopris Creek enters two miles downstream on the left, and Highway 82 runs farther from the river for the following 9 miles. A mile below Sopris Creek is a **RIVER ACCESS** at Hooks Bridge.

25 Steep **RIVER ACCESS** at Catherine Bridge. Most boaters avoid the next several miles, where the river runs through braided channels, making route-finding difficult.

29 Highway 133 crosses the river, leading to Carbondale a mile to the south. Just downstream on the right is a **RIVER ACCESS** at Groome's Campground (private, fee). A half mile farther downstream, beyond the railroad bridge, is another **RIVER ACCESS** at the old Sutank Bridge.

4. Carbondale to Glenwood Springs

29.5 **RIVER ACCESS** at Groome's Campground or Sutank Bridge (see above). Downstream the Crystal River, the Roaring Fork's largest tributary, enters from the left.

36 An old metal bridge crosses the river, and just downstream is the newer Westbank Bridge. **RIVER ACCESS** at either bridge. A frontage road leads to Highway 82. Many boaters put in here for the six-mile "Cemetery Run" down to Glenwood Springs. Below the bridges the river drops into a shallow canyon cut into the surrounding developed benchlands.

39.5 The river runs through a series of straightforward rapids with roller-coaster waves. The finale comes at **CEMETERY (II+; III at higher flows)**, a quarter mile of haystacks where the river winds around several shallow bends. Watch for a big hole at the top at high water. The rapid is named for Rosebud Cemetery, just downstream and out of sight above the right bank. A mile below the rapid, the Fourmile Road bridge crosses the river.

42.5 Veltus Park on the left offers a **possible take-out** (difficult for rafts). Downtown Glenwood Springs is on the right. Many boaters continue a half mile to the Colorado River confluence, then float a few hundred yards down the Colorado to an easier **TAKE-OUT** on the right at Two Rivers Park. Boaters may also continue down the Colorado (see the **Upper Colorado** chapter).

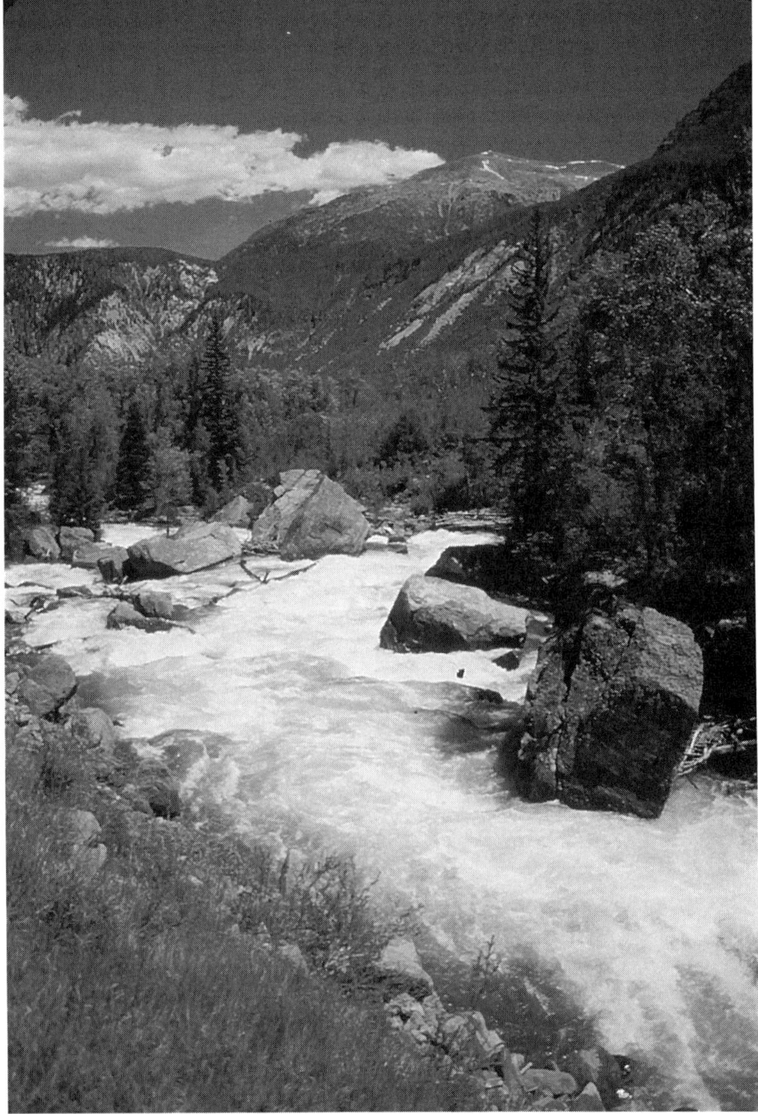

Meatgrinder Rapid, Crystal River *Bill Cross*

Crystal River

Rapid Creek Bridge to Carbondale

1. Rapid Creek Bridge (7,700') to Bogan Flats Campground.
IV (V at high flows); 2 miles; 100 ft./mi.

2. Bogan Flats Campground to Redstone Campground.
IVp (Vp at high flows); 8 miles; 50 ft./mi.

3. Redstone Campground to Avalanche Creek.
VI; 4 miles; 95 ft./mi.

4. Avalanche Creek to End of Canyon.
IV (V at high flows); 6 miles; 60 ft./mi.

5. End of Canyon to Carbondale (6,100').
II (III at high flows); 7 miles; 40 ft./mi.

Total Length: 27 miles. **Gradient:** 60 ft./mi.
Drainage Area and Average Annual Discharge: 167 sq. mi. and 221,000 af at Redstone.
Peak Recorded Flow: 4,180 cfs (June 25, 1983).
Season: May–late July.
Recommended Levels: 600–2,000 cfs.
Flow Information: "WaterTalk", (303) 831-7135; **5*12*** for flow at Redstone. Or call Aspen Kayak School, (303) 371-7739.
Special Hazards: Possible log hazards. Very cold water. Dangerous culverts below Bogan Flats Campground (*Run 2*). Meatgrinder Rapid (*Run 3*). Possible barbed wire fences (*Runs 2 and 5*). See **Mile Guide.**
Permits: Not presently required.
Managing Agency: Sopris RD, White River NF, P.O. Box 309, Carbondale, CO 81623; (303) 963-2266.

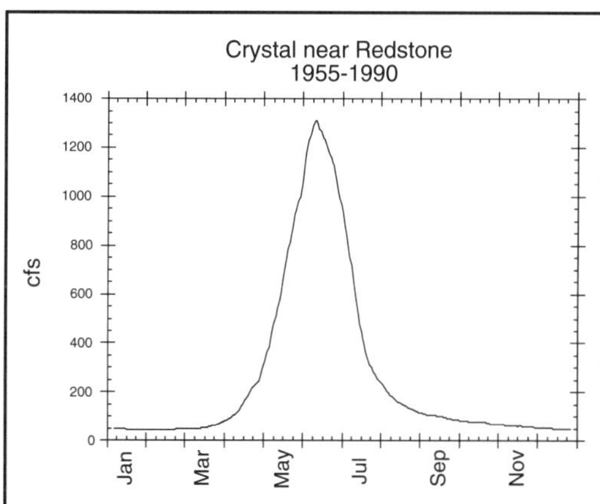

Commercial Raft Trips: None at this time.
Land Ownership: Mixed National Forest and private from Marble to the end of the canyon; private downstream.
Scenery: Excellent. Wooded mountain river on first four runs, open valley on last run.
Solitude: Fair to Good. Roads close by except first two miles.
Wilderness: No.
Fishing: Stocked rainbow trout.
Water: Ice cold and clear.
Camping: Several USFS campgrounds along the river (see **Mile Guide**).
Side Hikes: Trails into the Maroon Bells Snowmass Wilderness, including one up Avalanche Creek.
Side Excursions: Maroon Bells Snowmass Wilderness. Yule marble quarry outside Marble. USFS Road 314, which continues up the Crystal above Marble and becomes 4-wheel-drive as it climbs to Schofield Pass.
Guides and References:
- *A Guide to the Roaring Fork, Fryingpan, and Crystal Rivers* (USFS). Map-guide available from managing agency.
- Wheat, *Floater's Guide to Colorado.*

Maps:
- **USGS 7.5':** *Marble, Chair Mtn, Placita, Redstone, Mt. Sopris, Carbondale.*
- **USGS 1:100:** *Carbondale.*
- **USFS:** *White River NF.*

Logistics: Colorado Highway 133 and USFS Road 314 (Marble Road) follow the Crystal from Carbondale to the **uppermost put-in** near Marble, providing easy shuttles, good scouting and many accesses (including several in addition to those mentioned here). The **lowermost take-out** is just northwest of Carbondale, about a mile upstream from the Roaring Fork confluence at the bridge next to the Colorado Rocky Mountain School. For information on other accesses off Highway 133, refer to the **Mile by Mile Guide.** To reach Bogan Flats Campground and accesses above that point, follow Highway 133 south from the town of Redstone 5 miles and bear left onto USFS Road 314.

CRYSTAL

By geographic good luck, the Crystal has avoided most of the injuries civilization has inflicted on neighboring streams. Its sheltering mountains are far enough from Denver to discourage ski resort development. Its canyon offers no easy passage to any place in particular, sparing it from four-lane highways. Most important, the intervening Elk Mountains separate its watershed from the Continental Divide, leaving engineers with no easy way to divert the river's crystalline waters to Denver.[1]

From snowfields high in the Maroon Bells Snowmass Wilderness, the Crystal runs first west, then north to join the Roaring Fork near Carbondale. Though it carries some sediment at higher flows, the Crystal usually runs as clear as its name implies, thanks to low erosion rates in the hard limestone and marble bedrock of its upper watershed.

Local geology also explains much of the river's human history. The upper canyon's rich deposits of snow-white marble attracted miners, who established quarries around the town of Marble. The famous Yule Quarry produced flawless stone used in such national monuments as the Lincoln Memorial and the Tomb of the Unknown Soldier. The quarry was abandoned for many years but is back in operation today.

The Crystal is a classic high-mountain stream brimming with vigor, freshness, and purity. The short season, steep gradient, narrow V- shaped canyon, and numbingly cold water all contribute to its alpine flavor. Dark cloaks of evergreen and brilliant stands of aspen deck the riverside slopes. To complete the idyllic picture, the Crystal is relatively uncrowded by Colorado standards; most river runners and tourists stay on the well-beaten path that follows the Roaring Fork to the town of Aspen.

Nevertheless, a highway and a minor road run alongside the Crystal for most of its length, detracting from the solitude but providing frequent access. The river is sometimes confined between banks of rip-rap from the highway on one side and an old road bed on the other. In general the Crystal is quite swift and narrow. The channel is too constricted for large rafts in many places.

Although experts occasionally put in as far upstream as Marble, most regard the Rapid Creek Bridge some three miles below town as the upper limit of navigation. The first section below this bridge, known as "Marble Canyon" or "Bogans Canyon," offers continuous Class IV action in a secluded forest setting. Below Bogans Flat Campground the river moderates somewhat, but it remains challenging down to the resort community of Redstone. Boaters must portage around two dangerous highway culverts on this section and should scout them before putting in (see **Mile Guide**).

Below Redstone Campground the Crystal becomes temporarily unrunnable as it crashes through a stunning cascade known as Meatgrinder. (We classify this rapid as unrunnable rather than Class VI, though rumor has it that a few gonzo kayakers have negotiated it.)

The most popular stretch of the Crystal (and site of an annual downriver race) is the six miles from the mouth of Avalanche Creek to the end of the canyon (Class IV). Here the rapids are somewhat less demanding, and there are no portages. The final seven miles to Carbondale offer pleasant floating through more pastoral terrain with fine upstream views of Mt. Sopris, one of Colorado's most majestic peaks.

On all runs, but especially above Redstone, boaters should beware of possible sweepers and log jams in the narrow channel. Hypothermia is always a threat on this swift, ice-cold, high-elevation river.

---

[1]Dam builders have not forgotten the Crystal. Two water districts have frequently sought to block the river near Placita, a few miles above Redstone. Dams have also been proposed near Marble and in the narrow gorge above Avalanche Creek. The Crystal is a state Scenic Byway and should be a prime candidate for National Wild and Scenic protection, but as of 1993 no federal studies were under way. Among the groups working to preserve the Crystal is NORS (see appendix for address).

Mile by Mile Guide

0 — **PUT-IN** at Rapid Creek Bridge, where USFS Road 314 (Marble Road) crosses the river about 3 miles below the town of Marble. Just downstream the river enters a narrow canyon with over a mile of nonstop Class IV.

1.5 — Bogan Flats Campground (USFS) on the left, an unofficial **RIVER ACCESS.** (Boaters who aren't camping should park on the road, not in the campground.) Downstream, the rapids continue for over a mile, then ease momentarily as the Crystal runs through open meadows

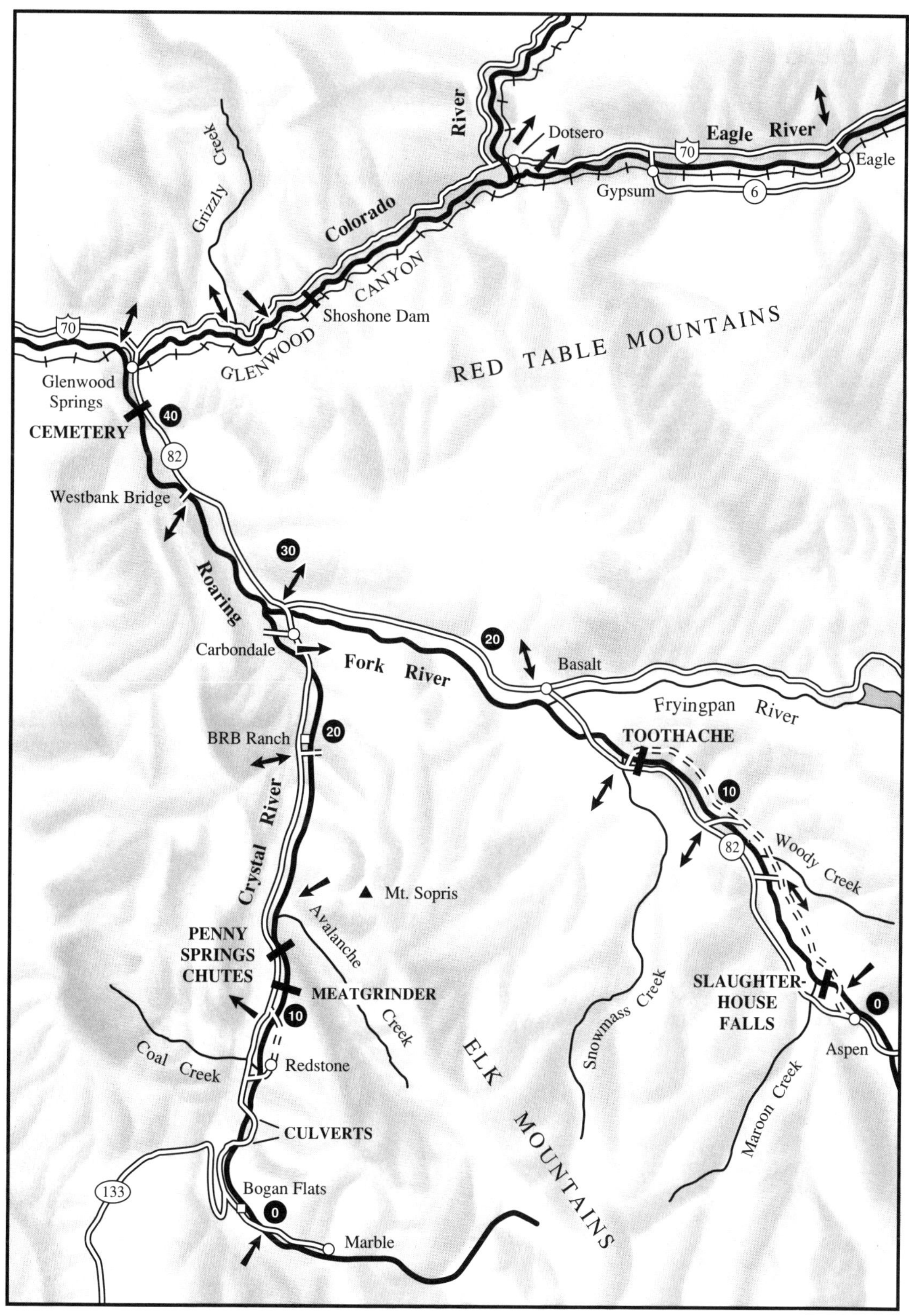

Eagle, Roaring Fork, and Crystal

near the ghost town site of Placita on the left at mile 4.2. *HAZARD.* As of 1993, a private residence here still had a **fence** strung across the river! Downstream, Highway 133 follows the river closely for several miles.

4.8 *HAZARD.* Shortly after the whitewater resumes below Placita, the river runs through a **dangerous culvert** under Highway 133. **A second dangerous culvert** is a mile farther downstream. **Portaging is strongly recommended for all craft at both culverts.** Scout carefully from the highway *before* making this run—the culverts are often clogged with brush and debris, and clearance is tight even for kayaks at most water levels. If you are not certain that you can catch an eddy above each culvert, do *not* attempt this section of river. A kayaker drowned here in 1990. Below the second culvert are a couple of miles of steep, rocky Class IV drops.

6.3 Hayes Creek enters on the left, with a scenic falls visible above the highway. Just downstream, Big Kline Creek enters on the right.

8.3 Redstone Bridge (possible **RIVER ACCESS**). Historic resort town of Redstone, with its famous inn, on the right. Coal Creek, a major tributary, enters on the left below the bridge. Downstream the river temporarily eases.

10 A bridge crosses the river from Highway 133 to Redstone Campground (USFS) on the right bank. *HAZARD.* This bridge is the **last take-out** before **MEATGRINDER (U), a mandatory portage** a few hundred yards downstream. Here the Crystal cascades more than 100 vertical feet in a half mile. The rapid is often clogged with debris, and the portage is long and difficult.

12.3 USGS gauging station on the right bank, opposite the highway, marks the first **RIVER ACCESS** below Meatgrinder. Before putting in here, carefully scout the half-mile-long Class V rapid just downstream. This drop, sometimes called **PENNY SPRINGS CHUTES** after a nearby hot springs, lies in a mile-long section of narrow canyon where the river is constricted by rip-rap on both sides. Boaters can avoid this difficult section by putting in farther downstream at Avalanche Creek.

13.5 Avalanche Creek, a major tributary, enters on the right. A jeep road and then a trail follow the creek up into the Maroon Bells Wilderness. Just downstream is a popular **RIVER ACCESS.** The next 6 miles are the most popular section of the Crystal. The gradient is still steep (60 ft./mi.), but the channel is less constricted. Some half dozen minor bridges cross the river between Avalanche Creek and the end of the canyon.

17 **MARBLE** (IV+), named for marble blocks in the river. This drop is only slightly tougher than other rapids in this stretch.

19 A minor bridge crosses the river just above the private BRB Ranch, a popular **RIVER ACCESS** on the left. Downstream, the canyon opens and the whitewater eases, though the Crystal continues to drop at a good clip (40 ft./mi.) down to the Roaring Fork. *HAZARD.* Possible barbed wire fences below this point.

23.5 Highway 133 crosses the river, providing a difficult **RIVER ACCESS** (swift water). Just downstream is another somewhat awkward **RIVER ACCESS** where a minor bridge crosses the river at a fish hatchery. A mile beyond the hatchery, the river begins to pass the outskirts of Carbondale on the right.

26.5 A bridge crosses the river at the Colorado Rocky Mountain School, providing the last **TAKE-OUT** before the confluence with the Roaring Fork half a mile downstream. A kayak slalom race is held each May on this section.

South Platte River

1. North Fork of the South Platte (Bailey Canyon): Bailey (7,700') to Pine.
IV+p; 12 miles; 82 ft./mi.

2. North Fork of the South Platte: Buffalo Creek Bridge (6,620') to Confluence.
III+; 11 miles; 51 ft./mi.

3. South Fork of the South Platte: Deckers (6,385') to Confluence.
II3; 15 miles; 20 ft./mi.

4. Urban South Platte: Chatfield Dam to Globeville Landing.
IIp; 19 miles; n.a.

Drainage Area and Average Annual Discharge: *North Fork:* 130 sq. mi. / 95,000 af above Bailey. *South Fork:* 1,752 sq. mi. / 122,400 af near Deckers.

Season: *North and South Forks:* Variable, May–Sept. *Urban South Platte:* April–Oct. Releases (controlled by Denver Water Board) may vary widely.

Recommended Levels: *North and South Forks:* 300–800 cfs. *Urban South Platte:* 400–3,000 cfs.

Flow Information: "Water Talk", (303) 831-7135; **1*42*** for North Fork at Grant (above Bailey); **1*40*** for South Fork near Deckers; **1*50*** for South Platte at South Platte (just below the confluence).

Special Hazards: Portages in Bailey Canyon.

Permits: Not presently required.

Managing Agency: The Forest Service has partial jurisdiction over the North and South Forks. For information contact South Platte RD, 11177 W. 8th Ave., Lakewood, CO 80225-0127; (303) 236-9431.

Commercial Raft Trips: Not at this time.

Land Ownership: North and South Forks are mixed National Forest and private. Urban South Platte is private with public parks and accesses.

Scenery: Excellent in Bailey Canyon (wooded gorge). Good on lower North Fork and South Fork (mountain valleys). Greenway on Urban South Platte.

Solitude: Excellent in Bailey Canyon, good to fair on South Fork.

Wilderness: Yes in Bailey Canyon, no on other runs.

Fishing: Excellent on both forks. South Fork is a Gold Medal Trout River.

Water: Cold and clear (but not recommended for drinking) on the North and South Forks. Water quality on the urban stretch is improving but still only fair.

Camping: USFS campground on South Fork.

Guides and References:

- Wheat, *Floater's Guide to Colorado.*

Maps:

- **USGS 7.5':** *North Fork:* Bailey, Pine, Platte Canyon. *South Fork:* Deckers, Platte Canyon. *Urban South Platte:* Littleton, Fort Logan, Englewood, Arvada, Commerce City.
- **USGS 1:100:** *Bailey* covers North and South Forks.
- **USFS:** *Pike NF* covers all but Urban South Platte.

Logistics: *North Fork:* To reach the **upper put-in,** follow U.S. 285 to Bailey, turn east on Wellington Lake Road, and drive a half mile downstream to the bridge over the river. To reach **Pine,** drive northeast on U.S. 285 to Pine Junction, then southeast on Colorado Highway 126 to Pine.

The **take-out** is at the minor bridge (private) about a quarter mile west of the town center. **Buffalo Creek** is located where Highway 126 crosses the river below Pine; a dirt road follows the left bank from the bridge to the confluence, providing frequent access and short shuttles.

South Fork: Popular **put-ins** are near Deckers where Highways 126 and 67 intersect along the river, or farther downstream at Bridge Crossing Picnic Ground. An unpaved road follows the river downstream to the North Fork confluence, providing alternate accesses and short shuttles.

Urban South Platte: Refer to Denver street map.

SOUTH PLATTE

The South Platte begins as a gathering of tributaries in South Park, a broad alpine basin 60 miles southwest of Denver. From these headwaters on the eastern slope of the Continental Divide, the river runs east and north, carving a long canyon through the Front Range of the Rockies. At one time the river emerged from its stony walls onto the vast expanses of the high plains, but today it courses through a man-made canyon of concrete and steel—Denver.

The South Platte, Denver's river, has served its master in many roles. It was long abused as a convenient storm drain, sewer, and dump. Recently, the city has recognized its potential as an urban parkway. Of course the South Platte has been heavily tapped for the city's water supply: six dams block the river above Denver. The most recent, Strontia Springs, completed in 1984, buried most of Waterton Canyon, a spectacular wilderness gorge just above Denver beloved by anglers and boaters.

Nor can the South Platte and its tributaries alone meet the tremendous demand for water. A complex of dams, tunnels, and ditches diverts nearly half a million acre-feet of water annually from the wetter west slope of the Rockies through the Continental Divide and into the South Platte.

For years the Denver Water Board and the Army Corps of Engineers have pursued the biggest project of all, Two Forks Dam, which would block the South Platte just below the confluence of the North and South Forks, create the biggest mountain reservoir in Colorado, and complete the conversion of this once wild river into a chain of placid artificial lakes.

In addition to flooding 15 miles of the South Fork and seven of the North Fork, Two Forks would destroy a Gold Medal Trout Fishery and wipe out canyons enjoyed by an estimated half million recreationists each year. The only way to fill this giant holding tank would be with increased diversions from the Upper Colorado basin on the west slope of the Divide.

This billion-dollar nightmare may never see the light of day. In 1990 the Environmental Protection Agency handed dam-builders one of their most stunning defeats in memory by vetoing the mammoth project. The EPA decision cited damage to fisheries and recreation as well as Denver's lack of a water conservation program. The EPA may not have the final word, however; the Two Forks project may be resurrected in the future.

South Platte River Guide

North Fork of the South Platte

Draining a small watershed along the Continental Divide near Mt. Evans, the North Fork was a relatively minor stream until 1964. In that year the Harold Roberts Tunnel began diverting water from Dillon Reservoir on the Blue River and shunting it through the Divide to the North Fork. The added 80,000 acre- feet per year helps maintain low but boatable flows (300 to 700 cfs) on the North Fork through most of the summer and into fall. July is often the month with the most water. The Blue and Upper Colorado Rivers pay the price.

North Fork: Bailey Canyon

About 15 miles below Roberts Tunnel lies the narrow, forested gorge of Bailey Canyon, a lovely but demanding Class IV wilderness run punctuated by three much bigger rapids. Most boaters portage at least two of these drops, but recognizing them from upstream isn't easy, so make your first trip with someone who knows the run. Much of the land along the river banks is private, and there have been reports of problems with property owners.

Class III warm-up rapids begin below Bailey (mile 0). At mile 3 the river turns northeast, leaves the road, and enters Bailey Canyon. A low bridge just above the canyon may require portage. An old railroad grade along the river allows easy scouting and portaging.

About a half mile into the canyon, just below some Class III water, the river slows briefly at a right bend and vaults over **FOUR FALLS (U/p)**, a series of steep drops that **should be portaged on the right.** Class III and IV water continues to **SUPER MAX (VI)**, mile 4.5. This rapid is roughly 200 yards below a 90° bend to the left. Swift Class III water leads into the drop, so start your **portage on the left** ***well upstream.***

Deer Creek enters on the left at mile 5.7, with **DEER CREEK RAPID (IV)** just downstream. In 1992 boaters at least partially removed a dangerous railroad tie that was lodged in the channel and made the rapid a mandatory portage. Scout on the left, portage if necessary.

Class III and IV rapids continue to the take-out, and the canyon opens up. Watch for Pine Valley Ranch on the left at mile 10—a small diversion **weir** above the main lodge **usually requires portage. Take out** at the private bridge just above Pine (mile 11.7). There is less interesting water between Pine and Buffalo Creek.

North Fork: Buffalo Creek to Confluence

The next popular section of the North Fork lies below the Highway 126 bridge (mile 0) at the town of Buffalo Creek. A dirt road follows the left bank, providing frequent access and convenient scouting. Easy Class III rapids begin about a mile and a half below the bridge as the canyon narrows. Technical water continues for about two miles, easing just above the hamlet of Foxton on the left (mile 3.7).

A mile below Foxton, Last Resort Creek enters on the left and the river turns sharply right. Downstream lie four miles of Class III+ pool-and-drop rapids. Be alert for at least one low bridge on the lower part of the run that may require portage. The rapids finally ease after the town of Longview (mile 8.5). **Take out** on the left at the South Fork confluence (mile 10.5).

South Fork of the South Platte*

Due to access problems, few boaters launch above the resort community of Deckers. The first few miles below Deckers run through largely private land, and some disputes with landowners have been reported.

Most boaters favor the 11 miles from Bridge Crossing Picnic Ground to the confluence, where more of the river banks are public and the whitewater and scenery are better. A riverside road provides easy access—not just for river runners but for anglers, sunbathers, innertubers, and tourists who flock here on summer weekends. Most of the rapids are Class II, with one Class III, **THE CHUTES**, eight miles below Bridge Crossing. **Take out** at the North Fork confluence.

*Technically, this isn't the South Fork; according to the maps, that tributary is far upstream near the Continental Divide. However, local boaters most commonly refer to this section of the South Platte above the North Fork confluence as either the "South Fork" or the "Deckers-to-confluence" section.

South Platte: Waterton Canyon

Below the confluence of the North and South Forks is a small remnant of Waterton Canyon, most of which is now buried by Strontia Springs Reservoir. For a mile and a half the South Platte tumbles through some half dozen rocky, technical Class IV drops before stilling in the reservoir. No boating is allowed on the reservoir, so river runners must haul their boats back up the foot trail along the left bank to the confluence.

Urban South Platte

Below Chatfield Reservoir the South Platte passes through several suburbs, then enters Denver. Here the river is an urban waterway, marred in places by pollution, channelizing, industrial development, and weirs. Until recently this section's only attraction was convenience for Denver boaters: where else could you go after work on a Wednesday evening?

But a fresh wind is blowing on the South Platte. In the mid-1970's a consensus began to emerge in favor of restoring the river banks to their former verdure and converting the flood plain to a string of city parks. Today, cement and iron are giving way to trees and ponds. Pollution has been reduced, and waterfowl and wildlife have begun to return. At some weirs runnable spillways have been installed, while other weirs are being replaced by artificial rapids. At one site a permanent slalom course has been added. Even the Army Corps of Engineers has been enlisted in the effort.

The first community to recognize the potential of a restored South Platte was Littleton, the suburb immediately below Chatfield Reservoir; today the park-lined reach through Littleton makes a thoroughly enjoyable suburban float. Continuing downstream as far as the Interstate 70 interchange, other sections of the South Platte are enjoying new-found popularity with canoeists, kayakers, and rafters. One of the most popular runs extends from the Eighth Avenue boat launch to the Globeville Landing just above I-70.

Arkansas River

Granite to Cañon City

1. Granite Canyon, Pine Creek, and The Numbers: Granite (8,920') to Railroad Bridge Recreation Site.
III–VIp; 11 miles; 65 ft./mi. overall (120 ft./mi. in Pine Creek Rapid).

2. Frog Rock and Milk Runs: Railroad Bridge Recreation Site to Ruby Mountain Recreation Site.
III+; 15 miles; 41 ft./mi. overall (50 ft./mi. first 9 miles, 30 ft./mi. downstream).

3. Browns Canyon and Salida Runs: Ruby Mountain Recreation Site to Salida.
III4 and II3; 21 miles; 27 ft./mi.

4. Arkansas River Canyon: Salida to Parkdale.
III4; 46 miles; 28 ft./mi.

5. Royal Gorge: Parkdale to Cañon City (5,360').
IV5; 10.5 miles; 46 ft./mi.

Drainage Area and Average Annual Discharge: 611 sq. mi. and 365,000 af at Buena Vista; 2,548 sq. mi. and 595,500 af at Parkdale.

Peak Recorded Flow: 3,950 cfs (June 11, 1980) at Buena Vista; 6,310 cfs (June 26, 1983) at Parkdale.

Season: May–August. Warm weather arrives late and departs early at these high elevations. Peak runoff is normally in late May and June. Flows are usually minimal by September.

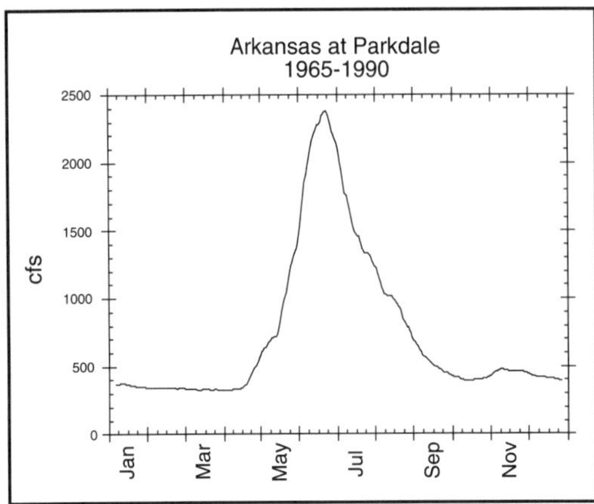

Recommended Levels: *Run 1:* 700–3,000 cfs at Wellsville; 1' to 4' on the Scott's Bridge gauge. *Runs 2–4:* 700–4,500 at Wellsville. *Run 5:* 700–3,000 at Wellsville.

Flow Information: WaterTalk, (303) 831-7135; 2*12* for flow near Wellsville, about 6 miles downstream from Salida. For readings on the informal gauge at Scott's Bridge on Run 1, call the managing agency.

Special Hazards: Pine Creek Rapid. Low bridges at high water. Remains of old bridges and diversion dams. Occasional logs.

Permits: Daily self-issued passes required; fees for camping and use of river access and recreation sites.

Managing Agency: Arkansas Headwaters Recreation Area (AHRA), P.O. Box 126, 307 W. Sackett, Salida, CO 81201; (719) 539-7289 or 539-7560.

Commercial Raft Trips: More than 60 outfitters; trips on every section of river. For references contact the managing agency.

Land Ownership: Mixed public and private.

Scenery: Good to excellent.

Solitude: Fair on popular sections (non-existent on summer weekends).

Wilderness: No. **Water:** Cold.

Fishing: Excellent. Mainly brown trout.

Camping: Public campsites (fee) at Ruby Mountain and Hecla Junction Recreation Sites (Browns Canyon); Rincon and Five Points Recreation Sites (Arkansas Canyon). Some commercial campsites along the river.

Side Excursions: Leadville. Princeton Hot Springs. Royal Gorge.

Guides and References:

- Staub, *The Upper Arkansas River: Rapids, History & Nature Mile by Mile.*
- Wheat, *Floater's Guide to Colorado.*
- Rampton, *River Runner's Guide to Brown's Canyon.*

Maps:

- **USGS 7.5':** *Granite to Salida:* Granite, South Peak, Harvard Lakes, Buena Vista West, Buena Vista East, Nathrop, Salida West. *Salida to Cañon City:* Salida East, Wellsville, Howard, Cotopaxi, Arkansas Mountain, Echo, McIntyre Hills, Royal Gorge, Cañon City.

- **USGS 1:100:** *Gunnison* sheet covers most of Granite to Salida section; *Cañon City* covers most of lower river.
- **USFS:** *San Isabel NF* covers most of run.
- Cassady and Calhoun, *Upper Arkansas River: Granite to Salida* and *Lower Arkansas River: Salida to Cañon City.*
- *Riverguide Bandana to the Arkansas* (Rivers & Mountains). Cloth map.

Auto Shuttles: Easy shuttles along highways; roughly same mileages as river.

Logistics: To reach the **put-in at Granite,** turn east off U.S. 24 onto County Road 397 and follow it to the bridge. **Scott's Bridge,** just below Number One Rapid (mile 6.3), is 10 miles north of Buena Vista off U.S. 24. To reach the current access, turn north on a dirt road just before crossing the bridge (contact the managing agency for updated information). To reach **Railroad Bridge Recreation Site** (mile 11), turn east off U.S. 24 some 8 miles north of Buena Vista onto County Road 371 toward Otero Pumping Station; cross the river, turn right (south), and drive just over 3 miles. There is private river access on the right bank at Johnson Village; inquire at Headwaters Equipment at this site, (719) 395-2409.

To reach **Fisherman's Bridge Recreation Site** (mile 24), turn east off U.S. 285 two miles north of Nathrop onto County Road 301, cross the river, and turn right at the top of the hill. **Ruby Mountain Recreation Site** (mile 26) is farther down the same road. To reach **Hecla Junction Recreation Site** (mile 34), turn east off U.S. 285 less than two miles north of the junction with Colorado Highway 291 onto County Road 194 and follow it about two miles. To reach **Stone Bridge,** turn east off 291 onto County Road 191. To reach **Big Bend Recreation Site** (mile 40), turn east off U.S. 285 four miles north of Poncha Springs onto County Road 165.

To reach **Salida** (mile 47), turn onto Colorado 291 from U.S. 285 or 50. The **Salida Boat Ramp** is upstream and **Riverside Park** is downstream from the F Street Bridge (both on the right bank). To reach **Vallie Bridge Recreation Site** (mile 65), turn east off U.S. 50 about two miles northwest of Coaldale onto County Road 45. The rest of the river accesses in the Arkansas Canyon are all on the right bank just off U.S. 50. The **put-in for the Royal Gorge, Parkdale Recreation Site** (mile 93.5), is two miles west of the Parkdale bridge, just off U.S. 50. To reach the **take-out at Centennial Park** (mile 104), exit U.S. 50 in Cañon City, turn south on Fourth Street, cross the river to the right bank, and turn right on Griffin Avenue. To reach the **lowermost take-out at the new River Station site,** turn south off U.S. 50 onto South Third Street.

The Arkansas is the nation's most popular whitewater river. Its fine variety of runs, good to excellent scenery, long season, and easy access attract hordes of boaters. More than 260,000 people floated the river in 1993, the great majority with the scores of commerical outfitters who operate an enormous flotilla of rafts. In addition, thousands of anglers and hikers enjoy the canyon.

The Arkansas also has America's most visible major whitewater, boasting more than 100 boatable miles within easy reach (and many within sight) of major highways flanking the river, which is less than three hours from Denver and one hour from Colorado Springs. The Arkansas can be dangerous at high water, but later in the summer, after peak runoff, moderate flows allow boaters of all skill levels to tackle its diverse rapids. Everyone will enjoy the splendid vistas of the many surrounding peaks more than 14,000' high.

The river's great surge in popularity over the last decade has led to some congestion, especially at popular accesses. A new managing agency, the Arkansas Headwaters Recreation Area (a partnership between the BLM and Colorado State Parks) is overseeing changes in access sites and regulations. Check with the managing agency for updated information and for new—or newly legal—access sites.

Much of the Arkansas' fame is due to its difficult rapids, which experts test at either end of the river: high up in Pine Creek Rapid and The Numbers, and far downstream in spectacular, sheer-walled Royal Gorge. But there is also whitewater for non-daredevils.

The most popular run is scenic Browns Canyon, where the river curves away from the highway and courses through rapids that are intermediate at low flows but require advanced skills at higher flows. Class III rapids dot the Salida-to-Cotopaxi stretch used for the annual FIB-Ark whitewater marathon. From Cotopaxi to Parkdale boaters will find intermediate water (more difficult at higher flows) and fine canyon scenery. The river has easy sections as well. The best are the short "Milk Run" from Johnson Village to Ruby Mountain Recreation Site and the 10-mile reach from Stone Bridge to Salida.

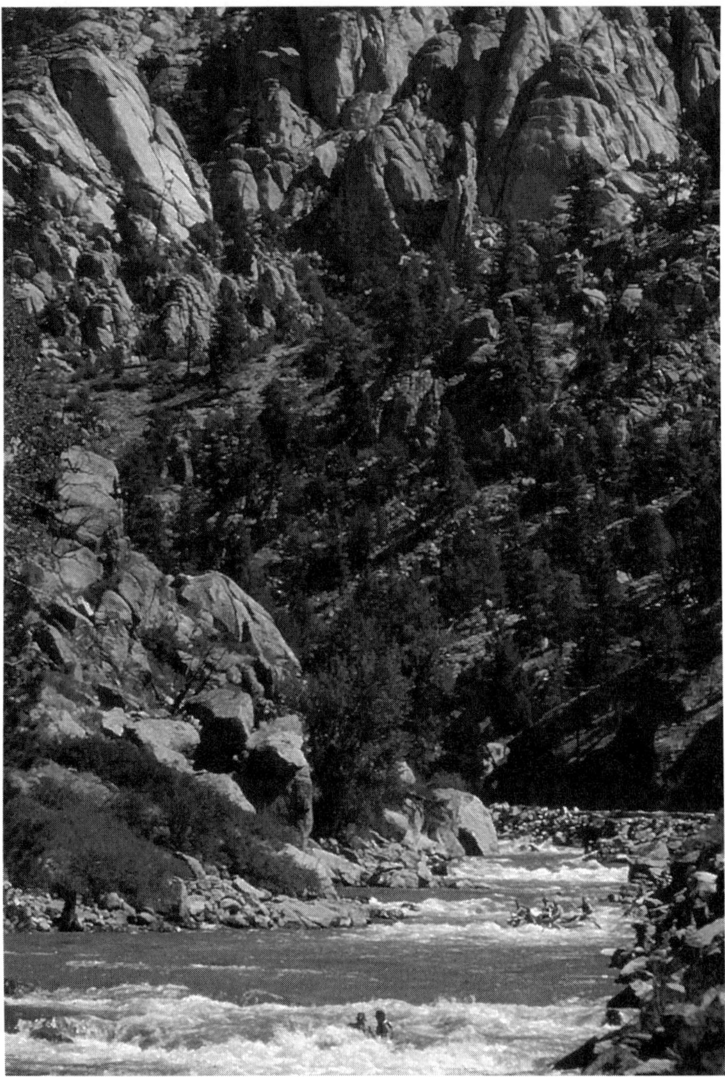
The Staircase, Browns Canyon, Arkansas River *Frank Staub*

For most of its 1,472-mile length the Arkansas[1] is a Great Plains river. It is the second-largest tributary of the Mississippi, after the Missouri. Whitewater boaters know only the uppermost sections of the Arkansas in the mountains west of Colorado Springs.

The Arkansas has long been an important travel route—first for Indians, then for explorers and wagon trains. Later came the railroads and today's busy highways. The first whites to explore the river were led by Zebulon Pike, an Army officer sent to map and explore the southwest reaches of the Louisiana Purchase in 1806.

The watershed of the upper Arkansas saw a brief gold rush around the time of the Civil War; then, in 1879, the discovery of rich silver deposits produced a period of more sustained mining activity centered around the boom town of Leadville near the river's headwaters. Shipping the ore out from Leadville proved quite difficult. The river was an obvious route, but the canyon was essentially impassable in many places—most notably at the dramatic vertical defile of Royal Gorge.

In the late 1870's two railroads, the Santa Fe and the Rio Grande, hungry for the tremendous profits that could be realized from the silver trade, began to push a rail line upstream through the Royal Gorge toward Leadville. Their bitter rivalry for exclusive control of the line up the Arkansas led to violence and sabotage. Ultimately, a compromise granted control to the Rio Grande Railroad. Today, this historic rail line follows the river all the way up to Leadville. The river-level stretch through the Royal Gorge still ranks as one of the world's most remarkable feats of railway engineering.

Fed by melting snow from the highest peaks of the Colorado Rockies, the Arkansas rises as a small mountain stream in a valley below Leadville. On either side tower the 14,000' peaks of the Sawatch and Mosquito Ranges. In its upper boatable reaches between Granite and Salida, the Arkansas runs south by southeast through rugged canyons formed where broad fans of gravel and cobble, extending outward from the Sawatch Range to the west, force the river to the east side of the valley. Here it cuts deep into the hard granitic bedrock of the Arkansas Hills and courses through challenging whitewater from Pine Creek through

[1]Arkansas, an Indian name meaning "bow on the smoky water," was applied to a tribe living far downstream in present-day Oklahoma and Arkansas.

Browns Canyon. Ice-age glaciers scoured the river's upper river valley and left a large terminal moraine. Today the river pours over the edge of that moraine at Pine Creek Rapid.

The Arkansas drains the drier east side of the Rockies, and the canyon is generally lightly forested, becoming semi-arid in its lower reaches near Cañon City. Tunnels and ditches divert additional water into the Arkansas drainage from the Eagle, Fryingpan, and Roaring Fork Rivers, tributaries of the Upper Colorado on the wetter west slope of the Divide. By the time the Arkansas reaches Browns Canyon, the combination of natural and diverted runoff has swollen the flow considerably.

Below Browns Canyon and Salida the river turns southeast through softer sedimentary strata. Then, just beyond Coaldale, it swerves northeast and crosses the Pleasant Valley Fault; suddenly, the geology and scenery change as the river carves into the basement rocks of the Lower Arkansas River Canyon. The river's final cut at the Royal Gorge, one of the West's most remarkable canyons, is the most spectacular of all. Here the Arkansas slices a narrow cleft over 1,000' deep though ancient granite and other hard rocks. Below Royal Gorge the river emerges onto the western edge of the Great Plains at Cañon City. As it reaches the plains, the Arkansas is extensively diverted for irrigation and municipal use.

The popularity of the Arkansas among recreational boaters doesn't mean the river's future is secure. True, the BLM is currently studying the Arkansas for designation as a recreational river in the National Wild and Scenic Rivers System. But in 1991 the national conservation organization American Rivers named the Arkansas one of the nation's ten most endangered rivers. The key threat is a proposal by the Colorado Springs Utility Department for a 135'-high dam at Elephant Rock, some four miles above Buena Vista, and another smaller dam not far upstream. In addition to flooding prime sections of river, these dams could seriously diminish downstream flows.[2]

Action starts at the little town of Granite. The 11 miles through Granite Canyon, Pine Creek, and The Numbers make up one of the West's most famous stretches of difficult whitewater. Boaters from around the world meet here to test their skills on some of the most formidable rapids in the Rockies. This continuous-gradient mountain torrent is no place for the inexperienced.

The opening rapids in Granite Canyon are not hard, but there are hazards and one portage. Then comes Pine Creek, a tough Class V at low and moderate flows and Class VI above 2,500 cfs. **Only top experts should attempt Pine Creek Rapid, and even they should avoid it at high flows.** Just downstream, the run through The Numbers is only slightly less difficult, rating Class IV (V at higher flows).

The next section, a scenic 15-mile stretch between The Numbers and Browns Canyon, is less frequently boated than it might be because access is limited by extensive private property along the banks. The upper run, called both the "Frog Rock Run" and "The Narrows," is a valuable training run for intermediate boaters. But at high water, the river develops big, powerful waves, and less seasoned boaters should stay away. At low levels, even novices can float the six-mile Class I–II "Milk Run" below the highway bridge at Johnson Village (mile 20).

For many recreational boaters, the Arkansas means Browns Canyon. It's not hard to see why this exhilarating ride has become one of the most popular whitewater runs in the country. Here the Arkansas plunges into a beautiful granite canyon, the highway disappears, and only the railroad follows the river. By this point the Arkansas has become a pool-and-drop river of considerable volume, swollen by creeks draining the Sawatch Range.

Boaters of varying skills enjoy this rare semi-wilderness section, which begins at Ruby Mountain Recreation Site. Advanced and expert kayakers and rafters aim for big water during peak runoff, while intermediates flock to the river later in the summer, when flows are lower and the weather is warmer. At any level, Browns Canyon is laced with tricky boulder gardens and challenging whitewater. Unguided novices should stay away.

Because the only legal access at the end of Browns Canyon—Stone Bridge, 11 miles below the Ruby Mountain put-in—is on private property, most boaters have taken out three miles upstream at Hecla Junction. That should change soon: AHRA, the managing agency, is purchasing a river access site at Stone Bridge. Boaters can also continue to Big Bend, three miles below Stone Bridge, or even on to Salida, seven

[2]For more information contact Friends of the Arkansas, P.O. Box 924, Buena Vista, CO 81211; or the National Organization for River Sports (see appendix for address).

miles farther, on a pleasant float with vistas of surrounding peaks. Here the canyon opens up, the river winds through a flood plain, and the main highways and railroad move well away from its banks. The stretch between Big Bend and Salida is very popular with anglers; please treat them with consideration (see appendix on **River Etiquette**).

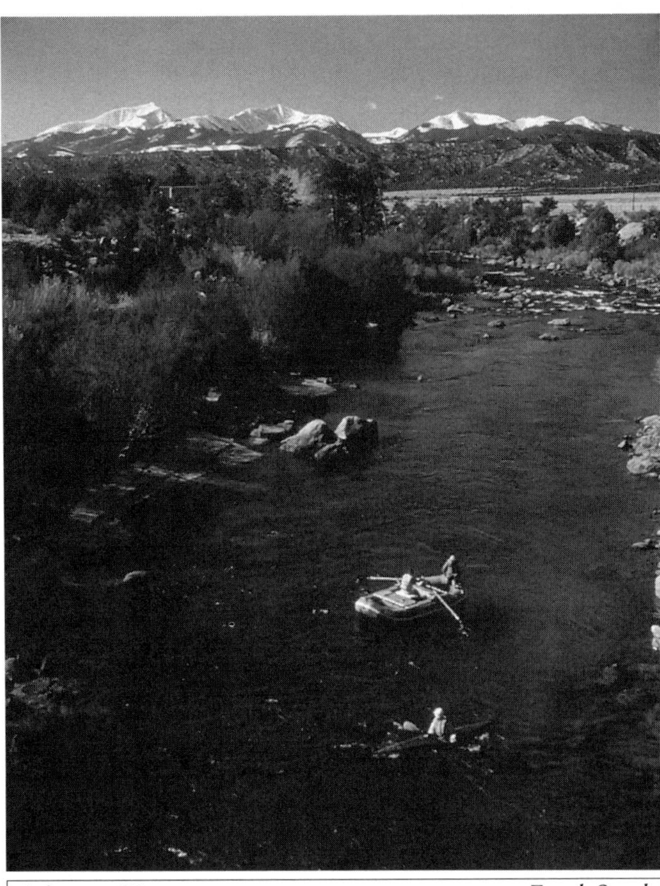
Arkansas River *Frank Staub*

Below Salida striking views of the Sangre de Cristo Mountains open to the south as the Arkansas flows through Pleasant Valley's aptly-named countryside. In this section, sometimes called the "Rincon Run" and recently named "Bighorn Sheep Canyon" by the Colorado Legislature, long calms are periodically interrupted by lively Class III rapids. (Bighorn sheep can indeed be seen on the canyon walls.)

Downstream from Coaldale, the river turns sharply northeast and enters the Lower Arkansas River Canyon (sometimes called the "Parkdale Run"). Here the rapids are more frequent and a little more difficult (IV above 3,000 cfs). Two miles above the Parkdale Bridge, the canyon opens up and the river flattens out. Don't miss the take-out at the Parkdale Recreation site; downstream, the river swings to the southeast and plunges into the rapids of the legendary Royal Gorge, site of the world's highest suspension bridge.

The Royal Gorge's continuous whitewater is the toughest on the Arkansas except for Pine Creek and The Numbers. In case of emergency, the only legal way out is by river. (The Denver & Rio Grande Western Railroad, for liability reasons, formally prohibits trespassing on the tracks on the left bank.) Little sunlight reaches the bottom of the narrow canyon, so wet suits are advised for boaters at any time of year.

Mile by Mile Guide

Note: River miles in left column sometimes start over at zero with put-in for a different section. Numbers in brackets show total miles from first put-in and correspond to mileages on our map.

Granite Canyon, Pine Creek, and The Numbers

0 **PUT-IN** on the left bank at the bridge in the town of Granite. The first Class III rapid is a mile downriver, just upstream from the entrance to Granite Canyon. More Class II and III rapids follow.

Open canoeists and novice kayakers might like the 6 miles of easy water upstream between the Pan-Ark Lodge Bridge and Granite. The only Class II rapid is about 4 miles below the Pan-Ark Bridge.

1.7 End of Granite Canyon. ***HAZARD. PORTAGE.*** Not far downstream, a short pool leads to a small dam with a cable strung across the bottom of a big drop. Portage on the right.

2.1 **RIVER ACCESS.** East Clear Creek Recreation Site is set back from the river on the right bank, not far from the Clear Creek Reservoir spillway. The river enters another small canyon.

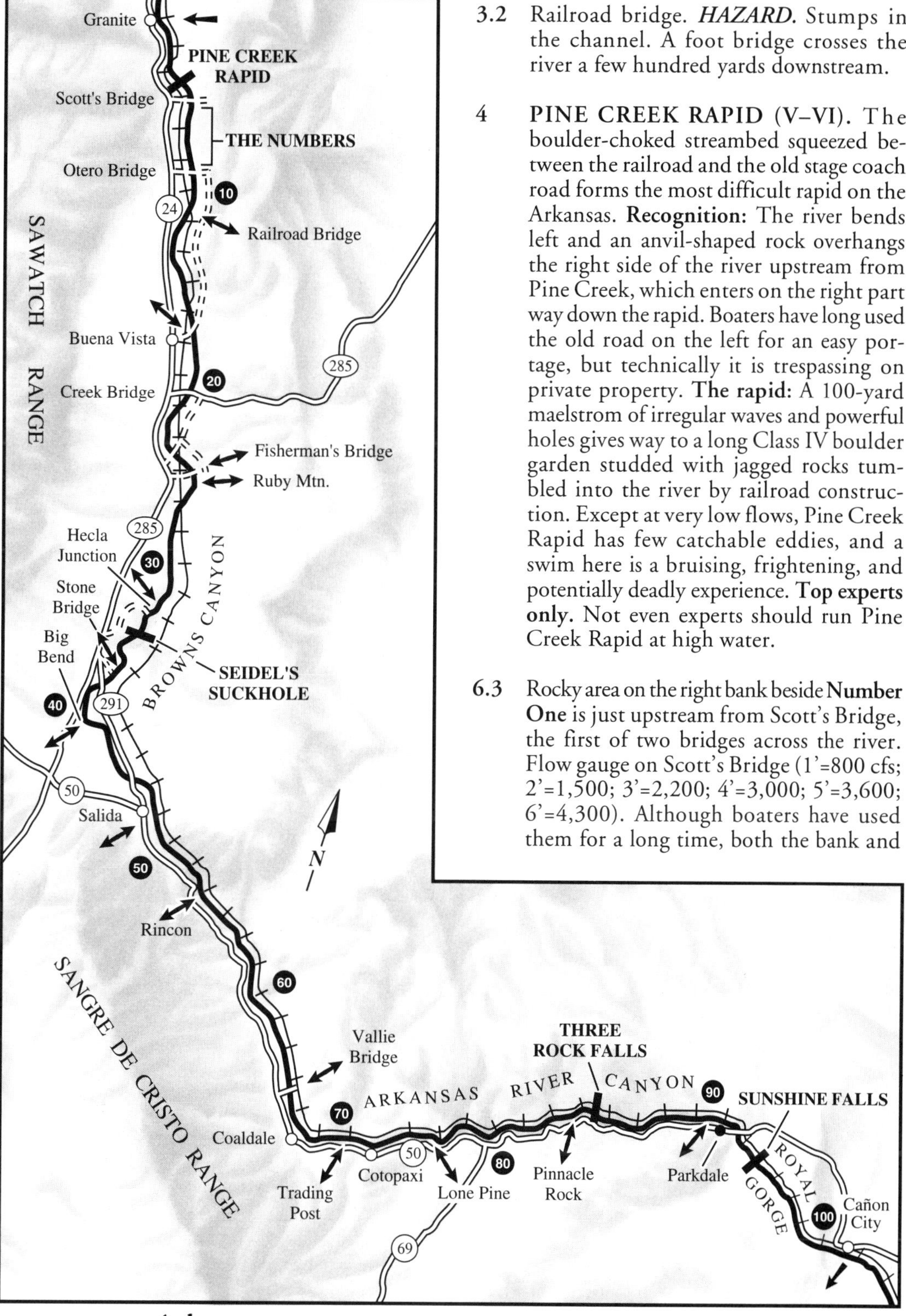

Arkansas

3.2 Railroad bridge. *HAZARD.* Stumps in the channel. A foot bridge crosses the river a few hundred yards downstream.

4 PINE CREEK RAPID (V–VI). The boulder-choked streambed squeezed between the railroad and the old stage coach road forms the most difficult rapid on the Arkansas. **Recognition:** The river bends left and an anvil-shaped rock overhangs the right side of the river upstream from Pine Creek, which enters on the right part way down the rapid. Boaters have long used the old road on the left for an easy portage, but technically it is trespassing on private property. **The rapid:** A 100-yard maelstrom of irregular waves and powerful holes gives way to a long Class IV boulder garden studded with jagged rocks tumbled into the river by railroad construction. Except at very low flows, Pine Creek Rapid has few catchable eddies, and a swim here is a bruising, frightening, and potentially deadly experience. **Top experts only.** Not even experts should run Pine Creek Rapid at high water.

6.3 Rocky area on the right bank beside **Number One** is just upstream from Scott's Bridge, the first of two bridges across the river. Flow gauge on Scott's Bridge (1'=800 cfs; 2'=1,500; 3'=2,200; 4'=3,000; 5'=3,600; 6'=4,300). Although boaters have used them for a long time, both the bank and the bridges are privately owned. (Contact the managing agency for updated information on access.) About 300 yards upstream is the site of the smaller of two dams proposed by Colorado Springs.

6.3 **NUMBER ONE (IV; V above 2,500 cfs)** begins above the two bridges. Like all the rapids in **The Numbers,** this one is a boulder-choked channel that demands technical maneuvering at low and moderate levels and becomes even more difficult when higher flows turn it into a boiling gauntlet of waves and holes. Not far downstream from this rapid is a big hole at high water, sometimes referred to as **NUMBER ONE AND A HALF (IV).**

6.7 **NUMBER TWO (IV).** A tricky S-turn laced with holes. It leads directly into **NUMBER THREE (IV),** a short, rocky pitch with a big hole in the middle.

7.2 **NUMBER FOUR (IV; V above 2,500 cfs).** Very difficult at high flows, when a big hole forms at the lower end of the initial chute. A 100-yard boulder slalom follows. Most boaters consider this one the toughest of The Numbers.

7.6 Ender Rock, a famous kayak play spot.

7.9 Bridge (County Road 371) to Otero Pumping Station, which diverts a maximum of 70 cfs from the Arkansas through a tunnel to the South Platte.

8 **NUMBER FIVE (IV; V above 3,000 cfs).** As the river bends right, boaters must maneuver into a sharp drop, then negotiate some powerful waves and holes.

9 **NUMBER SIX (IV; V above 3,000 cfs).** A zigzag route through big holes. Class III rapids the rest of the way, except for a half-mile-long Class IV- boulder maze, sometimes called **NUMBER SEVEN,** just above the take-out. **Alternate takeouts** on public land along the left bank. Avoid private property.

11 **TAKE-OUT** at Railroad Bridge Recreation Site on the left bank, just upstream from the railroad bridge across the river.

Frog Rock and Milk Runs

11 **PUT-IN.** Railroad Bridge Recreation Site (see above). Beginning of **Frog Rock Run,** also called **The Narrows.**

13 U.S. 24 comes close to the river, providing a popular informal put-in and takeout for kayakers, but access is too difficult for rafters and their gear.

14 **FROG ROCK (III+).** Medium-sized drop over boulders. Just downstream, Elephant Rock above the left bank guards the entrance to mile-long **Wildhorse Canyon,** which contains a quarter-mile-long Class III boulder field. Site of proposed Elephant Rock Dam (see essay). Below Wildhorse Canyon, several more Class III rapids dot the river all the way to Johnson Village.

16 Fourmile Bridge. Fourmile Creek enters on the left just downstream.

17 **HOUSE ROCK RAPID (III; IV above 3,000 cfs).** The canyon walls narrow, and a big boulder plugs the stream bed. Scout left to be sure no logs obstruct the channel.

17.9 **RIVER ACCESS** on the right at the Buena Vista River Park beyond the baseball field at the east end of Main Street.

19.2 **THE DAM (III).** The river pours over an old boulder dam into a powerful reversal. Runnable chute on the right is obstructed by a rock at the bottom at lower flows. Property owners on both banks do not allow scouting. Swift currents and Class III rapids continue downstream.

20.3 Johnson Village Bridge (U.S. Highways 24 and 285) and railroad bridge. Private **RIVER ACCESS** on the right (see **Logistics**). Beginning of **Milk Run.** Easier rapids (mostly Class I and II) from here to Browns Canyon.

23 Left channel is blocked by a new diversion dam. Stay right. Private road bridge just downstream.

24.3 **RIVER ACCESS.** Fisherman's Bridge Recreation Site on the left (County Road 301). Class II+ rapid just below the railroad bridge.

26.3 **TAKE-OUT.** Ruby Mountain Recreation Site on the left. To get here by car, cross Fisherman's Bridge (see above) and follow signs. Hamlet of Nathrop is downstream on the right, across the foot bridge. **Browns Canyon** begins 3 miles downstream, but the next river access is 8 miles downstream at Hecla Junction.

Browns Canyon and Salida Run

0 [26.3] **PUT-IN.** Ruby Mountain Recreation Site. For a longer float, put in two miles upstream at Fisherman's Bridge. Open country and Class I–II water for the next three miles. Chalk Creek enters on the right about half a mile downstream.

2.7 Railroad bridge. Cottonwood Creek enters on the left. Downstream the canyon narrows.

3 **CANYON DOORS** (III). Upper and Lower. Just downstream is **PINBALL** (III+), where boulders block the bottom of a series of ledges. Watch for a pourover at the top at high flows.

4 Browns Creek enters on the right. Just downstream is **ZOOM FLUME (III+)**, where a long chute becomes a ramp and ends in a hole. A boulder garden follows.

5.2 **BIG DROP** (III+). As the river bends right. Not far downstream is **THE STAIRCASE** (III+), also called **Giant Steps** and **Seven Falls,** a series of drops which get tougher toward the end.

6.2 **WIDOWMAKER** (III+). It's hard to find a clean route. A big recirculating hole in the middle is called **Devil's Punchbowl** or **Toilet Bowl.**

7.1 **RAFT RIPPER** (III+). Also called **Razor Rocks** and **Snake Slide.** After a drop, watch for sharp rocks on the left. Just downstream is **CEMETERY** (III), also called **Graveyard** and **Last Chance.**

7.8 [34.1] **RIVER ACCESS.** Hecla Junction Recreation Site (County Road 194) on the right. A dirt road leads to Highway 285. Some boaters take out here at high flows to avoid the big rapid downstream. Browns Canyon continues for another 3 miles to Stone Bridge, which has better road access and is being developed as a legal river access site.

9 **SEIDEL'S SUCKHOLE** (IV). Named for Erich Seidel, a champion East German boater whose foldboat collapsed on his first run of the rapid in 1952. Scout right. This river-wide drop has a nasty hole, often a "keeper," that is especially dangerous at high water. At low flows the rock at the bottom of the drop is exposed and a right-hand chute appears.

9.2 **TWIN FALLS** (III), also called **Double Drop.** Just downstream from another Fourmile Creek, which enters on the right. The canyon gradually begins to open up. Class II rapids from here to Stone Bridge.

11 [37.3] Stone Bridge (private bridge at end of County Road 191). ***HAZARD*** at high flows when boats have insufficient clearance. End of Browns Canyon and beginning of Salida Run. The managing agency is developing a legal **RIVER ACCESS** here. No river access at the Highway 291 bridge not far downstream.

13.8 **SQUAW CREEK,** the only Class III rapid on the Salida Run. Squaw Creek enters on the right.

14.3 **RIVER ACCESS.** Big Bend Recreation Site on the right.

17.8 ***HAZARD.*** Old diversion dam with a runnable chute on the left to allow boaters to avoid the dangerous reversal. Fish hatchery on the right half a mile downstream.

19.3 Highway 291 bridge. No river access at present here or at the County Road 175 bridge just downstream.

20.5 **TAKE-OUT.** Salida Boat Ramp (right bank). Rafts should take out here.

20.7 [47] **TAKE-OUT.** Riverside Park (right bank), downstream from Salida's F Street Bridge, is sometimes used by kayakers.

Arkansas River Canyon: Salida to Parkdale

0 [47] **PUT-IN** at Riverside Park or just upstream at the Salida Boat Ramp (see above). Every June, Salida rolls up its sleeves to host the FIB-Ark ("First in Boating–Arkansas") whitewater festival. The slalom competition centers around the F Street Bridge, while whitewater marathoners race from Salida to Cotopaxi. The Salida-to-Coaldale stretch is sometimes called the "Rincon Run."

2.5 **RIVER ACCESS.** Salida East Recreation Site.

3.3 **BEAR CREEK RAPID (III).** Big hole at higher flows. Scout from the right.

6 Wellsville Bridge. Flow gauge.

9.5 **RIVER ACCESS.** Rincon Recreation Site on the right.

10.2 **BADGER CREEK RAPID (III).** A large boulder blocks the river. Scout left. Another Class III rapid, **THE FLUME,** follows almost immediately.

12.5 Bridge at village of Howard.

14.7 **RIVER ACCESS.** Rocky Mountain Outdoor Center (right bank) upstream from a bridge. Two Class III rapids ahead: **TIN CUP**, about a mile downstream, and **RED ROCK,** about a mile beyond that.

18.5 [65.5] **RIVER ACCESS.** Vallie Bridge Recreation Site on the left.

20.8 Two bridges cross the river at Coaldale.

21.8 **COTTONWOOD RAPID (III+),** known for big standing waves at high water. Scout from the right. Downstream, Big Cottonwood Creek enters on the right, and the river swerves to the northeast.

22.3 **LITTLE COTTONWOOD RAPID (III).** The dread **Black Hole** lurks at the top left.

23.3 **RIVER ACCESS.** Trading Post Recreation Site on the right.

25 Town of Cotopaxi, named after a South American mountain, on the right. *HAZARD.* Low clearance under the bridge at flows above 4,000 cfs.

26.8 **RIVER ACCESS.** Lone Pine Recreation Site on the right.

32.5 *HAZARD.* Bridge abutment in the streambed just above **TEXAS CREEK RAPID (III).** Texas Creek enters from the right.

34.4 **MAYTAG (III).** Mediocre **RIVER ACCESS** at the Maytag Recreation Site.

37.2 **THREE FORKS (III).** Also called **Devil's Hole.** A boulder field becomes large waves and holes at higher flows. Watch for submerged rebar on the right.

38.2 **RIVER ACCESS.** Pinnacle Rock Recreation Site on the right. Popular put-in for the run to Parkdale.

39.4 **THREE ROCKS FALLS (IV). Recognition:** After a Class III rapid a few hundred yards upstream, stay left as the highway climbs well above the banks and the river S-curves to the right. Scout or portage on the left. **The rapid:** Probably the most difficult rapid between Salida and Parkdale. Three chutes to choose from.

39.8 **RIVER ACCESS.** Salt Lick Recreation Site on the right.

40 **FIVE POINTS RAPID (III).** No river access at Five Points Recreation Site on the right or at Floodplain Recreation Site about a mile downstream.

41.5 **RIVER ACCESS.** Spikebuck Recreation Site on the right.

42.2 **SPIKEBUCK (III–IV). Recognition:** Railroad markers labeled "Spikebuck." Scout right. **The rapid:** This long, boulder-choked passage is a negotiable slalom at low water but much tougher at high flows, when big holes block the channel.

43.5-44.5 **THE TUBE.** A series of Class III rapids called **SHARK'S TOOTH, DOUBLE DIP,** and **PUPPY.** Ruins on the left date from the 1878–1880 railroad wars.

46.5 [93.5] **TAKE-OUT.** Parkdale Recreation Site on the right. The canyon opens up and the river flows lazily through open country, most of it privately owned, for the next two miles. Farther downstream are the big rapids of the Royal Gorge.

Royal Gorge

0 [93.5] **PUT-IN** at the Parkdale Recreation Site (see above). Easy water for the first 4 miles.

1 Highway 50 bridge.

1.7 Old rock forts and breastworks on the left bank date from the 1878–1880 private railroad war between the Santa Fe and the Denver & Rio Grande. Several Class II and III rapids in the next mile.

2.7 Remains of an old diversion dam, dynamited in 1980, with a Class III rapid just below it.

3 **SUNSHINE FALLS** (V). Also called **Caretaker** or **White House. Recognition:** The rapid begins just downstream from a right-bank shack where the caretaker for the Cañon City Waterworks once lived. Scout right. **The rapid:** A technical entry leads to an abrupt drop and a river-wide hole. Usually portaged above 3,000 cfs, but the portage route along the railroad tracks is illegal.

3.2 **SLEDGEHAMMER (IV; V above 3,000 cfs).** A long, rocky ride with big holes at higher flows. The last drop is called **Clark's Hole** or **Three-Boat Suckhole.**

4.2 The river enters the heart of the Royal Gorge, and Class IV rapids come in quick succession. The first is **SQUEEZE BOX (IV)**, a long series of steep drops squeezed between the right-hand canyon wall and the railroad tracks on the left bank. At higher flows the drops combine into a long wave train.

4.7 Here the railroad tracks, somewhat misleadingly called the "Hanging Bridge," are bolted to the canyon wall above the river. Just downstream on the left is a refreshment stand at the foot of the Incline Railroad, a steep funicular that carries tourists into the gorge from the observation point above.

4.8 **BRIDGE RAPID** (IV). Also called **Wall Slammer.** Beneath the Royal Gorge Bridge a strong current pushes boats against the right wall.

5.3 **CORNER POCKET (IV; V above 3,000 cfs).** Also called **Boat Eater** for the big hole in the middle of the river.

5.7 **SODA FOUNTAIN ROCK** (IV). On a hard right turn, a big rock blocks the channel.

6 Watch for submerged rebar at an old bridge site, then a Class III rapid known as **PIPELINE** or **EXIT.** An old waterworks pipe crosses the river below this rapid. Only Class II and III downstream.

7.5 Tunnel Drive, a dirt road on the far side of the railroad tracks, runs along the left bank from here to Cañon City. Because the railroad prohibits trespassing, boaters should continue downstream. The canyon gradually opens up from this point on.

9.3 Grape Creek enters on the right.

9.8 Though boaters used it for years, there is no longer legal river access at the cottonwood grove at the end of Riverside Drive on the right bank. *HAZARD.* Just downstream is a dangerous diversion dam across the river with a newly-constructed runnable chute on the left.

10.5 [104] **TAKE-OUT** at Centennial Park on the right, just downstream from First Street Bridge in Cañon City. In the near future boaters will have a new take-out at the River Station, site of an old railroad depot just downstream on the left. For updated information, call Cañon City Dept. of Parks, (719) 269-9028.

Gunnison River

1. Gunnison Gorge:
Chukar Trail (5,370') to North Fork (5,090').
III+; 13 miles; 22 ft./mi.

2. Dominguez Canyon:
Delta (4,920') to Whitewater (4,610').
II-; 43 miles; 7 ft./mi. Shorter trips possible.

Drainage Area and Average Annual Discharge: 3,975 sq. mi. and 1,015,000 af near Gunnison Gorge put-in; 7,928 sq. mi. and 1,905,000 af at Dominguez Canyon take-out.

Season: *Run 1:* May–Sept. *Run 2:* April–Oct. Controlled by reservoir releases and diversions; rarely above 5,000 cfs or below 300. Typically peaks briefly in late May or early June, then settles to average summer flows of 800–1,200. Often rises again in the fall.

Recommended Levels: *Run 1:* 800–4,000 cfs. *Run 2:* 700–10,000 cfs.

Flow Information: Water Talk, (303) 831-7135; 4*6* for flow "below East Portal" (Run 1) or 4*8* for flow "near Grand Junction" (Run 2).

Permits: *Run 1:* Self-registration at put-in. Group size limit 12. *Run 2:* Not required.

Managing Agency: BLM, Uncompahgre Basin Resource Area, 2505 S. Townsend Ave., Montrose, CO 81401; (303) 249-6047. For the lower part of Dominguez Canyon beginning at Bridgeport, contact BLM, Grand Junction Resource Area, 2815 H Road, Grand Junction, CO 81506; (303) 244-3000.

Commercial Raft Trips: Yes, both runs. For a list of outfitters, contact the BLM's Uncompahgre Basin RA in Montrose (see above).

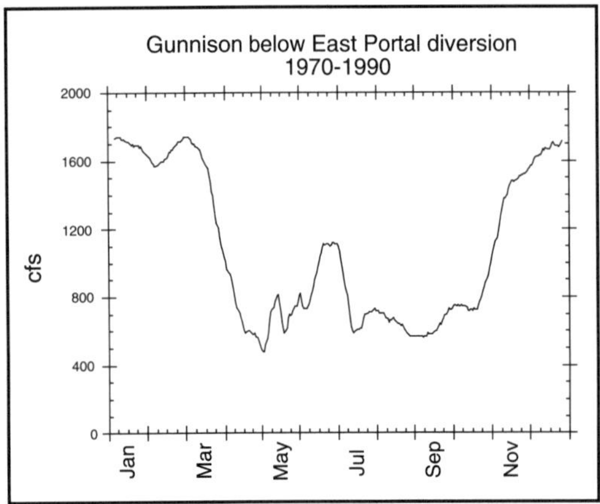

Land Ownership: *Run 1:* Almost all BLM. *Run 2:* Mixed BLM and private.

Scenery: Excellent. Transition from rocky gorge to sandstone canyon to high desert.

Solitude: Excellent.

Wilderness: *Run 1:* Yes. *Run 2:* Partial—railroad, minor roads, occasional ranches.

Fishing: Outstanding. Gunnison Gorge is a Gold Medal Trout Stream.

Water: Clear and cold. No drinking water at Chukar Trailhead.

Side Excursions: Overlooks in Black Canyon National Monument.

Guides and References:
- Wheat, *Floater's Guide to Colorado.*
- Nichols, *River Runners' Guide to Utah.* Gunnison Gorge only.
- Dolson, *Black Canyon of the Gunnison: A Story In Stone.* Human and natural history.
- BLM information sheets on both runs.

Maps:
- **USGS 7.5':** *Gunnison Gorge:* Red Rock Canyon, Black Ridge, Lazear. *Dominguez Canyon:* Delta, Roubideau, Point Creek, Dominguez, Triangle Mesa, Whitewater.
- **USGS 1:100:** *Gunnison Gorge:* Paonia. *Dominguez Canyon:* Delta.
- **BLM:** *Gunnison Gorge River Map.*
- **USFS:** *Uncompahgre NF* covers *Run 1; Grand Mesa NF* covers *Run 2.*

Logistics: *Gunnison Gorge:* To reach the **put-in,** drive about 12 miles south on U.S. 50 from Delta, Colorado. Just south of Olathe, turn east on Falcon Drive (paved, then dirt). After about 3.5 miles the name changes to Peach Valley Road; in another 1.5 miles bear right at the fork where a sign points to Chukar Trail. Follow this rough road (impassable when wet) about half a dozen miles to the picnic area at Chukar Trailhead. Many side roads can cause confusion; as a rule of thumb, bear left at road forks, staying on the most-used road. Better yet, call the BLM for detailed directions. A high clearance vehicle is required, and 4-wheel drive is preferred.

To reach the **take-out,** drive east from Delta on Colorado Highway 92. Just beyond the 14-mile marker, turn south onto an unpaved road at a sign marking the turnoff to Gunnison Forks, and drive about a mile to the confluence of the main stem and North Fork. Take out either at the BLM access on the North Fork just upstream from the confluence, or just below the confluence at the private Gunnison River Pleasure Park for a small fee. This private park also provides camping, cabins, and auto shuttles; phone (303) 872-2525. To hire pack animals, contact Ron Franks, (303) 323-5155.

Dominguez Canyon: To reach the **put-in** on the west side of the town of Delta, turn west off U.S. 50 about 100 yards south of the bridge over the Gunnison onto Gunnison River Drive, which leads about three quarters of a mile to Confluence Park on the left bank. A rarely-used intermediate access is at the County Road 1250 bridge, reached by turning south off U.S. 50 about 4 miles west of Delta. To reach the **popular acesss at Escalante Canyon Bridge,** turn southwest off U.S. 50 at a highway rest area 6 miles south of the Mesa/Delta County Line and 11 miles north of Delta. Follow the unpaved road roughly 3 miles to the bridge.

To reach the **Bridgeport access** (also called Deer Creek access), turn west off U.S. 50, one mile north of the Mesa County-Delta County Line and 11 miles south of Whitewater, onto an unpaved road that descends Deer Creek to the Gunnison. Though well known, this access, which involves getting rigged boats quickly across the railroad tracks and up or down a bank which lacks a true launch site, is of questionable legality. Contact the BLM in Grand Junction for more information on access problems both at Bridgeport and at the **lowermost take-out** at the Colorado Highway 141 bridge at Whitewater, 10 miles southeast of Grand Junction.

The Gunnison River is born full-fledged at the confluence of the Taylor and East Rivers near Gunnison, Colorado.[1] From here the river journeys some 160 miles across southwestern Colorado, growing steadily as it merges with abundant tributaries draining the Continental Divide, the Sawatch Range, and the Elk and San Juan Mountains. By the time it joins the Colorado at Grand Junction, the Gunnison is the state's second largest river after the Colorado itself. Among all the tributaries of the Colorado, only the Green is bigger.

The river and the town are named for Lieutenant John Gunnison, an engineer sent to survey a railroad route across the Rockies in 1853. Gunnison carefully scouted the river's upper and lower reaches but avoided the middle section. He knew that between the relative calm of the upper and lower river lay an impassable abyss more than 50 miles long: the Black Canyon of the Gunnison.

Downstream from the town of Gunnison, the river cuts through the hard, dark schist that gives the Black Canyon its name. At first the walls rise only 200' above the river, but they eventually climb to more than 2,000' in the heart of Black Canyon National Monument. At The Narrows the chasm is a nearly vertical slit, 350 yards across at the rim and 40' wide at river level.

The river's passage through this daunting defile is fierce and turbulent. The 12 miles within the National Monument boast an average gradient of 90 ft./mi., with a peak of 230 ft./mi. in the three miles beginning near The Narrows—an astonishing rate of descent for a river of this size. Cascading over vertical falls and churning through mazes of huge boulders, the river seems to defy all hope of human passage.

Yet the Black Canyon has been negotiated several times. The first known descent came in 1901, when William Torrence and Abraham Lincoln Fellows set out on foot to survey the river for a diversion tunnel. The men survived harrowing adventures to tell their story and to see the completion eight years later of what was then the world's longest irrigation tunnel—a six-mile shaft that still shuttles some 300,000 acre-feet of water each year from the Gunnison to the Uncompahgre Valley.

The controversy over who deserves credit for the first true boating descent is somewhat academic; any journey through Black Canyon is a mix of river running and rock climbing. Rope and basic climbing gear are essential. The long, arduous portages include one spot where the river is unrunnable for nearly a mile. In the runnable sections, pounding Class V drops challenge the finest of paddlers.

Even today only a handful of adventurers have made what may be the West's most de-

[1] For floats on major tributaries, see the write-ups on the **Taylor** (which also mentions an upstream run on the Gunnison itself) and the **Lake Fork of the Gunnison** in the **More Western Rivers** section.

manding river descent. **The Black Canyon run is only for teams of top-notch experts in superb condition using extreme caution.** In case of mishap, rescue would be very difficult.[2]

The heart of Black Canyon remains pristine, although the flow is diminished by diversions. Upstream, however, the Gunnison has not fared so well. The river's combination of sheer-walled dam sites and substantial water volume proved irresistible to engineers. Today, three dams block what was once one of Colorado's great wild rivers, taming its moods and flooding the upper half of Black Canyon. In the 1970's the most recent project, Crystal Reservoir, buried an 18-mile run from Cimmaron to East Portal—a section that Michael Jenkinson, in *Wild Rivers of North America,* praised as "one of the finest short wilderness whitewater runs to be found anywhere."

Not all the news is bad. In the 1980's the Chevron Corporation donated its right to 300 cfs of Gunnison water to the Nature Conservancy, which plans to enhance instream flows by leaving the water in the river. Chevron's gift, valued in the millions of dollars, is the first of its kind in the West, and conservationists are hopeful that similar rights can be obtained for other threatened rivers.

Gunnison Gorge

Fortunately for river runners, there remains one section of the Black Canyon with intermediate whitewater, no portages, and at least for the moment, no dams. The catch? You have to hike to the put-in. Two miles below the Black Canyon National Monument boundary, the steep Chukar (pronounced CHUCK-er) Trail leads one mile and 600 vertical feet down to the left bank. (Alternate upstream trails are more difficult and not recommended.)

The reward? Thirteen miles of outstanding wilderness scenery and excellent Class III–IV pool-and-drop whitewater through one of the most spectacular canyons in the Colorado Rockies. The run boasts superb fishing and abundant wildlife, including bighorn sheep, otters, eagles, falcons, and waterfowl. To top it off, this section sees only moderate use due to the difficult access and long drive from Denver. However, the number of boaters has increased substantially in the last few years.

The first five miles below the put-in are fairly straightforward. Then the river picks up steam, building to Class III+ or IV, depending on flow. The most difficult rapids lie about two thirds of the way through the run where a constricted gorge produces a series of challenging, rocky drops. Boaters making the run in one day should get an early start, while those willing to pack in more gear can savor a night at one of the canyon's unspoiled campsites.

In 1991 the national river conservation group American Rivers named the Gunnison one of the ten most endangered rivers in the nation. Gunnison Gorge is seriously threatened by two proposed diversions. One would take water from far upstream on the Taylor River, eliminating boating on that river and reducing flows on the Gunnison. This project, known by its fitting acronym "CRAP–UP" (Collegiate Range Aurora Project–Union Park), would shunt water east through a tunnel under the Continental Divide to Denver suburbs. The other proposal, called "AB Lateral," a hydropower scheme endorsed by the Bureau of Reclamation and Uncompahgre Valley water users, would significantly increase diversions through the existing East Portal tunnel just above Black Canyon, thereby reducing flows dramatically in Black Canyon and Gunnison Gorge.[3]

Gunnison Gorge River Guide

Put in where Chukar Trail reaches the left bank (mile 0). Boaters must sign a BLM register at the launch site. The first several miles are Class II to easy III, but watch for **IMPROVISE (II+)** at a sharp right bend at mile 1.5 (scout left). At mile 3.5 Duncan Trail climbs steeply from the left bank to a rough dirt road on the rim. Half a mile downstream, Long Gulch enters on the right, and the gorge opens for the next mile and a half, offering possible campsites. This section is known as Ute Park because Ute Indians are believed to have forded the river here. The Ute Trail follows the left bank briefly, but as the gorge closes in near mile 5, the trail leaves the river and climbs some 1,200' to the rim.

[2]If you're still interested, refer to Doug Wheat, *The Floater's Guide to Colorado,* and Scott Gerber, "The Portage: Three Days in the Black Canyon of the Gunnison" (*River Runner,* April 1988). Then contact the Park Service for a permit: Black Canyon National Monument, P.O. Box 1648, Montrose, CO 81402; (303) 249-7036.

[3]For information on the campaign to stop the diversions and secure National Wild and Scenic River status for 29 miles of the Gunnison, contact American Rivers, N.O.R.S. (see appendix for addresses), or the Western Colorado Congress, P.O. Box 472, Montrose, CO 81402; (303) 249-1978.

At mile 5.7 Red Canyon enters on the right at a rapid of the same name. Downstream, the river descends into a narrow inner gorge with the toughest rapids on the run. A ravine on the left at mile 7 marks **BOULDER GARDEN (III+)**. At mile 8.7 the river curves right through **THE SQUEEZE (III)**, a rocky drop with narrow runnable slots on the right. Just downstream is the steepest and most difficult section, a mile-long series of Class III+ to IV drops (depending on flow) separated by short pools.

CABLE (IV-), at mile 9.5, has a big wrap rock in the center; catch a small eddy on the right to scout. (The cable for which the rapid is named has been removed.) The last major drop is **GRAND FINALE (III+)**, a straightforward chute with big waves. Scout right. Look for a great surfing hole between Cable and Grand Finale.

The Smith Fork enters on the right at mile 10; its pools and waterfalls offer good side hikes. (Several dams have been proposed for the Gunnison at this site.) The final three miles are easy. The North Fork Gunnison enters on the right at mile 13.5; the **take-out** is on the right bank.

Some boaters continue below the North Fork take-out, floating an additional nine miles to Austin through more open country. This section also makes a good novice run, but beware of two possibly runnable diversion dams.

Dominguez Canyon

Below Austin the river flows through open and more developed terrain toward its confluence with the Uncompahgre River about a mile below the town of Delta. The Gunnison then winds across broad flats before gradually cutting into the eastern edge of the Uncompahgre Plateau. Downstream, the Gunnison meanders for more than 30 miles through scenic Dominguez Canyon,[4] where impressive walls of red and orange sandstone rise above the river. Here the Gunnison is gentle, with only a few easy riffles breaking the flatwater; this is an excellent novice float and an ideal setting for an extended open canoe trip. Two intermediate accesses within this 43-mile stretch—Escalante Canyon Bridge at mile 14.5 and Bridgeport at mile 28.5—make shorter runs possible, including long one-day floats.

The canyon has a near-wilderness feel, in spite of a railroad and occasional dirt roads and ranches. U.S. 50 is usually only two or three miles to the east, but the steep walls close out this and most other signs of civilization. In places the river curves around broad bars where cottonwoods shelter large heron rookeries. Mosquitoes can be a problem, especially in low-water years. Many side canyons, especially those draining the Uncompahgre Plateau on the left, offer good hiking. Anasazi petroglyphs add to the river's canyon country flavor.

The 14.5 miles from the Bridgeport access to the hamlet of Whitewater are much less frequently floated. Despite the name of the destination, there is no whitewater, and about halfway down this stretch the canyon opens up and the river flows through high desert.

Dominguez Canyon River Guide

The **put-in** is on the left bank of the Gunnison at Confluence Park in the town of Delta, about half a mile downstream from the U.S. 50 bridge. Another access point, infrequently used by boaters, is at the County Road 1250 bridge west of Delta (mile 3). The Gunnison winds across flats for the first few miles. Roubideau Creek enters on the left at mile 6.5 as the river gradually enters the canyon. Downstream, just below the railroad bridge across the river, is the first riffle on the run.

A popular **access** is at mile 14.5, where the Escalante Canyon Bridge crosses the river. Just downstream, Escalante Creek enters on the left at an easy riffle. Another riffle is at the mouth of Palmer Gulch, mile 17. Watch for a low rock **diversion weir** at mile 21. Near mile 26 the river flows through a long horseshoe bend to the right. Big Dominguez Creek (side hike) enters on the left in the middle of this bend, producing **DOMINGUEZ CREEK RAPID (II-)**. A bridge crosses the river below the rapid. Deer Creek at mile 28.5 marks the site of the **Bridgeport access.** Most boaters take out here.

A mile downstream, the railroad runs through a tunnel at a horseshoe bend. Kannah Creek enters on the right at mile 39. Two miles downriver is a proposed Bureau of Reclamation dam site. The final **take-out** is on the left at mile 43 where Colorado Highway 141 crosses the river at Whitewater. Legal access at this site is uncertain; contact the BLM in Grand Junction for current information before taking out here.

Downstream, the Gunnison runs another dozen miles through a shallower canyon to its confluence with the Colorado at Grand Junction. Private land, development, and diversions detract from this final stretch.

---

[4]The canyon is named for Fathers Dominguez and Escalante, who explored the area in 1777.

Upper San Juan River

Mesa Canyon

Difficulty: III-. **Gradient:** 33 ft./mi.
Length: 14 miles. Longer runs possible.
Put-in: Pagosa Springs (7,080').
Take-out: Above Trujillo (6,615').
Drainage Area and Average Annual Discharge: 298 sq. mi. and 278,000 af at put-in.
Season: May–early July.
Recommended Levels: 500–2,500 cfs. At high flows the roughest rapids are III+ to IV-.
Flow Information: WaterTalk, (303) 831-7135; 7*22* for flow at Pagosa Springs.
Permits: No boating permits, but request permission to use Indian Reservation lands (beginning near mile 5) from Southern Ute Tribe, Ignacio, CO 81137; (303) 563-4525.
Commercial Raft Trips: Yes. For references contact managing agency or Pagosa Springs Chamber of Commerce (see **Piedra** chapter).
Managing Agency: Pagosa Springs RD, San Juan NF, P.O. Box 310, Pagosa Springs, CO 81147; (303) 264-2268.
Land Ownership: Mixed private, National Forest, and Southern Ute Indian Reservation.
Scenery: Excellent. Partially forested canyon.
Solitude: Excellent.
Wilderness: Yes in the heart of Mesa Canyon. Lightly-used road below the canyon.
Water: Cold and relatively clear.
Side Excursions: Pagosa Hot Springs. Treasure Falls, just off U.S. 160 about 15 miles north of Pagosa Springs.
Guides and References:
- Wheat, *Floater's Guide to Colorado.*

Maps:
- **USGS 7.5':** *Pagosa Springs, Oak Brush Hill, Trujillo.*
- **USFS:** *San Juan NF.*
- **AAA:** *Indian Country.*

Auto Shuttle: 14–16 miles (half an hour) one way. Mostly unpaved. Contact Pagosa Rafting, (303) 731-4081.
Logistics: The best **put-in** is on the left bank just above the U.S. 160 bridge over the river at Pagosa Springs. An **alternate put-in** is half a mile downstream at the city park. To reach the **take-out,** drive west on U.S. 160; at the public library turn left on South 8th Street, which becomes Trujillo Road (County Road 500). Drive south some 12 miles to an easy access where the road comes close to the right bank just below the Trujillo Road 12-mile marker (river mile 14). An **alternate take-out** is two miles farther downstream at the bridge over the river at the hamlet of Trujillo. Trujillo Road continues downriver, providing other access points.

Most boaters know the San Juan as a silt-laden Canyon Country river that winds through spectacular gorges in southeastern Utah. But near its headwaters in the Colorado Rockies, the San Juan shows another face. Between the Continental Divide and the New Mexico border, the river is born as a sparkling mountain torrent and quickly ages into a muddy denizen of the desert.

The Upper San Juan offers everything from crystalline Class V cataracts to chocolate-brown flatwater. This guide covers the scenic intermediate stretch that features Mesa Canyon, but boaters can find more difficult rapids upstream or easier water downstream on the way to Navajo Reservoir. Whichever stretch they choose, they will likely enjoy the solitude, which is remarkable considering the easy vehicle access. Boating use is light on the Upper San Juan, due both to its distance from large cities and to the many other fine rivers nearby.

The river rises in the deep snows of the Continental Divide near Wolf Creek Pass, high in the San Juan Mountains of southwestern Colorado. Like its sister streams to the west, the Animas and Piedra, the San Juan drains the southern side of the range. But the San Juan encounters little resistant rock, so it carves no dramatic chasms to compare with the Animas Gorge or the Box Canyons of the Piedra. For most of its length, the Upper San Juan cuts steadily through softer sedimentary strata, producing gentler canyons and milder whitewater.

The only exceptions are near the headwaters, close to the junction of the river's East and West Forks about 10 miles northeast of Pagosa Springs. Here, hard volcanic rock produces the most difficult whitewater on the length of the

San Juan.[1] Class V rapids on the lower three miles of the East Fork occasionally draw expert boaters, but the short season, skimpy flows and frequent log hazards keep use light. A few boaters run the intermediate section below the confluence of the East and West Forks, which begins with Class III+ rapids and gets progressively easier as the river approaches Pagosa Springs. However, the run has several drawbacks, including access and landowner problems, fences, and check dams. Neither run is covered in this guide.

Mesa Canyon, the unheralded gem of the Upper San Juan, lies below Pagosa Springs. For more than a dozen miles the river has incised a narrow, shallow canyon into the sandstones of Eight Mile Mesa. Rapids occur primarily where dikes of volcanic rock protrude through the soft sedimentary deposits, forming resistant ledges across the river (notably near Squaw Creek, mile 8). The whitewater is mostly Class II to III-, reaching Class III+ only at high flows.

In Mesa Canyon the San Juan makes its transition from the mountains to the high desert, with one foot in the Colorado Rockies and one in Canyon Country. Riverside vegetation forms a mosaic of species common to both zones; an open forest of Ponderosa pines on moister and shadier sites, a scattering of pinyon and juniper on drier, sunnier slopes. The semiarid environment has thwarted most efforts at homesteading or ranching, so Mesa Canyon remains almost wilderness.

[1]With the exception of the Class VI waterfall that developed far downstream in 1991, when prolonged drought exposed a section of the Lower San Juan that is normally covered by Powell Reservoir. For more on that story, see the sidebar in the **Lower San Juan** chapter.

Below Mesa Canyon

Downstream from Trujillo, the river turns southwest through the Southern Ute Reservation. After 28 miles it stills in Navajo Reservoir, which has covered the San Juan's confluence with the Piedra since the early 1960's.

Below Mesa Canyon the Upper San Juan flows easily down a broad valley with lush stands of cottonwood and a few riverside ranches. In July and August this stretch has low but runnable flows and pleasantly warm water. From Trujillo to Pagosa Junction the water is mostly Class I+ with a few II's. The final stretch below Pagosa Junction is even milder. Though the easy rapids make for a good open canoe run, this stretch sees even less use than Mesa Canyon. An unpaved road along the right bank provides easy access and scouting and intrudes only slightly on the canyon's remote flavor.

Since 1971, trans-mountain diversions to the Rio Chama on the eastern side of the Continental Divide have drained most of the flow from two of the Upper San Juan's largest tributaries, the Rio Blanco and the Navajo River. At one time the Navajo was a fine canoe run, but today it is almost never boatable.

Mile by Mile Guide

0 **PUT-IN** on the left bank just above the U.S. 160 bridge in Pagosa Springs. An **alternate put-in** is half a mile downstream on the right at the city park. Then the river passes under a bridge and curves around Pagosa Hot Springs on the left. The scenery begins to improve farther downstream.

2.5 Water cascades from a generator building on the left at the mouth of Mill Creek. Unpaved road on the left ends a half mile below the creek. The rapids become more challenging downstream as the river gradually descends into Mesa Canyon.

4.8 The river enters the Southern Ute Indian Reservation. A mile downstream, the wooded mouth of Echo Canyon opens on the left. The rapids become longer and more difficult.

8.3 Squaw Canyon enters on the left, just above a sharp right bend. A long, technical rapid known as **THE ROCK GARDEN (III-)** begins above Squaw Canyon and extends a short way downstream. Soon the canyon walls give way to an open valley with mostly easier rapids.

10 **GRAND SLAM (II+)**. Just beyond an old gravel pit on the right. The river slides past a shale cliff on the right. Much of the current pours into a big reversal. Below the rapid a tumbledown bridge crosses the river at a private ranch on the right.

11.5 Trujillo Road approaches the right bank and follows the river downstream. Burns Canyon enters on the right a mile farther.

14 Easy **TAKE-OUT** where the road comes very close to the right bank. Half a mile downstream, the Rio Blanco—a major tributary depleted by trans-Divide diversions—enters on the left. The valley widens below this point.

16 **ALTERNATE TAKE-OUT** at the bridge at Trujillo (left bank). More alternate take-outs downstream as far as Navajo Reservoir (see essay).

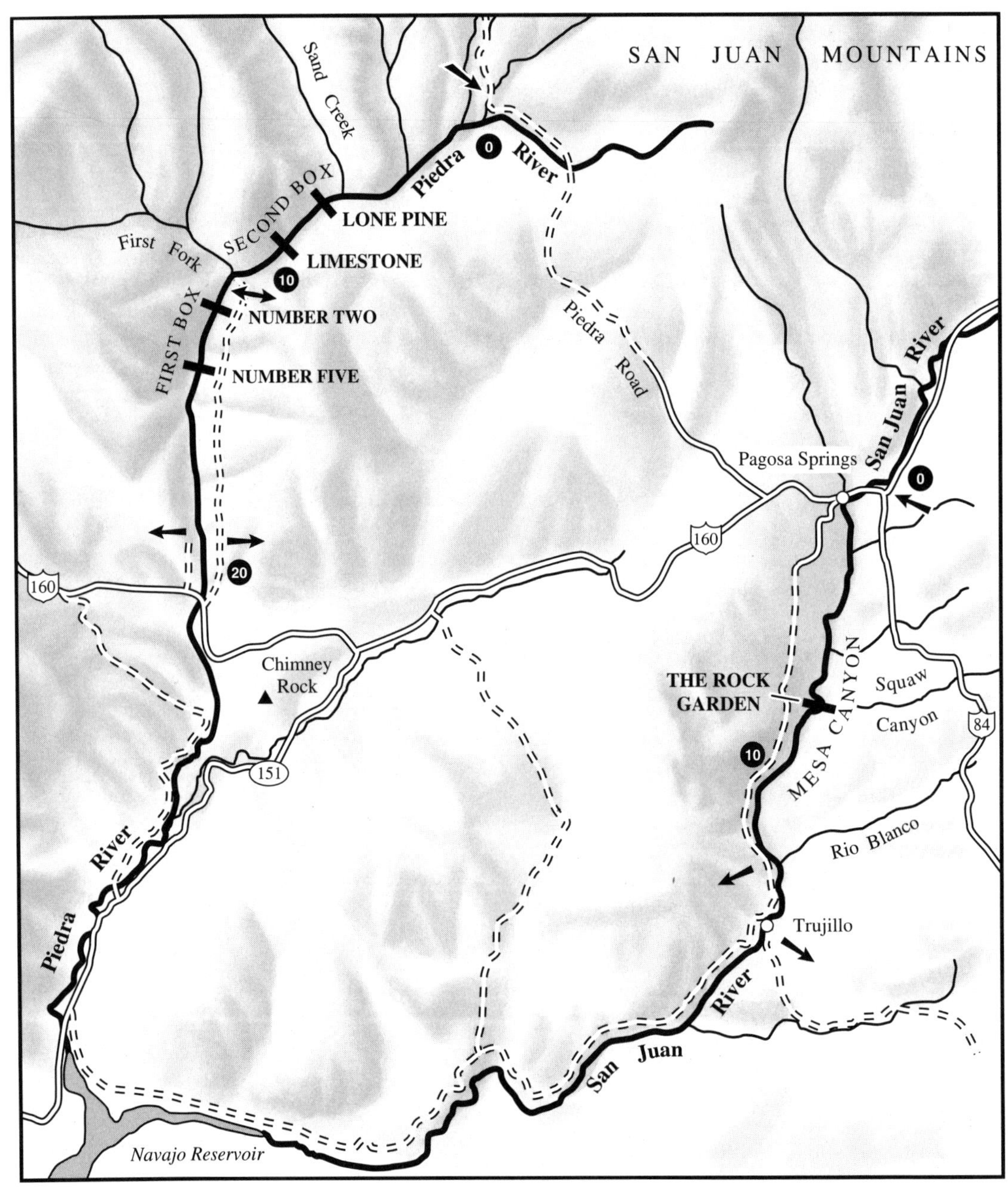

Piedra and Upper San Juan

Piedra River

Second and First Box Canyons

Difficulty: *Second Box:* III+ (IV above 1,500 cfs). *First Box:* IV+ (V above 1,500 cfs).
Length: 20 miles. Shorter runs possible.
Gradient: 53 ft./mi.
Put-in: Piedra Road Bridge (7,610').
Take-out: Lower Piedra Campground (6,580').
Drainage Area: 80 sq. mi.at put-in (est.); 470 at take-out.
Average Annual Discharge: 304,000 af.
Season: May–June. Typically peaks in late May. Lower run (First Box) is usually runnable for a couple of weeks longer than upper run (Second Box).
Recommended Levels: 700–2,000 cfs.
Flow Information: No reliable gauge. For current conditions call the managing agency or Four Corners River Sports in Durango, (303) 259-3893.
Special Hazards: Numerous logs. Difficult scouting and portages. Difficult to hike out in case of emergency. Landslides can alter rapids at any time.
Permits: Not presently required. (For Lower Piedra, see end of essay.)
Managing Agency: Pagosa Springs RD, San Juan NF, P.O. Box 310, Pagosa Springs, CO 81147; (303) 264-2268.
Commercial Raft Trips: Yes. For references contact managing agency or Chamber of Commerce, 402 San Juan St., Pagosa Springs, CO 81147; (800) 252-2204.
Land Ownership: Mostly National Forest.
Scenery: Excellent. Narrow forested canyon.
Solitude: Excellent. **Wilderness:** Yes.

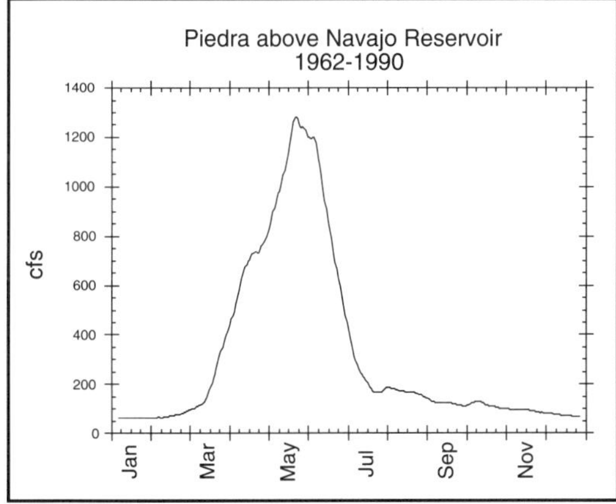

Fishing: Good for trout when water is clear.
Wildlife: Abundant.
Water: Cold. Muddy when high, clears as flows drop. Purify side creek water for drinking.
Camping: Many sites except in the box canyons. Most two-day trips camp at First Fork CG. USFS campgrounds at put-in and take-out.
Side Hikes: USFS trails climb some side creeks. A right-bank trail follows the upper half of the run, allowing boaters to see Second Box Canyon before (or instead of) running it.
Side Excursions: Weminuche Wilderness Area above the put-in. Chimney Rock (1200') and the Chimney Rock Archaeological Area with more than 100 Anasazi ruins; both are a few miles southeast of the take-out (contact USFS for information and tour reservations).
Guides and References:
- Wheat, *Floater's Guide to Colorado.*
- Rennicke, *Rivers of Colorado.*

Maps:
- **USGS 7.5':** *Oakbrush Ridge, Bear Mtn, Devil Mtn, Chimney Rock.*
- **USGS 1:100:** *Durango.*
- **USFS:** *San Juan NF* also covers Lower Piedra.
- **AAA:** *Indian Country.*

Auto Shuttle: About 50 miles (1 to 1.5 hours) one way for the full run.
Logistics: To reach the **put-in,** turn north off U.S. 160 two miles west of Pagosa Springs onto Piedra Road (USFS Road 631—paved, then dirt) and drive some 16 miles to the bridge near Piedra Picnic Ground. To reach the **take-out,** return to U.S. 160, drive west 19 miles, cross the Piedra, and half a mile farther, turn right on unpaved USFS Road 621, which leads over a mile up the right bank to Lower Piedra CG. To get to the **easier take-out** on the left bank opposite the campground, turn right on First Fork Road (USFS Road 622) just *before* (east of) the U.S. 160 bridge. To reach the **intermediate access** at First Fork CG (sometimes called Hunter CG), turn onto First Fork Road as above, but continue up the canyon all the way to the campground and river. This road is sometimes washed out near the end and may require 4-wheel drive; inquire locally about current conditions.

PIEDRA

From the Continental Divide in southwestern Colorado, the Piedra flows south some 60 miles to its confluence with the San Juan River near the New Mexico border, now covered by the waters of Navajo Reservoir. The Piedra watershed, lying on the southwest flank of the San Juan Mountains, is somewhat warmer in summer than others in the Colorado Rockies. In winter, however, it often accumulates one of the region's heaviest snowpacks. The upper watershed is protected by the Weminuche Wilderness.

For most of its length the Piedra courses through a sloping canyon draped in pine, fir, and spruce. Wildlife abounds, and civilization seems far away.[1] The rapids in these forest reaches are lively but by no means intimidating.

But in the middle of its course, the Piedra reveals the other side of its character. In two narrow defiles known as the Second and First Box Canyons, the Piedra passes out of softer sedimentary strata and cuts deep, sheer-sided trenches through massive blocks of ancient metamorphic rock that were thrust up into the river's eventual path some 40 to 70 million years ago. The Piedra canyon itself, including the box canyons, has been cut in the last two million years.

The river's name apparently comes from these towering canyon walls. In 1776 the exploring Spanish Fathers Dominguez and Escalante named it "El Rio de la Piedra Parada," or "The River of the Stone Wall." (Whether the Fathers saw these soaring ramparts themselves or simply heard rumor of them from the Utes or other Indians, no one can say.) Today, the river is known simply as the Piedra.

The First Box Canyon (the downstream canyon)[2] is decidedly more difficult than the Second. **The First Box should be attempted only by experts, and even they should stay away at high water.** Enormous blocks of rock have tumbled from the walls into the river, creating turbulent falls and boulder gardens. In places the vertical walls rise directly from the water, making scouting or portaging difficult and leaving no way out but downstream.

Those who would like to sample the Piedra at a lesser risk can use the intermediate access at First Fork Campground (sometimes called Hunter Campground) to take out just above the First Box. The campground is also popular with groups making a full two-day run; camping there makes it unnecessary to carry overnight gear down the river.

Two more factors add to the difficulty and uncertainty of running the Box Canyons. First, the canyon walls are unstable. Landslides can create new rapids or alter old ones at any time. As recently as 1979, a major slide near the mouth of First Box produced the most treacherous rapids on the run. Second, the combination of dense forest and unstable soils means lots of logs in the river—serious hazards that can change from one season to the next. Always inquire locally before running the Box Canyons.

Below U.S. 160 the Piedra leaves its mountain canyons and flows more easily across a gradually widening flood plain. The gradient soon drops to 25 ft./mi., and the river winds among gravel islands where towering cottonwoods partially screen several riverside ranches.

Eight miles below U.S. 160, the river leaves San Juan National Forest and enters the Southern Ute Indian Reservation (tribal use permit required; for address, see **Lower Animas**). Colorado Highway 151 joins the left bank at the reservation boundary and follows the river for eight more miles to the backwaters of Navajo Reservoir, providing several possible take-outs. Although the run below U.S. 160 is generally flat with easy riffles, boaters should watch for barbed wire, strainers, and possible irrigation diversions.

---

[1]The Piedra is a candidate for National Wild and Scenic protection, but Congress has so far failed to act.

[2]To boaters traveling downstream, it seems odd that the Second Box Canyon comes first. But the river was originally explored on foot by people headed upstream.

Mile by Mile Guide

See map at end of ***Upper San Juan*** *chapter.*

0 **PUT-IN** at Piedra Road Bridge. Three big tributaries entering from the north in the first 6 miles add substantially to the flow. A trail follows the right bank downstream to First Fork Campground. Not far below the put-in is a short but lovely mini-gorge with undercut sandstone walls.

1.7 Williams Creek enters on the right.

3.2 A foot bridge crosses the river. Half a mile downstream, Weminuche Creek enters on the right.

6 Sand Creek enters on the right (side hike). Half a mile downstream, the walls close in and the trail climbs high on the right as the river enters two-mile-long **Second Box Canyon.** The action starts with **LONE PINE (III+)**, a long rapid peppered with holes. More Class III+ rapids (IV at higher flows) follow.

8.5 **LIMESTONE (III+, IV at higher flows).** As the Second Box begins to open up, the river drops sharply over ledges and piles into the left wall. Below this rapid the river eases to Class II and III.

10.5 A bridge crosses the river as First Fork, a major tributary, enters on the right. First Fork Campground is on the left. **RIVER ACCESS** via First Fork Road, which climbs the slope and follows the river high above the left bank to U.S. 160.

Just downstream the Piedra enters **First Box Canyon,** a sheer-walled chasm filled with pounding, boulder-strewn drops. An extremely constricted channel and a steep gradient (80 ft./mi.) magnify the river's power dramatically. Vertical walls often rise directly from the water, hampering scouting and portaging. Even so, many boaters portage at least once, especially at higher flows. *Climbing out of First Box would be extremely difficult.* ***If in doubt, scout from shore first by hiking down the left bank.***

Some boaters refer to the rapids in First Box as **NUMBER ONE** through **NUMBER SIX,** while others use a variety of sometimes overlapping popular names. **NUMBER TWO,** also known as **First Box Falls,** is a steep, challenging Class IV+ drop against the left wall. More Class IV rapids follow.

At mile 12 the river begins to emerge from the box, but the biggest drop waits half a mile downstream. **NUMBER FIVE,** also called **Mudslide** or **Eye of the Needle,** is a difficult Class IV+ rapid (up to V+ at high flows) created by a landslide on the right. Debris from the slide forces the river against the left wall; there, it squeezes into a narrow funnel between big boulders and crashes over a treacherous drop. The runout is poor: immediately downstream is the final rapid, a complex boulder garden known by various names, including **NUMBER SIX** and **LUCIFER'S.** Scout right and, if necessary, attempt a very difficult portage. *HAZARD. These final rapids, formed by the 1979 landslide, may change at any time and could become even more difficult.* Below the last rapid the whitewater eases.

14.2 Sheep Creek enters on the right (side hike). Class II below this point. Downstream a foot bridge crosses the river, and a trail climbs the steep left slope to a spur road that connects with First Fork Road. Indian Creek (side hike) enters on the right three quarters of a mile farther downriver.

18 Tres Piedras Ranch (private) on the right.

19.5 **TAKE-OUT.** Lower Piedra Campground, a possible take-out on the right bank. Easier take-out on the left opposite the campground. (See **Logistics.**) A mile downstream, U.S. 160 crosses the river.

Animas River

1. Upper Animas: Mineral Creek (9,240') to Tacoma (7,240') or Rockwood (7,090').
V (VI at high water); 25 or 28 miles; 78 ft./mi.

2. Lower Animas: Trimble Bridge (6,560') to North Durango (6,520').
I+; 11 miles; 4 ft./mi.

3. Lower Animas: South Durango (6,480') to Bondad Bridge (5,980').
III-, I+; 20 miles; 25 ft./mi.
Shorter runs possible.

Drainage Area and Average Annual Discharge: *Upper:* 140 sq. mi. (est.) at put-in; 400 sq. mi. and 500,000 af (est.) at take-out. *Lower:* 692 sq. mi. and 617,000 af.

Season: *Upper:* May–July. Peak snowmelt in late May or early June. Best flows are usually from mid-June on, except in wet years when they may be too high until late June. Summer rains can swell the river suddenly. At any level, flows increase rapidly below the put-in and triple or quadruple by the take-out. *Lower:* April–August.

Recommended Levels: *Upper:* Roughly 200–800 cfs at the put-in or 800–3,000 cfs on the Durango gauge downstream from the take-out. *Lower:* 400–4,000 cfs.

Flow Information: WaterTalk, (303) 831-7135; 7*2* for flow at Durango.

Special Hazards: *Upper Animas:* **Entire run** (see essay). Someone who knows the river well should be on every trip. Boaters unfamiliar with the run may miss mandatory scouts or the take-out. **Do *not* attempt the unrunnable Lower Box.** Know where to take out *before* you put in. *Lower Animas:* Strainers and fences on Run 2.

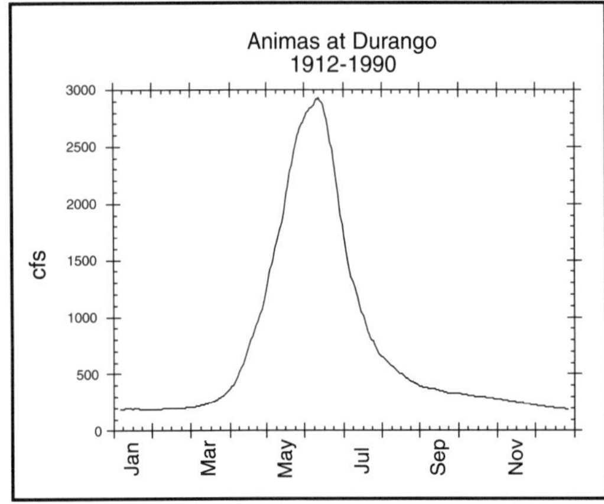

Permits: *Upper:* Not presently required. *Lower:* Required to take out on Souther Ute Reservation (see end of chapter).

Managing Agency: San Juan NF, 701 Camino Del Rio, Durango, CO 81301; (303) 247-4874.

Commercial Raft Trips: Yes. For references contact managing agency or Durango Area Chamber Resort Assn., 111 S. Camino Del Rio, Durango, CO 81301; (303) 247-0312.

Land Ownership: *Upper:* USFS and BLM; scattered private land. *Lower:* Mostly private to about 5 miles below Durango; Southern Ute Indian Reservation thereafter.

Scenery: *Upper:* Excellent. Dramatic, rugged alpine peaks and canyon. *Lower:* Good.

Solitude: *Upper:* Excellent. Narrow-gauge railway follows the river. *Lower:* Fair to good.

Wilderness: No.

Fishing: *Upper:* Fair for trout below Elk Creek.

Weather: Cold due to high elevation. Snow is possible into June.

Water: Very cold. Clear except at high flows.

Camping: *Upper:* Good riverside sites. Several USFS campgrounds in the area.

Side Hikes: *Upper:* The Durango & Silverton Railroad can drop off and pick up backpackers and day hikers in the canyon; call the railroad for details. The popular Purgatory Trail leads from Purgatory Campground on U.S. 550 down Cascade Creek, then follows the Animas upstream to Needleton. A steep trail leads from Needleton up into Chicago Basin and the Weminuche Wilderness.

Side Excursions: Historic Silverton. Durango & Silverton Railroad. Mesa Verde National Park, 35 miles west of Durango.

Guides and References:
- Wheat, *Floater's Guide to Colorado.*
- A good local source for information is Four Corners River Sports in Durango, (303) 259-3893.

Maps:
- **USGS 7.5':** *Upper:* Silverton, Snowdon Peak, Mountain View Crest, Electra Lake, Hermosa.
- **USGS 1:100:** *Silverton, Durango* (covers end of Upper and all of Lower Animas).
- **USFS:** *San Juan NF.*
- **AAA:** *Indian Country.*

Logistics: *Upper Animas:* **Put-ins** at Silverton include (1) right bank of the Animas at a gravel quarry downstream from the railroad station; (2) right bank of Mineral Creek below the U.S. 550 bridge; (3) right bank of the Animas below Mineral Creek.

There are two options for take-outs. The legal choice is to take out on the left bank opposite Tacoma Powerhouse and ride out on the Durango & Silverton Railroad. Tickets must be purchased and arrangements made *in advance*; call (303) 247-2733.

Another—the Rockwood take-out—is illegal, potentially dangerous, and not recommended, but boaters have used it for years. They float 2.5 miles past the Powerhouse take-out to a small ravine on the right, then scramble up to the railroad. They can cross the tracks, continue up the slope, and follow a trail that bypasses the Rockwood Cut, a cleft carved through the canyon wall where the rail line enters the gorge. However, some hike the last quarter mile along the tracks through the narrow cut, and they must *not* be on or near the tracks when trains are due. **Anyone hiking along the tracks should know the train schedule.** It would be safest to wait until the last train of the afternoon has passed. **The cut is private property, so boaters could be cited for trespassing.** *Note that using the Rockwood take-out adds very difficult rapids below Tacoma Bridge and presents the danger of missing the take-out and being swept into the unrunnable gorge downstream.*

To drive to this take-out, follow U.S. 550 south to the Rockwood turnoff (some 3 miles south of the Haviland Lake turnoff). Turn east and drive down to the railway buildings (private property). For shuttles contact Four Corners River Sports in Durango.

Lower Animas: Many alternate accesses; only the most popular are listed here. Runs of almost any length are possible. *Run 2:* To reach the **put-in** at Trimble Bridge, drive north from Durango some 7 miles on U.S. 550 and turn east on Trimble Lane. The **take-out** is on the left bank just above the 32nd Street bridge at the north end of Durango. *Run 3:* The **put-in** is on the right bank at the upstream end of Schneider Park, above the 9th Street bridge in Durango. For **alternate accesses** see the essay below. The **last take-out** is on the left about half a mile above Bondad (U.S. 550) Bridge. This site is reached by a short, unmarked spur road off U.S. 550.

Towering over southwestern Colorado are the lofty San Juan Mountains, boasting some of the state's most rugged and beautiful peaks. This great spur of the Rockies gives birth to a half dozen remarkable rivers, including the Rio Grande, San Juan, Piedra, Dolores, and San Miguel. Yet even in the midst of such shining company, one river—the Animas—stands above the rest for its breathtaking whitewater and superb scenery.

The Animas flows just over 100 miles from its icy headwaters near Silverton to the San Juan confluence in the high desert of New Mexico. The river, which is the largest tributary of the San Juan, is most famous for its upper reaches. The put-in for the Upper Animas is above 9,000', the shuttle road climbs above 10,000', and peaks over 14,000' are all around. In the Animas Gorge just below Silverton, continuous Class V whitewater brings the term "limits of navigability" to life. Of the rivers in this guide book that are regularly boated, this is one of the most hazardous. **The Upper Animas is emphatically for experts only.** Downstream from Durango, the Lower Animas is much milder.

Animas country has a history as rich as any in the Colorado Rockies region. Until a little over a hundred years ago, the river and its canyon were home to the Ute Indians. Spanish explorers seeking gold and riches hurried past the Animas without attempting to probe its upper reaches. Finding the jagged canyons ominous and forbidding, they named the river "El Rio de las Animas Perdidas en Purgatorio," or "The River of Lost Souls in Purgatory." In later years the name was shortened to "Animas."

The Spaniards marched right past some of the West's richest mining territory. Gold was discovered here in 1870—inconvenient timing, since just two years earlier the U.S. had granted the Utes these lands in perpetuity. For a few years conflicts with the Indians kept most miners away. In 1874, however, the government redefined "perpetuity" and forced the Utes to relinquish some 4,500 square miles of land for roughly 12 cents an acre.[1]

[1] In 1880, after the so-called "Meeker Massacre," the Utes were pushed out of the mountains and sent to high-desert reservations along the Colorado-New Mexico border.

With the way now opened for a rush of miners into the region, dozens of small camps and towns sprang into life. To link the mines along the upper river with processing mills downstream, the Denver & Rio Grande Railroad pushed a narrow-gauge spur line upriver through the rugged Animas Gorge. Even by modern standards the railroad was a remarkable feat of engineering.[2]

In 1882 the train carried its first load of ore from Silverton down to Durango. Silver mining boomed for ten years; then the bottom fell out when the government stopped buying silver to support the U.S. currency. Soon, however, gold and other metals picked up some of the slack, carrying the boom for another three decades before it finally faded. In the last 25 years mining has had a minor resurgence; Colorado's largest present-day gold mine operates not far from Silverton.

Now the Durango & Silverton Railroad carries a different load up and down the Animas Gorge. Three or four times a day, a steam locomotive hauls tourists along the upper river, treating them to some of the most spectacular mountain scenery in America: snow-covered peaks towering over a dramatic canyon, alpine forest punctuated by side creek waterfalls, and always, at the bottom, the raging river.

If they're lucky, the sightseers may get a glimpse of that most exotic denizen of the Animas, the whitewater lunatic. And lunatic it must seem from a comfortable seat on the train to venture onto that turbulent torrent. Few rivers can match the Upper Animas for heart-stopping whitewater action. In the 30-mile-long Animas Gorge—a deep, jagged slot carved through the ancient metamorphic bedrock of the San Juan Mountains—the river drops 2,450'. The scenery is among the finest in this guide, but river runners will find little time to gaze at snow-covered peaks. With a steep, continuous gradient, few eddies, several Class V rapids, and an unrunnable gorge below the take-out, the Animas is a non-stop challenge. **Only experts in kayaks or self-bailing rafts should try this one.**

Beyond its whitewater, the Upper Animas presents a host of difficulties that can make the run a true purgatory for the unprepared. *Altitude:* At 9,240' the Silverton put-in is, along with the Upper Rio Grande, the highest in this book. Boaters must be in top condition and well acclimated. *Cold:* The water is shocking, and sometimes the air isn't much warmer. Dry suits or wet suits are essential, and even then hypothermia is a serious threat. *Variable flows:* At the put-in the Animas is an overgrown mountain stream, but within a quarter mile Mineral Creek more than doubles the flow. The flow nearly doubles again before the take-out—unless rainstorms swell it even more—so the river's power increases throughout the run. *Isolation:* The terrain is extremely rugged, and evacuation may be difficult in an emergency. The railroad cannot be relied on for help.

Finally, there is the infamous Lower Box. Just before it flattens out above Durango, the Animas crashes through an unrunnable, unportageable, sheer-sided gorge with a gradient of more than 200 ft./mi. Even the railroad skirts this impassable section, and boaters must do likewise. Since no road penetrates the Animas Gorge, river runners are obliged to leave the canyon via the railroad, either by riding the train or by walking the tracks through the Rockwood Cut. The former method is logistically complex and a bit expensive but legal. The latter is illegal (see **Logistics**).

An overnight run is possible either by packing very light or by having overnight gear hauled in by the railway to Needleton, near the halfway point. River runners can end their trips at the take-out opposite Tacoma Powerhouse (mile 25) and take the train back to the put-in. Those who float the full 28-mile stretch to the

The Animas-La Plata Project

The Animas is one of the few rivers on the west slope of the Rockies that is not depleted by trans-Divide diversions. But its good luck could run out. In 1968 Congress authorized the Animas-La Plata Project to divert up to 200,000 acre-feet each year from the river near Durango and pump it into the adjacent La Plata basin. The project, whose current price tag is $641 million, has been stalled many times but never stopped. In 1991 the Animas-La Plata Irrigation District held a ceremonial ground-breaking. If it is completed, the diversion could reduce flows in the Lower Animas by several hundred cfs, significantly shortening the summer boating season and damaging wildlife and fish populations (particularly the threatened Colorado squawfish).

[2]The engineers who designed nearby U.S. 550, famous as the "Million Dollar Highway," made no attempt to follow the precipitous riverside route from Silverton to Durango. (The price tag for 50 miles of highway was about $1 million, but that was back when a buck was still worth a dollar.)

(illegal) Rockwood take-out must carry boats and any overnight gear out of the canyon, so most of those groups try to make the run in one long day. However, the difficult whitewater, constant scouting, probable portage(s), and strenuous take-out make this a demanding feat with little margin for error. A two-day run lowers the strain a notch and allows boaters to linger a bit on one of the world's finest whitewater rivers.

Upper Animas Mile Guide

0 **PUT-IN** on either the Animas or Mineral Creek about a quarter mile above their confluence (see **Logistics**). The river and the creek have nearly equal flows. The railroad crosses the creek just above the confluence. The Animas falls 65 ft./mi. in the first 5 miles to Elk Park.

1.2 Railroad crosses the river on a low bridge. ***HAZARD.*** A fence under the bridge may require portage. Downstream, the walls of the gorge close in and the gradient increases. Many side creek waterfalls plunge into the river in this section.

5.5 The walls recede as the river enters Elk Park, a more open area with easier whitewater. A foot bridge crosses the river at mile 5.8, serving a steep trail that leads two miles from the right bank up to the highway. **If in doubt, hike out: the river becomes much more difficult downstream.** Elk Creek enters on the left about a third of a mile below the foot bridge. A pack trail follows the creek upstream from the foot bridge.

6.7 The railway crosses the river. Just downstream the canyon walls close in again, and powerful rapids begin about a mile below the railroad bridge.

8.7 **GARFIELD SLIDE** (V), also known as **Tenmile.** A quarter-mile-long rapid formed by slides from steep slopes on the left. Metal debris in the current on the right adds to the difficulty and danger. Scout carefully from the right bank. Tenmile Creek enters on the left a half mile downstream. Continuous whitewater from here to No Name Falls.

10.8 **NO NAME FALLS** (V+). The most difficult rapid on the run. **Recognition:** The

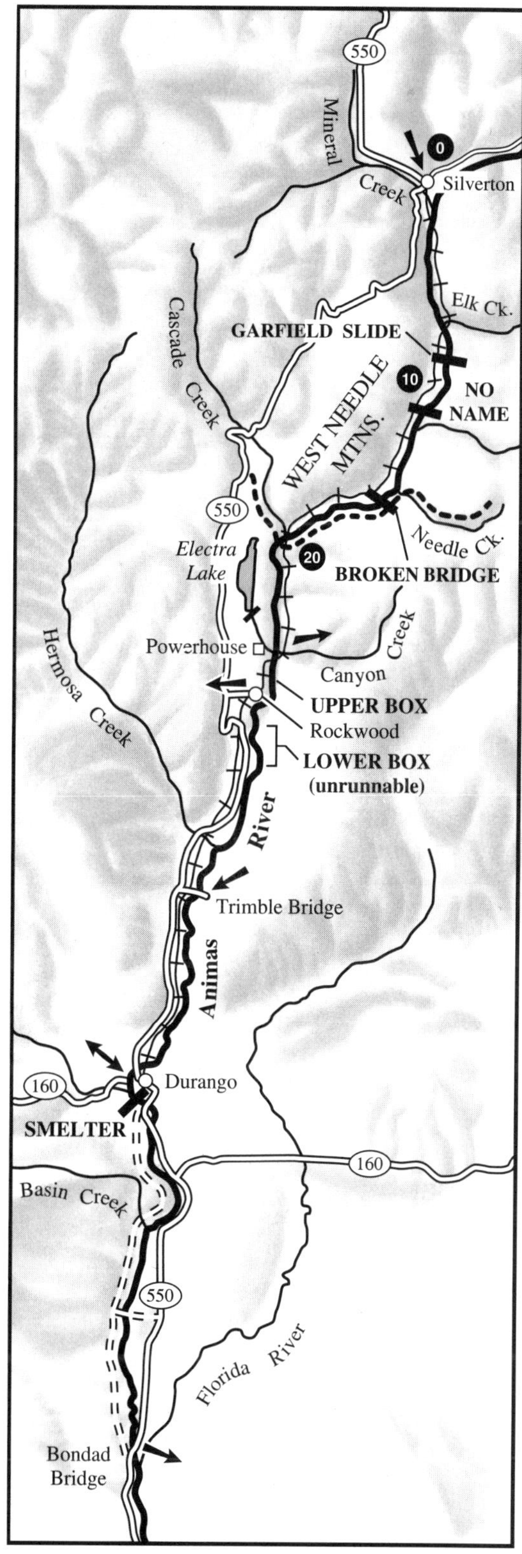

Animas

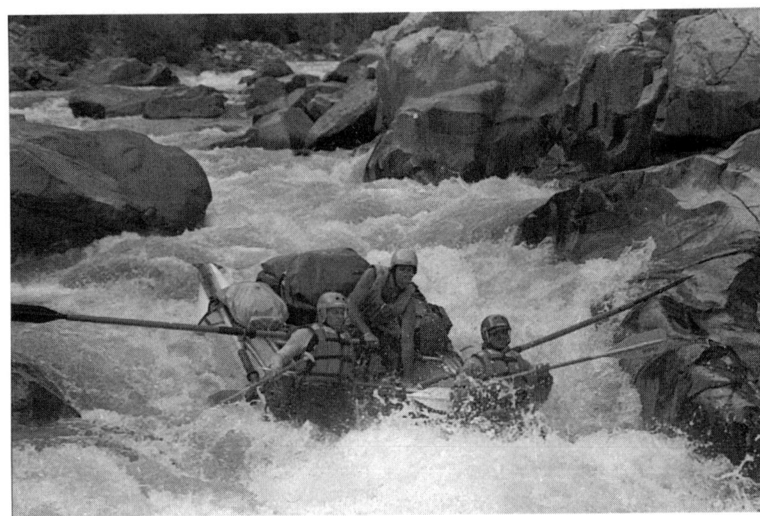

Upper Animas River *Jack Klopfer*

rapid is after a right-hand bend, but challenging whitewater just upstream makes recognition difficult. Approach this entire section of river with caution, scouting frequently. **The rapid:** The river squeezes between large granite boulders and drops abruptly through churning, irregular holes and side curlers. The run-out is poor, with a Class IV drop just 50' downstream. Scout and, if in doubt, portage on the right. Below the rapid No Name Creek enters on the left. Downstream, Class IV rapids continue for 3 miles as the Animas cuts between the 13,000' to 14,000' spires of the East and West Needle Mountains.

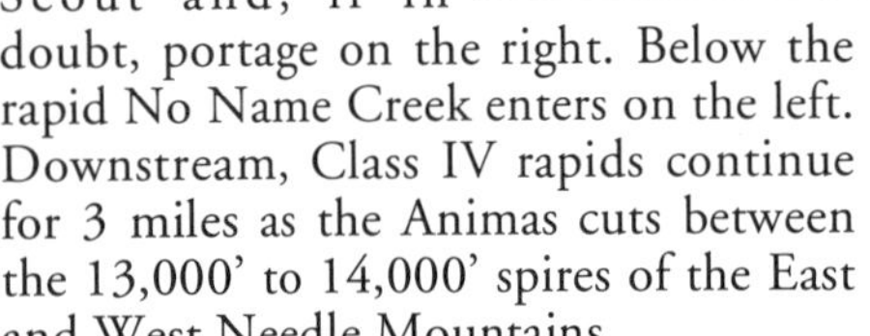

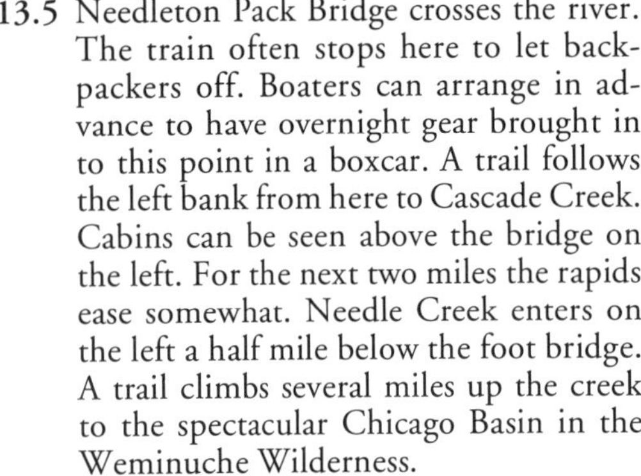

13.5 Needleton Pack Bridge crosses the river. The train often stops here to let backpackers off. Boaters can arrange in advance to have overnight gear brought in to this point in a boxcar. A trail follows the left bank from here to Cascade Creek. Cabins can be seen above the bridge on the left. For the next two miles the rapids ease somewhat. Needle Creek enters on the left a half mile below the foot bridge. A trail climbs several miles up the creek to the spectacular Chicago Basin in the Weminuche Wilderness.

15.5 **BROKEN BRIDGE RAPID** (V), also known as **Chicago Bridge Rapid.** The remains of a steel foot bridge across the river signal the entrance to a long, pounding rapid littered with big boulders and holes. Scout carefully on the right.

19 The railway crosses from right bank to left. Cascade Creek, a major tributary, enters on the right just downstream. The Purgatory Trail crosses the river on a foot bridge and follows the creek about 4 miles up to the highway, providing a possible emergency exit. Below Cascade Creek the gradient moderates slightly (65 ft./mi.) and the rapids shift to more of a pool-drop nature. Challenging Class IV chutes lurk in several mini-gorges.

23 Ah Wilderness Trails Ranch (private) on the left. A half mile downstream is a difficult Class IV drop with a powerful reversal.

25 **TAKE-OUT** on the left bank, opposite Tacoma Powerhouse, which generates electricity with water from Electra Lake. Boaters can take out here if they have arranged in advance to be picked up by the train.

26 The railway crosses to the right bank over the high Tacoma trestle. In the past some boaters have taken out here and hiked two miles down the tracks to Rockwood, but this involves trespassing along a hazardous stretch of railway and is strongly discouraged. Downstream lies the extremely challenging **Upper Box Canyon,** where the river drops 100 ft./mi. through a steep-walled inner gorge filled with Class IV+ and V- rapids. A particularly difficult drop with a river-wide hole (typically run far right) guards the entrance to the gorge. After one mile the canyon opens again, and the last possible take-out is about half a mile downstream. High above the right bank, the railway curves west to leave the canyon.

27.5 **ALTERNATE TAKE-OUT** on the right, about half a mile below the end of the Upper Box, at the foot of a small ravine or draw. This critical spot is not distinctive and, as of this writing, is not marked. Those unfamiliar with the run should hike in and scout the take-out carefully *before* running the Animas. From the river boaters scramble up the ravine to the railroad, then carry out along the trail above the Rockwood Cut (or along the cut itself). This access is illegal (see **Logistics**).

HAZARD. **Don't miss the take-out.** Downstream, the Animas plunges into **Lower Box Canyon,** a mile-and-a-half-long death trap of unrunnable rapids in a narrow, log-choked chasm with a gradient of over 200 ft./mi. Vertical walls make scouting, lining, and portaging impossible. Several lives have been lost here.

Lower Animas River Guide

Below the cataracts of the Lower Box the Animas abruptly changes character. The railroad and the highway rejoin the right bank as the river emerges from its dark gorge of hard metamorphic rock into softer sedimentary strata. Here the Lower Animas spreads out onto a broad flood plain. The river has partially filled its original valley with glacial debris, creating a mile-wide flat between steep mountain slopes on the way to Durango. Below Durango the river courses some 50 miles across the high desert to its confluence with the San Juan at Farmington, New Mexico.

Trimble Bridge to North Durango

The Animas meanders slowly across its flat flood plain, offering 11 miles of Class I water below the **put-in** at Trimble Bridge. Dozens of oxbow lakes and cutoff bends attest to a constantly shifting channel. Cottonwoods and willows harbor abundant bird life and give a sense of isolation despite the highway and the railroad. Most boaters **take out** at the 32nd Street bridge at the north end of Durango, but some follow the curving 2.5-mile stretch through town to Schneider Park, put-in for the next run.

South Durango to Bondad Bridge

Below Durango the Animas offers 20 miles of intermediate to novice boating through a shallow, semi-arid canyon. Commercial outfitters run frequent trips on portions of this reach.

The most popular **put-in** for intermediate boaters is Schneider Park near the south end of Durango (mile 0). About a mile downstream is the biggest rapid on the Lower Animas, **SMELTER (III-)**, an S-curve that develops big waves at high flows. Smelter is the site of the slalom event at the annual Animas River Days, one of the West's top whitewater rodeos. **Alternate accesses** are on the left bank at Durango Whitewater Park, both above and below the rapid.

Several smaller rapids follow in the next mile. **SANTA RITA HOLE,** at mile 1.5 just below the highway bridge, is the site of the Animas River Days hole-riding contest. The next easy **access** is at a city park behind Four Corners River Sports (mile 2.5). The highway crosses the river for the last time at mile 3.5 (**alternate access** on the left just below the bridge). A mile farther is another **access** on the right at a site known as the "Purple Cliffs," reached via La Posta Road (County Road 213). This site is private; inquire locally about permission to use it. Be advised that at present, *all access below this point is "iffy"*—but it is a nice float.

Downstream, the river is Class II or easier. At mile 5.5 the Animas enters the Southern Ute Indian Reservation. The Southern Utes do not require permits to float through their lands, but they do reuquire permits for take-outs (vehicle access) inside their borders, and they prosecute trespassers. To buy a permit or get updated information contact the Southern Ute Tribe, Ignacio, CO 81137; (303) 563-4525.

Soon the highway turns away from the river for more than ten miles. A permit from the Utes is necessary to use Weaselskin Bridge, which crosses the river at mile 11.5, for **river access.** The last good **take-out** is at mile 19.5, on the left bank a half mile upstream from Bondad Bridge (U.S. 550). This site, which has a gravel road, is private; inquire locally about permission to use it. Few boaters take out at Bondad Bridge because of the difficult clamber up to the highway.

Rio Grande

Lobatos Bridge to Taos County Line

1.Ute Mountain Run:
Lobatos Bridge (7,430') to Lee Trail.
II; 24.5 miles; 7 ft./mi.

2. Upper Box:
Lee Trail to Little Arsenic Springs.
III–VIp; 13 miles; 20–120 ft./mi.
Shorter runs possible.

3. La Junta Run:
Little Arsenic Springs to John Dunn Bridge.
II–III; 9.5 miles; 11 ft./mi.

4. Taos Box:
John Dunn Bridge to Taos Junction Bridge.
IV (IV+ above 3,000 cfs); 15 miles; 30 ft./mi.

5. State Park Run:
Taos Junction Bridge to Pilar.
II; 6.5 miles; 9 ft./mi. Shorter runs possible.

6. Racecourse Run:
Pilar to Taos County Line (5,865').
III (IV above 4,000 cfs); 4.5 miles; 34 ft./mi.
Shorter runs possible.

Drainage Area and Average Annual Discharge: 7,700 sq. mi. / 613,000 af at Lobatos Bridge.

Peak Recorded Flow: 13,200 cfs at Lobatos Bridge (June 8, 1905).

Season: *Run 1:* June–early July (closed April 1–May 31 to protect nesting birds). *Runs 2–4:* Mid-April–mid-July. *Runs 5 & 6:* April–Oct.

Recommended Levels: *Run 1:* 500–5,000 cfs. *Run 2:* 500–2,000 (**experts only**). *Run 3:* 800–5,000. *Run 4:* 800–5,000. *Runs 5 & 6:* 400–5,000.

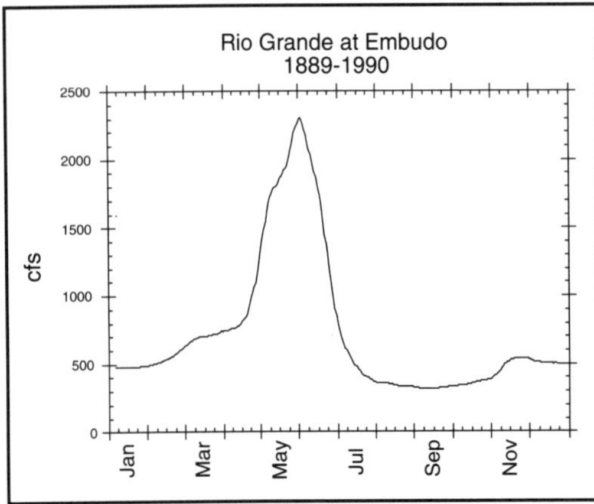

Flow Information: WaterTalk, (303) 831-7135; 3*13* for flow at Lobatos Bridge. BLM, (505) 758-8148, gives flows at John Dunn Bridge and Taos Junction Bridge. USGS, (505) 262-5388, gives flows at Lobatos Bridge, Embudo, and Otowi Bridge.

Special Hazards: Extremely hazardous rapids in Upper Box, which is for seasoned experts only. Remote area (Runs 1–3).

Permits: *Runs 1, 3, & 4:* Self-registration at put-ins. *Run 2:* Not required, but for safety notify BLM of trips. *Runs 5 & 6:* Not presently required. Contact BLM for updated information.

Managing Agency: BLM, Taos Resource Area, 224 Cruz Alta Road, Taos, NM 87571; (505) 758-8851.

Commercial Raft Trips: Popular on the Taos Box and Racecourse Runs; some trips on La Junta Run. For references contact the managing agency or Taos County Chamber of Commerce, P.O. Drawer 1, Taos, NM 87571; (800) 732-8267.

Land Ownership: Mixed BLM, National Forest, and private.

Scenery: Generally excellent. Includes several sheer-walled canyons cut into volcanic rock.

Solitude and Wilderness: Vary with run. See essay.

Fishing: Good for trout at lower flows.

Wildlife: Abundant birds on Run 1.

Water: Cold and turbid at high flows; cool in summer. A few springs in the upper canyons provide drinking water; downstream, be sure to carry your own.

Camping: *Run 1:* A few riverside campsites. *Run 2:* Some shelters along the left bank near Big and Little Arsenic Springs. Developed campsites and BLM Visitors' Center (camping information) in Rio Grande Wild River Recreation Area along the canyon rim above the Upper Box. *Runs 3 & 4:* Few boaters stop overnight on the La Junta Run or in the Taos Box, although there are a few small campsites. There are campsites in Orilla Verde Recreation Area downstream from the Taos Box take-out. *Run 5:* Several developed campsites in Orilla Verde Recreation Area (formerly Rio Grande Gorge State Park). *Run 6:* No riverside campsites. Camp upstream at Orilla Verde.

Side Excursions: Hike down from the rim to look at the Upper Box.

Guides and References:

- DeVries & Maurer, *Guide to the Wild and Scenic Rio Grande.* To be published in 1994.
- *New Mexico Whitewater: A Guide to River Trips* (New Mexico State Parks).
- Maurer, *Guide To New Mexico's Popular Rivers and Lakes.*
- Wheat, *Floater's Guide to Colorado.*
- Cassady & Calhoun, *Rio Grande Whitewater Map and Guide.*
- *Riverguide Bandana to the Rio Grande* (Rivers & Mountains). Cloth map.
- Jenkinson, *Wild Rivers of North America.* Boating guide, river history.
- Hillerman & Reynolds, *Rio Grande.* Coffee table book with spectacular photos and excellent text.

Maps: USGS 7.5': *Kiowa Hill, Sky Valley Ranch, Ute Mtn, Sunshine, Guadalupe Mtn, Arroyo Hondo, Los Cordovas, Taos SW, Carson, Trampas, Velarde.*

- **USGS 1:100:** *Wheeler Peak, Taos* (cover New Mexico sections only).
- **USFS:** *Carson NF.*

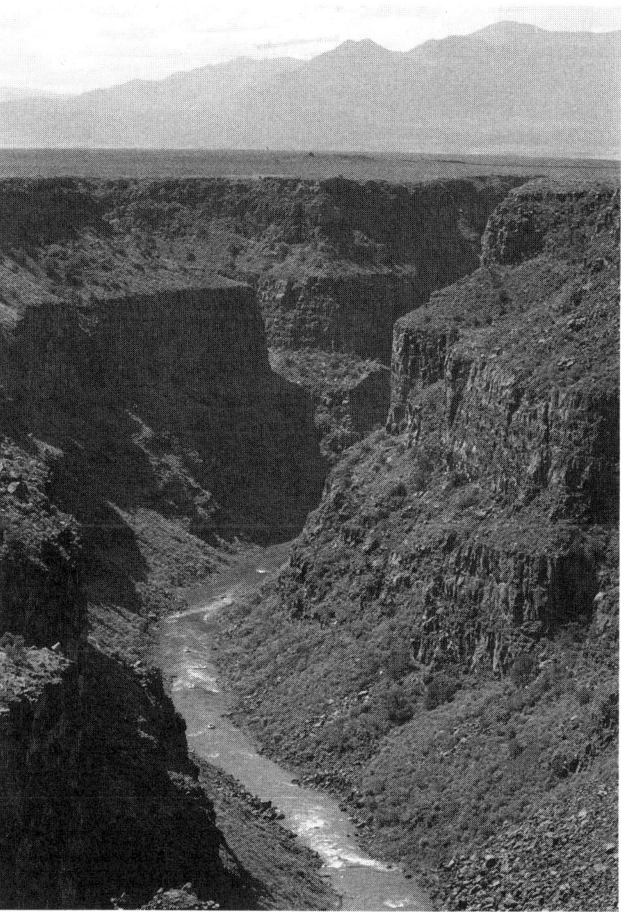

Taos Box — *Greg Moore*

Logistics: *Runs 1–3:* To reach **Lobatos Bridge**,turn west off Colorado 159 about 7 miles north of the New Mexico border onto Colorado 248. Just past Mesita the pavement ends and the main road heads south; 1.3 miles farther, turn west toward Lobatos Bridge, 6 miles away. To reach the rim-to-river trails near the end of the Ute Mountain Run, turn west off New Mexico 522 about 10 miles south of the Colorado border onto Sunshine Valley Road, an unmarked dirt road (paralleled by power line poles) that leads 6 miles to the rim and the head of Sunshine Trail. The road turns south for an additional 4 miles; at its end a sign marks the head of **Lee Trail.**

To reach the trails to the Upper Box and La Junta Runs, turn west off New Mexico 522 about 3 miles north of Questa onto New Mexico 378, which runs first west, then south to trailheads at four campgrounds along the rim: **Chiflo, Big Arsenic Springs, Little Arsenic Springs,** and **La Junta.** The head of a somewhat easier trail to the Red River confluence starts at **Cebolla Mesa CG,** reached by a rough dirt road (difficult when wet) running west off New Mexico 522 about 5 miles south of Questa.

Run 4: To reach the **put-in,** turn west off New Mexico 522 at Arroyo Hondo and drive 3 miles to John Dunn Bridge. The bridge can also be reached via a dirt road intersecting Highway 522 a mile and a half south of Arroyo Hondo. To reach the **take-out,** drive about 16 miles southwest of Taos on New Mexico 68 to Pilar, turn right onto New Mexico 567, and drive nearly 5 miles back upstream to Taos Junction Bridge (also the put-in for Run 5). Though heavily used, this access is on private property; the BLM is negotiating to acquire it. (New Mexico 570 is closed north of Taos Junction Bridge.)

Runs 5 & 6: See just above for directions to the Run 5 put-in. New Mexico 570 is alongside this run and provides frequent access. The take-out (also the put-in for Run 6) is at Quartzite Recreation site just south of Pilar. New Mexico 68 parallels Run 6, offering frequent and easy access. The take-out is at the Taos County Line Recreation Site.

RIO GRANDE

The Rio Grande rises along the eastern flank of the Continental Divide in southern Colorado. From its headwaters on the slopes of 13,000' peaks in the San Juan Mountains, it flows 1,887 miles to the Gulf of Mexico. Among rivers in the United States, only the Mississippi-Missouri system is longer. In 1598 scouts of Spanish explorer Don Juan Oñate named it "El Rio Bravo del Norte"—"The Wild River of the North." But *norteamericanos* now call it the Rio Grande and usually (mis)pronounce it as "REE-oh GRAND" instead of "REE-oh GRAHN-day."

The Rio Grande Valley offered an early route for Spanish and Mexican exploration and colonization of the American interior. The original inhabitants included the various Pueblo tribes, still present in the area, as well as Utes, Comanches, and Apaches. Over the centuries, the tribes staged several uprisings against the colonial powers. Mexico was forced to cede the territory to the U.S. in 1848. Gold fever struck the upper Rio Grande in the 1860's; the boom town of Creede, high in the Rockies, survives to this day, though the gold rush subsided long ago.

Geologists tell us that the headwaters of the ancestral Rio Grande once flowed eastward. Now the river runs south, following a system of interconnected rift valleys where the earth's crust has subsided along fault zones. In the last few million years, volcanoes filled parts of the valleys with lava flows, and the river began to cut its spectacular, sheer-sided box canyons in what is now southern Colorado and northern New Mexico.

Today, much of the river's flow is diverted for irrigation, especially in southern Colorado's San Luis Valley. In dry years the Rio Grande is nearly dewatered. The river is usually replenished below Alamosa, Colorado by a major tributary, the Conejos, which drains the southeastern flank of the San Juans. Except in dry years, there is enough water for river running downstream on the Rio Grande. The vast majority of boaters are to be found on either the Taos Box or the Racecourse Run below Pilar.

Those whose skills match the demands of the box canyons of the Rio Grande will find a dramatic wilderness, a major bird sanctuary, and some of the finest whitewater in this guide book.[1] Others should be content simply to hike in and admire the setting. Here, where the Rio Grande has carved its dramatic canyons through the flat lava flows of the Taos Plateau, the sheer black basalt walls of the narrow Upper and Taos Boxes rise to heights of 700' to 800'. Small stands of Ponderosa pine and Douglas-fir dot the otherwise barren river banks beginning around Big Arsenic Springs.

New Mexico's premier run is the Taos Box (also known as the Lower Box), a splendid 15-mile Class IV reach from John Dunn Bridge to Taos Junction Bridge. The Taos Box offers ideal conditions for advanced boating: challenging rapids, good road access at the put-in and take-out, and a beautiful wild canyon where only a few trails reach the river. Action is fast and nearly continuous in the "Rio Bravo" stretch near the end of the run. Both private boaters and guests on commercial raft trips flock to the Taos Box in good snowpack years.

If the Taos Box is the most famous section of the New Mexico Rio Grande, the Upper Box is the most notorious. This is an extremely hazardous and rarely-boated stretch of river. The danger is compounded by the fact that it is accessible only by long, steep trails. Rescue in case of injury or emergency would be very difficult. For years only a few veteran kayakers ventured into the Upper Box. It was first rafted successfully in 1986. Today, when flows allow, several hundred experts kayak it annually.

The Upper Box has three distinct sections. The first part, known as the Razor Blade Run for its sharp volcanic rocks, is Class II–III for the first five miles; then comes a long, tough Class IV rapid. Two steep trails to campgrounds on the rim offer boaters a chance to hike out before they enter the seven-mile heart of the Upper Box. **Only the most seasoned experts should attempt the Upper Box, and only at low and moderate flows.** Those running the Upper Box should be prepared for difficult portages around some of the short, steep falls. Boaters unfamiliar with the river should consult local kayakers before making this run; ask the managing agency for references.

A couple of miles below the biggest rapids, the Red River joins the Rio Grande, announcing the end of the heart-stopping whitewater and the beginning of the last section of the Upper Box. This increasingly popular stretch is called the La Junta Run, the Red River Conflu-

[1]For other boatable sections of the river, see the **Lower Rio Grande** in the Southwestern Border region and the **Upper Rio Grande** in the **More Western Rivers** section. The Rio Grande is one of the charter members of the National Wild and Scenic Rivers System. The protected stretch runs from the Colorado-New Mexico border to Taos Junction Bridge.

ence Run, and occasionally the Middle Box. ("Junta" means "confluence" in Spanish.) Boaters who want to put in at the confluence will have to hike down one of the steep trails from campgrounds on the rim. Those who wish to run an additional Class III rapid above the confluence take the trails from Little Arsenic or La Junta Campground. Using the somewhat easier trail from Cebolla Mesa Campground allows boaters to put in below this rocky rapid and to float the river at flows down to 300 cfs. There is only one more Class III rapid in the last 8.5 miles from the Red River to John Dunn Bridge. Some boaters—including commercial rafters who use pack trains to get their gear down the trail—combine the La Junta Run with the Taos Box just downstream.

Ute Mountain Run

Upstream from the Upper Box is a rewarding but little-known and very isolated stretch of river known as the Ute Mountain Run. At the Lobatos Bridge put-in, nine miles north of the Colorado-New Mexico border, the Rio Grande canyon is only a small notch, but its walls soon rise to hundreds of feet. There are few campsites. The river's gradient increases and Class II rapids appear more frequently toward the end of the run.

Eagles, falcons, owls, geese, and mergansers are more common here than kayakers and canoeists. Many more lovers of bird life, solitude, and high desert scenery would float this section of the Rio Grande if it weren't for the tough climb up steep Lee Trail (mile 24.5), the last take-out above the Upper Box. **Don't miss the take-out and enter the Upper Box by mistake.** Because of its remote location and the difficult hike out at its end, only seasoned wilderness boaters should attempt the Ute Mountain Run. At present this run is the exclusive preserve of hardy souls who can carry their boats up the trail (500 yards long; 220 vertical feet). The difficult access more or less rules rafters out unless they plan to run the Upper Box.

State Park and Racecourse Runs

Boaters who like their scenery without too much nerve-wracking action should consider one or more sections of the Lower Gorge of the Rio Grande between Taos Junction Bridge and Velarde. Taos Junction Bridge, where trips down the Taos Box end, is the start of the State Park Run, a relatively easy 6.5-mile float through Orilla Verde Recreation Area (formerly Rio Grande Gorge State Park). Black basalt walls enclose the canyon but do not reach the river, and developed campsites may be found along the banks in the recreation area. New Mexico 570 follows the left bank, but much of this stretch of highway is closed. Downstream from the recreation area, around Pilar, private property lines both banks, and the first river access is half a mile south of the town.

Below Pilar the action picks up again in the Racecourse Run, site of a traditional whitewater competition held every Mother's Day. Good road access via New Mexico 68 makes this the most popular stretch of the Rio Grande. The sprightly Class III rapids are less abrupt than the sharp drops of the Taos Box, and all can be scouted from the highway. At higher flows big holes develop and the whitewater becomes continuous Class IV, so any swim could be a long one. The run ends at the Taos County Line.

Downstream Runs

Downstream from the county line is the 8.5-mile Velarde Run—not covered in this chapter, but shown on the map. Easy Class I and II water and convenient road access make this a good run for open canoeists and novice kayakers. The Velarde Run is especially scenic in the fall, when the cottonwoods change their colors. The 15-mile stretch below Velarde is not recommended because of numerous diversion dams and fences across the river.

Farther downstream, below Otowi Bridge on New Mexico 502, the Rio Grande enters lovely White Rock Canyon, a 24-mile Class II–III wilderness run past Bandelier National Monument. This stretch was once very popular with capable canoeists, but its lower reaches are now partially flooded and silted up by Cochiti Reservoir. A few stubborn boaters persist in running White Rock Canyon, but they have to face upriver winds and miles of flatwater paddling across the upper end of the reservoir. Taking out on the left at Frijoles Canyon in Bandelier National Monument shortens the trip by about 10 miles and avoids the flatwater.[2]

[2]For information on conservation issues affecting the Rio Grande and other New Mexico rivers, contact Adobe Whitewater Club in Albuquerque and/or Amigos Bravos–Friends of the Wild Rivers in Taos (see appendix for addresses).

Mile by Mile Guide

River miles in left column sometimes start over at zero with put-in for a different section. Numbers in brackets show total miles from first put-in and correspond to mileages on the map.

Ute Mountain Run

0 **PUT-IN** on the left bank downstream from Lobatos Bridge.

9.1 Colorado-New Mexico border. Ute Mountain, an old lava cone, dominates the left (east) bank for the next 8 miles.

10.3 Costilla Creek enters on the left. Small campsite, short side hike.

14 Small left-bank campsite at the mouth of a side canyon. A crude trail leads to a 4-wheel-drive road on the rim that eventually reaches Sunshine Valley Road.

18 The river turns right, with a natural amphitheater on the left. An emergency trail leads from the left bank to the rim road.

21.5 Sunshine Trail (left bank) leads to the rim and a dirt road.

24.5 **TAKE-OUT.** Lee Trail reaches the left bank downstream from a grassy flat with a big boulder by the river's edge. ***HAZARD.*** Don't miss the take-out. **The Upper Box, an extremely difficult stretch of whitewater for experts only, is downstream.**

Upper Box

24.5-29.5 The first 7 miles are known as the Razor Blade Run because of sharp volcanic rocks in the channel. Class II and III rapids for the first 5 miles.

29.5 **RAZOR BLADE (IV).** A three-quarter-mile descent through powerful hydraulics and big boulders fallen from the sides of the gorge. Razor Blade Rock is halfway down in the narrowest section.

30.5 Trail (left bank) to Sheep Crossing Campground on the rim.

31.5 Trail (left bank) to Chiflo Campground on the rim. ***HAZARD.*** **Stop here unless you plan on running through the heart of the treacherous Upper Box.** Class III and IV rapids the next two miles.

33.3 Bear Trail (left bank) provides emergency access to the canyon rim.

33.5 **UPPER POWERLINE (V).** A power line across the river at one of the canyon's narrowest points marks the first in a mile-long series of very difficult Class V and VI rapids. Scout frequently and be prepared to portage. Then comes a half mile of flatwater known as "The Great Calm."

36.4 **BIG ARSENIC FALLS (VI/p).** The river turns sharply left into the biggest rapid in the Upper Box. Don't be swept into the falls by mistake. ***Difficult but near-mandatory portage at both Big and Little Arsenic.*** The water of Big Arsenic Springs (downstream on the left) is drinkable; long ago, a hermit misnamed the springs to keep others away. A trail on the left bank climbs from Big Arsenic Springs to Big Arsenic Campground on the rim. A branch trail well above river level heads half a mile downstream to **LITTLE ARSENIC RAPID (VI/p).**

La Junta Run

37.4 Little Arsenic Springs. Metal camping shelter (left bank); more shelters about 1/4 mile downstream. Trail from Little Arsenic Campground on the rim reaches the river here; "River Trail" follows the left bank downstream to the mouth of the Red River. The La Junta Run begins either here or a bit downstream.

38.1 **RED CONFLUENCE RAPID (III).** A boulder slalom just above the mouth of the Red River. A steep trail climbs from the left bank to La Junta Campground and the end of the rim road. This is another put-in for the La Junta Run.

38.3 The Red River, a major tributary, emerges from its narrow canyon on the left. Just downstream, a somewhat easier trail climbs from the left bank to Cebolla Mesa Campground on the rim. Putting in here for the La Junta Run avoids the rocky Class III rapid upstream. Downstream the gradient slackens; with one exception, the rapids ease to Class II for the next 10 miles. Benches above the river furnish several campsites along the way. A few crude trails reach the river from the rim.

44 San Cristobal Creek enters from the left. Small campsite. Indian petroglyphs on polished basalt boulders beside the river. About a mile downstream is **HORSETHIEF SHORTY (III).**

46.8 **TAKE-OUT.** John Dunn Bridge. Take out upstream on the right bank when you can see the steel-truss bridge.

Taos Box

0 [46.8] **PUT-IN.** John Dunn Bridge. Class I and II rapids the first 4 miles.

0.5 Small hot spring on the right bank is covered by the river except at low water.

2 Manby Hot Springs and a small campsite on the left bank. An old stage coach road leads up to the rim, where a dirt road heads east to the highway.

3.8 **SKI JUMP RAPID (III+).** Debris from a side canyon constricts the river channel. Scout on the right. Small campsite on the right bank just downstream from the rapid is the best in the Taos Box.

4.8 **HIGH BRIDGE RAPID (III).** Beneath the highway bridge, which is 650' above the river. No river access from bridge.

6 **YELLOW BAND RAPID (III+);** also called **Yellow Bank.** Named for the horizontal stripe in the rock on the left bank. Scout on the right. The current pushes boats toward a boulder obstructing the exit from the rapid. More difficult, and sometimes portaged, at low water.

6.2–10.8 In this stretch, known as "The Playground," frequent Class II and III rapids are formed by fallen boulders in the dark, narrow inner canyon.

10.8 **DEAD CAR RAPID (III+).** This technical rapid signals the beginning of more difficult whitewater. Look for a 1959 Pontiac in the talus slope on the right bank. Scout on the right.

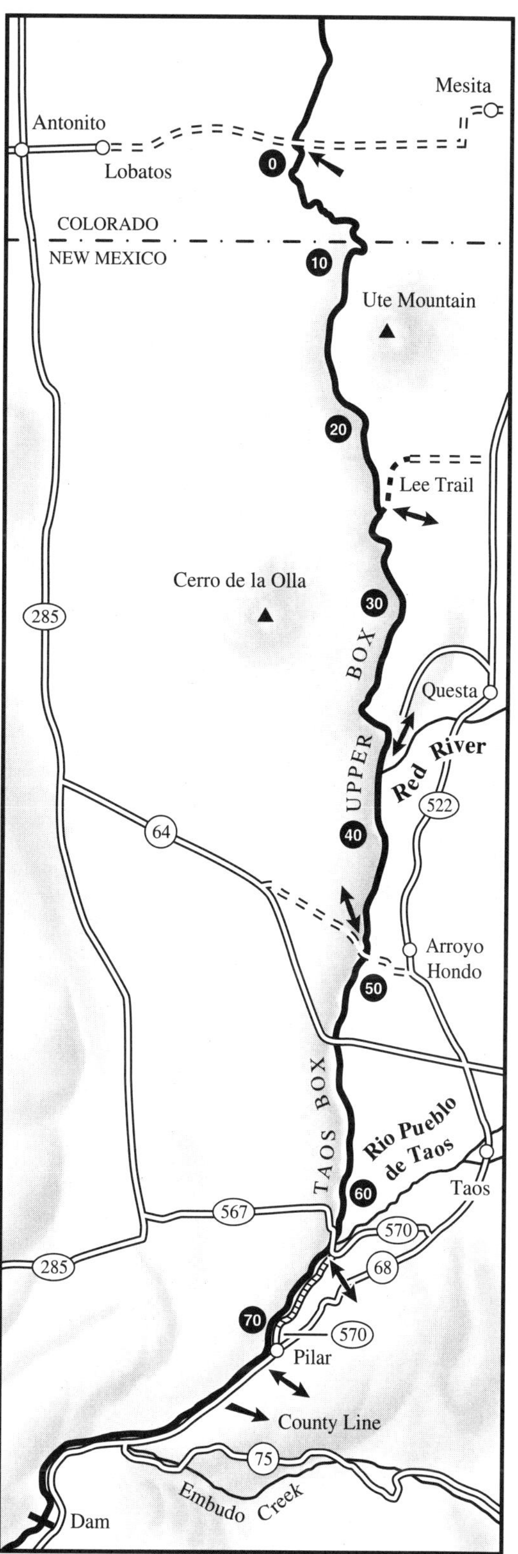

Rio Grande

11.6 **POWERLINE FALLS (III+).** Just downstream from a power line across the gorge, the river plunges down a steep chute dotted with huge boulders. At low water there is a very difficult portage along the right bank. A steep, crude trail on the right could be used as an emergency exit.

12– 14.5 **Rio Bravo section (IV).** Difficult, concentrated whitewater as the river drops at a rate of 40 ft./mi. Steep boulder slaloms come fast and furious, requiring skilled technical maneuvering at low water. At higher flows big waves and holes appear and some of the rapids run together, so trouble could lead to a long, dangerous swim. In short succession come rapids named **PINBALL, ROCK GARDEN, BUZZ SAW, THE CLEAVER, BOAT REAMER, THE GUT, PUNK ROCK, SCREAMING LEFT TURN, BOULDER FIELD,** and **SCREAMING RIGHT TURN.** Then the rapids begin to ease, but one more big one waits downstream.

15 **SUNSET (IV).** Also known as **Taos Junction Rapid.** The rapid begins at the mouth of the Rio Pueblo de Taos, a tributary on the left. Scout on the left. This rapid can also be scouted from the road.

15.2 **TAKE-OUT** on the left bank just downstream from Taos Junction Bridge.

State Park Run

0 [62] **PUT-IN.** Taos Junction Bridge.

1.9 **GAUGING STATION RAPID (II).** The first Class II rapid in this section is just downstream from the gauging station and an overhead cable.

3.8 **S-TURN (II).** Debris from an arroyo on the left constricts the river. **RIVER ACCESS** on the left just below the rapid.

4.6 Orilla Verde Campground (left bank), formerly a popular take-out, is no longer a river access point.

5.1 As the river leaves Orilla Verde Recreation Area, there is **RIVER ACCESS** at Pilar Campground. No river access from the highway for over a mile because of private property on both banks.

5.5 Village of Pilar. Low bridge is a ***HAZARD*** at high water; around 4,000 cfs and up, a **portage** is necessary. Not far downstream, a diversion dam creates a Class II surfing wave for kayakers. No river access from the highway.

6.5 **TAKE-OUT** on the left at Quartzite Recreation Site (BLM), downstream from the intersection of New Mexico 68 and 570. (This site was formerly known as Fishing Hole.) Many boaters continue downriver for the next run.

Racecourse Run

6.5 [68.5] **PUT-IN** at Quartzite Recreation Site (see above).

7–8 The canyon narrows and the gradient steepens as the river, crowded by the highway on the left bank, plunges through a mile of continuous Class III rapids: **ALBERT FALLS, HERRINGBONE, EYE OF THE NEEDLE, BOULDER FIELD, THE NARROWS,** and **DEAD FOOT.** At higher flows these rapids run together into a mile-long Class IV gauntlet.

8.5 *HAZARD. POSSIBLE PORTAGE.* Glen Woody Bridge, a dilapidated wooden structure hanging low above the river, may require portaging at high flows. Scout from the left, where the clearance is greatest.

8.7 **BIG ROCK (III).** Large boulders form big holes at high water and narrow, technical passages at low flows.

9.1 **SLEEPING BEAUTY (III).** The tongue leads to a "sleeper" pourover in midstream.

9.5 **SOUSE HOLE (III; IV at higher flows).** The river bends right, and a large hole blocks the middle of the channel. At higher flows the hole becomes a big wave. Downstream, the river flattens out as the canyon walls open slightly.

10.8 [72.8] **TAKE-OUT** at the Taos County Line Recreation Site (BLM) on the left. For downstream runs, see end of essay.

Rio Chama

Chama Canyon

Put-in: El Vado Ranch (6,710').
Take-out: Big Eddy above Abiquiu Reservoir (6,240').
Difficulty: II+.
Length: 31 miles. Shorter runs possible.
Gradient: 15 ft./mi.
Drainage Area and Average Annual Discharge: 877 sq. mi. and 355,000 af at put-in.
Peak Recorded Flow: 9,000 cfs (May 22, 1920).
Season: April–June (runoff season) and weekends from midsummer through August (dam release season). Spring snowmelt often produces flows of 1,000 to 2,500 cfs with occasional peaks of 4,000 or more. Flows typically drop to unrunnable levels around mid-June. As of this writing, releases from El Vado Dam of 500 to 1,000 cfs begin around the third week in July and continue for about six weeks through August. Call managing agency for updates; release schedule can change at any time.
Recommended Levels: 800–2,500 cfs.
Flow Information: BLM tape, (505) 758-8148, gives release from El Vado and projected flows and releases. USGS tape, (505) 262-5388, gives flow above Abiquiu Reservoir.
Permits: Required on the upper river (above mile 22). Not required on the lower river. Permits are issued for two distinct periods, the natural runoff season and the dam release season. Call or write in the fall to request information; the BLM mails out packets beginning in December. Group limit 16 on the upper river.
Managing Agency: BLM, Taos Resource Area, 224 Cruz Alta Rd., Taos, NM 87571; (505) 758-8851.
Commercial Raft Trips: Yes. For a list of outfitters, contact the BLM.
Land Ownership: Mostly BLM and National Forest; scattered private holdings.
Scenery: Excellent. Colorful, partially forested desert canyon.
Solitude: Excellent on weekdays, very good on weekends.
Wilderness: Yes for the first 22 miles. Rough dirt road follows the last 9 miles.
Fishing: Good for trout down to Rio Nutrias (mile 3); fair to Rio Cebolla (mile 13.5). Water is muddier downstream.
Wildlife: Abundant raptors and waterfowl.
Water: Usually muddy most of the way. Best to pack in all drinking water.
Camping: Many fine sites. Avoid private land.
Side Hikes: Several (see **Mile Guide**).
Side Excursions: Ghost Ranch Museum on U.S. 84. Cumbres & Toltec Scenic Railway from Chama, NM to Antonito, Colorado.
Guides and References:
- Maurer, *Guide to Wild and Scenic Rio Chama.* Southwest Natural & Cultural Heritage Assn., Drawer E, Albuquerque, NM 87103; (505) 345-9498.
- *Rio Chama: A Wild & Scenic River* (BLM). Map-guide.
- Wheat, *Floater's Guide to Colorado.*
- Verne Huser essay in Rennicke, *River Days.*

Maps:
- **USGS 7.5':** *El Vado, Navajo Peak, Laguna Peak, Echo Amphitheater.*
- **USGS 1:100:** *Chama, Abiquiu.*
- *Santa Fe NF* (omits first 5 miles of run).
- **AAA:** *Indian Country.*

Auto Shuttle: About 45 miles one way; partly paved. For shuttle services contact El Vado Ranch, (505) 588-7354.
Logistics: To reach the **put-in,** turn west off U.S. 84 just north of Tierra Amarilla (90 miles northwest of Santa Fe) onto New Mexico Route 112, drive southwest about 15 miles, then turn left on the short spur road to El Vado Ranch (fee for parking and put-in).

To reach the **take-out,** return to U.S. 84, turn right, and drive south roughly 27 miles. About 1.5 miles south of the turnoff to Echo Amphitheater Campground, turn right (west) onto USFS Road 151. (Ghost Ranch Living Museum is ¾ mile south of this turnoff.) Follow this dirt road (impassable when wet) 5 miles southwest to the Big Eddy take-out, just beyond the Adobe Ruins. The road continues up the left bank to the popular Chavez Canyon access (river mile 22) and ends at the Christ in the Desert Monastery (private).

RIO CHAMA

El Rio Chama[1] is one of New Mexico's best-loved rivers—not for its whitewater, though the rapids are pleasant enough, but for its tranquil beauty. This is a mellow, scenic stream, prized by open canoeists and others looking more for relaxation than for thrills and spills. Chama Canyon, the run featured in this chapter, is a V-shaped valley bounded by cliffs of pale orange, creamy yellow, light rose, and muted gray. Open, airy stands of Ponderosa pine add soft tones of green and brown, and an azure sky usually caps the scene.

Sound like a painting? It should. The great artist Georgia O'Keefe spent many of her 98 years at the Ghost Ranch near Chama Canyon. She also kept a small house in the village of Abiquiu, overlooking the pastoral valley of the lower Chama. O'Keefe's paintings evoke the spirit and charm of Chama country by capturing the clean, undiluted light and the subtle pastels of a magical landscape. Here, the state slogan "Land of Enchantment" seems most appropriate.

The Chama rises on the east slope of the Continental Divide in southern Colorado's San Juan Mountains . Its southerly course into New Mexico is carved through colorful layers of sedimentary rock. Just below El Vado Reservoir the river makes its deepest cut, Chama Canyon, where the walls rise as high as 1,500'. When the canyon finally opens up, the Chama, now thick with sediment, glides southeastward through an open, bluff-lined valley toward its confluence with the Rio Grande northwest of Santa Fe.

Though its canyons seem timeless, the Chama has seen profound changes in the last half century, beginning with the construction of El Vado Reservoir in the 1930's. In the early 1960's the Corps of Engineers built Abiquiu Dam 45 miles downstream, flooding the lower end of Chama Canyon. The Corps justified Abiquiu (pronounced "Abbey-Q") as a flood control project, but many believe the primary goal was to trap silt that was rapidly filling downstream reservoirs on the Rio Grande.

In 1971 the San Juan-Chama project began to divert 100,000 acre-feet of water per year from the upper San Juan basin, on the west side of the Continental Divide, through a tunnel to Heron Reservoir on a tributary of the Chama just above El Vado Reservoir. The diversion reduces flows to the Navajo River and Rio Blanco, tributaries of the San Juan, but increases summer releases on the Chama.

For years the run covered in this chapter was the center of controversy. Albuquerque and the Army Corps of Engineers hoped to raise the height of Abiquiu Dam and flood four more miles of river, while preservationists sought to head off more dam-building. After years of grassroots campaigns, in 1988 Congress declared the Chama a National Wild and Scenic River, protecting 25 miles of river below El Vado Dam. An additional four-mile stretch is under study for possible Wild and Scenic designation; unless it is also granted permanent protection, it will remain at risk of flooding by the enlargement of Abiquiu Dam.[2]

Each spring and summer, boaters, anglers, hikers, and campers head for Chama country. The wilderness run through Chama Canyon is a favorite of open canoeists, but almost any type of river boat is suitable. At higher flows caution is needed: eddies become scarce, waves get big enough to cause trouble for open canoes, and the water is very cold. Even at these levels, however, the roughest spots can be portaged.

Below El Vado Dam the Chama cuts through soft strata at a relatively constant gradient. The first five miles are fairly flat; then, as the walls of Chama Canyon rise, Class II rapids appear here and there. The upper 22 miles from El Vado Ranch to just below Christ in the Desert Monastery are wilderness, while a rough dirt road follows the final nine miles. Because most of the whitewater is in the lower stretch, many use the road to make one-day runs.

During spring snowmelt, the Chama generally carries more runoff than El Vado Reservoir can store, and the dam spills water. June is often an ideal time for boaters to enjoy both good weather and good flows before the river recedes again. Summer flows are closely regulated by El Vado Dam. Under an agreement being negotiated among various water and land agencies, mid- and late-summer releases are being scheduled to produce a second boating season beginning around mid-July. In recent years the Chama's popularity has increased dramatically, and in 1991 the BLM began restricting use under a new permit system.

---

[1]In his *Guide to the Wild and Scenic Rio Chama,* Stephen Maurer says "Chama" is a Spanish approximation of a Tewa Indian word that has been translated as meaning either "red" or "fighting around place."

[2]For more information on efforts to preserve the Chama, contact Adobe Whitewater Club, P.O. Box 3835, Albuquerque, NM 87110; and/or Amigos Bravos, Friends of the Wild Rivers, P.O. Box 238, Taos NM 87571, (505) 758- 3874.

Upstream Runs

Boaters occasionally run the Chama above El Vado Reservoir. Here the river is steeper and has a shorter season (in an average year, May and early June). The uppermost stretch, between the Colorado-New Mexico border and Los Ojos, is rarely boated due to scanty flows and a short season. The most commonly run section is between Los Ojos and El Vado Reservoir. From the New Mexico Highway 95 bridge just below the confluence with the Rio Brazos, the Chama flows for some 13 miles at a gradient of 28 ft./mi. The first several miles are through more open terrain where **fences across the river present the major hazard.** The run can be shortened by putting in on the left at La Puente near Plaza Blanca, three miles below the Highway 95 bridge, or at a gauging station on the right bank less than four miles downstream. Be alert for a **diversion dam** near the gauging station.

Below the diversion dam the Chama gradually enters a narrow, scenic canyon which climaxes just above El Vado Reservoir as a V-shaped gorge some 1,500' deep. The technical, rocky Class III and IV rapids become more difficult toward the end of the run. Boaters can take out on the right at Heron Dam (which blocks a tributary, not the main river) by carrying their boats several hundred feet up an access road. Or they can continue downstream through easier water to the backwaters of El Vado Reservoir. Take out where an unpaved spur road from Highway 95 reaches the north shore of the reservoir. Auto shuttles are via Highway 95.

Mile by Mile Guide

0 **PUT-IN.** El Vado Ranch on the left bank (private, fee). Parking, camping, lodging, shuttles. El Vado Dam is a mile upstream, and a gauging station is on the left just downstream. El Vado means "the ford."

3 The Rio Nutrias enters on the left.

3.7 Abandoned Ward Ranch on the right. Hot springs just downstream on the left.

6 Arroyo del Puerto Chiquito enters on the right in a more open section. A dirt road reaches the right bank here. Downstream, the canyon walls begin to rise. At mile 8 watch for **SLEEPER (II),** where a rock appears at moderate and lower flows.

10 Aragon Canyon enters on the right. Class II riffle. A steep hike leads less than a mile up the canyon to Aragon Springs. Two miles downstream is another Class II.

13 **DARK CANYON (II+).** This long rock garden—the biggest rapid between El Vado and the Monastery—is located where Dark Canyon enters on the right. Half a mile downstream the Rio Cebolla ("Onion River") enters on the left. The Chama Wilderness Area begins here and continues for the next 6 miles. Three major trails branch off from a junction about ¼ mile from the river: the Navajo Peak, Hart Canyon, and Rio Cebolla Trails. Side hikes on these trails include two five-hour loops. Half a mile farther downstream, Mine Canyon enters on the right, creating a Class II riffle.

16.8 Small canyon and campsite on the right. Good, short side hike.

18 Huckaby Canyon enters on the left. Short hike up this box canyon. Just downstream is a 4-mile section closed to camping.

21.2 Christ in the Desert Monastery, a private Benedictine facility, is on the left where the canyon begins to open. Please respect the solitude of this place by keeping noise down as you pass it. Visitors are asked to enter the monastery grounds only via the road (not via the river). A half mile downstream the Rio Gallina ("Hen River") enters on the right, often carrying a heavy load of sediment.

22.3 **RIVER ACCESS.** Chavez Canyon Access on the left is the standard put-in for one-day runs on the lower river and the take-out for overnight runs on the upper river when flows are low (500–800 cfs). USFS Road 151 follows the left bank for the next 9 miles. Downstream the rapids are more difficult, beginning with **MEANDERING RAPID (II+ to III-),** sometimes called **Island,** near mile 24. This long washboard around a gravel island is usually tougher at low flows. Some boaters may want to scout.

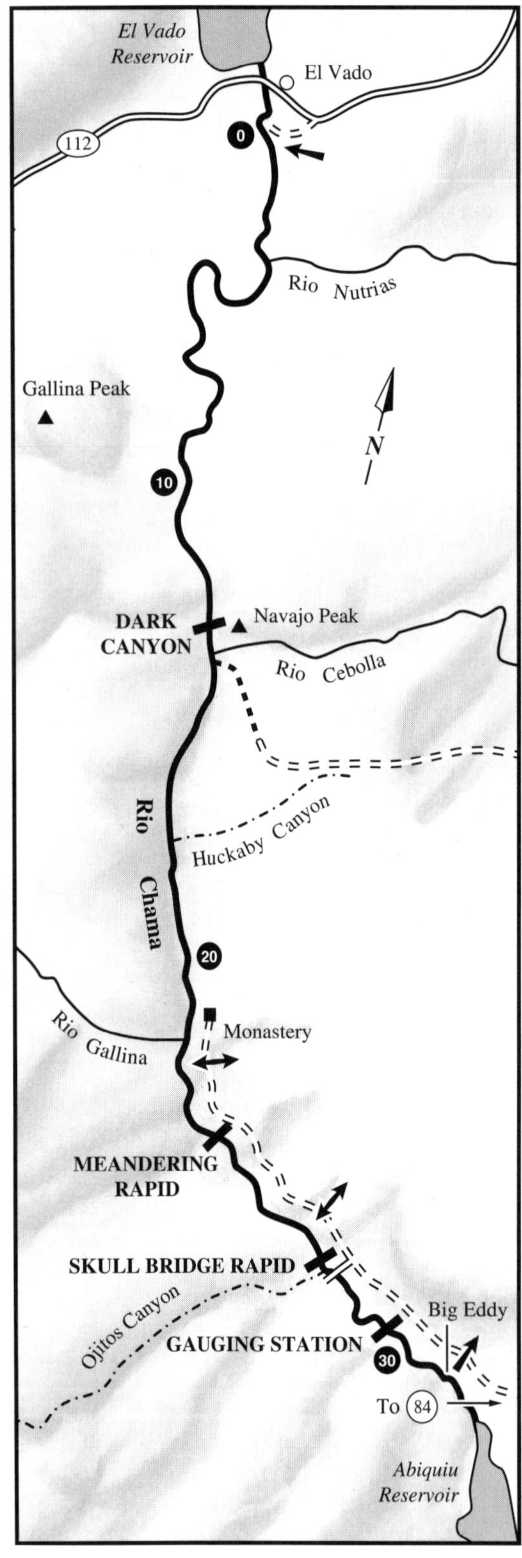

Rio Chama

27.3 **SKULL BRIDGE RAPID (II)**, a long rapid with good waves. The bridge in the middle of this rapid was once much lower and created a major hazard at higher flows until the Forest Service raised it in 1990. **RIVER ACCESS** on the left about ¾ mile above the bridge.

29.5 **GAUGING STATION (II+)**, where the river undercuts the left wall. More difficult at moderate flows, when a hole develops near the wall. The gauge on the left marks the approximate upstream limit of Abiquiu Reservoir at maximum level. Half a mile downstream is **BANK SHOT (II+ to III-)**, also known as **Screaming Left**, where the river turns sharply left and undercuts the right wall. The wall is usually hardest to avoid at moderate flows.

31 **TAKE-OUT.** Big Eddy on the left. Downstream the road leaves the river and the Chama stills in the backwaters of Abiquiu Reservoir. Boaters who continue downstream may have to paddle as much as 5 miles of flatwater to the next possible access at a camping area on the reservoir.

Region III. Canyon Country

Utah, Colorado, Arizona

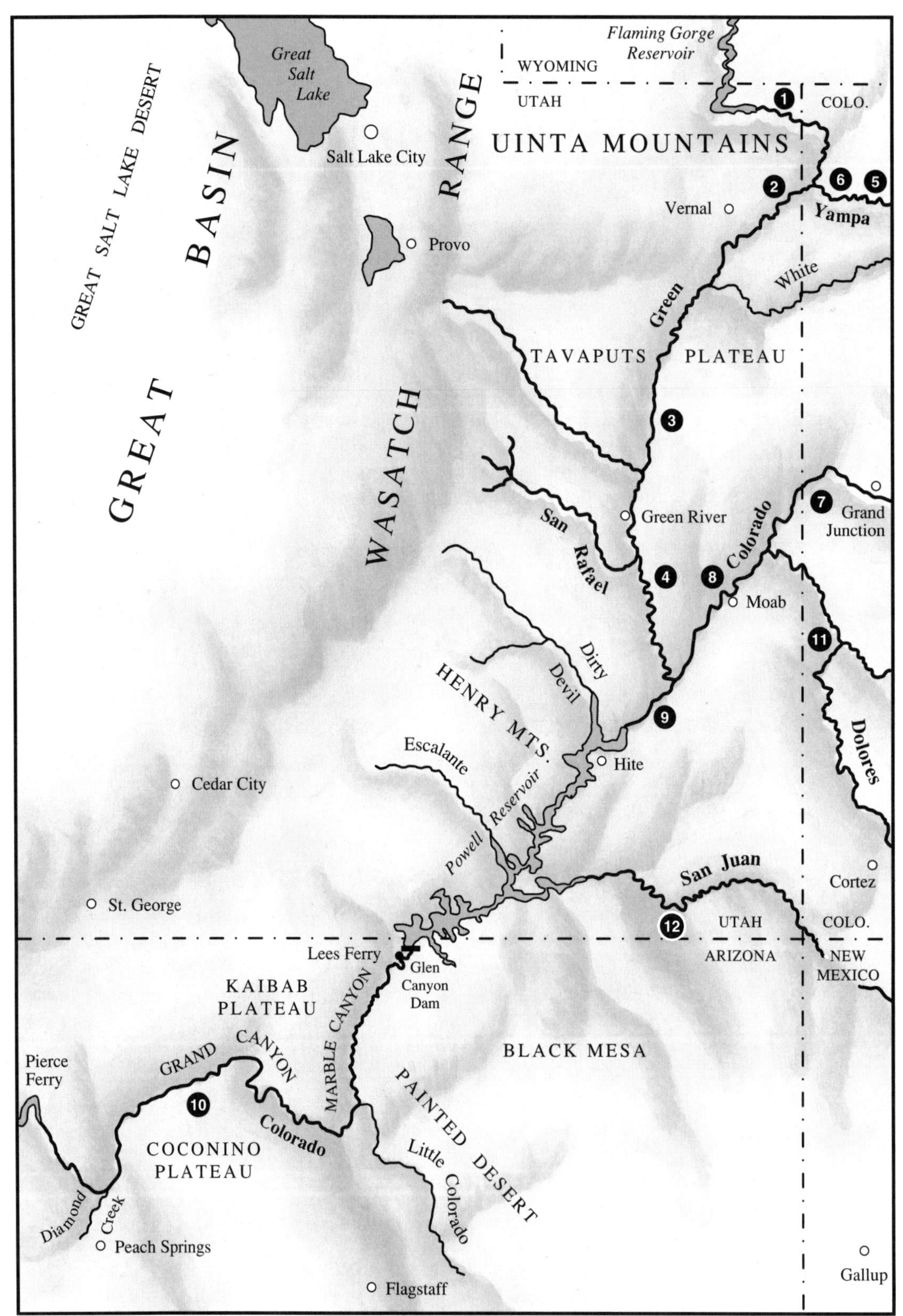

Canyon Country

Rivers of the Canyon Country

1. Green: Red and Swallow Canyons
2. Green: Lodore, Whirpool, and Split Mountain Canyons
3. Green: Desolation and Gray Canyons
4. Green: Labyrinth and Stillwater Canyons
5. Upper Yampa
6. Lower Yampa
7. Colorado: Horsethief and Ruby Canyons
8. Colorado: Westwater Canyon
9. Colorado: Cataract Canyon
10. Grand Canyon of the Colorado
11. Dolores
12. Lower San Juan

Canyon Country

When people think of the American West, they usually call to mind the Canyon Country—a land of barren red rock, broad muddy rivers, and deep, sheer-walled chasms. At the heart of the Canyon Country is the grandfather of all Western rivers, the Colorado, with its magnificent canyons and thundering brownwater rapids. Since John Wesley Powell's epic voyage in 1869, the Colorado has stood as the archetypal Western river. Even today, a journey through the Grand Canyon represents the supreme river running experience for whitewater boaters everywhere.

The unifying feature of the Canyon Country is its unique and spectacular geology. The foundation of the entire region is the Colorado Plateau, a vast uplifted section of the earth's surface that covers parts of four states: western Colorado, northwestern New Mexico, northern Arizona, and southern and eastern Utah. The plateau consists of dozens of layers of sedimentary rock that formed on ancient sea floors, beaches, dune fields, deltas, and flood plains and that have now been pushed far above sea level. Major rivers cut deeply into these relatively soft deposits, exposing colorful layers of sandstone, limestone, and other rock.

The Canyon Country itself is a desert, with less than 10" of annual precipitation in most places. Summer temperatures are scorching, though the elevation is high enough to make winters too cold for boating. The region's major rivers—the Colorado and Green and their larger tributaries—get virtually all their water from snowmelt along the Continental Divide in the distant Rocky Mountains of Colorado and Wyoming. Local rivers like the Escalante and San Rafael are small and ephemeral. The southern end of the region is influenced by the Sonoran Desert climate with its late summer thundershowers and flash floods.

The entire region is a testament to the erosive power of water. As the rivers scour downward, they entrench themselves ever deeper in their ancient courses, producing tortuous, steep-walled canyons. Local rainfall races off the barren, rocky terrain, producing flash floods that carry huge amounts of sand and silt down side canyons and into the rivers. Before Glen Canyon Dam was built, the mighty Colorado transported an average of 168 million tons of sediment every year through the Grand Canyon. This silt now settles in "Lake" Powell; it will eventually fill the reservoir completely.

Rapids on Canyon Country rivers usually form where flash floods wash debris down side canyons into the main river. The river soon carries away the finer sediments, but the larger rocks and boulders remain to block the river's flow and form a rapid. Two of the region's most famous big drops—Warm Springs Rapid on the Yampa and Crystal Rapid in the Grand Canyon—were created by side canyon flash floods in 1965 and 1966, respectively.

Canyon Country is the only region in this guide that lies entirely within one river basin. All the major rivers flowing into the region—the Green, Yampa, White, Upper Colorado, Gunnison, Dolores, and San Juan—are bound for one point: the mouth of the Colorado in northern Mexico. Today, of course, the Colorado is so thoroughly dammed and diverted that virtually none of its water finds its way to this natural outlet.

This region is home to some of the most ambitious, awe-inspiring, controversial, and destructive water projects ever built. Chief among these are two giant dams on the Colorado: Hoover Dam, which forms Mead Reservoir; and Glen Canyon Dam, which creates Powell Reservoir. For many, Glen Canyon is the ultimate symbol of the loss and destruction of Western rivers. Together these impoundments can store over 50 million acre-feet of water—equivalent to roughly four years' average flow on the Colorado.

Canyon Country rivers continue to be threatened. For more than a decade, "peaking power" operations at Glen Canyon Dam eroded beaches and destroyed wildlife habitat in the Grand Canyon (see **Grand Canyon** chapter). McPhee Dam was completed on the Dolores River in 1984, largely dewatering one of the region's loveliest runs. New dams have been proposed for the Yampa, White, Escalante, Colorado, Gunnison, and others.

The history of Western river running begins here, with Major John Wesley Powell's exploration of the Green and Colorado Rivers in 1869. Though a few adventurers challenged portions of these rivers before him, Powell's journey marks the first complete descent. The saga of his voyage through this un-

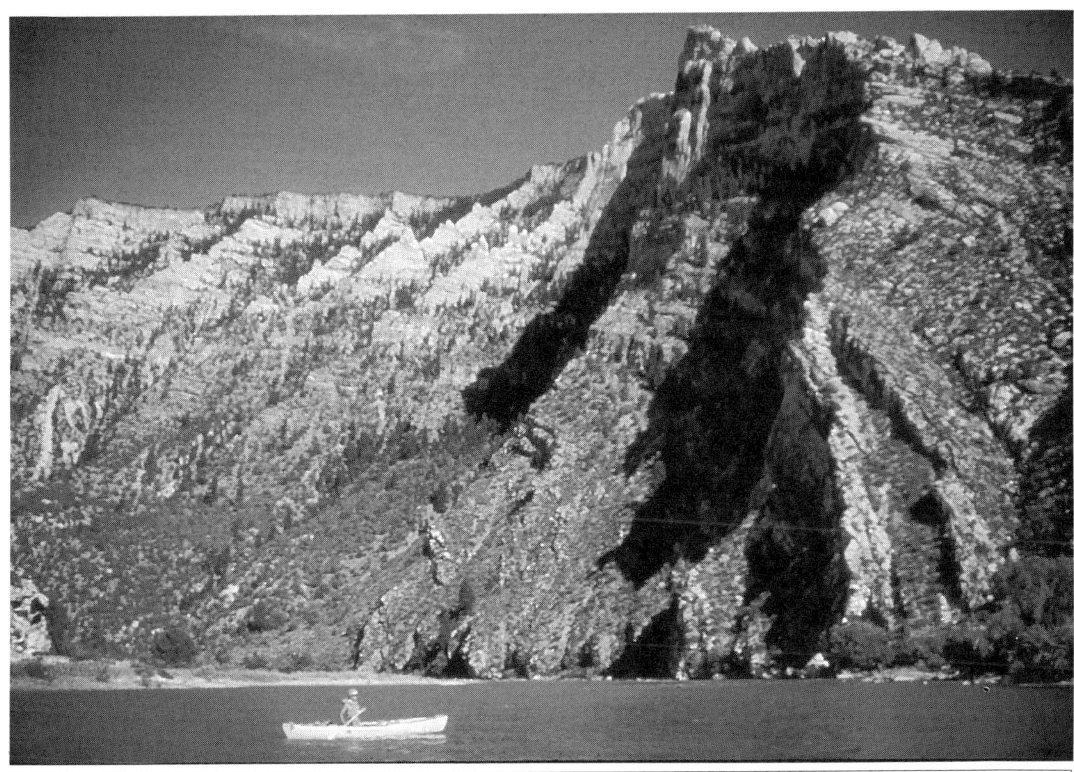

Steamboat Rock, Confluence of Green and Yampa Rivers *David Symonik*

charted terrain is one of the most dramatic stories in the history of whitewater boating.

Following Powell, other early river runners developed new techniques and better craft: "Nat" Galloway, Ellsworth and Emery Kolb, Norm Nevills, Bert Loper, Otis "Dock" Marston, and many others. In 1936 Bus Hatch started commercial trips on the Green, spawning an entire industry. In the late 1940's military surplus rafts began to replace wooden boats; soon, growing numbers of commercial passengers were running the big drops of the Grand Canyon.

Today, Canyon Country is still primarily a realm of big-water boating. The principal whitewater challenges are usually in the form of massive waves and monster holes rather than technical chutes and steep gradients. Large rafts, especially big oar rigs, are truly in their element here.

But the attraction of Canyon Country rivers goes far beyond huge roller-coaster rapids. Many of the West's longest wilderness runs are here, offering boaters a chance to escape from civilization for two or three weeks at a time. The rivers' heavy sediment loads produce broad camping beaches of clean, water-washed sand. The hiking is almost certainly the finest in the West, with countless side canyons inviting exploration. Many trips offer a glimpse of ruins and pictographs left by the Anasazi and other early inhabitants.

More than any other part of the West, the Canyon Country draws boaters from outside the region. River runners from throughout the West, around the nation, and even overseas come to experience these remarkable rivers. Many runs are popular enough to require permits and lotteries for launch dates; the waiting list for the Grand Canyon is notoriously long. Most trips eventually find their way to one of the region's old-time boating towns—Moab, Flagstaff, Green River, and others—all of which harbor large communities of local river rats.

Green River

Beginning as a Rocky Mountain stream amid deep snows and alpine lakes in western Wyoming's Wind River Range, the Green River courses generally south through Utah—and some of the most magnificent desert canyons in the West—to its confluence with the Colorado.

The Green's headwaters are on the western slope of the Continental Divide just 50 miles southeast of Jackson. Snowmelt from mountains including 13,804' Gannett Peak, the highest point in Wyoming, gathers in Green River Lakes. Leaving the lakes, the river briefly heads north, then buttonhooks south out of the mountains and into a long run through sagebrush-covered plateau country. Here, the Upper Green offers some 200 miles of runnable river—mostly flatwater, but with some Class II and III whitewater in the upper reaches. All of these sections receive very light use; most of the river traffic is local canoeists and fishermen.[1]

Downstream from the town of Green River, Wyoming, the river pauses in Flaming Gorge Reservoir, which extends across the Wyoming-Utah border and floods several lovely canyons named by Major Powell during his 1869 expedition down the Green and the Colorado. Below Flaming Gorge Dam in northeastern Utah, boaters can still enjoy the remaining half of Red Canyon and all of Swallow Canyon, both of which have fine scenery and easy rapids.

Below Swallow Canyon the Green wanders placidly eastward across the open flats of Browns Park and into the northwestern corner of Colorado. Then the river turns south by southwest into the heart of the Uinta Mountains and Dinosaur National Monument. This stretch of the Green, which begins with a run through the spectacular Canyon of Lodore, is one of the West's most renowned river trips. Except at rare high water, the rapids are of only moderate difficulty.

At the end of Lodore is the confluence with the undammed Yampa River, which during peak snowmelt adds 10,000 to 15,000 cfs to the Green's dam-controlled flow. Downstream lie Whirlpool and Split Mountain Canyons. The 44-mile trip through Dinosaur National Monument ends near Jensen, Utah.

Below Dinosaur the Green winds through open terrain in the Uinta Basin. Soon after the White and Duschene Rivers join the Green near Ouray, Utah, the river slices southward into the broad uplift of the Tavaputs Plateau. The ensuing run down Desolation and Gray Canyons is one of the Canyon Country's best wilderness floats, offering superb scenery and easy to moderate whitewater. The 84-mile run ends at the town of Green River in east central Utah.

The last 120 miles of the Green are calm and quiet. This is one of the West's finest flatwater wilderness trips, well suited for open canoes except at high water. Labyrinth and Stillwater Canyons require little in the way of whitewater skills, but basic boating ability, thorough planning, and solid outdoor experience are essential for a successful journey through these remote gorges.

This run also provides a popular approach to the big rapids of Cataract Canyon on the Colorado. Many Cataract trips launch at the last road access at Mineral Bottom, near the end of 70-mile-long Labyrinth Canyon, and float 50 miles of flatwater to the Colorado confluence. Below Mineral Bottom the Green enters Canyonlands National Park and eventually Stillwater Canyon. At the end of Stillwater the Green meets the Colorado at one of the West's most imposing confluences. Flatwater boaters can float less than four miles of the Colorado to Spanish Bottom and then use motors or a jet boat tow to make their way back up the Green or up the Colorado to Moab. Whitewater boaters can continue downstream through the much tougher whitewater of Cataract Canyon, provided they have the necessary skills, equipment, and permit.

---

[1]Dan Lewis, *Paddle and Portage: The Floater's Guide to Wyoming Rivers* covers all these upper runs in detail.

Green River

Red and Swallow Canyons

Difficulty: II to Taylor Flat Bridge (mile 16); I and I+ downstream.

Length: 7 miles to Little Hole; 16 to Bridge Hollow; 26 to Swallow Canyon; 46 to Lodore.

Gradient: 9 ft./mi. to Swallow Canyon; 2 ft./mi. thereafter.

Drainage Area and Average Annual Discharge: 19,350 sq. mi. / 1,580,000 af at the put-in.

Put-in: Flaming Gorge Dam (5,605').

Take-outs: Little Hole Boat Ramp (5,530'), Bridge Hollow Boat Ramp (5,440'), Swallow Canyon Boat Ramp (5,375'), or Lodore Boat Ramp (5,335').

Season: April–Oct. Year-round boatable flows (minimum release from Flaming Gorge Dam is 800 cfs). Spring releases range up to 4,700 cfs (and occasionally higher), then taper off beginning around mid-June. Typical flows from July through October are 800–1,500 cfs. See hydrograph in next chapter.

Recommended Levels: 800–6,000 cfs.

Flow Information: NWS tape, (801) 539-1311; release from Flaming Gorge Dam.

Permits: Not presently required.

Managing Agency: Flaming Gorge RD, Ashley NF, P.O. Box 278, Manila UT 84046; (801) 784-3445.

Commercial Raft Trips: Yes. For a list of outfitters, contact the managing agency.

Land Ownership: Almost all National Forest, BLM, or state-owned.

Scenery: Excellent. Colorful canyons first 14 miles, more open country downstream.

Solitude: Generally very good. Heavy use down to Little Hole (mile 7), lighter use thereafter.

Wilderness: Mostly. A few ranches and access roads.

Fishing: Excellent for trout in the first 16 miles (above Bridge Hollow Boat Ramp); good from there to Swallow Canyon Boat Ramp.

Water: Cold and clear. Sediment is trapped by Flaming Gorge Reservoir.

Side Excursions: Red Canyon Visitor Center, overlooking the site of Ashley Falls (now under Flaming Gorge Reservoir). Self-guided tours of Flaming Gorge Dam. Dam Overlook just off the road to the put-in.

Guides and References:

- Evans and Belknap, *Dinosaur River Guide.*
- Nichols, *River Runners' Guide to Utah.*
- Zwinger, *Run, River, Run.* Geology, natural and human history.
- *For more references see the next chapter.*

Maps:

- **USGS 7.5':** *Dutch John, Goslin Mtn, Clay Basin, Warren Draw, Swallow Canyon.*
- **USGS 1:100:** *Dutch John.*
- **USFS:** *Ashley NF* covers run to Bridge Hollow Boat Ramp (mile 16).

Logistics: To reach the **put-in** at Spillway Boat Ramp on the left (north) bank of the Green, drive about 45 miles north of Vernal, Utah on U.S.191, cross Flaming Gorge Dam, and turn right (east) onto the spillway access road. To reach **Little Hole Boat Ramp,** drive north on U.S.191 about two more miles, then turn right about ¼ mile beyond the Dutch John junction and follow the paved road past town some 7 miles to the river. To reach **downstream access points,** drive north on U.S.191; just past the Wyoming border, turn east at the Clay Basin turnoff and follow signs 29 miles to Browns Park. Turn right (upstream) on the access road to **Bridge Hollow Boat Ramp at Taylor Flat Bridge.** Or continue southeast on the Clay Basin Road about 5 miles to Willow Creek and **Swallow Canyon Boat Ramp.** For auto shuttles contact Flaming Gorge Lodge, (801) 889-3773, or Flaming Gorge Flying Service, (801) 885-3338.

Red Canyon, the uppermost remaining canyon on the Green, lives in the shadow of far more famous runs on the Green and Yampa in nearby Dinosaur National Monument. As a result, this delightful Utah river trip attracts mostly local boaters or passing tourists and remains little known outside the immediate area.

At one time Red Canyon was just one of a series of spectacular gorges on the Green between the town of Green River, Wyoming, and the Canyon of Lodore in Colorado. In 1869 Major John Wesley Powell's expedition named six major canyons: Flaming Gorge and Red Canyon for their "flaring, brilliant red" walls; Horseshoe and Hideout Canyons after their striking form and character; and Kingfisher and Swallow Canyons for their winged inhabitants.

Today only Red and Swallow Canyons remain; Flaming Gorge Dam flooded the four upstream gorges beginning in 1962. In fact, the 502'-high concrete arch blocks the Green near the heart of Red Canyon, burying more than half of this spectacular gorge as well. The 3.5 million acre-foot reservoir also covers the Green's roughest rapid above Lodore: Ashley Falls, named by Major Powell for an even earlier explorer, General William H. Ashley, who made the first descent of the Green in 1825.[2]

Every year, thousands of river runners enjoy the last remnants of these majestic canyons. Scenery is the main attraction. The easy-to-moderate whitewater consists mostly of straightforward, washboard-style riffles at the mouths of side canyons. Even so, this is not a run for first-timers. Less experienced boaters can put in at Bridge Hollow Boat Ramp (mile 16), below the most difficult whitewater.

Recently, the release pattern at Flaming Gorge Dam was changed to protect native fish endangered by the fluctuating daily flows and the cold water released from the base of the dam. Now, except when the reservoir is too full, spring flows are to be maintained at 4,700 cfs. Summer flows will continue to fluctuate daily according to the demand for electrical power, but warmer water will be released.

---

[2] For more on Green River history, see the sidebar in the next chapter and Roy Webb, *If We Had A Boat.*

Red and Swallow Canyons River Guide

The first seven miles are through lower Red Canyon. Iron oxides give the 1,500' walls a vibrant vermilion hue, in vivid contrast to the scattered evergreens that cling to the cliffs and river banks. The uppermost reach from Spillway Boat Ramp (left bank, mile 0) to Little Hole Boat Ramp (left bank, mile 7) is by far the most popular, thanks to outstanding scenery, Class II rapids, fine trout fishing, and a short shuttle. Private boaters share the river with commercial rafts and self-guided rental boats. A trail follows the left bank. No overnight camping or fires are allowed between the dam and Little Hole.

At Little Hole the canyon opens briefly. Downstream, the river is much less crowded due to long shuttles on unpaved roads. Soon, the walls close in again and the rapids resume, peaking at mile 11 where the river bends right and Red Creek enters on the left. Debris from the creek forms **RED CREEK RAPID (II+)**, the roughest whitewater between Flaming Gorge Dam and Lodore. This rocky drop is more difficult at low flows, and scouting is recommended. Downstream, the Green is Class I and I+ all the way to Lodore.

The walls of Red Canyon open for the last time at mile 13. A popular **alternate access** is at Indian Crossing Campground and Boat Ramp on the left between miles 15 and 16. Taylor Flat Bridge crosses the river at mile 16; immediately downstream on the right is the popular **access** at Bridge Hollow Boat Ramp, where less experienced boaters often put in. Below this point the river gradient remains moderate—about 9 ft./mi.—for about eight miles, then diminishes rapidly.

After Red Canyon the Green flows for more than 30 miles through Browns Park, a broad basin filled with deposits of sand, sediment, and volcanic ash. Waterfowl thrive in marshy flats next to the river, and much of this section is protected as wildlife refuge. Occasional ranches and unpaved roads intrude only slightly on the solitude.

Aside from a riffle just below Sears Creek (mile 22), the Green flows placidly through Browns Park, which extends from the foot of Red Canyon to the Gates of Lodore a mile below the take-out. This open section is broken only by a two-mile passage between the vertical walls of Swallow Canyon (miles 24–26). Above Swallow Canyon the river has a moderate gradient and current, but in the 20 miles below the canyon it slows to a lazy crawl. Upstream winds can be a problem. Open canoes are probably the best craft for this section.

Many boaters take out at Swallow Canyon Boat Ramp (mile 26) at the foot of Swallow Canyon. Two miles downstream, the river crosses into Colorado. Another intermediate access is Refuge Campground at mile 37. All boaters must take out at Lodore Boat Ramp at mile 46. (All of these access points are on the left bank.) A permit is required to float on through the Canyon of Lodore, where the difficulty increases dramatically.

The placid waters and pastoral scenery of Browns Park belie a violent past, for the basin was once home to some of the most notorious outlaws in the West. In the late nineteenth century, cattle rustlers and other criminals—including Butch Cassidy and the Wild Bunch—often holed up here. Sheriffs with a mind to reaching retirement generally avoided this remote stronghold.

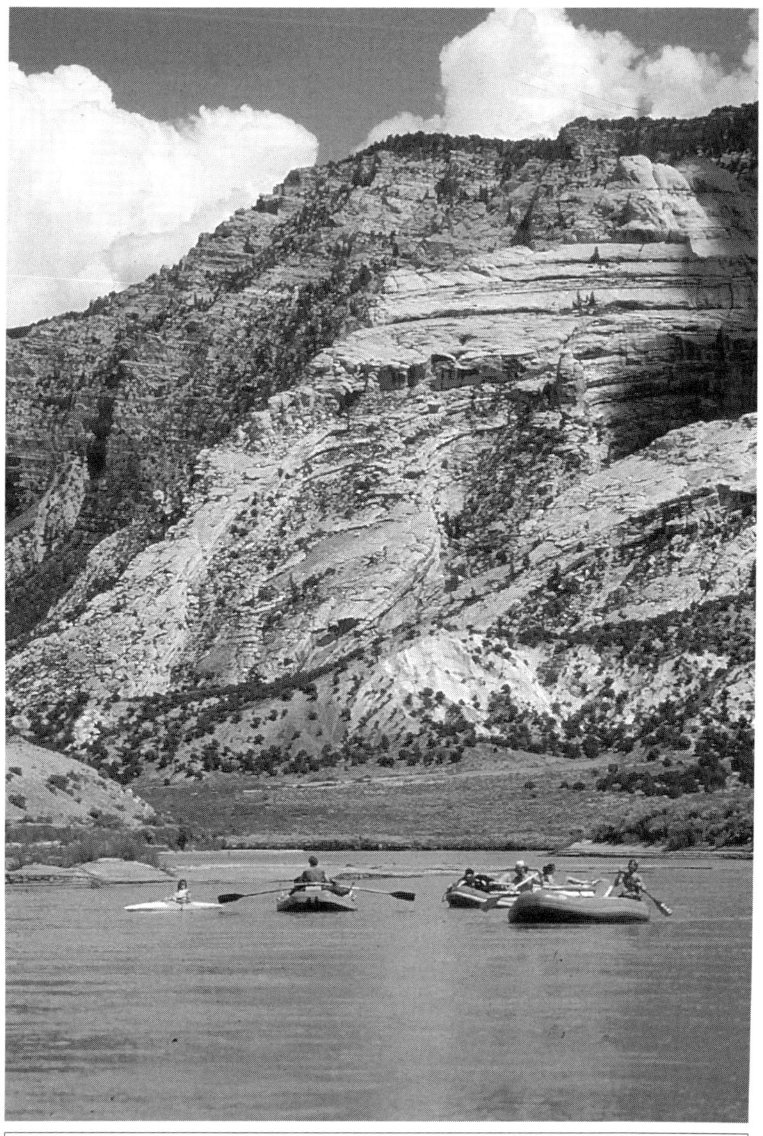

Island Park, Green River *Bill Cross*

Green River

Lodore, Whirpool, and Split Mountain Canyons

Difficulty: III; some IV at rare high water.
Length: 44 miles. Shorter runs possible.
Gradient: 13 ft./mi.
Drainage Area and Average Annual Discharge: 19,350 sq. mi. and 1,581,000 af at Flaming Gorge above put-in. 29,660 sq. mi. and 3,298,000 af at Jensen below take-out.
Put-in: Lodore Boat Ramp (5,335').
Take-out: Split Mountain Boat Ramp (4,780').
Peak Recorded Flow: 19,600 cfs at Flaming Gorge; 40,000 cfs (May 18, 1984) at Jensen.
Season: April–Oct. Year-round boatable flows. Controlled by Flaming Gorge Dam, but the undammed Yampa adds considerable flow at mile 19 during spring snowmelt. Spring dam releases range up to 4,700 cfs (and occasionally higher), then taper off beginning in mid-June. Typical releases from July through October of 800–2,000 cfs.
Recommended Levels: 800–6,000 cfs.
Flow Information: NWS tape, (801) 539-1311, gives the release from Flaming Gorge Dam (put-in), the Yampa flow at its mouth (added to the Green at mile 19), and the Green flow at Jensen (take-out).
Special Hazards: Peak runoff on the Yampa can create big waves on the lower part of this run.
Permits: Required year-round. Much sought after and difficult to get. Group limit 25. For high-use season (second Monday in May to second Friday in September), apply Dec. 1–Jan. 31 for lottery held in February. Odds are worst for launch dates in May and June, much better in late summer or off-season. No waiting list; call after March 1 for unused dates or cancellations, which account for about a third of the starts. For low-use season, call for dates on a first-come, first-served basis beginning March 1. Apply separately for one-day, 8-mile runs through Split Mountain Gorge.

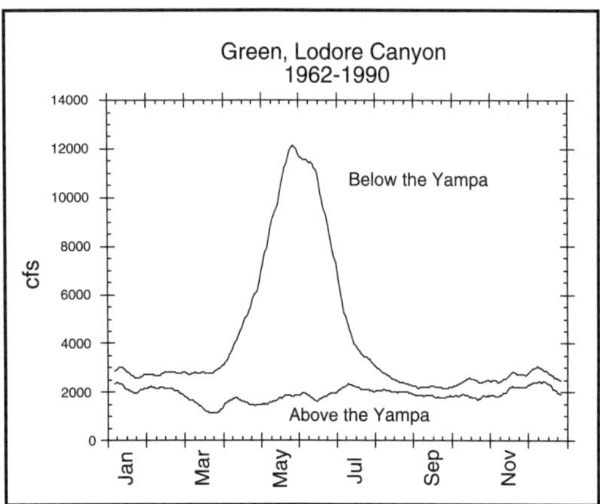

Managing Agency: River Office, Dinosaur National Monument, P.O. Box 210, Dinosaur, CO 81610; (303) 374-2468.
Commercial Raft Trips: Yes. For a list contact the managing agency.
Land Ownership: Public; mostly National Park.
Scenery: Excellent, varied. Three distinct high-desert sandstone canyons.
Solitude: Very good in high-use season; excellent at other times.
Wilderness: Yes.
Fishing: Fair for catfish and trout.
Wildlife: Bighorn sheep, reintroduced in the 1950's, are commonly seen. Also deer, beaver, raptors.
Weather: Early season (through May) can be cold and rainy; occasional snow. Summers are warm to hot; occasional thundershowers.
Water: Flaming Gorge Dam releases cold, desilted water that should be considered undrinkable. The Yampa adds a heavy load of sediment in spring and early summer. Purify water from side streams and/or pack water and refill at Echo Park (mile 19).
Camping: Excellent, but allowed only at established campsites (which are assigned during high-use season). Only one overnight stop allowed between Echo Park and the Split Mountain take-out.
Side Hikes: Of special note are Pot Creek, Rippling Brook, Echo Park and especially Jones Hole.
Side Excursions: Superb fossil exhibits at Dinosaur Quarry near the take-out. Several scenic viewpoints along Harper's Corner Road and Trail, including a panoramic overlook more than 2,000' above Echo Park and Whirlpool Canyon. (Follow Harper's Corner Road from Dinosaur National Monument Headquarters on U.S. 40). Outlaw Trail and Diamond Mountain Route (see **Logistics**).

Guides and References:

- Evans and Belknap, *Dinosaur River Guide.*
- Gernant, Hinton, & Hughes, *The Canyons of Dinosaur.*
- Wheat, *Floater's Guide to Colorado.*
- Nichols, *River Runners' Guide to Utah.*
- *Riverguide Bandana to the Green and Yampa* (Rivers & Mountains). Cloth map.
- Hayes & Simmons, *River Runners' Guide to Dinosaur National Monument and Vicinity.* Detailed geologic river log.
- Hagood, *Dinosaur: The Story Behind the Scenery.* Geology, fossils.
- Webb, *If We Had A Boat.* History and exploration of Upper Green.
- Zwinger, *Run, River, Run.* Personal essays, natural history.
- Stegner, *This Is Dinosaur.* Geology, human and natural history.
- Collins & Nash, *The Big Drops.* Essays on Hell's Half Mile and other famous Western rapids, emphasizing early boating history.
- Rennicke, *Rivers of Colorado* and *River Days.* Essays on this and other Colorado rivers.

Maps:

- **USGS 7.5'**: *Canyon of Lodore North, Canyon of Lodore South, Jones Hole, Island Park, Split Mtn, Dinosaur Quarry.*
- **USGS:** *Dinosaur National Monument* sheet, the best overall map, covers the entire run plus Yampa Canyon at 1:62,500.

Auto Shuttle: About 135 miles (3–4 hours) one way. For shuttle services contact River Runner's Transport, P.O. Box 1361, Vernal UT 84078; (801) 781-1180.

Logistics: To reach the **put-in** in the northwestern corner of Colorado, turn northwest off U.S. 40 onto Colorado Route 318 just west of Maybell, Colorado. Drive roughly 40 miles and turn left onto a dirt road, marked "Gates of Lodore," which leads about 10 miles to Lodore Campground and Boat Ramp.

To reach the **take-out** in the northeastern corner of Utah, return to U.S. 40, turn right (west) and drive about 80 miles to Jensen, Utah. Turn right (north) onto Utah Route 149 and drive beyond the Dinosaur Quarry to Split Mountain Campground and Boat Ramp. An alternate and shorter shuttle route, the beautiful Diamond Mountain Route through Crouse Canyon, runs west of the Green on unpaved roads and follows the Outlaw Trail. It is shown on the Dinosaur National Monument visitor information map and should be attempted only in dry weather.

To reach the **intermediate access at Rainbow Park** (put-in for one-day runs of Split Mountain Gorge), follow Utah 149 north from Jensen about 2.5 miles, then bear left on Brush Creek Road (impassable when wet) and follow signs to Island Park and Rainbow Park.

Since William Ashley's first descent in 1825, the Green River through today's Dinosaur National Monument has become known as one of the West's great river trips. True, the whitewater on the Green has been partially tamed by Flaming Gorge Dam. But the scenery is every bit as breathtaking as when Ashley and Powell explored here (see sidebar).

The three canyons featured in this chapter present a constantly changing panorama, from precipitous walls of red sandstone in Lodore to dramatically folded layers of grey limestone and pale sandstone in Split Mountain. Side canyons hold more intimate wonders: the cool rock sanctuary of Winnies Grotto, the delicate cascades of Rippling Brook, the lush verdure of Jones Hole, and much more. The open flats of Browns Park, Island Park, and Rainbow Park offer stunning views of some of the most dramatic and abrupt canyon entrances in the West.

The Green's flow within Dinosaur National Monument is controlled by Flaming Gorge Dam some 46 miles upstream from the Lodore put-in. River runners negotiating Disaster Falls and Hells Half Mile at low summer flows may wonder why these seemingly moderate rapids inspired such fear in early explorers. However, those who have seen the river during its rare modern periods of high water have a better appreciation for the hazards faced by boaters before Flaming Gorge Dam was built. In 1983 a record snowpack pushed flows above 10,000 cfs. In 1984 a brief flood forced a commercial trip to do the unthinkable: portage Hells Half Mile.

Below Lodore boaters sometimes get a feel for what the untamed Green was like. At peak runoff the Yampa can add 10,000 to 15,000 cfs at Echo Park, transforming normally mild Whirlpool Canyon into a cauldron of swirling,

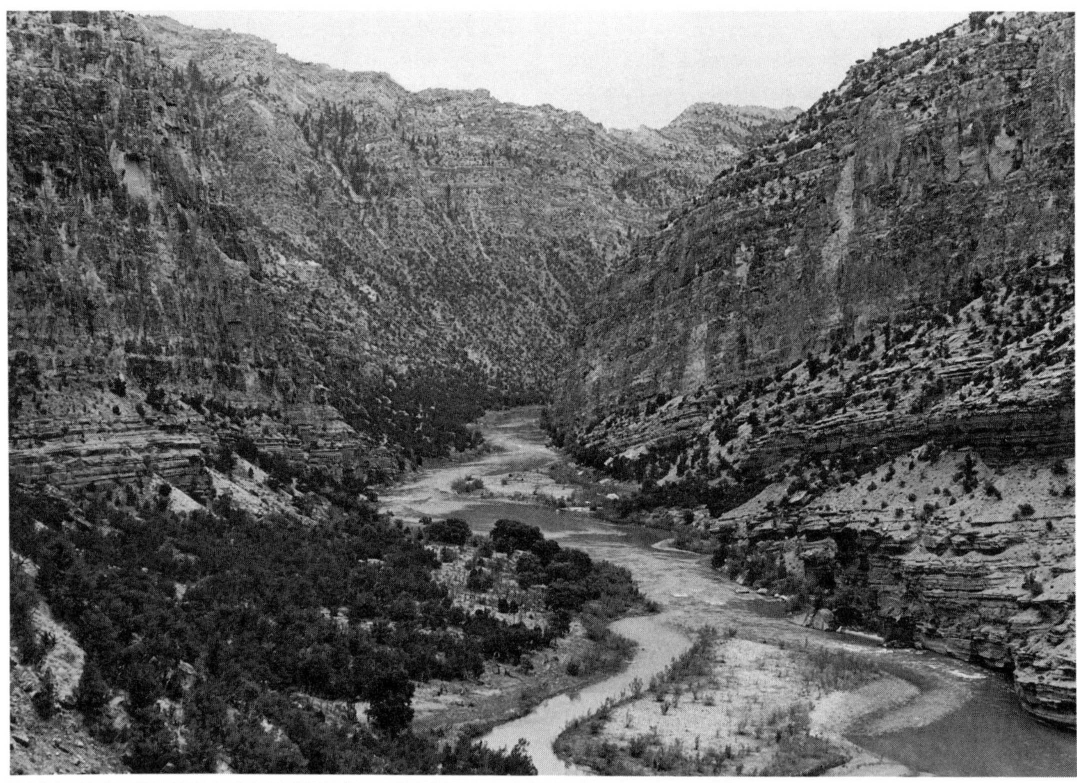

Canyon of Lodore, Green River *David Symonik*

turbulent currents, and turning Split Mountain's easy Class III rapids into a wild joyride down big, chocolate-brown waves. In an average year the Yampa actually carries more water than the Green at their confluence; however, the undammed Yampa yields most of its water in one relatively brief pulse of snowmelt, so at most times boaters find more water in the Green.

The popularity of the Lodore stretch of the Green has brought about a permit frenzy for high-use season trips. Commercial and private groups each get half the launch dates, and the daily number of put-ins is restricted to avoid crowding. It's not easy, but private boaters who persist can usually land a permit, either in the initial draw or by calling in for unused or cancelled dates.

Fifteen million years ago there was no Canyon of Lodore. From the broad flats of Browns Park along what is now the Utah-Colorado border, the ancestral Green River flowed east to join the North Platte and Missouri Rivers. The uplift of the Rockies along the Continental Divide forced the Green to change its course to the south. Then the Uinta Mountains began to rise in the river's new path. This time the river held firm, carving steadily downward as the mountain range grew around it.

One result of this process is the Canyon of Lodore, a narrow cleft incised deep into colorful sedimentary rocks. A brief opening at Echo Park separates Lodore from the next chasm, Whirlpool Canyon. Below Whirlpool the broad flats of Island Park and Rainbow Park divide the upper canyons from their smaller cousin, Split Mountain Canyon. At Split Mountain the Green slices directly through an isolated bulge in the earth's crust, taking a seemingly illogical course through, rather than around, a 7,600' peak. Here, as at Lodore, the ancient Green predates the younger mountain in a classic example of what geologists call antecedence.

On August 17, 1909 the southern slope of Split Mountain was the stage for one of the greatest scientific discoveries of all time, when paleontologist Earl Douglass found eight tail bones from the dinosaur Brontosaurus exposed in a bed of Morrison Sandstone. Further excavations over the next 14 years unearthed some 350 tons of fossils. Scientists concluded that 140 million years ago this incredibly rich site had been a riverside sandbar where dead dinosaurs drifted to shore, decayed, and were buried by sediments. In 1915 President Woodrow Wilson designated the quarry a national monument, and in 1938 President Franklin Roosevelt expanded the preserve to include the canyons of the Green and Yampa. The Dinosaur Quarry Visitor Center makes a fascinating side excursion for river runners.

Despite the fact that they run through a National Monument, the Green and Yampa Rivers were nearly destroyed in the 1950's. As part of the Colorado River Storage Project, the Bureau of Reclamation proposed a dam just below the Green-Yampa confluence in Echo Park. It would have flooded the Yampa all the way to Deerlodge (46 miles) and the Green all the way to Flaming Gorge Dam (67 miles). The fledgling conservation movement fought Echo Park Dam as a dangerous precedent of a major water project encroaching on a National Park. In a compromise still debated today, Glen Canyon of the Colorado River was essentially traded for the Green River in Dinosaur: the former was flooded and the latter was saved.

Early Descents of the Green River

Western whitewater boating grew up in the Canyon Country, and the roots of river running go deepest in the Canyon of Lodore. Boaters passing through the canyon's rocky portals retrace a path first followed more than 165 years ago. Downstream lies a timeless realm where rocks and rapids still echo with a rich history of exploration and adventure.

In 1825 a fur-trapping expedition led by General William H. Ashley made the first descent of the Green. After passing through difficult rapids and imposing canyons farther upstream, the men came suddenly upon the towering rock walls later named the Gates of Lodore. On May 8 the expedition entered the canyon, not knowing what might lie downstream but imagining the worst. Ashley wrote, "I was forcibly struck with the gloom which spread over the countenances of my men; they seemed to anticipate (and not too far distant, too) a dreadful termination of our voyage." Nevertheless, after an arduous descent marked by strenuous portages, the men came through safely.

In 1849 the California gold rush inspired another adventurer, William Manly, to head West. Accustomed to river travel in his native Michigan, Manly determined to reach California by descending the Green to its mouth—though at the time no one was certain just where the river reached the ocean, or what it did along the way. In a salvaged 12' ferry boat, Manly and six companions made a harrowing but successful descent of Lodore and other canyons before leaving the Green near the mouth of the Uinta River. Reports of hostile Indians farther downstream convinced them to continue their journey by land.

It was another 20 years before Major John Wesley Powell ran the Green on his way to the Colorado. Though many people mistakenly believe his was the first descent, in fact Powell's was simply the most well-documented and scientifically accurate exploration to date. Powell and his men named many rapids and landmarks. The "Canyon of Lodore" was inspired by a then-popular English poem describing a waterfall of the same name. As it had for previous adventurers, Lodore proved to be the greatest test Powell and his men faced on the Green. The expedition lost one of its four boats, the ***No Name****, at a rapid they dubbed Disaster Falls.*

Later adventurers included Nathaniel Galloway, who ran the river in the early 1900's, and the Kolb brothers, Ellsworth and Emery, who led a photographic expedition down the Green and the Colorado in 1911. By the mid-1930's Bus Hatch and his crew were taking passengers on 10-day runs from Green River, Wyoming to Jensen, Utah for $65 a head. By the 1950's he was using military surplus rafts for scheduled trips. His descendants still operate the family business in Vernal, Utah.[1]

[1]For more on Galloway and the Kolbs, see the chapter on the **Grand Canyon of the Colorado**. For more on Hatch, see Roy Webb, *Riverman: The Story of Bus Hatch.*

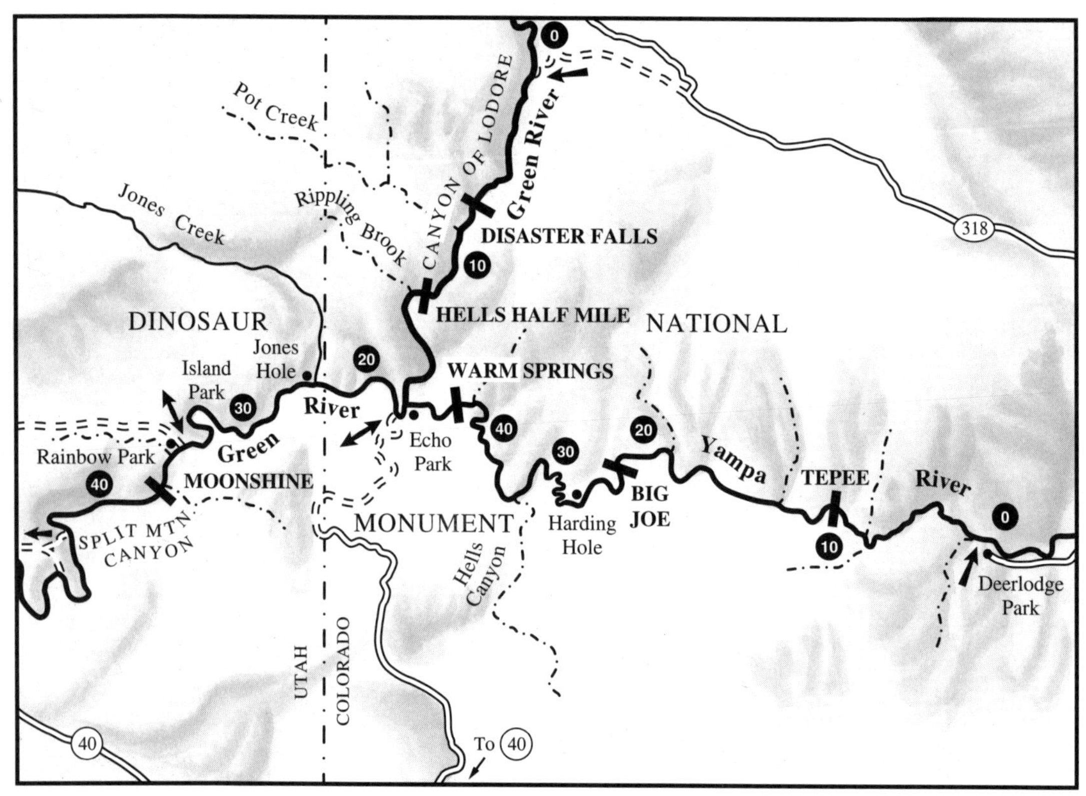

Green (Lodore) and Lower Yampa

Green River Mile Guide

0 **PUT-IN.** Lodore Boat Ramp, Campground, and Ranger Station on the left bank. Drinking water, overnight camping. A mile downstream, the Green glides through the Gates of Lodore and plunges into the Uinta Mountains. Rock beds tilt upward as the river moves downstream toward the highest point of the uplift.

2.7 Wade and Curtis Campground on the right. Just under a mile downstream is Winnies Grotto, a narrow side canyon. A small riffle at the Grotto signals the beginning of the whitewater, which builds over the next few miles.

6.7 **UPPER DISASTER FALLS** (III), a short drop between boulders and through a wave, followed by the long washboard of **LOWER DISASTER FALLS** (III). Difficult scout from the right. Named by Powell's expedition for the loss of the *No Name* here: "*... she swings around and is carried down at a rapid rate, broadside on, for a few yards, when striking amidships on another rock with great force, she is broken quite in two and the men are thrown into the river.*"

8 Zenobia Creek enters on the left. Half a mile downstream, Pot Creek enters on the right. Riverside campground; trail up the creek.

10 **HARP FALLS** (III-). Scout on the left. Just over a mile downstream is **TRIPLET FALLS** (III), which entails a move to the left in the middle of the rapid to avoid boulders and the canyon wall. Scout on the left.

12 **HELLS HALF MILE** (III+, IV- **at high water**), the toughest rapid of the trip and a bad place to take a swim. **Recognition:** A rocky horizon line at the end of a large pool. **The rapid:** Manuever among boulders at the top, line up for a steep center slot that feeds into a chain of waves, then negotiate a quarter-mile-long washboard of rocks, waves, and holes where the river

splits around islands. Below the rapid easy riffles continue for a couple of miles, followed by some half dozen miles of mostly flatwater to Whirlpool Canyon.

13.2 Rippling Brook enters on the right. River campground. Side hike to falls. Lodore Canyon reaches its greatest depth here—more than 3,000'. Downstream, the walls recede as the rock beds dip downward.

18.7 The Yampa River enters from the left in Echo Park, an open section that marks the end of the Canyon of Lodore. Massive Steamboat Rock is on the right. Echo Park Ranger Station and Campground are on the left below the Yampa; boaters can refill water jugs but may not camp. A road leads 38 miles to U.S. 40 but includes 1.5 miles of steep switchbacks, so Echo Park is not a recommended river access point. At the lower end of Echo Park, Pool Creek enters on the left, offering a short hike to petroglyphs near Whispering Cave.

21 The Green enters Whirlpool Canyon. This was the site proposed for Echo Park Dam. Although Whirlpool Canyon has no significant rapids, the river is swirly and turbulent, especially when the Yampa adds significant flow.

24.5 Colorado-Utah border. State Line River Campground on the right.

25 Jones Hole and Jones Hole Creek on the right. Ranger station. This very popular campground is often crowded, especially when the Yampa is running. Jones Hole Creek flows down a broad valley from the north. A beautiful two-mile hike up the creek leads to superb petroglyphs. Downstream, the canyon walls diminish as the rock beds slope downward again.

26.5 Sage Creek enters on the right.

29.5 Whirlpool Canyon ends spectacularly as the rock strata dive below the surface. The Green enters Island Park, splitting into channels as it drifts placidly around large wooded islands. Look for petroglyphs on the left a little over a mile into the park. Downstream, Island Park blends imperceptibly into another flatwater section, Rainbow Park.

36 **RIVER ACCESS.** Rainbow Park Boat Ramp on the right. This is the put-in for one-day runs of Split Mountain Canyon and the take-out for those (primarily an occasional Yampa trip) who wish to avoid the rapids downstream.

36.5 The Green abruptly enters Split Mountain Canyon. The gradient increases to 20 ft./mi. as the river rolls through several straightforward rapids with big waves. A mile into the canyon, where Moonshine Draw enters on the right, is **MOONSHINE (III)**, a long, fast washboard with big holes and waves in the center about halfway down. Scout left. A mile below Moonshine is **S.O.B.** (III-). A mile farther downstream at **SCHOOLBOY** (II+), the river sweeps into a cliff on the left.

40 Mitten Canyon enters on the right. Hot spring 100 yards up the canyon.

41.2 **INGLESBY** (III-). Large boulder in mid-channel.

44.2 **TAKE-OUT.** The canyon ends, and Split Mountain Boat Ramp appears on the right. Downstream, the river is smooth for over 100 miles. (See next chapter.)

Green River

Desolation and Gray Canyons

Difficulty: II+3. **Length:** 84 miles.
Gradient: 1 ft./mi. to Jack Creek (mile 26); 6 ft./mi. thereafter.
Put-in: Sand Wash Beach (4,650').
Take-out: Swasey's Beach (4,095').
Drainage Area and Average Annual Discharge: 44,850 sq. mi. and 4,648,000 af at Green River, Utah.
Peak Recorded Flow: 68,100 cfs (June 27, 1917).
Season: April–Oct. Typically peaks (often above 15,000 cfs) in late May or early June. Drops to 2,000–6,000 by late July and to 1,500–4,000 in September.
Recommended Levels: 1,000–20,000 cfs. Shallow and rocky below 2,000, big waves over 15,000.
Flow Information: NWS tape, (801) 539-1311; flow at Green River, Utah, near the take-out.
Special Hazards: Remote area.
Permits: Required year-round. Available for the asking off season; advance reservation, fee required for launch dates April 1–Oct. 31. Applications accepted Dec. 1–Jan. 31 for lottery held in February. Those not drawn in the lottery can often get a permit by calling after March 1 for unused dates, cancellations, or places on the waiting list. Group limit 25. No permit required for the one-day, 8-mile float below Nefertiti Rapid (mile 75).
Managing Agency: BLM, Price River RA, 900 N. 700 E., Price, UT 84501; (801) 637-4591.
Commercial Raft Trips: Yes. Contact the BLM for a list of outfitters.
Scenery: Excellent. Contrasting desert canyons.

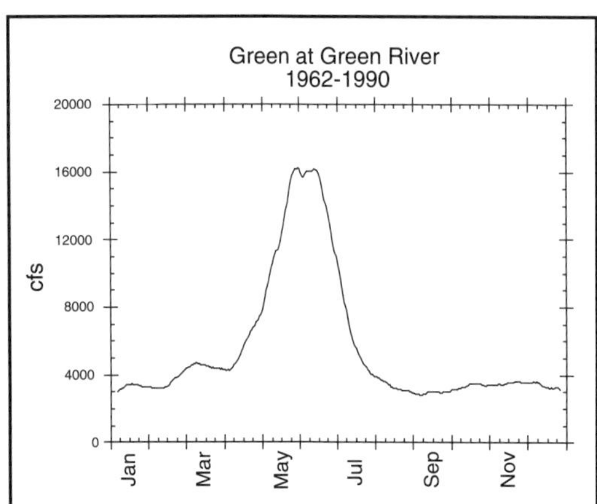

Solitude: Excellent, although river traffic is fairly heavy mid-May through July and in October (see essay).
Land Ownership: Right bank is almost all BLM. Left bank is BLM first 7.5 miles and last 14 miles, Uintah and Ouray Indian Reservation in between. See **Camping** below.
Wilderness: Yes.
Fishing: Catfish in the river, trout in the side creeks.
Wildlife: Bighorn sheep, deer, birds.
Weather: Variable in spring; occasional snow. Very hot in summer; occasional thunderstorms, possible flash floods in side canyons.
Water: Warm and murky in summer; undrinkable without puriying and filtering. Better to carry drinking water. A few side creeks (notably Rock Creek) offer refill sites, but purify the water. No drinking water at put- in.
Camping: Many broad beaches, especially in Desolation Canyon; fewer at high water. Permit required to camp or hike on Uintah and Ouray Indian Reservation land (left bank, miles 7.5–70); contact the BLM for details.
Side Hikes: Many excellent side canyons. See **Camping** (above) and **Mile Guide.**
Side Excursions: John Wesley Powell River History Museum in the town of Green River. Crystal Geyser just below the town.
Guides and References:

- Evans & Belknap, *Desolation River Guide.*
- Rampton, *River Guide to Desolation and Gray Canyons.*
- Nichols, *River Runners' Guide to Utah.*
- Wheat, *Floater's Guide to Colorado.*
- Zwinger, *Run, River, Run.* Essays, human and natural history.
- Webb, *If We Had A Boat.* History of boating and exploration.
- Mutschler, *River Runners' Guide to the Canyons of the Green and Colorado Rivers, With Emphasis on Geologic Features.* Detailed geologic river log.

Maps:

- **USGS** 7.5': *Nutters Hole, Duches Hole, Firewater Canyon North, Cedar Ridge Canyon, Steer Ridge Canyon, Chandler Falls, Three Fords Canyon, Butler Canyon, Tusher Canyon.*

- **USGS 1:100:** *Seep Ridge, Price, Huntington.*
- *Northeastern Utah.* Order from Utah Travel Council, Council Hall–Capitol Hill, Salt Lake City, UT 84114; (801) 533-5681.

Auto Shuttle: About 190 miles (4–5 hours) one way. For shuttle service contact Castle Country Travel Council, (801) 637-2788.

Air Shuttle: Boaters can hire a plane from the town of Green River to an airstrip near Sand Wash. Same contact as above.

Logistics: There are two routes to the **put-in.** The **preferred route** is smoother and less complicated but slightly longer: a couple of miles west of the town of Myton, which is located some 90 miles southwest of Vernal in northeastern Utah, turn south off U.S. 40 at a marked turnoff on the first paved road (becomes dirt). The road forks frequently, so follow signs carefully 52 miles to Sand Wash Boat Ramp. (The last 9 miles are in the wash; be aware of flash flood danger.) A rough alternate route, which leads north off U.S. 191/6 a few miles east of Wellington, is not recommended. Part of it is called the "Wrinkles Road" for good reason, and it saves 50 miles but little time.

To reach the **take-out,** return to U.S. 40, turn west to Duschene, then south on U.S. 191 to I-70, then east on I-70 and U.S. 50 to the town of Green River. About half a mile past the bridge over the Green, turn left on Hastings Road (first paved, then dirt) and drive up the left (east) bank of the river about 10 miles to the take-out below Swasey's Rapid. (Bear right at the second cattle guard.) The rough road continues upstream as far as Nefertiti Rapid, providing access for one-day trips.

"After dinner we pass through a region of the wildest desolation. The canyon is very tortuous, the river very rapid, and many lateral canyons enter on either side. These usually have their branches, so that the region is cut into a wilderness of gray and brown cliffs . . . We are minded to call this the Canyon of Desolation." —John Wesley Powell

Today, the ramparts of Desolation and Gray Canyons look much as they did when Major Powell and his men first ran the river in 1869. These stark chasms remain virtually untouched by civilization. Boaters embarking on this section of the Green step back into a primordial era where time is measured not in minutes, but in millennia.

Below Dinosaur National Monument and the town of Jensen, Utah, the Green winds through open terrain in the Uinta Basin. Soon after the White and Duschene Rivers join the Green near the town of Ouray, the river slices southward into the broad uplift of the Tavaputs Plateau. Over millions of years, the river maintained its course and cut steadily downward as the earth rose around it. The north-south gash of Desolation and Gray Canyons cleaves the Tavaputs into eastern and western halves for nearly a hundred miles. In places the canyon is 5,000' deep.

The human history of this rugged land is sparse but intriguing. Pottery, petroglyphs, ruins, and arrowheads offer mute reminders of the Fremont culture, which flourished here some 800 years ago. More recently, Ute Indians occupied the region before being forced onto reservations. In the early 1800's an occasional trapper wandered here, including the mysterious Frenchman Denis Julien, a wanderer who carved his initials at many points along the canyons of the Green and Colorado.

For the most part whites viewed these canyons as an impediment to travel. Few had reason to venture here when the Green offered easy crossings to the north and south. Eventually a few ranchers and homesteaders settled at flats or "holes" along the river, struggling against the harsh climate and difficult terrain. Near the turn of the century, Butch Cassidy and his bunch favored Gray Canyon as a hideout, and gang member George "Flat Nose" Curry got a fatal dose of Western justice near Rattlesnake Rapid in 1900. Today the homesteads and ranches are mostly abandoned.

Desolation and Gray Canyons have so far escaped dams. But they could be threatened by proposed dams on the Yampa River, the Green's largest tributary. Since Flaming Gorge Dam blocked the Green 200 miles above Sand Wash in 1962, Desolation and Gray have gotten much of their spring high water—and the sediment to replenish their beaches—from the free-flowing Yampa. Dams on the Yampa would seriously harm this pristine reach of the Green.

River running in Desolation and Gray has increased more slowly over the years than on a number of other Canyon Country runs. For many who don't know these canyons, their names may conjure up a mistaken image of a drab and lifeless realm. (Some commercial outfitters prefer to call this stretch the "Green River Wilderness.")

The reality is far from drab. By any name the Desolation–Gray float is one of the Canyon Country's finest, with excellent scenery, superb side hikes, expansive campsites, abundant wildlife (especially in spring), and above all, serenity and solitude. The only drawback is occasional early-summer problems with mosquitos in the first flat miles below Sand Wash.

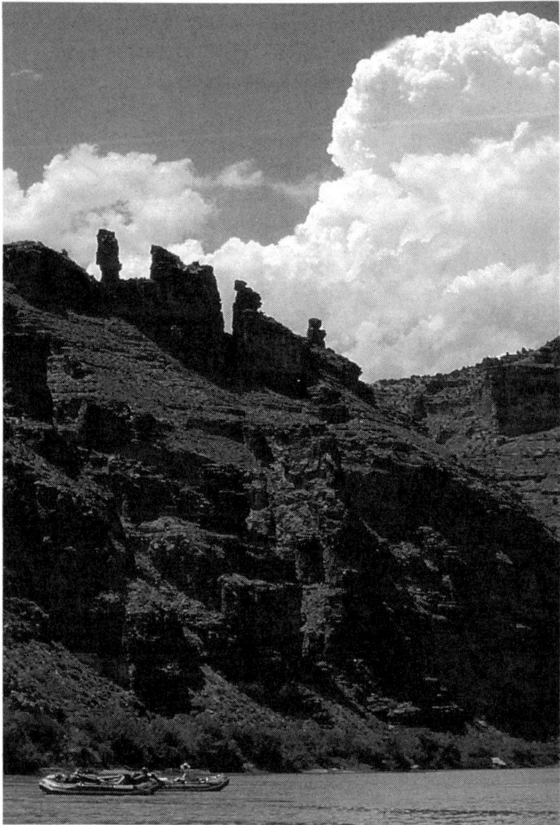

Desolation Canyon, Green River *Diane Cross*

Below Sand Wash the walls of Desolation Canyon rise gradually as the river glides southward. A profound sense of isolation grows with every mile. Slowly the desert vegetation gives way to a sparse forest of pinyon and juniper, which cling tenaciously to slopes and cliffs of gray or red-brown sedimentary rock. "Hoodoos"—curious pillars formed where a hard stone cap protects softer rock underneath from erosion—stand like silent sentinels above the river.

After some 60 miles, a short open valley separates Desolation Canyon from Gray Canyon, named by Powell for its pale sandstones and shales. Gray Canyon, shorter and smaller than Desolation, ends abruptly a few miles above the town of Green River.

The first 26 miles of Desolation Canyon are smooth and sometimes slow, especially when headwinds develop. The rapids finally begin at Jack Creek and appear every half mile or mile, usually where side canyons wash debris into the river. The whitewater generally grows rougher as the run progresses. Gray Canyon is more challenging than Desolation, though its rapids are fewer and farther between.

In all the Green rolls through some 40 moderate rapids and many smaller riffles, making this a good open canoe trip *for those with the necessary skills.* Beware of high water, which produces waves big enough to swamp open boats, and low water, when many canoes run into trouble. Raft support makes canoe trips easier. This is *not* a novice run, and the remote location dictates caution.

The last stretch of Gray Canyon offers half a dozen rapids and riffles that make a short, pleasant one-day run. A rough dirt road follows the left bank from Nefertiti Rapid (mile 75.5) to Swasey's Beach (mile 84). No permits are presently required for these day trips.

Upstream Runs

Those with a taste for flatwater and wildlife—and a tolerance for mosquitos—may enjoy the 33 miles upstream from Ouray to Sand Wash. Below the put-in at the Utah Route 88 bridge, the Green winds peacefully through gentle terrain. The scenery improves as the river approaches Desolation Canyon. There are 50 more miles even farther upstream, from Jensen to Ouray. Though the flat terrain is not terribly scenic, birdwatchers will enjoy floating through the Ouray National Waterfowl Refuge.[1]

[1] All these runs are covered in Evans and Belknap, *Dinosaur River Guide.* Rampton, *River Guide to Desolation and Gray Canyons,* covers Ouray to Sand Wash.

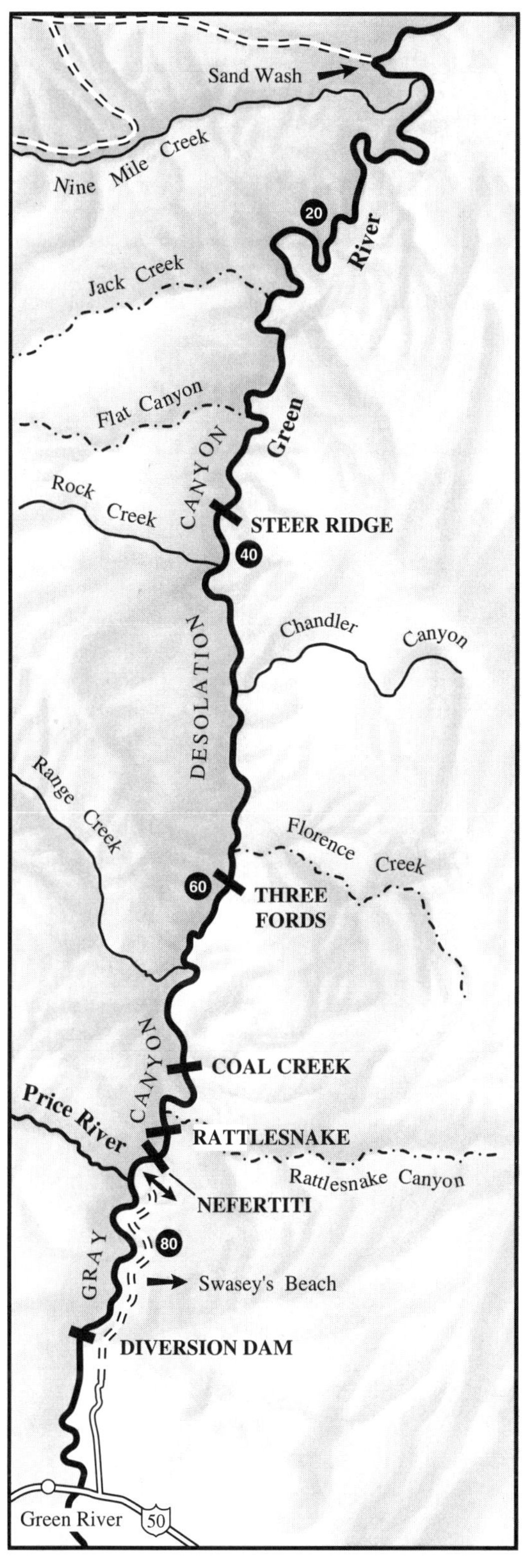

Green: Desolation and Gray Canyons

Mile by Mile Guide

0 **PUT-IN** at Sand Wash Boat Ramp on the right bank of the Green. BLM ranger station and dirt airstrip nearby. No drinking water. A ferry operated here in the first half of the century. Nine Mile Creek enters on the right two miles downstream. Few good campsites in the first dozen miles due to thick brush along the shore. No significant whitewater for 26 miles.

7.5 Uintah and Ouray Indian Reservation on the left bank from here to Coal Creek, mile 70. Permit required for camping and hiking (see **Camping**).

24 Light House Rock towers above the right bank, announcing the approach of whitewater. Two miles downstream, Jack Creek enters on the right. Debris from the creek forms **JACK CREEK RAPID** (II-). Downstream, the whitewater gradually increases in difficulty.

30 Firewater Canyon enters on the left. A half-mile hike up a small tributary canyon leads to an old bootlegger's cabin. Just over two miles downstream, look for superb petroglyphs on the right bank a few hundred yards above the mouth of Flat Canyon. A mile below Flat Canyon is the lovely glen of Dripping Springs high on the left. Hike to the springs offers a good view.

39 **STEER RIDGE** (II+) appears suddenly at a left bend. Beware of logs that often lodge on midstream rocks. Most boaters run left. Steer Ridge Canyon enters on the right.

41.5 Rock Creek, a beautiful tributary, enters on the right at the canyon's deepest point. A Class II- rapid is below the creek. No camping along the river within half a mile of the creek. Purify creek water before drinking. Good two-mile hike to petroglyphs on the north side of the creek. Just downstream on the right is abandoned Rock Creek Ranch.

44.5 **SNAP CANYON RAPID** (II). A two-part rapid where Snap Canyon enters on the left.

47 **BELKNAP FALLS (II).** A minor riffle until 1987, when a side canyon flash flood made it tougher.

48.5 Chandler Canyon enters on the left at **CHANDLER FALLS (II-).** Near the river boaters can find the inscription "DJ" (Denis Julien), which is over 150 years old. Side hike up the jeep trail, the first of two jeep trails which reach the river before the take-out.

54 **JOE HUTCH CREEK RAPID (II).** A mile downstream is **JOE HUTCH CANYON RAPID (II).**

56 Florence Creek Ranch and Ouray Lodge on the left. Florence Creek enters on the left ¾ mile downstream, just above a rapid of the same name. A hike up the creek leads to Indian granaries and petroglyphs. Downstream, Desolation Canyon ends, separated from Gray Canyon by a short, open valley.

59 Just below a tight right bend is **THREE FORDS (II+)**, where outwash from a side canyon on the left forces the river to the right. Rocky and more difficult at low water. Scout right.

64 **RANGE CREEK RAPID (II)** at the mouth of Range Creek, which enters on the right. Wilcox Ranch (private) is 6 miles up the creek.

69.5 Coal Creek enters on the left. **COAL CREEK RAPID (III-)** is usually the biggest of the run. Rocky at low flows, big waves and holes at higher levels. Avoid the far right. Scout right. Indian Reservation (left bank) ends. In 1911 an attempt was made to dam the Green below Coal Creek Rapid, but the river washed out the rock barrier.

73.5 **RATTLESNAKE (II+).** Avoid the far right, and watch for house rocks at the bottom.

75.5 **NEFERTITI (II-).** A rough, narrow dirt road (impassable when wet) from the town of Green River ends here on the left bank, providing **RIVER ACCESS.** The road follows the river to the Swasey's Beach take-out, allowing one-day floats of this section. No permits are currently required for day trips. Contact the BLM for regulations on overnight trips.

77.5 The Price River enters on the right. In times past, ranchers and outlaws made their way to Gray Canyon by following a trail down the Price.

84 **TAKE-OUT.** Swasey's Beach on the left, just below the foot of **SWASEY'S (II-).** Downstream, the Green flows out of Gray Canyon, past Gunnison Butte, and into the broad Gunnison Valley above the city of Green River. There is an **alternate take-out** 10 miles downstream at Green River State Park, on the right bank just below the I-70 bridge. If you float this stretch, beware of a potentially dangerous diversion dam 3 miles below Swasey's Beach.

Green River

Labyrinth and Stillwater Canyons

Difficulty: I+. Flatwater after first 10 miles.
Length: 120 miles to Colorado confluence, 123.5 to Spanish Bottom. Shorter trips possible: 68 miles from put-in to Mineral Bottom; 52 from Mineral Bottom to confluence.
Gradient: 1.5 ft./mi.
Drainage Area and Average Annual Discharge: 44,850 sq. mi. and 4,648,000 af.
Put-in: Green River State Park (4,040').
Take-out: Mineral Bottom at mile 68 (3,920'). No access at Colorado River confluence (3,870'). Boaters can stop just downstream at Spanish Bottom and either return upriver by jet boat tow or (with permit) continue 45 miles down Cataract Canyon to Hite, Utah.
Season: April–Nov. Boatable flows year-round. Typically peaks in late May or early June from 10,000–35,000 cfs. Drops to 2,000–6,000 by late July and to 1,500–4,000 in September. (See hydrograph in previous chapter.) Many prefer to boat before or after midsummer heat.
Recommended Levels: 1,000–20,000 cfs.
Flow Information: NWS tape, (801) 539-1311; flow at the town of Green River (put-in).
Special Hazards: Remote area.
Permits: (1) Not presently required above Mineral Bottom, but may be required in the near future. Contact BLM for updated information. (2) Required below Mineral Bottom; no use limits or fee at present. Contact Canyonlands National Park.
Managing Agencies: (1) BLM, San Rafael RA, 900 N. 700 E., Price, UT 84501; (801) 637-4591. (2) Canyonlands National Park, Moab UT 84532; (801) 259-3911.
Commercial Raft and Canoe Trips: Yes. For a list of outfitters, contact a managing agency.
Land Ownership: Mostly private first 23 miles; mostly BLM miles 23–72; all National Park thereafter.
Scenery: Excellent. Sandstone canyons.
Solitude: Very good. Some motorboats, notably on Memorial Day weekend when hundreds make the "Friendship Cruise" from the town of Green River to Moab.
Wilderness: Yes.
Weather: Variable in spring and fall; sometimes cold. Very hot in midsummer. Some thunderstorms in late summer; flash flood hazard in side canyons.
Water: Silty and undrinkable. Very warm in summer. Virtually no running side streams. Springs at Three Canyon, Anderson Bottom, and Water Canyon.
Camping: Good except at high water, when many sites are flooded.
Side Hikes: Excellent side canyons and Anasazi sites (see **Mile Guide**).
Side Excursions: Canyonlands National Park. Deadhorse Point State Park.
Guides and References:

- Baars, *A River Runner's Guide to Cataract Canyon and Approaches.*
- Belknap, *Canyonlands River Guide.*
- Kelsey, *River Guide to Canyonlands National Park and Vicinity.*
- Wheat, *Floater's Guide to Colorado.*
- Nichols, *River Runners' Guide to Utah.*
- *Calm Water Float Trips on the Green and Colorado Rivers.* Pamphlet available from Canyonlands National Park.
- Zwinger, *Run, River, Run.* Essays.

Maps:

- **USGS 7.5':** *Green River, Horse Bench East, Green River SE, Tenmile Point, Bowknot Bend, Mineral Canyon, Horsethief Canyon, Cleopatras Chair, Upheaval Dome, Turks Head, Spanish Bottom.*
- **USGS 1:100:** *San Rafael Desert, Moab, Hanksville, La Sal.*
- **USGS:** *Canyonlands National Park and Vicinity* covers last 70 river miles at 1:62,500.
- *Southeastern Utah* road map. Utah Travel Council, Council Hall–Capitol Hill, Salt Lake City UT 84114; (801) 533-5681.

Auto Shuttle: 68 miles one way to Mineral Bottom. For references for shuttle and jet boat services, contact a managing agency or Grand County Travel Council, P.O. Box 550, 210 N. 100 W., Moab, UT 84532; (801) 259-8825.
Logistics: The **uppermost put-in** is at Green River State Park (fee), on the right bank in the town of Green River in east central Utah. To reach an **alternate put-in** 23 miles downstream on the left bank at Ruby Ranch (private, fee), follow I-70 east about 13 miles

from Green River, take exit 173, and drive southwest on an unpaved road roughly 14 miles. Call in advance for permission, (801) 564-3538.

To reach the **take-out at Mineral Bottom**, drive east from Green River on I-70 about 20 miles to Crescent Junction, then south on U.S. 191 about 20 miles. Turn right onto Utah Route 313 for some 13 miles, then right again onto unpaved Mineral Canyon Road—don't confuse it with Mineral Point Road, which comes first—for the final 17 miles to the Green. The last two miles are steep switchbacks, impassable when wet.

Labyrinth and Stillwater received their very descriptive names from Major John Wesley Powell and his men on their 1869 expedition down the Green and the Colorado. Though the lack of a strong current compelled them to labor at their oars, they savored the respite from the whitewater of Desolation and Gray Canyons just upstream. In his journal Powell writes of Stillwater Canyon:

> "In many places the walls, which rise from the water's edge, are overhanging on either side. The stream is still quiet, and we glide along through a strange, weird, grand region. The landscape everywhere, away from the river, is of rock—cliffs of rock, tables of rock, plateaus of rock, terraces of rock, crags of rock—ten thousand strangely carved forms; rock everywhere, and no vegetation, no soil, no sand. In long, gentle curves the river winds about these rocks."

Today, river runners find a landscape virtually unaltered since Powell's day. Colorful sandstone walls reflect in the broad river, while more intimate wonders await hikers in dozens of intricately carved side canyons. River runners will find evidence of previous residents and voyagers, including Indian petroglyphs and inscriptions carved by nineteenth-century explorers and early river runners. (Please don't add your own etchings or graffiti to those already here.) Numerous Anasazi ruins, especially in Stillwater Canyon, remind boaters of the mysterious civilization that flourished here before dying out some 800 years ago.

Floating these canyons imparts a profound sense of isolation and peace. An occasional motorboat or another river trip may briefly break the silence, but for the most part the noiseless river and silent side canyons weave a spell of tranquility and quiet awe. In *Run, River, Run,* Ann Zwinger observes, "An afternoon in Labyrinth Canyon has a panoramic quality, as if the raft stands still and the landscape is pulled by."

This is one of the West's best wilderness trips for open canoes—except at high water. Because the area is so remote, it is recommended only for boaters with good wilderness skills. Rafts often have trouble with upstream winds, but many make the trip anyway—notably those using the Green as an approach to Cataract Canyon on the Colorado.

Most boaters launch at Green River State Park in the town of Green River, Utah, ten miles below the last rapid of Gray Canyon. Downstream the river is virtually flat: after a few small riffles in the first ten miles, the Green remains calm for its final 110 miles. The first section runs through an open valley with occasional ranches. After the San Rafael River enters at mile 23, the walls of Labyrinth Canyon gradually rise to enclose the Green for many sinuous miles. A rough dirt road provides a popular access at Mineral Bottom (mile 68). Many Cataract Canyon trips launch here, floating 50 miles of flatwater to the Colorado confluence.

Below Mineral Bottom the Green enters Canyonlands National Park for the remainder of the run. Here the river winds through a region of geologic wonders that the Indians called "Land of Standing Rocks." To the west lies the wild landscape of "The Maze," to the east the dramatic highlands of "Island in the Sky." Labyrinth Canyon opens up around mile 84. The river glides past the Buttes of the Cross, which rise above the right bank a few miles downstream, then enters Stillwater Canyon. Finally, after 120 miles, the Green meets the Colorado at one of the West's most imposing confluences.

Once past the last road access at Mineral Bottom, river runners face a logistical problem because there is no take-out at the confluence. They must decide in advance among three alternatives: (1) Continue down the Colorado through Cataract Canyon, provided they have the necessary skills, equipment, and permit. (2) Hire a jet boat to meet them at Spanish Bottom, 3.5 miles downstream on the Colorado, and tow them up the Colorado to Moab or up the Green to Mineral Bottom or to the town of Green River. (3) Bring their own motors and putt laboriously back upstream.

Mile by Mile Guide

*See map in chapter on **Colorado River: Cataract Canyon.***
The map does not show the upper 18 miles of the Labyrinth Canyon run.

0 **PUT-IN** at the boat ramp on the right bank in Green River State Park. Camping, drinking water. Small riffles in the first 10 miles.

4.5 On the left is Crystal Geyser, now inactive, created by an oil well drilled in 1936. About 4 miles downstream are the largest riffles of the run.

18 The Anvil, also called Dellenbaugh's Butte, on the left.

23 The San Rafael River enters on the right. **RIVER ACCESS.** Alternate put-in on the left at Ruby Ranch (private, fee). Downstream, the walls of Labyrinth Canyon slowly rise.

30 Trin-Alcove Bend. Excellent side hikes up the arms of Three Canyon, which enters on the right. Spring water can be found up the side canyon.

39.5 Tenmile Canyon on the left. Three miles downstream on the left is the River Register, where early river runners carved their names. Please don't write on the rocks; if you wish, register your visit in the ammo box provided.

50 The river enters Bowknot Bend, returning in 7 miles to within a few hundred yards of itself. Boaters can scramble up to the saddle, which overlooks the river on both sides. A poor dirt road connecting to Utah Route 313 reaches the river at Spring Canyon, mile 52.5, then follows the left bank for several miles.

63.5 Hell Roaring Canyon on the left. A short hike up the canyon leads to the inscription "D. Julien 3 Mai 1836." French trapper Denis Julien left his name or initials here and elsewhere along the Green and Colorado. A dirt road follows the left bank from here to Mineral Bottom.

68 Mineral Bottom, at the mouth of Mineral Canyon on the left. Popular **RIVER ACCESS** where a dirt road reaches the river from Utah Highway 313 and U.S. 191. Five miles downstream, the Green enters Canyonlands National Park.

79 Gooseneck meander at Fort Bottom creates a giant moat around an Anasazi ruin. Abandoned "Outlaw Cabin" on the left.

84 Labyrinth Canyon gradually opens up and comes to an end. A few miles downstream on the right are the Buttes of the Cross. Stillwater Canyon begins just above Anderson Bottom.

89 Anderson Bottom, a "rincon" or cut-off meander, is on the right at a sharp left bend. Side hikes, campsites and a reliable spring.

97 Turks Head rock formation on the right as the river sweeps through a long right bend.

105.5 Horse Canyon on the right.

116 Water Canyon on the right. Side hike, spring water.

120 Confluence with the Colorado. Downstream, the Colorado flows smoothly for 3.5 miles to Spanish Bottom on the right bank, the last stopping point before the big rapids of Cataract Canyon. See the **Colorado: Cataract Canyon** chapter.

Upper Yampa River

1. Little Yampa Canyon (Duffy Canyon): Yampa Project Pump Station (6,140') to Government Bridge (5,980').
I+; 38 miles; 4 ft./mi.

2. Juniper Canyon: Government Bridge to U.S. 40 (5,905').
II3; 13 miles; 6 ft./mi.

3. Cross Mountain Gorge: Canyon Entrance (5,815') to Lily Park (5,640').
IV+ (V above 3,000 cfs); 4 miles; 45 ft./mi. (60 ft./mi. in canyon).

Drainage Area and Average Annual Discharge: 3,410 sq. mi. and 1,150,000 af at Maybell, near end of Run 2.

Season: April–July. Low-water runs possible through September. This undammed river typically peaks in late May or early June at 6,000–12,000 cfs, diminishing to late summer lows of around 200 by August. Still, kayaks and canoes can often scrape down into October.

Recommended Levels: *Runs 1 & 2:* 1,000–5,000 cfs. *Run 3 (Cross Mountain Gorge):* 800–3,000. **Experts only above 3,000 cfs.**

Flow Information: Flow at Maybell is on NWS tape, (801) 539-1311, and WaterTalk, (303) 831-7135, **6*12*.**

Special Hazards: Isolation. High water on Run 3.

Permits: Not presently required.

Managing Agency: BLM, Little Snake RA, 1280 Industrial Ave., Craig, CO 81625; (303) 824-4441.

Commercial Raft Trips: Yes; raft and canoe outfitters. Contact the BLM for a list.

Land Ownership: Mostly BLM in the canyons, mostly private between.

Scenery: Excellent. Sandstone canyons.

Solitude: Excellent. Light boating use, though weekend traffic is increasing.

Wilderness: Yes. Railroad for several miles in Little Yampa Canyon (Run 1).

Side Excursions: Scenic, challenging hikes to the rims of Cross Mountain Gorge and Little Yampa Canyons. Contact BLM for details.

Guides and References:

- Kruse, *Yampa River Guide.* Runs 1 & 2.
- "Floating the Yampa River" (BLM). Runs 1 & 2. Pamphlet from managing agency.
- Wheat, *Floater's Guide to Colorado.* All runs.
- Nichols, *River Runners' Guide to Utah.* Covers Cross Mountain Gorge.
- A good local source of information is Buggy Whips, 435 Lincoln Ave., P.O. Box 770479, Steamboat Springs, CO 80477; (303) 879-8033 or (800) 759-0343.

Maps:

- **USGS 7.5':** *Run 1:* Round Bottom, Horse Gulch, Juniper Hot Springs. *Run 2:* Juniper Hot Springs, Juniper Mtn, Maybell. *Run 3:* Cross Mountain Canyon, Twelvemile Mesa.
- **USGS 1:100:** *Meeker, Canyon of Lodore, Rangely.*

Auto Shuttle: For references contact Moffat County Visitor Center, 360 E. Victory Way, Craig, CO 81625; (800) 864-4405.

Logistics: The BLM is developing new access points on the Yampa; contact the managing agency for updated information. *Runs 1 and 2:* To reach the **put-in for Run 1,** follow Colorado Higway 13 to the bridge over the Yampa 3 miles south of U.S. 40 near Craig in northwestern Colorado. Put in on the left below the bridge at the pumping station. (An **alternate put-in** is 5 miles upstream at Loudy Simpson County Park near the Colorado Route 394 bridge). To reach **Government Bridge,** drive west on U.S. 40 to the hamlet of Lay, turn south on County Road 17, and drive some 6 miles to the bridge over the Yampa. The **alternate access at Juniper Hot Springs** can be reached from U.S. 40 or County Road 17. The **take-out for Juniper Canyon** is at the U.S. 40 bridge 3 miles east of Maybell.

Run 3 (Cross Mountain Gorge): Some 15 miles west of Maybell, turn north off U.S. 40 onto County Road 85. After about 2.5 miles, turn left onto BLM Road 1551 and follow signs another 2.5 miles to the river access, which is about 3/4 mile upstream from the canyon entrance. On this rough dirt road (impassable when wet), high clearance is a must, and 4-wheel drive is recommended. Ask the BLM or inquire locally about road conditions. **To reach the take-out,** return to U.S. 40, drive west a couple of miles, bear right at the Deerlodge Park turnoff, and drive to the picnic area on the left bank at the foot of the gorge.

The Yampa is the last major river in the entire Colorado Basin with no large dams and reservoirs. It runs wild and free for almost its entire 300-mile length. The river is a recreational paradise, boasting one of the West's most famous floats, Yampa Canyon (covered in the next chapter), as well as three lesser-known trips discussed here. In addition, there are some 100 boatable miles of Class I water upstream, beginning at Steamboat Springs. Unfortunately, the Yampa continues to be one of the nation's most threatened rivers (see below).

Near its beginnings the Yampa is very much a river of the Colorado Rockies. Rising as sparkling snowmelt high on the White River Plateau in northwestern Colorado, the Yampa flows north to the famous ski resort of Steamboat Springs, then turns west toward its ultimate destination, the confluence with the Green in Dinosaur National Monument.[1]

In Steamboat Springs local boaters enjoy a half-mile run through Yampa River Park, where boulders placed in the river provide endless play opportunities and fine surfing. There is a permanent slalom course, and each June the Yampa River Festival is held here. Boaters also occasionally run easy, meandering stretches of the Yampa in the Steamboat Springs area.[2]

Below Steamboat Springs the Yampa changes its stripes, metamorphosing from a Rocky Mountain river into a Canyon Country classic. Downstream from Craig, the river picks up a thick load of silt as it slices through a series of four sandstone canyons. By far the most famous of these is the final 45-mile cut through Yampa Canyon in Dinosaur National Monument, but just upstream lie three lesser-known canyons—covered in this chapter—that offer excellent and varied boating.

Little Yampa Canyon

The first and longest canyon begins a few miles below Craig. In Little Yampa Canyon, also known as Duffy Canyon, the river winds through entrenched meanders where sloping sandstone walls rise more than 500' on either side. Here the Yampa is smooth and peaceful, with only one riffle rating Class I+. This is one of the West's finest open canoe runs. Boaters in all manner of craft enjoy the fine scenery, excellent campsites, and abundant wildlife. (Anglers should know that the Yampa is home to four endangered or threatened species of fish that must be released immediately if caught.)

One of Little Yampa Canyon's chief attractions is solitude. Though interest in the run is increasing, use is still relatively light, and midweek boaters often have the river to themselves. Except for a recently-constructed railroad, the run is nearly wilderness, broken only by an occasional ranch or jeep trail. The railway, built to haul coal from mines to the south, follows only the beginning of the run.

Below the **put-in** at the Yampa Project Pump Station (mile 0), the Yampa flows for five miles through open terrain to the Williams Fork confluence, which marks the canyon entrance. (River access may be possible here in the future). The canyon opens briefly at Round Bottom (miles 10–11.5), then closes in again. At mile 15.5 the railroad leaves the canyon to climb up Milk Creek. About mile 18 the river enters a series of entrenched meanders that continue for some 15 miles.

The "whitewater" comes at mile 26.5, at the end of a long right bend where a diversion for the Duffy Tunnel creates a Class I+ riffle. Five miles downstream, the river returns to within a half mile of this point and the tunnel, which runs through the narrow gooseneck, emerges on the left. A half mile below the tunnel outlet, the walls recede and the old Morgan Gulch take-out appears on the left (mile 32.5); this access has been closed due to concerns for endangered fish that congregate here, but the BLM is planning a new one just downstream. The river then winds 5.5 miles through pastoral landscape to the **Government Bridge take-out.** Boaters can continue downstream.

Juniper Canyon

The next canyon on the Yampa is short but beautiful and offers a bit more whitewater. Juniper Canyon makes a fine run by itself, or boaters can combine Little Yampa and Juniper for a continuous 50-mile float lasting three to five days. This second canyon sees even lighter use than the first, in part because of access problems. Boaters using the **put-in at Govern-**

[1]Trappers and early explorers mistranslated the Ute word "Yampa" as "Bear." As a result the river was long called the Bear, and its largest headwater stem above Steamboat Springs still carries that name. "Yampa" is actually the Ute word for an edible plant that grows along the river.

[2]Anderson and Hopkinson, *Rivers of the Southwest*, has more information on these runs, but it is out of print.

ment Bridge must cross eight miles of flatwater through open terrain to reach the canyon entrance. There is an **alternate put-in** at Juniper Canyon Access, seven miles below Government Bridge.

The canyon begins abruptly two miles below Juniper Hot Springs (private). The walls reach their greatest height just a mile downstream as Little Juniper Mountain rises above the right bank. A rock diversion weir for the Maybell Ditch creates the biggest whitewater on the run (Class II+ to III, depending on flow). The weir is just under a mile below the canyon entrance, where the river begins to curve left after a right bend. Scout left. Portaging is very difficult, especially at high water.

Downstream is busy Class II water. A mile below the weir, the Maybell Ditch crosses the river on a flume, and the canyon begins to open. The standard **take-out is at the U.S. 40 bridge** seven miles below Juniper Hot Springs.

Cross Mountain Gorge

For 30 miles below Juniper Canyon, the Yampa wanders peacefully westward past hills, mesas, and ranches as it gradually approaches Cross Mountain, a rugged 7,000' north-south barrier rising abruptly in the river's path. The river plows directly into the mountain, carving a dramatic gash three miles long and a thousand feet deep.

Cross Mountain Gorge is by far the toughest section of the Yampa. At low and moderate flows (500–3,000 cfs) the run is very technical, with enormous boulders, tight drops, and narrow chutes that challenge experts in kayaks or self-bailing rafts. At flows over 3,000 cfs this run, even more demanding and still quite technical, is for **experts only.** At about 5,000 cfs the house rocks submerge, and the gorge becomes a raging torrent of massive hydraulics runnable by none but daring top experts.

The standard **put-in** is only 3/4 mile above the jaws of the gorge. Just below the entrance is the biggest drop, **OSTERIZER,** also known as **Mammoth Falls.** This is a steep Class IV+ at moderate flows and rates up to VI (portage) at high water when a huge river-wide reversal develops. Scout, sneak, or portage on the right.

Below Osterizer is about half a mile of Class IV rapids leading up to **THE SNAKE PIT (IV+, V at higher flows)**, where a fence of house rocks nearly blocks the river. At most flows boaters start far right, immediately make the infamous "Death Ferry" all the way to the left to avoid another pile of boulders, then finish with a flush down a steep, angled flume.

Easier water follows until, a mile and a half into the canyon, the Yampa curves left and thunders through **POUROVER CITY (III+ below 3,000 cfs, IV+ above)**, also called **Browns Bend,** where a potentially lethal reversal waits in river center. Sneak routes may be possible down either side. Portage, if necessary, on the right; the left bank is a cliff. Downstream, the walls begin to lower, and the rapids ease somewhat. But toward the end of the run, be alert for **SHERM'S HOLE,** a big hydraulic in river center just below a right bend. Most boaters sneak it on the right.

Suddenly, just three miles after it began, Cross Mountain Gorge ends and the river emerges onto the broad plain of Lily Park. **Take out** on the left at the picnic area on Deerlodge Park Road.

The Yampa's Uncertain Future

In the 1950's the Yampa barely escaped being dammed at its mouth in Echo Park. Today, dam-builders are looking farther upstream. The proposed Juniper-Cross Mountain Project would dam the Yampa at both Juniper Canyon and Cross Mountain Gorge, flooding the three runs covered here. Conservation efforts and concerns for endangered fish have pushed this project onto a back burner, but the Colorado River Water Conservation District continues to urge that the two dams be built. The same water district has been looking for a new reservoir site above Craig. In addition to flooding a portion of the upper river, such a dam would harm downstream runs by reducing flows, ravaging beaches, and devastating fisheries.[3]

---

[3]Support for a free-flowing Yampa is growing. The BLM is working to expand recreation opportunities, with plans for improved boating access and a foot trail running the length of the river. Conservationists are urging permanent protection for the Yampa as a National Wild and Scenic River. In 1991 the BLM began to study the 83 miles from Williams Fork to Dinosaur National Monument for possible Wild and Scenic designation. The 47 miles in Dinosaur National Monument have already been recommended for "Wild" status, and some are urging that the National Monument become a National Park. For more information, contact American Rivers or the National Organization for River Sports. (See appendix for addresses.)

Lower Yampa River

Yampa Canyon

Difficulty: II+4-. **Gradient:** 12 ft./mi.
Length: 71 miles (46 on Yampa, 25 on Green).
Put-in: Deerlodge Park (5,595').
Take-out: Split Mountain Boat Ramp, Green River (4,780').
Drainage Area and Average Annual Discharge: 7,660 sq. mi. / 2,279,000 af at Deerlodge Park.
Peak Recorded Flow: 33,200 cfs (May 18, 1984).
Season: Prime season is early May to late June, though boating is often possible at other times. Flows vary widely, from a typical peak of over 10,000 cfs in late May to under 250 cfs in August. In some years canoes and kayaks can scrape down into August.
Recommended Levels: 800–6,000 cfs.
Flow Information: National Weather Service tape, (801) 539-1311, has the flow at Echo Park. WaterTalk has the flow at Deerlodge Park: (303) 831-7135, **6*16***.
Special Hazards: Warm Springs Rapid. High water in May and June.
Managing Agency: River Office, Dinosaur National Monument, P.O. Box 210, Dinosaur, CO 81610; (303) 374-2468.
Permits: Required year-round. Hard to get due to short season and high demand. For high-use season (second Monday in May to July 15), apply Dec. 1–Jan. 31 for February lottery. No waiting list; call beginning March 1 for unused or cancelled dates. For low-use season (both before and after high-use season), call for dates on a first-come, first-served basis beginning March 1.

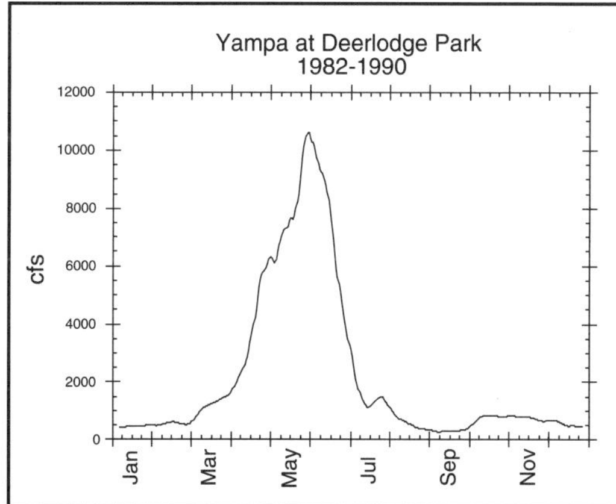

Commercial Raft Trips: Yes. For a list of outfitters, contact the managing agency.
Land Ownership: Mostly National Park; one private ranch.
Scenery: Excellent. Slickrock sandstone canyon.
Solitude: Very good in high-use season; excellent at other times.
Wilderness: Yes.
Wildlife: Bighorn sheep, deer, beaver, peregrine falcon.
Weather: Rain and snow possible early in the season. Hot in midsummer.
Water: Silty and undrinkable. Purify water from side streams. No drinking water at the put-in.
Camping: Excellent at established sites (pre-assigned in high use season).
Side Hikes: Mantle Cave. Several side canyons.
Side Excursions: Dinosaur Quarry near Jensen, Utah. Canyon overlooks on Harpers Corner Road and Trail (see **Logistics**).
Guides and References:

- Evans & Belknap, *Dinosaur River Guide.*
- Gernant, Hinton, & Hughes, *The Canyons of Dinosaur.*
- Wheat, *Floater's Guide to Colorado.*
- Nichols, *River Runners' Guide to Utah.*
- *Riverguide Bandana to the Green and Yampa* (Rivers & Mountains). Cloth map.
- Hayes & Simmons, *River Runner's Guide to Dinosaur National Monument and Vicinity.* Geologic river logs for Yampa and Green.
- Collins & Nash, *The Big Drops.* Includes essay on Warm Springs Rapid and Yampa.
- Stegner, *This Is Dinosaur.* Geology, natural and human history.
- Hagood, *Dinosaur: The Story Behind The Scenery.* Geology, prehistory.
- Rennicke, *River Days* and *The Rivers of Colorado.* Essays on Western rivers.
- Webb, *Riverman: The Story of Bus Hatch.*

Maps:

- **USGS 7.5'**: *Indian Water Canyon, Haystack Rock, Tanks Peak, Zenobia Peak, Hells Canyon, Canyon of Lodore South.*
- **USGS 1:100:** *Canyon of Lodore, Rangely.*
- **USGS:** *Dinosaur National Monument* is best overall map. Covers entire run at 1:62,500.

Auto Shuttle: 90 miles (two hours) one way. Contact River Runner's Transport, P.O. Box 1361, Vernal UT 84078; (801) 781-1180.

Logistics: To reach the **put-in,** turn north off U.S. 40 in northwestern Colorado onto a paved road about 16 miles west of Maybell and 7 miles east of Elk Springs. Follow this road 14 miles, first north toward the Yampa, then west (downstream) along the left bank to Deerlodge Park. To reach the **take-out,** return to U.S. 40 and drive west some 60 miles to Jensen in northeastern Utah. Turn right (north) onto Utah Route 149 and drive beyond the Dinosaur Quarry to Split Mountain Campground and Boat Ramp.

The intermediate access at Echo Park (mile 46) is rarely used because the final 1.5 miles of the rough dirt access road consist of steep switchbacks (impassable when wet). To get there, turn north at Dinosaur National Monument Headquarters onto Harper's Corner Road (paved) for some 26 miles, then turn right onto Echo Park Road and drive about 13 miles to Echo Park.

Of the Yampa's nearly 300 miles, most river runners know only the final 46, where the Yampa carves one of the West's loveliest canyons as it passes through Dinosaur National Monument. Known as Yampa Canyon and sometimes as Blue Mountain Canyon, this beautiful 2,500'-deep cut through the Uinta Mountains is one of the West's most popular river trips, overshadowing some fine runs just upstream (covered in the previous chapter).

Whitewater is not the key to Yampa Canyon's popularity. There are just three rapids of note and only one that rates above Class II+. Boaters spend more time looking up than ahead, admiring a breathtaking panorama of sheer cliffs, rounded buttes, and slickrock walls. At times the river slides dreamily beneath overhanging alcoves of sandstone striped by desert varnish.[1] Towering above the river in places are curious pinnacles known as "hoodoos," formed where a cap of harder stone protects softer underlying rock from erosion.

For some 25 miles below Deerlodge Park, the Yampa follows a relatively straight course, descending at a moderate pace between walls of red sandstone and gray limestone. Only two moderate rapids break the calm of this section.

Below Harding Hole the canyon's character changes as the Yampa enters a deep layer of pale sandstone (called Weber Sandstone). The current slows as the river winds through sinuous entrenched meanders. Boaters can hike up intimate side canyons or wonder at striking rock formations with names like Cleopatra's Couch and Katy's Nipple. At Mantle Cave river runners can explore a cavern that yielded one of the region's most remarkable archaeological finds, a perfectly preserved Indian headdress over a thousand years old.

Just when it seems that the flatwater reverie could go on forever, the river erupts. Four miles above the Green River confluence, the Yampa thunders through one of the West's most famous rapids, Warm Springs.

Before 1965 only a small riffle marked the mouth of Warm Springs Draw, but in June of that year a flash flood roared down the side canyon and out into the river, filling the channel with huge boulders and temporarily damming the Yampa. The following morning a commercial trip, expecting smooth sailing all the way to the Green, unwittingly floated into the new rapid. One boatman, wearing cowboy boots and caught sitting on his life jacket, was drowned. (See story.) Warm Springs instantly acquired an undeserved reputation as one of the West's most dangerous rapids.

A quarter of a century later, Warm Springs is still the biggest action on either the Yampa or the Green in Dinosaur National Monument. A long, somewhat technical approach leads directly into huge holes at the foot of the rapid. At high water perhaps half the boats running Warm Springs emerge upside down. Nevertheless, the rapid's reputation is less fearsome than it once was, for a number of reasons. There is a good stretch of calm water downstream for recovery, so over the years boaters have learned that a flip here is far from fatal. (In fact, that first drowning was the only one in this rapid until 1993.) Moreover, river running skills and equipment have advanced dramatically since 1965, and the high-water years of the early 1980's seem to have softened this relatively new rapid somewhat.

Not far below Warm Springs, the Yampa merges with the Green at Echo Park. Although

[1] The "varnish" is a thin, dark film of iron or manganese oxides produced by bacterial action when mineral-rich water trickles down the stone.

a few boaters take out here, most prefer to continue down the Green River—either 17 relatively easy miles to Rainbow Park, or the full 25 miles to Split Mountain Boat Ramp. The latter course includes eight miles of Class II and III water in Split Mountain Canyon (see the **Green: Lodore** chapter).

Before the creation of Warm Springs Rapid in 1965, Yampa Canyon was one of the Canyon Country's mildest runs. When legendary river explorer Nathaniel Galloway[2] made the first descent in 1909, he brought along his 10-year-old son. Even so, the river's wildly fluctuating flows troubled many parties, most notably a team of four *Denver Post* reporters sent to make another "first descent" in 1928. On August 19 the team launched two 16' wooden boats on what must have been an oversized creek. (Galloway had had the sense to run in the spring, when flows were adequate.) For two weeks they bumped and splintered their way downstream. The river destroyed one boat, and the reporters abandoned the other. Still, the expedition was a huge success: front-page stories of harrowing adventure sold lots of newspapers.

Today, the Yampa—the only major river in the Colorado Basin with no large dams or reservoirs[3]—still surges through a wide range of flows each season. Spring runoff can quickly push the river to dangerous levels, while in midsummer upstream diversions reduce the river to a tepid trickle. Boaters who run the Yampa at low water should expect much higher flows (and colder water) below the confluence with the dam-controlled Green.

---

[2]For more on Galloway, see the chapter on the **Grand Canyon of the Colorado.**

[3]For information on dam threats to the Yampa, see the previous chapter.

Mile by Mile Guide

See map in ***Green: Lodore*** *chapter.*

0 **PUT-IN.** Deerlodge Park Boat Ramp and Campground on the left bank. No drinking water. A mile and a half downstream, the river enters Yampa Canyon.

4.7 Anderson Hole campground on the right. The Stubs Cabin is just downstream.

7.5 Thanksgiving Gorge enters on the left. A half mile downstream, Corral Springs Draw enters on the right.

10.2 **TEPEE (II+)**, created by debris washed into the river down Tepee Draw on the right. Boulders divide the current at low water and create big waves and a hole at high flows. Scout right. River campground on the right. The Yampa drops swiftly for the next two and a half miles.

12 Haystack Rock on the left. Browns Draw enters on the right a mile and a half downstream.

17.5 Bower Draw enters on the right. A little over a mile downstream, Dry Woman Canyon enters on the left.

20 Five Springs Draw enters on the right, forming a Class II rapid.

22.5 **BIG JOE (II+).** Starvation Valley enters on the right, pushing debris into the river. Scout on the right. Campground on the right.

26–27 Soon after Johnson Canyon enters on the left (side hike) the main canyon opens briefly at scenic Harding Hole. River campgrounds are on the left bank, and a short hike leads to viewpoints above the campsites. Downstream, the river winds through a series of entrenched meanders, advancing less than two air miles in the next 7 river miles.

28.5 Mathers Hole river campground on the left.

31.5 Grand Overhang, where a pebble dropped from the lip of the undercut wall on the left would land on the right bank.

34.5 The canyon opens at Castle Park. Mantle Ranch (private) is on the left. Just downstream, Hells Canyon enters on the left. The rough Mantle Ranch Road leads up Hells Canyon, providing a possible emergency access (private, permission required). Mantle Cave, once used by local Indians, is several hundred yards below Hells Canyon up a small draw on the left.

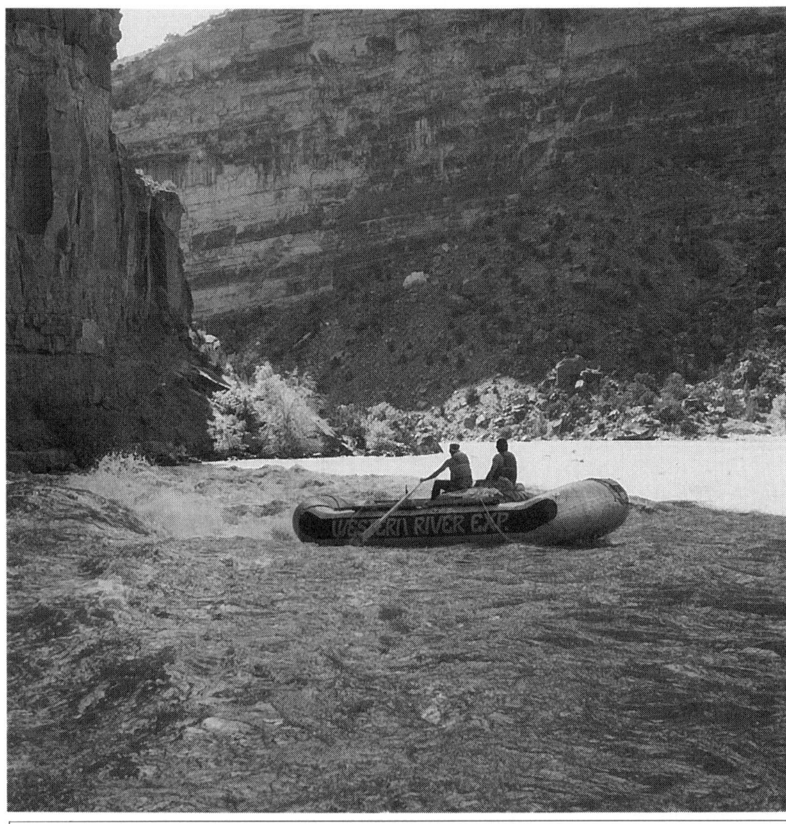

Warm Springs Rapid, Yampa River *Verne Huser*

36 Laddie Park river campground on the right. Just downstream, Red Rock Canyon enters on the left, and a little over a mile farther downriver boaters pass an undercut cliff on the left known as the "Tiger Wall" for its dramatic stripes of desert varnish. The current is weak in this section because it is backed up for several miles by the natural dam at Warm Springs Rapid.

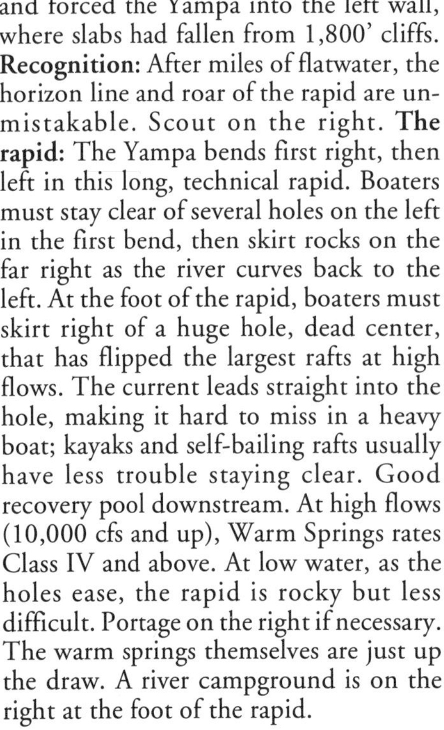

42 **WARM SPRINGS (IV-).** In 1965 a flash flood on Warm Springs Draw (on the right) filled the river channel with rocks and forced the Yampa into the left wall, where slabs had fallen from 1,800' cliffs. **Recognition:** After miles of flatwater, the horizon line and roar of the rapid are unmistakable. Scout on the right. **The rapid:** The Yampa bends first right, then left in this long, technical rapid. Boaters must stay clear of several holes on the left in the first bend, then skirt rocks on the far right as the river curves back to the left. At the foot of the rapid, boaters must skirt right of a huge hole, dead center, that has flipped the largest rafts at high flows. The current leads straight into the hole, making it hard to miss in a heavy boat; kayaks and self-bailing rafts usually have less trouble staying clear. Good recovery pool downstream. At high flows (10,000 cfs and up), Warm Springs rates Class IV and above. At low water, as the holes ease, the rapid is rocky but less difficult. Portage on the right if necessary. The warm springs themselves are just up the draw. A river campground is on the right at the foot of the rapid.

44 Box Elder Park and river campground on the right. A mile downstream, Sand Canyon enters on the left, marking an old proposed dam site.

46 Confluence with the Green, which joins the Yampa from the right. Echo Park Ranger Station and Campground are on the left below the confluence; drinking water available, but no camping by boaters. A road leads 38 miles to U.S. 40 but includes steep switchbacks (see **Logistics**), so Echo Park is rarely used as an **alternate access.**

For the next 25.5 miles on the Green, including Whirlpool and Split Mountain Canyons, see the **Mile Guide** in the **Green: Lodore** chapter.

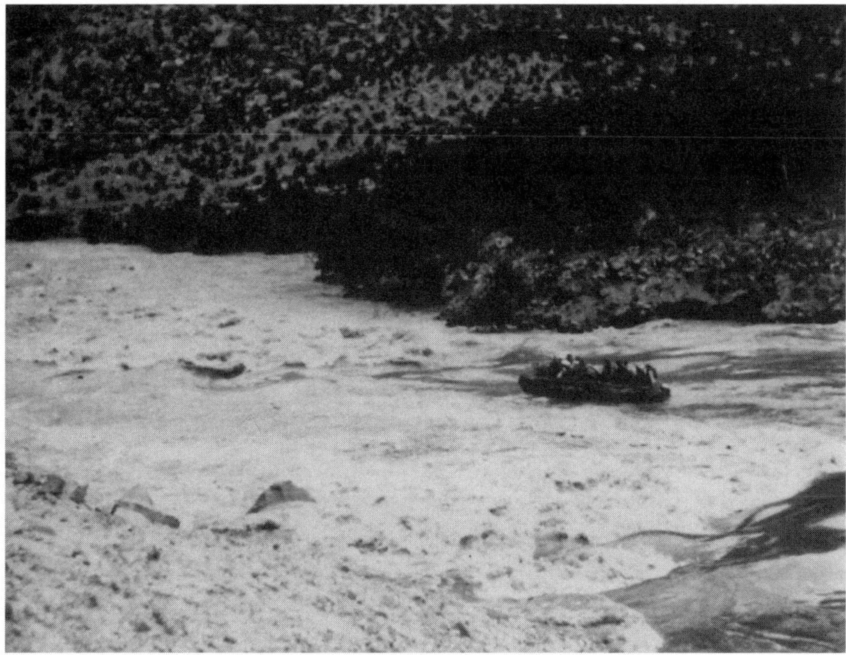

Warm Springs Rapid, Yampa River, 1965 *Hatch River Expeditions*

Bad Day at Warm Springs

As the Hatch crew drifted past Mantle's Ranch, the river slowed almost to a standstill. Something was wrong, but they didn't know what. They rowed on downstream.

There were only two rubber rafts on this early-season float down the Lower Yampa in spring 1965, but they were enormous 27' pontoon rigs with 12' oars. And everyone knew there were no rapids worthy of the name between Mantle's Ranch and Echo Park.

A couple of miles farther, the current disappeared. The river was like a lake. The boatmen, Al Holland and a young trainee, Les Oldham, rowed on through the calm. Eventually they heard a muffled roar in the distance. Puzzled, they peered downstream, trying to figure out the mystery. They didn't bother to land and walk ahead. The noise didn't make sense. Life vests weren't even required on this known flatwater stretch. Oldham had taken his off. He was also wearing cowboy boots.

The roar grew louder, and the river disappeared beyond a horizon line. Before they could see what awaited them, the boatmen were committed to the tongue of a huge pour-over. Below was something new for the Yampa—a cauldron of gigantic red boulders and leaping whitewater.

Down they went. Holland's raft somehow avoided the worst of the holes and rocks and reached the foot of the rapid. But along the way, Holland had caught a glimpse of Oldham catapulted out of his own raft when he tried to hang on to an oar caught in the churning water. At the bottom of the rapid everyone looked around in terror. They landed and searched, but in vain. Oldham's body surfaced three days later at Island Park downstream on the Green River.

This unlucky boating party was the first to run the newly-created Warm Springs Rapid, which had been formed by boulders washed down the side creek in a flash flood a day or two earlier. Warm Springs Rapid no longer has the fury those unsuspecting river runners faced that day, although at high flows it still makes you sit up and take notice. The Yampa has been rearranging the furniture ever since the rapid's birth. Most notably, the big house rock has been broken up and rolled from the top to the bottom of the rapid. The rapid will keep on changing, and some day another new one may be born somewhere on the river. Let's hope the first boater to find it has on a life vest.

—Don Hatch

Colorado River

Horsethief and Ruby Canyons

Put-in: Loma Boat Ramp (4,440').
Take-out: Westwater Ranger Station (4,305').
Difficulty: I+. One Class II at higher flows.
Length: 25 miles. **Gradient:** 5 ft./mi.
Drainage Area and Average Annual Discharge: 17,843 sq. mi. and 4,600,000 af near take-out.
Season: April–Nov. Typically peaks in late May or June at 15,000–30,000 cfs, then gradually recedes to late summer lows of 2,000–4,000. See hydrograph in next chapter.
Recommended Levels: 2,000–20,000 cfs.
Flow Information: NWS tape, (801) 539-1311, gives the flow at Westwater.
Permits: Not presently required.
Managing Agency: BLM, Grand Junction District, 2815 H Road, Grand Junction, CO 81506; (303) 244-3000. *Note:* BLM refers to both canyons together as Ruby Canyon.
Commercial Raft Trips: Some Westwater Canyon outfitters offer trips here. For references contact Visitor & Convention Bureau, 360 Grand Ave., Grand Junction, CO 81501; (303) 244-1480.
Land Ownership: Mostly BLM, some private.
Scenery: Excellent. Colorful sandstone canyons.
Solitude: Good. Railway with occasional train. A few motorboats.
Wilderness: Yes first 8 miles; railroad thereafter.
Side Excursions: Colorado National Monument. Arches National Park.
Guides and References:

- Nichols, *River Runners' Guide to Utah.*
- Wheat, *Floater's Guide to Colorado.*

Maps:

- **USGS 7.5':** *Mack, Ruby Canyon, Bitter Creek Well, Westwater.*
- **BLM:** *The Colorado River: Ruby/Westwater Canyons.* Best all-around river map. Free.

Auto Shuttle: About 40 miles (one hour) one way.
Logistics: To reach the **put-in,** follow I-70 to the Loma Exit, 16 miles west of Grand Junction, Colorado. Turn south, cross over the freeway, take the first dirt road on the left, and drive a little over half a mile (first east, then south and downhill) to the Loma Boat Ramp. To reach the **take-out,** drive west on I-70, then follow directions in the next chapter to Westwater Ranger Station (put-in for the Westwater Canyon run).

Horsethief and Ruby Canyons mark the Colorado River's entrance into Canyon Country. Though the run begins in the state of Colorado, the river no longer has the feel of the Rockies. The stream is broad and muddy, swollen by its confluence with the Gunnison River just upstream, and its mirror-smooth waters reflect colorful formations of slickrock sandstone. This is no longer the Upper Colorado; here, finally, is the mighty Colorado, master stream of the Southwest.

The Colorado, known to millions as a fearsome and turbulent desert giant, is gentle in Horsethief and Ruby Canyons—mostly flatwater with some scattered riffles. At times, upstream winds pose the only serious challenge to navigation. The run is quiet and forgiving, well suited to open canoes. The diciest stretch for these craft is a section of Ruby Canyon known as Black Rocks, where the current stirs into swirling boils and spinning eddies. Yet even here the river is relatively placid, and Black Rocks Rapid merits a Class II rating only at high flows.

In these canyons the Colorado at last gets a respite from civilization.[1] For more than 120 miles upstream, beginning with the Eagle River confluence at Dotsero, the Colorado is closely followed by Interstate 70. Finally, 15 miles below Grand Junction, the river shakes free of its concrete companion.

Downstream from the town of Loma, the Colorado winds peacefully through the quiet beauty of Horsethief and Ruby Canyons. The solitude is broken only occasionally by a motorboat or a train on the railroad that follows the

[1] Horsethief and Ruby Canyons are eligible for Wild and Scenic River status, but Congress has not yet acted. Unless this stretch of the river is protected, the Horsethief Canyon hydropower project may one day be resurrected. This proposed dam west of Grand Junction would flood nine miles of the river. For more information, contact American Rivers or the National Organization for River Sports. (See appendix for addresses.)

lower two thirds of the run. Towering cottonwoods shade spacious beaches, and numerous side canyons invite exploration. The main canyon hosts an abundance of waterfowl during spring and fall migrations. Best of all, the river is seldom crowded, and no permit is required.[2]

At the heart of Ruby Canyon is a shallow gorge of dark, polished stone called the Black Rocks. Here the Colorado exposes ancient basement rock, the same formation seen in the Vishnu Schist of the Grand Canyon and the dark rocks that form the inner gorge of Westwater Canyon. Over millennia the river has sculpted the stone into sinuous curves and intriguing forms. The inky, intricately-carved rocks along the river contrast with smooth walls of vermilion sandstone above.

Horsethief and Ruby River Guide

*See map in **Colorado: Westwater** chapter.*

The **put-in** is at the Loma Boat Ramp on the right bank. (No drinking water available.) A mile downstream, the river enters Horsethief Canyon. Rattlesnake Canyon enters on the left at mile 3.5. The entrance of Salt Creek on the right at mile 8.5 marks the end of Horsethief Canyon and the beginning of Ruby Canyon, so-named for colorful slickrock formations of Wingate and Entrada Sandstone. The Denver & Rio Grande Railroad enters the canyon at Salt Creek and follows the right bank for the rest of run.

At mile 14 Mee Canyon enters on the left. Two miles downstream, the river bends left and enters the Black Rocks reach. The swirly water here is the trickiest of the trip. Moore Canyon enters on the left at mile 17 (large, popular campsite). About a mile farther downstream, McDonald Canyon enters on the right, followed by Knowles Canyon on the left. At mile 19 the State Line gauge is on the right, and a mile and a half downstream the river crosses into Utah. Look for Anasazi toeholds in the cliff on the right near the border. **Take out** on the right at Westwater Ranger Station (mile 25). A permit is required to boat downstream in Westwater Canyon (see next chapter).

[2]The rapids may be mild, but beware of the alligator. In July 1991 two alligators named Ralph and Ed escaped from a roadside zoo in Grand Junction and slipped into the Colorado. Rangers recaptured Ralph five days later, but at last report Ed was unaccounted for. Think about *that* the next time you get the urge for a cool dip in the Colorado.

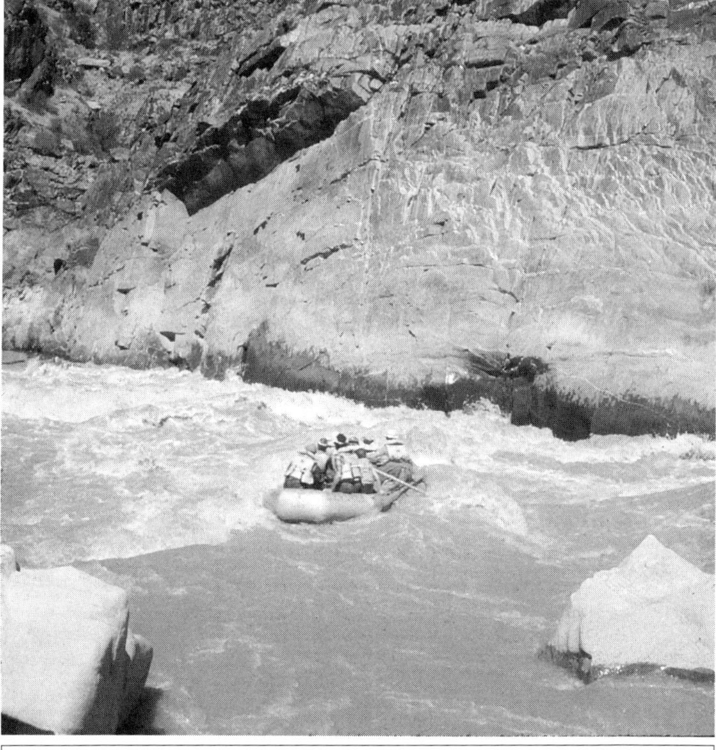

Skull Rapid, Westwater Canyon *Verne Huser*

Colorado River

Westwater Canyon

Difficulty: III+4 (IV+ at high flows). Difficulty varies widely at different flows.

Length: 17 miles. Longer trips possible.

Gradient: 10 ft./mi. Maximum is 20 ft./mi. for 2.5 miles below Marble Canyon (mile 8.5).

Put-in: Westwater Ranger Station (4,305').

Take-out: Rose Ranch (4,140').

Drainage Area and Average Annual Discharge: 17,843 sq. mi. and 4,630,000 af at State Line, just above the put-in.

Peak Recorded Flow: 69,800 cfs (May 27, 1984).

Season: April–Nov. Typically peaks in June at 15,000–30,000 cfs, then recedes to late summer and autumn lows of 2,000–4,000. Never too low.

Recommended Levels: 2,000–20,000 cfs. Technical below 2,000; challenging and semi-continuous above 8,000; very big and continuous over 15,000.

Flow Information: For the flow at State Line, just above the put-in, call NWS, (801) 539-1311, or WaterTalk, (303) 831-7135, **5*10***.

Special Hazards: Skull Rapid. High flows, when boaters may face icy water, continuous big rapids, long swims, and floating trees or other debris.

Permits: Required April 1–Oct. 31. Applications accepted Dec. 1–Jan. 31 for lottery held in early February. Odds are best for smaller groups, weekdays, and early or late season. Beginning in early March, boaters can call for unused dates, cancellations, and spots on the waiting list. Maximum group size 25. Off-season permits not presently required.

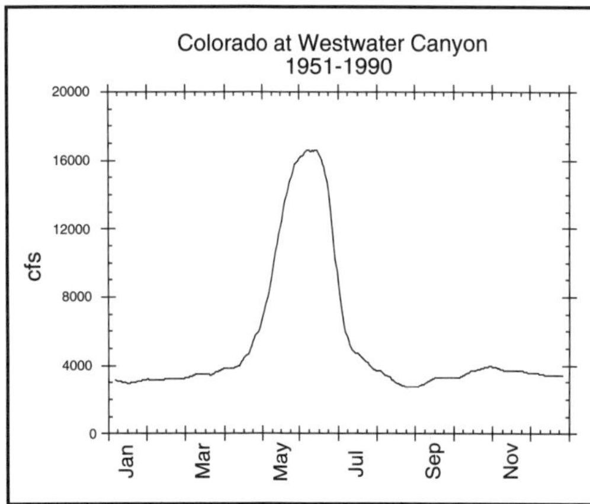

Managing Agency: BLM, Grand Resource Area, 885 S. Sand Flats Rd., Moab, UT 84532; (801) 259-4421.

Commercial Raft Trips: Yes; many outfitters. For a list contact the BLM.

Land Ownership: BLM at put-in, from mile 2.5 to mile 15.5, and at take-out.

Scenery: Excellent. Narrow, colorful desert canyon.

Solitude: Excellent except for heavy boating use on summer weekends.

Wilderness: Yes.

Wildlife: Mule deer, waterfowl, eagle, beaver, occasional bighorn sheep.

Water: Muddy and undrinkable. No reliable side streams. Best to bring all water. No drinking water at put-in.

Camping: Limited number of designated sites; assigned at put-in. Only one night allowed between canyon entrance (mile 3) and Cottonwood Wash (mile 12). Little Dolores campsite (mile 7.3) is excellent but usually crowded.

Side Hikes: Side canyons include Little Dolores, Big Hole, and Marble Canyon.

Side Excursions: Arches and Canyonlands National Parks.

Guides and References:

- Belknap, *Canyonlands River Guide.*
- *Guide to Westwater* (BLM).
- Nichols, *River Runners' Guide to Utah.*
- Wheat, *Floater's Guide to Colorado.*
- Rennicke, *River Days.* Essays on this and other Western river trips.

Maps:

- **USGS** 7.5': *Westwater, Agate, Big Triangle.*
- **BLM:** *The Colorado River: Ruby/Westwater Canyons.* Best all-around river map.

Auto Shuttle: Roughly 30 miles (one hour) one way. For shuttle references contact Grand County Travel Council, P.O. Box 550, Moab UT 84532; (801) 259-8825.

Logistics: To reach the **put-in,** follow I-70 to the Westwater Exit (exit 225, about 6 miles west of the Colorado-Utah border). A paved road leads generally south a little more than half a dozen miles to Westwater Ranger Station. Some signs are posted along the way. After crossing the railroad tracks bear left, follow the tracks about a mile, then bear right to the put-in. To reach the **take-out,** return to I-70, drive west about 12 miles, take the Cisco exit (exit 212), and drive to the southeast corner of town. Follow unpaved Pumphouse Road southeast about 3 miles to a "Y," then bear left and drive another two miles to the Cisco Landing–Rose Ranch boat ramp. To reach the **alternate take-out** at Fish Ford, bear right at the "Y."

Here in Westwater Canyon, one of the roughest reaches of the Colorado is sandwiched between some of its quietest stretches. Westwater lies just west of the Colorado-Utah border, below placid Horsethief and Ruby Canyons and upstream from the easy water between Rose Ranch and Moab.

In Ruby Canyon just upstream, the Colorado gives a hint of things to come as it swirls quietly but ominously through a short gorge of polished stone known as the Black Rocks. This same layer of ancient black schist, similar to the famous Vishnu Schist of the Grand Canyon, appears again in Westwater Canyon; but this time it rises much higher and forms a true inner gorge. Steep walls constrict the Colorado and massive ebony boulders litter the riverbed.

The rapids in Westwater come and go as this formation appears and disappears. The whitewater climaxes where the inner walls rise highest (about 200') at Skull Rapid, then fades as the somber ramparts recede again. Westwater is sometimes called "Granite Canyon" after the dark rocks of the inner gorge.[1]

In this narrow, V-shaped inner gorge, rapids change radically with the flow. At low water steep, sharp drops and narrow, rocky passages are separated by short pools. At high flows the two and a half miles from Marble Canyon to Star Canyon become an almost continuous maelstrom of violent hydraulics and big waves that have flipped the largest rafts. Eddies dwindle and disappear, and at peak flow the river often carries logs and other dangerous debris. Trouble in the first big rapid can mean a long, nasty swim.

Up-to-date flow information is essential for boaters planning Westwater trips. In spite of numerous dams in the Upper Colorado basin, the river has a fairly natural runoff pattern: a sharp snowmelt peak, usually in late May or early June, followed by a steep decline to late summer lows. Yet it never falls too low for boating. The most popular (and crowded) season for Westwater is late summer, when many other rivers in the area are too low.

[1]The name "Westwater" is taken from the old railroad stop near the put-in.

At almost any water level the action peaks at Skull Rapid, one of the most famous pieces of rough water in Canyon Country. Skull throws up a variety of obstacles, including a remarkable whirlpool-like eddy known as the Room of Doom. The rapid's alternate name, Dead Sheep, refers to livestock seen floating and bloating in this eddy in the past. Boats and swimmers have also been trapped here.

Besides its challenging rapids, Westwater has some of the finest scenery on the Colorado. The walls of the inner gorge are a study in contrast, with smooth red Wingate Sandstone sitting directly atop jagged black schist. Away from the river, enchanting side canyons invite exploration. Although Westwater can be run in one day, many parties prefer to linger. For a longer trip, boaters can start 25 miles upstream at Loma and run through Horsethief and Ruby Canyons. They can also continue downstream on runs described later in this essay.

Westwater was one of the last stretches of the Colorado to be boated. Until 1889 no one had fully explored the river between Grand Junction, Colorado and the Green River confluence. In that year engineer Frank Kendrick led a railway survey down the river; however, the expedition portaged Westwater, which Kendrick dubbed "Hades Canyon." In 1916 explorers Ellsworth Kolb and Bert Loper shot Westwater in a small wooden boat.

Westwater's popularity as a recreational run also came relatively late. Use was only sporadic before the early 1970's. But interest boomed in the next 20 years: the BLM reported 17,500 user-days in 1992. In that year, when the permit season extended only through September, more than 700 private boaters launched on the first Saturday in October. As a result the managing agency now includes October in the permit period.

A BLM study has found Westwater eligible for Wild and Scenic River designation, but so far Congress has not acted.[2]

[2]For more information, contact American Rivers or the National Organization for River Sports. (See appendix for addresses.)

Downstream: Rose Ranch to Moab

The Colorado offers many miles of outstanding scenery and good boating below Westwater Canyon. The 46 miles from Rose Ranch to Moab make an excellent supplement to a Westwater trip or a fine run in their own right. This portion of the Colorado is popular with canoeists, though open boats may face sizeable waves at high water. Camping is good and permits are not presently required.[3]

Easy access allows boaters to choose shorter runs. The first and last sections are flat, while Class II rapids and lesser riffles punctuate the middle stretches. The most popular run is a 13-mile Class II reach known as the "Colorado River Daily," which extends from Hittle Bottom to "Take-Out Beach."

Few boaters float the first 16 miles below Rose Ranch (mile 0), where the flat, slow river divides frequently around islands. At mile 12 Utah Highway 128 (Dewey Road) joins and follows the right bank. Two miles downstream, the Dolores River enters from the left. At mile 16 the highway crosses the river at **Dewey Bridge**, a popular **alternate put-in.**

Utah 128 generally follows the left bank from Dewey Bridge to Moab, providing easy shuttles and frequent access (though road and river diverge at times). Just below Dewey Bridge, Ninemile Canyon's sheer sandstone walls close in for about six miles. Then the river enters the open flats of Richardson Amphitheater and Professor Valley, where boaters enjoy breathtaking views of Fisher Towers and the distant La Sal Mountains.

Hittle Bottom, an **access** on the left bank at mile 23, serves as the put-in for the "Colorado River Daily" run and marks the beginning of the whitewater. Onion Creek enters on the left at mile 25, washing debris into the river and creating the first noteworthy rapid. Rapids and riffles continue for the next dozen miles, mostly at the mouths of side canyons. At mile 33, just below Castle Creek Rapid, the valley ends and sandstone walls close in again. A couple of miles into this canyon, Salt Wash enters on the right. Downstream on the left is a popular **access at "Take-Out Beach"** (mile 36), end of the "Colorado River Daily" run.

At mile 38 the Colorado winds through Big Bend. The riffles end a couple of miles farther downstream, and smooth water continues to the **U.S. 191 bridge** near Moab (mile 46). Boaters can **take out** above the bridge on the right, or continue an additional 16 flat miles to the **last possible take-out at the Potash access,** the standard put-in for Cataract Canyon.

[3]For more information contact the BLM in Moab and refer to Belknap, *Canyonlands River Guide.*

Westwater Canyon Mile Guide

0 **PUT-IN** on the right bank at Westwater Ranger Station (BLM). No drinking water available. Camping OK here; reserve downstream sites with BLM rangers April–Oct. This is the take-out for Horsethief and Ruby Canyons just upstream.

3 Westwater Creek enters on the right. Cliffs closing in from the right mark the entrance to Westwater Canyon. Easy riffles in the next 4 miles.

3.5 Miner's Cabin (left bank) was built in the early 1900's by gold prospectors. Look for sluice boxes below the cabin. Not far downstream, black schist appears at river level.

7.3 The Little Dolores River enters on the left. Popular and overused campsite at the mouth. A short side hike leads to a seasonal waterfall and swimming hole. Rocks washed out of the creek into the riverbed form **LITTLE DOLORES (III-).** Just downstream, the river bends left; Hades Bar on the right is the last campsite before the bigger rapids begin. Below Hades on the left is Outlaw Cave, where two robbers allegedly hid out for a year and a half after hitting a bank in Vernal.

8.5 Marble Canyon enters on the left (difficult but rewarding side hike), and the real action begins right away. The walls close in and the river drops 55' in 2.5 miles, with several Class III's and one Class IV. **MARBLE CANYON (III),** longest in the series, begins at the mouth of the side canyon. Just downstream are the big standing waves of **STAIRCASE (III-).** Above 10,000 cfs these first two rapids wash out somewhat. A half mile farther at a right bend, watch for **BIG HUMMER (III)** with a large rock in the channel (big waves at high water).

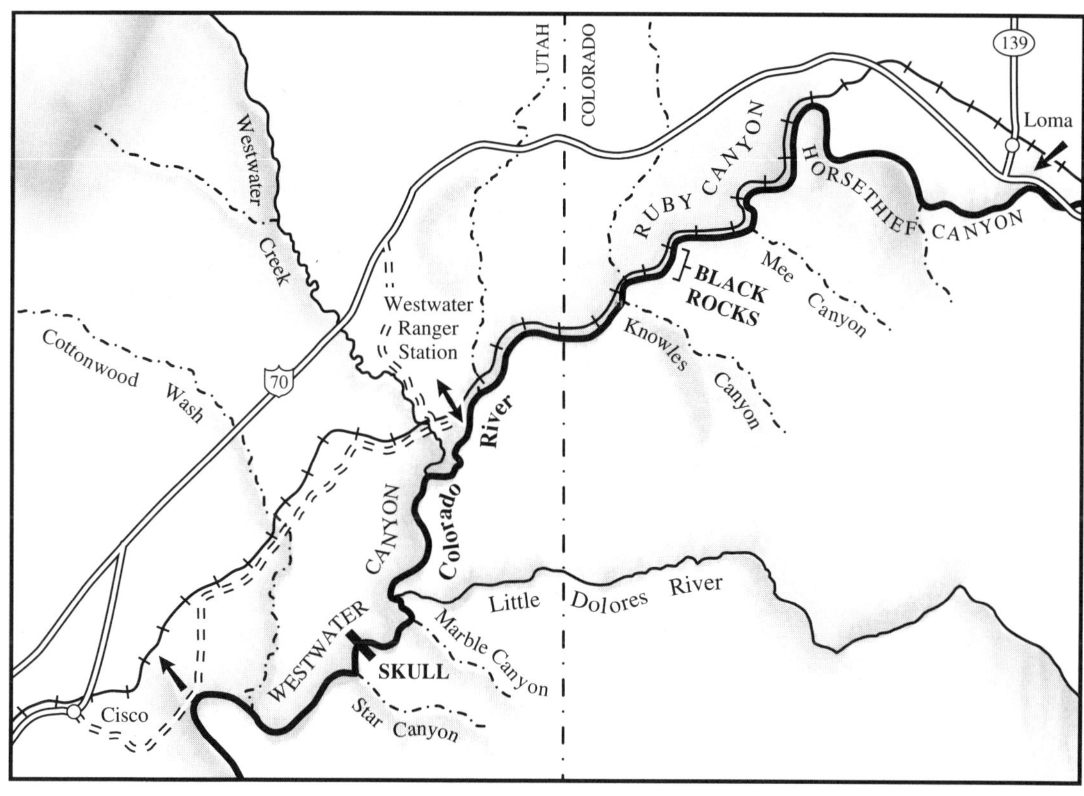

Colorado: Horsethief, Ruby, and Westwater Canyons

9.5 Immediately below Big Hummer is **FUNNEL FALLS (III+)**, a sharp drop between boulders with big V-waves that lead unwary boats into the right wall. Two smaller rapids follow, **SURPRISE** and an unnamed drop that appears at low flows.

10.2 **SKULL (IV)**. Toughest at extreme high and low flows. The Colorado churns down the right wall and into (or over) a house rock that forms a nasty hydraulic above about 3,000 cfs. Skirt to the left. Next, the river runs headlong into a cliff and splits. The main flow exits stage left, and the remainder surges into a deep recess in the right wall where it swirls and circles endlessly in the infamous eddy called the "Room of Doom." Stay left. Hapless boaters have been trapped in the "Room" and unable to break out across the eddy fence, especially at higher flows when it becomes almost a whirlpool. To scout the rapid, catch the small eddy at the top left. (The scouting eddy is washed out at higher flows.)

10.4–11 The river eases, but a few Class II's and III's remain. At low and moderate flows, a superb endo hole forms at **BOWLING ALLEY.** A quarter mile downstream, a sharp drop creates a big cresting wave (washed out at higher flows) at **SOCK-IT-TO-ME.** Then comes **LAST CHANCE,** where a big boulder (wave or hole around 5,000 cfs) blocks the channel. Below Last Chance, Star Canyon enters on the left. Six scenic miles of flatwater continue to the take-out. As the rugged inner gorge gradually gives way to a more open sandstone canyon, the riverbed widens, and beaches and cottonwood trees reappear.

12 Big Hole Canyon, an abandoned meander or "rincon" on the right. Good side hike.

15.5 Cottonwood Wash enters on the right as Westwater Canyon ends.

17 **TAKE-OUT** on the right at Cisco Landing/Rose Ranch Boat Ramp. Or continue downstream (see end of essay).

Colorado River

Cataract Canyon

Difficulty: I to Spanish Bottom (mile 51.5); IV- in Cataract Canyon.
Length: 96 miles. Shorter trip possible (to Spanish Bottom).
Gradient: 1 ft./mi. first 48 miles; 16 ft./mi. in Cataract Canyon.
Put-in: Potash Launch Site (3,925').
Take-out: Hite Marina (3,700').
Drainage Area and Average Annual Discharge: (est.) 72,000 sq. mi. / 10,500,000 af at take-out.
Peak Recorded Flow: 130,100 cfs (July 1917).
Season: April–Nov. Typically peaks between late May and late June at 30,000–80,000 cfs, but varies widely and can be even higher. Recedes to low flows (occasionally below 5,000) in August and September. Never too low.
Recommended Levels: 2,000–20,000 cfs. Often boated at higher levels. Rapids become more turbulent and continuous as flows increase. Ratings would be about III+ at low flows but IV+ above 40,000 and V over 60,000.
Flow Information: NWS tape, (801) 539-1311, gives estimated flow in Cataract Canyon and flow at Cisco, upstream from the put-in.
Open Canoes: OK to Spanish Bottom (return by jet boat). Specific regulations below Spanish Bottom; contact managing agency.
Special Hazards: Huge hydraulics at high water. Isolated, rugged canyon.
Permits: Required year-round below Spanish Bottom. Available for the asking in the off-season but limited April 15–Oct. 14. Apply on a first-come, first-served basis starting Jan. 1. (July and August are the most popular months.) Those on the waiting list often get permits. Group limit 40. Special regulations when flows are over 60,000 cfs. Backcountry permits for trips on the flatwater section above Spanish Bottom are available for the asking year round.

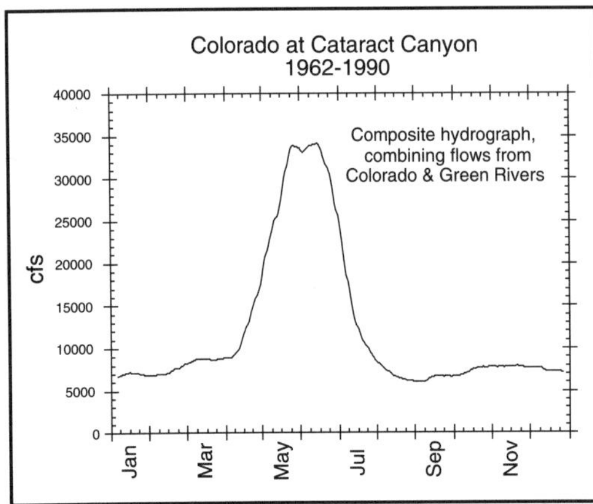

Managing Agency: Canyonlands National Park, Moab UT 84532; (801) 259-3911.
Commercial Raft Trips: Yes. For a list of outfitters, contact the managing agency.
Land Ownership: Almost all public. Private land at and near put-in.
Scenery: Excellent. Deep, rugged desert canyon.
Solitude: Good above Green River confluence; some motorboat traffic. Excellent in Cataract Canyon.
Wilderness: Yes.
Fishing: Not an attraction; catfish.
Wildlife: Bighorn sheep, mule deer, coyote.
Weather: Very hot in midsummer. Some thunderstorms in late summer (side canyon flash flood hazard).
Water: Muddy and undrinkable. Bring water or purify. No drinking water at the put-in.
Camping: Excellent; broad beaches. Many sites are flooded at high water.
Side Hikes: Many outstanding hikes (see **Mile Guide**).
Side Excursions: Canyonlands National Park.
Guides and References:

- Baars, *River Runner's Guide to Cataract Canyon and Approaches.*
- Belknap, *Canyonlands River Guide.*
- Kelsey, *River Guide to Canyonlands National Park and Vicinity.*
- Nichols, *River Runners' Guide to Utah.*
- *Calm Water Float Trips on the Green and Colorado Rivers* (National Park Service). Helpful pamphlet for trips from Potash to Spanish Bottom.
- Baars & Molenaar, *Geology of Canyonlands and Cataract Canyon.*
- Mutschler, *River Runners' Guide to Canyonlands National Park and Vicinity.* Geologic river log.
- Collins & Nash, *The Big Drops.* Essays on famous Western rapids and early boating history.

Maps:
- **USGS:** *Canyonlands National Park and Vicinity* covers the run (except for the last 10 miles of reservoir) at 1:62,500.
- *Southeastern Utah* road map. Utah Travel Council, Council Hall–Capitol Hill, Salt Lake City UT 84114; (801) 533-5681.

Auto Shuttle: 160 miles (3–4 hours) one way. Contact Canyonlands National Park for a list of shuttle and jet boat tow services. To hire reservoir tow-outs, contact Del Webb Co., (800) 528-6154.

Logistics: To reach the **put-in:** U.S. 191 crosses the Colorado some 4 miles northwest of Moab. About a mile west of the U.S. 191 bridge, turn south onto Utah 279 and drive some 15 miles downriver to the Potash Boat Ramp, about a mile past the Texas-Gulf potash plant. To reach the **take-out,** return to U.S. 191, drive north to I-70, then west to Utah 24, then south to Hanksville. Turn left onto Utah 95 and drive some 40 miles to Hite Marina on the south shore of Powell Reservoir. There is a longer alternate shuttle route via U.S. 191 and Utah 95.

For early river runners, Cataract Canyon was a fearsome stretch of water. Between placid Labyrinth and Stillwater Canyons upstream on the Green and gentle Glen Canyon downstream on the Colorado, Cataract lay waiting to crush the unlucky and the foolhardy. For years this 36-mile gauntlet claimed lives and boats at an alarming rate and developed a reputation as the "Graveyard of the Colorado."

John Wesley Powell's expedition made the first descent of Cataract in 1869. For eight toilsome days the men rowed, portaged, and lined their way downstream. Awed by the biggest, most continuous rapids they had seen thus far in their journey down the Green and Colorado, they named the place Cataract Canyon.

Major Powell's journal reveals both wonder at the spectacular slickrock landscape and anxiety in the face of unrelenting rapids and dwindling provisions. At one point he imagines the worst: "may be we shall come to a fall in these canyons which we cannot pass, where the walls rise from the water's edge, so that we cannot land, and where the water is so swift that we cannot return." Yet his first expedition came through almost unscathed, with only one swamping and the loss of a few oars. In 1871 Powell made a second successful descent.

But the next two attempts to run Cataract ended in disaster. In 1889 a railroad survey party led by Frank Brown and Robert Brewster Stanton nearly starved after losing a supply raft and two boats. The men barely escaped Cataract with their lives, only to have the expedition end in tragedy farther downstream when Brown and two others drowned in Marble Canyon. (See the **Grand Canyon** chapter.)

Two years later, prospector James Best and his party of nine pinned a boat irretrievably in Cataract's Mile Long Rapid and had to squeeze into the one remaining boat for the rest of the journey to Hite. The expedition commemorated its hardship with an inscription on a nearby boulder, the first of several etchings left by Cataract's battered adventurers. Many inscriptions, including the one by Best, are still visible today. From 1896 to 1908 several parties passed safely—or at least without loss of life—through the canyon, but a rash of at least seven deaths in the next five years ensured Cataract's reputation as the Colorado's watery grave.

Why should Cataract wreck more boats and claim more lives than the Grand Canyon, which has more difficult rapids? Most likely for the simple reason that Cataract had the first shot at unskilled or ill-equipped boaters, weeding them out before they ever reached Lee's Ferry. A contributing factor may be the more continuous nature of Cataract's whitewater.

The frequent rapids result from Cataract Canyon's unique geology. Extensive faulting has fractured the riverside cliffs into discrete blocks, many of which have sheared away. These rockfalls and landslides constrict the river and occasionally pitch massive boulders into the current. No doubt more rapids will form here in the future in this way. Cataract is the only stretch of the desert Colorado where the major rapids were not formed by debris flows from side creeks.

Sadly, more than half of Cataract's magnificent whitewater lies buried beneath Powell Reservoir. Of the 52 rapids identified by surveyor William Chenoweth in 1921, only half remain. The reservoir covers 23 of the original 36 miles of whitewater, reaching to within a half mile of the largest rapid, Big Drop. Nevertheless, the surviving remnant of Cataract Canyon still stands as one of the West's grandest river trips.

The Colorado above Powell Reservoir has not been entirely tamed by dams on the upstream river and its tributaries. In fact, Cataract Canyon experiences a remarkably wide range of flows within each season and from one year to the next. In dry years the river may be sluggish and rocky, but in wet years a heavy snowmelt can send more than 70,000 cfs roaring through the canyon as a continuum of heart-stopping waves and mind-boggling holes. Boaters should choose a starting date carefully, then keep track of snowpack and runoff. Many launch in July and August to avoid May and June high water.

There is another consideration for Cataract trips: when Powell Reservoir is full, flatwater begins 34 miles above the take-out. Few attempt to paddle or row this distance; the effort is likely to take more than one day, campsites are few and far between, and upstream winds can make the experience a living hell. Most groups bring a motor or arrange to be towed out by a motorboat or houseboat from Hite Marina.

Since Cataract Canyon lies just below the Green-Colorado confluence, boaters can approach it on either river. Both are essentially flat for many miles above the confluence. Most Cataract trips launch at the Potash access on the Colorado and drift 48 miles to the confluence, while a smaller number start from various sites on the Green and float anywhere from 52 to 120 miles to the same point. (See the **Green: Labyrinth and Stillwater** chapter.) All trips eventually find their way to the confluence of the Green and the Colorado, one of the most majestic meetings of waters in the West and, in Ute Indian mythology, the center of the universe.

Boaters who prefer scenery to whitewater can take out at Spanish Bottom (mile 51.5) and return to the put-in with the aid of a jet boat hired in advance. This is a popular option for open canoeists in particular. The flatwater section in the run down to the confluence offers some of the finest side hiking in the Canyon Country, combining outstanding scenery and fascinating geology. Boaters can explore dramatic side canyons, the marvelous rock formations of the Doll House and the Needles, and numerous Anasazi ruins. The mile guide lists the best-known hikes.

Cataract Canyon begins at the Green River confluence, but for the next four miles the Colorado keeps its composure. Then "Cat," as river guides know it, erupts into ten miles of big-water rapids. At low flows boaters may count 26 distinct drops, though some are only Class II. At high water many of the rapids blend together in a pounding millrace.

Many rapids are known only by the numbers that Mr. Chenoweth and the U.S. Geological Survey assigned them, but the larger drops have acquired various nicknames over the canyon's 120-year boating history. Though some of the overlapping names have fallen into disuse, others persist, and things can get confusing when boaters use different names for the same rapid.

At peak runoff, Cataract Canyon runs brimful with the original, undiluted Canyon Country brew: a frothy concoction of muddy water, some of the biggest waves on the Colorado—up to 15'—and monster holes that can flip the largest rafts. The sneak chutes are often comfortably wide, but a few passages demand skillful maneuvering in very heavy surf.

The opening five miles of rapids are a good warm-up; then comes a short breather before the big test. The first real challenge comes at Mile Long (Rapids 13 through 18 combined). The Colorado saves the best for last as it thunders through renowned Big Drop just above Powell Reservoir. Here Rapids 21 through 23 combine in one of the West's most famous whitewater gauntlets.

Mile by Mile Guide

0 **PUT-IN** at the Potash launch site on the right bank a mile below the Texas-Gulf potash mine. Camping permitted.

9 Abandoned oil drilling equipment on the right. About a mile downstream, Dead Horse Point overlook appears on the north rim, 1,700' above the river.

16.5 The river enters Canyonlands National Park. A mile downstream, Little Bridge Canyon enters on the right, offering an easy side hike.

21 Lockhart Canyon on the left. Lathrop Canyon on the right 3 miles downstream, across the river from Indian ruins and pictographs. A jeep track climbs Lathrop Canyon to the White Rim Jeep Trail.

30.5 Indian Creek enters on the left. Short hike to Anasazi granaries; a waterfall is

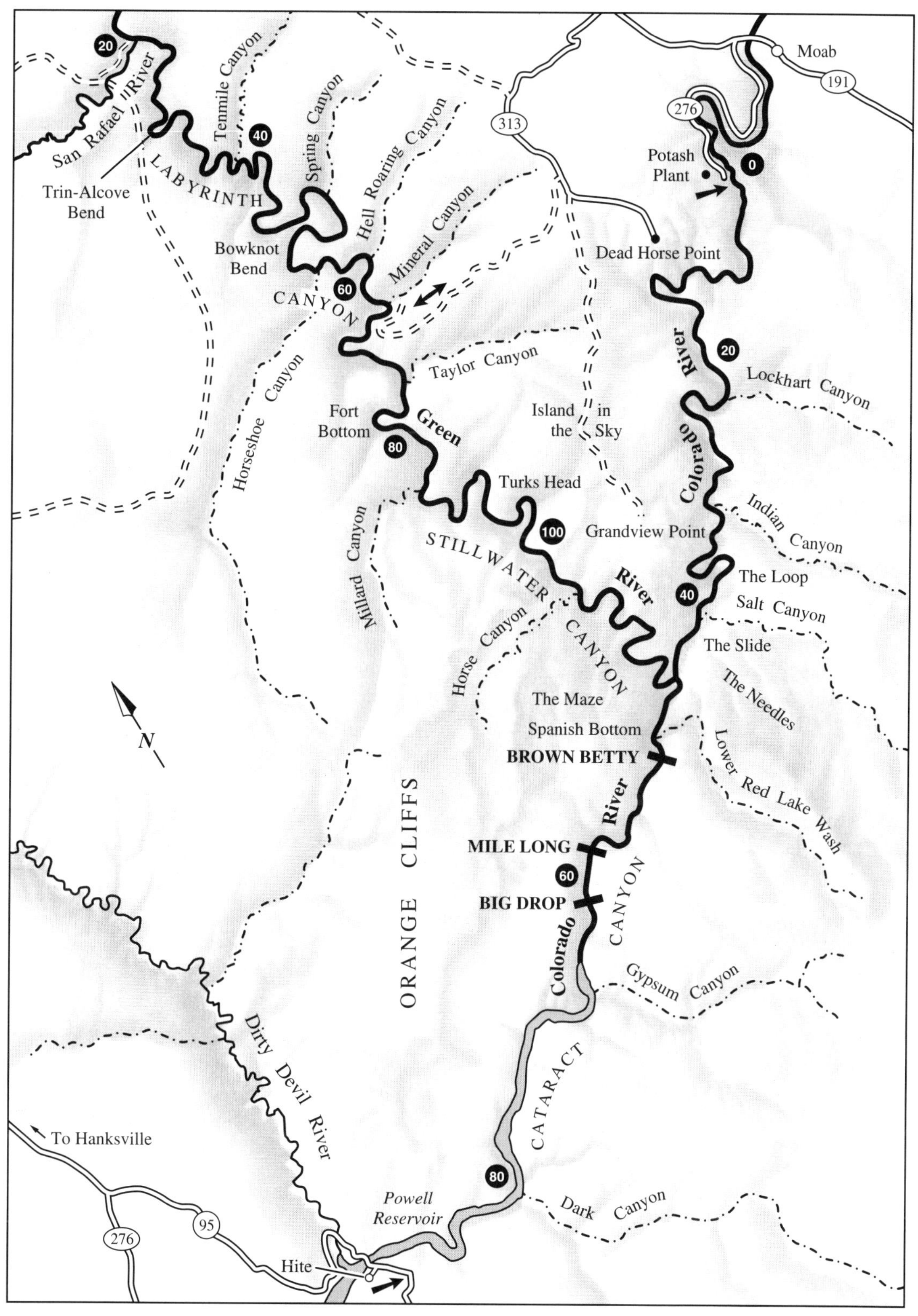

Colorado (Cataract) and Green (Labyrinth and Stillwater)

farther up the creek. About a mile downstream, Monument Creek enters on the right; side hike to a 300' stone spire known as the Totem Pole.

36 The river enters "The Loop," a double gooseneck that winds 6 river miles to advance one air mile. Some boaters can hike half a mile across the first gooseneck while others float 4 miles to meet them.

44 Salt Creek enters on the left. Two miles downstream, a landslide from the right bank forms a minor riffle known as **THE SLIDE**, which in 1905 thwarted an attempted upstream run by the steamboat *City of Moab.*

47.5 Confluence of the Colorado and Green.

51.5 Spanish Bottom, a large flat on the right. Flatwater trips can meet jet boats here for the tow back to Moab. An old trail crosses the river: from the right bank it climbs to spectacular mesa-top formations in the Doll House; from the left bank it winds 4 miles up Lower Red Lake Canyon to the Needles area, then joins a 4-wheel-drive road that runs 9 more miles to Needles District Campground (possible emergency exit).

Below Spanish Bottom the fun begins: the river drops 170' from here to the reservoir. First up is **RAPID 1** or **Brown Betty** (III-), named for the ill-fated kitchen boat on the 1889 Brown-Stanton expedition. Rapids in the next 4 miles are mostly minor, but scout **RAPID 5** at low water, and watch for **RAPID 7** (III) at mile 54. At higher flows Rapids 7 and 8 combine into a challenging Class III+. Downstream, the rapids ease for a couple of miles.

58.7– **MILE LONG** (III+), **Rapids 13–19.**
60.2 Continuous and over a mile long. Rapid 15, known as **CAPSIZE**, is the toughest. **Recognition:** After Rapid 12 the river is smooth for almost two miles, then curves left into Mile Long. While scouting on the right, look for the Best expedition's 1891 inscription.

60.7 **RAPID 20** (III-), also called **Been Hurt.** A difficult passage at very low flows.

61– **BIG DROP, Rapids 21–23.** Three dis-
61.8 tinct drops at low water, each larger than the one before, blend together as flows approach 40,000 cfs. Usually referred to as **BIG DROP 1, 2, and 3,** but known by many other names (individual waves and holes even have nicknames). **Recognition:** The first drop begins where Teapot Canyon (Calf Canyon) enters on the right.

BIG DROP 1 (III), also known as **Upper Big Drop,** can be scouted on the left. In **BIG DROP 2** (IV-), also called **Satan's Seat,** two huge boulders (holes above 35,000 cfs) flank a runnable center channel. The right-hand hole is known as "Little Niagara." Scout left. A pool separates this rapid from **BIG DROP 3** (IV), also known as **Satan's Gut,** but at high water the pool disappears and waves connect the two rapids. Rockfalls from both walls constrict the river. Boaters must avoid house rocks (holes around 10,000 cfs and up) on the left and massive "Frogg Hole" on the right. Scout right.

62.5 When full, Powell Reservoir begins a half mile below Big Drop. Campsites are scarce downstream because the reservoir fills the canyon from wall to wall.

67.5 Gypsum Canyon enters on the left. Side hike leads about 4 miles to a waterfall and plunge pool. Major Powell claimed he outran a flash flood here in 1869. Downstream, the reservoir enters a deep, narrow gorge. Log jams sometimes develop here during spring runoff, but the channel generally remains passable. Ice jams often close the channel in winter.

72 Clearwater Canyon enters on the right. Good side hike.

81 Dark Canyon enters on the left. Good side hike to pools and falls. Dark Canyon Rapid, one of the most feared in Cataract Canyon, is buried beneath the reservoir. Six miles farther on is the former site of Cataract's last rapid, number 52.

93.5 U.S. 95 crosses the river. A mile below the bridge, the Dirty Devil River canyon opens on the right. Continue down the left shore of the reservoir to the **TAKE-OUT** at Hite Marina, mile 96.

Grand Canyon of the Colorado

Lees Ferry to Diamond Creek or Pierce Ferry

Difficulty: IV+5.
Length: 225 or 280 miles.
Put-in: Lees Ferry (3,107').
Take-out: Diamond Creek (1,350') or Pierce Ferry on "Lake" Mead (includes up to 40-odd miles of flatwater on reservoir).
Gradient: 7.8 ft./mi. to Diamond Creek.
Drainage Area: 111,800 sq. mi. at put-in.
Average Annual Discharge: 12 to 13 million af.
Peak Recorded Flow: *Pre-Dam:* 220,000 cfs (June 18, 1921). *Post-Dam:* 97,300 cfs (June 29, 1983). Both at Phantom Ranch (mile 88).
Season: All year.
Recommended Levels: 5,000–40,000 cfs. More difficult at low water; more dangerous at high flows. High-float life vests recommended.
Flow Information: Glen Canyon Dam tape, (800) 752-8525.
Special Hazards: Remote area (commercial rafters carry emergency radios). Cold water makes hypothermia a danger even in summer; consider donning a wet suit for the biggest rapids. Flash floods (see **Camping**).
Permits: Required year-round. Only one private launch per day April 16–Oct. 15. Maximum group size 16. Maximum trip duration to Diamond Creek: 18 days (April 16–Oct. 15), 21 days (Oct. 16–Nov. 30 and March 1–April 15), or 30 days (Dec. 1–Feb. 29). It takes about 7 years to move to the top of the waiting list. Applications accepted only in February. You must confirm your position on the waiting list by mail every year between Dec. 15 and Jan. 31. Anyone on the waiting list may call for canceled dates.

Note: You must also obtain a permit (substantial fee) to take out at Diamond Creek. Contact Hualapai Tribal Council, Peach Springs, AZ 86434; (602) 769-2216.

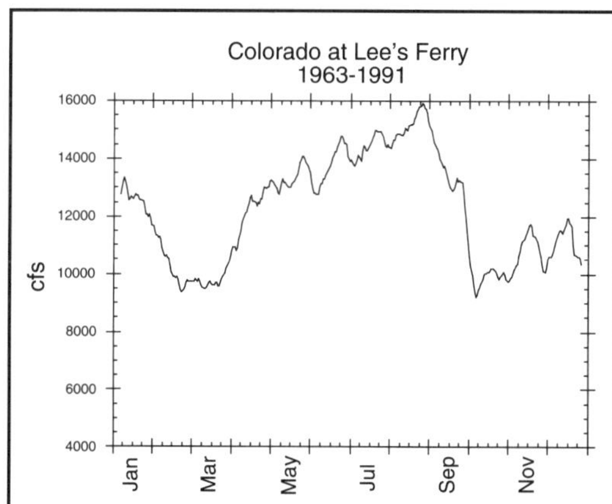

Managing Agency: National Park Service, River Permit Office, Grand Canyon National Park, P.O. Box 129, Grand Canyon, AZ 86023; (602) 638-7888 or 638-7843.
Commercial Raft Trips: Yes, both oar- and motor-powered. For a list contact the managing agency. Up to 5 commercial trips daily during peak season (May 1–Sept. 30). No motors Sept. 16–Dec. 15.
Scenery: Unsurpassed. **Wilderness:** Yes.
Solitude: Good during peak season; excellent off season.
Fishing: Fair for trout in some of the larger side creeks. Fair to good for trout in the river itself above the Little Colorado (mile 61). The upstream stretch between Glen Canyon Dam and Lees Ferry is one of the Southwest's best trout fisheries (introduced, non-native trout).
Water: Very cold. Fairly clear and green unless turned brown by muddy tributaries. Filter and purify river water before drinking. Side creek water should also be treated.
Camping: Excellent beaches in many stretches, although fluctuating dam releases have eroded them in the upper part of the run (see essay). Little shade. Campsites are scarce in some sections—part of Marble Canyon (miles 11-38), Upper Granite Gorge, Havasu area, and below Diamond Creek. Negotiations with other boating parties are advised to prevent conflicts over sites. Gathering of firewood prohibited May 1–Sept. 30. Use caution in camping near the mouths of side canyons; **flash floods** can begin far upstream in the creek drainage and take you unawares. Permits necessary for off-river camping; contact Back Country Reservations Office, Grand Canyon National Park, P.O. Box 129, Grand Canyon, AZ 86023; (602) 638-7888. For camping on the Havasu Reservation, see **Mile Guide** entry on Havasu Creek.

Side Hikes: Excellent. Almost every side canyon could be an adventure. John Annerino, *Hiking the Grand Canyon* (Sierra Club), has a section on side hikes from the river.

Guides and References:

- Stevens, *Colorado River in Grand Canyon.*
- Belknap & Evans, *Grand Canyon River Guide.*
- Ghiglieri, *Canyon.* Veteran guide's book includes everything from whitewater tales to geology, history, and wildlife.
- Lavender, *River Runners of the Grand Canyon.*
- Crumbo, *River Runner's Guide to the History of the Grand Canyon.*
- Powell, *Exploration of the Colorado River and Its Canyons.*
- Stegner, *Beyond The Hundredth Meridian: John Wesley Powell and the Second Opening of the West.* Puts Powell's explorations and later career in context and corrects the mistakes—intentional and otherwise—in Powell's published diary.
- Dellenbaugh, *A Canyon Voyage.* First-hand account of Powell's second expedition.
- Stanton, *The Colorado River Survey.* First-hand account of the 1889-1890 float trip.
- Stanton, *Colorado River Controversies.* An early Canyon boater tries to get to the bottom of questions such as why Powell's crew members hiked out at Separation Rapid.
- Lucchitta, *Canyon Maker: A Geological History of the Colorado River.*
- Collier, *Introduction to Grand Canyon Geology.*
- Chronic, *Pages of Stone: Geology of Western National Parks,* vol. 4: *Grand Canyon and the Plateau Country.*
- Hughes, *The House of Stone and Light.* Humans and the Grand Canyon.
- Hoffman, *Grand Canyon Visual.* Photos and some text on geology and natural and human history.
- Abbey, *The Hidden Canyon: A River Journey.* Photos by John Blaustein.
- Fradkin, *A River No More: The Colorado River and the West.* History, politics, economics, and environmental consequences of water development.
- Carothers & Brown, *The Colorado River through Grand Canyon: Natural History and Human Change.* Emphasizes changes since Glen Canyon Dam.
- Brian, *River to Rim: A Guide to Place Names in the Grand Canyon.*

Maps:

- **USGS 7.5':** Not recommended; dozens of sheets necessary to cover the run.
- **USGS 1:100:** *Glen Canyon Dam, Tuba City, Grand Canyon, Mount Trumbull, Peach Springs.*
- **USGS 1:250:** *Marble Canyon, Grand Canyon, Williams.*
- **USGS:** *Grand Canyon National Park and Vicinity* (38" x 60") covers miles 35–155 at the same scale as 15' maps (1:62,500). *Grand Canyon National Monument* (33" x 42") covers miles 144–188 at 1:48,000. Neither map is folded.
- *Grand Canyon Geologic Map* (Grand Canyon Natural History Association).

Auto Shuttle: *To Diamond Creek:* About 260 miles; 6-7 hours one way. *To Pierce Ferry:* About 355 miles; 8-9 hours one way. For a list of shuttle and/or reservoir tow-out services, contact the managing agency.

Logistics: To reach the **put-in at Lees Ferry,** turn north off U.S. 89A about 120 miles north of Flagstaff at the village of Marble Canyon, just west of the Navajo Bridge. A road leads 5 miles down to the river and a nearby parking lot. Check with the ranger about camping near (but not *at*) the put-in.

To reach the **take-out at Diamond Creek** (fee; see **Permits**), drive south to Flagstaff on U.S. 89, turn west on I-40, and exit about 70 miles farther at Seligman. Drive about 40 miles west on U.S. 66; at Peach Springs turn right onto Diamond Creek Road (dirt), which leads 22 miles to the river.

To reach **Pierce Ferry,** drive about 150 miles west on I-40 from Flagstaff. Just past Kingman, turn right on U.S. 93 and follow it northwest 26 miles. Then turn right and follow signs past Dolan Springs and Meadview some 52 miles to Pierce Ferry on Lake Mead. The last 3 miles are unpaved. To reach **South Cove,** take the left fork of the road at Meadview and follow signs.

An **alternate shuttle route to Pierce Ferry** saves about 40 miles and one hour but is partly dirt. Follow the directions toward Diamond Creek, but instead of turning off U.S. 66 at Peach Springs, continue west about 24 miles to Hackberry. About 5 miles past Hackberry, turn right (north) onto a dirt road (muddy after rains) leading 32 miles to the Dolan Springs-Meadview road. Turn right and follow signs to Pierce Ferry or South Cove.

For most people, floating the Grand Canyon of the Colorado—usually referred to simply as "the Canyon"—is the river trip of a lifetime. The four million tourists who peek over the rim each year get only a glimpse of the Canyon's awesome vastness and come away with little notion of its breathtaking variety. But the 21,000 who boat the river each year get a good close look.

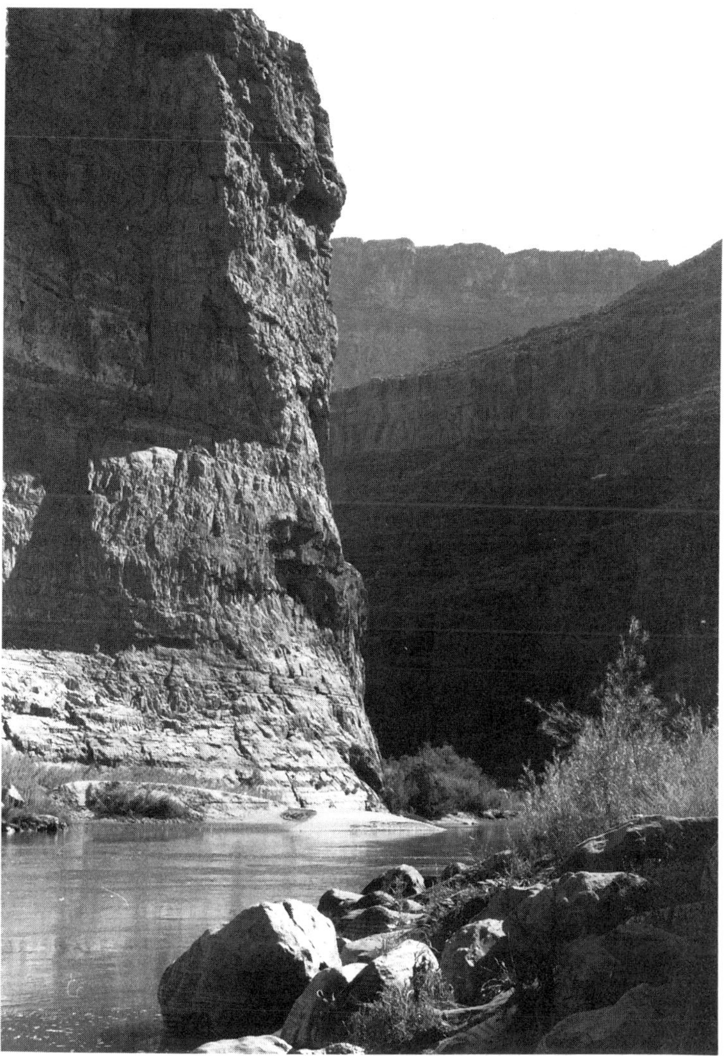

Marble Canyon *Kathryn Cahill*

Around every bend is a splendid new vista. Unforgettable hikes up side creeks reveal wonders with each twist and turn. The big, boiling rapids are no longer considered the ultimate whitewater test, but they're not to be taken lightly. Crystal and Lava Falls still strike fear into the hearts of most boaters.

A Grand Canyon float trip is also the geology lesson of a lifetime. All but the most incurious will want to know a little about what they are seeing as they move down the river and backward in time. The river slices gradually downward through the gently dipping sedimentary strata of the southern Colorado Plateau. The 250 million-year-old Kaibab Limestone that appears at river level just below the Lees Ferry put-in rises quickly to form the rim rock of the canyon. Only 30 miles downstream it towers 2,500' above the river. It is succeeded at river level by older formations which appear one after another and climb ever higher.

In the heart of the Canyon, over a mile below the rim, the dark, twisted walls of the V-shaped Granite Gorge are made of 1.7 billion-year-old metamorphic rock: black Vishnu Schist and pink Zoroaster Granite, the roots of a great mountain range that rose and was eroded away before the North American continent took shape.

Though the rocks are old, the deep cut of the Colorado River that made the Grand Canyon is relatively young. It is the result of the rapid uplift of the southern Colorado Plateau, a rough ellipse of about 130,000 square miles centered around the Four Corners area. From roughly 17 million to about 5 million years ago, the plateau rose some 4,000'.

The uplift of the river's largely arid watershed produced massive erosion, and the enormous amount of debris carried by the river greatly increased the cutting force with which it carved its canyon ever deeper into the rising rock strata.[1] As the uplift tapered off, the river's

[1]The story may be even more complex. Major Powell's theory was that the river was already in its present path before the uplift and simply cut down through the rising plateau. Today, some geologists believe that the ancestral Colorado River was what is now the Little Colorado and that it did not carve its present course south to the Gulf of California until it was forced that way by the uplift. One theory is that before the uplift, the river found its outlet to the north, along the path (but in the opposite direction) of Kanab Creek.

cutting action declined and the Canyon assumed largely the shape it presents today. The Colorado's riverbed is only about 50' lower than it was a million years ago.

Human habitation of the Grand Canyon area dates back about 4,000 years to the Desert Culture of the prehistoric American Indians. The people that left the most evidence of their presence were the Anasazi, who lived in and around the Canyon from about 700 to 1200 A.D. during periods when the climate was wet enough to permit agriculture. Anasazi ruins dot the Canyon and are clearly in evidence in the Nankoweap and Unkar areas. Two later-arriving Indian tribes, the Havasupai and the Hualapai, have reservations in the Grand Canyon. The Canyon also holds the most sacred sites of the Hopi, who have lived nearby for a thousand years. (See sidebar.)

Europeans had no impact on this remote region until after the American Civil War. Two brief visits by the Spanish, in the sixteenth and again in the eighteenth century, left no traces. But the arrival of English-speaking Americans in the last half of the nineteenth century—explorers, prospectors, pioneer settlers—was a different matter. Where the Indians had seen a place of refuge and the Spaniards an impassable obstacle, expansion-minded Americans envisioned a source of natural wealth. Some even dreamed of using the Colorado River as a thoroughfare between East and West (see sidebar on Captain Samuel Adams in the **Upper Colorado** chapter).

Still, by the end of the Civil War, the Colorado remained largely unexplored above the Grand Wash Cliffs at the western end of the Grand Canyon. It took the historic river journeys of Major John Wesley Powell, a Union officer who lost his right arm in the Civil War, to shed the first real light on the nature of the canyon. Powell was a sort of Renaissance man of the West—geologist, paleontologist, ethnologist, and cartographer—who explored the headwaters of the Colorado and the Green in 1867-68. On May 24, 1869, his party of ten set off from Green River, Wyoming, in four wooden boats on an expedition down the Green and Colorado and through the unknown expanses of the Grand Canyon (a name he helped to make popular).

The story of Powell's trip should be savored in more detail than space allows here, and his published diary—though not entirely reliable—makes good reading on a Canyon float. Suffice it to say that after much hardship, the loss of a boat, and one defection, Powell and his crew reached the mouth of the Paria River (later the site of Lees Ferry) on August 4 and Bright Angel Creek in the heart of the Upper Granite Gorge on August 15. They struggled on to Separation Rapid (mile 239), where on August 28 three more crew members walked out. Abandoning one boat, the rest of the party continued downstream, emerged from the Canyon at the Grand Wash Cliffs, and floated down to a Mormon settlement at the mouth of the Virgin River.

In 1871 and 1872 Powell led a second expedition from Green River, Wyoming that made its way much more slowly downriver because of extensive surveying and mapping. Powell called the trip off at Kanab Creek, about halfway through the Grand Canyon.

Powell's expeditions were headline news, and with some of the blanks on the map filled in, prospectors rushed into the Canyon. Gold was found at Kanab Creek in 1871. Mining of various minerals has continued on a modest scale ever since but has rarely proven profitable.

Powell's explorations proved that the Colorado through the Grand Canyon was no river highway like the Mississippi. But in spite of his description of the rugged and often vertical canyon walls, railroad builders still had their eyes on the Canyon. The 1889 Brown-Stanton railroad survey party, floating in especially flimsy wooden boats, saw three men drowned in the first 25 miles below Lees Ferry—including Frank Brown, president of the railroad, who had refused to buy life vests for the expedition. Engineer Robert Stanton abandoned the trip and led the survivors out of the Canyon. Returning the following year with better boats and new cork life jackets, he made his way successfully (though with great difficulty) through the Canyon to the Gulf of California. Stanton remained convinced that a railroad could be built along the route but was unable to persuade enough investors.

Those remarkable journeys are only the opening chapters in the long history of Grand Canyon river running. In 1897 trapper and boatman Nathaniel Galloway demonstrated a key conceptual breakthrough by taking his wooden "cataract boat" stern-first through the Canyon—facing downstream, not upstream as previous oarsmen had done. In 1911 photographers Emery and Ellsworth Kolb rowed two boats from Green River, Wyoming all the way to Needles, California on the Lower Colorado and filmed their own expedition. A float trip by the U.S. Geological Survey in 1923, with Emery Kolb as head boatman, resulted in the first accurate topographical map of the Canyon.

By the turn of the twentieth century, the Canyon was becoming a major tourist attraction. The arrival of the railroad at the south rim in 1901 brought hordes of sightseers. The Grand Canyon, under federal protection for a century, has been a National Park since 1919.[2]

The Canyon's first commercial river runner was Norman Nevills, who rowed guests down the Colorado in wooden boats beginning in 1938. In 1941 a Nevills customer, Alexander

[2]The Grand Canyon was declared a National Park in 1919, but the park boundaries included only 82 miles of the river corridor. Left outside the park were the first 52 miles below Lees Ferry (most of the stretch which Powell named Marble Canyon) and everything below Tapeats Creek (mile 134). In 1969, after the threat of Marble Canyon Dam was beaten back, Marble Canyon was made a National Monument. In 1975 the various components were consolidated as Grand Canyon National Park, which now covers nearly 1,900 square miles and the entire river from Lees Ferry to Pierce Ferry (including 40-plus miles usually under "Lake" Mead).

Human History in the Grand Canyon

The first humans in this part of the Colorado Plateau were prehistoric hunter-gatherers of the Desert Culture. Their 4,000-year-old willow-twig figurines of game animals have been found in caves inside the Grand Canyon as well as beyond both of its rims. It is not known whether they actually lived inside the Canyon or just visited it. They are thought to have vanished by around 1,000 B.C.

More is known about the Anasazi, Indians of the Pueblo culture who inhabited Southwestern plateaus and canyons from about 600 to 1200 A.D. ("Anasazi" means "ancestral enemies" in Navajo.) The Kayenta branch began to farm the rims of the Grand Canyon between 700 and 850 and eventually moved onto the Canyon floor in the Nankoweap, Little Colorado, Unkar, Phantom Ranch, and Tapeats Creek areas around 1050. Slight changes in climate made the Canyon first hospitable to crops, then inhospitable; this cycle was repeated several times. The Anasazi abandoned the floor of the Canyon around 1200 because the climate turned dry again—this time for good.

*The Hopi,[1] who still inhabit the high mesas about 100 miles east of the Grand Canyon, may have taken in some of the migrating Kayenta Anasazi when they left the Grand Canyon. The most sacred sites of the Hopi are in the Canyon and the Little Colorado drainage (see **Mile Guide**).*

About the time the Anasazi were withdrawing from the Grand Canyon, people from the Cerbat culture appeared in the area. Their present-day descendants are the Havasupai ("people of the blue-green waters"), a small tribe of hunter-farmers who still live on their 185,000-acre reservation up Havasu Creek.

Beginning around 1300 A.D. the Southern Paiutes, a branch of the Shoshone, roamed the north rim of the Grand Canyon for five centuries or more. In 1885, after years of Paiute hostilites—both with the Navajo[2] and with white settlers—the U.S. Government moved them to reservations just north of the Kaibab Plateau.

In 1540 the first Europeans gazed in wonder at the Grand Canyon. They were part of a detachment dispatched by the Spanish explorer Coronado to investigate reports of an Indian tribe (probably the Havasupai) who lived near a great river to the west. (Coronado was searching for the fabled "Seven Cities of Cibola," which turned out to be adobe pueblos with no streets of gold.) The Spaniards finally arrived at the south rim and tried unsuccessfully to descend to the river, which they judged to be about two yards wide. After three difficult days they gave up, concluding that the river was much farther away, and the scale of the Canyon far greater, than they had imagined.

No European returned to the Grand Canyon for over two centuries. In 1846 the region fell into American hands as a prize of the war with Mexico. After the Civil War, Major Powell's river explorations brought the Grand Canyon into the public consciousness for good.

[1]"Hopi" is short for "Hopitu Shinumo" or "the peaceful ones." The Hopi are descendants of the Anasazi, Mogollon, and Sinaguan peoples.

[2]The Navajo arrived in the Southwest around 1600 A.D. In the nineteenth century their violent resistance to white settlement ended in surrender and the infamous "Long Walk," a 300-mile death march to imprisonment in Fort Sumner, New Mexico. In 1868 they were granted a large reservation in the Four Corners area.

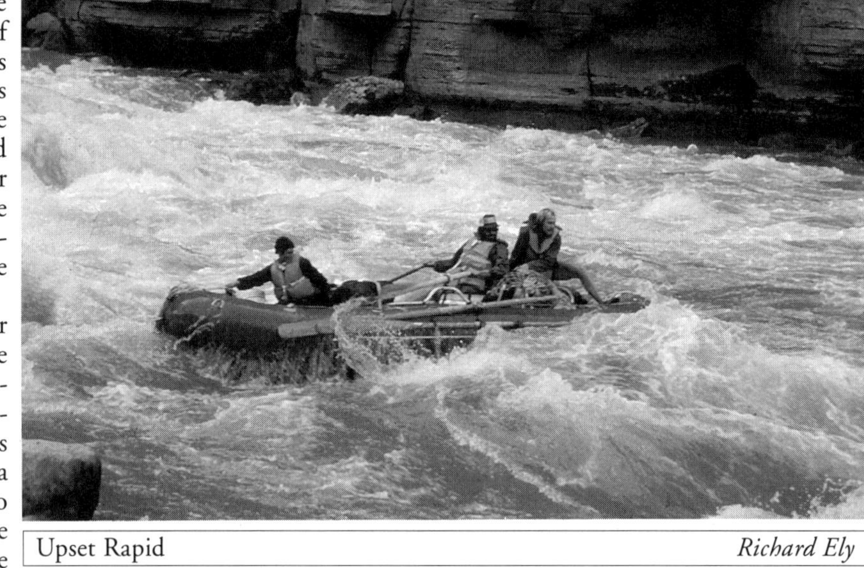

Upset Rapid *Richard Ely*

"Zee" Grant, was the first to kayak the Canyon, but he portaged some of the rapids in his wood-and-canvas craft. Still, by the end of the Second World War, fewer than 100 people (including Powell) had floated the Grand Canyon.

As on other Western rivers, the availability of surplus military inflatable pontoons after the war was a major stimulus to boating. In the Canyon they were often coupled with outboard motors. Georgie White Clark pioneered large-scale river trips in the 1950's with her motor-powered "G-rigs," three rafts lashed side by side. Then came Don and Ted Hatch, Jack Curry, Ron Smith, and Don Harris with their "snout rigs" or "J-rigs," 38' bridge pontoons attached to a frame. More commercial outfitters, some running oar-powered float trips in inflatable rafts, continued to appear on the Colorado. Renowned boater Walt Kirschbaum made the first kayak run without portage in a canvas-decked craft in 1960.

Boating in the Grand Canyon mushroomed in the 1960's. By the early 1970's more than 16,000 people floated the river annually, and the Park Service began to limit both commercial and private trips. Today, commercial rafting accounts for 80 percent of the user-days. Permits for private floats are highly prized and require many years on the waiting list. Preparing for a private trip down the Canyon is a major logistical operation. Large rafts (or many smaller ones) are advisable simply to provide capacity for carrying in all the food and supplies and hauling out all the waste.[3]

May through September is peak boating season in the Grand Canyon. June and July are the hottest months, with air temperatures regularly surpassing 100°. But the river is so cold that wet suits are sometimes advisable. Thunderstorms break the heat in late July and August (the latter is the rainiest month of the year). Flash floods in side canyons can be a hazard, especially at this time.

Late September and October trips usually have the best daytime weather, though autumn days grow short and nights can be chilly. Some tough-hided boaters run the Canyon in winter, braving cold rain and even snow. Springtime weather is variable with average daily highs in the 70's. Upstream winds are common, and rowing or paddling a heavily-laden raft against the wind through the long, slack pools requires plenty of exertion. Kayaks, of course, have far less trouble with wind and flatwater.

Some busy people who can't take off two weeks or more to float the entire Grand Canyon settle for a partial trip beginning at Phantom Ranch (mile 88). A few hardy souls even end their trips there, but it's easier to hike *down* the 9.5-mile Bright Angel Trail from the South Rim than to hike *up* it—especially with gear. Still, someone has to take the boats all the way down the river. It's best to make time for the entire trip, at least to Diamond Creek.

The Colorado in the Grand Canyon is a classic pool-and-drop river. Its rapids are caused by debris washed down the side canyons

[3]Businesses in the Flagstaff area will do almost everything for private Grand Canyon trips: rent rafts and other river gear (including portable toilets); drive shuttles; plan menus and purchase and pack food for the trip. Some commercial outfitters offer special trips providing raft support for kayakers and canoeists. For information contact the managing agency.

The Impact of Glen Canyon Dam

The Colorado River that flows through the Grand Canyon today is very different from the untamed behemoth of yesteryear. Still, the fact that it flows at all represents a victory for lovers of wilderness everywhere.

In 1956 Congress authorized a massive system of hydroelectric dams and reservoirs called the Colorado River Storage Project. Six of the dams were eventually built—including the largest, Glen Canyon, which towers above the Colorado some 16 miles upstream from Lees Ferry. "Lake" Powell, its 26 million acre-foot reservoir, stretches 186 miles back up the Colorado.

Two other proposed dams could have turned all but a hundred miles of the Grand Canyon into slackwater reservoirs. Marble Canyon Dam at mile 39 would have drowned the river all the way back to Glen Canyon Dam. Hualapai Dam at mile 237 would have flooded the Canyon back to Kanab Creek (mile 143). A media campaign mounted by David Brower and the Sierra Club, including several full-page newspaper ads that compared the proposal to flooding the Sistine Chapel, aroused so much public outrage that the government abandoned the Marble Canyon project. The proposed Hualapai Dam has been on the back burner ever since, although some Arizona congressmen occasionally try to resurrect it.

Until 1963, when Glen Canyon Dam plugged the river, the Colorado ran wild and free through the Grand Canyon and into "Lake" Mead (the huge 1936 reservoir behind Hoover Dam which flooded the lower 40 miles of the Canyon). Average flows in the undammed Canyon ranged from a winter low of about 5,000 cfs to a high of around 125,000 cfs, usually in June. Water temperatures varied from just above freezing in winter and spring to an average high of over 80° in late summer and early fall.

During most of the year the sediment-laden river was a muddy reddish-brown—hence the name "Colorado," which means "reddish" in Spanish. Every year, the river washed away the sandy beaches with high flows. Then, as the water dropped in the summer, it re-created them by depositing fresh sediment carried from far upstream. This natural cycle was interrupted by Glen Canyon Dam and replaced by a computer-driven schedule of releases determined by the hourly demand for electricity.[1] *No longer is the Colorado allowed to replenish its beaches. The sediment it carries is deposited in the upper reaches of the reservoir. Now, beaches washed away by high flows simply disappear.*

Fluctuating daily "peaking power" dam releases have greatly accelerated the erosion of the beaches, especially in the upper part of the run. Such releases were standard operating procedure from 1981, when the enormous reservoir first filled, until 1991. During daytime hours when electrical demand was highest, peak flows of up to 31,500 cfs surged through the canyon, washing away beaches and destroying fish and wildlife habitat. Dam operators then turned the river almost completely off later in the day and on weekends when power demand declined. Within a few hours, flows fell as low as 1,000 to 3,000 cfs. The pace of the devastation was accelerated by occasional flood releases which resulted from keeping Powell Reservoir too full. In 1983 an unexpectedly large runoff due to late spring snowstorms in the Rockies threatened to overtop the dam. To avert this disaster, the dam operators opened the spillways and released more than 90,000 cfs, scouring out even more beaches. A similar but less severe situation the following year resulted in emergency releases of 50,000 cfs.

Water temperature was also changed radically by the dam. The intake structures for its turbines are located far below the surface of the reservoir, so the river in the Grand Canyon is now cold all year long.[2] *Water temperature at Lees Ferry ranges from roughly 45° in winter to 56° in summer. The water usually warms up about 4° to 6° by the time it reaches Diamond Creek 225 miles downstream.*

In 1989 the Department of the Interior yielded to years of public pressure by calling for a formal Environmental Impact Study (EIS) of Glen Canyon Dam operations. In 1991 the Department imposed an "interim flow regime" of moderated releases for the duration of the EIS process, and in late 1992 the federal Grand (cont.)

---

[1]The electricity generated at Glen Canyon Dam and other hydroelectric facilities in the federal Colorado River Storage Project is sold to preferred customers—publicly-owned utilities, agricultural irrigation districts, and rural electrical cooperatives—in 15 Western states at subsidized, bargain-basement prices that are only a fraction of market rates.

[2]Native fish have had enormous difficulty adapting to the year-round cold water, fluctuating flows, and loss of habitat. Two species, the bony-tailed chub and the Colorado River squawfish, are now extinct in the Grand Canyon, though they cling to life elsewhere in the Colorado River. Another fish unique to the Colorado and Little Colorado Rivers, the humpback chub, is on the endangered species list.

by flash floods. In just this fashion in 1966, Crystal changed overnight from a negligible drop into one of the canyon's most feared passages.

Aside from Lava Falls, the biggest rapids today are in the Upper Granite Gorge. (Two of the Canyon's most imposing rapids, Separation and Lava Cliff, are now under the waters of Mead Reservoir.) The drops are often quite substantial—15 or 20 vertical feet, sometimes more, over a hundred yards or so.[4]

Most rapids in the Canyon require only one or two maneuvers; a few are more complex. Kayakers will find the maneuvers simple enough, but they need a strong brace and a good roll. Big-water experience is essential for all boaters. Even lesser rapids contain holes strong enough to flip incautious boats. On the positive side, most of the whitewater is fairly straightforward fun.[5] Kayakers will revel in the marvelous surfing in rapid after rapid.

When dam releases fluctuate, boaters need to be aware of when the water rises and falls in the various parts of the Canyon—not just for running rapids, but also for deciding where to make camp and tie boats.[6] (In general, heavy rafts should be tied where sand drops off into deep water.) The **Mile Guide** includes information on typical flow patterns in various parts of the canyon *based on traditional peaking power releases.* However, future release patterns are uncertain (see sidebar on Glen Canyon Dam), so don't expect the river necessarily to behave as we say.

(cont.) *Canyon Protection Act gave the new flows temporary legal status. This regime will likely be modified after the EIS is finished in 1994. For now, maximum releases have been lowered to 20,000 cfs, while minimum releases have been increased to 8,000 during the day and 5,000 at night. Daily flows may not vary more than 5,000 to 8,000 cfs. Perhaps most important of all, changes in flows must now be gradual.*[3]

The EIS is considering long-term alternatives for Glen Canyon Dam operations ranging from traditional peaking power releases to steady flow schedules. Ultimately, more public pressure and perhaps further legislation may be necessary to ensure that future dam operations will protect, not degrade, the river corridor.[4] *The Grand Canyon is too important a part of our national heritage to be sacrificed to a power plant.*

[3] Sudden changes in flows, like those in peak power operations, undercut existing beaches and leave sand and other sediment trapped on the canyon walls where wind and later high flows disperse it. Gradual changes in flows, like those mandated by the interim flow regime, allow sediment a chance to settle at riverside in traditional beach locations downstream.

[4] The least damaging alternatives for the river corridor would eliminate peaking power operations at the dam. The same total amount of electricity would be produced, but at different times of the day: less during peak hours and more during off-peak hours than at present. Some utilities would have to buy more of their peak power on the open market, which would mean a small rise in the cost of their operations. Typical residential customers would probably see an increase of much less than a dollar a month in their electricity bills. These customers are now, and still would be, paying far less than the average American for their power.

For more information, contact Colorado River Studies Office (BuRec), 125 South State St., Salt Lake City, UT 84147; Grand Canyon Trust, Route 4, Box 718, Flagstaff, AZ 86001, (602) 774-7488; Environmental Defense Fund, 5655 College Ave., Suite 304, Oakland, CA 94618, (510) 658-8008; Friends of the River, 128 J St., Sacramento, CA 95814; (916) 442-3155.

[4] For years Lava Falls' overall drop was said to be 37', the greatest in the Canyon. Recent measurements have shown it to be only 13'—but it isn't any easier. Hance Rapid has the biggest overall drop, 30'.

[5] How good do you have to be to run the Grand Canyon? The following story, told by Fletcher Anderson and Ann Hopkinson in their *Rivers of the Southwest,* may not be the last word, but it does provide food for thought. In 1977 a raft on a commercial trip worked loose from its tether near Nankoweap (mile 52) and disappeared downstream. It was found floating in an eddy above Havasu Creek (mile 156), still right side up with all its gear in place, including some life jackets that weren't tied in. It is not known what routes the unmanned raft took at big rapids like Hance, Horn, Granite, and Crystal.

[6] In a section of the canyon where the water drops overnight, boaters may find their heavily-loaded rafts stranded high and dry 10' above the river. If the water rises at night, they may awaken to find an imprudently selected campsite about to be flooded and boats in danger of being swept away. (Both problems are especially keen in campsites just above rapids, where the level of the pool rises radically as the flow increases.) The problems are less acute under the interim flow regime (see sidebar on Glen Canyon Dam), which limits the volume and rate of changes in dam releases considerably more than in the past.

Mile by Mile Guide

Rapids for which no rating is shown are Class III or less. Geology notes are in italics. Information on flow patterns (times of day when the river rises or falls in various parts of the canyon) is based on traditional peaking power releases and is not accurate when other release schedules are in effect.

0 **PUT-IN** on the right bank at Lees Ferry near the mouth of the Paria River. With typical peaking power dam releases, water begins to rise in mid-morning and starts to drop in late afternoon.

The Chocolate Cliffs and Vermillion Cliffs downstream on the right, composed of younger rock formations than those found in the Grand Canyon, soon recede from view. Layers of sedimentary rock appear in rapid succession downstream—Kaibab and Toroweap Limestone at miles 1 and 1.7 and Coconino Sandstone near mile 4. They soon form a sheer cream-colored wall that rises quickly to imposing heights.

4.3 Navajo Bridge (U.S. 89A) arches more than 450' above the river. *About a mile downstream, Hermit Shale appears at river level and soon forms its characteristic red slope at the base of the upper wall.*

7.8 **BADGER (III+)**, the first sizeable rapid, at the mouths of Badger Canyon on the right and Jackass Creek on the left. More difficult at lower flows. Scout left. Large campsites on both banks below the rapid. Explorer Jacob Hamblin is said to have shot a badger somewhere up this creek.

11.2 **SOAP CREEK (III)**. Campsites above and below the rapid on the right. Here, Hamblin tried to boil the badger he shot upstream, but it was so fat that he ended up with a kettle of soap. About half a mile downstream on the left is a rock with an inscription marking the drowning of Frank Brown in Soap Creek Rapid during the 1889 Brown-Stanton railroad survey float trip. *The Supai Group's first layer, a light-colored sandstone, emerges just below the rapid and rises quickly to form jagged walls downstream. The canyon rim is now more than 1,000' above the river.*

17 **HOUSE ROCK (III+)**, at the mouth of Rider Canyon on the right. Moving to the right of the big boulder is more difficult at moderate flows (about 10,000–15,000 cfs). Scout on either side. Named not for the boulder but for House Rock Wash, which drains into Rider Canyon (good side hike). In this section of the canyon, water rises in mid- to late afternoon.

20.5 North Canyon on the right. Side hike. Rapids are more frequent for the next several miles, beginning with **21 MILE RAPID**, in a stretch known (with some exaggeration) as the **Roaring Twenties.**

Redwall Limestone appears near **23 MILE RAPID.** *Thinking the rock, polished smooth by the river, was marble, Powell gave the name Marble Canyon to the next stretch down to the Little Colorado. When it first appears, the limestone is gray; downstream, its spectacular cliffs take on their characteristic red hue due to staining by iron oxide washed down from the Hermit Shale and the Supai Group above.*

24 **24 MILE RAPID**, which appeared in 1989, is worth scouting below 10,000 cfs.

24.5 **24½ MILE RAPID (III+)**, at the mouth of a small wash entering from the left. Big hole is harder to miss at higher flows. Scout left. **25 MILE RAPID** just downstream can be a problem at low flows. In this section flows are typically low all day and rise in the early evening.

29 Shinumo Wash enters from the left, with **29 MILE RAPID** at its mouth. Short hike to spectacular Silver Grotto, a large cavern in the Redwall. "Shinumo" is a Paiute word for the Anasazi.

31.6 South Canyon (also called Paradise Canyon) on the right. Campsite, side hike to Anasazi ruins. Just downstream on the right is Vasey's Paradise (named for Powell's botanist), where lush plants, including watercress, monkey flowers, and **poison ivy**, flourish beneath the crystalline waters flowing from a spring in the limestone wall. *The top of the canyon wall—the same Kaibab Limestone exposed at river level a mile below Lees Ferry—is now 2,500' above the river.*

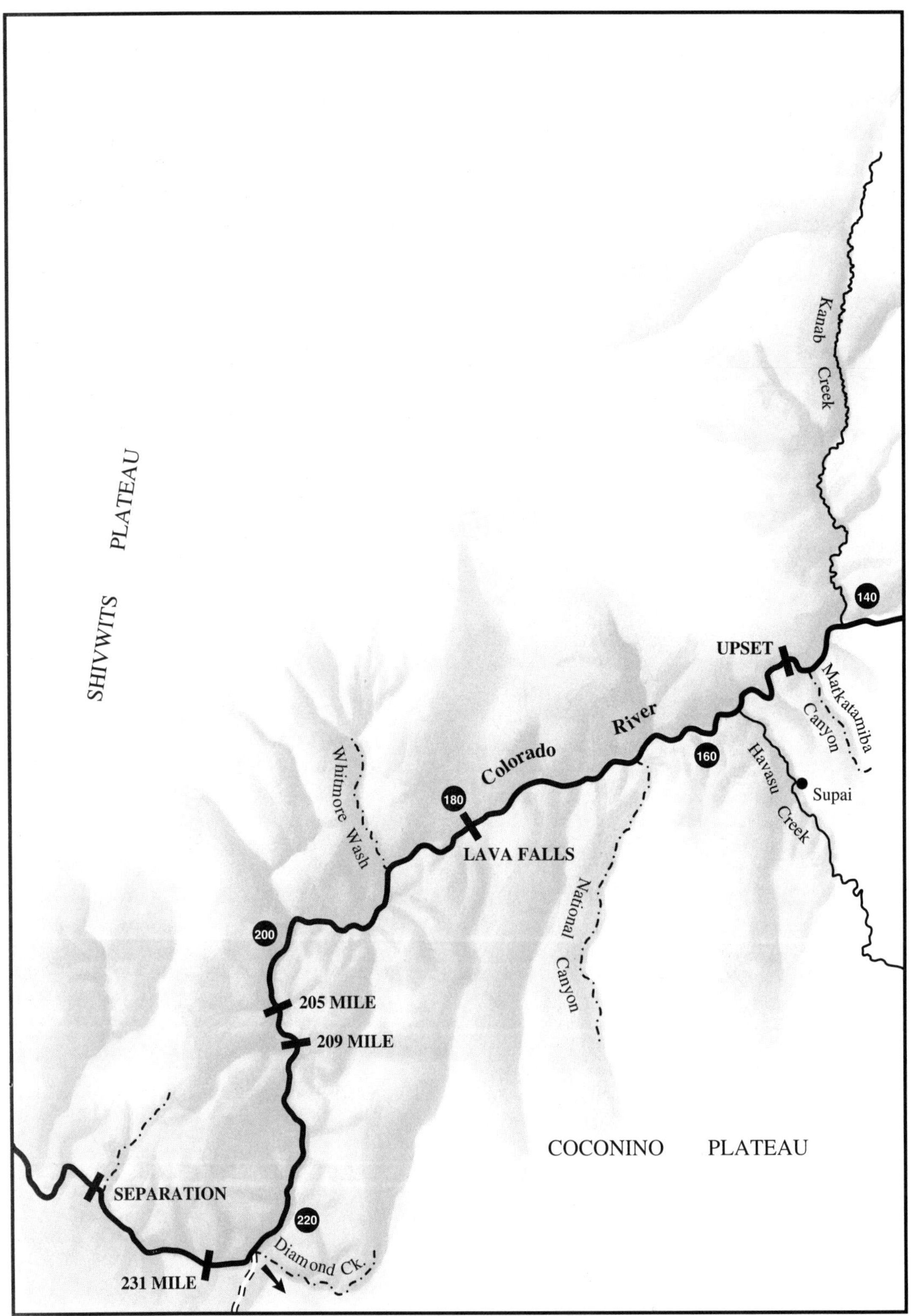

Grand Canyon (West)

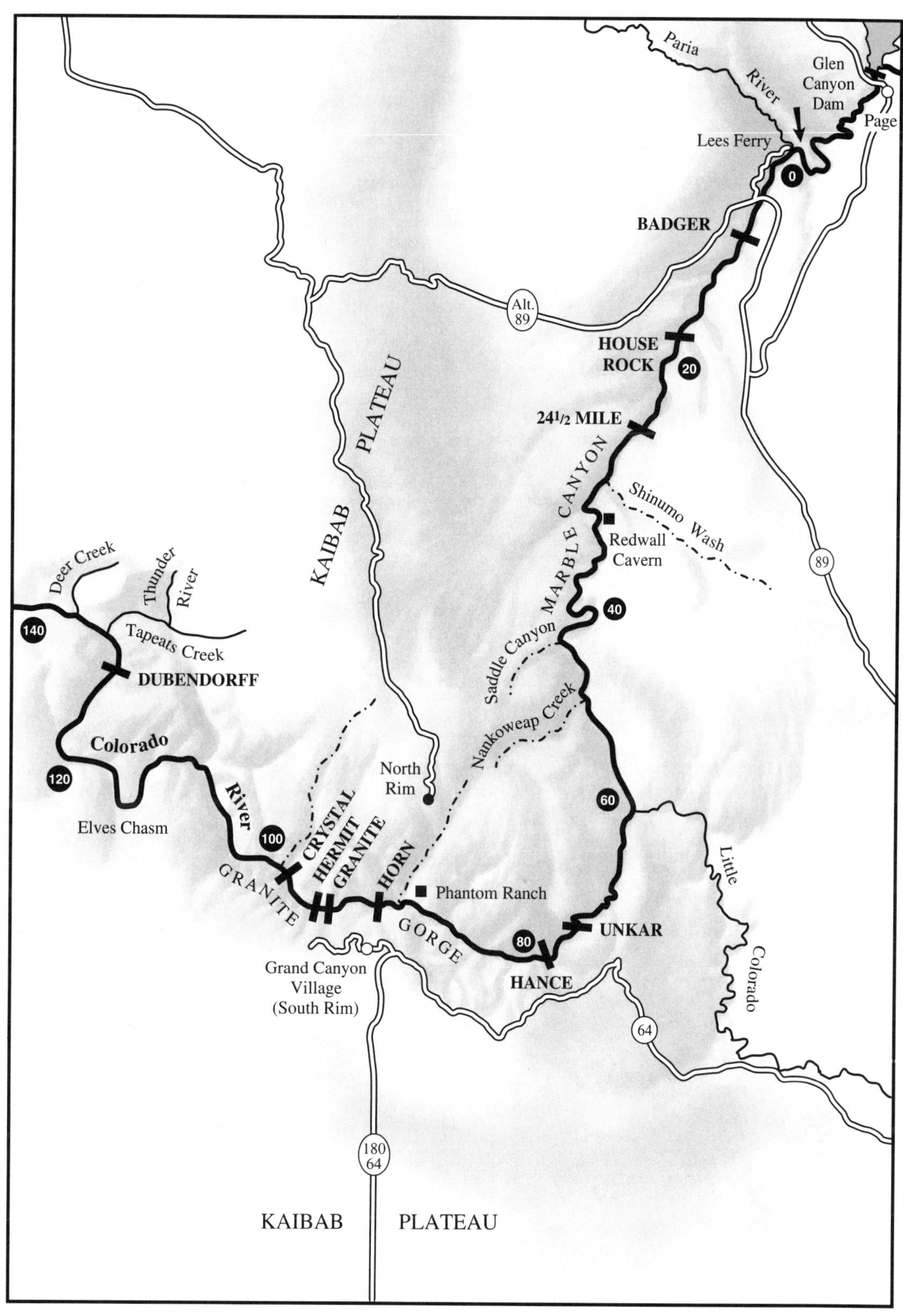

Grand Canyon (East)

33 Redwall Cavern on the left. This huge natural amphitheater is one of the most-photographed places in the Grand Canyon, and deservedly so. Great place for lunch or a rest stop, but no camping allowed. *The cavern was not carved by the river but is the biggest of the many "solution caverns" hollowed out by interaction of water and the almost pure calcium carbonate of the Redwall Limestone.*

34.8 Nautiloid Canyon on the left. Small campsite. Short hike reveals large fossils of nautiloids, ancient squid-like creatures, in the limestone of the creek bed. *Muav Limestone emerges about a mile upstream.*

39 Site of Marble Canyon Dam, proposed by the Bureau of Reclamation in 1950 (see essay) and marked by test holes drilled in the walls. Buck Farm Canyon (side hike) is a mile downstream on the right. *Temple Butte Limestone, which appears near mile 38, can sometimes be seen beneath the Redwall and above the Muav Limestone in this stretch.*

43 Anasazi wooden pole bridge high above the right bank. (The fragile site is closed to visitors.) Campsites just downstream on the left. The river flows through a great horseshoe bend around spectacular Point Hansborough. **PRESIDENT HARDING RAPID,** near the apex of the curve, features a giant boulder in midstream. Many campsites in this stretch.

47 Saddle Canyon on the right. Campsite, side hike.

52 Nankoweap Canyon on the right. Several campsites along the right bank. One of the Grand Canyon's best-known side hikes leads to Anasazi granaries high above the river. Many more archaeological sites farther up Nankoweap Canyon. *By now the canyon has begun to open up. Redwall Limestone forms the towering walls of the inner gorge, but the north rim is about 7 miles from the river while the south rim is only half a mile away. Bright Angel Shale appears at river level a couple of miles upstream. This is the easily eroded tan, olive, and purple formation that, farther downstream, makes up the sprawling slopes of the Tonto Platform above the Granite Gorge.*

56 **KWAGUNT (III)**, at the mouth of Kwagunt Creek, which enters from the right. Campsite, side hike. The many large campsites in the next few miles are much sought after by boating parties who want to hike the Little Colorado the next day. *The north rim is more than a mile above the river. Tapeats Sandstone emerges about 3 miles downstream.*

61.5 Little Colorado River enters on the left. Eddy up above its mouth. No camping. No fishing in the Little Colorado or near its mouth in the main river.

Vista of Chuar Butte across the Colorado. Long hike up the Little Colorado, whose water—if upstream rains haven't muddied it—is a marvelous turquoise. Pink-hued travertine in the streambed adds more magic to the sight. The water, rich in calcium carbonate, is not recommended for drinking. After a big storm the Little Colorado can carry an awesome volume of thick, brown water. Several miles up the right bank is the sacred Hopi site Sipapu, a spring atop a huge travertine dome; Hopi belief holds that mankind emerged from this fissure in the rock. The tribe asks visitors not to disturb this site.

Many campsites downstream on the Colorado. The sacred Hopi salt mines are on the left bank near mile 64; no stopping allowed. The river's course turns toward the southwest.

65.4 Lava Canyon on the right. Campsites on the right above **LAVA CANYON (CHUAR) RAPID** and on the left below it, near the site of Seth Tanner's pioneer-era mine. He helped rebuild an old Indian trail, now called the Tanner Trail, leading from the south rim to the mouth of Tanner Canyon, 4 miles downstream on the left. *The Great Unconformity first appears a couple of miles upstream, but the best views come in the next three miles as the river passes through Furnace Flats. The tilted red strata beneath the unconformity are the easily eroded shales and siltstones of the Dox Formation, part of the Grand Canyon Series (also called the Grand Canyon Supergroup); they are some 600 million* *years older than the horizontal Tapeats Sandstone strata just above. Downstream the south rim, capped by steep cliffs called the Palisades of the Desert, recedes from the river.*

70.8 Cardenas Creek on the left, named for one of Coronado's lieutenants who explored the south rim near here in 1540. Side hike leads high above the left bank to ruins of an Anasazi fort atop the bluff overlooking Unkar Rapid.

72.4 **UNKAR (III+).** A boulder-strewn pitch (more difficult at lower flows) where the river swings right around the broad delta at the mouth of Unkar Creek on the right. Campsites on both banks above the rapid. Site of the largest known Anasazi settlement in the Canyon, dating back to around 950 A.D. Ruins at the base of the bluff on the north side of the creek. *A couple of miles downstream, light-colored Shinumo Quartzite, the most resistant rock in the Grand Canyon, appears at river level. The red-orange Hakatai Shale appears a mile beyond that.* **NEVILLS RAPID,** 3 miles below Unkar, has big pourovers or holes in the center. In this stretch the water typically rises early in the morning and begins to drop late in the afternoon.

76.5 **HANCE (IV+)**, at the mouth of Red Canyon on the left. A long, wide, complex boulder slalom. Scout either side. Routes vary with the flow. At higher flows many boaters run left to avoid the huge midstream holes at the bottom. Miner and tour guide John Hance, the first permanent white inhabitant of the Grand Canyon, built the Old Hance and Red Canyon (New Hance) Trails from the south rim to the river.

At Hance, the first of the big rapids, the Colorado turns west-northwest into the **Upper Granite Gorge.** Campsite on the left above the rapid. Campsites are scarce in the gorge. *A 1.1 billion-year-old basaltic dike intrudes at a sharp angle into the overlying Hakatai Shale on the right bank just above the rapid. Black Vishnu Schist and pink Zoroaster Granite, among the Canyon's oldest rocks, appear downstream and soon form the walls of the narrow V-shaped gorge.*

78.6 **SOCKDOLAGER (IV)**, at the mouth of Hance Creek on the left, less than half a mile downstream from a sharp right bend. Named by the second Powell expedition with a slang term meaning a wallop or hard blow. That is just what boats get if they follow the tongue into the big, staggered V-waves that wait left of center. Difficult scout on the right.

81.5 **GRAPEVINE (III+)**, at the mouth of Grapevine Creek, which enters from the left. Most of the trouble is on the left. More difficult at lower flows. Big, popular campsite above the rapid is the last good site for miles. Don't plan on finding it vacant late in the day.

84.1 Clear Creek enters on the right. Pretty side hike ultimately leads to Chevaya Falls, 12 miles up the creek. **ZOROASTER RAPID,** half a mile downstream on the right, is a problem only at low flows. Small campsite across the river. *Good view of Zoroaster Granite at river level.* In this part of the canyon, the water typically starts to drop in the early evening.

85.8 Cremation Creek on the left. Two small campsites about a mile downstream on the left are the last above Phantom Ranch and should be used only by parties planning to exchange personnel the next day.

87.8 Bright Angel Canyon on the right. Anasazi ruins just upstream on river right near Kaibab Bridge (painted black), where the Kaibab Trail crosses the river. Short hike up Bright Angel Canyon leads to Phantom Ranch. Food, supplies, phone, showers, rooms by advance reservation, post office (ask for hand canceling with the Phantom Ranch postmark), hikes or mule rides to and from the south rim. No camping for boating parties. Bright Angel Bridge (painted silver) crosses the Colorado to Bright Angel Trail, which leads 9.5 miles up to Grand Canyon Village on the south rim. *The V-shaped Granite Gorge is now 1,500' deep.*

90.2 **HORN (IV+)**, at the mouth of Horn Creek on the left. A short, sharp drop guarded by horn rocks on either side. When flows are high enough to cover the left horn, many boaters run directly over it. One of the Canyon's most difficult rapids at low flows, when more rocks are exposed and a big hole blocks the bottom right. Scout either side.

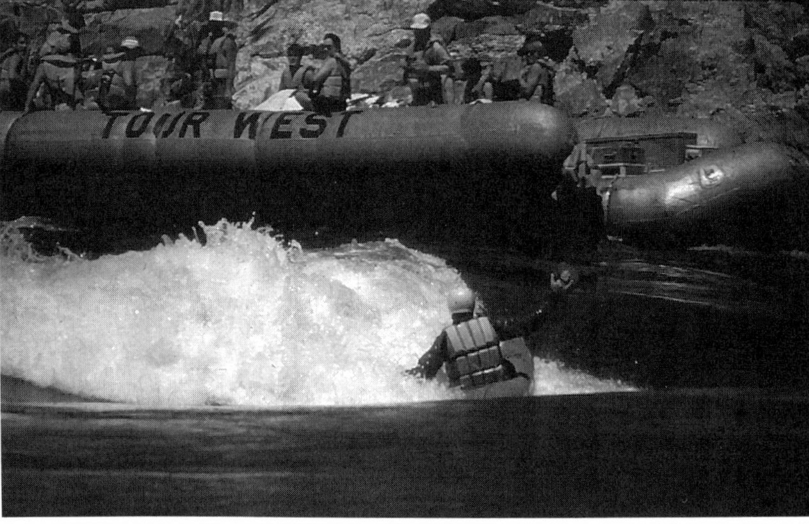

Hand-paddling kayaker meets motor rig at Elves Chasm *Curt Smith*

93.4 **GRANITE** (IV+), at the mouth of Monument Creek on the left. A rough pitch curving slightly left, with powerful laterals coming off the right wall. If possible, stay left of the island at the bottom. Scout left. Campsite above the rapid; side hike leads 3 miles to the spire for which Monument Creek is named.

95 **HERMIT** (III), at the mouth of Hermit Creek on the left. Huge roller-coaster waves provide one of the most enjoyable rides on the run, but they will flip poorly-handled boats. Small campsites on each bank a mile downstream. The rapid and creek are named for "the hermit," prospector Louis Boucher, who lived in the canyon for years before 1912.

98 **CRYSTAL** (IV+), at the mouths of Crystal Creek on the right and Slate Creek on the left, is the climax of the run through the Granite Gorge. Scout right. A smooth tongue leads into big standing waves and a violent hole. The usual run is to the right except at lower flows, when some boaters run left. Crystal is no place for a swim; the rapid continues for several hundred rough, rocky yards, splitting around a boulder-strewn gravel bar.

This was an unimportant rapid until a flash flood on Crystal Creek in December 1966 washed big boulders into the river channel. Emergency dam releases in 1983 and 1984 altered it somewhat, making it a little easier at low and moderate flows and even more difficult at high flows. Some say that above 25,000 cfs Crystal is the toughest rapid in the Canyon.

Campsite on the right above the rapid; side hike. Rapids become easier after Crystal. In this part of the canyon, the water starts to drop in the evening.

101.2 **SAPPHIRE** (III+), which has big waves at high flows, is one of the "Jewel" rapids. **AGATE** is about a mile upstream, **TURQUOISE** is 3/4 mile downstream, **RUBY** (III+) is about half a mile downstream from **104 MILE RAPID**, and **SERPENTINE**, at mile 106, has a huge hole at the upper right. It is prudent to scout these rapids, especially at low water. *Much more granite in the canyon walls in this stretch.*

107.7 **BASS RAPID** at the mouth of Hotauta Canyon on the right, just downstream from Bass Canyon on the left (small campsite). Larger campsite on the right about half a mile downstream. Few campsites between miles 109 and 120.

In the 1880's prospector William Bass built a trail to the river from his tourist camp on the south rim to another camp in the Shinumo Creek drainage downstream on the right (no camping at the mouth). **WALTENBERG RAPID** (III+) at mile 112.2 should be scouted from the right at low water. It was named for a sometime partner of Bass.

Some of the Grand Canyon Series, including its oldest formation, Bass Limestone, is exposed at river level from miles 107 to 110. The walls of schist and granite grow ever lower until the river leaves the Upper Gran-

ite Gorge around mile 115.5, and Tapeats Sandstone descends to river level.

116.5 Elves Chasm (left bank), a refreshing oasis where moss and ferns luxuriate in the sparkling cascades of Royal Arch Creek. A clamber up the right bank of the creek leads to another waterfall. Downstream the river passes through the monumental Stephen and Conquistador Aisles, familiar from countless postcards. Campsites become more plentiful beginning just above Blacktail Canyon (mile 120; side hike). In this stretch the water starts to rise before noon. *Below mile 122 Bright Angel Shale descends to river level.*

125 **FOSSIL RAPID** is at the mouth of Fossil Canyon on the left. Side hike. Few campsites from here to mile 131. *Not far downstream, dark schist reappears and the river enters the* ***Middle Granite Gorge.*** At mile 129, **SPECTER (III+)** is worth scouting (from the left) at low flows.

130.5 **BEDROCK (III+)**, at the mouth of Bedrock Canyon on the right. The river splits around a house-sized slab of rock. More difficult at lower flows. Recommended route is to the right; the left-side run is blind and narrow. Small campsite half a mile downstream on the right. In this stretch the water typically rises in the early afternoon.

131.8 **DUBENDORFF (IV)**, at the mouth of Galloway Canyon on the right. A long boulder slalom around a gradual left curve. More difficult at low flows. Scout from either bank. Side canyon is named for legendary boatman "Nat" Galloway. Rapid is named for Galloway's companion who flipped here in 1909. Campsite just downstream on the right, below the mouth of Stone Creek; short hike up the creek to a lovely waterfall. Downstream the Colorado's general course changes from northwest to west-southwest.

133.8 Tapeats Creek, the biggest tributary originating within the Grand Canyon, enters on the right. Campsites above and below the mouth of the creek and **TAPEATS RAPID.** Side hike is one of the Canyon's best. The trail begins with a potentially dangerous scramble up a steep cliff on the right (west) bank of the creek, then crosses the creek twice. About 4 miles from the mouth, a steep trail heads left up the right bank of the short, spectacular Thunder River, a tributary of Tapeats Creek which cascades almost straight down from Thunder Spring in the limestone wall. Just across the top of the saddle near Thunder Spring, a trail leads through Surprise Valley and down Deer Creek. Some boaters arrange to make this hike, even camping overnight, and have their companions pick them up at the mouth of Deer Creek. *Note:* Permit necessary to camp in Tapeats side canyon or at Thunder River. (See **Camping.**)

136.2 Deer Creek enters on the right. Short hike to a spectacular, much-photographed waterfall. (Watch for **poison ivy.**) No camping. Several campsites on the left bank of the Colorado in this stretch. *Granite Narrows, which includes the river's narrowest point (variously estimated at 35' to 76'), begins upstream at mile 135 and ends below mile 138, where Tapeats Sandstone appears at river level. The gentle slopes of the Esplanade (part of the Supai Group) atop the Redwall Limestone widen to as much as 3 miles.*

143.5 Kanab Creek, a major tributary, enters on the right. Good, long side hike. Powell ended his second expedition here. "Kanab" is a Paiute word for willow.

145.5 Olo Canyon on the left. Remarkable sight, but the hike quickly becomes a dangerous rope-assisted climb.

148 Matkatamiba Canyon on the left. Memorable wet-footed side hike and clamber up the sinuous curves of the limestone canyon. Small campsite downstream on the left where the river turns sharply right. *The sheer wall on river left is over 2,000' high.*

149.8 **UPSET (IV)**, at the mouth of 150 Mile Canyon on the right, just after a sharp left bend. Long, wide, rocky pitch requires maneuvering around boulders and holes. Big hole at bottom right. Tougher at low flows. Usually scouted from the right, but scout left for the left-side run at flows up to 10,000 cfs. Named for a flip by head boatman Emery Kolb on the 1923 U.S.

Geological Survey expedition. Campsites are scarce for the next 15 miles or so.

156.8 Havasu Creek, a major tributary, enters on the left. The name means "blue-green waters," but don't drink the creek water. Great side hike, although a flash flood in 1990 washed away many of the trees along the creek. No camping at the creek mouth; competition is keen for small campsites like "Last Chance" and "Last Last Chance" on the right about a half mile and a quarter mile upstream, respectively.

Havasupai Reservation begins at Beaver Falls, 4 miles up the creek. Spectacular Mooney Falls is 3 miles farther. The trail leads 2.5 more miles to Supai Village, the principal Havasupai settlement, then 7 miles to the south rim. Some boaters contact the reservation, (602) 448-2121, months in advance of their float trips to reserve campsites above Mooney Falls, then turn this day hike into an overnighter. (No camping below Mooney.)

Few campsites downstream on the Colorado for the next 10 miles. Left bank is Hualapai Indian Reservation beginning at mile 164.7, just downstream from Tuckup Canyon on the right. In this stretch the river is typically low in the morning and rises in the afternoon.

166.5 National Canyon on the left. Two campsites; side hike. Another campsite and side hike at Fern Glen Canyon 1.5 miles downstream on the right. Campsites are more frequent downstream.

178 Vulcan's Forge (also called Vulcan's Anvil), a huge neck of basalt in the river, announces that Lava Falls is not far downstream. Boaters often touch it for luck. *The rock is the solid core of a volcano that erupted through a vent in the riverbed. The million-year-old Lava Cascades that flowed from volcanos on the Esplanade and filled Toroweap Canyon can be seen downstream on the right. Evidence of other lava flows on both sides. Lava flows extend 75 miles downstream. These lava flows repeatedly dammed the river, flooding the Canyon to a depth of more than 1,000' and creating natural lakes that reached upstream beyond present Glen Canyon Dam. Vulcan's Throne, one of the more recent volcanos, perches on the very rim of the inner gorge (right bank).*

179.3 LAVA FALLS (V). The most famous rapid in the Canyon. **Recognition:** Horizon line across the river; mouth of Prospect Canyon (campsite) on the left; Lava Cascades on the right. Stop well upstream to scout via right-bank trail. **The rapid:** A churning river-wide reversal is broken only on the right, where huge V-waves lead to an exploding hole beside a looming black lava boulder. The right side is the standard run and at lower flows, the only run. At medium and high flows sneak routes can be found down the far left. (A nervy middle run is sometimes used by larger rafts at moderate flows: boats follow a bubble line on the inside right of the tongue to "The Slot," marked by a spouting rooster tail. If all goes well, they squirt through the reversal right side up.) Lava is a bad place to swim; below the big drop the rapid continues for another 150 rough yards. In this stretch the river is typically low in the morning and rises in the late afternoon.

The untrained mind wants to accept Powell's view of the rapid's genesis, but geologists now say that Lava Falls is not a result of the huge lava flows that dammed the river here a million years ago; the Colorado has long since cut through those rocks. Like all Grand Canyon rapids, it is caused by debris washed into the river channel from a side canyon—in this case, Prospect Canyon.

No more big rapids for the next 25 miles. The Colorado flows through more open country; both rims of the canyon are well back from the river. Many campsites. *Striking columnar basalt formations are evidence of old lava flows.*

188 Whitmore Wash, a lava-filled canyon similar to Toroweap, on the right. Large campsite, side hike. Many guests on commercial floats end their trips just upstream, flying out on helicopters from the helipad on the left bank. There is a one-mile hike up the Whitmore Trail on the right bank opposite the helipad.

198.5 Parashant Wash on the right. Large campsite, side hike. The general course of the river changes to southerly. Boaters can finish fast from here on because the water is typically high most of the day.

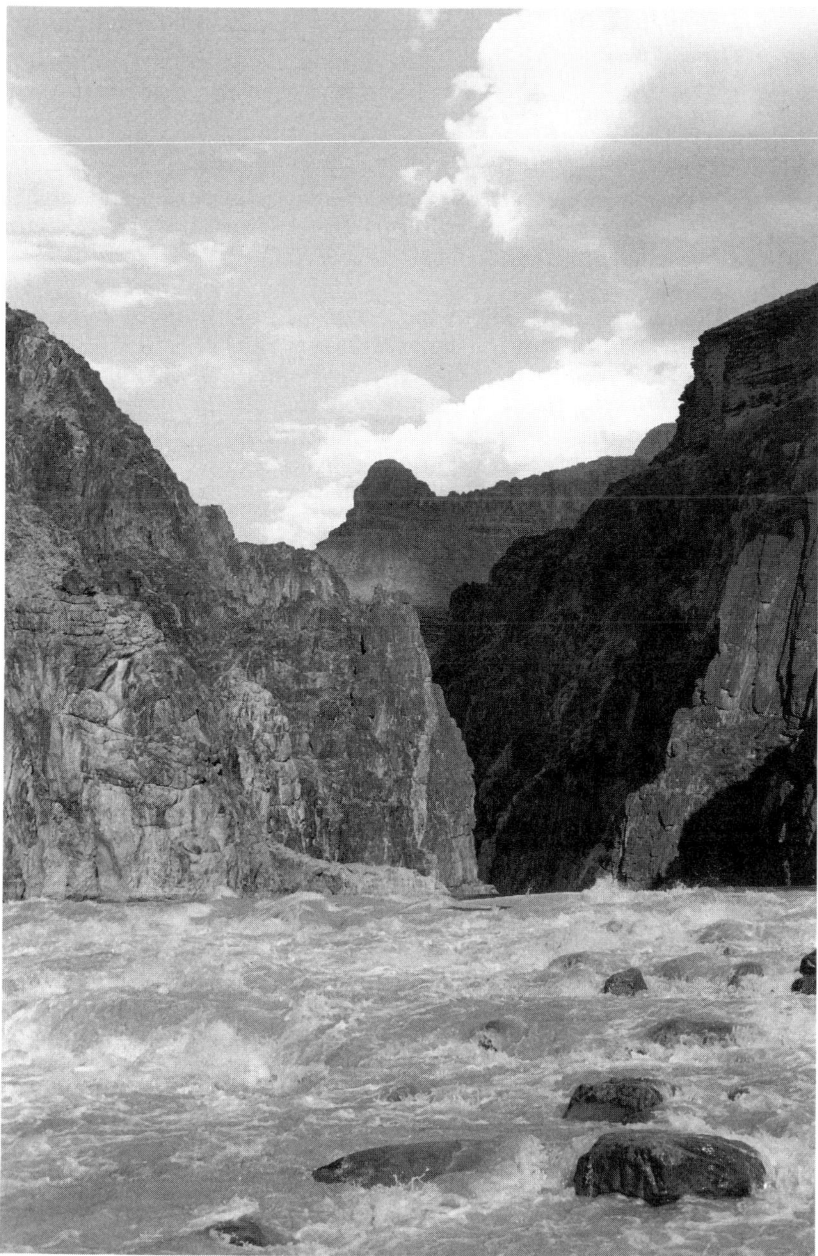

Lava Falls *Don Briggs*

right. A big hole lurks at the bottom of the tongue; most try to skirt it on the left.

212.2 **212 MILE RAPID,** a sharp drop at low flows, is about 3/4 mile below the mouth of Fall Canyon, which enters from the right. Less than a mile downstream at the left edge of the river is Pumpkin Spring, a huge travertine bowl formed by calcium carbonate precipitating from the bitter spring water. *In the canyon walls Tapeats Sandstone has descended to river level.*

215.6 Three Springs Canyon on the left. Just downstream is the **Lower Granite Gorge.**

217.3 **217 MILE RAPID (III).** Big waves at top.

220.4 Granite Spring Canyon on the left, just downstream from 220 Mile Canyon on the right. Soon the prominent pyramid of Diamond Peak (left bank) comes into view.

205.4 **205 MILE RAPID (III+),** also called **Kolb Rapid** in honor of early Canyon boatman Emery Kolb. Watch for a big hole, and avoid the right wall at the bottom.

209 **209 MILE RAPID (III),** at the mouths of 209 Mile Canyon on the right and Granite Park Canyon on the left. The river splits around a gravel bar, with most of the current—and most boats—going

225.5 **RIVER ACCESS** at Diamond Creek on the left. Eddy up above **DIAMOND CREEK RAPID.** Take-out fee (see **Permits**). A rough dirt road leads 22 miles up Diamond Creek and Peach Springs Wash to U.S. 66. Most parties take out here, but more of the Grand Canyon lies downstream and is definitely worth seeing. However, boats will usually have to negotiate many miles of flatwater to reach the next take-out at Pierce Ferry (mile 280); arranging to be towed out by a motorboat is advisable (see **Logistics**). Few campsites in the next 10 miles. Not far downstream, the Colorado starts its long right-hand curve around the Shivwits Plateau.

229 Travertine Canyon on the left. *Large travertine deposits along the wall of the side canyon. Below its cap of Tapeats Sandstone, the Lower Granite Gorge is over 1,000' deep in this stretch.* The course of the river is now westward. About 1.5 miles downstream on the left, Travertine Falls, fed by a bitter spring, is visible from the river. **231 MILE RAPID,** a little farther downstream, is more difficult at lower flows. Scout **232 MILE RAPID** at low water; the current pushes boats toward "The Fingers," protruding rocks on the right.

235.2 Mouth of Bridge Canyon on the left. Campsite. The river is now heading generally northwest. When Mead Reservoir is full to the brim, it extends this far upriver, though the normal high-water mark is a couple of miles downstream. When the reservoir is very low, the current continues beyond Pierce Ferry. Rapids from here on, including **BRIDGE CANYON,** have been silted up. Gneiss Canyon is on the left a mile downstream. Site of proposed Hualapai Dam (see essay) is at mile 237.

239.6 Separation Canyon on the right. Site of **SEPARATION RAPID,** where three of Powell's crew left his expedition and hiked up the side canyon to the rim, apparently to meet their deaths at the hands of Indians. A bronze plaque commemorates the incident.

248.3 Surprise Canyon on the right.

259.5 Burnt Spring Canyon on the right. Quartermaster Canyon on the left just downstream.

266.2 Bat Cave on the right. Costly attempt to mine it for guano in the late 1950's failed. Towers high on the south rim anchored a cable used to transport the guano out of the Canyon.

273.3 Hualapai Reservation (left bank) ends.

276 Grand Wash Cliffs mark the western end of the Grand Canyon and the Colorado Plateau and the beginning of the Basin and Range country. End of Grand Canyon National Park and beginning of Lake Mead National Recreation Area. Before Hoover Dam was built, this was the place where the Colorado emptied onto the desert floor. Downstream, the drowned river's path curves left (west) and the reservoir waters widen.

280 **TAKE-OUT** on the left at Pierce Ferry, the first sign of civilization since Phantom Ranch. A 52-mile road leads southwest to U.S. 93 between Las Vegas and Kingman, Arizona. When the reservoir is low, Pierce Ferry turns into mud flats, and most parties take out at South Cove, 16 miles downstream on the left.

"A hole big enough to swallow a school bus." We've all heard that. But on this day in June 1983, the hole at Crystal Rapid was big enough to gulp down two or three school buses at once.

We'd been scouting Crystal for half an hour. Some other guides had been staring at it even longer. By Park Service mandate, all the passengers on commercial rowing trips, including ours, had to walk around the rapid. Now, while those with cameras busily snapped away at the huge exploding hole, we boatmen jostled each other on a high promontory to get a clear view.

No one standing on that crumbling cliff had ever seen the Colorado flowing at 100,000 cfs. No one in history had ever seen the new Crystal Rapid (b. 1966) at such a flow. The hydraulic jump was a good 20' high. All this was because Glen Canyon Dam operators had allowed Powell Reservoir to fill before inflow from the Colorado had peaked. Now the release was an official 97,300 cfs. Add some water from tributaries and the total flow may have reached six figures.

But our problem wasn't arithmetic, it was physics. Or hydrodynamics. Even aesthetics. In other words, living through this run, staying right side up, and—if possible—looking good while doing it.

We watched as the first group of guides filed back to their orange 18' Rogue River rafts and pushed off. They headed for the far right and crashed down a roaring sluice over boulders that normally would have been high and dry a good stone's throw from the river's edge. Tamarisk trees bent forward under the rafts, then snapped back into place. The last boat went even farther right, uprooted a tamarisk, and then slammed to a dead stop atop a boulder with too little water flowing over it. RIIIIP... the floor parted as if a Stephen King demon were slicing it with a switchblade from the nether world. Still, all the boats had avoided that monstrous hole.

Stomachs churning, we returned to our rafts, coiled our bowlines, gave each other the "thumbs-up" signal, and rowed out into the river—but not far. We quickly crossed the right edge of the tongue and rowed up Crystal Creek, threading our way through the willows. Finally, we dropped over the boulder field and shot toward the biggest hole in North America.

Oddly enough, this run had seemed harder two weeks earlier at "only" 70,000 cfs. Now my yellow 18' Domar felt light without its passengers, and the route seemed as wide as an L.A. freeway. My raft accelerated as it bumped and ground down the pourovers. The eater of school buses loomed ever closer. Suddenly my boat hit slack water, and I pulled hard right into a genuine eddy rocked by heavy surf.

I was happy. My passengers were waiting on the shore. Everyone else made the eddy, and we celebrated by having lunch—and a beer—right on the spot while the other trip's crew repaired the floor of their damaged raft. We even pounded our chests a bit. It would be two more weeks before we had to face Crystal again.

Both trips pushed off at the same time, dotting the river with orange and yellow boats. I stayed right of center. The waves in Lower Crystal were huge. Just upstream of where "Thank God Eddy" normally gives haven to the successful, I saw a huge wave. We were headed straight for it. "Hold on," I yelled, but I was really thinking "No sweat" as we climbed this mountain of green water.

Abruptly, as we reached the crest, a hydraulic surge from the right shore turned us over in the blink of an eye. The boat had neither stalled nor pivoted, and it had been pointed directly into the wave. Yet here it was flipping sideways. "What?" I asked myself as we went over. "How could—" Then I was in the water.

When I fought to the surface and started counting heads, I saw only two, and I forgot all about figuring out why we had flipped. This was every guide's nightmare: the missing passenger (a 14-year-old) must be caught under the boat, possibly trapped by a rope or a strap. I felt for my knife and reached under the boat for a line to haul myself underneath. Instead, I felt an arm. I grabbed it and yanked its owner out into the air and sunlight. He sputtered, looked around, and then grinned idiotically. So did I.

All of us clambered onto the floor of my flipped raft. Bruce Helin rowed up to us. He had never looked so good. My passengers climbed aboard his raft—and then he rowed away, calling "See ya" with a smile. Towing my upside-down boat into an eddy turned out to be a major pain, even with two rafts trying to control it. Alistair Bleifuss and Brian Dierker, each in his own raft, threw me lines and fought the monster current for two or three miles before they managed to haul me into an eddy below Agate Rapid. Then it took a dozen of us to flip my boat back over. As it turned out, I lost only a bailing bucket—and a lot of my cockiness.

—Michael P. Ghiglieri

Dolores River

Bradfield Bridge to Colorado River Confluence

1. Dolores Canyon: Bradfield Bridge (6,460') to Slick Rock (5,465').
III4; 47 miles; 21 ft./mi.

2. Little Glen and Slick Rock Canyons: Slick Rock to Bedrock (4,950').
III-; 50 miles; 10 ft./mi.

3. Paradox and Mesa Canyons: Bedrock to Gateway (4,550').
III, II; 45 miles; 9 ft./mi.

4. Gateway Canyon: Gateway to Colorado River Confluence (4,090').
II+4; 33 miles; 14 ft./mi.

Total Length: 175 miles.

Drainage Area: 2,024 sq. mi. at Bedrock (mile 97); 4,580 sq. mi. near mouth.

Average Annual Discharge: 360,000 af at Bedrock.

Season: Variable; depends on releases from McPhee Dam. Under current management there may be up to 6 weeks of boatable releases in an average year at any time from mid-April to mid-June. In dry years there will likely be no boatable releases; in wet years they may continue to early July. For information call the Bureau of Reclamation, Cortez Project Office, (303) 565-0500 or 565-0531. The lower Dolores (Mesa and Gateway Canyons) has a longer, more reliable season thanks to the added flow of the San Miguel River.

Recommended Levels: 1,000–4,000 cfs.

Flow Information: BLM tape, (303) 882-7600; BuRec, (303) 656-0500; NWS tape, (801) 539-1311 (flows at Bedrock and Cisco). WaterTalk, (303) 691-4393 7*5* (flow below McPhee). Use the Cisco reading to judge flows in Mesa and Gateway canyons.

Permits: Not currently required except on Run 4 (Gateway Canyon). No use limits on any run. Sign in to document use.

Managing Agency: *Runs 1 & 2:* BLM, San Juan RA, 701 Camino del Rio, Durango, CO 81301; (303) 247-4082; *Runs 3 & 4:* BLM, 764 Horizon Dr., Grand Junction, CO 81501; (303) 243-6552. *Run 4:* BLM, Grand RA, 885 S. Sand Flats Rd., Moab, UT 84532; (801) 259-4421.

Commercial Raft Trips: Yes. Contact the managing agency for a list of outfitters.

Land Ownership: *Runs 1 & 2:* Mostly public. *Runs 3 & 4:* Mixed public and private.

Scenery: Excellent. Sandstone canyons—forested at first, slickrock later.

Solitude: Excellent except in the stretch followed by the highway (most of Run 3 and beginning of Run 4).

Wilderness: *Runs 1 & 2:* Yes. *Run 3*: No. *Run 4:* Mostly (some ranches).

Water: Silty and undrinkable. Purify water from side streams. Drinking water available at Bradfield put-in.

Camping: Varies. Excellent on Run 1, good on Run 2. Camping allowed at Bradfield put-in.

Side Hikes: Many, especially Bull and Spring Canyons (see below).

Side Excursions: Dolores Canyon Overlook (east of Dove Creek on Colorado 502).

Guides and References:

- DeVries and Maurer, *Dolores River Guide.*
- Wheat, *Floater's Guide to Colorado.*
- Nichols, *River Runners' Guide to Utah.*

Maps:

- **USGS 7.5':** *Run 1:* Trimble Point, Yellow Jacket, Doe Canyon, The Glade, Secret Canyon, Joe Davis Hill, Hamm Canyon, Horse Range Mesa. *Run 2:* Horse Range Mesa, Hamm Canyon, Anderson Mesa, Paradox. *Run 3:* Paradox, Davis Mesa, Red Canyon, Roc Creek, Juanita Arch, Gateway. *Run 4:* Gateway, Dolores Point North, Steamboat Mesa, Fisher Valley, Blue Chief Mesa, Dewey.
- **USGS 1:100:** *Dove Creek, Nucla, Delta, Moab.*
- **USFS:** *San Juan NF* covers to mile 32.
- **AAA:** *Indian Country* shows roads for Runs 1 & 2.

Logistics: *Runs 1 & 2:* To reach the **put-in near Bradfield Bridge**, turn east off U.S. 666 onto Colorado 505 just north of Pleasant View, about 20 miles northwest of Cortez in the southwestern corner of Colorado. Drive some 6 miles to the river and launch at Bradfield Recreation Site, several hundred yards downstream from the bridge on the left bank. The **Mountain Sheep Point access,** located on the left bank at river mile

19 near the Dove Creek Pumping Station, is reached via a rough dirt road off U.S. 666 at Dove Creek. The **Slick Rock access** (river mile 47) is on the right bank above the Colorado 141 bridge over the Dolores between the towns of Dove Creek and Naturita (private access, no parking; pay to park at the cafe west of the bridge).

The **Gypsum Valley access,** on the right bank at mile 61, is reached by turning off Colorado 141 onto unpaved Road 20R, then driving some 11 miles to the river. The **Bedrock access** (mile 97) is on the left bank about a half mile upstream from where Colorado 90 crosses the Dolores some 20 miles west of Naturita. To reach the access, turn south on a dirt road about 1/4 mile west of the highway bridge.

Run 3: Colorado 141 follows the Dolores for most of this run, providing several access points. *Run 4:* The **Gateway access** (mile 142) is near the Highway 141 bridge at the town of Gateway, Colorado. The final access is at **Dewey Bridge** (Utah 128) on the Colorado River south of Cisco, Utah, a couple of miles downstream from the Dolores confluence. There are several alternate shuttle routes for Run 4—one long and paved, two shorter and dirt. Check with the BLM for directions and road conditions.

Here is an exquisite river devastated only a few years ago by the Bureau of Reclamation's McPhee Dam. Before the dam was completed in 1984, the Dolores[1] was one of the longest undammed rivers in the lower 48 states and one of the finest runs in the Canyon Country. In 1982 it was Colorado's fourth most popular river, and use was increasing rapidly. If not for the dam, the Dolores would today be one of the Canyon Country's longest and most popular floats.

McPhee Reservoir drowned a lovely stretch of the river so that diversions to the adjacent San Juan basin could be dramatically increased. Today the Dolores loses an average of some 100,000 acre-feet each year to irrigation withdrawals and trans-basin diversions.[2]

The result? Below the dam the Dolores is a shadow of its former self, reduced to a trickle and only briefly rising to boatable levels for much of its length. Yet the Dolores is not entirely dead. Its canyons are among the most beautiful in the West, and the river needs only to have some of its water restored to become one of the Canyon Country's greatest runs once again. The public can someday reclaim this outstanding river by demanding increased releases from McPhee Dam.[3]

The Dolores has been severely diminished but not destroyed. True, McPhee Dam is required to release only a relative trickle (as little as 20 cfs in a dry year, although that minimum may soon be increased to 50 cfs for the sake of downstream fish). But as a practical matter, the reservoir cannot contain all the snowmelt runoff in an average year.

So except in dry years, there should be a brief boating season in late spring and very early summer when water spills from the dam. In dry years the dam will release only minimum flows, precluding boating on the best runs in the upper canyons. Even at these times, however, the lower canyons (Mesa and Gateway) should

[1] El Rio de Nuestra Señora de los Dolores—The River of Our Lady of Sorrows—was named by Fathers Escalante and Dominguez, leaders of a Spanish expedition that explored the Four Corners region in 1776. According to some accounts, the name commemorates the drowning of one of the expedition's members in the river; others say that the drowning occurred on the Piedra, and that the Dolores was named for the "Feast of Our Lady of Sorrows," which the Fathers celebrated on the day they reached the river. In the late 1800's and early 1900's the River of Sorrows earned its name again, when mining for gold, silver, and uranium polluted its waters.

[2] At one time there was hope for stopping the dam. In the early 1970's President Carter recommended the Dolores for designation as a National Wild and Scenic River. But local agriculture and development interests, with their eyes on subsidized water, had the ear of Congress and demanded a cynical compromise whereby the river could be designated Wild and Scenic only if construction of McPhee Dam were allowed. As Doug Wheat observes in *The Floater's Guide to Colorado,* the Dolores thereby became "America's first Wild and Scenic Dry Gulch." As of 1993 the section from Bradfield Bridge to Bedrock was still under consideration for Wild and Scenic status but had not yet been designated.

[3] American Outdoors, a commercial outfitters' group, is doing just that. For more information, contact them at P.O. Box 1348, Knoxville, TN 37901; (615) 524-4814.

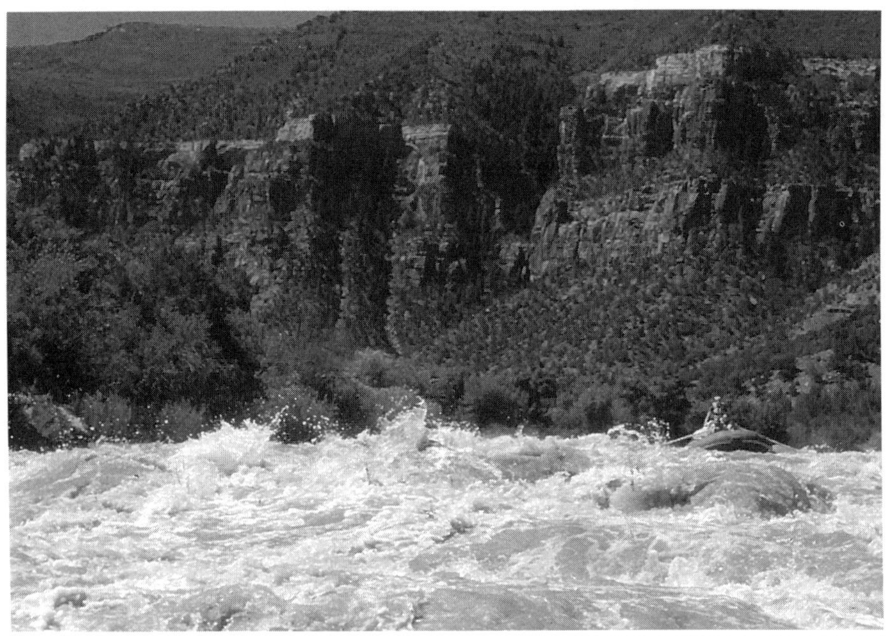
Snaggletooth Rapid, Dolores River *Martha Moran*

have a brief season sometime in May and/or June, thanks to the added flow of the Dolores' largest tributary, the San Miguel River.

The headwaters of the Dolores spring from snowmelt on the San Miguel Mountains, a lofty spur of the San Juan Range in southwestern Colorado. From here the river runs some 250 miles—first southwest, then north for most of its length to join the Colorado River near Moab, Utah. In its course along the western flank of the Uncompahgre Plateau, the Dolores carves six spectacular canyons: Dolores, Little Glen, Slick Rock, Paradox, Mesa, and Gateway. The first of these isolated gorges has some of the high-altitude feel of the Colorado Rockies, with steep slopes lightly clad in pine and fir. But for most of its length, the Dolores is a classic Canyon Country river winding through superb slickrock scenery.

The Dolores also offers excellent side hiking, intriguing Anasazi ruins, fine camping, and good Class II to III whitewater with two widely separated Class IV rapids: the famous Snaggletooth in Dolores Canyon and Stateline in Gateway Canyon nearly 125 miles downstream. Boaters can choose from a variety of runs, from one-day drifts to the full 185-mile journey from McPhee Dam to the Colorado River. In fact, they can tack on an additional 30 miles down the Colorado River to Moab. The upper canyons above Bedrock (Dolores, Little Glen, and Slick Rock) are the most popular, while the lower river sees only light use.

Dolores River Guide

The first 12 miles below McPhee Dam offer easy Class I+ water in a scenic, forested canyon. An unpaved road follows the right bank, providing access for one-day runs. This section sees relatively light use.

Dolores Canyon

The river's most popular float begins a dozen miles below McPhee Dam, at **Bradfield Recreation Site** (mile 0) on the left bank downstream from Bradfield Bridge. Although this section holds the most challenging rapids, the trip begins with a relatively quiet Class II passage through scenic Ponderosa Gorge, where green pines contrast with red sandstone. By mile 10, where a power line crosses overhead, the canyon has deepened to 2,000'.

Glade Canyon enters on the right at a left-hand bend (mile 15), forming a long Class II to II+ rapid. Dolores Canyon Overlook is 1,800' above the left bank. Look for Anasazi ruins on the right near mile 18.5, just before the river bends sharply to the right around Mountain Sheep Point and Secret Canyon enters on the left. A half mile downstream, Big Canyon enters on the left. Just downriver are the Dove Creek pumping station and **Mountain Sheep Point Boat Launch** on the left (mile 19). This **alternate access,** located where a rough dirt road reaches the left bank, is sometimes used as a take-out for short runs from Bradfield. A rough jeep road follows the left bank for the next 15 miles. Downstream the rapids get rougher; there are several Class II–III drops in the next half-dozen miles.

At mile 26.5 boaters encounter **LITTLE SNAG (III),** also called **Molar.** A mile downstream at the canyon's deepest point, the whitewater climaxes at **SNAGGLETOOTH (IV; more difficult at high flows),** the Dolores' biggest rapid. There are no prominent landmarks—just a calm, flat pool preceding the drop. Stop on the left bank to scout and/or portage along the jeep road. At Snaggletooth the Dolores drops some 20' in a couple of hundred yards, first through rocks and waves, then down a washboard of holes, and finally into a pointed rock that cleaves the current right of center. A big hole and more rocks follow. The rapid is quite technical at low flows and hazardous—approaching Class V—at high water. Not only is the river more powerful at high flows, but chances for recovery below the rapid also recede. Swift whitewater continues for nearly half a mile downstream, ending at **THE WALL (III),** sometimes called **Cannonball,** where boaters must avoid the dangerously undercut right bank.

Below Snaggletooth the Dolores enters drier terrain: pinyon and juniper replace pine and fir, and cactus and desert shrubs appear. At mile 30, two miles below Snaggletooth, the Dolores sweeps through a horseshoe bend to the left. Near mile 33 the river enters **THREE MILE:** semi-continuous Class III drops (big waves at high water) that go on for, yes, three miles. The road along the left bank ends near mile 35. At about mile 36 the whitewater eases, and near mile 39 the canyon begins to open. Disappointment Creek enters on the right at mile 42, and Colorado 141 crosses the river at mile 47. The popular **Slick Rock access** is on the right above the bridge, and the settlement of the same name is on the left. This access is on private land; ask permission and pay fees at the cafe across the bridge. No overnight parking.

Little Glen and Slick Rock Canyons

Below Slick Rock the rapids are fewer and easier, but the scenery remains spectacular as the river winds through impressive sandstone gorges. The canyons from Slick Rock to Bedrock are being considered for official wilderness designation. **These middle sections of the Dolores are popular with open canoeists, but several spots in Slick Rock Canyon require strong intermediate skills.** Between rapids the current is often slow, especially in Little Glen Canyon, whose placid waters produce annoying mosquitos and no-see-ums in summer. An intermediate access at Gypsum Valley allows separate runs of either canyon.

Five miles below the Slick Rock access at mile 47 (see above), the Dolores enters lovely **Little Glen Canyon,** cutting through the same sandstone strata that form the walls of Glen Canyon of the Colorado. After five miles the river emerges into Big Gypsum Valley, where Big Gypsum Creek enters on the right. **Gypsum Valley Recreation Site** (BLM) provides an **alternate access** on the right at mile 61. It can be reached via unpaved Road 20R off Colorado 141.

At mile 63.5 the Dolores abruptly leaves the valley and enters tortuous **Slick Rock Canyon,** where it winds through more than 30 miles of entrenched meanders to advance just ten air miles. The red sandstone walls soar to heights of over 1,000' and in some places overhang the river. The current is stronger than in Little Glen Canyon, and several rapids and undercut bends present more challenges.

At mile 66.5 Bull Canyon enters on the right, offering a fine side hike and creating a Class II rapid. A mile downstream is another moderate rapid. Between miles 73 and 76 the river winds through an entrenched meander known as "The Cloverleaf," where boaters often hike to the saddle of the gooseneck. At mile 82 Spring Canyon enters on the right, offering another good hike and creating **SPRING CANYON RAPID (III-),** which features an undercut wall. Coyote Wash enters on the left at mile 85, and a mile downstream boaters can hike to the saddle of the Mule Shoe Bend gooseneck.

Downstream, although the canyon opens a bit, several rapids lie ahead. They include **ONE HOLER (III)** at mile 92, where the river splits at an island (common run is down the left side); **LA SAL (III-),** about three quarters of a mile farther down, just above where La Sal Creek enters on the left; and **S-CURVE (III),** a right-left bend a mile below La Sal. The standard **take-out** is the **Bedrock access** on the left at mile 97. Just downstream, the Dolores emerges from the canyon into Paradox Valley (so named because the river flows across rather than down it). At mile 98 Colorado 90 crosses the river; the hamlet of Bedrock is west of the bridge.

Paradox and Mesa Canyons

Below Bedrock the river flows placidly through open ranch country for some five miles before entering scenic **Paradox Canyon,** where the current accelerates and the whitewater builds to Class III at times. A rough dirt road follows the right bank through the canyon, providing shuttle and accesses.

Near mile 107 is **CONFLUENCE (III).** Just downstream, the San Miguel River enters on the right, marking the end of Paradox Canyon and the beginning of **Mesa Canyon.** A dirt road down the San Miguel from Colorado 141 reaches the right bank here. Boaters sometimes use this road as an **alternate access** and launch at the confluence. When the Dolores itself is too low in late spring or early summer, the San Miguel sometimes adds enough water to make the Dolores boatable from this point on.

Downstream, Colorado Highway 141 enters the main canyon high above the right bank and follows the Dolores—often well above the river—for 35 miles to Gateway, providing several access points along the way. Below the confluence the remains of an old mining flume can be seen on the cliff face on the right.

Mesa Canyon's rapids are mostly Class II to II+, depending on the flow. At mile 118 the highway crosses the river where Roc Creek enters on the left. Maverick Canyon enters on the right at mile 132; a side hike of about a mile and a half leads to Juanita Arch. Just downstream, Salt Creek enters on the left, creating a long Class II rapid. Watch for a Class II+ where Cave Canyon enters on the left at mile 138. At mile 142 the highway crosses the river near the town of Gateway on the right (**river access**).

Gateway Canyon

For several miles below Gateway, where the river leaves the highway, the Dolores flows through open bottomlands with dirt roads and ranches on both banks. At mile 151 the right-bank road ends, and the Dolores crosses into Utah. Here lies the river's second big rapid, **STATELINE (IV),** a long washboard that splits around an island. Scout on either side. Most of the run is down the right, but boaters must first avoid a small vertical fall at the top right created by an old irrigation diversion structure. A flat spot in the middle of the rapid allows time to move right. Watch for sweepers. Stateline is rocky and technical at low flows and develops big waves and holes at high water. Easier rapids follow.

Below Stateline the Dolores leaves civilization behind and enters **Gateway Canyon.** This run offers excellent scenery and fine hiking as well as a longer and more reliable season, thanks to the flow added upstream by the San Miguel. Nevertheless, Gateway gets relatively light use, in part due to its long shuttle.

At mile 154 watch for **BEAVER CREEK (III-)** where Beaver Creek enters on the left. Just downstream, the river turns north and enters an impressive gorge. The canyon continues until Granite Creek enters on the right at mile 162, after which the walls recede and the Dolores winds more gently through more open country to its confluence with the Colorado. Near mile 166 the Dolores runs through its last rapid at **BIG ROCK (II+).** The Dolores meets the Colorado at mile 174; a good **take-out** is a mile downstream where **Dewey Bridge** (Utah 128) crosses the Colorado. Those looking for a longer trip can continue up to 30 miles down the Colorado to Moab (see chapter on **Colorado: Westwater Canyon**).

Upstream Runs

Boaters sometimes find enough water above McPhee Reservoir for tiny, technical runs on the river's swift upper reaches. Roads along these mountain sections allow scouting and access. Be alert for log jams, fences, and weirs. For information contact San Juan National Forest, (303) 882-7296.

The river's main stem tumbles at some 50 ft./mi. through nearly continuous Class III–IV whitewater for 25 miles from Rico (elevation 9,000') to the West Fork confluence. The main stem has a short season, typically in June. The smaller and more densely forested West Fork has an earlier season. Floating is possible on the West Fork for some 12 miles from the Road 686 bridge to the confluence with the main stem of the Dolores. Several Forest Service campgrounds provide intermediate access points along the way. The 15-mile stretch from this confluence to the town of Dolores has a longer season, but weirs and fences detract from this run. For more information see Wheat, *Floater's Guide to Colorado.*

> Why yes, the Dolores, too, is scheduled for damnation. Only a little dam, say the politicians, one little earth-fill dam to irrigate the sorghum and alfalfa plantations.... True, only a little dam. But dammit, it's only a little river.
>
> —Edward Abbey, *Down The River*

The last time I saw Ed Abbey was outside the Bedrock General Store. He'd just bought me a case of beer and was telling me how he couldn't stay with our boating party on our way down the Dolores and the Colorado to Moab and perhaps beyond.

We had met Abbey about a week earlier. The three of us—Ann, Kathy, and I—had put in at the town of Dolores. We had two rafts and provisions for at least a couple of weeks. The weather was cool, crisp, and sunny. It was early spring runoff in April 1979, and the Dolores was flowing at maybe a thousand cfs. At the time, it was one of the last remaining wild rivers in the Canyon Country.

That first day, we floated through the fertile riverbottom pastures where, a thousand years ago, Anasazi had settled for a couple of centuries before they moved twenty miles south to Mesa Verde. Archaeologists had recently been busy surveying and mapping the important sites. Within a few years McPhee Dam would be completed. Slack reservoir waters would flood the idyllic valley behind the dam, and diversions from the reservoir to the San Juan watershed would dry up the river below it.

We camped just below the dam site in a canyon brimming with budding scrub oak. Next morning we floated on down the river and joined up with a dozen rafts and two dozen river rats, including a bunch of rookies and one Edward Abbey, who was certainly no stranger to Western waters. As it turned out, Abbey floated with Ann most of the trip. She was willing to let him take over occasionally. That gave him a chance to flail about with the oars and almost get her boat into trouble a few times.

At the Ponderosa Grove campsite the night before we ran Snaggletooth, I chatted with Abbey about books and writers, rivers and dams. He talked about the heartbreak of losing Glen Canyon and of watching one river after another disappear. I offered him a beer. He said he was trying to dry out, but he still wanted to work out a deal. He would drink my Jim Beam and beer with me, and then he would buy me a case of cold ones when we got to Bedrock, a hundred miles downstream.

So we spent the better part of a week together, floating down the Dolores. The last night before Paradox Valley and Bedrock, we camped at Coyote Wash. In a magazine article Abbey wrote not long afterward, he recounted the incident that took place there:

> After dark, a member of the crew, a pyromancer, climbs a 500-foot bluff above camp and builds a bonfire of old juniper and piñon pine. He is joined by a second dark figure, dancing around the flames. As the flames die, the two shove the mound of glowing coals over the edge. A cascade of fire streams down the face of the cliff. Clouds of sparks float on the darkness, slowly flickering out as they sink into oblivion. A few tiny spot fires burn among the boulders at the base of the cliff, then fade. The end of something. A gesture—but symbolizing what? In [the trip leader's] view it is an act of childish vandalism; he will not speak to the two when they return to camp. I do not blame him much. ["Floating the River of the Mind," *Rocky Mountain Magazine*, April 1980.]

Well, I can tell you that Abbey was the chief pyromancer in that little episode. His celebratory frenzy may not have been ecologically correct, but it had a raw, primal beauty and passion.

At Bedrock those of us continuing downstream invited Abbey to join us, but he had obligations. We stayed in touch later, and when I moved to New York he arranged for me to meet his son. I never saw the old man of the river again, but I can still hear his harmonica's sweet lament for the River of Our Lady of Sorrows.

—Mark S. McCaffrey

Lower San Juan River

Bluff to Clay Hills

Difficulty: II. **Gradient:** 8 ft./mi.
Length: 84 miles. Shorter trips of 27 and 57 miles possible using intermediate access at Mexican Hat.
Put-in: Sand Island Recreation Area (4,270').
Take-out: Clay Hills Crossing (3,680').
Drainage Area and Average Annual Discharge: 23,000 sq. mi. and 1,886,000 af at Mexican Hat.
Peak Recorded Flow: 70,000 cfs (Sept. 10, 1927).
Season: April–Sept. Often boatable earlier and later if weather permits. Much of the water released from Navajo Dam, which blocks the Upper San Juan and Piedra, is diverted to towns and farms in northern New Mexico, but enough often remains in the Lower San Juan to provide year-round boatable flows. Snowmelt runoff, primarily from the free-flowing Animas, usually peaks in late May or early June. Midsummer flows are sometimes too low for rafts, but August and September thunderstorms usually add water.
Recommended Levels: 800–12,000 cfs.
Flow Information: NWS tape, (801) 539-1311, or BLM, (801) 672-2222; flow "at Bluff" (Mexican Hat gauge).
Special Hazards: Remote area. Side canyon flash floods.
Permits: Required year-round. Applications accepted Dec. 1–Jan. 31 for peak season permits (April 1–Oct. 31); lottery held in February. Off-season permits issued first-come, first-served beginning Jan. 1. Competition is heaviest for May and June starts from Sand Island.

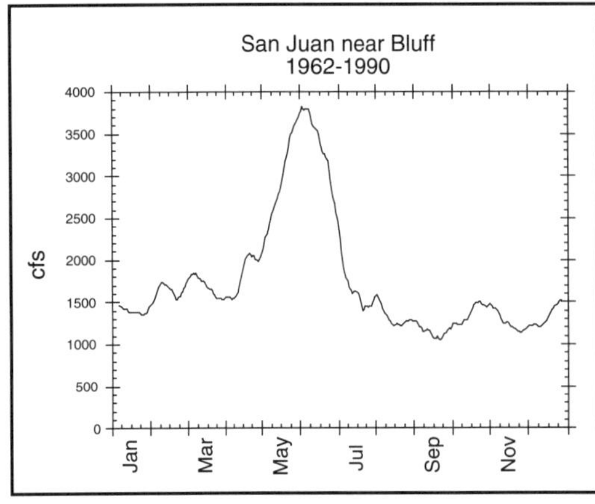

Managing Agency: BLM, San Juan RA, P.O. Box 7, Monticello, UT 84535; (801) 587-2144.
Commercial Raft Trips: Yes. For a list of outfitters, contact the BLM.
Land Ownership: Left bank is Navajo Indian Reservation. Right bank is mostly BLM and Glen Canyon National Recreation Area.
Scenery: Excellent. Deep desert canyons.
Solitude: Excellent.
Wilderness: Yes.
Wildlife: Bighorn sheep in stretch from Sand Island to Mexican Hat.
Weather: Midsummer is very hot. Late summer thunderstorms may cause flash floods in side canyons. Early season can be cold.
Water: Silty and undrinkable. Side creeks are unreliable. Best to pack in water. No drinking water at Sand Island or Mexican Hat accesses. Ask permission before using private spigots; there is often a small fee.
Camping: Excellent. Some sites are flooded at high water. Permit required from Navajo tribe (see **Side Hikes**) to camp on reservation (left bank of river). From May 1–Sept. 30 only one night is allowed at Slickhorn Canyon (mile 66; 3 sites) and Grand Gulch (mile 70). Sign up for these sites on a first-come, first-served basis at a register a few miles below Mexican Hat. Limited camping below Grand Gulch. River level can vary dramatically with rain or snowmelt—tie boats securely and camp high.
Side Hikes: Many excellent hikes, including Honaker Trail, Johns Canyon, Slickhorn Canyon, Grand Gulch, and Steer Gulch (see **Mile Guide**). Permit required from Navajo tribe to hike anywhere on reservation; call (602) 871-6647. Good hiking map is *Grand Gulch Plateau* (Trails Illustrated).
Side Excursions: Goosenecks Overlook near Mexican Hat. Natural Bridges National Monument just off shuttle route. Monument Valley to the south.
Guides and References:

- Baars & Stevenson, *San Juan Canyons: A River Runner's Guide.*
- Zwinger, *Wind In The Rock.* Personal essays, natural history.

- *Geology of the Canyons of the San Juan River* (Four Corners Geological Society).
- Aitchison, *Naturalist's San Juan River Guide.*
- Wilde, *The San Juan: The Four Corners River.* (Vol. 62, No. 4 of Museum of Northern Arizona's *Plateau* magazine).
- Abbey, *Down The River.* Includes an essay describing a San Juan trip.

Maps:

- **USGS 7.5'**: *Bluff, White Rock Point, San Juan Hill, Mexican Hat, The Goosenecks, Goulding NE, Slickhorn Canyon East, Slickhorn Canyon West, Whirlwind Draw, Mikes Mesa.*
- **USGS 1:100:** *Bluff, Navajo Mtn.*
- **AAA:** *Indian Country* road map.
- *Southeastern Utah* (Utah Travel Council).

Auto Shuttle: About 95 miles (3 hours) one way from Sand Island put-in to Clay Hills. Contact the BLM for shuttle references.

Logistics: The **Sand Island put-in** is ust north of the U.S. 191 bridge across the San Juan, 3 miles west of Bluff in the southeastern corner of Utah. **Accesses at Mexican Hat** are upstream from the U.S. 163 bridge. To reach the **take-out at Clay Hills Crossing,** drive north from Bluff on U.S. 191 about 22 miles, then west on Utah 95 about 38 miles, then southwest on Utah 276 some 19 miles, then turn left onto unpaved Clay Hills Road and drive 11 rough miles to Powell Reservoir. The shuttle from Sand Island to Mexican Hat is roughly 23 miles via U.S. 163. The shuttle from Mexican Hat to Clay Hills is about 80 miles via Utah 261 and 276.

The San Juan is a river of many faces. Rising among 13,000' peaks along the Continental Divide in the San Juan Mountains of southwestern Colorado, the San Juan begins its 400-mile journey to its confluence with the Colorado as a sparkling torrent plunging down forested alpine valleys. Joined by the Piedra, Animas, and other mountain tributaries, the San Juan quickly swells to become one of the West's master streams and the third largest branch of the Colorado.

As it dips south into New Mexico, the San Juan metamorphoses into a sandy desert river and is swallowed up in Navajo Reservoir. Below Navajo Dam the river winds westward in shifting channels across sagebrush plains as it heads toward Four Corners, where the states of Utah, Colorado, New Mexico and Arizona meet.

In its lower reaches, covered in this chapter, the river is transformed once more. Below the hamlet of Bluff in the southeastern corner of Utah, the Lower San Juan winds through two magnificent canyons, carving a spectacular, twisting passage between towering walls of ancient stone. The scenery turns suddenly rugged, yet the river remains relatively gentle. For 84 miles the sandy riverbed and gentle gradient produce no rapids above Class II+ (except at high flows). This makes the Lower San Juan something of an exception in river running territory dominated by the thundering whitewater of Cataract Canyon and the Grand Canyon.

In fact, aside from outstanding canyon scenery the Lower San Juan bears little resemblance to its more famous neighboring runs. The water is often bathtub warm by early summer, and motorized trips are relatively rare. The Lower San Juan is ideal for those seeking a taste of Grand Canyon scenery without Lava Falls, for families introducing children to the river, or for veteran boaters on vacation from the Class V circuit.[1]

At one time the San Juan ran free all the way to its confluence with the Colorado. Until about 30 years ago, the standard trip was a remarkable 235-mile journey: 140 miles from Bluff to the Colorado, then nearly 100 miles down the Colorado through Glen Canyon to Lees Ferry. Sadly, the San Juan's lower 56 miles suffered the same fate as Glen Canyon, drowned in the 1960's by Powell Reservoir (euphemistically known as "Lake" Powell).

Upstream in New Mexico, Navajo Dam blocks the Upper San Juan below its confluence with the Piedra. Navajo Reservoir floods some 30 miles of the river and partially tames the wild fluctuations that earned the San Juan its Navajo name "Pawhuska," or "mad river." (The modern name dates to 1776, when the exploring Spanish Fathers Dominguez and Escalante named the river for St. John the Baptist.)

Though its length is curtailed by Powell Reservoir and its flow is diminished along the way by diversions for irrigation, industry, and towns in northern New Mexico, what remains

[1]If you prefer a working vacation, consider entering the Goosenecks Classic, a one-day, 84-mile race down the San Juan. The course record is 7 hours, 10 minutes.

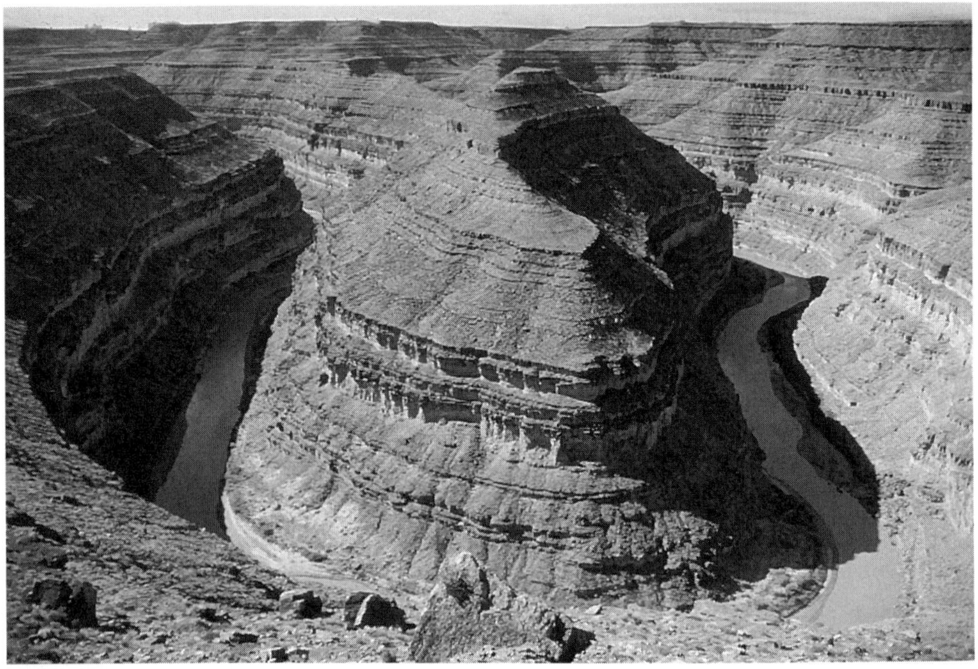

Goosenecks of the San Juan *Curt Smith*

of the Lower San Juan still ranks as one of the West's great wilderness river trips. These days, river runners float the 27-mile upper canyon from Sand Island (near Bluff) to Mexican Hat and/or the lower canyon from Mexican Hat to Clay Hills (57 miles). Sand Island launches outnumber Mexican Hat starts by more than three to one.[2]

The San Juan's fascinating geology appeals to experts and casual observers alike. Below Sand Island the river carves deep into a plateau of sedimentary rock known as the Monument Upwarp. Colorful layers of sandstone and limestone rise a quarter mile above the river in places. Downstream from Mexican Hat, a tortuous series of entrenched meanders, the famous Goosenecks of the San Juan, send river runners looping through 13 miles of twisting canyon to gain just three air miles.

The river's human history is equally rich. For more than a thousand years the San Juan and its side canyons were home to the Anasazi, whose culture disappeared about 1,300 A.D. Today, their cliff dwellings, petroglyphs, and scattered artifacts can be found throughout the canyons. (Please respect these fragile ancient sites.) The Navajo tribe has occupied the region since the middle of the nineteenth century, and the Lower San Juan now marks the northern boundary of their reservation.

The history of San Juan river running begins with Norman Nevill's pioneering 1934 descent from Mexican Hat in a wooden boat built with planks from an old outhouse. Two years later, Nevills and a partner began guiding commercial trips down the canyon.[3] Ken Ross established the first modern rafting outfit in 1957. The following three decades saw a steady increase in interest until finally, in the mid-1980's, the BLM began limiting use through a permit system.

For many, the biggest attraction of a San Juan trip is the superb side hiking: the lovely swimming holes of Slickhorn Canyon, the Anasazi ruins and dramatic slickrock in Grand Gulch, and the rugged solitude of Steer Gulch. Hikers with a head for heights will enjoy the Honaker Trail, which climbs 2.5 miles from the river to the rim at the canyon's deepest point.[4]

---

[2]Spring and early summer flows on the Lower San Juan would be severely curtailed if part of the water of its free-flowing tributary, the Animas, were diverted for irrigation. See the sidebar on the Animas-La Plata Project in the **Animas** chapter.

[3]Wallace Stegner, *The Sound of Mountain Water,* includes an essay on running the San Juan and Glen Canyon with Nevills.

[4]Ann Zwinger's *Wind in the Rock* describes these treks in captivating detail.

The Lower San Juan is easy enough that the rugged side hikes and searing summer heat are probably the greatest hazards boaters face. But what the river lacks in whitewater, it makes up for with its famous sand waves. Occasionally seen on other rivers, sand waves are common on the sediment-laden San Juan at high water.

With no apparent cause, a chain of standing waves two to (rarely) eight feet high slowly rises in a stretch of smooth water. The waves are short-lived, lasting only a few seconds or minutes before fading away. The secret behind this conjurer's trick lies hidden beneath the surface: the waves form when temporary ripples or bulges develop in the sandy riverbed, then disappear as the rushing water smooths the sand again. Though this spectacle can be a little unnerving, the waves are basically benign (except perhaps for open canoes). In fact, they are ideal for surfing—if you can catch them while they last.

The same heavy sediment load that creates the sand waves eventually finds its way to "Lake" Powell, where it settles out to produce vast silt beds. When the reservoir is full to the brim, slack water begins at Grand Gulch and boaters must struggle across 13.5 miles of flatwater to reach the Clay Hills take-out.[5]

In 1991, after several dry years, the mild-mannered San Juan gave birth to one of the West's most dramatic rapids. As Powell Reservoir receded below Clay Hills Crossing, the river cut down into the deep silt beds that the river had deposited when the reservoir was full. A couple of miles below Clay Hills, the river wandered from its original course and began pouring over a rock outcropping on one side of the canyon. What began as a 4' drop soon developed into a mighty waterfall as the San Juan eroded away the silt on the downstream side of the ledge.

As of 1993 the near-vertical waterfall had reached some 35' in height and stood temporarily unrivaled as the biggest drop in the entire Colorado River system. It is absolutely unrunnable and virtually impossible to portage due to a lack of eddies on the approach and thickets of tamarisk on the bank. **Until further notice no one should boat below the Clay Hills Crossing take-out.** In the future the river may abandon the falls and resume its original placid course. But until then, or until the reservoir again covers this spot, no one should consider the option of continuing downstream to the former alternate take-out at Paiute Farms.

[5]As of 1993 the reservoir had reached that level only once, during the high-water year of 1983-84. After that the level dropped some 70'—to well below Clay Hills—due to the West's prolonged drought. Contact the BLM for up-to-date information on the reservoir level, and enjoy the current as long as it lasts.

At high water the Lower San Juan has been estimated to be roughly three parts water to one part sand. On a single day at peak flood level in October 1941, the river moved 12 million tons of sediment in 24 hours. At the present rate of deposition in Powell Reservoir, much of this run will one day be silted up.

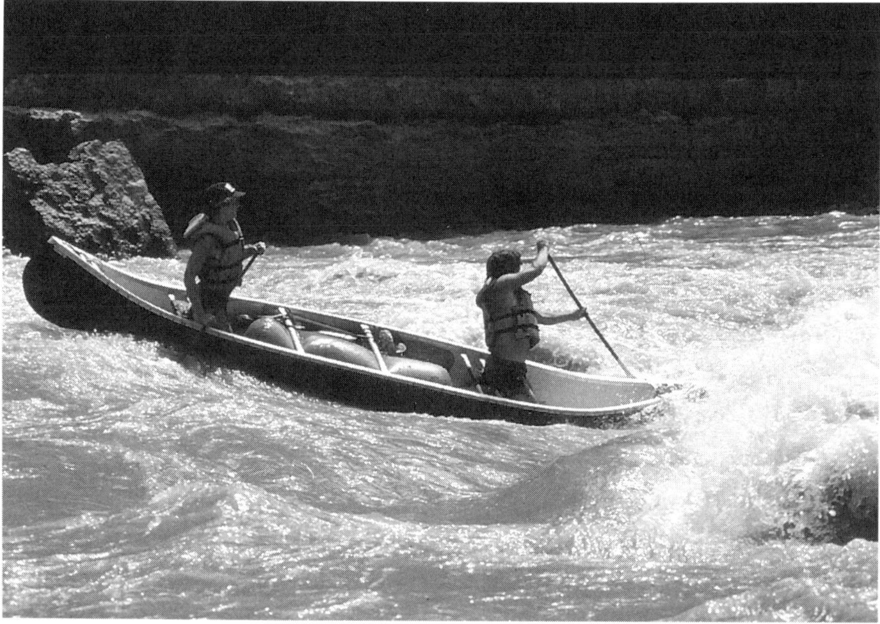

Tandem open canoe on the San Juan *Bill Cross*

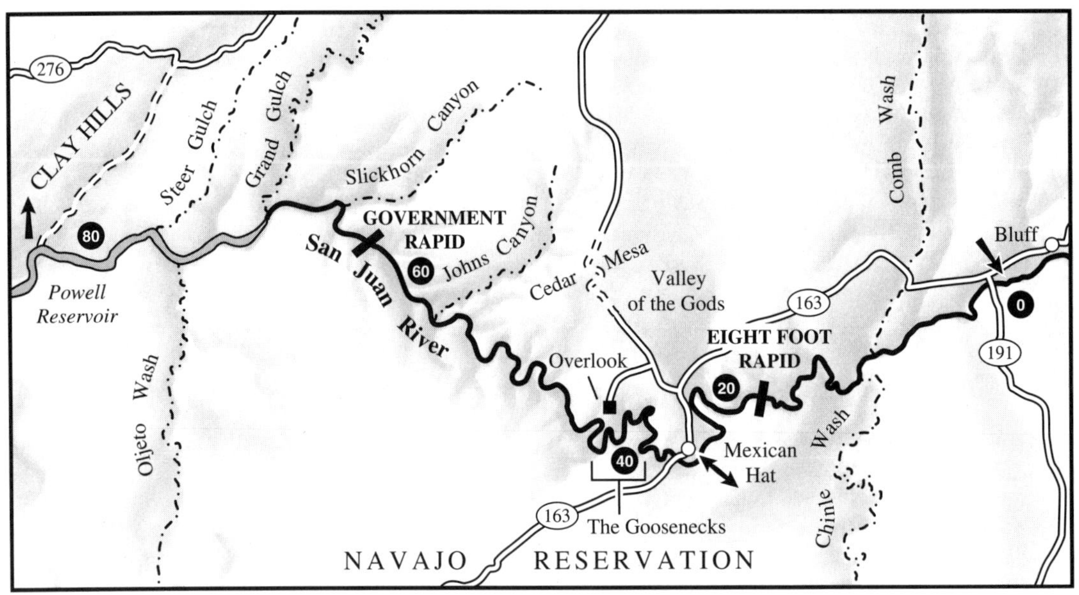

Lower San Juan

Mile by Mile Guide

0 **PUT-IN** on the right bank at Sand Island Recreation Area, near the U.S. 191 bridge 3 miles west of Bluff. The left bank is Navajo Indian Reservation.

4 Butler Wash enters on the right. Just downstream on the right are outstanding petroglyphs on a cliff of Navajo Sandstone (no camping). Sad to say, they were defaced and vandalized in 1991. Downstream on the right is private land; please do not trespass.

6 Well back from the right bank is the River House Ruin, reached by hiking a third of a mile north across sand flats. Just downstream, Comb Wash enters on the right.

8.5 Chinle Wash enters on the left, with Anasazi ruins less than a mile up the wash. (A permit is required from the Navajo tribe to hike here; see **Side Hikes.**) Downstream, the river cuts into a steep anticline (upwardly folded rock beds) and abruptly enters San Juan Canyon, whose walls rise more than 1,000'. Campsites become harder to find. About two miles into the canyon is the first riffle, **FOUR-FOOT RAPID (I+)**.

12.5 Abandoned river meander or "rincon" on the right.

17 **EIGHT-FOOT RAPID (II)**, followed by the mile-long Upper Narrows. Look for **LEDGE RAPID (II-)** below the Narrows at mile 19.

20.5 The canyon ends suddenly as the rock beds dip down. Three miles downstream, Mexican Hat Rock is on the right.

26.5 Mexican Hat **RIVER ACCESS** on the right. Water and limited services in the hamlet of Mexican Hat. Just downstream is a Class II riffle where Gypsum Creek enters on the left. Gauging station on the left at the foot of the riffle. A few hundred yards below the gauge, U.S. 163 crosses the river. The **alternate access** on the right above the bridge is the last possible take-out above Clay Hills Crossing, nearly 60 miles downstream. Downstream the canyon deepens rapidly.

30 The river enters Mendenhall Loop, with the ruins of Walter Mendenhall's stone cabin atop the saddle of the gooseneck. The campsite register for Slickhorn Canyon and Grand Gulch (see **Camping**) is on the downstream side of the loop on the right.

34 The river meanders around a rock formation known as The Tabernacle. A couple

of miles downstream, the San Juan enters the Second Narrows.

37 The river enters The Goosenecks. Boaters advance just one air mile in the next 5.5 river miles. Look for the Goosenecks Overlook on the canyon rim—first directly astern, later straight ahead.

42.5 As the Goosenecks end, a small canyon enters on the left, creating a riffle. Campsites are easier to find again in the next few miles.

44 At a right bend the Honaker Trail, built in 1904 by prospectors, climbs some 2.5 miles and 1,300' to the rim, offering superb views. This is the canyon's deepest point, though the walls remain high for 20 more miles.

52 **ROSS (II)**. A large rock forms a good wave at higher flows. Named for longtime local river runner and archaeologist Ken Ross.

58.5 Johns Canyon enters on the right, just above a small riffle. Good camp; short side hike to a beautiful plunge pool.

63.5 **GOVERNMENT RAPID (II+)**, just below a right-hand bend. Scout left.

66 Slickhorn Canyon enters on the right, creating **SLICKHORN (II)**. Campsites above and below the creek must be reserved in advance. One night only in peak season. Excellent side hike up the creek to warm plunge pools.

70 Grand Gulch enters on the right. Only one campsite (reserve in advance) and only one night in peak season. A side hike up the winding gulch leads to warm pools (in season) and, several miles farther, Anasazi ruins. When full, Powell Reservoir extends upstream to this point. Campsites beyond this point are limited, especially if the reservoir is full.

75.5 Oljeto Wash (Moonlight Creek) enters on the left. About two miles farther, Steer Gulch enters on the right (side hike). In another mile and a half, Whirlwind Draw enters on the right.

84 **TAKE-OUT.** Clay Hills Crossing on the right. ***HAZARD.*** Do not continue downriver. Just over two miles downstream is a lethal waterfall (see essay).

Even in the colorful canyon of the Lower San Juan, the flash of fluorescent orange was hard to miss. I pulled to shore to investigate. Lodged behind a boulder was a 6' by 6' plywood highway sign, wedged in such a way that passing boaters couldn't see its urgent message emblazoned in foot-high letters across a brilliant orange diamond: **DANGER!**

It was an incongruous warning on the mellow San Juan. I considered the possibilities. Was this simply what it appeared to be—a highway sign washed downriver by a flash flood? Or was it in fact a "sign," a mysterious message from the next dimension, warning of unknown dangers lurking around the bend?

Whatever its meaning, the sign was hard to ignore. And hard to leave behind, too. I always try to clean up any trash I find along shore, and an obscenely bright 36-square-foot highway sign definitely qualifies as trash. I decided to tow it downriver and out of the canyon. As I rowed down to our camp at Slickhorn Canyon, another thought struck me: maybe the sign was telling me that I needed more "danger" in my humdrum existence. If so, then I should go for the gusto the next chance I got.

My opportunity came the next morning as we launched our boats above Slickhorn Rapid. Why run the drop in a raft or a kayak, I thought? Those were known quantities—reliable and predictable vehicles for timid souls. Instead, I resolved to shoot Slickhorn on my highway sign ... or die in the attempt. Brandishing my kayak paddle, I kneeled carefully on the sign. It sank slowly to the bottom under my weight. Concluding that a bit more flotation was in order, I grabbed our innertube and lashed it to the underside. Eureka! The combination rig was an instant success, and with it I bagged the first—and presumably only—descent of Slickhorn Rapid on a highway sign.

I towed the sign as far as Grand Gulch, but when I hit the slack water of Powell Reservoir the drag was too much. So, with a fond farewell, I set my sign free. For all I know it's still out there, spreading its big, bright message of risk and adventure among the houseboaters.

—Bill Cross

Region IV. Southwestern Border

New Mexico, Arizona, Texas

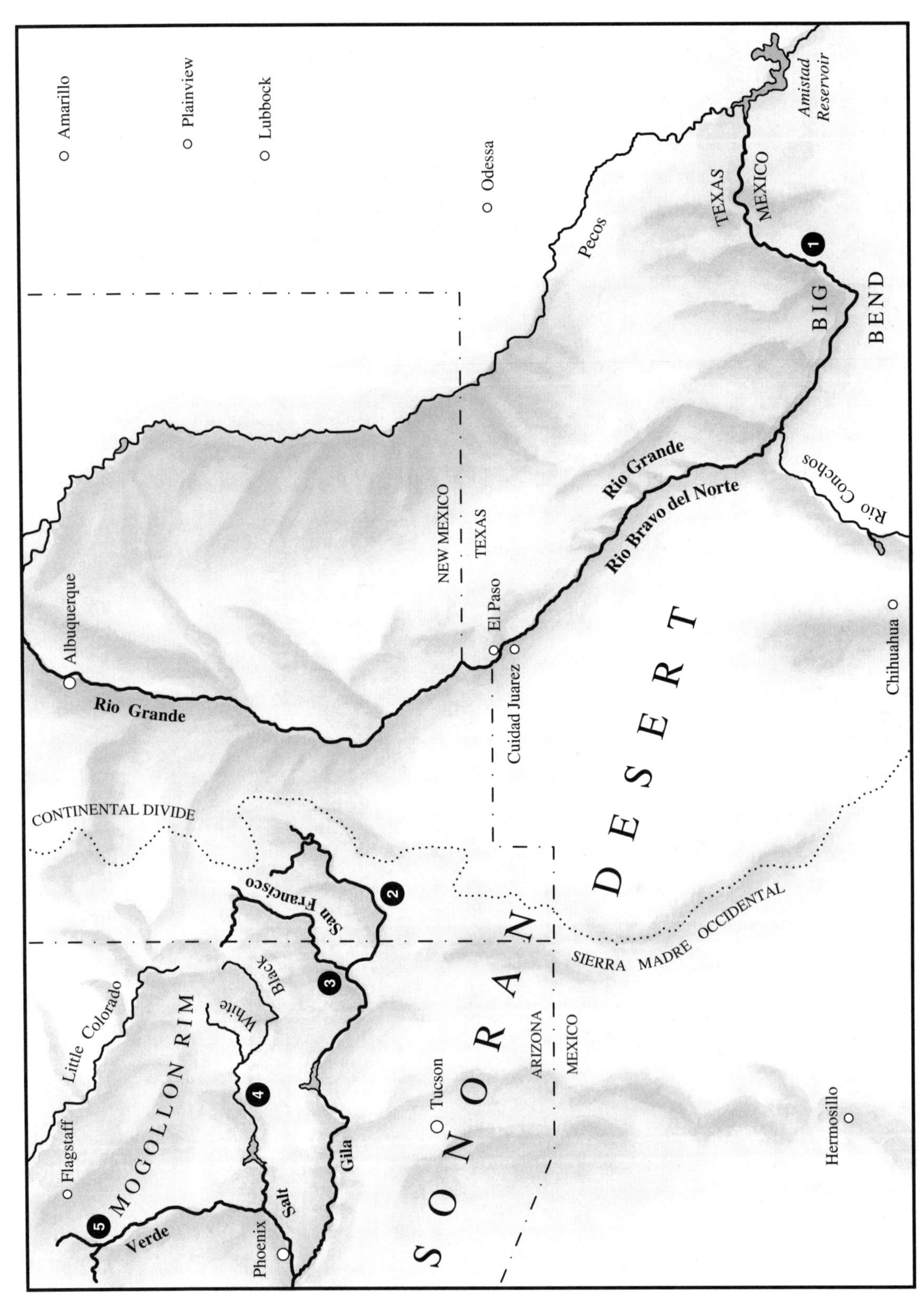

Southwestern Border

Rivers of the Southwestern Border

1. Lower Rio Grande
2. Gila
3. San Francisco
4. Salt
5. Verde

Southwestern Border

The Southwestern Border region is a land of little water and few rivers. Here, close to the Mexican frontier, most places receive less than 10" of precipitation in an average year. Temperatures are scorching from late spring to early fall. Two major deserts—the Sonoran to the west and the Chihuahuan to the east—cover much of the area.

Rivers in this region share a desert character with those of the Canyon Country, but the Southwestern Border lacks the Canyon Country's key unifying feature—the dramatic sedimentary geology of the Colorado Plateau. Also, the climate here is more strongly influenced by the Gulf of Mexico. In late summer, humid air sweeping in off the Gulf produces a local "monsoon" season with intense thundershowers and occasional severe flash floods.

The Continental Divide's north-south trace through this region follows several relatively low ranges that mark an indistinct southern extension of the Rocky Mountains. On the east side of the Divide, the Rio Grande and the Pecos bring some of their water from Colorado and New Mexico mountain ranges north of the region. On the west side of the Divide, the Gila and its tributaries carry the scanty runoff from mountains in western New Mexico and eastern Arizona toward the Gila's confluence with the Lower Colorado at the extreme western edge of the region.

The most significant river in the Southwestern Border region is the Lower Rio Grande, which marks the boundary between Texas and Mexico. With its dramatic gorges and parched desert surroundings, the Rio Grande in many ways resembles a Canyon Country river, yet it lies more than 600 miles southeast of the Grand Canyon. The Rio Grande's low elevation, southern latitude, and massive drainage area make it boatable year-round.

The rivers of the Gila drainage—the Salt, Verde, San Francisco, and Gila—all drain westward toward the Sonoran Desert and the Colorado River. All have short, unpredictable snowmelt seasons in early spring, often followed by brief periods of runnable flows in late summer during the "monsoon" season.

In this land of scarce water and booming cities, rivers are often dammed and diverted until they run dry. The Rio Grande is normally a dry wash by the time it reaches West Texas, where it is replenished by the added flow of a major Mexican tributary, the Rio Conchos. The Gila, Salt, and Verde are almost entirely used up in their passage through the rapidly-growing metropolis of Phoenix, while the Lower Colorado is drained empty by pumps and canals feeding cities and farms in Southern California, Arizona, and Mexico.

Nevertheless, the Southwestern Border boasts several outstanding stretches of free-flowing rivers that draw boaters from throughout the West and around the nation. A key attraction is the mild off-season weather, which allows boaters to enjoy river running when conditions farther north are too harsh. In addition, these rivers offer outstanding desert scenery, a wide range of whitewater difficulty, and several long wilderness trips.

Lower Rio Grande

Rancherias Canyon to Dryden Crossing

1. Colorado Canyon: Rancherias Canyon (2,410') to Madera Canyon (2,340'). II+; 9.5 miles; 8 ft./mi.	**5. Mariscal Canyon: Talley to Solis (1,890').** II+; 10 miles; 6 ft./mi.
2. Madera Canyon to Lajitas (2,280'). II+; 11.5 miles; 5 ft./mi.	**6. San Vicente and Hot Springs Canyons: Solis to Rio Grande Village (1,820').** I+; 18.5 miles (shorter runs possible); 4 ft./mi.
3. Santa Elena Canyon: Lajitas to below Terlingua Creek (2,140'). II+4; 20 miles; 7 ft./mi.	**7. Boquillas Canyon: Rio Grande Village to Stillwell Crossing or La Linda (1,675').** I+; 27.5 or 33 miles; 4 ft./mi.
4. Terlingua Creek to Talley (1,950'). I+; 45.5 miles; 5 ft./mi.	**8. Lower Canyons: La Linda to Dryden Crossing (1,285').** III4; 83 miles (longer runs possible); 5 ft./mi.

Drainage Area and Average Annual Discharge: 67,760 sq. mi. and 960,000 af near Santa Elena Canyon.

Peak Recorded Flow: 71,900 cfs (Sept. 30, 1978).

Season: All year, though summer can be unbearably hot (see **Weather**). Early fall usually sees good flows and cooler weather. Winter flows are adequate, but weather may be chilly. Mild weather makes March and April very popular; flows are low but boatable. From May through October, flows are variable with occasional rain-induced floods. Flows typically peak in late summer and/or early fall.

Recommended Levels: 500–5,000 cfs. Generally, boating is better above 1,000 cfs.

Flow Information: Big Bend National Park, (915) 477-2251 or 477-2393, can give readings from five different gauges. Most of the water comes from Mexico's dam-controlled Rio Conchos.

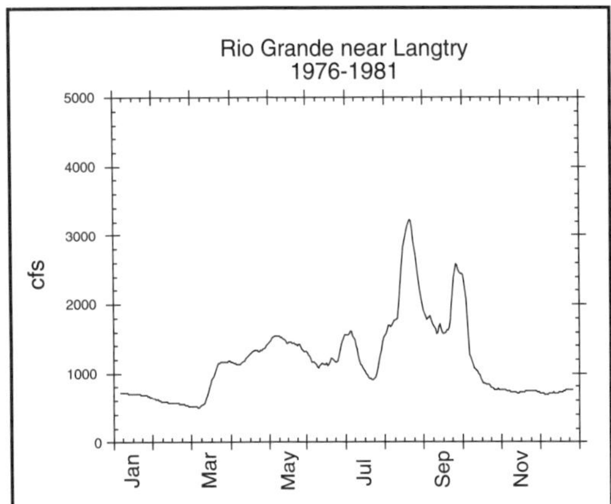

Special Hazards: The Rockslide in Santa Elena Canyon. Isolation, especially in Lower Canyons. Flash floods. Vandalism and theft; don't leave boats, gear, or vehicles unattended.

Permits: Required year-round; available for the asking. Contact appropriate managing agency.

Managing Agencies: *Colorado Canyon:* Big Bend Ranch State Natural Area, P.O. Box 1180, Presidio, TX 79845; (915) 358-4444. *Other runs:* NPS, Big Bend National Park, TX 79834; (915) 477-2251.

Commercial Raft Trips: Yes. For references contact the managing agencies.

Land Ownership: *Left bank:* Mostly State Natural Area in Colorado Canyon; National Park from below Lajitas to Stillwell Crossing; mostly private thereafter. *Right bank:* Mostly private Mexican land. Please respect property rights.

Scenery: Excellent. Dramatic desert canyons separated by stretches of open terrain.

Solitude: Excellent. River traffic is heaviest in Santa Elena and Boquillas Canyons, especially around Easter (spring break) and Thanksgiving.

Wilderness: Mostly. Occasional ranches, roads, or settlements between canyons.

Fishing: Good for catfish.

Wildlife: Abundant waterfowl. Also beaver, javelina, bobcat.

Weather: Summers are extremely hot (June average high: 103°). Thunderstorms are common from midsummer to early fall (flash flood hazard). Winter days are generally mild, but nights are often frosty, and weather can suddenly become freezing (January averages: high 66°, low 32°).

Water: Below 50° in winter, above 80° in summer. Silty and undrinkable. Side streams unreliable. Bring water or refill and purify at springs.

Camping: Many excellent sites. Camp high; the river can rise rapidly. Beware of side canyon flash floods.

Side Hikes: Many, especially in Boquillas and Lower Canyons.

Side Excursions: Big Bend National Park and Big Bend Ranch State Natural Area.

Guides and References:

- *River Guide to the Rio Grande* (Big Bend Natural History Assn.). Map-guides and mile-by-mile notes cover all runs.
- Aulbach & Butler, *Lower Canyons of the Rio Grande.* Detailed maps and mile-by-mile. Best guide to the Lower Canyons.
- Kirkley, *A Guide to Texas Rivers and Streams.*
- *Riverguide Bandana to the Rio Grande* (Rivers & Mountains). Cloth map.
- Jenkinson, *Wild Rivers of North America.* History, whitewater information.
- Parent, *Big Bend of the Rio Grande.* Photo journey.
- Horgan, *Great River: The Rio Grande in North American History.* Two volumes.

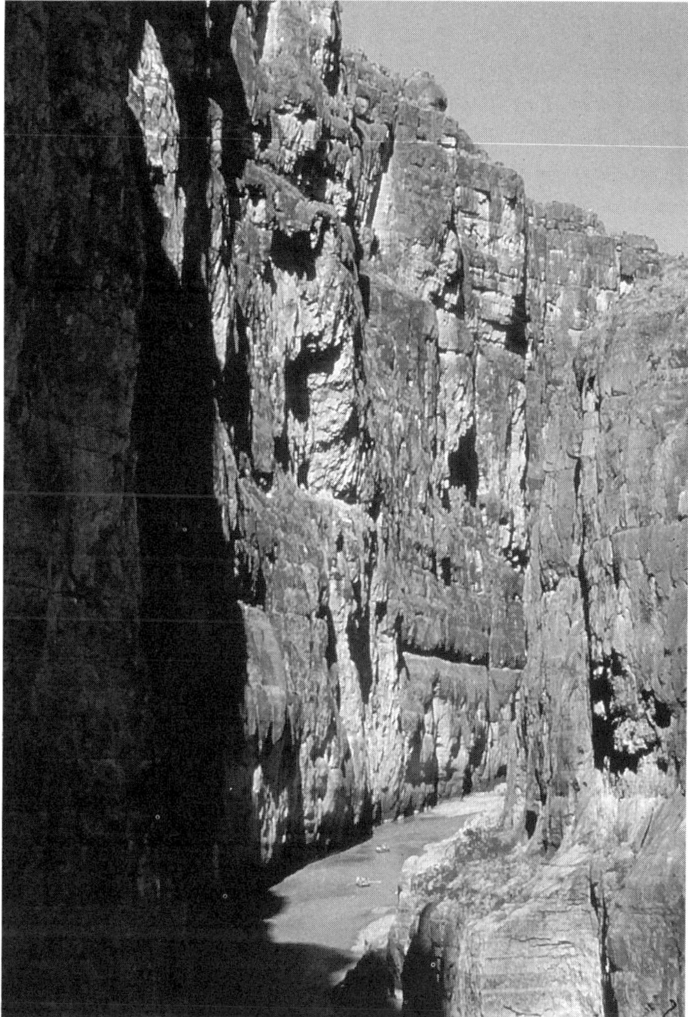

Santa Elena Canyon *Tracy Lynch*

Maps:

- **USGS 1:100:** *Lower Canyons:* Boquillas, Dove Mtn, Comstock.
- **USGS 7.5':** *Colorado Canyon:* Santana Mesa, Lajitas. *Santa Elena:* Lajitas, Mesa De Anguila, Castolon. *Mariscal:* Mariscal Mtn, Solis. *Boquillas:* Boquillas, Ernst Valley, Stillwell Crossing. These maps do not cover the Mexican side.
- **USGS** *Big Bend National Park* sheet shows Lajitas to Stillwell Crossing at 1:100,000. Does not cover the Mexican side.
- National Park Service's *Big Bend* map shows roads and accesses.
- *Big Bend National Park* (Trails Illustrated). Hiking map also shows Mexican side.

Auto Shuttle: *Santa Elena:* 35–60 miles depending on route, all or part paved. *Mariscal:* 20 miles. *San Vicente and Hot Springs:* 20 miles, part paved. *Boquillas:* 80 miles, paved. *Lower Canyons:* 160 miles, mostly paved. Contact Park Service for shuttle service references.

Logistics: Many shuttles are on remote dirt roads; contact Park Service regarding road conditions, and carry water, shovel, tools, etc. Park Service has maps showing shuttle routes and mileages. Private accesses—including Lajitas, Stillwell Crossing, and Dryden Crossing—require permission and may involve fees but provide more security. Vehicle break-ins have occurred at some public accesses; try not to leave cars unattended.

The **Rancherias Creek, Madera Canyon, Grassy Banks, and Lajitas accesses** are on or near Texas 170 between Terlingua and Red-ford. The **Santa Elena Canyon take-out** and the **Talley, Solis, and Rio Grande Village accesses** are in Big Bend National Park; refer to Park Service maps for directions. The unpaved road to Talley is very rough.

To reach **La Linda,** take Texas 385 south from Marathon. Just before the north entrance to Big Bend National Park, turn east on Road 2627 and drive some 28 miles to Gerstacker Bridge. Mexican officials allow boaters to drive to the right bank from 7 a.m. to 6 p.m. The Park Service plans to develop a new access here on the U.S. side, to be called Ten Eyck Landing. To reach **the access upstream at Stillwell Crossing (private, fee),** follow the directions above, but after about 22 miles on Road 2627, turn right on the unpaved road to Adams Ranch and drive about 8 rough miles to the river. For permission call Lee Roberts, (915) 376-2212 or 2215.

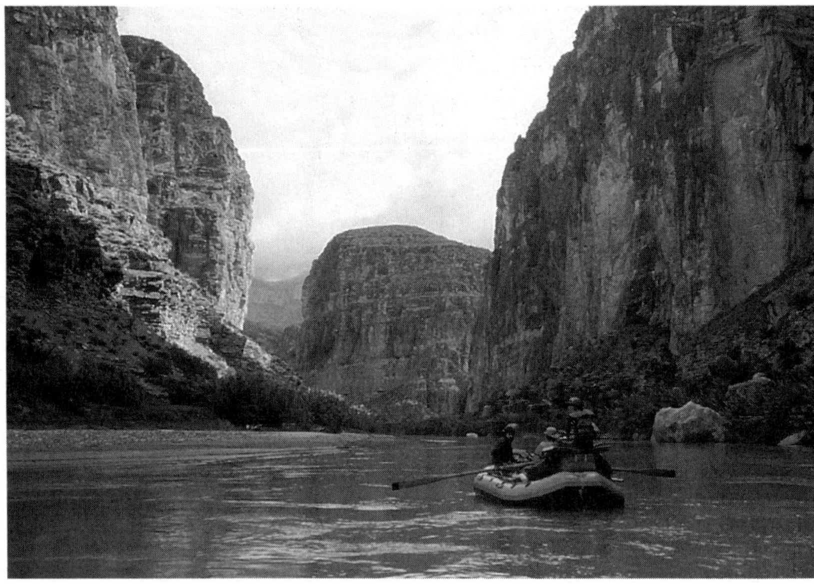

Mariscal Canyon *Tracy Lynch*

The **Dryden Crossing access** is on private property at John's Marina. Boaters must pay a fee, get maps and directions, and be given the combination to a padlocked gate. For information call Dudley Motors in Sanderson, (915) 345-2503, or Scott Shuttle Service in Marathon, (915) 386-4574.

The Lower Rio Grande is the classic off-season wilderness float in the United States. Both private boaters and guests on commercial trips enjoy the spectacular scenery in these remote reaches along the Texas-Mexico border. In the Big Bend region, river runners can choose one or more consecutive sections through a series of dramatic desert canyons, each with its own individual character. Farther downstream and far less known are the Lower Canyons, where deep, narrow gorges alternate with open desert and rugged hills on one of the remotest river runs in the country.

The Rio Grande,[1] the second longest river in the United States, runs some 1,900 miles from the snow-capped Rocky Mountains of southern Colorado to the balmy beaches of the Gulf of Mexico. The river flows south through New Mexico, then turns southeast near El Paso and for the next 1,250 miles marks the boundary between Mexico and the U.S. Along the way, the Rio Grande traces a giant, 200-mile S-curve known as the Big Bend. Here the river winds through rugged peaks and broad plateaus that are part of a southeastern extension of the Rocky Mountains known in Mexico as the Sierra Madre Oriental. The river, older than the mountains, has held to its course and carved deep chasms as the land has risen around it.

The Lower Rio Grande lies farther east and south than any other major run in this guide.[2] Clocks are set to Central Time here, and the latitude of the run is south of New Orleans.

---

[1]To Americans this is the Rio Grande—the "Great River"—but the Mexicans know it as El Rio Bravo. In 1598, scouts for Spanish explorer Don Juan Oñate, who was seeking the fabled Seven Cities of Cibola, came upon the river in spring flood and named it El Rio Bravo del Norte—the "Wild River of the North."

[2]Of the rivers in this book, only the rarely-floated Pecos, a tributary of the Rio Grande, lies farther east.

The climate and vegetation—marked by the extreme heat and aridity of the Chihuahuan Desert with its mesquite, creosote bush, and cacti—are distinct from those on other Western American rivers.

The water in the river is largely of Mexican origin. By the time it reaches El Paso, the Rio Grande has been sucked almost dry for irrigation in Colorado and New Mexico. The Lower Rio Grande is boatable downstream thanks to releases from a dam on a large Mexican tributary, the Rio Conchos, which enters the main river near Presidio, upstream from the Big Bend. Thus boaters on the lower river are usually riding a stream of runoff born in Mexico's high Sierra Madre Oriental. ("Usually" because the river sometimes rises due to muddy rain runoff from the watersheds of smaller tributaries). On average, only four percent of the water flowing through the Big Bend comes from the Rio Grande itself.[3]

Still, the Lower Rio Grande is a distinctly Western American river. Vertical limestone canyons recall the desert gorges of Arizona and Utah. Enticing hot springs and intriguing side canyons abound. The rapids are Southwestern classics, born of landslides and flash floods. (They are also the first whitewater to break the Rio Grande's smooth flow in more than 600 miles. The nearest rapids upriver are in northern New Mexico.) Finally, the extreme isolation is unmistakably Western.

From Colorado Canyon to Dryden Crossing, the Lower Rio Grande offers 230 miles of continuous floating, though this distance is divided among a number of canyons separated by open desert or low hills. Few boaters make the complete trip. The longest run most parties consider is 145 miles from the head of Mariscal Canyon to Dryden Crossing. Many sections are fine open canoe runs.[4]

Colorado Canyon, the first run, is upstream from Big Bend National Park. Just under ten miles long, it is a popular one-day trip with easy access and enjoyable Class II rapids against a background of rugged, reddish walls. This is the only gorge on the Lower Rio Grande carved through volcanic—as opposed to sedimentary—rock. Colorado Canyon was recently made part of the Big Bend Ranch State Natural Area. For longer trips, boaters can add 3.5 miles by putting in upriver at Tapado Canyon and 11.5 miles by continuing downstream through more open terrain to Lajitas.

Below Lajitas the river flows for 118 miles along the boundary of the National Park. Big Bend's first and most popular canyon, Santa Elena, is an eight-mile-long vertical slot cut through the Mesa de Anguila. Sheer limestone walls soar 1,500' high. Santa Elena has the best-known rapid on the Lower Rio Grande—The Rockslide—where a huge section of cliff has fallen into the river and created a maze of narrow channels between enormous boulders.

Nearly 50 miles of open desert and easy water separate Santa Elena from its downstream cousin, Mariscal Canyon. Here, at the southern tip of the Big Bend, the Rio Grande turns northeast and cuts its most imposing gorge (sometimes called "the Grand Canyon of Texas") through Mariscal Mountain. Like Santa Elena, Mariscal Canyon is an impressive vertical limestone defile with rapids formed by rockfalls. But Mariscal is shorter, has easier rapids, and is less heavily used. Many boaters make a day trip of this 10-mile run from Talley to Solis, while others combine it with downstream reaches.

After Mariscal the river makes two shorter, shallower cuts through San Vicente and Hot Springs Canyons. Overshadowed as they are by larger canyons above and below, these scenic sections are less heavily used and are most often floated in conjunction with other runs.

Continuing along the east side of the National Park, the Rio Grande carves deep into the Sierra del Carmen mountain range through beautiful Boquillas Canyon, the longest and mildest in the park. For 33 miles the river flows

[3]Could Mexico deplete the Rio Conchos as America has the Upper Rio Grande and the Lower Colorado, thereby threatening boating on the Lower Rio Grande? In an article for *Texas Monthly*, writer Griffin Smith jr. comments: "Although a minimum supply of water is presently guaranteed by international treaty, the desperate agricultural needs of Mexico's burgeoning population may soon require all the water the Conchos can provide. Treaties have been known to yield to less."

The Rio Conchos is threatened by timber and pulp mill development, and the resulting pollution will obviously affect the Rio Grande downstream. In 1992 the Rio Grande topped the list of North America's most endangered rivers drawn up by the conservation organization American Rivers—partly because of agricultural diversions and pollution from mines upstream in the United States, and partly because of industrial pollution and untreated human waste in the river along the Texas-Mexico border.

[4]For local canoe rentals, contact Scott Shuttle Service, P.O. Box 477, Marathon, TX 79842; (915) 386-4574.

through nothing but small riffles and one easy Class II rapid, making this a fine run for less experienced boaters or anyone more interested in scenery than whitewater. Unlike Santa Elena and Mariscal, Boquillas is sloping rather than sheer-sided, with many intriguing side canyons where limestone fossils and caves are among the sights awaiting hikers.

Below Boquillas Canyon and the Mexican village of La Linda, the river leaves the Big Bend and any remaining semblance of civilization far behind. Its course through open desert and rugged hills is punctuated here and there by the Lower Canyons of the Rio Grande,[5] steep-sided gorges laced with enticing side canyons. Use is gradually increasing, but the Lower Canyons are still rarely floated; only about 700 people per year make the trip. Boaters may go days without seeing any people other than those in their party. The combination of extreme isolation and scattered challenging rapids (up to Class III+ at most flows) demands careful preparation and extra caution. Many open canoeists portage a few rapids, including Upper and Lower Madison Falls.

On any float on the Lower Rio Grande, whether in the Big Bend or the Lower Canyons, river runners must prepare for isolation, extreme heat, changeable weather, and fluctuating flows. Sudden summer and fall rainstorms can cause flash floods in side canyons and rapid changes in the river level.[6] Winter weather can shift dramatically, from hot and dry to cold wind and rain, in just a few hours. Plan carefully for adequate drinking water, both on the river and on remote shuttle roads.

[5]Though they lie outside the National Park, the Lower Canyons are within the 191 miles of the Lower Rio Grande, from just above Mariscal Canyon to below Dryden Crossing, designated as a National Wild and Scenic River in 1978.

[6]As you snuggle into your sleeping bag at night, consider this: in the June 1954 flood, flows at Langtry (just below the Lower Canyons) surged from less than 1,000 to 169,000 cfs in four hours.

Mile by Mile Guide

Note: River miles in left column start at zero with each put-in. Numbers in brackets show total miles from first put-in, Rancherias Canyon. Numbers in parentheses indicate frequently-used International Boundary & Water Commission mileage, measured upstream from mouth.

Colorado Canyon

0 (925) **PUT-IN** on the left bank of the Rio Grande at the mouth of Rancherias Canyon. An alternate private put-in 3.5 miles upstream at Tapado Canyon adds a scenic Class III reach known as the "Hoodoos" section. Debris from Rancherias Canyon creates a Class II+ rapid. Two more Class II+ rapids in the next 2.5 miles.

6 Unusual cliffs on the right as the canyon walls recede. Downstream is **PANTHER (III-)** at the mouth of Panther Canyon, which enters on the left.

9.5 (915.5) Madera Canyon **RIVER ACCESS.** After a mile-long cut through Big Hill, the canyon opens, allowing Highway 170 to reach the river. The access is on the left, a quarter mile below the concrete tepees at the roadside park. Downstream is **LEDGEROCK (II+)**. From here to Lajitas the terrain is mostly hills or open desert, with one short cut through Black Rock Canyon at mile 19.

12.7 Grassy Banks, a popular **RIVER ACCESS** on the left. A little over a mile downstream, Fresno Creek enters on the left. Outwash from the creek pushes the river against the right wall and creates **FRESNO (II+).**

21 Lajitas **RIVER ACCESS** (private) on the left as the river bends right above the town. Short dirt road leads to Highway 170.

Santa Elena Canyon

0 [21] (904) **PUT-IN** on the left just upstream from Lajitas. Downstream, take the main channel on the right when the river splits. Big Bend National Park on the left bank begins about two miles below the put-in and continues for 118 miles. The terrain becomes more rugged, and there are several rapids in the 9 miles from the park boundary to the canyon entrance.

3.5 **MATADERO (III-)**, where Arroyo Matadero enters on the right.

8 The Sentinel, a conical peak, appears 3 miles ahead on the Mexican side.

11 Arroyo San Antonio enters on the right, creating a Class II rapid. Below the rapid is the awesome vertical entrance of Santa Elena Canyon. Just inside, the swift current undercuts the walls; use caution.

12.7 About a mile below the canyon entrance lies **THE ROCKSLIDE (IV)**, the toughest rapid in the Big Bend.

Recognition: A small rockfall on the right precedes the big slide, and a few big house rocks divide the current at this point. Boaters can maneuver around these initial boulders and land on the right bank at the head of the rapid. **Scouting mandatory.** Scout from the right-bank trail that climbs to the top of the main slide. Use this trail for a difficult portage, if necessary, or at lower flows consider lining and portaging down the left. **The rapid:** A massive rockfall on the right forces the river into the left wall and fills the channel with enormous boulders for a quarter mile. At low flows some slots are too narrow for most boats; at high flows big hydraulics develop. Strainers and debris can lodge in the chutes. Boaters should memorize their route; once in the rapid, boulders block the view downstream.

The rest of Santa Elena is mostly easy water, but **beware of undercut walls.**

16 Arch Canyon enters on the right, followed by Fern Canyon, where boaters can climb to lush pools. A mile downstream, high on the right, is Smugglers Cave.

19 Just as the canyon reaches its maximum depth of 1,500', the walls abruptly end and Terlingua Creek enters on the left. Take out a mile downstream at a **RIVER ACCESS** on the left, or 5.5 miles farther on the left at Blue Creek. Few boaters float the 40 miles of easy water and open terrain from here to Mariscal Canyon.

Mariscal Canyon

0 [86.5] (838.5) **PUT-IN** on the left at Talley, an abandoned ranch. Downstream, the walls rise as the river cuts into Mariscal Mountain.

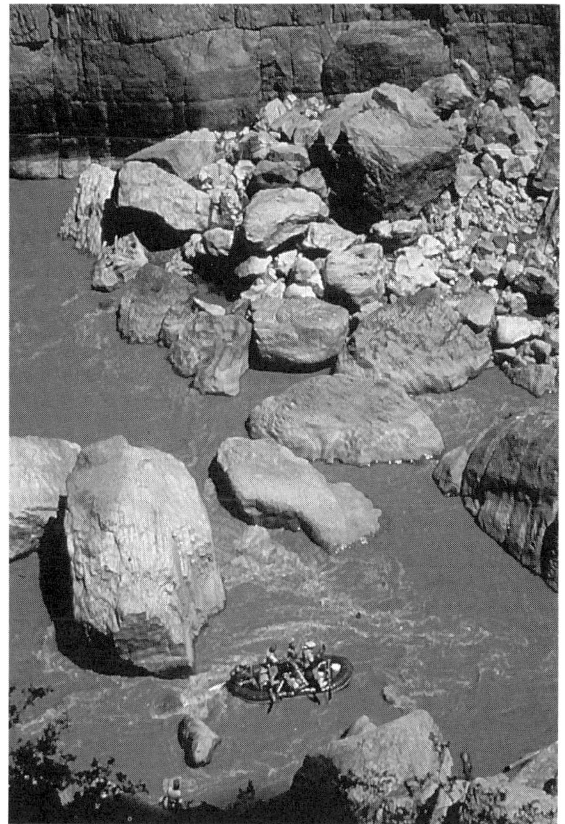

The Rockslide, Rio Grande *Tracy Lynch*

2.5 Entrance to Mariscal Canyon. Just downstream, a left bend marks the southernmost point in Big Bend, and just below this curve is **ROCKPILE (II+)**, where big boulders split the current. About a half mile below Rockpile and a mile into the canyon is **TIGHT SQUEEZE (II–III)**, where a huge block of stone divides the river into a 5'-wide channel on the left and a 10'-wide channel on the right. Scout on the right. At high water this rapid can be hazardous, and at extreme flows the big rock becomes a massive reversal. The rest of Mariscal has only easy riffles.

8 The canyon ends abruptly, but rugged hills continue for two miles.

10 Solis **RIVER ACCESS** at a break in the vegetation on the left.

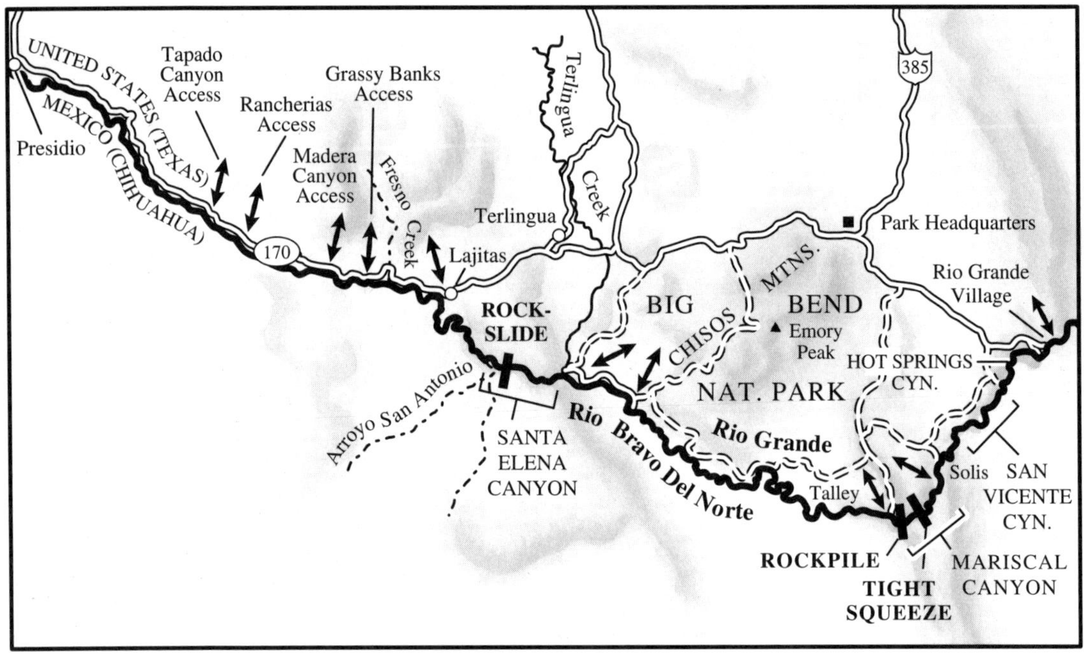

Lower Rio Grande (West)

San Vicente and Hot Springs Canyons

0 [96.5] (828.5) **PUT-IN** at Solis Landing on the left. A mile and a half downstream, Fresno Creek enters on the left, and the rugged slopes of San Vicente Canyon close in.

5.5 The canyon walls recede. Just ahead, Glenn Draw enters on the left. Debris from the draw creates a small rapid. Two miles downstream, look for the ruins of Casa de Piedra on the left (emergency access).

9.5 The village of San Vicente appears on the right. No camping within half a mile of either side of the village. A ford at mile 12.5 is known as San Vicente Crossing.

14.5 Gravel pit on the left bank is a common **RIVER ACCESS.** Two miles downstream, Tornillo Creek enters on the left, creating a small rapid and marking another **RIVER ACCESS** at the former site of Langford Hot Spring resort. Hot springs can be found here and just downriver. Downstream, the walls of Hot Springs Canyon close in for about 1.5 miles.

18.5 Boat ramp on the left at Rio Grande Village is a popular **RIVER ACCESS.** Ranger station, campground, and services.

Boquillas Canyon

0 [115] (810) **PUT-IN** at the boat ramp on the left bank at Rio Grande Village, behind the group campground.

5 Entrance to Boquillas Canyon. Boquillas Canyon trail ends here on the left.

8 Cañon Puerto Rico enters on the right, followed by another side canyon 1.5 miles downstream. Both offer good hikes.

13.5 The Marufo Vega pack trail reaches the left bank.

15.5 Arroyo Venado enters on the left, creating a small riffle. A large side canyon enters on the right less than a mile downstream.

18.5 Cow Canyon enters on the left. Downstream, two more canyons enter on the Mexican side (good hiking), and a rock formation known as the Rabbit Ears comes into view on the left.

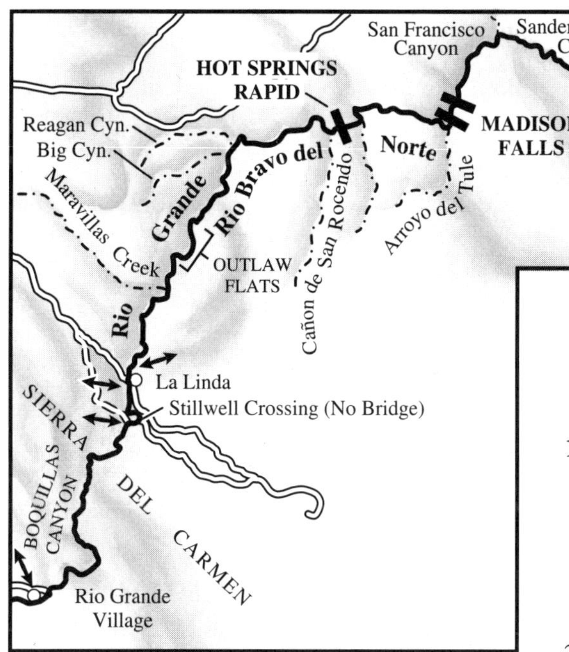

Lower Rio Grande (East)

21.5 Boquillas Canyon ends abruptly.

25.5 Big Bend National Park ends on the left. Downstream, the Texas shore is private for several miles, though the river is still Wild and Scenic.

27.5 Stillwell Crossing **RIVER ACCESS** on the left, on private land belonging to Adams Ranch. Fee. (See **Logistics.**)

30.5 Arroyo del Veinte enters on the right, creating a Class II rapid.

33 Gerstacker Bridge. **RIVER ACCESS.** Town of La Linda on the right. The Park Service plans to develop a new take-out on the left bank above the bridge. The old site is on the right. (See **Logistics.**)

Lower Canyons

0 [148] (777) **PUT-IN** at Gerstacker Bridge. Black Gap Wildlife Management Area begins on the left bank and continues to mile 27.

11.5 Maravillas Creek enters on the left, creating a riffle. Good campsite on the right. A road up the creek leads some 17 miles to the wildlife area headquarters—the last emergency access for miles. Developed campsites can be seen on the left in the next ten miles through the wildlife area.

15 The canyon gradually opens and the river flows placidly through Outlaw Flats for some 10 miles. A flat-topped butte known as Cerro el Sombrero ("Hat Rock") or Castle Butte rises on the Mexican side.

27 Big Canyon enters on the left, creating a Class II rapid. Three quarters of a mile farther, Reagan Canyon enters on the left, creating another riffle. Downstream the steep walls of the Lower Canyons close in for more than 40 miles, and the whitewater becomes more difficult.

34 Two side canyons enter on the left. Two miles farther, a cavern known as Cueva de la Puerta Grande appears on the right.

38 Good springs on both banks. The remains of a water works are on the left.

40.5 **HOT SPRINGS (III). Recognition:** The river bends left, and the wide opening of Cañon de San Rocendo can be seen ahead on the right. **The rapid:** The river drops steeply through a washboard of rocks and holes, and a big slanted house rock protrudes on the left. Sharp rocks wait at the bottom. Scout and, if necessary, portage on the right. A large warm (not hot) spring is near the foot of the rapid on the right.

43 Cañon Caballo Blanco enters on the right. A mile downstream, a jeep trail reaches the left bank. A little farther downstream, the river curves right and cuts through the Bullis Gap Range, deepest point in the Lower Canyons. Watch for a Class II to II+ rapid in this narrow cut. Palmas

Canyon enters on the left at mile 45.5, creating another Class II rapid. Scout left.

50 Arroyo de Complejo del Caballo enters on the right in a narrow section, creating **RODEO (III)**, where big waves develop at high flows. Scout right.

55 **UPPER MADISON FALLS (III–IV)**, the biggest rapid on the Lower Rio Grande. Tougher at high and low flows. **Recognition:** A third of a mile above the rapid, the river curves left around prominent Burro Bluff. Stop on the right at the mouth of the Arroyo El Tule to scout or portage. **The rapid** has two parts: a fairly straightforward upper section and a more difficult lower falls. At some levels boaters may be able to run the first drop, then catch an eddy on the left to scout the lower falls. At most flows the lower drop divides around a rocky island, and boaters typically take the left channel.

57 **LOWER MADISON FALLS (III-)**, also known as **Horseshoe Falls.** A rockfall from the right wall partially blocks the river. Scout left. Boaters usually run down the chute on the left. Look for springs on the left below the rapid.

61 Panther Canyon enters on the left (side hike). Frequent flash floods have created **PANTHER (II+)**, where a deep, swift channel undercuts the left bank. Scout left. A few hundred yards below the rapid on the left is the last reliable spring for the rest of the trip (submerged at higher flows).

66.5 San Francisco Canyon, a major side canyon, enters on the left. Frequent flash floods have created **SAN FRANCISCO (II+)**. New floods may alter this rapid, but the main channel normally undercuts the left bank. Downstream are easy riffles and flatwater as the canyon walls gradually recede.

79 Sanderson Canyon enters on the left. Class II rapid.

82.5 [230.5] (694.5) Arroyo de Agua Verde enters on the right. Class II rapid. A third of a mile downstream, a gauging station appears on the left, and just beyond is the popular Dryden Crossing **TAKE-OUT** at John's Marina on the left. In earlier times, this famous ford was used by Apaches and Comanches moving between Texas and Mexico.

The very rarely boated stretch of river downstream is broken by occasional riffles and a couple of larger rapids as it runs through hills, open desert, and grazing lands. One final gorge, Martin Canyon, closes in from about mile 90 to mile 98; watch for an intermediate rapid with an undercut wall just below the canyon entrance. Another Class III rapid is at the mouth of Lozier Canyon, mile 115. ***HAZARD.*** A 5' weir at Foster's Ranch (mile 120) should not be run. An alternate take-out may be possible at this ranch. The last take-out is at Langtry, mile 138. When it is full, Amistad Reservoir's backwaters extend several miles upstream from Langtry.

Gila River

1. Wilderness Run: Grapevine CG (5,525') to Mogollon Creek (4,640').
III; 41 miles; 22 ft./mi.

2. Middle Box:
USFS Road 809 (4,340') to Redrock (4,015').
III (IV above 500 cfs); 18 miles; 18 ft./mi.

3. Lower Box:
Redrock to New Mexico 92 Bridge (3,770').
I+p; 20 miles; 12 ft./mi.

4. Arizona Gila Box: Old Safford-Clifton Road (3,340') to Bonita Creek (3,115').
II; 19 miles; 12 ft./mi.

5. Lower Gila.
Below Coolidge Dam; see essay.

Drainage Area and Average Annual Discharge: 1,864 sq. mi. and 108,000 af near Mogollon Creek; 4,010 sq. mi. and 143,500 af at put-in for Arizona Gila Box.

Season: Usually boatable during brief period of peak snowmelt, typically some time between mid-March and mid-April, but ranging as widely as early March or late May. Late summer rains often raise the river briefly to boatable levels.

Flow Information: USGS in Albuquerque, (505) 262-5388, has readings "near Gila" (Wilderness Run take-out) and "near Redrock" (Middle and Lower Boxes). USGS in Tucson, (602) 670-6671, has readings "near Virden" (gauge #09432000), above Arizona Gila Box put-in; "at head of Safford Valley" (#09448500), near Arizona Gila Box take-out; and "below Coolidge Dam" (#09469500).

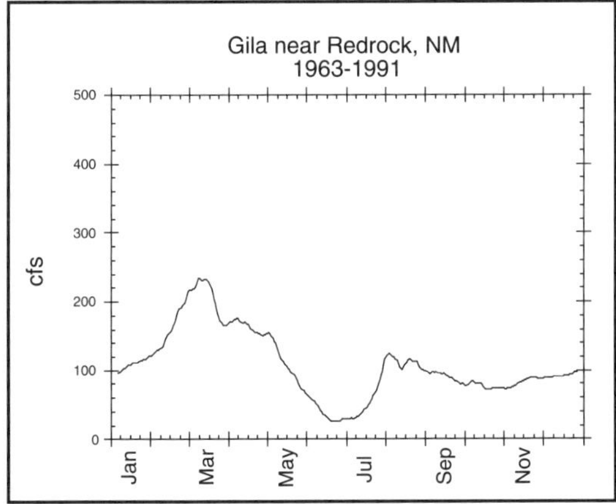

Irrigation diversions may deplete the river, so at times flows may be lower on downstream runs than on upstream runs.

Special Hazards: Fences and diversion dams. Strainers and log hazards. Sudden floods. Private property owners.

Permits: Not presently required.

Managing Agencies: *Wilderness Run:* Wilderness RD, Gila NF, Route 11, Box 100, Silver City, NM 88061; (505) 536-9461. *Middle Box:* Silver City RD, Gila NF, 2915 Highway 180 East, Silver City, NM, 88061; (505) 538-2771. *Lower Box:* BLM, Las Cruces District, 1800 Marquess St., Las Cruces, NM 88005; (505) 525-8228. *Arizona Gila Box:* BLM, Safford District, 711 14th Ave., Safford, AZ, 85546; (602) 428-4040.

Commercial Raft Trips: Yes in Arizona Gila Box and below Coolidge Dam. For a list of outfitters, contact the BLM in Safford. None at present on the New Mexico runs.

Land Ownership: *Wilderness Run:* Almost all National Forest. *Middle Box:* National Forest first 10 miles, then private. *Lower Box:* Mixed BLM and private. *Arizona Gila Box:* Mostly BLM.

Scenery: Very good to excellent. Varied; see essay.

Solitude: Excellent.

Wilderness: Yes in the canyons; no between them.

Side Excursions: Gila Cliff Dwellings National Monument and Gila Hot Springs near the Wilderness Run put-in.

Guides and References:
- *New Mexico Whitewater* (New Mexico State Park Division). Covers Runs 1–3.
- *Arizona Rivers and Streams Guide* (Arizona State Parks). Covers Runs 4 & 5.
- Information sheets from BLM and USFS.
- M. H. Salmon, *Gila Descending.* Essays on a canoe trip down the Gila.

Maps:
- **USGS 7.5':** *Wilderness Run:* Gila Hot Springs, Little Turkey Park, Granny Mtn, Canyon Hill, Canteen Canyon. *Middle Box:* Mangas Springs, Brushy Mtn, Redrock. *Lower Box:* Redrock, Nichols Canyon, Canador Peak. *Arizona Gila Box:* Guthrie, Gila Box.
- **USGS 1:100:** *Wilderness Run:* Mogollon Mtns. *Middle and Lower Box:* Silver City.

Arizona Gila Box: Safford. *Lower Gila:* Globe, Mammoth, Mesa.
- **USFS:** *Gila NF* covers Wilderness Run and Middle Box.
- **BLM:** *Safford District* covers Arizona Box.

Logistics: *Note:* Vandalism of parked vehicles has been reported at some accesses.

Wilderness Run: Shuttle is roughly 75 miles one way, mostly paved. To reach the **put-in,** follow U.S. 180 to Silver City, NM, then drive north on NM 15 toward Gila Hot Springs and Gila Cliff Dwellings. The put-in is a mile short of Gila Hot Springs at Grapevine Campground, near the bridge over the Gila at the confluence of the East and West Forks. To reach the **take-out at Mogollon Creek,** return to U.S. 180, drive west and north some 30 miles to the town of Cliff, turn right for a mile on NM 211, then bear left on Route 293 and drive up the west side of the river. After about 5 miles this road crosses the Gila NF boundary and becomes unpaved USFS Road 755, which leads roughly another 1.5 miles to the take-out on the right bank near the mouth of Mogollon Creek. (The last portion of road may be impassable at times.) The **alternate take-out at Turkey Creek** is reached by a much rougher road on the east side of the river, USFS Road 155, which may be impassable when wet. Contact Gila NF for information.

Middle Box: To reach the **put-in,** turn southwest off U.S. 180 on USFS Road 809 about 4 miles south of Cliff, NM. Follow this unpaved road (high clearance recommended) down the east bank roughly 5.5 miles to the Gila NF boundary, then continue down to a suitable put-in point. **Do not launch above the Forest boundary due to a dangerous diversion.** Two alternate routes lead to the **take-out at the bridge north of Redrock:** (1) a long paved route (about 100 miles one way) on U.S. 180, NM 90, U.S. 70, and NM 464; (2) an alternate route (45 miles one way) over USFS Road 851, which may be impassable when wet. Contact Gila NF for more information.

Lower Box: To reach the **put-in,** follow NM 464 north from U.S. 70 to Redrock. Launch at the bridge north of town. To reach the **take-out,** follow U.S. 70 to NM 92, then drive north to the highway bridge over the Gila southeast of Virden, NM, just a few miles east of the Arizona border.

Arizona Gila Box: Shuttle is about 50 miles one way, partly paved. To reach the **put-in,** follow U.S. 191 north from Guthrie, AZ across the Gila some 5.5 miles to where the divided highway ends and becomes a two-lane highway. Turn left, cross the highway onto a small dirt road (Old Safford-Clifton Road), and drive south 4 miles to the bridge over the Gila. To reach the **take-out,** follow U.S. 70 to Solomon, AZ, some 5 miles east of Safford. Turn north on Sanchez Road, cross the Gila, and bear right (still on Sanchez Road), then follow BLM signs to the Bonita Creek take-out. Along the way to Bonita Creek are short spur roads to the **alternate accesses** at Dry Canyon and Spring Canyon. Contact the BLM for details. High clearance vehicles recommended. For shuttles on this section, try Joe Castaneda in Clifton, (602) 865-2354.

Few people know that the Gila[1] is one of the longest rivers in the West. From the Continental Divide in southwestern New Mexico, the river runs some 500 miles west to the Colorado River near Yuma, Arizona. Major tributaries include the Salt and San Francisco Rivers. The Gila also drains one of the West's largest basins. Its watershed comprises nearly 60,000 square miles of New Mexico, Arizona and northern Mexico—an area larger than the entire Green River basin and more than four times as big as the drainage of Idaho's Salmon River.

In spite of these impressive statistics, the Gila is one of the West's most obscure rivers, almost unknown outside Arizona and New Mexico. The reasons are simple. First, the basin is the driest in this guide, taking in the greater part of the Sonoran Desert where rainfall generally averages less than 10" per year. Even near its mountain headwaters—a relatively moist region compared to the rest of the basin—the Gila carries little water. The 1,800-square mile upper watershed produces just over 100,000

[1]Pronounced "HEE-lah." Origins of the name are murky; the Spanish may have garbled an Indian name for the river—perhaps a shortened version of the Yuma Indians' "hah-quah-sa-eel" ("running salt water").

acre-feet of water each year.[2] Second, the river's scanty natural endowment is almost entirely used up by humans along the way; the Gila is normally drained dry before the halfway mark in its journey.

But in western New Mexico and eastern Arizona, the Upper Gila still flows free,[3] and in most years it has enough water to float small boats through some of the loveliest canyons in the Southwest. Its headwater streams gather light snowmelt from high peaks some 150 miles southwest of Albuquerque: the East Fork Gila drains the Black Range along the Continental Divide, while the Middle and West Forks tumble out of the Mogollon[4] Mountains. Boating begins after the three forks join in Gila National Forest and continues intermittently to within 50 miles of Phoenix. This 350-mile section contains five runs, only two of which—the Middle and Lower Boxes in New Mexico—are contiguous. The first four runs are through deep canyons separated by broad, open agricultural valleys where hazardous barbed-wire fences and irrigation diversions are common.

The Gila has an extremely variable and unpredictable season. The river normally rises to boatable levels only during a brief runoff peak in early spring or after unpredictable late summer rains. It rarely has enough water for rafts longer than 14', and in some years it barely rises high enough for canoes. Weather is a critical variable on early season-runs, when sudden rain and snow are possible. Heavy rains, especially during the late summer "monsoon" season, can produce sudden, dangerous floods.

The whitewater is mostly moderate. **Ranch fences, brush strainers, and irrigation diversions pose the greatest hazards.** This guide notes only a few of the worst spots, but boaters will probably encounter others. Log and brush hazards can change from year to year or even from storm to storm. Be alert for strainers and fences on all runs. Scout blind corners before running them. Be prepared to make several short portages if necessary.

The canyon sections of the Gila encompass a varied landscape: open Ponderosa pine forest in the Wilderness Run; pinyon and juniper woodland in the Middle Box; palo verde and mesquite in the Arizona Gila Box. Yet the canyons have much in common, most notably a sense of deep wilderness. The Gila region was one of the last portions of the lower 48 states to be settled, and large tracts of land bear little mark of civilization.

For roughly a thousand years the Mogollon and Anasazi peoples lived on or near various sections of the upper Gila and its tributaries, building imposing structures like those at Gila Cliff Dwellings National Monument. During this same period, the Hohokam practiced irrigation farming along the lower reaches of the Gila and Salt Rivers in Central Arizona. About 1400 A.D., for reasons unknown, all of these peoples abruptly disappeared.

By the time Spanish explorers arrived, Apache tribes dominated the region. In 1540, Spanish explorer Francisco Coronado crossed the lower Gila in search of the fabled Seven Cities of Cibola. The warlike Apaches fiercely resisted Spain's attempts to establish a permanent presence in the region. Following the conclusion of the Mexican-American war in 1848, the Gila River briefly marked the southern boundary of the United States. However, when the Americans realized that the best transportation routes lay south of the river, they acquired additional lands via the Gadsden Purchase of 1853, which resulted in the modern border between the two nations.

[2]In contrast, the Wynoochee River in Washington's Olympic Peninsula, with the wettest basin in this guide, carries 385,000 acre-feet per year from an upper watershed of only 41 square miles.

[3]Though the Gila's upper reaches in New Mexico and eastern Arizona are still free-flowing (aside from irrigation diversions), these sections have been threatened by dam proposals in the past and could be again in the future. The Lower Box and Arizona Gila Box are being studied for possible National Wild and Scenic designation. For more information, contact: (1) In New Mexico: Amigos Bravos, P.O. Box 238, Taos, NM 87571, (505) 758-3874; (2) In Arizona: American Rivers Arizona, 3601 N. 7th Ave., Phoenix, AZ 85013, (602) 264-1823.

[4]Locally pronounced "MUGGY-uhn." Named for Don Juan Ignacio Flores Mogollon, an early governor of Spain's New World territories.

Gila River Guide

Wilderness Run

Here, where the Gila carves a pristine passage between the Mogollon Mountains to the north and the Pinos Altos Range to the south, is one of the gems of Southwestern boating. For 34 miles the river flows through the southern corner of the 600,000-acre Gila Wilderness,[5] a remote region whose abundant wildlife includes bear, javelina, elk, eagle, and wild turkey. The river supports healthy populations of trout, smallmouth bass, and catfish.

The Gila follows a tortuous course through this wilderness, winding 35 miles to cover just 18 as the crow flies. Though the whitewater is generally moderate, an abundance of log and brush hazards can pose serious dangers. At times, downed trees may completely block the channel, requiring portage. Boaters should also be alert for possible fences across the river. Sharp, right-angle turns in the narrow streambed can force unwary boaters into rock headwalls.

Put in at Grapevine Campground where New Mexico Highway 15 crosses the river just below the confluence of the Gila's East and West Forks (mile 0). Downstream, the river enters the Gila Wilderness. A trail follows the river all the way to Turkey Creek (mile 35). A hot springs is on the left at mile 2. Sycamore Canyon enters on the right at mile 10.5. At mile 16.5 the Gila winds through a gooseneck bend to the right and shifts from a generally southwesterly course to a westerly one. Sapillo Creek enters on the left in the middle of the gooseneck, and a trail (possible emergency exit) leads up the north side of the creek about six miles to Highway 15.

The river leaves the wilderness area at mile 33.5. Turkey Creek, a major tributary, enters on the right a mile downstream. A trail leads up the creek some three miles to a hot springs. Downstream, the river again trends southwest. Not far below Turkey Creek is an **alternate take-out** where a rough dirt road reaches the left bank. A half dozen miles farther downstream is the **primary take-out** where USFS Road 755 reaches the right bank at the mouth of **Mogollon Creek** (see **Logistics**).

[5]Designated in 1924 as the world's first primitive area, thanks to the pioneering efforts of conservationist Aldo Leopold.

Downstream from Mogollon Creek, the Gila flows through open ranch and farm land for some nine miles to the U.S. 180 bridge near Cliff, New Mexico. Below U.S. 180 the terrain is open for several miles, gradually becoming more rugged as it approaches the Middle Box. **Boating is not recommended from Mogollon Creek to the Middle Box due to barbed-wire fences and irrigation diversions.**

Middle Box

About eight miles south of Cliff, New Mexico, the river reenters Gila National Forest and gradually descends into a narrow, seldom-run canyon. Boaters can launch below the Forest boundary on the left bank near the end of USFS Road 809 (mile 0). It may be possible to put in farther upstream, but **a diversion some two miles above the Forest boundary presents a hazard.**

Downstream, the walls slowly close in. In the Middle Box the river carves a very narrow passage between walls of dark metamorphic bedrock rising 100' to 200' above the stream. The resistant rock produces some of the toughest rapids on the Gila—Class III at most flows, more demanding at high water. Watch for challenging drops near the head of the box where side canyons have washed debris into the river. The inner gorge lies within an isolated canyon forested in pinyon and juniper. Birds abound along the riverbank, and angling is good for bass and catfish. Camping is limited in the last five miles of the canyon due to the sheer walls.

Near mile 10 the river leaves Gila National Forest and enters BLM and private lands. Near mile 12, a USGS gauging station appears on the left. **Watch for fences and diversions below this point.** A mile beyond the gauge, the canyon opens and the river flows over an open flood plain for five miles to the bridge just north of Redrock (mile 18).

Lower Box

With less dramatic scenery and no real whitewater, this stretch gets even less use than the infrequently-run Middle Box. The first several miles pass through open ranching country, where boaters should watch for **diversions and fences.** Then the river enters the scenic Lower Box, with red-and-white cliffs on both sides. Birds are abundant, and anglers may have luck

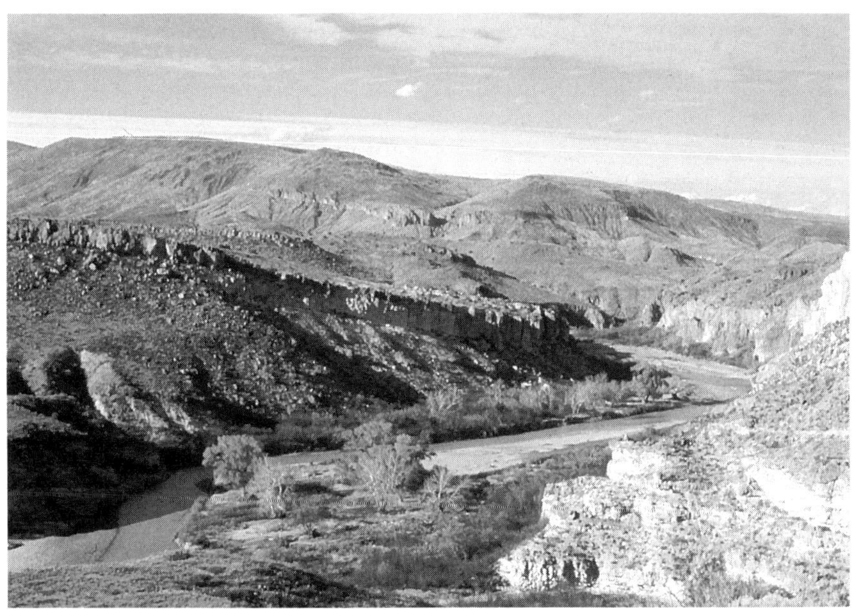
Lower Box, Gila River *M.H. Salmon*

catching catfish. This section has been recommended for designation as a wilderness and is under study for National Wild and Scenic River protection.

Put in at the bridge just north of Redrock (mile 0). The first seven miles are fairly open, then the canyon closes in. A dirt road reaches the left bank at the mouth of Nichols Canyon, mile 10 (private land). The canyon narrows again just downstream. Cottonwood Canyon enters on the left at mile 16.5. Not far downstream is a **mandatory portage at a diversion dam**; portage on the left (south) bank. Below the dam the Box opens, and the river runs through an open valley to the **take-out at the New Mexico Highway 92 bridge** (mile 19.5). Below Highway 92 the river flows through broad valleys and farmland for some 35 miles to the U.S. 666 bridge south of Clifton, Arizona.

Arizona Gila Box

After crossing into Arizona and wandering for many miles through open valleys, the Gila runs through one final canyon, often called simply the "Gila Box." (We usually refer to it as the "Arizona Gila Box," to avoid confusion with the two New Mexico boxes.) Here, the Gila Mountains to the north and the Black Hills to the south rise above the river's deep cut. The canyon walls, which rise several hundred feet in places, are clad in cactus and desert shrubs, while scattered cottonwood, ash, and willow cling to the banks of the river. Wildlife abounds, including bighorn sheep, deer, javelina, and many kinds of birds. Camping is excellent.

This remote, roadless reach is currently (1993) under study as a possible National Wild and Scenic River. In addition, the canyon was designated as a Riparian National Conservation Area in 1990. Despite this protection, however, there is continuing controversy over proposals to allow off-road vehicles to drive in the riverbed during times of lowest flows.

Upstream diversions often reduce flows on this stretch of the Gila, but near the head of the canyon, the San Francisco River usually adds considerable water—sometimes carrying more than the Gila. In fact, many boaters approach the Gila Box by floating the last section of the San Francisco below Clifton. This alternate approach is often preferable because it avoids private land and fences on the Gila above the San Francisco confluence. However, the San Francisco itself may have fences. Refer to the chapter on the **San Francisco** for more information.

The rapids in the Gila Box are generally Class II or less, with one Class II+ passage at Black Canyon. In several places the current runs directly into headwalls, creating potential problems for less experienced boaters. As on other Gila runs, **several hazardous fences may require portage.** Contact the BLM in Safford for an up-to-date map showing the exact location of fences. (In 1992 there were five: four above the San Francisco River, and one below.)

Put in on the right bank at the **Old Safford-Clifton Road bridge** (mile 0). Downstream, the canyon narrows. Treat private land in this section with plenty of respect; in the past, boaters have had problems with landowners. **Watch out for fences across the river.** The first likely encounter with a fence is at Subia Ranch, a little over a mile below the put-in. Be alert for more downstream. The San Francisco

River enters on the right at mile 6 as the walls of the Gila Box close in. Eagle Creek, a large tributary canyon, enters on the right at mile 9. This could be a good campsite and side hike, but it is private property.

A steep orange-brown layer of sedimentary rock, the remains of a prehistoric lake bed, towers over the right bank at mile 15.5. This deposit serves as a landmark for the toughest whitewater on the run, a Class II+ rapid half a mile downstream where Black Canyon enters on the left. Downstream, the walls slowly recede. Watch for another fence about two miles below Black Canyon. The large side canyon of **Bonita Creek** opens on the right at mile 19. **Take out here,** or continue to **alternate takeouts:** Spring Canyon Picnic Area, about two miles downstream on the right, and the Dry Canyon access, about half a mile farther on the right. Below Spring Canyon are several **hazardous diversion dams** as the river flows out into a broad, shallow valley.

Lower Gila

More than 60 miles downstream from the Gila Box and some 80 miles east of Phoenix, Coolidge Dam blocks the Gila, creating San Carlos Reservoir. Irrigation releases from the dam provide boatable flows on the Lower Gila from April or May through September in most years.

Unfortunately, **much of the river below the dam is rendered unrunnable by an impenetrable tangle of trees and brush.** These strainers are the result of inadequate flows below the dam. The tightly-controlled releases prevent the high flows that would naturally sweep out much of the vegetation. In recent years, outfitters working with the BLM have cleared the worst strainers from some portions of the lower river. As a result, some sections are now being run. In January 1993 major flooding on the Gila resulted in unprecedented releases of about 30,000 cfs from Coolidge Dam. These flows cleared out many of the strainers and brush hazards on the sections of the river below the dam. **However, because new brush hazards can develop at any time, boaters should inquire locally and with the managing agency before attempting these sections.**

HAZARD. Immediately below Coolidge Dam the Gila cuts through a canyon known as **Needle's Eye. Do not attempt this section.** Although the gradient in this 20-mile stretch is only 15 ft./mi., it is **unrunnable due to deadly strainers.** There have been several deaths here. Also, access is problematic since the left bank is in the San Carlos Apache Indian Reservation, which does not allow public use of the road leading to the base of Coolidge Dam.

Some 20 miles below Coolidge Dam, Arizona Highway 77 joins the river at Dripping Springs Wash and follows the right bank some nine miles to the town of Winkelman. This section has been partially cleared of strainers, allowing boaters to enjoy a Class I+ run with a gradient of 12 ft./mi. Despite the low difficulty rating, **boaters should remain alert for strainers and brush hazards,** especially after periods of high water. This stretch is popular with innertubers, and several commercial outfitters offer trips here. For more information, contact the BLM in Safford.

Boating is not recommended on the ten miles from Winkelman to Kearny. This section is plagued by **strainers.** It is also less scenic, with Arizona Highway 177 along the right bank.

Below Kearny the river leaves the highway and follows an isolated course through rolling desert hills. The 19 miles from the small town of Kelvin (a few miles below Kearny) to Ashurst-Hayden Dam offer quiet floating (the gradient is only 9 ft./mi.) and good birdwatching. **Be alert for strainers and fences on this seldom-run section.** For more information contact the Phoenix office of the BLM, 2015 W. Deer Valley Road, Phoenix, AZ 85027; (602) 863-4464). Below Ashurst-Hayden Dam the river is normally drained dry by diversions.

An unusual hazard may loom over the entire Lower Gila. There has been considerable controversy regarding the safety of Coolidge Dam. Studies in 1979 and 1989 revealed several safety concerns, including weaknesses in the bedrock that some believed could lead to a dam failure and devastating flood. As of 1993 the Bureau of Reclamation was repairing and reinforcing the dam, with work scheduled to be completed by mid-1995. In the meantime, sirens have been set up at the dam and in downstream towns to alert residents to evacuate in the event of a disaster. If you hear a siren while boating, head for the hills!

In his book *Gila Descending*, M.H. "Dutch" Salmon recounts a trip down the Gila with his dog and cat in a 13' Coleman canoe. These excerpts describe their misadventures on the Wilderness Run.

Even before rounding the bend I could tell there was a big sycamore down in the water. I assumed I'd get around it somehow so I didn't pull in to scout the route. Of course when you can't see around a bend you have no business assuming anything. I didn't get around it. There was no way. I backpaddled hard to limit the force of the collision but I still hit the trunk hard enough to bounce the dog off the front seat into the stream. It wasn't a rapids right there, just the Gila's regular current, or I could have gone over and under and been in lots of trouble. Rojo swam ashore. I got out on the tree and led the canoe back around the stump, picked up the dog, and away we went. Nobody needed to be there to tell me I'd made a mistake, not with the paddle but in judgment.

We ran a few more, going along good. The cat had showed no signs, since his first attempt, at jumping ship. I got to feeling sorry for the little guy, leashed up like he was, and I unclipped the lead.

From the first—and no matter how calm the current—I had to be alert all the time because Rojo was rather like packing a sixty pound bowling ball in the front seat. He was unceasingly fascinated by the Great Blue Herons that frequented the shoreline; their stilted walk always set him to whining and prancing in place, putting the entirety on a tightrope of sorts. Whenever he'd put his weight on one gunwhale or another I'd roll my own weight in the stern to compensate. It had come to seem a natural enough way to travel but, still, I had to be alert, and when we came to the first really heavy whitewater I put him ashore, shot through, then picked him up down below. He was glad for the run.

We came to this nasty, twisty, narrow stretch—not whitewater but fast and deep with a bunch of brush and branches hanging over the channel. It was pretty wild there for a little bit. I worked the paddle hard to make it through and somewhere along in there a branch grabbed my hat and dropped it into the river. When I got into the regular current down below I put in at a sand beach, got out real quick and climbed up on a rock. Pretty soon here comes my hat, floating just under the surface. I ran down the beach, waded out and picked it up. It wasn't till I got back to the boat that I realized the cat was gone.

At first I thought he'd hopped out after I'd put ashore but I looked and couldn't find him anywhere around. I had no recollection of him going over the side—had no idea whether he'd jumped out or had been taken out like my hat—but somewhere up in that fast water I'd lost him. I worked the shoreline upstream, searching among the big cottonwoods, and I called out a bunch of times: "Come back, Cat... Goddammit!" But he didn't show. I looked downstream too, but he didn't show there either. I walked back to the canoe again. I didn't know what to do.

Drowned? Not likely. I knew he could swim. Like an otter. One day weeks before I'd taken him up to Bear Canyon Lake for testing. After paddling out into the lake I set him over the side, then raced him to the shore. Cats can swim awfully fast, probably because they can't wait to get out. He fairly planed a wake—he could damn near walk on water—and he got there before I did. It wasn't likely he'd drown in the Gila where it wasn't twenty yards across.

He wasn't dead, but he sure was gone, and I'll confess my concern and sense of loss was tinctured by a certain ambivalence, a creeping, cryptic exaltation. Ours was a relationship that had never entirely worked. There was an inherent personality clash that rather balanced the restrained affection we felt for one another; if he had chosen freedom and hunting in the Sierra del Gila over canoeing with me, I couldn't blame him; perhaps we were both better off. He was certainly capable of taking care of himself in the wilderness and if he got lonesome, in time he'd make his way to a ranch downstream. Or drop onto some unsuspecting rafters. But I would give him more time. I took a pinch of Beech-Nut, got out my spinning rod, and started to fish.

Rojo saw him first. He whined and wagged his tail and was looking downstream and here comes that cat, walking up the bank on the far side, wet, besotted (they sure look scrawny soaked down like that) and mad enough to spit. He must have had quite a ride. I swam over, picked him up, and with a long arm in a long arc, gave a heave. He landed on his feet on the sand beach and immediately sat and began licking himself dry. Rojo ran tight circles and pranced all around him. That did make me feel pretty bad. Rojo's feelings about that cat are not ambivalent at all, and what kind of a man would leave a dog's favored friend alone in the wilds?

With everyone back together I took the time to make a cheese sandwich for lunch. I fished for a while and had what looked to be a rainbow on but I lost him. I loaded everybody up, leashed the cat, and shoved off.

Little by little the Gila was turning into a whitewater river. Approaching a rapids I'd stand in the boat, take a quick look and make a decision. Sometimes it was a short straight run and I'd pick a route and shoot on through. Often a blind corner accompanied the roar of whitewater and I'd have to stop, walk downstream and scout the run. Occasionally, there'd be a long stretch of whitewater and I'd have to stop and look it over even though there were no blind corners to contend with. Where possible, I'd let Rojo run the bank while I ran the wilder rapids. It wasn't always possible; in places he could only run so far before canyon walls left him bluffed up. I didn't want him swimming any rapids in an attempt to follow so wherever it looked like he might get bluffed up ashore I had to keep him in the boat and let him ride on through....

With a flow of less than 1,000 cfs none of these rapids were all that awesome—nothing like I'd seen in Quebec—but blind corners, narrow canyons, rocks and boulders sticking up all over and trees across the river made it plenty treacherous and, like I said, it was getting worse all the time....

My next mistake had more serious consequences. I stood up in the boat and looked down a straight run of whitewater, maybe fifty yards at most, no big rocks that I could see but some big standing waves (haystacks) right at the end. I'd come upon this all of a sudden. There was just time enough to pull into the left bank and unload the dog; I could pick him up down below. I chose to run it, as is. Those big standing waves picked the bow up into the air to where, briefly, I couldn't see a thing ahead of the boat. Rojo and the cat were still in place as we came down in a shower of river water; it was ankle deep in the boat as we shot on through.

The current eddied out quickly down below into a manageable flow as the river made a right angle turn to the left up against a rock wall. We were setting awfully low in the water. I wanted to get to shore wherever I could. I pried the bow around with a hard backpaddle on the left side, then tried to paddle on by that rock wall by pulling hard on the right. This took too long (with only one paddler you can't pry around and pull through a turn at the same time) and our momentum took us up against the bluff. We didn't hit very hard—just a tap—but it was enough; the dog ("Rojo you son-of-a-bitch!") lost his balance, stepped onto the left gunwhale, tipping the gunwhale into the current, broadside; the boat filled like a glass and over we went.

I was kneeling to shoot these rapids, my feet braced under the seat, and after we went over I had a devil of a time, hanging upside down under water, getting my feet loose. When I did, the current took me up against the rock wall. I got back to the surface by springing off the bottom, grabbed for air, and there was Rojo climbing out on the left bank, and there was the canoe, headed for Arizona with a good lead, bottom up, with a cat tied up inside.

I knew I could catch the boat before it got down into the next rapids. I didn't know if I could catch it in time to keep a cat from drowning. I was not wearing a PFD [life jacket]; I'd been kneeling on it. Not too bright, except in this case it left me a faster swimmer.

I don't know how long it took me to catch the canoe but I remember thinking as I did: if that cat's still alive he's got gills! I rolled the canoe over out in the channel. It lay there swamped, just under the surface, and a tomcat appeared from under the tarp, broke for air, and climbed up onto the load. He sneezed a couple of times as I was swimming the outfit ashore (even in times of great stress there's nothing sillier than a tomcat sneezing) but otherwise gave no indication that he'd taken on any water.

I placed the little guy on a flat rock in the sun and everywhere I moved hard, green eyes were staring me down. Can't say as I blamed him. Over on the other side Rojo was running the bank, whining and howling like a whipped dog. With the boat full of water and who knows what all lost or ruined, you're asking yourself about then: what kind of a sock-and-shoe outfit is this?

I swam across and retrieved the dog, made apologies to the cat. I found I'd tied the load down well. The only things I'd lost were my hat, one paddle, and the trotline, which was wrapped around a chunk of driftwood. There was nothing ruined, nothing wet but what would dry off. I dumped out a boatful of water, reset the load, and decided that I was going to try hard to be a brighter boy from here on in.

San Francisco River

1. San Francisco Hot Springs (4,555') to Clifton (3,435').
53 miles; III-; 21 ft./mi.
Shorter runs may be possible.

2. Clifton to Bonita Creek on Gila River (3,115').
25 miles (including 13 on the Gila); II; 14 ft./mi. on San Francisco, 12 ft./mi. on Gila.

Drainage Area and Average Annual Discharge: 1,653 sq. mi. / 60,930 af at Hot Springs; 2,766 sq. mi. / 153,600 af at Clifton.
Season: Usually runnable during a brief snowmelt peak—typically in March or April—or after unpredictable late summer rains. Run 2 has a longer season than Run 1.
Recommended Levels: 300–2,000 cfs. Minimum 600 for rafts (small rafts only).
Flow Information: USGS in Albuquerque, (505) 262-5388, has the flow at Hot Springs put-in. USGS in Tucson, (602) 670-6671, has flow at Clifton (ask for gauge #09444500).
Special Hazards: Many brush and log hazards. Fences. Weirs. Diversion dam at Martinez Ranch. Flash floods.
Permits: Not presently required.
Managing Agencies: (1) *Hot Springs to New Mexico border:* Glenwood RD, Gila NF, P.O. Box 8, Glenwood, NM 88039; (505) 539-2481. *Arizona state line to Clifton:* Clifton RD, Apache-Sitgreaves NF, P.O. Box 698, Clifton, AZ 85533; (602) 865-4129. *(2) Clifton to Gila River:* BLM, Safford District, 711 14th Ave., Safford, AZ 85546; (602) 428-4040.
Commercial Raft Trips: No above Clifton. Yes from Clifton through Gila Box; contact the BLM in Safford for references.
Land Ownership: *Run 1:* Mainly National Forest. *Run 2:* Mixed BLM and private.
Scenery: Excellent. High desert canyon.
Solitude: Excellent. Both runs are virtually roadless and little used.
Wilderness: Yes. One or two ranches.
Side Excursions: Whitewater Canyon, just east of U.S. 180 at Glenwood.
Guides and References:
- *New Mexico Whitewater* (New Mexico State Parks).
- *Arizona Rivers and Streams Guide* (Arizona State Parks).
- **BLM:** Brochure on the Gila Box, which is part of Run 2 (free from Safford office).

Maps:
- **USGS 7.5':** *Run 1:* Wilson Mtn, Harden Cienega, Dix Creek, Mitchell Peak, Clifton. *Run 2:* Clifton, Guthrie, Gila Box.
- **USGS 1:100:** *Mogollon Mtns, Clifton.*
- **USFS:** *Gila NF* and *Apache-Sitgreaves NF* together cover Run 1.

Auto Shuttle: One possibility is Joe Castaneda in Clifton, (602) 865-2354. For other references contact the managing agencies.
Logistics: *Note:* Vehicle break-ins have been reported at access points.

Run 1: To reach the **Hot Springs put-in,** follow U.S. 180 to Pleasanton, NM, some 60 miles northwest of Silver City. Roughly a mile south of Pleasanton, turn southwest onto unpaved USFS Road 519, which leads to several put-ins on the left bank near the hot springs. To reach the **take-out,** drive south on U.S. 180, west on State Highway 78, and north on U.S. 191 to Clifton, Arizona. Accesses in Clifton are near the U.S. 191 bridge. Another is about 3 miles upstream at a picnic area on the right bank; follow unpaved USFS Road 212 upstream from Clifton.

Intermediate access may (or may not) be possible via a difficult, 12-mile-long, 4-wheel-drive road (impassable when wet) that reaches the left bank at mile 30 at **Martinez Ranch** (private; advance permission required). For more information refer to the *Apache NF* map and contact the Clifton Ranger District.

Run 2: For access points in or near Clifton, see above. To reach the most popular **put-in** at the **Phelps-Dodge San Francisco River picnic site,** drive northwest from Clifton toward Morenci on U.S. 191. As the road tops a hill, turn hard left onto Mountain View Road, which climbs briefly and turns right into a residential area. Stay on the main road as it passes a school on the right, then leaves the residential area and passes some corrals, and finally descends to the picnic site on the river. (Locals advise against leaving cars overnight at this site.) For directions to the **Bonita Creek take-out,** refer to **Logistics** in the **Gila** chapter. The shuttle is via U.S. 191 and U.S. 70.

River runners are accustomed to losing rivers, as dams, diversions, and other developments continue to reduce boating opportunities throughout the West. The San Francisco is a rare example of a river regained. Until recently the river was closed to boating every year from March 15 to July 15—a policy established by the Forest Service to protect the rare Mexican Black Hawk, which nests in the area. Unfortunately, the closure period included the entire boatable season in most years, effectively eliminating river running on the San Francisco.

Happily, recent Forest Service studies have determined that non-motorized traffic poses no threat to the hawks, especially since most of the nesting sites are in small side canyons and not along the main river. As a result, in 1989 the San Francisco was officially opened to river running once again. Nevertheless, boaters must avoid disturbing the birds, making too much noise, and especially hiking or camping near nesting sites. The river could be closed again in the future if the Forest Service feels that boaters pose a threat to either the Black Hawks or other threatened and endangered birds that nest here, including Peregrine Falcons.

Although it is only a small river by the standards of wetter regions, the San Francisco ranks as a significant watercourse in the arid Southwest. Lying between the Salt River basin to the west and the Upper Gila River watershed to the east, the San Francisco and its principal tributary, the Blue River, drain the semi-arid San Francisco and Blue Mountains along the Arizona-New Mexico border. From headwaters just inside Arizona the river runs first eastward into New Mexico, then generally southwest back into Arizona, eventually emptying into the Gila near the head of the Gila Box.

In its middle reaches the San Francisco picks up added flow from the west slope of the high Mogollon Mountains (locally pronounced MUGGY-uhn), the same range that gives birth to the Upper Gila. Below Pleasanton, New Mexico, the San Francisco runs through a remote, beautiful wilderness canyon that offers fine boating during brief periods of adequate flow—either during snowmelt runoff in early spring, or after unpredictable summer rains.

The whitewater on the San Francisco is relatively mild and probably merits only a Class II rating at most flows. However, **numerous strainers and log hazards pose a serious and ever-changing danger.** Downed trees often completely block the channel, requiring portages. Boaters must be constantly alert for brush and log hazards and should scout frequently, especially around blind corners. The San Francisco is a very small river with many sharp, blind turns that require extra skill and caution. **Fences, weirs, and a diversion dam also pose potential hazards.** Finally, weather can be a complicating factor: storms and snow are possible during the early season snowmelt window, and heavy rains at other times can produce sudden high water and flash floods. For all of these reasons we rate the run above Clifton III- at low flows, and the rating increases to III+ above 1,000 cfs. Anyone attempting this trip should have strong wilderness boating skills.

The upper run on the San Francisco is 53 miles from San Francisco Hot Springs (near the New Mexico towns of Pleasanton and Glenwood) to Clifton, Arizona. It may (or may not) be possible to shorten the trip by using a difficult intermediate access at Martinez Ranch, near the halfway point (see **Logistics** and **River Guide**). The Blue River joins the San Francisco below the ranch, and the added flow may allow boating on the lower 24 miles when conditions are marginal on the upper part of the run.

Between San Francisco Hot Springs and Clifton, the San Francisco cuts a scenic canyon through various types of rocks including limestone, sandstone, basalt, and granite. Intriguing caves and cliff formations are common. For the most part the slopes are clad in high desert chaparral, while sycamores, cottonwoods, and willows thrive along the river and side creeks. In this nearly roadless area, wildlife is abundant: a wealth of bird life, deer, turkey, bighorn sheep, and occasional bear and mountain lion. Catfish thrive in the river.

Below Clifton, the final 12 miles of the San Francisco offer an alternate approach to the (Arizona) Gila Box. Many boaters prefer this way to start a Gila Box run because it avoids private land and fences on the Gila above the confluence. (However, boaters should also be alert for possible fences on the San Francisco.) Moreover, while the San Francisco's total average flow is less than that of the Gila, it sometimes carries more water, due mostly to extensive agricultural diversions from the Gila.

San Francisco River Guide

Hot Springs to Clifton

The **put-in** is on the left bank near San Francisco Hot Springs (mile 0). Downstream, the canyon closes in. More hot springs are on the right in the first half mile. Big Dry Creek, which enters on the left at mile 2.5, is about the only way out of the canyon other than downriver. Table Top Spring Creek enters via a beautiful falls on the right bank at mile 10. A mile farther, Mule Creek enters on the left (side hike). A rough trail, not marked on maps, climbs out of the canyon at this point, providing a possible emergency exit. Look for the trail on a hill on the left (south) side of the river, immediately below (west of) the mouth of Mule Creek. The trail eventually reaches Harden Cienega Road, which in turn leads to Highway 78.

Below Mule Creek the whitewater becomes more challenging, and **brush and log hazards are even more of a problem. Scout frequently and proceed with caution.** At mile 18 watch for what may be the run's most challenging rapid, a rocky drop located where the river bends right and a powerline comes into view downstream. Scout on the right. The power line marks the New Mexico-Arizona border. Good rapids continue downstream.

At mile 28 the left side of the canyon opens at Harden Cienega, and then the river bends right. Just downstream is a 4' **diversion dam**: approach with caution and portage on the right. On the left for the next mile or so is Martinez Ranch (private). Although access *may* be possible here via a 4-wheel drive road from the south, some boaters have reported serious problems with the landowner. Inquire locally and ask permission *before* landing here or attempting to use this spot as an access. At mile 29.5 Dix Creek enters on the left near the downstream end of the ranch.

Below Martinez Ranch the canyon closes in again. Again, be alert for **strainers, fences, and weirs.** A cliff dwelling is above the right bank at mile 31. The Blue River enters on the right (side hike) at mile 32, adding substantial flow. Sardine Creek enters on the right at mile 38.5. The river leaves the National Forest at mile 42.5, but BLM land continues for about three miles before the river enters mostly private land. The final miles are more open and less scenic. A pumping station is on the right at mile 49, and a dirt road follows the river from here to Clifton. A mile downstream, boaters can **take out at a picnic area** on the right where the dirt road crosses the river. Or they can continue three more miles to **alternate take-outs** near the U.S. 191 bridge in Clifton (mile 53).

Clifton to Bonita Creek

You can launch in Clifton near the U.S. 191 bridge or at various nearby private sites. Most boaters launch some four miles downstream at the **Phelps-Dodge San Francisco River picnic site** on the right bank. **Be alert for possible fences across the river in this section.** Some may have to be portaged. The old tailings of the Smuggler Mine can be seen on the right three miles below the Phelps-Dodge put-in. Four miles farther downstream—12 miles below Clifton—the San Francisco merges with the Gila River, which enters from the left in a narrow section of canyon. Refer to the **Gila** chapter for information on the remainder of the run through Gila Box to Bonita Creek.

Other Runs

Boaters may want to consider upstream runs on the San Francisco, beginning as much as 45 miles above San Francisco Hot Springs at Frisco Springs, near San Francisco Plaza. These sections of river are very rarely run due to very limited flows and **numerous fence and strainer hazards.** For more information refer to *New Mexico Whitewater* (listed above), and contact Gila National Forest.

Salt River

Highway 60 to Highway 288

Difficulty: IVp. **Gradient:** 22 ft./mi.

Length: 52 miles. Shorter runs possible.

Drainage Area and Average Annual Discharge: 4,306 sq. mi. and 654,000 af at take-out.

Put-in: Salt River Canyon (U.S. 60) Bridge (3,340').

Take-out: Arizona Highway 288 Bridge (2,205').

Peak Recorded Flow: 144,000 cfs (Jan. 8, 1993) at take-out.

Season: Very hard to predict. Any time from February to early June, depending on snowpack and weather. Peak flows often come during winter storms; early spring often brings steadier high flows from snowmelt. Prime boating window is usually mid-March to late April. Kayaks and small inflatables can often scrape down into early summer and beyond.

Recommended Levels: 800–3,000 cfs. Small rafts only below 1,200 cfs.

Flow Information: Salt River Project tape, (602) 236-8888, gives flows at Salt River Canyon (put-in) and Roosevelt Lake (take-out).

Special Hazards: Quartzite Falls. Diversion dam below take-out. Sudden high water and floods.

Permits: Required by White Mountain Apache Tribe on Fort Apache Reservation. Available (fee) at Salt River Canyon Store near U.S. 60 bridge. No use limits. Group size limit 25 in the first 20 miles, 15 downstream in Salt River Canyon Wilderness.

Managing Agencies: (1) White Mountain Apache Tribe Game & Fish, P.O. Box 220, White River, AZ 85941, (602) 338-4385. (2) Tonto NF, P.O. Box 5348, Phoenix, AZ 85010, (602) 225-5200.

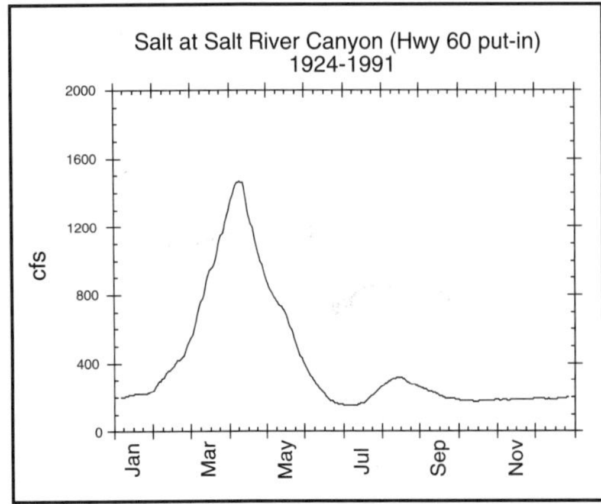

Commercial Raft Trips: Yes. For a list of outfitters, contact Tonto NF.

Land Ownership: Indian Reservations on both banks to mile 4 and on the right bank to mile 29.5. Otherwise almost all National Forest.

Scenery: Excellent. Rugged desert canyon.

Solitude: Excellent except for heavy boating use on weekends in peak season.

Wilderness: Yes.

Fishing: Good for catfish.

Wildlife: Many birds, including bald eagles. Rattlesnakes, coral snakes, and Gila monsters are venomous but usually shy.

Water: Cold and silty during runoff. Undrinkable. Purify water from side streams. Drinking water available at Salt River Canyon Store near put-in.

Camping: Many sites. Permit required to camp on Fort Apache Reservation (covered by boating permit). Primitive campgrounds along the dirt road below U.S. 60.

Guides and References:

- Rink, ed., *A Guide to Salt River Canyon: Natural History and River Running.*
- *Upper Salt River: Recreation Opportunity Guide* (USFS). Maps and mile guide. Available from Tonto NF.
- Hollister, *A Riverrunner's Guide to the Salt River.*
- *Arizona Rivers and Streams Guide* (Arizona State Parks). Includes brief coverage of the Lower Salt.

Maps:

- **USGS 7.5':** *Mule Hoof Bend, Picacho Colorado, Haystack Butte, Dagger Peak, Meddler Wash, Salt River Peak.*
- **USGS 1:100:** *Seneca.*
- **USFS:** *Tonto NF* covers all but the first mile.

Auto Shuttle: 65 miles one way; about 1.5 hours. For shuttle references contact Globe-Miami Chamber of Commerce, 1360 N. Broad, Globe, AZ 85501; (602) 425-4495.

Logistics: To reach the **put-in,** follow U.S. 60 to the Salt River Canyon Bridge some 40 miles northeast of Globe in eastern Arizona. About 100 yards north of the bridge, turn west (downstream) on an unpaved road that follows the right bank. Some boaters launch just below the highway bridge, but the **main put-in** is about 1/4 mile downstream at **Mule Hoof Campground No. 1.** Farther down the road are more accesses, among them Exhibition Campground, Cibeque Creek, and Salt River Draw. (The last site is more difficult, and it is usable only if Cibeque Creek can be forded.) These downstream sites can serve as alternate put-ins for multi-day trips or as take-outs for one-day runs beginning at Mule Hoof. See the **Mile Guide** for details.

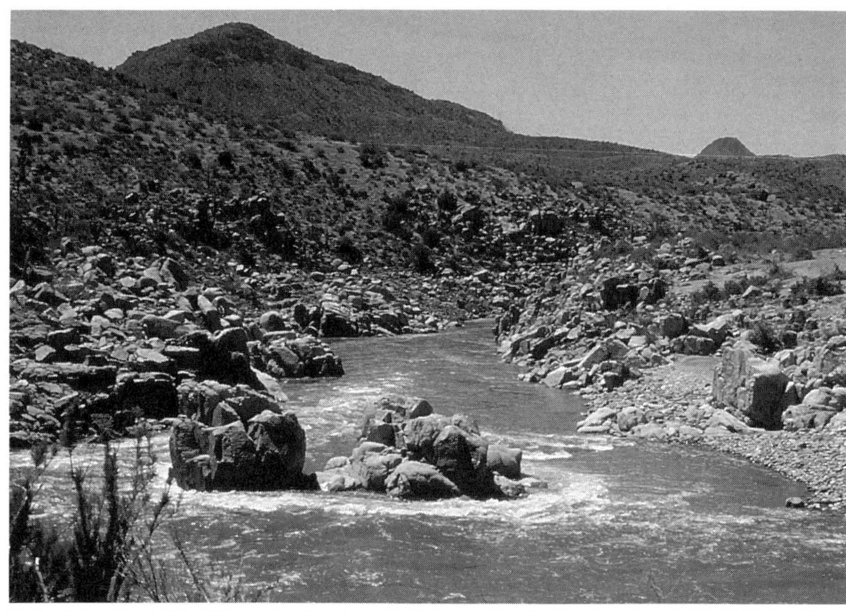
Salt River *Thor Lane*

To reach the **take-out,** follow U.S. 60 to about 3 miles west of Globe. Turn north on Arizona 88, drive 15 miles, bear right on Arizona 288, and drive some 4.5 miles to the bridge over the Salt. The take-out is on the left (south) bank just downstream from the bridge. For routes to the **alternate accesses** at Gleason Flat (mile 20) and Horseshoe Bend (mile 39), refer to the USFS *Upper Salt River* guide. Contact the Forest Service for current road conditions.

Tumbling out of the White Mountains in eastern Arizona, the Salt plunges through nearly 90 miles of wild desert canyons and spectacular gorges that contain one of the Southwest's finest wilderness runs. The river has plenty of challenges, but the trickiest part is catching it at the right level. Good boating flows usually last only a few weeks, and "average" seasons are rare because the delicate interaction of snowpack and weather in this semi-arid region produces variable and unpredictable runoff. But those who arrive at the opportune moment will be richly rewarded.

The Salt's headwaters are some 150 miles east of Phoenix. Here in the White Mountains, the White and Black Rivers collect the melting snow on 11,403' Baldy Peak, Arizona's second highest summit.[1] The two streams descend through the rugged, lightly forested Fort Apache and San Carlos Indian Reservations and merge to form the Salt, the largest river entirely within Arizona. Downstream from the White-Black confluence, the Salt flows westward, first through these Apache reservations, then through Tonto National Forest. When at last the river emerges from the mountains it is swallowed alive by a series of reservoirs, dams, and pipes that divert virtually the entire flow to feed the faucets of Arizona's largest city. Just west of Phoenix the Salt yields what little water it may still hold to the Gila River.

But above Theodore Roosevelt "Lake," the first in this chain of reservoirs, the Salt flows wild and free, virtually untouched by civilization. The Apaches still control much of the river's rugged mountain drainage, and boaters must pay access fees to the tribe. Despite a recent surge in the Salt's popularity, as of 1993

[1]This upper watershed is the wettest spot in an arid state. The White Mountains typically get three to four times as much precipitation as nearby Phoenix, which receives only 11" in an average year.

neither the Apaches nor the Forest Service places limits on boating use. However, use restrictions and private permits may be in store in the future as more river runners discover this fine run.[2]

The run (sometimes referred to as the "Upper Salt") starts below the Salt River Canyon Bridge on U.S. Highway 60.[3] Downstream the river winds for more than 50 miles through a canyon of ever-changing beauty. There are many challenging rapids and one big, dangerous drop that should not be run. Good camping beaches invite boaters to stretch the float to a leisurely four or five days. High-desert wildlife, including bald eagles, is an added attraction.

In addition to the rapids, boaters on the Salt must contend with variable flows, isolation, and a portage at Quartzite Falls. Those making this run for the first time should shoot for flows of 1,000 to 2,000 cfs. The river is very tight and rocky below 800 and much more powerful and difficult above 3,000. Weather during the prime early spring season ranges from sunshine to snow showers.

According to local river runners, the record floods of January 1993 made no major changes in the Salt's rapids. However, the receding floodwaters deposited large amounts of sand and gravel in the flatter sections of the river, especially below Horseshoe Bend and in the pools above some rapids in the upper portions of the run. Until the river reworks and channels these new sediments, low-water runs will be a bit more difficult because the river tends to spread out and become shallower as it flows over the sand and gravel bars.

The run begins with moderate rapids as the Salt carves a 2,000'- deep canyon through soft sedimentary rock. Cactus, yucca, mesquite, juniper, and pinyon pine form a sparse cover on the rocky slopes, while willow, tamarisk and an occasional cottonwood dot the banks. Many boaters enjoy a one-day Class III run of the first six or seven miles below U.S. 60 (see **Mile Guide** and **Logistics**); as a result, this is the most crowded section of the river.

Both rapids and scenery turn rugged near mile 14 as the river enters the first of three narrow gorges carved into older, harder rock. Massive granite boulders and sculptured walls force the river through twisting passages and jarring, boulder-studded drops. Below Gleason Flat the whitewater climaxes as the river cuts into ancient bedrock. At Quartzite Falls, the biggest drop on the run, boaters must portage (except at lower flows, when it may be possible to line the drop). Running the falls entails very serious risks, even for top experts, and is definitely not recommended. Two boaters drowned here in 1993.

Downstream the Salt leaves its gorges and glides gently through an open valley for the final 15 miles. At this lower elevation Sonoran Desert vegetation predominates, with giant saguaro cactus towering over smaller ocotillo and palo verde. The remaining whitewater is Class II or easier. By using a rough, difficult access at Horseshoe Bend, less experienced boaters can run the last 13 miles to Highway 288.

Lower Salt

Flatwater enthusiasts may be interested in a 14-mile stretch of the Lower Salt just east of Phoenix, from Stewart Mountain Dam to Granite Reef Dam. Because it offers summer-long flows in the middle of a scorching desert next to a major city, this section gets an astounding amount of use: an estimated one million user-days per year. On summer weekends it's wall-to-wall innertubes and floating beer parties. On weekdays and in the off-season, however, use is lighter and boaters can enjoy the pleasant scenery at a relaxing pace. Access is easy and frequent. For more information contact Tonto National Forest and refer to the *Arizona Rivers and Streams Guide* listed above.

---

[2]Much of the run is protected as part of the Salt River Canyon Wilderness Area. The Arizona Rivers Coalition has proposed that this stretch of the Salt be added to the National Wild & Scenic Rivers System.

[3]Above U.S. 60 is an isolated and extremely demanding 40-mile stretch of river known as the "Upper Upper" Salt. The Apaches prohibit all boating on this section. But even if the Apaches were to lift their ban, most boaters would be deterred by this run's treacherous whitewater and a long, arduous portage.

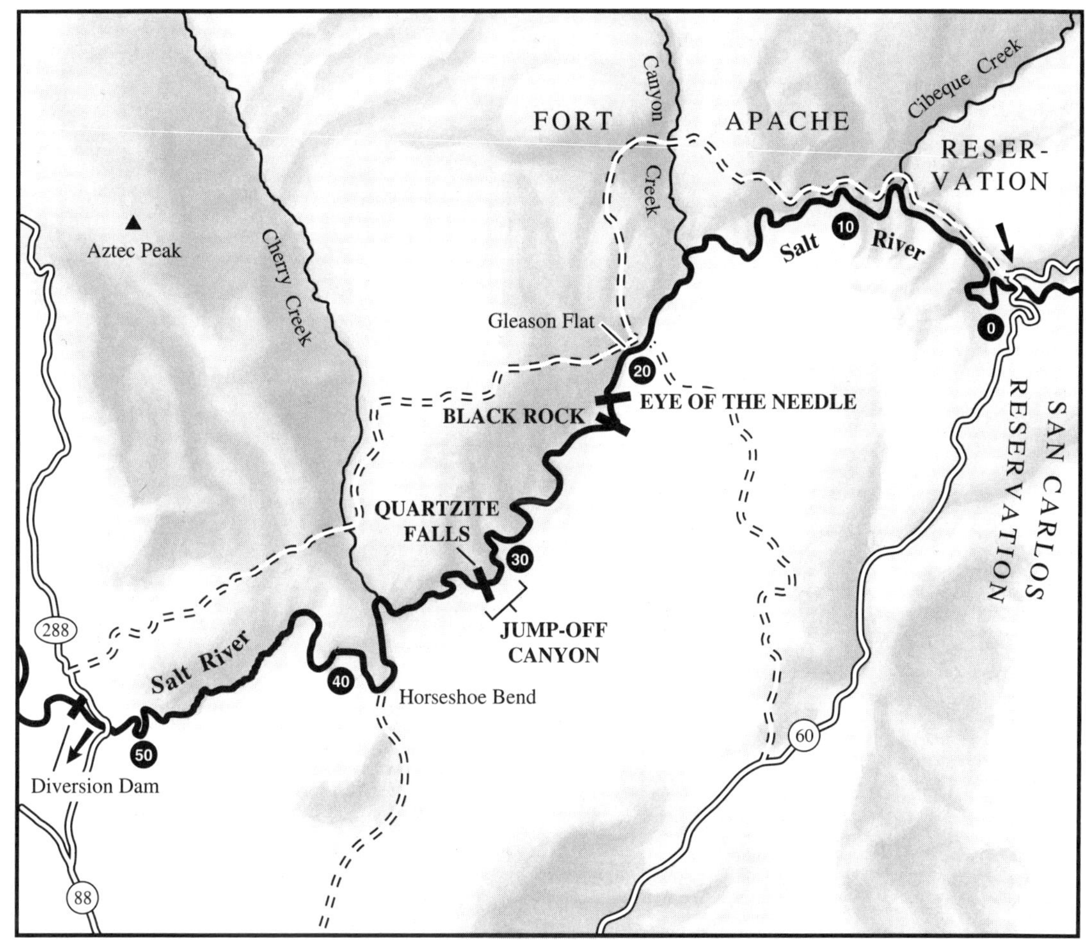

Salt

Mile by Mile Guide

Note: Two mileages appear for each entry. The first mileages are measured downstream from the Salt River Canyon Bridge. The second, in brackets, are measured upstream from Roosevelt Reservoir (actually, from the point where the reservoir level reaches the elevation of 2,120') and are provided here because they are used in the Forest Service guide and some other guides.

0 [59.8] Salt River Canyon Bridge (U.S. Highway 60). **Alternate RIVER ACCESS.** Some boaters start here, but most launch half a mile downstream at Mule Hoof Campground, thereby avoiding **ISLAND RAPID** (which can be nearly impassable at low and moderate flows). Downstream, an unpaved road follows the right bank for 10 miles. The right bank is Fort Apache Indian Reservation (White Mountain Apache Tribe).

0.5 [59.3] **PUT-IN.** Mule Hoof Campground No. 1, the most popular access, on the right bank below Island Rapid. Downstream the river winds through Mule Hoof Bend (miles 2–3), an entrenched meander with several rapids including **MAYTAG (III-)**, generally run right of the island; **REFORMA (III)**, whose big holes are often sneaked on the right; and **OVERBOARD (III)**, where huge waves develop at higher flows.

4.2 [55.6] The left bank changes from San Carlos Indian Reservation to Tonto National Forest.

5.8 [54] Exhibition Campground No. 2, an **alternate RIVER ACCESS** on the right. Immediately downstream is **EXHIBITION (III)**, with big waves at high water.

A mile below the rapid, Cibeque Creek enters on the right, with an **alternate RIVER ACCESS** just above the creek. The road on the right bank is often impassable beyond this point.

8.4 [51.4] Salt River Draw on the right. Possible **alternate access** by carrying boats up to the road. Half a mile below the draw, watch for **LOWER SALT RIVER DRAW RAPID (III)**, also called **Mescal Falls.**

10.2 [49.6] On the right are the Salt Banks, orange-stained deposits that may have given the river its name. Until the 1940's Indians gathered salt here, and the site continues to have spiritual meaning for the Apaches. No camping. Just upstream is a possible emergency take-out known as the **Salt Banks access.** This is the last possible access above Gleason Flats, but the road is very rough.

10.9 [48.9] **LEDGES (III).** The river drops over quartzite ledges, producing good play holes at moderate levels and a big reversal at high water. Cliff dwelling on the right. Picturesque Walnut Creek Falls is a third of a mile downstream on the left (side hike). At mile 12.5 a tough scramble leads to another ruin on the right. Please do not disturb these sites.

13.8 [46] **RAT TRAP (III).** Just downstream around a sharp right bend, **WHITE ROCK (III-)** marks the entrance to a narrow 5-mile-long defile with polished boulders and swirling currents.

16.1 [43.7] Canyon Creek enters on the right. A quarter mile downstream is **GRANITE (III)**, where boaters can skirt around either side of a big boulder.

18–21.3 [41.8–38.5] Gleason Flat, an open area where rough roads provide **RIVER ACCESS** on both banks (see **Logistics**). Downstream, the left bank enters the Salt River Canyon Wilderness.

21.6 [38.2] As the canyon walls close in, boaters encounter **EYE OF THE NEEDLE (IV-).** Very narrow passages at low water. Stop well upstream on the left to scout. A half mile downstream at the end of a right bend is **BLACK ROCK (IV)**, a 6' drop into river-wide reversals that get worse at low water. Scout on the right.

25.5 [34.3] Hess Canyon enters on the left, with a good side hike up a narrow wash. About a mile below the canyon is **PENDEJO (III-).**

28.9 [30.9] **LOWER CORRAL (III)** at a sharp left bend. Watch for a big rock (hole at high water) in the center. This drop marks the beginning of **Jump-Off Canyon,** with fast water and many rapids. Fort Apache Reservation ends on the right bank; both banks are now Salt River Canyon Wilderness and Tonto National Forest. Just below Lower Corral is **PINBALL (III-)**, which continues down to **THE MAZE (IV)**, a difficult boulder garden (holes at high water) at a right bend.

31.5 [28.3] **QUARTZITE FALLS (VI/p).** *HAZARD.* **Recognition:** A sign on the left warns "Danger, Falls ¼ mile." **The rapid:** A double falls drops 15' over ledges into a dangerous river-wide reversal. Short, strenuous portage on the left: boaters must catch a small eddy guarded by rocks about 10 yards above the first drop, then lower boats over a ledge into the pool below. At low water boaters can line or portage on the right by beaching farther upstream at the top of a small gravel bar (covered at higher flows). **CAUTION: The left-hand eddy above the falls is small and can be filled up by only a few boats.** To avoid a forced run of the falls, stop above the warning sign and make sure there is room in the eddy. If possible, plan your trip to avoid arriving at the falls on prime-season weekends, when the most serious traffic jams occur.

The falls have been run, often successfully below 800 cfs. But portaging or lining is recommended—not least because a long, turbulent rapid, **CORKSCREW (IV)**, is just downstream. Its runout continues into Class III water where a hole called "The Sleeper" can catch boaters unawares. Downstream, the river gradually leaves Jump-Off Canyon and enters gentler terrain.

34.1 [25.7] **CLIFFHANGER (II+)**, where the current piles into the canyon wall. Below this point the river is Class II or less all the way to the take-out. A mile and a half downstream, Cherry Creek enters on the right.

37.5 [22.3–19.8] Horseshoe Bend. **Alternate**
–40 **RIVER ACCESS** on the left at mile 39. Steep carry from road to river. See **Logistics.** Downstream, miles 41.2–42.5 [18.6–17.3], is a bald eagle nesting area. Boaters are asked not to stop in this area from Dec. 1 through June 30 in order to leave the eagles undisturbed. A bit farther downstream, the river curves around Redmond Flat, an open area on the left.

51.7 [8.1] Highway 288 bridge. The **TAKE-OUT** is just downstream from the bridge on the left (south) bank. ***HAZARD.*** Half a mile downstream is a **dangerous diversion dam,** a mandatory portage for anyone continuing downriver to Roosevelt Reservoir.

The Salt River in Human History

For over 1,000 years, beginning around 300 A.D., the Hohokam culture flourished in the lower Salt River valley and developed what may have been the first agricultural civilization in North America. The Hohokam irrigated crops with water from the Salt, Verde, and Gila Rivers, using an elaborate canal system that would have impressed even the Bureau of Reclamation; the largest canal was over 30 feet wide and 15 miles long. About 1400 A.D. the Hohokam abruptly disappeared, possibly the victims of catastrophic flood or drought, but more likely felled by a more mundane disaster: salt buildup in the soil due to excessive irrigation.

By the time Spanish explorer Francisco Coronado arrived in 1540, fierce Apache tribes were firmly in control of the rugged upper watershed. The Spanish settled in the lower valley and named the river "Rio Salado" or "Salty River," possibly after salt banks along the present whitewater run. The Apaches periodically swept down from their mountain strongholds on raids.

After the Mexican-American War the region fell under U.S. control. In the late nineteenth century the Army tried to force the Apaches onto reservations, but legendary leaders like Cochise and Geronimo mounted a fierce resistance in what was to be America's last great Indian uprising. Some 75 Apaches were killed in an assault on Fort Apache, a U.S. outpost established in 1870 along the White River some 20 miles upstream from the Black River confluence.

In the 1860's American settlers began to revive some of the abandoned Hohokam canals to irrigate crops with Salt River water. A local farming center developed at the town of Pumpkinville, which in 1870 changed its name to Phoenix. By the turn of the century nearly 200,000 acres were being irrigated, but the Salt's variable flow led farmers to seek help from the federal government to build storage reservoirs.

The result was the Salt River Project, first of the West's major reclamation projects. Centerpiece of the project is Roosevelt Dam, completed in 1911 and dedicated by President Theodore Roosevelt. It was the largest masonry dam ever built, constructed entirely of granite blocks quarried on-site by imported Italian workers. Over the next two decades three more major dams were built farther downstream.

All told, the Salt River Project uses seven dams and some 1,300 miles of canals to subdue the Salt and its main tributary, the Verde, and to distribute their water. Below the last dam the Salt is almost always dry, completely used up by Phoenix. Nevertheless, the river occasionally brings the city more water than it knows what to do with: in February 1980 an astonishing 180,000 cfs roared down the lower river's normally dry channel and flooded part of the city.

Verde River

Camp Verde to Horseshoe Reservoir

Difficulty: I+ from Camp Verde to Beasley Flat (mile 9); III, Beasley to Childs Powerhouse (mile 26.5); II, Childs to Sheep Bridge.
Length: 59 miles. Shorter runs possible.
Gradient: 17 ft./mi.
Put-in: Camp Verde Bridge (3,050').
Take-out: Sheep Bridge (2,040').
Drainage Area and Average Annual Discharge: 5,872 sq. mi. and 410,800 af at take-out.
Peak Recorded Flow: 127,000 cfs (Jan. 8, 1993) at take-out.
Season: March–early May, but quite variable depending on snowpack and weather. In dry years the river may not rise high enough to boat. The season is typically a week or two longer on the lower river below Childs due to added flow from Childs Powerhouse and some tributary flow.
Recommended Levels: 300–2,000 cfs.
Flow Information: Salt River Project tape, (602) 236-5929, gives flows "at Camp Verde" (put-in) and "near Horseshoe Lake" (take-out).
Special Hazards: Brush hazards (strainers).
Permits: Not presently required.
Managing Agencies: (1) Verde RD, Prescott NF, P.O. Box 1674, Camp Verde, AZ 86322; (602) 567-4121. (2) Tonto NF, P.O. Box 5348, Phoenix, AZ 85010; (602) 225-5237.
Commercial Raft Trips: Yes. Contact the Forest Service for references.
Land Ownership: Mostly private first 8 miles, almost all National Forest thereafter.
Scenery: Good. Shallow desert canyon.
Solitude: Excellent. **Wilderness:** Yes.

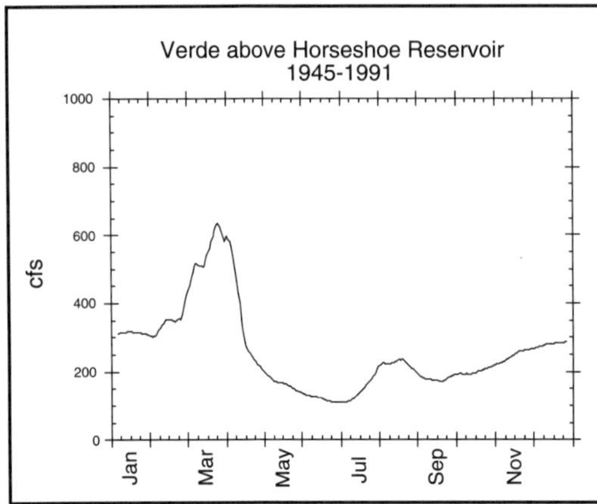

Side Excursions: Montezuma Castle National Monument, a cliff dwelling along a tributary near Camp Verde, just off I-17. City of Sedona. Oak Creek Canyon, West Clear Creek, and other streams along the Mogollon Rim.
Guides and References:

- Slingluff, *Verde River Recreation Guide.* Includes upstream and downstream runs.
- *River Runners Guide to the Verde River* (USFS). Free from the Forest Service.
- *Arizona Rivers and Streams Guide* (Arizona State Parks).

Maps:

- **USGS 7.5:** *Camp Verde, Horner Mtn, Hackberry Mtn, Verde Hot Springs, Wet Bottom Mesa, Chalk Mtn.*
- **USFS:** *Tonto NF* map covers mile 7 to take-out. For first 7 miles refer to *Coconino NF* or *Prescott NF* map.

Logistics: The **Camp Verde put-in** is just east of I-17, some 80 miles north of Phoenix and 55 miles south of Flagstaff. Cross Camp Verde Bridge at the southeast corner of town and put in on USFS land on the left bank. To reach the **alternate put-in at Beasley Flat,** follow Salt Mine Road (USFS Road 574) downstream from Camp Verde along the west (right) bank roughly 8 miles, then turn left on USFS Road 529 and drive about two miles to the right-bank access at the end of the road. To reach the **intermediate access at Childs Powerhouse,** follow the General Crook Highway (Arizona 260) east from Camp Verde about 7 miles, turn right on unpaved USFS Road 708, and drive southwest roughly 14 miles. Bear right on Child Road (USFS Road 502) and follow it to the river; just before reaching the powerhouse, bear left on a short, steep spur road that descends to the left bank. The **take-out at Sheep Bridge,** at the top of Horseshoe Reservoir, is reached via unpaved USFS Road 269 from the west. A couple of different approaches are possible; contact the Forest Service for advice. Shuttle roads may be impassable when wet; contact the Forest Service regarding road conditions. For auto shuttles inquire at canoe rental outfits in Camp Verde or ask Forest Service for advice.

The Verde River cannot be traced to a single source. It grows gradually as central Arizona's sparse precipitation gathers into small rivulets which coalesce into creeks and streams. The Verde first becomes recognizable as a river about 30 miles southwest of Flagstaff, though in wetter regions it would still be dismissed as an oversized creek. It grows large enough for whitewater boating near the middle of its 180-mile journey southward. By the time the Verde merges with the Salt River just east of Phoenix, it ranks as the Salt's largest tributary.

The Verde has always been overshadowed by its larger cousin, the Salt. With less water,[1] a gentler canyon, and easier rapids, the Verde is sometimes seen—unfairly—as a second-choice trip by local river runners. Most out-of-state boaters have never even heard of it. In 1984 the Verde got overdue recognition when Congress designated most of the boatable reach as Arizona's first (and, as of 1993, only) National Wild and Scenic River. The protection culminated a long battle in which environmentalists fought a proposed Bureau of Reclamation dam that would have flooded miles of scenic canyon and wiped out precious bald eagle nesting habitat. In 1992 the Arizona Rivers Coalition proposed that Wild and Scenic protection be extended to additional sections of the Verde.

Though the Verde is still primarily a local run for Flagstaff and Phoenix boaters, more river runners from outside the area are coming to appreciate the river's desert scenery, its mild to moderate whitewater, and especially its early season. The Verde's brief surge of spring runoff comes when rivers in adjoining regions are still locked in winter's icy grip. Even so, the Verde is not a guaranteed cure for the off-season blues: its season is short and variable—in some years it never gets high enough to boat—and early spring weather is unpredictable, with rain and even snow possible into early May. Nights are usually chilly during the boating season.

According to local boaters, the record 1993 flood on the Verde rearranged many sections of the river channel, entirely eliminated one Class II rapid, and deposited large amounts of sand and gravel in the riverbed. Until the Verde reworks these new sediments, the river will spread out and become shallower as it passes over the new sand and gravel bars, making low-water runs more difficult than in the past.

For the most part the Verde flows through moderate pool-and-drop whitewater, cutting a fairly forgiving passage through soft, easily eroded limestone. In most sections **strainers are the greatest hazard**; boatable flows come only at peak runoff, when the river overflows its banks and washes through riverside trees. High flows also mean cold water and fewer eddies, increasing the risks of hypothermia in the event of a swim. At these times the Verde becomes a muddy, silt-laden torrent that belies the translation of its Spanish name, "Green River."

The chief whitewater hazard lies a dozen miles below Camp Verde, where dark volcanic rock intrudes into the canyon. Here the river carves a jarring passage through hard basalt and plunges over the 5' vertical drop of Verde Falls. Below the intermediate access at Childs (mile 26.5), the Verde is flatter and milder.

The Verde's desert canyon, while relatively open, is nevertheless quite rugged in places. The vegetation is mostly scrub and cactus, except for a strip of lush riparian growth along the banks. Though Phoenix is nearby, the river flows through isolated terrain, and much of the canyon below Childs is protected by the Mazatzal Wilderness, largest in Arizona. Birds—especially waterfowl—are the most conspicuous wildlife. Hiking opportunities include side canyons as well as trails that climb nearby ridges. In order not to disturb eagle nesting sites, from December 1 to June 15 boaters are not permitted to stop or to make excessive noise in a designated two-mile stretch between Verde Falls and Sycamore Canyon. More such protected nesting areas may be designated in the future.

The region's earliest known inhabitants, the Hohokam, irrigated fields with water from the Verde and Salt Rivers for hundreds of years before they mysteriously disappeared about 1,400 A.D. Later, the Sinagua built Montezuma Castle and other cliff dwellings that can still be seen in the canyons of the Verde and its tributaries. When Coronado arrived in 1540, fierce Apaches dominated the region.

After the U.S. annexed the Southwest in 1848, friction between Indians and whites increased. It reached a climax in 1872 when General George Crook, based at Camp Verde, led a campaign against the Tonto Apaches and the neighboring Yavapai tribe. In the twentieth century, the public works frenzy of the Depression years brought major changes: the construction of Bartlett Dam in 1939 and Horseshoe Dam farther upstream in 1946.

[1] Their watersheds are of nearly equal size, but the Salt's higher-elevation basin produces over 50% more water.

Verde River Guide

Camp Verde to Beasley Flat

Put in on the left bank at **Camp Verde Bridge** (mile 0), where General Crook Highway (Arizona 260) crosses the river. The first nine miles—relatively slow and flat, with a gradient of only 11 ft./mi.—are well suited to less experienced boaters. The Verde winds easily through open rural land (mostly private).

Beasley Flat to Childs

Many boaters put in at the **alternate access** at **Beasley Flat** (mile 9, right bank), where Forest Service lands and the Wild and Scenic stretch begin. Downstream, the gradient increases and the whitewater becomes considerably more difficult. About a mile below Beasley Flat, the canyon walls begin to close in. The bedrock soon shifts from limestone to basalt.

At mile 11.5 Cottonwood Creek enters on the left, creating the first Class II rapid, **OFF THE WALL** or **Numero Tres.** A few hundred yards downstream, eddy out on the left to scout **PRE-FALLS** and the biggest drop on the river, **VERDE FALLS (III+)**. At Pre-Falls the river splits around an island; the larger drop is in the left channel. Just downstream, below the island, is Verde Falls itself, a 5' drop into jarring reversals. The runout below the falls is narrow and swift. Long swims are a risk at higher flows. *Note: To protect critical eagle nesting habitat, from Dec. 1 to June 15 boaters are asked not to stop, camp, or make excessive noise between Verde Falls and the mouth of Sycamore Canyon (about two miles downstream on the left).*

Around mile 16.5 watch for **PUNK ROCK (III-)**, called **Turkey Gobbler** in the Forest Service guide, where the river piles up against boulders along the steep right bank. A midstream rock at the foot of the rapid—"Punk Rock"—creates a big hole at higher flows. A mile downstream, Gap Creek enters on the right; **river access** is possible via a quarter-mile-long trail up the creek to USFS Road 574. A trail generally parallels the left bank of the Verde, sometimes up to a mile away from the river, for the rest of the run.

Below Gap Creek on the right is Brown Springs Ranch (private). Below the ranch the Verde turns sharply right and runs through **BUSHMAN (II+)**, where a tree and reversals demand careful maneuvering. The last significant rapid is **WHITE FLASH (II+)**, mile 20. At mile 25.5 a rough road fords the river (no access). Just downstream, the river splits around a long island; Verde Hot Springs is down the right channel. The Childs Powerhouse appears on the left at mile 26.5. Here, roughly 70 cfs diverted from Fossil Creek flows into the Verde. **River access** is possible via a dirt road that reaches the left bank a couple of hundred yards below the powerhouse.

Childs to Sheep Bridge

Immediately below the access point at Childs is a Class II rapid. Power lines crossing the river mark the upstream boundary of the Mazatzal Wilderness. Fossil Creek enters on the left at mile 30, and a few hundred yards downstream is the former site of **NASTY LITTLE DOGLEG,** a Class II rapid that was eliminated by the 1993 flood. The East Verde River, a major tributary, enters on the left at mile 33.5. Watch for possible **strainers** below the confluence. A gauging station appears at mile 36.5. Three quarters of a mile farther is **RED WALL (II),** named for a bluff on the right, followed by **TREE ROW (II).**

From mile 43.5 to 46 the river winds through an entrenched meander at Mule Shoe Bend. At mile 48.5 is **MELL OF A HESS (II),** and a mile farther Red Creek enters on the right, creating **RED CREEK (II)**. A rough 4-wheel-drive road descends Red Creek to the river, providing a **possible access.** A mile below Red Creek is **WET ASS (II)**. Tangle Creek enters on the right at mile 58.5; half a mile downstream, Sycamore and Horse Creeks enter on the left. Immediately below Horse Creek, Sheep Bridge crosses the river. A hot springs is on the right just above the bridge. The **take-out is below Sheep Bridge** on the right. The backwaters of Horseshoe Reservoir begin just downstream. Those who enjoy flatwater paddling can continue eight miles to an alternate take-out at Horseshoe Dam.

Other Runs

Boating is possible on other sections of the Verde: above Camp Verde; from Horseshoe Dam to Bartlett Dam; and from Bartlett Dam to the Salt River. These stretches get even less use. For more information see Jim Slingluff, *Verde River Recreation Guide,* and the *Arizona Rivers And Stream Guide.*

Region V. California

Ashland
Klamath Falls
OREGON
CALIFORNIA
NEVADA
CASCADE RANGE
Klamath
Smith
Scott
Mt. Shasta
Salmon
Eureka
Eel
Trinity
Shasta Reservoir
Redding
Mt. Lassen
SIERRA
Sacramento
Feather
Yuba
Reno
N. Fk. American
Carson City
E. Fk. Carson
COAST
Cache Creek
S. Fk. American
Sacramento
Stanislaus
PACIFIC OCEAN
Mono Lake
Tuolumne
El Sobrante
Berkeley
San Francisco
Merced
NEVADA
Kings
Fresno
Mt. Whitney
RANGE
Kern
Bakersfield
Los Angeles

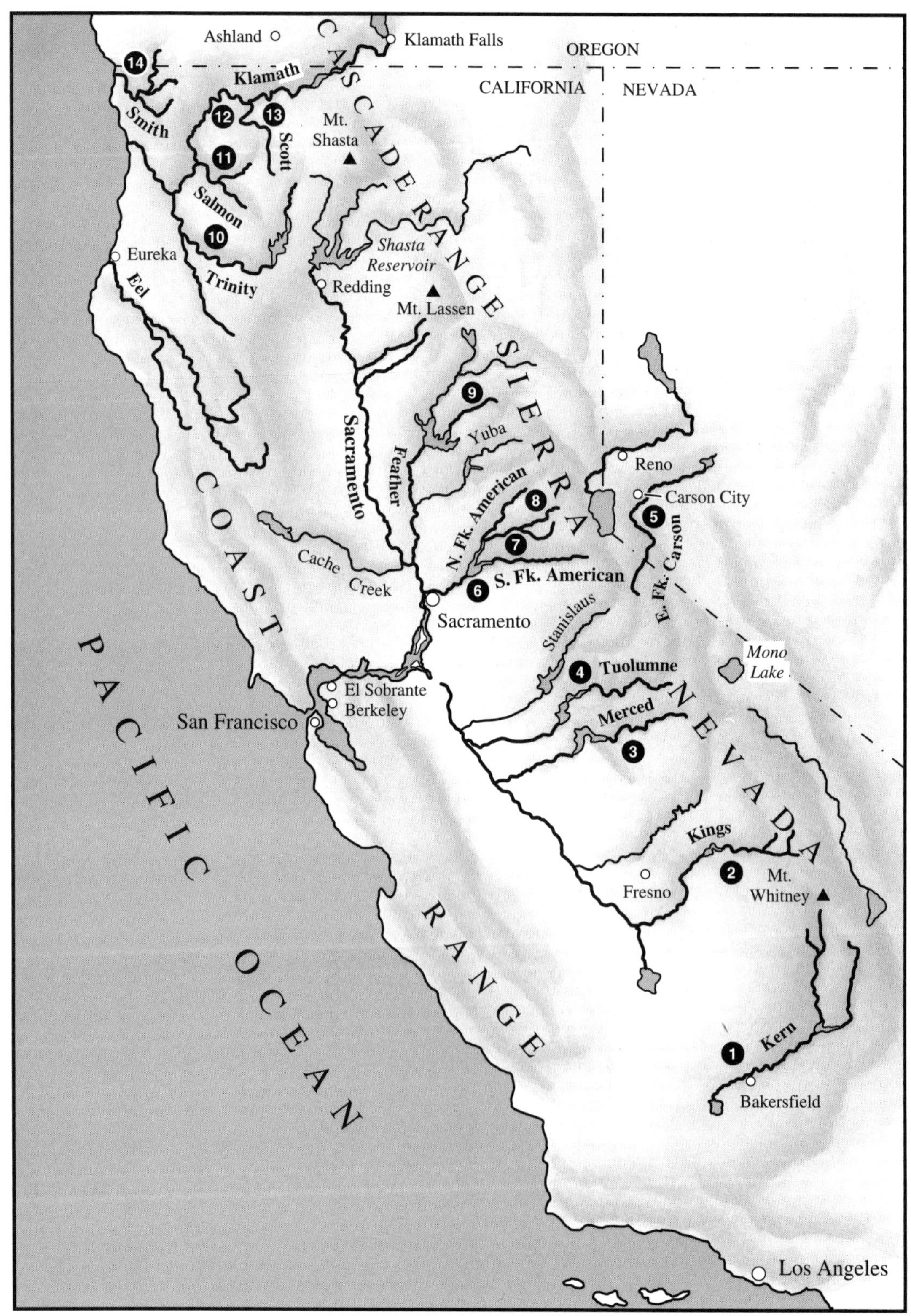

California

Rivers of California

1. Kern
2. Kings
3. Merced
4. Tuolumne
5. East Fork Carson
6. South Fork American
7. Middle Fork American
8. North Fork American
9. Middle Fork Feather
10. Trinity
11. Salmon
12. Klamath
13. Scott
14. Smith

California

California, the most populous state in the nation, is a river running region unto itself. By sheer weight of numbers, whitewater boating is bigger in California than anywhere else in the West. Though boaters make up a smaller percentage of the population here than in most other Western states, California—in particular the northern half of the state—is nonetheless home to the West's largest concentration of river runners.

The Golden State also boasts a superb collection of whitewater rivers born of four major mountain ranges: the Sierra Nevada and southern Cascades, which run north and south for almost the entire length of California; and the Coast Ranges and Klamath Mountains, which together form an uninterrupted mountainous zone in the northwestern quarter of the state. Winter storms sweeping in off the Pacific drop much of their moisture on these four ranges, each of which spawns its own distinctive group of rivers.

The Sierra Nevada is the West's longest continuous mountain range as well as one of its youngest and most rugged. The high ramparts of the Sierra crest stand directly across the path of incoming Pacific storms, leaving the few and relatively small rivers on the Sierra's extremely steep eastern slope in a strong rain shadow. These east-slope watersheds are part of the landlocked Great Basin; with no outlet to the sea, eastern Sierra rivers empty into vast, shallow lakes in the high desert of eastern California and western Nevada.

The bulk of the Sierra runoff—and almost all the river running—is found on the range's slightly less abrupt western flank. All but the southernmost rivers on the west slope descend to the Central Valley as tributaries of the Sacramento and San Joaquin Rivers, which merge in the Delta and then flow into San Francisco Bay.

Sierra rivers are the steepest in the Western United States, dropping from high mountaintops to near sea level in just a few dozen miles. The Kings River, steepest in this guide, plummets from 14,000' to under 1,000' in less than 40 miles. Due to their extreme gradients, most Sierra rivers are too difficult to run high in the mountains. Whitewater boating generally begins only after the rivers have dropped to under 2,000' elevation. (Rivers on the east side of the range are an exception to this rule.)

The tallest Sierra peaks rise gradually from around 8,000' north of Lake Tahoe to 14,495' Mt. Whitney in the south. Though the southern Sierra is higher, precipitation there is lower: 40" in an average year compared to 80" at the northern end of the range. Draining wetter, lower-elevation watersheds, northern Sierra rivers generally carry more water and have earlier boating seasons than their southern counterparts.

The natural flow pattern for undammed Sierra rivers is a big peak in spring or early summer, followed by a rapid decline to very low flows from midsummer through early fall. During the dry season—typically about mid-May to mid-October—almost no rain or snow falls to replenish the rivers. Water tends to run off the Sierra's solid granite bedrock rather than soak into the ground, so springs and groundwater seepage contribute very little to river flows during the long, hot summer.

On the north the Sierra Nevada blends into the southern reaches of the Cascade Range, which extends northward into Oregon and Washington. The short California section of the Cascades includes 14,162' Mt. Shasta, the second-highest peak in the entire range. In contrast to the granitic Sierra, the Cascades are built of highly porous volcanic rock that soaks up water and releases it steadily throughout the year, often via big springs.

California's North Coast Ranges are a wet, heavily forested region of moderate-elevation mountains north of San Francisco. Like the Cascades, the coastal mountains continue on into the Pacific Northwest. Average annual precipitation is very heavy, especially in the lush northwest corner of the state: nearly 100" at the headwaters of the Smith River near the Oregon border. Most of this moisture falls as rain during the winter, producing strong seasonal runoff; in the dry summers flows dwindle to almost nothing. Rivers like the Smith and the Eel are popular for rainy-season (winter and early spring) boating. The combination of low elevations and the moderating influence of the nearby Pacific Ocean keeps air temperatures reasonable during much of the winter.

Just inland from the Coast Range, and blending imperceptibly with it, are the Klamath Mountains. Like the Rockies, the Klamaths are a collection of subranges: the Trinity Alps, the Salmon Mountains, and the

Marble Mountains, as well as the Siskiyous which extend northward into Oregon. Almost all the runoff from these ranges finds its way to the Klamath, California's second-largest river. Several pockets of higher-elevation peaks with relatively heavy snowpacks help to keep rivers like the Salmon and Trinity runnable well after their Coast Range neighbors have fallen too low.

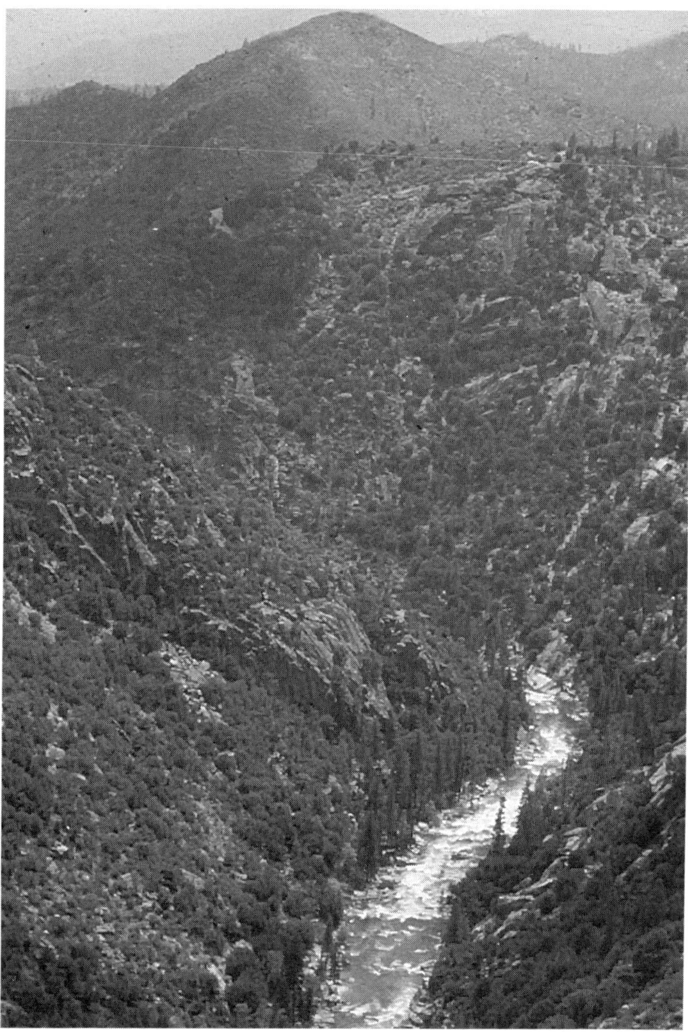

Forks of the Kern *Curt Smith*

In California, even more than elsewhere in the West, humans have altered the natural riverscape. Both the federal and the state government have constructed a remarkably complex system for the storage and distribution of water. Enormous canals shunt water all the way to southern California, where the bulk of the state's inhabitants live. But the lion's share of the water is siphoned off en route by farms. More than 80 percent of the water in California harnessed for direct or indirect human use goes to agriculture.

True, it is hard to imagine our society without dams and hydroelectric installations. But did we—and do we—need all of the 1,200 dams now in place on California rivers and streams? Justified or not, the toll has been staggering. There is only one river system in the state, the Smith, left entirely undammed. From high in the mountains to the floor of the Central Valley, most Sierra rivers wear reservoirs and dams like beads on a string.

Hundreds of miles of spectacular canyons and superb whitewater have been lost. The most recent was the Stanislaus—once the West's most popular whitewater river—which was drowned in the early 1980's by New Melones Reservoir.[1] Native salmon runs have been driven to the brink of extinction. Though the dam-builders' momentum has been curtailed in this era of economic austerity, some projects continue to be proposed, including the nightmarish Auburn Dam, an enormous boondoggle which still threatens the American River.

The bright side is that California's large and committed boating community has spearheaded the West's growing river conservation movement. Activists have fought to protect the undammed remnants of great rivers like the Tuolumne and the South Fork American, and they have sought to preserve intact some of the state's least-developed river systems, notably the lightly-dammed Klamath and the undammed Smith. Another cause for guarded optimism is the potential introduction of market forces into water allocation—allowing farmers to sell part or all of their water rights—which could lessen the pressure to dam more rivers.

[1]During the six-year drought that ended in 1993, the famous Camp Nine Run of the Stanislaus emerged from the dwindling backwaters of the reservoir. More than a few private and commercial boaters took advantage of the reappearance of this old friend, somewhat the worse for wear but still runnable. See **Stanislaus** write-up in our **More Western Rivers** section.

Kern River

The Kern is a mountain river on the edge of the desert. The scorched wastes of Death Valley lie only 50 miles east of its headwaters on the western slopes of California's tallest peak, Mt. Whitney (14,495'). The Mojave Desert is less than 60 miles from Bakersfield, where the lower Kern flows out of its canyon into the sun-baked San Joaquin Valley. The Kern is also a wild river nearly on the threshold of the West's biggest metropolis: Los Angeles is only 100 miles and three hours' drive to the south.

The Kern's north-south path—unusual in the Sierra Nevada—was established more than 80 million years ago, making this one of the oldest rivers in California. Its deep gorge, cut into the uplifted granite bedrock of the southern Sierra, is parallel to and a couple of miles west of the great Kern Canyon Fault. Before it reaches civilization at Johnsondale Bridge, the Kern flows almost due south through more than 60 miles of pristine wilderness. Twenty miles downstream, its confluence with the South Fork is now buried by Isabella Reservoir.[1] Here the river turns southwest through the Greenhorn Mountains toward the valley and its final destination, Buena Vista Lake.

The Kern is south of the main winter storm tracks and within a partial rain shadow created by the high peaks of the Great Western Divide. But its watershed is both the largest in the Sierra and so high that the river is amply fed by melting snow until early July in average years, longer in wet years. Its tremendous descent from Mt. Whitney to the valley qualifies as the greatest vertical drop of any Western river.

Civilization has intruded heavily on the Kern, which now spins turbines at five powerhouses. In 1953 the Corps of Engineers built Isabella Dam to store water for summer irrigation releases to valley farms. These releases provide the Lower Kern with boatable flows all summer in most years. Downstream, after the Kern leaves its canyon, agricultural diversions consume most its water.

Today, conservationists are struggling to save the remaining free-flowing sections of river. In 1987, the Forks of the Kern and the Upper Kern (along with the South Fork Kern, which is not in this book) were added to the National Wild and Scenic Rivers System. But in 1989 a new hydroelectric project essentially dewatered the Rio Bravo run just below the canyon's mouth. Another proposed hydro diversion threatens the very popular Lower Kern.

The Kern is the longest river in the Sierra, yet it offers few easy stretches: only the short Powerhouse Run on the Upper Kern and the last two miles of the Rio Bravo run on the valley floor. (The latter can be extended for ten more miles of Class I and II water). The longest mild section was buried by Isabella Reservoir. The remaining segments add up to more than 50 miles and range from Class III+ to Class VI.

The jewel in the Kern's crown is the dazzling wilderness run known as the Forks of the Kern, whose pristine mountain scenery and pounding rapids make it one of the West's finest rivers. Below Johnsondale Bridge a road is usually nearby, but the whitewater remains excellent. Both the Upper and Lower Kern are studded with very difficult rapids—some of which should be portaged—and dangerous brush.

Between the end of the Lower Kern run and the mouth of the canyon, the river plummets at more than 100 ft./mi. over awesome cataracts. Their sight alone should be enough to scare off anyone, yet over the years dozens of swimmers, innertubers and fishermen have drowned here and upstream. More people have died on the "Killer Kern" than on any other whitewater river in the state, but few if any were wearing life jackets. Organized boating on the Kern—with examples of good gear and correct safety measures—has helped to reduce the death rate.[2]

[1]The main stem above Isabella Reservoir is sometimes referred to as the North Fork, but most boaters call it the Upper Kern.

[2]The Kern has long been recognized as a dangerous river. The Spanish called it El Rio Bravo ("The Wild River") because it was so difficult to cross. Explorer John C. Fremont named the river in 1845 for his geographer, Edward Kern, who almost drowned trying to ford it. Contemporary writer Tim Hillmer, a former guide on the Kern, sets his novel *The Hookmen* on the Kern; the title characters use ropes and grappling hooks to help search-and-rescue teams recover drowning victims from the river.

Forks of the Kern

Little Kern Confluence to Johnsondale Bridge

Difficulty: V. **Gradient:** 55 ft./mi.
Length: 17 miles.
Put-in: Little Kern Confluence (4,680').
Take-out: Johnsondale Bridge (3,740').
Drainage Area and Average Annual Discharge: 846 sq. mi. and 570,000 af.
Peak Recorded Flow: 60,000 cfs (Dec. 6, 1966).
Season: May–mid-July. Flows typically peak in late May or early June, then drop fairly quickly to late-summer lows of a few hundred cfs.
Recommended Levels: 800–3,000 cfs.
Flow Information: DWR tape, (916) 653-9647, gives the flow at Kernville, which slightly overestimates flow on this run.
Rafts: ***Experts only.*** Self-bailing rafts preferred. Travel light; portages may be necessary, and most groups hire pack animals to carry their gear down the trail to the put-in. Horses and mules can carry rafts, but frames and oars must break down or be carried by hand. Allow a full day for the put-in. For details contact Golden Trout Wilderness Pack Trains, P.O. Box 756, Springville, CA 93265; (209) 539-2744 (all year) or 542-2816 (summer only).
Kayaks: ***Experts only.*** Kayakers can avoid the hassle and expense of pack animals by carrying their gear down the two-mile put-in trail. One-day runs are possible with a *very* early start and a minimum of playing.
Open Canoes: A few top experts have made the run.
Special Hazards: At some flows certain drops may require portage or lining, notably Vortex (mile 11.4) and Carson Falls (mile 16.3). Long, nasty swims possible. Wet suits mandatory. Remote wilderness; rescue difficult.

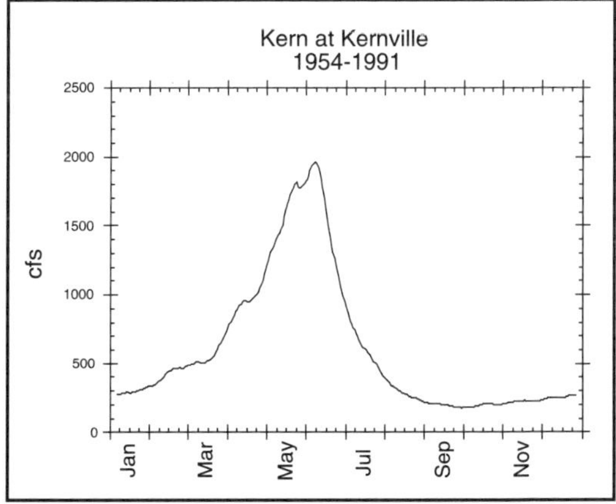

Permits: Required May 15–Sept. 15. Group limit 15. New lottery system as of 1994; contact managing agency for application dates and details.
Managing Agency: Cannell RD, Sequoia NF, 105 Whitney Rd., P.O. Box 6, Kernville, CA 93238; (619) 376-3781.
Commercial Raft Trips: Yes. Expensive because of complex logistics, but worth the money. Only one commercial launch per day. For a list, contact the managing agency.
Land Ownership: All National Forest.
Scenery: Excellent. Dramatic alpine canyon.
Solitude: Excellent. **Wilderness:** Yes.
Fishing: Excellent for trout.
Wildlife: Abundant.
Weather: Usually hot days and chilly nights.
Water: Cold and clear.
Camping: Superb sites along the river.
Side Hikes: Many excellent side creeks; see **Mile Guide.**
Side Excursions: Freeman Creek Grove, the southernmost stand of giant redwoods, is a couple of miles from the Lloyds Meadow Trailhead.
Guides and References:

- Cassady & Calhoun, *California Whitewater: A Guide to the Rivers.*
- Holbek & Stanley, *A Guide to the Best Whitewater in the State of California.*

Maps:

- **USGS 7.5':** *Hockett Peak, Durrwood Creek, Fairview.*
- **USFS:** *Sequoia NF.*
- **AAA:** *Sequoia.*
- *Forks of the Kern* (Cassady & Calhoun). Detailed map-guide; waterproof paper.

Auto Shuttle: 25 miles (one hour) one way.
Logistics: To reach the **take-out at Johnsondale Bridge,** drive northeast from Bakersfield on California Highway 178 about 40 miles to the town of Lake Isabella. Turn left on California 155 for 7 miles to Wofford Heights. Bear right on Burlando Road 4 miles to Kernville. Sierra Way (Mountain Road 99) leads 20 miles upstream to Johnsondale Bridge. An **alternate take-out**

is two miles downstream at the end of the Limestone Run (see **Upper Kern** chapter). To reach the **put-in,** continue up Mountain 99 beyond Johnsondale Bridge. Just past the abandoned logging town of Johnsondale, turn right onto a paved road heading north toward Lloyds Meadow. Follow this road 15 miles, then turn right onto a dirt road marked by a sign reading "Fork of the Kern 4." The road ends two miles ahead, at the top of a well-maintained two-mile trail leading down into the canyon.

The Forks of the Kern, with its sparkling water and relentless rapids, is one of the finest expert runs in the West. Part of the magic—and danger—of this run is its remote location, high in the southern Sierra where few trails penetrate. Hiking down to the put-in, boaters enter the Golden Trout Wilderness, home of the official state fish. The pristine alpine scenery is unsurpassed. Pines line the ridge tops while great slabs of granite form the canyon walls. Few rivers in California are runnable at such a high elevation.

The name "Forks of the Kern" is fairly recent. Before whitewater boaters arrived, this reach was known as Durrwood Canyon, and the confluence of the Kern and Little Kern was referred to as the "fork" of the Kern. Apparently, early kayakers mistakenly called it "Forks of the Kern," and the name stuck. Pioneering kayakers on this run include Doug Carson and Dennis Johnson. In 1980 Jim Cassady and Bill McGinnis of Whitewater Voyages were the first rafters to run all the rapids and prove that the river could be floated by commercial outfitters.

The 17-mile run includes many Class IV rapids, most unnamed; a number of long Class IV+ passages; and half a dozen Class V's, two of which are rated VI at certain flows. The **Mile Guide** below lists only the toughest spots.

Mile by Mile Guide

0 **PUT-IN** on the right bank of the Kern just below the Little Kern confluence, or just upstream on the Little Kern. Class III and IV rapids for the first 3.5 miles.

3.5 Freeman Creek enters on the right. A hundred yards up the creek is a lovely 20' falls. Eddy out above the creek; a major rapid is just downstream.

3.6 **UPPER FREEMAN CREEK FALLS** (IV+). Look for a runnable chute near the right bank. Just downstream is **LOWER FREEMAN CREEK FALLS** (V), where the river crashes through big boulders, then turns sharply left into a large hole. A third of a mile farther is **WRAPID** (IV+), an S-turn through huge boulders. Difficult scout on the left.

5.5 **NEEDLEROCK FALLS** (IV+). Boaters usually run a steep, narrow chute on the far right. Just downstream, Needlerock Creek cascades into the river. A crude emergency trail leads up to the road from the right bank. Needle Camp (left bank) offers stunning views of the Needles—granite pinnacles towering 3,000' above the right bank. After a short pool the river races through **DOWNHILL** (IV+), a long boulder garden laced with sharp drops.

6.1 **SLALOM** (IV+). If you can, eddy out on the left below **Downhill** to look at this, a shorter version of the same rapid. At high flows rapids are more or less continuous from **Needlerock Falls** through **Slalom.**

8 Poker Flats Camp (left bank) offers fine views of the Needles. A quarter mile downstream, Durrwood Creek enters on the left. Not far below the creek on the left is Durrwood Lodge, a former hunting outpost. Ask permission before looking around. Trails lead from the left bank up to Rincon Trail and from the right bank down to Peppermint Creek and out of the canyon.

9.5 Peppermint Creek enters on the right. Good campsite. A trail up the creek leads to spectacular falls and provides a possible emergency exit.

10 **LITTLE BEAN** (IV), a challenging boulder garden. Hike down the right bank to the foot of the rapid to plan your exit above **Big Bean** just downstream. Between the

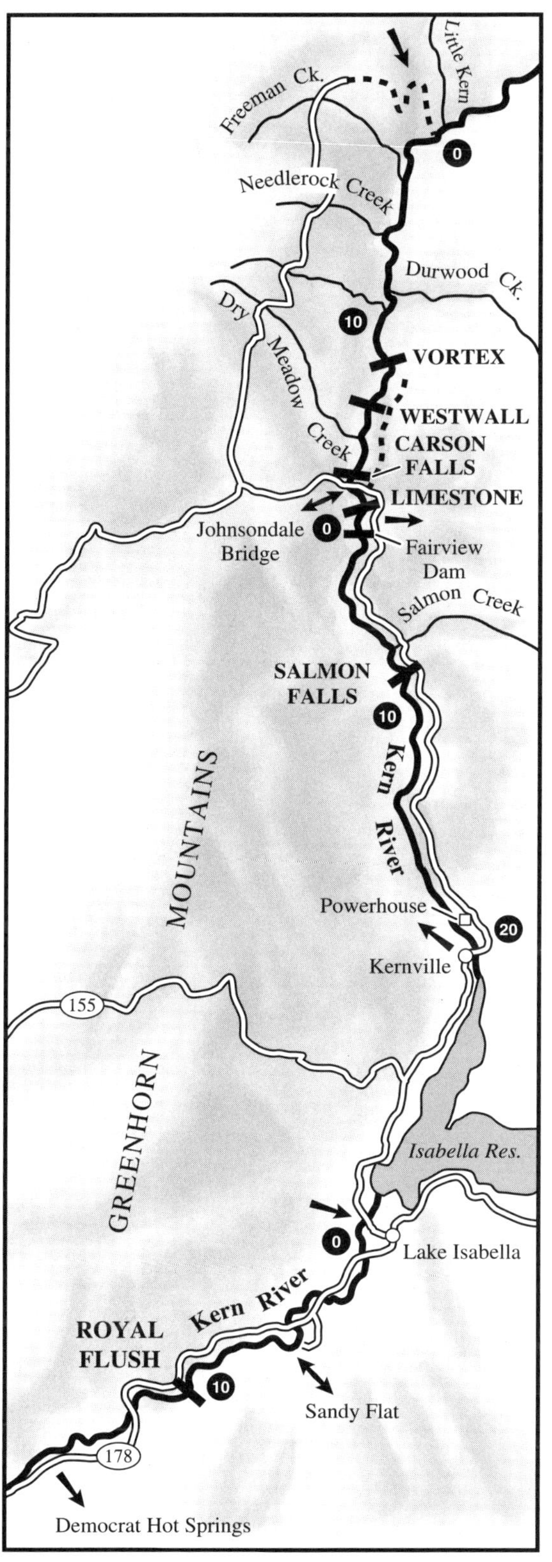

Kern

two rapids on the right bank is Bean Camp, one of the last good camps for nearly 3 miles. Downstream, the walls steepen, the gradient increases, and the really tough rapids begin. Just below Bean Camp is **BIG BEAN** (V), a long, violent run through powerful holes and sharp drops.

11.5 VORTEX (V–VI). *POSSIBLE PORTAGE.* **Recognition:** A large granite dome on the right with fallen debris at its base. Stop well upstream to scout on the right. There is a campsite just above the rapid. **The rapid:** Above about 1,300 cfs a runnable route on the right offers a way over the intimidating big drop at the top. Under 1,300 cfs, when the right chute becomes too shallow and the middle chute drops into a dangerous keeper, boaters should portage on the left. Below the first drop are more than 200 yards of continuous Class V rapids known as **The Gauntlet.**

12.8 FOUR MILE (IV+). The river bends right into this rocky rapid, which has big, unavoidable holes toward the bottom. A good hiking trail begins here on the left bank and continues downriver to Johnsondale Bridge.

13–13.7 RINCON AISLE (IV+). Three continuous Class IV+ rapids—**RINCON, METAMORPHOSIS,** and **BASALT**—make up a very tough stretch at high flows. Volcanic basalt can be seen at the top of the ridge above the right bank; upstream, folded rocks near the Kern Canyon Fault are visible. After the river bends left, half a mile of Class III–III+ rapids follow.

14.3 WESTWALL (V). The river bends back to the right and plunges down a spectacular quarter-mile-long rapid. A long stretch of boulder dodging leads to an 8' vertical drop with a wrap rock lurking below. Scout carefully, and station rescue parties downstream.

14.8 Dry Meadow Creek drops 15' into the river on the right. A difficult scramble up the creek leads to lovely waterfalls and pools.

15.2 RESPECT (IV+). Big boulders block the river. Boaters must negotiate several treacherous drops and holes. At the bottom right, Maytag Hole has held rafts for more than 5 minutes.

16.3 CARSON FALLS (V–VI). *POSSIBLE PORTAGE.* **Recognition:** Abandoned mine on the right well above river level. **The rapid:** A short rock garden leads to a 12' vertical drop. If running waterfalls isn't your idea of fun, consider portaging or lining on the left. Neither task will be easy.

16.8 Johnsondale Bridge. Take out on either bank, or float two more miles of Class IV water to an easier take-out above Fairview Dam (see Limestone Run of the **Upper Kern**).

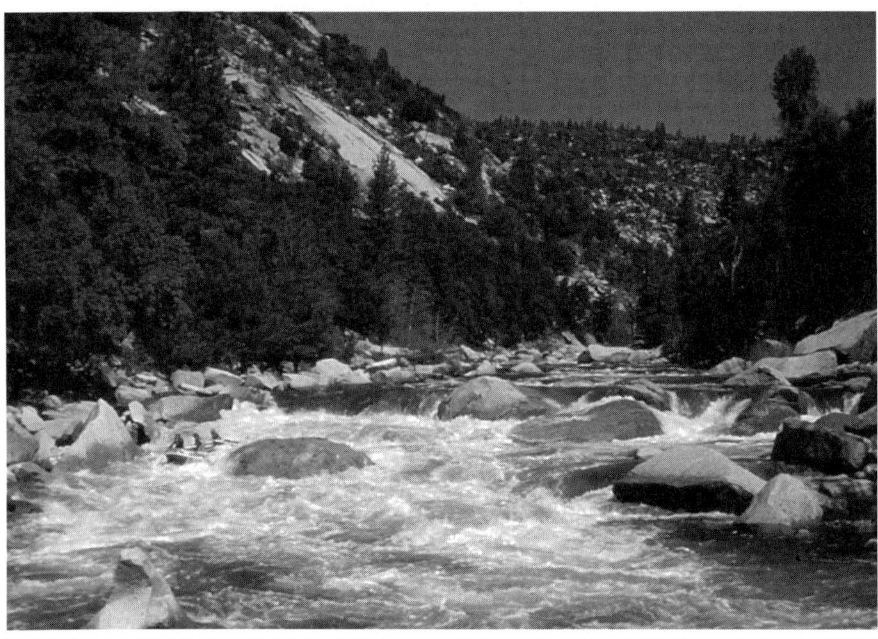

Vortex Rapid, Forks of the Kern *Bill Cross*

The raft rocked slowly in the eddy while I leaned on the oars and caught my breath. I had just rowed the most difficult rapid in my six years of river running, and I knew a worse one was downstream. "What's between here and Carson Falls?" I called to the trip leader.

"Nothing," he grinned as he muscled his raft back into the current. "Just follow me."

Thirty seconds later, his boat was upside down, its three occupants were bobbing in the cold, swift current, and I was desperately trying to keep my own raft from flipping at the same spot. Whitewater boating is full of surprises, I thought.

That run down the Forks of the Kern in June 1982, my first time on a true Class V river, was a real eye-opener. After more than a dozen floats on the Tuolumne and a trip down the Grand Canyon, I still wasn't prepared for the intensity and the fury of the rapids on the Forks. Part of the problem was that the river was high—nearly 4,000 cfs—but the intrepid journalists for whom we planned the trip hadn't been interested when I proposed a less intimidating river. Judging by an article she wrote later, one of them changed her mind right away.

As it turned out, we were lucky. We suffered some anxious moments, with one raft flipped, another swamped, and a third stuck in a reversal and shedding passengers for five minutes. Somehow, though, we gathered everyone up without injury and lost only a few oars. But by the time we reached Carson Falls late in the afternoon and stared at the huge vertical drop, most of us had lost our nerve as well. The passengers hiked the short distance to the Johnsondale Bridge while the other two boatmen, Jim Cassady and Andy Sninsky, took turns running all three rafts over the falls—successfully. That was the first time I ever refused to take my own boat down a rapid someone else was willing to float. It probably won't be the last.

—Fryar Calhoun

Upper Kern River

1. Limestone Run.
Johnsondale Bridge to Fairview Dam.
IV; 2.4 miles; 44 ft./mi.

2. Fairview Run (Calkins Flat Run).
Fairview Dam to Calkins Flat.
III; 2.8 miles; 35 ft./mi.

3. Chamise Gorge.
Calkins Flat to above Salmon Falls.
IV+; 2.2 miles; 60 ft./mi.

4. Gold Ledge Run.
Ant Canyon to Camp 3 Campground.
V; 7 miles; 65 ft./mi.

5. Camp 3 Run.
Camp 3 Campground to the Powerhouse.
IV; 2.4 miles; 50 ft./mi.

6. Powerhouse Run.
Powerhouse to Riverside Park, Kernville.
III-; 2 miles; 30 ft./mi.

Upper Put-in: Johnsondale Bridge (3,740').
Lower Take-out: Kernville (2,620').
Drainage Area and Average Annual Discharge: 1,009 sq. mi. and 677,000 af at Kernville.
Peak Recorded Flow: 74,000 cfs (Dec. 6, 1966).
Season: *Runs 1 & 6:* April–July. *Runs 2–5:* May–June. See hydrograph in **Forks of the Kern** chapter.
Recommended Levels: *Run 1:* 800–3,000 cfs. *Run 2:* 1,500–4,000. *Runs 3 & 4:* 1,500–3,000. *Run 5:* 1,500–4,000. *Run 6:* 600–6,000. *Note:* All these levels refer to flow at Kernville. Flow is actually 500 cfs less on Runs 2–5.
Flow Information: DWR tape, (916) 653-9647; flow at Kernville.
Special Hazards: Fairview Dam, just below the Limestone run take-out. **Salmon Falls (VI)** between the Chamise Gorge and Gold Ledge runs.
Permits: Required May 15–Sept. 15. Available for the asking from the managing agency.
Managing Agency: Cannell RD, Sequoia NF, 105 Whitney Rd., P.O. Box 6, Kernville, CA 93238; (619) 376-3781.
Commercial Raft Trips: Yes. For references contact the managing agency.
Land Ownership: Mostly National Forest except the Powerhouse Run, which is through mainly private land. Refer to *Sequoia NF* map.
Scenery: Good. Steep, dry canyon.
Solitude: Fair. Good in Chamise Gorge, where the road leaves the river.
Wilderness: No.
Water: Cold and clear. Drinking water available at several campgrounds.
Camping: Many USFS campgrounds and primitive sites along the river.
Guides and References:
- Cassady & Calhoun, *California Whitewater: A Guide to the Rivers.*
- Holbek & Stanley, *A Guide to the Best Whitewater in the State of California.*

Maps:
- **USGS 7.5':** *Fairview, Kernville.*
- **USFS:** *Sequoia NF.*
- **AAA:** *Sequoia.*
- *Upper Kern River* (Cassady & Calhoun). Detailed map-guide; waterproof paper.
- *Riverguide Bandana to the Upper Kern* (Rivers & Mountains). Cloth map.

Logistics: To reach the **take-out at Kernville,** drive northeast from Bakersfield on California Highway 178 about 40 miles to Lake Isabella. Turn left on California 155 and drive 7 miles to Wofford Heights, then bear right on Burlando Road 4 miles to Kernville. Sierra Way (Mountain Road 99) leads 20 miles upstream to the **put-in at Johnsondale Bridge,** passing various **access points** along the way. Shuttles are short and easy along Sierra Way/Mountain 99.

From its first contact with civilization at Johnsondale Bridge to Isabella Reservoir 20 miles downstream, the Kern drops over 1,100' through a high desert canyon surrounded by 8,000' granite peaks. The Upper Kern's wide range of whitewater attracts boaters from all over Southern California. All but a few of the rapids can be seen from the road (Sierra Way/Mountain 99) that leads upriver from Kernville.

Most of the Upper Kern is as challenging as any boater could want. Outfitters train guides for the Forks of the Kern on the Upper Kern's toughest segments, the Class IV–IV+

Limestone and Chamise Gorge Runs and the Class V Gold Ledge section. On the other hand, the Powerhouse Run near Kernville is a traditional learning stretch for novices.

We have split the Upper Kern into six runs, divided either by a dramatic change in difficulty, by unrunnable rapids, or by Fairview Dam. Scout each stretch carefully from the road, and be sure you can recognize your take-out from the river.

Because 500 cfs are diverted at the dam and returned to the river at the powerhouse, the first and last sections have longer seasons than the four middle runs. In wet years, Limestone and Powerhouse may be raftable into August and runnable in kayaks all year; in dry years, they may be boatable only into June. In wet years, the other runs can be boated from April to mid-July; in dry years, they may never be runnable.[1]

[1]It is possible that increased instream flows will be required when the dam is relicensed. For more information contact Friends of the River (see appendix for address).

Mile by Mile Guide

See map in ***Forks of the Kern*** *chapter.*

Limestone Run

This is the most popular advanced run on the Upper Kern because of its powerful rapids longer season, and striking scenery. The narrow canyon is named for limestone outcroppings in the granite walls. This run is especially dangerous at high water. It becomes Class V above 4,000 cfs.

0 **PUT-IN** on the right bank at Johnsondale Bridge. About two thirds of a mile downstream, Brush Creek enters on the left at **BRUSH CREEK RAPID (III).**

1 **LIMESTONE (IV).** The river drops sharply right at Limestone Campground (left bank), then turns left and pours into a big hole that becomes a monster at higher flows. **Dangerous at high water.** Scout from the campground before you put in, and station rescue parties downstream. The next big drop is just around the corner.

1.2 **JOE'S DINER (IV).** A boat-stopping hole on the right can be avoided by running left at lower flows. At higher flows holes appear everywhere.

2.4 **TAKE-OUT** at a turnout beside the road a few hundred yards above Fairview Dam. Limited parking space. ***HAZARD*** Don't float downstream over the dam!

Fairview Run (Calkins Flat Run)

This pretty stretch of river is much easier than those just above and below. It makes a good warm-up for the demanding Chamise Gorge run immediately downstream.

3 **PUT-IN** at a turnout where the river and road bend sharply left, 0.4 miles below Fairview Dam and just below **BOMBS AWAY (V).**

4.3 Fairview Campground (left bank). Downstream, a foot bridge crosses the river.

5.8 **TAKE-OUT** at Calkins Flat on the left, or continue downstream. Much tougher rapids are right around the corner.

Chamise Gorge

The river turns away from the road into a short, beautiful gorge. Most boaters combine this with the Fairview run. Continuous rapids begin immediately. The two listed below are very big—be sure you can handle them; stay away at high flows. ***HAZARD.*** Scout the take-out *before* you put in, and don't miss it when you're on the river. Just below it is **Salmon Falls,** half a mile of dangerous Class VI drops.

5.8 **PUT-IN.** Calkins Flat Primitive Camping Area (left bank). Just downstream is **ENTRANCE (IV+),** a long, difficult boulder slalom.

7.6 **SATAN'S SLOT (IV+).** Scout from the left where the road returns to the bank. The river crashes through two narrow channels, with difficult maneuvering above and below.

7.8 **TAKE-OUT** on the left just below Satan's Slot. **Alternate take-out** on the left a couple of hundred yards downstream. **HAZARD.** Don't float beyond these take-outs into **SALMON FALLS (VI).**

Gold Ledge Run

Experts only. This run is the most difficult on the Upper Kern. Even experts should avoid it at high flows. Scout the entire stretch carefully from the road before you put in. This guide lists only the biggest rapids; there are many difficult, unnamed, and unmentioned passages and numerous alternate accesses. Survivors can combine this stretch with the Camp 3 and Powerhouse runs for nearly a dozen continuous miles down to Kernville.

9.4 Ant Canyon Primitive Camping Area is a convenient **PUT-IN.** A mile downstream on the left is Gold Ledge Campground; beyond it are difficult boulder gardens.

11.5 Springhill Primitive Camping Area (left bank). About two thirds of a mile downstream is Corral Creek Picnic Grounds (left bank).

12.6 Corral Creek enters on the left. A quarter mile downstream is **SQUASHED PADDLER (V)**, where big holes block the river. A quarter mile farther, just after the river turns away from the road, is **SOCK-'EM-DOG (V).** Here the river drops into a wall and turns sharply left. Look for big holes before and after the turn.

14.5 Hospital Flat Campground (left bank). A half mile downstream is **THE FLUME (IV+)**, where the river squeezes into a narrow channel and over a big drop. Scout left. A few hundred yards farther is **FENDER BENDER (V)**, a dangerous maze of rocks and brush. Scout from the road.

16.2 **THE CABLE (IV).** Technical, heavily obstructed boulder garden; unrunnable holes at higher flows. Boaters on the Camp 3 Run often put in just above this rapid.

16.5 **TAKE-OUT** at Camp 3 Campground on the left, or continue downstream.

Camp 3 Run

Here the river calms down a bit, but there is still plenty of challenging whitewater. This stretch can be combined with the Powerhouse Run downstream.

16.6 **PUT-IN** at the lower end of Camp 3 Campground. Just downstream at **THE WALL (IV)**, the river cascades into the right bank, then bends sharply left.

17 **TOMBSTONE (IV).** A boulder-choked left bend. Just downstream on the left is Headquarters Campground.

17.5 **BUZZARD'S PERCH (III+).** At higher flows, trees present a serious hazard toward the end of this left-bending rapid. Not far downstream the river splits: the left channel, **TEQUILA CHUTE (IV)**, is more difficult; the right channel, **PEPSI CHALLENGE (III)**, is the usual route.

18.5 **POWERHOUSE (III+).** Rocks and big holes for over a quarter mile.

19 **TAKE-OUT** just below the powerhouse on the left, or continue downstream.

Powerhouse Run

This is Southern California's best novice run and the site of the Kernville Whitewater Races every April.

19 A short paved road leads to the **PUT-IN** on the left below the powerhouse. A half mile downstream is **BIG DADDY (III-)**, a swift chute down the right.

20.7 **EWING'S (III-).** Beneath Ewing's Restaurant the river drops between large boulders. A good play spot for kayakers.

21 **TAKE-OUT** on the right at Riverside Park in Kernville. Slalom competitions are held here during the annual whitewater races. If the reservoir is low, you can boat up to two more miles of very brushy Class II, but the take-outs are somewhat inconvenient. One possibility is just past the golf course on the right.

Lower Kern River

Main Dam Campground to Democrat Picnic Area

Difficulty: IVp. **Gradient:** 28 ft./mi.
Length: 18 miles. Shorter runs possible.
Put-in: Below Main Dam Campground (2,360').
Take-out: Democrat Picnic Area (1,855').
Drainage Area and Average Annual Discharge: 2,258 sq. mi. and 750,000 af.
Peak Recorded Flow: 40,000 cfs (Nov. 19, 1950).
Season: June–August.
Recommended Levels: 1,000–3,000 cfs.
Flow Information: DWR tape, (916) 653-9647; release from Isabella Dam.
Rafts: Because of the portage at **Royal Flush,** it's best not to take much gear downriver.
Kayaks: Because Borel Powerhouse (mile 6) usually releases 600 cfs year round, kayakers can run the lower dozen miles in any season.
Special Hazards: Brush and trees in the river. Royal Flush, a Class V–VI rapid that is usually portaged.
Permits: Required May 15–Sept. 15. Available for the asking from the managing agency.
Managing Agency: Sequoia NF. Either Greenhorn RD, 15701 Highway 178, P.O. Box 6129, Bakersfield, CA 93386, (805) 871-2223; or Cannell RD, 105 Whitney Rd., P.O. Box 6, Kernville, CA 93238, (619) 376-3781.
Commercial Raft Trips: Yes. For a list of outfitters, contact the managing agency.
Land Ownership: Mostly National Forest with a few private parcels.
Scenery: Good. Deep, arid canyon.
Solitude: Good. **Wilderness:** No.
Water: Warm and undrinkable.

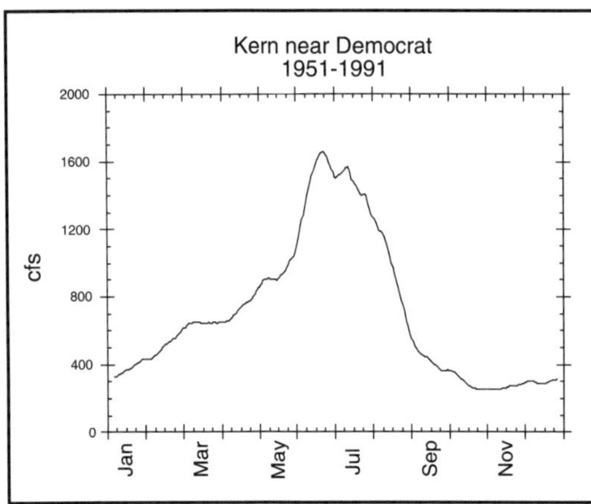

Camping: Because of the portage, it's best not to take camping gear downriver. Two-day trips can camp with river access to vehicles at Sandy Flat (mile 6.3) or Miracle Hot Springs campground (private, mile 7.3). Also in the area is Main Dam Campground (USFS), on Highway 155 at Isabella Dam.

Guides and References:
- Cassady & Calhoun, *California Whitewater: A Guide to the Rivers.*
- Holbek & Stanley, *A Guide to the Best Whitewater in the State of California.*

Maps:
- **USGS 7.5':** *Lake Isabella North, Lake Isabella South, Miracle Hot Springs, Democrat Hot Springs.*
- **USGS 1:100:** *Isabella Lake.*
- **USFS:** *Sequoia NF.*
- **AAA:** *Kern County; Sequoia.*
- *Lower Kern River* (Cassady & Calhoun). Detailed map-guide; waterproof paper.
- *Riverguide Bandana to the Lower Kern* (Rivers & Mountains). Cloth map.

Logistics: Follow California Highway 178 northeast from Bakersfield into the Kern canyon and past several miles of unrunnable cataracts. About two miles after the road begins to climb higher above the river, a dirt road leads down to the **take-out at Democrat Picnic Area.** To reach the **put-ins,** continue up Highway 178 to the town of Lake Isabella and turn left on California 155. About a quarter mile before the highway crosses the Kern, just opposite the road leading to Corps of Engineers headquarters, a dirt road on the left leads to a **put-in** about half a mile downstream on the left bank. To reach two **alternate put-ins** on the right bank, cross the Kern on Highway 155 and turn left on Keysville Road (paved) opposite Main Dam Campground. After three quarters of a mile, turn left onto a dirt road that leads down toward the river. Another put-in at mile 2 is reached by continuing on Keysville Road another half mile or less and turning left onto a two-mile dirt road. This put-in is under the Highway 178 bridge but cannot be reached from that highway.

Below Isabella Reservoir the Kern turns southwest and cuts a deep canyon through the Greenhorn Mountains. This stretch is surprisingly secluded despite a highway perched on the canyon wall. The Lower Kern has excellent advanced whitewater below Miracle Hot Springs (mile 7.3), which is used as a put-in for one-day runs. One big rapid, **Royal Flush,** is almost always portaged. Below the take-out is a lethal diversion dam and a long series of deadly waterfalls.

The wide, shallow reservoir above Isabella Dam stores runoff eight or nine months a year, releasing only a relative trickle to the first six miles of the Lower Kern. This allows trees and brush to grow in the river—a serious boating hazard. About 600 cfs are diverted at the dam and returned to the river at Borel Powerhouse (mile 6).[1] The boating season (June–August in average years, May–September in wet years) coincides with summer irrigation releases, which usually range from 1,000 to 3,000 cfs. Unlike many other dam-controlled rivers, the Lower Kern does not drop at night or on weekends.[2]

Rio Bravo Run

Below the mouth of the canyon and downstream from the last unrunnable cataract lies the Rio Bravo run, a short stretch of fine Class III and IV water. Sadly, this reach was devastated by the completion in 1989 of the privately-owned Rio Bravo project, which diverts 1,600 cfs from the river below the old powerhouse and pipes it to a new powerhouse 2.2 miles downstream. The operators guarantee an instream flow of only a miserly 50 cfs, leaving the first two miles of the Rio Bravo run too low for boating except in years wet enough for releases from Isabella Dam to exceed 2,200 cfs.

The Rio Bravo run always included one mandatory portage at a brush-clogged spot known as **Helicopter Island,** 1.7 miles below the original put-in near the old powerhouse. Now, drastically reduced flows in the dewatered section will allow brush and trees to grow into the channel, making strainers an even more serious hazard on the rare occasions when this section has sufficient water for boating.

The first possible access below the new powerhouse is the Rancheria Road bridge, 2.8 miles into the original run and below all of the best rapids. Only one Class III remains, about a quarter mile below the bridge; otherwise the river is Class II. The next access is two miles below Rancheria Road at Kern River Group Picnic Area on the left. Downstream are ten miles of Class I and II water that draw hordes of innertubers on summer weekends.

---

[1]There is a chance that increased instream flows will be required if deferred relicensing flow issues are reconsidered. For information contact Friends of the River (see appendix for address).

[2]In the 1980's the Kern County Water Agency and a private investor proposed to build Hobo Dam around mile 7.5 on the Lower Kern. The dam would divert up to 1,200 cfs into a pipeline, dewatering the next 11 miles of the Lower Kern and returning the water to the river at a powerhouse to be built near the take-out (mile 18). Presently dormant, the Hobo project could be revived in the future. If it were built, the best boaters could hope for would be a short summer season during which minimum flows, just adequate for low-water rafting, would be released for a few hours each day. During dry years, instream flows would likely be too low for any boating. But the marginal economics of this project could lead its owners to seek bigger daytime diversions and reduced instream flows that would wipe out most of the Lower Kern run, just as the first part of the Rio Bravo Run downstream has been reduced to fish flows. Friends of the River is working to keep the Hobo project from coming to life again (see appendix for address).

Mile by Mile Guide

*See map in **Forks of the Kern** chapter.*

0 PUT-IN on either bank about half a mile below the Highway 155 bridge. **The major hazard for the first eight miles or so is brush and trees in the river.**

0.8 WALLOW ROCK (III+). A big boulder blocks the channel. A mile downstream boaters can hike to Indian pictographs high on the right wall, inscribed by the Tubatulabal Indians ("Pine Nut Eaters") around 1500 A.D.

2 RIVER ACCESS on the right under the Highway 178 bridge.

2.7 DILLY (III). Avoid the big hole at the bottom left. Not far downstream is OSCAR'S NIGHTMARE (III+), a blind left turn with wrap rocks in the center. Scout on the left.

3.6 Highway 178 crosses overhead. No vehicle access.

6 Just below another bridge, Borel Powerhouse (left bank) adds 600 cfs.

6.3 **RIVER ACCESS** at Sandy Flat, an undeveloped camping area on the left.

6.9 Hobo Campground (left bank). No access at present—check with the Forest Service for changes. Just downstream is **HOBO (III)**, a brushy left curve.

7.3 **RIVER ACCESS** at Miracle Hot Springs campground (private) on the left. Often used as a put-in for one-day runs. For information and reservations call (619) 379-8350. The springs are still there, but a hotel where many came for cures in the nineteenth century burned down in 1975. Site of proposed Hobo Dam is just downstream. Below this point, year-round flows from Borel Powerhouse help thin out the trees and brush somewhat, but they remain a hazard. The rapids become more difficult.

8.6 Remington Hot Springs (left bank).

8.9 **WHITE MAIDENS' WALKAWAY (IV)**, the first big rapid. Skirt holes and watch for a big rock dead center at the bottom.

9.4 **SUNDOWN FALLS (III+)**. Steep but straightforward. Downstream is a stretch of continuous Class III known as **SILVER STAIRCASE.**

10.6 **DEAD MAN'S CURVE (IV)**. A right-left jog with big holes. Scout right. Below the rapid is River Camp, an unimproved site on the left. Emergency access via a dirt road leading down from the Old Kern Canyon Road (locked gate).

11.5 **FALSE FLUSH (III; IV above 2,800 cfs).** Big boulders block the channel. Dangerous at high water because boats and swimmers can be swept into the big one just downstream. Run left of the big hole in the middle, then move quickly right to eddy out before **Royal Flush.**

11.7 **ROYAL FLUSH (V–VI).** ***PORTAGE.*** The river drops into a big hole, piles into a ledge blocking the center, then surges into the left wall and over the final drop. Most boaters should portage on the right. Even experts should not attempt the rapid above 2,400 cfs, when water washes over the dangerous ledge in the center.

13.5 Delonegha Hot Springs (right bank), where an old resort hotel once stood.

14 Highway 178 bridge. No river access at present—check with the Forest Service for changes. Just downstream, Mill Creek enters on the left.

14.7 **SURPRISE (III+)**. A big rock hides in the last standing wave. Surprise!

15.1 **HARI-KARI (IV)**. A horizon line at the end of a long pool warns of this sharp drop into a right-hand turn. Difficult scout on the right.

15.4 **HORSESHOE FALLS (IV)**. The toughest rapid on the run after **Royal Flush.** Three drops around a right turn. The second has a big hole that is hard to miss above 2,400 cfs.

16.1 **SIDEWINDER (III+)**. Also known as **Bailmore** and **Patch Corner.** S-turns and big drops. Over the next mile the river curves around a large peninsula, China Gardens, where Asian laborers and prospectors lived in the last century.

17.6 **PINBALL (IV)**. A difficult boulder garden. Scout left.

18 **TAKE-OUT.** Democrat Picnic Area on the left. ***HAZARD.*** Upstream, the river splits around an island: **take the left channel!** If you go right, you will miss the take-out. Downstream, the river drops over a deadly 30' diversion dam (mile 18.8) into an unrunnable gorge. Except in emergencies, do not take out at Democrat Hot Springs (mile 18.3), which is guarded private property.

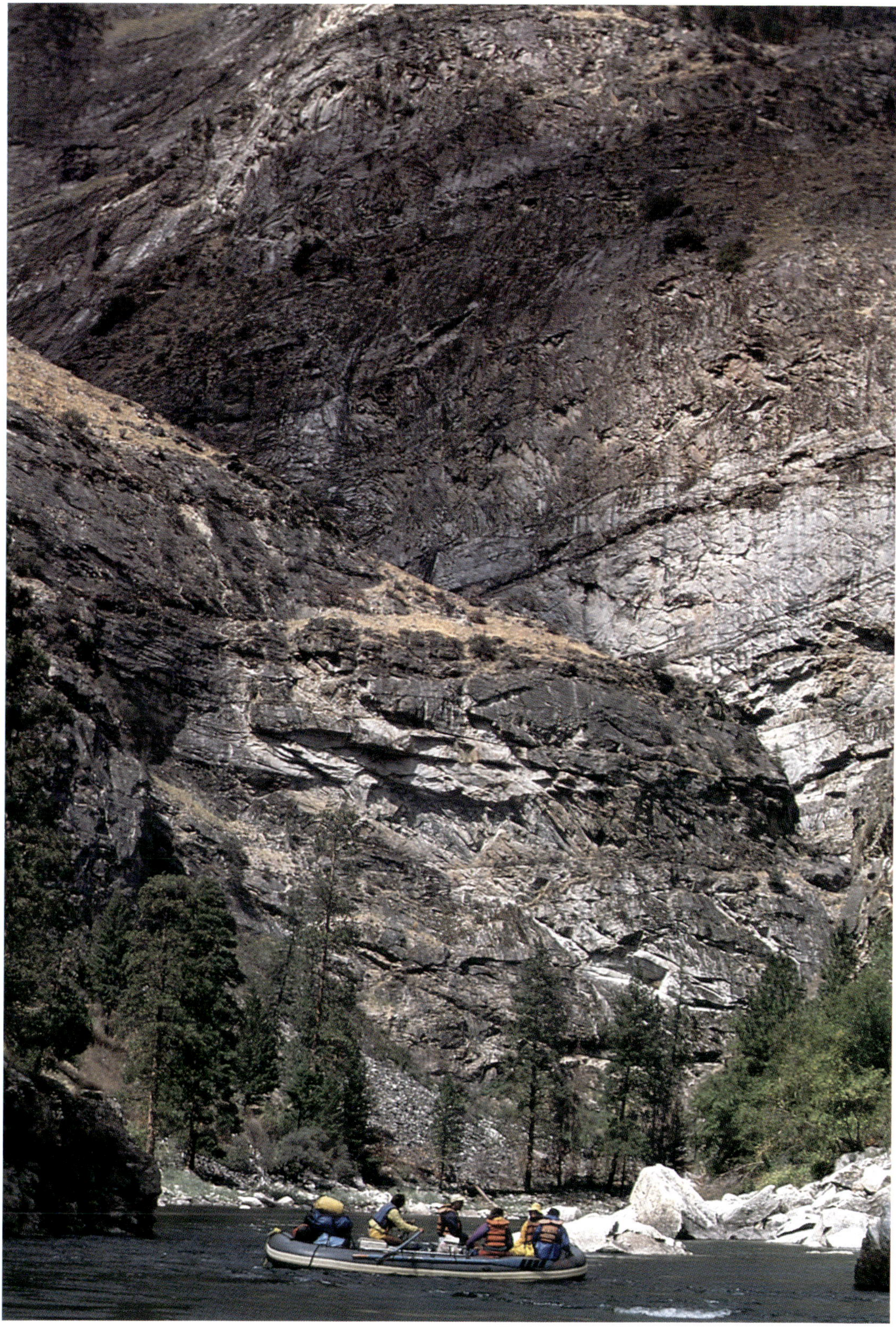

Middle Fork Salmon River *Larry Harrel / Echo*

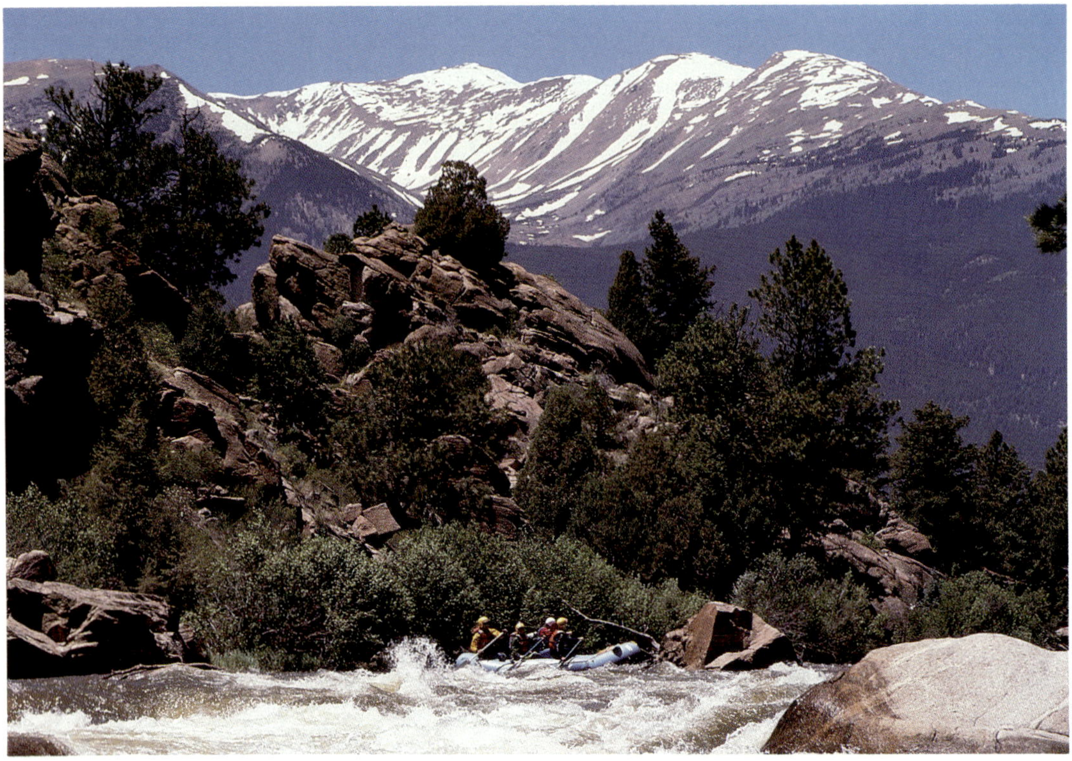

Browns Canyon, Arkansas River *Tim Brown / ProFiles West*

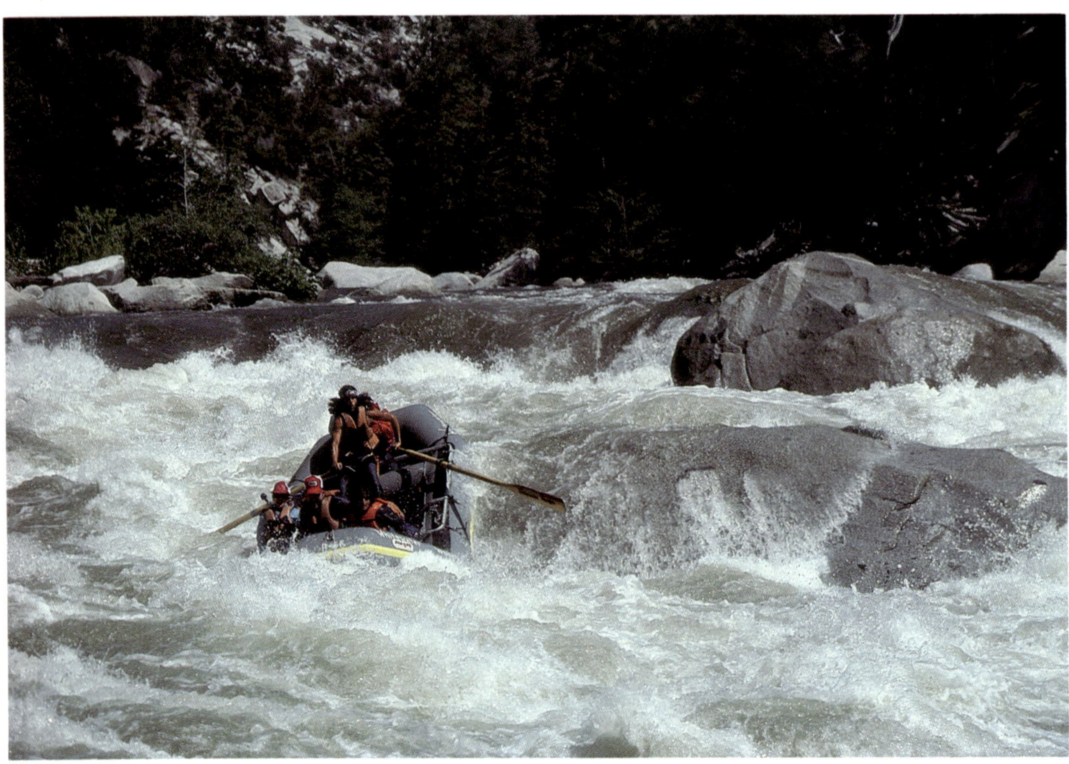

Vortex Rapid, Forks of the Kern *Curt Smith*

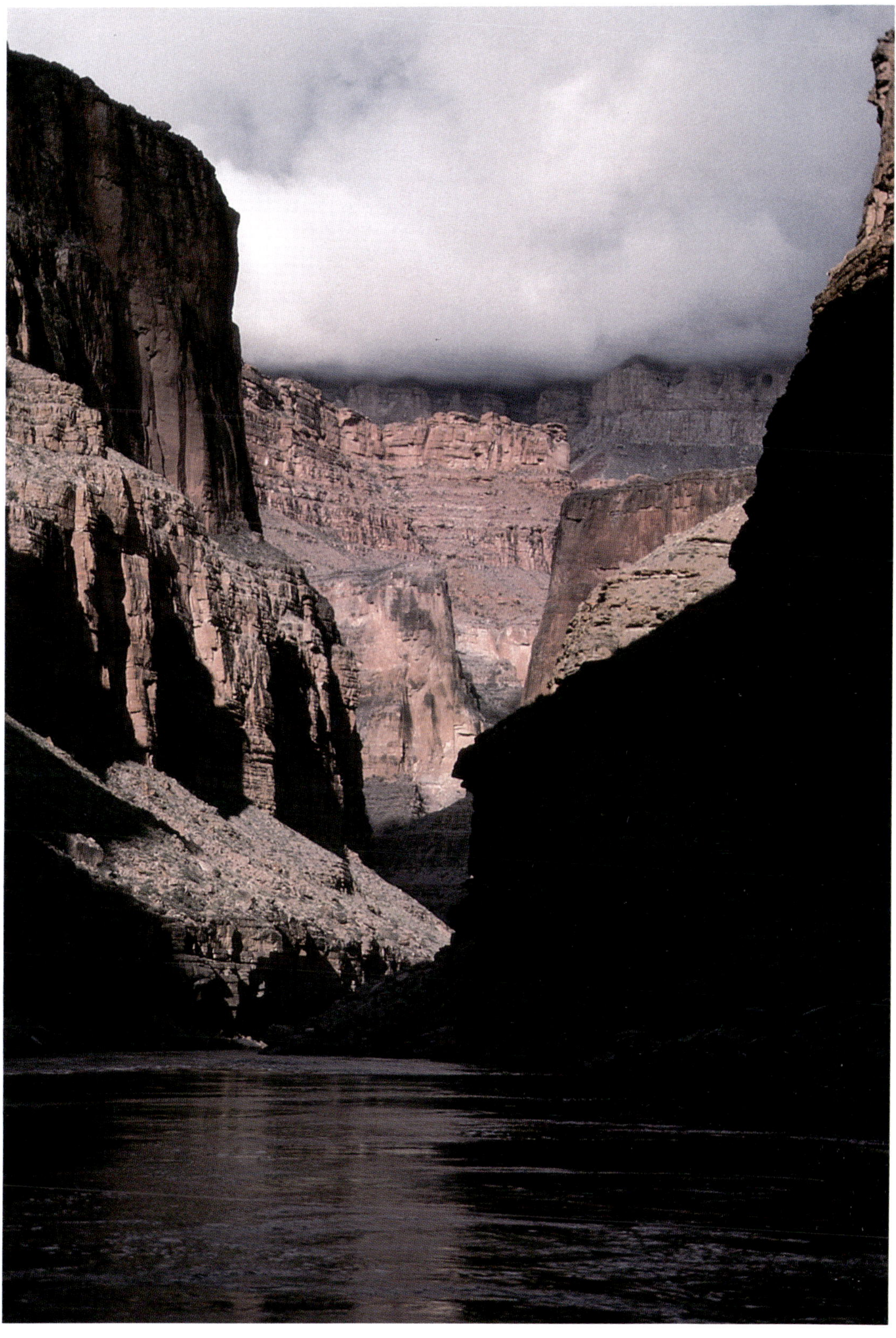

Grand Canyon above Havasu Creek *Michael P. Ghiglieri*

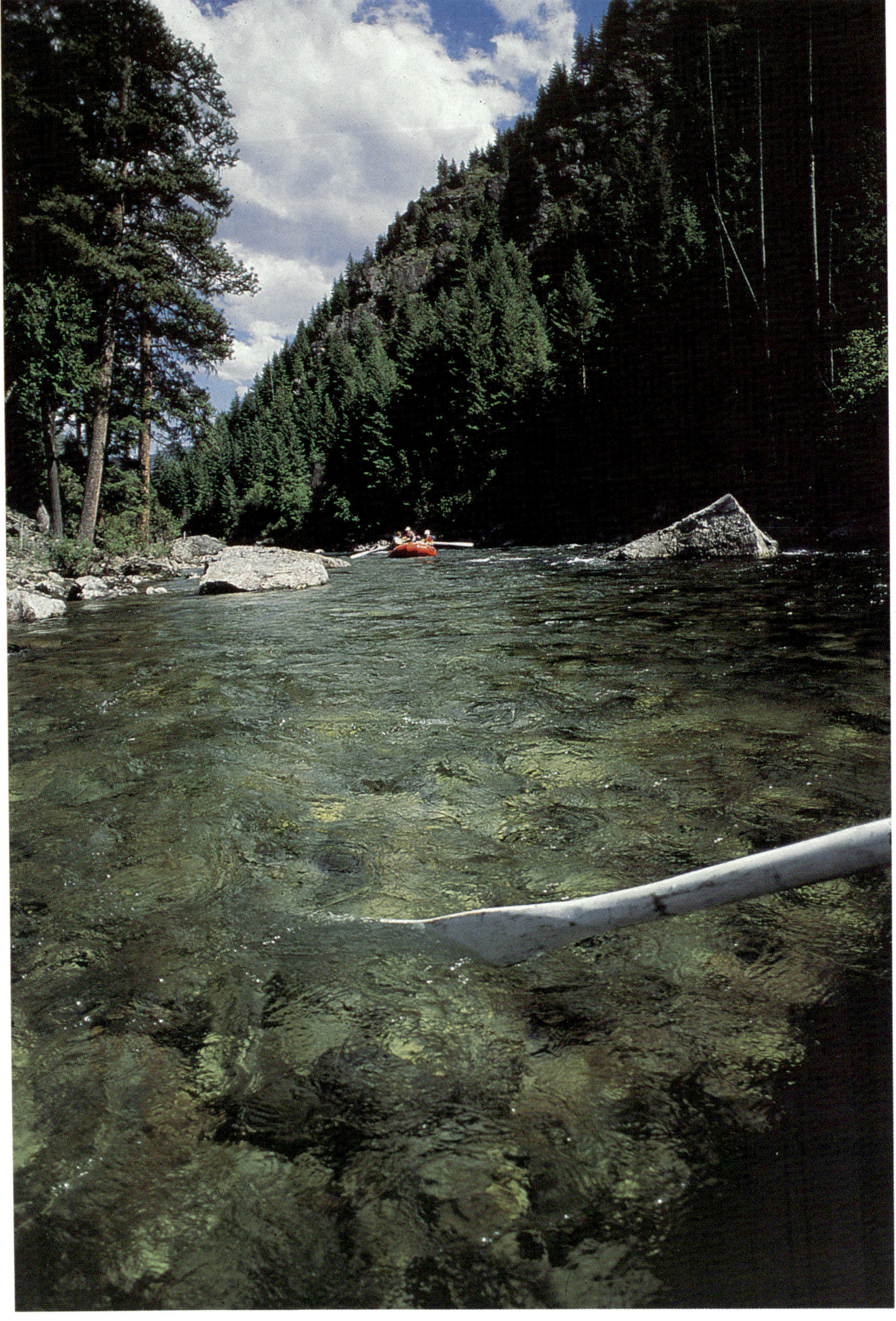

Selwway River *Steve Bly*

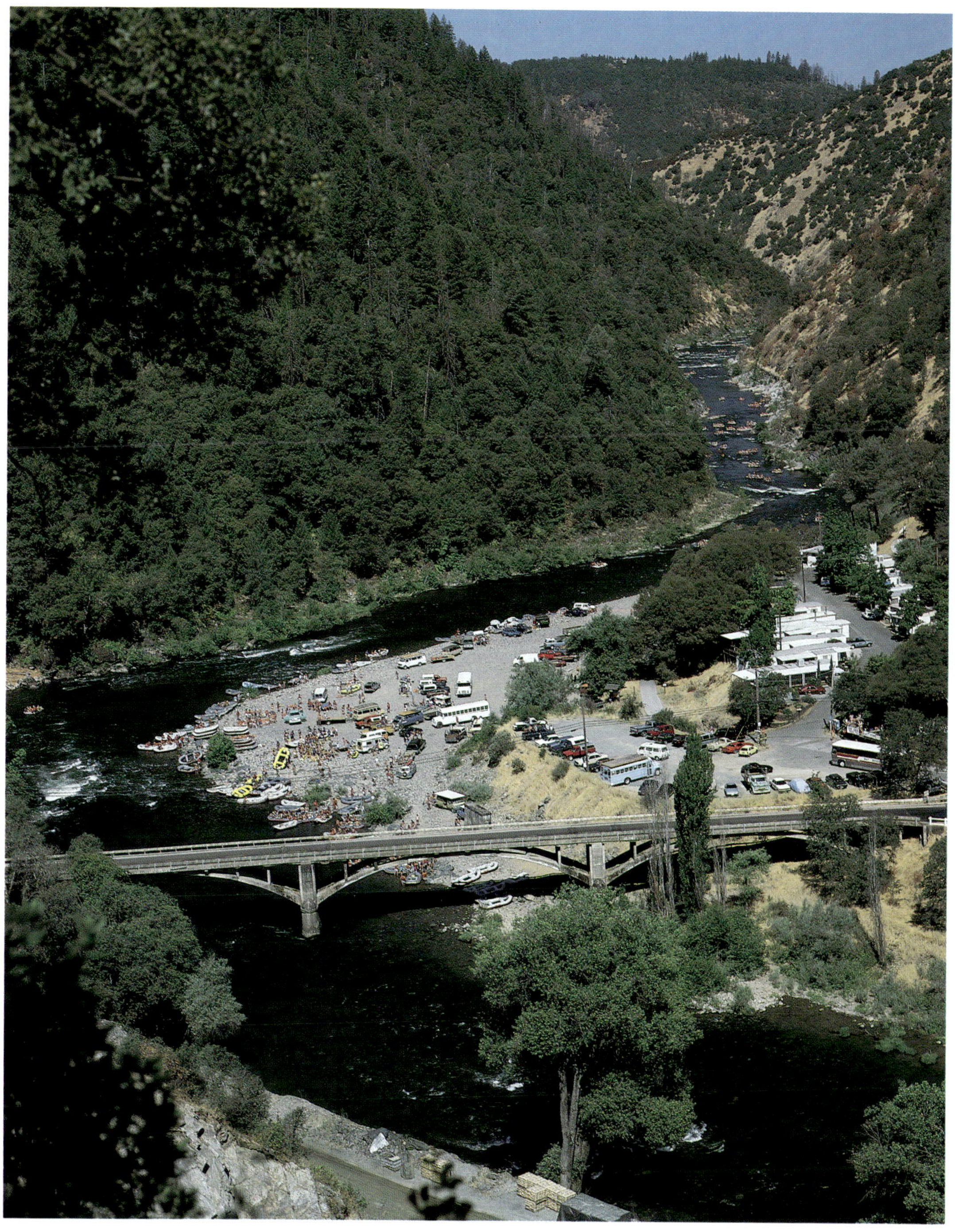

Chili Bar, South Fork American River *Mark Leder-Adams / Rapid Shooters*

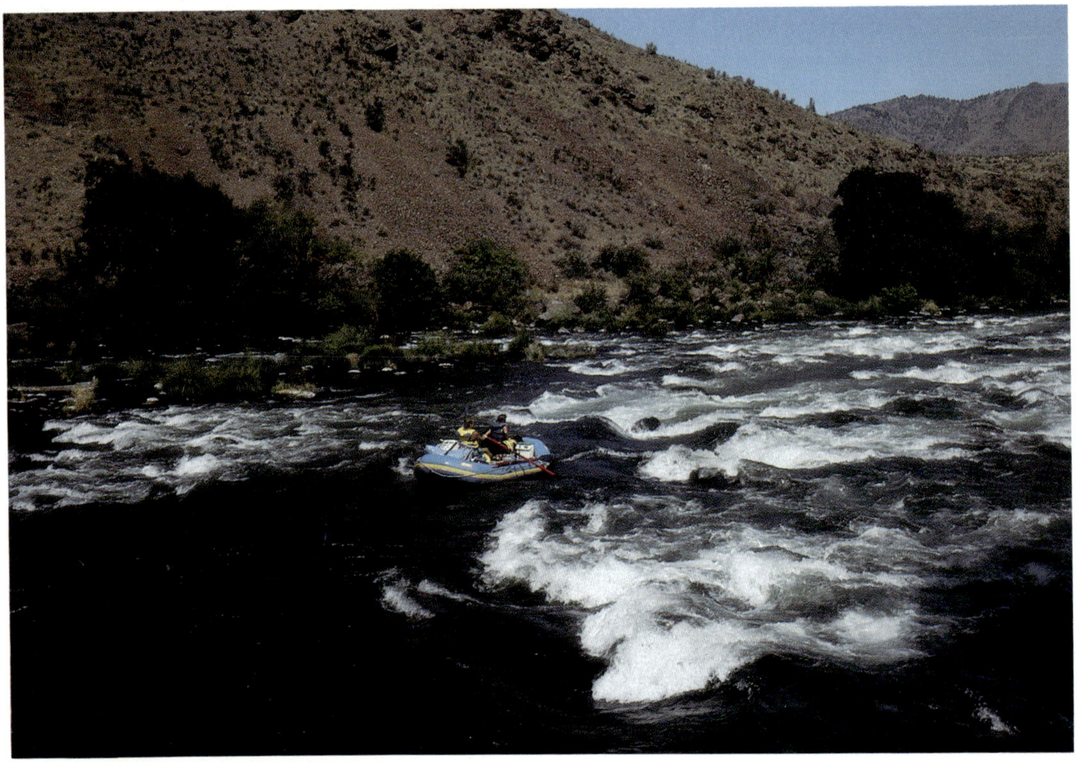

Boxcar Rapid, Deschutes River *Martha Moran*

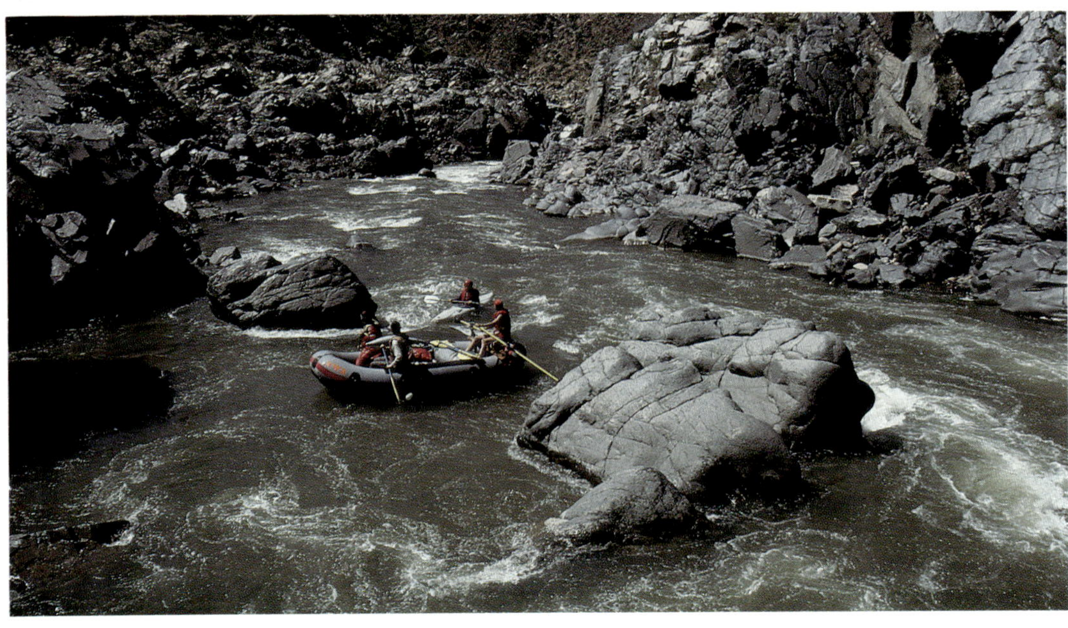

Salt River *Steve Miller*

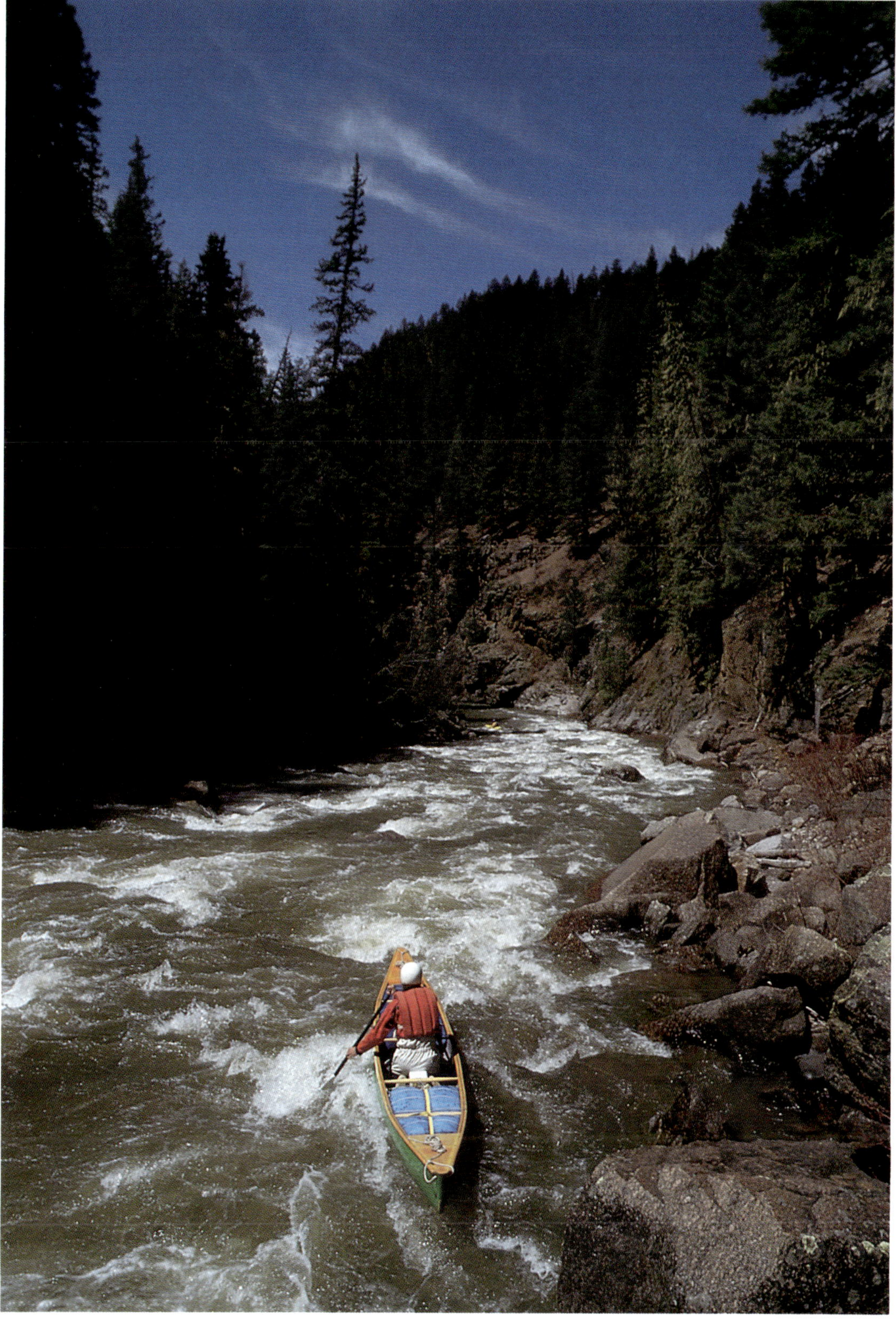

Piedra River *Amy Wiley & Chuck Wales / ProFiles West*

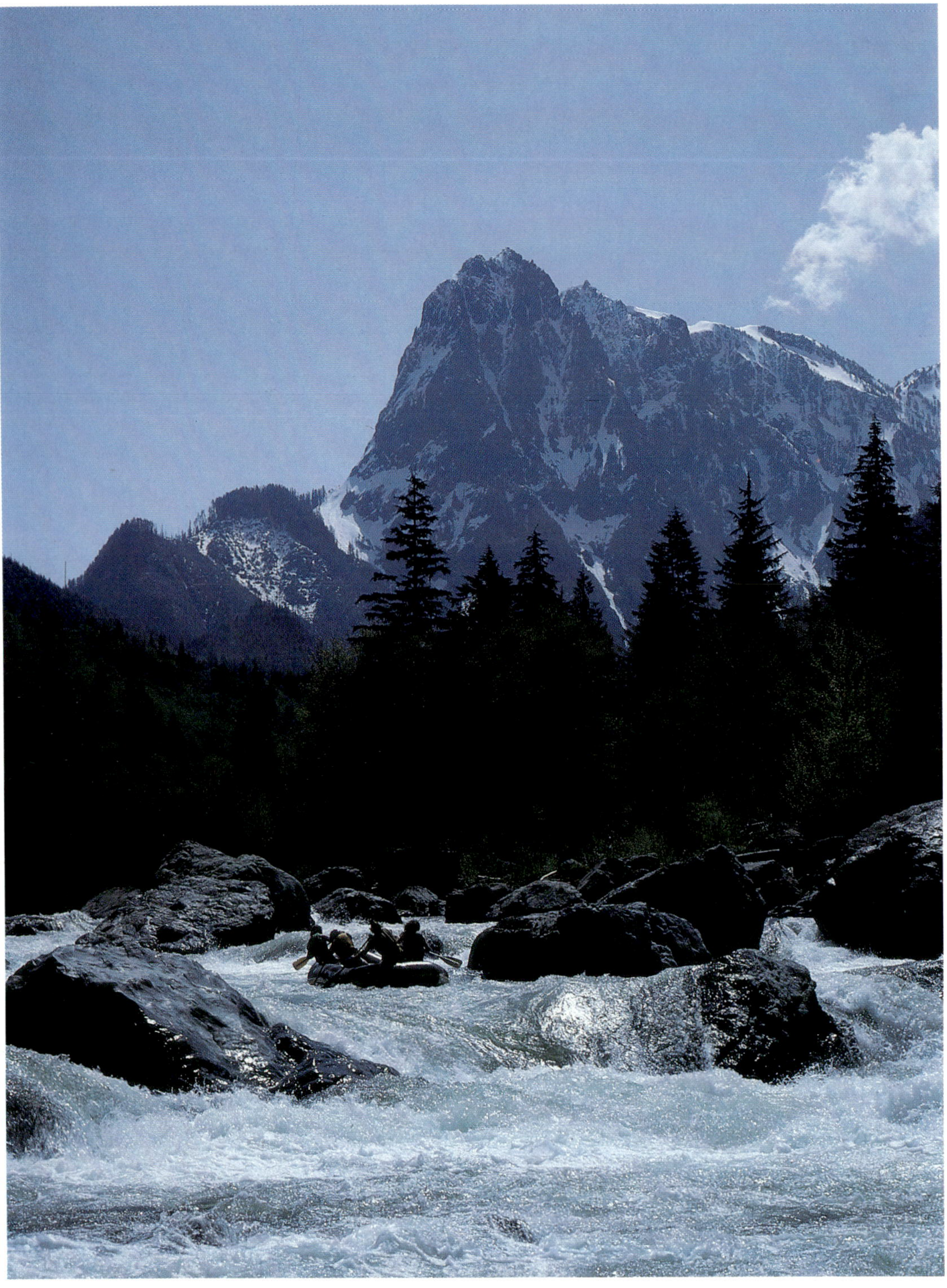

Skykomish River and Mt. Index *Verne Huser*

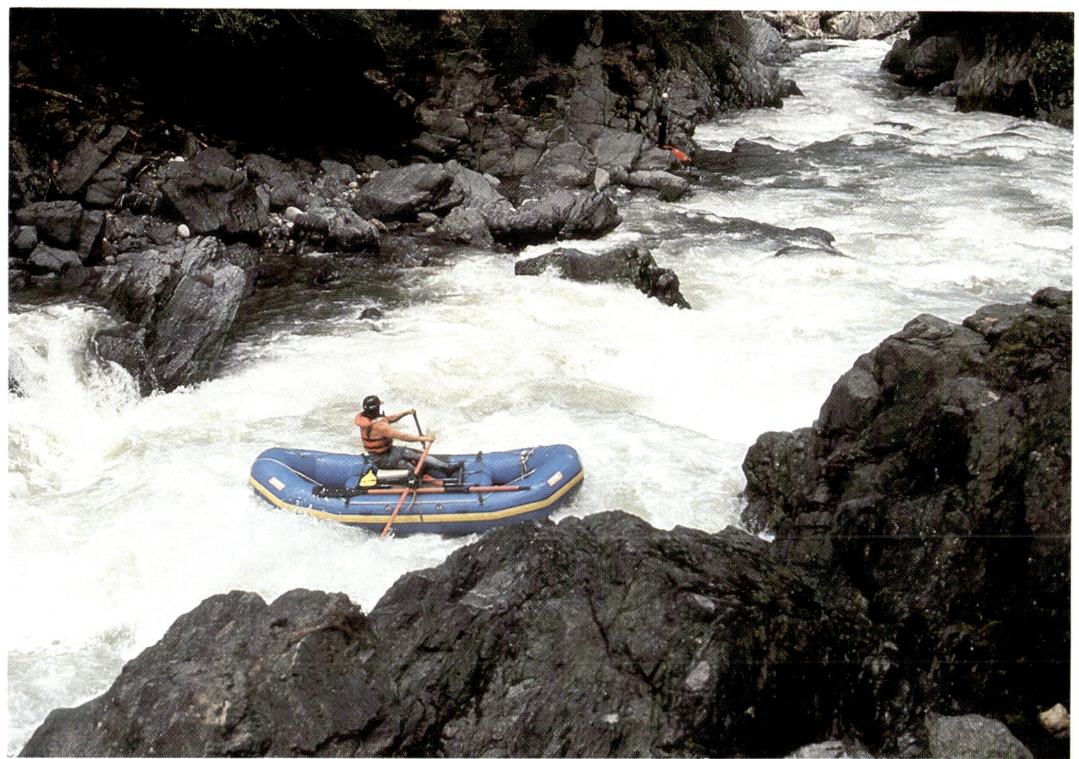

Robe Canyon, South Fork Stillaguamish River *Jeff Bennett*

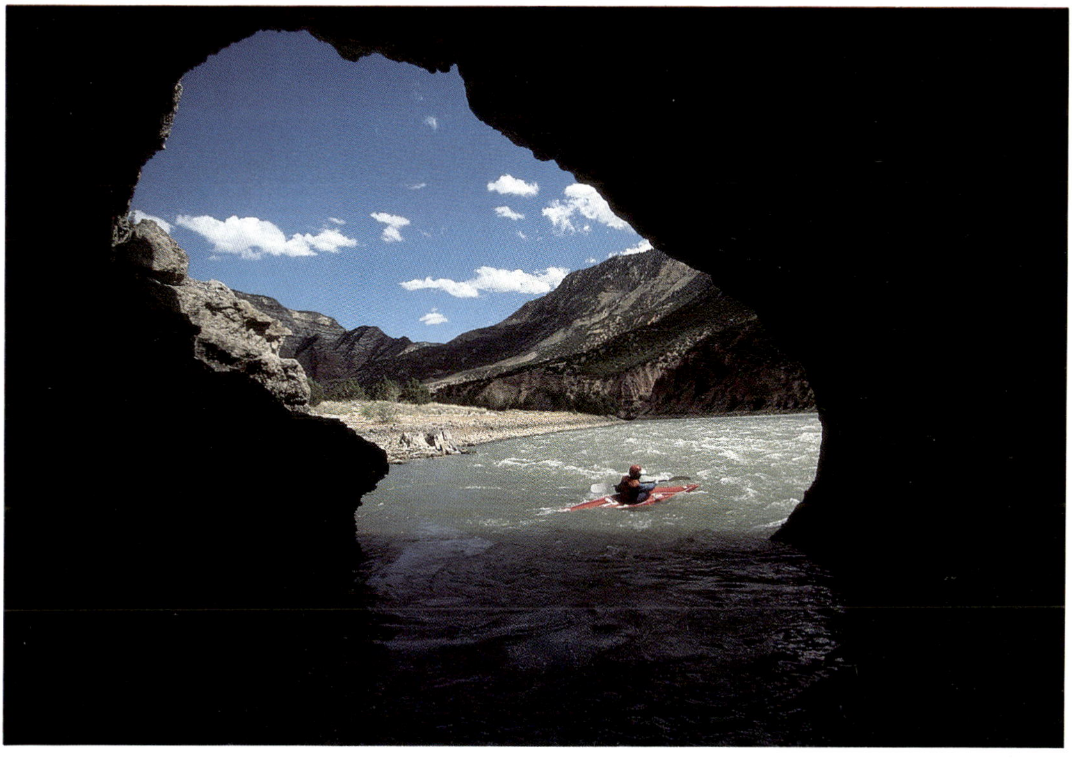

Split Mountain Canyon, Green River *Steve Miller*

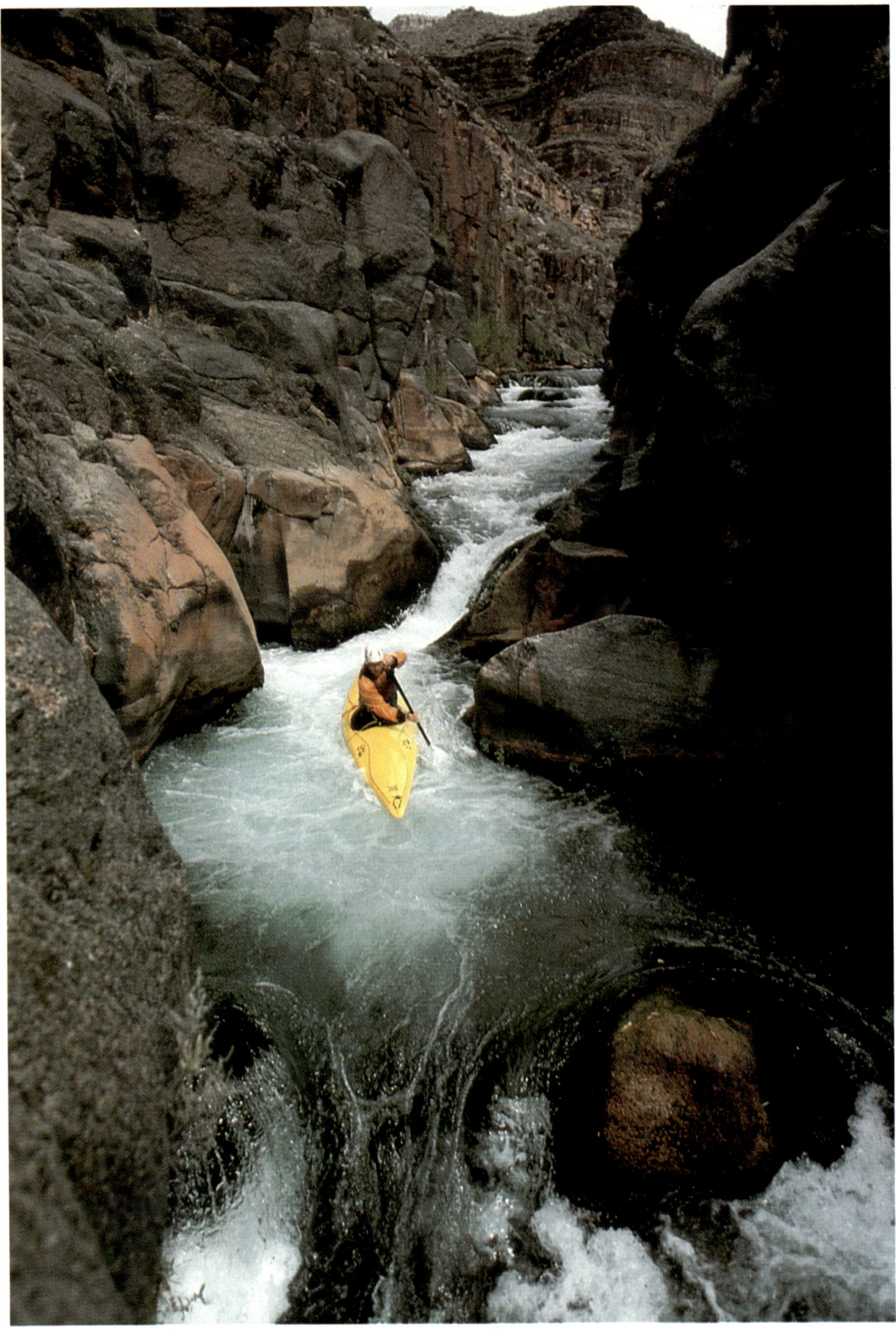

C-1 on Tapeats Creek, Grand Canyon *Daniel Bolster*

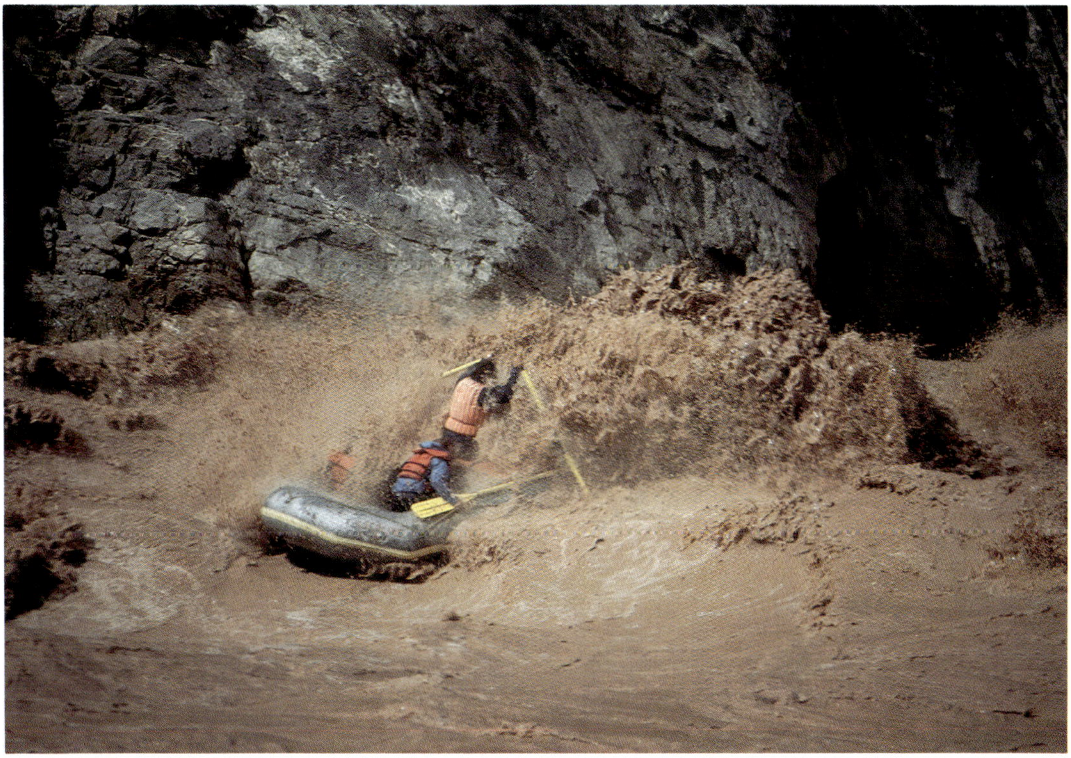

Crystal Rapid, Grand Canyon *Curt Smith*

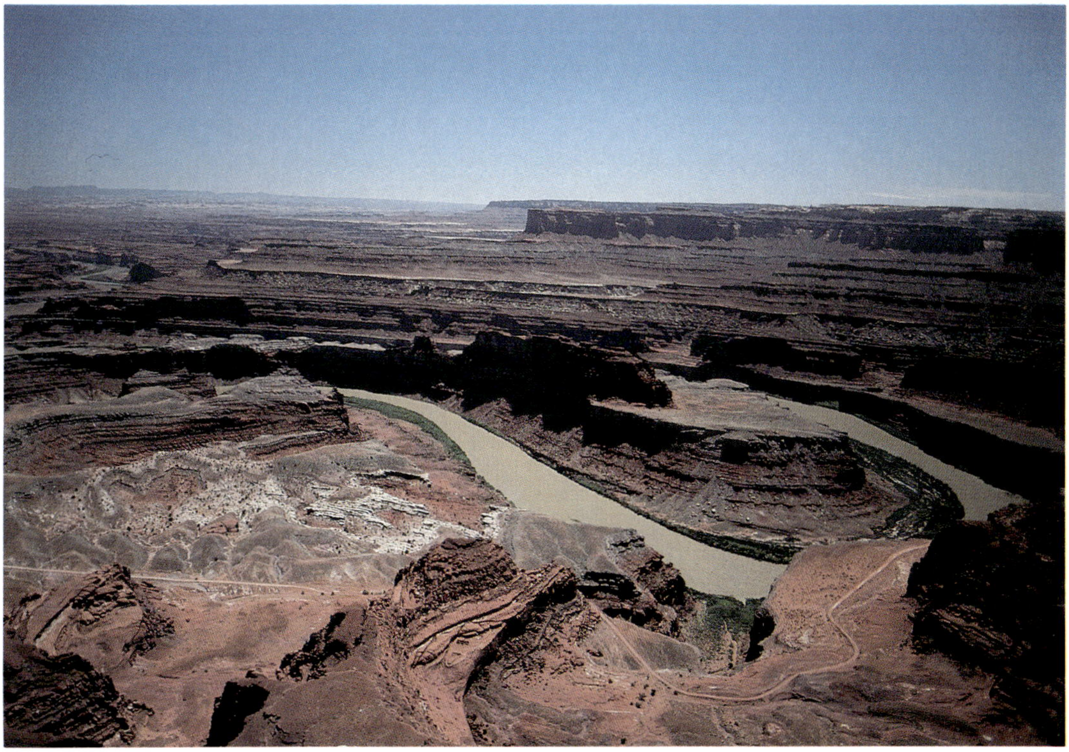

Meander Canyon from Dead Horse Point, Colorado River *Bill Cross*

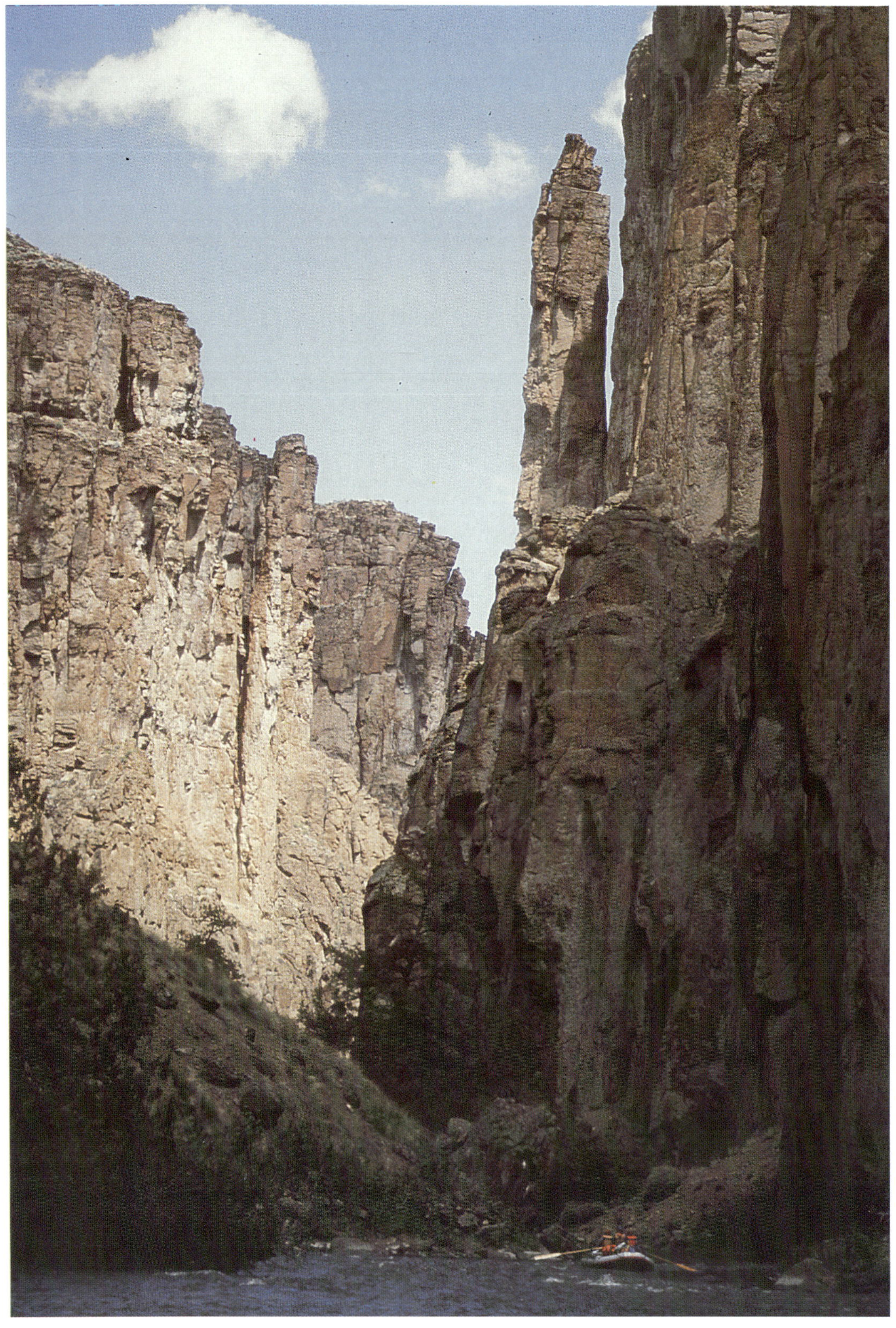

Bruneau River *Steve Bly*

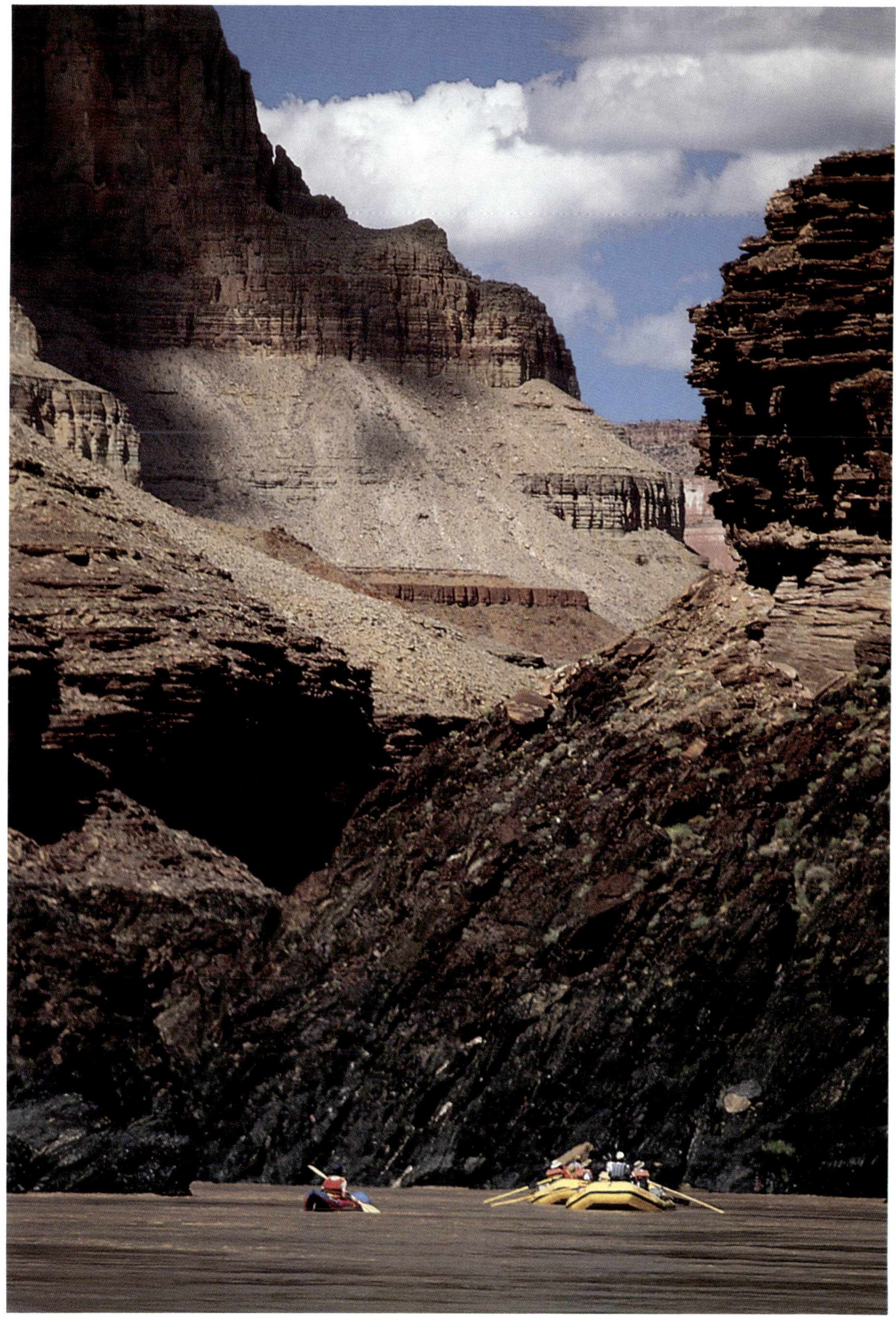

Middle Granite Gorge, Grand Canyon *Liz Hymans*

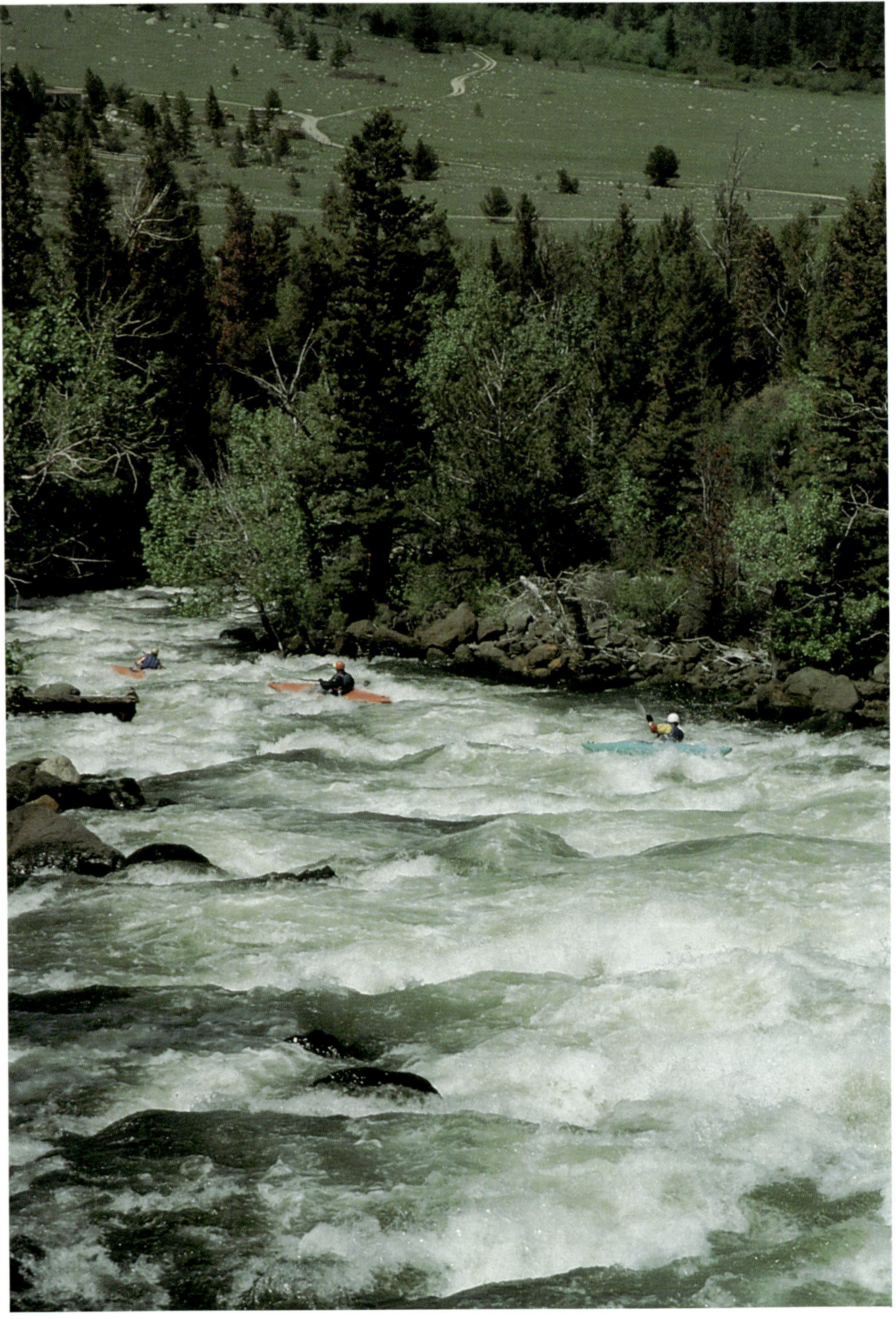

Lower Chrome Mine Chute, Stillwater River *Ron Lodders*

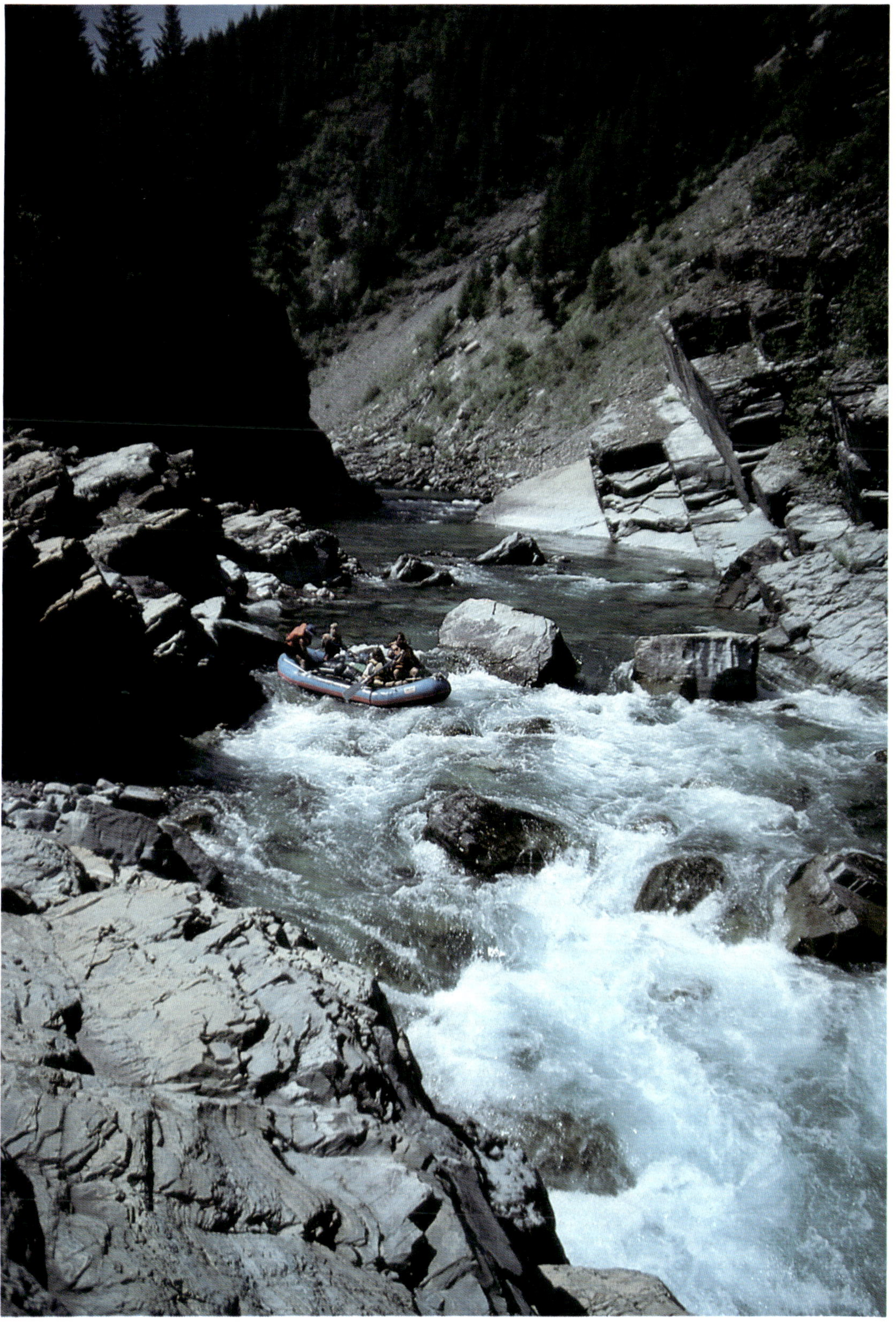

Upper Middle Fork Flathead River *Glacier Raft Co.*

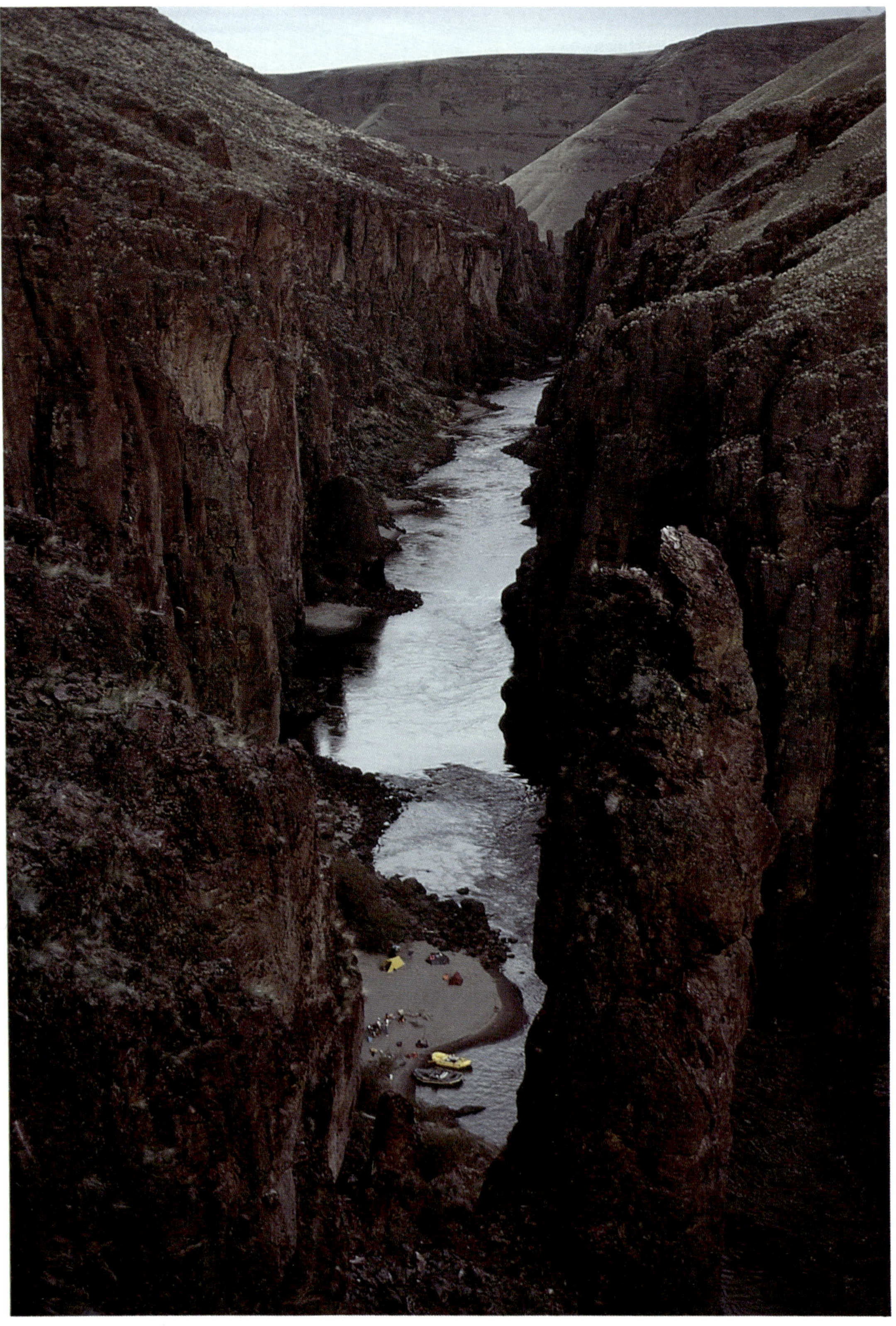

Beam Camp Pinnacle, Owyhee River *Ted Weigold*

Kings River

1. Upper Kings: Confluence of Middle and South Forks (2,240') to Garnet Dike Campground (1,280').
V+p; 100 ft./mi.; 10 miles.

2.Main Kings: Garnet Dike Campground to Kirch Flat Campground (950').
III; 9.5 miles; 35 ft./mi.
Shorter runs possible.

Drainage Area and Average Annual Discharge: 950 sq. mi. and 1,300,000 af (est.) at Rodgers Crossing on Run 2.

Season: *Upper Kings:* About a month sometime in the summer, often from late June to late July. Usually too high or too low for boating, so the season is short. *Main Kings:* April–late July.

Recommended Levels: *Upper Kings:* 800–2,000 cfs. *Main Kings:* 1,500–8,000 cfs.

Flow Information: DWR tape, (916) 653-9647; flow at Rodgers Crossing (3 miles above the lowermost take-out at Kirch Flat). Flow at Upper Kings put-in is a bit less.

Special Hazards: *Upper Kings:* Remote, inaccessible wilderness canyon. Rescue would be difficult or impossible.

Permits: Not presently required.

Managing Agency: Kings River RD, Sierra NF, Trimmer Route, Sanger, CA 93657; (209) 855-8321.

Commercial Raft Trips: *Upper Kings:* No. *Main Kings:* Yes. For references contact the managing agency.

Land Ownership: All National Forest.

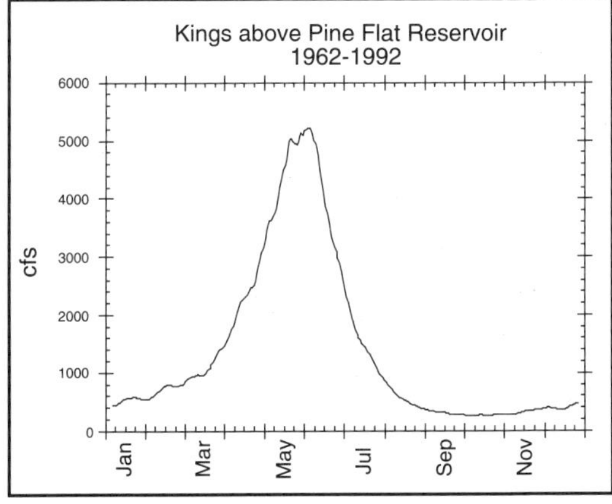

Scenery: *Upper Kings:* Excellent. Deep, dramatic granite canyon. *Main Kings:* Very good. Deep foothills canyon.

Solitude: *Upper Kings:* Excellent. *Main Kings:* Good.

Wilderness: *Upper Kings:* Yes. *Main Kings:* No. Dirt road, campgrounds.

Guides and References:
- Cassady & Calhoun, *California Whitewater: A Guide to the Rivers.*
- Holbek & Stanley, *A Guide to the Best Whitewater in the State of California.*

Maps:
- **USGS 7.5':** *Wren Peak, Hume, Verplank Ridge, Luckett Mtn.*
- **USFS:** *Sequoia NF* and *Sierra NF.*
- **AAA:** Sequoia.

Logistics: To reach the Main Kings run and the take-out for the Upper Kings, drive 18 miles east of Fresno on California Highway 180. At Centerville turn left on slow, winding Trimmer Springs Road and follow it past Piedra and around the north side of Pine Flat Reservoir to **Kirch Flat Campground, take-out for the Main Kings.**

To reach **Garnet Dike Campground, put-in for the Main Kings and take-out for the Upper Kings,** continue upriver. The road crosses the river twice, becomes dirt, and then deteriorates, becoming very rough as you approach the access point just below Garnet Dike CG (called Upper Kings CG on USFS maps). The Garnet Dike-Kirch Flat shuttle is 9.5 miles (30 to 45 minutes) one way.

To reach the **put-in for the Upper Kings,** follow California Highway 180 east from Fresno toward Kings Canyon National Park. If you're driving from the take-out at Garnet Dike CG, you can save some miles by turning south at Piedra onto Elwood Road, which connects with Highway 180. Stop at Yucca Point, some 16 miles northeast of Grant Grove Village, and descend a 2-mile trail to the put-in. Although Highway 180 crosses the South Fork 3.5 miles upstream, do *not* attempt to put in there: the South Fork drops more than 200 ft./mi. and includes unrunnable sections that can't be scouted or portaged. The shuttle for the Upper Kings is 50 or 80 miles (2.5 hours) one way.

KINGS

The Kings is one of California's biggest rivers. Its large, high-elevation watershed[1] near the southern end of the Sierra Nevada holds its deep snowpack well into summer, giving the Kings[2] the longest boating season of any undammed river in the state. During spring snowmelt the Kings has the highest flows of any California river. (Flows rise even higher on the biggest North Coast rivers, the Klamath and the Eel, but only during the winter rainy season.) The Kings is also the steepest river in this book, dropping down the west slope of the Sierra from around 14,000' to 1,000' in less than 40 miles.

Before the white man arrived with plow and shovel, the Kings emptied into a vast marsh known as Tulare Lake, which covered some 700 square miles of the Central Valley. At one time this huge wetland supported the most abundant concentration of wildlife in the state, including enormous numbers of waterfowl, herds of Tule Elk, and even roaming grizzly bears. In the late nineteenth century, farmers began digging irrigation canals in the Kings River Delta and in the valley near Fresno, reducing inflows to Tulare Lake and causing it to shrink. In this century, as agriculture demanded still more land, much of Tulare Lake was drained and cultivated. In 1954 the Army Corps of Engineers built Pine Flat Dam on the Kings to store water for irrigation.

Today the Kings faces new threats. The Corps' proposed raising of Pine Flat Dam by 20' would flood the lower portion of the Main Kings run. Because National Wild and Scenic protection extends only part way down the main stem, much of the river is still vulnerable. If wholesale electricity prices rise, the Kings River Conservation District may ask Congress for permission to build a 600'-high dam at Rodgers Crossing, which would flood the lower four miles of the Upper Kings and most of the Main Kings below Garnet Dike Campground.[3]

The Main Kings means big water. In May and June of a wet year, when a heavy snowpack combines with warm weather to swell the river, the Kings gives California boaters a chance to test their skills against hydraulics on the scale of the Grand Canyon. The riverbed in this ten-mile stretch just above Pine Flat Reservoir is wide and not heavily obstructed, so even at high flows the Main Kings isn't exceptionally hazardous. Of course, big water always calls for extra precautions. Most of the rapids can be seen and scouted from the road.[4]

The Main Kings rolls through a deep, dry foothill canyon. In spring the riverside slopes put on a dazzling display of wildflowers. This is a popular meeting place for boaters from northern and southern California. Kayak races are often held here in the spring, and commercial outfitters run daily raft trips throughout most of the summer. Camping is good at numerous undeveloped sites along the river, and a lightly-used road follows the entire run. If time allows, consider hiking five miles up the trail above the put-in to peer over the rim of the canyon where Garlic Falls plummets a thousand feet into the Upper Kings.

Upstream, in a deep, spectacular canyon just downstream from the confluence of the Middle and South Forks, is the rarely attempted Upper Kings run—emphatically **for daring experts only.** The Upper Kings is among the most difficult runs in the West. It is for fearless, seasoned, top-notch boaters who don't mind carrying their gear down a two-mile trail, portaging several rapids, and running many others at the limits of navigability. Only expert kayakers and rafters have seen this remote, rugged stretch of river. Even hikers and fishermen can reach only the area around the put-in at the end of the trail, which drops about 2,000' to the river.

Still, the fantastic whitewater and the spectacular virgin wilderness lure boaters from time to time. Roger Paris, Maynard Munger, and Bryce Whitmore made the first kayak descent —portaging frequently—in 1960, when most top kayakers were content with running Class III and IV rivers. Jim Cassady led the first raft descent in 1981 (see story). Now, every year, a few parties of experts make this very demanding run, usually portaging some rapids.

---

[1]Most of the watershed is protected by Kings Canyon National Park, the John Muir Wilderness, the High Sierra Primitive Area, and the Kings River Special Management Area. In 1987, Congress added several sections of the Kings to the National Wild and Scenic Rivers System: the South and Middle Forks and the first six miles of the Upper Kings above Garlic Spur.

[2]The river was named "El Rio de los Santos Reyes"—The River of the Holy Kings—when it was first seen by Spanish explorers in 1805 on the feast day of the biblical wise men.

[3]For more information, contact Friends of the River. See appendix for address.

[4]There is also a Class I–II canoe float on the Lower Kings below the reservoir which is not covered in this book.

Upper Kings River Guide

Experts only. Plan to scout frequently. Depending on the flow and your skills, more rapids than the few mentioned below may require portaging.

Put in where a two-mile trail from Yucca Point reaches the left bank at the confluence of the Middle and South Forks of the Kings. The first three miles are Class IV, except for one Class V passage near mile 2. Then survival boating begins; the river drops 160 ft./mi. for two miles, with at least three or four possible portages in that short stretch. At mile 4.5, near where Rough Creek enters on the right via a spectacular waterfall, there is another possible portage. There is yet another possible portage a few hundred yards downstream, near one of the few good campsites in this rugged canyon (right bank).

At mile 5 spectacular Garlic Falls cascades down the right wall. In the remaining five miles the gradient "eases" to 90 ft./mi., but the river is still laced with Class V rapids that must be scouted as well as one or two more that may need to be portaged. Garnet Dike Campground is on the right at mile 10. **Take out** at an open spot about 100 yards downstream, or continue downriver (see next Kings run).

Main Kings River Guide

Put in on the right bank about a hundred yards below Garnet Dike Campground, or at alternate sites all along the road that follows the run. A quarter mile below the upper put-in is **BANZAI (III+)**, the toughest drop. At lower flows watch for a boat-eating hole in the center; at higher flows this hole washes out, but other, bigger holes appear elsewhere in the rapid.

At mile 2.8 is **MULE ROCK (III)**, where the current piles into a midstream rock (hole above 3,000 cfs). A mile farther down is **FANG TOOTH (III)**, a long boulder garden. Mill Flat Creek enters on the left at mile 4.5 (side hike, good campsite). At mile 6.5 is Rodgers Crossing, site of the proposed dam. A mile farther downstream, a bridge crosses the river and the North Fork of the Kings enters on the right.

A quarter mile below the North Fork is **SIDEWINDER (III)**, with a large rock on the left that becomes a big hole at higher water. A third of a mile below Sidewinder is the last Class III, **RANCH RAPID,** also known as **Rooster Tail** (mile 8.2). Here the river splits, with most of the water turning left into a sharp drop. At higher flows the right channel is a "chicken route." A quarter mile downstream, a bridge crosses the river, and a mile below the bridge is the **take-out on the right at Kirch Flat Campground** (mile 9.5).

It was July 1981. Our group was made up of seven river guides—all tired from working commercial trips the previous day—in two small, conventional Avon rafts. One was rigged as an oar boat; the other, for a paddle crew. We got around to shopping so late for our planned two-day float that we had to buy our provisions from a liquor store. At least we knew to pack light. After all, this was the fearsome Upper Kings, and we planned to do some portaging.

On the morning of the first day, we hiked our gear down the trail and put in around noon. The going was slow, with one big drop following another and everyone peering around the corners in expectation of even worse rapids. We camped around mile 3. The next day was even slower, as we made our way down the Rough Creek-Garlic Meadow Creek section that drops at 160 feet per mile. The current was so swift at 1,800 cfs that we had to take emergency measures so our boats could stop between rapids. We ran one raft at a time, and members of our team were stationed downstream to throw lines from shore and pull them into the tiny eddies. Even without serious problems, we covered only two miles.

We were so far behind schedule that we had to ration our food. But we camped just upstream from one of the most gorgeous spots in the Sierra, Garlic Meadow Creek's thousand-foot waterfall. The sight of the moon rising over the canyon wall and the knowledge that few humans had ever been there were worth all the trouble. We made it out the next day. By the next time I ran the Upper Kings, in 1984, I had helped design and develop a self-bailing raft, partly with this river in mind.

—Jim Cassady

Merced River

Red Bud to Bagby

Difficulty: IVp; II from mile 9 to mile 16.
Length: 29 miles. Shorter runs possible.
Gradient: 34 ft./mi.
Put-in: Red Bud Picnic Area (1,700').
Take-out: Bagby (715').
Drainage Area: 691 sq. mi. at Briceburg.
Season: March–June. Typically peaks in May and drops quickly after mid-June. Kayaks and small rafts can often run well into July.
Recommended Levels: 800–5,000 cfs.
Flow Information: DWR tape, (916) 653-9647; inflow to McClure Reservoir. This reading slightly overestimates flows on the Merced run because it includes the North Fork. The hydrograph below, based on the El Portal gauge over 30 miles upstream, underestimates flows on most of the run.
Special Hazards: Portage at North Fork Falls (mile 22.8). At higher flows it is dangerous to run Quarter Mile Rapid (mile 22.3) because boats could be swept over the falls. When flows exceed 4,000 cfs, taking out at the end of the road (Railroad Flat Campground, mile 20.5) is recommended.
Permits: Not required unless group exceeds 24.
Managing Agency: BLM, Folsom RA, 63 Natoma Street, Folsom, CA 95630; (916) 985-4474.
Commercial Raft Trips: Yes. For a list of outfitters contact the BLM.
Land Ownership: Mixed BLM, National Forest, and private.
Scenery: Very good.
Solitude: Good despite the highway. Very good below Briceburg, where only a dirt road follows the river.

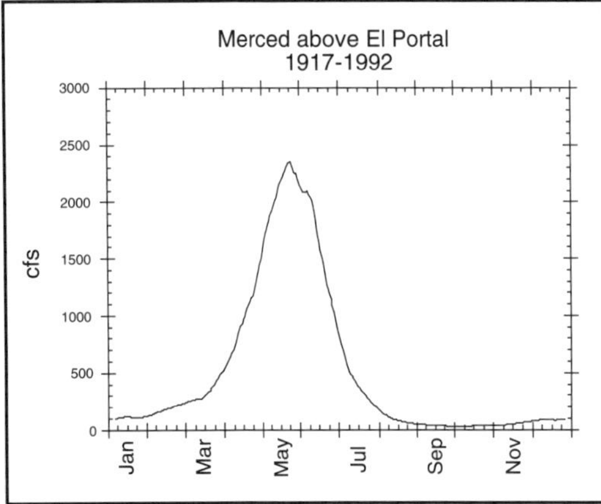

Wilderness: No. **Fishing:** Good for trout.
Water: Cold during peak snowmelt, warmer as flows drop in midsummer.
Camping: Public and private campgrounds along the highway are crowded on spring weekends and all week in the summer. Below Briceburg boaters can find campsites on both banks; those on the left are more secluded.
Side Hikes: South and North Forks of the Merced (see **Mile Guide**).
Side Excursions: Yosemite National Park.
Guides and References:

- Cassady & Calhoun, *California Whitewater: A Guide to the Rivers.*
- Holbek & Stanley, *A Guide to the Best Whitewater in the State of California.* Includes a hairball upstream run and the South Fork Merced.
- Orr & Orr, *Rivers of the West: A Guide to the Geology and History.*

Maps:

- **USGS 7.5':** *El Portal, Kinsley, Feliciana Mtn, Bear Valley, Buckhorn Peak, Hornitos.*
- **USGS 1:100:** *Yosemite Valley, Oakdale.*
- **USFS:** *Sierra NF* covers Red Bud to Briceburg.
- **AAA:** *Yosemite.*

Logistics: The **put-in** for private boaters is on the right bank at Red Bud Launch Site, across Foresta Bridge from Red Bud Picnic Area, 29 miles east of Mariposa on California Highway 140 and a few miles west of the El Portal entrance to Yosemite Park. There are many alternate accesses between the put-in and mile 20. At higher flows boaters may want to avoid the first 3 miles by launching at Cranberry Gulch (see **Mile Guide** for this and other alternate accesses). Shuttles are quick and easy down to Briceburg (mile 15) via Highway 140. The lowest take-out is near the recreational settlement of Bagby at the upper end of McClure Reservoir. To reach **the take-out at Bagby,** drive 18 miles north of Mariposa on California Highway 49 and turn right on a dirt road leading up the left (south) shore of the reservoir. The shuttle from Red Bud to Bagby is about 45 miles (1 hour 15 minutes) one way.

Fifteen miles west of its headwaters on the glacier-studded slopes of Mt. Lyell (13,114'), the Merced drops down the spectacular cataracts of Nevada and Vernal Falls into Yosemite Valley, where for a time it becomes a peaceful, meandering stream. Thanks to the popularity of Yosemite, which became a national park in 1890, the Merced[1] is one of the few Sierra rivers left undammed in its upper reaches.

Just west of the park the river surges forward again, falling off the edge of the glacial moraine that forms Yosemite Valley and tumbling down several miles of breathtakingly steep chutes and falls along Highway 140. The gradient gradually begins to slacken above the little settlement of El Portal and continues to decrease down to the Red Bud put-in.

The Merced's cold, clear, free-flowing waters peak in May and, except in years of heavy snowfall, drop quickly after mid-June. By late July in most years the river dwindles to a tepid trickle, though kayaks and small rafts can often scrape down at this time. The Merced is at its best in spring, when redbuds and poppies splash the rugged hillsides with bright colors and Yosemite Park is not yet spilling over with tourists.

The boating season may be short, but it is intense. At El Portal, where some experts start their runs, the gradient is over 120 ft./mi.; a mile downstream at the Highway 140 bridge, another alternate put-in, the stream is dropping at 100 ft./mi.; and at Red Bud, the most popular starting point, the gradient is still 75. Below the South Fork (mile 6) the pace slackens a bit, but several major rapids still lie in wait. Toughest among them is **Quarter Mile** (mile 22.3), a long, rough boulder slalom that should not be run at high water because of the danger of being swept over unrunnable North Fork Falls just downstream. The portage around the falls is strenuous, and boaters running this lower section are advised to pack lightly.

The river also has its calm stretches, especially between the foot bridge (mile 9) and Briceburg (mile 15)—a section that makes an excellent float for less experienced boaters. At Briceburg (a historical site, not a town) the highway leaves the river, but a dirt road follows the right bank for five more miles. Even after the road ends, the abandoned road bed of the old Yosemite Railroad—defunct since 1945—follows the right bank all the way to McClure Reservoir, providing a good way to hike out in case of emergency.

The final 8 miles from Railroad Flat to Bagby require considerably more effort than the upper 20 miles. In addition to the mandatory portage at North Fork Falls, the lower section entails a longer shuttle and a flatwater paddle of up to a mile and a half across the backwaters of McClure Reservoir.[2] Nevertheless, the challenging whitewater and excellent scenery make this section well worth the effort.

The Merced above Briceburg and its South Fork have been National Wild and Scenic Rivers since 1987, but the section below Briceburg was endangered by the Merced Irrigation District's proposal to build a dam at Bagby. After years of lobbying, in late 1992 Congress added the eight-mile stretch between Briceburg and the reservoir to the National Wild and Scenic System, ending the threat to the river.

Other Runs

The National Park Service now permits Class I flatwater floats through Yosemite Valley, where the Merced winds quietly through some of the world's most famous scenery. Rubber duckies (tiny lightweight rafts) can be rented in the park. The run ends near Yosemite Lodge, above a Class III stretch known as the El Capitan run where boating is not permitted. Below this stretch the river drops off the edge of the moraine and down deadly waterfalls.

Expert boaters may be interested in the last few miles of the South Fork Merced, which meets the main stem 5.6 miles below Red Bud. Difficult access (hike to the put-in) and a short season are major disadvantages. A good trail follows the right bank for the lower four miles of the run. Adding three more miles of river by putting in farther upstream involves a long shuttle.[3] A few daring experts have made a very exotic, 22-mile, multi-day low-water run down the South Fork all the way from Highway 41 to Highway 140. This steep, dangerous run involves many difficult portages and an illegal put-in in Yosemite Park, so it cannot be recommended.

[1]Merced means "mercy" in Spanish. A 1774 expedition led by explorer Juan Bautista de Anza named the river for "Nuestra Señora de la Merced" ("Our Lady of Mercy"). Yosemite was inhabited by the Awani Indians before whites routed them in the early years of the Gold Rush. The new arrivals thought "Yosemite" was the Indians' tribal name, but it apparently meant "grizzly bear" in their language.

[2]McClure Reservoir, with a capacity of 1 million acre-feet, is formed by New Exchequer Dam, built in 1966 to furnish water and power for the Merced Irrigation District.

[3]See the Holbek & Stanley guide listed above.

Mile by Mile Guide

*See map in **Tuolumne** chapter.*

0 **PUT-IN.** Red Bud Launch Site (right bank). Experts sometimes start upstream at the Highway 140 bridge to run an extra mile of continuous Class IV rapids that are not visible from the highway. Really salty boaters occasionally launch near the cafe and gas station at El Portal, another mile upstream (continuous Class IV+). The first mile below Red Bud is continuous Class III–IV, with few eddies except at lower flows.

1.2 **NIGHTMARE ISLAND (IV). Recognition:** The river jogs right, then splits around an island as it bends sharply left. Scout this rapid and **Chipped Tooth** at the same time, from either bank. **The rapid:** Above 3,000 cfs most boaters run down the left. However, at lower flows this channel ends in a nasty boulder sieve, and boaters usually run the sharp, narrow drops on the right.

1.4 **CHIPPED TOOTH (IV).** A short staircase with a sizable rock (hole at higher flows) in the middle. At higher flows this rapid merges with the one above. From here to mile 6 are numerous unnamed Class II–III rapids, frequent at first but less so downstream as the gradient eases. The river occasionally splits around brushy islands.

2.5 **RIVER ACCESS.** Cranberry Gulch, an alternate put-in on the left. Recommended at high flows to avoid the rapids upstream. Cedar Lodge is on the left.

5.6 The South Fork of the Merced enters on the left. Good side hike.

7.5 **NED'S GULCH (IV). Recognition:** The river bends left at Ned's Gulch, a small draw on the right marked by a house and other signs of habitation. Scout from the right. **The rapid:** A staircase rapid; the third and last drop is the biggest. At high water the holes turn into huge but runnable waves.

9 **RIVER ACCESS.** A foot bridge crosses the river. Alternate access on the steep left bank. Easy Class II and a gradient of only 20 ft./mi. for the next six miles.

15 **RIVER ACCESS.** Briceburg—a historical site, not a town. No camping. Bear Creek enters on the left. Highway 140 leaves the river here, but a bridge crosses to the right bank and a dirt road continues downstream, providing frequent access for the next 5 miles.

17.2 **SPLIT ROCK (IV).** A huge rock (hole at higher flows) blocks the center of the river. Scout this rapid and the next at the same time from the right. Just downstream at **CORNER POCKET (IV)**, the river turns sharply right, and most of the current pours into a strong reversal on the left.

20.2 **RIVER ACCESS.** Railroad Flat CG (right bank). End of the road. A trail continues downstream along the old rail bed. Take out here at higher flows (4,000–5,000 cfs and up) to avoid the risk of running **Quarter Mile Rapid** unsuccessfully and being swept into North Fork Falls.

21.8 An old 4' weir spanned the river here until the BLM dynamited it some years ago. It's still a good idea to stop upstream and scout it at low flows. Eddy out just below the weir on the right to scout Quarter Mile Rapid.

22 **QUARTER MILE (IV+).** Longer than its name indicates. A complex boulder slalom at lower flows; big, powerful waves and holes at higher flows. Scout carefully from the right bank, memorizing your entire route. Station rescue parties with throw bags downstream. Check the short pool separating the end of the rapid from North Fork Falls. **If you're not sure you can stop in time, don't run this rapid.** Holbek and Stanley's guide book (see **Guides and References**) includes a hair-raising story about a kayaker who didn't make this must-catch eddy.

22.8 **NORTH FORK FALLS (U).** *PORTAGE.* A 25' near-vertical drop decorated with huge boulders. Sure, a few crazies have run the far left side, but that's no reason for you to try it. Use the boat ramps on the right to make the strenuous portage. The falls form where the harder bedrock that produces Quarter Mile suddenly ends. The cascading river cuts deeply into the softer rock on the downstream side. Just downstream, the North Fork of the Merced enters on the right (side hike). Class II rapids from here on.

26.8 High-water mark of McClure Reservoir.

28.3 **TAKE-OUT** on the left at the end of the dirt road leading up from Bagby. A small fee is required to use the road.

29 Highway 49 bridge across the reservoir at Bagby.

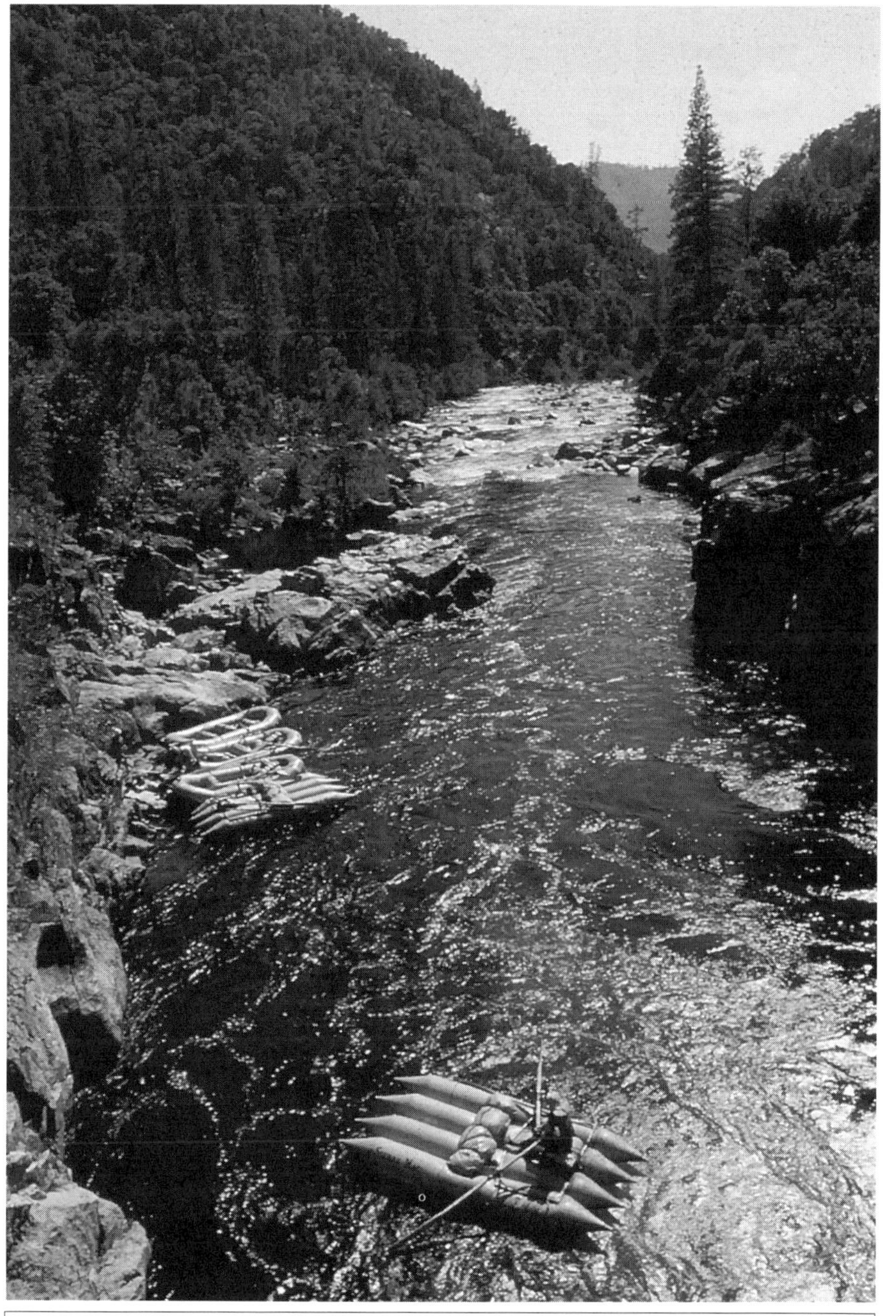

Tuolumne below Lumsden Falls *Brian Fessenden / Sierra Mac River Trips*

Tuolumne River

Cherry Creek to Ward's Ferry

1. Upper Tuolumne:
Cherry Creek (2,240') to Meral's Pool (1,430').
Vp; 9 miles; 93 ft./mi.

2. Main Tuolumne:
Meral's Pool to Ward's Ferry (750').
IV+; 18 miles; 38 ft./mi.

Drainage Area and Average Annual Discharge: 723 sq. mi. and 950,000 af at Cherry Creek confluence. 1,350 sq. mi. and 1,205,000 af at Ward's Ferry.

Season: March–Oct. Often too high during peak snowmelt in late May and part or all of June. After peak snowmelt, flows are largely controlled by upstream hydro plants. Summer releases usually range from 900 to 1,300 cfs weekdays, 600 to 800 Saturdays, and 500 or less Sundays. Water comes up slowly in the morning and drops early in the evening.

Recommended Levels: *Upper Tuolumne:* 700–2,000 cfs. *Main Tuolumne:* 1,000–5,000 cfs.

Flow Information: DWR tape, (916) 653-9647. Flow at Meral's Pool includes Cherry Creek, the main Tuolumne, and the South Fork, which enters just above Meral's Pool. Hydrograph below does not take daily fluctuations into account. Daytime summer flows are usually higher than graph indicates.

Special Hazards: *Upper Tuolumne:* Lumsden Falls and Flat Rock Falls.

Permits: Required May 1–Sept. 30. First come, first served. Request form from Forest Service after Jan. 1 and return form with fee. Advance reservations confirmed by mail. No advance phone reservations. Limit 6 trips per person per season. Group limit 26. Call for unused or cancelled dates and pick up permit at ranger station.

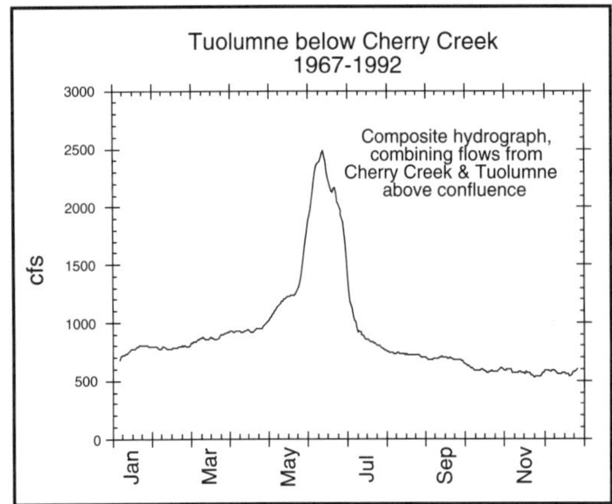

Managing Agency: Groveland RD, Stanislaus NF, 24545 Highway 120, Groveland, CA 95321; (209) 962-7825.

Commercial Raft Trips: Yes. For a list of outfitters contact the managing agency.

Land Ownership: Almost all National Forest.

Scenery: Excellent. **Solitude:** Excellent.

Wilderness: *Upper:* Partial. Lightly-used dirt road follows the lower part of the run. *Main:* Yes.

Fishing: Very good for trout.

Wildlife: Abundant. Deer, coyote, bobcat, otter, raptors, waterfowl.

Water: Cold and clear.

Camping: *Upper:* Don't try to carry camping gear downriver; camp at Lumsden Bridge CG or other nearby sites. *Main:* Large sites are fairly scarce above mile 15, presumably due to the trapping of sand and sediment by upstream reservoirs. Some sites are reserved for commercial use, some for private.

Side Hikes: *Main:* Clavey River, North Fork Tuolumne, others.

Side Excursions: Yosemite National Park.

Guides and References:

- Cassady & Calhoun, *California Whitewater: A Guide to the Rivers.*
- Holbek & Stanley, *A Guide to the Best Whitewater in the State of California.*
- Cassidy, ed., *A Guide to Three Rivers: The Stanislaus, Tuolumne and South Fork of the American.* Flora, fauna, geology, history.
- Wright, *Rocks and Rapids of the Tuolumne River: Guide to Human and Natural History.*
- Orr & Orr, *Rivers of the West: A Guide to the Geology and History.*

Maps:

- **USGS 7.5':** *Upper:* Cherry Lake South, Duckwall Mtn, Jawbone Ridge. *Main:* Jawbone Ridge, Groveland, Tuolumne, Standard.
- **USGS 1:100:** Oakdale.
- **USFS:** *Stanislaus NF.*
- **AAA:** *Yosemite.*
- *Tuolumne River* (Cassady & Calhoun). Main Tuolumne run. Waterproof paper.

• *Riverguide Bandana to the Tuolumne* (Rivers & Mountains). Cloth map.

Logistics: To reach **Meral's Pool, take-out for the Upper Tuolumne and put-in for the Main Tuolumne,** drive east on California Highway 120 into the Sierra foothills. About 7.5 miles east of Groveland, turn left onto Ferretti Road (paved). After about a mile, just past the second cattle guard, turn right onto Lumsden Road, which descends 5 steep, rough miles to the river. Meral's Pool is a couple of hundred yards downstream from Lumsden Campground. Another campground is about two miles upstream, just below Lumsden Bridge.

To reach the **Cherry Creek put-in for the Upper Tuolumne,** continue upstream on Lumsden Road. About 4 miles beyond Lumsden Bridge, turn right at a T-intersection, ford Jawbone Creek, continue two miles and turn right onto a paved road. Almost immediately, turn right again onto Cherry Lake Road, drive to the bridge across Cherry Creek, then continue about another 1.5 miles and turn right onto a steep, unmarked paved road that leads to the put-in just downstream from the powerhouse. (If you cross the main stem of the Tuolumne, you've gone too far.)

If you're driving to the **Upper Tuolumne put-in** first, there's a quicker route: continue on Highway 120 toward Yosemite and at the San Jose Camp, 14 miles east of Groveland, turn north onto Cherry Oil Road (USFS Road 1N07). Bear left when the road forks and follow signs toward Cherry Lake. Seven miles from the highway, the road crosses the Tuolumne at Early Intake Powerhouse. About 1.5 miles beyond this bridge, turn left onto a steep, unmarked paved road that leads to the put-in on Cherry Creek. The shuttle for the Upper Tuolumne is 12 miles (up to an hour) one way.

To reach the **Ward's Ferry take-out for the Main Tuolumne,** turn north off Highway 120 at Big Oak Flat (two miles west of Groveland) onto Ward's Ferry Road (paved) and drive 7 miles to the bridge across the upper end of New Don Pedro Reservoir. Shuttle drivers can save a few minutes by taking Deer Flat Road, which connects Ward's Ferry Road with the highway just west of Groveland. The Main Tuolumne shuttle is about 25 miles (one hour) one way. *Note:* If you descend from the foothills on Highway 120, do not take steep, dangerous Old Priest Grade, which can burn out the brakes on many vehicles. New Priest Grade (the main stem of the highway) is safer.

California's premier whitewater river, the Tuolumne, courses through outstanding rapids in a spectacular wild canyon in the central Sierra. Many of California's best rafters and kayakers cut their teeth on the exciting, boulder-strewn rapids from Meral's Pool to Ward's Ferry. Until more difficult runs were opened in the late 1970's and early 1980's, this section of the Tuolumne was considered the state's prime test of technical boating, and it remains one of the West's best river trips.

Upstream, the river is truly fierce. Clavey Falls, the biggest drop below Meral's Pool, would be just an average rapid on the Cherry Creek run. The Upper Tuolumne is one of the toughest stretches of regularly-boated whitewater in the country. Commercial raft trips have been offered since 1981, and the run grows more and more popular.

The river's upper watershed makes up a larger portion of Yosemite Park than that of the Merced, which flows through Yosemite Valley just to the south. The Tuolumne[1]—known affectionately as the "T" among river runners—drains the western slopes of the Sierra crest from an area southwest of Mono Lake northward to the Emigrant Wilderness. North of Tuolumne Meadows, the great granite walls of the Grand Canyon of the Tuolumne open onto Hetch Hetchy Valley, described by John Muir as "another Yosemite Valley."

Much of that valley has long been buried under the waters of Hetch Hetchy Reservoir, a San Francisco city project approved by Congress in 1913 over the objections of Muir's young Sierra Club. Hetch Hetchy is the only sizable commercial reservoir in the country permitted in a national park. O'Shaughnessy Dam, completed in 1923 and named for its designer, is relatively small: maximum reservoir capacity is only 360,000 acre-feet. The City of San Francisco not only drinks the Tuolumne

[1]"Tuolumne" is an attempt at "talmalamne," or "people of the stone dwellings," and was the name of Miwok Indians who lived, perhaps in caves, near this river and the nearby Stanislaus. For more on the natural and human history of the Tuolumne, see John Cassidy, *A Guide to Three Rivers.*

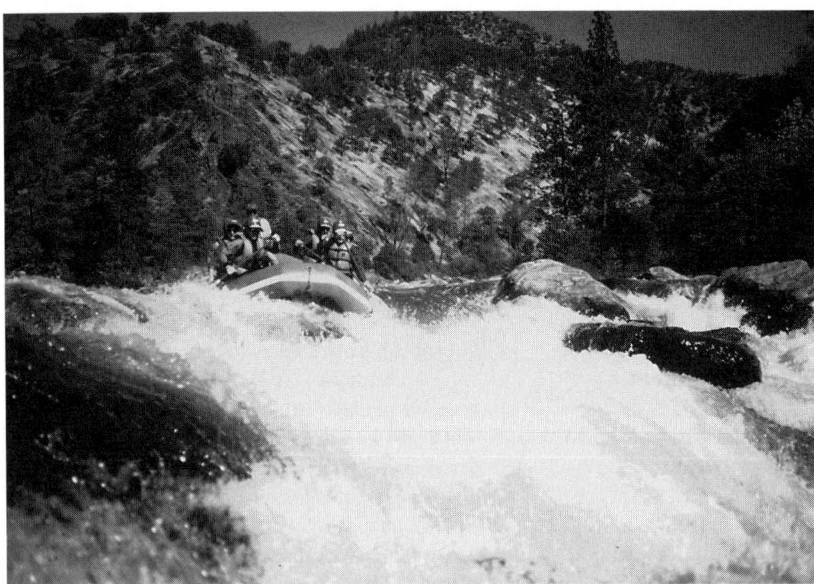

Clavey Falls, Tuolumne River *Doug Robinson*

but realizes about $25 million a year by selling Hetch Hetchy power. Such is the price of another Yosemite Valley.[2]

Between Hetch Hetchy and the backwaters of New Don Pedro Reservoir some 36 miles downstream, the Tuolumne flows like a wild river in winter and spring and at the behest of dam operators from about midsummer on. San Francisco also operates reservoirs and powerhouses on two major tributaries, Cherry Creek and Eleanor Creek, and another powerhouse downstream on Moccasin Creek. Below Ward's Ferry the Tuolumne has been harnessed again by New Don Pedro Dam, owned by the Modesto and Turlock irrigation districts.

What remains of the Tuolumne was admitted to the National Wild and Scenic Rivers System in September 1984 over the opposition of the Modesto and Turlock irrigation districts, who along with their political allies have prevented the river's friends from passing a bill to protect more of the watershed. Even though the Tuolumne already supplies their customers with cheap, plentiful water and electricity, the irrigation districts are studying a project for a dam and powerhouse on the Clavey River.[3] This beautiful major tributary, a favorite of hikers and anglers, is being boated by a growing number of daring experts and is briefly covered in the **More Western Rivers** section of this book.

Upper Tuolumne

The Cherry Creek run of the Tuolumne, also known as the "Upper T," is the most popular Class V run in California. Excellent scenery, outstanding whitewater, and a long boating season—all within a relatively easy drive of the Bay Area and Sacramento—make this one of the most frequently-boated expert runs in the West.

Tackling the Cherry Creek run puts boaters on the leading edge of the sport. Here in Jawbone Canyon, the Tuolumne plummets at an average rate of more than 90 ft./mi. over granite boulders torn from the Sierra bedrock. In one mile-long section the river falls 200'. **The Upper Tuolumne is for experts only, and then only at low flows.** The rapids are separated by very short pools; kayakers must have a bomb-proof roll, and rafters should use self-bailers since a swamped boat can get into trouble in a hurry.

The mile guide in this chapter lists only the very toughest rapids on the "Upper T." Aside from Lumsden Falls, the three most feared by boaters are Mushroom, Lewis's Leap, and Flat Rock Falls. But there are plenty of others difficult enough to cause trouble. Stop and scout whenever possible, even though this probably means contact with poison oak—another good reason to wear a wet suit even in the heat of summer. Don't get overconfident when you make it to the halfway point: the pools grow shorter and the rapids even more difficult the rest of the way. Be sure you recognize Flat Rock Falls (mile 6.8); most boaters wisely portage

[2]For a full discussion of Hetch Hetchy and more recent conservation issues on the Tuolumne, see Tim Palmer, *Endangered Rivers and the Conservation Movement.*

[3]The completion of massive New Don Pedro Reservoir (2 million acre-feet) in 1970 flooded the end of the Main Tuolumne run as well as a fine six-mile float below Ward's Ferry. For updated information on the Clavey River project, contact Friends of the River (see appendix for address).

this dangerous drop. Lumsden Falls is even worse and should be considered unrunnable.

Though relatively short, this run takes all of a long day due to the slow shuttle, frequent scouting, and likely portages. Get an early start. If darkness catches you on the river, tie up the boats, climb up the right bank to the road, and finish the run in the morning.

Kayakers Dick Sunderland and Gerald Meral were the first to run the "Upper T" in 1968. Marty McDonnell and Walt Harvest made the first raft trip in 1973 (see story), and McDonnell's company, Sierra Mac River Trips, pioneered commercial rafting here in 1981.

Main Tuolumne

The "T" is perhaps the best-loved river trip in the state. The reasons are simple: it offers an overnight float in a region where extended trips are rare; the scenery is striking and the wilderness solitude is deep and unspoiled; the river is within a relatively easy drive of the Bay Area and Sacramento; and the whitewater is sublime. This is a challenging run for advanced boaters at any level, and for **experts only above 4,000 cfs.** More than a dozen drops rated Class IV or higher dot the run, and there are many unnamed Class III and III+ rapids.

When kayakers and rafters first began tackling this run in the 1960's, they usually portaged its biggest rapid, Clavey Falls. First to run all the rapids was solo kayaker Noel DeBord in 1965, but early descents by Dick Sunderland, Gerald Meral, and Jim Morehouse had more to do with turning boaters' attention to the "T." In 1968 Bryce Whitmore and Marty McDonnell made the first raft run without portages.

The Tuolumne's popularity soared as whitewater sport took off during the late 1970's and early 1980's. Though the river is sometimes too high to run from late May to early July, some 6,000 people float the Tuolumne every year, and that number would be considerably higher without the Forest Service's fairly tight restrictions on both private and commercial boaters.

Upper Tuolumne Mile Guide

0 **PUT-IN** on the right bank of Cherry Creek just below the bridge, or at a primitive campsite on the left bank. **Experts only.** After midsummer most of the Tuolumne's flow is released down Cherry Creek from Holm Powerhouse, so boaters put in on the creek and float a mile of continuous Class IV rapids down to the river.

1 Confluence of Cherry Creek and the Tuolumne, which enters from the left.

2 **CORKSCREW** (V), marked by a horizon line. Avoid an undercut rock at the bottom left. Scout left. Less than half a mile downstream, boulders block the channel at **JAWBONE** (V), where Jawbone Creek enters on the right. Scout right.

3.2–3.4 **MUSHROOM** (V). Just beyond a sharp right turn. Scout left. The river drops 30' in the first 50 yards—over ledges, into holes, and against a huge flake of rock that has split away from the right wall. The flake divides a sharp vertical drop onto a big boulder. Just downstream, a final Class V vertical, **TOADSTOOL,** splits around another big rock that catches much of the current. An eddy on the left above this final drop is hard to escape. Downstream, half a mile of Class IV boulder gardens that can be seen from the road continue to the next big rapid.

3.9 **CATAPULT** (V). Also called **Unknown Soldier.** As a cable crosses the river and the road comes into view high on the right, the river surges down a rocky slalom and into a sharp drop down a right-hand chute. Scout the final drop, either from the right bank before you enter the rapid or from one of the small eddies on either side just above the drop.

4–5 **MIRACLE MILE** (V). Continuous action as the river drops 200' in a mile. A gulch on the right (mile 4.3) announces **JUST A SLALOM** (also called **Gar's Lunch**), a brutal quarter-mile boulder garden laced with steep drops. The worst ones are near the top, so a mistake could mean a nasty swim. Scout right. Around mile 4.7 comes **BLIND FAITH,** a steep, rough chute leading to a tiny pool. Then the current piles into **Coffin Rock.** Most boaters avoid it by running far right behind a big boulder. Scout on either side.

5–6 Another mile of continuous Class V: a boulder slalom; then a wide, shallow rock garden; next a set of wrap rocks. Near the end the river turns right, and **Christmas Hole,** an 8' vertical, is just downstream.

6.1 AIRPLANE TURN (V). After flowing through a large pool, the river turns left and drops into a very sticky hole. Scout on the right.

6.4 LEWIS'S LEAP (V). Also called **Number Two.** Sharp drops and boulder dodging lead up to the leap into a huge, river-wide hole. Amazingly, most boats emerge upright. No guarantees. Scout right.

6.7 ALTERNATE TAKE-OUT. Boaters often take out above **Flat Rock Falls,** but it's very difficult. The choices: scramble up the steep right slope to the road, carry gear out via a long trail on the left that has lots of poison oak, or line some parts and run some parts of the rapid.

6.8 FLAT ROCK FALLS (V-VI). P*OSSIBLE PORTAGE.* A boulder garden leads to a 10' fall onto a severely undercut rock. Swimmers trapped in the reversal could drown. Portage recommended at most flows. Some boaters flirt with disaster to reach a slightly less intimidating vertical chute on the right. Scout either side. Portage (a tough one) on the left.

7 LUMSDEN FALLS (U). *PORTAGE.* ALTERNATE TAKE-OUT. Look at this one from the bridge. You may think you see a way down this long, turbulent rapid's shelves and ledges, but don't even think about testing your theory. Portage or take out on the left.

7.1 RIVER ACCESS. Lumsden Bridge. Access at the Forest Service campground just downstream on the right.

7.5 AGAINST THE WALL (IV). A right turn leads to a hole in the middle of the river. Just downstream is HORSESHOE FALLS (IV+), a staircase rapid with the second drop the biggest. Scout from the island on the right.

8.3 South Fork Tuolumne enters on the left. Just downstream on the left is Lumsden Campground; kayakers sometimes take out or put in here. Below the campground is MERAL'S POOL TABLE (IV), a rock garden with an undercut ledge on the left at lower flows.

8.6 TAKE-OUTon the left at Meral's Pool.

Main Tuolumne Mile Guide

0 PUT-IN on the left bank at Meral's Pool. A flow gauge is nearby. Kayakers can launch upstream at Lumsden Campground, but it's tough for rafts. Another access point is farther upstream, just below Lumsden Bridge (see **Upper Tuolumne**). Just below Meral's Pool is ROCK GARDEN (IV), a boulder slalom that is toughest at low water, when rafts usually have to cross from right to left part way down. At high flows there is a dangerous reversal at the bottom.

0.4 NEMESIS (IV). Another low-water nightmare just after a sharp left bend. The **Nemesis,** a big boulder pile halfway down, is usually skirted on the left.

0.8 SUNDERLAND'S CHUTE (IV+). At the end of a short pool, the river bends right and tumbles down a rough chute. The current pushes boats toward a big rock (hole at higher flows) on the right. Difficult scout on the right; keep your life jacket on. Not far below Sunderland's is HACKAMACK HOLE (IV), a sharp drop divided by two big rocks. At high flows the rocks form a river-wide hole.

1.5 RAM'S HEAD (IV; **V above 3,500 cfs**). The river bends left down a rocky pitch with a boulder (big hole at medium and high flows) at the end. Good recovery pool. Scout on either bank. A half mile downstream are INDIA and LOWER INDIA (IV-), two short chutes separated by a small pool. Both end with sharp drops plugged by big rocks/holes. Scout left.

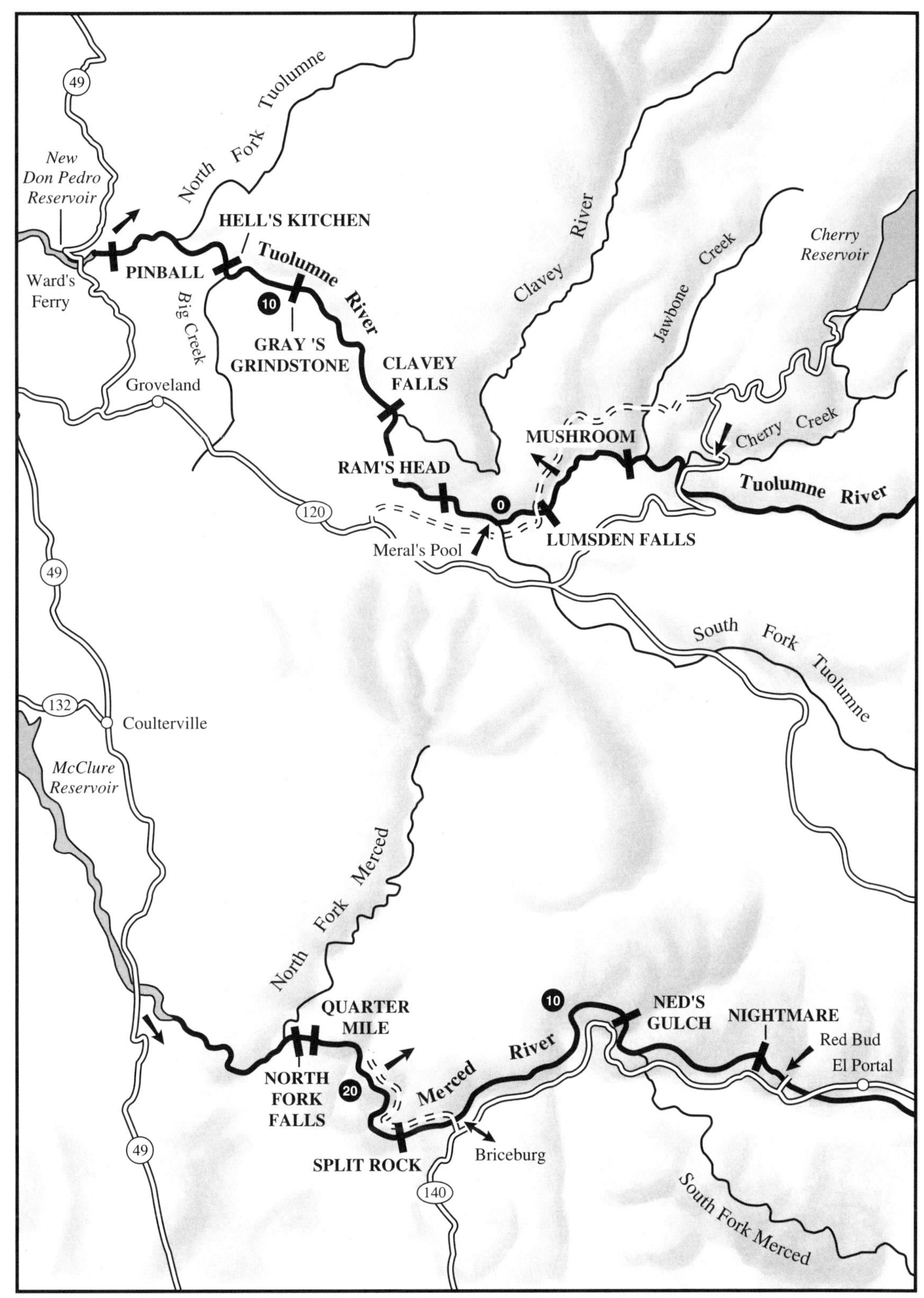

Tuolumne and Merced

3.3 Tin Can Cabin Camp (left bank). A steep trail climbs to Lumsden Road.

4.4 **STERN (IV-)**, also called **The Squeeze.** More difficult at low flows, when big boulders blocking the river create a bridging hazard for rafts, which must run a narrow slot between the left wall and a big rock. A quarter mile downstream is **EVANGELIST (IV)**, where the river bends right into a series of short drops with a big rock/hole right center.

5.4 The Clavey River enters on the right, and the Tuolumne turns sharply left into Clavey Falls, the biggest rapid on the run. A trail leads from the left bank downstream and out of the canyon. Good hiking and fishing up the Clavey (dangerous at high water). When the Clavey is running high, it can be difficult to get rafts across its mouth to eddy out on the right bank of the Tuolumne above the falls.

5.4 **CLAVEY FALLS (V).** The first two drops in this dramatic staircase rapid are the biggest. The first—"The Falls"—pushes boats toward the left wall. The second drop features a boat-eating hole across the left half of the river. Rafts have trouble avoiding it above 2,000 cfs; kayaks can usually find sneak routes. Station rescue parties downstream. Portage on the right if necessary.

5.9 The trail that begins above Clavey Falls climbs out of the canyon to Ferretti Road from above the left bank.

7.5 Powerhouse Campsite on the right. The powerhouse provided electricity for mines early in the century and was destroyed by flood in 1937. A trail on the left bank leads downstream to Indian Creek and then out of the canyon.

7.9 Grapevine Creek enters on the right. A third of a mile downstream, Indian Creek enters on the left, and below the creek an old road grade climbs out of the canyon.

9.5 **GRAY'S GRINDSTONE (IV).** At the end of a long pool, boulders block the left side of the river at the beginning of this thousand-yard maze. At high flows a big hole lurks in the standing waves near the top of the rapid.

11 **THREAD THE NEEDLE (IV).** Rocks block most of the river. Most boaters should take the "Chicken Shot" on the left, rather than attempting to "thread the needle" between the rocks in the center.

12.6 **CABIN (IV).** The river bends right and drops down a curving chute with a big rock/hole just below the entrance. Big Humbug Creek enters on the left.

12.8 Big Creek enters on the left. Short hike up the creek to a waterfall. Just downstream is **HELL'S KITCHEN (IV)**, where boulders extending from the right bank nearly block the river. There is a runnable slalom down the left, made even tighter for many years by a snag caught on a rock.

14.4 An old suspension bridge marks the site of two abandoned mines. The Mohican Trail leads out of the canyon on the left.

15.1 The North Fork of the Tuolumne enters on the right, with a side hike up to a narrows known as Devil's Gate. Better campsites from here on. Just over a half mile downstream is the high-water mark of New Don Pedro Reservoir.

17.5 **PINBALL (IV).** One of the best rapids on the run, almost in sight of the take-out, but usually covered by the reservoir. Scout left.

18 **TAKE-OUT** on the right at Ward's Ferry Bridge.

I've seen a lot of changes in whitewater boating in California. Back in the early sixties, when I first started floating rivers, the South Fork American and the Stanislaus were the hot runs, and it was rare to see a kayaker wearing a helmet or a rafter wearing a life jacket. By the late sixties, when boaters started running the main Tuolumne below Lumsden Campground, techniques, equipment, and safety procedures had improved considerably. Then, running the main "T" was putting yourself out on the leading edge of the sport, and Clavey Falls was the ultimate rapid.

When I heard about the first kayak run of the Upper Tuolumne in 1969, I was intrigued. The Tuolumne was a candidate for Wild and Scenic status on the one hand and for more dams on the other. Jerry Meral and Dick Sunderland wanted to show that there was another boatable section of the river. They took a couple of days to float the eight miles down to Lumsden Falls, and they portaged a lot of rapids, but they made their point.

For the next few years I fantasized about rafting that stretch, but I figured it was too tough. Eventually, though, we learned enough on the main Tuolumne to think we had a chance. We had developed boats appropriate for the run: modified Huck Finns, which we called "spider boats" or "catarafts" because they had only two tubes, one on each side, held together by rowing frames and rigging. They were light, quick, and impossible to swamp, though they would flip.

In April 1973 Walt Harvest, one of the strongest and shrewdest kayakers and rafters I've ever known, joined me for a first raft run of the Cherry Creek stretch. We each rowed a spider boat with one experienced river runner as a passenger—Mark DuBois with me, Fred Dennis with Walt. (Being a passenger on a spider boat is a very active job, because these light rafts need vigorous high-siding and counterbalancing to prevent flips. Now we use stabler boats, full Huck Finns or a newer type of self-bailing raft.) We wore helmets—unusual for rafters in those days—and took climbing gear in case we needed to line our boats through rapids or belay them down the steep canyon walls if we portaged.

We found our way to the put-in at night and lowered the boats over a sheer 60-foot cliff down to the river. If the put-in was this tough, we thought, how bad would the river be? We couldn't help feeling apprehensive. By dawn we were on the water, picking our way down the boulder gardens, with first one raft leading the way, then the other. Our plan was to spend a couple of days on the river, since we were scouting every rapid. But we made much better time than we had expected. We were nearly two miles downstream, scouting a rapid we later named Corkscrew, when the sun finally appeared above the canyon wall.

It was like a dream come true. To our amazement, we found that we were able to run one after another of these fearsome chutes and drops. The rapids that later became Mushroom, Lewis's Leap, and Flat Rock Falls caused us the most hesitation. (At the time, we referred to them as Numbers One, Two, and Three.) But we made it every time, and at the bottom of the rapid we'd just look at each other and laugh. We could hardly believe we were really doing it.

Our euphoria almost ran away with us, and we started talking about running Lumsden Falls as well. But when we finally got there and looked at this dangerous pitch, we sobered up soon enough. Lumsden Falls has no feasible entrance, a very tough boulder field in the middle, and a bad exit that takes boats toward an undercut ledge. So we quit while we were ahead and hauled the rafts up the steep bank to the road.

We ran the Upper "T" twice more that spring, and by the time summer came around, our concept of rafting had been transformed. After that, though we continued to respect it, the main Tuolumne run looked almost flat.

—Marty McDonnell

East Fork Carson River

Cave Rock to Ruhenstroth Dam

1. Upper East Fork: Cave Rock (6,000') to Hangman's Bridge (5,500').
III; 7 miles; 68 ft./mi.
Shorter runs possible.

2. Wilderness Run: Hangman's Bridge to Ruhenstroth Dam (4,950').
II; 20 miles; 27 ft./mi.

Drainage Area and Average Annual Discharge: 276 sq. mi. and 272,500 af near Hangman's Bridge.
Season: May and June.
Recommended Levels: 600–3,000 cfs.
Flow Information: DWR tape, (916) 653-9647. Flow near Gardnerville.
Special Hazards: Deadly waterfall over the 30' diversion dam a few hundred yards below the Wilderness Run take-out. Possible log hazards.
Permits: Voluntary registration at the put-in for the Wilderness Run.
Managing Agency: Carson RD, Toiyabe NF, 1536 S. Carson, Carson City, NV 89701; (702) 822-2766.
Commercial Raft Trips: Yes. For a list of outfitters, contact the managing agency.
Land Ownership: Mostly BLM and National Forest, with a few private parcels.
Scenery: Excellent. Dry alpine canyon.
Solitude: Good on Upper, excellent on Wilderness Run.
Wilderness: No on Upper, yes on Wilderness.
Side Excursions: Grover Hot Springs outside Markleeville.
Guides and References:

- Cassady & Calhoun, *California Whitewater: A Guide to the Rivers.*
- Holbek & Stanley, *A Guide to the Best Whitewater in the State of California.*
- Murphy, *Lore and Legend of the East Fork: A Historical Guide for Floating the East Carson River.*
- Orr & Orr, *Rivers of the West: A Guide to the Geology and History.*

Maps:

- **USGS 7.5':** *Heenan Lake, Markleeville, Carters Station.*
- **USFS:** *Toiyabe NF—Carson RD.*
- **AAA:** *Lake Tahoe.*

Logistics: Markleeville is southeast of Lake Tahoe. To reach **Hangman's Bridge, take-out for the Upper East Fork and put-in for the Wilderness Run,** drive southeast from Markleeville about two miles on combined California Highways 4 and 89 to the bridge over the river. To reach the **upper put-in at Cave Rock,** drive upstream (south) from Hangman's Bridge, following Highway 4 when it splits from 89. About 3 miles beyond (south of) this junction, turn left on Wolf Creek Road (which follows the river while the highway turns up Silver Creek). Put in about a mile and a half up Wolf Creek Road, just before the road leaves the river. An **alternate put-in** is on Silver Creek just below the Wolf Creek Road bridge.

To reach the **take-out at Ruhenstroth Dam,** drive 7 miles north from Markleeville on Highway 89, turn right on Highway 88, follow it for 14 miles, and turn right (south) on Highway 395. About 5 miles south of Gardnerville, Nevada, turn right onto a dirt road leading to the take-out and parking area on the right bank just upstream from Ruhenstroth Dam. **Look at the take-out carefully to be sure you recognize it from the river;** it's worth your life if you miss it.

The East Fork Carson is one of the best easy float trips in California. Superb scenery, fine camping, a luxurious hot spring, and continuous but forgiving rapids make the East Carson a perennial favorite. It is one of the few overnight wilderness trips in the Sierra with relatively mild whitewater.

From headwaters at the base of 11,000' Sonora Peak north of Yosemite, the East Carson[1] drops steeply down the east slope of the Sierra toward the high desert of western Nevada. The river flows freely until well after it crosses the border into Nevada, where diversions irrigate the Carson Valley and provide water to the river's namesake, Carson City. Below Carson City the river meanders north

[1]The river was named by John C. Fremont for Kit Carson, who guided him across the Sierra in 1844.

and east across the desert toward the Carson Sink, the mostly dry bed of a large glacial-era lake.

Rivers that drain the steep eastern side of the Sierra Nevada—notably the Carson, Walker, and Truckee—contrast sharply with the bigger, more numerous rivers flowing down the wetter and more gradual west slope. Since their watersheds lie in the partial rain shadow of the Sierra crest, east slope streams carry less water and have shorter seasons. They fall quickly and steadily down the steep "back" side of the range, and their nearly continuous rapids are less severe than those of pool-and-drop rivers on the west side. East slope rivers are also runnable at much higher elevations than their west slope counterparts.

Two different runs await boaters on the East Carson. The upper section features seven miles of continuous Class III rapids in a mile-high pine forest with Highway 89 close by. The lower or Wilderness Run takes boaters through 20 miles of rugged back country where the river plunges from alpine forest to high desert. At times boaters catch glimpses of the snow-capped Sierra crest. In spite of a respectable gradient of 27 ft./mi., Wilderness Run rapids are only Class II. Bring wet suits and warm clothing; the river is icy, and nights are generally cold at these elevations. The weather is usually too cold for boating until May.

In recent years the Carson has been the scene of two important conservation victories. In 1989 the ten miles from Hangman's Bridge to the Nevada border were added to the California Wild and Scenic Rivers System. In 1991 Congress ordered the Department of Interior to restore a major wetlands once nourished by the river. Until this century the vast 100,000-acre Stillwater Marsh in Carson Sink supported massive numbers of birds migrating on the Pacific Flyway. Then the Bureau of Reclamation's Newlands Irrigation Project diverted water from the Carson and Truckee Rivers to farms in the erstwhile desert, depriving the marsh of water and shrinking it to just 3,100 acres by 1991. Needless to say, bird populations plummeted. The new law calls for Stillwater Marsh to be restored to 14,000 acres, marking the first time that water from a U.S. "reclamation" project has been returned to save a wetlands.

East Carson River Guide

Upper East Fork

Put in at any convenient spot downstream from Cave Rock (mile 0). Don't venture farther upstream; the rapids are treacherous. Downstream, the river is continuous Class III all the way to take-out, with several narrow spots.

Silver Creek enters on the left at mile 1.2. An **alternate put-in** is just up Silver Creek at the Wolf Creek Road bridge. Another **alternate access** is on the main river at mile 1.6 where the Centreville Bridge (Highway 4) crosses the river. At mile 3.7 Monitor Creek enters from the right, marking the junction of Highways 4 and 89. **Take out** on the right at Hangman's Bridge (mile 7.3).

Wilderness Run

Put in at Hangman's Bridge (mile 0). Local vigilantes claimed that they lynched a confessed murderer here in 1874 in order to save the county the cost of a trial. Downstream are nearly continuous Class I and II rapids throughout the run. At mile 1.6, where Markleeville Creek enters on the left, is the best upriver view of the spectacular Sierra crest.

At mile 8 Cottonwood Creek enters on the right, and a few hundred yards downstream at a left bend is **SIDEWINDER (II+)**, probably the toughest rapid on the run (open canoeists and novice rafters and kayakers may want to scout). Not far below this rapid on the left is a very popular hot spring (about 104°). The river crosses into Nevada at mile 11.

Near mile 15.5 the canyon narrows, marking the proposed site of a 300'-high dam. Fortunately, this Army Corps of Engineers scheme—which would have wiped out most of the run—has been shelved.

Downstream the river carves a lovely canyon around Horseshoe Bend. **Take out** on the right at mile 20. ***HAZARD.*** Don't miss the take-out; just downstream is a deadly **30' waterfall over the dam.**

American River

The American is California's classic Gold Country river. Its three forks rise along the Sierra crest in the Desolation Wilderness west of Lake Tahoe, flow down the west slope through the rich foothills of the Mother Lode between Auburn and Placerville, then empty into Folsom Reservoir. Downstream, the American merges with the Sacramento River not far from the State Capitol.

In 1848 James Marshall discovered gold at John Sutter's mill on the South Fork and touched off the great invasion that made California irretrievably American. Yet the river's name stems from a case of mistaken identity. Western explorer Jedediah Smith called it the "Wild River" in 1828, but later it was dubbed "Rio de los Americanos" by Spanish-speaking Indians because Canadian trappers forded the river a few miles upstream from Sutter's fort at Sacramento. In 1841 Sutter translated the Spanish name for a map, and it stuck.

The American River is also the birthplace of whitewater boating in California. In the 1950's and 1960's early kayakers practiced on the easy rapids of the Coloma-to-Lotus run on the South Fork American before advancing to the Chili Bar and Gorge runs and other rivers. Now, the South Fork between Chili Bar and Salmon Falls (Class III) is one of the most popular whitewater rivers in the country. But that is not all the American offers. The Middle and North Forks are considerably more challenging (Class IV–V) and have attracted increasing numbers of boaters in recent years. The South Fork itself has more whitewater upstream between Kyburz and Riverton. The placid Lower American attracts many first-time boaters.

Like other Sierra rivers, the American and its tributaries have their share of dams. The largest, Folsom Dam, a 1956 federal hydroelectric and irrigation project, backs up water into both the main stem and the South Fork. Dam builders continue to have designs on what is left of the American. More than two decades ago, the Bureau of Reclamation announced plans for a 700'-high concrete arch dam near Auburn, just downstream from the confluence of the North and Middle Forks. In 1975 work on its foundations was under way when a sizable earthquake (5.7 on the Richter scale) shook nearby Oroville and proved that faults in the Sierra foothills, including some at the Auburn Dam site, were potentially active. Critics warned that if Auburn Dam failed, Sacramento would be flooded in a matter of hours, with extensive loss of life and damage in the billions of dollars. Some feared that the reservoir itself could trigger a quake. Work was abandoned.

American River: Guides and References

Mandel, *The American River: North, Middle and South Forks* (PARC; see note 1 for address).

Cassady & Calhoun, *California Whitewater: A Guide to the Rivers.*

Holbek & Stanley, *A Guide to the Best Whitewater in the State of California.*

Orr & Orr, *Rivers of the West: A Guide to the Geology and History.*

More specific guides are listed in the individual chapters.

But like a recurring nightmare, Auburn Dam refuses to go away. The project has been redesigned and resurrected several times. Where once its proponents argued water and power (of which the dam would have delivered very little), they now talk flood control, with the encouragement of downstream developers who would profit from building in the river's flood plain. How much flood control the dam would provide in case of a big earthquake is, of course, debatable.

If Auburn Dam is ever built, the reservoir behind it will wipe out as much as 20 miles of the North Fork American and the entire 25-mile stretch of the Middle Fork now enjoyed by boaters. Their living canyons will become narrow fingers of stagnant water whose level will fluctuate wildly each year, exposing large bathtub rings of dirt, rock, dead vegetation, and debris. Experience has shown that the recreational value of such artificial lakes is vastly overrated by dam proponents. In contrast, conservationists are not only coordinating opposition to the dam, but also proposing an alternative: the creation of a National Recreation Area encompassing the canyons of the North and Middle Forks of the American River.[1]

[1]For more information contact Friends of the River (see appendix for address) and PARC (Protect American River Canyons), P.O. Box 9312, Auburn, CA 95604.

South Fork American River

Chili Bar and Gorge Runs

Difficulty: III. **Gradient:** 23 ft./mi.
Length: 20 miles. Shorter runs possible.
Put-in: Chili Bar (930').
Take-out: Salmon Falls Bridge (460').
Drainage Area and Average Annual Discharge: 673 sq. mi. and 1,172,000 af near Lotus (mile 9).
Peak Recorded Flow: 64,500 cfs (Nov. 21, 1950).
Season: All year. Flows controlled by several upstream reservoirs.
Recommended Levels: 1,000–5,000 cfs.
Flow Information: DWR tape, (916) 653-9647. Release from Chili Bar Dam. Hydrograph below does not take daily fluctuations into account. Actual daytime flows—especially in summer—are usually higher than the graph indicates.
Permits: May be required in the future. Currently, private boats must display use tags (available at major access points).
Managing Agencies: (1) El Dorado County Dept. of Parks & Recreation, 360 Fair Lane, Placerville CA 95667; (916) 621-5353. (2) BLM, 63 Natoma St., Folsom, CA 95630; (916) 985-4474.
Commercial Raft Trips: Yes, many outfitters. For a list contact El Dorado County Parks.
Land Ownership: Mostly private; some BLM.
Scenery: Very good. Lightly forested foothill canyon. **Wilderness:** No.
Solitude: Good above Coloma and below Lotus, except summer weekends when river traffic is very heavy.
Water: Releases from bottoms of upstream reservoirs keep river cold all summer. Undrinkable.

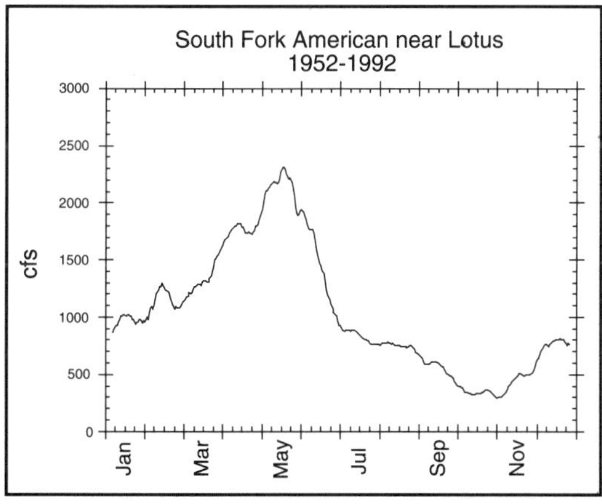

Camping: Several private campgrounds with river access: Chili Bar (put-in), Camp Coloma (mile 5), Coloma Resort (mile 5.5), Point Pleasant (mile 6), and Camp Lotus (mile 9); reserve sites in advance. BLM lands in the lower half of the run are open for camping; small fee (contact the BLM).
Side Excursions: Sutter Gold Discovery site and the American River Land Trust and Nature Center, both in Coloma.
Guides and References: (See also general American River essay.)

- *South Fork of the American River: Information Guide to Whitewater Boating* (El Dorado County). Map-pamphlet available at launch sites or county offices.
- *Riverguide Bandana to the South Fork American* (Rivers & Mountains). Cloth map.
- Wright, *Geology and Rapids, South Fork American River.* Mile guide and geology notes.
- David Bolling essay in Rennicke, *River Days.*

Maps:

- **USGS 7.5':** *Garden Valley, Coloma, Pilot Hill.*
- **AAA:** *Lake Tahoe.*
- *South Fork American River* (Cassady & Calhoun). Map-guide; water-resistant paper.

Auto Shuttle: 25 miles (1 hour plus) one way.
Logistics: To reach the **Chili Bar put-in,** take U.S. 50 to Placerville, turn north on California 49, drive to the north side of town, bear right on California 193, and descend 3 miles to the bridge over the South Fork at Chili Bar. Put in below the bridge on the right bank (private, fee). To reach the **Salmon Falls take-out,** return to Placerville on Highway 193, turn right on Highway 49, and follow it north through Coloma. About 7 miles after Highway 49 crosses the river, turn left onto Salmon Falls Road, then turn left again, still on Salmon Falls Road, and follow it about 7 miles to the take-out on the right bank of Folsom Reservoir just above Salmon Falls Bridge. This take-out can also be reached directly from U.S. 50 by taking the El Dorado Hills exit and driving north on El Dorado Hills Blvd. and Salmon Falls Road.

Intermediate access is possible at several sites near Coloma and Lotus, including:

Marshall Gold Discovery State Park (put-ins only; no take-outs allowed); the Highway 49 bridge at Coloma; Henningsen-Lotus County Park; and Camp Lotus (private). To reach **Camp Lotus,** turn south off Highway 49 onto Lotus Road, drive a mile, turn right on Bassi Road, go another mile, and look for signs to Camp Lotus on the right. See the **Mile Guide** for exact locations of other alternate accesses.

The South Fork American, California's most popular whitewater river, provides 100,000 people a year with a thrilling ride through the heart of Gold Rush Country. Below the Chili Bar put-in the South Fork drops quickly through a remote, steep-walled canyon cut into metamorphic volcanic rock. Five miles farther, where the canyon opens up into the gentle Coloma Valley, Troublemaker Rapid provides the climax of the Chili Bar stretch. Civilization is close at hand for the next four easy miles between Coloma and Lotus. Then the river heads into back country again, winding through foothills and finally plunging into the exhilarating, nearly continuous rapids of the South Fork Gorge before stilling in Folsom Reservoir.

Dam-controlled flows often make the South Fork runnable year round. On summer weekends the river is very crowded. But weekday boaters enjoy the scenery and the bouncy but forgiving rapids in relative solitude. The Chili Bar and Gorge runs are considerably more difficult at flows over 3,000 cfs, but they are tough enough even at low and moderate levels to get the inexperienced into trouble. Beginners and novices should stick to the Class II stretch from Coloma to Lotus, or the Class I–II run on the Lower American below Folsom Reservoir.

The South Fork runs are on a small remnant of river bounded by Chili Bar Dam upstream and Folsom Reservoir downstream. Even so, additional dams have been proposed, including one at the site of Troublemaker Rapid. After negotiations involving river runners, landowners, and El Dorado County, in 1982 the California Legislature passed a bill to delay new dam proposals for at least ten years if a series of dam and diversion projects were approved for the upper South Fork above Kyburz. As of 1992 none of these projects had been built, and it was uncertain whether dam proposals on the South Fork would be renewed. The river is also threatened by an El Dorado County proposal to divert 20,000 acre-feet from the upper South Fork. Such a diversion would severely restrict instream flows and hamper boating. (For updated information contact Friends of the River; see appendix for address.)

Another problem is the extensive private property along much of the river below Chili Bar—an important factor in El Dorado County's abortive attempt to prohibit whitewater sport on the South Fork in the early eighties. After the courts ruled that the public had the right to run the river, El Dorado County took over the task of regulating boating. The county now patrols the river, requires private river runners to register at put-ins, and asks all boaters to observe a "quiet zone" between miles 4.4 and 11.5. Use fees from commercial rafting outfitters provide the county with a tidy sum.

With so much private land, the South Fork faces a grave threat from the tremendous growth of greater Sacramento. New houses are appearing in previously undeveloped sections of the canyon. Leading the effort to protect the river from uncontrolled growth is the American River Land Trust, which has purchased sensitive parcels in the South Fork Gorge and is working to buy more riverside land in the Chili Bar stretch. The Trust's office and Nature Center in Coloma is well worth a visit (see **Side Excursions**).

Upstream Runs

The South Fork offers some boating—primarily for experts only—above Chili Bar Reservoir. U.S. Highway 50 follows much of the upper river, offering easy access but detracting from the solitude. The most common run on the upper river is 7 miles of Class IV–V water from Kyburz to Riverton. Just above Riverton the South Fork cuts a steep chute through sharp rocks where a landslide bocked the highway and temporarily plugged the river in 1983. The run can be extended another 3.5 miles by continuing past Riverton to the Peavine Ridge Road bridge. Below Peavine the South Fork roars down an extremely steep Class VI gorge that drops more than 200 ft./mi. in places. This stretch is known as the Golden Gate Run because boating it is nearly as suicidal as jumping off the Golden Gate Bridge. (For more information on the upper river, refer to the guide books by Cassady and Calhoun or Holbek and Stanley listed earlier.)

Mile by Mile Guide

*See map in **North Fork American** chapter.*

0 **PUT-IN** at Chili Bar (fee) on the right bank just downstream from the Highway 193 bridge. Overnight camping (fee); phone (916) 642-1667. Though misspelled, Chili Bar was named for Chilean miners who worked here during the Gold Rush.

0.6 **MEATGRINDER (III).** A long rock garden with big waves and holes and a boulder at the bottom. Continuous at high water. Scout on the right.

1.3 **RACEHORSE BEND (II+).** A sharp left bend forces boats toward the right wall. A few hundred yards downstream is **MAYA (II–III)**, which poses no problem at low water but develops big, dangerous holes across most of the channel at high flows.

3 Site of old miner's cabin (right bank). Just downstream is **TRIPLE THREAT (III)**, three widely-spaced drops with exposed rocks at low water and strong hydraulics at high flows.

4.4 Indian Creek enters on the left. Private homes and campgrounds appear. El Dorado County asks boaters to observe a "quiet zone" from here to mile 11.5.

5.1 **TROUBLEMAKER (III+).** Biggest rapid on the Chili Bar reach. A river-wide ledge strewn with boulders; almost always run on the far left. Scout on the left, but stay close to the river and avoid walking through the private campsites. Spectators crowd the shore on summer weekends.

5.2–10.6 Below the town of Coloma (left bank), easy Class I and II rapids continue for more than five miles.

5.7 **RIVER ACCESS.** Marshall Gold Discovery State Park (left bank). A stone monument marks the site of Sutter's Mill, where the Gold Rush started. A replica of the mill is nearby, and a mining museum is across the highway. Boaters may put in at the northern (downstream) end of the park (fee). Take-outs are not allowed.

7.1 **OLD SCARY (II).** Once the most difficult rapid on the Coloma-Lotus stretch, it was rearranged into a moderate riffle by high water in winter 1982.

7.4 **RIVER ACCESS** on the right just below the Highway 49 bridge (no fee). No parking. A half mile downstream is another **RIVER ACCESS** on the left at Henningsen-Lotus County Park (fee).

9 **RIVER ACCESS.** Camp Lotus (left bank; fee), a popular overnight camp, has long been a favorite meeting place for boaters on the South Fork. Store, hot showers, toilets. Reserve sites in advance; (916) 622-8672.

9.8 BLM land on the right is set aside as campsites for non-commercial boaters.

10.6 **CURRENT DIVIDER (II+).** Rocky chute with a wrap rock in the center. A half mile downstream is **HIGHWAY RAPID (II+)**, a long, curving rock garden.

11.5 Greenwood Creek enters on the right. End of "quiet zone." A half mile downstream is the first of two short stretches of BLM land on both banks (miles 12.1–12.3 and miles 12.7–13.5). Portable toilets on the right.

15 Downstream, the "Lollipop Tree" can be seen on a hilltop. This well-known landmark signals that the South Fork Gorge is less than a mile ahead.

15.8 **FOWLER'S ROCK (III).** First big rapid in the gorge deserves special respect at high water. Scout left if desired. The river bends left into a short pool, then turns right past a house rock on the right. **Fowler's** is the wrap rock in the left center just below the house rock; a second sharp drop is just downstream. Downstream, the river narrows as it cuts a shallow gorge through hard metamophic rock.

16.9 **SATAN'S CESSPOOL (III+).** The biggest rapid in the gorge. At the end of a long pool, the river pours over a sharp drop known as **Lost Hat,** then bends left and right into a bigger drop against the left wall. The rapid can be scouted on the left, but most boats end up running the big drop anyway. A rock on the left above the drop offers a good vantage point. Just downstream is a small eddy on the left; if you miss it, watch out for **Dead Man's Drop** (II+) just below. Stay right.

17.4 **SCISSORS (III).** The river turns left down a narrow, rocky chute with big, irregular waves, then squeezes through a tight constriction.

17.6 **LOWER HAYSTACK CANYON (II+).** Big waves and short drops in a narrow section of the gorge. Just downstream is a short stretch of BLM land on both banks. Weber Creek enters on the left at mile 18.1, offering a half-mile hike before you reach private property.

18.2 **BOUNCING ROCK (II+).** Big but runnable hole on the far right.

18.6 **HOSPITAL BAR (III).** Named for a medical tent set up here in the Gold Rush. This is the last big ride in the gorge—a rocky chute that bends left, then rushes into a steep drop with big cresting waves. Just downstream is **RECOVERY ROOM (II+)**, with nice waves and a hole in the right center. When full, Folsom Reservoir extends upstream to this point. In dry years or at other times when the reservoir is low, Class II+ rapids continue to the take-out.

20.5 **TAKE-OUT.** Salmon Falls Bridge. Take out on the right bank upstream from the bridge. Salmon Falls, a two-tiered falls located about a mile downstream, is now covered by the reservoir.

Lower American River

Nimbus Dam to Sacramento River Confluence

Difficulty: I+2. **Season:** All year.
Length: 23 miles. Shorter runs possible.
Flow Information: DWR tape, (916) 653-9647. Release from Nimbus Dam.
Guides and References:
- *A Boating Trail Guide to the American River Parkway* (California Dept. of Boating & Waterways, 1629 S St., Sacramento, CA 95814; (916) 445-2615. Excellent map shows all roads and accesses.

Other sources for more information:
- Sacramento County Parks Department, (916) 366-2072.
- Local whitewater shops California Canoe & Kayak, (916) 381-6636, and Wilderness Sports, (916) 985-3555.

Below Folsom and Nimbus Dams the Lower American courses through central Sacramento, forming a green oasis in the heart of California's busy and booming capital. Here is a remarkable success story among urban rivers: the Lower American is protected as both a National and State Wild and Scenic River, and as the heart of the American River Parkway—a lush 23-mile-long public park that attracts boaters, hikers, swimmers, bicyclists, birdwatchers, and many others. The dam-controlled river usually has adequate flows year-round.

The Lower American offers fine novice boating in this stretch, which features miles of fairly swift flatwater and two small Class II rapids. Local boating clubs and whitewater instructors often use this reach to introduce beginners to moving water.

More than a dozen possible launch sites allow trips of almost any length. Floating begins as high as the Sailor Bar boat launch, about a half mile below Nimbus Dam. Four miles downstream is San Juan Rapids, and five miles farther down is a Class II- ledge drop at Arden Rapids. The remaining 13 miles to the Sacramento River confluence are all Class I to I+.

Middle Fork American River

Oxbow Bend to Highway 49 Bridge

Difficulty: IVp; II from Greenwood Bridge site to Mammoth Bar (miles 16–23).
Length: 25 miles. Shorter runs possible.
Gradient: 22 ft./mi.
Put-in: Oxbow Bend (1,100').
Take-out: Highway 49 Bridge (550').
Drainage Area and Average Annual Discharge: 524 sq. mi. and 877,000 af near put-in.
Peak Recorded Flow: 310,000 cfs (Dec. 23, 1964).
Season: May–September. Dam-controlled.
Recommended Levels: 800–2,000 cfs.
Flow Information: DWR tape, (916) 653-9647. Release from Oxbow Powerhouse.
Rafts: Long portage at Ruck-A-Chucky.
Special Hazards: Tunnel Chute (mile 2.5). Ruck-A-Chucky (mile 14.5). Difficulties with miners and private landowners.
Permits: Not presently required.
Managing Agencies: (1) California Dept. of Parks & Recreation, P.O. Box 3266, Auburn, CA 95604; (916) 885-5648. (2) Tahoe NF, 22830 Foresthill Rd., Foresthill, CA 95631; (916) 367-2224. (3) El Dorado NF, 7600 Wentworth Springs Rd., Georgetown, CA 95634; (916) 333-4312).
Commercial Raft Trips: Yes. For references contact the Dept. of Parks & Recreation.
Land Ownership: Mixed National Forest, BLM, and private.
Scenery: Excellent. Steep, forested canyon.
Solitude: Excellent.
Wilderness: Mostly. Occasional dirt road.
Water: Cold and relatively clear. Not drinkable.
Camping: Because of portages in the first 15 miles, few boaters carry overnight gear downriver. Instead, they often drive it in to the Greenwood Bridge site (mile 16).

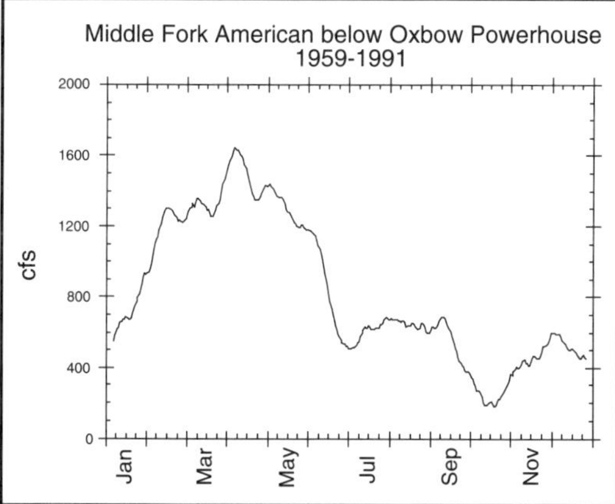

Side Hikes: Several side creeks, especially American Canyon (mile 19).
Guide and References: (See also general American River essay.)

- *A Boating Trail Guide to the North and Middle Forks of the American River* (California Dept. of Boating & Waterways, 1629 S St., Sacramento, CA 95814; (916) 445-2615.
- *Riverguide Bandana to the North and Middle Forks of the American* (Rivers & Mountains). Cloth map.

Maps:

- **USGS 7.5':** *Michigan Bluff, Foresthill, Georgetown, Auburn, Greenwood.*
- **AAA:** *Lake Tahoe.*
- *American River Recreation Area* (Friends of the River; see appendix for address).

Auto Shuttle: 25 miles (1.5 hours) one way for the entire run.
Logistics: To reach the **put-in,** take the Foresthill exit from I-80 near Auburn and follow the Auburn-Foresthill Road east about 17 miles. At the town of Foresthill, turn right and follow Mosquito Ridge Road down to and across the North Fork of the Middle Fork American. About two miles beyond this tributary, turn right and drive down to the Middle Fork put-in, just downstream from Oxbow Powerhouse.

The **Greenwood Bridge site** (mile 16) is best reached via unpaved Drivers Flat Road, which turns south off Auburn-Foresthill Road about 7 miles east of I-80 (10 miles west of Foresthill) and descends steeply to the river. A 4-wheel-drive road that leads upriver from Greenwood to Ruck-a-Chucky Rapid may be blocked off. **Mammoth Bar** is reached via unpaved Mammoth Bar Road, which turns off Old Foresthill Road about halfway between the junction with Highway 49 and the junction with the Auburn-Foresthill Road. The access is on the right bank at the upstream end of the bar. The **lowermost take-out** is 3 miles southeast of Auburn at the confluence with the North Fork American, not far above the Highway 49 bridge over the river.

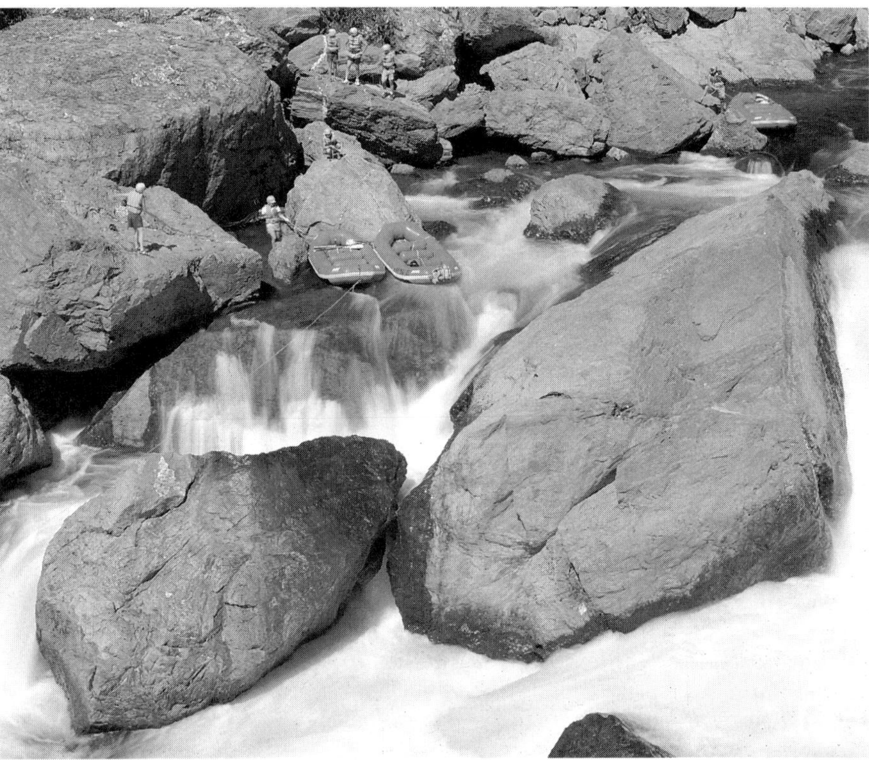

Ruck-a-Chucky, Middle Fork American *Mark Leder-Adams / Rapid Shooters*

The Middle Fork American is a legendary Gold Rush river. In the nineteenth century mining towns sprang up along its banks and forty-niners worked claims that covered almost every foot of the river. It is said that more gold has been found in the Middle Fork canyon than in any other. Even today, successful mining and dredging operations continue.

In many places the miners diverted the Middle Fork completely out of its bed. The most dramatic example is at Horseshoe Bend, where the river once flowed in a circuitous loop three quarters of a mile long around a steep granite ridge. The miners blasted a short tunnel through the ridge, diverted the river through the tunnel, then gleaned gold from the dry streambed. Today, boaters pass through this historic tunnel just below Tunnel Chute rapid.

The Middle Fork rises on the west side of the Sierra crest just west of Squaw Valley. The Rubicon River, its principal tributary, drains the northern part of the Desolation Wilderness and peaks west of Alpine Meadows. Both streams are dammed high up. In December 1964, when the Placer County Water Agency was building Hell Hole Dam on the Rubicon, flood waters swept it away and knocked out downstream bridges all the way to Folsom Reservoir. The agency promptly rebuilt the rockfill barrier. Another Placer County project in the mid-1960's was Anderson Dam, an earthfill structure which created French Meadows Reservoir on the upper Middle Fork.

Though it is only 140 miles from the Bay Area and offers runnable flows throughout most summers, the Middle Fork sees only moderate boating traffic. The shuttle is long and slow, and then there are the portages: mandatory at Ruck-a-Chucky; optional but recommended at Tunnel Chute, Murderer's Bar, and—at high water—Cartwheel. Boaters willing to deal with these difficulties will enjoy a much more challenging and secluded summer run than the nearby South Fork American.

Middle Fork whitewater is all or nothing, with a handful of extremely challenging and hazardous drops, long stretches of mild Class I and II water, and relatively few sections of intermediate rapids. On occasion, boaters on the Middle Fork have run afoul of private landowners and miners; some years ago a caretaker brandished a shotgun to emphasize his point. Nevertheless, the law upholds the public's right to boat on navigable rivers. If you have to portage, be quick and polite about it. Stay close to the river itself. And never argue with a shotgun.

Novices or anyone looking for a mild float can enjoy a secluded, scenic seven-mile Class II stretch from Greenwood Bridge site (mile 16) to Mammoth Bar (mile 23). This reach is popular with open canoeists and anglers. But keep in mind that summer releases from Oxbow Powerhouse do not reach the Greenwood Bridge site until relatively late in the day.

Mile by Mile Guide

*See map in **North Fork American** chapter.*

0 Oxbow Bend. **PUT IN** just below the Oxbow Powerhouse penstock. A mile downstream, the North Fork of the Middle Fork enters on the right.

2.5 **TUNNEL CHUTE (V–VI).** Also known as **Kanaka Falls.** *POSSIBLE PORTAGE.* A dangerous passage. The tunnel blasted by miners through a narrow ridge is flat and easy. But the dynamited chute leading down to it has sharp sides that can damage boats and people, and it ends in a big drop with a powerful reversal. Portaging the chute on the left is easy, but above 2,000 cfs it is hard to launch boats again above the tunnel. **This is why we do not recommend running the Middle Fork above 2,000 cfs.** A private 4-wheel-drive road—for emergencies only—leads out of the canyon from this point.

2.7–4.7 Numerous Class III rapids.

5 **CARTWHEEL (IV+; V above 1,500 cfs).** *POSSIBLE PORTAGE.* At the end of a large pool, the river tumbles off to the right. Several big reversals obstruct the channel, and at the bottom the current sweeps boats toward the right wall. Easy scout and portage on the left.

5.2–14.2 A pleasant nine-mile stretch of Class I and II rapids and fine scenery.

6 **RIVER ACCESS.** Cash Rock. A poor 4-wheel-drive road used mainly by miners leads from the left bank to Volcanoville.

14.2 **RIVER ACCESS.** Rough dirt road leads downstream to the Greenwood Bridge site and better roads out of the canyon. If your vehicle is up to it, and if the road is open, you can avoid the portage by taking out here.

14.3 **UPPER RUCK-A-CHUCKY (IV).** This is the beginning of **Ruck-a-Chucky,** named by miners in the last century. You can shorten the portage by running this drop, but don't try it if the flow is too high. The next drop is just downstream, and it is definitely unrunnable. Station rescuers downstream. Scout on the right.

14.5 **RUCK-A-CHUCKY (U).** *PORTAGE.* Even crazed daredevils don't attempt this one. The river drops 20' through a sieve of huge boulders. Difficult portage on the right. Many of the rocks are severely undercut. Extend your portage far enough downstream to bypass all the dangers.

14.7 **LOWER RUCK-A-CHUCKY (IV).** Begins just below the 6' drop that ends **Ruck-a-Chucky** proper. Scout left. Boaters usually start down a narrow, runnable chute in the center, then move left.

14.8–16 Enjoyable Class III rapids.

16 **RIVER ACCESS.** Site of Greenwood Bridge, washed out when Hell Hole Dam gave way in 1964. Primitive campsite on the right. Roads lead out of the canyon.

16–23 A lovely stretch of wilderness and Class II rapids.

19 American Canyon on the left. Fine side hike to falls and swimming holes.

23.1 **RIVER ACCESS.** Mammoth Bar (right bank). A dirt road leads to the old Auburn-Foresthill Road. Take out here to avoid **Murderer's Bar Rapid** just downstream.

23.2 **MURDERER'S BAR (V-VI).** *POSSIBLE PORTAGE.* The rapid is upstream from Murderer's Bar, so stop at Mammoth Bar and walk down to scout it. **Very difficult portage;** it's better to take out at Mammoth Bar. Murderer's Bar was so named because five Oregonians were killed here in 1849 by Indians as an act of vengeance. Downstream, the rest of the run is Class II.

25.3 **TAKE-OUT.** Confluence of Middle and North Forks of the American. Take out on the right just above the confluence. Downstream, Highway 49 crosses the river; don't float below the bridge, or you'll have to paddle 10 miles of Folsom Reservoir to the next take-out. Worse, only 3 miles below the bridge, water is diverted around the Auburn Dam site through a very dangerous half-mile-long tunnel that is illegal to run.

North Fork American River

Eucre Bar to Clementine Reservoir

1. Giant Gap: Eucre Bar (1,890') to Colfax-Iowa Hill Road (1,110').
V; 14 miles; 55 ft./mi.

2. Chamberlain Falls Run: Colfax-Iowa Hill Road to Shirttail Canyon (900').
IV+; 5 miles; 42 ft./mi.

3. Big Bend Run: Shirttail Canyon to Ponderosa Way (790').
II; 4.5 miles; 25 ft./mi.

4. Ponderosa Way to Clementine Reservoir (715').
II-; 4.5 miles; 17 ft./mi.

Drainage Area and Average Annual Discharge: About 200 sq. mi. at Eucre Bar. 342 sq. mi. and 620,200 af at Clementine Reservoir.
Peak Recorded Flow: 65,400 cfs (Dec. 23, 1964).
Season: *Giant Gap:* April–early June. *Other runs:* March–mid-June.
Recommended Levels: *Giant Gap:* 500–2,000 cfs. *Other runs:* 500–3,000 cfs. The narrow streambed produces severe hydraulics at what might appear to be moderate flows.
Flow Information: DWR tape, (916) 653-9647. Inflow to Clementine Reservoir. This is close to the actual flow on Runs 2–4. For Giant Gap, take about three quarters of this figure.
Special Hazards: *Giant Gap:* Rugged, isolated canyon; little chance of help in case of trouble.
Permits: Not presently required.
Managing Agencies: *Giant Gap:* BLM, 63 Natoma St., Folsom, CA 95630; (916) 985-4474. *Other runs:* California Dept. of Parks & Recreation, P.O. Box 3266, Auburn, CA 95604; (916) 885-5648.

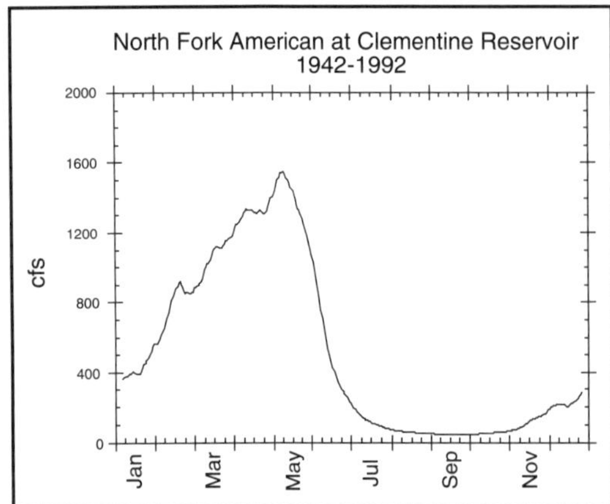

Commercial Raft Trips: Yes. For a list of outfitters, contact the managing agency.
Land Ownership: Mixed BLM, state, and private.
Scenery: Excellent. Steep, forested canyon.
Solitude: *Giant Gap:* Excellent. *Other runs:* Excellent on weekdays and early in the season; very good on weekends (more river traffic).
Wilderness: Yes. Occasional dirt roads.
Water: Cold and clear. Purify to be safe.
Camping: Many excellent sites along the river, except in narrow Giant Gap.
Guides and References: See **Middle Fork American** chapter and general American River essay.
Maps:
- **USGS 7.5':** *Run 1:* Dutch Flat, Foresthill, Colfax. *Runs 2 & 3:* Colfax. *Run 4:* Greenwood.
- **USGS 1:100:** Truckee (shows all but Run 4).
- **AAA:** *Lake Tahoe.*
- *American River Recreation Area* (Friends of the River; see appendix for address).

Logistics: To reach **Eucre Bar,** take the Alta exit from I-80 about 30 miles northeast of Auburn. Turn south on Casa Loma Road and drive about 3 miles to a sign marking the trailhead. A wide trail descends two miles to the put-in, just downstream from a foot bridge across the river.

To reach the **Colfax-Iowa Hill Road bridge,** take the Colfax exit from I-80 about 16 miles northeast of Auburn. Cross to the southeast side of the freeway, turn right on Canyon Way for a short distance, then turn left on Colfax-Iowa Hill Road and descend to the bridge over the river.

To reach **Shirttail Canyon,** drive south from Colfax (or north from Weimar) on Canyon Way and turn left (or right, coming from Weimar) on Yankee Jim's Road (a sign reads "Foresthill 13 mi."). Descend this steep road to the bridge across the river. The access is on the left bank upstream from the bridge. To reach the **Ponderosa Way access,** take the Weimar Cross Road exit from I-80 about 12 miles northeast of Auburn. Turn left on Canyon Way, then right on Ponderosa Way, which descends to a bridge over the river. The access is on the right bank below the bridge. To reach the **Clementine Reservoir access,** take the Foresthill exit from I-80 near Auburn. Drive east on the new Auburn-Foresthill Road about 6 miles, then bear left on Upper Clementine Road and descend to the access on the left bank near the top of the reservoir. This access is closed from about October to April.

From the bottom of the North Fork American's steep-walled canyon, it looks like a long way back to civilization. Yet busy Interstate 80 climbs toward Lake Tahoe along a ridgetop only a few miles away, and Sacramento is less than an hour to the west. Here and there country roads cross the river, providing boaters with access to its banks and dividing the North Fork into runs of varying difficulty.

In the past 15 years, as whitewater sport has exploded, the North Fork has evolved from a little-known kayaking run to one of the state's most popular rivers in spring and early summer. The North Fork offers outstanding scenery, near-wilderness solitude, and a wide variety of whitewater runs. 38 miles of this pristine river are protected as part of the National Wild and Scenic Rivers System.

In the 28 miles described the North Fork changes from a steep, cascading High Sierra river to a mild, easy-going foothill stream. The uppermost common run is Giant Gap, where the river cuts a sheer-walled chasm through Giant Gap Ridge and cascades down a continuous series of thundering drops that comprise one of the toughest runs in this book. Below the Colfax-Iowa Hill Road bridge, where the Chamberlain Falls run begins, the North Fork's clear, green waters flow through several miles of exhilarating Class IV and IV+ rapids. Downstream from Shirttail Canyon the river eases to Class II, and below Ponderosa Way it becomes even easier before stilling in Clementine Reservoir. With several alternate accesses, boaters can choose the sections that best fit their skills.

Because the headwaters of the North Fork rise at only 8,500', its boating season is shorter and more variable than that of most other Sierra rivers. In dry years the season may begin and end in April. Even in wet years, the river drops too low for rafts by the end of June, though kayakers can scrape down for a few more weeks. Spring flows usually peak in April or early May.

If it weren't for North Fork Dam, which creates Clementine Reservoir, the North Fork would be entirely free-flowing, and river runners could extend the Chamberlain Falls-Big Bend runs all the way to the confluence with the Middle Fork American at Auburn, 10 miles below the Ponderosa Way take-out. This old debris dam, built by the WPA in 1939 to catch rocks and sludge from upstream mining, was rendered unnecessary when large-scale hydraulic mining never resumed and became doubly useless when Folsom Dam was finished in 1956. Unfortunately, the old dam is still in place, and the waters of tiny Clementine Reservoir cover five miles of the North Fork canyon. The dam produces no hydroelectric power and provides no flood control or water storage.

But North Fork Dam is a minor problem compared to the behemoth proposed for a site farther downstream. Auburn Dam would wipe out the Chamberlain Falls and Big Bend runs, the Middle Fork run, and North Fork Dam, not to mention archaeological sites along the rivers. A far better alternative is the National Recreation Area proposed for the North and Middle Forks of the American. (See general essay on the American River.)

Giant Gap

Giant Gap is one of the most spectacular river canyons in California. Narrow rock walls tower more than 2,000' above the clear, green stream as it splashes down steep rapids choked by huge boulders. This stretch became a target for top kayakers and rafters in the 1980's. **Experts only.** The run is long and difficult, so get an early start. Almost all boaters plan a one-day run to avoid carrying overnight gear down the steep put-in trail. For the same reason, rafters generally favor paddle boats to avoid having to carry rowing frames and oars down the trail. Self-bailing rafts recommended.

The three-mile gorge itself, where the river cuts through Giant Gap Ridge, is inaccessible except by boat. However, hikers and river runners whose skills aren't up to the demands of this run can get a taste of the upper North Fork American by hiking down the trails to Eucre Bar, Green Valley, Pickering Bar, and Tommy Cain Ravine. The latter two trails are not marked on USGS topo maps.

Chamberlain Falls and Big Bend Runs

Just downstream from the Colfax-Iowa Hill Road bridge, take-out for Giant Gap and put-in for the Chamberlain Falls run, the North Fork plunges into a narrow gorge. Big rapids follow in quick succession for most of the next five miles. At moderate and high flows eddies become scarce and hard to catch, and boats must negotiate some big holes—especially at Chamberlain Falls and Staircase. Below Staircase (mile 3.3) the river eases a bit, but a couple of unnamed Class III rapids can surprise the unwary boater.

At Shirttail Canyon (mile 5) the river changes into a Class II float. Novice and intermediate boaters often put in here for the Big Bend run, which officially ends 4.5 miles downstream at Ponderosa Way. However, boaters can double the length of the run by continuing to the lowermost take-out on Clementine Reservoir.

Giant Gap Mile Guide

0 **PUT-IN.** Eucre Bar. Put in just downstream from the foot bridge. Nice swimming hole at low water. The first mile has Class IV rapids in a scenic gorge.

1–2.5 Green Valley. The canyon opens up and the rapids ease. Several trails lead out of the canyon from the right bank.

2.5–5.5 Giant Gap, a narrow chasm between spectacular 2,000' walls. There are several Class V rapids in this stretch. Even experts should make their first trips at flows below 1,000 cfs; above that level, the pools between drops are so swift that rescue is very difficult. Scout at every opportunity.

3.2 **NUTCRACKER (V).** *POSSIBLE PORTAGE.* The river narrows into a violent, rocky chute. Scout, and portage if necessary, on the left.

3.5 **LOCOMOTIVE FALLS (V–V+).** *POSSIBLE PORTAGE.* A sharp 6' vertical drop into a big reversal. Scout, and portage if necessary, on the right. Difficult both to scout and to run above 2,000 cfs.

5 **DOMINATOR (V).** *POSSIBLE PORTAGE.* A complex entry leads to a tough final drop. Many possible routes. Scout and/or portage on the right.

5.5 Canyon Creek enters on the right, offering a short side hike to waterfalls. Class IV–V rapids for the next mile and a half.

6 Pickering Bar (left bank). A trail leads out of the canyon on the right.

7 Tommy Cain Ravine on the right. A trail leads out from the right bank. Class III–IV rapids for the next 7 miles.

13.9 **PINBALL (IV+).** A tough technical test at a left-hand bend.

14.2 **TAKE-OUT.** Colfax-Iowa Hill Road bridge. Take out on the left above the bridge or on the right below it.

Mile Guide: Chamberlain Falls and Big Bend Runs

Note: Mileages in brackets represent total miles from the Giant Gap put-in, as shown on the map.

0 [14.2] **PUT IN** on either bank at the Colfax-Iowa Hill Road bridge. Not quite half a mile downstream is **SLAUGHTER'S SLUICE (IV)**, a boulder slalom whose entry is obscured by a huge midstream rock. Scout on the left. Enter right, then work quickly left behind the rock. Drops continue to **Chamberlain Falls.**

0.8 [15] **CHAMBERLAIN FALLS (IV+).** A narrow slot with an 8' vertical drop and a big reversal. If you run too far left, you may be caught by a violent eddy between the reversal and the left bank. At certain flows the only way to rescue boats from this eddy is to drag them out with a line. Scout on the left, but remember that the small eddy above the rapid is hard to catch at high water.

1.1 [15.3] **TONGUE AND GROOVE (IV-),** marked by a horizon line. The tongue on the left is easier, the groove (left center)

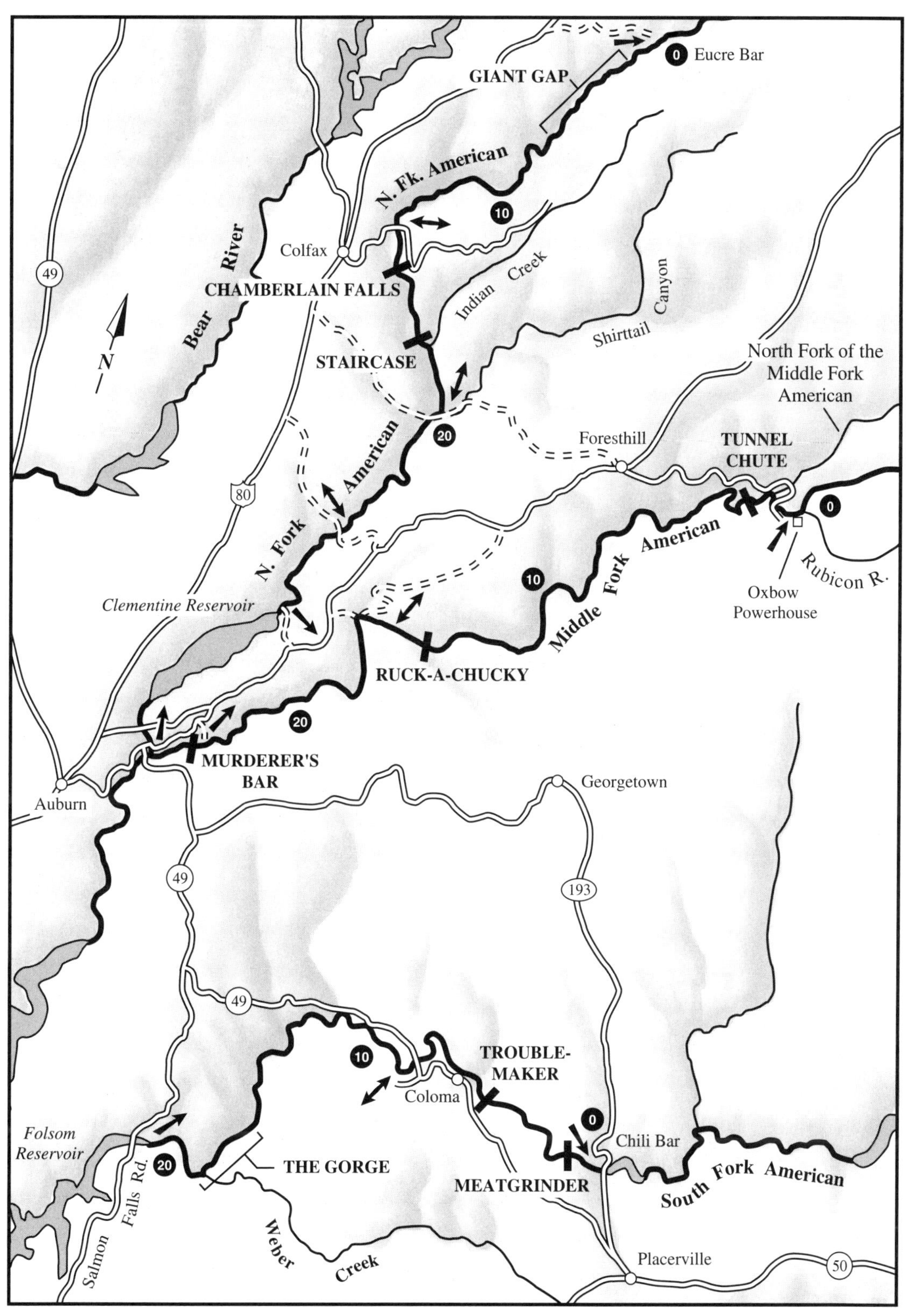

American: North, Middle, and South Forks

requires maneuvering. A half mile downstream is **ZIG-ZAG** (IV), with a tricky boulder-dodging route that starts center, moves right, then shifts back left.

2.4 [16.6] **ACHILLES' HEEL** (IV). Another boulder slalom, toughest at low water when the right side gets very rocky. A quarter mile downstream is **BOGUS THUNDER** (IV), with a big reversal in the center. Scout from either bank.

3 [17.2] **GRAND SLALOM** (IV). Huge boulders form a long, technical maze. Scout from the right.

3.3 [17.5] **STAIRCASE** (IV+). Three river-wide ledges, with a vicious keeper hole below the second. At very low flows (400 cfs and below), rocks on the left below the second drop have fatally entrapped swimmers. Scout right. Class III rapids from here to Shirttail Canyon.

3.8 [18] Indian Creek enters on the left. Nice falls about a quarter mile up the creek.

5 [19.2] **RIVER ACCESS.** Shirttail Canyon Creek enters on the left, just above the suspension bridge. Put in or take out on the left bank upstream from the bridge. The Big Bend run begins here.

6.5 [20.7] Brushy Creek enters on the right. A mile downstream is Big Bend, where the river makes a long horseshoe meander to the right.

9.5 [23.7] **TAKE-OUT.** Ponderosa Way bridge. The take-out is just downstream on the right. Mild Class I and easy II water continues another 4.5 miles to the final access on Clementine Reservoir (see **Logistics**).

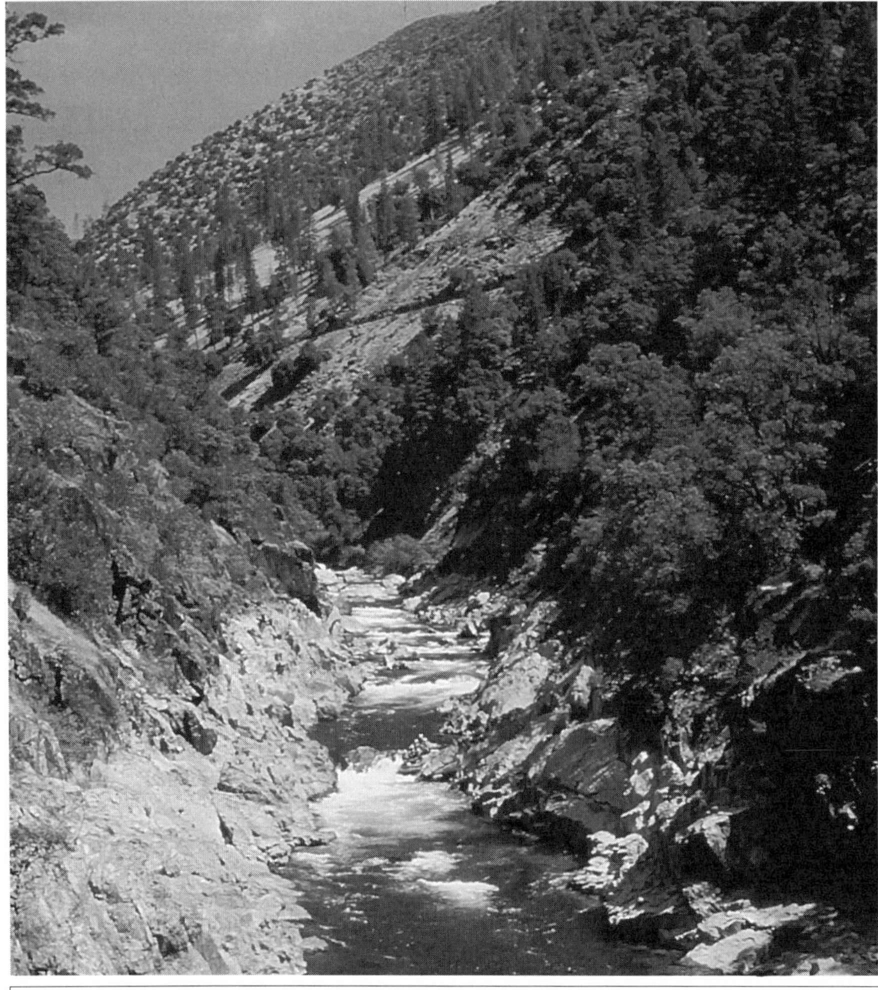

Chamberlain Falls, North Fork American *Mark Leder-Adams / Rapid Shooters*

Middle Fork Feather River

Middle Fork Gorge

Difficulty: V+p. **Gradient:** 75 ft./mi.
Length: 32 miles.
Put-in: Nelson Point (3,900').
Take-out: Milsap Bar (1,500').
Season: Late May–early July.
Recommended Levels: 400–1,000 cfs at the put-in, which is usually around 1,000–2,500 cfs at the take-out.
Flow Information: No gauge reading available. As a very rough estimate, take three quarters of the inflow to New Bullards Bar Reservoir on the nearby North Fork Yuba, given on the DWR tape, (916) 653-9647.
Special Hazards: Mandatory portage at mile 29; many other portages likely. Remote wilderness canyon; rescue difficult.
Permits: Not required.
Managing Agency: Plumas NF, 159 Lawrence St., Box 1500, Quincy, CA 95971; (916) 283-2050.
Commercial Raft Trips: None at this time.
Land Ownership: All National Forest.
Scenery: Excellent. Steep-walled, forested canyon.
Solitude: Excellent. **Wilderness:** Yes.

Guides and References:
- Cassady & Calhoun, *California Whitewater: A Guide to the Rivers.*
- Holbek & Stanley, *A Guide to the Best Whitewater in the State of California.*

Maps:
- **USGS 7.5':** *Blue Nose Mtn, Onion Valley, Dogwood Peak, Haskins Valley, Cascade, Brush Creek.*
- **USGS:** *Plumas NF.*
- **AAA:** *Feather-Yuba Region.*

Logistics: The town of Quincy is about 85 miles northwest of Lake Tahoe. To reach the **put-in at Nelson Point,** drive 3 miles east of Quincy on combined California Highways 89 and 70, turn south on La Porte Road, and drive 7 miles to the put-in on the left bank just downstream from the bridge. To reach the **take-out,** return to Oroville on California 70, drive northeast on California 162 to Brush Creek, turn south on Galen Ridge Road for a few hundred yards, then turn left on Milsap Bar Road and descend to the bridge across the Middle Fork.

The gorge of the Middle Fork Feather is one of the most spectacular and difficult rivers in the West. **Only teams of experts in kayaks or self-bailing rafts should attempt this run, and then only at low and moderate water levels.**[1] They should be prepared for a long, multi-day descent through pounding Class V—and worse—rapids in a remote, steep-walled wilderness canyon. In the gorge the river drops at an average rate of 75 ft./mi., with a peak gradient of well over 100 ft./mi. in the middle of the 32-mile run.

The Feather is the northernmost of the Sierra rivers. It drains a lush, moderate-elevation watershed whose heavy runoff long ago attracted the interest of dam-builders. Oroville Dam—the world's biggest earthfill dam and the centerpiece of the California State Water Project—blocks the Feather's main stem and backs water up all three forks. Only the Middle Fork runs free above Oroville Reservoir, thanks to its 1968 designation as a charter member of the National Wild and Scenic Rivers System. Below Nelson Point is the Middle Fork Gorge, where the river carves a deep, forested canyon through solid Sierra granite. The scenery and solitude are unexcelled.

The Middle Fork Feather is one of the remotest rivers in California. Only a few footpaths and jeep trails reach the bank at isolated points. In many places, rescue would be virtually impossible in the event of a mishap. Carry good maps, and note all possible emergency trails leading out of the canyon—our **Mile Guide** below includes only a selected few.

The gorge presents a host of technical challenges. Class IV and V rapids are scattered through the run. Most of the Class V+ drops and portages are below Onion Valley Creek (mile 14.5). The most obvious mandatory portage is Granite Dome Falls (mile 29), a staircase of Class V drops that climaxes in a lethal jumble of boulders.

[1] Intermediate boaters occasionally run the English Bar reach upstream, an eight-mile Class III stretch between Sloat and Nelson Point.

The river is generally runnable during spring snowmelt, but it should be attempted only when flows at the put-in are low. Keep in mind that numerous side creeks swell the river over the course of this run, doubling or even tripling the flow between put-in and take-out. Take a close look at the flow at Milsap Bar before committing to the run.

Middle Fork Feather River Guide

Note: This is only a general guide; its mileages are very approximate, and it lists only a few of the numerous Class V and V+ rapids and possible portages on this extremely demanding run. ***Scout frequently, and portage if in doubt.***

Put in on the right bank at Nelson Point. **Experts only.** A mile and a half downstream, Nelson Creek enters on the left. After three miles of Class III and IV, the difficulty increases to solid Class V from mile 3 to mile 9. Watch for a rocky 6' ledge drop in this section that should probably be portaged. Below mile 9 the rapids ease to Class IV for a time. An emergency trail climbs out of the canyon on the right at mile 9.5. Around mile 10 the river winds around Horseshoe Bend. A jeep trail reaches the left bank near mile 12.

Onion Valley Creek enters on the left at mile 14.5, and the Pacific Crest Trail crosses overhead on a foot bridge. Downstream is Franklin Canyon, a long stretch of turbulent Class V+ rapids and possible portages with a gradient of over 100 ft./mi. The first big rapid, just a few hundred yards below Onion Valley Creek, should probably be portaged. Just downstream is Class V+ **HOLE-IN-THE-BOX** (mile 15), where a narrow chute drops into a big hole. Very difficult water continues. Around mile 15.5 Dogwood Creek plunges down a beautiful waterfall on the left. Near mile 22 another foot bridge crosses the river at Hartman's Bar.

The Middle Fork enters dramatic **Devil Canyon** around mile 28, and massive granite walls rise abruptly from the river. The gradient is "only" 80 ft./mi., with major rapids formed by huge chunks of granite that have broken off the walls and dropped into the river. Side streams have by now significantly increased the river's flow, adding to the difficulty of this final stretch. Be alert for possible portages.

A mile into Devil Canyon is the long, strenuous **mandatory portage at GRANITE DOME FALLS,** which comes at the end of a big pool where the river bends right and a huge granite dome towers over the left bank. A mile below this rapid the canyon begins to open, but difficult rapids continue. **Take out** on the right bank above the Milsap Bar Road bridge.

Below Milsap Bar lies infamous **Bald Rock Canyon,** the last 7 miles of the Middle Fork above Oroville Reservoir. Here the river plummets over massive slabs of granite at a rate of 110 ft./mi., with a peak gradient of 200. Bald Rock Canyon has been run by only a handful of expert kayakers, including Lars Holbek and Chuck Stanley, who relate their adventures in the guide book listed above and in *First Descents: In Search of Wild Rivers,* edited by Cameron O'Connor and John Lazenby.

On our exploratory raft run down the Middle Fork Feather in July 1983, we had just begun our third day on the river when we met veteran innertuber Don Turner and some other adventurous souls near Hartman's Bar. Unlike most innertubers, who account for the vast majority of drownings on American rivers, Turner and his friends know what they're doing. They wear wet suits and life jackets and carry gear in backpacks strapped to extra tubes. They float through the calm pools and portage or line the big rapids. Turner has been navigating stretches of the Middle Fork in this manner for years—including Bald Rock Canyon, downstream from this run and even more difficult. On this occasion he was on the fifth day of a six-day, six-mile trip from Stag Point to Hartman's Bar.

We left the tubers behind and kept going. By the time we got to Granite Dome Falls, our paddle crew was getting pretty cocky. Thanks in part to our self-bailing raft, we had run 29 miles of outrageous river with no portages and no major problems. But there was a moment when common sense almost turned to putty. After looking over the horrors of the falls, half the crew wanted to run it. For a moment we were tempted. One of the crazies signaled "Let's go!" to our two kayakers, who were scouting from the other bank. They looked at us for a moment across the roaring chute. Then, in unison, each pointed to the frightening drop at the bottom of the rapid with one hand and put the other to his head like a gun. We portaged.

—Jim Cassady

Trinity River

1. North Fork Confluence (1,390') to China Slide (900').
III+ to mile 5.2; II+ thereafter.
25 miles; 19 ft./mi.

2. Burnt Ranch Gorge: China Slide to Hawkins Bar (570').
V; 8.5 miles; 39 ft./mi.
(100 ft./mi. between miles 1.5 and 3.5).

3. Lower Trinity: Hawkins Bar to Weitchpec (200').
II3; 39 miles; 9 ft./mi.
Shorter runs possible.

4. South Fork Trinity: Highway 36 (2,300') to Low Level Bridge Site (525').
Vp; 48 miles; 37 ft./mi.
Shorter runs possible.

Drainage Area and Average Annual Discharge: 1,439 sq. mi. / 1,314,000 af near Burnt Ranch. *South Fork:* 764 sq. mi. / 1,111,000 af near Hyampom (mile 30).

Peak Recorded Flow: 172,000 cfs (Dec. 22, 1955).

Season: *Runs 1 & 3:* All year, but best in late spring and summer. *Run 2 (Burnt Ranch Gorge):* Summer, after high water is over. Trinity flows are partially controlled by Lewiston Dam upstream. *Run 4 (South Fork):* April–May; to late June in wet years.

Recommended Levels: *Run 1:* 500–5,000 cfs. *Run 2:* 500–2,000 cfs. *Run 3:* 800–8,000 cfs. *Run 4:* 600–3,000 cfs.

Flow Information: DWR tape, (916) 653-9647. Take the flow at Hoopa, then estimate as follows: *Run 1:* About 60% of the flow at Hoopa. *Run 2:* About 90%. *Run 3:* 100%. *Run 4:* 25%. *Note:* The hydrograph on this page does not fully reflect increased releases from Lewiston Dam since 1981.

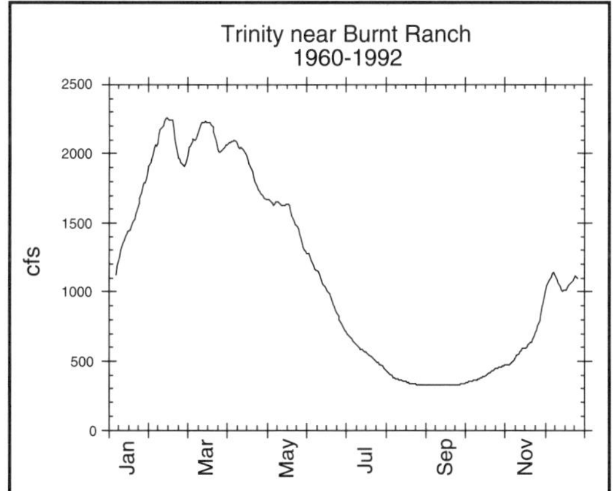

Special Hazards: *Run 2:* Most of Burnt Ranch Gorge, especially at higher flows. *Run 4:* Very difficult rapids and tough portages below Winton Flat (mile 22.5) and in the Big Slide area (mile 31).

Permits: Not presently required.

Managing Agencies: *Runs 1 & 2:* Big Bar RD, Shasta-Trinity NF, Star Route 1, Box 10, Big Bar, CA 96010; (916) 623-6106. *Run 3:* Lower Trinity RD, Six Rivers NF, P.O. Box 668, Willow Creek, CA 95573; (916) 629-2118. *Run 4, miles 0–35:* Hayfork RD, Shasta-Trinity NF, P.O. Box 159, Hayfork, CA 96041; (916) 628- 5227. *Run 4, miles 35–48:* Same as Run 3.

Commercial Raft Trips: *Runs 1–3:* Yes. For references contact the Forest Service. *Run 4:* No.

Land Ownership: *Runs 1–3:* Mostly National Forest; some private parcels. Lower half of Run 3 is Hoopa Valley Indian Reservation. *Run 4:* Mixed National Forest and private.

Scenery: *Runs 1 & 3:* Very good. *Run 2:* Excellent; highway is far above. *Run 4:* Excellent.

Solitude: *Run 1:* Fair; highway nearby. *Run 2:* Excellent. *Run 3:* Good. *Run 4:* Excellent.

Wilderness: *Run 1:* No. *Run 2:* Yes. *Run 3:* Partial. *Run 4:* Mostly. Occasional dirt road, town, or campground.

Fishing: Excellent for salmon and steelhead.

Water: *Runs 1–3:* Clear and warm in summer. *Run 4:* Clear except after heavy rains. On all runs, purify side streams for drinking.

Camping: *Runs 1 & 3:* Excellent riverside sites, plus many USFS campgrounds on the river (see **Mile Guide.**) *Run 2:* USFS campgrounds on Highway 299. Carrying camping gear downriver in Burnt Ranch Gorge is not recommended. *Run 4:* Superb riverside sites. USFS campgrounds at put-in and mile 31.

Guides and References:

- Cassady & Calhoun, *California Whitewater: A Guide to the Rivers.*
- Holbek & Stanley, *A Guide to the Best Whitewater in the State of California.*
- Alt & Hyndman, *Roadside Geology of Northern California.*

Maps:

- **USGS 7.5':** *Run 1:* Helena, Hayfork Bally, Big Bar, Del Loma, Ironside Mtn. *Run 2:* Ironside Mtn, Hennessy Peak. *Run 3:* Salyer, Willow Creek, Hoopa, Weitchpec. *Run 4:* Naufus Creek, Sportshaven, Hyampom, Hyampom Mtn, Sims Mtn, Hennessy Peak.
- **USGS 1:100:** *Runs 1 & 2:* Hayfork. *Run 3:* Hayfork, Hoopa. *Run 4:* Hayfork, Garberville.
- **USFS:** *Runs 1 & 2:* Shasta-Trinity NF. *Runs 2 & 3:* Six Rivers NF. *Run 4:* Either.
- **AAA:** *Northwestern California.*

Logistics: *Main Trinity (Runs 1–3):* All accesses are on or near California Highways 299 and 96, which follow the river and provide many accesses in addition to those listed here (see **Mile Guide** and USFS maps).

The **upper put-in at Pigeon Point** is about 80 miles east of Arcata and 15 miles west of Weaverville on Highway 299. The access at **Cedar Flat** is about 3 miles upriver from the hamlet of Burnt Ranch, on the right bank just upstream from the highway bridge over the river. The turnoff to **China Slide** is a little over a mile downriver from the Cedar Flat bridge; turn north toward the China Slide Dump and follow this side road to the end. **Hawkins Bar** is about 10 miles east of Willow Creek; turn north off 299 onto a dirt road just west of Hawkins Bar Trailer Park and drive to the river. The final take-out at **Weitchpec** is 22 miles north of Willow Creek on Highway 96.

South Fork (Run 4): The **put-in** is at the USFS campground at Forest Glen, where California Highway 36 crosses the river. To reach the **take-out,** turn south off California 299 about 8 miles east of Willow Creek onto South Fork Road (just east of the bridge across the South Fork). Stay on the main road for 6.8 miles, then take a right fork down to the river and the site of a washed-out bridge. The only other good access is in Hyampom Valley (miles 25–30). Poor access, in case of emergency, may be found at Klondike Mine (mile 4.4), Oak Flat (mile 20.4), Underwood Creek (mile 36), and Surprise Creek (mile 42). There are two long shuttle routes. *The 100-mile route:* Nine miles east of Forest Glen, turn north onto California Highway 3, then turn west on California 299 at Douglas City. The *145-mile route:* drive west to U.S. 101, north to Eureka, and east on 299. Both shuttles take several hours one way.

The Trinity, the Klamath's largest tributary, rises some 20 miles west of Mt. Shasta, near the headwaters of the Sacramento and Scott Rivers. At first a small river, the Trinity runs south, then west and north through rugged terrain as it loops south of the snow-covered Trinity Alps. By the time it joins the Klamath at Weitchpec, the Trinity is a big river winding through a lush, green canyon. The Trinity and its North and South Forks are part of the National Wild and Scenic Rivers System.

The Trinity—called the "Hoopa" by local Indians—was given its present name by a pioneer who mistakenly thought it flowed into Trinidad Bay. The man who misnamed the river, Pierson B. Reading, found gold along its banks in July 1848, just six months after Marshall's discovery at Sutter's Mill on the American. By 1851, 10,000 men were mining the Trinity and its side creeks. Huge placer operations left mountains of rock tailings, many still visible along the upper Trinity. Hydraulic mining washed away entire mountainsides, and dredging operations reworked the river bed. The Trinity has been dramatically altered by mining, but the runs recommended in this guide are downstream from most of the damage.

The river has also been hard hit by modern water projects. The biggest is Trinity Dam northeast of Weaverville, completed by the Bureau of Reclamation in 1960. Its reservoir, now called Clair Engle "Lake," is California's third largest, capturing runoff from the Trinity's upper watershed. Just downstream, smaller Lewiston Dam diverts 80 percent of this water through a tunnel to the Sacramento basin and the Central Valley.

Until 1981 these dams reduced flows on the Trinity to 150 cfs nine months of the year—far too little for downstream fish and water quality. At that time a decision by outgoing Interior Secretary Cecil Andrus required the Bureau to release more water from Lewiston Dam. Since then, the Bureau has varied releases depending on runoff and the status of downstream fisheries. The highest releases (800 to 3,000 cfs) have usually been in late May and early June, to wash smolts (young salmon and steelhead) downstream. Except in very dry years, releases are unlikely to fall below 300 even in late summer. Flows downstream are somewhat higher due to tributaries. Boaters can take advantage of two days of higher flows (1,200 cfs) in early September during the annual Hoopa Indian White Deerskin Boat Dance.

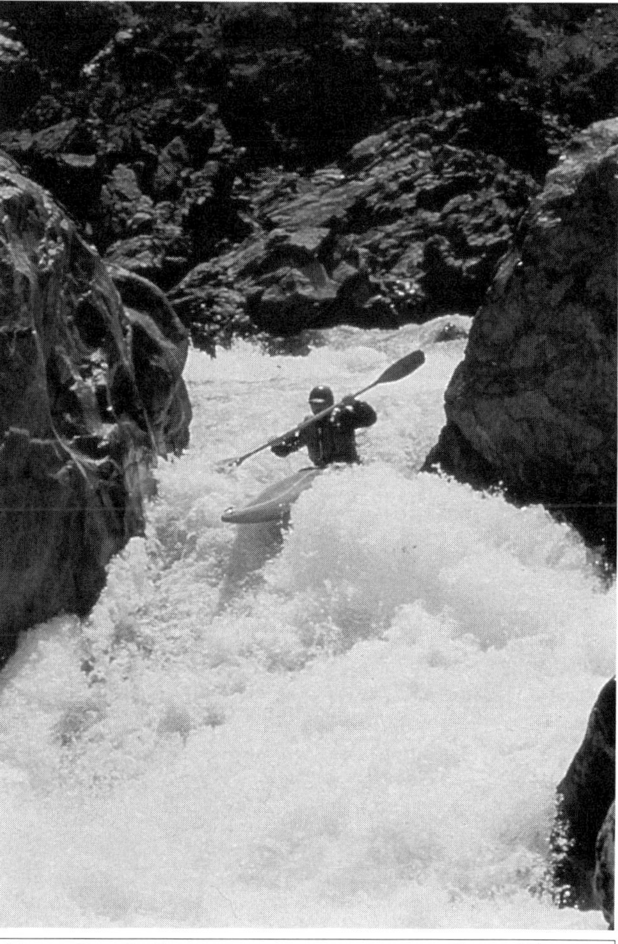

Burnt Ranch Gorge *James Thomson*

Upper and Main Trinity

The upper Trinity drains the drier eastern slope of the Coast Range and remains a small river from its headwaters all the way to the confluence with the North Fork. Still, the upper river offers a dozen miles of Class III whitewater above Clair Engle Reservoir and 37 miles of Class I and II floating between Lewiston and the North Fork confluence.

The Trinity is at is best downstream, where the river leaves behind the worst scars of the gold-mining era and flows through wetter country. Canyon Creek and the North Fork Trinity drain the southern slopes of the Trinity Alps, adding considerably to the main river's flow. Soon the canyon narrows, the vegetation becomes lusher, and the rapids grow more difficult.

The first run recommended in this guide begins at the mouth of the North Fork. On this scenic stretch of the Trinity, sometimes called the Pigeon Point Run, frequent vehicle access makes it possible to start and end the float at many different points—far more than those indicated in this guide. Most rapids can be seen from the nearby highway.

Burnt Ranch Gorge

Farther west, the river changes as it slices through the Ironside Mountain Batholith, a massive granite intrusion formed 150 million years ago. This is Burnt Ranch Gorge, one of the best expert runs in the west—eight miles of Class V whitewater in a steep-walled canyon inaccessible except by boat.

Though the overall gradient is moderate, this pool-and-drop run is laced with major rapids and is definitely **for experts only.** Help is hard to come by because few trails penetrate the sheer-walled canyon. Don't hesitate to portage the biggest rapids, and don't make the mistake of attempting Burnt Ranch Gorge at high water. Wait for low summer flows, when Lewiston Dam far upstream furnishes most of the water. The actual flow in Burnt Ranch Gorge is somewhat higher than the dam releases because of tributaries downstream from the dam.

Lower Trinity

Below Hawkins Bar is a scenic, easy float past the mouth of the South Fork, through the Hoopa reservation, and on to the Klamath confluence at Weitchpec. Here in the western part of the Coast Range the Trinity has become a large river, its lush mountain setting much like the Lower Klamath's. This is a fine summer run for boaters who enjoy Class II whitewater; most of the more challenging rapids are in the first 8 miles below Hawkins Bar. Upstream winds make the Lower Trinity less popular with rafters than with kayakers and canoeists.

The Lower Trinity has several wilderness sections where the highway and other traces of civilization are far away: from Hawkins Bar to the mouth of the South Fork (miles 0–8.4); from Riverdale Park to Tish Tang Campground (18.4–22.9); and from Hoopa to Weitchpec (30.9–39). The final cut through Weitchpec Gorge is spectacular. Around mile 23 the river enters the Hoopa Valley Indian Reservation. If you want to run a shorter stretch, be sure to pick one of the wilderness sections.

South Fork Trinity

The South Fork Trinity rises in the Coast Range on the northern slopes of the Yolla Bolly Mountains, whose tallest peaks approach 8,000' and retain their snow cover well into summer. The river flows northwest toward its confluence with the main Trinity at Salyer. Much of the watershed has been logged, but few of the scars are visible from the river, which is one of the most scenic in California. The South Fork was among the North Coast rivers that flooded in December 1964, and its streambed is still partially choked by boulders and slides from that record runoff. The lower part of the canyon has numerous sand and gravel bars that provide excellent campsites.

Experts only. In spite of its moderate gradient, the South Fork has plenty of very difficult, boulder-strewn rapids. The most challenging sections include the first four miles, the stretch just below mile 22.5, and the first seven miles of the run below Big Slide Campground (mile 30.9). Rafters in particular should consider the tough portages before committing to a run. Because of its relatively short season, remote location, and tough whitewater, few boaters know this river. Boaters looking for a more placid alternative can enjoy a lovely Class I float down the last eight miles of the South Fork.

Trinity River Mile Guide

North Fork Confluence to China Slide

0 PUT-IN. Pigeon Point Campground, just below the North Fork Trinity confluence.

2.2 THE SLOT (III). Also called **Z-Drop.** Above 1,200 cfs the reversal at the bottom gets very big, and many boaters portage.

3.2 HELL HOLE (III+). Steep vertical drop, washed out above 1,500 cfs. May require portage during fall salmon runs, when crowds of anglers dangle lines into the rapid. Three quarters of a mile downstream is **SAILOR'S BAR (III)**, a recently formed rapid with a big hole.

5.1 FISH TAIL (III). A boulder garden. Fishing lines can be a problem during salmon runs. Rapids ease below this point.

5.2 RIVER ACCESS. Big Flat Campgrounds on the right—one private, one USFS. Popular take-out for those running only the more challenging upper section.

8 Bridge across the river. Big Bar Campground is on the left, a short ways up the road. USFS ranger station on the right, across the highway.

13.5 French Bar. The river bends left around a peninsula where gold miners dug a tunnel in an attempt to divert the river and mine its bed. Big French Creek enters from the right at the tip of the peninsula, just above a Class II+ rapid.

16.9 Hayden Flat Campground (right bank). The stretch from Big Flat (mile 5.2) to this point is less regularly boated, but the run from here to Cedar Flat (mile 23.6) is popular.

18.2 The Trinity enters a mini-gorge with two Class II+ rapids.

23.6 TAKE-OUT. Cedar Flat. Take out on the right above the highway bridge. An alternate—and less inviting—take-out is a mile and a half downstream at the China Slide dump; however, a gate on the road leading to the dump is sometimes locked. **Experts only downstream in Burnt Ranch Gorge.**

Burnt Ranch Gorge

0 China Slide. Put in here or at Cedar Flat, 1.5 miles upstream. In 1890 heavy rains caused a huge landslide off the south canyon wall that killed two Chinese miners and temporarily blocked the river, backing water 12 miles upstream. A quarter

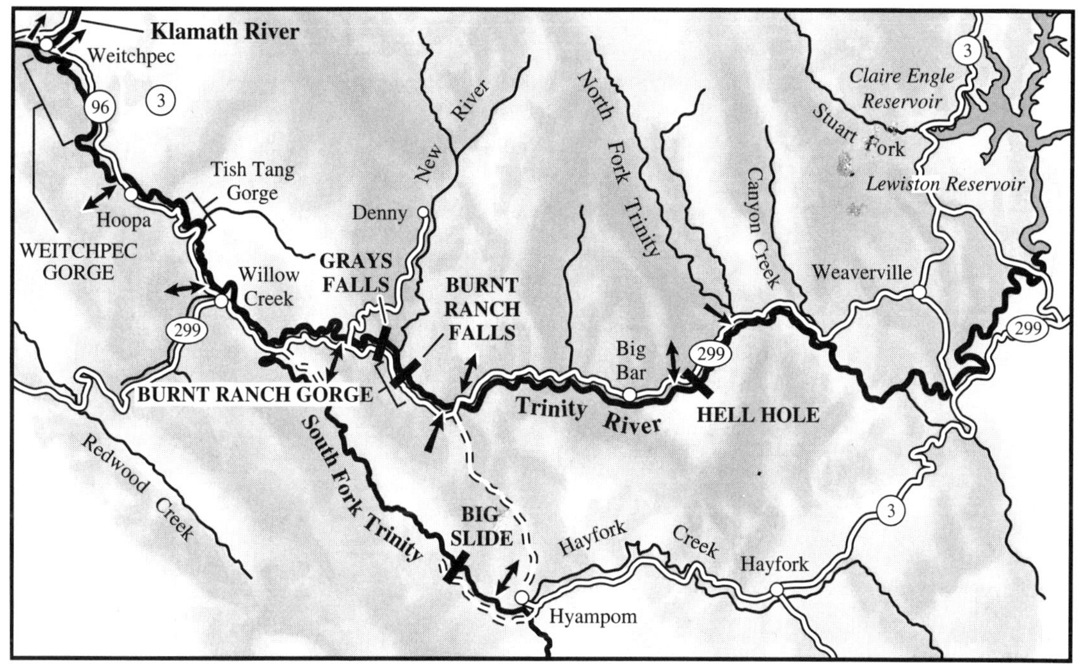

Trinity

mile downstream around a left bend is **CHINA SLIDE RAPID** (IV), a shallow, rocky chute with tight maneuvering. Next is **PEARLY GATES** (IV+), an 8' drop that announces the beginning of Box Canyon. Scout right. Flatwater through the rest of Box Canyon.

1.5 **TIGHT SQUEEZE** (IV+). Big rocks constrict the river to a narrow run down the middle. Scout left. The next two miles drop 200'. Scout frequently.

2.7 **UPPER BURNT RANCH FALLS** (V). Also called **Jaws.** A simple chute leads to three monoliths blocking the river. Boaters have successfully run the 10' falls between the two left-hand boulders. Depending on flow, the slot is 5' to 7' wide. Scout and portage on the left.

3 **MIDDLE BURNT RANCH FALLS** (V). The river surges down a jumbled slide with a total drop of 20'. Scout, and portage if necessary, on the left. Downstream, a trail leads from the left bank up to Burnt Ranch Campground and the highway.

3.1 **LOWER BURNT RANCH FALLS** (V). Formerly the toughest rapid in the gorge, but rearranged in 1991. Still formidable, with a steep drop into a large pool. Strenuous portage on the left is still the wisest choice for many boaters.

3.3 **HENNESSY FALLS** (V), a right-left zigzag at the end of a long pool. Not far downstream is **ORIGAMI** (V), with turbulent holes at the bottom that can fold a raft like Japanese paper. Above 1,200 cfs look for a sneak route on the left. Scout, and portage if necessary, on the left. Next up is **TABLE ROCK** (IV–VI), where a dangerously undercut flat rock waits at the bottom of a chute. Below 1,000 cfs the slower current allows boaters to move right of the rock. At higher flows consider the easy portage on the left.

5 The New River enters on the right. A mile downstream is the last big drop, **GRAY'S FALLS** (V), where big boulders block the river. Scout left. A trail leads up the left bank to Gray's Falls Campground. The river is Class II from here to take-out.

8.5 **TAKE-OUT** on the left at the Hawkins Bar River Access, downstream from the Hawkins Bar bridge. This is the put-in for the Lower Trinity run.

Lower Trinity

0 **PUT-IN.** Hawkins Bar. The first 8 miles have frequent Class II and II+ rapids. Formerly, the highway was well above the river, but new construction may bring the road closer in places, increasing access and reducing solitude.

4.2 Devil's Elbow, a crook in the river. A quarter-mile trail leads from a beach on the left to Tunnel Flat Road, off Highway 299, making this an alternate access for lightweight craft.

7.2 Bridge across the river. Hamlet of Salyer high on the left.

8.4 South Fork Trinity enters on the left, adding considerable flow. The river also grows wider. **RIVER ACCESS** on the left just above the confluence, via a trail up to Highway 299. Downstream, the canyon begins to open and the rapids ease.

13.7 Bridge across the river at the town of Willow Creek on the left. Just downstream Willow Creek enters on the left. **RIVER ACCESS** below the creek on the left at Big Rock, near the gravel pit and airstrip.

18.4 **RIVER ACCESS.** Riverdale Park and Trinity River Rafting Center on the left. Camping and river access for small fees. The next four miles are through a beautiful gorge with the highway far away.

19.8 Horse Linto Creek enters on the right. A mile downstream is **SUGAR BOWL (II+)**, a small ledge. Scout on the right.

22.9 Tish Tang Campground on the left. **RIVER ACCESS** at a nearby gravel bar. Just downstream, Tish-Tang-a-Tang Creek, named for a former Hoopa Indian village, enters on the right. Below this point the river runs through the Hoopa Valley Indian Reservation, home to the Hoopa and Yurok tribes.

28.2 Highway 96 bridge over the river. **RIVER ACCESS** just downstream on the left. Additional accesses can be found a mile downstream where Hostler Creek enters on the right, and at mile 31 where Mill Creek enters on the right.

33 The river enters Weitchpec Gorge, with the road far up on the wall.

38.4 **WEITCHPEC FALLS (III).** The rapid changes from year to year, and its difficulty varies with the flow. Scout on either side, and portage on the right if necessary.

39 **TAKE-OUT.** Just above the Klamath confluence on the right, a steep trail leads up to the hamlet of Weitchpec. An alternate take-out requires boaters to make a strong ferry across the Klamath to its right bank—a difficult move at high flows—where there is vehicle access on Martin's Ferry Road.

South Fork Trinity River Guide

Experts only. Rapids on this run are especially liable to change, and new ones can form. Scout often and be prepared to portage. Note: The map in this chapter shows only the lower part of this run.

A convenient **put-in** is on the right bank at Forest Glen Campground just east of the Highway 36 bridge. (To reach an alternate put-in 1.5 miles upstream, drive south on a USFS road that intersects the highway a mile east of the bridge. The one big rapid in this upper stretch can be portaged.) The first 4 miles below the bridge drop steeply at 90 ft./mi., and Class V rapids come in clusters. Some may require portage. At mile 4.4, a trail climbs several hundred yards up the left bank to rough Klondike Mine Road, which leads to Highway 36. The river eases, with only Class II and III rapids to mile 22.5.

Plummer Creek enters on the right around mile 11.5. The first **river access** below the put-in is at Oak Flat (mile 20.4). On the right St. John Road (dirt) leads north to Hyampom Road two miles east of Hyampom. A mile downstream, Butter Creek enters on the right. ***HAZARD.*** A cabin on the left at Winton Flat (mile 22.5) signals a difficult section just ahead: steep Class V–VI drops with **dangerous undercut rocks.** Possible emergency river access at the cabin (private property; ask permission).

There is **river access** around mile 25 as the canyon opens into lovely Hyampom Valley. Class I for the next five miles. A mile downstream Hayfork Creek, the South Fork's biggest tributary, enters on the right and adds substantial flow. Below the creek on the right is the hamlet of Hyampom, another **possible river access.** A bit past mile 29, the canyon narrows again, but the rapids remain easy for another mile and a half.

Big Slide Campground (mile 30, left bank) is the last good **river access** for 17 miles—and a warning of the falls ahead. (To reach the campground by road, cross to the left bank at Hyampom and turn north on Lower South Fork Road.) ***HAZARD.*** About a mile below the campground is a mandatory ***PORTAGE*** at **BIG SLIDE FALLS (VI).** Huge boulders and landslide debris create fearsome chutes. Scout and portage on the left. The next three miles are Class III and IV except for one big **unnamed Class V–VI drop** about a mile and a half below Big Slide where the river drops left, then right down a bedrock staircase. The major problem is a dangerous undercut rock in the bottom center. Easy scout and portage on the right.

Watch for **POWER LINE FALLS (V),** marked by power lines on the hills ahead, around mile 34.5. Scout right. The river passes through a boulder field, then drops over a wide ledge choked with big rocks. Some boaters negotiate a tricky S-turn on the far right, and at higher flows a sneak route appears even farther right. Below this drop is a short pool followed by more Class IV and V rapids.

Underwood Creek enters on the right around mile 36. Just downstream is a foot bridge. On the left, a precarious road (for emergency access only) comes fairly close to the river. (To reach this spot, follow Lower South Fork Road six miles beyond Big Slide Campground—see above—pass under the power lines, and take the second right, Gates Road, down toward the river.) Grouse Creek enters on the left over a mile downstream. A third of a mile farther, after a left bend, the river drops down a 200'-long **unnamed Class V+ rapid** cluttered with big boulders and nasty holes. Scout and portage either side. Below this drop are Class III and IV rapids in a deep, lush canyon.

Downstream from Coon Creek and Surprise Creek, which enter from the right around mile 42, a cable crosses the river to a lone house on the left. The canyon begins to open up slightly. Poor **river access** via South Fork Road. At mile 45.8, watch for **THE THREE BEARS (IV+). Papa** and **Mama** require tricky maneuvering around big boulders. **Baby Bear** (mile 46.4), a wrap rock, is hard to miss at low flows. **Take out** on the right at mile 48 at the remains of a washed-out low-water bridge. Or continue down eight miles of beautiful Class I to the confluence with the Main Trinity at Salyer.

"Why has God done this to me?" I thought, as I dragged my inflatable kayak over yet another enormous boulder. Then I remembered: this wasn't God's idea—it was Cassady's.

Jim Cassady had tricked me into this 17-mile, all-day portage fest on the uppermost South Fork Trinity. He had cleverly played on my weakness for stunning scenery by telling me that Dick Schwind's classic out-of-print guide book, West Coast River Touring, rated this run Class IV for whitewater and "AA" for scenery.

If I had consulted my own copy, I'd have seen that Cassady had neglected to mention the first sentence of Schwind's write-up: "The many portages make this run unrewarding—in fact, unrunnable for all but those who love to portage."

Most sane people would see that and think, "Not my idea of a good time." Not Cassady. He was convinced that Schwind's "portages" might turn out to be runnable Class V's. It had been 15 years since Schwind's run, and techniques and equipment had improved dramatically, right?

As it turned out, the only techniques and equipment that would have made any difference were a knowledge of demolitions and a lot of TNT. It was a gorgeous run, but we spent more time out of our boats than in them, struggling over massive piles of boulders where the river churned through rock sieves and death traps.

By late afternoon we were utterly sapped, and I was dehydrated. Our canteens were long since empty, but I wouldn't drink the river for fear of giardia. Here I was, dying of thirst with water all around. Death was even beginning to sound like a reasonable option.

Darkness was falling, and I was just debating whether to use the last of my strength to save myself or to kill Cassady, when the take-out came into sight. We dragged ourselves up the bank, crawled into the car, and drove away looking like two people who had just witnessed a nuclear blast from ground zero.

We got about a quarter mile before I asked Cass to pull over so I could barf. I didn't even have the strength to get out of the car—just opened the door and hung my head out.

—Bill Cross

Salmon River

Forks of Salmon to Somes Bar

Difficulty: V; II+ above mile 4.3 and below mile 14.
Length: 19 miles. Longer and shorter runs possible.
Gradient: 31 ft./mi.
Put-in: Forks of Salmon (1,200').
Take-out: Somes Bar (610').
Drainage Area and Average Annual Discharge: 750 sq. mi. and 1,330,000 af.
Peak Recorded Flow: 133,000 cfs (Dec. 22, 1964).
Season: April–June. Heavy rains produce runnable flows through much of the winter and spring, then comes a short snowmelt season in late spring and early summer.
Recommended Levels: 600–3,000 cfs.
Flow Information: DWR tape, (916) 653-9647; flow at Somes Bar.
Permits: Not presently required.
Managing Agency: Klamath NF, 1312 Fairlane Road, Yreka, CA 96097; (916) 842-6131.
Commercial Raft Trips: Yes. For a list of outfitters, contact the Forest Service.
Land Ownership: Mostly private first 3 miles, almost all National Forest thereafter.
Scenery: Excellent. Heavily forested canyon.
Solitude: Very good. The road is usually high above the river.
Wilderness: No.
Water: Clear and cold. Purify before drinking.
Camping: Few sites in the gorge (miles 5–14). There is road access at Butler Creek (mile 10.5), so some groups leave boats there and camp elsewhere.
Side Hikes: Some nice trails, especially up Wooley Creek.

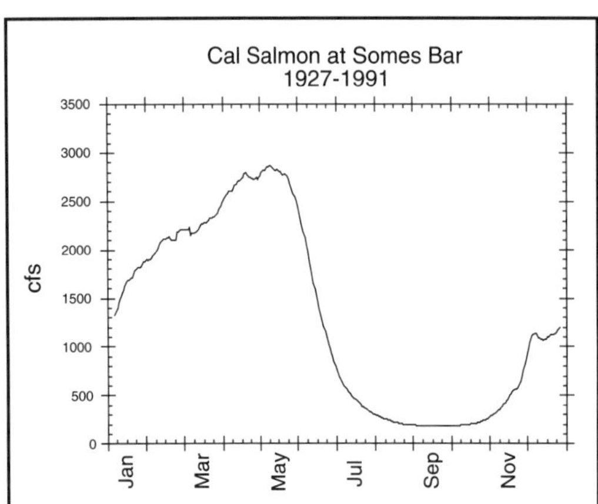

Side Excursions: Ishi Pishi Falls, a long Class VI cataract on the Klamath just upstream from the confluence with the Salmon.
Guides and References:
- Cassady & Calhoun, *California Whitewater: A Guide to the Rivers.*
- Holbek & Stanley, *A Guide to the Best Whitewater in the State of California.* Includes upstream runs on North and South Forks.

Maps:
- **USGS 7.5':** *Forks of Salmon, Orleans Mtn, Somes Bar.*
- **USFS:** *Klamath NF.*
- **AAA:** *Northwestern California.*

Logistics: Somes Bar is on Highway 96 at the confluence of the Klamath and Salmon. To reach the most popular **take-outs** upstream along the Salmon, turn east off California Highway 96 onto Salmon River Road. See the **Mile Guide** for details on possible take-outs. To reach the **put-in,** continue upriver some 17 miles to the little town of Forks of Salmon. The shuttle takes about half an hour one way.

California's Salmon River, a major tributary of the Klamath, rises in the Salmon-Trinity Alps Primitive Area, one of the most isolated regions in the state. Here, icy melt from Sawtooth, the only glacier in California's Coast Range, combines with abundant rain and snowmelt to produce a surge of runoff each winter and spring. Water gathers into two major tributaries, the North and South Forks of the Salmon, which join at the hamlet of Forks of Salmon.[1]

The "Cal Salmon"—so called to distinguish it from the larger and better-known Salmon River in Idaho—is one of the finest whitewater rivers in the West. Though boaters occasionally tackle sections of the small, steep North and South Forks, the Cal Salmon's most popular run is below their confluence, where strong flows and a steep gradient combine to produce powerful whitewater.

[1]The Salmon, its North and South Forks, and Wooley Creek are all part of the National Wild and Scenic Rivers System.

The heart of the run described here is the beautiful Salmon River gorge. Boaters will discover an intimate, steep-walled canyon where sparkling green waters splash through an exhilarating series of Class IV and V rapids separated by deep, quiet pools. A road through the canyon is usually unobtrusive and provides several alternate accesses for shorter runs. Less experienced boaters can float the first and last parts of the full 19-mile run, above and below the gorge.

Heavy precipitation—80" a year on average—produces lush forests along the Cal Salmon and feeds brilliant side creeks that often drop down spectacular cascades into the river. Keep in mind that Somes Bar is only 30 miles from the Pacific and that even in June, storms can move in quickly. Boaters should be prepared for cold water and possible cold weather.

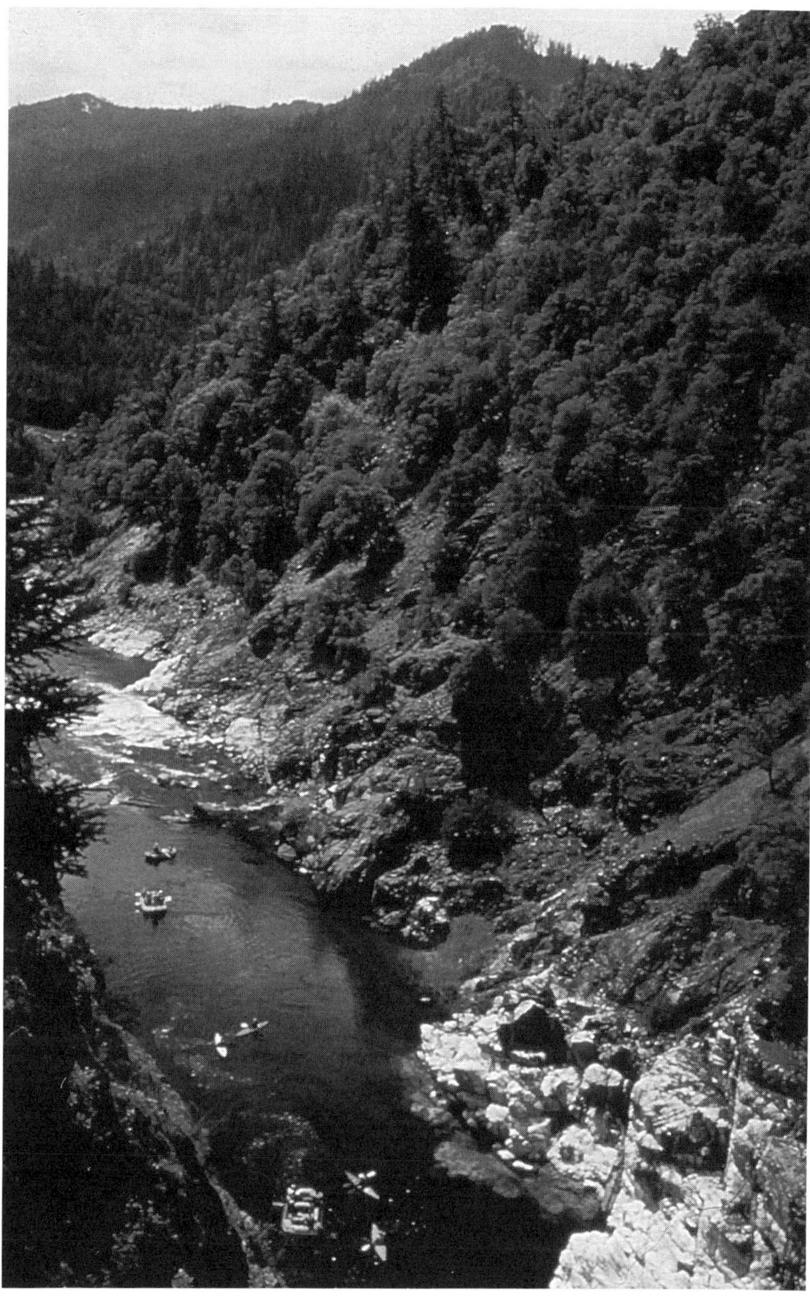

Cal Salmon *James Thomson*

The run can be extended by putting in at Methodist Creek on the South Fork, six miles above Forks of Salmon, and by continuing past the take-out down the Ikes section of the Klamath to an access near Orleans. Additional upstream runs are possible on both the North and South Forks of the Salmon, with steep gradients, difficult whitewater and relatively short seasons. (For details on the upstream runs, refer to the guidebook by Holbek and Stanley listed above.)

Mile by Mile Guide

*See map in **Klamath** chapter.*

0 **PUT-IN** at a gravel bar just downstream from the public school in Forks of Salmon. Two miles downriver is the Otter Bar Lodge kayak school. The first five miles are Class II+ through scenic open country.

4 The road crosses from the right to the left bank just above Crapo Creek.

4.3 **RIVER ACCESS.** Nordheimer Creek enters from the left. Nordheimer Flat Campground is just downstream on the left. *Note:* **At high flows most boaters avoid the difficult stretch of river just downstream and put in farther downstream at Butler Creek** (mile 10.7).

5 BLOOMER FALLS (IV). A sharp drop at a right turn. At lower flows the current forces boats toward a rock at the bottom right. Scout left. Bloomer Falls has quite a history. In the great December 1964 flood, a landslide blocked the river here. When a channel was dynamited, **Bloomer Falls,** one of California's most dangerous rapids, was created. An expert kayaker drowned here in 1982. In 1983 the state Department of Fish and Game dynamited the falls again—officially to ease the way for salmon migrating upstream, but probably to reduce the danger as well. Thus a manmade Class V–VI rapid became a manmade Class IV. Then nature added a touch in March 1993, when flood-level flows lodged a huge tree trunk across the river at the very top of the rapid. The log forms a dramatic entrance gate well above river level and out of the way of boats.

5.1 THE MAZE (IV). A long, nearly continuous zigzag through rocks and boulders.

6 LEWIS CREEK FALLS (IV). Lewis Creek enters on the left. The river turns sharply right and piles into a rock. The Salmon River gorge begins here.

6.5 Morehouse Creek enters on the right. A quarter mile downstream at **AIRPLANE TURN (IV+)**, the river turns right into a channel obstructed by big boulders. Scout left.

8 Portuguese Creek enters on the right at a Class III rapid.

8.5 CASCADE (V). Also called **Steelhead Falls.** The river plunges through a boulder maze with several channels, none of them easy. Scout left. A couple of hundred yards downstream is **ACHILLES HEEL (IV+),** also called **Cataract,** another boulder-choked drop with somewhat easier passages. Scout from either side.

9.7 WHIRLING DERVISH (IV+), a tricky rapid at a right bend. The **Dervish** is a big boulder in the center. The right channel is obstructed by large holes, and the left channel leads toward a slightly undercut wall. Scout left.

10.2 LAST CHANCE (V). A moderate rapid leads into a fearsome river-wide hole that must be negotiated successfully to avoid swimming the next big drop. The hole gets worse at higher flows. Scout on the right, and station rescue parties downstream (difficult trail on the right). Line or portage if necessary. Just downstream around a sharp left bend is **FREIGHT TRAIN** (V), a long, difficult rapid that makes a nasty swim. This rapid, also called **Grant Bluff** after a high bluff on the left bank, is visible from a turnout on the road atop the bluff.

10.7 **RIVER ACCESS** above **BUTLER CREEK LEDGE (IV–V).** Butler Creek enters on the left and the road approaches the river, providing an access just upstream. The rapid consists of a river-wide ledge and a powerful reversal that surfs boats into a big rock just below. There is often a tiny runnable slot at the far left end of the ledge. At higher flows boaters can sneak down a side channel even farther left. **Consider portaging** if this chicken route is unavailable.

11 DOUBLE HOLE (IV). Two big drops. Frequent Class III and IV rapids from here to Wooley Creek (mile 14).

13 **MARBLE (IV+).** Also called **Gaping Maw** or **The Maw.** This long, complex maze of boulders (holes at higher flows) begins just after a sharp right bend. Scout from the left. Look for a cave on the left below the rapid.

14.1 Wooley Creek, a superb salmon stream, enters on the right, and the gorge begins to open. Class II and II+ from here to the Klamath. No river access at the bridge just upstream.

14.5 **RIVER ACCESS.** Bridge across the river. The road is close by for the next 4 miles, providing several **alternate take-outs or put-ins.**

16 **RIVER ACCESS.** Many boaters take out at Oak Bottom Campground (Forest Service) on the right. There are a few more possible take-outs in the next couple of miles. Below mile 18.5 the road leaves the river and there is very limited access the rest of the way to the confluence.

19 Klamath confluence. Somes Bar is on the hill between the Highway 96 bridge and the confluence. Boaters can continue down the next five miles of the Klamath on the Ikes run; see **Klamath** chapter.

The problem isn't so much that Last Chance eats you. It's that it feeds you right into Freight Train. Just as it had done with Marty and his crew of strong paddlers sixty minutes and a thousand years ago.

Our best guide had rowed the oar boat through, and Jeff and I had scrambled over the rocks to set up protection before Marty's run. Suddenly, we were fishing people out of the river with throw lines and Steve was sacrificing himself and the oar boat to Freight Train to snatch three swimmers out of the rapid even as they were swept into its gullet.

Oar boat gone to an unknown and uncertain fate, empty paddle boat hot on its trail, extra bodies shivering on the banks, and Jeff and I, the two remaining guides, just kind of looking at each other and saying nothing.

Just staring at Last Chance. Thinking. Thinking too much, thinking too long, thinking of all the wrong things. Remembering how Jeff and I had trained together: Class III, then Class IV, then Class V. Confident on Class IV. Not so confident on Class V, but big ego boost to be accepted as qualified. Been having kind of a rough run today, though. Timing must be off a little. Been trying too hard, maybe. Even million-dollar baseball stars go into slumps and take weeks to get out of them. But they won't die if they don't.

I could just line the boat. Paddlers would be disappointed big time. No party at Oak Bottom tonight. Maybe I'm just not a Class V guide. Yes, I am. No, I've just been faking it all this time. Don't endanger your paddlers. Don't disappoint your paddlers. Hell, why is everyone looking at me? Have I been staring at the hole that long?

Into the boat. Uncharacteristically terse instructions to my paddlers. If you swim, don't even think of holding on to your paddle. Swim as hard as you can for river right. If you don't make it, remember to keep your feet up and pointed downstream.

Push off. Zen drifting. A little steering. Pick up a little speed. Left side of the tongue, slight left ferry angle: just right, ready for the killer backpaddle we will need in a few seconds. A little faster, faster, tongue turns white, bouncy. BIG bounce. LEFT TURN! BACKPADDLE! BACKPADDLE, BACKPADDLE, BACKPADDLE! LEFT TURN! BACKPADDLE, HARDER! Oh, no! We're going in!

Hanging above the hole, boat turned sideways, time stops. Then time starts again, but it's damaged, somehow too slow. Paddles flexing, paddlers grunting, no rhythm, just raw power, nothing exists but that paddle. Wonderful, incredible, strong, motivated paddlers, holding us back and yes, we are moving, moving ever so slowly to the right, defying current, rejecting gravity, crossing back over the River Styx, returning to the land of the living. Straighten out, left tube through the side of the hole, but that blessed, glorious right tube is riding the chute and we are through.

Quick, pull into the eddy before Freight Train gobbles us. No shouts of exuberance; too stunned for joy. Collapse on the floor, weak high-fives. Just saving our strength for the party at Oak Bottom tonight.

—Tony Finnerty

Klamath River

Iron Gate Dam to Weitchpec

1. Iron Gate Dam (2,165') to Scott River.
II+; 47 miles; 13 ft./mi.

2. Scott River to Happy Camp.
III-; 36 miles; 14 ft./mi.

3. Happy Camp to Green Riffle.
III; 37.5 miles; 14 ft.mi.
Note: Take out above **Ishi Pishi Falls (VI).**

4. Ikes Run: Salmon River to Trinity River Confluence near Weitchpec (200').
III4; 24 miles; 17 ft./mi.

Length: 148 miles. **Gradient:** 13 ft./mi.
Drainage Area and Average Annual Discharge: 4,630 sq. mi. and 1,672,000 af at Iron Gate; 8,475 sq. mi. and 6,080,000 af at Orleans.
Peak Recorded Flow: 29,400 cfs at Iron Gate and 307,000 cfs at Orleans (Dec. 22, 1964).
Season: All year. Sometimes too high for safe boating in winter.
Recommended Levels: 1,500–15,000 cfs at Orleans.
Flow Information: DWR tape, (916) 653-9647; release from Iron Gate (mile 0) and flow at Orleans (mile 132).
Special Hazards: High water in rainy season. Ishi Pishi Falls (mile 124).
Permits: Not presently required.
Managing Agencies: *(1) Iron Gate to Somes Bar (mile 125):* Klamath NF, 1312 Fairlane Rd., Yreka, CA 96097; (916) 842-6131. *(2) Somes Bar to Weitchpec:* Six Rivers NF, 507 F St., Eureka, CA 95501; (707) 442-1721.
Land Ownership: Mixed National Forest and private.

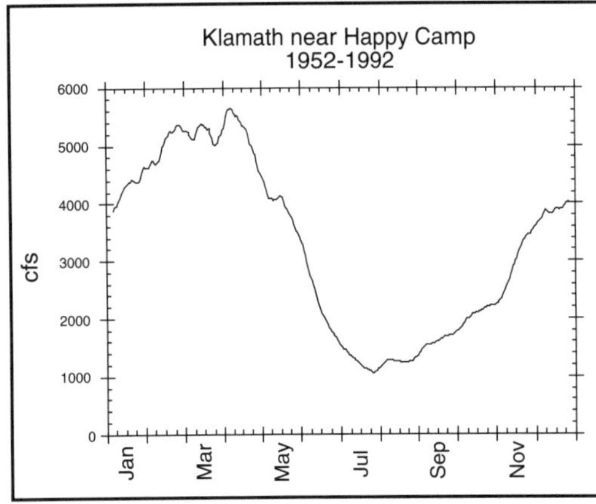

Commercial Raft Trips: Yes, plus inflatable kayak and drift boat fishing trips. For a list of outfitters, contact the managing agency.
Scenery: Very good to excellent. Transition from semi-arid volcanic canyon to lush forest.
Solitude: Very good. Highway 96 follows the river but is often high on the bank.
Wilderness: No.
Fishing: Excellent for steelhead and salmon, though the runs have suffered in recent years.
Wildlife: Abundant. Deer, bear, otter, and remarkable bird life including heron, osprey, waterfowl, and raptors.
Water: Usually warm and murky in summer.
Camping: Numerous developed and primitive sites along the river and highway. Many large beaches.
Side Hikes: Numerous. Among the best is Ukonom Creek (mile 101).
Side Excursions: Scott and Salmon Rivers. Marble Mountain Wilderness. Ishi Pishi Falls. The Indian Creek Cafe in Happy Camp boasts an eclectic menu more than 18 pages long.
Guides and References:

- Quinn & Quinn, *Handbook to the Klamath River Canyon.*
- Cassady & Calhoun, *California Whitewater: A Guide to the Rivers.* Covers miles 48–148.
- Schwind, *West Coast River Touring.* Out of print and somewhat out of date, but the only guide that covers the lowermost run from Weitchpec to the Pacific.
- Orr & Orr, *Rivers of the West: A Guide to the Geology and History.*

Maps:

- **USGS 7.5':** Not recommended (19 sheets).
- **USGS 1:100:** *Yreka, Happy Camp, Hoopa.*
- **USFS:** *Klamath NF.*
- **AAA:** *Northwestern California.*

Auto Shuttle: Roughly same mileages as river; paved. For shuttle references contact the Forest Service in Happy Camp, (916) 493-2243, or the nearby Klamath Inn Motel & RV Park, (916) 493-5377 or 493-2860.
Logistics: To reach the **upper put-ins at Iron Gate Dam and Klamathon Bridge (mile 5.5),** take the Hornbrook exit from I-5 and drive upriver on Copco Road. All other accesses

are on or near California Highway 96, which generally follows the Klamath from the I-5 bridge (mile 11) to Weitchpec. Highway 96 may be approached at the upstream end by turning west off I-5 about 8 miles north of Yreka, or at the downstream end by following California 299 east from Arcata or west from Redding and turning north at Willow Creek. Highway 96 provides numerous alternate accesses—refer to the **Mile Guide** for a listing of the major sites.

The Klamath is California's longest and biggest whitewater river,[1] with 184 runnable miles and an average flow at its mouth that surpasses that of the Colorado in the Grand Canyon. Though boaters—even Californians—sometimes overlook it, the Klamath offers a variety of excellent one-day and overnight trips on the longest Wild and Scenic River segment in the state. The river's unique combination of moderate rapids, warm water (in summer), easy access, superb scenery, abundant wildlife, excellent camping, and fairly light use make it one of the state's best floats.

The Klamath's enormous watershed—as big as Massachusetts and Connecticut combined—begins just east of Crater Lake in southern Oregon. Snowmelt from the east slope of the Cascade Range gathers in broad, shallow Upper Klamath Lake, then spills southwest and cuts through the Cascades in a rugged volcanic canyon where the Upper Klamath whitewater run is located (see Pacific Northwest region).

After crossing into California, the Klamath leaves the Cascades and enters the Klamath Mountains, a broad uplift that includes several major subranges: the Siskiyous, the Salmon Mountains, the Marble Mountains, the Scott Bar Mountains, and the lofty Trinity Alps. Below the Trinity River confluence at the town of Weitchpec, the Klamath turns northwest, flows through the Coast Range, and finally empties into the Pacific south of Crescent City.

As it cuts through California's rugged northwest corner, the Klamath makes a gradual transition from the dry east side of the mountains to the wet coastal climate. With each mile the canyon grows greener, and the vegetation steadily shifts from a sparse cover of juniper and even prickly pear cactus to dense stands of coast redwood near the river's mouth. In between are slopes clad in a mixed forest of pine, oak, madrone, fir, hemlock, cedar, and other trees.

The Klamath's major tributaries—the Shasta, Scott, Salmon, and Trinity Rivers—mirror this progression. Each brings more water than the one before, swelling the Klamath from a year-round average flow of 2,300 cfs at Iron Gate Dam to 5,000 near Happy Camp and 18,000 below the Trinity confluence. (Of course, flows are considerably lower than these averages in summer and much higher during the wet winter months).

In a state where the emphasis is usually on the new and the transitory, the Klamath seems ancient and timeless. Indeed, the river's course was well established some 10 million years ago, prior to most of the volcanic activity that formed the Cascade Range and before the last major uplift of the Klamath Mountains and the emergence of the Coast Range. The Klamath held to its course as the mountains grew around it, and today it is one of only three rivers that cut through both the Cascade and Coast Ranges. (The others are the Columbia and the Sacramento-Pit system.)

Civilization retains only a small foothold in the largely unpopulated Klamath region. The largest town along the river is Happy Camp with about 800 inhabitants. Were it not for the two-lane highway that follows the river, the canyon would probably be almost deserted. At most any hamlet along the river, one can still hear tales of Bigfoot, the hulking, hairy humanoid reputed to live in the remote forests that surround the Klamath canyon.

Before white settlement the Klamath was home to several groups of Indians, including a tribe of Modocs known as the Klamath—or Tlamatl, a closer approximation of the word's pronunciation—after whom the river is named. The word means "swiftness" in the Chinook tongue. Other tribes living along the river and its tributaries included the Shasta, the Karok (whose name means "upstream"), and the Yurok ("downstream").

The life of these Indians, who depended primarily on the river's plentiful salmon and steelhead for subsistence, was profoundly dis-

[1] Among California rivers only the Sacramento below Shasta Reservoir carries more water, and the Lower Sacramento is predominantly flat.

rupted after 1850 when gold-seeking whites overran their remote homelands. Dam building, dredging, and other mining operations dumped tons of rock and dirt into the river and cut the fish off from some of their best spawning grounds. The native Indian population dropped sharply.

Early in this century, the Klamath's prolific fisheries suffered another blow with the advent of large-scale water development. In 1917 the completion of Pacific Power and Light's Copco Dam and hydroelectric plant just south of the Oregon border blocked the upper reaches of the Klamath and drastically altered the river's flow. The plant's "peaking power" schedule called for alternating high and low releases that often left fish high and dry and made sport and commercial fishing much more dangerous.

Since then, things have improved. In 1924 California voters passed an initiative to protect the rest of the fishery by prohibiting dams on the Klamath downstream from its confluence with the Shasta River, 175 miles from the Pacific and about 20 miles below Copco. In the 1950's the state Department of Fish and Game began to tear down abandoned mining dams and construct fish ladders around obstacles. The program reopened hundreds of miles of streams where adult salmon and steelhead can spawn and where fry still too small for the journey to the sea can grow unmolested. In 1961, PP&L built Iron Gate Dam about six miles downstream from Copco; although the new dam flooded an additional section of river, it did smooth out the upper dam's irregular releases. Iron Gate also produces power and has a fish hatchery. Below Iron Gate the Klamath runs unimpeded to the Pacific.

All these efforts would have been for naught if the Bureau of Reclamation had succeeded in its proposal to dam the Klamath. The sidebar tells the story of how the Klamath escaped being flooded by one of the biggest reservoirs ever proposed in the West. In 1980 the California section of the Klamath was finally placed off limits to further dams when it was added to the National Wild and Scenic Rivers System.

Still, the Klamath is a troubled river. The outstanding Upper Klamath whitewater run in Oregon—above Copco Reservoir—is threatened by the Salt Caves hydroelectric project. (see the **Upper Klamath** chapter in the Pacific Northwest region). Downstream in California, the Klamath's renowned salmon and steelhead fishery suffers from a host of insults, including upstream dams and irrigation diversions, overlogging, road-building, and pollution.

Nevertheless, for whitewater boaters the Klamath remains one of California's finest and most reliable rivers. It is never too low to boat; even in California's severe drought in the late 1980's and early 1990's, the river had plenty of water. In summer Upper Klamath Lake acts as a giant solar water heater, spilling water at around 70°—ideal for kayakers learning their rolls or for thrill-seekers on body boards. The Klamath may be California's best river for open canoes; at lower summer flows, its long stretches of moderate rapids are well suited to these craft. Thanks to its relatively low elevation, the Klamath also remains boatable in winter. Heavy rains produce high flows and some of the biggest water in the state—at times, much too big for safe boating.

Few boaters run the full section described here. In fact, a continuous run is impossible without an arduous portage at dangerous Ishi Pishi Falls. The most popular section of river is the 36-mile (or shorter) Class III run from Happy Camp to a few miles above Ishi Pishi. Elsewhere, boaters can find lightly-used sections with rapids to suit any skill level from beginner to advanced. Highway 96 is generally nearby, though usually unobtrusive, providing frequent access and allowing boaters to choose sections that suit their tastes and skills.

The run can be extended to 184 miles by floating 36 miles below Weitchpec to Klamath Glen, only a few miles above the river's mouth. The first 18 miles below Weitchpec (to the end of Martin's Ferry Road) are especially scenic and make a rewarding float. However, this lower reach has some problems: below the Trinity confluence the Klamath turns northwest into strong prevailing winds—particularly tough for rafts—and Class III rapids soon give way to small riffles and a relatively lazy current. Also, the shuttle to Klamath Glen is quite long.

Mile by Mile Guide

Note: This guide lists only the most significant rapids and access points. The map does not show the first 40 miles.

0 **PUT-IN** on the right bank below Iron Gate Dam. Downstream is swift Class I and II water. Rolling hills and open terrain for the first 9 miles.

5.5 **RIVER ACCESS** on the right bank at Klamathon Bridge. Use caution downstream where old bridge piers divide the current just above the railroad bridge.

9 Interstate 5 briefly joins the right bank as the river enters a dry volcanic canyon.

11 **RIVER ACCESS.** I-5 bridge. Downstream, Highway 96 follows the river. The canyon narrows and deepens, and Class II and II+ rapids become more frequent.

13 Highway 263 bridge. Just downstream, the Shasta River enters on the left. Two miles farther is the old Ash Creek bridge at a Class II+ rapid.

18.5 **RIVER ACCESS.** Tree of Heaven Campground and boat ramp on the right.

22 **RIVER ACCESS.** Skeahan Bar on the right. The next two miles have two or three tougher Class II+ drops, notably **DUTCH CREEK** and **HONOLULU.**

29 Beaver Creek enters on the right. Downstream is the little town of Klamath River. Easy water and more houses from here to Horse Creek.

34 Walker Bridge, one of only a few that predate the great 1964 flood.

41 Highway 96 bridge. A mile down on the left is the town of Horse Creek (access).

46 **RIVER ACCESS.** Blue Heron boat access.

47 The Scott River enters on the left. **RIVER ACCESS** a mile downstream at Sarah Totten Campground on the left.

49 **HAMBURG (III).** Big boulders in the channel at a sharp right bend. The town of Hamburg (left bank) was a mining center in the late 1800's. Downstream are several miles of Class II water.

57.5 Highway 96 bridge. Downstream, the Klamath flows briefly through open Seiad Valley, where Seiad Creek enters on the right and Grider Creek on the left. As the canyon narrows again, watch for big waves at **SLUICE BOX (II+).**

62 **RIVER ACCESS** on the right at Portuguese Creek.

64.5 **UPPER SAVAGE (III-).** Holes and boulders block the channel. Well-known surfing hole just downstream. A mile below Upper Savage, big slabs of rock divide the river at **OTTER'S PLAY PEN (III-).**

67 Thompson Creek enters on the right. Legend has it that the first "Bigfoot" was sighted near here by Chinese workers. A mile downstream is the Seattle Creek **RIVER ACCESS** on the right. Mostly Class I+ for the next 16 miles.

72 **RIVER ACCESS.** China Point on the right. The highway leaves the river for the next 8 miles as the Klamath flows through beautiful and peaceful **Cade Canyon.** Gordons Ferry **RIVER ACCESS** is on the right at mile 77.

83 Bridge over the river at Happy Camp, largest town on the Klamath. As the name implies, gold miners found what they were looking for. Many commercial and private trips start here. Below the bridge Indian Creek enters on the right at a popular **RIVER ACCESS.** An **alternate access** is just downstream on the left at Curley Jack Campground. Just downstream, Elk Creek enters on the left; farther downstream, the rapids become more difficult.

87 **KANAKA FALLS (III),** also called **Rattlesnake,** at a sharp left bend. A big hole lurks in the center; boats can usually sneak down the left. Downstream is a series of Class II+ drops, including **MIXMASTER, FUNNEL** and **THE TRENCH.**

91 Clear Creek enters on the right. *For the next three miles, both banks are ceremonial grounds sacred to the Karok Indians.* Every

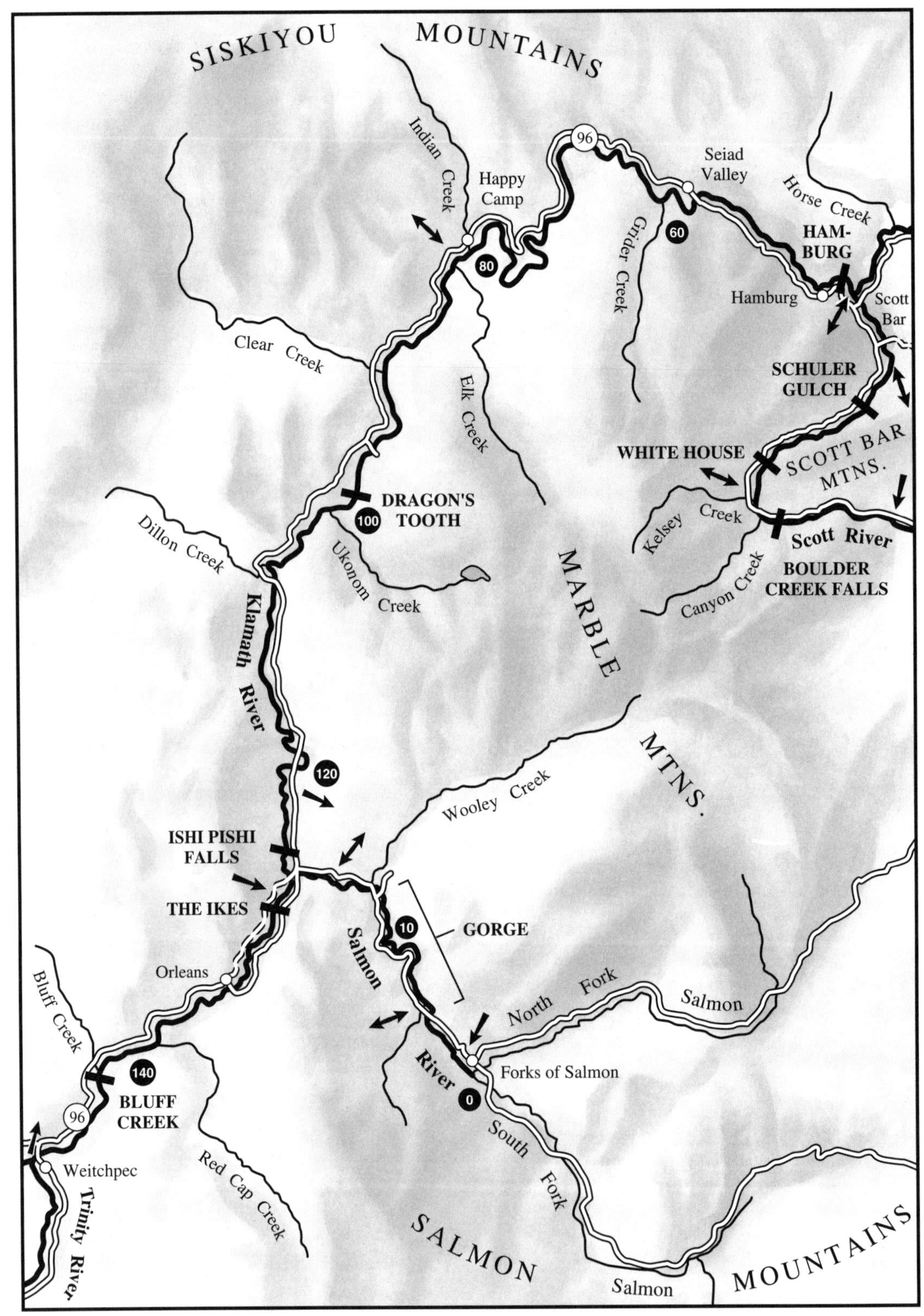

Klamath, Salmon, and Scott

year the Karok hold their World Renewal Ceremony here. During this 5-week period no camping is allowed in this stretch, and boaters should not stop along the bank.

94 **RIVER ACCESS.** Ferry Point on the right. Just downstream is a Class II+ rapid.

96 **RIVER ACCESS.** Bridge over the Klamath at a Class II rapid where Independence Creek enters on the left. Downstream, the highway climbs high above the right bank.

99.5 **DRAGON'S TOOTH (III+).** Also called **Little Blossom.** Big boulders block the channel, and the current plows into the biggest—the tooth. Routes and difficulty vary with the flow. Scout right. The rapid is not visible from the highway.

Escaping Ah Pah Dam

In water-hungry California the Klamath's prodigious flow did not escape the dam-builders' notice. Marc Reisner's acclaimed book on Western water, Cadillac Desert, *chronicles the Bureau of Reclamation's 1964 idea of constructing massive Ah Pah Dam 12 miles above the river's mouth, despite a long-standing California law prohibiting additional dams on the Klamath. This 813'-high plug would have backed water some 70 miles up the river—nearly to Happy Camp—and far up the Trinity and Salmon Rivers as well. At 15 million acre-feet, the reservoir would have dwarfed Shasta Dam's 4 million acre-foot capacity, which is the state's largest.*

To get all that water through several intervening mountain ranges to the Sacramento River, whence it could be diverted south to irrigate fields and water lawns in central and southern California, the Bureau proposed to dig a tunnel of unprecedented size: 60 miles long and nearly 40' in diameter.

Fortunately, the budgetary and political landscape changed before the Bureau could break ground on Ah Pah. But the Klamath's hairbreadth escape may have spelled doom for many other California rivers. Reisner quotes a Bureau official: "In California, you had two choices: you could build a lot of little projects on tributaries of the Sacramento and the San Joaquin, or you could build one huge project on the Klamath. I don't know whether it made better sense to do one or the other."

101 Ukonom Creek, named after a Karok chief, enters on the left. Popular campsite; excellent side hike up the creek to Twin Falls. A mile downstream is Coon Creek **RIVER ACCESS** on the right. Not far below the access is **BLUE SWILLUP RAPID (II+)**, after which the rapids ease somewhat for several miles.

107 Steep **RIVER ACCESS** on the right just below the mouth of Dillon Creek. Downstream is a highway bridge (no access).

109 **RIVER ACCESS.** Persido Bar on the left.

118.5 The highway crosses the river, then recrosses a mile downstream.

120.5 **TAKE-OUT.** Green Riffle access on the left, **the last possible take-out above Ishi Pishi Falls,** which is 3.5 miles downstream.

124 **ISHI PISHI FALLS (VI).** ***PORTAGE.*** If you don't take out upstream, this is a long, mandatory portage. Ishi Pishi means "end of the trail" to the Karok and refers to their arrival at this, their new home, after a long migration across the ocean. Somes Bar and Ukonom Ranger Station are above the highway on the left. Sugarloaf Mountain on the left is sacred to the Karok; souls of the dead climb to its top and depart for their next lives.

125 **PUT-IN.** The Salmon River enters on the left, just below a high bridge. Put in under the bridge on the Klamath's right bank, or upstream on the Salmon.

125.7 **The Ikes.** The first rapid, **LITTLE IKE (III-)**, with a big rock outcrop in the middle of the river, warns boaters that **BIG IKE (IV)** is just ahead. Above 12,000 cfs Big Ike can be a Class V much like Crystal in the Grand Canyon: powerful currents sweep boats directly toward a giant hole in the center. At lower flows boats can sneak down the right, but there have been fatal entrapments here. Scout on the left at high water, on the right at lower flows. Last in the series is **SUPER IKE (III+)**, which has big standing waves at high water and becomes a more difficult ledge drop at lower flows.

130.5 **RIVER ACCESS.** Dolan Bar on the left.

132 Highway bridge. Town of Orleans is on the right. Two miles downstream, Camp Creek enters on the right. Red Cap Creek enters on the left at mile 138.

141.5 BLUFF CREEK RAPID (III), a river-wide ledge where Bluff Creek enters on the right. Scout left. A Class II+ follows.

148 TAKE-OUT. The Trinity River, the Klamath's largest tributary, enters on the left. Access on the right just below the confluence. Weitchpec is half a mile upstream on the right. Highway 96 crosses the Klamath and follows the Trinity up to the town of Willow Creek, while Highway 169 follows the Klamath northwest another 18 miles. Downstream, after a few Class II+ to III rapids in the first few miles below Weitchpec, the river widens and the gradient and rapids ease. Strong upstream winds deter most boaters from floating these final 36 miles below Weitchpec, which flow through the Hoopa Indian Reservation to the town of Klamath Glen on U.S. 101.

I had been guiding Class IV and V runs on the Kern River all summer, so working a trip on the Lower Klamath sounded like a vacation. Little did I know, this was The Commercial Raft Trip From Hell.

Day One: *My sister, also a guide, gets stung by hornets while scouting a rapid. Within minutes, anaphylaxis sets in and Diane swells up like a blowfish. One customer, a nurse, asks if anyone has drugs that might slow the allergic reaction. The other passengers rummage through their ditty bags and come up with quite a selection: illegal white powder and green herbs, legal Valium and little yellow pills ... Now I understand why they're having so much trouble learning right and left turns in the paddle boat! One woman asks whether vaginal itching cream would help.*

We flag down a car and get Diane to Happy Camp, where a doctor reverses the reaction with epinephrine. She's pretty woozy, though, and in no shape to row. Back at the river we prop her up in the baggage raft, and she mumbles directions to my romantic interest and future wife, Polly, who has never rowed a raft. At each rapid Diane rouses herself to moan, "More on the right oar, the ***right*** *oar ... Oh, God!"*

Day Two: *I decide to row lead in the baggage raft, and since this is the Mellow Klamath, I'm fairly casual about tying in my load. Polly sits atop the gear and we make eyes at each other. The trouble starts when I fix on the idea of snagging the prime campsite at Ukonom Creek. We're just ahead of another commercial group, who probably have the same plan. When we stop for lunch and they pass us, my heart sinks: surely they'll go straight down and stake out Ukonom.*

But after lunch, we pass the other group having ***their*** *lunch. This is our chance! There's only one problem: just downstream is the biggest rapid on the run, Dragon's Tooth. We should stop and scout—especially since I've only seen it a couple of times, and at much higher flows. But what if the other group decides to run it without scouting? They'll get that camp. I remember Dragon's Tooth as an easy right-side run. So I cruise past the scouting eddy.*

As I round the bend and Dragon's Tooth comes into view my confidence begins to erode. Things don't look quite the way I remember. I try to pull to the right bank, but there's no eddy and the big baggage raft handles like the Queen Mary. I struggle at the oars, but still we're being dragged in. As we pass the point of no return, I utter my famous last words: "It's O.K., Polly, there's only one way to run this rapid anyway."

By the time I realize that it's ***not*** *OK, because there* ***is*** *no right-side run at this water level, it's too late to move left. There is only time to square up and hit the big house rock head on. The bow rides straight up the rock like a breaching whale. Polly looks down from eight feet above me with an expression that asks "Is* ***this*** *the run you were talking about?"*

"Hang On!" I shout, but Polly is no fool; she jumps ship. Next moment I am squashed like a bug as Big Bertha and the personal baggage of 25 people come down on my head. Everything I had neglected to tie in securely—fire pan, dutch oven, guide book, my best sweater—answers the call of gravity and makes a swift, one-way Voyage To The Bottom Of The Klamath.

I would never have guessed that my first and only oar-boat flip would come on the Mellow Klamath. But then, as my literary wife would be quick to remind me, pride goeth before a flip.

—Bill Cross

Scott River

Canyon Entrance to Klamath Confluence

Difficulty: V (III- below mile 18).
Length: 21.5 miles. Shorter runs possible.
Gradient: 52 ft./mi.
Put-in: Canyon Entrance (2,600').
Take-out: Klamath River Confluence (1,480').
Drainage Area and Average Annual Discharge: 653 sq. mi. and 490,000 af at put-in.
Season: April–late June.
Recommended Levels: 800–3,000 cfs.
Flow Information: DWR tape, (707) 443-9305.
Permits: Not presently required.
Managing Agency: Klamath NF, 1213 Fairlane Road, Yreka, CA 96097; (916) 842-6131.
Commercial Raft Trips: Yes. For references contact the Forest Service.
Land Ownership: Mostly National Forest; some private.
Scenery: Very good. Steep, forested canyon.
Solitude: Very good.
Wilderness: No.
Side Hikes: Kelsey Creek (mile 7.5).
Guides and References:
- Cassady & Calhoun, *California Whitewater: A Guide to the Rivers.*
- Holbek & Stanley, *A Guide to the Best Whitewater in the State of California.*

Maps:
- **USGS 7.5':** *Scott Bar, Hamburg.*
- **USFS:** *Klamath NF.*
- **AAA:** *Northwestern California.*

Logistics: To reach the **take-out** at the Klamath confluence, drive 35 miles west on California Highway 96 from I-5 about 10 miles north of Yreka. To reach the **put-in,** turn south off Highway 96 onto Scott River Road and drive upriver some 20 miles. There are several possible put-ins upstream from the Kelsey Creek bridge. The shuttle takes about 40 minutes one way.

The Scott River, a tributary of the Klamath, drains the east side of the Marble Mountain Wilderness and the northern and eastern slopes of the Salmon-Trinity Alps, with headwaters at about 8,000'. Because it lies in a partial rain shadow created by these mountains, the Scott drainage is drier than the nearby Salmon River watershed, and the Scott's season is usually a bit shorter than the Salmon's. The Scott is part of the National Wild and Scenic Rivers System.

The Scott[1] is small and steep above the town of Callahan, but soon the river slows as it passes through ranchlands in broad Scott Valley. Open canoeists occasionally run up to 30 miles of easy water in the valley, enjoying views of snow-capped peaks in the distance. Intensive cattle ranching in Scott Valley harms the river's water quality, and the Scott is often murky by the time it reaches the more difficult runs downstream.

Some ten miles west of Fort Jones, the river plunges into a deep, heavily forested canyon—the setting for the run described below. This challenging section was long known only to a few expert kayakers, but in the 1980's it began to receive attention from expert rafters. Regular commercial trips began in 1983.

The first three miles are less ferocious (Class III and IV), and the final 3.5 miles from Scott Bar to the Klamath are Class III-. However, **most of the Scott canyon is for experts only.** Tough rapids are almost continuous, with short pools separating sharp, boulder-choked drops. From Indian Scotty Campground (mile 4.5) to Tompkins Creek (mile 10), the gradient averages 90 ft./mi. Many boaters avoid Boulder Creek Falls, where a portage is often the right choice, by putting in at a side road bridge at mile 6 or at Bridge Flat Campground at mile 7.5. Scott River Road follows the run, often high above the river.

[1]The river is named for John Scott, who discovered gold here in 1850.

Scott River Guide

*See map in **Klamath** chapter.*

Put in on the right bank at any of several sites between the canyon entrance and the gauging station, where the rapids begin. The first 3.5 miles are Class III to moderate Class IV. Jones Beach Picnic Area is on the right at mile 3.5. Downstream, the rapids become more difficult.

Below Indian Scotty Campground (mile 4.5) the gradient increases markedly, with extremely difficult rapids for the next nine miles. *Note: Only the biggest rapids are mentioned here.*

The toughest drop is **BOULDER CREEK FALLS (V–VI)**, a **probable portage** at mile 5.8 where huge rocks block the channel. Immediately downstream is **CANYON CREEK RAPID (V)**, where the river bends right and plunges down several hundred yards of churning foam. Canyon Creek enters on the left.

Many boaters avoid Boulder Creek Falls by launching at one of **two alternate put-ins:** (1) on the left bank at mile 6, just below Canyon Creek Rapid and just above a side road bridge over the river; (2) 1.5 miles downstream—not far below where Kelsey Creek enters on the left—where the main road crosses the river at Bridge Flat Campground. The access is on the left just below the bridge. There is a fine side hike on a trail that leads several miles up scenic Kelsey Creek.

Below Bridge Flat are many difficult drops in quick succession. At mile 9.2, just below where Middle Creek enters on the left, is **WHITE HOUSE (V)**, marked by (what else?) a white house between the road and the river. Here the Scott plunges through a boulder sieve into a river-wide reversal. At mile 10 watch for **TOMPKINS CREEK RAPID (V)**, a 200-yard gauntlet of rocks and holes just above the mouth of Tomkpins Creek, which enters on the left. Below this rapid the road begins to climb away from the river. The last big drop is **SCHULER GULCH (V)**, located at a left bend at mile 13.5 where Schuler Gulch enters on the right. Downstream, the canyon begins to open, and the rapids ease somewhat.

A bridge crosses the river at Scott Bar (mile 18). An **alternate access** above the bridge on the right is popular as a take-out for the preceding expert run, or as a put-in for the short intermediate run downstream. Class II and easy Class III rapids continue to the Highway 96 bridge and Klamath River confluence at mile 21.5. **Take out** at the highway bridge, or continue down the Klamath to Sarah Totten Campground.

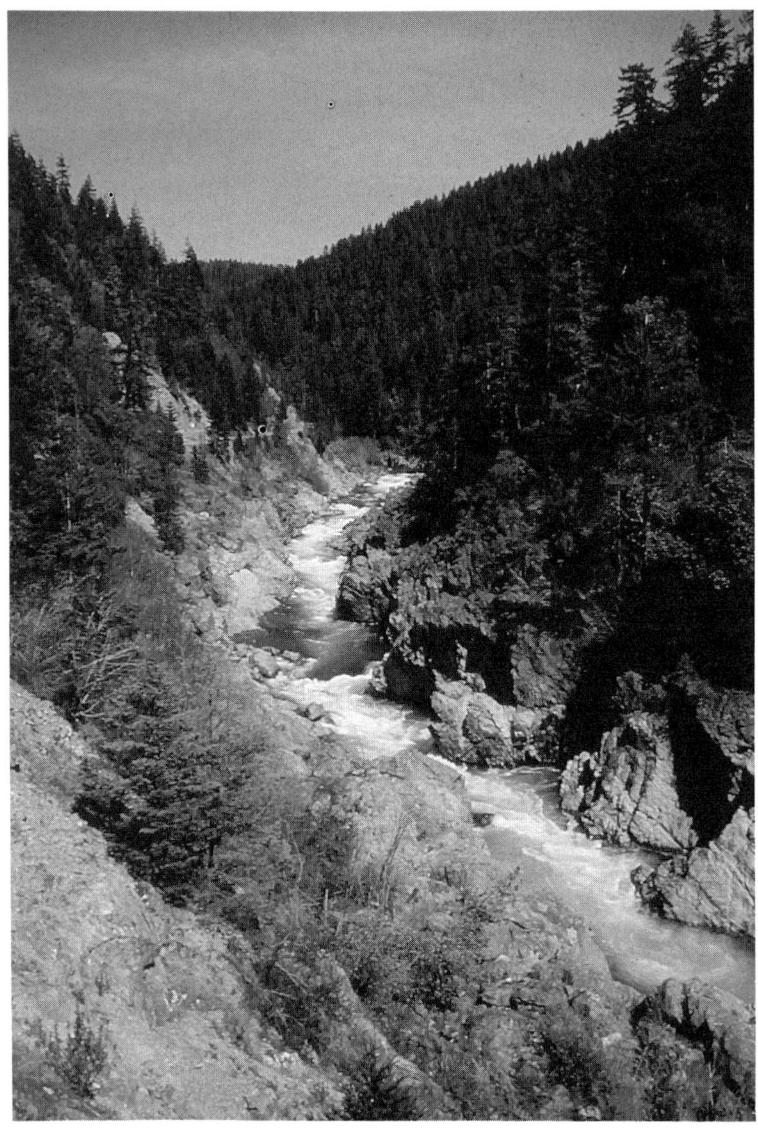

Oregon Hole Gorge, Smith River *Bill Cross*

Smith River

North Fork, Main Smith, and South Fork

1. North Fork Smith: Low Divide Road (880') to Middle Fork Confluence (310').
IV; 13 miles; 44 ft./mi.

2. Main Smith: Gasquet (310') to South Fork Confluence (105').
II+ first 6 miles, V in mile-long Oregon Hole Gorge; 7.7 miles; 27 ft./mi. Longer and shorter runs possible.

3. South Fork Smith: South Fork Road (510') to Main Smith Confluence (105').
III first 12 miles, V in mile-long South Fork Gorge; 13 miles; 30 ft./mi. Longer and shorter runs possible.

Drainage Area: *Run 1:* 157 sq. mi. *Run 2:* 287 sq. mi. *Run 3:* 291 sq. mi. All figures are at or near take-outs.

Season: *Run 1:* November–May. *Run 2:* November–May or June. *Run 3:* October–mid-June. On all runs, occasional heavy rains in the off-season can produce boatable flows for a few days.

Recommended Levels: *Run 1:* 500–2,000 cfs (2,000–7,000 cfs on Jed Smith gauge). *Runs 2 & 3:* 500–3,000 (1,000–6,000 on Jed Smith gauge).

Flow Information: DWR tape, (916) 653-9647. Flow at Jedediah Smith State Park. Estimate as follows: *Run 1:* One third to one quarter of the flow at Jed Smith. *Run 2:* About half. *Run 3:* About half.

Special Hazards: *Run 2:* Oregon Hole Gorge; **experts only below mile 6.2.** *Run 3:* South Fork Gorge; **experts only below mile 11.7.**

Permits: Not presently required on any runs.

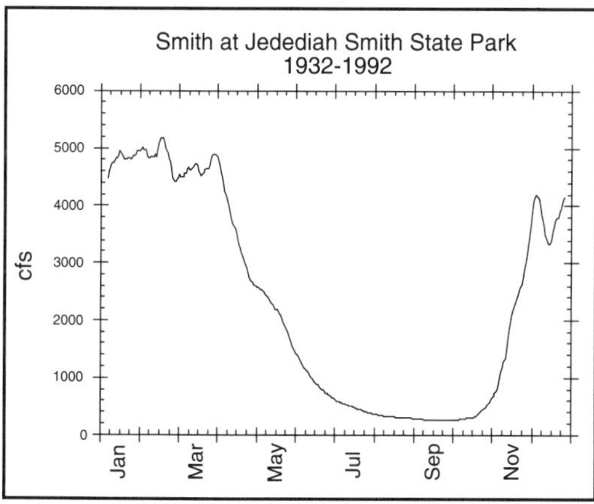

Managing Agency: Gasquet RD, Six Rivers NF, P.O. Box 228, Gasquet, CA 95543; (707) 457-3131.

Commercial Raft Trips: None now. For updates contact the Forest Service.

Side Excursions: Jedediah Smith State Park and other state parks on the coast.

Guides and References:
- Cassady & Calhoun, *California Whitewater: A Guide to the Rivers.*
- Holbek & Stanley, *A Guide to the Best Whitewater in the State of California.*
- *Soggy Sneakers Guide to Oregon Rivers* (Willamette Kayak and Canoe Club).

Land Ownership: Almost all National Forest; a few small private parcels.

Scenery: Excellent.

Solitude: *Run 1:* Excellent. *Run 2:* Good. Highway 199 is usually nearby. *Run 3:* Very good. Road is lightly used and usually high above the river.

Wilderness: *Run 1:* Yes. *Runs 2 & 3:* No.

Maps:
- **USGS 7.5':** *Run 1:* High Plateau Mtn, High Divide, Gasquet. *Run 2:* Gasquet, Hiouchi, Smith River. *Run 3:* Cant Hook Mtn, Hiouchi.
- **USFS:** *Six Rivers NF.*
- **AAA:** *Northwestern California.*

Logistics: *Run 1 (North Fork):* To reach the **put-in**, follow U.S. 199 to the junction with California Highway 197 in Jedediah Smith State Park, some 8 miles east of Crescent City. Turn north on 197, drive 2.5 miles, and turn right on Low Divide (Wimer) Road. Veer right 9.5 miles later at the intersection with Rowdy Creek Road and continue 13 more miles to the put-in at the bridge over the North Fork. There are **two alternate take-outs in Gasquet,** which is located on U.S. 199 some 20 miles east of Crescent City. The **upper take-out** is at the confluence of the North and Middle Forks: turn north off U.S. 199, cross the Middle Fork, then walk down a trail from a turnout on the north side of the bridge to the confluence. An **easier take-out** is 1.5 miles downriver, on the left bank just downstream from a trailer park at the lower end of Gasquet where U.S. 199 joins the river. This access, though commonly used, is on private land. The shuttle is 34 miles one way (22 on a winding dirt road) and takes 1.5 to 2 hours. To hire drivers, ask around in Gasquet (try the Gasquet Store) or Hiouchi.

Run 2 (Main Smith): The **two alternate put-ins at Gasquet** are the same as the take-outs for the North Fork (see above). To reach the **take-out above Oregon Hole Gorge,** drive about 6 miles west of Gasquet on U.S. 199 and find a turnout near Caltrans highway marker 9.09. A short trail leads down to the river. **Scout this spot carefully to be sure you will recognize it from the river.** Experts running the gorge can take out just downstream from the South Fork Road bridge across the main river. Vehicle access is via either of two rough dirt roads: one begins at the intersection of the highway and South Fork Road, the other intersects South Fork Road several hundred yards below the bridge across the Smith.

Run 3 (South Fork): Three miles east of Jedediah Smith State Park, turn south off U.S. 199 onto South Fork Road and drive about 13 miles upstream to the **put-in** at the fourth bridge over the South Fork. (Don't count the bridge over the Main Smith just off U.S. 199.) **Alternate put-ins** are at the second and third bridges, near mile 6. For those not running South Fork Gorge, the **take-out** is reached via a trail from a turnout on South Fork Road a little over a mile above the first bridge over the South Fork (about two miles from U.S. 199). **Scout this spot carefully to be sure you recognize it from the river.** Experts running the gorge may choose among several take-outs: a difficult scramble up a trail on the right bank of the South Fork just downstream from the South Fork Road bridge below the gorge; the State Park campground 2.5 miles downriver; and the U.S. 199 bridge a mile farther down.

Among all of California's significant river systems, only the Smith remains entirely undammed. The main Smith[1], its four forks, and dozens of smaller tributaries—some 3,100 miles of pure, rushing water in all—flow freely down the western slopes of the Siskiyou Mountains in the far northwestern corner of California. This remote watershed receives some 100" of precipitation annually, producing lush riverside forests and one of the state's finest stands of old-growth redwoods in Jedediah Smith State Park.[2] The Smith's outstanding scenery, challenging whitewater, ancient forests, and thriving fisheries have long attracted a small but loyal following of boaters.

In 1990, after decades of struggle, the Smith was permanently protected by a 305,000-acre National Recreation Area. The Smith had previously been protected as a National Wild and Scenic River, but the new designation includes large portions of the watershed not previously protected from destructive logging and other abuses.[3]

The Smith offers whitewater to suit almost every taste and skill level. This guide concentrates on three runs: the North Fork, a Class IV wilderness float; the main Smith, a Class II+ run along U.S. Highway 199 from Gasquet to the South Fork confluence; and the South Fork, a Class III run with an unobtrusive road usually high on the canyon slope. Both the main Smith and the South Fork abruptly change character a mile above their respective take-outs, ending in steep, narrow gorges strewn with Class V rapids. **Only experts should attempt Oregon Hole and South Fork Gorges.** In each case, alternate take-outs enable river runners to avoid these sections if they wish.

Other runs attract some boating. There are ten miles of Class I+ water on the Main Smith from the South Fork confluence through Jedediah Smith State Park, and there is an eight-mile run on the Middle Fork above Gasquet (III4). Highly-skilled whitewater adven-

[1]The river is named for Jedediah Smith (1799-1831), the premier western explorer of his day. Smith tried to hang his name on what is now the lower Klamath, but after decades of confusion, the next river north of the Klamath became the Smith.

[2]This grove was the setting for the spectacular hovercraft chase in the Star Wars film "Return of the Jedi."

[3]In recent years the Smith was seriously threatened by a strip mining proposal by Cal Nickel Corporation. Though the NRA designation does not specifically prohibit this type of mining, it significantly reduces the threat by limiting the price that Cal Nickel can obtain for the minerals.

turers may want to explore the relatively uncharted upper reaches of the North Fork, Middle Fork, Siskiyou Fork, and South Fork.

North Fork Smith

The little-known North Fork Smith, one of California's loveliest wilderness whitewater runs, is lightly used because of its remote location and because summer flows are too low for boating. It is even more a rainy-season river than the other forks of the Smith because its upper watershed, which lies below 5,000', is more than 1,000' lower than the others'. The North Fork rises in southern Oregon near the headwaters of the Chetco River, not far from the Illinois and Rogue drainages. The put-in is just a mile south of the Oregon-California border, deep in virgin forest.

Much of the North Fork's watershed is underlain by old ocean crust that has been scraped up by the thrusting edge of the continent. The local bedrock, known as peridotite, produces soil that is deficient in certain trace elements. Consequently, the trees are stunted and of little economic value, and the North Fork has never been logged. All but the lower reaches of the rocky, rugged canyon are sparsely forested.

The nutrient-poor soil favors the proliferation of unusual plants, notably epiphytes (often called "air" plants because they take most of their sustenance from the air rather than the soil) and the bizarre carnivorous pitcher plant, which can be seen in large numbers along the North Fork, clinging to moist spots on the canyon walls. (Don't worry: they prefer insects and consume boaters only when their regular fare is in short supply.)

One of the North Fork's most outstanding attributes is its crystalline water, which runs clear even after rainstorms—perhaps due to the lack of logging. Countless pristine side creeks cascade into the river, increasing the flow considerably between put-in and take-out. The lack of sediment probably accounts for the scarcity of camping beaches; nevertheless, a few good campsites can be found, and an overnight trip is well worth the effort. One-day trips require an early start due to the long shuttle.

Main Smith

The Smith River proper begins at the confluence of the North and Middle Forks. Though Highway 199 follows this run, the canyon remains beautiful. This is a lovely setting for low-water floats in late spring and early summer, but most boaters should take out above the difficult section known as Oregon Hole Gorge. The Class V rapids in this narrow gorge look much smaller from the highway than they do at river level.

Upstream and Downstream Runs: Downstream from the South Fork confluence are ten miles of Class I and II water through first-growth redwoods in Jedediah Smith State Park. There are several alternate accesses in this section, including the final take-out at the U.S. 101 bridge. This is the lowermost run in the Smith system, and it has the longest boating season.

Another run is upstream on the Middle Fork from Patrick Creek to Gasquet. These eight miles are primarily Class III with one or two Class IV's. U.S. 199 parallels this run, detracting from the scenery and solitude.

South Fork Smith

The South Fork, largest of the Smith's branches, rises near Bear Paw Mountain in the Siskiyou Wilderness. For most of its distance it flows through moderate rapids in a beautiful, heavily forested canyon. Just above its confluence with the main stem, however, the South Fork cuts into the same rock that forms Oregon Hole Gorge on the Main Smith. This resistant bedrock produces South Fork Gorge, a dramatic mile-long canyon laced with Class IV and V rapids.

Though not as pristine as the North Fork, the South Fork Smith's watershed has been only slightly affected by man. Here and there, a logging road or cabin attests to civilization's presence; otherwise, the canyon is much as it has been for thousands of years. All that could change if the proposed Gasquet-Orleans Road becomes a reality. Timber interests want a paved route to connect Elk Valley Road, in the Klamath drainage, with the watershed of the South Fork Smith. In addition to bringing in its wake extensive logging, the road would cut across lands sacred to local Indians.

Boaters on South Fork can enjoy nearly a dozen miles of Class III whitewater before they approach **South Fork Gorge, which is for experts only.** (Other boaters should scout the upstream take-out at mile 11.6 carefully and memorize landmarks so they won't miss it and end up running the gorge.) Most of the gorge can be scouted by scrambling down from the road along the left bank. Small variations in flow can produce dramatic changes in this constricted section. Be alert for brush and snags in the channel, especially after winter rains and floods.

North Fork Smith River Guide

Note: This log contains only very general information about the run. The North Fork is laced with small gorges and frequent Class III and IV rapids. Stop to scout when you can't see a clear route, and remember that winter floods can rearrange rapids and lodge fallen trees across the river.

Put in on the left bank at the Low Divide Road bridge (mile 0). Just over a mile downstream, Diamond Creek, the North Fork's largest tributary, enters on the left. Several hundred yards farther, the North Fork enters the first and probably most difficult of some half-dozen small gorges. Still Creek enters on the right at mile 3.5, offering a good campsite. Downstream, another gorge begins.

Peridotite Canyon enters on the left at mile 8.5, and at mile 11.7 Stony Creek enters on the left. At mile 13 boaters reach the confluence with the Middle Fork, which enters from the left at Gasquet. **Take out** here (carry up to the road) or continue 1.5 miles down the main Smith to the **alternate take-out.**

Main Smith River Guide

Note: This guide does not list specific rapids. Scout carefully; the most difficult spots are hard to see from the highway.

Put in at the confluence of the Middle and North Forks (mile 0), or a mile and a half downstream where U.S. 199 approaches the river at the lower end of Gasquet (see **Logistics**). At mile 2.5 the highway crosses the river, and a mile downstream Hardscrabble Creek enters on the right. The highway leaves the river at mile 4.5, returning again just above the gorge. At mile 6.2 watch for the **alternate take-out**; to avoid running the gorge, take out on the right bank where a short trail leads up to the highway. **Experts only downstream.** At mile 6.5 the river enters narrow, steep-walled **Oregon Hole Gorge** (V). Below the gorge the South Fork Road bridge crosses the river. **Take out** here on either bank, or continue downstream on the Main Smith (Class I+).

South Fork Smith River Guide

Note: This log does not list individual rapids among the many Class II and III passages on the South Fork. Most are technical rock gardens at low and moderate flows.

Put in at the South Fork Road bridge (mile 0). At mile 2.5 Gordon Creek enters on the right. Watch for a more difficult rapid where big boulders divide the current just below a sharp right bend at mile 4; this drop can be seen from the road on the way to the put-in.

Rock Creek enters on the left at mile 5, and about a mile downstream two new bridges cross the river, providing **alternate accesses.** Coon Creek enters on the right at mile 8.5 as the river loops through a horseshoe bend to the left. At mile 11.5 Craigs Creek enters on the right, signalling the **alternate take-out** just downstream where a trail climbs the left bank to the road. **Experts only downstream.**

A quarter mile below the alternate take-out, the river enters beautiful but very difficult **South Fork Gorge** (V). At one point the river drops 80' in less than half a mile.

At mile 13, just below the end of the gorge, South Fork Road crosses overhead; **take out** here via a steep trail up the right bank, or continue to **easier take-outs** at the State Park campground 2.5 miles downstream or at the U.S. 199 bridge a mile farther downriver. The South Fork joins the Main Smith just a few hundred yards below the South Fork Road bridge.

Region VI. Pacific Northwest

Oregon, Washington

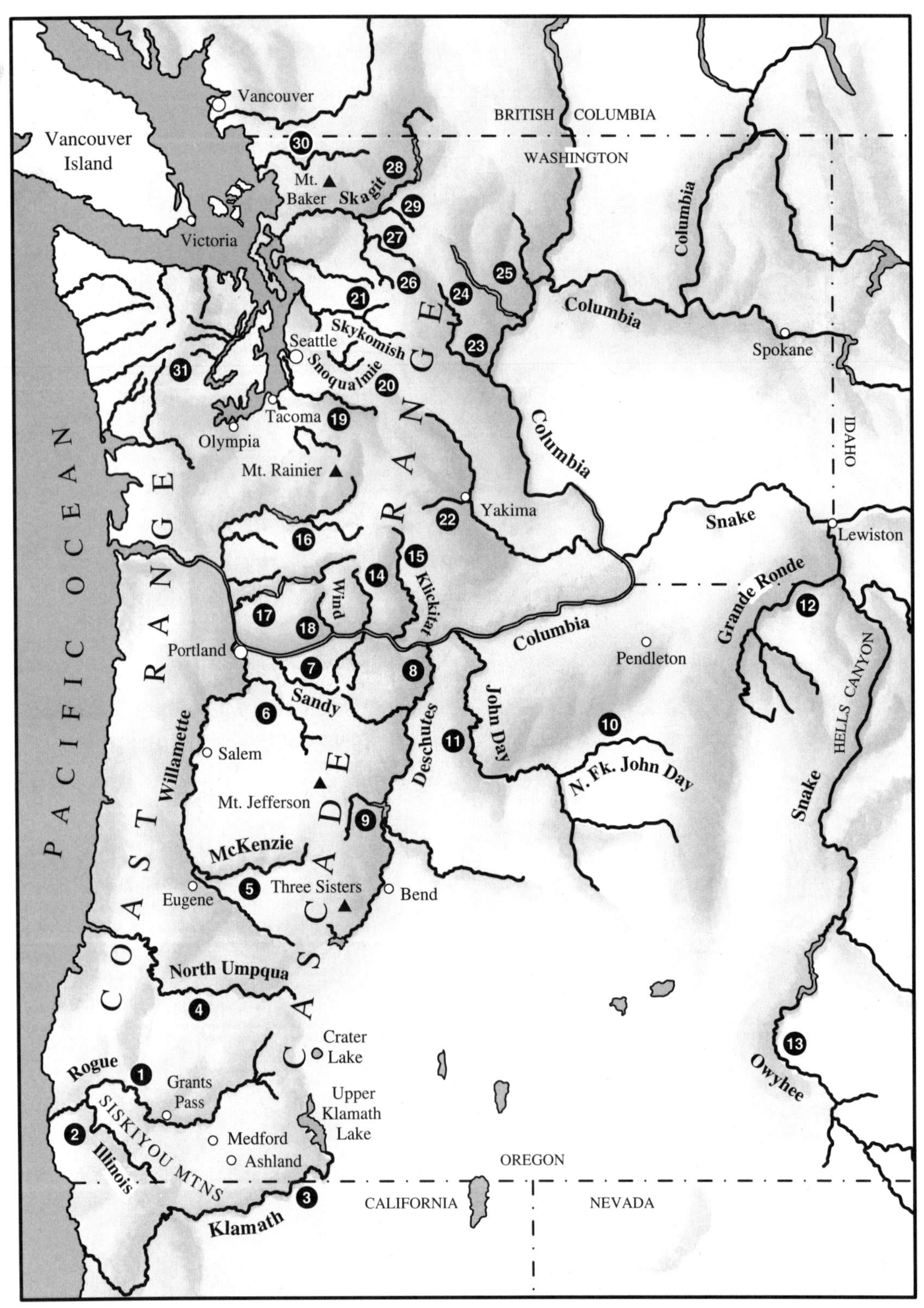

Pacific Northwest

Rivers of the Pacific Northwest

1. Rogue
2. Illinois
3. Upper Klamath
4. North Fork Umpqua
5. McKenzie
6. Clackamas
7. Sandy
8. Deschutes
9. Metolius
10. North Fork John Day
11. Main John Day
12. Grande Ronde
13. Owyhee
14. White Salmon
15. Klickitat
16. Cispus
17. Lewis
18. Wind
19. Green
20. Snoqualmie
21. Skykomish
22. Tieton
23. Wenatchee
24. Chiwawa
25. Methow
26. Sauk
27. Suiattle
28. Skagit
29. Cascade
30. North Fork Nooksack
31. Olympic Peninsula

Pacific Northwest

The Pacific Northwest is a land of contrasts, home to the widest variety of landscapes and rivers in the West. Oregon and Washington seem to have everything: lush rain forests and barren deserts; fiery volcanoes and icy glaciers; small, cascading mountain torrents and the biggest river in the West.

Within this wondrously varied geography, one key feature stands out—the Cascades, the great north-south chain of volcanic peaks that runs more than 500 miles from southern British Columbia to northern California. The Cascades divide the Pacific Northwest into two radically different sections. The western third of Oregon and Washington is by far the wettest region in the West. Frequent Pacific storms drop over 100" of precipitation per year in parts of Washington. Lands east of the Cascades lie in a strong rain shadow, with some desert areas getting as little as 8" of annual precipitation.

With glacier-studded pinnacles rising from a rolling sea of evergreen forest, the Cascades are perhaps the most visually dramatic mountains in the West. Yet they are a relatively low-elevation range. Only nine summits in the Oregon-Washington section of the Cascades exceed 10,000', and only three—Mt. Hood, Mt. Adams and Mt. Rainier—top 11,000'. Most of the range is well below timberline, and all but a few of the passes are under 5,000'. The West's other two great ranges, the Sierra Nevada and the Rockies, are far higher; in Colorado alone, 52 summits top 14,000'.

In spite of the relatively low elevation of the mountains, several factors combine to give many Cascade rivers some of the longest and most consistent seasons in the West. Many areas on the west slope, particularly in northern Oregon and Washington, get occasional summer rain. Also, glaciers on the higher peaks produce steady streams of ice melt in summer. But the most important factor is the porous volcanic rock that underlies most of the range. Water from rain and snowmelt percolates into these rocks, then reemerges through large, steady springs that nourish rivers all year long. The Deschutes and Metolius Rivers in central Oregon are famous for their consistent flows of cold, clear spring water.

The only major break in the Cascades is the Columbia River Gorge, where the West's largest river cleaves a spectacular passage directly through the mountain barrier. The Columbia, the Klamath, and the Pit-Sacramento system are the only rivers that cut through the Cascades. All three predate the mountains and held to their courses when the range began rising about seven million years ago.

The Cascades are not the only mountains in the Pacific Northwest; several other ranges produce outstanding whitewater rivers. In southwestern Oregon the Siskiyou Mountains are home to the region's most famous river trip, the Wilderness Run of the Rogue. In the northeastern corner of the state are the Blue and Wallowa Mountains, which boast fine wilderness rivers like the John Day and Grande Ronde. Running north and south along the western edge of Oregon and Washington, the lush Coast Range produces dozens of short, rainy-season runs. Finally, in northwestern Washington the rain-drenched Olympic Mountains spawn more rivers and more runoff than any area of similar size in the U.S.

Most of the extended wilderness trips in the Pacific Northwest are located in Oregon, while whitewater boating in Washington is primarily limited to one-day trips. Many Washington rivers run down dramatic, U-shaped glacial valleys that are extremely steep in their upper reaches and relatively flat on the valley floors. In between, boaters often find only short stretches of runnable whitewater.

Particulary in Washington, boaters sometimes have more water than they know what to do with. Floods are not uncommon, and many rivers are too high for safe boating during normal peak runoff. River runners visiting Washington from drier parts of the West are often surprised to find that flows they would regard as high back home are considered "low water" on many Washington rivers.

The Pacific Northwest holds the only heavily populated area in the West where people and water are both concentrated in the same place: the wet west side of the Cascades. For drinking water the region's major cities rely primarily on relatively small dams on local rivers. Trans-basin diversions—a commonplace in Colorado and California—are rare in the Pacific Northwest.

Hydropower is the rationale for the region's big dams. The rivers of the Pacific Northwest can generate a staggering amount of electricity. The biggest of all, the Columbia, with an average flow of 250,000 cfs at its mouth, was an early target. Massive hydroelectric dams have turned the river into little more than a chain of reservoirs. Dozens of smaller hydro projects now block rivers throughout Washington and Oregon. Hundreds of miles of outstanding river have been flooded, and native salmon runs that once numbered in the millions have in many cases dwindled to a handful.

At long last a strong local river conservation movement is flexing its muscle in the Pacific Northwest. In 1988 Oregon led the way for other states by adding more than 40 rivers to the National Wild and Scenic Rivers System. Today, a hot topic of debate in the Pacific Northwest is existing dams and their devastating effects on native fish runs. Conservationists are proposing that many dams be altered, and some even removed, in an effort to save the once-abundant salmon. The Elwha River in Washington may become the first in the West to have a major dam torn down.

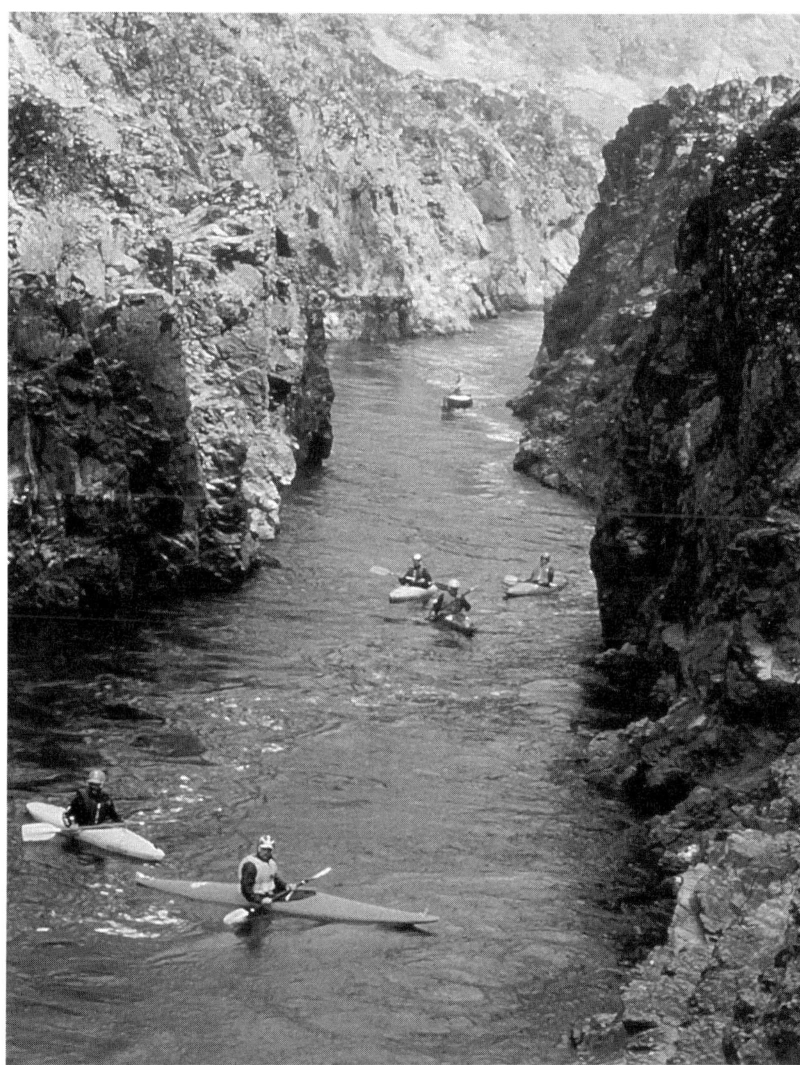

Mule Creek Canyon, Rogue River *James Thomson*

River running in the Pacific Northwest has a long history, beginning with early guides using drift boats (dories) on famous Oregon fishing rivers like the Rogue and McKenzie in the 1920's and 1930's. After the Second World War the popularity of Pacific Northwest rivers increased dramatically, to the point that in 1978 a permit system was instituted to ease crowding on the famous Rogue River. Today, interest has expanded far beyond the Rogue to include many rivers that were virtually unknown to boaters just a decade ago.

Rogue River

Wilderness Run

Difficulty: III+, plus Rainie Falls (V/p).
Length: 34 miles. **Gradient:** 14 ft./mi.
Put-in: Grave Creek (625').
Take-out: Foster Bar (150').
Drainage Area and Average Annual Discharge: 3,940 sq. mi. and 4,798,000 af near take-out.
Peak Recorded Flow: 290,000 cfs (Dec. 23, 1964).
Season: All year. Frequent high water in winter and spring. Never too low. Partially controlled by upstream reservoirs.
Recommended Levels: 1,000–5,000 cfs.
Flow Information: NWS tape, (503) 249-0666, gives the flow at Agness below the take-out. For the flow near the put-in, call NWS tape, (503) 476-5256; NWS staff, (503) 773-1067; or managing agency (see below). For upstream runs call the Army Corps of Engineers, (800) 472-2434, for the inflow and outflow at Lost Creek Reservoir.
Special Hazards: Rainie Falls. Black bears are sometimes a problem.
Permits: Required May 15–Oct. 15 from Grave Creek to Foster Bar. Limited June 1–Sept. 15; available for the asking otherwise. Request information after Sept. 15; applications accepted Jan. 1–mid-Feb.; lottery in early March. Odds of success average roughly one in 9. Odds are worst for large groups on July and August weekends and better for (1) small groups, (2) dates near the beginning and end of the control period, and (3) Sunday–Wednesday start dates. No waiting list; call for unused dates or cancellations beginning the first weekday in April. About 40% of starts go to boaters who call in. Group limit 20. Maximum trip length 7 days.

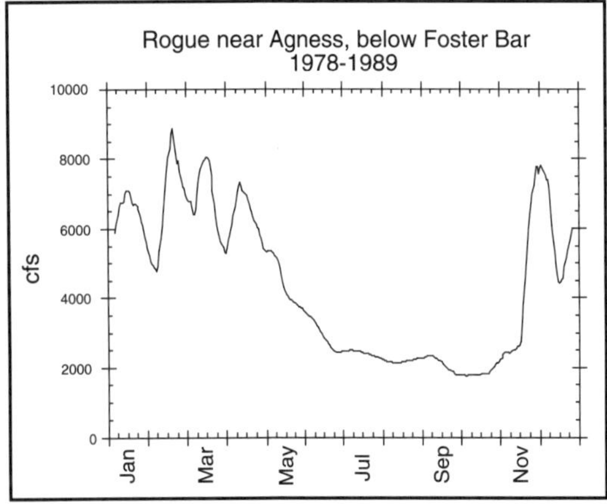

Managing Agency: River Permits Office, 14335 Galice Road, Merlin, OR 97532; (503) 479-3735. Jointly managed by Forest Service and BLM.
Commercial Raft Trips: Yes, many outfitters. Also drift boat fishing trips and a kayak school. Contact the River Permits office for references.
Land Ownership: Almost all National Forest and BLM; a few private parcels.
Scenery: Excellent. Forested canyon becomes very lush toward take-out.
Solitude: Excellent except for heavy boating traffic in summer.
Wilderness: Yes. A few private lodges.
Fishing: Famous steelhead and salmon runs have declined in recent years.
Wildlife: Abundant. Deer, bear, otter, raptors, waterfowl.
Weather: Generally hot in summer, though mornings can be misty. Strong afternoon upstream winds are common. Quite rainy late fall through spring. Generally cooler, cloudier, and rainier as you head downriver toward the coast.
Water: Green and sometimes murky. Purify water from numerous clear side streams.
Camping: Many excellent sites with heavy use; refer to *Rogue River Float Guide* listed below. Outhouses at larger sites. Competition for sites is most intense immediately above Mule Creek Canyon. *Note:* Bears are often problems on lower portions of the run, especially at Tate Creek, Solitude, and Brushy Bar.
Side Hikes: Many lovely side creeks. Lower Rogue Trail follows the right bank of the river.
Side Excursions: Southern Oregon coast. Crater Lake National Park. Hiking along Upper Rogue. Shakespeare Festival in Ashland.
Guides and References:

- *Rogue River Float Guide* (USFS/BLM). Purchase from managing agency. Covers river from Grants Pass to the Pacific.
- *Soggy Sneakers Guide to Oregon Rivers* (Willamette Kayak and Canoe Club).
- Garren, *Oregon River Tours.*

- Quinn, Quinn, & King, *Handbook to the Rogue River Canyon.*
- Kovalik, *Rogue River Guide: Natural and Human History.*
- Purdom, *Guide to the Geology and Lore of the Wild Reach of the Rogue River, Oregon.*
- Arman & Wooldridge, *The Rogue: A River To Run.* Engaging personal history by the Rogue's pioneering river runner.
- Collins & Nash, *The Big Drops.* Essay on Rainie Falls and river history.
- Atwood, *Illahe: The Story of Settlement in the Rogue River Canyon.*
- Orr & Orr, *Rivers of the West: A Guide to The Geology and History.*
- Jackman & Bernstein, *Hip-Pocket Naturalist: A Guide to Oregon's Rogue River Basin.*
- Zane Grey, *Forlorn River; Rogue River Feud; Tales of Fresh Water Fishing.*

Maps:

- **USGS 7.5':** *Mt. Reuben, Bunker Creek, Kelsey Peak, Marial, Illahe.*
- **USFS:** *Kalmiopsis Wilderness/Wild Rogue Wilderness,* which covers miles 12–34; and *Siskiyou NF,* useful for the shuttle.
- *Riverguide Bandana to the Rogue.* (Rivers & Mountains). Cloth map.

Auto Shuttle: Roughly 50 miles (two hours) one way. For shuttle service references, contact the managing agency.

Logistics: To reach the **put-in,** take the Merlin exit (# 61) from I-5 just north of Grants Pass and drive west on Merlin-Galice Road, which reaches the Rogue in about 8 miles, crosses the river, and then follows the left bank downstream. Three miles beyond the hamlet of Galice, pick up your permit at the Rand Visitor Center. About 4.5 miles farther downstream, the road crosses the Rogue on Grave Creek Bridge. Put in just below the bridge on the right bank. Many **alternate put-ins** are farther upstream, notably Almeda Bar some 4 miles above Grave Creek.

To reach the **take-out,** return upstream to Galice and turn right (west) on paved BLM Road 34-8-36 (becomes USFS Road 23), which runs some 35 miles over a 5,000' divide and returns to the Rogue just above the hamlet of Agness. Upon reaching the river turn right on the paved road, drive upstream a mile and a half, cross the Rogue, bear right again, and drive upstream about 3 more miles to the hamlet of Illahee and the Foster Bar take-out.

Note: A free shuttle map is available from the managing agency. Snow often blocks the shuttle road until late spring. A long alternate shuttle, open year round, follows U.S. Highways 199 and 101 through Crescent City, California and Gold Beach, Oregon.

> The dark green slopes, the darker green river, sliding, whirling, foaming around the shaded bend, the grand bronze and fern festooned cliffs, the black rocks that were sections of a splintered mountain.... These seemed alive under the purple mantle of the lifting mist, gleaming in that subdued and supernatural light like the strange glow of low clouds before a storm.
>
> —Zane Grey, *Rogue River Feud*

Oregon's Rogue River is one of the West's most famous and enchanting waterways. Its canyon is a Pacific Coast wonderland of deep green pools, lush forests, and sparkling waterfalls. In its wilderness ancient forces still hold sway. The canyon's dark forests shelter an abundance of wildlife, while the river itself has long been famous for world-class fishing and fine whitewater boating. In 1968 the Rogue's surpassing beauty earned it a place among the eight charter members of the National Wild and Scenic Rivers System. Sad to say, the river's famous salmon and steelhead runs have declined in recent years. Possible causes include dams, drought, logging, pollution, and overfishing.

From its headwaters along the crest of the Cascade Range near Crater Lake in southwestern Oregon, the Rogue runs generally west some 200 miles to the Pacific. In its volcanic upper watershed, lava flows have created natural dams across the river's path; here, the Rogue alternates between placid pools and violent cataracts. In its middle reaches the river flows more gently through the open terrain of the Rogue Valley, famous as a fruit growing center and retirement mecca. Finally, below the city of Grants Pass, the river begins cutting its lower canyons through the Coast Range.

The wilderness run featured in this chapter is the heart of the oldest and most famous river trip in the Pacific Northwest. (It is also called the Wild Rogue, Lower Rogue, Rogue River Canyon, and—by some locals—"The Canyon.") In the 1920's and 1930's the Rogue's superb salmon and steelhead runs began to attract anglers. Later, river runners came to "shoot the rapids" in small wooden boats, foldboats, and military surplus rafts. In those early days of whitewater boating, the Rogue developed a fearsome reputation as one of the West's most dangerous rivers. Rainie Falls, by far the biggest rapid on the run, was considered one of the most lethal of the West's "Big Drops."

Things have changed. Today the Rogue, with exciting but generally forgiving rapids at moderate summer flows, is regarded as a classic family float. Even Rainie Falls is now run fairly frequently. For the vast majority who still take a sneak chute around Rainie, the biggest challenge comes at Blossom Bar, a Class IV-boulder garden. Elsewhere the rapids are Class III or easier, and they are often separated by long, placid pools.

The Rogue's historical descent down the scale of difficulty from fearsome to friendly is not entirely the result of improved whitewater skills and equipment. In fact, early boaters faced a much more dangerous river than the one we know today. Upstream dams have taken much of the fierceness out of the Rogue, not only by taming its periodic wild floods[1] but also by capturing logs washed down from the heavily forested upper watershed. Log jams were once among the Rogue's biggest hazards, especially in the narrow confines of Mule Creek Canyon.

Even more significant was the wholesale dynamiting of the Rogue's rapids by early river runners. Using explosives supplied free by the Forest Service, they blasted dozens of boulders out of the main channel. The result was the smooth, glassy drops that seem so easy today. Due to the dynamiting, the Rogue's difficulty increases less at higher flows than that of most other rivers: with fewer big boulders in the channel, not so many large hydraulics form at high water. Before the dams and the blasting, the Rogue was probably closer in appearance and difficulty to its largest tributary, the Class IV+ Illinois River.

Upstream dams have also contributed to the decline of the river's famous salmon and steelhead fishery, in spite of the Army Corps' construction of Oregon's largest fish hatchery to offset lost spawning habitat. Lost Creek Dam, biggest in the Rogue drainage, flooded ten of the Rogue's best miles, burying outstanding scenery and fine intermediate whitewater.

Dams and dynamite notwithstanding, the Rogue remains a beauty by any measure. The canyon from Grave Creek to Foster Bar is an unspoiled wilderness except for occasional rustic riverside lodges[2] which detract little from the deep sense of isolation and solitude. Hikes up crystalline side creeks lead to lovely waterfalls and deep swimming holes. An unbroken forest mantles the steep canyon—lush green Douglas Fir on shadier sites, oak and madrone on drier slopes. Wildlife is remarkably abundant, and deer, otter, eagle, osprey, heron, and **bear**[3] are common.

Every year some 6,000 boaters apply for 650 private boating permits on the Rogue. The 120 river runners allowed to launch each day (60 commercial, 60 private) share the Rogue with hikers, anglers and others. In fall and winter fishing dories ("drift boats") outnumber rafts and kayaks. In the summer big jet boats ply the river above Grave Creek and below Blossom Bar, whisking sightseers down from Grants Pass or up from the coast. Jet boats have a long history on the Rogue, beginning early in the twentieth century when they delivered mail and supplies to remote riverside homesteads. Not all river runners appreciate these noisy craft, but relations are generally courteous. Etiquette calls for river runners to yield the main

[1]The Rogue's most famous flood occurred in December 1964, when warm, torrential rains melted a heavy snowpack. Not far below the take-out, the raging waters swept away a bridge perched 90' above normal river level.

[2]Some lodges take reservations from private boaters. Contact the River Permits office for information.

[3]Alhough they are not considered dangerous (unless provoked), black bears can be a major nuisance. In recent years sloppy camping habits have encouraged more brazen assaults on coolers and food boxes. At least one bear actually boarded a boat and punctured it in the process—so storing food overnight on rafts floating in eddies is discouraged. Boaters should be extra careful with food and garbage, maintain a clean campsite, and consider avoiding camps with a history of problems (see **Camping** and contact the River Permits office). One good anti-bear method is to seal coolers and boxes tightly with cam straps, then tie them all together to create a big, awkward bundle. Other methods recommended by local boaters include placing a bowl of ammonia on or near garbage and food containers and keeping a lantern burning all night. Although the bears were here first, if push comes to shove it is unfortunately the bears who will lose. So avoiding contact is the best way to protect them.

channel where possible; in return the jetboat will slow down, if it can, to reduce its wake.

Rogue River country's earliest inhabitants were Indians of the Takelma and Tutuni cultures, who subsisted primarily on fish from the river. Exploration by whites brought conflict and friction, and early French trappers were soon referring to the local Indians as "coquins"—rogues—and the river as "La Rivière aux Coquins." Anglo settlers later translated the name and shortened it to Rogue River.[4]

White settlement boomed after a local gold discovery in 1851, and within four years the conflict between whites and Indians reached a climax. In the Rogue River Wars of 1855-56, the U.S. Army and local volunteers invaded the canyon from both ends, trapping and eventually defeating the Indians. Of an Indian population of 10,000 before the whites arrived, only 2,000 remained at the end of the war. Most were sent to reservations in northern Oregon.[5]

In this century the Rogue became a popular vacation spot. In the 1920's and 1930's writer Zane Grey retreated here, fishing and gathering material for his tales. President Herbert Hoover and many Hollywood stars fished the river and sometimes shot the rapids. As commercial and private river running increased, the Rogue developed a rich boating history. Many stories from the early days can be found in *A River to Run,* the personal history of the Rogue's most famous early boater (and dynamiter), Glen Wooldridge.

Master Blasters on the Rogue

Experienced boaters notice that the Rogue has a number of suspiciously clean rapids—broad, glassy tongues rolling down into big, harmless symmetrical waves. The abundance of forgiving roller-coaster chutes is no fluke. Almost every major rapid on the river was blasted to some extent in the 1930's and 1940's by early boaters trying to smooth out the rough passages.

The method was simple enough: fill a sack with explosives, weight it with stones, row up to the offending rock, light the fuse, drop the sack, and "row like hell." Sometimes the rock didn't move; sometimes it ended up in an even worse spot. But with persistence and dynamite, the blasters could make almost any drop runnable. Early photos of Blossom Bar show a completely impenetrable boulder maze before early river runners blew out enough obstacles for small jet boats to negotiate the rapid.

Pioneer boater Glen Wooldridge participated in much of the dynamiting and described the efforts in his book A River to Run. *"We worked on the river a lot. Any place of consequence that gave us any trouble at all, we blasted the rocks out.... I remember one time at Blossom Bar we shot a fifty pound box of powder at one shot. That kind of shook things up a bit. There were three big boulders leaning together with a big hole in the middle. We just put in fifty pounds of powder and eliminated all three of them. Andy Huggins, who lived at the top of Devil's Stair and on the other side of the river, about a quarter of a mile away, came down and complained that we had shot a boulder into his yard.... Powder wasn't much of a problem, because the Forest Service was furnishing it. I remember they delivered a thousand pounds to me at one time, at Blossom Bar .... We done a lot of work at Kelsey Falls. We changed the channel from one side of the river to the other.... Then we came on up to Horseshoe Bend, and Jenny Creek ... bombed Hell out of that." And on and on. Black Bar Falls, Tyee, Wildcat, Grave Creek Falls—nearly every major rapid on the run.*

Upper Rogue

There is boatable water in a number of sections of the Upper and Middle Rogue, upstream from the Wild Rogue stretch featured in this chapter. Refer to the *Rogue River NF* map.

The scenic, heavily forested reach above Lost Creek Reservoir in Rogue River National Forest was added to the National Wild and Scenic River System in 1988. Expert boaters sometimes run short sections of the Upper Rogue, but the river is peppered with lethal waterfalls, unrunnable gorges, and severe log hazards. **With one exception, the Upper Rogue is for adventurous experts only.** Even they must avoid many unrunnable sections. Most boaters should be content with hiking the scenic Forest Service trail that follows the river. Those considering runs should scout carefully first from this trail.

The exception to the experts-only rule is a delightful five-mile stretch of intermediate to

[4]Our information on the meaning of this and other Oregon river names comes from Lewis McArthur, *Oregon Geographic Names.*

[5]For more on the Rogue River Wars, refer to Frank Walsh, *Indian Battles Along the Rogue River* (North Bend, OR: Te-Cum-Tom Publications, 1972).

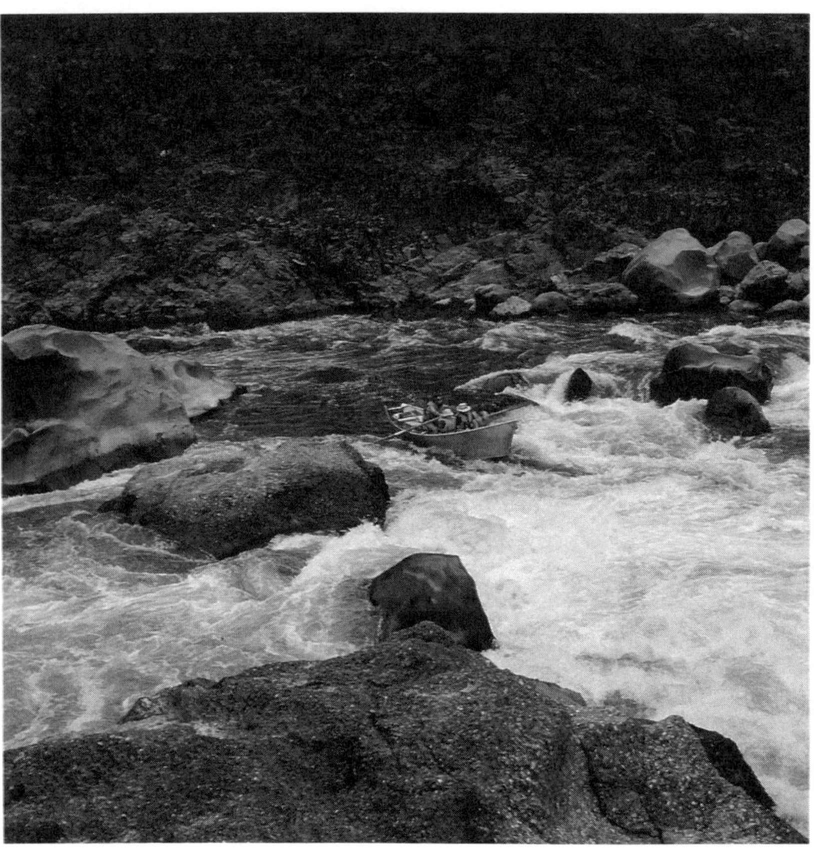

Blossom Bar, Rogue River *Dennis Sammut*

advanced water which starts at the bridge near River Bridge Campground and ends just above a diversion dam near the hamlet of Prospect. **Be especially alert for log hazards.** Above River Bridge Campground are the scenic narrows of Class V **Takelma Gorge,** occasionally run by expert boaters.

Middle Rogue

The Rogue's middle reaches offer several popular runs. Pleasant Class II water extends some 25 miles from the base of Lost Creek Dam to Tou Velle State Park above Gold Ray Dam. Frequent access and proximity to the city of Medford make this a popular local float. Riverside houses detract from the gentle scenery near the town of Shady Cove.

Two challenging rapids lie between Gold Ray Dam and the town of Gold Hill. Some three miles below the dam, the river splits around a rocky island at **NUGGET FALLS (III+).** Take the left channel, which narrows to a steep chute with strong reversals. Scout left. Below the falls a mile-long pool leads to a **river-wide weir. Approach with caution,** especially at higher flows.

Immediately below the weir is **POWERHOUSE (IV),** where the river divides into many narrow, rocky chutes. Scout this rapid carefully before running the weir; the route is hard to see from upstream. For more information refer to the *Soggy Sneakers Guide to Oregon Rivers.*

Hog Creek Run

Class II water extends for 30 miles from the outskirts of Grants Pass to the head of the permit section at Grave Creek. Here the river begins cutting into the Coast Range, its canyon growing steadily deeper and narrower. With fine scenery, frequent access, Wild and Scenic recognition, and proximity to Grants Pass, this section is very popular—especially the 16 miles from Hog Creek Landing to Grave Creek. This stretch is covered in detail in *Rogue River Float Guide* (USFS/BLM) and Michael Walker, *Handbook to the Rogue River's Hog Creek Float.*

Mile by Mile Guide

0 **PUT-IN.** Grave Creek Boat Ramp on the right bank, just below Grave Creek Bridge. No drinking water at this site. Many **alternate put-ins** farther upstream. The Lower Rogue Trail begins on the right bank and follows the entire run. Class III- whitewater begins immediately downstream with **GRAVE CREEK** and **GRAVE CREEK FALLS.**

1 The river splits around a large island. At the foot of the island, a sign high on the right wall next to the trail marks the crest of the December 1964 flood.

1.7 **RAINIE FALLS (V).** Named for "Old Man Rainie" who lived here and gaffed salmon at the falls. **Recognition:** A horizon line at the end of a long pool warns boaters to pull over. Scout from either bank; the left offers better views, but boaters must then ferry back to the right to run, line, or portage. **The rapid:** Most of the river drops over a 12' ledge on the left into a chaotic hydraulic. Though boaters occasionally run the main falls, most pick one of two alternate chutes to the right. The "Fish Ladder," an artificial channel blasted down the far right, is shallow and rocky but provides a route for running or lining moderate-sized boats (difficult at low flows). Portages are along its right bank. The middle chute, a narrow Class IV staircase, carries enough water for larger boats, but its tricky entrance involves a close approach to the worst part of the main falls. Above 2,000 cfs or so the risk of being swept over the main falls increases. Scout carefully from shore; the middle chute's entrance is difficult to see from river level. Also, beware of bridging in its abrupt, jarring drops.

3 Whiskey Creek enters on the right and Rum Creek on the left. Short hike up Whiskey Creek to a mining cabin built around 1880. Just downstream is Big Slide, where in the late 1800's a massive landslide briefly blocked the river, backing water more than 15 miles upstream.

4.5 **TYEE (III)**, a left bend studded with rocks and holes, with a house rock on the left. The name is an Indian word for "chief." Just downstream at **WILDCAT (III-)**, the river splits into two long, rocky channels. A mile farther, Howard Creek enters on the left. Many Class II rapids in the following two miles.

8 Big Windy Creek enters on the left. Just downstream is **UPPER BLACK BAR FALLS (III-)**, a rock garden where the current sweeps into the right wall. Scout right. More difficult at higher flows, when a big hole develops. **LOWER BLACK BAR FALLS (II+)** is about 100 yards downstream, and Black Bar Lodge is out of sight above the left bank.

10.5 Horseshoe Bend. Class II and III- rapids as the river turns right, then sweeps through a long bend to the left.

12–13 **Kelsey Canyon.** Sculpted rock walls close in, stirring the river into boils and small waves. Then as the walls recede, Kelsey Creek enters on the right.

14 Battle Bar, site of an 1856 skirmish between the U.S. Cavalry and Rogue Indians. More than 500 troops under Colonel Kelsey occupied the right bank, firing at some 200 Indians, mostly women and children, on the left bank. 20 to 30 Indians died; only one soldier was killed. A mile downstream on the right is Winkle Bar, site of Zane Grey's cabin (private property, but tourists are welcome).

19.5 Mule Creek enters on the right. Very popular campsites on the right offer the last good camping before Mule Creek Canyon. Rogue River Ranch, with its beautifully restored turn-of-the-century home, sits back on the grassy bench above the right bank. Marial Lodge is on the right a half mile below the creek. The small settlement of Marial lies hidden in the trees on the right. Unpaved Marial Road ends here (**emergency access**).

20.8–21.5 **Mule Creek Canyon.** Two house rocks in the channel mark the entrance to this impressive defile. Fluted vertical walls of hard, metamorphosed volcanic rock close in, churning the current into boils, whirlpools, and diagonal waves, making this a

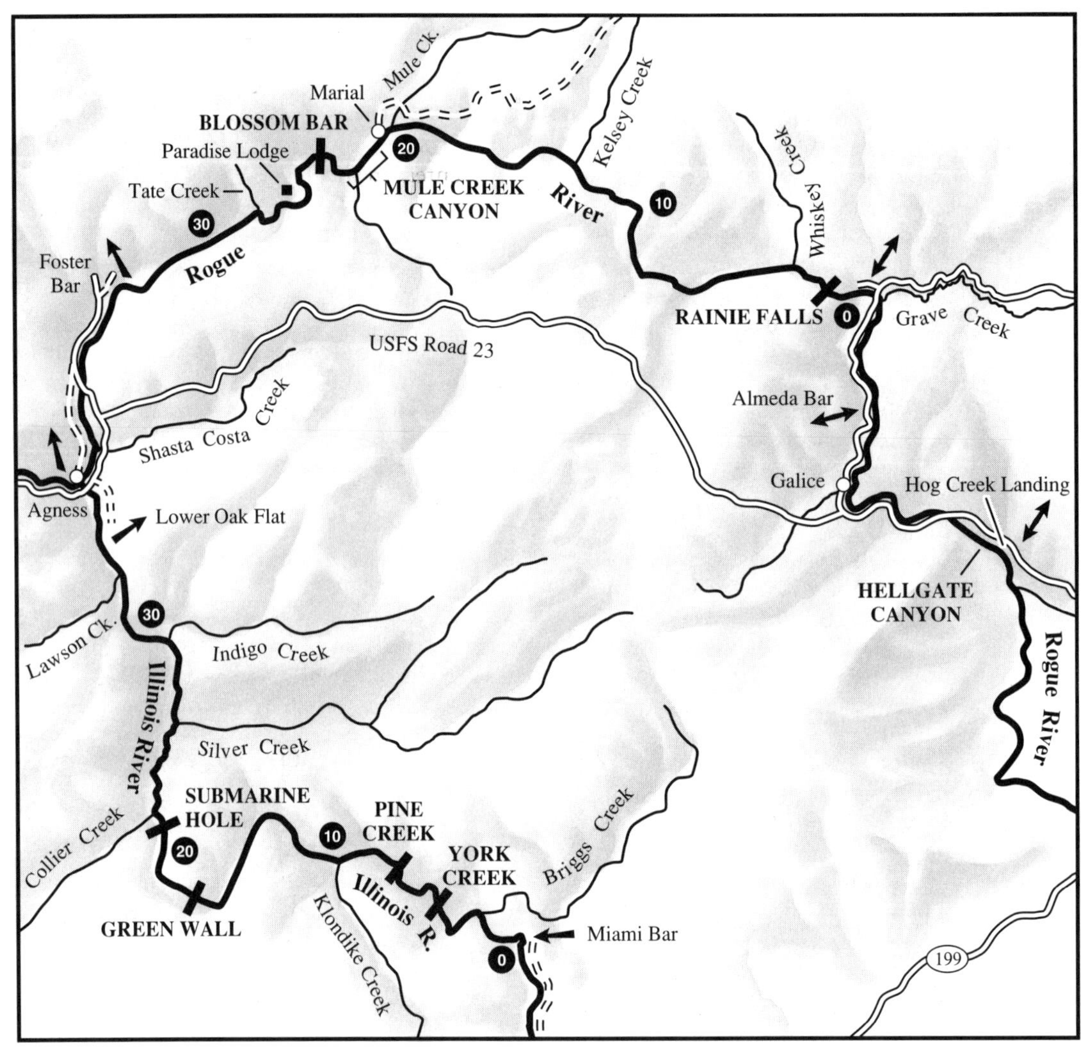

Rogue and Illinois

Class III passage. At one point the river is less than 10' wide. In the constricted section called **Coffee Pot,** the turbulence can be especially powerful. In case of mishap, long swims are possible since the walls are mostly sheer. The entire canyon can be scouted from the trail on the right. Near the end of the canyon, Stair Creek enters in a beautiful falls on the left. Difficult but rewarding side hike up the creek.

22.5 **BLOSSOM BAR** (IV-), named for wild azaleas blooming here. Since most boaters choose not to run Rainie Falls, this long, technical boulder garden is usually the biggest rapid of the trip. **Recognition:** many house rocks appear as the river bends left through flat, moving water. **Mandatory scout,** even for those who know the rapid, from the rocky bluff high on the right. Frequent mishaps and poor rescue techniques can result in rescue lines being strung across the runnable channels. **The rapid:** In the standard run, boaters catch a critical eddy behind a house rock at the top left, move quickly to the center, and then rock-hop their way down various alternate routes. Those who miss the eddy at the top are either swept down a nasty left-hand chute or hung up on a row of rocks known as the "Picket

Fence." At high flows this rapid develops big hydraulics and is more difficult.

Just downstream is **DEVILS STAIRCASE (II+)**, where a long chain of waves washes into a rock spur jutting from the right wall. Downstream the gradient decreases, the current slows, and the rapids are all Class II to II+. Jet boats, which can ascend the river to the foot of Blossom Bar, may be seen at any time.

23.5 Paradise Lodge high on the right. Cold drinks, airstrip, emergency radio. Just downstream on the left, steep stairs climb to Half Moon Bar Lodge (airstrip).

28 Tate Creek enters on the right, with a popular side hike to a sliding rock. Downstream the canyon shifts from hard volcanic rocks to softer sedimentary strata: sandstone, siltstone, shale, and conglomerates. Three quarters of a mile below Tate Creek, Clay Hill Lodge appears on the right. Just below the lodge is **CLAY HILL (II+)**, followed by a beautiful pool known as Clay Hill Stills. Nearly two miles long, this calm can be exhausting when upstream winds kick up in the afternoon.

30.5 Flora Dell Creek enters on the right, with a beautiful falls up near the hiking trail. A mile below the creek, Wild River Lodge appears on the left.

32.5–33.5 Big Bend, a long curve to the left. Site of the final conflict of the Rogue River Wars in May 1856.

34 **TAKE-OUT.** Foster Bar Boat Ramp on the right. Camping. The Rogue continues 35 more miles through Class I and II water to the Pacific Ocean at Gold Beach. A paved road follows this final reach, which passes magnificent stands of old-growth Douglas-fir and Port Orford cedar.

There's something about a bloodcurdling scream of terror that puts a damper on things; particularly honeymoon kinds of things. It was two nights before our long-awaited nuptial trip down the Rogue: just me and Bill, and all the makings for heavy romance—no schedule to keep or other people to suit, perfect weather, and clear starry nights with meteor showers predicted.

On our way to the Rogue we stopped to camp along the Scott River on a secluded beach a short hike down from the road. It was perfect timing. Just as we were snuggling into our bags the still night air was ripped apart by the snarls and grunts of an attack followed by the aforementioned bloodcurdling scream. A very big something was enjoying dinner, a scant distance across the very low, narrow, late-season river. We of course did what any sensible piece of meat would do in the face of a hungry carnivore—we ran. We spent the rest of the sleepless night huddled in the cab of our pickup, scared witless.

Feeling like utter fools in the next morning's warm sunshine, we each pretended that we had only slept in the pickup to keep the other company. Laughing the incident off—and hardly believing it had really happened, since the Beast had left no bloody tracks—we soon dismissed it and continued on our way up north.

Little did we realize the mythic proportions The Scream would assume on our little love cruise that week. Bears are an accepted fact of life along the Rogue, and, for most boaters, merely a tolerable nuisance. But with imaginations fueled by The Scream, the bears metamorphosed into monstrously huge demons, flesh-eating maniacs armed tooth and claw and bent on our slaughter.

By wit and ingenuity, we survived. Among other survival tactics, we armed ourselves nightly with camera flashes, air horns and Buck knives; deluded ourselves that our tiny nylon pup tent was a fortress; further deluded ourselves by camping one night on an island (fact: bears can swim); kept the kerosene lantern burning all night and slept fitfully between false alarms (fact: the rustling noises outside your tent are more likely to be deer and squirrels than bears).

So ... did we see any bears on our trip? No. Did we feel like gutless fools at take-out? (Hint: we rowed furiously from Marial to Foster Bar, to hasten take-out by a day in order to avoid the bear paradise of Brushy Bar.) Yes, gutless fools, and worse. Conclusion? Disastrous honeymoons are at least good for a laugh (post-mortem) and can even be more valued in the long run than the predictable week in Hawaii. And how often do you hear a bear story that doesn't feature an actual bear?

—Polly Greist

Illinois River

Miami Bar to Lower Oak Flat

Difficulty: IV+ (V above 3,000 cfs).
Length: 32 miles. **Gradient:** 24 ft./mi.
Put-in: Miami Bar (870').
Take-out: Lower Oak Flat (115').
Drainage Area and Average Annual Discharge: 988 sq. mi. and 3,234,000 af near take-out.
Peak Recorded Flow: 225,000 cfs (Dec. 22, 1964).
Season: Nov.–May. Extremely variable; mostly rain runoff. Best conditions are often from early March to late May.
Recommended Levels: 600–2,000 cfs on the Kerby gauge.
Flow Information: NWS tape, (503) 249-0666, or NWS staff, (503) 773-1067. Flow at Kerby, 15 miles above the Miami Bar put-in. Flows are somewhat higher at the put-in and usually significantly higher (up to three times) at the take-out.
Special Hazards: Unpredictable and variable flows and weather. Remote area. Cold water. Green Wall Rapid.
Permits: Unlimited; available at Selma Market (see **Logistics**).
Managing Agency: (1) River Permits Office, 14335 Galice Road, Merlin OR 97532; (503) 479-3735. (2) Gold Beach RD, Siskiyou NF, 1225 S. Ellensburg, Box 7, Gold Beach, OR 97444; (503) 247-6651.
Commercial Raft Trips: Yes, three outfitters. Contact Siskiyou NF for references.
Land Ownership: Almost all National Forest.
Scenery: Excellent. Steep, heavily forested canyon. Recent fire scars.
Solitude: Excellent. Very little boating traffic.
Wilderness: Yes.

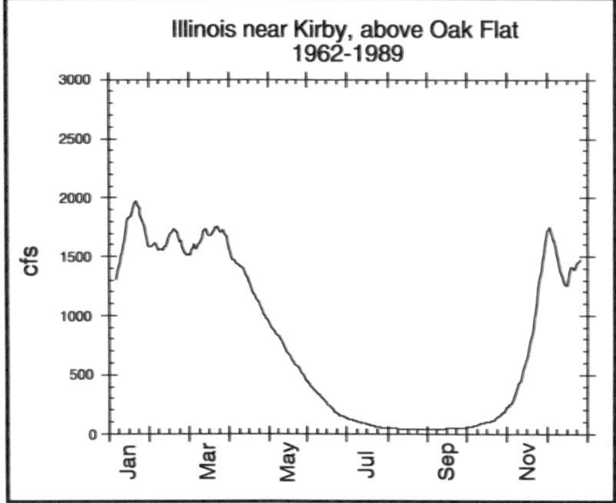

Weather: Variable and unpredictable; often cold and rainy.
Water: Cold and clear. Don't drink river water (upstream agriculture); purify water from side streams.
Camping: Sites are sparse and limited, sometimes with difficult access. Few good riverside sites. Most are on benches above steep, rocky banks. Some long stretches have almost no good spots, so plan carefully. Camp high; the river can rise rapidly. Refer to *Floating the Illinois River* and/or the Quinn *Handbook to the Illinois* listed below.
Side Hikes: Limited due to steep terrain. Some trails are mentioned in the **Mile Guide.**
Side Excursions: Oregon Caves National Monument. Oregon coast. Illinois River Falls, a waterfall about 5 miles above the put-in.
Guides and References:

- *Floating the Illinois River* (Oregon State Parks). Small map-pamphlet.
- Quinn, Quinn, & King, *Handbook to the Illinois River Canyon.*
- *Soggy Sneakers* (Willamette Kayak and Canoe Club).
- Garren, *Oregon River Tours.*
- Jackman & Bernstein, *Hip-Pocket Naturalist: A Guide to Oregon's Rogue River Basin.*

Maps:

- **USGS 7.5':** *Pearsoll Peak, York Butte, Silver Peak, Tincup Peak, Horse Sign Butte, Agness.*
- **USFS:** *Kalmiopsis Wilderness/Wild Rogue Wilderness.* Best all-around map for this run; available from Siskiyou NF.
- **USFS:** *Siskiyou NF* also covers the run.

Auto Shuttle: 95–160 miles (3–6 hours) one way, depending on route. For shuttle service references contact the River Permits office in Galice.
Logistics: To reach the **put-in,** follow U.S. 199 to Selma, Oregon (about 23 miles southwest of Grants Pass). Drive west on Illinois River Road (USFS Road 3504), which eventually becomes dirt and may require 4-wheel drive when wet. About 7 miles from Selma, take the left (downhill) fork. Nine miles farther, the road descends steeply to the right bank at the Miami Bar put-in.

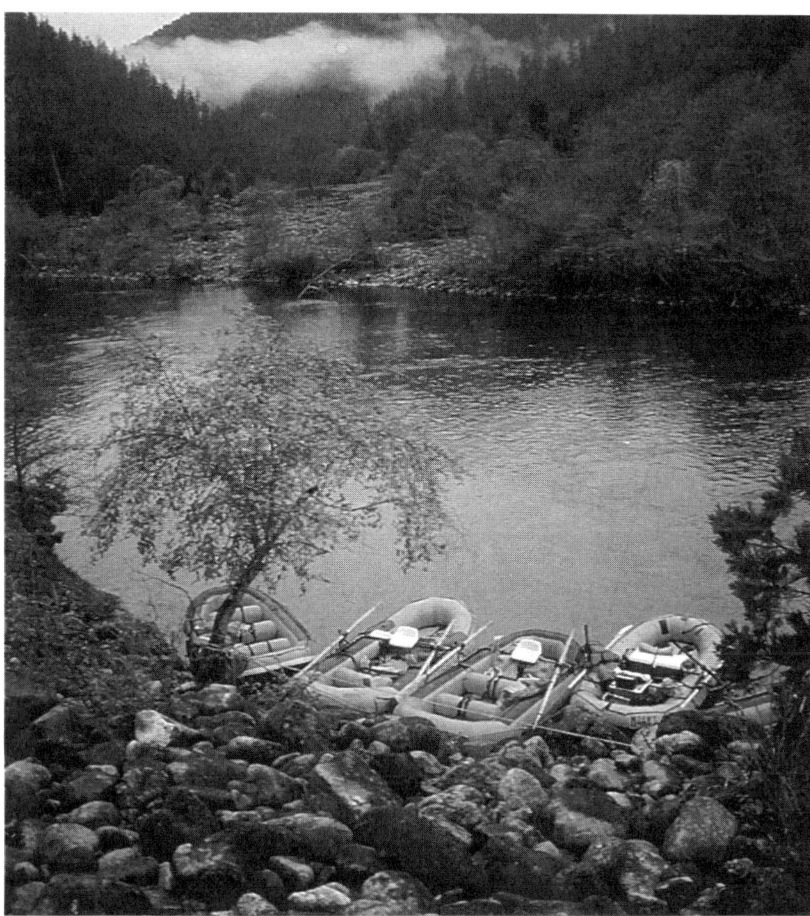

Illinois River *Pete Gillette*

Among river runners in southern Oregon and northern California, the suggestion "Let's do the Illinois this year" is the equivalent of "Let's do lunch" in Hollywood. Everybody talks about running this exotic coastal river, but somehow the trips just don't seem to come together very often. Despite its excellent name recognition and location within a day's drive of some of the West's biggest boating communities, the Illinois usually sees only a few hundred boaters—commercial and private—each year.

The reasons are simple: weather and water. Most of the Illinois' relatively low-elevation basin in the Siskiyou Mountains along the Oregon-California border lies below 4,000', so it rarely has enough snowpack to extend boating much beyond the spring rainy season. Furthermore, the watershed's relatively impervious soils shed rainwater quickly, producing sudden fluctuations in river level with each fresh storm. In other words, you have to boat when the weather is usually lousy, and you can't predict what the flow will be from one day to the next.

In fact, the river may rise or fall significantly between the time you leave your home and the time you put in, or—worse yet—between the time you put in and the time you take out. More than a few boaters have been stranded halfway down the run by sudden high water. Even when conditions don't change, the numerous tributaries along the way can double or triple the flow by the take-out.

Nevertheless, the Illinois remains near the top of the "to-do" list for many West Coast boaters, and for good reason. In its northwesterly passage through the rugged coastal mountains of southwest Oregon, this largest tributary

There are two alternate routes to the **take-out.** The shorter is often snowed in until late spring; contact the Forest Service for road conditions.

Short route: From Selma drive northeast on U.S. 199 to Grants Pass and I-5, then follow the Rogue shuttle route, taking BLM Road 34-8-36 (which becomes USFS Road 23) from Galice to the Rogue about two miles upstream from the Illinois confluence. Drive down the Rogue about 1.5 miles, turn left on Road 450, and drive about 4 miles up the Illinois to Lower Oak Flat. To reach the **alternate take-out at Agness,** from Road 23 drive about 1.5 miles up the Rogue, cross the river, turn left, and double back downstream.

Long Route: From Selma drive southwest on U.S. 199 to U.S. 101, turn north on 101 some 50 miles to Gold Beach, then drive up the left (south) bank of the Rogue about 34 miles, cross the bridge over the mouth of the Illinois, and turn right on Road 450 to Lower Oak Flat.

of the Rogue thunders over dozens of technical rapids in a remote canyon of stunning beauty. For more than 20 miles the Illinois flows through a corner of the vast Kalmiopsis Wilderness Area.[1] Mosses and ferns thrive in this wet coastal climate, crowding into niches on the craggy riverside walls. The lush forest and steep surrounding slopes harbor abundant wildlife. Boating use is light, so most groups have the river to themselves. And when the sun does shine, the canyon is as close to paradise as you are likely to find.

Frequent landslides account for most rapids on the Illinois. The steep canyon slopes have little topsoil and become unstable after heavy rains. Each slide leaves a boulder dam across the river's path, giving the whitewater its technical pool-and-drop character. The biggest rapid, Green Wall, presents a serious challenge for boaters in any craft. Many rapids become much more difficult with modest increases in flow, and long swims are a threat at high water. Boaters must be prepared for variable flows, unpredictable weather, and extreme isolation.

Though the broad, fertile upper Illinois Valley has a rich history, the rugged Illinois Canyon has seen relatively little traffic over the years. Before whites arrived, small bands of local Indians lived, fished, and hunted in the canyon. At the height of the local gold rush, only a few prospectors tried their luck in the rugged canyon below Upper Oak Flat. The river was named by two brothers from Peoria, Illinois, who discovered gold in the upper valley.

In 1968 the Illinois was one of the original rivers listed for study as a possible addition to the National Wild and Scenic Rivers System. Two years later, the state of Oregon made the Illinois a State Scenic Waterway, but Congress didn't get around to giving it National Wild and Scenic designation until 1984. Federal protection finally laid to rest plans for the proposed Buzzards Roost Dam, which would have flooded the run described here.

Nearly 100,000 acres of the Kalmiopsis region burned in the enormous Silver Fire in 1987. The Illinois Canyon itself was affected from just below Pine Flat almost to the mouth of Silver Creek. However, much of this area was only lightly burned; the heaviest burns were between Klondike Creek and Collier Creek. Fortunately, light but steady rains the following year held post-fire erosion to a minimum, and riverside slopes are now returning to their former green splendor.

[1]Named for a rare member of the heath family. The Kalmiopsis Wilderness is considered by botanists to be the richest, most diverse plant habitat in the Northwest.

Upstream Runs

Two one-day runs above Miami Bar offer good scenery and intermediate to advanced whitewater. The first is an eight-mile stretch from the USFS Road 4201 bridge below Little Illinois River Falls to a take-out on the right bank above Illinois River Falls. Scout the take-out very carefully; **unrunnable Illinois River Falls** is only half a mile downstream. This take-out is along Illinois River Road some ten miles west of U.S. 199 at Selma, about a mile before the turnoff to McCaleb Ranch.

The second run begins a third of a mile downstream from Illinois River Falls at the low bridge at McCaleb Ranch. The take-out is 4.5 miles downstream at Miami Bar. To reach McCaleb Ranch, follow Illinois River Road west from Selma some 11 miles, then bear left down a steep road leading to the low-water bridge over the Illinois. Use caution; the last part of this steep road may be impassable.

Mile by Mile Guide

*See map in **Rogue** chapter. Note: This mile guide lists only some, not all, of the major rapids.*

0 — **PUT-IN** on the right bank at Miami Bar. Overnight camping. No drinking water. A mile downstream on the right is Upper Oak Flat. A trail follows the right bank, usually high above the river, from Upper Oak Flat to Pine Flat.

2.5 — Briggs Creek enters on the right. A half mile downstream, Panther Creek enters on the right. The Kalmiopsis Wilderness begins a half mile below Panther Creek. Downstream the whitewater becomes more difficult. In the first mile below Panther Creek lie two Class III- rapids, **LABRADOR CREEK** and **NOME CREEK,** followed in a third of a mile by two closely-spaced Class III+ drops known as **ROCKY TOP.**

4.7 **YORK CREEK** (IV). Just below the mouth of York Creek, which enters on the right. The current sweeps along the left wall and rushes down a tight slot between a hole on the left and a large boulder on the right, then continues past another hole, and finally pours over a sharp drop at the bottom.

5.5 **CLEAR CREEK** (IV-). A long, technical boulder garden, most challenging at the bottom. Clear Creek enters on the right at the foot of rapid.

8 **PINE CREEK** (IV). Located in a more open section of canyon just below the mouth of Pine Creek on the right. Scout right. The river bends left, and most of the current sweeps to the right down a chute between a big boulder and rocks projecting from the right shore. Watch for a nasty hole in this slot. A sneak route is often available on the far left, along the bank. Below the rapid on the right is Weaver Ranch. Downstream the rapids are Class II and III for 9 miles.

10 Klondike Creek enters on the left. Good campsite. Another good camp is 2.5 miles downstream at Deadman Bar.

17.2 Red Rock Bar. The river turns sharply right, and a creek enters on the left. Corner Camp on the right is the last large site for many miles.

17.8 **PRELUDE** (IV-). A rock garden at a right bend ends in a sharp drop among big boulders. Also known as **Fawn Falls.**

18 **THE GREEN WALL** (V-), named for a mossy rock wall on the right. **Recognition:** Located at the end of the pool below Prelude. Eddy out on the left *above* the entrance rock garden to scout. **The rapid:** The river sweeps into a rock garden at a right-hand bend, then straightens and thunders down a steep 100-yard gauntlet of huge boulders, drops, and holes along the right wall. The most treacherous obstacles are the big holes along the wall, notably the first and last drops. High water produces enormous hydraulics here. If necessary, make a very difficult portage on the left through giant boulders and poison oak. Boaters may also consider running the upper rock garden, eddying out on the left, then portaging the lower drops. Difficult rapids continue downstream.

19 **LITTLE GREEN WALL** (IV), often called **Ain't Over Yet** or **Big Mac,** located a quarter mile below a side creek waterfall on the left. Boulders from a landslide on the left force the river against the right wall. Scout left. There are several Class III and IV rapids in the next mile and a half.

21 **SUBMARINE HOLE** (IV). Rock outcrops on both sides constrict the river at the bottom of this rapid, and a big boulder sits squarely in the main channel, nearly blocking the river at lower flows and producing a fierce hole at higher water levels. Scout left. Downstream the canyon broadens and the whitewater eases to Class II and III. A mile below the rapid Collier Creek enters on the left.

25 A trio of waterfalls appears on the left bank. Not far downstream Silver Creek enters on the right, and a half mile farther the river leaves the Kalmiopsis Wilderness. A trail follows the right bank for the next two miles.

28.5 Indigo Creek enters on the right. A half mile downstream is the old Buzzard's Roost Dam Site.

32 **TAKE-OUT** at Lower Oak Flat on the right, not far below where Lawson Creek enters on the left. Or continue 3 miles down to the Rogue confluence and take out at Agness boat landing on the right bank of the Rogue, opposite the mouth of the Illinois.

Upper Klamath River

Hell's Corner Run

Difficulty: IV+. **Gradient:** 40 ft./mi.
Length: 11 or 17 miles.
Put-in: John Boyle Powerhouse (3,300').
Take-out: Copco Reservoir (2,620').
Drainage Area and Average Annual Discharge: 4,080 sq. mi. and 1,400,000 af at put-in.
Season: April–October.
Recommended Levels: 1,400–3,000 cfs. When one generator at the powerhouse is running (typical summer conditions), the flow is usually about 1,500 cfs. When both generators are running (winter, spring, sometimes fall), the flow rises to about 2,700. Higher flows occur only during major storms or on rare occasions when upstream reservoirs are full.
Flow Information: DWR tape, (916) 653-9647, or Pacific Power & Light tape, (800) 547-1501. Release from Boyle Powerhouse.
Special Hazards: Sharp volcanic rocks.
Permits: Not presently required. Self-registration at put-in.
Managing Agency: BLM, Klamath Falls Resource Area, 2795 Anderson Avenue, Building 25, Klamath Falls, OR 97603; (503) 883-6916.
Commercial Raft Trips: Yes. For a list of outfitters contact the BLM.
Land Ownership: Mostly BLM with scattered utility company parcels.
Scenery: Very good. Semi-arid volcanic canyon.
Solitude: Very good. **Wilderness:** Partial.
Water: Carry your own. The undrinkable river water comes from shallow upstream reservoirs and is warm and algae-laden in summer. No usable side streams.
Camping: Most boaters on overnight trips camp on the right bank within the first 5 miles of this run, where a dirt road follows the river, and send their gear out by car before entering the gorge. There are some good wilderness campsites for those willing to carry gear. Topsy Campground, on Topsy Road just off Oregon Highway 66, is 2.5 miles from the put-in.
Guides and References:

- Cassady & Calhoun, *California Whitewater.*
- Holbek & Stanley, *A Guide to the Best Whitewater in the State of California.*
- *Soggy Sneakers Guide to Oregon Rivers* (Willamette Kayak and Canoe Club).
- Garren, *Oregon River Tours.*
- Quinn & Quinn, *Hell's Corner Gorge of the Upper Klamath.*
- Quinn & Quinn, *Handbook to the Klamath River Canyon.* Also includes the Main and Lower Klamath down to Weitchpec.
- Orr & Orr, *Rivers of the West: A Guide to the Geology and History.*

Maps:

- **USGS 7.5':** *Chicken Hills (OR), Mule Hill (OR), Secret Spring Mtn (CA), Copco (CA).*
- **USGS 1:100:** *Medford, Yreka.*
- **USFS:** *Klamath NF.* Covers all but beginning of run.

Auto Shuttle: Roughly 80 miles (2 hours) one way. For shuttle references call the Copco Lake Store, (916) 459-3655.
Logistics: To reach the **take-outs,** follow I-5 to the Henley-Hornbrook turnoff, 7 miles south of the Oregon-California border. Drive east about 3 miles, turn right on Ager Road and cross the Klamath, drive about 3.5 more miles, then turn left on Ager-Beswick Road and drive about 15 miles to where the Klamath flows into the upper reaches of Copco Reservoir. At the top end of the reservoir, a side road turns left and crosses a bridge. Turn left on this road to reach an excellent private take-out on the north shore at Copco Lake Store (fee), or continue straight and drive up the south bank (river left) another half mile to a BLM take-out at Fishing Access 1 (river mile 17). To shorten the river run by 6 miles, continue up the south bank to an alternate take-out at the BLM's Stateline River Access near the Oregon border (river mile 11). The last section of road down to this upper access is quite rough but may be improved in the future. **Do not use any other river or fishing accesses to take out; they are reserved for anglers.**

To reach the **put-in,** return to I-5, drive north across the Oregon border to Ashland, take Exit 14 and drive east on Oregon Highway 66 for some 43 miles to John Boyle Reservoir. Before crossing the reservoir, turn right on an unpaved road that leads downstream a little under 5 miles to John Boyle Powerhouse. A sign marks the put-in a quarter of a mile downstream from the powerhouse on the right bank. This once-difficult put-in has now been improved by the BLM. The unpaved road continues down the right bank for several miles, providing alternate accesses farther downstream.

Until recently boaters could shorten the shuttle considerably by driving directly north on Copco Road from Copco Reservoir to Oregon Highway 66. Unfortunately, a rancher on Copco Road—apparently upset about dust raised by passing vehicles—has blocked the road with locked gates. The legality of this action is questionable, but for now this shorter shuttle route is closed. For current information contact the BLM.

Some private groups and several commercial outfits make a one-day run from Frain Ranch to the Stateline Access by shuttling on the old Topsy Grade, which follows the left (southeast) side of the canyon. This very rough and slow dirt road is not suitable for standard passenger vehicles.

The Upper Klamath River on the Oregon-California border is a fairly recent whitewater discovery. Until 1979 it was known only to a private river runner from Oregon, Jack LeRoy. That year Dean Munroe, head of Wilderness Adventures of Redding, California, floated the river and spread the word that the "Hell's Corner Run"—a name of his own invention[1]—was as tough as the Tuolumne or the Illinois. Within a couple of years, dozens of outfitters were applying for commercial permits. Today the Upper Klamath is a standard run for river runners from Oregon's Rogue Valley, and it draws many California boaters as well.

The Upper Klamath watershed takes in a wide area to the south and east of Crater Lake in southwestern Oregon. Snowmelt from the east slope of the Cascades, combined with groundwater flow from a wide area, gathers in broad, shallow Upper Klamath Lake. Near the city of Klamath Falls the river leaves the lake and winds for several miles through open agricultural lands. Soon the river turns southwest and heads for California. Along the way it cuts directly through the rugged Cascade Range, where hard volcanic bedrock churns the river to froth in the Upper Klamath whitewater run.

Actually, "whitewater" is a misnomer: the river is more the color of ale, due to a heavy load of algae from Upper Klamath Lake. In fact, the Upper Klamath's powerful rapids act as an enormous blender, whipping this organic matter into a sudsy froth that collects as a mat of foam in the eddies below some rapids. Many boaters find that the dark water adds considerably to the challenge of reading rapids, as it obscures many sharp rocks just below the surface. The river and side creeks are undrinkable, so be sure to carry plenty of drinking water.

The Upper Klamath run, which features a concentrated dose of tough rapids in a five-mile gorge just north of the Oregon-California border, is for advanced and expert boaters only. When both generators are running at Boyle Powerhouse and the river is flowing at 2,700 cfs or more, the action is fast and furious. Lower flows aren't so easy, either. The sharp volcanic rocks cluttering the river bed are unforgiving to boats and swimmers alike. In fact, many boaters wear wetsuits even in hot weather to help protect their hides in the event of a swim.

A key attraction of the Upper Klamath is its relatively reliable flows, which normally hold up all the way through late summer and early fall. The river's rugged high desert canyon offers good scenery and solitude. It is on the Pacific Flyway, a major migratory route for a wide variety of birds. River runners may see bald and golden eagles, falcons, ospreys, herons, cormorants, Canadian geese and even pelicans. The canyon is also rich in history, and boaters can explore the remains of Indian settlements, old mines, ranches, and mills.

Upstream Run

In the spring boaters can enjoy a fine six-mile Class III+ run from Keno Dam to John Boyle Reservoir. Here the Upper Klamath has carved a scenic, intimate volcanic gorge as it makes its first cut west into the Cascades. Highway 66 provides a short paved shuttle (in contrast to the long shuttle for the Hell's Corner run downstream). The gradient averages 50 ft./mi., and the most difficult rapids are near the end of the run, just above the reservoir. For details, refer to the *Soggy Sneakers Guide to Oregon Rivers.*

[1]Munroe also named most of the rapids and even wrote a song about the run.

Upper Klamath River Guide

Put in on the right bank below Boyle Powerhouse (mile 0). The first 5.7 miles are moderate—nothing above Class III. The dirt road follows the right bank in this reach, providing alternate accesses. This first section has several good campsites. Frain Ranch is on the left at mile 5.5. Built by an early settler on the site of an old Indian village, it is worth a stop.

Below Frain Ranch the dirt road ends on the right and the Klamath plunges into a five-mile gorge. Campsites are scarce below this point. **This guide lists only the biggest rapids in the gorge.** The gradient steepens to 75 ft./mi. for nearly four miles. The first big rapid is **CALDERA (IV+)** (mile 5.7), where the river drops down a 150-yard, boulder-choked chute. Like all major rapids in the gorge, Caldera is the result of large landslides dating back 20,000 to 30,000 years. Scout on the left.

A mile downstream is **SATAN'S GATE (IV)**, a sharp right turn into a series of rocky drops. Catch an eddy at the bottom left (difficult at higher flows) to scout the next rapid, **HELL'S CORNER (IV+)**. Walk the entire length of this sinuous 600-yard rapid before you run it. Watch for a sharp submerged rock about 15 yards off the right bank near the top. The river bends first left, then right, and the current sweeps boats left toward big boulders. Boaters try to stay right and catch an eddy before the final drop, called **The Dragon.** The teeth of the beast are two submerged rocks at the bottom.

Two-thirds of a mile below Hell's Corner is **AMBUSH (IV)**, where the current accelerates, splits around a shallow island, then turns sharply right into the **Ambush,** where wrap rocks block the center and left. Stop well upstream to scout on the left. A half mile downstream look for the Salt Cave on the left. Home to a rare species of bat, the cave is off limits to visitors.

At mile 10 the river splits at **SNAG ISLAND FALLS (III+)**, the last big rapid. Most boaters take the right channel. The remains of an old bridge mark the California border at mile 11. Just downstream is **STATELINE FALLS (III)**, with a sharp ledge drop in the center. The upper BLM take-outs are on the left just above and below the rapid. (The lower is more popular.) The next half dozen miles are scenic floating through private land, with a few Class II+ drops over old diversion dams. The canyon opens and ranches appear. Shovel Creek enters on the left at mile 13.8, and an old log chute is on the right at mile 14.5. **Take out** at Fishing Access 1 (mile 17, left bank), or a third of a mile farther down at an improved take-out at Copco Lake Store (small fee).

A Threatened River

The Upper Klamath is one of the nation's most endangered rivers. The city of Klamath Falls has tenaciously pursued plans to build the Salt Caves hydroelectric project, which would devastate this last significant free-flowing section of the Upper Klamath, despite the 1988 approval by Oregon voters of an initiative that added it to the State Scenic Waterways. But state protection cannot stop a federally-licensed project. So Klamath Falls—with the cooperation of its bureaucratic ally, the Federal Energy Regulatory Commission (FERC)—has persevered.

In the latest gambit, the city has scrapped plans to build a high dam and proposed instead to divert water directly out of the tailrace of Boyle Powerhouse and run it through a series of ditches and pipes to a new powerhouse just above the California border. The city has misleadingly dubbed this proposal the "no-dam alternative." In fact, the plan simply makes use of the existing Boyle Dam to dewater 11 miles of river.

In a major setback for the city, the Oregon Department of Environmental Quality refused in 1991 to issue a water quality certification for the project, citing its adverse effects on water temperature. Without this permit, the project is dead. However, the city is has indicated its willingness to appeal even to the U.S. Supreme Court.

The surest protection for the Upper Klamath would be Congressional designation as a National Wild and Scenic River, which in 1993 was recommended by the BLM and the Governor of Oregon. The Lower Klamath in California is already protected in this way. For current information contact the Pacific Rivers Council (see appendix for address) and/or Save Our Klamath River, P.O. Box 1956, Klamath Falls, OR 97601, (503) 882-6841.

North Fork Umpqua River

Boulder Flat to Cable Crossing

Difficulty: III4-.
Length: 32 miles. Shorter runs possible.
Gradient: 26 ft./mi.
Put-in: Boulder Flat Campground (1,600').
Take-out: Cable Crossing (780').
Drainage Area and Average Annual Discharge: 475 sq. mi. and 1,127,000 af near put-in.
Season: All year. Usually peaks in May and early June, then drops to late summer lows from August through October. Rarely below 700 cfs at the put-in.
Recommended Levels: 800–2,500 cfs.
Flow Information: Douglas County Water Resources, (503) 440-4255, can provide the flow "below Steamboat" (near mile 20). NWS tape, (503) 249-0666, gives the flow at Winchester, 30 miles below the take-out. This reading significantly overestimates flows at the Boulder Flat put-in.
Special Hazards: Narrow chutes. Cold water. Possible log hazards. Rock Creek Falls (also called Deadline Falls) below the Cable Crossing take-out.
Permits: Not presently required for private boaters. Voluntary closures on some sections to reduce conflict with anglers. Group size limit 20.
Managing Agency: North Umpqua RD, Umpqua NF, 18782 North Umpqua Highway, Glide, OR 97443; (503) 496-3532.
Commercial Raft Trips: Yes. Contact the managing agency for references.
Land Ownership: Mostly National Forest and BLM, with a few private parcels.
Scenery: Excellent. Lush, forested canyon; interesting rock formations.
Solitude: Good in spite of highway.
Wilderness: No.
Fishing: One of the nation's top steelhead streams. Best July–Oct. Fly angling only.
Side Excursions: Crater Lake National Park. Local waterfalls (see essay).
Guides and References:

- Corliss & Chase, *Backpaddlers Guide to the North Umpqua River* (3 books). Covers Soda Springs Dam to Winchester Dam.
- An informative *User's Guide,* available from the Forest Service, includes boating information and details on boating closures.
- *Soggy Sneakers Guide to Oregon Rivers* (Willamette Kayak & Canoe Club). Includes downstream runs.
- Garren, *Oregon River Tours.*
- Alt and Hyndman, *Roadside Geology of Oregon.* Covers Highway 138 along river.
- Crawford, *North Umpqua Angler's Guide.*

Maps:

- **USGS 7.5':** *Illahee Rock, Steamboat, Mace Mtn, Old Fairview.*
- **USFS:** *Umpqua NF.*

Auto Shuttle: All on paved roads; mileages are roughly the same as river miles.
Logistics: Oregon Highway 138 follows the river, offering frequent access and short shuttles. The **Cable Crossing take-out** (marked by a small blue and white sign) is on the right bank roughly 25 miles east of Roseburg and about 1.5 miles downstream from Richard Baker Wayside (County Park). **Scout this take-out carefully! A Class V–VI falls is just downstream.**

A very popular intermediate access, **Gravel Bin,** is some 17 miles upriver from Cable Crossing on the right bank, about three quarters of a mile upstream from Steamboat Creek (roughly midway between highway mile posts 39 and 40). The **Boulder Flat put-in** is about 12.5 miles farther upriver on the left bank at the upstream end of Boulder Flat Campground (near highway mile post 52).

Alternate accesses include (in downriver order, with approximate highway mile posts in parentheses): Soda Springs Powerhouse (54); access road to Horseshoe Bend Campground (46.2); adjacent to Bogus Creek Campground (34.7); Wright Creek Bridge (33.8); Susan Creek Recreation Site (28.4); Richard Baker Wayside (22.9). More information on these accesses is in the **River Guide** section below.

NORTH FORK UMPQUA

In a state packed with excellent rivers, the North Fork of the Umpqua has sometimes been overlooked. Located in a lightly populated region and pinched between Oregon's two most famous rivers—the Willamette to the north and the Rogue to the south—the Umpqua, well known to fishermen, saw only light boating use until recently. But river runners in increasing numbers are discovering that the North Umpqua is one of Oregon's loveliest whitewater streams. The entire run covered here was added to the National Wild and Scenic Rivers System in 1988.

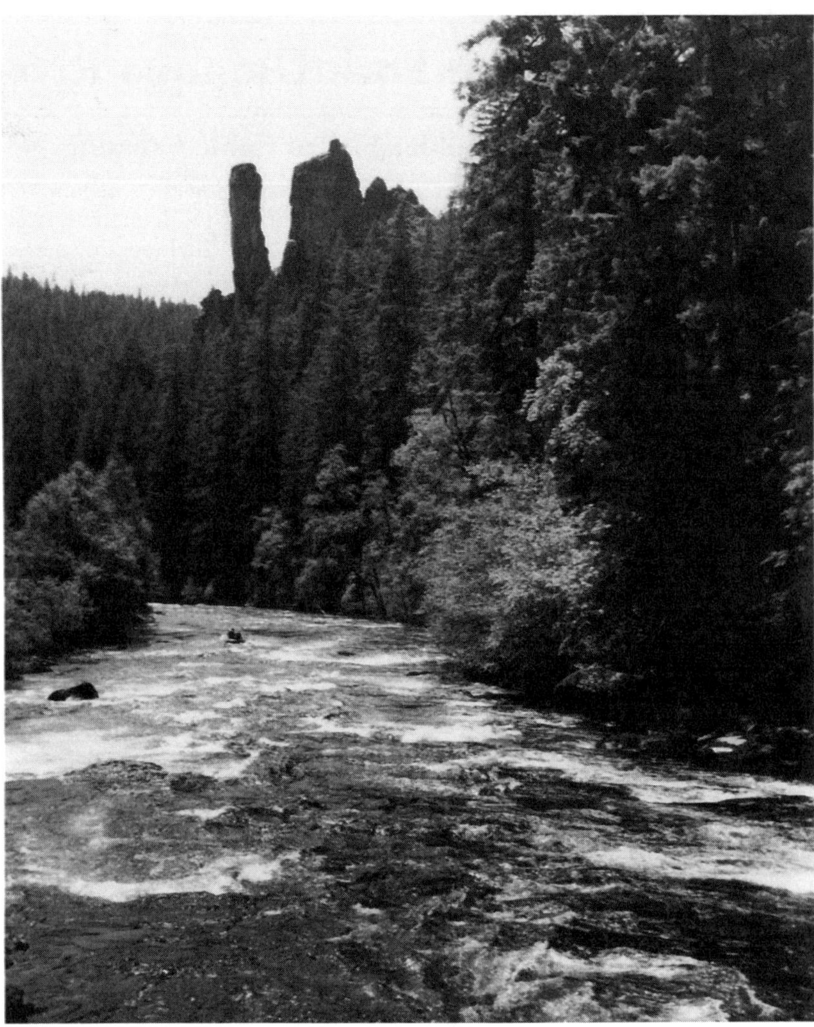

North Fork Umpqua River *Polly Greist*

From its headwaters near Crater Lake in southwest Oregon, the North Umpqua flows down the west slope of the Cascade Range to Roseburg. There it joins with the South Umpqua before cutting through the Coast Range to the Pacific. In its upper reaches in the Cascades, the North Umpqua offers lush scenery and fairly reliable summer weather. A dark mantle of Douglas-fir cloaks the steep canyon slopes, while trees on the river bank help screen the highway that parallels the run. Here and there, dramatic basalt spires tower above the river, attesting to the region's fiery volcanic past. Volcanic formations also account for the watershed's abundance of large waterfalls, including Toketee and Lemolo Falls on the upper North Fork, and 272' Watson Falls on a tributary stream. After all, "Umpqua" is an Indian name meaning "Thunder Water."

Local geology explains the pure water and summer-long flows of the North Umpqua. Volcanic eruptions—including the cataclysmic explosion of Mt. Mazama that created nearby Crater Lake some 7,000 years ago—laid down vast deposits of pumice and ash in the upper watershed. Rain and snowmelt percolate through these natural filters and emerge at springs whose steady flows of pure, icy water help keep the river above minimum levels even in late summer.

Minerals in the groundwater probably account for the North Umpqua's breathtaking color, a deep aquamarine. It is best seen when sunlight shines through wave tips or into the turbulence of a reversal. There is a disadvantage: steady flows and lack of sediment mean the river has virtually no camping beaches. Fortunately, the Forest Service maintains many fine riverside campgrounds.

The North Umpqua's technical pool-and-drop whitewater demands skill and precision. Most of the larger rapids are Class III; one or two rate IV-. Higher flows generally present greater challenges. At low flows several spots—notably Pinball and Bathtub—become narrow enough to cause problems.

At the Boulder Flat put-in the river is small and steep, dropping at about 40 ft./mi. The gradient gradually diminishes to about half that rate as pools begin to separate the rapids. Always be alert for **possible log hazards** in the river's narrow chutes.

The 32 miles covered here divide easily into shorter runs. The first six miles from Boulder Flat to Horseshoe Bend are steep and fairly continuous. The next eight miles from Horseshoe Bend to Gravel Bin (Steamboat Creek) take on more of a pool-and-drop nature. This stretch includes Pinball, a Class IV- rock garden. Below Gravel Bin the canyon begins to broaden and the pools become even longer, but lots of good rapids remain. Many alternate accesses allow boaters to choose among the sections.

While the North Umpqua's whitewater is gaining in popularity, the river is still better known to anglers than boaters. Despite some damage to the fishery from past logging and road building, both of which increased sediment loads and caused other changes, the North Umpqua remains a world-famous steelhead stream. When the big ones are running, the river can be an obstacle course of fishing lines. The native steelhead migrate primarily to spawning grounds on the North Fork's major tributary, Steamboat Creek. The fish tend to cluster in the river below the mouth of Steamboat, and since the creek itself is off limits to fishing, anglers congregate here as well.

Needless to say, these folks aren't always thrilled when boaters splash through their favorite fishing pools. To reduce conflicts, the Forest Service has instituted limited voluntary boating closures for peak steelhead season: no boating on the five miles between Gravel Bin (just above Steamboat Creek) and Bogus Creek Campground July 15–October 31, and no boating before 10 a.m. or after 6 p.m. July 1–October 31 on any section. Dates and regulations may change, so contact the Forest Service for current information.

Even with these restrictions boaters are likely to encounter anglers. A combination of common courtesy and etiquette can keep these meetings positive. (See appendix on **River Etiquette.**)

North Umpqua River Guide

Boulder Flat to Gravel Bin

The uppermost **put-in** commonly used by river runners is **at the upstream end of Boulder Flat Campground** (mile 0). Boaters can add a mile and a half by starting at a more difficult access farther upstream at Soda Springs Dam and Powerhouse (reached by USFS Road 4775 off Highway 138).

Technical Class III water begins immediately below Boulder Flat. Soon the basalt spires of Old Man Rock, Eagle Rock and Rattlesnake Rock appear, towering high above the right bank. Copeland Creek enters on the left at mile 1. The highway crosses the river at mile 3 (steep **alternate access**) and stays on the right for the rest of the run. At mile 6 a minor bridge crosses the river, and Calf Creek enters on the left. Just below the bridge is **WEIRD WEIR,** a river-wide ledge where most of the flow funnels into a narrow slot on the right. About 50 yards downstream is an **alternate access** on the right where a wide, graveled foot path leads to the access road serving Horseshoe Bend Campground.

Downstream is Horseshoe Bend itself, a mile-long gooseneck meander to the right where the highway leaves the river and a campground appears on the right bank. Below Horseshoe Bend the difficulty increases, with longer pools separating bigger drops. About three quarters of a mile below Horseshoe Bend, a log spans the right channel high overhead, left there by the 1964 flood. About a mile downstream watch for a long Class III rapid, **AFRICAN QUEEN.**

Panther Creek enters on the left at mile 10; just downstream, the Apple Creek Bridge crosses the river (**alternate access**). About a quarter mile below the bridge at a right bend is **PINBALL (IV-)**, a tight, technical 100-yard boulder garden that cannot be seen from the highway. Scouting from the left bank is strongly recommended; however, boaters may have trouble catching an eddy, especially at higher flows when the long gravel island on the left above the rapid is covered. If in doubt, start moving to shore well upstream. Alternatively, scout Pinball before boating this section by turning off the highway just downstream from Apple Creek Campground, crossing the Apple Creek Bridge, and then hiking downstream along the left bank trail.

The **Gravel Bin access** is on the right at mile 14, just past Island Campground. Take out here when boating closures are in effect.

Gravel Bin to Cable Crossing

Below Gravel Bin the gradient decreases to 21 ft./mi., with long, slow pools separating the mainly Class III rapids. Half a mile below Gravel Bin, a historic wooden bridge crosses the river; just downstream, Steamboat Creek, the North Umpqua's largest tributary, enters on the right. The canyon gradually widens and the river becomes broader below this point. Flows on Steamboat Creek fluctuate much more than those on the relatively constant North Umpqua; as a result, the river has greater seasonal flow variations below this confluence.

Just below Steamboat Creek is a challenging rapid with a swift chute down the left. On the right bank is the Steamboat Inn (a good spot for dinner with a view of the river). Cougar Creek enters on the left at mile 18.5. About a quarter mile downstream at a right-hand bend is the **Bogus Creek river access.** A short graveled foot path leads up the right bank to a highway turnout near the entrance to Bogus Creek Campground, which is on the opposite side of the highway. At mile 19.5 the Wright Creek Bridge crosses the Umpqua (**alternate access** on the left).

A quarter mile below Wright Creek Bridge is **BATHTUB (IV-; more difficult at low flows)**, also called **Drop-Off.** At low water the chutes here are very narrow and sometimes impassable for rafts. Kayaks and canoes may face a bridging hazard. Scout on either side and portage, if necessary, on the left (easy carry at low flows). About a mile downstream at a left bend is **CURL BACK,** an easier rapid with a standing wave. Fall Creek enters inconspicuously on the right at mile 21; a scenic Forest Service trail begins on the far side of the highway and leads a mile up the creek to a waterfall.

At mile 22 imposing cliffs rise on both banks, marking an old dam site (look for numbers painted high on the left wall). These cliffs signal the approach of **ISLAND (III)**, which begins about 300 yards downstream where the river divides around a long, rocky island. Most of the flow, and most boaters, go to the right. A rocky drop in the right channel at the head of the island presents the greatest challenge, but be alert for a steep chute at the bottom end as well. Most of this rapid is visible from the highway.

At mile 25.5 Susan Creek Recreation Site (BLM) offers an **alternate access** via a short trail up the right bank. (No access is allowed at the BLM's Susan Creek CG half a mile upstream.) The next four miles are slow and mild.

Another **alternate access** is at the upstream end of Richard Baker Wayside (County Park) at mile 30. Below this access is the short, sharp drop of **BAKER FALLS (III-).** The **final take-out is at the Cable Crossing access** on the right bank at mile 32. **Do not miss this take-out!**

HAZARD. A third of a mile below Cable Crossing, the river vaults over **ROCK CREEK FALLS (V–VI)**, also called **Deadline Falls.** This 9' vertical drop features a nasty keeper reversal and, for most boaters, should be a scenic attraction only. It's a great spot to watch steelhead trying to leap upstream. A mile below the falls, the river surges through two Class IV to IV+ drops in **THE NARROWS.** Boaters interested in running these drops should be forewarned: this section is often a maze of fishing lines. The **next good access** is about four miles below The Narrows at a boat ramp on the left bank, **just upstream from Idleyld Park.**

Downstream Runs

Below Idleyld Park the river eases to Class II and II+ for about 40 miles, and the canyon scenery gives way to pastoral hill country. Farther downstream, below the confluence of the North and South Forks, the main Umpqua runs through nearly 100 miles of pastoral scenery and Class I and I+ water to the Pacific. For more information on these sections, refer to the *Soggy Sneakers Guide to Oregon Rivers.*

McKenzie River

Olallie Campground to Helfrich Landing

1. Olallie Campground (1,915') to Paradise Campground (1,520').
III; 8 miles; 50 ft./mi.

2. Paradise CG to Blue River (1,030').
II+; 14.5 miles; 35 ft./mi.

3. Blue River to Prince Helfrich Boat Landing (795').
II3; 13 miles; 18 ft./mi.

Drainage Area and Average Annual Discharge: 185 sq. mi. and 780,000 af near Olallie; 950 sq. mi. and 2,956,000 af near Helfrich Landing.
Peak Recorded Flow: 64,400 cfs (Dec. 28, 1945) near Helfrich Landing.
Season: March–November. Adequate flows all year. Rarely too high or low.
Recommended Levels: 1,000–5,000 cfs at Vida gauge.
Flow Information: Eugene Water and Electric Board tape, (503) 341-1860, gives the flow at Trail Bridge (just above the Olallie put-in), Leaburg Dam (not far below the Helfrich Landing take-out), and Partridge Lane (near Eugene). NWS tape, (503) 249-0666, gives flows at Vida (near Helfrich Landing) and Trail Bridge (near Olallie). Flows are also listed in Eugene newspapers.
Special Hazards: Cold water. Log jams and strainers.
Permits: Not presently required.
Managing Agency: McKenzie RD, Willamette NF, McKenzie Bridge, OR 97413; (503) 822-3381.

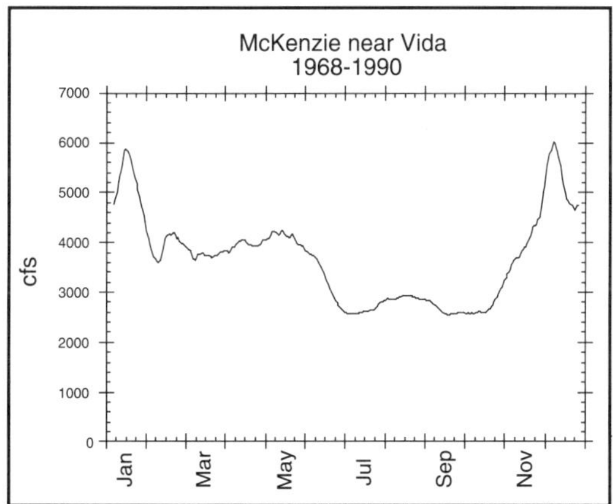

Commercial Raft Trips: Yes. For references contact the managing agency.
Land Ownership: All National Forest first 5 miles; mixed public and private thereafter.
Scenery: Excellent. Forested valley; some riverside cabins and development.
Solitude: Very good on Run 1; good on other runs. Heavy boating use on summer weekends, especially below Blue River (mile 23).
Wilderness: No. Road, campgrounds, houses.
Fishing: Excellent for trout, steelhead, and chinook salmon.
Water: Cold, clear, ice-blue. Drinking water available at many campgrounds along the river.
Camping: Few beaches and limited camping on the banks. USFS and private campgrounds along the river.
Side Excursions: Sahalie Falls (140') and Koosah Falls (80'), just off Highway 126 some 7 miles above the Olallie put-in.
Guides and References:

- *Soggy Sneakers Guide to Oregon Rivers* (Willamette Kayak and Canoe Club). Includes downstream and tributary runs.
- Crawford, *Driftboater's Guide to the Upper McKenzie: Olallie to Leaburg Lake.* Emphasis on dory boating and fishing. Mile guide, aerial photos, maps.
- Garren, *Oregon River Tours.* Covers below Blue River (mile 23).
- Alt & Hyndman, *Roadside Geology of Oregon.*

Maps:

- **USGS 7.5':** *Tamolitch Falls, Belknap Springs, McKenzie Bridge, Blue River, Mt. Hagan, Nimrod, Vida.*
- **USGS 1:100:** *McKenzie River.* Also covers downstream runs.
- **USFS:** *Willamette NF.*
- *McKenzie River Recreation Map.* Available locally. Includes the lower river from Leaburg Dam to Eugene.
- *Riverguide Bandana to the McKenzie* (Rivers & Mountains). Cloth map.

Auto Shuttle: About the same as river miles. For shuttle services contact Gardner's Leaburg Store, (503) 896-3215; Nimrod Store, (503) 822-3500; or local outfitters.

Logistics: Oregon Highway 126 parallels the McKenzie east of Eugene, providing many accesses in addition to the four mentioned below. Several alternate sites are listed in the **Mile Guide.** For more information refer to the *McKenzie River Recreation Map* listed above, or contact the Forest Service.

The **lowermost take-out** is at Prince Helfrich Boat Landing on the right bank of the McKenzie about two miles east of the town of Vida. To get there, turn south off Highway 126 onto Thompson Lane. The **Blue River access,** known as Forest Glen Boat Landing, is just off Highway 126 on the right bank about a third of a mile upstream from the Blue River confluence, at the east end of the small town of Blue River. **Paradise Campground** (USFS) is on the left bank just off Highway 126, about 3.5 miles east of the bridge over the river at the town of McKenzie Bridge. **The put-in at Olallie Campground** (USFS) is on the left bank just off Highway 126, about 8 miles upriver from Paradise Campground and 16 miles south of the junction of Highway 126 and U.S. 20 (put in at the downstream end of the campground).

Rising on the western slopes of the Three Sisters and Mt. Washington Wilderness Areas, the McKenzie River drains the heart of the Oregon Cascades, a land of fire and ice. The ice is plain to see in the several glaciers that adorn the 10,000' Sisters peaks, while the vast and inhospitable lava fields of Mt. Washington attest to the fiery origins of this watershed.

The river's true headwaters lie far beneath the lava, buried but not obliterated by the forces that built the peaks. Rainwater and snowmelt percolating down through porous, fractured volcanic rock still find their way along ancient channels far beneath the surface. Fortunately for river runners, a lava dam intersects this underground flow about eight miles from Mt. Washington, forcing the water to the surface at Great Springs near Clear Lake. Here, in a phenomenon seen elsewhere in the Cascades, a full-fledged river materializes from a lake with few visible tributaries.

From Clear Lake the McKenzie runs south and then west for 91 miles to its confluence with the Willamette, passing first through lush forests and later through fertile bottomlands. At the upstream end boaters will find a river that looks and acts like an oversized stream, racing at 60 ft./mi. through busy, continuous, shallow Class II and III rapids. Just 60 miles downstream, the river meanders at less than 10 ft./mi., ideal for lazy Class I canoeing. In between, easy and frequent access from Oregon Highway 126 lets boaters choose the runs that suit them best.

Close to Eugene and not too far from other Oregon cities, the McKenzie is one of the state's most popular rivers. Use is especially heavy below Blue River. Excellent trout and salmon fishing draws scores of anglers, including many in dories or "drift boats." River runners looking for more solitude and quite a bit more challenge might consider runs on the South Fork McKenzie or the Blue River, but catching these tributaries with enough water in them can be difficult.

The 36 miles described here can be divided into any number of shorter runs. The first section, from Olallie Campground to Paradise Campground, has very little riverside development and offers the most seclusion. Here the river is narrow and intimate and has no real flood plain due to its relatively steady flow. The whitewater on this upper reach—much more continuous than on the downstream runs—provides a good test of intermediate rock-dodging and "read-and-run" skills.

The lower runs are slower and have more of a pool-and-drop nature. For the most part these sections are milder than the upper reach, but boaters should not be entirely lulled. Even as the gradient steadily diminishes, the volume greatly increases: the average flow at the Helfrich Landing take-out is nearly four times that at the Olallie put-in. A Class III drop near the end of the third run often causes trouble for the unwary. The lower runs are also more open and developed than the upper run, with a wider riverbed and many cabins and houses scattered along the shore.

Although the McKenzie's rapids are generally forgiving, the river must be approached with caution. **Logs and strainers are a serious potential hazard, especially on the upper run.** Also, the swift, icy water poses a hypothermia threat even in midsummer. Boating begins just ten miles from the Cascade crest, and the water looks and feels like freshly melted ice.

River running has a long history on the McKenzie.[1] As on the Rogue, shooting the rapids was at first a necessity incidental to the primary purpose of fishing. In the early 1900's local boatmen developed the McKenzie Drift Boat, a flat-bottomed fishing dory that later became popular on many other rivers. The most famous of these early boatmen was Prince Helfrich, who began guiding trips in heavy wooden drift boats in the mid-1920's. Today his sons and grandsons are outfitters on the McKenzie.

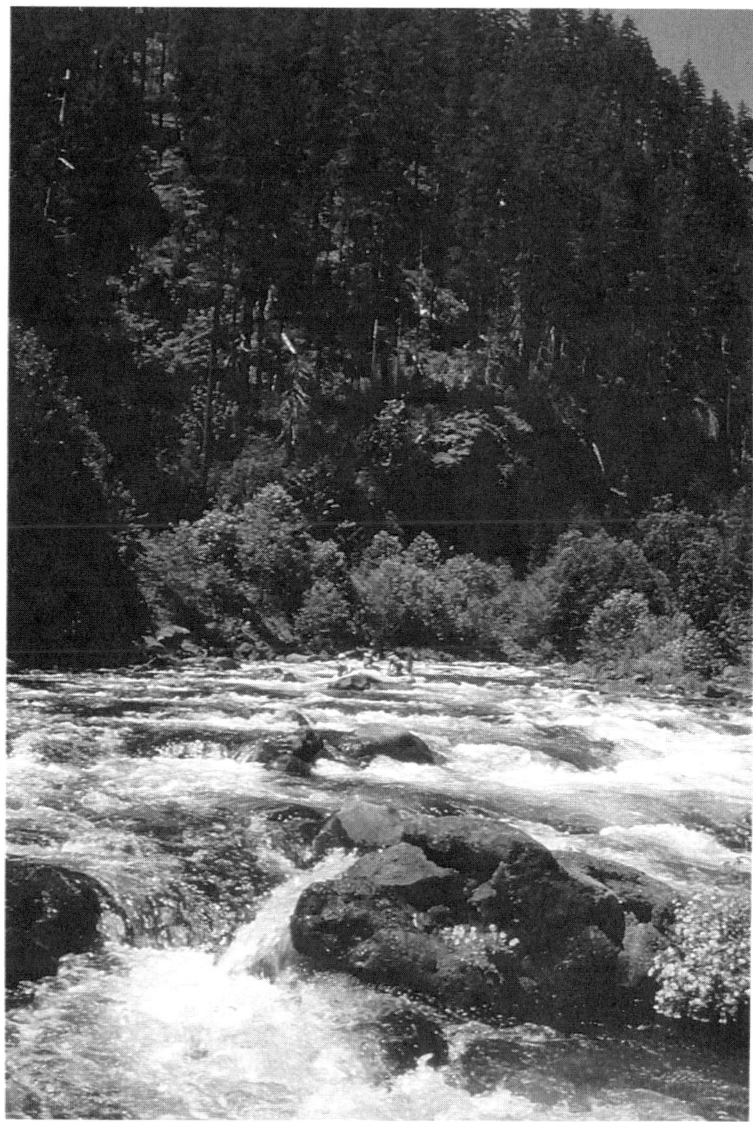

Fish Ladder Rapid, McKenzie *Martha Moran*

Two relatively small dams block the river above and below the run described here. At one time the Army Corps of Engineers had plans for a major dam at Quartz Creek, not far below Blue River, which would have flooded most of the upper McKenzie. Local residents stopped the dam, however, and two major tributaries, the Blue River and the South Fork McKenzie, were flooded instead.

In 1988 13 miles of the McKenzie were designated a National Wild and Scenic River, and Oregon voters added the McKenzie to the State Scenic Waterways System. However, much of the river remains vulnerable to development. The Pacific Rivers Council is one of the groups working to preserve the river. (See appendix for address.)

Downstream Runs

Not far below Helfrich Landing the McKenzie slows above Leaburg Dam. Below the dam boaters can enjoy some 30 miles of easy water all the way to Eugene. Open canoeists, drift boaters, and beginning kayakers favor this section. The pastoral, rolling countryside and diminishing current and gradient lend a relaxed, peaceful atmosphere to the reach. The first 20 miles from the dam to Hayden Bridge are generally Class II. Watch for Hayden Bridge Rapid at the very end of this section. The final ten miles down to Armitage Park in Eugene are mild Class I, suitable for novices. Several alternate accesses allow shorter runs. For more information see the *Soggy Sneakers Guide to Oregon Rivers.*

[1]The river is named for Donald McKenzie, who explored the upper Willamette River region in 1812 as a trader with John Jacob Astor's Pacific Fur Company. McKenzie first called the river the East Fork of the Willamette, but others later changed the name to McKenzie's Fork of the Willamette, which was in turn shortened to McKenzie.

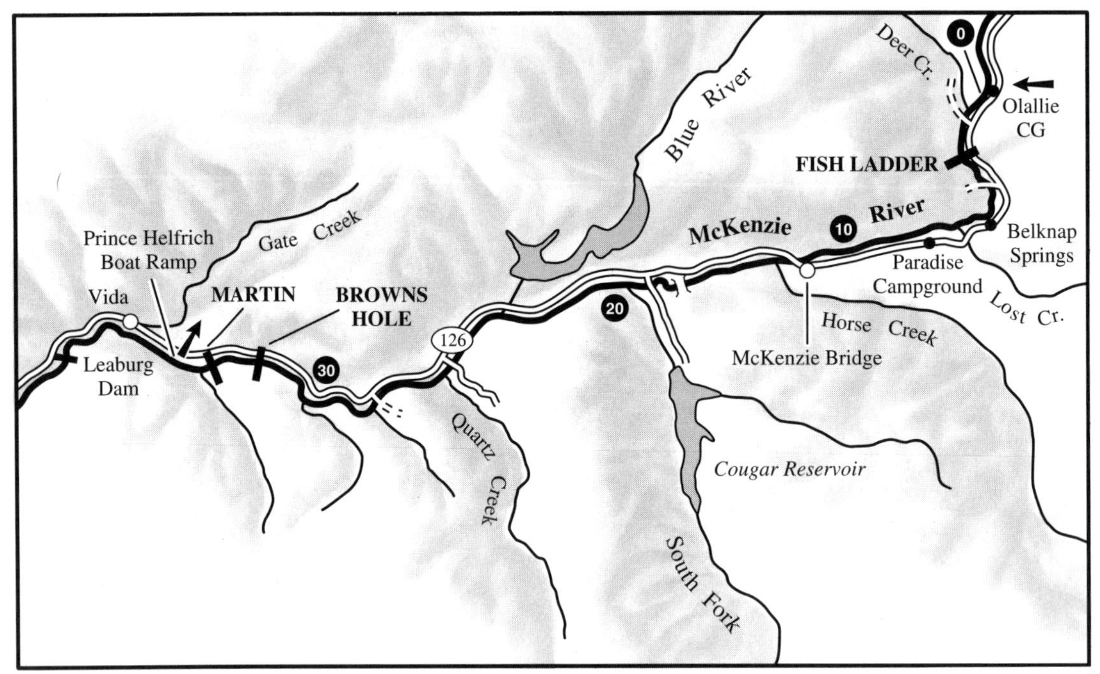

McKenzie

Mile by Mile Guide

0 **PUT-IN.** Olallie Campground (left bank). The first 5 miles are almost constant Class II+ to III with a 50 ft./mi. gradient. The McKenzie River Trail follows first the right, then the left bank for the next 10 miles. A little over a mile below the put-in, a minor bridge crosses the river as Deer Creek enters on the right. Just downstream is **DEER CREEK (III).**

3 **FISH LADDER (III).** One of the most challenging rapids on the run. Not visible from the highway. **Recognition:** The river bends left, and power lines cross overhead. Scout from the dirt road on the right. **The rapid:** The river sweeps around a left bend into a long rock garden. A mile below the rapid, a minor bridge crosses the river.

5.5 Belknap Hot Springs (private) on the right, with a lodge on the left. Just downstream is **SALT SPRINGS (III-)**, also called **Belknap.** The McKenzie changes course from south to west.

8 **RIVER ACCESS** at Paradise Campground on the left. The gradient eases to 40 ft./mi.

10 Gauging station on the left. McKenzie River Trail ends on the left. Cabins and other signs of civilization are more common below this point.

12 Highway 126 crosses the river at the town of McKenzie Bridge. A good **RIVER ACCESS** is a half mile downstream on the right at McKenzie River Campground.

15.7 Belknap Covered Bridge, sometimes called Rainbow Bridge. Just downstream, the river splits around Dearborn Island. The standard run is down the right channel. A steel bridge connects the island to the right bank.

17.5 USFS Road 19 crosses the river. A half mile downstream is the old Redsides log scaling station on the right. Kayakers often park here and launch their boats to surf a great ender wave.

19.5 **RIVER ACCESS.** Hamlin Boat Landing on the right. A half mile downstream, the South Fork McKenzie enters on the left.

22.5 **RIVER ACCESS.** Forest Glen Boat Landing on the right. The next half dozen miles are easy Class II. A half mile downstream, the Blue River enters on the right.

25.5 Finn Rock rises on the right and a bridge crosses the river. **RIVER ACCESS** on the left above the bridge. Downstream, Quartz Creek enters on the left.

28.3 Rosboro Bridge crosses the river above the settlement of Nimrod on the right. **RIVER ACCESS** on the left below the bridge. Nearby is a good surfing wave known as **Clover Point.** A half mile downstream is a Class II rapid named **EAGLE ROCK** for a cliff on the left.

30 Silver Creek Boat Ramp on the right. A mile downstream, Deer Creek enters on the left.

31.5 The river splits around an island and runs through an easy Class II rapid. On the right at mile 32 is a popular **RIVER ACCESS,** Rennie Landing. A mile below the access Bear Creek enters on the right, creating a shallow rapid.

33.5 A sticky reversal called **BROWNS HOLE (II+)** blocks the left side of the river. Though it is easy to skirt on the right, the hole is hard to see from upstream.

34.8 **RIVER ACCESS.** Boat ramp on the right at Ben and Kay Dorris State Park. A few hundred yards downstream is **MARTIN (III)**, the biggest rapid on the lower run. Large boulders divide the river into several channels and a big hole waits near the bottom. Scout right.

35.7 **TAKE-OUT.** Prince Helfrich Boat Landing on the right where a foot bridge crosses the river about half a mile below Martin Rapid. Boaters may continue another four miles through mostly flat water and one noteworthy rapid, **GATE CREEK (II+)**, to a boat ramp above Leaburg Dam.

Clackamas River

Upper and Lower Clackamas

Upper Clackamas

1. Killer Fang Run: Collawash River (1,465') to Three Lynx (1,110').
IV5+; 9 miles; 40 ft./mi.

2. Three Lynx Run: Three Lynx to North Fork Reservoir (680').
IV-; 13 miles; 33 ft./mi.

Lower Clackamas

3. McIver Park (300') to Barton Park (150').
II; 9 miles; 17 ft./mi.

Drainage Area and Average Annual Discharge: 479 sq. mi. and 1,456,000 af at Three Lynx.

Peak Recorded Flow: 68,200 cfs (Dec. 22, 1964).

Season: *Run 1:* Nov.–mid-June (rainy season and spring snowmelt); a bit longer for kayaks. Weather and road access may be problems in winter. *Run 2:* All year. Flows peak in winter or early spring, then recede to lows of 700 cfs or less in late summer. Rain usually raises flows again in late autumn. *Run 3:* All year, partially controlled by reservoirs which cause flow fluctuations in summer. Typically peaks in midwinter at over 5,000 cfs at Estacada, recedes to lows of 1,000 cfs or less in August and September.

Recommended Levels: *Upper:* 1,000–4,000 cfs. Much more powerful above 5,000 cfs. *Lower:* 1,000–5,000 cfs.

Flow Information: NWS tape, (503) 249-0666, gives the flow at Three Lynx and Estacada. The Three Lynx gauge (Upper Clackamas) is below the power plant; flows above this point (on Run 1) are roughly 300 cfs less. The Estacada gauge is just above the Lower Clackamas put-in. The Estacada flow is also given as the flow "below River Mill Dam" on Portland General Electric's recorded "Fish Line," (800) 632-3474.

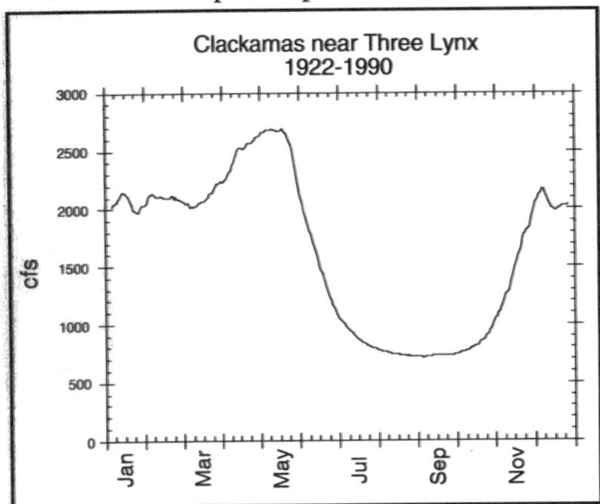

Special Hazards: New Fang Rapid on Run 1. Logs, especially on Run 1. Cold water.

Permits: Not presently required.

Managing Agency: Estacada RD, Mt. Hood NF, 595 NW Industrial Way, Estacada, OR 97023; (503) 630-6861.

Commercial Raft Trips: Not currently allowed. Contact the Forest Service for updated information.

Land Ownership: *Upper:* All National Forest. *Lower:* Private except parks and river accesses.

Scenery: *Upper:* Excellent; lush forested canyon. *Lower:* Very good; wooded bluffs and pastoral rolling hills.

Solitude: *Run 1:* Excellent. *Run 2:* Very good, despite a riverside road. Boating use is heavy on summer weekends. *Lower:* Good. Heavy river traffic on summer weekends.

Wilderness: No, but upper run is very secluded.

Water: Clear except during storms.

Camping: *Upper:* USFS campgrounds along the river; refer to *Mt. Hood NF* map. *Lower:* McIver Park.

Side Excursions: Austin and Bagby Hot Springs.

Guides and References:

- *Soggy Sneakers Guide to Oregon Rivers* (Willamette Kayak and Canoe Club).
- Garren, *Oregon River Tours.*

Maps:

- **USGS 7.5':** *Upper:* Fish Creek Mtn, Three Lynx, Bedford Point. *Lower:* Estacada, Redland, Damascus.
- **USFS:** *Mt. Hood NF.*

Auto Shuttle: *Upper:* Paved, same length as river miles. *Lower:* Paved, about 12 miles (15 minutes) one way.

Logistics: *Upper:* From the town of Estacada, roughly 30 miles southeast of Portland, follow Oregon Highway 224 upstream along the right bank of the Clackamas to the upper end of North Fork Reservoir. The **lowermost take-out for the Three Lynx Run is at Memaloose Scaling Station,** located about two miles beyond Promontory Park. A dirt road reaches the river across the highway from the scaling station. **Alternate take-outs** are Bob's Hole and Big Eddy Picnic Area, 3 and 4 miles upstream from the scaling station, respectively. To reach the **put-ins for the Three Lynx Run,** continue upstream on Highway 224 to Three Lynx power station. The highway crosses the river above and below the powerhouse, providing two possible accesses. The upper bridge serves as **take-out for the Killer Fang Run.** To reach the **put-ins for the Killer Fang Run,** continue upstream another 4 miles, cross the Oak Grove Fork of the Clackamas, bear right on USFS Road 46, and drive another 3 miles to Riverside Campground on the right bank, or one additional mile to the Clackamas-Collawash confluence.

Lower: The **put-in** is on the left bank at the upstream end of Milo McIver State Park, a half mile below River Mill Dam. There is an **alternate access** at a picnic area and parking lot at the lower end of the park. To reach the park, follow signs from the bridge over the Clackamas at the south end of Estacada. To reach the **take-out,** return to Estacada, drive 5 miles north on combined Highways 211/224 to Eagle Creek, then 3 miles northwest on Highway 224 to Barton. Turn left and follow signs to Barton County Park Boat Ramp (right bank).

In its journey northwest from the Cascades to its confluence with the Willamette River south of Portland, the Clackamas passes through two distinct sections separated by dams. In its upstream reaches the river tumbles over challenging rapids in a heavily forested canyon, cutting deep into hard formations of volcanic andesite and basalt. Below the dams, by contrast, the Clackamas is a river of easy rapids and light riffles, winding through open terrain as it sculpts a relatively smooth channel in deep sedimentary deposits.

Although its headwaters lie between 10,497' Mt. Jefferson and 11,239' Mt. Hood, the Clackamas[1] receives no snowmelt or glacial runoff from these imposing peaks, which are just outside the river's watershed. This leaves the Clackamas only a relatively gentle 30-mile stretch of the Cascade crest in its drainage. Most of this upper watershed is below 5,000', so the Clackamas has a somewhat earlier and shorter season than other large rivers that drain the west slope of the Cascades. Sudden rainstorms can send a surge of runoff down the river, raising flows dramatically in just a few hours.

The Clackamas is one of Oregon's most popular rivers, offering a variety of whitewater and scenery, easy access, short shuttles, fine fishing and camping, and—above all—convenience for Portland boaters. Unfortunately, the easy access and near-urban location also make the Clackamas one of the state's deadliest rivers: on average, roughly a dozen people become statistics here each year. Most of the drownings involve alcohol, and virtually all could be prevented by proper use of life jackets.

Upper Clackamas

Southeast of Estacada the Clackamas runs through more than 20 miles of excellent whitewater in a steep, fir-mantled canyon above North Fork Reservoir.[2] Sheer cliffs tower over the river in places, sometimes forming headwalls where the current rushes directly into the rock face. In general the upper river becomes less popular the farther upstream one goes, due to increasing difficulty and decreasing flows. In 1988, 47 miles of the Upper Clackamas above North Fork Reservoir were added to the National Wild and Scenic Rivers System.

Killer Fang Run: This very demanding near-wilderness stretch begins at the Collawash River confluence and extends nine miles to the Three Lynx power station. The run is named for Killer Fang Rapid, which was at one time a death trap and mandatory portage. However, in 1991 a huge landslide reduced Killer Fang to Class III and created a **dangerous new Class V–VI rapid** just downstream. See the **Mile Guide** for details.

[1]The river is named for an Indian tribe that lived along its banks, but the meaning of the word has been lost.

[2]Adventurous boaters occasionally explore runs upstream from the two described here. Those with a taste for intimate, technical, high-gradient boating sometimes tackle an eight-mile stretch of the Clackamas immediately above the Collawash River confluence. Challenges here include low flows, frequent log hazards, numerous Class III to III+ rapids, and at least one Class IV drop. USFS Road 46 follows the right bank, allowing easy access and scouting. For more information on this section refer to the *Soggy Sneakers Guide*.

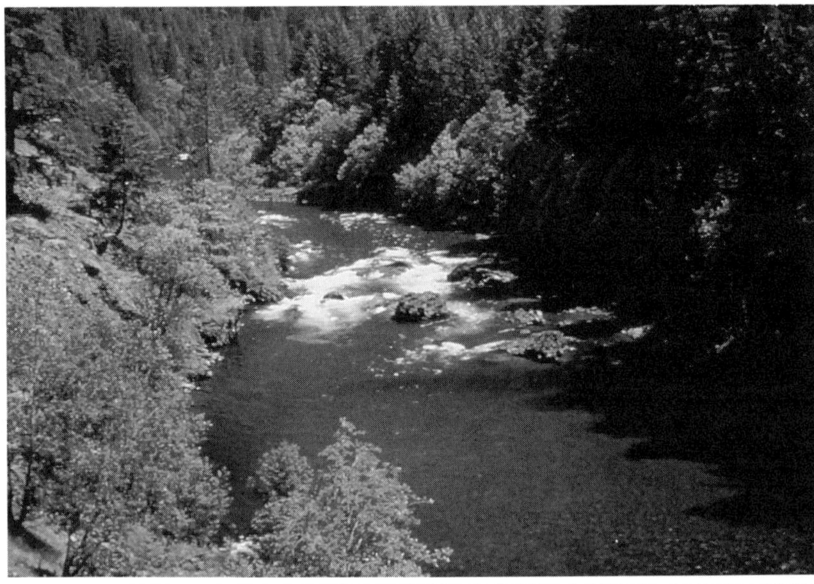
Clackamas River *Tom Iraci / USFS*

The Killer Fang Run's relatively moderate gradient is deceiving: the river is pool-and-drop, losing most of its elevation in a handful of very demanding drops. **Logs are a major potential hazard** on this section; many of the rapids have narrow chutes that can easily be blocked. Boaters should scout whenever they cannot see clearly to the bottom of a drop.[3]

Three Lynx Run: The 13 miles from Three Lynx to North Fork Reservoir are by far the most popular section of the Upper Clackamas. This reach offers a winning combination of powerful intermediate to advanced whitewater, fine scenery, good camping, and a relatively long season. Well-known rapids include Hole In The Wall, Carter Bridge Rapid, Toilet Bowl, and Bob's Hole, a renowned kayak play spot and site of an annual whitewater rodeo. Another whitewater festival, including a raft race, is held every year on the Three Lynx Run. Logs can still be a hazard on this section, so stay alert. Oregon Highway 224 follows this reach closely, offering frequent access and allowing boaters to choose the sections best suited to their skills.

The Upper Clackamas ends where the river stills in North Fork Reservoir. In the next ten miles, three dams block the Clackamas. The middle of these, Cazadero Dam, collapsed in the December 1964 flood, sending a torrent of water down on the town of Estacada.

Lower Clackamas

Below the third reservoir, formed by River Mill Dam near Estacada, the Clackamas flows freely through scenic pastoral terrain for some 22 miles to its confluence with the Willamette. Although a few Class II rapids punctuate this section, at moderate flows the Lower Clackamas is generally forgiving and well suited to less experienced boaters. The river divides frequently around islands as it reworks its gravelly channel. In winter and spring, high flows produce bigger waves and greater turbulence which make this section considerably more difficult, especially for open boats. At these times boaters must be especially aware of hypothermia risks and strainer hazards.

Most of the whitewater is concentrated near the beginning of this section, and boaters often repeat a short run of the first couple of miles within McIver Park. Downstream the river is milder, and several accesses allow boaters to choose sections appropriate to their abilities. Below Barton Park the river banks are more developed and roads are closer to the water, though the scenery remains pleasant. For more information on the lower river, refer to the guide books listed above.

[3]For up-to-date information on this run, contact Alder Creek Kayak Supply, 250 NE Tomahawk Island Dr., Portland, OR 97217; (503) 285-0464.

Mile by Mile Guide

Upper Clackamas

Killer Fang Run

0 **PUT-IN** on the right bank of the Clackamas at the confluence with the Collawash, which enters from the left. **Alternate put-in** a mile downstream at Riverside Campground. The first two miles are Class II–III. A trail follows the right bank from Riverside Campground to the Oak Grove Fork.

2.5 The whitewater becomes more difficult as the Clackamas drops 40' in a half mile. At **THE GATES (III+)** big boulders are strewn across the channel. Not far downstream, watch for a big hole on the left.

4 The Oak Grove Fork of the Clackamas enters on the right.

4.5 **ROCKY'S (III+)**. The river careens into the left wall and veers right. Downstream on the right is Alder Flat Campground, where a long trail leads up to the road (difficult access). Below the campground the whitewater gets rougher, beginning with **DROP STOPPER (IV)**, where a big midstream rock sits at the foot of the rapid.

6.3 **PRELUDE (III+; IV at higher flows)**. Just above this drop the river surges into a headwall on the left. The drop itself consists of two chutes. ***HAZARD.*** As of 1993 the right-hand chute was blocked by a log, and at most flows only the left chute was passable. Approach this drop with caution, and proceed carefully downstream. This section of the canyon is unstable, and rapids can change at any time.

6.4 **KILLER FANG (III)**, once a mandatory portage, was transformed into an intermediate boulder garden in 1991 when the "Killer Fang," a big boulder, was displaced—perhaps by vibrations from a left-bank landslide. ***HAZARD.*** Eddy out in the pool below Killer Fang for a mandatory scout—and possible portage—of the new rapid just downstream.

NEW FANG (V–VI). ***POSSIBLE PORTAGE.*** Immediately below Killer Fang is a very dangerous new rapid created by the 1991 landslide. The river plunges nearly 20' into thundering holes, and the drop is littered with trees, brush, and other debris. This rapid is unstable and could change at any time. If in doubt, portage.

6.7 A couple of hundred yards below New Fang, the river bends sharply to the right and tumbles through **THE SIEVE (IV; IV+ at higher flows)**, a complex boulder garden. Difficult scout on the left. **Be alert for logs and brush** which often jam up here. This threat is even greater since debris may be washed down from the new rapid just upstream. Not far downstream is the last big rapid, **RIVER'S REVENGE (IV; IV+ at higher flows)**, another boulder-choked drop where logs often jam. Difficult scout on the right.

8.5 **TAKE-OUT.** Highway 224 crosses the river at Sandstone Bridge. Take out on the left bank just above the bridge, or continue downstream.

Three Lynx Run

Note: Mileages in brackets are cumulative from the Collawash River confluence.

0 [8.5] **RIVER ACCESS** on the left bank at the upper Highway 224 bridge (Sandstone Bridge). **Alternate access** a mile downstream at the next highway bridge. A trail follows the left bank for several miles downstream. Boaters may want to scout the first few hundred yards before launching. Below the first bridge the river splits around an island, with most of the current flowing down the right side into a wrap rock known as **Pancake Rock.** Just downstream is **POWERHOUSE (III+)**, sometimes called **Three Lynx**, where the river bends gradually to the right, then sharply back to the left as it piles into the right bank. Stay left at the bottom to avoid hitting the wall or getting trapped in a powerful eddy on the right. Just below the rapid on the right is the Three Lynx power station, which adds an average of about 300 cfs to the river.

1 [9.5] The highway recrosses the river, providing an **alternate RIVER ACCESS.**

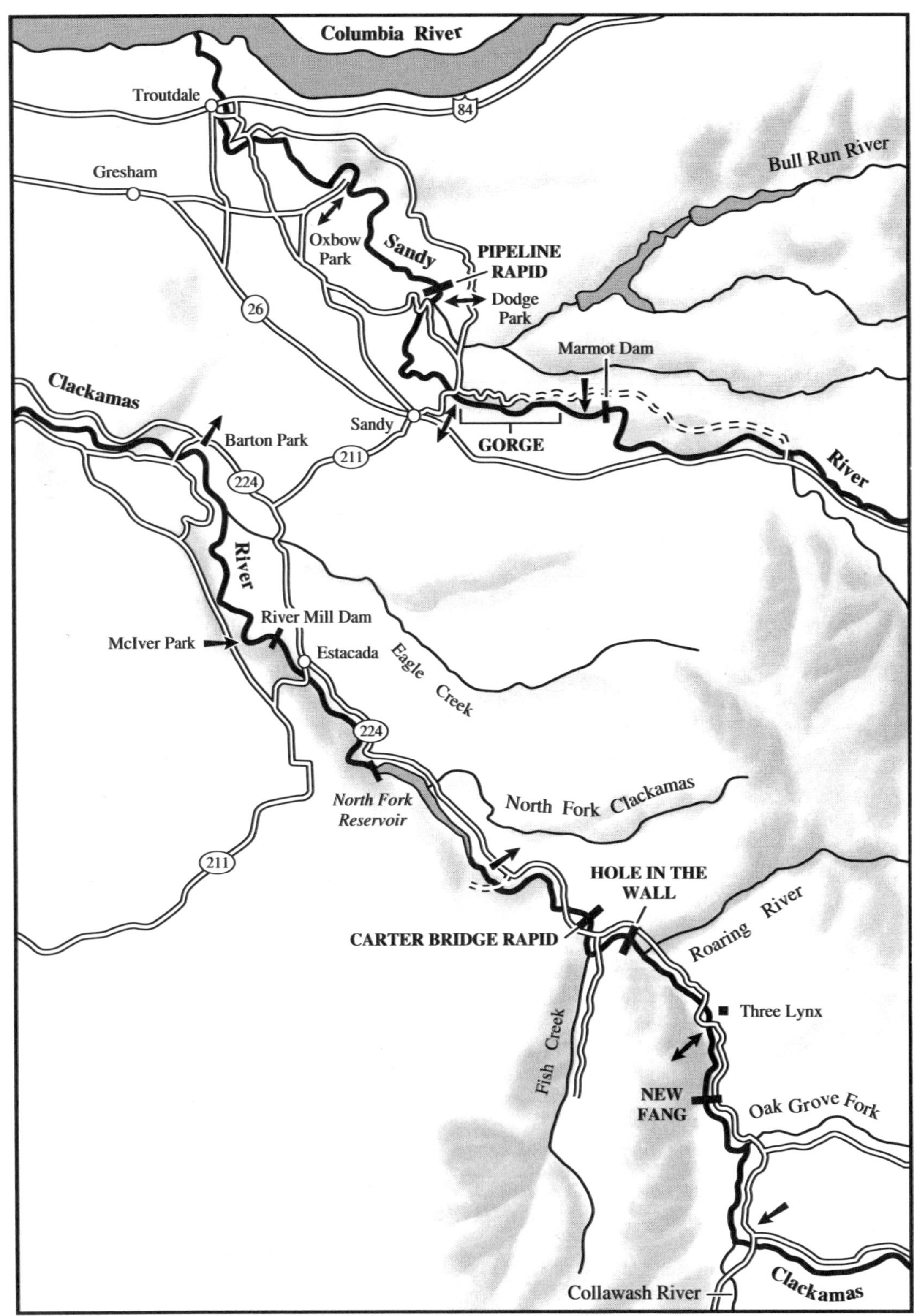

Clackamas and Sandy

2.3 [10.8] **THE NARROWS (III).** The river narrows to about 15', then races down a beautiful rock-walled mini-gorge.

4 [12.5] **ROARING RIVER RAPID (III).** A rock garden leads into a 5' drop. Common runs are down the center or left. More difficult at low water. Roaring River Campground is on the right, and the Roaring River enters on the right just downstream.

5 [13.5] **HOLE IN THE WALL (IV),** also called **Headwall.** Scouting recommended on the right. The river funnels down a steep, rocky chute on the left and plunges into a headwall on the left bank that divides the current. Stay right; the tongue leads left into a swirling, turbulent eddy/whirlpool with sheer walls. Boats and swimmers can be trapped here, and there have been deaths in the past. At higher flows this rapid can be sneaked down the right, but at lower flows boats often hit the wall. In the mid-1980's a chain ladder was bolted to the rock wall in the "hole" to allow swimmers to haul themselves out of the eddy. This has made the rapid less dangerous, but it's a good idea to scout this spot from the shuttle road before launching to be sure the ladder is in place.

7 [15.5] A minor bridge crosses the river, just above the mouth of Fish Creek on the left and Fish Creek Campground on the right. Kayakers often launch here. Three more Forest Service campgrounds line the riverbank in the next mile. Just below Fish Creek the river bends right and splits around an island: go left, but watch out for a big hole (boulder at lower flows) at the bottom.

7.9 [16.4] **CARTER BRIDGE RAPID (IV-). Recognition:** Below Fish Creek the highway crosses the river twice in the space of a half mile, first at mile 7.5 (Armstrong Bridge), and again at mile 8 (Carter Bridge). The rapid is just above the second bridge. Scout left, or scout from the shuttle road before boating. **The rapid:** The river drops sharply over an angled ledge, with the safest route on the far left. More difficult at higher flows.

9.3 [17.8] **BIG EDDY (III).** Just downstream, Big Eddy Picnic Area offers a possible **alternate RIVER ACCESS** on the right. Immediately below is **ROCK AND ROLL (III+).** A couple of hundred yards farther downstream, the river sweeps around a right bend into **TOILET BOWL (III),** where huge lateral waves develop at the bottom at high water. A third of a mile below Toilet Bowl is **BOB'S HOLE (III),** a famous kayak play spot and site of a whitewater rodeo each May. Kayakers sometimes take out on the right at Bob's Hole.

12.8 [21.3] A minor road bridges the river. **RIVER ACCESS.** The last possible take-out is about a quarter mile downstream, where a dirt road reaches the right bank across the highway from the Memaloose Scaling Station. A half mile downstream, the river enters the backwaters of North Fork Reservoir.

Lower Clackamas

0 **PUT-IN.** McIver State Park Boat Ramp (left bank). River Mill Dam is about half a mile upstream. The largest rapid on the run, **McIVER (II+, III at high flows),** is just downstream and can be scouted from the put-in. The drop has several standing waves and develops a sizable hole at higher flows. Class II rapids continue downstream.

2 Alternate **RIVER ACCESS** on the left at a parking lot and picnic area at the downstream end of McIver Park. Put in here to avoid the first rapid. Easy Class II from here on.

5.5 Eagle Creek, a major tributary, enters on the right. A mile downstream, several power lines cross the river.

9 **TAKE-OUT.** Barton County Park Boat Ramp (right bank). Or continue downstream through up to 13 additional miles of Class II water to the Willamette River. Accesses below Barton Park include Carver County Park on the left bank at mile 14; Riverside Park on the right at mile 17.5; and Clackamette Park at the Willamette confluence, mile 22.

Sandy River

Sandy Gorge and Lower Sandy

1. Sandy Gorge: Below Marmot Dam (630') to Revenue Bridge (435').
IV+ (V above 2,500 cfs); 5 miles; 40 ft./mi.

2. Lower Sandy: Dodge Park (245') to Oxbow Park (75').
II+; 7 miles; 25 ft./mi.

Longer runs possible on both sections.

Drainage Area and Average Annual Discharge: 262 sq. mi. and 1,002,000 af near put-in.

Season: *Run 1:* Nov.–May. *Run 2:* Oct.–July. Usually peaks in midwinter, then drops to low flows in August. Fall rains often raise the river to boatable levels again.

Recommended Levels: *Run 1:* 800–2,000 cfs. *Run 2:* 1,000–3,000 cfs.

Flow Information: NWS tape, (503) 249-0666, gives the flow "near Bull Run." This gauge is located a half mile below Dodge Park, the put-in for Run 2, and includes the flow of the Bull Run River, a major tributary. Flows on Run 1 are usually much less.

Rafts: Run 1 is very rarely rafted due to difficult accesses, numerous log hazards, and possible portages.

Special Hazards: Very serious log hazards on Run 1.

Permits: Not presently required.

Commercial Raft Trips: None at this time.

Land Ownership: Almost all private except for river accesses and some BLM land between Dodge Park and Oxbow Park.

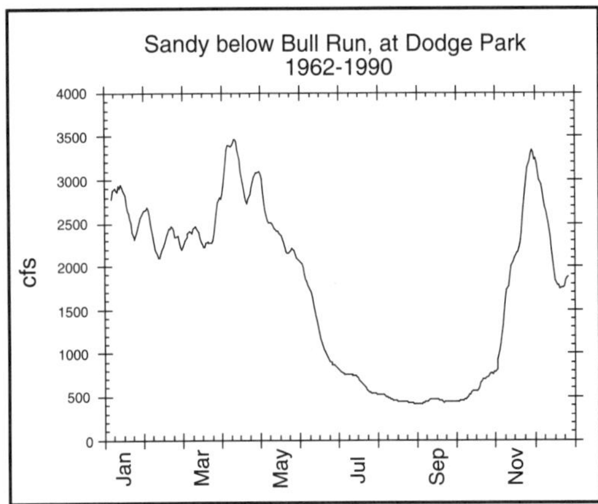

Scenery: Excellent. Run 1 is a lush, narrow gorge. Run 2 is through forested hills.

Solitude: *Run 1:* Excellent. *Run 2:* Very good, though boating use is heavy.

Wilderness: Yes.

Water: Very cold and relatively clear except at very low flows.

Guides and References:

- *Soggy Sneakers Guide to Oregon Rivers* (Willamette Kayak and Canoe Club). Also covers upstream and downstream runs.
- Garren, *Oregon River Tours.* Covers Run 2 and downstream runs.

Maps:

- **USGS** 7.5': *Bull Run, Sandy.*
- **USFS:** *Mt. Hood NF.*

Logistics: *Run 1:* Follow U.S. 26 to the town of Sandy, roughly 20 miles southeast of Portland. A few blocks east of Oregon Highway 211, turn north on Teneyck Road (marked by a sign for Bull Run). In about half a mile, Teneyck Road turns hard left; continue a little over a mile to Revenue Bridge. The **take-out** is a steep trail on the left bank. Consider hiking upstream from this take-out to scout **Revenue Bridge Rapid** before you run.

To reach the **put-in,** cross the Sandy and drive roughly 8 miles east on the paved road, staying right at all main intersections. About 300 yards past the end of the pavement, bear right onto a gated dirt road (Portland General Electric sign) and descend a little over a mile to a turnout on the right. A steep trail leads several hundred yards downhill across a flume to the put-in on the right bank, just over a mile downstream from Marmot Dam. Boaters can put in upstream at Wildcat Creek, but this means a portage of Marmot Dam.

Run 2: From I-84 east of Portland, take Exit 17, turn south on 257th for 4 miles, turn left on Division (which becomes Oxbow Parkway), and follow signs some 7 miles to the **take-out** on the left bank near the upstream end of Oxbow County Park. To reach the **put-in,** exit the park and drive south a half mile on Hosner Road, turn left on Lusted Road, and drive roughly 5 miles upriver to the bridge over the Sandy. Just beyond the bridge, turn left into Dodge Park.

From icy beginnings among glaciers on the west face of 11,239' Mt. Hood, Oregon's highest peak, the Sandy traces a short course northwest toward the Columbia River through a variety of landscapes. In its upper reaches the Sandy is a swift, technical mountain stream rushing through a steep, forested canyon. Near the middle of its journey, the river churns through dramatic rapids in a narrow volcanic gorge.

As it approaches the Columbia, the Sandy meanders gently through deep woods where civilization seems far away. In its lower reaches the river winds in shifting channels over thick deposits of sand and gravel. When this sediment eventually reaches the Columbia, it forms large sandbars at the river's mouth. When Lewis and Clark saw these deposits in 1805, they dubbed the river the "Quicksand." Later settlers modified to the name to "Sandy."

Even more than the Clackamas, the Sandy is Portland's backyard river. The Lower Sandy offers a variety of convenient day trips less than an hour's drive from a large urban boating community. Unlike many rivers near metropolitan areas, it has fine scenery in a near-wilderness setting. Here river runners can escape the metropolitan hustle and bustle and let the river restore their city-weary souls.

Hard-core boaters can take on something far more serious: the Sandy Gorge above Revenue Bridge. This five-mile section below Marmot Dam has the best scenery but also the toughest and most dangerous whitewater on the river. It is almost exclusively the domain of expert kayakers; rafters are usually deterred by the steep access trails, narrow chutes, log jams, and possible portages.

The Sandy Gorge is an intimately-scaled chasm carved in deposits of compressed volcanic ash. In places the river has gouged deep overhangs into the walls, creating shady recesses where ferns and mosses thrive. Rivulets and side streams descend from the surrounding forested valley and cascade over cliffs into the verdant inner gorge.

The most difficult rapids form where large boulders have tumbled into the gorge, dividing the river into steep, narrow chutes that become much more difficult at higher flows. Logs often lodge in these constricted slots, creating the biggest hazards on the run. Boaters must be especially cautious after heavy storms because high water can shift the logs into new positions. To complicate matters, the narrow canyon hampers scouting and portaging. **At times there may be rapids that are both unrunnable and unportageable.**

Taken together, these factors argue for first inquiring locally about river conditions, then running the gorge with an experienced local boater who has seen the river recently.[1]

Below Revenue Bridge the gorge opens and the Sandy runs through more open terrain. Relatively few boaters float the five miles from Revenue Bridge to Oxbow Park, the most developed and least secluded reach of the Sandy. Below Oxbow Park a sense of near-wilderness seclusion returns as the river flows easily through forested bottomlands and hills. Wildlife is abundant, and civilization seems far away despite the proximity to Portland. The run below Dodge Park is popular with campers, anglers, and river runners alike. Controlled releases down the Bull Run River, a major tributary, keep this section boatable for much of the summer. The Lower Sandy is all Class II+ or easier, ideal for less experienced boaters provided they remain alert for possible log hazards and strainers.

Some 29 miles of the Sandy were added to the National Wild and Scenic Rivers System in 1988: a 12-mile stretch below Dodge Park plus some 17 miles near the headwaters in Mt. Hood National Forest. Unfortunately, 35 miles of the river's middle reaches—including the spectacular gorge below Marmot Dam—were not included.[2]

Downstream Runs

Below Oxbow Park, the take-out for the run covered here, the Lower Sandy offers several more miles of seclusion and pleasant floating on Class I+ and II water. Popular downstream accesses are Dabney Park on the right bank 5.5 miles below Oxbow, and Lewis and Clark State Park three miles farther downstream, just above the river's mouth. Drift boaters, rafters, canoeists, anglers, and innertubers all enjoy the light riffles and fine scenery of this final quiet reach.

---

[1]For up-to-date information on this run, contact Alder Creek Kayak Supply, 250 NE Tomahawk Island Dr., Portland, OR 97217; (503) 285-0464.

[2]The Pacific Rivers Council (see appendix for address) and Friends of the Sandy (P.O. Box 23, Sandy, OR 97055) are working to protect more of this fine river.

Upstream Runs

The Upper Sandy has some 18 boatable miles above Marmot Dam, ranging from extremely steep Class IV+ whitewater in the upper reaches to generally milder rapids as the river approaches Marmot Dam—with the notable exception of Class IV Alder Creek Rapids about three miles above the dam. These upstream sections are runnable only during the rainy season. For more information refer to the *Soggy Sneakers Guide to Oregon Rivers.* Be aware that Marmot Dam is a mandatory portage for those continuing below the alternate access at Wildcat Creek.

Mile by Mile Guide

See map in Clackamas chapter.

Marmot Dam to Revenue Bridge

0 **PUT-IN** on the right bank a little over a mile below Marmot Dam at the foot of a trail (on Portland General Electric property; see **Logistics**). The Sandy Gorge begins immediately downstream. *HAZARD.* Be alert for **"The '64 Log Jam,"** a dangerous tangle in the Class IV+ rapid just below the put-in. There may be a sneak route down the right, but scout carefully from the right bank before running, and portage if necessary.

3–4.5 This mile-and-a-half stretch in the heart of the gorge features four major rapids. Approach each drop with caution, scout carefully, be constantly alert for log hazards, and portage if in doubt.

First comes **BOULDER (IV+)**, which **may be unrunnable,** especially for rafts, depending on **log hazards. Recognition:** As the canyon narrows, look for an overhanging cliff and waterfall on the left. **The rapid:** Huge boulders constrict the river and divide it into narrow channels. Logs often block the only runnable channel, and an undercut creates an additional hazard on the right. Very difficult portage on the left under the overhang.

Next up is **RASP ROCK (IV)**, a long rapid with big holes and two boulders at the bottom that divide the river into narrow chutes where boats could bridge. Much more difficult at high flows; pinning hazards in low water. Logs can jam in the chutes at the end of the rapid. Scout carefully from the right bank before running. Portage if necessary.

The third big drop is **DRAIN HOLE (IV+).** *POSSIBLE PORTAGE* at higher flows. Three house rocks block the left two thirds of the river, and most of the current rushes into an undercut on the left. A small chute on the far right may be runnable. Logs can jam in the chutes between the boulders. Much more difficult at higher flows. Scout on the right; portage if necessary.

The last big rapid is **REVENUE BRIDGE (IV+)** at mile 4.5. **Recognition:** As the river curves gradually to the right, the bridge comes into view downstream through the trees. Scout, and portage if necessary, on the left. Better yet, scout this one *before* you run this stretch by hiking upstream from the take-out. **The rapid:** A long, technical boulder garden. About halfway down, the current slams into the right wall, then drops into two huge holes at the bottom. Most boaters try to skirt left of the second hole.

4.8 Revenue Bridge. Difficult **RIVER ACCESS** up a steep trail on the left. Boaters may float some 5 miles of milder water to an **easier take-out at Dodge Park.**

Dodge Park to Oxbow Park

0 **PUT-IN.** Dodge Park on the right bank, not far below a bridge across the river. At the end of the park the Bull Run River enters on the right, adding considerable flow. Not far below this confluence is **PIPELINE (III-)**, a rock garden where a pipeline bridges the river. More Class II rapids follow.

1.5 **BLUE HOLE (II+)**, a long boulder garden ending in a wave/hole on the left.

3.5 Indian John Island. The left channel is the usual route.

7 **TAKE-OUT.** Oxbow Park Boat Ramp on the left. Take out or continue downstream (see essay).

Deschutes River

1. U.S. Highway 26 (1,350')
to above Sherars Falls (725').
III; 53 miles; 12 ft./mi.

2. Below Sherars Falls (705')
to Columbia River Confluence (165').
III; 42.5 miles; 12 ft./mi.

Many shorter runs possible on both sections.

Drainage Area and Average Annual Discharge: 10,500 sq. mi. and 4,230,000 af at mouth.
Peak Recorded Flow: 75,500 cfs (Dec. 22, 1964).
Season: All year. Flows regulated by Pelton and Round Butte Dams. Typical winter peak of 6,000–7,500 cfs in May, with summer flows usually 3,500–5,000 cfs.
Recommended Levels: 2,000–8,000 cfs.
Flow Information: NWS tape, (503) 249-0666; flow at Moody (river mouth). Portland General Electric "fish line," (800) 632-3474; release from Pelton Dam (put-in).
Special Hazards: Sherars Falls, a mandatory portage between the two runs.
Permits: Not required as of 1993. Boating regulations are under a three-year review; contact the managing agency for current information. As of 1993 Oregon requires a "boater pass"; annual passes also available. Also, boats must display an ID tag. Group size limit 16 on all sections except from Deschutes Club Locked Gate (Run 1, mile 37) to Sherars Falls (Run 1, mile 53), where the limit is 24.
Managing Agency: BLM, Prineville District, P.O. Box 550, Prineville, OR 97754; (503) 447-4115.

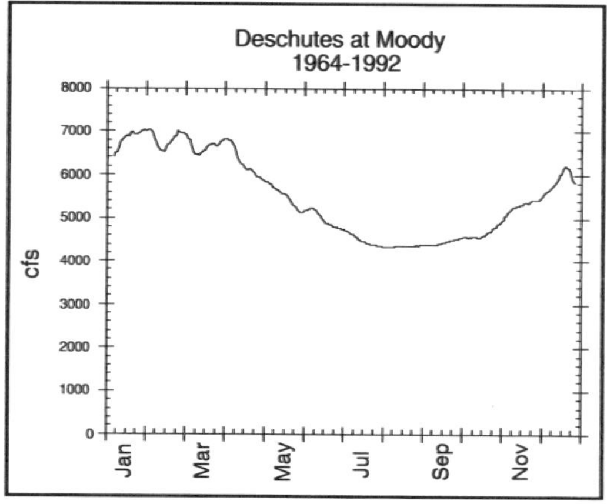

Commercial Raft Trips: Yes, many outfitters. For a list contact the BLM.
Land Ownership: Mixed BLM, Warm Springs Indian Reservation, state, and private. More public land on the lower section.
Scenery: Good to fair. Dry, grassy canyon.
Solitude: Good on weekdays and in the off-season. Very poor on summer weekends when river traffic is heaviest. Some power boats, especially below Macks Canyon (Run 2, mile 18.5). Railroad follows the entire run.
Wilderness: No. Railroad, several minor roads.
Fishing: Excellent for trout and steelhead. Steelhead run begins in late July.
Water: Always cold, fairly clear. Bring water or purify water from side streams.
Camping: Good riverside camping, though shade is scarce. Many sites have toilets. Competition for sites in peak season. No camping on Warm Springs Indian Reservation (see **Mile Guide**).
Guides and References:

- *Soggy Sneakers Guide to Oregon Rivers* (Willamette Kayak and Canoe Club). Also covers upstream runs.
- Garren, *Oregon River Tours.*
- Quinn, Quinn, & King, *Handbook to the Deschutes River Canyon.* Also covers upstream runs.
- Richmond, *Fishing in Oregon's Deschutes River.*
- Orr & Orr, *Rivers of the West.* Local history and geology.
- Hughes, *Deschutes.* Emphasis on angling.
- A good local source of information is Bend Whitewater Supply, P.O. Box 461, 55 NW Wall St., Bldg. C, Bend, OR 97709; (503) 389-7191.

Maps:

- **BLM:** *Lower Deschutes River.* Best all-around map; includes topography. Available from the managing agency.
- *Oregon Fishing Map: Lower Deschutes River* (Frank Amato Publications). Available locally. Shows rapids, accesses, etc.
- *Whitewater Map of the Deschutes River* (Scott Vollstedt). Available locally.
- *Riverguide Bandana to the Deschutes* (Rivers & Mountains). Cloth map.

Auto Shuttle: *Run 1:* About 75 miles one way, all paved. *Run 2:* About 55 miles one way, mostly paved. Contact the managing agency for advice on shuttle services.

Logistics: Contact the managing agency for current information regarding river accesses.

Run 1: The **put-in** is on the right bank just above the U.S. 26 bridge, about 12 miles northwest of Madras. The present **take-out** above Sherars Falls is on the left just off Oregon Highway 216, roughly 7 miles east of U.S. 197 at Tygh Valley. **Scout this take-out carefully!** Shuttle via U.S. 26, U.S. 97, U.S. 197 and Oregon 216. In the future the Sherars Falls take-out will be closed, and boaters will have to take out at the **Sandy Beach access** on the right bank about a mile and a half upstream. Sandy Beach can be reached by following the right bank road downstream from Maupin or upstream from Highway 216. Many **alternate accesses,** including Gateway (Trout Creek), South Junction, and several more below the Locked Gate above Maupin (reached by a dirt road that follows the right bank upstream from Maupin). Refer to the **Mile Guide** and consult the BLM map.

Run 2: To reach the **put-in below Sherars Falls,** follow Oregon 216 east about 8 miles from U.S. 197 near Tygh Valley. Cross the Deschutes, drive about ¾ mile downstream, and bear left on an unpaved road along the left bank. The most common put-in is at **Buck Hollow,** a half mile down this road, just above Elder Creek. An **alternate put-in** is about 2.5 miles farther down the road at the **Pine Tree access.** For more alternate accesses see the **Mile Guide** and the BLM map. The **take-out at the Heritage Landing Boat Ramp** on the left bank is off I-84 about 13 miles east of the U.S. 197 junction. Shuttle via Oregon 216, U.S. 197, and I-84.

The Deschutes is Oregon's most popular whitewater river, thanks to a long season, fun but forgiving rapids, convenient location for urbanites, and sunny weather—a key factor in the drizzly Pacific Northwest. (The Wenatchee is Washington's favorite river for the same reasons.) Palefaced Portlanders flock to the Deschutes, seeking adventure and the perfect sunburn. Despite crowds, middling scenery, and noisy power boats in some sections, the popularity of the Deschutes is booming: 60,000 user-days in 1975; 90,000 in 1982; 138,000 in 1990.[1]

Oregon's second-longest river after the John Day, the Deschutes runs north some 250 miles from headwaters southeast of Bend to the Columbia River near The Dalles. Along the way several major tributaries draining the east slope of the Cascades enter from the west: the Little Deschutes, Metolius, Warm Springs, and White Rivers. Only one major tributary, the Crooked River, drains the semi-arid lands east of the Deschutes.

The Deschutes is fed primarily by groundwater flowing from porous volcanic rock in the upper watershed. The river can be traced upstream only as far as Lava Lake, five miles east of the Cascade crest, where it emerges full-fledged from a lake with no above-ground tributaries. The groundwater flow is so steady that, according to the USGS, "the Deschutes has a more nearly uniform flow than any other river of its size in the United States." Though some incorrectly give credit to reservoirs for the year-round boating season, in fact groundwater provides adequate flows in even the driest years. The cold, clear water also supports a rich trout fishery, making the Deschutes very popular with anglers.

The most popular section of the river is the 97-mile Lower Deschutes, which is featured in this chapter. This is a long Class III stretch from the last dam near Madras to the confluence with the Columbia. Sherars Falls, a Class VI cataract, divides this section roughly in half. In 1988 Congress designated the Lower Deschutes a National Wild and Scenic River. Though some refer to the 53-mile reach above Sherars Falls as the "Upper Deschutes," this is a misnomer: the Upper Deschutes is actually the section near Bend in central Oregon. Some boating takes place on the Upper Deschutes, and readers will find brief information on these runs at the end of this chapter.

[1]The BLM's 1993 management plan calls for limiting total boating use to near 1990 levels and an additional effort to reduce peak weekend use. During an initial three-year trial period, the BLM will use voluntary methods to limit and redistribute use; if that program is unsuccessful, it may use mandatory restrictions.

Whitewater on the Lower Deschutes is generally forgiving and enjoyable for intermediates. The rapids are mostly wide open, with room for maneuvering. Cold water is of some concern, though most of the rapids have good runouts in the event of a mishap. The bulk of the rougher water is concentrated near the end of each of the two main sections. Alternate accesses allow boaters to choose from a variety of shorter runs.

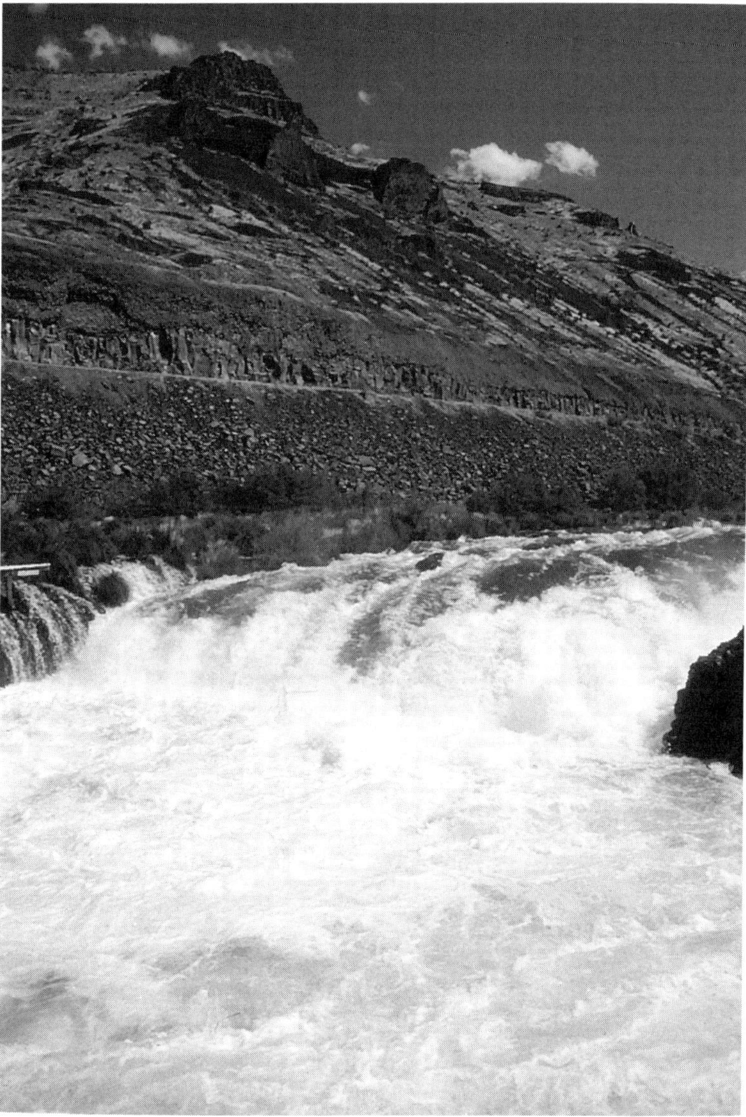

Sherars Falls, Deschutes River *Bill Cross*

Entertaining rapids, good fishing, and easy access mean big crowds in peak season. The most popular reach—the 16 miles from the Deschutes Club Locked Gate above Maupin (see mile by mile) to Sherars Falls—can be packed with 2,500 boaters or more on hot July and August weekends. The next most popular section is the 37 miles above the Locked Gate. Boaters can find more privacy, and do their bit to ease crowding, by sticking to weekdays, the off-season, or the run below Sherars Falls.

Unfortunately, power boats detract from the solitude below the falls. Until recently they were allowed everywhere except the first 28 miles of the upper run. By 1996 the BLM plans to prohibit them altogether above Sherars Falls and to allow them only in the off-season in the first 18 miles below the falls. They will still be common on the second stretch below Macks Canyon.

Scenery, like solitude, is not the Lower Deschutes' strongest suit. Lying in a strong rain shadow east of the Cascades, the canyon generally gets less than 10" of rain per year. Grasslands predominate and trees are few and far between, though recent efforts to fence out cattle and replant riparian trees have helped regreen the canyon somewhat. If the canyon looks windswept, there's a reason: the same powerful winds that delight boardsailors in the Columbia Gorge continue right on up the Deschutes, and on some afternoons these gusts pose a real obstacle for river runners.

Local geology contributes to the Deschutes' stark landscape. At first the river flows through soft, sometimes colorful deposits of volcanic ash and other sediments. Near mile 40 of Run 1, the river enters hard, dark lavas that dominate the rest of the way to the Columbia. These layered deposits, formed by eruptions some 15 million years ago, do not produce dramatic gorges like those on the Crooked or Owyhee Rivers. Nevertheless, boaters can admire fine formations of columnar basalt and explore several lava tubes and caves.

DESCHUTES

The Deschutes[2] was once home to the Tenino Indians, who called the river "Towornehiooks." The Tenino subsisted primarily on fish from the Deschutes and Columbia. Celilo Falls, one of the world's greatest natural fishing sites, was located on the Columbia just above the mouth of the Deschutes. The great Columbia narrowed to 150', then plunged over a thunderous 50' drop. Incredible numbers of migrating salmon congregated here, and the Indians harvested thousands using dip nets. Today this natural wonder is gone, buried by the Army Corps of Engineers' Dalles Dam.

Early in the twentieth century, rival rail barons fought to be the first to complete a line up the Lower Deschutes to Bend. Crews under James Hill laid tracks up the west bank, while teams under Edward Harriman raced up the east. Despite frequent mutual sabotage, both sides soon pushed tracks 70 miles upriver, from which point a joint line continued to Bend. Both railroads operated for a time, but eventually the east-bank line was abandoned and partially converted to roads. Burlington Northern trains still run on the west bank.

In this century engineers discovered the Deschutes, taking advantage of its steady flow and sudden drops to generate hydropower. The river's largest dam, Round Butte, was built in 1964 to create Billy Chinook Reservoir (named after a Wasco Indian chief). The dams have devastated fish runs on the Deschutes as well as its tributaries, the Crooked and Metolius.

---

[2]According to Lewis McArthur, *Oregon Geographic Names,* Lewis and Clark saw the Deschutes in 1805 and named it Clarks River. Later, French trappers with the Hudson's Bay Company called it "Rivière des Chutes" or "River of Falls." The name was not a reference to cataracts on the Deschutes itself, but rather to Celilo Falls on the Columbia.

Lower Deschutes Mile Guide

Note: mileages in brackets are measured upstream from the mouth. These figures are commonly used by local boaters.

U.S. 26 to Sherars Falls

0 [97] **PUT-IN** on the right bank just above the U.S. 26 bridge. **Alternate put-in** at Mecca Flat 1.5 miles downriver on the right. Left bank to mile 28 is Warm Springs Indian Reservation; no camping allowed. First 10 miles are Class I to I+. A trail follows the right bank from Mecca Flat to Trout Creek.

6.5 [90.5] Side hike to Frog Springs on the right.

9 [88] **RIVER ACCESS.** Gateway Recreation Site on the right. A rough dirt road leads to Madras. Downstream, Trout Creek enters on the right, followed by **TROUT CREEK (II+)** at a right bend. Below the rapid the railway joins the right bank. The next 8 miles are more open.

12.5 [84.5] South Junction railroad siding on the right. Warm Springs River enters a half mile downstream on the left. A rough **RIVER ACCESS** is a half mile downstream on the right. Easy water next 8 miles.

18 [79] The summer homes of Kaskela appear on the right. Downstream the canyon deepens as the river cuts through the Mutton Mountains.

21 [76] **WHITEHORSE (III)**, a long washboard at a right bend. Scout right. The first 150 yards or so are the steepest, but Class II water continues for over a mile.

24.5 [72.5] North Junction railroad bridge. The tracks follow the left bank from here to Sherars Falls, while a rough dirt road follows the right bank on the old railway grade (no public access). Easy water for the next 9 miles.

28 [69] End of Warm Springs Indian Reservation (left bank).

33 [64] **BUCKSKIN MARY (II+)**, a straight shot through standing waves. Class II riffles for the next mile or so.

37 [60] Deschutes Club Locked Gate on the right bank road. Downstream the road is open, with **many alternate accesses.** The most popular sites—Nena, Devil Canyon, Rainbow Bend, and Harpham Flat—are between the gate and Wapinitia Rapids. From here to Sherars Falls is the river's most popular stretch.

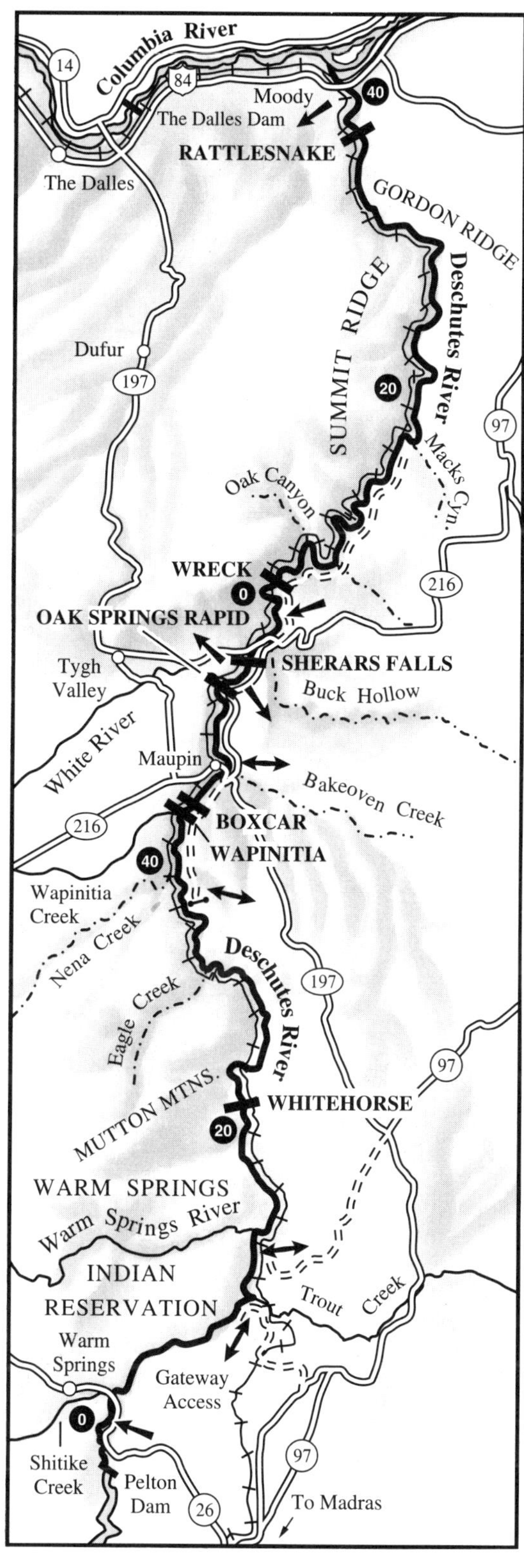

Deschutes

42.5 [54.5] **WAPINITIA (III-)**, a long rapid at a right bend where Wapinitia Creek enters on the left. Rocks block the center, and the typical run is down the right. The name is pronounced "Wa-pin-NEESH-a." About three quarters of a mile downstream is **BOXCAR (III)**, named for a 1950's train wreck. A ledge creates a steep drop. Watch for a big hole on the left. Scout on the left. This rapid is sometimes called **Lower Wapinitia.**

45.5 [51.5] U.S. 197 bridge at Maupin. RIVER ACCESS (fee) at the city park on the right below the bridge. A paved road follows the right bank from here to Sherars Falls.

49.5 [47.5] **OAK SPRINGS (III)**, at a right bend below a fish hatchery on the left. Two rock outcrops divide the river; big hole on the right. A mile downstream, the White River enters on the left at a Class II+ rapid. The glacier-fed White turns milky in late summer. Good side hike up the White to White River Falls.

51.5 [45.5] **Alternate TAKE-OUT** on the right at the **Sandy Beach access,** just above **OSBORNE (II+).** In the future, this will be the last possible take-out above Sherars Falls.

53 [44] Mandatory **TAKE-OUT** on the left where Highway 216 approaches the river. *HAZARD.* SHERARS FALLS (VI) is just downstream. This take-out will be closed in the future when the upstream take-out at Sandy Beach is improved. Sherars Falls is named for a turn-of-the-century toll bridge operator. Indians fish here with nets from rickety wooden platforms. Highway 216 crosses the river below the falls. Boaters making the long portage around the falls can launch again just above the bridge.

Sherars Falls to Columbia River

0 [42.5] **PUT-IN.** Buck Hollow access on the right. Two rapids, **UPPER BRIDGE** (III-) and **LOWER BRIDGE** (III), can be added by using a more difficult put-in just over a mile upstream, above the Highway 216 bridge on the right. A road follows the right bank for the next 20 miles, providing alternate accesses. The railroad follows the left bank for the entire run.

1.5–2.5 [41–40] The railroad crosses the Deschutes twice at a mile-long horseshoe bend to the right. Below the second bridge is **WRECK** (III-), named for a head-on train collision in 1949. **RIVER ACCESS** is possible at Pine Tree Campground, below the rapid on the right; this access avoids the rapids just upstream. No significant whitewater for over 30 miles.

10–11.5 [32.5–31] The river makes a sweeping right bend around a low peninsula known as "The Beavertail." **RIVER ACCESS** on the right at Beavertail Recreation Area.

18.5 [24] Macks Canyon Campground and **RIVER ACCESS** on the right. Power boats are common below this point. Half a mile downstream, the right bank road ends where Macks Canyon enters on the right.

30.5 [12] Harris Canyon enters on the right. An old water tank is nearby.

35 [7.5] Freebridge. The piers are all that remain of a former toll-free county bridge which stood here until 1914.

36.5–39.5 [6–3] A series of strong rapids beginning with **GORDON RIDGE** (II+), where the river drops over a ledge of columnar basalt just below a sharp right bend. A mile and a half downstream is **COLORADO** (III-), with big standing waves and a reversal on the left. Just downstream, Gordon Canyon enters on the right. Below the canyon at "The Narrows," the river splits around grass-topped rocks. Below these rocks is the largest rapid, **RATTLESNAKE** (III), where the river drops over a broad ledge with a big reversal on the right.

42.5 [0] **TAKE-OUT.** Heritage Landing on the left. The Deschutes is flat here, backed up by The Dalles Dam, 13 miles downstream on the Columbia.

Upper Deschutes River Guide

In its upper reaches near Bend, the Deschutes flows through young volcanic terrain where recent lava flows influence the river's course. Ramparts of jagged black rock form natural dams over which the river pours in spectacular falls. The flat areas behind many of these dams have filled with silt, and above several falls the Deschutes winds placidly through verdant meadowlands—a reminder of the eventual fate of all reservoirs. Much of the upper river was added to the National Wild and Scenic Rivers System in 1988.

The Upper Deschutes is definitely a pool-and-drop river, switching abruptly from mirror-smooth Class I to thundering Class VI. Between the falls boaters enjoy superb flatwater floats and a sprinkling of intermediate-to-expert runs. **Take-outs should be scouted carefully and memorized.** Boaters *must* be certain that they put in and take out at the correct points. (In 1993 two rafters were killed when they accidentally launched above Dillon Falls and blundered into that huge drop.) **Be alert for log hazards throughout.** For detailed information refer to the *Deschutes NF* map, *Handbook to the Deschutes River Canyon,* and the *Soggy Sneakers Guide.*[3]

Wickiup Dam to Benham Falls

This 43-mile section above the most recent lava flows offers pleasant Class I floating except for one Class IV rapid and one big log jam. Frequent access allows boaters to choose from a variety of runs. The first 17 miles to La Pine State Recreation Area offer forest solitude and stronger current, while the following 26 miles are generally slower and more open, with occasional roads and houses.

A very scenic eight-mile Class I run begins on the left bank at Wickiup Dam, some 30 miles southwest of Bend. Here the Upper

---

[3]A good local source for information on the Upper Deschutes is Bend Whitewater Supply (see **Guides and References**).

Deschutes flows smoothly through an open forest where osprey abound. After eight miles look for Wyeth Campground on the left; take out here to avoid Pringle Falls just downstream. Below the campground Class II water leads around a left bend, under a bridge and directly into Class IV Pringle Falls, where strainers often lodge.

Class I boating resumes at Pringle Falls Campground, below the falls on the left. Four miles downstream, Tetherow Log Jam requires a short portage on the right. Boaters can avoid the portage by using an alternate put-in on the right bank below the jam. Three miles below the jam, La Pine State Recreation Area offers another alternate access on the right.

Below La Pine the current slackens and the river meanders across open marsh and meadow. **Alternate downstream accesses** include Big River Campground, Harper Bridge (USFS Road 40), and Besson Camp (8, 16, and 17.5 miles below La Pine, respectively). Houses dot the bank from Big River to Harper Bridge, while Sunriver Resort is on the right for six miles below Harper Bridge. The **mandatory take-out** is at Benham Falls Boat Ramp on the right bank, 26 miles below La Pine and just upstream from a foot bridge and log jam. The falls are a half mile downstream.

Benham Falls to Lava Island Falls

At Benham Falls the Deschutes encounters fresh lava less than 2,000 years old. The river thunders over three major falls in the next five miles: Benham, Dillon, and Lava Island. Few boaters make the two-mile advanced run from below Benham Falls to above Dillon Falls.

By contrast, the two miles from below Dillon Falls to above Lava Island Falls are the most popular on the upper river. Known as the Big Eddy Run, this Class III quickie has the Upper Deschutes' only intermediate whitewater.

The run begins on the left bank at Aspen Campground. After an initial mile of Class II, the river bends right, pauses in a placid pool, then rolls through the big waves and holes of **BIG EDDY.** The **mandatory take-out** is on the left bank above Lava Island Falls.

Below Lava Island Falls are two expert runs leading down to the outskirts of Bend. Though still lightly used, these runs have recently been getting more attention from local expert kayakers. These sections include very difficult rapids, sharp rocks, log hazards, and a diversion dam. Inquire locally for detailed information before attempting these runs.

Riverhouse Run

Below Bend, irrigation diversions leave the Deschutes too low for boating in summer. In the off-season, however, the irrigation canals are dry and the river is full. From mid-October to mid-April, boaters can make a six-mile Class IV run (gradient: 60 ft./mi.) from Bend to Tumalo State Park. This reach is known as the "Riverhouse Run" after a resort hotel at the put-in on the north side of Bend. If summer flows could be restored to the Riverhouse Run, it would quickly become one of Oregon's most popular river trips. For more details consult the *Soggy Sneakers Guide* and Bend Whitewater Supply (see **Guides and References**). Boating may also be possible below Tumalo State Park, but inquire locally first; this section is punctuated by unrunnable falls.

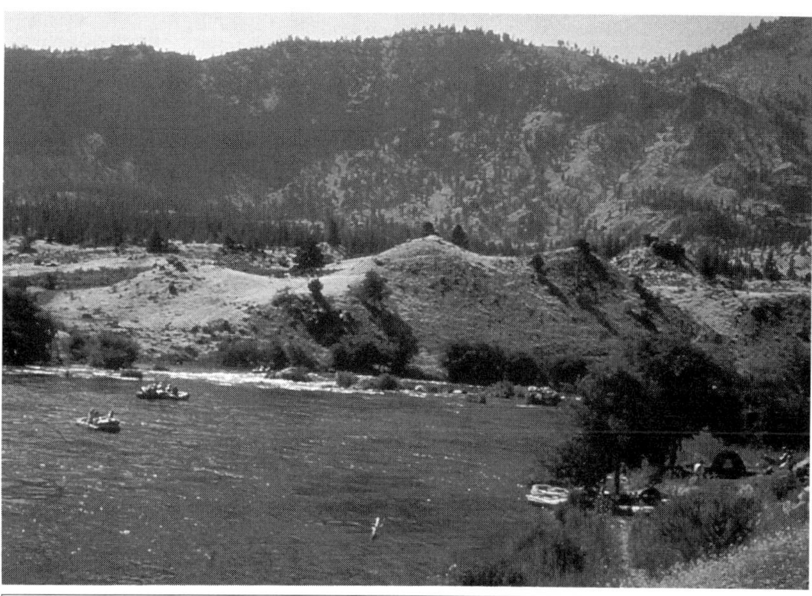

Whitehorse stretch, Deschutes River *BLM, Prineville District*

Metolius River

Lower Bridge to Monty Campground

Difficulty: III. **Gradient:** 45 ft./mi.
Length: 17 mi. Longer trips possible.
Put-in: Lower Bridge (2,710').
Take-out: Monty Campground (1,980').
Drainage Area and Average Annual Discharge: 316 sq. mi. and 1,085,000 af at take-out.
Season: April–Nov. Runnable flows all year.
Recommended Levels: 1,000–2,500 cfs.
Flow Information: Not available and normally not needed. This spring-fed river usually varies only slightly from its average flow of 1,480 cfs at the take-out. Flows are almost never below 1,100 cfs or above 2,500 cfs. Variations are caused by side creeks below the springs, but even during major storms these feeders very rarely push the flow at take-out above 4,000 cfs.
Special Hazards: Icy water. Very few eddies. Frequent log hazards.
Permits: Not presently required. Contact managing agency for updated information.
Managing Agency: Sisters RD, Deschutes NF, P.O. Box 249, Sisters, OR 97759; (503) 549-2111.
Commercial Raft Trips: Not permitted.
Land Ownership: Below Lower Bridge is National Forest on the right and Warm Springs Indian Reservation on the left. Camping and shore use (landing) are prohibited on the reservation. Above Lower Bridge is mostly National Forest.
Scenery: Excellent. Open forest, sloping volcanic canyon.
Solitude: Excellent.
Wilderness: Not quite. A seldom-used dirt road follows much of the run.

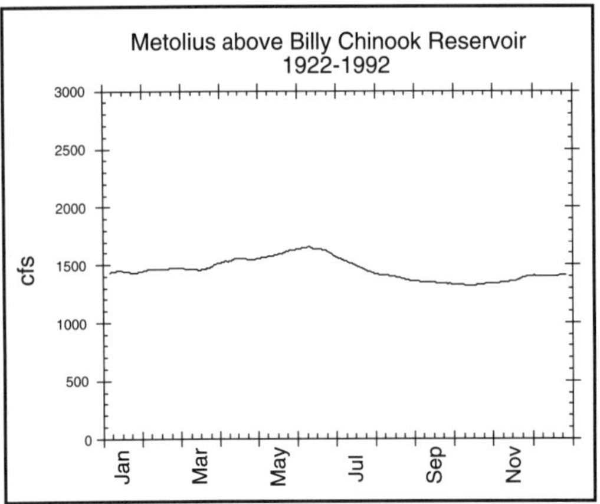

Side Excursions: "Head of the Metolius" (see **Logistics** and essay).
Guides and References:

- Garren, *Oregon River Tours.*
- *Soggy Sneakers Guide to Oregon Rivers* (Willamette Kayak and Canoe Club).

Maps:

- **USGS 7.5':** *Prairie Farm Spring, Shitike Butte, Metolius Bench, Fly Creek.*
- **USGS 1:100:** *Madras.* Covers entire run.
- **USFS:** *Deschutes NF.*

Auto Shuttle: About 23 miles one way. Only 45 minutes to an hour in good weather, but difficult in wet weather. Roads over Green Ridge are usually closed by snow until late spring. A long alternate paved route follows Oregon Highways 97 and 126 through Redmond and Sisters. For more information contact the managing agency.
Logistics: Due to the many intersecting dirt roads, boaters are strongly advised to have a *Deschutes NF* map when running the shuttle.

To reach the **put-in,** follow U.S. 20 to the Metolius River/Camp Sherman turnoff between Santiam Pass and the town of Sisters. (Sisters is 22 miles northwest of Bend.) Turn north and drive 2.5 miles, bear right at the "Y," and continue about a mile to the turnoff to "Head Of The Metolius." (Short side trip leads to springs where the river emerges from the ground.) Continue past this turnoff about 9 miles, driving downstream along the river's east bank on paved USFS Road 14. Put in on the right bank where the road crosses the river at Lower Bridge, adjacent to Lower Bridge Campground. (Many locals refer to Lower Bridge as "Bridge 99.")

To reach the **take-out** from Lower Bridge, drive back toward Camp Sherman about half a mile, then turn left on unpaved USFS Road 1490. Note your mileage. Drive uphill to the top of Green Ridge (enjoying stunning views of Mt. Jefferson along the way), then near mile 6 bear left on USFS Road 1140. In another 1.3 miles continue straight through an intersection, staying on the main dirt road which now becomes USFS Road 1180. Drive east another 3.5 miles, then continue straight through another intersection as the main road becomes USFS Road

1170. In another 5 miles, Road 1170 ends at a "T" intersection. Turn left, following signs toward "Forest Campgrounds," and drive the final 7 rough miles to Monty Campground. Turn into the campground, drive to the west (upriver) end, and park. When you take out, you must carry all gear about 100 yards up the old road that leads from the take-out (at the flat area beside the gauging station on the right bank of the river) to the parking area. The road has been blocked off to vehicles. **Scout the take-out very carefully!** The water is swift, and missing the landing means continuing 4 miles across the upper end of Billy Chinook Reservoir to the next possible access at Perry South Campground.

One of the West's most beautiful and enigmatic waterways, the Metolius River traces a scenic course down the east slope of the Cascade Range northwest of Bend, Oregon. This major tributary of the Deschutes presents something of a puzzle—a picture that doesn't look quite right. The Metolius is a powerful river that flows through a relatively shallow canyon whose banks are lined with large pines and other well-established vegetation. No gravel bars can be seen, and there is no evidence of a flood plain. Bridges are built daringly low to the water, while houses and cabins are sited as little as a foot above the river.

The answer to the riddle? The Metolius is almost entirely spring-fed, flowing at a nearly constant rate year-round. At the "Head of the Metolius" the river rises quietly from one of the West's largest springs, which yields some 300–350 cfs, or about 2,500 gallons per second. Additional springs on side streams soon add to the flow, which averages 1,200–1,400 cfs some 30 miles downstream at the take-out. Yet the river's above-ground drainage area at the take-out measures only 316 square miles—much too small to account for so much water, and insufficient to produce floods that would deepen the canyon, clear out the pines, deposit gravel bars, wipe out bridges, and wash away houses.

In fact, the greater part of the river's drainage lies hidden beneath the surface. Over millions of years, an ancient depression along the Cascade crest south of Mt. Jefferson was filled by lava flows. The porous lava acts like a gigantic underground sponge, soaking up rain and snowmelt from both sides of the crest. To the west, faults block much of the subterranean flow and force it back to the east. As a result, a good deal of water falling on the west side of the Cascades eventually finds its way—probably over a period of years—to the "Head of the Metolius" on the east side.

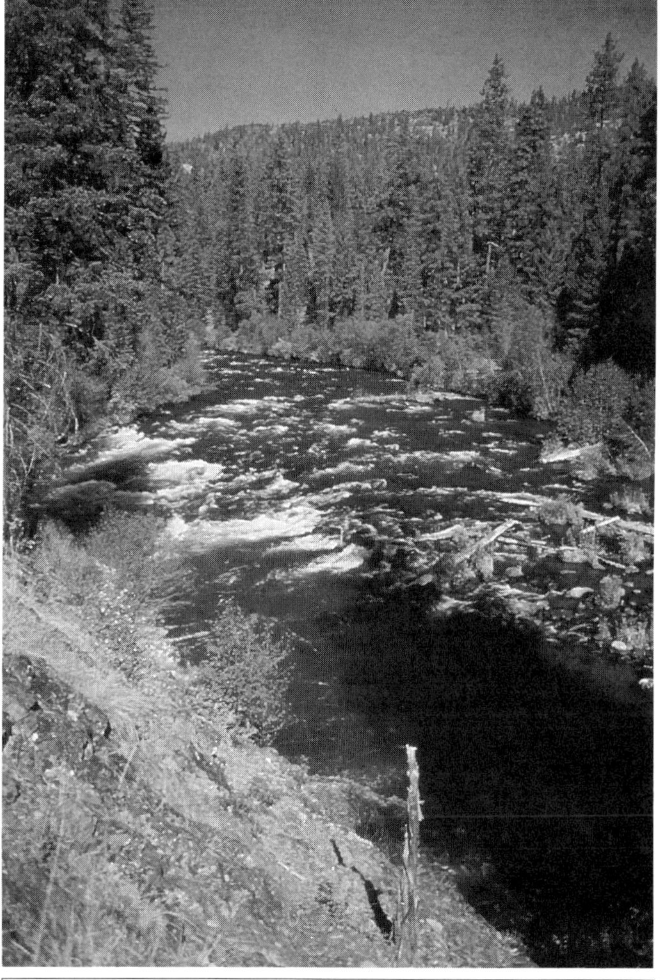

Metolius River *Bill Cross*

For river runners this means that the Metolius always has a boatable flow of crystal-clear, ice-cold water. (The water has a breathtaking ice-blue hue when sunlight shines through wave tips or into reversals.) The lowest flow since record-keeping began in 1910 was 1,080 cfs; the highest was a modest 7,530 cfs during the deluge of December 1964 that saw devastating floods on many other Pacific Northwest rivers. Almost all the variation in the Metolius' flow comes from feeder streams entering below the constant headwater springs.

In addition to marvelous water and reliable flows, the Metolius offers good weather, fine scenery, and near-wilderness solitude. When Portland and the west side of Cascades are socked in, boaters on the Metolius often enjoys sunny skies and crisp mountain air as the river winds through an open forest of pine, fir, and cedar. In late spring and summer wildflowers abound on the riverbanks and midstream rock islands; in autumn the shore is dotted with colorful maples and ash. Below the last crossing, Lower Bridge, the river runs through 17 miles of near-wilderness country where boating use is relatively light (but increasing).

For whitewater boaters the Metolius is essentially one long rapid. Beginning with the first Class III drop about a mile below Lower Bridge, the river rushes down a 16-mile continuum of Class II- to III+ whitewater, broken only occasionally by short stretches of swift but smooth water. The entire 17-mile run can easily flash by in just three or four hours.

Only one passage—a Class III+ about three quarters of the way down, sometimes called Whitewater River Rapid—stands out above the rest. Because it is so swift, the Metolius is normally run as a one-day trip. Camping is possible along the undeveloped right bank, but most groups choose to overnight at Forest Service campgrounds along the upper river (above Lower Bridge) or at the take-out.

Despite its moderate rating, this run demands extra caution: the water is extremely cold, the current is swift and nearly continuous, and eddies are small and *very* scarce. Long swims are possible, and hypothermia is a threat even in warm weather. Also, without the benefit of periodic floods the river may take years to clear out any trees that fall into the channel. As a result, **logs are a very serious hazard.** In the past, sweepers have blocked the entire channel in places. A boater in an inflatable kayak was swept into a strainer and killed in 1992. Swimmers are at risk from submerged logs hidden beneath the surface. In short, although the rapids on the Metolius may not seem too threatening, the consequences of a mistake can be disastrous.

Though the Metolius is gaining popularity among river runners, it is still best known as a world-class trout stream. The pure, icy water supports a remarkable abundance of rainbow and bull trout, drawing anglers from around the nation. Needless to say, the anglers aren't always thrilled when boaters splash through their favorite fishing holes. Please be considerate; a little courtesy now can avert problems down the road (see appendix on **River Etiquette**). Boaters can greatly reduce conflicts by avoiding early-morning and late-afternoon floating through the most popular fishing reaches: the entire upstream run (from Lower Canyon Campground to Lower Bridge; see below) and the first few miles of the main run.

In addition to resident trout, the Metolius once supported rich runs of migratory salmon and steelhead. In fact, the river's name comes from a Warm Springs Indian word meaning "white salmon" or "spawning salmon." Unfortunately, the river's steep gradient and steady flows proved irresistible to hydro developers: in 1964 Round Butte Dam was built not far below the confluence of the Metolius and the Deschutes. The resulting reservoir, named Billy Chinook after a Wasco Indian who lived in the area in the nineteenth century, flooded many miles of the Deschutes and the lower 15 miles of the Metolius, eliminating the salmon and steelhead runs. Fortunately, what is left of the river is now off limits to dam builders: Congress added the remaining free-flowing reach of the Metolius to the National Wild and Scenic Rivers System in 1988.[1]

[1] In 1993 the Warm Springs Indian tribe, whose reservation covers the left bank, formally prohibited all boating on the Metolius (though as of late 1993 the tribe had made no attempt physically to stop boaters from using the river, and boaters had continued to make the run). The tribe's legal right to ban boating is highly questionable. Contact the Forest Service for updated information.

Metolius River Guide

Put in on the right bank just above **Lower Bridge** (mile 0). A rough dirt road follows the right bank for the first nine miles. A mile of swift, easy water below the bridge leads to the first Class III rapid at a shallow left bend where Candle Creek Campground can be seen on the left bank. Below the campground Jefferson Creek enters on the left, bringing melted snow and ice from 10,497' Mt. Jefferson to the west. The river runs through almost continuous Class II and III rapids for the rest of the run.

Below Jefferson Creek the left bank is part of the Warm Springs Indian Reservation, which is closed to camping and shore use, including landing boats. Please respect this regulation.

At about mile 9 the rough dirt road along the right bank ends, though a trail continues. The Whitewater River enters on the left at mile 12, carrying milky meltwater from glaciers on Mt. Jefferson. The Metolius' ice-blue clarity diminishes below this point. A little over half a mile downstream is the most serious whitewater on the run, a Class III+ washboard sometimes called **WHITEWATER RIVER RAPID.** This rapid features a long series of holes and waves, with the strongest hole near the bottom right. As of 1993 a barely submerged log spanned the river near the head of this rapid, creating an extra hazard. Scout from the right shore.

An unpaved road follows the right bank for the remainder of the run. A gauging station appears on the right at mile 16.7, immediately above the **take-out at Monty Campground.** *Don't miss this landing!* The current is swift. This is the last road access above Billy Chinook Reservoir, which begins about a mile downstream. The next possible access is four miles across the reservoir at Perry South Campground.

Upstream Run

Boaters can run five additional miles of the Metolius by starting farther upstream at Lower Canyon Creek Campground. Boating is not recommended above this point due to several low bridges and more frequent encounters with anglers and cabin owners who are sometimes less than cordial.

This upper section is slower and easier—Class II to II+ with a gradient of 28 ft./mi.—and marks the river's transition from open flats to deeper canyon. This reach is more popular for fishing than the lower river. The scenic West Metolius Trail follows the left bank through this section. Boaters can take out on the right at Lower Bridge or continue down the main run.

HAZARD. One spot on this upstream run deserves extra caution. Some two miles below Lower Canyon Creek Campground, the river surges down a narrow channel at Wizard Falls. Though the "Falls" themselves are not particularly treacherous, immediately downstream is a **dangerous low bridge** at Wizard Falls Fish Hatchery. The bridge may be passable for kayaks, but it is a **mandatory portage for rafts.** Because the approach to the bridge is so swift, **all boaters should stop well upstream to scout** and consider portaging. The hatchery is open to the public and makes an interesting stop.

North Fork John Day River

Dale to Monument

Difficulty: II. **Length:** 42 miles.
Gradient: 18 ft./mi. (30 ft./mi. near put-in, 10 ft./mi. near take-out).
Put-in: U.S. 395 bridge (2,770').
Take-out: Monument Bridge (1,975').
Drainage Area and Average Annual Discharge: 2,520 sq. mi. and 892,600 af at take-out.
Season: April through May, sometimes into early June depending on snowpack. Generally peaks in early to mid-spring, then recedes quickly, often dropping below 500 cfs by mid-June.
Recommended Levels: 1,000–5,000 cfs.
Flow Information: NWS tape, (503) 249-0666, gives the flow at Monument, which includes the Middle Fork of the John Day. For a rough estimate of flows above the Middle Fork, which enters at mile 28, take ⅔ to ¾ of the flow at Monument.
Special Hazards: Isolation.
Permits: Not presently required.
Managing Agency: BLM, Prineville District, P.O. Box 550, Prineville, OR 97754; (503) 447-4115.
Commercial Raft Trips: Yes. Contact the BLM for current information.
Land Ownership: Mixed private and BLM.
Scenery: Excellent. Varies among canyon, open forest, and grasslands.
Solitude: Very good where dirt roads follow the river (about half of trip), otherwise excellent. Light boating use.
Wilderness: Partial. Dirt road first 19 and last 7 miles. A few houses and cabins.
Guides and References:

- Garren, *Oregon River Tours.*
- *Soggy Sneakers Guide to Oregon Rivers* (Willamette Kayak and Canoe Club).

Maps:

- **USGS 7.5':** *Dale, Bridge Creek, Deerhorn Creek, Meadow Brook Summit, Ritter, Slickear Mtn, Johnny Cake Mtn, Monument.*
- **BLM:** *Upper John Day River: Public Lands.* Best all-around map. Includes topography; 1:100,000 scale. $4 from managing agency.
- **USFS:** *Umatilla NF.*

Auto Shuttle: 50 miles (about 75 minutes) one way, paved. To hire shuttles, try the Monument Store or contact the BLM for advice.

Logistics: There are several alternate **put-ins** near Dale in northeastern Oregon. U.S. 395 follows the river for 3 miles from the bridge just north of Dale to the Camas Creek confluence; many possible accesses in this stretch. The BLM recommends a site on the left bank, opposite the highway. To get there, turn south off the highway about ¾ mile upstream from Camas Creek, cross the river on a one-lane bridge, and drive upstream a couple of hundred yards to the put-in. There are more **alternate accesses** below Camas Creek, where a dirt road follows the right bank.

To reach the **take-out,** follow U.S. 395 south from Dale roughly 25 miles to the settlement of Long Creek, then turn west and drive some 22 miles to the bridge over the North Fork at Monument. The lower take-out is just above this bridge on the right bank. An **alternate take-out** farther upstream can be reached by following an unpaved road north some 3 miles from Monument. The access is on BLM land on the right (west) bank near River Mile 39.

One river does the work, the other gets the glory. The North Fork of the John Day carries twice as much water as the "main" John Day where they meet, but by geographic convention the longer "main" stem gets to be called the John Day above the confluence.

What's in a name, anyway? In this case, perhaps, the difference between obscurity and popularity. The main John Day is one of Oregon's favorite easy floats, while the North Fork—despite what many consider its better scenery and whitewater—remains little used. More people might float this fine river if they thought of it simply as the "Upper John Day" instead of an obscure tributary. Of course, most of those who *have* discovered this excellent run don't mind the obscurity one bit. [1]

From 8,000' headwaters in the Blue Mountains of northeastern Oregon, the North

[1] 54 miles of the North Fork John Day were added to the National Wild and Scenic Rivers System in 1988. Unfortunately, the protection covers only the upper North Fork and ends near the put-in for the run covered here.

Fork John Day flows west and southwest through a remote canyon dotted with Ponderosa pine. Layered formations of dark basalt testify to the landscape's volcanic origins. As the North Fork approaches its confluence with the main stem, the terrain becomes drier. Grasslands and juniper dominate in the lower portion of the run described here.

Though little visited and sparsely settled today, the North Fork drainage was once home to hundreds of prospectors seeking their fortunes in gold. Near the turn of the century, mining claims stretched along most of the river and up several major tributaries. Old cabins and placer mining scars can still be seen in places. Today, the canyon's main treasure is fish. The John Day—in particular the North Fork—has the largest spawning population of salmon in the entire Columbia River basin.

The North Fork's boating season coincides with a brief surge of snowmelt, usually in late spring; then the river subsides to a tepid trickle. The impervious soils of its drainage soak up little water during snowmelt, allowing peak flows to reach surprisingly high levels for a river of this size. These same soils yield little groundwater to maintain flows during the summer.

At most water levels the North Fork offers easy intermediate whitewater. High flows can cause problems for less experienced boaters: the river becomes swift and icy, and waves grow big enough to cause trouble. At low flows the river can be rocky and technical. Most of the whitewater comes in the first 15 miles; the gradient and difficulty gradually ease and the current diminishes throughout the trip. Boaters should be prepared for isolation, changeable flows, and unpredictable weather.

North Fork John Day River Guide

Boaters can choose from a number of alternate put-ins (see **Logistics**). We use the U.S. 395 bridge as mile 0. The highway follows the right bank from this bridge to Camas Creek, which enters on the right at mile 3. Below Camas Creek a dirt road follows the right bank for another 19 miles. Watch for a long, rocky Class II rapid three miles below Camas Creek at a left bend. Several Class II drops follow in the next half dozen miles, after which the river is generally milder.

Stony Creek enters on the right near mile 15, and the right bank road crosses the creek on a wooden bridge. Potamus Creek enters on the right at about mile 21.5. Not far downstream, a bridge crosses the river and the right bank road ends. Mallory Creek enters on the right a half mile below the bridge, and Ditch Creek enters on the right two miles farther downstream. At mile 28 the Middle Fork John Day enters on the left, usually with about a quarter the flow of the North Fork.

Near mile 33 Johnny Cake Mountain and Neal Butte rise on the right. Wall Creek enters on the right around mile 37.5. Below the creek a dirt road follows the right bank most of the way to Monument. From about mile 38 to mile 39.5, the river passes through BLM land, allowing an **alternate take-out** along the right bank (see **Logistics**). Near mile 42 the canyon opens, and soon Deer Creek enters on the left. The **final take-out** is on the right bank at mile 44, just above the bridge at Monument.

Below Monument the North Fork flows through open terrain for some 16 miles to its confluence with the main John Day at Kimberly. This reach is rarely run due to its lower gradient, less inspiring scenery, agricultural diversions, and paved road.

Upstream Runs

USFS Roads 55 and 5506 provide access along the right bank for some 15 miles above Dale, allowing boaters to extend upstream the run described here when water conditions permit. The scenery in much of this section still bears the scars of intensive placer mining in the 1940's and 1950's.

Adventurous low-flow fanatics might consider a wilderness hike-in run even farther upstream, beginning at the confluence with Granite Creek (elevation 3,940') and extending to Big Creek or Oriental Creek for trips of 11 or 14 miles, respectively. A trail follows the right bank, allowing advance scouting of this **experts-only** section. The North Fork here is really just an oversized creek, cutting a deep, narrow canyon through the North Fork John Day Wilderness Area. The gradient averages 50 ft./mi., but the first two miles drop at 80 ft./mi. There is reportedly at least one Class V rapid, just below Granite Creek, and many other very tough drops. **Logs are a major potential hazard,** and some jams would probably have to be portaged.

John Day River

Service Creek to Cottonwood Bridge

1. Service Creek (1,650') to Clarno (1,260').
II; 47 miles; 8.5 ft./mi.

2. Clarno to Cottonwood Bridge (525').
II3; 68 miles; 11 ft./mi.

Drainage Area and Average Annual Discharge: 5,090 sq. mi. and 1,332,000 af at Service Creek.

Season: April–June. After a snowmelt peak in late April or early May, the river quickly drops to unrunnable summer lows, typically by early July. Autumn rains sometimes resurrect the river. The prime—and most crowded—season is usually late May and early June, when weather is fairly reliable and water temperature is rising.

Recommended Levels: 1,200–6,000 cfs.

Flow Information: NWS tape, (503) 249-0666; flow at Service Creek.

Special Hazards: Isolation. Cold water during peak runoff.

Permits: Not presently required.

Managing Agency: BLM, Prineville District, P.O. Box 550, Prineville, OR 97754; (503) 447-4115.

Commercial Raft Trips: Yes, many outfitters. For a list contact the BLM.

Land Ownership: Mixed private and BLM.

Scenery: Very good. Colorful desert canyon with interesting rock formations.

Solitude: Very good; better below Clarno. Heavy river traffic on holidays.

Wilderness: Mostly, especially below Clarno. Scattered ranches, dirt roads.

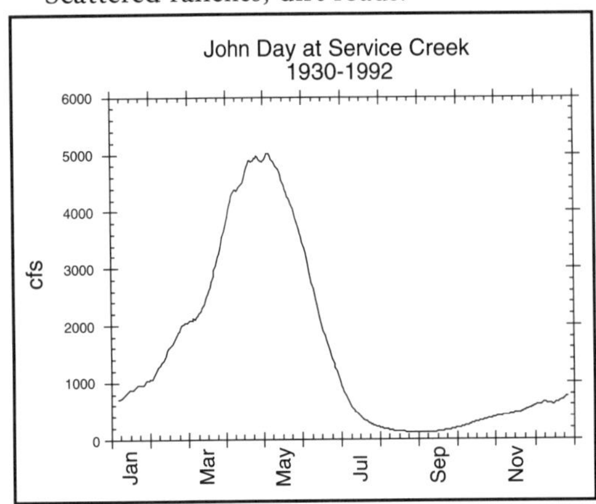

Water: Murky and undrinkable. Most side streams are tainted by grazing. Purify water from side streams or—better—pack in water. Some springs provide possible refill sites, especially below Clarno.

Camping: Good on benches above the river where scattered trees provide some shade. Signs of grazing cattle detract from some sites.

Side Excursions: John Day Fossil Beds National Monument near Clarno.

Guides and References:
- Campbell, *John Day River Drift and Historical Guide.*
- *Floating the John Day River* (BLM). Small map-pamphlet.
- *Soggy Sneakers Guide to Oregon Rivers* (Willamette Kayak and Canoe Club).
- Garren, *Oregon River Tours.*
- Orr & Orr, *Rivers of the West.* Local history and geology.

Maps:
- **BLM:** *Lower John Day River: Public Lands.* Best all-around map. Includes topography; 1:100,000 scale. Order from managing agency.

Auto Shuttle:

Run 1: About 40 paved miles via Oregon Highways 218 and 19.

Run 2: Roughly 65 paved miles via Oregon Highways 206, 19, and 218. Contact the BLM for shuttle driver references.

Logistics: The hamlet of **Service Creek** is located at the intersection of Oregon Highways 19 and 207, roughly 45 miles from U.S. 26 in north central Oregon. The **put-in** is about a quarter mile south of the highway junction, on the right bank upstream from the Highway 207 bridge over the John Day.

The **Clarno access** is on the right bank below the Oregon 218 bridge over the John Day.

The **Cottonwood Bridge take-out** is on the right bank below the Oregon 206 bridge over the river.

At 280 free-flowing miles, the John Day is the longest undammed river in the Pacific Northwest.[1] It also offers the region's longest continuous river trip. The John Day—especially its North Fork—supports the largest remaining spawning population of salmon and other anadromous fish in the entire Columbia River basin above Bonneville Dam near Portland. In 1988 Congress designated 148 miles of the main John Day (including the run covered here) and 101 miles of the North and South Forks as National Wild and Scenic Rivers.

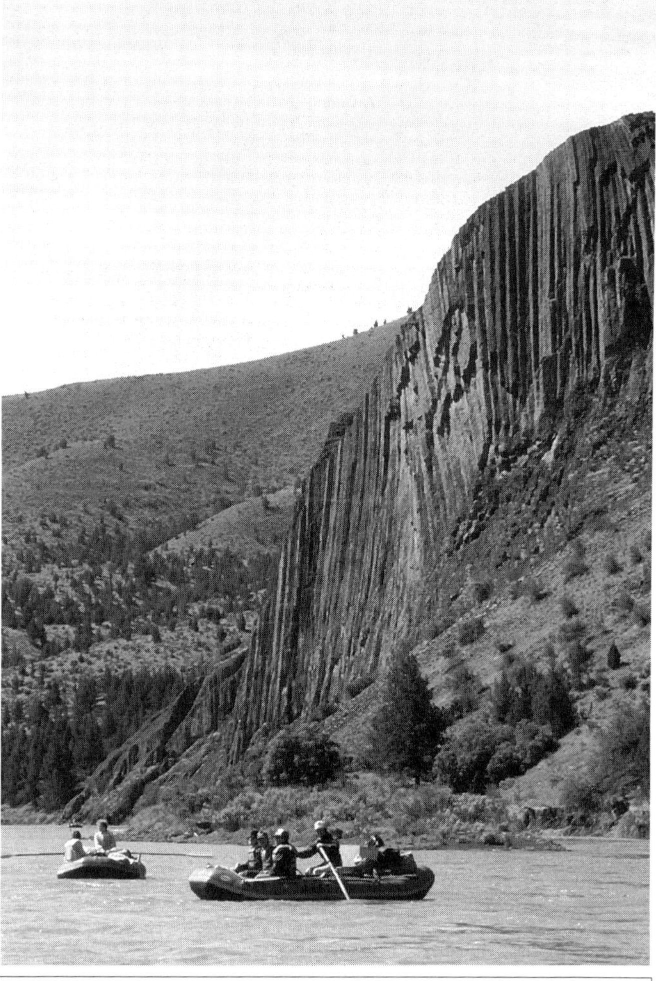

John Day River *Verne Huser*

The John Day[2] drains a large, semi-arid watershed in northeastern Oregon, gathering snowmelt from the Blue Mountains and the Strawberry Range. After its four forks merge, the river flows through a giant dogleg—first west, then north to the Columbia.

The lower John Day is nearly parallel to the Deschutes, which lies some 25 to 50 miles to the west. But the two rivers are very different. The Deschutes' volcanic watershed yields a steady flow of clear spring water, while the John Day's sedimentary geology produces dramatic flow fluctuations and turbid runoff. In fact, the John Day is Oregon's siltiest river, scouring an average of 100 tons of sediment from each square mile of its watershed in a typical year. The Deschutes rarely drops below 4,000 cfs at its mouth, while the John Day, with few year-round springs and heavy irrigation withdrawals, recedes to a couple of hundred cfs in midsummer.

Although the Deschutes surpasses its neighbor in length of season and total flow, the John Day gets the nod from most river runners for scenery and solitude. Portland boaters seeking an escape from the fog and drizzle typically head for the Deschutes, the first river east of the Cascades. The relative few who journey the extra miles to the John Day discover a geologic wonderland born of a fiery volcanic past. In some places the river cuts through dark, imposing basalt canyons up to 2,000' deep; elsewhere it winds through valleys carved from colorful deposits of volcanic ash tinted red, buff, cream, or pale green.

Not far below the Service Creek put-in, the river exposes layers of ash famous for abundant fossils. Buried here some 30 to 40 million years ago, the fossils include countless plants and an

[1] John Day Dam, located on the Columbia River just downstream from the mouth of the John Day, backs water up the last few miles of the John Day.

[2] The murky history of the river's name features several conflicting versions of the following story. In 1811 (or, some say, 1812) a young man from Virginia named John Day came west, bound for Astoria (or, as some would have it, The Dalles). His emigrant party either ran short of provisions or got lost and decided to split up. Near the river's mouth John Day and another man were beset by Indians, who took their belongings and clothing but let them go—or, according to some versions, beat them savagely and left them to die.

The Indians in this story were probably members of the Tenino tribe, who had many settlements along the river. Today river runners will find their petroglyphs at Clarno, Muddy Creek, and other sites.

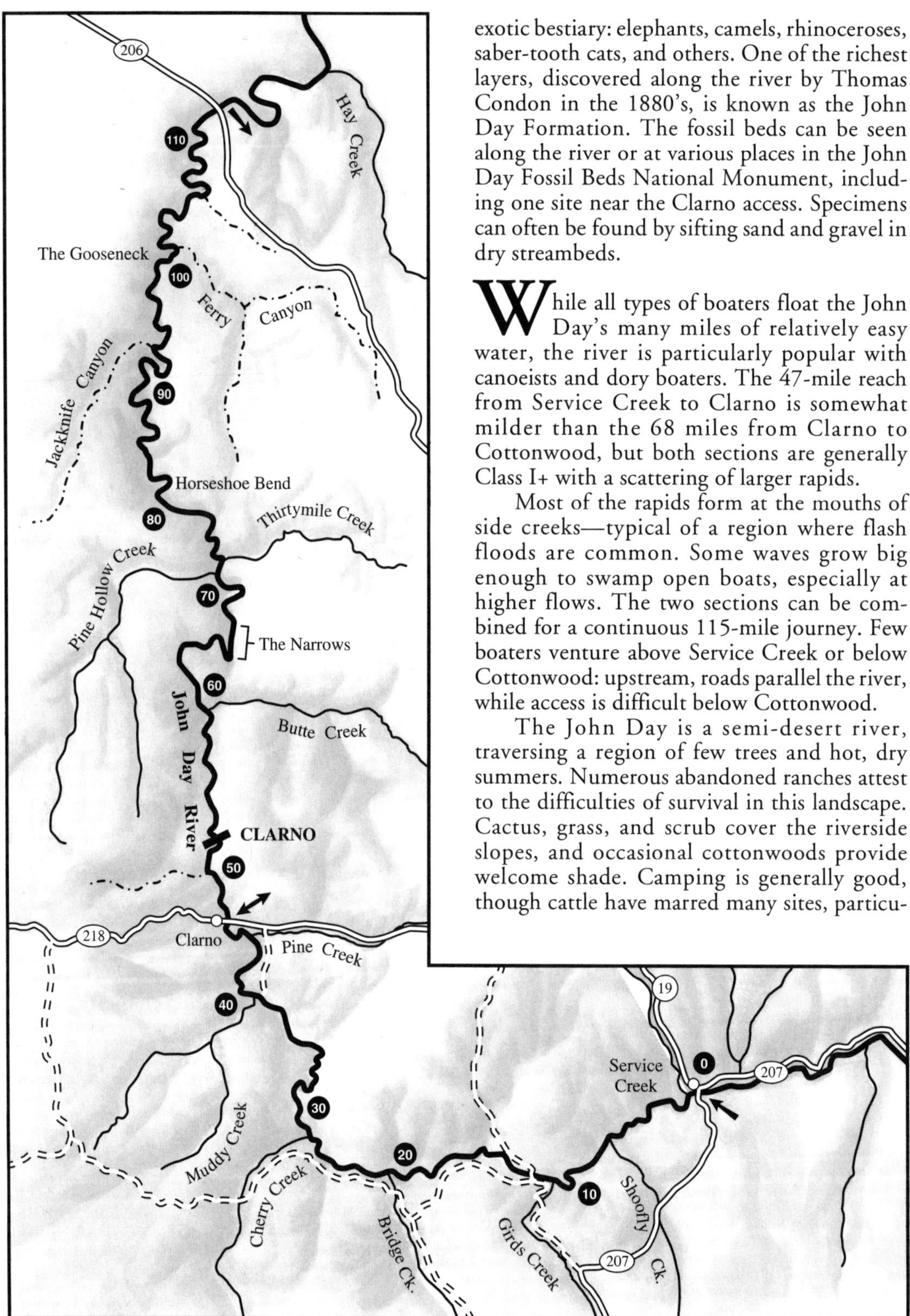

John Day

exotic bestiary: elephants, camels, rhinoceroses, saber-tooth cats, and others. One of the richest layers, discovered along the river by Thomas Condon in the 1880's, is known as the John Day Formation. The fossil beds can be seen along the river or at various places in the John Day Fossil Beds National Monument, including one site near the Clarno access. Specimens can often be found by sifting sand and gravel in dry streambeds.

While all types of boaters float the John Day's many miles of relatively easy water, the river is particularly popular with canoeists and dory boaters. The 47-mile reach from Service Creek to Clarno is somewhat milder than the 68 miles from Clarno to Cottonwood, but both sections are generally Class I+ with a scattering of larger rapids.

Most of the rapids form at the mouths of side creeks—typical of a region where flash floods are common. Some waves grow big enough to swamp open boats, especially at higher flows. The two sections can be combined for a continuous 115-mile journey. Few boaters venture above Service Creek or below Cottonwood: upstream, roads parallel the river, while access is difficult below Cottonwood.

The John Day is a semi-desert river, traversing a region of few trees and hot, dry summers. Numerous abandoned ranches attest to the difficulties of survival in this landscape. Cactus, grass, and scrub cover the riverside slopes, and occasional cottonwoods provide welcome shade. Camping is generally good, though cattle have marred many sites, particularly on the upper run. Below Clarno the river has more wilderness flavor.

In spring, unpredictable weather is a complicating factor; snow is possible until June. In summer strong upstream winds often develop in the afternoon, making downstream progress a struggle, especially for rafts.

Mile by Mile Guide

Service Creek to Clarno

0 **PUT-IN** on the right bank above the Highway 207 bridge near Service Creek.

6.3 **RUSSO** (II), at a left bend just below the mouth of Shoofly Canyon on the left. A rock garden leads into a wall on the bottom left. About 1.5 miles downstream, the fossil-rich John Day Formation appears at river level.

12.5 Twickenham Bridge. Private property, but boaters sometimes launch here. Unpaved roads lead to Highways 207 or 19. The next 3 miles are open ranching terrain with a rough road along the left bank.

18 **WRECK** (II), also called **Fossil** or **Homestead.** The current washes into the bluff on the right.

21.5 Bridge Creek enters on the left. About 3/4 mile downstream on the left is Burnt Ranch. A rough dirt road generally follows the left bank for the next 5 miles.

24 **BURNT RANCH** (II). Three miles downstream, Cherry Creek enters on the left. Below the creek is Big Bend, a small gorge.

37.5 Pictographs under an overhang on the right, just after a sharp left bend.

39 A dirt road on the right (may be gated) leads to Highway 218. Just downstream, Muddy Creek enters on the left.

47 **RIVER ACCESS** on the right below the Highway 218 bridge. Clarno is on the left.

Clarno to Cottonwood Bridge

Mileages below Clarno in brackets are cumulative from Service Creek and correspond to mileages on the map.

0 [47] **RIVER ACCESS.** Clarno. Next several miles are open ranchland with occasional dirt roads.

4.5 [51.5] **CLARNO** (III). Class II riffles lead around a sweeping left bend into this long rapid. The biggest drop is halfway down, just below some islands. The standard run is left of the islands. Scout left. The John Day Queen, a 50' stern-wheel steamer used as a ferry at Clarno, was wrecked here in 1909.

12 [59] Butte Creek enters on the right.

15 [62] **BASALT** (II), a long rapid where black boulders divide the current. Easier water from here on. About two miles downstream is Red Wall, an imposing cliff on the left.

20 [67] The Narrows, a basalt gorge.

24 [71] Pine Hollow Creek enters on the left, and a natural gas pipeline crosses the river. Thirtymile Creek enters on the right 3/4 mile downstream. A long, rough road leads up the creek to Highway 19.

34–35.5 [81–82.5] Horseshoe Bend, a long, sweeping left curve that returns to within about 100 yards of itself. The section below the bend is known as Great Basalt Canyon. A mile below Horseshoe Bend, look for petroglyphs on the right near the mouth of Potlatch Canyon.

47.5 [94.5] Jackknife Canyon enters on the left. A mile and a half downstream, look for Hoot Owl Rock above the right bank.

54.5 [101.5] The river enters a sharp left-hand meander known as The Gooseneck. Ferry Canyon enters on the right near the middle of the bend. A ferry operated here at the turn of the twentieth century.

68 [115] **TAKE-OUT** on the right below Cottonwood Bridge (Highway 206).

Grande Ronde River

1. Minam (2,530') on the Wallowa River to Powwatka Bridge (1,720').
II+; 39 miles; 21 ft./mi.

2. Powwatka Bridge to Boggan's Oasis (1,240').
II; 26 miles; 18 ft./mi.

3. Boggan's Oasis to Snake River Confluence (820').
II3; 26 miles; 16 ft./mi.

Drainage Area and Average Annual Discharge: 3,275 sq. mi. and 2,303,000 af at Troy, 7 miles below Powwatka Bridge.

Season: April–July. The high watershed has a fairly late snowmelt. Flows usually peak in May above 6,000 cfs (Troy gauge), then recede to less than 1,000 cfs by late summer. Often too low for rafts and drift boats from late July to autumn. Kayakers and canoeists can scrape down all summer.

Recommended Levels: 1,200–8,000 cfs on the Troy gauge. Below 1,500 rafts may have trouble getting down the Wallowa at the outset of Run 1. Above 8,000 there are few eddies, and some campsites are under water.

Flow Information: NWS tape, (503) 249-0666; BLM, (503) 437-5580; or Army Corps of Engineers, (509) 522-6603. Flow at Troy. Flows on the Wallowa River are usually roughly half the Troy reading.

Permits: Not presently required.

Managing Agencies: Walla Walla RD, Umatilla NF, 1415 W. Rose Street, Walla Walla, WA 99362; (509) 522-6278; and BLM, Baker RA, P.O. Box 987, Baker, OR 97814; (503) 523-6391.

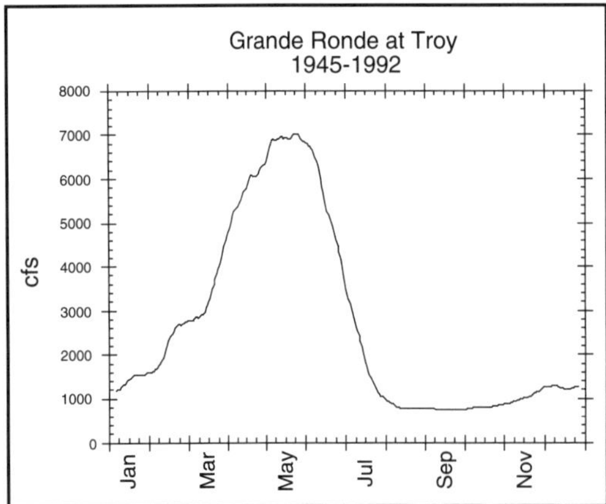

Commercial Raft Trips: Yes. For references contact the Forest Service.

Land Ownership: Mixed National Forest, BLM, and private.

Scenery: Excellent. Volcanic canyon becomes drier downstream.

Solitude: Excellent on Runs 1 and 3; very good on run 2 (dirt road). Heavy boating use on holidays.

Wilderness: Mostly. Railroad first 10 miles; dirt road along Run 2.

Fishing: Steelhead in spring and fall, trout in summer.

Water: Cold and fairly clear but undrinkable (towns and grazing). Purify side stream water.

Camping: Excellent, mostly on riverside benches. Best on Run 1.

Side Excursions: Wallowa Mountains (Eagle Cap Wilderness). Hells Canyon.

Guides and References:

- *Soggy Sneakers Guide to Oregon Rivers* (Willamette Kayak and Canoe Club).
- Garren, *Oregon River Tours.* Runs 1 and 2.
- North, *Washington Whitewater.* Runs 2 and 3.
- Bennett, *Guide to the Whitewater Rivers of Washington.* Runs 2 and 3.
- *The Grande Ronde River* (USFS and BLM). Order from managing agencies.
- Orr & Orr, *Rivers of the West.* History, geology.

Maps:

- **USGS 7.5':** *Run 1:* Minam, Howard Butte, Rondowa, Fry Meadow, Deep Creek, Elbow Creek, Promise, Eden, Troy. *Run 2:* Troy, Mountain View. *Run 3:* Mountain View, Flora, Field Spring, Black Butte, Limekiln Rapids.
- **USGS 1:100:** *Runs 1 & 2:* Wallowa. *Runs 2 & 3:* Clarkston.
- **USFS:** *Umatilla NF* covers Runs 1 and 2. *Wallowa-Whitman NF, North Half* shows shuttle for Run 1.

Auto Shuttle: Length depends on route. For shuttles contact Joining Waters Shuttle Service at the Minam Motel, (503) 437-4475 or 437-1111; Boggan's Oasis, (509) 256-3372. For more references contact the managing agencies.

Logistics: These are the simplest routes. Many alternate routes, but some are complicated and involve rough dirt roads. Contact managing agencies for more information.

The **Minam** access is on the left bank below the Oregon Highway 82 bridge over the Wallowa River, some 34 miles northeast of La Grande in the northeastern corner of the state. Alternate access *may* be possible at Rondowa at the Wallowa-Grande Ronde confluence via dirt roads from the east; contact the USFS for more information.

To reach **Powwatka Bridge,** follow Highway 82 east from Minam to Enterprise, turn north on Oregon Highway 3 for about 34 miles, then turn west about 3 miles to Flora. In Flora turn right at signs for the Grande Ronde and Troy; then, just north of town, bear left and drive to the bridge at Troy (**alternate access** here on the right bank). Cross the river, turn left, and drive upstream a little under 7 miles to an access about a quarter mile upstream from a U.S. Fish & Wildlife station and fish ladder. Access is also possible half a mile farther upstream at Powwatka Bridge itself.

Boggan's Oasis is on the right bank just above the Washington Highway 129 bridge over the Grande Ronde, about 4 miles north of the state line. An unpaved road on the left bank connects this access with Troy.

The **Snake River access** is at Hellers Bar on the left bank of the Snake a half mile below the mouth of the Grande Ronde. From Boggan's Oasis follow Washington Highway 129 steeply north to Rattlesnake Summit. Not far beyond the summit, a mile and a half south of the town of Anatone, turn right on Montgomery Ridge Road. Drive some 15 miles to the Snake, then turn right and drive 10 miles up the Snake to Hellers Bar. An **alternate take-out** is 3 miles up the Grande Ronde, on the left bank at a bridge.

Fed by melting snows from the Elkhorn Range and the lofty Wallowa Mountains—second-highest peaks in Oregon—the Grande Ronde River curves 185 miles through northeastern Oregon and the southeastern corner of Washington to meet the Snake River. In the lower half of its journey the Grande Ronde glides through one of the most scenic river trips in the Pacific Northwest.[1]

Most boaters begin a Grande Ronde trip by floating the last ten miles of the Wallowa River, the Grande Ronde's biggest tributary. The Wallowa (wah-LAW-wah) is actually the larger river in terms of flow, but geographers give the name to the longer Grande Ronde. Not far above the put-in the Wallowa flows through a broad, fertile valley that was once home to the Nez Perce Indians.[2] In 1877, less than 20 years after whites settled in the valley, the Nez Perce were driven out and relocated to reservations. The Indians' resistance and retreat under the brilliant leadership of Chief Joseph and others is briefly recounted elsewhere in this guide.[3]

In the canyons of the Wallowa and the Grande Ronde, river runners can explore a land of gentle beauty and abundant wildlife. Bald eagles soar overhead while deer and elk browse beneath ponderosa pines. To most, the scenery is more reminiscent of Idaho rivers to the east than of Oregon rivers to the west. The volcanic canyon is composed of horizontal basalt ledges, which alternate with grassy or forested slopes to give the landscape a terraced appearance. The ledges are actually individual lava flows laid down one on top of another.

Below Powwatka Bridge the character of the canyon slowly changes as the forest gradually gives way to grass and cactus in the drier lower elevations. The walls become steeper and the volcanic rock formations become more rugged, especially below the popular Boggan's Oasis access. Not far above the Snake confluence, an ancient lava flow constricts the river, creating the Grande Ronde's only Class III rapid—The Narrows. Aside from this drop, however, the two lower runs offer less whitewater than the uppermost section.

With its more frequent whitewater and greener canyon, the upper run from Minam to Powwatka is the most popular stretch. As a result, the Grande Ronde below Powwatka offers considerably more solitude at peak season for those who appreciate its arid beauty. By running all three sections continuously, boaters can enjoy 91 miles of continuous floating—one of the region's longest river trips.

---

[1] In 1988 Congress added 44 miles of the Grande Ronde, from the confluence with the Wallowa to the Washington state line, to the National Wild and Scenic Rivers System. Congress also designated the Wallowa as a study river. The Grande Ronde in Washington is eligible for Wild and Scenic designation.

[2] "Wallowa" is a Nez Perce term for a tripod of sticks used to anchor a fish trap in the river.

[3] See the **Lower Salmon** chapter in Region I.

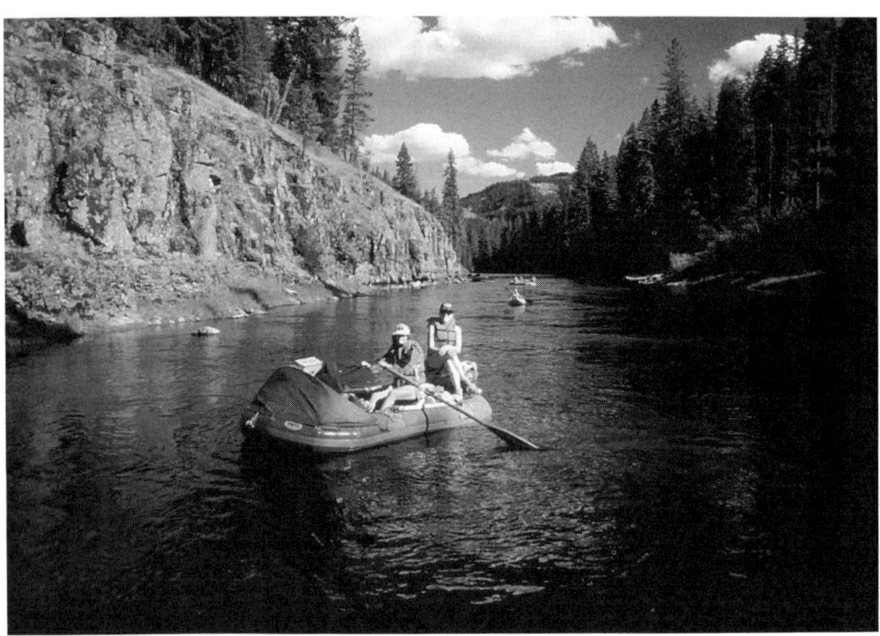

Grande Ronde River *Bill Cross*

from Oregon, Idaho, Washington, and other states.

Upstream Runs

The Grande Ronde is boatable off and on for some 80 miles above the Wallowa confluence. Frequent access allows boaters to choose from a wide range of runs—from steep Class III and IV to lazy flatwater floats. One of these sections—a sinuous, meandering reach in a broad valley below La Grande, Oregon—gave the river its name: French trappers called it Grande Ronde, or "Great Round," in reference either to the bowl-shaped valley or the river's winding course. For more information on upstream runs on the Grande Ronde, refer to the *Soggy Sneakers Guide to Oregon Rivers.* For information on an upstream run on the Minam River, see the **More Western Rivers** section of this book.

With the exception of The Narrows, the runs covered here present nothing above Class II+ at most flows. Even so, the canyon's remote location dictates caution. All boaters should be wary of high water, when the river is icy and swift and eddies are scarce. Weather ranges from hot in July and August to unpredictable and sometimes very cold in spring and fall. Rain and snow are possible into early June. In spite of its isolation, the upper river can be crowded on holiday weekends, drawing boaters

Mile by Mile Guide

Minam to Powwatka Bridge

0 **PUT-IN** on the left bank of the Wallowa, below the Highway 82 bridge and the Minam River confluence. The hamlet of Minam consists of a store and motel. A dirt road follows the left bank for a mile and a half. A rarely-used rail line follows the right bank for 10 miles. Fast Class II water downstream.

1.5 **MINAM ROLLER** (II–III-) at a sharp right bend. A modest rapid at low to moderate flows, but above about 2,500 cfs a big reversal develops on the left. Downstream on the left is Minam State Park. About a mile below the park is **RED ROCK** (II), also called **House Rock Drop**, which features a steep drop to the left of a big boulder.

5.5 **VINCENT FALLS** (II+), also called Blind Falls. **Recognition:** Power lines cross the canyon above the rapid. **The rapid:** A series of rocky drops with a blind ledge part way down.

10 The Grande Ronde River enters on the left. The hamlet of Rondowa is on the right (possible access; see **Logistics**). Two bridges—one partly washed out—cross the river. The railroad heads up the Grande Ronde.

11.5 Sheep Creek enters on the left at a right bend. A quarter mile downstream at a left bend is **SHEEP CREEK RAPID** (II+), a

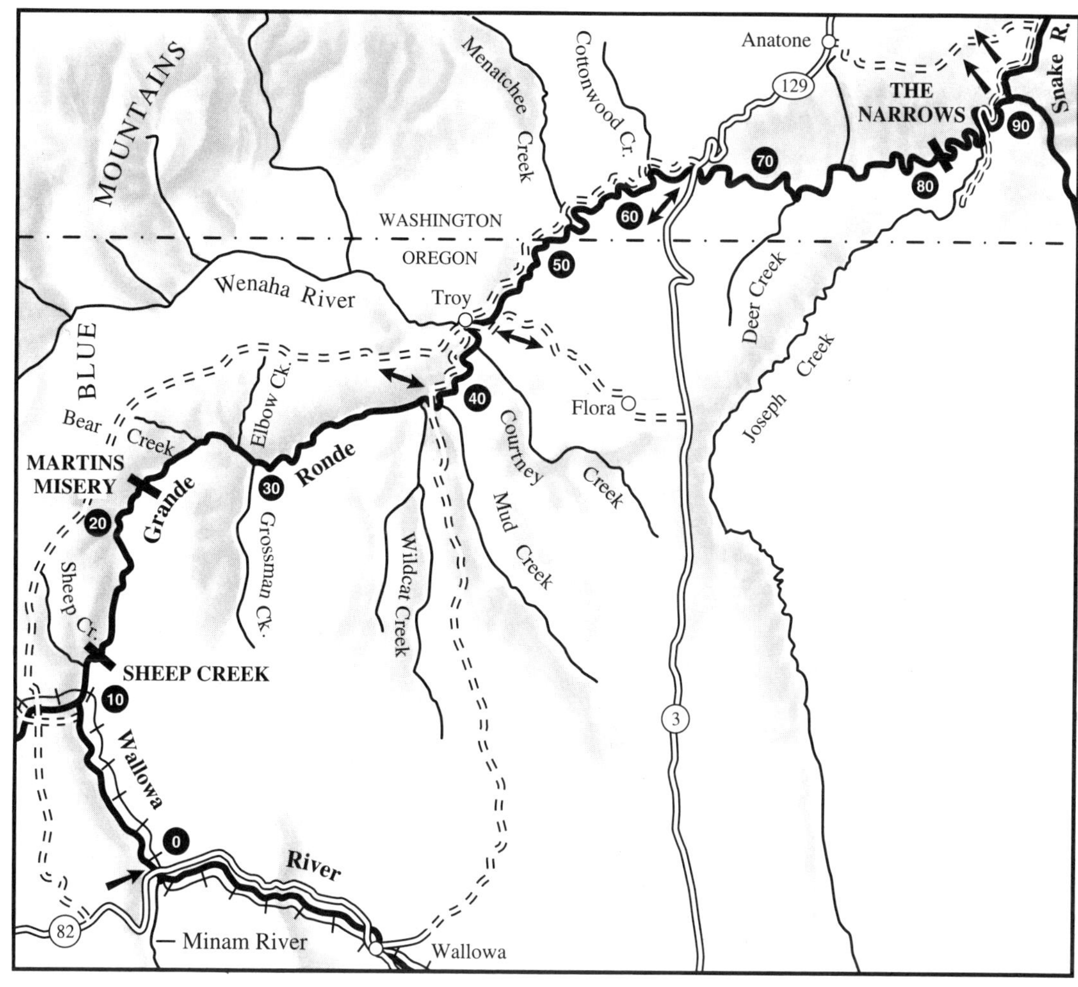

Grande Ronde

long, broad washboard. Class I+ next 10 miles. The next 18 miles run through Umatilla National Forest.

16 Clear Creek enters on the right. Campsite, side hike.

20.5 Alder Creek enters on the left. A half mile downstream the river bends right through a long Class II+, then sharply left through MARTINS MISERY (II+). Downstream the whitewater is Class II except for The Narrows.

25.5 Bear Creek enters on the left. Another 1.5 miles downstream, Elbow Creek enters on the left, followed 1.5 miles later by Grossman Creek on the right. Below Grossman Creek the National Forest ends, and much of the land is private.

33 Sickfoot Creek on the right. Side hike.

38 Wildcat Creek enters on the right. Powwatka Bridge is a half mile downstream. **TAKE-OUT** on the right below the bridge. **Alternate TAKE-OUT** a half mile farther on the left, opposite the mouth of Mud Creek. Or continue downstream. *(See next page.)*

Powwatka Bridge to Boggan's Oasis

Mileages in brackets are cumulative from Minam and correspond to mileages on the map.

0 [39] **PUT-IN** at Powwatka Bridge or Mud Creek (see above). A gravel road follows the left bank to Boggan's Oasis. Boats should stay to the right at the fish hatchery below Mud Creek.

5.5 [44.5] Courtney Creek enters on the right. A half mile downstream is **Double Eddy**, where strong turbulence forms at high water.

7 [46] **RIVER ACCESS** on the right bank just below the bridge across the river. Town of Troy on the left. The Wenaha River enters on the left.

13 [52] Washington state line. Downstream the river enters Horseshoe Bend, a long meander to the left. Below the bend Menatchee Creek enters on the left.

23.5 [62.5] Cottonwood Creek enters on the left.

26 [65] **TAKE-OUT.** Boggan's Oasis. Access on the right above the Highway 129 bridge. Or continue downstream. Rattlesnake Creek enters on the left.

Boggan's Oasis to Snake River

0 [65] **PUT-IN** on the right (see above). Narrow canyon first 10 miles.

7 [72] Deer Creek enters on the right just above a sharp left bend.

10.5 [75.5] Shumaker Creek enters on the left in an open section of canyon.

16 [81] Cliffs on the left. Two miles downstream, the river splits around a large island. Below the island are 9 miles of sinuous meanders.

21.5 [86.5] **THE NARROWS (III)**, where basalt ledges constrict the river. **Recognition:** The rapid is at the end of a right bend where the river starts to curve left again. Scout on the left. **The rapid:** At moderate flows entry waves lead into a channel on the left with a big breaking wave. At low flows this channel dwindles to only 8' to 10' wide. At high flows big waves develop, and the rapid rates III+. Below the rapid Joseph Creek enters on the right.

23.5 [88.5] **Alternate TAKE-OUT** on the left at a bridge. Watch for a strong Class II rapid here.

26 [91] Snake River confluence. The **TAKE-OUT** at Hellers Bar is half a mile down the Snake on the left.

Owyhee River

Three Forks to Leslie Gulch

1. Middle Owyhee:
Three Forks (3,950') to Rome (3,360').
IV5; 37 miles; 16 ft./mi.

2. Lower Owyhee:
Rome to Leslie Gulch (2,670').
III; 65 mi. (up to 10 on reservoir); 13 ft./mi.

Alternate take-out at Birch Creek, 17 miles above Leslie Gulch, avoids the reservoir.

Drainage Area and Average Annual Discharge: 8,000 sq. mi. and 730,000 af at Rome.
Peak Recorded Flow: 41,400 cfs (Feb. 19, 1986).
Season: Generally April–early June, but varies widely with snowpack and weather. In some years there is virtually no boating season; in others flows fluctuate wildly.
Recommended Levels: *Middle:* 900–3,000 cfs. *Lower:* 800–5,000 cfs.
Flow Information: NWS tape, (503) 249-0666, or BLM, (503) 586-2612. Flow at Rome.
Special Hazards: *Middle:* Difficulty hiking out. Widowmaker Rapid (possible portage). *Both runs:* Extreme isolation. Rattlesnakes. Changeable weather.
Permits: Self-registration boxes at put-ins.
Managing Agency: BLM, Vale District, 100 Oregon St., Vale, OR 97918; (503) 473-3144.
Commercial Raft Trips: Yes. For a list of outfitters, contact the BLM.
Land Ownership: *Middle:* Mostly BLM. *Lower:* Mixed private and BLM.
Scenery: Excellent. High desert canyons; some open sections on Lower.

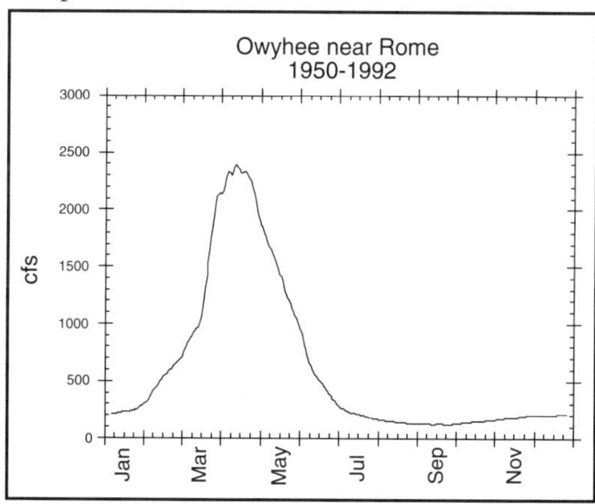

Solitude: Excellent. Heaviest boating use is Memorial Day weekend.
Wilderness: Yes, both runs. A few ranches on the Lower.
Water: Silty and undrinkable. Side creeks are unreliable, but several springs provide possible refill sites. Water available at Rome access.
Camping: Excellent on beaches and bars. Very few sites on the reservoir.
Side Excursions: Overlook on the Middle Owyhee shuttle (see **Logistics**).
Guides and References:
- *The Lower Owyhee: A River Runner's Guide* and *A River Runner's Guide to the Middle Owyhee: Three Forks to Rome* (River Graphics). Waterproof map-guides. See **Bibliography** for ordering information.
- Garren, *Oregon River Tours.*
- *Soggy Sneakers Guide to Oregon Rivers* (Willamette Kayak and Canoe Club).
- *Owyhee National Wild River Boating Guide* (BLM).
- Moore & McClaran, *Idaho Whitewater.* Covers Middle Owyhee and upstream runs.
- Amaral, *Idaho: The Whitewater State.* Covers Middle Owyhee and upstream runs.
- Orr & Orr, *Rivers of the West.* History and geology.

Maps:
- **USGS 7.5'**: *Middle:* Three Forks, Whitehorse Butte, Skull Creek, Indian Fort, Dry Creek Rim, Scott Reservoir. *Lower:* Rome, Owyhee Butte, Lambert Rocks, Rinehart Canyon, The Hole In The Ground, Jordan Craters North, Diamond Butte, Rooster Comb.
- **USGS 1:100:** *Jordan Valley* (both runs), *Mahogany Mtn* (Lower).

Auto Shuttle: *Middle:* 51 miles (1.5 hours) one way. *Lower:* 75 miles (two hours) one way. For shuttle and reservoir tow-out references, contact the BLM or ask around Jordan Valley.
Logistics: The hamlet of Rome is in the southeastern corner of Oregon.To reach the **Rome** access, midway point of the two runs, turn south (upstream) on a gravel road at the east end of the U.S. 95 bridge over the Owyhee at Rome. Drive about a quarter mile to a parking area and boat ramp on the right bank.

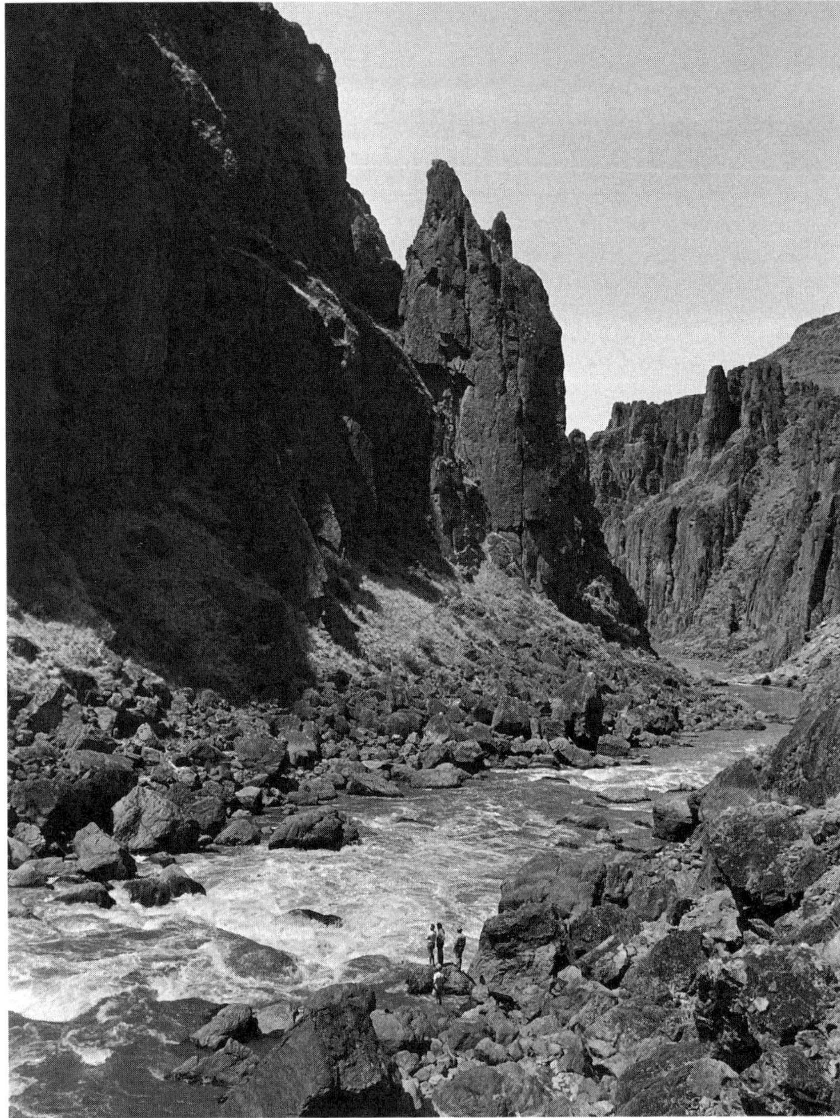
Widowmaker Rapid, Middle Owyhee *Ted Weigold*

To reach **Three Forks,** put-in for the Middle Owyhee, drive east from Rome on U.S. 95 about 17 miles and turn south on Three Forks Road. (The turnoff is 16 miles west of Jordan Valley, Oregon, a hamlet near the Idaho border.) Follow this unpaved road some 32 miles to the canyon rim, then descend a steep mile and a half to the put-in at the confluence of the North Fork and main Owyhee. Three Forks Road is often impassable when wet, especially the last section. High-clearance vehicles recommended. Be sure to stop at the Owyhee Canyon Overlook; turn west on a very short spur road some 17 miles south of U.S. 95. For road information on the Upper Owyhee, contact the BLM.

To reach **Leslie Gulch,** take-out for the Lower Owyhee, drive east from Rome on U.S. 95 some 32 miles to Jordan Valley, then north 18 miles to Succor Creek Road. Turn left and drive 8 miles to the hamlet of Rockville. Just beyond an abandoned school turn left, drive a quarter mile, turn right (just past a small bridge), drive a mile and a half, then turn left at a sign for Leslie Gulch and drive the final 15 miles to the reservoir.

An **alternate take-out** for the Lower Owyhee is at **Birch Creek Ranch.** Roads leading to this access are impassable when wet, and 4-wheel drive is strongly recommended at all times. Some 7 miles north of Jordan Valley, turn left off U.S. 95 onto an unpaved road (known locally as Cow Creek Road) at a sign for Jordan Craters. Drive some 11 miles to a fork in the road, bear right, drive 12 more miles to another fork, bear right again, drive a mile to the canyon rim, then make the final steep 4-mile descent into the canyon down Birch Creek.

It has been called the loneliest river in the U.S. outside Alaska. This comment isn't meant to characterize boating use, for while the Owyhee is far from crowded, it does have its own loyal following. Rather, the Owyhee is the loneliest river because of its remote, isolated, back-of-beyond, middle-of-nowhere location.

In 400 miles from its headwaters in northern Nevada to its confluence with the Snake River on the Oregon-Idaho border, the Owyhee passes just one town: Rome, Oregon, estimated population 50. The Owyhee's 11,000-square-mile watershed has more cattle than people—and probably as many rattlesnakes as cattle. Most of the region gets less than 10" of rain in an average year, making this a tough place to carve out a life. The USGS didn't even bother to print maps for much of the area until the late 1980's.

So why is this, the driest river in the Pacific Northwest, named after a tropical paradise? Indeed, Owyhee (Oh-WYE-hee) is just an old-fashioned spelling of Hawaii. It seems that in the early 1800's, "Owyhans" often came to the continent seeking work with trapping or exploring expeditions. In 1819 three islanders joined a party under Donald McKenzie (of McKenzie River fame). Accounts vary, but one way or another the Owyhans wound up missing and presumed dead in the vicinity of the river. Some say they were killed by Indians, others assert that McKenzie sent them off downstream and they never returned. In any case their surviving comrades named the river after them. (Boaters may also wonder why Rome, Oregon was named for the great world city; apparently, early travelers crossing the Owyhee thought the eroded white bluffs along the river resembled Roman columns.)

Geographically and geologically, the Owyhee is a close cousin of the Jarbidge-Bruneau River system in southwestern Idaho. Like its neighbors, the Owyhee rises from headwaters in arid northern Nevada and flows for much of its length through a slot-like chasm in a relatively flat volcanic plateau. From above Three Forks—where the Middle Fork, North Fork, and main stem of the Owyhee join—to Rome, the Middle Owyhee is almost entirely confined by sheer thousand-foot walls of hard metamorphic rhyolite and volcanic basalt. Rockfalls from the steep walls form natural dams, giving the river its pool-and-drop character. The Lower Owyhee, in contrast, alternates between dark volcanic gorges and open valleys of softer ash or sedimentary rock. Numerous hot springs attest to fiery forces lingering beneath the surface—forces that produced eruptions as recently as 5,000 years ago.

The Owyhee offers a wide variety of river trips. On almost all runs boaters will discover hot springs, caves, abandoned ranches, and a variety of desert wildlife, including abundant rattlesnakes. Various sections can be combined to create some of the Pacific Northwest's longest river trips—up to 200 miles. The two runs featured in this chapter, if run continuously, add up to more than 100 miles.

The most popular stretch is the Lower Owyhee from Rome to Owyhee Reservoir, with intermediate whitewater and dramatic wilderness scenery that includes narrow gorges, badlands, and open sagebrush valleys. Fewer boaters venture down the much more challenging Middle Owyhee from Three Forks to Rome. (Until recently the stretch beginning at Three Forks was commonly called the Upper Owyhee. But with more boaters running the upper main stem above Three Forks, it is more aptly called the Middle Owyhee—not to be confused with the Middle Fork of the Owyhee.) Though use is increasing, many boaters are deterred by Widowmaker, an intimidating drop (and possible portage) near the middle of this spectacular slot canyon.

The big obstacle facing Owyhee boaters is flow. The arid, moderate-elevation basin receives only a modest snowpack, which then melts in an unpredictable fashion. The Owyhee has one of the most variable seasons of any snowmelt river in this guide. About the best one can say is that in most years the river gets one or more surges of runoff sometime between February and May, then recedes to unboatable levels by mid-June. Some years the river has no season at all, some years it stays runnable through early July, and some years the runoff pattern is so fluky that the hydrograph looks like the Dow Jones Industrials Average.

The Middle Owyhee is for advanced and expert river runners only. The moderate gradient is deceptive because the river stores up most of its energy in long pools, then loses its elevation in a few big drops. Intermediate boaters should stick to the Lower Owyhee with its relatively forgiving rapids. In general, the Middle Owyhee is tougher at high water when big hydraulics develop, while the Lower gets trickier at low flows when abrasive rocks clog the channels. A key concern for both runs is the extreme

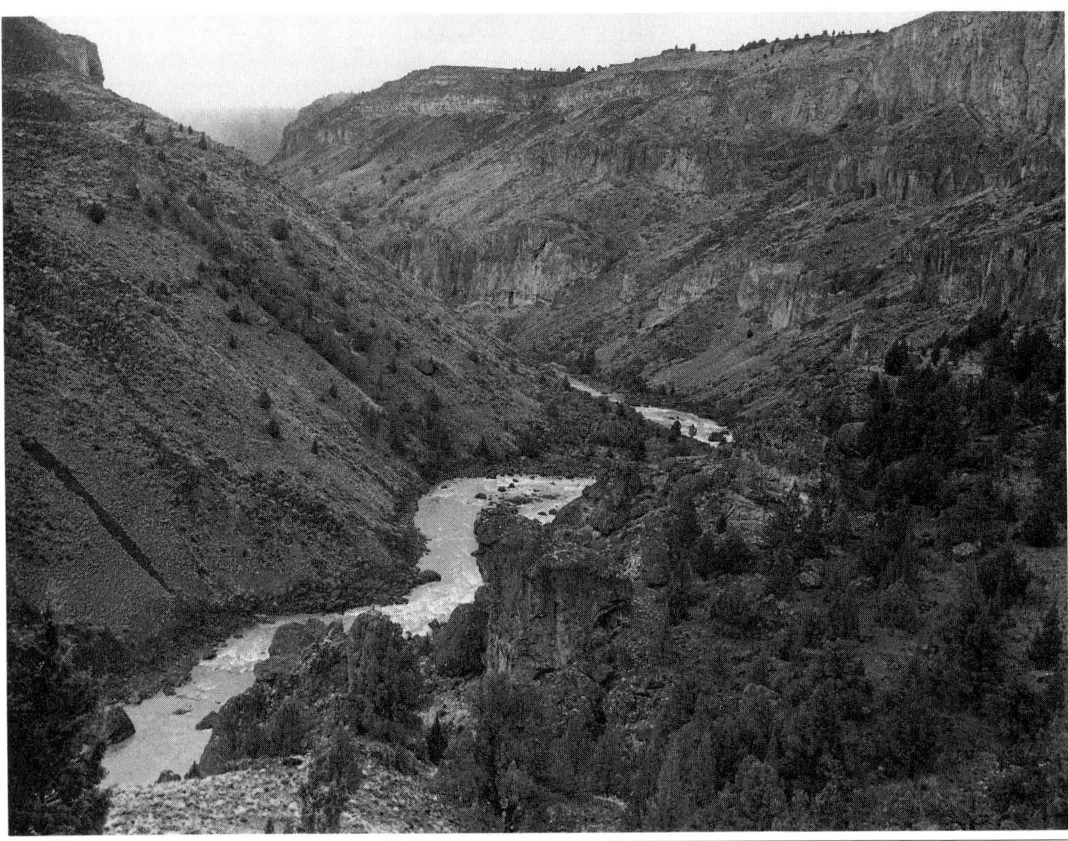

Middle Fork Owyhee above Three Forks *Ted Weigold*

isolation and difficulty hiking out in the event of a mishap; this is especially critical on the Middle Owyhee and upstream runs (discussed below). What's more, weather early in the season can change quickly from oven-like heat to snow.

Though first run commercially in 1951 by famous Oregon outfitter Prince Helfrich, the Owyhee remained relatively undiscovered until the mid-1970's. In 1984 Congress added some 120 miles of the main stem to the National Wild and Scenic Rivers System. Portions of the North Fork and West Little Owyhee were added in 1988.[1]

Upper Owyhee and Tributaries

Only a relative handful of adventurous boaters explore the Owyhee watershed above Three Forks. This small but growing band can choose among a bewildering array of little-known but outstanding runs on the Upper Owyhee and its many forks and tributaries—the South, East, and North Forks and Deep Creek. The runs range from mild floats to demanding expert floats with lots of portages.

Most of these isolated runs are located in southwestern Idaho. Access is often poor, sometimes requiring 4-wheel drive and permission from private landowners. Some runs can be combined, and all eventually lead to Three Forks and points downstream—that is, all rivers lead to Rome! Whitewater difficulty varies widely, and seasons are generally shorter and earlier than on the main runs. Elevations range from 4,000' to 5,000', and the weather can be very cold.[2]

The East Fork of the Owyhee and Deep Creek are threatened by a proposed Air Force bombing range in southwestern Idaho (see the **Jarbidge and Bruneau** chapter in Region I). Both streams have been proposed for National Wild and Scenic Rivers status.

[1]In 1992 the BLM found 223 miles of the Upper Owyhee and its tributaries in Idaho eligible for National Wild and Scenic designation.

[2]For more information on the Upper Owyhee and its tributaries, refer to any or all of the following: Amaral, *Idaho: The Whitewater State*; Moore & McClaran, *Idaho Whitewater*, and *Owyhee River Boating Guide* (BLM), available from the Boise District Office, 3948 Development Ave., Boise, ID 83705; (208) 384-3300.

Mile by Mile Guide

Middle Owyhee

0 Three Forks. **PUT-IN** on the right bank at the confluence of the North Fork and the main stem of the Owyhee. The Middle Fork joins the North Fork a half mile upstream. Camping allowed at the put-in. Downstream the canyon narrows rapidly.

1.5 **THE LEDGE** (IV). First the river bends right around a rockslide and plunges over a steep pourover chute between big boulders; then it churns down a long boulder garden. Not a good place to swim. Scout from the left bank; at low water, from the right. Porcupine Canyon enters on the left. A mile and a half downstream an abandoned cabin is on the right, with a hot springs nearby.

5 The river enters a more open section of canyon known as Deary Pasture.

10.3 **HALF MILE** (IV). A long S-turn rapid, more difficult at higher flows. **Recognition:** The small drainage of Indian Canyon enters on the right about three quarters of a mile above the rapid. At the top of the rapid, the river bends right and splits around a rocky island (which may be covered at high flows). Stop above this island on the right to scout. **The rapid:** Below the island is a short, swift pool, followed by a difficult rock garden with nasty boulders at the bottom right. At higher flows the upper and lower parts of the rapid run together, and the entire rapid should be scouted from the right before entering. At lower flows boaters can stop in the slow water between the two parts to scout the second section separately.

10.7 Immediately below Half Mile is **RAFT FLIP** (III), a short rapid with a strong reversing wave at the bottom. Boats can sneak down the left side at higher flows when the wave is bigger. **At low flows this passage becomes an unrunnable rock sieve; portage on the right.** The next 3 miles have several easy Class III rapids. Owyhee Canyon Overlook is high on the right at mile 13.

15 **SUBTLE HOLE** (III), which begins as a wide, rocky washboard and narrows at the bottom. Immediately downstream is **BOMBSHELTER DROP** (III+), a similar rapid which becomes more difficult at higher flows. It is named for a big cave on the left just downstream.

17 Skull Creek enters on the left. Just downstream, avoid the rocks at **SHARKS TOOTH** (II+), also called **FINGER ROCK.** Despite its modest difficulty, this rapid causes trouble for many boaters.

19.5 Soldier Creek, a large side canyon, enters on the right at a big gravel bar. Good side hike. Campsites above and below the creek are the last large ones above Widowmaker. A mile downstream, the canyon walls close in as the climax approaches. The river drops 80' between miles 20 and 22.

21 **WIDOWMAKER** (V). ***POSSIBLE PORTAGE.*** **Recognition:** About a mile below Soldier Creek, the river runs through three Class II–III rapids while the canyon narrows and bends to the left. After the third drop the canyon opens slightly, and the river straightens before accelerating toward a Class I–II riffle that marks the entrance to Widowmaker. The safest approach is to eddy out on the right above the riffle to scout. Many groups line or portage on the right. Huge boulders make the portage very difficult for large craft. **The rapid:** Boulders tumbled from the canyon walls create a treacherous rapid with two big drops and one giant boulder in between. At high flows this spot gets very nasty, and even most experts portage. The runout is poor, leading into a rocky intermediate rapid.

After a few Class III rapids in the next four miles, the river settles down to Class II and easier as the rock shifts from rhyolite to basalt. Below mile 25 the canyon walls lower rapidly.

31 Sand Hollow opens on the left. A little over two miles downstream, the river eases through its last Class II riffle at a diversion site. The final three and a half miles are through open terrain.

37 **TAKE-OUT** on the right a quarter mile upstream from the U.S. 95 bridge, or continue downstream on the Lower Owyhee. The hamlet of Rome is on the left.

Lower Owyhee

0 **PUT-IN** on the right above the U.S. 95 bridge in Rome. The river flows gently through an agricultural valley for the first 5 miles, sometimes splitting around islands. Two miles downstream, Jordan Creek enters on the right.

6 Crooked Creek enters on the left as the river enters a narrow canyon. After a mile and a half, the canyon opens and the first riffles begin.

9 A side canyon enters on the left as the river makes two sharp bends to the right. Downstream, Class II rapids appear as the canyon narrows and the gradient increases.

12 **UPSET (II; III at high flows)**, marked by a big boulder on the left bank. The river bends left, and boulders (holes at higher flows) block the right and center. Half a mile downstream, just below a sharp right bend, the river surges into big midstream boulders at **BULLSEYE (II+; more difficult at low water)**. At low flows this rapid is quite challenging. Below Bullseye the river enters a more open section and the gradient diminishes.

17 The canyon closes in again. Look for Weeping Wall, a lovely set of springs on the left where water jugs can be filled. Not far downstream the canyon opens again; more campsites below this point.

21 **ARTILLERY (II+)**, where the river narrows to a chute on the left. About a mile downstream, look for a hot springs on the right. A bit farther up the bank are abandoned stone corrals and the so-called Rustler's Cabin.

24–26 Lambert Rocks, a jagged basalt formation on the right. On the opposite shore are the eroded badlands of the Chalk Basin Rocks, with a formation known as Pruitt's Castle. Good hiking.

26.5 Bogus Creek and Bogus Falls (when running) on the right.

28 Bull Creek on the left after a sharp right-hand bend. Just downstream is **DOGLEG,** a rocky Class II that gets tougher at low water. Three quarters of a mile downstream, a jeep trail reaches the right bank (possible emergency access over private land). Downstream the river enters a narrow red-rock canyon.

30.3 **WHISTLING BIRD (III).** Scout left. Debris washed down a draw on the left forces the river into the steep right bank, where a large rock slab has fallen into the river. Avoid this hazard to the left. At low water this rapid is very tight and more difficult. Good camping and side hiking here. A mile downstream, the river cuts into a spectacular, sheer-walled rhyolite canyon. Watch for a boulder-strewn Class II known as **Rock Trap.**

32.5 **MONTGOMERY (III+)**, sometimes called **Iron Point** after a rock formation high on the left. The toughest drop on the lower river; more difficult at low flows. **Recognition:** Just upstream, the canyon turns abruptly left and the river runs through **TIGHT SQUEEZE**, a Class II slot between a cliff on the left and a gravel bar on the right. Eddy out on the left just below the "squeeze" to scout. **The rapid:** The river drops through a constriction and plows into midstream rocks. A mile below the rapid, the canyon opens somewhat.

37 Jackson Creek enters on the left in an open area known as Jackson Hole. Good camping and hiking. A mile and a half downstream, the falls of spring-fed Rinehart Creek appear on the left. Just below the creek is **MORCUM DAM (III-)**, also called **Rock Dam,** an old diversion structure for Hole-In-The-Ground Ranch that creates a rocky, difficult obstacle at low water. Scout left. Downstream, the canyon opens and the whitewater diminishes to Class II.

39.5 Hole-In-The-Ground Ranch on the right (private). Emergency access via dirt roads may be possible with permission. About a mile below the ranch, look for petro-

Owyhee Reservoir
Leslie Gulch
60
Cedar Mountain
Rinehart Canyon
Hole in the Ground
Jackson Creek
Mahogany Mountain
50
40
Birch Cr.
MORCUM DAM
Birch Creek Ranch
Bull
Owyhee
MONTGOMERY
30
WHISTLING BIRD
Creek
Bogus Creek
Lower
Lambert Rocks
Ryegrass Creek
20
Weeping Wall
Lower Owyhee
95
Jordan Valley
10
Creek
Jordan
Rome
0
Owyhee River
30
20
Crooked Creek
WIDOWMAKER
Soldier Creek
Overlook
HALF MILE
10
THE LEDGE
Three Forks
0
North Fork
Middle Fork

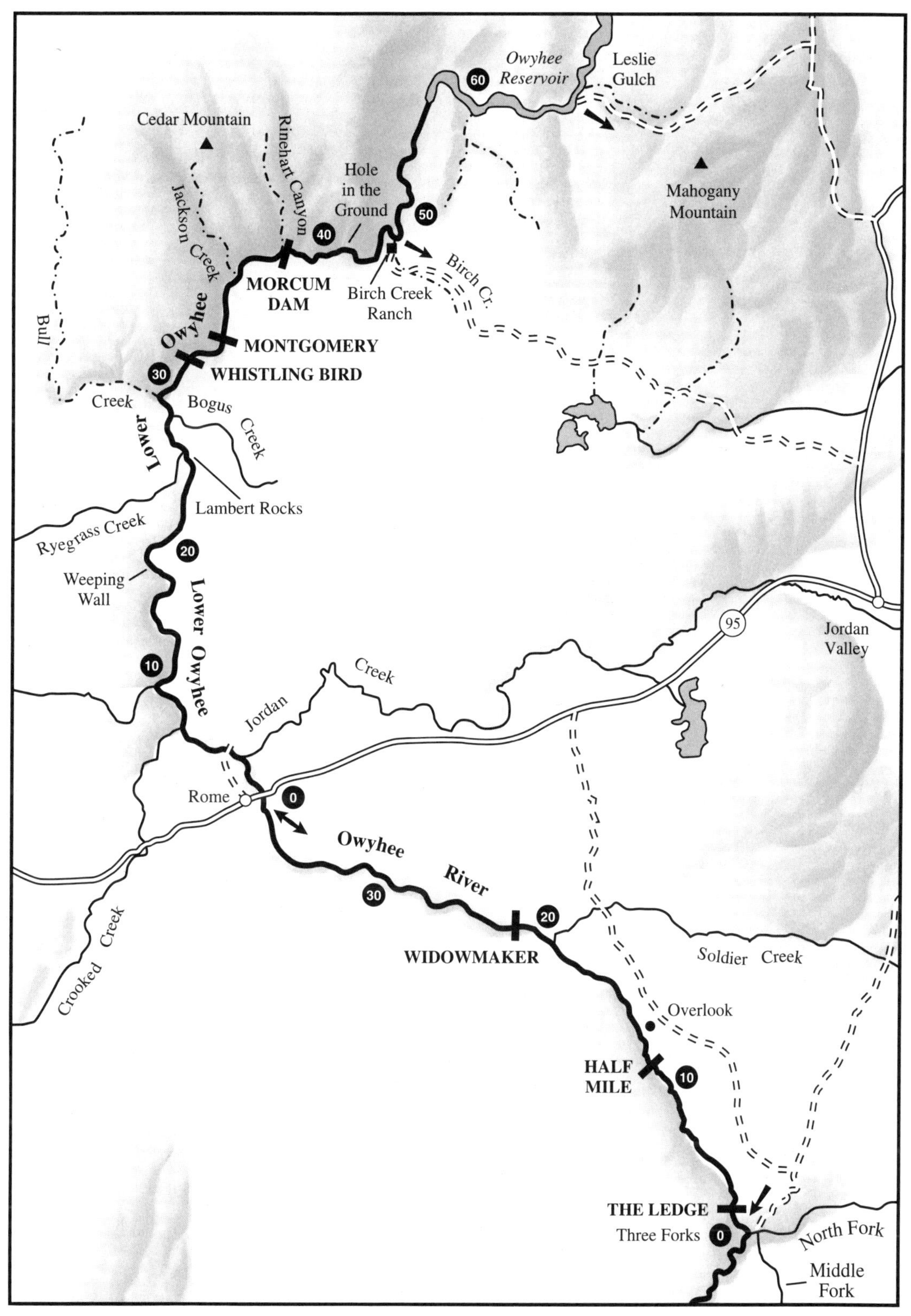

Owyhee

glyphs on boulders on the left. (Don't touch.) Roughly two miles below the petroglyphs, look for a hot spring tub in a grassy spot low on the left.

48 **RIVER ACCESS.** BLM campsite on the right about a quarter mile upstream from Birch Creek and Birch Creek Historic Ranch. A rough dirt road leads east to U.S. 95. (See **Logistics.**) Below the ranch buildings on the right is a large water wheel. Flatwater below this point, with jeep trails on both banks for several miles. Another water wheel is on the right at mile 53. When full, Owyhee Reservoir begins at mile 55, 10 miles above the take-out. Upstream winds are common here, and campsites are scarce.

65 **TAKE-OUT.** Leslie Gulch on the reservoir's right shore.

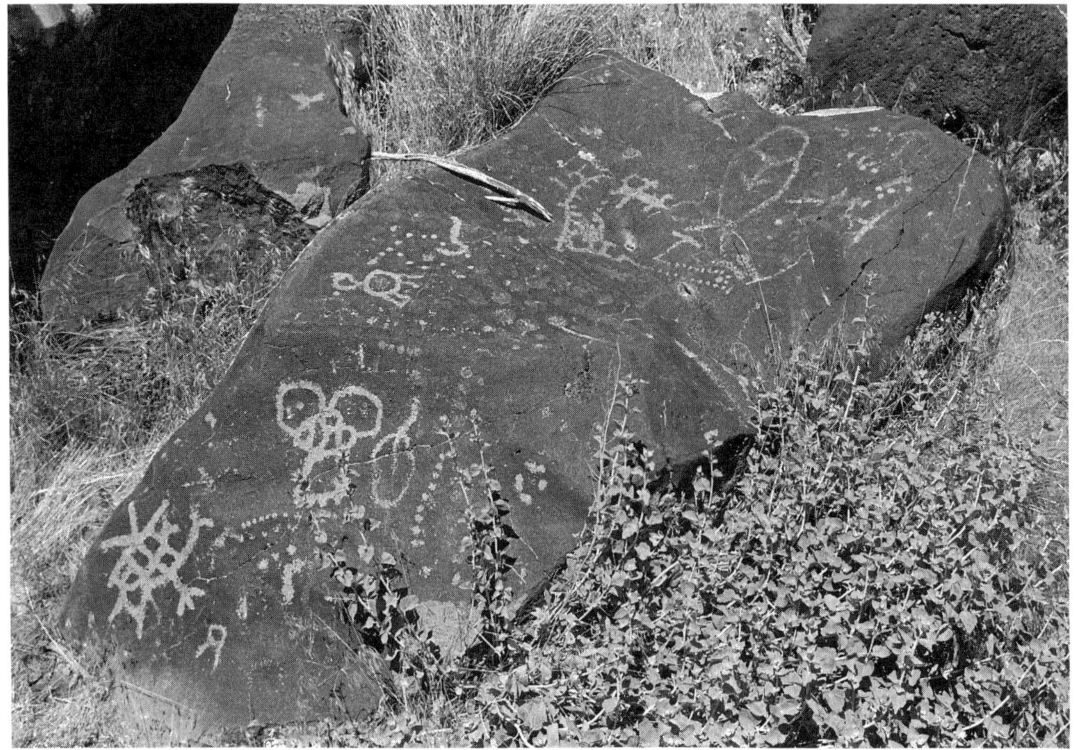

Petroglyphs on the Lower Owyhee *Ted Weigold*

Rivers of the Mt. Adams Area

Mt. Adams is southern Washington's forgotten mountain. At 12,307' it is the second-highest peak in the Pacific Northwest after Mt. Rainier. Yet locals and outsiders alike are more familiar with its nearest neighbors, 8,365' Mt. St. Helens to the west and 11,235' Mt. Hood to the south in Oregon.

For knowledgeable river runners Mt. Adams is one of the most significant peaks in the Pacific Northwest. The mountain's snowfields and glaciers feed four major rivers: the White Salmon to the south, the Klickitat to the east, the Lewis to the west, and the Cispus to the northwest. Most of these names are unfamiliar outside the immediate vicinity. Together they constitute one of the finest collections of lesser-known boating streams in the Pacific Northwest. To this group we have added the small Wind River, which is in the area but whose drainage is cut off from Mt. Adams by the adjacent White Salmon and Lewis watersheds. The Wind is for experts only.

With one exception, these rivers are relatively obscure and lightly boated, thanks to their location away from major cities in a region traversed by minor roads. Only the White Salmon, which drains the southern slopes of Mt. Adams, sees heavy whitewater traffic. Of these rivers, it is the closest to Portland and the only run near an interstate highway. The White Salmon, a tributary of the Columbia, features a short, scenic Class III+ run with one Class V drop, Husum Falls, that can be portaged.

The Klickitat, a bigger and longer river, rises well to the north and, on its way to the Columbia, collects tributaries draining Mt. Adams' eastern slopes. Because of its sprightly intermediate whitewater and the beauty of its canyon, the Klickitat is finally beginning to receive more attention.

The Cispus, a tributary of the Cowlitz, drains the northern slopes of Mt. Adams as well as other Cascade peaks farther north. The whitewater rates Class IV on the nine-mile Upper Cispus and III on the 11-mile Lower Cispus. Logs are the principal hazard.

Just south of the Cispus is the watershed of the Lewis River, which rises on the western slopes of Mt. Adams and runs west by southwest toward its confluence with the Columbia. The Lewis features a 12-mile Class IV run which also has significant log hazards as well as a major obstruction, Big Creek Gorge, which is impassable to all but small craft. For this reason, the extraordinarly lush and lovely canyon of the Lewis remains primarily the province of kayakers and other hardshell boaters.

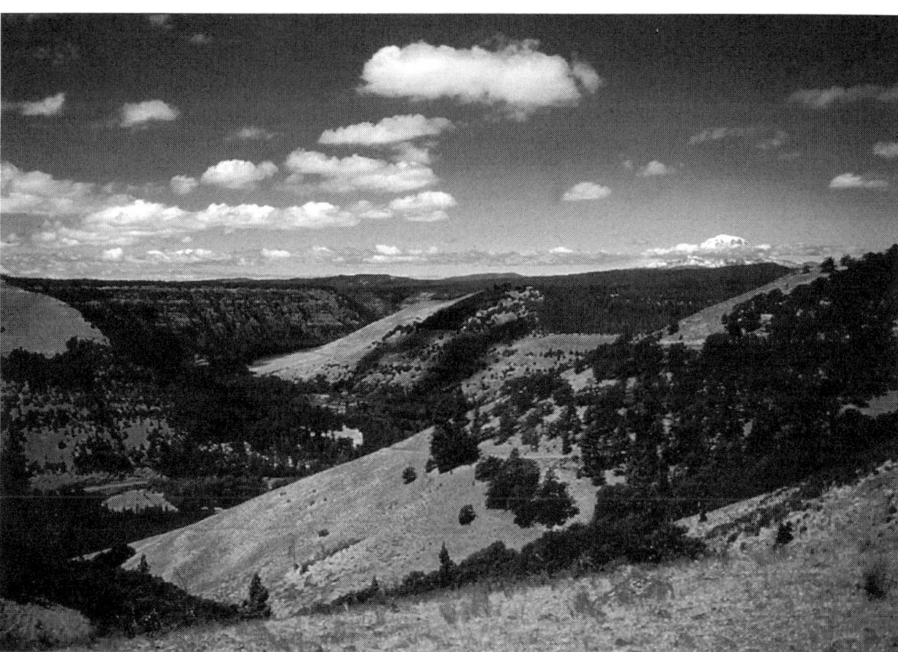

Klickitat Valley below Mt. Adams *Bill Cross*

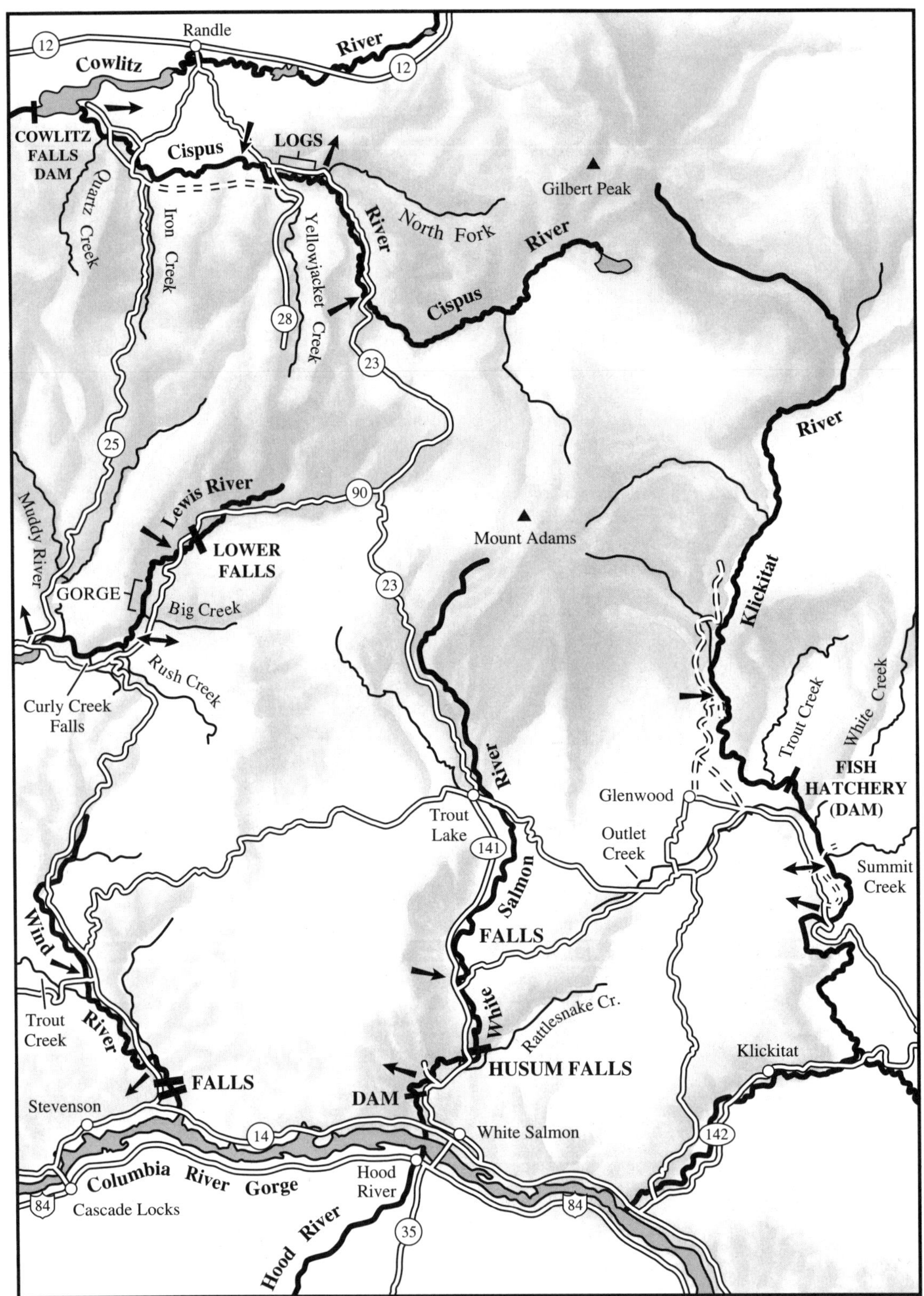

Rivers of the Mt. Adams Area
White Salmon, Klickitat, Cispus, Lewis, and Wind

White Salmon River

BZ Corner to Northwestern Reservoir

Difficulty: III+5.
Length: 7.5 miles. Shorter runs possible.
Gradient: 45 ft./mi. (55 first 5 miles).
Put-in: BZ Corner (640').
Take-out: Northwestern Reservoir (295').
Drainage Area and Average Annual Discharge: 386 sq. mi. and 817,200 af.
Peak Recorded Flow: 15,300 cfs (Jan. 15, 1974).
Season: April–Oct. Prime season May through July. Glacial melt and flow from springs usually provide minimum runnable flows year-round. Flows typically peak in late winter and spring, then recede slowly to late summer and early autumn lows of 400 to 700 cfs.
Recommended Levels: 700–1,500 cfs. Much pushier above 1,500 cfs.
Flow Information: NOAA Whitewater Hotline, (206) 526-8530; flow at Underwood, just downstream from Northwestern Reservoir. At times, releases from the reservoir differ from flows on the upper river.
Rafts: Small boats only at low flows.
Special Hazards: Husum Falls. Possible log hazards.
Permits: Not presently required.
Managing Agency: Columbia River Gorge National Scenic Area, 902 Wasco Ave., Hood River, OR 97031; (503) 386-2333.
Commercial Raft Trips: Yes. For a list of outfitters, contact the managing agency.
Land Ownership: Almost all private.
Scenery: Excellent. First 4 miles are through a lush, narrow volcanic canyon.

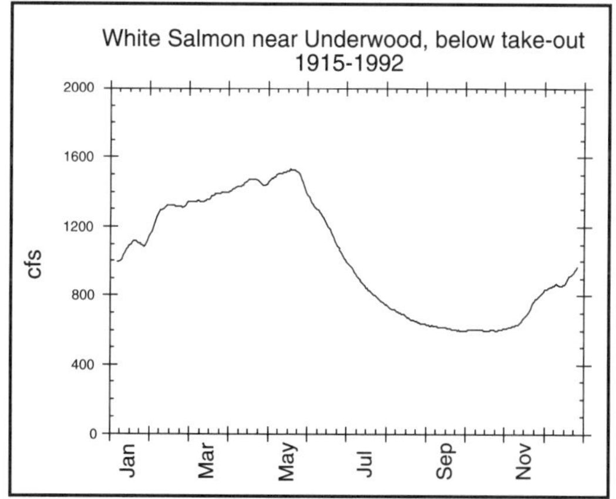

Solitude: Very good. Highway and houses are generally away from the river.
Wilderness: No.
Water: Cold. Some glacial flour in summer.
Camping: USFS campgrounds about 20 miles away in Gifford Pinchot NF.
Side Excursions: Mt. Adams. Mt. St. Helens. Columbia River Gorge.
Guides and References:

- *White Salmon River User Guide* (Columbia River Gorge National Scenic Area).
- Bennett, *Guide to the Whitewater Rivers of Washington.* Includes upstream runs.
- North, *Washington Whitewater.*
- *Soggy Sneakers Guide to Oregon Rivers* (Willamette Kayak and Canoe Club). Includes upstream runs.

Maps:

- **USGS 7.5':** *Northwestern Lake, Husum.*
- **USGS 1:100:** *Hood River.*
- **USFS:** *Gifford Pinchot NF.*

Auto Shuttle: About 6 miles one way.
Logistics: The primary **take-out** is at the upstream end of Northwestern Reservoir. From the town of White Salmon on the north bank of the Columbia River about 55 miles east of Portland, follow Washington Highway 141 north about 5 miles, turn left on Northwestern Lake Road, and drive about a quarter mile to a bridge over the reservoir. Just beyond the bridge, turn left into Northwestern Park (operated by Pacific Power & Light Co.). A boat ramp is just below the bridge on the right bank.

Two **intermediate accesses** are located near Husum Falls, a little over halfway through the run. To reach these accesses, continue up Highway 141 some two miles beyond the Northwestern Lake turnoff to the bridge over the river at Husum Falls. An **alternate put-in,** used to run only the milder lower portion of the river, is located on the left bank just below the bridge and the falls (private, fee; inquire at the Whitewater Market in Husum). An **alternate take-out** for the upper river is on the right bank just above the falls.

To reach the **put-in,** follow Highway 141 north (upstream) another 4 miles to the hamlet of BZ Corner. Signs advertise a private access on the right bank, just upstream from a secondary road bridge over the White Salmon. (No access at the bridge.) Fee; call in advance for information: (509) 493-3691.

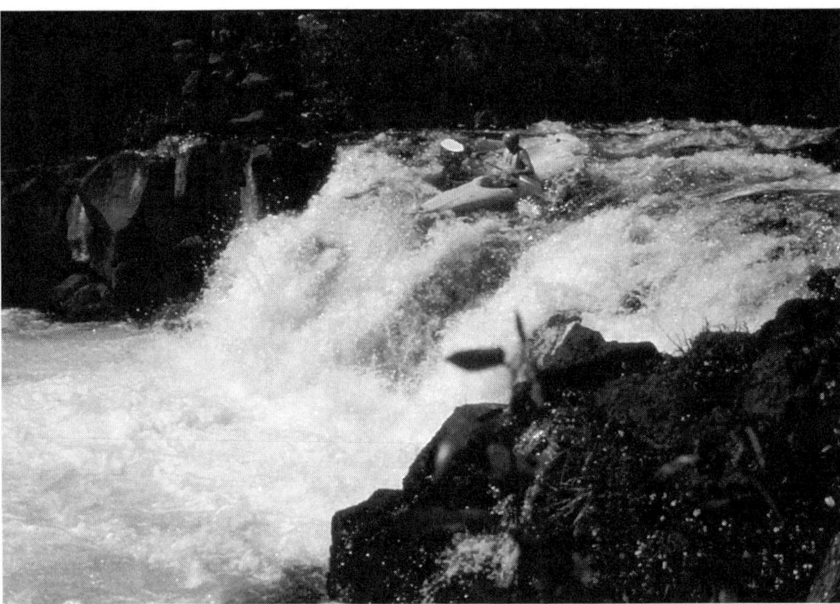

Husum Falls, White Salmon *Jeff Bennett*

High on the southwest face of Mt. Adams, meltwater from the Avalanche and White Salmon glaciers gathers into milky rivulets that coalesce to form the White Salmon River. In its southerly course the river grows rapidly as abundant springs and side streams add clear, icy water to the glacial melt. Breathtakingly steep and peppered with waterfalls over much of its length, the White Salmon drops from 12,000' headwaters to its confluence with the Columbia River in only 40 miles. As a result most of the river is either unrunnable or for experts only. Fortunately, in its lower reaches the White Salmon offers a less difficult run through an enchanting volcanic gorge.

The White Salmon, a Washington river, is heavily used by boaters from nearby Portland as a convenient one-day run. The river's popularity has skyrocketed in recent years: 1,800 user-days in 1984, 6,000 in 1988, and 12,000 in 1992. Roughly three quarters are passengers on commercial raft trips. Weekends are, of course, the busiest times.

A key to the river's popularity is the generally reliable summer weather. Located slightly east of the Cascade crest, the White Salmon lies in a partial rain shadow and offers more sunshine than other Portland area rivers like the Sandy and Clackamas. Precipitation in the relatively small watershed produces only moderate runoff, but glacial melt and spring flow help to maintain minimum boatable flows throughout most summers.

For much of its length the White Salmon flows through a narrow, slot-like canyon incised within a broader volcanic valley. Though the rugged walls often rise no more than 100' on either side, they hold civilization at bay and give the river an intimate, secluded feel. Farms and homes are usually just out of sight beyond the canyon rim. The inner gorge stays shady and cool even in summer, providing a moist refuge for ferns and mosses.

The most popular run begins at the hamlet of BZ Corner, about 12 miles above the river's mouth. Here the canyon walls are nearly vertical and unbroken, making the put-in a challenge. Boaters must use a private access where the landowner maintains a steep trail and a cable system for lowering rafts more than 100' to the river. Kayaks can be carried.

The White Salmon offers no warm-up at all: right at the put-in is a Class IV- rapid, followed by a long section of non-stop Class III action. The gorge remains steep and narrow for the first few miles, producing constricted rapids that become much more difficult as flows increase. Even in summer boaters should prepare for cold conditions; the water is always icy, and direct sunlight is limited in the gorge.

Surprisingly, the whitewater climaxes only after the White Salmon leaves its narrow inner canyon. At Class V Husum Falls, site of an annual whitewater competition, the river tumbles over a resistant ledge of basalt into a powerful hydraulic that many boaters portage. Accesses above and below the big drop allow boaters to run only the upper or lower sections and avoid the falls if they wish. Less experienced boaters favor the final three miles below the falls, where the river runs through gentle rapids and flatwater in a scenic forest.

The run ends at the backwaters of Northwestern Reservoir, formed by Pacific Power & Light's Condit Dam. Some years ago, hydroelectric dams and diversions were also proposed on the run featured in this chapter. Fortunately, grassroots efforts helped win National Wild and Scenic River protection for this reach in 1986. As of 1993 Congress was considering the 30 miles of river above BZ Corner for Wild and Scenic designation.

At one time the White Salmon was a major spawning stream for salmon and steelhead. Early settlers to the area remarked on the enormous concentrations of migrating fish that gathered near the river's mouth. Because spawning salmon often turn a pale whitish color, the settlers named the river "White Salmon." The bountiful fish runs were devastated by the construction of Condit Dam in the early twentieth century.

Today, with increasing concern for endangered fish runs and a growing appreciation for river recreation, a movement is afoot to modify or even tear down Condit Dam. Environmental groups and public agencies have called on Pacific Power & Light and the Federal Energy Regulatory Commission to study alternatives that would be less harmful to fish, including complete removal of the dam. FERC has recently agreed to consider this option in its environmental impact study on relicensing the dam.

Removal of Condit Dam would benefit more than just the fishery. Once the dam and its hydroelectric diversion were out of the way, river runners would have an additional five miles of river to enjoy, all the way to the Columbia River confluence if desired. With an average gradient of 60 ft./mi., this lost section of the White Salmon would no doubt offer plenty of excitement. Nothing could do more to ease overcrowding on this much-loved river than to reclaim five miles of outstanding whitewater.[1]

Upstream Runs

Expert river runners occasionally tackle very difficult sections of the upper White Salmon above BZ Corner, including the infamous Zig Zag Canyon. However, difficult access and mandatory portages around waterfalls keep use light on these thrilling and spectacular reaches. For further information refer to Jeff Bennett, *A Guide to the Whitewater Rivers of Washington.*

[1]Anyone interested in joining this effort should contact the Rivers Council of Washington (see appendix for address).

Mile by Mile Guide

See map just before this chapter.

0 **PUT-IN** on the right bank at BZ Corner (private, fee). At the put-in is **MAYTAG** (IV-), the second roughest drop on the run. There is a big keeper hole directly underneath the cable and another hole at the bottom. Most boaters avoid the first hole by launching just downstream. Scout Maytag from the right before putting in, and portage or line on the right if necessary. Just below Maytag the BZ Corner Bridge crosses high overhead (no access). Boaters can get a bird's-eye view of the put-in and Maytag by walking out on this bridge before launching. Not far below the bridge, watch for a dangerous undercut on the right as the river bends left. More undercuts are downstream.

0–1 The first mile below the bridge is fairly continuous Class III, beginning with **SHARK'S TOOTH, GRASSHOPPER,** and **SIWASH.** Next up are two slightly tougher drops. First is **CORKSCREW,** a sharp drop at a right bend that has big hydraulics at high flows and is tight and challenging at low water. Then comes **WATERSPOUT,** which develops big waves and a nasty hole at high flows. Most boaters try to stay left to avoid the hole. Downstream the gorge opens somewhat, and the rapids ease for a little over a mile.

2.8 **STAIRSTEP (III+)**, a series of four sharp drops. The rapid is half a mile below an old powerhouse on the left bank.

4.3 **HUSUM FALLS (V).** *POSSIBLE PORTAGE.* **Recognition:** Near mile 4 the canyon opens somewhat, a few houses appear, and Highway 141 approaches the right bank. **The rapid:** An 8' drop over a river-wide ledge into a strong reversal. Much more turbulent and difficult above about 1,400 cfs. Boaters can get a good look at the falls from the highway bridge before boating. Experts run the drop at some levels, but most boaters portage (or line) along a trail on the left bank. Boaters can avoid the falls altogether by taking out at an **alternate RIVER ACCESS** about 50 yards upstream on the right.

Just below the falls Highway 141 crosses the river, offering an **alternate RIVER ACCESS** on the left (private, fee; inquire at the Whitewater Market in Husum). Less experienced boaters often start here and run the final section down to Northwestern Reservoir. A couple of hundred yards downstream, a second bridge crosses the river to the town of Husum on the right bank. Rattlesnake Creek enters on the left below the second bridge, and in the next mile the river runs through several Class II to II+ rapids. The final two miles are easy floating through a scenic forest away from the highway.

7.5 **TAKE-OUT.** As the river enters the backwaters of Northwestern Reservoir, Buck Creek enters on the right and a bridge crosses overhead. Take out at the boat ramp on the right just below the bridge.

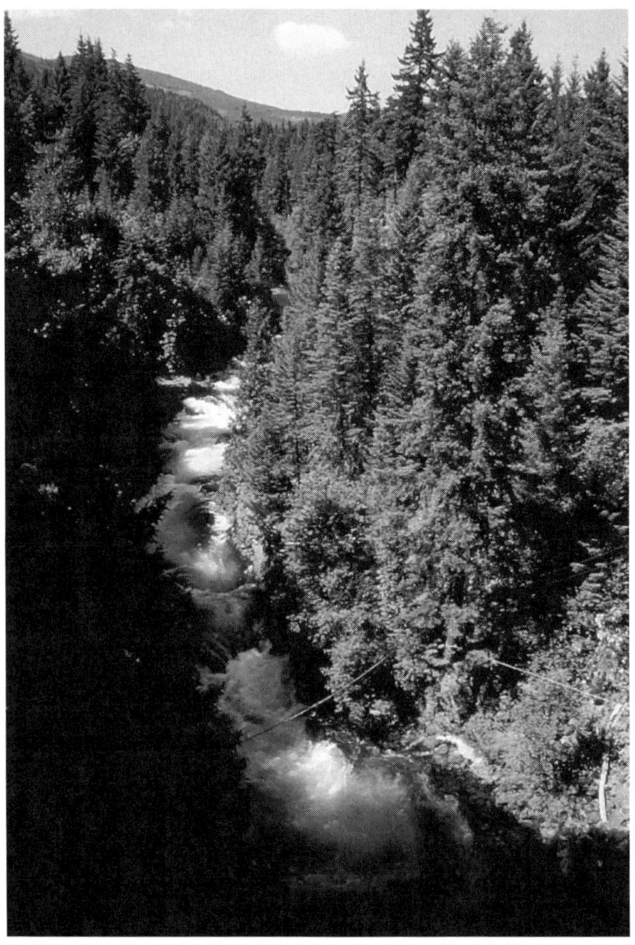

White Salmon just above BZ Corner *Bill Cross*

Klickitat River

Gauging Station to Leidl Bridge

Difficulty: III; IV above about 3,000 cfs.
Length: 19 miles. Longer and shorter runs possible.
Gradient: 45 ft./mi. (60 first 8 miles, then 35).
Put-in: Gauging Station (1,700').
Take-out: Leidl Bridge (850').
Drainage Area and Average Annual Discharge: 1,297 sq. mi. and 1,195,000 af at Pitt, 25 miles below take-out.
Season: April–July. After the rainy season the river typically has a snowmelt peak sometime in May, then recedes slowly to September and October lows. Glacial melt and spring flow help maintain minimum boatable flows through July in most years.
Recommended Levels: 750–3,000 cfs (actual flow; for conversion from Pitt gauge, see below). The river can be run at higher flows, but the upper section is virtually continuous above 3,000 and should be considered Class IV.
Flow Information: NOAA Whitewater Hotline, (206) 526-8530; flow at Pitt, 25 miles below the take-out. This reading, which includes many downstream tributaries, overestimates flows on the run described here—especially in the rainy season. Convert as follows: in April, divide the Pitt figure roughly in half; in May, take about 2⁄3 of the Pitt flow; in June and July, about 3⁄4.
Special Hazards: Log hazards. Cold water. Weir at fish hatchery (mile 8).
Permits: No boating permits presently required, but a Washington Dept. of Wildlife license is necessary to use the Leidl Bridge take-out. For information call (206) 753-5719.

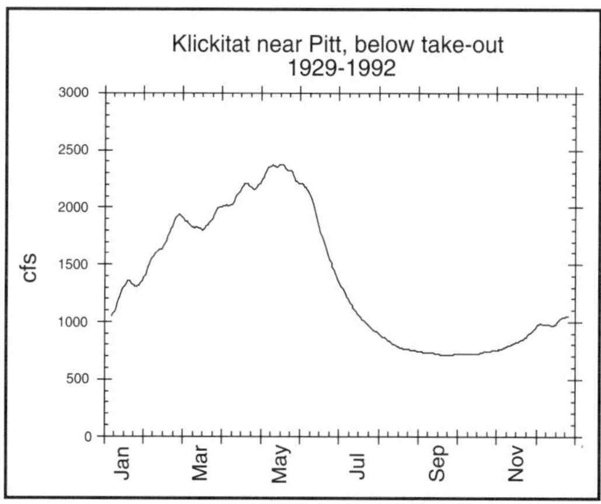

Managing Agency: Columbia River Gorge National Scenic Area, 902 Wasco Ave., Hood River, OR 97031; (503) 386-2333.
Commercial Raft Trips: Yes, several outfitters. For references contact the managing agency.
Land Ownership: Mostly private.
Scenery: Excellent. Narrow volcanic canyon in semi-forested plateau.
Solitude: Excellent first 8 miles; very good thereafter (minor road).
Wilderness: Partial. Roadless first 8 miles, riverside road thereafter.
Water: Silty during spring runoff; glacial flour in summer. Always cold. No drinking water at the put-in. Purify water from side streams or bring water.
Camping: A few area campgrounds, including Leidl Campground at the take-out.
Side Excursions: A good viewpoint overlooks the river at mile 11; turn north off the shuttle road onto a short dirt spur road midway between Leidl Bridge and Glenwood (about 6.5 miles from either point).
Guides and References:

- Bennett, *Guide to the Whitewater Rivers of Washington.* Includes downstream runs.
- North, *Washington Whitewater.* Includes downstream runs.
- *Soggy Sneakers Guide to Oregon Rivers* (Willamette Kayak and Canoe Club).

Maps:

- **USGS 7.5':** *Glenwood, Outlet Falls, Dead Canyon, Grayback Mtn.*
- **USGS 1: 100:** *Mt. Adams, Hood River.*

Auto Shuttle: Just under 20 miles (about 45 minutes) one way. To hire shuttles, try the Shade Tree Inn or the Flying L Ranch in Glenwood.
Logistics: To reach the **take-out,** from the Columbia River some 60 miles east of Portland, take Washington State Highway 141 north about 9 miles to BZ Corner, turn right across the White Salmon River, and drive roughly 18 miles to Glenwood. Continue east about 12 miles to the boat ramp on the right bank of the Klickitat below Leidl Bridge (license required; see **Permits**).

An **alternate take-out** at Summit Creek is on private logging company land, but it is frequently used by boaters. Turn left one mile west of Leidl Bridge onto an unpaved logging road, then drive upriver about 3 miles to Summit Creek Bridge.

To reach the **put-in**, drive east from Glenwood about 3.5 miles or west from Leidl Bridge about 9 miles to the turnoff to the Klickitat Fish Hatchery (Don't take that turnoff unless you want to use the **alternate access** at the hatchery.) About 100 yards west of the hatchery turnoff, turn north at another turnoff and drive about 8 miles. Bear right onto unpaved Road K1400 (about ¾ mile past the Road K1300 turnoff). Drive downhill about ¾ mile, turn right on K1410, drive another 1.5 miles downhill, then bear left and drive half a mile to an abandoned gauging station on the right bank. The last section of road may be impassable. Also, the roads to this and the alternate upstream put-in can be blocked by snow until mid-May.

To reach the **alternate upstream put-in,** continue past the K1400 turnoff to the Yakima Indian Reservation boundary; stop at the sign and make a very long, very difficult scramble down to the right bank.

Among Washington rivers, the Klickitat offers a nearly unique combination of fine scenery, near-wilderness seclusion, light to moderate use, and reliable summer weather.

From headwaters in the Goat Rocks Wilderness, the Klickitat[1] sweeps south across a forested volcanic plateau in the vast Yakima Indian Reservation. Near the reservation's southern boundary, as the river passes Mt. Adams, several tributaries bring meltwater from snowfields and glaciers on the peak's eastern face. Over the milennia this added flow has helped the Klickitat to cut deeper into the plateau, and the river has carved out a scenic canyon on its way south toward its confluence with the Columbia River.[2]

Below the Yakima Reservation lie miles of unspoiled scenery and intermediate whitewater. For most of the run described here, the Klickitat tumbles through a narrow gorge cut into a volcanic plateau. Steep, rocky slopes rise several hundred feet from the river, giving the Klickitat a remote, intimate flavor. In places the river runs headlong into dramatic cliffs of columnar basalt. Ferns and mosses thrive in shady spots and near springs, but most of the canyon is clad in an open, airy forest of pine, fir, and oak.

The Klickitat lies in a strong rain shadow east of the Cascades crest, and summer days are usually sunny and warm. Like other Mt. Adams rivers, the Klickitat enjoys an extended summer season thanks to glacial melt and abundant spring flow from the porous volcanic rock.

The first half of the run is much steeper than the lower section, with nearly continuous Class III action at tight, rocky drops. **Log hazards** and cold water present additional dangers. Boaters should scout any time they cannot see clearly to the bottom of a drop. High flows demand more caution: eddies disappear, constricted rapids become much more difficult, and long, cold swims become a serious threat. The upper portion of the run should be considered Class IV above 3,000 cfs or so. Finally, a 3' fish hatchery **weir** near the halfway mark in the run **must be portaged or lined** (see **Mile Guide**). Or boaters can use an alternate take-out just above the weir.

Boaters who don't mind arduous put-ins can extend the run upriver some 3.5 miles by launching at the Yakima Indian Reservation boundary. (The tribe prohibits boating within the reservation.) In this short section the Klickitat tumbles at 80 ft./mi. through almost continuous Class III to IV rapids in a narrow, scenic gorge. Unfortunately, the access road is 400' above the put-in, and the informal "trail" to the river is more of a slide—steep, brushy, and difficult.

The standard take-out is at Leidl Bridge. Some boaters take out five miles upstream at Summit Creek Bridge, although this alternate access is on private logging company land.

[1] The unusual name comes from a Chinook Indian word meaning "beyond." The Chinook, a coastal people, apparently referred to the people of this region east of the Cascades as the Klickitat, or "people beyond the mountains." Our information on the meaning of this and many other Washington river names comes from James Phillips, *Washington State Place Names.*

[2] The lower 11 miles of the Klickitat were added to the National Wild and Scenic Rivers System in 1986, and the upper sections of the river are under study for similar designation.

Downstream Runs

Leidl Bridge to Klickitat Springs: Below Leidl Bridge the valley widens and the forest becomes more open, giving way to grassland in places. The broader channel and 25-ft./mi. gradient produce fairly easy Class II water, though **sweepers and log jams add an ever-changing hazard.** A private, unpaved logging road follows the right bank, detracting only slightly from the scenery and solitude. This section runs through a State Wildlife Area. Washington Highway 142 joins the river 12 miles below Leidl Bridge. A good **take-out** is at the fishing access at Klickitat Springs, about a mile downriver from the hamlet of Wahkiacus and two miles upriver from the town of Klickitat.

Klickitat Springs to Above Lyle Gorge: Below Klickitat Springs the highway and a railroad follow the river as it runs through Class II and III rapids. An old **weir** about two miles below Klickitat Springs should be scouted carefully.

The **take-out** is at a picnic area and fishing access on the left bank, some 11 miles below Klickitat Springs and 5 miles above Lyle. A few hundred yards above this take-out is the biggest rapid on this section, a Class III+ drop where Dillacort Canyon enters on the left. ***HAZARD.* Do not float past the take-out!** A couple of miles downstream is **Lyle Gorge**, where the Klickitat makes its final dramatic plunge to the Columbia River near the town of Lyle. The gorge begins with an unrunnable waterfall and continues with furious Class V rapids in a sheer-walled chasm. It's worth stopping along Highway 142 for a look down into the chasm.

Mile by Mile Guide

*See map just before **White Salmon** chapter.*

0 **PUT-IN** on the right bank at an abandoned gauging station. Difficult **alternate put-in** 3.5 miles upstream (see **Logistics**). A mile downstream, the river splits around islands, and logs sometimes lodge in the channels.

2 Bacon Creek enters on the right. A half mile downstream the Class III action begins with **RATTLER.** Downstream the canyon narrows, and in the next mile the river makes several sharp turns as it encounters steep headwalls.

4 Deer Creek enters on the left via a small waterfall. Just downstream, the river splits around an island, marking the beginning of two miles of challenging and continuous Class III (IV above about 3,000 cfs). At the end of this steep section, the canyon opens somewhat.

7 Power line across the river. Half a mile downstream, Trout Creek enters on the left.

8 **HATCHERY DROP (III)**, a right-left S-turn. About 300 yards downstream, a foot bridge crosses the river at the state fish hatchery. **Alternate RIVER ACCESS** above the foot bridge where Hatchery Road approaches the right bank. *HAZARD.* The hatchery weir is 100 yards below the foot bridge at a right bend. Debris and logs often lodge here, and there is exposed metal. **Portage or line on the left.** Below the dam is **BORDE (III)**, after which the river eases to Class II for a couple of miles. A road follows the left bank beginning about a mile below the dam.

11 Outlet Creek enters on the right, just below a spring-fed waterfall on the right. A quarter mile downstream White Creek, a major tributary, enters on the left. About half a mile below White Creek are the final Class III rapids, **BOUNDARY** (named for the original Indian Reservation boundary) and an unnamed drop. Class II water continues to Leidl Bridge.

13.5 Summit Creek Bridge; road crosses to the right bank. **RIVER ACCESS.** Some boaters take out on the right below the bridge, though this is private logging company land. Summit Creek enters on the left.

16 High cliffs on both banks force the river through a left-right jog. Downstream the road climbs away from the right bank.

18.7 **TAKE-OUT.** Leidl Bridge across the river. Leidl Campground on the right. Take out on the right below the bridge (license required—see **Permits**).

Cispus River

1. Upper Cispus: Road 23 Bridge (1,840') to North Fork (1,345').
IV; 9 miles; 55 ft./mi.

2. Lower Cispus: Tower Rock Bridge (1,250') to Crystal Creek Bridge (940').
III; 11 miles; 28 ft./mi. Shorter runs possible.

Drainage Area and Average Annual Discharge: 321 sq. mi. / 970,000 af at Tower Rock Bridge.

Season: *Upper:* April through June. *Lower:* April to mid-July. Flows typically peak in May or early June, then decline to September lows of under 500 cfs.

Recommended Levels: *Upper:* 1,000–2,500. *Lower:* 1,300–4,000. The Upper Cispus becomes much more difficult at higher flows, when strong hydraulics develop and eddies disappear. The broad lower river gets shallow in places below about 1,300 cfs.

Flow Information: NOAA Whitewater Hotline, (206) 526-8530, gives the flow "near Randle"—actually a gauge at Tower Rock near the Lower Cispus put-in. Flows on the upper run are roughly ⅔ to ¾ of this reading.

Special Hazards: Changeable log hazards; scout all blind drops.

Permits: Not presently required.

Managing Agency: Randle RD, Gifford Pinchot NF, Randle, WA 98377; (206) 497-7565.

Commercial Raft Trips: Yes. For a list of outfitters, contact the managing agency.

Land Ownership: *Upper:* All National Forest. *Lower:* Mostly National Forest to Iron Creek (some private near Tower Rock), all private thereafter.

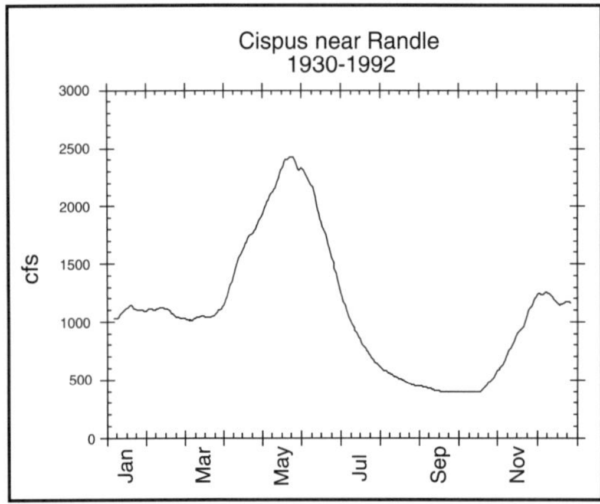

Scenery: *Upper:* Excellent; narrow, forested valley. *Lower:* Very good; open, forested valley with some logging scars, especially below Iron Creek Campground.

Solitude: *Upper:* Excellent. *Lower:* Very good; campgrounds, cabins. Roads are usually inconspicuous on both runs. Light river traffic.

Wilderness: No. Minor roads nearby.

Water: Cold and fairly clear.

Camping: Many USFS campgrounds, including several on the river.

Side Excursions: Mt. St. Helens. Mt. Adams. Goat Rocks Wilderness.

Guides and References:
- Bennett, *Guide to the Whitewater Rivers of Washington.* Includes upstream runs.
- North, *Washington Whitewater.*

Maps:
- **USGS 7.5':** *East Canyon Ridge, Blue Lake, Tower Rock, Greenhorn Buttes, Cowlitz Falls.*
- **USGS 1:100:** *Mt. Adams, Mt. St. Helens.*
- **USFS:** *Gifford Pinchot NF.*

Auto Shuttle: Roughly same mileages as runs.

Logistics: The many shuttle roads and accesses can be confusing; refer to the *Gifford Pinchot NF* map. There are several alternate accesses and shuttle routes besides those listed below. Contact the USFS for more detailed information.

Follow U.S. 12 to Randle in southwestern Washington. Turn south on combined USFS Roads 23 and 25 (a sign reads "To Mt. St. Helens"). This road immediately crosses the Cowlitz River. About ¾ mile beyond the bridge, the shuttle routes diverge as Roads 23 and 25 split:

1. To reach the Lower Cispus take-out at Crystal Creek Bridge, bear right on Road 25 and drive roughly 6 miles, then bear right on an unpaved road and drive downriver two miles to where a side road branches left and crosses the bridge over the Cispus.

An alternate take-out may—or may not—be possible two miles farther downstream at a new access provided by the Lewis County Public Utilities District (PUD). The PUD access is reached by continuing down the road along the north (right) bank. However, this road runs through land owned by Champion Lumber, and as of

1993 Champion has gated and locked the access road. For current information contact the managing agency or the Rivers Council of Washington (see appendix for address).

2. To reach the Lower Cispus put-in at Tower Rock Bridge, bear left on Road 23 and drive roughly 9 miles. Bear right on USFS Road 2306, drive 0.9 mile, then turn sharply left and drive ⅓ mile to the bridge (closed). Access is on the right bank.

3. For Upper Cispus accesses bear left on Road 23 and drive 10 miles to the intersection with Road 28. Stay left on Road 23. Two miles past this intersection, a small spur road turns off to the right and leads to the **take-out** just below the mouth of the North Fork. To reach the **Upper Cispus put-in,** continue up Road 23 some 8 more miles to the bridge over the Cispus (about ¾ mile past the Road 21 intersection).

Situated midway between Seattle and Tacoma to the north and Portland to the south, the Cispus, a major tributary of the Cowlitz, is often overlooked by urban boaters seeking runs closer to home. Yet the Cispus offers miles of exciting boating in a scenic forest setting. River runners can choose from two very different stretches, often referred to as the Upper and Lower Cispus. The upper run offers more challenge and seclusion than the lower.

The Cispus really has two headwaters. One branch of the upper river begins in the 7,000' Goat Rocks, a cluster of rugged volcanic peaks on the Cascade crest southeast of Mt. Rainier. The other drains the north face of 12,276' Mt. Adams, where glacial meltwater gives the Cispus most of its summer flow. Both runs described here are below the confluence of the two branches, where the Cispus flows westward down a gradually widening glacial valley.

On both runs, but especially on the upper one, **logs are a major potential hazard.** At times they have completely blocked the channel, forcing boaters to portage or even abandon the river. Inquire locally before attempting a run. Jams are especially prevalent in the four to five miles of broad, shallow river below the upper run's take-out at the North Fork confluence. This obstructed reach—sometimes called "Okefenokee" after the well-known swamp—separates the two runs described here and prevents a continuous float. Jams may also extend into the first portion of the Lower Cispus.

The Upper Cispus challenges boaters with steep, technical Class IV rapids that become much more difficult at higher flows. The river courses down a narrow, heavily forested valley and through two lush mini-gorges. The Lower Cispus, by contrast, runs down a broader channel in a wide glacial valley where increased flow has less effect on the rapids. Tower Rock dominates the scenery on much of the Lower Cispus, rising more than 2,000' above the river. Clearcuts mar some slopes, especially in the final stretch outside the National Forest boundary.

Until recently, boaters on the lower run could float all the way to the mouth of the Cispus, then continue down the Cowlitz River to take-outs above or below the powerful drop of Cowlitz Falls. However, a Lewis County Public Utilities District hydro dam is now being built at Cowlitz Falls. Scheduled for completion in 1994, the dam will flood the final 1.5 miles of the Cispus and 10.5 miles of the Cowlitz.

Hydro developers are now proposing another project that would divert almost all the water from the last five miles of the Lower Cispus run. The Forest Service has recommended much of the Cispus for addition to the National Wild and Scenic Rivers System, but as of 1993 Congress has not acted to protect the river. To help, contact the Rivers Council of Washington (see appendix for address).

Expert boaters occasionally attempt to navigate beautiful but dangerous reaches of the Cispus above the Upper Cispus run described here. These uppermost reaches hold frequent log hazards and many mandatory portages. For more information consult Jeff Bennett, *A Guide to the Whitewater Rivers of Washington.*

Upper Cispus Mile Guide

See map just before ***White Salmon*** *chapter.*

0 PUT-IN on the left below the USFS Road 23 bridge. ***HAZARD.*** A mile downstream the channel splits, and the left side is often jammed by logs.

1.8 Juniper Creek enters on the left. Just downstream is **PICKY PICKY (III)**, a long boulder garden that marks the beginning of more difficult whitewater. The river drops 180' in the next two miles.

3 **BIG BEND (IV).** The Cispus drops over ledges and among boulders as it cuts into a short, beautiful mini-gorge. **Recognition:** A quarter mile above the rapid the river bends right, then sharply left just above the drop. Scout on the left at the left bend.

3.6 **WHITE LIGHTNING (IV).** Sharp staircase drops over boulders, then large runout waves. Scout either side. Another short mini-gorge encloses the river here.

4.2 Blue Lake Creek enters on the right. Easier water and lower gradient for the next 1.5 miles. Tongue Mountain rises more than 3,000' on the left.

5.7 **SMOOTHROCK FALLS (IV-; IV at higher flows).** A 4' drop over a riverwide ledge creates a dangerous reversal at higher flows. A runnable chute can usually be found on the right. Scout right. Easier water ahead.

7.3 **Alternate RIVER ACCESS** as Road 2801 approaches the left bank at a right-hand bend (long, difficult carry for rafts). Another possible alternate take-out is on the right about a half mile downstream.

9 North Fork Cispus enters on the right. Primary **TAKE-OUT** is downstream on the right at a gravel bar, where a short road leads to USFS Road 23. ***HAZARD.*** Downstream, the current slows and **log jams** become a major problem as the Cispus enters the "Okefenokee" section. **Boating below the North Fork is not recommended** due to numerous log jams and portages in the 2.5 miles down to the Road 28 bridge.

Lower Cispus Mile Guide

See map just before ***White Salmon*** *chapter.*

0 **PUT-IN** on the right at the old Tower Rock Bridge (closed). Tower Rock soars 2,000' above Tower Rock Campground on the left bank (**alternate access**). The Randle gauging station is on the left bank just above the bridge. A Forest Service road generally follows the left bank for the next 8 miles. The first two miles are through mostly private land. (An alternate **put-in** is two miles upstream at the USFS Road 28 bridge. However, logs stranded in this stretch may require portage.)

2 Private land ends, Class II riffles begin, and the scenery improves. A mile downstream Greenhorn Creek enters on the left, and a spur road off USFS Road 76 reaches the left bank (**alternate RIVER ACCESS.**)

6.5 Twin Cedars, a popular **alternate RIVER ACCESS** at a beach on the left (reached via USFS Road 76). Downstream is **IRON CREEK (III)**, a pair of drops marking the start of some 3 miles of busy Class II+ to III water. Below the rapid Iron Creek, a major tributary, enters on the left.

7.5 Iron Creek Campground on the left. Not far downstream, the river splits around an island at **LET'S MAKE A DEAL (III-)**: the left side is steep and rocky, the right is easier. A bit farther is **HELL HOLE (III)**, also called **Roller Coaster,** usually the roughest drop on the run. At lower flows the river plunges into a big, hard-to-miss hole on the bottom right. At higher levels standing waves develop.

8.5 **Alternate RIVER ACCESS.** USFS Road 25 bridge, known as Huffaker Bridge.

9.2 The river bends right and runs through **AGITATOR (III-).** About ¾ mile downstream is **LIONS JAW (III-).** Woods Creek enters on the right, after which the whitewater eases somewhat.

11 **TAKE-OUT** at a minor bridge across the river a few hundred yards upstream from Crystal Creek. It may—or may not—be possible to continue another 2.5 miles to a new PUD access on the right bank, just above the backwaters of the new Cowlitz Falls Reservoir. (See **Logistics**.) The final 2.5 miles include **DOUBLE TROUBLE (III-)** at mile 13.3.

Lewis River

1. Crab Creek Bridge (1,410')
to Road 9039 Bridge (1,115').
IV; 8 miles; 37 ft./mi.
Possible portages in **Big Creek Gorge.**

2. Road 9039 Bridge to Road 90 Bridge
at Eagle Cliff (1,020').
III-; 3.5 miles; 27 ft./mi.

Drainage Area and Average Annual Discharge: 150 sq. mi. / 800,000 af at Cussed Hollow (est.).
Season: April–mid-July, depending on rainfall.
Recommended Levels: *Run 1:* 1,000–2,000 cfs. *Run 2:* 1,000–5,000 cfs.
Flow Information: No gauge. For a rough estimate, call the NOAA Whitewater Hotline, (206) 526-8530, and convert from the Randle gauge reading on the nearby Cispus River as follows: in March and April, take 90% of the Cispus flow; in May, 80%; in June, 70%; in July, 60%.
Rafts: Small paddle rafts only on upper run due to very narrow passages at Big Creek Gorge.
Kayaks: Bridging hazards in Big Creek Gorge.
Special Hazards: Log hazards. Big Creek Gorge.
Permits: Not presently required.
Managing Agency: Gifford Pinchot NF, Mt. St. Helens National Volcanic Monument, 42218 N.E. Yale Bridge Rd., Amboy, WA 98601; (206) 750-3900.
Commercial Raft Trips: None at this time.
Land Ownership: All National Forest.
Scenery: Excellent. Heavily forested canyon.
Solitude: Excellent. Road is usually well away from the river. **Wilderness:** No.
Water: Cold, sometimes silty from glacial melt.
Camping: Several USFS campgrounds. Lower Falls CG is just upstream from the put-in.
Side Hikes: A trail (good for mountain bikers as well as hikers) follows the run and also leads upstream from the put-in (or Lower Falls CG) to three falls on the Upper Lewis. Side hike up Big Creek (see **Mile Guide**).
Side Excursions: Big Creek Falls viewpoint on the shuttle road. Mt. St. Helens National Monument. Mt. Adams.
Guides and References:
- Bennett, *Guide to the Whitewater Rivers of Washington.* Covers both runs.
- North, *Washington Whitewater.* Covers Run 2.

Maps:
- **USGS 7.5':** *Spencer Butte, Burnt Peak, Mt. St. Helens SE.*
- **USFS:** *Gifford Pinchot NF.*

Auto Shuttle: Roughly same mileages as river.
Logistics: To reach the **take-out at Eagle Cliff Bridge,** follow I-5 to Woodland in southwestern Washington, then drive east about 30 miles on Washington Highway 503 to Cougar. Continue east some 20 miles on USFS Road 90 to the Eagle Cliff Bridge over the Lewis (a couple of miles upstream from Swift Reservoir).

To reach the **intermediate access,** follow Road 90 upstream 5.5 miles from the Eagle Cliff take-out, turn left onto Road 9039, and drive ¼ mile. Access is on the right bank above the bridge; leave vehicles in the parking area on the left (south) side of the river.

To reach the **put-in at Crab Creek Bridge,** continue up Road 90 some 6.5 miles past Rush Creek to where the road crosses the river at Cussed Hollow. Be sure to stop at Big Creek Falls Viewpoint on the way.

The Lewis is a river caught between two volcanic giants. Rising among glaciers and snowfields on the northwest face of Mt. Adams (12,276'), the Lewis—sometimes called the North Fork Lewis— runs westward toward the Columbia River, passing just 10 miles south of the shattered summit of Mt. St. Helens (8,365'). In this land of fire and ice the Lewis River canyon is a garden oasis. Boaters enjoying the lush scenery and icy rapids may find it hard to imagine the cataclysmic eruption of May 1980 that blew 1,300' off St. Helens' summit.

The run described here was largely unaffected by the eruption, but enormous mudflows devastated two large tributaries—Muddy River and Pine Creek. A mixture of melted ice and snow, ash, soil, trees, and debris tore down these canyons and surged into the Lewis not far above Eagle Cliff Bridge. The mudflows wiped out the bridge (since rebuilt), then thundered into Swift Reservoir. Today, signs of the eruption are visible below the Muddy River confluence, but this section is quickly restoring itself.

Above the Muddy River confluence the Lewis boasts some of Washington's finest river scenery: narrow gorges, fern-decked cliffs, lush forests, and one of the West's loveliest side creek waterfalls, Curly Creek, which plunges 70' directly into the river, passing under two natural bridges as it falls. Many smaller waterfalls adorn the canyon, while the Lewis itself plummets over three major cataracts not far above the Cussed Hollow put-in.

The upper run holds the more difficult rapids, with the major challenge in a roughly 100-yard stretch of Big Creek Gorge near mile 4. Here huge blocks of columnar basalt have tumbled into the river, dividing the current into narrow, turbulent passages. At lower flows some chutes are only 5' or 6' wide, making the gorge impassable even for medium-sized rafts. Only kayaks, small paddle rafts, and possibly open canoes in the hands of true experts can attempt this short section—and even they may have to make some portages.

Though the whitewater itself rates Class IV, the dangers of Big Creek Gorge make the upper stretch an **experts-only** run. Even experts should think twice before running the gorge at higher or lower levels than our recommended range (1,000–2,000 cfs). Undercut boulders are more dangerous at lower levels. **Stay constantly alert for log hazards on this run.**

Boaters can launch at an intermediate access at the Road 9039 bridge to avoid the difficult water upstream. Those floating this lower section will enjoy seeing Curly Creek Falls and running one Class III drop near the Eagle Cliff take-out. **Beware of log hazards.**

Three hydroelectric dams have already flooded some 40 miles of the Lewis, and Pacific Power & Light's proposed Muddy Project would drown this run by damming the river at Eagle Cliff. Fortunately, this proposal appears to be dead, and the outlook is now brighter for saving the free-flowing upper river. The Forest Service has recommended National Wild and Scenic protection from the headwaters to Swift Reservoir, including the run covered here, but Congress has not acted.

East Fork Lewis

The smaller, steeper East Fork of the Lewis (Class III to V) is much closer to urban centers and attracts lots of boaters—mainly kayakers—from the Portland area. For more information refer to the Bennett guide book listed above.

Mile by Mile Guide

0 **PUT-IN** on the right bank above the Crab Creek (Road 90) bridge. A USFS trail follows the entire run, first on the right bank, later on the left. Class II and III rapids first 1.5 miles.

1.5 **SPENCER (IV).** Boulders clog the center and right channels. **Recognition:** Near mile 1.3 the canyon narrows, then the river sweeps through a sharp left bend. The drop is at the end of the bend. Scout right.

3.8 **BIG CREEK GORGE (IV)** begins just below a shallow right bend and continues for ⅓ mile. Scout carefully and watch for logs. ***POSSIBLE PORTAGES,*** especially in a 100-yard stretch in the middle of the gorge. Small boats only due to narrow passages. Below the gorge Big Creek enters on the left. Spectacular hike (no trail) up the creek to Big Creek Grotto.

6 A steep, rough dirt road leads from the left bank up to Road 90 (emergency **RIVER ACCESS**). Rush Creek enters downstream on the left. Class II and II+ rapids for the next two miles.

7.5 The river gradually enters a narrow inner gorge that runs for over a mile.

8 **RIVER ACCESS** on the right above the Road 9039 bridge. Trail crosses to the left bank for the remainder of the run. Downstream, Curly Creek Falls cascades into the river on the left, followed by smaller Miller Creek Falls, also on the left.

10.5 The Muddy River, a major tributary, enters on the right, creating a **Class III-rapid.** Half a mile farther, Pine Creek enters on the right at another **Class III-rapid.** Just below this rapid is the final whitewater, **EAGLE CLIFF (III)**, with numerous waves and reversals.

11.5 **TAKE-OUT** on the right just below the Eagle Cliff (Road 90) Bridge, just below Eagle Cliff Rapid. Downstream are the backwaters of Swift Reservoir.

Wind River

Stabler to High Bridge

Difficulty: V- below 1,500 cfs; V to V+ at higher flows.
Length: 6.5 miles.
Gradient: 80 ft./mi.
Put-in: Hemlock Road bridge (915').
Take-out: Old Detour above High Bridge (365').
Season: Rainy season through May, sometimes into June.
Recommended Levels: 500–1,500 cfs. Very demanding above 1,500.
Flow Information: No gauge, but flows should be adequate when Oregon's Clackamas River has a reading of 2,000 cfs or more at Three Lynx. The Three Lynx flow is on the NWS tape, (503) 249-0666.
Permits: Not presently required.
Land Ownership: Mostly private but undeveloped.
Scenery: Excellent. Lush, narrow volcanic gorge.
Solitude: Excellent. Steep walls screen out civilization.
Wilderness: No.

Guides and References:
- Bennett, *A Guide to the Whitewater Rivers of Washington.* Includes downstream run.
- *Soggy Sneakers Guide to Oregon Rivers* (Willamette Kayak and Canoe Club).

Maps:
- **USGS 7.5:** *Stabler, Big Huckleberry Mtn.*
- **USFS:** *Gifford Pinchot NF.*

Logistics: Access is via Wind River Highway, which leads north from Washington Highway 14 near Carson, about 40 miles east of Portland.

To reach the **take-out,** turn left on High Bridge Road, two miles north of Carson and about ⅓ mile before the highway crosses the Wind, then bear right on Old Detour Road and descend to the take-out on the right bank.

To reach the **put-in,** return to Wind River Highway, drive north about 5.5 miles to Stabler, turn left on Hemlock Road, and put in at the bridge.

The Wind is another Washington river whose proximity to Portland (within an hour's drive) makes it a backyard run for boaters from that city. In this case, though, the boaters should be **experts only.**

This relatively small river drains a moderate-elevation watershed (almost entirely below 4,000') on the north side of the Columbia River Gorge. The Wind's headwaters are cut off from the glaciers and snowfields of nearby Mt. Adams and Mt. St. Helens by the neighboring White Salmon and Lewis drainages. Despite the lack of significant snowpack, the Wind has a surprisingly long season thanks to the steady release of groundwater from the porous volcanic rock. Boatable flows typically extend from the first heavy rains of autumn through May and sometimes into June.

The Wind runs generally south on its short course to meet the Columbia River near Cascade Locks. The run described here takes in most of the river's final plunge down a lush, narrow chasm incised in dark volcanic rock on the way to the Columbia Gorge. Steep walls give boaters a sense of near-wilderness seclusion despite a highway well above the left bank.

At flows above 1,500 cfs, the Wind's demanding whitewater should be attempted only by teams of experts. Rafters should run this river only in agile self-bailing boats. The most difficult whitewater is concentrated near the beginning of the run. At some levels several of the rapids become nearly continuous, raising the prospect of long, nasty swims and possible hypothermia. High water dramatically increases the difficulty of this narrow river.

Wind River Guide

*See map just before **White Salmon** chapter.*

Put in at Hemlock Road bridge in Stabler (mile 0). The initial rapids are Class III to IV. The heavy whitewater begins about three quarters of a mile into the run, where Trout Creek (referred to in some guides as Rock Creek) enters on the right. Stop on the right bank just

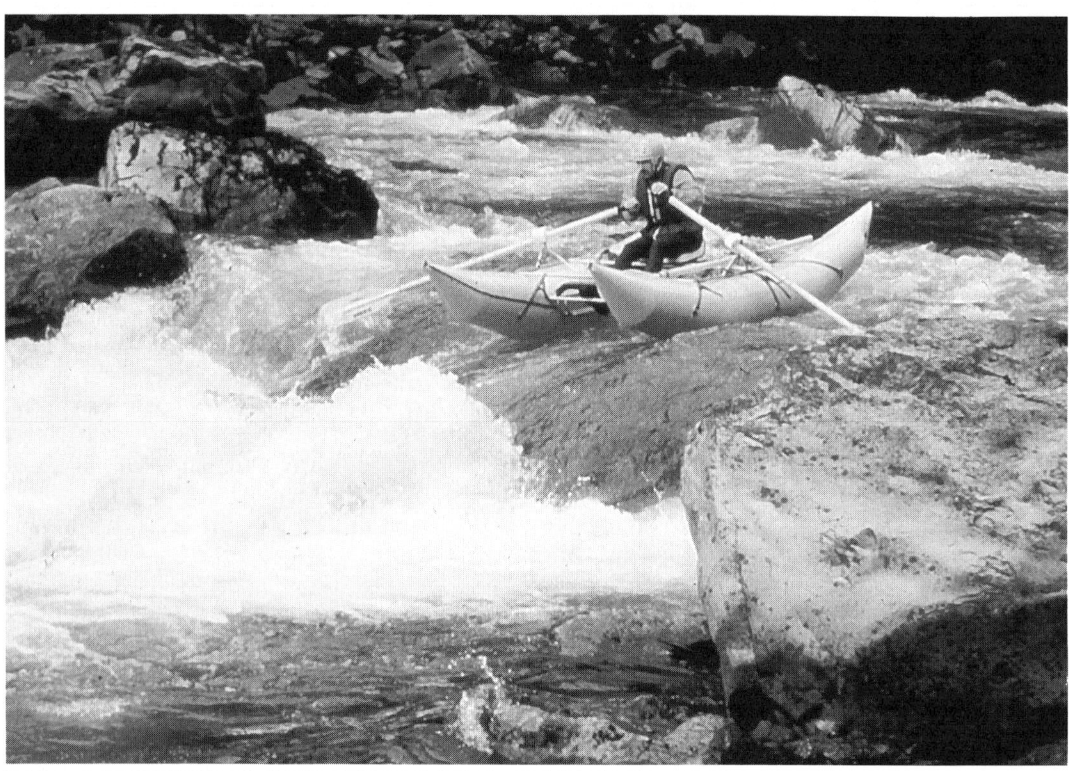

Cataraft on the Wind River *Jeff Bennett*

below the creek to scout. The Wind drops 125' in the next mile. The first major rapid, **INITIATION (IV+)**, is immediately below the creek. In the half mile below Initiation the river plunges headlong through almost continuous drops, culminating with a dramatic rapid known as **RAM'S HORN (V-; V at higher flows)**, which features two powerful holes that become enormous at high flows. Scout on the left. Just downstream is a small waterfall on the right.

In the mile below Ram's Horn the whitewater eases temporarily, only to erupt again in the biggest rapid of the run, **CLIMAX (V-; V at higher flows)**. Located at the end of a short pool at about mile 2.7, Climax has a nasty reversal that could hold swimmers at some levels (scout from either bank). The final four miles below Climax are milder but still challenging, with several technical Class III and IV rapids and a gradient of 65 ft./mi. **Take out** on the right at the old bridge site.

Hard-core experts occasionally tackle the final 4.5 miles from the High Bridge down to the Columbia River. However, this very difficult section includes two portages, one of which is a hellish carry around a 50' cascade known as **Shipherd Falls**, located about 3 miles below High Bridge. Those who want to see the falls without running this stretch can hike down a steep trail on the right (west) side of the canyon about a mile northeast of Carson.

Green River

Kanaskat-Palmer State Park to Flaming Geyser State Park

Difficulty: IV. **Gradient:** 45 ft./mi.
Length: 12 miles. Longer, shorter runs possible.
Put-in: Kanaskat-Palmer State Park (730').
Take-out: Flaming Geyser State Park (205').
Drainage Area and Average Annual Discharge: 231 sq. mi. and 715,000 af at put-in.
Season: Nov.–mid-June. Dam-controlled, but flows are quite variable. Typically peaks in winter and spring, then declines rapidly to unboatable summer lows of less than 400 cfs, which continue until autumn rains bring the river up again.
Recommended Levels: 800–3,000 cfs. High water begins around 2,500 cfs. Very powerful above 4,000 cfs.
Flow Information: Howard Hanson Dam releases change daily. Call Army Corps of Engineers weekdays 7 a.m.–4 p.m., (206) 764-6702, for expected releases; call Friday for weekend estimates. NOAA Whitewater Hotline, (206) 526-8530, is usually updated every Wednesday, so its reading is frequently out of date.
Permits: Not presently required.
Managing Agencies: (1) Kanaskat-Palmer State Park, 32101 Kanaskat-Cumberland Rd., Ravensdale, WA 98051; (206) 886-0148. (2) Flaming Geyser State Park, 23700 SE Flaming Geyser Rd., Auburn, WA 98002; (206) 931-3930.
Commercial Raft Trips: Yes. For a list of outfitters, contact a managing agency.
Land Ownership: Mostly state; some private.
Scenery: Excellent. Lush, narrow, winding gorge.
Solitude: Very good. Heavy river traffic on spring weekends.
Wilderness: No, but very secluded.

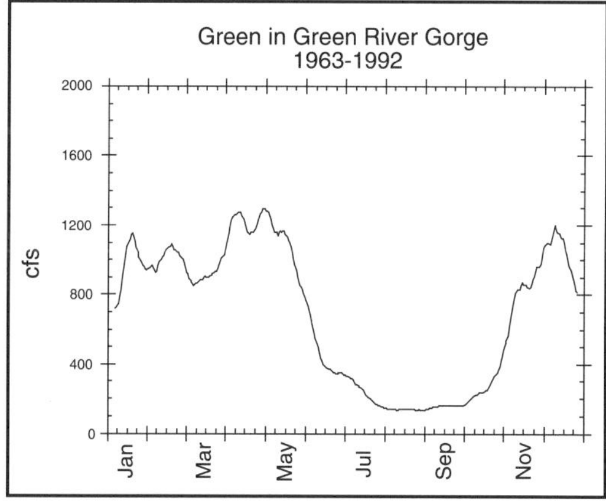

Guides and References:
- North, *Washington Whitewater.*
- Bennett, *Guide to the Whitewater Rivers of Washington.*

Maps:
- **USGS 7.5':** *Cumberland, Black Diamond.*

Auto Shuttle: Roughly 20 paved miles (30 minutes) one way.
Logistics: The **take-out** is at a picnic area on the left (south) bank at **Flaming Geyser State Park.** Coming from the east, follow Washington Highway 169 south two miles from Black Diamond, or north 6 miles from Enumclaw, to S.E. Green Valley Road (3/4 mile north of the Highway 169 bridge over the Green). Drive west on Green Valley 2.5 miles to the park entrance, then another 1.5 miles to the take-out. The park can also be reached from the west by following S.E. Green Valley Road east from Auburn.

To reach the **put-in at Kanaskat-Palmer State Park,** return to Highway 169, drive about 1.5 miles north to Black Diamond, then turn right (east) on Green River Gorge Road for 4 miles to Franklin Bridge over the Green. (Tough intermediate access for a fee at Green River Gorge Resort on the south side of this bridge; see **Mile Guide.**) Cross the bridge, drive 0.4 miles, then turn sharply left and drive roughly two more miles to Kanaskat-Cumberland Road. Turn left again, drive northeast a little over two miles, and turn left into the State Park. Bear left at the first intersection, then bear right and follow signs to the upper boat launch. Another more difficult put-in within the park is a half mile downstream.

A popular **alternate put-in** on the left bank some 3 miles upstream allows more warm-up before the largest rapids. Follow directions above to Kanaskat-Palmer State Park, but continue on Kanaskat-Cumberland Road 0.4 miles beyond the State Park turnoff, then bear right on a paved road where a sign indicates "Green River Headworks" (this turnoff is a few hundred yards south of the bridge over the Green). Drive upriver just over a mile, then cut down to a parallel road closer to the river and drive another hundred yards to the launch site.

GREEN

Washington's Green River is a glittering emerald in an unlikely setting. Just 25 miles from downtown Seattle and Tacoma, this near-wilderness gem runs 12 miles through a narrow, twisting gorge decked with ferns, mosses, and towering old-growth evergreens. Dozens of seeps and small waterfalls decorate the lush canyon. The Green's tortuous course enhances the sense of isolation and intimacy: boaters are usually out of sight and sound from one another.

With its solitude, outstanding scenery, advanced whitewater, and near-urban location, the Green has become one of Washington's most popular floats. In fact, if summer flows were higher, the Green would be one of the Pacific Northwest's most popular rivers. However, the Green's small, moderate-elevation watershed produces adequate runoff only during the rainy season. (Small boats may scrape down into early summer.)

The Green relinquishes a good part of its already low summertime flows to the city of Tacoma, and the river stands to lose more water as local population booms. In the future, a proposed pipeline and the possible expansion of Howard Hanson Dam upstream could mean less water in the river. The best hope for boaters may be mitigation to guarantee minimum recreational releases. Local groups are also working to gain State Scenic River designation. For more information contact the Rivers Council of Washington (see appendix for address).

The Green drains a relatively gentle portion of the Cascades between Mt. Rainier to the south and the high Alpine Lakes region to the north. The river runs generally west to the Seattle suburb of Auburn, then turns north through Seattle's industrial south side. Tacoma controls the upper watershed, and entry is restricted. In this upper reach the Army Corps of Engineers' Howard Hanson Dam blocks the Green and regulates downstream flows. Tacoma's water intake and purification plant are a few miles below the dam. Below these facilities the river is open to the public.

The Green River Gorge begins roughly three miles below the purification plant as the river gradually enters a shallow but steep-walled slot cut into a broad plateau of sedimentary rock. The most popular put-in is at Kanaskat-Palmer State Park, though alternate launch sites are available.

Technical Class IV whitewater begins just below the Park put-in as the gorge quickly deepens to 150' to 250'. Advanced boaters find plenty of action in the 5.5 miles to Franklin Bridge, with several rapids that demand scouting. Below Franklin Bridge the difficulty eases considerably. Some boaters use a more difficult access at Green River Gorge Resort near the bridge to avoid the rough water upstream.

Dam-controlled flows on the Green are variable and subject to change with little or no notice. Beware of high water, since increased flows in the constricted gorge make the rapids much more difficult and hazardous. Also, because the Green is runnable only during the

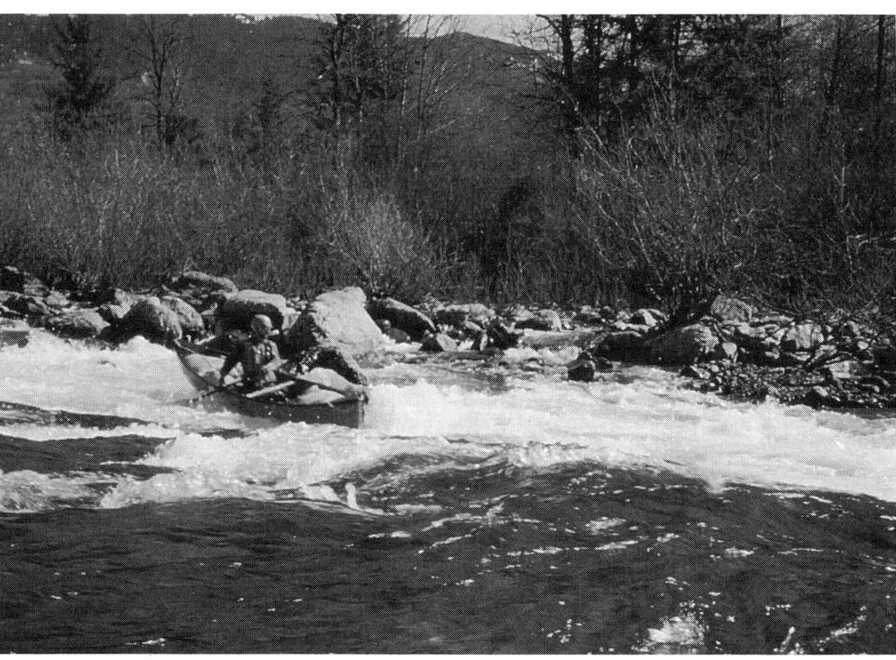

Ledge 1, Green River *Jon Almquist*

rainy season, conditions are often cold and damp. Even on sunny days little direct sunlight penetrates to the river, and the water is always cold. Although local boaters usually head home for a hot soak after a day on the Green, overnight camping is available at state parks.

In the early 1900's the area surrounding Green River Gorge was known primarily as a coal region. Several mining operations produced coal for the local market until they were idled by the advent of less expensive petroleum. Today, place names like Black Diamond recall the coal era. The "Flaming Geyser" near the take-out is also an artifact of earlier times. It is not a geyser at all; in the 1920's a test hole drilled here in search of coal punctured a pocket of methane gas that continues to burn.

Green River Guide

Put in on the left bank at Kanaskat-Palmer State Park (mile 0), across from a fish hatchery on the right bank (see Logistics for alternate put-ins). Just downstream the river bends left into **LEDGE 1 (III).** Like the other rapids in the Green River Gorge, this one gets much rougher at higher flows. Many are difficult to scout because of sheer walls and/or heavy underbrush.

The next two miles contain many Class III rapids, including **LEDGE 2,** just below a right bend at mile 0.8. The usual run is along the left wall. At a right bend at mile 2 is **PIPELINE (IV),** where a rocky bar on the right forces the river left and into a rocky drop. At the bottom left is a big hole or wave (depending on flow). Several hundred yards downstream at a right bend is **LEDGE 3 (III+).**

About half a mile farther, the gorge narrows and a power line crosses overhead—a warning to stop and scout the two roughest rapids just downstream. **Recognition:** Below the power line the river bends left, splits around a small island (take the right channel), then splashes through a short Class III. Pull out in a small eddy on the left just below the Class III to scout. **The rapids:** First is **MERCURY (IV),** a rocky drop (big waves at high flows) that is typically run left of center. After a short stretch of swift water comes **THE NOZZLE (IV),** where three big boulders block the river and most of the flow churns into the middle rock. Boaters must run a narrow chute between the left and middle boulders without getting pinned or wrapped. Approach this pair of rapids with extra caution above 2,500 cfs. At high flows a nasty hole forms on the left just downstream.

The next 2.5 miles hold almost constant Class III action. About a quarter mile below **The Nozzle,** boulders divide the channel into three slots. At mile 5.5 Franklin Bridge crosses the river, marking the end of the more difficult water; downstream the rapids are Class III or easier. Just below the bridge on the left is the Green River Gorge Resort (**alternate access**). Boaters who wish to launch or take out here may pay a fee to use a steep access trail (difficult for rafts). Just downstream is **PARADISE LEDGE,** a favorite play spot.

At mile 6.5 a foot bridge crosses the river not far from a warm spring on the left. A mile farther, **SLIDE (III)** appears at a sharp right bend. Here the river has undercut the left bank, triggering a landslide that has filled the channel with rocks and logs. Though the river has gradually worn a wider passage through the blockage, **scouting is recommended;** the site is unstable, and new slides or logs could appear at any time. At mile 9.5 Highway 169 crosses the river (high bridge, no access). Class II water continues to the **take-out** on the left at the Flaming Geyser State Park picnic area (mile 12).

Downstream Runs

The Green is boatable for over 30 miles below the standard take-out at Flaming Geyser. Frequent access allows runs of varying length and difficulty. The first three miles to Whitney Bridge are Class II with good scenery; this section is known as the "Yo-Yo" run because boaters often repeat it. The following seven miles to the Highway 18 bridge are Class I+ (with possible log or brush hazards) in a semi-rural setting. Below Highway 18 is flatwater, frequently with riprapped banks, in a suburban or urban setting. For more information on the lower Green, refer to Huser, Paddle Routes of Western Washington, LeRoux and Rudersdorf, Paddle Washington, and Furrer, Water Trails of Washington.

Snoqualmie River

North and Middle Forks

Middle Fork Snoqualmie

1. Upper Middle: Taylor River (1,010') to Concrete Bridge (810').
II+; 9 miles; 22 ft./mi.

2. Middle Middle: Concrete Bridge to Tanner (525').
III4 (IV above 3,000 cfs); 7 miles; 40 ft./mi.

North Fork Snoqualmie

Deep Creek (1,275') to Swinging Bridge Site (1,020').
III; 6 miles; 40 ft./mi.

Drainage Area and Average Annual Discharge: *Middle Fork:* 154 sq. mi. and 907,000 af near Tanner. *North Fork:* 64 sq. mi. and 362,000 af.

Season: *Middle Fork:* Nov.–early July. *North Fork:* Nov.–late June. Both forks typically have high water in winter and again in mid- to late spring. Middle Fork generally peaks in late May or early June, then recedes to less than 500 cfs in August and September. North Fork usually peaks in May, then recedes to below 500 cfs by early July.

Recommended Levels: *Middle Fork:* 1,000–4,000 cfs. *North Fork:* 600–2,000 cfs.

Flow Information: NOAA Whitewater Hotline, (206) 526-8530. Flows on the Middle Fork near Tanner and on the North Fork.

Special Hazards: Log hazards, especially on the North Fork.

Permits: Not presently required.

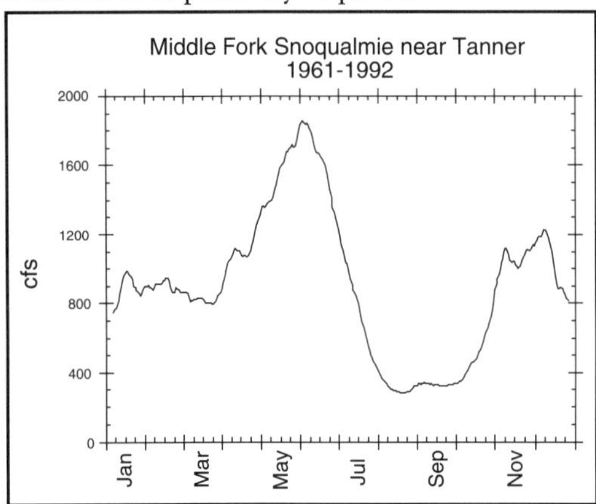

Managing Agency: North Bend RD, Mt. Baker-Snoqualmie NF, 42404 SE North Bend Way, North Bend, WA 98045; (206) 888-1421.

Commercial Raft Trips: Yes on the Middle Fork. Contact the USFS for a list of outfitters.

Land Ownership: *Middle Fork:* Mixed National Forest and private first 5 miles, private thereafter. *North Fork:* All private.

Scenery: Very good. Dense forest, some mountain views.

Solitude: Very good. Dense vegetation screens roads.

Wilderness: No.

Water: Cold and clear.

Camping: Campground at Mine Creek on the Middle Fork. Few sites on the river banks.

Side Hikes: A trail up 4,167' Mt. Si offers good views of both forks of the Snoqualmie.

Side Excursions: Snoqualmie Falls on the river's main stem. Mt. Rainier.

Guides and References:
- Bennett, *Guide to the Whitewater Rivers of Washington.*
- North, *Washington Whitewater.*
- Huser, *Paddle Routes of Western Washington.* Downstream runs.

Maps:
- **USGS 7.5':** *Middle Fork:* Lake Philippa, Mt. Si, Chester Morse Lake. *North Fork:* Mt. Si.
- **USGS 1:100:** *Middle Fork:* Skykomish River, Snoqualmie Pass. *North Fork:* Skykomish River.
- **USFS:** *Mt. Baker-Snoqualmie NF.*
- **AAA:** *Mt. Rainier.*

Logistics: *Middle Fork:* Status of the Tanner take-out is currently unclear due to problems with landowners (see essay and footnote; call for current information). To reach the **take-out** near the town of Tanner, take exit 34 from I-90 east of North Bend. Drive briefly north on Edgewick Road, turn left on the frontage road along I-90, drive 1.5 miles, turn right on SE Tanner Road, drive a half mile, then turn left on a short spur road to the river (may be gated). Park on the main road. This take-out is on private land. For **upstream accesses** return to Edgewick Road, turn left, drive 0.4 miles and bear right on Middle Fork Road (becomes USFS Road 56), which passes Mine Creek Campground (an **alternate access**) and eventually crosses the Middle Fork. Access is possible at this bridge but may be difficult for rafts. To reach the **Upper Middle Fork put-in**, continue just over 6 miles past the bridge, then turn right onto an unmarked spur road to the river. This turnoff is about 0.6 miles before Road 56 crosses the Taylor River.

North Fork: The river and shuttle roads pass through Weyerhaeuser Corporation land, and a crucial road is blocked by a locked gate. As of 1993 Weyerhaeuser was allowing boaters to borrow a key. For current information contact the Rivers Council of Washington (see footnote in essay below), which hopes to work out an access arrangement with the corporation. **Directions:** Take Exit 31 from I-90 and drive west on Washington Highway 202 into North Bend. Turn right on North Bend Way, then left on Ballarat Avenue North. Follow this road out of town and across the Middle and North Forks, after which it becomes North Fork Road. Bear left 1.5 miles past the North Fork bridge. In another 1.4 miles, at the end of a left curve, a spur road turns sharply right. To reach the **take-out,** take this road (gated as of 1993), drive a half mile, bear left at the "Y," drive another 0.8 miles, bear right, then in 200 yards continue straight down a hill to the end of the road. Park and hike to the river. **Scout this take-out carefully! Downstream are very hazardous rapids and falls.**

To reach the **put-in,** return to North Fork Road and continue 2.5 miles to a four-way intersection. The road to the right (gated as of 1993) leads to an alternate access at Spur 10 Bridge (see **Mile Guide**). Continue straight just over 5 miles to the little bridge over Deep Creek. Half a mile past the bridge, park and carry your gear down a short trail to the right bank. **Do not put in above this point—Class VI Wagner Falls is just upriver!** (If you come to a big bridge over the North Fork, you've gone too far. The North Fork bridge is upstream from Wagner Falls, a mandatory portage.)

Despite their location less than an hour's drive—traffic permitting—from downtown Seattle, the North and Middle Forks of the Snoqualmie[1] offer some of Washington's most secluded and scenic river running. Yet the Middle Fork take-out is just five minutes off busy I-90. A dense forest of cedar and fir blankets these rain-drenched watersheds, and thick riverbank vegetation helps screen out civilization. Though gravel roads are nearby, boaters have a sense of near-wilderness isolation.

The Middle Fork, the larger of the two streams, drains snowy 6,000' and 7,000' peaks along the Cascade crest in the Alpine Lakes Wilderness east of Seattle. From these headwaters the Middle Fork flows westward down a gradually widening, U-shaped glacial valley bounded by spectacular granite ridges and spires. Boaters enjoy dramatic mountain scenery in the first third of the run below the Taylor River confluence. Rugged peaks tower up to 4,000' above the river. For most of the run described here, the Middle Fork cascades over granite bedrock, but in its lower reaches the river glides more easily over deep deposits of gravel, cobble, and other glacial debris.

The smaller North Fork drains a narrow pocket of moderate-elevation terrain. Its headwaters are pinched off from the Cascade crest by the neighboring watersheds of the Middle Fork Snoqualmie and South Fork Skykomish. As a result the North Fork has lower flows and a shorter season than the Middle Fork, and its water level fluctuates more with rainfall. This branch of the river also affords fewer mountain views. Instead, boaters enjoy the beauty of a narrow, boulder-strewn channel flanked by towering evergreens.

Not far below the town of North Bend, the North, Middle, and South Forks join to form the main stem of the Snoqualmie. A few miles below their confluences, the combined waters plunge over 268' Snoqualmie Falls, one of the most impressive waterfalls in the Pacific Northwest. Below the falls the Snoqualmie meanders north to meet its sister stream, the Skykomish. The two rivers join to form the Snohomish River, which empties into Puget Sound at Everett, Washington.

[1]The name apparently referred to a local Indian tribe, and is thought to mean "people of the moon."

Today the Snoqualmie faces development threats, including logging plans in the Middle Fork watershed and a proposed dam on the North Fork. Boaters and conservationists have stalled the dam, but only National Wild and Scenic designation will provide long-term protection. The Forest Service is recommending designation for 12 miles of the North Fork and 40 miles of the Middle Fork.[2]

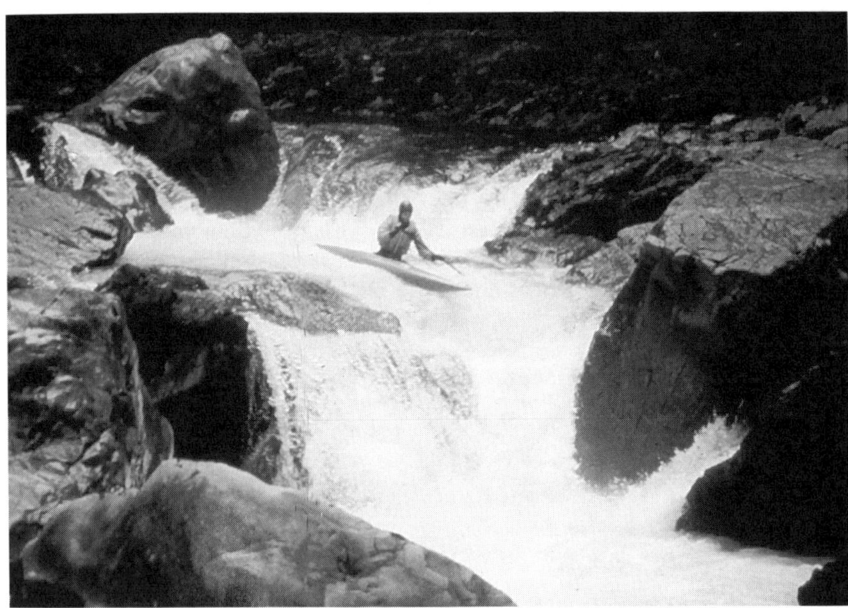

Ernie's Canyon, North Fork Snoqualmie *Jeff Bennett*

Other Runs

South Fork Snoqualmie: Boaters interested in a short, moderate run can consider a four-mile float on the South Fork Snoqualmie, from Twin Falls State Park to the 436th Avenue S.E. Bridge south of North Bend. This rocky Class II to II+ run has a shorter season than the Middle Fork, but it is popular thanks to its pleasant scenery and easy access. The short shuttle is via I-90. Beware of a **weir** near the end of the run, about a third of a mile below a railroad bridge. For details refer to Jeff Bennett, *A Guide to the Whitewater Rivers of Washington.*

Lower Snoqualmie: The main stem of the Snoqualmie is runnable for 40 miles from the powerhouse below Snoqualmie Falls to the confluence with the Skykomish River near Munroe. However, rapids are found only in the first few miles below the powerhouse.

The most popular whitewater run is one mile of Class II to II+ water from the powerhouse to Plum's Landing. Both accesses are on the right bank, and both are reached via Fish Hatchery Road off Highway 202 east of Fall City. This short stretch, known as the "Powerhouse Run," is a favorite training section for less experienced boaters, many of whom come after work on summer evenings.

Below Plum's Landing the river quickly eases to II-, then I+. Below Fall City the Snoqualmie is all flatwater, but several sections offer pleasant pastoral scenery. For more information refer to Verne Huser, *Paddle Routes of Western Washington.*

Middle Fork Snoqualmie

The first nine miles of the Middle Fork below the Taylor River confluence have mostly easy rapids that allow time for admiring the mountain scenery. But below the bridge at mile 9, all eyes shift to the river as the whitewater increases to rocky, technical Class III and one Class IV. The milder stretch above the bridge is often referred to as the "Upper Middle Snoqualmie," while the rougher and rockier section downstream is called the "Middle Middle." At higher flows the "Middle Middle" is peppered with powerful holes and hydraulics. A good alternate access at the bridge allows boaters to choose the run best suited to their skills.

Below the Tanner take-out is the "Lower Middle Snoqualmie." The four-mile Class II run (gradient: 25 ft./mi.) from Tanner to the 428th Avenue bridge at North Bend is a popular training run for local paddling clubs and is commonly known as the "Club Stretch." This section offers enjoyable floating but much less seclusion. Boaters may also consider the next

[2]For more information contact the Rivers Council of Washington (see appendix for address.)

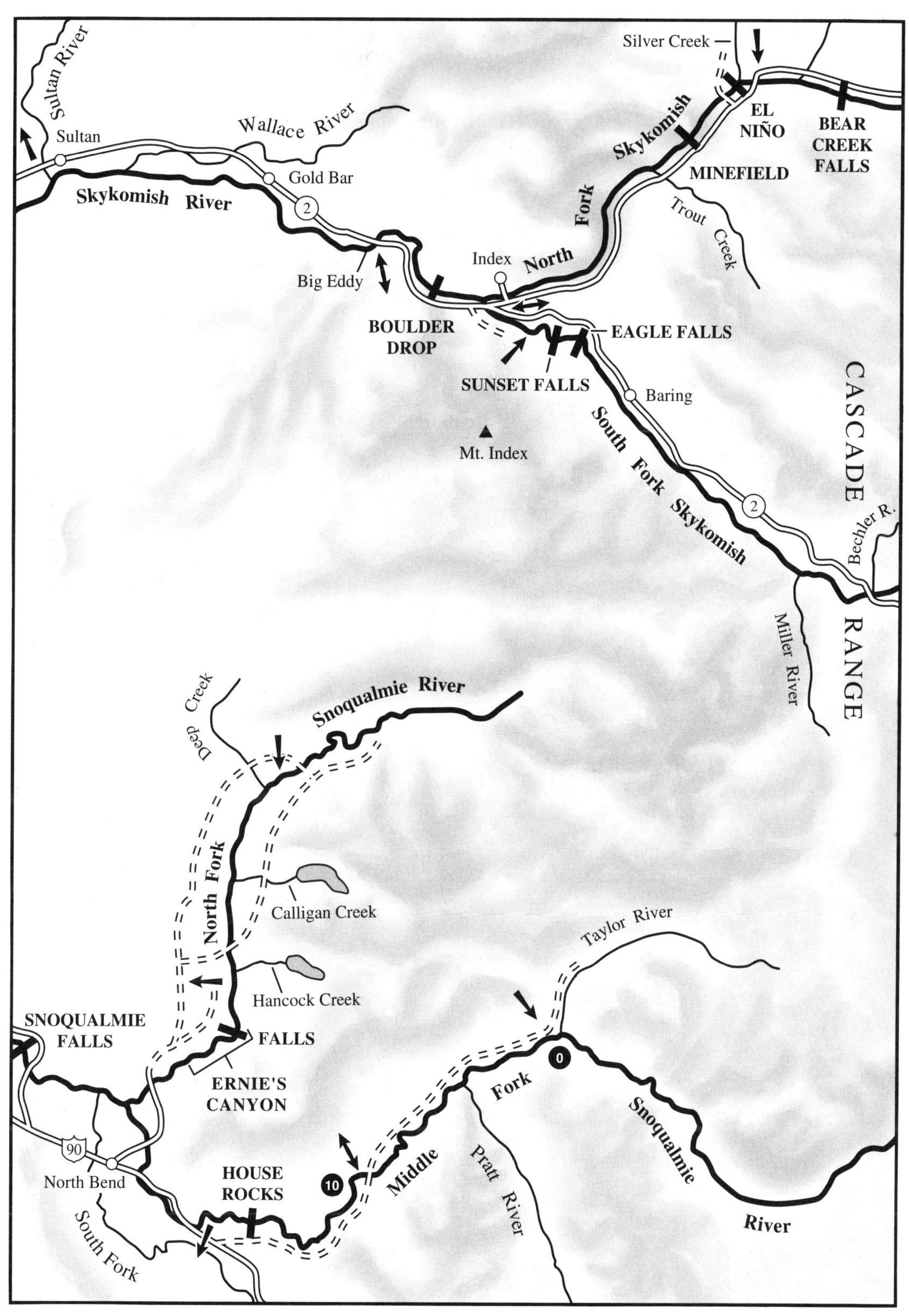

Snoqualmie and Skykomish

four miles from the North Bend bridge to an access on the right bank off Mill Pond Road, just above the Washington Highway 202 bridge. In this section the North and South Forks join the Middle Fork to form the Main Snoqualmie. **Do not float beyond the Highway 202 bridge—Snoqualmie Falls is just downstream.**

In 1992 the Tanner access was the focus of controversy among boaters, a private landowner, and governement agencies. At the landowner's request, the county installed a locked gate on the access road, and river runners were forced to park on the main road and carry equipment about 100 yards to or from the river—more of a problem for rafters than for kayakers. The Rivers Council of Washington and other groups are working to restore full access at this site.[3]

[3]For current information contact the Council (see appendix for address).

Middle Snoqualmie Mile Guide

Upper Middle Snoqualmie

0 **PUT-IN** on the right bank below the mouth of the Taylor River, a major tributary. Three quarters of a mile downstream is **RAINY CREEK DROP (II+)**, where the river bends left down a long washboard, then accelerates down a fast chute into a headwall on the left. Stay right at the bottom to avoid the wall. Class II from here to the bridge at mile 9.

4 The Pratt River enters inconspicuously on the left. Downstream on the left is Russian Butte.

6 A beach on the right marks a **possible alternate RIVER ACCESS** where a rough spur road leads to USFS Road 56. This is private land, but public use has been tolerated in the past. Just downstream Gifford Creek enters on the left.

9 **RIVER ACCESS** at the Road 56 bridge. May be difficult for rafts.

Middle Middle Snoqualmie

9 **RIVER ACCESS.** Road 56 bridge. A mile downstream, just beyond a sharp right bend, watch for **CABLE DROP (III)**, a long series of boulder-strewn ledges marked by a gauging station cable across the river. Mine Creek Campground provides an **alternate RIVER ACCESS** on the left about 3⁄4 mile downstream. Below the campground the river splits at **ISLAND DROP (III)**, where most of the water goes to the right. Watch for a big boulder and a sharp drop at the bottom.

12 The channel gets steeper and rockier as the river enters a 2.5-mile stretch of Class III's and one IV. The appearance of a cabin downstream at mile 12.5 signals **A-FRAME DROP (III)**, where the river surges into a headwall on the left and turns sharply right. Watch for a log jam on the right. About 3⁄4 mile downstream, the river bends sharply left and runs through **SURPRISE (III)**, where a big reversal waits at the bottom center.

14 At a shallow left bend watch for **RIGHT ANGLE DROP (III)**. A quarter mile downstream is the biggest rapid on the Middle Fork, **HOUSE ROCKS (IV)**. Scout left. The rapid features a big reversal at the top right and boulders in the center. Boaters typically skirt right of the big rocks. After one or two more Class III's, the river moderates to Class II.

16 Tanner **TAKE-OUT** on the left, at the end of a long left bend where power lines cross overhead. Boaters may continue downstream. See essay for downstream runs and for problems with Tanner take-out.

North Fork Snoqualmie

In contrast to the Middle Fork, which can be navigated in a variety of craft, the North Fork is almost exclusively a kayaker's river. Low flows, possible portages around log hazards, and long carries at the put-in and take-out deter most rafters and canoeists. **Strainers and sweepers are always a threat** on this narrow, low-volume river which passes through heavily logged forest terrain. As of 1993 access to the North Fork was problematic due to road closures by Weyerhauser Corporation, which owns virtually all the land along the river (see **Logistics**).

The main whitewater challenge comes in two steep stretches of nearly continuous Class III rapids near either end of the run. Trouble here could mean a long, cold swim. Boaters who run the North Fork frequently report that the rapids often change from one season to the next, making it prudent to inquire locally before boating and scout frequently.

Scout the put-in and take-out for this run carefully. Above the put-in are unrunnable rapids. Below the take-out—which is hard to recognize from the river—the North Fork plunges into Ernie's Canyon (also known as Black Canyon), a fearsome Class V+p stretch that includes several mandatory portages and a 30' falls. Though this section has been run, even experts should think twice before making an attempt. For more information refer to Jeff Bennett, *A Guide to the Whitewater Rivers of Washington.*

North Snoqualmie Mile Guide

0 PUT-IN on the right bank about a half mile *below* Wagner Bridge. **Do not launch above this point:** unrunnable, log-choked rapids lie between the bridge and the put-in. Not far below the put-in, Deep Creek enters on the right, followed by a Class III rapid of the same name—watch for a sharp drop at the bottom. Downstream the river runs through a half mile of nearly continuous Class III rapids. Gauging station (on the left as rapids ease) has gauge quoted on Whitewater Hotline tape.

3 Calligan Creek enters on the left. Half a mile downstream watch for a Class III with strong reversals.

4.8 Spur 10 Bridge across the river. Difficult alternate take-out; road gated as of 1993. Half a mile downstream Hancock Creek enters on the left, followed by the boulders of **HANCOCK DROP (III)**, which is usually run down the far right. Class III water continues almost all the way to the take-out.

6 TAKE-OUT on the right. ***HAZARD.*** The take-out is very hard to recognize. Do not miss it! Downstream is the Class V+p gorge known as Ernie's Canyon.

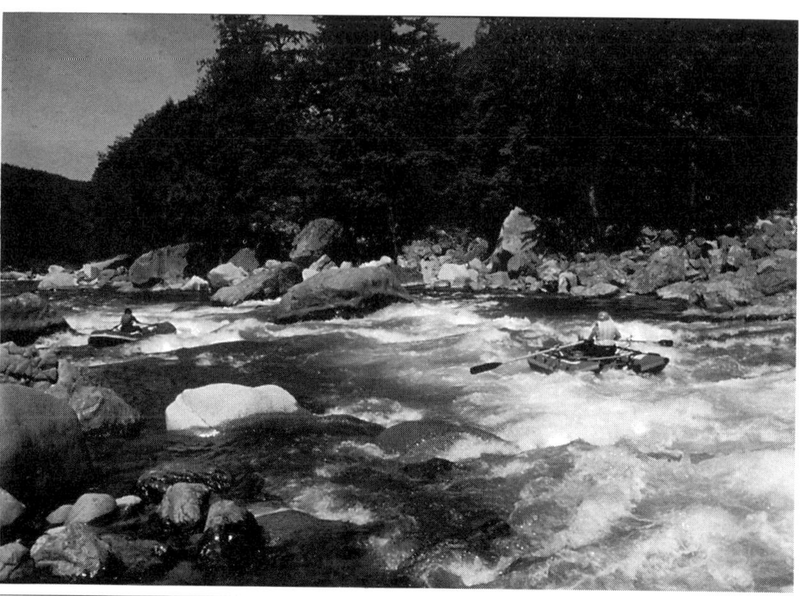

Boulder Drop, Skykomish River *Steve Stroud*

Skykomish River

1. Main Skykomish: Index (480') to Gold Bar (Big Eddy) (225').
III5 (IV5 over 5,000 cfs); 6.5 miles; 40 ft./mi.
Longer runs possible.

2. North Fork: Galena (1,140') to Index (530').
IV-; 9.5 miles; 65 ft./mi.
Longer runs possible.

Drainage Area and Average Annual Discharge: 535 sq. mi. and 2,858,000 af at Big Eddy.
Peak Recorded Flow: 102,000 cfs (Nov. 24, 1991) at Big Eddy.
Season: *Main:* Oct.–early August. *North Fork:* roughly April–mid-July. Peaks in winter, again in late spring/early summer. Snowmelt runoff on main stem usually peaks in May and June. Flows then decline rapidly to August and September lows of less than 1,000 cfs.
Recommended Levels: *Main:* 1,800–6,000 cfs. *North Fork:* 1,500—5,000 cfs.
Flow Information: NOAA Whitewater Hotline, (206) 526-8530; flow at Gold Bar, take-out for the main stem. For the North Fork, estimate roughly 1/4 to 1/3 of this figure.
Special Hazards: High water. Boulder Drop. Log hazards, especially on the North Fork.
Permits: Not presently required. Helmets and life jackets required for all boaters.
Managing Agency: Skykomish RD, Mt. Baker-Snoqualmie NF, P.O. Box 305, Skykomish, WA, 98288; (206) 677-2414.
Commercial Raft Trips: Yes. Many outfitters on the main stem, a few on the North Fork. For references contact the managing agency.

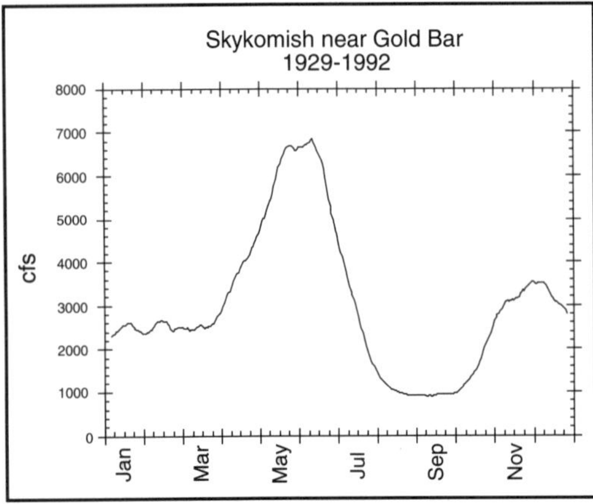

Land Ownership: *Main:* Mostly private with scattered public access. *North Fork:* Mixed National Forest and private.
Scenery: Excellent. Forested banks, spectacular mountain views.
Solitude: *Main:* Good. Vegetation helps screen the highway and railroad. Heavy river traffic. *North Fork:* Very good. Cabins, minor road, light river traffic.
Wilderness: No. Highway, railroad.
Weather: Typical of Washington's West Cascades: rainy from late fall through spring, intermittently clear in summer.
Water: Cold and clear, but don't drink it. Purify water from side streams or bring water.
Camping: USFS campgrounds near U.S. Highway 2 above Index and on the North Fork above Galena.
Side Excursions: Wallace Falls on the Wallace River just outside Gold Bar.
Guides and References:
- Bennett, *Guide to the Whitewater Rivers of Washington.*
- North, *Washington Whitewater.*
- Huser, *Paddle Routes of Western Washington.* Downstream runs.
- Rennicke, *River Days.* Essay by Bill Stewart on Main Skykomish.
- Alt & Hyndman, *Roadside Geology of Washington.* Brief coverage of Main Skykomish.

Maps:
- **USGS 7.5':** *Main:* Index, Gold Bar. *North Fork:* Monte Cristo, Baring, Index.
- **USGS 1:100:** *Skykomish River.* Covers both runs.
- **USFS:** *Mt. Baker-Snoqualmie NF.*
- **AAA:** *Mt. Rainier.*

Auto Shuttle: Roughly same mileages as runs.
Logistics: *Main:* To reach the **take-out,** follow U.S. Highway 2 east from Gold Bar about two miles to the bridge over the Skykomish. Just east of the bridge, turn right (south) on a short dirt road leading to the Big Eddy access on the left bank just downstream from the bridge. To reach the **put-in,** drive upriver (east) on U.S. 2 just under 5 miles. Just before the next bridge over the Skykomish (near Index), turn right on Mt. Index Road, drive about half a mile, park, and then follow a path down to the left bank. This put-in

is just upstream from power lines across the river. To launch on the North Fork, see directions to the take-out for that run (below).

North Fork: To reach the **take-out** (alternate put-in for the Main "Sky"), follow U.S. 2 to the Index turnoff ⅓ mile east of the highway bridge over the South Fork. Drive northeast just under a mile; then, where the road bears left and crosses the North Fork, look for the access on the left bank on the upstream side of the bridge. To reach the **put-in,** proceed upriver along the left bank a little over 9 miles to where the road crosses a bridge over the river just upstream from the hamlet of Galena. The put-in is about 500' above the bridge on the right bank.

Alternate put-ins include a side road bridge over the river about a mile downstream (see **Mile Guide**). Experts may launch up to a mile above the recommended put-in—but be extremely cautious and scout carefully from shore first: big Class IV and V rapids are just upstream. Also, be aware that two miles above the recommended put-in is **Bear Creek Falls, an unrunnable Class VI gorge.** Do *not* launch at or above this rapid.

The Skykomish River from Index to Gold Bar is the best-known advanced whitewater run in Washington. With easy access from Seattle, stunning mountain scenery, a nearly year-round season, good Class III whitewater, and one big Class IV+ to V drop, the Skykomish has long been one of the Evergreen State's most popular river trips. Local boaters know it as the "Sky"—an appropriate nickname given the river's clear, blue-green waters.[1]

The Skykomish drains the wet west slope of the Cascades between the Snoqualmie basin to the south and the Sauk drainage to the north. From headwaters among 6,000' and 7,000' granite peaks in the Alpine Lakes and Henry M. Jackson Wilderness Areas, the river's North and South Forks tumble down deep, U-shaped glacial valleys. Near the town of Index the two forks join to form the main stem of the Skykomish, which runs generally west toward Monroe where it joins with the Snoqualmie River to form the Snohomish.

Local geology explains much of the river's whitewater character. Above the town of Gold Bar,[2] the Skykomish and its two tributary forks cut through hard igneous and metamorphic rocks that produce a rugged, constricted riverbed littered with large, resistant boulders. In places, especially along the South Fork, the river thunders over dramatic waterfalls. Below Gold Bar, in contrast, the river glides easily through deposits of soft sedimentary sandstone and mudstone with few resistant boulders in a broad, gentle channel.

The Index-to-Gold Bar run on the main stem of the Skykomish gets heavy commercial and private use. Boating begins just above the confluence of the North and South Forks. Most river runners launch on the South Fork, but some prefer to start on the smaller North Fork when flows are adequate. Below the confluence lie nearly three miles of good Class III rapids, punctuated by a long Class IV–V passage known as Boulder Drop. Technical and challenging at low and moderate flows, Boulder Drop gets big and intimidating at higher levels.

The Skykomish is extremely seasonal, and big spring peaks of 10,000 cfs or more are not uncommon. Boaters must use extra caution during high water; the river gets pushy, and long swims are possible. Frequently poor weather increases the risk of hypothermia.

In addition to exciting whitewater, boaters on the main stem enjoy outstanding mountain scenery. Rugged peaks rim the glacial valley, with the soaring pinnacles of Mt. Index (5,979') and Mt. Persis (5,464') dominating the view from the river. The sheer north face of Mt. Index provides a favorite challenge for rock climbers. In the foreground, a lush forest of fir, hemlock, cedar, alder, and maple lines the river banks. The trees help to screen U.S. Highway 2 and the Burlington Northern Railroad, which parallel the South Fork and the Main Sky.

The Skykomish was the first river to be included in Washington's State Scenic River sys-

[1]Outsiders often reveal themselves as such by confusing the Skykomish with similar-sounding Washington rivers like the Skokomish, Snohomish, Stillaguamish or Snoqualmie. All of these names are of Indian origin. Skykomish apparently means either "Inland People" or "River People".

[2]Geology also accounts for part of the local history: Gold Bar, Index, and other towns began as prospecting camps during a brief gold rush in the late nineteenth and early twentieth centuries.

tem. The Forest Service has recommended National Wild and Scenic River status for almost the entire Skykomish River system, including the North Fork, South Fork, and main stem. In addition to preventing dams and diversions (which have recently threatened the North Fork in particular), Wild and Scenic status would improve public access and help preserve the river's excellent scenery and fine fishing.

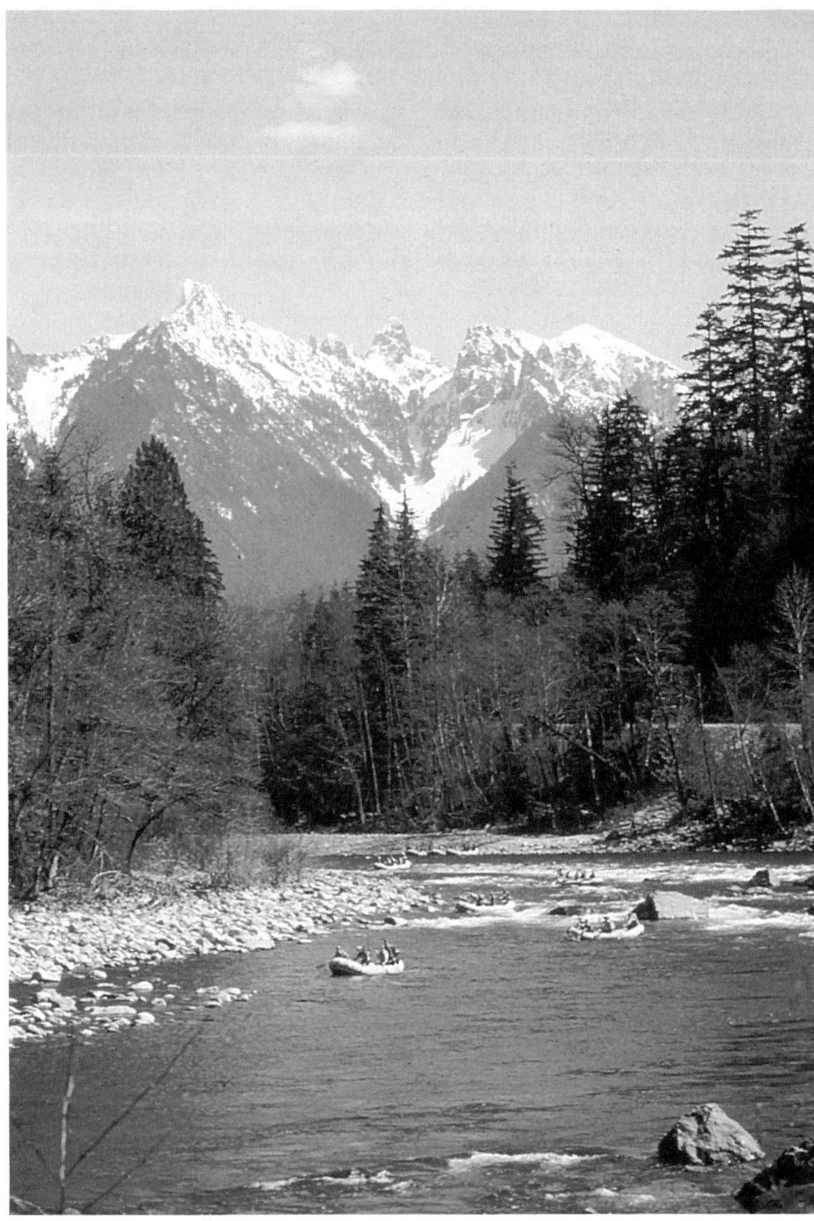

Skykomish River *Cliff Hollenbeck*

North Fork Skykomish

With no highway or railroad along its banks, the North Skykomish offers a secluded contrast to the South Fork and Main Sky. Above the town of Index, only a lightly-used county road follows the left bank, and it is usually screened from the river by dense vegetation. Like the main stem, the North Fork offers many stunning mountain views. Occasional cabins and other structures dot the bank. When water conditions permit, boaters can make a continuous float of the North Fork and Main Sky.

The North Fork is steeper and narrower than the main stem, with nearly continuous Class III whitewater and a couple of larger Class IV- drops. The rapids are mostly long, technical rock and hole gardens where the river drops steeply through fields of polished granite boulders. **Logs are a major potential hazard**, and anyone contemplating a run should inquire with local boaters or outfitters first.

The North Fork's rapids generally become more difficult the farther upstream one goes. Boaters can avoid some of the rougher water by choosing among several alternate put-ins below the first one listed in this guide. Boaters launching at the highest access listed in the **Mile Guide**—near the bridge just above the hamlet of Galena—should scout the first Class IV- drop, El Niño, from the shuttle road on the way to the put-in.

Experts can add about a mile of big Class IV and V action by launching a bit farther upstream. However, just two miles above the recommended put-in is an **unrunnable Class VI gorge known as Bear Creek Falls, which should not be attempted.** Do *not* launch at or above this rapid. For more details on alternate accesses, see **Logistics** and the **Mile Guide.**

South Fork Skykomish

Well above the cataracts of Eagle and Sunset Falls, the South Fork Skykomish offers fine intermediate water. Boating typically begins at the U.S. Highway 2 bridge at the Beckler River confluence, just east of the town of Skykomish. Downstream the South Fork runs through ten miles of Class II and II+ rapids with a gradient of 25 ft./mi. This section offers fine mountain views, though the highway is never far away. The common take-out is about 1.5 miles west of the town of Baring, where Barclay Creek enters on the right. **Do not float past this take-out; unrunnable waterfalls are downstream.**

Below Baring the South Fork thunders over the dramatic cascades of Eagle Falls and Sunset Falls. The latter is a dramatic 45° slide down a polished granite face, with a total vertical drop of 104'. Unbelievably, Sunset Falls was successfully run by professional daredevil Al Fausset in a home-made wooden canoe in 1926. Some 3,000 spectators paid a dollar a head to witness the spectacle. In subsequent years Fausset ran several other major waterfalls, including 212' Shoshone Falls on the Snake River.

Several major tributaries of the South Fork also offer boating. These include the Tye, Foss, Beckler, and Rapid Rivers. For more information on these rivers, consult Jeff Bennett, *Guide to the Whitewater Rivers of Washington.*

Downstream Runs

Below Gold Bar the main stem of the Skykomish broadens, flowing between wooded banks in a wide valley. The nine miles from Gold Bar to Sultan are swift (gradient: 35 ft./mi.) but relatively easy. The largest rapid is a Class II immediately below the put-in at Big Eddy (take-out for the Sunset Falls run). Another strong riffle comes at mile 4.5 where the river runs through waves along a cut bank on the left.

The river often splits around islands, particularly in the middle of the run. Tall trees generally screen the highway and railroad, though some houses appear in the lower reaches. In good weather boaters enjoy upstream views of Mt. Index and other peaks. The standard take-out is a park at the confluence with the Sultan River. The next nine miles from the park to Monroe offer easy Class I+ drifting, with pleasant scenery and good steelhead fishing. This section is especially popular with drift boats (dories). Access is possible at the Highway 203 bridge near Monroe. For more information on these runs, refer to Verne Huser, *Paddle Routes of Western Washington.*

Main Skykomish Mile Guide

*See map in **Snoqualmie** chapter.*

0 **PUT-IN** on the South Fork Skykomish, where a good path reaches the left bank just upstream from power lines across the river. Alternate put-ins on the North Fork near Index. Sunset Falls is a mile upstream.

Immediately downstream is **POWERLINE (III)**, also called **Cable Drop**, which has a big rock or reversal at the top center. About 1/3 mile below the rapid, U.S. Highway 2 crosses the river, followed immediately by the confluence with the North Fork, which enters from the right. Some 3/4 mile below the confluence, watch for a long, rocky Class III known as **THE MAZE** or **Guardian.**

1.6 **ANDERSON HOLE (III)**, where Anderson Creek enters on the left. Big boulder and reversal in the center. When you pass them (most boaters run right), get ready to eddy out on the right above **Boulder Drop**, which is just 500' downstream.

1.8 **BOULDER DROP (IV+ to V, depending on flow)**. A long, steep, complex boulder field. More difficult above about 6,000 cfs. Scout carefully on the right, and portage or line on this side if desired. The rapid's nature and difficulty vary widely with water level, from rocky and technical at low flows to very powerful and turbulent at higher levels. Always a bad place to swim.

The initial drop is typically run on the right through holes and waves. In the middle of the rapid a line of big rocks known as the "Picket Fence" divides the river into several chutes. Depending on water levels, most boaters choose one of three passages through the fence. At high flows (above about 6,000 cfs) the common run is down the "Mercy Chute" on the far right. At moderate levels (roughly 3,000–6,000) the most common run is "The Needle"—a steep, sharp, narrow drop between two boulders in river center, where the outwash flushes into a rock on the left. At lower flows (below about 3,000) most boaters choose the "Airplane Turn" on the far left. The rapid ends with a final dose of waves, holes, and boulders.

Just below Boulder Drop is **THE LEDGE (III)**, a 4' drop that develops a powerful reversal on the right at higher flows.

2.3 Below The Ledge the river runs through three closely spaced Class III's: **MARBLE SHOOT**, also called **Banzai**, with a big hole in river center; **LUNCH HOLE**, with big reversals; and **DÉJA VU**, also called **Aquagasm**, where a big reversal forms left of center at higher flows. Class II and III rapids continue downstream, becoming more widely spaced.

3.2 The railroad crosses the river. Difficult **alternate RIVER ACCESS** just below the bridge where a steep path reaches the left bank. Some ¾ mile below the bridge at a left bend is **FISHERMEN'S (III).** Proctor Creek enters on the left at mile 5.5.

6.5 **TAKE-OUT.** U.S. 2 crosses the Skykomish. Big Eddy take-out is immediately below the bridge on the left bank. See the essay for continuing downstream runs.

North Fork Skykomish Mile Guide

0 **PUT-IN** on the right bank just above the bridge above the hamlet of Galena. Nearly continuous Class III to IV- rapids begin immediately. The river drops at 80 ft./mi. for the first 4 miles.

Alternate put-ins are possible up to a mile upstream, but the accesses and the whitewater are much more difficult above this point. Anyone heading farther upriver should scout carefully from the road first. ***HAZARD.*** Be certain that you do *not* launch at or above unrunnable **BEAR CREEK FALLS (VI)**, roughly two miles above the Galena put-in.

0.8 Silver Creek enters on the right. Hamlet of Galena on the right. About 250 yards below the creek lies **EL NIÑO (IV-)**, a long boulder field. The road runs close to the left bank here, so this rapid can be scouted on the way to the put-in.

1.3 Below El Niño a bridge crosses the river. **Alternate RIVER ACCESS** on the left bank below the bridge near the mouth of Howard Creek. Not far below the creek, the river churns down a newly cut, unstable section of channel. The flow may split around an island. Be alert for possible log hazards. Salmon Creek enters on the right in this section.

3.5 **THE MINEFIELD (IV-).** A long, steep rock garden with several strong reversals that get very big at high flows. Scout left.

4.3 Trout Creek enters on the left. Boaters sometimes use an alternate river access just above the creek, but this is private land. Downstream, buildings dot the left bank. The gradient eases somewhat and the river often splits around islands.

8.5 Buildings first on the left, then on both banks as the river approaches Index.

9.5 **TAKE-OUT** on the left bank just above the bridge over the river at Index. Or continue downstream through a mile and a half of Class III water to the confluence with the South Fork. However, since there is no access at the confluence, boaters who continue below Index must run at least the first three miles of the main stem, including Boulder Drop.

Tieton River

Rimrock to Windy Point

Difficulty: III; III+ above 2,000 cfs. One possible portage at some flows.
Length: 12 miles. Longer and shorter runs possible.
Gradient: 54 ft./mi.
Put-in: Rimrock (2,640').
Take-out: Windy Point Campground (2,010').
Drainage Area and Average Annual Discharge: 187 sq. mi. and 342,000 af.
Season: September irrigation releases. Dam spillover in June of wet years.
Recommended Levels: 900–2,500 cfs.
Flow Information: NOAA Whitewater Hotline, (206) 526-8530, or BuRec tape, (509) 575-5854; flow at Rimrock (put-in).
Special Hazards: Diversion weir at mile 5.7. Log hazards.
Permits: Not presently required.
Managing Agency: Naches RD, Wenatchee NF, 10061 Highway 12, Naches, WA 98937; (509) 653-2205.
Commercial Raft Trips: Yes. For a list of outfitters, contact the managing agency.
Land Ownership: Mostly National Forest.
Scenery: Very good. Lightly forested canyon, becoming drier downstream.
Solitude: Fair. Highway follows the river; heavy commercial rafting use.
Wilderness: No.
Guides and References:

- North, *Washington Whitewater.*
- Bennett, *Guide to the Whitewater Rivers of Washington.*

Maps:

- **USGS 7.5':** *Tieton Basin, Weddle Canyon.*
- **USFS:** *Wenatchee NF.*

Logistics: U.S. Highway 12 follows the river, providing easy access and shuttles. Boaters can approach from the east or west, but the most common route is to follow I-82 to Yakima, then drive west on U.S. 12.

The Windy Point Campground **take-out** is 8 miles west (upriver on the Tieton) on U.S. 12 from its junction with Washington Highway 410. To reach the **put-ins**, continue west (upstream) 9 miles to an easy access at Hause Creek Campground, or two more miles to where a dirt road descends to a steep access on the right bank half a mile east of Rimrock.

For eleven months of the year, Washington boaters neglect the Tieton. But come September, when the Bureau of Reclamation releases irrigation water stored behind Tieton Dam, river runners by the thousands flock to this small river to finish off their paddling seasons with a bang. At a time when most other Washington rivers have been reduced to a trickle, the Tieton (TIE-uh-tahn) offers reliable flows, good weather, enjoyable scenery, easy access, and exciting intermediate whitewater.

The Tieton drains a relatively small watershed on the east slope of the Cascades south of Mt. Rainier. Its upper reaches are flooded by reservoirs, and below Tieton Dam the river flows eastward for only 20 miles before joining the Naches River west of Yakima. The high Cascade crest to the west produces a strong rain shadow that accounts for the Tieton's generally sunny summer weather.

Don't go to the Tieton expecting solitude. U.S. Highway 12 follows the left bank, while the river is packed with commercial rafters and private boaters of all stripes. Most of the riverside land is National Forest; as a result the Tieton offers more undeveloped forest scenery than other popular east-slope rivers like the Wenatchee and Methow. The scenic canyon is lightly forested near the beginning of the run and becomes drier and brushier toward the end.

Despite its moderate difficulty rating, the Tieton must be approached with caution. The river is steep and swift, with fairly continuous Class III whitewater and few eddies. Rescue can be difficult in the event of a mishap. Wet suits are a good idea, since long swims are a real possibility. Because flows are tightly controlled, brush grows thickly along the banks, and **strainers and log hazards** are always a potential danger. Historically, the most significant hazard on the Tieton was a dangerous weir at mile 5.7 that required a short portage. The dam has been altered, however, and can now be navigated at most flows (see below).

In most years the Tieton is boatable only during September irrigation releases. But in wet years when spring snowmelt produces more runoff than the reservoirs can hold, the dam may spill excess water, producing a brief boatable window, often in June.

Tieton River Guide

The highest common **put-in** is half a mile west of the town of Rimrock where a short dirt spur road off U.S. 12 leads to a steep access on the left bank (mile 0). There is no warm-up; Class III rapids begin immediately. A minor bridge crosses the river a mile and a half downstream. Two miles below the upper put-in, Hause Creek Campground (USFS) offers an easier **alternate put-in** on the left. Wild Rose Campground is on the left at mile 4.

HAZARD. Be alert for a **diversion dam** at mile 5.7. (Warning signs may be posted upstream.) The dam is located immediately below a sharp left bend, and a foot bridge spans the river just above the lip. Once a mandatory portage, the dam has been altered to make it navigable at most flows. (The left side of the dam usually offers the best run.) Nevertheless, boaters should approach it with caution and scout to be sure it is runnable. A strong, potentially dangerous reversal can still form here at higher flows. If in doubt, make a short, easy portage on the left. The current leading up to the weir is swift, and the eddy on the left above the dam is small and can be filled to capacity with rafts, especially on weekends.

A mile below the dam, several dwellings appear on the left. Just downstream is a challenging Class III rapid, followed by a minor road bridge over the river. Busy Class III water continues for several miles. At mile 11 the highway crosses the river twice as the Tieton bends to the right around Windy Point. The **take-out** is a third of a mile below the second highway bridge, on the left bank at Windy Point Campground (mile 11.7).

Although it is possible to continue another nine miles down the Tieton to the Naches River confluence, **frequent log hazards** deter most boaters from attempting this section. In some years river-wide log jams have precluded any boating on this lower reach. Anyone considering this section should inquire locally first. **Do not continue down the Naches itself; a dangerous diversion weir is located immediately below the Tieton confluence.**

Wenatchee River

Upper and Lower Wenatchee

1. Upper Wenatchee: Lake Wenatchee (1,865') to Highway 2 (1,660').
II; 19 miles; 11 ft./mi.
Shorter trips possible.

2. Lower Wenatchee: Leavenworth (1,095') to Monitor (680').
III; 18 miles; 23 ft./mi.
Shorter trips possible.

Drainage Area and Average Annual Discharge: 1,000 sq. mi. and 2,240,000 af at Peshastin.

Peak Recorded Flow: 40,000 cfs (Nov 25, 1991).

Season: *Upper:* April–Oct. Fairly low July onward. *Lower:* April–mid-August. Lower river typically peaks sometime from late May to late June, often above 10,000 cfs, then recedes to late summer lows of under 1,000 cfs. Autumn rains boost the flows again.

Recommended Levels: *Upper:* 1,000–10,000 cfs. *Lower:* 2,000–20,000 cfs.

Flow Information: NOAA Whitewater Hotline, (206) 526-8530; flow at Peshastin, not far below the Lower Wenatchee put-in.

Special Hazards: *Lower:* Mandatory portage at weir near Dryden (mile 7).

Permits: Not presently required. On the Lower Wenatchee, a Washington Dept. of Wildlife license is necessary to use the right-bank take-out at Monitor or the alternate access upstream at Peshastin. Buy license at outdoor stores or call (206) 753-5719 for information.

Managing Agency: *Upper:* Lake Wenatchee RD, Wenatchee NF, 22976 Highway 207, Leavenworth, WA 98826; (509) 763-3103. *Lower:* None.

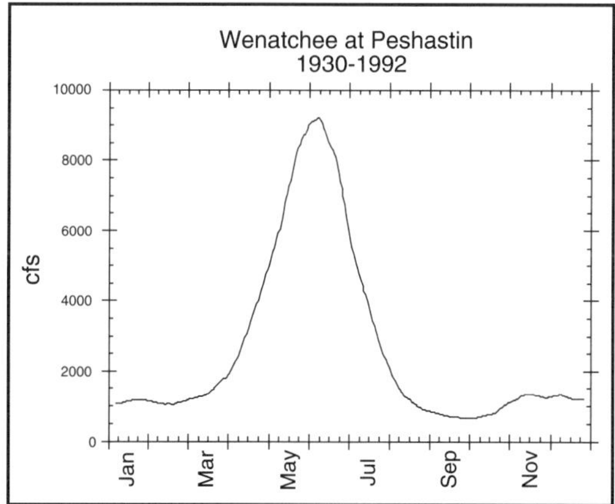

Commercial Raft Trips: *Upper:* No. *Lower:* Yes, many outfitters. For a list contact the USFS or the Leavenworth Chamber of Commerce, (509) 548-5807.

Land Ownership: *Upper:* Mixed National Forest and private. *Lower:* Almost all private.

Scenery: *Upper:* Very good; open, forested valley. *Lower:* Good near put-in (mountain views); fair downstream (open valley, orchards, towns).

Solitude: *Upper:* Very good; a few houses and minor roads. *Lower:* Fair. Highway, railroad, houses, very heavy river traffic on summer weekends.

Wilderness: No, though portions of the upper river are quite secluded.

Fishing: Trout in summer, steelhead and salmon in fall and early winter.

Weather: Usually sunny, sometimes hot in summer.

Water: Clear.

Camping: Campgrounds along Icicle Creek, in Tumwater Canyon, on the Chiwawa River, and at Lake Wenatchee. Wenatchee River County Park at Monitor.

Side Excursions: Glacier Peak. Henry M. Jackson and Alpine Lakes Wildernesses. Icicle Creek canyon near Leavenworth. Tumwater Canyon.

Guides and References:

- Bennett, *Guide to the Whitewater Rivers of Washington.* Covers all runs.
- North, *Washington Whitewater.* Covers Lower Wenatchee.
- Furrer, *Water Trails of Washington.* Brief coverage of Upper Wenatchee.
- Alt & Hyndman, *Roadside Geology of Washington.* Brief coverage along U.S. 2.

Maps:

- **USGS 7.5':** *Upper:* Plain, Winton. *Lower:* Leavenworth, Peshastin, Cashmere, Monitor.
- **USGS 1: 100:** *Chelan* (covers upper and most of Lower).
- **USFS:** *Wenatchee NF.* Covers both runs.
- **AAA:** *Mt. Rainier.*
- *Riverguide Bandana to the Wenatchee* (Rivers & Mountains). Cloth map.

Auto Shuttle: All short, paved. For shuttle references contact the USFS. For the Upper Wenatchee contact Leavenworth Outfitters, (509) 763-3733 or (800) 347-7934.

Logistics: *Upper:* To reach the **put-in,** follow U.S. 2 to Coles Corner, which is about 35 miles northwest of the city of Wenatchee and roughly halfway between Stevens Pass and the town of Leavenworth. Turn north on Washington Highway 207 and drive just under 3 miles, then turn left at the sign for the South State Park Day Use Area. Follow this paved road about a mile, through the state park entrance and down to the boat ramp on the right bank near the lake outlet. To reach the **alternate put-in** a half mile farther downstream, simply stay on Highway 207 and drive to the bridge over the river.

To reach the **intermediate access at the town of Plain,** continue north on Highway 207 a fifth of a mile past the State Park turnoff mentioned above, then turn right on Washington Highway 209 and drive about 4.5 miles to the access on the left bank above the bridge over the Wenatchee. The **take-out** is on the right bank at Tumwater Campground, where U.S. 2 crosses the Wenatchee at the head of Tumwater Canyon.

Lower: To reach the **put-in,** follow U.S. 2 to Leavenworth. Just east of the bridge over the Wenatchee, turn southwest on East Leavenworth Road and drive upriver a little over half a mile. Then, as the road bends left, bear right on a short dirt spur road to the access on the right bank. The **alternate put-in** is 5 miles downriver on School Street in Peshastin.

To reach the **take-out,** drive downriver (east and southeast) on U.S. 2 roughly 14 miles from Leavenworth and take the Monitor turnoff. Accesses are on the left bank at Wenatchee River County Park and across the river at a Department of Wildlife access above the bridge. An **alternate take-out** is 4 miles upstream in Cashmere, on the right bank below the Division Street bridge.

The Lower Wenatchee River has a lot in common with Los Angeles: great weather, freeways, big crowds, and roller-coaster rapids right out of Disneyland. Heck, there's even a cute Bavarian theme town at the put-in: Leavenworth, Washington, has some of the West's best examples of neo-Hansel and Gretel architecture. Of course there are a few key differences from the real Disneyland. You can take a deep breath on the Wenatchee without turning green (as long as your head is above water) and, as anyone who has run the river at high water knows, the boats are definitely not on a track.

The Lower Wenatchee is Washington's most popular river. With nearly 20,000 user-days annually, the Wenatchee accounts for roughly half of all commercial rafting use in the state. Columns of weekend warriors stream east on U.S. Highway 2, seeking escape from the often damp and dreary weather on the west side of the Cascades. A strong rain shadow on the east side keeps things hot and dry much of the time. Even so, the Wenatchee's large watershed provides enough runoff for a long boating season and some of the biggest peak flows in the Pacific Northwest.

Snowmelt from the Cascade crest gathers in five-mile-long Lake Wenatchee, then glides down the gentle, forested Upper Wenatchee. Suddenly the river turns due south into narrow, rugged Tumwater Canyon's Class V+ rapids. At the town of Leavenworth the Wenatchee abruptly emerges from Tumwater and turns east.[1] For the final 30 miles to the Columbia River confluence near the city of Wenatchee, the river rolls through big, playful rapids in a broad pastoral valley. In addition to providing whitewater chills and spills, the Lower Wenatchee supplies irrigation water for the area's famous apple orchards.[2]

May and June are the big water months. At peak runoff flows often rise above 10,000 cfs, and sometimes top 20,000. At these times the lower river is at its best, with deep, roller-coaster rapids providing plenty of excitement without too much risk. In fact, although the waves and holes get bigger at higher flows, the river's overall difficulty does not increase dramatically. Many rapids develop wide sneak

[1] "Wenatchee," the name of a local Indian tribe, has been variously translated as "great opening in the mountains" or "river flowing from the canyon." Both may be references to the mouth of Tumwater Canyon.

[2] Portions of the Wenatchee and its tributaries have been recommended for protection under the National Wild and Scenic Rivers System.

chutes at high flows. The biggest threat at these times—one that should be taken seriously—is the possibility of a long, cold swim. At any water level, boaters should portage a diversion weir at Dryden.

River lovers come to the Lower Wenatchee for superb whitewater and reliable weather, not for scenery and solitude. The view begins with nice upstream panoramas of nearby mountains but quickly shifts to a semi-rural landscape of small towns and orchards for most of the run. A busy four-lane highway and a railroad parallel the river as it winds down its broad, semi-arid valley.

As a side excursion, boaters might enjoy a tour of a local apple orchard and tasting room or perhaps a stop in Leavenworth. Charming and quaint to some, hopelessly tacky to others, this erstwhile logging and railroad town responded to a sagging lumber industry in the late 1960's by converting its business district into a Little Switzerland.

In many respects the Upper Wenatchee is the exact opposite of the lower river; about the only thing the two sections have in common is reliable summer weather. For 19 miles below the outlet of Lake Wenatchee the upper river winds easily through a secluded pine forest in a scenic, gentle valley. The Upper Wenatchee is a quiet float much favored by open canoeists. Its most challenging passages are a few mild Class II rapids.

The first six miles to the confluence with the Chiwawa River are especially gentle, with a gradient of 5 ft./mi. Much of the land along the river banks is private, and vacation cabins dot the shore in the upper portion of the run. Intermediate access is possible at the Highway 209 bridge near Plain (mile 7.5). Below this point the river offers somewhat more challenge and solitude.[3] Boaters can also approach the Upper Wenatchee via the Chiwawa River, which is covered in the next chapter.

[3]The best local source for information on the upper river is Leavenworth Outfitters, a canoeing and rafting outfit that offers rentals, shuttles, information, and possibly an alternate put-in as well; call (509) 763-3733 or (800) 347-7934.

Upper Wenatchee River Guide

The **uppermost put-in** is on the right bank at the State Park boat ramp at the outlet of Lake Wenatchee. Half a mile downstream, the river passes under Highway 207 (**alternate access**) as Nason Creek enters on the right. The Chiwawa River enters from the left at mile 5.5. All the land is private for seven miles below this confluence.

Near mile 7 the river runs up against a steep bluff on the left, marking a section of rocky Class II rapids where the current splits around islands. Highway 209 crosses the river at mile 7.5; a good **intermediate access** is above the bridge on the left. Another bridge is about 300 yards downstream. The small settlement of Plain is off to the left. An unpaved road generally follows the right bank for several miles below the second bridge.

Below Plain the river is somewhat more challenging, with several short Class II sections. The Burlington Northern Railroad crosses the river at mile 12. At mile 15 a power line crosses the river; nearby is an unimproved camping area on USFS land on the right. The final four miles are through a more rugged canyon with a wilderness feel. At mile 18.5 Chiwakum Creek enters on the right. Not far downstream, the **Tumwater Campground take-out** appears on the right, just above the U.S. Highway 2 bridge. **Do not continue downstream: below the bridge is Class V+ Tumwater Canyon.**

Tumwater Canyon

Below the U.S. 2 bridge—take-out for the Upper Wenatchee run—the river enters a narrow, V-shaped cleft known as Tumwater Canyon. Tumwater, a Chinook word meaning "Rough Water," is an appropriate name for this dramatic gorge where the walls rise 3,500'. Here the Wenatchee's large volume combines with a gradient of 60 to 80 ft./mi. to produce big, continuous Class IV to V+ rapids, many of which cannot be seen from the nearby highway. **A treacherous dam (mandatory portage)** is thrown in at no extra charge. The canyon continues for roughly eight miles before opening suddenly at the confluence with Icicle Creek near Leavenworth. **Though experts have run Tumwater Canyon, boating here is not advised.** Anyone considering it should refer to the Bennett book listed above.

White River

Flatwater enthusiasts looking for fine scenery and a quiet, secluded float may enjoy the White River, one of the major streams flowing into Lake Wenatchee. (This river should not be confused with the White River in Oregon, which is covered in **More Western Rivers** toward the back of this book.)

The White rises on the southern flank of 10,541' Glacier Peak, where meltwater from the White River Glacier produces a heavy load of glacial flour that gives the river its milky color and its name. The White offers fine alpine scenery, good wildlife viewing, and excellent canoeing for nine miles from Napeequa Campground (USFS) to Lake Wenatchee. This section may have log jams, especially in the first couple of miles.[4]

[4]For more information contact Leavenworth Outfitters; see previous footnote.

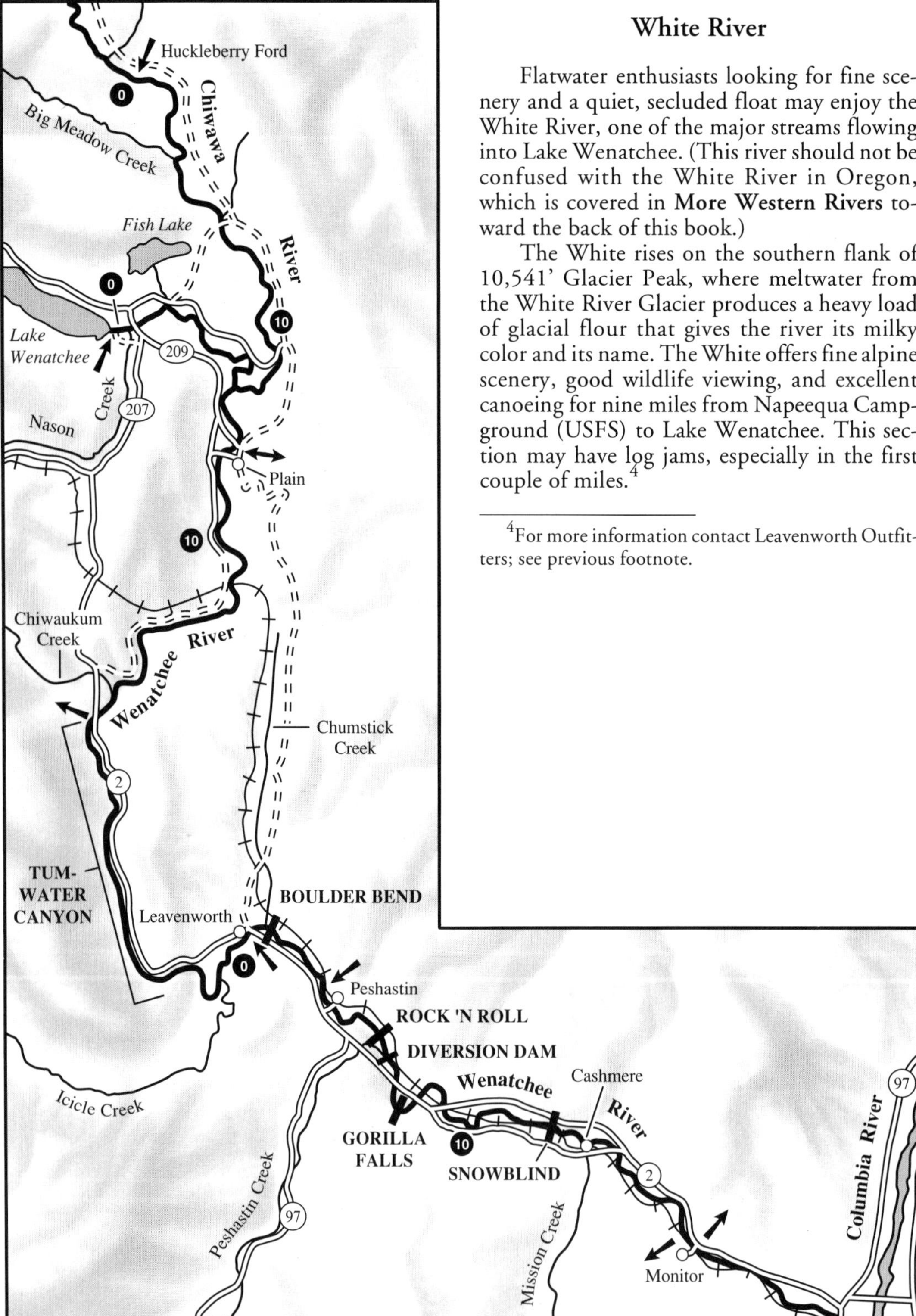

Wenatchee and Chiwawa

Lower Wenatchee Mile Guide

0 **PUT-IN** on the right bank opposite the town of Leavenworth. Just over half a mile downstream, U.S. 2 crosses the river. Not far below the bridge, Chumstick Creek enters on the left at a right-hand curve, marking the site of **BOULDER BEND (III)** (also called **Chumstick, Rock Garden,** and **Hobo Gulch**). Scout right if desired. The river bends right and splits around a rock island (hole at higher flows), and most of the current surges into rocks and holes on the left at the outside of the curve. Boaters often sneak down the right.

4.7 Bridge over the river at the town of Peshastin on the left. **RIVER ACCESS** at School Street about a third of a mile downstream on the left. License required to use this site (see **Permits**).

6.2 The river splits around an island. Most of the flow goes to the right into a long Class III known as **ROCK 'N ROLL.** The rapid is rocky at low water and filled with big waves and holes at moderate and high flows. At moderate flows a big reversal known as "Satan's Eyeball" develops in the right center near the top of the rapid. Scout from the island. About a quarter mile below the rapid, Peshastin Creek enters on the right. ***HAZARD.*** Below the creek, near mile 7, a river-wide diversion weir creates a potentially deadly keeper hydraulic. ***MANDATORY PORTAGE*** on a maintained trail on the right bank.

7.5 About half a mile below the weir, the river passes under U.S. 2 and through the holes and waves of **GORILLA FALLS (III).** Downstream the river curves left and U.S. 2 crosses again, followed by another road and railroad bridge serving the town of Dryden on the right.

9.7 The railroad and highway cross the river, and about a mile downstream the railroad crosses again. A few hundred yards past the second railroad bridge, steep bluffs on the left mark the site of **DRUNKARD'S DROP (III)**, a short, sharp, unobstructed fall over a river-wide ledge and into big waves.

13 A minor bridge crosses the river. A quarter mile downstream lies **SNOWBLIND (III)**, a series of good waves and reversals. A little over a half mile farther down is **GRANNY (II+)**, where an enormous back-curler known as "The Suffocator" forms at higher flows. Below this rapid the Division Street bridge crosses the river, serving the city of Cashmere on the right bank. An **alternate TAKE-OUT** is on the right just below the bridge. The rest of the run is Class II and easier.

18.4 **TAKE-OUT** on the right bank above the bridge at Monitor (license required—see **Permits**) or on the left at Wenatchee River County Park.

Chiwawa River

Huckleberry Ford to Wenatchee Confluence

Difficulty: III.
Length: 15 miles (2 miles on Wenatchee). Longer and shorter runs possible.
Gradient: 37 ft./mi. (45 ft./mi. first 9 miles).
Put-in: Huckleberry Ford (2,370').
Take-out: Highway 209 bridge near Plain (1,805').
Drainage Area and Average Annual Discharge: 190 sq. mi. and 450,000 af (est.).
Season: May–mid-July. Snowmelt runoff typically peaks sometime between late May and mid-June, then quickly recedes to unrunnable levels by about mid-July.
Recommended Levels: 800–3,000 cfs.
Flow Information: No gauge. As a rough estimate, take 20% of the flow on the Wenatchee at Peshastin, given on the NOAA Whitewater Hotline, (206) 526-8530.
Special Hazards: Log hazards, which may shift at any time; inquire locally before running, and always scout if in doubt. Continuous whitewater and few eddies, so long, cold swims are a danger.
Permits: Not presently required.
Managing Agency: Lake Wenatchee RD, Wenatchee NF, 22976 Highway 207, Leavenworth, WA 98826; (509) 763-3211.
Commercial Raft Trips: Yes. Contact the managing agency for references.
Land Ownership: National Forest first 9 miles, mostly private thereafter.
Scenery: Excellent. Heavily forested valley.
Solitude: Excellent except for houses and roads below mile 10.
Wilderness: No.
Water: Silty at high water, very clear at moderate and low flows.
Side Excursions: Great scenery and camping in the Chiwawa valley above the put-in.
Guides and References:

- North, *Washington Whitewater.*
- Bennett, *A Guide to the Whitewater Rivers of Washington.*

Maps:

- **USGS 7.5':** *Chikamin Creek, Plain.*
- **USGS 1:100:** *Chelan.*
- **USFS:** *Wenatchee NF.*
- **AAA:** *Mt. Rainier.*

Auto Shuttle: About 16 paved miles (30 minutes) one way.
Logistics: Shuttles and accesses are best understood with the help of a *Wenatchee NF* map. To reach the **take-out** on the Wenatchee River near Plain, follow U.S. Highway 2 to the Washington Highway 207 turnoff. Drive north on 207 roughly 3.5 miles, bear right on Washington 209, and drive about 4.5 miles to the take-out on the left bank just above the bridge over the Wenatchee.

To reach the Huckleberry Ford **put-in,** return to Highway 207, turn right, drive just over a half mile (across the Wenatchee), bear right on Chiwawa Loop Road, drive a mile and a half, and turn left on Chiwawa River Road (USFS Road 62). Drive 4 miles to the bridge over the Chiwawa (**alternate access,** river mile 6). A half mile past this bridge, stay left on Road 62 at an intersection, then drive upriver another 4.5 miles to the Grouse Creek Group Campground turnoff. Continue up the main road roughly 100 yards past this turnoff, then bear left on an unmarked dirt spur road that leads about 400 yards to the put-in on the left bank.

To reach the **alternate take-out** at river mile 11, begin by following the directions to the put-in as above, but do not turn off Chiwawa Loop Road onto Chiwawa River Road. Instead, continue on the Loop Road a little over 3 miles to the bridge over the Chiwawa.

The Chiwawa River, once an obscure east slope stream, is fast gaining popularity among Washington river runners. This major tributary of the Wenatchee lures boaters with its combination of reliable weather, near-wilderness seclusion, superb forest scenery, enjoyable Class II to III+ whitewater, and a location less than three hours from Seattle. Some river runners come for quick day trips, but most enjoy a longer stay, overnighting at one of the area's excellent forest service campgrounds and perhaps enjoying a run of the nearby Wenatchee.

The Chiwawa drains one of a series of parallel glacial valleys on the eastern side of the Cascades near Glacier Peak Wilderness. The first few miles below the headwaters are steep and furious, but soon the river eases into a long, meandering glide to the southeast down a trough-shaped valley some 25 miles long and half a dozen miles wide. The thick forest and low gradient in this upper section produce numerous **log jams** that deter most river runners. Inflatable kayaks—small and easy to portage—would probably be the best craft for the slow but beautiful section above Huckleberry Ford.

Near Huckleberry Ford the valley narrows and the gradient suddenly increases. Downstream the Chiwawa[1] descends swiftly through nearly a dozen miles of almost continuous Class II to III whitewater. Although they are less common in this fast-moving stretch, **logs still pose a potential hazard.** Inquire locally before making this run, and stay alert. Continuous rapids, cold water, and lack of eddies means that long, cold swims are also a significant risk.

Even after the whitewater eases around mile 10, the gradient remains steep and the current swift and strong all the way to the confluence with the Wenatchee. Most boaters continue about two miles down the Wenatchee to take out at the Highway 209 bridge near Plain. Several alternate accesses allow river runners to choose among different sections, though most of the stretches are roughly the same level of difficulty. If they wish, boaters can make a continuous 27-mile float from Huckleberry Ford to Tumwater Campground on the Upper Wenatchee (see **Wenatchee** chapter).

The first ten miles below Huckleberry Ford are intimate and secluded, as the river courses between towering ranks of fir and cedar. Alders and other riparian trees lean out over the water in places, searching for sunlight. The lush forest screens nearby dirt roads, giving boaters a sense of near-wilderness isolation.[2] In the final three miles private land predominates and many houses are visible, but in general the view from the river remains lush and pleasant.

Chiwawa River Guide

*See map in **Wenatchee** chapter.*

The **put-in** is on the left bank at Huckleberry Ford (mile 0). Class II to II+ rapids begin just downstream. In the first mile Gate Creek and Grouse Creek enter on the left. Below Grouse Creek the canyon narrows and the difficulty increases to Class III, with over a mile of nearly continuous whitewater. **Be alert for log hazards,** and watch for a **low cable across the river** about 3⁄4 mile below Grouse Creek.

At mile 3.5 Big Meadow Creek Campground (good **alternate access**) and Big Meadow Creek appear on the right, signaling another Class III stretch just downstream. The canyon begins to open somewhat around mile 5, and at mile 6, just below the mouth of Alder Creek on the left, the Chiwawa River Road crosses overhead (**alternate access**—see **Logistics**).

Goose Creek enters on the left near mile 7, marking the beginning of two miles of narrower canyon and fairly continuous Class III whitewater. The rapids here are rockier and more demanding, and eddies are scarce. Around mile 9 the canyon opens again and a small irrigation diversion appears on the left. Downstream the rapids ease to Class II. The land is mostly private below this point, with houses and minor roads. Chiwawa Loop Road crosses the river at mile 11, providing a more difficult **alternate access** on the right (see **Logistics**).

The last two miles of the Chiwawa are swift but easy, with the exception of a **potentially dangerous weir** a mile below the Loop Road Bridge and immediately below a series of cabins on the right bank. ***HAZARD.*** The weir is designed to be runnable at higher flows, but at low and moderate water levels boaters should portage on the right. Approach this obstacle with caution at all flows, and stop well upstream to scout carefully.

At mile 13 the much larger Wenatchee River flows in from the right. The float on the Wenatchee begins easily, but in a mile and a half a bluff appears on the left, marking a short section of Class II rapids. The whitewater continues to the **take-out** on the left bank just above the Highway 209 bridge near Plain (mile 15). If you continue downstream, refer to the **Wenatchee** chapter.

---

[1]No, it's not the name of a small, hyperactive Mexican dog. The river's name derives from an Indian word, "Ch'wah." According to some the word means "talking water," while others believe it means "last canyon next to the mountains" (a remarkable amount of information for such a short word). The Indians used the Chiwawa as a travel route, both for journeys across the Cascades as well as for annual treks in late summer to rich huckleberry fields in the surrounding mountains. They crossed the river at Huckleberry Ford.

[2]The Forest Service, recognizing the Chiwawa's great beauty, historical importance, and superb recreational qualities, has recommended the river for National Wild and Scenic River designation.

Methow River

Carlton to Pateros

Difficulty: II first 11 miles, III next 16 miles.
Length: 27 miles. Shorter runs possible.
Gradient: 22 ft./mi.
Put-in: Carlton (1,385').
Take-out: Pateros (790').
Drainage Area and Average Annual Discharge: 1,772 sq. mi. / 1,155,000 af near take-out.
Season: Late April–mid-July.
Recommended Levels: 2,000–11,000 cfs.
Flow Information: NOAA Whitewater Hotline, (206) 526-8530; flow at Pateros (take-out).
Special Hazards: Cold water. Strainers at high flows.
Permits: Not presently required. A State Dept. of Wildlife conservation license is necessary to use the Carlton put-in and the alternate put-in at mile 11; purchase at outdoor stores or call (206) 753-5719 for information.
Commercial Raft Trips: Yes. For a list of outfitters, refer to Armstead, *Whitewater Rafting in Western North America.*
Land Ownership: Almost all private.
Scenery: Good. Lightly forested hills and canyon. Ranches and orchards.
Solitude: Fair. Highway follows run; heavy commercial raft traffic.
Wilderness: No.
Guides and References:
- Bennett, *Guide to the Whitewater Rivers of Washington.*
- North, *Washington Whitewater.*

Maps:
- **USGS 7.5':** *Methow, Cooper Mtn, Pateros.*
- **USFS:** *Okanogan NF.*

Logistics: The Methow is in north central Washington just east of Lake Chelan. Washington Highway 153 follows the river between Twisp (where it becomes Washington Highway 20) and U.S. Highway 97 at Pateros, where the Methow joins the Columbia. The upper **put-in** is on the left bank just upstream from the Highway 153 bridge over the river at Carlton. A popular **intermediate access** is at river mile 11, on the left bank just above the Highway 153 bridge some 2.5 miles upstream from the town of Methow. The common **take-out** is on the right (south) bank just off Highway 153, a short way upstream from the U.S. 97 bridge near the Methow-Columbia confluence at Pateros.

The Methow has much in common with the Wenatchee to the south: both are Columbia River tributaries draining big watersheds on the east slope of the Cascades, both offer big-water boating along busy highways in semi-arid pastoral valleys, and both attract lots of commercial rafters. The main difference is scale: the Methow[1] and its highway are smaller, and it is a bit less crowded than the Wenatchee.

Boating is generally limited to the Methow's final 27 miles, from Carlton to the Columbia confluence near Pateros. Washington Highway 153 follows this section closely. Few boaters venture above Carlton due to frequent log hazards and diversion dams.

The Methow is known for its big Class III rapids. Above about 5,000 cfs the river features roller-coaster rapids with large waves and holes. Most of the action is confined to a seven-mile stretch below the town of Methow, where the resistant rocks of Black Canyon produce a series of big Class III rapids in quick succession.

Boaters come to the Methow primarily for thrills and for the sunshine provided by the strong rain shadow of the high North Cascades. The riverside scenery in the lightly forested valley ranges from farmlands and ranches to scattered cliffs and rock formations.

Chewuch River

The Methow's largest tributary, the Chewuch, offers good boating during a somewhat shorter season. The most popular section is the 13-mile run from Camp Four to Five-Mile Bridge. Here the Chewuch tumbles through numerous Class III rapids (and one III+) in a scenic, forested canyon. Be alert for **log hazards and a diversion dam** on this run. The Chewuch (pronounced CHEE-wuck and spelled "Chewack" on older maps) is also boatable above and below this popular section. To reach the Chewuch, turn north off Highway 20 just west of Winthrop onto County Road 1213 (West Chewuch Road). For more information refer to the *Okanogan NF* map and the guide books by Bennett and North listed above.

---

[1]The name comes from an Indian word meaning "salmon falls river" and is pronounced "MET-ow" (rhymes with "bet now").

Methow River Guide

The **upper put-in** is on the left bank just above the Highway 153 bridge near Carlton (mile 0). A license is required to use this site (see **Permits**). The first 11 miles are Class I and II as the river winds swiftly down a broad flood plain lined by orchards and ranches. Highway 153 crosses at mile 4.3, mile 7, mile 10.3, and mile 11. The fourth highway bridge (mile 11) marks a popular **alternate access** where boats can be carried or lowered down a steep trail on the left bank above the bridge (license also required at this site). Boaters can put in here to avoid the long stretch of easier water upstream.

At mile 13.3 the highway crosses the river again. The town of Methow is on the right at mile 15. Below Methow the highway rejoins the right bank, and a third of a mile downstream boaters encounter the first larger rapid, **ENGLE'S SLIDE (III)**, a long series of big waves.

Downstream the canyon gradually narrows, but the rapids remain moderate for the next three miles. Near mile 18 the river passes a cliff on the left, followed by a long left curve. Just downstream is the biggest whitewater on the run, **BLACK CANYON (III+)**, where the river rushes past cliffs on the left. The biggest obstacle is a boat-eating hole on the left side. Big waves and holes continue over the next mile as the river surges through **STAIRCASE (III)** and **CORNER (III)**.

About a mile below Corner Rapid is an island just above a foot bridge; beware of a big hole if you take the right channel. A half mile below the foot bridge are the big waves of **ROADSIDE ATTRACTION (III)**. A third of a mile farther (mile 22.3), the highway crosses the river, warning of **GREEN BRIDGE RAPID (III)** just below the bridge.

The highway crosses the river for the last time at mile 23. A few hundred yards downstream is the last potentially serious whitewater challenge—a big rock on the right, known as "The Meteorite," that forms a huge hole at high flows. Downstream the river eases to Class II, then becomes flat as it stills in the backwater formed by Wells Dam on the Columbia River. **Take out** on the right bank opposite the town of Pateros.

Rivers of the Northwest Cascades

With their high elevation, deep west-slope snowpacks, and copious rainfall (more than 100" of average annual precipitation), the Northwest Cascades produce some of the heaviest river runoff in the United States. Stretching some 65 miles from Glacier Peak in the south to the Canadian border in the north, this line of lofty summits wrings moisture from storm clouds streaming in off the Pacific. Rivers are high from winter through late spring; then, in summer and early fall, meltwater from numerous glaciers keeps many of them flowing strong.

Almost all this water eventually finds its way to the Skagit River, the region's master stream, which in an average year carries some 12 million acre-feet to the Pacific—an average flow of 16,500 cfs. That's about the same average flow as the Colorado in Grand Canyon, from a watershed one-thirtieth the size. The Skagit system's five main branches drain all but a small part of the Northwest Cascades: the upper Skagit taps lofty peaks in southern British Columbia and Washington's North Cascades National Park; the Cascade drains snowy summits and glacial cirques just to the south; the Suiattle and Sauk spring from ice fields on 10,568' Glacier Peak; and the Baker River drains 10,778' Mt. Baker.

Of these five rivers, only the Baker lacks any boatable sections, having been converted almost entirely to reservoirs. The remaining four offer a wide variety of river trips, from Class V cataracts to flatwater floats. All share some qualities: very cold water, numerous log hazards, and frequently damp and cloudy weather. Though these rivers do have their sunny days, those looking for reliable sunshine would do better to head for the east slope. On the other hand, the hardy and well-equipped can boat some of these runs even in winter, thanks to the relatively low elevations and mild maritime climate.

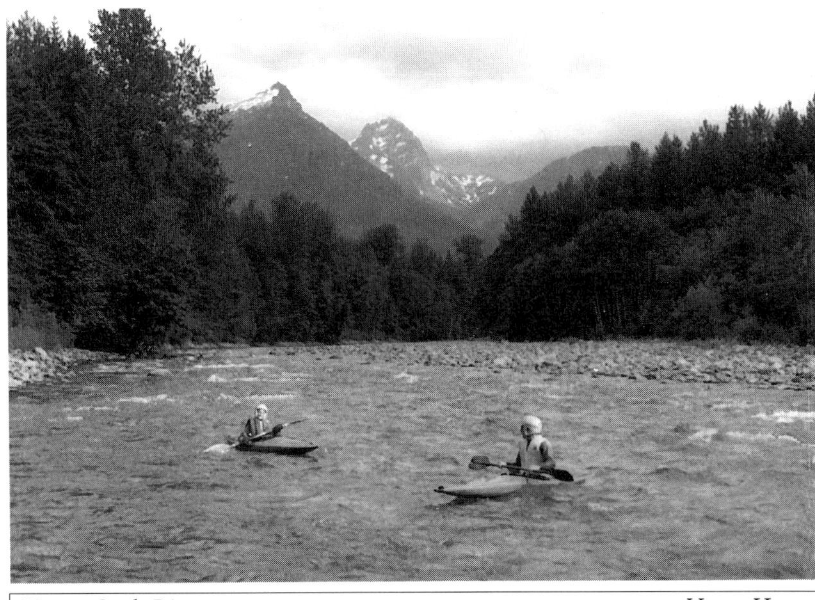

Upper Sauk River *Verne Huser*

The Northwest Cascades are a world apart. Rivers here have their own unique character. Many seem more remote than they really are, because the wet climate produces a forest so dense and lush that nearby roads and buildings are often invisible from the river. Above the wall of green is a primordial world of fire and ice: lofty volcanos capped by blue-white glaciers and wreathed in shreds of cloud.

The Skagit and its tributaries were added to the National Wild and Scenic Rivers System in 1978.

Northwest Cascades — General Data

Maps:

- **USFS:** *Mt. Baker-Snoqualmie NF* covers all runs described here. In addition, *The Skagit Wild And Scenic River System* shows shuttles, accesses, etc. on all rivers. Order from USFS (see individual chapters for addresses).
- **USGS:** *North Cascades National Park* shows the Suiattle, Skagit, and Cascade at 1:100,000 scale.
- **AAA:** *Mt Baker.*

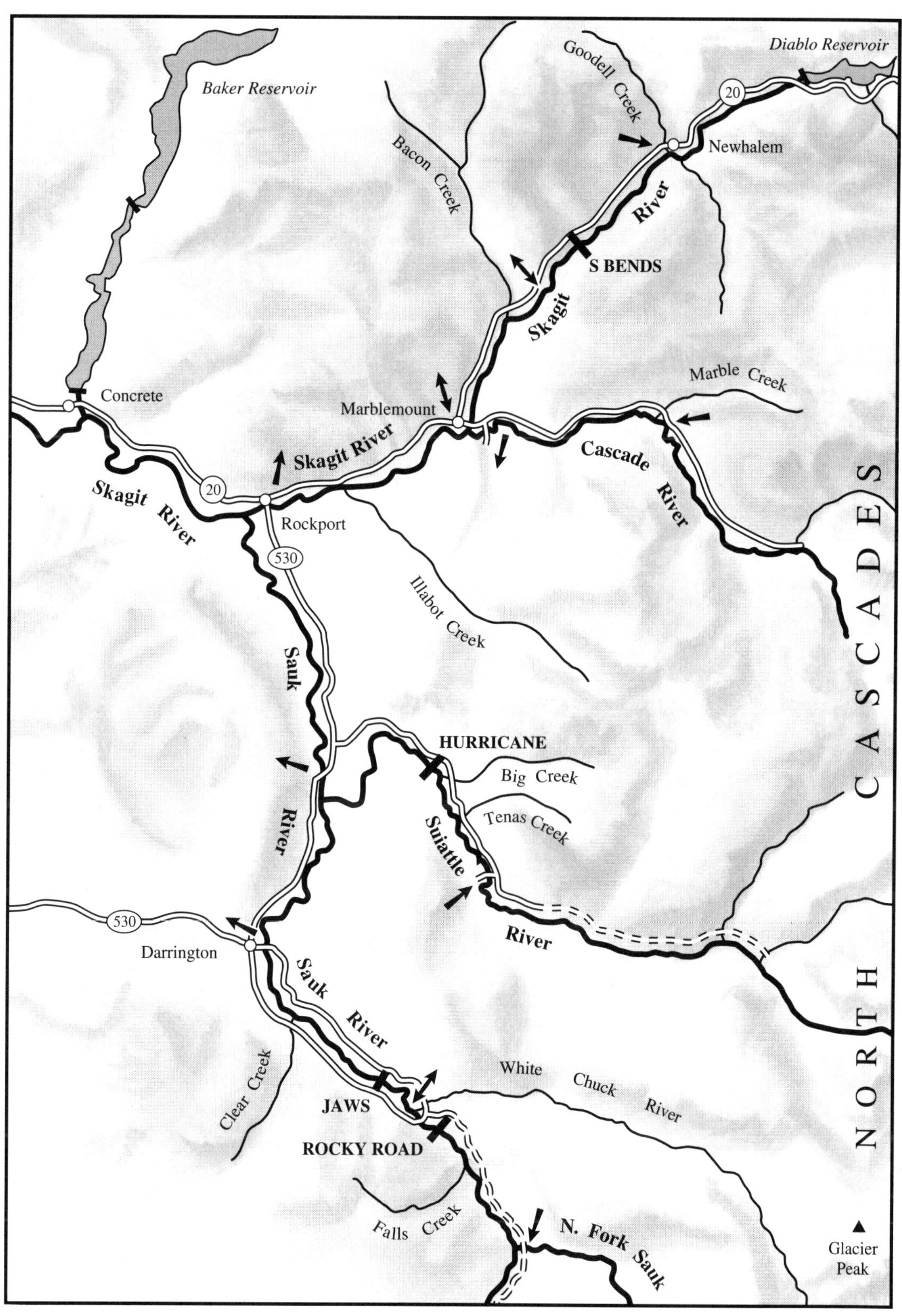

Northwest Cascades: Sauk, Suiattle, Skagit, Cascade

Sauk River

Bedal Campground to Darrington

1. Upper Sauk: Bedal CG (1,215') to White Chuck River (905').
II+; 8 miles; 37 ft./mi.

2. Middle Sauk: White Chuck River to Darrington (500').
III+ (IV at high flows); 10.5 miles; 39 ft./mi. (60 ft./mi. maximum).

Drainage Area and Average Annual Discharge: 240 sq. mi. / 1,600,000 af on Middle Sauk (est.).

Season: *Upper:* Nov.–late July. *Middle:* Nov.–mid-August. Flows are variable but typically peak in June and drop to 1,500 cfs or less by mid-August. Rain or warm weather can cause flows to rise rapidly, especially in spring.

Recommended Levels: *Upper:* 750–2,500 cfs (roughly 3,000–10,000 cfs on Sauk gauge). *Middle:* 1,000–4,500 cfs (roughly 2,000–9,000 cfs on the gauge). Above 5,000 cfs (about 10,000 cfs on the gauge), the Middle Sauk's rating rises to Class IV.

Flow Information: NOAA Whitewater Hotline, (206) 526-8530, gives the flow "near Sauk," which overestimates flows for these runs. (The gauge is far downstream and includes the Suiattle River.) For the *Upper Sauk,* take roughly a quarter of the Sauk reading (slightly more in spring, a bit less in late summer). For the *Middle Sauk,* take about half the Sauk reading (again, a bit more in spring, slightly less in late summer). The hydrograph below is for Run 1 only.

Special Hazards: Numerous log hazards, which may shift at any time—inquire locally before running, and scout when in doubt. Flow fluctuations. Very cold water.

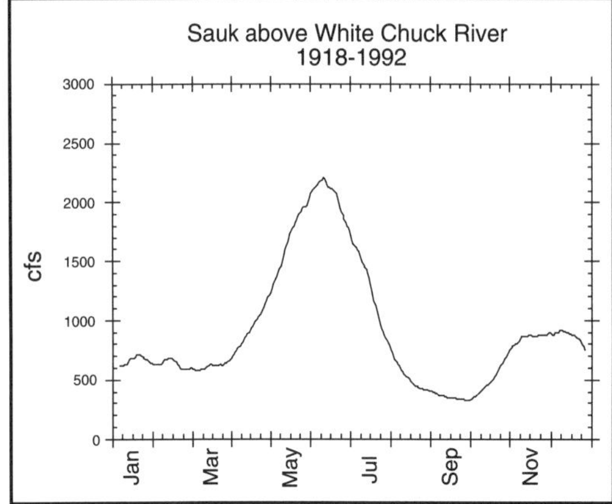

Permits: Unlimited self-registration permits at put-ins.

Managing Agency: Darrington RD, Mt. Baker-Snoqualmie NF, 1405 Emmens St., Darrington, WA 98241; (206) 436-1155.

Commercial Raft Trips: Yes. For references contact the managing agency.

Land Ownership: All National Forest except last 3 miles.

Scenery: Excellent. Lush, forested valley with mountain views.

Solitude: Excellent, except last 3 miles of Middle Sauk. Lush vegetation screens nearby roads.

Wilderness: No.

Water: Very cold. Clear on Upper, milky on Middle. Purify water from side streams for drinking.

Camping: Many USFS campgrounds along the river and in the area.

Side Excursions: Waterfall on the North Fork Sauk about two miles upstream from Bedal Campground put-in, just off USFS Road 49. Also, trails ascending the North Fork Sauk and White Chuck River into Glacier Peak Wilderness.

Guides and References:

- North, *Washington Whitewater.*
- Bennett, *Guide to the Whitewater Rivers of Washington.*
- *Sauk River: White Chuck to Suiattle* (USFS). Free brochure shows shuttles, accesses.
- Huser, *Paddle Routes of Western Washington.* Downstream runs below Darrington.
- Furrer, *Water Trails of Washington.* Brief notes on upper and lower Sauk.

Maps:

- **USGS 7.5':** *Bedal, White Chuck Mtn, Helena Ridge, Darrington.*
- **USGS 1:100:** *Sauk River.*

Auto Shuttle: About same mileages as river.

Logistics: Follow Washington Highway 530 (northeast of Seattle) to Darrington. The **Middle Sauk take-out** is on the left bank at Darrington Bridge where Sauk Prairie Road crosses the Sauk about a third of a mile east of Darrington Ranger Station. For upstream accesses drive upstream (south) from

Darrington on Mountain Loop Road (USFS Road 20). A good **alternate take-out** is on the left bank at Backman County Park about two miles south of town. About 8 miles south of Darrington, Mountain Loop Road crosses the Sauk. (If you are running the Upper Sauk, be sure to stop and scout Rocky Road Rapid from this bridge). To reach the **White Chuck access,** turn left about 200 yards past the bridge onto USFS Road 22, then drive a short distance to the launch site on the right bank just below the confluence of the Sauk and the White Chuck. To reach the **Bedal put-in,** continue upriver on Mountain Loop Road some 7 more miles, then bear right into Bedal Campground.

The Sauk, the Skagit's largest tributary, is a river with two distinct headwaters. One stem of the river—the one that carries the name "Sauk" [1]—drains the north face of a snowy ridge that separates the Sauk basin from the Skykomish watershed to the south. The other major branch, the White Chuck River, carries meltwater from glaciers on the western flank of 10,568' Glacier Peak. Together, these very different branches give the Sauk's two whitewater runs their distinct characters.

The Upper Sauk run begins near the confluence of the North and South Forks and extends to the White Chuck confluence. Fed by snowmelt and rainfall, the Upper Sauk runs clean and clear. Its steep gradient produces a strong, swift current, but the relatively small water volume and few rocky obstacles make this a fairly forgiving section—except for one challenging rapid just above the take-out.

At the White Chuck confluence everything changes. The White Chuck, running thick and milky with its heavy load of glacial flour, turns the Sauk from translucent emerald to opaque jade. This major tributary also adds substantial flow, giving the Middle Sauk more power than the Upper. Finally, the White Chuck brings obstacles to the Sauk: over thousands of years, volcanic eruptions at Glacier Peak have sent violent flows of mud and rubble down the White Chuck.[2] Below the confluence the gradient suddenly increases as the Sauk tumbles over and around rocks and boulders.

Taken together, these factors make the Middle Sauk more difficult than the Upper. Above about 5,000 cfs (roughly 10,000 on the Sauk gauge), the Middle Sauk is peppered with powerful holes and hydraulics and rates Class IV. The turbid water is more difficult to read at these times. Use extra caution at higher flows.

Despite their differences, these two sections of the Sauk also have much in common. Both are subject to **very serious log hazards,** which shift from year to year and may require portaging at times. Inquire locally before boating, and always scout when in doubt. In addition, the water in both reaches is perpetually cold, and the weather is often poor—factors that increase the risk of hypothermia. Both stretches are subject to sudden flow fluctuations induced by rain or warm weather.

On the brighter side, both sections flow down moist, densely forested valleys where wildlife abounds. Thick riverbank vegetation almost completely screens nearby roads, giving a sense of near-wilderness seclusion; maple and alder lean out over the water in search of sunlight, while towering evergreens close ranks behind. Finally, both runs offer occasional views of spectacular snow-clad peaks.

The Middle Sauk sees more use than the Upper—in part because many prefer the more challenging rapids on the Middle Sauk, and in part because the added flow of the White Chuck gives this section a longer season. Glacial melt begins in earnest in midsummer, just as snowmelt is fading on the Upper Sauk. Boaters can make a continuous run of both sections.

Lower Sauk

Below Darrington the Sauk, with a gradient of 15 ft./mi., offers up to 21 miles of swift floating through wooded bottomlands with views of distant peaks. Roads are busier and more apparent here; Highway 530 parallels most of the run. The river winds over a gravelly bed, splitting frequently around islands where logs are often stranded. The riffles are generally

[1] The name, according to James Phillips, *Washington State Place Names,* comes from the Sah-kee-ma-hu branch of the Skagit tribe.

[2] Geologists believe that volcanic eruptions at Glacier Peak altered the Sauk's course. The Sauk originally ran almost due west to the Stillaguamish River, but beginning perhaps 15,000 years ago a series of eruptions blocked the riverbed with mud and debris, forcing the Sauk northward on its present course to the Skagit.

Class II- or easier, but boaters should **stay alert for frequent sweepers.** The Suiattle River joins the Sauk about eight miles below Darrington, adding considerable flow and a heavy load of glacial silt. Lower Sauk accesses include Darrington bridge (left bank, mile 0), just above the Highway 530 bridge (right bank, mile 8.5), and Sauk County Park (left bank, mile 15).

Few boaters float the final six miles from the County Park to the Skagit River confluence, though this section offers pleasant scenery, good fishing, and abundant wildlife. The next possible take-out is about five miles down the Skagit. For more information on the Lower Sauk, refer to Verne Huser, *Paddle Routes of Western Washington.*

Upper Sauk Mile Guide

See map just before this chapter.

0 **PUT-IN.** Bedal Campground on the right bank of the North Fork Sauk. About ⅓ mile downstream, where the river splits around an island, the South Fork Sauk enters from the left. For the first 4 miles the river drops steeply (45 ft./mi.) through swift Class II whitewater, with one Class II+ at mile 1.7 just above some cabins on the right.

2.8 A headwall on the left bank forces the river sharply right.

4 The gradient eases to 30 ft./mi. with easy riffles for the next 4 miles. Falls Creek enters on the left at mile 5.2.

8 Gauging station on the right; cable across the river. 300 yards downstream at a right bend is the roughest rapid on the Upper Sauk, **ROCKY ROAD** (III-). This steep rock garden continues around the bend to the Mountain Loop Road bridge and can be scouted from the bridge on the drive to the put-in. To avoid the rapid, make a difficult take-out just upstream on the right and carry boats several hundred yards to Mountain Loop Road. Below the bridge and rapid the White Chuck River enters on the right, substantially increasing the flow. **TAKE OUT** on the right or continue downstream.

Middle Sauk Mile Guide

0 **PUT-IN** on the right bank just below the confluence of the Sauk and White Chuck. Class III rapids begin immediately. The river drops at almost 60 ft./mi. for the first 3 miles. About a mile below the put-in, at the end of a sweeping left bend, is **ALLIGATOR** (III+), where a big hole forms in the center at higher flows.

2 **JAWS** (IV-), at a shallow left bend. **Recognition:** The rapid begins with a long, narrow island near the right shore; almost all of the water goes down the left side through a series of big reversals. Stop well upstream to scout from the right shore or from the island itself, if possible. Rapids continue downstream, making Jaws a bad place to swim. **The rapid:** Below the island watch for a broad rock (the "Demon Seed") in the right center. At most flows boaters usually skirt this rock on the right, then move quickly back to the center to avoid logs on the right just downstream. At high flows the Demon Seed is covered and creates a huge reversal.

2.8 The river curves left and plunges through **WHIRLPOOL** (III-), where boaters must avoid a steep headwall (and possible log jam) on the left that forces the river to the right. Downstream the gradient eases, and Murphy Creek enters on the left.

4 **POPEYE** (III+). Big waves, especially at high water. Beware of an undercut rock just downstream. Easier water for the next 3 miles.

6.7 Clear Creek enters on the left, just above Clear Creek Campground. Houses appear on the left.

7.5 **RIVER ACCESS.** Good alternate take-out on the left at Backman County Park. Not far downstream is a Class III- drop. Soon the valley opens to the left, with the town of Darrington well back from the river on the left bank.

10.5 **TAKE OUT** on the left at the Sauk Prairie Road bridge at Darrington, or continue downstream (see section on **Lower Sauk** at end of essay above).

Suiattle River

Boundary Bridge to Highway 530 Bridge

Difficulty: III-. **Gradient:** 30 ft./mi.
Length: 13 miles. Longer runs possible.
Put-in: Boundary Bridge (750').
Take-out: Highway 530 bridge (370').
Drainage Area and Average Discharge: 360 sq. mi. and 1,750,000 af (est.).
Season: Generally all year, though occasionally too low in September. Flows typically peak in June, then recede gradually to late summer lows of roughly 1,000 cfs.
Recommended Levels: 1,000–5,000 cfs.
Flow Information: No gauge. NOAA Whitewater Hotline, (206) 526-8530, gives the flow on the Sauk "near Sauk." On average the Suiattle supplies roughly half this flow, but since the Suiattle drains a higher-elevation watershed than the upper Sauk, it contributes less than half the flow early in the season and more than half late in the season.
Special Hazards: Numerous shifting log hazards; inquire locally before boating, and scout when in doubt. Very cold water.
Permits: Not presently required.
Managing Agency: Darrington RD, Mt. Baker-Snoqualmie NF, 1405 Emmens St., Darrington, WA 98241; (206) 436-1155.
Commercial Raft Trips: Yes. For a list of outfitters, contact the managing agency.
Land Ownership: Mostly private.
Scenery: Very good. Forested valley, mountain views, some logging scars.
Solitude: Very good. Lush vegetation screens nearby road.
Wilderness: No.
Water: Glacial melt, very cold and quite silty. Purify water from side streams for drinking.
Camping: Three USFS campgrounds on or near the river.
Side Excursions: USFS trail up the upper Suiattle into Glacier Peak Wilderness.
Guides and References:

- Bennett, *Guide to the Whitewater Rivers of Washington.* Includes upstream run.
- Harris, *Fire Mountains of the West.* Geology of Glacier Peak.

Maps: USGS 7.5': *Lower:* Prairie Mtn, Darrington.

- **USGS 1:100:** *Sauk River.*

Auto Shuttle: About 10 miles, mostly paved.

Logistics: The **take-out** is at the State Highway 530 bridge over the Sauk River (right bank, upstream side of bridge), about 7 miles north of Darrington or 12 miles south of Highway 20 at Rockport in northwestern Washington. An **alternate take-out** is on the left bank of the Sauk at the Sauk-Suiattle confluence, reached by driving half a mile south on Highway 530 from the bridge.

To reach the **put-in,** drive east on Highway 530 just 300 yards from the Sauk River Bridge take-out, then stay right on USFS Road 26 as the highway veers left. Follow this road up the left bank of the Suiattle (the river is rarely visible through the trees) some 10 miles to the intersection with Road 25, then turn right on Road 25 and immediately cross Boundary Bridge (also known as Rat Trap Bridge). The put-in is on the left bank on the downstream side of the bridge.

The Suiattle (pronounced "Sue-attle") is both a glacial river and a volcanic river, born among ice fields on the north and east flanks of the North Cascades' second-highest volcano, Glacier Peak. Towering more than 2,000' above any other peak in the watershed, Glacier Peak defines the landscape and shapes the Suiattle's course and character.

The Suiattle carries the heaviest load of glacial silt of any river in this guide. Glaciers grind and pulverize underlying rock into a fine powder or "flour," which is then carried downstream as the ice melts. Several of the Suiattle's upstream tributaries run thick with sediment, earning names like Chocolate Creek, Dusty Creek and Milk Creek. This glacial runoff gives the Suiattle one of the longest boating seasons in Washington, providing minimum runnable levels even in the driest period of the year, from midsummer to autumn. At these times the Suiattle runs brown and muddy, undiluted by the clean rainwater and snowmelt that contribute much of its flow at other times.

Ice is not the only force shaping the Suiattle: fire has played a role as well. Over thousands of years, eruptions at Glacier Peak have sent violent flows of mud and debris down the river, filling its original bed with deep deposits of mud, ash, and sediment.[1] Today the Suiattle meanders in shifting, sometimes braided channels across these loose, unconsolidated deposits. As the river cuts new channels it frequently undermines trees, felling them into the river where they create serious hazards for boaters.

Due to the lack of exposed bedrock, the Suiattle's rapids are generally mild; only one or two rate a full Class III. Even so, the numerous log hazards and perpetually cold water demand extra caution. Also, the river's braided channels and frequent islands may test water-reading skills. Like the Sauk, the Suiattle runs through a heavily forested valley where lush vegetation screens out civilization. When weather permits, views of the surrounding mountains are stunning. For most boaters, scenery rather than whitewater is the primary attraction on the Suiattle.

The Suiattle, the largest tributary of the Sauk, actually carries slightly more water than its parent river. In addition to the ice fields of Glacier Peak, the Suiattle drains snowfields on 7,000' and 8,000' peaks along the Cascade crest. The Sauk and Suiattle join a few miles north of Darrington. The trip described here takes in the last 12 miles of the Suiattle and ends on the Sauk about a mile below the confluence.

[1]Though Glacier Peak is momentarily quiet, it is almost certain to erupt again in the not-too-distant future, producing potentially catastrophic mudflows.

Upstream Runs

It is possible to add up to 14 miles of river above the run described here, with put-ins as far upriver as Sulphur Creek Campground near the Glacier Peak Wilderness boundary. However, extensive and frequent log jams deter most boaters. Inquire with local river runners before considering any run above Boundary Bridge. Most of this upper section is Class III to III+, including some very swift sections with few eddies. Heavy riverbank vegetation precludes scouting most of this section from the road. A new access has recently been proposed some three miles upstream from Boundary Bridge. Contact the Forest Service for current information. For more whitewater information on this upstream section, refer to the guide book by Jeff Bennett listed above.

Suiattle Mile Guide

*See map before **Sauk** chapter.*

0 **PUT-IN** on the left bank just downstream from Boundary Bridge (also called Rat Trap Bridge) on USFS Road 25.

2 Site of washed-out Tenas Creek bridge. Stay left to avoid metal debris on the right. Tenas Creek enters on the right.

3.7 **COYOTE CROSSING (III-)**. A quarter mile downstream Big Creek, a major tributary, enters on the right.

4.2 A quarter mile below Big Creek at a right bend is **HURRICANE (III)**. The river drops through two swift chutes peppered with holes. Scout left if desired. The next two miles have many Class II+ rapids, including **SHIPWRECK** and **PORCUPINE.**

7 The Suiattle makes a long curve to the left, flowing past Dearinger State Park on the left. Watch for a final Class III- at the end of the bend (about mile 8). Downstream the valley opens and the Suiattle winds through Class II riffles and many islands. Watch for log jams in this lower section.

12 **RIVER ACCESS.** Confluence with the Sauk River, which enters from the left. Alternate access on the left bank of the Sauk (see **Logistics**).

13 **TAKE-OUT.** Highway 530 bridge over the Sauk. Take out on the right just above the bridge, or continue downstream (see **Sauk** chapter).

Skagit River

Goodell Creek to Rockport

1. Goodell Creek CG (475')
to Copper Creek (355').
II+; 9 miles; 14 ft./mi.

2. Copper Creek to Marblemount (315').
II-; 6 miles; 7 ft./mi.

3. Marblemount to Rockport (215').
I+; 10 miles; 9 ft./mi.

Drainage Area and Average Annual Discharge: 1,175 sq. mi. and 3,225,000 af at Newhalem near the upper put-in.

Season: All year. Typically peaks at moderate levels in June or July and slowly recedes to low but runnable flows (rarely below 1,800 cfs) in September and October. Upstream dams dampen seasonal flow variations but may produce daily fluctuations; releases vary with electricity demands.

Recommended Levels: 1,200–8,000 cfs.

Flow Information: NOAA Whitewater Hotline, (206) 526-8530; flow at Newhalem, near the Goodell Creek put-in.

Special Hazards: Cold water. Occasional log hazards. Flow fluctuations.

Permits: *Run 1:* Unlimited, self-issued permits (required) at Goodell Creek put-in. *Runs 2 & 3:* Not required. Contact managing agency about possible future winter boating restrictions to protect eagles.

Managing Agencies: *Run 1:* North Cascades National Park, Marblemount, WA 98267; (206) 873-4590. *Runs 2 & 3:* Mt. Baker RD, Mt. Baker-Snoqualmie NF, 2105 Highway 20, Sedro Woolley, WA 98284; (206) 856-5700.

Commercial Raft Trips: Yes. For references contact the NPS or USFS.

Land Ownership: *Run 1:* All public. *Runs 2 & 3:* Mostly private.

Scenery: Very good. Forested glacial valleys, mountain views.

Solitude: Good. Highway 20, which follows all runs, is less conspicuous below Marblemount.

Wilderness: No.

Fishing: Excellent for steelhead (fall and winter) and trout (June 1–Mar. 1).

Wildlife: Famous for bald eagles in winter.

Water: Clear and very cold.

Camping: *Run 1:* No on-river camping; campground at put-in. *Runs 2 & 3:* Camping on midstream islands is discouraged (private property). Campground at Steelhead Park take-out in Rockport.

Side Excursions: North Cascades National Park.

Guides and References:
- Bennett, *Guide to the Whitewater Rivers of Washington.* Covers Runs 1 & 3.
- North, *Washington Whitewater.* Covers Run 1.
- Huser, *Paddle Routes of Western Washington.* Runs 2 and 3.
- LeRoux & Rudersdorf, *Paddle Washington.* Runs 2 and 3.
- Alt & Hyndman, *Roadside Geology of Washington.* Geology of Highway 20 corridor.

Maps:
- **USGS 7.5':** *Run 1:* Mt. Triumph, Big Devil Peak. *Run 2:* Marblemount. *Run 3:* Marblemount, Illabot Peaks, Rockport.
- **USGS 1:100:** *Mt. Baker* sheet covers Runs 1 and 2.

Auto Shuttle: About the same mileages as river, all paved.

Logistics: All shuttles and accesses are via Washington Highway 20, which follows the north bank of the Skagit. The following popular accesses are listed in ascending (upstream) order. **Rockport:** on the right bank at Howard Miller Steelhead Park, just below the Highway 530 bridge. **Marblemount:** just east of town on the left bank at the Cascade Road bridge over the Skagit. **Copper Creek:** on the right bank, reached via a very short dirt road that turns off Highway 20 about 6 miles upriver from Marblemount. (The turnoff is about 0.8 miles east of the Highway 20 bridge over Bacon Creek.) **Goodell Creek:** on the right bank at Goodell Creek Campground, just west of Newhalem.

The headwaters of the Skagit—western Washington's largest river after the Columbia—lie across the border in southern British Columbia, high in the Canadian Cascades where some of the world's deepest snowpacks accumulate. From here the river runs south into Washington, gathering more snowmelt from lofty granite peaks in North Cascades National Park. Then the Skagit turns southwest through the Cascade foothills and finally due west to Puget Sound.

Today, reservoirs cover most of the Skagit's upper reaches. Between 1924 and 1949 Seattle built three hydroelectric dams to harness the river's mighty flow. The largest impoundment, Ross Reservoir, extends more than 25 miles up a long glacial valley, backing water across the Canadian border. With a combined storage of some 1.5 million acre-feet, these reservoirs dampen the river's natural seasonal flow pattern, reducing the spring highs and augmenting the late summer lows.

Seattle continues to push for a fourth dam that would flood ten more miles of river and bury the only remaining whitewater run—Run 1 in this chapter. Unfortunately, this section was not designated as a Wild and Scenic River when the rest of the Skagit was protected in 1978. To help save this section, please contact the Rivers Council of Washington (see appendix for address).

For the moment the Skagit still runs free from the last dam near Newhalem to Puget Sound. Though all 90 miles are boatable, the first 25 down to the Sauk River confluence hold the most interest for river runners. The three back-to-back runs described below offer a variety of whitewater and scenery, and they can be combined for longer trips.

Goodell Creek to Copper Creek

Here the Skagit courses swiftly down a narrow, heavily forested glacial valley that provides frequent views of nearby snow-capped summits. The river is ice cold and clear, and on sunny days the water is an intense and beautiful blue-green. The first ten miles to Bacon Creek hold the Skagit's only whitewater, making this section popular with commercial and private rafters, kayakers, and some open canoeists. Most of the action is limited to a short Class II+ gauntlet where the river cuts a narrow passage through granite bedrock. The difficulty increases at higher flows. Highway 20 follows the run closely, allowing boaters to scout the roughest spots from the road before running. This section has the only **Mile Guide** in this chapter (see below).

Copper Creek to Marblemount

A mile below Copper Creek the Skagit runs through one final Class II riffle at Bacon Creek, then settles into a swift but gentle glide down a gradually widening flood plain. Soon the river begins meandering in shifting channels over deep deposits of gravel and cobble, the legacy of an ice-age glacier that once filled the valley and extended all the way to Puget Sound. This stretch of the lower Skagit is popular with canoeists, who enjoy many views of snowy peaks and, late in the season, spectacular fall colors. Highway 20 follows most of this section closely, and some houses dot the shore. **Take out** at Cascade Bridge, just upstream from the Cascade River confluence.

Marblemount to Rockport

Below Cascade Bridge and Marblemount the Skagit valley widens and the channel becomes broader, splitting occasionally around large islands. This section enjoys a little more solitude: the river occasionally winds away from the highway, and dense vegetation provides some privacy. In autumn the riverside foliage turns to blazing yellow and orange. **Take out** just above the Sauk River confluence at Steelhead Park in Rockport.

This stretch is perhaps best known for its annual gathering of bald eagles. Each winter hundreds of the great birds come south from Alaska and Canada, drawn to the Skagit by throngs of migrating salmon and steelhead. The eagles in turn attract bird-watchers, making the Skagit a favorite midwinter river trip. Commercial companies offer eagle-watching tours from December to February—a time when most river runners are more likely to be cross-country skiing or soaking in a hot bath. Between eagle-watching and heavy fishing use by dory boaters, the lower Skagit sees more traffic in winter than summer. To reduce disturbance of the birds, boaters should launch only after 11 a.m., pass by as quietly as possible, and not land on shore.[1]

---

[1]Even though the eagle population is growing, the Forest Service is considering restrictions on boating. Contact the managing agency for updated information.

Skagit Mile Guide

*See map before **Sauk** chapter.*

Goodell Creek to Copper Creek

0 **PUT-IN.** Goodell Creek Campground (right bank). A mile upstream, water is released into the river at the Gorge Powerhouse above Newhalem. An easy Class II lies just below the put-in, followed by 4 miles of Class I+.

5 Damnation Creek enters on the right. Downstream the canyon narrows and the highway runs close above the right bank. A half mile below the creek, the river accelerates into a pair of Class II+ drops known as **S-BENDS** or **S-CURVES** at a right-left crook. Scout from the highway before running (near milepost 114). Difficulty increases at higher flows.

6 A power line crosses overhead, then recrosses a half mile downstream. A gauging station is on the right at mile 6.8. Half a mile below the gauge, the river bends sharply right and runs through **WAVY TRAIN (II).**

8.7 **TAKE-OUT.** A mile below Wavy Train, Copper Creek enters on the left. Take out on the right where a dirt spur road reaches the river, or continue downstream (see essay; no **Mile Guide** for Runs 2 & 3).

The Skagit River Valley has been a magnet for explorers, trappers, prospectors, adventurers, and fortune-seekers for almost two centuries. The late nineteenth century saw several gold rushes and a silver rush on tributaries of the Skagit. In the early twentieth century, the Skagit itself became the precious resource as entrepreneurs dammed the river to produce power (and wealth). Between 1924 and 1961 they erected three dams in the Skagit Gorge.

Fortunately, the lower river has survived and flourished. From Marblemount to Rockport the Skagit still flows broad and deep, with emerald pools that hint at the river's glacial origins. It is in this section that the Skagit Bald Eagle Recreation Area has been set aside as a protected wintering site for large populations of the magnificent birds.

In the winter of 1984 I met friends at Rockport for a day of peaceful drifting and eagle-watching. We were dressed to stay warm and dry on the river, armed with cameras, and twitching with excitement at the prospect of seeing the birds in their natural habitat. But as the late arrivals straggled in, the day grew unusually sunny, and talk turned from eagles to whitewater. As the weather continued to improve, the entertaining intermediate section above Marblemount was beckoning us .

Should we run the rapids upstream or watch the eagles downstream? As we struggled with the decision, an adult eagle suddenly swooped within 20 feet of our heads, taking all of us by surprise. A minute later, a second eagle flew by, skimming low above the river, and then flapped back up to his perch. In the next half hour we spotted three more eagles. That made up our minds.

We had come to see eagles, and we had been rewarded with five sightings—all without getting our feet wet! True, this visual feast was only a hors d'oeuvre compared to the average 25 to 100 sightings typical of a midwinter float down the Skagit below Marblemount. But we wanted to have our cake and eat it too, so we headed upstream for the Goodell Creek put-in. By the end of the day, we had seen another four or five eagles, enjoyed the fun run through the S-Bends, and picked up a bit of a midwinter tan on our faces.

—Jeff Bennett

Cascade River

Marble Creek to Fish Hatchery

Difficulty: V, with possible portages.
Length: 7.5 miles.
Gradient: 85 ft./mi. (peaks at 130 ft./mi. from miles 1–4).
Put-in: Marble Creek Campground (970').
Take-out: Fish Hatchery Bridge (330').
Drainage Area and Average Annual Discharge: 140 sq. mi. / 850,000 af at Marble Creek (est.).
Season: Mid-June to mid-August.
Flow Information: No gauge. See immediately below.
Recommended Levels: 600–2,000 cfs. An informal gauge is spray-painted on the bridge at the take-out, and at most recent report local boaters preferred levels in the 1' to 2' range on this gauge. However, the significance of these figures could change at any time as the riverbed changes.
Special Hazards: Numerous log hazards. The Monster (see **River Guide** below).
Permits: Not presently required.
Managing Agency: Mt. Baker RD, Mt. Baker-Snoqualmie NF, 2105 Highway 20, Sedro Woolley, WA 98284; (206) 856-5700.
Commercial Raft Trips: Yes. For references contact the managing agency.
Land Ownership: Mostly private.
Scenery: Excellent. Steep, forested valley with mountain views.
Solitude: Excellent first 3 miles, good thereafter.
Wilderness: No.
Water: Very cold and clear.
Camping: USFS campgrounds at Marble Creek and Mineral Park.
Side Hikes: Upstream from this run, trails ascend Kindy Creek and the South and Middle Forks of the Cascade into Glacier Peak Wilderness. A steep trail climbs from Cascade Road a mile below the put-in to Lookout Mountain.
Guides and References:

- Bennett, *Guide to the Whitewater Rivers of Washington.*

Maps:

- USGS 7.5': *Big Devil Peak, Marblemount.*

Auto Shuttle: About the same mileages as river.
Logistics: Follow Washington Highway 20 to Marblemount. Just east of town, where the highway turns sharply left (north), continue straight (east) on Cascade Road and cross the Skagit River. Half a mile past this bridge, turn right and drive 100 yards to a bridge over the Cascade River near the state fish hatchery. The **take-out** is on the left bank above the bridge. To reach the **put-in,** return to Cascade Road and drive upriver some 7.5 miles to Marble Creek Campground. Launch at the downstream end of the campground.

The Cascade River offers by far the most challenging whitewater in the Skagit system. A steep gradient and big, boulder-choked drops make the Cascade a great run—**for experts only.** Adding to the difficulty and danger are ice-cold water and numerous, ever-shifting log hazards. Portages may be necessary around rapids, strainers, and log jams. A favorite among expert kayakers, the Cascade has more recently gained popularity with expert rafters as well.

The Cascade drains a small, scenic alpine watershed between the Suiattle and Skagit basins. The river originates in snowfields and glaciers in North Cascades National Park and Glacier Peak Wilderness, then tumbles north and west to join the Skagit River near Marblemount. The free-flowing Cascade is typically runnable only during a relatively brief snowmelt window. However, at peak snowmelt flows are usually too high, so in most years boaters have to catch the river near the beginning or end of the melt.

Action begins not far below the put-in at Marble Creek Campground where the river tumbles over the lip of an ancient glacial moraine. In the next three miles the Cascade plummets 390 vertical feet, crashing through elaborate mazes of granite boulders. Though the run is only eight miles long, boaters should allow plenty of time for careful scouting and possible portaging.

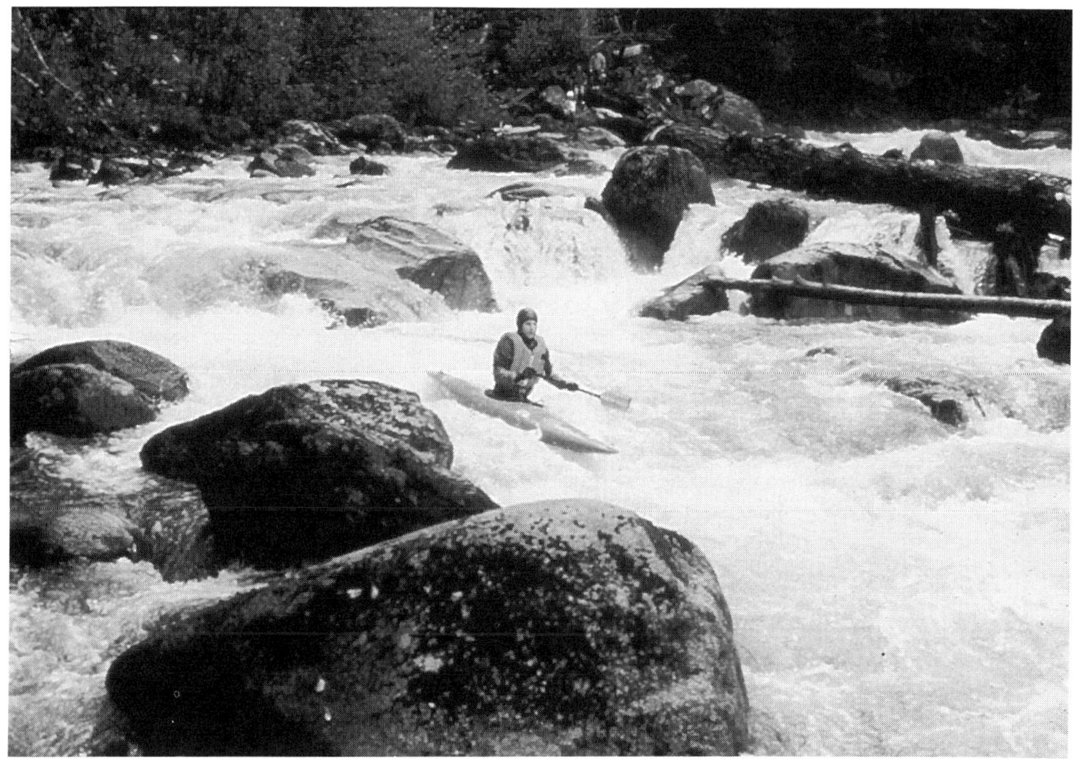

C-1 on the Cascade River *Jeff Bennett*

Cascade River Guide

See map before the ***Sauk*** *chapter. This guide provides only the briefest overview of the river and lists only a few of the largest rapids. For more detailed information consult local river runners and the guide book by Jeff Bennett listed earlier.*

Put in on the right bank at Marble Creek Campground (mile 0). **Do not attempt to launch above this point due to severe log hazards upstream.** Marble Creek, a major tributary, enters downstream on the right. Below the creek the canyon narrows and the gradient and difficulty suddenly skyrocket as the river drops over a glacial moraine.

The first big rapid, **STARTS WITH A BANG (V)**, is a 500-yard-long gauntlet at a left bend about half a mile into the run. Scout this one in its entirety before running it. Difficult rapids continue, leading up to the climax at **THE MONSTER** (V+) near mile 2. Here the river churns among enormous granite boulders, dividing into narrow chutes where logs often lodge. Scout carefully from, and consider portaging on, the left.

Downstream from The Monster look for Irene Creek, which enters as a lovely waterfall on the left. More big rapids follow, including **SHARK'S TOOTH** (V) near mile 3. Below this point the canyon opens slightly, but the gradient remains quite steep for another mile. A minor bridge crosses the river at mile 4.5 (private, no access), and the gradient finally begins to ease. The last three miles are much more open, leading down to the **take-out** on the left just above the fish hatchery bridge at mile 7.5.

North Fork Nooksack River

Douglas Fir Campground to Maple Falls

Difficulty: III.
Length: 8 miles. Shorter and longer runs possible.
Gradient: 52 ft./mi.
Put-in: Douglas Fir Campground (975').
Take-out: Maple Falls (560').
Drainage Area and Average Annual Discharge: 105 sq. mi. / 562,000 af near Douglas Fir CG.
Season: May through August. The North Fork typically peaks between late May and mid-June, then recedes gradually to September and October lows of less than 600 cfs.
Runnable Levels: 600–3,000 cfs.
Flow Information: NOAA Whitewater Hotline, (206) 526-8530; flow at North Fork Gauge near put-in.
Special Hazards: Log hazards, which may shift at any time; inquire locally before running, and scout if in doubt. Very cold water.
Permits: Not presently required.
Managing Agency: Mt. Baker RD, Mt. Baker-Snoqualmie NF, 2105 Highway 20, Sedro Woolley, WA 98284; (206) 856-5700.
Commercial Raft Trips: Yes. For references contact Mt. Baker RD in Sedro Woolley (for address, see **Cascade** chapter).
Land Ownership: Mixed National Forest and private.
Scenery: Excellent. Forested canyon, narrow gorges, mountain views.
Solitude: Very good.
Wilderness: No. Highway, campgrounds, small town.
Side Excursions: Horseshoe Bend Interpretive Trail follows the right (north) bank for about a mile and a half above the Highway 542 bridge near Douglas Fir Campground.

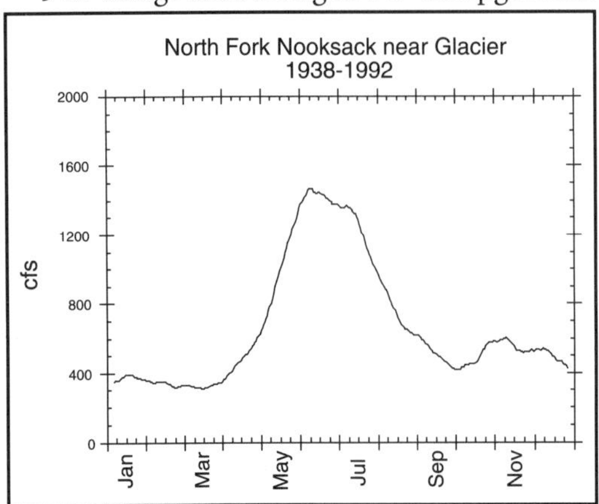

Expert boaters can use this trail to scout the Class V gorge below Horseshoe Bend. Spectacular Nooksack Falls (170') is just upstream from Excelsior Campground.
Guides and References:
- North, *Washington Whitewater.*
- Bennett, *Guide to the Whitewater Rivers of Washington.*

Maps:
- **USGS 7.5':** *Bearpaw Mtn., Glacier, Maple Falls.*
- **USGS 1:100:** *Mt. Baker.*
- **USFS:** *Mt. Baker-Snoqualmie NF.*

Auto Shuttle: Highway 542 follows the runs, providing short, paved shuttles. Mileages are roughly the same as river.
Logistics: The Maple Falls **take-out** on the right bank is reached via a short dirt spur road off State Highway 542 about 1.5 miles east of the town of Maple Falls in the northwestern corner of Washington. This take-out is on private land, but many boaters have used this site in the past. The Douglas Fir **put-in** is on the right bank at the campground, just downstream from the Highway 542 bridge two miles east of Glacier.

The North Fork of the Nooksack, the northernmost river in Washington, lies just half a dozen miles south of the Canadian border. Draining a small watershed between the Skagit River to the south and British Columbia's Fraser River to the north, the North Fork gets most of its flow from melting glaciers on the north faces of 10,778' Mt. Baker and 9,127' Mt. Shuksan. From summer through autumn, the North Nooksack[1] is milky gray with a heavy load of glacial flour. The abundant supply of ice-cold glacial meltwater gives the Nooksack a much longer season than rivers fed by snow or rain alone.[2]

---

[1]The river's unusual name is an Indian word meaning "mountain men," an apparent reference to a local branch of the Suquawmish tribe.

[2]The Forest Service has recommended that the North Fork Nooksack be designated a National Wild and Scenic River, but Congress has not acted.

Dominating the North Nooksack landscape is Mt. Baker, generally considered the Cascade's most active and dangerous volcano after Mt. St. Helens. Frequent eruptions in the last few hundred years have produced massive mudflows on the mountain's south and east flanks. The North Fork Nooksack has been shaped as much by Mt. Baker's fire as by its ice.

The most popular whitewater run begins at Douglas Fir Campground. Almost all the action is compressed into the first couple of miles where the river drops steeply through a lush, narrow gorge strewn with nearly continuous Class III rapids. Farther downstream the river presents nothing above Class II as it flows swiftly down braided channels in an open valley. This lower section offers spectacular vistas of nearby Mt. Baker and other snowy summits. **Log hazards** are a major concern on all sections of this heavily forested river. Also, the extremely cold water and frequently poor weather combine to increase the hypothermia risk.

Washington Highway 542 follows both runs, often away from the river and screened by trees. Boaters can camp overnight at any of three Forest Service campgrounds along the river. Little boating takes place below Maple Falls due to the slow current and more frequent log problems. Near the town of Deming the North, Middle, and South Forks of the Nooksack join, and the combined waters flow gently to the Pacific Ocean near Bellingham.

Expert boaters can attempt a Class V gauntlet known as **Horseshoe Bend** just upstream from Douglas Fir Campground. Here the Nooksack thunders through a dramatic mile-long gorge which, though remarkably lush and beautiful, is also very demanding and dangerous. The gradient is extremely steep: the river drops a total of 150' feet in just over a mile. Prospective boaters—**experts only**—should scout the gorge carefully from a trail along the north bank before considering this section. Logs lodged in rapids here could prove lethal.

North Nooksack River Guide

Put in on the right bank at the upstream end of Douglas Fir Campground, just below the Highway 542 bridge. Just above the bridge is a Class III rapid that is the site of an annual slalom competition.

In the first two miles below Douglas Fir the Nooksack drops at 60 ft./mi. through a narrow gorge with almost continuous Class III action. Noteworthy spots in this stretch include **LANDSLIDE (III)** at mile 1.5, where a slide on the right forces the river left. At mile 1.8 Glacier Creek, a major tributary, enters on the left. Just downstream is **GALLOP (III)** with a big reversal at the bottom right. Watch for a wrap rock about a mile below Glacier Creek.

Below this point the valley opens, the gradient eases, and the Nooksack throttles back to Class II for the remainder of the run. The river now splits frequently around islands, and the wider channel affords excellent mountain views for the remainder of the run. Highway 542 crosses the river at mile 4.5 (**alternate access**), just below the mouth of Canyon Creek on the right.

The common **take-out** is 3.5 miles downstream at an unmarked site on the right bank, about three quarters of a mile below the mouth of Boulder Creek on the right. Though this access is on private land, it has been commonly used by boaters for years.

Rivers of the Olympic Peninsula

If you think you've seen every river under the sun ... if you've run the Escalante and the Yaak and the San Francisco and you're wondering if there's anything left to explore ... then it's time to head for the Olympic Peninsula, the West's final whitewater frontier.

The wettest place in the continental U.S., the peninsula also has the West's greatest concentration of whitewater: dozens of boatable rivers in an area slightly larger than Yellowstone National Park. A whitewater junkie could spend an entire season here, sampling everything from expert runs down glacier-fed torrents to placid floats through towering rain forests, and still not exhaust the possibilities.

The Olympic Peninsula, an isolated spur roughly 60 miles wide by 80 long surrounded on three and a half sides by water, lies just west of Seattle and south of Vancouver Island. The peninsula is most famous as the site of Olympic National Park, which forms a protective circle around the snow-capped Olympic Mountains. Unlike the Cascades, the young, jagged Olympics are not volcanic; they are the product of an ongoing collision between two massive tectonic plates. Their highest point, Mt. Olympus, rises 7,965' above the nearby Pacific Ocean.[1]

Despite their moderate elevations, the Olympics catch enormous quantities of moisture from air streaming in off the Pacific. Mt. Olympus is the wettest spot in the continental U.S., with some 200" (over 16') of average annual precipitation. The heaviest rain and snowfall is on the southwest flank of the mountains, while the leeward side basks in a relatively sunny rain shadow: Sequim on the northeast coast gets only 17" of rain in an average year.

Water defines and shapes the peninsula, with rivers radiating from the central mountains like the spokes of a wheel. In the alpine region rivers carry meltwater from glaciers and snowfields, while at lower elevations they brim with a constant surplus of clean, clear rainwater.[2] The amount of fresh water running off the peninsula is staggering: from a basin of just 250 square miles, the Hoh River gathers as much water as the Canyon Country's San Juan collects from nearly 25,000 square miles. The 50-mile-long Queets River, largest on the peninsula, carries as much water as the combined Green and Yampa Rivers in Dinosaur National Monument.

The pristine Olympic rivers are famous for their rich runs of salmon and other migratory fish. Anglers flock to the remaining undammed rivers, in many cases outnumbering whitewater boaters. Ongoing efforts to restore one of the peninsula's fisheries could result in the historic removal of two major dams on the Elwha.

Before whites settled here, local tribes thrived on the natural bounty of migrating fish. Most Olympic rivers carry Indian names—usually that of the nearest tribe—and the list includes some of the most unusual and intriguing names in the West: Duckabush, Dosewallips, Soleduck, Humptulips, Wynoochee, and so on.

Rivers on the west side of the peninsula, like the Hoh and the Queets, cut through the heart of one of the world's rare temperate rain forests. The combination of heavy rainfall, coastal fog, and low elevation produces a profusion of vegetation unmatched outside the tropics. A towering canopy of Sitka spruce, Douglas-fir, western hemlock, and western red cedar intercepts almost all direct sunlight. Below, a jungle-like understory of mosses, ferns, creepers, and vines thrives in perpetual twilight.

For river runners the profusion of trees also means **an abundance of log hazards.** No stream on the peninsula is free of them; on many they present a much greater hazard than the whitewater. Always scout when in doubt, and inquire locally before launching—especially if you plan to use a boat that would be tough to portage. Additional challenges include cold water, typically wet weather, and limited information on flows.

---

[1] Namesake of the Greek mountain, this inspiring peak almost had a decidedly less lofty title. In the 1830's Pacific Northwest residents lobbied unsuccesfully to have the Cascade Range relabeled the President Range, with prominent peaks taking the names of chief executives. Under this plan Mt. Olympus—althought not part of the Cascades—was to be renamed Mt. Van Buren.

[2] Efforts are currently under way to win National Wild and Scenic River protection for many rivers on the Peninsula. For more information on these and other local river conservation issues contact the Olympic Rivers Council and/or the Rivers Council of Washington. See appendix for addresses.

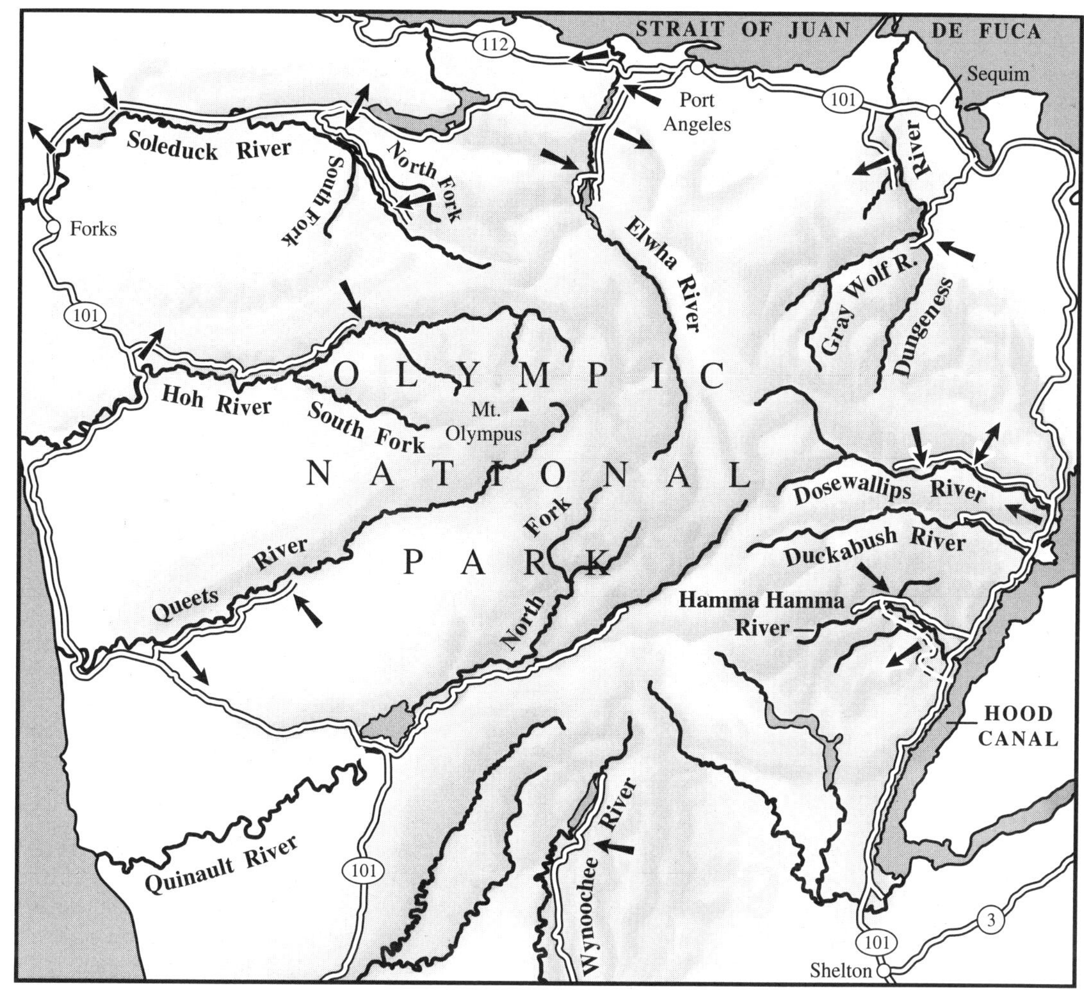

Rivers of the Olympic Peninsula

The rivers we discuss in this section are only a tiny sample of the Olympic Peninsula's vast whitewater offerings—not to mention the numerous flatwater floats. For more, consult Gary Korb's excellent book, *A Paddler's Guide to the Olympic Peninsula,* which covers 69 runs on 41 rivers. Because roads penetrate only a short way into the National Park, many miles of Olympic rivers remain largely unexplored. Seasoned veterans willing to pack in hardshell boats or lightweight inflatables can use the park's excellent trail system to explore new runs.

Managing Agency: (1) Olympic National Park, 600 East Park Ave., Port Angeles, WA 98362, (206) 452-4501. (2) Olympic NF, 1835 Black Lake Blvd., Olympia, WA 98512-5623, (206) 956-2300.

Permits: Not required on any Olympic river.

Commercial Raft Trips: Only on a few of the best-known rivers. For references contact Olympic National Park; and/or Chamber of Commerce, 121 E. Railroad, Port Angeles, WA 98362, (206) 452-2363; and/or Forks Visitors Center, (800) 443-6757.

Guides and References:

- Korb, *Paddler's Guide to the Olympic Peninsula.* By far the best source. 69 runs.
- North, *Washington Whitewater.* Elwha, Soleduck.
- Huser, *Paddle Routes of Western Washington.* Lower Hoh, Lower Wynochee, Queets.
- LeRoux & Rudersdorf, *Paddle Washington.* Lower Soleduck, Queets, others.

Maps:

- **USGS:** *Olympic National Park and Vicinity* covers the following at 1:125,000: Hoh, Soleduck, Elwha, Dungeness, Queets.
- **USFS:** *Olympic NF.*

Hoh River

Difficulty: II.
Length: 21 miles. Shorter and longer runs possible.
Gradient: 20 ft./mi.
Put-in: Hoh Ranger Station (590').
Take-out: Oxbow Recreation Area (170').
Drainage Area and Average Annual Discharge: 253 sq. mi. and 1,841,000 af.
Season: All year, though sometimes too low late August–October. More water below the South Fork confluence (mile 6).
Flow Information: NOAA Whitewater Hotline, (206) 526-8530; flow "below Tom Creek," near put-in (does not include South Fork).
Wilderness: No.
Logistics: The **take-out** at Oxbow Recreation Area is just northeast of the U.S. 101 bridge over the Hoh. To reach the **put-in,** drive 1.5 miles north on 101, turn right on Upper Hoh Road, and drive 18 miles to Hoh Ranger Station. **Alternate access** just inside the National Park below the South Fork.

The free-flowing Hoh River, famous for its salmon and steelhead, springs from glaciers on the north face of Mt. Olympus and runs 55 miles west to the Pacific. Even in summer the river water is ice cold and tinted milky gray by glacial flour. The Hoh Rain Forest is one of Olympic National Park's top attractions. The west-facing valley funnels moist air off the Pacific, producing 150" to 180" of annual rainfall.

Most boating takes place in the 21 miles from Hoh Ranger Station to U.S. Highway 101. **Logs are by far the biggest hazard.** The first six miles to the South Fork are often choked with log jams, so portages are likely. An alternate put-in is just below the South Fork near the National Park boundary. Below the confluence the valley widens, the current eases, log hazards diminish, and ranches occasionally come into view. Class II rapids occur sporadically through the run, which also has some long flat stretches.

There are flatwater runs on the broad lower river below the U.S. 101 bridge. Those making the full 14-mile run to the ocean need permission to take out on the Hoh Reservation at the mouth. The Hoh tribe once occupied the entire lower valley. Traditionally, the tribe avoided the upper river, believing it to be the realm of Thunderbird, a great god who sometimes sent icefalls crashing down from Mt. Olympus.

Boaters may enjoy hiking the rain forest around Hoh Ranger Station. A trail ascends the Hoh all the way to its headwaters. Adventurers with lightweight boats can do pack-in trips on the upper river, risking severe log hazards and the wrath of Thunderbird. (Guidebook author Gary Korb reports that many Class V sections of the Upper Hoh have already been explored.)

Soleduck River

1. **Sol Duc Hot Springs (1,610') to Fibreboard Bridge (1,020').** IV5; 9 miles; 65 ft./mi.

2. **Fibreboard Bridge to Hatchery (380').** III; 24 miles; 27 ft./mi. Shorter runs possible.

3. **Hatchery to Salmon Drive (260').** II+; 8 miles; 14 ft./mi.

Season: Nov.–July. Varies with weather. Shorter season for Run 1. **Wilderness:** No.
Logistics: Salmon Drive turns off U.S. 101 about 6.5 miles west of Sappho. To reach the **Hatchery,** turn south off U.S. 101 about 0.3 mile west of Sappho.

To reach **Fibreboard Bridge,** turn south off U.S. 101 4 miles west of Fairholm onto South Fork Soleduck Road and drive upriver 3 miles.

To reach the **Hot Springs,** turn south off 101 onto Sol Duc Hot Springs Road some two miles west of Fairholm.

Alternate accesses just off U.S. 101 include Bear Creek Boat Ramp, 2.5 miles east of Sappho, and Klahowya Campground, midway between Sappho and Fairholm.

The crystal-clear Soleduck River flows through a lush rain forest in the northwestern corner of the Olympic Peninsula. From 5,000' peaks on High Divide the Soleduck winds westward to the Pacific. Rich runs of steelhead and salmon draw both eagles and fishermen to the lower reaches. The Indian name, sometimes spelled Sol Duc, translates as "sparkling water"—a reference to hot springs on the upper river which local tribespeople believed held medicinal powers.[1]

The uppermost run listed here is for adventurous experts only. The stretch beginning at Sol Duc Hot Springs includes numerous portages around log jams in the first couple of miles, long sections of Class IV rapids, and a thundering Class V drop called **SALMON CASCADE** (mile 6) where coho salmon leap in late summer. A road follows the right bank, allowing scouting and providing alternate accesses. Many boaters launch below Salmon Cascade. Near the end of the run the North and South Forks of the Soleduck enter, boosting flows on downstream runs.

Below Fibreboard Bridge is intermediate water. U.S. 101 follows these lower sections, providing easy access but remaining fairly unobtrusive thanks to dense vegetation. Alternate accesses include Klahowya Campground and Bear Creek Boat Ramp, 9 and 18 miles below Fibreboard Bridge, respectively. A low dam at the hatchery divides the two lower runs. Boaters can combine them by navigating a boat chute at the dam; they should scout this slot carefully for debris or other hazards.

Boating continues below the Salmon Drive take-out; downstream is mostly Class I+ water with a few rocky riffles. The lower Soleduck is very popular with anglers, both on shore and in drift boats; river runners should strive to avoid conflicts. Fishing use is heaviest below Klahowya Campground from late spring through midsummer and again in winter.

A side excursion leads to dramatic Soleduck Falls, where the upper river plunges down a narrow slot deep in the rain forest. Drive to the end of Sol Duc Hot Springs Road, then hike in about a mile.

[1]Our information on the meaning of this and several other local river names comes from James Phillips, *Washington State Place Names.*

Elwha River

1. Upper Elwha Dam (400') to USGS gauge (225').
III4; 4.5 miles; 35 ft./mi.

2. Aldwell Reservoir (90') to River Mouth (0').
II; 5 miles; 18 ft./mi.

Drainage Area and Average Annual Discharge: 269 sq. mi. and 1,095,000 af.
Season: All year, but flows are fairly low in late summer.
Flow Information: NOAA Whitewater Hotline, (206) 526-8530.
Wilderness: No.
Logistics: *Run 1:* From the east end of the U.S. 101 bridge over the Elwha (southwest of Port Angeles), turn south for nearly a mile, then turn right on a spur road to the gauging station **take-out.** To reach the **put-ins,** continue up the main road 3.5 miles to a bridge. (Alternate put-ins here or at Altaire Campground just downstream). To reach the **upper put-in,** continue ¾ mile to a spur road with a sign "Authorized Vehicles Only." Boaters usually carry down this road to the river.

Run 2: A steep trail leads to the **put-in** at the base of Lower Elwha Dam, reached via a spur road off Washington Highway 112. The **take-out** is at the river's mouth at the end of Elwha Dike Road, reached via Highway 112 and Place Road.

From 6,000' headwaters east of Mt. Olympus, the Elwha runs north to the Strait of Juan de Fuca near Port Angeles. The river's lower reaches offer good rapids and fine scenery. Trails follow the steep upper river deep into Olympic National Park. The watershed is moist but not as wet as the west side of the Peninsula.

The Elwha[1] is best known for its dams: two controversial concrete plugs in the lower reaches of this otherwise free-flowing river. The dams devastated the river's salmon and steel-

[1]The river's name is from an Indian word for elk, which winter in the valley.

head fisheries, which at one time produced runs estimated at 400,000 fish annually, and destroyed what may have been the Peninsula's best extended whitewater run.

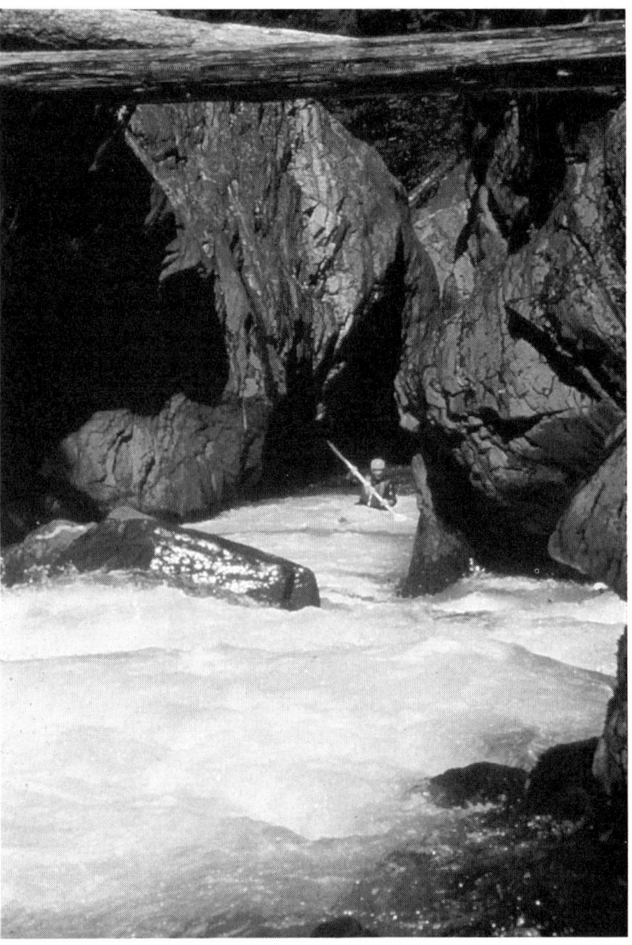

Elwha River *Gary Korb*

The Elwha Today

Upper Run:[2] Below Upper Elwha Dam the river drops steeply through a scenic, mile-long gorge that holds the run's toughest drop, **GORGE RAPID (IV)**, a half mile below the put-in around a sharp left bend. Scout this one from shore before launching (short hike off the shuttle road). Boaters can avoid this rapid by putting in a mile downstream at the bridge or Altaire Campground (see **Logistics**). Below the bridge is mostly Class II with a little Class III. The easier water lets boaters admire the lush forest, deep valley and mountain views. At mile 3.5 the river leaves the National Park, the valley widens and the current slows. **Take out** on the right at the gauging station (mile 4.5) or continue another mile to an alternate access at Elwha Resort (private, permission required) on the right below the U.S. 101 bridge. Be alert for log hazards on the entire run.

Lower Run: Below Lower Elwha Dam is a short float to the ocean. Though not recommended for large rafts due to the difficult put-in, the Lower Elwha is ideal for kayaks. In the first mile paddlers enjoy mild rapids in a narrow canyon. Then comes a quick drop over a low weir, followed by three miles of flatwater to the ocean.

The Elwha of the Future

With a little luck, the Elwha's dams may soon fall victim to the wrecker's ball. The Elwha may again flow free, fish may again run upriver, and whitewater enthusiasts may for the first time see five miles of reclaimed river and enjoy an uninterrupted 15-mile float to the sea.

The dams' only purpose is to generate one third of the electricity needed by a pulp mill in Port Angeles. The dams provide no flood control and no water storage. The 100'-high Lower Dam was built in 1912, while the 200'-high Upper Elwha Dam, also known as Glines Canyon Dam, was built in 1926. Neither dam has a fish ladder.

In 1987, eco-saboteurs from the environmental group Earth First! made headlines by painting "Free The Elwha!" on the upper dam. In 1990 the National Park Service, U.S. Fish and Wildlife Service, and Bureau of Indian Affairs declared that the dams should be removed to restore fish runs. In 1991 the Department of the Interior followed suit. The economic and aesthetic benefits of tearing down the dams far outweigh the costs. The restored fishery and whitewater run would have enormous recreational value, while the Elwha Klallam Indians, who once harvested the river's bounty of fish, could reclaim a former way of life.[3]

[2]Gary Korb's guide book describes a memorable Class V hike-in run upstream from Upper Elwha Dam.

[3]To help, contact Friends of the Earth, (206) 633-1661; Rivers Council of Washington; or Olympic Rivers Council (see appendix for addresses and phones).

Dungeness River

Difficulty: III+. **Gradient:** 55 ft./mi.
Length: 6 miles.
Put-in: Dungeness Forks Campground (805').
Take-out: Fish Hatchery (480').
Drainage Area and Average Annual Discharge: 156 sq. mi. and 282,600 af.
Season: Nov.—June. **Wilderness:** Yes.
Logistics: To reach the **take-out,** follow U.S. 101 to the bridge over the Dungeness west of Sequim. Some 300 yards west of the bridge, turn south on Taylor Cutoff, drive almost 3 miles, jog left on May Road, then turn right on Hatchery Road and drive a mile to the hatchery. Ask permission to take out here. To reach the **put-in,** follow 101 east from Sequim about 3 miles, drive south on Palo Alto Road about 8 miles, then follow signs to Forks Campground. Launch on the Gray Wolf River immediately above the Dungeness confluence.

The Dungeness River watershed, driest on the Peninsula, lies in a strong rain shadow northeast of the Olympic Mountains. The river's headwater peaks rise 6,000' to 7,000' but receive a relatively light dusting of snow. The town of Sequim (pronounced "Skwim") near the river's mouth has an average annual rainfall of just 17", and the Dungeness' year-round average flow is less than 400 cfs.

Fortunately, the river does rise to higher levels, primarily during winter storms and spring snowmelt. The best time for boating is usually late spring. Trips begin at the confluence of the Dungeness and its largest tributary, the Gray Wolf River. From here the Dungeness runs swiftly north down one of the few wilderness canyons on the peninsula. The shuttle road does not parallel the river.

The Dungeness flows through a deep, forested valley for six miles below the put-in. Boaters face intermediate whitewater and **numerous log hazards.** Several portages will probably be necessary—a fact which, combined with the relatively skimpy flows, makes this run best suited to kayaks and small inflatables.

The mouth of Canyon Creek on the left at mile 5.5 signals the end of the canyon and the approach of the **take-out** on the left at a fish hatchery. Two irrigation diversions in the final mile attest to the semi-arid local climate.

Dosewallips River

1. Elkhorn CG (680') to USFS Road 2620 (260').
V; 5.5 miles; 75 ft./mi.

2. Road 2620 to River Mouth (0').
III; 6.5 miles; 40 ft./mi.

Season: November–early July.
Wilderness: No.
Logistics: The **lower take-out** is at Dosewallips State Park, just south of the U.S. 101 bridge over the river near Brinnon. Upstream access is via Dosewallips Road, which turns east off U.S. 101 about ¾ mile north of the 101 bridge. Drive upriver 6 miles to the Road 2620 turnoff, then turn south for about 200 yards to the bridge. This access is quite steep; an alternate access is a couple of hundred yards past the bridge on the left. To reach the Elkhorn Campground **put-in,** return to Dosewallips Road and continue 5 miles upriver.

The Dosewallips River[1] drains 6,000' and 7,000' peaks near the eastern edge of Olympic National Park and runs east into Hood Canal, a long inland finger of the Pacific. A trail follows the steep upper river all the way to its headwaters. The lower 12 miles, outside the National Park, offer expert to intermediate boating in a deep, forested valley. Be alert for **log hazards** on all runs.

[1]The river is named for a character in local Indian mythology who was transformed into a mountain near the river's headwaters.

Upper Run: The upper **experts-only** run of the Dosewallips drops 180' in the first two miles. A few hundred yards below the put-in lies the toughest rapid, **THE MAZE (V)**, a long series of steep drops that many elect to portage. Downstream the gradient and difficulty ease slightly, only to increase again around mile 5. Just above the Road 2620 bridge take-out, the river plunges through **THE PINCH (IV)**, a constricted slot that poses a bridging hazard for kayaks and could prove too narrow for most rafts.

Lower Run: Below Road 2620 the valley widens somewhat and the gradient diminishes. The first stretch below the bridge holds most of this section's more challenging rapids. Three miles below the bridge, Rocky Brook enters on the left. Just downstream, the river bends right and plunges into a lovely gorge with several good rapids. As the gorge opens, the rapids fade and the Dosewallips flows easily through an open valley for two miles to the ocean.

Hamma Hamma River

Difficulty: III4+ **Gradient:** 45 ft./mi.
Length: 4.5 miles. **Wilderness:** No.
Put-in: Cabin Creek Bridge (555').
Take-out: Above the gorge (350').
Drainage Area: 51 sq. mi. near put-in.
Season: Nov.–mid-June. No large rafts.
Logistics: Follow U.S. 101 to the intersection with Hamma Hamma Road, about two miles north of the 101 bridge over the river mouth. Drive upriver about 6 miles; not far beyond Hamma Hamma CG, bear left to the **put-in** at Cabin Creek bridge. To reach the **take-out**, continue across the bridge, drive downriver just under 4 miles, then turn hard left onto a rough dirt road that descends a little over a half mile to the river. **Scout this take-out carefully; an unrunnable gorge is downstream.**

From 6,000' peaks along the eastern edge of Olympic National Park, the Hamma Hamma makes a short but very steep descent to Hood Canal, a fjord-like finger of the Pacific. The section described here is sandwiched between unrunnable gorges; just below the take-out, the river plummets 300' in less than a mile through cataracts that even salmon cannot leap. The river's Indian name means "stinky stinky"—presumably referring to dying fish trapped at the base of the lower gorge.

The Hamma Hamma is a challenging, technical river best suited for small craft. Be alert for **log hazards.** At the put-in the river is narrow and shallow, but Jefferson Creek adds substantial flow at mile 2. Below the creek lies the roughest water: from mile 3 to mile 4 are several difficult rapids including **U-TURN (IV–V)**, located just below a left bend. This long, steep rapid may require a difficult portage on the right. A half mile downstream is the **mandatory take-out** on the right, **just above an unrunnable gorge.** Boaters considering the Hamma Hamma should consult Gary Korb's guide book (listed earlier) and contact local river runners.

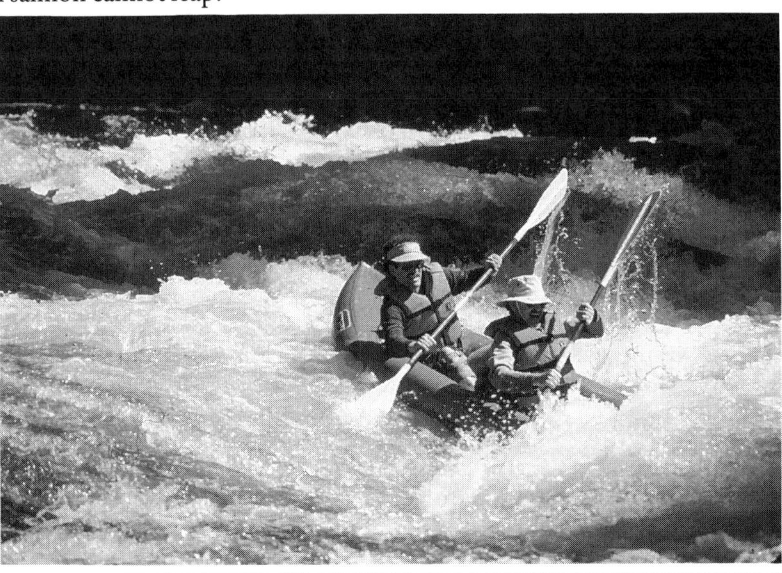

Inflatable kayak (IK-2) *Jock Montgomery*

Wynoochee River

Difficulty: III5p first 11 miles; I+ thereafter.
Length: 31 miles. Normally divided into shorter trips.
Gradient: 15 ft./mi.
Put-in: Wynoochee Dam (640').
Take-out: Carter Creek (155').
Drainage Area: 74 sq. mi at mile 11.
Average Discharge: 600,000 af.
Season: All year, but often very low in late summer. Dam-controlled.
Special Hazards: Portage at fish dam. New rapid formed by 1986 landslide.
Wilderness: No.
Logistics: About 10 miles east of Aberdeen, at the town of Montesano, turn north (upriver) onto Wynoochee Valley Road. Some 5.5 miles past the Wishkah-Wynoochee Road turnoff, the Carter Creek **take-out** is on the left. To reach the **put-in**, continue upriver, turn left at signs for Wynoochee Dam, drive to the river, and put in on the left bank below the bridge. Many alternate accesses; refer to Gary Korb's guide (listed earlier).

The Wynoochee River drains a moderate-elevation watershed south of Olympic National Park and offers a variety of runs through scenic gorges and lush valleys. The upper reaches are small and generally best suited to narrow, nimble craft. Releases from Wynoochee Dam usually maintain boatable flows year-round, though by late summer flows can get as low as the minimum release of 200 cfs.

The 31 miles briefly covered here can be divided into several sections using alternate accesses, including more than those mentioned here. The first stretch, from the bridge below Wynoochee Dam (mile 0) to a fish dam at mile 2, offers Class II water in a scenic gorge. Boaters can take out above the dam or portage it and continue downstream.

The next five miles are mild and meandering. One **alternate access** is on the left bank at mile 6. Below "The Oxbow," a meander at mile 7, the river plunges into a narrow, spectacular gorge filled with steep Class III rapids and one bigger drop. Just below the entrance is a very difficult rapid formed by a landslide in 1986. At last report this was a Class V, but it may change at any time. Scout carefully and **consider portaging.** The gorge continues to about mile 11, where a gauging station on the right bank marks an **alternate access** on the left. Downstream the river is placid Class I+ in a broad valley. For information on the lower river, refer to Verne Huser, *Paddle Routes of Western Washington.*

Queets River

Difficulty: II. **Gradient:** 15 ft./mi.
Length: 12 miles. Shorter trips possible.
Put-in: Queets Campground (280').
Take-out: Below Lyman Rapids (85').
Drainage Area and Average Annual Discharge: 445 sq. mi. and 3,084,000 af.
Season: Glacial melt provides minimum flows year-round. Low in late summer.
Wilderness: No.
Logistics: Some 7.5 miles east of the U.S. 101 bridge over the Queets, turn north onto Queets River Road. After two miles the road approaches the left bank, marking the **take-out** two miles below Lyman Rapids. To reach the **put-in,** continue upriver 12 miles to Queets CG. There are two good intermediate accesses along the way (see below).

The Queets, largest of the Olympic Peninsula rivers, rises among glaciers on the south face of Mt. Olympus and flows southwest to the Pacific. The river cuts through the heart of the rain forest, where some 150" to 200" of annual precipitation produce enormous runoff from a relatively small drainage. The Queets' renowned runs of steelhead, salmon, and cutthroat trout draw throngs of anglers and many fishing dories.

Olympic National Park protects almost all of the Queets, but only a narrow corridor of park land shelters the lower reaches described here. The landscape is a contrast of pristine rain forest in the foreground and clear cuts in the background. The protected strip is impressive and harbors abundant wildlife, however, and

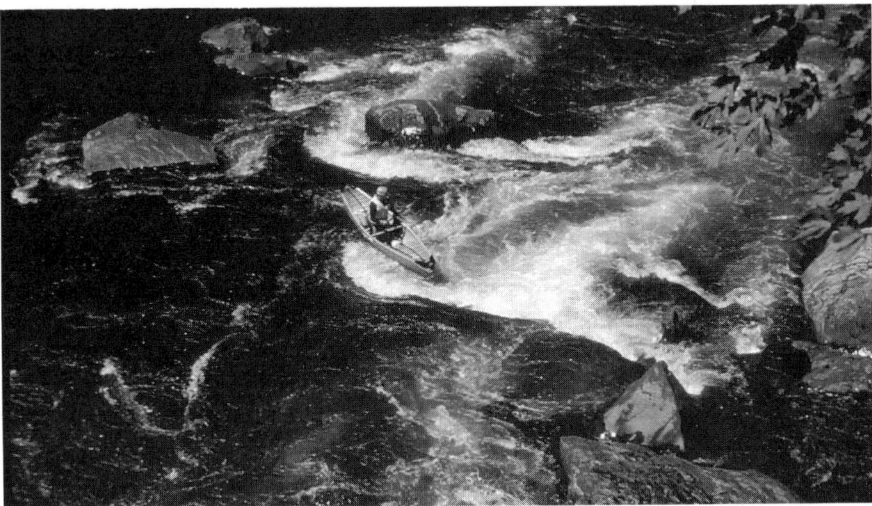

Whitewater canoe — Dave Ewoldt

launch above or below the rapid. The other rocky spot, **LYMAN RAPIDS,** is at mile 10 just below the mouth of Tacoma Creek on the right. Be alert for **log hazards,** which sometimes block the main channel. Inquire locally, especially before launching large boats that would be hard to portage. **Intermediate access** is possible at Streater Crossing (mile 6) and River View (mile 8), both on the left bank. Boating is prohibited on the last section of river through the Quinault Indian Reservation. The river is named for the Quaitso Indian tribe.

the heavy vegetation helps screen the shuttle road. To see untouched rain forest, hike up the trail above the put-in.

The run from Queets Campground (mile 0) to Hartzell Creek (mile 12) has two Class II rapids and miles of Class I+. The first rough spot, **SAM'S RAPID,** is right at the put-in; boaters can scout first and decide whether to

In June 1984 Paul Thompson arrived from Las Vegas for some boating. Since I had to work that week, we ran some Olympic rivers in the evenings. I told him about how I'd portaged the "U-Turn" on a solo run of the Hamma Hamma and how I wanted to go back and run it.

We arrived at the put-in about 6 p.m. with hours of daylight left, so we decided to walk the four-mile shuttle after the run. We played our way down, making the most of this beautiful little river. Scouting the "U-Turn" isn't easy; it probably took us half an hour. We decided on our routes, climbed into our boats, and headed down. Once through the three drops of the "U," I started to surf at the bottom. Paul wanted to surf, too, and tried to eddy out, but he was swept into the wall and knocked over. He fell out and swam the rest of the gorge. When he got to shore, he was without his paddle. It had SUNK! We could see it through the clear water, lying on the bottom.

We probed at it with some sticks, but the water was about 15 feet deep and fairly swift. Paul decided to dive for it. His first try was comical: he went upstream, dived from a rock, and bobbed along the surface in his wetsuit and life jacket. So he removed his life jacket, found about a 25-pound rock, and dived in head first with it. He went straight to the bottom, released the rock, and groped around unsuccessfully for his paddle. But after a few more tries Paul had his method worked out: he could just walk along the bottom holding a big rock. The trouble was that by this time, it was so dark we couldn't see anything.

I rummaged through the driftwood and found a flat piece of cedar and a branch suitable for a shaft. I split the branch and inserted the flat piece, then lashed them together with rope. It worked. We paddled the last mile in the dark, portaging the chute above the take-out.

When we got back to the car it was nearly midnight. I got home and went to bed at 2:30 a.m. When I got up at 6:00 a.m. to go to work, I had to laugh—because tonight after work, "we're going to go run the Dosewallips!"

—Gary Korb

More Western Rivers

Idaho and the Northern Rockies

Moyie River

Difficulty: II+ first 13 miles, IV- last 7 miles.
Length: 20 miles. Shorter runs possible.

Along with the North Fork of the Flathead in Montana, the lovely but little-known Moyie is the northernmost run in this guide. The Moyie is a small, short-season river that rises in southern British Columbia and flows southward into Idaho. After crossing into the U.S., the Moyie runs for some 25 miles through the Purcell Mountains along the eastern edge of the Idaho panhandle. Then the river stills behind Moyie Falls Dam before joining the mighty Kootenai near Bonners Ferry, Idaho.

The Moyie divides conveniently into two runs. The easier upper run begins at the Copper Creek Campground **put-in** just south of the Canadian border. To reach this access, turn east off U.S. 95 just north of the bridge over the Moyie (a mile south of the border) and drive downstream about a mile and a half to the campground.

For a dozen miles below Copper Creek, the Moyie drops at 20 ft./mi. through relatively easy intermediate whitewater in a lush, gradually deepening valley. An unpaved road and the Union Pacific Railroad follow the river through this section, crossing it several times. This road also serves as the shuttle road. Common **take-outs** are at the Meadow Creek Bridge (mile 13) or a mile downstream on the right at Meadow Creek Campground (USFS).

Meadow Creek Campground serves as the **put-in** for the more difficult lower Moyie run. Downstream the river rushes for seven miles through a narrower and rockier canyon at a gradient of about 40 ft./mi. The whitewater rates about Class III+ to IV, depending on flow, with two rapids standing out above the rest. Two miles after passing the mouth of Deer Creek on the left, boaters encounter the first big drop at the abandoned **EILEEN DAM.** The dam has been breached on the left side, but it still creates a challenging rapid. This drop should be scouted, though the steep canyon walls may make this difficult. The second big rapid, **HOLE-IN-THE-WALL,** should also be scouted. The **take-out** is on the right at the backwaters of the small lake formed by Moyie Falls Dam.

The Moyie is normally runnable during a fairly short snowmelt season in May and June. Idaho DWR, (208) 327-7900, may be able to quote flows for the gauge near Eastport. For more information, refer to Amaral, *Idaho: The Whitewater State* or Moore and McClaran, *Idaho Whitewater.* Also contact the USFS, Bonners Ferry RD, Route 4, Box 4860, Bonners Ferry, ID 83805; (208) 267-5561. The best map for the run is the Forest Service's *Idaho Panhandle National Forest (Kanisku NF).*

Yaak River

1. Spread Creek to Yaak Falls.
II–III; 16 miles.

2. Yaak Falls to Kootenai River.
V; 9 miles.

The Yaak, one of the West's least-known rivers, carves its course through the remote northwestern corner of Montana. From headwaters along the Canadian border, the Yaak flows southwest toward its confluence with the Kootenai River near the Montana-Idaho state line. Like its sister stream the Moyie ten to 20 miles west in the Idaho panhandle, the Yaak tumbles through a lush, densely forested canyon in the Purcell Mountains. Also like the Moyie, the Yaak begins gently but becomes much steeper and more difficult as it approaches the deep Kootenai valley.

In addition to boating, the Yaak offers excellent fishing for rainbow and brook trout, good camping at USFS campgrounds along the river, and scenic hiking on a number of USFS trails. Though the river's name conjures up images of woolly Himalayan beasts, according to Roberta Cheney, *Names on the Face of Montana,* it is an Indian word meaning "arrow." The Yaak is being considered for National Wild and Scenic River designation.

The Yaak is lightly used by kayakers and very rarely run by rafters. Boating is possible on the low-gradient upper river, but the most common runs are below Spread Creek, which enters the Yaak from the right some eight miles downstream from the remote riverside settlement of Yaak. Below Spread Creek the river turns south and the gradient increases.

The 16 miles from Spread Creek to Yaak Falls offer primarily Class II and III rapids with an average gradient of 25 ft./mi. The first two miles below Spread Creek and the last 3.5 miles from Seventeenmile Bridge to the falls are steeper than the rest of the run and hold most of the whitewater action. The final two miles above the falls drop 110', and some boaters may want to take out above this steep section. Those making the full run should **scout the take-out very carefully—Yaak Falls is beautiful but definitely unrunnable.** USFS Road 508 follows the right bank closely through this section, providing alternate accesses and an easy shuttle.

Below Yaak Falls the road leaves the right bank while the Yaak plunges down a spectacular nine-mile-long wilderness canyon. With a gradient of 91 ft./mi., **the lower Yaak is a difficult Class V run that should be attempted by experts only, and even they should be alert for possible portages.** The gorge, extremely narrow in places, continues all the way to the take-out. Boaters are committed once they launch; there is no access between the **put-in** (about a quarter mile below the falls on the right) and the **take-out** (at Yaak River Campground at the Kootenai confluence). The short shuttle is via U.S. 2 and USFS Road 508.

The Yaak is generally runnable in late spring and early summer, typically peaking in May. Beware of high water and possible **log hazards,** especially below Yaak Falls. For more information refer to Thompson, *Floating and Recreation on Montana Rivers,* consult the *Kootenai NF* map, and contact Three Rivers RD, 1437 North Highway 2, Troy, MT 59935; (406) 295-4693. For flow information, call the USGS, (406) 449-5263, and ask for the Yaak flow "near Troy."

Priest River

Difficulty: III-. **Length:** 44 miles.

The Priest traces a leisurely course through the lush glacial terrain of northern Idaho. From headwaters near the Canadian border the Priest flows south through the Selkirk Mountains near the western edge of the Idaho panhandle. Around the midpoint in its journey the river pauses in Priest Lake, one of the largest in Idaho. Below the lake the Priest meanders through 44 miles of gentle valley and scenic wetlands on the way to its confluence with the Pend Oreille River. Much of the run is through National and State Forest lands.

Despite the moderate terrain and mild gradient (7 ft./mi.), the Priest offers enjoyable whitewater. Rapids are few and widely spaced, but at least two spots rate up to Class III at higher flows. The river peaks in late spring, but small boats can run it into midsummer in most years. At lower water levels the rapids and riffles rate only Class II. Early autumn is an ideal floating time: flows increase as more water is released to lower the level of Priest Lake, and the forest puts on a brilliant show of fall color. Ask the Idaho DWR, (208) 327-7900, for the flow "at Priest River" (near the mouth).

Six public river accesses along the run allow a variety of one-day and overnight trips. The upper half of the river is generally more secluded than the lower section; lightly-used roads and an occasional house will be seen below the confluence with the East River, some 21 miles below the lake.

The best whitewater is in the short stretch from the **put-in** (a quarter mile below the outlet dam of Priest Lake) to Dickensheet Campground, a popular access on the left bank near mile 5. The largest rapid, **BINARCH (III)**, is located some two miles below the dam. Below Dickensheet the river is flatter, but includes three rapids of note: **CHIPMUNK (II)**, about 8.5 miles below the lake; **MCABEE FALLS (II)**, about 25 miles below the lake and just below a bridge over the river; and **EIGHTMILE (III-)**, near mile 31.

The **lowermost take-out** is at Priest River Recreation Area, near the Highway 2 bridge at the city of Priest River. To reach Dickensheet Campground, follow Idaho Highway 57 north some 22 miles, then bear right and drive a mile to the campground and bridge over the Priest. To reach the **uppermost put-in** just below the lake outlet, continue up Highway 57 some 3 miles past the Dickensheet turnoff. At least three alternate accesses are available. For more information contact Priest Lake Ranger Station, Kanisku NF, HCR5, Box 207, Priest River, ID 83856; (208) 443-2512. Be sure to request their free map-pamphlet, *Priest River Float Trips.* Also refer to the USFS *Idaho Panhandle National Forests (Kanisku NF)* map.

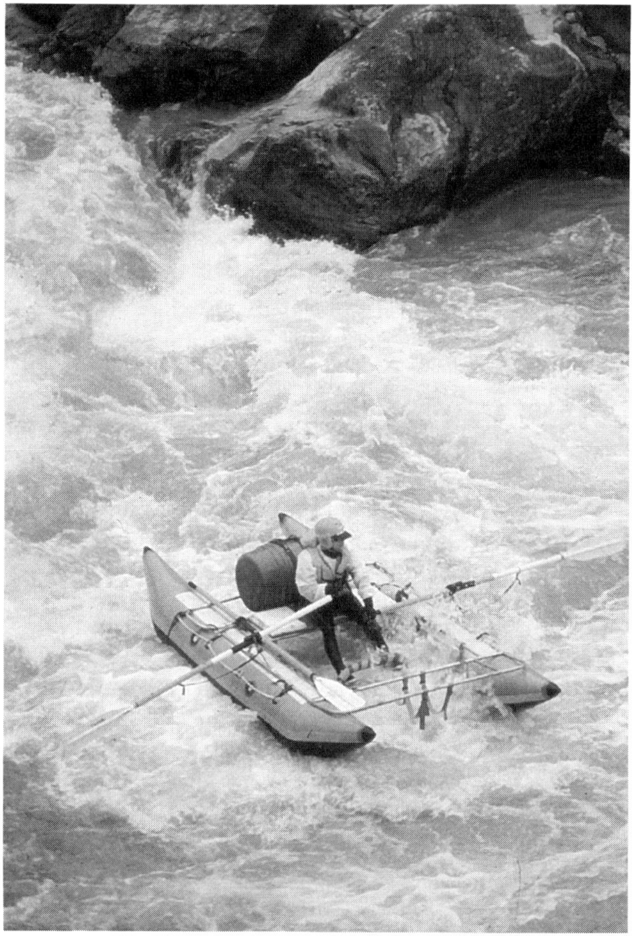

Cataraft *Dan Lewis*

Boise River

The Boise River offers backyard boating for river runners in Boise and southwestern Idaho. The river's three forks drain a large watershed east of the Idaho capital, carrying snowmelt from the jagged Sawtooth Range down to downtown Boise and, eventually, the Snake River. Three major dams flood sections of the river, and a fourth has been proposed, but several excellent free-flowing stretches remain.

South Fork

The most popular run on the Boise is a 16-mile Class III+ section of the South Fork that offers a long season due to late summer releases from Anderson Ranch Dam. The trip begins at Danskin Bridge, 11 miles below Anderson Ranch Dam, and ends at Neal Bridge just above Arrowrock Reservoir. The scenery is excellent in the river's narrow, rugged canyon cut into volcanic rock. The 26 ft./mi. gradient produces numerous Class II and easy Class III rapids, plus two larger drops, **RASPBERRY** (mile 9) and **DEVILS HOLE** (mile 10), which rate about Class III+ at moderate flows.

Though dirt roads are rarely far away, the South Fork's intimate canyon provides a near-wilderness feel. Boaters should get an early start for this long one-day run. Bring cold-weather gear, even in summer; the steep walls cast long shadows, and the water is icy. The shuttle is east of the river on Roads 189 (Upper Blacks Creek Road) and 113, which intersect near the small hamlet of Prairie. The river can be reached from I-84 to the west or U.S. 20 to the south. For details on accesses and shuttles, refer to the *Boise NF* map.

The South Fork usually has good flows during snowmelt runoff in spring and early summer, with a peak sometime in late May or early June. Flows then drop to low but usually still boatable levels in July and early August. Around mid-August, Anderson Ranch Dam begins releasing more water—usually about 1,600 cfs, the capacity of the dam's generators. The Idaho DWR tape, (208) 327-7865, has the flow below Anderson Ranch Dam.

Less experienced boaters can run 11 miles of mostly Class II- water just upstream from the section described above. This mild run begins at Anderson Ranch Dam and ends at Danskin Bridge (put-in for the standard run). Watch for one full Class II rapid a mile above the take-out.

North and Middle Forks

Though less popular than the South Fork, these tributaries offer good boating during spring snowmelt.[1] The North Fork is the more challenging run: eight miles of steep (60 ft./mi.) Class III+ to IV water from Black Rock Campground to the Middle Fork confluence. **Log jams** and a long, dusty shuttle keep use light on this scenic wilderness reach.

---

[1]A proposed dam threatens these sections in spite of a 1993 state law prohibiting the project. The Federal Energy Regulatory Commission, which is considering the proposal, sees the state's position as only advisory.

Below the confluence of the North and Middle Forks are eight miles of easy intermediate water—Class II+ to III at most flows—to Badger Creek Campground, not far above Arrowrock Reservoir. A dirt road follows this section, providing frequent access. With the combined flow of the two forks, this section has a longer season than the North Fork. Local boaters and guide books refer to this stretch as the Middle Fork of the Boise, but the USGS and the Idaho DWR consider it the main stem; so the DWR recording (see above) gives the flow for this section as "Boise River near Twin Springs."

For more information on all runs in the Boise system, refer to Amaral, *Idaho: The Whitewater State* and/or Moore and McClaran, *Idaho Whitewater.* A good local source of information is Idaho River Sports, 1521 N. 13th, Boise, ID 83702; (208) 336-4844.

Fall River

Difficulty: IVp.
Length: 21 miles. Shorter runs possible.

The Fall River rises in the southwestern corner of Yellowstone National Park. Fed largely by springs bubbling from porous volcanic rock, the river tumbles over waterfalls where it encounters fractures in the lava bedrock. From its forested upper reaches the Fall[2] descends westward to the semi-arid plains of southeastern Idaho, where it joins the Henrys Fork of the Snake.

Excellent scenery on the Fall ranges from a forested wilderness canyon in the upper reaches to a tight basalt gorge farther downstream. The first 12 miles are through Targhee National Forest, while land along the lower river is mostly private. Boating use is light, and the trout fishing is excellent. The Fall is being considered for National Wild and Scenic status.

Unfortunately, when a new, privately-owned "cash register" hydro project begins to produce electricity in 1994, it will divert 500 cfs from the river at Marysville (mile 9.5). This will reduce the season on the best stretch of the Fall, the Canyon Run, to five or six weeks of snowmelt runoff in an average year.

The undammed upper river normally has good flows from May to September. Runoff usually peaks in June. For flow information call the Idaho DWR, (208) 327-7900.

Because of several **mandatory portages** around waterfalls and diversion dams, the Fall is more popular with kayakers than with rafters. A 45 ft./mi. gradient keeps things busy. Much of the whitewater on the upper stretch comes in **unrunnable falls** which, along with **diversion dams and logs,** constitute the run's main hazards. The 21 miles described here can be divided at the "CCC bridge" at mile 15.

Put in at Cave Falls Campground just south of the Yellowstone Park boundary. Be prepared for **portages.** Three miles downstream is Cavern Falls, an easy portage on the left. At mile 6 is Sheep Falls, a longer portage on the right. Some boaters run the Yellowstone Canal Diversion Dam (mile 9.5), but it is more prudent to portage—an easy carry on the left.

At mile 14 make an easy portage on the left at the Marysville Diversion Dam. A mile below this dam is the **alternate access** at the "CCC Bridge" (also called "Squirrel Bridge" for the nearby hamlet of the same name).

Below the bridge the Fall enters the **Canyon Run,** a basalt gorge with rapids that are rougher than the runnable drops on the upper section. Watch for a **diversion dam at mile 5—portage** on the right. A mile below the dam is the Kirkham Bridge **take-out.** Water from the Marysville diversion is returned to the river through a penstock just upstream. Boaters can continue another six miles to the U.S. 20 bridge; however, this less scenic run involves two portages around diversion dams.

To reach all accesses, begin at U.S. 20 in Ashton. Drive east on Idaho Highway 47 for a mile, then south on Idaho 32 for a mile, then east on Road 1200 N for four miles to **Kirkham Bridge.** From here continue east five miles, then turn left on Road 4525 E and drive a mile to the **CCC Bridge.** To reach the **upper put-in,** continue north one mile, then turn right on Cave Falls Road and drive to the campground. Snow usually blocks this road until June.

For further information contact Ashton RD, Targhee NF, Ashton, ID 83420; (208) 652-7442. Consult the *Targhee NF* map and Amaral, *Idaho: The Whitewater State.*

[2]In local usage the river has always been called the "Fall." The USGS introduced some confusion by publishing maps naming it the "Falls." In 1992 the USGS rectified the error, so everyone now agrees on "Fall."

Bitch Creek

Difficulty: V-. More difficult at higher flows.
Length: 13 miles (last 5 miles on Teton River). Longer runs possible.

Bitch Creek is one of Idaho's most scenic expert runs. From headwaters in Wyoming's Teton Range, this small tributary of the Teton River tumbles westward down a lovely wilderness canyon. Also known as the North Fork of the Teton, Bitch Creek came by its name when early American trappers corrupted the original French name "Biche," or "Doe."

Most boating takes place in the creek's lower reaches, where it runs through a narrow, spectacular basalt gorge. The creek, generally boatable from May through July, usually peaks in June. This low-volume river is not only extremely technical, it also has a huge number of nasty **log jams and strainers which change position frequently. Several may require portage.** For these reasons, Bitch Creek is almost exclusively the domain of expert kayakers.

The most common run begins where Highway 32 crosses the creek southeast of Ashton. **Experts only.** The first eight miles are on Bitch Creek, while the final five are on the Teton River. The canyon is deep and secluded, with a strong wilderness flavor despite the proximity of agricultural lands above the rim on either side. Bitch Creek itself is fast and furious, with several long boulder-strewn Class IV to V rapids and an average gradient of 68 ft./mi. The whitewater reaches full throttle just over a mile into the run at **DRISCOLLS DROP.**

The five miles on the Teton are pool-and-drop, with a milder 25-ft./mi. gradient. This section was inundated by the ill-fated Teton Dam before its collapse in 1976; in fact, the Spring Hollow take-out is the site of a boat ramp built to serve the short-lived reservoir. The **take-out** can be hard to find, and the access road may require 4-wheel drive. From the put-in drive west on Highway 32 about 7.5 miles, then at a right-hand curve make a shallow left onto an unpaved road, drive southwest some 4 miles to the old boat ramp, and continue down to the river (if the road is passable).

Upper run: Boaters sometimes run the 11 miles above Highway 32, where the creek runs through a wooded canyon in Targhee National Forest. However, difficult access and constant log hazards keep use light on this section. The **put-in** involves a two-mile hike from the end of USFS Road 265 at Coyote Meadows. Boating begins where the trail reaches Bitch Creek at the confluence with Crater Creek. The rapids are milder than on the lower run, and the gradient is a less frenetic 55 ft./mi. However, boaters must be alert for **frequent log jams, many of which will require portage.** This section could be combined with the lower run.

For more information on Bitch Creek, see Moore and McClaran, *Idaho Whitewater,* and/or Amaral, *Idaho: The Whitewater State.* Also, contact the USFS (see **Fall River** above for address and phone). The *Targhee NF* map shows all shuttle roads and most of the creek.

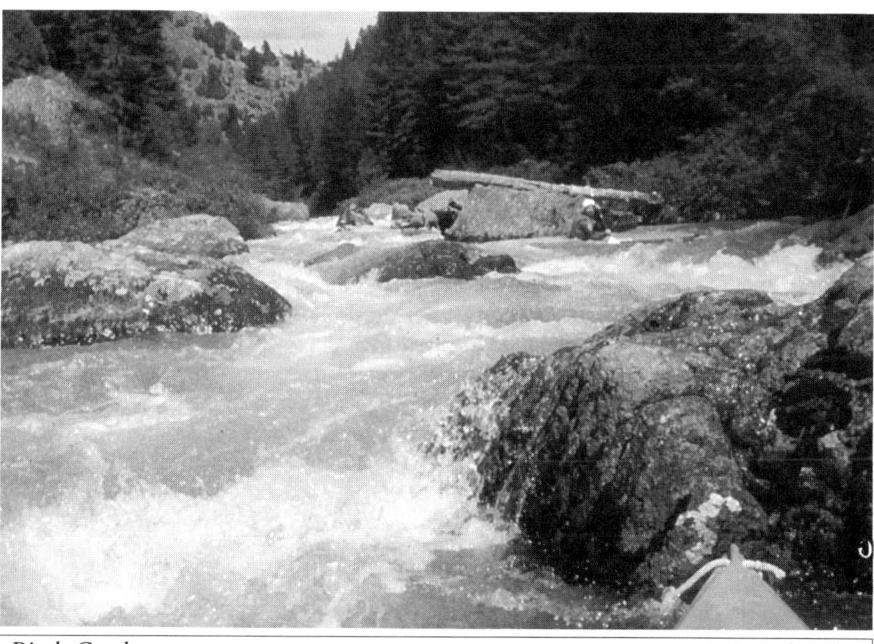
Bitch Creek — *Tom Whittaker*

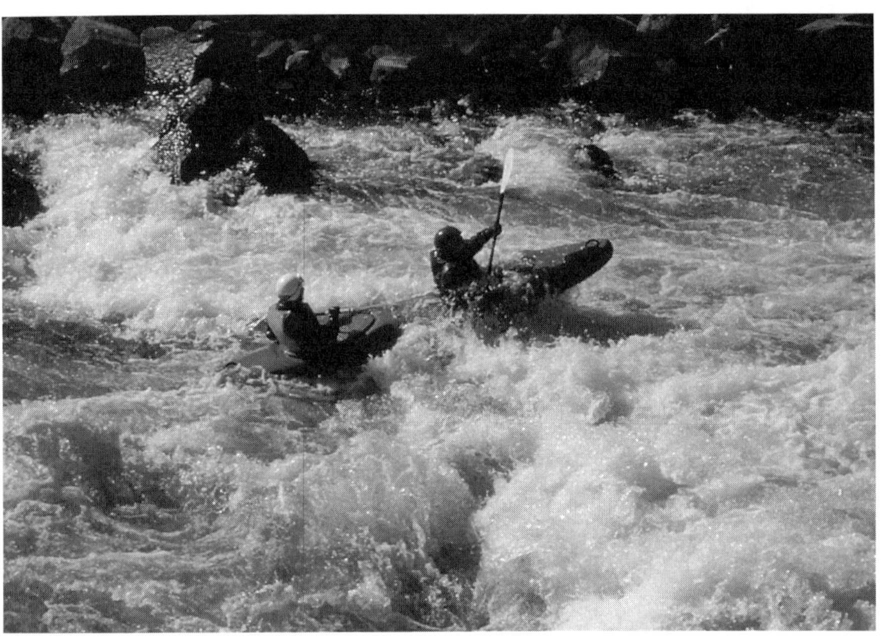

Duo Topolino (K-2) *Ron Lodders*

Clarks Fork of the Yellowstone

Difficulty: VI, IV.
Length: 25 miles in several shorter sections.

The Clarks Fork of the Yellowstone may be the most spectacular and difficult whitewater river in the West. Often called simply the Clarks Fork,[1] this major river cuts a chasm more than 4,000' deep in the Beartooth Mountains of northwestern Wyoming. The heart of the canyon is The Box, a sheer-walled defile just east of Yellowstone National Park where the river plunges 1,200 vertical feet in only six miles.

The Clarks Fork begins and ends in Montana. It rises on the south face of 12,799' Granite Peak, highest point in the state, and empties into the Yellowstone River near Billings. In between, the river loops southward into Wyoming,[2] and it is here that the big whitewater action lies.

The **put-in** for the uppermost run is at a turnout on Wyoming Highway 296 (Sunlight Basin Road) 2.5 miles southeast of the U.S. 212 junction. Class II floating is possible above this point, but numerous **log hazards** deter most boaters. The 2.5 miles from the highway turnout to Hunter Peak Campground are mostly Class III and IV, punctuated by two much bigger drops: the second rapid on this stretch is an **unrunnable narrows (mandatory portage)**, while a big Class V to V+ known as **ADRENALIN** waits near the end of the run. Most boaters **take out** at Hunter Peak Campground, though some continue another mile and a half to the Highway 296 bridge.

Below the Highway 296 bridge the Clarks Fork descends into a spectacular alpine canyon that echoes with the roar of major rapids. **Experts only.** The bridge serves as **put-in** for either of two runs: the 2.5-mile Honeymoon Run (sometimes called the Upper Honeymoon Run), or an 18-mile expedition through The Box itself. These runs are best attempted when flows have dropped to around 1,000 cfs at the highway bridge.

The short **Honeymoon Run** begins with several Class IV to IV+ rapids and advances to Class V and V+. About a mile and a half below the highway bridge, Beartooth Creek enters as a spectacular waterfall on the left. Half a mile below the creek are three big drops: **BIG NASTY,** a Class V–VI passage that is commonly portaged; **TRIXI** (V–V+); and **CRANDALL CREEK** (V-), located where Crandall Creek enters on the right. A quarter mile below Crandall Creek, a 4-wheel drive road off Highway 296 comes to within a couple of hundred yards of the right bank, offering a **possible take-out.** This difficult access marks the end of the (Upper) Honeymoon Run.

Only seasoned, daring experts should boat below this point. Anyone continuing down-

---

[1]The river is named for Captain William Clark of the Lewis and Clark expedition. It is often confused with the **Clark Fork** in western Montana (see Region I).

[2]In 1991 the Clarks Fork of the Yellowstone became Wyoming's first National Wild and Scenic River. Some 20 miles were designated, including the Honeymoon Run, the Box, and a bit of the lower river.

stream is committed to running The Box. Just downstream from this access point is a long mandatory portage on the right bank known as "The Green Monster." Boaters make this portage to avoid a **deadly, unrunnable stretch** about three quarters of a mile long called "The Corral Creek Strainer." (Experts who know the river well can run one short Class V drop before beginning the portage, but most boaters should begin the portage *immediately after the Upper Honeymoon Run take-out.*) **Missing the portage and continuing downstream would be fatal.**

Below this portage the river widens and flows easily for some six miles at an average gradient of less than 20 ft./mi. Then, ten miles downstream from the Highway 296 bridge, the Clarks Fork plunges into **The Box,** an indescribable sheer-walled gorge with *the most difficult whitewater in this book.* The Box was not successfully run in its entirety until 1984.[3] For six miles the Clarks Fork drops at an average of 200 ft./mi.—an astounding gradient for a river this large. In one remarkable mile the river plunges more than 300 vertical feet between sculpted bedrock walls. The worst rapids, both blind Class V's, are **DELIBERATION CORNER** and **ROCK OF DOOM FALLS.**

Numerous grueling portages are required, including some that demand strong climbing skills. This should be regarded as a Class VI run. It is emphatically **only for daring teams of top experts in superb condition and using extreme caution.** In case of mishap, rescue would be difficult: only a couple of steep, rough trails climb the canyon walls.

Finally, some 18 miles below the Highway 296 bridge, The Box ends and the canyon opens a bit. A rough 4-wheel drive road begins on the left and continues downstream, gradually improving and eventually leading to Highway 296. It is possible to use this road to take out at the end of The Box, but most boaters who have come this far continue down the Lower Clarks Fork.

The **Lower Clarks Fork** is the river's most popular section, with three miles of classic big-water boating in a scenic high desert canyon. Snowmelt runoff produces powerful waves and big hydraulics: the run rates Class IV at levels up to about 6,000 cfs, and becomes a full Class V as flows approach 10,000 cfs. This section is usually boatable into late summer.

The put-in for the Lower Clarks Fork is on the left bank upstream from Cyclone Bar. The action begins immediately at **ZONA,** followed by a flatwater stretch, then **CYCLONE, SLAM DUNK,** and **MIKE'S MOTEL** (where the standard run is on the right). The whitewater climaxes at **UPPER** and **LOWER TWIN PIN.** The **take-out** is on the left bank where a fence marks the Shoshone National Forest boundary.

Boaters looking for easier water may be interested in a seldom-run Class II stretch below the Lower Clarks Fork take-out, continuing as far as Edelweiss on Wyoming Highway 120. A fishing access near the middle of this section allows shorter runs. The first half of the run offers the best scenery as the river passes through desert badlands dotted with wild rose bushes.

The Clarks Fork is shown on the *Shoshone NF (North Half)* map. For more information refer to Lewis, *Paddle and Portage,* and contact Clarks Fork RD, Shoshone NF, 1002 Road 11, Powell, WY 82435; (307) 754-7207.

[3]Yvon Chouinard describes this run in *First Descents: In Search of Wild Rivers,* edited by Cameron O'Connor and John Lazenby.

Boulder River

Difficulty: V–II+. **Length:** Varies.

The Boulder, which rises in the high country just north of Yellowstone National Park in south central Montana, has much in common with its nearest neighbor, the Stillwater to the east (see Region I). Both drain the richly forested Absaroka Beartooth Wilderness, and both are major tributaries of the Yellowstone River. However, the Boulder watershed is only about half the size of the Stillwater's, and has fewer high peaks. As a result, the Boulder is smaller and has a shorter boating season.

In recent years the Boulder has become a favorite of kayakers in Billings and Bozeman. Local boaters divide the Boulder into four major runs, which in general become easier and less technical as one moves farther downstream. Access to all runs is via County Road 298, which leads south from Big Timber. This road becomes USFS Road 6639, the "Main Boulder Road," where it crosses into Gallatin National Forest. Runs and shuttles are best understood by referring to the *Gallatin NF* map.

The Boulder is generally boatable from about mid-May to mid-July. For flow information call the USGS, (406) 449-5263, or the NWS,

(406) 657-6988. Both quote the Big Timber gauge near the mouth. Flows on the upper river are much lower. The minimum recommended flow is roughly 3' at Big Timber, though some boaters scrape down at levels as low as 2'.

This very challenging river should be approached with caution. **Log hazards** are always a threat on this heavily forested stream, especially on the upper runs. High water can be dangerous: eddies disappear and long, cold swims are a serious risk. Be especially careful to avoid trespassing; there have been some problems with landowners in the past. For more information refer to Thompson, *Floating and Recreation on Montana Rivers.* A good local source for information on the Boulder is Northern Lights Trading Co., 1716 West Babcock, Bozeman, MT 59715; (406) 586-2338.

The uppermost run is **Hells Canyon,** 2.5 miles of very demanding **experts-only** water where the road is away from the river. To make this spectacular run, boaters must put in at the bridge across Fourmile Creek, a little over a mile upstream from Hells Canyon Campground, and float a short distance on the creek to the Boulder. ***HAZARD. PORTAGE.*** After a short stretch of flatwater, a horizon line across the Boulder warns boaters to portage on the left to avoid the **Gates of Hell,** a deadly series of waterfalls. (Until recently, boaters could put in on the Boulder itself about 3/4 mile above Hells Canyon Campground by hiking down a trail from the road. The trail, which crosses private property, was closed in 1993. For updated information contact Big Timber RD, Gallatin NF, P.O. Box 196, Big Timber, MT 59011; (406) 932-5155.

After the portage, warm-up water leads down to Hawley Creek, which enters on the right. Below the creek is **Hells Canyon,** a mile and a half of nearly continuous, highly technical Class V rapids with an astounding 190 ft./mi. gradient. At high flows (around 5' and above at Big Timber) Hells Canyon is continuous Class V+. In the heart of the canyon is **THE BOX,** a cliff-lined rapid that cannot be portaged at high flows. The run ends where the road returns to the river and the Miminagish Bible Camp appears on the left. Ask permission to use the Bible Camp as an access.

The **Bible Run** begins at Miminagish Bible Camp and extends five miles to Chippy Park Campground. This Class III+ section can be scouted from the road, which crosses the river at Fleming Bridge near the midpoint of the run. A short canyon below Fleming Bridge has the most difficult rapids in this stretch.

Below Chippy Park Campground is the **Middle Boulder,** a five-mile Class II run with one Class III rapid, which can be scouted from the road. Both the Bible Run and Middle Boulder pass through a scenic, heavily forested canyon. The **take-out** for the Middle Boulder is at Falls Creek Campground. **Boating is not recommended below this point** due to flat water, private land, fences, and a **lethal waterfall** a few miles downstream.

About half a dozen miles below Falls Creek Campground, the bedrock shifts from hard granite to soft limestone. The river has cut deeply into the limestone, producing a 100' vertical plunge known as Natural Bridge Falls. The falls make an excellent scenic side excursion, though the natural bridge collapsed a few years ago. Below the falls is the last short stretch of canyon, a treacherous three-quarter mile reach where the river cuts numerous underground passages through the limestone. Although this short section has been run under carefully selected conditions by a few daring experts, it is **not recommended for boating** due to the deadly hazard posed by the underground passages.

Below the canyon mouth the Boulder is flat for about a dozen miles. Rapids finally resume at McLeod Fishing Access, just below the confluence with the West Fork Boulder. McLeod is the put-in for the **Lower Boulder,** ten miles of popular Class II and III water through pastoral foothill country. Road 298 crosses the river twice in this run: once at mile 4, where it offers an alternate access, and again at Eightmile Bridge, the **recommended take-out.** At high flows this wide-open stretch has many play spots.

An eight-mile Class III run is possible on the West Fork Boulder from Schoolhouse Bridge to McLeod. This short-season run is boatable at flows above about 4' on the Big Timber gauge. Beware of **log hazards.**

Colorado Rockies

Clear Creek

Difficulty: V+p. **Length:** 15 miles.

Clear Creek, one of Colorado's better-known expert runs, features intense whitewater for those with the necessary skills. Rising on the Continental Divide west of Denver, this relatively small tributary of the South Platte plummets down an extremely steep, narrow, and spectacular canyon carved into the bedrock of the Front Range (a subrange of the Rockies). The action doesn't let up until the creek reaches the city of Golden at the edge of the Great Plains, where it supplies the "Rocky Mountain Water" used to make Coors beer.

I-70 follows the upper reaches of Clear Creek, while U.S. Highway 6 follows its lower course. Whitewater boating is generally limited to the 15-mile stretch along Highway 6. The highway affords frequent access and easy scouting but detracts substantially from the solitude. In addition, sharp rocks tumbled into the river during highway construction add to the difficulty and danger.

With an average gradient of 98 ft./mi., Clear Creek is a non-stop millrace of boulder-choked Class IV, V, and even Class VI rapids—depending on the flow. This very tight and extremely technical run is almost exclusively the domain of expert kayakers, though successful descents have been made in nimble self-bailing rafts. Anyone considering the run should scout carefully from the highway before making an attempt. Boaters should be alert for possible **log hazards** and be prepared for **possible portages at the biggest drops.**

The uppermost **put-in** (mile 0) is on the left bank not far below the junction of U.S. 6 and I-70. The most extreme whitewater begins near mile 6 and continues nearly to mile 11, after which it eases only slightly. Numerous highway bridges and tunnels provide good landmarks and help boaters track their progress. Be alert for a **mandatory portage at a dangerous diversion dam** near mile 14, just upstream from Highway Tunnel #1 (the tunnels are numbered upstream from Golden, so this is the first tunnel encountered when driving upriver). At mile 15 the canyon suddenly opens and the run ends as Clear Creek reaches the outskirts of Golden.

Clear Creek typically peaks in June, often at levels too high for boating. More reasonable flows usually come in May and July, before and after peak snowmelt. At other times the creek is generally too low. Clear Creek's natural runoff is supplemented by trans-Divide diversions. For flow information call Water Talk, (303) 831-7135; **1*22*** for the flow at Golden. For more information refer to Wheat, *Floater's Guide to Colorado.*

Elk River

Difficulty: III. **Length:** 9 miles.

The Elk is the backyard run for local boaters from Steamboat Springs. This major tributary of the upper Yampa drains the high peaks of the Park Range in the Mt. Zirkel Wilderness. Below the wilderness the river thunders down a spectacular box canyon, then emerges into a forested valley near the confluence of the Middle and North Forks.

Downstream from the **put-in** at Box Canyon Campground, the Elk provides good intermediate boating in most years from roughly late May to early July—a little longer below the South Fork confluence a few miles into the run. The river is steep and continuous, with few eddies and an average gradient of nearly 65 ft./mi. The whitewater is generally tougher toward the beginning of the run. Be especially alert for **log hazards**—inquire locally, and scout carefully from the dirt road that follows the river.

The **take-out** is at the Colorado Highway 129 bridge over the Elk at the hamlet of Glen Eden, some 20 miles north of Steamboat Springs. To reach the **put-in,** turn east up Road 400 and drive to the launch site at the *bottom* end of Box Canyon Campground. Along the way are several alternate accesses. Experts can launch a mile *above* Box Canyon Campground for a short Class IV+ to V run, including some very challenging water going past the campground itself. However, beware of a nasty Class V+ drop at the top of the campground (portage recommended).

Boating is less rewarding on most of the lower river below the Glen Eden **take-out,** with the exception of a short novice run just above Mad Creek where the river passes briefly through Forest Service lands.

For more information see Wheat, *Floater's Guide to Colorado.* The *Routt NF* map covers the entire run. For flow information call WaterTalk, (303) 831-7135; **6*3*** for the flow "at Clark," which is at the Glen Eden (Highway 129) bridge.

South Fork White River

Difficulty: IV to VI, with portages.
Length: 14 miles from Budge's Resort to South Fork Campground. Shorter run possible.

The South Fork of the White is one of the most obscure rivers in the Colorado Rockies. Few people outside the region have even heard of the White River, let alone this small upstream tributary. Nevertheless, on a few occasions experts from Steamboat Springs and Glenwood Springs have tackled this outstandingly scenic stream. (For information on the very mellow lower **White River,** see the **Canyon Country** section of **More Rivers.**)

The South Fork White begins high in the Flat Tops Wilderness on the broad White River Plateau in northwestern Colorado. Just across the ridge are the headwaters of the Yampa. For perhaps a dozen miles the South Fork flows across pure alpine wilderness to Budge's Resort, a high-country lodge located at the end of USFS Road 600—the only point where the South Fork touches the wilderness boundary. Here boaters—**experts only**—can launch their craft on this oversized mountain stream and begin one of the most scenic and challenging descents anywhere in the Rockies.

If exploring new runs at the very edge of navigability is your idea of a good time, consider the following facts. The elevation at Budge's Resort is nearly 9,000'. The drainage area is a mere 52 square miles. The next possible take-out is 14 miles downstream at South Fork Campground; in between, only a trail follows the right bank. Meanwhile, the South Fork drops 1,400' through four distinct canyons at an average gradient of 100 ft./mi. The season is short, and in dry years there is no season at all. The shuttle is monstrous. There are portages, log jams, and endless Class IV to VI rapids. And the forested alpine scenery is breathtakingly beautiful.

If you're still intrigued—and if your skills are up to the run—ask around in Steamboat Springs or Glenwood Springs, get the topos and Forest Service maps, and contact White River NF. (Don't be surprised if they refer you to a suicide prevention hotline.) Those who want to see the scenery but avoid the hair-raising rapids are in luck: a fine Forest Service trail follows the whole run.

A much larger number of expert boaters tackle the last four miles of the run described above, thereby avoiding the low flows and horrible shuttle that the full run entails. Lightweight boats can be carried up the trail from South Fork Campground, located at the wilderness boundary southeast of Buford, Colorado. A four-mile hike brings boaters to the launch point at the junction with Lost Solar Creek, which enters from the north. Don't be fooled, though: the whitewater is still Class IV to VI. For more on this lower run, refer to Wheat, *Floater's Guide to Colorado.* The *White River NF* map covers the run.

Taylor River

Difficulty: II to V-, depending on run.
Length: 17 miles. Shorter runs possible.

Born on the west slope of the Continental Divide in Colorado's lofty Sawatch Range, the Taylor descends briefly through a narrow, forested canyon before merging with the East River at Almont, Colorado to form the Gunnison River. Though small, the Taylor offers a wide range of excellent whitewater as well as outstanding alpine scenery and abundant wildlife. The river is lightly used, mostly by local kayakers and a handful of commercial outfitters in nearby Gunnison and Crested Butte.

Flows are regulated by Taylor Park Dam, which normally releases 200 to 400 cfs through summer and early fall. In wet years the reservoir may spill 1,000 cfs or more, making many sections of the Taylor extremely dangerous. Most of the time, however, the river is tiny and technical, suitable only for small craft. Be alert for possible **log hazards.** A highway follows the river, providing frequent access and scouting. To reach the river follow U.S. 50 to Gunnison, then Colorado Highway 135 to Almont.

The river is boatable from Taylor Park Dam to Almont. However, access problems keep most boaters from running the first four miles of Class III water from the dam to Lottis Creek. The riverbed and banks here are private, and the landowner has erected fences and intimidating signs to keep boaters out. Below Lottis Creek the difficulty suddenly jumps to Class IV–V, then decreases gradually over the next 17 miles, easing to Class II by Almont.

Only experts should try the demanding two-mile **Staircase Run** from Lottis Creek (mile 0) to Lodgepole Campground; the river drops 210' in two miles through a continuum of steep, technical and very narrow Class IV–V rapids. At Lodgepole Campground (mile 2) the gradient eases to 70 ft./mi., and the next four miles hold many Class IV rapids, as well as possible fences and diversions. Watch for **THE SLOT (IV)** not far below Crystal Creek, which enters on the left at mile 4.3. After passing the Whitewater Ranch Resort (private), the Taylor returns to the road and public land at mile 6 (river access).

The stretch from below Whitewater Ranch to Taylor Canyon Picnic Ground (mile 9.5) is Class III with a gradient of 60 ft./mi. Access is possible at the picnic ground and at both the Rosy Lane and Onemile Campgrounds (USFS). Two major tributaries, Spring Creek and Beaver Creek, join the Taylor near the picnic area, boosting the flow in early summer. The final seven miles to Almont are Class III- to II (gradient: 45 ft./mi.). Many boaters **take out** where Colorado Highway 306 crosses the river (mile 12).

Boaters may continue below the East River confluence at Almont, floating the uppermost portion of the Gunnison, which—after a few Class II riffles—meanders through ranchlands. If they wish, boaters may continue all the way to the backwaters of Blue Mesa Reservoir. Watch for **fences and diversions.**

For flow information call WaterTalk, (303) 831-7135; **4*23*** for the release from Taylor Park Reservoir, or **4*22*** for the flow at Almont (above the East River confluence). The managing agency is Gunnison NF, 2250 Highway 50, Delta, CO 81416; (303) 874-7691. The USFS *Gunnison Basin Area* map covers the Taylor. For more information see Wheat, *Floater's Guide to Colorado.*

The Taylor is seriously threatened by a proposed water diversion. The project, known by its fitting acronym "CRAP-UP" (Collegiate Range Aurora Project–Union Park), would shunt water east from the Taylor through a tunnel under the Continental Divide to suburbs around Denver. In addition to eliminating boating on the Taylor, the diversion would seriously reduce flows farther downstream on the Gunnison. For more information contact the National Organization for River Sports (see appendix for addresses).

Slate River

Adventurous experts may be interested in a short but intense run on the nearby Slate River. The Slate, a tributary of the East River, has three miles of Class V to V+ whitewater upstream from the ski resort town of Crested Butte. **Experts only.** The Slate is extremely steep and narrow, peppered with tight, technical Class V drops. The season for this tiny alpine river is short—sometime in May and/or June of most years. Anyone interested in the run should inquire locally in Crested Butte.

Lake Fork of the Gunnison

Difficulty: III- first 19 miles, V- last 5 miles.
Length: 24 miles. Shorter runs possible.

The Lake Fork of the Gunnison rises along the Continental Divide in southwestern Colorado's San Juan Mountains, not far from the headwaters of the Animas and the Rio Grande. This major tributary of the Gunnison flows freely all the way to Blue Mesa Reservoir, which floods the lower eight miles of the Lake Fork and covers its confluence with the main stem.

Despite good scenery and a variety of whitewater, the Lake Fork gets only light use. Snowmelt from the north slope of the San Juans produces runnable flows until mid- to late July in average years. The river offers two very distinct sections: upstream, a 19-mile Class II and easy III reach with a fairly continuous gradient of 35 ft./mi.; downstream, five miles of Class IV to V action with a gradient of 55 ft./mi. Nearby roads allow shorter runs within these stretches, or the two sections can be combined for a continuous float of 24 miles. Because of problems with private landowners on the upper run, most boaters with the necessary skills favor the lower stretch, below Red Bridge Campground, where the Lake Fork passes through more remote public lands.

Both runs are covered in Wheat, *Floater's Guide to Colorado.* Refer to the USFS *Gunnison Basin Area* map for accesses, shuttles, and land ownership. No flow information is currently available.

Independence Gulch to Red Bridge CG

Although Colorado Highway 149 follows most of this section, it is usually out of sight on a shelf above the river. Much of this stretch is through private land, and there are **occasional fences across the river.** Please respect private property; boaters have had problems with landowners here. The first several miles below Lake City are not recommended. **Put in** about five miles below town where there is access on public land along the highway, not far below the mouth of Independence Gulch.

For the next 19 miles the Lake Fork runs swiftly down a small canyon cut into a broader valley. Elk Creek enters on the left about mile 4.5. The highway crosses the river at mile 10. About 2.5 miles below this highway bridge, the river cuts through a narrows known as The Gate. Downstream, the highway leaves the river. A gauging station at mile 17 must be **portaged.** Near this point the highway leaves the canyon, and downstream access is via a dirt road along the right bank. **Take out** on the right at Red Bridge Campground, mile 19.

Red Bridge CG to Blue Mesa Reservoir

Below Red Bridge Campground the Lake Fork cuts into the same hard, dark rock that forms the Black Canyon of the Gunnison on the main stem. The sudden geologic shift produces a radical change in scenery and whitewater: in its final five miles the Lake Fork tumbles through a narrow, rugged gorge peppered with Class IV and V pool-and-drop rapids. The biggest drop, **RATTLESNAKE (V)**, comes about halfway through this section and includes a vertical plunge of nearly 10'. Scout this entire section carefully from the dirt road along the right bank. The run ends near Gateview Campground, where the Lake Fork stills in the backwaters of Blue Mesa Reservoir.

Upper Rio Grande

Difficulty: IV. **Length:** 6.5 miles.

The box canyon of the Upper Rio Grande in southwestern Colorado is a little-known but rewarding run at the extreme upstream limits of navigation on America's second-longest river. The Rio Grande springs from an alpine bowl on the east slope of the Continental Divide in the San Juan Mountains, a major subrange of the Rockies. Snowmelt gathers in Rio Grande Reservoir, then spills downstream through the highest-elevation run in this guide, with the put-in at 9,500'.

The **put-in** (mile 0) is at River Hill Campground some two miles below the reservoir. A couple of miles downstream, the Rio Grande accelerates into the rugged, narrow, thickly-forested gorge, where steep ridges tower as much as 1,700' above the river. The river tumbles at about 50 ft./mi. through numerous Class III rapids and a few Class IV drops (V at higher flows). As on other alpine runs, high altitude and cold water add to the difficulty. Dangerous **log hazards** are always a possibility on this narrow river.

From miles 2 through 6 the river runs through a corner of the vast Weminuche Wilderness Area. Those lucky enough to make an overnight trip through this rarely-visited canyon can enjoy unsurpassed camping and utter isolation. Anglers may catch their dinners from the sparkling water. All too soon, the canyon ends as the Rio Grande suddenly turns smooth and enters a broad valley. The first possible **take-out** is at a low-water bridge at the mouth of the box canyon (mile 6.5).

In addition to short mileage, this run also has a very short season—usually sometime from May to late June. These factors, plus the distance from population centers, keep boating use light on the Upper Rio Grande.

For flow information call WaterTalk, (303) 831-7135; **3*14*** for the flow at Thirty Mile Bridge, just above the put-in. The managing agency is Creede RD, Rio Grande NF, Box 270, Creede, CO 81130; (719) 658-2556. The *Rio Grande NF* map covers this run.

To reach the **take-out,** follow Colorado Highway 149 to the intersection with USFS Road 520, roughly midway between Creede and Spring Creek Pass. Turn west onto Road 520, drive one mile, and bear left on an unpaved road that leads just over a mile south to the low-water bridge. To reach the **put-in,** return to Road 520, bear left, and drive roughly eight miles to River Hill Campground.

Downstream Runs

Below its box canyon the Rio Grande offers easier boating through less rugged scenery. Highway 149 follows these sections, providing frequent access, short shuttles, and easy scouting. Watch for fences on these stretches. A pleasant Class II–III run begins near Rio Grande Campground and extends some six miles to the Highway 149 bridge above Creede.

A more popular run begins farther downstream at Wagon Wheel Gap; most boaters **put in** where Highway 149 crosses the river about seven miles southeast of Creede, or at alternate sites just downstream. Be alert for **hazardous bridges** on this run. The gap itself is a narrower section of canyon where the gradient increases to produce several Class II rapids. An annual raft race is held here. The river shares its canyon with a highway, a railroad, and several small mountain resorts. Most boaters **take out** at the Highway 149 bridge about a mile above the confluence with the South Fork Rio Grande.

For more information refer to Wheat, *Floater's Guide to Colorado.*

San Miguel River

Difficulty: III.
Length: 24 miles. Shorter runs possible.

The San Miguel, largest tributary of the Dolores, rises among spectacular peaks around Telluride in southwestern Colorado's San Juan Range. Colorado Highway 145 follows the upper river for many miles west from Telluride, but just east of the small town of Norwood, the highway crosses the river and climbs out of the canyon. Downstream the San Miguel tumbles through lively Class III rapids in a scenic, roadless sandstone canyon known as Norwood or San Miguel Canyon. This section sees only light boating use from private boaters and outfitters based in Telluride.

The standard **put-in** is Norwood Bridge (Highway 145), with an alternate access about two miles upstream opposite the mouth of Beaver Creek. A minor road follows the right bank for four miles below Norwood Bridge. Horsefly Creek enters on the right at mile 9 (good side hike). About a mile and a half below the creek is a **diversion weir** that must often be lined or portaged on the left. The diversion reduces downstream flows somewhat, shortening the boatable season below this point. A rough road begins on the right at the weir.

A section of good Class III rapids signals the approach of Piñon Bridge (old Highway 90) at mile 16. Although the bridge is on private land, boaters sometimes take out here. A legal access is about half a mile upstream on BLM land along the right bank. (Follow the dirt road up the right bank from the bridge; the powerline marks the approximate beginning of BLM land.) From Norwood to Piñon the river drops at 45 ft./mi.

Below Piñon Bridge the canyon opens and the gradient eases to 35 ft./mi. The remaining eight miles have several small **diversions,** some of which may require portage. The river banks are mostly private in this lower section. The best **take-out** is at a bridge four miles upstream from Naturita. Immediately below the bridge is a power plant, followed by a **dangerous weir** that would be very tough to portage. To reach this bridge, turn north off Highway 141 onto old Highway 90 about three miles east of Naturita (half a mile west of the Highway 145 junction), then drive about 1.5 miles to the river.

Though the rapids in Norwood Canyon are mostly Class III, beware of high water and log hazards. The season is roughly May to early July; for flow information call WaterTalk, (303) 831-7135; **4*17*** for the flow "near Placerville," a half dozen miles above Norwood Bridge. For more information refer to the *Uncompahgre NF* map and contact the BLM at 2505 S. Townsend Ave., Montrose, CO 81401; (303) 249-7791.

Boaters also run various stretches of the San Miguel above Norwood Bridge—as far upstream as the South Fork confluence, a couple of miles below the upper Highway 145 bridge. These steep, swift sections feature continuous whitewater. Scout from Highway 145, which closely follows the right bank. The Bureau of Reclamation has a long-standing proposal to dam this reach of the San Miguel at a site some ten miles above Norwood Bridge.

Canyon Country

White River

Difficulty: II.
Length: Up to 160 miles. Shorter runs possible.

From headwaters on the White River Plateau in northwestern Colorado, the White runs west into Utah, joining the Green River near the head of Desolation Canyon. Snowmelt from the plateau gives rise not only to the White but also to its more famous northern sister, the Yampa.

The little-known White has a growing following among open canoeists and boaters looking for desert canyon scenery with minimal whitewater. The river is boatable for most of its distance below the confluence of the North and South Forks east of Meeker, Colorado. (For more on the very difficult **South Fork White,** see the write-up a few pages back in the Colorado Rockies section.)

The first few miles of the White below this confluence are fairly swift. Then the river slows as it winds through open terrain above Meeker; this flat stretch also has numerous irrigation **diversions.** Better boating can be found farther downstream, beginning at the Colorado Highway 13 bridge below Meeker and running through Rio Blanco State Recreation Area. For some 65 miles the river provides flatwater canoeing to the backwaters of Kenney Reservoir east of Rangely. Colorado Highway 64 follows this section, providing alternate accesses. (Please respect private land.)

The most popular floating sections are below Rangely in scenic and largely roadless canyons, where a gradient of 7 ft./mi. produces several Class II rapids. Though all 100 miles from Rangely to the Green River are boatable, most river runners avoid the first few miles below Rangely and concentrate on more scenic reaches farther downstream. Several alternate accesses allow runs ranging from seven to 100 miles and from one day to five or more.

A partly paved, partly dirt road follows the left bank for some ten miles below Rangely, allowing a **put-in** near the head of the canyons. A few miles downstream, the river passes into Utah. The next access is at Cowboy Canyon, located on the right bank some 30 miles below Rangely and reached by a very rough road leading east from Bonanza, Utah. Rapids are more frequent below this point.

Bonanza Bridge (Utah Highway 45) crosses the river nine miles below Cowboy Canyon, providing a good access. This is the put-in for the most popular run, often referred to simply as the **White River Canyon.** Only a few dirt roads reach the river in the 39 miles from Bonanza Bridge to the popular access point and usual **take-out** at Mountain Fuel Bridge. (This access is on the Ute Reservation; a permit is required to leave a car here.) Below Mountain Fuel Bridge the White meanders slowly (gradient: 3 ft./mi.) for 22 miles through more open terrain to its confluence with the Green.

The White is a relatively small river, about half the size of the Yampa. It is typically boatable between mid-May and early July. Call the NWS tape, (801) 539-1311, for the flow "at Watson"; this reading is from the gauge at Bonanza Bridge, 48 miles below Rangely. For the upper river call WaterTalk, (303) 831-7135; **6*11*** for the flow near Meeker.

For advice on accesses (including several not listed above), road conditions, flows, etc., contact the BLM. *For the Colorado sections:* BLM, White River Resource Area, P.O. Box 928, Meeker, CO 81641-0928; (303) 878-3601. *For the Utah sections:* BLM, 170 South 500 East, Vernal, UT 84078; (801) 789-1362. Ask for a copy of their map-pamphlet "Floating the White River." For more information refer to Nichols, *River Runners' Guide to Utah and Adjacent Areas.*

Until recently the White was one of the last free-flowing tributaries in the Colorado River system. Then, in the mid-1980's, Taylor Draw Dam was built a few miles above Rangely for a municipal and recreational water supply. The future may hold even bigger dams for the White if oil companies seek to tap the area's rich deposits of oil shale. Extraction of the oil requires enormous amounts of water, and the White is a tempting source. During the synthetic fuels boom of the 1970's and early 1980's, a large dam was proposed for a site a few miles below Bonanza Bridge in the very heart of White River Canyon. As interest in oil shale faded, the dam project was moved to a back burner. If interest revives, the White may be threatened again.

San Rafael River

1. Little Grand Canyon:
Fullers Bottom to San Rafael CG.
I+; 15 miles.

2. First and Second Black Box:
San Rafael CG to I-70.
IVp; 42 miles. Shorter runs possible.

The San Rafael rises among high peaks on the east slope of the Wasatch Plateau in central Utah. Southeast of the town of Castle Dale, three large tributary creeks join to form the San Rafael, which winds some 100 miles to meet the Green River near the head of Labyrinth Canyon. Along the way this small, short-season river cuts a series of dramatic canyons through a broad uplift of the earth's crust known as the San Rafael Swell.

The river's initial cut into the swell, known as the **Little Grand Canyon,** offers spectacular wilderness scenery and easy boating. A good **put-in** is at Fullers Bottom, reached by a spur road off the dirt road that runs from Castle Dale to San Rafael Campground. The 15 miles from Fullers Bottom to the campground are remarkably lovely, with sheer and even overhanging walls of Navajo sandstone. There are plenty of campsites (except at high flows), and the side hiking is excellent. The **take-out** is at the bridge near San Rafael Campground. For more information on this run contact the BLM, Price River Resource Area, 900 North 700 East, Price, UT 84501; (801) 637-4584. Also consult Michael Kelsey, *Hiking and Exploring Utah's San Rafael Swell.*

Below the bridge at San Rafael Campground lies one of the most demanding and little-known wilderness runs in the Canyon Country, the **Black Box Canyons** of the San Rafael. Here the river cuts through the heart of the San Rafael Swell. Extreme constriction and a high gradient (over 50 ft./mi. in places) combine to produce a very challenging and **potentially dangerous run, suitable only for experts in small craft.** A rough access road between the two boxes allows boaters to run either or both. The First Black Box contains at least one mandatory portage, and both boxes hold numerous difficult Class IV drops. The best **take-out** is near the I-70 bridge, some 12 miles west of the city of Green River.

The San Rafael is typically boatable in late May or early June of good snowpack years. Call the NWS tape, (801) 539-1311, for the San Rafael flow "at Green River." **Do not attempt the Black Box runs at flows above 1,000 cfs.**

As with other obscure Canyon Country runs, the Black Boxes of the San Rafael attract more hikers than boaters. The best boating information is found in Nichols, *River Runners' Guide to Utah and Adjacent Areas.* (The cover photo of this fine book is a shot from the Second Black Box.) For a hiker's perspective, try the Kelsey book mentioned above.

Dirty Devil River

Difficulty: II-.
Length: 53 miles to Poison Spring Canyon; or 67 miles to Powell Reservoir, then 18 miles on reservoir.

The Dirty Devil is an obscure Colorado River tributary formed by the confluence of the Fremont River and Muddy Creek near Hanksville in south central Utah. Like the Escalante, its sister stream to the west, the Dirty Devil is a scenic, remote wilderness run with a very short and unpredictable season. The river may have a brief runnable window—for small craft only—sometime in May or early June of good snowpack years. In some years the water never gets high enough for boating; during rare flash floods, the flow can exceed 10,000 cfs.

The Dirty Devil owes its unflattering name to William Dunn, a member of the 1867 Powell expedition. Seeing the river at its mouth, where it joins the Colorado just below Cataract Canyon, Dunn remarked that it was "a dirty devil," and the name stuck. Modern boaters find the river just as silty today; in fact, boaters are advised to bring all their own drinking water, since clear water to purify may not be available.

Boating begins at the Utah Highway 24 bridge, which crosses both Muddy Creek and the Fremont River just outside Hanksville. In less than a mile the two tributaries join to form the Dirty Devil. For the first several miles the river spreads out over a wide, shallow channel in barren, open terrain. Below mile 8 it gradually enters a scenic sandstone canyon for the remainder of the run. Numerous spectacular side canyons invite exploration.

Below Happy Canyon (mile 46) riffles are more frequent. At mile 53, a mile above the mouth of Poison Spring Canyon, a 4-wheel-

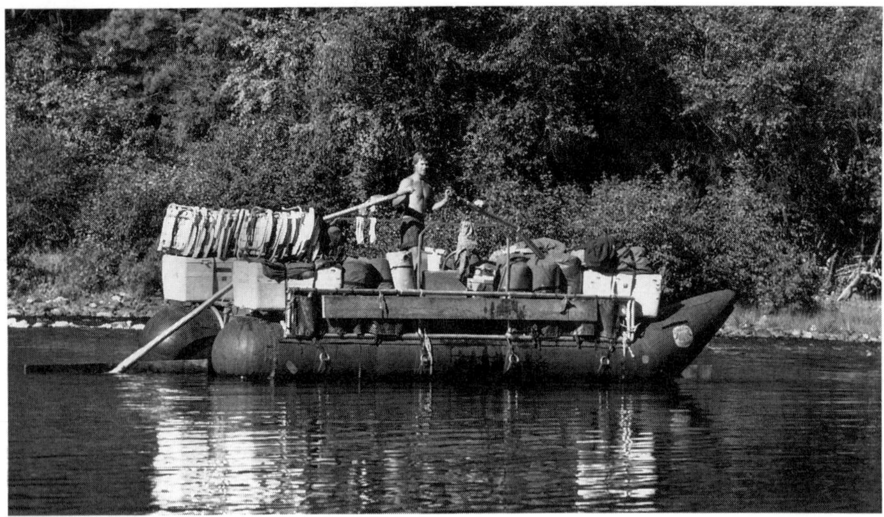

J-rig sweep boat *Jock Montgomery*

Areas. For flow information and other advice, contact the BLM in Hanksville, (801) 542-3461 (see below for address). The flow may also be quoted on the NWS tape, (801) 539-1311.

drive road reaches the right bank, offering **possible river access.** The road climbs Poison Spring Canyon to Utah Highway 95.

Boaters who continue downstream have another 14 miles of slightly faster current before reaching the high-water mark of Powell Reservoir. When full, the huge reservoir backs a narrow finger of flatwater some 18 miles up the Dirty Devil. Boaters can **take out** near the high-water mark of the reservoir where a dirt road leading from Highway 95 descends to the right bank. When the reservoir is low, several more miles of river are exposed. For information on the reservoir level, contact the BLM (address below) or Glen Canyon National Recreation Area (address in **Glen Canyon** write-up in the following pages). Boaters can row or paddle out or arrange a tow to Hite Marina, located across from the mouth of the Dirty Devil on the south shore of the reservoir (see the **Colorado: Cataract Canyon** chapter).

Though the Dirty Devil's moderate gradient (8 ft./mi.) produces only mild riffles, the run must be approached with caution and careful planning due to the extreme isolation and lack of river traffic. The best reference is Nichols, *River Runners' Guide to Utah and Adjacent*

[1]The Fremont River, the other major tributary, has two boatable sections: an **experts-only** upper wilderness run of nine miles (gradient: 130 ft./mi., with portages) and a short lower run (gradient: 55 ft./mi.) along Utah Highway 24 in Capitol Reef National Park. A proposed hydro project would put a 108'-high dam near the bottom of the upper run. For more information on the run, see the Nichols book mentioned above. For more information on the hydro project, contact the National Organization for River Sports (see appendix for address).

Muddy Creek

A few boaters have run various sections of Muddy Creek, one of the Dirty Devil's two main tributaries.[1] Floating begins as far upstream as the I-70 bridge some 60 miles west of the town of Green River. The gauge just below this bridge gives a good indication of flow, with 2.2 feet considered the approximate minimum. The whitewater (or, more accurately, brownwater) on these stretches ranges from Class I+ to II, but **only seasoned adventurers should attempt these runs** through very remote and rugged terrain. The sandstone canyon scenery is outstanding, but the boating season is very short.

The first 11 miles from the I-70 bridge **put-in** to Lone Tree Crossing (a dirt road ford) are swift and winding. Below the crossing the river slows and the canyon narrows and deepens. At mile 30 the canyon opens briefly at Tomsich Butte, where a rough road provides **river access** on the left (some groups put in here). About four miles downstream, the river enters The Chute, where swift water runs between sheer walls over 200' high. **Hazards** here include bridging (the slot is under 10' wide in places) and **log jams.**

Below The Chute is a stretch of Class II water with a gradient of over 30 ft./mi. At mile 45 is an access where a road reaches the left bank at Hidden Splendor Mine, a common **take-out** for groups launching at Tomsich Butte. Below the mine the creek cuts through the plunging rock beds of the San Rafael Reef and emerges onto open terrain at about mile 49. In another mile a dirt road fords the river, offering a good **take-out** on either bank. Few boaters continue downstream. Most of the remaining 22 miles to Highway 24 near Hanksville are slower (gradient: 13 ft./mi.) With the exception of one short canyon, the lower stretch is through open terrain.

For more information refer to the Nichols book mentioned above. Michael Kelsey's *Hiking and Exploring Utah's San Rafael Swell* was written for backpackers, but it contains good information on Muddy Creek. Also contact the BLM: for the upper sections, Price River Resource Area (see **San Rafael** write-up above for address and phone); for the lower runs, Henry Mountain Resource Area, P.O. Box 99, Hanksville, UT 84734, (801) 542-3461.

Escalante River

Difficulty: III. **Length:** 71 miles.

The Escalante is probably the most exotic river in the Canyon Country. From headwaters in the semi-arid Escalante Mountains of southern Utah, the river cuts southwest, winding in entrenched meanders toward its confluence with the Colorado in Glen Canyon, now covered by Powell Reservoir.

Below the **put-in** at the Utah Highway 12 bridge east of the town of Escalante, the river carves one of the West's most remote and enchanting canyons, a slickrock wonderland of orange and pink sandstone. Natural bridges and arches abound along the main river and in innumerable tributary canyons. The side hiking is probably the finest in the region.

The Escalante canyon is beyond the back of beyond: completely uninhabited, far removed from settlements or roads, and only occasionally traversed by cattle and backpackers. In fact, the Escalante was reportedly the last river in the United States to be discovered by whites—in 1872. The river is named for Father Francisco Silvestre de Escalante, co-leader of a Spanish expedition to the Southwest in 1776.

In spite of its outstanding solitude and scenery, the Escalante is almost never run—for two simple reasons. First, it almost never has enough water. Second, the take-out logistics are monstrous.

In good snowpack years the river may briefly reach boatable levels any time from early May to mid-June. But in many years the river never gets high enough to boat. Even with good runoff the Escalante is best suited to small, lightweight boats. (Most of the year, the craft of choice is a pair of hiking boots.) Call the BLM in Escalante for flow information; note that Boulder Creek adds water about six miles below the gauge at the Highway 12 put-in.

An equally tough nut to crack is the **take-out.** When it is full, Powell Reservoir covers the lower 17 miles of the Escalante, and the nearest road access on the reservoir is another 40 miles up the main arm at Bullfrog Marina. The shuttle to Bullfrog is very long.

If a 60-mile flatwater paddle doesn't sound like your idea of fun, consider the alternative: a grueling three-mile hike and climb out of the canyon at Coyote Gulch (mile 71), near the reservoir's backwaters. After hauling themselves and their gear up sand dunes, talus slopes, and cliffs, boaters must find their way out on a rough 4-wheel-drive track that connects with the Hole-In-The-Rock Road, which in turn leads to Highway 12. The preferred take-out method, for those with the means, is to hire a motorboat tow up the reservoir to Bullfrog Marina.

For anyone who can overcome these obstacles—plus the challenge of provisioning a 71-mile trip through arid wilderness in small boats—the whitewater shouldn't prove too daunting. The gradient averages 21 ft./mi., and the last 20 miles are the steepest and roughest. Most of the drops rate Class II to II+, but watch for **SCORPION RAPID,** not far below Scorpion Gulch (mile 51). Downstream are several other obstructed, rocky drops and at least one possible portage. Overall, the run probably merits a Class III rating, given the extreme isolation and lack of any river traffic to help in the event of a mishap. What's more, the river's widely varying flows mean that rapids are constantly changing, and reliable information is tough to come by. Weather can sometimes be a factor, given the early season and relatively high elevation (5,200' at the put-in).

The best reference is Nichols, *River Runners' Guide to Utah and Adjacent Areas.* Also, pick up copies of Rudi Lambrechtse, *Hiking the Escalante* and Verne Huser, *Canyon Country Paddles.* For mouth-watering photos, have a look at *Slickrock* by Edward Abbey and Philip Hyde. The best maps are the USGS quads; Utah Travel Council, *Southeastern Utah*; and BLM, *Escalante Resource Area.* For more information contact BLM, P.O. Box 225, Escalante, UT 84726; (801) 826-4291.

Colorado: Glen Canyon

Difficulty: I. **Length:** 15 miles.

"The features of this canyon are greatly diversified. We have a curious ensemble of carved walls, royal arches, glens, alcove gulches, mounds and monuments. From which of these shall we select a name? We decide to call it Glen Canyon."

—John Wesley Powell, August 3, 1869

At one time the Colorado River flowed free and smooth for some 175 miles from the end of Cataract Canyon to Lee's Ferry at the head of Grand Canyon. This was Glen Canyon, the longest stretch of flat water on the river and one of the loveliest canyons in the West. This reach of the Colorado was buried by Glen Canyon Dam and "Lake" Powell in the early 1960's.[1]

What many people don't know is that not quite all of Glen Canyon was flooded. There remains a placid and strikingly beautiful 15-mile run from the base of Glen Canyon Dam to Lee's Ferry. Here boaters can get a brief glimpse of the enchanting scenery and quiet majesty that was the focus of one of the West's greatest conservation struggles. The river is broad, deep and uncharacteristically peaceful, carrying boaters smoothly past soaring walls of orange and pink sandstone, intimate side canyons, petroglyphs, dripping springs, and inviting campsites. The stillness in this roadless canyon is broken only occasionally by small motorboats and the large motorized pontoon rafts that carry sightseers from the dam to Lees Ferry.

The Colorado is unnaturally clear and *very* cold as it emerges from the bottom of Powell Reservoir—making hypothermia a real possibility in the event of a swim, despite the often searing air temperatures. Also, beware of fluctuating releases from the dam (see the **Grand Canyon** chapter); camp high and tie boats securely. Last but not least, don't forget your fishing pole: the icy water supports one of Arizona's best trout fisheries (introduced, non-native trout).

The main drawback to floating this section is the complicated logistics. Since the boat ramp area below the dam was wiped out by the extreme high water of 1983, launching at the base of the dam has been tightly restricted. The sole commercial raft outfitter on this section holds an exclusive permit to launch at the dam.

The alternative is to come up from Lee's Ferry (1) under paddle or oar power (recommended only at lower flows, when the current is easier to overcome) or (2) with a tow from one of the local fishing guides licensed to operate motorboats on this reach. Arranging a tow can be cumbersome, but it does eliminate the need for a vehicle shuttle. For a list of these guides, and for more information on this section of river, contact NPS, Glen Canyon National Recreation Area, P.O. Box 1507, Page, AZ 86040; (602) 645-2471.

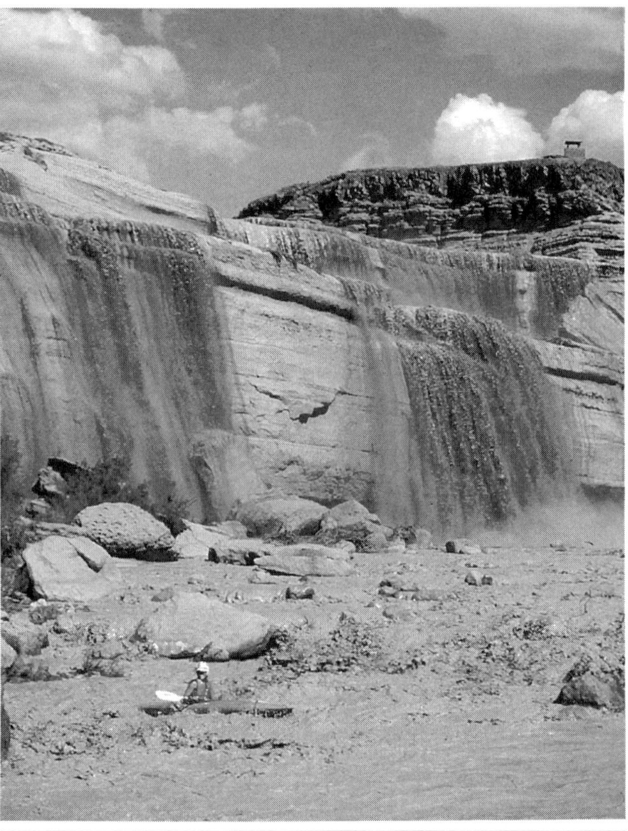

Grand Falls, Little Colorado *Curt Smith*

[1]Glen Canyon and Glen Canyon Dam are the subjects of many fine books. Eliot Porter, *The Place No One Knew: Glen Canyon on the Colorado River*, offers a magnificent photographic glimpse of what Glen Canyon was like. Edward Abbey, *Desert Solitaire*, includes an essay about a lazy float down Glen Canyon. Russell Martin, *A Story That Stands Like a Dam: Glen Canyon and the Struggle for the Soul of the West*, is a superb account of the construction of Glen Canyon Dam.

Southwestern Border

Pecos River

Difficulty: II. **Length:** 60 miles.

The Pecos River has been called the boundary of the West, where the canyons of the Southern Rockies meet the vast flatlands of the Great Plains. Inhabitants of the hill country of central Texas might object—with some reason—that they too are part of the West. Still, there is truth in this characterization of the Pecos, especially as it applies to rivers. Moving from west to east, the Pecos is the last significant river with a Western character,[1] so it is also the easternmost river in this book.

As one of the Rio Grande's major tributaries, the Pecos mimics its big sister in many respects. It has a short, steep upper stretch in the Rocky Mountains; a long, flat, middle reach where much of its flow is diverted for irrigation; and a final scenic canyon in Texas. River runners focus on the two ends of the river: a stretch near the headwaters in New Mexico's Sangre de Cristo Range and the lower 60 miles where the isolated canyon of the Pecos approaches its confluence with the Rio Grande near Langtry, Texas. (The confluence is now buried by Amistad Reservoir.) Open canoeists in particular enjoy the lower river's long, mild wilderness run.

The Pecos drainage is even drier than that of the Rio Grande. This fact, combined with irrigation withdrawals, means that flows rarely exceed 1,000 cfs. Nevertheless, for much of the year the Pecos has enough water for small boats. July is typically the month with the lowest flows, but most boaters avoid the searing heat of midsummer anyway. Spring and fall are the best times for boating; winter runs are possible, but the weather can be chilly. Thunderstorms and flash floods are possible at any time, but the danger is highest from August through October. For current flow information contact the Border Water Commission at (512) 775-2437.

[1]We discarded the notion of including the Guadalupe River in our book, mainly because this lovely little hill country stream in the Austin area has been so overwhelmed by hordes of beer-guzzling party types in innertubes and rubber duckies that it resembles a frat rat's vision of Disneyland more than a Western river.

The most common run on the lower Pecos begins with a **put-in** at Pandale Crossing, where an unpaved road crosses the river just south of the tiny hamlet of Pandale. The Pecos slips into its remote canyon very gradually; the final 25 miles are the most isolated and scenic. The rapids are generally Class I+ to II, becoming stronger over the course of the run (average gradient: 12 ft./mi.). Watch for a bigger rapid at mile 39, where Cold Water Canyon enters on the left. A **weir** near mile 50 requires a short **portage.**

When Amistad Reservoir is full, it backs a narrow finger of flatwater up to nine miles above the take-out at U.S. 90. Strong headwinds are common in this final reach. For these reasons, boaters may want to inquire locally about permission to take out on private land above the reservoir. The standard **take-out** is at the old U.S. 90 crossing, not far from the new U.S. 90 high bridge.

Although the river banks are entirely private, the land is sparsely populated and the run is through virtual wilderness. A good local source for more information is Triple RRR Canoe Service in Langtry, (915) 291-3348. Good coverage of this run can be found in Gene Kirkley, *A Guide to Texas Rivers and Streams.*

Lower Colorado River

Difficulty: I+ in Black Canyon, I on lower runs.
Length: *Black Canyon:* 12 miles. *Topock Gorge:* 16 miles. Up to 75 miles of downstream runs.

Most river runners assume that the Colorado River ends at "Lake" Mead—at least as far as non-motorized boating is concerned. The Lower Colorado has a reputation as a hangout for jet boaters, water skiers, and gamblers from southern California. Yet the Lower Colorado also holds several remote desert river trips, including two of the Southwest's best short flatwater floats—Black Canyon and Topock Gorge.

The Lower Colorado, ideal for open canoes, is at its best in spring and fall, when rivers elsewhere are too low or too cold. Midwinter runs are possible, though temperatures may dip below freezing at night. Summer can be astoundingly hot (over 110°), and the river may be crowded. Flows are more than adequate year-round. A good local source for more information is Jerkwater Canoe Co., P.O. Box 800, Topock, AZ 86436; (602) 768-7753. Jerkwater also offers rentals, shuttles, and maps.

Black Canyon

Black Canyon is the last great gorge on the Colorado's journey to the Gulf of California. Here the river squeezes between towering walls of craggy black volcanic andesite, carving a gunsight notch that engineers long ago recognized as one of the West's premier dam sites. In just two years beginning in 1933, Hoover Dam was built a mile and a half below the head of Black Canyon, creating the vast, 110-mile-long reservoir called "Lake" Mead.

Below the dam the Colorado courses smoothly for a dozen miles through the remainder of Black Canyon, offering outstanding flatwater boating along the Arizona-Nevada border just 30 miles southeast of Las Vegas and a few hours' drive from Los Angeles. Attractions include spectacular wilderness scenery, hot springs, side canyons, desert wildlife, and historic sites.

Launch permits are required from the Bureau of Reclamation, (702) 293-3856, which operates Hoover Dam and allows two non-commercial put-ins daily. Call at least two weeks in advance (earlier for popular Saturday starts). Boaters are escorted down a white-knuckle road to the launch site near the base of the awesome 726'-high concrete arch dam.[1] This site is closed to the public except for commercial trips and pre-arranged private launches. First, call the BuRec to reserve a date. Then, for additional information and helpful pamphlets, contact Lake Mead National Recreation Area, 601 Nevada Highway, Boulder City, NV 89005-2426; (702) 293- 8907.

Black Canyon makes a good overnight trip, but be alert for flow fluctuations: camp high and tie boats securely. The water is swift, cold, and clear. The only "whitewater" is Class I+ **RINGBOLT RAPIDS,** 3.5 miles into the run—the final riffle on the Colorado. The rapid is named for a large iron ring, still visible on the Arizona side, that was once used to winch steamboats up through the swift water. Most groups take out at Willow Beach on the Arizona side (left bank) 12 miles below the dam. Downstream the river slows in the backwaters of "Lake" Mojave, another reservoir.

[1]Hoover was the tallest dam in the world at the time of its construction. It was also the first structure in the Western world to exceed the bulk of Egypt's 4,500-year-old Great Pyramid of Cheops.

Topock Gorge

Below Lake Mojave the river runs free again, offering many miles of flatwater boating from Bullhead City down to the next impoundment at "Lake" Havasu. Within this section the most scenic and popular reach is Topock Gorge, a 16-mile float featuring striking red rock buttes and abundant wildlife. Much of this section, which also runs along the California-Arizona border, is protected by the Havasu National Wildlife Refuge. Campfires, camping, and power boats are prohibited; for information call (619) 326-3853.

The standard **put-in** is Park Moabi, a mile north of the I-40 bridge on the California side (right bank) near the town of Needles. The **take-out** is at Castle Rock on the Arizona side, reached by a spur road from Arizona Highway 95. For more information on this section, refer to *A Boating Trail Guide to the Colorado River: Davis Dam to Parker Dam,* published by the California Dept. of Boating and Waterways, 1629 S St., Sacramento, CA 95814; (916) 445-2616.

Blythe to Imperial Dam

Below Blythe the river runs unimpeded for about 75 miles. Numerous accesses allow shorter trips within this section. Some 16 miles below Blythe, the river begins to pass through three wildlife refuges where waterfowl and other animals thrive in marshes, sloughs, and small lakes just off the main channel. No camping is allowed in the refuges. For detailed coverage of this section, refer to the *Boating Trail Guide to the Colorado* listed just above.

California

Clavey River

Difficulty: V+p.
Length: 18 miles (plus 12 on Tuolumne). Shorter run possible.

The Clavey, a major tributary of the Tuolumne, has long been known as a superb native trout stream. In the 1980's some leading-edge expert kayakers began to run it, and an all-female paddle crew made the first raft descent. Now, a fair number of daring experts run the Clavey every year. Anyone with lesser skills and less nerve should definitely stay away—or admire the Clavey and its waterfalls by hiking up from the Tuolumne (only when the Clavey is running low).

Boaters willing to undertake the challenge will find nearly non-stop Class V and V+ rapids—and usually a fair number of portages—throughout the 18-mile run. The Clavey plunges through a succession of well-formed mini-gorges which have unusually few brush hazards, perhaps due to the river's mainly north-south course which exposes the banks and streambed to the searing summer sun.

The put-in is where paved Cottonwood Road crosses the Clavey deep in the Sierra foothills between the town of Sonora and Cherry "Lake," one of the reservoirs on the Tuolumne. A dirt road crosses the Clavey about halfway down, and most boaters split their trips here. Even the first half, with all the scouting and portaging, can make a very full day. The second half of the run is usually considered a bit more difficult than the upper stretch. At its end, boaters face 12 miles on the Tuolumne beginning with famed Clavey Falls, but the "T" is going to look pretty easy to anyone who's made it down the Clavey. For the take-out, see the **Tuolumne** chapter in Region V.

The Clavey is in danger. In spite of the Tuolumne's hard-won National Wild and Scenic River status, local irrigation districts are going ahead with plans to build a big hydroelectric dam on the Clavey despite the damage it would cause to fishing and recreation. For information on conservationists' campaign against this highly questionable project and for Wild and Scenic status for the Clavey, contact Friends of the River (see appendix for address).

Stanislaus River

1. North Fork: Sourgrass CG to Calaveras Big Trees State Park.
IV+5 (V above 2,000 cfs); 5 miles.

2. Camp Nine Run: Camp Nine to Parrott's Ferry.
III4; 9 miles (some or all on reservoir).

3. Lower Stanislaus: Goodwin Dam to Knight's Ferry.
V (III–IV with several portages); 4 miles.

From headwaters draining 9,000' and 10,000' peaks along the crest of the central Sierra Nevada, the Stanislaus flows southwest toward its confluence with the San Joaquin in California's Central Valley. Along its way, the Stanislaus is interrupted by 14 major dams. The infamous New Melones Dam, whose reservoir covers the Camp Nine Run except during extended droughts, is the latest and biggest.

Yet there is still boatable whitewater on the Stanislaus[1] even when New Melones Reservoir is full. Well upstream, the North Fork Stanislaus runs through an alpine canyon cloaked in pine and cedar. Downstream, the Lower Stanislaus flows through a low-elevation gorge in the Sierra foothills just before it empties onto the valley floor. Both are much more difficult than the Camp Nine stretch, although a few portages can turn the Lower Stan into a high intermediate run.

For flow information call the DWR tape, (916) 653-9647, or staff, 653-9647. *North Fork:* Flow at McKays Point. *Camp Nine:* Flow below Camp Nine. *Lower:* Flow at Orange Blossom Bridge. For more whitewater information refer to Cassady and Calhoun, *California Whitewater,* and/or Holbek and Stanley, *Guide to the Best Whitewater in the State of California.* For history and geology, see *Guide to Three Rivers* (John Cassidy, ed.) and Orr, *Rivers of the West.*

---

[1]Named for Estanislao, a young California Indian who led a band of rebel Indians in guerrilla warfare against the Mexican authorities in the 1820's.

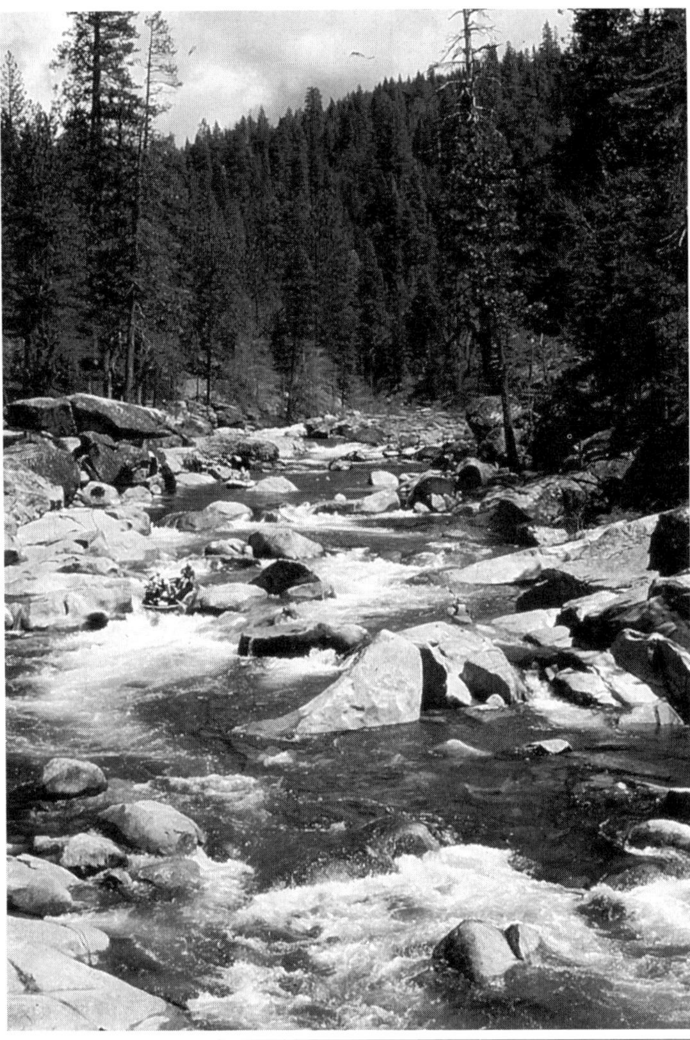

North Fork Stanislaus *Mark Leder-Adams / Rapid Shooters*

North Fork Stanislaus

This small, steep river (gradient: 70 ft./mi.) has become popular in recent years for its fine high-elevation scenery (4,000' at the put-in) and lively advanced whitewater. River access is quick and easy on paved roads leading a few miles off California Highway 4 near the central Sierra town of Arnold. Boaters can view majestic giant sequoias in Calaveras Big Trees State Park just a short way from the take-out. Flows are usually good in April and May. Depending on how recently-enlarged Spicer Reservoir is managed, low but boatable dam releases are possible during part or all of the summer.

The Sourgrass Campground **put-in** (left bank, just above the bridge) allows no warm-up before boaters face the biggest drop of the run, **SOURGRASS RAVINE** (V), a long, complex rapid just below the bridge. To avoid this drop, carry down to an alternate launch site on the right bank at the base of the rapid.

Downstream from Sourgrass the North Fork Stanislaus is technical and challenging, with a number of solid Class IV and IV+ drops. The whitewater peaks again at the end of the run with **UPPER** and **LOWER SEQUOIA (IV+)** just above the bridge in Calaveras Big Trees State Park. The **take-out** is on the right below the bridge.[2]

The North Stan's future may be all or nothing. While the Forest Service has recommended it for National Wild and Scenic status, a local water district and a power agency are proposing an upstream hydro project that would dewater the run described here. For more information, contact Friends of the River (see appendix for address).

Camp Nine Run

In May 1982 one of the loveliest rivers in the country, the Stanislaus below Camp Nine, disappeared under the rising waters of New Melones Reservoir. Sixteen miles of living river canyon were drowned by a dam of questionable necessity—New Melones, one of the largest earth-and-rock dams in the world. The struggle to save the Stan went on for more than a decade.[3] Though the campaign ended in defeat, it gave birth to Friends of the River and quickly led to the coming of age of the California river conservation movement. Other dams continue to be proposed—and opposed—but since New Melones, no more big dams have been constructed in the state.

As California suffered through a long drought in the late 1980's, the Camp Nine stretch began to emerge from the receding res-

[2]Experts have run the next 2.5 miles—continuous Class V, with a gradient over 100 ft./mi.—but most boaters shouldn't even consider it. The road to the take-out at McKays Point is bad and sometimes impassable or closed by a locked gate.

[3]For a full account see Tim Palmer, *Stanislaus: The Struggle for a River.*

ervoir waters. By 1987 enough of the river was exposed to tempt boaters into making the run again. In the early 1990's, as the drought continued and the flatwater at the end of the run grew shorter, commercial rafting outfitters brought paying customers back to the Stanislaus. It now appears that whenever the reservoir is low enough to expose most of the river, some boaters will include Camp Nine on their itineraries.

Though the river banks are dotted with dead trees and, in the lower stretches, badly silted up, the trip is definitely worthwhile. The canyon itself is still beautiful, and making this run provides a first-hand look at what a reservoir does to a river. A side hike up Rose Creek (mile 2.5, left bank) quickly leads above the high-water mark of the reservoir and into unspoiled territory. When you're in Coral Cave (mile 4.6, right bank) you can briefly forget the dam was ever built.

The whitewater is still good. In fact, the toughest rapid on the run, **BIG DOG (IV)**, just below the right-bank **put-in,** is unfamiliar to old Stan hands. It was created when big boulders were tumbled into the river during construction of the new high bridge above the top end of the reservoir. Most of the action is in the first 2.5 miles above Rose Creek, where short pools alternate with a series of exhilarating Class III rapids: **ROCK GARDEN, DEATH ROCK, DEVIL'S STAIRCASE, BAILEY FALLS,** and **WIDOWMAKER.**

Below Rose Creek the pools grow longer, and most of the rapids are only Class II. The series of easy III's that used to mark the last couple of miles are now usually either covered by the reservoir or silted up. The **take-out** is on the left at the old (low) Parrott's Ferry bridge, on Parrott's Ferry Road between California Highways 4 and 49. The Camp Nine Road to the put-in heads east from Parrott's Ferry Road a few miles north of the river and about six miles east of the town of Angels Camp.

Lower Stanislaus

As it descends to the eastern edge of the Central Valley, the Stanislaus flows through a small, steep-sided gorge known as Goodwin Canyon. Here, only 100 miles from the Bay Area, boaters can run the river's final rapids. Releases from Goodwin Dam just upstream provide the Lower Stan with boatable flows in the summer and sometimes all year. Goodwin Canyon is much smaller and less imposing than the Stanislaus canyon upstream, but the scenery in this tiny near-wilderness is very good. The river flows through striking granite formations capped here and there by the remnants of old lava flows.

The overall gradient is moderate (30 ft./mi.), but the Lower Stan is an extreme pool-and-drop river. Some of the tight, rocky rapids are very steep, and a few are nothing short of dangerous. Deadly mishaps have occurred here in recent years. Yet if boaters are willing to make a few easy portages, the river's difficulty drops to Class III–IV. At certain flows one or more portages may be required, even for experts.

The **put-in** is on the left bank a half mile below Goodwin Dam (take Tulloch Road off California Highway 108/120 east of Oakdale). A half mile downstream is **MR. TOAD'S (V),** where big holes and a **dangerous undercut boulder** dictate a careful scout and possible portage on the right. A quarter mile farther is **OFF-RAMP (V–VI),** a **probable portage** where a river-wide ledge forms a **deadly reversal at higher flows,** followed by **PINBALL (III–IV)** at mile 2.

The last big rapid on the run is **HAUNTED HOUSE (V)** at mile 2.3, a 5' drop onto a submerged boulder and into a powerful reversal. Scout carefully, and consider making the easy portage on the right. The last two miles are much easier, with only one Class IV. The **take-out** is on the right at Knight's Ferry, just beyond the covered bridge (reached via a side road off Highway 108/120).

Both this and downstream runs will be eliminated if, as seems likely, San Joaquin Valley irrigation districts are permitted to divert water upstream from Goodwin Dam. As of 1993 they had spent some $70 million building canals and tunnels to carry the water. For more information contact Friends of the River (see appendix for address).

Downstream Runs

Below Knights Ferry are up to 45 miles of scenic novice boating with reliable summer flows down to the San Joaquin River confluence west of Modesto. Here the Lower Stanislaus winds quietly through lush riparian woodlands where bird life abounds. Beginners should beware of Class II **RUSSIAN RAPID,** located just below Knight's Ferry; portage on the left if necessary. Below Orange Blossom Bridge, some 7 miles below Knight's Ferry, the Stanislaus is Class I with a few small riffles.

Numerous public parks along the lower river allow a variety of one-day runs and even overnight trips. A good local source for information and canoe rentals is Sunshine River Adventures in Oakdale, (209) 881-3236. Boats can also be rented at River Journey, (916) 847-4671.

North Fork Yuba River

Difficulty: III–V.
Length: 19 miles. Shorter trips possible.

From headwaters at Yuba Pass in the northern Sierra Nevada, the North Fork of the Yuba runs southwest down a steep, scenic canyon. Plentiful rainfall and a relatively high elevation (about 3,000') give the North Yuba a lushness seen on few Sierra rivers. Mossy rocks and dense stands of pine, fir, and cedar mark this transition zone between the drier central Sierra to the south and the wet Cascades to the north.

At one time the North Yuba was one of the most productive placer mining rivers in the state. Even today, miners work the riverbed with gasoline-powered dredges. The historic gold rush town of Downieville sits at the confluence of the North Yuba and its largest tributary, the Downie River.

The North Yuba flows freely all the way to New Bullards Bar Reservoir and generally has sufficient water for boating from April through June. California Highway 49 follows the run closely, offering frequent access and short, easy shuttles. Several sections are for experts only, and some of the big rapids could require portage, depending on flow.

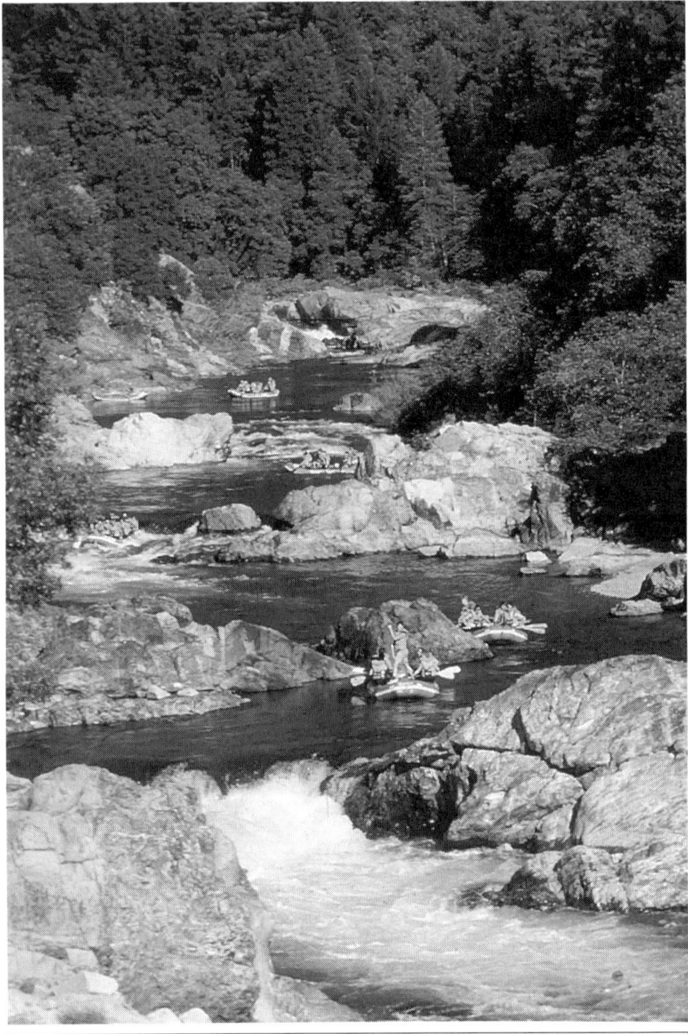

North Fork Yuba River *Erik Simonson*

The Downieville Run—the first 10 miles from Union Flat Campground to Goodyears Bar—is for **experts only.** The whitewater is continuous, the gradient is steep (80 ft./mi.), and the run has almost constant Class IV and V drops plus a mile of solid Class V in **Moss Canyon,** which begins two miles below Union Flat. Six miles below Union Flat the Downie River enters from the right at Downieville, nearly doubling the flow. Just under a mile downstream is a mile-long Class V section called **Rossasco Ravine.**

A popular access at mile 10 is on the left just below the Goodyears Bar bridge. This is the **put-in** for the Goodyears Bar Run, which has a more moderate gradient (50 ft./mi.) and generally milder Class III and IV rapids. The main exception is **MAYTAG,** a big Class V located six miles below Goodyears Bar at a right bend where Humbug Creek enters on the left. The river drops into a powerful reversal, followed by a nasty Class IV run-out.

Take out at the Highway 49 bridge or at Fiddle Creek Campground just under a mile upstream. Boaters may consider running the final six miles of the

North Fork below the bridge, down to New Bullards Bar Reservoir. This beautiful roadless section has many Class IV to IV+ rapids; however, at the end lie 12 miles of flatwater to the first possible take-out on the reservoir at Dark Day Boat Ramp. Try to hire a tow locally. At the opposite end of the river, experts sometimes tackle 8 miles of very difficult Class V water above Union Flat, beginning at Haypress Creek. Flows are usually skimpy this far upstream, and the gradient is a daunting 110 ft./mi.

The fate of the North Yuba hangs in the balance, with river conservation groups calling for National Wild and Scenic designation even as hydropower developers propose at least two new dams. Friends of the River (see appendix for address) is working to preserve this outstanding Sierra river.

For more information refer to Cassady and Calhoun, *California Whitewater* and/or Holbek and Stanley, *Guide to the Best Whitewater in the State of California.* For flows call the DWR tape, (916) 653-9647, and check the inflow to New Bullards Bar Reservoir. For an estimate of the flow on the North Yuba above the Downie River, take about two thirds of the inflow; below the Downie, about three quarters. For maps and information contact Tahoe NF, Highway 49 and Coyote St., Nevada City, CA 95959; (916) 265-4531.

Eel River

Difficulty: II–IV+5 (various forks).

The Eel is the biggest and most diverse of California's North Coast rivers, draining a large section of the wet western slope of the Coast Range north of San Francisco. The river's three forks and main stem offer good boating during the winter and spring rainy season. Runs range from Class II to Class IV+ (with one bigger rapid on the Middle Fork) and last from one to several days. In 1980 much of the Eel was added to the National Wild and Scenic Rivers System.

Eel River country is a land of heavy rain, floods, and landslides. In an average year the watershed gets 50" to 90" of precipitation, almost entirely from November through April. The awesome "thousand- year" flood of December 1964 was the biggest on any California river since stream flows have been measured. In that deluge the Eel peaked at 752,000 cfs near its mouth, and even today the river is still laboring to remove immense gravel bars deposited by the flood. Heavy erosion means that rapids change frequently, and new ones are occasionally formed by landslides. The watershed has few high peaks to hold a snowpack, so the river drops quickly when the rains stop.

The descriptions below are necessarily brief. The most comprehensive source for more information is Dick Schwind's classic guide book, *West Coast River Touring.* Unfortunately, this 1974 publication is out of print and somewhat out of date. For current information refer to the Cassady-Calhoun and/or Holbek-Stanley guide books listed earlier. The Eel is popular with Bay Area boaters, and good advice can be found at local whitewater shops. For flow information call the DWR tape, (916) 653-9647.

Main Eel

The uppermost commonly-run stretch of the main Eel is the Class III+ **Pillsbury Run,** which begins just below Scott Dam northeast of Ukiah and extends six or nine miles, depending on the take-out. The moderate gradient (30 ft./mi.) produces technical rapids, and the forest scenery is excellent. Downstream the river stills in Van Arsdale Reservoir, where water is diverted south to the Russian River drainage.

Below Van Arsdale Dam the main Eel runs free all the way to the Pacific. The heart of the river is the 46-mile **Dos Rios to Alderpoint Run.** Here boaters find rugged scenery, fine beaches, and a few Class III rapids as the river follows a northwesterly course some 10 to 20 miles east of U.S. 101. The canyon is essentially roadless; only a lightly-used rail line follows the run.

Boaters can put in farther upstream at alternate sites, adding up to 34 miles of Class II+ water. However, these upper sections are usually dried up by diversions beginning in April. Boaters can also continue downstream past Alderpoint. Or they can combine a Middle Fork float with the Dos Rios run for a 77-mile trip.

Dos Rios is north of Ukiah and 13 miles east of U.S. 101 at Laytonville. Alderpoint is about 21 miles east of 101 at Garberville.

North Fork Eel

This little-known branch drains a beautiful portion of the Coast Range between Round Valley and Six Rivers National Forest. Adventurous boaters occasionally enjoy a scenic eight-mile Class III run from Hulls Creek to Mina Road. (There have been access problems with local property owners at the Hulls Creek put-in.) Below the take-out the river carves through Split Rock Ridge, dropping more than 100 ft./mi. in the last four miles of its plunge to the main Eel confluence. **Boating the Split Rock stretch is not recommended.**

Middle Fork Eel

The Middle Eel is one of the best wilderness runs in California: 30 miles of outstanding scenery and challenging whitewater that can be run alone or combined with the Dos Rios section of the main Eel (see above). Only a difficult passage at Coal Mine Falls—a major obstacle that is often portaged—keeps the Middle Eel from becoming more popular. Due to its higher watershed, the Middle Fork enjoys a longer season than other Eel runs.

Most boating begins at the confluence with the Black Butte River, reached via Mendocino Pass Road from the small town of Covelo, which is about 20 miles northeast of Dos Rios (see **Main Eel** above). For 24 miles boaters enjoy rolling hills and Class II water. Then the Middle Fork changes character, and they face **SKINNY CHUTES (IV)** and **COAL MINE FALLS** (mile 26), a V–VI passage with a **very tough portage.** Below this rapid the river enters a deep gorge that continues to the **take-out** at the Main Eel confluence at Dos Rios.

South Fork Eel

The South Fork's small, low-elevation watershed produces boatable flows only during the rainy season, making this Class IV+ run popular with San Francisco Bay Area boaters who can drive up on short notice. The run is even more demanding than the rating of its rapids indicates. Its length—the vast majority of boaters try to make it in one day—its isolation, and its availability only during the rainy season make this an **experts-only** run.

The heart of this run is the seven-mile South Fork Gorge, laced with Class IV and IV+ drops and one larger rapid—**DOUBLE DROP**—that is often portaged. The gorge begins where Tenmile Creek joins the South Fork northwest of Laytonville and a few miles west of U.S. 101. However, there is no road access at the confluence, so boaters descend either the South Fork or Tenmile Creek to reach this point; the former offers six miles of Class II water, while the latter drops through difficult rapids that approach Class V as the creek nears the confluence. Either way, the South Fork run totals 16 miles. The standard **take-out** is at Big Bend Lodge (right bank, private) off U.S. 101. Downstream are miles of scenic Class II water, including sections through magnificent redwood groves. Access and shuttle logistics for the South Fork are complicated; refer to the Cassady-Calhoun guide book listed above.

Upper Sacramento River

Difficulty: III–IV5.
Length: 36 miles. Shorter runs possible.

Humans haven't been good to the Upper Sacramento. First came Shasta Dam in 1949, then Box Canyon Dam in 1969. There was the construction of Interstate 5 in the 1960's and 1970's, a chemical spill in 1976, and in 1991 a disastrous train derailment that dropped a tank car full of toxic weed killer into the river. This calamity wiped out all life in 34 miles of the Upper Sacramento, including its world-class trout fishery.

After all this, one might think that the river was hardly worth a second look. Remarkably, however, the "Upper Sac" is back, offering excellent whitewater and outstanding scenery to those willing to give it another chance. The fishery may take years to recover from the spill, and wildlife is only slowly returning. But the river is running pure once again, vegetation appears to have suffered only minimal damage, and the rapids are as good as ever. The river deserves Wild and Scenic designation.

Boating begins a dozen miles south of Mt. Shasta, where the Sacramento is a small mountain river, not the enormous valley waterway it becomes after merging with the larger McCloud and Pit Rivers at a confluence now covered by Shasta Reservoir.[1] I-5 and the Southern Pacific Railroad follow the river much of the way, reducing the solitude but providing numerous accesses—many more than are mentioned below. The most popular sections are the first

[1] Surprisingly, most of the water in Shasta Reservoir comes from the Pit River, which has over four times the volume of the Upper Sacramento. Despite its name the Pit, which drains a vast watershed that extends to headwaters in the extreme northeastern corner of the state, is clearly the main stem of the Sacramento system.

six miles from Box Canyon Dam to above Dunsmuir (Class IV), where I-5 is away from the river; and the last 14 miles from Sims Flat to Dog Creek (IV).

The season is roughly April to mid-June, and the river sometimes rises again in late fall. For flow information call the DWR tape, (916) 653-9647; the "Delta Gauge" gives the flow just above Shasta Reservoir.

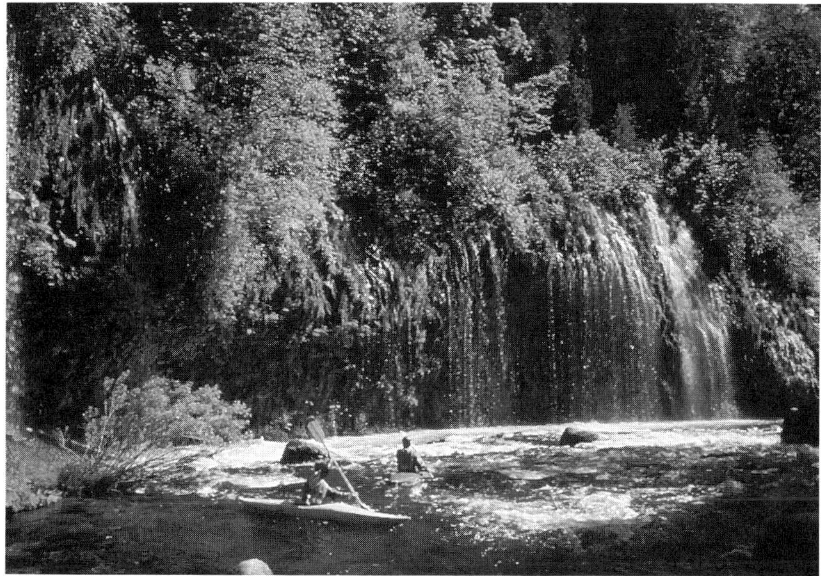

Box Canyon, Upper Sacramento *Bill Cross*

The uppermost reach is what remains of very beautiful Box Canyon, where the river cuts a narrow gorge through lava erupted from Mt. Shasta. The put-in (mile 0) is just below Box Canyon Dam; behind the dam is Siskiyou Reservoir and most of Box Canyon.[2] The dam builders provided plentiful access to the reservoir, but not even a trail down to the river; as a result, the put-in is unimproved, steep, arduous, and potentially dangerous. Gear must be lowered part way, limiting the run to small, lightweight craft. The put-in can be hard to find, and a proposed subdivision could change the shuttle directions—it's best to ask locally. (This put-in may be greatly improved in the near future by a bungee-jumping operation.)

Box Canyon is worth the effort: near-vertical walls rise on either side as the river tumbles through steep, closely-spaced Class IV drops at 100 ft./mi. This spectacular gorge ends all too soon—near mile 2 where Stink Creek enters on the right. The scenery remains excellent, however, as the river flows down a deep, lush V-shaped canyon that continues to Shasta Reservoir. Downstream the gradient averages 45 to 55 ft./mi.

[2]Box Canyon Dam is one of the more unnecessary dams in a state rife with unnecessary dams. Lake Siskiyou is too small to provide significant water storage or flood control (five years after the dam was built the downstream town of Dunsmuir suffered the worst inundation in its history), and recreation has never lived up to initial predictions due to the proximity of Shasta, the state's largest and most popular reservoir.

Those wishing to avoid the difficult Box Canyon put-in can use an alternate access on the left at mile 2.1, just above the Cantara Loop railroad bridge—site of the 1991 toxic spill. (Follow Old South Stage Road to Cantara Road, then descend to the river.)

The rest of the run to Dunsmuir is rocky and challenging Class IV. The first river access is on the left at mile 6, at the Prospect Street access at the upstream end of Dunsmuir. The next access is under the I-5 overpass at mile 7.5.

Floating the following stretch through Dunsmuir is less scenic at first, but below town boaters have spectacular upstream views of Mt. Shasta. Near mile 13 the granite spires of Castle Crags appear on the right. At mile 16 is a popular access at the Sweetbriar Bridge. Downstream the rapids become more difficult.

Near mile 20 the railroad crosses the river, passes through a tunnel, then recrosses, signalling the approach of **MEARS CREEK FALLS** (V) at mile 21. Sometimes called **Triple Drop**, this is the biggest rapid on the river. It is toughest at high flows. Portage or line if necessary.

The next access is Sims Flat, mile 22, on the left bank below Sims bridge (reached via Sims Road from I-5). Downstream is the most popular section of the Upper Sacramento, with consistent Class III and IV rapids and a slightly longer season. Boaters usually run either 10.5 miles to a **take-out** on the right at Lamoine, where Slate Creek enters; or 14 miles to **another take-out** on the left at Dog Creek, just below the Fender Ferry Road bridge. Downstream the river stills in Shasta Reservoir.

For detailed information see the Cassady-Calhoun and/or Holbek-Stanley guide books listed earlier. The *Shasta-Trinity NF* map covers the run. The best map for access and shuttles is *Upper Sacramento River Fishing Access* (Streamtime, P.O. Box 7093, Cotati, CA 94931), which is sold in local shops. A good local source for information is Turtle River Rafting Co. in the town of Mt. Shasta, (916) 926-3223.

McCloud River

Difficulty: III.
Length: 10 miles (7 on river, 3 on reservoir).

The McCloud, a classic river of the Cascade Range, drains the southern flank of Mt. Shasta. The porous volcanic rock soaks up rain and melted snow like a sponge and then releases it steadily through springs. Consequently, the McCloud shows much less variation in flow than other California rivers. (There's a catch: since the river rarely gets high enough to move them aside, fallen trees pose a potential hazard.)

At Big Springs a cascade of some 500 cfs of icy groundwater instantly transforms the McCloud from a creek into a river. Unfortunately, boaters can't get *to* Big Springs, thanks to the extensive and exclusive landholdings of the Hearst Corporation, present-day repository of some of California's oldest and biggest money. The Hearsts have been unable to stop boating on the river where it passes through their land; legally, they can only prevent boaters from stepping on shore. As a result, river runners float right past the Hearst family's secluded riverside estate at Wyntoon.

At most flows the best **put-in** is about a mile below Fowler's Campground, just above the Hearst property, where an unmarked trail descends steeply to the river from a dirt road above the right bank. It's a mile and a half from here to Big Springs, and flows on this section are usually very skimpy after late spring—often, there is more dragging and carrying than floating, so lightweight craft are preferred.

At higher flows boaters can launch half a mile upstream, just below Lower Falls near Fowler's Campground. (There is a series of falls; be sure to launch below the *last* one.) Be alert: the gradient in the first mile below Lower Falls is 130 ft./mi., and this stretch is Class IV at higher flows. Fowler's Campground is reached via an unpaved side road off California Highway 89 east of the town of McCloud.

A small spring adds a little flow about a half mile below the lower put-in, but the real relief comes at Big Springs. From here on the river always has enough water, running ice cold and crystal clear all year. The next 2.5 miles are swift, continuous Class III with a gradient of 70 ft./mi. Then a log bridge crosses the river; downstream, the gradient and rapids ease as the geology shifts from volcanic bedrock to softer deposits of ash and pumice. The lush forest scenery is outstanding.

Four miles below Big Springs, boaters come upon one of the most bizarre sights on any western river—Wyntoon. This private Hearst estate features two clusters of palatial houses in a variety of themes: Bavarian Cottage, Cape Cod, Log Cabin, and Medieval Castle. Just below the second compound the river stills in the backwaters of McCloud Reservoir. From here it's a slow three-mile flatwater paddle to the boat ramp at Tarantula Gulch (reached by taking Squaw Valley Road south from the town of McCloud). Boaters could take out at the top of the reservoir were it not Hearst property.[1]

The McCloud has some of the finest forest scenery on any California river. Conservationists are pushing the Forest Service to recommend the river for Wild and Scenic status—over the objections of the Hearst Corporation, the timber industry, and private fishing clubs.

Experts might want to tackle a more difficult (Class IV–V) run on the Lower McCloud from McCloud Dam to Gilman Road on the upper reaches of Shasta Reservoir. The Lower McCloud has a very short spring season because of upstream hydroelectric diversions. An even more challenging route is to float Squaw Valley Creek down to its confluence with the McCloud—a Class V stretch with some waterfalls that must be portaged.

[1] Boaters will notice that Huckleberry Creek, which enters on the right at the top of the reservoir, carries a heavy load of light-colored silt from glacial runoff on Mt. Shasta. The silt doesn't originate in Huckleberry Creek, which is spring-fed and would normally run clear. The silt comes from Mud Creek, which is supposed to enter the McCloud well upstream, over two miles above Wyntoon. The Hearsts wanted a clear river running past their estate, so they tidied things up by having Mud Creek's naturally silty water ditched and diverted over to Huckleberry Creek.

Pacific Northwest

Crooked River

Difficulty: IV first 17 miles, III+p last 7 miles.
Length: 26 miles. Shorter runs possible.

The Crooked, a major tributary of the Deschutes, drains a large, semi-arid basin in central Oregon's Ochoco Mountains. Boating takes place in the lower reaches north of Bend where the river cuts through a rugged volcanic gorge.

The section described here divides easily into two runs: (1) 17 miles from Lone Pine Road bridge to Crooked River Ranch, and (2) nine miles from the ranch to Opal Springs at the upper end of Billy Chinook Reservoir. The gradient on both runs is 35 to 40 ft./mi. Steep canyon walls provide seclusion, though civilization is not far away. The upper reach is usually boatable only during a brief snowmelt window, typically sometime between mid-April and early May. Springs augment flows and extend the season on the lower run. The lower reach was designated a National Wild and Scenic River in 1988.

The upper run, from Lone Pine Road bridge to Crooked River Ranch, holds demanding, technical Class IV whitewater and the spectacular scenery of Smith Rocks State Park, one of the Northwest's foremost rock-climbing sites. The **put-in** is about five miles east of Terrebone and U.S. 97. The run begins fairly mildly as the gorge gradually deepens. At mile 2.5 a flume crosses the river, signaling the beginning of a long stretch of continuous Class IV. Near mile 4 the river turns suddenly placid as it enters Smith Rocks, drifting lazily past soaring spires and walls.

Below the park, near mile 7, Class III and IV rapids resume for the rest of the trip. The gorge continues to deepen, and Highway 97 and the Burlington Northern Railway cross high overhead at mile 11.5 (no access). Just beyond a difficult rapid known as **CHINESE DAM** is a **river access (take-out for the upper run)** on the left bank at Crooked River Ranch, a private resort at mile 17 (permission required).

Boaters may continue downstream or put in (with permission) at the ranch for the lower run to Opal Springs. Whitewater continues as the gorge reaches its greatest depth of about 800'. A difficult **portage** is required at Opal Springs Dam, five miles below Crooked River Ranch. Look for water flowing in from Opal Springs on the right below the dam. Most boaters **take out** at Opal Springs. (The access site should be open on weekdays, but the gate may be locked on weekends, so inquire locally.) When Billy Chinook Reservoir is full, it extends upstream almost to this point. Boaters who continue must cross three miles of flatwater to the next possi-

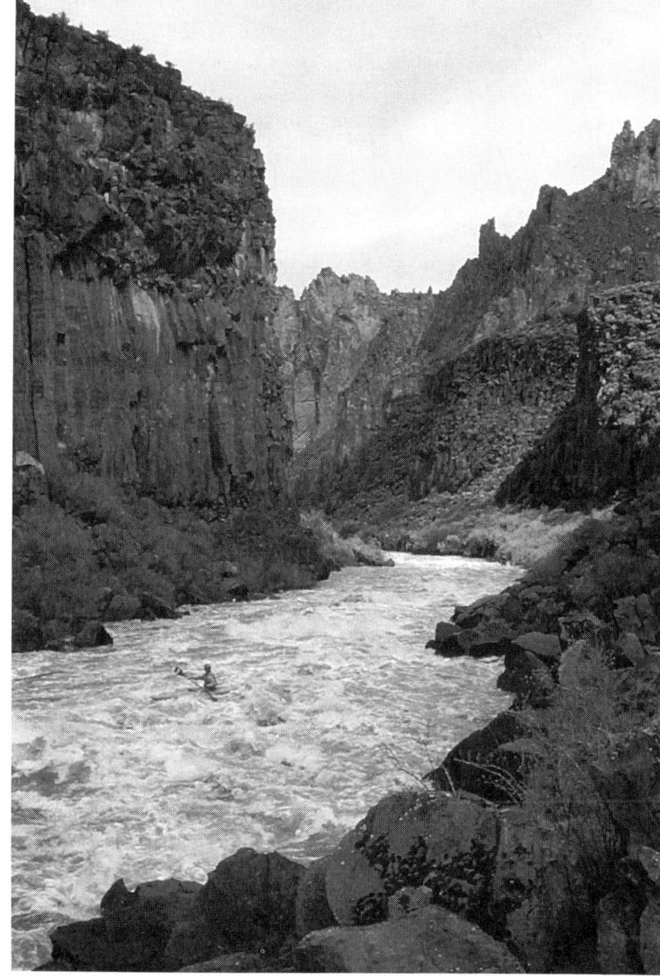

Crooked River *Hayden Glatte*

ble take-out. (For more information on these runs, refer to the *Soggy Sneakers Guide to Oregon Rivers* and the *Deschutes NF* map.)

North Fork Crooked

Adventurous experts only may consider a 26-mile Class IV+p wilderness run down the North Fork of the Crooked, a tributary rising among old-growth Ponderosa pines in Ochoco National Forest. The boatable window during spring snowmelt is extremely brief; in dry years it never opens. The North Fork Crooked was added to the National Wild and Scenic Rivers System in 1988.

The run from Deep Creek Campground (mile 0) to the confluence with the main stem follows a twisting course through remote basalt canyons peppered with rocky, technical rapids and possible log hazards. The moderate average gradient of 33 ft./mi. disguises several much steeper sections. There are **two mandatory portages:** first at **UPPER FALLS,** eight miles below Deep Creek (rough access may be possible here); and again at **LOWER FALLS** (mile 17) in the deepest part of the canyon at the end of a long gooseneck bend to the right.

The three miles below Lower Falls drop at 60 ft./mi. **River access** may be possible at mile 21 via a jeep track that approaches the right bank near the mouth of Committee Creek above Teaters Ranch. Boaters who continue below Committee Creek should beware of **barbed wire fences and an earthen dam** across the river. A **take-out** at the river's mouth (mile 26) requires landowner permission.

For more information contact Ochoco NF, Prineville, OR 97754, (503) 447-6247, and BLM, Prineville District, P.O. Box 550, Prineville, OR 97754, (503) 446-8717.

White River

Difficulty: IV, III.
Length: 30 miles. Shorter runs possible.

Named for the milky appearance of its glacial meltwater, Oregon's White River begins on the south face of 11,235' Mt. Hood, 50 miles east of Portland. In its journey down the Cascade's east slope, this tributary of the Deschutes makes a transition from forested alpine canyon to semi-arid volcanic gorge. The White, which was added to the National Wild and Scenic Rivers System in 1988, offers excellent scenery and good seclusion.

The main reason the White does not see more use is **numerous and dangerous log hazards.** Boaters must be constantly alert for strainers and jams, some of which will likely require portage. For this reason small, lightweight craft are preferred. The steep but constant gradient produces almost continuous advanced and intermediate rapids. The White is boatable during spring snowmelt; call the River Forecast Center, (503) 249-0666, for the flow at Tygh Valley. Flows diminish the farther upstream one goes.

Alternate accesses at miles 7 and 18.5 allow boaters to divide the White into three very different sections. The first stretch, from the **put-in** at Barlow Crossing (USFS Road 43 bridge) to Keeps Mill Campground (where Keeps Mill Road crosses the river), begins at an elevation of 3,000' and passes through lovely forest scenery. However, the very small drainage means skimpy flows and a short season. The whitewater is moderate at first, but after a couple of miles the canyon narrows and the river accelerates into continuous Class III to IV whitewater. The gradient steadily increases to 90 ft./mi. near the end of the stretch.

Near Keeps Mills Campground (**alternate access,** mile 7) two major tributaries add to the flow: Clear Creek on the right, followed by Boulder Creek on the left. Technical Class III to IV whitewater continues as the gradient holds at 80 to 90 ft./mi. and the canyon deepens and narrows. At mile 11 the river leaves the National Forest and soon begins to cut through drier foothill terrain. At mile 18.5 White River Crossing Road crosses the river, providing an **alternate access** (about 4 miles north of Highway 216 and reached via Victor Road).

In the final 11 miles to Tygh Valley the gradient diminishes to 40 ft./mi. and the whitewater eases to Class II+ to III at most flows, with one or two more difficult spots. The now-arid canyon remains narrow and scenic. Rock Creek enters on the left at mile 24. Threemile Creek enters on the left at mile 28.5 as the canyon opens. **Take out** one mile downstream in Tygh Valley. **Do not float beyond U.S. 197;** about two miles downstream, the White plunges over a **lethal waterfall** just above its confluence with the Deschutes. For more information consult the *Soggy Sneakers Guide to Oregon Rivers* and the *Mt. Hood NF* map.

Hood River

Difficulty: IVp, IV-.
Length: 7–14 miles.

From glaciers on the northern face of Oregon's 11,235' Mt. Hood, the Hood River plummets to near sea level and its confluence with the Columbia in just 20 miles. The relatively small upper watershed produces strong flows only until about late June, but glacial melt allows hardy boaters to scrape down at minimum flows throughout the summer. The most common runs on the Hood are a seven-mile section of the West Fork and a seven-mile combination run of the East Fork and main stem.

The West Fork run begins at White Bridge Park, located roughly five miles southwest of Dee on the Dee-Lost Lake Road. This scenic and secluded springtime run includes many Class IV rapids and a **mandatory portage** about three miles below the put-in where a fish ladder bypasses a waterfall. The river is very steep, with an average gradient of nearly 100 ft./mi. Just upstream from the confluence with the East Fork is **PUNCHBOWL FALLS,** a powerful ledge drop into a beautiful round pool (a popular swimming hole in summer). Boaters can **take out** just above the East Fork confluence, via a difficult trail up the right bank, or continue downstream on the main stem.

The more popular East Fork-Main Hood run offers somewhat easier whitewater and less demanding logistics. Most of the rapids are Class III to III+, with a scattering of easy Class IV drops. The run begins near the bridge over the East Fork at Dee. A mile and a half downstream the West Fork enters, roughly doubling the flow. Below the confluence the Hood has a continuous gradient of over 60 ft./mi. for six miles down to Tucker Bridge, a popular **takeout** on the right bank about a mile downstream from Tucker Park. (To reach the bridge, drive south from the city of Hood River on Tucker Road.) Below the bridge the river eases as it passes through a lovely valley. A **dam** a mile and a half below the bridge requires a **portage.** Four miles below the dam, the Hood passes the town of Hood River on the left, flows under I-84, and empties into the broad Columbia.

For more information see the *Soggy Sneakers Guide to Oregon Rivers* and/or Garren, *Oregon River Tours.* Call the River Forecast Center in Portland, (503) 249-0666, for the flow at Tucker Bridge; each fork has about half. The *Mt. Hood NF* map covers all runs.

Minam River

Difficulty: III. **Length:** 23 miles.

The Minam, a major tributary of the Wallowa River in the northeastern corner of Oregon, drains 8,000' peaks in the Wallowa Mountains. It may be familiar to Grande Ronde boaters, who usually launch at the Minam-Wallowa confluence. But that brief glimpse of the Minam's last few hundred yards gives only a hint of its enchanting wilderness course farther upstream. The Minam was designated a National Wild and Scenic River in 1988.

Those willing to pack or fly their boats to the remote put-in in the Eagle Cap Wilderness will discover a pristine river that few boaters have seen. The Minam ("MY-num") rushes at 50 ft./mi. down a deep canyon carved from layers of dark basalt. Stands of Ponderosa pine alternate with open grassland, and wildlife is abundant. The Nez Perce tribe knew this canyon as "E-mi-ne-mah," or "valley of the roots," after an edible plant.

The Minam's continuous, technical whitewater rates Class III at most flows, but that does not convey the serious challenges and dangers of the run. Eddies are scarce and the water is icy, making hypothermia a serious threat. Abundant logs and **log jams** pose a major and constantly shifting hazard; portages are likely, and eddies may be hard to catch above the danger spots. Anyone considering the Minam should inquire locally first, then scout the entire river first by air or trail. Melting snow generally provides boatable flows sometime from about May to mid-June.

The run begins at either Red's Horse Ranch or Minam Lodge, located a half mile apart and accessible only by pack trail or light plane. Both offer lodging, meals, and pack service. At the **put-in** (3,600' elevation) the Minam makes the transition from its granitic upper watershed to its volcanic lower canyon. A trail follows the right bank downstream, providing a scouting route.

Below the put-in the canyon narrows and the gradient slowly increases. The Little Minam River enters on the left at mile 5. A trail leads up the Little Minam, and a steep side branch climbs some four miles to a Forest Service road, providing a possible alternate access route. The half-dozen miles below the Little Minam are the steepest of the run. At mile 10.5 Murphy Creek enters on the right, followed at mile 13 by Trout Creek on the right. A mile below Trout Creek the river leaves the Eagle Cap Wilderness. The gradient the rest of the way averages 40 ft/mi. At mile 19 a private road crosses the river. Highway 82 soon appears high on the left, gradually descending to the Minam-Wallowa confluence at mile 23. **Take out** below the highway bridge on the left.

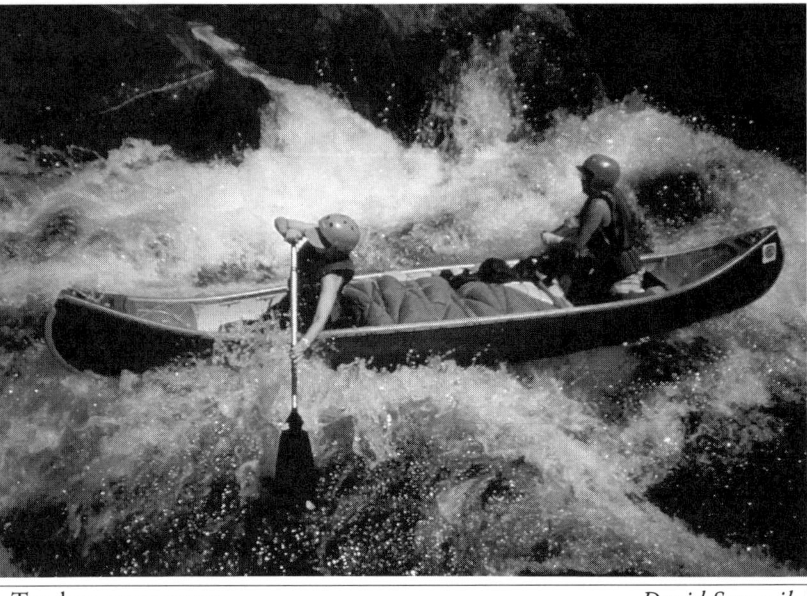
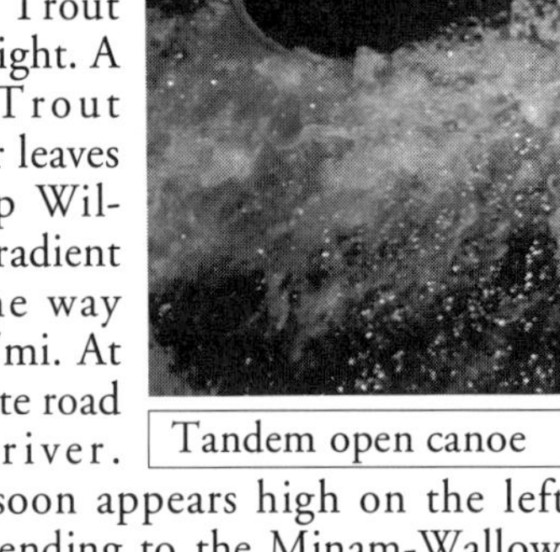

Tandem open canoe *David Symonik*

For more information contact Wallowa-Whitman NF, Eagle Cap RD, 888401 Highway 82, Enterprise, OR 97828; (503) 426-4978. Refer to the *Wallowa-Whitman NF (North Half)* and *Eagle Cap Wilderness* maps and to Garren, *Oregon River Tours.*

Kalama River

1. Upper: Below Upper Kalama Falls to above Gobar Creek.
III4; 15 miles.

2. Middle: Above Gobar Creek to above Lower Kalama Falls.
III; 9.5 miles.

3. Lower: Indian Creek to Modrow Bridge.
II; 5 miles.

The Kalama, a scenic rainy-season run in southwestern Washington, is popular with Portland boaters, for whom it is a quick drive north on I-5. Rising low on the southwestern flank of Mt. St. Helens, the Kalama flows west to meet the Columbia near Longview. The Kalama usually has good flows during the rainy season about November through May (dates vary). The NOAA Whitewater Hotline, (206) 526-8530, gives the flow near the mouth.

In keeping with its Indian name, which means "pretty maiden," the Kalama is a river of gentle beauty, flowing through a thickly forested low-elevation canyon. Though logging scars mar the scenery in places, dense riverside vegetation and occasional passages between rocky walls give a sense of solitude. Houses dot the shore in the lower sections, and a road follows the right bank the entire way, often well above the river.

A good access divides the Upper and Middle runs, while **unrunnable Lower Kalama Falls** divides the Middle from the Lower. **Logs are a possible hazard on all runs.** Three local guide books provide details: Bennett, *Guide to the Whitewater Rivers of Washington,* covers the Upper and Middle; North, *Washington Whitewater,* covers the Middle; Huser, *Paddle Routes of Western Washington,* covers the Lower.

All accesses are via Kalama River Road, which follows the right bank upstream from I-5 (exit 32). Several are reached by turning onto spur roads. **Common accesses,** in ascending order, are: Modrow Bridge, take-out for the Lower run, just over a mile east of I-5; Indian Creek, some 5 miles east of I-5; Kalama Falls Salmon Hatchery, just above Lower Kalama Falls, 8 miles east of I-5; the bridge above Gobar Creek, 8 miles above the Salmon Hatchery; Road 7300 bridge, 11.5 miles farther upstream.

The **Upper Kalama put-in** is either at the bridge just below Upper Kalama Falls or at the Road 7300 bridge (easier access) some three miles downstream. Below the upper put-in lie

15 miles of Class III water (overall gradient: 55 ft./mi.) with one tougher spot, **DOUBLE DROP (IV)**, at mile 13. Double Drop is about 1.5 miles below the Jacks Creek bridge, a spur road bridge where Jacks Creek enters on the left (steep alternate access). The run ends at the spur road bridge above Gobar Creek.

The **Middle Kalama** begins at the bridge above Gobar Creek. The next 9.5 miles are mostly Class II and III (gradient: 30 ft./mi.) with one rougher spot, **LEADER (III+, IV at high water)**. This long rock garden is half a mile below the Summers Creek bridge. Below Leader is Class II water down to the **mandatory take-out** on the right at Kalama Falls Salmon Hatchery. **Don't miss the take-out! Just downstream is unrunnable Lower Kalama Falls.**

Below Lower Kalama Falls is the **Lower Kalama,** which is mostly Class II. The first couple of miles below the falls hold much stronger rapids, but difficult access below the falls deters most boaters. A more common **put-in** is near Indian Creek, below which the Kalama runs through easy Class II riffles at 10 ft./mi. **Take out** at Modrow Bridge near the canyon mouth, or continue down three more miles of flatwater to the Columbia confluence.

Toutle River

Difficulty: III4.
Length: 9.5 miles.

Washington's Toutle River rises on the northwest face of 8,365' Mt. St. Helens, then flows west into the Cowlitz River. The Toutle offers good whitewater and a look at the lingering effects of the Mt. St. Helens eruption of 1980. The river's convenient location—near I-5, midway between Portland, Oregon and Olympia, Washington—makes it popular with boaters from both states. The river is runnable during the rainy and snowmelt seasons, roughly November to early July, with the prime season April through June. Beware of high flows during and after storms. The NOAA Whitewater Hotline, (206) 526-8530, gives the flow at the take-out.

The cataclysmic 1980 eruption sent a massive mudflow down the North Fork Toutle. The slurry of melted snow and ice, mud, ash, and logs took out seven bridges and dozens of homes. The flood crested at 50' at the Highway 504 bridge (put-in for the run). In many places the old riverbed was buried by a deep deposit of sediment. As of 1993 the Toutle has cleared out much of the mud, particularly in narrow, rocky reaches. The river still runs thick with sediment, however, and in flatter sections winds in shifting channels across broad silt flats. Even so, the Toutle offers good scenery; rock-walled gorges twice close in on the river. These constrictions hold almost all the whitewater. The gradient in the gorges is much steeper than the 30 ft./mi. average.

The **put-in** is on the right bank above the Highway 504 bridge, near the confluence of the North and South Forks. Downstream the canyon narrows. A half mile below the bridge is **STAIRCASE** or **STAIRSTEPS (III)**, and in another half mile the river curves left into **TEAPOT,** a rocky Class III (scout left). After a few more rapids the canyon opens and the rapids ease.

From mile 2.5 to mile 6 the Toutle runs in braided, shifting channels through an open area filled with sediment. Around mile 6 the walls of Hollywood Gorge close in and the rapids resume. Near the top of the gorge a big midstream boulder marks **HOLLYWOOD GORGE FALLS (IV)**, where the river drops over a ledge and rushes toward a big hole at the bottom. Scout right. After a little more Class III the walls open and the whitewater fades. **Take out** on the left at Tower Road Bridge.

To reach the Toutle run, take exit 49 from I-5 and drive east two miles on Highway 504 to the junction with Tower Road. Here the routes diverge: bear left on Tower Road three miles to take-out, or right on Highway 504 nine miles to the put-in. The precise put-in is uncertain, as the old site has been blocked off in preparation for construction of a trailer park. For detailed information refer to Bennett, *Guide to the Whitewater Rivers of Washington* and/or North, *Washington Whitewater.*

Cowlitz River

Difficulty: II. **Length:** 8 miles.

The Cowlitz, one of Washington's largest rivers, begins among glaciers on the southeast face of 14,410' Mt. Rainier, then jogs south and west toward its confluence with the Columbia River at Longview. Though many stretches are boatable, the Cowlitz[1] has little whitewater and is more famous for steelhead than rapids. The run described here, from La Wis Wis Campground to Packwood, is generally boatable from about November through July. The NOAA Whitewater Hotline, (206) 526-8530, gives the flow at Packwood. U.S. Highway 12 follows the left bank through this section, often well away from the river and screened by lush vegetation. Be alert for possible **log hazards.**

The La Wis Wis Campground **put-in** is at the confluence of the Ohanapecosh River and the Clear Fork of the Cowlitz. For two miles the Cowlitz runs clean and pure, dancing through Class II riffles in a lush forest setting. At mile 2, just below Jody's Bridge (USFS Road 1270), the Muddy Fork of the Cowlitz enters from the right, carrying a heavy load of silt and glacial flour. Downstream the Cowlitz winds murkily over a gravel riverbed where channels shift frequently. The foreground scenery loses much of its appeal, but boaters enjoy fine backdrop views of Mt. Rainier. At mile 8 the **take-out** appears on the left at the Skate Creek Road bridge, just west of Packwood. Boaters who prefer the scenery above the Muddy Fork can take out at Jody's Bridge (mile 2) and drive back up Highway 12 to repeat the first part of the run. For more information refer to North, *Washington Whitewater* and/or Bennett, *Guide to the Whitewater Rivers of Washington.*

Downstream Runs

Until recently boaters could enjoy the big water of the Cowlitz Falls run, located many miles below Packwood, just below the Cispus River confluence. Sadly, that section has been lost to a hydroelectric dam scheduled for completion in 1994. Below Cowlitz Falls two more dams inundate many miles of river. Finally, below Mayfield Dam the Cowlitz again runs free, offering some 20 miles of good novice water and pleasant woodland scenery down to the I-5 bridge near Toledo. Boating begins just below the Cowlitz Salmon Hatchery, about three miles below Mayfield Dam. Several downstream accesses allow runs of varying length and difficulty, with the upper sections presenting more challenge. For detailed information refer to Huser, *Paddle Routes of Western Washington.*

---

[1]J.E.D. Garoutte II, *Place Names of the Big Bottom/Rainey Valley Region,* indicates that Cowlitz is an Indian name meaning "capturing the medicine spirit."

Carbon River

Difficulty: V+p. **Length:** 9 miles.

This hairball section of the Carbon River—emphatically for daring experts only—is the toughest run in the Pacific Northwest section of this guide and one of the most difficult runs in the entire book. Only the most confident and skilled experts should get any closer than just reading about the run.

The Carbon is a relatively small river, rising at the base of the Carbon Glacier on the northwest flank of towering Mt. Rainier. After a short but tumultuous descent the Carbon joins the Puyallup River southeast of the city of Puyallup, not far from the metropolis of Tacoma. The river's name dates to the discovery of coal along its banks in 1876.

As it leaves Mt. Rainier National Park the Carbon is relatively mild, but below the Highway 165 bridge near Fairfax the river plunges into an outstandingly spectacular and highly constricted gorge studded with pounding Class V–VI drops. Challenges include **difficult portages, nearly unportageable waterfalls, potentially lethal log hazards, and very difficult scouting.** At times the gradient approaches 200 ft./mi. Climbing out of this sheer-walled slot would be impossible in most places.

This run should be attempted only by fearless experts at moderate to low water levels. In late spring and early summer, snowmelt runoff is usually too heavy; better conditions come later in the summer when water levels have fallen. Even at these times, however, experts will face major hazards.

The **put-in** is about three miles upstream from the Highway 165 bridge over the Carbon, on the south (left) bank near the old town site of Fairfax. (About a half mile past the bridge, bear left at the "Y," then after about two miles bear left again on Fairfax-Burnett Road, which descends to the river.) Survivors can **take out** at the end of 177th Street East. (Follow Highway 162 to the bridge over the river between the towns of Orting and South Prairie; just south of the bridge turn east on 177th St. East; the take-out is at the end of the road.)

For more information refer to Bennett, *Guide to the Whitewater Rivers of Washington.* For a flow estimate, call the NOAA Whitewater Hotline, (206) 526-8530, and take roughly a quarter to a third of the reading on the nearby White River above Mud Mountain Dam.

South Fork Stillaguamish

1. River Bar to Verlot.
III; 7 miles.

2. Verlot to above Granite Falls.
Vp; 12 miles.

3. Below Granite Falls to Jordan.
IV first mile, then II; 9 miles.

4. Jordan to Arlington.
I; 8 miles.

The South Fork of the Stillaguamish River drains the west slope of the Cascades near Everett, Washington. The river's headwaters do not extend to the Cascade crest; the watershed is pinched off by the adjoining drainages of the Sauk and Skykomish Rivers. The highest peaks in the watershed rise to only about 6,000', so the river is runnable only during the rainy season or the early part of the snowmelt season. Beware of **log hazards.**

The South Stillaguamish offers a wide variety of runs. Few boaters launch farther upstream than the Mountain Loop Highway bridge at River Bar, located about 15 miles east of the town of Granite Falls. The seven miles to Verlot hold several intermediate rapids, including **WILEY CREEK** about three miles below River Bar. The next access is at Verlot Campground.

The second run—for experts only—begins innocently enough with five miles of Class II- water below Verlot. Then the canyon walls suddenly close in, and the river plunges into treacherous **Robe Canyon,** where the gradient increases to over 100 ft./mi. The first major rapid is **TUNNEL,** followed by frequent Class IV to V drops. Scout frequently, using an old railroad grade that follows the run, and be ready to portage. **LANDSLIDE,** about halfway through the canyon, is almost always portaged. **Take out** (difficult carry) at the Mountain Loop Highway bridge **just upstream of unrunnable Granite Falls.**

Boaters can begin floating again at the base of Granite Falls by carrying down a trail from the highway. The first mile below the falls has a steep gradient and advanced water. The river eases to Class II by the time it reaches an easier alternate access a mile downstream on the right bank at the Jordan Road bridge (a mile northwest of the town of Granite Falls). Canyon Creek enters on the right just above the bridge, adding considerable flow. Below Jordan Bridge are eight miles of swift Class II water down to an access at the town of Jordan.

Below Jordan the river is Class I, broader, and less secluded. Take-outs are located at River Meadows County Park (five miles below Jordan on the right bank) and three miles farther downstream in the city of Arlington.

"Stillaguamish," or "river people," is the name of a local Indian tribe. Local boaters know the river as the "Stilly." For more information, refer to Bennett, Guide to the Whitewater Rivers of Washington (Runs 1–3) or Huser, Paddle Routes of Western Washington (Runs 3 and 4). The NOAA Whitewater Hotline, (206) 526-8530, gives the flow near Granite Falls.

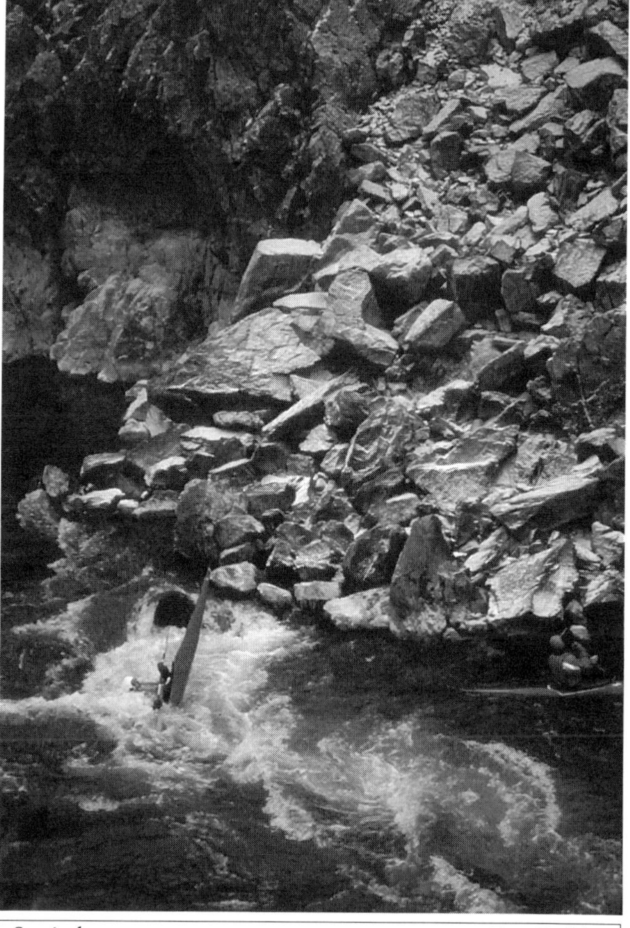

Squirtboats *Ron Lodders*

Stehekin River

Difficulty: II4. The Class IV rapid (at the start of the run) can be avoided.
Length: 10 miles.

The Stehekin River, one of Washington's most remote and scenic waterways, is unique among Western rivers in that it can be reached only by ferry boat. From headwaters in the dramatic high country of the Glacier Peak Wilderness and North Cascades National Park, the Stehekin runs its short course of less than 30 miles and empties into the upper end of spectacular Lake Chelan, Washington's largest natural lake and the second-deepest lake in North America. The run described here covers the river's last ten miles above the lake.

Lake Chelan is basically a freshwater fjord—55 miles long and rarely more than a mile wide—that fills a deep glacial valley on the east slope of the Cascades in north central Washington. At its lower end, near the Columbia River, the lake is accessible via U.S. 97. But roads extend only a short way up the steep shore, and the only way to get farther up is by boat or small plane. Most people take a ferry to the little hamlet of Stehekin[1] at the head of the lake, enjoying a scenic ride that begins in open, grassy hills and ends in tall forests surrounded by glacier-studded peaks.

Unfortunately, no hardshell boats are allowed on the ferries. Deflated rafts and other inflatable or collapsible boats are permitted within certain weight restrictions. For complete information contact the Lake Chelan Boat Company, (509) 682-4584, which operates the ferries, *Lady of the Lake* and the newer and faster *Lady Express.* Kayakers and canoeists who would rather fight than switch to an inflatable can try either to ship their boats up the lake on a freight barge (which operates only sporadically) or find a power boat to make the trip on their own.

The ferries drop boaters at Stehekin Landing, about a mile from the river's mouth. Paradoxically, a road follows the river upstream from this point, even though there is no way to drive here from the outside world. To get to the put-in, boaters usually ride upriver on a shuttle van operated by the National Park Service. The van will not carry kayaks or canoes, and advance reservations may be required. For details contact Lake Chelan National Recreation Area, (509) 682-2549.

Boaters **put in** on the left bank at one of two alternate sites, either just above or just below **CASCADE (IV)**, a difficult rapid located ten miles above the lake. The upper access is not far below the High Bridge over the Stehekin; it is a little below the mouth of Agnes Creek, a major tributary that enters on the opposite (right) bank. The lower site is half a mile downstream on the left, below Cascade Rapid. Below the lower put-in the river is all Class II or easier. Anyone considering the upper put-in should scout Cascade carefully from shore first.

Below the lower put-in the river, swift at first, gradually slows as it approaches the lake. (Average gradient for the full 10-mile run is 40 ft./mi.) The scenery is outstanding as the Stehekin runs easily down a broad-bottomed glacial valley bounded by steep, forested slopes. Harlequin Bridge crosses the river at mile 6, and about a mile downstream, 312' Rainbow Falls can be seen off to the left. The river glides into the lake at mile 10. A superb boat-in campsite is on the lake shore just west of the river's mouth.

The Stehekin has a long snowmelt season, usually peaking in late May or June and gradually diminishing to unrunnable levels by late August. At peak flows the river can be dangerous, with fast, icy water and few eddies. At any level, be alert for possible **log hazards.** For flow information call the NOAA Whitewater Hotline, (206) 526-6087, for the flow at Stehekin.

For more information on this run, refer to North, *Washington Whitewater,* and/or Bennett, *Guide to the Whitewater Rivers of Washington.* The *Wenatchee NF* map covers the run. A good local source of information is the Stehekin Adventure Company, (509) 682-4677, a commercial raft outfitter with a small office near Stehekin Landing.

[1]Stehekin, pronounced "Stuh-HEE-kin," is from an Indian word meaning "the way through" and probably refers to a relatively easy east-west route over the mountains at Cascade Pass near the river's headwaters.

Bibliography

Some of the books listed here are out of print. For current information, refer to *Books In Print.* We list addresses for some small publishers whose books are not easily found in stores. For more bibliographical information on river running books, refer to Ronald Ziegler, *Wilderness Waterways: The Whole Water Reference for Paddlers,* an excellent source book with complete annotations (see below: **Other Source Books, General**). For local maps and for guides published by government agencies, see the specific river chapter. For books on river conservation and water politics, see the end of **Appendix V.**

1. River Guides

General

Jenkinson, Michael. *Wild Rivers of North America.* 2d ed. New York: Dutton, 1981. 409 pp.

Penny, Richard. *The Whitewater Sourcebook: A Directory of Information on American Whitewater Rivers.* 2d ed. Birmingham: Menasha Ridge Press, 1991. 375 pp.

River Information Digest, Western Region. American River Management Society (P.O. Box 621911, Littleton, CO 80162), 1992. 204 pp.

Idaho and Northern Rockies

Amaral, Grant. *Idaho—The Whitewate State: A Guidebook.* Watershed Books (P.O. Box 721, Boise, ID 83701), 1990. 315 pp.

Belknap, Buzz and Verne Huser. *Snake River Guide.* Boulder City, NV: Westwater Books, 1972. 72 pp.

Fischer, Hank. *The Floater's Guide to Montana.* 2d ed. Billings, MT: Falcon Press, 1986. 152 pp.

Garren, John. *Idaho River Tours: A Guide to Touring Idaho's Most Popular Wilderness Whitewater Rivers.* Garren Publishing (01008 SW Comus, Portland, OR 97219), 1987. 125 pp.

Geier, Dick and Todd Graeff. *A River Runners Guide to Idaho.* Boise: Idaho Dept. of Parks and Recreation & BLM, 1980. 47 pp.

Lewis, Dan. *Paddle and Portage: The Floater's Guide to Wyoming Rivers.* The Wyoming Naturalist (P.O. Box 863, Douglas, WY 82633), 1991. 185 pp.

Moore, Greg and Don McClaran. *Idaho Whitewater: The Complete River Guide for Canoeists, Rafters and Kayakers.* Class VI Whitewater (P.O. Box 1794, McCall, ID 83638), 1989. 220 pp.

Nichols, *River Runners' Guide to Utah and Adjacent Areas.* Full listing in **Canyon Country** region.

Quinn, James M., James W. Quinn, and James G. King. *Hells Canyon of the Snake River.* Portland: Frank Amato Publications, n.d.

Quinn, James M., James W. Quinn, and James G. King. *Handbook to the Middle Fork of the Salmon River.* Portland: Frank Amato Publications, 1981. 186 pp.

Schafer, *Canoeing Western Waterways: The Mountain States.* Full listing in **Colorado Rockies** region.

Thompson, Curt. *Floating and Recreation on Montana Rivers. Curt Thompson (P.O. Box 392, Lakeside, MT 59922), 1993. 370 pp.*

Three Forks of the Flathead River Floating Guide. Glacier Natural History Assn. (P.O. Box 327, West Glacier, MT 59936), 1989. 36 pp.

Colorado Rockies

Anderson and Hopkinson, *Rivers of the Southwest.* Full listing in **Canyon Country** region.

Cassady, Jim and Fryar Calhoun. *Upper Arkansas River: Whitewater Map and Guide.* North Fork Press, 1987. Distributed by Rivers & Mountains, 862 San Antonio Ave., Palo Alto, CA 94306; (415) 424-1213.

Cassady, Jim and Fryar Calhoun. *Lower Arkansas River: Whitewater Map and Guide.* North Fork Press, 1987. Distributed by Rivers & Mountains (see above).

Cassady, Jim and Fryar Calhoun. *Rio Grande Whitewater Map and Guide.* North Fork Press, 1987. Distributed by Rivers & Mountains (see above).

DeVries, Ralph and Stephen Maurer. *Dolores River Guide.* Southwest Natural & Cultural Heritage Assn. (Drawer E, Albuquerque, NM 87103). Expanded 1993 edition. 73 pp.

DeVries, Ralph and Stephen Maurer. *Guide to the Wild and Scenic Rio Grande.* Southwest Natural & Cultural Heritage Assn. (Drawer E, Albuquerque, NM 87103). Publication in spring 1994.

Lewis, *Paddle and Portage.* Full listing in **Idaho and Northern Rockies** region.

Maddox, Bryan Green. *River Guide to the Cache la Poudre River.* Bellevue, CO: Maddog Publishing, 1993. 73 pp.

Maurer, Stephen G. *Guide to New Mexico's Popular Rivers and Lakes.* Heritage Associates (P.O. Box 6291, Albuquerque, NM 87197), 1983. 53 pp.

Maurer, Stephen G. *Guide to Wild & Scenic Rio Chama.* Southwest Natural & Cultural Heritage Assn. (Drawer E, Albuquerque, NM 87103), 1991. 28 pp.

New Mexico Whitewater: A Guide to River Trips. New Mexico State Parks Division (Natural Resources Dept., 141 East De Vargas, P.O. Box 1147, Santa Fe, NM 87503), 1983. 69 pp.

Perry, Earl. *Rivers of Colorado: Ten Easy River Trips in the Mountains, Canyons and Plains of Colorado.* Colorado Springs, CO: National Organization for River Sports, 1978. 60 pp.

Rampton, Thomas G. *River Runner's Guide to Brown's Canyon.* Thomas G. Rampton (Box 601, Buena Vista, CO 81211), 1987. 57 pp.

Schaefer, Ann. *Canoeing Western Waterways: The Mountain States.* New York: Harper & Row, 1978. 279 pp.

Staub, Frank. *The Upper Arkansas River: Rapids, History & Nature Mile By Mile.* Golden, CO: Fulcrum, 1988. 265 pp.

Stohlquist, Jim. *Colorado Whitewater: A Guide to the Difficult Rivers and Streams of the Rocky Mountain State Region.* Buena Vista, CO: Colorado Kayak Supply, 1982. 157 pp.

Wheat, Doug. *The Floaters' Guide to Colorado.* Billings, MT: Falcon Press, 1983. 296 pp.

Canyon Country

Aitchison, Stewart. *A Naturalist's San Juan River Guide.* Boulder, CO: Pruett Publishing, 1983. 57 pp.

Anderson, Fletcher and Ann Hopkinson. *Rivers of the Southwest: A Boaters Guide to the Rivers of Colorado, New Mexico, Utah and Arizona.* 2d ed. Boulder, CO: Pruett Publishing, 1982. 135 pp.

Baars, Don. *A River Runner's Guide to Cataract Canyon and Approaches.* Lawrence, KS: Cañon Publishers, 1987. 81 pp.

Baars, Don and Gene Stevenson. *San Juan Canyons: A River Runner's Guide.* Lawrence, KS: Cañon Publishers, 1986. 65 pp.

Belknap, Bill, Buzz Belknap, and Loie Belknap Evans. *Canyonlands River Guide: Westwater, Lake Powell, Canyonlands National Park.* Boulder City, NV: Westwater Books, 1991. 72 pp.

Belknap, Buzz and Loie Belknap Evans. *Dinosaur River Guide.* Boulder City, NV: Westwater Books, 1993. 64 pp.

Belknap, Buzz and Loie Belknap Evans. *Grand Canyon River Guide.* Boulder City, NV: Westwater Books, 1989. 96 pp.

DeVries, Ralph and Stephen G. Maurer. *Dolores River Guide.* Albuquerque, NM: Southwest Natural & Cultural Heritage Assn. (Drawer E, Albuquerque, NM 87103), 1993. 96 pp.

Evans, Loie Belknap and Buzz Belknap. *Desolation River Guide: Green River Wilderness.* Boulder City, NV: Westwater Books, 1992. 56 pp.

Gernant, Bob, Barbara Hinton, and Mel Hughes. *The Canyons of Dinosaur National Monument: A River Runners' Guide and Natural History of the Green and Yampa River Canyons.* Lawrence, KS: Cañon Publishers, 1992. 96 pp.

Hayes, Philip T. and George C. Simmons. *River Runner's Guide to Dinosaur National Monument and Vicinity, With Emphasis on Geologic Features.* Rev. ed. Denver: Powell Society, 1973. 78 pp.

Huser, Verne. *Canyon Country Paddles: A Practical, Informative, and Entertaining Guide to River Running Using the Kayak, Canoe, or Rubber Raft in Southeastern Utah.* Canyon Country Guide Book No. 12. Salt Lake City: Wasatch Publishers, 1978. 96 pp.

Kelsey, Michael R. *River Guide to Canyonlands National Park and Vicinity.* Kelsey Publishing (456 E 100. N., Provo, UT 84606), 1991. 256 pp.

Kruse, Dale. *Yampa River Guide: Craig to Maybell.* Dale Kruse, 1991. 17 pp. (Order from Museum of Northwest Colorado, 590 Yampa Ave., Craig, CO 81625.)

Mutschler, Felix E. *River Runner's Guide to Canyonlands National Park and Vicinity, with Emphasis on Geologic Features.* Rev. ed. Denver: Powell Society, 1977. 99 pp.

Mutschler, Felix E. *River Runner's Guide to the Canyons of the Green and Colorado Rivers, with Emphasis on Geologic Features; Desolation and Gray Canyons.* River Runners' Guides, vol. 4. Denver: Powell Society, 1969. 85 pp.

Nichols, Gary C. *River Runners' Guide to Utah and Adjacent Areas.* Rev. ed. Salt Lake City: Univ. of Utah, 1986. 168 pp.

Perry, *Rivers of Colorado.* Full listing in **Colorado Rockies** region.

Rampton, Thomas G. *River Guide to Desolation and Grays Canyons on the Green River, Utah: A Mile by Mile Guide to the Green River Between the Towns of Ouray and Green River.* Blacktail Enterprises (14800 County Rd. 270, Nathrop, CO 81236), 1992. 68 pp.

Schafer, *Canoeing Western Waterways: The Mountain States.* Full listing in **Colorado Rockies** region.

Simmons, George C. and David L. Gaskill. *Marble Gorge and Grand Canyon.* River Runners' Guides, vol. 3. Denver: Powell Society, 1969. 132 pp.

Stevens, Larry. *The Colorado River in Grand Canyon: A Comprehensive Guide to Its Natural and Human History.* 3d ed. Red Lake Books (P.O. Box 1315, Flagstaff, AZ 86002), 1987. 115 pp.

Wheat, *The Floaters Guide to Colorado.* Full listing in **Colorado Rockies** region.

Southwestern Border

Anderson and Hopkinson, *Rivers of the Southwest.* Full listing in **Canyon Country** region.

Arizona Rivers & Streams Guide. Arizona State Parks (800 W. Washington, Suite 145, Phoenix, AZ 85007), 1989. 182 pp.

Aulbach, Louis and Joe Butler. *The Lower Canyons of the Rio Grande: La Linda to Dryden Crossing—Maps and Notes for River Runners.* Houston: Wilderness Area Map Service, 1988. (Available from Louis Aulbach, 3002 Helberg Road, Houston, TX 77092.) 91 pp.

A Boating Trail Guide to the Colorado River: Davis Dam to Parker Dam. California Dept. of Boating & Waterways, 1629 S St., Sacramento, CA 95814; (916) 445-2616.

Hollister, Dana. *A Riverrunner's Guide to the Salt River.* Dana Hollister (P.O. Box 56784, Phoenix, AZ 85079). 30 pp.

Humphrey, Mary E. *Running the Rio Grande: A Floaters Guide to the Big Bend.* Austin, TX: AAR/Tantalus, 1981. 66 pp.

Kirkley, Gene. *A Guide to Texas Rivers and Streams: Floating, Fishing, and Fun on Texas Waterways.* Lone Star Books (P.O. Box 2608, Houston, TX 77252), 1983. 107 pp.

Maurer, *Guide to New Mexico's Popular Rivers and Lakes.* Full listing in **Colorado Rockies** region.

New Mexico Whitewater: A Guide to River Trips. New Mexico State Parks Division. Full listing in **Colorado Rockies** region.

Nolen, Ben and Bob Marramore. *Texas Rivers and Rapids: Canoe and Backpack Guide Book.* Ben Nolen and Bob Narramore (3610 Maruis Drive, Garland, TX 75042), 1987. 164 pp.

Rink, Glenn, ed. *A Guide to Salt River Canyon: Natural History and River Running.* Worldwide Exploration, Inc. (P.O. Box 686, Flagstaff, AZ 86002), 1990. 73 pp.

River Guide to the Rio Grande: Colorado Canyon through Santa Elena Canyon. Vols. 1–4. John Pearson, ed. Big Bend Natural History Assn. (P.O. Box 68, Big Bend National Park, TX 79834), 1982.

Slingluff, Jim. *Verde River Recreation Guide.* Golden West Publishers (4113 N. Longview Ave., Phoenix, AZ 85014), 1990. 173 pp.

California

Cassady, Jim and Fryar Calhoun. *California Whitewater: A Guide to the Rivers.* 2d rev. ed. Berkeley: North Fork Press, 1990. 299 pp. Available from Rivers & Mountains, 862 San Antonio Avenue, Palo Alto, CA 94306; (415) 424-1213.

Cassady, Jim and Fryar Calhoun. *South Fork American River Whitewater Map and Guide.* North Fork Press, 1983. Available from Rivers & Mountains (see above).

Cassady, Jim and Fryar Calhoun. *Tuolumne River Whitewater Map and Guide.* North Fork Press, 1983. Available from Rivers & Mountains (see above).

Cassady, Jim and Fryar Calhoun. *Lower Kern River Whitewater Map and Guide, Upper Kern River Whitewater Map and Guide,* and *Forks of Kern Whitewater Map and Guide.* North Fork Press, 1983. Available from Rivers & Mountains (see above).

Cassidy, John. *A Guide To Three Rivers: The Stanislaus, Tuolumne and South Fork of the American.* San Francisco: Friends of the River Books, 1981. 295 pp.

Dwyer, Ann. *Canoeing Waters of California.* Kentfield, CA: GBH Press, 1973. 95 pp.

Dwyer, Ann. *California Paddle Trails.* Windsor, CA: GBH Press. Scheduled for 1994 publication.

Holbek, Lars and Chuck Stanley. *A Guide To The Best Whitewater In The State Of California.* 2d ed. San Francisco: Friends of the River Books, 1988. 281 pp.

Quinn, James M. and James W. Quinn. *Handbook to the Klamath River Canyon.* Portland: Frank Amato Publications, 1983. 181 pp.

Martin, Charles. *Sierra Whitewater: A Paddler's Guide to the Rivers of California's Sierra Nevada.* Charles Martin (P.O. Box 57, Wayland, MA 01778), 1974. 192 pp.

Murphy, Shane. *The Lore & Legend of the East Fork: A Historical Guide For Floating The East Carson River.* Carson River Conservation Fund (P.O. Box 1221, Dephyr Cove, NV 89448), 1982. 74 pp.

Schafer, Ann. *Canoeing Western Waterways: The Coastal States.* New York: Harper & Row, 1978. 272 pp.

Schwind, Dick. *West Coast River Touring: Rogue River Canyon & South.* Beaverton, OR: Touchstone Press, 1974. 225 pp.

The American River: North, Middle & South Forks. Wilderness Conservancy. Protect American River Canyons (Box 9312, Auburn, CA 95604), 1989. 320 pp.

Wright, Terry. *Guide to Geology and Rapids, South Fork American River.* Wilderness Interpretation Publications (P.O. Box 279-P, Forestville, CA 95436), 1981.

Wright, Terry. *Rocks and Rapids of the Tuolumne River: A Guide to Natural and Human History.* Wilderness Interpretation Publications (see above), 1983. 88 pp.

Pacific Northwest

A River-Runner's Guide to the Middle Owyhee: Three Forks to Rome. River Graphics (P.O. Box 3427, Breckenridge, CO 80424), 1988.

Arighi, Scott and Margaret S. Arighi. *Wildwater Touring: Techniques and Tours.* New York: Macmillan, 1974. 334 pp.

Bennett, Jeff. *A Guide to the Whitewater Rivers of Washington.* Swiftwater Publishing (P.O. Box 3031, Portland, OR 97208), 1991. 304 pp.

Campbell, Arthur. *John Day River Drift and Historical Guide.* Portland: Frank Amato Publications, 1980. 90 pp.

Corliss, Ralph, and Richard Chase. *Backpaddlers Guide to the North Umpqua River. Book 1: Soda Springs Dam to Gravel Bin; Book 2: Gravel Bin to Cable Crossing; Book 3: Cable Crossing to Winchester Dam.* Walk on Water Publications (646 SE Jackson, Roseburg, OR 97470), 1990, 1993.

Crawford, Doc. *Driftboater's Guide to the Upper McKenzie: Olallie to Leaburg Lake.* Northwest Rivers Publishing (2133 Centennial Plaza, Eugene, OR 97401), 1986. 86 pp.

Furrer, Werner. *Water Trails of Washington.* Signpost Books (8912 192d SW, Edmonds, WA 98020), 1979. 96 pp.

Garren, John. *Oregon River Tours.* Rev. ed. Portland: Garren Publishing (01008 SW Comus, Portland, OR 97219), 1991. 270 pp.

Huser, Verne. *Paddle Routes of Western Washington: 50 Flatwater Trips for Canoe and Kayak.* Seattle: The Mountaineers, 1990. 240 pp.

Jones, Philip N. *Canoe Routes: Northwest Oregon.* Seattle: The Mountaineers, 1982. 157 pp.

Kovalik, Vladimir. *The Rogue River Guide: A Comprehensive Guide to the Natural and Human History of the Rogue River.* Vladimir Kovalik (12035 Galice Road, Merlin, OR 97532). 85 pp.

Korb, Gary. *A Paddler's Guide to the Olympic Peninsula.* 2d ed. Gary Korb (4930 Geiger Rd., Port Orchard, WA 98366), 1992. 216 pp.

LeRoux, Dave and Martha Rudersdorf. *Paddle Washington: Water Trips for Canoes and Sea Kayaks.* Seattle: Neah Bay Books, 1984. 163 pp.

North, Douglass A. *Washington Whitewater: The 34 Best Whitewater Rivers.* Seattle: The Mountaineers, 1992. 304 pp.

Quinn and Quinn, *Handbook to the Klamath River Canyon.* Full listing in **California** region.

Quinn, James M., James W. Quinn, and James G. King. *Handbook to the Rogue River Canyon.* Portland: Frank Amato Publications, 1978. 133 pp.

Quinn, James M., James W. Quinn, and James G. King. *Handbook to the Deschutes River Canyon.* Portland: Frank Amato Publications, 1979. 148 pp.

Quinn, James M, James W. Quinn, and James G. King. *Handbook to the Illinois River Canyon.* Portland: Frank Amato Publications, 1979. 162 pp.

Quinn, James M., James W. Quinn, and James G. King. *Hells Corner Gorge of the Upper Klamath.* Portland: Frank Amato Publications, n.d.

Schafer, *Canoeing Western Waterways: The Coastal States.* Full listing in **California** region.

Schwind, *West Coast River Touring: Rogue River Canyon & South.* Full listing in **California** region.

Soggy Sneakers Guide to Oregon Rivers. Willamette Kayak & Canoe Club, ed. 3d ed. Seattle: The Mountaineers, 1994. 304 pp.

The Lower Owyhee: A River Runner's Guide. River Graphics (P.O. Box 3427, Breckenridge, CO 80424), 1986.

Walker, Michael L. *Handbook to the Rogue River's Hog Creek Float.* White Water Flips (850 Three Pines Road, Grants Pass, OR 97526), 1989. 127 pp.

2. Other Source Books

General

America's Wild and Scenic Rivers. Washington, D.C.: The National Geographic Society, 1983. 199 pp.

Amos, William H. *The Infinite River: A Biologist's Vision of the World of Water.* New York: Ballantine, 1970. 267 pp.

Armstead, Lloyd D. *Whitewater Rafting in Western North America.* Chester, CT: Globe Pequot Press, 1990. 331 pp.

Bangs, Richard. *Whitewater Adventure: Running America's Great Scenic Rivers.* San Diego: Thunder Bay Press, 1990. 144 pp.

Bardach, John. *Downstream: A Natural History of the River from its Source to the Sea.* New York: Grosset & Dunlap, 1964. 278 pp.

Barrow, Pope, ed. *The American Whitewater Affiliation Nationwide Whitewater Inventory.* American Whitewater Affiliation (P.O. Box 85, Phoenicia, NY 12464), 1990.

Bartlett, Richard A., ed. *Rolling Rivers: An Encyclopedia of America's Rivers.* New York: McGraw-Hill, 1984. 398 pp.

Bennett, Jeff. *Rafting! The Complete Guide to Whitewater Rafting Techniques and Equipment.* Swiftwater Publishing (P.O. Box 3031, Portland, OR 97208-3031), 1993.

Collins, Robert and Roderick Nash. *The Big Drops: Ten Legendary Rapids.* San Francisco: Sierra Club Books, 1978. 215 pp.

Fradkin, Philip L. *A River No More: The Colorado River and the West.* New York: Knopf, 1968, 1981. 360 pp.

Harder, Kelsie P., ed. *Illustrated Dictionary of Place Names, United States and Canada.* New York: Van Nostrand Reinhold, 1976. 631 pp.

Hodgson, Michael. *America's Secret Recreation Areas: Your Guide to the Unexplored Lands of the Bureau of Land Management.* San Francisco: Foghorn Press, 1993. 512 pp.

Huser, Verne, ed. *River Reflections: An Anthology.* Charlotte, NC: East Woods Press. 268 pp.

Norton, Boyd. *Rivers of the Rockies.* Chicago: Rand McNally, 1975. 160 pp.

O'Connor, Cameron and John Lazenby. *First Descents: In Search of Wild Rivers.* Birmingham: Menasha Ridge Press, 1989. 163 pp.

Orr, Elizabeth and William Orr. *Rivers of the West: A Guide to the Geology and History.* Elizabeth and William Orr (P.O. Box 5286, Eugene, OR 97405), 1985. 334 pp.

McGinnis, William. *Whitewater Rafting.* New York: Quadrangle/New York Times, 1975. 361 pp.

Rennicke, Jeff, ed. *River Days: Travels on Western Rivers.* Golden, CO: Fulcrum, Inc., 1988. 174 pp.

Thomas, Bill. *American Rivers: A Natural History.* New York: Norton, 1978. 221 pp.

Waldman, Carl. *Encyclopedia of Native American Tribes.* New York: Facts on File, 1988. 293 pp.

Ziegler, Ronald. *Wilderness Waterways: The Whole Water Reference for Paddlers.* Canoe America Associates (P.O. Box 3146, Kirkland, WA 98083), 1991. 177 pp.

Idaho and the Northern Rockies

Alt, David and Donald W. Hyndman. *Roadside Geology of Montana.* Missoula, MT: Mountain Press, 1986. 427 pp.

Ashworth, William. *Hells Canyon: The Deepest Gorge on Earth.* New York: Hawthorne, 1977. 246 pp.

Boone, Lalia Phipps. *Idaho Place Names: A Geographical Dictionary.* Moscow, ID: Univ. of Idaho Press, 1988. 413 pp.

Brooks, Charles. *The Living River: A Fisherman's Intimate Profile of the Madison River Watershed—Its History, Ecology, Lore and Angling Opportunities.* New York: Nick Lyon Books, 1979. 207 pp.

Carrey, Johnny and Cort Conley. *River of No Return.* Backeddy Books (P.O. Box 301, Cambridge, ID 83610), 1978. 319 pp.

Carrey, Johnny and Cort Conley. *The Middle Fork: A Guide.* Backeddy Books (see above), 1990.

Carrey, Johnny, Cort Conley, and Ace Barton. *Snake River of Hells Canyon.* Backeddy Books (see above), 1979. 399 pp.

Cheney, Roberta Carkeek. *Names on the Face of Montana.* Missoula, MT: Mountain Press, 1983. 324 pp.

DeVoto, Bernard, ed. *The Journals of Lewis and Clark.* Boston: Houghton Mifflin Co., 1953.

DuBois, Eliot. *An Innocent on the Middle Fork: A Whitewater Adventure in Idaho's Wilderness.* Seattle: The Mountaineers, 1987. 187 pp.

Fritz, William J. *Roadside Geology of the Yellowstone Country.* Missoula, MT: Mountain Press, 1985. 144 pp.

Gildart, Bert. *Flathead Country.* Helena: Montana Magazine/American Geographic, 1986. 104 pp.

Hughes, Dave. *The Yellowstone River and Its Angling.* Portland: Frank Amato Publications, 1992. 96 pp.

Krakel, Dean II. *Downriver: A Yellowstone Journey.* San Francisco: Sierra Club Books, 1987. 250 pp.

Lageson, David and Darwin Spearing. *Roadside Geology of Wyoming.* Missoula: Mountain Press, 1988. 273 pp.

Lavender, David. *The Way to the Western Sea.* New York: Harper & Row, 1988. 444 pp.

Lavender, David. *Let Me Be Free: The Nez Perce Tragedy.* New York: Harper Collins, 1992. 403 pp.

Neihardt, John G. *The River and I.* Lincoln: Univ. of Nebraska Press, 1968; reprint of original 1910 book. 325 pp.

Palmer, Tim. *The Snake River: Window to the West.* Washington, D.C./Covelo, CA: Island Press, 1991. 322 pp.
Schultz, James W. *Floating on the Missouri.* Norman: Univ. of Oklahoma Press, 1979. 142 pp.
Urbanek, Mae. *Wyoming Place Names.* Missoula, MT: Mountain Press, 1988. 233 pp.
Vestal, Stanely. *The Missouri.* Lincoln: Univ. of Nebraksa Press, 1945. 368 pp.

Colorado Rockies

Chronic, Halka. *Roadside Geology of Colorado.* Missoula, MT: Mountain Press, 1980. 322 pp.
Chronic, Halka. *Roadside Geology of New Mexico.* Missoula, MT: Mountain Press, 1987. 255 pp.
Davis, Clyde Brian. *The Arkansas.* New York: Farrar & Rinehart, 1940. 340 pp.
Dolson, John. *The Black Canyon of the Gunnison: A Story In Stone.* Boulder, CO: Pruett Publishing, 1982. 55 pp.
Dorset, Phyllis Flanders. *The New El Dorado: The Story of Colorado's Gold and Silver Rushes.* New York: Macmillan, 1970. 434 pp.
Lavender, David. *The Rockies.* New York: Harper & Row, 1968. 404 pp.
Lavender, David. *Colorado River Country.* New York: E.P. Dutton, 1982. 238 pp.
Rennicke, Jeff. *The Rivers of Colorado.* Billings, MT: Falcon Press, 1985. 112 pp.
Waters, *The Colorado.* Full listing in **Canyon Country** region.

Canyon Country

Abbey, Edward. *Desert Solitaire: A Season in the Wilderness.* New York: McGraw-Hill, 1968. 320 pp.
Abbey, Edward and Philip Hyde. *Slickrock.* Layton, UT: Peregrine Smith, 1987. 143 pp.
Abbey, Edward, *The Hidden Canyon: A River Journey.* Photos by John Blaustein. New York: Viking, 1977. 135 pp.
Baars, D. L., ed. *Geology of the Canyons of the San Juan River.* Durango, CO: Four Corners Geological Society, 1973. 94 pp.
Baars, D. L. and C. M. Molenaar. *Geology of Canyonlands and Cataract Canyon.* Four Corners Geological Society, 1971. 99 pp.
Barnes, Frank A. *Canyon Country Hiking and Natural History.* Salt Lake City: Wasatch Publishers, 1977. 176 pp.
Barnes, Frank A. *Canyon Country Geology.* Salt Lake City: Wasatch Publishers, 1978. 160 pp.
Barnes, Frank A., and Michaelene Pendleton. *Canyon Country Prehistoric Indians: Their Cultures, Ruins, Artifacts and Rock Art.* Salt Lake City: Wasatch Publishers, 1979. 256 pp.
Beal, Merrill D. *Grand Canyon: The Story Behind the Scenery.* 3rd ed. K. C. Publications (P.O. Box 14447, Las Vegas, NV 89114), 1989. 64 pp.
Brian, Nancy. *River to Rim: A Guide to Place Names along the Colorado River in Grand Canyon from Lake Powell to Lake Mead.* Flagstaff: Earthquest Press (P.O. Box 1391, Flagstaff, AZ 86002-1391), 1992. 176 pp.
Carothers, Steven and Bryan Brown. *The Colorado River through Grand Canyon: Natural History and Human Change.* Tucson: Univ. of Arizona Press, 1991. 235 pp.
Chronic, Halka. *Pages of Stone: Geology of Western National Parks, 4: Grand Canyon and the Plateau Country.* Seattle: The Mountaineers, 1988. 184 pp.
Chronic, Halka. *Roadside Geology of Utah.* Missoula: Mountain Press, 1990. 336 pp.
Clark, Georgie White and Duane Newcomb. *Georgie Clark: Thirty Years of River Running.* San Francisco: Chronicle Books. 165 pp.
Cooley, John. *The Great Unknown: The Journals of the Historic First Expedition Down the Colorado River.* Northland Publishing (P.O. Box 1389, Flagstaff, AZ 86002), 1988. 207 pp.
Collier, Michael. *An Introduction to Grand Canyon Geology.* Grand Canyon Natural History Assn. (P.O. Box 399, Grand Canyon, AZ 86023), 1980. 42 pp.

Crumbo, Kim. *A River Runner's Guide to the History of the Grand Canyon.* Johnson Books (1880 South 57th Court, Boulder, CO 80301), 1981. 61 pp.

Dellenbaugh, Frederick. *A Canyon Voyage: The Narrative of the Second Powell Expedition.* Tucson: Univ. of Arizona Press, 1991. Reprint of a 1908 book. 277 pp.

Ghiglieri, Michael P. *Canyon.* Tucson: Univ. of Arizona Press, 1992. 311 pp.

Hagood, Allen, and Linda West. *Dinosaur: The Story Behind the Scenery.* Rev. ed. K. C. Publications (P.O. Box 14447, Las Vegas, NV 89114), 1990. 48 pp.

Hamblin, W. Kenneth, and J. Keith Rigby. *Guidebook to the Colorado River, Parts 1 & 2.* Provo, UT: Brigham Young Univ. Press, 1968.

Hoffman, John F. *Grand Canyon Visual.* San Diego; Scenic Visuals Publications, 1987. 80 pp.

Hughes, J. Donald. *In the House of Stone and Light: A Human History of the Grand Canyon.* Grand Canyon Natural History Assn. (P.O. Box 399, Grand Canyon, AZ 86023), 1978. 137 pp.

Kelsey, Michael. *Hiking and Exploring Utah's San Rafael Swell.* 2d ed. Kelsey Publishing (456 E. 100 N., Provo, UT 84606), 1990. 160 pp.

Kolb, E. L. *Through the Grand Canyon from Wyoming to Mexico.* Tucson: Univ. of Arizona Press, 1989; reprint of original 1914 book. 344 pp.

Lambrechtse, Rudi. *Hiking the Escalante.* Salt Lake City: Wasatch Publishers, 1985. 192 pp.

Lavender, David. *River Runners of the Grand Canyon.* Grand Canyon Natural History Assn. (P.O. Box 399, Grand Canyon, AZ 86023), 1985. 147 pp.

Lucchitta, Ivo. *Canyon Maker: A Geological History of the Colorado River.* Special edition of *Plateau,* vol. 59, no. 2 (1988), Museum of Northern Arizona Press (Rt. 4, Box 720, Flagstaff, AZ 86001). 32 pp.

Martin, Russell. *A Story That Stands Like A Dam.* New York: Henry Holt and Co., 1989. 354 pp.

Porter, Eliot. *The Place No One Knew: Glen Canyon on the Colorado River.* San Francisco: Sierra Club Books, 1963.

Powell, John Wesley. *The Exploration of the Colorado River and its Canyons.* New York: Dover, 1961; reprint of original 1875 book. 400 pp.

Rigby, J. Keith et. al. *Guidebook to the Colorado River, Part 3: Moab to Hite, Utah through Canyonlands National Park.* Provo, UT: Brigham Young Univ., 1971. 91 pp.

Stanton, Robert B. *The Colorado River Survey.* Salt Lake City: Howe Bros., 1987. Reprint. 319 pp.

Stanton, Robert B. *Colorado River Controversies.* James M. Chalfant, ed. Boulder City, NV: Westwater Books, 1982. New edition of a 1932 book.

Stegner, Wallace, ed. *This Is Dinosaur: Echo Park Country and Its Magic Rivers.* Boulder, CO: Roberts Rinehart, 1983; reprint of original 1955 book. 93 pp.

Stegner, Wallace. *Beyond The Hundredth Meridian: John Wesley Powell and the Second Opening of the West.* Lincoln: Univ. of Nebraska Press, 1982; reprint of original 1953 book. 438 pp.

Waters, Frank. *The Colorado.* New York: Rinehart, 1946. 400 pp.

Watkins, T.H. et al. *The Grand Colorado: The Story of a River and Its Canyons.* American West Publishing, 1969. 310 pp.

Webb, Roy. *If We Had A Boat: Green River Explorers, Adventurers and Runners.* Salt Lake City: Univ. of Utah Press, 1986. 194 pp.

Webb, Roy. *Riverman: The Story of Bus Hatch.* Labyrinth Publishing (P.O. Box 246, Rock Springs, WY 82902), 1989. 158 pp.

Wilde, Kathryn. *The San Juan: The Four Corners River.* Museum of Northern Arizona (Route 4, Box 720, Flagstaff, AZ 86001), 1991. 32 pp.

Zwinger, Ann. *Wind in the Rock.* New York: Harper & Row, 1978. 258 pp.

Zwinger, Ann. *Run, River, Run: A Naturalist's Journey Down One of the Great Rivers of the West.* Tucson: Univ. of Arizona Press, 1984. 317 pp.

Southwestern Border

Barnes, William Croft. *Arizona Place Names.* Rev. and enlarged by Byrd H. Granger. Tucson: Univ. of Arizona Press, 1960. 519 pp.

Calvin, Ross. *River of the Sun: Stories of the Storied Gila.* Albuquerque: Univ. of New Mexico Press, 1946. 153 pp.

Chronic, Halka. *Roadside Geology of Arizona.* Missoula: Mountain Press, 1983. 320 pp.

Hillerman, Tony and Robert Reynolds. *Rio Grande.* Portland: Charles H. Belding Graphic Arts Center, 1975. 127 pp.

Horgan, Paul. *Great River: The Rio Grande in North American History.* New York: Holt, Rinehart & Winston, 1954. 2 vols.

Larson, Peggy, with Lane Larson. *A Sierra Club Naturalist's Guide to the Deserts of the Southwest.* San Francisco: Sierra Club Books, 1977. 285 pp.

Parent, Laurence. *Big Bend of the Rio Grande.* Big Bend Natural History Assn. (P.O. Box 68, Big Bend National Park, TX 79834). Scheduled for 1994 publication.

Salmon, M.H. *Gila Descending: A Southwestern Journey.* 2d ed. San Lorenzo, NM: High Lonesome Books (P.O. Box 878, Silver City, NM 88062), 1986. 221 pp.

California

Alt, David D. and Donald W. Hyndman. *Roadside Geology of Northern California.* Missoula, MT: Mountain Press, 1975. 244 pp.

The California Water Atlas. Sacramento: State of California, 1978. 118 pp.

Dana, Julian. *The Sacramento: River of Gold.* New York: Farrar & Rinehart, 1939. 294 pp.

Farquhar, Francis P. *History of the Sierra Nevada.* Berkeley: Univ. of California Press, 1965. 262 pp.

Gudde, Erwin Gustav. *California Place Names: The Origin and Etymology of Current Geographical Names.* 3d ed. Berkeley: Univ. of California Press, 1969. 416 pp.

Harris, Stephen L. *Fire Mountains of the West.* Full listing in Pacific Northwest region.

Hart, James D. *A Companion to California.* New York: Oxford Univ. Press, 1978. 504 pp.

Palmer, Tim. *Stanislaus: The Struggle for a River.* Berkeley: Univ. of California Press, 1982. 297 pp.

Whitney, Stephen. *A Sierra Club Naturalist's Guide to the Sierra Nevada.* San Francisco: Sierra Club Books, 1979. 526 pp.

Pacific Northwest

Alt, David D. and Donald W. Hyndman. *Roadside Geology of Oregon.* Missoula, MT: Mountain Press, 1978. 272 pp.

Alt, David D. and Donald W. Hyndman. *Roadside Geology of Washington.* Missoula, MT: Mountain Press, 1984. 282 pp.

Atwood, Kay. *Illahe: The Story of Settlement in the Rogue River Canyon.* Kay Atwood (120 So. Pioneer, Ashland, OR 97520), 1978. 251 pp.

Crawford, Doc. *North Umpqua Angler's Guide.* Portland: Frank Amato Publications, 1989. 96 pp.

Harris, Stephen L. *Fire Mountains of the West: The Cascade and Mono Lake Volcanoes.* Missoula: Mountain Press, 1988. 379 pp.

Helfrich, Prince. *Tales of the Oregon Cascades.* Natural World Press (47227 Goodpasture Rd., Vida OR 97488), 1990. 224 pp.

Hughes, David. *Deschutes.* Frank Amato Publications (P.O. Box 82112, Portland, OR 97282), 1990. 95 pp.

Jackman, Andrew, and Art Bernstein. *The Hip-Pocket Naturalist: A Guide to Oregon's Rogue River Basin.* Magnifica Press (1450 NE A St., Grants Pass, OR 97526), 1989. 272 pp.

Lavender, *The Way to the Western Sea.* Full listing in **Idaho and Northern Rockies** region.

McArthur, Lewis L. *Oregon Geographic Names.* 4th ed. Portland: Oregon Historical Society, 1974. 835 pp.

McNulty, Tim and Pat O'Hara. *Washington's Wild Rivers: The Unfinished Work.* Seattle: The Mountaineers, 1990. 144 pp.

Phillips, James W. *Washington State Place Names.* Seattle: Univ. of Washington Press, 1971. 167 pp.

Purdom, William B. *Guide to the Geology and Lore of the Wild Reach of the Rogue River Oregon.* Eugene: Univ. of Oregon, Museum of Natural History Bulletin No. 22, May 1977. 67 pp.

Richmond, Scott. *Fishing in Oregon's Deschutes River.* Scappoose, OR: Four Rivers Press / Flying Pencil Publications (33126 Callahan Rd., Scappoose, OR 97056), 1993. 173 pp.

Whitney, Stephen. *A Sierra Club Naturalist's Guide to the Pacific Northwest.* San Francisco: Sierra Club Books, 1989. 342 pp.

Wooldridge, Glen, with Florence Arman. *The Rogue: A River to Run.* Wildwood Press (209 SW Wildwood Ave., Grants Pass, OR 97526), 1982. 276 pp.

Appendix I.
Sources for River Running Equipment

This list of well-established Western sources for river equipment generally follows the geographical sequence of chapters in this book. (If the list is not complete, we apologize to companies whom we inadvertently omitted.) Most of the suppliers listed here specialize in whitewater gear. You can usually find some gear at general outdoor stores like REI.

Companies marked with an asterisk (*) provide instruction in river running in addition to selling and/or renting equipment. For specialized river running schools, see the next appendix.

Idaho and Northern Rockies

Northwest River Supplies
2009 S. Main
Moscow, ID 83843-8913
(800) 635-5202

Gravity Sports
503 Pine St.
P.O. Box 1717
McCall, ID 83638
(208) 634-8530

Idaho River Sports
1521 N. 13th
Boise, ID 83702
(208) 336-4844

Boise Army/Navy
4924 Chinden Blvd.
Boise, ID 83714
(208) 322-0660

Canyon Whitewater Supply
P.O. Box 51443
450 S. Yellowstone
Idaho Falls, ID 83405
(208) 522-3932

Teton Aquatic Supply
145 W. Gill
Jackson, WY 83001
(307) 733-3127

Technical Sports
1035 W. Broadway, P.O. Box 8695
Jackson, WY 83001
(307) 733-2471

Wyoming River Raiders
601 SE Wyoming Blvd.
Casper, WY 82609
(307) 235-8624

Northern Lights Trading Co.
1716 West Babcock
Bozeman, MT 59715
(406) 586-2225

Stillwater Kayaks
1035 O'Malley Drive
Billings, MT 59102
(406) 248-6987

Sunshine Sports
1144 Grand Ave.
Billings, MT 59102
(406) 252-3724

The Trail Head
110 E. Pine
Missoula, MT 59802
(406) 543-6966

Colorado Rockies

Boulder Outdoor Center*
2510 N. 47th
Boulder, CO 80301
(303) 444-8420

Down River Equipment
12100 West 52nd Ave., #101
Wheat Ridge, CO 80033
(303) 467-9489

Colorado Kayak Supply
P.O. Box 3059
Buena Vista, CO 81211
(719) 395-2422

Headwaters*
12844 Highway 285
Johnson Village, CO 81211
(719) 395-2409

Phoenix Rafting
2481 River Road # H
Grand Junction, CO 81505
(303) 243-4424

Whitewater West
339 Ute Ave.
Grand Junction, CO 81501
(303) 241-0441

Four Corners River Sports*
P.O. Box 379
Durango, CO 81302-0379
(800) 426-7637; (303) 259-3893

Mountains and Rivers
2320 Central S.E.
Albuquerque, NM 87106
(505) 268-4876

Canyon Country and Southwestern Border

Canyon R.E.O.
P.O. Box 3493
Flagstaff, AZ 86003
(800) 637-4604

Canyon Supply
P.O. Box 1969 / 1855 W. Kaibab
Flagstaff, AZ 86001
(602) 779-0624

Expeditions
625 N. Beaver Street
Flagstaff, AZ 86001
(602) 779-3769

PRO
P.O. Box 635
Flagstaff, AZ 86002
(602) 779-1512

Waters Edge*
546 W. Lester St.
P.O. Box 50272
Tucson, AZ 85703
(800) 999-RAFT; (602) 884-7080

California

Long Beach Water Sports
730 E. 4th Street
Long Beach, CA 90802
(310) 432-0187

Southwind Kayak Center
17855 Sky Park Circle # A
Irvine, CA 92714
(714) 261-0200

Sierra South*
1300 Kernville Rd.
P.O. Box Y
Kernville, CA 93238
(619) 376-3745; (619) 376-4875

Western Mountaineering
840 Town & Country Village
San Jose, CA 95128
(408) 984-7611

Pacific River Supply
3675 San Pablo Dam Road
El Sobrante, CA 94803
(510) 223-3675

California Canoe & Kayak*
409 Water Street
Oakland, CA 94607
(510) 893-7833

California Canoe & Kayak*
8631 Folsom Blvd.
Sacramento, CA 95826
(916) 381-6636

Wilderness Sports*
12401 Folsom Blvd.
Rancho Cordova, CA 95742
(916) 985-3555 or (800) 985-3555

Rescue Source
(Specialty Rescue Equipment)
P.O. Box 519
Elk Grove, CA 95759-0519
(800) 457-3728

The River Store
1032 Lotus Road
Lotus, CA 95651
(916) 626-3435

Clavey Equipment
P.O. Box 1149 / 11431 Highway 1
Pt. Reyes Station, CA 94956
(800) 832-4226; (415) 663-1921

California Rivers
10070 Old Redwood Highway
P.O. Box 1140
Windsor, CA 95492
(707) 838-8919

Chico Canoe & Kayak*
641 Nord Ave. # D
Chico, CA 95928
(916) 343-6474

Northern Mountain Supply
125 W. 5th Street
Eureka, CA 95501
(707) 445-1711

Adventures Edge
650 10th St.
Arcata, CA 95521
(707) 822-4673

Pacific Northwest

McKenzie Outfitters
130 East 8th
Medford, OR 97501
(503) 773-5145

Cascade Outfitters*
145 Pioneer Parkway East
Springfield, OR 97477
(800) 223-RAFT (223-7238)
(503) 747-2272

Bend Whitewater Supply
55 NW Wall Street, Bldg. C
Bend, OR 97709
(503) 389-7191

Andy & Bax
324 SE Grand Ave.
Portland, OR 97213
(503) 234-7538

Alder Creek Kayak Supply*
250 NE Tomahawk Island Drive
Portland, OR 97217
(503) 285-0464

Swiftwater
4235 Fremont Ave. N.
Seattle, WA 98103
(206) 547-3377

Pacific Water Sports*
16055 Pacific Highway South
Seattle, WA 98188
(206) 246-9385

Northwest Outdoor Center*
2100 Westlake Ave.
Seattle, WA 98109
(206) 281-9694

Watershed
16241 Cleveland
Redmond, WA 98052
(206) 869-6871

Northwest Kayaks
15145 N.E. 90th
Redmond, WA 98052
(206) 869-1107

Olympic Outdoor Center*
18971 Front St.
Poulsbo, WA 98370
(206) 697-6095

Appendix II.
River Running Instruction

Equipment suppliers who also offer instruction are marked with an asterisk (*) in the previous appendix.

In addition to the professional schools listed below, a number of universities have programs that include kayak, canoe, and raft instruction. Many commercial rafting outfitters also offer guide schools; for references, contact the outfitters' association: America Outdoors, (800) 524-4814.

If this list of schools is not complete, we apologize to those whom we inadvertently omitted.

Kayaking and Canoeing

Cascade Kayak and Canoe School
P.O. Box 6
Garden Valley, ID 83622
(800) 292-RAFT; (208) 462-3292

Jackson Hole Kayak School
P.O. Box 8695
Jackson, WY 83001
(307) 733-2471

Snake River Kayak and Canoe School
P.O. Box 3482
Jackson, WY 83001
(800) 824-5375

Rocky Mountain Outdoor Center
10281 Highway 50
Howard, CO 81233
(303) 942-3214

Aspen Kayak School
P.O. Box 1520
Aspen, CO 81611
(303) 925-6248

Otter Bar Kayak School
P.O. Box 210
Forks of Salmon, CA 96031
(916) 462-4772

Sundance Expeditions, Inc.
14894 Galice Road
Merlin, OR 97532
(503) 479-8508

Rafting

Running Wild Whitewater School
P.O. Box 658
Ashland, OR 97520
(503) 482-WAVE (482-9283)

Safety and Rescue

Rescue 3
P.O. Box 519
Elk Grove, CA 95759-0519
(800) 457-3728

Canyons Inc.
P.O. Box 823
McCall, ID 83638
(208) 634-4303

Appendix III. River Photographers

This is a list of photographers whose photos appear in this book and whose work is available to the public.

Almquist, Jon
1261 S.W. 152d St.
Seattle, WA 98166

Bennett, Jeff
P.O. Box 3031
Portland, OR 97208-3031

Bly, Steve
2334 S. Swallowtail Ln.
Boise, ID 83706

Bolster, Daniel
802 Eastman
Boise, ID 83702

Briggs, Don
398 11th St.
San Francisco, CA 94103

Brown, Tim
See ProFiles West

Cahill, Kathryn
12 Ocean Blvd.
Point Lookout, NY 11569

Cross, Diane
17655 Lazy Dog Ave.
Nevada City, CA 95959

Fessenden, Brian
368 50th St.
Oakland, CA 94609

Ghiglieri, Michael P.
814 N. Leroux
Flagstaff, AZ 86001

Glacier Raft Co.
P.O. Box 218
West Glacier, MT 59936

Glatte, Hayden
2025 Tolman Creek Rd.
Ashland, OR 97520

Harrel, Larry
917 Hearst Ave.
Berkeley, CA 94710

Hollenbeck, Cliff
2223 Second Ave.
Seattle, WA 98121

Huser, Verne
7106 Coors Trail NW
Albuquerque, NM 87120

Hymans, Liz
P.O. Box 1245
Flagstaff, AZ 86002

Korb, Gary
4930 Geiger Rd.
Port Orchard, WA 98366

Lane, Thor
P.O. Box 50272
Tucson, AZ 85703

Leder-Adams, Mark
See Rapid Shooters

Lewis, Dan
P.O. Box 863
Douglas, WY 82633

Lynch, Tracy
P.O. Box 315
Terlingua, TX 79852

Miller, Steve
Route 5, Box 302-A
Santa Fe, NM 87501

Montgomery, Jock
Bogan Road
Monson, MA 01507

Moore, Greg
212 W. Cheyenne Mtn. Blvd.
Colorado Springs, CO 80906

Moran, Martha
P.O. Box 8
Alma, CO 80420

ProFiles West
210 East Main
Buena Vista, CO 81211

Rapid Shooters
7221 Highway 49
Lotus, CA 95651

Robinson, Doug
7 David St.
Mascot, NSW 2020
Australia

Salmon, M.H.
P.O. Box 878
Silver City, NM 88062

Smith, Curt
600 Western Ave.
Petaluma, CA 94952

Spiker, Scott
P.O. Box 2509
Columbia Falls, MT 59912

Staub, Frank
P.O. Box 50801
Tucson, AZ 85703

Stroud, Steve
4427 Glasgow Way
Anacortes, WA 98221

Symonik, David
139-B Southampton Ln.
Santa Cruz, CA 95062

Theodorson, Judy
210 E. Olive
Bozeman, MT 59715

Thomson, James
P.O. Box 463
Ashland, OR 97520

Wales, Chuck
See ProFiles West

Weigold, Ted
P.O. Box 476
Boise, ID 83701

Whittaker, Tom
220 Grove Ave.
Prescott, AZ 86301

Wiley, Amy
See ProFiles West

Appendix IV. River Running Etiquette

Boaters' watchwords should be safety first, minimum impact on the environment, and courteous relations with others on and around the rivers. For our comments on safety, see the *Introduction* and *How to Use This Guide* at the beginning of this book. In this section we address the other two issues.

River running is potentially one of the outdoor sports with the lowest impact on the environment. Water craft can pass through wild lands leaving only a ripple on the water, and careful boaters can leave nothing but their footprints.

On the other hand, river runners always follow the same routes through the countryside, so the effects of their journeys are concentrated and intensified within the narrow river corridors. Even seemingly minor individual actions, when multiplied by the growing number of boaters in the last couple of decades, can have damaging cumulative effects.

There are practical reasons for minimizing our impact on the river environment. We would all like to see as much wildlife and as little trash as possible, and we would like to enjoy the best possible relations with other users of the river corridor. The reverse of the coin is that nothing will lead more quickly to restrictions on boating than abuse of the land, the wildlife, or other river users.

There are also ethical reasons. Rivers are not theme parks, and they are much more than roller coaster rides. These delicate ecosystems are ribbons of life in the natural fabric of our country. They deserve our respect and care—not only for the joy they bring us, but also because they are such a vital part of our environment.

Minimum-Impact River Running

Pride in caring for the river should be one of the real pleasures of a float trip. Even if it means a little extra effort, every boater should help to maintain the river environment in as pristine a condition as possible. Here are some guidelines:

Leave Nothing Behind: Pack out all garbage. If fires are permitted in the river corridor, paper and burnables (*not* plastic) can be burned, but the ashes should be packed out (see **Campfires** below). Before leaving, make a sweep through your entire camp. Keep a trash bag handy during the day to collect your own litter as well as that left by others, whether thoughtlessly or accidentally. Leave the river canyon cleaner than you found it.

Make Campfires with Care: Use a fire pan. Don't buld fire rings. Best is a fire pan with legs, so the pan itself doesn't touch the ground. If the pan is going to touch the ground, before you place it on soil, dig up an inch or two of topsoil (if any), set it aside, and replace it when you break camp. Alternatively—or in addition—set a fire blanket under the pan to insulate the soil. Otherwise, the heat will kill plants and microscopic life and leave the soil sterile.

If collecting firewood is permitted, be sure to gather only driftwood and "dead and down" wood. Standing dead wood, snags, and dead limbs are part of the canyon setting; leave them alone. When you break camp, scatter any unused firewood to leave the site in a more natural state. If the ground under the fire pan is still hot when you pack the pan away, mark the site with sticks to make sure no bare feet get burned accidentally.

Keep a close eye on your fire, and have sand, shovel, and water nearby. Make sure the fire is completely extinguished. Carry out charcoal and partially burned wood as you would garbage. A benefit of "ash in the trash" is that it absorbs garbage odors on long trips.

Dispose of Human Waste Properly: If possible—and it usually is—carry all solid human waste (feces) out of the river canyon. This is a requirement on some rivers. It is highly desirable on most, whether it is required or not. Many river canyons have little or no topsoil near the river, and feces does not decompose in sand, so burying human waste is *not usually recommended.* If you have no other choice, and if suitable soil is available, make sure your latrine is at least 8" deep, 100' from any side streams, and well above the river's high-water line. Toilet paper should be packed out or burned in the campfire.

For many years, river runners carried human waste in watertight ammo cans lined with plastic and doused with lime or some other deodorant. However, legally disposing of these bags is now more or less impossible. As requirements grow more stringent, new technologies are coming into play on some rivers. Among the developments are "scat machines" which clean unlined ammo boxes and portable toilets that can be emptied at RV dump stations. Be sure you know what is required when you plan your next trip.

Be Careful with Soap: Use biodegradable, phosphate-free soap to wash yourself and your dishes at least 100' from the river and any side streams. Pour dirty dishwater through a strainer into a hole dug at a site away from campsites. Put the food particles caught in the strainer into the trash.

Keep Wildlife in Mind: Dozens of species dwell in the critical riparian zone, and others come to the river to drink, hunt, and/or breed. Making noise or approaching too closely to observe wildlife or snap a photo can disturb nesting birds and other animals. Some nesting birds will even abandon their nests if frightened. A pair of binoculars or a telephoto lens will give you a front-row view from a respectful distance. Please respect closures of sensitive sites, and keep your noise down when you pass them. Choose camps and lunch stops with the needs of wildlife in mind.

In camp maintain a clean and secure kitchen. Food and garbage attract animals, who then associate people with food, hang around the campsites, and become "repeat offenders." Animals who become dependent on people for food may starve in winter when boaters no longer come by. What's more, animals such as skunks and especially bears can be most unwelcome midnight visitors. (See the footnote about bears in the **Rogue** chapter in Region VI.)

Respect Historical Sites: Pictographs, petroglyphs, artifacts, and dwellings of earlier inhabitants are an irreplaceable part of the river's history. Please be careful when you explore these sites. Leave everything in its place.

Limit Groups to a Moderate Size: Smaller groups have less impact—both on the environment and on the wilderness experience of other boaters.

Use Extra Care at Fragile or Heavily-Used Sites: River access points, popular campsites, favorite side hikes, legendary hot springs—all of these get intensive use, so more effort is necessary to keep them clean and healthy.

Respecting Other River Users

Rivers attract a wide variety of people: boaters, fishermen, campers, hikers, swimmers, serious prospectors and amateur gold-panners, photographers, sunbathers, and others. All of them have the right to privacy, quiet, and solitude; please respect that right.

Other Boaters: Make room for others at heavily-used river access points. At busy put-ins and take-outs, load and unload right away and move your boats and vehicles out of the way as quickly as possible.

Choose campsites and lunch spots well away from where others have stopped. Friendly discussion of upcoming campsites with other boating parties can avoid conflicts later in the day.

When your group is following another party, give them plenty of room when they head into rapids; this is a matter of safety as well as courtesy. If you want to pass them, do so in a smooth stretch of water if possible. If another group needs to pass you, try to pull over or even eddy out to let them by.

Boaters playing a wave should yield to others coming downstream. Don't be a "hole hog."

Anglers: When approaching a fisherman, try to hold back and ask where to pass. Use and look for hand signals rather than talking. If in doubt, stay to the far side of the channel and move through as smoothly and quietly as possible, keeping oar or paddle splashes to a minimum. If an angler has hooked a fish, try to wait upstream until the fish has been landed.

Quiet can be important to a fisherman, so let the angler decide whether to talk. A friendly wave and smile make a sufficient greeting.

Campers: At river access points, do not park in campsites. Walk around, not through, occupied campsites.

Private Property: Respect property rights. Keep noise to a minimum when riverside homes are nearby. Always ask permission if you want to use private land for river access or camping.

Appendix V.
River Conservation

"A river is more than an amenity, it is a treasure."

—Oliver Wendell Holmes

"Our world is so full of beautiful things ... A virtual Paradise. But even Paradise can be damned, flooded, overrun, generally mucked up by fools in pursuit of paper profits and plastic happiness."

—Edward Abbey, *Down The River.*

"In the West, of course, where water is concerned, logic and reason have never figured prominently in the scheme of things."

—Marc Reisner, *Cadillac Desert.*

When white settlers arrived in the West they found wild, untamed rivers that rose and fell according to their own ancient rhythms and followed age-old courses to the ocean without regard for human needs or wants. The pioneers sought to control and redirect these rivers, building structures to subdue floods, harness hydropower, "reclaim" deserts through irrigation, and keep precious water from "wasting to the sea."

Succeeding generations pursued this task with incredible vigor, damming almost every river in the West—some many times over. The results have been remarkable: decades of effort and massive government investments in water projects have produced an elaborate plumbing system that has helped transform the West into a flourishing land of cities and farms—at least for a time.

While much was created, much was also lost along the way. Those same dams destroyed fisheries, inundated farms and towns, wiped out wildlife habitat, obliterated outstanding scenery and silenced whitewater. Wild western rivers—once a natural treasure in abundance—became a rare and vanishing breed.

Many of the dams were, and are, essential structures. It is impossible to imagine our society without reservoirs and hydroelectric installations. But we have enough. In fact, we have more than enough. Many existing dams are obsolete, while others should never have been built in the first place. You can't construct as many dams as we have—1,200 in California alone—without building some mistakes.

River conservation has usually been a rearguard action—an attempt to cut losses to a minimum and to save first one, then another river. But in the last decade or so, successes have begun to outnumber failures by a wide margin. With time and with the growing strength of the conservation movement has come a greater public recognition of the aesthetic and economic values of free-flowing rivers.

It is now up to the river conservation movement to make a convincing case to the public that we can protect the quality and even increase the number of our free-flowing rivers without harming our standard of living. Essential to the success of this effort is the widespread conservation of water and power, which will not only eliminate the need for new dams, but also allow us to remove or modify some existing dams and diversions. Perhaps the twenty-first century will be an era of restoration and true "reclamation" for Western rivers.

River Conservation Organizations

Listed below are national, regional, and state organizations working to preserve the West's free-flowing rivers. This list does not include the dozens of local groups working to protect individual rivers; those groups are mentioned in the individual river chapters. The River Network in Portland (see below) can refer readers to local river conservation organizations through its River Clearinghouse program. A complete listing of river conservation groups can also be found in the *River Conservation Directory,* published by the National Park Service and National Association for State River Conservation Programs, and available from American Rivers in Washington, D.C. (see below).

National

American Rivers
801 Pennsylvania Ave. SE, Suite 400
Washington, D.C. 20003
(202) 547-6900

River Network
P.O. Box 8787
Portland, OR 97207
(503) 241-3506; (800) 423-6747

NORS
(National Organization for River Sports)
212 W. Cheyenne Mountain Blvd.
Colorado Springs, CO 80906
(719) 579-8759

American Whitewater Affiliation
P.O. Box 85
Phoenicia, NY 12464
(914) 688-5569

Idaho and Northern Rockies

Idaho Rivers United
P.O. Box 633
Boise, ID 83701
(208) 343-7481

Colorado Rockies and Southwestern Border

NORS (see above)

Adobe Whitewater Club
P.O. Box 3835
Albuquerque, NM 87110

Amigos Bravos—Friends of the Wild Rivers
P.O. Box 238
Taos, NM 87571
(505) 758-3874

American Rivers Arizona
3601 North 7th Ave.
Phoenix, AZ 85013
(602) 264-1823

California

Friends of the River
128 J St.
Sacramento, CA 95814
(916) 442-3155

Friends of the River
Building C, Fort Mason Center
San Francisco, CA 94123
(415) 771-0400

Pacific Northwest

Pacific Rivers Council
P.O. Box 309
Eugene, OR 97440
(503) 345-0119

Rivers Council of Washington
1731 Westlake Ave. N., Suite 202
Seattle, WA 98109-3043
(206) 283-4988

International

International Rivers Network
300 Broadway, Suite 2B
San Francisco, CA 94133
(415) 986-4693

Suggested Reading

Ashworth, William. *Nor Any Drop to Drink.* New York: Summit Books, 1982. 272 pp.

Bolling, David. *How To Save A River: A Guide to Citizen Action.* Washington, D.C./Covelo, CA: Island Press/The River Network. Scheduled for 1994 publication. About 250 pp.

Curtis, Christopher. *Grassroots River Protection: Saving Rivers under the National Wild and Scenic Rivers Act through Community-Based River Protection Strategies and State Action.* Washington, D.C.: American Rivers, 1992. 147 pp.

Dennis, Harry. *Water and Power: The Peripheral Canal and Its Alternatives.* San Francisco: Friends of the Earth Books, 1981. 167 pp.

Gottlieb, Robert. *A Life of Its Own: The Politics and Power of Water.* San Diego: Harcourt Brace Jovanovich, 1988. 332 pp.

High Country News. *Western Water Made Simple.* Washington, D.C./Covelo, CA: Island Press, 1987. 231 pp.

Hunt, Constance E., with Verne Huser. *Down by the River: The Impact of Federal Water Projects and Policies on Biological Diversity.* Washington, D.C./Covelo, CA: Island Press, 1988. 260 pp.

1992 River Conservation Directory. Washington, D.C.: National Park Service and American Rivers, 1992. 143 pp.

Palmer, Tim. *Endangered Rivers and the Conservation Movement.* Berkeley: Univ. of California Press, 1986. 316 pp.

Palmer, Tim. *The Wild and Scenic Rivers of America.* Washington, D.C./Covelo, CA: Island Press, 1993. 339 pp.

Powledge, Fred. *Water.* New York: Farrar, Strauss, and Giroux, 1982. 423 pp.

Reisner, Mark. *Cadillac Desert: The American West and its Disappearing Water.* New York: Viking Penguin, 1986. 582 pp.

Reisner, Mark and Sarah Bates. *Overtapped Oasis: Reform or Revolution for Western Water.* Washington, D.C./Covelo, CA: Island Press, 1990. 200 pp.

Worster, Donald. *Rivers of Empire: Water, Aridity and the Growth of the American West.* New York: Pantheon Books, 1985. 402 pp.

Index of Stories

Regional Index of Easier Runs

This is an index of rivers in this book which are rated Class II+3 and below (at low and moderate flows only). They are listed in the geographical order followed by this book, with the briefer entries from our **More Western Rivers** section mixed in with the featured rivers which have their own chapters. In addition to covering the featured runs, many chapters also mention easy upstream and downstream runs (and even runs on tributaries); those runs are not listed in this index. (S) means shorter runs possible.

The term "easier" doesn't mean that these runs are without hazard. "Easier" refers only to the difficulty of the whitewater. Some of these runs are remote, some have log hazards, and so on. Take all necessary precautions. Note that runs rated Class II+ occasionally include one or two Class III rapids.

I. Idaho and Northern Rockies

II. Colorado Rockies

3. Canyon Country

4. Southwestern Border

5. California

6. Pacific Northwest

Alphabetical Index of Rivers

About the Authors

Jim Cassady (b. 1945), a native of Maryland, first dug a paddle into whitewater as a canoeist on Eastern and Midwestern creeks and rivers. After he migrated to southern California, where he taught social science in a Long Beach high school, he learned to kayak and later became a professional rafting guide. He led the first raft trips down some of California's toughest rivers, including Burnt Ranch Gorge of the Trinity, the Upper Kings, the North Fork Mokelumne, and the Forks of the Kern. He now lives in the San Francisco Bay Area and has a daughter, Grace. Cassady is founder and co-owner of Pacific River Supply in El Sobrante. He designed the SOTAR self-bailing raft produced by Whitewater Manufacturing of Grants Pass, Oregon. Cassady, who has boated more than 200 rivers in the U.S. and abroad, is co-author (with Fryar Calhoun) of *California Whitewater: A Guide to the Rivers* and a number of whitewater map-guides.

Bill Cross (b. 1959) began his whitewater career in an unlikely setting: the gutter outside his boyhood home in Los Angeles, where he sent twig boats sailing down the miniature rapids created by suburban street runoff. He got his first taste of full-scale whitewater as a commercial passenger on a Grand Canyon trip in the early 1970's. After attending a whitewater school in 1978, he worked as a professional rafting guide and whitewater instructor, and he has boated recreationally throughout the West. Today, Bill and his wife, Polly Greist, operate their own whitewater instruction outfit, Running Wild Whitewater School, based in Ashland, Oregon. They have two sons, Gregory and Nicholas. Bill has studied ecology, hydrology, and water resources and is active in river conservation efforts. He has written articles on river-related subjects for *Paddler, Canoe, Headwaters, Outdoor Family, California Explorer,* and other publications.

Fryar Calhoun (b. 1942) grew up in the flat, dry West Texas Panhandle, far from whitewater rivers. Later he lived and studied on the East Coast and in Europe, then spent a number of years teaching history at the University of California at Berkeley. Until 1976, when a friend took him on a raft trip down the Salmon River in Idaho, he thought the outdoors meant playing golf or tennis. Since then he has run rivers throughout the Western U.S., organized a private whitewater rafting cooperative, worked as a professional rafting guide, and published articles on rivers, dams, and other subjects in magazines like *New West, California, Texas Monthly, Success, Sacramento,* and *Motorland,* and in newspapers including the *San Francisco Chronicle, San Jose Mercury-News, Sacramento Bee, Peninsula Times-Tribune,* and *Arkansas Democrat.* Fryar lives in Berkeley with his wife Caroline Sutour. He is publisher and co-author (with Jim Cassady) of *California Whitewater: A Guide to the Rivers* and a number of whitewater map-guides.

Also by Cassady and Calhoun: Detailed guides with shaded-relief river maps to eight of the best-known whitewater runs in California and the West: the **Tuolumne** (Meral's Pool to Ward's Ferry), **South Fork American, Forks of the Kern, Upper Kern, Lower Kern, Upper Arkansas, Lower Arkansas,** and **Rio Grande** (including the Taos Box).

North Fork Press
P.O. Box 3580
Berkeley, CA 94703
(510) 540-0800